2015

FREE RANGE?
NOT SO MUCH,
THESE HENS
ARE KEPT
BEHIND BARS

The Good Pub Guide 2015

Edited by Alisdair Aird and Fiona Stapley

Associate Editor: Patrick Stapley

Editorial Research: Fiona Wright
Office Manager: Sarah White
Administrative Assistant: Jan Jones

EBURY PRESS
LONDON

Please send reports on pubs to:

The Good Pub Guide
FREEPOST RTJR-ZCYZ-RJZT, Perrymans Lane, Etchingham TN19 7DN

or **feedback@goodguides.com**

or visit our website: **www.thegoodpubguide.co.uk**

If you would like to advertise in the next edition of *The Good Pub Guide*,
please email **goodpubguide@tbs-ltd.co.uk**

10 9 8 7 6 5 4 3 2 1

Published in 2014 by Ebury Press, an imprint of Ebury Publishing

A Random House Group Company

Addresses for companies within the Random House Group can be found at
www.randomhouse.co.uk

A CIP catalogue record for this book is available from the British Library

The Random House Group Limited supports The Forest
Stewardship Council (FSC®), the leading international forest
certification organisation. Our books carrying the FSC label are printed
on FSC® certified paper. FSC is the only forest certification scheme
endorsed by the leading environmental organisations, including
Greenpeace. Our paper procurement policy can be found
at www.randomhouse.co.uk/environment

To buy books by your favourite authors and register for offers,
visit www.randomhouse.co.uk

Typeset from authors' files by Jerry Goldie Graphic Design
Project manager and copy editor Cath Phillips
Proofreader Tamsin Shelton

Printed and bound by CPI Group (UK) Ltd, Croydon, CR0 4YY

ISBN 9780091958084

Cover design by Two Associates
Cover photographs reproduced by kind permission of the pubs:
Front cover: Red Lion; *Spine:* Bolingey Inn, Perranporth, Cornwall;
Back cover (left–right, clockwise): Queen's Arms, Litton, Yorkshire; Gurnards Head
Hotel, Gurnards Head, Cornwall; Dirty Habit, Hollingbourne, Kent; Angel & Blue Pig,
Lymington, Hampshire; Malt Shovel; Black Bull.

Contents

Introduction & The Good Pub Guide Awards 2015

The pub scene has changed utterly from the days of decrepit boozers with dull beer and freezer-pack food to a thriving industry that's now finding ingenious ways of pleasing millions of new customers. And this transformation has taken place against a background of hard economic times that have driven many less alert pub businesses to the wall. A handful of people have played vital roles in this. The following seven men, each at the forefront of a key development that has proved crucial to the new mood of forward-looking confidence in the pub world, are today's Pub Superheroes.

We first came across **Bill Sharp** in 1994, when he was delivering a keg of a beer we'd never heard of to a little Cornish pub. We tried that beer and liked it a lot. Bill had just started a small brewery in the nearby village of Rock, and was beginning to attract a keen local following. The business grew, and was sold in 2003 and again in 2011 – but Bill Sharp's beers have stayed the same. On the quality foundations he'd laid down, Sharps Doom Bar has become a top seller, found in pubs throughout Britain. His success has been an inspiration to hundreds of other brewers, now producing literally thousands of different beers – a revolution in drinks choice for pub lovers.

Another success story is Greene King, a brewer on an altogether bigger scale, and one that owns a flourishing pub chain. Its achievement is down to **Rooney Anand**, chief executive since 2005 (and manager of the brewing side before that). He steered the business through the credit crunch by avoiding the debt pitfalls that sank some other pubcos, and is growing it by focusing sharply on what customers want. Under his guidance, good value food has become a central part of the mix. Providing proper jobs for over 20,000 people, he's proved that sound management pays off.

Greene King's growth has brought under its wing several other beer and pub companies. One of these is Ridleys, a small chain of Essex pubs. **Jocelyn Ridley** has since then bought one of his family's former pubs, the Compasses at Littley Green, and runs it as the very archetype of an unspoilt country tavern. Concentrating on a truly warm-hearted atmosphere, simple traditional furnishings, honest hearty food and well kept beers (including one brewed nearby by his brother), he's shown that a cheerful pub can win plenty of happy customers without a fancy menu or fashionable trappings.

The Wetherspoons chain has nearly 1,000 pubs. When we started this *Guide* in 1983, **Tim Martin**, the chain's founder and boss, then still in his twenties, had just four pubs but had already found the formula that has driven his success – good motivated staff, cheap beer, remarkable value food, plenty of space and character, and usually no piped music.

The pubs that don't just survive but really thrive, are those that keep evolving, anticipating what customers will want. More and more, this means nibbles, tapas-like small dishes and 'sharing boards', with anything from baby honey and mustard bangers through mini barbecued ribs to wild boar and quail egg scotch eggs. **Andres Alemany** of the Purefoy Arms at Preston Candover in Hampshire is a past master at this art of creating mouth-watering tapas – it is after all in his spanish heritage. See right for his easy-to-follow recipe for squid with romesco sauce.

Back in the 1980s, **Jerry Brunning** and his business partner **Graham Price** had a dim view of prevailing pub standards. Instead, they tried to create a pub that was more attractive compared to what people could get at home – real comfort, inviting décor, appetising and interesting food, good but not expensive wine and a better range of beers and other drinks than those offered by the competition. We're always impressed, too, by their exemplary staff. This formula has fuelled the successful growth of the Brunning & Price group, now with over 40 pubs.

To recap, these are the Pub Superheroes:

- Bill Sharp – inspiring a new generation of craft brewers
- Rooney Anand – showing how a national brewer with 1,600 pubs can flourish
- Tim Martin – a powerful force in giving us good value food and drink.

Squid with romesco sauce

Sauce
150ml spanish extra-virgin olive oil, plus extra for coating the vegetables
1 red pepper
6 ripe plum tomatoes
1 head garlic, halved, papery outer skin removed
1 spanish onion
3 ñora chilli peppers (or other dried sweet chilli pepper)
50g blanched almonds
25g white bread, crust removed
1 tbsp sherry vinegar
1 tsp pimentón (spanish sweet paprika)
0.5 teaspoon salt

Brush a thin film of oil over the pepper, tomatoes, garlic and onion and lay them in a roasting pan. Roast for about 25 minutes, until soft. Remove from the oven and, once cool enough to handle, peel them all. De-seed the pepper and tomatoes and cut off their tops. Meanwhile, place the chillis in a bowl, cover with hot water and soak for 15 minutes. Strain, remove the seeds, place the flesh in a blender and purée. Pass the purée through a fine-mesh sieve into a bowl and set aside.

Heat 1 tbsp of oil in a small pan over a low heat. Add the almonds and sauté until just browned, about 1 minute. Transfer to a bowl and set aside. Raise the heat to medium, add the bread to the same pan and toast until a nice brown colour, about 30 seconds on each side. Remove the bread and set aside. Add the puréed chillis to the pan, cook for 30 seconds, then remove the pan from the heat.

Place the peeled roasted vegetables into the blender. Add the almonds, bread, chilli paste, vinegar, pimentón and the remaining olive oil. Blend into a thick sauce, add salt to taste, then pour into a bowl and set aside.

Squid
vegetable oil (for deep-frying)
500g squid, cleaned (ask your fishmonger to do this)
spanish frying flour
generous pinch sea salt
1 lemon, cut into wedges, to serve

(To dust the squid, we use a special flour from southern spain called *farina especial para freir*, available from good Spanish delis. If unavailable, substitute with equal amounts of plain flour and breadcrumbs mixed together.)

Preheat the oil in a deep-fat fryer to 180°C. Rinse the squid, carefully pat dry with kitchen paper, then cut into 1.5cm rings and set aside, with the tentacles.

Tip plenty of flour (or flour/breadcrumb mix) into a large bowl. Toss a large handful of squid in the flour to coat, gently shake off any excess and add carefully to the hot oil. Deep-fry for 3 minutes or until crisp and golden, then drain on kitchen paper. Repeat, cooking the squid in batches, then sprinkle with a little salt and lemon juice. Serve immediately with the lemon wedges and romesco sauce.

Andres Alemany, Purefoy Arms, Preston Candover, Hampshire

- Jocelyn Ridley – champion of the unspoilt traditional pub
- Andres Alemany – top of the new tapas tree
- Jerry Brunning and Graham Price – pub visionaries, never satisfied with less than all-round excellence.

Drinks: the search for fair prices and top quality

Our national survey of beer prices shows a whopping 76p-a-pint difference between Herefordshire, the cheapest county, and London, the most expensive area. The average price for a pint of beer in Britain is now £3.31. How does your area rank? Here are the details, in average price order:

Bargain beer
Herefordshire, Worcestershire, Derbyshire, Cumbria, Staffordshire, Northamptonshire, Northumbria, Yorkshire
Fair priced beer
Wales, Shropshire, Cornwall, Somerset, Lancashire, Nottinghamshire
Average priced beer
Cheshire, Leicestershire and Rutland, Devon, Gloucestershire, Lincolnshire, Bedfordshire, Wiltshire, Cambridgeshire, Essex, Dorset, Suffolk, Isle of Wight, Warwickshire, West Midlands, Scotland, Hampshire, Norfolk
Expensive beer
Oxfordshire, Buckinghamshire, Scottish Islands, Kent, Hertfordshire, Sussex, Berkshire
Rip-off beer
Surrey, London

In 1981, Norfolk brewery Woodfordes produced their first commercial brew of Wherry Bitter. Since then, they've won many well deserved awards and demand for their carefully crafted ales has meant a move to their current premises in Woodbastwick. They have their own bore hole and use local barley and quite an array of whole hops to achieve their distinctive ales. All can be tasted in their brewery tap, the Fur & Feather, next to the brewery. Woodfordes is our **Brewery of the Year 2015**.

In this edition, we've picked 329 pubs that qualify for one of our Beer Awards – each is outstanding for the quality and, often, the range of what they sell.

This year's Top Ten Beer Pubs are the Bhurtpore in Aston and Mill in Chester (Cheshire), Watermill at Ings (Cumbria), Tom Cobley at Spreyton (Devon), Old Spot in Dursley (Gloucestershire), Malt Shovel in Northampton (Northamptonshire), Fat Cat in Norwich (Norfolk), Fat Cat in Ipswich (Suffolk), Nags Head in Malvern (Worcestershire) and Kelham Island Tavern in Sheffield (Yorkshire). Genuinely welcoming and full of character, the Nags Head in Malvern is **Beer Pub of the Year 2015**.

Pubs brewing their own beer – as 24 in this edition do – typically save you 45p a pint, compared to the average. Our Top Ten Own-Brew Pubs are the Brewery Tap in Peterborough (Cambridgeshire), Beer Hall at Hawkshead Brewery in Staveley and Watermill at Ings (Cumbria), Old Poets Corner at Ashover (Derbyshire), Church Inn at Uppermill (Lancashire), Grainstore in Oakham (Leicestershire), Dipton Mill Inn at Diptonmill and Ship in Newton-by-the-Sea (Northumbria), Three Tuns at Bishop's Castle (Shropshire) and Weighbridge Brewhouse in Swindon (Wiltshire). For its fantastic and interesting choice, the Church Inn at Uppermill is **Own-Brew Pub of the Year 2015**.

Many pubs really care about the wines they stock, and 358 qualify for our Wine Award. Our Top Ten Wine Pubs are the Old Bridge Hotel in Huntingdon (Cambridgeshire), Nobody Inn at Doddiscombsleigh (Devon), Yew Tree at Clifford's Mesne (Gloucestershire), Inn at Whitewell (Lancashire), Olive Branch at Clipsham (Leicestershire and Rutland), Woods at Dulverton (Somerset), Crown at Southwold and Crown at Stoke-by-Nayland (Suffolk), Inn at West End (Surrey) and Vine Tree at Norton (Wiltshire). With 400 wines from an extraordinary choice (they'll open any of them just for a glass), Woods in Dulverton wins again and is **Wine Pub of the Year 2015**.

Of the many pubs that stock a fine choice of malt whiskies, our Top Ten Whisky Pubs are the Nobody Inn at Doddiscombsleigh (Devon), Bhurtpore at Aston and Old Harkers Arms in Chester (Cheshire), Angel at Larling (Norfolk), Black Jug in Horsham (Sussex), Pack Horse in Widdop (Yorkshire) and Bow Bar in Edinburgh, Bon Accord in Glasgow and Sligachan Hotel and Stein Inn on the Isle of Skye (Scotland). With its phenomenal choice of 400, and perfect scenery in which to sample them, the Sligachan Hotel is **Whisky Pub of the Year 2015**.

Pub food: looking for value and flavour

It's been really hard in these tough times for pubs to keep prices for meals as fair as they can. Even so, 106 pubs hold one of our Bargain Meals Awards, meaning they offer interesting cooking that gives real value, typically with a tempting choice for under £10. Our Top Ten Value Pubs are the Church Inn at Chelmorton (Derbyshire), Yew Tree at Lower Wield (Hampshire), Ring o' Bells at Lathom (Lancashire), Butcher & Beast at Heighington (Lincolnshire), Dipton Mill Inn at Diptonmill (Northumbria), Old Castle in Bridgnorth (Shropshire), Square & Compass at Ashill (Somerset), Lord Nelson in Southwold (Suffolk), Six Bells at Chiddingly (Sussex) and Lamb in Marlborough (Wiltshire). The Ring o' Bells at Lathom is **Value Pub of the Year 2015**.

The ten pubs in this list represent the best pubs in Britain for a special meal. They are the Cock in Hemingford Grey (Cambridgeshire), Treby Arms at Sparkwell (Devon), Feathered Nest at Nether Westcote (Gloucestershire), Wellington Arms at Baughurst (Hampshire), Stagg at Titley (Herefordshire), Assheton Arms at Downham (Lancashire), Plough at Kingham (Oxfordshire), Lord Poulett Arms at Hinton St George (Somerset), Horse Guards at Tillington (Sussex) and Pipe &

Glass at South Dalton (Yorkshire). For beautifully presented, seriously good food from an interesting menu, the Pipe & Glass in South Dalton is **Dining Pub of the Year 2015**.

The country's top pubs

Set up in 2010 by Michael Ibbotson and Chris Blundell, Provenance Inns in Yorkshire has six pubs. Their ideal is a proper pub with top class food and beer – and not just restaurants in pubs' clothes. Both men are passionate about keeping everything local, from food to ales, from producers to tradesmen. This theory has worked out so well for their customers that Provenance Inns is **Pub Group of the Year 2015**.

There are many genuinely unchanging and unpretentious pubs that rely on their landlords and landladies to keep them that way, and on their strength of character rather than their food. Our Top Ten Unspoilt Pubs are the Harrington Arms at Gawsworth (Cheshire), Barley Mow at Kirk Ireton (Derbyshire), Rugglestone near Widecombe (Devon), Digby Tap in Sherborne and Square & Compass at Worth Matravers (Dorset), Viper at Mill Green (Essex), Harrow at Steep and White Horse near Petersfield (Hampshire), and Crown at Churchill and Halfway House at Pitney (Somerset). The Square & Compass in Worth Matravers is **Unspoilt Pub of the Year 2015**.

Pubs in towns are always popular locally, but to be able to extend that genuine welcome to visitors too is a special quality. Our Top Ten Town Pubs are the Park in Bedford (Bedfordshire), Old Harkers Arms in Chester (Cheshire), Eight Bells in Chipping Campden (Gloucestershire), Wykeham Arms in Winchester (Hampshire), Kings Arms in Woodstock and Lamb in Burford (Oxfordshire), Old Green Tree in Bath (Somerset), Crown in Southwold (Suffolk), Old Joint Stock in Birmingham (Warwickshire) and Olde Mitre in central London. For its lively atmosphere and fine range of drinks and food, the canalside Old Harkers Arms in Chester is **Town Pub of the Year 2015**.

Think of a lovely place to relax in after a perfect country walk, and you've probably got a good country pub in mind: roaring log fires in winter and pretty gardens in summer; honest, hearty food and delicious thirst-quenchers; and a genuinely warm welcome. Our Top Ten Country Pubs are the White Horse at Hedgerley (Buckinghamshire), Pheasant at Burwardsley (Cheshire), Duke of York at Iddesleigh (Devon), Brace of Pheasants at Plush (Dorset), Butchers Arms at Sheepscombe

(Gloucestershire), English Partridge at Bighton and Royal Oak at Fritham (Hampshire), Hatchet at Lower Chute and Malet Arms at Newton Tony (Wiltshire), and Harp at Old Radnor (Wales). New to us this year, and one of our loveliest recent finds, the English Partridge at Bighton is **Country Pub of the Year 2015**.

We've found 121 new pubs that we're really happy with this year, ranging from simple places through to smart dining pubs. Our Top Ten New Pubs are the Church Inn at Mobberley (Cheshire), Tudy Inn at St Tudy (Cornwall), Stapleton Arms at Buckhorn Weston (Dorset), English Partridge at Bighton (Hampshire), Assheton Arms at Downham and Old Hall at Worsley (Lancashire), Lord Crewe Arms at Blanchland (Northumbria), Lion & Pheasant in Shrewsbury (Shropshire), Kingsdon Inn at Kingsdon (Somerset) and Bell at Ramsbury (Wiltshire). With bags of character, the nicely traditional Church Inn at Mobberley is **New Pub of the Year 2015**.

Staying at a really well run inn with lovely bedrooms and a cheerful bar is becoming increasingly popular. Our Top Ten Inns are the New Inn at Coleford and Rock at Haytor Vale (Devon), New Inn at Cerne Abbas (Dorset), Kings Head at Bledington (Gloucestershire), Mill at Gordleton near Hordle and Wellington Arms at Baughurst (Hampshire), Inn at Whitewell, Whitewell (Lancashire), Crown in Southwold (Suffolk)), Red Lion at Long Compton (Warwickshire) and Blue Lion at East Witton (Yorkshire). A beautifully refurbished 16th-c former coaching inn, the New Inn at Cerne Abbas is **Inn of the Year 2015**.

To run a great pub, you have to be completely dedicated to both your pub and your customers, be prepared to work really hard for up to 18 hours a day –

and keep smiling! Our Top Ten Licensees of the Year are Philip and Lauren Davison of the Fox at Peasemore (Berkshire), Tim Wilkes of the Spyway at Askerswell (Dorset), Colin Hayling of the Crown at Little Walden (Essex), Tim Gray of the Yew Tree at Lower Wield (Hampshire), Glenn Williams of the Bell at Tillington (Herefordshire), Julie Barclay and Robert Windeler of the Queens Head at Bulwick (Northamptonshire), Peter and Veryan Graham of the George at Croscombe and Stephen, Sally, Richard and Leonie Browning of the Rose & Crown at Stoke St Gregory (Somerset), the Mainey family of the Crown at Roecliffe (Yorkshire) and the Key family of the Nags Head in Usk (Wales). The Mainey family who run the Crown at Roecliffe so superbly are **Licensees of the Year 2015**.

Certain pubs stand out over the year as places that are truly special, featuring again and again in our readers' warmest reports. For the sheer enjoyment they give their customers, these Top Ten Pubs are listed below in county order. Run with such care and love by Mr and Mrs Goodrich, the **Rose & Crown** in Snettisham is **Pub of the Year 2015**.

TOP TEN PUBS 2015
(in county order)

Royal Standard of England
in Forty Green (Buckinghamshire)

Crown at Little Walden (Essex)

Olive Branch at Clipsham
(Leicestershire and Rutland)

Rose & Crown at Snettisham (Norfolk)

Woods in Dulverton (Somerset)

Horse Guards at Tillington (Sussex)

Bell in Welford-on-Avon (Warwickshire)

Compasses at Chicksgrove (Wiltshire)

Nags Head in Malvern (Worcestershire)

Crown at Roecliffe (Yorkshire)

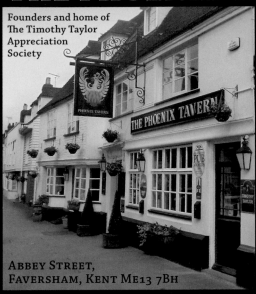

The best bread and beer pairings ever

By **James Morton**

There's been a concerted attempt by many beer advocates to turn beer into the next wine – to highlight its superior variability and thus its ability to complement more starters, mains and desserts than wine ever could. I've been a big champion of this change. Many foods will be better represented paired with the most appropriate beers rather than the most appropriate wines.

But most of the times I drink beer, I'm not really thinking about the food. The beer is the showstopper. The beer is the starter, main course and dessert – and I don't want a meal to distract from its beauty. I simply want sustenance to serve alongside.

Pubs serve nuts or crackling or crisps. Even chips. And these are fine. They may scratch away at the lining of your mouth, but their salty hit makes you want to take another drink, and another. But my nagging feeling is that these are physiological sides served for the purpose of profit, rather than as the supreme supplement to beer.

Bread. Butter. Salt. This is how you'll get the best out of your beer. Yes, there's still the functional aspect to this: the thirst-inducing salt inside and on top of the bread. The butter that satisfies that greasy urge we all get when we drink. Even the mastication required to get us through a hunk of chewy crust makes the next sip more inviting. For me, the marrying of beer and bread is a true, spiritual experience.

Consider too that bread and beer are made in the same way. I make lots and lots of both, and can testify that both are just grain that's soaked in water and fermented with yeast. Baker's and brewer's yeast are even the same species. This gives an essential overlap in flavours, which means that when you drink the beer you can perhaps pick up a few more of the subtleties of the bread. But the amplification of the beer's flavour is altogether more profound.

While 'researching' (drinking) for this article, I discovered a rule of contrasts. This surprised me. No, clean lagers didn't go with plain white breads. Big, dark belgian beers didn't go with raisin-filled brioches. My first revelation was that the beer I found went best with dense, crumbly pumpernickel (rye bread) was the much-underrated Munich helles. New brewers are so much about hybrid pilsners and dry-hopped american lagers that this sensationally drinkable example from Bavaria has been largely overlooked. My favourite example is from Augustiner-Bräu and is available in many independent beer shops around the UK. Its flawless cleanliness and good malt backbone wash over the rye superbly.

If you're going to have one bread-basket on a bar or one loaf to share among friends when tasting a selection of beers, then go for a baguette or two, properly made by a proper bakery. The crust should be dark and thick with the middle (the 'crumb') chewy and holey. Baguettes are slowly fermented, giving them a tang as the natural bacteria of the flour infect the dough in delicious ways. These notes complement any beer. Serve with good, french unsalted butter. Then sprinkle with english sea salt on top. Bliss.

When it comes to more aggressive, hoppier styles, it's harder to find bread that truly adds to them. In these situations, I think a simple interruption is needed to provide occasional relief from their overwhelming nature. And solace comes in the milk loaf. This traditional english white bread is made with milk, butter and a touch of sugar, and is soft-fleshed and indulgent. In imperial IPAs, such as Stone Ruination IPA or BrewDog Jack Hammer, the hop bitterness swamps the taste buds, rendering any subsequent delicacies pathetic. The very slight sweetness of the milk loaf, though, intensifies the dry bitterness of these beers and teases you into taking sip upon sip while still allowing them to do all the singing and dancing.

With the darker styles, I had some problems pairing. I was testing against what I believe is the UK standard for stouts: Sam Smiths Oatmeal Stout. This is one of my favourite beers coming out of the UK right now. I found white breads slightly cloying and Italian breads far too greasy for its viscosity. This needed bite. The evident choice was to go for a crusty wholemeal, and not for healthiness's sake – the gritty nuttiness goes so well with the roasted notes of the beer. It just works. I'd recommend serving wholegrain with any stout, imperial stout or porter.

In fact, I include at least a little wholegrain in most of my breads for that extra dimension of flavour, along with another ingredient: sourdough starter. Sourdough is spontaneously fermented bread that takes its flavour from the many species of wild yeast and bacteria that populate the dough. It has an equivalent in beer: the hugely sour and divisive lambic. The classical aromas are 'funk' and 'barnyard' (among many more derogatory), so it's not to everyone's taste at first. Persist, though, for maybe the second or third time you try one, you'll have an epiphany.

The most traditional and best lambic comes from a brewery in Brussels called Cantillon. Their gueze, available seasonally but across the UK, cuts through any flavours that might have been lingering to completely whitewash your palate. Use this to showcase with a well made sourdough, such as a massive miche, made with a mix of white and rye flour. Moreover, the acidity of the bread quantifies the puckering of the beer to help open up more of the flavour.

Lambic is awesome, but I'll leave you with my very favourite bread/beer combination: a scone, apricot jam and clotted cream served with a super-strong dark beer. I'd recommend any old or scotch ale above 8% or so – try Harviestoun Ola Dubh or Orkney Dark Island Reserve, both aged in scotch whisky casks for that extra layer of lush. This will be the best afternoon tea you ever have. I believe Mary Berry would approve. 99

James Morton was runner-up in the BBC's *The Great British Bake Off* in 2012 and is the author of *Brilliant Bread* (Ebury, 2013). **Favourite pub** BrewDog in Glasgow.

THE COCK

The Cock
Free House

Like craft beer? Make your own! The Tom Ditto IPA story

By **Danny Wallace**

66 Here's the thing: I enjoy beer, and I enjoy pubs – real pubs, with history and stories and their own identity. I especially like the **Dog & Duck** in London's Soho, with its tiled floors and narrow bar, and its outdoor drinkers caught between Frith and Dean Streets. And the **Coal Hole** on the Strand, which is like drinking on a galleon, and where Gilbert & Sullivan used to go through their songs and rehearse. And the **Bear & Staff** just by Leicester Square, where Charlie Chaplin drank, and where my mate Steve reckons he once saw Lionel Blair. There's a sense that you're a part of history when you're in a pub like these.

Nicholson's pubs in London are just the sort of pubs I like, and recently someone from the company noticed I'd been mentioning a few of their pubs in my articles and books. The man from Nicholson's said: 'Brew us a beer and base it on one of your books!' He sounded insane. I asked for ID. But it all checked out, so I said yes.

The beer needed to taste of London, with a little bit of New York streets. Obviously, that sounds disgusting. But Nicholson's set me up with the legendary Truman's Brewery in the East End of London, and it all fell into place. Their head brewer, Ben, had laid out some hops for me to smell. Some were American hops. Some were British hops. Some were so new they hadn't even been named yet. And there was beer: pint after pint for us to taste and take inspiration from. We combined a never-before-combined mixture of high-quality hops into one very special secret recipe: Tom Ditto IPA. It was as golden as the sun, as light as a feather, as smooth and drinkable as... well... liquid, and yet packed a powerful punch.

I'm genuinely proud that Truman's are brewing it. I hope that if you're old enough, you enjoy a taste of it this summer. **99**

Danny Wallace is a *Sunday Times*-bestselling author who lives in London. His first book, *Join Me,* was described as 'one of the funniest stories you will ever read'; his second, *Yes Man*, became a hugely successful film with Jim Carrey in the lead role. His latest novel, *Who is Tom Ditto?*, was published by Ebury in 2014.

What is a good pub?

The Main Entries in this *Guide* have been through a two-stage sifting process. First of all, some 2,000 regular correspondents keep in touch with us about the pubs they visit, while double that number report occasionally. We also get a flow of reports sent to us at feedback@goodguides.com or via our website, www.thegoodpubguide.co.uk. This keeps us up to date about pubs included in previous editions: it's their alarm signals that warn us when a pub's standards have dropped (after a change of management, say) and it's their continuing approval that reassures us about keeping a pub as a full entry for another year.

New Entries

Particularly important are the reports we receive on pubs we don't know at all. It's from these new discoveries that we create a shortlist, to be considered for possible inclusion as new Main Entries. The more people that report favourably on a new pub, the more likely it is to win a place on this shortlist – especially if some of the reporters belong to our hardcore of trusted correspondents whose judgement we have learned to rely on. These are people who have each given us detailed comments on dozens of pubs, and shown that (when we ourselves know some of those pubs too) their judgement is closely in line with our own.

This brings us to the acid test. As well as inspection, the editors have to find some special quality that would make strangers enjoy visiting it. What often marks out the pub for special attention is good value food (and that might mean anything from a well made sandwich, with good fresh ingredients at a low price, to imaginative cooking outclassing most restaurants in the area). The drinks may be out of the ordinary – maybe several hundred whiskies, remarkable wine lists, interesting ciders, a wide range of well kept real ales (perhaps even brewed by the pub itself) or bottled beers from all over the world. Perhaps there's a special appeal about it as a place to stay, with good bedrooms and obliging service. Maybe it's the building itself (from centuries-old parts of monasteries to extravagant Victorian gin-palaces), or its surroundings (lovely countryside, attractive waterside, extensive well kept garden), or what's inside it (charming furnishings, extraordinary collections of bric-a-brac).

Above all, though, what makes the good pub is its atmosphere. You should be able to feel at home there, and feel not just that you're glad you've come but that they're glad you've come. A good landlord or landlady makes a huge difference here – they can make or break a pub.

It follows from this that a great many ordinary local pubs, perfectly good in their own right, don't earn a place in the *Guide*. What makes them attractive to their regular customers (an almost clubby chumminess) may even make strangers feel rather out of place.

Another important point is that there's not necessarily any link between charm and luxury. A basic unspoilt village tavern, with hard seats and a flagstone floor, may be worth travelling miles to find, while a deluxe pub-restaurant may not be worth crossing the street for.

Those pubs featured with Main Entries do pay a fee, which helps to cover the *Guide*'s research and production costs. But no pub can gain an entry simply by paying a fee. Only pubs that have been inspected anonymously, and approved as meeting our very high standards, are invited to join.

A woman's take on beer

By **Hannah Rhodes**

" There are many things I absolutely love about beer: you can try the very best beers in the world for less than a budget bottle of wine; you can get hands-on with raw ingredients making a brew from scratch; or explore the variety of flavour, aroma and colour that can be found across the world's wildly varied beer styles. This last point leads to another favourite thing: introducing people (beer and non-beer drinkers alike) to a new beer that they absolutely love.

That was certainly the way it went for me many years ago. I didn't think I liked beer, but what I meant was: 'I don't like fizzy flavourless lager or flat watery ales'! At my first beer tasting, after trying just a red ale and an amber lager, I was hooked, as well as amazed that I'd not tried these delicious malty beers sooner. For something so simple and pleasurable, and that's such a huge part of our culture, economy and heritage, we know very little about beer as a nation, including which beers we actually like.

The great news is, things are changing. Increased consumer demand for quality and flavoursome beer, alongside the drive for innovation and experimentation on the brewing side means that the better pubs now offer a decent range of local brews, real ales and craft beers, cask, bottled and draught. They're as proud of their beer selection as they are of their food and wine, making this the perfect time to try some new beer styles and breweries.

Even if you're a seasoned beer drinker, familiarise yourself with a few different beer styles. Hoppy IPAs to malty lagers, best bitters to wheat beers, honey beers to smoked bocks – they're as different in flavour, colour and aroma as chalk and cheese. Developing familiarity across styles will enable you to identify your preferred brewer for that particular ale or lager. A good beer can be soothing, refreshing, enjoyed as an aperitif or to bring out extra flavour in a meal; hundreds of great beers do this, and can suit any mood. Most importantly, though, a beer is to be enjoyed. If you don't like a particular beer, just move on to the next! "

Hannah Rhodes spent five years at one of London's first craft breweries, where she learnt about quality beer and launched one of the country's biggest-selling craft lagers. She's since discovered urban beekeeping and realised her dream of starting her own beer brand. Hiver, the honey beer launched in September 2013, is the winner of Ocado's Britain's Next Top Supplier 2014.
Favourite pub Roebuck, 50 Great Dover Street, London, SE1.

Handpicked London pubs perfect for walkers

By Euan Ferguson

A pub crawl shouldn't be embarked upon unless under specific circumstances (rugby club social, stag do… that's it), but a walk punctuated by a good pub or two is a civilised way to spend an afternoon. In colder months, a wrapped-up hike over crunching ground is eased by the thought of a seat by the fire and a pint of something dark and reassuring; when summer comes, a waterside amble becomes more agreeable when a verdant pub garden hoves into view.

In London, the Thames provides fine opportunities for rambling and refreshment. In a quiet bit of Docklands hides the **Gun**, a gastropub with a long nautical history. The Sunday lunch is pricey but splendid, with the likes of roast middlewhite pork and sage gravy, but even as a stop-off there's plenty to recommend. A couple of changing ales and an extensive wine list, for starters, but what makes the Gun special is its position on a wide river bend complete with epic skies not usually seen in the city.

Four miles upriver in Wapping, the perambulating pub-goer is spoilt for choice. The **Prospect of Whitby** is the oldest pub on the Thames, with 500 years on the clock; inside, it's dim and atmospheric, while the terrace has views to Rotherhithe and Canary Wharf. It's a Taylor Walker house, so expect the usual Adnams and Greene King ales, but there's often a beer from smaller local breweries.

From here the Thames Path runs through central London, but it's best futher west when the river narrows, the air freshens and branches dip to the water. In bucolic Barnes is the imposing **White Hart**, which welcomes footsore walkers and lunchers who've just stepped out of their Range Rovers. Upstairs in the smart Terrace Kitchen, the definitely-not-pub-grub includes smoked egg toast with duck hearts, but traditionalists will be delighted with lancashire hotpot or fish and chips on the bar menu as well as well kept Youngs ales.

At 130 metres above London, Hampstead Heath's slopes are packed in fair weather. As are the local pubs – to avoid the masses, step away from Hampstead village to the **Southampton Arms**. Food is restricted to meaty treats like pork pies, but it's one of the capital's foremost craft beer, ale and cider bars – on the 18 taps is the cream of small independent british brewers (many within the M25), and the minimal interior manages to be warm and earnest at the same time.

Although Greenwich Park isn't the largest green space in London, its sweeping vistas attract millions of walkers every year; the proximity to the National Maritime Museum and Greenwich Market helps too. In the Old Royal Naval College, Meantime's **Old Brewery** is quite probably the best pub in the area – it stocks the full range from the pioneering producer, including the toasty chocolate porter. Some beers find their way into the inventive modern british food; terrine of oxtail and pilsner with piccalilli beats a bag of smoky bacon any day.

Euan Ferguson has been principal bars and pubs reviewer at *Time Out London* for the last four years, visiting just about every establishment in the capital during this time. He writes about drinks for various other publications, and is the author of *Drink London: The 100 Best Bars and Pubs* (Frances Lincoln, 2014).
Favourite pub Wenlock Arms, London, N1.

Whose craft beer is it anyway?

By **Andy Hamilton**

" A wag once told me that real ale is made with four ingredients and craft beer with six. Real ale is made with water, hops, malt and yeast; craft beer has two extra ingredients: Twitter and Facebook. It's a neat little joke as it helps to illustrate that sometimes there's little discernible difference between them, other than perhaps their approaches to marketing. It's no wonder so many of us are scratching our heads and wondering, just what is craft beer and where did it come from?

The first reference I've found for 'craft beer' dates from 1995, when *New York* magazine refers to it as 'a rarefied name for beer that has no cruddy adjuncts'. Since then it's become such an institution in the US that, courtesy of the Brewers Association and the IRS, it now has a legal definition. Craft beer has to come from a small brewery with an 'annual production of six million barrels of beer or less'; these 'small' breweries also have to be independent, with no more than 25 per cent of the brewery controlled by larger non-craft breweries or drinks concerns.

These craft breweries (often referred to as microbreweries) started to appear across the US in the late 1970s and '80s. They were set up by home-brewers fed up with the bland mass-produced beer that seemed to be the only stuff available, and who often turned to UK ales for influence. They grew in number and by the '90s almost every american was within drinking distance of a decent brewery.

One of the major strengths of these craft brewers is their inclusion and openness. Unlike the bigger breweries, they freely share information and brewing techniques: it's a win-win, as brewers get good very quickly and punters can rely on good beer.

American craft brewers will take influence from historic beers, just as they might from international brewing techniques. This pushes the boundaries of beer-making to its limits. Take, for example, a black imperial saison. A saison is a belgian farmhouse style characterised by the peppery, almost cidery, fruit flavour derived from the yeast. It's normally cloudy and pale, but here the black colour is influenced by the black IPAs that have been popularised recently by craft brewers; imperial means it's strong in alcohol, like the drinks brewed for the russian imperial court in the 19th century. As you can imagine, craft beers can never be called bland!

In the past few years, craft beer has travelled from the US and its influence can be felt across the beer-drinking world. This has caused a problem for some traditionalists in the UK, due to one issue: the keg. In the States, the cask is rarely used and instead they favour (or should that be, favor) the keg. Cask beers use natural carbonation while keg beers use forced carbonation, pumped into the beer from a canister when it's served. Back in the 1970s, when CAMRA launched, all the mass-produced, pasteurised, bland beer they were fighting against was being served from a keg. This distinction made it very easy to champion cask beers and vilify the keg.

There's been much debate on the cask vs keg issue, and CAMRA's stand against the keg even when it's full of amazing beer. I find CAMRA's stance odd, especially as they'll happily champion cider, which last time I checked wasn't made with hops or malt – in fact, don't they use apples? In CAMRA's defence, cask beer is considered very british and it would indeed be a shame if this method disappeared for the sake of a trend.

Petty arguments aside, british craft beer pretty much mirrors american craft beer. The people creating it are enthusiastic brewers, working out of small-barrel plants. They make highly innovative, interesting beers with care and attention. If your local brewer matches this description, then you have a craft brewer.

However, craft beer is under attack in the UK – or rather, the term is, as many of the huge breweries are getting in on the act and creating new styles that they're calling 'craft beers'. This muddies the water, especially as the UK has no legal definition for craft beer. If this trend continues, I imagine the term will have to evolve to match. Already, drinkers are just referring to 'really good beer' and there's even an organisation called CAMRGB (Let's Campaign for Really Good Beer) to reflect this trend.

Perhaps the term will change as, like a bad beer, it continues to be watered down. For now, most will agree that craft beer is a style of beer typified by innovative styles and great brewing practices, something that came over from the US and yet was influenced by the UK. If you haven't tried a pint, I'd urge you to seek out your local craft ale pub, as it's the best thing to happen to beer since Enki (the god that first created beer).

Andy Hamilton is the author of *Brewing Britain* (Bantam Press, 2013).
Favourite pub impossible to choose between the Lamplighter, Northampton and Royal Naval Volunteer, Bristol.

Charting the journey to the pub of the humble gin & tonic

By **Jack Adair-Bethan**

❝ The extraordinary history of the gin and tonic began in Holland in the 17th century. Like many of our favourite drinks, gin was born from the hand of a chemist and was originally intended as a remedy for medical problems ranging from gallstones to gout. Key ingredients were juniper, anise, caraway and coriander, and in its native land it was known as genever, a name that would evolve into gin in England.

The changes in duty after William of Orange claimed the british throne in 1688 meant that gin became very affordable. When the government decided it was a good idea to allow unlicensed gin production, and financially obstruct all imports of spirits, something rather predictable happened. The public made their own, and lots of it. This period, known as the Gin Craze, lasted the best part of 30 years. Parliament passed five acts designed to reduce the consumption of the drink; one in 1736 led to mass rioting, the final act in 1751 seemed to stem the flow of gin and by 1757 the craze had all but passed.

The Victorians made great advancements in distillation using 'continuous stills', and there was a resurgence in gin consumption. The first 'gin palaces' were built in the early 19th century: glittering cathedrals of gin, gas-lit and ever so fashionable. These licensed premises also sold ale and wine and their particular style of décor went on to influence the design we would associate with Victorian pubs. To appreciate the look, visit the Princess Louise in London's Holborn, run by the Samuel Smith Brewery. Expect ornate mirrors and dramatic tiling.

If we now turn our attention from the cities of Queen Victoria's realm to the far-flung corners of her empire, we'll see that officers in India began to mix their gin ration with sugar, water, quinine and lime. The antimalarial properties of quinine, the bark of the cinchona tree, had been discovered a century earlier. Trust the british to turn it into a cocktail. The addition of lime, as well as being a crowning feature, is thought to owe its inclusion to an attempt to stave off scurvy. The non-alcoholic element of the drink – the tonic – started out as a concoction mixed by the officers, but evolved and became an industry, with the first commercial 'indian tonic water' patented by Erasmus Bond in 1858. Schweppes followed in 1870, along with other companies offering their own recipes.

The G&T, which began life as a bitter liquid swipe at malaria, was carried in the coat-tails of the officer class to the tables of clubs and lounge bars and by the outbreak of World War I was 'the usual' for many. Imagine Major Gowen of Fawlty Towers for a fitting picture of our drinker. Gin enjoyed a prominent drinks position until the 1970s when its younger cousin vodka began to steal the show. But there's no denying it became a ubiquitous offering, albeit neglected, on pub lists. We've all experienced a bad G&T, a stained highball glass, a cube and a half of ice (if you're lucky), 25ml of house gin, a petrified slice of lemon and a grudging squirt of corn syrup tonic from a gun. This is not the way of the G&T, my good people.

There are four crucial elements to the perfect classic. First, the glass must be large and clean. Take a good-sized red wine glass and fill two-thirds with ice (ideally, this should be twice-frozen but we mustn't be too picky). Choose your gin carefully – the selection will influence your decision on the garnish. Williams Chase Elegant Gin, for example, pairs incredibly well with a slice of bramley apple as it accentuates the flavour of the gin. This principle applies in general: identify the botanicals in the gin and include them in the garnish. If in doubt, a slice of fresh lime is just the ticket. Finally, top with tonic. Pick one that complements the ingredients so far, as a delicate gin will be overpowered by a strong-flavoured tonic.

The good news is that a great number of pubs now take this historic drink very seriously. One is the **Pump House** in Bristol, which boasts a list of over 120 gins and six tonics. They offer a selection of garnishes based on the gin chosen, and also run five-course food-and-gin pairing evenings. The **Cholmondeley Arms** in Cheshire is a kindred spirit, creeping ahead with nearly 200 gins. The landlord also invites customers to 'Bring Gin to the Inn': bring a gin that's not available in the UK to the pub in exchange for the cost of the bottle plus a gift voucher.

The gin craze is back, and it's infinitely more refined. 99

Jack Adair-Bethan is a mixologist fascinated by food history. He is co-author, with Paûla Zarate and Matthew and Iain Pennington, of *The Ethicurean Cookbook*, and co-founder of the restaurant of the same name at Wrington, near Bristol. **Favourite pub** Crown, Churchill, Somerset.

Using the *Guide*

The Counties

England has been split alphabetically into counties. Each chapter starts by picking out the pubs that are currently doing best in the area, or are specially attractive for one reason or another.

The county boundaries we use are those for the administrative counties (not the old traditional counties, which were changed back in 1976). We have left the new unitary authorities within the counties that they formed part of until their creation in the most recent local government reorganisation. Metropolitan areas have been included in the counties around them – for example, Merseyside in Lancashire. And occasionally we have grouped counties together – for example, Rutland with Leicestershire, and Durham with Northumberland to make Northumbria. If in doubt, check the Contents pages.

Scotland, Wales and London have each been covered in single chapters. Pubs are listed alphabetically (except in London, which is split into Central, East, North, South and West), under the name of the town or village where they are. If the village is so small that you might not find it on a road map, we've listed it under the name of the nearest sizeable village or town. The maps use the same town and village names, and additionally include a few big cities that don't have any listed pubs – for orientation.

We list pubs in their true county, not their postal county. Just once or twice, when the village itself is in one county but the pub is just over the border in the next-door county, we have used the village county, not the pub one.

Stars ★

Really outstanding pubs are awarded a star, and in one case two: these are the aristocrats among pubs. The stars do NOT signify extra luxury or specially good food – in fact, some of the pubs that appeal most distinctively and strongly are decidedly basic in terms of food and surroundings. The detailed description of each pub shows what its particular appeal is, and this is what the stars refer to.

Food Award 🏵️

Pubs where food is really outstanding.

Stay Award 🛏️

Pubs that are good as places to stay at (obviously, you can't expect the same level of luxury at £60 a head as you'd get for £100 a head). Pubs with bedrooms are marked on the maps as a square.

Wine Award ♀

Pubs with particularly enjoyable wines by the glass – often a good range.

Beer Award ◖

Pubs where the quality of the beer is quite exceptional, or pubs that keep a particularly interesting range of beers in good condition.

Value Award £

This distinguishes pubs that offer really good value food. In all the award-winning pubs, you will find an interesting choice at under £10.

Recommenders

At the end of each Main Entry we include the names of readers who have recently recommended that pub (unless they've asked us not to use their names).

Important note: the description of the pub and the comments on it are our own and not the recommenders'.

Also Worth a Visit

The Also Worth a Visit section at the end of each county chapter includes brief descriptions of pubs that have been recommended by readers in the year before the *Guide* goes to print and that we feel are worthy of inclusion – many of them, indeed, as good in their way as the featured pubs (these are picked out by a star). We have inspected and approved nearly half of these ourselves. All the others are recommended by our reader-reporters. The descriptions of these other pubs, written by us, usually reflect the experience of several different people.

The pubs in Also Worth a Visit may become featured entries in future editions. So do please help us know which are hot prospects for our inspection programme (and which are not!), by reporting on them. There are report forms at the back of the *Guide*, or you can email us at feedback@goodguides.com, or write to us at

The Good Pub Guide, FREEPOST RTJR-ZCYZ-RJZT,
Perrymans Lane, Etchingham TN19 7DN.

Locating Pubs

To help readers who use digital mapping systems we include a postcode for every pub. Pubs outside London are given a British Grid four-figure map reference. Where a pub is exceptionally difficult to find, we include a six-figure reference in the directions. The Map number (Main Entries only) refers to the maps at the back of the *Guide*.

Motorway Pubs

If a pub is within four or five miles of a motorway junction we give special directions for finding it from the motorway. The Special

Interest Lists at the end of the book include a list of these pubs, motorway by motorway.

Prices and Other Factual Details

The *Guide* went to press during the summer of 2014, after each pub was sent a checking sheet to get up-to-date food, drink and bedroom prices and other factual information. By the summer of 2015 prices are bound to have increased, but if you find a significantly different price please let us know.

Breweries or independent chains to which pubs are 'tied' are named at the beginning of the italic-print rubric after each Main Entry. That generally means the pub has to get most if not all its drinks from that brewery or chain. If the brewery is not an independent one but just part of a combine, we name the combine in brackets. When the pub is tied, we have spelled out whether the landlord is a tenant, has the pub on a lease, or is a manager. Tenants and leaseholders of breweries generally have considerably greater freedom to do things their own way, and in particular are allowed to buy drinks including a beer from sources other than their tied brewery.

Free houses are pubs not tied to a brewery. In theory they can shop around, but in practice many free houses have loans from the big brewers, on terms that bind them to sell those breweries' beers. So don't be too surprised to find that so-called free houses may be stocking a range of beers restricted to those from a single brewery.

Real ale is used by us to mean beer that has been maturing naturally in its cask. We do not count as real ale beer that has been pasteurised or filtered to remove its natural yeasts.

Other drinks. We've also looked out particularly for pubs doing enterprising non-alcoholic drinks (including good tea or coffee), interesting spirits (especially malt whiskies), country wines, freshly squeezed juices and good farm ciders.

Bar food usually refers to what is sold in the bar; we do not describe menus that are restricted to a separate restaurant. If we know that a pub serves sandwiches, we say so – if you don't see them mentioned, assume you can't get them. Food listed is an example of the sort of thing you'd find served in the bar on a normal day.

Children. If we don't mention children at all, assume that they are not welcome. All but one or two pubs allow children in their garden if they have one. 'Children welcome' means the pub has told us that it lets them in with no special restrictions. In other cases, we report exactly what arrangements pubs say they make for children. However, we have to note that in readers' experience some pubs make restrictions that they haven't told us about (children only if eating, for example). If you come across this, please let us know, so that we can clarify with the pub concerned for the next edition. The absence of any reference to children in an Also Worth a Visit entry means we don't know either way. Children's Certificates exist, but in practice children are allowed into some part of most pubs in this *Guide* (there is no legal restriction on the movement of children over 14 in any pub). Children under 16 cannot have alcoholic drinks. Children aged 16 and 17 can drink beer, wine or cider with a meal if it is bought by an adult and they are accompanied by an adult.

Dogs. If Main Entry licensees have told us they allow dogs in their pub or bedrooms, we say so; absence of reference to dogs means dogs are not welcome. If you take a dog into a pub you should have it on a lead. We also mention in the text any pub dogs or cats (or indeed other animals) that we've come across ourselves, or heard about from readers.

Parking. If we know there is a problem with parking, we say so, otherwise assume there is a car park.

Credit cards. We say if a pub does not accept them; some that do may put a surcharge on credit card bills, to cover charges made by the card company. We also say if we know that a pub tries to retain customers' credit cards while they are eating. This is a reprehensible practice, and if a pub tries it on you, please tell them that all banks and card companies frown on it – and please let us know the pub's name, so that we can warn readers in future editions.

Telephone numbers are given for all pubs that are not ex-directory.

Opening hours are for summer; we say if we know of differences in winter, or on particular days of the week. In the country, many pubs may open rather later and close earlier than their details show (if you come across this, please let us know – with details). Pubs are allowed to stay open all day if licensed to do so. However, outside cities many pubs in England and Wales close during the afternoon. We'd be grateful to hear of any differences from the hours we quote.

Bedroom prices normally include full english breakfasts (if available), VAT and any automatic service charge. If we give just one price, it is the total price for two people sharing a double or twin-bedded room for one night. Prices before the '/' are for single occupancy, prices after it for double.

Meal times. Bar food is commonly served from 12-2 and 7-9, at least from Monday to Saturday. We spell out the times if they are significantly different. To be sure of a table it's best to book before you go. Sunday hours vary considerably from pub to pub, so it's advisable to check before you leave.

Disabled access. Deliberately, we do not ask pubs about this, as their answers would not give a reliable picture of how easy access is. Instead, we depend on readers' direct experience. If you are able to give us help about this, we would be particularly grateful for your reports.

Electronic Route Planning

Microsoft® AutoRoute™, a route-finding software package, shows the location of pubs in *The Good Pub Guide* on detailed maps and includes our text entries for those pubs on screen.

Our website (www.thegoodpubguide.co.uk) includes every pub in the *Guide*.

iPhone and iPad

You can search and read *The Good Pub Guide* both on our website (www.thegoodpubguide.co.uk) and as a download on your smartphone or iPad. They contain all the pubs in this *Guide*. You can also write reviews and let us know about undiscovered gems.

There are apps available for iPhone and iPad – and the *Guide* can be downloaded as an eBook to your reader.

Changes during the year – please tell us

Changes are inevitable during the course of the year. Landlords change, and so do their policies. We hope that you will find everything just as we say, but if not please let us know. You can find out how by referring to the Report Forms section at the end of the *Guide*.

Editors' acknowledgements

We could not produce the *Guide* without the huge help we have from the many thousands of readers who report to us on the pubs they visit, often in great detail. Particular thanks to these greatly valued correspondents: George Atkinson, Richard Tilbrook, Phil and Jane Hodson, Chris and Angela Buckell, Tony and Wendy Hobden, Roger and Donna Huggins, Paul Humphreys, Michael Doswell, Gordon and Margaret Ormondroyd, John Wooll, Clive and Fran Dutson, Brian and Anna Marsden, Michael and Jenny Back, Gerry and Rosemary Dobson, Jeremy King, Ann and Colin Hunt, Dr Kevan Tucker, R K Phillips, Val and Alan Green, Steve Whalley, Michael Butler, John Pritchard, Tracey and Stephen Groves, Taff Thomas, David Jackman, Sara Fulton, Roger Baker, Mrs Margo Finlay, Jörg Kasprowski, Simon and Mandy King, Ian Phillips, Liz Bell, Susan and John Douglas, Peter Meister, Phil Bryant, J F M and M West, Brian Glozier, Ian Herdman, Derek and Sylvia Stephenson, Dave Braisted, Dr W I C Clark, Martin and Pauline Jennings, Comus and Sarah Elliott, Ross Balaam, Pat and Tony Martin, Richard Kennell, B and M Kendall, Edward Mirzoeff, John and Sylvia Harrop, Tom and Jill Jones, Tony and Jill Radnor, Sheila Topham, Mike and Mary Carter, R T and J C Moggridge, Nigel Espley, Giles and Annie Francis, John Evans, Bob and Margaret Holder, John Beeken, Guy Vowles, Di and Mike Gillam, Mr and Mrs P R Thomas, Dr D J and Mrs S C Walker, Eddie Edwards, Robert W Buckle, John and Eleanor Holdsworth, Dennis Jones, M G Hart, Simon Collett-Jones, Iain Clark, Nigel Espley, Ray and Winifred Halliday, Dennis and Doreen Haward, Roy Hoing, Mike and Eleanor Anderson, R L Borthwick, R C Vincent, David Hunt, Richard Stanfield, Neil and Angela Huxter, Mike and Wena Stevenson, R Anderson, Tony Tollitt, Christian Mole, Lynda and Trevor Smith, Tim Brogan, Adrian Stone, Rich Frith, David M Smith, Tina and David Woods-Taylor, David Fowler, Pat and Stewart Gordon, Neil and Anita Christopher, Steve and Claire Harvey, Theocsbrian, PLC, John T Ames, Hugh Roberts, Dr J Barrie Jones, Patrick and Daphne Darley, Alan Thwaite, GSB, Ron Corbett, Jill and Julian Tasker, Alex and Hazel Evans, Bruce Jamieson, Katharine Cowherd, Stanley and Annie Matthews, David Jackson, Richard and Patricia Jefferson, Brian and Janet Ainscough, Hunter and Christine Wright, S Holder, P and J Shapley, P Dawn, Steve and Liz Tilley, Howard and Margaret Buchanan, the Dutchman, Revd R P Tickle, Adrian Johnson, Colin McKerrow, David and Julie Glover, J R Wildon, Philip and Susan Philcox, Barry Collett, Malcolm, Robert Wivell, Pete Flower, Lois Dyer, C and R Bromage, Glenwys and Alan Lawrence, Nigel and Jean Eames, Peter Grant, Geoffrey Kemp, Wendda and John Knapp, Richard Ecclestone, Nick Lawless, Michael Mellers, John Boothman, Nigel and Sue Foster, Gene and Tony Freemantle, Ryta Lyndley, Gerry Price, J A Snell, Conrad Freezer, Robert and Sarah Milne, Kay and Alistair Butler, Martin and Karen Wake, W K Wood, Mike and Jayne Bastin, Phil and Jane Villiers, Michael Sargent

Thanks, too, to the ladies at The Book Service for their cheerful dedication: Maria Tegerdine, Michele Csaforda, Kerry Rusch and Carol Bryant. And particularly to John Holliday of Trade Wind Technology, who built and looks after our all-important database.

Alisdair Aird and Fiona Stapley

ENGLAND

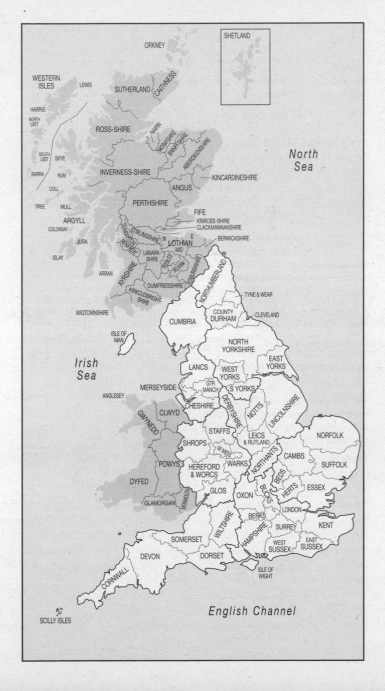

SHETLAND

ORKNEY

WESTERN ISLES

LEWIS

HARRIS

NORTH UIST

SUTHERLAND

CAITHNESS

ROSS-SHIRE

NAIRN

MORAYSHIRE

BANFFSHIRE

ABERDEENSHIRE

SOUTH UIST

SKYE

INVERNESS-SHIRE

KINCARDINESHIRE

North Sea

BARRA

RUM

COLL

ANGUS

TIREE

MULL

PERTHSHIRE

FIFE

ARGYLL

COLONSAY

JURA

STIRLINGSHIRE

W

KINROSS-SHIRE

CLACKMANNANSHIRE

ISLAY

DUNBARTON

RENFREW

LANARK-SHIRE

E

LOTHIAN

MID

BERWICKSHIRE

AYRSHIRE

PEEBLES

SELKIRK

ROXBURGHSHIRE

ARRAN

DUMFRIESSHIRE

NORTHUMBERLAND

TYNE & WEAR

KIRKCUDBRIGHT-SHIRE

WIGTOWNSHIRE

CUMBRIA

COUNTY DURHAM

CLEVELAND

ISLE OF MAN

NORTH YORKSHIRE

Irish Sea

LANCS

WEST YORKS

EAST YORKS

MERSEYSIDE

GTR MANCH.

S YORKS

ANGLESEY

CHESHIRE

DERBYSHIRE

NOTTS

LINCOLNSHIRE

GWYNEDD

CLWYD

STAFFS

NORFOLK

LEICS & RUTLAND

POWYS

SHROPS

W.MIDS

WARKS

NORTHANTS

CAMBS

SUFFOLK

DYFED

HEREFORD & WORCS

BEDS

HERTS

ESSEX

MONMOUTH

GLOS

OXON

BUCKS

GLAMORGAN

LONDON

BERKS

SURREY

KENT

WILTSHIRE

HAMPSHIRE

WEST SUSSEX

EAST SUSSEX

SOMERSET

DORSET

DEVON

SUSSEX

ISLE OF WIGHT

CORNWALL

SCILLY ISLES

English Channel

Bedfordshire

KEY	★ Star Pub	🍽️ Top Quality Food	🍺 Great Beer
	♇ Good Wines	£ Bargain Meals	🛏️ Good Bedrooms	🍴 Serves Food

AMPTHILL   TL0338   Map 5
Prince of Wales
Bedford Street (B540 N from central crossroads); MK45 2NB

Civilised with contemporary décor and up-to-date food; bedrooms

Once inside this traditional-looking red-brick town house, the stylish and comfortable interior comes as a pleasant surprise. Set on two levels, it's more of an open-plan bar-brasserie than a straightforward pub, with good lighting and modern prints on mainly cream walls (dark green and maroon accents at either end). The slightly sunken flagstoned area with a log fire in the exposed brick fireplace leads to a partly ply-panelled dining room with dark leather dining chairs set around a mixed batch of sturdy tables, and there are plenty of church candles and big leather deco-style armchairs and sofas at low tables on wood-strip flooring; background music. Wells & Youngs Bombardier and Eagle on handpump, plenty of wines by the glass and good coffee. The nicely planted two-level lawn has picnic-sets, with more on a terrace by the car park.

🍴 The thoughtful choice of good food includes sandwiches, baguettes and wraps, coconut tempura prawns with sweet chilli, sausages of the week with red onion gravy, vegetarian quiche and pasta dish, Jack Daniels-marinated barbecue ribs with southern fries, ham-wrapped chicken with a tomato, olive and basil sauce, bass fillets with prawns, lemongrass and mango salsa, and puddings such as banoffi pie and crème brûlée of the day; Thursday is steak night. *Benchmark main dish: fillet steak wellington £24.00. Two-course evening meal £18.00.*

Wells & Youngs ~ Lease Richard and Neia Heathorn ~ Real ale ~ (01525) 840504 ~ Open 11-11 (midnight Fri, Sat); 12-5 (8 in summer) Sun ~ Bar food 12-2.30 (3 weekends), 6.30-9 (9.30 Fri, Sat); not Sun evening ~ Restaurant ~ Children welcome ~ Dogs allowed in bar and bedrooms ~ Wi-fi ~ Bedrooms: £55/£70 ~ www.princeofwales-ampthill.com
Recommended by Ruth May, Pip White

BEDFORD   TL0550   Map 5
Park ♇
Corner of Kimbolton Road (B660) and Park Avenue, out past Bedford Hospital; MK40 2PA

Civilised and individual oasis – a great asset for the city

Open and offering food all day, this relaxing pub appeals to a wide group of customers. You can choose your mood, from the more or less conventional bar with its heavy beams, panelled dado and leaded lights in big windows, or the light and airy conservatory sitting room with easy chairs well spread on a carpet, or the extensive series of softly lit rambling dining areas, carpeted or flagstoned. The décor is appealing throughout – all sorts of thoughtful touches without being too obtrusive. Neat efficient staff serve Wells & Youngs Eagle, Bombardier and Bitter with a guest such as Holts Two Hoots from handpump, inventive bar nibbles and an excellent choice of wines by the glass; well reproduced background music. The sheltered brick-paved terrace has good timber furniture, some under dark red canopies, and attractive shrub plantings.

With everything made in-house and using home-grown herbs, the imaginative food includes red onion, chilli and fennel tarte tatin with pulled lamb and pomegranate dressing, sharing platters, a home-made pasta dish and a risotto of the day, blue cheese and sweet potato wellington with cheese sauce, guinea fowl breast with celeriac and apple rösti, pork fillet with honey, sesame seeds and a carrot and ginger sauce, and puddings such as apple and rhubarb cobbler and bubble gum-flavoured panna cotta. *Benchmark main dish: steak and coriander burger with swiss cheese, bacon and chips £11.75. Two-course evening meal £20.00.*

Front Line Inns ~ Lease Alan Smith ~ Real ale ~ (01234) 273929 ~ Open 11.30-11.30 (midnight Fri, Sat); 12-11 Sun ~ Bar food 12-3, 6.30-10; 12-10 Sat; 12-8 Sun ~ Restaurant ~ Children in one bar and restaurant ~ Dogs allowed in bar ~ Wi-fi ~ Comedy Sun evening every two months ~ www.theparkbedford.co.uk
Recommended by Emma Scofield, Pip White

FLITTON TL0535 Map 5
White Hart ♀
Village signed off A507; MK45 5EJ

Simply furnished and friendly village pub with bar and dining area, real ales, interesting food, and seats in the garden

The rewarding food in this friendly pub continues to draw in plenty of cheerful customers. The minimally decorated front bar has dark leather tub chairs around low tables, contemporary leather and chrome seats at pedestal tables, and Farrow & Ball painted walls. B&T Dragon Slayer and a guest such as Buntingford Twitchell on handpump and 20 wines – as well as champagne and prosecco – by the glass; TV. Steps lead down to a good-sized, simply furnished back dining area with red plush seats and banquettes on dark wooden floorboards. The nice garden has neat shrub borders, and teak seats and tables on a terrace shaded by cedars and weeping willows. This is a quiet village and the pub is between the 13th-c church and Flitton Moor.

The often enterprising food includes their famous steaks, as well as toasted ciabatta with toppings, fig, mozzarella and parma ham, whitebait with gremolata mayonnaise, ham and free-range eggs, barbecued pork belly with sweetcorn purée and wholegrain mustard sauce, lamb shank with sweet potato and root vegetable mash, and puddings such as rum and raisin crème brûlée and lemon, lime and ginger posset; they also offer a two- and three-course set menu (not Monday and Sunday or Friday and Saturday evenings). *Benchmark main dish: aberdeen angus steak with home-made chips £15.95. Two-course evening meal £20.00.*

Free house ~ Licensees Phil and Clare Hale ~ Real ale ~ (01525) 862022 ~ Open 12-2.30, 6-midnight; 12-3, 6-1am Sat; 12-5 Sun; closed Sun evening, Mon ~ Bar food 12-2 (2.30 Sun), 6.30-9 (9.30 Fri, Sat) ~ Restaurant ~ Children welcome ~ Dogs allowed in bar ~ Wi-fi ~ www.whitehartflitton.co.uk *Recommended by Richard and Liz Thorne*

IRELAND
Black Horse ⚫ 🍷
Off A600 Shefford–Bedford; SG17 5QL

Bedfordshire Dining Pub of the Year

Contemporary décor in old building, impressive food, good wine list and lovely garden with attractive terraces; bedrooms

Of course, it's the first class, imaginative food that most customers are here to enjoy, but they do serve Adnams Bitter, Fullers London Pride and Sharps Doom Bar on handpump, 24 wines by the glass, a dozen malt whiskies, Weston's cider and good coffee from the long green-slate bar counter. It's a 17th-c building and the low ceilings, beams, timbering and inglenook fireplaces complement the contemporary furnishings rather well. There are leather armchairs and comfortable wall seating, a mix of elegant wooden and high-backed leather dining chairs around attractive tables on polished oak boards or sandstone flooring, original artwork, and fresh flowers on each table. French windows open on to various terraces with individual furnishings and pretty flowering pots and beds. The refurbished, well equipped bedrooms are across the courtyard in a separate building; continental breakfasts are included. The Birch at Woburn is under the same ownership.

 As well as lunchtime ciabattas, the enticing food includes lemon, pea and basil risotto, sharing platter of nibbles, chickpea and cumin flatcake with lemon- and honey-roasted vegetables, free-range chicken with thyme boulangère, chestnut-stuffed onions and porcini gravy, gressingham duck breast with potato and pistachio rösti, smoked pancetta and orange caramel jus, a lamb dish of the day, and puddings such as salted toffee tart with crème fraîche sorbet and chocolate and pecan nut pudding with chocolate sauce. *Benchmark main dish: pork belly, ham terrine, black pudding, crackling, apple sauce and pea purée £16.95. Two-course evening meal £22.00.*

Free house ~ Licensee Darren Campbell ~ Real ale ~ (01462) 811398 ~ Open 11.30-3.30, 6-11; 12-6 Sun; closed Sun evening ~ Bar food 12-2.30, 6.30-10; 12-5 Sun ~ Restaurant ~ Children welcome ~ Wi-fi ~ Bedrooms: /£75 ~ www.blackhorseireland.com
Recommended by Andy Lickfold, Edward Heaney, Mark Barker, Martin and Clare Warne

OAKLEY
Bedford Arms 🍷
High Street; MK43 7RH

Updated 16th-c village inn with several individual rooms, real ales and wines by the glass, fish and other popular food in two dining rooms and seats in the garden

There's plenty of space for both drinking and dining in this updated 16th-c village pub. The contemporary décor is different in each of the interconnected rooms. The pubbiest part, with a baby grand piano, has straightforward wooden furniture on bare boards, flower prints on the walls, daily papers, a decorative woodburning stove with a flat-screen TV above it, and Courage Directors, Wells & Youngs Eagle IPA and Special and a guest beer on handpump and around two dozen wines and champagne by the glass; darts. The four cosy, individually decorated rooms leading off the main bar are the nicest places for a drink and chat. One has a large circular pine table (just right for a private party), the second has farmhouse chairs and a cushioned pew beside a small fireplace, another has ladder-back chairs and shiny tables on ancient floor tiles, and the last is very much

Victorian in style. The stone-floored dining rooms have tartan-covered seating or wicker chairs and the light, airy conservatory overlooks the pretty garden where there are seats for warm-weather meals.

🍴 They specialise in fresh fish, with dishes such as tiger prawns in thai broth, white crabmeat and smoked salmon tagliatelle and fresh, daily changing specials. Also, lunchtime sandwiches, home-cooked ham and eggs, burger with bacon, cheese and chips, chicken caesar salad, a pie of the day, steak, kidney and oyster pudding, lamb rump with mint hollandaise, and puddings. *Benchmark main dish: home-made pies such as lamb and rosemary £11.95. Two-course evening meal £21.00.*

Wells & Youngs ~ Tenants Tim and Yvonne Walker ~ Real ale ~ (01234) 822280 ~ Open 12-11 (10.30 Sun) ~ Bar food 12-2.30, 6-9.30; 12-5 Sun ~ Restaurant ~ Children welcome ~ Dogs allowed in bar ~ Wi-fi ~ www.bedfordarmsoakley.co.uk
Recommended by Richard and Karen Clark, Harvey Brown

RAVENSDEN
Horse & Jockey 🏮○🍷

TL0754 Map 5

Village signed off B660 N of Bedford; pub at Church End, off village road; MK44 2RR

Contemporary comfort, with enjoyable food and good range of drinks

All are welcomed at this enjoyable, carefully run pub and there's a good mix of customers. The refurbished interior is pleasantly modern with a quiet colour scheme of olive greys and dark red, careful lighting, modern leather easy chairs in the bar, a wall of meticulously arranged old local photographs, a rack of recent *Country Life* issues and daily papers; background music and board games. Service is charming, and there are some 30 wines by the glass and Adnams Bitter, Sharps Doom Bar and a couple of guest beers on handpump. The bright dining room has nice chunky tables and high-backed seats, well lit prints and a contemporary etched glass screen; it overlooks a sheltered terrace with smart modern tables and chairs under cocktail parasols, a few picnic-sets on the grass beside. The handsome medieval church with churchyard is further off.

⭐ The highly rewarding food includes lunchtime open sandwiches, duck terrine with home-made fruit chutney, fresh crab with sugar-cured lemon and pea shoots, aubergine parmigiana, steak burger with relish and chips, coq au vin, catalan fish stew, venison pie, and puddings such as pear tarte tatin or chocolate mousse with sponge and orange jelly. *Benchmark main dish: smoked haddock florentine with fries £13.50. Two-course evening meal £20.50.*

Free house ~ Licensees Darron and Sarah Smith ~ Real ale ~ (01234) 772319 ~ Open 12-3, 6-11; 12-midnight Sat; 12-10 Sun ~ Bar food 12-2, 6-9; 12-6 Sun ~ Restaurant ~ Children welcome ~ Dogs allowed in bar ~ Wi-fi ~ www.horseandjockey.info
Recommended by Michael Sargent

SOULDROP
Bedford Arms 🍺 £

SP9861 Map 4

Village signposted off A6 Rushden–Bedford; High Street; MK44 1EY

Proper country tavern with good value homely food in cottagey dining area

Our readers enjoy their visits to this honest pub with its traditional décor – the games room was once a brew house – easy-going atmosphere and lively, welcoming licensees. As well as bar chairs against the counter (liked by chatty regulars), there are a few more seats in the small low-beamed room, including a table in a snug, low-ceilinged alcove. Black Sheep, Copper Kettle Cornucopia (brewed just a mile away), Greene King IPA, Hopping Mad Brainstorm and Phipps Red Star on handpump, several wines by the glass and local farm cider from Evershed's. The cottagey dining area has more low beams (one route through is potentially a real head-cracker) and a central fireplace – and, like the rest of the pub, broad floorboards, shelves of china, and original artwork (for sale). In the evenings and at weekends, the roomy, mansard-ceilinged public area comes to life, with table skittles, darts, games machine, juke box, shove-ha'penny, TV and board games; it has a big inglenook fireplace, and opens on to a neat garden with a pétanque court.

The generously served food includes sandwiches, baguettes and ciabattas, home-made pâté, prawn cocktail, cottage pie, vegetable lasagne, liver, bacon and onions, sausage and mash with onion gravy, cheese-stuffed chicken wrapped in bacon, and puddings. *Benchmark main dish: steak in ale pie £10.25. Two-course evening meal £14.25.*

Free house ~ Licensees Fred and Caroline Rich ~ Real ale ~ (01234) 781384 ~ Open 12-3, 6-11; 12-midnight Fri, Sat; 12-10 Sun; closed Mon except bank holidays ~ Bar food 12-2, 6.30-9; 12-4 Sun ~ Restaurant ~ Children welcome ~ Dogs allowed in bar ~ Wi-fi
Recommended by Edward Heaney, George Atkinson

STEPPINGLEY   TL0135   Map 5
French Horn ♀
Off A507 just N of Flitwick; Church End; MK45 5AU

Comfortable pub with modern touches to the thoughtfully prepared food

The newish landlord in this attractive old pub has no plans to radically change much in the characterful and interconnected bar rooms. The eclectic mix of chesterfield sofas and leather armchairs, cushioned antique dining chairs and other new and old furniture works well with the stippled beams, standing posts and wall timbers – there are even two armchairs tucked into an old brick inglenook (the other houses a woodburning stove). Some nice pews, lamps, cushions, paintings on the wonky walls and rugs on flagstones or floorboards keep it homely and welcoming. Greene King IPA and Abbot on handpump, 11 wines by the glass from a very good list and an interesting selection of malt whiskies; background music and TV. The dining room is softly lit and elegantly furnished.

The inviting food includes lunchtime sandwiches, scallops with crispy bacon and puréed cauliflower, devilled kidneys on fried bread, butternut squash and sage risotto, chicken kiev with coleslaw, smoked haddock with bubble and squeak and a poached egg, a pie of the day, and puddings such as chocolate fondant and golden syrup sponge pudding. *Benchmark main dish: burger with cheese, chips and harissa mayonnaise £9.95. Two-course evening meal £18.00.*

Greene King ~ Lease Richard Hargroves ~ Real ale ~ (01525) 720122 ~ Open 12-midnight (1am Sat, 11 Sun) ~ Bar food 12-3, 6-10; 12-10 Sat; 12-9 Sun ~ Restaurant ~ Children welcome ~ Dogs allowed in bar ~ Wi-fi ~ www.frenchhornpub.co.uk
Recommended by Caroline Prescott, Piotr Chodzko-Zajko

> 'Children welcome' means the pub says it lets children inside without any special restriction. If it allows them in, but to restricted areas such as an eating area or family room, we specify this. Some pubs may impose an evening time limit. We do not mention limits after 9pm as we assume children are home by then.

SUTTON
TL2247 Map 5

John o'Gaunt ⭐ ♀
Off B1040 Biggleswade–Potton; SG19 2NE

Bustling friendly pub run by first class licensees, with smashing food, attractive bars and seats in garden

The food here, cooked by the landlord, is extremely highly thought of, but this isn't a straightforward dining place. It's a proper pub with bar skittles and pétanque teams, real ale and a friendly, welcoming atmosphere. There are beams and timbering, red-painted or pretty wallpapered walls, paintings by local artists (for sale), and fresh flowers and house plants. The bar has plush, striped, cushioned wall seats and stools, and leather tub chairs around pubby tables, tiles and carpeting, and stools against the counter where they keep Adnams Ghost Ship and Woodfordes Wherry on handpump and ten wines by the glass; background music. The dining rooms have all sorts of chairs, from elegant high-backed and black cushioned, dark leather or carved ones around a medley of tables on bare boards. You can sit outside in the well sheltered garden. To reach the pub you have to drive through a shallow ford by a humpbacked 14th-c packhorse bridge.

⭐ Using local produce with own-made bread and ice-cream, the appealing food includes open sandwiches, tempura king prawns and squid with soy sauce, chilli and lime, chicken liver parfait with onion marmalade, wild mushroom risotto with white truffle oil, rump burger with cheddar, tomato chutney and chips, daily fresh fish dishes, pheasant with smoked bacon, mushrooms and roasted garlic mash, and puddings such as vanilla crème brûlée and caramelised lemon tart. *Benchmark main dish: home-made pie of the day £12.30. Two-course evening meal £21.00.*

Free house ~ Licensees Jago and Jane Hurt ~ Real ale ~ (01767) 260377 ~ Open 12-3, 6-11; 12-6 Sun; closed Sun evening, all day Mon except bank holidays ~ Bar food 12-2, 6.30-9; 12-3 Sun; not Sun evening ~ Children welcome ~ Dogs allowed in bar ~ Wi-fi ~ www.johnogauntsutton.co.uk *Recommended by D C Poulton, Isobel Mackinlay*

WOBURN
SP9433 Map 4

Birch ⭐ ♀
3.5 miles from M1 junction 13; follow Woburn signs via A507 and A4012, right in village then A5130 (Newport Road); MK17 9HX

Well run dining establishment with focus on imaginative food, good wines and attentive service

Thoughtfully and carefully run for both regulars and visitors, this edge-of-town pub continues to get deservedly high praise from our readers. There are quite a few individually and elegantly furnished linked rooms with contemporary décor and paintwork. The upper dining area has high-backed leather or wooden dining chairs around tables on stripped and polished floorboards, while the lower part is in a light and airy conservatory with a pitched glazed roof, ceramic floor tiles, light coloured furnishings and original artwork and fresh flowers. The bustling bar is similarly furnished and has a few high bar stools against the sleek, smart counter where they serve Adnams Bitter and Sharps Doom Bar on handpump, 15 good wines by the glass, a dozen malt whiskies and quite a few teas and coffees; unobtrusive background music. There are tables out on a sheltered deck, and in summer the front of the pub has masses of flowering hanging baskets and tubs. The Black Horse at Ireland is under the same ownership.

⭐ Using local seasonal produce, the tempting food includes meat and fish cooked to your specification on an open griddle, plus pork and liver terrine with glazed apple and shallot salad, roasted squash risotto with lemon mascarpone, a daily changing vegetarian platter, free-range chicken with confit leg and tarragon and truffle jus, local venison with honey-glazed pear, braised chicory, creamed blue cheese and redcurrant vinaigrette, and puddings such as blackberry soufflé and apple ice-cream and white chocolate brûlée. *Benchmark main dish: griddled bass fillets with warm shellfish salsa £16.95. Two-course evening meal £23.00.*

Free house ~ Licensee Mark Campbell ~ Real ale ~ (01525) 290295 ~ Open 11.30-3.30, 6-11; 12-6 Sun; closed Sun evening ~ Bar food 12-2.30, 6.30-10; 12-5 Sun ~ Restaurant ~ Children welcome ~ www.birchwoburn.com *Recommended by Roy Hoing, Michael Sargent, Barbara and Peter Kelly, Richard Kennell*

Also Worth a Visit in Bedfordshire

Besides the fully inspected pubs, you might like to try these pubs that have been recommended to us and described by readers. Do tell us what you think of them: feedback@goodguides.com

---

AMPTHILL TL0337
Albion (01525) 634857
Dunstable Street; MK45 2JT Drinkers' pub with up to 12 well kept real ales including local B&T and Everards, three ciders and a perry, friendly knowledgeable staff, no food apart from lunchtime rolls, traditional music night second Sat of month; dogs welcome, beer garden, open all day. *(G Holmes)*

BEDFORD TL0549
Embankment (01234) 261332
The Embankment; MK40 3PD Neatly kept mock-Tudor hotel adjacent to the river, airy L-shaped front bar with mix of modern furniture on wood floor, pretty blue-tiled fireplace, Wells & Youngs ales and several wines by the glass, good choice of food from sandwiches and deli boards up, cheerful helpful service, restaurant; background music; children welcome, seats out on front terrace, 20 bedrooms (best ones with river views), good breakfast, open all day. *(Harvey Brown, George Atkinson)*

BIDDENHAM TL0249
Three Tuns (01234) 354847
Off A428; MK40 4BD Refurbished part-thatched village dining pub with new restaurant extension, good varied menu (not Sun evening, Mon) from traditional favourites to more ambitious modern cooking, lunchtime and evening set menus (Tues-Fri), extensive wine list, well kept Greene King ales, fast friendly service; spacious garden with picnic-sets, more contemporary furniture on terrace and decked area, open all day. *(Michael Sargent, Susan and Jeremy Arthern)*

BLETSOE TL0157
⭐**Falcon** (01234) 781222
Rushden Road (A6 N of Bedford); MK44 1QN Refurbished 17th-c building with comfortable opened-up bar, low beams and joists, seating from cushioned wall/window seats to high-backed settles, woodburner in double-sided fireplace, snug with sofas and old pews, panelled dining room, enjoyable fairly traditional food plus some interesting specials, Wells & Youngs and a guest ale, decent choice of wines by the glass and good coffee, daily papers; unobtrusive background music; decked and paved terrace in lovely big garden down to the Ouse, open all day. *(Edward Heaney)*

BOLNHURST TL0858
⭐**Plough** (01234) 376274
Kimbolton Road; MK44 2EX Stylish conversion of ancient building with a thriving atmosphere, charming staff and top-notch food (must book Sat night), real ales such as Adnams and Hopping Mad, good carefully annotated wine list (including organic vintages) with over a dozen by the glass, home-made summer lemonade and tomato juice, airy dining extension, log fires; children welcome, dogs in bar, attractive tree-shaded garden with decking overlooking pond, remains of old moat, closed Sun evening, Mon and for 2 weeks after Christmas. *(Edward Heaney, Ryta Lyndley, Michael Sargent and others)*

BROOM TL1743
Cock (01767) 314411
High Street; from A1 opposite Biggleswade turn-off, follow Old Warden 3, Aerodrome 2 signpost, first left signed Broom; SG18 9NA Unspoilt village-green pub under newish ownership (no longer tied to Greene King); four changing ales tapped

from casks by cellar steps off central corridor (no counter), Potton Press cider, traditional food such as steak and kidney pudding, original latch doors linking one quietly cosy little room to the next (four in all), low ceilings, stripped panelling, farmhouse tables and chairs on old tiles, open fires, bar skittles; children and dogs welcome, picnic-sets on terrace by back lawn, open all day. *(Anon)*

CARDINGTON   TL0847
★ **Kings Arms** (01234) 838533
The Green; off A603 E of Bedford; MK44 3SP Much-extended Mitchells & Butlers village dining pub with interestingly furnished linked rooms; easy-going bar with cushioned wall seats, tub chairs around trestle-style or copper-topped tables, driftwood mirrors, Adnams, Everards and Purity from rustic counter, dining room with church chairs and white-painted tables on coir, sepia photographs of airships, good choice of food from light lunches up, set menu too, good tea and coffee, more formal room with Victorian furniture, portraits and unusual log-end wallpaper, comfortable end room with leather banquettes and big log fire; background music, small TV; well behaved children and dogs welcome, disabled facilities, modern seats on terrace, picnic-sets under willows to one side. *(Mark Barker)*

CLOPHILL   TL0837
★ **Flying Horse** (01525) 860293
The Green; MK45 4AD Refurbished and extended Mitchells & Butlers dining pub, split-level beamed bar with log fire in old brick fireplace, comfortable armchairs, tub chairs and cushioned stools around small copper-topped tables on stripped boards, church candles and contemporary woodblock bird paintings, Purity Pure Ubu and Sharps Doom Bar, several wines by the glass, enjoyable food including fixed-price weekday deal till 6pm, friendly young staff, open-plan timbered dining area with raised central log fire (huge conical hood), white-painted chairs around pale tables, lower dining area too; children and dogs (in bar) welcome, disabled access, seats under parasols on side terrace and out in front, open (and food) all day. *(D C Poulton, Ruth May, Toby Jones)*

CLOPHILL   TL0838
Stone Jug (01525) 860526
N on A6 from A507 roundabout, after 200 yards, second turn on right into backstreet; MK45 4BY Secluded old stone-built local (originally three cottages), cosy and welcoming, with traditional old-fashioned atmosphere, popular good value pubby lunchtime food (not Sun, Mon), friendly service, well kept local ales such as B&T Shefford, various rooms around L-shaped bar, darts in small games extension; background music; children welcome,

roadside picnic-sets and pretty little back terrace, open all day Fri-Sun. *(N R White)*

GREAT BARFORD   TL1351
Anchor (01234) 870364
High Street; off A421; MK44 3LF Refurbished open-plan Wells & Youngs pub by medieval arched bridge and church, their ales and guests kept well, good sensibly priced food (all day Sat, Sun) from snacks up, river views from main bar, back restaurant (children welcome here); background music; picnic-sets overlooking Great Ouse, three bedrooms, open all day weekends. *(Mark Barker)*

HARLINGTON   TL0330
Old Sun (01525) 877330
Sundon Road, by Methodist church; LU5 6LS Traditional 18th-c village pub, friendly and welcoming, with up to five well kept ales including Harveys and St Austell, good value home-made food (Tues and Fri evenings, Sun lunchtime), log fires; children and dogs welcome, not good for wheelchairs, open all day. *(Anon)*

HENLOW   TL1738
Crown (01462) 812433
High Street; SG16 6BS Recently refurbished beamed dining pub; good choice of popular food including children's menu, several wines by the glass, well kept Caledonian Flying Scotsman, Courage Directors and a guest, daily newspapers, woodburners (one in inglenook); background music, free wi-fi; terrace and small garden, open (and food) all day. *(Harvey Brown)*

HENLOW   TL1738
★ **Engineers Arms** (01462) 812284
A6001 S of Biggleswade; High Street; SG16 6AA Spotless traditional village pub, up to a dozen changing ales plus good choice of ciders/perries, bottled belgian beers and wines by the glass, helpful knowledgeable staff, limited range of good value snacks, comfortable carpeted front room with old local photographs on fleur-de-lys wallpaper, bric-a-brac collections and good log fire, smaller tiled inner area and another comfortable carpeted one, beer/cider/country wine festivals, occasional live music, board games; sports TVs, juke box and silenced fruit machine; dogs allowed in bar, plenty of outside seating, open all day. *(George Atkinson)*

HOUGHTON CONQUEST   TL0441
★ **Knife & Cleaver** (01234) 930789
Between B530 (old A418) and A6, S of Bedford; MK45 3LA Refurbished and extended 17th-c village dining pub opposite church, good variety of well liked food from separate bar and restaurant menus, extensive choice of wines by the glass including champagne, Courage, Wells & Youngs and a guest, friendly helpful staff, free

wi-fi; children welcome, no dogs inside, nine chalet bedrooms arranged around courtyard and garden, good breakfast, free charging of electric cars for guests, open all day from 7am (8am weekends), till 8pm Sun.
(D C Poulton, Vikki and Matt Wharton)

KEYSOE   TL0763
★**Chequers** (01234) 708678
Pertenhall Road, Brook End (B660); MK44 2HR Good value tasty home-made food from sandwiches to blackboard specials in peaceful down-to-earth village local, friendly long-serving licensees, two homely, comfortably worn-in beamed rooms divided by stone-pillared fireplace, beers such as Bass, Boddingtons and McEwans, Weston's cider, reasonably priced wines; background music/radio, no credit cards; children welcome, wheelchair access through side door, seats on front lawn and on terrace behind, play area, closed Mon evening, Tues. *(Michael and Jenny Back and others)*

LITTLE GRANSDEN   TL2755
Chequers (01767) 677348
Main Road; SG19 3DW Village local in same family for 60 years and retaining 1950s feel; simple bar with coal fire, darts and framed historical information about the pub, step down to cosy snug with another fire and bench seats, comfortable back lounge with fish tank, interesting range of own-brewed Son of Sid ales, no food apart from good fish and chips Fri evening (must book); open all day Fri, Sat. *(Roger Fox)*

MAULDEN   TL0538
★**Dog & Badger** (01525) 860237
Clophill Road, E of village, towards A6/A507 junction; MK45 2AD Attractive neatly kept bow-windowed cottage, family run and friendly, with good well priced food (booking advised weekends) including sharing boards, pizzas and grills, set lunch Mon-Sat and other deals, beams and exposed brickwork, high stools on bare boards by carved wooden counter serving Wells & Youngs and guests, mix of dining chairs around wooden tables, double-sided fireplace, steps down to two carpeted areas and restaurant; background music, sports TV; children welcome, tables and smokers' shelter in front, back garden with sturdy play area, open all day Fri-Sun. *(Harvey Brown)*

MAULDEN   TL0537
White Hart (01525) 406118
Ampthill Road; MK45 2DH Modernised 17th-c thatched and beamed pub, enjoyable nicely presented food from pubby choices up, friendly helpful service, a couple of ales such as Wells & Youngs, good choice of wines by the glass, large well divided dining area; background music; children welcome, plenty of tables in sizeable gardens with pleasant back decking, play area, open all day.
(Harvey Brown)

NORTHILL   TL1446
★**Crown** (01767) 627337
Ickwell Road; off B658 W of Biggleswade; SG18 9AA Prettily situated refurbished village pub; cosy flagstoned bar with copper-topped counter, heavy low beams and bay window seats, woodburner here and in restaurant with modern furniture on light wood floor, steps up to another dining area with exposed brick and high ceiling, good brasserie-style food (not Sun evening) including lunchtime baguettes and panini, Greene King and guests, plenty of wines by the glass; soft background music; children welcome, no dogs inside, tables out at front and on sheltered side terrace, more in big back garden with good play area, open all day Fri-Sun. *(Anon)*

ODELL   SP9657
Bell (01234) 720254
Off A6 S of Rushden, via Sharnbrook; High Street; MK43 7AS Popular thatched village pub with several low-beamed rooms around central servery, mix of old settles and neat modern furniture, open fires, well kept Greene King ales and good choice of fairly priced standard food (all day Sun till 7pm) from lunchtime sandwiches and baked potatoes up, good friendly service; background music; children welcome away from counter, delightful big garden backing on to River Ouse, handy for Harrold-Odell Country Park, open all day Fri-Sun.
(Philip Sewell)

RISELEY   TL0462
Fox & Hounds (01234) 709714
Off A6 from Sharnbrook/Bletsoe roundabout; High Street, just E of Gold Street; MK44 1DT Village pub dating from the 16th c and revamped under present licensees; low beams, stripped boards and imposing stone fireplace, Wells & Youngs Bombardier and Eagle, steaks cut to weight and other food, separate dining room; children and dogs (in bar) welcome, seats out in front and in back garden with terrace, open (and food) all day. *(Michael Sargent, Mrs Margo Finlay, Jörg Kasprowski)*

SALFORD   SP9339
Swan (01908) 281008
Not far from M1 junction 13 – left off A5140; MK17 8BD Popular Edwardian country dining pub (Peach group), good choice of well liked food and wine, set menu Mon-Thurs 12-7pm, Sharps Doom Bar and Cornish Coaster, friendly staff, refurbished interior with drinking area to right of central servery, sofas and leather chairs on wood floor, restaurant to left with modern country cottage feel and window view into kitchen; background music; children welcome, dogs in bar, seats out on decking, kitchen garden, smokehouse and own chickens, open all day.
(S Holder)

SOUTHILL
TL1441
White Horse (01462) 813364
Off B658 SW of Biggleswade; SG18 9LD
Comfortable well run country pub with
extensive eating area, enjoyable generous
pubby food from baguettes up, friendly staff,
good choice of changing ales and decent
wines; background music; children welcome,
lots of tables in big neatly kept garden with
play area. *(Lois Dyer, D C Poulton)*

STAGSDEN
SP9848
Royal George (01234) 823299
High Street; MK43 8SG Village pub
with cleanly refurbished modern interior,
enjoyable food including signature pizzas
from open kitchen, beers such as Greene
King Abbot and Sharps Doom Bar, friendly
attentive staff; children welcome, small lawn
at the back and terrace, local walks, open all
day weekends. *(S Holder)*

STUDHAM
TL0215
Red Lion (01582) 872530
Church Road; LU6 2QA Character
community pub with hands-on landlord,
public bar and eating areas filled with
pictures and bits and pieces collected over
many years, house plants, wood flooring,
carpeting and old red and black tiles,
open fire, ales such as Adnams, Fullers,
Greene King and Timothy Taylors, enjoyable
pubby food (not evenings Sun, Mon, Tues);
background music; green picnic-sets in front
under pretty window boxes, more on side
grass, open all day Fri-Sun. *(Anon)*

TILSWORTH
SP9824
Anchor (01525) 411404
Just off A5 NW of Dunstable; LU7 9PU
19th-c red-brick village pub with three well
kept real ales and enjoyable food including
good steaks, friendly efficient service, dining
conservatory; children welcome, picnic-sets
in large garden with play area, open all day.
(Ross Balaam)

TOTTERNHOE
SP9721
★Cross Keys (01525) 220434
*Off A505 W of A5; Castle Hill Road;
LU6 2DA* Well restored thatched and
timbered two-bar pub below remains of a
motte and bailey fort, low beams and cosy
furnishings, good straightforward food,
several real ales including well kept Adnams
Broadside, friendly service, dining room; big-

screen TV; good views from large attractive
garden. *(Ross Balaam)*

TURVEY
SP9352
★Three Fyshes (01234) 881463
*A428 NW of Bedford; Bridge Street,
W end of village; MK43 8ER*
Refurbished early 17th-c beamed pub, big
inglenook with woodburner, mix of easy
and upright chairs around tables on tiles
or ancient flagstones, good interesting
home-made food (all day weekends), friendly
attentive service, ales such as Banks's,
Greene King and Marstons, decent choice of
wines, daily papers, extended side restaurant;
background music; dogs welcome, children
in eating area, decking and canopy in
charming garden overlooking bridge and mill
on the Great Ouse, car park further along the
street, open all day. *(George Atkinson)*

WOBURN
SP9433
Bell (01525) 290280
Bedford Street; MK17 9QJ Small beamed
bar area, longer bare-boards dining lounge up
steps, pleasant décor and furnishings, decent
good value food all day including set menu,
friendly helpful service, Greene King ales,
good choice of wines by the glass, nice coffee;
background music, games; children welcome,
back terrace, hotel part across busy road,
handy for Woburn Park. *(Mrs Margo Finlay,
Jörg Kasprowski, Brian and Jean Hepworth)*

WOBURN
SP9330
Flying Fox (01525) 290444
*Sheep Lane (actually A5 Bletchley–
Hockcliffe, well away from village);
MK17 9HD* Relaxed Vintage Inn dining pub
with linked beamed areas, open fires (one in
two-way hearth), enjoyable reasonably priced
food including fixed-price menu Mon-Sat till
5pm, good choice of wines by the glass and
a couple of ales such as Adnams and Purity,
efficient friendly service; background music;
children welcome, tables out on lawn, open
all day. *(Ross Balaam)*

WOOTTON
TL0046
Legstraps (01234) 854112
Keeley Lane; MK43 9HR Refurbished
dining pub under new management, good if
pricey restaurant-style food (also lunchtime
sandwiches), changing ales and plenty of
wines by the glass including champagne; dogs
in bar area, open all day Sat, till 6pm Sun,
closed Mon. *(D C Poulton)*

Post Office address codings confusingly give the impression that some pubs
are in Bedfordshire, when they're really in Buckinghamshire or Cambridgeshire
(which is where we list them).

Berkshire

KEY ★ Star Pub   🍽 Top Quality Food   🍺 Great Beer

🍷 Good Wines   £ Bargain Meals   🛏 Good Bedrooms   🍴 Serves Food

---

BRAY   SU9079   Map 2

Crown 🍽 🍷

1.75 miles from M4 junction 9; A308 towards Windsor, then left at Bray signpost on to B3028; High Street; SL6 2AH

Ancient low-beamed pub with knocked-through rooms, enjoyable food, real ales and plenty of outside seating

The atmosphere in this 16th-c pub is surprisingly pubby, given that the owner is Heston Blumenthal. The partly panelled main bar has heavy old beams – some so low you may have to mind your head – plenty of timbers handily left at elbow height where walls have been knocked through, two winter log fires and neatly upholstered dining chairs and cushioned settles. Courage Best and Directors and a couple of changing guest beers on handpump and around 17 wines by the glass; board games. There are modern slatted chairs and tables in the covered and heated courtyard and plenty of picnic-sets in the large, enclosed back garden; croquet and aunt sally.

🍽 Good food includes lunchtime sandwiches, chicken liver parfait with sweet and sour onions, potted Morecambe Bay shrimps, pork, black pudding and cider sausages with port sauce, fish and chips, pasta with cheese sauce, leeks and beetroot, salmon fillet with celeriac purée and salmon sauce, and puddings such as earl grey tea panna cotta with lemon crumble and syrup baked apple with honey ice-cream; takeaway burgers and fish and chips are available. *Benchmark main dish: irish steak burger with burger sauce and fries £14.50. Two-course evening meal £21.00.*

Scottish Courage ~ Lease Shakira Englefield ~ Real ale ~ (01628) 621936 ~ Open 11.30-11; 12-10.30 Sun ~ Bar food 12-2.30 (3 Sat), 6-9.30 (10 Fri, Sat); 12-8 Sun ~ Children welcome ~ Dogs allowed in bar ~ Wifi ~ www.thecrownatbray.co.uk
Recommended by Ruth May

BRAY   SU9079   Map 2

Hinds Head 🍽 🍷

High Street; car park opposite (exit rather tricky); SL6 2AB

First class food in top gastropub, traditional surroundings, local ales, fine wines by the glass and quite a choice of other drinks too

This is just as much a place for a pint and a chat as it is for an accomplished meal. It's a handsome old pub with an informal and welcoming atmosphere, and the thoroughly traditional L-shaped bar has dark beams and panelling, polished oak parquet, blazing log fires, red cushioned built-in wall seats and studded leather carving chairs around small round tables, and latticed windows. They keep beers from local breweries such as Rebellion and Windsor & Eton and a changing guest on handpump, 19 wines by the glass from an extensive list, 18 malt whiskies, and a dozen specialist gins with interesting ways of serving them. Heston Blumenthal is the owner.

 The enterprising food includes tea-smoked salmon with sour cream butter, hash of snails, bubble and squeak with a slow-cooked egg, oxtail and kidney pudding, fillet of bream with crab and mussel broth, breast of pigeon with braised leg and pigeon and date sauce, and puddings such as treacle tart with milk ice-cream and rhubarb trifle. *Benchmark main dish: veal steak with cabbage and soused onion and sauce 'reform' £29.95. Two-course evening meal £33.00.*

Free house ~ Licensee Kevin Love ~ Real ale ~ (01628) 626151 ~ Open 11-11; 12-7 Sun ~ Bar food 12-2.30, 6.15-9.30; 12-3.30 Sun ~ Restaurant ~ Children welcome ~ Dogs allowed in bar ~ Wi-fi ~ www.hindsheadbray.com *Recommended by Ruth May*

COMPTON
SU5180 Map 2

Swan
High Street; RG20 6NJ

Plenty of room in neatly kept inn for both dining and drinking, original features mixing with contemporary touches, several real ales and wines, enjoyable food and seats in pretty garden; bedrooms

Handy for Newbury Racecourse or after a walk along the Ridgeway, this neatly kept pub is popular with both diners and drinkers. The bar has high tables surrounded by equally high stools, cushioned wall seating, wooden, tub or unusual hooded wicker chairs around all sorts of tables on big flagstones. There's Greene King Morlands Original and Yardbird, plus a beer named for the pub, on handpump and 18 wines by the glass, served from an attractively carved counter. Two dining rooms have contemporary wallpaper or pale paintwork, pen and ink cartoons and hunting prints, high-backed brown leather and antique, cushioned dining chairs and dark tables on bare boards, modern chandeliers and an open log fire. There's also a comfortable end room with sofas and books on shelves; TV and background music. The pretty garden has one big table and chairs under cover, and picnic-sets and more tables and chairs on the lawn. The bedrooms are well equipped and up-to-date. This is sister pub to the Black Boy in Headington (in Oxfordshire).

Good food includes a grazing, tapas-like menu with deep-fried coconut-scented prawns, lamb koftas with dill crème fraîche and hummus with chilli oil, plus black pudding with pancetta and soft boiled egg, mushroom and champagne risotto, pizzas, sausage and mash with beer onion jus, steak and kidney pie, slow-roast pork belly with garlic and thyme mash and cider jus, and puddings such as iced white chocolate and raspberry mousse and sticky toffee pudding with caramel sauce. *Benchmark main dish: bavette steak with confit tomatoes, chips and béarnaise or pepper sauce £16.95. Two-course evening meal £23.00.*

Free house ~ Licensees Abigail Rose and Chris Bentham ~ Real ale ~ (01635) 579400 ~ Open 12-3, 5.30-11; 12-11 Sat, Sun ~ Bar food 12-2.45, 6-9.15 ~ Restaurant ~ Children welcome ~ Dogs allowed in bar ~ Wi-fi ~ Bedrooms: /£90 ~ www.thecomptonswan.com *Recommended by Harvey Brown, Caroline Prescott*

We mention bottled beers and spirits only if there is something unusual about them – imported belgian real ales, say, or dozens of malt whiskies; so do please let us know about them in your reports.

COOKHAM DEAN

SU8785   Map 2

Chequers ♀

Dean Lane; follow signpost Cookham Dean, Marlow; SL6 9BQ

Friendly, civilised dining pub with neat, comfortable bar and restaurant, airy conservatory, first rate food and three real ales

Helpful, professional staff in this civilised place will make you feel just as welcome if it's a pint and a chat that you want rather than a full meal – though most customers are here for the imaginative food. The busy little bar has a relaxed atmosphere, comfortable old sofas on flagstones, Rebellion IPA and Smuggler on handpump and ten good wines by the glass. Assorted dining tables on either side of the bar have crisp white linen and fresh flowers; maybe background music. The area on the left, with an open stove in its big brick fireplace, leads back to a conservatory that overlooks the neat sloping lawn. There are plenty of picnic-sets under smart green parasols on grass at the front.

First class food includes confit duck terrine with fig chutney, seared scallops, pea purée and pancetta, open ratatouille lasagne with pesto, fillet of salmon, crayfish risotto and confit fennel, lamb pie, calves liver and bacon with red wine jus, and puddings such as chocolate brownie and coconut panna cotta with berry compote; they also offer a two- and three-course set lunch. *Benchmark main dish: pork platter: belly, tenderloin, black pudding and apple sauce £15.95. Two-course evening meal £25.00.*

Free house ~ Licensee Peter Roehrig ~ Real ale ~ (01628) 481232 ~ Open 12-3, 5.30-11; 12-5 Sun ~ Bar food 12-2.30, 6.30-9.30; 12-5 Sun ~ Children welcome ~ Wi-fi ~ www.chequersbrasserie.co.uk *Recommended by Harvey Brown, R K Phillips*

EAST GARSTON

SU3676   Map 2

Queens Arms ♀ ⇌

3.5 miles from M4 junction 14; A338 and village signposted Gt Shefford; RG17 7ET

Smart but chatty dining pub with good food and friendly country bar

This well run, warmly friendly pub is right at the heart of racehorse-training country, so much of the local chat is about horse racing. The spacious opened-up bar has plenty of antique prints (many featuring jockeys), daily papers on a corner table (the most prominent being the *Racing Post*), wheelbacks and other dining chairs around well spaced tables on a wooden floor, Ramsbury Flint Knapper and Gold and Sharps Doom Bar on handpump, ten wines by the glass, a fair choice of whiskies, and a farm cider. Background music and live horse racing on TV. Opening off on the right is a lighter dining area with bigger horse and country prints and a pleasing mix of furniture. There are seats on a sheltered terrace. This is an enjoyable place to stay, with spacious, spotlessly clean and attractively decorated bedrooms and very good breakfasts. They can arrange fly-fishing and shooting and there are lots of surrounding downland walks.

Rewarding food includes gin-cured salmon with pickled fennel, beetroot, pickled egg and crème fraîche, goats cheese and roasted fig salad, butternut squash three-ways with toasted pumpkin seeds, sausages with red onion gravy, burger with mushrooms, onions, cheddar, coleslaw and chips, steak in ale pie, smoked haddock and salmon fishcakes with wilted spinach, poached egg and hollandaise, and puddings such as apple sponge and lemon meringue pie. *Benchmark main dish: beer-battered haddock and triple-cooked chips £12.00. Two-course evening meal £22.00.*

Free house ~ Licensee Zdenka Antoniaziova ~ Real ale ~ (01488) 648757 ~
Open 11-11 (10.30 Sun) ~ Bar food 12-2.30, 6.30-9.30; 12-3, 7-9 Sun ~ Restaurant ~
Children welcome ~ Dogs allowed in bar and bedrooms ~ Wi-fi ~ Bedrooms: /£110 ~
www.queensarmshotel.co.uk *Recommended by Simon Lewis, Richard Tilbrook*

FRILSHAM
SU5573 Map 2
Pot Kiln 🍺

*From Yattendon take turning S, opposite church, follow first Frilsham
signpost, but just after crossing motorway go straight on towards Bucklebury,
ignoring Frilsham signposted right; pub on right after about half a mile; RG18 0XX*

**Country dining pub with bustling small bar, local beers, imaginative
food and suntrap garden**

A real country pub and 'as lovely as ever', says a reader with enthusiasm.
There's always a good mix of locals and visitors and the atmosphere
remains genuinely pubby despite an emphasis on the interesting food. The
little bar has West Berkshire Brick Kiln Bitter, Mr Chubbs Lunchtime Bitter,
Maggs Magnificent Mild and a guest beer on handpump, several wines by
the glass and maybe a couple of ciders. The main bar area has dark wooden
tables and chairs on bare boards and a winter log fire, while the extended
lounge is open-plan at the back and leads into a large, pretty dining room
with a nice jumble of old tables and chairs and an old-looking stone
fireplace; darts. It's in an idyllic spot with wide, unobstructed views from
seats in a big suntrap garden and there are plenty of walks in the nearby
woods.

The good, popular food includes ciabatta rolls, venison scotch egg with pickles,
a sharing platter, beef and venison burger with bacon, cheese and coleslaw,
confit gressingham duck leg with puy lentils and cavolo nero, lamb rump with
pea purée and crispy shallots, and puddings such as rice pudding with rhubarb
compote and a changing crumble; they also offer a two- and three-course set
menu. *Benchmark main dish: peppered venison with peppercorn sauce and puréed
potatoes £25.50. Two-course evening meal £19.50.*

Free house ~ Licensees Mr and Mrs Michael Robinson ~ Real ale ~ (01635) 201366 ~
Open 12-3, 6-11; 12-11 Sat; 12-9.30 Sun; closed Tues ~ Bar food 12-2.30, 6-9 (6.30-9 Sat)
~ Restaurant ~ Children welcome ~ Dogs allowed in bar ~ Wi-fi ~ www.potkiln.org
Recommended by Robert Watt, Alistair Forsyth, Pat and Tony Martin

HARE HATCH
SU8077 Map 2
Horse & Groom 🍷 🍺

A4 Bath Road W of Maidenhead; RG10 9SB

**Spreading pub with attractively refurbished, timbered rooms, friendly
staff, enjoyable food, a fine range of drinks and seats outside**

This handsome old coaching inn has lots of interest in several
interconnected rooms. There are beams and timbering, a pleasing
variety of well spread individual tables and chairs on mahogany-stained
boards, oriental rugs and some carpet to soften the acoustics, open fires in
attractive tiled fireplaces, a profusion of mainly old or antique prints and
mirrors, book-lined shelves and house plants. The long bar counter has a
splendid choice of drinks served by well trained, courteous staff, including
a good changing range of 15 wines by the glass, Brakspears Bitter and
Oxford Gold and changing guests such as Brakspears Special, Jennings
Cumberland and Wychwood Hobgoblin on handpump, Weston's farm cider,
lots of spirits including 77 malt whiskies, and several coffees; also several

daily papers. A sheltered back garden has picnic-sets and the front terrace has teak tables and chairs under parasols.

 Quite a choice of popular food includes sandwiches, chicken livers with mushrooms, spinach and sherry jus, smoked mackerel pâté with tempura samphire, chilli crab and prawn linguine, honey and mustard roast ham with free-range eggs, thai green vegetable curry, beef bourguignon with horseradish mash, and puddings such as chocolate cheesecake and black cherry compote and crème brûlée. *Benchmark main dish: chicken, leek and ham pie £13.50. Two-course evening meal £20.00.*

Brunning & Price ~ Manager Mark Hider ~ Real ale ~ (0118) 940 3136 ~ Open 11.30-11 (10.30 Sun) ~ Bar food 12-10 (9.30 Sun) ~ Well behaved children welcome ~ Dogs allowed in bar ~ Wi-fi ~ www.horseandgroom-harehatch.co.uk
Recommended by Paul Humphreys, DHV, John Boothman

HUNGERFORD   SU3368 Map 2
Plume of Feathers 🌟◉ ♀
High Street; street parking opposite; RG17 0NB

Right at the heart of a bustling little town with well liked bar food and a relaxed family atmosphere

A ll are warmly welcomed by the friendly licensees and their cheerful staff in this particularly well run town pub – and that includes dogs too; the pub labrador is called Tosh. The unspoilt open-plan rooms stretch from the smallish bow-windowed façade around the island bar to an open fire in the stripped fireplace at the back. There are armchairs and a black leather sofa around low tables under low beams on the left at the front, and a mix of tables with padded chairs or cushioned small pews on bare boards elsewhere. A beer named for the pub from Greene King, Ruddles Best and a guest from maybe Brentwood Brewery on handpump, a dozen wines by the glass, and good coffee. The sheltered back courtyard isn't large but is well worth knowing about on a warm day: it's prettily planted, with a swing seat as well as green-painted metal tables and chairs.

 Consistently good, well priced food includes sandwiches and ciabatta rolls, pigeon breast with crispy bacon and poached egg, mixed home-made goujon platter, burger with melted cheese, onion rings, barbecue sauce and fries, spicy mixed bean tortilla wrap with salsa and sour cream, thai chicken green curry, and gammon and free-range eggs, and puddings. *Benchmark main dish: beer-battered fresh cod and chips £11.20. Two-course evening meal £18.00.*

Greene King ~ Lease Haley and James Weir ~ Real ale ~ (01488) 682154 ~ Open 11-3, 5.30-11; 12-4 Sun; closed Sun evening ~ Bar food 12-2.30, 7-9 ~ Children welcome ~ Dogs welcome ~ Wi-fi ~ www.theplumehungerford.co.uk *Recommended by Mike and Mary Carter, Mr and Mrs P R Thomas, Martin Day, Richard Tilbrook, Susan and Nigel Brookes, JPC*

INKPEN   SU3564 Map 2
Swan
Lower Inkpen; coming from A338 in Hungerford, take Park Street (first left after railway bridge); RG17 9DX

Extended country pub with rambling rooms, traditional décor, friendly staff, real ales and plenty of seats outside; comfortable bedrooms

L ocal, organic beef farmers own this much-extended country pub and you can buy their produce (and ready-made meals and groceries) in the interesting farm shop next door. The rambling beamed rooms have cosy corners, traditional pubby furniture, eclectic bric-a-brac and three log fires, and there's a flagstoned games area plus a cosy restaurant. Friendly helpful staff serve Butts Jester and Traditional and a changing summer guest on handpump, several wines by the glass and home-made sloe gin; darts, shut the box and board games. The bedrooms are quiet and comfortable. There are picnic-sets on tiered front terraces overlooking a footpath and nearby walks on the North Wessex Downs.

Made with their own farm produce, the tasty food includes sandwiches, beef ravioli in tomato sauce, chicken liver pâté, home-made sausages with mash, thai green chicken curry, vegetarian cannelloni, beer-battered cod and chips, steak pie with onion gravy, and puddings such as chocolate fudge cake and lemon cheesecake. *Benchmark main dish: organic local burger with chips £12.95. Two-course evening meal £21.00.*

Free house ~ Licensees Mary and Bernard Harris ~ Real ale ~ (01488) 668326 ~ Open 12-2.30, 7-11; 12-11 Sat; 12-4 Sun; closed Sun evening ~ Bar food 12-2 (4 Sun), 7-9 ~ Restaurant ~ Children welcome ~ Wi-fi ~ Bedrooms: £70/£85 ~ www.theswaninn-organics.co.uk *Recommended by Mr and Mrs P R Thomas, Terry Mercy*

KINTBURY   SU3866   Map 2

Dundas Arms �♟ ⇔

Village signposted off A4 Newbury–Hungerford about a mile W of Halfway; Station Road – pub just over humpback canal bridge, at start of village itself; RG17 9UT

Carefully updated inn with relaxed informal bar, good two-level restaurant, and lovely waterside garden; comfortable bedrooms

On what amounts to an island on the Kennet & Avon Canal, this is a handsome Georgian inn with picnic-sets on decking overlooking the water. The large, pretty back garden (water on each side) has plenty of well spaced tables on grass among shrubs and trees. This is overlooked by the big windows of the smart two-level restaurant. At the other end is a smallish bar, taking its relaxed informal mood from the cheerful helpful staff; there are sporting prints above a high oak dado, neat little cushioned arts-and-crafts chairs around a few stripped or polished tables on broad floorboards, and high chairs by the counter. Tutts Clump farm cider is on handpump as well as Flack Manor Flack Catcher, Upham Punter and two or three ales from West Berkshire, and 14 wines by the glass. Between the bar and restaurant is a cosy tartan-carpeted sitting room with wing chairs and a splendid leather and mahogany settee, daily papers, a good winter log fire flanked by glazed bookcases, and big silhouette portraits on topiary-print wallpaper. Pleasant nearby walks.

Tempting food includes baked goats cheese with poached pear and chicory salad, king scallops wrapped in pancetta with roasted hazelnut dressing, sausages of the day, sweet potato gnocchi with spinach and ricotta, beer-battered fish of the day, crispy pork belly with black pudding and tarragon jus, and puddings such as white chocolate and raspberry cheesecake bread and butter pudding; they also offer a two- and three-course set lunch menu. *Benchmark main dish: burger with smoked cheese, bacon and fries £12.75. Two-course evening meal £20.00.*

Free house ~ Licensee Tom Moran ~ Real ale ~ (01488) 658263 ~ Open 12-11 (10.30 Sun) ~ Bar food 12-3, 6-9; 12-10 Sat; 12-9 Sun ~ Restaurant ~ Children welcome ~ Dogs allowed in bar and bedrooms ~ Wi-fi ~ Bedrooms: £80/£120 ~ www.dundasarms.co.uk *Recommended by Alex Macdonald, Mrs P Sumner, Stella and Geoffrey Harrison*

NEWBURY   SU4767   Map 2

Newbury ⭐ 🍷 🍺

Bartholomew Street; RG14 5HB

Berkshire Dining Pub of the Year

Lively pub open for morning coffee, brunch and interesting meals, thoughtful choice of drinks, horse-racing artwork and plenty of bar and dining space

This stylish and cheerful pub in the middle of town opens at 10am for morning coffees and teas, and starts serving weekend brunches at that time too. The bar has an assortment of wooden dining chairs around sturdy farmhouse and other solid tables on bare boards, comfortable leather sofas, church candles and a fantastic choice of drinks: Timothy Taylors Landlord, Two Cocks Cavalier and Roundhead, and West Berkshire Good Old Boy on handpump, a farm cider, 70 malt whiskies, shots and cocktails, and around 15 wines by the glass. Light and airy, the dining rooms have benches and church chairs around more rustic tables on bare boards, horse-racing artwork and shelves full of cookery books. As we went to press, refurbishments were taking place inside and out.

⭐ Cooked in an open kitchen using seasonal produce from small growers, the imaginative food includes sandwiches, crab with soft herbs and brown meat dressing, herb gnocchi with jerusalem artichokes and garlic sauce, braised ox cheek with girolle mushrooms and snail bordelaise, burger with stilton, gherkins and triple-cooked chips, 32oz T-bone for two with Marmite butter, roasted root vegetables and horseradish, and puddings such as clementine panna cotta with cranberry biscotti and spiced chocolate sauce and baked alaska with smoked chocolate. *Benchmark main dish: rack of lamb, faggots, mash and salsa verde £19.50. Two-course evening meal £30.00.*

Free house ~ Licensees Clarke Oldfield and Peter Lumber ~ Real ale ~ (01635) 49000 ~ Open 12-midnight; 10am-1am Sat; 10am-11pm Sun ~ Bar food 12-3, 5.30-10; 10-4, 5.30-10 weekends; not Sun evening ~ Restaurant ~ Children welcome ~ Dogs allowed in bar ~ Wi-fi ~ Regular live music ~ www.thenewburypub.co.uk *Recommended by Harvey Brown, Alfie Bayliss*

PEASEMORE   SU4577   Map 2

Fox

4 miles from M4 junction 13, via Chieveley: keep on through Chieveley to Peasemore, turning left into Hillgreen Lane at small sign to Fox Inn; village also signposted from B4494 Newbury–Wantage; RG20 7JN

Friendly downland pub on top form under its expert licensees

This enjoyable, bustling, carefully opened-up place is run by first class licensees. The long bare-boards bar has strategically placed high-backed settles, with comfort guaranteed by plenty of colourful cushions, a warm woodburning stove in a stripped-brick chimney breast and, for real sybarites, two luxuriously carpeted end areas, one with velour tub armchairs. Friendly and efficient black-clad staff serve Butts Traditional, West Berkshire Good Old Boy and a weekly guest on handpump and 15 wines by the glass; faint nostalgic pop music. This is downland horse-training country, and a couple of picnic-table sets at the front look out to the rolling fields beyond the quiet country lane – on a clear day as far as the Hampshire border hills some 20 miles south. There are more picnic-sets on a smallish sheltered back terrace.

The enjoyable food includes lunchtime sandwiches and baguettes, cajun tiger prawns with sweet chilli, red onion and goats cheese tart with a trio of sauces, sharing platters, lambs liver and bacon with caramelised onion gravy, coq au vin, fish pie, pheasant breast with port game jus, and puddings such as vanilla crème brûlée and praline cheesecake with hazelnut sauce; they also offer a two- and three-course set midweek menu. *Benchmark main dish: fillet of beef wellington with port and stilton sauce £18.95. Two-course evening meal £21.50.*

Free house ~ Licensees Philip and Lauren Davison ~ Real ale ~ (01635) 248480 ~ Open 12-2.30, 6-11; 12-11 Sat; 12-10.30 Sun; closed Mon (except bank holidays), Tues ~ Bar food 12-2.30, 6-9; 12-9 Sat; 12-5 Sun ~ Restaurant ~ Children welcome ~ Dogs allowed in bar ~ Wi-fi ~ Live entertainment bank holiday Sun ~ www.foxatpeasemore.co.uk
Recommended by Ruth May, Ian Herdman

RUSCOMBE SU7976 Map 2

Royal Oak 🌟 ◀

Ruscombe Lane (B3024 just E of Twyford); RG10 9JN

Wide choice of popular food at welcoming pub with interesting furnishings and paintings, local beer and wine

The open-plan, carpeted bars here are cleverly laid out so that each area is fairly snug, but the overall feel is of a lot of people enjoying themselves. A good variety of furniture runs from dark oak tables to big chunky pine ones with mixed seating to match – the two sofas facing one another are popular. As a contrast to the old exposed ceiling joists, mostly unframed modern paintings and prints decorate the walls, which are mainly dark terracotta over a panelled dado. Binghams (the brewery is just across the road) Space Hoppy and Twyford Tipple and Fullers London Pride on handpump, 13 wines by the glass (they stock wines from the Stanlake Park Vineyard in the village), several malt whiskies and attentive service. Picnic-sets are ranged around a venerable central hawthorn in the garden behind (where there are ducks and chickens); summer barbecues. The pub (known locally as Buratta's, so don't drive past) is on the Henley Arts Trail. Do visit the landlady's antiques and collectables shop which is open during pub hours.

 Good, popular food includes sandwiches and paninis, field mushroom stuffed with stilton mousse, crayfish cocktail, sharing platters, ham and egg, bangers and mash with onion gravy, thai green vegetable curry, chicken in mushroom, brandy and mustard sauce, calves liver and bacon, confit of duck with bacon and flageolet beans, and puddings. *Benchmark main dish: monkfish wrapped in parma ham with green peppercorn sauce £13.00. Two-course evening meal £21.00.*

Enterprise ~ Lease Jenny and Stefano Buratta ~ Real ale ~ (0118) 934 5190 ~ Open 12-3, 6-11; 12-4 Sun; closed Mon and Sun evenings ~ Bar food 12-2.30, 6-9.30; 12-3 Sun ~ Restaurant ~ Children welcome ~ Dogs allowed in bar ~ Wi-fi ~ www.burattas.co.uk
Recommended by Paul Humphreys

SHEFFORD WOODLANDS SU3673 Map 2
Pheasant

Under 0.5 miles from M4 junction 14 – A338 towards Wantage, first left on B4000; RG17 7AA

Bustling bars, a separate dining room, enjoyable food and beer and seats outside; bedrooms

If you're fed up with the busy M4, head to this friendly, bustling inn. The various interconnecting bar rooms have plenty of horse-related prints, photos and paintings (including a huge mural) – the owners are keen racegoers – as well as a warm fire in a little brick fireplace, a mix of elegant wooden dining chairs and settles around all sorts of tables, and big mirrors here and there. One snug little room, with log-end wallpaper, has armchairs, a cushioned chesterfield and a flat-screen TV. There's also a separate dining room; background music. Ramsbury Gold and two guests such as Two Cocks Cavalier and Upham Tipster on handpump and quite a few good wines by the glass. Seats in the garden have attractive views. The comfortable modern bedrooms are in a separate extension; the continental breakfast (cooked is also available) is good.

The reliably good food includes lunchtime baguettes, crispy salt and pepper squid with garlic mayonnaise, goats cheese croquettes with red pepper purée, burger with smoked cheese, bacon and fries, butternut squash, pine nut and parmesan risotto, venison, steak and kidney pudding with horseradish mash, fish pie, and puddings such as apple and berry crumble and sticky toffee pudding. *Benchmark main dish: lemon and herb chicken schnitzel with fries and parmesan sauce £14.50. Two-course evening meal £21.50.*

Free house ~ Licensee Rupert Fowler ~ Real ale ~ (01488) 648284 ~ Open 7.30am (8.30am Sat)-11pm; 8.30am-10.30pm Sun ~ Bar food 12-2.30, 6.30-9.30 (9 Sun) ~ Children welcome ~ Dogs allowed in bar and bedrooms ~ Wi-fi ~ Bedrooms: /£85 ~ www.thepheasant-inn.co.uk *Recommended by Pip White, Mr and Mrs P R Thomas, Katharine Cowherd*

SONNING
Bull

SU7575   Map 2

Off B478, by church; village signed off A4 E of Reading; RG4 6UP

Pretty timbered inn in attractive spot near Thames, plenty of character in old-fashioned bars, Fullers beers, friendly staff and good food; bedrooms

There's a lot of character in this picture-postcard 16th-c inn and it's a comfortable and well equipped place to stay too. The building looks its best when the wisteria is flowering and the courtyard is full of bright flower tubs. The two old-fashioned bar rooms have low ceilings and heavy beams, cosy alcoves, leather armchairs and sofas, cushioned antique settles and low wooden chairs on bare boards, and open fireplaces. Fullers Chiswick, HSB, Honey Dew, London Pride and a couple of guests on handpump served by helpful staff, 16 good wines by the glass and a farm cider. The dining room has a mix of wooden chairs and tables, rugs on parquet flooring and shelves of books. If you bear left through the ivy-clad churchyard opposite, then turn left along the bank of the River Thames, you come to a very pretty lock. The Thames Valley Park is close by.

Highly thought-of food includes sandwiches, chicken and duck liver parfait with port and clementine jelly, mussels in cider and cream, jerk spiced ham with poached duck egg and pineapple salsa, chilli con carne, butternut squash gnocchi with wild mushrooms and tomatoes, fish casserole, pheasant stew, and puddings such as ginger panna cotta with rhubarb compote and sticky toffee pudding. *Benchmark main dish: pheasant casserole with herb dumplings £16.00. Two-course evening meal £21.00.*

Fullers ~ Manager Dennis Mason ~ Real ale ~ (0118) 969 3901 ~ Open 11-11 (11.30 Sat); 12-11 Sun ~ Bar food 10-9.30 ~ Restaurant ~ Children welcome ~ Dogs allowed in bar ~ Wi-fi ~ Tribute acts monthly ~ Bedrooms: /£99 ~ www.fullershotels.com *Recommended by John Saville, Susan and John Douglas, M A Borthwick*

STANFORD DINGLEY SU5771 Map 2

Old Boot

Off A340 via Bradfield, coming from A4 just W of M4 junction 12; RG7 6LT

Country furnishings and open fires in welcoming beamed bars, a choice of bar food, real ales, and seats in the garden

There's always a good mixed crowd at this stylish pub – all are made welcome by the friendly landlord and his staff. The beamed bar has fine old pews, settles, country chairs and polished tables, as well as some striking pictures and hunting prints, boot ornaments and fresh flowers; two open fires (one in an inglenook) keep things cosy in winter. West Berkshire Good Old Boy and a guest such as Fullers London Pride or Upham Punter on handpump and several wines by the glass. There's also a conservatory-style restaurant. The large quiet garden has picnic-sets on a terrace and pleasant rural views; a swing and a slide for children. More picnic-sets at the front are dotted between the flowering tubs.

Quite a choice of food includes lunchtime sandwiches and burgers, salmon and dill fishcake with hollandaise, an antipasti plate, sausages with onion sauce, burger with bacon, cheese and straw fries, a pie of the day, lamb shank with mash, slow-cooked pork belly with apple gravy, seafood linguine, and puddings such as banoffi pie and chocolate and whiskey terrine. *Benchmark main dish: beer-battered fish and chips £10.95. Two-course evening meal £16.00.*

Free house ~ Licensee John Haley ~ Real ale ~ (0118) 974 4292 ~ Open 11-3, 5-11; 11-11 Sat, Sun ~ Bar food 12-2, 6-9 ~ Restaurant ~ Children welcome ~ Dogs allowed in bar ~ Wi-fi ~ www.oldbootinn.co.uk *Recommended by Harvey Brown, Mike Swan*

SWALLOWFIELD SU7364 Map 2

George & Dragon ⬤ ▽

Church Road, towards Farley Hill; RG7 1TJ

Busy country pub with good nearby walks, enjoyable bar food, real ales, friendly service and seats outside

With good food and a warm welcome from the long-serving licensees, this comfortable, well run pub continues to attract plenty of customers. The various interconnected rooms have a lot of character: as well as beams (some quite low) and standing timbers, there's a happy mix of nice old dining chairs and settles around wooden tables, rugs on flagstones, lit candles, a big log fire and country prints on red or bare brick walls; background music. Fullers London Pride, Ringwood Best and Sharps Doom Bar on handpump, quite a few wines by the glass and several gins and whiskies. There are picnic-sets on gravel or paving in the garden. Their website has details of a circular 4-mile walk that starts and ends at the pub.

Good, interesting food includes lunchtime ciabattas, barbecue baby back ribs, whole baked camembert with apricot and chilli jam, venison and porter sausages with bubble and squeak and gravy, wild mushroom and tarragon risotto, corn-fed chicken with panzanella salad and pesto, smoked haddock with wilted spinach and a poached egg, and puddings such as lemon crème brûlée and knickerbocker glory. *Benchmark main dish: slow-roasted half shoulder of english lamb with garlic mash and rosemary sauce £14.95. Two-course evening meal £21.50.*

Free house ~ Licensee Paul Dailey ~ Real ale ~ (0118) 988 4432 ~ Open 12-11 (midnight Sat) ~ Bar food 12-2.30 (3 Sun), 7-9.30 (10 Fri, Sat, 9 Sun) ~ Restaurant ~ Children welcome ·· Dogs allowed in bar ~ www.georgeanddragonswallowfield.co.uk *Recommended by Ian Herdman, Mrs P Sumner, John Pritchard*

UPPER BASILDON
Red Lion ♀ ⬤

SU5976   Map 2

Off A329 NW of Pangbourne; Aldworth Road; RG8 8NG

Laid-back country pub with friendly family atmosphere, popular food and a good choice of drinks

M any customers are here for the interesting food, but drinkers are welcomed too and they keep Courage Directors, Sharps Doom Bar, West Berkshire Good Old Boy and a weekly changing guest on handpump, a dozen wines from an extensive list and a farm cider. There's a relaxed atmosphere, chapel chairs, a few pews and miscellaneous stripped tables on bare floorboards, a green leather chesterfield and armchair, and pale blue/grey paintwork throughout – even on the beams, ceiling and some of the top-stripped tables. Beyond a double-sided woodburning stove, an area with a pitched ceiling has much the same furniture on cord carpet, but a big cut-glass chandelier and large mirror give it a slightly more formal dining feel. The *Independent* and *Racing Post*, occasional background music and regular (usually jazz-related) live music. There are sturdy picnic-sets in the sizeable enclosed garden, and summer barbecues and hog roasts.

Tempting food includes lunchtime sandwiches and baguettes, country terrine with tomato chutney, baked camembert with cranberry sauce, home-cooked ham and eggs, pork and leek sausages with onion gravy, lamb and mint burger with tzatziki and feta, slow-cooked pork belly with bacon and cabbage and cider jus, and puddings such as treacle tart and rhubarb and apple crumble. *Benchmark main dish: seafood spaghetti £14.50. Two-course evening meal £19.50.*

Enterprise ~ Lease Alison Green ~ Real ale ~ (01491) 671234 ~ Open 11-3, 5-11; all day weekends ~ Bar food 12-2.30 (3 Sun), 6-9 (9.30 Sat, 8.30 Sun) ~ Restaurant ~ Children welcome ~ Dogs allowed in bar ~ Wi-fi ~ www.theredlionupperbasildon.co.uk
Recommended by Simon Grigg

WHITE WALTHAM
Beehive ⬤

SU8477   Map 2

Waltham Road (B3024 W of Maidenhead); SL6 3SH

Traditional village pub with welcoming staff and enjoyable food and drink; seats outside

O ur readers very much enjoy their visits to this deservedly popular and consistently well managed pub. It's run by a courteous, hospitable landlord and his efficient staff and the atmosphere is bustling and friendly. To the right, several comfortably spacious areas have leather chairs around sturdy tables; to the left is a neat bar brightened up by cheerful scatter cushions on comfortable built-in wall seats and captain's chairs. Brakspears Bitter, Fullers London Pride, Greene King Abbot and a changing guest from Loddon or Rebellion on handpump, ten wines by the glass and a good choice of soft drinks. A brick-built room has glass doors opening on to the front terrace (the teak seats and picnic-sets here take in the pub's rather fine topiary). Background music and board games. A good-sized sheltered back lawn has seats and tables. Disabled access and facilities.

Reliably good food includes sandwiches (the hot ones come with fries), portobello mushrooms stuffed with stilton, crispy ham and herbs, scallops with chorizo, home-baked ham and eggs, chicken with a whisky, wild mushroom and bacon sauce, a pie of the day, thai-style fishcakes with sweet chilli dip, calves liver and bacon with red wine jus, and puddings such as treacle sponge and apple crumble. *Benchmark main dish: smoked haddock with spinach mash, poached egg and beurre blanc £12.95. Two-course evening meal £21.00.*

Enterprise ~ Lease Guy Martin ~ Real ale ~ (01628) 822877 ~ Open 11-3, 5-11; 11-11 Sat; 12-10 Sun ~ Bar food 12-2.30, 5.30-9.30; 12-9.30 Sat; 12-7.30 Sun ~ Restaurant ~ Children welcome ~ Dogs allowed in bar ~ Wi-fi ~ www.thebeehivewhitewaltham.co.uk
Recommended by Paul Humphreys, Susan and John Douglas, John Pritchard, Richard and Liz Thorne, Roger and Donna Huggins, Nigel and Sue Foster

WOOLHAMPTON
Rowbarge ♀ ◧

SU5766 Map 2

Station Road; RG7 5SH

Refurbished canalside pub with lots of outside seating, rambling rooms full of interest, six real ales and good bistro-style food

The six beamed and timbered rambling rooms in this fine old place are connected by open doorways and knocked-through walls: plenty of nooks and crannies, open fires, and décor that's gently themed to represent the nearby canal. There are oars on the walls and hundreds of prints and photographs (some of rowers and boats), old glass and stone bottles, fresh flowers, big house plants and evening candles; the many large mirrors create an impression of even more space. Throughout there are antique dining chairs around various nice old tables, settles, built-in cushioned wall seating, armchairs, a group of high stools around a huge wooden barrel table, and rugs on polished boards, stone tiles or carpeting. Friendly, helpful staff serve Phoenix Brunning & Price Original plus guests such as Itchen Valley Tea Clipper, Milestone Loxley, Ramsbury Flint Knapper, Tring Side Pocket for a Toad, Upham Stakes and Wild Weather Stormbringer on handpump, 20 wines by the glass and 60 malt whiskies; background music and board games. There are wooden chairs and tables on a decked terrace and picnic-sets among trees beside the Kennet & Avon Canal.

 Attractively presented food includes sandwiches, potted smoked mackerel pâté with prune chutney, moules marinière, honey-roast ham and free-range eggs, wild mushroom, spinach and hazelnut quiche, steak burger with bacon, cheese, coleslaw and chips, salmon fillet with herb crust and saffron and chive sauce, and puddings such as chocolate and ginger torte and mulled pear and apple crumble. *Benchmark main dish: lamb shoulder with dauphinoise potatoes and rosemary gravy £16.95. Two-course evening meal £20.00.*

Brunning & Price ~ Manager Stephen Butt ~ Real ale ~ (0118) 971 2213 ~ Open 11-11 (10.30 Sun) ~ Bar food 12-10 (9 Sun) ~ Restaurant ~ Children welcome ~ Dogs allowed in bar ~ Wi-fi ~ www.rowbarge.hcpr.co.uk *Recommended by John Pritchard, Ron Corbett*

YATTENDON
Royal Oak ⍟ ♀ ⇌

SU5574 Map 2

The Square; B4009 NE from Newbury; right at Hampstead Norreys, village signed on left; RG18 0UG

Handsome old inn with beamed and panelled rooms, lovely flowers, local beers and imaginative food, and seats in pretty garden; comfortable bedrooms

This is a comfortable place to stay with the light and attractive bedrooms overlooking the garden or village square; breakfasts are good. The charming, civilised bar rooms have plenty of space for an enjoyable meal or a quiet drink; with the West Berkshire brewery actually in the village, the four real ales on handpump are on tiptop form, and the ten wines by the glass are well chosen. There are beams and panelling, an appealing choice of wooden dining chairs around interesting tables, some half-panelled wall seating, rugs on quarry tiles or wooden floorboards, plenty of prints on brick, cream or red walls, lovely flower arrangements and four log fires. Under the trellising in the walled back garden are wicker armchairs and tables, while at the front there are picnic-sets under parasols. The pub is only ten minutes from Newbury Racecourse and gets pretty busy on race days.

The seasonally focused menu includes sandwiches, scallops and crevettes in corn chowder with saffron oil, a charcuterie plate, cauliflower, artichoke and shallot gratin, chicken and mushroom pie, tagliatelle with wild boar ragout, braised ox cheek with celeriac mash, honey-roast ham with chive mash and parsley sauce, and puddings such as chocolate and almond tart and apple and soured cherry crumble. *Benchmark main dish: rib steak on the bone with chips and béarnaise or peppercorn sauce £24.00. Two-course evening meal £23.50.*

Free house ~ Licensee Rob McGill ~ Real ale ~ (01635) 201325 ~ Open 11-11; 12-10.30 Sun ~ Bar food 12-2.30 (3 weekends), 6.30-9.30(9 Sun) ~ Children welcome ~ Dogs welcome ~ Wi-fi ~ Bedrooms: £90/£110 ~ www.royaloakyattendon.co.uk
Recommended by Neil and Angela Huxter, Wendy Breese

Also Worth a Visit in Berkshire

Besides the fully inspected pubs, you might like to try these pubs that have been recommended to us and described by readers. Do tell us what you think of them: feedback@goodguides.com

ALDWORTH   SU5579
★**Bell** (01635) 578272
A329 Reading–Wallingford; left on to B4009 at Streatley; RG8 9SE Unspoilt and unchanging (in same family for over 250 years), simply furnished panelled rooms, beams in ochre ceiling, ancient one-handed clock, woodburner, glass-panelled hatch serving Arkells, West Berkshire and a monthly guest, Upton cider, nice house wines, maybe winter mulled wine, good value rolls, ploughman's and winter soup, traditional pub games, no mobile phones or credit cards; can get busy weekends; well behaved children and dogs welcome, seats in quiet, cottagey garden by village cricket ground, animals in paddock behind pub, maybe Christmas mummers and summer morris, closed Mon (open lunchtime bank holidays). *(Alfie Bayliss)*

ALDWORTH   SU5579
★**Four Points** (01635) 578367
B4009 towards Hampstead Norreys; RG8 9RL Attractive 17th-c thatched roadside pub with low beams, standing timbers and panelling, nice fire in bar with more formal seating area to the left and restaurant at back, good value home-made food from baguettes up, local Two Cocks and Wadworths 6X, friendly helpful young staff; children welcome, garden over road with play area. *(Paul Humphreys)*

ARBORFIELD CROSS   SU7667
Bull (01189) 762244
On roundabout; RG2 9QD Light open-plan dining pub with good popular food including some french dishes (best to book at busy times), well priced house wines, good service; children welcome, closed Mon, otherwise open all day. *(Paul Humphreys)*

ASHMORE GREEN   SU4969
Sun in the Wood (01635) 42377
B4009 (Shaw Road) off A339, right to Kiln Road, left to Stoney Lane; RG18 9HF Refurbished under newish licensees; high-beamed front bar with mix of tables and cushioned chairs on wood floor, Wadworths ales and good choice of wines by the glass, enjoyable food (not Sun evening) from sandwiches and sharing boards up, more beams in big back dining area, conservatory; children and dogs welcome, terrace and woodside garden with play area, closed Mon. *(Anon)*

ASTON   SU7884
★**Flower Pot** (01491) 574721
Off A4130 Henley–Maidenhead at top of Remenham Hill; RG9 3DG Roomy popular country pub with nice local feel, roaring log fire, array of stuffed fish and fishing prints in airy country dining area, enjoyable food from baguettes to fish and game, well kept

ales including Brakspears, quick friendly service, snug traditional bar with more fishing memorabilia; very busy with walkers and families at weekends; lots of picnic-sets giving quiet country views from big, dog-friendly orchard garden, side field with poultry, Thames nearby, bedrooms. *(Susan and John Douglas, DHV, Roy Hoing)*

CHARVIL   SU7776
Lands End (0118) 934 0700
Lands End Lane/Whistley Mill Lane near Old River ford; RG10 0UE Friendly 1930s Tudor-style pub with reasonably priced food from baguettes to blackboard specials, well kept Brakspears and a dozen wines by the glass, open-plan bar with log fire, separate restaurant, various stuffed fish (good fishing nearby); children welcome, sizeable garden with terrace picnic-sets. *(Paul Humphreys)*

CHEAPSIDE   SU9469
★Thatched Tavern (01344) 620874
Off A332/A329, then off B383 at Village Hall sign; SL5 7QG Civilised dining pub with a good deal of character and plenty of room if you just want a drink; interesting up-to-date food (can be pricey) along with one or two pub staples, competent friendly staff, good choice of wines by the glass, Fullers London Pride, a beer named for the pub and a guest ale, Weston's cider, big inglenook log fire, low beams and polished flagstones in cottagey core, three smart dining rooms off; children welcome, dogs in bar, tables on terrace and attractive sheltered back lawn, handy for Virginia Water, open all day weekends and busy on race days. *(Susan and John Douglas)*

CHIEVELEY   SU4773
★Olde Red Lion (01635) 248379
Handy for M4 junction 13 via A34 N-bound; Green Lane; RG20 8XB Attractive village pub with friendly landlord and helpful staff, three well kept Arkells beers, nice varied choice of generously served food from good sandwiches and baguettes up, reasonable prices, low-beamed carpeted L-shaped bar with panelling and hunting prints, log fire, extended back restaurant; background music, games machine, TV; wheelchair accessible throughout, small garden, five bedrooms in separate old building, open all day weekends. *(Phil and Jane Hodson)*

COOKHAM   SU8985
★Bel & the Dragon (01628) 521263
High Street (B4447); SL6 9SQ Smartly refurbished 15th-c inn with panelling and heavy Tudor beams, log fires, bare boards and simple country furnishings in two-room front bar and dining area, hand-painted cartoons on pastel walls, more modern bistro-style back restaurant, helpful friendly staff, good food cooked to order including cheaper lunchtime menu, Rebellion IPA and

a local guest, good choice of wines; children welcome, dogs in bar, well tended garden with terrace tables, five bedrooms, Stanley Spencer Gallery almost opposite, open all day. *(Brian Glozier)*

COOKHAM   SU8985
Ferry (01628) 525123
Sutton Road; SL6 9SN Splendidly placed riverside pub/restaurant with relaxing contemporary décor, wide choice of food all day including sharing plates and fixed-price menu (Mon-Fri 12-7pm), good service, Sharps Doom Bar and a guest, some interesting lagers, comprehensive wine list, light and airy Thames-view dining areas upstairs and down, sofas and coffee tables by fireplace, small servery in beamed core; background music; children welcome, extensive terrace overlooking river with slipway. *(Martin and Karen Wake, Alistair Forsyth, Ian Phillips)*

COOKHAM   SU8885
★White Oak (01628) 523043
The Pound (B4447); SL6 9QE Bustling pub with emphasis on airy back dining area: three rows of light wood tables in varying sizes, comfortably cushioned or upholstered chairs and brown leather wall banquettes, polished boards, white-framed mirrors on grey walls, end french windows, linked front bar with armchairs, other seats on slightly raised platform, cosier areas at each side, interesting well liked food cooked by landlord, Greene King Abbot and good choice of wines, friendly staff; free wi-fi; children welcome, sturdy wooden furniture on sheltered back terrace and steps up to white wirework tables on grass, closed Sun evening, otherwise open all day. *(Alfie Bayliss, Harvey Brown, Simon Collett-Jones)*

COOKHAM DEAN   SU8785
★Jolly Farmer (01628) 482905
Church Road, off Hills Lane; SL6 9PD Traditional pub owned by village consortium; old-fashioned unspoilt bars with open fires, five well kept ales including Brakspears, Courage and Rebellion, local cider (apples from the pub's garden) and decent wines, sensibly priced popular food (not Sun or Mon evenings) from baguettes up, pleasant attentive staff, good-sized more modern eating area and small dining room, old and new local photographs, pub games; well behaved children and dogs welcome (friendly resident black lab called Czar), tables out in front and on side terrace, nice garden with play area, open all day. *(Susan and John Douglas)*

COOKHAM DEAN   SU8785
Uncle Toms Cabin (01628) 483339
Off A308 Maidenhead–Marlow; Hills Lane, towards Cookham Rise and Cookham; SL6 9NT Welcoming small-roomed local with simple, sensitively modernised interior, four well kept

mainstream ales and enjoyable fairly traditional food from good sandwiches up, low beams, wood floors and sage-green panelling, gleaming horsebrasses, open fire; children in eating areas, dogs in bar, seats out at front and in sheltered sloping back garden, peaceful country setting, closes at 9pm Sun and Mon. *(Paul Humphreys, Susan and John Douglas and others)*

EAST ILSLEY   SU4981

★**Crown & Horns** (01635) 281545

Just off A34, about 5 miles N of M4 junction 13; Compton Road; RG20 7LH Civilised Georgian pub in horse-training country, rambling beamed rooms, log fires, enjoyable home-made food from sandwiches, pizzas and pub favourites up including good Sun lunch, five real ales, friendly efficient staff; background music; children, dogs and muddy boots welcome, tables in pretty courtyard, modern bedroom extension, open all day from 10am. *(R T and J C Moggridge)*

HAMPSTEAD NORREYS   SU5376

White Hart (01635) 202248

Church Street; RG18 0TB Friendly and relaxed low-beamed village pub with three linked rooms, fireside seating and good-sized dining area, enjoyable sensibly priced home-made food, a couple of well kept Greene King ales and a guest, well chosen wines, quiz first Sun of the month; children and dogs (in bar) welcome, back terrace and garden, open all day weekends. *(Anon)*

HARE HATCH   SU8078

Queen Victoria (0118) 940 3122

Blakes Lane; just N of A4 Reading–Maidenhead; RG10 9TA Cottagey early 18th-c country pub, two low-ceilinged carpeted rooms with small conservatory to one side, well kept Brakspears, generous helpings of enjoyable good value pubby food from sandwiches up, open fire; dogs welcome, a few picnic-sets out in front, open all day weekends. *(John Pritchard)*

HENLEY   SU7682

★**Little Angel** (01491) 411008

Remenham Lane (A4130, just over bridge E of Henley); RG9 2LS Civilised dining pub, more or less open-plan but with distinct seating areas, bare boards throughout, little bar with leather cube stools, tub and farmhouse chairs, woodburner, other parts with mix of dining tables and chairs, artwork on Farrow & Ball paintwork, contemporary food (all day weekends), Brakspears ales and several wines by the glass, pleasant attentive service, airy conservatory; soft background music; well behaved children allowed, dogs in bar, tables on sheltered floodlit back terrace looking over to cricket pitch, open all day. *(Ian Phillips, Simon Collett-Jones, DHV, Tom and Ruth Rees)*

HOLYPORT   SU8977

George (01628) 628317

1.5 miles from M4 junction 8/9, via A308(M)/A330; The Green; SL6 2JL Attractive old pub with colourful history, open-plan low-beamed interior, cosy and dimly lit, with nice fireplace, good choice of enjoyable food from baguettes up, well kept ales such as Fullers London Pride and Rebellion IPA, several wines by the glass, ebullient landlord and friendly helpful service; background music; picnic-sets on attractive terrace, lovely village green. *(Alistair Forsyth, Paul Humphreys, Simon Collett-Jones)*

HUNGERFORD NEWTOWN SU3571

Tally Ho (01488) 682312

A338 just S of M4 junction 14; RG17 0PP Traditional red-brick beamed pub owned and recently refurbished by the local community, four local ales including Siren, enjoyable pubby food (not Sun evening), log fire; children welcome, picnic-sets out in front, open all day. *(Mr Jim Allen)*

HURLEY   SU8281

Dew Drop (01628) 824327

Small yellow sign to pub off A4130 just W; SL6 6RB Old flint and brick pub tucked way in nice rustic setting, well liked fairly traditional food from lunchtime sandwiches (not weekends) up, Brakspears and a guest ale, friendly staff, Tues quiz; children and dogs welcome, french windows to terrace, pleasant views from landscaped back garden, good local walks, open all day Sat, till 6pm Sun, closed Mon evening. *(Paul Humphreys)*

HURLEY   SU8382

Red Lyon (01628) 823558

A4130 SE, just off A404; SL6 5LH Large pub with several linked low-beamed areas, stone floors and panelling, log fires, good food from sandwiches and deli boards up using local produce (some home-grown), ales such as Rebellion and White Horse; children welcome, picnic-sets in good-sized pretty garden (summer hampers and rugs available). *(Paul Humphreys)*

HURST   SU7973

★**Castle** (0118) 934 0034

Church Hill; RG10 0SJ Popular old dining pub still owned by the church opposite; very good well presented food (not Sun evening, Mon) including daily specials, well kept Binghams Twyford Tipple and a couple of local guests, nice wines by the glass (their house wines are particularly good), well trained helpful staff, bar and two restaurant areas, beams, wood floors and old brick walls, some visible wattle and daub; children welcome, dogs in bar, garden picnic-sets, open all day weekends, closed Mon lunchtime. *(Paul Humphreys, DHV and others)*

HURST
SU8074
Green Man (0118) 934 2599
Off A321 just outside village; RG10 0BP
Partly 17th-c pub with good value food from
baguettes and sharing plates to steaks and
blackboard specials, weekday set menu
choices too, well kept Brakspears, pleasant
attentive service, bar with dark beams and
standing timbers, cosy alcoves, wall seats and
built-in settles, hot little fire in one fireplace,
old iron stove in another, dining area with
modern sturdy wooden tables and high-
backed chairs on solid oak floor; children
welcome, sheltered terrace, picnic-sets under
big oak trees in large garden with play area,
open (and food) all day weekends. *(Paul
Humphreys)*

INKPEN
SU3764
Crown & Garter (01488) 668325
*Inkpen Common: Inkpen signposted
with Kintbury off A4; in Kintbury turn
left into Inkpen Road, then keep on
into Inkpen Common; RG17 9QR* The
long-serving landlady has left this tucked-
away country pub (a previous Main Entry),
but it should have reopened after major
refurbishment by the time you read this
– reports please. *(Mrs J A Taylar, Mrs Julie
Thomas, David and Judy Robison, Mrs P Sumner)*

KNOWL HILL
SU8178
★ Bird in Hand (01628) 826622
*A4, handy for M4 junction 8/9; RG10
9UP* Relaxed, civilised and roomy, with cosy
alcoves, heavy beams, panelling and splendid
log fire in tartan-carpeted main area, wide
choice of popular home-made food (special
diets catered for), four well kept mainly
local ales and good choice of other drinks,
much older side bar, smart restaurant; soft
background music, free wi-fi; tables on front
terrace and in neat garden, summer weekend
barbecues, 22 bedrooms (some in separate
block), open (and food) all day. *(Susan and
John Douglas, DHV)*

KNOWL HILL
SU8279
Royal Oak (01628) 822010
Pub signed off A4; RG10 9YE Welcoming
village pub smartened up under newish local
management; L-shaped room with central
bar and log fire, Brakspears, Rebellion and
Sharps, enjoyable reasonably priced pubby
food including good choice of sandwiches,
morning coffee and danish pastries; free
wi-fi; children, walkers and dogs welcome,
good-sized informal garden overlooking
fields, annual steam fair, open all day.
(Paul Humphreys)

LAMBOURN
SU3180
Malt Shovel (01488) 73777
Upper Lambourn; RG17 8QN Décor
and customers reflecting racing-stables
surroundings, traditional locals' bar,
enjoyable home-made food in smart modern

dining extension including evening specials,
well kept Box Steam and a guest, nice
choice of wines by the glass; sports bar with
pool, TVs for racing, weekend live music;
children welcome, garden with play area, five
bedrooms, open all day. *(Michael Sargent)*

LECKHAMPSTEAD
SU4376
Stag (01488) 638436
Shop Lane; RG20 8QG Comfortable old
pub in quiet village, enjoyable attractively
priced food including good ploughman's,
well kept West Berkshire ale; nice local
walks. *(David and Judy Robison, Dr David and
Mrs Clare Gidlow)*

LITTLEWICK GREEN
SU8379
Cricketers (01628) 822888
*Not far from M4 junction 9; A404(M)
then left on to A4 – village signed on left;
Coronation Road; SL6 3RA* Welcoming
village pub in charming spot opposite
cricket green (can get crowded); well kept
Badger ales and good choice of wines by the
glass, enjoyable pub food from lunchtime
sandwiches and baguettes to specials,
traditional interior with huge clock above
brick fireplace; background music, Tues quiz;
children and dogs (they have their own)
welcome, a few tables out in front, open all
day, closed Mon in winter. *(Paul Humphreys)*

MARSH BENHAM
SU4267
Red House (01635) 582017
Off A4 W of Newbury; RG20 8LY
Attractive thatched dining pub with good
fairly traditional food with a twist from
french chef/owner including set menu
choices (Mon-Sat till 6.30pm), West
Berkshire and a guest ale, lots of wines by
the glass, afternoon tea, roomy flagstoned/
wood floor bar with woodburner, refurbished
restaurant; background music; children and
dogs welcome, terrace and long lawns sloping
to water meadows and the River Kennet,
open all day. *(Phoebe Peacock)*

NEWBURY
SU4767
Lock Stock & Barrel (01635) 580550
Northbrook Street; RG14 1AA Popular
modern pub standing out for canalside
setting, with partly flagstoned bar, suntrap
balcony and terrace looking over a series of
locks towards handsome church, low ceiling
and panelling, lots of windows, varied choice
of enjoyable sensibly priced food all day,
well kept Fullers and a guest such as West
Berkshire, efficient friendly staff, Tues poker
night, Sun quiz, live music Sun afternoon;
free wi-fi; children welcome, canal walks,
open till midnight Fri, Sat. *(Cliff Sparkes)*

OAKLEY GREEN
SU9276
★ Greene Oak (01753) 864294
*Off A308 Windsor–Maidenhead at
Twyford (B3024) signpost; Dedworth
Road; SL4 5UW* Several rambling eating
areas with variety of dining chairs and

wall banquettes around unusual green-painted kitchen-style tables, dark boards or flagstones, country-landscape wallpaper and floral blinds, enjoyable traditional and modern food from changing menu, inner back bar counter serving Greene King IPA and Abbot, plenty of wines by glass, friendly helpful staff; soft background music, free wi-fi; children welcome, sizeable paved and gravelled terrace behind, heated smokers' shelter, open all day (till 9pm Sun). *(Simon Collett-Jones)*

PALEY STREET   SU8675
Bridge House (01628) 623288
B3024; SL6 3JS Extended low-beamed cottage with comfortable traditional log-fire bar, friendly helpful landlady, four well kept ales including Rebellion and Fullers London Pride, decent reasonably priced pubby food (all day weekends) from shortish menu, pleasant back dining room; background music, TV, Weds quiz; children welcome, gardens front and back, two smokers' shelters, open all day. *(Dave Braisted)*

PALEY STREET   SU8676
★Royal Oak (01628) 620541
B3024 W; SL6 3JN Attractively modernised 17th-c restauranty pub owned by Sir Michael Parkinson and son Nick; highly regarded british cooking (not cheap) and most here to eat, good attentive service, dining room split by brick pillars and timbering with mix of well spaced wooden tables and leather chairs on bare boards or flagstones, smallish informal beamed bar with open fire, leather sofas and cricketing prints, Fullers London Pride and wide choice of wines by the glass including champagne; background jazz; children welcome (no pushchairs in restaurant), closed Sun. *(Tracey and Stephen Groves)*

PANGBOURNE   SU6376
Cross Keys (0118) 984 3268
Church Road, opposite church; RG8 7AR Refurbished 18th-c pub with linked split-level beamed rooms, simple bar on right, neat dining area to the left, two Greene King ales with a guest such as Brentwood, enjoyable food including lunchtime set menu (Mon-Thurs), friendly helpful staff; background music; children and dogs welcome, streamside terrace at back with covered seating area, paid daytime parking some way off, open all day. *(N R White, Paul Humphreys)*

READING   SU7173
★Alehouse (0118) 950 8119
Broad Street; RG1 2BH Cheerful no-frills drinkers' pub with eight well kept quickly changing ales and a couple of craft beers, also lots of different bottled beers, czech lager on tap, farm ciders and perry; small bare-boards bar (no mobile phones, children or dogs) with raised seating area, hundreds of pump clips on walls and ceiling, corridor to several appealing little panelled rooms, some

little more than alcoves, no food; background music, TV and quiz first Mon of month; open all day. *(John Pritchard)*

READING   SU7174
Moderation (0118) 375 0767
Caversham Road; RG1 8BB Modernised airy Victorian pub with some eastern influences, enjoyable reasonably priced food including thai/indonesian choices, pleasant prompt service, four well kept changing ales; enclosed garden behind, open all day. *(C and R Bromage, Dave Braisted)*

READING   SU7073
Nags Head 07765 880137
Russell Street; RG1 7XD Largish drinkers' pub just outside town centre attracting good mix of customers, a dozen well kept changing ales and 13 real ciders, baguettes and pies, open fire, darts and cribbage; background and occasional live music, TV for major sporting events; beer garden, open all day. *(John Pritchard)*

READING   SU7173
★Sweeney & Todd (0118) 958 6466
Castle Street; RG1 7RD Pie shop with popular bar/restaurant behind (little changed in 30 years), warren of private period-feel alcoves and other areas on various levels, good home-made food all day including their range of pies such as venison and wild boar, cheery service, small bar with four well kept ales including Wadworths and Adnams, Weston's cider and decent wines; children welcome in restaurant area, open all day (closed Sun evening and bank holidays). *(Pete Walker, John Pritchard, Simon Collett-Jones)*

READING   SU7173
Zero Degrees (0118) 959 7959
Bridge Street; RG1 2LR Modern bar/restauarant over three floors with welcoming staff and cheerful mix of customers, own-brew beers and enjoyable food including pizzas, pasta and mussels done in different ways; open all day. *(David M Smith)*

SHINFIELD   SU7367
★Magpie & Parrot (0118) 988 4130
2.6 miles from M4 junction 11, via B3270; A327 just SE of Shinfield on Arborfield Road; RG2 9EA Unusual homely little roadside cottage with warm fire, lots of bric-a-brac (miniature and historic bottles, stuffed birds, dozens of model cars, veteran AA badges and automotive instruments) in two cosy spic-and-span bars, Fullers London Pride and local guests from small corner counter, weekday lunchtime snacks and evening fish and chips (Thurs, Fri), hospitable landlady; no credit cards or mobile phones; pub dog (others welcome), seats on back terrace and marquee on immaculate lawn, open 12-7.30, closed Sun evening. *(Anon)*

SHURLOCK ROW   SU8374
★ **Shurlock Inn** (0118) 934 9094
*Just off B3018 SE of Twyford; The Street;
RG10 0PS* Cosy village-owned pub with
good food (all day Sun) from pubby choices
up, four local ales including West Berkshire
Mr Chubb and nice house wines, log fire in
double-sided fireplace dividing bar and larger
dining room, new oak flooring, panelling
and one or two old beams; background
music; children welcome, dogs in bar, black
metal furniture on side and back terraces,
garden with picnic-sets under parasols and
fenced play area, open all day Fri, Sat, till
9pm Sun. *(Paul Humphreys, Susan and John
Douglas, Charlotte)*

STREATLEY   SU5980
Bull (01491) 872392
Reading Road (A417/B4009); RG8 9JJ
Refurbished pub dating from Tudor times,
half a dozen well kept mainly Marstons-
related ales, enjoyable reasonably priced
food from sandwiches up including range of
curries, good service; tables in tree-sheltered
garden, nice walks (on Ridgeway Trail), five
bedrooms, open all day. *(Ross Balaam)*

SUNNINGHILL   SU9367
Carpenters Arms (01344) 622763
Upper Village Road; SL5 7AQ Restauranty
village pub run by french team, good
authentic french country cooking, not cheap
but they do offer a reasonably priced set
lunch (Mon-Sat), nice wines, Sharps Doom
Bar; no children in the evening, terrace
tables, open all day and best to book.
(Phoebe Peacock)

SUNNINGHILL   SU9367
Dog & Partridge (01344) 623204
Upper Village Road; SL5 7AQ
Modern feel with emphasis on good home-
made food (all day Sun till 7pm) including
set lunch, friendly helpful staff, Fullers
London Pride and Sharps Doom Bar, good
range of wines; background and some live
music; children and dogs welcome, disabled
facilities, sunny courtyard garden with
fountain, play area, open all day Fri-Sun,
closed Mon. *(Anon)*

THEALE   SU6471
★ **Fox & Hounds** (01189) 302295
*2 miles from M4 junction 12; best to
bypass restricted-access town centre –
take first left at town-edge roundabout,
then at railway turn right into Brunel
Road, then left past station on Station
Road; keep on over narrow canal bridge
to Sheffield Bottom S of town; RG7 4BE*
Large neatly kept dining pub, friendly and
relaxed, with well priced food (all day Fri,
Sat, not Sun evening) from baguettes and
pizzas to blackboard specials, several well
kept Wadworths ales, Weston's cider, decent
wines and coffee, L-shaped bar with dividers,

traditional mix of furniture on carpet or bare
boards including area with modern sofas
and low tables, two open fires, daily papers;
pool and darts, Sun quiz; children and dogs
welcome, outside seating at front and sides,
lakeside bird reserve opposite, open all day
Fri-Sun. *(John Pritchard)*

THEALE   SU6168
Winning Hand (0118) 930 2472
*A4 W, opposite Sulhamstead turn; handy
for M4 junction 12; RG7 5JB* Good
choice of enjoyable bar and restaurant food
including well priced set menu, friendly
efficient service, two changing ales and
varied wine list, dining room with stripped-
pine furniture and church candles on brass
or wrought-iron stands, further eating area
with modern furniture on light wood floor
and contemporary artwork; quiet background
music, no dogs; children welcome, tables on
front and back terraces, closed Sun evening,
Mon. *(John Pritchard)*

THREE MILE CROSS   SU7167
Swan (0118) 988 3674
*A33 just S of M4 junction 11;
Basingstoke Road; RG7 1AT* Smallish
traditional pub built in the 17th c and later
a posting house, six well kept ales including
Fullers London Pride, Loddon Hoppit and
Timothy Taylors Boltmaker, enjoyable fairly
standard home-made food at reasonable
prices, friendly staff, beams, inglenook with
hanging black pots, old prints and some
impressive stuffed fish; large well arranged
outside seating area behind (also home to
wolfhound Mr Niall, the London Irish RFC
mascot), near Madejski Stadium and very
busy on match days, open all day weekdays,
closed Sun evening. *(John Pritchard)*

TIDMARSH   SU6374
Greyhound (0118) 984 3557
A340 S of Pangbourne; RG8 8ER
Prettily restored old thatched and beamed
pub, warm and friendly, with good choice
of enjoyable food including two-course deal
(Mon-Thurs), pleasant service, Fullers ales
and several wines by the glass, two carpeted
bars, back dining extension; background
music, free wi-fi; good walks nearby, open all
day (till 9pm Sun). *(Harvey Brown)*

WALTHAM ST LAWRENCE   SU8376
★ **Bell** (0118) 934 1788
B3024 E of Twyford; The Street; RG10 0JJ
Welcoming 14th-c village local with well
preserved beamed and timbered interior,
cheerful landlord and chatty regulars,
good home-made blackboard food (not Sun
evening) from bar snacks including own
pork pies up, friendly service, well kept
Binghams and local guests such as West
Berkshire (summer beer festival), real cider,
plenty of malt whiskies and nice wines, warm
log fires, compact panelled lounge, daily
papers; children and dogs welcome, pretty

back garden with extended terrace and shady trees, open all day weekends. *(Paul Humphreys, N R White, Susan and John Douglas and others)*

WARGRAVE   SU7878
Bull 0843 289 1773
Off A321 Henley–Twyford; High Street; RG10 8DE Low-beamed 15th-c coaching inn recently refurbished and back under former landlady; main bar with inglenook log fire, two dining areas (one up steps for families), enjoyable traditional home-made food from baguettes up, Brakspears ales and a guest, friendly helpful staff; background music, free wi-fi; well behaved dogs welcome, walled garden behind, four bedrooms, open all day weekends. *(Paul Humphreys)*

WEST ILSLEY   SU4782
Harrow (01635) 281260
Signed off A34 at E Ilsley slip road; RG20 7AR Appealing country pub in peaceful spot overlooking cricket pitch and pond, Victorian prints in deep-coloured knocked-through bar, some antique furnishings, log fire, good choice of enjoyable sensibly priced home-made food (not Sun or Mon evenings), well kept Greene King ales and nice selection of wines by the glass, afternoon teas; children in eating areas, dogs allowed in bar, big garden with picnic-sets, more seats on pleasant terrace, handy for Ridgeway walkers, may close early Sun evening if quiet. *(Helen and Brian Edgeley, David and Judy Robison, M and GR)*

WINDSOR   SU9676
Carpenters Arms (01753) 863739
Market Street; SL4 1PB Nicholsons pub rambling around central servery with good choice of well kept ales and several wines by the glass, reasonably priced pubby food all day from sandwiches up including range of pies, friendly helpful service, sturdy pub furnishings and Victorian-style décor with two pretty fireplaces, family areas up a few steps, also downstairs beside former tunnel entrance with suits of armour; background music, no dogs; tables out on cobbled pedestrian alley opposite castle, no nearby

parking, handy for Legoland bus stop. *(Ian Herdman, George Atkinson)*

WINDSOR   SU9676
Two Brewers (01753) 855426
Park Street; SL4 1LB In the shadow of Windsor Castle with three compact unchanging bare-board rooms, well kept Fullers London Pride and a couple of guests, good choice of wines by the glass, enjoyable food (not Fri-Sun evenings) from shortish menu, friendly efficient service, thriving old-fashioned pub atmosphere, beams and open fire, enamel signs and posters on walls, daily papers; background music, no children inside; dogs welcome, tables and attractive hanging baskets out by pretty Georgian street next to Windsor Park's Long Walk, open all day. *(Ian Herdman, Richard Stanfield)*

WINDSOR   SU9576
Vansittart Arms (01753) 865988
Vansittart Road; SL4 5DD Friendly three-room Victorian pub, interesting local prints, some old furniture and cosy corners, open fires, well kept Fullers ales and enjoyable good value home-made food (all day weekends); background music, sports TV, pool, free wi-fi; children and dogs welcome, good-sized beer garden with heated smokers' area, summer barbecues, open all day. *(Anon)*

WINTERBOURNE   SU4572
Winterbourne Arms (01635) 248200
3.7 miles from M4 junction 13; at A34 turn into Chieveley Services and follow Donnington signs to Arlington Lane, then follow Winterbourne signs; RG20 8BB This nice old bustling pub (a former popular Main Entry) will have new licensees by the time you read this – reports please; has had traditionally furnished bars with mix of pine tables and chairs, beers such as Ramsbury Gold and good choice of wines, big windows give peaceful rural views, and there are seats in the big landscaped side garden; pretty village with lovely surrounding walks. *(Ian Herdman, David Fowler, Martin Day, Alistair Forsyth, R K Phillips, D and M T Ayres-Regan and others)*

Post Office address codings confusingly give the impression that some pubs are in Berkshire, when they're really in Buckinghamshire, Oxfordshire or Hampshire (which is where we list them).

Buckinghamshire

KEY  ★ Star Pub   🌟 Top Quality Food   🍺 Great Beer

🍷 Good Wines   £ Bargain Meals   🛏 Good Bedrooms   🍴 Serves Food

---

 ADSTOCK   SP7330   Map 4

Old Thatched Inn 🍺

Main Street, off A413; MK18 2JN

Pretty thatched dining pub with keen landlord, friendly staff, five real ales and enjoyable food

---

Deservedly popular, this is a very well run and pretty thatched dining pub with warmly friendly and efficient staff. The bustling front bar area has low beams, flagstones, high bar chairs and an open fire, and they keep Fullers London Pride, Hook Norton Hooky Bitter, Sharps Doom Bar, Timothy Taylors Landlord and a guest or two on handpump, 15 wines by the glass, a dozen malt whiskies and three ciders. A dining area leads off with more beams and a mix of pale wooden dining chairs around miscellaneous tables on a stripped wooden floor; background music. There's also a modern conservatory restaurant at the back with well spaced tables on bare boards. The sheltered terrace has tables and chairs under a gazebo. This is an attractive village.

🍴 As well as a weekday two- and three-course set menu, the attractively presented, popular food includes chicken liver parfait, devilled kidneys on toast, free-range chicken with tomato provençale, cumberland sausages with red wine gravy, steak in ale pie, duck breast and confit leg with butternut purée and potato croquette, and puddings such as white chocolate mousse and apple crumble tart with caramel ice-cream. *Benchmark main dish: crispy calamari and bass risotto £13.95. Two-course evening meal £20.50.*

Free house ~ Licensee Andrew Judge ~ Real ale ~ (01296) 712584 ~ Open 12-11 (midnight Sat, 10.30 Sun) ~ Bar food 12-2.30, 6-9.30; 12-8 Sun ~ Restaurant ~ Well behaved children welcome ~ Dogs allowed in bar ~ www.theoldthatchedinn.co.uk
Recommended by Harvey Brown, George Atkinson

 AYLESBURY   SP8113   Map 4

Kings Head 🍺

Kings Head Passage (off Bourbon Street), also entrance off Temple Street; no nearby parking except for disabled; HP20 2RW

Handsome town centre pub with civilised atmosphere, good local ales (used in the food too) and friendly service

---

The pub in this rather special 15th-c building is just one part – the others being a coffee shop, arts and crafts shop, Tourist Information Office and conference rooms. It's such a surprise, tucked away as it is in a modern town centre, with its particularly beautiful early Tudor windows and stunning 15th-c stained glass in the former Great Hall showing the Royal Arms of Henry VI and Margaret of Anjou. Three timeless rooms have been restored with careful and unpretentious simplicity – stripped boards, cream walls with little decoration, gentle lighting, a variety of seating which includes upholstered sofas and armchairs, cushioned high-backed settles and some simple modern pale dining tables and chairs dotted around. Most of the bar tables are of round glass, supported on low cask tops. It's all nicely low-key – not smart, but thoroughly civilised. The neat corner bar has Chiltern Ale and Beechwood Bitter (they're the brewery tap for Chiltern) and a couple of guests on handpump and some interesting bottled beers. Service is friendly and there's no background music or machines. The atmospheric medieval cobbled courtyard has teak seats and tables, some beneath a pillared roof, and a second-hand bookshop. The place is owned by the National Trust. Disabled access and facilities.

Tasty lunchtime food includes sandwiches, bubble and squeak with bacon and free-range egg, beef in ale stew with dumplings, a pie of the week, wild mushroom and goats cheese wellington, and puddings such as chocolate sponge with chocolate sauce and banoffi pie. *Benchmark main dish: beer-battered haddock and chips £11.50.*

Chiltern ~ Manager George Jenkinson ~ Real ale ~ (01296) 718812 ~ Open 11-11; 12-10.30 Sun ~ Bar food 12-2; 12-3 weekends ~ Children welcome ~ Wi-fi ~ www.farmersbar.co.uk *Recommended by Tim and Ann Newell, Tony and Wendy Hobden*

BOVINGDON GREEN
Royal Oak ⭐ ♀ SU8386 Map 2

0.75 miles N of Marlow, on back road to Frieth signposted off West Street (A4155) in centre; SL7 2JF

Civilised dining pub with nice little bar, a fine choice of wines by the glass, real ales, good service and imaginative food

---

With a fine choice of drinks – Rebellion IPA and Zebedee on handpump, 24 wines by the glass (plus pudding wines), several gins and farm cider – and highly thought-of food, this friendly little whitewashed pub is popular with both regulars and visitors. The low-beamed cosy snug, closest to the car park, has three small tables and a woodburning stove in an exposed brick fireplace (with a big pile of logs beside it). Several other attractively decorated areas open off the central bar with half-panelled walls variously painted in pale blue, green or cream (though the dining room ones are red). Throughout, there's a mix of church chairs, stripped wooden tables and chunky wall seats, with rugs on the partly wooden, partly flagstoned floors, co-ordinated cushions and curtains, and a very bright, airy feel. Thoughtful extra touches enhance the tone: a bowl of olives on the bar, carefully laid-out newspapers and fresh flowers or candles on the tables. Board games and background music. A sunny terrace with good solid tables leads to an appealing garden; there's also a smaller side garden, a kitchen herb garden and a pétanque court. Red kites regularly fly over.

Beautifully presented food includes lunchtime sandwiches (not weekends), potted salmon and smoked haddock with brown butter vinaigrette, bubble and squeak with oak-smoked bacon and free-range poached egg, spiced chickpea, sweetcorn and onion burger with chips, duck breast with bombay parsnip pickle and tamarind caramel, crispy skinned sea bream with horseradish mash, pressed beetroot and dill sauce, and puddings such as rhubarb and custard crème brûlée and baked chocolate soup with salted caramel and nut ice-cream.

Benchmark main dish: maple syrup-glazed pork belly with crackling £14.75.
Two-course evening meal £21.00.

Salisbury Pubs ~ Lease Matt Burchell ~ Real ale ~ (01628) 488611 ~ Open 11-11;
12-10.30 Sun ~ Bar food 12-2.30 (3 Sat, 4 Sun), 6.30-9.30 (10 Fri, Sat) ~ Restaurant ~
Children welcome ~ Dogs allowed in bar ~ Wi-fi ~ www.royaloakmarlow.co.uk
Recommended by Martin and Karen Wake, Di and Mike Gillam, Dave Braisted, Richard and
Liz Thorne

DENHAM
Swan 🌟 🍷
TQ0487   Map 3

Village signed from M25 junction 16; UB9 5BH

**Double-fronted dining pub in quiet village with interesting furnishings
in several bars, open fires, good food, and a fine choice of drinks**

In warm weather, the extensive garden behind this civilised old pub is
a big draw (it's also floodlit at night) and there are seats and tables on
a sheltered terrace, with more on a spacious lawn; the wisteria is lovely in
May. Inside, the bar rooms are stylishly furnished with a nice mix of antique
and old-fashioned chairs and solid tables, individually chosen pictures on
cream and warm green walls, rich heavily draped curtains, inviting open
fires, newspapers to read and fresh flowers. Caledonian Flying Scotsman
and Rebellion IPA on handpump, 24 wines by the glass (plus pudding
wines) and a good choice of vodkas and liqueurs; background music.
It can get busy at weekends, when parking may be tricky.

 Using the best local produce, the inventive food includes duck faggot with
caramelised rhubarb and honey-braised beetroot, mussels in white wine,
tomatoes and saffron, free-range sausages of the day, chestnut mushroom, spinach
and goats cheese wellington with puy lentil stew, venison burger with root vegetable
chips, salmon with lemon thyme ratatouille and roast garlic oil, and puddings such
as brioche apple doughnuts with custard dip and chocolate and peanut bread and
butter pudding. *Benchmark main dish: slow-cooked beef cheek with cottage pie and
cheddar mash £13.50. Two-course evening meal £21.00.*

Salisbury Pubs ~ Lease Mark Littlewood ~ Real ale ~ (01895) 832085 ~ Open 11-11;
12-10.30 Sun ~ Bar food 12-2.30 (3 Sat), 6.30-9.30 (10 Fri, Sat); 12-9 Sun ~ Restaurant ~
Children welcome ~ Dogs allowed in bar ~ Wi-fi ~ www.swaninndenham.co.uk
Recommended by Alfie Bayliss, Phoebe Peacock

EASINGTON
Mole & Chicken 🌟 🍷 🛏
SP6810   Map 4

*From B4011 in Long Crendon follow Chearsley, Waddesdon signpost into
Carters Lane opposite indian restaurant, then turn left into Chilton Road; HP18 9EY*

**Country views from decking and garden, an inviting interior, real ales
and enjoyable food and drink; nice bedrooms**

At the back of this creeper-clad pub is a raised terrace and decked area
with views over fine rolling countryside – a lovely place for a summer's
lunch or sunset drink. The opened-up interior is arranged so that the
different parts seem quite snug and self-contained without being cut off
from the relaxed sociable atmosphere. The heavily beamed bar curves
around the serving counter in a sort of S-shape, and there are cream-
cushioned farmhouse chairs around oak and pine tables on flagstones or
tiles, a couple of dark leather sofas, church candles and good winter log
fires. Vale Best Bitter and a guest on handpump, several wines by the glass

and quite a few malt whiskies; background music. This is a civilised place to stay in cosy and comfortable bedrooms, and the breakfasts are good too.

 Enticing food includes scallops with black pudding and samphire risotto, confit duck salad with thai herbs and cashew nuts, crispy poached duck egg with asparagus, pea and broad bean risotto, chicken with smoked aubergine and tomato ragout with chive linguine, rump burger with cheese, bacon and chips, lamb shoulder with bubble and squeak and mint jus, and puddings such as chocolate fondant with honeycomb ice-cream and vanilla crème brûlée; they also offer a two- and three-course set menu and a sharing menu. *Benchmark main dish: 28-day-aged rib-eye steak with choice of sauce and chips £19.50. Two-course evening meal £28.00.*

Free house ~ Licensee Steve Bush ~ Real ale ~ (01844) 208387 ~ Open 11-11 ~ Bar food 12-2.30 (4 Sun), 6-9.30 (9 Sun) ~ Children welcome ~ Wi-fi ~ Bedrooms: £85/£110 ~ www.themoleandchicken.co.uk *Recommended by Roger and Anne Newbury, Richard Kennell*

FINGEST
SU7791 Map 2
Chequers
Off B482 Marlow–Stokenchurch; RG9 6QD

Friendly, spotlessly kept old pub with big garden, real ales and interesting food

There are plenty of good walks surrounding this white-shuttered brick and flint pub with quiet pastures sloping up to beechwoods; dogs are allowed in the bar. There's an unaffected public bar with real country charm plus other neatly kept old-fashioned rooms that are warm, cosy and traditional, with large open fires, horsebrasses, pewter tankards, and pub team photographs on the walls. Brakspears Bitter and Special and a guest such as Ringwood Boondoggle on handpump alongside quite a few wines by the glass and several malt whiskies; board games and a house cat and dog. French doors from the smart back dining extension open to a terrace (plenty of picnic-sets), which leads on to the big, beautifully tended garden with fine views over the Hambleden valley. Over the road is a unique Norman twin-roofed church tower – probably the nave of the original church.

Good, enjoyable food includes lunchtime sandwiches, king prawns in garlic and chilli, welsh rarebit, local sausages with onion rings, white bean cassoulet, lemon sole with lemon butter, venison loin with braised red cabbage, and puddings such as banoffi cheesecake and hot chocolate fondant. *Benchmark main dish: beef or venison burger with fries and salad £11.95. Two-course evening meal £20.00.*

Brakspears ~ Tenants Jaxon and Emma Keedwell ~ Real ale ~ (01491) 638335 ~ Open 12-3, 5.30-11; 12-11 Sat; 12-10.30 Sun ~ Bar food 12-2 (3 Sat, 4 Sun), 7-9 (9.30 Fri, Sat) ~ Restaurant ~ Children welcome ~ Dogs allowed in bar ~ www.chequersfingest.com *Recommended by Tracey and Stephen Groves, Ms Caroline Heaney*

FORTY GREEN
SU9291 Map 2
Royal Standard of England
3.5 miles from M40 junction 2, via A40 to Beaconsfield, then follow sign to Forty Green, off B474 0.75 miles N of New Beaconsfield; keep going through village; HP9 1XT

Full of history and character, fascinating antiques in rambling rooms, and good choice of drinks and food

'A wonderful muddle of ancient things in a fascinating warren of rooms,' is how one reader happily describes this ancient place. It's been trading for nearly 900 years (the leaflet documenting the pub's history is very interesting) and there are some fine old features to look out for. The rambling rooms have huge black ship's timbers, lovely worn floors, carved old oak panelling, roaring winter fires with handsomely decorated iron firebacks and cluttered mantelpieces, and there's a massive settle apparently built to fit the curved transom of an Elizabethan ship. Nooks and crannies are filled with a collection of antiques, including rifles, powder-flasks and bugles, ancient pewter and pottery tankards, lots of tarnished brass and copper, needlework samplers and richly coloured stained glass. As well as brewing their own Britannia Pale and Gold, they keep six changing guests from other breweries such as Brakspears, Chiltern, Rebellion, Vale and Windsor & Eton; there's also a carefully annotated list of bottled beers and malt whiskies, farm ciders, perry, somerset brandy and around a dozen wines by the glass. You can sit outside in a neatly hedged front rose garden or under the shade of a tree; look out for the red gargoyle on the wall facing the car park. The inn is used regularly for filming television programmes such as *Midsomer Murders*. They also own the Red Lion at Penn.

As well as a weekday two- and three-course set lunch, the good, popular, fairly priced food includes lunchtime sandwiches and baguettes, chicken liver pâté, moules marinière, walnut, apple and stilton salad, chicken, leek and mushroom pie, a fish dish of the day, duck in orange sauce, lambs liver and bacon, and puddings such as treacle sponge pudding and custard and chocolate mousse. *Benchmark main dish: cod and chips £12.50. Two-course evening meal £19.50.*

Own brew ~ Licensee Matthew O'Keeffe ~ Real ale ~ (01494) 673382 ~ Open 11-11; 12-10.30 Sun ~ Bar food 12-10 ~ Children welcome ~ Dogs allowed in bar ~ Wi-fi ~ www.rsoe.co.uk *Recommended by Dave Braisted, Susan and John Douglas, Simon Collett-Jones, Tracey and Stephen Groves, N R White, Roy Hoing, Paul Humphreys, Gordon and Jenny Quick, Richard and Liz Thorne, D J and P M Taylor, Richard Tilbrook*

FULMER
Black Horse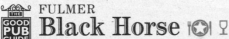

SU9985 Map 2

Village signposted off A40 in Gerrards Cross, W of its junction with A413; Windmill Road; SL3 6HD

Appealingly reworked dining pub, friendly and relaxed, with enjoyable up-to-date food, exemplary service and pleasant garden; bedrooms

Even when coping with crowds of drinkers and diners, staff in this 17th-c pub remain friendly and efficient. The building has been gradually extended over the years to form a charming and thoughtfully run country pub with a lot of character. There's a proper bar in the middle and two cosy areas to the left with low black beams, rugs on bare boards, settles and other solid pub furniture and several open log fires. Greene King IPA and H&H Olde Trip and a changing guest beer on handpump, and most of the wines on their list are available by the glass; background music. The main area on the right is set for dining and leads to the good-sized suntrap back terrace. They now have two stylish, well-equipped bedrooms. This is a charming conservation village.

Good, interesting food includes sandwiches (until 6pm), sticky pork ribs, spiced lamb koftas with tzatziki, interesting salads, red pepper, sweetcorn, chilli and spring onion risotto, burger with cheddar, gherkins, coleslaw and chips, marmalade-braised pork belly, confit cabbage and potato and apple terrine, whole lemon sole with chilli, anchovies and toasted almond, and puddings such as bakewell tart with amaretti crème fraîche and chocolate brownie. *Benchmark main dish: beer-battered haddock and chips £13.00. Two-course evening meal £20.00.*

Greene King ~ Lease David Webster ~ Real ale ~ (01753) 663183 ~ Open 8.30am-11pm; 12-10.30 Sun ~ Bar food 8.30am-9.30pm (10pm Sat, 7pm Sun) ~ Restaurant ~ Children welcome ~ Dogs allowed in bar ~ Wi-fi ~ Bedrooms: /£110 ~ www.theblackhorsefulmer.co.uk *Recommended by R K Phillips, M G Hart, Simon Collett-Jones*

GREET MISSENDEN

SP9000 Map 4

Nags Head

Old London Road, E – beyond Abbey; HP16 0DG

Well run and pretty inn with beamed bars, an open fire, a good range of drinks and modern cooking; comfortable bedrooms

There's no doubt that most customers in this quietly civilised and neatly kept place are here to enjoy the tempting food, but they do keep Rebellion IPA and a couple of guests from Chiltern, Tring or Vale on handpump from the unusual bar counter (the windows behind face the road), 25 wines by the glass from an extensive list and half a dozen vintage Armagnacs. There's a low-beamed area on the left, a loftier part on the right, a mix of small pews, dining chairs and tables on the carpet, Quentin Blake prints on cream walls and a log fire in a handsome fireplace. There's an outside dining area under a pergola and seats on the extensive back lawn. The beamed bedrooms are well equipped and comfortable, and the breakfasts are very good. Roald Dahl used this as his local and the Roald Dahl Museum & Story Centre is just a stroll away.

 Imaginative food includes chicken liver parfait with pear chutney, cornish crab with home-smoked salmon with chive cream and blinis, sausages of the day with red wine gravy, guinea fowl breast with pheasant sausage and liver mousse feuilletée and thyme jus, mini pork and cider pie with pork fillet and black pudding and wholegrain mustard jus, and puddings such as sticky toffee pudding with date mascarpone and apple and red fruit crumble. *Benchmark main dish: crab and home-smoked salmon with chive cream £8.65. Two-course evening meal £25.*

Free house ~ Licensee Adam Michaels ~ Real ale ~ (01494) 862200 ~ Open 11-11 ~ Bar food 12-2.30, 6.30-9.30 ~ Restaurant ~ Children welcome ~ Dogs allowed in bar ~ Wi-fi ~ Bedrooms: £75/£95 ~ www.nagsheadbucks.com *Recommended by Ruth May, Alfie Bayliss, Tracey and Stephen Groves*

HAMBLEDEN

SU7886 Map 2

Stag & Huntsman

Off A4155 Henley–Marlow; RG9 6RP

Friendly inn with chatty bar, plenty of dining space and very good food, welcoming staff and country garden; bedrooms

In a pretty Chilterns village, this handsome brick and flint pub has been refurbished by the Culden Faw Estate. The little bar has the atmosphere of a thriving local with plenty of chatty regulars plus walkers and their dogs (they keep a laminated book showing local hikes): stools against the counter, built-in cushioned wall seating, simple tables and chairs, bare floorboards. Loddon Hoppit and Rebellion IPA on handpump and several wines by the glass, served by warmly friendly staff. There's also a sizeable open-plan room with armchairs beside a woodburning stove in a brick

---

Real ale may be served from handpumps, electric pumps (not just the on-off switches used for keg beer) or – common in Scotland – tall taps called founts (pronounced 'fonts') where a separate pump pushes the beer up under air pressure.

fireplace, and a sofa and stools around a polished chest on more boards; this leads into the dining room with all sorts of wooden or high-backed red leather dining chairs around a variety of wooden tables, and hunting prints and other pictures on floral wallpaper. The bedrooms are warm and comfortable and the breakfasts good. There are seats in the country garden which is just a field away from the river.

🍴 Enjoyable food includes sandwiches, ham hock terrine, deep-fried sweetbreads with tomato and chilli jam, butternut squash risotto, slow-cooked beef pie, corn-fed chicken breast with savoury bread pudding, smoked bacon gravy and sage and onion pesto, pollock, chorizo, chickpea and tomato stew, and puddings such as crème brûlée and rhubarb and apple crumble. *Benchmark main dish: beer-battered fish and chips £12.95. Two-course evening meal £20.00.*

Free house ~ Licensee Jaxon Keedwell ~ Real ale ~ (01491) 571227 ~ Open 11-11 ~ Bar food 12-2.30, 6-9.30; 12-3.30, 6-9 ~ Restaurant ~ Children welcome ~ Dogs allowed in bar ~ Wi-fi ~ Bedrooms: /$100 ~ www.thestagandhuntsman.co.uk
Recommended by Susan and John Douglas, John Pritchard

HEDGERLEY
White Horse ★ ◧ £
SU9687 Map 2

2.4 miles from M40 junction 2; at exit roundabout take Slough turn-off following alongside M40; after 1.5 miles turn right at T junction into Village Lane; SL2 3UY

Old-fashioned drinkers' pub with lots of beers tapped straight from the cask, regular beer festivals, home-made lunchtime food and a cheery mix of customers

Even when this charming country gem is packed there's always a good-natured, convivial atmosphere – and a fantastic choice of up to eight real ales. As well as Rebellion IPA, they keep up to seven daily changing guests, sourced from all over the country and tapped straight from casks kept in a room behind the tiny hatch counter. Their Easter, May, Spring and August bank holiday beer festivals (they can get through about 130 beers during the May event) are highlights of the local calendar. This marvellous range of drinks extends to three farm ciders, still apple juice, a perry, belgian beers, eight wines by the glass, 12 malt whiskies and winter mulled wine. The cottagey main bar has plenty of unspoilt character, with lots of beams, brasses and exposed brickwork, low wooden tables, standing timbers, jugs, ballcocks and other bric-a-brac, a log fire, and a good few leaflets and notices about village events. A little flagstoned public bar on the left has darts and board games. The canopied extension leads out to the garden where there are tables and the occasional barbecue, and lots of hanging baskets; a few tables in front of the building overlook the quiet road. Good walks nearby, and the pub is handy for the Church Wood RSPB reserve and popular with walkers and cyclists; it's often crowded at weekends.

🍴 Lunchtime bar food includes good sandwiches, a salad bar with home-cooked quiches and cold meats, and changing hot dishes such as soup, sausages, smashing steak and mushroom pie, lamb casserole and proper puddings such as plum sponge and bread and butter pudding. *Benchmark main dish: home-made pies £7.45.*

Free house ~ Licensees Doris Hobbs and Kevin Brooker ~ Real ale ~ (01753) 643225 ~ Open 11-2.30, 5-11; 11-11 Sat; 12-10.30 Sun ~ Bar food 12-2 (2.30 weekends) ~ Children in canopied extension area ~ Dogs allowed in bar *Recommended by N R White, Susan and John Douglas, Tracey and Stephen Groves, Roy Hoing*

LEY HILL
SP9901 Map 4

Swan 🍺

Village signposted off A416 in Chesham; HP5 1UT

Charming, old-fashioned pub with friendly licensees, chatty customers, four real ales and quite a choice of popular food

Once three cottages, this attractive little place – carefully refurbished recently – dates from the 16th c and has plenty of original features and a lot of character. The hands-on, friendly licensees keep it all spic and span, and the main bar is cosily old-fashioned with black beams (mind your head) and standing timbers, an old range, a log fire, a nice mix of old furniture and a collection of old local photographs. St Austell Tribute, Timothy Taylors Landlord, Tring Side Pocket for a Toad and a guest such as Black Sheep Best on handpump and several wines by the glass. The dining section is light and airy with a raftered ceiling, cream walls, red and gold curtains and all sorts of old tables and chairs on timber floors. It's worth wandering over to the common (where there's a cricket pitch and a nine-hole golf course) opposite this little timbered inn to turn back and admire the very pretty picture it makes, with picnic-sets among tubs of flowers and hanging baskets (there are more in the large back garden).

🍴 Good food includes crab cakes with sweet chilli dip, lambs kidneys and mushrooms on toasted ciabatta, burger with cheddar, mustard mayonnaise and chips, steak and kidney in Guinness pie, chicken stuffed with sun-dried tomatoes and wrapped in bacon with red wine jus, vegetarian tagliatelle, creamy seafood pot, and puddings such as raspberry and white chocolate cheesecake and sticky toffee and date pudding with toffee sauce. *Benchmark main dish: slow-cooked pork belly with red wine jus and apple purée £13.95. Two-course evening meal £20.50.*

Free house ~ Licensee Nigel Byatt ~ Real ale ~ (01494) 783075 ~ Open 12-2.30, 5.30-11; 12-4 Sun; closed Sun evening, Mon ~ Bar food 12-2.30 (3 Sun), 6-9 ~ Restaurant ~ Children welcome until 9pm ~ www.swanleyhill.com *Recommended by Ross Balaam, Isobel Mackinlay, John and Penny Wheeler*

LITTLE MARLOW
SU8787 Map 2

Queens Head 🍴⭐

Village signposted off A4155 E of Marlow near Kings Head; bear right into Pound Lane cul-de-sac; SL7 3SR

Charmingly tucked away country pub, with good food and beers, friendly staff and seats in an appealing garden

Once again, this consistently well run and highly enjoyable pub comes in for warm praise from our readers. The friendly and unpretentious main bar has simple but comfortable furniture on polished boards and leads back to a sizeable squarish carpeted dining extension with good solid tables. Throughout are old local photographs on cream or maroon walls, panelled dados painted brown or sage, and lighted candles. On the right is a small, quite separate, low-ceilinged public bar with Fullers London Pride and Rebellion IPA and Roasted Nuts on handpump, several wines by the glass, quite a range of whiskies and good coffee; neatly dressed efficient staff and unobtrusive background music. On a summer's day, the garden in front of this pretty tiled cottage is a decided plus, though not large:

We checked prices with the pubs as we went to press in summer 2014.
They should hold until around spring 2015.

---

sheltered and neatly planted, it has teak tables and quite close-set picnic-sets, and white-painted metal furniture in a little wickerwork bower.

 Extremely popular, good food includes lunchtime sandwiches, ham hock terrine with home-made piccalilli, scallops on sweetcorn pancakes with red pepper coulis, spicy bean burger with virgin mary sauce, corn-fed chicken with black pudding purée and sweet potato hash, fishcake with lobster sauce, pickled shallot salad and lemon crème fraîche, and puddings such as orange chocolate cheesecake and frozen strawberry and poached summer fruit trifle. *Benchmark main dish: beer-battered fish and chips £10.95. Two-course evening meal £22.50.*

Punch ~ Lease Daniel O'Sullivan and Chris Rising ~ Real ale ~ (01628) 482927 ~ Open 12-2.30 (4 Sat, Sun), 6.30-9.30 ~ Bar food 12-2.30 (4 Sat, Sun), 6.30-9.30 ~ Restaurant ~ Children welcome ~ Wi-fi ~ www.marlowslittlesecret.co.uk *Recommended by Martin and Karen Wake, Paul Humphreys, D and M T Ayres-Regan, Simon Collett-Jones, Gerald and Brenda Culliford*

 LITTLE MISSENDEN   SU9298 Map 4

Crown  £

Crown Lane, SE end of village, which is signposted off A413 W of Amersham; HP7 0RD

Long-serving licensees and pubby feel in little brick cottage, with several real ales and traditional food; attractive garden

A favourite with both loyal regulars and visitors, this traditional brick-built local has been run by the same family for over 90 years, and the cheerfully chatty and friendly landlord keeps everything spic and span. There are old red flooring tiles on the left, oak parquet on the right, built-in wall seats, studded red leatherette chairs and a few small tables and a winter fire. Adnams Bitter, St Austell Tribute and a guest or two such as Rebellion IPA and West Berkshire Maggs Magnificent Mild on handpump or tapped from the cask, farm cider, summer Pimms and several malt whiskies; darts and board games. The large attractive sheltered garden behind has picnic-sets and other tables, and there are also seats out in front. Bedrooms are in a converted barn (continental breakfasts in your room only). The interesting church in the pretty village is well worth a visit.

🍴 Honest lunchtime food (not Sunday) includes their famous bucks bite, sandwiches, filled baked potatoes, pasty with beans, field mushrooms stuffed with bacon and brie, salads and steak and kidney pie. *Benchmark main dish: bucks bite £7.50.*

Free house ~ Licensees Trevor and Carolyn How ~ Real ale ~ (01494) 862571 ~ Open 11-2.30 (3 Sat), 6-11; 12-3, 7-11 Sun ~ Bar food 12-2; not Sun ~ Wi-fi ~ Bedrooms: £70/£85 ~ www.the-crown-little-missenden.co.uk *Recommended by Roy Hoing, Edward May, Toby Jones*

LONG CRENDON   SP6908 Map 4

Eight Bells £

High Street, off B4011 N of Thame; car park entrance off Chearsley Road, not 'Village roads only'; HP18 9AL

Good beers and sensibly priced pubby food in nicely traditional village pub with charming garden

In an interesting old village (known to many from TV's *Midsomer Murders*), this unassuming pub is friendly and unchanging. The little bare-boards bar on the left has Ringwood Best and a beer named for the pub plus a couple of guests such as Springhead Outlawed and White Horse

Village Idiot on handpump or tapped from the cask, and a decent choice of wines by the glass; service is cheerful. A bigger low-ceilinged room on the right has a log fire, daily papers and a pleasantly haphazard mix of tables and simple seats on ancient red and black tiles; one snug little hidey-hole with just three tables is devoted to the local morris men – frequent visitors. Darts, board games and background music. The little back garden is a joy in summer and there are well spaced picnic-sets among a colourful variety of shrubs and flowers; aunt sally.

As well as their new weekend breakfast menu (from 10am), the fairly priced food includes sandwiches, ham hock croquettes, potted rabbit, pizzas, chargrilled polenta with roasted vegetables, feta and a raisin and pine nut dressing, chicken, ham, leek and cheddar pie, bass fillets with jerusalem artichoke and broad bean risotto, and puddings such as chocolate and honeycomb cheesecake with salted caramel sauce and rhubarb tartlet with custard. *Benchmark main dish: steak burger with smoked cheese, bacon, horseradish mayonnaise and chips £11.20. Two-course evening meal £16.75.*

Free house ~ Licensee Paul Mitchell ~ Real ale ~ (01844) 208244 ~ Open 12-11 ~ Bar food 12-9 (4 Sun) ~ Restaurant ~ Children welcome ~ Dogs allowed in bar ~ Wi-fi ~ Quiz night every second Tuesday ~ www.eightbellspub.com *Recommended by Mel Smith, John Branston, David Jackman*

MILTON KEYNES
SP8939   Map 4
Swan ♀
Broughton Road, Milton Keynes village; MK10 9AH

Plenty of space in well thought-out rooms, contemporary furnishings, open fires in inglenooks, enjoyable food and drink and seats outside

Cleverly done, mixing original features with contemporary furnishings, this is an attractive thatched pub with plenty of space both inside and out, and the interconnecting rooms have an easy-going and friendly atmosphere. The beamed main bar area has an open fire in an inglenook fireplace with logs piled up neatly on each side and two striped plush armchairs in front, several high tables and chairs dotted about, a cushioned wall banquette with scatter cushions, and wooden dining chairs and chunky tables on flagstones; Hydes Finest, Wells & Youngs Bitter and Bombardier and a guest beer on handpump, 30 wines by the glass, good coffees and large glass jars of nuts; courteous service. Leading off to the left is a cosy room with a gas stove, more cushioned banquettes and similar tables and chairs on parquet flooring, bookcase-effect wallpaper, some photos of the pub and a TV. The spreading, partly beamed restaurant with views of the open kitchen has all manner of wooden and pretty fabric-covered dining chairs, cushioned settles and wall seats and a few curved banquettes (creating snug, private areas) on floorboards, and a woodburning stove. Steps lead up to an airy room that overlooks the garden, where there are seats and picnic-sets on grass.

Enjoyable food using local producers and home-grown herbs includes lunchtime sandwiches, salmon and halibut gravadlax with beetroot salad, sharing platters, a pasta dish and a pie of the day, sausages with mash and onion gravy, vegetable and date terrine with lemon and thyme couscous, apple-stuffed chicken with dauphinoise potatoes and red wine jus, and puddings such as panettone and dark chocolate pudding and crumble of the day. *Benchmark main dish: chargrilled local steak with garlic butter or peppercorn sauce and chunky chips £19.25. Two-course evening meal £19.50.*

Front Line Inns ~ Manager Becky Voce ~ Real ale ~ (01908) 665240 ~ Open 11-11 (midnight Fri, Sat); 12-10.30 Sun ~ Bar food 12-3, 6-9.30; 12-10 Fri, Sat; 12-8 Sun ~ Restaurant ~ Children welcome ~ Dogs allowed in bar ~ Wi-fi ~ Regular comedy nights Sun ~ www.theswan-mkvillage.co.uk *Recommended by Isobel Mackinlay, Toby Jones, Edward May*

PENN
SU9093 Map 4
Old Queens Head 🌟 ♀

Hammersley Lane/Church Road, off B474 between Penn and Tylers Green; HP10 8EY

Stylishly updated pub with interesting food, a good choice of drinks, and woodland walks nearby

All are welcomed in this extended dining pub, and dogs might be offered a biscuit. The open-plan rooms have lots of different areas to sit in, all with different aspects, and are decorated in a stylish mix of contemporary and chintz. There are well spaced tables, a modicum of old prints and comfortably varied seating on flagstones or broad dark boards. Stairs lead up to an attractive (and popular) two-level dining room, partly carpeted, with stripped rafters. The active bar side has Greene King IPA and Ruddles County on handpump, 24 wines by the glass (plus pudding wines) and quite a few liqueurs; the turntable-top bar stools let you swivel to face the log fire in the big nearby fireplace; daily papers and well reproduced background music. The sunny terrace overlooks the church of St Margaret's and there are picnic-sets on the sheltered L-shaped lawn. You can walk through the nearby ancient beechwoods of Common or Penn Woods.

 Interesting food using seasonal produce includes lunchtime sandwiches (not weekends), mussels in cider and shallots, chicken liver parfait with rhubarb chutney, spaghetti with clams and chilli, free-range sausages of the day, cod fillet with mustard puy lentils, parmentier potatoes and tomato oil, slow-cooked pork belly with apple mash and rosemary jus, and puddings such as chocolate, cardamom and cranberry brownie and rhubarb and custard crème brûlée. *Benchmark main dish: slow-roast lamb faggot with garlic mash and minted gravy £11.50. Two-course evening meal £21.00.*

Salisbury Pubs ~ Lease Tina Brown ~ Real ale ~ (01494) 813371 ~ Open 11-11; 12-10.30 Sun ~ Bar food 12-2.30 (3 Sat), 6.30-9.30 (10 Fri, Sat); 12-9 Sun ~ Restaurant ~ Children welcome ~ Dogs allowed in bar ~ Wi-fi ~ www.oldqueensheadpenn.co.uk *Recommended by I D Barnett, Edward Mirzoeff, Richard Kennell*

PENN
SU9093 Map 4
Red Lion 🍺

Elm Road, B474; HP10 8LF

Bustling village pub with lots to look at in character rooms, a good mix of customers, well kept ales and tasty, pubby food; seats outside

All kinds of customers are welcomed here including dogs and ducks – the village pond is opposite. It's a proper local with original 17th-c features here and there in the various bar rooms, and some fine old pieces of furniture: a happy mix of rustic tables all set with a candle in a nice old brass candlestick, chairs ranging from cushioned mates' ones to leather and brass-studded dining chairs, all sorts and sizes of settles (the curved one beside the woodburner in the main bar is noteworthy), various homely sofas and armchairs and rugs on ancient parquet flooring or old quarry tiles. The walls are covered with a fantastic collection of British Empire prints and paintings, the beams are draped with hops, and the window sills and mantelpieces are crammed with Staffordshire china dogs and plates and stone and glass bottles; it's all really friendly and relaxed. Efficient staff serve Aylesbury Pure Gold, Chiltern Beechwood Bitter and Windsor & Eton Zinzan's Drop on handpump, farm cider and wines by the glass; TV and board games. There are wooden and metal seats and tables on the front terrace and settles lined up against the walls facing the pond. The pub is under the same ownership as the Royal Standard of England at Forty Green.

As well as lunchtime baguettes, the tasty food includes salt and pepper squid, chicken liver parfait, sausages with onion gravy, vegetarian lasagne, gammon and eggs, liver and bacon, beer-battered cod and chips, seasonal game dishes, and puddings such as lemon tart and ginger crème brûlée. *Benchmark main dish: steak in ale pie £11.50. Two-course evening meal £16.00.*

Free house ~ Licensee Matthew O'Keeffe ~ Real ale ~ (01494) 813107 ~ Open 11-11 (10 Sun) ~ Bar food 12-10 (9 Sun) ~ Restaurant ~ Children welcome ~ Dogs welcome ~ Wi-fi ~ www.redlionpenn.co.uk *Recommended by Harvey Brown, Paul Humphreys, Tracey and Stephen Groves*

PRESTWOOD

SP8799   Map 4

Polecat 🏅🍴 🍷

170 Wycombe Road (A4128 N of High Wycombe); HP16 0HJ

Enjoyable food, real ales and a chatty atmosphere in several smallish civilised rooms; attractive sizeable garden

Even on a miserable winter Monday evening you'll find plenty of chatty customers in this civilised, well run pub. Several smallish rooms, opening off the low-ceilinged bar, have a slightly chintzy décor: an assortment of tables and chairs, various stuffed birds, stuffed white polecats in one big cabinet, small country pictures, rugs on bare boards or red tiles, and a couple of antique housekeeper's chairs by a good open fire. Adnams Broadside, Brakspears Bitter, Ringwood Best and Skinners Betty Stogs on handpump, 16 wines by the glass, 15 malt whiskies and home-made summer elderflower pressé. They don't take bookings at lunchtime (except for groups of six or more) so you do need to arrive promptly at weekends to be sure of a table. The garden is most attractive with lots of spring bulbs, colourful summer hanging baskets and tubs and plenty of herbaceous plants; there are picnic-sets under parasols on neat grass out in front beneath a big fairy-lit pear tree, and more on a big well kept back lawn.

Well liked food includes lunchtime sandwiches, chicken liver and pistachio pâté with apricot chutney, twice-baked stilton soufflé, steak, mushroom and ale pie, mushroom and courgette rissoles with grain mustard dip, pheasant, bacon and root vegetable casserole, salmon with spinach mousse in filo pastry with watercress sauce, and puddings such as sherry trifle and profiteroles with chocolate sauce. *Benchmark main dish: chicken forestière £12.80. Two-course evening meal £17.00.*

Free house ~ Licensee John Gamble ~ Real ale ~ (01494) 862253 ~ Open 11.30-2.30, 6-11; 12-3 Sun; closed Sun evening ~ Bar food 12-2, 6.30-9; 12-2 Sun ~ Children allowed in gallery or drovers' bar only ~ Dogs allowed in bar
Recommended by Peter and Jan Humphreys, Mel Smith, Roy Hoing, David and Sue Smith, Tracey and Stephen Groves

SEER GREEN   SU9691 Map 2
Jolly Cricketers ⭐ 🍺
Chalfont Road, opposite the church; HP9 2YG

Bustling and friendly village pub with cricketing paraphernalia, a thoughtful choice of drinks, enjoyable food and seats on a back terrace

Just the place for a pint and a newspaper or a highly enjoyable meal, this red-brick pub appeals to all with its gently civilised and chatty atmosphere. The two rooms of the parquet-floored bar are divided by a big chimney, with a woodburning stove in each room, nice cushioned seats in bow windows, a mix of pale farmhouse and antique dining chairs around wooden and painted tables, candles and fresh flowers, and plenty of old cricketing photos, prints and bats on the walls. The stools at the bar are well used by locals, and friendly, helpful staff serve Fullers London Pride, Rebellion IPA and Ankle Tap, Skinners Betty Stogs and Vale VPA on handpump (they hold regular beer festivals), 16 good wines by the glass, 20 malt whiskies and home-made sloe gin and blackberry vodka; big glass jars of nuts and dried fruit behind the bar, board games and background music. The separate restaurant is similarly furnished and has a tiny little cushioned settle, teddy bears in cricket gear, a basket of cricket bats and a chandelier over the table by the window. There's a handsome wisteria at the front and picnic-sets on a back terrace; occasional live music.

 Impressive food using some home-grown produce includes crispy squid with thai basil and chilli, pork terrine with golden raisin chutney, corn-fed chicken, bacon and avocado salad, burger with cheddar, aioli and chips, honey and mustard ham shank with parsley sauce, stone bass with wild mushrooms, braised fennel in orange and saffron with potato galette, and puddings such as vanilla cheesecake with poached rhubarb and rhubarb sorbet and treacle tart with drunken oranges. *Benchmark main dish: pork belly with local black pudding, apple purée, coriander potato cake and yuzu dressing £15.50. Two-course evening meal £23.00.*

Free house ~ Licensees Amanda and Chris Lillitou ~ Real ale ~ (01494) 676308 ~ Open 12-11.30 (midnight Fri, Sat); 12-10.30 Sun ~ Bar food 12-2.30 (3 Sat, 4 Sun), 6.30-9; not Sun evening ~ Restaurant ~ Live music once a month ~ Dogs allowed in bar ~ Wi-fi ~ www.thejollycricketers.co.uk *Recommended by Tracey and Stephen Groves, Edward May*

STOKE MANDEVILLE   SP8310 Map 4
Bell 🍽 🍷
Lower Road; HP22 5XA

Buckinghamshire Dining Pub of the Year

Friendly landlord and staff in extended red-brick Victorian pub, with a relaxed atmosphere, a fine choice of drinks and interesting food and seats outside

Open from 10am for morning coffee and speciality teas, this extended red-brick Victorian pub is run by a friendly landlord of high repute. The interconnected bar and dining areas have flagstones or polished pine floorboards, dark blue dado with prints, drawings and maps of local interest and hunting prints on the walls above, and an easy-going atmosphere. High stools line the counter where they keep Chiltern Ale and Wells & Youngs Bombardier and Eagle on handpump and 20 wines (including sweet wines) by the glass; there are some equally high stools and tables opposite. Throughout are high-backed cushioned wooden and farmhouse chairs, wall settles with scatter cushions, and rustic benches around a medley of tables, some painted beams, and a woodburning stove; a snug alcove has just one table surrounded by cushioned wall seats. Quiet background music. The little side terrace has picnic-sets and there are more on grass beside a weeping birch.

Using the best local, seasonal produce, the interesting food includes sandwiches, parma ham-wrapped chicken and leek terrine with spiced pear, langoustine and smoked red pepper open ravioli, goats cheese and beetroot pearl barley risotto, burger with onion rings, coleslaw and chips, slow-roast lamb shank with flageolet bean and chorizo cassoulet, guinea fowl with creamed cabbage and ceps, and puddings such as pecan, date and honey pudding with yoghurt sorbet and apple tarte tatin with cinnamon cream. *Benchmark main dish: pork belly, roast tenderloin, parmentier potatoes and honey and thyme jus £14.50. Two-course evening meal £20.25.*

Wells & Youngs ~ Lease James Penlington ~ Real ale ~ (01296) 612434 ~ Open 10am-11pm; 12-10.30 Sun ~ Bar food 12-9.30; 12-4, 6.30-8.30 Sun ~ Restaurant ~ Children welcome ~ Dogs allowed in bar ~ Wi-fi ~ www.bellstokemandeville.co.uk
Recommended by Kate Day, Alexander Attridge, Jerry Scales, Sharon Cottle

WENDOVER
SP8609 Map 4

Village Gate

Aylesbury Road (B4009); HP22 6BA

Well run country pub with plenty of outside seating, friendly bar and several dining rooms, real ales and good, interesting food

You can pop into this carefully updated place from 10am for daily papers and a coffee and they offer some kind of food all day. The interconnected rooms have an easy-going, friendly atmosphere, contemporary paintwork and furnishings, and the bar has red leather tub chairs around log tables with polished tops, a woodburning stove in a brick fireplace, chunky leather stools and an assortment of dining chairs around various wooden tables, and animal prints above the half-panelling. High leather bar chairs sit against the modern bar counter with its unusual metal decoration, and they keep Brakspears Bitter, St Austell Tribute and Sharps Doom Bar on handpump. The other rooms are laid out for eating with high-backed plush, wooden or leather dining chairs around a mix of tables on oak boarding (some carpeting and stone tiling too); one room has rafters and beams in a very high ceiling and long swagged curtains. In warm weather there's plenty of outside seating on a roped-off decked area covered by a giant parasol, on terracing, on a raised decking and on gravel; long-reaching country views.

Rewarding food includes ham hock terrine with pickled vegetables and piccalilli, bubble and squeak with parma ham, hollandaise and a poached egg, sharing platters, a changing vegetarian risotto, burger with interesting toppings, a pie of the day, thai chicken curry, rack of ribs with coleslaw and cajun fries, and puddings such as crumble of the week and sticky toffee pudding. *Benchmark main dish: bass with fennel, spinach and olives in a citrus beurre blanc £13.95. Two-course evening meal £16.50.*

Free house ~ Licensee Jacob Wankowicz ~ Real ale ~ (01296) 623884 ~ Open 12-11 ~ Bar food 12-10 ~ Restaurant ~ Children welcome ~ Dogs allowed in bar ~ Wi-fi ~ Live music Friday evenings ~ www.villagegatewendover.com *Recommended by Ruth May, Taff Thomas*

WOOBURN COMMON
SU9187 Map 2

Chequers ♀ ⌂

From A4094 N of Maidenhead at junction with A4155 Marlow road keep on A4094 for another 0.75 miles, then at roundabout turn right towards Wooburn Common and into Kiln Lane; if you find yourself in Honey Hill, Hedsor, turn left into Kiln Lane at the top of the hill; OS Sheet 175 map reference 910870; HP10 0JQ

Busy, friendly hotel with a bustling bar, four real ales, bar food and more elaborate dishes in smart restaurant; comfortable bedrooms

Despite quite an emphasis on the hotel and restaurant side here, the friendly bar is the heart of the place and has plenty of chatty locals. It feels nicely pubby with low beams, standing timbers and alcoves, characterful rickety furniture and comfortably lived-in sofas on bare boards, a bright log-effect gas fire, pictures, plates, a two-man saw and tankards. In contrast, the bar to the left, with its dark brown leather sofas at low tables on wooden floors, feels plain and modern; the smart restaurant has high-backed black leather dining chairs around white-clothed tables. Rebellion IPA and Smuggler and St Austell Tribute on handpump, a good sizeable wine list (with a dozen by the glass), and a fair range of malt whiskies and brandies; background music. The spacious garden, set away from the road, has seats around cast-iron tables and summer barbecues.

Highly thought-of food includes sandwiches, chicken and ham hock with fig chutney, scallops with confit pork belly and champagne butter sauce, cumberland sausage with onion gravy, venison with celeriac rösti and blackberry jus, sea bream with mussel, leek and spiced crab broth, and puddings such as bakewell tart with caramelised cherries and sticky toffee pudding; they also offer a two- and three-course set lunch and afternoon teas (must book in advance). *Benchmark main dish: beer-battered fish and chips £10.95. Two-course evening meal £27.50.*

Free house ~ Licensee Peter Roehrig ~ Real ale ~ (01628) 529575 ~ Open 10am-11pm; 12-11 Sun ~ Bar food 12-2.30, 6-9.30 (light snacks all day); all day weekends ~ Restaurant ~ Children welcome ~ Dogs allowed in bar ~ Wi-fi ~ Bedrooms: £99.50/£107.50 ~ www.chequers-inn.com *Recommended by R K Phillips, Roy Hoing*

Also Worth a Visit in Buckinghamshire

Besides the fully inspected pubs, you might like to try these pubs that have been recommended to us and described by readers. Do tell us what you think of them: feedback@goodguides.com

AMERSHAM   SU9597
Swan (01494) 727079
High Street; HP7 0ED Refurbished Mitchells & Butlers pub/restaurant on two floors, contemporary bar with comfortable chairs and low tables, decent choice of food all day from sharing plates up, children's menu, several wines by the glass, well kept beers such as Fullers and Rebellion; tables out on front cobbles and in pleasant garden behind. *(Roy Hoing)*

ASKETT   SP8105
★**Three Crowns** (01844) 347166
W off A4010 into Letter Box Lane; HP27 9LT Handsome, well run pub in small hamlet among the Chiltern Hills; main emphasis on the particularly good interesting food, but also real ales such as Vale from herringbone-brick counter, good wine list, two contemporary-styled beamed dining rooms with mix of high-backed pale wood or black leather chairs around dark wood tables, light flooring, minimal décor; some

---

You can send reports directly to us at feedback@goodguides.com

picnic-sets outside under parasols, pretty front flower beds and baskets, closed Sun evening, Mon. *(Peter and Jan Humphreys, Mel Smith)*

BEACONSFIELD · SU9490
Royal Saracens (01494) 674119
1 mile from M40 junction 2; London End (A40); HP9 2JH Striking timbered façade (former coaching inn) with well updated open-plan interior, comfortable chairs around light wood tables, massive beams and timbers in one corner, log fires, welcoming efficient young staff, wide choice of enjoyable food including shared dishes and fixed-price weekday menu (busy at weekends when best to book), well kept ales such as Fullers London Pride and Sharps Doom Bar, quite a few wines by the glass, large back restaurant; attractive sheltered courtyard, open (and food) all day. *(Gordon and Jenny Quick)*

BENNETT END · SU7897
Three Horseshoes (01494) 483273
Horseshoe Road; from Radnage on unclassified road towards Princes Risborough, left into Bennett End Road, then right into Horseshoe Road; HP14 4EB Country pub in lovely quiet spot – seemingly off the beaten track but close to M40; well kept Rebellion IPA and a guest, several wines by the glass, good choice of food including some traditional options (not cheap and service charge added), flagstoned softly lit snug bar with log fire in raised fireplace, original brickwork and bread oven, two further sitting areas, one with long winged settle, the other enclosed by standing timbers, stone-floor dining room with big windows overlooking garden, red telephone box half submerged in duck pond, unspoilt valley beyond; can be busy on warm summer's day; children welcome till 9pm, dogs in bar, six bedrooms, closed Sun evening, Mon lunchtime. *(Roy Hoing)*

BLEDLOW RIDGE · SU7997
Boot (01494) 481499
Chinnor Road; HP14 4AW Refurbished village pub under newish management, clean and tidy with a contemporary look, good food from sandwiches, sharing plates and pub favourites up (best to book weekends), well kept Rebellion, Sharps Doom Bar and a guest, several wines by the glass from extensive list, friendly staff; children and dogs welcome, terrace and in sizeable lawned garden, open all day Fri-Sun (till 7pm Sun), closed Mon. *(Anon)*

BOURNE END · SU8987
Bounty (01628) 520056
Cock Marsh, actually across the river along the Cookham towpath, but shortest walk – still about 0.25 miles – is from Bourne End, over the railway bridge; SL8 5RG Welcoming take-us-as-you-find-us pub tucked away in outstanding setting on bank of the Thames and accessible only by foot or boat; collection of flags on ceiling and jumble of other bits and pieces, well kept Rebellion ales from boat counter, basic standard food including children's meals, back dining area, darts and bar billiards; background music inside and out; dogs and muddy walkers welcome, picnic-sets with parasols on front terrace, play area to right, open all day in summer (may be boat trips), closed winter weekdays. *(N R White)*

BRADENHAM · SU8297
Red Lion (01494) 562212
A4010, by Walters Ash turn-off; HP14 4HF Welcoming NT-owned pub with small simple bar and good-sized low-beamed dining room, three or four well kept Rebellion ales, enjoyable home-made food from good baguettes up; children, walkers and dogs welcome, picnic-sets on terrace and lawn, pretty village green nearby, closed Sun and Mon evenings. *(Bob Dizon)*

BRILL · SP6514
★Pheasant (01844) 239370
Windmill Street; off B4011 Bicester– Long Crendon, HP18 9TG More or less open-plan with raftered bar area, leather tub seats in front of woodburner, well kept Vale and a guest, enjoyable food served by friendly helpful staff, dining areas with high-backed leather or dark wooden chairs, attractively framed prints, books on shelves; background music; children and dogs (in bar) welcome, seats out on raised deck with steps down to garden, fine views over post windmill (one of the oldest in working order), four comfortable bedrooms (two in former bakehouse), good breakfast, open all day. *(Paul Bates, John Evans, Neil and Angela Huxter, Alan Weedon)*

BUCKINGHAM · SP6933
Villiers (01280) 822444
Castle Street; MK18 1BS Pub part of this large comfortable hotel with own courtyard entrance, big inglenook log fire, panelling and stripped masonry in flagstoned bar, beers from Hook Norton and Black Sheep, reliably good food from shortish menu (also set choices Mon-Fri), competent friendly staff, sofas and armchairs in more formal front lounges, restaurant with two large tropical fish tanks; no dogs; children welcome till 9pm, terrace, tables, open all day. *(Anon)*

BUTLERS CROSS · SP8407
Russell Arms (01296) 624411
Off A4010 S of Aylesbury, at Nash Lee roundabout; or off A413 in Wendover, passing station; Chalkshire Road; HP17 0TS Refurbished village-owned pub, a former 18th-c coaching inn and servants' quarters for nearby Chequers; beamed bar with woodburner and open fire, separate light and roomy dining room, well kept ales

such as Aylesbury, Chiltern, Rebellion and Vale, good wine choice, enjoyable food from bar snacks to restaurant choices including good value weekday set lunch, village shop; background music, sports TV; children welcome, small sheltered garden, well placed for Chilterns walks, closed Sun evening, Mon. *(Anon)*

CADSDEN   SP8204
Plough (01844) 343302
Cadsden Road; HP27 0NB Extended former 16th-c coaching inn with airy open-plan bar/dining area, clean and bright, with well spaced pine tables on flagstones, exposed brick and some faux beams, very popular with families and Chilterns ramblers, good choice of real ales, well presented home-made food (not especially cheap), cherry pie festival (first Sun in Aug), efficient service; lots of tables in delightful quiet front and back gardens, some woodland seating, pretty spot on Ridgeway path (shoe covers for walkers), bedrooms, open all day weekends (no food Sun evening). *(Mel Smith, Roy Hoing)*

CHALFONT ST GILES   SU9895
★ Ivy House (01494) 872184
A413 S; HP8 4RS Old brick and flint beamed coaching inn tied to Fullers, interesting range of enjoyable if not particularly cheap food (not Sun evening, Mon), decent wines by the glass and over 30 whiskies, friendly young staff, some refurbishment in elegantly cosy L-shaped bar and lighter flagstoned dining extension; dogs allowed in bar, pleasant terrace and sloping garden (traffic noise), five bedrooms. *(Roy Hoing)*

CHALFONT ST GILES   SU9893
Milton's Head (01494) 872961
Deanway; HP8 4JL Popular little pub/restaurant with good mainly italian food cooked by sardinian landlord, also pizza menu and traditional Sun roasts, reasonable prices, nice italian wines and coffee, no real ales but Peroni on draught; children and dogs welcome, small side terrace, handy for John Milton's Cottage, closed Sun evening, Mon. *(Dr Paul Glover)*

CHEARSLEY   SP7110
Bell (01844) 208077
The Green; HP18 0DJ Cosy traditional thatched and beamed pub on attractive village green, Fullers beers and good wines by the glass, enjoyable sensibly priced home-made food (not Sun or Mon evenings), efficient friendly service, inglenook with big woodburner; children in eating area, dogs welcome, plenty of tables in spacious back garden with heated terrace and play area. *(Anon)*

CHENIES   TQ0298
Red Lion (01923) 282722
2 miles from M25 junction 18; A404

towards Amersham, then village signposted on right; Chesham Road; WD3 6ED* Long-serving licensees in proper village pub with loyal local following, traditional and unpretentious L-shaped bar, comfortable built-in wall benches and other straightforward seats and tables, old photographs of village and traction engines, small back snug and neat dining extension with more modern décor, Rebellion, Thwaites and Wadworths, ten wines by glass, enjoyable food including good Sun roasts; no children, dogs welcome in bar, pretty hanging baskets and window boxes, picnic-sets on small side terrace, good local walks, open (and food) all day weekends. *(Nick Gill, John Branston, Roy Hoing, John Boothman, Mrs Margo Finlay, Jörg Kasprowski)*

CHESHAM   SP9703
Black Cat (01494) 773966
Lycrome Road, Lye Green; HP5 3LF Friendly local with Timothy Taylors Landlord, Wells & Youngs Bitter and a guest, ten malt whiskies, ample helpings of well priced honest food including breakfast from 9am (not Sun), eggs for sale at the counter, carpeted beamed bar with old Guinness adverts, cat clock and small brick fireplace; sports TV, Thurs quiz, darts, crib and dominoes; children and dogs welcome, good sized garden with play area, open all day weekends, shuts 7pm Mon. *(Roger and Donna Huggins)*

CHESHAM   SP9604
Black Horse (01494) 784656
Vale Road, N off A416 in Chesham; HP5 3NS Popular neatly extended black-beamed country pub, good choice of enjoyable food including meal deal Weds and Thurs, Fullers London Pride, Tring Side Pocket for a Toad and a couple of guests, decent wines, good friendly service, inglenook log fire; fortnightly Mon quiz; children and dogs welcome, picnic-sets out in front and on back grass, closed Sun evening. *(Anon)*

CHESHAM   SP9501
Queens Head (01494) 778690
Church Street; HP5 1JD Popular well run Fullers corner pub, two traditional beamed bars with scrubbed tables and log fires, their ales and a guest kept well, good thai food along with modest range of pub staples, restaurant, friendly staff and chatty locals; sports TV; children welcome, tables in small courtyard used by smokers, next to little River Chess, open all day. *(Paul A Moore)*

COLESHILL   SU9594
★ Harte & Magpies (01494) 726754
E of village on A355 Amersham–Beaconsfield, by junction with Magpie Lane; HP7 0LU Friendly roadside dining pub with wide mix of customers; big open-plan interior with rambling collection of

pews and high-backed booths making for plenty of snug corners, some quite distinctive furniture, patriotic antique prints, candles in bottles, Chiltern Ale, Rebellion Smuggler and a guest, good choice of other drinks, popular food from extensive menu, friendly service; live music Sat, free wi-fi; children and dogs welcome (pub labrador is Scrumpy Jack), terrace and big sloping informal garden with play area, good nearby walks, open (and food) all day. *(Brian Glozier, Susan and John Douglas, Alistair Forsyth, Richard and Liz Thorne)*

COLNBROOK   TQ0277
Ostrich (01753) 682628
1.25 miles from M4 junction 5 via A4/ B3378, then 'village only' road; High Street; SL3 0JZ Spectacular timbered Elizabethan building (with even longer gruesome history – tales of over 60 murders); contemporary interior with comfortable sofas on stripped wood and a rather startling red plastic/stainless steel bar counter, three well kept ales (one badged for them) and good choice of wines by the glass including champagne, enjoyable sensibly priced food from sandwiches and pub favourites up, good value set lunch Mon-Sat, efficient friendly service, attractive restaurant with open fire; soft background music, comedy and live music nights upstairs; children welcome, open all day Sun. *(Susan and John Douglas, Nigel and Sue Foster)*

CUBLINGTON   SP8322
Unicorn (01296) 681261
High Street; LU7 0LQ Extended low-beamed 17th-c village pub with popular sensibly priced food from interesting menu, Sharps, Shepherd Neame, XT and guests (May, Aug beer festivals), handsome fireplace at one end, Mon quiz and some live music; big enclosed garden behind, open all day. *(Mel Smith, Graham and Carol Parker)*

CUDDINGTON   SP7311
★ Crown (01844) 292222
Spurt Street; off A418 Thame–Aylesbury; HP18 0BB Convivial refurbished thatched cottage with chatty mix of customers, comfortable pubby furnishings including cushioned settles in two low-beamed linked rooms, big inglenook log fire, well kept Fullers and guests, around 20 wines by the glass, good home-cooked food (not Sun evening), competent friendly service, carpeted two-room back dining area with country-kitchen chairs around nice mix of tables; children welcome; neat side terrace with modern garden furniture and planters, picnic-sets in front. *(Mel Smith, Dave Braisted, Dennis and Doreen Haward)*

DINTON   SP7610
Seven Stars (01296) 749000
Signed off A418 Aylesbury–Thame, near Gibraltar turn-off; Stars Lane; HP17 8UL Pretty 17th-c community-owned pub with french landlady and well supported locally, inglenook bar, beamed lounge and dining room, a couple of well kept ales (one local), plenty of wines by the glass, enjoyable food cooked to order from pub staples up, friendly service; tables in sheltered garden with terrace, pleasant village, open all day weekends. *(Mel Smith, David Lamb, Graham and Carol Parker)*

DORNEY   SU9279
Palmer Arms (01628) 666612
2.7 miles from M4 junction 7, via B3026; Village Road; SL4 6QW Modernised and extended dining pub in attractive conservation village, good popular food (best to book) from snacks and pub favourites to more restauranty dishes, friendly efficient service, Greene King ales, lots of wines by the glass and nice coffee, open fires in civilised front bar and back dining room, daily newspapers; background music; children and dogs (in certain areas) welcome, disabled facilities, terrace overlooking mediterranean-feel garden, enclosed play area, good riverside walks nearby, open (and food) all day. *(Cliff Sparkes, I D Barnett, Alistair Forsyth)*

DORNEY   SU9279
Pineapple (01628) 662353
Lake End Road; 2.4 miles from M4 junction 7; left on A4 then left on B3026; SL4 6QS Nicely old-fashioned pub, shiny low Anaglypta ceilings, black-panelled dados, leather chairs around sturdy country tables (one very long, another in big bow window), woodburner and pretty little fireplace, china pineapples and other decorations on shelves in one of three cottagey carpeted linked rooms on left, well kept Fullers London Pride, Sharps Doom Bar and Windsor & Eton Guardsman, up to 1,000 varieties of sandwiches in five different fresh breads; background music, games machine; children and dogs welcome, rustic seats on roadside verandah, round picnic-sets in garden, fairy-lit decking under oak tree, some motorway noise, open all day. *(Anon)*

FORD   SP7709
Dinton Hermit (01296) 747473
SW of Aylesbury; HP17 8XH Carefully extended 16th-c stone inn in quiet hamlet; bar with scrubbed tables on black and white tiles, uneven stone walls, old print of John Bigg (supposed executioner of King Charles I and later known as the Dinton Hermit), huge inglenook fireplace, back dining area with similar furniture on quarry tiles, Adnams and a guest from Vale, several wines by the glass; children and dogs (in bar) welcome, pretty summer window boxes and tubs, picnic-sets under parasols in quiet back garden, comfortable modern bedrooms (some in converted barn), open all day (Sun till 8.30pm in winter). *(Mel Smith, David Lamb)*

BUCKINGHAMSHIRE | **91**

FRIETH　　　　　　　　　SU7990
Prince Albert　(01494) 881683
Off B482 SW of High Wycombe; RG9 6PY
Friendly cottagey Chilterns local with low
black beams and joists, high-backed settles,
big black stove in inglenook and log fire
in larger area on right, decent lunchtime
food from sandwiches up (also Fri and Sat
evenings), well kept Brakspears and guests,
quiz and folk nights; children and dogs
welcome, nicely planted informal side garden
with views of woods and fields, good walks,
open all day. *(Anon)*

GAWCOTT　　　　　　　　SP6831
Crown　(01280) 822322
Hillesden Road; MK18 4JF Welcoming
traditional beamed village pub, good value
popular food including carvery Weds and Sun,
well kept ales such as Sharps Doom Bar from
herringbone-brick counter, restaurant area;
background music, Sky TV, pool; children
welcome, long back garden with swings, open
all day (no food Mon). *(Anon)*

GERRARDS CROSS　　　　TQ0089
Three Oaks　(01753) 899016
*Austenwood Lane, just NW of junction
with Kingsway (B416); SL9 8NL* Well
run civilised dining pub facing Austenwood
Common; welcoming neatly dressed staff,
two-room front bar with fireside bookshelves,
tartan wing armchairs, sturdy wall settles
and comfortable banquettes, Fullers and
Rebellion ales, several wines by the glass,
dining part with three linked rooms, well
thought-of food; soft background music,
free wi-fi; children welcome, sturdy wooden
tables on flagstoned side terrace; open all
day. *(Caroline Prescott, Harvey Brown, Simon
Collett-Jones)*

GREAT HAMPDEN　　　　SP8401
★Hampden Arms　(01494) 488255
*W of Great Missenden, off A4128;
HP16 9RQ* Friendly village pub opposite
cricket pitch, good mix of locals and visitors,
comfortably furnished rooms (back one more
rustic with big woodburner), Adnams, Hook
Norton and a guest from Vale, several wines
by the glass and maybe Addlestone's cider
from small corner bar, reasonably priced
pubby food including one or two greek dishes,
cheerful efficient service; children and dogs
welcome, seats in tree-sheltered garden,
good Hampden Common walks. *(N R White,
David Lamb, John Wooll)*

GREAT KINGSHILL　　　SU8798
★Red Lion　(01494) 711262
A4128 N of High Wycombe; HP15 6EB
Refurbished village pub with contemporary
décor and relaxed informal atmosphere,
generous well cooked brasserie-style food
including set menus, local beers and good
value wine list, 'lobby' and cosy little
flagstoned bar with leather tub chairs by

log fire, spacious candlelit dining room;
well behaved children welcome, closed Sun
evening, Mon. *(Tracey and Stephen Groves)*

GREAT LINFORD　　　　SP8542
Nags Head　(01908) 607449
High Street; MK14 5AX Thatched 15th-c
pub with big inglenook in low-beamed
lounge, several ales including Fullers, Tetleys
and Sharps, straightforward inexpensive
food, friendly staff coping well when busy,
darts in public bar, some live music; children
welcome, picnic-sets outside, pleasant walks
(next to park and canal), open all day. *(Paul
Rampton, Julie Harding, Peter Martin)*

GREAT MISSENDEN　　　SP8901
★Cross Keys　(01494) 865373
High Street; HP16 0AU Relaxed and
friendly village pub, unspoilt beamed bar
divided by standing timbers, traditional
furnishings including high-backed settle,
log-effect gas fire in huge fireplace, well
kept Fullers ales and often an unusual guest,
enjoyable fairly priced food from sandwiches
and pizzas up, cheerful helpful staff, spacious
beamed restaurant; children and dogs
welcome, picnic-sets on back terrace, open
all day. *(Roger and Donna Huggins)*

GROVE　　　　　　　　　SP9122
★Grove Lock　(01525) 380940
*Pub signed off B488, on left just S
of A505 roundabout (S of Leighton
Buzzard); LU7 0QU* Overlooking Grand
Union Canal and usefully open all day; open
plan with lofty high-raftered pitched roof
in bar, squashy brown leather sofas on oak
boards, eclectic mix of tables and chairs
including butcher's block tables by bar, big
open-standing log fire, steps down to original
lock-keeper's cottage (now a three-room
restaurant area), enjoyable food from
sandwiches to daily specials, Fullers ales
and lots of wines by the glass; background
music, free wi-fi; children welcome, seats
on canopied deck and waterside lawn by
Lock 28. *(Mel Smith, Taff Thomas)*

HADDENHAM　　　　　　SP7408
Green Dragon　(01844) 690345
*Village signposted off A418 and A4129,
E/NE of Thame; then follow Church End
signs into Churchway; HP17 8AA*
Shuttered 18th-c village pub under new
management; open-plan modernised interior
with two log fires, well kept Sharps, St Austell
and XT, enjoyable home-made food (not Sun
evening, Mon), friendly staff; children and
dogs welcome, big sheltered gravel terrace,
picnic-sets in appealing garden, open all day
in summer. *(Anon)*

HAWRIDGE COMMON　　SP9406
★Full Moon　(01494) 758959
*Hawridge Common; left fork off A416 N
of Chesham, follow for 3.5 miles towards
Cholesbury; HP5 2UH* Welcoming 18th-c

pub with low-beamed little bar, ancient flagstones and chequered floor tiles, built-in floor-to-ceiling oak settles, hunting prints and inglenook fireplace, Adnams, Fullers London Pride, Timothy Taylors Landlord and Sharps Doom Bar, several wines by the glass, popular bar food from sandwiches up, friendly young staff; background music; seats in pleasant garden or on heated covered terrace with views over fields and windmill beyond, paddock for hitching horses, walks on common, open all day. *(Mel Smith, R Anderson)*

HUGHENDEN VALLEY   SU8697
★ **Harrow** (01494) 564105
Warrendene Road, off A4128 N of High Wycombe; HP14 4LX Small cheerful brick and flint roadside cottage surrounded by Chilterns walks; traditionally furnished with tiled-floor bar on left, black beams and joists, woodburner in big fireplace, pewter mugs, country pictures and wall seats, similar but bigger right-hand bar with sizeable dining tables on brick floor, carpeted back dining room, tasty pub food (not Sun evening) from sandwiches up including meal deal Mon-Weds, Courage Best, Fullers London Pride and Shepherd Neame Spitfire, friendly staff; Tues quiz; children and dogs welcome, disabled access, plenty of picnic-sets in front with more on back lawn, play area, open all day. *(David Lamb)*

HYDE HEATH   SU9300
Plough (01494) 774408
Off B485 Great Missenden–Chesham; HP6 5RW Prettily placed pub overlooking village green, traditional bare-boards bar and carpeted dining extension, good value food including some thai dishes, Fullers London Pride and St Austell Tribute, real fires; background music, TV; open all day Fri-Sun. *(Roy Hoing)*

ICKFORD   SP6407
Rising Sun (01844) 339238
E of Thame; Worminghall Road; HP18 9JD Pretty thatched local with cosy low-beamed bar, friendly staff and regulars, usually four ales including Black Sheep, simple reasonably priced home-made food; pleasant garden with picnic-sets, may be red kites overhead, handy for Waterperry Gardens. *(David Lamb)*

IVINGHOE ASTON   SP9518
Village Swan (01525) 220544
Aston; signed from B489 NE of Ivinghoe; LU7 9DP Friendly rather eccentric village-owned pub, swagged curtains, glitzy chandeliers, candelabras etc at odds with the traditional beamed interior, enjoyable home-made pub food including Sun carvery, three real ales and nice wines by the glass, quiz first Mon of month; soft background music, free wi-fi; children welcome, covered outside area and garden, handy for Ivinghoe Beacon

and Icknield Way, open all day Sun, closed Mon. *(Alan Weedon)*

LACEY GREEN   SP8200
Black Horse (01844) 345195
Main Road; HP27 0QU Friendly mix of customers in this two-bar beamed country local, popular good value home-made food (not Sun evening, Mon) from baguettes up, breakfast from 9am Tues-Sat, four real ales including Brakspears, nice choice of wines by the glass, quotations written on walls, inglenook woodburner, darts; sports TV; children welcome, picnic-sets in garden with play area and aunt sally, closed Mon lunchtime, open all day Thurs-Sun. *(Mel Smith, Paul Humphreys)*

LACEY GREEN   SP8201
Pink & Lily (01494) 489857
A4010 High Wycombe–Princes Risborough, follow Loosley sign, then Gt Hampden, Great Missenden sign; HP27 0RJ Friendly 18th-c pub reopened in 2013 after lengthy closure; enjoyable food from sandwiches and traditional choices up, five changing mainly local ales (plans for own microbrewery) and several wines by the glass, pubby furniture and open fire in airy main bar, cosier side areas and conservatory-style extension with big arches, small tap room with built-in wall benches on red tiles, old wooden ham rack hanging from ceiling, framed Rupert Brooke poem about the pub (he used to drink here) and broad inglenook, games room; occasional background music, free wi-fi; children, dogs and muddy walkers welcome, big garden with heated deck, play area and barbecue, open all day. *(James)*

LACEY GREEN   SP8100
Whip (01844) 344060
Pink Road; HP27 0PG Cheery and attractive hilltop local welcoming walkers, mix of simple traditional furnishings in smallish front bar and larger downstairs dining area, popular good value food from sandwiches to daily specials (booking advised weekends), six interesting well kept/priced ales and a couple of proper ciders, beer festivals (May and Sept) with live jazz, good landlord and friendly helpful service; TV, fruit machine; tables in mature sheltered garden looking up to windmill, open all day. *(Mel Smith, Tracey and Stephen Groves)*

LANE END   SU8091
Grouse & Ale (01494) 882299
High Street; HP14 3JG Welcoming beamed pub with good food from standards up, helpful friendly staff, great range of wines by the glass including champagne, well kept changing ales, comfortable bar and smartly laid out restaurant with flowers on tables, log fires, newspapers and books; soft background music, free wi-fi; children welcome and toys provided, seats outside. *(D and M T Ayres-Regan, Gordon and Jenny Quick)*

LEDBURN   SP9022
Hare & Hounds (01525) 373484
Off B488 Ivinghoe–Leighton Buzzard,
S of Linslade; LU7 0QB 18th-c dutch-
gabled brick pub surrounded by farmland,
bare-boards bar with log fire, back dining
area, good choice of food including specials,
Greene King ales, friendly service, Great
Train Robbery memorabilia; children
welcome, pleasant back garden with play
area, handy for Ascott (NT). *(David Lamb)*

LITTLE KINGSHILL   SU8999
Full Moon (01494) 862397
Hare Lane; HP16 0EE Picturesque
brick and flint village pub with good choice
of popular well presented food, well kept
Adnams, Fullers London Pride, Wells &
Youngs and a guest, nice wines, friendly
helpful service from busy staff, traditional
beamed and quarry-tiled bar with open fire,
bigger dining room, live music first and third
Mon of month; children and dogs welcome,
round picnic-sets out at front, lawned garden
with swings, good walks. *(Anon)*

LITTLE MARLOW   SU8788
★Kings Head (01628) 484407
Church Road; A4155 about 2 miles E of
Marlow; SL7 3RZ Long, flower-covered
local with open-plan bar, low beams,
captain's chairs and other traditional
seating around dark wood tables, cricketing
memorabilia (pitch opposite), log fire, half
a dozen well kept ales such as Adnams
Broadside and Wychwood Hobgoblin, popular
pubby blackboard food from sandwiches up
(booking advised weekends), evening deals
Mon and Thurs, free bar nibbles Sun, helpful
friendly service, gingham-clothed tables in
attractive dining room; big walled garden
with modern terrace furniture, open all
day. *(Paul Humphreys, D and M T Ayres-Regan*
and others)

LITTLE MISSENDEN   SU9298
★Red Lion (01494) 862876
Off A413 Amersham–Great Missenden;
HP7 0QZ Unchanging pretty 15th-c
cottage with long-serving landlord; small
black-beamed bar, plain seats around
elm pub tables, piano squashed into big
inglenook beside black kitchen range
packed with copper pots, kettles and rack
of old guns, little country dining room with
pheasant décor, well kept Greene King
IPA, Marstons Pedigree and Wadworths 6X,
fairly priced wines, good coffee, enjoyable
inexpensive pubby food and good friendly
service, live music Tues and Sat; children
welcome, dogs in bar (there's a friendly
pub dog), picnic-sets out in front and on
grass behind wall, back garden with little
bridge over River Misbourne, some fancy
waterfowl, stables farm shop, open all day
Fri, Sat. *(Roy Hoing)*

LITTLEWORTH COMMON   SP9386
Blackwood Arms (01753) 645672
3 miles S of M40 junction 2; Common
Lane; SL1 8PP Small 19th-c brick pub in
lovely spot on edge of beechwoods with good
walks, sturdy mix of furniture on bare boards,
roaring log fire, enjoyable home-made food
(not Sun evening), well kept Brakspears
and guests, friendly staff; children and dogs
welcome, nice garden with paved area, closed
Mon, otherwise open all day (Sun till 9.30pm
– earlier winter). *(Cliff Sparkes)*

LITTLEWORTH COMMON   SU9386
Jolly Woodman (01753) 644350
2 miles from M40 junction 2; off A355;
SL1 8PF Welcoming red-brick country pub
with enjoyable reasonably priced home-
made food including range of pies, five well
kept changing ales, rambling multi-level
beamed and timbered areas including snug,
central woodburner, jazz Mon night (can
get busy); children and dogs welcome, small
front terrace and nice garden, good site
by Burnham Beeches, closed Sun evening,
otherwise open all day. *(Anon)*

LUDGERSHALL   SP6617
★Bull & Butcher (01844) 238094
Off A41 Aylesbury–Bicester; bear left to
The Green; HP18 9NZ Nicely old-fashioned
welcoming country pub facing village green,
bar with low beams in ochre ceiling, wall
bench and simple pub furniture on dark tiles
or flagstones, inglenook log fire, back dining
room, decent bar food from shortish well
priced menu, a couple of changing ales, aunt
sally and dominoes teams, quiz (second Sun
of month); children welcome, picnic-sets on
pleasant front terrace, play area on green,
open all day weekends, closed Mon.
(David Lamb)

MAIDS MORETON   SP7035
Wheatsheaf (01280) 822903
Main Street, just off A413 Towcester–
Buckingham; MK18 1QR Attractive 17th-c
thatched and low-beamed local smartened
up and thriving under enthusiastic new
owners; good food including some interesting
choices, ales such as Courage, Everards,
Tring and Sharps, bar with bare boards and
tiled floors, old settles and two inglenooks,
conservatory restaurant; seats on front
terrace, hatch service for pleasant enclosed
back garden. *(George Atkinson)*

MARLOW   SU8486
★Hand & Flowers (01628) 482277
West Street (A4155); SL7 2BP Restaurant
rather than pub owned by celebrity chef
Tom Kerridge; nice informal atmosphere
in three linked beamed rooms all set for
dining, high-backed leather-seated chairs
and brown suede wall seats around chunky
tables, bare boards or flagstones, fresh
flowers and candles, first class food and

professional service, new extension with stools at counter for dining and drinking plus more set tables, Greene King, Rebellion and a beer named for the pub, lots of good wines by the glass from fine list and specialist gins; children welcome, comfortable character bedrooms, Thames walks nearby, closed Sun evening. *(Pip White, Ruth May, Tracey and Stephen Groves)*

MARLOW   SU8586
★ **Two Brewers** (01628) 484140
St Peter Street, first right off Station Road from double roundabout; SL7 1NQ Well liked beamed pub being renovated after major fire – news/reports please. *(David Fowler)*

MARLOW BOTTOM   SU8588
Three Horseshoes (01628) 483109
Signed from Handy Cross roundabout, off M40 junction 4; SL7 3RA Welcoming much-extended former coaching inn tied to nearby Rebellion, their full range kept well, brewery photographs, knowledgeable helpful uniformed staff, extensive choice of reasonably priced generous blackboard food (not Sun evening), good value wines, comfortable traditional furnishings on different levels, beams and log fires; children and dogs welcome, big back garden, good walks nearby, open all day Fri, Sat. *(Tony and Wendy Hobden, Alicia Garrett)*

MARSWORTH   SP9114
Red Lion (01296) 668366
Vicarage Road; off B489 Dunstable–Aylesbury; HP23 4LU Partly thatched 18th-c pub close to impressive flight of locks on Grand Union Canal; plain public bar on right with quarry tiles, straightforward furniture and small coal fire, Fullers London Pride and good selection of guests, traditional food at low prices, friendly service, raised ceiling area with red leather stools and sofas, multi-level lounge to left with comfortable sofas in one part and various knick-knacks, two-roomed games area (bar billiards, darts and juke box); children and dogs welcome, picnic-sets out in front, back terrace with heated smokers' gazebo, steps up to sizeable garden, more seats on village green opposite with old stocks. *(Susan and John Douglas, Alan Weedon)*

MOULSOE   SP9141
Carrington Arms (01908) 218050
1.25 miles from M1 junction 14: A509 N, first right signed Moulsoe; Cranfield Road; MK16 0HB Wide choice of well liked food including chargrilled meats and fish sold by weight from refrigerated display, up to three changing ales, friendly helpful staff, open-plan layout with mix of wooden chairs and cushioned banquettes; children allowed, long pretty garden behind, 16 bedrooms in two adjacent blocks, open all day. *(John Saville)*

NEWPORT PAGNELL   SP8743
Cannon (01908) 211495
High Street; MK16 8AQ Friendly bay-windowed drinkers' pub with military theme, four well kept/priced ales including Banks's and Marstons, regular live music in room behind; small back terrace and heated smokers' shelter, open all day. *(David John)*

NEWTON LONGVILLE   SP8431
★ **Crooked Billet** (01908) 373936
Off A421 S of Milton Keynes; Westbrook End; MK17 0DF Thatched pub with good enterprising restauranty food along with some cheaper pub favourites including sandwiches, set menu choices too (Tues-Sat lunch, Tues-Thurs dinner), Greene King ales, extensive choice of wines by the glass, modernised extended pubby bar, log fire in dining area; background and monthly live music, no dogs; children welcome away from bar, tables out on lawn, closed Mon. *(Toby Jones)*

OLNEY   SP8851
Bull (01234) 711470
Market Place/High Street; MK46 4EA Former 18th-c coaching inn with sofas and other seats in three smallish front rooms, varnished tables in big airy eating area on right, popular food (not Sun evening) from bar snacks up including mussels done six-ways, set menu choices lunchtime/early evening, pleasant service, well kept Wells & Youngs and guests (Aug Bank Holiday festival), good coffee, open and log-effect gas fires; children and dogs welcome, seats in courtyard and big back garden with climbing frame, start of the famous Shrove Tuesday pancake race, Sept food festival in square, open all day from 10am. *(Jeremy King)*

OLNEY   SP8851
★ **Swan** (01234) 711111
High Street S; MK46 4AA Friendly beamed and timbered linked rooms, good food (not Sun evening, Mon) from sandwiches up, at least three well kept changing ales and plenty of wines by the glass, quick helpful service, rather close-set pine tables, log fires, small back bistro dining room (booking advised for this); courtyard tables, open all day (Sun till 6pm). *(S Holder)*

PENN STREET   SU9295
★ **Hit or Miss** (01494) 713109
Off A404 SW of Amersham, keep on towards Winchmore Hill; HP7 0PX Traditional pub with friendly licensees, heavily beamed main bar with leather sofas and armchairs on parquet flooring, horsebrasses, open fire, two carpeted rooms with interesting cricket and chair-making memorabilia, more sofas, wheelback and other dining chairs around pine tables, Badger ales (summer beer festival), interesting if not cheap food; background

music, free wi-fi; children welcome, dogs in certain areas, picnic-sets on terrace overlooking pub's cricket pitch, open all day. *(Roy Hoing)*

PENN STREET   SU9295
Squirrel (01494) 711291
Off A404 SW of Amersham, opposite the Common; HP7 0PX Friendly sister pub to nearby Hit or Miss, open-plan bar with flagstones, log fire and mix of furniture including comfortable sofas, reasonably priced home-made pubby food from baguettes up (not Sun evening), good children's meals too, up to six well kept ales such as Rebellion, Tring and XT, Weston's cider, bric-a-brac and cricketing memorabilia, sweets in traditional glass jars, live acoustic music Fri; covered outside deck with logburner, good play area in big garden with village cricket view, lovely walks, closed Mon lunchtime, otherwise open all day. *(Anon)*

POUNDON   SP6425
Sow & Pigs (01869) 277728
Main Street; OX27 9BA Small beamed village local with L-shaped bar, Brakspears ales and maybe a Marstons-related guest, good value straightforward food from short menu; Sky TV; children and dogs welcome, tables in good-sized back garden, open from 4pm weekdays, all day Sat, till 6pm Sun. *(David Lamb)*

SKIRMETT   SU7790
★Frog (01491) 638996
From A4155 NE of Henley take Hambleden turn and keep on; or from B482 Stokenchurch–Marlow take Turville turn and keep on; RG9 6TG Pretty pub in Chilterns countryside; nice public bar with log fire, prints on walls, cushioned sofa and leather-seated stools on wood floor, high chairs by counter, Rebellion IPA, Gales Seafarer and a changing guest, 18 wines by the glass including champagne, 24 malt whiskies, two dining rooms in different styles – one light and airy with country kitchen furniture, the other more formal with dark red walls, smarter furniture and candlelight, good interesting food (not always cheap) from baguettes and deli boards up, friendly efficient staff offering free coffee refills; background music; children welcome, dogs in bar (their black lab is Belle), side gate to lovely garden with unusual five-sided tables, attractive valley views and farmland walks, Chiltern Valley Winery & Brewery nearby, three comfortable bedrooms, closed Sun evening Oct-May. *(Ian Herdman, R T and J C Moggridge, Paul Humphreys, Simon Rodway, David Jackman and others)*

STOKE GOLDINGTON   SP8348
★Lamb (01908) 551233
High Street (B526 Newport Pagnell– Northampton); MK16 8NR Chatty village

pub with friendly helpful licensees, up to four interesting changing ales including Tring, real ciders and good range of wines, enjoyable generous home-made food (all day Sat, not Sun evening) from baguettes to good value Sun roasts, lounge with log fire and sheep decorations, two small pleasant dining rooms, darts and table skittles in public bar; may be soft background music, TV; children and dogs welcome, terrace and sheltered garden behind with play equipment, bedrooms in adjacent cottage, open all day Sat, till 7pm Sun, closed Mon lunchtime. *(Anon)*

STOKE MANDEVILLE   SP8310
★Woolpack (01296) 615970
Risborough Road (A4010 S of Aylesbury); HP22 5UP Thatched Mitchells & Butlers pub with boldly decorated contemporary interior, Brakspears, Purity Pure UBU and Sharps Doom Bar, several wines by the glass, cocktails, good choice of food including fixed price weekday menu (till 7pm), efficient service; well behaved children allowed, seats in back garden and on the heated front terrace, open all day. *(Mel Smith, Tracey and Stephen Groves)*

STONE   SP7912
Bugle Horn (01296) 747594
Oxford Road, Hartwell (A418 SW of Aylesbury); HP17 8QP Long 17th-c stone-built former farmhouse (Vintage Inn), comfortable linked rooms with mix of furniture, their usual choice of reasonably priced food including fixed-price menu till 5pm, three real ales and lots of wines by the glass, log fires, conservatory; children welcome, attractive terrace, lovely trees in big garden with pastures beyond, open (and food) all day. *(Mel Smith)*

STONY STRATFORD   SP7840
Old George (01908) 562181
High Street; MK11 1AA Attractive beamed and timbered inn dating from the 16th c, enjoyable good value food from sandwiches and wraps up, quick friendly staff, real ales such as Marstons, Ringwood and Wychwood, back dining room; background and some live music, quiz nights; upstairs lavatories; tables in courtyard behind, 11 bedrooms, parking nearby can be tricky. *(George Atkinson)*

THE LEE   SP8904
★Cock & Rabbit (01494) 837540
Back roads 2.5 miles N of Great Missenden, E of A413; HP16 9LZ Stylish place run for over 25 years by same friendly italian family, although much emphasis on the good italian cooking they do keep Flowers and a guest ale and are happy to provide lunchtime baps, good value set menu Mon-Fri (must book), carefully decorated plush-seated lounge, cosy dining room and larger restaurant; seats outside on verandah, terraces and lawn, good walks. *(Roy Hoing)*

THE LEE   SP8904
★ **Old Swan** (01494) 837239
*Swan Bottom, back road 0.75 miles
N of The Lee; HP16 9NU* Welcoming
tucked-away 16th-c dining pub with three
attractively furnished linked rooms, low
beams and flagstones, log fire in inglenook
cooking-range, enjoyable sensibly priced food
(not Sun evening, Mon) from pub favourites
up, Weds set deal, well kept Chiltern,
Sharps Doom Bar and an occasional guest,
attentive service; children welcome, big back
garden with play area, good walks, open all
day Fri, Sat and till 7pm Sun, closed Mon
lunchtime. *(Anon)*

TURVILLE   SU7691
★ **Bull & Butcher** (01491) 638283
*Valley road off A4155 Henley–Marlow at
Mill End, past Hambleden and Skirmett;
RG9 6QU* Popular black and white pub
in pretty village (famous as film and TV
setting), two traditional low-beamed rooms
with inglenooks, wall settles in tiled-floor
bar, deep well incorporated into glass-topped
table, Brakspears ales kept well and decent
wines by the glass, enjoyable traditional food
including lunchtime sandwiches, friendly
staff; background and some live music;
children and dogs welcome, seats by fruit
trees in attractive garden, good walks, closed
Sun evening in winter otherwise open all
day. *(Gordon Neighbour)*

WADDESDON   SP7316
Long Dog (01296) 651320
High Street; HP18 0JF Well renovated
village pub with good varied choice of
food cooked in open-view kitchen, friendly
accommodating service, well kept ales and
nice choice of wines by the glass, bar area
with open fire; background music, live jazz
every other Tues; children and dogs welcome
(resident dachshund), tables out front and
back, very handy for Waddesdon Manor (NT),
open (and food) all day. *(Colin McKerrow)*

WEEDON   SP8118
Five Elms (01296) 641439
Stockaway; HP22 4NL Welcoming two-bar
cottagey thatched pub, low beams and log
fires, ample helpings of good traditional food
cooked by landlord (best to book), Tring Side
Pocket for a Toad or Skinners Betty Stogs
kept well, good reasonably priced wines,
old photographs and prints, separate dining
room, games such as shove-ha'penny; a few

picnic-sets out in front, pretty village, closed
Sun evening. *(Chris Birks, Taff Thomas)*

WESTON UNDERWOOD   SP8650
Cowpers Oak (01234) 711382
*Signed off A509 in Olney; High Street;
MK46 5JS* Wisteria-clad beamed pub
with enjoyable country cooking (all day
weekends), Hopping Mad, Sharps Doom Bar,
Woodfordes Wherry and a guest, friendly
helpful staff, nice mix of old-fashioned
furnishings including pews, painted
panelling and some stripped stone, two open
fires, back restaurant; background music;
children and dogs welcome, small suntrap
front terrace, more tables on back decking
and in big orchard garden, fenced play
area, pretty thatched village, open all day
weekends. *(George Atkinson)*

WINCHMORE HILL   SU9394
Plough (01494) 259757
The Hill; HP7 0PA Village pub/restaurant
with italian-influenced food including
good pizzas (landlord is from Campania),
flagstones, low beams and open fires, linked
dining area with polished wood floor, real
ales and imported lagers, nice coffee, little
shop selling italian wines and other produce;
children welcome, tables on terrace and
lawn, pleasant walks nearby, open all day
from 9.30am for breakfast. *(C and R Bromage)*

WING   SP8822
Queens Head (01296) 688268
High Street; LU7 0NS Welcoming
refurbished 16th-c pub, enjoyable freshly
cooked food (not Sun evening) in bar,
restaurant or snug, well kept Wells & Youngs
and local guests, decent wines, afternoon tea
with home-made scones, log fires; children
welcome, disabled facilities, sunny terrace
and garden, open all day Fri-Sun, closed Mon.
(Anon)

WORMINGHALL   SP6308
Clifden Arms (01844) 339273
Clifden Road; HP18 9JR Beamed and
timbered 16th-c thatched dining pub in
attractive village, good imaginative food
cooked by landlord-chef along with more
traditional choices, ales such as Fullers,
Sharps and XT, friendly young staff,
fortnightly Sun quiz; children and dogs
(in bar) welcome, nice garden with
vegetables growing around terrace, play
area, open all day Fri-Sun (no food Sun
evening), closed Mon. *(Anon)*

Post Office address codings confusingly give the impression that some pubs
are in Buckinghamshire, when they're really in Bedfordshire or Berkshire
(which is where we list them).

Cambridgeshire

BALSHAM
TL5850   Map 5

Black Bull 🍺 🛏

Village signposted off A11 SW of Newmarket, and off A1307 in Linton; High Street; CB21 4DJ

Pretty thatched pub with bedroom extension – a good all-rounder – enjoyable food too

Dating from the 16th c, this is a neatly kept thatched inn that's been carefully refurbished while preserving its original features. The beamed bar spreads around a central servery where they keep their own-label Red & Black Ale (from Growler) plus Adnams Bitter, Brandon Rusty Bucket, Woodfordes Wherry and a guest beer on handpump, 12 wines by the glass from a good list, a dozen malt whiskies, draught lager and interesting juices. Dividers and standing timbers break up the space, which has an open fire (and leather sofas in front of it), floorboards, and low black beams in the front part; furniture includes small leatherette-seated dining chairs. A restaurant extension has a high-raftered oak panelled roof and a network of standing posts and steel ties. The front terrace has teak tables and chairs by a long, pleasantly old-fashioned verandah and there are more seats in a small sheltered back garden. Smart, comfortable bedrooms are in a neat single-storey extension. This pub has the same good owners as the Red Lion at Hinxton.

🍴 As well as their highly popular four daily pies with four types of potato and four gravies, the rewarding food includes sandwiches and baguettes, chicken liver parfait with toasted brioche, grilled prawns with lobster bisque and mozzarella and potato fondue, burger with smoked cheese, tomato chutney and chips, curried butternut squash risotto with coconut, monkfish and parma ham with madeira velouté, and puddings such as orange and cinnamon tart with mango coulis and raspberry sorbet and berry granola crumble. *Benchmark main dish: venison loin with beetroot crisps and purée and veal jus £20.00. Two-course evening meal £24.00.*

Free house ~ Licensee Alex Clarke ~ Real ale ~ (01223) 893844 ~ Open 7.30am-11.30pm; 8.30am-11.30pm Sat; 8.30am-10.30pm Sun ~ Bar food 12-2 (2.30 Fri-Sun), 6.30-9 (9.30 Fri, Sat); 7-9 Sun ~ Restaurant ~ Well behaved children welcome ~ Dogs welcome ~ Jazz singer first Sat of month ~ Bedrooms: $85/$109 ~ www.blackbull-balsham.co.uk *Recommended by Dave Braisted, Caroline Prescott*

> The letters and figures after the name of each town are its Ordnance Survey map reference. Using the Guide at the beginning of the book explains how it helps you find a pub, in road atlases or large-scale maps as well as in our own maps.

BRANDON CREEK
Ship

TL6091 Map 5

A10 Ely–Downham Market; PE38 0PP

Bustling pub in fine riverside spot with plenty of outside seating, cosy snug and busy bar, four ales and nine wines by the glass, and well liked food

---

This 17th-c pub is in a fine spot where the Great Ouse is met by the Little Ouse, and seats on the terrace and in the riverside garden make the most of its position. Run by a father and son team who offer a friendly welcome to all their customers, it has a carefully modernised bar at the centre of the building, with massive stone masonry in the sunken former forge area, a big log fire at one end with a woodburning stove at the other, interesting old photographs and prints and Adnams Bitter and Woodfordes Wherry and a couple of changing guest beers on handpump, nine wines by the glass and farm cider; board games and background music. There's a cosy snug on the left with another open fire and a restaurant overlooking both rivers.

Using their own beef and lamb and also gluten-free ingredients, the well thought-of food includes sandwiches and baguettes, mushrooms in vermouth with a poached egg, paprika-dusted whitebait with home-made tartare sauce, a pie of the day, leek and mushroom crumble, beef or chicken burgers with cheese, bacon, onion rings and chips, gressingham duck with orange and port jus, venison loin with red wine reduction, and puddings. *Benchmark main dish: slow-roasted pork belly with cider jus £12.95. Two-course evening meal £18.00.*

Free house ~ Licensee Mark Thomas ~ Real ale ~ (01353) 676228 ~ Open 12 (11 weekends)-11 (10 winter) ~ Bar food 12-3, 6-9; 12-9 Sat; 12-8 Sun ~ Restaurant ~ Children welcome ~ Dogs allowed in bar ~ Wi-fi ~ Live music Fri evening and first Weds evening of month ~ www.theshipbrandoncreek.co.uk *Recommended by Deborah Watson*

DUXFORD
John Barleycorn

TL4746 Map 5

Handy for M11 junction 10; right at first roundabout, then left at main village junction; CB22 4PP

Pretty pub with friendly staff, attractive beamed interior, real ales and good wines, enjoyable food, and seats on terrace and in garden; bedrooms in converted barn

---

With welcoming staff and a lovely atmosphere, this charming 17th-c inn looks very much like a perfect english country pub with its thatched roof and shuttered windows. Inside, standing timbers and brick pillars create alcoves and different drinking and dining areas: hops on heavy beams and nice old floor tiles, log fires, all manner of seating from rustic blue-painted cushioned settles through white-painted and plain wooden dining chairs to some rather fine antique farmhouse chairs and quite a mix of wooden tables. There's also a lot to look at, including china plates, copper pans, old clocks, a butterchurn, a large stuffed fish, and plenty of pictures on blue or pale yellow walls. Greene King Abbot and IPA and guests such as Butcombe Matthew Pale Ale and St Austell Proper Job on handpump and ten wines by the glass; background music. There are blue-painted picnic-sets beside pretty hanging baskets on the front terrace and more picnic-sets among flowering tubs and shrubs in the back garden. This is a comfortable place to stay. The pub was used by the young airmen of Douglas Bader's Duxford Wing during World War II. The Air Museum is close by.

🍴 Good, popular food includes sandwiches (until 6pm), kipper and whisky pâté, pancetta-seared scallops, a pie of the day, cherry tomato and rocket risotto with parmesan, spiced lamb koftas with apricot couscous, sausages with onion gravy, supreme of soy-marinated, honey-glazed salmon with lime rice, and puddings such as sticky toffee pudding and crème brûlée. *Benchmark main dish: bass with fennel velouté and chargrilled fennel £16.25. Two-course evening meal £17.50.*

Greene King ~ Tenant Nicholas Kersey ~ Real ale ~ (01223) 832699 ~ Open 11-11 (10.30 Sun) ~ Bar food 12-3, 5-9.30; 12-10 Fri, Sat; 12-8.30 Sun ~ Children welcome ~ Dogs allowed in bar ~ Wi-fi ~ Bedrooms: /£79.50 ~ www.johnbarleycorn.co.uk
Recommended by Mrs Margo Finlay, Jörg Kasprowski, Mr and Mrs M Walker, Gordon and Margaret Ormondroyd, Pat and Stewart Gordon

ELTON
Crown 🎗️ ⚐ 🛏️
TL0894 Map 5

Off B671 S of Wansford (A1/A47), and village signposted off A605 Peterborough–Oundle; Duck Street; PE8 6RQ

Carefully refurbished restaurant in pretty stone and thatched pub, interesting food, several real ales, well chosen wines and a friendly atmosphere; stylish bedrooms

Just a short walk from Elton Mill and Lock, this is a lovely thatched stone inn in a charming village. The airy dining extension has been carefully refurbished recently and the softly lit beamed bar has an open fire in a stone fireplace, good pictures and pubby ornaments on pastel walls and leather and antique dining chairs around a nice mix of chunky tables on bare boards. The beamed main dining area has fresh flowers and candles and similar tables and chairs on stripped wooden flooring. High bar chairs against the counter are popular with locals, and they keep Golden Crown (brewed for them by Tydd Steam), Grainstore Phipps IPA, Greene King IPA and a guest or two such as Digfield Fools Nook and Oakham JHB on handpump, well chosen wines by the glass and farm cider; board games, background music and TV. There are tables outside on the front terrace. The bedrooms are smart, comfortable and well equipped and the breakfasts are especially good.

🍴 Enjoyable food cooked by the landlord includes sandwiches, braised oxtail and wild mushroom tortellini with smoked bacon and tomato sauce, fishcakes with caper butter, omelettes, local sausages with onion gravy, faggot with bubble and squeak and shallot jus, burger with dry-cured bacon, cheddar and chips, hake with pea purée, prawns and shellfish sauce, and puddings such as Baileys crème brûlée and dark chocolate torte with white chocolate ice-cream. *Benchmark main dish: venison cottage pie £13.95. Two-course evening meal £20.90.*

Free house ~ Licensee Marcus Lamb ~ Real ale ~ (01832) 280232 ~ Open 12-11 ~ Bar food 12-2 (3 Sun), 6.30-9; not Sun evening ~ Restaurant ~ Children welcome ~ Dogs allowed in bar ~ Wi-fi ~ Bedrooms: £75/£110 ~ www.thecrowninn.org
Recommended by Howard and Margaret Buchanan, Lesley Dick, Barry Collett, George Atkinson

FEN DRAYTON
Three Tuns 🍺
TL3468 Map 5

Off A14 NW of Cambridge at Fenstanton; High Street; CB24 5SJ

Lovely old pub, traditional furnishings in bar and dining room, real ales, tasty food and seats in garden

This charming building may have been the medieval guild hall for the pretty village, and its heavy-set moulded Tudor beams and timbers were certainly built to last. The three rooms are more or less open-plan with a mix of burgundy cushioned stools, nice old dining chairs and settles in the friendly bar, and wooden dining chairs and tables on the red-patterned carpet in the dining room; framed prints of the pub too. The open fires in each room help create a warm and relaxed atmosphere – all helped along by the friendly licensees. Greene King IPA and Old Speckled Hen, a beer named for the pub and guests such as Rudgate Ruby Mild and St Austell Proper Job on handpump and 13 wines by the glass. A well tended lawn at the back has seats and tables, a covered dining area and a play area for children.

Using good local produce, the fairly priced food includes lunchtime sandwiches, peppered mackerel pâté with wholegrain mustard cream, garlic mushrooms with garlic mayonnaise, vegetarian enchiladas, beer-battered haddock and chips, sausages with onion gravy, cajun chicken, gammon with egg or pineapple, and puddings such as crumble of the day and dark chocolate délice with hazelnut praline and chantilly cream. *Benchmark main dish: pie of the day £9.25. Two-course evening meal £15.00.*

Greene King ~ Tenant Sam Fuller ~ Real ale ~ (01954) 230242 ~ Open 12-2 (3 Sat), 6-11; 12-3 Sun; closed Sun evening ~ Bar food 12-2, 6.30-9 (9.30 Sat); 12-3 Sun ~ Restaurant ~ Children welcome ~ Dogs allowed in bar ~ Wi-fi ~ www.the3tuns.co.uk
Recommended by Jeremy King, R L Borthwick, R T and J C Moggridge, Pat and Graham Williamson

GREAT WILBRAHAM
TL5558   Map 5
Carpenters Arms
Off A14 or A11 SW of Newmarket, following The Wilbrahams signposts; High Street; CB21 5JD

Inviting village pub with traditional bar, good food in both the bar and back restaurant; nice garden

To be sure of a table, it's best to book in advance as this bustling, friendly pub is always deservedly popular. The properly pubby, low-ceilinged village bar on the right has their own-brewed Crafty Beers Carpenters Cask and Sauvignon Blonde on handpump, a carefully chosen wine list (strong on the Roussillon region), a sturdy settle by the big inglenook with its woodburning stove, copper pots and iron tools, and cushioned pews and simple seats around the solid pub tables on floor tiles; bar billiards and background music. Service is spot on: thoughtful, helpful and cheerful. On the left, a small, cosy, carpeted dining area has another big stone fireplace and overflowing bookshelves; this leads through to a sitting area with comfortable sofas and plenty of magazines. The light and airy extended main dining room has country kitchen chairs around chunky tables. A huge honeysuckle swathes the tree in the pretty back courtyard, and, further on, an attractive homely garden, with fruit and vegetables, has round picnic-sets shaded by tall trees.

 Using home-grown produce and other local ingredients, the excellent food cooked by the landlady includes sandwiches, country terrine with home-made chutney, seared scallops, smoked salmon and dill and ricotta fritters, beer-battered fish of the day, beef in ale pie, pheasant supreme stuffed with chestnut and bacon with port reduction sauce, and puddings such as orange and chocolate tart and crumble of the day. *Benchmark main dish: slow-roast pork belly with cinnamon and apple sauce £14.50. Two-course evening meal £21.50.*

Free house ~ Licensees Rick and Heather Hurley ~ Real ale ~ (01223) 882093 ~ Open 11.30-3, 6.30-11; 11.30-3 Sun; closed Sun evening, Tues ~ Bar food 12-2.15, 7-9 ~ Restaurant ~ Children welcome ~ Wi-fi ~ www.carpentersarmsgastropub.co.uk
Recommended by M and GR, R P Knight, Paul and Corinna Goldman, Steve and Sue Griffiths

HEMINGFORD ABBOTS
TL2870 Map 5

Axe & Compass

High Street; village signposted off A14 W of Cambridge; PE28 9AH

Thatched pub in charming village with several linked rooms, a good range of drinks and food served by friendly staff, and seats and a play area outside

In a lovely village, this partly 15th-c pub has all sorts of linked rooms with plenty of space for both drinkers and diners. The simple public bar has beams, mate's chairs and stools around wooden tables on lovely ancient floor tiles, and an open two-way fireplace (not in use) into the family room next door where there's a woodburning stove. The main room has more beams and standing timbers, tweed tartan-patterned chairs and armchairs and cushioned wall seating around nice old tables on wood floors, local photographs, a TV at each end and stools against the counter where they serve Adnams Lighthouse, Sharps Doom Bar and Timothy Taylors Landlord on handpump and 12 wines by the glass; there's a second woodburner in a small brick fireplace. The long dining room has more photographs on green walls and high-backed dark leather dining and other chairs around pale wooden tables. The garden, between the pretty thatched pub and the tall-spired church, has a fenced-off area with play equipment, contemporary seats and tables on the terrace and picnic-sets on grass. Disabled facilities.

Well liked food includes lunchtime sandwiches, salt and pepper calamari, scotch egg with piccalilli, sharing platters, burger with cheese, bacon, salad and chips, chicken and mushroom pie, sausages and mash with gravy, beer-battered cod and chips, and puddings such as sticky toffee pudding and apple crumble with cinnamon ice-cream. *Benchmark main dish: pie of the day £12.50. Two-course evening meal £17.00.*

Enterprise ~ Lease Emma Tester ~ Real ale ~ (01480) 463605 ~ Open 12-11 (10 Sun, Mon) ~ Bar food 12-2.30, 6-9; 12-9 Sat; 12-5 Sun ~ Restaurant ~ Children welcome ~ Dogs allowed in bar ~ Wi-fi ~ www.axeandcompass.co.uk *Recommended by Toby Jones*

HEMINGFORD GREY
TL2970 Map 5

Cock 🌟 🍴 ♀ 🍺

Village signposted off A14 eastbound, and (via A1096 St Ives road) westbound; High Street; PE28 9BJ

Cambridgeshire Dining Pub of the Year

Imaginative food in pretty pub with extensive wine list, four interesting beers, a bustling atmosphere and a smart restaurant

This continues to be a first class pub with delicious food and drinks all served by lovely staff. The bar rooms have fresh flowers and church candles, artwork here and there, dark or white-painted beams, lots of contemporary pale yellow and cream paintwork, and throughout a really attractive mix of old wooden dining chairs, settles and tables. They've sensibly kept the traditional public bar on the left for drinkers only: an open woodburning stove on a raised hearth, bar stools, wall seats and a carver, and steps that lead down to more seating. Brewsters Hophead, Great Oakley Harpers, Milton Pegasus and Nethergate IPA on handpump, 18 wines by the glass mainly from the Languedoc-Roussillon region, Calvors (an East Anglian lager) and Cromwell cider (made in the village); they hold a beer festival every August Bank Holiday weekend. In marked contrast, the stylishly simple, newly refurbished restaurant on the right – you must book to be sure of a table – is set for dining, with flowers on each table, pale wooden floorboards and another woodburning stove. There are seats and tables among stone troughs and flowers on a new terrace and in the neat garden, and pretty hanging baskets.

The impressive, seasonally inspired food includes duck parcel with sweet and sour cucumber, potted rabbit with beetroot relish, broccoli and blue cheese risotto, pork honey and wholegrain mustard sausages with a choice of mash and sauces, slow-roasted goat shoulder with onion sauce, chicken stuffed with tarragon mousse with red wine sauce, and puddings such as earl grey crème brûlée and double chocolate and macadamia nut brownie with salt caramel and vanilla ice-cream; they hold a steak and chop night on Tuesdays and also offer a two- and three-course weekday lunch. *Benchmark main dish: bass fillets with squash purée, crab potato cake, pickled cabbage and fennel marmalade £16.50. Two-course evening meal £23.00.*

Free house ~ Licensees Oliver Thain, Richard Bradley ~ Real ale ~ (01480) 463609 ~ Open 11.30-3, 6-11; 11.30-11 Sat; 12-10.30 Sun ~ Bar food 12-2.30, 6.30 (6 Fri, Sat)-9; 12-2.45, 6.30-8.30 Sun ~ Restaurant ~ Children allowed in bar lunchtime only; over-5s only in restaurant in evening ~ Dogs allowed in bar ~ www.cambscuisine.com
Recommended by John Saville, S Holder, Gordon and Margaret Ormondroyd, Revd R P Tickle

HINXTON
Red Lion

TL4945   Map 5

2 miles off M11 junction 9 northbound; take first exit off A11, A1301 N, then left turn into village – High Street; a little further from junction 10, via A505 E and A1301 S; CB10 1QY

16th-c pub with friendly staff, interesting bar food, real ales and a big landscaped garden; comfortable bedrooms

At the heart of a pretty conservation village and handy for the M11, this is a pink-washed inn with a good range of drinks and sophisticated food. The low-beamed bar has oak chairs and tables on bare boards, two leather chesterfield sofas, an open fire in a dark green fireplace, an old wall clock and a relaxed, friendly atmosphere. Their own-label Red & Black Ale (from the local Growler Brewery) plus Adnams Bitter, Woodfordes Wherry and a guest such as Crafty Beers Sauvignon Blonde on handpump, 20 wines by the glass, a dozen malt whiskies and first class service. An informal dining area has high-backed settles, and the smart restaurant (with oak rafters and traditional dry peg construction) is decorated with various pictures and assorted clocks. The neatly kept big garden has a pleasant terrace with teak tables and chairs, picnic-sets on grass, a dovecote and views of the village church; another terrace just outside the porch has a huge parasol for sunny days. The bedrooms are in a separate flint and brick building. They also own the Black Bull in Balsham just up the road.

Creative food includes sandwiches, confit duck terrine with celeriac rémoulade, braised pork cheeks with toffee apples, root vegetable purée and tomato jus, wild mushroom risotto, steak in ale pie, smoked haddock with poached egg and wholegrain mustard sauce, a burger board with local beef, lamb, venison and partridge with a choice of three cheeses and three chutneys, maple-glazed goose breast with horseradish jus and parsnip fondants, and puddings such as vodka and lime burnt cream and chocolate torte with honeycomb marshmallow and caramel nest. *Benchmark main dish: bass fillets and scallops with orange butter sauce and lemongrass £18.00. Two-course evening meal £22.00.*

Free house ~ Licensee Alex Clarke ~ Real ale ~ (01799) 530601 ~ Open 7.30am (8.30am weekends)-11pm (10.30pm Sun) ~ Bar food 12-2 (2.30 Fri, Sat), 6.30-9 (9.30 Fri, Sat), 12-2.30, 7-9 Sun ~ Restaurant ~ Well behaved children welcome ~ Dogs allowed in bar ~ Bedrooms: £90/£115 ~ www.redlionhinxton.co.uk *Recommended by Charles Gysin, Mrs Margo Finlay, Jörg Kasprowski, Tom and Ruth Rees, Gerry and Rosemary Dobson*

HUNTINGDON
TL2471 Map 5

Old Bridge Hotel

1 High Street; ring road just off B1044 entering from easternmost A14 slip road; PE29 3TQ

Georgian hotel with smartly pubby bar, splendid range of drinks, first class service and excellent food; fine bedrooms

As always, our readers love their visits to this extremely civilised but warmly welcoming place, where they can be sure of first class food, drinks and service. And while the hotel side clearly dominates, there's a wide mix of customers who very much enjoy the traditional pubby bar. This has a log fire, comfortable sofas and low wooden tables on polished floorboards and Adnams Bitter and City of Cambridge Hobson's Choice on handpump. They also have an exceptional wine list (up to 36 by the glass in the bar) and a wine shop where you can taste a selection of the wines before you buy. Food is available in the big airy Terrace (an indoor room, but with beautifully painted verdant murals suggesting the open air) or in the slightly more formal panelled restaurant. There are seats and tables on the terrace by the Great Ouse, and they have their own landing stage. This is a lovely place to stay and some bedrooms overlook the river.

 Excellent food includes sandwiches, pigeon breast with puy lentils and crisp cavolo nero, cured trout with pea and radish salad, crab linguine with chilli, pork and leek sausages with onion and mustard sauce, corn-fed chicken with girolle mushrooms, confit potatoes and soft herbs, venison cottage pie, slow-cooked lamb shank with ratatouille and garlic mash, and puddings such as crème brûlée with champagne rhubarb and bakewell tart with blackberry jam ripple ice-cream; they also offer a two- and three-course set menu (not Saturday evening). *Benchmark main dish: aberdeen angus steak sandwich on ciabatta with caramelised onions and grain mustard £9.95. Two-course evening meal £24.45.*

Huntsbridge ~ Licensee John Hoskins ~ Real ale ~ (01480) 424300 ~ Open 9am-11pm ~ Bar food 9am-10pm ~ Restaurant ~ Children welcome ~ Dogs welcome ~ Wi-fi ~ Bedrooms: £99/£180 ~ www.huntsbridge.com *Recommended by Martin and Pauline Jennings, Michael Sargent, Mrs Margo Finlay, Jörg Kasprowski*

KEYSTON
TL0475 Map 5

Pheasant

Just off A14 SE of Thrapston; brown sign to pub down village loop road, off B663; PE28 0RE

Good civilised country dining pub with appealing décor and attractive garden

Our readers return regularly to this picture-book-pretty pub with its neat thatch, as you can be sure of an excellent meal and a genuine welcome. The main bar has pitched rafters high above, with lower dark beams in side areas, and the central serving area has padded stools along the leather-quilted counter and dark flagstones, with hop bines above the handpumps for Adnams Southwold and Broadside and Nene Valley NVB, and a tempting array of 17 wines by the glass. Nearby are armchairs, a chesterfield, quite a throne of a seat carved in 17th-c style, other comfortable seats around low tables, and a log fire in a lofty fireplace. The rest of the pub is mostly red-carpeted with dining chairs around a variety of polished tables, and large sporting prints – even hunting-scene wallpaper in one part. Lighted candles and tea-lights throughout, and the attentive attitude of neat friendly staff, add to the feeling of well-being. The attractively planted and well kept garden behind has tables on lawn and terrace, and there are picnic-sets in front; the car park has been enlarged. This is a quiet farming hamlet.

Cooked by the licensee, the imaginative food includes rabbit and hare beef terrine with apple and celeriac rémoulade, salmon tempura with nori seaweed and asian dipping sauce, butternut squash, savoy cabbage and pine nut pudding with beetroot sauce, free-range pork sausages with red wine sauce, corn-fed chicken with borlotti beans, pancetta and confit celeriac, sea trout with gnocchi, fennel, clams and fish cream, and puddings such as sticky toffee pudding and baked chocolate tart with orange sauce; they also offer a two- and three-course set menu (not Saturday evening, Sunday or Monday). *Benchmark main dish: braised ox cheek and chargrilled beef fillet, smoked mash, braised leeks and artichokes £22.95. Two-course evening meal £21.00.*

Free house ~ Licensee Simon Cadge ~ Real ale ~ (01832) 710241 ~ Open 12-3, 6-11; 12-11 Fri, Sat; 12-5 Sun; closed Sun evening, Mon ~ Bar food 12-2, 6-9.30; 12-3.30 Sun ~ Restaurant ~ Children welcome ~ Dogs allowed in bar ~ Wi-fi ~ www.thepheasant-keyston.co.uk *Recommended by Ryta Lyndley, J F M and M West, Michael Sargent, Alex and Hazel Evans*

KIMBOLTON TL0967 Map 5

New Sun
High Street; PE28 0HA

Interesting bars and rooms, tapas menu plus other good food, and a pleasant back garden

There's always a friendly crowd of customers in this interesting old place, and everyone is served quickly by the efficient, welcoming staff; it's right on the attractive high street, so people tend to pop in and out all day from morning coffee onwards. The cosiest room is perhaps the low-beamed front lounge with a couple of comfortable armchairs and a sofa beside a log fire, standing timbers and exposed brickwork, and books on shelves. This leads into a narrower locals' bar with Wells & Youngs Bombardier and Eagle and a weekly changing guest on handpump, and 14 wines by the glass (including champagne and pudding wines); background music, board games, piano and quiz machine. The traditionally furnished dining room opens off here. The airy conservatory with high-backed leather dining chairs has doors leading to the terrace where there are smart seats and tables under giant umbrellas. Note that some of the nearby parking spaces have a 30-minute limit.

Reliably good food includes popular tapas such as marinated anchovies, spanish meats, manchego, and fried squid with aioli, as well as sandwiches, home-cooked ham and free-range eggs, mushroom stroganoff, slow-cooked lamb with parsnip purée and braising juices, fish pie, duck breast, confit leg and port jus, and puddings such as Malteser cheesecake and fruit oat crumble and clotted cream ice-cream. *Benchmark main dish: steak and kidney pudding £10.95. Two-course evening meal £18.00.*

Wells & Youngs ~ Lease Stephen and Elaine Rogers ~ Real ale ~ (01480) 860052 ~ Open 11.30-11; 12-10.30 Sun; 11.30-2.30, 5-11 Mon-Thurs in winter ~ Bar food 12-2.15

(2.30 Sun), 7-9.30; not Sun or Mon evenings ~ Restaurant ~ Children welcome ~ Dogs allowed in bar ~ Wi-fi ~ www.newsuninn.co.uk *Recommended by Alan Sutton, Ryta Lyndley*

PETERBOROUGH

Brewery Tap ◀ £

TL1899 Map 5

Opposite Queensgate car park; PE1 2AA

Fantastic range of real ales including their own brews, and popular thai food, in huge conversion of old labour exchange

The very good Oakham ales brewed in this striking modern conversion of an old labour exchange are as first class as ever – and, perhaps surprisingly, go very well with their popular thai food. The open-plan contemporary interior has an easy-going and relaxed feel, with an expanse of light wood and stone floors and blue-painted iron pillars holding up a steel-corded mezzanine level. It's stylishly lit by a giant suspended steel ring with bulbs running around the rim and steel-meshed wall lights. A band of chequered floor tiles traces the path of the long sculpted pale wood bar counter, which is boldly backed by an impressive display of bottles in a ceiling-high wall of wooden cubes. There's also a comfortable downstairs area, a big-screen TV for sporting events, background music and regular live bands and comedy nights. A two-storey glass wall divides the bar from the brewery, giving fascinating views of the ten-hectolitre microbrewing plant. They produce their Oakham beers (Bishops Farewell, Citra, Inferno, JHB, Scarlet Macaw and seasonal ales) and also keep up to eight guests; quite a few whiskies and several wines by the glass. It gets very busy in the evening.

The thai food remains incredibly popular. As well as set menus and specials, you might find tom yum soup, chicken, beef, pork, prawn, duck and vegetable curries, stir-fried crispy chilli beef, talay pad cha (prawns, squid and mussels with crushed garlic, chilli and ginger), various noodle dishes, all sorts of salads and stir-fries and five kinds of rice. *Benchmark main dish: pad thai £7.25. Two-course evening meal £15.00.*

Own brew ~ Licensee Jessica Loock ~ Real ale ~ (01733) 358500 ~ Open 12-11 ~ Bar food 12-2.30, 5.30-10.30; 12-10.30 Fri, Sat; 12-3.30, 5.30-9.30 Sun ~ Restaurant ~ Children welcome during food service times only ~ Dogs allowed in bar ~ Wi-fi ~ Jazz and open mike first and third Sat, live bands last Fri of month ~ www.thebrewery-tap.com
Recommended by Pat and Tony Martin, Martin Jones

STILTON
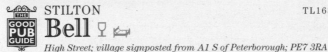

Bell ♀ ⇌

TL1689 Map 5

High Street; village signposted from A1 S of Peterborough; PE7 3RA

Fine coaching inn with several civilised rooms including a residents' bar, bar food using the famous cheese, and seats in a very pretty courtyard; bedrooms

Customers return to this lovely 17th-c coaching inn on a regular basis and it's very handy for the A1. The left-hand side is a civilised hotel, but the two neatly kept right-hand bars (which have the most character) are where our readers tend to head for. There are bow windows, sturdy upright wooden seats on flagstone floors, plush button-back built-in banquettes and a good big log fire in one handsome stone fireplace; one bar has a large cheese press. The partly stripped walls have big prints of sailing and winter coaching scenes and a giant pair of blacksmith's bellows hangs in the middle of the front bar. Digfield Fools Nook, Greene King IPA, Hook Norton

Old Hooky and Oakham Bishops Farewell on handpump, quite a few malt whiskies and around a dozen wines by the glass; service is helpful and welcoming. Other rooms include a residents' bar, a bistro and a restaurant; background music and TV. Through the fine coach arch is a very pretty sheltered courtyard with tables, and a well that dates from Roman times.

They make their own version of the famous cheese, which is used in the enjoyable food: stilton pâté with apple and cinnamon chutney, moules marinière with Guinness bread roll, stilton, red onion and chestnut tart, beer-battered fresh haddock and chips, salmon escalope with pumpkin and parsley risotto, beef in ale casserole with stilton dumplings, and puddings such as sticky toffee pudding and white chocolate rice pudding. *Benchmark main dish: beef burger with Jack Daniels barbecue sauce, stilton, coleslaw and chips £13.25. Two-course evening meal £20.00.*

Free house ~ Licensee Liam McGivern ~ Real ale ~ (01733) 241066 ~ Open 12-2.30, 6-11; 12-3, 6-midnight Sat; 12-10.30 Sun ~ Bar food 12-2.15 (3 Sat), 6-9.30 (9 Sun) ~ Restaurant ~ Children welcome ~ Wi-fi ~ Bedrooms: £80/£108 ~ www.thebellstilton.co.uk *Recommended by Aimee, J F M and M West, B and M Kendall, Lee and Liz Potter, Margaret and Peter Staples, Mrs J Kavanagh*

SUTTON GAULT
TL4279 Map 5

Anchor ⭐ ▽ 🛏
Bury Lane off High Street (B1381); CB6 2BD

Tucked-away inn with charming candlelit rooms, inventive food, real ales and thoughtful wine list; bedrooms

'This pub ticks every box,' says one reader, who stayed overnight in this particularly well run inn; the bedrooms are comfortable and well equipped and overlook the river, and breakfasts are imaginative. Most customers are here to enjoy the lovely food, but this is more than a restaurant. Although space for drinkers only may be limited on Friday and Saturday evenings and Sunday lunchtime, at other times you can pop in for a pint of Nethergate Growler tapped from the cask or one of the dozen wines by the glass. The four heavily timbered rooms are stylishly simple, with two log fires, antique settles and wooden dining chairs around scrubbed pine tables, set with candles and nicely spaced on gently undulating old floors; good lithographs and big prints hang on the walls. Service is helpful and friendly. There are seats outside and you can walk along the high embankment where the bird-watching is said to be good.

As well as a two- and three-course weekday set lunch, the excellent food includes king scallops with puréed smoked corn and sea vegetables, loin of rabbit with crispy leg, apple purée and candied walnuts, coq au vin, tempura vegetables with sweet potato purée and chimichurri sauce, duck three-ways (seared breast, leg terrine, gizzard sausage) with celeriac and apricot, and puddings such as apple crumble and chocolate délice with sour cherry purée and cherry sorbet. *Benchmark main dish: Estate venison with spiced ragoût and bitter chocolate £18.95. Two-course evening meal £25.00.*

Free house ~ Licensee Jeanene Flack ~ Real ale ~ (01353) 778537 ~ Open 12-2, 7-9 (6-9.30 Sat); 12-2.30, 6.30-9 Sun ~ Bar food 12-2 (2.30 weekends), 7-9 (6-9 Sat, 6.30-9 Sun) ~ Restaurant ~ Children welcome ~ Wi-fi ~ Bedrooms: £59.50/£79.50 ~ www.anchor-inn-restaurant.co.uk *Recommended by Andrew Conway, Mrs Margo Finlay, Jörg Kasprowski, Sally Anne and Peter Goodale, Margaret Tait, M and GR, Ryta Lyndley, George Atkinson, Mr and Mrs P R Thomas*

If you know a pub is ever open all day, please tell us.

WHITTLESFORD
Tickell Arms 🏅 ♈

TL4648 Map 5

2.4 miles from M11 junction 10: A505 towards Newmarket, then second turn left signposted Whittlesford; keep on into North Road; CB22 4NZ

Light and refreshing dining pub with good enterprising food and pretty garden

Painted a distinctive blue, this carefully run place does have a proper bar, despite most emphasis being on the interesting modern food. Set on the left, this L-shaped room with floor tiles has some mementoes of the legendarily autocratic regime of Wagner-loving former owner Kim Tickell; three porcelain handpumps from his era are now orphaned and decorate a high 'counter' that's suspended between a pair of ornate cast-iron pillars and lined with bentwood bar stools. Brewsters Hophead, Buntingford Twitchell, Milton Pegasus and Nethergate Old Growler on handpump and a good range of fairly priced wines by the glass including champagne, served by neatly dressed and friendly staff. Through an ornate glazed partition on the right is the dining room, containing tables varying from sturdy to massive, with leather-cushioned bentwood and other dining chairs and one dark pew, and fresh minimalist décor in palest buff. This opens into an even lighter limestone-floored conservatory area, partly divided by a very high-backed ribbed-leather banquette. The side terrace has comfortable tables, and the secluded garden beyond has pergolas and a pond.

🌟 Using seasonal local produce, the modern british food includes venison scotch egg with cider-pickled onions, ham hock and foie gras terrine, curried cauliflower risotto, slow-cooked ox cheek with crushed jerusalem artichokes, duck breast with parsnip and vanilla purée and honey-glazed chicory, chicken with salsify and mushroom broth, a daily fresh fish dish, and puddings such as chocolate fondant and chocolate sauce and vanilla crème brûlée; they also offer a two- and three-course weekday set menu. *Benchmark main dish: hanger steak with caramelised onions and chips £21.00. Two-course evening meal £21.00.*

Free house ~ Licensees Oliver Thain, Richard Bradley, Max Freeman ~ Real ale ~ (01223) 833025 ~ Open 12-3, 6-11; may open all day weekends; 12-3, 6-10.30 Sun ~ Bar food 12 2.30, 6.30-9 (9.30 Fri); 12-3, 6-9.30 Sat; 12-3, 6-8 Sun ~ Restaurant ~ Children welcome, over-10s only in pub, over-5s only in restaurant in evening ~ Dogs allowed in bar ~ www.cambscuisine.com/the-tickell-whittlesford
Recommended by Giles and Annie Francis

Also Worth a Visit in Cambridgeshire

Besides the fully inspected pubs, you might like to try these pubs that have been recommended to us and described by readers. Do tell us what you think of them: feedback@goodguides.com

ABBOTS RIPTON TL2377
Abbots Elm (01487) 773773
B1090; PE28 2PA Open-plan thatched dining pub reconstructed after major fire (was the Three Horseshoes); good food from bar meals to interesting restaurant dishes, set menus too, extensive choice of wines by the glass including champagne, three well kept ales; children and dogs welcome, three bedrooms, open all day Fri, Sat, till 5pm Sun. *(Anne Morton)*

ABINGTON PIGOTTS TL3044
Pig & Abbot (01763) 853515
High Street; SG8 0SD Spotless Queen Anne local with two small traditional bars and restaurant, good choice of enjoyable home-cooked food at reasonable prices, friendly efficient staff, well kept Adnams Southwold, Fullers London Pride and guests, log fires; back terrace, pretty village with good walks, open all day weekends – very busy then. *(Lucien Perring)*

BARRINGTON TL3849
Royal Oak (01223) 870791

Turn off A10 about 3.7 miles SW of M11 junction 11, in Foxton; West Green; CB22 7RZ Rambling thatched Tudor pub with tables out overlooking classic village green, heavy low beams and timbers, mixed furnishings, a beer named for the pub from Greene King along with Adnams, Twitchell and Woodfordes, Aspall's and Thatcher's cider, enjoyable food from pub favourites up, good wine list, efficient friendly service, airy dining conservatory; background music, free wi-fi; children welcome, classic car club first Fri of month, open all day Sun till 10pm. *(Mr and Mrs M Walker)*

BOURN TL3256
★Willow Tree (01954) 719775

High Street, just off B1046 W of Cambridge; CB23 2SQ Light and airy dining pub with relaxed informal atmosphere despite the cut-glass chandeliers, sprinkling of Louis XVI furniture and profusion of silver-plate candlesticks; accomplished restaurant-style cooking (all day Sun till 8pm), Milton and Woodfordes ales, several wines by the glass and inventive cocktails, friendly efficient staff; children welcome, smart tables and chairs on back deck with extendable canopy, grassed area beyond car park with fruit trees and huge weeping willow acting as the 'pole' for circular tent, open all day. *(Mike and Mary Carter, John Saville, Evelyn and Derek Walter, Mrs Margo Finlay, Jörg Kasprowski)*

BOXWORTH TL3464
Golden Ball (01954) 267397

High Street; CB23 4LY Attractive partly thatched building with contemporary open-plan bar and three-part restaurant in original core, friendly helpful staff, popular food (all day Sun till 8pm) from baguettes through suet puddings and pies to grills, well kept Courage and Wells & Youngs, good whisky choice; children welcome, nice garden and heated terrace, pastures behind, 11 quiet bedrooms in adjacent block, open all day. *(Jeremy King, John Gibbon)*

BRAMPTON TL2170
Black Bull (01480) 457201

Church Road; PE28 4PF 16th-c and later with updated low-ceilinged interior, stripped-wood floor and inglenook woodburner in split-level main bar, restaurant area with light wood furniture on tiles, enjoyable well priced food (not Sun evening) including own sausages and pies, four real ales, alcoholic milkshakes, friendly staff; children welcome and dogs (home-made treats for them), garden play area, open all day (till 9pm Sun). *(Anon)*

BROUGHTON TL2877
★Crown (01487) 824428

Off A141 opposite RAF Wyton; Bridge Road; PE28 3AY Attractively tucked away opposite church, fresh and airy décor, sturdy furnishings including nicely set dining end, good well presented food, friendly service, real ales such as Church End and Growler; disabled access and facilities, tables out on big stretch of grass behind, open all day Sun till 8pm. *(Roy Shutz)*

BUCKDEN TL1967
★George (01480) 812300

High Street; PE19 5XA Handsome and stylish Georgian-faced hotel with bustling informal bar, fine fan beamwork, leather and chrome chairs, log fire, Adnams Southwold and a changing guest from chrome-topped counter, lots of wines including champagne by the glass, teas and coffees, popular brasserie with smart cream dining chairs around polished tables, good modern food served by helpful enthusiastic young staff; background music; children and dogs welcome, tables under large parasols on pretty sheltered terrace with box hedging, charming bedrooms, open all day. *(David and Ruth Hollands, J F M and M West, Ryta Lyndley, Michael Sargent)*

BUCKDEN TL1967
★Lion (01480) 810313

High Street; PE19 5XA Partly 15th-c coaching inn, black beams and big inglenook log fire in airy bow-windowed entrance bar with plush bucket seats, wing armchairs and sofas, enjoyable food from lunchtime sandwiches up, fine choice of wines, Adnams Southwold and two guests, prompt friendly staff, panelled back restaurant beyond latticed window partition; children welcome, back courtyard, 14 bedrooms, open all day. *(Toby Jones)*

CAMBRIDGE TL4458
Anchor (01223) 353554

Silver Street; CB3 9EL Refurbished pub/ restaurant in beautiful riverside position by punting station, fine river views from upper dining room and suntrap terrace, five well kept beers and plenty of wines by the glass, nice variety of food (fairly priced for the area), friendly service; popular with tourists and can get very busy; children welcome, open all day. *(Dave Braisted)*

CAMBRIDGE TL4658
★Cambridge Blue (01223) 471680

85 Gwydir Street; CB1 2LG Nice little backstreet local, knowledgeable landlord and a dozen or more interesting ales (some tapped from the cask – regular festivals), 200 bottled beers and over 20 malt whiskies, good choice of well priced traditional food served promptly, attractive conservatory and extended bar area with lots of breweriana and old advertising signs, board games; free wi-fi; children and dogs welcome, seats in surprisingly rural-feeling back garden bordering cemetery, open all day and can get very busy at weekends. *(Tony Hobden, John Saville)*

CAMBRIDGE   TL4558

Cambridge Brew House

(01223) 855185 *King Street; CB1 1LH*
Contemporary open-plan pub visibly brewing its own beers (plenty of guest ales/craft beers on tap too), enjoyable food from open kitchen including british tapas, sharing boards and own-smoked meats and fish, friendly staff, sports TV in upstairs bar; open (and food) all day. *(Anon)*

CAMBRIDGE   TL4459

Castle (01223) 353194

Castle Street; CB3 0AJ Full Adnams beer range and several interesting guests in big airy bare boards bar, five pleasantly simple rooms, scrubbed tables, wide range of good value quick pubby food from sandwiches up, friendly young staff, peaceful upstairs (downstairs can be louder, with background music); picnic-sets in good walled back courtyard, open all day Fri, Sat. *(Roger Fox)*

CAMBRIDGE   TL4657

Devonshire Arms (01223) 316610

Devonshire Road; CB1 2BH Popular Milton-tied pub with two cheerful chatty linked bars, their well kept ales and guests, real cider, also great choice of bottled beers, decent wines and a dozen malts, low-priced food from sandwiches and pizzas to steaks, creaky wood floors, mix of furniture including long narrow refectory tables, architectural prints and steam engine pictures, woodburner in back bar; disabled access, handy for the station, open all day. *(Chris and Angela Buckell, Mr and Mrs M Walker)*

CAMBRIDGE   TL4458

★Eagle (01223) 505020

Bene't Street; CB2 3QN Go for the original architectural features (this was once the city's most important coaching inn); rambling rooms with two medieval mullioned windows and the remains of possibly medieval wall paintings, two fireplaces dating from around 1600, lovely worn wooden floors and plenty of pine panelling, dark red ceiling left unpainted since World War II to preserve signatures of british and american airmen made with Zippo lighters, candle smoke and lipstick, Greene King ales including Eagle DNA (Crick and Watson announced their discovery of DNA's structure here in 1953) and two guests, decent choice of enjoyable food served efficiently considering the crowds; children welcome, disabled facilities, heavy wooden seats in attractive cobbled and galleried courtyard, open all day. *(Chris and Angela Buckell, Jim and Nancy Forbes, Roger Fox, John Wooll, Mrs Sally Scott and others)*

CAMBRIDGE   TL4558

Elm Tree (01223) 502632

Orchard Street; CB1 1JT Traditional one-bar backstreet drinkers' pub, ten well kept ales including B&T and Wells & Youngs, good range of continental bottled beers, local ciders/perries usually poured from the barrel, friendly knowledgeable staff, no food, nice unspoilt interior with breweriana, some live music; a few tables out at side, open all day. *(Chris and Angela Buckell)*

CAMBRIDGE   TL4559

Fort St George (01223) 354327

Midsummer Common; CB4 1HA Picturesque old pub (reached by foot only) in charming waterside position overlooking ducks, swans, punts and boathouses; extended around old-fashioned Tudor core, good value bar food including traditional Sun lunch, well kept Greene King ales and decent wines, cheery helpful young staff, oars on beams, historic boating photographs, stuffed fish etc; children and dogs welcome, wheelchair access via side door, lots of tables outside. *(John Wooll)*

CAMBRIDGE   TL4558

★Free Press (01223) 368337

Prospect Row; CB1 1DU Unspoilt little backstreet pub with interesting décor, including old newspaper pages and printing memorabilia recalling its time as a print shop for a local paper; Greene King IPA, Abbot and Mild plus regularly changing guests, 25 malt whiskies, lots of gins and rums, tasty good value food served by friendly staff, log fire, board games; children and dogs (in bar) welcome, wheelchair access, small sheltered paved garden behind, open all day Fri, Sat. *(Chris and Angela Buckell, Roger Fox, Roy Shutz)*

CAMBRIDGE   TL4657

★Kingston Arms (01223) 319414

Kingston Street; CB1 2NU Victorian backstreet pub with well kept interesting ales from 11 handpumps, over 50 bottled beers and good choice of wines by the glass, enjoyable freshly prepared food including some bargains, discounts for students, companionably big plain tables and basic seating, thriving chatty atmosphere; free wi-fi; children and dogs welcome, back beer garden (torch-lit, heated and partly covered), open all day Fri-Sun. *(Tony Hobden)*

CAMBRIDGE   TL4557

Live & Let Live (01223) 460261

Mawson Road; CB1 2EA Popular backstreet alehouse, friendly and relaxed, with well kept Growler Umbel and half a dozen guests, lots of bottled belgians, local cider and over 120 rums, good value bar food, heavily timbered brickwork rooms with sturdy varnished pine tables on bare boards, country bric-a-brac and some steam railway and brewery memorabilia, gas lighting (not always lit), cribbage and dominoes; children and dogs welcome, disabled access is awkward but possible. *(Chris and Angela Buckell)*

CAMBRIDGE   TL4458
Mill (01223) 311829
Mill Lane; CB2 1RX Pleasant refurbished pub in picturesque spot overlooking mill pond where punts can be hired; seven mainly local ales and proper cider, reasonably priced pubby food (all day weekends) including children's choices, Mon quiz; open all day. *(John Wooll)*

CAMBRIDGE   TL4458
Mitre (01223) 358403
Bridge Street, opposite St Johns College; CB2 1UF Popular Nicholsons pub close to the river, spacious rambling bar on several levels, their usual good value food cooked well and served all day including fixed-price menu from 5pm, good selection of well kept ales, farm cider, reasonably priced wines by the glass, good friendly service; background music, free wi-fi; children welcome, disabled access. *(Revd R P Tickle)*

CAMBRIDGE   TL4559
★ Old Spring (01223) 357228
Ferry Path; car park on Chesterton Road; CB4 1HB Extended Victorian pub, roomy and airy, with smartly old-fashioned scrubbed-wood décor, bare boards, lots of old pictures, enjoyable well priced home-made food from pub staples to more enterprising dishes, friendly efficient service, well kept Greene King IPA, Abbot and four guests, plenty of wines by the glass and good coffee, two log fires, long back conservatory; background music; well behaved children welcome, dogs outside only, disabled facilities, seats out in front and on large heated back terrace, open all day. *(Anon)*

CAMBRIDGE   TL4459
Pickerel (01223) 355068
Magdalene Street, opposite the college; CB3 0AF Nicely old-fashioned multi-roomed coaching inn close to the river, popular with locals and students (can get crowded evenings – 20% student discount), bars front and back, low beams and some dark panelling, well kept Theakstons, Woodfordes and five quickly changing guests, plenty of wines by the glass, good value Taylor Walker menu till 9pm, friendly staff; background music, free wi-fi; children and dogs welcome, wheelchair access with help, heated courtyard, open all day. *(M and J White)*

CAMBRIDGE   TL4459
★ Punter (01223) 3633221
Pound Hill, on corner of A1303 ring road; CB3 0AE Former coaching house (sister pub to the Punter in Oxford); rambling series of informal rooms with

pleasing choice of pews, elderly dining chairs and wicker easy seats on dark boards, old prints and paintings, small area down a few steps with candles on scrubbed tables, interesting food from daily changing menu served promptly by friendly staff, Adnams Ghost Ship and a beer from Growler named for the pub, plenty of wines by the glass; background and occasional acoustic music (Sun); children and dogs welcome, seats on mainly covered flagstoned coachyard, raftered barn bar (similar in style) with big-screen TV, open all day. *(Martin Jones)*

CASTOR   TL1298
★ Prince of Wales Feathers
(01733) 380222 *Off A47; PE5 7AL*
Friendly stone-built local with well kept Adnams, Castor, Woodfordes and interesting guests (festivals in May and Oct), farm cider and perry too, good value food cooked by landlady (not weekend evenings) including popular Sun roasts, open-plan interior with dining area to the left; pool (free Thurs), Sat live music, Sun quiz, Sky TV and games machines; children and dogs welcome (their friendly setter is Maddy), new disabled facilities, attractive front terrace and another at the back with large smokers' shelter, open all day, till late weekends. *(David Moody)*

DUXFORD   TL4745
Plough (01223) 833170
St Peters Street; CB22 4RP Popular early 18th-c thatched pub, clean bright and friendly, with enjoyable home-made food from shortish reasonably priced menu, Everards, Adnams and guests kept well, music and quiz nights, darts, dominoes and crib; handy for Air Museum, open all day (no evening food Sun-Tues). *(Gordon and Margaret Ormondroyd)*

ELTISLEY   TL2759
Eltisley (01480) 880308
The Green; village signposted off A428 Cambridge–St Neots; PE19 6TG Village-green inn with all sorts of rambling areas, grey-painted walls and beams, bare boards and flagstones, leatherette wall seats, curved high-backed settles and easy chairs by cast-iron stove in massive central chimneypiece, Wells & Youngs Eagle and decent wines by the glass, enjoyable food, cosy low-beamed library down some steps, more formal raftered dining room; background music; children and dogs welcome, canopied deck in sheltered back area, six stylish bedrooms in separate block, open all day Sat, closed Sun evening, Mon. *(Lucien Perring, Michael Sargent)*

ELTON   TL0893
Black Horse (01832) 281222
Overend; B671 off A605 W of Peterborough and A1(M); PE8 6RU
Honey-stone and beamed dining pub neatly refurbished and opened up under present licensees, enjoyable food from sandwiches and pub favourites to daily specials, Adnams,

Digfield and a guest, decent wines and good coffee, friendly staff; children welcome, clean dogs in bar area, terrace and garden with views across to Elton Hall park and village church, open all day. *(Anon)*

ELY   TL5479
★**Cutter** (01353) 662713
Annesdale, off Station Road (or walk S along Riverside Walk from Maltings); CB7 4BN Beautifully placed contemporary riverside pub with carpeted dining bar and smart restaurant, enjoyable promptly served food from sandwiches up including good value Sun roasts, well kept Sharps Doom Bar and Woodfordes Wherry from boat-shaped bar, nice wines by the glass, decent coffee, good views from window seats and front terrace. *(John Saville, Ryta Lyndley, Val and Alan Green, J F M and M West)*

ELY   TL5480
Lamb (01353) 663574
Brook Street (Lynn Road); CB7 4EJ Good choice of food in popular hotel's panelled lounge bar or restaurant, friendly welcoming staff, Greene King ales and plenty of wines by the glass, decent coffee; children welcome, close to cathedral, 31 clean comfortable bedrooms, good breakfast. *(Dave Braisted)*

ETTON   TF1406
Golden Pheasant (01733) 252387
Just off B1443 N of Peterborough, signed from near N end of A15 bypass; PE6 7DA Yellow-brick Georgian pub revamped under newish owners, country-style panelled restaurant next to bare-boards bar with open fire, Greene King, Grainstore, Oakham and a couple of interesting small brewery guests, decent choice of wines and spirits, good food (not Sun night) including competitively priced weekday set menu (lunchtime/early evening), perhaps live music on Sat; children and dogs welcome, big tree-sheltered garden with play area, table tennis and table football in marquee, vintage car meetings, on Green Wheel cycle route, bedrooms planned, open all day Fri-Sun, closed Mon lunchtime. *(Howard and Margaret Buchanan)*

FEN DITTON   TL4860
Plough (01223) 293264
Green End; CB5 8SX Big Mitchells & Butlers riverside dining pub with good choice of food and extensive wine list (many by the glass), well kept Adnams and guests, pleasant service, split-level interior with rowing décor; background music; children welcome, tables out on deck and waterside lawns, nice walk from town, open (and food) all day. *(Jeremy King)*

FOWLMERE   TL4245
★**Chequers** (01763) 208558
B1368; SG8 7SR Popular 16th-c coaching

inn refreshed under enthusiastic new landlady: two comfortable downstairs rooms, long cushioned wall seats, dining chairs around dark tables, log fire, good traditional food served by pleasant staff, Greene King IPA and two guests, several wines by the glass, attractive upstairs beamed and timbered dining room with interesting moulded plasterwork above one fireplace, spacious conservatory (children welcome here); no dogs; terrace and garden with tables under parasols. *(Roy Hoing)*

GRANTCHESTER   TL4355
★**Blue Ball** (01223) 840679
Broadway; CB3 9NQ Character bare-boards local rebuilt 1900 on site of much older pub (cellars still remain), Adnams Southwold and a guest kept in top condition by veteran hands-on landlord (there's a list of previous publicans back to 1767), good log fire, cards and traditional games including shut the box and ring the bull, lots of books; no food; dogs welcome, tables on small terrace with lovely views to Grantchester Meadows, good heated smokers' shelter, nice village, open from 2pm (midday weekends), till 7pm Sun. *(Stuart Gideon, Mrs Catherine Simmonds)*

GREAT CHISHILL   TL4239
★**Pheasant** (01763) 838535
Follow Heydon signpost from B1039 in village; SG8 8SR Popular old split-level flagstoned pub with beams, timbering, open fires and some elaborately carved (though modern) seats and settles, good freshly made food (not Sun evening) using local produce, welcoming friendly staff, two or three ales including one for the pub from Growler, good choice of wines by the glass, small dining room (best to book), darts, cribbage, dominoes; no under-14s inside; dogs allowed, charming secluded back garden with small play area, open all day weekends. *(Mrs Margo Finlay, Jörg Kasprowski)*

GREAT GRANSDEN   TL2655
Crown & Cushion (01767) 677214
Off B1046 Cambridge–St Neots; West Street; SG19 3AT Small thatched and beamed local much improved and thriving under welcoming newish owners, two or three interesting changing ales kept well, authentic Indonesian cooking from landlady (Fri evening, Sat, Sun), live music; small garden, pretty village, open all day weekends, closed Mon. *(Roger Fox)*

HARDWICK   TL3758
Blue Lion (01954) 210328
Signed off A428 (was A45) W of Cambridge; Main Street; CB23 7QU Attractive old dining pub, beams and timbers, leather armchairs by copper-canopied inglenook, good food from landlord-chef in bar and extended dining area with conservatory, friendly young uniformed staff,

Greene King IPA and guest ales; children welcome, pretty roadside front garden, more seats on decking and lawn with play area, handy for Wimpole Way walks, open all day. *(Anon)*

★ King William IV (01763) 838773

HEYDON   TL4339

Off A505 W of M11 junction 10; SG8 8PW Rambling dimly lit rooms with fascinating rustic jumble (ploughshares, yokes, iron tools, cowbells and so forth) along with copperware and china in nooks and crannies, log fire, Fullers, Greene King and Timothy Taylors ales, good varied choice of well presented food including proper home-made pies, helpful staff; background music; children and dogs (in bar) welcome, teak furniture on heated terrace and in pretty garden, four bedrooms in separate building, open all day weekends. *(Anon)*

★ Red Lion (01223) 564437

HISTON   TL4363

High Street; CB24 9JD Impressive choice of draught and bottled beers along with farm cider and perry (festivals Easter/early Sept), ceiling joists in L-shaped main bar packed with hundreds of beer mats and pump clips among hop bines and whisky-water jugs, fine collection of old brewery advertisements, traditional pub food with a twist (all day Sat, not Mon, Fri, Sun evenings), cheerful efficient service, comfortable brocaded wall seats, matching mate's chairs and pubby tables, log fires, nice working antique one-arm bandit, extended bar on left (well behaved children allowed here) with darts, TV and huge collection of beer bottles; mobile phones discouraged, no dogs inside; disabled access/facilities, picnic-sets in neat garden, limited parking, open all day. *(Martin Jones)*

★ Hole in the Wall (01223) 812282

LITTLE WILBRAHAM   TL5458

High Street; A1303 Newmarket Road to Stow cum Quy off A14, then left at The Wilbrahams signpost, then right at Little Wilbrahams signpost; CB1 5JY Tucked-away pub/restaurant with cosy carpeted ochre-walled bar on right, log fire in big brick fireplace, 16th-c beams and timbers, snug little window seats and other mixed seating around scrubbed kitchen tables, similar middle room with fire in open range, rather plusher main dining room with another fire, really good inventive cooking including evening tasting menu (set lunch menu is more affordable), Fellows ales and guests, ten wines by the glass and some unusual soft drinks; well behaved children allowed, dogs in bar, neat side garden with good teak furniture and small verandah, interesting walk to nearby unspoilt Little Wilbraham Fen, closed Sun evening, all day Mon and for two weeks in Jan. *(Mr and Mrs T R Leighton, John Saville, R J Shears)*

Three Horseshoes (01954) 210221

MADINGLEY   TL3960

High Street; off A1303 W of Cambridge; CB23 8AB Civilised thatched restauranty pub – most customers come here for the inventive if not cheap italian-influenced food; there is, though, a small pleasantly relaxed bar, with simple wooden furniture on bare boards and open fire (can be a bit of a crush at peak times), a couple of real ales and plenty of wines by the glass from excellent list, friendly service, pretty dining conservatory; children welcome, picnic-sets under parasols in sunny garden. *(Anon)*

★ Pike & Eel (01480) 463336

NEEDINGWORTH   TL3571

Pub signed from A1123; Overcote Road; PE27 4TW Peacefully placed old riverside hotel with spacious lawns and small marina; plush bar opening into room with easy chairs, sofas and big open fire, civilised eating area (also separate smart restaurant) in light and airy glass-walled block overlooking water, boats and swans, good food and service, Adnams, Black Sheep and Greene King IPA, nice wines and coffee; background music; children welcome, 12 clean simple bedrooms, good breakfast. *(Ryta Lyndley)*

★ Queens Head (01223) 870436

NEWTON   TL4349

2.5 miles from M11 junction 11; A10 towards Royston, then left on to B1368; CB22 7PG Lovely traditional unchanging pub run by same welcoming family for many years – lots of loyal customers; peaceful bow-windowed main bar with crooked beams in low ceiling, bare wooden benches and seats built into cream walls, curved high-backed settle, paintings and big log fire, Adnams ales tapped from the cask, farm cider and simple hearty food, small carpeted saloon, traditional games including table skittles, shove-ha'penny and nine men's morris; no credit cards; children on best behaviour allowed in games room only, dogs welcome, seats out in front by vine trellis. *(Toby Jones)*

Horseshoe (01480) 810293

OFFORD D'ARCY   TL2166

High Street; PE19 5RH Extended former 17th-c coaching house with two bars and restaurant, emphasis on good food including popular Sun carvery, friendly service, up to five changing ales and well chosen wines, beams and inglenooks; children welcome, lawned garden with play area, open all day Fri-Sun. *(Anon)*

Chequers (01223) 207840

ORWELL   TL3650

Town Green Road; SG8 5QL Much improved under new owners, enjoyable food (not Sun evening) including popular themed nights, well kept ales such as St Austell Tribute and Sharps Doom Bar, decent choice of wines by the glass, pleasant helpful staff; children and dogs (in bar) welcome, disabled facilities, closed Mon, otherwise open all day. *(Anon)*

PAMPISFORD   TL4948

★**Chequers** (01223) 833220

2.6 miles from M11 junction 10: A505 E, then village and pub signed off; Town Lane; CB22 4ER Traditional neatly kept old pub with friendly licensees, low beams and comfortable old-fashioned furnishings, booth seating on pale ceramic tiles in cream-walled main area, low step down to bare-boards part with dark pink walls, Greene King IPA, Woodfordes Wherry and two guests, good fairly priced food including themed nights, Sun carvery and OAP lunch Weds, good service; TV; children and dogs welcome (their collie is Snoopy), picnic-sets in prettily planted small garden lit by black street lamps, parking may be tricky, open all day (till 4pm Sun). *(David Jackman, D and M T Ayres-Regan, Roy Hoing)*

PETERBOROUGH   TL1998

★**Charters** (01733) 315700

Town Bridge, S side; PE1 1FP Interesting conversion of dutch grain barge moored on River Nene; sizeable timbered bar on lower deck with a dozen real ales including Oakham (regular beer festivals), restaurant above serving good value pan-asian food, lots of wooden tables and pews; background music, live bands (Fri and Sat after 10.30pm, Sun from 3.30pm); children welcome till 9pm, dogs in bar, huge riverside garden (gets packed in fine weather), open all day. *(Pat and Tony Martin)*

PETERBOROUGH   TL1897

Coalheavers Arms (01733) 565664

Park Street, Woodston; PE2 9BH Friendly old-fashioned 19th-c flagstoned local, well kept Milton and guest beers, farm cider, good range of continental imports and malt whiskies, basic snacks, Sun quiz; near football ground and busy on match days; pleasant garden, closed lunchtime Mon-Weds, open all day Fri-Sun. *(Anon)*

PETERBOROUGH   TL1898

Drapers Arms (01733) 847570

Cowgate; PE1 1LZ Roomy open-plan Wetherspoons in sympathetically converted draper's, fine ale range, low-priced promptly served food all day; can get very busy Fri, Sat evenings; children welcome, open from 9am. *(Roger Fox)*

REACH   TL5666

Dyke's End (01638) 743816

From B1102 follow signpost to Swaffham Prior and Upware; village signposted; CB25 0JD Welcoming 17th-c farmhouse with simply decorated bar, kitchen chairs and heavy pine tables on

dark boards, panelled section on left and step down to carpeted part with servery, Adnams, Purity and a couple of guests (they no longer brew their own beer), good food (not Sun evening, Mon) from pub favourites up; children and dogs welcome, picnic-sets on front grass, attractive spot next to church and village green, open all day weekends, closed Mon lunchtime. *(Caroline Prescott)*

SPALDWICK   TL1372

George (01480) 890293

Just off A14 W of Huntingdon; PE28 0TD Friendly well run 16th-c pub, stylish décor, sofas in bar, larger bistro area, nice food from good value bar snacks up, local real ales; children welcome. *(Roy Shutz)*

ST NEOTS   TL1761

Eaton Oak (01480) 219555

Just off A1, Great North Road/Crosshall Road; PE19 7DB Under same ownership as the Rose at Stapleford; wide choice of popular food including grills, fresh fish and very good value early evening deal for two (Mon-Fri), Wells & Youngs ales and maybe a guest, good friendly service, plenty of nooks and crannies in older part, light airy dining area, conservatory; children and dogs (in bar) welcome, disabled access throughout, tables outside under parasols, smokers' shelter, nine bedrooms, open all day (breakfast for non-residents). *(Michael and Jenny Back and others)*

STAPLEFORD   TL4651

★**Rose** (01223) 843349

London Road; M11 junction 11; CB22 5DG Comfortable sister pub to the Eaton Oak at St Neots, emphasis on dining and can get very busy, wide choice of good reasonably priced food including weekday early-bird deal, pleasant uniformed staff, Wells & Youngs Best and Bombardier, small low-ceilinged lounge with inglenook woodburner, roomy split-level dining area; faint background music; picnic-sets on back grass, open (and food) all day Sun. *(Michael and Jenny Back)*

STILTON   TL1689

Stilton Cheese (01733) 240546

Signed off A1; North Street; PE7 3RP Welcoming former coaching inn with wide range of good food from sandwiches to fish specials, a couple of ales such as Adnams Broadside and Timothy Taylors Landlord, decent wines, old interior with roaring log fire in central bar, four linked dining rooms; no dogs; children welcome, tables out in back garden with sheltered deck, six barn-conversion bedrooms, closed Sun evening and lunchtimes Mon, Tues. *(M and GR)*

STOW CUM QUY   TL5260

White Swan (01223) 811821

Off A14 E of Cambridge, via B1102; CB25 9AB Cosy 17th-c beamed village pub-restaurant under newish licensees, five well kept ales, Weston's cider and several wines by the glass, enjoyable home-made food from bar snacks and pubby choices to more ambitious restaurant dishes, big fireplace, friendly atmosphere; children and dogs welcome, terrace picnic-sets, handy for Anglesey Abbey (NT), open all day. *(Mrs M Baxter, Hazel Miller, M and GR, Chris and Angela Buckell)*

THORNEY   TL2799
Dog in a Doublet (01733) 202256
B1040 towards Thorney; PE6 0RW Friendly dining pub across from river, good bar food and more upmarket restaurant menu (some produce from own farm), well kept ales, deli counter, open fire; children and dogs (in bar) welcome, handy for Hereward Way walks, four bedrooms and camping, open all day Fri-Sun, closed Mon, Tues lunchtime. *(Middlemass Ryan)*

THRIPLOW   TL4346
Green Man (01763) 208855
3 miles from M11 junction 10; A505 towards Royston, then first right; Lower Street; SG8 7RJ Refurbished little roadside pub owned by the village, enjoyable food from shortish menu and four well kept changing ales, efficient friendly service; children welcome, picnic-sets on small grassy triangle in front, open all day (Sun till 4pm). *(Mrs Margo Finlay, Jörg Kasprowski, Alex and Hazel Evans)*

TILBROOK   TL0769
White Horse (01480) 860764
High Street (B645); PE28 0JP Welcoming and relaxed beamed country pub with cosy bar, dining lounge and conservatory, Courage and Wells & Youngs ales, enjoyable reasonably priced food (not Sun evening, Mon) and nice range of coffees, good service, pub games including table skittles; popular live music first Mon of month, free wi-fi; big garden with play equipment, goats, chickens and ducks, closed Mon lunchtime, otherwise open all day. *(Ryta Lyndley)*

UFFORD   TF0904
★White Hart (01780) 740250
Main Street; S on to Ufford Road off B1443 at Bainton, then right; PE9 3BH Friendly village pub dating from the 17th c, informal, chatty bar with wood floor and exposed stone walls, railway memorabilia, farm tools and chamber pots, high-backed settles and leather sofa by woodburner, well kept Oakham JHB, Sharps Doom Bar and a couple of guests, several wines by the glass, good food from varied menu, beamed restaurant and small orangery; children and dogs welcome, three acres of gardens, six comfortable bedrooms, good breakfast, open all day (till 9pm Sun). *(Michael Doswell, Gordon and Margaret Ormondroyd)*

WANSFORD   TL0799
Paper Mills (01780) 782328
London Road; PE8 6JB Attractively refurbished old bay-windowed stone pub with friendly atmosphere, Fullers London Pride and a couple of guests, good wine selection, enjoyable popular food from changing menu, good sandwiches too, beamed and flagstoned bar with fireplaces either side, conservatory; children and dogs welcome, tables in nicely tended terrace garden, open all day. *(G Jennings, Lois Dyer)*

WARESLEY   TL2454
Duncombe Arms (01767) 650265
Eltisley Road (B1040, 5 miles S of A428); SG19 3BS Comfortable welcoming old pub, well managed with some emphasis on eating, long main bar with fire at one end, reliably good pub food including specials, well kept Greene King ales, efficient friendly service, back room and restaurant; children welcome, picnic-sets in shrub-sheltered garden. *(Roger Fox)*

WHITTLESFORD   TL4648
Bees in the Wall (01223) 834289
North Road; handy for M11 junction 10 and Duxford Air Museum; CB22 4NZ Village-edge local with comfortably worn-in split-level timbered lounge, polished tables and country prints, small tiled public bar with old wall settles, darts, decent good value food (not Sun or Tues evenings) from sandwiches up, well kept Timothy Taylors Landlord and guests, open fires; may be background music, games machine, no dogs; picnic-sets in big paddock-style garden with terrace, bees still in the wall (here since the 1950s), closed Mon. *(Martin Jones)*

WICKEN   TL5670
Maids Head (01353) 720727
High Street; CB7 5XR Old thatched dining pub in village-green setting, good choice of enjoyable home-made food all day (till 6pm Sun), Greene King IPA and three guests, fairly priced house wines, unpretentious beamed bar with pool and darts, restaurant (children welcome here), two open fires, occasional quiz nights; dogs allowed in bar, picnic-sets out in front, handy for Wicken Fen nature reserve (NT), open all day (till 1am Fri, Sat). *(Anon)*

WOODDITTON   TL6558
Three Blackbirds (01638) 731100
Signed off B1063 at Cheveley; CB8 9SQ Popular two-bar thatched pub, low 17th-c beams, mix of old country furniture on bare boards, pictures and knick-knacks, open fires, enterprising food together with pub favourites and lunchtime sandwiches, Adnams, Timothy Taylors and changing local guests, plenty of wines by the glass including champagne, restaurant; children welcome, garden picnic-sets, open all day Sun till 7pm. *(Michael and Jenny Back)*

Cheshire

ALDFORD   SJ4259   Map 7

Grosvenor Arms ★  ♀ ◖

B5130 Chester–Wrexham; CH3 6HJ

Spacious place with impressive range of drinks, wide-ranging imaginative menu, good service, suntrap terrace and garden

Just a few miles from Chester with all its attractions, this is a sizeable Victorian brick and half-timbered pub with a buoyantly chatty atmosphere and genuinely friendly, attentive staff. The various rooms have plenty of interest and individuality. Spacious cream-painted areas are sectioned by big knocked-through arches with a variety of wood, quarry tile, flagstone and black and white tile floor finishes – some richly coloured turkish rugs look well against these natural materials. Good solid pieces of traditional furniture, plenty of interesting pictures and attractive lighting keep it all intimate. A handsomely boarded panelled room has tall bookshelves lining one wall; good selection of board games. Phoenix Brunning & Price Original, Weetwood Eastgate and four quickly changing guests are served from a fine-looking bar counter and they offer 20 wines by the glass, over 80 whiskies and distinctive soft drinks such as peach and elderflower cordial and Willington Fruit Farm pressed apple juice. Lovely on summer evenings, the airy terracotta-floored conservatory has lots of gigantic low-hanging flowering baskets and chunky pale wood garden furniture. It opens out to a large elegant suntrap terrace and a neat lawn with picnic-sets.

 Good food from an interesting menu includes sandwiches, potted mackerel and shrimp with horseradish butter, venison and pancetta meatballs in juniper and blueberry sauce, cheese, potato and onion pie with home-made baked beans, chicken breast wrapped in pancetta with wild mushroom and barley risotto and red wine sauce, braised ox cheek with white onion purée, malaysian fish curry, and puddings such as peanut butter and chocolate cheesecake and glazed lime tart. *Benchmark main dish: pork belly, chorizo and black pudding salad with garlic croutons and cumberland dressing £12.95. Two-course evening meal £20.50.*

Brunning & Price ~ Manager Tracey Owen ~ Real ale ~ (01244) 620228 ~ Open 11-11 (10.30 Sun) ~ Bar food 12-9.30 (10 Fri, Sat; 9 Sun) ~ Children welcome ~ Dogs allowed in bar ~ Wi-fi ~ www.grosvenorarms-aldford.co.uk *Recommended by Claes Mauroy, Clive Watkin, Mike and Wena Stevenson, Stephen Shepherd*

Post Office address codings give the impression that some pubs are in Cheshire, when they're really in Derbyshire (and therefore included under that chapter) or in Greater Manchester (see the Lancashire chapter).

ALLOSTOCK   SJ7271   Map 7

Three Greyhounds ♀

4.7 miles from M6 junction 18: A54 E then forking left on B5803 into Holmes Chapel, left at roundabout on to A50 for 2 miles, then left on to B5082 towards Northwich; Holmes Chapel Road; WA16 9JY

Relaxing, civilised and welcoming, with enjoyable food all day

Our readers enjoy their visits to this prominent former farmhouse – it's the caring, attentive service and interesting food that get mentioned first and foremost. The various rooms are interconnected by open doorways and the décor throughout is restful: thick rugs on quarry tiles or bare boards, candles and soft lighting, dark grey walls (or interesting woven wooden ones) hung with modern black-on-white prints, three open fires, and an appealing variety of wooden dining chairs, cushioned wall seats, little stools and plenty of deep purple scatter cushions around all sorts of tables – do note the one made from giant bellows. A good choice of drinks includes 15 interesting wines by the glass, 50 brandies and three house ales – Almighty Allostock Ale (from Mobberley), Biley Bomber (from Caledonian) and Three Greyhounds Bitter (from Weetwood) – plus three quickly changing guests on handpump; unobtrusive background music. The big side lawn has picnic-table sets under cocktail parasols, with more tables on the decking of a Perspex-roofed side verandah. Just across the road is Shakerley Mere, with a nature reserve walk. The pub is owned by Tim Bird and Mary McLaughlin.

 Rewarding food using local produce is served all day: sandwiches, beetroot-cured sea trout with fennel and apple salad, potted confit of duck with orange marmalade, sharing platters, pork and leek sausages with wholegrain mustard mash, root vegetable and chickpea casserole, lancashire hotpot, smoked haddock and salmon fishcakes with lemon mayonnaise, and puddings such as dark and white chocolate cheesecake and spiced sherry plum crumble; they also hold themed cheese and brandy tasting evenings. *Benchmark main dish: beer-battered haddock and chips £11.95. Two-course evening meal £18.00.*

Free house ~ Licensee James Griffiths ~ Real ale ~ (01565) 723455 ~ Open 12-11 (10.30 Sun) ~ Bar food 12-9.15 (9.45 Fri, Sat, 8.45 Sun) ~ No under-10s after 7pm ~ Dogs allowed in bar ~ Wi-fi ~ Jazz Fri evenings ~ www.thethreegreyhoundsinn.co.uk
Recommended by Caroline Prescott, David Heath

ASTBURY   SJ8461   Map 7

Egerton Arms £ 🛏

Village signposted off A34 S of Congleton; CW12 4RQ

Friendly and cheery pub with popular bar food, four real ales and large garden; nice bedrooms

The jovial hands-on landlord and his attentive staff remain as friendly as ever to both regulars and visitors at this partly 16th-c village pub. The pubby cream-painted rooms are decorated with newspaper cuttings relating to 'Grace' (the landlady's name), the odd piece of armour, shelves of books and quite a few mementoes of the Sandow Brothers (one of whom was the landlady's father) who performed as 'the World's Strongest Youths'. In summer, dried flowers replace the fire in the big fireplace; background music and TV. Robinsons Dizzy Blonde, Double Hop, Unicorn and a guest beer on handpump, 11 wines by the glass, 16 malt whiskies and alcoholic winter warmers. Well placed tables outside enjoy pleasant views of the church opposite, and a play area has a wooden fort; handy for Little Moreton Hall (National Trust).

🍴 The popular, fairly priced food includes sandwiches and baps, salt and pepper whitebait, duck pâté, cumberland sausage with red wine gravy, vegetable curry, lambs liver and onions in rich gravy, a choice of roasts, huge cod fillet (battered or grilled), and puddings such as raspberry cheesecake and syrup pudding. *Benchmark main dish: braised steak and onions in ale £10.75. Two-course evening meal £16.25.*

Robinsons ~ Tenants Allen and Grace Smith ~ Real ale ~ (01260) 273946 ~ Open 11.30-11 (10.30 Sun) ~ Bar food 11.30-2, 6-9; 12-8 Sun ~ Restaurant ~ Children welcome ~ Wi-fi ~ Bedrooms: £60/£70 ~ www.egertonarms.co.uk *Recommended by Paul Humphreys, Dr D J and Mrs S C Walker, Mike and Wena Stevenson, Dave Webster, Sue Holland, John Wooll, Roger and Anne Newbury*

ASTON
SJ6146 Map 7
Bhurtpore ★ ♀ ☖ £
Off A530 SW of Nantwich; in village follow Wrenbury signpost; CW5 8DQ

Fantastic range of drinks (especially real ales) in warm-hearted pub with some unusual artefacts; big garden

'A beer drinker's dream' says one reader enthusiastically, and the fact that they get through more than 1,000 different ales a year reinforces his comment. They usually keep 11 on at any one time, sourced from all over the country, such as Abbeydale Absolution, AllGates Ostara, Blue Monkey Ape Ale, Buntingford Full Tilt, Coach House Squires Gold, Dark Star Revelation, Hook Norton Hooky Mild, Redwillow Soulless, Salopian Automaton, Spitting Feathers 1862 and Wychwood Piledriver. They also stock dozens of unusual bottled beers and fruit beers, a great many bottled ciders and perries and farm cider, over 100 different whiskies, carefully selected soft drinks and wines from a good list; summer beer festival. The pub name commemorates the siege of Bhurtpore (a town in India) during which local landowner Sir Stapleton Cotton (later Viscount Combermere) was commander in chief. The connection with India also explains some of the quirky artefacts in the carpeted lounge bar – look out for the sunglasses-wearing turbanned figure behind the counter; also good local period photographs and some attractive furniture in the comfortable public bar; board games, pool, TV and games machine. Weekends tend to be pretty busy.

🍴 Quite a choice of tasty food includes sandwiches and toasties, smoked haddock in a herby pancake with cheese and leek sauce, steak in ale pie with mushroom dumplings, gammon with free-range eggs or pineapple, lamb shoulder in mint and sherry gravy, quite a range of curries, and puddings such as belgian waffle with toffee sauce and chocolate fudge cake. *Benchmark main dish: pie of the day £10.50. Two-course evening meal £17.00.*

Free house ~ Licensee Simon George ~ Real ale ~ (01270) 780917 ~ Open 12-2.30, 6.30-11.30; 12-midnight Fri, Sat; 12-11 Sun ~ Bar food 12-2, 6.30-9.30; 12-9.30 Sat; 12-9 Sun ~ Restaurant ~ Children welcome ~ Dogs allowed in bar ~ Wi-fi ~ Monthly folk music ~ www.bhurtpore.co.uk *Recommended by Dave Webster, Sue Holland*

BUNBURY
SJ5658 Map 7
Dysart Arms 🏵 ♀ ☖
Bowes Gate Road; village signposted off A51 NW of Nantwich; and from A49 S of Tarporley – coming in this way on northernmost village access road, bear left in village centre; CW6 9PH

Civilised chatty dining pub attractively filled with good furniture in thoughtfully laid-out rooms, with enjoyable food and a lovely garden with pretty views

'I'd move house to make this my local' – a lovely comment from a reader on this bustling and very well run pub. The interior has been opened up, but the neatly kept rooms still retain a cottagey feel as they ramble around the pleasantly lit central bar. Cream walls keep it all light, clean and airy, with deep venetian red ceilings adding cosiness; each room (some with good winter fires) is nicely furnished with an appealing variety of well spaced sturdy wooden tables and chairs, a couple of tall filled bookcases and just the right amount of carefully chosen bric-a-brac, properly lit pictures and plants. Flooring ranges from red and black tiles to stripped boards and some carpet. Phoenix Brunning & Price Original, Timothy Taylors Landlord and three guests such as Adnams, Caledonian Deuchars IPA and Fullers London Pride on handpump, alongside a good selection of 17 wines by the glass and just over 20 malts. Sturdy wooden tables on the terrace and picnic-sets on the lawn in the neatly kept slightly elevated garden are lovely in summer, with views of the splendid church at the end of this pretty village, and the distant Peckforton Hills beyond.

 Quality food from a well judged menu includes twice-baked blue cheese soufflé with a spiced walnut and chicory salad, venison and rabbit faggots in rich gravy, steak burger with bacon, cheese and chips, vietnamese king prawn and rice noodle salad with mint, coriander, chilli and lime dressing, game hotpot, cajun chicken on apple, celeriac and pecan salad, and puddings such as vanilla crème brûlée and pear tarte tatin with liquorice and blackberry ice-cream. *Benchmark main dish: steak in ale pie £11.95. Two-course evening meal £19.50.*

Brunning & Price ~ Manager Kate John ~ Real ale ~ (01829) 260183 ~ Open 11.30-11; 12-10.30 Sun ~ Bar food 12-9.30 (9 Sun) ~ Children welcome ~ Dogs allowed in bar ~ Wi-fi ~ www.dysartarms-bunbury.co.uk *Recommended by Claes Mauroy, Mike and Wena Stevenson, Dave Webster, Sue Holland, CES*

BURLEYDAM
Combermere Arms 🌟 🍺
SJ6042 Map 7

A525 Whitchurch–Audlem; SY13 4AT

Roomy and attractive beamed pub successfully mixing a good drinking side with imaginative all-day food

With a fine choice of drinks served by first class staff, super food and plenty of character, this extended pub with a 16th-c heart remains on top form. The many rambling yet intimate-feeling rooms are attractive and understated, and the various nooks and crannies are filled with all sorts of antique cushioned dining chairs around dark wood tables, rugs on wood (some old, some new oak) and stone floors, prints hung frame-to-frame on cream walls, bookshelves, deep red ceilings, panelling and open fires. You'll get an equally nice welcome whether drinking or dining, with both aspects of the business doing well. Phoenix Brunning & Price Original, Joules Pale Ale and Weetwood Cheshire Cat with guests such as Salopian Shropshire Gold, Wadworths 6X and Wincle Waller on handpump, 100 malt whiskies, 14 wines by the glass from an extensive list and three farm ciders; board games and background music. Outside there are good solid wood tables and picnic-sets in a pretty, well tended garden.

 Imaginative, contemporary brasserie-style dishes include sandwiches, chicken liver pâté with apricot and carrot chutney, scallops with caramelised cauliflower purée, air-dried ham and caper dressing, open vegetable samosa with tandoori paneer cheese, steak burger with bacon, cheese, coleslaw and chips, smoked haddock and salmon fishcakes, duck three-ways with parsnip purée and port jus, and puddings such as white chocolate and Baileys cheesecake and crème brûlée. *Benchmark main dish: lamb shoulder with dauphinoise potatoes and gravy £16.95. Two-course evening meal £20.45.*

Brunning & Price ~ Manager Lisa Hares ~ Real ale ~ (01948) 871223 ~ Open 11.30-11 ~ Bar food 12-9.30 (10 Thurs-Sat, 9 Sun) ~ Children welcome ~ Dogs allowed in bar ~ Wi-fi ~ www.combermerearms-burleydam.co.uk *Recommended by Roger Fox, Brian and Anna Marsden*

BURWARDSLEY
SJ5256   Map 7

Pheasant ★ ♀ ⇐

Higher Burwardsley; signposted from Tattenhall (which itself is signposted off A41 S of Chester) and from Harthill (reached by turning off A534 Nantwich–Holt at the Copper Mine); follow pub's signpost uphill from Post Office; OS Sheet 117 map reference 523566; CH3 9PF

Fantastic views and enjoyable food at this fresh conversion of an old heavily beamed inn; open all day

To make the most of the fine walking around this half-timbered and sandstone inn (the scenic Sandstone Trail along the Peckforton Hills is close by) you could stay overnight in the comfortable bedrooms – the breakfasts are good too. The attractive low-beamed interior is airy and modern-feeling in parts, and the various separate areas (gently refurbished this year) have nice old chairs spread spaciously on wooden floors and a log fire in a huge see-through fireplace. Local Weetwood Best and Eastgate, plus guests such as Beartown Kodiak Gold and Weetwood Old Dog, on handpump, a dozen wines by the glass, several malt whiskies and local farm cider served by friendly, helpful staff; quiet background music and daily newspapers. A big side lawn has picnic-sets. The views right across the Cheshire plains from seats on the terrace are glorious; on a clear day with the telescope you can see as far as the pier head and cathedrals in Liverpool. Sister pubs are the Fishpool in Delamere and Bears Paw at Warmingham.

Sourcing the best local produce, the good, interesting food includes sandwiches (until 6pm), crispy beef hash with a fried egg and beetroot ketchup, moules marinière, sharing boards, coriander and chilli gnocchi with caramelised orange and pesto, corn-fed chicken breast with chive butter sauce and rissole potatoes, gressingham duck, toulouse sausage, haricot beans and parmesan, and puddings such as glazed lemon tart and spotted dick and custard. *Benchmark main dish: pie of the day £13.00. Two-course evening meal £22.00.*

Free house ~ Licensee Andrew Nelson ~ Real ale ~ (01829) 770434 ~ Open 11-11 (10.30 Sun) ~ Bar food 12-9.30 (10 Fri, Sat, 9 Sun) ~ Restaurant ~ Children welcome ~ Dogs allowed in bar and bedrooms ~ Wi-fi ~ Bedrooms: £75/£85 ~ www.thepheasantinn.co.uk *Recommended by Claes Mauroy, Dave Webster, Sue Holland, S Holder*

CHESTER
SJ4066   Map 7

Albion ★ ◧ £

Albion Street; CH1 1RQ

Strongly traditional pub with comfortable Edwardian décor and captivating World War I memorabilia; pubby food and good drinks

An attractive way to reach this pub is along the city wall, coming down at Newgate/Wolfsgate and walking along Park Street. It remains a genuinely friendly, old-fashioned pub with charming licensees who have been here for over 40 years. Over this time they have gathered an absorbing

collection of World War I memorabilia; in fact, this is an officially listed site
of four war memorials to soldiers from the Cheshire Regiment. The peaceful
rooms are filled with big engravings of men leaving for war and similarly
moving prints of wounded veterans – as well as flags, advertisements and
so on. There are also leatherette and hoop-backed chairs around cast-iron-
framed tables, lamps, an open fire in the Edwardian fireplace and dark floral
William Morris wallpaper (designed on the first day of World War I). You
might even be lucky enough to hear the vintage 1928 Steck pianola being
played; there's an attractive side dining room too. Adnams and a couple of
guests from brewers such as Hook Norton and Titanic on handpump, new
world wines, fresh orange juice, organic bottled cider and fruit juice, over
25 malt whiskies and a good selection of rums and gins. Bedrooms are small
but comfortable and furnished in keeping with the pub's style (free parking
for residents and a bottle of house wine if dining).

Even the trench rations (helpings are so generous they don't offer starters)
are in period: sandwiches, corned beef hash with pickled cabbage, lambs liver
and bacon in cider gravy, cumberland sausages with apple sauce, haggis and tatties,
and gammon and pease pudding with parsley sauce. *Benchmark main dish:
cottage pie £9.95.*

Punch ~ Lease Mike and Christina Mercer ~ Real ale ~ No credit cards ~ (01244)
340345 ~ Open 12-2.30, 5 (6 Sat)-11; 12-3 Sun; closed Sun evening ~ Bar food 12-2, 5-8;
12-2.30, 6-8.30 Sat; 12-2 Sun ~ Restaurant ~ Dogs allowed in bar ~ Wi-fi ~ Bedrooms:
$75/$85 ~ www.albioninnchester.co.uk *Recommended by David H Bennett, Simon J Barber,
Dave Webster, Sue Holland, Roger and Anne Newbury, Pat and Tony Martin*

CHESTER
Architect ♀ ◀

SJ4066 Map 7

Nicholas Street (A5268); CH1 2NX

**Bustling pub by the racecourse, with interesting furnishings and
décor, attentive staff, a good choice of drinks and super food**

This interesting Georgian pub, by Roodee racecourse, is almost two
separate places connected by a glass passage. The pubbiest part, with
more of a bustling feel, is the garden room, where they serve Phoenix
Brunning & Price Original and Weetwood Eastgate and guests such as
Conwy Infusion, Montys Moonrise, Moorhouses Black Cat and Ticketybrew
Pale Ale on handpump, 17 wines by the glass, 74 whiskies and farm cider.
Throughout there are elegant antique dining chairs around a mix of nice
old tables on rugs or bare floorboards, hundreds of interesting paintings
and prints on green, cream or yellow walls, house plants and flowers on
windowsills and mantelpieces, and lots of bookcases. Also, open fires,
armchairs in front of a woodburning stove or tucked into cosy nooks,
candelabra and big mirrors, and a friendly, easy-going atmosphere. Big
windows and french doors look over the terrace, where there are plenty
of good quality wooden seats and tables under parasols.

Good, rewarding food includes sandwiches, chicken liver pâté with apricot
and carrot chutney, venison, rabbit and thyme faggot with juniper sauce,
wild mushroom, lemon and parsley pasta with confit tomatoes, lamb and mint pie,
duck breast with a sweet and sour orange sauce, plaice fillet with smoked salmon
and prawn mousse and creamy mussel sauce, and puddings such as cherry and
almond tart with cherry crumble ice-cream and sticky toffee pudding with toffee
sauce. *Benchmark main dish: poached cod with rice noodles and asian broth
£14.50. Two-course evening meal £21.00.*

Brunning & Price ~ Manager Jon Astle-Rowe ~ Real ale ~ (01244) 353070 ~ Open 10.30am-11pm; 10.30-10.30 Sun ~ Bar food 12-10 (9.30 Sun) ~ Restaurant ~ Children welcome ~ Dogs allowed in bar ~ Wi-fi ~ www.architect-chester.co.uk
Recommended by Isobel Mackinlay, Wendda and John Knapp

 ## CHESTER
Mill £

SJ4166 Map 7

Milton Street; CH1 3NF

Big hotel with huge range of real ales, good value food and cheery service in sizeable bar

They always have at least ten (and up to 16) beers on handpump in this smart, modern hotel – and get through more than 2,000 guest beers a year. Weetwood Best and Mill Premium (brewed for them by Coach House) are on all the time, with other regulars being from Elland, Cheshire, Copper Dragon, Peerless, Rudgate, Stonehouse and Titanic; also, a dozen wines by the-glass, two farm ciders and 25 malt whiskies. You'll find a real mix of customers in the neatly kept bar which has some exposed brickwork and supporting pillars, local photographs on cream-papered walls, contemporary seats around marble-topped tables on light wooden flooring, and helpful, friendly staff. One comfortable area is reminiscent of a bar on a cruise liner; quiet background music and unobtrusively placed big-screen sports TV. Converted from an old mill, the hotel straddles either side of the Shropshire Union Canal, with a glassed-in bridge connecting the two sections. The bedrooms are comfortable and rather smart.

As well as a three-course lunch deal (not Sunday) and several other menus, the bar food includes sandwiches, chicken caesar salad, lamb burger with coleslaw and chips, sausage with mash, bacon and onion gravy, vegetable curry, chilli con carne, steak in ale pie, and puddings such as black forest trifle and syrup sponge pudding. *Benchmark main dish: a changing curry £12.50. Two-course evening meal £19.50.*

Free house ~ Licensee Gordon Vickers ~ Real ale ~ (01244) 350035 ~ Open 10am-midnight ~ Bar food 11.30-11; 12-10 Sun ~ Restaurant ~ Children welcome ~ Bedrooms: £73/£95 ~ www.millhotel.com *Recommended by Dave Webster, Sue Holland*

CHESTER
Old Harkers Arms ♀ ◗

SJ4166 Map 7

Russell Street, down steps off City Road where it crosses canal; CH3 5AL

Well run, spacious, canalside building with a lively atmosphere, a great range of drinks (including lots of changing real ales) and tasty food

With a cheerful atmosphere, this clever conversion of an early Victorian warehouse is right by the Shropshire Union Canal – you can watch the boats from the tall windows that run the length of the main bar. The striking industrial interior with its high ceilings is divided into user-friendly spaces by brick pillars. Walls are covered with old prints hung frame-to-frame, there's a wall of bookshelves above a leather banquette at one end, the mixed dark wood furniture is set out in intimate groups on stripped-wood floors, and attractive lamps lend some cosiness; board games. Cheerful staff serve up to nine real ales on handpump including Phoenix Brunning & Price Original, Weetwood Cheshire Cat and half a dozen regularly changing guests from brewers such as Bradfield, Lancaster, Salopian and Titanic; also, 130 malt whiskies, 24 wines from a well described list and six farm ciders.

Good enjoyable food includes sandwiches, pigeon breast with beetroot risotto and game reduction, crab and avocado salad with lemon crème fraîche, honey-glazed ham with free-range eggs, venison rump with bacon and juniper juice, slow-braised lamb shoulder with redcurrant gravy, moroccan-spiced cod with chickpea tagine, and puddings such as hot waffle with butterscotch sauce and apple and rhubarb crumble. *Benchmark main dish: beef and stilton pudding £12.95. Two-course evening meal £19.00.*

Brunning & Price ~ Manager Paul Jeffery ~ Real ale ~ (01244) 344525 ~ Open 10.30am-11pm; 12-10.30 Sun ~ Bar food 12-9.30 ~ Children welcome but no babies, toddlers or pushchairs ~ Dogs allowed in bar ~ Wi-fi ~ www.harkersarms-chester.co.uk
Recommended by David H Bennett, Simon J Barber, Dr Kevan Tucker, Dave Webster, Sue Holland, Roger and Anne Newbury, Wendda and John Knapp

CHOLMONDELEY   SJ5550   Map 7

Cholmondeley Arms

Bickley Moss; A49 5.5 miles N of Whitchurch; SY14 8HN

Imaginatively converted high-ceilinged schoolhouse with a decent range of real ales and wines, well presented food and a sizeable garden

Our readers enjoy their visits to this former schoolhouse very much – all citing the knowledgeable, helpful and friendly staff and impressive food. The rooms, with their lofty ceilings and high gothic windows, have a great deal of individuality, and the huge old radiators and school paraphernalia (hockey sticks, tennis rackets, trunks and so forth) are all testament to its former identity. Also, armchairs by the fire with a massive stag's head above, big mirrors, all sorts of dining chairs and tables, warmly coloured rugs on bare boards, fresh flowers and church candles; background music. Cholmondeley Best and Headmasters Ale (both Weetwood beers) and three guests such as Salopian Shropshire Gold, Tatton Best and Wincle Waller on handpump, 15 wines by the glass and an amazing range of 200 gins. There's plenty of seating outside on the sizeable lawn, which drifts off into open countryside, and more in front overlooking the quiet road. The pub (owned by Tim Bird and Mary McLaughlin) is handily placed for Cholmondeley Castle Gardens.

A thoughtful choice of enticing food using local game and farm produce includes sandwiches, duck liver and foie gras pâté with grape chutney, ale-battered haddock and chips, wild boar faggots with cider and puy lentil stew, smoked chicken, ham and treacle pudding, spinach, mushroom and blue cheese pancakes, duck breast with parsnip cream, pastrami duck leg hash and cherry gravy, and puddings such as milk chocolate brownie with peanut praline and apple and amaretti pancakes. *Benchmark main dish: steak and kidney pie £13.95. Two-course evening meal £18.00.*

Free house ~ Licensee Steven Davies ~ Real ale ~ (01829) 720300 ~ Open 12-11 (10.30 Sun) ~ Bar food 12-9.30 (9.45 Sat, 8.45 Sun) ~ No under-10s after 7pm ~ Dogs welcome ~ Wi-fi ~ Live jazz monthly Sun, quiz monthly winter ~ Bedrooms: £59.95/£79.95 ~ www.cholmondeleyarms.co.uk *Recommended by David and Lin Short, Claes Mauroy, Steve Whalley, Dave Webster, Sue Holland, R T and J C Moggridge, Ray and Winifred Halliday, Peter Harrison*

COTEBROOK
Fox & Barrel 🅖🏵 ♉

SJ5765   Map 7

A49 NE of Tarporley; CW6 9DZ

Attractive building with stylishly airy décor, an enterprising menu and good wines

At peak times especially, you'll have to book a table in advance in this bustling place as the excellent food is so popular. But this is no straightforward dining pub, and drinkers feel happily at home perched on the high chairs against the counter or on cushioned benches and settles enjoying a chat and a pint of Caledonian Deuchars IPA, Weetwood Eastgate and a couple of guests from brewers such as Black Sheep and Lancaster on handpump. They also have a good array of wines including about 20 by the glass. A big log fire dominates the bar while a larger uncluttered beamed dining area has attractive rugs and an eclectic mix of period tables on polished floorboards, with extensive wall panelling hung with framed old prints. The terrace has plenty of smart tables and chairs, picnic-sets on grass and some nice old fruit trees.

 Impressive food from a wide menu includes sandwiches, ham hock and cheshire cheese terrine with piccalilli, scallops, crispy beef and hoisin dressing on chinese salad, steak burger with mozzarella and chips, lamb rump with crispy breast and red pepper risotto, black bream fillet with king prawn cannelloni and thai broth, honey-glazed gammon with egg and pineapple, and puddings such as rhubarb panna cotta and dark, milk and white chocolate mousse. *Benchmark main dish: beer-battered fish and chips £12.75. Two-course evening meal £21.00.*

Free house ~ Licensee Gary Kidd ~ Real ale ~ (01829) 760529 ~ Open 12-11 (10.30 Sun) ~ Bar food 12-9.30 (9 Sun) ~ Children welcome ~ Dogs allowed in bar ~ Wi-fi ~ www.foxandbarrel.co.uk *Recommended by Dennis Jones*

DELAMERE
Fishpool ♉ 🍺

SJ5667   Map 7

Junction A54/B5152 Chester Road/Fishpool Road, a mile W of A49; CW8 2HP

Something for everyone in extensive, interestingly laid out pub, with a good range of food served all day

Great style and wit have been used in the clever layout here, which combines an open main section, large, bright and happy, with plenty of other snug and intimate smaller areas. And you'll be warmly greeted by the efficient, neatly dressed staff. Throughout, furnishings are carefully chosen and rather unusual, with lots of variety: a lofty central part, partly skylit and full of contented diners, has a row of booths facing the long bar counter, and plenty of other tables with banquettes or overstuffed small armchairs on pale floorboards laid with rugs; then a conservatory overlooking picnic-table sets on a flagstone terrace, and a lawn beyond. Off on two sides are many rooms with much lower ceilings, some with heavy dark beams, some with bright polychrome tile or intricate parquet flooring, William Morris wallpaper here, dusky paintwork or neat bookshelves there, sofas, armchairs, a twinkling fire in an old-fashioned open range, lots of old prints, and some intriguing objects including carved or painted animal skulls. They have a dozen wines by the glass and five real ales such as Weetwood Best, Cheshire Cat and Eastgate plus guests from Privateer and Tatton on handpump; unobtrusive background music; upstairs lavatories.

Sister pubs are the Pheasant in Burwardsley and the Bears Paw in Warmingham.

🍴 As well as flatbreads and pizzas, and grills from a special charcoal oven, the wide choice of food includes sandwiches (until 6pm), crayfish, prawn and lobster cocktail, crispy lambs tongue with shiso mayonnaise, mediterranean vegetable lasagne, corn-fed chicken stuffed with spinach mousse with an onion and pancetta port wine reduction, beef bourguignon, and puddings such as whiskey ginger cheesecake and double chocolate brownie. *Benchmark main dish: pie of the week £11.95. Two-course evening meal £20.00.*

Free house ~ Licensee Andrew Nelson ~ Real ale ~ (01606) 883277 ~ Open 11-11 ~ Bar food 12-9.30 (10 Fri, Sat, 9 Sun) ~ Restaurant ~ Children welcome ~ Dogs allowed in bar ~ Wi-fi ~ www.thefishpoolinn.co.uk *Recommended by Harvey Brown, Malcolm and Pauline Pellatt*

EATON
SJ8765 Map 7
Plough 🛏
A536 Congleton–Macclesfield; CW12 2NH

Neat and cosy village pub with up to four interesting beers, bar food, and views from big attractive garden; good bedrooms

From the big tree-filled garden behind this red-brick 17th-c pub you get fine views of the fringes of the Peak District, and there are picnic-sets on the lawn and a covered decked terrace with heaters. Inside, the carefully converted traditional bar has plenty of beams and exposed brickwork, a couple of snug little alcoves, comfortable armchairs and cushioned wooden wall seats on red patterned carpets, long red curtains, leaded windows and a woodburning stove in the big stone fireplace. Service is friendly and attentive, and they keep Storm Desert Storm and Cheshire Engine Vein and a couple of guest beers on handpump, and several wines by the glass from a decent list; background music and occasional TV. Moved here piece by piece from its original home in Wales, the heavily raftered barn at the back makes a striking restaurant. The appealingly designed bedrooms are in a converted stable block. Dogs are allowed at the management's discretion.

🍴 Using as much local produce as possible, the good, honest food includes mussels with cider, bacon and cream, chicken liver pâté with home-made chutney, corned beef hash with a free-range egg, cheshire cheese and vegetable omelette, sausages with onion gravy and mash, chargrilled barbecue chicken and chips, gammon with egg or pineapple, steak burger with various toppings, and puddings; they also offer a two-course set lunch. *Benchmark main dish: special lasagne £9.95. Two-course evening meal £17.00.*

Free house ~ Licensee Thomas Philip McCumesky ~ Real ale ~ (01260) 280207 ~ Open 12-11 ~ Bar food 12-2.30, 6-9.30; 12-9.30 Sat; 12-8 Sun ~ Restaurant ~ Children welcome ~ Dogs allowed in bedrooms ~ Wi-fi ~ Bedrooms: £60/£75 ~ www.theploughinncheshire.com *Recommended by Richard and Penny Gibbs*

GAWSWORTH
SJ8869 Map 7
Harrington Arms
Off A536; Congleton Road/Church Lane; SK11 9RJ

Helpful, friendly staff in unspoilt gem with simply furnished original rooms, Robinsons ales and good food

Once a farmhouse, this three-storey handsome brick house is still part of a working farm. It's simply furnished and has kept many of its original early 18th-c features such as low beams, snug corners, open fires and tiled and flagstoned floors. The serving counter is in a narrow space on the right as you enter, with people leaning on it and filling the bench opposite; several rooms laid off with scatter cushions on old settles, an eclectic collection of tables and chairs, lots of pictures on red or pale-painted walls, and a chatty, relaxed atmosphere. Robinsons 1892, Dizzy Blonde, Unicorn and a guest beer on handpump, several wines by the glass and 13 malt whiskies; background music. The lane leads to one of Cheshire's prettiest villages, with a fine black and white timbered Hall and Old Rectory.

As well as hot and cold sandwiches, the well liked food includes chicken liver pâté, leek, potato and cheese crumble, local sausages with onion gravy, parmesan-coated chicken with wild mushroom sauce, pork chop with black pudding hash and leek, cider and cream sauce, and daily specials. *Benchmark main dish: rabbit or steak and kidney pie £10.50. Two-course evening meal £15.00.*

Robinsons ~ Licensees Andy and Caroline Wightman ~ Real ale ~ (01260) 223325 ~ Open 12-3, 5-11.30 (midnight Fri); 12-11.30 Sat; 12-11 Sun ~ Bar food 12-2.30, 5-8.30 (9 Fri); 12-9 Sat; 12-8 Sun ~ Children welcome ~ Dogs allowed in bar ~ Wi-fi ~ www.harringtonarmsgawsworth.robinsonsbrewery.com *Recommended by Dr D J and Mrs S C Walker, Claes Mauroy*

KETTLESHULME
SJ9879 Map 7

Swan ✪

B5470 Macclesfield–Chapel-en-le-Frith, a mile W of Whaley Bridge; SK23 7QU

Charming 16th-c cottagey pub with enjoyable food (especially fish), good beer and an attractive garden

A lovely place and handy for walks in the relatively unfrequented north-west part of the Peak District National Park, this is a pretty white cottage clad in wisteria with friendly, polite staff. The interior is snug and cosy, with latticed windows, very low dark beams hung with big copper jugs and kettles, timbered walls, antique coaching and other prints and maps, ancient oak settles on a turkish carpet and log fires. Marstons Bitter on handpump with a couple of guest beers from breweries such as Marble and Osset, and 12 wines by the glass. The front terrace has teak tables, another two-level terrace has further tables and steamer benches under parasols, and there's a sizeable streamside garden.

Good, enjoyable food includes sandwiches, monkfish cheeks with wild mushrooms and chilli, chinese-style guinea fowl with hoisin sauce and cucumber salad, bouillabaisse, cheese and onion pie, kleftiko (greek-style slow-roast lamb shoulder), beef and stilton pudding, monkfish and tiger prawns in hot red thai coconut curry, and puddings such as chocolate brownie and sticky toffee pudding. *Benchmark main dish: parsley-battered haddock and chips £12.00. Two-course evening meal £20.50.*

Free house ~ Licensee Robert Cloughley ~ Real ale ~ (01663) 732943 ~ Open 12-11 (midnight Sat); closed Mon lunchtime ~ Bar food 12-8.30 (9 Thurs-Sat) ~ Children welcome ~ Dogs allowed in bar ~ Wi-fi ~ www.verynicepubs.co.uk/swankettleshulme *Recommended by Richard and Penny Gibbs, David Cotterill, John William Isaacson, Dr Kevan Tucker, Malcolm and Pauline Pellatt, Roger Yates*

If a compulsory service charge is mentioned prominently on a menu or accommodation terms, you must pay it if service was satisfactory. If service is really bad, you are legally entitled to refuse to pay some or all of the service charge as compensation for not getting the service you might reasonably have expected.

LOWER WITHINGTON
Black Swan

SJ8268 Map 7

Trap Street; SK11 9EQ

Neatly kept and well run pub with character rooms, cottagey décor, enjoyable food and seats outside

There's a great deal of individual character here and a sense of fun. Friendly staff welcome you into several cottagey rooms: chesterfield sofas with brightly patterned scatter cushions, wooden and prettily upholstered chairs around scrubbed pine and painted tables, walls of red or green paintwork, bare brick or with all manner of cheerful wallpaper, assorted lighting from hanging floral lampshades to table lamps, and fresh flowers on windowsills. Also, open fires, antlers, decorative plates and prints – it's all very light and airy and easy-going. Jennings Cumberland and guests from breweries such as Redwillow and Merlins on handpump, and a dozen wines by the glass. Outside there are green-painted picnic-sets and other seats on a side terrace and under a gazebo, and they have a summer pizza oven; boules. A gentle one-hour walk for dogs leads through the fields opposite. This is sister pub to the Swan at Newby Bridge (in our Cumbria chapter).

Food is served all day, from bacon butties through home-made cakes to enjoyable main dishes, such as crab and coriander tian with lemongrass, tea and ginger dressing, chicken liver parfait with apple and damson chutney, spicy lentil stew, barbecued half-chicken with caesar salad and french fries, beer-battered fish and chips, pork belly with caramelised apples, and puddings such as Malteser cheesecake and cherry bakewell tart. *Benchmark main dish: burger with cheese, home-made onion rings, pickles and french fries £11.95. Two-course evening meal £19.00.*

Free house ~ Licensee Sarah Gibbs ~ Real ale ~ (01477) 571770 ~ Open 11-11; 10-midnight Fri, Sat; 10-10 Sun ~ Bar food 12-9 ~ Children welcome ~ Dogs allowed in bar ~ Wi-fi ~ www.blackswancheshire.com *Recommended by Roger and Anne Newbury*

MACCLESFIELD
Sutton Hall

SJ9271 Map 7

Leaving Macclesfield southwards on A523, turn left into Byrons Lane signposted Langley, Wincle, then just before canal viaduct fork right into Bullocks Lane; OS Sheet 118 map reference 925715; SK11 0HE

Historic building set in attractive grounds, with a fine range of drinks and impressive food

Ideal for customers of all ages (the lovely garden is liked by families), this fine 16th-c manor house remains as well run and friendly as ever. The original hall that forms the heart of the building is highly impressive, particularly the entrance space. A charming series of bar and dining areas, some divided by tall oak timbers, are cosy with plenty of character, antique oak panelling, warmly coloured rugs on broad flagstones, bare boards and tiles, lots of pictures placed frame to frame, and a raised open fire. The atmosphere is nicely relaxed and a good range of drinks includes Phoenix Brunning & Price Original, Flowers Original, Wincle Lord Lucan and a couple of guests from brewers such as Beartown and Tatton on handpump, 18 wines by the glass from an extensive list and 30 malt whiskies. The pretty gardens have spaciously laid out tables, some on their own little terraces, sloping lawns and fine mature trees.

🍴 Interesting food includes sandwiches, asian-spiced duck in seaweed wrap with crispy noodles, cajun-spiced king prawns with jambalaya fritters, moules marinière, pork and leek sausages with onion gravy, lamb and mint pudding, rosemary and garlic chicken with bacon, wild mushrooms and pasta, and puddings such as rhubarb and ginger sponge with ginger custard and sugared cinnamon waffle with caramelised sauce. *Benchmark main dish: beer-battered fish and chips £12.25. Two-course evening meal £19.00.*

Brunning & Price ~ Manager Syd Foster ~ Real ale ~ (01260) 253211 ~ Open 11-11 (10.30 Sun) ~ Bar food 12-10 (9.30 Sun) ~ Children welcome ~ Dogs allowed in bar ~ Wi-fi ~ www.suttonhall.co.uk *Recommended by Claes Mauroy, Michael Butler, Pat and Tony Martin, Brian and Anna Marsden, Dr Kevan Tucker, John Wooll*

MARTON
SJ8568 Map 7

Davenport Arms ⬢ £

A34 N of Congleton; SK11 9HF

Handsome pub with welcoming bar, comfortable restaurant, good food and drink, and good-sized sheltered garden

The two linked front bar rooms have a good traditional feel and a welcoming atmosphere. There's a woodburning stove, ticking clock, comfortably cushioned wall settles, wing armchairs and other hand-picked furnishings on patterned carpet, old prints on the cream walls, and colourful jugs hanging from sturdy beams. You can eat (or just have a drink or coffee), and there's also a pleasantly light and airy more formal dining area behind; background music. Courage Directors, Theakstons Black Bull and a couple of guests from brewers such as Cottage and Moorhouses on handpump, and staff are friendly and helpful. Outside is a terrace with metal garden furniture, a fairy-lit arbour and a timber shelter, well spaced picnic-sets and a set of swings in the garden beyond, and a substantial separate play area. The 14th-c timbered church just opposite is well worth a look. They do take caravans but you must book.

🍴 Good, popular food includes lunchtime baguettes and wraps, smoked salmon and prawn mousse parcel, giant scotch egg with piccalilli, fresh pasta with tomatoes and mediterranean vegetables, home-baked ham and eggs, rack of ribs with slaw and very good chips, pheasant and duck hotpot, fishcakes with citrus mayonnaise, and puddings; Tuesday is curry night. *Benchmark main dish: beef bourguignon £14.95. Two-course evening meal £16.60.*

Free house ~ Licensees Ron Dalton and Sara Griffith ~ Real ale ~ (01260) 224269 ~ Open 12-3, 6-11; 12-11 Sat; 12-10.30 Sun; closed Mon lunchtime except bank holidays ~ Bar food 12-2.30; 6-9; 12-9 Sat; 12-8 Sun ~ Restaurant ~ Children welcome ~ Dogs allowed in bar ~ Wi-fi ~ www.thedavenportarms.co.uk *Recommended by Mike and Wena Stevenson, Dr D J and Mrs S C Walker*

MOBBERLEY
SJ7879 Map 7

Bulls Head 🍴 ♦ ⬢

Mill Lane; WA16 7HX

Terrific all-rounder with interesting food, just over 6 miles from the M6

Our readers enjoy their visits to this particularly well run, welcoming pub very much and return on a regular basis. It's been kept nice and pubby with just a touch of modernity, and there's plenty of room round the counter where they serve four Weetwood beers (named for the pub)

and three local guests from brewers such as Beartown, Coach House and
Wincle on handpump (useful tasting notes too), 15 wines by the glass and
80 malt whiskies; dogs are made equally welcome, with the friendly staff
dispensing doggie biscuits from a huge jar. Several rooms are furnished
quite traditionally, with an unpretentious mix of wooden tables, cushioned
wall seats and chairs on fine old quarry tiles, black and pale grey walls
contrasting well with warming red lampshades, pink stripped-brick walls
and pale stripped-timber detailing, and there are lots of mirrors, hops,
candles and open fires; background music and board games. Behind
the bar are leaflets of popular walks. This pub is owned by Tim Bird and
Mary McLaughlin.

From a thoughtful menu, the highly popular food includes nibbles and sharing
platters, seafood pot in creamy dill and white wine sauce, duck terrine with
spicy orange chutney, burger with bacon, cheddar, coleslaw and chips, beer-battered
haddock and chips, slow-braised lamb shoulder with redcurrant and rosemary gravy,
and puddings such as chocolate brownie with chocolate sauce and whiskey sticky
toffee pudding; they do regular themed food evenings. *Benchmark main dish: steak
in ale pie £13.95. Two-course evening meal £21.00.*

Free house ~ Licensee Barry Lawlor ~ Real ale ~ (01565) 873395 ~ Open 12-11 (10.30
Sun) ~ Bar food 12-9.15 (9.45 Sat, 8.45 Sun) ~ Children welcome but no under-10s after
7pm ~ Dogs allowed in bar ~ Wi-fi ~ Live jazz every second Sun; quiz monthly winter
~ www.thebullsheadpub.co.uk *Recommended by Michael and Angela Prior, Mike and Wena
Stevenson, Dave Webster, Sue Holland, Jim Tassell, Brian and Anna Marsden, Nigel and Sue Foster*

MOBBERLEY   SJ7980 Map 7
Church Inn ★ ♀ ◖

Brown sign to pub off B5085 on Wilmslow side of village; Church Lane;
WA16 7RD

**Nicely traditional friendly country pub, with bags of character
and good food and drink**

Candlelight, low ceilings, small snug interconnected rooms and
friendly young staff quickly make you feel not just at home but
rather cosseted and special. Dogs too – who get not just a tub of snacks
on the counter, but even the offer of a meaty 'beer'. The real beers, on
handpump, are brewed locally: Beartown Bear Ass and Ginger Bear,
and Tatton Church Ale-Alujah and Mallorys Mobberley Best (George
Mallory, lost near Everest's summit in 1924, was buried at the church
across the lane when his body was finally found in 1999). They also have
unusual and rewarding wines, including plenty by the glass. The décor in
soothing greys and dark green, with some oak-leaf wallpaper, is perked
up by a collection of stuffed grouse and their relatives and a huge variety
of pictures; perhaps well reproduced piped pop music. A side courtyard
has extremely sturdy tables and benches, and a sunny back garden
snakes down to the old bowling green with lovely pastoral views; they
give out a leaflet detailing a good four-mile circular walk from the pub,
passing its sibling, the Bulls Head, en route.

Two of the rooms give a glimpse of the busy kitchen team preparing rewarding
food that includes sandwiches (weekdays till 5.30), pig cheek slow-cooked
in cider with herby barley salad, crayfish and avocado salad, shepherd's pie,
field mushrooms stuffed with ricotta, basil, lemon and chilli with creamy white
wine sauce, chicken with celeriac dauphinoise, lamb burger topped with feta,
caramelised onion chutney, pickled cucumber and chips, and puddings such as
sticky date bread and butter pudding and millionaire's shortbread cheesecake;

they also offer Sunday brunch (from 10.30am) and themed food evenings. *Benchmark main dish: pork belly with parsnip purée, port and prune sauce and crackling £14.95. Two-course evening meal £21.00.*

Free house ~ Licensee Simon Umpleby ~ Real ale ~ (01565) 873178 ~ Open 12-11; 10.30-10.30 Sun ~ Bar food 12-3, 5.30-9.15; 12-9.45 Sat; 10.30-8.45 Sun ~ Restaurant ~ Children welcome but no under-10s after 7pm ~ Dogs allowed in bar ~ Wi-fi ~ www.churchinnmobberley.co.uk *Recommended by Caroline Prescott*

MOTTRAM ST ANDREW   SJ8878 Map 7
Bulls Head ♀ ◖

A538 Prestbury–Wilmslow; Wilmslow Road/Priest Lane; E side of village; SK10 4QH

Superb country dining pub, an excellent retreat at any time of day

At the heart of this sizeable dining pub is the bustling bar with its cheerful, efficient staff and large and thoughtful choice of drinks: Phoenix Brunning & Price Original, Wincle Sir Philip and guests from breweries such as Cheshire, Kelham Island and Tatton on handpump, around 20 wines by the glass, a fine range of spirits, and an attractive separate tea and coffee station with pretty blue and white china cups, teapots and jugs. But perhaps the star feature is the dining zone at the far end. Four levels stack up, each with a distinctive décor and style, from the informality of a sunken area with rugs on a tiled floor, through a comfortable library/dining room, to one with an upstairs conservatory feel and another, higher-windowed, with more of a special-occasion atmosphere. The rest of the pub has an appealing mix of abundant old prints and pictures, and comfortable seating in great variety, with a coal fire in one room, a blazing woodburning stove in a two-way fireplace dividing two other rooms, an antique black kitchen range in yet another; background music, daily papers and board games. There are picnic-table sets under cocktail parasols out on the lawn.

Good, tempting food includes sandwiches, lime-cured smoked salmon with wasabi crème fraîche and sesame shrimp toast, venison, duck and rabbit terrine with home-made gooseberry chutney, honey-roast ham and free-range eggs, mexican three-bean lasagne with sour cream and avocado and sweetcorn salad, miso-braised beef with stir-fried noodles and honey and lime dressing, chicken, ham and leek pie, and puddings such as glazed lemon tart with blackcurrant sorbet and dark chocolate marquis. *Benchmark main dish: lamb shoulder with dauphinoise potatoes and rosemary gravy £16.95. Two-course evening meal £21.00.*

Brunning & Price ~ Manager Andrew Coverley ~ Real ale ~ (01625) 828111 ~ Open 10.30am-11pm; 12-10.30 Sun ~ Bar food 12-10 (9.30 Sun) ~ Children welcome ~ Dogs allowed in bar ~ Wi-fi ~ www.bullshead-mottram.co.uk *Recommended by Toby Jones, Brian and Anna Marsden, John Wooll, Pat and Tony Martin*

NETHER ALDERLEY   SJ8576 Map 7
Wizard ✪

B5087 Macclesfield Road, opposite Artists Lane; SK10 4UB

Bustling pub with interesting food, real ales, a friendly welcome and relaxed atmosphere

On National Trust land in Windmill Wood and with a good mix of diners and drinkers, this is a well run pub with plenty of seats in the sizeable back garden – perfect after a walk along Alderley Edge. Inside, the various rooms are connected by open doorways and are cleverly done up in a mix of modern rustic and traditional styles: beams and open fires, antique dining chairs (some prettily cushioned) and settles around all sorts of tables, rugs on pale floorboards, prints and paintings on contemporary paintwork and decorative items ranging from a grandfather clock to staffordshire dogs and modern lampshades; fresh flowers and plants dotted about. Thwaites Wainwright and a guest from Storm on handpump and quite a few wines by the glass; background music. The pub is part of the Ainscoughs group.

Attractively presented food includes lunchtime sandwiches, wild mushrooms on toast with a poached egg and mustard cream, smoked trout fishcakes with citrus crème fraîche, sharing platters, sausages with chive mash and onion gravy, roasted butternut squash, lentil and spinach casserole with an onion fritter, burger with cheese, bacon and triple-cooked chips, roasted cod loin with chorizo cream sauce, and puddings such as crème brûlée and sticky toffee pudding. *Benchmark main dish: trio of lamb with garlic fondant potato £15.95. Two-course evening meal £20.00.*

Free house ~ Licensee Jamie Stuart ~ Real ale ~ (01625) 584000 ~ Open 12-3, 5.30-11; 12-11 Sat; 12-10 Sun ~ Bar food 12-3, 6-9.30; 12-9 weekends ~ Children welcome ~ Dogs allowed in bar ~ Wi-fi ~ Live pianist Fri evenings ~ www.ainscoughs.co.uk
Recommended by David Cotterill

SANDBACH
SJ7560   Map 7

Old Hall

1.2 miles from M6 junction 17: A534 – ignore first turn into town and take the second – if you reach the roundabout double back; CW11 1AL

Stunning mid 17th-c hall-house with impressive original features, plenty of drinking and dining space, six real ales and imaginative food

There are many wonderful original architectural features in this glorious 17th-c manor house – particularly in the room to the left of the entrance hall, which is much as it's been for centuries, with a Jacobean fireplace, oak panelling and a priest's hole. This leads into the Oak Room, divided by standing timbers into two dining areas, with heavy beams, oak flooring and reclaimed panelling. Other rooms in the original building have more hefty beams and oak boards, three open fires and a woodburning stove; the cosy snugs are carpeted. The Garden Room is big and bright, with reclaimed quarry tiling and exposed A-frame oak timbering, and opens on to a suntrap back terrace with teak tables and chairs among flowering tubs. Throughout, the walls are covered with countless interesting prints, there's an appealing collection of antique dining chairs and tables of all sizes, and plenty of rugs, bookcases and plants. From the handsome bar counter, efficient and friendly staff serve Phoenix Brunning & Price Original, Redwillow Feckless and Three Tuns XXX with three guests such as Dickensian Ale of Two Cities Bitter, Peerless Crystal Maze and Woodlands Oak Beauty on handpump, 15 good wines by the glass, 50 malt whiskies and farm cider; board games. There are picnic-sets in front of the building by rose bushes and clipped box hedging.

Modern brasserie-style food includes sandwiches, whiskey-cured salmon with celeriac rémoulade, duck liver pâté with juniper and pear chutney, sharing platters, potato, thyme and parmesan gnocchi with sage cream sauce, spiced chicken and vegetable empanada with roast pepper salad and chimichurri sauce, beef stroganoff with wild mushrooms, fish stew with spicy sausage, and puddings such as almond florentine tart with toffee sauce and passion-fruit and mango pavlova. *Benchmark main dish: grilled salmon niçoise with crispy duck egg and french dressing £14.95. Two-course evening meal £21.00.*

Brunning & Price ~ Manager Chris Button ~ Real ale ~ (01270) 758170 ~ Open 10.30am-11pm; 12-10.30 Sun ~ Bar food 12-10 (9 Sun) ~ Restaurant ~ Children welcome ~ Dogs allowed in bar ~ Wi-fi ~ www.oldhall-sandbach.co.uk *Recommended by Brian and Anna Marsden, Dr and Mrs A K Clarke, Mike and Wena Stevenson, Dave Webster, Sue Holland, R Anderson, R T and J C Moggridge, Hugh Roberts, JPC*

SPURSTOW
SJ5657 Map 7

Yew Tree ★ 🌟 ♀ ◧

Off A49 S of Tarporley; follow Bunbury 1, Haughton 2 signpost into Long Lane; CW6 9RD

Plenty of individuality, smashing food and drinks and a bouncy atmosphere

At any time of day this entertaining place is buzzing with locals and diners, all efficiently looked after by the energetic young staff. Décor is quirky and individual: nicely simple pale grey, off-white and cream surfaces explode into striking bold wallpaper; there's a magnified hunting tapestry and surprisingly angled bright tartans. An elegant mix of nice old tables and chairs mix with Timorous Beasties' giant bees papered on to the bar ceiling and a stag's head that looms out of the wall above a log fire. And the doors to the loos are quite a puzzle – which of the many knobs and handles actually work?! Elland Best Bitter, Heavy Industry Nos Smoked Porter, Lytham Fettlers Ale, Phoenix White Monk and Stonehouse Station Bitter on handpump, 20 malt whiskies, 15 wines by the glass from an interesting list and 15 gins. A more dining-oriented area shares the same feeling of relaxed bonhomie – a favourite table is snugged into a stripped-wood alcove resembling a stable stall; background music. A terrace outside has teak tables, with more on the grass.

🌟 Championing the best local produce, the impressive food includes sandwiches, slow-braised pig cheeks with crispy pancetta and apple and sage compote, ham hock and cheddar terrine with apricot chutney, spiced butternut squash and chickpea tagine with red onion and tomato sambals, a pie of the day, burger with cheese, bacon, sautéed onions and chips, naturally smoked haddock with soft poached egg and light mustard cream sauce, and puddings such as cherry bakewell tart and vanilla panna cotta. *Benchmark main dish: fresh and smoked fish pie £12.00. Two-course evening meal £20.00.*

Free house ~ Licensees Jon and Lindsay Cox ~ Real ale ~ (01829) 260274 ~ Open 12-11 (10.30 Sun) ~ Bar food 12-9.30 (10 Fri, Sat, 9 Sun) ~ Children welcome ~ Dogs welcome ~ Wi-fi ~ Live acoustic music last Fri of month ~ www.theyewtreebunbury.com
Recommended by Jane Taylor and David Dutton, Dave Webster, Sue Holland, Steve Whalley

SWETTENHAM
SJ7967 Map 7

Swettenham Arms 🌟

Off A54 Congleton–Holmes Chapel or A535 Chelford–Holmes Chapel; CW12 2LF

Big old country pub in a fine setting with shining brasses, five real ales and tempting food

The hard-working licensees run this former nunnery with much care and thought for both their customers and their pub; they've been here 21 years now. The three linked areas – gently refurbished this year and with contemporary paintwork – are still nicely traditional, with individual furnishings on a sweep of fitted turkey carpet (the bar now has a wooden floor), dark heavy beams, a polished copper bar, three welcoming open fires, plenty of shiny brasses and a variety of old prints – military, hunting, old ships, reproduction Old Masters and so forth. Friendly efficient staff serve Beartown Best Bitter, Moorhouses Pride of Pendle, Storm Hurricane Hubert, Timothy Taylors Landlord and a guest beer on handpump, 14 wines by the glass, several malt whiskies and winter mulled wine and cider. Outside there are tables on a back lawn that merges into a lovely sunflower and lavender meadow. There are walks in the delightful surrounding countryside and Quinta Arboretum is close by. Do visit the interesting village church which dates in part from the 13th c.

Using some home-grown vegetables and eggs from their free-range hens, the reliably good food includes sandwiches, chicken livers in madeira sauce, smoked trout, dill and crème fraîche pâté, steak and mushroom in ale pie, bream with chargrilled mediterranean vegetables and basil and tomato dressing, slow-roasted pork with apple and sage potato cake and calvados jus, and puddings such as mango crème brûlée and orange and almond cake with rhubarb and ginger crumble. *Benchmark main dish: beer-battered cod and chips £11.50. Two-course evening meal £20.00.*

Free house ~ Licensees Jim and Frances Cunningham ~ Real ale ~ No credit cards ~ (01477) 571284 ~ Open 11.30-11 (midnight Sat); 12-10 Sun; 11.30-3.30, 6-11 in winter ~ Bar food 12-9.30; 12-2.30, 6-9.30 in winter ~ Restaurant ~ Children welcome ~ Dogs allowed in bar ~ Wi-fi ~ www.swettenhamarms.co.uk *Recommended by Mike and Wena Stevenson, Hilary Forrest, Mr and Mrs R Shardlow*

THELWALL
Little Manor ♀
SJ6587   Map 7

Bell Lane; WA4 2SX

Restored manor house with lots to look at, plenty of space, well kept ales and interesting bistro-style food; seats outside

Although this carefully renovated handsome old house is pretty big, the nooks and crannies with plenty of character have been carefully preserved. The six beamed rooms, linked by open doorways and standing timbers, have an appealing variety of antique dining chairs around small, large, circular or square tables, flooring that ranges from rugs on bare boards through carpeting to some fine old black and white tiles, and leather armchairs by open fires (note the lovely carved wooden one); background music. There are metal chandeliers, wall lights and standard lamps, and the décor includes hundreds of interesting prints and photographs, books on shelves and lots of old glass and stone bottles on windowsills and mantelpieces; plenty of fresh flowers and house plants too. Phoenix Brunning & Price Original and Coach House Cromwells Best Bitter with guests from Hawkshead, Tatton and Wincle on handpump, around 15 wines by the glass and 60 whiskies; the young staff are consistently helpful. In fine weather you can sit at the chunky teak chairs and tables on the terrace; some are under a heated shelter.

Contemporary brasserie dishes include sandwiches, warm pickled mackerel with caraway vinaigrette, a charcuterie plate, honey-roast ham with free-range eggs, aubergine and courgette curry, beef and onion or fish pie, chicken breast with confit leg, potato and globe artichoke stew and red wine sauce, lamb rump with ratatouille, parsley purée and rosemary jus, and puddings such as blood orange cheesecake with orange gel and crème brûlée. *Benchmark main dish: beer-battered haddock and chips £21.75. Two-course evening meal £21.00.*

Brunning & Price ~ Manager Jill Dowling ~ Real ale ~ (01925) 212070 ~ Open 10.30am-11; 12-10.30 Sun ~ Bar food 12-10 (9.30 Sun) ~ Children welcome ~ Dogs allowed in bar ~ Wi-fi ~ www.littlemanor-thelwall.co.uk *Recommended by Dr and Mrs A K Clarke, David Jackman, R T and J C Moggridge*

WARMINGHAM
SJ7161 Map 7

Bears Paw 🍴 🛏

School Lane; CW11 3QN

Nicely maintained place with enjoyable food, half a dozen real ales and well equipped bedrooms

Plenty of individual character remains in the maze of linked refurbished rooms in this extensive Victorian inn, and you'll find several cosy places to sit. We particularly like the two little sitting rooms with their panelling, fashionable wallpaper, bookshelves and slouchy leather furniture with plumped-up cushions comfortably arranged by magnificent fireplaces with woodburners; stripped wood flooring and a dado keep it all informal. There's an eclectic mix of old wooden tables and some nice old carved chairs well spaced throughout the dining areas, with lofty windows providing a light and airy feel and big pot plants adding freshness. There are stools at the long bar counter where cheerful and efficient staff serve Mobberley Barn Buster, Rudgate Ale and Hearty, Spitting Feathers Empire IPA, and Westwood Best Bitter, Cheshire Cat and Eastgate on handpump, ten wines by the glass and quite a few malt whiskies; background music. There are tables in a small front garden by the car park. The bedrooms are well equipped and comfortable, and the breakfasts very good. This is sister pub to the Pheasant in Burwardsley and the Fishpool at Delamere.

🍴 Using produce from local farms and fishing boats where possible, the well presented food includes sandwiches (until 6pm), spicy, sizzling king prawns, potted rabbit with caramelised fig and pear chutney, various deli boards, open vegetable lasagne, salmon and smoked haddock fishcake with a poached egg and hollandaise, chicken wrapped in parma ham with sweet potato and madeira jus, calves liver with smoked bacon and lentil jus, and puddings such as treacle tart with honeycomb ice-cream and vanilla crème brûlée. *Benchmark main dish: steak in ale pie £12.95. Two-course evening meal £19.50.*

Free house ~ Licensee Andrew Nelson ~ Real ale ~ (01270) 526317 ~ Open 11-11 (10.30 Sun) ~ Bar food 12-9.30 (10 Fri, Sat, 9 Sun) ~ Restaurant ~ Children welcome ~ Dogs allowed in bar and bedrooms ~ Wi-fi ~ Bedrooms: £95/£105 ~ www.thebearspaw.co.uk
Recommended by Richard and Penny Gibbs, Dave Webster, Sue Holland, David Jackman

WHITELEY GREEN
SJ9278 Map 7

Windmill 🍷 🍴

Brown sign to pub off A523 Macclesfield–Poynton, just N of Prestbury; Hole House Lane; SK10 5SJ

Extensive relaxed country dining bar with big sheltered garden and enjoyable food

The pub is up a long quiet lane in deepest leafy Cheshire countryside, and its spreading lawns, surrounded by a belt of young trees, provide plenty of room for well spaced tables and picnic-sets, and even a maze to baffle children. The interior spreads around a big bar counter faced with maroon leather padding, its handpumps serving well kept Sharps Doom Bar and local guests such as Storm Bosley Cloud and Hurricane Hubert, and Tatton Ale. Most of the pub is given over to dining tables, mainly in a pleasantly informal, painted base/stripped top style, on bare boards. One area has several leather sofas and fabric-upholstered easy chairs; another by a log fire in a huge brick fireplace has more easy chairs and a squishy suede sofa. Staff are friendly and organise events most weeks (one local regular holds bee-keeping taster courses here); piped pop music, daily papers. The pub is just a stroll from Middlewood Way (a sort of linear country park) and Macclesfield Canal (Bridge 25).

🍴 Good, well presented food includes sandwiches, corned beef hash cake with a poached egg, scallops with tempura black pudding and pea purée, leek and goats cheese pie, hake fillet with courgette noodles and chilli and saffron consommé, loin of lamb with slow-braised shoulder parcel and spring onion potato cake, and puddings such as sticky toffee pudding and chocolate brownie with double chocolate ice-cream; the first Wednesday of the month is steak night. *Benchmark main dish: beer-battered haddock and chips £10.00. Two-course evening meal £19.50.*

Mitchells & Butlers ~ Lease Peter Nixon ~ Real ale ~ (01625) 574222 ~ Open 12-11 (10.30 Sun) ~ Bar food 12-2.30, 5-9.30; 12-9.30 Sat; 12-8 Sun ~ Restaurant ~ Children welcome ~ Dogs allowed in bar ~ Live music every second and last Fri of month ~ www.thewindmill.info *Recommended by Dr Kevan Tucker, Adam Macintosh*

Also Worth a Visit in Cheshire

Besides the fully inspected pubs, you might like to try these pubs that have been recommended to us and described by readers. Do tell us what you think of them: feedback@goodguides.com

ACTON BRIDGE   SJ5974
Hazel Pear (01606) 853195
Hill Top Road; CW8 3RA Revamped country pub with enjoyable freshly made food from good sandwiches to steaks, up to six ales including local brews such as Coach House, Mobberley and Weetwood, lots of wines by the glass, friendly service, good mix of tables and chairs on wood or tiled floors, woodburners; free wi-fi; children (till 8pm) and dogs welcome, tables outside, own bowling green, open all day. *(Harvey Brown)*

ALLGREAVE   SU9767
Rose & Crown
A54 Congleton–Buxton; SK11 0BJ Small pub in remote upland spot with good Dane Valley views and walks; under new ownership as we went to press (landlord previously at the Hanging Gate in Langley) – reports please. *(Anon)*

ALPRAHAM   SJ5759
Travellers Rest (01829) 260523
A51 Nantwich–Chester; CW6 9JA Unspoilt four-room country local in same friendly family for three generations, well kept Tetleys and Weetwood, no food, leatherette, wicker and Formica, some flock wallpaper, fine old brewery mirrors, darts and dominoes; may be nesting swallows in the outside gents'; dogs welcome, back bowling green, 'Hat Day' last Sun before Christmas with locals sporting unusual headgear, closed weekday lunchtimes. *(Claes Mauroy)*

BARBRIDGE   SJ6156
Barbridge Inn (01270) 528327
Just off A51 N of Nantwich; CW5 6AY Open-plan family dining pub by lively marina at junction of Shropshire Union and Middlewich canals, enjoyable food from sandwiches to steaks served by friendly staff, local Woodlands beers, conservatory; background music, no dogs inside; waterside garden with play area, open (and food) all day. *(Dave Webster, Sue Holland)*

BARTHOMLEY   SJ7752
★**White Lion** (01270) 882242
M6 junction 16, B5078 N towards Alsager, then Barthomley signed on left; CW2 5PG Charming 17th-c tavern (rethatched and carefully restored after 2013 fire), straightforward tasty food (lunchtime only) and six well kept Marstons-related ales, friendly main bar with latticed windows, heavy low beams, moulded black panelling and good log fire, steps up to room with another fire, more panelling and a high-backed winged settle; children (away from

---

Though we don't usually mention it in the text, most pubs will now make coffee or tea – it's always worth asking.

bar) and dogs welcome, seats out on cobbles overlooking attractive village and early 15th-c red sandstone church, open all day and can get busy. *(Claes Mauroy, B J Thompson, Mike and Wena Stevenson, Dave Webster, Sue Holland)*

BARTON   SJ4454
★**Cock o' Barton** (01829) 782277
Barton Road (A534 E of Farndon); SY14 7HU Stylish contemporary décor in bright open skylit bar, good choice of well liked up-to-date food (children eat for free Sun), cocktail menu and plenty of wines by the glass, ales such as Spitting Feathers and Stonehouse, neat courteous staff; background and some live music; tables in sunken heated inner courtyard with canopies and modern water feature, picnic-sets on back lawn, closed Mon, otherwise open (and food) all day. *(Anon)*

BIRKENHEAD
Refreshment Rooms
(0151) 644 5893 *Bedford Road E; CH41 1LS* Bow-fronted former 19th-c refreshment rooms for the Mersey ferry; three rooms with fascinating collection of old photographs and other memorabilia, good selection of mainly local ales such as Liverpool Organic, Peerless and a house beer from Lees (HMS Conway), Rosie's welsh cider and a couple of interesting lagers, good competitively priced food from home-made scouse to oriental spiced bass fillets, Sat evening set bistro menu, charming prompt service; quiz Weds, live music last Fri of month, pool; children and dogs welcome, beer garden at back with play area, open (and food) all day. *(Tom and Jill Jones)*

BOLLINGTON   SJ9377
Church House (01625) 574014
Church Street; SK10 5PY Welcoming village pub with good reasonably priced home-made food including OAP menu, efficient friendly service, well kept frequently changing ales (often Adnams and Thwaites), roaring fire, separate dining room; good place to start or end a walk, bedrooms. *(Dr D J and Mrs S C Walker)*

BOLLINGTON   SJ9477
Poachers (01625) 572086
Mill Lane; SK10 5BU Stone-built village local prettily set in good walking area, comfortable and welcoming, with five well kept ales including Storm and Weetwood, good pubby food including bargain lunches, daily newspapers; sunny back garden, open all day Sun, closed Mon lunchtime. *(Anon)*

BOLLINGTON   SJ9377
Vale (01625) 575147
Adlington Road; SK10 5JT Friendly tap for Bollington Brewery in three converted 19th-c cottages, their full range and a couple of local guests (tasters offered), good range of enjoyable freshly made food, efficient

---

knowledgeable young staff, interesting photos, newspapers and books, roaring fire; picnic-sets behind overlooking cricket pitch, near Middlewood Way and Macclesfield Canal, open all day Fri-Sun. *(Mike and Wena Stevenson)*

BRERETON GREEN   SJ7764
Bears Head (01477) 544732
Handy for M6 junction 17; set back off A50 S of Holmes Chapel; CW11 1RS Beautiful 17th-c black and white timbered Vintage Inn with civilised linked rooms, low beams, log fires and old-fashioned furniture on flagstones or bare boards, enjoyable well prepared food served promptly by friendly staff, Sharps Doom Bar, Thwaites Wainwright and a guest; 25 bedrooms in modern Innkeepers Lodge, open (and food) all day. *(Dr D J and Mrs S C Walker)*

BURTONWOOD   SJ5692
Fiddle i'th' Bag (01925) 225442
3 miles from M62 junction 9, signposted from A49 towards Newton-le-Willows; WA5 4BT Eccentric place (not to everyone's taste) crammed with bric-a-brac and memorabilia, three well kept changing ales and enjoyable uncomplicated home-made food, friendly staff; may be nostalgic background music; children welcome, open all day weekends. *(Harvey Brown)*

CHELFORD   SJ8175
★**Egerton Arms** (01625) 861366
A537 Macclesfield–Knutsford; SK11 9BB Cheerful rambling old village pub, beams and nice mix of furniture including carved settles, wooden porter's chair by grandfather clock, Copper Dragon Golden Pippin, Wells & Youngs Bombardier and five guests, good food and service, restaurant, steps down to little raftered games area with pool and darts; background music (live jazz last Fri of month), sports TV; children and dogs welcome, picnic-sets on canopied deck, more on grass and toddlers' play area, adjoining delicatessen, open (and food) all day. *(David Cotterill, Dr D J and Mrs S C Walker)*

CHESTER   SJ4065
★**Bear & Billet** (01244) 351002
Lower Bridge Street; CH1 1RU Handsome 17th-c timbered Okells pub with four changing guest ales, belgian and american imports and nice range of wines by the glass, reasonably priced home-made pubby food, interesting features and some attractive furnishings in friendly and comfortable open-plan bar with fire, sitting and dining rooms upstairs; sports TVs; pleasant courtyard, open all day. *(Dave Webster, Sue Holland)*

CHESTER   SJ4065
Brewery Tap (01244) 340999
Lower Bridge Street; CH1 1RU Tap for Spitting Feathers Brewery in interesting

Jacobean building with 18th-c brick façade, steps up to lofty bar (former great hall) serving their well kept ales plus mainly local guests, real cider and good choice of wines, hearty home-made food using local suppliers including produce from Spitting Feathers farm (rare-breed pork); open all day. *(David H Bennett, Simon J Barber, Dave Webster, Sue Holland, Allan and Joan Spencer)*

CHESTER SJ4166
Cellar (01244) 318950

City Road; CH1 3AE Laid-back Canal Quarter bar with four well kept changing ales and good selection of interesting imported beers, some good value food including burgers, live music Fri and Sat (can get packed), basement bar for private functions; closed weekday lunchtimes, open all day weekends (till 2.30am Fri, Sat). *(Anon)*

CHESTER SJ4066
Coach House (01244) 351900

Northgate Street; CH1 2HQ Refurbished 19th-c coaching inn by town hall and cathedral, comfortable lounge with central bar, Bass, Thwaites and guests, decent choice of locally sourced food from semi-open kitchen, afternoon tea with home-made scones, prompt friendly service; children and dogs welcome, tables out in front, eight bedrooms, open all day from 9am for breakfast. *(David H Bennett)*

CHESTER SJ4066
Olde Boot (01244) 314540

Eastgate Row N; CH1 1LQ Good value in lovely 17th-c Rows building, heavy beams, dark woodwork, oak flooring, flagstones, some exposed Tudor wattle and daub, old kitchen range in lounge beyond, old-fashioned settles and oak panelling in upper area, well kept bargain Sam Smiths, cheerful service and bustling atmosphere; no children. *(David H Bennett)*

CHESTER SJ4066
Pied Bull (01244) 325829

Upper Northgate Street; CH1 2HQ Old beamed and panelled coaching inn with roomy open-plan carpeted bar, good own-brewed ales along with guests, enjoyable fairly priced traditional food from sandwiches and baked potatoes up, friendly staff and locals, imposing stone fireplace with tapestry above, divided inner dining area; background music, games machines; children welcome, handsome Jacobean stairs to 13 bedrooms, open (and food) all day. *(Derek Wason, Dave Webster, Sue Holland)*

CHESTER SJ4066
Telfords Warehouse (01244) 390090

Tower Wharf, behind Northgate Street near railway; CH1 4EZ Well kept interesting ales in large converted canal building, generous fresh up-to-date food including good sandwich menu, efficient staff, bare boards, exposed brickwork and high pitched ceiling, big wall of windows overlooking the water, some old enamel signs and massive iron winding gear in bar, steps up to heavily beamed area with sofas, artwork and restaurant; late-night live music, bouncers on the door; tables out by water, open all day (till late Weds-Sun). *(Isobel Mackinlay)*

CHURCH MINSHULL SJ6660
Badger (01270) 522607

B5074 Winsford–Nantwich; handy for Shropshire Union Canal, Middlewich branch; CW5 6DY Refurbished 18th-c coaching inn in pretty village next to church, good imaginative food from sharing boards up (pub favourites too), Tatton ales and guests, Thatcher's cider, interesting range of wines and several malt whiskies, friendly helpful staff, bar and spacious lounge leading to back conservatory; children till 6pm, five bedrooms, good breakfast, open (and food) all day. *(Leo and Barbara Lionet, John and Hazel Sarkanen)*

COMBERBACH SJ6477
★**Spinner & Bergamot** (01606) 891307

Warrington Road; CW9 6AY Comfortable 18th-c beamed village pub (named after two racehorses) with two-room carpeted lounge, good home-made bar and restaurant food (12-7.30pm Sun) including fresh fish, friendly attentive service, well kept Robinsons ales and good wines, log fires, hunting prints, toby jugs and brasses, some Manchester United memorabilia, daily papers, pitched-ceiling timber dining extension, simple tiled-floor public bar; unobtrusive background music; children and dogs welcome, picnic-sets on sloping lawn, lots of flowers, small verandah, bowling green, open all day. *(Simon J Barber, Mike and Wena Stevenson, Tom and Jill Jones)*

CONGLETON SJ8659
Horseshoe (01260) 272205

Fence Lane, Newbold Astbury, between A34 and A527 S; CW12 3NL Former 18th-c coaching inn set in peaceful countryside; three small carpeted rooms with decorative plates, copper and brass and other knick-knacks (some on delft shelves), mix of seating including plush banquettes and iron-base tables, log fire, well kept predominantly Robinsons ales, popular hearty home-made food at reasonable prices, friendly staff and locals; no dogs; children welcome, rustic garden furniture, adventure play area with tractor, good walks. *(Dr D J and Mrs S C Walker)*

CONGLETON SJ8762
Queens Head (01260) 272546

Park Lane (set down from flyover); CW12 3DE Friendly local by Macclesfield Canal, quaint dark interior with open fire, up to eight well kept ales and good selection of malt whiskies, reasonably priced hearty pub food (not Sun evening), friendly staff, table skittles, darts and pool; sports TV, quiz Mon, poker Tues; children and dogs welcome, steps up from towpath to nice garden with play area and boules, three bedrooms, useful for station, open all day. (Dr Kevan Tucker)

CREWE   SJ7055
Borough Arms (01270) 748189
Earle Street; CW1 2BG Own microbrewery and lots of changing guest ales, good choice of continental beers too, friendly staff and regulars, two small rooms off central bar and downstairs lounge; occasional sports TV; picnic-sets on back terrace and lawn, open all day Fri-Sun, closed lunchtime other days. (Dave Webster, Sue Holland)

FADDILEY   SJ5852
★**Thatch** (01270) 524223
A534 Wrexham–Nantwich; CW5 8JE Attractive, thatched, low-beamed and timbered dining pub carefully extended from medieval core, open fires, raised room to right of bar, back barn-style dining room (children allowed here), well kept ales such as Salopian and Weetwood, good choice of enjoyable popular food (booking advised weekends), friendly helpful service, relaxing atmosphere; soft background music; charming country garden with play area, open all day weekends, closed Mon and Tues lunchtimes. (Anon)

FIVECROSSES   SJ5276
Travellers Rest (01928) 735125
B5152 Frodsham–Kingsley; WA6 6SL Modernised and extended roadside dining pub, good food (booking advised) from lunchtime sandwiches and pub staples up, well kept Black Sheep and two guests, efficient pleasant service; free wi fi; children welcome, superb views across Weaver Valley, open all day (food till 6pm Sun). (Isobel Mackinlay)

FRODSHAM   SJ5276
Travellers Rest (01928) 735125
Kingsley Road; WA6 6SL Popular family-run pub with emphasis on good fairly priced food (not Sun evening, booking advised) from sandwiches and pub favourites up including fresh fish/seafood, well kept Black Sheep and a couple of guests, good selection of wines, friendly attentive service; children welcome, open all day. (Dave Jackson)

FULLERS MOOR   SJ4954
Sandstone (01829) 782333
A534; CH3 9JH Light and airy dining pub with wide choice of good sensibly priced fresh food (all day weekends) from sandwiches and snacks up, well kept local ales such as Beartown, Coach House, Stonehouse and Weetwood, friendly staff, modern décor, woodburner, dining conservatory, Tues quiz; children and dogs

(in bar) welcome, spacious garden with lovely views, handy for Sandstone Trail, open all day. (Tom Barton, Lucy Charles)

GOOSTREY   SJ7770
Crown (01477) 532128
Off A50 and A535; CW4 8PE Refurbished and extended 18th-c village pub, beams and open fires, good choice of enjoyable food with many main courses available in smaller sizes, friendly efficient service, well kept ales including locals such as Tatton and Weetwood; close to Jodrell Bank, open all day. (Malcolm and Pauline Pellatt)

GRAPPENHALL   SJ6386
★**Parr Arms** (01925) 212120
Near M6 junction 20 – A50 towards Warrington, left after 1.5 miles; Church Lane; WA4 3EP Charming refurbished black-beamed pub in picture-postcard setting with picnic-sets out on cobbles by church, more tables on small canopied back terrace, reasonably priced food from ciabattas up, friendly helpful service, well kept Robinsons from central bar, log fires, Weds quiz; children and dogs welcome, open all day Fri-Sun. (Anon)

GREAT BUDWORTH   SJ6677
George & Dragon (01606) 892650
Signed off A559 NE of Northwich; High Street opposite church; CW9 6HF Smartly refurbished building owned by Lees and dating in parts from the 1720s; their beers kept well and plenty of wines by the glass, welcoming friendly young staff, good choice of enjoyable reasonably priced food from lunchtime sandwiches and baguettes to specials, dark panelled bar with log fire, grandfather clock and leather button-back banquettes, back area more restaurant with tables around central woodburner; children and dogs (in bar) welcome, delightful village, open all day Fri-Sun. (Mike and Wena Stevenson, Simon J Barber)

HASLINGTON   SJ7356
Hawk (01270) 582181
A534 Crewe–Sandbach; CW1 5RG Cosy old timbered coaching inn with several small rooms including notable oak-panelled back one, beams and open fires, more modern restaurant, Robinsons ales, good value pub food; beer garden with smokers' shelter, open all day. (Anon)

HOLLINS GREEN   SJ6991
Black Swan (0161) 222 4444
Just off A57 Manchester–Warrington, 3 miles from M6 junction 21; WA3 6LA Refurbished and extended 17th-c coaching inn, enjoyable fairly traditional food cooked to order, half a dozen changing ales and good choice of wines from reasonably priced list; events such as poker and quiz nights, monthly farmers' market; children welcome, sizeable garden with terrace, duck pond and

play area, 14 bedrooms, local walks (leaflets available), open (and food) all day. *(Martin and Patricia Forest)*

KELSALL   SJ5268
Farmers Arms (01829) 751784
Chester Road (SE off A54 dual carriageway); CW6 0SJ Traditional pub (at top of hill on village outskirts) improved under current landlord, four well kept Weetwood ales and enjoyable generously served pubby food, main bar, snug and tap room, beams and some stripped stone, comfortable banquettes and mix of tables and chairs, friendly efficient staff. *(Dennis Jones)*

KNUTSFORD   SJ7578
Cross Keys (01565) 750404
King Street; WA16 6DT Timber-fronted former coaching inn, six well kept ales including Copper Dragon, Jennings, Timothy Taylors and local Tatton, enjoyable traditional lunchtime food, pleasant service, steps down to cellar dining room; children welcome, 13 bedrooms, open all day Fri-Sun, closed Mon lunchtime. *(W D Christian)*

KNUTSFORD   SJ7578
Lord Eldon (01565) 652261
Tatton Street, off A50 at White Bear roundabout; WA16 6AD Old brick-built coaching inn with four comfortable rooms, much bigger inside than it looks, friendly staff and locals, beams, brasses and large open fire, well kept local ales, no food; music nights; back garden but no car park, handy for Tatton Park (NT). *(Pat and Tony Martin)*

KNUTSFORD   SJ7578
Rose & Crown (01565) 652366
King Street; WA16 6DT Beamed and panelled 17th-c inn with bar and Chophouse restaurant, good food from extensive menu, Black Sheep, Shepherd Neame Spitfire and a couple of guests, plenty of wines by the glass including champagne, good personable service; children welcome, nine bedrooms, open (and food) all day. *(W D Christian)*

LANGLEY   SJ9569
★Hanging Gate (01260) 252238
Meg Lane, Higher Sutton; OS Sheet 118 map reference 952696; SK11 0NG New licensees for this remote old place close to the moors – wonderful distant views to Liverpool Cathedral and even Snowdonia; three cosy little low-beamed simply furnished rooms, log fires, Hydes and a couple of guests, good choice of wines by the glass and quite a few malt whiskies, food from pub favourites

up, board games and books; background music; children in 'blue room' only, dogs in bar, has been open all day Fri-Sun. *(David Crook)*

LANGLEY   SJ9471
★Leather's Smithy (01260) 252313
Off A523 S of Macclesfield; OS Sheet 118 map reference 952715; SK11 0NE Isolated stone-built pub in fine walking country next to reservoir, well kept Theakstons and two or three guests, lots of whiskies, good food from sandwiches to blackboard specials such as pheasant and wild boar, good welcoming service, beams and log fire, flagstoned bar, carpeted dining areas, interesting local prints and photographs; unobtrusive background music; children welcome, no dogs but muddy boots allowed in bar, picnic-sets in garden behind and on grass opposite, lovely views, open all day weekends. *(David Cotterill, John Wooll)*

LITTLE BOLLINGTON   SJ7387
★Swan with Two Nicks
(0161) 928 2914 *2 miles from M56 junction 7 – A56 towards Lymm, then first right at Stamford Arms into Park Lane; use A556 to get back on to M56 westbound, WA14 4TJ* Extended village pub full of beams, brass, copper and bric-a-brac, some antique settles and roaring log fire, welcoming helpful staff, good choice of enjoyable generously served food from baguettes up including popular Sun lunch (best to book), several well kept ales, decent wines and coffee; children and dogs welcome, tables outside, attractive hamlet by Dunham Massey (NT) deer park, walks by Bridgewater Canal, open all day. *(Mike and Wena Stevenson, Gerry and Rosemary Dobson, Hilary Forrest)*

LITTLE BUDWORTH   SJ5965
Egerton Arms (01829) 760424
Pinfold Lane; CW6 9BS Welcoming 18th-c country local reopened under new family management, enjoyable home-made food and six real ales, also selection of bottled beers and interesting cocktails; outside gents'; children and dogs welcome, closed Mon, otherwise open all day (till 1am Fri, Sat). *(Anon)*

LITTLE LEIGH   SJ6076
Holly Bush (01606) 853196
A49 just S of A533; CW8 4QY Ancient thatched and timbered pub, spotlessly clean, with good choice of enjoyable well priced food including several vegetarian options, charming helpful staff, Tetleys and a couple of mainstream guests, restaurant; children

welcome, no dogs inside, wheelchair access, courtyard tables and garden with play area, 14 bedrooms in converted back barn, open all day weekends. *(Mike and Wena Stevenson, Tom and Jill Jones)*

LOWER PEOVER   SJ7474
★ **Bells of Peover** (01565) 722269
Just off B5081; The Cobbles; handy for M6 junction 17; WA16 9PZ Lovely old building in charming spot on quiet cobbled lane next to fine black and white 14th-c church; modern furnishings with contrasting original panelling, beams and open fires, emphasis on food (all day weekends) from lunchtime sandwiches and pub standards to more inventive dishes (not particularly cheap), Robinsons ales, guest beers and several wines by the glass, helpful friendly staff; background music; children welcome, no dogs inside, disabled facilities, front terrace and big side lawn with trees, outside summer bar and barbecues, open all day but may close for weddings and private functions. *(Trevor Swindells, Hugh Roberts)*

LOWER WHITLEY   SJ6178
Chetwode Arms (01925) 730203
Just off A49, handy for M56 junction 10; Street Lane; WA4 4EN Rambling low-beamed dining pub dating from the 17th-c, good food with some south african and austrian influences including early-bird deal (before 7pm), also steaks cooked on a hot stone, welcoming efficient service, solid furnishings all clean and polished, small front bar with warm open fire, Adnams and a local guest, good wines by the glass; well behaved children allowed but best to ask first, limited wheelchair access, bowling green, closed lunchtimes apart from Sun. *(Harvey Brown)*

LYMM   SJ7087
Barn Owl (01925) 752020
Agden Wharf, Warrington Lane (just off B5159 E); WA13 0SW Comfortably extended popular pub in nice setting by Bridgewater Canal, Marstons and four guest ales, decent wines by the glass, reasonable choice of good value all-day pub food including OAP deals, efficient service even when busy, friendly atmosphere; children welcome, disabled facilities, may be canal trips, moorings (space for one narrowboat). *(Anon)*

MACCLESFIELD   SJ9273
Puss in Boots (01625) 263378
Buxton Road; SK10 1NF Unpretentious Victorian stone pub by bridge over Macclesfield Canal, public bar, lounge and dining area, decent food including good value Sun carvery, Bollington and Greene King ales, hospitable staff; sports TV, games machine, occasional live bands; children welcome, seats in garden and by canal, play area, open all day (till 1am Fri, Sat). *(John Wooll)*

MACCLESFIELD   SJ9173
Waters Green Tavern
(01625) 422653 *Waters Green, opposite station; SK11 6LH* Half a dozen quickly changing and interesting largely northern ales in roomy L-shaped open-plan local, good value home-made lunchtime food (not Sun), friendly staff and regulars, back pool room. *(Anon)*

MOBBERLEY   SJ8179
★ **Plough & Flail** (01565) 873537
Off B5085 Knutsford–Alderley Edge; at E end of village turn into Moss Lane, then left into Paddock Hill Lane (look out for small green signs to pub); WA16 7DB Extensive family dining pub tucked down narrow lanes; bar with plain cream walls and panelled dado, chunky cushioned dining chairs around stripped tables, low beams and flagstones, Joules and Lees ales and good choice of wines by the glass, handsomely floored side area with low sofas and sports TV, well liked all-day food (till 8pm Sun) including set menus, comfortable airy dining room and conservatory; nostalgic background music, teak tables on heated terraces, picnic-sets on neat lawns, play area, open all day. *(Michael Butler, Dr and Mrs A K Clarke, W K Wood)*

MOULDSWORTH   SJ5170
Goshawk (01928) 740900
Station Road (B5393); CH3 8AJ Comfortable family dining pub (former station hotel); mix of furniture in extensive series of rooms including small 'library' area, masses of pictures, double-sided log fire, good popular food from sandwiches to restaurant dishes, cheerful attentive uniformed staff, half a dozen well kept ales including Spitting Feathers, Weetwood and a couple of house beers, good wines by the glass; background music; dogs allowed in bar, disabled facilities, good spot near Delamere Forest with big outdoor space including play area and bowling green, open all day. *(Simon J Barber)*

NANTWICH   SJ6452
★ **Black Lion** (01270) 628711
Welsh Row; CW5 5ED Old black and white building smartened up but keeping beams, timbered brickwork and open fire, good food from short interesting menu, three well kept Weetwood ales and three regularly changing guests, good service, upstairs rooms with old wooden tables and sumptuous leather sofas on undulating floors; open all day. *(Dave Webster, Sue Holland)*

NANTWICH   SJ6551
Globe (01270) 623374
Audlem Road; CW5 7EA Victorian red-brick pub with full range of well kept Woodlands ales and guests, ten wines by the glass and enjoyable home-made food

(lunchtime deals), friendly helpful staff, comfortable open-plan layout keeping distinct areas, occasional live music; children welcome, garden tables, open all day till midnight. *(Dave Webster, Sue Holland)*

NANTWICH SJ6552
Vine (01270) 624172
Hospital Street; CW5 5RP Fairly straightforward black and white fronted pub dating from the 17th c, modernised interior stretching far back with dimly lit quiet corners, five well kept ales including Hydes, friendly staff and locals, pubby food from lunchtime sandwiches and baked potatoes up (not Sun evening, Mon), raised seating areas, darts and dominoes; background music, sports TV; children welcome, small outside seating area behind, open all day till midnight. *(Clive and Fran Dutson)*

NESTON SJ2976
Harp (0151) 336 6980
Quayside, SW of Little Neston; keep on along track at end of Marshlands Road; CH64 OTB Tucked-away two-room country local with well kept Holts, Peerless, Timothy Taylors and two guests, decent choice of bottled beers, wines and some good malt whiskies, no food, woodburner in pretty fireplace, pale quarry tiles and simple furnishings, interesting old photographs, hatch servery to lounge; children and dogs allowed, garden behind, picnic-sets on front grassy bank facing Dee Marshes and Wales, glorious sunsets with wild calls of wading birds, open all day. *(Tony Tollitt)*

PARKGATE SJ2778
Boathouse (0151) 336 4187
Village signed off A540; CH64 6RN Popular black and white timbered pub with attractively refurbished linked rooms, wide choice of good food (booking advised) from snacks up, cheerful attentive staff, well kept changing ales such as local Brimstage, several wines by the glass and nice coffee, big conservatory with great views to Wales over silted Dee estuary (RSPB reserve), may be egrets and kestrels. *(Mike and Wena Stevenson)*

PARKGATE SJ2778
Ship (0151) 336 3931
The Parade; CH64 6SA Bow-window estuary views from hotel's refurbished bar, well kept Marstons Pedigree with guests such as Brimstage, Spitting Feathers and Woodlands, several wines by the glass and over 50 whiskies, good reasonably priced home-cooked food including daily specials and popular Sun roasts, afternoon tea, good helpful service, log fire, Weds quiz; children welcome, no dogs inside, a few tables out at front and to the side, 25 bedrooms, open all day. *(Justin Lang, Paul Whitehead, Gillian Turner, Geoff Jones, Paul Humphreys, John and Gwyn Brignal and others)*

PEOVER HEATH SJ7973
⋆ Dog (01625) 861421
Wellbank Lane; OS Sheet 118 map reference 794735; the pub is often listed under Over Peover instead; WA16 8UP Traditional country pub refurbished under newish management, popular interesting food (all day weekends), five ales including Dunham Massey and Weetwood, decent choice of wines by the glass and malt whiskies, tap room where dogs allowed; children welcome, picnic-sets out in front and in pretty back garden, can walk from here to the Jodrell Bank Discovery Centre and Arboretum, six bedrooms, open (and food) all day. *(Brian and Anna Marsden, Mike and Wena Stevenson, Gerry and Rosemary Dobson)*

PLUMLEY SJ7275
Golden Pheasant (01565) 722125
Plumley Moor Road (off A556 by the Smoker Inn); WA16 9RX Well extended country pub with good food including Sun carvery, friendly efficient service, three Lees ales, traditional panelled bar and comfortable lounge areas, roomy restaurant, conservatory, locals' bar with darts, open fires; background music, free wi-fi; children and dogs (in bar) welcome, spacious gardens with play area, regular classic car meetings, six bedrooms (two with four-posters), open (and food) all day. *(Leo and Barbara Lionet)*

PLUMLEY SJ7075
Smoker (01565) 722338
2.5 miles from M6 junction 19: A556 towards Northwich and Chester; WA16 OTY Neatly kept 400-year-old thatched coaching inn with three lounges, old-fashioned feel with dark panelling, deep sofas and other comfortable seats, decorative plates and copperware, open fires in period fireplaces, generous reasonably priced bar food (all day Sun) including weekday deals, five Robinsons beers and a good choice of wines and whiskies, friendly competent service; background music; children welcome away from bar, sizeable garden with roses and play area, open all day weekends. *(Andy Dolan, Paul Humphreys, Dennis Jones, Adrian Johnson)*

POYNTON SJ9483
Boars Head (01625) 876676
Shrigley Road N, Higher Poynton, off A523; SK12 1TE Some recent refurbishment at this welcoming Victorian country pub, good value straightforward home-made food including speciality pies, four well kept ales such as Black Sheep and Jennings, warm woodburner; walkers and dogs welcome, next to ex-railway Middlewood Way and close to Macclesfield Canal moorings, also handy for Lyme Park (NT), open all day weekends. *(Dr D J and Mrs S C Walker)*

POYNTON   SJ9283
Cask Tavern (01625) 875157
Park Lane; SK12 1RE Refurbished by
Bollington (their third pub) and back to its
previous name – was the Red Rock; five of
their well kept ales and a guest, real ciders,
several wines by the glass including draught
prosecco, no food; dogs allowed, open all day
Fri-Sun, from 4pm other days. *(Anon)*

PRESTBURY   SJ9077
Admiral Rodney (01625) 829484
New Road; SK10 4HP Comfortable old
beamed pub with well kept Robinsons ales
and enjoyable simple food from good barm
cakes to hotpots, prompt friendly service,
warming winter fire, daily newspapers; open
all day. *(Dr D J and Mrs S C Walker)*

PRESTBURY   SJ8976
Legh Arms (01625) 829130
A538, village centre; SK10 4DG Smart
beamed hotel with divided-up bar and
lounge areas, Robinsons ales, decent wines,
enjoyable bar food and more elaborate
restaurant choices, soft furnishings,
ladder-back chairs around solid dark tables,
brocaded bucket seats, stylish french prints
and italian engravings, staffordshire dogs on
mantelpiece, cosy panelled back part with
narrow offshoot, open fire, daily papers;
background music; children and dogs
welcome, seats on heated terrace, bedrooms,
good breakfast, open all day. *(John Wooll)*

STOAK   SJ4273
Bunbury Arms (01244) 301665
*Little Stanney Lane; a mile from M53
junction 10, A5117 W then first left;
CH2 4HW* Big but cosy beamed lounge with antique
furniture, pictures and books, small snug,
wide choice of enjoyable generously served
food (all day Sun) from sandwiches to
interesting specials including fresh fish, good
changing ales, extensive wine list, open fires,
board games and Mon quiz; can get busy;
garden tables (some motorway noise), short
walk for Shropshire Canal users (Bridge
136 or 138), also handy for Cheshire Oaks
shopping outlet, open all day. *(Tony Tollitt,
Roger and Anne Newbury)*

STYAL   SJ8383
Ship (01625) 444888
B5166 near Ringway Airport; SK9 4JE
Refurbished 17th-c pub under same
ownership as the Dog at Peover, good food
and well kept ales including Dunham Massey
and Weetwood, plenty of wines by the glass;
children welcome, attractive NT village with

good walks on the doorstep, open (and food)
all day. *(Dr D J and Mrs S C Walker)*

TARPORLEY   SJ5562
★ Rising Sun (01829) 732423
*High Street; village signposted off A51
Nantwich–Chester; CW6 0DX* The friendly
long-serving licensees at this well liked down-
to-earth pub are retiring, so things may have
changed by the time you read this; plenty
of character in the low-ceilinged prettily
furnished interior, eye-catching old seats and
tables including creaky 19th-c mahogany and
oak settles, attractive kitchen range next to
gleaming old cupboard doors, sporting and
other old-fashioned prints on cream walls,
Robinsons ales, fair-priced popular food,
sports TV in tiny side bar; background music,
no credit cards; children welcome, open
(and food) all day weekends. *(Mike Proctor,
Caroline Prescott)*

WHITEGATE   SJ6268
Plough (01606) 889455
*Beauty Bank, Foxwist Green; OS Sheet
118 map reference 624684; off A556 just
W of Northwich, or A54 W of Winsford;
CW8 2BP* Comfortable country pub with
bar and extended dining area, wide choice
of good home-made food (best to book)
from panini and baked potatoes up, cheerful
efficient service, four well kept Robinsons
ales and plenty of wines by the glass;
background music, free wi-fi; no under-14s,
well behaved dogs allowed in tap room,
disabled access, picnic-sets out at front and
in back garden, colourful window boxes and
hanging baskets, popular walks nearby, open
(and food) all day. *(James Morrell)*

WILLINGTON   SJ5367
★ Boot (01829) 751375
Boothsdale, off A54 at Kelsall; CW6 0NH
Attractive hillside dining pub in row of
converted cottages, views over Cheshire
plain to Wales, popular food from pub
staples to daily specials, local Weetwood
ales and decent choice of wines and malt
whiskies, friendly staff, small opened-up
unpretentiously furnished rooms, lots of
original features, woodburner, extension with
french windows overlooking garden, pub
cat, dog and donkey; well behaved children
welcome (no pushchairs), dogs outside only,
picnic-sets on raised suntrap terrace, open
all day. *(Caroline Prescott)*

WILMSLOW   SJ8282
Honey Bee (01625) 526511
Altrincham Road, Styal; SK9 4LT Large
red-brick Vintage Inn (former retirement
home) with several linked rooms around

Anyone claiming to arrange, or prevent, inclusion of a pub in the Guide is a fraud.
Pubs are included only if recommended by genuine readers and if our own anonymous
inspection confirms that they are suitable.

central bar, well kept Sharps Doom Bar, Thwaites Wainwright and a guest, their usual choice of enjoyable food including popular Sun roasts, open fires; children welcome, no dogs inside, terrace and garden seating, open all day. *(Michael Butler)*

WINCLE   SJ9665
★ **Ship** (01260) 227217
Village signposted off A54 Congleton–Buxton; SK11 0QE Friendly 16th-c stone-built country pub, bare-boards bar leading to carpeted dining room, old stables area with flagstones, beams, woodburner and open fire, good generously served food (not Sun evening) from varied menu, three Lees ales and a dozen wines by the glass, quick attentive service; children and dogs (in tap room) welcome, tables in small side garden, good Dane Valley walks, open all day weekends, closed Mon. *(David Cotterill)*

WRENBURY   SJ5947
★ **Dusty Miller** (01270) 780537
Cholmondeley Road; village signed from A530 Nantwich–Whitchurch; CW5 8HG Well converted 19th-c corn mill with fine canal views from gravel terrace and series

of tall glazed arches in bar, spacious modern feel, comfortably furnished with tapestried banquettes, oak settles and wheelback chairs around rustic tables, quarry-tiled area by bar with oak settle and refectory table, old lift hoist up under the rafters, four Robinsons beers, farm cider, enjoyable generously served food (all day weekends), good friendly service; background music; children and dogs welcome, closed Mon, otherwise open all day. *(Mike and Wena Stevenson, Dave Webster, Sue Holland)*

WYBUNBURY   SJ6949
Swan (01270) 841280
Main Road (B5071); CW5 7NA Bow-windowed beamed pub with nooks and crannies in comfortable rambling lounge, pleasant public bar, some bric-a-brac, woodburners, good selection of Robinsons ales and wines by the glass, enjoyable pubby food from sandwiches and sharing boards up, friendly helpful staff; background and some live music, TV, games machine, pool; tables in garden by beautiful churchyard with leaning tower, summer Fig Pie Wakes (200-year-old pie rolling competition), seven bedrooms, open all day. *(Anon)*

Cornwall

BLISLAND
Blisland Inn 🍺 £

SX1073 Map 1

Village signposted off A30 and B3266 NE of Bodmin; PL30 4JF

Village local by the green with fine choice of real ales, beer-related memorabilia, pubby food and seats outside

The fine range of real ales and genuinely warm welcome continue to draw the many customers to this old-fashioned, traditional pub. Every inch of the beams and ceiling is covered with beer badges (or their particularly wide-ranging collection of mugs), and the walls are similarly filled with beer-related posters and the like. Tapped from the cask or on handpump, the ales include two named for the pub by Sharps – Blisland Special and Bulldog – as well as Harbour Double IPA No 3, Holsworthy Tamar Black, St Austell Dartmoor Best Bitter, Sharps Winter Berry Ale and Kite Try Time; also, farm cider, fruit wines and real apple juice; good service. The carpeted lounge has several barometers on the walls, toby jugs on the beams and a few standing timbers, while the family room has pool, table skittles, euchre, cribbage and dominoes; background music. Plenty of picnic-sets outside. The popular Camel Trail cycle path is close by – though the hill up to Blisland is pretty steep. As with many pubs in this area, the approach by car involves negotiating several single-track roads.

🍴 Honest, home-cooked food includes lunchtime baps, chicken livers with bacon, cream and whisky, leek and mushroom bake, moroccan-style lamb with couscous, gammon and egg, and puddings such as fruit crumble or syrup sponge. *Benchmark main dish: steak in ale pie £8.95. Two-course evening meal £15.00.*

Free house ~ Licensees Gary and Margaret Marshall ~ Real ale ~ (01208) 850739 ~ Open 11.30-11.30 (midnight Sat); 12-10.30 Sun ~ Bar food 12-2, 6.30-9; not Sun evening ~ Restaurant ~ Children in family room only ~ Dogs welcome ~ Live music every second Sat *Recommended by P and J Shapley, Fiona Loram, B J Thompson, Paul and Karen Cornock, Mark Flynn, John and Bernadette Elliott*

BOSCASTLE
Cobweb

SX0991 Map 1

B3263, just E of harbour; PL35 0HE

Heavy beams and flagstones, lots of old jugs and bottles, a cheerful atmosphere, several real ales and friendly staff

The two interesting bars in this tall stone pub have heavy beams hung with hundreds of bottles and jugs, lots of pictures of bygone years, quite a mix of seats (from settles and carved chairs to more pubby furniture) and cosy log fires. They keep four real ales such as St Austell Tribute, Sharps Doom Bar, Tintagel Cornwalls Pride and a guest on handpump and a local cider and there's a cheerful, bustling atmosphere, especially at peak times; games machine, darts, a juke box and pool. The restaurant is upstairs. There are picnic-sets and benches outside, some under cover. A self-catering apartment is for rent.

 Straightforward food includes lunchtime sandwiches, garlic mushrooms, deep-fried whitebait, gammon with pineapple and egg, beer-battered fish and chips, lasagne, vegetarian bake, mixed grill, steaks, and puddings such as a crumble or cheesecake. *Benchmark main dish: steak in ale pie £9.80. Two-course evening meal £15.00.*

Free house ~ Licensees Ivor and Adrian Bright ~ Real ale ~ (01840) 250278 ~ Open 10.30am (12.30 Sat)-11.30pm ~ Bar food 11.30-2.30, 6-9.30 ~ Restaurant ~ Children welcome ~ Dogs allowed in bar ~ www.cobwebinn.co.uk *Recommended by George Atkinson, John and Bernadette Elliott*

CADGWITH
Cadgwith Cove Inn
SW7214 Map 1

Down very narrow lane off A3083 S of Helston; no nearby parking; TR12 7JX

Traditionally furnished bars, real ales, all-day food and fine coastal walks; bedrooms

With wonderful coastal walks in either direction, it's useful that this little pub offers some kind of food all day. The two front rooms have bench seating and tables on parquet flooring, a log fire, lots of local photographs and memorabilia such as naval hat ribands, fancy knot-work and compass binnacles; some of the dark beams have blue spliced rope hand-holds. Otter Bitter, St Austell Tribute, Sharps Doom Bar and Skinners Betty Stogs on handpump; background music, darts, board games, euchre, TV and Monday evening quiz. A back bar has a huge and colourful fish mural. Seats on the good-sized front terrace look down to the fish sheds by the bay, and the comfortable refurbished bedrooms overlook the sea. It's best to park at the top of the village and meander down through the thatched cottages, but it's quite a steep hike back up again. They now have a Kellys ice-cream parlour in the back bar.

 As well as all-day cream teas, the tasty food includes lunchtime sandwiches, pasties, moules marinière, ham and eggs, a pie and a vegetarian dish of the day, burger with home-made chutney and chips, seasonal crab salad with asian-style salad, local seafood medley, and puddings such as chocolate fondant and eton mess; they also offer afternoon tea. *Benchmark main dish: beer-battered fish and chips £10.70. Two-course evening meal £18.50.*

Punch ~ Lease Garry and Helen Holmes ~ Real ale ~ (01326) 290513 ~ Open 11am-midnight ~ Bar food 12-9 ~ Restaurant ~ Children welcome ~ Dogs welcome ~ Wi-fi ~ Folk night Tues, local singers Fri ~ Bedrooms: $56/$97 ~ www.cadgwithcoveinn.com *Recommended by Adrian Johnson*

CONSTANTINE
Trengilly Wartha ♀ 🛏
SW7328 Map 1

Nancenoy; A3083 S of Helston, signposted Gweek near RNAS Culdrose, then fork right after Gweek; OS Sheet 204 map reference 731282; TR11 5RP

Well run inn surrounded by big gardens, with a friendly welcome for all, an easy-going atmosphere and popular food and drink; bedrooms

Readers enjoy staying at this tucked-away inn: the cottagey bedrooms are comfortable, the breakfasts very good and there are lots of surrounding walks. It's a welcoming place with courteous licensees and helpful staff, and the long low-beamed main bar has a sociable feel (especially in the evening when the locals drop in). There are all sorts of tables and chairs, a woodburning stove, cricket team photos on the walls, Keltic Light, Penzance Crowlas and Potion No 9, and Sharps Own on handpump, up to 20 wines by the glass, 50 malt whiskies and quite a choice of gins and rums. Leading off the bar is the conservatory family room and there's also a cosy bistro. The six acres of gardens are well worth a wander and offer plenty of seats and picnic-sets under large parasols.

Good, popular food includes sandwiches, devilled crab pot, local mussels in piri-piri sauce, pork and garlic sausages with onion gravy and mustard mash, chicken and leek pie, mushroom and cheese risotto, braised pig cheeks on black pudding mash with blackberry sauce, shredded duck in filo pastry in madeira sauce, and puddings. *Benchmark main dish: local whole grilled plaice £14.00. Two-course evening meal £21.50.*

Free house ~ Licensees Will and Lisa Lea ~ Real ale ~ (01326) 340332 ~ Open 11 (12 Sun)-3.15, 6-11 ~ Bar food 12-2.15, 6.30-9.30 ~ Restaurant ~ Children welcome away from bar area ~ Dogs allowed in bar and bedrooms ~ Wi-fi ~ Live music Weds evening ~ Bedrooms: £60/£84 ~ www.trengilly.co.uk *Recommended by John and Bryony Coles, Chris and Angela Buckell, Tony and Rachel Schendel, Colin McKerrow, Alison Ball, Ian Walton*

DEVORAN
Old Quay

SW7938 Map 1

Devoran from new Carnon Cross roundabout A39 Truro–Falmouth, left on old road, right at mini-roundabout; TR3 6NE

Light and airy bar rooms in friendly pub with four real ales, good wine and imaginative food and seats on pretty back terraces; bedrooms

Just up the hill from Devoran Quay, this easy-going, airy pub is at the end of a quiet residential terrace. The roomy bar has an interesting 'woodburner' set halfway up one wall, a cushioned window seat, wall settles and a few bar stools around just three tables on the stripped boards, and bar chairs by the counter (much favoured by the friendly locals), where Otter Bitter, Sharps Doom Bar, Skinners Betty Stogs and a guest such as Timothy Taylors Landlord on handpump and good wines by the glass are served by cheerful, helpful staff; you can buy their own jams and chutneys. Off to the left is an airy room with pictures by local artists (for sale) on white walls, built-in, cushioned wall seating, plush stools and a couple of big tables on the dark slate floor. To the other side of the bar is another light room with more settles and farmhouse chairs, attractive blue and white striped cushions and more sailing photographs; darts and board games. As well as some benches at the front that look down through the trees to the water, there's a series of snug little back terraces with picnic-sets and chairs and tables. Nearby parking is limited unless you arrive early. There is wheelchair access through a side door. The pub is next to the coast-to-coast Portreath to Devoran Mineral Tramway path.

The high quality food includes dishes such as lunchtime sandwiches, ham hock and chorizo terrine with home-made apricot jam, local mussels in shallot, parsley and garlic cream sauce, turmeric, dill and beer-battered fish and chips, vegetable risotto, home-roasted cola ham and egg, beef or cajun chicken burgers, rabbit or venison pie, and puddings such as profiteroles with chocolate sauce and Baileys cheesecake. *Benchmark main dish: hake on bubble and squeak with creamy mussel sauce £14.00. Two-course evening meal £18.75.*

Punch ~ Tenants John and Hannah Calland ~ Real ale ~ (01872) 863142 ~ Open 11-11 ~ Bar food 12-3, 6-9 ~ Restaurant ~ Children welcome ~ Dogs allowed in bar ~ Wi-fi ~ Bedrooms: £55/£75 ~ www.theoldquayinn.co.uk *Recommended by Pete Walker, Chris and Angela Buckell, Ian Herdman*

 GURNARDS HEAD   SW4337   Map 1

Gurnards Head Hotel 🍽 ♟ 🛏

B3306 Zennor–St Just; TR26 3DE

Interesting inn close to the sea, lots of wines by the glass, good inventive food and fine surrounding walks; comfortable bedrooms

The comfortable bedrooms here, with views of rugged moors or the sea, make a fine base from which to explore this wild coastline. It's a civilised but informal inn, just 500 metres from the Atlantic, and the bar rooms are painted in bold, strong colours; there are paintings by local artists, open fires and all manner of wooden dining chairs and tables on stripped boards. St Austell Tribute, Skinners Betty Stogs and a guest on handpump, ten wines by the glass and a couple of ciders; background music, darts and board games. The large back garden has plenty of seats. This is under the same ownership as the Griffin at Felinfach (see Wales) and Old Coastguard in Mousehole, also in Cornwall.

 From a sensibly short menu, the impressive food includes crab tartlet with sorrel hollandaise, duck liver parfait with pickled fig and hazelnut granola, herb gnocchi with courgettes, pine nuts, capers and tomato, chicken breast with cheese and potato mousseline and truffle jus, brill with spinach, mussel and dill cream, and puddings such as frozen calvados parfait with crumble and apple sorbet and brioche and butter pudding with marmalade ice-cream. *Benchmark main dish: pork cheek with parsnip purée, shallots and apple £16.95. Two-course evening meal £21.75.*

Free house ~ Licensees Charles and Edmund Inkin ~ Real ale ~ (01736) 796928 ~ Open 10am-midnight ~ Bar food 12-2.30, 6-9.30 ~ Restaurant ~ Children welcome ~ Dogs allowed in bar and bedrooms ~ Wi-fi ~ Bedrooms: £85/£110 ~ www.gurnardshead.co.uk *Recommended by M A Borthwick, Clifford Blakemore, Pete Walker, J D and A P, Stephen Shepherd, J R Wildon*

HELFORD PASSAGE   SW7626   Map 1

Ferryboat

Signed from B3291; TR11 5LB

Plenty of seats outside look over a sandy beach and the river – extremely popular in fine weather; pubby food (including fish dishes) and St Austell ales

Seats on the terrace (bookable in advance) in front of this 300-year-old pub look over a sandy beach where you can hire small boats and arrange fishing trips – it's a lovely spot. There's also a summer ferry from Helford village. The interior isn't huge, with just one bar room, and there are farmhouse and blue-painted kitchen chairs and built-in cushioned wall seats around stripped wooden tables on grey slates, and mirrors above a woodburning stove. An arched doorway leads to the games room with pool, darts, board games and a leather sofa. St Austell Proper Job, Tribute and a guest on handpump, a dozen wines by the glass and farm cider. The walk down from the car park is quite steep.

🍴 Using local produce, the tasty food includes lunchtime sandwiches, fishcakes with lemon mayonnaise, smoked mackerel pâté, hot chorizo, blue cheese and little gem salad, battered haddock and chips, beetroot, cheese and roast walnut risotto, ox cheeks with pickled red cabbage and boulangère potatoes, and puddings such as crème brûlée and apple and blackberry crumble and custard. *Benchmark main dish: burger with special sauce, home-made coleslaw and chips £10.00. Two-course evening meal £18.00.*

St Austell ~ Tenant Ben Wright ~ Real ale ~ (01326) 250625 ~ Open 10am-11pm ~ Bar food 12-3, 6-9.30 ~ Children welcome ~ Dogs allowed in bar ~ Wi-fi ~ Live bands Fri evenings ~ www.thewrightbrothers.co.uk *Recommended by Edward May, Belinda May*

HELSTON
SW6522 Map 1

Halzephron 🍷 🛏️

Gunwalloe, village about 4 miles S but not marked on many road maps; look for brown sign on A3083 alongside perimeter fence of RNAS Culdrose; TR12 7QB

Bustling pub in lovely spot with tasty bar food, local beers and good nearby walks; bedrooms

This bustling inn is in such a fine spot – Gunwalloe fishing cove is just 300 metres away and Church Cove with its sandy beach is nearby – so it makes good sense (and is useful) that it's open all day. The neatly kept bar and dining areas have an informal, friendly atmosphere, comfortable seating, a warm winter fire in the woodburning stove, Sharps Doom Bar, Skinners Betty Stogs and a guest such as Otter Bitter on handpump, nine wines by the glass, 41 malt whiskies and summer farm cider. The dining Gallery seats up to 30 people; darts and board games. Picnic-sets outside look across National Trust fields and countryside and there are lovely coastal walks in both directions.

🍴 Good food includes sandwiches, salmon and dill fishcakes with cucumber and chilli salsa, ham hock and parma ham terrine with red onion marmalade, a casserole of the day, beer-battered fish of the day with chips, root vegetable and sweet potato stew, cottage pie, guinea fowl with dauphinoise potatoes, and puddings such as black cherry and almond flan and chocolate and amaretto truffle torte. *Benchmark main dish: bass with roasted vegetables and anya potatoes £14.95. Two-course evening meal £20.00.*

Free house ~ Licensee Claire Murray ~ Real ale ~ (01326) 240406 ~ Open 10.30am-11pm; 12-10.30 Sun ~ Bar food 12-2 (3 Sun), 6-9 ~ Restaurant ~ Children welcome ~ Dogs allowed in bar ~ Bedrooms: £55/£94 ~ www.halzephron-inn.co.uk *Recommended by Paul Rampton, Julie Harding, Nigel Morton, Dave Webster, Sue Holland, Ian and Rose Lock*

LANLIVERY
SX0759 Map 1

Crown 🛏️

Signposted off A390 Lostwithiel–St Austell (tricky to find from other directions); PL30 5BT

Chatty atmosphere in nice old pub, traditional rooms and well liked food and drink; bedrooms

Just ten minutes from the Eden Project, this ancient place has real character. The main bar has a log fire in a huge fireplace, traditional settles on big flagstones, some cushioned farmhouse chairs, church and other wooden chairs around all sorts of tables, old yachting photographs, and beams in the boarded ceilings. Harbour Amber and Skinners Betty Stogs and Ginger Tosser on handpump and several wines by the glass.

A couple of other rooms are similarly furnished (including a dining conservatory) and there's another open fire. The porch has a huge lit-up well with a glass top and the quiet, pretty garden has picnic-sets. The bedrooms have all been redecorated over the last year or so; breakfasts are good.

Using local, seasonal produce, the tasty food includes sandwiches, crab gratin, salt and pepper squid, lasagne, mushroom stroganoff, seafood tagliatelle, chicken with thyme and lemon butter, and puddings such as layered chocolate cheesecake and nutty treacle tart. *Benchmark main dish: moules marinière £11.95. Two-course evening meal £16.00.*

Wagtail Inns ~ Licensee Nigel Wakeman ~ Real ale ~ (01208) 872707 ~ Open 11-11; 12-10.30 Sun ~ Bar food 12-2.30, 6-9 ~ Restaurant ~ Children welcome away from bar ~ Dogs allowed in bar and bedrooms ~ Wi-fi ~ Bedrooms: /£70 ~ www.wagtailinns.com
Recommended by Robert Parker, Richard Stanfield

LOSTWITHIEL
Globe ♀ ◧
SX1059 Map 1

North Street (close to medieval bridge); PL22 0EG

Unassuming bar in traditional local, interesting food and drinks, and friendly staff; suntrap back courtyard with outside heaters

As always, this bustling town pub is reliably well run and our readers continue to enjoy their visits very much. You can be sure of a friendly welcome in the unassuming bar, which is long and somewhat narrow with a mix of pubby tables and seats, local photographs on pale green plank panelling at one end and nice, more or less local prints (for sale) on canary yellow walls above a coal-effect stove at the snug inner end; there's also a small red-walled front alcove. The ornately carved bar counter, with comfortable chrome and leatherette stools, dispenses Sharps Doom Bar, Skinners Betty Stogs and a changing guest on handpump, plus 11 reasonably priced wines by the glass, 20 malt whiskies and two local ciders; background music, darts, board games and TV. The sheltered back courtyard is not large but has some attractive and unusual plants, and is a real suntrap (with an extendable awning and outside heaters). You can park in several of the nearby streets or the (free) town car park. The 13th-c church is worth a look and the ancient river bridge, a few yards away, is lovely.

Very popular food includes sandwiches, moules marinière, mushroom, stilton and port pot, chilli con carne, pasta with smoked bacon and parma ham in creamy white wine and mushroom sauce, a vegetarian roast, sausages with onion gravy, home-made pie of the day, slow-roasted lamb shoulder with rosemary and mint, and puddings such as caramel apple pie and raspberry cheesecake. *Benchmark main dish: seafood chowder £9.95. Two-course evening meal £20.00.*

Free house ~ Licensee William Erwin ~ Real ale ~ (01208) 872501 ~ Open 12-2.30, 6 (5 Fri)-11 (midnight Fri, Sat) ~ Bar food 12-2, 6.30-9 ~ Restaurant ~ Children welcome but no pushchairs in restaurant ~ Dogs allowed in bar ~ Wi-fi ~ Live music Fri, quiz Sun ~ Bedrooms: /£70 ~ www.globeinn.com *Recommended by Peter Salmon, Mr and Mrs Richard Osborne, R K Phillips, Dr and Mrs S G Barber, B and M Kendall, Stephen Shepherd*

People named as recommenders after the full entries have told us that the pub should be included. But they have not written the report – we have, after anonymous on-the-spot inspection.

MORWENSTOW
Bush
SS2015 Map 1
Signed off A39 N of Kilkhampton; Crosstown; EX23 9SR

**Ancient pub in fine spot, character bar, several dining rooms
and outside dining huts and well liked food; bedrooms**

There are fantastic walks all around this 13th-c former smugglers' inn
(good surfing beaches too) and, usefully, some sort of food is served all
day. The character bar has traditional pubby furniture on big flagstones, a
woodburner in a big stone fireplace, horse tack and copper knick-knacks
and St Austell HSD and Tribute and a guest from Forge on handpump, eight
wines by the glass, several whiskies and farm cider; background music,
games machine, darts and board games. One beamed dining room has tall
pale wooden dining chairs and tables on bare boards, small prints on cream-
painted walls, fresh flowers and another woodburning stove; a second has
big windows overlooking the picnic-sets and heated dining huts. The neat
bedrooms have lovely views and breakfasts are seved until 11am.

 Well liked food includes creamy garlic mushrooms, beetroot and goats cheese
salad with balsamic syrup, beef or chicken burger with bacon, cornish yarg,
tomato relish and chips, butternut squash, red onion and blue cheese risotto, rump
steak with herb butter, and puddings such as lemon and sherry syllabub and dark
chocolate brownie with chocolate sauce. *Benchmark main dish: beer-battered local
fish and chips £11.00. Two-course evening meal £15.50.*

Free house ~ Licensees Colin and Gill Fletcher ~ Real ale ~ (01288) 331242 ~ Open
10am-midnight ~ Bar food 11-9 ~ Restaurant ~ Children welcome away from restaurant
~ Dogs allowed in bar and bedrooms ~ Wi-fi ~ Live music Sat evening ~ Bedrooms:
$50/$90 ~ www.thebushinnmorwenstow.com *Recommended by Toby Jones, Edward May,
Ryta Lyndley*

MOUSEHOLE
Old Coastguard
SW4726 Map 1
The Parade (edge of village, Newlyn coast road); TR19 6PR

**Lovely position for carefully refurbished inn, a civilised, friendly
atmosphere, character furnishings, a good choice of wines and first
rate food; bedrooms with sea views**

Most of the comfortable bedrooms here look over the sea to St
Michael's Mount and the Lizard; the seats on the terrace have the
same marvellous view. The garden, with its tropical palms and dracaena,
is charming and a path leads down to rock pools below. The bar rooms
have boldly coloured walls hung with paintings of local scenes and sailing
boats, stripped floorboards and an atmosphere of informal but civilised
comfort. The Upper Deck houses the bar and the restaurant, with a nice
mix of antique dining chairs around oak and distressed pine tables, lamps
on big barrel tables and chairs to either side of the log fire, topped by
a vast bressumer beam. St Austell Tribute and Skinners Betty Stogs on
handpump, 16 wines by the glass, a farm cider and a good choice of soft
drinks. The Lower Deck has glass windows running the length of the
building, several deep sofas and armchairs, and shelves of books and
games; background music. This is sister pub to the Gurnards Head (also
Cornwall) and the Griffin at Felinfach (Wales).

Good, interesting food includes duck livers with beetroot and walnuts, smoked
cods roe with a soft boiled egg and capers, butternut squash and spinach lasagne,

plaice with jerusalem artichoke and brown shrimp butter, slow-cooked lamb shoulder with anchovy and black olive butter, venison ragu with tagliatelle, and puddings such as chocolate mousse and banana cake with brandy prunes and brown bread ice-cream. *Benchmark main dish: fish stew £12.50. Two-course evening meal £18.00.*

Free house ~ Licensees Charles and Edmund Inkin ~ Real ale ~ (01736) 731222 ~ Open 10am-11.30pm ~ Bar food 12.30-2.30, 6.30-9 (9.30 Fri, Sat) ~ Restaurant ~ Children welcome ~ Dogs allowed in bar and bedrooms ~ Wi-fi ~ Bedrooms: /£145 ~ www.oldcoastguardhotel.co.uk *Recommended by Ian and Rose Lock, Alison Ball, Ian Walton, Peter Andrews, Geoff and Linda Payne*

MOUSEHOLE
SW4626 Map 1
Ship 🛏
Harbourside; TR19 6QX

Bustling harbourside local in pretty village; bedrooms

There's a good mix of locals and visitors in this bustling pub just across the road from the harbour. The opened-up main bar has black beams and panelling, built-in wooden wall benches and stools around low tables, sailors' fancy ropework, granite flagstones and a cosy open fire. St Austell HSD, Trelawny and Tribute on handpump, several wines by the glass and maybe background music. The bedrooms are above the pub or in the cottage next door and some overlook the water. It's best to park at the top of the village and walk down (traffic can be a bit of a nightmare in summer). The elaborate harbour lights at Christmas are well worth a visit.

Tasty food includes sandwiches, moules marinière, smoked salmon and crème fraîche roulade, honey-roast ham and eggs, burger with cheese, onion rings and chips, local whitemeat crab salad, lamb stew in cider and tomatoes, smoked haddock fishcakes with shellfish mayonnaise, and puddings. *Benchmark main dish: beer-battered fresh local fish and chips £10.50. Two-course evening meal £16.00.*

St Austell ~ Manager Melanie Matthews ~ Real ale ~ (01736) 731234 ~ Open 11-11; 11-10.30 Sun ~ Bar food 12-2.30, 6-8.30 ~ Restaurant ~ Children welcome ~ Dogs allowed in bar and bedrooms ~ Wi-fi ~ Quiz Thurs evening ~ Bedrooms: /£110 ~ www.shipinnmousehole.co.uk *Recommended by Isobel Mackinlay, Pete Walker, Ian and Rose Lock, Alan Johnson*

MYLOR BRIDGE
SW8137 Map 1
Pandora ♀
Restronguet Passage: from A39 in Penryn, take turning signposted Mylor Church, Mylor Bridge, Flushing and go straight through Mylor Bridge following Restronguet Passage signs; or from A39 further N, at or near Perranarworthal, take turning signposted Mylor, Restronguet, then follow Restronguet Weir signs, but turn left down hill at Restronguet Passage sign; TR11 5ST

Beautifully placed waterside inn with seats on long floating pontoon, lots of atmosphere in beamed and flagstoned rooms, and some sort of food all day

This is a special pub, both inside and out, and you'll need to get here early to bag a seat as they only take bookings for the upstairs restaurant. The thatched medieval building is in an idyllic sheltered waterside position, with picnic-sets at the front and on the long floating jetty – at high tide, many customers do arrive by boat. There's a back cabin bar with pale farmhouse chairs, high-backed settles and a model galleon in a big glass cabinet. Several other rambling, interconnecting rooms have low beams, beautifully polished big flagstones, cosy alcoves, cushioned built-in wall seats and pubby tables and chairs, three large log fires in high hearths (to protect them against tidal floods) and maps, yacht pictures, oars and ship's wheels; church candles help with the lighting. St Austell HSD, Proper Job, Trelawny and Tribute on handpump, 17 wines by the glass and 18 malt whiskies served by friendly, efficient staff. Upstairs, the attractive dining room has exposed oak vaulting, dark tables and chairs on pale oak flooring and large brass bells and lanterns. Because of the pub's popularity, parking is extremely difficult at peak times; wheelchair access.

Some sort of highly thought-of food – including afternoon cream teas – is served all day: sandwiches (until 5pm), smoked mackerel pâté, local mussels in white wine, garlic and cream, a sharing tapas board, burger with bacon, mustard coleslaw and chips, vegetable and blue cheese bubble and squeak with a poached duck egg, slow-roasted pork belly with braised pig cheek, black pudding faggot and toffee apple, and puddings such as sugar-dusted home-made doughnuts with berry milkshake and marzipan ice-cream and lemon posset. *Benchmark main dish: beer-battered fish and chips £11.75. Two-course evening meal £20.00.*

St Austell ~ Tenant John Milan ~ Real ale ~ (01326) 372678 ~ Open 10.30-11 ~ Bar food 10.30-9.30 ~ Restaurant ~ Children welcome away from bar area ~ Dogs allowed in bar ~ Wi-fi ~ www.pandorainn.com *Recommended by Chris and Angela Buckell, Pat and Tony Martin, R Elliott, Mick and Moira Brummell, John and Bernadette Elliott, Colin McKerrow*

PENZANCE
SW4730 Map 1
Turks Head

At top of main street, by big domed building, turn left down Chapel Street; TR18 4AF

Cheerfully run pub with a good, bustling atmosphere and popular food and beer

This bustling town pub is just the place to drop into on a wet and windy day – there's always a lively mix of locals and visitors, and the landlord and his staff offer a friendly welcome to all. The bar has old flat irons, jugs and so forth hanging from the beams, pottery above the wood-effect panelling, wall seats and tables and a couple of elbow-rests around central pillars; background music. Sharps Doom Bar, Skinners Betty Stogs and guests such as Greene King Abbot and Wadworths 6X on handpump, a dozen wines by the glass and 12 malt whiskies. The suntrap back garden has big urns of flowers. There's been a Turks Head here for over 700 years – though most of the original building was destroyed by a Spanish raiding party in the 16th c.

Tasty food includes lunchtime sandwiches, panko-breadcrumbed king prawns with chilli jam, chicken caesar salad, sausages of the day with caramelised red onion, port and redcurrant gravy, chicken, beef or bean burgers with chips or spicy cajun potato wedges, beef casserole, fish pie, and puddings. *Benchmark main dish: seafood in a crab velouté pie with cheese topping £13.50. Two-course evening meal £18.00.*

Punch ~ Lease Jonathan and Helen Gibbard ~ Real ale ~ (01736) 363093 ~ Open 11.30am-midnight; 12-midnight Sun ~ Bar food 12-2.30, 6-9.30 (10 in summer) ~ Restaurant ~ Children welcome ~ Dogs allowed in bar ~ Wi-fi ~ www.turksheadpenzance.co.uk *Recommended by Alan Johnson, Alison Ball, Ian Walton*

If you have to cancel a reservation for a bedroom or restaurant, please telephone or write to warn them. You may lose your deposit if you've paid one.

PERRANUTHNOE

SW5329   Map 1

Victoria 🏆

Signed off A394 Penzance–Helston; TR20 9NP

Cornwall Dining Pub of the Year

Carefully furnished inn close to Mount's Bay beaches, friendly welcome, local beers, interesting fresh food, and seats in pretty garden; bedrooms

The Dining Pub of the Year Award here is well deserved and our readers remain as enthusiastic as ever about the food; you'll get a warm welcome too. The L-shaped bar has a bustling atmosphere, a cheerful mix of customers, an attractive array of dining chairs around wooden tables on oak flooring, various cosy corners, exposed joists and a woodburning stove; also, all sorts of artwork on the walls and fresh flowers. The restaurant is separate. Sharps Doom Bar and Rebel Cornish Sunset on handpump and several wines by the glass; background music. The pub labrador is Bailey. The pretty tiered garden has rattan chairs around wooden tables, and the beaches of Mount's Bay are a couple of minutes' stroll away. The bedrooms are light and airy, and they also have a flat for rent in Porthleven.

 Using top quality, local ingredients, the highly enjoyable food includes lunchtime sandwiches, crispy squid and tiger prawn tempura with spicy vegetable salsa and coriander dressing, ham and free-range eggs with home-made ketchup, risotto of mushroom and local greens with cheese and truffle oil, slow-braised duck and prune faggots with onion gravy, hake with mussels and a caper and parsley dressing, and puddings such as fruit and almond crumble with calvados ice-cream and dark chocolate and tiramisu pot with salted caramel sauce and Tia Maria ice-cream. *Benchmark main dish: slow-cooked pork belly £14.95. Two-course evening meal £21.00.*

Pubfolio ~ Lease Anna and Stewart Eddy ~ Real ale ~ (01736) 710309 ~ Open 12-3, 5.15-midnight; 12-2.30 Sun; closed Sun evening, Mon ~ Bar food 12-2, 6.15-9; 12-2.30 Sun ~ Restaurant ~ Children welcome ~ Dogs allowed in bar ~ Wi-fi ~ Bedrooms: /£75 ~ www.victoriainn-penzance.co.uk *Recommended by R and S Bentley, Pete Walker, Brian and Anna Marsden, Alison Ball, Ian Walton, Di and Mike Gillam*

PERRANWELL

SW7739   Map 1

Royal Oak

Village signposted off A393 Redruth–Falmouth and A39 Falmouth–Truro; TR3 7PX

Welcoming and relaxed pub, with well liked food and real ales

The hub of the village and warmly friendly to all, this is a small, traditional pub surrounded by walks and cycle paths in attractive countryside. The carpeted bar, with a relaxed atmosphere, horsebrasses on black beams and paintings by local artists on the walls, rambles around beyond a big stone fireplace to a snug room, behind which more candlelit tables can be found. St Austell Tribute, Sharps Doom Bar, Skinners Betty Stogs and a guest ale on handpump, as well as good

---

Please let us know what you think of a pub's bedrooms: feedback@goodguides.com or (no stamp needed) *The Good Pub Guide*, FREEPOST RTJR-ZCYZ-RJZT, Perrymans Lane, Etchingham TN19 7DN.

wines by the glass and farm cider. There are picnic-sets in front of the
building and more seats in the garden.

🍴 As well as daily specials, the reliably good food includes sandwiches, scallops
with chorizo, sherry and cream, whole baked goats cheese with onion
marmalade, beer-battered cod and chips, mushroom stroganoff, duck leg confit with
tomato and red onion reduction, haddock, lemon sole and monkfish meunière, and
puddings. *Benchmark main dish: crab bake topped with grilled cheese £13.75.
Two-course evening meal £19.00.*

Free house ~ Licensees Tim Cairns and Lizzie Archer ~ Real ale ~ (01872) 863175 ~
Open 11-3.30, 6 (5 Fri)-midnight; 11-midnight Sat; 12-11.30 Sun ~
Bar food 12-2.30, 6.30-9.30 ~ Children welcome ~ Dogs allowed in bar ~ Wi-fi ~
www.theroyaloakperranwellstation.co.uk *Recommended by Gene and Tony Freemantle,
John Marsh, John and Susan Miln, Ian and Rose Lock*

POLPERRO
Blue Peter ◑ £
SX2050   Map 1

Quay Road; PL13 2QZ

**Friendly pub overlooking pretty harbour, with fishing paraphernalia,
paintings by local artists and carefully prepared food**

There's usually a good mix of customers of all ages in this bustling little
harbourside pub – though families must use the upstairs room. The
cosy low-beamed bar has a chatty, relaxed atmosphere, St Austell Tribute,
Sharps Own and guests such as Bays Gold and Cornish Crown St Michaels
Bitter on handpump, and traditional furnishings that include a small winged
settle and a polished pew, wooden flooring, fishing regalia, photographs
and pictures by local artists, lots of candles and a solid wood bar counter.
One window seat looks down on the harbour, while another looks out past
rocks to the sea; background music and board games. There are a few seats
outside on the terrace and more in an upstairs amphitheatre-style area. It
gets crowded at peak times. Usefully, they have a cash machine (there's no
bank in the village).

🍴 Good value food includes sandwiches, chicken liver pâté, fishcake of the day
with sweet chilli, honey-roasted ham and eggs, chicken tikka masala, steak in ale
pie, moroccan vegetable tagine, seafood pasta of the day, and puddings. *Benchmark
main dish: tempura-battered fish and chips £9.95. Two-course evening meal £16.50.*

Free house ~ Licensees Steve and Caroline Steadman ~ Real ale ~ (01503) 272743
~ Open 10am-11pm; 10am-10.30pm Sun ~ Bar food 12-3, 6-9; all day in summer peak
season ~ Restaurant ~ Children in upstairs family room only ~ Dogs allowed in bar ~
Wi-fi ~ Live music Fri and Sat evenings in summer ~ www.thebluepeter.co.uk
Recommended by Ruth Mann, Adrian Johnson, Peter Thornton, Richard Tilbrook

PORT ISAAC
Port Gaverne Inn 🛏
SX0080   Map 1

*Port Gaverne signposted from Port Isaac and from B3314 E of Pendoggett;
PL29 3SQ*

**Busy small hotel near the sea and fine cliff walks, with a lively bar and
well liked food and drink; bedrooms**

Customers tend to come back to this 17th-c inn year after year. It's
a comfortable place to stay, close to the sea, and the bar is always
full of lively chat. There are low beams, flagstones and carpeting, some
exposed stone, and a big log fire; the lounge has some interesting old local

photographs. You can eat in the bar or in the 'Captain's Cabin' – a little room where everything is shrunk to scale (old oak chest, model sailing ship, even the prints on the white stone walls). St Austell Tribute, Sharps Doom Bar and Skinners Betty Stogs on handpump, a decent choice of wines and several whiskies; cribbage and dominoes. There are seats in the terraced garden and splendid clifftop walks all around.

 The long-serving chef uses the best local produce: sandwiches, crab soup, smoked mackerel pâté, ham and eggs, roasted stuffed peppers, a pie of the week, honey-roasted duck with brandy, cream and green peppercorn sauce, monkfish with tomato, orange and basil sauce, and puddings with clotted cream. *Benchmark main dish: beer-battered fish and chips £11.25. Two-course evening meal £16.00.*

Free house ~ Licensee Graham Sylvester ~ Real ale ~ (01208) 880244 ~ Open 11-11; 12-10.30 Sun ~ Bar food 12-2 (2.30 weekends and in peak season), 6.30-9 ~ Restaurant ~ Children welcome ~ Dogs welcome ~ Wi-fi ~ Bedrooms: /£75 ~ www.port-gaverne-hotel.co.uk *Recommended by John and Bernadette Elliott, Phil and Helen Holt*

PORTHLEVEN
Ship
SW6225   Map 1

Mount Pleasant Road (harbour) off B3304; TR13 9JS

Friendly harbourside pub with fantastic views, pubby furnishings, real ales and tasty food and seats on terrace

A friendly new landlord has taken over this fishermen's pub right by the harbour entrance (it's interestingly floodlit at night) and there has been some gentle refurbishment. If you arrive early enough you can bag a window seat in the bar and look across to the sea just yards away – the candlelit dining room has the same view. There are open fires in stone fireplaces, cushioned settles, mate's chairs and other wooden dining chairs and plush stools around all sorts of tables on floorboards or flagstones, banknotes and beermats on the ceilings and walls, various lamps and pennants and a bustling, cheerful atmosphere. Hancocks HB, Sharps Doom Bar and Special, Skinners Porthleven and Rebel Bal Maiden on handpump; background music. More of the terraced garden has been opened up, with plenty of seats looking over the water.

 Well liked food includes sandwiches, moules marinière, beef, chicken and bean burgers with coleslaw and french fries, sausage cassoulet, barbecue ribs, a changing vegetarian dish, beef in ale pie, a fish dish of the day with caper and crayfish butter, and puddings. *Benchmark main dish: fish pie £11.95. Two-course evening meal £15.00.*

Free house ~ Licensee Christian Waite ~ Real ale ~ (01326) 564204 ~ Open 11-11; 12-10.30 Sun ~ Bar food 12-9; 12-2, 6.30-9 in winter ~ Well behaved children welcome ~ Dogs allowed in bar ~ Wi-fi ~ www.theshipinncornwall.co.uk
Recommended by Clifford Blakemore, Geoff and Linda Payne

PORTHTOWAN
Blue
SW6948   Map 1

Beach Road, East Cliff; car park (fee in season) advised; TR4 8AW

Informal, busy bar right by a wonderful beach, with modern food and drinks; lively staff and customers

The fantastic beach next door to this bustling bar attracts a wide mix of cheerful customers from serious surfers to dog walkers to families. They all pile in here throughout the day and the atmosphere is easy and informal; big picture windows look across the terrace to the huge expanse of sand and sea. The front bays have built-in pine seats, while the rest of the large room has wicker and white chairs around pale tables on grey-painted floorboards, cream or orange walls, several bar stools and plenty of standing space around the counter; ceiling fans, some big ferny plants and fairly quiet background music. St Austell Tribute and Sharps Doom Bar on handpump, several wines by the glass, cocktails and shots, and all kinds of coffees, hot chocolates and teas served by perky, helpful young staff.

 Food is served all day from 10am: starters to share include nachos and chips with chilli jam and other dips, aioli, hummus or sour cream with chives, plus main dishes such as beef, free-range chicken or burgers, beer-battered fish of the day, tasty daily specials, and puddings such as sticky toffee pudding and belgian waffles with clotted cream ice-cream. *Benchmark main dish: mussels in cream, garlic and white wine £13.00. Two-course evening meal £15.00.*

Free house ~ Licensees Tara Roberts and Luke Morris ~ Real ale ~ (01209) 890329 ~ Open 10am-11pm (10pm Sun) ~ Bar food 10am-9pm ~ Children welcome ~ Dogs allowed in bar ~ Wi-fi ~ Acoustic music Sat evening, comedy night monthly ~ www.blue-bar.co.uk *Recommended by Edward May, Toby Jones*

PORTLOE
SW9339 Map 1
Ship
At top of village; TR2 5RA

Cheerful, traditional local in charming village, friendly atmosphere, traditional furnishings, good ales and food, and seats in garden; bedrooms

Set in a lovely little fishing village, this is a well run, traditional 17th-c inn with a cheerful atmosphere. The L-shaped bar has tankards hanging from beams, nautical bric-a-brac and local memorabilia, an amazing beer bottle collection, straightforward dark farmhouse and high-backed brown leather seats around a nice medley of wooden tables on red carpet, and stools by the counter where friendly staff serve St Austell Dartmoor Best and Tribute on handpump, six wines by the glass, cider and perry; background music. Across the lane is an attractive sloping streamside garden with picnic-sets under umbrellas. The bedrooms are clean and comfortable, and the beach is just five minutes away.

 Popular, generously served food includes excellent crab sandwiches, tomato, goats cheese and basil salad, whitebait with garlic mayonnaise, broccoli and stilton tart, specially made sausages with herb mash and red onion gravy, steak in ale pie, steamed hake with garlic oyster mushrooms, and puddings such as double chocolate brownie and fruit crumble with clotted cream. *Benchmark main dish: beer-battered fish and chips £11.95. Two-course evening meal £19.00.*

St Austell ~ Tenant Mark Swannell ~ Real ale ~ (01872) 501356 ~ Open 12-3, 6-11 ~ Bar food 12-2.30, 6-9 ~ Children welcome ~ Dogs allowed in bar ~ Wi-fi ~ Bedrooms: £60/£80
Recommended by John and Sharon Hancock, Barry Collett, Richard Tilbrook, Chris and Angela Buckell

ST MAWGAN
SW8765 Map 1
Falcon
NE of Newquay, off B3276 or A3059; TR8 4EP

Warmly friendly village inn with a compact, simply furnished bar and dining room, four ales, good food and seats in pretty garden; bedrooms

Try to visit this attractive 16th-c pub when the wisteria is in blossom – it's a beautiful sight. What shines through here is the genuinely friendly welcome for both visitors and regulars: it really is the hub of this pretty village. The bar has a big fireplace with large stone bottles on each side (there's a log fire in winter, fresh flowers in summer), farmhouse and cushioned wheelback chairs around an assortment of tables on patterned carpeting, blue plush stools, antique coaching prints and falcon pictures. There's a beer named for the pub from Penpont plus guests such as Abbeydale Hells Bells, Cornish Crown St Michaels Bitter and Cotleigh Tawny Owl on handpump; darts. The compact stone-floored dining room has similar furnishings. The peaceful flower-filled back garden has solid chairs and benches around tables under umbrellas and a wishing well, and there's a cobbled front courtyard too. Bedrooms are comfortable and handy for nearby Newquay Airport. The Japanese garden just down the road is worth a visit.

Good food includes lunchtime sandwiches and pasties, spicy crab and peanut cakes with sweet chilli sauce, pâté of the day, sausages and smoked cheese mash with gravy, butternut squash and parmesan risotto, steak and kidney pie, lamb curry, beer-battered haddock and chips, chicken with white bean and chorizo cassoulet, and puddings. *Benchmark main dish: locally smoked haddock with bubble and squeak and poached duck egg £14.95. Two-course evening meal £20.00.*

St Austell ~ Managers David Carbis and Sarah Lawrence ~ Real ale ~ (01637) 860225 ~ Open 11-11 (midnight Fri, Sat); 12-11 Sun; 11-3, 5.30-11 (midnight Fri) weekdays in winter ~ Bar food 12-2.30 (2 in winter, 3 Sun), 5.30 (6 winter Sun)-9.30 ~ Restaurant ~ Children welcome away from the bar ~ Dogs allowed in bar ~ Wi-fi ~ Bedrooms: £50/£90 ~ www.thefalconinnstmawgan.co.uk *Recommended by Brian and Anna Marsden, Richard Stanfield*

ST MERRYN
Cornish Arms
Churchtown (B3276 towards Padstow); PL28 8ND

SW8874 Map 1

Busy roadside pub, liked by locals and visitors, with bar and dining rooms, real ales, good pubby food, friendly service and seats outside

This roadside pub is packed with holidaymakers in summer, but is quieter and more relaxed out of season, with a warm log fire and Friday fish nights, Saturday curries and Sunday roasts. The main door leads into a sizeable informal area with a pool table and plenty of cushioned wall seating; to the left, a light, airy dining room overlooks the terrace. There's an unusual modern upright woodburner (with tightly packed logs on each side), photographs of the sea and former games teams, and pale wooden dining chairs around tables on quarry tiles. This leads to two more linked rooms with ceiling joists; the first has pubby furniture on huge flagstones, while the end room has more cushioned wall seating, contemporary seats and tables and parquet flooring. St Austell Proper Job, Trelawny and Tribute on handpump, 16 wines by the glass, a farm cider, friendly service, background music and TV. The window boxes are pretty and there are picnic-sets on a side terrace and more on grass.

Popular food includes sandwiches, blue cheese tart, field mushrooms with parmesan and aioli, vegetable curry, ham and egg, burger with cheese, chipotle relish and chips, pork sausages with mash and gravy, grilled hake with mushy peas and tartare sauce, and puddings such as apple and almond sponge with custard and sticky toffee pudding with clotted cream. *Benchmark main dish: moules frites £12.95. Two-course evening meal £18.50.*

St Austell ~ Tenant Luke Taylor ~ Real ale ~ (01841) 532700 ~ Open 11.30-11 ~
Bar food 12-3, 5-9 ~ Restaurant ~ Children welcome ~ Dogs welcome ~ Wi-fi ~
www.rickstein.com/the-cornish-arms.html *Recommended by Robert Watt, Chris and*
Val Ramstedt, Alison Ball, Ian Walton

ST TUDY

SX0676 Map 1

Tudy Inn ♀

Off A391 near Wadebridge; PL30 3NN

**Refurbished pub with friendly licensees, several bars and dining
rooms, good wines by the glass, enjoyable food and seats outside**

Run by highly professional and warmly friendly licensees – Mrs Stratton-
Downes also runs the kitchen – this is a carefully refurbished pub
with a good mix of both locals and visitors. The main bar has a lovely
old and very high-backed settle beside the log fire in a raised fireplace
(horsebrasses on the bressumer beam), shelves of tankards, jars and
antique china, and wooden stools, mate's chairs and smaller settles on the
newish slate floor. Sharps Doom Bar and Wadworths 6X on handpump and
17 carefully chosen wines by the glass. The dining rooms are relaxed and
informal, with a mix of dark farmhouse, wheelback and elegant wooden
chairs and tables on bare boards or rugs, modern art on red walls, big
house plants, a second fireplace (one fire is lit all year round) and a sizeable
carved sideboard topped with lilies. As well as picnic-sets beneath parasols
at the front, there's a back terrace too.

Rewarding food includes sandwiches, thai fishcakes with peanut chilli sauce,
crispy-coated camembert with cranberry sauce, three-egg omelettes, beer-
battered cod and chips, smoked haddock with gruyère sauce and fried quails eggs,
duck leg confit with smoked bacon and flageolet beans, and puddings. *Benchmark
main dish: steak and kidney pie £10.95. Two-course evening meal £18.00.*

Free house ~ Licensees Paul and Jo Stratton-Downes ~ Real ale ~ (01208) 850656 ~
Open 12-3, 6-11; 12-3 Sun; closed Sun evening, Mon ~ Bar food 12-2, 7-9 ~ Restaurant ~
Well behaved children welcome ~ Dogs allowed in bar ~ Wi-fi ~ www.tudyinn.co.uk
Recommended by Jason Caulkin, Mrs Jill Silversides, Barry Brown

TREVAUNANCE COVE

SW7251 Map 1

Driftwood Spars 🍺 🛏

Off B3285 in St Agnes; Quay Road; TR5 0RT

**Friendly old inn with plenty of history, own-brew beers,
a wide range of other drinks and popular food, and beach nearby;
attractive bedrooms**

As this busy pub is just up the lane from a dramatic cove and beach,
it's always full of customers – usefully, they're open all day. The
bars are timbered with massive ships' spars (the masts of great sailing
ships, many of which were wrecked along this coast), and there are dark
wooden farmhouse and tub chairs and settles around a mix of tables,
padded bar stools by the counter, old ship prints, lots of nautical and wreck
memorabilia and woodburning stoves. It's said that an old smugglers'
tunnel leads from behind the bar up through the cliff. Seven real ales on
handpump might include their own Driftwood Alfies Revenge, Blackheads
Mild and Lou's Brew with guests such as St Austell Tribute, Sharps Doom
Bar and Tintagel Cornwalls Pride; they hold two beer festivals a year. Also,
25 malt whiskies, ten rums, seven gins and several wines by the glass; table
football and pool. The modern dining room overlooks the cove. Service is

friendly and helpful. There are pretty hanging baskets in summer and seats in the garden, and many of the attractive bedrooms overlook the coast.

🍴 As well as cakes and coffee all day (not Sunday), the popular food includes lunchtime ciabattas, a meze sharing platter, burger with bacon, cheese, chutney and fries, aubergine parmigiana, fish and chips, sausages with mash and onion gravy, and puddings such as chocolate and pistachio torte and sticky toffee pudding with clotted cream. *Benchmark main dish: fresh local mackerel with slow-roasted tomatoes £7.95. Two-course evening meal £16.00.*

Own brew ~ Licensee Louise Treseder ~ Real ale ~ (01872) 552428 ~ Open 11-11 (1am Sat); 11-10.30 Sun ~ Bar food 12-2, 6-9 ~ Restaurant ~ Children welcome ~ Dogs welcome ~ Wi-fi ~ Live music Sat evenings, open mike first and third Sun of month ~ Bedrooms: £55/£75 ~ www.driftwoodspars.com *Recommended by Tracey and Phil Eagles, Edward May*

WAINHOUSE CORNER
SX1895 Map 1
Old Wainhouse
A39; EX23 0BA

Cheerful pub, open all day, with friendly staff and a good mix of customers, plenty of seating space, real ales and tasty food

Handy for walkers on the South West Coast Path, this cream-painted and black-shuttered pub offer some kind of food all day. The main bar has an easy-going, cheerful atmosphere, an attractive built-in settle, stripped rustic farmhouse chairs and dining chairs around a mix of tables on enormous old flagstones, a large woodburner with stone bottles on the mantelpiece above it, and beams hung with scythes, saws, a horse collar and other tack, spiles, copper pans and brass plates; do note the lovely photograph of a man driving a pig across a bridge. Off here is a simpler room with similar furniture, a pool table, a flat-screen TV and background music. The dining room to the left of the main door has elegant high-backed dining chairs around pale wooden tables, another woodburner and more horse tack. Sharps Cornish and Doom Bar on handpump and friendly service. Outside, a grass area to one side of the building has picnic-sets. Bedrooms are clean and comfortable.

🍴 Using as much local produce as possible, the tasty food includes wild boar terrine with apple and cider chutney, prawn cocktail, beer-battered haddock and chips, lentil or beef burgers with toppings, gammon with free-range egg and pineapple, and puddings such as plum crumble and chocolate brownie with chocolate sauce. *Benchmark main dish: 21-day-aged sirloin steak with a choice of sauces £17.50. Two-course evening meal £18.50.*

Enterprise ~ Lease Peter Owen ~ Real ale ~ (01840) 230711 ~ Open 10am-midnight ~ Bar food 10-9 ~ Restaurant ~ Children welcome ~ Dogs welcome ~ Wi-fi ~ Bedrooms: £55/£90 ~ www.oldwainhouseinn.co.uk *Recommended by Mick and Moira Brummell, Toby Jones*

'Children welcome' means the pub says it lets children inside without any special restriction. If it allows them in, but to restricted areas such as an eating area or family room, we specify this. Some pubs may impose an evening time limit. We do not mention limits after 9pm as we assume children are home by then.

Also Worth a Visit in Cornwall

Besides the fully inspected pubs, you might like to try these pubs that have been recommended to us and described by readers. Do tell us what you think of them: feedback@goodguides.com

ALTARNUN SX2280
Kings Head (01566) 86241
Five Lanes; PL15 7RX Old stone-built beamed village pub, Greene King Abbot and guests such as Dartmoor and local Penpont, Weston's cider, generous reasonably priced pubby food from sandwiches and baguettes up including popular Sun carvery, carpeted lounge set for dining with big log fire, slate floor restaurant and public bar with another fire; background music, TV, pool; children and dogs welcome, picnic-sets on front terrace and in small raised garden, four bedrooms, handy for A30, open all day. *(Anon)*

ALTARNUN SX2083
★ Rising Sun (01566) 86636
NW; village signed off A39 just W of A395 junction; PL15 7SN Tucked-away 16th-c pub with traditionally furnished L-shaped main bar, low beams, slate flagstones and coal fires, good choice of food including excellent local seafood and generous Sun roasts, Penpont and Skinners ales, farm cider, good friendly service; background music; dogs and well behaved children allowed in bar but not restaurant, seats on suntrap terrace and in garden, pétanque, camping field, nice village with beautiful church, open all day weekends. *(David Crook, John and Bernadette Elliott, Alison Ball, Ian Walton)*

BODINNICK SX1352
Old Ferry (01726) 870237
Across the water from Fowey; coming by road, to avoid the ferry queue, turn left as you go downhill – car park on left before pub; PL23 1LX Old inn just up from the river with lovely views from terrace, dining room and some of its 12 bedrooms; traditional bar with nautical memorabilia, old photographs and woodburner, back room hewn into the rock, well kept Sharps and enjoyable food from lunchtime sandwiches up including children's menu; good circular walks, lane by pub in front of ferry slipway is extremely steep and parking limited, open all day. *(Dave Webster, Sue Holland, Peter J and Avril Hanson, Di and Mike Gillam)*

BODMIN SX0467
Borough Arms (01208) 73118
Dunmere (A389 NW); PL31 2RD Roomy 19th-c roadside pub with good value food including daily carvery, Bass, Dartmoor and St Austell, cheerful staff, partly panelled stripped-stone walls, lots of railway photographs and posters, snug corners, open fire, family room and separate dining

room; background music, quiz machine; dogs allowed in bar, picnic-sets among shady apple trees, two play areas, on Camel Trail, open (and food) all day. *(Mick and Moira Brummell)*

BOSCASTLE SX0990
★ Napoleon (01840) 250204
High Street, top of village; PL35 0BD Welcoming 16th-c thick-walled white cottage at top of steep quaint village (fine views halfway up); slate floors and cosy rooms on different levels including small evening bistro, oak beams and log fires, interesting Napoleon prints and lots of knick-knacks, good food from daily changing menu, well kept St Austell tapped from casks, decent wines and coffee, traditional games; background music (live Fri, sing-along Tues); children and dogs welcome, small covered terrace and large sheltered garden, open all day. *(Stanley and Annie Matthews)*

BOSCASTLE SX0991
Wellington (01840) 250202
Harbour; PL35 0AQ Old hotel's long carpeted beamed bar, good fairly priced food from new chef, ales such as Skinners and St Austell kept well, nice coffee, roaring log fire, upstairs gallery area and separate evening restaurant; children welcome, big secluded garden, comfortable bedrooms. *(Ryta Lyndley)*

BOTALLACK SW3632
★ Queens Arms (01736) 788318
B3306; TR19 7QG Honest old pub with good home-made food including local seafood, meat sourced within 3 miles, well kept Sharps and Skinners, good service, log fires (one in unusual granite inglenook), dark wood furniture, tin mining and other old local photographs on stripped-stone walls, family extension; dogs welcome, tables out in front and pleasant back garden, wonderful clifftop walks nearby, lodge accommodation, open all day. *(Pete Walker)*

BREAGE SW6128
Queens Arms (01326) 573485
3 miles W of Helston just off A394; TR13 9PD Village pub under new management, long carpeted bar with plush banquettes and fire at either end, up to seven real ales, home-cooked food (not Sun evening, Mon lunchtime) including daily specials, small restaurant area, games room with pool and TV; background and live music, quiz nights, free wi-fi; children and dogs welcome, some picnic-sets outside, covered smokers' shelter with logburner, medieval wall paintings in church opposite, open all day. *(Pat and Tony Martin)*

BUDE   SS2006
Brendon Arms (01288) 354542
Falcon Terrace; EX23 8SD Popular pub (particularly in summer) near canal, two big friendly pubby bars and back family room, well kept ales such as St Austell and Sharps, decent wines by the glass, enjoyable food from doorstep sandwiches up, bargain OAP lunch Tues, nice coffee and maybe hot spicy apple juice; juke box, sports TV, pool and darts; dogs allowed in public bar, disabled access, picnic-sets on front grass, heated smokers' shelter, bedrooms and holiday apartments, good walks nearby. *(Mike and Wena Stevenson)*

BUDE   SS2006
Falcon (01288) 352005
Breakwater Road; EX23 8SD Popular 19th-c hotel overlooking canal, enjoyable good value food in carpeted bar with lots of plush banquettes and fire, good friendly service, well kept St Austell Tribute and a couple of guests, restaurant; free wi-fi; attractive well maintained gardens, comfortable bedrooms, good breakfast, open all day in summer, all day weekends in winter. *(Ryta Lyndley)*

CALSTOCK   SX4368
★ Tamar (01822) 832487
The Quay; PL18 9QA Cheerful relaxed local dating from the 17th c, just opposite the Tamar with its imposing viaduct, dark stripped stone, flagstones, tiles and bare boards, pool room with woodburner, more modern fairy-lit back dining room, good generous straightforward food and summer cream teas, well kept Sharps Doom Bar and other cornish ales, good service from cheery young staff and reasonable prices, some live music; children away from bar and well behaved dogs welcome, nicely furnished terrace, heated smokers' shelter, hilly walk or ferry to Cotehele (NT). *(Giles and Annie Francis, Ian Herdman)*

CAWSAND   SX4350
Cross Keys (01752) 822706
The Square; PL10 1PF Welcoming pub in little village square, slate-floored traditional locals' bar with some cask tables, steps up to carpeted dining room with nautical décor, enjoyable home-made food including fish/seafood specials, reasonable prices, Dartmoor Legend or Wooden Hand plus summer guests, friendly helpful service; background music (live Sun afternoon), big TV, free wi-fi; children welcome, towels provided for wet dogs, self-catering apartment, no parking close by, open all day, closed Mon Jan-Mar. *(Simon J Barber)*

CHAPEL AMBLE   SW9975
Maltsters Arms (01208) 812473
Off A39 NE of Wadebridge; PL27 6EU Country pub-restaurant with good food including Sun lunchtime carvery, friendly accommodating staff, St Austell Tribute and Sharps Doom Bar, Weston's cider, log fire, beams, painted half-panelling, stripped stone and some slate flagstones, modern back extension, Weds quiz and fortnightly live music; children welcome, seats outside. *(Anon)*

CHARLESTOWN   SX0351
Rashleigh Arms (01726) 73635
Quay Road; PL25 3NX Modernised early 19th-c pub with nautical touches, public bar, lounge and dining area, well kept St Austell range, good wine choice and coffee, enjoyable fairly priced food all day including popular Sun carvery, friendly obliging service; background music, fortnightly live bands Fri, trad jazz second Sun of month, free wi-fi; children welcome, dogs in bar, disabled facilities, front terrace and garden with picnic-sets, eight bedrooms (some with sea views), Grade II listed car park (site of old coal storage yards), attractive harbour with tall ships. *(Robert Watt, Taff Thomas)*

COMFORD   SW7339
Fox & Hounds (01209) 820251
Comford; A393/B3298; TR16 6AX Attractive rambling low-beamed pub; stripped stone and painted panelling, high-backed settles and cottagey chairs on flagstones, some comfortable leather seating too, three woodburners, generous helpings of enjoyable fairly traditional food, St Austell ales, newspapers, darts and board games; background music; children and dogs (in bar) welcome, disabled facilities, nice floral displays in front, picnic-sets in back garden, open all day weekends, closed Mon. *(Anon)*

COVERACK   SW7818
Paris (01326) 280258
The Cove; TR12 6SX Comfortable Edwardian seaside inn above harbour in beautiful fishing village, carpeted L-shaped bar with well kept St Austell ales and Healey's cider, large relaxed dining room with white tablecloths and spectacular bay views, wide choice of interesting if not inexpensive food including good fresh fish, Sun lunchtime carvery, helpful friendly service, model of namesake ship (wrecked nearby in 1899), popular Weds quiz; children welcome, more sea views from garden and four bedrooms, limited parking. *(Stanley and Annie Matthews, Tom and Jill Jones)*

CRACKINGTON HAVEN   SX1496
★ Coombe Barton (01840) 230345
Off A39 Bude–Camelford; EX23 0JG Much-extended old inn in beautiful setting overlooking splendid sandy bay, modernised pubby bar with plenty of room for summer crowds, welcoming young staff, wide range of simple bar food including local fish, popular carvery Sun lunchtime, Sharps, St Austell and good wine choice, lots of local pictures,

surfboard hanging from plank ceiling, big plain family room, restaurant; darts, pool, fruit machines, background music and TV; dogs allowed in bar, side terrace with plenty of tables, fine cliff walks, roomy bedrooms, good breakfast, open all day in season. *(Anon)*

CRAFTHOLE   SX3654
Finnygook (01503) 230338

B3247, off A374 Torpoint road; PL11 3BQ 15th-c coaching inn with beams and joists in smart bar, long cushioned settles and carved cushioned dining chairs around wooden tables on bare boards, central log fire, high chairs and tables near counter serving Bays Topsail, Harbour IPA and St Austell Tribute, decent choice of wines by the glass, ten malt whiskies and a real cider, record player (bring your own vinyl), dining room with fine views, unusual log-effect gas fire in big cabinet, dining library, enjoyable interesting food and friendly attentive service; live music last Fri of month, free wi-fi; children and dogs welcome, good surrounding walks, bedrooms, closed Mon Oct-Apr, otherwise open all day. *(M G Hart, John and Sharon Hancock, Ian and Rose Lock, Susan and Jeremy Arthern)*

CREMYLL   SX4553
Edgcumbe Arms (01752) 822294

End of B3247; PL10 1HX Splendid setting by Plymouth foot-ferry with great Tamar views and picnic-sets out by the water; attractive layout and décor, slate floors, big settles and comfortably old-fashioned furnishings including fireside sofas, old pictures and china, well kept St Austell ales and reasonably priced food from sandwiches up, lunchtime carvery (evenings Fri-Sun), good family room/games area; pay car park some way off; children in eating area, dogs allowed in one bar (most tables here too low to eat at), four bedrooms, open all day. *(David Crook, Simon J Barber)*

CROWS NEST   SX2669
Crows Nest (01579) 345930

Signed off B3264 N of Liskeard; OS Sheet 201 map reference 263692; PL14 5JQ Old-fashioned 17th-c pub with good traditional food and well kept St Austell ales, attractive furnishings under bowed beams, big log fire, chatty locals; children and dogs welcome, picnic-sets on terrace by quiet lane, handy for Bodmin Moor walks. *(John and Bernadette Elliott)*

CUBERT   SW7857
★**Smugglers Den** (01637) 830209

Off A3075 S of Newquay; TR8 5PY Big open-plan 16th-c thatched pub tucked away in small hamlet; good locally sourced food and four well kept beers (May pie and ale festival), plenty of wines by the glass, efficient friendly young staff, neat ranks

of tables, dim lighting, stripped stone and heavy beam and plank ceilings, west country pictures and seafaring memorabilia, steps down to section with huge inglenook, another step to big side dining room, also a little snug area with woodburner and leather armchairs; background music; children and dogs welcome, small front courtyard, terrace with nice country views, sloping lawn and play area, camping opposite, open all day summer, closed Mon-Weds lunchtime in winter. *(P and J Shapley, John Coatsworth)*

DULOE   SX2358
Plough (01503) 262556

B3254 N of Looe; PL14 4PN Popular restaurant pub with three country-chic linked dining rooms all with woodburners, dark polished slate floors, a mix of pews and other seats, good fairly priced locally sourced food (must book weekends) including some imaginative cooking, also lunchtime sandwiches and snacks such as duck scotch eggs, well chosen reasonably priced wines, well kept St Austell Tribute, Sharps Doom Bar and local guests, friendly service; unobtrusive background music; children and dogs welcome, picnic-sets out by road, open all day in summer, all day Sun in winter. *(Paul Bonner)*

EDMONTON   SW9672
★**Quarryman** (01208) 816444

Off A39 just W of Wadebridge bypass; PL27 7JA Welcoming busy family-run pub adjoining small separately owned holiday courtyard complex; three-room beamed bar with interesting decorations including old sporting memorabilia, pubby food from shortish menu including good individual dishes such as sizzling steaks and portuguese fish stew, quick friendly service, well kept Otter, Skinners and two guests, seven wines by the glass, no mobile phones or background music; well behaved children and dogs allowed, disabled access (but upstairs lavatories), picnic-sets in front and courtyard behind, self-catering apartment, open all day. *(Pete Walker)*

FALMOUTH   SW8132
★**Chain Locker** (01326) 311085

Custom House Quay; TR11 3HH Busy old-fashioned place in fine spot by inner harbour with window tables and lots more seats outside, good selection of Sharps and Skinners ales, well priced generous food from sandwiches and baguettes to fresh local fish and interesting vegetarian choices (they also cater for smaller appetites), cheery young staff, nooks and crannies, bare boards and masses of nautical bric-a-brac, darts alley; background music, games machine; well behaved children and dogs welcome, self-catering accommodation, open all day. *(Simon J Barber, Comus and Sarah Elliott, Ken Parry, Ian Herdman)*

FALMOUTH   SW8132
Front (01326) 212168
Custom House Quay; TR11 3JT Bare-
boards drinkers' pub with good changing
selection of ales, some tapped from the cask,
also foreign beers and ciders/perries, friendly
knowledgeable staff, no food but can bring
your own (good fish and chip shop above),
mix of customers from students to beards;
seats outside, open all day. *(Mike and Eleanor
Anderson, Comus and Sarah Elliott, Phil and Jane
Villiers)*

FALMOUTH   SW8032
Seven Stars (01326) 312111
The Moor (centre); TR11 3QA Quirky
17th-c local, unchanging and unsmart (not
to everyone's taste), friendly atmosphere
and chatty regulars, no gimmicks, machines
or mobile phones, up to five well kept ales
tapped from the cask including Bass, Sharps
and Skinners, bar snacks (maybe oysters),
big key ring collection, quiet back snug;
corridor hatch serving roadside courtyard,
open all day. *(Anon)*

FLUSHING   SW8033
Seven Stars (01326) 374373
Trefusis Road; TR11 5TY Old-style
waterside pub with welcoming local
atmosphere, well kept ales and pubby food,
coal fire, separate dining room, darts and pool;
dogs welcome, pavement picnic-sets, great
views of Falmouth with foot-ferry across, open
all day. *(Mike and Eleanor Anderson)*

FOWEY   SX1251
Galleon (01726) 833014
*Fore Street; from centre follow car-ferry
signs; PL23 1AQ* Superb spot by harbour
and estuary, good beer range (local/national)
and decent choice of wines, well liked pubby
food from extensive reasonably priced menu,
friendly attentive service, modern nautical
décor and lots of solid pine, dining areas off,
Sun lunchtime jazz, live bands Fri evening;
pool, big-screen TV, free wi-fi; children
welcome, disabled facilities, attractive
extended waterside terrace and sheltered
courtyard with covered heated area, estuary-
view bedrooms, open all day. *(Mick and Moira
Brummell, Dave Webster, Sue Holland)*

FOWEY   SX1251
★ King of Prussia (01726) 833694
Town Quay; PL23 1AT Handsome
quayside building with roomy neatly kept
upstairs bar, bay windows looking over
harbour to Polruan, good welcoming service,
nice choice of enjoyable food from good crab
sandwiches and tapas boards up, well kept
St Austell ales and sensibly priced wines,
side restaurant; background music, pool, free
wi-fi; children and dogs welcome, six pleasant
bedrooms (all with views), open all day in
summer. *(John Edwell, Ian Herdman, Mr and
Mrs A H Young, B and M Kendall, Monica Shelley)*

FOWEY   SX1251
Lugger (01726) 833435
Fore Street; PL23 1AH Centrally
placed St Austell pub with unpretentious
bar and small back dining area, good
mix of locals and visitors (can get busy),
enjoyable food including local fish; children
welcome, pavement tables, open all day in
summer. *(Dave Webster, Sue Holland)*

FOWEY   SX1251
Safe Harbour (01726) 833379
Lostwithiel Street; PL23 1BP Welcoming
19th-c coaching inn set away from main
tourist part; lounge/dining area and lower-
level regulars' bar, good value home-made
food and well kept/priced St Austell ales, old
local prints, upstairs overflow dining room;
pool, darts, games machine; heated side
terrace, seven bedrooms and a self-catering
apartment, open all day till midnight.
(Dave Webster, Sue Holland, Ian Herdman)

FOWEY   SX1251
★ Ship (01726) 832230
Trafalgar Square; PL23 1AZ Bustling
local with generous helpings of good sensibly
priced food from sandwiches up, well kept
St Austell ales, log fire and banquettes in
tidy bar with lots of yachting prints and
nauticalia, newspapers, steps up to family
dining room with big stained-glass window,
pool/darts room; background music, sports
TV; dogs allowed, comfortably old-fashioned
bedrooms, some oak-panelled. *(Ian Herdman,
Mr and Mrs A H Young)*

GERRANS   SW8735
Royal Standard (01872) 580271
The Square; TR2 5EB Friendly little
local (a quieter alternative to the nearby
Plume of Feathers) with narrow doorways
linking carpeted rooms, up to three well
kept local ales, Sharp's cider and Skinners
lager, short choice of well chosen wines,
enjoyable pub food from sandwiches to
local fish, old photographs on white plaster
or black boarded walls, brass shell cases
and kitchen utensils, woodburner, lakeland
terrier called Millie; children welcome
away from bar, disabled access, sunny beer
garden, opposite interesting 15th-c church
(rebuilt in 19th c after fire). *(Chris and
Angela Buckell)*

GOLANT   SX1254
★ Fishermans Arms (01726) 832453
Fore Street (B3269); PL23 1LN Bustling
partly flagstoned small waterside local with
lovely views across River Fowey from front
bar and terrace, good value generous home-
made food including nice crab sandwiches
and seafood, efficient friendly service, up
to five well kept cornish ales (tasting trays
available), good wines by the glass, log fire,
interesting pictures; children and dogs
welcome, pleasant garden, open all day in

summer, all day Fri-Sun in winter.
(B and M Kendall)

GORRAN CHURCHTOWN SW9942
Barley Sheaf (01726) 843330
Follow Gorran Haven signs from Mevagissey; PL26 6HN Built in 1837 by local farmer and now owned and extensively refurbished by his great (x3) grandson; good home-made food including popular Sun lunch, well kept Sharps Doom Bar and guests, local cider, friendly staff, Tues quiz and some live music; children and dogs welcome, well tended sunny beer garden. *(Jeremy Whitehorn, Stephen and Judy Parish, Nick Lawless, Martin and Sue Radcliffe)*

GRAMPOUND SW9348
Dolphin (01726) 882435
A390 St Austell–Truro; TR2 4RR Friendly St Austell pub with their well kept ales and decent choice of wines, good generous pub food, two-level bar with black beams and some panelling, polished wood or carpeted floors, pubby furniture with a few high-backed settles, pictures of old Grampound, log fire; pool, Thurs quiz; children welcome, dogs in bar, wheelchair access from car park, beer garden, smokery opposite, handy for Trewithen Gardens, open all day Sat. *(Chris and Angela Buckell)*

GULVAL SW4831
Coldstreamer (01736) 362072
Centre of village by drinking fountain; TR18 3BB Welcoming place (sister pub to the Dolphin in Penzance) with good food including fresh Newlyn fish, a couple of well kept local ales and guests, traditional bar with woodburner, old photographs and traditional games, restaurant with modern pine furniture on wood floor, local artwork; children welcome, quiet pleasant village very handy for Trengwainton Garden (NT), comfortable bedrooms, open all day. *(Pete Walker)*

HARROWBARROW SX4069
Cross House (01579) 350482
Off A390 E of Callington; School Road – towards Metherell; PL17 8BQ Substantial stone building (former farmhouse) with spreading carpeted bar, some booth seating, cushioned wall seats and stools around pub tables, enjoyable reasonably priced home-made food, well kept St Austell ales and nice wines by the glass, friendly smiling service, open fire and woodburner, darts area, restaurant; children and dogs (in bar) welcome, disabled facilities, plenty of picnic-sets on good-sized lawn, play area, handy for Cotehele (NT), open all day. *(John and Nan Hurst)*

HELFORD SW7526
Shipwrights Arms (01326) 231235
Off B3293 SE of Helston, via Mawgan; TR12 6JX Thatched 18th-c pub by beautiful wooded creek, at its best at high tide, terraces making the most of the view, plenty of surrounding walks and summer foot-ferry from Helford Passage; run by local consortium and refurbished in simple contemporary style, woodburner, Sharps Doom Bar and a couple of cornish guest ales, good locally sourced food (booking advised) including fresh fish from daily changing menu, nice crab sandwiches using landlady's organic bread, friendly helpful young staff, occasional live music; children, dogs and muddy boots welcome, small car park (parking nearby may be tricky), pontoon mooring, open all day. *(Henry Fryer)*

HELSTON SW6527
★ Blue Anchor (01326) 562821
Coinagehall Street; TR13 8EL Many (not all) love this no-nonsense, highly individual, thatched 15th-c pub; quaint rooms off corridor, flagstones, stripped stone, low beams and well worn furniture, family room, traditional games and skittle alley, ancient back brewhouse still producing distinctive and very strong Spingo IPA, Middle and seasonals such as Bragget with honey and herbs, no food but can bring your own (good pasty shop close by), friendly local atmosphere; regular live music, Mon quiz; seats out behind (some under cover), four bedrooms in house next door, big breakfast, open all day. *(Phil and Jane Hodson)*

HESSENFORD SX3057
Copley Arms (01503) 240209
A387 Looe–Torpoint; PL11 3HJ 17th-c village pub with slightly old-fashioned feel, popular with families and passing tourists, enjoyable reasonably priced food from sandwiches to grills in linked carpeted areas, friendly service, well kept St Austell ales and nice choice of wines, variety of teas and coffee, log fires, tables in cosy booths, one part with sofas and easy chairs, big family room; background and some live music, Thurs quiz; dogs allowed in one area, a few roadside picnic-sets by small River Seaton, fenced play area, five bedrooms, open all day. *(Adrian Johnson)*

HOLYWELL SW7658
St Pirans (01637) 830205
Holywell Road; TR8 5PP Great location backing on to dunes and popular with holidaymakers, friendly helpful staff, well kept ales such as St Austell and Sharps, decent wines, enjoyable pub food with blackboard specials; children and dogs welcome, tables on large back terrace, open all day, but closed out of season. *(Alison Ball, Ian Walton)*

HOLYWELL SW7658
Treguth (01637) 830248
Signed from Cubert, SW of Newquay; TR8 5PP Ancient whitewashed stone and thatch pub near big beach, cosy low-beamed carpeted bar with big stone fireplace,

larger dining room at back, three real ales and enjoyable home-cooked food, friendly service; Weds quiz, pool; children and dogs welcome, handy for campsites and popular with holidaymakers, open all day weekends. *(Richard Stanfield)*

KINGSAND   SX4350
Devonport (01752) 822869
The Cleave; PL10 1NF Character pub with lovely bay views from front bar, three changing local ales and good choice of enjoyable well priced food, friendly service, scrubbed floorboards and Victorian décor, lots of ship photographs and bric-a-brac, mix of cast-iron-framed pub furniture with window seats and pine settles, log fire, back snug; dogs welcome, tables out by sea wall, good value bedrooms. *(Suzy Miller)*

LELANT   SW5436
Old Quay House (01736) 753445
Griggs Quay, Lelant Saltings; A3047/ B3301 S of village; TR27 6JG Large pub in great spot for bird sanctuary estuary; enjoyable home-made pub food including Sun carvery, Sharps and Skinners ales, dining area off wide divided open-plan bar, upstairs restaurant; children and dogs (in bar) welcome, garden and small roof terrace with views over saltings, play area, nine motel-type bedrooms, open all day. *(Anon)*

LELANT   SW5436
Watermill (01736) 757912
Lelant Downs; A3074 S; TR27 6LQ Mill-conversion family dining pub; working waterwheel behind with gearing in dark-beamed central bar opening into brighter airy front extension, upstairs evening (and Sun lunchtime) restaurant, Sharps Doom Bar, Skinners Betty Stogs and a guest, enjoyable food served by friendly staff; free wi-fi; dogs welcome, good-sized pretty streamside garden, open all day. *(Anon)*

LERRYN   SX1356
Ship (01208) 872374
Signed off A390 in Lostwithiel; Fore Street; PL22 0PT Lovely spot especially when tide's in, well kept local ales, farm cider, good wines (including country ones) and whiskies, sensibly priced food from traditional choices up, cheerful service, huge woodburner, adults-only attractive dining conservatory (booked quickly evenings and weekends), games room with pool; children welcome, dogs on leads (friendly resident black lab), picnic-sets and pretty play area outside, near famous stepping stones and three well signed waterside walks, decent bedrooms in adjoining building and self-catering cottages, open all day Fri-Sun. *(Anon)*

LIZARD   SW7012
Top House (01326) 290974
A3083; TR12 7NQ Neat clean pub with friendly staff and regulars, good local food from sandwiches and snacks up including fresh fish, children's meals and cream teas, well kept ales such as St Austell Tribute and Skinners Betty Stogs, lots of good local sea pictures, fine shipwreck relics and serpentine craftwork (note the handpumps), warm welcoming log fire; sheltered terrace, eight bedrooms in adjoining building (three with sea views), open all day in summer, all day weekends in winter. *(M P Mackenzie, Dave Webster, Sue Holland, Clifford Blakemore)*

LIZARD   SW7012
Witchball (01362) 290662
Lighthouse Road; TR12 7NJ Small friendly beamed pub popular with locals, good food including fresh fish and seafood, Sun carvery, ales such as Chough, St Austell and Skinners, cornish cider, cheerful helpful staff, Sat quiz; children and dogs welcome, terrace tables, open all day summer, closed winter lunchtimes Mon-Weds. *(Dave Webster, Sue Holland, Ian and Rose Lock)*

LOOE   SX2553
Olde Salutation (01503) 262784
Fore Street, East Looe; PL13 1AE Good welcoming bustle in big squareish slightly sloping beamed and tiled bar, reasonably priced straightforward food from notable crab sandwiches to Sun roasts, well kept Sharps Doom Bar, friendly service, red leatherette seats and neat tables, blazing fire in nice old-fashioned fireplace, lots of local fishing photographs, side snug with olde-worlde harbour mural, step down to simple family room; may be background music, no credit cards; dogs welcome, lots of hanging baskets, handy for coast path, forget about parking, open all day. *(George Atkinson)*

LUDGVAN   SW5033
★White Hart (01736) 740574
Off A30 Penzance–Hayle at Crowlas; TR20 8EY Appealing old village pub, friendly and welcoming, with well kept Sharps Doom Bar and a guest tapped from the cask, own summer cider and premium range of spirits, enjoyable blackboard food from pub standards up including good value Sun lunch, small unspoilt beamed rooms with wood and stone floors, nooks and crannies, woodburners, quiz first Weds of month; dogs welcome, beer garden and little decked area at back, interesting church next door, two bedrooms, open all day Fri-Sun. *(R and S Bentley)*

Half pints: by law, a pub should not charge more for half a pint than half the price of a full pint, unless it shows that half-pint price on its price list.

MARAZION   SW5130
Godolphin Arms (01736) 888510
West End; TR17 0EN Extensively
refurbished former coaching inn with
wonderful views across to St Michael's
Mount, light contemporary décor and modern
furnishings, good food from sandwiches and
sharing plates up, St Austell and Skinners
ales, lots of wines by the glass and good
coffee, helpful friendly staff; children
welcome, beachside terrace, ten stylish
bedrooms (most with sea view, some with
balconies), good breakfast, open all day
from 8am. *(Anon)*

MARAZION   SW5130
Kings Arms (01736) 710291
The Square; TR17 0AP Old one-bar pub
in small square, comfortable and welcoming
with warm woodburner, good well presented
food including local fish from regularly
changing menu, well kept St Austell ales,
considerate staff; children and dogs welcome,
picnic-sets out in front, open all day.
(Alan Johnson)

MAWNAN SMITH   SW7728
Red Lion (01326) 250026
*W of Falmouth, off former B3291
Penryn–Gweek; The Square; TR11 5EP*
Old thatched and beamed pub with cosy
series of dimly lit rooms including raftered
bar, enjoyable food from open-view kitchen,
good fresh fish and other daily specials,
quick friendly service, plenty of wines by
the glass and three well kept changing ales,
good coffee, daily papers, woodburner in
huge stone fireplace, dark woodwork, country
and marine pictures, plates and bric-a-brac;
background music, TV; children (away from
bar) and dogs welcome, disabled access,
picnic-sets outside, handy for Glendurgan
(NT) and Trebah Gardens, open all day.
(R Elliott)

MENHENIOT   SX2862
Golden Lion (01209) 860332
Top of village by reservoir; TR16 6NW
Tucked-away stone pub in nice spot by
Stithians Reservoir; fires in beamed bar and
snug, St Austell ales and good selection of
wines by the glass, enjoyable generous food
(all day weekends) from pub favourites up,
friendly staff, restaurant with lake view, folk
night third Sat of month; children and dogs
welcome, attractive garden with heated
shelter, good walks, camping, open (and
food) all day weekends. *(Mick and Moira
Brummell)*

MEVAGISSEY   SX0144
★ Fountain (01726) 842320
*Cliff Street, down alley by Post Office;
PL26 6QH* Popular low-beamed fishermen's
pub, slate floor, some stripped stone and
a welcoming coal fire, old local pictures,
piano, well kept St Austell ales, good food

at reasonable prices including local fish/
seafood (particularly good fish stew),
friendly staff, back bar with glass-topped pit,
small upstairs evening restaurant; children
and dogs welcome, pretty frontage with
picnic-sets, two bedrooms, open all day in
summer. *(Henry Fryer, Martin Lewis, Di and
Mike Gillam, Stephen and Judy Parish)*

MEVAGISSEY   SX0144
Ship (01726) 843324
Fore Street, near harbour; PL26 6UQ
16th-c pub with interesting alcove areas
in big open-plan bar, low beams and
flagstones, nautical décor, woodburner,
cheery uniformed staff, fairly priced pubby
food including good fresh fish, small helpings
available, St Austell ales kept well, back
pool table; games machines, background
and some live music; dogs allowed, children
welcome in two front rooms, five bedrooms,
open all day in summer. *(Anon)*

MINIONS   SX2671
Cheesewring (01579) 362321
Overlooking the Hurlers; PL14 5LE
Popular well run village pub useful for
Bodmin Moor walks, well kept ales including
Sharps and good choice of reasonably
priced home-made food, lots of brass and
ornaments, chatty locals; children and dogs
welcome, bedrooms, open all day. *(Anon)*

MITCHELL   SW8554
★ Plume of Feathers (01872)
510387/511125 *Off A30 Bodmin–
Redruth, by A3076 junction; take
southwards road then first right;
TR8 5AX* Relaxed well run 16th-c
coaching inn with several linked bar and
dining rooms, appealing contemporary
décor with local artwork on pastel walls,
stripped beams and standing timbers,
painted dados and two open fires, good
food including pub standards, Sharps,
Skinners and St Austell, several wines by
the glass, impressive dining conservatory;
background music; children (away from
bar) and dogs welcome, picnic-sets under
parasols in well planted garden areas,
comfortable stable-conversion bedrooms,
open all day from 8am. *(Bernard Stradling,
David Elfman, Pete Walker, R J Herd, Tom and
Jill Jones and others)*

MITHIAN   SW7450
★ Miners Arms (01872) 552375
Off B3285 E of Street Agnes; TR5 0QF
Cosy old stone-built pub with traditional
small rooms and passages, pubby furnishings
and open fires, fine old wall painting of
Elizabeth I in back bar, popular good
value food, Sharps and Skinners ales kept
well, friendly helpful staff, board games;
background music; children welcome, dogs in
some rooms, seats on sheltered front cobbled
forecourt, back terrace and in garden, open
all day. *(Anon)*

MULLION   SW6719
Old Inn (01326) 240240
*In small one-way street opposite church
– not down in the cove; TR12 7HN*
Thatched and beamed 16th-c pub with nice
home-made food including good value light
lunch menu, well kept St Austell ales and a
guest, decent wines, friendly obliging staff,
narrowish bar with linked eating areas,
lots of brasses, plates, clocks, nautical bits
and old wreck pictures, big inglenook; TV;
children and dogs welcome, picnic-sets
on terrace and in garden, five bedrooms,
open all day (till midnight Fri, Sat). *(Paul
Rampton, Julie Harding, Ian and Rose Lock)*

MYLOR BRIDGE   SW8036
Lemon Arms (01326) 373666
Lemon Hill; TR11 5NA Popular and
friendly traditional village pub, opened-up
bar area with stripped stone walls and
panelling, well kept St Austell ales, enjoyable
generously served food at fair prices (no
credit cards); children and dogs welcome,
wheelchair access with help, picnic-
sets on back terrace, good coastal walks
nearby. *(Anon)*

NEWLYN   SW4629
★**Tolcarne** (01736) 363074
Tolcarne Place; TR18 5PR Traditional
17th-c quayside pub redecorated under new
landlord/chef, very good food (not Mon) from
daily changing menu with much emphasis
on local fish/seafood, friendly efficient
service, St Austell Tribute, Skinners Betty
Stogs and maybe a local microbrew, live jazz
Sun lunchtime; children and dogs welcome,
terrace (harbour wall cuts off view), good
parking. *(Anon)*

NEWLYN EAST   SW8256
Pheasant (01872) 510237
Churchtown; TR8 5LJ Friendly traditional
village pub in quiet backstreet, enjoyable
reasonably priced food including popular Sun
carvery, Dartmoor and Sharps beers, good
service; not far from Trerice (NT). *(Stanley
and Annie Matthews)*

NEWQUAY   SW8061
Fort (01637) 875700
Fore Street; TR7 1HA Massive recently
built pub in magnificent setting high above
surfing beach and small harbour, decent
food all day from sandwiches, hot baguettes
and baked potatoes up, open-plan areas
well divided by balustrades and surviving
fragments of former harbourmaster's house,
good solid furnishings from country kitchen
to button-back settees, soft lighting, friendly
staff coping well at busy times, full St Austell
range, games part with two pool tables,

excellent indoor children's play area; great
views from long glass-walled side section
and sizeable garden with multi-level terrace
and further play areas, open all day. *(Alan
Johnson, Richard Stanfield)*

NEWQUAY   SW8061
Lewinnick Lodge (01637) 878117
*Pentire headland, off Pentire Road;
TR7 1NX* Modern flint-walled bar-
restaurant built into bluff above the sea
– big picture windows for the terrific views;
light and airy bar with wicker seating,
spreading dining areas with contemporary
furnishings on light oak flooring, popular
bistro-style food from shortish menu,
good service, three or four well kept ales
and several wines by the glass, pleasant
relaxed atmosphere even when busy;
children welcome, modern seats and tables
on terraces making the most of stunning
Atlantic views, ten bedrooms, open all
day; same management as the Plume of
Feathers in Mitchell. *(Peter Humble)*

PADSTOW   SW9175
★**Golden Lion** (01841) 532797
Lanadwell Street; PL28 8AN Old inn
dating from the 14th c, cheerful black-
beamed locals' bar and high-raftered back
lounge with plush banquettes, Sharps Doom
Bar, Skinners Betty Stogs and Tintagel Castle
Gold, reasonably priced simple bar lunches
including good crab sandwiches, evening
steaks and fresh fish, friendly staff, coal
fire and woodburner; pool in family area,
background music, sports TV; dogs welcome,
colourful floral displays at front, terrace
tables, three bedrooms, open all day. *(Anon)*

PADSTOW   SW9175
Harbour Inn (01841) 533148
Strand Street; PL28 8BU Attractive
pub set just back from the harbour and a
quieter alternative; long room with nautical
bric-a-brac, front area with comfy sofas,
woodburner, well kept St Austell ales,
enjoyable home-made food including daily
specials, good coffee, friendly helpful staff;
children and dogs welcome, open all day.
(Anon)

PADSTOW   SW9175
London (01841) 532554
Llanadwell Street; PL28 8AN Intimate
proper fishermen's local with lots of
pictures and nautical memorabilia, mix of
tables, chairs and built-in benches, friendly
ex-merchant navy landlord, half a dozen well
kept St Austell ales and decent choice of malt
whiskies, good value bar food including fresh
local fish, more evening choice, back dining
area (arrive early for a table), two log fires;
can get very busy, background and some live

We say if we know a pub allows dogs.

music; children and dogs welcome (resident boxer is Pixie), three refurbished bedrooms, open all day. *(Pete Walker, Tony Tollitt)*

PADSTOW SW9275
Old Custom House (01841) 532359
South Quay; PL28 8BL Large, bright and airy open-plan seaside bar, comfortable and well divided, with rustic décor and cosy corners, beams, exposed brickwork and bare boards, raised section, big family area and conservatory, good food choice from baguettes up, four local ales including St Austell, efficient service (they swipe your card if running a tab), adjoining fish restaurant; background and live music, TV, machines, pool; good spot by harbour, attractive sea-view bedrooms, open all day and can get very busy. *(Ted George, Brian and Anna Marsden)*

PELYNT SX2054
⋆ Jubilee (01503) 220312
B3359 NW of Looe; PL13 2JZ Popular early 17th-c beamed inn with wide range of locally sourced home-made food (best to book in season) from good sandwiches up including Sun roasts, well kept St Austell ales, good wines by the glass, friendly helpful young staff, spotless interior with interesting Queen Victoria mementoes (pub renamed in 1897 to celebrate her diamond jubilee), some handsome antique furnishings, log fire in big stone fireplace, separate bar with darts, pool and games machine; children and dogs welcome, disabled facilities, large terrace, 11 comfortable bedrooms, open all day weekends. *(Peter Thornton, Stanley and Annie Matthews)*

PENDOGGETT SX0279
Cornish Arms (01208) 880263
B3314; PL30 3HH Old beamed coaching inn with traditional oak settles on front bar's polished slate floor, Sharps Doom Bar and a couple of local guests, decent wines by the glass, enjoyable food and friendly helpful service, comfortably spaced tables in small carpeted dining room, proper back locals' bar with woodburner and games; provision for children, dogs welcome in bars, disabled access, terrace with distant sea view, bedrooms, open all day. *(R T and J C Moggridge)*

PENELEWEY SW8140
Punch Bowl & Ladle (01872) 862237
B3289; TR3 6QY Thatched dining pub in same small group as the Pandora at Mylor Bridge (see Main Entries); enjoyable home-made food from fairly traditional menu including good sandwiches, helpful chatty service, four St Austell ales, Healey's cider and good wine and whisky selection, black beams, some white-painted stone walls and oak panelling, big sofas and rustic bric-a-brac, steps down to lounge/dining area, restaurant; soft background music,

free wi-fi; children (away from bar) and dogs welcome, wheelchair access (not from small side terrace), handy for Trelissick Garden (NT), open all day. *(Paul Rampton, Julie Harding, Chris and Angela Buckell, Mick and Moira Brummell)*

PENTEWAN SX0147
Ship (01726) 842855
Just off B3273 St Austell–Mevagissey; West End; PL26 6BX 17th-c beamed pub opposite tiny village's harbour, comfortable and clean with bar, snug and lounge/dining area, lots of dark timbers, open fire, up to four well kept St Austell ales, Healey's cider, decent reasonably priced pub food including good fish and chips, Sun carvery, prompt service; background and some live music; children and dogs welcome, picnic-sets in small garden across road overlooking water, near good sandy beach and big caravan park, open all day summer, all day weekends winter (till 7pm Sun, closed Mon evening). *(Stephen Funnell, Brian and Anna Marsden)*

PENZANCE SW4730
Admiral Benbow (01736) 363448
Chapel Street; TR18 4AF Wonderfully quirky pub, full of atmosphere and packed with interesting nautical gear, friendly staff, good value above-average food including local fish, well kept ales such as Sharps, Skinners and St Austell, cosy corners, fire, downstairs restaurant in captain's cabin style, upper floor with pool, pleasant view from back room; children and dogs welcome, open all day in summer. *(Tom and Jill Jones)*

PENZANCE SW4730
Crown (01736) 351070
Victoria Square, Bread Street; TR18 2EP Friendly little backstreet corner local with neat bar and snug dining room, own-brewed Cornish Crown beers plus Otter, several wines by the glass, enjoyable good value home-made food (not Sun evening, Mon or Tues) chalked on blackboard, Mon acoustic music, Tues quiz, board games (beat the landlady at Snatch for a free pint); children and dogs welcome, seats outside, open all day. *(Anon)*

PENZANCE SW4729
⋆ Dolphin (01736) 364106
Quay Street, opposite harbour after swing-bridge; TR18 4BD Well run old pub (under same ownership as the Coldstreamer at Gulval), enjoyable good value food including fresh fish, up to four well kept St Austell ales and good wines by the glass, roomy bar on different levels, nautical memorabilia, three resident ghosts; pool and juke box; children and dogs welcome, pavement picnic-sets, two bedrooms (harbour views), no car park (public one not far away), handy for Scillies ferry, open (and food) all day. *(Mr and Mrs C F Turner, Pete Walker)*

PERRANARWORTHAL   SW7738
Norway (01872) 864241
A39 Truro–Penryn; TR3 7NU Large
beamed pub with half a dozen linked areas,
good choice of food including daily specials
and carvery (all day Sun, Tues lunchtime),
St Austell ales and several wines by the
glass, friendly service, open fires, panelling
and mix of furniture on slate flagstones,
restaurant; background music, free wi-fi;
children and dogs welcome, tables outside,
four bedrooms, open (and food) all day.
(M J Winterton)

PHILLEIGH   SW8739
★Roseland (01872) 580254
*Between A3078 and B3289, NE of St
Mawes just E of King Harry Ferry;
TR2 5NB* In a small hamlet and handy for
the King Harry Ferry and Trelissick Garden
(NT); two cosy black-beamed bar rooms,
one with flagstones, the other carpeted,
wheelbacks and built-in red cushioned seats,
old photographs and some giant beetles and
butterflies in glass cases, woodburner, tiny
lower area for locals, side restaurant too, well
kept Skinners Betty Stogs and own-brewed
Cornish Shag, nice wines, enjoyable food
including local fish/seafood, prompt friendly
service; children and dogs welcome, seats
on paved front terrace, open all day school
summer holidays. *(Mr and Mrs Richard
Osborne, Chris and Angela Buckell, R K Phillips,
Comus and Sarah Elliott, Phil and Jane Villiers
and others)*

PILLATON   SX3664
★Weary Friar (01579) 350238
*Off Callington–Landrake back road;
PL12 6QS* Tucked-away welcoming 12th-c
inn, good generously served food from wide-
ranging menu in bar and restaurant (best
to book), friendly helpful staff, well kept
St Austell and Sharps, farm cider, knocked-
together carpeted rooms, dark beams, copper
and brass, log fires in stone fireplaces; no
dogs inside; children welcome, tables out in
front and behind, church next door (Tues
evening bell-ringing), 14 bedrooms, open all
day. *(Ted George)*

POLGOOTH   SW9950
Polgooth Inn (01726) 74089
*Well signed off A390 W of St Austell;
Ricketts Lane; PL26 7DA* Big welcoming
country pub, separate servery for good
generous food from doorstep sandwiches
up (only roasts on Sun), children's helpings
and reasonable prices, well kept St Austell
ales and good wine choice, eating area
around sizeable bar with woodburner, good
big family room, live music; fills quickly in
summer (handy for nearby caravan parks);
dogs welcome, steps up to play area, tables
out on terrace and grass, pretty countryside,
open all day. *(P and J Shapley, Stephen
Funnell)*

POLKERRIS   SX0952
Rashleigh (01726) 813991
*Signposted off A3082 Fowey–St Austell;
PL24 2TL* Beachside pub with wonderful
terrace views towards the far side of
St Austell and Mevagissey bays; cosy beamed
bar with comfortable chairs around dark
wood tables, local photographs on stone
walls, log fire, ales such as Bath, Otter,
Timothy Taylors and Wooden Hand, two
farm ciders and several wines by the glass,
good choice of food from ciabattas to daily
specials, afternoon cream teas and snacks
too, sea-view restaurant; children and dogs
(in bar) welcome, good walks (local section
of the coast path is renowned for its striking
scenery), open all day. *(David and Sue
Atkinson, Paul Rampton, Julie Harding, Paul and
Karen Cornock, Dave Webster, Sue Holland, Di and
Mike Gillam, Ian Herdman and others)*

POLPERRO   SX2051
Crumplehorn Mill (01503) 272348
*Top of village near main car park;
PL13 2RJ* Converted mill and farmhouse
keeping beams, flagstones and some stripped
stone, snug lower bar leading to long main
room with cosy end eating area, well kept
cornish ales, wide choice of enjoyable
good value food from snacks to blackboard
specials (booking advised), friendly speedy
service, log fire; children welcome, outside
seating and working mill wheel, refurbished
bedrooms, self catering, open all day. *(Robert
Turnham)*

POLPERRO   SX2050
Three Pilchards (01503) 272233
Quay Road; PL13 2QZ Small low-beamed
local behind fish quay, good choice of
reasonably priced food all day from baguettes
to fresh fish, St Austell Tribute and Sharps
Doom Bar, efficient obliging service even
when busy, lots of black woodwork, dim
lighting, simple furnishings, open fire in big
stone fireplace; children and dogs welcome,
picnic-sets on upper terrace up steep steps,
open all day. *(Anon)*

POLRUAN   SX1250
Lugger (01726) 870007
*The Quay; back roads off A390 in
Lostwithiel, or foot-ferry from Fowey;
PL23 1PA* Popular and friendly waterside
pub recently refurbished under newish
management; steps up to beamed bar with
open fire and woodburner, restaurant on
upper level, good food from bar snacks
to fresh local fish, Sun carvery, well kept
St Austell ales; children, dogs and muddy
boots welcome, good local walks, limited
parking, open all day. *(Monica Shelley)*

PORT ISAAC   SW9980
★Golden Lion (01208) 880336
Fore Street; PL29 3RB 17th-c pub with
friendly local atmosphere in simply furnished

old rooms, bar and snug with open fire, window seats and balcony tables looking down on rocky harbour and lifeboat slip far below, upstairs restaurant, straightforward food including good local fish, St Austell ales, darts and dominoes; background music – live in cellar bar (open mainly weekends), games machine; children and dogs welcome, dramatic cliff walks, open all day. *(Anon)*

PORTHALLOW   SW7923
Five Pilchards (01326) 280256
SE of Helston; B3293 to St Keverne, then village signed; TR12 6PP Sturdy old-fashioned stone-built local in secluded cove right by shingle beach, lots of salvaged nautical gear, interesting shipwreck memorabilia and model boats, woodburner, cornish ales and enjoyable reasonably priced straightforward food including local fish, friendly chatty staff, conservatory; children and dogs welcome, seats out in sheltered yard, refurbished bedrooms, in winter closed Sun evening, Mon lunchtime, all day Tues. *(Henry Fryer, Fran Ward)*

PORTHLEVEN   SW6325
Atlantic (01326) 562439
Peverell Terrace; TR13 9DZ Friendly buzzy pub in great setting up above harbour, good value tasty food, real ales including Skinners and St Austell from boat-shaped counter, big open-plan lounge with well spaced seating and cosier alcoves, good log fire in granite fireplace, dining room with amazing trompe l'oeil murals; lovely bay views from front terrace, open all day. *(Simon Lindsey, Rose Rogers)*

PORTHLEVEN   SW6225
Harbour Inn (01326) 573876
Commercial Road; TR13 9JB Large neatly kept pub-hotel in outstanding harbourside setting, well organised friendly service, expansive lounge and bar with impressive dining area off, big public bar with panelling, well kept St Austell ales, good range of pubby food including catch of the day and nice pasties, carvery Wed lunchtime and Sun; quiet background music (live Sat), Thurs quiz, free wi-fi; children welcome, picnic-sets on big quayside terrace, 15 well equipped bedrooms, some with harbour view, good breakfast, open all day. *(Pat and Tony Martin, Tom and Jill Jones, Alison Ball, Ian Walton, M J Winterton)*

PORTSCATHO   SW8735
Plume of Feathers (01872) 580321
The Square; TR2 5HW Cheerful largely stripped-stone coastal village pub under newish management (some redecoration), well kept St Austell ales and good reasonably priced food, sea-related bric-a-brac and pictures in two comfortable linked areas, also small side bar and separate restaurant; background music, free wi-fi; children, dogs and muddy boots welcome, disabled access

(steps to restaurant and gents'), picnic-sets under awning, lovely coast walks, open all day in summer (other times if busy). *(Chris and Angela Buckell, Robert Watt)*

PRAZE AN BEEBLE   SW6335
St Aubyn Arms (01209) 831425
The Square; TR14 0JR Welcoming refurbished pub with two bars and contemporary restaurant, well kept Otter, St Austell and Skinners, enjoyable food with emphasis on local steaks, attentive friendly service, Tues quiz; background music; children and dogs welcome, picnic-sets in large attractive garden. *(Anon)*

ROSUDGEON   SW5529
Falmouth Packet (01736) 762240
A394; TR20 9QE Comfortably modernised old pub with bare-stone walls, slate/carpeted floors and open fire, good food using local produce (booking advised), own pickles, relishes etc for sale, well kept Penzance ales and guests, family run and good friendly service, conservatory; tables out at front and in garden, self-catering cottage, open all day Fri, till 7pm Sun. *(Anon)*

RUAN LANIHORNE   SW8942
Kings Head (01872) 501263
Village signed off A3078 St Mawes Road; TR2 5NX Country pub in quiet hamlet with interesting church nearby; relaxed small bar with log fire, Skinners and a guest, maybe farm cider, well liked food especially local fish, dining area to the right divided in two, lots of china cups hanging from ceiling joists, cabinet filled with old bottles, hunting prints and cartoons, separate restaurant to the left; background music; well behaved children allowed in dining areas, dogs in bar only, terrace across road and nice lower beer garden, walks along Fal estuary, closed Sun evening and Mon in winter. *(M Mossman, Martin Lewis, Barry Collett, R and S Bentley)*

ST DOMINICK   SX4067
Who'd Have Thought It
(01579) 350214 *Off A388 S of Callington; PL12 6TG* Large, comfortable and welcoming country pub under mother and daughter (chef) management, wide choice of enjoyable food from generous sandwiches to blackboard specials, well kept St Austell ales, decent wines, superb Tamar views especially from conservatory, cosily plush lounge areas with open fires; dogs allowed in public bar, garden tables, handy for Cotehele (NT). *(Peter Thornton, John Evans, Ted George)*

ST ISSEY   SW9271
Ring o' Bells (01841) 540251
A389 Wadebridge–Padstow; Churchtown; PL27 7QA Traditional slate-clad 18th-c village pub with open fire at one end of beamed bar, pool the other, well kept Courage Best, Sharps

Doom Bar and a guest, good choice of
wines and whiskies, friendly service,
enjoyable sensibly priced local food (own
vegetables and pork) in long narrow side
dining room, live folk first Sat of month;
can get packed in summer; children
and dogs welcome, decked courtyard,
hanging baskets and tubs, four bedrooms,
car park across road, open all day
weekends. *(Stephen Green)*

ST IVES   SW5140
Lifeboat (01736) 794123
Wharf Road; TR26 1LF Thriving family-
friendly beamed quayside pub, wide choice
of good value generously served pubby food,
well kept St Austell ales, spacious interior
with harbour-view tables and cosier corners,
nautical theme including lifeboat pictures,
friendly helpful staff, Sept music festival;
sports TV, fruit machine, no dogs; disabled
access/facilities, open (and food) all day.
(Anon)

ST IVES   SW5441
Pedn Olva (01736) 796222
The Warren; TR26 2EA Hotel not pub, but
has well kept reasonably priced St Austell
ales in roomy bar, panoramic views of sea
and Porthminster beach (especially from
tables on roof terrace), all-day bar food
and separate restaurant, good service;
comfortable bedrooms. *(Alan Johnson)*

ST IVES   SW5441
Queens (01736) 796468
High Street; TR26 1RR Late Georgian
inn with relaxed open-plan bar, mix of
chairs around scrubbed tables on wood
floor, some comfy leather armchairs, tartan
banquettes either side of Victorian fireplace,
wall of barometers, St Austell ales from
marble-topped counter, good interesting
food along with more standard pubby dishes,
friendly helpful staff; background and some
live music; children welcome, ten good
bedrooms. *(Anon)*

ST IVES   SW5140
★Sloop (01736) 796584
The Wharf; TR26 1LP Busy, low-beamed,
panelled and flagstoned harbourside pub
with bright St Ives School pictures and
attractive portrait drawings in front bar,
booth seating in back bar, good value food
from sandwiches and interesting baguettes
to lots of fresh local fish, quick friendly
service even though busy, ales including
Greene King Old Speckled Hen and Sharps
Doom Bar, good coffee; background
music, TV; children in eating area, a few
beach-view seats out on cobbles, open all
day (breakfast from 9am), cosy bedrooms,
handy for Tate gallery. *(Stanley and Annie
Matthews, Clifford Blakemore, Richard Tilbrook,
Ian and Rose Lock, Alan Johnson, Brian and
Anna Marsden and others)*

ST IVES   SW5140
Union (01736) 796486
Fore Street; TR26 1AB Popular and
friendly low-beamed local, roomy but cosy,
with good value food from sandwiches to
local fish, well kept Sharps Doom Bar and
Weston's Old Rosie cider, decent wines
and coffee, small hot fire, leather sofas
on carpet, dark woodwork and masses of
ship photographs; background music; dogs
welcome. *(Alan Johnson)*

ST JUST IN PENWITH   SW3731
Kings Arms (01736) 788545
Market Square; TR19 7HF Three
separate carpeted areas, granite walls and
beamed and boarded ceilings, open fire and
woodburner, shortish menu of good home-
made food (not Sun evening), helpful caring
service, well kept St Austell ales; background
music (live Sun), Weds quiz, TV; children and
dogs welcome, tables out in front.
(Alan Johnson)

ST JUST IN PENWITH   SW3731
★Star (01736) 788767
Fore Street; TR19 7LL Relaxed and
informal low-beamed two-room local, friendly
landlord, five well kept St Austell ales, no
food (bring your own lunchtime sandwiches
or pasties), dimly lit main bar with dark walls
covered in flags and photographs, coal fire,
sleepy pub cat, darts and euchre, nostalgic
juke box, live celtic music Mon, open mike
Thurs; tables in attractive backyard with
smokers' shelter, open all day. *(Alan Johnson)*

ST KEW   SX0276
★St Kew Inn (01208) 841259
*Village signposted from A39 NE of
Wadebridge; PL30 3HB* Popular grand-
looking 15th-c pub with neat beamed bar,
stone walls, winged high-backed settles
and more traditional furniture on tartan
carpeting, all sorts of jugs dotted about,
roaring log fire in stone fireplace, three
dining areas, St Austell beers from cask and
handpump, good choice of enjoyable well
presented food (not Sun evening in winter),
friendly attentive service, live music every
other Fri; children (away from bar) and dogs
welcome, pretty flowering tubs and baskets
outside, picnic-sets in garden over road, open
all day in summer. *(Chris and Val Ramstedt,
J D and A P, Edna Jones)*

ST MAWES   SW8433
Rising Sun (01326) 270233
The Square; TR2 5DJ Light and airy pub
across road from harbour wall; relaxed bar
on right with end woodburner, sea-view bow
window opposite, rugs on stripped wood, a
few dining tables, sizeable carpeted left-hand
bar with dark wood furniture, well prepared
tasty food including good fish and chips
served by friendly young staff, well kept
St Austell ales and nice wines by the glass,

wood-floored conservatory; background music; awkward wheelchair access, picnic-sets on sunny front terrace, comfortable bedrooms, open all day. *(Stanley and Annie Matthews, John and Sharon Hancock, Phil and Jane Villiers, Comus and Sarah Elliott)*

ST MAWES   SW8433
Victory (01326) 270324
Victory Hill; TR2 5DQ Popular pub tucked up from the harbour and still for sale; slate floor locals' bar on left, carpeted dining area to the right, more formal upstairs restaurant with balcony, well kept Otter, Sharps and Skinners, good food including plenty of local fish, log fires, friendly staff; background music, no wheelchair access; children welcome, one or two picnic-sets outside, two good value bedrooms, open all day. *(Henry Fryer, Barry Collett, Comus and Sarah Elliott)*

STITHIANS   SW7640
Cornish Arms (01872) 863445
Frogpool, not shown on many road maps but is NE of A393, ie opposite side to Stithians itself; TR4 8RP Unspoilt 18th-c village pub run by brother-and-sister team (he cooks), long beamed bar with fires either end, cosy snug, low-priced wholesome food (not Mon) from sandwiches and four types of ploughman's up, local ales and ciders; pool (free Tues), euchre; well behaved children and dogs welcome, closed Mon lunchtime. *(John Marsh)*

TIDEFORD   SX3459
Rod & Line (01752) 851323
Church Road; PL12 5HW Small old-fashioned local set back from road up steps, friendly lively atmosphere, Greene King Abbot and St Austell Tribute kept well, lots of fish from local market including good crab and scallops, angling theme with rods etc, low-bowed ceiling, settles, good log fire; children and dogs welcome, tables outside, open all day. *(Anon)*

TOWAN CROSS   SW4078
Victory (01209) 890359
Off B3277; TR4 8BN Comfortable roadside local with above-average good value food, four ales including Skinners, helpful staff; pool, euchre and Tues quiz; children and dogs welcome, beer garden, camping, handy for good uncrowded beaches, open all day. *(John Marsh)*

TREBARWITH   SX0586
Mill House (01840) 770200
Signed off B3263 and B3314 SE of Tintagel; PL34 0HD Former 18th-c corn mill wonderfully set in own steep woods above the sea; bar with white-painted beams, Delabole flagstones and mix of furniture including comfortable sofas, light and airy restaurant with pitched ceiling, enjoyable bar food and more upmarket evening restaurant menu, friendly staff, up to four local ales,

decent wines by the glass and good coffee; background and live music; children and dogs welcome, sunny terrace and streamside garden, eight bedrooms, open all day. *(Ryta Lyndley)*

TREBARWITH   SX0585
Port William (01840) 770230
Trebarwith Strand; PL34 0HB Lovely seaside setting with glorious views and sunsets, waterside picnic-sets across road and on covered terrace, maritime memorabilia and log fires inside, well kept St Austell ales, enjoyable food from sandwiches and baked potatoes to local lobster; background music; children and dogs welcome, eight well equipped comfortable bedrooms, open all day. *(D B Mines)*

TREBURLEY   SX3477
Springer Spaniel (01579) 370424
A388 Callington–Launceston; PL15 9NS Relaxed country dining pub under new management (same owners as the Treby Arms, Sparkwell – see Devon Main Entries); traditional bar with high-backed settle by woodburner, further cosy room set for dining and restaurant up some steps, very good attractively presented food from imaginative menu, Dartmoor Jail and three St Austell ales, eight wines by the glass, efficient aproned staff; background music, free wi-fi; children and dogs (in bar) welcome, picnic-sets on side terrace, closed Mon, otherwise open all day. *(Stanley and Annie Matthews, Giles and Annie Francis)*

TREEN   SW3923
★ Logan Rock (01736) 810495
Just off B3315 Penzance–Land's End; TR19 6LG Low-beamed traditional bar with well kept St Austell ales, tasty food from sandwiches and pasties up, good vegetarian options too, inglenook fire, small back snug with excellent cricket memorabilia (welcoming landlady eminent in county's cricket association), family room (no under-14s in bar); dogs welcome on leads (resident cat), pretty split-level garden behind with covered area, good coast walks including to Logan Rock itself, handy for Minack Theatre, open all day in season and can get very busy. *(David Crook)*

TREGADILLETT   SX2983
★ Eliot Arms (01566) 772051
Village signposted off A30 at junction with A395, W end of Launceston bypass; PL15 7EU Creeper-covered with series of small rooms, interesting collections including 72 antique clocks, 700 snuffs, hundreds of horsebrasses, barometers, old prints and shelves of books/china, fine mix of furniture on Delabole slate from high-backed settles and chaises longues to more modern seats, open fires, well kept St Austell Tribute, Wadworths 6X and a guest, good value generous food, friendly service; background

music, games machine, darts; children and dogs welcome, seats out front and back, lovely hanging baskets and tubs, two bedrooms, open all day. *(John and Bernadette Elliott, Peter Salmon)*

TREGONY   SW9244
Kings Arms   (01872) 530202
Fore Street (B3287); TR2 5RW Light and airy 16th-c coaching inn, long traditional main bar and two beamed and panelled front dining areas, St Austell ales, Healey's cider/perry, nice wines, good quality reasonably priced pub food using local produce, tea and coffee, welcoming prompt service and chatty landlord, two fireplaces, one with huge cornish range, pubby furniture on carpet or flagstones, old team photographs, back games room; well behaved children welcome, disabled access, tables in pleasant suntrap garden, charming village. *(Chris and Angela Buckell, Phil and Jane Hodson)*

TRURO   SW8244
Market   (01872) 277214
Lemon Quay; former Market Tavern; TR1 2LW Good tapas bar run by two spaniards, local ales and nice spanish wines, friendly service; seats outside (and seagulls). *(Comus and Sarah Elliott)*

TRURO   SW8244
★ Old Ale House   (01872) 271122
Quay Street; TR1 2HD Town-centre tap for Skinners brewery, five of their ales (samples offered) plus guests, some from casks behind bar, several wines by the glass including country ones, tasty bargain food such as sizzling skillets from open kitchen, good cheerful service, dimly lit beamed bar with engaging mix of furnishings, sawdust on the floor, beer mats on walls and ceiling, some interesting 1920s bric-a-brac, life-size cutout of Betty Stogs, daily newspapers, free monkey nuts, upstairs room with table football; juke box; children (away from bar) and dogs welcome, open all day. *(Alan Johnson, B and M Kendall)*

TRURO   SW8244
White Hart   (01872) 277294
New Bridge Street (aka Crab & Ale House); TR1 2AA Compact old city-centre pub with nautical theme, friendly landlord and locals, five well kept ales including Greene King Abbot, St Austell Tribute and Sharps Doom Bar, good helpings of enjoyable reasonably priced pub food; background music, disco Sat, quiz Thurs; children welcome, open all day. *(Stanley and Annie Matthews, Alan Johnson)*

TYWARDREATH   SX0854
New Inn   (01726) 813901
Off A3082; Fore Street; PL24 2QP Timeless 18th-c local, friendly and relaxed, with Bass tapped from the cask and St Austell ales on handpump, caring friendly

landlord, open fires; recently started doing food – reports please; children welcome, large secluded garden behind, nice village setting, open all day. *(Anon)*

VERYAN   SW9139
New Inn   (01872) 501362
Village signed off A3078; TR2 5QA Comfortable and homely one-bar beamed local, straightforward good value food from sandwiches up (can get busy in evenings so worth booking), St Austell ales, Healey's cider and decent wines by the glass, friendly attentive service, inglenook woodburner, polished brass and old pictures; background music; dogs and well behaved children welcome, wheelchair access with help, secluded beer garden behind, two bedrooms, interesting partly thatched village not far from nice beach, nearby parking unlikely in summer. *(M Mossman, Chris and Angela Buckell, R K Phillips, Richard Tilbrook)*

WATERGATE BAY   SW8464
Beach Hut   (01637) 860877
B3276 coast road N of Newquay; TR8 4AA Great views from bustling modern beach bar with customers of all ages, surfing photographs on planked walls, cushioned wicker and cane armchairs around green and orange tables, weathered stripped-wood floor, unusual sloping bleached-board ceiling, big windows and doors opening to glass-fronted deck looking across sand to the sea, simpler end room, three real ales including Skinners, decent wines by the glass and lots of coffees and teas, good modern food served by friendly young staff; background music; dogs welcome in bar, easy wheelchair access, open 8.30am-11pm, 10.30am-5pm in winter. *(Chris and Val Ramstedt, Jason Caulkin)*

WATERGATE BAY   SW8464
Phoenix   (01637) 860353
Trevarrian Hill; TR8 4AB Popular surfers' haunt with great coast and sunset views from open balcony, enjoyable food including burgers and pizzas in upstairs dining room, downstairs bar with well kept St Austell ales and decent wines, sensible prices and good friendly service; live music, TV and pool; well behaved children and dogs welcome, disabled facilities, plenty of outside seating, new bedrooms, open all day weekends. *(Anon)*

WENDRON   SW6731
New Inn   (01326) 572683
B3297; TR13 0EA Friendly little 18th-c granite-built country pub, up to four well kept changing ales and good reasonably priced food cooked by landlady; children and dogs welcome, garden behind with valley views, closed Mon lunchtime. *(Anon)*

ZELAH   SW8151
Hawkins Arms   (01872) 540339
A30; TR4 9HU Homely 18th-c stone-built beamed local, well kept Tintagel Castle Gold

and one or more guests, tasty well presented food from sandwiches to blackboard specials, nice coffee, friendly landlord and staff, copper and brass in bar and dining room, woodburner in stone fireplace; children and dogs welcome, back and side terraces. *(Stanley and Annie Matthews)*

ZENNOR ☆ Tinners Arms SW4538 (01736) 796927

B3306 W of St Ives; TR26 3BY Friendly welcome and good food from ploughman's with three cornish cheeses to fresh local fish, long unspoilt bar with flagstones, granite, stripped pine and real fires each end, back dining room, well kept St Austell and Sharps ales, farm cider, sensibly priced wines and decent coffee, quick service even when busy, nice mix of locals and visitors, Thurs folk night; children, muddy boots and dogs welcome, tables in small suntrap courtyard, lovely peaceful windswept setting near coast path and by church with 15th-c carved mermaid bench, bedrooms in building next door, open all day. *(David and Sue Atkinson, Richard Tilbrook, Pete Walker)*

ISLES OF SCILLY

ST AGNES ☆ Turks Head SV8808 (01720) 422434

The Quay; TR22 0PL One of the UK's most beautifully placed pubs, idyllic sea and island views from garden terrace, can get very busy on fine days, good food from pasties to popular fresh seafood (best to get there early), well kept ales such as Skinners Betty Stogs, proper cider, friendly licensees and good cheerful service; children and dogs welcome, closed in winter, otherwise open all day. *(Michael Butler, Stephen Shepherd)*

ST MARY'S ☆ Atlantic Inn SV9010 (01720) 422323

The Strand; next to but independent from Atlantic Hotel; TR21 0HY Spreading and hospitable dark bar with well kept St Austell ales, good range of food including daily specials, sea-view restaurant, low beams, hanging boat and other nauticalia, mix of locals and tourists – busy evenings, quieter on sunny lunchtimes; darts, pool, games machines, background and live music, Thurs quiz; nice raised verandah with wide views over harbour, good bedrooms in adjacent hotel. *(Michael Butler, Neil and Anita Christopher, Stephen Shepherd)*

ST MARY'S Mermaid SV9010 (01720) 422701

The Bank; TR21 0HY Splendid picture-window views across town beach and harbour from back restaurant extension, unpretentious dimly lit bar with lots of seafaring relics and ceiling flags, stone floor and rough timber, woodburner, steps down to second bar with tiled floor, boat counter and another woodburner, large helpings of enjoyable well priced food including children's choices, Sun carvery, well kept Ales of Scilly, Sharps and Skinners; background music, pool; children and dogs (in bar) welcome, packed Weds and Fri when the gigs race, open all day. *(Michael Butler)*

ST MARY'S Old Town Inn SV9110 (01720) 422301

Old Town; TR21 0NN Nice local feel in welcoming light bar and big back dining area, wood floors and panelling, enjoyable food (not Mon-Weds in winter) cooked by landlady including good pizzas, well kept Ales of Scilly, Sharps Doom Bar and guests, monthly folk club; pool and darts; children and dogs welcome, tables in tidy garden behind, three courtyard bedrooms, handy for airport, open all day in summer (from 5pm weekdays, all day weekends in winter). *(Anon)*

TRESCO ☆ New Inn SV8815 (01720) 423006

New Grimsby; TR24 0QG Handy for ferries and close to the famous gardens; main bar with comfortable old sofas, banquettes, planked partition seating and farmhouse tables and chairs, a few standing timbers, boat pictures, collection of old telescopes and large model yacht, pavilion extension has cheerful yellow walls and plenty of seats on blue-painted floors, Ales of Scilly and Skinners, a dozen good wines by the glass, quite a choice of spirits and several coffees, enjoyable food including daily specials; background music, board games, darts and pool; children and dogs (in bar) welcome, seats on flower-filled sea-view terrace, bedrooms, open all day in summer. *(David and Katharine Cooke, Bernard Stradling, R J Herd and others)*

Cumbria

AMBLESIDE
NY3704   Map 9

Golden Rule

Smithy Brow; follow Kirkstone Pass signpost from A591 on N side of town; LA22 9AS

Simple town local with a cosy, relaxed atmosphere, and real ales

This no-frills local doesn't change at all, which is how its regular customers like it; but there's a warm welcome too for walkers and their dogs after a day on the fells. The bar area has built-in wall seats around cast-iron-framed tables (one with a local map set into its top), horsebrasses on black beams, assorted pictures on the walls, a welcoming winter fire and a relaxed atmosphere. Robinsons 1892, Dizzy Blonde, Double Hop, Hannibals Nectar, Hartleys Cumbria Way, Hartleys XB and Hatters Dark Mild on handpump and Weston's cider. A brass measuring rule hangs above the bar (hence the pub's name). There's also a back room with TV (not much used), a room on the left with darts and a games machine, and another room, down a couple of steps on the right, with lots of seating. The backyard has benches and a covered heated area, and the window boxes are especially colourful. There's no car park.

There might be scotch eggs and pies but they tend to run out fast, so don't assume you'll be able to get something to eat.

Robinsons ~ Tenant John Lockley ~ Real ale ~ No credit cards ~ (015394) 32257 ~ Open 11am-midnight ~ Children welcome away from bar and must leave by 9pm ~ Dogs welcome ~ Wi-fi ~ www.goldenrule-ambleside.co.uk *Recommended by G Jennings, Chris Johnson, Mike and Eleanor Anderson*

AMBLESIDE
NY3703   Map 9

Wateredge Inn

Borrans Road, off A591; LA22 0EP

Family-run inn in beautiful Lake Windermere spot, plenty of room both inside and out, six ales on handpump and enjoyable all-day food; comfortable bedrooms

The modernised bar here – originally two 17th-c cottages – has splendid views through big windows looking over the sizeable garden that runs down to Lake Windermere. There's an easy-going, bustling atmosphere, a wide mix of customers, leather tub chairs around wooden tables on flagstones and several different areas leading off with similar furniture, exposed stone or wood-panelled walls and interesting old photographs and paintings. A cosy and much favoured room has beams and timbering, sofas, armchairs and an open fire. The six real ales on handpump served by friendly, cheerful staff come from breweries such as Barngates, Cumberland, Jennings, Theakstons and Tirril and they have lots of wines by the glass; quite a choice of coffees too. Background music and TV. Plenty of seats outside, and their own moorings. Many of the stylish and comfortable bedrooms have water views.

Using local, seasonal produce and offering some food all day, the popular dishes include lunchtime sandwiches, chicken liver pâté with cumberland sauce, ploughman's platter, baby pork ribs with a sweet chilli glaze, sausage with onion and red wine gravy, pea and mint risotto, free-range chicken curry, a pie of the day, and puddings such as chocolate fudge cake and lemon and lime cheesecake. *Benchmark main dish: tempura-battered fresh haddock and chips £12.50. Two-course evening meal £18.40.*

Free house ~ Licensee Derek Cowap ~ Real ale ~ (015394) 32332 ~ Open 11-11 ~ Bar food 12-9.30 ~ Children welcome ~ Dogs allowed in bar and bedrooms ~ Wi-fi ~ Singer Fri evening ~ Bedrooms: £55/£104 ~ www.wateredgehotel.co.uk
Recommended by Ruth May, Caroline Prescott, Comus and Sarah Elliott

BASSENTHWAITE LAKE

NY1930 Map 9

Pheasant ★ ⊙ ⅂ ⇔

Follow Pheasant Inn sign at N end of dual carriageway stretch of A66 by Bassenthwaite Lake; CA13 9YE

Delightful, old-fashioned bar in smart hotel, with enjoyable bar food and a fine range of drinks; comfortable bedrooms

It's still a surprise for newcomers to find this quite unchanging and charming little bar of proper character at the heart of a rather smart and civilised hotel. Nicely old-fashioned and much used by chatty locals, it has mellow polished walls, cushioned oak settles, rush-seat chairs and library seats, and hunting prints and photographs. Coniston Bluebird, Cumberland Corby Ale and Eden Dark Knight on handpump, a dozen good wines by the glass, over 60 malt whiskies and several gins and vodkas, all served by friendly, knowledgeable staff. There's a front bistro, a formal back restaurant overlooking the garden and several comfortable lounges with log fires, beautiful flower arrangements, fine parquet flooring, antiques and plants. The garden has seats and tables and is surrounded by attractive woodland; there are plenty of walks in all directions.

You can eat in the bar, bistro or lounges at lunchtime, and in the bistro and restaurant only in the evening: lunchtime open sandwiches, potted shrimps on toast, chicken liver pâté with red onion marmalade, guinea fowl with cep butter stuffing and creamed brussels sprouts, lemon sole with caper and parsley brown butter, chicken, leek and mushroom pie, daily specials, and puddings such as glazed apple tart with chantilly cream and sticky toffee pudding; they also offer a two- and three-course set lunch. *Benchmark main dish: beer-battered haddock and triple-cooked chips £13.50. Two-course evening meal £19.00.*

Free house ~ Licensee Matthew Wylie ~ Real ale ~ (017687) 76234 ~ Open 11.30-11; 12-11 Sun ~ Bar food 12-2.30, 6-9.30 ~ Restaurant ~ Children over 8 only ~ Dogs allowed in bar and bedrooms ~ Bedrooms: £95/£110 ~ www.the-pheasant.co.uk
Recommended by Colin McLachlan, Hugh Roberts, Martin Day, Hilary De Lyon and Martin Webster

---

Bedroom prices are for high summer. Even then you may get reductions for more than one night, or (outside tourist areas) weekends. Winter special rates are common, and many inns cut bedroom prices if you have a full evening meal.

BOWLAND BRIDGE
Hare & Hounds 🌟 ⊘ ♀ 🛏

SD4189   Map 9

Signed from A5074; LA11 6NN

17th-c inn in quiet spot with a friendly, cheerful landlady, real ales, popular food and fine views; comfortable bedrooms

Away from the crowds and in a peaceful location, this handsome 17th-c former coaching inn is run by exceptionally friendly people. There's a little bar with a log fire, daily papers to read and high chairs by the wooden counter where they serve Hare of the Dog (named for the pub by Tirril) and guests such as Coniston Bluebird and Hesket Newmarket Haystacks on handpump, a farm cider from half a mile away, and a dozen wines by the glass. Leading off here, other rooms are appealingly furnished with a mix of interesting dining chairs around all sorts of tables on black slate or old pine-boarded floors, numerous hunting prints on painted or stripped-stone walls, a candlelit moroccan-style lantern in a fireplace with neatly stacked logs to one side, and a relaxed atmosphere; background music and board games. The collie is called Murphy. There are teak tables and chairs under parasols on the front terrace, with more seats in the spacious side garden and fine valley views. The comfortable bedrooms make this a good base for the area – Lake Windermere is just three miles away.

 Good, enjoyable food includes lunchtime sandwiches, twice-baked cheese soufflé with creamy chive sauce, smoked mackerel and celeriac pâté, lamb hotpot topped with dauphinoise potatoes, beer-battered haddock and chips, spiced potato rösti with roasted mixed vegetable ratatouille, burger of the day with cheese, dill pickle and chips, bass with basil pesto cream, and puddings such as chocolate terrine with raspberry coulis and sticky ginger pudding. *Benchmark main dish: steak in ale pie £11.75. Two-course evening meal £18.00.*

Free house ~ Licensee Kerry Parsons ~ Real ale ~ (015395) 68333 ~ Open 12-11 (10.30 Sun) ~ Bar food 12-2, 6-9; all day weekends ~ Children welcome ~ Dogs welcome ~ Wi-fi ~ Bedrooms: /£85 ~ www.hareandhoundsbowlandbridge.co.uk *Recommended by R J Herd, David Heath, Michael Doswell, David Jackman*

BOWNESS-ON-WINDERMERE
Hole in t' Wall ◖

SD4096   Map 9

Fallbarrow Road, off St Martins Parade; LA23 3DH

Lively and unchanging town local with popular ales and friendly staff

Full of interest and character, this is the sort of place where both locals and visitors mingle quite happily – the friendly licensees offer a warm welcome to all. It's the town's oldest pub and the split-level rooms have beams, stripped stone and flagstones, lots of country knick-knacks and old pictures, and a splendid log fire beneath a vast slate mantelpiece; the upper room has some noteworthy plasterwork. Robinsons Dizzy Blonde, Hannibals Nectar, Hartleys XB and Unicorn on handpump and 20 malt whiskies; juke box in the bottom bar. The small flagstoned front courtyard has sheltered picnic-sets and outdoor heaters.

🍴 Bar food includes pâté, fish pie, curries of the day, scampi and chips, and puddings such as chocolate sponge and sticky toffee pudding. *Benchmark main dish: beef in Guinness pie £9.95. Two-course evening meal £16.00.*

Robinsons ~ Tenant Susan Burnet ~ Real ale ~ (015394) 43488 ~ Open 11-11 (11.30 Fri, Sat); 12-11 Sun ~ Bar food 12-2.30, 6-8.30; 12-8 Fri, Sat; 12-5 Sun ~

Children welcome ~ Live music Fri evening, Sun 12-4.30 ~
www.newhallinnbownessonwindermere.robinsonsbrewery.com *Recommended by Roger and Donna Huggins*

BRIGSTEER   SD4889   Map 9
Wheatsheaf ♀
Off Brigsteer Brow; LA8 8AN

Newly refurbished inn surrounded by pretty countryside, with interestingly furnished and decorated rooms, a good choice of food and drink, and seats outside; luxury bunkhouse bedrooms

Reopened after a careful and thoughtful refurbishment, this is a place of proper character. There are various rooms and cosy corners for both eating and drinking, and the atmosphere is friendly and relaxed. The bar has a two-way log fire, carved wooden stools against the counter and Hawkshead Bitter, Lancaster Celtic Rose and Thwaites Lancaster Bomber and Wainwright on handpump, 16 wines by the glass and eight malt whiskies. Throughout, an appealing variety of cushioned dining chairs, carved and boxed settles and window seats are set around an array of tables on either flagstones or floorboards, walls with pale-painted woodwork or wallpaper are hung with animal and bird sketches, cartoons and interesting clock faces, and the lighting is both old-fashioned and contemporary. Outside, there are seats and tables along the front of the building and picnic-sets on raised terracing. Their Lumley Fee luxury bunkhouse has five ensuite rooms and fine country views; breakfasts are hearty.

 As well as sandwiches and nibbles, the tasty food includes prawn cocktail, chicken liver pâté with seasonal chutney, sharing boards, butternut squash and sage risotto, pizzas and flatbreads with several toppings, cumberland sausages with apple and grain mustard mash and gravy, a pie of the day, beer-battered fresh haddock and chips, and puddings such as lemon posset with raspberry coulis and sticky toffee pudding. *Benchmark main dish: slow-cooked brisket of beef £13.50. Two-course evening meal £17.50.*

Individual Inns ~ Managers Nicki Higgs and Tom Roberts ~ Real ale ·· (015395) 68938 ~ Open 10am-11pm ~ Bar food 10-9; 12-8 Sun ~ Restaurant ~ Children welcome ~ Dogs allowed in bar ~ Wi-fi ~ Bedrooms: /£70 ~ www.thewheatsheafbrigsteer.co.uk
Recommended by Ray and Winifred Halliday, Peter Andrews

BROUGHTON MILLS   SD2190   Map 9
Blacksmiths Arms ⓞ
Off A593 N of Broughton-in-Furness; LA20 6AX

Friendly little pub with rewarding food, local beers and open fires; fine surrounding walks

After a day on the fells, the thought of the roaring open fires and enjoyable food in this charming little pub is most heart-warming. The four small bars have warm log fires, a relaxed, friendly atmosphere and are simply but attractively decorated with straightforward chairs and tables on ancient slate floors. Barngates Cracker, Hawkshead Bitter and Tirril Nameless Ale on handpump, ten wines by the glass and summer farm cider; darts, board games and dominoes. The hanging baskets and tubs of flowers in front of the building are very pretty in summer, and there are seats and tables under parasols on the back terrace.

The highly thought-of food includes lunchtime sandwiches, confit of shredded duck salad with hoisin sauce, honey-roast ham with poached egg, cumberland sausage with black pudding and red onion gravy, wild mushroom and parmesan risotto with truffle oil, burger with crispy pancetta, cheese and chips, pork fillet wrapped in parma ham with chorizo and chickpea casserole, and puddings such as lime and ginger crème brûlée and dark chocolate brownie with chocolate sauce. *Benchmark main dish: slow-braised lamb shoulder with mint gravy and dauphinoise potatoes £13.95. Two-course evening meal £18.00.*

Free house ~ Licensees Mike and Sophie Lane ~ Real ale ~ (01229) 716824 ~ Open 12-2.30, 5-11; 12-11 Sat, Sun; closed Mon lunchtime ~ Bar food 12-2, 6-9; not Mon ~ Restaurant ~ Children welcome ~ Dogs welcome ~ www.theblacksmithsarms.com
Recommended by Tina and David Woods-Taylor

CARLETON
NY5329 Map 9

Cross Keys ◀
A686, off A66 roundabout at Penrith; CA11 8TP

Friendly refurbished pub with several connected seating areas, real ales and popular food

With the surrounding countryside enjoyed by walkers, cyclists and nature lovers, this well run pub is always deservedly busy. The beamed main bar has a friendly, bustling atmosphere, pubby tables and chairs on light wooden floorboards, modern metal wall lights and pictures on bare stone walls, and Tirril 1823 and a guest such as Timothy Taylors Landlord on handpump. Steps lead down to a small area with high bar stools around a high drinking table and then upstairs to the restaurant: a light, airy room with big windows, large wrought-iron candelabras hanging from the vaulted ceiling, solid pale wooden tables and chairs, and doors to a verandah. At the far end of the main bar, there's yet another couple of small connected bar rooms with darts, games machine, pool, juke box and dominoes; TV and background music. There are fell views from the garden. This is under the same ownership as the Highland Drove in Great Salkeld.

Popular food includes warm baguettes and sandwiches, chicken liver pâté with onion and apricot chutney, prawn cocktail, sharing platters, beer-battered haddock and chips, wild mushroom pasta, cumberland sausage with mash, chicken wrapped in bacon with barbecue sauce, and puddings such as chocolate brownie with chocolate sauce and rhubarb and ginger crème brûlée. *Benchmark main dish: steak in ale pie £10.95. Two-course evening meal £16.50.*

Free house ~ Licensee Paul Newton ~ Real ale ~ (01768) 865588 ~ Open 12-3, 5-midnight; 12-1am Sat; 12-midnight Sun ~ Bar food 12-2.30, 6 (5.30 Fri, Sat)-9 (8.30 Sun) ~ Restaurant ~ Children welcome ~ Dogs allowed in bar ~ Wi-fi ~ www.kyloes.co.uk *Recommended by Gregg Davies, Comus and Sarah Elliott, Richard J Holloway, Kim Skuse*

CARTMEL
SD3778 Map 7

Kings Arms ◀

The Square; LA11 6QB

Bustling village pub with five real ales and well liked food

Right in the middle of an historic village, this 18th-c former coaching inn has seats and picnic-sets out in front facing the lovely square. Inside, the cosy bars have beams, open log fires, flagstones and wooden floorboards and an attractive range of seats, from nice old wooden or leather and brass-studded dining chairs around a mix of wooden tables, to comfortable leather armchairs. Bass and Hawkshead Bitter, Brodies Prime, Lakeland Gold and Windermere Pale on handpump served by friendly staff. There's a notable priory church and good surrounding walks.

🍴 Attractively presented, the good food includes sandwiches, mussels in white wine and cream, smoked haddock fishcakes with thai cucumber salad, game sausages with mash, slow-braised beef in ale, vegetarian tagine, grilled loin of cod with parsley mash, smoked bacon and peas, and puddings such as white chocolate panna cotta and sticky toffee pudding; they also offer a two-course menu (Sun-Thurs). *Benchmark main dish: asian platter £14.95. Two-course evening meal £18.00.*

Enterprise ~ Lease Karen Lyons ~ Real ale ~ (015395) 33246 ~ Open 10am-midnight (1am Fri, Sat) ~ Bar food 12-10 ~ Restaurant ~ Children welcome ~ Dogs welcome ~ Wi-fi ~ Live bands Fri and Sat evenings ~ www.thekingsarmscartmel.com
Recommended by Pauline Fellows and Simon Robbins, Adrian Johnson

CARTMEL FELL
Masons Arms 🏵️ 🍷 🍺

SD4189   Map 9

Strawberry Bank, a few miles S of Windermere between A592 and A5074; perhaps the simplest way of finding the pub is to go uphill W from Bowland Bridge (which is signposted off A5074) towards Newby Bridge and keep right, then left at the staggered crossroads – it's then on your right, below Gummer's How; OS Sheet 97 map reference 413895; LA11 6NW

Stunning views, beamed bar with plenty of character, interesting food and real ales plus many foreign bottled beers; self-catering cottages and apartments

As this particularly well run inn is so popular all year round, you'll need to book a table in advance if you want to eat. Whatever the season, you can enjoy stunning views over the Winster Valley to the woods below Whitbarrow Scar from windows in the pub, and from the rustic benches and tables on the heated terrace. The main bar has plenty of character, with low black beams in the bowed ceiling, and country chairs and plain wooden tables on polished flagstones. A small lounge has oak tables and settles to match its fine Jacobean panelling. There's also a plain little room beyond the serving counter with pictures and a fire in an open range, a family room with the atmosphere of an old parlour, and an upstairs dining room; background music and board games. Cumbrian Legendary Loweswater Gold, Hawkshead Bitter, and Thwaites Nutty Black and Wainwright on handpump, quite a few foreign bottled beers, 12 wines by the glass, ten malt whiskies and farm cider; service is friendly and helpful. The stylish and comfortable self-catering cottages and apartments also have fine views.

⭐ Highly enjoyable food includes lunchtime sandwiches, twice-baked goats cheese soufflé with pickled pears, country pork pâté with mustard pickle, a pie of the day, spiced root vegetable, chickpea and lentil casserole with herb dumplings, cumberland sausage ring with apple and cider, smoked haddock and scampi fishcakes with creamy chive sauce, and puddings such as sticky toffee pudding and chocolate torte. *Benchmark main dish: battered fresh haddock and chips £12.95. Two-course evening meal £17.50.*

Individual Inns ~ Managers John and Diane Taylor ~ Real ale ~ (015395) 68486 ~ Open 11-11; 12-10.30 Sun ~ Bar food 12-2.30, 6-9; 12-9 weekends and in summer ~ Restaurant ~ Children welcome ~ Dogs allowed in bedrooms ~ Wi-fi ~ www.strawberrybank.com
Recommended by Tina and David Woods-Taylor, Mr and Mrs P R Thomas, Pauline Fellows and Simon Robbins, Roger Fox, Adrian Johnson, Ray and Winifred Halliday, Christian Mole

CLIFTON

NY5326 Map 9

George & Dragon 🔘 ⚫ 🍷 🛏

A6; near M6 junction 40; CA10 2ER

Former coaching inn with attractive bars and sizeable restaurant, local ales, well chosen wines, imaginative food and seats outside; smart bedrooms

---

For a civilised break from the nearby M6, this carefully restored 18th-c inn is just perfect. There's a relaxed reception room with leather chairs around a low table in front of an open fire, bright rugs on flagstones, a table in a private nook to one side of the reception desk (just right for a group of six) and a comfortable bed for Porter, the pub's patterdale terrier. Through some wrought-iron gates is the recently redecorated main bar area, with additional cheerful rugs on flagstones, assorted wooden farmhouse chairs and tables, grey panelling topped with yellow-painted walls, photographs of the Lowther Estate and of the family with hunting dogs, various sheep and fell pictures and some high bar stools by the panelled bar counter. Cumberland Corby Blonde, Eden Gold and Hawkshead Bitter on handpump, 16 wines by the glass from a well chosen list and home-made soft drinks. An additional room with another open fire is similarly furnished. The sizeable restaurant to the left of the entrance consists of four open-plan rooms: plenty of old pews and church chairs around tables set for dining, a woodburning stove and a contemporary open kitchen. Outside, there are tables on the decoratively paved front area and in a high-walled enclosed courtyard; there's also a herb garden. Bedrooms are stylish and comfortable and breakfasts are first class.

 Using produce reared and grown on the Lowther Estate to which this inn belongs, the accomplished cooking from an interesting menu includes a bap of the day, eggs benedict, twice-baked cheese soufflé with white wine and chive sauce, butternut squash, sage and brown butter risotto with a poached egg, a pie of the day, venison casserole, monkfish with pak choi dressing, and puddings such as baked alaska with lemon meringue ice-cream and apple and treacle toffee crumble. *Benchmark main dish: Estate burger with chips £12.95. Two-course evening meal £20.50.*

Free house ~ Licensee Charles Lowther ~ Real ale ~ (01768) 865381 ~ Open 12-midnight ~ Bar food 12-2.30, 6-9 ~ Restaurant ~ Children welcome ~ Dogs allowed in bar and bedrooms ~ Wi-fi ~ Regular live band ~ Bedrooms: £79/£95 ~ www.georgeanddragonclifton.co.uk *Recommended by Chris Hoyer Millar, Pat and Stewart Gordon, Steve Whalley, David and Katharine Cooke, John and Eleanor Holdsworth, Kim Skuse, David Heath*

CONISTON

SD3098 Map 9

Sun 🍽 🛏

Signed left off A593 at the bridge; LA21 8HQ

Lovely position for extended old pub with a lively bar, plenty of dining space, real ales, well liked food and seats outside; comfortable bedrooms

---

The position of this 16th-c inn is spectacular, with views of dramatic bare fells from the quiet, comfortable bedrooms and from the seats and tables on the terrace and in the big tree-sheltered garden. At the heart of the pub is a cheerful bar, with a good mix of customers (and their dogs), exposed stone walls, beams and timbers, flagstones and a Victorian-style range. Also, cask seats, old settles and cast-iron-framed tables and quite a few Donald Campbell photographs (this was his HQ during his final attempt on the world water-speed record). A fine range of up to eight real ales on handpump might include Barngates Tag Lag, Coniston Bluebird Bitter, Old Man Ale and XB, Cumbrian Legendary Loweswater Gold, Hawkshead Bitter, Hesket Newmarket Skiddaw Special Bitter and Ulverston Lonesome Pine; the friendly staff also keep eight wines by the glass and 20 malt whiskies. Above the bar is another room, with extra seating for families and larger groups, and there's also a sizeable side lounge that leads into the dining conservatory; pool, darts, TV and maybe background music.

 The standard of food is high and the menu includes ham hock terrine with honey and mustard dressing, crayfish salad in dill and chive mayonnaise, sweet-cured gammon and free-range eggs, steak in ale pie, roast vegetable and tomato spaghetti, home-smoked chicken with orange and thyme gravy, lamb and black pudding hotpot, and puddings such as apple pie and chocolate tart. *Benchmark main dish: cumberland sausage and mash £8.95. Two-course evening meal £14.00.*

Free house ~ Licensee Alan Piper ~ Real ale ~ (015394) 41248 ~ Open 11am-midnight ~ Bar food 12-2.30, 5.30-8.30; 12-8.30 Fri-Sun ~ Restaurant ~ Children welcome ~ Dogs allowed in bar and bedrooms ~ Bedrooms: /£50 ~ www.thesunconiston.com
Recommended by Roger Fox

CROSTHWAITE
SD4491   Map 9
Punch Bowl
Village signed off A5074 SE of Windermere; LA8 8HR

Cumbria Dining Pub of the Year

Smart dining pub with a proper bar and several other elegant rooms, real ales, a fine wine list, impressive food and friendly staff; seats on terrace overlooking the valley; comfortable, stylish bedrooms

Many customers come to this civilised inn for an excellent meal or to stay overnight in the lovely, well equipped bedrooms, but there's a proper bar too, liked by locals for a pint and a chat. There's a relaxed and nicely uncluttered feel throughout, and the public bar has rafters, a couple of eye-catching rugs on flagstones, bar stools by the slate-topped counter, Barngates Cracker and Tag Lag and Coniston Bluebird on handpump, 16 wines and two sparkling wines by the glass, 15 malt whiskies and local damson gin. To the right are two linked carpeted and beamed rooms with well spaced country pine furniture of varying sizes, including a big refectory table, and walls that are painted in restrained neutral tones with an attractive assortment of prints; winter log fire, woodburning stove, lots of fresh flowers and daily papers. On the left, the wooden-floored restaurant area (also light, airy and attractive) has comfortable high-backed leather dining chairs; background music. There are some tables on a terrace stepped into the hillside overlooking the lovely Lyth Valley.

 Using the best seasonal, local produce, the enterprising modern food includes sandwiches, hand-dived scallops with white chocolate and truffle risotto, black pudding with bubble and squeak, an egg and apple caramel, wild mushroom and ricotta ravioli with cep purée, slow-cooked beef with roast garlic mash, bone marrow and dates, brill fillet with smoked salmon and caper butter and potato rösti, and puddings such as yoghurt panna cotta with cinammon doughnut, blood orange and sesame, and dark chocolate délice with passion fruit and fennel. *Benchmark main dish: loin of rabbit with crayfish mousse, leg croquette and apricot £16.50. Two-course evening meal £23.50.*

Free house ~ Licensees Richard Rose and Abi Lloyd ~ Real ale ~ (015395) 68237 ~ Open 11-11 ~ Bar food 12-9; 12-4, 5.30-9 weekends ~ Restaurant ~ Children welcome ~ Dogs allowed in bar ~ Bedrooms: £95/£140 ~ www.the-punchbowl.co.uk
Recommended by Joss Mitchell, G Jennings, Richard Tilbrook, Pat and Tony Martin, Peter and Josie Fawcett, Colin McLachlan, Ray and Winifred Halliday, Pat and Graham Williamson

ELTERWATER   NY3204   Map 9
Britannia 🍺 🛏
Off B5343; LA22 9HP

Much loved inn surrounded by wonderful walks and scenery; up to six real ales and well liked food; refurbished bedrooms

The very high standards here are kept year after year, and our readers love the place. It's at the heart of the Lake District, close to Langdale and the central lakes, and there are walks of every gradient right from the front door; it does get packed at peak times. The atmosphere is friendly and old-fashioned and the little front bar has beams and a couple of window seats that look across to Elterwater through the trees. The small back bar is traditionally furnished: thick slate walls, winter coal fires, oak benches, settles, windsor chairs and a big old rocking chair. A couple of beers are named for the pub – Britannia Special (from Coniston) and Britannia Gold (from Eden) – plus Coniston Bluebird, Jennings Sneck Lifter and Derwent Whitwell & Mark Pale Ale on handpump, and 15 malt whiskies. The lounge is comfortable, and there's also a hall and dining room. Plenty of seats outside, and morris, and step and garland, dancers in summer.

🍴 Enjoyable and generously served (book in advance to be sure of a table), the food includes lunchtime sandwiches, cumberland pâté with port sauce, grilled haggis with plum jam, sausages with mash and onion gravy, wild and button mushroom stroganoff, chicken, ham and leek pie, bass fillet with lemon and chervil butter, and puddings such as sticky toffee pudding and profiteroles with hot chocolate sauce. *Benchmark main dish: lamb shoulder braised in mint and honey £15.00. Two-course evening meal £19.50.*

Free house ~ Licensee Andrew Parker ~ Real ale ~ (015394) 37210 ~ Open 10.30am-11pm ~ Bar food 12-5, 6-9 ~ Restaurant ~ Children welcome ~ Dogs allowed in bar and bedrooms ~ Wi-fi ~ Bedrooms: £89/£115 ~ www.britinn.co.uk *Recommended by Tina and David Woods-Taylor, G Jennings*

GREAT SALKELD   NY5536   Map 10
Highland Drove ⭐
B6412, off A686 NE of Penrith; CA11 9NA

Bustling place with a cheerful mix of customers, good food in several dining areas, fair choice of drinks, and fine views from the upstairs verandah; bedrooms

Customers of all ages really enjoy their visits to this well run and welcoming old place – it's a nice play to stay overnight too. The spotlessly kept, chatty main bar has sandstone flooring, stone walls, cushioned wheelback chairs around a mix of tables and an open fire in a raised stone fireplace. The downstairs eating area has more cushioned dining chairs around wooden tables on pale wooden floorboards, stone walls and ceiling joists, and a two-way fire in a raised stone fireplace that separates this room from the coffee lounge with its comfortable leather chairs and sofas. There's also an upstairs restaurant – it's best to book to be sure of a table. A beer named for the pub from Eden, Theakstons Black

Bull and a guest ale on handpump, a dozen wines by the glass and 28 malt whiskies; background music, darts, pool and dominoes. The lovely views over the Eden Valley and the Pennines are best enjoyed from seats on the upstairs verandah; there are also seats on the back terrace. This is under the same ownership as the Cross Keys in Carleton.

 As well as lunchtime sandwiches and rolls, the good, popular food includes pork rillettes with sage mayonnaise, various platters, three-egg omelettes, burgers with cheese and bacon, steak in ale pie, beer-battered haddock and chips, venison curry, duck breast with celeriac and olive mash and port and red onion sauce, and puddings such as glazed lemon tart with raspberry coulis and chocolate brownie with chocolate sauce. *Benchmark main dish: steak in ale pie £10.95. Two-course evening meal £16.00.*

Free house ~ Licensees Donald and Paul Newton ~ Real ale ~ (01768) 898349 ~ Open 12-3, 6-11; 12-midnight Sat; 12-3, 6-11 Sun; closed Mon lunchtime ~ Bar food 12-2, 6-9 ~ Restaurant ~ Children welcome ~ Dogs allowed in bar ~ Wi-fi ~ Bedrooms: £42.50/£75 ~ www.kyloes.co.uk *Recommended by Richard J Holloway, Dave Braisted, Kim Skuse*

INGS
SD4498 Map 9

Watermill 🍺 🛏

Just off A591 E of Windermere; LA8 9PY

Busy, cleverly converted pub with fantastic range of real ales including own brews, and well liked food; bedrooms

Many people here are repeat customers keen to try the fantastic range of changing real ales. At peak times, there may be up to 16 beers on handpump – including their own brews: Watermill A Bit'er Ruff, Blackbeard, Collie Wobbles, Dogth Vader, Isle of Dogs, Windermere Blonde, Ruff Justice and W'ruff Night – plus guests such as Coniston Bluebird, Cumbrian Legendary Loweswater Gold, Fell Robust Porter and Unsworths Yard Cartmel Peninsula and Crusader Gold. Also, scrumpy cider, a huge choice of foreign bottled beers and 40 malt whiskies. The building, cleverly converted from a woodmill and joiner's shop, has plenty of character and the bars have an assortment of chairs, padded benches and solid oak tables, bar counters made from old church wood, open fires and interesting photographs and amusing cartoons by a local artist. The spacious lounge bar, in much the same traditional style as the other rooms, has rocking chairs and a big open fire; darts and board games. There are seats in the gardens and lots to do nearby. Dogs may get free biscuits and water. It's also a smashing place to stay.

Generous helpings of good, popular food includes sandwiches, creamy garlic mushrooms, deep-fried king prawns with chilli mayonnaise, mushroom stroganoff, chicken caesar salad, gammon with free-range egg and pineapple, beer-battered fish and chips, cumberland sausage with beer and onion gravy, and puddings such as sticky toffee pudding and hot chocolate fudge cake. *Benchmark main dish: beef in ale pie £10.75. Two-course evening meal £16.00.*

Own brew ~ Licensee Brian Coulthwaite ~ Real ale ~ (01539) 821309 ~ Open 11.15-11 (10.30 Sun) ~ Bar food 12-9 ~ Children welcome ~ Dogs allowed in bar and bedrooms ~ Wi-fi ~ Storytelling monthly ~ Bedrooms: £46/£77 ~ www.lakelandpub.co.uk
Recommended by Tina and David Woods-Taylor, Dave Webster, Sue Holland, David Fowler, Ray and Winifred Halliday, Dennis Jones

---

The star-on-a-plate award, 🌟, distinguishes pubs where the food is of exceptional quality. The knife-and-fork symbol just means the pub serves food.

LANGDALE   NY2806 Map 9

Old Dungeon Ghyll ◖ £

B5343; LA22 9JY

Straightforward place in lovely position with real ales, traditional food and fine surrounding walks; bedrooms

Even on particularly sodden and chilly days there's always a boisterous atmosphere and plenty of fell walkers and climbers in this straightforward local. It's right at the heart of the Great Langdale Valley and has plenty of character; the vibe is basic but cosy, so there's no need to remove boots or muddy trousers – you can sit on seats in old cattle stalls by the big warming fire and enjoy the fine choice of six real ales on handpump: Jennings Cumberland, Theakston Old Peculier, Yates Best Bitter and three quickly changing guests. It's a good place to stay, with warm bedrooms and highly rated breakfasts. It may get lively on a Saturday night (there's a popular National Trust campsite opposite).

Decent helpings of honest food include their own bread and cakes, lunchtime sandwiches, garlic mushrooms, chicken liver pâté, vegetable and bean goulash, chicken in creamy peppercorn sauce, baked ham with cumberland sauce, and puddings such as fruit crumble and sticky toffee pudding. *Benchmark main dish: home-made pies £10.95. Two-course evening meal £15.00.*

Free house ~ Licensee Neil Walmsley ~ Real ale ~ (015394) 37272 ~ Open 11-11 (10.30 Sun) ~ Bar food 12-2, 6-9 ~ Restaurant ~ Children welcome ~ Dogs allowed in bar and bedrooms ~ Wi-fi ~ Live music Weds evening ~ Bedrooms: /£106 ~ www.odg.co.uk
Recommended by Dave Braisted, Comus and Sarah Elliott

LEVENS   SD4987 Map 9

Strickland Arms �glass ◖

4 miles from M6 junction 36, via A590; just off A590, by Sizergh Castle gates; LA8 8DZ

Friendly, open-plan pub with popular food, local ales and a fine setting; seats outside

Even on a wet and dreary Monday lunchtime, this civilised place is deservedly busy and our readers love the place. It's largely open-plan with a light and airy feel; the bar on the right has oriental rugs on flagstones, a log fire, Black Swan Blonde Ale, Cumberland Corby Ale, Old School Blackboard, Thwaites Wainwright and a guest beer on handpump, several malt whiskies and nine wines by the glass. On the left are polished boards and another log fire, and throughout there's a nice mix of sturdy country furniture, candles on tables, hunting scenes and other old prints on the walls, curtain in heavy fabric and some staffordshire china ornaments. Two of the dining rooms are upstairs; background music and board games. The flagstoned front terrace has plenty of seats; disabled access and facilities. Sizergh Castle, a lovely partly medieval house with beautiful gardens run by the National Trust, is open in the afternoon (not Friday or Saturday) from April to October. The pub is part of the Ainscoughs group.

Good food includes sandwiches, welsh rarebit, potted shrimps, sausages with onion gravy, burger (using their own organic beef) with cheese and bacon, vegetable hotpot, steak in ale pie, seafood risotto, chicken fillets in beer and grain mustard sauce, and puddings such as plum and ginger crumble and white chocolate and Baileys cheesecake. *Benchmark main dish: sea trout with chorizo £12.95. Two-course evening meal £18.25.*

Free house ~ Licensee Nicola Harrison ~ Real ale ~ (015395) 61010 ~ Open 12-11 (10.30 Sun) ~ Bar food 12-2, 6-9; 12-8.30 weekends ~ Children welcome ~ Dogs welcome ~ Wi-fi ~ www.thestricklandarms.com *Recommended by Mr and Mrs P R Thomas, John and Sylvia Harrop, W K Wood, Ray and Winifred Halliday*

LITTLE LANGDALE
Three Shires

NY3103 Map 9

From A593 3 miles W of Ambleside take small road signposted The Langdales, Wrynose Pass; then bear left at first fork; LA22 9NZ

Fine valley views from seats on the terrace, local ales, quite a choice of food and comfortable bedrooms

Lots of tired, hungry and sometimes wet walkers are accommodated with good humour and a cheerful welcome in this reliably well run inn. It's in a lovely spot, with views over the valley from seats on the terrace to the partly wooded hills below; there are more seats on a neat lawn behind the car park, backed by a small oak wood, and award-winning summer hanging baskets. Inside, the comfortably extended back bar has green Lakeland stone and homely red patterned wallpaper, stripped timbers and a stripped beam-and-joist ceiling, antique oak carved settles, country kitchen chairs and stools on big dark slate flagstones, and Lakeland photographs. Coniston Old Man, Cumbrian Legendary Loweswater Gold, Hawkshead Red and Jennings Cumberland on handpump, over 50 malt whiskies and a decent wine list. The front restaurant has chunky leather dining chairs around solid tables on wood flooring, wine bottle prints on the dark red walls, and fresh flowers; a snug leads off here; darts, TV and board games. The three shires are the historical counties of Cumberland, Westmorland and Lancashire, which meet at the top of the nearby Wrynose Pass.

Using fresh local produce, the very good, popular food includes lunchtime sandwiches (the soup and sandwich deal is well liked), hot grilled smoked salmon with cucumber and mint sorbet, a charcuterie plate, cumberland sausage with beer-battered onion rings, wild mushroom and thyme risotto, lamb rump with sweet potato and garlic mash and redcurrant sauce, bass fillets with herb mash and garlic prawns, and puddings such as maple crème brûlée and lemon curd and sultana roly-poly with custard. *Benchmark main dish: beer-battered haddock and chips £13.50. Two-course evening meal £21.00.*

Free house ~ Licensee Ian Stephenson ~ Real ale ~ (015394) 37215 ~ Open 11-10.30 (11 Fri, Sat); 12-10.30 Sun; 11-3; 6-11 Fri-Sun in winter; closed 3 weeks Jan ~ Bar food 12-2, 6-9 ~ Restaurant ~ Children welcome ~ Dogs allowed in bar ~ Wi-fi ~ Bedrooms: /£100 ~ www.threeshiresinn.co.uk *Recommended by Christian Mole, Tina and David Woods-Taylor, G Jennings, Barry Collett, J R Wildon, Hugh Roberts*

LOWESWATER
Kirkstile Inn

NY1421 Map 9

From B5289 follow signs to Loweswater Lake; OS Sheet 89 map reference 140210; CA13 0RU

A lovely location for this well run, popular inn with busy bar, own-brewed beers, good food and friendly welcome; bedrooms

With its cosy atmosphere and roaring log fire, this friendly little pub is a haven for walkers; there are marvellous hikes of all levels nearby. The bustling main bar has low beams and carpeting, comfortably cushioned small settles and pews, partly stripped stone walls, board games and a slate shove-ha'penny board. As well as their own-brewed Cumbrian Legendary

Esthwaite, Langdale and Loweswater Gold, they keep a guest such as Watermill Collie Wobbles on handpump; nine wines by the glass and ten malt whiskies. The stunning views of the surrounding peaks can be enjoyed from picnic-sets on the lawn, from the very attractive covered verandah in front of the building and from the bow windows in one of the rooms off the bar; if you're lucky, you might spot a red squirrel. Dogs are allowed only in the bar and not during evening food service.

🍴 Championing local produce, the highly thought-of food includes lunchtime sandwiches, chicken liver pâté with plum and port chutney, wild mushroom risotto, omelette arnold bennett, steak in ale pie, slow-cooked marinated lamb shoulder in rosemary, red wine and orange jus, salmon fillet with spring onion and cheddar mash and white wine cream sauce, and puddings such as sticky toffee pudding with toffee sauce and cheesecake of the day. *Benchmark main dish: steak in ale pie £10.50. Two-course evening meal £17.50.*

Own brew ~ Licensee Roger Humphreys ~ Real ale ~ (01900) 85219 ~ Open 11-11; 12-11 Sun ~ Bar food 12-9; light meals and afternoon tea 2-4.30 ~ Restaurant ~ Children welcome ~ Dogs allowed in bar ~ Bedrooms: £63.50/£99 ~ www.kirkstile.com
Recommended by Martin Day, Christian Mole, Comus and Sarah Elliott, Margaret and Peter Staples

NEAR SAWREY
SD3795 Map 9

Tower Bank Arms

B5285 towards the Windermere ferry; LA22 0LF

Well run pub with several real ales, tasty bar food and a friendly welcome; nice bedrooms

This friendly, bustling pub backs on to Beatrix Potter's farm and features in *The Tale of Jemima Puddle-Duck*, so it gets pretty packed at weekends during the school holidays and you'll need to book a table in advance at those times. The low-beamed main bar has plenty of rustic charm, with a rough slate floor, game and fowl pictures, a grandfather clock, a log fire and fresh flowers; there's also a separate restaurant. Barngates Cracker Ale, Cumbrian Legendary Langdale and Loweswater Gold and Hawkshead Bitter and Brodies Prime on handpump, several wines by the glass, 16 malt whiskies and Weston's organic perry; board games and darts. There are pleasant views of the wooded Claife Heights from seats in the extended garden. This is an enjoyable place to stay and the breakfasts are particularly good.

🍴 Good quality food generously served includes lunchtime sandwiches, black pudding and pancetta tower with whisky and honey mustard cream, crayfish tails in marie rose sauce, mixed pepper and pine-nut risotto, gammon and egg, haggis-stuffed chicken wrapped in pancetta with a wild mushroom and tarragon sauce, leg of lamb with black pepper mash and rosemary and redcurrant sauce, and puddings such as lemon sherbert and basil cheesecake and bread and butter pudding. *Benchmark main dish: beef in ale stew with herb dumplings £12.50. Two-course evening meal £19.50.*

Free house ~ Licensee Anthony Hutton ~ Real ale ~ (015394) 36334 ~ Open 11.30-11; 12-10.30 Sun; may close on winter afternoons if quiet; closed 1 week mid Jan ~ Bar food 12-2, 6-9 (8 Sun, winter Mon-Thurs and bank holidays) ~ Restaurant ~ Children welcome ~ Dogs allowed in bar and bedrooms ~ Wi-fi ~ Bedrooms: /£95 ~ www.towerbankarms.com *Recommended by Christian Mole, Ian and Rose Lock, Roger Fox*

The 🍺 symbol shows pubs that keep their beer unusually well, have a particularly good range or brew their own.

NEWBY BRIDGE
Swan 🛏
SD3686 Map 9

Just off A590; LA12 8NB

Riverside hotel with bustling bar, a good mix of customers, helpful staff, bold fabrics and décor, real ales, wines by the glass and seats on a waterside terrace; comfortable bedrooms

---

Beside a five-arch bridge on the banks of the River Leven at the southern tip of Lake Windermere, this family-run, extended former coaching inn has been offering hospitality to travellers since the 17th c. Its heart, as it's always been, is the bar, where you'll find locals, hotel guests and boating folk all mingling happily. There are low ceilings, cheerful floral-print upholstered dining chairs around scrubbed tables on bare floorboards, window seats, a log fire in a little iron fireplace, pictures and railway posters on the grey-green walls, and stools at the long bar counter. Jennings Cumberland, Cumbrian Legendary Loweswater Gold and a guest beer on handpump, served by smart, friendly staff; background music. Towards the back is another log fire with a sofa and upholstered pouffes around a low table, and a similarly furnished further room; the front snug is cosy. In the main hotel off to the left are two sizeable restaurants (upstairs and downstairs). Original features mix well with the bold fabrics and wallpaper, fresh flowers, nice old pieces of china and modern artwork – it's all been done with a great deal of thought and care. Plenty of pretty ironwork tables and chairs line the riverside terrace. The contemporary bedrooms are comfortable and well equipped; some overlook the water.

 With some kind of food offered all day, the interesting menu includes sandwiches, crispy salt and pepper squid with chorizo and aioli, pork croquette with cabbage, pancetta and apple cider, rotisserie chicken with aioli and french fries, roasted beetroot with lentil, feta and mint salad and a pomegranate and orange dressing, hake fillet with salsa verde, lamb koftas with lime and red pepper couscous and tzatziki, and puddings such as chocolate and salted caramel pot and pear, plum and cinnamon crumble. *Benchmark main dish: burger with cheddar, onion rings, pickles and french fries £12.95. Two-course evening meal £20.00.*

Free house ~ Licensee Sarah Gibbs ~ Real ale ~ (015395) 31681 ~ Open 10am-11pm; 12-10.30 Sun ~ Bar food 10-9.30 ~ Restaurant ~ Children welcome in restaurant and eating area of bar until 9pm ~ Dogs allowed in bar ~ Wi-fi ~ Bedrooms: /£129 ~ www.swanhotel.com *Recommended by Margaret and Jeff Graham, Caroline Prescott*

RAVENSTONEDALE
Black Swan 🔯 🛏
NY7203 Map 10

Just off A685 SW of Kirkby Stephen; CA17 4NG

Bustling hotel with thriving bar, several real ales, enjoyable food and good surrounding walks; comfortable bedrooms

---

You can be sure of a genuinely warm welcome from the helpful staff at this smart, neatly kept Victorian hotel. A popular place, it has a bustling U-shaped bar, quite a few original period features, stripped-stone walls, plush stools by the counter, a comfortable green button-back banquette, various dining chairs and little stools around a mix of tables and fresh flowers; you can eat here or in two separate restaurants. Black Sheep Ale and Bitter, John Smiths and a couple of changing guests such as Cumberland Corby Ale and Thwaites Nutty Black on handpump, ten wines by the glass, more than 30 malt whiskies and a good choice of fruit juices and pressés; background music, TV, darts, board games and newspapers and magazines. There are picnic-sets in the tree-sheltered streamside garden across the road and lots of good walks from the door; they have leaflets describing some routes. This is an enjoyable place to stay with individually decorated bedrooms (some have disabled access, others are dog friendly) and big breakfasts. They also run the village store, which has café seating outside.

Using local farm produce in seasonal menus, the good, popular food includes ox tongue terrine with caramelised sweet garlic, smoked tuna with lime and dill potato salad, butternut squash, coconut and peanut curry, steak in ale pie, chargrilled chicken on sweet red onion rösti, beer-battered haddock and chips, lambs liver and pancetta in creamy peppercorn sauce, and puddings. *Benchmark main dish: monkfish and ham hock croquette with pea purée £15.95. Two-course evening meal £17.95.*

Free house ~ Licensees Louise and Alan Dinnes ~ Real ale ~ (015396) 23204 ~ Open 11am-midnight (1.30am Sat); 12-midnight Sun ~ Bar food 12-9 ~ Restaurant ~ Children welcome ~ Dogs allowed in bar and bedrooms ~ Wi-fi ~ Bedrooms: £65/£75 ~ www.blackswanhotel.com *Recommended by Claes Mauroy, J R Wildon, Kim Skuse, Steve and Liz Tilley, Michael Butler*

RAVENSTONEDALE
NY7204 Map 10

Kings Head 🏆 ⛏

Pub visible from A685 W of Kirkby Stephen; CA17 4NH

Riverside inn with beamed bar and adjacent dining room, attractive furniture on flagstones or wood, fresh flowers, three real ales and interesting food; comfortable bedrooms

Beside a bridge over the River Lune, this is a nicely opened-up village inn. The beamed bar rooms have lovely big flagstones, assorted rugs, a wing chair by a log fire in a raised fireplace, an attractive array of fine wooden chairs and cushioned settles around various tables, a few prints on grey-painted walls and an old yoke above the double-sided woodburner and bread oven. Dent Porter, Eden Gold and Jennings Cumberland on handpump and eight wines by the glass, served by friendly staff; background music and a games room with pool and local photographs. The dining room is similarly furnished, but with some upholstered chairs on wooden floors, tartan curtains, fresh flowers and a few prints. There are picnic-sets by the water in a nicely fenced-off area. Bedrooms are comfortable and breakfasts hearty. Plenty of good surrounding walks.

Rewarding food includes sandwiches, potted confit pork with apple and cinnamon compote, black pudding with duck egg, air-dried ham and mustard cream, cumberland sausage with red wine jus, coq au vin, mushroom and leek pudding with chive cream, sea bream fillet with parsley risotto and garlic crayfish, and puddings such as peanut mousse with peanut brittle and caramel banana and lemon panna cotta with poached rhubarb. *Benchmark main dish: home-made pies £12.95. Two-course evening meal £20.00.*

Free house ~ Licensee Beverley Fothergill ~ Real ale ~ (015396) 23050 ~ Open 11-11 (1.30am Sun) ~ Bar food 12-2.30, 6-9; light snacks in afternoon ~ Restaurant ~ Children welcome ~ Dogs allowed in bar ~ Wi-fi ~ Bedrooms: £75/£98 ~ www.kings-head.com *Recommended by Gary Topham*

Anyone claiming to arrange, or prevent, inclusion of a pub in the *Guide* is a fraud. Pubs are included only if recommended by genuine readers and if our own anonymous inspection confirms that they are suitable.

STAVELEY   SD4798 Map 10

Beer Hall at Hawkshead Brewery

Staveley Mill Yard, Back Lane; LA8 9LR

Hawkshead Brewery showcase plus a huge choice of bottled beers, brewery memorabilia, knowledgeable staff and ever-changing tapas

Don't expect your usual pub experience in this spacious and modern glass-fronted building, but it's an interesting place with the full range of Hawkshead Brewery ales and regular beer festivals. From the 14 handpumps there might be Bitter, Brodies Prime, Cumbrian Five Hop, Dry Stone Stout, Lakeland Gold and Lager, Red, Windermere Pale and seasonal beers. They also offer an extensive choice of bottled beers and whiskies with an emphasis on independent producers – all served by friendly, interested staff. The main bar is on two levels with the lower level dominated by the stainless-steel fermenting vessels. There are high-backed chairs around light wooden tables, benches beside long tables, nice dark leather sofas around low tables (all on oak floorboards) and a couple of walls are almost entirely covered with artistic photos of barley and hops and the brewing process; darts. You can buy T-shirts, branded glasses and polypins and there are brewery tours. Parking can be tricky at peak times.

A choice of up to 14 tapas might include scotch egg and piccalilli, sweetcorn and coriander fritters and duck and chilli sausages. More substantial dishes include cumberland sausage and mash, yorkshire pudding filled with local beef and topped with horseradish sauce, beer-battered fish and chips, venison and damson casserole with dumplings, and puddings such as cherry bakewell tart and sticky toffee pudding. *Benchmark main dish: platter of pie, sausages, parma ham, black pudding, ribs, pickles and chutney £14.50.*

Own brew ~ Licensee Alex Brodie ~ Real ale ~ (01539) 825260 ~ Open 12-5 Mon; 12-6 Tues-Thurs; 12-11 Fri, Sat; 12-8 Sun ~ Bar food 12-3; 12-8 Fri, Sat; 12-6 Sun ~ Children welcome away from bar until 8pm ~ Dogs allowed in bar ~ Wi-fi ~ www.hawksheadbrewery.co.uk *Recommended by Michael Doswell, Caroline Prescott, Dennis Jones, Kay and Alistair Butler*

STAVELEY   SD4797 Map 9

Eagle & Child £

Kendal Road; just off A591 Windermere–Kendal; LA8 9LP

Welcoming inn with warming log fires, a good range of local beers and enjoyable food; bedrooms

Our readers enjoy their visits to this lively and friendly pub very much and return regularly. It's in a lovely spot, with walks along the Dales Way and more that fan out from the recreation ground just across the road. The bar has a log fire beneath an impressive mantelbeam and the L-shaped flagstoned main area has plenty of separate parts, furnished with pews, banquettes, bow window seats and high-backed dining chairs around polished dark tables. Also, police truncheons and walking sticks, some nice photographs and interesting prints, a few farm tools, a delft shelf of bric-a-brac and another log fire. The five real ales on handpump might be Barngates Pale, Cumbrian Legendary Loweswater Gold, Dent Flock & Roll, Jennings Cocker Hoop and Yates Bitter, and they keep several wines by the glass, 20 malt whiskies and farm cider; background music, darts and board games. An upstairs barn-themed dining room has its own bar for functions.

There are picnic-sets under cocktail parasols in a sheltered garden by the River Kent, with more on a good-sized back terrace and a second garden behind. The bedrooms are comfortable and the breakfasts very generous.

🍴 There's Lunch for a Fiver deal (not Sunday). Other highly thought-of dishes include lunchtime sandwiches, chicken liver pâté with chutney, thai-style salmon fishcakes with chilli and basil dip, vegetable curry, chicken wrapped in bacon with barbecue sauce, moroccan-style lamb, beer-battered haddock and chips, and puddings such as apple crumble and sticky ginger pudding. *Benchmark main dish: steak in ale pie £9.95. Two-course evening meal £15.00.*

Free house ~ Licensees Richard and Denise Coleman ~ Real ale ~ (01539) 821320 ~ Open 11-11; 12-10.30 Sun ~ Bar food 12-2.30, 6-9; 12-9 weekends ~ Restaurant ~ Children welcome ~ Dogs allowed in bar ~ Wi-fi ~ Bedrooms: £60/£80 ~ www.eaglechildinn.co.uk *Recommended by G Jennings, Tina and David Woods-Taylor, David Jackman, Roger and Donna Huggins*

STONETHWAITE   NY2513   Map 9

Langstrath 🍺 🛏

Off B5289 S of Derwentwater; CA12 5XG

Civilised little place in lovely spot, traditional food with a modern twist, four real ales, good wines and malt whiskies, and seats outside; bedrooms

You can be sure of a warm welcome from the friendly licensees at this civilised little inn surrounded by the steep fells above Borrowdale. There are fine walks nearby and both the Cumbrian Way and the Coast to Coast path are not far. The neat, simple bar (at its pubbiest at lunchtime) has a welcoming log fire in a big stone fireplace, rustic tables, plain chairs and cushioned wall seats, and walking cartoons and attractive Lakeland mountain photographs on its textured white walls. Four real ales on handpump such as Jennings Cumberland Ale and Cocker Hoop, Keswick Gold and Theakstons Old Peculier, 30 malt whiskies and several wines by the glass; background music and board games. The small room on the left (actually the original cottage built around 1590) is a residents' lounge; the restaurant has fine views. Outside, a big sycamore shelters several picnic-sets with views up to Eagle Crag.

🍴 Attractively presented, the all-day food includes lunchtime sandwiches, potted local brown shrimps, welsh rarebit with fruit chutney, steak burger with chunky chips, ham and free-range eggs, butternut squash, tomato and parmesan risotto, cumberland sausage with wholegrain mustard mash and onion gravy, a fish dish of the day, and puddings such as vanilla crème brûlée and white chocolate panna cotta with dark chocolate mousse. *Benchmark main dish: slow-cooked local lamb with rich gravy £17.95. Two-course evening meal £19.00.*

Free house ~ Licensees Guy and Jacqui Frazer-Hollins ~ Real ale ~ (017687) 77239 ~ Open 12-10.30; closed Mon ~ Bar food 12-4, 6-9 ~ Restaurant ~ Children over 10 in restaurant until 7.30pm ~ Dogs allowed in bar ~ Wi-fi ~ Bedrooms: £75/£110 ~ www.thelangstrath.com *Recommended by Graham and Jane Bellfield, Stephen Funnell, Tina and David Woods-Taylor, Graham and Elizabeth Hargreaves*

TALKIN   NY5457   Map 10

Blacksmiths Arms 🍷 🛏

Village signposted from B6413 S of Brampton; CA8 1LE

Neatly kept and welcoming with tasty bar food, several real ales and fine nearby walks; bedrooms

In attractive countryside with good surrounding walks, this is a friendly 18th-c former blacksmiths. Several neatly kept, traditionally furnished bars include a warm lounge on the right with a log fire, upholstered banquettes and wheelback chairs around dark wooden tables on patterned red carpeting, and country prints and other pictures on the walls. The restaurant is to the left and there's also a long lounge opposite the bar, with a step up to another room at the back. A beer named for the pub, Geltsdale Cold Fell, Yates Bitter and a guest ale on handpump, 15 wines by the glass and 25 malt whiskies; background music, darts and board games. There are a couple of picnic-sets outside the front door and more in the back garden. This is a quiet and comfortable place to stay.

Reliably good food includes sandwiches and paninis, deep-fried brie with cranberry sauce, smoked haddock and spring onion fishcakes with chilli dip, vegetable curry, chicken curry, local cumberland sausage and egg, specials such as barbecue ribs, salmon in white wine, cream and lemon sauce, liver, bacon and onion casserole, and puddings. *Benchmark main dish: steak and kidney pie £8.95. Two-course evening meal £15.00.*

Free house ~ Licensees Donald and Anne Jackson ~ Real ale ~ (016977) 3452 ~ Open 12-midnight ~ Bar food 12-2, 6-9 ~ Restaurant ~ Children welcome ~ Bedrooms: £55/£75 ~ www.blacksmithstalkin.co.uk *Recommended by Ruth May, Dr Kevan Tucker*

TIRRIL
NY5026 Map 10

Queens Head

B5320, not far from M6 junction 40; CA10 2JF

18th-c Lakeland pub with two bars, real ales, speciality pies and seats outside; bedrooms

Our readers enjoy staying in this well run, busy inn and the breakfasts are highly rated. The place dates from 1719: the oldest parts of the main bar have original flagstones and floorboards, low beams and black panelling, and there are nice little tables and chairs on either side of the inglenook fireplace (always lit in winter). Another bar to the right of the entrance has pews and chairs around sizeable tables on a wooden floor, and candles in the fireplace, while the back locals' bar has heavy beams and a pool table; there are three dining rooms too. Robinsons Cumbria Way, Dizzy Blonde and Unicorn and a guest beer on handpump and several wines by the glass. Outside, there are picnic-sets at the front, and modern chairs and tables under cover on the back terrace. The hard-working licensees also run the Pie Mill (you can eat their pies here) and the village shop. The pub is very close to several interesting places, including Dalemain at Dacre, and Ullswater is nearby.

As well as the eight popular pies, food includes sandwiches, creamy garlic mushrooms and bacon, chorizo and black pudding salad, vegetable lasagne, honey-roast ham and egg, a curry of the day, cod topped with king prawns in parsley butter, duck with honey, port and coriander reduction, and puddings such as a fruit pie of the day and sticky toffee pudding; they also offer a two-course menu. *Benchmark main dish: sirloin steak with onion rings, mushrooms and chips £16.95. Two-course evening meal £16.00.*

Robinsons ~ Tenants Margaret and Jim Hodge ~ (01768) 863219 ~ Open 11-11 (midnight Sat); 12-10.30 Sun ~ Bar food 12-2.30, 5-8.30 ~ Restaurant ~ Children welcome ~ Dogs allowed in bar and bedrooms ~ Wi-fi ~ Bedrooms: £50/£75 ~ www.queensheadinn.co.uk *Recommended by Rosie Fielder, Roger and Donna Huggins*

ULVERSTON
Bay Horse ♀ 🛏
SD3177 Map 7

Canal Foot signposted off A590, then wend your way past the huge Glaxo factory; LA12 9EL

Civilised waterside hotel with lunchtime bar food, three real ales and a fine choice of wines; smart bedrooms

Many of our readers stay at this civilised and friendly hotel, where the bedrooms have french windows that open on to a terrace with a panoramic view of the Leven Estuary; the bird life is wonderful and the breakfasts excellent. The bar (at its most informal at lunchtime) has a relaxed atmosphere despite its smart furnishings: new cushioned teak dining chairs, paisley-patterned built-in wall banquettes, glossy hardwood traditional tables, a huge stone horse's head, black beams and props, and lots of horsebrasses. Magazines are dotted about, there's an open fire in the handsomely marbled, grey slate fireplace and decently reproduced background music; board games. Jennings Cocker Hoop and Cumberland and a guest beer on handpump, 16 wines by the glass (including champagne and prosecco) from a carefully chosen, interesting list and several malt whiskies. The conservatory restaurant has lovely views over Morecambe Bay and there are some seats outside on the terrace.

Featuring their own bread and delicious shortbread, the consistently good food includes lunchtime dishes such as sandwiches, as well as chicken liver pâté with cranberry and ginger purée, deep-fried chilli prawns with sweet and sour sauce, pork, leek and cheese in a madeira sauce, lamb shank with orange, ginger and red wine, naturally smoked haddock with mushroom and onion pâté and creamy herb sauce, and puddings; in the evening, the emphasis is on the restaurant and light snacks only are available in the bar. *Benchmark main dish: crab and salmon fishcakes on white wine and herb cream sauce £14.95. Two-course evening meal £21.50.*

Free house ~ Licensee Robert Lyons ~ Real ale ~ (01229) 583972 ~ Open 9am-11pm (10.30pm Sun) ~ Bar food 12-3 (2 Mon, 4 weekends), 7-9 ~ Restaurant ~ Children welcome but over-9s only after 7pm or in bedrooms ~ Dogs allowed in bar and bedrooms ~ Wi-fi ~ Bedrooms: £80/£100 ~ www.thebayhorsehotel.co.uk *Recommended by John and Sylvia Harrop, W K Wood, Hugh Roberts*

WINSTER
Brown Horse ◀
SD4193 Map 9

A5074 S of Windermere; LA23 3NR

Refurbished inn in pretty valley with old and new features mixing well, own-brewed beers and lagers, and enjoyable food; bedrooms

Set in a pretty country valley, this traditional 19th-c coaching inn has been carefully refurbished. The chatty bar has mate's chairs, church pews and one lovely tall settle around all sorts of tables on flagstones, and their own-brewed Winster Valley ales: Best Bitter, Chaser, Dark Horse, Hurdler, Lakes Blonde, Lakes Lager and Lakes Pilsner. Also, guest beers, several wines by the glass and ten malt whiskies. The candlelit dining room – painted green above a panelled dado – has chairs ranging from white-painted and distressed to high-backed leather to cushioned antiques around a medley of wooden tables, with coppper implements, old skis, carpet beaters, horse prints, hunting horns and antlers as decoration. There are seats and tables among flowering tubs and window boxes at the front, with more on a raised terrace. As well as contemporary-style bedrooms, several self-catering properties are available.

🍴 Using home-grown produce, the popular food includes sandwiches and ciabattas, chicken liver parfait with house chutney, poached pear, blue cheese and toasted walnut dressing, a rack of barbecued ribs, burger with cheese, bacon, coleslaw and frites, gammon steak with pineapple fritter and free-range eggs, sticky corn-fed poussin with thai curried rice, mango and coconut, and puddings. *Benchmark main dish: slow-cooked lamb in mint and honey £15.95. Two-course evening meal £21.50.*

Free house ~ Licensees Karen and Steve Edmondson ~ Real ale ~ (015394) 43443 ~ Open 11-11 ~ Bar food 12-2, 6-9 ~ Restaurant ~ Children welcome ~ Dogs allowed in bar ~ Bedrooms: /£95 ~ www.thebrownhorseinn.co.uk *Recommended by Tina and David Woods-Taylor, Hugh Roberts*

WITHERSLACK
SD4482   Map 10
Derby Arms 🏵️ 🍺 🛏️
Just off A590; LA11 6RH

Bustling country inn with half a dozen ales, good wines, particularly good food and a friendly welcome; reasonably priced bedrooms

This is a comfortable and fairly priced base for exploring the Southern Lakes and Dales, and also handy for Levens Hall with its topiary garden and for Sizergh Castle (National Trust). The main bar has an easy-going atmosphere, lots of sporting prints on pale grey walls, elegant old dining chairs and tables on large rugs over floorboards, some hops above the bar counter and an open fire. A fine choice of drinks served by friendly, courteous staff includes up to six real ales on handpump, such as Black Swan Blonde Ale, Cumberland Corby Ale, Prospect Nutty Slack, Thwaites Wainwright and a couple of guests; also, 11 wines by the glass and 22 malt whiskies. A larger room to the right is similarly furnished (with the addition of some cushioned pews), and has numerous political cartoons and local castle prints, a cumbrian scene above another open fire, and alcoves in the back wall full of nice bristol blue glass, ornate plates and staffordshire dogs and figurines. Large windows lighten up the rooms, helped at night by candles in brass candlesticks; background music, TV and pool. There are two additional rooms – one with dark red walls, a red velvet sofa, more sporting prints and a handsome mirror over the fireplace. This is part of the Ainscoughs group.

🏵️ Using beef from their own organic farm, the enjoyable food includes sandwiches, smoked salmon and crayfish salad, black pudding with a mustard cream sauce and crispy boiled egg, beef in ale pie, vegetable hotpot, cumberland sausage with onion gravy, rosemary and garlic lamb chops with dauphinoise potatoes, and puddings such as chocolate torte with damson ice-cream and sticky toffee pudding; they also offer a two-course weekday set menu. *Benchmark main dish: venison suet pudding £11.95. Two-course evening meal £18.00.*

Free house ~ Licensee Jessica Brown ~ Real ale ~ (015395) 52207 ~ Open 12-11 (10.30 Sun) ~ Bar food 12-2.30, 6-9.30; all day weekends ~ Children welcome ~ Dogs allowed in bar and bedrooms ~ Wi-fi ~ Bedrooms: £60/£80 ~ www.thederbyarms.co.uk *Recommended by Hugh Roberts, David Heath, Kay and Alistair Butler, Peter Andrews*

YANWATH
NY5128   Map 9
Gate Inn 🏵️ 🍷
2.25 miles from M6 junction 40; A66 towards Brough, then right on A6, right on B5320, then follow village signpost; CA10 2LF

Emphasis on imaginative food but with local beers and well chosen wines, a pubby atmosphere and a warm welcome from helpful staff

A favourite with many of our readers, this is a civilised and immaculately kept 17th-c dining pub with a warm welcome for all. Despite the emphasis on the impressive cooking, locals do drop in for a chat and a beer from breweries such as Barngates, Tirril and Yates on handpump – there's also a dozen or so good wines by the glass, 12 malt whiskies and Weston's Old Rosie cider. A cosy bar of charming antiquity has country pine and dark wood furniture, lots of brasses on the beams, church candles on all the tables and a good log fire in the attractive stone inglenook; staff are courteous and helpful. Two restaurant areas have oak floors, panelled oak walls and heavy beams; background music. There are seats on the terrace and in the garden. They have a self-catering cottage to let, and the pub is handy for Ullswater and the M6.

Using top quality ingredients, the accomplished cooking includes dishes such as weekday open sandwiches, mussels with chorizo, chilli, garlic and tomato sauce, ham hock terrine with home-made piccalilli, sweet potato and butternut squash tagine with apricot and toasted almond couscous, venison with spiced poached pear, dauphinoise potatoes and redcurrant jus, wild line-caught bass with tiger prawn and chive risotto, and puddings such as chocolate tart with mascarpone cream and sticky date pudding with toffee sauce. *Benchmark main dish: local steak with three-bean ragout and onion mash £19.95. Two-course evening meal £24.00.*

Free house ~ Licensee Matt Edwards ~ Real ale ~ (01768) 862386 ~ Open 12-11 ~ Bar food 12-2.30, 6-9 ~ Restaurant ~ Children welcome ~ Dogs allowed in bar ~ Wi-fi ~ www.yanwathgate.com *Recommended by Tina and David Woods-Taylor, Walter and Susan Rinaldi-Butcher, Dr and Mrs A K Clarke, Pat and Stewart Gordon, Michael Doswell, David and Katharine Cooke, Roger and Donna Huggins, Clifford Blakemore*

Also Worth a Visit in Cumbria

Besides the fully inspected pubs, you might like to try these pubs that have been recommended to us and described by readers. Do tell us what you think of them: feedback@goodguides.com

ALLITHWAITE   SD3876
Pheasant (015395) 32239
B5277; LA11 7RQ Welcoming family-run pub with enjoyable freshly cooked food including good Sun roasts, reasonable prices and prompt friendly service, Thwaites Original and four other local beers, log fire, Thurs quiz; children welcome (not in conservatory), dogs in bar, outside tables on deck with Humphrey Head views, open (and food) all day. *(David Cannings)*

AMBLESIDE   NY4008
★ **Kirkstone Pass Inn** (015394) 33888
A592 N of Troutbeck; LA22 9LQ Lakeland's highest pub, in grand scenery, with flagstones, stripped stone and dark beams, lots of old photographs and bric-a-brac, open fires, good value pubby food and changing Cumbrian ales, hot drinks, daily papers; soft background music, they may ask to keep a credit card while you eat; well behaved children and dogs welcome, tables outside with incredible views to Windermere, bedrooms, bunkhouse and camping field, open all day in summer (till 6pm Sun). *(Simon J Barber)*

APPLEBY   NY6819
★ **Royal Oak** (01768) 351463
B6542/Bongate; CA16 6UN Attractive old beamed and timbered coaching inn on edge of town, popular generously served food including early-bird and OAP deals, friendly efficient young staff, log fire in panelled bar, lounge with easy chairs and carved settle, traditional snug, restaurant; background music, TV; children and dogs welcome (menus for both), terrace tables, 11 bedrooms and self-catering cottage, good breakfast, open all day from 8am. *(Jane Bailey, Comus and Sarah Elliott, Richard and Penny Gibbs)*

ARMATHWAITE   NY5046
Dukes Head (016974) 72226
Off A6 S of Carlisle; right at T junction; Front Street; CA4 9PB Refurbished Eden Valley inn under newish management; enjoyable good value pub food, Black Sheep, Lancaster and a guest, cheerful helpful service, comfortable lounge/dining area divided by central stone fireplace, settles and mix of tables and chairs on carpet or bare boards, some upholstered wall benches,

small public bar with pool; background music, free wi-fi; children and dogs welcome, seats on paved area, decking and back lawn, five bedrooms (three ensuite), closed Mon lunchtime (weekday lunchtimes in winter). *(Isobel Mackinlay)*

ARMATHWAITE   NY5045
★**Fox & Pheasant** (016974) 72400
E of village, over bridge; CA4 9PY
Well run friendly old coaching inn with lovely River Eden views, well kept Robinsons ales and decent wines by the glass, good freshly made food, log fire in main beamed and flagstoned bar, converted stables dining bar with exposed stone walls and woodburner, also a small more formal Victorian dining room; picnic-sets outside, comfortable bedrooms. *(Jean and Douglas Troup, Lucien Perring)*

ASKHAM   NY5123
Punch Bowl (01931) 712443
4.5 miles from M6 junction 40; CA10 2PF
Attractive 18th-c village pub with spacious beamed main bar, locals' bar, snug lounge and dining room, open fires, Thwaites Wainwright and two or three other beers, decent choice of food from pub standards up, friendly staff; children and dogs welcome, picnic-sets out in front, on edge of green opposite Askham Hall, six bedrooms, open all day. *(Roger and Donna Huggins)*

ASKHAM   NY5123
Queens Head (01931) 712225
Lower Green; off A6 or B5320 S of Penrith; CA10 2PF Traditional 17th-c beamed pub with enjoyable good value wholesome food (all day) including gluten-free choices, well kept beers such as Black Sheep, friendly landlady, banquettes and other red upholstered seating, dark wood tables, brasses and old photographs, open fires, games room with pool and TV, yorkshire terrier called Oscar; background music, free wi-fi; children welcome, tables out at front and in pleasant garden, four bedrooms. *(David and Katharine Cooke)*

BAMPTON GRANGE   NY5218
Crown & Mitre (01931) 713225
Opposite church; CA10 2QR Old inn set in attractive country hamlet (*Withnail and I* was filmed around here); opened-up interior with comfortable modern décor, some leather sofas by log fire, substantial helpings of high quality home-made food from pub favourites up, four well kept beers such as Black Sheep and Hesket Newmarket, good coffee, efficient friendly young staff; children and dogs welcome, walks from the door, eight

bedrooms and a self-catering apartment, open all day in summer, from 5pm weekdays, midday weekends in winter. *(Stephen Funnell, Tina and David Woods-Taylor)*

BASSENTHWAITE   NY2332
Sun (017687) 76439
Off A591 N of Keswick; CA12 4QP
White-rendered village pub under newish management; rambling bar with low 17th-c black beams, blazing winter fires in two stone fireplaces, built-in wall seats and heavy wooden tables, two Jennings ales and a guest, generous food served by friendly staff, cosy dining room; children and dogs welcome, terrace with views of the fells and Skiddaw, open all day weekends, from 4pm other days. *(Christian Mole, Mr N and Mr G Webb, Annette Nicolle)*

BAYCLIFF   SD2872
Fishermans Arms (01229) 869133
A5087 Barrow–Ulverston; LA12 9RJ
Updated 1930s hotel, big spotless bar/dining area with black and white check carpet and slightly raised balustraded area, varied choice of appealing fairly priced food (all day) from lunchtime sandwiches up, decent wine selection, real ales such as local Greenodd from light oak counter, snug with comfortable armchairs and leather chesterfield, restaurant, good welcoming service; children allowed, playground next door, six comfortable bedrooms (some with Morecambe Bay views). *(J B Taylor)*

BEETHAM   SD4979
Wheatsheaf (015395) 62123
Village (and inn) signed off A6 S of Milnthorpe; LA7 7AL Striking old building with fine black and white timbered cornerpiece, handily positioned on the old road to the Lake District; traditionally furnished rooms, opened-up lounge with exposed beams and joists, main bar (behind on the right) with open fire, two upstairs dining rooms, residents' lounge, Cross Bay Nightfall, Thwaites Wainwright and maybe a guest ale, several wines by the glass and quite a few malt whiskies, decent choice of food including deals, friendly if not always quick service; children welcome, dogs in bar, plenty of surrounding walks, pretty 14th-c church opposite, five bedrooms, open all day. *(David and Katharine Cooke, Roger and Anne Newbury)*

BOOT   NY1701
Boot Inn (019467) 23711
Aka Burnmoor; signed just off the Wrynose/Hardknott Pass road; CA19 1TG
Refurbished beamed pub with three or

Please tell us if any pub deserves to be upgraded to a featured entry – and why: feedback@goodguides.com, or (no stamp needed) The Good Pub Guide, FREEPOST RTJR-ZCYZ-RJZT, Perrymans Lane, Etchingham TN19 7DN.

more real ales, decent wines and enjoyable locally sourced home-made food, log-fire bar, conservatory; children and dogs welcome, garden with play area, lovely surroundings and walks, nine bedrooms, open all day. *(Anon)*

BOOT   NY1701
★ **Brook House** (019467) 23288

From Ambleside, W of Hardknott Pass; CA19 1TG Good views and walks, friendly family service, wide choice of enjoyable sensibly priced country cooking including some interesting dishes and unusual sandwiches, over 160 whiskies and good range of well kept ales such as Barngates, Cumbrian, Hawkshead and Yates, Weston's farm cider or perry, decent wines, relaxed and comfortable raftered bar with woodburner and stuffed animals, smaller plush snug, peaceful separate restaurant; children and dogs welcome, tables on flagstoned terrace, eight reasonably priced bedrooms, good breakfast (for nearby campers too), mountain weather reports, excellent drying room, handy for Eskdale railway terminus, open all day. *(Hugh Roberts, Kay and Alistair Butler)*

BOOT   NY1901
Woolpack (019467) 23230

Bleabeck, midway between Boot and Hardknott Pass; CA19 1TH Last pub before the notorious Hardknott Pass; refurbished and welcoming with main walkers' bar and more contemporary café bar, also an evening restaurant (Fri, Sat), good home-made food including wood-fired pizzas, pies, steaks and daily specials, up to eight well kept ales, real cider and vast range of vodkas and gins, June beer festival, pool room, some live music; children and dogs welcome, mountain-view garden with play area, eight bedrooms, plans for a shop, open (and food) all day. *(Alan Eaves, Sarah Flynn)*

BOUTH   SD3285
★ **White Hart** (01229) 861229

Village signed off A590 near Haverthwaite; LA12 8JB Cheerful bustling old inn with Lakeland feel, six changing ales and 25 malt whiskies, popular generously served food (all day Sun), good friendly service, sloping ceilings and floors, old local photographs, farm tools and stuffed animals, collection of long-stemmed clay pipes, two woodburners; background music; children welcome, no dogs at mealtimes, seats outside and fine surrounding walks, five comfortable bedrooms, open all day. *(Anon)*

BOWNESS-ON-WINDERMERE   SD4096
Royal Oak (015394) 43970

Brantfell Road; LA23 3EG Handy for steamer pier, interconnecting bar, dining room and big games room, lots of bric-a-brac, open fire, well kept ales such as Coniston, Jennings, Sharps and Timothy Taylors, generous reasonably priced pub food from baguettes to specials, friendly efficient service; pool, darts and juke box; children welcome, tables out in front, eight bedrooms, open all day. *(Dennis Jones)*

BRAITHWAITE   NY2323
Royal Oak (017687) 78533

B5292 at top of village; CA12 5SY Bustling local atmosphere, four well kept Jennings ales and hearty helpings of traditional food (children's servings available), prompt helpful service, well worn-in flagstoned bar, restaurant; background music, Sky TV; no dogs at mealtimes, bedrooms, open all day. *(Michael Butler)*

BROUGHTON-IN-FURNESS   SD2187
Manor Arms (01229) 716286

The Square; LA20 6HY End-of-terrace drinkers' pub on quiet sloping square, up to eight well priced changing ales and good choice of ciders, flagstones and nice bow-window seat in front bar, coal fire in big stone fireplace, chiming clocks, old photographs, limited food such as toasties; pool, free wi-fi; children and dogs allowed, bedrooms, open all day. *(Dr Peter Crawshaw)*

CARLISLE   NY4056
Kings Head (01228) 533797

Fisher Street (pedestrianised); CA3 8RF Heavy 17th-c beams, lots of old local prints, drawings and black and white photographs, friendly bustling atmosphere, Yates and two or three guests, generous bargain pub lunches, raised dining area; background and live music, TV, silent fruit machine, no children or dogs; partly covered courtyard and historical plaque outside explaining why Carlisle is not in the Domesday Book, open all day. *(Jeremy King, Eric Larkham, Dave Braisted)*

CARTMEL   SD3778
Cavendish Arms (015395) 36240

Cavendish Street, off the Square; LA11 6QA Former coaching inn with simply furnished open-plan beamed bar, roaring log fire (even on cooler summer evenings), three or four ales featuring a house beer from Cumberland, several wines by the glass and decent coffee, friendly attentive staff, ample helpings of enjoyable food from shortish menu including lunchtime sandwiches and good steak and ale pie, restaurant; children welcome, dogs in bar, tables out in front and behind by stream, nice village with notable priory church, good walks, ten bedrooms – three more above their shop in the square, open (and food) all day. *(Steve and Claire*

If we know a pub has an outdoor play area for children, we mention it.

Harvey, Dennis Jones, Adrian Johnson, Kay and Alistair Butler, John and Sylvia Harrop)

CARTMEL   SD3878
Pig & Whistle (015395) 36482
Aynesome Road; LA11 6PL Traditional village pub now under same local ownership as L'Enclume and Rogan & Company restaurants; simple bar and lounge/dining area, Robinsons and local guest ales, food can be very good (all day Sun, not Mon, Tues), pleasant staff, open mike night Thurs; sports TV; children, dogs and muddy boots welcome, garden tables, lovely views, open all day (till 2am Fri, Sat). *(Michael Butler)*

CARTMEL   SD3778
Royal Oak (015395) 36259
The Square; LA11 6QB Low-beamed flagstoned local under same management as the Kings Arms next door (see Main Entries); cosy nooks and big log fire, good value food including traditional choices, home-made pizzas, pasta and grills, Thwaites and two changing local guests; welcoming helpful staff; background and weekend live music, two sports TVs; children and dogs welcome, nice big riverside garden with heated terrace, four bedrooms, open all day (till 1am Fri, Sat). *(Kay and Alistair Butler)*

CASTERTON   SD6379
★ Pheasant (015242) 71230
A683; LA6 2RX Refurbished 18th-c family-run inn with neat beamed rooms, good interesting food alongside traditional favourites, three well kept changing local ales and several malt whiskies, welcoming helpful staff, arched and panelled restaurant; background music, free wi-fi; children and dogs welcome, a few roadside seats, more in pleasant garden with Vale of Lune views, near church with Pre-Raphaelite stained glass and paintings, ten bedrooms, closed Mon lunchtime, otherwise open all day. *(John and Bridget Dean)*

CASTLE CARROCK   NY5455
Duke of Cumberland
(01228) 670341 *Geltsdale Road; CA8 9LU* Popular cleanly refurbished village-green pub with friendly family owners, upholstered wall benches and mix of pubby furniture on slate floor, coal fire, dining area with old farmhouse tables and chairs, well kept Geltsdale ales and a guest, enjoyable nicely presented pub food at reasonable prices; children welcome, no dogs inside, open all day. *(Dr Kevan Tucker)*

CHAPEL STILE   NY3205
Wainwrights (015394) 38088
B5343; LA22 9JH Popular white-rendered former farmhouse, half a dozen changing ales and plenty of wines by the glass, enjoyable well priced pubby food from good sandwiches up, friendly helpful service, roomy new-feeling bar welcoming walkers and dogs, slate floor and good log fire, other spreading carpeted areas with beams, some half-panelling, cushioned settles and mix of dining chairs around wooden tables, old kitchen range; background music, TV and games machines, Weds quiz; children welcome, terrace picnic-sets, fine views, open all day. *(G Jennings, Comus and Sarah Elliott)*

COCKERMOUTH   NY1230
1761 (01900) 829282
Market Place; CA13 9NH Handsome old building with shopfront windows, well kept Yates and two local guests, good choice of foreign beers and wines by the glass, real cider, fairly priced interesting light snacks, two (gas) woodburners (one in back room with some ancient stripped brick), slate flagstones by counter on left, bare boards on right, polychrome tiles of a former corridor floor dividing the two, cushioned window seats and a couple of high-backed settles, big Lakeland landscape photographs, traditional pub games; background music, free wi-fi; children and dogs (in bar) welcome, disabled facilities, back courtyard below lawn sloping up to church, open from 3pm. *(Anon)*

COCKERMOUTH   NY1130
Bush (01900) 822064
Main Street; CA13 9JS Traditional 18th-c two-bar beamed pub with friendly staff and locals, full Jennings range and a guest kept well (tasters offered), enjoyable straightforward lunchtime food, bare boards and slate floors, some stripped stone and half-panelling, banquettes, log fires, occasional acoustic live music; sports TV; children and dogs welcome, open all day. *(Mike and Eleanor Anderson, Comus and Sarah Elliott)*

COCKERMOUTH   NY1230
Castle Bar 07765 696679
Market Place; CA13 9NQ Renovated 16th-c pub on three floors, beams, timbers and other original features mixing with modern furnishings, five well kept local beers including Cumberland Legendary and Jennings (happy hour 4-7pm Mon-Fri, 12-8.30pm Sun), Weston's cider, good choice of enjoyable food in upstairs dining room or in any of the three ground-floor areas, friendly young staff; sports TV; children and dogs (downstairs) welcome, seats on back tiered terrace, open all day. *(Mike and Eleanor Anderson)*

CONISTON   SD3097
Black Bull (015394) 41335/41668
Yewdale Road (A593); LA21 8DU Bustling 17th-c beamed inn brewing its own good Coniston beers; back area (liked by walkers and their dogs) with slate floor, more comfortable carpeted front part has log fire and Donald Campbell memorabilia, enjoyable food including daily specials, lounge with 'big toe' of Old Man of Coniston (large piece

of stone in the wall), restaurant; they may ask to keep a credit card if you run a tab; children welcome, plenty of seats in former coachyard, 15 bedrooms, open (and food) all day from 8am, parking not easy at peak times. *(Robin Constable)*

CROOK   SD4695
★**Sun** (01539) 821351
B5284 Kendal–Bowness; LA8 8LA
Comfortable welcoming atmosphere in low-beamed bar with two dining areas off, good generously served traditional food, reasonable prices, prompt cheerful service, well kept ales such as Coniston and Hawkshead, good value wines, roaring log fire; children and dogs (in bar) welcome, open all day weekends (food all day then too). *(Isobel Mackinlay)*

CROSBY-ON-EDEN   NY4459
Stag (01228) 573455
A689 NE of Carlisle; CA6 4QN Friendly beamed village pub with three small rooms, variety of good value food including thai along with pub favourites, two Jennings ales, pleasant service, nice open fire; children welcome, tables outside, on Hadrian's Wall path and cycle way. *(Dr Kevan Tucker)*

DENT   SD7086
George & Dragon (01539) 625256
Main Street; LA10 5QL Two-bar corner pub in cobbled street, the Dent Brewery tap, with their full range kept well plus real cider and perry, old panelling, partitioned tables and open fire, enjoyable food from snacks up, prompt friendly service, steps down to restaurant, games room with pool and juke box; sports TV; children, walkers and dogs welcome, ten bedrooms, lovely village, open all day. *(Claes Mauroy, Comus and Sarah Elliott)*

ENNERDALE BRIDGE   NY0716
Fox & Hounds (01946) 861373
High Street; CA23 3AR Popular community-owned pub, smart and clean with flowers on tables, five well kept ales including local Ennerdale and Jennings, tasty reasonably priced home-made food; picnic-sets in streamside garden, three bedrooms, substantial breakfast, handy for walkers on Coast to Coast path, open all day. *(Stephen Funnell, Tina and David Woods-Taylor)*

ENNERDALE BRIDGE   NY0615
Shepherds Arms (01946) 861249
Off A5086 E of Egremont; CA23 3AR Friendly well placed walkers' inn by car-free dale, bar with log fire and woodburner, up to five local beers and good choice of generous home-made food, can provide packed lunches, panelled dining room and conservatory; free wi-fi; children welcome, seats outside by beck, eight bedrooms. *(Anon)*

ESKDALE GREEN   NY1200
Bower House (01946) 723244
0.5 miles W of Eskdale Green; CA19 1TD Old-fashioned 17th-c stone-built inn (plans for refurbishment by new local owners) extended around beamed and alcoved core, log fires, local ales such as Jennings and good choice of freshly made food in bar and biggish restaurant, friendly atmosphere; nicely tended sheltered garden by cricket field, charming spot with great walks, bedrooms, open all day. *(Tina and David Woods-Taylor, Martin Day)*

ESKDALE GREEN   NY1400
King George IV (01946) 723470
E of village; CA19 1TS Cheerful beamed and flagstoned bar with log fire, good range of well kept ales and over 100 malt whiskies, sensibly priced plentiful food from sandwiches to daily specials, friendly staff, restaurant, games room with pool; free wi-fi; children and dogs welcome, fine views from garden tables (road nearby), lots of good walks, bedrooms and self-catering accommodation. *(Margaret and Jeff Graham)*

FAUGH   NY5054
String of Horses (01228) 670297
S of village, on left as you go downhill; CA8 9EG Welcoming 17th-c coaching inn with cosy communicating beamed rooms, log fires, oak panelling and some interesting carved furniture, tasty traditional food alongside central american/mexican dishes, two Geltsdale beers, restaurant; free wi-fi; children welcome, a few tables out in front, 11 comfortable bedrooms, good breakfast, closed lunchtimes and all day Mon. *(Anon)*

FOXFIELD   SD2085
★**Prince of Wales** (01229) 716238
Opposite station; LA20 6BX Cheery bare-boards pub with half a dozen good changing ales including bargain beers brewed here and at their associated Tigertops Brewery, bottled imports and real cider too, huge helpings of enjoyable home-made food (lots of unusual pasties), good friendly service and character landlord, hot coal fire, pub games including bar billiards, daily papers and beer-related reading matter; children (games for them) and dogs welcome, four reasonably priced bedrooms, open all day Fri-Sun, from mid-afternoon Wed, Thurs, closed Mon, Tues. *(Pauline Fellows and Simon Robbins, Sarah Flynn)*

'Children welcome' means the pub says it lets children inside without any special restriction; some may impose an evening time limit earlier than 9pm – please tell us if you find this.

GOSFORTH NY0703

Gosforth Hall (019467) 25322

Off A595 and unclassified road to Wasdale; CA20 1AZ Friendly well run Jacobean inn with interesting history, beamed and carpeted bar (popular with locals) with fine plaster coat of arms above woodburner, lounge/reception area with huge fireplace, ales such as Hawkshead, Keswick and Yates, enjoyable home-made food including good range of pies, restaurant; TV; nice big side garden, 22 bedrooms (some in new extension), open all day, food from 5pm (not Sun). *(Clifford Blakemore)*

GREAT URSWICK SD2674

General Burgoyne (01229) 586394

Church Road; LA12 0SZ Flagstoned early 17th-c village pub overlooking small tarn, four cosy rambling rooms with beams and log fires (look for the skull in a cupboard), three Robinsons ales, creative cooking from landlord/chef along with pub favourites, dining conservatory; children and dogs welcome, picnic-sets out at front, closed lunchtimes Mon and Tues, otherwise open all day. *(Caroline Prescott)*

GREYSTOKE NY4430

Boot & Shoe (01768) 483343

By village green, off B5288; CA11 0TP Cosy two-bar 17th-c inn by green in pretty 'Tarzan' village; low ceilings, exposed brickwork and dark wood, good generously served traditional food, well kept Black Sheep and local microbrews, bustling friendly atmosphere, live music; children and dogs welcome, seats out at front and in back garden, on national cycle route, bedrooms, open all day. *(Anon)*

HARTSOP NY4013

Brotherswater Inn (01768) 482239

A592; CA11 0NZ Walkers' and campers' pub in magnificent setting at the bottom of Kirkstone Pass, local ales including Jennings and good choice of malt whiskies, generous helpings of enjoyable reasonably priced food, friendly staff; free wi-fi; dogs welcome, beautiful fells views from picture windows and terrace tables, six bedrooms, bunkhouse and campsite, open all day (from 8am for breakfast). *(Tina and David Woods-Taylor)*

HAWKSHEAD NY3501

★ Drunken Duck (015394) 36347

Barngates; the pub is signposted from B5286 Hawkshead–Ambleside, opposite the Outgate Inn; or take the first right from B5286, after the wooded caravan site; OS Sheet 90 map reference 350013; LA22 0NG Civilised inn – at its most informal at lunchtime – with small smart bar, leather club chairs, beams and oak boards, photographs, coaching prints and hunting pictures, stools by slate-topped counter serving own good Barngates ales, 17 wines by the glass from fine list, malt whiskies, lunchtime food plus first class evening dishes in three elegant areas, efficient service; children allowed, dogs in bar, tables and benches on grass opposite with spectacular fell views, profusion of spring and summer bulbs, lovely bedrooms with own balcony (book in advance), open all day. *(Colin McLachlan, John Evans, Dave Webster, Sue Holland, J R Wildon, Michael Doswell, Christian Mole)*

HAWKSHEAD SD3598

Queens Head (015394) 36271

Main Street; LA22 0NS Timbered pub in charming village, low-ceilinged bar with heavy bowed black beams, red plush wall seats and stools around hefty traditional tables, decorative plates on panelled walls, open fire, snug little room off, several eating areas, Robinsons ales and a guest, good wine and whisky choice, enjoyable bar food and more elaborate evening meals, friendly helpful staff; background music, TV, darts; children and dogs welcome, seats outside and pretty window boxes, 13 bedrooms, open all day. *(Dave Webster, Sue Holland, B J Harding)*

HAWKSHEAD SD3598

Red Lion (015394) 36213

Main Street; LA22 0NS Friendly old inn with good selection of well kept local ales including Hawkshead, enjoyable traditional home-made food, original panelling and good log fire; dogs allowed, eight bedrooms (some sloping floors), open all day. *(Richard Tilbrook)*

HESKET NEWMARKET NY3438

★ Old Crown (016974) 78288

Village signed off B5299 in Caldbeck; CA7 8JG Straightforward co-operative-owned local in attractive village, small bar with bric-a-brac, mountaineering kit and pictures, log fire, own good Hesket Newmarket beers (can book brewery tours) and generous helpings of good value freshly made pub food, friendly prompt service, dining room and garden room, folk night first Sun of month; juke box, pool and board games; children and dogs welcome, lovely walking country away from Lake District crowds, near Cumbria Way, closed lunchtimes Mon-Thurs (Mon, Tues in school holidays). *(Dr Kevan Tucker, Hilary De Lyon and Martin Webster)*

HIGH NEWTON SD4082

Crown (015395) 30613

Just off A590 Lindale–Newby Bridge, towards Cartmel Fell; LA11 6JH Friendly 17th-c coaching inn with beamed and flagstoned bar, log fire in stone fireplace, local ales such as Cumbrian Legendary and Hawkshead, decent wines by the glass and enjoyable home-made food from pub standards up, sizeable restaurant; children and dogs welcome, beer garden, good local walks and fishing, seven bedrooms, open (and food) all day weekends, closed lunchtimes Mon and Tues. *(Walter and Susan Rinaldi-Butcher)*

KESWICK   NY2623
★ **Dog & Gun** (017687) 73463

Lake Road; off top end of Market Square; CA12 5BT Unpretentious town pub with good mix of customers in friendly bustling bar, low beams and timbers, part slate, part wood, part carpeted flooring, fine collection of striking mountain photographs, brass and brewery artefacts, reasonably priced hearty food including signature goulash in two sizes, half a dozen well kept ales, log fires; dogs (menu for them) and muddy boots welcome, children before 9pm if eating, open (and food) all day, can get very busy in season. *(John and Gloria Isaacs, Eddie Edwards, Adrian Johnson, Dave Webster, Sue Holland)*

KESWICK   NY2623
George (017687) 72076

St Johns Street; CA12 5AZ Handsome 17th-c coaching inn with open-plan main bar and attractive traditional dark-panelled side room, old-fashioned settles and modern banquettes under black beams, log fires, daily papers, four Jennings ales and a couple of guests kept well, plenty of wines by the glass, generous home-made food including signature cow pie, prompt friendly service, restaurant; background music, Tues quiz; children welcome in eating areas, dogs in bar, 13 bedrooms, open all day. *(Eddie Edwards)*

KESWICK   NY2421
Swinside Inn (017687) 78253

Newlands Valley, just SW; CA12 5UE Lovely peaceful valley setting and some recent refurbishment; carpeted beamed coal-fire bar with well kept ales including Theakstons Best, decent choice of reasonably priced food, stripped-floor area beyond with central woodburner and back games part; background and occasional live music, Sky TV, free wi-fi; children and dogs welcome, tables in garden and on upper and lower terraces giving fine views across to the high crags and fells around Rosedale Pike, six bedrooms, open all day. *(David Heath, Tina and David Woods-Taylor)*

KIRKBY LONSDALE   SD6178
Orange Tree (015242) 71716

Fairbank B6254; LA6 2BD Family-run inn acting as tap for Kirkby Lonsdale brewery, well kept guest beers too and good choice of wines, beams, sporting pictures and old range, enjoyable food in back dining room served by friendly staff; pool, darts, background music; children and dogs welcome, comfortable bedrooms (some in building next door), open all day. *(Anon)*

KIRKBY LONSDALE   SD6278
Red Dragon (015242) 71205

Main Street; LA6 2AH Recently refurbished by Robinsons, their well kept ales and wide choice of generously served home-cooked food, beams and flagstones, matching wooden furniture including a couple of high-backed settles, log fire and woodburner; children and dogs welcome, bedrooms, open (and food) all day. *(Ray and Winifred Halliday)*

KIRKBY LONSDALE   SD6178
★ **Sun** (015242) 71965

Market Street (B6254); LA6 2AU Cheerful busy 17th-c inn striking good balance between pub and restaurant; unusual-looking building with upper floors supported by three sturdy pillars above pavement, attractive rambling beamed bar with flagstones and stripped oak boards, pews, armchairs and cosy window seats, big landscapes and country pictures on cream walls, two log fires, comfortable back lounge and modern dining room, good contemporary food (booking advised), well kept Hawkshead, Thwaites and a guest, friendly helpful service; background music; children and dogs welcome, nice bedrooms, no car park, open all day from 9am, closed Mon till 3pm. *(Caroline Prescott)*

KIRKOSWALD   NY5641
Fetherston Arms (01768) 898284

The Square; CA10 1DQ Busy old stone inn with cosy bar and various dining areas, enjoyable food at reasonable prices including good home-made pies, interesting range of well kept changing beers, friendly helpful staff; bedrooms, nice Eden Valley village. *(David Heath)*

LANGDALE   NY2906
Sticklebarn (015394) 37356

By car park for Stickle Ghyll; LA22 9JU Glorious views from this roomy and busy Langdale Valley walkers'/climbers' bar owned and run by the NT; up to five well kept changing ales and a real cider, home-made locally sourced food (meat from next-door farm), mountaineering photographs, two woodburners, upstairs bar with pool; background music (live Sat); children, dogs and boots welcome, big terrace with inner verandah, outside pizza oven, open (and food) all day. *(Dr and Mrs Leach, Comus and Sarah Elliott)*

LEVENS   SD4885
Hare & Hounds (015395) 60004

Off A590; LA8 8PN Welcoming smartened-up village pub handy for Sizergh Castle (NT), five well kept changing local ales and good home-made pub food including pizzas, partly panelled low-beamed lounge bar, front tap room with coal fire, further room down steps; Weds quiz in winter;

children and dogs welcome, good views from front terrace, open all day Fri-Sun, closed Mon and till 4pm Tues-Thurs. *(Anon)*

LORTON   NY1526
★**Wheatsheaf** (01900) 85199
B5289 Buttermere–Cockermouth; CA13 9UW Friendly local atmosphere in neatly furnished bar with two log fires and vibrant purple walls, affable hard-working landlord, Jennings ales and regular changing guests, several good value wines, popular home-made food (all day Sun) from sandwiches up, curry night Weds, fresh fish Thurs and Fri evenings, smallish restaurant (best to book), good friendly service, occasional live music; children and dogs welcome, tables out behind and campsite, open all day weekends, closed lunchtimes Tues, Weds (Mon-Fri lunchtimes in winter). *(Anon)*

LOWICK GREEN   SD3084
Farmers Arms (01229) 861277
Just off A5092 SE of village; LA12 8DT Stable bar with heavy black beams, huge slate flagstones and log fire, cosy corners, some interesting furniture and pictures in plusher hotel lounge/dining area, tasty reasonably priced food (all day Fri-Sun) from sandwiches and basket meals up, Thwaites Wainwright, Fullers London Pride and three guests, decent choice of wines by the glass, good friendly service; pool and darts, Sky TV, background music, free wi-fi; children and dogs welcome, ten comfortable bedrooms, good breakfast, closed Mon lunchtime, otherwise open all day. *(Derek and Margaret Senior)*

LUPTON   SO5581
★**Plough** (015395) 67700
A65, near M6 junction 36; LA6 1PJ Carefully refurbished inn, comfortable and relaxing, with spreading open-plan bars – sister pub to the Punch Bowl at Crosthwaite (see Main Entries); beams, hunting prints and Punch cartoons on contemporary grey paintwork, rugs on wooden floors, some antique tables and chairs, leather sofas and armchairs by woodburner, good interesting food served by neat staff, ales such as Coniston, Hawkshead, Jennings and Kirkby Lonsdale, several wines by the glass; background music, daily papers; children and dogs (in bar) welcome, rustic seats under parasols behind white picket fence, more in back garden, good surrounding walks, bedrooms, open (and food) all day. *(David Heath, Kay and Alistair Butler, Ray and Winifred Halliday, Ian Herdman)*

MUNGRISDALE   NY3630
★**Mill Inn** (017687) 79632
Off A66 Penrith–Keswick, 1 mile W of A5091 Ullswater turn-off; CA11 0XR Part 17th-c pub in fine setting below fells with wonderful surrounding walks,

neatly kept bar, log fire in stone fireplace, old millstone built into counter serving Robinsons Dizzy Blonde, Hartleys Cumbria Way, Hartleys Cumbrian XB and a guest beer, traditional dark wood furnishings, hunting pictures on walls, quite a choice of food using local produce, separate dining room, darts, winter pool, dominoes; children and dogs welcome, seats in garden by river, six bedrooms, open all day. *(Isobel Mackinlay, David Jackman, Martin Day)*

NETHER WASDALE   NY1204
★**Strands** (01946) 726237
SW of Wast Water; CA20 1ET Lovely spot below the remote high fells around Wast Water, own-brew beers and popular good value food, well cared-for high-beamed main bar with woodburner, smaller public bar with pool, separate dining room, pleasant staff and relaxed friendly atmosphere; background music; children and dogs welcome, neat garden with terrace and belvedere, 14 bedrooms, open all day. *(Isobel Mackinlay)*

NEWBIGGIN   NY5649
Blue Bell (01768) 896615
B6413; CA8 9DH Tiny L-shaped one-room pub with two local ales and decent pubby food, friendly atmosphere, fireplace on right, pool; good Eden Valley walks. *(Dr Kevan Tucker)*

PENRITH   NY5130
Moo Bar (01768) 606637
King Street; CA11 7AY Bare-boards bar opened 2012 (originally a 19th-c cattle house), ever-changing range of six local ales, craft beers such as BrewDog and over 100 bottled imports, friendly knowledgeable staff and good mix of customers, no food, upstairs 'Udder Room' with sofas and sports TV, Mon folk night; well behaved dogs welcome, open all day. *(Geoff O'Connell)*

PENRUDDOCK   NY4227
★**Herdwick** (01768) 483007
Off A66 Penrith–Keswick; CA11 0QU Attractively cottagey and sympathetically renovated 18th-c inn, warm welcoming atmosphere, well kept Jennings and summer guests from unusual curved bar, decent wines, enjoyable sensibly priced pubby food, Sun carvery, friendly efficient staff, good open fire, stripped stone and white paintwork, nice dining room with upper gallery, games room with pool and darts; children in eating areas, five good value bedrooms, open all day weekends. *(Alan Eaves)*

POOLEY BRIDGE   NY4724
Sun (017684) 86205
Centre of village (B5320); CA10 2NN Friendly roadside local in row of whitewashed cottages, well kept Jennings and guests, decent choice of enjoyable fairly traditional food, two bars with steps between (dogs allowed in lower one), restaurant; may

be background music; children welcome, picnic-sets in garden with play fort, nine bedrooms. *(Steve and Liz Tilley, David Heath)*

RAVENSTONEDALE NY7401
Fat Lamb (015396) 23242
Crossbank; A683 Sedbergh–Kirkby Stephen; CA17 4LL Isolated inn surrounded by great scenery (good walks), pews in comfortable beamed bar with fire in traditional black inglenook range, good local photographs and bird plates, propeller from 1930s biplane over servery, friendly helpful staff, wide choice of good proper food from filled baguettes to enjoyable restaurant meals, well kept Black Sheep, decent wines and around 60 malts; children and dogs welcome, disabled facilities, tables out by nature-reserve pastures, 12 bedrooms, open all day. *(Comus and Sarah Elliott)*

ROSTHWAITE NY2514
Scafell (017687) 77208
B5289 S of Keswick; CA12 5XB Hotel's big tile-floored back bar useful for walkers, weather forecast board and blazing log fire, up to eight well kept ales in season, enjoyable food from sandwiches up, afternoon teas, also appealing cocktail bar/sun lounge and dining room, friendly helpful staff; background music, pool; children and dogs welcome, tables out overlooking beck, 23 bedrooms, open all day. *(Anon)*

RULEHOLME NY5060
Golden Fleece (01228) 573686
Signed off A689; CA6 4NF Welcoming inn with good food and a couple of local ales, friendly attentive service; children welcome, seven comfortable bedrooms. *(Malcolm)*

RYDAL NY3606
Glen Rothay Hotel (015394) 34500
A591 Ambleside–Grasmere; LA22 9LR Attractive small 17th-c hotel with up to five well kept changing local ales in back bar, banquettes and stools, some badger pictures, good choice of enjoyable locally sourced food from sandwiches up, beamed and panelled dining lounge with open fire, restaurant, helpful friendly staff, acoustic music first Weds of month; walkers and dogs welcome, tables in pretty garden, eight comfortable bedrooms, open all day. *(Anon)*

SANDFORD NY7316
★ Sandford Arms (01768) 351121
Village and pub signposted just off A66 W of Brough; CA16 6NR Neat former 18th-c farmhouse in peaceful village, enjoyable food (all day weekends Apr-Oct) from chef/landlord, L-shaped carpeted main bar with stripped beams and stonework, well kept ales including a house beer from Tirril, comfortable raised and balustraded eating area, more formal dining room and second flagstoned bar, woodburner; background music; children and dogs welcome, seats in front garden and covered courtyard, three bedrooms and self-catering cottage, closed Tues, lunchtime Weds. *(Caroline Prescott)*

SANTON BRIDGE NY1101
Bridge Inn (01946) 726221
Off A595 at Holmrook or Gosforth; CA19 1UX Old inn set in charming riverside spot with fell views, bustling beamed and timbered bar, log fire, some booths around stripped-pine tables, Jennings and other Marstons-related beers, traditional food including blackboard specials, Sun carvery, separate dining room, friendly helpful staff, small reception hall with log fire and daily papers; background music, free wi-fi; children and dogs (in bar) welcome, seats outside by quiet road, plenty of walks, 16 bedrooms, open all day from 8am (breakfast for non-residents). *(Anon)*

SATTERTHWAITE SD3392
Eagles Head (01229) 860237
S edge of village; LA12 8LN Pretty and prettily placed on the edge of beautiful Grizedale Forest (visitor centre nearby); welcoming newish management, low black beams and comfortable furnishings, various odds and ends including antlers, horsebrasses, decorative plates and earthenware, woodburner, ales such as Barngates, Hawkshead and Cumbrian Legendary, enjoyable pubby food, occasional live music; children, dogs and muddy boots welcome, picnic-sets in attractive tree-shaded courtyard garden with pergola, open all day summer, closed Mon in winter. *(Isobel Mackinlay)*

SEATHWAITE SD2295
★ Newfield Inn (01229) 716208
Duddon Valley, near Ulpha (not Seathwaite in Borrowdale); LA20 6ED Friendly 16th-c cottage with good local atmosphere in slate-floored bar, wooden tables and chairs, interesting pictures, woodburner, three changing local beers and good straightforward food, comfortable side room, games room; children and dogs welcome, tables in nice garden with hill views and play area, good walks, two self-catering flats, open all day. *(Anon)*

SEDBERGH SD6592
Red Lion (015396) 20433
Finkle Street (A683); LA10 5BZ Cheerful beamed local, down to earth and comfortable, with good value generous home-made food (meat from next-door butcher), well kept Jennings and other Marstons-related beers, good coal fire, quiz and music nights; sports TV, free wi-fi, no dogs; open all day weekends when it can get very busy, no food Mon. *(Derek Stafford)*

ST BEES NX9711
Queens (01946) 822287
Main Street; CA27 0DE Friendly 17th-c two-bar pub with well kept Jennings and

good reasonably priced home-made food, dining area and conservatory, log fires, Thurs quiz and monthly live music; two-tier garden behind, good walks (Coast to Coast one starts/ends here), 14 bedrooms, good breakfast. *(Stephen Funnell, Frank Gorman)*

THRELKELD NY3225
★**Horse & Farrier** (017687) 79688
A66 Penrith–Keswick; CA12 4SQ Popular 17th-c inn with linked mainly carpeted rooms (some flagstones), mix of furniture from comfortably padded seats to pubby chairs and wall settles, candlelit tables, beams and open fires, well cooked/ presented local food such as Morecambe Bay scallops and Penruddock duck, good selection of Jennings ales, partly stripped-stone restaurant; children welcome, dogs allowed in one part of bar, disabled facilities, a few picnic-sets outside and fine views towards Helvellyn range, walks from the back door, bedrooms, open all day. *(Tina and David Woods-Taylor, WAH, Martin Day, Christian Mole, Margaret and Peter Staples, Chris and Val Ramstedt)*

TORVER SD2894
Wilson Arms (01539) 441237
A593; LA21 8BB Old family-run roadside inn, beams, nice log fire and some modern touches, well kept Cumbrian ales and good locally sourced food cooked to order (more evening choice) in bar or dining room, friendly service; free wi-fi; children and dogs welcome, hill views (including Old Man of Coniston) from tables outside, deli, seven bedrooms and three holiday cottages, open (and food) all day. *(Jane Walker)*

TROUTBECK NY4103
Mortal Man (015394) 33193
A592 N of Windermere; Upper Road; LA23 1PL Beamed and partly panelled bar with cosy room off, log fires, well kept local ales including a house beer from Hawkshead, several wines by the glass, well liked food in bar and picture-window restaurant, folk night Sun, quiz Weds; free wi-fi; children and dogs welcome, great views from sunny garden, lovely village, bedrooms, open all day. *(Ian and Rose Lock)*

TROUTBECK NY4103
Queens Head (015394) 32174
A592 N of Windermere; LA23 1PW This popular 17th-c beamed coaching inn was badly damaged by fire as we went to press – owners Robinsons say they will fully restore it.

TROUTBECK NY3827
Troutbeck Inn (017684) 83635
A5091/A66; CA11 0SJ Former railway hotel with small bar, lounge and log-fire restaurant, good food cooked by proprietor, a couple of Jennings ales, efficient friendly service; children and dogs (in bar) welcome, seven bedrooms, four self-catering cottages in converted stables, open all day spring/ summer. *(Graham and Elizabeth Hargreaves)*

ULVERSTON SD2878
★**Farmers Arms** (01229) 584469
Market Place; LA12 7BA Convivial attractively modernised town pub, front bar with comfortable sofas, contemporary wicker chairs and original fireplace, daily newspapers, quickly changing ales and a dozen wines by the glass, good choice of interesting fairly priced food including fish specials, second bar leading to big raftered dining area (children here only); unobtrusive background music, Thurs quiz; seats on attractive heated front terrace, lots of colourful tubs and hanging baskets, Thurs market day (pub busy then), bedrooms and self-catering cottages, open all day from 9.30am. *(Anon)*

WASDALE HEAD NY1807
Wasdale Head Inn (019467) 26229
NE of Wast Water; CA20 1EX Mountain hotel worth knowing for its stunning fellside setting; roomy walkers' bar with nice fire, enjoyable home-made food, several local ales and good choice of wines; residents' bar, lounge and panelled restaurant; children welcome, dogs in bar, nine bedrooms, also nine apartments (six self-catering) in converted barn, camping, open all day. *(Margaret and Jeff Graham, Martin Day)*

Derbyshire

KEY ★ Star Pub 🌟 Top Quality Food ◀ Great Beer

🍷 Good Wines £ Bargain Meals 🛏 Good Bedrooms 🍴 Serves Food

ALDERWASLEY
SK3153 Map 7
Bear ★ 🍷 ◀

Left off A6 at Ambergate on to Holly Lane (turns into Jackass Lane),
then right at end (staggered crossroads); DE56 2RD

**Unspoilt country inn with beamed cottagey rooms, good range of
real ales, tasty food and a peaceful garden; bedrooms**

In warm weather, try to bag one of the well spaced picnic-sets in the
lovely garden with its wonderful country views. Inside is popular too,
so it's best to book a table in advance. There's no obvious front door – you
get in through the plain back entrance by the car park. One little room has
a large glass chandelier over assorted high-backed chairs around a single
vast table; another has tartan-covered wall banquettes, ladderback chairs
around a big square table and large antlers hanging from the ceiling; and
a third room has beams, a double-sided woodburner and assorted plates
on a dresser. Other décor includes staffordshire china ornaments, old
paintings and engravings and a grandfather clock. Sharps Doom Bar,
Thornbridge Jaipur, Timothy Taylors Landlord and guests such as Blue
Monkey BG Sips and 99 Red Baboons on handpump, several wines by
the glass from a decent list, and malt whiskies.

🍴 Generous helpings of tasty food includes sandwiches, pigeon with bacon lardons
with anchovy and red wine vinaigrette, arancini filled with tomato and thyme
with parmesan crisps, steak in ale pie, spinach, courgette and goats cheese lasagne,
chicken with smoked pancetta and ceps in brandy jus, and puddings such as sticky
toffee pudding and cheesecake of the day. *Benchmark main dish: burger with
smoked cheese with Jack Daniel's sauce and chips £12.95. Two-course evening
meal £20.00.*

Free house ~ Licensee Keith Marshall-Clarke ~ Real ale ~ (01629) 822585 ~ Open 11-11
~ Bar food 12-2.30, 6-9; 12-9 Fri, Sat, until 8.30 Sun ~ Restaurant ~ Children welcome ~
Dogs allowed in bar ~ Wi-fi ~ Bedrooms: /£65 ~ www.bear-hotel.co.uk
Recommended by Richard Cole, Peter F Marshall, Stephen Shepherd, Dennis Jones

ASHOVER
SK3462 Map 7
Old Poets Corner ◀ £ 🛏

Butts Road (B6036, off A632 Matlock–Chesterfield); S45 0EW

**A fine range of interesting real ales (some own brew) and ciders in
characterful village pub with enthusiastic owners; hearty, reasonably
priced food**

The fine range of around ten real ales on handpump remains a huge draw to this cheerful village local. Four are from their own microbrewery (Ashover Light Rale, Coffin Lane Stout, Hydro and Poets Tipple – you can do a brewery tour) alongside guests from breweries such as Abbeydale, Batemans, Blue Monkey, Kelham Island, Oakham, Roosters, Salopian, Sarah Hughes and Slaters; also, a terrific choice of eight farm ciders, a dozen fruit wines, 20 malt whiskies and belgian beers. They also hold regular beer festivals. The informal bar has an easy-going atmosphere and a mix of chairs and pews, while a small room opening off the bar has a stack of newspapers and vintage comics; background music. French doors lead to a tiny balcony with a couple of tables. They hold regular acoustic, folk and blues sessions, and posters advertise forthcoming events, which might include quiz nights, poetry evenings and morris dancers. The bedrooms are attractive, and there's also a holiday cottage sleeping up to eight.

Fairly priced pubby dishes include baguettes, creamy garlic mushrooms on toasted sourdough, home-cooked ham and eggs, chilli con carne, chicken wrapped in bacon with cheese and barbecue sauce, vegetable lasagne, beef stew, quite a choice of sausages with mash, liver and onions in stout, and puddings; Sunday is curry night. *Benchmark main dish: beer-battered fish and chips £9.95. Two-course evening meal £15.25.*

Own brew ~ Licensees Kim and Jackie Beresford ~ Real ale ~ (01246) 590888 ~ Open 12-11 ~ Bar food 12-2 (3 Sat), 6-9 (9.30 Fri, Sat); 12-4, 7-9 Sun ~ Restaurant ~ Children welcome away from bar ~ Dogs allowed in bar and bedrooms ~ Wi-fi ~ Acoustic evenings Tues, Sun; live bands monthly ~ Bedrooms: £55/£80 ~ www.oldpoets.co.uk
Recommended by Ken and Lynda Taylor, Laurence Sillars, Peter F Marshall, Derek and Sylvia Stephenson, D B Mines

BRASSINGTON
Olde Gate £

SK2354 Map 7

Village signed off B5056 and B5035 NE of Ashbourne; DE4 4HJ

Lovely old interior, candlelit at night, with tasty, fairly priced food, real ales and country garden

This unspoilt old place with mullioned windows has bags of character. It's full of fine furnishings: a venerable wall clock, rush-seated old chairs and antique settles (note the ancient one in black solid oak), a 17th-c kitchen range with gleaming copper pots, beams hung with pewter mugs and shelves lined with embossed Doulton stoneware flagons. There's a panelled Georgian room and, to the left of a small hatch-served lobby, a cosy beamed room with stripped panelled settles, scrubbed-top tables and a blazing fire under a huge mantelbeam. Jennings Cumberland and Ringwood Boondoggle on handpump; cribbage, dominoes, cards and maybe boules on Sunday evenings in summer. The inviting garden has tables that look out to idyllic silvery-walled pastures, and there are benches in the small front yard.

Popular, reasonably priced food includes lunchtime sandwiches and baguettes, warm goats cheese en croûte with pear and walnut salad, creamed garlic mushrooms on crusty bread, trio of sausages with onion gravy, chicken with tarragon sauce, vegetarian curry, bass with herb and lemon sauce, and puddings such as white chocolate and raspberry brioche bread and butter pudding and sticky toffee pudding. *Benchmark main dish: steak in Guinness pie £9.95. Two-course evening meal £19.00.*

Marstons ~ Lease Peter Scragg ~ Real ale ~ No credit cards ~ (01629) 540448 ~ Open

12-2.15 (3 Sat), 6-11; 12-4, 7-11 Sun; closed Mon except bank holiday lunchtimes, Tues
lunchtime (may open then in summer) ~ Bar food 12-1.45 (2.30 Sat), 6-9; 12-3 Sun ~
Restaurant ~ Well behaved children welcome ~ Dogs allowed in bar ~ Wi-fi ~
www.oldgateinnbrassington.co.uk *Recommended by Ann and Colin Hunt, Peter F Marshall*

BRETTON

SK2078 Map 7

Barrel

*Signposted from Foolow, which itself is signposted from A623 just E of
junction with B6465 to Bakewell; can also be reached from either the B6049 at Great
Hucklow, or the B6001 via Abney, from Leadmill just S of Hathersage; S32 5QD*

**Remote dining pub with traditional décor, popular food and
friendly staff**

This pub is in a tremendous spot in excellent walking country, with
unparalleled views – you can see five counties when the weather
is right. The outdoor seats (on the front terrace by the road and in a
courtyard garden) are nicely sheltered from the inevitable breeze at this
height. Inside, everything is spic and span and the friendly staff are smartly
dressed. Stubs of massive knocked-through stone walls divide the place
into several areas. The cosy dark oak-beamed bar is charmingly traditional,
with gleaming copper and brass, a warming fire, patterned carpet, low
doorways and stools lined up at the counter. There's Marstons Pedigree
and EPA and Wychwood Hobgoblin on handpump, 28 malt whiskies, a farm
cider and wines by the glass; background radio.

 Well liked food includes sandwiches, stilton mushrooms, chicken liver pâté with
curried rhubarb chutney, courgette, spring onion and pea risotto, beer-battered
fish and chips, fish crumble, lambs liver with onions, venison pie, and puddings such
as sticky toffee and bakewell puddings. *Benchmark main dish: steak in ale pie
£11.95. Two-course evening meal £21.00.*

Free house ~ Licensee Philip Cone ~ Real ale ~ (01433) 630856 ~ Open 11-3, 6-11
(may open all day in high summer); 11-11 Sat, Sun ~ Bar food 12-2, 6-9; 12-9 Sun ~
Well behaved children welcome ~ Wi-fi ~ Bedrooms: /$85 ~ www.thebarrelinn.co.uk
Recommended by Dennis Jones

CHELMORTON

SK1170 Map 7

Church Inn ♨ £ ⇌

*Village signposted off A5270, between A6 and A515 SE of Buxton; keep on up
through village towards church; SK17 9SL*

**Cosy, convivial, traditional inn beautifully set in High Peak walking
country; good value food**

The chatty, low-ceilinged bar in this bustling inn has a warming fire and
is traditionally furnished with built-in cushioned benches and simple
chairs around polished cast-iron-framed tables (a couple still have their
squeaky sewing treadles). Shelves of books, Tiffany-style lamps and house
plants in the curtained windows, atmospheric Dales photographs and
prints, and a coal-effect stove in the stripped-stone end wall all add a cosy
feel. Adnams Bitter, Marstons Bitter and Pedigree and a couple of guests
such as Thornbridge Kipling and Timothy Taylors Landlord on handpump;
darts in a tiled-floor games area on the left; TV, darts and board games. The
inn is opposite a mainly 18th-c church and is prettily tucked into woodland,
with fine views over the village and hills beyond from good teak tables
on a two-level terrace. The cottagey bedrooms are comfortable and the
breakfasts good.

As well as hot and cold baps, the fairly priced food includes black pudding fritters with spiced chutney, creamy garlic mushrooms, chickpea tagine, gammon with egg and pineapple, lasagne, steak and kidney pie, chicken in stilton sauce, pork stroganoff, beer-battered fresh haddock and chips, and puddings. *Benchmark main dish: rabbit pie £12.75. Two-course evening meal £14.00.*

Free house ~ Licensees Julie and Justin Satur ~ Real ale ~ (01298) 85319 ~ Open 12-3, 6-11; 12-11 Sat, Sun ~ Bar food 12-2.30, 6-8.30; 12-8.30 Fri-Sun ~ Children welcome ~ Dogs allowed in bar ~ Wi-fi ~ Bedrooms: £55/£80 ~ www.thechurchinn.co.uk
Recommended by Greg Lawton, Ann and Colin Hunt, Mike and Margaret Banks, Peter F Marshall, John Wooll

CHINLEY   SK0382   Map 7
Old Hall ★ ◧ ⌂

Village signposted off A6 (very sharp turn) E of New Mills; also off A624 N of Chapel-en-le-Frith; Whitehough Head Lane, off B6062; SK23 6EJ

Charming small Peak District inn with great range of beers and ciders, good country food and striking ancient dining hall; comfortable bedrooms

Even if you've come to this 16th-c stone-built inn just for a drink or bar meal, do poke your nose into the dining room, which is surprisingly grand with a great stone chimney soaring into high eaves, refectory tables on a parquet floor, lovely old mullioned windows and a splendid minstrels' gallery. The warm bar – basically four small friendly rooms opened into a single area tucked behind a massive central chimney – contains open fires, some broad flagstones, red patterned carpet, sturdy country tables, a couple of long pews and various other seats including a leather chesterfield and a wing armchair. The beers are exceptional and might include Happy Valley Lazy Daze, Hop Back Entire Stout, Marstons Bitter, Redwillow Directionless, Storm Bosley Cloud and Thornbridge Hopton and Jaipur IPA on handpump, as well as Thatcher's farm cider, some interesting lagers on tap, 21 malt whiskies and a rare range of bottled ciders and (mostly belgian) beers; beer festivals with music are held in late February and September. Also, mainly new world wines by the glass and friendly, helpful service. The pretty walled garden has picnic-sets under sycamore trees.

Quite a choice of enjoyable food includes sandwiches, smoked salmon and cream cheese pâté, antipasti plate to share, wild mushroom risotto, home-roasted ham and free-range eggs, cumberland pork sausages with onion gravy, chilli burger with gruyère, bacon, coleslaw and chips, steak in ale pudding, cod loin with brown shrimp butter, and puddings such as bitter chocolate tart and lemon and lime panna cotta. *Benchmark main dish: steak in ale pudding £12.00. Two-course evening meal £18.00.*

Free house ~ Licensee Daniel Capper ~ Real ale ~ (01663) 750529 ~ Open 12-12 ~ Bar food 12-2, 5-9 (9.30 Fri, Sat); 12-7 Sun ~ Restaurant ~ Children welcome ~ Dogs allowed in bar ~ Wi-fi ~ Bedrooms: £75/£89 ~ www.old-hall-inn.co.uk
Recommended by Hawtins, Mike Swan

FENNY BENTLEY   SK1750   Map 7
Coach & Horses
A515 N of Ashbourne; DE6 1LB

Cosy former coaching inn with pretty country furnishings, roaring open fires and food all day

Our readers enjoy their visits to this welcoming and comfortable coaching inn, with the food and ales coming in for particular praise. The traditional interior has all the trappings you'd expect of a country pub, from roaring log fires, exposed brick hearths and flagstone floors to black beams hung with pewter mugs, and hand-made pine furniture that includes wall settles with floral-print cushions. There's also a conservatory dining room and a cosy front dining room. Marstons Pedigree and a guest such as Church End Goats Milk on handpump, and the landlord is knowledgeable about malt whiskies – he stocks just under two dozen; quiet background music. There are tables in a side garden by an elder tree (with views across fields), as well as modern tables and chairs under cocktail parasols on a front roadside terrace. It's a few minutes' walk to the Tissington Trail, a popular cycling/walking path along a former railway line that is best joined at the nearby picturebook village of Tissington.

Good, popular food at fair prices includes hot and cold sandwiches (until 5pm), ham hock terrine with apricot and chilli chutney, a deli board to share, wild mushroom and leek stroganoff, toulouse sausages with tomato and garlic sauce, chicken korma, beer-battered fresh haddock and chips, lamb casserole with herby dumplings, and puddings. *Benchmark main dish: duck breast with black cherry and vodka sauce £14.00. Two-course evening meal £18.00.*

Free house ~ Licensees John and Matthew Dawson ~ Real ale ~ (01335) 350246 ~ Open 11-11; 12-10.30 Sun ~ Bar food 12-9 ~ Restaurant ~ Children welcome ~ Wi-fi ~ www.coachandhorsesfennybentley.co.uk *Recommended by Ann and Colin Hunt, Dave Webster, Sue Holland, J and E Dakin, Tracey and Stephen Groves, P Dawn, Brian BT, Fiona Todd, Jill and Julian Tasker, Dennis Jones*

GREAT LONGSTONE
Crispin
SK1971 Map 7

Main Street; village signed from A6020, N of Ashford in the Water; DE45 1TZ

Spotless traditional pub with emphasis on good, fairly priced pubby food; good drinks choice, too

The family running this well established pub offer a genuinely warm welcome to all their customers. Décor throughout is thoroughly traditional: brass or copper implements, decorative plates, a photo collage of regulars, horsebrasses on the beams in the red ceiling, cushioned built-in wall benches and upholstered chairs and stools around polished tables on red carpet, and a fire. A corner area is snugly partitioned off, and there's a separate, more formal dining room on the right; darts, board games and maybe faint background music. Cheerful staff serve a good choice of wines and whiskies, as well as Robinsons Dizzy Blonde, Double Hop, Hannibals Nectar, Trooper and Unicorn on handpump and Weston's Old Rosie cider. There are picnic-sets out in front, set well back above the quiet lane, and more in the garden. This is excellent walking country.

Tasty straightforward food includes sandwiches, chicken liver pâté with cumberland sauce, mussels in cider and garlic, vegetable shepherd's pie topped with goats cheese mash, burger with cheddar, mushrooms, tomato salsa and chips, slow-roasted pork shoulder with marsala gravy, bass with sauce vierge, and puddings such as tiramisu and apple and berry crumble; they also offer a two- and three-course set menu and an OAP lunch menu. *Benchmark main dish: steak and kidney in ale pie £12.95. Two-course evening meal £19.00.*

Robinsons ~ Tenant Paul Rowlinson ~ Real ale ~ (01629) 640237 ~ Open 12-3, 6-midnight; 12-midnight Sat; 12-10.30 Sun ~ Bar food 12-2.30, 6-9 ~ Restaurant ~ Children welcome ~ Dogs welcome ~ Wi-fi ~ www.thecrispin.co.uk *Recommended by David Eberlin*

HASSOP
SK2272 Map 7

Eyre Arms

B6001 N of Bakewell; DE45 1NS

Comfortable, neatly kept pub with decent food and beer, and pretty views from the garden

The delightful garden with its gurgling fountain looks straight out to fine Peak District countryside, and the summer hanging baskets are lovely. The low-ceilinged beamed rooms of this 17th-c former coaching inn are snug and cosy, with cheery log fires. Traditional furnishings include cushioned oak settles, comfortable plush chairs, a longcase clock, old pictures and lots of brass and copper. The small public bar has an unusual collection of teapots, as well as Black Sheep, Peak Ales Swift Nick and a guest from Bradfield on handpump, eight wines by the glass and 25 malt whiskies; darts and dominoes. The dining room is dominated by a painting of the Eyre coat of arms above the stone fireplace.

Using some home-grown produce, food includes lunchtime sandwiches and toasties, deep-fried garlic mushrooms, thai-style crab cakes with sweet pepper sauce, aubergine and mushroom lasagne, steak and kidney pie, venison pie, salmon with orange and basil sauce, spicy lamb with coconut, and puddings such as bakewell pudding and eton mess. *Benchmark main dish: chicken stuffed with leeks and stilton in a creamy sauce £13.40. Two-course evening meal £17.25.*

Free house ~ Licensees Nick and Lynne Smith ~ Real ale ~ (01629) 640390 ~ Open 11.30-3, 6-11; closed Mon evening Oct-Easter ~ Bar food 12-2 (2.30 weekends), 6-9 ~ Children welcome ~ Dogs allowed in bar ~ www.eyrearms.com *Recommended by Caroline Prescott, Emma Scofield*

HATHERSAGE
SK2380 Map 7

Plough

Leadmill; B6001 towards Bakewell; S32 1BA

Derbyshire Dining Pub of the Year

Comfortable dining pub usefully placed for exploring the Peak District, with good food, beer and wine, and seats in the waterside garden; comfortable bedrooms

With unfailingly helpful, friendly staff, good food and well equipped beamed bedrooms in a barn conversion, this thoughtfully run and spotlessly kept inn is much enjoyed by our readers. The cosy, traditionally furnished rooms have rows of dark wooden chairs and tables (with cruets showing the emphasis on dining) and a long banquette running almost the length of one wall, on bright tartan and oriental patterned carpets. Also, a big log fire and a woodburning stove, decorative plates on terracotta walls and pewter tankards hanging from a dark beam; the neat dining room is slightly more formal. They have a good wine list (with 21 by the glass), 17 malt whiskies, and Bass, Black Sheep, Bradfield Farmers Blonde and Greene King Old Speckled Hen on handpump; quiet background music. The nine-acre grounds are on the banks of the River Derwent – the pretty garden slopes down to the water – and there's a terrace with wonderful valley views.

Good, interesting food includes sandwiches, smoked bacon velouté with black pudding toastie, scallops with chorizo three-ways, wild mushroom and artichoke pizzetta with tomato and olive fondue, sausages with onion jus and champ, linguine with king prawns and chilli, corn-fed chicken with sun-dried tomato and rosemary beurre blanc, pork belly and pressed ham hock with cabbage and celeriac cannelloni and sage cream, and puddings. *Benchmark main dish: beef in Guinness pie with honey-roast parsnips £14.00. Two-course evening meal £20.00.*

Free house ~ Licensees Bob, Cynthia and Elliott Emery ~ Real ale ~ (01433) 650319 ~ Open 11-11; 12-10.30 Sun ~ Bar food 11.30-9.30; 12-9 Sun ~ Restaurant ~ Children welcome ~ Dogs welcome ~ Wi-fi ~ Pianist Fri evenings ~ Bedrooms: £80/£105 ~ www.theploughinn-hathersage.co.uk *Recommended by Mike and Mary Carter, R L Borthwick, David Cochrane, Richard Cole, Jill and Julian Tasker, David Carr, Dr Kevan Tucker*

HAYFIELD
SK0388 Map 7

Lantern Pike

Glossop Road (A624 N) at Little Hayfield, just N of Hayfield; SK22 2NG

Relaxing retreat from the surrounding moors of Kinder Scout, with reasonably priced food; bedrooms

You'll get a friendly welcome from the licensees and their staff at this homely place in the Peak District National Park. Tables on the stone-walled terrace look over a big-windowed weaver's house towards Lantern Pike hill. The traditional red plush bar proudly displays photos of the original *Coronation Street* cast, many of whom were regulars here, along with Tony Warren (the series creator) who based his characters on some of the locals. It's quite possible that the interior hasn't changed much since those days. There's a warm fire, an array of antique clocks and a montage of local photographs. Theakstons Black Bull and Timothy Taylors Landlord on handpump; TV and background music. Dogs may be allowed in at the licensees' discretion, and if clean.

Chalked up on boards, the menu includes pâté, garlic mushrooms, various platters, home-made pork sausages with apple sauce, shepherd's pie, sage-cooked chicken, fidget pie, vegetarian bake, and puddings such as jam roly-poly and blackcurrant cheesecake. *Benchmark main dish: lamb kebabs £14.50. Two-course evening meal £15.50.*

Enterprise ~ Lease Stella and Tom Cuncliffe ~ Real ale ~ (01663) 747590 ~ Open 12-3, 5-11; 12-11 Sat, Sun; closed Mon lunchtime ~ Bar food 12-2.30, 5-8.30; all day weekends ~ Restaurant ~ Children welcome ~ Dogs allowed in bar ~ Wi-fi ~ Bedrooms: £53/£66 ~ www.lanternpikeinn.co.uk *Recommended by Stuart Paulley, Dean Johnson*

HAYFIELD
SK0387 Map 7

Royal 🛏

Market Street; SK22 2EP

Big, bustling inn with fine panelled rooms, friendly service and thoughtful choice of drinks and food; bedrooms

The recently upgraded bedrooms in this handsome 18th-c stone-built former coaching inn are spotlessly clean and comfortable, and breakfasts are good. The oak-panelled bar and lounge areas (attracting a good mix of both locals and visitors) have open fires and a fine collection of seats, from long settles with pretty scatter cushions through elegant upholstered dining chairs to tub chairs and chesterfields, around an assortment of solid tables on rugs and flagstones; house plants, daily papers. There's Thwaites Original and guests such as Dark Star Hophead, Happy Valley Sworn Secret, Holdens Black Country Bitter and Thwaites Wainwright on handpump (they hold a beer festival in October) and three farm ciders; background music, TV and board games. The sunny front terrace has plenty of seats.

Quite a choice of food includes sandwiches and wraps, prawn and crayfish cocktail, fresh and smoked salmon fishcakes with sweet chilli dip, sharing platters, chicken, mushroom and leek pie, macaroni cheese, sausages with onion gravy, burger (beef and horseradish or chicken) with bacon, cheese and chips, beef bourguignon, and puddings such as apple crumble and chocolate fudge cake; they also offer a two- and three-course set menu. *Benchmark main dish: beer-battered fish and chips £9.50. Two-course evening meal £14.25.*

Free house ~ Licensees Mark Miller and Lisa Davis ~ Real ale ~ (01663) 742721 ~ Open 10am-11pm (11.30 Sat); 12-10.30 Sun; 11am opening in winter ~ Bar food 10-8.30 (9 Sat, 7 Sun); no food 2.30-6 weekday afternoons in winter ~ Restaurant ~ Children welcome ~ Dogs allowed in bar and bedrooms ~ Wi-fi ~ Live folk Thurs evenings ~ Bedrooms: $60/$80 ~ www.theroyalathayfield.com *Recommended by Ruth May, P Dawn*

HURDLOW
SK1265 Map 7
Royal Oak
Monyash–Longnor Road, just off A515 S of Buxton; SK17 9QJ

Bustling, carefully renovated pub in rural spot with beamed rooms, friendly staff and tasty, all-day food

Just the place for tired walkers craving a well earned pint and an honest meal, or for families on a day out, this remains a hospitable, thoughtfully run pub. The two-roomed beamed bar has an open fire in a stone fireplace, lots of copper kettles, bed warming pans, horsebrasses and country pictures, cushioned wheelback chairs and wall settles around dark tables, and stools against the counter where friendly, helpful staff serve Buxton Best, Sharps Doom Bar, Thornbridge Wild Swan and Whim Hartington Bitter and IPA on handpump, nine wines by the glass and several malt whiskies; background music and board games. The attractive dining room has country dining chairs, more wheelbacks and a cushioned pine settle in one corner on bare floorboards, pretty curtains and another open fire. For large groups, there's also a flagstoned cellar room with benches on either side of long tables. The terraced garden has plenty of seats, including picnic-sets on grass. A self-catering barn has bunk bedrooms and there's a campsite too.

 Nicely presented all-day food includes sandwiches, mexican prawns with spicy salsa, chicken liver pâté with tomato chutney, gammon and eggs, burger with bacon, stilton, coleslaw and chips, butternut squash, spinach and walnut lasagne, pork fillet in Grand Marnier cream with black pudding mash, lambs liver with bacon, onion and red wine gravy, fisherman's platter, and puddings such as banoffi pie and white chocolate cheesecake. *Benchmark main dish: beef and stilton pie £11.95. Two-course evening meal £18.00.*

Free house ~ Licensee Justin Heslop ~ Real ale ~ (01298) 83288 ~ Open 10am (8.30am weekends)-11pm ~ Bar food 12-9 ~ Children welcome ~ Dogs welcome ~ Wi-fi ~ www.peakpub.co.uk *Recommended by Graham and Carol Parker*

INGLEBY
SK3427 Map 7
John Thompson 🛑 £ 🛏
NW of Melbourne; turn off A514 at Swarkestone Bridge or in Stanton by Bridge; can also be reached from Ticknall (or from Repton on B5008); DE73 7HW

Own-brew pub that strikes the right balance between attentive service, roomy comfort and good value lunchtime food

This friendly, down-to-earth own-brew pub is the longest established microbrewery in the county and has appeared in every edition of this *Guide* since it started in 1983. The simple but comfortable and immaculately kept modernised lounge has ceiling joists, some old oak settles, button-back leather seats, sturdy oak tables, antique prints and paintings and a log-effect gas fire; background music. A couple of smaller, cosier rooms open off; piano, games machine, board games, darts, TV, and pool in the conservatory. Friendly staff serve some of their own John Thompson brews, such as JTS XXX, St Nick, Summer Gold and Rich Porter, alongside a guest such as Timothy Taylors Landlord. There are lots of tables by flower beds on the neat lawns or you can sit on the partly covered terrace, surrounded by pretty countryside. Breakfast is left in your fridge if you stay in one of the self-catering chalet lodges.

Straightforward lunchtime food includes sandwiches, baked potatoes, salads, cheese and broccoli pasta bake, a carvery, and puddings such as crumbles and their famous bread and butter pudding – a speciality of the pub for the past 40 years. *Benchmark main dish: roast beef £8.95.*

Own brew ~ Licensee Nick Thompson ~ Real ale ~ (01332) 862469 ~ Open 11-2.30, 6-11; 11-11 Sat; 12-10.30 Sun; closed Mon lunchtime except bank holidays ~ Bar food 12-2 ~ Restaurant ~ Children welcome in main bar till 6pm, in conservatory till 9pm ~ Dogs allowed in bar ~ Wi-fi ~ www.johnthompsoninn.com *Recommended by Tracey and Stephen Groves, Stephen Shepherd, Dr D J and Mrs S C Walker, Michael Butler*

KIRK IRETON   SK2650   Map 7
Barley Mow
Village signed off B5023 S of Wirksworth; DE6 3JP

Welcoming old inn that focuses on real ale and conversation; bedrooms

'This is everything a pub should be – it's a gem.' We agree heartily with this enthusiastic comment from a reader, because this is a special place with a long-serving and kindly landlady who's been here well over 30 years. An inn since around 1800, it evokes how some grander rural pubs might have looked a century or so ago. The small main bar has a relaxed, very pubby feel, with a roaring coal fire, antique settles on tiles or built into panelling, four slate-topped tables and shuttered mullioned windows. Another room has built-in cushioned pews on oak parquet and a small woodburning stove; a third has more pews, low beams and big landscape prints. In casks behind a modest wooden counter are five well kept ales, such as Abbeydale Daily Bread, Froth Blowers Piffle Snonker, Northumberland Bosuns Bitter, Thornbridge Lumford and Whim Hartington IPA; french wines and farm cider too. There are two pub dogs. Outside, you'll find a good-sized garden, a couple of benches out in front, and a shop in what used to be the stable. This hilltop village is very pretty and within walking distance of Carsington Water. Bedrooms are comfortable, and readers enjoy the good breakfasts served in the stone-flagged kitchen.

Very inexpensive lunchtime filled rolls are the only food; the decent evening meals (no choice) are for overnight guests.

Free house ~ Licensee Mary Short ~ Real ale ~ No credit cards ~ (01335) 370306 ~ Open 12-2, 7-11 (10.30 Sun) ~ Bar food lunchtime rolls only ~ Children welcome ~ Dogs allowed in bedrooms ~ Bedrooms: £45/£65 *Recommended by Edward May, Emma Scofield*

It's very helpful if you let us know up-to-date food prices when you report on pubs.

LADYBOWER RESERVOIR SK1986 Map 7
Ladybower Inn

A57 Sheffield–Glossop, just E of junction with A6013; S33 0AX

Comfortable, proper pub nestling above reservoir in good walking country; good value bedrooms

They serve food all day in this well run, friendly inn, which is very helpful for those visiting the huge reservoir nearby. The various carpeted areas are homely with traditional furnishings that take in peach cottagey wallpaper and curtains, little pictures, cast-iron fireplaces, wall banquettes, captain's and country kitchen chairs and the like. The most relaxed place in which to eat is down at the end on the right, with leather-padded traditional dining chairs around heavier tables, lancaster bomber pictures recalling the Dambusters' practice runs on the reservoir, and a coal-effect fire; unobtrusive background music and darts. Cheerful, helpful staff serve Acorn Barnsley, Bradfield Farmers Blonde, Greene King Ruddles County and a guest such as Bradfield Yorkshire Farmer on handpump, and decent wines by the glass. If you stay in the annexe bedrooms, you won't be disturbed by traffic noise – but the road is busy, so crossing from the car park opposite needs care; picnic-sets out in front.

 Generously served food includes hot and cold sandwiches, potted duck rillettes, curried crab and watermelon salad, spinach and goats cheese lasagne, shepherds pie, free-range gammon with eggs and pineapple, scampi and chips, tandoori salmon with raita, duck with plum and ginger sauce, and puddings. *Benchmark main dish: beef in ale pie £10.50. Two-course evening meal £18.00.*

Free house ~ Licensee Deborah Wilde ~ Real ale ~ (01433) 651241 ~ Open 10am-11pm ~ Bar food 12-9 ~ Restaurant ~ Children welcome ~ Dogs allowed in bar ~ Wi-fi ~ Bedrooms: $45/$80 ~ www.ladybower-inn.co.uk *Recommended by Richard and Andrea Bion*

LADYBOWER RESERVOIR SK2084 Map 7
Yorkshire Bridge

A6013 N of Bamford; S33 0AZ

Handy for the reservoir with several real ales, friendly staff, tasty food and fine views; bedrooms

The cosy bar in this pleasantly genteel inn has countless tankards hanging from beams, lots of china plates, photographs and paintings on red walls, horsebrasses and copper items, red plush dining chairs around a mix of tables on red patterned carpeting, and a woodburning stove. There's lots more space in several other rooms – including a light and airy garden room with fine valley views – with an assortment of seating ranging from wicker and metal through bentwood-style chairs around quite a choice of wooden tables, on more carpeting or flagstones, plus many more decorative plates and photographs. Friendly staff serve Blue Bee Rugbee Rugbee Rugbee, Bradfield Farmers Blonde, Peak Bakewell Best Bitter and a guest beer on handpump, and nine wines by the glass. Dogs are allowed in some bedrooms, but not in the bar at mealtimes.

 With some dishes available in smaller helpings, the choice of food includes sandwiches, giant yorkshire pudding with white onion sauce and gravy, garlic mushrooms in creamy stilton sauce, lasagne, chilli con carne, sausage and mash, battered haddock and chips, minted lamb chops, and puddings such as a hot sponge of the day and a daily changing cheesecake. *Benchmark main dish: steak and kidney pie £10.95. Two-course evening meal £15.75.*

Free house ~ Licensee John Illingworth ~ Real ale ~ (01433) 651361 ~ Open 11-11 (10.30 Sun) ~ Bar food 12-2.30, 6-9 (9.30 Fri, Sat); 12-8.30 Sun ~ Children welcome ~ Dogs allowed in bedrooms ~ Bedrooms: £60/£75 ~ www.yorkshire-bridge.co.uk
Recommended by Caroline Prescott

 ## LITTON   SK1675   Map 7
Red Lion
Village signposted off A623, between B6465 and B6049 junctions; also signposted off B6049; SK17 8QU

Unspoilt charm in this friendly village pub with cosy bars, real ales and well liked food

Walkers, fresh from hikes in the nearby Dales, crowd into this friendly village pub at lunchtime. Converted from farm cottages, the two linked front rooms are homely, with low beams and panelling, cushioned settles and wall seats around pubby tables, paintings, horsebrasses and open fires. Abbeydale Absolution, Peak Bakewell Best Bitter and a guest beer on handpump, 11 decent wines by the glass and several malt whiskies. There's also a bigger stripped-stone back room; darts and evening TV. As well as seats and tables out in front, there are more on the village green.

The tasty, generously served food includes sandwiches, chicken liver pâté, mushroom and black pudding on toast, vegetarian sausage and mash, beer-battered haddock and chips, a roast of the day, burger with bacon, cheese and onion marmalade, cumin and chilli chicken with bombay potatoes, lambs liver, onion and bacon, and puddings such as chocolate tart and ginger sponge; they also offer a two- and three-course set menu. *Benchmark main dish: steak and kidney pie £10.95. Two-course evening meal £17.00.*

Enterprise ~ Lease Louise Parker ~ Real ale ~ (01298) 871458 ~ Open 12-11 (midnight Fri, Sat); 12-10.30 Sun ~ Bar food 12-9 (8 Sun) ~ Children over 6 welcome ~ Dogs allowed in bar ~ www.theredlionlitton.co.uk *Recommended by David Hunt, David and Jenny Billington, Mike and Wena Stevenson, Barry Collett, Alan Johnson, Dennis Jones*

 ## OVER HADDON   SK2066   Map 7
Lathkil
Village and inn signposted from B5055 just SW of Bakewell; DE45 1JE

Traditional pub well placed for Lathkill Dale, with super views, good range of beers and well liked food

Not surprisingly, this unpretentious hotel is very popular with walkers as it's at the heart of the Peak District National Park; dogs are welcome, but muddy boots must be left in the lobby. The spectacular views can be enjoyed from seats in the walled garden – and from windows in the bar. The airy room on the right as you enter has a nice fire in an attractively carved fireplace, old-fashioned settles with upholstered cushions, chairs, black beams, a delft shelf of blue and white plates and some original prints and photographs. On the left, the sunny spacious dining area doubles as an evening restaurant. Blue Monkey Right Turn Clyde, Everards Tiger, Peak Swift Nick, Storm Bosley Cloud and Whim Hartington IPA on handpump, a reasonable range of wines (including mulled wine) and a decent selection of malt whiskies; background music, darts, TV and board games. The bedrooms are warm and comfortable and the breakfasts hearty.

Lunch (served buffet-style) includes filled rolls, pâté of the day, lasagne, chicken and stilton pie, mediterranean vegetable hotpot and venison casserole, with evening choices such as mini whole camembert, warm smoked duck salad with blackcurrant vinaigrette, salmon parcel with tomato pesto, loin of lamb with redcurrant and port sauce, mixed grill, and puddings. *Benchmark main dish: beef in ale casserole £8.95. Two-course evening meal £17.25.*

Free house ~ Licensee Alice Grigor-Taylor ~ Real ale ~ (01629) 812501 ~ Open 11-11; 12-10.30 Sun ~ Bar food 12-2 (2.30 weekends), 6.30-8.30 ~ Restaurant ~ Children welcome but over-10s only in bar ~ Dogs allowed in bar and bedrooms ~ Wi-fi ~ Bedrooms: £60/£75 ~ www.lathkil.co.uk *Recommended by Dennis Jones, Kim Skuse, Derek and Sylvia Stephenson*

REPTON
SK3026 Map 7

Bulls Head
High Street; DE65 6GF

Lively pub in attractive village, with interesting décor, solid wooden furniture in various rooms, wide choice of drinks and impressive food

Carefully reworked a few years ago, this lively place is popular with a good mixed crowd of customers. The various interconnected downstairs bars have beams and pillars, all manner of chunky tables surrounded by ornately carved or plain wooden dining chairs, settles and built-in wall seats with scatter cushions, squashy sofas, bare boards or flagstones, open fires and woodburning stoves; there are driftwood sculptures, animal hide décor, arty bulls heads and – in the restaurant – big gilt-edged mirrors on ornate wallpaper. Greene King Old Speckled Hen, Jennings Cumberland, Marstons Pedigree and guests such as Dancing Duck Ay Up and Nice Weather on handpump, 15 wines by the glass and 20 malt whiskies, served by cheerful staff; background music. The sizeable, heated terrace has neatly set tables and chairs under big parasols.

Rewarding food using local, seasonal produce includes lunchtime sandwiches and wraps, mussels in white wine and cream, deep-fried panko-crumbed brie and caramelised red onion jam, sharing platters, spanish chicken and mushroom pie, steak burgers with several toppings, pumpkin, cranberry and red onion tagine, honey and mustard-glazed gammon and free-range eggs, and puddings such as banana sponge pudding with caramel sauce and crème brûlée. *Benchmark main dish: beef stroganoff £12.50. Two-course evening meal £17.00.*

Free house ~ Licensees Richard and Loren Pope ~ Real ale ~ (01283) 704422 ~ Open 12-midnight ~ Bar food 12-10 ~ Restaurant ~ Children welcome ~ Dogs allowed in bar ~ Wi-fi ~ www.thebullsheadrepton.co.uk *Recommended by Casper Leaver, Stephen Shepherd*

STANTON IN PEAK
SK2364 Map 7

Flying Childers ■ £
Village signposted from B6056 S of Bakewell; Main Road; DE4 2LW

Top-notch beer and inexpensive simple bar lunches in a warm-hearted, unspoilt pub – a delight

There are some fine walks surrounding this homely village pub and both walkers and their dogs are warmly welcomed; they keep doggy treats behind the bar. The friendly landlord keeps Wells & Youngs Bombardier and a couple of guests such as Abbeydale Deception and Black Sheep on handpump, and wines by the glass. The best room in which to enjoy them is the snug little right-hand bar, virtually built for chat, with its dark beam-and-plank ceiling, dark wall settles, single pew, plain tables, a hot coal and log fire, a few team photographs, dominoes and cribbage; background music. There's a bigger, equally unpretentious bar on the right. The well tended garden at the back has picnic-sets, and there's a couple more out in front; this beautiful steep stone village overlooks a rich green valley.

🍴 Using some home-grown produce and prepared by the landlady, the food – served at lunchtime only – includes filled rolls and toasties, ploughman's and maybe weekend game casseroles, sausages, and liver and bacon.

Free house ~ Licensees Stuart and Mandy Redfern ~ Real ale ~ No credit cards ~ (01629) 636333 ~ Open 12-2 (3 weekends), 7-11; closed Mon and Tues lunchtimes ~ Bar food 12-2 ~ Children in lounge bar only ~ Dogs allowed in bar ~ Live accoustic music first Thurs of month ~ www.flyingchilders.com *Recommended by Edward May, Caroline Prescott*

Also Worth a Visit in Derbyshire

Besides the fully inspected pubs, you might like to try these pubs that have been recommended to us and described by readers. Do tell us what you think of them: feedback@goodguides.com

ASHFORD IN THE WATER SK1969
⭐ **Ashford Arms** (01629) 812725
Church Street; DE45 1QB
Attractive 18th-c inn set in pretty village, ample choice of good quality reasonably priced food including Weds steak night (32oz rump if you're really hungry), well kept Black Sheep and two local guests such as Peak, nice wines, friendly staff, restaurant and dining conservatory; children and dogs welcome, plenty of tables outside, eight comfortable bedrooms, open all day Sun (food till 5pm). *(Peter F Marshall)*

ASHFORD IN THE WATER SK1969
⭐ **Bulls Head** (01629) 812931
Off A6 NW of Bakewell; Church Street (B6465, off A6020); DE45 1QB
Traditional 17th-c village pub under new licensees (but still in same family that has run it since 1953); cosy two-room beamed and carpeted bar with fires, one or two character gothic seats, spindleback and wheelback chairs around cast-iron-framed tables, local photographs and country prints on cream walls, daily papers, three Robinsons ales and good choice of traditional home-made food (not Tues evening), friendly efficient service; background music; children welcome, dogs in bar, overshoes for walkers, hardwood tables and benches in front and in good-sized garden behind with boules and Jenga. *(Anon)*

ASTON-UPON-TRENT SK4129
Malt (01332) 792256
M1 junction 24A on to A50, village signed left near Shardlow; The Green (one-way street); DE72 2AA Comfortably revamped village pub with enjoyable good value food and well kept ales such as Bass, Marstons and Sharps, friendly atmosphere; children and dogs welcome, back terrace. *(Brian and Jean Hepworth)*

BAKEWELL SK2168
Castle Inn (01629) 812103
Bridge Street; DE45 1DU Bay-windowed, Georgian-fronted pub dating from the 17th c, well kept Greene King ales and a guest, good competitively priced straightforward food, three candlelit rooms with two open fires, flagstones, stripped stone and lots of pictures, good friendly service; background music and fruit machine; dogs welcome, level inside for wheelchairs but steps at front, tables out by road, gets busy Mon market day, four bedrooms. *(David and Jenny Billington, Derek and Sylvia Stephenson, Paul Goldman, David Carr)*

BAMFORD SK2083
Anglers Rest (01433) 659317
A6013/Taggs Knoll; S33 0BQ Friendly community-owned pub with good local beers and tasty food, café part and post office; children, walkers and dogs welcome. *(Phil Taylor)*

BASLOW SK2572
Wheatsheaf (01246) 582240
Nether End; DE45 1SR Cheerful Marstons inn (former coaching house) with comfortable carpeted interior, popular choice of reasonably priced food including good children's menu, four well kept ales, good friendly service; free wi-fi; plenty of seats outside and play area, bedrooms, open all day. *(Ms Edna M Jones, Derek and Sylvia Stephenson, John Wooll)*

BEELEY SK2667
⭐ **Devonshire Arms** (01629) 733259
B6012, off A6 Matlock–Bakewell; DE4 2NR Lovely 18th-c stone inn; original part with black beams, flagstones, stripped stone and cheerful log fires, contrasting ultra-modern bistro/conservatory, up to six well kept changing ales, several wines by the glass and good range of malt whiskies, food

has been imaginative including seasonal game (reports please); background music; children welcome, dogs allowed in bedrooms but not bar, attractive Peak District village near Chatsworth, open all day. *(Andy Dolan, Di and Mike Gillam, Tracey and Stephen Groves, Stephen Shepherd)*

BELPER   SK3349
Bulls Head (01773) 824900
Belper Lane End; DE56 2DL Friendly village local with own Shottle Farm ales (brewed nearby) and enjoyable straight-forward food, small simple front bar with beams, flagstones and stripped wood, larger back bar with comfortable sofas and open fire, sizeable dining conservatory, music and quiz nights; picnic-sets out in front, big lawned garden, open all day weekends, closed weekday lunchtimes. *(Richard Stanfield)*

BIRCHOVER   SK2362
★Druid (01629) 653836
Off B5056; Main Street; DE4 2BL 17th-c stone pub under new ownership; traditional quarry-tiled bar with open fire, dining areas either side plus more modern downstairs restaurant with wood-strip floor, good varied menu changing regularly including some unusual choices, no food Mon lunchtime but curry in evening, up to four very well kept changing ales (tasters offered), some live folk and jazz; background music, free wi-fi; children welcome, dogs in bar, tables out in front on two levels, good area for walks, Nine Ladies stone circle nearby, open all day. *(Tracey and Stephen Groves)*

BIRCHOVER   SK2362
Red Lion (01629) 650363
Main Street; DE4 2BN Friendly early 18th-c stone-built pub with popular good value italian-influenced food (landlord is from Sardinia), also make their own cheese and have a deli next door, Sun carvery, well kept ales (up to five in summer), four ciders, microbrewery still planned, glass-covered well inside, woodburners; children and dogs welcome, nice rural views from outside seats, popular with walkers, open all day weekends, closed Mon, Tues in winter. *(Anon)*

BONSALL   SK2758
★Barley Mow (01629) 825685
Off A5012 W of Cromford; The Dale; DE4 2AY Basic one-room stone-built local with friendly colourful atmosphere, beams, character furnishings and coal fire, pictures and bric-a-brac, well kept local ales and real ciders, microbrewery planned, hearty generously served food (be prepared to share a table), live music Fri and Sat; short walk

out to lavatories; children and dogs welcome, nice little front terrace, events such as hen racing and world-record-breaking day, popular with UFO enthusiasts, walks organised from the pub, camping, open all day weekends, closed Mon and lunchtimes Tues-Fri. *(Anon)*

BRACKENFIELD   SK3658
Plough (01629) 534437
A615 Matlock–Alfreton, about a mile NW of Wessington; DE55 6DD Much modernised 16th-c former farmhouse in lovely setting, welcoming three-level beamed bar with cheerful log-effect gas fire, well kept ales and plenty of wines by the glass, good popular food including lunchtime set deal (Mon-Fri), appealing lower-level restaurant extension; children welcome, large neatly kept gardens with terrace, open all day (till 6pm Sun), closed Mon in winter. *(Anon)*

BUXTON   SK0573
Old Hall (01298) 22841
The Square, almost opposite Opera House; SK17 6BD Large usefully placed hotel with bar, wine bar doing good value, enjoyable food (all day weekends), various lounges and a more formal restaurant, well kept ales such as Buxton, Sharps and Thornbridge, good choice of wines by the glass; 38 bedrooms, open all day. *(Brian and Jean Hepworth)*

BUXTON   SK0573
★Old Sun (01298) 23452
High Street; SK17 6HA Charming old building with several cosy and interesting traditional linked areas, well kept Marstons-related ales and good choice of wines by the glass, simple bargain home-made food from good sandwiches up, low beams, bare boards or tiles, soft lighting, old local photographs, open fire; background music and some live acoustic evenings, Sun quiz, no dogs; children till 7pm, roadside garden, open all day. *(Ann and Colin Hunt, Barry Collett, Tracey and Stephen Groves)*

BUXWORTH   SK0282
Navigation (01663) 732072
S of village towards Silkhill, off B6062; SK23 7NE Friendly inn by restored canal basin, six well kept ales including Robinsons Unicorn and Timothy Taylors Landlord, good value pubby food from sandwiches up, cheery welcoming staff, linked low-ceilinged rooms, canalia, brassware and old photographs, open fires, games room with pool and darts, Thurs quiz; background music; children allowed away from main bar, dogs in some areas, disabled access, tables on sunken flagstoned terrace, play area, five bedrooms, breakfast

---

If you stay overnight in an inn or hotel, they are allowed to serve you an alcoholic drink at any hour of the day or night.

8-11am (non-residents welcome), open all day. *(Brian and Anna Marsden)*

CALVER   SK2374
Derwentwater Arms (01433) 639211
In centre, bear left from Main Street into Folds Head; Low Side; S32 3XQ Largely bright and modern inside, big windows looking down from village-centre knoll across car park to cricket pitch, good fairly priced food including specials, some choices in smaller helpings, three well kept ales such as Acorn, Adnams and Peak (tasting tray available); children and dogs welcome, terraces on slopes below (disabled access from back car park), boules, self-catering cottage, open (and food) all day weekends. *(Brian and Anna Marsden)*

CASTLETON   SK1582
Bulls Head (01433) 620256
Cross Street (A6187); S33 8WH Imposing building spreading through several attractive linked areas, handsome panelling and pictures, appealing mix of comfortable seating including sofas and easy chairs, heavy drapes and coal fires, well kept Robinsons ales, food from sandwiches and hot ciabattas to pub standards and specials, helpful friendly service; background music, no dogs; some roadside picnic-sets, five bedrooms. *(Anon)*

CASTLETON   SK1482
★ Castle Hotel (01433) 620578
High Street/Castle Street; S33 8WG Roomy and welcoming Vintage Inn with usual good choice of well priced food all day from sandwiches up, Leeds, Marstons, Sharps and three guests, plenty of wines by the glass, decent coffee, friendly efficient staff even at busy times, log fires, stripped-stone walls, beams and some ancient flagstones; background music; children and dogs (in designated area) welcome, seats out in front and on heated terrace, 16 comfortable bedrooms, good breakfast, open all day. *(Anon)*

CASTLETON   SK1482
★ George (01433) 620238
Castle Street; S33 8WG Busy but relaxed old pub with flagstoned bar and restaurant, well kept Courage, Wells & Youngs and a guest, good choice of malts, enjoyable home-made food at reasonable prices, decent coffee, friendly staff, ancient beams and stripped stone, copper and brass, log fires; children and dogs welcome, tables out at front and back, castle views, good walks, bedrooms, open all day in summer. *(Anon)*

CASTLETON   SK1583
Olde Cheshire Cheese
(01433) 620330 *How Lane; S33 8WJ* Family-run 17th-c inn with two linked beamed and carpeted areas, cosy and spotless, with six well kept ales such as

Acorn, Bradfield and Peak, good range of reasonably priced wholesome food and decent house wines, quick friendly service, two gas woodburners, lots of photographs, toby jugs, plates and brassware, back dining room where children welcome; background music, free wi-fi; dogs allowed in bar, ten bedrooms, parking across road, open (and food) all day. *(Eddie Edwards, David and Jenny Billington, Dennis Jones)*

CASTLETON   SK1582
★ Olde Nags Head (01433) 620248
Cross Street (A6187); S33 8WH Small solidly built hotel dating from the 17th c, interesting antique oak furniture and coal fire in civilised beamed and flagstoned bar, adjoining snug with leather sofas, steps down to restaurant, well kept Black Sheep, Sharps Doom Bar and guests, nice coffee and good locally sourced food, friendly helpful staff; live music Sat; children and dogs (in bar) welcome, nine comfortable bedrooms, good breakfast, open all day. *(Anon)*

CHESTERFIELD   SK3871
Chesterfield Arms (01246) 236634
Newbold Road (B6051); S41 7PH Restored 19th-c pub with up to 16 ales including Everards, Fullers London Pride and three house beers from Leatherbritches, six ciders and good choice of wines and whiskies, basic snacks along with Mon pie night and Thurs curry, open fire, oak panelling and stripped wood/flagstoned floors, new conservatory linking weekend barn room, beer festivals, some live music and Weds quiz; outside tables on decking, open all day. *(Andrew Bosi, P Dawn)*

CHESTERFIELD   SK3670
Rose & Crown (01246) 563750
Old Road (A619); S40 2QT Brampton Brewery pub with their full range plus Everards and two changing guests, Weston's cider, enjoyable home-made food (not weekend evenings), spacious traditional refurbishment with leather banquettes, panelling, carpet or wood floors, brewery memorabilia and cast-iron Victorian fireplace, cosy snug area, quiz nights, trad jazz first Sun of month; free wi-fi; tables outside, open all day. *(Anon)*

CHINLEY   SK0482
Paper Mill (01663) 750529
Whitehough Head Lane; SK23 6EJ Former Oddfellows Arms refurbished and under same management as next door Old Hall (see Main Entries); good selection of ales and craft beers including Thornbridge, plenty of bottled belgians too, simple bar snacks including cheeseboards and mini ploughman's, also a raclette room (must book in advance – minimum eight people), good choice of teas and coffees, friendly helpful service, flagstones, woodburners and open fire, local artwork for sale; TV for major

sporting events; children, walkers and dogs welcome, seats out at front and on split-level back terrace, plenty of good local walks, four bedrooms, closed weekdays till 5pm, open all day weekends. *(Sally Barnett, Richard Newman, Elizabeth Land, Sue Kennerley, James Cadman, T Matthews)*

CLIFTON   SK1645
Cock (01335) 342654
Cross Side, opposite church; DE6 2GJ
Unpretentious two-bar beamed village local, comfortable and friendly, with jovial landlord, enjoyable reasonably priced home-made pub food from baguettes up, well kept Marstons Pedigree, Timothy Taylors Landlord and a couple of guests, decent choice of wines by the glass, separate dining room, darts, quiz first Tues of month; children, dogs and walkers welcome, garden with play equipment, closed Mon lunchtime. *(Simon Cattley, Pete and Jan Woods)*

COMBS   SK0378
Beehive (01298) 812758
Village signposted off B5470 W of Chapel-en-le-Frith; SK23 9UT
Roomy, neat and comfortable, with emphasis on good freshly made food (all day Sun) from baguettes to steaks and interesting specials, also very good value weekday set menu, ales including Marstons Pedigree and a house beer from Wychwood, good choice of wines by the glass, log fire, heavy beams and copperware; background music, TV, Tues quiz; plenty of tables out in front, by lovely valley tucked away from main road, good walks, one-bed holiday cottage next door, open all day. *(Anon)*

CRICH   SK3454
Cliff (01773) 852444
Cromford Road, Town End; DE4 5DP
Unpretentious little two-room pub with well kept ales such as Blue Monkey, Buxton, Dancing Duck and Sharps, straightforward reasonably priced food (not weekend evenings or Mon), welcoming staff and friendly regulars, two woodburners, Sun folk night; children and dogs welcome, great views and walks, handy for National Tramway Museum, open all day weekends, closed Mon lunchtime (weekday lunchtimes in winter). *(Anon)*

CROWDECOTE   SK1065
Packhorse (01298) 83618
B5055 W of Bakewell; SK17 0DB
Small three-room 16th-c pub in lovely setting, welcoming landlord and staff, good reasonably priced home-made food from weekday light bites and sandwiches up, four changing well kept ales, split-level interior with brick or carpeted floors, stripped-stone walls, open fire and two woodburners, pool room; tables out behind, beautiful views, popular walking route, closed Mon, Tues. *(Graham and Carol Parker)*

DERBY   SK3538
Abbey Inn (01332) 558297
Darley Street; DE22 1DX Former abbey gatehouse opposite Derwent-side park (pleasant riverside walk from centre), massive 15th-c or older stonework remnants, brick floor, studded oak doors, coal fire in big inglenook, stone spiral staircase to upper bar (open weekends, and Tues and Fri evenings) with oak rafters and tapestries, bargain Sam Smiths and reasonably priced bar food; the lavatories with their beams, stonework and tiles are worth a look too; children and dogs (downstairs) welcome, open all day. *(Anon)*

DERBY   SK3635
Alexandra (01332) 293993
Siddals Road; DE1 2QE Imposing Victorian pub, popular locally; two simple rooms with traditional furnishings on bare boards or carpet, railway prints/memorabilia, well kept Castle Rock ales and quickly changing microbrewery guests, lots of continental bottled beers with more on tap, snack food such as pork pies and cobs; background music; children and dogs welcome, nicely planted backyard, four bedrooms, open all day. *(P Dawn)*

DERBY   SK3535
Babington Arms (01332) 383647
Babington Lane; DE1 1TA Large well run open-plan Wetherspoons with 16 real ales and four proper ciders, good welcoming service, usual well priced food, comfortable seating with steps up to relaxed back area; attractive verandah, open all day from 8am for breakfast. *(Anon)*

DERBY   SK3536
Brewery Tap (01332) 366283
Derwent Street/Exeter Place; DE1 2ED Updated Derby Brewing Co corner pub (aka Royal Standard), ten ales including five of their own from curved brick counter, lots of bottled imports, decent good value food all day (till 5pm Sun) from sandwiches and baked potatoes up, open-plan bare-boards interior with two drinking areas, small upstairs room and roof terrace overlooking the Derwent, live music and quiz nights; open all day (till 1am Fri, Sat). *(P Dawn)*

DERBY   SK3635
★Brunswick (01332) 290677
Railway Terrace; close to Derby Midland Station; DE1 2RU One of Britain's oldest railwaymen's pubs, 16 ales including Brampton and four from own microbrewery, eight ciders, good choice of bottled beers and malt whiskies, cheap traditional lunchtime food, welcoming high-ceilinged panelled bar, snug with high-backed wall settle by coal fire, chatty front family parlour, wall displays showing history and restoration of building, interesting old train photographs and prints, quiz Mon, jazz upstairs Thurs evening, darts;

TV, games machine, free wi-fi; dogs welcome, walled beer garden and side terrace, open all day (till midnight Fri, Sat). *(P Dawn)*

DERBY   SK3435
Exeter Arms (01332) 605323
Exeter Place; DE1 2EU Victorian survivor amid 1930s apartment blocks and car parks; recently extended into next door cottage, but keeping its traditional character including tiled-floor snug with curved wall benches and polished open range, friendly staff, well kept Dancing Duck, Marstons and two guests, good pubby food with a twist served all day (till 4pm Sun), quiz Mon, live music Weds and Sat; small garden with outside bar for beer festivals, open all day (till midnight Fri, Sat). *(P Dawn)*

DERBY   SK3534
Falstaff (01332) 342902
Silver Hill Road, off Normanton Road; DE23 6UJ Friendly straightforward local (aka the Folly), brewing its own good value ales, recently refurbished main bar with new slate floor and log-effect gas fire, left-hand bar with games, coal fire and brewery memorabilia in quieter lounge; open all day. *(Anon)*

DERBY   SK3436
Five Lamps (01332) 348730
Duffield Road; DE1 3BH Traditionally refurbished corner pub with opened-up but well divided interior around central servery, wood-strip or carpeted floors, panelling, leather button-back bench seats, small balustraded raised section, nine or so well kept local ales including Buxton, Everards, Oakham, Peak, Whim and a house beer from Derby, real ciders, decent good value pubby food (not Sun evening); background music, TV, games machines; a few picnic-sets outside, open all day (till midnight Fri, Sat). *(P Dawn)*

DERBY   SK3436
Mr Grundys Tavern (01332) 349806
Georgian House; Ashbourne Road; DE22 3AD Hotel bar serving own Mr Grundys ales (brewed here) and plenty of guests, two inviting dimly lit rooms, coal fires, panelling, old bench seating, superb collection of hats, a wall of classic film-star pictures, lots of breweriana and an old red telephone box, decent food (not Sun evening); children and dogs welcome, garden picnic-sets, 17 bedrooms, open all day. *(Anon)*

DERBY   SK3536
Old Silk Mill (01332) 369748
Full Street; DE1 3AF Refurbished keeping traditional feel, cosy inside with two open fires, nine changing ales from main bar including a house beer from Blue Monkey, second bar strung with hops (open Thurs and Fri evenings, all day Sat, Sun lunchtime)

with usually four cask-tapped beers, friendly service, regular live music; open all day. *(P Dawn)*

DERBY   SK3536
Olde Dolphin (01332) 267711
Queen Street; DE1 3DL Quaint 16th-c timber-framed pub just below cathedral, four small dark unpretentious rooms including appealing snug, big bowed black beams, shiny panelling, opaque leaded windows, lantern lights and coal fires, half a dozen predominantly mainstream ales (good July beer festival), cheap simple food all day, upstairs steak bar (not always open); no under-14s inside; sizeable outside area for drinkers/smokers, open all day. *(P Dawn)*

DERBY   SK3335
Rowditch (01332) 343123
Uttoxeter New Road (A516); DE22 3LL Popular character local with own microbrewery, well kept Marstons Pedigree and guests too, country wines, friendly landlord, attractive small snug on right, coal fire, pianist first and third Sat of month; no children or dogs; pleasant back garden, closed weekday lunchtimes. *(Anon)*

DERBY   SK3436
Standing Order (01332) 207591
Irongate; DE1 3GL Cavernous Wetherspoons in grand and lofty-domed former bank, main part with large island bar, booths down each side, handsome plasterwork, pseudo-classical torsos, high portraits of mainly local notables, good range of ales, standard food, reasonable prices; TVs for news, daily papers and free wi-fi; good disabled facilities, open all day from 7am. *(Anon)*

DUFFIELD   SK3543
Pattern Makers Arms
(01332) 842844 *Crown Street, off King Street; DE56 4EY* Welcoming Edwardian backstreet local with well kept Bass (from the jug), Marstons, Timothy Taylors and guests, bargain lunchtime food (under-10s eat free Mon-Sat), pubby furniture on wood or carpeted floors, upholstered banquettes, some stained-glass and etched windows, darts, pool and other games, Sun quiz; background music, TV; beer garden behind, open all day Fri-Sun. *(Andrew Bosi)*

EARL STERNDALE   SK0966
★ Quiet Woman (01298) 83211
Village signed off B5053 S of Buxton; SK17 0BU Old-fashioned unchanging country local in lovely Peak District countryside, simple beamed interior with plain furniture on quarry tiles, china ornaments and coal fire, character landlord serving well kept Marstons Pedigree and guests, own-label bottled beers (available in gift packs), good pork pies, family room with pool, skittles and darts; picnic-sets out

in front along with budgies, hens, turkeys, ducks and donkeys, you can buy free-range eggs, local poetry books and even hay, good hikes across nearby Dove Valley towards Longnor and Hollinsclough, small campsite next door, caravan for hire. *(Ann and Colin Hunt, Barry Collett)*

EDALE SK1285
Old Nags Head (01433) 670291
Off A625 E of Chapel-en-le-Frith; Grindsbrook Booth; S33 7ZD Relaxed well used traditional pub at start of Pennine Way, food from sandwiches up including new carvery, four well kept local ales, friendly service, log fire, flagstoned area for booted walkers, airy back family room; TV, pool and darts; dogs welcome, front terrace and garden, two self-catering cottages, closed Mon and Tues out of season, otherwise open all day, can get very busy weekends. *(Anon)*

ELMTON SK5073
Elm Tree (01909) 721261
Off B6417 S of Clowne; S80 4LS Softly lit popular country pub with good food all day (till 6pm Sun) including lunchtime set menu, well kept Black Sheep plus one or two guests, wide choice of wines, quick friendly service, stripped stone and panelling, log fire, back barn restaurant (mainly for functions); children very welcome, garden tables, play area, closed Tues. *(Mr and Mrs R Shardlow, Derek and Sylvia Stephenson)*

ELTON SK2260
★ Duke of York (01629) 650367
Village signed off B5056 W of Matlock; Main Street; DE4 2BW Unspoilt local kept spotless by long-serving amiable landlady (here since 1968), bargain Marstons Burton Bitter, lovely little quarry-tiled back tap room with coal fire in massive fireplace, glazed bar and hatch to corridor, prints and more fires in the two front rooms – one with pool table, the other with darts and dominoes, friendly chatty locals; outside lavatories; children and dogs welcome, charming village, open 8.45pm-11pm and Sun lunchtime, closed Mon, no food. *(Anon)*

FOOLOW SK1976
★ Bulls Head (01433) 630873
Village signposted off A623 Baslow–Tideswell; S32 5QR Friendly pub by green in pretty upland village; simply furnished flagstoned bar with interesting collection of photographs including some saucy Edwardian ones, Black Sheep, Peak and two guests, over 30 malts, good food (all day Sun) with more elaborate evening choices, OAP weekday lunch deal, step down

to former stables with high ceiling joists, stripped stone and woodburner, sedate partly panelled dining room with plates on delft shelves; background music (live Fri evening); children, walkers and dogs welcome (resident westies Holly and Jack, and shih tzu Daisy), side picnic-sets with nice views, paths from here out over rolling pasture enclosed by dry stone walls, three refurbished bedrooms, closed Mon. *(Ann and Colin Hunt, Dr Kevan Tucker)*

FROGGATT EDGE SK2476
★ Chequers (01433) 630231
A625, off A623 N of Bakewell; S32 3ZJ Roadside country dining pub with opened-up bar and eating areas, cushioned settles, farmhouse and captain's chairs around mix of tables, antique prints, longcase clock and woodburner, interesting food (all day weekends) along with more traditional choices, Bradfield, Peak and a guest ale, eight wines by the glass, friendly helpful staff; background music; children welcome, no dogs inside, garden with Froggatt Edge up through woods behind, comfortable clean bedrooms and good breakfast, open all day. *(Emma Scofield, Caroline Prescott, Stephen Shepherd)*

FROGGATT EDGE SK2577
Grouse (01433) 630423
Longshaw, off B6054 NE of Froggatt; S11 7TZ Nicely old-fashioned beamed pub in same family since 1965, carpeted front bar with wall benches and other seating, log fire, back bar with coal-effect gas fire, small conservatory, enjoyable hearty home-made food (smaller helpings available) from nice sandwiches to blackboard specials, four well kept Marstons-related beers and over 40 malt whiskies, friendly prompt service; children and dogs welcome, terrace seating, lovely views and good moorland walks, open all day weekends. *(Anon)*

GLOSSOP SK0394
Star (01457) 853072
Howard Street; SK13 7DD Unpretentious corner alehouse opposite station with four well kept ales and Weston's cider, no food (you can bring your own), interesting layout including flagstoned tap room with hatch service, old local photographs; background music; open all day from 2pm (4pm Mon, Tues, noon Sat, Sun). *(Anon)*

HARDSTOFT SK4463
Shoulder (01246) 850276
B6039/Deep Lane; S45 8AE Modernised country inn with comfortable linked areas, Greene King Abbot and Ruddles plus four guest beers kept well, decent pub food

---

Places with gardens or terraces usually let children sit there – we note in the text the very few exceptions that don't.

including daily specials, friendly young staff, woodburner and open fire, soft lighting and lots of pictures; TV, free wi-fi; children and dogs welcome, handy for Hardwick Hall (NT) and Five Pits Trail, not far from M1 (junction 29), four clean bedrooms, closed Mon and Tues lunchtimes in winter, otherwise open all day. *(Comus and Sarah Elliott)*

HARDWICK HALL   SK4663
★**Hardwick Inn** (01246) 850245
Handy for M1 junction 29; S44 5QJ
Golden-stone building dating from the 15th c at the south gate of Hardwick Park; several busy linked rooms including proper bar, open fires, fine range of some 220 malt whiskies and plenty of wines by the glass, well kept Black Sheep, Peak, Theakstons and a Brampton ale badged for the pub, popular well priced bar food served all day, carvery restaurant, long-serving licensees and efficient friendly staff; unobtrusive background music; children allowed, dogs in area of bar, tables out in front and in pleasant back garden, open all day.
(Andy Dolan, Comus and Sarah Elliott, Edward Mirzoeff)

HARTINGTON   SK1260
Charles Cotton (01298) 84229
Market Place; SK17 0AL Popular four-square stone-built hotel in attractive village centre; large comfortable bar-bistro with open fire, good food from lunchtime sandwiches and snacks up (more restaurant evening choice), up to five ales including local Whim, bottled beers and real cider, nice wines and italian coffee, friendly helpful service, restaurant and summer tearoom; background and some live music; children welcome, dogs in bar, seats out at front and in small back garden, 17 bedrooms, open all day. *(Ann and Colin Hunt, J and E Dakin, Dennis Jones)*

HARTINGTON   SK1260
Devonshire Arms (01298) 84232
Market Place; SK17 0AL Traditional unpretentious two-bar pub in attractive village, welcoming landlord, ales including Marstons Pedigree, generous home-made food, log fires; may be background music; children and dogs welcome, tables out in front facing duck pond, more in small garden, good walks, open (and food) all day weekends. *(Alan Johnson)*

HARTSHORNE   SK3220
Bulls Head (01283) 215299
Woodville Road; DE11 7ET Welcoming popular local dating in part from 1600, big helpings of good value freshly cooked food including daily specials, meal deals, well kept Marstons Pedigree and a guest, helpful friendly staff, lots of beams and shelves of bric-a-brac; background music, free wi-fi; children welcome, clean comfortable bedrooms. *(Mike and Wena Stevenson)*

HATHERSAGE   SK2381
★**Scotsmans Pack** (01433) 650253
School Lane, off A6187; S32 1BZ Bustling inn equally popular with drinkers and diners; dark panelled rooms with lots of interesting knick-knacks, upholstered gingham stools and dining chairs, cushioned wall seats and assortment of tables, woodburner, well kept Black Sheep, Jennings, Marstons and a couple of guests, enjoyable food including daily specials board; background music (live first Fri of month), TV, darts; picnic-sets on terrace overlooking trout stream, plenty of surrounding walks, bedrooms, open (and food) all day in summer, all day Fri-Sun in winter. *(Dennis Jones)*

HAYFIELD   SK0486
Sportsman (01663) 741565
Off A624 Chapel-en-le-Frith–Buxton; Kinder Road, up past the Royal, off Market Street; SK22 2LE Good choice of enjoyable generously served food in roomy and neatly kept traditional inn, beams, carpet and open fires, friendly staff, well kept Thwaites, decent wines and lots of malt whiskies; children and dogs welcome, lovely location (handy for Kinder Scout walks), outside area with rustic furniture, bedrooms could do with updating. *(P Dawn)*

HEAGE   SK3750
Black Boy (01773) 856799
Old Road (B6013); DE56 2BN Recently refurbished village pub-restaurant with welcoming licensees, popular good value food including fish specials in bar and upstairs dining area, a house beer brewed by Marstons and well kept regularly changing guests, upholstered settles, decorative copperware and jugs, open fire; TV for major sports events, no dogs; children welcome, small outside seating area, open all day.
(John Beeken)

HEANOR   SK4445
Marlpool Ale House (01773) 711285
Breach Road; DE75 7NJ Tiny old-fashioned alehouse in former butcher's shop, own good Marlpool beers and a couple of guests served from pulpit counter, cheery atmosphere and some impromptu acoustic music; dogs welcome, open 2-10pm Fri, 12-10pm Sat, Sun. *(Frank Hazeldine)*

HOGNASTON   SK2350
★**Red Lion** (01335) 370396
Off B5035 Ashbourne–Wirksworth; DE6 1PR Traditional 17th-c inn with open-plan beamed bar, three fires, attractive mix of old tables, curved settles and other seats on ancient flagstones, friendly licensees, good well presented home-made food from shortish menu in bar and conservatory restaurant, nice wines by the glass, Marstons Pedigree and guests; background music;

picnic-sets in field behind, boules, handy for
Carsington Water, three good bedrooms, big
breakfast. *(Anon)*

HOLBROOK   SK3645
★**Dead Poets** (01332) 780301
*Chapel Street; village signed off A6 S of
Belper; DE56 OTQ* Unchanging drinkers'
local with up to nine ales (some served
from jugs), real cider and country wines,
filled cobs and good value weekday bar food,
simple cottagey décor with beams, stripped-
stone walls and broad flagstones, high-
backed settles forming booths, big log fire,
plenty of tucked-away corners, woodburner in
snug, children allowed in back conservatory
till 8pm; quiet background music, no credit
cards; dogs welcome, seats out at back, open
all day Fri-Sun. *(Anon)*

HOPE   SK1783
★**Cheshire Cheese** (01433) 620381
Off A6187, towards Edale; S33 6ZF
16th-c traditional stone inn with snug
oak-beamed rooms on different levels,
open fires, red carpets or stone floors,
straightforward furnishings and gleaming
brasses, friendly staff serving up to four ales
including Bradfield and Peak, a dozen malts,
pubby food from sandwiches up, folk night
first Thurs of month; children welcome,
dogs allowed in bar, good local walks in the
summits of Lose Hill and Win Hill or the cave
district around Castleton, four bedrooms,
limited parking, open all day weekends,
in summer, closed Mon. *(Brian and Anna
Marsden, John Wooll, Dennis Jones)*

HORSLEY WOODHOUSE   SK3944
Old Oak (01332) 881299
*Main Street (A609 Belper–Ilkeston);
DE7 6AW* Busy roadside local linked
to nearby Bottle Brook and Leadmill
microbreweries, their ales and guests plus
weekend back bar with another eight well
priced beers tapped from the cask, farm
ciders, good basic snacks (can also bring your
own food), beamed rooms with blazing coal
fires, chatty friendly atmosphere, occasional
live music; children and dogs welcome, hatch
to covered courtyard tables, nice views,
closed weekday lunchtimes till 4pm, open all
day weekends. *(Anon)*

ILKESTON   SK4742
Dewdrop (0115) 932 9684
*Station Street, Ilkeston junction, off
A6096; DE7 5TE* Large Victorian corner
local in old industrial area, not strong on bar
comfort but popular for its well kept beers
(up to eight) including Blue Monkey, Castle
Rock and Oakham, simple bar snacks, back
lounge with fire and piano, connecting lobby
to front public bar with pool, darts and TV,

some Barnes Wallis memorabilia; sheltered
outside seating at back, walks by former
Nottingham Canal, open all day weekends,
closed weekday lunchtimes. *(P Dawn)*

ILKESTON   SK4641
Spanish Bar (0115) 930 8666
South Street; DE7 5QJ Busy bar with well
kept and well priced changing ales, bottled
belgians, friendly efficient staff, evening
overspill room, Tues quiz night; small back
garden and skittle alley, open all day.
(P Dawn)

LITTLE LONGSTONE   SK1971
Packhorse (01629) 640471
*Off A6 NW of Bakewell via Monsal Dale;
DE45 1NN* Three comfortable linked
beamed rooms, pine tables on flagstones, well
kept Thornbridge ales and a guest, popular
locally sourced food (all day weekends) from
daily changing blackboard, good value wine
list, coal fires, Thurs quiz; children, dogs and
hikers welcome (on Monsal Trail), terrace in
steep little back garden. *(J and E Dakin)*

LULLINGTON   SK2513
Colvile Arms (01827) 373212
*Off A444 S of Burton; Main Street;
DE12 8EG* Popular 18th-c village pub with
high-backed settles in simple panelled bar,
cosy comfortable beamed lounge, pleasant
atmosphere and friendly staff, well kept Bass,
Marstons Pedigree and a guest, no food apart
from cobs; soft background music; picnic-
sets on small sheltered back lawn, closed
lunchtimes apart from Sun. *(Anon)*

MAKENEY   SK3544
★**Holly Bush** (01332) 841729
*From A6 heading N after Duffield, take
first right after crossing River Derwent,
then first left; DE56 0RX* Down-to-earth
two-bar village pub (former farmhouse) with
three blazing coal fires (one in old-fashioned
range by snug's curved high-backed settle),
flagstones, beams, black panelling and tiled
floors, lots of brewing advertisements, half
a dozen or so well kept changing ales (some
brought from cellar in jugs), real cider,
cheap food including rolls and pork pies,
may be local cheeses for sale, games lobby
with hatch service (children allowed here),
regular beer festivals; picnic-sets outside,
walkers and dogs welcome, open all day.
(Cliff Sparkes)

MATLOCK   SK2960
Thorn Tree (01629) 580295
Jackson Road, Matlock Bank; DE4 3JQ
Superb valley views to Riber Castle from this
homely 19th-c stone-built local, Bass, Greene
King, Timothy Taylors Landlord and four
guests, simple well cooked food (Tues-Fri

Pubs close to motorway junctions are listed at the back of the book.

lunchtimes, Sun 5-6.30pm, Weds pie night), friendly staff and regulars; free wi-fi; dogs welcome, closed Mon lunchtime, open all day Fri-Sun. *(Anon)*

MILFORD   SK3545
King William IV (01332) 840842
Milford Bridge; DE56 0RR Friendly and relaxing stone-built pub across from the River Derwent; long room with low beams, bare boards and quarry tiles, old settles and a blazing coal fire, well kept Greene King, Sharps, Timothy Taylors and a couple of guests, simple food, music and quiz nights; dogs welcome, three bedrooms, closed weekday lunchtimes, open all day weekends. *(Anon)*

MILLERS DALE   SK1473
Anglers Rest (01298) 871323
Just down Litton Lane; pub is PH on OS Sheet 119 map reference 142734; SK17 8SN Creeper-clad pub in lovely quiet riverside setting on Monsal Trail, two bars and dining room, log fires, Adnams, Storm and two usually local guests, enjoyable simple food, cheery helpful service, reasonable prices, darts, pool, muddy walkers and dogs (they have their own) in public bar; children welcome, wonderful gorge views and river walks, self-catering apartment, open all day Sat, till 9pm Sun. *(Anon)*

MONSAL HEAD   SK1871
★ Monsal Head Hotel (01629) 640250
B6465; DE45 1NL Outstanding hilltop location for this friendly inn, cosy stables bar with stripped timber horse-stalls, harness and brassware, cushioned oak pews, farmhouse chairs and benches on flagstones, big open fire, ales such as Bradfield, Buxton, Oakwell and Wincle, german bottled beers, several wines by the glass, enjoyable locally sourced food from lunchtime sandwiches up (they may ask to keep your credit card while you eat), elegant restaurant; children (over 3), well behaved dogs and muddy walkers welcome, big garden, stunning views of Monsal Dale with its huge viaduct, seven comfortable bedrooms, open all day till midnight. *(Dennis Jones, Emma Scofield, Edward May, Kay and Alistair Butler)*

MONYASH   SK1566
★ Bulls Head (01629) 812372
B5055 W of Bakewell; DE45 1JH Rambling stone pub with high-ceilinged rooms, straightforward traditional furnishings including plush stools lined along bar, horse pictures and a shelf of china, log fire, Black Sheep and a couple of guests, restaurant more cottagey with high-backed dining chairs on heated stone floor, popular fairly traditional food (all day weekends) from sandwiches and baked potatoes up, small back room with darts, board games and pool; background music; children and dogs welcome, plenty of picnic-sets under parasols in big garden, gate leading to well equipped public play area, good surrounding walks, open all day Fri-Sun. *(Derek and Sylvia Stephenson)*

NEW MILLS   SJ9886
Fox (0161) 427 1634
Brook Bottom Road; SK22 3AY Tucked-away unmodernised country local at end of single-track road, Robinsons ales and good value basic food (not Tues evening) including sandwiches, log fire, darts and pool; no credit cards; children and dogs welcome, lots of tables outside, good walking area, open all day Fri-Sun. *(Brian and Anna Marsden)*

NEWTON SOLNEY   SK2825
Brickmakers Arms (01283) 703170
Main Street (B5008 NE of Burton); DE15 0SJ Friendly beamed village pub owned by Burton Bridge Brewery; their ales kept well and occasional guests, plenty of bottled beers too, no food, two rooms off bar, one with original panelling and a delft shelf displaying jugs and plates, pubby furniture, built-in wall seats and open fires, area with piano and books; Mon quiz; tables on terrace and a little shop, open all day Sat, closed lunchtimes during the week. *(Anon)*

OCKBROOK   SK4236
Royal Oak (01332) 662378
Off B6096 just outside Spondon; Green Lane; DE72 3SE 18th-c village local run by same friendly family since 1953, good value honest food (not weekend evenings) from good lunchtime cobs to steaks, well kept Bass and interesting guest beers, tile-floor tap room, carpeted snug, inner bar with Victorian prints, larger and lighter side room, nice old settle in entrance corridor, open fires, darts and dominoes, some live music; children welcome, dogs in the evening, sheltered cottage garden and cobbled front courtyard, separate play area, open all day Sun. *(Anon)*

OSMASTON   SK1943
Shoulder of Mutton (01335) 342371
Off A52 SE of Ashbourne; DE6 1LW Down-to-earth red-brick pub with three well kept ales including Marstons Pedigree, enjoyable generous home-made food and good friendly service; attractive garden, farmland views, peaceful pretty village with thatched cottages, duck pond and good walks. *(MP)*

PARWICH   SK1854
★ Sycamore (01335) 390212
By church; DE6 1QL Chatty old country pub well run by cheerful welcoming landlady, generous wholesome food lunchtimes and most Weds-Sat evenings, Robinsons ales, good log fire in neat traditional back bar, pool in small front hatch-served games room, another room serving as proper village shop; children welcome, tables in front courtyard, picnic-sets on neat side grass, good walks, open all day in summer. *(Ann and Colin Hunt)*

PENTRICH   SK3852

★**Dog** (01773) 513360

*Main Road (B6016 N of Ripley);
DE5 3RE* Extended pub popular for
its good variety of food including daily
specials, Bass, Sharps Doom Bar and a
guest from carved church-look counter,
nice wines by the glass, woodburner, pubby
bar furniture, smarter modern dining area
beyond part with leather sofas; background
music; well behaved children allowed if
eating (not Fri, Sat evenings), extensive
garden behind, nice views and good walks,
open all day (food all day Fri, Sat, till 6pm
Sun). *(John Boothman)*

PILSLEY   SK2371

★**Devonshire Arms** (01246) 583258

*Village signposted off A619 W of
Baslow, and pub just below B6048;
High Street; DE45 1UL* Civilised little
country inn on the Chatsworth Estate;
gentle contemporary slant with flagstoned
bar and several fairly compact areas off
(each with own character), log fires in
stone fireplaces, comfortable seating
and big modern paintings, four local ales
and several wines by the glass, food from
sandwiches up using Estate produce;
children welcome, a few tables outside,
Chatsworth farm shop at the top of lane,
bedrooms, open all day. *(J R and P D Holt)*

RIPLEY   SK3950

Talbot Taphouse (01773) 742626

Butterley Hill; DE5 3LT Full range of local
Amber ales and changing guests kept well by
knowledgeable landlord, farm ciders, draught
belgians and bottled beers too, long narrow
panelled room with new bar counter, comfy
chairs, open fire in brick fireplace, friendly
atmosphere; open all day weekends, from
5pm other days. *(Anon)*

ROWSLEY   SK2565

Grouse & Claret (01629) 733233

A6 Bakewell–Matlock; DE4 2EB
Attractive family dining pub in old stone
building, spacious, clean and comfortable,
with welcoming licensees and friendly
staff, enjoyable low-priced food (all day
weekends) from sandwiches up, well
kept Jennings Cumberland and Marstons
Pedigree, decent wines, open fires, tap
room popular with walkers; tables outside,
play area, good value bedrooms, campsite,
open all day. *(David Carr)*

ROWSLEY   SK2565

★**Peacock** (01629) 733518

Bakewell Road; DE4 2EB Civilised small
17th-c country hotel, comfortable seating

in spacious modern lounge, inner bar with
log fire, bare stone walls and some Robert
'Mouseman' Thompson furniture, enjoyable
if not cheap food from lunchtime sandwiches
to restaurant meals, Peak ales, good wines
and well served coffee, pleasant helpful staff;
attractive riverside gardens, trout fishing,
14 good bedrooms. *(Anon)*

SHARDLOW   SK4430

Malt Shovel (01332) 792066

*3.5 miles from M1 junction 24, via A6
towards Derby; The Wharf; DE72 2HG*
Canalside pub in 18th-c former maltings,
interesting odd-angled layout with cosy
corners, Marstons-related ales, good value
tasty home-made food from lunchtime
sandwiches and baked potatoes up (evening
food Thurs, Fri only), quick friendly service,
beams, panelling and central open fire, live
music Sun; dogs welcome, lots of terrace
tables by Trent & Mersey Canal, pretty
hanging baskets, open all day. *(Anon)*

SHARDLOW   SK4429

Old Crown (01332) 792392

*Off A50 just W of M1 junction 24;
Cavendish Bridge, E of village;
DE72 2HL* Good value pub with great range
of Marstons-related ales and guests all kept
well, nice choice of malt whiskies, pubby food
(not Sun evening, Mon) from sandwiches and
baguettes up, beams with masses of jugs and
mugs, walls covered with other bric-a-brac
and breweriana, big inglenook; quiz Mon,
fortnightly live music Tues; children and
dogs welcome, garden with play area, open
all day. *(Stephen Shepherd)*

SHELDON   SK1768

★**Cock & Pullet** (01629) 814292

*Village signed off A6 just W of Ashford;
DE45 1QS* Charming no-frills village
pub with low beams, exposed stonework,
flagstones and open fire, cheerful mismatch
of furnishings, large collection of clocks and
various representations of poultry (some
stuffed), well kept Black Sheep, Sharps
and Timothy Taylors, good simple food from
shortish menu, reasonable prices, pool and
TV in plainer public bar; quiet background
music, no credit cards; children and dogs
welcome, seats and water feature on pleasant
back terrace, pretty village just off Limestone
Way and popular all year with walkers, clean
bedrooms, open all day. *(Peter F Marshall,
Ian and Suzy Masser, J and E Dakin, Sara Fulton,
Roger Baker, Dennis Jones)*

SHIRLEY   SK2141

Saracens Head (01335) 360330

Church Lane; DE6 3AS Modernised late
18th-c dining pub in attractive village; good

Post Office address codings confusingly give the impression that a few pubs are in
Derbyshire, when they're really in Cheshire (which is where we list them).

range of interesting well presented food from pubby to more expensive restaurant dishes, four Greene King ales, speciality coffees, simple country-style dining furniture and two pretty working art nouveau fireplaces; background music; children and dogs (in bar area) welcome, picnic-sets out in front and on back terrace, self-catering cottage, open all day Sun. *(Anon)*

SMISBY   SK3419
Smisby Arms (01530) 412677
Nelsons Square; LE65 2UA Low-beamed village local serving generous helpings of good reasonably priced food, friendly helpful service, two well kept changing ales, bright little dining extension down steps; no dogs; children welcome, a few tables out in front, open all day Sun. *(Anon)*

SPONDON   SK3935
★Malt Shovel (01332) 674203
Off A6096 on edge of Derby, via Church Hill into Potter Street; DE21 7LH Homely traditional pub with several well kept mainly Marstons-related ales (some tapped from the cask) in tiny bar or from hatch in tiled corridor, various other little rooms, old-fashioned décor and a huge inglenook, generous inexpensive home-cooked food (not weekend evenings), friendly helpful staff, steps down to big games bar with darts and pool; children welcome, lots of picnic-sets, some under cover, in large back garden with play area, open all day Fri-Sun. *(Anon)*

STONEDGE   SK3367
Red Lion (01246) 566142
Darley Road (B5057); S45 0LW Revamped bar-bistro (former 17th-c coaching inn) on edge of the Peak District; good attractively presented food from sandwiches up using local ingredients including own vegetables, fresh fish/shellfish counter, real ales and good choice of wines, bare stone walls, flagstones and wood floors, some substantial timbers, lounge area with comfortable seating and open fire; picnic-sets out under parasols at back, 27 bedrooms in adjacent modern hotel, open all day. *(Carl Riley)*

SUTTON CUM
DUCKMANTON   SK4371
Arkwright Arms (01246) 232053
A632 Bolsover–Chesterfield; S44 5JG Friendly mock-Tudor pub with bar, pool room (dogs allowed here) and dining room, all with real fires, good choice of well priced food (not Sun evening), up to 16 changing ales including local Raw, ten real ciders and four perries (beer/cider festivals Easter/

Aug bank holidays); TV, games machine; children welcome, seats out at front and on side terrace, attractive hanging baskets, play equipment, open all day. *(Anon)*

TICKNALL   SK3523
★Wheel (01332) 864488
Main Street (A514); DE73 7JZ Stylish contemporary décor in bar and upstairs restaurant, enjoyable interesting home-made food (all day weekends), friendly staff, well kept Marstons Pedigree and a guest; children welcome, no dogs inside, nice outside area with café tables on raised deck, near entrance to Calke Abbey (NT). *(Anon)*

TIDESWELL   SK1575
Horse & Jockey 0845 498 9009
Queen Street; SK17 8JZ Friendly and relaxed family-run local reworked in old-fashioned style, with beams, flagstones, cushioned wall benches and coal fire in small public bar's traditional open range, bare boards, button-back banquettes and woodburner in lounge, ales such as Bradfield, Sharps, Tetleys and Thornbridge, decent modestly priced food, stripped stone and flagstones in sparely decorated dining room; children and dogs welcome, five bedrooms, good walks, open all day. *(David Hunt, Derek and Sylvia Stephenson)*

WARDLOW   SK1875
★Three Stags Heads (01298) 872268
Wardlow Mires; A623/B6465; SK17 8RW Basic unchanging pub (17th-c longhouse) of great individuality, flagstoned floors, old country furniture, heating from cast-iron kitchen ranges, old photographs, long-serving plain-talking landlord, locals in favourite corners, well kept Abbeydale ales including house beer Black Lurcher (brewed at a hefty 8% ABV), lots of bottled beers, hearty seasonal food on home-made plates (licensees are potters and have a small gallery), may be free roast chestnuts or cheese on the bar, folk music Sun afternoon; no credit cards; well behaved children and dogs welcome, hill views from front terrace, good walking country, only open Fri evening and all day weekends. *(Dennis Jones)*

WHITTINGTON MOOR   SK3873
★Derby Tup (01246) 454316
Sheffield Road; B6057 just S of A61 roundabout; S41 8LS Spotless no-frills Castle Rock local with up to a dozen well kept interesting ales from long line of gleaming handpumps, farm cider and irish whiskeys too, friendly service, simple furniture, coal fire and lots of standing room as well as two small side rooms, daily papers,

---

Please let us know what you think of a pub's bedrooms: feedback@goodguides.com or (no stamp needed) The Good Pub Guide, FREEPOST RTJR-ZCYZ-RJZT, Perrymans Lane, Etchingham TN19 7DN.

no food (sandwiches from nearby deli); can get very busy weekend evenings and on match days, no children; dogs welcome, open all day Fri-Sun, closed Weds lunchtime. *(P Dawn)*

WILLINGTON SK2928

Dragon (01283) 704795

The Green; DE65 6BP Refurbished pub backing on to Trent & Mersey Canal, enjoyable well cooked food (all day Fri-Sun) from sandwiches and sharing boards to pub favourites and grills, Marstons Pedigree, Sharps Doom Bar, Timothy Taylors Landlord and local guests, quiz and music nights; free wi-fi; children welcome, picnic-sets out overlooking canal, moorings, open all day. *(Anon)*

WINSTER SK2460

★**Bowling Green** (01629) 650219

East Bank, by NT Market House; DE4 2DS Traditional old stone pub with good chatty atmosphere, character landlord and welcoming staff, enjoyable reasonably priced home-made food, at least three well kept changing local ales and good selection of whiskies, end log fire, dining area and family conservatory (dogs allowed here too); nice village, good walks, closed Mon, Tues and lunchtimes apart from Sun. *(Anon)*

WINSTER SK2360

Miners Standard (01629) 650279

Bank Top (B5056 above village); DE4 2DR Simply furnished 17th-c stone local, relaxed at lunchtime, livelier in the evening, well kept Brampton, Marstons Pedigree and guests, good value honest pub food, big woodburner, lead-mining photographs and minerals, lots of brass, backwards clock, ancient well, snug and restaurant; background music; children allowed away from bar, attractive view from garden, campsite next door, interesting

stone-built village below, open all day weekends. *(Anon)*

WIRKSWORTH SK2854

Royal Oak (01629) 823000

North End; DE4 4FG Friendly old-fashioned little terraced local, five well kept ales including Bass, Timothy Taylors Landlord and Whim Hartington, some bric-a-brac and interesting old photographs, pool room; only open evenings from 8pm and Sun lunchtime. *(Cliff Sparkes)*

WOOLLEY MOOR SK3661

★**White Horse** (01246) 590319

Badger Lane, off B6014 Matlock–Clay Cross; DE55 6FG Attractive and welcoming old dining pub in rolling countryside, neatly updated uncluttered rooms with rows of furniture (including a leather sofa) on stone or bare boards, boldly patterned curtains and blinds, chatty tap room with Peak Ales and a guest, well thought of food including good value weekday set menu, conservatory; background music; children welcome, sloping garden with picnic-sets and play area, boules, close to Ogston Reservoir, closed Sun evening, Mon. *(Derek and Sylvia Stephenson, M G Hart)*

YOULGREAVE SK2164

George (01629) 636292

Alport Lane/Church Street; DE45 1WN Old bay-windowed inn opposite Norman church, comfortably worn inside, with banquettes running around three sides of main bar, flagstoned tap room (walkers and dogs welcome) and games room, generous helpings of reasonably priced home-made food from extensive menu including children's choices, Theakstons Black Bull and a couple of guests, friendly service; free wi-fi; roadside tables, attractive village handy for Lathkill Dale and Haddon Hall, simple bedrooms, open (and food) all day. *(Dennis Jones)*

Devon

BEESANDS
Cricket 🛏

SX8140 Map 1

About 3 miles S of A379, from Chillington; in village turn right along foreshore road; TQ7 2EN

Welcoming pub with plenty of fish dishes and real ales; clean, airy bedrooms

With a relaxed atmosphere, chatty locals and friendly licensees, this well run pub gets busy at peak times. The light, airy décor is new england in style, with dark wood or leather chairs around big, solid light wood tables on stripped-wood flooring by the bar and light brown patterned carpet in the restaurant. Big TV screens at either end roll through old local photographs, sport or the news. Otter Ale and Bitter and St Austell Tribute on handpump, 14 wines by the glass and local cider; background music. The cheerful black labrador is called Brewster. There are picnic-sets beside the sea wall (a little bleak but essential protection) with pebbly Start Bay beach just over the other side. The South West Coast Path runs through the village.

🍴 Using crab, scallops and lobster caught in the bay, the changing food includes sandwiches, crab soup, cornish sardines, mushroom, blue cheese and walnut linguine, mussels of the day with skinny fries, burger with bacon, gruyère, onion rings and chips, rosemary cod loin with curried seafood risotto and crispy ham, and puddings such as chocolate fondant and bubblegum baked alaska with fruit coulis. *Benchmark main dish: seafood pancake £12.00. Two-course evening meal £22.00.*

Heavitree ~ Tenant Nigel Heath ~ Real ale ~ (01548) 580215 ~ Open 12-10 ~ Bar food 12-2.30, 6-8.30; 12-8.30 high summer ~ Restaurant ~ Children welcome ~ Dogs allowed in bar ~ Wi-fi ~ Bedrooms: £80/£90 ~ www.thecricketinn.com *Recommended by S Holder, Roy Hoing, Peter Travis, Jane and Kai Horsburgh*

BRAMPFORD SPEKE
Lazy Toad 🎖

SX9298 Map 1

Off A377 N of Exeter; EX5 5DP

Well run dining pub in pretty village with delicious food, real ales, friendly service and pretty garden; bedrooms

With two dog-friendly bedrooms in an annexe and plenty of nearby walks, our readers and their hounds enjoy this friendly 18th-c inn (though dogs must be kept on a lead in the bar). The interconnected rooms have beams, standing timbers and slate floors, a comfortable sofa and rocking chair (much prized in winter) by the open log fire, and cushioned wall settles and high-backed wooden dining chairs around a mix of tables; the cream-painted brick walls are hung with lots of pictures and there's a rather fine grandfather clock. Otter Bitter and St Austell Tribute on handpump, 18 wines by the glass and home-made cordials are served by attentive staff; the resident cocker spaniel is called Sam. There are green-painted picnic-sets in the courtyard (once used by the local farrier and wheelwright) and the walled garden. The comfortable, pretty bedrooms are in the main building and an annexe. The charming village with its thatched cottages is well worth wandering around and there are fine walks beside the River Exe and on the Exe Valley Way and Devonshire Heartland Way.

Using some home-grown produce, their own eggs, home-reared lamb, and home-smoking fish and meat, the highly rewarding food might include black pudding scotch duck eggs, home-smoked pigeon, bacon and crouton salad, beetroot and blue cheese risotto, sausages with onion gravy, plaice with caper nut brown butter, steak and kidney pie, coq au vin, and puddings such as amaretti chocolate mousse cake and turkish delight syllabub with Cointreau and marshmallow. *Benchmark main dish: hake, chickpea and chorizo with mediterranean tomato fondue £17.95. Two-course evening meal £21.00.*

Free house ~ Licensees Clive and Mo Walker ~ Real ale ~ (01392) 841591 ~ Open 11.30-2.30, 6-11; 12-3 Sun; closed Sun evening, Mon, last three weeks Jan ~ Bar food 12-2, 6.30-9; 12-2.30 Sun ~ Children welcome till 7pm but over-12s only in bedrooms ~ Dogs allowed in bar and bedrooms ~ Wi-fi ~ Bedrooms: £58/£85 ~ www.thelazytoadinn.co.uk
Recommended by Jan and Alan Summers

BRANSCOMBE
Fountain Head ◀ £

SY1888 Map 1

Upper village, above the robust old church; village signposted off A3052 Sidmouth–Seaton, then from Branscombe Square follow road uphill towards Sidmouth and after about a mile turn left after the church; OS Sheet 192 map reference SY188889; EX12 3BG

Old-fashioned and friendly stone pub with own-brewed beers and reasonably priced, well liked food

Our readers always enjoy their visits to this genuinely welcoming and quite unchanging 14th-c pub. The atmosphere is nicely old-fashioned, with no background music, TV or games machines. The room on the left (formerly a smithy) has forge tools and horseshoes on high oak beams, cushioned pews and mate's chairs and a log fire in the original raised firebed with its tall central chimney. They keep their own-brewed Branscombe Vale Branoc and Summa That plus a changing guest beer on handpump, several wines by the glass and local cider – there's also a beer festival in June. On the right, an irregularly shaped, more orthodox snug room has another log fire, a white-painted plank ceiling with an unusual carved ceiling rose, brown-varnished panelled walls and a flagstone and lime ash floor. Local artists' paintings and greeting cards are for sale; darts and board games. You can sit outside on the front loggia and terrace listening to the little stream gurgling beneath the flagstoned path. The surrounding walks are very pleasant.

Good, fairly priced food includes sandwiches, mussels in white wine and cream, spiced chicken, ham hock and pistachio terrine with home-made piccalilli, home-cooked honey-roast ham and eggs, fresh fish of the day, steak in ale pie, walnut-coated brie on roasted vegetables, pork belly with sweet red wine dressing and pineapple salsa, and puddings. *Benchmark main dish: beer-battered fresh cod and chips £10.50. Two-course evening meal £16.75.*

~ Licensees Jon Woodley and Teresa Hoare ~ Real ale ~ (01297) 680359 ~ Open 11-3,
6-11; 12-10.30 Sun ~ Bar food 12-2, 6.30-9 ~ Restaurant ~ Children welcome away from
main bar area ~ Dogs allowed in bar ~ Live entertainment Sun evenings in summer ~
www.fountainheadinn.com *Recommended by R K Phillips, George Atkinson, Kerry Law, Patrick
and Daphne Darley, Pete Walker, Roger and Donna Huggins, Nigel Williams, Revd R P Tickle*

BRANSCOMBE

Masons Arms 🛏️

SY2088 Map 1

Main Street; signed off A3052 Sidmouth–Seaton, then bear left into village;
EX12 3DJ

**Rambling low-beamed rooms, woodburning stoves, a fair choice of
real ales, popular food and seats on quiet terrace and in garden;
cottagey bedrooms**

This is a nice place to stay, with bedrooms in the pub itself or in
converted cottages overlooking the gardens (dogs can stay in these
rooms); the sea is just a stroll away and the pretty village is well worth
exploring. The rambling main bar is the heart of the place; with a good mix
of locals and visitors, you can be sure of a cheerful, bustling atmosphere
and a warm welcome from the licensees. There are comfortable seats and
chairs on slate floors, ancient ships' beams, a log fire in a massive hearth,
St Austell Proper Job and Tribute and guest beers such as Branscombe Vale
Branoc and Otter Bitter on handpump and ten wines by the glass. A second
bar also has a slate floor, a fireplace with a two-sided woodburning stove
and stripped pine; there are also two dining rooms. A quiet flower-filled
front terrace, with thatched-roof tables, extends into a side garden. It's best
to arrive early to be sure of a parking space.

🍴 As well as ciabatta sandwiches and ploughman's (served until 6pm), the reliably
good food includes pâté with tomato chutney, mussels in white wine, garlic and
cream, beer-battered fish and chips, sausages with caramelised onions and red wine
sauce, pasta with roasted peppers, red pesto and cheese, a pie of the day, burger
with gruyère, bacon and chips, chargrilled chicken with couscous, chilli and toasted
peanuts, and puddings. *Benchmark main dish: local crab ploughman's £14.50.
Two-course evening meal £20.00.*

St Austell ~ Managers Simon and Alison Ede ~ Real ale ~ (01297) 680300 ~ Open 11-11;
12-10.30 Sun ~ Bar food 12-2.15, 6.30-9 ~ Restaurant ~ Children welcome in bar area ~
Dogs allowed in bar and bedrooms ~ Wi-fi ~ Bedrooms: /$85 ~ www.masonsarms.co.uk
Recommended by Pete Walker

BUCKLAND BREWER

Coach & Horses

SS4220 Map 1

*Village signposted off A388 S of Monkleigh; OS Sheet 190 map reference
423206; EX39 5LU*

**Friendly old village pub with a mix of customers, open fires and real
ales; good nearby walks**

The friendly and polite licensees have been running this thatched 13th-c
inn for over 25 years, and it's somewhere our readers return to again
and again. The heavily beamed bar (mind your head on some of the beams)
has comfortable seats, a handsome antique settle and a woodburning stove
in an inglenook; there's also a good log fire in the big stone inglenook of the
small lounge. A little back room has darts and pool; the three-legged cat is
called Marmite. Cotleigh Golden Seahawk, Otter Ale and Sharps Doom Bar
on handpump, Winkleigh cider and several wines by the glass; skittle alley

(which doubles as a function room), background music, games machine, darts, pool table and occasional TV for sports. There are picnic-sets on the front terrace and in the side garden. They have a holiday cottage to rent next door. The RHS garden Rosemoor is about five miles away.

From a sizeable menu, the food includes sandwiches, deep-fried breaded camembert with apple and redcurrant jelly, chicken liver pâté, burger with bacon and cheese, five different curries, beer-battered fish and chips, spinach, stilton and mushroom pasta bake, bacon-wrapped chicken with wild mushroom sauce, and puddings such as fruit crumble and banana, cream and toffee pie. *Benchmark main dish: steak in Guinness pie £9.50. Two-course evening meal £17.00.*

Free house ~ Licensees Oliver and Nicola Wolfe ~ Real ale ~ (01237) 451395 ~ Open 12-3, 5.30 (6 Sun)-midnight ~ Bar food 12-2, 6.30-9.30 ~ Restaurant ~ Children welcome ~ Dogs allowed in bar ~ Wi-fi ~ www.coachandhorsesbucklandbrewer.co.uk
Recommended by Ryta Lyndley, John Marsh, Pat and Tony Martin

BUCKLAND MONACHORUM   SX4968   Map 1
Drake Manor ♨ £ 🛏
Off A386 via Crapstone, just S of Yelverton roundabout; PL20 7NA

Nice little village pub with snug rooms, popular food, quite a choice of drinks and pretty back garden; bedrooms

With its lovely local atmosphere, good food and warm welcome from the long-serving landlady, this bustling old pub remains a favourite with our readers. The heavily beamed public bar on the left has brocade-cushioned wall seats, prints of the village from 1905 onwards, horse tack and a few ship badges, and a woodburning stove in a very big stone fireplace; a small door leads to a low-beamed cubbyhole. The snug Drakes Bar has beams hung with tiny cups and big brass keys, a woodburning stove in another stone fireplace, horsebrasses and stirrups, and a mix of seats and tables (note the fine stripped-pine high-backed settle with hood). On the right is a small beamed dining room with settles and tables on flagstones. Shove-ha'penny, darts, euchre and board games. Dartmoor Jail Ale, Otter Amber and Sharps Doom Bar on handpump, 12 wines by the glass and 20 malt whiskies. There are picnic-sets in the prettily planted and sheltered back garden and the front floral displays are much admired; morris men perform regularly in summer. The bedrooms are comfortable and they also have an attractive self-catering apartment. Buckland Abbey (National Trust) is close by.

Using local produce, the enjoyable food includes lunchtime baguettes, ham hock terrine with piccalilli, salmon and prawn fishcakes with horseradish and lemon mayonnaise, gammon and free-range eggs, chicken with chilli and lime rub and yoghurt and lemon dip, wild boar and pear burger topped with brie, wild mushroom risotto, specials such as venison pie and hake fillet with chive butter sauce, and puddings. *Benchmark main dish: steak in ale pie £9.95. Two-course evening meal £15.50.*

Punch ~ Lease Mandy Robinson ~ Real ale ~ (01822) 853892 ~ Open 11.30-2.30, 6.30-11; 11.30-11.30 Fri, Sat; 12-11 Sun ~ Bar food 11.30-2 (2.30 weekends), 7-9.30 (10 Fri, Sat) ~ Restaurant ~ Children allowed in restaurant and area off main bar ~ Dogs allowed in bar ~ Wi-fi ~ Bedrooms: /£90 ~ www.drakemanorinn.co.uk *Recommended by Maureen Wood, Suzy Miller, Di and Mike Gillam, Stephen Shepherd*

CHAGFORD
Three Crowns 🛏

SX7087 Map 1

High Street; TQ13 8AJ

**13th-c thatched inn on the edge of Dartmoor National Park; stylishly
refurbished bar and lounges, conservatory restaurant, good food and
thoughtful choice of drinks; smart bedrooms**

After a major refurbishment cleverly blending the ancient (this is, after
all, a 13th-c former manor house) with the modern, this interesting
place offers plenty of space for both cosy fireside drinks and candlelit
meals. The bar has leather armchairs and stools in front of a big log fire,
built-in panelled wall seats with bright scatter cushions, a few leather tub
chairs and pretty curtains with tassled tie-backs. St Austell HSD, Proper
Job and Tribute on handpump and several wines by the glass, served by
friendly, efficient staff. The dining lounges have all sorts of leather, plush
or carved wooden chairs and settles around an assortment of tables, and
big gilt-edged mirrors over fireplaces. Throughout these rooms are painted
beams, standing timbers, pale flagstones, rugs, exposed stone walls hung
with photographs and prints, and various copper kettles, pots and warming
pans. There's also a conservatory-style dining area with varied furnishings;
the courtyard has sturdy tables and chairs among box topiary. Bedrooms
are stylish, well equipped and comfortable and breakfasts good and
generous. Parking is limited, but there's more in a nearby pay-and-display
car park.

Using local, seasonal produce, the enjoyable food includes sandwiches (until
5pm), mussels in white wine and cream, chicken and pistachio terrine with fruit
chutney, butternut squash risotto, burger with gruyère, crispy pancetta, coleslaw and
fries, corn-fed chicken with truffled mash, and puddings such as crème brûlée and a
platter of chocolate torte, lemon posset and eton mess. *Benchmark main dish:
beer-battered fish and chips £10.25. Two-course evening meal £18.00.*

St Austell ~ Manager Jared Lothian ~ Real ale ~ (01647) 433444 ~ Open 9am-10.45pm ~
Bar food 12-2.30, 6-9 (9.30 Fri, Sat) ~ Restaurant ~ Children welcome ~ Dogs allowed in
bar and bedrooms ~ Wi-fi ~ Bedrooms: £89/£99 ~ www.threecrowns-chagford.co.uk
Recommended by Di and Mike Gillam

CLAYHIDON
Merry Harriers ♀

ST1817 Map 1

*3 miles from M5 junction 26: head towards Wellington; turn left at first
roundabout signposted Ford Street and Hemyock, then after a mile turn left signposted
Ford Street; at hilltop T junction, turn left towards Chard – pub is 1.5 miles on right;
at Forches Corner NE of the village itself; EX15 3TR*

**Bustling and friendly dining pub with several real ales and quite a few
wines by the glass; sizeable garden**

New licensees have taken over this cheerful pub with its friendly
atmosphere. There are several small linked carpeted areas with
comfortably cushioned pews and farmhouse chairs, a woodburning
stove, tables set with candles, and work by local artists. Two dining areas
have quarry tiles, beams and lightly timbered white walls. Clarks Heroes,
Exmoor Ale and Otter Head on handpump, 12 wines by the glass and
several malt whiskies; skittle alley and board games. The sizeable garden
and terrace have plenty of tables and chairs and there's a wendy house and
other play equipment for children; good surrounding walks.

As well as lunchtime sandwiches and ploughman's, the popular food includes chicken liver parfait, whitebait with tartare sauce, ham and eggs, steak and kidney pie, beer-battered fresh cod and chips, gammon and egg, chicken and mushrooms in a red wine sauce, and puddings such as apple and blackberry crumble and crème brûlée. *Benchmark main dish: steak and kidney pie £10.50. Two-course evening meal £17.80.*

Free house ~ Licensees Reg and Lesley Payne ~ Real ale ~ (01823) 421270 ~ Open 11-11; 11.30-10.30 Sun; 12-3, 6-11 in winter; closed Sun evening and Mon in winter ~ Bar food 12-2 (2.15 Sun), 6.30-9 ~ Restaurant ~ Children welcome ~ Dogs allowed in bar ~ Wi-fi *Recommended by R T and J C Moggridge, Paul Humphreys, Paul Bonner, PLC, Bob and Margaret Holder, Comus and Sarah Elliott*

COCKWOOD
Anchor ♀ 🍺

SX9780 Map 1

Off, but visible from, A379 Exeter–Torbay road, after Starcross; EX6 8RA

Busy dining pub specialising in seafood (other choices available), with up to six real ales

Fronting the little harbour with its bobbing boats, swans and ducks, this incredibly popular dining pub has tables on a sheltered verandah overlooking the water; you'll need to arrive early to bag one and there are often queues to get in. As well as an extension made up of mainly reclaimed timber and decorated with over 300 ship emblems, brass and copper lamps and nautical knick-knacks, there are several small, low-ceilinged, rambling rooms with black panelling and good-sized tables in various nooks; the snug has a cheerful winter coal fire. Dartmoor Jail Ale, Otter Ale and St Austell Proper Job plus a couple of guest beers on handpump (beer festivals at Easter and Halloween), several wines by the glass and 50 malt whiskies; background music, darts, cards and board games.

 A huge range of fish dishes includes 28 ways of serving River Exe mussels and six ways of serving local scallops, as well as crab and brandy soup, sharing platters, seafood mornay, bass fillets on leeks with white wine and cream and paprika cod loin wrapped in smoked bacon. Non-fishy dishes include sandwiches, steak in ale pie, local sausages with onion gravy and spicy chicken in sweet pepper sauce, and there are puddings such as lemon and lime syllabub and sticky toffee pudding. *Benchmark main dish: 28 varieties of mussels £14.95. Two-course evening meal £22.00.*

Heavitree ~ Lease Malcolm and Katherine Protheroe, Scott Hellier ~ Real ale ~ (01626) 890203 ~ Open 11-11; 11.30-10.30 Sun ~ Bar food 12-10 (9.30 Sun) ~ Restaurant ~ Children welcome if seated and away from bar ~ Dogs allowed in bar ~ www.anchorinncockwood.com *Recommended by Adrian Johnson, Dr and Mrs J D Abell*

COLEFORD
New Inn

SS7701 Map 1

Just off A377 Crediton–Barnstaple; EX17 5BZ

Ancient thatched inn with interestingly furnished areas, well liked food, real ales and welcoming licensees; bedrooms

We've had plenty of warmly enthusiastic comments from readers about staying overnight in this genuinely friendly 13th-c inn. The bedrooms are well equipped and comfortable and the breakfasts particularly good. The U-shaped building has the servery in the 'angle' with interestingly furnished areas leading off it: ancient and modern settles, cushioned stone wall seats, some character tables (a pheasant worked into the grain of one) and carved dressers and chests. Also, paraffin lamps, antique prints on the white walls, landscape-decorated plates on one beam and pewter tankards on another. Captain, the chatty parrot, may greet you with a 'hello' or even a 'goodbye'. Otter Ale and Sharps Doom Bar on handpump, local cider, wines by the glass and a dozen malt whiskies; background music, TV, darts and board games. There are chairs and tables on decking beneath a pruned willow tree by the babbling stream, and more in a covered dining area.

 Good food using carefully sourced local produce includes baguettes, stilton soufflé with walnut and apple salad, gammon and egg, aubergine, sweet potato, tomato and feta moussaka, sausages on spring onion mash, cajun chicken with sweet chilli sauce and yoghurt, slow-cooked lamb shank in rosemary, garlic and thyme, pork belly with black pudding in cider sauce, and puddings. *Benchmark main dish: local mussels £11.25. Two-course evening meal £19.50.*

Free house ~ Licensees Carole and George Cowie ~ Real ale ~ (01363) 84242 ~ Open 12-3, 6-11; 12-3.30, 6-10.30 Sun ~ Bar food 12-2, 6.30-9.30 ~ Restaurant ~ Children welcome ~ Dogs allowed in bar ~ Wi-fi ~ Bedrooms: £69/£89 ~ www.thenewinncoleford.co.uk
Recommended by S G N Bennett, P and J Shapley, R Elliott, Nick Lawless, Michael Butler, J R Wildon

DALWOOD   ST2400 Map 1
Tuckers Arms

Village signposted off A35 Axminster–Honiton; keep on past village; EX13 7EG

13th-c thatched inn with friendly, hard-working young licensees, real ales and interesting bar food

'Just what every pub lover would want; I can't wait to go back,' says one of our more discerning readers. And this pretty thatched longhouse is always full of repeat customers – locals or holidaymakers – all keen to enjoy the relaxed, happy atmosphere. The beamed and flagstoned bar has traditional furnishings including assorted dining chairs, window seats and wall settles, and a log fire in an inglenook fireplace with lots of horsebrasses on the wall above. The back bar has an enormous collection of miniature bottles and there's also a more formal dining room; lots of copper implements and platters. Branscombe Vale Branoc, Otter Bitter and a changing local guest beer on handpump, several wines by the glass and up to 20 malt whiskies; background music and a double skittle alley. In summer, the hanging baskets are pretty and there are seats in the garden. Apart from the church, this is the oldest building in the parish.

 Good, enterprising food using local ingredients includes sandwiches, smoked haddock and leek gratin, an antipasti sharing board, butternut squash and goats cheese lasagne, rare-breed pork sausages with onion gravy, beer-battered line-caught pollack and chips, lemon and herb chicken in lemony sauce, tagine of pulled lamb with apricots, raisins and cucumber and cashew nut rice, and puddings such as dark chocolate and Tia Maria cheesecake and apricot and almond frangipane with custard. *Benchmark main dish: pot-roast loin of pork £16.00. Two-course evening meal £22.00.*

Free house ~ Licensee Tracey Pearson ~ Real ale ~ (01404) 881342 ~ Open 11.30-3, 6.30-11.30 ~ Bar food 12-2, 6.30-9 ~ Restaurant ~ Well behaved children in restaurant ~ Dogs allowed in bar ~ Wi-fi ~ Bedrooms: £45/£69.50 ~ www.thetuckersarms.co.uk
Recommended by Guy Vowles, Patrick and Daphne Darley, Nick Lawless

---

Cribbage is a card game using a block of wood with holes for matchsticks or special pins to score with; regulars in cribbage pubs are usually happy to teach strangers how to play.

 DARTMOUTH   SX8751   Map 1

Floating Bridge

Opposite Upper Ferry, use Dart Marina Hotel car park; Coombe Road (A379); TQ6 9PQ

Quayside pub with seats by the water and on rooftop terrace, some boating memorabilia and friendly staff

This bustling pub is right beside the River Dart, so you can watch all the comings and goings of boats in the marina, as well as the busy little car ferry. There are tables and chairs on the sizeable roof terrace and plenty of seats including picnic-sets on the quayside. The bar has lots of stools by the windows to make the most of the waterside view, oak chairs and tables, black and white photographs of local boating scenes, St Austell Tribute and Sharps Doom Bar plus guests such as Dartmoor Jail Ale and Timothy Taylors on handpump and several wines by the glass; background music and board games. The dining room on the left is brighter, with leather-backed dining chairs around a mix of wooden tables on bare boards. The window boxes are pretty against the white-painted building.

Well liked food includes sandwiches and baguettes, hoisin duck with cucumber and spring onion, creamy stilton mushrooms on toast, steak and kidney pie, home-cooked ham and eggs, burger with cheese, bacon, coleslaw and chips, spicy moroccan-style lamb with cumin gravy, seared tuna steak with stir-fried vegetables, and puddings. *Benchmark main dish: bouillabaisse £17.50. Two-course evening meal £18.50.*

Enterprise ~ Lease Alison Hogben ~ Real ale ~ (01803) 832354 ~ Open 11 (12 Sun)-11 ~ Bar food 12-9 ~ Restaurant ~ Children welcome ~ Dogs allowed in bar ~ Wi-fi ~ www.thefloatingbridge.co.uk *Recommended by Peter Harrison*

 DARTMOUTH   SX8751   Map 1

Royal Castle Hotel 🛏

The Quay; TQ6 9PS

350-year-old hotel by the harbour with two quite different bars, a genuine mix of customers, real ales and good food; comfortable bedrooms

There's a great deal of character and many original features in this bustling 17th-c inn – some of the beams are said to have come from the wreckage of the Spanish Armada. The two ground-floor bars are quite different. The traditional Galleon bar (on the right) has a log fire in a Tudor fireplace, some fine antiques and maritime pieces, quite a bit of copper and brass and plenty of chatty locals. The Harbour Bar (to the left of the flagstoned entrance hall) is contemporary in style and rather smart, with a big-screen TV and live acoustic music on Thursday evenings. The more formal restaurant looks over the river; background music. Dartmoor Jail Ale, Otter Amber and Sharps Doom Bar on handpump and 28 wines by the glass. Some of the stylish bedrooms overlook the water; dogs, welcome in all rooms, get treats and a toy. The inn was originally two Tudor merchant houses (though the façade is Regency) and overlooks the inner harbour; they have their own secure parking.

Using long-standing local suppliers and offering some kind of food from 8am to 10pm, options include sandwiches, leeks, sun-dried tomato and porcini tartlet with a poached egg and truffle oil, sharing platters, honey-roast pork sausages with onion gravy, a pie of the week, burger with bacon, mozzarella and skinny fries, salmon linguine puttanesca with anchovies and olives, and puddings such as mascarpone and raspberry trifle and a trio of apple (toffee apple cake, apple tarte tatin, apple and calvados bavarois); Tuesday is curry night. *Benchmark main dish: seafood chowder £14.95. Two-course evening meal £20.00.*

Free house ~ Licensees Nigel and Anne Way ~ Real ale ~ (01803) 833033 ~ Open 8am-11pm; 8.30-10.30 Sun ~ Bar food 11.30-10 ~ Restaurant ~ Children welcome ~ Dogs allowed in bar ~ Wi-fi ~ Live acoustic music Thurs evening, jazz Sun afternoon ~ Bedrooms: £120/£170 ~ www.royalcastle.co.uk *Recommended by Peter Harrison, Mrs Sally Scott*

DODDISCOMBSLEIGH   SX8586   Map 1

Nobody Inn ♀

Off B3193; EX6 7PS

Busy old pub with plenty of character, a fine range of drinks, well liked bar food and friendly staff; bedrooms

There's always a good mix of regulars and visitors at this 17th-c inn – all are welcomed by the licensees and their friendly staff. The beamed lounge bar of two character rooms contains handsomely carved antique settles, windsor and wheelback chairs, all sorts of wooden tables, guns and hunting prints in a snug area by one of the big inglenook fireplaces, and fresh flowers. They keep a fantastic range of drinks, including a beer named for the pub from Branscombe Vale and two changing guests such as Bays Up and Under and Cotleigh Harrier on handpump, 32 wines by the glass from a list of 200, 262 whiskies and a farm cider. The restaurant is more formal. There are picnic-sets in the pretty garden with views of the surrounding wooded hill pastures. The medieval stained glass in the local church is some of the best in the west country.

As well as pubby favourites such as game terrine or cumin and honey-glazed ham and free-range eggs, the inventive choices might include rabbit tortellini with bacon and tarragon foam and pancetta crisps, panko-crumbed goats cheese crottin with beetroot and carrot salad, walnut and sultana dressing and popping candy, fish of the day, herb-crusted pork fillet with crisp belly and black pudding, and puddings such as apple tart with crème anglaise and calvados cream, and dark chocolate mousse with earl grey ice-cream. *Benchmark main dish: steak in ale pie £12.95. Two-course evening meal £22.00.*

Free house ~ Licensee Susan Burdge ~ Real ale ~ (01647) 252394 ~ Open 11-11; 12-10.30 Sun ~ Bar food 12-2, 6.30-9 (9.30 Fri, Sat); 12-3, 7-9 Sun ~ Restaurant ~ Children welcome away from main bar; no under-5s in restaurant ~ Dogs allowed in bar ~ Wi-fi ~ Bedrooms: £65/£90 ~ www.nobodyinn.co.uk *Recommended by B J Thompson, Ian and Rose Lock, Stephen Shepherd*

EXMINSTER   SX9686   Map 1

Turf Hotel 🍺

From A379 S of village follow the signs to the Swan's Nest, then continue to end of track, by gates; park and walk right along canal towpath – nearly a mile; EX6 8EE

Remote but very popular waterside pub with fine choice of drinks, super summer barbecues and lots of space in a big garden

Half the fun of this charming family-run pub is actually getting there. You have to walk (about 20 minutes along the ship canal), cycle or catch the 60-seater boat down the Exe estuary from Topsham Quay (15-minute trip, adult £4.50, child £2); and for customers arriving in their own boat there's a large pontoon and several moorings. Inside are various little bars: the end room has a slate floor, pine walls, built-in seats, a woodburning stove and lots of photographs of the pub; along a corridor (with a dining room to one side) is a simply furnished room with wood-plank seats around tables on a stripped wood floor. Exeter Avocet, Otter Ale and Bitter and O'Hanlons Yellowhammer on handpump, local cider and juices, ten wines by the glass (and local wines too) and jugs of Pimms; background music and board games. Plenty of picnic-sets are spread around the big garden; the sea and estuary birds are fun to watch at low tide. Arrive early in fine weather, when it's particularly popular.

Using local suppliers, the interesting food includes toasties, fresh crab on toast with lemon mayonnaise, beer-battered fresh fish of the day with chips, tamarind dhal with carrot chutney and crispy squash patties, slow-cooked lamb in moroccan spices with hummus and pitta bread, flat-iron steak with red onion marmalade, chips and coleslaw, daily specials and puddings; they still do their smashing summer barbecues (and you can cook your own for a private party). *Benchmark main dish: local moules marinière £11.95. Two-course evening meal £17.00.*

Free house ~ Licensees Clive and Ginny Redfern ~ Real ale ~ (01392) 833128 ~ Open 11-11 (10.30 Sun); closed Jan, Feb ~ Bar food 12-2.30 (3 weekends), 6.30-9 (9.30 Fri, Sat) ~ Children welcome ~ Dogs welcome ~ Bedrooms: £50/£80 ~ www.turfpub.net
Recommended by Richard and Penny Gibbs

FROGMORE
Globe 🛏

SX7742   Map 1

A379 E of Kingsbridge; TQ7 2NR

Extended and neatly refurbished inn with a bar and several seating and dining areas, real ales and nice wines by the glass, helpful staff, popular food and seats outside; comfortable bedrooms

This is a lovely area to explore and the surrounding South Hams countryside is very pretty – so it makes good sense to use this white-painted inn, with its lovely flowering window boxes, as a comfortable base. The bedrooms are light, airy and well equipped and the breakfasts hearty. The neatly kept bar has a double-sided woodburner with horsebrass-decorated stone pillars on either side, another fireplace filled with logs, cushioned settles, chunky farmhouse chairs and built-in wall seating around a mix of tables on wooden flooring, and a copper diving helmet. Attentive staff serve Otter Ale, Skinners Betty Stogs and South Hams Eddystone on handpump and several wines by the glass. The slate-floored games room has a pool table and darts. There's also a comfortable lounge with an open fire, cushioned dining chairs and tables on red carpeting, a big leather sofa, a model yacht and a large yacht painting – spot the clever mural of a log pile. Teak tables and chairs sit on the back terrace, with steps leading up to another level with picnic-sets.

As well as lunchtime baguettes and baked potatoes, the well liked food includes beer-battered mushrooms with garlic mayonnaise, chicken liver and mushroom pâté, vegetable lasagne, chicken curry, home-cooked ham and egg, burger with red onion marmalade and chips, guinea fowl with bacon and wild mushroom jus, and puddings. *Benchmark main dish: local fish pie £9.95. Two-course evening meal £15.00.*

Free house ~ Licensees John and Lynda Horsley ~ Real ale ~ (01548) 531351 ~ Open 12-11; closed Mon lunchtime in winter ~ Bar food 12-2, 6-9 ~ Restaurant ~ Children welcome ~ Dogs allowed in bar and bedrooms ~ Wi-fi ~ Live folk first Tues and third Thurs of month ~ Bedrooms: £60/£85 ~ www.theglobeinn.co.uk
Recommended by B J Harding

GEORGEHAM

SS4639 Map 1

Rock 🏵 🍷

Rock Hill, above village; EX33 1JW

Beamed family pub with good food cooked by the landlord, five real ales, plenty of room inside and out and a relaxed atmosphere

'An excellent pub' is how our readers describe this well run, neatly kept place and, although there's quite an emphasis on the particularly good food, drinkers feel very much at home too. The sizeable, heavy beamed bar is divided in two by a step. The pubby top part has half-planked walls, an open woodburning stove in a stone fireplace and captain's and farmhouse chairs around wooden tables on quarry tiles; the lower area has panelled wall seats, some built-in settles forming a cosy booth, old local photographs and ancient flat-irons. Leading off here is a red-carpeted dining room with attractive black and white photographs of North Devon folk. Friendly young staff serve Exmoor Gold, Greene King Abbot, St Austell Tribute and Sharps Doom Bar on handpump and 14 wines by the glass; background music and board games. The light and airy back dining conservatory has high-backed wooden or modern dining chairs around tables under a growing vine, with a little terrace beyond. There is wheelchair access. Next to the pretty hanging baskets and tubs in front of the pub are some picnic-sets.

 High standards of cooking include dishes such as lunchtime sandwiches, salt and pepper chilli squid, sharing platters, burger with tomato and chilli jam, coleslaw and chips, honey-glazed ham and free-range eggs, wild mushroom risotto, tagliatelle with salmon, crayfish and tarragon cream sauce, specials such as dressed local crab with aioli, and puddings. *Benchmark main dish: own-made Gloucester Old Spot sausages with mash £10.95. Two-course evening meal £18.00.*

Punch ~ Lease Daniel Craddock ~ Real ale ~ (01271) 890322 ~ Open 11 (12 Sun)-11.30 ~ Bar food 12-2.30, 6-9.30; 12-9 Sun ~ Restaurant ~ Children welcome ~ Dogs welcome ~ Wi-fi ~ www.therockgeorgeham.co.uk *Recommended by Stephen Shepherd, Stephen and Judith Thomas, Bob and Margaret Holder*

HAYTOR VALE

SX7777 Map 1

Rock ★ 🏵 🍷 🛏

Haytor signposted off B3387 just W of Bovey Tracey, on good moorland road to Widecombe; TQ13 9XP

Civilised Dartmoor inn at its most informal at lunchtime; super food, real ales and seats in pretty garden; comfortable bedrooms

The consistently high standards in all areas at this notably well run, civilised inn continue to draw high praise from our readers. It's at its most informal at lunchtime (good for walkers in Dartmoor National Park), when there's a fine value two- and three-course weekday set menu. Dartmoor IPA and Jail Ale on handpump, 15 wines (plus champagne and sparkling rosé) by the glass and 16 malt whiskies. The two neatly kept, linked, partly panelled bar rooms have lots of dark wood and red plush, polished antique tables with candles and fresh flowers, old-fashioned prints and decorative plates, and warming winter log fires (the main fireplace has a fine Stuart fireback). There's also a light and spacious dining room in the lower part of the inn and a residents' lounge. The large, pretty garden opposite has some seats, with more on the little terrace next to the pub. You can park at the back of the building. Some of the smart, beamed bedrooms are up steep stairs; the breakfasts are excellent.

The enticing, first class food includes lunchtime baguettes, local mussels with white wine, cream and garlic, twice-baked cauliflower cheese soufflé, asparagus, spring onion and pea risotto, steak in ale pie, salmon tagliatelle in creamy white wine and chive sauce, duck breast with honey-glazed salsify, sauce d'epice and confit garlic, and puddings such as mocha and rum cheesecake with raspberry sorbet and chocolate and coriander tart with home-made rum and raisin ice-cream; Tuesday is fresh fish night and they also offer a two- and three-course set menu. *Benchmark main dish: lamb rump with dauphinoise potatoes, jerusalem artichoke purée and red wine sauce £16.95. Two-course evening meal £23.50.*

Free house ~ Licensee Christopher Graves ~ Real ale ~ (01364) 661305 ~ Open 10am-11pm; 12-10.30 Sun ~ Bar food 12-2, 7-9 ~ Restaurant ~ Children welcome away from main bar ~ Dogs allowed in bedrooms ~ Wi-fi ~ Bedrooms: £79/£89 ~ www.rock-inn.co.uk
Recommended by John and Gloria Isaacs, Philip Crawford, Dr and Mrs J D Abell, B J Harding, J R Wildon

HORNDON   SX5280 Map 1
Elephants Nest 🍺 £ 🛏

If coming from Okehampton on A386, turn left at Mary Tavy Inn, then left after about 0.5 miles; pub signposted beside Mary Tavy Inn, then Horndon signposted; on OS Sheet it's named as the New Inn; PL19 9NQ

Isolated old inn surrounded by Dartmoor walks, with some interesting original features, real ales and changing food; comfortable bedrooms

Originally three 16th-c miners' cottages, this isolated pub is on the lower slopes of Dartmoor, where there are plenty of walks. It's run by a charming landlord. The main bar has lots of beer pump clips on the beams, high bar chairs by the bar counter, Dartmoor Jail Ale, Otter Amber, Palmers IPA and Tavy Best on handpump, a couple of farm ciders, several wines by the glass and 15 malt whiskies. Two other rooms have an assortment of wooden dining chairs around a mix of tables, and throughout there are bare stone walls, flagstones, horsebrasses and three woodburning stoves. The spreading, attractive garden (with an area reserved for adults only) has picnic-sets under parasols and looks across dry stone walls to pastures and rougher moorland above. The bedrooms are attractively furnished and comfortable and the breakfasts very good.

Using fresh, local produce, the food includes some good value lunchtime dishes (hence the Bargain Meals award): baguettes and tortilla wraps, pork terrine with cumberland sauce, burger with red onion marmalade and french fries, beer-battered fresh haddock, a pie of the day, chicken stuffed with taleggio cheese and wrapped in pancetta with creamy sauce, pork escalope with sage, parma ham and marsala wine, and puddings such as mixed fruit crumble and chocolate mousse. *Benchmark main dish: steak and kidney pudding £12.95. Two-course evening meal £19.00.*

Free house ~ Licensee Hugh Cook ~ Real ale ~ (01822) 810273 ~ Open 12-3, 6.30-11 (10.30 Sun) ~ Bar food 12-2.15, 6-9 ~ Restaurant ~ Children welcome ~ Dogs welcome ~ Wi-fi ~ Bedrooms: £77.50/£87.50 ~ www.elephantsnest.co.uk *Recommended by M G Hart, P and J Shapley, Simon Lindsey, Rose Rogers, Phil and Jane Villiers, Stephen Shepherd, J R Wildon*

IDDESLEIGH   SS5608 Map 1
Duke of York 🛏

B3217 Exbourne–Dolton; EX19 8BG

Unfussy and exceptionally friendly, with simply furnished bars, popular food and a fair choice of drinks; charming bedrooms

Thriving under its present landlord, this charming little local always has a bustling, friendly atmosphere and a good mix of customers. The unspoilt bar has plenty of homely character: rocking chairs, cushioned benches built into the wall's black-painted wooden dado, stripped tables and other simple country furnishings, banknotes pinned to beams, and a large open fireplace. Adnams Broadside, Cotleigh Tawny Owl and a changing guest beer such as Bays Topsail tapped from the cask and a dozen wines by the glass. It can get pretty cramped at peak times. The dining room has a huge inglenook fireplace. Through a small coach arch is a little back garden with some picnic-sets. Three bedrooms are in the pub, with three more just a minute's walk away. Michael Morpurgo, author of *War Horse*, got the inspiration to write the novel after talking to World War I veteran Wilfred Ellis in front of the fire here almost 30 years ago.

As well as pubby choices listed on a board, the well liked food includes scallops in crispy bacon, garlic mushrooms with stilton, game pie, spinach and mushroom tagliatelle, slow-cooked lamb shanks with rosemary and mint, pork belly with apple, honey and cider sauce, whole lemon sole with white wine and dill, and puddings. *Benchmark main dish: steak and kidney pudding £12.95. Two-course evening meal £18.00.*

Free house ~ Licensee John Pittam ~ Real ale ~ (01837) 810253 ~ Open 11-11 (midnight); 12-11 Sun ~ Bar food 12-9.30 ~ Restaurant ~ Children welcome ~ Dogs allowed in bar and bedrooms ~ Wi-fi ~ Bedrooms: $45/$75 ~ www.dukeofyorkdevon.co.uk
Recommended by Peter Thornton, Anita French, Mark Flynn, S G N Bennett, Ron Corbett

KING'S NYMPTON   SS6819   Map 1
Grove 🏨⭐🍺
Off B3226 SW of South Molton; EX37 9ST

Thatched 17th-c pub in remote village with local beers, highly thought-of bar food and cheerful licensees

Very much off the tourist route, this is a 17th-c thatched pub in a lovely conservation village. The low-beamed bar has lots of bookmarks hanging from the ceiling, simple pubby furnishings on flagstones, bare stone walls and a winter log fire. The particularly friendly landlord tries to source his ales as locally as possible, so there might be Cottage Old Hooker, Exmoor Ale, Forge Hawkers and Teignworthy Reel Ale on handpump (they hold a beer festival in July); also, 25 wines (and champagne) by the glass, 65 malt whiskies, local cider, darts and board games. They have a self-catering cottage to rent, and the pub is surrounded by quiet rolling and wooded countryside.

Enjoyable food using carefully sourced, local produce includes sandwiches, duo of trout with horseradish cream, scotched free-range egg, root vegetable stew with herb dumplings, chicken stuffed with blue cheese, parma ham and thyme, veal burger with cheese and chips, steak and kidney pudding with mustard mash, cod with rapeseed mash and green sauce, and puddings such as warm treacle tart with clotted cream and white chocolate cheesecake with rhubarb compote. *Benchmark main dish: individual beef wellington £17.00. Two-course evening meal £16.75.*

Free house ~ Licensees Robert and Deborah Smallbone ~ Real ale ~ (01769) 580406 ~ Open 12-3, 6-11; 12-4, 7-10 Sun; closed Mon lunchtime except bank holidays ~ Bar food 12-2, 6.45-9; 12-3 Sun ~ Restaurant ~ Well behaved children welcome ~ Dogs allowed in bar ~ Wi-fi ~ www.thegroveinn.co.uk *Recommended by Tony and Jill Radnor, Mark Flynn, John Evans*

KINGSBRIDGE   SX7344 Map 1
Dodbrooke Inn ▮ £
Church Street, Dodbrooke (parking some way off); TQ7 1DB

Bustling local with friendly licensees, chatty locals and well thought-of food and drink

This small terraced pub in a quiet residential area has long-serving, hands-on licensees who keep everything running smoothly. The traditional bar has quite a mix of customers of all ages, built-in cushioned stall seats and plush cushioned stools around pubby tables, some horse harness, local photographs and china jugs, a log fire and an easy-going atmosphere. Bass, Greene King IPA and Sharps Doom Bar on handpump, local cider and several wines by the glass. You can sit in the covered courtyard, which might be candlelit in warm weather.

Tasty food includes sandwiches, home-made pâté, scallops and bacon, steak and kidney pie, beer-battered fresh cod and chips, stuffed peppers, bass and grilled lemon sole, and puddings such as treacle tart and melting chocolate puddings. *Benchmark main dish: charcoal steaks £13.50. Two-course evening meal £18.50.*

Free house ~ Licensees Michael and Jill Dyson ~ Real ale ~ (01548) 852068 ~ Open 12-2, 5-11; 12-2, 7-10.30 Sun; closed Mon and Tues lunchtimes ~ Bar food 12-1.30, 5-8.30; 12-1.30, 7-8 Sun ~ Children welcome if over 5 ~ Dogs allowed in bar
Recommended by Peter Brix, Edward May

KINGSKERSWELL   SX8666 Map 1
Bickley Mill
Bickley Road, SW of Kingskerswell; TQ12 5LN

Friendly inn surrounded by lovely countryside with bustling bars, attractive furnishings and enjoyable food and drink; contemporary bedrooms

The restful, well equipped bedrooms in this former flour mill are modern and comfortable, and the breakfasts good. The friendly licensees have decorated the place with style: the rambling beamed rooms have an appealing variety of seating from rustic chairs and tables through settles to sofas piled with cushions, as well as rugs on wooden floors, three open fires, black and white photos or modern art on the stone walls, and an easy-going atmosphere. Bays Devon Dumpling and Gold on handpump, and 14 wines by the glass, served by helpful, courteous staff. Outside, there are seats on a big terrace and a subtropical hillside garden. The surrounding countryside is lovely.

Interesting food from a thoughtful menu includes sandwiches, smoked salmon roulade with lemon and caper dressing, thai-style fishcakes with coriander and chilli sauce, chicken, leek and bacon pie with madeira sauce, vegetable curry, lamb rump with roasted black pudding, swede purée and red wine sauce, cod with a walnut, lemon and parmesan crust and sauce vierge, and puddings such as honeycomb cheesecake with chocolate sauce and passion-fruit crème brûlée. *Benchmark main dish: burger with gruyère, chutney and chips £10.95. Two-course evening meal £18.50.*

Free house ~ Licensees Vanessa and James Woodleigh-Smith ~ Real ale ~ (01803) 873201 ~ Open 11-11; 12-10.30 Sun ~ Bar food 12-2.30, 6-9; 12-3, 6-8 Sun ~ Children welcome ~ Dogs allowed in bar ~ Wi-fi ~ Bedrooms: £75/£90 ~ www.bickleymill.co.uk *Recommended by Mike and Mary Carter*

LUSTLEIGH   SX7881 Map 1
Cleave

Off A382 Bovey Tracey–Moretonhampstead; TQ13 9TJ

**Thatched pub in popular beauty spot with a roaring log fire and
popular food and drink; pretty summer garden**

A lways deservedly busy – it's best to arrive early – this is a picture-
postcard pretty thatched pub in a lovely village. The low-ceilinged
beamed bar has a roaring log fire, granite walls and attractive antique
high-backed settles, cushioned wall seats and wheelback chairs around
the tables on red patterned carpet. Otter Ale and Bitter and a guest such as
Dartmoor Jail Ale on handpump and several wines by the glass. At the back
(formerly the old station waiting room) is a light and airy bistro with pale
wooden tables and chairs on a wood-strip floor and candlelight; doors from
here open to an outside eating area. The lovely sheltered garden has plenty
of seats and lots of hanging baskets and flower beds; good walks in the
surrounding Dartmoor National Park.

Some sort of tasty food is usefully served all day: baguettes, rabbit terrine with
damson chutney, local mussels, vegetable lasagne, whole rack of ribs, steak
and Guinness pudding, Martinique-style fruity chicken curry, and puddings such as
chocolate lime torte and bread and butter pudding. *Benchmark main dish: locally
caught fish and shellfish stew £14.95. Two-course evening meal £22.00.*

Heavitree ~ Tenant Ben Whitton ~ Real ale ~ (01647) 277223 ~ Open 11-11 ~ Bar food
12-9 (7 Sun) ~ Restaurant ~ Children welcome ~ Dogs allowed in bar ~ Wi-fi ~
www.thecleavelustleigh.com *Recommended by B J Harding, Julie and Bill Ryan, Mike and
Mary Carter*

MARLDON   SX8663 Map 1
Church House

Off A380 NW of Paignton; TQ3 1SL

**Spreading bar plus several other rooms in this pleasant inn,
particularly good food, fine choice of drinks and seats on
three terraces**

B uilt around 1400 to house artisans working on the nearby church, this
is a neatly kept and friendly pub overlooking the village cricket field.
The attractively furnished, spreading bar with its woodburning stove
has several different areas radiating off the big semicircular bar counter:
unusual windows, some beams, dark pine and other nice old dining chairs
around solid tables, and yellow leather bar chairs. Leading off here is a
cosy little candlelit room with four tables on bare boards, a dark wood
dado and stone fireplace. There's also a restaurant with a large stone
fireplace and, at the other end of the building, a similarly interesting room,
split into two, with a stone floor in one part and a wooden floor (and big
woodburning stove) in the other. The old barn holds yet another restaurant,
with displays by local artists. Dartmoor Best and Jail Ale, St Austell Tribute
and Teignworthy Gun Dog on handpump, 18 wines by the glass, ten malt
whiskies and a farm cider; background music. There are picnic-sets on
three carefully maintained grassy terraces behind the pub.

If we don't specify bar meal times for a featured entry, these are normally 12-2
and 7-9; we do show times if they are markedly different.

Tempting food from a well judged menu includes lunchtime sandwiches and baguettes, pork, apple and sage pâté with spicy fruit chutney, salmon and cod fishcakes with salsa verde, wild mushroom, cheese and spinach pasta with walnut pesto, pork loin on red cabbage stir-fry with plum sauce, corn-fed chicken stuffed with spinach and pine nut mousse with pancetta and parmesan sauce, and puddings. *Benchmark main dish: slow-cooked lamb shoulder with port, redcurrant and rosemary sauce £15.75. Two-course evening meal £22.50.*

Enterprise ~ Lease Julian Cook ~ Real ale ~ (01803) 558279 ~ Open 11.30-2.30, 5-11; 11.30-3, 5.30-11.30 Sat; 12-3, 5.30-10.30 Sun ~ Bar food 12-2, 6.30-9.30; 12-2.30, 6.30-9 Sun ~ Restaurant ~ Children welcome ~ Dogs allowed in bar ~ www.churchhousemarldon.com *Recommended by B J Harding, Mike and Mary Carter*

MORETONHAMPSTEAD
SX7586   Map 1

Horse

George Street; TQ13 8NF

Hard-working, hands-on licensees at this simply furnished town pub, with a good choice of drinks, well liked food and mediterranean-style courtyard

The enthusiastic landlady and her chef husband continue to run this simply furnished and warmly friendly town pub with great energy; there's always something going on, from live bands to art shows. The bar has leather chesterfields and deep armchairs in front of a woodburning stove, all manner of wooden chairs, settles and tables on carpet or wooden floorboards, rustic tools and horse tack alongside military and hunting prints on the walls, a dresser offering home-made cakes and local cider and juice for sale, and stools by the green planked counter where they serve Dartmoor IPA and Legend and Otter Ale on handpump, a dozen wines by the glass, ten malt whiskies, two farm ciders and quite a few coffees. A long light room leads off from here, and there's also a high-ceilinged barn-like back dining room too. The sheltered inner courtyard, with metal tables and chairs, is popular in warm weather.

The interesting food is cooked by the landlord: gourmet sandwiches, venison bresaola with wild mushroom pickle, antipasti sharing plates, several frittatas, moules frites, chicken caesar salad, crab linguine, lots of pizzas, lamb shank and lamb sausage cassoulet, and puddings such as panettone bread and butter pudding and dark chocolate marquise. *Benchmark main dish: thin-based pizzas £10.00. Two-course evening meal £18.00.*

Free house ~ Licensees Nigel Hoyle and Malene Graulund ~ Real ale ~ (01647) 440242 ~ Open 12-midnight (in winter 5-10 Mon, Sun; 12-3.30, 5-midnight Tues-Sat) ~ Bar food 12-2.30, 6.30-9; pizzas only Sun and Mon evenings ~ Restaurant ~ Children welcome ~ Dogs allowed in bar ~ Wi-fi ~ Live folk last Mon of month, blues third Thurs of month ~ www.thehorsedartmoor.co.uk *Recommended by Isobel Mackinlay, Emma Scofield*

PARKHAM
SS3821   Map 1

Bell

Rectory Lane; EX39 5PL

A proper village pub with chatty locals, welcoming landlord, neatly kept bars, four real ales and well liked food

There are always plenty of chatty locals in this honest thatched pub, which is very much the heart of the village. The three communicating rooms are spotlessly kept, with beams and standing timbers hung with horsebrasses, a woodburning stove in the main bar and a small coal fire in the lower one, brass and copper jugs, nice old photos of the pub and the village, a grandfather clock, and pubby tables and seats (mate's and other straightforward chairs and burgundy or green plush stools) on red patterned carpet. Model ships and lanterns hang above the bar, where there's Exmoor Fox, Otter Ale and Sharps Doom Bar on handpump and a dozen malt whiskies; darts. The covered back terrace has picnic-sets and fairy lights.

🍴 Popular food includes sandwiches and baguettes, creamy garlic mushrooms, prawn and avocado cocktail, ham or sausage and egg, timbale of rice topped with roast vegetables in cider and tomato sauce, venison sausages with port and cranberry sauce, a pie of the day, beer-battered cod and chips, duck breast in orange and Grand Marnier sauce, and puddings. *Benchmark main dish: chicken with blue cheese and crispy bacon £10.95. Two-course evening meal £15.00.*

Free house ~ Licensees Michael and Rachel Sanders ~ Real ale ~ (01237) 451201 ~ Open 12-2, 5.30-11; 12-10 Sun ~ Bar food 12-1.30, 6-8.30; 12-8.30 Sun ~ Restaurant ~ Well behaved children welcome ~ Dogs allowed in bar ~ Wi-fi ~ www.thebellinnparkham.co.uk *Recommended by C and R Bromage, Kim Skuse*

PORTGATE
🏠 GOOD PUB GUIDE
Harris Arms ♀
SX4185 Map 1

Leave A30 E of Launceston at Broadwoodwidger turn-off (with brown sign to Dingle Steam Village) and head S; Launceston Road (old A30 between Lewdown and Lifton); EX20 4PZ

Enthusiastic, well travelled licensees in roadside pub with exceptional wine list and interesting food

Wine lovers should head to this bustling pub. The licensees, Mr and Mrs Whiteman, are award-winning wine-makers and around 20 of their favourite wines are available by the glass with detailed, helpful notes; you can also buy to take home – and they're growing 24 of their own vines. The bar has a woodburning stove, burgundy end walls and cream ones in between, and afghan saddle-bag cushions scattered around a mix of dining chairs and along a red plush built-in wall banquette. On the left, steps lead down to the dining room with elegant beech dining chairs (and more afghan cushions) around stripped-wood tables. Bays Topsail and Frys Frydeal on handpump, local cider and Luscombe organic soft drinks; there may be a pile of country and food/wine magazines. In warm weather, try to bag one of the seats among the pots of lavender on the heated decking behind the pub – the views over the rolling hills are very pretty; plenty of picnic-sets in the sloping garden too.

🍴 Using local farmers and producers and artisan cheeses, the enjoyable food includes baguettes, slow-cooked pork cheeks with sweet potato and mushroom hash with cider sauce, prawns piri-piri, home-cooked ham and eggs, vegetarian shepherd's pie, beer-battered fish and chips, trio of local sausages with mash and onion gravy, fish of the day with a seasonally changing sauce, confit duck leg with chorizo and haricot bean ragoût and red wine sauce, and puddings such as treacle sponge, dark chocolate truffle with ice-cream and white chocolate cheesecake. *Benchmark main dish: pan-roasted fillet of cod with tomato, basil, olive and caper sauce £15.95. Two-course evening meal £20.00.*

Free house ~ Licensees Andy and Rowena Whiteman ~ Real ale ~ (01566) 783331 ~ Open 12-3, 6.30-11; 12-3 Sun; closed Sun evening, Mon ~ Bar food 12-2, 6.30-9 ~ Restaurant ~ Well behaved children welcome ~ Dogs allowed in bar ~ www.theharrisarms.co.uk *Recommended by M G Hart, R T and J C Moggridge*

POSTBRIDGE   SX6780 Map 1

Warren House

B3212 0.75 miles NE of Postbridge; PL20 6TA

Straightforward old pub, relaxing for a drink or meal after a Dartmoor hike

After a cold walk on Dartmoor you can be sure of a friendly welcome in this isolated pub – and open fires (one of which is said to have been kept alight since 1845). There's a lot of local character and the place is something of a focus for the scattered moorland community. The cosy bar is straightforward, with simple furnishings such as easy chairs and settles beneath the beamed ochre ceiling, old pictures of the inn on partly panelled stone walls and dim lighting (powered by the pub's own generator); there's also a family room. Butcombe Haka, Otter Ale and Summerskills Start Point on handpump, local farm cider and malt whiskies; background music. The picnic-sets on both sides of the road have moorland views.

Well liked, honest food includes sandwiches, moules marinière, chicken, leek and tarragon pie, meat or vegetarian lasagne, cajun chicken, smoked haddock fishcakes and chips, gammon and pineapple, lamb shank in red wine and rosemary, and puddings. *Benchmark main dish: steak in ale pie £12.50. Two-course evening meal £.16.00*

Free house ~ Licensee Peter Parsons ~ Real ale ~ (01822) 880208 ~ Open 11 (12 Sun in winter)-11 (10.30 Sun); 11-3 Mon, Tues in winter ~ Bar food 12-9 (8.30 Sun) ~ Restaurant ~ Children in family room only ~ Dogs allowed in bar ~ www.warrenhouseinn.co.uk *Recommended by Robert Watt, Christian Mole, David Crook*

RATTERY   SX7461 Map 1

Church House

Village signposted from A385 W of Totnes, and A38 S of Buckfastleigh; TQ10 9LD

One of Britain's oldest pubs with plenty to look at, a friendly landlord, a good range of drinks and popular bar food; peaceful views

This fine old place is described by our readers as 'a gem' and, with its nice, chatty landlord and friendly, attentive service, we agree. Parts of the original building, dating from around 1030, still survive – notably the spiral stone steps behind a little stone doorway on the left. The rooms have plenty of character: massive oak beams and standing timbers in the homely open-plan bar, large fireplaces (one with a cosy nook partitioned off around it), traditional pubby chairs and tables on patterned carpet, some window seats, and prints and horsebrasses on plain white walls. The dining room is separated by heavy curtains and there's a lounge too. Dartmoor Jail Ale and Legend, Exe Valley Bitter and St Austell Tribute on handpump, 18 malt whiskies and ten wines by the glass. The garden has picnic-sets on the large hedged-in lawn and peaceful views of the partly wooded surrounding hills.

As well as generous sandwiches, the well liked food includes devilled whitebait, spicy crab cakes, homity pie, beer-battered cod and chips, moussaka, duck with orange sauce, and puddings such as blackberry and raspberry brûlée and bread and butter pudding. *Benchmark main dish: steak in ale pie £10.95. Two-course evening meal £16.00.*

The details at the end of each featured entry start by saying whether the pub is a free house, or if it belongs to a brewery or pub group (which we name).

Free house ~ Licensee Ray Hardy ~ Real ale ~ (01364) 642220 ~ Open 11-2.30, 6-11; 12-3, 6-10.30 Sun ~ Bar food 11.30 (12 Sun)-2, 6.30-9 ~ Restaurant ~ Children welcome ~ Dogs allowed in bar ~ Wi-fi ~ www.thechurchhouseinn.co.uk
Recommended by B J Harding, John Evans, Roger and Donna Huggins

SANDFORD
SS8202 Map 1

Lamb

The Square; EX17 4LW

Bustling, friendly 16th-c inn with beams and standing timbers, four real ales and decent wines by the glass, very good food and seats in garden; well equipped bedrooms

There's always something going on in this charming village pub, whether it's Sunday curry night, a mini beer festival, quiz and open mike evenings or their free weekend cinema. It's all very easy-going and friendly. The beamed bar has a log fire in a stone fireplace with red leather sofas beside it, cushioned window seats, a settle and various dining chairs around a few tables on patterned carpet; towards the back is a handsome carved chest, a table of newspapers and magazines and a noticeboard of local news and adverts. Dartmoor IPA, Otter Bitter, O'Hanlons Yellowhammer and Skinners Hunny Bunny on handpump, nine wines by the glass, cocktails, farm cider and 20 malt whiskies. The linked dining area has a woodburning stove, a cushioned wall pew, all manner of nice old wooden dining chairs and tables (each with a church candle) and similarly heavy beams; the landlord's wife created the large animal paintings (also in the bedrooms). There's also a simpler public bar and a skittle alley; the jack russell is called Tiny, the collie, Bob. The informal cobbled garden has fairy lights and simple seats and tables, and there are picnic-sets on grass beyond the hedge. The bedrooms are comfortable, modern and well equipped. Nearby parking is at a premium but the village car park is just a few minutes' walk up the small lane to the right.

Using home-grown and local produce, the sensibly short choice of rewarding food includes duck liver parfait with red onion marmalade, crab and scallop lasagne with shellfish bisque, beetroot pearl barley risotto with goats cheese beignet, sausage and mash with onion gravy, chicken leg stuffed with roast chestnuts and apricots, and puddings such as chocolate fondant and spiced poached pear with salted caramel mousse. *Benchmark main dish: venison haunch with home-cured bacon and truffled mash £12.25. Two-course evening meal £20.00.*

Free house ~ Licensee Mark Hildyard ~ Real ale ~ (01363) 773676 ~ Open 10.30am-11pm (midnight Fri, Sat) ~ Bar food 12.30-2.15, 6.30-9.15 ~ Restaurant ~ Children welcome ~ Dogs welcome ~ Wi-fi ~ Live music and regular open mike sessions ~ Bedrooms: £69/£130 ~ www.lambinnsandford.co.uk *Recommended by Richard and Penny Gibbs*

SIDBURY
SY1496 Map 1

Hare & Hounds

3 miles N of Sidbury, at Putts Corner; A375 towards Honiton, crossroads with B3174; EX10 0QQ

Large, well run roadside pub with log fires, beams and attractive layout, popular daily carvery and a big garden

Even though this is a pretty big place, it does get packed at peak times and you should book in advance to be sure of a seat. It's not a straightforward pub – many customers are here to enjoy the exceptionally popular carvery – but they do keep Otter Bitter and Ale and St Austell Tribute tapped from the cask and eight wines by the glass. There are two log fires (and rather unusual wood-framed leather sofas complete with pouffes), heavy beams and fresh flowers, and red plush-cushioned dining chairs, window seats and leather sofas around plenty of tables on carpeting or bare boards. The newer dining extension, with a central open fire, opens out on to a decked area; the seats here, and the picnic-sets in the big garden, have marvellous views down the Sid Valley to the sea at Sidmouth.

As well as a highly thought-of carvery using the best local meat, they also offer a wide choice of dishes such as sandwiches and baguettes, garlic mushrooms with cream and sherry, a combo platter, burger with coleslaw and chips, roasted vegetable and lentil lasagne, three different sausages with red wine and onion gravy, steak and kidney pudding, poached salmon with lemon and white wine sauce, and puddings. *Benchmark main dish: daily carvery £10.25. Two-course evening meal £14.50.*

Heartstone Inns ~ Managers Graham Cole and Lindsey Chun ~ Real ale ~ (01404) 41760 ~ Open 10am-11pm ~ Bar food 12-9 ~ Children welcome ~ Dogs allowed in bar ~ www.hareandhounds-devon.co.uk *Recommended by George Atkinson, Geri Eld, John and Susan Miln, Roy Hoing*

SLAPTON
Tower

SX8245 Map 1

Off A379 Dartmouth–Kingsbridge; TQ7 2PN

Bustling inn with friendly young owners, beams and log fires, good beers and wines and a pretty back garden; bedrooms

A short stroll from several miles of beautiful beach backed by Slapton Ley nature reserve, this family-run inn makes a good base for the area; the comfortable bedrooms are reached via an external stone staircase. With a relaxed and informal atmosphere, the low-ceilinged beamed bar has armchairs, low-backed settles and scrubbed oak tables on flagstones or bare boards, open log fires and a genuine core of chatty locals; Butcombe Bitter, Otter Bitter, St Austell Proper Job and Sharps Doom Bar on handpump, and several wines by the glass. Picnic-sets on the neat lawn in the pretty garden behind the pub are overlooked by the ivy-covered ruins of a 14th-c chantry. The lane up to the pub is very narrow and parking can be tricky at peak times.

As well as fresh fish caught in the bay, the seasonal dishes include lunchtime sandwiches, confit duck with sweet and sour dressing and roasted squash, mussels with chorizo, tomato and basil broth, home-made corned beef with fries, beetroot and goats cheese 'speltotto', bouillabaisse, duo of venison with sweet potato mash and smoked bacon, and puddings. *Benchmark main dish: côte du boeuf for two £45.00. Two-course evening meal £22.00.*

Free house ~ Licensee Dan Cheshire ~ Real ale ~ (01548) 580216 ~ Open 12-3, 6-11 (10.30 Sun); closed Sun evening in winter, first two weeks Jan ~ Bar food 12-2.30, 6.30-9.30 ~ Children welcome ~ Dogs allowed in bar and bedrooms ~ Wi-fi ~ Bedrooms: £60/£80 ~ www.thetowerinn.com *Recommended by Paul Humphreys, Peter Travis, David Gunn*

Real ale to us means beer that has matured naturally in its cask – not pressurised or filtered. We name all real ales stocked. We usually name ales preserved under a light blanket of carbon dioxide too, though purists – pointing out that this stops the natural yeasts developing – would disagree (most people, including us, can't tell the difference!).

SOUTH POOL SX7740 Map 1

Millbrook 🌟

Off A379 E of Kingsbridge; TQ7 2RW

Delightful village local by the Salcombe estuary, with local ales, very good food and a warm welcome for all

This charming creekside pub is so small it can be a bit of a squash at weekends, when both locals and visitors want to enjoy the easy-going atmosphere and particularly good food. There are several little beamed bars, with the main one having a log fire in an inglenook fireplace, a couple of settles and a blanket box on turkey rugs, and stools against the counter where they keep three ales on handpump – Red Rock Drift Wood, another from Red Rock named for the pub, and a guest – and several local farm ciders; daily papers. The dining area to the right has a woodburning stove, settles and wheelback chairs around scrubbed wooden tables, and stone and cream walls decorated with maps, some old pictures, a barometer and a brass clock; this leads to another small dining area and there's also a simply furnished Top Bar for families. Seats on the terrace outside overlook the water and there are mooring facilities for small boats. An honesty Veg Shed sells fresh vegetables and local sausages and bacon.

 Using the best local meat and fish, the impressive country cooking includes warm duck gizzard, smoked duck, black pudding and duck egg salad, potted crab with orange and pickled fennel, honey-roast ham hock with red cabbage and piccalilli, a seasonally changing pearl barley risotto, monkfish osso bucco with gremolata, pheasant kiev, and puddings such as chocolate fondant and a changing panna cotta; they also offer a two- and three-course menu of the day. *Benchmark main dish: bouillabaisse £20.00. Two-course evening meal £24.00.*

Free house ~ Licensees Ian Dent and Diana Hunt ~ Real ale ~ (01548) 531581 ~ Open 12-11 (10.30 Sun) ~ Bar food 12-2 (3 Sun), 7-9; no food Mon in winter ~ Restaurant ~ Children welcome ~ Dogs allowed in bar ~ Live jazz; check website for dates ~ www.millbrookinnsouthpool.co.uk *Recommended by Mark Davidson, Caroline Prescott*

SPARKWELL SX5857 Map 1

Treby Arms 🌟

Off A38 at Smithaleigh, W of Ivybridge, Sparkwell signed from village; PL7 5DD

Devon Dining Pub of the Year

Little village pub offering delicious food, real ales and a friendly welcome

The imaginative food in this little village pub – cooked by *MasterChef* winner Anton Piotrowski – remains so popular that you may have to book a table some time in advance. The bar area, used by locals for a pint and a chat, has stools against the counter, simple wooden dining chairs and tables, a built-in cushioned window seat and a woodburning stove in a stone fireplace with shelves of cookery and guide books piled up on either side. Dartmoor Jail Ale and St Austell Tribute on handpump and several good wines by the glass from a list with helpful notes, served by friendly, competent staff. Off to the right is the dining room, with another woodburning stove, old glass and stone bottles on the mantelpiece and captain's and wheelback chairs around rustic tables; there's another carpeted dining room upstairs. The sunny front terrace has seats and tables.

Exceptional, beautifully presented food using the best local suppliers includes bar snacks such as house terrine with toast, ploughman's, ham hock, egg, pineapple and triple-cooked chips, as well as scallops with black pudding crumble, pork belly and pea purée, venison and pork pie with piccalilli, beetroot risotto with herb-crusted goats cheese bonbons, white wine-battered fish and chips, pork fillet with ham hock, fried egg and red pepper ketchup, and puddings such as layered carrot cake with popping candy and chocolate 'soil' and earl grey panna cotta with lemon-curd polenta cake; there's also a three-course set lunch. *Benchmark main dish: cocoa-marinated venison with pickled apple and feta £21.00. Two-course evening meal £28.00.*

Free house ~ Licensees Anton and Clare Piotrowski ~ Real ale ~ (01752) 837363 ~ Open 12-3, 6-11; 12-11 Sat; 12-10.30 Sun; closed Mon ~ Bar food 12-2, 6-9; 12-2.30, 6-8 Sun; bar snacks 12-9 Fri-Sun ~ Restaurant ~ Children welcome ~ Dogs allowed in bar ~ Wi-fi ~ www.thetrebyarms.co.uk *Recommended by Brian and Maggie Woodford, John Evans*

SPREYTON — Tom Cobley 🍺

SX6996 Map 1

Dragdown Hill; W out of village; EX17 5AL

Huge range of quickly changing real ales and ciders in friendly and busy village pub; quite a choice of food too; bedrooms

The hard-working staff in this friendly, family-run inn continue to keep the wonderful range of up to 14 real ales on handpump or tapped from the cask. Changing daily, these might include Black Tor Dartmoor Pale Ale, Country Life Black Boar, Dartmoor Jail Ale, Holsworthy Muck 'n Straw and Tamar Black, Otter Ale, St Austell Proper Job and Tribute, Skinners Betty Stogs and Teignworthy Gun Dog; also, up to 14 real ciders and perries and quite a range of malt whiskies. The comfortable little bar has straightforward pubby furnishings and an open fire, and local photographs, country scenes and prints of Tom Cobley (who was born in the village) on the walls. A large back dining room has beams and background music. There are seats in the tree-shaded garden and more out in front by the quiet street. Some of the good value bedrooms have shared facilities.

 Honest, traditional food includes lunchtime sandwiches and toasties, pâté and toast, home-made pasties, butternut squash and goats cheese lasagne, liver, bacon and onions, bacon-wrapped chicken with cheese and barbecue sauce, smoked haddock, mozzarella and spring onion fishcakes with sweet chilli sauce, steak and kidney pudding, duck in orange sauce, and puddings. *Benchmark main dish: home-made pies £9.50. Two-course evening meal £17.00.*

Free house ~ Licensees Roger and Carol Cudlip ~ Real ale ~ (01647) 231314 ~ Open 6.30-11 Mon; 12-3, 6-11 (1am Fri, Sat); 12-4, 7-11 Sun; closed Mon lunchtime ~ Bar food 12-2, 7-9 ~ Restaurant ~ Children welcome ~ Dogs allowed in bar ~ Bedrooms: £40/£80 ~ www.tomcobleytavern.co.uk *Recommended by Peter Thornton, Jeremy Whitehorn*

TIPTON ST JOHN — Golden Lion

SY0991 Map 1

Pub signed off B3176 Sidmouth–Ottery St Mary; EX10 0AA

Friendly village pub with three real ales, well liked bar food, a good mix of customers and plenty of seats in the attractive garden

Locals and diners from further afield mix happily in this bustling village pub. The main bar, split into two, has a comfortable, relaxed atmosphere, as does the back snug, and throughout are paintings by west country artists, art deco prints, Tiffany lamps and, hanging from the beams, hops, copper pots and kettles. A few tables are kept for those just wanting a pint and a chat. Bass and Otter Ale and Bitter on handpump and 13 wines by the glass; maybe background music and cards. There are seats on the terracotta-walled terrace with outside heaters and grapevines, and more seats on the grass edged by pretty flowering borders. Dog walkers and smokers may use a verandah.

🍴 Popular food includes lunchtime sandwiches, moules marinière, home-smoked duck salad, home-cooked ham and egg, vegetable lasagne, steak and kidney pudding, slow-roasted lamb shank, venison pie, plaice with garlic butter, and puddings such as fruit crumble and lemon brioche pudding. *Benchmark main dish: chunky bouillabaisse £7.95. Two-course evening meal £22.00.*

Heavitree ~ Tenants François and Michelle Teissier ~ Real ale ~ (01404) 812881 ~ Open 12-2.30, 6-10 (11 Fri, Sat); closed Sun evening ~ Bar food 12-2, 6.30-8.30 ~ Children welcome ~ Live jazz summer Sun lunchtime ~ www.goldenliontipton.co.uk
Recommended by Edward May

TORQUAY
SX9265 Map 1

Cary Arms 🍷 🛏

Beach Road: off B3199 Babbacombe Road, via Babbacombe Downs Road; turn steeply down near Babbacombe Theatre; TQ1 3LX

Interesting bar in secluded hotel with lovely sea views, plenty of outside seating, enjoyable if not cheap food, real ales and friendly service; sea-view bedrooms

This charming higgledy-piggledy hotel is a civilised and genuinely friendly place to stay; the boutique-style bedrooms are very special, and they also have four self-catering properties. The glorious views over Babbacombe Bay can be enjoyed from the bedrooms, as well as from the outdoor seats (picnic-sets on terraces, teak chairs and tables on gravel) and from windows in the bar; there's a barbecue, pizza oven and outside bar, and steps lead down to the quay. The beamed, grotto-effect bar has rough pink granite walls, alcoves, rustic hobbit-style red leather cushioned chairs around carved wooden tables on slate or bare boards, an open woodburning stove with a ship's wheel above it, and some high bar chairs beside the stone bar counter. Bays Topsail, Otter Ale and Red Rock Devon County on handpump, nine good wines by the glass and two local ciders; cheerful young staff. There's also a small, glass-enclosed entrance room with large ship lanterns and cleats; darts and board games. There are six mooring spaces and they can arrange a water taxi for guests arriving by boat. The lane down to the hotel is tortuously steep and not for the faint-hearted.

🍴 Making impressive use of local ingredients, the highly enjoyable food includes lunchtime sandwiches (the white crabmeat and lemon mayonnaise is delicious), moules marinière with cream, asparagus and brie risotto with cumberland sauce, lunchtime burger with home-made tomato relish and fries, lamb rump with thyme fondant potato and redcurrant jus, and puddings such as lemon grass and lime panna cotta with mango compote and rhubarb and vanilla crème brûlée. *Benchmark main dish: Brixham battered fish and chips £13.50. Two-course evening meal £22.00.*

Free house ~ Licensee Felicia Crosby ~ Real ale ~ (01803) 327110 ~ Open 12-11 ~ Bar food 12-3, 6-9.30 ~ Children welcome ~ Dogs allowed in bar and bedrooms ~ Wi-fi ~ Occasional live music evenings ~ Bedrooms: £156/£195 ~ www.caryarms.co.uk
Recommended by K B Ohlson

TOTNES
SX8059 Map 1

Steam Packet

St Peters Quay, on W bank (ie not on Steam Packet Quay); TQ9 5EW

Seats outside overlooking quay, attractive layout and décor inside, and well liked food and drink; bedrooms

The seats on the front terrace overlooking the River Dart get snapped up pretty fast – best to arrive early in warm weather. The pub is interestingly laid out, with bare stone walls, wooden flooring, an open log fire at one end, a squashy leather sofa with lots of cushions against a wall of books, a similar seat built into a small curved brick wall (which breaks up the room) and a TV. The main bar has built-in wall benches and plenty of stools and chairs around traditional pub tables; another area has a coal fire and dark wood furniture. Dartmoor Jail Ale, Sharps Doom Bar and a guest from Red Rock on handpump, a dozen wines by the glass and farm cider; background music and board games. The conservatory restaurant has high-backed leather dining chairs around wooden tables, and smart window blinds. If the parking area is full, there's a pay-and-display car park nearby.

As well as lunchtime sandwiches, the good popular food includes plaice goujons with tartare sauce, mushrooms in garlic, white wine and cream, a pie of the day, pulled pork shoulder with borlotti stew and glazed root vegetables, thai green fish curry, goats cheese and vegetable risotto, salmon niçoise, and puddings such as blackberry cheesecake and banoffi tart. *Benchmark main dish: beer-battered haddock and chips £10.95. Two-course evening meal £17.50.*

Buccaneer Holdings ~ Manager Richard Cockburn ~ Real ale ~ (01803) 863880 ~ Open 11-11; 12-10.30 Sun ~ Bar food 12-2.30 (3 Sat), 6-9.30; 12-8 Sun ~ Restaurant ~ Children welcome ~ Dogs allowed in bar ~ Wi-fi ~ Bedrooms: £85/£105 ~ www.steampacketinn.co.uk *Recommended by Keith and Sandra Ross, Dave Webster, Sue Holland, N R White*

WIDECOMBE
SX7276 Map 1

Rugglestone

Village at end of B3387; pub just S – turn left at church and NT church house, OS Sheet 191 map reference 720765; TQ13 7TF

Unspoilt local with a couple of bars, cheerful customers, friendly staff, four real ales and traditional pub food

In complete contrast to the nearby tourist village, this is a simple little place with plenty of charm. The unspoilt bar has just four tables, a few window and wall seats, a one-person pew built into the corner by a nice old stone fireplace (with a woodburner) and a good mix of customers. The rudimentary bar counter dispenses Bays Gold, Dartmoor Legend, Otter Bitter and a beer named for the pub from Teignworthy tapped from the cask; local farm cider and a decent small wine list. The room on the right is slightly bigger and lighter in feel, with beams, another stone fireplace, stripped-pine tables and a built-in wall bench; there's also a small dining room. There are seats in the field across a little moorland stream, and tables and chairs in the garden. A holiday cottage is for rent.

Quite a choice of tasty food includes baguettes, good pasties, smoked duck with chutney, cheese and spinach cannelloni with herby tomato sauce, burger with cheese, bacon and chips, lambs liver with bacon and onion gravy, fish pie topped with cheese, spicy meatballs with potato wedges, and puddings. *Benchmark main dish: steak and stilton pie £10.50. Two-course evening meal £16.50.*

Free house ~ Licensees Richard and Vicki Palmer ~ Real ale ~ (01364) 621327 ~ Open 11.30-3, 6-11.30 (5-midnight Fri); 11.30am-midnight Sat; 12-11 Sun ~ Bar food 12-2, 6.30-9 ~ Restaurant ~ Children allowed away from bar area ~ Dogs welcome ~ www.rugglestoneinn.co.uk *Recommended by Nigel and Sue Foster, John and Gloria Isaacs, Julie and Bill Ryan, Mr Yeldahn*

WOODBURY SALTERTON
Diggers Rest
SY0189 Map 1

3.5 miles from M5 junction 30: A3052 towards Sidmouth, village signposted on right about 0.5 miles after Clyst St Mary; also signposted from B3179 SE of Exeter; EX5 1PQ

Bustling village pub with real ales, well liked food and country views from the terraced garden

Our readers enjoy their visits to this thatched Tudor pub (easy to find from the M5), where friendly staff offer a warm welcome to all. The main bar has antique furniture, local art on the walls and a cosy seating area by the open fire. The modern extension is light and airy and opens on to the garden, which has contemporary garden furniture under canvas parasols on the terrace, and lovely countryside views. Bays Topsail and Otter Ale and Bitter on handpump, 13 wines by the glass and Weston's cider; service is attentive and efficient. Background music, darts, TV and board games. The window boxes and flowering baskets are pretty, and there are lots of good walks surrounding this quiet village.

Using seasonal local produce, the tasty food includes honey-glazed ham hock with hash potato and soft poached egg, roast garlic ribs with chilli and spring onion salad, beer-battered fish and chips, pot-roast chicken with pancetta croquette, thai pork salad, roasted vegetable lasagne, steak in ale pie, and puddings such as sticky toffee pudding with butterscotch sauce. *Benchmark main dish: pork belly with black pudding galette and cider jus £12.95. Two-course evening meal £19.00.*

Heartstone Inns ~ Licensee Marc Slater ~ Real ale ~ (01395) 232375 ~ Open 11-3, 5.30-11; 11-11 Sat, Sun ~ Bar food 12-2.15, 6-9 ~ Restaurant ~ Children welcome ~ Dogs allowed in bar ~ Live music; check website for dates ~ www.diggersrest.co.uk *Recommended by John Evans, Rich Frith, M G Hart, John Wooll, Katharine Cowherd, Roy Hoing*

Also Worth a Visit in Devon

Besides the fully inspected pubs, you might like to try these pubs that have been recommended to us and described by readers. Do tell us what you think of them: feedback@goodguides.com

ABBOTSKERSWELL SX8568
Court Farm (01626) 361866
Wilton Way; look for the church tower; TQ12 5NY
Attractive neatly extended 17th-c longhouse tucked away in picturesque hamlet, various rooms off long beamed and paved main bar, good mix of furnishings, well priced popular food from sandwiches to steaks, friendly helpful staff, several ales including Bass and Otter, farm cider and decent wines, woodburners; background music, pool and darts; children welcome, picnic-sets in pretty lawned garden, open all day (food all day Thurs-Sun). *(Anon)*

APPLEDORE SS4630
Beaver (01237) 474822
Irsha Street; EX39 1RY Relaxed harbourside pub with lovely estuary view from popular raised dining area, well priced food especially fresh local fish, prompt friendly service, good choice of west country ales, farm cider, decent house wines and great range of whiskies; background and some live music including jazz, pool in smaller games room, TV; children and dogs

welcome, disabled access (but no nearby parking), tables on small sheltered water-view terrace. *(Paul Bonner)*

ASHPRINGTON
SX8056
Watermans Arms (01803) 732214
Bow Bridge, on Tuckenhay Road; TQ9 7EG New licensees for this 17th-c creekside inn; beamed and quarry-tiled main bar area, built-in cushioned wall seats and wheelbacks around stripped tables, woodburner, dining room with fishing-related décor, comfortable area down steps and front bar with log fire, Palmers ales and several wines by the glass, good choice of traditional food from sandwiches and baked potatoes up; children and dogs welcome, seats out by the water and in garden, bedrooms (some in purpose-built annexe), open all day. *(David Jackman)*

AVONWICK
SX6958
★ Turtley Corn Mill (01364) 646100
0.5 miles off A38 roundabout at SW end of South Brent bypass; TQ10 9ES Converted watermill with individually decorated linked rooms, bookcases, church candles and oriental rugs in one area, dark flagstones by the bar, woodburner, mix of comfortable dining chairs around heavy rustic tables, array of prints and some framed 78rpm discs, Dartmoor, St Austell, Sharps and Summerskills, several wines by the glass and around 30 malt whiskies, good choice of food including weekday set menu, friendly staff coping well when busy; children welcome, dogs in bar, extensive garden with plenty of well spaced picnic-sets, giant chess set and small lake, bedrooms, open all day from 8.30am (11am Sun) for breakfast. *(Colin and Angela Boocock, Helen and Brian Edgeley, John Evans, Christian Mole, Nicki Spicer, Lynda and Trevor Smith and others)*

AXMOUTH
SY2591
★ Harbour Inn (01297) 20371
B3172 Seaton–Axminster; EX12 4AF Family-run thatched pub by estuary; two heavily beamed bar rooms with brass-bound cask seats, settles and all manner of tables on bare boards, pots hanging in huge inglenook, lots of model boats and accounts of shipwrecks, glass balls in nets and a large turtle shell, more heavy beams in two dining rooms, snug alcove leading off with nautical bric-a-brac, Badger ales and several wines by the glass, good choice of enjoyable food from sandwiches and deli boards up, pool, skittle alley; children and dogs (in bar) welcome, modern furniture on terrace, picnic-sets on grass, open (and food) all day from 9am. *(Jonathan Alexander)*

BAMPTON
SS9520
★ Exeter Inn (01398) 331345
A396 some way S, at B3227 roundabout; EX16 9DY Long low roadside pub under welcoming new owners; stone-built with

several updated linked rooms, mainly flagstoned, two log fires and woodburner, large restaurant, wide choice of good generous food at sensible prices including fresh fish, friendly efficient service, Cotleigh, Exmoor and guests tapped from the cask, daily papers; children and dogs welcome (pub yorkie is Oscar), disabled facilities, tables out in front, ten bedrooms, fairly handy for Knightshayes (NT), open all day. *(Anon)*

BAMPTON
SS9622
Quarrymans Rest (01398) 331480
Briton Street; EX16 9LN Bustling village pub under new management; beamed and carpeted main bar, leather sofas in front of inglenook woodburner, dining chairs and some housekeepers' chairs around wooden tables, good home-made food and four well kept west country ales, steps up to comfortable stripped-stone dining room with high-backed leather chairs and heavy pine tables; pool and games machines; children and dogs welcome, picnic-sets in pretty back garden, more seats in front, four bedrooms, open all day. *(Anon)*

BAMPTON
SS9522
Swan (01398) 332248
Station Road; EX16 9NG Refurbished beamed village inn with spacious bare-boards bar, woodburners in two inglenooks, three changing local beers and good home-made food (not Mon), efficient service; children and dogs welcome, good modern bedrooms, big breakfast, closed Mon lunchtime, otherwise open all day. *(Anon)*

BANTHAM
SX6643
★ Sloop (01548) 560489
Off A379/B3197 NW of Kingsbridge; TQ7 3AJ Friendly 14th-c pub close to fine beach and walks, good mix of customers in black-beamed bar with stripped-stone walls and flagstones, country tables and chairs, woodburner, well kept St Austell ale and a guest ale, enjoyable food from good sandwiches to fresh fish, friendly efficient service, restaurant; background music; children and dogs welcome, seats out at back, five bedrooms, open all day in summer. *(Lynda and Trevor Smith, Roy Hoing, Peter Travis and others)*

BARNSTAPLE
SS5533
Panniers (01271) 329720
Boutport Street; EX31 1RX Centrally placed Wetherspoons (close to Panniers Market), busy and reliable, with good range of beers and decent food served promptly by pleasant staff, family area; free wi-fi; open all day from 7am. *(Derek and Sylvia Stephenson)*

BEER
ST2289
Anchor (01297) 20386
Fore Street; EX12 3ET Sea-view dining pub with wide choice of enjoyable food including good local fish, Greene King and

Otter, good value wines, rambling open-plan layout with old local photographs, large eating area; sports TV, background music; children well looked after, lots of tables in attractive clifftop garden over road, delightful seaside village, reasonably priced bedrooms. *(Patrick and Daphne Darley)*

BEER SY2289
Dolphin (01297) 20068
Fore Street; EX12 3EQ Hotel's recently refurbished lounge bar with comfortable banquettes on wood or carpeted floors, also long public bar with darts, pool and machines, well kept ales such as Bays, Cotleigh, Fullers and Skinners, decent wine and coffee, enjoyable food including fresh local fish (scallops and bacon the signature dish), friendly service, large back restaurant; background and live music; children and dogs welcome, sunny back terrace, 22 bedrooms, open all day. *(Anon)*

BELSTONE SX61293
Tors (01837) 840689
A mile off A30; EX20 1QZ Small Victorian granite pub/hotel in peaceful Dartmoor-edge village, family-run and welcoming, with long carpeted bar divided by settles, well kept ales such as Dartmoor and Sharps, over 50 malt whiskies and good choice of wines, enjoyable well presented food from sandwiches to specials, cheerful prompt service, restaurant; children and dogs (they have their own) welcome, disabled access, seats out on nearby grassy area overlooking valley, good walks, bedrooms, open all day in summer. *(Chris and Angela Buckell)*

BERE FERRERS SX4563
Old Plough (01822) 840358
Long dead-end road off B3257 S of Tavistock; PL20 7JL 16th-c pub with stripped stone and panelling, low beam-and-plank ceilings, slate flagstones and open fires, enjoyable good value home-cooked food, well kept Sharps Doom Bar and a couple of guests, farm cider, warm local atmosphere, steps down to cosy restaurant; some live music; garden overlooking estuary, secluded village, open all day weekends. *(Anon)*

BERRYNARBOR SS5546
Olde Globe (01271) 882465
Off A399 E of Ilfracombe; EX34 9SG Rambling dimly lit rooms geared to family visitors (cutlasses, swords, shields and rustic oddments), good choice of reasonably priced straightforward food, Sharps Doom Bar and a couple of guests, friendly service, ancient walls and flagstones, high-backed oak settles and antique tables, lots of old pictures, open fire and woodburner, more modern family room, play areas inside and out; background and summer live music; dogs welcome, tables on paved front terrace and side lawn, pretty village, open (and food) all day in season from 9am. *(Anon)*

BIDEFORD SS4526
Kings Arms (01237) 475196
The Quay; EX39 2HW Popular old-fashioned 16th-c pub with Victorian harlequin floor tiles in alcovey front bar, friendly staff, well kept west country ales and reasonably priced pubby food all day, back raised family area; background music; dogs welcome, tables out on pavement, three bedrooms, handy for Lundy ferry. *(Anon)*

BISHOP'S TAWTON SS5629
★**Chichester Arms** (01271) 343945
Signed off A377 outside Barnstaple; East Street; EX32 0DQ Friendly 15th-c cob and thatch pub, good generous well priced food from baguettes to fresh local fish and seasonal game, quick obliging service even when crowded, St Austell Tribute, Wells & Youngs Bombardier and a guest, decent wines, heavy low beams, large stone fireplace, restaurant; children welcome, awkward disabled access but staff very helpful, picnic-sets on front terrace and in back garden, open all day. *(Mark Flynn)*

BLACKAWTON SX8050
★**Normandy Arms** (01803) 712884
Signposted off A3122 W of Dartmouth; TQ9 7BN Clean and airy restauranty pub refurbished under present owner; most people here for the very good if not cheap food in two main dining areas, high-backed chairs around wooden tables on slate floors, drinkers' area with tub leather chairs and sofas by woodburner, a couple of local ales, good wines by the glass and cocktails; benches out in front and picnic-sets in small garden across lane, pretty village (May worm-charming competition), three bedrooms, closed Sun, Mon and lunchtimes Tues, Weds. *(Anon)*

BRANDIS CORNER SS4103
Bickford Arms (01409) 221318
A3072 Hatherleigh–Holsworthy; EX22 7XY Friendly 17th-c beamed village pub (rebuilt after 2003 fire); wide choice of enjoyable locally sourced food cooked to order, west country ales such as Skinners, slate-floor bar with woodburner in large stone fireplace, carpeted restaurant; well behaved children welcome if eating, garden with round picnic-sets, attractive countryside, five comfortable bedrooms, good breakfast. *(J V Dadswell)*

BRAYFORD SS7235
★**Poltimore Arms** (01598) 710381
Yarde Down; 3 miles towards Simonsbath; EX36 3HA Ivy-clad 17th-c beamed pub – so remote it generates its own electricity and water is from a spring; refurbished and extended under present licensee, good home-made food including daily specials (best to book) and two or three changing ales tapped from the cask,

friendly helpful staff, traditional furnishings, woodburner in inglenook, two attractive restaurant areas separated by another woodburner, good country views; children and dogs welcome, picnic-sets in side garden, open all day. *(Anon)*

BRENDON SS7547
★ Rockford Inn (01598) 741214
Rockford; Lynton–Simonsbath Road, off B3223; EX35 6PT Homely and welcoming small 17th-c beamed inn surrounded by fine walks and scenery; neatly linked rooms with cushioned settles, wall seats and other straightforward furniture, country prints and horse tack, open fires, good helpings of enjoyable well priced pubby food, Clearwater, Cotleigh and Exmoor tapped from the cask, farm cider, decent wines by the glass, lots of pump clips and toby jugs behind counter, board games; background music; children and dogs (in bar) welcome, seats out overlooking East Lyn river, well appointed bedrooms, open all day (afternoon break Sun). *(Sheila Topham)*

BRENDON SS7648
Staghunters (01598) 741222
Leedford Lane; EX35 6PS Idyllically set family-run hotel with gardens by East Lyn river, good choice of enjoyable reasonably priced food, well kept Cotleigh and Exmoor ales, friendly efficient staff, bar with woodburner, restaurant; can get very busy, though quiet out of season; walkers and dogs welcome, riverside tables, 12 good value bedrooms. *(Bob and Margaret Holder)*

BRIXHAM SX9256
Blue Anchor (01803) 859373
Fore Street/King Street; TQ5 8AH Friendly harbourside pub of some character, plenty of nautical hardware, banquettes and log fire, up to four well kept ales and enjoyable generously served food from good sandwiches to bargain Sun lunch, two small dining rooms – one a former chapel down steps, interesting old photographs, regular live music; dogs welcome, open all day. *(Paul Humphreys)*

BRIXHAM SX9256
★ Maritime (01803) 853535
King Street (up steps from harbour – nearby parking virtually non-existent); TQ5 9TH Single bar packed with bric-a-brac, chamber-pots hanging from beams, hundreds of key fobs, cigarette cards, pre-war ensigns, toby jugs, mannequins, astronomical charts, even a binnacle by the door, friendly long-serving landlady, Bays Best and Hunters Half Bore and Pheasant

Plucker, over 80 malt whiskies, no food or credit cards, lively terrier called George, and Mr Tibbs the parrot; background music, small TV, darts and board games; well behaved children and dogs allowed, fine views over harbour, six bedrooms (not ensuite), closed lunchtime. *(Mrs Sally Scott)*

BROADCLYST SX9897
Red Lion (01392) 461271
B3121, by church; EX5 3EL Refurbished 16th-c pub now under same owners as the Hunters at Newton Tracey; heavy beams, flagstones and log fires, St Austell, Sharps and a guest, enjoyable well priced traditional food (special diets catered for) in bar and restaurant, good cheerful service; children and dogs welcome, picnic-sets out in front below wisteria, more in small enclosed garden across quiet lane, nice village and church, not far from Killerton (NT), may have bedrooms, open all day weekends. *(Gene and Tony Freemantle)*

BROADHEMBURY ST1004
Drewe Arms (01404) 841267
Off A373 Cullompton–Honiton; EX14 3NF Extended partly thatched family-run pub dating from the 15th c; carved beams and handsome stone-mullioned windows, woodburner and open fire, mix of furniture (some perhaps not matching age of building), modernised bar area, five local ales and seven wines by the glass, enjoyable pubby food (all day weekends) including Thurs early-bird offer, friendly helpful service, skittle alley; terrace seats, more up steps on tree-shaded lawn, nice setting near church in pretty village, open all day. *(Peter Kirkman)*

BUDLEIGH SALTERTON SY0681
Feathers (01395) 442042
High Street; EX9 6LE Old town-centre inn with bustling local atmosphere in long beamed bar, well kept St Austell Tribute and three west country guests, enjoyable reasonably priced pubby food (not Sun evening) including specials, more intimate softly lit dining lounge, friendly staff; Sun quiz, pool, darts; children and dogs welcome, four bedrooms, open all day. *(S Holder)*

BURGH ISLAND SX6444
Pilchard (01548) 810514
300 metres across tidal sands from Bigbury-on-Sea; walk, or summer sea tractor if tide's in; TQ7 4BG Sadly, the splendid beamed and flagstoned upper bar with its lanterns and roaring log fire is reserved for locals and guests at the associated flamboyantly art deco hotel, but

---

A star symbol before the name of a pub shows exceptional character and appeal. It doesn't mean extra comfort. Even quite a basic pub can win a star, if it's individual enough.

the more utilitarian lower bar is still worth a visit for the unbeatable setting high above the sea swarming below this tidal island; well kept Sharps, Thwaites and an ale named for the pub, real cider, good local oysters and lunchtime baguettes, Fri curry night; dogs welcome, tables outside, some down by beach. *(Anon)*

BUTTERLEIGH   SS9708
Butterleigh Inn   (01884) 855433
Off A396 in Bickleigh; EX15 1PN Small-roomed heavy-beamed country pub, friendly and relaxed with good mix of customers, enjoyable reasonably priced pubby food (not Mon, Sun evening), Sun carvery, four well kept ales including Cotleigh and Otter, good choice of wines, unspoilt lived-in interior with two big fireplaces, back dining room; children welcome, picnic-sets in large garden, four comfortable bedrooms, closed Mon lunchtime and winter Sun evening. *(Jeremy Whitehorn)*

CADELEIGH   SS9107
★ Cadeleigh Arms   (01884) 855238
Village signed off A3072 W of junction with A396 Tiverton–Exeter at Bickleigh; EX16 8HP Attractive and friendly old pub owned by the local community, well kept Cotleigh, Dartmoor, St Austell and a guest, fresh locally sourced food (not Sun evening, Mon) from favourites up, Thurs curry night, carpeted room on left with bay-window seat and ornamental stove, flagstoned room to the right has high-backed settles and log fire in big fireplace, airy dining room down a couple of steps with valley views, local artwork, games room (pool and darts) and skittle alley; background music; children and dogs welcome, picnic-sets on gravel terrace with barbecue, more on gently sloping lawn, closed Mon lunchtime. *(Jeremy Whitehorn)*

CALIFORNIA CROSS   SX7053
California   (01548) 821449
Brown sign to pub off A3121 S of A38 junction; PL21 0SG Neatly modernised 18th-c or older dining pub with beams, panelling, stripped stone and log fire, wide choice of enjoyable food from baguettes to steaks in bar and family area, popular Sun lunch (best to book), separate evening restaurant (Weds-Sun) and small snug, St Austell Tribute, Sharps Doom Bar and a local guest, farm cider and decent wines by the glass; background music; dogs welcome, attractive garden and back terrace, open all day. *(S Holder, M G Hart, Bob and Margaret Holder)*

CHAGFORD   SX7087
Ring o' Bells   (01647) 432466
Off A382; TQ13 8AH Welcoming old pub with beamed and panelled bar, four well kept ales including Dartmoor, traditional fairly priced home-made food, good friendly service, woodburner in big fireplace, some

live music; dogs and well behaved children welcome, sunny walled garden, nearby moorland walks, four bedrooms, open all day. *(Anon)*

CHALLACOMBE   SS6941
Black Venus   (01598) 763251
B3358 Blackmoor Gate–Simonsbath; EX31 4TT Low-beamed 16th-c pub with friendly helpful staff, two or three well kept changing ales and Thatcher's cider, enjoyable fairly priced food from sandwiches to popular Sun lunch, pews and comfortable chairs, woodburner and big fireplace, roomy attractive dining area, games room with pool and darts; free wi-fi; children and dogs welcome, garden play area, lovely countryside and good walks from the door, open all day in summer. *(Anon)*

CHERITON BISHOP   SX7792
★ Old Thatch Inn   (01647) 24204
Off A30; EX6 6JH Attractive thatched village pub doing well under present landlord, welcoming relaxed atmosphere, rambling beamed bar separated by big stone fireplace, Otter, Dartmoor and other well kept local ales, good freshly prepared food from baguettes up, restaurant, efficient friendly service; free wi-fi; children and dogs welcome, nice sheltered garden, two comfortable clean bedrooms, closed Sun evening, Mon. *(Maureen Wood)*

CHITTLEHAMHOLT   SS6420
★ Exeter Inn   (01769) 540281
Off A377 Barnstaple–Crediton, and B3226 SW of South Molton; EX37 9NS Spotless 16th-c thatched coaching inn with friendly staff and long-serving licensees, good food (should book weekends) from sandwiches and traditional choices up, ales such as Exmoor and Otter (some tapped from the cask), local ciders and good wine choice, barrel seats by open stove in huge fireplace, beams spotted with hundreds of matchboxes, shelves of old bottles, traditional games, lounge with comfortable seating and woodburner, dining room and barn style conservatory; background music; children and dogs welcome, gravel terrace, three bedrooms and four self-catering units. *(Mark Flynn)*

CHULMLEIGH   SS6814
Red Lion   (01769) 580384
East Street; EX18 7DD Nicely refurbished and well divided 17th-c coaching inn, beams and open fires, enjoyable fairly priced food including pasta dishes, pizzas and grills, St Austell, Sharps and guest, friendly service; children welcome, five bedrooms, open all day Fri-Sun, closed Mon lunchtime. *(Anon)*

CHURCHSTOW   SX7145
Church House   (01548) 852237
A379 NW of Kingsbridge; TQ7 3QW Attractive old building dating from the

13th c, heavy black beams and stripped stone, enjoyable home-made food including daily specials and popular carvery (Weds-Sat evenings, Sun lunchtime, booking advised), St Austell ales and decent wines, friendly staff, back conservatory with floodlit well; children welcome, dogs in certain areas, tables on big terrace. *(B J Harding, Helen and Brian Edgeley)*

CLAYHIDON ST1615
Half Moon (01823) 680291
On main road through village; EX15 3TJ Attractive old village pub with warm friendly atmosphere, wide choice of enjoyable home-made food including good smoked fish platter, well kept Otter and a couple of guests, farm cider, good wine list, comfortable bar with inglenook log fire, some live music; children and dogs welcome, picnic-sets in tiered garden over road, valley views. *(Guy Vowles)*

CLOVELLY SS3225
New Inn (01237) 431303
High Street; car-free village, visitors charged £6.50 (£4 children) to park and enter; EX39 5TQ Quaint peaceful 17th-c inn halfway down the steep cobbled street and under same management as the harbourside Red Lion; Arts & Crafts décor, simple lower bar with flagstones and bric-a-brac (narrow front part has more character than back eating room), well kept local Country Life and maybe a guest, short choice of good value bar food, upstairs restaurant; great views, small garden behind, nice bedrooms. *(Pete Walker)*

CLOVELLY SS3124
Red Lion (01237) 431237
The Quay; EX39 5TF Rambling 18th-c building in lovely position on curving quay below spectacular cliffs, beams, flagstones, log fire and interesting local photographs in character back bar (dogs on leads allowed here), well kept Country Life and Sharps Doom Bar, bar food and upstairs restaurant, efficient service; great views, 11 attractive bedrooms (six more in Sail Loft annexe), open all day. *(Anon)*

CLYST HYDON ST0201
★ Five Bells (01884) 277288
W of village, just off B3176 not far from M5 junction 28; EX15 2NT Thatched and beamed dining pub now under same owners as the Jack in the Green at Rockbeare; smartly refurbished interior with several different areas including raised dining part, woodburner in large stone fireplace, really good attractively presented food served

by efficient friendly staff, four local ales including Otter, games room with pool and sports TV; children welcome, lovely cottagey garden with thousands of spring and summer flowers, country views. *(Keith Hannaford)*

COCKWOOD SX9780
★ Ship (01626) 890373
Off A379 N of Dawlish; EX6 8NU Comfortable traditional 17th-c pub set back from estuary and harbour – gets very busy in season; good value freshly made food including good fish dishes and puddings, Thurs pie night, OAP lunch deal Fri, Butcombe and Sharps Doom Bar, friendly staff and locals, partitioned beamed bar with big log fire and ancient oven, decorative plates and seafaring memorabilia, small restaurant; background music; children and dogs welcome, nice steep-sided garden. *(Adrian Johnson, Gavin and Helle May)*

COMBE MARTIN SS5846
Pack o' Cards (01271) 882300
High Street; EX34 0ET Unusual 'house of cards' building constructed in the late 17th c to celebrate a substantial gambling win – four floors, 13 rooms and 52 windows; snug bar area and various side rooms, St Austell Tribute, Wells & Youngs Bombardier and a guest, enjoyable inexpensive pub food including children's choices and good Sun roast, friendly helpful service, restaurant; pretty riverside garden with play area, six comfortable bedrooms, generous breakfast, open all day. *(Anon)*

COMBEINTEIGNHEAD SX9071
★ Wild Goose (01626) 872241
Off unclassified coast road Newton Abbot–Shaldon, up hill in village; TQ12 4RA Rambling pub with five mainly local ales and at least one real cider in spacious back beamed lounge, wheelbacks and red plush dining chairs, agricultural bits and pieces, pubby food, front bar with more beams, standing timbers and some flagstones, step down to area with big old fireplace and another cosy room with comfortable sofa and armchairs, bar billiards, darts and board games; background music (live on Fri), Sat quiz, TV; children in dining areas only, dogs in bar, garden with nice country views. *(Anon)*

COUNTISBURY SS7449
Blue Ball (01598) 741263
A39, E of Lynton; EX35 6NE Beautifully set rambling heavy-beamed pub, friendly licensees, good range of generous local food in bar and restaurant, three ales including one badged for the pub, decent

---

A few pubs try to make you leave a credit card at the bar, as a sort of deposit if you order food. This is a bad practice, and the banks and credit card firms warn you not to let your card go like this.

wines and proper ciders, handsome log fires; background music; children, dogs and walkers welcome, views from terrace tables, good nearby cliff walks (pub provides handouts of four circular routes), comfortable bedrooms, open all day. *(Lynda and Trevor Smith, Mr and Mrs D J Nash)*

CREDITON   SS8300
Crediton Inn (01363) 772882
Mill Street (follow Tiverton sign); EX17 1EZ Small friendly local with long-serving landlady, well kept O'Hanlons Yellow Hammer and up to nine quickly changing guests (Nov beer festival), cheap well prepared weekend food, home-made scotch eggs other times, back games room/skittle alley; free wi-fi; open all day Mon-Sat. *(Anon)*

CROYDE   SS4439
Manor House Inn (01271) 890241
Street Marys Road, off B3231 NW of Braunton; EX33 1PG Friendly family pub with cheerful efficient service, three well kept west country ales, good choice of enjoyable fairly priced food from lunchtime sandwiches to blackboard specials, carvery Weds and Sun, cream teas, restaurant and dining conservatory; background and live music, sports TV, games end; skittle alley, disabled facilities, attractive terraced garden with good big play area, open all day. *(Pat and Tony Martin)*

CROYDE   SS4439
Thatch (01271) 890349
B3231 NW of Braunton; Hobbs Hill; EX33 1LZ Lively thatched pub near great surfing beaches; cheerful efficient young staff, laid-back feel (can get packed in summer); rambling and roomy, with beams, open fire, settles and good seating, enjoyable sensibly priced pubby food from sandwiches up, well kept changing local ales, morning coffee, teas, smart restaurant with dressers and lots of china; background music; children in eating areas, tables on flower-filled suntrap terraces, large gardens shared with neighbouring Billy Budds, good play area, bedrooms simple but clean and comfortable, open (and food) all day. *(Pat and Tony Martin)*

CULMSTOCK   ST1013
★Culm Valley (01884) 840354
B3391, off A38 E of M5 junction 27; EX15 3JJ Friendly old dining pub, a touch eccentric and with a slightly off-beat but charming landlord; informal lively atmosphere, bar has hotchpotch of modern and unrenovated furnishings, paintings and knick-knacks, big fireplace, well liked imaginative food, up to nine quickly changing ales tapped from the cask, local ciders (also somerset cider brandies), wines from smaller french vineyards imported by landlord's brother, dining room and small front conservatory, large back room with

paintings for sale by local artists, folk night first Weds of month; outside gents', free wi-fi; children allowed away from main bar, dogs welcome (theirs are Lady and Spoof), outside tables overlooking bridge and River Culm, three bedrooms sharing two bathrooms, open all day Fri-Sun. *(Hugo Jeune, Guy Vowles, Mark Flynn)*

DARTINGTON   SX7861
Cott (01803) 863777
Cott signed off A385 W of Totnes, opposite A384 turn-off; TQ9 6HE Long 14th-c thatched pub with heavy beams, flagstones, nice mix of old furniture and two inglenooks (one with big woodburner), good home-made locally sourced food from traditional choices up in bar and restaurant, three ales including local Hunters and Greene King, Ashridge cider, nice wines by the glass, good service, live music Sun; children and dogs welcome, wheelchair access (with help into restaurant), picnic-sets in garden and on pretty terrace, five comfortable bedrooms, open all day. *(Paul Humphreys, John Evans)*

DARTMOUTH   SX8751
★Cherub (01803) 832571
Higher Street; walk along river front, right into Hauley Road and up steps at end; TQ6 9RB Ancient building (Dartmouth's oldest) with two heavily timbered upper floors jutting over the street and many original interior features, oak beams, leaded lights, tapestried seats and big stone fireplace with photo of pub ghost above, up to six well kept ales including St Austell in bustling bar, low-ceilinged upstairs restaurant, good food from pub favourites to fish specials, efficient friendly service; background music; children welcome (no pushchairs), dogs in bar, open all day. *(Simon Lindsey, Rose Rogers, Richard Tilbrook)*

DARTMOUTH   SX8751
Dartmouth Arms (01803) 832903
Lower Street, Bayard's Cove; TQ6 9AN Friendly local with tables out in prime harbour-wall spot overlooking estuary (Pilgrim Fathers set sail from here), well kept beers such as Sharps Doom Bar and enjoyable good value food including pizzas, panelling and boating memorabilia, log fire; children and dogs welcome, next door apartment with bay view, open all day. *(Anon)*

DARTMOUTH   SX8751
Dolphin (01803) 833698
Market Street; TQ6 9QE Interesting building in picturesque part of town, quirky and laid-back, with own Bridgetown beer (brewed in Totnes) and St Austell Tribute, good food including well priced fish platters, friendly staff; background and live music; children and dogs welcome, open all day. *(Anon)*

DAWLISH WARREN
SX9778
Mount Pleasant (01626) 863151
Mount Pleasant Road; EX7 0NA
Expansive sea views from large recently
refurbished inn (run by same family for
over 30 years), carpeted heavily beamed
lounge and linked rooms, well kept Otter
ales, wide choice of fairly standard home-
cooked food including children's, friendly
service and good mix of customers, skittle
alley; terrace tables, handy for coast path
and nature reserve, bedrooms, open all day.
(N R White)

DITTISHAM
SX8654
★ **Ferry Boat** (01803) 722368
*Manor Street; best to park in village car
park and walk down; TQ6 0EX*
Cheerful riverside pub with lively mix of
customers; beamed bar with log fires and
straightforward pubby furniture, lots of
boating bits and pieces, tide times chalked
on wall, flags on ceiling, picture-window view
of the Dart, at least three ales such as Dorset,
Otter and Sharps, a dozen wines by the glass,
good range of home-made food including pie
of the day and various curries; background
and some live music; children and dogs
welcome, moorings for visiting boats on
adjacent pontoon and bell to summon ferry,
good walks, open all day. *(Lynda and Trevor
Smith, Ken Parry, Bruce Jamieson)*

DITTISHAM
SX8654
Red Lion (01803) 722235
The Level; TQ6 0ES Lovely location
looking down over attractive village and River
Dart; welcoming atmosphere, decent food
including daily specials, Dartmoor, Palmers
and a summer guest, good italian coffee and
morning pastries, carpeted bar, restaurant,
open fires; also houses village store, tiny post
office, library and craft shop; children and
dogs welcome, eight bedrooms (some with
river view), free wi-fi, open from 8.30am, may
shut Weds and weekend afternoons
in winter. *(Bruce Jamieson)*

DREWSTEIGNTON
SX7390
Drewe Arms (01647) 281409
*Off A30 NW of Moretonhampstead;
EX6 6QN* Pretty thatched village pub
under new management; unspoilt room on
left with basic wooden wall benches, stools
and tables, original serving hatch, ales
such as Dartmoor and Otter from tap room
casks, local cider, enjoyable sensibly priced
pubby food including daily specials, two
dining areas, one with Rayburn and history
of Britain's longest serving landlady (Mabel
Mudge), another with woodburner, darts
and board games, live music and quiz nights
in back Long Room; free wi-fi; children and
dogs welcome, seats under umbrellas on
front terrace and in garden, pretty flowering
tubs and baskets, two four-poster bedrooms,
four bunk rooms, on Dartmoor Trail and

handy for Castle Drogo (NT), open (and
food) all day in summer. *(Barry Collett)*

EAST ALLINGTON
SX7648
Fortescue Arms (01548) 521215
*Village signed off A381 Totnes–
Kingsbridge, S of A3122 junction;
TQ9 7RA* Pretty family-run village pub;
two-room bar with mix of wooden tables and
chairs on black slate floor, some brewery
memorabilia, three Dartmoor ales and eight
wines by the glass, restaurant with own bar,
Farrow & Ball paintwork and high-backed
dining chairs around painted tables, well
liked freshly made food including pizzas;
background and occasional live music, free
wi-fi; children and dogs welcome, seats at the
front with more on sheltered terrace, open
all day during school holidays (closed Mon,
lunchtimes Tues-Thurs at other times).
(Anon)

EAST DOWN
SS5941
Pyne Arms (01271) 850055
*Off A39 Barnstaple–Lynton near
Arlington; EX31 4LX* Old village pub
under newish licensees, cosy carpeted
bar with lots of alcoves, woodburner,
sensibly priced traditional food and daily
blackboard specials, two Exmoor ales and
good choice of wines, flagstoned area with
sofas, conservatory; background music;
children and dogs welcome, small enclosed
garden, good walks, handy for Arlington
Court (NT), open (and food) all day
weekends. *(Geof Cox)*

EAST PRAWLE
SX7836
Pigs Nose (01548) 511209
Prawle Green; TQ7 2BY Relaxed and
quirky three-room 16th-c pub with low
beams and flagstones, local ales tapped from
the cask, farm ciders and enjoyable simple
pubby food, lots of interesting bric-a-brac
and pictures, mix of old furniture, jars of
wild flowers and candles on tables, open fire,
small family area with unusual toys, pool and
darts, friendly dogs (others welcome – even
a menu for them); unobtrusive background
music, hall for live bands (friendly landlord
was 1960s tour manager); tables outside,
pleasant spot on village green. *(David
Jackman, Richard Tilbrook)*

EXETER
SX9292
Chaucers (01392) 422365
*Basement of Tesco Metro, High Street;
EX4 3LR* Steps down to this large, dimly
lit olde-worlde-style pub/bistro/wine bar;
beamed low ceiling and timber-framed walls,
wood floors, several levels with booths and
alcoves, comfortable furnishings, Marstons-
related ales and well priced wines (plenty
by the glass), cocktails, enjoyable good value
food from snacks to specials, quick friendly
service; background music, silent games
machines, no under-14s; open all day (till
4pm Sun). *(Jeremy King)*

EXETER   SX9192
Fat Pig (01392) 437217
John Street; EX1 1BL Popular refurbished
Victorian corner pub (same owners as the
Rusty Bike in Howell Road), welcoming and
relaxed, with focus on dining, good food
from daily changing blackboard menu using
local produce (some from owner's farm),
home-smoked meats, own ales (brewed in
the cellar), real ciders and good wine choice,
light and airy stripped-pine interior with
nice fire, small conservatory-style room,
Mon quiz; children in heated courtyard, open
all day Sat, till 5pm Sun, closed weekday
lunchtimes. *(Phil Bryant)*

EXETER   SX9193
Great Western (01392) 274039
St David's Hill; EX4 4NU Up to nine well
kept ales including Branscombe, Dartmoor
and RCH in this large commercial hotel's well
worn-in plush-seated bar, friendly efficient
staff, fresh good value pubby food from
sandwiches up (kitchen also supplies hotel's
restaurant), daily papers; may be background
music, sports TV, free wi-fi; children and dogs
welcome, 35 bedrooms, handy for station,
pay parking, open all day (till 1am Fri, Sat).
(Pete Walker)

EXETER   SX9292
★ Hour Glass (01392) 258722
*Melbourne Street; off B3015 Topsham
Road; EX2 4AU* Old-fashioned bow-
cornered pub tucked away in surviving
Georgian part above the quay; good inventive
food including vegetarian from shortish
regularly changing menu, up to five well kept
ales (usually one from Otter) and extensive
range of wines and spirits, friendly relaxed
atmosphere, beams, bare boards and mix of
furnishings, assorted pictures on dark red
walls and various odds and ends including
a stuffed badger, open fire in small brick
fireplace; background and live music;
children away from bar and dogs welcome
(resident cats), open all day weekends,
closed Mon lunchtime. *(Jeremy Whitehorn)*

EXETER   SX9193
★ Imperial (01392) 434050
*New North Road (above St David's
Station); EX4 4AH* Impressive 19th-c
mansion in own six-acre hillside park with
sweeping drive, various different areas
including two clubby little side bars, fine
old ballroom with elaborate plasterwork
and gilding, light and airy former orangery
with unusual mirrored end wall, interesting
pictures, up to 14 real ales, standard good
value Wetherspoons menu; can get very busy
and popular with students; plenty of picnic-

sets in grounds and elegant garden furniture
in attractive cobbled courtyard, open all day.
*(Tony and Wendy Hobden, Pete Walker, Roger and
Donna Huggins)*

EXETER   SX9292
Old Fire House (01392) 277279
New North Road; EX4 4EP Compact
relaxed city-centre pub in Georgian building
behind high arched wrought-iron gates, up to
ten ales including Otter, several real ciders
and good choice of bottled beers and wines,
bargain food including late evening pizzas,
friendly efficient staff, dimly lit beamed
rooms with simple furniture; background
music, live weekends and popular with young
crowd (admission charge Fri, Sat night);
picnic-sets in front courtyard, open all day
till late. *(Anon)*

EXETER   SX9293
Rusty Bike (01392) 214440
Howell Road; EX4 4LZ Individual
backstreet pub with pine tables, pews and
bench seating on stripped boards in large
open bar, big black and white photographs,
table football, adjoining snug and dining
area, own range of beers (brewed at sister
pub the Fat Pig in John Street), traditional
cider and good wine choice, well liked
interesting blackboard food, good service,
broad mix of customers including students;
background and some live music, projector
for live sport and film nights; courtyard
seating, limited parking, open all day Sun,
closed lunchtimes other days. *(Jo McCreedie)*

EXETER   SX9292
Well House (01392) 223611
*Cathedral Yard (attached to Royal
Clarence Hotel); EX1 1HB* Splendid
position with big windows looking across
to cathedral in partly divided open-plan
bar, good choice of real ales and ciders
(festivals), eight wines by the glass, quick
friendly service, enjoyable food from hotel's
kitchen, lots of Victorian prints, daily papers,
Roman well below (can be viewed by prior
arrangement), live music last Sun of month;
open all day. *(Phil and Jane Villiers, Michael
Butler, Ken Parry)*

EXMOUTH   SX9980
Grapevine (01395) 222208
Victoria Road; EX8 1DL Popular
refurbished red-brick corner pub (calls itself
a pub-bistro); light and spacious with mix
of wooden tables and seating, rugs on bare
boards, local modern artwork, good range
of changing west country ales and bottled
imports, interesting well presented food
including daily specials and weekday set
deal (till early evening), friendly service and

Children – if the details at the end of a featured entry don't mention them,
you should assume that the pub does not allow them inside.

pleasant relaxed atmosphere, popular with younger crowd; background music, live bands Fri, charity quiz Mon, free wi-fi; children welcome, open all day from 9am, till 4pm Sun. *(N R White)*

EXMOUTH   SY9980
Grove (01395) 272101

Esplanade; EX8 1BJ Roomy Victorian pub set back from beach, traditional furnishings, caricatures and local prints, enjoyable pubby food all day including local fish specials, friendly staff, Wells & Youngs and guests kept well, decent house wines, attractive fireplace at back, sea views from appealing upstairs dining room and balcony; background music (live jazz first Sun of month), quiz Thurs; children welcome, picnic-sets in front garden. *(Roger and Donna Huggins, PL)*

FOLLY GATE   SX5798
Crossways (01837) 52088

A386 Hatherleigh–Okehampton; EX20 3AH Friendly beamed village pub with homely comfortable atmosphere, enjoyable food including Fri curry night and roasts Weds/Sun, well kept west country ales; garden picnic-sets, closed Mon in winter. *(Simon and Angela Thomas)*

GEORGEHAM   SS4639
Kings Arms (01271) 890240

B3231 (Chapel Street) Croyde– Woolacombe; EX33 1JJ Welcoming comfortably updated pub with red walls, slate floors and leather sofas by big woodburner, good freshly cooked food using local ingredients, efficient friendly service, St Austell Tribute and a couple of local guests, good choice of wines, upstairs dining area with tables out on sunny balcony, some traditional pub games; background and live music; children and dogs welcome, small front terrace screened from road, open all day. *(Stephen Shepherd)*

HARTLAND   SS2524
Hart (01237) 441474

The Square; EX39 6BL Old village pub with good freshly made food from interesting varied menu, ales such as Sharps and Skinners, reasonably priced wines; closed Sun evening, Mon. *(Nick and Nikki Wright)*

HATHERLEIGH   SS5404
George (01837) 811612

A386 N of Okehampton; Market Street; EX20 3JN Completely rebuilt after original 15th-c thatched and timbered pub burnt down in 2008; old-style interior with lots of reclaimed timbers and other old materials, mix of furniture (some new) on carpet, wood and tiled floors, open fires, enjoyable home-made food including daily specials and Sun carvery, well kept Courage Directors, St Austell Tribute and a guest, nice coffee, friendly helpful staff; 13 bedrooms, open all day. *(Anon)*

HEMYOCK   ST1313
Catherine Wheel (01823) 680224

Cornhill; EX15 3RQ Village pub with cosy refurbished bar, sofas and woodburner, fresh flowers on tables, enjoyable interesting local food (sometimes foraged), ales such as Sharps Doom Bar, friendly landlord; children welcome. *(Richard and Patricia Jefferson)*

HOLNE   SX7069
★Church House (01364) 631208

Signed off B3357 W of Ashburton; TQ13 7SJ Medieval inn in quaint moorland hamlet surrounded by slopes of Dartmoor where *War Horse* was filmed; lower bar with stripped pine panelling and 18th-c curved elm settle, heavy 16th-c oak partition separating it from lounge bar, candles and log fires, ales from Dartmoor and St Austell, real cider, several wines by the glass, hearty food (not Sun evening); background and monthly live music, board games; children and dogs welcome, fine views from the pillared porch, good walks (on Two Moors Way), bedrooms, the church with its fine medieval rood screen is also worth a visit. *(Anon)*

HOLSWORTHY   SS3304
Rydon Inn (01409) 259444

Rydon (A3072 W); EX22 7HU Comfortably extended family-run dining pub, clean and tidy, with enjoyable food and well kept ales such as Otter and Sharps, good friendly service, raftered bar with thatched servery, woodburner in stone fireplace; background music; children and dogs welcome, disabled facilities, views over lake from conservatory and deck, well tended garden, open all day. *(Ryta Lyndley)*

HONITON   ST1599
Heathfield (01404) 45321

Walnut Road; EX14 2UG Ancient thatched and beamed pub in contrasting residential area, well run and spacious, with Greene King ales and good value reliable food from varied menu including the Heathfield Whopper (20oz rump steak), Sun carvery, cheerful prompt service, skittle alley; children welcome, seven bedrooms, open all day Fri-Sun. *(Bob and Margaret Holder, Colin McKerrow)*

HONITON   SY1198
★Holt (01404) 47707

High Street, W end; EX14 1LA Charming little bustling pub run by two brothers, relaxed and informal, with just one room downstairs, chunky tables and chairs on slate flooring, brown leather sofas, a coal-effect woodburner, shelves of books, full range of Otter beers (the family founded the brewery), bigger brighter upstairs dining room with similar furniture on pale floorboards, attractive musician prints, very good tapas and other inventive food, friendly service; background music; well behaved children welcome, dogs in bar, music festival four times a year, closed Sun, Mon. *(Guy Vowles, Michael Butler, Revd R P Tickle, Mike and Jayne Bastin)*

HOPE COVE   SX6740
Hope & Anchor (01548) 561294
Tucked away by car park; TQ7 3HQ
Bustling unpretentious inn, friendly and comfortably unfussy, in lovely seaside spot, good open fire, helpful amiable young staff, good value straightforward food including lots of fish, well kept St Austell Dartmoor and a beer named for the pub, reasonably priced wines, flagstones and bare boards, dining room views to Burgh Island, big separate family room; background music; dogs welcome, sea-view tables out on decking, great coast walks, bedrooms, good breakfast, open all day. *(Peter Travis)*

HORNS CROSS   SS3823
★Hoops (01237) 451222
A39 Clovelly–Bideford, W of village; EX39 5DL Pretty thatched inn with good bustling atmosphere; traditionally furnished bar has china hanging from beams, log fires in sizeable fireplaces and some standing timbers and partitioning, more formal restaurant with attractive mix of tables and chairs, some panelling, exposed stone and another open fire, Hoops Bitter (from Country Life) and Hoops Best and Light (from Forge), over a dozen wines by the glass, enjoyable fairly straightforward food using local suppliers, friendly helpful staff; may be background music; children and dogs welcome, picnic-sets under parasols in enclosed courtyard, more seats on terrace and in two acres of gardens, well equipped bedrooms, open all day. *(C and R Bromage)*

HORSEBRIDGE   SX4074
★Royal (01822) 870214
Off A384 Tavistock–Launceston; PL19 8PJ Dimly lit ancient local with dark half-panelling, log fires, slate floors, scrubbed tables and interesting bric-a-brac, good reasonably priced home-made food including plenty of fish, friendly landlord and staff, well kept Dartmoor, St Austell and Skinners poured from the cask, Rich's farm cider, café-style side room; no children in evening; picnic-sets on front and side terraces and in big garden, quiet rustic spot by lovely old Tamar bridge, popular with walkers and cyclists. *(Giles and Annie Francis, Peter Thornton)*

IDE   SX8990
★Poachers (01392) 273847
3 miles from M5 junction 31, via A30; High Street; EX2 9RW Cosy and welcoming beamed pub in quaint village, good home-made food, Branscombe Vale Branoc and four changing west country guests from ornate curved wooden bar, mismatched old chairs and sofas, various pictures and odds and

ends, big log fire, restaurant; dogs welcome (they have a boxer), tables in pleasant garden with barbecue, three comfortable bedrooms, open all day (till late Fri, Sat). *(Anon)*

IDEFORD   SX8977
★Royal Oak (01626) 852274
2 miles off A380; TQ13 0AY
Unpretentious little 16th-c thatched and flagstoned village local, friendly helpful service, Courage and guests, generous helpings of tasty well priced food, navy theme including interesting Nelson and Churchill memorabilia, beams, panelling and big open fireplace; children and dogs welcome, tables out at front and by car park over road, closed Mon. *(Martin and Ruth Lucas)*

ILFRACOMBE   SS5247
George & Dragon (01271) 863851
Fore Street; EX34 9ED One of the oldest pubs here (14th c) and handy for the harbour, clean and comfortable with friendly local atmosphere, ales such as Exmoor, Sharps and Shepherd Neame, decent wines, traditional home-made food including local fish, beams, stripped stone and open fireplaces, lots of ornaments, china etc, no mobile phones; background music, quiz nights; dogs welcome, open all day and can get very busy weekends. *(Dave Braisted)*

ILFRACOMBE   SS5247
Ship & Pilot (01271) 863562
Broad Street, off harbour; EX34 9EE
Bright yellow pub near harbour with friendly mix of regulars and visitors, six well kept changing ales (usually have Bass), two proper ciders and a perry, no food apart from rolls, traditional open-plan interior with lots of old photos, darts and juke box, weekend live music; a couple of TVs for sport; tables outside, open all day. *(Anon)*

ILSINGTON   SX7876
Carpenters Arms (01364) 661629
Old Town Hill; TQ13 9RG Pretty, unspoilt 18th-c local next to church in quiet village, beams and flagstones, country-style pine furniture, brasses, woodburner, enjoyable generous home-made food and well kept changing ales, friendly atmosphere, darts; children, well behaved dogs and muddy boots welcome, tables out at front, good walks, no car park, open all day weekends. *(David Jackman)*

INSTOW   SS4730
Boat House (01271) 861292
Marine Parade; EX39 4JJ Modern high-ceilinged bar-restaurant with huge tidal beach just across lane and views to Appledore, wide choice of good food including plenty of fish/seafood, two well kept local ales and decent wines by the glass, friendly prompt service, lively family bustle; background music; roof terrace. *(Anon)*

INSTOW
SS4730
Wayfarer (01271) 860342
Lane End; EX39 4LB Unpretentious locals' pub tucked away near dunes and beach, well kept ales tapped from the cask, maybe winter mulled wine, good choice of enjoyable generous home-made food using local fish and meat, quick cheerful service; children and dogs welcome, enclosed garden behind, six bedrooms (some with sea view), open all day. *(Anon)*

KILMINGTON
SY2698
New Inn (01297) 33376
Signed off Gammons Hill; EX13 7SF Traditional thatched pub, originally three 14th-c cottages but carefully rebuilt after 2004 fire; spotless pine-clad bar with stools, dark wood furniture, patterned carpet and banquettes, Palmers ales kept in tip-top condition by long-serving landlord, enjoyable no-nonsense home-made food, friendly service, skittle alley; picnic-sets in large garden with tree-shaded areas. *(Pete Walker)*

KILMINGTON
SY2798
★ Old Inn (01297) 32096
A35; EX13 7RB Thatched 16th-c pub, beams and flagstones, welcoming licensees and nice bustling atmosphere, enjoyable good value food using local supplies, well kept ales such as Butcombe, Cotleigh and Otter, good choice of wines, small character front bar with traditional games (there's also a skittle alley), back lounge with leather armchairs by inglenook log fire, small restaurant; children welcome, beer gardens. *(Pete Walker, Phil and Jane Villiers)*

KINGSBRIDGE
SX7343
Crabshell (01548) 852345
Embankment Road, edge of town; TQ7 1JZ Great waterside position, charming when tide is in, with lovely views from big windows and outside tables, emphasis on food including good fish/seafood, nice crab sandwiches too, friendly staff, well kept local Quercus ales, feature open fire; children welcome, open all day. *(Peter Travis)*

KINGSTON
SX6347
★ Dolphin (01548) 810314
Off B3392 S of Modbury (can also be reached from A379 W of Modbury); TQ7 4QE Cosy and peaceful 16th-c inn run by two brothers; knocked-through beamed rooms with pubby furniture and cushioned wall seats on red carpeting, open fire and woodburner in inglenook fireplaces, well kept ales such as Otter, St Austell, Sharps and Timothy Taylors, farm cider and decent wines by the glass, well liked food using local suppliers, good friendly service; free wi-fi; children and dogs welcome, seats in garden, pretty tubs and window boxes, quiet village with several tracks leading down to the sea, three bedrooms in building across lane, good breakfast, closes some Sun evenings in winter. *(Steve Whalley, Simon Lindsey, Rose Rogers, B J Harding)*

KINGSWEAR
SX8851
★ Ship (01803) 752348
Higher Street; TQ6 0AG Attractive old beamed local by the church, plenty of atmosphere and kind cheerful service, well kept Adnams, Otter, Wadworths and guests from horseshoe bar, Addlestone's cider and nice wines, popular food including good fresh fish (best views from restaurant up steps), nautical bric-a-brac and local photographs, tartan carpets and two log fires, occasional live music; big-screen sports TV; dogs welcome, a couple of river-view tables outside, open all day Fri-Sun and in summer (when can get very busy). *(Richard Tilbrook)*

LAKE
SX5288
★ Bearslake (01837) 861334
A386 just S of Sourton; EX20 4HQ Rambling low thatched stone pub, leather sofas and high bar chairs on crazy-paved slate floor at one end, three more smallish rooms with woodburners, toby jugs, farm tools and traps, stripped stone, well kept ales such as Otter and Teignworthy, good range of spirits and whiskies, decent wines and enjoyable food, beamed restaurant; free wi-fi through most of the building; children allowed, large sheltered streamside garden, Dartmoor walks, six comfortable bedrooms, generous breakfast, closed Sun evening, otherwise open all day. *(Anon)*

LANDSCOVE
SX7766
Live & Let Live (01803) 762663
SE end of village by Methodist chapel; TQ13 7LZ Friendly open-plan village local, good freshly made food and well kept ales such as Teignworthy, log fire; children and dogs welcome, tables on small front deck and in little orchard across lane, good walks, closed Mon. *(J D O Carter)*

LEE
SS4846
Grampus (01271) 862906
Signed off B3343/A361 W of Ilfracombe; EX34 8LR Attractive unpretentious 14th-c beamed pub, friendly and relaxed, with good range of well kept ales and local ciders, reasonably priced traditional food (not Sun evening), tea room (in season) and shop, skittles, pool and darts, live music Fri; dogs very welcome, lots of tables in appealing sheltered garden, short stroll from sea – superb coast walks, open all day summer weekends. *(Eddie Edwards)*

You can send reports directly to us at feedback@goodguides.com

LIFTON   SX3885

★**Arundell Arms** (01566) 784666

Fore Street; PL16 OAA Good interesting lunchtime food in substantial country-house fishing hotel, warmly welcoming and individual, with rich décor, nice staff and sophisticated service, good choice of wines by the glass, morning coffee with home-made biscuits, afternoon tea, restaurant; also adjacent Courthouse bar, complete with original cells, doing good fairly priced pubby food (not Mon evening), well kept St Austell Tribute and Dartmoor Jail; can arrange fishing tuition – also shooting, deer-stalking and riding; 21 bedrooms, useful A30 stop. *(A E Forbes)*

LITTLEHEMPSTON   SX8162

Pig & Whistle (01803) 863733

Newton Road (A381); TQ9 6LT Large welcoming former coaching inn, enjoyable traditional food and ales such as Dartmoor and Teignworthy, long bar with beams and stripped stone, extensive dining area; free wi-fi; children welcome, decked front terrace, two bedrooms, open all day. *(Anon)*

LITTLEHEMPSTON   SX8162

Tally Ho (01803) 862316

Off A381 NE of Totnes; TQ9 6LY Old community-owned pub opposite church, neat and cosy, with low black beams and stripped stone walls, traditional food from sandwiches to steaks, ales from Bays, Dartmoor and Hunters, friendly atmosphere; children welcome, picnic-sets on flower-filled terrace, open all day Sun (food till 6pm), closed Mon. *(Anon)*

LOWER ASHTON   SX8484

Manor Inn (01647) 252304

Ashton signposted off B3193 N of Chudleigh; EX6 7QL Well run country pub under friendly hard-working licensees, good quality sensibly priced food including lunchtime set menu, well kept ales such as Otter and Teignworthy, good choice of wines, open fires in both bars, back restaurant in converted smithy; dogs welcome, disabled access, garden picnic-sets with nice rural outlook, open all day Sun, closed Mon. *(Anon)*

LUPPITT   ST1606

★**Luppitt Inn** (01404) 891613

Back roads N of Honiton; EX14 4RT Unspoilt basic farmhouse pub tucked away in lovely countryside, an amazing survivor, with chatty long-serving landlady, tiny room with corner bar and a table, another not much bigger with fireplace, cheap Otter tapped from the cask, intriguing metal puzzles made by a neighbour, no food or

music, lavatories across the yard; closed lunchtime and Sun evening. *(Anon)*

LUTON   SX9076

★**Elizabethan** (01626) 775425

Haldon Moor; TQ13 0BL Tucked-away much-altered low-beamed dining pub (once owned by Elizabeth I); wide choice of good well presented food including daily specials and popular Sun lunch, three well kept ales and several reasonably priced wines by the glass, friendly efficient service and thriving atmosphere; children welcome, pretty front garden, open all day weekends. *(Anon)*

LYDFORD   SX5184

Castle Inn (01822) 820241

Off A386 Okehampton–Tavistock; EX20 4BH Tudor inn owned by St Austell, friendly helpful staff, traditional twin bars with big slate flagstones, bowed low beams and granite walls, high backed settles and four inglenook log fires, notable stained-glass door, good popular food, restaurant; free wi-fi; children and dogs welcome in certain areas, seats out at front and in sheltered back garden, lovely NT river gorge nearby, eight bedrooms, open all day. *(M G Hart)*

LYMPSTONE   SX9884

Swan (01395) 272644

The Strand, by station entrance; EX8 5ET Well cared for pub with nice old-fashioned décor, split-level panelled dining area with leather sofas by big fire, enjoyable home-made food including local fish, well kept ales such as Otter, Palmers, St Austell and Wadworths, short interesting wine list, welcoming helpful staff, games room with pool, some live music; children welcome, picnic-sets out at front and smokers' area, popular with cyclists (bike racks provided), open all day. *(Peter Salmon, Mrs Jo Rees)*

LYNMOUTH   SS7249

Rising Sun (01598) 753223

Harbourside; EX35 6EG Wonderful position overlooking harbour; bustling beamed and stripped-stone bar with good fire, four Exmoor ales, popular food from comprehensive menu (emphasis on fish), upmarket hotel side with attractive restaurant; background music; dogs welcome, gardens behind, bedrooms in cottagey old thatched building, parking can be a problem – expensive during the day, sparse at night. *(Taff Thomas, Lynda and Trevor Smith)*

MEAVY   SX5467

★**Royal Oak** (01822) 852944

Off B3212 E of Yelverton; PL20 6PJ Partly 15th-c pub taking its name from 800-year-old oak tree on green opposite;

Half pints: by law, a pub should not charge more for half a pint than half the price of a full pint, unless it shows that half-pint price on its price list.

heavy-beamed L-shaped bar with church pews, red plush banquettes, old agricultural prints and church pictures, smaller locals' bar with flagstones and big open-hearth fireplace, separate dining room, well liked food and good friendly service, Dartmoor ales and guests, farm ciders, a dozen wines by the glass and several malt whiskies, cribbage and board games; background music; children and dogs (in bar) welcome, picnic-sets out in front and on green, pretty Dartmoor-edge village, open all day in summer, all day weekends in winter. *(Hugh Roberts)*

MILTONCOMBE   SX4865
★ **Who'd A Thought It** (01822) 853313
Village signed off A386 S of Yelverton; PL20 6HP Attractive 16th-c whitewashed pub; black-panelled bar with interesting bric-a-brac, woodburner, barrel seats and high-backed winged settles, two separate dining areas, good home-made food from pub favourites up using local produce including own pork, friendly efficient staff, Sharps Doom Bar and three other west country ales, farm ciders, decent choice of wines; background music; children and dogs welcome, a few tables out in front, more in back beer garden with stream, flaming torches may light your way from car park on summer nights, two bedroom in converted hayloft, open all day weekends summer (all day Sun winter). *(Jan Gould)*

MOLLAND   SS8028
London (01769) 550269
Village signed off B3227 E of South Molton; EX36 3NG Proper Exmoor inn at its busiest in the shooting season; two small linked rooms by old-fashioned central servery, local stag-hunting pictures, cushioned benches and plain chairs around rough stripped trestle tables, Exmoor Ale, attractive beamed room on left with famous stag story on wall, panelled dining room on right with big curved settle by fireplace (good hunting and game bird prints), enjoyable home-made food using fresh local produce including seasonal game, small hall with stuffed birds and animals; fine Victorian lavatories; children and dogs welcome, picnic-sets in cottagey garden, untouched early 18th-c box pews in church next door, two bedrooms. *(Jeremy Whitehorn)*

MONKLEIGH   SS4520
Bell (01805) 938285
A388; EX39 5JS Well looked after thatched and beamed 17th-c village pub, carpeted bar and small restaurant, three real ales, enjoyable reasonably priced food including daily specials and Sun carvery, friendly staff; background music, darts; children welcome (till 9pm) and dogs (treats for good ones), wheelchair access, garden with raised deck, views and good walks, closed Mon. *(Phil and Jane Hodson)*

MORCHARD BISHOP   SS7607
London Inn (01363) 877222
Signed off A377 Crediton–Barnstaple; EX17 6NW Prettily placed 16th-c village coaching inn, helpful friendly service (mother and daughter licensees), good generous home-made food (best to book weekends), Fullers London Pride and a guest, low-beamed open-plan carpeted bar with woodburner in large fireplace, thriving local atmosphere, pool, darts and skittles, small dining room; children and dogs welcome. *(Anon)*

MORTEHOE   SS4545
Chichester Arms (01271) 870411
Off A361 Ilfracombe–Braunton; EX34 7DU Blue-shuttered former 16th-c vicarage, enjoyable local food including good crab, well kept west country ales, quick friendly service, panelled lounge, dining room and pubby locals' bar with darts and pool, interesting old local photographs; skittle alley and games machines in summer children's room, dogs welcome in bar, tables out in front and in paved side garden, lovely coast walk, open all day. *(Dr D J and Mrs S C Walker)*

NEWTON ABBOT   SX8671
★ **Olde Cider Bar** (01626) 354221
East Street; TQ12 2LD Basic old-fashioned cider house with plenty of atmosphere; around 30 interesting reasonably priced farm ciders (helpful long-serving landlord may offer tasters – some very strong), a couple of perries, more in bottles, good country wines from the cask too, baguettes, pasties etc, stools made from cask staves, barrel seats and wall benches, flagstones and bare boards; small back games room with bar billiards and machines; terrace tables, open all day. *(Anon)*

NEWTON ABBOT   SX8671
Richard Hopkins (01626) 323930
Queen Street; TQ12 2EH Big partly divided open-plan Wetherspoons, busy and friendly, with ten real ales, proper cider and their usual good value food; covered tables out at front, open all day from 8am. *(Anon)*

NEWTON ABBOT   SX8468
Two Mile Oak (01803) 812411
A381 2 miles S, at Denbury/ Kingskerswell crossroads; TQ12 6DF Appealing beamed coaching inn, log fires, black panelling, traditional furnishings and candlelit alcoves, well kept Bass, Otter and guests tapped from the cask, nine wines by the glass, enjoyable well priced pubby food from sandwiches and baked potatoes up (special diets catered for), decent coffee, cheerful staff; background music; children and dogs welcome, round picnic-sets on terrace and lawn, open all day. *(Anon)*

NEWTON FERRERS   SX5447
Dolphin (01752) 872007
Riverside Road East: Newton Hill off Church Park (B3186) then left; PL8 1AE Shuttered 18th-c pub in attractive setting; L-shaped bar with a few low black beams, pews and benches on slate floors and some white plank panelling, open fire, three well kept Badger ales and decent wines by the glass, enjoyable traditional food including good fish and chips and daily specials, friendly staff; children and dogs welcome, terraces over lane looking down on River Yealm and yachts, open all day in summer when it can get packed, parking limited. *(M J Winterton, Mrs Carole Baldock)*

NEWTON ST CYRES   SX8798
Beer Engine (01392) 851282
Off A377 towards Thorverton; EX5 5AX Friendly former railway hotel brewing its own beers since the 1980s, wide choice of good home-made food including local fish and popular Sun lunch; children welcome, decked verandah, steps down to garden, open all day. *(Anon)*

NEWTON TRACEY   SS5226
★ Hunters (01271) 858339
B3232 Barnstaple–Torrington; EX31 3PL Extended 15th-c pub with massive low beams and two inglenooks, good reasonably priced freshly made food from pub standards up, two well kept St Austell ales and Jollyboat Mainbrace, decent wines, efficient friendly service; soft background music; children and dogs welcome, disabled access using ramp, skittle alley popular with locals, tables on small terrace behind, open all day. *(Dr D J and Mrs S C Walker, Mr and Mrs P R Thomas, Theocsbrian)*

NOMANSLAND   SS8313
Mount Pleasant (01884) 860271
B3137 Tiverton–South Molton; EX16 8NN Informal country local with good mix of customers, huge fireplaces in long low-beamed main bar, well kept ales such as Cotleigh, Exmoor and Sharps, several wines by the glass, Weston's cider, good freshly cooked hearty food all day from baguettes up, friendly attentive service, happy mismatch of simple well worn furniture including comfy old sofa, candles on tables, country pictures, daily papers, cosy dining room (former smithy with original forge), darts in public bar; background music; well behaved children and dogs welcome, picnic-sets in back garden. *(Jeremy Whitehorn)*

NORTH BOVEY   SX7483
★ Ring of Bells (01647) 440375
Off A382/B3212 SW of Moretonhampstead; TQ13 8RB Bulgy-walled thatched inn dating from the 13th c, low beams, flagstones, big log fire, sturdy rustic tables and winding staircases, good imaginative local food, well kept St Austell, Teignworthy and guests, plenty of wines by the glass from good list, charming licensees and friendly staff, carpeted dining room and overspill room; children and dogs (in bar) welcome, garden by lovely tree-covered village green below Dartmoor, good walks, five big clean bedrooms, open all day. *(Julie and Bill Ryan, B J Harding)*

NOSS MAYO   SX5447
★ Ship (01752) 872387
Off A379 via B3186, E of Plymouth; PL8 1EW Charming setting overlooking inlet and visiting boats, thick-walled bars with bare boards and log fires, six well kept west country beers including local Summerskills, good choice of wines and malt whiskies, popular food all day from wide-ranging menu, friendly efficient service, lots of local pictures and charts, books, newspapers and board games, restaurant upstairs; can get crowded in good weather, parking restricted at high tide; children and dogs (downstairs) welcome, plenty of seats on heated waterside terrace. *(John Evans, Christian Mole, Lynda and Trevor Smith, Roy Hoing and others)*

OAKFORD   SS9121
Red Lion (01398) 351592
Rookery Hill; EX16 9ES Friendly 17th-c village coaching inn (partly rebuilt in Georgian times) refurbished under new owner, well kept Otter ales and reasonably priced pubby food including OAP lunch deal Thurs, woodburner in big inglenook; bedrooms, open all day Sun till 10pm, closed Mon lunchtime. *(Anon)*

OTTERTON   SY0885
Kings Arms (01395) 568416
Fore Street; EX9 7HB Big open-plan carpeted pub dating from the 1700s and handy for families from extensive nearby caravan site, enjoyable pubby food from baguettes up including good fresh fish, Sun carvery, fast friendly service even when busy, O'Hanlons and Otter, reasonable prices, restaurant, darts, pool and good skittle alley doubling as family room; TV, free wi-fi; dogs welcome, beautiful evening view from attractive back garden with play area, also a covered terrace, 12 bedrooms, charming village, open all day. *(George Atkinson, Roger and Donna Huggins)*

PAIGNTON   SX8860
Isaac Merritt (01803) 556066
Torquay Road; TQ3 3AA Spacious well run Wetherspoons conversion of former shopping arcade, good range of ales and usual low-priced food all day, friendly welcoming service, cosy alcoves and comfortable family dining area, air conditioning; covered area at back for smokers, good disabled access, open from 8am. *(Anon)*

PARRACOMBE   SS6644
⋆**Fox & Goose** (01598) 763239
Off A39 Blackmoor Gate–Lynton;
EX31 4PE Popular rambling Victorian
pub, hunting and farming memorabilia
and interesting old photographs, well kept
Cotleigh and Exmoor, farm cider, good
choice of wines by the glass, generous well
prepared food from imaginative menu,
friendly staff, log fire, separate dining
room; children and dogs welcome, small
front verandah, riverside terrace and
garden room, three bedrooms, open all day
in summer. *(Anon)*

PETER TAVY   SX5177
⋆**Peter Tavy Inn** (01822) 810348
Off A386 near Mary Tavy, N of Tavistock;
PL19 9NN Old stone village inn tucked
away at end of little lane, bustling low-
beamed bar with high-backed settles on
black flagstones, mullioned windows, good
log fire in big stone fireplace, snug dining
area with carved wooden chairs, hops on
beams and plenty of pictures, up to five well
kept west country ales, Winkleigh's cider,
good wine and malt whisky choice, well
liked food including vegetarian options,
quick friendly service, separate restaurant;
children and dogs welcome, picnic-sets
in pretty garden, peaceful moorland
views. *(Stephen Shepherd, Helen and Brian*
Edgeley, Christian Mole, Roy Hoing)

PLYMOUTH   SX4953
Bridge (01752) 403888
Shaw Way, Mount Batten; PL9 9XH
Modern two-storey bar-restaurant with
terrace and balcony overlooking busy
Yacht Haven Marina, enjoyable food
from sandwiches and pub favourites up
including good value set menu, nice choice
of wines by the glass, St Austell Tribute
and Sharps Doom Bar, impressive fish tank
upstairs; children welcome, well behaved
dogs downstairs, open all day from 9am
(8.30am weekends) for breakfast. *(Anon)*

PLYMOUTH   SX4854
China House (01752) 661592
Sutton Harbour, via Sutton Road off
Exeter Street (A374); PL4 0DW
Attractive Vintage Inns conversion of
Plymouth's oldest warehouse, lovely boaty
views, dimly lit and inviting interior with
beams and flagstones, bare slate and
stone walls, two good log fires, interesting
photographs, their usual food including
good value set menu, Butcombe, St Austell
Tribute and a guest, plenty of wines by the
glass; background music, no dogs; children
welcome, good parking and disabled

access/facilities, tables out on waterside
balconies, open all day. *(Roger and Donna*
Huggins)

PLYMOUTH   SX4854
Dolphin (01752) 660876
Barbican; PL1 2LS Unpretentious chatty
local with good range of well kept cask-
tapped ales including Bass and St Austell,
open fire, Beryl Cook paintings (even one
of the friendly landlord), no food but can
bring your own; dogs welcome, open all day.
(Anon)

PLYMOUTH   SX4555
Lounge (01752) 561330
Stopford Place, Stoke; PL1 4QT
Old-fashioned panelled corner local with
cheery landlord and chatty regulars, well
kept Bass and guests, decent lunchtime
pubby food; busy on match days; dogs
welcome, open all day weekends, closed
Mon lunchtime. *(Anon)*

PLYMOUTH   SX4853
Thistle Park (01752) 204890
Commercial Road; PL4 0LE Welcoming
bare-boards pub near National Maritime
Aquarium, well kept South Hams ales (used
to be brewed here) and guests, Thatcher's
cider, lunchtime bar food and evening thai
restaurant (upstairs), interesting décor,
open fire, back pool room, juke box, live
music at weekends; no children, dogs in
bar, roof garden and smokers' shelter, open
all day till midnight (2am Fri, Sat). *(Anon)*

PLYMTREE   ST0502
Blacksmiths Arms (01884) 277474
Near church; EX15 2JU Friendly 19th-c
beamed and carpeted pub with reasonably
priced home-made food (takeaways
available), three well kept changing local
ales and decent choice of wines by the glass,
pool room and skittle alley; children welcome
and dogs (theirs is called Jagermeister),
garden with boules and play area, open
all day Sat, till 4pm Sun and from 6pm
weekdays. *(Anon)*

POUNDSGATE   SX7072
Tavistock Inn (01364) 631251
B3357 continuation; TQ13 7NY
Picturesque old pub liked by walkers (plenty
of nearby hikes), beams and other original
features like narrow-stepped granite spiral
staircase, original flagstones, ancient log
fireplaces, Courage, Otter and Wychwood,
traditional bar food; children and dogs
welcome, tables on front terrace and in quiet
back garden, pretty flower boxes, open (and
food) all day in summer. *(Simon Lindsey,*
Rose Rogers)

By law, pubs must show a price list of their drinks. Let us know if you're
inconvenienced by any breach of this law.

PUSEHILL   SS4228
Pig on the Hill (01237) 459222
Off B3226 near Westward Ho!;
EX39 5AH Extensively refurbished
restauranty pub (originally a cowshed)
reopened 2013 under new owners; good
choice of fresh well presented food (booking
advised evenings and weekends), friendly
service, Country Life and local guests, games
room with skittle alley; background music;
children and dogs (in bar) welcome, disabled
facilities, good views from terrace tables and
picnic-sets on grass, play area, boules, open
all day. *(Anon)*

RINGMORE   SX6545
Journeys End (01548) 810205
Signed off B3392 at Pickwick Inn,
St Anns Chapel, near Bigbury; best to
park opposite church; TQ7 4HL Ancient
village inn with friendly chatty licensees,
character panelled lounge and other linked
rooms, Sharps Doom Bar and local guests
tapped from the cask, farm cider, decent
wines, well executed nicely presented food
from good shortish menu (not Sun evening,
best to book in summer), good value set
lunch, log fires, family dining conservatory
with board games; dogs welcome, pleasant
big terraced garden with boules, attractive
setting near thatched cottages and not far
from the sea, open all day weekends, closed
Mon. *(Christian Mole, MP, Tracey and Phil*
Eagles, Peter Travis)

ROBOROUGH   SS5717
New Inn (01805) 603247
Off B3217 N of Winkleigh; EX19 8SY
Tucked-away 16th-c thatched village pub
under new management, cheerful and busy,
with well kept ales and enjoyable not over-
ambitious food, beamed bar with woodburner,
tiny back room leading up to dining room;
seats on sunny front terrace. *(Mark Flynn)*

ROCKBEARE   SY0195
★ Jack in the Green (01404) 822240
Signed from A30 bypass E of Exeter;
EX5 2EE Neat welcoming dining pub
run well by long-serving owner; flagstoned
lounge bar with comfortable sofas, ales
such as Butcombe, Otter and Sharps, local
cider, a dozen wines by the glass (over
100 by the bottle), popular top notch food
and emphasis on larger dining side with
old hunting/shooting photographs and
leather chesterfields by big woodburner,
good friendly service; background music;
well behaved children welcome, no dogs
inside, disabled facilities, plenty of seats
in courtyard, open all day Sun, closed 25
Dec-5 Jan, quite handy for M5. *(John Evans,*

Stephen Shepherd, Mrs J Ekins-Daukes, David
and Helena Johnson)

SALCOMBE   SX7439
Fortescue (01548) 842868
Union Street, end of Fore Street;
TQ8 8BZ Proper pub with five linked
nautical-theme rooms, enjoyable good value
food served promptly by cheerful helpful
staff, well kept ales such as Bass, Courage
and Otter, decent wines, good woodburner,
old local black and white shipping pictures,
big public bar with games, small dining
room; children welcome, courtyard picnic-
sets. *(Anon)*

SALCOMBE   SX7439
★ Victoria (01548) 842604
Fore Street; TQ8 8BU Attractive 19th-c
pub opposite harbour car park, neat nautical
décor, comfortable furnishings and big open
fires, enjoyable sensibly priced home-made
food, well kept St Austell ales, decent wines,
friendly enthusiastic service, separate family
area; background music, can get busy at
weekends; dogs welcome, large sheltered
tiered garden behind with good play area and
chickens, bedrooms. *(Ken Parry)*

SAMPFORD COURTENAY   SS6300
New Inn (01837) 82247
B3072 Crediton–Holsworthy; EX20 2TB
Attractive 16th-c thatched restaurant and
bar, nice choice of good interesting food from
landlord-chef at reasonable prices, local ales
and cider, relaxed atmosphere with candlelit
tables, beams and log fires; garden picnic-
sets, picturesque village. *(D P and M A Miles)*

SAMPFORD PEVERELL   ST0314
★ Globe (01884) 821214
A mile from M5 junction 27, village
signed from Tiverton turn-off; Lower
Town; EX16 7BJ Spacious and comfortable
village inn backing on to Grand Western
Canal; enjoyable good value pub food (all
day weekends) from baguettes to grills and
popular Sun carvery, lunchtime deal (Mon-
Thurs), four well kept ales including Otter
and Sharps Doom Bar, good wine choice,
friendly efficient staff, cosy beamed lounge
with boothed eating area, back restaurant;
background and some live music, free
wi-fi; children and dogs welcome, disabled
facilities, courtyard and enclosed garden with
play equipment, six bedrooms (breakfast for
non-residents too), open all day. *(Mr and Mrs*
Richard Osborne, Tina and David Woods-Taylor)

SANDY PARK   SX7189
Sandy Park Inn (01647) 433267
A382 Whiddon Down–Moretonhampstead;
TQ13 8JW Welcoming little thatched inn,

If you report on a pub that's not a featured entry, please tell us any lunchtimes or
evenings when it doesn't serve bar food.

beams and flagstones, varnished built-in wall settles around nice tables, high stools by counter, Dartmoor, Otter and a guest ale, good food from sensibly short menu including pizzas and a vegetarian choice, small dining room on left, inner snug; open mike night third Sun of month; children and dogs welcome, big garden with fine views, smokers' shelter, four comfortable bedrooms, open all day. *(Anon)*

SCORRITON
SX7068
Tradesmans Arms (01364) 631206
Main road through village; TQ11 0JB Welcoming open-plan Dartmoor-edge pub, tasty well presented local food, Dartmoor, Otter and guests, friendly service, fresh flowers and woodburner, wonderful rolling hill views from conservatory and garden, Thurs quiz; dogs welcome, bedrooms, open all day Sun. *(Anon)*

SHALDON
SX9372
Clifford Arms (01626) 872311
Fore Street; TQ14 0DE Attractive 18th-c open-plan pub on two levels, clean and bright, with good range of home-made blackboard food (not mid Jan), up to five mainly local ales, eight wines by the glass, low beams and stone walls, wood or carpeted floors, log fire, live jazz Sun and Mon; children over 5 welcome, front terrace and decked area at back with palms, pleasant seaside village. *(Anon)*

SHALDON
SX9472
London Inn (01626) 872453
Bank Street/The Green; TQ14 8AW Popular bustling pub opposite bowling green in pretty waterside village, good generous reasonably priced food using local suppliers (excellent mussels), Otter and St Austell ales, friendly efficient service; background music, pool; children and dogs (in bar) welcome, open all day. *(J D O Carter)*

SHALDON
SX9272
Shipwrights Arms (01626) 873232
B3195 to Newton Abbot; TQ14 0AQ Friendly two-bar end of terrace village pub under newish licensees, open fires, three well kept local ales such as Otter, enjoyable food from short menu, some live music; dogs welcome, River Teign view from walled back terrace. *(Anon)*

SHEBBEAR
SS4309
★ Devils Stone Inn (01409) 281210
Off A3072 or A388 NE of Holsworthy; EX21 5RU Neatly kept 17th-c beamed village pub reputed to be one of England's most haunted; seats in front of open woodburner, long L-shaped pew and second smaller one, flagstone floors, St Austell Tribute and other west country beers, decent wines, enjoyable food in dining room across corridor, plain back games room with pool and darts; picnic-sets on front terrace and in

garden behind, right by actual Devil's Stone (turned by villagers on 5 Nov to keep the devil at bay), eight bedrooms (steep stairs to some), fishing and shooting organised, open all day weekends. *(J V Dadswell)*

SHEEPWASH
SS4806
★ Half Moon (01409) 231376
Off A3072 Holsworthy–Hatherleigh at Highampton; EX21 5NE Ancient inn loved by anglers for its 12 miles of River Torridge fishing (salmon, sea trout and brown trout), small tackle shop and rod room with drying facilities; simply furnished main bar, lots of beams, log fire in big fireplace, well kept St Austell, Sharps and a local guest, several wines by the glass, wide choice of enjoyable food including blackboard specials, friendly service (may slow at busy times), separate extended dining room, bar billiards; children and dogs welcome, 13 bedrooms (four in converted stables), generous breakfast, tiny Dartmoor village off the beaten track. *(J V Dadswell, Roy Hoing)*

SIDFORD
SY1389
★ Blue Ball (01395) 514062
A3052 just N of Sidmouth; EX10 9QL Handsome thatched pub in same friendly family for over 100 years and restored after 2006 fire; central bar with three main areas each with log fire, pale beams, nice mix of wooden dining chairs around circular tables on patterned carpet, prints, horsebrasses and plenty of bric-a-brac, well kept Bass, Otter, St Austell and Sharps, popular bar food, pleasant attentive service, chatty public bar, darts, board games, skittle alley; background music and games machine; children and dogs welcome, terrace and flower-filled garden, smokers' gazebo, coastal walks close by, bedrooms, open all day from 8am for breakfast. *(Dennis and Doreen Haward, Phil and Sally Gorton, Neil and Heather Cross, Roger and Donna Huggins)*

SIDFORD
SY1390
Rising Sun (01395) 513722
School Street; EX10 9PF Friendly two-bar traditional pub, Bass, local Branscombe and a guest, well priced pubby menu including OAP weekday lunch deal, mix of tables and chairs on wood floors, old local photographs on white walls, pool and darts, monthly quiz; children welcome away from bar, resident chihuahua Tammy, steep garden behind, car parking at nearby Spar (free after 6pm), open all day weekends (no food Sun evening). *(Roger and Donna Huggins)*

SIDMOUTH
ST1287
Anchor (01395) 514129
Old Fore Street; EX10 8LP Welcoming family-run pub popular for its fresh fish and other good value food, well kept Caledonian ales including one named for them, decent

choice of wines, good service, large carpeted L-shaped room with nautical pictures, steps down to restaurant; tables out in front, more in back beer garden with stage for live acts, open (and food) all day. *(Roger and Donna Huggins)*

SIDMOUTH   SY1287
Dukes (01395) 513320

Esplanade; EX10 8AR More brasserie than pub, but long bar on left has Branscombe Vale and a couple of guests, enjoyable food all day specialising in local fish (best to book in the evening), efficient young staff, daily papers, linked areas including conservatory and flagstoned eating area (once a chapel), smart contemporary décor; big-screen TV, may be summer queues; children welcome, disabled facilities, prom-view terrace tables, bedrooms in adjoining Elizabeth Hotel, open, all day. *(Guy Vowles, Michael Butler, Roger and Donna Huggins)*

SIDMOUTH   SY1287
★**Swan** (01395) 512849

York Street; EX10 8BY Cheerful old-fashioned town-centre local, well kept Wells & Youngs and good value blackboard food from sandwiches up, friendly staff, lounge bar with interesting pictures and memorabilia, darts and woodburner in bigger light and airy public bar with boarded walls and ceilings, daily newspapers, separate dining area; no under-14s, dogs welcome, flower-filled garden with smokers' area, open all day. *(Phil and Sally Gorton, Roger and Donna Huggins)*

SILVERTON   SS9503
Lamb (01392) 860272

Fore Street; EX5 4HZ Flagstoned local run well by friendly landlord, Exe Valley, Otter and a guest tapped from stillage casks, inexpensive home-made pubby food including specials, separate eating area, skittle alley; handy for Killerton (NT), open all day weekends. *(Anon)*

SLAPTON   SX8245
★**Queens Arms** (01548) 580800

Sands Road corner, before church; TQ7 2PN Smartly kept one-room village local with welcoming staff and locals, good straightforward inexpensive food, four ales including Dartmoor and Otter, snug comfortable corners, fascinating World War II photos and scrapbooks, dominoes and draughts; children and dogs welcome, lots of tables in lovely suntrap stepped garden. *(Steve Whalley)*

SOURTON   SX5390
★**Highwayman** (01837) 861243

A386, S of junction with A30; EX20 4HN Unique place – a fantasy of dimly lit stonework and flagstone-floored burrows and alcoves, all sorts of things to look at, one room a make-believe sailing galleon; a couple of local ales and farm cider, organic wines,

good proper sandwiches and home-made pasties, friendly chatty service, nostalgic background music; children allowed in certain areas, outside fairy-tale pumpkin house and an old-lady-who-lived-in-the-shoe house, period bedrooms with four-posters and half-testers, bunkrooms for walkers/cyclists. *(Anon)*

SOUTH BRENT   SX6960
Oak (01364) 72133

Station Road; TQ10 9BE Friendly village pub with well priced traditional and modern food, three well kept local ales, good choice of wines by the glass, welcoming helpful service, comfortable open-plan bar with some leather sofas, restaurant, Weds folk night; children and dogs welcome, small courtyard, five bedrooms, little nearby parking. *(David Jackman)*

SOUTH ZEAL   SX6593
★**Oxenham Arms** (01837) 840244

Off A30/A382; EX20 2JT Wonderful building first licensed in 1477 – before that a monastery built around a Neolithic standing stone that still survives here; heavily beamed and partly panelled front bar with elegant mullioned windows and Stuart fireplaces, mix of seats around oak tables on bare boards, small inner room with another open fire, Dartmoor, Exmoor, Teignworthy and a Red Rock beer named for them, traditional cider and nice wines by the glass, good popular seasonal food including special of the day; regular live folk and jazz; children welcome, dogs in bar, curved stone steps up to four-acre garden with fine views, walks from the door, bedrooms, open all day Sat in summer. *(David and Stella Martin, Ian Herdman)*

STAPLE CROSS   ST0320
Staplecross Inn (01398) 361374

Holcombe Rogus–Hockworthy; TA21 0NH Traditional family-run village local, well cooked pubby food including blackboard specials, Otter, St Austell and a guest beer, three linked rooms with quarry tiles, stripped stone, beams and substantial woodburners in big fireplaces; well behaved children and dogs welcome, open all day weekends, from 4pm weekdays, closed Mon. *(Anon)*

STAVERTON   SX7964
★**Sea Trout** (01803) 762274

Village signposted from A384 NW of Totnes; TQ9 6PA Welcoming partly 15th-c inn with good mix of customers, neat rambling beamed lounge with fishing theme, elegant wheelbacks and mix of tables on carpet or wood floors, simple locals bar with stag's head, horsebrasses and large stuffed fish above woodburner, Palmers ales, good interesting food as well as pub standards, smartly furnished panelled restaurant, conservatory; children and dogs (in bar) welcome, attractive terrace garden behind, well equipped bedrooms, fishing available on nearby River Dart, open all day from 8am. *(Paul Humphreys, Lynda and Trevor Smith)*

STICKLEPATH   SX6494
★ **Devonshire** (01837) 840626

Off A30 at Whiddon Down or Okehampton; EX20 2NW Welcoming old-fashioned 16th-c thatched village local next to Finch Foundry museum (NT); low-beamed slate-floor bar with big log fire, longcase clock and easy-going old furnishings, key collection, sofa in small snug, well kept low-priced ales tapped from the cask, farm cider, good value sandwiches, soup and home-made pasties from the Aga, games room, lively folk night first Sun of month; dogs welcome (pub has its own), wheelchair access from car park, good walks, bedrooms, open all day Fri, Sat. *(Chris and Angela Buckell)*

STOKE FLEMING   SX8648
Green Dragon (01803) 770238

Church Street; TQ6 0PX Popular and friendly village pub with yachtsman landlord, well worn-in interior with beams and flagstones, boat pictures and charts, sleepy dogs and cats, snug with sofas and armchairs, grandfather clock and open fire, well kept ales including Otter, Addlestone's and Aspall's ciders, good choice of wines by the glass, enjoyable range of local food including good fish soup; tables out on partly covered heated terrace, lovely garden, handy for coast path. *(Richard Tilbrook)*

STOKE GABRIEL   SX8457
★ **Church House** (01803) 782384

Off A385 just W of junction with A3022; Church Walk; TQ9 6SD Friendly and popular early 14th-c pub; lounge bar with fine medieval beam-and-plank ceiling, black oak partition wall, window seats cut into thick butter-coloured walls, woodburner in huge fireplace, ancient mummified cat, well kept Bass, Sharps Doom Bar and a guest, enjoyable good value food, little locals' bar; background music, Sun quiz; no under-14s, dogs welcome in bar, picnic-sets on small front terrace, old stocks (can use them if you wish), limited parking, open all day. *(Paul Humphreys, Eddie Edwards)*

STOKENHAM   SX8042
Church House (01548) 580253

Opposite church, N of A379 towards Torcross; TQ7 2SZ Attractive extended old pub overlooking common, three open-plan areas, low beams, mix of seating on flagstones and lots of knick-knacks, Greene King, Otter and guests, local organic cider, several wines by the glass, well liked food from good sandwiches up using local produce, dining conservatory, live music; children and dogs (in bar) welcome, picnic-sets on lawn with play area, interesting church next door. *(Anon)*

STOKENHAM   SX8042
Tradesmans Arms (01548) 580996

Just off A379 Dartmouth–Kingsbridge; TQ7 2SZ Picturesque partly thatched 14th-c pub overlooking village green, good attractively presented food using local ingredients, sensible wine list and well kept local beers, traditional low-beamed cottagey interior, log fire, restaurant; children and dogs welcome, nice bedrooms. *(Simon Lindsey, Rose Rogers, Lynda and Trevor Smith)*

STRETE   SX8446
Kings Arms (01803) 770377

A379 SW of Dartmouth; TQ6 0RW Popular former 1830s hotel refurbished by present licensees; bar with dining area up steps, log fire, good home-made food from regular changing menu, Otter and St Austell ales; well behaved children and dogs welcome, back terrace and garden with lovely views over Start Bay, open all day weekends, closed Mon. *(Ron and Val Broom)*

THORVERTON   SS9202
Thorverton Arms (01392) 860205

Village signed off A396 Exeter–Tiverton; EX5 5NS Spacious 16th-c coaching inn with five adjoining areas including log-fire bar and restaurant, good well presented home-made food at reasonable prices, three real ales, welcoming landlord and efficient friendly staff; pool; children and dogs (in bar) welcome, wisteria-draped terrace and sunny garden, pleasant village, six comfortable bedrooms, nice breakfast. *(R T and J C Moggridge)*

THURLESTONE   SX6743
Village Inn (01548) 563525

Part of Thurlestone Hotel; TQ7 3NN Small 16th-c pub attached to smart family-run hotel, good food from sandwiches to blackboard specials, well kept local beers, beams and comfortable country-style furnishings, central fireplace with gas fire, quiz Tues, some live music; free wi-fi; children and dogs welcome, picnic-sets out at front, handy for coast path, open all day Fri, Sat and in high season. *(B J Harding)*

TOPSHAM   SX9688
★ **Bridge Inn** (01392) 873862

2.5 miles from M5 junction 30: Topsham signposted from exit roundabout; in Topsham follow signpost (A376) Exmouth, on the Elmgrove Road, into Bridge Hill; EX3 0QQ Very special old drinkers' pub (16th-c former maltings) with up to nine well kept ales and in landlady's family for five generations; quite unchanging and completely unspoilt with friendly staff and locals, character small rooms and snugs, traditional furniture including a nice high-backed settle, woodburner, the 'bar' is landlady's front parlour (as notice on the door politely reminds customers), simple food, live folk and blues; no background music, mobile phones or credit cards; children and dogs welcome, picnic-sets overlooking weir. *(Peter Thornton)*

TOPSHAM   SX9687
⋆ **Globe** (01392) 873471
Fore Street; 2 miles from M5 junction 30; EX3 0HR Substantial inn dating from the 16th c, some refurbishment but keeping cosy traditional feel, heavy-beamed bow-windowed bar with open fire, well kept St Austell ales and good interesting home-made food from sandwiches and snacks up, restaurant, daily newspapers and nice relaxed atmosphere; children welcome, dogs in bar, 19 attractive bedrooms (some in courtyard), parking can be tricky, open all day. *(Phil and Sally Gorton)*

TOPSHAM   SX9687
⋆ **Lighter** (01392) 875439
Fore Street; EX3 0HZ Big busy pub looking over quay, quickly served food from good sandwiches and light dishes to fresh fish, three Badger ales kept well, nautical décor, old local photographs, panelling and large central log fire, friendly staff, good children's area; games machines, background music; lots of waterside tables (bird views at half tide), handy for antiques centre but little nearby parking. *(David Crook)*

TOPSHAM   SX9688
Passage House (01392) 873653
Ferry Road, off main street; EX3 0JN Relaxed 18th-c pub with traditional black-beamed bar and slate-floored lower drinking area, good food from sandwiches to local fish, well kept ales and decent wines, friendly service; peaceful terrace looking over moorings and river (lovely at sunset) to nature reserve beyond. *(Mrs Jo Rees, Peter Andrews)*

TORBRYAN   SX8266
⋆ **Old Church House** (01803) 812372
Pub signed off A381; TQ12 5UR 13th-c former farmhouse with attractive bar, lots of locals' benches built into fine panelling, settle and other seats by big log fire, Hunters Pheasant Plucker, Skinners Betty Stogs, St Austell Tribute and changing guest on handpump, several wines by the glass and around 35 malt whiskies, tasty food, helpful staff; comfortable and discreetly lit lounges, one with a splendid deep Tudor inglenook fireplace; background music; comfortable bedrooms (one has woodburner) and good breakfasts. *(David and Angela George, M G Hart, Michael Butler)*

TORCROSS   SX8242
Start Bay (01548) 580553
A379 S of Dartmouth; TQ7 2TQ More fish and chip restaurant than pub but does sell Bass, Otter, local wine and cider; very much set out for eating and exceptionally busy at peak times with staff coping well, food is enjoyable and sensibly priced; wheelback

chairs around dark tables, country pictures, some photographs of storms buffeting the pub, winter coal fire, small drinking area by counter, large family room; no dogs during food times, seats outside (highly prized) looking over pebble beach and wildlife lagoon, open all day. *(Mark Lubienski)*

TORQUAY   SX9166
Crown & Sceptre (01803) 328290
Petitor Road, St Marychurch; TQ1 4QA Two-bar local in 18th-c stone-built beamed coaching inn, five real ales including St Austell, Otter and Wells & Youngs, interesting naval memorabilia and chamber-pot collection, friendly long-serving licensees, basic good value lunchtime food, snacks any time, live jazz Tues, folk Fri; children and dogs welcome, two gardens, open all day Fri-Sun. *(Anon)*

TORQUAY   SX9163
Hole in the Wall (01803) 200755
Park Lane, opposite clock tower; TQ1 2AU Ancient two-bar local near harbour, reasonably priced usual food including good fresh fish, several well kept ales such as Bays, Butcombe and Sharps, Blackawton cider, smooth cobbled floors, low beams and alcoves, lots of nautical brassware, ship models, old local photographs, chamber-pots, restaurant/function room (band nights); can get very busy weekends; some seats out at front, open all day. *(Mrs Sally Scott, Dr and Mrs A K Clarke)*

TOTNES   SX8060
Albert (01803) 863214
Bridgetown; TQ9 5AD Unpretentious slate-hung pub near the river, small bar and two other rooms, low beams, flagstones, panelling, some old settles and lots of knick-knacks, friendly landlord brewing his own good Bridgetown ales, plenty of whiskies, friendly local atmosphere, Albert the pub dog, quiz and music nights, darts; free wi-fi; paved beer garden behind. *(David Jackman)*

TOTNES   SX7960
Bay Horse (01803) 862088
Cistern Street; TQ9 5SP Traditional two-bar inn dating from the 15th c, friendly community-spirited licensees, four well kept changing local ales (regular beer festivals) and good choice of ciders (maybe a winter mulled one), lunchtime bar snacks such as pasties and ploughman's; background music and regular live music including good Sun jazz; children and dogs welcome, nice garden behind, two comfortable bedrooms, good breakfast, open all day. *(Anon)*

TOTNES   SX7960
⋆ **Kingsbridge Inn** (01803) 863324
Leechwell Street; TQ9 5SY Attractive rambling 17th-c pub-restaurant, black beams, timbering and white-painted stone walls, big woodburner, good variety of highly

regarded freshly cooked food including blackboard specials and popular Sun roasts, well kept Otter and nice choice of wines, good friendly service, live music and other events in upstairs Piano Bar, resident ghost; open all day in summer (afternoon break Mon). *(Bruce Jamieson, Richard Tilbrook)*

TOTNES   SX8060
★Royal Seven Stars (01803) 862125
Fore Street, The Plains; TQ9 5DD Exemplary town-centre bar and coffee bar in well run civilised old hotel, friendly and easy-going, with well kept ales and enjoyable generously served food all day from breakfast on, separate brasserie/grill room with adjoining champagne bar; heated tables out in front, river across busy main road, bedrooms. *(Dave Webster, Sue Holland, Michael and Lynne Gittins)*

TRUSHAM   SX8582
Cridford Inn (01626) 853694
Off B3193 NW of Chudleigh, just N of big ARC works; TQ13 0NR Interesting 14th-c thatched pub – Norman in parts, with UK's oldest domestic window, lots of stripped stone, flagstones and stout timbers, inglenook woodburner, low-beamed Vanilla Pod restaurant, well kept ales and decent choice of wines by the glass, food cooked by landlord-chef can be good; children in eating area, nice sunny terrace, outside pizza oven, bedrooms and self-catering cottages, open all day weekends in summer, closed Sun evening in winter. *(M J Winterton)*

TUCKENHAY   SX8156
★Maltsters Arms (01803) 732350
Ashprington Road, off A381 from Totnes; TQ9 7EQ Popular old pub in lovely quiet spot by wooded creek, good food from bar snacks up, well kept west country ales and farm ciders, great range of wines by the glass, friendly service, creek-view restaurant; children and dogs welcome, waterside terrace with open-air bar and summer barbecues, six pleasantly refurbished bedrooms, open all day. *(David Gunn)*

UGBOROUGH   SX6755
Anchor (01752) 690388
Off A3121; PL21 0NG Newly revamped 17th-c beamed village dining pub, interesting menu including one or two pub favourites (no food Sun evening, Mon), bar snacks in separate log-fire bar with ales such as Bass and Sharps Doom Bar, friendly helpful staff, light contemporary décor with local artwork for sale, cookery classes; six bedrooms, open all day. *(Anon)*

UGBOROUGH   SX6755
Ship (01752) 892565
Off A3121 SE of Ivybridge; PL21 0NS Friendly dining pub extended from cosy 16th-c flagstoned core, well divided open-plan eating areas a step down from neat bar

with woodburner, good choice of enjoyable home-made food including some interesting blackboard specials (plenty of fish), cheerful service, well kept Palmers, St Austell and a local guest, nice house wines; background music; children welcome, dogs in bar, tables out in front, open all day Fri-Sun in summer. *(M G Hart, David Jackman, John and Susan Miln, Lynda and Trevor Smith)*

WEARE GIFFARD   SS4722
Cyder Press (01237) 425517
Tavern Gardens; EX39 4QR Welcoming local in pretty village overlooking River Torridge, three real ales including Dartmoor and St Austell, local ciders, enjoyable fairly standard food from baguettes up, inglenook woodburner, darts in public bar, separate dining area; children welcome, garden with play area, beautiful countryside and handy for Tarka Trail, two bedrooms. *(Mark Flynn)*

WEMBURY   SX5349
Odd Wheel (01752) 863052
Knighton Road; PL9 0JD Modernised village pub with well kept west country ales and good reasonably priced fairly traditional food from sandwiches and panini up, good service, restaurant, pool in bar; children welcome, seats out on decking, fenced play area, open (and food) all day weekends. *(Hugh Roberts, Mo and David Trudgill)*

WEMBWORTHY   SS6609
★Lymington Arms (01837) 83572
Lama Cross; EX18 7SA Large early 19th-c beamed dining pub in pleasant country setting, clean and bright, with wide choice of reliably good food including some interesting specials, good service from character landlady and friendly staff, well kept Sharps Doom Bar and Skinners Betty Stogs, Winkleigh farm cider, decent wines, comfortably plush seating and red tablecloths in partly stripped-stone bar, big back restaurant; children welcome, picnic-sets outside, closed Sun evening, Mon and Tues. *(Anon)*

WESTON   ST1400
★Otter (01404) 42594
Off A373, or A30 at W end of Honiton bypass; EX14 3NZ Big busy family pub with heavy low beams, enjoyable good value food (best to book) from light dishes up including lots of vegetarian options, good Sun carvery, OAP specials and other deals, cheerful helpful staff, well kept Cotleigh and Otter ales, good log fire; background music; disabled access, picnic-sets on big lawn leading to River Otter, play area, open all day. *(Bob and Margaret Holder)*

WHIDDON DOWN   SX6992
Post (01647) 231242
Exeter Road, off A30; EX20 2QT Welcoming beamed local with enjoyable good value home-made food in bar and large dining area, Sun carvery, friendly prompt

service, well kept local ales, darts; dogs welcome, small garden with lovely Dartmoor view. *(Mike and Liz Burns)*

WHIMPLE   SY0497
New Fountain (01404) 822350
Off A30 Exeter–Honiton; Church Road; EX5 2TA Unassuming two-bar beamed village pub with friendly local atmosphere, good inexpensive home-made food (not Mon lunchtime) from short unfussy menu, well kept changing beers including O'Hanlons brewed in the village, woodburner; well behaved dogs welcome, some outside seating. *(Michael and Lynne Gittins)*

WONSON   SX6789
★ **Northmore Arms** (01647) 231428
Between Throwleigh and Gidleigh; EX20 2JA Far from smart and a favourite with those who take to its idiosyncratic style (not all do); two simple old-fashioned rooms, log fire and woodburner, low beams and stripped stone, well kept ales such as Dartmoor tapped from the cask, farm cider and decent house wines, good honest home-made food (all day Mon-Sat), darts and board games; children and dogs welcome, picnic-sets outside, bedrooms, beautiful remote walking country, normally open all day. *(Anon)*

WOOLACOMBE   SS4543
Red Barn (01271) 870264
Barton Road/Challacombe Hill Road; EX34 7DF Popular modern seaside bar-restaurant looking out on superb beach, food all day from sandwiches and ciabattas up, well kept St Austell and guest ales, efficient staff coping well when busy, surfing pictures

and memorabilia, live music; children and dogs welcome. *(Eddie Edwards)*

YEALMPTON   SX5851
Rose & Crown (01752) 880223
A379 Kingsbridge–Plymouth; PL8 2EB Central bar counter, all dark wood and heavy brass, solid leather-seated stools, mix of furnishings, stripped-wood floor and open fire, carpeted dining areas, emphasis on popular bar and restaurant food including good value lunchtime/early evening set menu, efficient service even at busy times, three St Austell ales, quite a few wines by the glass and nice coffee; children welcome, dogs in bar, tables in walled garden with pond, also a lawned area, open all day. *(John Evans)*

LUNDY

LUNDY   SS1344
★ **Marisco** (01271) 870870
Get there by ferry (Bideford and Ilfracombe) or helicopter (Hartland Point); EX39 2LY One of England's most isolated pubs (yet busy most nights), great setting, steep trudge up from landing stage, galleried interior with lifebelts and shipwreck salvage, open fire, two St Austell ales named for the island and its spring water on tap, Weston's cider and reasonably priced house wines, good basic food using Lundy produce and lots of fresh seafood, friendly staff, books and games; children welcome, tables outside, souvenir shop, and doubles as general store for the island's few residents, open (and food) all day from breakfast on. *(Stephen and Judith Thomas)*

Dorset

 ASKERSWELL   SY5393 Map 2

Spyway £

Off A35 Bridport–Dorchester; DT2 9EP

Family-run country inn with friendly welcome, unspoilt décor, real ales, well liked food and fine views; bedrooms

This is a lovely pub and our readers continue to enjoy their visits here very much. A simple inn run by a genuinely friendly landlord, it has plenty of customers, fair value food and comfortable bedrooms; breakfasts are good too. The unspoilt little rooms are cosily filled with old-fashioned high-backed settles, cushioned wall and window seats and some tub chairs. Old photos of the pub and rustic scenes are displayed on the walls, and jugs hang from the beams; the warm Rayburn is a bonus on chilly days. Otter Ale and Bitter and a guest such as Butcombe on handpump, ten wines by the glass and farm cider are served by friendly staff. The dining area has old oak beams and timber uprights, red cushioned dining chairs around dark tables on patterned carpet, horse tack and horsebrasses on the walls and a woodburning stove. Two smaller rooms lead off from here. There are marvellous views of the downs and coast from seats on the back terrace and in the garden, and a small children's play area. The pub's steep lane continues up Eggardon Hill, one of the highest points in the region.

Good, popular food includes creamy baked mushrooms with home-made bread, chicken liver and orange pâté, mixed bean chilli, wild boar sausages and mash, fish of the day with chips, corn-fed chicken with wild mushroom and madeira sauce, slow-roasted pork belly with black pudding and mash, and puddings such as sticky toffee pudding and crème brûlée. *Benchmark main dish: pie of the day £10.00. Two-course evening meal £15.00.*

Free house ~ Licensee Tim Wilkes ~ Real ale ~ (01308) 485250 ~ Open 12-3, 6-11 ~ Bar food 12-3, 6-9 ~ Restaurant ~ Children welcome ~ Wi-fi ~ Occasional summer harpist or guitarist ~ Bedrooms: £50/£80 ~ www.spyway-inn.co.uk *Recommended by Itsguy, Dru and Louisa Marshall, Pete Flower, B and M Kendall, Katharine Cowherd*

 BRIDPORT   SY4692 Map 1

Bull

East Street B3162; DT6 3LF

Bustling inn with plenty of room to sit and chat, real ales, lots of coffees, good food and helpful, friendly staff; bedrooms

At any time of day you can be sure of a friendly welcome and an easy-going atmosphere in this former coaching inn. Morning coffee and afternoon tea are popular, and if you're lucky you can grab one of the comfortable squashy armchairs by the warm open fire in the reception area. The bustling bar has another open fire, dark turquoise wall banquettes and white-painted dining chairs around dark tables on wooden floors, flowers and candlelight, and an unusual sculpture of a child lying on the back of a bellowing bull. Cheerful, helpful staff serve Otter Bitter and Ale on handpump, good wines by the glass and ten malt whiskies. French windows lead out to a sheltered courtyard with seats and benches under parasols, and lots of pretty flowers. The relaxed, informal dining room is similarly furnished to the bar, and doubles as the breakfast room; it's incredibly popular in the evening, so booking is essential. Those in the know head upstairs to the tucked-away, cosy, candlelit Venner Bar, which is great fun with its leather chesterfields, ornate gilt-edged period chairs, rugs on floorboards, big mirrors, a large central chandelier and a huge choice of cocktails. The bedrooms are comfortable and the breakfasts extremely good, with home-made bread and conserves.

🍴 As well as sandwiches and rustic bread and chutney with deli items, the popular food includes mussels with chilli, coriander and lemon, spinach and taleggio arancini with basil aioli, burger with cheese and chips, butternut squash, celeriac and thyme risotto with mascarpone, tempura-battered fish and chips, pheasant with red wine jus, and puddings such as rhubarb custard, eton mess and dark chocolate and orange tart with Cointreau syrup and blood orange jelly; they also offer a two- and three-course set lunch. *Benchmark main dish: steak and chips £12.00. Two-course evening meal £19.75.*

Free house ~ Licensees Nikki and Richard Cooper ~ Real ale ~ (01308) 422878 ~ Open 8am-11pm ~ Bar food 12-3, 6.30-9.30 ~ Restaurant ~ Children welcome ~ Dogs allowed in bar ~ Wi-fi ~ Bedrooms: £90/£100 ~ www.thebullhotel.co.uk *Recommended by Ruth May, Harvey Brown, Dr D J and Mrs S C Walker*

BRIDPORT
Stable
At the back of the Bull Hotel; DT6 3LF

SY4692 Map 1

Lots of draught ciders and perry, freshly made pizzas and friendly, helpful service in big, buzzy place

This isn't a proper pub – it's a lively cider and pizza bar tucked away behind the Bull Hotel on the High Street – and much enjoyed by a good mix of customers of all ages. The lofty barn-like room is rustic in design: rough planked walls and ceiling, some big steel columns, two long rows of pale wooden tables flanked by wide benches, hefty wooden candlesticks holding fat candles, and steps up to a raised end area with cushioned red wall benches and brass-studded red leather dining chairs around a few tables. They have St Austell Proper Job on handpump, over 57 varieties of cider (plus lots of bottled cider) and six wines by the glass. It's the easy-going, young-at-heart atmosphere, and music to match, that pulls it all together. An upstairs room (not always open) is similar in style. There are sister operations in Bath, Bristol, Poole and Weymouth.

🍴 As well as a dozen freshly made pizzas, the popular food includes a range of pies (pork; spinach, pumpkin and feta; beef and horseradish; ham, cheese and chutney), salads such as free-range chicken or Rosary goats cheese, and puddings such as apple crumble and warm chocolate brownie with clotted cream. *Benchmark main dish: pizzas £12.50. Two-course evening meal £15.00.*

Free house ~ Licensee Nikki and Richard Cooper ~ Real ale ~ (01308) 426876 ~ Open 12-11; closed weekday lunchtimes in winter ~ Bar food 12-9; 5.30-9 in winter ~

Children welcome ~ Dogs allowed in bar ~ Wi-fi ~ Bedrooms: £90/$100 ~
www.thestabledorset.co.uk *Recommended by Ruth May, Pete Flower*

 BUCKHORN WESTON   ST7524   Map 2
Stapleton Arms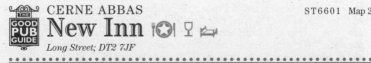
Church Hill; off A30 Shaftesbury–Sherborne via Kington Magna; SP8 5HS

**Handsome old building with a sizeable, civilised bar and separate
dining room, good choice of real ales and wines by the glass, enjoyable
food and friendly service; bedrooms**

With entrance pillars and elegant metal tables and chairs on York
flagstones and gravel, this is a civilised yet informal inn with a friendly
atmosphere and courteous, helpful staff. The large bar has several different
seating areas with dark slate flagstones or floorboards, vases of lilies and
church candles. To the left, leather or pink hessian sofas face one another
across a low table in front of a log fire in a fine stone fireplace, some high
stools are grouped around an equally high shelf, and a circular corner table
comes with chapel chairs. A squashy leather sofa in the centre, with a big
trunk as a table, seems a much prized place to sit, while off to the right is
a long L-shaped wall seat with sizeable cushions, as well as farmhouse and
chapel chairs around wooden tables. Modern art adorns the dark red walls.
Butcombe Bitter, Moor Revival, Plain Hairy Hooker and Keystone Bedrock
on handpump, 32 wines by the glass, farm cider and 16 malt whiskies.
The separate restaurant (with shutters and carpet) has big candles in
the fireplace and in glass jars on the window sills, walls painted blue or
mushroom, and elegant Victorian-style dining chairs around dark tables.
The back garden is charming. The well equipped bedrooms are decorated
in both antique and contemporary style; great breakfasts too. Wincanton
Racecourse is nearby and this is a lovely area for walking; they can provide
boots, maps and picnics.

The particularly good food includes lunchtime sandwiches and baps, ham
hock terrine with piccalilli, crab cakes with chilli and lime mayonnaise,
beer-battered line-caught haddock with triple-cooked chips, chicken breast with
parma ham and spring onion risotto, bream with a red wine glaze and cavolo nero,
and puddings such as steamed orange and treacle sponge and cinnamon crème brûlée
with caramelised apples. *Benchmark main dish: burger using local beef with
bacon, cheese and triple-cooked chips £12.00. Two-course evening meal £20.00.*

Free house ~ Licensee Victoria Reeves ~ Real ale ~ (01963) 370396 ~ Open 10-3, 6-11;
11-11 Sat; 12-10 Sun ~ Bar food 12-3, 6-10 ~ Restaurant ~ Children welcome ~ Dogs
allowed in bar ~ Bedrooms: £70/£90 ~ www.thestapletonarms.com
Recommended by Mark Flynn

 CERNE ABBAS   ST6601   Map 2
New Inn
Long Street; DT2 7JF

Dorset Dining Pub of the Year

**Carefully refurbished former coaching inn with character bar
and two dining rooms, friendly licensees, local ales and inventive
food; fine bedrooms**

Several of our readers describe their visits to this lovely place as 'a real
treat' – and it really is a first class all-rounder. It was sympathetically
refurbished a couple of years ago by the friendly, hands-on licensees, who

have carefully kept many of its original features and much of its character. The bar has a solid oak counter, an attractive mix of old dining tables and chairs on slate or polished wooden floors, settles built into various nooks and crannies, and a woodburner in the opened-up York stone fireplace; there are lovely mullioned windows and heavy oak beams throughout. Palmers Copper, Dorset Gold and IPA on handpump, a dozen wines by the glass, ten malt whiskies and local cider. The two dining rooms are furnished in a similar style. There are seats on the terrace, and picnic-sets beneath mature fruit trees and parasols in the back garden. The smart, well equipped bedrooms are found in both the charming 16th-c main building and the converted stable block. You can walk from the attractive stone-built village to the prehistoric Cerne Abbas Giant chalk carving and on to other nearby villages.

The delicious and accomplished food includes pork and ginger terrine with asian salad, twice-baked goats cheese soufflé with olive tapenade, truffle-roasted chicken breast with madeira cream, line-caught cod with marinated peppers and lemon jam, local venison with roast garlic and potato gratin, and puddings such as white chocolate and fig cheesecake and warm treacle tart with orange sauce and clotted cream. *Benchmark main dish: slow-roast pork belly and crackling with apple sauce and champ £15.00. Two-course evening meal £24.00.*

Palmers ~ Tenant Jeremy Lee ~ Real ale ~ (01300) 341274 ~ Open 12-3, 6-11 ~ Bar food 12-2.15, 7-9 ~ Children welcome ~ Dogs allowed in bar ~ Wi-fi ~ Bedrooms: £85/£95 ~ www.thenewinncerneabbas.co.uk *Recommended by Alan Johnson, M G Hart, Michael Doswell, Richard Tilbrook, Patrick and Daphne Darley, John and Sarah Perry*

CHIDEOCK
George
A35 Bridport–Lyme Regis; DT6 6JD

SY4292 Map 1

Comfortably traditional local with a thriving atmosphere and well liked food and drink

Popular and always busy with a cheerful mix of holidaymakers and locals, this heavily thatched 17th-c village inn has a nicely traditional interior and friendly, efficient staff. The cosy, low-ceilinged carpeted bar is just as you'd hope, with Palmers 200, Copper, Dorset Gold and IPA on handpump, several wines by the glass and farm cider, warm log fires, and brassware and pewter tankards hanging from dark beams. There are wooden pews and long built-in tongue-and-groove banquettes, cream walls hung with old tools and high shelves of bottles, plates and mugs; background music, TV, bar billiards, darts and board games. The garden room opens on to a pretty walled garden with a terrace and a much used wood-fired oven.

The short menu is topped up by lots of highly thought-of daily specials: lunchtime sandwiches (not Sun), home-made chorizo scotch egg, burgers topped with cheese and bacon, home-cooked local ham and free-range eggs, linguine with home-made pesto and goats cheese, chicken with leeks, bacon and brie sauce, and puddings such as Baileys crème brûlée and chocolate brownie. *Benchmark main dish: beer-battered local fish of the day with chips £10.50. Two-course evening meal £16.50.*

Palmers ~ Tenants Mr and Mrs Steve Smith ~ Real ale ~ (01297) 489419 ~ Open 12-3, 6-11 ~ Bar food 12-2.30, 6-9.30 ~ Restaurant ~ Children welcome ~ Dogs allowed in bar ~ Wi-fi ~ Live music Weds and Sat evenings in summer ~ www.georgeinnchideock.co.uk *Recommended by George Atkinson, Brian and Anna Marsden, Paul Humphreys, Pete Flower*

CHURCH KNOWLE
SY9381 Map 2

New Inn ♀

Village signed off A351 N of Corfe Castle; BH20 5NQ

Partly thatched former farmhouse with plenty of seating in various rooms, open fires, a thoughtful choice of drinks, good food and a cheerful landlord

There's so much to look at in the connected character bar rooms here: brass and copper measuring jugs, bed warmers, pots and pans, horsebrasses, elderly board games and books, stone jars, china plates, a glass cabinet filled with household items from years ago, tilley lamps, the odd mangle and set of scales, a coastguard flag and an old diver's helmet. The main bar has an open fire in a stone fireplace, high-backed black leather dining chairs and cushioned wall settles around heavy rustic tables on the red-patterned carpet, and quite a few stools against the counter. Butcombe Bitter, Dorset Jurassic and Sharps Doom Bar on handpump, eight wines by the glass and farm cider; there's a wineshack from which you can choose your own wines, and also a wide choice of teas, coffees and local soft drinks. The dining room leads off here; it has similar furnishings, a serving counter with hot plates, two fireplaces (one with church candles, the other with a stove) and a dark red dado. Outside are picnic-sets on the lawn. The ruins of Corfe Castle are nearby.

 A wide choice of food includes lunchtime sandwiches, toasted goats cheese on marinated tomato and onion salad with home-made banana chutney, game pâté with cranberry jelly, home-cooked ham and farm eggs, local game pie, lots of fish dishes such as fresh crab soup, fillet of yellowfin sole with leeks and bacon in a cream sauce, seasonal mussels, lobster, skate and dover sole, and puddings such as lemon crunch and hot chocolate sponge. *Benchmark main dish: roast of the day £9.95. Two-course evening meal £19.50.*

Punch ~ Tenants Maurice and Rosemary Estop ~ Real ale ~ (01929) 480357 ~ Open 10-3, 6-11; 12-3.30, 6-11 Sun; closed Mon in Jan, Feb, Nov ~ Bar food 12-2.15, 6-9.15 ~ Restaurant ~ Children welcome ~ Wi-fi ~ www.newinn-churchknowle.co.uk
Recommended by Nick and Sylvia Pascoe, George Atkinson, Wendy Breese, Eddie Edwards

CRANBORNE
SU0513 Map 2

Inn at Cranborne 🛏

Wimborne Street (B3078 N of Wimborne); BH21 5PP

Neatly refurbished old inn with bustling friendly atmosphere in bars and dining areas, good choice of drinks, highly rated food and seats outside; comfortable bedrooms

Set on the edge of Cranborne Chase, this 17th-c inn has several historic associations. 'Hanging Judge' Jeffries stayed here, Thomas Hardy visited while writing *Tess of the D'Urbervilles*, and Rupert Brook wrote a poem about the place. The rambling character bars have heavy beams, open doorways and the odd standing timber, and the atmosphere is relaxed and chatty. The main bar area, divided into two by a partition, is our favourite place to sit: it has grey-planked and tartan-cushioned built-in wall seats lined with big scatter cushions, assorted chairs (farmhouse, wheelback, ladderback) on parquet flooring, flagstones or rugs, nightlights on each table and a woodburner in the inglenook fireplace, with George the pub dog's bed beside it. Badger First Gold and Tanglefoot and a guest beer on handpump and several wines by the glass; background music, TV, darts and board games. The dining areas lead back from here, with similar furnishings and a little brick fireplace piled with logs; there's also a second bar with white-painted or wooden furniture and another woodburning stove. Plenty of coaching prints on grey walls above a darker grey dado, and church candles. Outside, you'll find plenty of benches, seats and tables on neat gravel. The comfortable, well equipped bedrooms are individually furnished and the breakfasts very good.

🍴 Quite a choice of food includes open sandwiches, potted treacle-cured salmon and brown shrimp with pickled cucumber, pressed local pork and apple with piccalilli, ham hock and free-range eggs with triple-cooked chips, butternut squash, parmesan and sage risotto, breast and leg of pheasant with black pudding and chestnuts, trio of local pork (fillet, belly, shoulder fritter) with creamed cauliflower, and puddings such as apple trifle with cider granita and custard-filled doughnuts, and sticky toffee and date pudding with toffee sauce. *Benchmark main dish: burger with cheese, tomato relish and skinny fries £12.95. Two-course evening meal £20.00.*

Badger ~ Tenant Jane Gould ~ Real ale ~ (01725) 551249 ~ Open 11-11 (10 Sun) ~ Bar food 12-2, 6-9; 12-2.30, 6-9.30 Fri, Sat; 12-3, 6-9 Sun ~ Restaurant (evening only) ~ Children welcome ~ Dogs welcome ~ Wi-fi ~ Live music last Fri of month ~ Bedrooms: £75/£99 ~ www.theinnatcranborne.co.uk *Recommended by Judith and Barry McCormick, David Guest*

EVERSHOT
Acorn 🍷 🛏
Off A37 S of Yeovil; DT2 0JW

ST5704   Map 2

A 400-year-old inn in a pretty village, with plenty of character in several rooms, log fires and knick-knacks, and friendly licensees; bedrooms

Each of the attractive bedrooms here is individually decorated and has a Thomas Hardy theme – this prettily placed inn is immortalised as the Sow & Acorn in *Tess of the D'Urbervilles*. It's a cheerful, warmly welcoming place. The public bar has chatty locals, a log fire, lots of beer mats on beams, big flagstones and high chairs against the counter where they serve Otter Ale and Wooden Hand Cornish Buccaneer on handpump, 39 wines by the glass and 100 malt whiskies; dogs are looked after with a bowl of water, and biscuits behind the bar. A second bar has comfortable beige leather wall banquettes and little stools around tables set with fresh flowers, and a turkish rug on nice old quarry tiles. This leads to a bistro-style dining room with ladderback chairs around red gingham and beige-clothed tables; the slightly more formal restaurant is similarly furnished. There's also a comfortable lounge with armchairs, board games, shelves of books and a skittle alley. Throughout are open fires, wood panelling, pretty knick-knacks, all manner of copper and brass items, water jugs, wall prints and photographs; background music, TV and darts. The walled garden has picnic-sets under a fine beech tree, and there are numerous walks nearby.

🍴 Using local, seasonal produce, the enjoyable food includes sandwiches, crab and chilli linguine with peanut sauce, potted confit duck with black cherry chutney and home-made crackers, good burgers with interesting toppings, open lasagne of wild mushrooms and blue cheese, beef with shallot purée, truffle polenta, red wine jus and seared foie gras, and puddings such as peanut butter parfait, raspberry sorbet and tempura banana, and white chocolate fondant with dark chocolate tart and chocolate ice-cream. *Benchmark main dish: beer-battered local fish with triple-cooked chips £12.95. Two-course evening meal £20.00.*

Free house ~ Licensee Alex Mackenzie ~ Real ale ~ (01935) 83228 ~ Open 11am-11.30pm; 12-10.30 Sun ~ Bar food 12-2, 7-9 ~ Restaurant ~ Children welcome ~

Dogs allowed in bar and bedrooms ~ Wi-fi. ~ Bedrooms: £89/£109 ~ www.acorn-inn.co.uk
Recommended by Alan Johnson

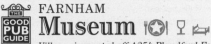

FARNHAM ST9515 Map 2
Museum 🌟 🍷 ⌂
Village signposted off A354 Blandford Forum–Salisbury; DT11 8DE

Partly thatched and rather smart inn with appealing rooms, inventive modern cooking, real ales and fine wines, and seats outside; lovely bedrooms

The proper little bar here remains the heart of this rather civilised 17th-c inn and there's a thoughtful choice of drinks too: it has beams and flagstones, a big inglenook fireplace, quite an assortment of dining chairs around plain or painted wooden tables and bar stools against the counter. Friendly, helpful staff serve Ringwood Best and Waylands Sixpenny 6D Best and a changing guest from Waylands on handpump, several wines by the glass and a dozen malt whiskies. Leading off here is a simply but attractively furnished dining room with cushioned window seats, a long, dark leather button-back wall seat, similar chairs and tables on bare floorboards and quite a few photographs on the patterned wallpaper; there's also a quiet lounge with armchairs around a low table in front of an open fire, books on shelves and board games. This leads to an outside terrace with cushioned seats and tables under parasols. The stylish, well equipped bedrooms are in the main building and in converted stables, and they also have a self-catering cottage.

🌟 Using the best regional produce, the delicious food includes lunchtime sandwiches, local snails on cheese rarebit with prosciutto crisp, scallops with pea purée and chorizo, open vegetable lasagne with basil pesto and halloumi, clove and honey-baked ham and eggs, burger with pickled cucumber, bacon, cheese and fries, pheasant, chestnut, orange and brandy pie, bream with cockle and saffron sauce, and puddings such as dark chocolate and Guinness torte with Jaffa cake shot and vanilla bean ice-cream and lemon tart with berry compote. *Benchmark main dish: calves liver with bacon and champ £15.95. Two-course evening meal £22.00.*

Free house ~ Real ale ~ (01725) 516261 ~ Open 8am-11pm ~ Bar food 8-10, 12-2.30 (3 weekends), 6-9 (9.30 Sat) ~ Restaurant ~ Children welcome ~ Dogs welcome ~ Wi-fi ~ Bedrooms: £80/£90 ~ www.museuminn.co.uk *Recommended by Charlie May, Peter Brix*

MELPLASH SY4897 Map 2
Half Moon 🌟
A3066 Bridport–Beaminster; DT6 3UD

Creative food using local, seasonal produce and cooked by the landlord, Palmers ales and an easy-going atmosphere

This thatched and shuttered 18th-c dining pub is extremely popular for its creative and enjoyable food, cooked by the landlord. It's a simply furnished place with beams and a log fire, dark wood mate's and other sturdy chairs around straightforward tables on patterned carpeting, a couple of hunting horns and a few country-style pictures. Palmers Best and 200 on handpump and wines by the glass served by friendly staff; background music. There are picnic-sets in the mature back garden.

🌟 Interesting, tasty food using local Estate game and West Bay shellfish includes sandwiches, seared squid with kohlrabi and celeriac slaw and a curried dressing, scallops with black pudding beignet and chorizo jam, saffron tagliatelle with wild mushrooms, spinach, poached duck egg and parmesan, calves liver with pancetta, truffled mash and port wine and shallot sauce, hake with mussels and fennel and crab ravioli, venison burger with vintage cheddar and chips, and puddings such as toffee apple sponge with salted caramel and rosemary-scented chocolate terrine. *Benchmark main dish: fresh local fish dishes £15.00. Two-course evening meal £18.00.*

Palmers ~ Tenants Dan and Jenny Clarke ~ Real ale ~ (01308) 488321 ~ Open 12-3, 6-11; 12-3 Sun; closed Sun evening, Mon ~ Bar food 12-2, 6-9; 12-2.30 Sun ~ Children welcome ~ Dogs allowed in bar ~ Wi-fi ~ www.palmersbrewery.com/2013/01/half-moon
Recommended by Bruce Jamieson, B and M Kendall, Richard Wyld

MIDDLEMARSH   ST6607   Map 2

Hunters Moon 🛏

A352 Sherborne–Dorchester; DT9 5QN

Plenty of bric-a-brac in several linked areas, reasonably priced food and quite a choice of drinks; comfortable bedrooms

With first class service and a warm welcome for all, this busy former coaching inn remains as good as ever. The traditional beamed bar rooms are cosily filled with a great variety of tables and chairs on red patterned carpet, an array of ornamentation from horsebrasses up, and lighting in the form of converted oil lamps; the atmosphere is properly pubby. Booths are formed by some attractively cushioned settles, walls are of exposed brick, stone and some panelling and there are three log fires (one in a capacious inglenook); background music, children's books and toys and board games. Butcombe Bitter and a couple of guests such as Adnams Best and Timothy Taylors Landlord on handpump, farm cider and 16 wines by the glass. A neat lawn has picnic-sets, including some circular ones.

Highly popular food includes lunchtime sandwiches, scallops and bacon in lemon and pea cream, farmhouse pâté with date and plum chutney, sharing platters, a pie of the day, several pizzas, vegetable wellington with tomato ragoût, burgers with toppings such as egg, onion, bacon and cheese, a curry of the week, chicken in mustard, mushroom and tarragon sauce, and puddings. *Benchmark main dish: beer-battered cod and chips £11.75. Two-course evening meal £20.00.*

Enterprise ~ Lease Dean and Emma Mortimer ~ Real ale ~ (01963) 210966 ~
Open 10.30-2.30, 6 (5 Fri)-11; 10.30am-11pm Sat, Sun ~ Bar food 12-2, 6-9; all day weekends ~ Children welcome ~ Dogs welcome ~ Wi-fi ~ Bedrooms: £65/£75 ~
www.hunters-moon.org.uk *Recommended by H J Reynolds, R J and G M Townson, Gene and Tony Freemantle*

MUDEFORD   SZ1792   Map 2

Ship in Distress

Stanpit; off B3059 at roundabout; BH23 3NA

Wide choice of fish dishes, quirky nautical décor and friendly staff in a cheerful cottage pub

This former smugglers' pub is handy for Mudeford Quay and Stanpit Marsh Nature Reserve and is just the place for a fresh fish lunch. It's full of entertaining seaside bits and pieces: brightly painted fish cutouts swimming across the walls, rope fancywork, brassware, lanterns and oars, an aquarium, model boats and the odd piratical figure; darts, games machine, board games, big-screen TV, background music and a winter woodburning stove. As well as several boat pictures, the room on the right has tables with masses of snapshots (under the glass tabletops) of locals caught up in various waterside japes. Ringwood Best and a guest or two such as Dartmoor Jail Ale and Sharps Doom Bar on handpump, alongside several wines by the glass. A spreading and bustling two-room restaurant area has a fish tank, contemporary works by local artists for sale and a light-hearted mural giving the impression of a window opening on to a sunny boating scene. There are seats and tables on the suntrap back terrace and a covered heated area for chilly evenings.

Using locally caught fresh fish, the good food might include cockles, whelks, oysters, mussels, crab, lobster, fish soup with rouille, whole mackerel, and black bream with scallops and creamy mustard sauce. A few non-fishy choices include sandwiches, duck and orange pâté, cottage pie, gammon and egg, and puddings such as lemon posset and crème brûlée with berries; they also offer a two-course set lunch. *Benchmark main dish: whole lemon sole with fries £16.50. Two-course evening meal £21.75.*

Punch ~ Lease Maggie Wheeler ~ Real ale ~ (01202) 485123 ~ Open 11am-midnight (11pm Sun) ~ Bar food 12-2.30, 6.30-9 ~ Restaurant ~ Children welcome ~ Dogs allowed in bar ~ Wi-fi ~ Bingo Weds evening ~ www.ship-in-distress.co.uk *Recommended by Denise Flack, Tom Evans, Katharine Cowherd*

 NETTLECOMBE   SY5195   Map 2

Marquis of Lorne ◀

Off A3066 Bridport–Beaminster, via West Milton; DT6 3SY

Attractive country pub with enjoyable food and drink, friendly licensees and seats in big garden; bedrooms

The countryside around this former farmhouse is particularly lovely, and the big mature garden really comes into its own in warm weather with its pretty herbaceous borders, picnic-sets under apple trees and a rustic-style play area. Inside, the comfortable, bustling main bar has a log fire, mahogany panelling, old prints and photographs and neatly matching chairs and tables. Two dining areas lead off, the smaller of which has another log fire. The wooden-floored snug (liked by locals) has board games, table skittles and background music, and they keep Palmers Copper, IPA and 200 on handpump, with a dozen wines by the glass from a decent list. The pub is within strolling distance of Eggardon Hill, one of Dorset's most evocative Iron Age hillfort sites.

Using home-grown and other local produce, the rewarding food includes sandwiches, duck liver pâté with spiced pears, scallops and black pudding with garlic cream, mustard and sugar-baked ham with eggs and home-made piccalilli, vegetable lasagne, sticky beef with indonesian-style salad, bass with creamed prawn velouté, and puddings such as triple chocolate cheesecake and lemon and lime sponge. *Benchmark main dish: lambs liver with bacon and mustard mushrooms £11.50. Two-course evening meal £18.00.*

Palmers ~ Tenants Stephen and Tracey Brady ~ Real ale ~ (01308) 485236 ~ Open 12-2.30, 6-11 ~ Bar food 12-2, 6-9.30 ~ Restaurant ~ Children welcome ~ Dogs allowed in bar ~ Wi-fi ~ Bedrooms: £80/£90 ~ www.themarquisoflorne.co.uk *Recommended by David and Julie Glover, Dr D J and Mrs S C Walker*

Bedroom prices are for high summer. Even then you may get reductions for more than one night, or (outside tourist areas) weekends. Winter special rates are common, and many inns cut bedroom prices if you have a full evening meal.

PLUSH   ST7102   Map 2

Brace of Pheasants 🎯 ♀ 🛏

Village signposted from B3143 N of Dorchester at Piddletrenthide; DT2 7RQ

16th-c thatched pub with friendly service, three real ales, lots of wines by the glass, generously served food and decent garden; comfortable bedrooms

They take extra care at this 16th-c thatched inn to welcome both visitors and locals (often with their dogs) and the atmosphere throughout is bustling and friendly. The beamed bar has windsor chairs around good solid tables on patterned carpeting, a few standing timbers, a huge heavy-beamed inglenook at one end with cosy seating inside, and a good warming log fire at the other. Flack Manor Double Drop, Palmers Best and Ringwood Best are tapped from the cask by the helpful licensees, and they offer a fine choice of wines with 18 by the glass, and two proper farm ciders. A decent-sized garden includes a terrace and a lawn sloping up towards a rockery. The pub is well placed for walks – an attractive bridleway behind the building leads to the left of the woods and over to Church Hill – and is also a nice place to stay. Attractively fitted out and comfortable, the bedrooms are in a converted bowling alley; each has a little outside terrace.

 With suppliers listed on the menu, the thoughtful choice of good food includes baguettes, spicy breaded pheasant strips with lemon and worcestershire mayonnaise, crab, dill and cheddar tartlet, beer-battered fish of the day, warm goats cheese salad with walnuts and croutons, venison burger with wild garlic mayonnaise and chips, smoked chicken with madeira and blue cheese sauce, and puddings such as walnut and fig cake and sticky toffee pudding with caramel sauce. *Benchmark main dish: trio of wild boar and apple sausages with caramelised red onion gravy and bubble and squeak £12.95. Two-course evening meal £20.50.*

Free house ~ Licensees Phil and Carol Bennett ~ Real ale ~ (01300) 348357 ~ Open 12-3, 7-11 (10.30 Sun) ~ Bar food 12-2, 7-9 ~ Children welcome ~ Dogs allowed in bar ~ Wi-fi ~ Bedrooms: £105/£115 ~ www.braceofpheasants.co.uk *Recommended by Steve Whalley, R Elliott, Barry Collett, M G Hart, David and Stella Martin, Alan Johnson, Phil Bryant*

SHERBORNE   ST6316   Map 2

Digby Tap 🍺 £

Cooks Lane; park in Digby Road and walk round corner; DT9 3NS

Regularly changing ales in simple alehouse, open all day with very inexpensive beer and food

Much loved by a very wide mix of customers, this remains a delightfully simple backstreet tavern with a genuine welcome, a lively local atmosphere and no frills whatsoever. The straightforward flagstoned bar, with its cosy corners, is full of understated character; the small games room has a pool table and a quiz machine, and there's also a TV room. Otter Bitter, Teignworthy Neap Tide, Yeovil Glory and a guest such as Exmoor Fox on handpump, several wines by the glass and a choice of malt whiskies. There are some seats outside, and beautiful Sherborne Abbey is a stroll away.

Generous helpings of incredibly good value, straightforward food – lunchtime only – includes sandwiches and toasties, three-egg omelettes, sausages with free-range eggs, burgers and specials such as sausage casserole, fish pie and a mixed grill. *Benchmark main dish: ham, egg and chips £5.00.*

Free house ~ Licensees Oliver Wilson and Nick Whigham ~ Real ale ~ No credit cards ~
(01935) 813148 ~ Open 11-11; 12-11 Sun ~ Bar food 12-2; not Sun ~ Children welcome
before 6pm ~ Dogs allowed in bar ~ Wi-fi ~ www.digbytap.co.uk *Recommended by Barrie
and Mary Crees, Mark Flynn, Tony and Wendy Hobden*

SHROTON
Cricketers

ST8512   Map 2

*Off A350 N of Blandford (village also called Iwerne Courtney); follow signs;
DT11 8QD*

**Country pub with real ales, well liked food and pretty garden;
nice views and walks nearby**

This red-brick country pub sits on the Wessex Ridgeway and is
overlooked by the formidable grassy Iron Age ramparts of Hambledon
Hill, which gradually descends to become the village cricket pitch in front
of the pub. Walkers are welcome if they leave their muddy boots outside.
The bright, divided bar has a woodburning stove in a stone fireplace,
cushioned high-backed windsor and ladderback chairs in one area and
black leather ones in another, all sorts of tables, a settle with scatter
cushions, and red or cream walls decorated with cricket bats and photos
of cricket teams; there's also a cosy little alcove and a spreading dining
area towards the back. There are lots of cheerful locals, and service is
friendly. They keep Butcombe Bitter, Otter Amber and Salisbury English
Ale on handpump (and hold a beer festival on the early May Bank Holiday
weekend) and several wines by the glass; background music. There's a
couple of circular picnic-sets at the front of the building, plus a secluded
and pretty back garden with more seats on a terrace and a lawn.

 Popular food includes lunchtime sandwiches, twice-baked cheddar and stilton
soufflé with apple and brandy cream, duck liver mousse with port jelly, moules
frites, a pie of the day, cauliflower, aubergine and sweet potato curry, crispy confit
duck leg with spiced rice and plum sauce, pork and home-made chorizo cassoulet, and
puddings such as passion fruit, coconut and rum trifle and treacle tart. *Benchmark
main dish: rare-breed pork belly with mustard coleslaw, sour cream and potato
wedges £12.50. Two-course evening meal £18.00.*

Heartstone Inns ~ Licensees Joe and Sally Grieves ~ Real ale ~ (01258) 860421 ~ Open
12-3, 6-11; 12-10.30 Sun ~ Bar food 12-2.30, 6.30-9; 12-2.30 Sun (12-2.30, 6-8 in summer)
~ Children welcome ~ Wi-fi ~ www.thecricketsshroton.co.uk *Recommended by Robert
Watt, Michael and Sheila Hawkins*

TARRANT MONKTON
Langton Arms 🏅 🍺 🛏

ST9408   Map 2

Village signposted from A354, then head for church; DT11 8RX

**Charming thatched pub in pretty village, with friendly staff, real ales,
good food, plenty of dining space and seats outside; bedrooms**

If you can't find this popular thatched pub, just head for the church. The
bars have a few beams, high-backed tartan dining chairs around wooden
tables on carpeting, a cushioned window seat, a few high chairs against
the light oak counter and Flack Manor Double Drop and a guest such as
Dorset Piddle Jimmy Riddle on handpump. The two connected, beamed
dining rooms, furnished with cushioned wooden chairs around white-
clothed tables, lead into a light and airy conservatory; country prints, dried
flower arrangements, background music, TV and board games. In fine
weather, you can sit out in front or at teak tables in the flower-filled back

garden; there's also a well equipped children's play area. The comfortable bedrooms occupy brick buildings around the attractive courtyard, with four in a neighbouring cottage.

From a seasonally changing menu, the attractively presented food includes baguettes, duck liver parfait with plum chutney, creamy garlic mushrooms topped with brie, sharing platters, twice-baked cheese soufflé, ham and free-range eggs, thai green chicken curry, burger with mozzarella, onion rings and chips, home-made faggot with horseradish mash and onion gravy, and puddings such as fruit crumble and vanilla crème brûlée. *Benchmark main dish: steak in red wine and port pie £15.50. Two-course evening meal £20.50.*

Free house ~ Licensee Barbara Cossins ~ Real ale ~ (01258) 830225 ~ Open 11am-midnight; 12-11 Sun ~ Bar food 12-2.30, 6-9.30 (10 Fri); all day weekends ~ Restaurant ~ Children welcome ~ Dogs allowed in bar and bedrooms ~ Wi-fi ~ Bedrooms: £70/£90 ~ www.thelangtonarms.co.uk *Recommended by Leslie and Barbara Owen, Howard and Margaret Buchanan, Stewart Harvey, Steve Whalley*

TRENT
ST5818 Map 2

Rose & Crown
Opposite the church; DT9 4SL

Character thatched pub in pretty rural position with friendly owners and staff, cosy rooms, open fires, a good choice of drinks and well thought-of food; bedrooms

The hands-on landlady and her friendly staff make all their customers feel welcome here and the atmosphere is relaxed and chatty. The cosy little bar on the right has big, comfortable sofas and stools around a low table in front of an open fire (the logs are neatly piled on each side right to the ceiling), fresh flowers and candlelight. The bar opposite is popular with cheerful locals (often with their dogs) and is furnished with nice old wooden tables and chairs on quarry tiles, and stools against the counter where they serve Wadworths IPA, 6X and Horizon and guests such as Butcombe Bitter and Hardys & Hansons Olde Trip on handpump, and 13 wines by the glass. Two further connected rooms have similar wooden tables and chairs, settles and pews, a grandfather clock, pewter tankards, and church candles in fireplaces. Throughout are all sorts of pictures, including Stuart prints commemorating the fact that Charles II sort refuge in this village after the Battle of Worcester. The simply furnished back dining room has doors leading to the garden, which has seats and tables and fine views (and sunsets); there are some picnic-sets at the front. The pretty bedrooms are in a converted byre. The church opposite is lovely.

Creative food includes sandwiches, treacle-cured salmon with soft shell crab, oriental salad and passion fruit, crispy pigs head with rhubarb and warm malt-glazed pigs cheeks, macaroni cheese with wild mushrooms and butternut squash, veal cottage pie, guinea fowl with onion and cep purée and herb gnocchi, and puddings such as brown sugar parfait with raspberry vinegar jelly and hazelnut praline and lemon posset with berry compote. *Benchmark main dish: duck breast with dauphinoise potatoes, bacon and cabbage £16.50. Two-course evening meal £19.50.*

Wadworths ~ Tenant Nick Lamb ~ Real ale ~ (01935) 850776 ~ Open 11-11 ~ Bar food 12-2.30, 6-9 ~ Children welcome ~ Dogs welcome ~ Wi-fi ~ Bedrooms: £65/£95 ~ www.roseandcrowntrent.co.uk *Recommended by Ruth May, Emma Scofield, Gene and Tony Freemantle*

The star-on-a-plate award, 🟊, distinguishes pubs where the food is of exceptional quality. The knife-and-fork symbol just means the pub serves food.

WEST BAY   SY4690   Map 1

West Bay ⭐◎ 🛏

Station Road; DT6 4EW

Relaxed seaside inn with emphasis on seafood; bedrooms

Set at the western end of Chesil Beach within strolling distance of the busy little harbour, this popular inn with quiet and comfortable bedrooms makes an obvious base. The fairly simple front part, with bare boards, a coal-effect gas fire and a mix of sea and nostalgic prints, is separated by an island servery from the cosier carpeted dining area, which has more of a country kitchen feel; background music and board games. Though its spaciousness means it never feels crowded, booking is essential in season. Palmers 200, Best, Copper Ale and Dorset Gold are served on handpump alongside good house wines (including eight by the glass) and several malt whiskies. There are tables in a small side garden, and more in the large main garden. Several local teams meet to play in the pub's 100-year-old skittle alley.

 Using fresh fish and seafood from local boats, the highly rated food includes crab pâté, smoked haddock and chorizo fishcakes, spinach crêpes stuffed with ratatouille, twice-cooked pork belly with sage, black pudding and cider jus, free-range chicken wrapped in bacon with a spring onion and sunblush tomato sauce, duck breast with chasseur sauce, surf 'n' turf, and puddings. *Benchmark main dish: trio of fish with shellfish and bacon velouté £17.95. Two-course evening meal £21.00.*

Palmers ~ Tenant Samuel Good ~ Real ale ~ (01308) 422157 ~ Open 12-11 (midnight Sat, 10 Sun); 12-3, 6-11 Nov-Mar ~ Bar food 12-3, 6-9 ~ Children welcome till 8pm ~ Dogs allowed in bar ~ Wi-fi ~ Bedrooms: £75/£100 ~ www.thewestbayhotel.co.uk
Recommended by Pat and Tony Martin, Dave Braisted, Charlie May, Phil Bryant

WEST STOUR   ST7822   Map 2

Ship ♀ 🛏

A30 W of Shaftesbury; SP8 5RP

Civilised and pleasantly updated roadside dining inn, offering a wide range of food

If you stay in the attractive and comfortable bedrooms in this 18th-c former coaching inn, you'll get pastoral views and a particularly good and hearty breakfast. It's run by a convivial, hands-on landlord. The neatly kept rooms include a smallish but airy bar on the left with cream décor, a mix of chunky farmhouse furniture on dark boards and big sash windows that look beyond the road and car park to rolling pastures. The smaller flagstoned public bar has a good log fire and low ceilings. Butcombe Bitter, Shepherd Neame Spitfire and Timothy Taylors Landlord on handpump, 14 wines by the glass and four farm ciders. During their summer beer festival they showcase a dozen beers and ten ciders, all from the West Country. On the right, two carpeted dining rooms with stripped pine dado, stone walls and shutters are similarly furnished in a pleasantly informal style, and have some attractive contemporary cow prints; TV, lots of board games and background music. The bedlington terriers are called Douglas and Toby.

🍴 From a thoughtful menu, the enjoyable food includes lunchtime sandwiches, pâté of the day, devilled kidneys on toasted brioche, broccoli, leek, lentil and butternut squash crumble, ginger beer-battered cod and chips, spicy lime chicken with a crayfish and peanut cream sauce, maple-glazed pork fillet stuffed with pear and black pudding with a saffron and cider cream, venison burger with bacon, cheese and chilli mayonnaise, and puddings. *Benchmark main dish: scallop, tiger prawn, salmon and smoked haddock pie £14.95. Two-course evening meal £21.25.*

Free house ~ Licensee Gavin Griggs ~ Real ale ~ (01747) 838640 ~ Open 12-3, 6-11.30 (midnight Sat); 12-11 Sun ~ Bar food 12-2.30, 6-9; not Sun evening ~ Restaurant ~ Well behaved children in restaurant and lounge ~ Dogs allowed in bar ~ Wi-fi ~ Bedrooms: £60/£90 ~ www.shipinn-dorset.com *Recommended by S J and C C Davidson, Leslie and Barbara Owen, Hugh Roberts*

WEYMOUTH
SY6878   Map 2
Red Lion ◖ £
Hope Square; DT4 8TR

Cheery place with sunny terrace, smashing range of drinks, popular food and lots to look at

There's an impressive range of drinks in this lively and handsome Victorian pub in the now pedestrianised Old Harbour: Dorset Jurassic, Hop Back Summer Lightning, Lifeboat Bitter (named for the pub, brewed by Otter) and Sharps Doom Bar on handpump, over 80 rums (with a rum 'bible' to explain them) and 12 wines by the glass; service is helpful and friendly. The refurbished bare-boards interior, kept cosy with candles, has all manner of wooden chairs and tables, cushioned wall seats, some unusual high, maroon-cushioned benches beside equally high tables, the odd armchair here and there, numerous pictures and artefacts to do with the lifeboat crews and their boats (this is the closest pub to Weymouth RNLI) and other bric-a-brac on stripped brick walls. Some nice contemporary touches include the woven timber wall and loads of mirrors wittily overlapped; daily papers, board games and background music. There are plenty of seats outside that stay warmed by the sun well into the evening. This is part of the Cheshire Cat Pubs & Bars group, which also includes the Three Greyhounds in Allostock, Cholmondeley Arms at Bickley Moss and Bulls Head and Church Inn in Mobberley (all in our Cheshire chapter).

Quite a choice of popular food includes sandwiches, kipper hash with bacon, egg and HP Sauce, mussels in white wine, shallots and cream, various sharing boards, sausages with onion gravy, steak or sweet potato and cheddar pies, local ale-battered haddock and chips, and puddings such as toffee apple cake and chocolate brownie; the Bargain Meals award is for the handful of dishes under £10. *Benchmark main dish: fish pie £11.95. Two-course evening meal £15.50.*

Free house ~ Licensee Brian McLaughlin ~ Real ale ~ (01305) 786940 ~ Open 11-11 (midnight Sat); 12-10.30 Sun; 12-10.30 (11 Fri, Sat) Mon-Thurs in winter ~ Bar food 12-9; 12-3, 6-9 in winter ~ Children welcome until 7pm ~ Wi-fi ~ Live music outside Sun afternoons in summer ~ www.theredlionweymouth.co.uk *Recommended by Victoria Cotton, B and M Kendall, Phil and Jane Villiers*

WIMBORNE MINSTER
SZ0199   Map 2
Green Man ◖ £
Victoria Road, at junction with West Street (B3082/B3073); BH21 1EN

Cosy, warm-hearted town pub with simple food at bargain prices

A delightful little pub at any time of year (though the award-winning summer flowering tubs, hanging baskets and window boxes are fantastic), this place is always full of locals and visitors and the landlord offers a friendly welcome to all. The four small linked areas have maroon

plush banquettes and polished dark pub tables, copper and brass
ornaments, red walls, Wadworths IPA, 6X and a guest beer on handpump
and a farm cider. One room has a log fire in a sizeable brick fireplace,
another has a coal-effect gas fire, and there are two dart boards, a silenced
games machine, background music and TV; the Barn houses a pool table.
Their little border terrier is called Cooper. The heated back terrace has
seats and more lovely flowers.

 The traditional food, served lunchtimes only, is amazing value: sandwiches and
toasties, beans on toast, full english breakfast, thai-style fishcakes, lasagne,
meat or vegetarian burgers, fish and chips and lamb shank. *Benchmark main dish:
Sunday roast £7.95.*

Wadworths ~ Tenant Andrew Kiff ~ Real ale ~ (01202) 881021 ~ Open 10am-11.30pm
(12.30 Sat) ~ Bar food 10-2 ~ Restaurant ~ Children welcome until 7.30pm ~ Dogs
allowed in bar ~ Wi-fi ~ Live music Fri-Sun evenings ~ www.greenmanwimborne.com
Recommended by Dr and Mrs A K Clarke, Tom Evans, B and M Kendall

WORTH MATRAVERS   SY9777   Map 2
Square & Compass ★ ◖
At fork of both roads signposted to village from B3069; BH19 3LF

**Unchanging country tavern with masses of character, in the same
family for many years; lovely sea views and fine nearby walks**

'Wonderful atmosphere' and 'my absolute favourite' are just two
comments from readers on this basic and unchanging little place
that's been in the Newman family for more than a century. The simple
offerings are not to everyone's taste – to this day, there's no bar counter.
Palmers Copper, guests from brewers such as Cottage, Frys and Otley, and
up to ten ciders are tapped from a row of casks and passed through two
serving hatches to customers in the drinking corridor; also, a dozen malt
whiskies. A couple of unspoilt rooms have straightforward furniture on
flagstones, a woodburning stove and a loyal crowd of friendly locals; darts
and shove-ha'penny. From the benches of local stone out in front there's
a fantastic view over the village rooftops down to the sea. There may be
free-roaming chickens and other birds clucking around and the small
(free) museum exhibits local fossils and artefacts, mostly collected by the
friendly current landlord and his father. Wonderful walks lead to some
exciting switchback sections of the coast path above St Aldhelm's Head
and Chapman's Pool – you'll need to park in the public car park (£2 honesty
box) 100 metres along the Corfe Castle road.

 Bar food is limited to home-made pasties and pies.

Free house ~ Licensees Charlie Newman, Kevin Hunt ~ Real ale ~ No credit cards
~ (01929) 439229 ~ Open 12-11; 12-3, 6-11 Mon-Thurs in winter ~ Bar food all day ~
Children welcome ~ Dogs welcome ~ Live music some Fri, Sat evenings, Sun lunchtime
~ www.squareandcompasspub.co.uk *Recommended by Robert Watt, S J and C C Davidson, Alan
Johnson, Ian Phillips, David and Stella Martin, Wendy Breese, Eddie Edwards, Phil and Jane Villiers*

'Children welcome' means the pub says it lets children inside without any special
restriction. If it allows them in, but to restricted areas such as an eating area or family
room, we specify this. Some pubs may impose an evening time limit. We do not mention
limits after 9pm as we assume children are home by then.

Also Worth a Visit in Dorset

Besides the fully inspected pubs, you might like to try these pubs that have been recommended to us and described by readers. Do tell us what you think of them: feedback@goodguides.com

BISHOP'S CAUNDLE ST6913
White Hart (01963) 23301
A3030 SE of Sherborne; DT9 5ND
Smallish 17th-c roadside pub doing well under present licensees; reworked carpeted interior with moulded dark beams, panelling, stripped stone and log fire, good nicely presented food including daily specials, well kept Sharps Doom Bar and local guests, restaurant, skittle alley; children and dogs welcome, country views from garden, closed Sun evening, Mon. *(David and Stella Martin)*

BLANDFORD ST MARY ST8805
Hall & Woodhouse (01258) 455481
Bournemouth Road; DT11 9LS Visitor centre for Badger brewery, their full range in top condition including interesting bottled beers, decent lunchtime food from well filled baguettes up, friendly staff; spectacular chandelier made of beer bottles, lots of memorabilia in centre and upper gallery; popular tours of new brewery (not Weds, Sun), open lunchtimes only, closed Sun. *(Anon)*

BOURNEMOUTH SZ1092
Cricketers Arms (01202) 551589
Windham Road; BH1 4RN Well preserved Victorian pub near station, separate public and lounge bars, lots of dark wood, etched windows and stained glass, tiled fireplaces, Fullers London Pride and two quickly changing guests such as local Southbourne, food Sat and Sun lunchtimes only, Mon folk night; children and dogs welcome, picnic-sets out in front, open all day. *(Anon)*

BOURNEMOUTH SZ0891
Goat & Tricycle (01202) 314220
West Hill Road; BH2 5PF Interesting two-level rambling Edwardian local (two former pubs knocked together); Wadworths ales and guests from pillared bar's impressive rank of ten handpumps, real cider, reasonably priced pubby food, friendly staff; background music, Sun quiz, free wi-fi; no children; dogs welcome, good disabled access, part-covered yard, open (and food) all day. *(Dr and Mrs A K Clarke)*

BOURTON ST7731
★ White Lion (01747) 840866
High Street, off old A303 E of Wincanton; SP8 5AT Popular 18th-c low-beamed dining pub with welcoming landlord, three smallish opened-up rooms creating one well divided space, big flagstones, some stripped stone and half-panelling, bow-window seats and fine inglenook log fire, good well priced food

here or in large restaurant, neat friendly young staff, beers such as Otter and Sharps Doom Bar, Rich's and Thatcher's cider, nice wines; picnic-sets on back paved area and raised lawn, three bedrooms, open all day Fri-Sun. *(Edward Mirzoeff, Martin and Karen Wake)*

BRIDPORT SY4692
George (01308) 423187
South Street; DT6 3NQ Relaxed cheerful town pub refurbished under welcoming new licensees, enjoyable modern pub food from open kitchen, well kept Palmers and good choice of wines by the glass, efficient friendly service; children welcome, disabled facilities, open all day, from 10am market days (Weds, Sat) for popular brunch. *(Martin and Sue Radcliffe)*

BRIDPORT SY4692
Ropemakers (01308) 421255
West Street; DT6 3QP Welcoming town-centre pub, long and rambling, with lots of pictures and memorabilia, well kept Palmers ales and good value home-made food from nice sandwiches up, regular live music and other events; courtyard tables behind, open all day apart from Sun evening. *(Pete Walker, Val and Alan Green)*

BRIDPORT SY4692
Tiger (01308) 427543
Barrack Street, off South Street; DT6 3LY Cheerful and attractive open-plan Victorian beamed pub with well kept Sharps Doom Bar and three guests, real ciders, no food except breakfast for residents, skittle alley, darts; sports TV; seats in heated courtyard, five bedrooms, open all day. *(Michael and Lynne Gittins)*

BUCKLAND NEWTON ST6804
Gaggle of Geese (01300) 345249
Locketts Lane; E end of village; DT2 7BS Victorian country pub with enjoyable affordably priced home-made food, Ringwood, Yeovil and guests, log-fire in bar, dining room with mix of old and new furniture, skittle alley; children welcome and dogs (pub has its own), garden with terrace, orchard and pond, paddock with horses, closed Sun evening, Mon. *(Anon)*

BURTON BRADSTOCK SY4889
Anchor (01308) 897228
B3157 SE of Bridport; DT6 4QF Cheerful helpful staff in pricey but good seafood restaurant, other food including nice local steaks, refurbished village pub part too with blackboard choices from baguettes up,

ales such as Dorset, St Austell and Sharps, decent wines by the glass and several malt whiskies, table skittles, live music second Sun of month; children and dogs (in bar) welcome, two bedrooms, open all day Fri-Sun. *(Paul Humphreys)*

BURTON BRADSTOCK   SY4889
Three Horseshoes (01308) 897259
Mill Street; DT6 4QZ Traditional thatched pub handy for nearby sandy beach; pubby furniture on patterned carpet, brocaded built-in wall seats, one table made from an old bed with headrest still intact, photographs of the pub, horsebrasses and open woodburner, neat small dining room, Palmers ales and straightforward food; background music; children and dogs (in bar) welcome, picnic-sets on back grass and a few seats out in front, open all day in summer. *(B and M Kendall)*

CHARMOUTH   SY3693
Royal Oak (01297) 560277
Off A3052/A35 E of Lyme Regis; The Street; DT6 6PE Three-room split-level village local, popular and friendly, with enjoyable food and well kept Palmers ales, good service; quiz and music nights. *(Anon)*

CHEDINGTON   ST4805
Winyards Gap (01935) 891244
A356 Dorchester–Crewkerne; DT8 3HY Attractive dining pub surrounded by NT land with spectacular view over Parrett Valley and into Somerset; enjoyable good value food from sandwiches and ploughman's served on wooden boards to daily specials, four well kept beers including St Austell and Sharps Doom Bar, friendly staff and st bernard called Daisy, stylish dining room, skittle alley; children and dogs welcome, tables on front lawn under parasols, good walks, open all day weekends. *(Katie Collins)*

CHETNOLE   ST6008
★Chetnole Inn (01935) 872337
Village signed off A37 S of Yeovil; DT9 6NU Attractive inn with beams, huge flagstones and country kitchen décor, well kept Sharps Doom Bar and guests, 16 malt whiskies, central woodburner and modern leather seats in minimalist snug, log fire and pale wood tables on stripped boards in dining room with fresh flowers, candles and linen napkins, well liked interesting food served by friendly efficient staff, deli with small tearoom; dogs welcome in bar, picnic-sets out in front and in delightful back garden, three bedrooms overlooking old church, good breakfast, closed Sun evening, also Mon in winter; for sale so things may change. *(M G Hart, Ian Malone)*

CHIDEOCK   SY4191
★Anchor (01297) 489215
Off A35 from Chideock; DT6 6JU Dramatically set pub offering lovely sea

and cliff views from large terrace; close to the Dorset Coast Path. As we went to press the pub was closed for a massive refurbishment. *(Peter Meister, Paul Humphreys, Dru and Louisa Marshall, Pete Flower)*

CHIDEOCK   SY4192
Clockhouse (01297) 489423
A35 W of Bridport; DT6 6JW Friendly family-run thatched village local, well kept Otter and guests, enjoyable straightforward food, long main carpeted bar and raised dining area, huge collection of clocks, skittle alley/games room; children welcome, dogs in bar. *(J V Dadswell)*

CHILD OKEFORD   ST8213
★Saxon (01258) 860310
Signed off A350 Blandford–Shaftesbury and A357 Blandford–Sherborne; Gold Hill; DT11 8HD Welcoming 17th-c village pub, quietly clubby snug bar with log fire, two dining rooms, Butcombe, Ringwood and guests, nice choice of wines, enjoyable reasonably priced home-made food including good Sun roast, efficient service; children welcome, dogs in bar, attractive back garden, good walks on Neolithic Hambledon Hill, four comfortable bedrooms. *(Robert Watt)*

CHRISTCHURCH   SZ1593
Rising Sun (01202) 486122
Purewell; BH23 1EJ Sympathetically updated old pub specialising in authentic thai food, Flack Manor and Sharps Doom Bar from L-shaped bar, good choice of wines by the glass, pleasant helpful young staff; terrace with palms and black rattan-style furniture under large umbrellas. *(Anon)*

COLEHILL   SU0302
Barley Mow (01202) 882140
Colehill signed from A31/B3073 roundabout; Long Lane; BH21 7AH Part-thatched 16th-c pub with low-beamed main bar, brick inglenook and attractive oak panelling, library with tub chairs leading to restaurant and family area, three Badger ales, enjoyable freshly made food, friendly service; background music, quiz first Weds of month; dogs welcome, tethering for horses, seats out at front and in garden behind with decking, fenced part with kunekune pigs, also fields for various events such as farmers' market and lawnmower races, open all day weekends. *(Anon)*

CORFE CASTLE   SY9681
Castle Inn (01929) 480208
East Street; BH20 5EE Welcoming little two-room pub mentioned in Hardy's *Hand of Ethelberta*, good fairly priced food using local supplies including popular Fri fish night, competent service, Dorset and Ringwood ales, heavy black beams, exposed stone walls, flagstones and open fire; children welcome, back terrace and big sunny garden with mature trees. *(Anon)*

CORFE CASTLE SY9681
Fox (01929) 480449
West Street; BH20 5HD Old-fashioned take-us-as-you-find-us stone-built local, ales tapped from the cask and generous reasonably priced home-made food, good log fire in early medieval stone fireplace, glassed-over well in second bar; dogs but not children allowed, informal castle-view garden. *(Anon)*

CORFE CASTLE SY9682
★Greyhound (01929) 480205
A351; The Square; BH20 5EZ Bustling picturesque old pub in centre of this tourist village, three small low-ceilinged panelled rooms, steps and corridors, well kept ales such as Palmers, Ringwood and Sharps, local cider, wide choice of food from sandwiches and light dishes to good local seafood, efficient service, traditional games including Purbeck longboard shove-ha'penny, family room; background music – live on Fri; dogs welcome, garden with large decked area, great views of castle and countryside, pretty courtyard opening on to castle bridge, open all day weekends and in summer. *(Dr D J and Mrs S C Walker, Mrs Sally Scott, Eddie Edwards)*

CORFE MULLEN SY9798
Coventry Arms (01258) 857284
Mill Street (A31 W of Wimborne); BH21 3RH Refurbished 15th-c pub with bar and four dining rooms, low ceilings, eclectic mix of furniture on flagstones or wood flooring, large central open fire and a mummified cat to ward off evil spirits, Ringwood, Timothy Taylors Landlord and one or two cask-tapped guests, well liked fairly priced food from open kitchen, friendly helpful staff; background and occasional live music; children and dogs welcome, big waterside garden with terrace, open all day. *(Jenny and Brian Seller, Katharine Cowherd, Peter Salmon)*

DORCHESTER SY6990
★Blue Raddle (01305) 267762
Church Street, near central short-stay car park; DT1 1JN Cheery pubby atmosphere in long carpeted and partly panelled bar, well kept Butcombe, Fullers, Otter, St Austell and Sixpenny, local ciders, good wines and coffee, enjoyable simple home-made food at reasonable prices (not Sun, Mon or evenings Tues-Weds), coal-effect gas fires; background and live folk music (Weds fortnightly), no children; dogs welcome, good disabled access apart from one step, closed Mon lunchtime. *(Anon)*

DORCHESTER SY6990
Goldies (01305) 260252
High East Street; DT1 1HN Traditional beamed pub with eight real ales including Brakspears and Ringwood, live music and quiz nights; open all day. *(Richard Tilbrook)*

EAST LULWORTH SY8581
Weld Arms (01929) 400211
B3070 SW of Wareham; BH20 5QQ Thatched 17th-c cottage-row pub, civilised log-fire bar with sofas, ales such as Palmers and Sharps, Weston's cider and some nice wines by the glass, well liked home-made food from lunchtime sandwiches and baguettes up, friendly helpful service, two dining rooms; children and dogs welcome, picnic-sets out in big back garden with play area, open all day. *(Anon)*

EAST MORDEN SY9194
Cock & Bottle (01929) 459238
B3075 W of Poole; BH20 7DL Popular extended dining pub with wide choice of good if not cheap food (best to book), well kept Badger ales and nice selection of wines by the glass, efficient cheerful service; children and dogs allowed in certain areas, outside seating and pleasant pastoral outlook, closed Sun evening. *(Anon)*

EAST STOUR ST8123
Kings Arms (01747) 838325
A30, 2 miles E of village; The Common; SP8 5NB Extended dining pub with popular food from scottish landlord/chef including bargain lunch menu and all-day Sun carvery (best to book), Greene King IPA, St Austell Tribute and Sharps Doom Bar, decent wines and good selection of malt whiskies, friendly efficient staff, open fire in bar, airy dining area with light wood furniture, scottish pictures and Burns quotes; gentle background music; children welcome, dogs in bar, good disabled access, picnic-sets in big garden, bluebell walks nearby, three bedrooms, open all day weekends. *(Roy Hoing)*

FIDDLEFORD ST8013
Fiddleford Inn (01258) 475612
A357 Sturminster Newton–Blandford Forum; DT10 2BX Beamed roadside pub with three linked areas, old flagstones, carpets and some stripped stone, enjoyable pubby food, three well kept changing ales, good service even when busy; background and occasional live music; children and dogs welcome, picnic-sets in big fenced garden, two bedrooms, open all day. *(Robert Watt)*

FONTMELL MAGNA ST8616
★Fontmell (01747) 811441
A350 S of Shaftesbury; SP7 0PA Imposing dining pub with rooms, much emphasis on the enterprising modern cooking, but also some more straightforward reasonably priced dishes, charming service, good wine list, local ales including a house beer (Mallyshag) from Keystone, small bar area with stripy stools, comfy sofas and easy chairs, some bold colours, restaurant with shelves of books and wine bottles, windows overlooking fast flowing stream that runs

under the building; tables on small terrace, six comfortable well appointed bedrooms, open all day in summer, closed lunchtimes Mon, Tues at other times. *(Michael Doswell, George Atkinson)*

HIGHCLIFFE   SZ2193
Galleon (01425) 279855
Lymington Road; BH23 5EA Fresh contemporary refurbishment with leather sofas, light wood floors and open fires, well prepared food from snacks and pub favourites up, local ales including Ringwood, good service, conservatory opening on to terrace and sunny garden; background music – live most weekends; children welcome, summer barbecues, play area, open all day (till midnight Fri, Sat). *(June Asher)*

HINTON ST MARY   ST7816
White Horse (01258) 472723
Just off B3092 a mile N of Sturminster; DT10 1NA Traditional village pub doing well under friendly new licensees, good imaginatively presented food, well kept ales such as Sharps Doom Bar and decent house wines, unusual inglenook fireplace in cheerful bar, extended dining room with gingham tablecloths; children, walkers and dogs welcome, garden tables, attractive setting, open all day weekends. *(Anon)*

HURN   SZ1397
Avon Causeway (01202) 482714
Village signed off A338, then follow Avon, Sopley, Mutchams sign; BH23 6AS Roomy, civilised and comfortable hotel/dining pub, enjoyable food from well filled baguettes and pub favourites up, Sun carvery, well kept Wadworths ales, helpful staff, interesting railway decorations and Pullman-coach restaurant (breakfast served here) by former 1870s station platform; children and dogs welcome, disabled access, nice garden (some road noise) with play area, 12 bedrooms, near Bournemouth Airport (2 weeks free parking if you stay the night before you fly), open all day. *(Anon)*

IBBERTON   ST7807
Crown (01258) 817448
Village W of Blandford Forum; DT11 0EN Traditional village dining pub, flagstones, toby jugs and comfortable seats by inglenook woodburner, back eating area, ales such as Butcombe and Palmers from brick-faced bar, local cider, good variety of enjoyable freshly made food, friendly helpful staff; dogs on leads in bar and in lovely garden, beautiful spot under Bulbarrow Hill, good walks, closed Mon (also Tues lunchtime and Sun evening in winter). *(Anon)*

KINGSTON   SY9579
★Scott Arms (01929) 480270
West Street (B3069); BH20 5LH Extensively modernised old pub rambling through several levels, some sofas and easy chairs, beams, stripped stone, bare boards and log fires, good reasonably priced local food including fresh fish, well kept Dorset, Ringwood and a couple of local guests, decent wines, family dining area; dogs welcome, big attractive garden with outstanding views of Corfe Castle and the Purbeck Hills, summer barbecues, two well equipped bedrooms, good walks, open all day. *(Eddie Edwards)*

LYME REGIS   SY3391
Cobb Arms (01297) 443242
Marine Parade, Monmouth Beach; DT7 3JF Spacious place with well kept Palmers ales and decent wines, good choice of reasonably priced freshly cooked food (gluten-free options), cream teas, quick service, a couple of sofas, ship pictures and marine fish tank, open fire; pool, juke box, TVs; children and dogs welcome, disabled access (one step up from road), tables on small back terrace, next to harbour, beach and coastal walk, three bedrooms, open all day. *(Mrs Sally Scott)*

LYME REGIS   SY3391
★Harbour Inn (01297) 442299
Marine Parade; DT7 3JF More eating than pubby with thriving family atmosphere, attentive young staff, good food from lunchtime sandwiches to local fish (not cheap), good choice of wines by the glass, well kept Otter and local Town Mill, tea and coffee, clean-cut modern décor keeping original flagstones and stone walls (lively acoustic), paintings for sale, sea views from front windows; background music; dogs welcome, disabled access from street, verandah tables. *(Guy Vowles)*

LYME REGIS   SY3492
★Pilot Boat (01297) 443157
Bridge Street; DT7 3QA Popular modern all-day family food place near waterfront, neatly cared for by long-serving licensees, wide choice of good sensibly priced food cooked to order including local fish, nice crab sandwiches, well kept Palmers ales and several wines by the glass, efficient friendly service, plenty of tables in cheery nautically themed areas, skittle alley; quiet background radio; dogs welcome on the lead, terrace tables. *(David and Julie Glover, George Atkinson, B and M Kendall)*

LYME REGIS   SY3391
★Royal Standard (01297) 442637
Marine Parade, The Cobb; DT7 3JF Right on broadest part of beach, properly pubby bar with log fire, fine built-in stripped high settles, local photographs and even old-fashioned ring-up tills, quieter eating area with stripped brick and pine, well kept Palmers ales and good choice of wines by the glass, food from generous crab sandwiches up including local fish and good vegetarian choices, friendly helpful service; darts,

prominent pool table, background and some live music, free wi-fi; children and dogs welcome, good-sized suntrap courtyard with own servery and harbour views, open all day and gets very busy in season. *(Patrick and Daphne Darley, Dru and Louisa Marshall)*

LYME REGIS   SY3492
Volunteer (01297) 442214
Top of Broad Street (A3052 towards Exeter); DT7 3QE Cosy old-fashioned pub with long low-ceilinged bar, nice mix of customers (can get crowded), a well kept house beer from Branscombe tapped from the cask and two west country guests, enjoyable modestly priced food in dining lounge (children allowed here), friendly young staff, roaring fires; dogs welcome, open all day. *(Anon)*

LYTCHETT MINSTER   SY9693
★ **St Peters Finger** (01202) 622275
Dorchester Road; BH16 6JE Well run two-part beamed roadhouse with cheerful efficient staff, popular sensibly priced food from sandwiches and baguettes up, small helpings available, Badger ales and several wines by the glass, welcoming end log fire, cottagey mix of furnishings in different sections giving a cosy feel despite its size; good skittle alley, tables on big terrace, part covered and heated. *(Leslie and Barbara Owen, M G Hart)*

MANSTON   ST8116
Plough (01258) 472484
B3091 Shaftesbury–Sturminster Newton, just N; DT10 1HB Welcoming good-sized traditional country pub, Palmers ales and guests, enjoyable fairly priced standard food, beams, richly decorated plasterwork, ceilings and bar front, red patterned carpets, dining conservatory, some live music; garden picnic-sets, adjacent caravan site. *(Michael and Jenny Back)*

MARNHULL   ST7719
Blackmore Vale (01258) 820701
Burton Street, via Church Hill off B3092; DT10 1JJ Old village pub under welcoming new management; good freshly made traditional food from landlord-chef including two-course OAP lunch (not Sun), three Badger ales, good choice of reasonably priced wines, pleasantly opened-up beamed and flagstoned dining bar with woodburner, more flagstones and oak flooring in cosy smaller bar with log fire, skittle alley, fortnightly quiz Weds; background music; children welcome, dogs in bar, tables in reworked garden, open all day. *(Comus and Sarah Elliott)*

MARNHULL   ST7818
Crown (01258) 820224
About 3 miles N of Sturminster Newton; Crown Road; DT10 1LN Part-thatched inn dating from the 16th c (the Pure Drop Inn in Hardy's *Tess of the D'Urbervilles*); linked

rooms with oak beams, huge flagstones or bare boards, log fire in big stone hearth in oldest part, more modern furnishings and carpet elsewhere, Badger ales and enjoyable food, good friendly service, restaurant; children welcome, peaceful enclosed garden, bedrooms. *(S J and C C Davidson)*

MARTINSTOWN   SY6488
Brewers Arms (01305) 889361
Burnside (B3159); DT2 9LB Friendly family-run village pub, good reasonably priced food including specials, Palmers Copper and Sharps Doom Bar, restaurant, live music including folk night third Tues of month, Weds quiz; children and dogs welcome, garden picnic-sets, good local walks, two bedrooms, closed Sun evening, Mon. *(Ann Salmon)*

MILTON ABBAS   ST8001
Hambro Arms (01258) 880233
Signed off A354 SW of Blandford; DT11 0BP Refurbished pub in beautiful late 18th-c thatched landscaped village, two beamed bars and restaurant, well kept ales such as Dorset Piddle, Ringwood and Sharps Doom Bar, good food from ciabattas and panini up, prompt friendly service; children welcome, dogs in bar, tables on front terrace, four bedrooms, open all day weekends. *(Robert Watt)*

MOTCOMBE   ST8426
Coppleridge (01747) 851980
Signed from The Street, follow to Mere/ Gillingham; SP7 9HW Good food from sandwiches to speciality steaks and fresh fish, real ales including Butcombe, decent wines and welcoming service in former 18th-c farmhouse's bar and various dining rooms, some live music; children welcome, ten spacious courtyard bedrooms, 15-acre grounds, play area. *(Anon)*

NORDEN HEATH   SY94834
Halfway (01929) 480402
A351 Wareham–Corfe Castle; BH20 5DU Cosily laid out partly thatched pub with friendly staff, Badger beers, good wines by the glass and enjoyable food all day including children's choices, pitched-ceiling back serving bar where the locals congregate, front rooms with flagstones, log fires, stripped stonework, snug little side area; picnic-tables outside with play area, good nearby walks. *(Wendy Breese)*

OSMINGTON MILLS   SY7381
★ **Smugglers** (01305) 833125
Off A353 NE of Weymouth; DT3 6HF Bustling old partly thatched family-oriented inn, well extended, with cosy dimly lit timber-divided areas, woodburners, old local pictures, Badger ales and guests, several wines by the glass, good all-day food from varied well priced menu, friendly service; picnic sets on crazy paving by little stream,

thatched summer bar, play area, useful for coast path, four bedrooms, parking charge refunded at bar. *(Barrie and Mary Crees, Phil and Jane Hodson, Peter Salmon)*

PAMPHILL ST9900
★**Vine** (01202) 882259
Off B3082 on NW edge of Wimborne: turn on to Cowgrove Hill at Cowgrove sign, then left up Vine Hill; BH21 4EE Simple old-fashioned place run by same family for three generations and part of Kingston Lacy estate (NT); two tiny bars with coal-effect gas fire, handful of tables and seats on lino floor, local photographs and notices on painted panelling, narrow wooden stairs up to room with darts, Fullers London Pride and a guest, local cider and foreign bottled beers, lunchtime bar snacks; quiet background music, no credit cards, outside lavatories; children (away from bar) and dogs welcome, verandah with grapevine, sheltered gravel terrace and grassy area. *(Anon)*

PIDDLEHINTON SY7197
Thimble (01300) 348270
High Street (B3143); DT2 7TD Partly thatched pub with two handsome fireplaces and deep glazed-over well in low-beamed carpeted core, enjoyable freshly made food from sandwiches (home-baked bread) and one or two pub favourites up, well kept Palmers, good friendly service; background music, free wi-fi; children and dogs welcome, disabled facilities, garden with stream and little bridge, closed Mon. *(Robert Watt)*

PIMPERNE ST9009
★**Anvil** (01258) 453431
Well back from A354; DT11 8UQ Attractive 16th-c thatched family pub with good choice of enjoyable food from varied menus, well kept ales such as Butcombe, Salisbury and Sixpenny, cheerful efficient young staff, bays of plush seating in bright spacious bar, neat black-beamed dining areas; background music, games machines; dogs welcome in certain parts, good garden with fish pond and big weeping willow, 12 bedrooms, nice surroundings, open all day. *(Leslie and Barbara Owen)*

POOLE SZ0391
Bermuda Triangle (01202) 748087
Parr Street, Lower Parkstone (just off A35 at Ashley Cross); BH14 0JY Old-fashioned bare-boards local with four particularly well kept changing ales, two or three good continental lagers on tap and many other beers from around the world, friendly landlady and staff, no food, dark panelling, snug old corners and lots of nautical and other bric-a-brac, cloudscape ceiling, back room with sports TV; no children and a bit too steppy for disabled access; pavement picnic-sets, open all day weekends. *(Charles Carter, Kim Skuse)*

POOLE SZ0391
Cow (01202) 749569
Station Road, Ashley Cross, Parkstone; beside Parkstone Station; BH14 8UD Interesting open-plan pub with airy bistro bar, squashy sofas, leather seating cubes and low tables on stripped-wood floors, open fire in exposed brick fireplace, good modern food (not Sun evening) from sensibly short menu, up to four real ales and a dozen wines by the glass from extensive list, friendly welcoming staff, evening dining room, board games and newspapers; background music, discreet TV; children welcome till 7.30pm, dogs in bar, enclosed heated terrace, open all day. *(Anon)*

POOLE SZ0190
Poole Arms (01202) 673450
Town Quay; BH15 1HJ 17th-c waterfront pub looking across harbour to Brownsea Island, good fresh fish at reasonable prices, well kept Ringwood, one comfortably old-fashioned room with boarded ceiling and nautical prints, pleasant staff; outside gents'; picnic-sets in front of the handsome green-tiled façade, almost next door to the Portsmouth Hoy. *(David M Smith)*

POOLE SZ0090
Portsmouth Hoy (01202) 673517
The Quay; BH15 1HJ Harbourside pub with views to Brownsea Island, old-world atmosphere with dark wood, beams and bare boards, good value food including fresh fish and vegetarian choices, well kept Badger ales, friendly service, live music (jazz, blues, folk); children welcome, outside tables shared with the Poole Arms, open all day. *(David Hunt)*

POOLE SZ0190
Rising Sun (01202) 771246
Dear Hay Lane; BH15 1NZ Large modernised dining pub, good freshly cooked food from sandwiches up including weekday set menu and blackboard specials, friendly helpful staff, lots of wines by the glass, ales such as Ringwood, comfortable bar area with bucket chairs and some high tables and stools, restaurant; background music; children welcome, tables in attractive garden areas front and back. *(Lawrence Pearse)*

PORTLAND SY6873
Cove House (01305) 820895
Follow Chiswell signposts – is at NW corner of Portland; DT5 1AW Low-beamed 18th-c pub in superb position effectively built into the sea defences just above the end of Chesil Beach, great views from three-room bar's bay windows, Sharps Doom Bar and other well kept beers, pubby food (all-day weekends); background music, Mon quiz, steep steps down to gents'; children welcome, dogs in bar, tables out by seawall, open all day. *(Anon)*

PORTLAND
Royal Portland Arms
SY6873

(01305) 862255 *Fortuneswell; DT5 1LZ*
Friendly 18th-c stone-built local, homely and
unfussy, with well kept quickly changing ales
(some tapped from the cask), local ciders,
bar snacks, live music Fri and winter Sun
afternoon; dogs welcome, open all day, till
late Fri, Sat. *(Anon)*

POWERSTOCK
SY5196
⋆**Three Horseshoes** (01308) 485328
*Off A3066 Beaminster–Bridport via
West Milton; DT6 3TF* Tucked-away pub
surrounded by good walks; cheerful cosy
bar with flagstones and stripped panelling,
windsor and mate's chairs around assorted
tables, Palmers ales and eight wines by the
glass, nice food cooked by landlord, slightly
more formal dining room with local paintings
for sale; background music, board games;
children and dogs (in bar) welcome, picnic-
sets on back terrace with garden and country
views, two comfortable bedrooms, closed
Mon lunchtime. *(Itsguy, Caroline Prescott,
Emma Scofield, Dr D J and Mrs S C Walker, B and
M Kendall)*

PUDDLETOWN
SY7594
Blue Vinney (01305) 848228
The Moor; DT2 8TE Large modernised
village pub under newish management,
beamed oak-floor bar and restaurant, nice
variety of popular well presented food (not
Sun evening) from lunchtime baguettes up,
well kept Sharps, Youngs and a beer named
for the pub, friendly young staff; children
welcome, terrace overlooking garden with
play area, open all day Fri-Sun. *(Michael
Doswell)*

SANDFORD ORCAS
ST6220
⋆**Mitre** (01963) 220271
*Off B3148 and B3145 N of Sherborne;
DT9 4RU* Thriving tucked-away country
local with welcoming long-serving licensees,
three well kept ales such as Ringwood,
Sharps and Yeovil, wholesome home-
made food (not Mon) from good soup and
sandwiches up, flagstones, log fires and fresh
flowers, small bar and larger pleasantly
homely dining area; occasional open mike
and quiz nights; children and dogs welcome,
pretty back garden with terrace, closed Mon
lunchtime. *(B J Thompson)*

SHAFTESBURY
ST8622
Mitre (01747) 853002
High Street; SP7 8JE Imposing old
sandstone building, unpretentious inside,
with friendly efficient service, well kept Wells

& Youngs ales and a couple of guests, good
range of wines, enjoyable pub food including
well filled sandwiches, fine log fire, daily
papers, varied mix of tables, Blackmore Vale
views from back dining room and three-tier
suntrap decking; background music; children
and dogs welcome, open all day. *(Anon)*

SHAPWICK
ST9301
Anchor (01258) 857269
*Off A350 Blandford–Poole; West Street;
DT11 9LB* Welcoming red-brick Victorian
pub owned by village consortium; popular
freshly made food including set deals
(booking advised), ales such as Palmers,
Ringwood and Sharps, real cider, scrubbed
pine tables on wood floors, pastel walls
and open fires; children welcome, tables
out in front, more in attractive garden with
terrace behind, handy for Kingston Lacy
(NT). *(Anon)*

SHAVE CROSS
SY4198
Shave Cross Inn (01308) 868358
*On back lane Bridport–Marshwood,
signposted locally; OS Sheet 193 map
reference 415980; DT6 6HW* Former
medieval monks' lodging; small character
timbered and flagstoned bar with huge
inglenook, Branscombe Vale Branoc, Dorset
Marshwood Vale and pub's own-label
4Ms, farm ciders, vintage rums, attractive
restaurant with grandfather clock, pricey
caribbean-influenced food (also more
traditional bar menu), pleasant staff,
ancient skittle alley with pool, darts and a
juke box; background music; children and
dogs welcome, sheltered pretty garden with
thatched wishing-well, carp pool and play
area, seven recently built boutique bedrooms,
helipad, closed Sun evening, Mon. *(Peter
Meister, Pat and Tony Martin, Paul Humphreys)*

STOBOROUGH
SY9286
Kings Arms (01929) 552705
*B3075 S of Wareham; Corfe Road;
BH20 5AB* Part-thatched village pub
with up to five well kept changing ales,
Thatcher's cider, good choice of enjoyable
reasonably priced food in bar and restaurant,
live music Sat; children and dogs welcome,
disabled access, views over marshes to River
Frome from big terrace tables, open all day
Fri-Sat. *(Anon)*

STOKE ABBOTT
ST4500
⋆**New Inn** (01308) 868333
*Off B3162 and B3163 2 miles W of
Beaminster; DT8 3JW* Spotless 17th-c
thatched pub with friendly helpful staff, good
nicely presented food from varied menu using
local produce including own vegetables and

herbs, well kept Palmers ales, woodburner in big inglenook, beams, brasses and copper, some handsome panelling, flagstoned dining room, fresh flowers on tables; occasional background music; children welcome, wheelchair access, two lovely gardens, unspoilt quiet thatched village with good surrounding walks, street fair third Sat in July, closed Sun evening, Mon. *(Councillor Stephen Chappell)*

STOURTON CAUNDLE   ST7115
⋆ **Trooper**   (01963) 362405
Village signed off A30 E of Milborne Port; DT10 2JW Pretty little stone-built pub in lovely village setting, friendly staff and atmosphere, good simple food and well kept changing beers including own microbrews, reasonable prices, spotless tiny low-ceilinged bar, stripped stone dining room, darts, dominoes and shove-ha'penny, skittle alley; background and some live music (folk and jazz), sports TV, outside gents'; children and dogs welcome, a few picnic-sets out in front, pleasant side garden with play area, camping, closed Mon lunchtime. *(Anon)*

STRATTON   SY6593
Saxon Arms   (01305) 260020
Off A37 NW of Dorchester; The Square; DT2 9WG Traditional but recently built flint-and-thatch local, open-plan, bright and spacious with light oak tables and comfortable settles on flagstones or carpet, open fire, well kept Ringwood, Timothy Taylors Landlord and two guests, good value wines, tasty generous food including good choice of specials and winter lunchtime set deal (Mon-Fri), large comfortable dining section on right, traditional games; background music; children and dogs welcome, terrace tables overlooking village green, open all day Fri-Sun. *(Anon)*

STUDLAND   SZ0382
Bankes Arms   (01929) 450225
Off B3351, Isle of Purbeck; Manor Road; BH19 3AU Very popular spot above fine beach, outstanding country, sea and cliff views from huge garden over road with lots of seating; comfortably basic big bar with raised drinking area, beams, flagstones and good log fire, well kept changing ales including own Isle of Purbeck, local cider, nice wines by the glass, all-day food, darts and pool in side area; background music, machines, sports TV, can get very busy on summer weekends and parking complicated (NT car park); over-8s and dogs welcome, just off coast path, big comfortable bedrooms. *(R Elliott, Jenny and Brian Seller, S J and C C Davidson)*

STURMINSTER MARSHALL   SY9499
Black Horse   (01258) 857217
A350; BH21 4AQ Welcoming roadside country pub with enjoyable good value food from nice sandwiches up, Badger ales, long comfortable beamed and panelled bar;

children welcome, no dogs, closed Sun evening. *(Anon)*

STURMINSTER MARSHALL   SY9500
Red Lion   (01258) 857319
Opposite church; off A350 Blandford–Poole; BH21 4BU Attractive village pub opposite handsome church, bustling local atmosphere, wide variety of enjoyable food including set menu deal, special diets catered for, well kept Badger ales and nice wines, old-fashioned roomy U-shaped bar with log fire, good-sized dining room in former skittle alley; background music; children and dogs welcome, disabled access, back garden with wicker furniture and picnic-sets, open all day Sun, closed Mon. *(Robert Watt)*

STURMINSTER NEWTON   ST7813
Bull   (01258) 472435
A357, S of centre; DT10 2BS Thatched and beamed 16th-c riverside pub refurbished after recent flooding and under new management, Badger ales and good home-made food; children welcome, roadside picnic-sets, more in secluded back garden, open all day weekends. *(Sue Dean)*

SWANAGE   SZ0278
Red Lion   (01929) 423533
High Street; BH19 2LY Busy 17th-c low-beamed local, great choice of ciders and up to six well kept ales including Palmers, Ringwood, Sharps and Timothy Taylors, good value food from sandwiches and baked potatoes up; background and some live music, pool; children welcome, picnic-sets in garden with partly covered terrace, bedrooms in former back coach house, open all day. *(Anon)*

SYDLING ST NICHOLAS   SY6399
Greyhound   (01300) 341303
Off A37 N of Dorchester; High Street; DT2 9PD New landlady for this former coaching inn; beamed and flagstoned serving area with three real ales, carpeted bar with straightforward furniture and handsome Portland stone fireplace, covered well in cosy dining room, conservatory; children welcome, picnic-sets in little front garden, small but comfortable bedrooms, has closed Sun evening. *(Michael Doswell, Peter Brix)*

TARRANT KEYNSTON   ST9204
True Lovers Knot   (01258) 452209
B3082 Blandford–Wimborne; DT11 9JG Neatly kept corner pub with modernised largely carpeted bar, some beams and flagstones, woodburner, uncluttered dining extension, food from traditional dishes up including good Sun carvery, Badger ales, decent wines by the glass; children and dogs welcome, picnic-sets in big garden overlooking fields, four well equipped bedrooms, good breakfast, campsite. *(Anon)*

THREE LEGGED CROSS   SU0905
Three Legged Cross (01202) 812901
Ringwood Road, towards Ashley Heath and A31; BH21 6RE Picturesque thatched Vintage Inn, long and low, with pleasant rambling layout, their usual reasonably priced food and some interesting specials, ales such as Ringwood, decent wines; children welcome, lots of tables on attractive terrace and front lawn by fish pond, handy for Moors Valley Country Park, open all day. *(David Cannings)*

UPLODERS   SY5093
Crown (01308) 485356
Signed off A35 E of Bridport; DT6 4NU Refurbished stone village pub, log fires, dark low beams, flagstones and mix of old furniture including stripped-pine, traditional food, Palmers ales; background music; children and dogs welcome, tables in attractive two-tier garden. *(Dru and Louisa Marshall)*

UPWEY   SY6785
Old Ship (01305) 812522
Off A354; Ridgeway; DT3 5QQ Traditional 17th-c beamed pub (features in Hardy's *Under the Greenwood Tree*), alcoves and log fires, Ringwood and a couple of guests, enjoyable sensibly priced food including blackboard specials, friendly attentive staff, skittle alley; children and dogs welcome, picnic-sets in garden with terrace, interesting walks nearby, open all day Fri, Sat. *(Terry Townsend)*

WAREHAM   SY9287
Kings Arms (01929) 552503
North Street (A351, N end of town); BH20 4AD Traditional stone and thatch town local, well kept Ringwood and guests, decent good value pubby food, friendly staff, back serving counter and two bars off flagstoned central corridor, beams and inglenook, darts; children and dogs welcome, garden behind with picnic-sets, open all day. *(S J and C C Davidson)*

WAREHAM   SY9287
Old Granary (01929) 552010
The Quay; BH20 4LP Fine old brick building with riverside terrace; emphasis on dining but two small beamed rooms by main door for drinkers, enjoyable fairly standard food, well kept Badger ales and good wines by the glass, neat efficient young staff, airy dining room with leather high-backed chairs and pews around pale wood tables, brick walls and new oak standing timbers, two further rooms with big photographs of the pub, woodburners, nice relaxed atmosphere; quiet background jazz; children welcome, boats for hire over bridge, open all day from 9am (10am Sun). *(Patrick and Daphne Darley, Peter Salmon)*

WAREHAM   SY9287
Quay Inn (01929) 552735
The Quay; BH20 4LP Comfortable 18th-c inn in great spot by the water, enjoyable food including pubby favourites and cook-your-own meat on a hot stone, friendly attentive service, well kept Otter, Isle of Purbeck and Ringwood, reasonably priced wine list, flagstones and open fires; children welcome, terrace area and picnic-sets out on quay, boat trips, bedrooms, parking nearby can be difficult, market day Sat, open all day in summer. *(Anon)*

WAREHAM FOREST   SY9089
★ Silent Woman (01929) 552909
Wareham–Bere Regis; Bere Road; BH20 7PA Long neatly kept dining pub divided by doorways and standing timbers, good variety of enjoyable home-made food including daily specials, Badger ales kept well and plenty of wines by the glass, traditional furnishings, farm tools and stripped masonry; background music, no children inside; dogs welcome, wheelchair access, plenty of picnic-sets outside including a covered area, walks nearby; a popular wedding venue so best to check it's open. *(R Elliott, Leslie and Barbara Owen)*

WAYTOWN   SY4797
Hare & Hounds (01308) 488203
Between B3162 and A3066 N of Bridport; DT6 5LQ Attractive 18th-c country local up and down steps, friendly caring staff, well kept Palmers tapped from the cask, local cider, enjoyable good value food generously served including popular Sun lunch, open fire, two small cottagey rooms and pretty dining room; children and dogs welcome (there's a pub dog and treats on the bar), lovely Brit Valley views from sizeable well maintained garden, play area, occasional barbecues and live music. *(Peter Thornton, Will Hancox, Sancha Butcher)*

WEST BEXINGTON   SY5386
Manor Hotel (01308) 897660
Off B3157 SE of Bridport; Beach Road; DT2 9DF Relaxing quietly set hotel with long history and fine sea views; good choice of enjoyable food in beamed cellar bar, flagstoned restaurant or Victorian-style conservatory, well kept Otter, Thatcher's cider and several wines by the glass, friendly owners; children welcome, dogs on leads (not in restaurant), charming well kept garden, close to Chesil Beach, 13 bedrooms. *(Anon)*

WEST LULWORTH   SY8280
Castle Inn (01929) 400311
B3070 SW of Wareham; BH20 5RN Pretty 16th-c thatched inn in lovely spot near Lulworth Cove, good walks and lots of summer visitors; beamed flagstoned bar concentrating on wide choice of popular generously served food, well kept

changing local ales, 12 ciders/perries, maze of booth seating divided by ledges, cosy more modern-feeling lounge bar, pleasant restaurant; background music; children and dogs welcome, front terrace, long attractive garden behind on several levels, boules and barbecues, 12 bedrooms. *(Ian and Sharon Shorthouse)*

WEST LULWORTH
SY8280
Lulworth Cove (01929) 400333
Main Road; BH20 5RQ Modernised inn with good range of enjoyable food at reasonable prices, well kept Badger ales and several wines by the glass, helpful friendly service, seaside theme bar with bare boards and painted panelling; free wi-fi; children and dogs welcome, picnic-sets on sizeable terrace, short stroll down to cove, 12 bedrooms (some with sea view balcony), open (and food) all day. *(Pete Coates)*

WEST PARLEY
SZ0898
Curlew (01202) 594811
Christchurch Road; BH22 8SQ Refurbished Vintage Inn in early 19th-c farmhouse; beamed areas around central bar, mixed furnishings, candles on tables, two log fires, emphasis on enjoyable food including good value fixed price menu (till 5pm), well kept Ringwood, St Austell and a guest, good choice of wines, friendly courteous staff; unobtrusive background music, TV; picnic-sets in front garden, open all day. *(David and Sally Frost, Peter Salmon)*

WEST STAFFORD
SY7289
Wise Man (01305) 261970
Sgned off A352 Dorchester–Wareham; DT2 8AG 16th-c thatched and beamed pub near Hardy's Cottage (NT), open-plan interior with flagstone and wood floors, good well priced food from lunchtime ciabattas up including some interesting choices, Sun carvery, Butcombe, Dorset, Ringwood and St Austell from central bar, good choice of wines by the glass, friendly attentive staff; children and dogs welcome, disabled facilities, plenty of seats outside, lovely walks nearby, open all day weekends. *(R J and G M Townson)*

WEYMOUTH
SY6778
Boot 07809 440772
High West Street; DT4 8JH Friendly unspoilt old local near the harbour, comfortably lived in with beams, bare boards, panelling, hooded stone-mullioned windows and coal fires, cosy gently sloping snug, well kept Ringwood ales and guests from five brass handpumps, real cider and good selection of malt whiskies, no food apart

from pork pies and pickled eggs, live music Tues, quiz Weds; free wi-fi; disabled access, pavement tables, open all day. *(Anon)*

WEYMOUTH
SY6878
Nothe Tavern (01305) 839255
Barrack Road; DT4 8TZ Roomy and comfortable early 19th-c pub near Nothe Fort, wide range of good food including fresh local fish and good value Sun carvery, OAP weekday lunch deal too, friendly efficient service, two well kept Ringwood ales and a guest, decent wines and good choice of malt whiskies, lots of dark wood, whisky-water jugs on ceiling, interesting prints and photographs, restaurant with distant harbour glimpses; may be quiet background music; children and dogs welcome, more views from terrace, open all day weekends. *(Leslie and Barbara Owen, D J and P M Taylor)*

WEYMOUTH
SY6778
Royal Oak (01305) 761343
Custom House Quay; DT4 8BE Welcoming old harbourside local with good choice of beers and ciders; weekend live music; open (and food) all day. *(David and Sally Cullen)*

WEYMOUTH
SY6778
Ship (01305) 773879
Custom House Quay; DT4 8BE Neatly modern extended waterfront pub with several nautical-theme open-plan levels, well kept Badger ales from long bar, several wines by the glass, enjoyable good value usual food (upstairs only in the evening) from sandwiches and baguettes up, friendly helpful staff; unobtrusive background music; dogs welcome (biscuits for them), wheelchair access downstairs, some quayside seating and pleasant back terrace. *(Phil Bryant, E J Palmer)*

WEYMOUTH
SY6778
Wellington Arms (01305) 786963
St Alban Street; DT4 8PY Friendly backstreet pub with handsome 19th-c tiled façade, panelled and carpeted interior with banquettes, mirrors and lots of old local photographs, well kept Ringwood and other Marstons-related beers, good value pubby food, some live music; children welcome in back dining room, disabled access, open all day. *(Anon)*

WIMBORNE MINSTER
SU0000
Kings Head (01202) 880101
The Square; BH21 1JG Imposing recently refurbished 18th-c hotel (Old English Inn), good choice of enjoyable

---

If a compulsory service charge is mentioned prominently on a menu or accommodation terms, you must pay it if service was satisfactory. If service is really bad, you are legally entitled to refuse to pay some or all of the service charge as compensation for not getting the service you might reasonably have expected.

food in roomy bar or restaurant, Greene King ales and some nice wines, cheery helpful staff; free wi-fi; children welcome, comfortable reasonably priced bedrooms, good breakfast, open all day. *(Sue and Mike Todd)*

WIMBORNE MINSTER   SU0100
★ **Olive Branch** (01202) 884686
East Borough, just off Hanham Road (B3073, just E of its junction with B3078); has good car park; BH21 1PF
Handsome spacious town house undergoing extensive refurbishment as we went to press – news please. *(Leslie and Barbara Owen, Harvey Brown, Richard Tilbrook)*

WIMBORNE ST GILES   SU0212
Bull (01725) 517300
Off B3078 N of Wimborne; BH21 5NF
Nicely refurbished open-plan Edwardian dining inn, good if not particularly cheap food using fresh local ingredients (organic where possible), fine choice of wines by the glass, Badger ales, good friendly service, conservatory overlooking neatly kept garden; children and dogs welcome, five stylish bedrooms, closed Sun evening, Mon. *(Anon)*

WINTERBORNE STICKLAND   ST8304
Crown (01258) 881042
North Street; DT11 0NJ Welcoming thatched village local refurbished under newish licensees, two rooms separated by servery, smaller one with inglenook woodburner, high backed settle and dark tables and chairs on patterned carpet, the other with low beams, more tables and chairs and darts, well kept Ringwood ales, a local cider and enjoyable traditional food from sandwiches and light dishes up; live music Fri, free wi-fi; children welcome, pretty terrace garden, open all day Fri-Sun. *(Michael Doswell, Marina Reece)*

Post Office address codings confusingly give the impression that some pubs are in Dorset, when they're really in Somerset (which is where we list them).

Essex

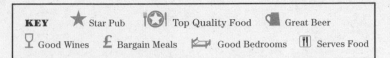

ARKESDEN   TL4834   Map 5

Axe & Compasses 🍷

Off B1038; CB11 4EX

Comfortably traditional pub with Greene King beers and decent food

There's always a good mix of both visitors and regulars in this rambling thatched pub. The oldest part (dating from the 17th c) is the traditionally carpeted lounge bar, with low-slung ceilings, polished upholstered oak and elm seats, sofas and a blazing fire; a smaller, quirky, uncarpeted public bar has built-in settles and darts. Throughout there are gleaming brasses, and a relaxed welcoming atmosphere created by the pleasant licensees and their staff. Greene King IPA, Hardys & Hansons Olde Trip and St Austell Proper Job on handpump, a very good wine list (with 15 by the glass) and around two dozen malt whiskies. The side terrace has seats and tables and pretty hanging baskets, and parking is at the back. This is a particularly lovely village.

🍴 Popular food includes lunchtime sandwiches (not Sunday), chicken liver pâté with cumberland sauce, fresh plaice with a mushroom, white wine and cream sauce, spinach, leek and stilton tart with a tomato and basil sauce, chicken and mushrooms wrapped in pastry with a wholegrain mustard cream, lambs liver and bacon, monkfish on roasted red pepper sauce, and puddings. *Benchmark main dish: steak, kidney and mushroom pie £13.95. Two-course evening meal £20.50.*

Greene King ~ Tenants Themis and Diane Christou ~ Real ale ~ (01799) 550272 ~ Open 11.30-2.30, 6-11; 12-3, 6-10.30 Sun ~ Bar food 12-2 (2.30 Sun), 6.30-9 ~ Restaurant ~ Children welcome ~ Dogs allowed in bar ~ www.axeandcompasses.co.uk
Recommended by Martin Jones, David Jackson

AYTHORPE RODING   TL5915   Map 5

Axe & Compasses 🌟 🍺

B184 S of Dunmow; CM6 1PP

Appealing free house, with nice balance of eating and drinking and a friendly welcome

There's always something going on at this lively, well run pub, such as pie and pint offers, two-for-one fish and chips on Wednesday evenings, quiz nights and music events. It's an attractive weatherboarded pub with views across open fields to a windmill, and there's always a good mix of customers of all ages – all welcomed by the friendly landlord and his staff. Everything is warm, cosy and neatly kept, with bent old beams and timbers in stripped red-brick walls, comfortable bar chairs at the counter, leatherette settles, stools and dark country chairs around a few pub tables on pale boards and turkish rugs. The original part (on the left) has a two-way fireplace marking off a snug little raftered dining area, which has sentimental prints on dark masonry and a big open-faced clock. Nethergate IPA, Sharps Doom Bar and guests such as Adnams Broadside, Colchester Romani Ite Domum and Wibblers Apprentice on handpump or tapped from the cask, 13 wines by the glass, and up to three Weston's farm ciders; background music and board games. The small back garden has stylish modern tables and chairs.

 A wide choice of good, popular food includes breakfast (from 9am), lunchtime sandwiches, chicken liver parfait with home-made chutney, smoked salmon and home-made blini, pies (including pork belly with cider, lamb shank in ale, rabbit), courgette and tomato bake, toad in the hole with gravy, barbecue beef or chicken burgers with toppings and chips, thai-style fishcakes with asian coleslaw, and puddings such as white chocolate and raspberry parfait and bakewell tart with custard; food deals are offered on Monday, Tuesday and Wednesday. *Benchmark main dish: steak in ale pie £11.95. Two-course evening meal £16.70.*

Free house ~ Licensee David Hunt ~ Real ale ~ (01279) 876648 ~ Open 9am-11pm (10.30pm Sun) ~ Bar food 9-2.30, 6-9.30; 9am-9.30pm Sat; 9-8 Sun ~ Restaurant ~ Children welcome ~ Dogs allowed in bar ~ Wi-fi ~ www.theaxeandcompasses.co.uk
Recommended by Alan Just, N R White, Mrs Margo Finlay, Jörg Kasprowski

CLAVERING
Cricketers
TL4832 Map 5

B1038 Newport–Buntingford; CB11 4QT

Busy dining pub with inventive food, real ales and a carefully chosen wine list; individually decorated bedrooms

'This ticks all the boxes' and 'I wish I lived nearer' are just two comments from enthusiastic readers about this neatly kept and carefully modernised pub. It's been owned by Jamie Oliver's parents for many years (signed books by Jamie are on sale) and has plenty of old-fashioned charm. The main area with its very low beams and big open fireplace has bays of deep purple button-backed banquettes and padded leather dining chairs on dark floorboards. The back part on the left is more obviously designed for eating: two fairly compact carpeted areas, with a step in between. The right side is similar: it's set more formally for dining, but is still traditional with some big copper and brass pans on dark beams and timbers; background music. Ales from Adnams, Nethergate and Saffron on handpump and 19 wines by the glass from a list with helpful notes. The attractive front terrace has wicker-look seats around teak tables among colourful flowering shrubs. The six bedrooms (cottagey or contemporary in style) are well equipped and comfortable. The pub is handy for Stansted Airport.

 Rewarding food includes weekday sandwiches, hot smoked salmon with a free-range poached egg and hollandaise, fresh oysters four-ways, home-made sausage bolognaise, spiced stuffed squash with halloumi, a pie of the day, a half-duck with confit leg and plum and star anise sauce, venison curry, and puddings such as sticky toffee pudding with vanilla ice-cream in a brandy snap basket. *Benchmark main dish: steak in ale pie £14.95. Two-course evening meal £21.50.*

Free house ~ Licensee Trevor Oliver ~ Real ale ~ (01799) 550442 ~ Open 7am-11pm ~ Bar food 12-2, 6.30-9.30; 12-8 Sun ~ Children welcome ~ Wi-fi ~ Bedrooms: £67.50/£95 ~ www.thecricketers.co.uk *Recommended by Mrs Margo Finlay, Jörg Kasprowski, Peter Rozée, M and G R*

DUNMOW
TL6222 Map 5

Angel & Harp

Church Road, Church End; B1057 signposted to Finchingfield/The Bardfields, off B184 N of town; CM6 2AD

Comfortable and relaxing, a good place to drop in any time of day

Open all day from 9am for breakfast, this bustling place rambles about through standing timbers and doorways and into all sorts of interconnected rooms. There's a good choice of seating from armchairs, sofas and banquettes to more upright dining chairs – or, for a very pubby feel, the bar stools along each side of the free-standing zinc 'counter' that spans two structural uprights. The low-ceilinged main area has a substantial brick fireplace and some fine old floor tiling as well as carpet. They keep Adnams Explorer, Nethergate IPA and a guest from Mauldons or Mighty Oak on handpump and eight wines by the glass, and there's a big espresso machine on a separate dresser. The atmosphere is friendly and informal and the staff neatly dressed and helpful; background music. Up a few steps, an interesting raftered room has Perspex chairs around one huge table. A glass wall gives tables in an attractive L-shaped extension a view over the flagstoned courtyard with its wishing fountain, cushioned metal chairs under big canopies, and picnic-table sets on the grass beyond.

 Reliably good food includes smashing breakfasts, sandwiches, prawn and crayfish salad, barbecue chicken wings with blue cheese dressing, pizzas from a woodburning oven, beef, chicken and vegetarian burgers with a choice of chips, calves liver and bacon with gravy, seafood thermidor, crispy lamb peking-style, and puddings such as banoffi sundae and chocolate brownie with chocolate sauce. *Benchmark main dish: rack of barbecue baby back ribs with coleslaw and chips £14.95. Two-course evening meal £16.00.*

Free house ~ Licensee David Hunt ~ Real ale ~ (01371) 859259 ~ Open 9am-11pm (10pm Sun) ~ Bar food 9am-9.30pm (till 8pm Sun) ~ Restaurant ~ Children welcome ~ Dogs allowed in bar ~ Wi-fi ~ Occasional live music plus monthly quiz ~ www.angelandharp.co.uk *Recommended by Ruth May, Caroline Prescott*

FEERING
TL8720 Map 5

Sun ◖ £

Just off A12 Kelvedon bypass; Feering Hill (B1024 just W of Feering proper); CO5 9NH

Striking timbered and jettied pub with six real ales, well liked food and pleasant garden

Handy for the A12, this handsome 16th-c pub is warmly welcoming to both locals and visitors. The spreading carpeted bar is relaxed, unpretentious and civilised, with two big woodburning stoves – one in the huge central inglenook fireplace, another by an antique winged settle on the left. Throughout are handsomely carved black beams and timbers galore, and attractive wildflower murals in a frieze above the central timber divider. There are half a dozen Shepherd Neame ales on handpump (Amber, Bishops Finger, Kents Best, Master Brew, Spitfire, Whitstable Bay Pale) plus monthly guests – as well as summer and winter beer festivals – and nine wines by the glass; cheerful service, daily papers, board games. A brick-paved back courtyard has tables, heaters and a shelter, and the garden beyond has tall trees shading green picnic-sets.

Well liked food includes sandwiches, baguettes and panini, prawn and crayfish cocktail, chicken and bacon terrine with apricot chutney, home-cooked ham and free-range eggs, beer-battered fresh haddock and chips, vegetarian tagine with herb couscous, slow-cooked pork belly with wholegrain mustard and cider cream, and puddings such as ginger sponge with lime syrup and crumble of the day. *Benchmark main dish: beef, mushroom and stilton pie £10.50. Two-course evening meal £16.50.*

Shepherd Neame ~ Tenant Andy Howard ~ Real ale ~ (01376) 570442 ~ Open 12-3, 5.30-11; 12-midnight Sat; 12-10.30 Sun ~ Bar food 12-2.30, 6-9.30; 12-8 Sun ~ Children welcome away from bar ~ Dogs welcome ~ Wi-fi ~ www.suninnfeering.co.uk
Recommended by Steve and Irene Homer, Edward Mirzoeff, N R White

FULLER STREET   TL7416   Map 5
Square & Compasses
Back road Great Leighs–Hatfield Peverel; CM3 2BB

Neatly kept country pub, handy for walks, with two woodburning stoves, four ales and enjoyable food

This is the sort of place we love having in our *Guide*. It's run with care for both the pub and its customers – and it shows; our readers come back regularly. The L-shaped beamed bar has two woodburning stoves in inglenook fireplaces, Adnams Best, Farmers Ales A Drop of Nelsons Blood and Wibblers Dengie IPA and Dengie Dark on handpump, Weston's cider and 18 wines by the glass, served by friendly staff. The dining room features shelves of bottles and decanters against timbered walls and an appealing variety of dining chairs around dark wooden tables set with linen napkins, on carpeting; there's a small extension for walkers and dogs. Background jazz. The tables out in front on decking offer gentle country views, and the Essex Way long-distance footpath is nearby.

 Enjoyable food includes sandwiches, mussels with smoked bacon, leeks and cream, home-cooked ham with free-range eggs, beer-battered fresh cod and chips, cumberland sausage ring with onion gravy, fresh crab cakes with chilli salsa, free-range chicken wrapped in parma ham with spiced pear chutney and red wine sauce, and puddings such as white and dark chocolate bread and butter pudding and lemon and lime cheesecake. *Benchmark main dish: steak in ale pie £11.95. Two-course evening meal £20.00.*

Free house ~ Licensee Victor Roome ~ Real ale ~ (01245) 361477 ~ Open 11.30-3, 5.30-midnight; 11.30am-midnight Sat; 12-11 Sun ~ Bar food 12-2 (2.30 Sat), 6.30-9.30; 12-6 Sun ~ Restaurant ~ Well behaved children welcome ~ Dogs allowed in bar ~ www.thesquareandcompasses.co.uk *Recommended by Mrs Margo Finlay, Jörg Kasprowski, Evelyn and Derek Walter, N R White*

FYFIELD   TL5706   Map 5
Queens Head ♀
Corner of B184 and Queen Street; CM5 0RY

Friendly old pub with seats in riverside garden, a good choice of drinks and highly thought-of food

On sunny days, it's best to arrive early to this neat 15th-c pub to bag a seat in the prettily planted back garden that runs down to the sleepy River Roding. Inside, the compact, low-beamed, L-shaped bar has exposed timbers, pretty lamps on nice sturdy elm tables and comfortable seating from wall banquettes to attractive, unusual high-backed chairs, some in a snug little side booth. In summer, two facing fireplaces have church candles instead of a fire; background music. The upstairs restaurant is more formal.

🍴 Tempting food using local ingredients includes devilled chicken livers and wild mushrooms on toast, mussels in cider with pancetta and leeks, chicken caesar salad, home-cured ham and duck egg, wild mushroom risotto with candied tomatoes, lambs liver and bacon, toad in the hole with caramelised onion gravy, soy-glazed salmon with spiced crab linguine and shellfish consommé, and puddings such as raspberry ripple cheesecake and chocolate mousse. They also offer a two- and three-course set menu (not Friday and Saturday evenings or Sunday). *Benchmark main dish: skate wing with brown caper butter and triple-cooked chips £18.50. Two-course evening meal £21.00.*

Free house ~ Licensee Daniel Lamprecht ~ Real ale ~ (01277) 899231 ~ Open 12-3.30, 6-11; 12-11 Sat; 12-10.30 Sun; closed Mon ~ Bar food 12-2.30 (4 Sat), 6.30-9.30; 12-6 Sun ~ Restaurant ~ Children welcome away from bar ~ Wi-fi ~ Folk music first Weds of month ~ www.thequeensheadfyfield.co.uk *Recommended by Mrs Margo Finlay, Jörg Kasprowski*

GOLDHANGER
TL9008 Map 5
Chequers 🍺
Church Street; off B1026 E of Heybridge; CM9 8AS

Cheerful and neatly kept pub with six real ales, traditional furnishings, friendly staff and tasty food

As well as holding spring and autumn beer festivals, this popular village pub keeps around half a dozen real ales on handpump, such as Adnams Ghost Ship, Crouch Vale Brewers Gold, Sharps Doom Bar and Wells & Youngs Bitter and guests such as Camerons Tontine and Great Western Moose River; also, 16 wines by the glass, ten malt whiskies and several farm ciders. The nice old corridor with its red and black floor tiles leads to six rambling rooms, including a spacious lounge with dark beams, black panelling and a huge sash window overlooking the graveyard, a traditional dining room with bare boards and carpeting, and a games room with bar billiards; woodburning stove, open fires, TV and background music. There are picnic-sets under umbrellas in the courtyard with its grapevine. Next door is a fine old church.

🍴 A wide choice of reliably good food includes sandwiches, duck and orange pâté with cumberland sauce, creamy baked stilton mushrooms, ham and free-range eggs, brie, courgette and almond crumble, chargrilled cajun chicken with coleslaw and fries, lamb and mint pudding, smoked haddock, king prawn and salmon pie, and puddings such as lemon meringue pie and pot au chocolat. *Benchmark main dish: steak in stout pie £11.25. Two-course evening meal £17.00.*

Punch ~ Lease Philip Glover and Dominic Davies ~ Real ale ~ (01621) 788203 ~ Open 11-11; 12-10.30 Sun ~ Bar food 12-3, 6.30-9; not Sun evening or Mon bank holiday evening ~ Restaurant ~ Children welcome except in tap room ~ Dogs allowed in bar ~ Wi-fi ~ www.thechequersgoldhanger.co.uk *Recommended by John Edwell, Caroline Prescott*

GOSFIELD
TL7829 Map 5
Kings Head £
The Street; CO9 1TP

Comfortable dining pub with proper public bar and good value food

They've cleverly mixed old beams, standing timbers and other original features with modernised touches and some bright splashes of paintwork. The softly lit beamed main bar, with red panelled dado and ceiling, has neat modern black leather armchairs, bucket chairs and a sofa, as well as sturdy pale wood dining chairs and tables on dark boards, and a log fire in a handsome old brick fireplace with big bellows. Black timbers mark off a dining area with red carpet, walls and furnishings that opens into a carpeted conservatory; background music, daily papers. Adnams Lighthouse, Fullers Brit Hop, Sharps Doom Bar and Timothy Taylors Landlord on handpump, 16 wines by the glass (including quite a few english ones), organic soft drinks and an impressive list of 70 malt whiskies – the well supported whisky club meets four times a year for tastings. The sizeable and quite separate public bar, with a purple pool table, games machine, darts and TV, has its own partly covered terrace; the main terrace has circular picnic-sets and there are more under parasols at the front.

The enterprising food includes mushroom and brie filo parcels with tomato chutney, green-lipped mussels with salsa and melted cheese, lamb hotpot, chicken, leek and stilton pie, duck breast in black bean sauce with stir-fried vegetables, gourmet burger with chips, skate wing with caper and lemon butter, and puddings such as mango and coconut cheesecake and raspberry crème brûlée. *Benchmark main dish: twice-cooked pork belly with cider jus and cheesy mash £11.95. Two-course evening meal £17.95.*

Enterprise ~ Lease Mark Bloomfield ~ Real ale ~ (01787) 474016 ~ Open 12-11 (1am Sat); 12-10.30 Sun ~ Bar food 12-2.30, 6-9.30; 12-6 Sun ~ Restaurant ~ Children welcome ~ Dogs allowed in bar ~ Wi-fi ~ www.thekingsheadgosfield.co.uk
Recommended by Mrs Margo Finlay, Jörg Kasprowski

GREAT CHESTERFORD   TL5142 Map 5
Crown & Thistle

1.5 miles from M11 junction 9A; pub signposted off B184, in High Street; CB10 1PL

Interesting ancient pub with good home cooking and local ales

Our readers enjoy their visits to this friendly and substantial village pub, and the food is very good indeed. There's some attractive decorative plasterwork, inside and out – particularly around the early 16th-c inglenook fireplace; do look out for the lovely old wooden benches too. The long, handsomely proportioned dining room has a striking photographic mural of the village; there's also a low-ceilinged, carpeted area by the bar, with bare boards behind. Served by helpful staff, the beers on handpump come from breweries such as Buntingford, Milton and Woodfordes and they keep ten wines by the glass. A suntrap back courtyard has picnic-sets.

Attractively presented and using seasonal produce, the food includes lunchtime sandwiches, duck and pheasant terrine, garlic king prawns, beer-battered fish and chips, halloumi with roasted vegetables, chicken, leek and mushroom pie, calves liver, bacon and onion, and puddings such as lemon tart and sticky toffee pudding. *Benchmark main dish: steak and kidney pudding £13.95. Two-course evening meal £20.00.*

Free house ~ Licensee Simon Clark ~ Real ale ~ (01799) 530278 ~ Open 12-3, 6-midnight; 12-6 Sun; closed Sun evening, Mon ~ Bar food 12-2.30, 6.30-9.30; 12-3.30 Sun ~ Children welcome ~ Dogs allowed in bar *Recommended by Ruth May, Harvey Brown, Mrs Margo Finlay, Jörg Kasprowski, David Jackman*

The letters and figures after the name of each town are its Ordnance Survey map reference. 'Using the *Guide*' at the beginning of the book explains how it helps you find a pub, in road atlases or large-scale maps as well as in our own maps.

 HATFIELD BROAD OAK TL5416 Map 5

Dukes Head ♀

B183 Hatfield Heath-Takeley; High Street; CM22 7HH

Relaxed, well run dining pub with enjoyable food and an attractive layout of nicely linked separate areas

Various cosy seating areas ramble pleasantly around the central woodburner and side servery, and the atmosphere is relaxed and easy-going. Seating consists mainly of good solid wooden dining chairs around a variety of chunky stripped tables, with a comfortable group of armchairs and a sofa at one end, and a slightly more formal area at the back on the right. Cheerful prints on the wall and some magenta panels in the mostly cream décor make for a buoyant mood. Greene King IPA, Sharps Doom Bar, Timothy Taylors Landlord and a guest such as Hop Back Summer Lightning on handpump and 25 wines by the glass from a good list, served by cheerful staff; background music and board games. Sam the dog welcomes other canines, and there are always dog biscuits behind the bar. The back garden, with its sheltered terrace and a wendy house at the end, has chairs around teak tables under cocktail parasols; there are also some picnic-sets in the front corner of the building, which has some nice pargeting.

Interesting food includes chicken liver pâté with fig jam, bubble and squeak with bacon, free-range poached egg and hollandaise, pumpkin and brie lasagne, beer-battered haddock with triple-cooked chips, sausages of the day with thyme and shallot gravy, maple-cured hot smoked salmon fishcake with cauliflower purée, pork belly with pea, broad bean and feta gnocchi with basil dressing, and puddings such as banana and walnut bread and butter pudding and Baileys cream and chocolate cheesecake; they also offer weekend brunches (from 10.30am Sat, 9am Sun). *Benchmark main dish: king prawn spaghetti £13.25. Two-course evening meal £20.00.*

Enterprise ~ Lease Liz Flodman ~ Real ale ~ (01279) 718598 ~ Open 11.30-11; 10.30am-11pm Sat, Sun ~ Bar food 12-2.30, 6-9.30 (10 Fri); all day weekends ~ Restaurant ~ Children welcome ~ Dogs allowed in bar ~ Wi-fi ~ www.thedukeshead.co.uk
Recommended by David Jackman, Grahame Brooks

 HORNDON-ON-THE-HILL TQ6783 Map 3

Bell 🍴⭐ ♀ ◧ 🛏

M25 junction 30 into A13, then left after 7 miles on to B1007, village signposted from here; SS17 8LD

Essex Dining Pub of the Year

Lovely historic pub with fine food and a very good range of drinks; attractive bedrooms

This is a super place to stay, with individually styled rooms of all sizes with up-to-date facilities and good breakfasts. Excellent food also plays a big role, but the heavily beamed bar still maintains a strongly pubby appearance. It's furnished with lovely high-backed antique settles and benches, with rugs on flagstones and highly polished oak floorboards. Look out for the curious collection of ossified hot cross buns hanging along a beam in the saloon bar. The first was put there in 1906 to mark the day (a Good Friday) that Jack Turnell became licensee; the tradition continues to this day, with the oldest available person in the village hanging the bun each year. The impressive range of drinks includes Crouch Vale Brewers Gold, Greene King IPA, Sharps

Doom Bar and a couple of changing guests on handpump and over 100 well chosen wines (14 by the glass). Two giant umbrellas cover the courtyard, which is very pretty in summer with hanging baskets.

 Using some home-grown produce, the enticing and attractively presented food includes sandwiches, chicken and apricot ballottine with curried crème fraîche, scallops with mussel and sweetcorn chowder and crispy squid, pork and leek sausages with caramelised onions, chargrilled truffled potatoes with tarragon mustard crème fraîche, feta and poached egg, calves liver and chorizo, duck with dauphinoise potatoes and orange marmalade, and puddings such as dark chocolate marquise with white chocolate sauce and mango and mascarpone cheesecake. *Benchmark main dish: suckling pig on creamed sweetcorn, sweet potato fondant and smoked bacon velouté £19.95. Two-course evening meal £22.00.*

Free house ~ Licensee John Vereker ~ Real ale ~ (01375) 642463 ~ Open 11-11; 12-10.30 Sun ~ Bar food 12-2, 6.30-10; not bank holiday Mon ~ Restaurant ~ Children welcome ~ Dogs allowed in bar and bedrooms ~ Wi-fi ~ Bedrooms: /£90 ~ www.bell-inn.co.uk
Recommended by Bob and Tanya Ekers, N R White

LITTLE WALDEN
Crown ▨ £
TL5441   Map 5

B1052 N of Saffron Walden; CB10 1XA

Bustling 18th-c cottage pub with a warming log fire, hearty food and bedrooms

Nothing is ever too much trouble for the particularly friendly and accommodating landlord and his helpful staff, and our readers love staying overnight here – the breakfasts are excellent. It's very much the hub of the local community, but visitors are never excluded from the cheerful chatter, and the low-ceilinged rooms have a cosy, welcoming atmosphere. Furnishings are traditional, with book-room-red walls, floral curtains, bare boards, navy carpeting, cosy warm fires and an unusual walk-through fireplace. A higgledy-piggledy mix of chairs ranges from high-backed pews to little cushioned armchairs spaced around a good variety of closely arranged tables, mostly big, some stripped. The small red-tiled room on the right has two small tables. Three changing beers – including Adnams Broadside, Greene King Abbot and Woodfordes Wherry – are tapped straight from casks racked up behind the bar; TV, disabled access. Tables on the terrace have views over the surrounding tranquil countryside.

Fairly priced, the well liked traditional food includes lunchtime sandwiches and baguettes, chicken liver pâté, devilled whitebait, spinach and ricotta cannelloni, honey-roast ham and eggs, chicken curry, moussaka, pork fillet in cajun sauce, and puddings such as treacle pudding and spicy apple crumble. *Benchmark main dish: steak and mushroom pie £10.95. Two-course evening meal £16.00.*

Free house ~ Licensee Colin Hayling ~ Real ale ~ (01799) 522475 ~ Open 11.30-2.30 (3 Sat), 6-11; 12-10.30 Sun ~ Bar food 12-2, 6.30-9; 12-3 Sun; not Sun and Mon evenings ~ Restaurant ~ Children welcome ~ Dogs allowed in bar and bedrooms ~ Wi-fi ~ Live jazz Weds evenings ~ Bedrooms: /£75 ~ www.thecrownlittlewalden.co.uk
Recommended by Mrs Margo Finlay, Jörg Kasprowski, Nick Clare, Sara Fulton, Roger Baker, Roger and Donna Huggins, Dave Braisted

---

Please tell us if the décor, atmosphere, food or drink at a pub is different from our description. We rely on readers' reports to keep us up to date: feedback@goodguides.com, or (no stamp needed) The Good Pub Guide, FREEPOST RTJR-ZCYZ-RJZT, Perrymans Lane, Etchingham TN19 7DN.

LITTLEY GREEN
TL6917 Map 5

Compasses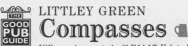

Village signposted off B1417 Felsted road in Hartoft End (opposite former Ridleys Brewery), about a mile N of junction with B1008 – former A130; CM3 1BU

Classic East Anglian traditional country local – a prime example of what is now an all too rare breed

The fine range of drinks in this charming brick tavern includes Bishop Nick Ridleys Rite (brewed in Felsted by the landlord's brother) as well as Cliff Quay Anchor Bitter, Roosters 41 Degrees South and weekend guest beers, all tapped from casks in a back cellar; in summer and at Christmas they hold beer festivals, with a choice of dozens of ales, alongside festivities that may include vintage ploughing in the field opposite. Also, Fosseway and Tumpy Ground farm ciders, perries from Cornish Orchards and Gwynt y Ddraig and eight wines by the glass. The bar is a companionable place, highly traditional – brown-painted panelling and wall benches, plain chairs and tables on quarry tiles, with chat and laughter rather than piped music, a piano, darts and board games in one side room, and decorative mugs hanging from the beams in another. There are picnic-sets out on the sheltered side grass and the garden behind, with a couple of long tables on the front cobbles by the quiet lane. Bedrooms are in a small newish block.

A big blackboard shows the day's range of huffers: big rolls with a hearty range of hot or cold fillings. They also serve ploughman's, baked potatoes, and a few sensibly priced hot dishes such as soup, chicken liver pâté, beer-battered fish and chips, gammon and egg, chicken curry, scampi and rib-eye steak. *Benchmark main dish: huffers £9.00. Two-course evening meal £14.50.*

Free house ~ Licensee Jocelyn Ridley ~ Real ale ~ (01245) 362308 ~ Open 12-3, 5.30-11.30; 12-11.30 Thurs-Sun ~ Bar food 12-2.30 (4 Sat, 5 Sun), 7-9.30 ~ Children welcome ~ Dogs welcome ~ Wi-fi ~ Live folk every third Mon ~ Bedrooms: £75/£85 ~ www.compasseslittleygreen.co.uk *Recommended by Harvey Brown, David Jackson*

MARGARETTING TYE
TL6801 Map 5

White Hart £

From B1002 (just S of A12/A414 junction) follow Maldon Road for 1.3 miles, then turn right immediately after river bridge, into Swan Lane, keeping on for 0.7 miles; The Tye; CM4 9JX

Fine choice of ales tapped from the cask in cheery country pub, with good food and a family garden

Always deservedly busy with locals and visitors, this is a particularly well run pub with a welcome for all. The open-plan but cottagey rooms have walls and wainscoting painted in chalky traditional colours that match well with the dark timbers and mix of old wooden chairs and tables; a stuffed deer head is mounted on the chimney breast above the woodburning stove. The neat carpeted back conservatory is similar in style, and the front lobby has a charity paperback table. They keep an impressive range of eight real ales tapped straight from the cask, such as Adnams Best and Broadside, Mighty Oak IPA and Oscar Wilde and changing guests from breweries such as Cottage, Franklins and Red Fox, a german wheat beer, interesting bottled beers and winter mulled wine; beer festivals in June and October feature around 60 different ales. Darts, board games and background music. There are plenty of picnic-sets out on grass and terracing around the pub, with a sturdy play area, a fenced duck pond and views across the fields; lovely sunsets.

🍴 Enjoyable food includes sandwiches, baked whole camembert with cranberry sauce, smoked salmon, crab and crayfish tian, creamy wild mushroom pasta, ham and free-range eggs, burger topped with bacon and stilton with chips and coleslaw, chicken provençale, a curry of the week, and puddings such as apple and rhubarb crumble and hot chocolate fudge cake. *Benchmark main dish: beer-battered haddock £13.50. Two-course evening meal £18.50.*

Free house ~ Licensee Elizabeth Haines ~ Real ale ~ (01277) 840478 ~ Open 11.30-3.30, 6-midnight; 11.30am-1am Sat, Sun ~ Bar food 12-2, 6-9 (9.30 Sat); 12-7.30 Sun ~ Well behaved children welcome in conservatory ~ Dogs welcome ~ Wi-fi ~ Bedrooms: /£80 ~ www.thewhitehart.uk.com *Recommended by John Saville, Ian Phillips, George Atkinson, John Boothman, Mrs Margo Finlay, Jörg Kasprowski, David Jackson*

MILL GREEN
TL6401 Map 5

Viper 🍺 £

The Common; from Fryerning (which is signposted off N-bound A12 Ingatestone bypass) follow Writtle signposts; CM4 0PT

Delightfully unpretentious, with local ales, simple pub food and no modern intrusions

In summer, try to grab one of the tables on the lawn overlooking the beautifully tended cottage garden – it's a dazzling mass of colour; the overflowing hanging baskets and window boxes at the front are lovely too. Tucked away in the woods, this remains a charming unspoilt local liked by a wide mix of customers, including regulars, cyclists, walkers with their dogs and families. The cosy, unchanging rooms have spindleback and country kitchen chairs and tapestried wall seats around neat little old tables, and a log fire. The fairly basic parquet-floored tap room is more simply furnished with shiny traditional wooden wall seats and a coal fire; beyond is another room with country kitchen chairs and sensibly placed darts. As well as a couple of beers named for the pub, there might be Crouch Vale Brewers Gold, Mighty Oak Oscar Wilde and Moles Rucking Mole on handpump, and Weston's scrumpy and perry. Live bands play at their Easter and August beer festivals, and morris dancers sometimes appear. The pub cat is called Millie, and the west highland terrier, Jimmy; dominoes and cribbage.

🍴 Simple lunchtime-only food served promptly includes sandwiches, baked potatoes, pâté with toast, cottage pie, sausages with beans and gravy, chicken curry, beef stew with dumplings, and puddings such as spotted dick with custard and apple crumble. *Benchmark main dish: steak in ale pie £7.50.*

Free house ~ Licensee Donna Torris ~ Real ale ~ (01277) 352010 ~ Open 12-3.30, 6-11; 12-11 Sat; 12-10.30 Sun ~ Bar food 12-2 (3 weekends) ~ Children allowed ~ Dogs allowed in bar ~ Wi-fi *Recommended by Mike Swan, Charlie May*

SOUTH HANNINGFIELD
TQ7497 Map 5

Old Windmill 🍽️ 🍷

Off A130 S of Chelmsford; CM3 8HT

Extensive, invitingly converted pub with interesting food and a good range of drinks

A forest of stripped standing timbers and open doorways create lots of cosy, rambling areas in this 18th-c pub. There's an agreeable mix of highly polished old tables and chairs, frame-to-frame pictures on cream walls, woodburning stoves and homely pot plants. Deep green or dark red dado and a few old rugs dotted on the glowing wood floors provide splashes of colour; other areas are more subdued, with beige carpeting. Phoenix Brunning & Price Original and five guests such as 1648 Ruby Mild, Brentwood Blonde, Crouch Vale Brewers Gold, Mighty Oak Captain Bob and St Austell Tribute on handpump, with a dozen wines by the glass, 70 malt whiskies and a good range of spirits; background music. A back terrace has tables and chairs and there are picnic-sets on the lawn and a few more seats out in front.

 Appealing and very good, the food includes sandwiches, braised ham hock terrine with chutney, crispy pea and mint risotto balls with oven-dried tomato dressing, artichoke pie with mushroom sauce, cumberland sausages with onion gravy, rosemary and garlic chicken with wild mushrooms, bacon, spinach and pasta, calves liver and crispy bacon, bass with crab and sweetcorn fritters and soy and mirin dressing, and puddings such as raspberry roulade with raspberry ripple ice-cream and chocolate brownie with chocolate sauce. *Benchmark main dish: beer-battered fish and chips £13.25. Two-course evening meal £20.00.*

Brunning & Price ~ Manager Nick Clark ~ Real ale ~ (01268) 712280 ~ Open 11.30-11; 12-10.30 Sun ~ Bar food 12-10 (9.30 Sun) ~ Restaurant ~ Children welcome ~ Dogs allowed in bar ~ Wi-fi ~ www.oldwindmillpub.co.uk *Recommended by Evelyn and Derek Walter, Tina and David Woods-Taylor, David Jackman, John Boothman, N R White*

WENDENS AMBO
Bell 🍺
TL5136 Map 5

B1039 W of village; CB11 4JY

Chatty local with lots going on, good ales and ciders, pubby food and big garden

All sorts of events are organised by the cheerful landlord here, there's plenty of lively banter from the friendly regulars and an easy-going atmosphere. The cottagey, bustling bars have low ceilings, brasses on ancient timbers, wheelback chairs at neat tables, a winter log fire and Growler Hound Dog and Priory Mild, Oakham JHB and Woodfordes Wherry on handpump, farm cider and perry, and several wines by the glass. There are seats under umbrellas on the paved terrace, which overlooks the three acres of gardens where there's a pond leading to the River Uttle, a woodland walk and a children's timber playground.

🍴 Popular food includes lunchtime sandwiches, chicken liver pâté with chutney, welsh rarebit, home-cooked ham and free-range eggs, stuffed peppers, beer-battered fresh haddock and chips, a curry of the day, lamb steak with garlic mash and minted gravy, and puddings such as apple and blackberry pie and warm chocolate brownie. *Benchmark main dish: steak in ale pie £9.95. Two-course evening meal £16.50.*

Free house ~ Licensee Simon Holland ~ Real ale ~ (01799) 540382 ~ Open 12-11 (11.30 Sat, 10.30 Sun); closed Mon lunchtime except bank holidays ~ Bar food 12-2 (2.30 Fri, Sat, 4 Sun), 6-9; not Mon ~ Restaurant ~ Children welcome ~ Dogs welcome ~ Wi-fi ~ www.thebellatwenden.co.uk *Recommended by Caroline Prescott, Mrs Margo Finlay, Jörg Kasprowski, Tony Hobden*

'Children welcome' means the pub says it lets children inside without any special restriction. If it allows them in, but to restricted areas such as an eating area or family room, we specify this. Places with separate restaurants often let children use them, and hotels usually let children into public areas such as lounges. Some pubs impose an evening time limit – let us know if you find one earlier than 9pm.

Also Worth a Visit in Essex

Besides the fully inspected pubs, you might like to try these pubs that have been recommended to us and described by readers. Do tell us what you think of them: feedback@goodguides.com

ARDLEIGH   TM0429
★**Wooden Fender**   (01206) 230466
A137 towards Colchester; CO7 7PA
Pleasantly extended and furnished old pub
with friendly attentive service, beams and log
fires, good choice of enjoyable food including
set lunch, Greene King and guests, decent
wines; children welcome in large dining area,
dogs in bar, good-sized garden with play area,
open all day Sat, till 9pm Sun. *(David and
Gill Carrington)*

ASHDON   TL5842
Rose & Crown   (01799) 584337
*Back Road Saffron Walden–Haverhill,
junction with back road to Radwinter;
CB10 2HB* Refurbished 17th-c beamed pub
under newish management, well kept ales
such as Black Sheep, Sharps and Woodfordes,
plenty of wines by the glass and good fairly
traditional food including daily specials,
friendly helpful service; no dogs inside, tables
in raised garden with boules. *(Anon)*

BELCHAMP ST PAUL   TL7942
Half Moon (01787) 277402
Cole Green; CO10 7DP Thatched 16th-c
pub overlooking green, well kept Greene
King IPA and guests, good choice of popular
home-made food (not Sun evening), friendly
staff, snug beamed interior with log fire,
restaurant, Aug beer/music festival; no
dogs inside; children welcome, tables out
in front and in back garden, open all day
weekends. *(Anon)*

BIRCHANGER   TL5122
★**Three Willows** (01279) 815913
*Under a mile from M11 junction 8:
A120 towards Bishop's Stortford, then
almost immediately right to Birchanger
Village; don't be waylaid earlier by the
Birchanger Services signpost; CM23
5QR* Welcoming dining pub feeling nicely
tucked away – some refurbishment from
present owners; spacious carpeted bar with
lots of cricketing memorabilia, Greene
King ales, well furnished smaller lounge
bar, good range of popular fairly traditional
food including plenty of fresh fish; children
welcome, dogs allowed in bar, picnic-sets
out in front and on lawn behind (some
motorway and Stansted Airport noise), good

play area, closed Sun evening. *(Roy Hoing,
Mrs Margo Finlay, Jörg Kasprowski and others)*

BOREHAM   TL7409
Lion   (01245) 394900
Main Road; CM3 3JA Stylish bistro/
bar with rooms, good well presented and
affordably priced food (order at bar) from
snacks to daily specials, several wines by
the glass, bottled beers and well kept ales
including one named for them, efficient
friendly staff, conservatory; children
welcome, no dogs, open all day. *(John Saville,
Tina and David Woods-Taylor)*

BRENTWOOD   TQ5993
Nags Head   (01277) 260005
*A1023, just off M25 junction 28;
CM14 5ND* Popular open-plan Mitchells
& Butlers dining pub with good food and
wine choice, well kept ales and snacks
in comfortable bar area, prompt friendly
service; pleasant garden, open all day. *(Anon)*

BULMER TYE   TL8438
★**Bulmer Fox**   (01787) 312277
A131 S of Sudbury; CO10 7EB Popular
pub-bistro with enjoyable fairly priced food,
neatly laid tables with forms to write your
order (can also order at the bar), Adnams
and Greene King IPA, help-yourself water
fountain, friendly well trained staff, bare
boards with one or two 'rugs' painted on
them, pastel colours and lively acoustics,
quieter side room and intimate central snug,
home-made chutneys, preserves etc for sale;
children welcome, sheltered back terrace
with arbour. *(Anon)*

BURNHAM-ON-CROUCH   TQ9495
★**White Harte** (01621) 782106
The Quay; CM0 8AS Cosy old-fashioned
17th-c hotel on water's edge with views from
garden of yacht-filled River Crouch; partly
carpeted bars with down-to-earth charm,
assorted nautical bric-a-brac and hardware,
other traditionally furnished high-ceilinged
rooms with sea pictures on brown panelled or
stripped brick walls, cushioned seats around
oak tables, enormous winter log fire, well
kept Adnams and Crouch Vale, good food and
friendly efficient service; children and dogs
welcome, bedrooms, open all day. *(Gwyn
Harries, N R White)*

A few pubs try to make you leave a credit card at the bar, as a sort of deposit if you
order food. This is a bad practice, and the banks and credit card firms
warn you not to let your card go like this.

BURTON END   TL5323
Ash (01279) 814841
Just N of Stansted Airport; CM24 8UQ
Popular thatched country pub with dining
extension, helpful cheerful staff, two or
three real ales, enjoyable all-day food from
lunchtime sandwiches and pubby choices
up, log fires; tables outside on deck and
grass, bedrooms in converted barn across
lane. *(Mrs Margo Finlay, Jörg Kasprowski)*

CASTLE HEDINGHAM   TL7835
Bell (01787) 460350
St James Street (B1058); CO9 3EJ
Beamed and timbered three-bar pub dating
from the 15th c, unpretentious and unspoilt
(well run by same family for over 45 years),
Adnams, Mighty Oak and guests served from
the cask (July/Nov beer festivals), popular
pubby food and turkish specials; background
and some live music (lunchtime jazz last Sun
of month); dogs welcome, children away from
public bar, garden, handy for Hedingham
Castle, open all day Fri-Sun. *(Anon)*

CASTLE HEDINGHAM   TL7835
Wheatsheaf (01787) 469939
Top end of Queen Street; CO9 3EX
Unassuming 15th-c local with welcoming
landlord, chatty regulars and two friendly
pub dogs, well kept Greene King ales
and generous helpings of straightforward
lunchtime (and Sat evening) food including
Sun roasts, moulded beams (some with floral
carvings), stag's head, brewery memorabilia
and other odds and ends, inglenook
woodburner, bar billiards; three bedrooms,
open all day. *(Dr W I C Clark)*

CHELMSFORD   TL7006
Queens Head (01245) 265181
Lower Anchor Street; CM2 0AS Lively
well run Victorian corner local with very
well kept Crouch Vale beers and interesting
guests, summer farm cider, good value
wines, friendly staff, bargain food weekday
lunchtimes from baguettes up, winter log
fires, Weds quiz; children welcome, picnic-
sets in colourful courtyard, handy for county
cricket ground, open all day. *(Anon)*

CHRISHALL   TL4439
Red Cow (01763) 838792
*High Street; off B1039 Wendens
Ambo–Great Chishill; SG8 8RN* Popular
refurbished 16th-c thatched pub with lots of
atmosphere; timbers, low beams, wood floors
and log fires, one half laid for dining, decent
choice of enjoyable food from simple bar
meals up including weekday set deals, well
kept Adnams, Greene King IPA and a guest,
interesting wine list, weekend newspapers,
board games; children and dogs welcome,
nice garden, old adjacent barn for functions,
handy for Icknield Way walkers, open all day
weekends, closed Mon. *(Mrs Margo Finlay,
Jörg Kasprowski)*

COGGESHALL   TL8224
★Compasses (01376) 561322
Pattiswick, signed off A120 W; CM77 8BG
More country restaurant than pub with well
presented food using local produce from
light lunches up, also weekday set deals and
children's meals, two well kept ales such as
Growler and Woodfordes Wherry, good wine
choice, cheerful attentive young staff, neatly
comfortable spacious beamed bars, barn
restaurant, some live music; plenty of lawn
and orchard tables, rolling farmland beyond,
open all day. *(Steve and Irene Homer)*

COLCHESTER   TM9824
Hospital Arms (01206) 542398
*Crouch Street (opposite hospital);
CO3 3HA* Friendly pub with several
small linked areas, good selection of well
kept Adnams ales and guests, enjoyable
inexpensive lunchtime food, quick cheerful
service; games machines; beer garden, open
all day. *(Anon)*

COLNE ENGAINE   TL8530
Five Bells (01787) 224166
*Signed off A1124 (was A604) in Earls
Colne; Mill Lane; CO6 2HY* Welcoming
and popular old village pub, good home-made
food (all day weekends) using local produce,
own-baked bread, six well kept changing ales
including Adnams (Nov festival), friendly
efficient service, bare boards or carpeted
floors, woodburners, old photographs,
high-raftered dining area (former
slaughterhouse), public bar with pool and
sports TV, some live music; children and dogs
welcome, disabled facilities, attractive front
terrace with gentle Colne Valley views, open
all day Thurs-Sun. *(Anon)*

COOPERSALE STREET   TL4701
★Theydon Oak (01992) 572618
*Off B172 E of Theydon Bois; or follow
Hobbs Cross Open Farm brown sign off
B1393 at N end of Epping; CM16 7QJ*
Attractive old weatherboarded dining pub,
very popular for its good food (all day Sun)
from varied menu, Fullers London Pride,
Greene King IPA and a guest, friendly
prompt service, beams and masses of
brass, copper and old brewery mirrors, two
woodburners; background music, no dogs;
children welcome, tables on side terrace and
in fenced garden with small stream, lots of
hanging baskets, separate play area, open
all day. *(Gordon Neighbour)*

CRANHAM   TQ5786
Jobbers Rest (01708) 250480
St Marys Lane; RM14 3LT Popular
beamed pub with well kept beers and
good reasonably priced food (not Sun
evening), pleasant service, sofas in bar area,
conservatory restaurant; children welcome,
garden with outside bar and play area.
(Robert Lester)

DANBURY   TL7705
Griffin   (01245) 222905
A414, top of Danbury Hill; CM3 4DH
Refurbished 16th-c pub with well divided
interior, beams and some carved woodwork,
mix of new and old furniture on wood, stone
or carpeted floors, log fires, enjoyable food
from pub standards, deli boards and pizzas
up, changing real ales and nice choice of
wines by the glass, good attentive service;
background music; children welcome,
terrace seating, views. *(Mrs Margo Finlay,
Jörg Kasprowski, John Boothman)*

DEDHAM   TM0533
★ Sun   (01206) 323351
High Street (B2109); CO7 6DF Stylish
old Tudor coaching inn opposite church;
good italian-influenced food using seasonal
local produce, also cheaper set menu (not
Fri, Sat or Sun lunchtime), impressive
wine selection (over 20 by the glass), well
kept Adnams, Crouch Vale and two guests,
Aspall's cider, friendly efficient young staff,
historic panelled interior with high carved
beams, handsome furnishings and splendid
fireplaces; background music, TV; children
welcome, dogs in bar, picnic-sets on quiet
back lawn with mature trees and view of
church, characterful panelled bedrooms,
good Flatford Mill walk, open all day.
*(Steve and Irene Homer, N R White, Roy Hoing
and others)*

DUTON HILL   TL6026
Three Horseshoes   (01371) 870681
*Off B184 Dunmow–Thaxted, 3 miles N of
Dunmow; CM6 2DX* Friendly traditional
village local, well kept Mighty Oak and
guests (late May Bank Holiday beer festival),
central fire, aged armchairs by fireplace in
homely left-hand parlour, lots of interesting
memorabilia, darts and pool in small public
bar, no food, folk club third Thurs of month;
dogs welcome, old enamel signs out at front,
garden with pond and nice views, closed
lunchtimes Mon-Thurs. *(Anon)*

EDNEY COMMON   TL6504
Green Man   (01245) 248076
Highwood Road; CM1 3QE
Comfortable country pub/restaurant,
good well presented food from interesting
changing menu cooked by chef-owners,
extensive wine list (several by the glass),
a couple of real ales, friendly staff, carpeted
interior with black beams and timbers;
tables out at front and in garden, closed Sun
evening, Mon. *(Anon)*

EPPING FOREST   TL4501
Forest Gate   (01992) 572312
Bell Common; CM16 4DZ Large friendly
open-plan pub dating from the 17th c and
run by the same family for over 50 years;
beams, flagstones and panelling, well kept
Adnams, Growler and guests from brick-
faced bar, some basic food; dogs welcome,
tables on front lawn, popular with walkers,
bedrooms and adjacent rather upmarket
restaurant. *(Anon)*

FINCHINGFIELD   TL6832
Fox   (01371) 810151
The Green; CM7 4JX Splendidly pargeted
16th-c building with spacious beamed bar,
exposed brickwork and central fireplace,
ales from Adnams and Growler, good choice
of wines by the glass, popular freshly made
food from sandwiches and pub favourites
up, pleasant staff; background and some live
music (may be Thurs jazz); children and dogs
welcome, picnic-sets in front overlooking
village duck pond, bedrooms, open all day
(closed Sun evening in winter). *(Lois Dyer)*

FINGRINGHOE   TM0220
Whalebone   (01206) 729307
*Off A134 just S of Colchester centre,
or B1025; CO5 7BG* Old pub geared
for dining, airy country-chic rooms with
cream-painted tables on oak floors, good
local food (not Sun evening) including some
interesting choices, nice sandwiches too, well
kept beers such as Adnams, barn function
room; background music; children and
dogs welcome, charming back garden with
peaceful valley view, front terrace, handy for
Fingringhoe Wick nature reserve, open all
day weekends. *(N R White)*

FYFIELD   TL5707
Black Bull   (01277) 899225
*Dunmow Road (B184), N end of village;
CM5 0NN* Traditional pub with generous
helpings of enjoyable food including good
fresh fish, Fullers London Pride, Greene
King IPA and Growler Priory, friendly staff,
heavy low beams and standing timbers
in comfortably opened-up pubby bar
and country-style dining area, open fire;
background music; tables in back garden by
car park, ten bedrooms in adjacent building,
open all day Sun. *(Richard Kennell)*

GESTINGTHORPE   TL8138
★ Pheasant   (01787) 461196
Off B1058; CO9 3AU Civilised country
pub with old-fashioned character in small
opened-up beamed rooms, settles and mix
of other furniture on bare boards, books
and china platters on shelves, woodburners
in nice brick fireplaces, Adnams, Crouch
Vale and a beer named for the pub, nine
wines by the glass, enjoyable food; children
and dogs (in bar) welcome, seats outside
under parasols with views over fields, stylish
bedrooms, open all day weekends, closed
first two weeks Jan. *(Walter and Susan Rinaldi-
Butcher, Mrs Margo Finlay, Jörg Kasprowski)*

GREAT HENNY   TL8738
Henny Swan   (01787) 269238
Henny Street; CO10 7LS Welcoming
smartly refurbished dining pub in great

location on the River Stour (summer boat trips); bar with open fire, more formal dining room, well-kept regularly changing ales, good variety of food from bar snacks and pubby choices to restaurant-style dishes, special diets and vegetarians catered for; children welcome, terrace and waterside garden, play area, closed Sun evening, otherwise open all day. *(Anon)*

HASTINGWOOD   TL4807
★ **Rainbow & Dove** (01279) 415419
0.5 miles from M11 junction 7;
CM17 9JX Pleasantly traditional low-beamed pub with three small rooms, built-in cushioned wall seats and mate's chairs around pubby tables, stripped stone and cream or green paintwork, golfing memorabilia, woodburner in original fireplace, Adnams, Oakham, Sharps and Timothy Taylors, 11 wines by the glass and enjoyable fairly priced food, friendly licensees and staff; background music, darts; children and dogs welcome, tables out under parasols, country views, closed Sun evening. *(John Saville)*

HATFIELD HEATH   TL5115
Thatchers (01279) 730270
Stortford Road (A1005); CM22 7DU
Thatched and weatherboarded 16th-c dining pub at end of large green, good popular food (best to book weekends) from varied menu including set lunch Mon-Fri, well kept St Austell Tribute, Sharps Doom Bar and two guests from long counter, several wines by the glass, woodburners, beams, some copper and brass and old local photographs; background music, no dogs; children in back dining area, tables in front under parasols, open all day weekends. *(Anon)*

HEMPSTEAD   TL6337
Bluebell (01799) 599199
B1054 E of Saffron Walden; CB10 2PD
Comfortable and attractive beamed bar with two rooms off and a restaurant, enjoyable food including popular Sun roasts, Adnams, Woodfordes and guests, Aspall's cider, friendly service, log fires, regular live music, classic car meetings (first Sat of month); children and dogs welcome, terrace and garden seating, play area. *(Mrs Margo Finlay, Jörg Kasprowski)*

HENHAM   TL5428
Cock (01279) 850347
Church End; CM22 6AN Welcoming old timbered place striking good balance between community local and dining pub, nice choice of well priced home-made food (not Sun evening), four ales including Saffron (brewed in the village), decent wines, good open fires, restaurant with leather-backed chairs on wood floor, sports TV in snug, live music last Sun of month; children welcome, dogs in bar, seats out at front and in tree-shaded garden, open all day Fri-Sun. *(Anon)*

HERONGATE   TQ6491
★ **Olde Dog** (01277) 810337
Billericay Road, off A128 Brentwood–Grays at big sign for Boars Head;
CM13 3SD Welcoming weatherboarded country pub dating from the 16th c, long attractive dark-beamed bar and separate dining areas, exposed brickwork and uneven floors, well kept Greene King, a house beer from Crouch Vale and guests tapped from the cask, popular food (all day weekends, Sun till 7pm), friendly staff; pleasant front terrace and neat sheltered side garden, open all day. *(N R White, A N Bance)*

HOWLETT END   TL5834
White Hart (01799) 599030
Thaxted Road (B184 SE of Saffron Walden); CB10 2UZ Comfortable pub/restaurant with two smartly set modern dining rooms either side of small tiled-floor bar, good food from sandwiches and light dishes up, Greene King IPA and local guests, nice choice of wines, friendly helpful service; children welcome, terrace and big garden, quiet spot, closed Sun evening, Mon. *(Anon)*

HULLBRIDGE   TQ8195
Anchor (01702) 230777
Ferry Road; SS5 6ND Extensively refurbished riverside pub/restaurant, always busy but enough staff to cope well, good bar and restaurant food, plenty of wines by the glass including champagne, real ales; children welcome, lots of seats outside overlooking River Crouch, summer barbecues, open all day. *(Bob and Tanya Ekers)*

INGATESTONE   TQ6499
Bell (01277) 353314
High Street; CM4 0AT Old Shepherd Neame pub with oak beams and three original fireplaces, pubby food from toasted panini up, good range of wines, friendly atmosphere and efficient service, live music and quiz nights, large TV in separate room; children welcome, big garden with play area, open all day. *(Robert Lester, Eddie Edwards)*

LANGHAM   TM0232
Shepherd (01206) 272711
Moor Road/High Street; CO4 5NR Recently refurbished village pub, wood floors and painted panelling, welcoming licensees, Adnams and a guest, plenty of wines by the glass and good selection of other drinks, enjoyable sensibly priced food, L-shaped bar with areas off, large OS map covering one wall, comfortable sofas, woodburner; children welcome, side garden, open all day from 9am (9.30am Sun) for breakfast. *(Malcolm)*

LEIGH-ON-SEA   TQ8385
★ **Crooked Billet** (01702) 480289
High Street; SS9 2EP Homely old pub with waterfront views from big bay windows, packed on busy summer days when service

can be frantic but friendly, well kept Adnams, Nicholsons, Sharps and changing guests including seasonals, enjoyable standard Nicholsons menu, log fires, beams, panelled dado and bare boards, local fishing pictures and bric-a-brac; background music; children allowed if eating but no under-21s after 6pm, side garden and terrace, seawall seating over road shared with Osborne's good shellfish stall (plastic glasses for outside), pay-and-display parking by flyover, open all day. *(George Atkinson, David Jackson, N R White)*

LITTLE BRAXTED   TL8413
⋆ **Green Man** (01621) 891659

Kelvedon Road; signed off B1389; OS Sheet 168 map reference 848133; CM8 3LB Homely and cottagey with windsor chairs on patterned carpets, mugs hanging from beams and some 200 horsebrasses, open fire in traditional little lounge, tiled public bar with darts and cribbage, Greene King ales and a guest, big helpings of good sensibly priced food, friendly helpful staff and nice chatty atmosphere; children till 8pm, dogs in bar, picnic-sets in pleasant sheltered garden, closed Sun evening. *(Anon)*

LITTLE BROMLEY   TM1028
Haywain (01206) 390004

Bentley Road; CO11 2PL Welcoming family-run 18th-c pub popular with locals and visitors, carpeted interior with various cosy areas leading off from main bar, beams, exposed brickwork and open fires, Adnams and guests like Colchester, Growler and Crouch Vale, generous helpings of enjoyable home-made food (booking recommended evenings/weekends); closed Sun evening, Mon, Tues lunchtime. *(N R White)*

LOUGHTON   TQ4296
Victoria (020) 8508 1779

Smarts Lane; IG10 4BP Welcoming flower-decked Victorian local with enjoyable home-made pubby food (large helpings), good range of fairly mainstream beers including Adnams and Greene King, chatty panelled bare-boards bar with small raised end dining area; pleasant neatly kept front garden, Epping Forest walks. *(Phil Bryant)*

MALDON   TL8407
⋆ **Blue Boar** (01621) 855888

Silver Street; car park behind; CM9 4QE Quirky cross between coaching inn and antiques or auction showroom, most showy in the main building's lounge and dining room, interesting antique furnishings and pictures also in the separate smallish dark-timbered bar and its spectacular raftered upper room, good Farmers ales brewed at the back, also

Adnams Southwold and a guest, enjoyable food from bar snacks to daily specials, friendly helpful staff; tables outside, 22 bedrooms (some with four-posters), good breakfast, car park fee refunded at bar, open all day. *(Anon)*

MATCHING GREEN   TL5310
Chequers (01279) 731276

Off Downhall Road; CM17 0PZ Civilised Victorian place reworked as contemporary upmarket pub/restaurant, not particularly cheap but very enjoyable traditional and mediterranean-style food from good lunchtime ciabattas up, also fixed-price weekday lunch and children's menu, friendly helpful staff, nice wines from comprehensive list, well kept Greene King IPA, occasional cabaret nights; disabled facilities, quiet spot overlooking pretty green with new cricket pavilion, nice local walks, open all day weekends, closed Mon. *(Tina and David Woods-Taylor)*

MESSING   TL8919
Old Crown (01621) 815575

Signed off B1022 and B1023; Lodge Road; CO5 9TU Attractive late 17th-c village pub refurbished under present owners; good interesting food (not Sun evening) from light lunches up, well kept Adnams, friendly helpful staff; near fine church, open all day. *(Steve and Irene Homer)*

MISTLEY   TM1131
⋆ **Thorn** (01206) 392821

High Street (B1352 E of Manningtree); CO11 1HE Popular for American chef/landlady's good food (especially seafood), but there's also a friendly all-day welcome if you just want a drink or coffee; high black beams give a clue to the building's age (Matthew Hopkins, the notorious 17th-c witchfinder general, based himself here), décor, though, is crisply up to date – comfortable basketweave chairs and mixed dining tables on terracotta tiles around horseshoe bar, cream walls above sage dado, colourful modern artwork, end brick fireplace with woodburner, good range of wines by the glass, newspapers and magazines, cookery classes; front terrace tables looking across to Robert Adam's swan fountain, interesting waterside village, ten comfortable bedrooms. *(Steve and Irene Homer, Kay and Alistair Butler)*

MOUNT BURES   TL9031
⋆ **Thatchers Arms** (01787) 227460

Off B1508; CO8 5AT Well run modernised pub with good local food (freshly prepared so may be a wait), midweek meal deals, well kept ales such as Adnams Mild and Bitter and Crouch Vale Brewers Gold, cheerful

---

If you have to cancel a reservation for a bedroom or restaurant, please telephone or write to warn them. You may lose your deposit if you've paid one.

efficient staff; background music; dogs welcome, plenty of picnic-sets out behind, peaceful Stour Valley views, open all day weekends, closed Mon. *(Alexandra Woolmore, N R White)*

ORSETT   TQ6483
Dog & Partridge   (01375) 891377
A128 S of Bulphan; RM16 3HU Roadside pub with good straightforward food and well kept beers, friendly helpful staff; large garden with duck pond. *(Tina and David Woods-Taylor)*

PAGLESHAM   TQ9492
Plough & Sail   (01702) 258242
East End; SS4 2EQ Relaxed 17th-c weatherboarded dining pub in pretty spot, popular fairly traditional food from sandwiches up, friendly service, well kept changing ales, decent house wines and local cider, low beams and big log fires, pine tables, lots of brasses and pictures, traditional games; background music; children welcome, front picnic-sets and attractive side garden, open all day Sun. *(N R White)*

PAGLESHAM   TQ9293
★ Punchbowl   (01702) 258376
Church End; SS4 2DP Weatherboarded 16th-c former sailmaker's loft with low beams and stripped brickwork, pews, barrel chairs and lots of brass, local pictures, lower room laid for dining, Adnams Southwold, Sharps Doom Bar and a couple of guests, straightforward fairly priced food including good OAP menu (Tues, Thurs), prompt friendly service, cribbage and darts; background music; children usually welcome but check first, lovely rural view from sunny front garden, open all day Sun. *(Gwyn Harries, N R White)*

PELDON   TM0015
★ Rose   (01206) 735248
B1025 Colchester–Mersea (do not turn left to Peldon village); CO5 7QJ Friendly old inn with dark bowed beams, standing timbers and little leaded-light windows, some antique mahogany and padded leather wall banquettes, arched brick fireplace, Adnams, Greene King and Woodfordes, several wines by glass and enjoyable food (not Sun evening), cosy restaurant and smart airy garden room; children welcome away from bar, plenty of seats in spacious garden with pretty pond, comfortable country-style bedrooms, open all day (till 7pm Sun in winter). *(Ryta Lyndley, Mike Swan, Charlie May)*

PURLEIGH   TL8401
Bell   (01621) 828348
Off B1010 E of Danbury, by church at top of hill; CM3 6QJ Cosy rambling beamed and timbered pub with fine views over the marshes and Blackwater estuary;

bare boards, hops and brasses, inglenook log fire, well kept ales such as Adnams and Mighty Oak, plenty of wines by the glass (some local), good sensibly priced home-made food including specials, friendly staff; cinema in adjoining barn; children welcome, picnic-sets on side grass, good walks (on St Peter's Way), closed Sun evening, Mon. *(Giles and Annie Francis)*

RICKLING GREEN   TL5129
Cricketers Arms   (01799) 543210
Just off B1383 N of Stansted Mountfichet; CB11 3YG Beamed dining pub under same management as the Eight Bells in Saffron Walden, enjoyable food from reasonably priced varied menu, good selection of wines and cheerful attentive staff, split-level modernised interior; nice position opposite cricket green, ten bedrooms. *(Charles Gysin)*

RIDGEWELL   TL7340
White Horse   (01440) 785532
Mill Road (A1017 Haverhill–Halstead); CO9 4SG Comfortable beamed village pub with Mighty Oak Oscar Wilde and guests tapped from the cask, real ciders and decent wines by the glass, good generous food from weekly changing bar and restaurant menus, friendly service; background music, no dogs; children welcome, tables out on terrace, modern bedroom block with good disabled access, closed Mon and Tues lunchtimes, otherwise open all day. *(Anon)*

ROXWELL   TL6508
Hare   (01245) 248788
Bishops Stortford Road (A1060); CM1 4LU Refurbished open-plan pub (Pie & Pint Inns); Golden Crust ales (brewed by Brentwood) and guests such as Adnams and Timothy Taylors, plenty of wines by the glass, good choice of traditional food with smaller helpings available, teas, coffee and home-made cakes, some timbers and log fire; children welcome, no dogs inside, terrace and garden with stream, farmland views, open all day. *(Anon)*

SAFFRON WALDEN   TL5338
Eight Bells   (01799) 522790
Bridge Street; B184 towards Cambridge; CB10 1BU Old refurbished beamed pub, open bar area with bare boards, leather armchairs and sofas, coal-effect gas fire in brick fireplace, back dining part in handsomely raftered and timbered 16th-c barn with modern dark wood furniture and log-effect end wall, good food from sandwiches and deli boards up, St Austell Tribute, Woodfordes Wherry and a guest, plenty of wines by the glass including champagne, helpful friendly staff; background music, DJ night last Fri of month; children welcome, dogs in bar, garden with raised deck, handy for Audley End, open all day. *(John Saville)*

SAFFRON WALDEN   TL5438
Old English Gentleman
(01799) 523595 *Gold Street; CB10 1EJ*
Busy 19th-c red-brick town-centre pub,
bare boards, panelling and log fires, plenty
of inviting nooks and crannies, well kept
Adnams, Woodfordes Wherry and a couple
of guests, several wines by the glass, good
choice of lunchtime food from sandwiches
and deli boards up; background and live
music; terrace tables, open all day (till 1am
Fri, Sat). *(Alcuin Bramerton)*

SOUTHMINSTER   TQ9699
Station Arms (01621) 772225
Station Road; CM0 7EW Popular
weatherboarded local with unpretentious
L-shaped bar, bare boards and panelling,
friendly chatty atmosphere, Adnams, Crouch
Vale, Mighty Oak and guests, beer festivals
(Jan, May) and some live music; back
courtyard, open all day Sat from 2pm.
(N R White)

STAPLEFORD TAWNEY   TL5001
★ Mole Trap (01992) 522394
*Tawney Common; signed off A113 N of
M25 overpass – keep on; OS Sheet 167
map reference 500013; CM16 7PU*
Popular unpretentious little country pub,
carpeted beamed bar (mind your head as you
go in) with brocaded wall seats and plain pub
tables, steps down to similar area, warming
fires, well kept Fullers London Pride and
changing guests, reasonably priced down-
to-earth food (not Sun and Mon evenings),
cheery swift service; no credit cards, quiet
background radio; children welcome away
from bar, small dogs allowed at quiet times,
seats outside. *(George Atkinson, David Jackson)*

STISTED   TL7923
Dolphin (01376) 321143
*A120 E of Braintree, by village turn;
CM77 8EU* Old mansard-roofed pub with
cheerful heavily beamed and timbered bar,
good value fairly straightforward food cooked
to order, Greene King ales tapped from
the cask, brasses, antlers and lots of small
prints, log fire, bright extended eating area
on left; background music; children and dogs
welcome, pretty back garden with covered
area, views over fields, open (and food)
all day. *(Anon)*

STOCK   TQ6999
★ Hoop (01277) 841137
*B1007; from A12 Chelmsford bypass
take Galleywood, Billericay turn-off;
CM4 9BD* Popular old weatherboarded

pub with cheery locals and down-to-earth
feel, open-plan bar with beams and standing
timbers (a hint at original layout as three
weavers' cottages), wooden tables and
brocaded settles, brick-walled fireplace,
well kept Adnams Southwold and three
guests, lots of wines by the glass and well
liked food (all day weekends), good service,
airy upstairs restaurant – very different in
style with own menu; free wi-fi; children (if
eating) and dogs (in bar) welcome, picnic-
sets on covered area and in big sheltered
garden, summer beer festival with 200 ales,
80 ciders/perries and hog roast, limited
parking, open all day. *(Brian Glozier)*

STOW MARIES   TQ8399
★ Prince of Wales (01621) 828971
*B1012 between South Woodham Ferrers
and Cold Norton Posters; CM3 6SA*
Cheery atmosphere in several little low-
ceilinged unspoilt rooms, bare boards and log
fires, conservatory dining area, half a dozen
widely sourced ales, bottled and draught
belgian beers including fruit ones, enjoyable
food (all day Sun) with some interesting
specials, home-made pizzas (winter Thurs)
from Victorian baker's oven, live jazz (third
Fri of month); children in family room,
terrace and garden tables, summer Sun
barbecues, converted stable bedrooms,
open all day. *(N R White)*

TAKELEY   TL5421
Green Man (01279) 879181
The Street; CM22 6QU Small well renovated
village pub, ales such as Sharps and Wells
& Youngs, nice wines by the glass and good
well presented food, also coffee shop serving
lovely cakes; free wi-fi; children and dogs
welcome, handy for Hatfield Forest (NT) and
Stansted Airport, five bedrooms, open all day.
(Mrs Margo Finlay, Jörg Kasprowski)

TENDRING   TM1523
Cherry Tree (01255) 830340
*Off A120 E of Colchester; B1035 junction
with Crow Lane, E of village centre;
CO16 9AP* Extended heavy-beamed, red-
brick dining pub, good food (not Sun evening,
booking advised weekends) including daily
specials and set lunch (Tues-Sat), helpful
friendly staff, high-backed black leather
chairs around compact pub tables on broad
polished boards, open fire, comfortable
chairs by counter serving Adnams, Greene
King and good value wines by the glass, two
areas set with white linen; disabled facilities,
teak tables under parasols on sheltered back
terrace, more tables on lawn behind tall
hedge, closed Mon. *(N R White)*

Please keep sending us reports. We rely on readers for news of new discoveries,
and particularly for news of changes – however slight – at the fully described pubs:
feedback@goodguides.com, or (no stamp needed) The Good Pub Guide,
FREEPOST RTJR-ZCYZ-RJZT, Perrymans Lane, Etchingham TN19 7DN.

THAXTED   TL6031
Swan (01371) 830321
Bull Ring; CM6 2PL Dark beamed Tudor
inn with long open bar, leather sofas and log
fire, well kept Greene King ales and good
choice of whiskies, pubby food served by
friendly staff, restaurant; roadside picnic-sets
overlooking lovely church (Holst was organist
here), windmill nearby, 20 bedrooms (back
ones quieter), open all day. *(Tina and David
Woods-Taylor)*

THEYDON BOIS   TQ4599
Queen Victoria (01992) 812392
Coppice Row (B172); CM16 7ES Nice
spot set back from green, cosy beamed and
carpeted traditional lounge, roaring log fire,
local pictures and mug collection, two further
bars, popular good value food including
children's menu, McMullens ales and decent
house wines, friendly efficient young staff,
end restaurant; background music; dogs
welcome, picnic-sets on well laid out front
terrace, open all day. *(Robert Lester, N R White)*

UPSHIRE   TL4100
Horseshoes (01992) 712745
*Horseshoe Hill, E of Waltham Abbey;
EN9 3SN* Welcoming Victorian pub with
small bar area and dining room, good freshly
made food (not Sun evening, Mon) from
chef/landlord with some emphasis on fish,
well kept McMullens and guests, friendly
helpful staff; children and dogs (in bar)
welcome, garden overlooking Lea Valley,
more tables out in front, good walks, open
all day. *(Joel Calhoun, David Jackson)*

WICKHAM ST PAUL   TL8336
★Victory (01787) 269364
SW of Sudbury; The Green; CO9 2PT
Attractive and spacious old dining pub,
interesting choice of good fresh food (not
Sun evening), friendly efficient service,
Adnams, Sharps Doom Bar and a guest from
brick-fronted bar, beams and timbers, leather
sofas and armchairs, inglenook woodburner;
background music, pool and darts; children
welcome, neat garden overlooking village
cricket green, open all day. *(Anon)*

WIDDINGTON   TL5331
★Fleur de Lys (01799) 543280
Signed off B1383 N of Stansted; CB11 3SG
Welcoming unpretentious low-beamed
and timbered village local, well prepared
generous food (not Mon, Tues evening) in

bar and dining room from sandwiches to Sun
roasts, children's helpings, well kept Adnams,
Sharps and two guests chosen by regulars,
decent wines, dim lighting and inglenook log
fire, pool and other games in back bar, Thurs
quiz; dogs welcome, picnic-sets in pretty
garden, open all day Fri-Sun. *(Anon)*

WIVENHOE   TM0321
Black Buoy (01206) 822425
Off A133; CO7 9BS Recently reopened and
fully refurbished by village consortium; open-
plan partly timbered bare-boards bar, well
kept ales such as Colchester, Mighty Oak and
Red Fox, Aspall's cider, several wines by the
glass and good sensibly priced home-made
food (not Sun evening), cheerful service,
open fires, upper dining area glimpsing river
over roofs; well behaved children and dogs in
certain areas, terrace seating, two bedrooms,
open all day. *(Anon)*

WOODHAM MORTIMER   TL8104
Hurdlemakers Arms
(01245) 225169 *Post Office Road;
CM9 6ST* Small quietly placed traditional
country local, flagstoned lounge with settles,
low ceiling, timbered walls and big open fire,
four well kept ales and enjoyable fresh food,
friendly efficient service, public bar; children
welcome, picnic-sets among trees and shrubs,
play area and summer barbecues. *(Natasha
Hoare)*

WRITTLE   TL6706
Wheatsheaf (01245) 420695
The Green; CM1 3DU Traditional little
19th-c two-room local, friendly and chatty,
with well kept Adnams, Farmers, Mighty Oak,
Sharps, Wibblers and two guests, lunchtime
baguettes and a couple of hot dishes (not
Sun), free bar nibbles, folk night third
Fri of month; terrace tables, open all day
weekends. *(Bob Hibberd)*

YOUNGS END   TL7319
Green Dragon (01245) 361030
*Former A131 Braintree–Chelmsford
(off new bypass), just N of Essex
Showground; CM77 8QN* Refurbished
beamed dining pub (part of the Old English
Inns group), enjoyable reasonably priced
food from sharing plates up, meal deals,
Greene King ales, friendly staff, leather
chairs by log fire, converted hayloft area;
background music; children welcome, picnic-
sets on terrace and back lawn. *(Mrs Margo
Finlay, Jörg Kasprowski)*

Gloucestershire

ASHLEWORTH
SO8125 Map 4

Queens Arms 🌟 🍷 🍺

Village signposted off A417 at Hartpury; GL19 4HT

Neatly kept pub with friendly licensees, a civilised bar, highly rated food, thoughtful wines and sunny courtyard

This 17th-c inn in a pretty village has been run by the same hard-working, hands-on south african licensees for 17 years. Everything is kept spic and span and the friendly, civilised main bar has an appealing variety of farmhouse and brocaded dining chairs around big oak and mahogany tables on green carpet, and numerous pictures and paintings on the faintly patterned wallpaper and red ochre walls; at night, it's softly lit by fringed wall lamps and candles. A little art gallery displays work by local artists. Brains The Rev James, Otter Ale and a summer guest such as Donnington BB on handpump, 15 wines by the glass including south african ones, 22 malt whiskies, winter mulled wine and summer home-made lemonade; background music. The friendly pub cat is called Talulah. The sunny courtyard has cast-iron chairs and tables and lovely flower beds in summer; two perfectly clipped mushroom-shaped yews dominate the front of the building. Wheelchair access.

🌟 Using seasonal local produce, the good, popular food includes lunchtime baguettes, filo prawns with sweet and sour sauce, pork and duck liver terrine, chicken with mozzarella in a creamy marsala sauce, rack of honey and barbecue spare ribs, greek lamb shank in a rich red wine gravy topped with mint yoghurt, bobotie (a spicy south african beef, fruit and nut dish), and puddings such as lemon cheesecake and cape brandy pudding (light sponge with brandy-soaked dates). *Benchmark main dish: steak and kidney pie £11.95. Two-course evening meal £22.00.*

Free house ~ Licensees Tony and Gill Burreddu ~ Real ale ~ (01452) 700395 ~ Open 12-3, 7-11; 12-3 Sun; closed Sun evening, Mon ~ Bar food 12-2, 7-9 ~ Restaurant ~ Well behaved children allowed ~ www.queensarmsashleworth.co.uk
Recommended by Bernard Stradling, Ian Wilson, Chris and Angela Buckell, P and J Shapley

BARNSLEY
SP0705 Map 4

Village Pub 🌟 🍷 🛏

B4425 Cirencester–Burford; GL7 5EF

Smart country pub with comfortable communicating rooms, candles and open fires, excellent food and a good choice of drinks, and seats in the back courtyard; individually decorated bedrooms

Our readers visit this bustling pub on a regular basis and very much enjoy the friendly welcome and rewarding food. The low-ceilinged bar rooms are smart and contemporary, with pale paintwork, flagstones and oak floorboards, heavy swagged curtains, oil paintings, plush chairs, stools and window settles around polished candlelit tables, three open fireplaces and country magazines and newspapers. There's always a cheerful mix of customers, from regulars (often with a dog in tow) to diners enjoying a delicious meal. Cotswold Lion Best in Show and Hook Norton Old Hooky on handpump, an extensive wine list with several by the glass, and farm cider. The sheltered back courtyard has solid wooden furniture under parasols, outdoor heaters and its own servery. This is an extremely comfortable and civilised place to stay and the breakfasts are very good, with local sausages, bacon and eggs and home-made bread and jam.

From a seasonally aware menu, the consistently excellent food includes nibbles such as quail and black pudding scotch eggs, fish soup with saffron mayonnaise and garlic croutons, twice-baked cheddar cheese soufflé, chicken kiev, pot-roasted brisket with dumplings, beetroot and horseradish purée, smoked haddock fishcakes with poached egg, spinach and lemon butter sauce, and puddings such as apple and treacle tart and hot chocolate mousse. *Benchmark main dish: slow-roast pork belly £15.00. Two-course evening meal £23.00.*

Free house ~ Licensee Michael Mella ~ Real ale ~ (01285) 740421 ~ Open 11-11 ~ Bar food 12-2.30 (3 weekends), 6-9.30 (10 Sat, 9 Sun) ~ Children welcome ~ Dogs welcome ~ Wi-fi ~ Bedrooms: $100/$135 ~ www.thevillagepub.co.uk *Recommended by Steve and Liz Tilley, Tracey and Stephen Groves*

BLAISDON
Red Hart ◖

SO7016   Map 4

Village signposted off A4136 just SW of junction with A40 W of Gloucester; OS Sheet 162 map reference 703169; GL17 0AH

Village pub with interesting bric-a-brac in attractive rooms, popular bar food and several real ales

In summer, the window boxes at the front of this bustling pub are very pretty and there are picnic-sets in the garden and a children's play area; the terrace hosts popular barbecues. The flagstoned main bar has cushioned wall and window seats, traditional pub tables, a log fire, four real ales from breweries such as Bespoke, Kingstone, Wells & Youngs and Wickwar on handpump, nine wines by the glass and local cider; background music and bar billiards. On the right is an attractive beamed restaurant with interesting prints and bric-a-brac; on the left, you'll find additional dining space for families. The little church above the village is worth a visit.

Using local produce and rearing their own pigs, the well liked food includes sandwiches, king prawns in garlic butter, chicken and leek terrine, ham, egg and bubble and squeak, steak and mushroom in ale pie, leek and parmesan risotto with a poached egg, poached salmon with herb and cheese polenta cake in rich tomato sauce, and puddings. *Benchmark main dish: home-reared slow-roast pork belly £13.00. Two-course evening meal £19.50.*

Free house ~ Licensee Sharon Hookings ~ Real ale ~ (01452) 830477 ~ Open 12-3, 6-11.30; 12-4, 7-11 Sun ~ Bar food 12-2, 7-9 ~ Restaurant ~ Children welcome ~ Dogs allowed in bar ~ Wi-fi ~ www.redhartinn.co.uk *Recommended by R T and J C Moggridge, Chris and Val Ramstedt*

BLEDINGTON

SP2422 Map 4

Kings Head

B4450; OX7 6XQ

Beams and atmospheric furnishings in 16th-c former cider house, super wines by the glass, real ales and delicious food; smart bedrooms

'At the top of its game – a wonderful all-rounder' is how a reader describes this particularly well run inn. The main bar remains the heart of the place and is full of ancient beams and other atmospheric furnishings (high-backed wooden settles, gateleg or pedestal tables) and has a warming log fire in a stone inglenook; sporting memorabilia of rugby, racing, cricket and hunting. To the left, a drinking area has built-in wall benches, stools and dining chairs around wooden tables, rugs on bare boards and a woodburning stove. Hook Norton Best and guests from breweries such as Butcombe, Oxfordshire Ales and Wye Valley on handpump, a super wine list with ten by the glass and 20 malt whiskies; background music. There are seats out in front and more in the back courtyard garden; resident ducks and chickens. This is a lovely place to stay and the bedrooms are elegantly simple and charming. The same first class licensees also run the Swan at Swinbrook (see our Oxfordshire chapter).

 Using local, organic produce from named suppliers, the accomplished and imaginative cooking includes lunchtime sandwiches, vodka and tonic deep-fried soft shell crab with saffron aioli, potted smoked shrimps with red pepper marmalade, cauliflower risotto with parmesan, line-caught fish and chips, pigeon breasts with puy lentil and carrot tart, and puddings such as rhubarb and walnut macaroon crumble and dark chocolate and orange tart with blood orange sorbet; Wednesday is burger night (roe deer, beef and lamb). *Benchmark main dish: chilli burger with montgomery cheddar, harissa mayonnaise and skinny chips £13.50. Two-course evening meal £22.00.*

Free house ~ Licensees Nicola and Archie Orr-Ewing ~ Real ale ~ (01608) 658365 ~ Open 11.30 (12 Sun)-11 ~ Bar food 12-2, 6.30-9 (9.30 Fri, Sat) ~ Restaurant ~ Children welcome ~ Dogs allowed in bar ~ Wi-fi ~ Bedrooms: £75/£95 ~ www.kingsheadinn.net
Recommended by Bernard Stradling, Tracey and Stephen Groves, Richard Tilbrook, Liz Bell

BOURTON-ON-THE-HILL

SP1732 Map 4

Horse & Groom

A44 W of Moreton-in-Marsh; GL56 9AQ

Handsome Georgian inn with a fine range of drinks, excellent food, friendly staff and lovely views from seats outside; smart bedrooms

This honey-coloured stone inn is a special place to stay, with individually styled, well equipped bedrooms and good breakfasts. The pubby bar is light and airy with a nice mix of wooden chairs and tables on bare boards, stripped-stone walls, a good log fire, Goffs Jouster and guests such as Stroud Budding and Wickwar BOB on handpump, 20 wines by the glass and farm cider. There are plenty of original features throughout; board games. The large back garden has lots of seats under parasols and fine views over the surrounding countryside. It's best to get here early to be sure of a space in the smallish car park. Batsford Arboretum is not far away.

 Cooked by the landlord, the inventive food includes sandwiches, deep-fried salt and pepper squid with vietnamese salad, twice-baked goats cheese and thyme soufflé, home-cured rare-breed ham and egg, smoked haddock, salmon and leek fishcakes with mustard cream sauce, butternut squash and mascarpone risotto with sage butter, rare-breed burger with horseradish mayonnaise, and puddings such as banana and hazelnut eton mess and damson jam bakewell tart. *Benchmark main dish: beer-battered fish and chips £13.25. Two-course evening meal £20.00.*

Free house ~ Licensee Tom Greenstock ~ Real ale ~ (01386) 700413 ~ Open 11-2.30 (3 Sat), 6-11; 12-3.30 Sun; closed Sun evening except bank holiday weekends ~ Bar food 12-2, 7-9.30 ~ Restaurant ~ Children welcome ~ Wi-fi ~ Bedrooms: $80/$120 ~ www.horseandgroom.info *Recommended by Simon Collett-Jones, Tracey and Stephen Groves, Richard Tilbrook, Di and Mike Gillam, Dr J J H Gilkes, Derek Thomas, Bernard Stradling, J R Wildon, P and J Shapley*

BROCKHAMPTON SP0322 Map 4
Craven Arms

Village signposted off A436 Andoversford–Naunton – look out for inn sign at head of lane in village; can also be reached from A40 Andoversford–Cheltenham via Whittington and Syreford; GL54 5XQ

Friendly village pub with tasty bar food, real ales and seats in a big garden

The large garden here has plenty of seats for use in warm weather and the views are lovely. An attractive 16th-c pub tucked away down a country lane with good surrounding walks, it draws a happy mix of both locals and visitors. The bars have low beams, thick roughly coursed stone walls and some tiled flooring; although it's largely been opened out to give a sizeable eating area off the smaller bar servery, there's a feeling of several communicating rooms. The furniture is mainly pine, with comfortable leather sofas, wall settles and tub chairs; also, gin traps and various stuffed animal trophies and a warm log fire. Otter Bitter, Butcombe Legless Bob (named for the landlord and 20p per pint goes to Diabetes UK), and Stroud Budding on handpump, eight wines by the glass and a farm cider; board games. The dog is called Max and the cat Polly.

Popular food includes duck liver parfait with truffle butter and Grand Marnier jelly, potted shrimps, ham and free-range eggs, sweet potato, butterbean, broccoli and stilton pie, beer-battered fresh fish and chips, steak in ale pie, barbecue-style 'hot rock' meat and fish choices, and puddings. *Benchmark main dish: slow-cooked lamb £16.95. Two-course evening meal £18.00.*

Free house ~ Licensees Barbara and Bob Price ~ Real ale ~ (01242) 820410 ~ Open 12-3, 6-11; 12-11 Sat; 12-6 Sun; closed Sun evening, Mon ~ Bar food 12-2 (2.30 Sat), 6.30-9; 12.30-3.30 Sun ~ Restaurant ~ Children welcome ~ Dogs allowed in bar ~ Wi-fi ~ www.thecravenarms.co.uk *Recommended by Neil and Anita Christopher, Dr A J and Mrs B A Tompsett, Mrs Jo Rees, Martin and Pauline Jennings*

CHELTENHAM SO9624 Map 4
Royal Oak ♀ ◀

Off B4348 just N; The Burgage, Prestbury; GL52 3DL

Bustling and friendly with popular food, several real ales and wine by the glass, and seats in the sheltered garden

There's always something going on in this bustling, friendly pub – beer and sausage or cider and cheese festivals, themed food nights (indian, italian, fish), whisky tastings and comedy evenings. The congenial low-beamed bar has fresh flowers and polished brasses, a comfortable mix of seating including chapel chairs on parquet flooring, some interesting pictures on the ochre walls and a woodburning stove in a stone fireplace.

Dark Star Hophead, Harveys Best, Otley O1, Timothy Taylors Landlord and Wye Valley Bitter on handpump and several wines by the glass; efficient, helpful service. Dining room tables are nicely spaced so that you don't feel crowded, and the skittle alley doubles as a function room. There are seats and tables under canopies on the heated terrace and in a sheltered garden. Sister pub is the Gloucester Old Spot in Coombe Hill.

Enjoyable food includes lunchtime baguettes and ciabattas, braised pig cheeks with chorizo and haricot beans, foie gras terrine with lightly curried chutney, pork and bacon hash with a free-range egg, panko-crumbed aubergine stuffed with goats cheese and chives with sweet potato mash and red pepper and harissa sauce, battered fresh fish of the day and chips, corn-fed chicken breast stuffed with gruyère and walnuts with leek and potato dauphinoise and porcini mushroom sauce, and puddings. *Benchmark main dish: roast lamb rump with dauphinoise potatoes and local wild garlic leaves £16.95. Two-course evening meal £20.00.*

Free house ~ Licensees Simon and Kate Daws ~ Real ale ~ (01242) 522344 ~ Open 11-11; 12-10.30 Sun ~ Bar food 12-2, 6.30-9; all day Sun ~ Restaurant ~ Children welcome in dining room and before 7pm in bar ~ Wi-fi ~ www.royal-oak-prestbury.co.uk
Recommended by Ian Herdman, Michael Sargent, R C Vincent, M G Hart

CHIPPING CAMPDEN   SP1539   Map 4

Eight Bells

Church Street (one way – entrance off B4035); GL55 6JG

Lovely inn with massive timbers and beams, log fires, quite a choice of bar food, real ales and seats in the large terraced garden; bedrooms

Always cheerfully busy with an interesting mix of customers, this is a handsome old inn that our readers enjoy very much. The candlelit bars have heavy oak beams, massive timber supports and stripped-stone walls with cushioned pews, sofas and solid dark wood furniture on broad flagstones, and log fires in up to three restored stone fireplaces. A glass panel in the dining room floor reveals the passage from the church by which Roman Catholic priests could escape from the Roundheads. Hook Norton Best, Goffs Jouster, Purity Mad Goose and a guest such as Wye Valley HPA on handpump from the fine oak bar counter, eight wines by the glass and two farm ciders; background music and board games. There's a large terraced garden with plenty of seats, and striking views of the almshouses and church. Attractive and comfortable bedrooms – and the breakfasts are well thought-of too. The pub is handy for the Cotswold Way walk, which leads to Bath.

Using seasonal local produce, the good food includes lunchtime ciabattas, prawn and spinach frittata, mackerel pâté, roast mediterranean vegetables on pasta with red pepper pesto, pork and leek sausages with home-made onion rings and wholegrain mustard jus, lamb chump with garlic and rosemary jus, chicken stuffed with wild mushroom and tarragon mousse and wrapped in streaky bacon with basil pesto, and puddings such as rhubarb panna cotta and sticky toffee pudding with butterscotch sauce. *Benchmark main dish: beer-battered fish and skin-on chips £13.75. Two-course evening meal £21.00.*

Free house ~ Licensee Neil Hargreaves ~ Real ale ~ (01386) 840371 ~ Open 12-11 ~ Bar food 12-2, 6.30-9; 12-2.30, 6.30-9.30 Fri, Sat; all day Sun ~ Restaurant ~ Well behaved children welcome in dining room after 6pm; over-7s only in bedrooms ~ Dogs allowed in bar ~ Wi-fi ~ Bedrooms: £65/£95 ~ www.eightbellsinn.co.uk *Recommended by Bernard Stradling, J Trevor Roberts, Simon Collett-Jones, Jim and Maggie Cowell, Clive and Fran Dutson, Paul Humphreys, Michael Sargent*

CIRENCESTER

SP0202 Map 4

Fleece 🛏

Market Place; GL7 2NZ

Carefully renovated inn with plenty of room in various bars and lounges, courteous staff, enjoyable food and drink and seats on terrace; character bedrooms

Carefully refurbished by Thwaites, this 17th-c former coaching inn is usefully open all day – and customers do drop in and out, creating a bustling, easy-going atmosphere. There's plenty of room in the various bars, lounges and airy dining areas, all different in style. Wheelback and mate's chairs and high bar stools and tables around the counter, wicker tub and high-backed yellow or orange dining chairs around an assortment of wooden tables, shelves of glassware and pottery, and french windows that open on to the terrace where there are white metal tables and chairs under parasols. Throughout, there are bare floorboards, contemporary pale paintwork, plenty of prints and fresh flowers and good lighting. Efficient, courteous staff serve Cotswold Lion Golden Fleece and Thwaites Lancaster Bomber and Wainwright on handpump, several wines by the glass and good coffees and teas. The comfortable, attractive and well equipped bedrooms – some with much character – make a good base for exploring the lovely town and surrounding countryside; breakfasts are hearty.

🍴 Some sort of good, enjoyable food is served all day: nibbles, sandwiches, deli boards, salt and pepper squid with aioli, butternut squash risotto with pine nuts and crispy sage, crab and chilli linguine, lamp rump with dauphinoise potatoes, free-range pork belly with black pudding fritter and celeriac purée, and puddings such as vanilla crème brûlée and gooseberry and elderflower fool with apple crisps; also, afternoon teas 2-6pm. *Benchmark main dish: beef or chicken burger with interesting toppings and fries £13.00. Two-course evening meal £20.20.*

Free house ~ Licensee Ricardo Canestra ~ Real ale ~ (01285) 658507 ~ Open 10.30am-11pm (10.30pm Sun) ~ Bar food 12-9 (8.30 Sun) ~ Restaurant ~ Children welcome ~ Dogs allowed in bar and bedrooms ~ Wi-fi ~ Bedrooms: /£102 ~ www.thefleececirencester.co.uk *Recommended by Mrs Jo Rees, Richard Tilbrook, Edward May*

CLIFFORD'S MESNE

SO6922 Map 4

Yew Tree ⭐ 🍷 🍺

From A40 W of Huntley, turn off at May Hill 1, Clifford's Mesne 2.5 signpost – pub eventually signed up steep narrow lane on left; Clifford's Mesne also signposted off B4216 S of Newent – pub then signed on right; GL18 1JS

Unusual dining pub nicely tucked away on slopes of May Hill, with inventive food and wine bargains

Just the place to end up at after a walk in the rolling countryside, this is an interesting dining pub with a fantastic choice of drinks. There's a remarkable choice of provincial french wines from small producers – all served by glass (three sizes), 500ml jug and bottle – and a seating area in the small informal wine shop; if you buy a bottle with your meal, the mark-up is £6, which is excellent value especially at the top end. Cottage DB5, Sharps Own and Wickwar Spring Ale on handpump, local farm cider and perry, 16 gins and good value winter mulled wine and cider; service is prompt and genial. The smallish two-room beamed bar has an attractive mix of small settles, a pew and character chairs around various tables including some antique ones, rugs on an unusual stone floor, and a warm woodburning stove. Up a few steps is a more formal carpeted dining room and, beyond, a sofa by a big log fire; newspapers and unobtrusive nostalgic pop music. The teak tables on the side terrace are best placed for the views, and steps lead down to a sturdy play area.

 As well as light lunches and smaller helpings for under £8 (Wednesday-Saturday lunchtimes), the thoughtful choice of often enterprising food includes nibbles, duck mousse with apple and elderberry jelly, pheasant goujons with redcurrant dip, aubergine, tomato and cream cheese gateau, chargrilled lemon chicken with rösti potato, cold pork loin with potato pancakes and warm tomato and onion relish, and puddings such as ginger sponge with chocolate fudge sauce and apple and date crumble. *Benchmark main dish: gloucester old spot loin steaks with apple and sage butter £16.00. Two-course evening meal £21.00.*

Free house ~ Licensees Mr and Mrs Philip Todd ~ Real ale ~ (01531) 820719 ~ Open 12-2.30, 6-11; 12-5 Sun; closed Sun evening, Mon, Tues lunch ~ Bar food 12-2, 6-9; 12-4 Sun ~ Children welcome ~ Dogs welcome ~ Wi-fi ~ www.yewtreeinn.com
Recommended by Eric and Mary Barrett, Guy Vowles

 COOMBE HILL   SO8926   Map 4
Gloucester Old Spot ★ ◖
A mile from M5 junction 10 (access only from southbound/to northbound carriageways); A4019 towards A38 Gloucester–Tewkesbury; GL51 9SY

The country local comes of age – a model for today's country pubs

Much bigger than it seems from outside, this thoughtfully restored country pub is handy for the M5 in both directions. The companionable quarry-tiled beamed bar has chapel chairs and other seats around assorted tables (including one in a bow-windowed alcove) and opens into a lighter, partly panelled area with cushioned settles and stripped kitchen tables. Purity Mad Goose, Severn Vale Severn Nations, Sharps Cornish Coaster and Wye Valley Butty Bach on handpump, seven decent wines by the glass, farm cider and perry; the young staff are friendly without being pushy. Decoration is in unobtrusive good taste, with winter log fires. A handsome separate dining room, with high stripped-brick walls, dark flagstones and candlelight, has similar country furniture. The garden has chunky benches and tables under parasols on the terrace, with some oak barrel tables on brickwork and pretty flowering vintage buckets and baskets; there are heaters for cooler weather. This is sister pub to the Royal Oak in Prestbury, near Cheltenham.

Using the best local seasonal ingredients, the enjoyable food includes lunchtime rolls, corn-fed chicken, leek and confit garlic terrine with fig chutney, crispy pressed pork shoulder with seared scallops, poached rhubarb and asparagus, tomato, basil and mozzarella tartlet with tomato vinaigrette, venison and oxtail pie, hazelnut-crusted cod with curried coconut mussels, spinach pakora and minted yoghurt, and puddings such as lemon and ginger cheesecake and brioche bread and butter pudding. *Benchmark main dish: pork mixed grill (braised cheek, crispy shoulder, chop, belly and toulouse sausage) £15.50. Two-course evening meal £21.00.*

Free house ~ Licensees Simon Daws and Hayley Cribb ~ Real ale ~ (01242) 680321 ~ Open 10am-11pm (10pm Sun) ~ Bar food 12-2, 6-9; 12-8 Sun ~ Restaurant ~ Children welcome ~ Dogs allowed in bar ~ Wi-fi ~ www.thegloucesteroldspot.co.uk
Recommended by Roger and Donna Huggins, M G Hart, Patrick and Daphne Darley

---

A star after the name of a pub shows exceptional quality. It means most people (after reading the report to see just why the star has been won) would think a special trip worthwhile.

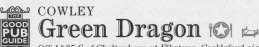

COWLEY   SO9714   Map 4

Green Dragon

Off A435 S of Cheltenham at Elkstone, Cockleford sign; OS Sheet 163 map reference 970142; GL53 9NW

17th-c stone-fronted inn with beamed bars, separate restaurant, popular food, real ales and seats on terraces; well appointed bedrooms

'It's so hard to leave,' says one of our readers about this attractive stone-fronted and particularly well run pub. The two beamed bars have plenty of character and a cosy, nicely old-fashioned feel, with big flagstones and wooden floorboards, candlelit tables and winter log fires in two stone fireplaces; staff are consistently friendly and helpful. Hook Norton Old Hooky, Sharps Doom Bar and guests such as Butcombe Bitter and Otter Bitter on handpump, a dozen wines by the glass and 11 malt whiskies; background music. The furniture and the bar itself in the upper Mouse Bar were made by Robert Thompson, and little mice run over the hand-carved tables, chairs and mantelpiece; there's also a small upstairs restaurant and a separate skittle alley. The bedrooms are comfortable and well appointed and breakfasts generous. There are seats outside on terraces and this is good walking country.

 As well as lunchtime sandwiches (not Sunday), the tempting food includes smoked salmon mousse with avocado and chive yoghurt, warm chicken liver and bacon salad with quail eggs and croutons, beer-battered fish and chips, mushroom ravioli with pesto cream sauce, lamb casserole in mint and red wine gravy, cod with creamy leek and bacon sauce, and puddings such as banoffi pie and crème brûlée. *Benchmark main dish: 28-day hung sirloin steak with peppercorn and brandy or stilton sauce £19.95. Two-course evening meal £22.25.*

Buccaneer Holdings ~ Managers Simon and Nicky Haly ~ Real ale ~ (01242) 870271 ~ Open 11-11; 12-10.30 Sun ~ Bar food 12-2.30 (3 Sat), 6-10; 12-3.30, 6-9 Sun ~ Restaurant ~ Children welcome ~ Dogs allowed in bar and bedrooms ~ Wi-fi ~ Bedrooms: £70/£95 ~ www.green-dragon-inn.co.uk *Recommended by Howard and Margaret Buchanan, Richard Tilbrook, Dr A J and Mrs B A Tompsett, Roy Shutz*

DURSLEY   ST7598   Map 4

Old Spot £

Hill Road; by bus station; GL11 4JQ

Unassuming and cheery town pub with up to 11 real ales, regular beer festivals and good value lunchtime food

A favourite with so many of our readers, this bustling town local is unfailingly well run. There's a genuinely happy atmosphere, and a fantastic choice of up to 11 real ales on handpump. Butcombe Bitter and Uley Old Ric are always available, as well as guests from breweries such as Bath, Church End, Cotswold, Dark Star, North Cotswold, Otter, Ramsbury and Severn Vale, and they hold a couple of annual beer festivals; 40 malt whiskies, half a dozen wines by the glass and a farm cider. The front door opens into a deep-pink small room with stools on shiny quarry tiles beside the pine-boarded bar counter, and old enamel beer signs on the walls and ceiling; there's a profusion of porcine paraphernalia. A small room leads off on the left, and the little wood-floored room to the right has a stone fireplace. A step goes down to a cosy Victorian tiled snug and (to the right) a meeting room. The heated and covered garden has seats. Wheelchair access.

Good value lunchtime food (and evening dishes on Monday) includes doorstep sandwiches (the soup-and-sandwich deal is popular), pork, apple and cider sausages with onion gravy, a pie of the day, chicken korma, mediterranean vegetable tart, and puddings such as blueberry cheesecake and a seasonal crumble. *Benchmark main dish: salmon and smoked haddock fishcakes £8.50.*

Free house ~ Licensee Ellie Sainty ~ Real ale ~ (01453) 542870 ~ Open 11-11; 12-11 Sun ~ Bar food 12-3; no evening meals except 6-9 Mon ~ Children welcome away from bar area before 9pm ~ Dogs welcome ~ Wi-fi ~ Folk music monthly ~ www.oldspotinn.co.uk
Recommended by Kerry Law, Mrs P Sumner, Dr and Mrs A K Clarke, Michael Snelgrove, PL

EASTINGTON
SO7705 Map 4

Old Badger ◀

Alkerton Road, a mile from M5 junction 13; GL10 3AT

Friendly, traditionally furnished pub with plenty to look at, five real ales, tasty food and seats in attractive garden

Renovated and extended by the owners of the fine Old Spot in Dursley, this is now a friendly pub with an easy-going, chatty atmosphere. The split-level connected rooms are traditionally furnished with built-in planked and cushioned wall seats, settles and farmhouse chairs around all sorts of tables on quarry tiles and floorboards, and feature two open fires. There are stone bottles, bookshelves, breweriana on red or cream walls, and even a stuffed badger. Badger (of course) IPA, Church End Goats Milk, Moles Tap, Otter Bright and Uley Bitter on handpump, 14 wines by the glass and three farm ciders, served by helpful, smiling staff. The nicely landscaped garden has benches and picnic-sets on the terrace, lawn and under a covered gazebo; the flowering tubs and window boxes are pretty.

 The popular food, using local produce, includes sandwiches, several tapas from patatas bravas through salt and pepper squid to pork meatballs in a creamy almond sauce, ham and egg, pesto linguine with sun-dried tomatoes, beer-battered haddock and chips, pancetta-wrapped chicken stuffed with garlic butter, and puddings such as tipsy tiramisu and rhubarb and custard tart. *Benchmark main dish: pie of the day £10.95. Two-course evening meal £15.00.*

Free house ~ Licensees Ellie Sainty and Julie Gilborson ~ Real ale ~ (01453) 822892 ~ Open 12-11.30 (10.30 Sun) ~ Bar food 12-2.30, 6-9; 12-3 Sun ~ Children welcome ~ Dogs welcome ~ Wi-fi ~ Live music monthly ~ www.oldbadgerinn.co.uk *Recommended by Neil and Anita Christopher, Michael Snelgrove*

FORD
SP0829 Map 4

Plough ◀ 🛏

B4077 Stow–Alderton; GL54 5RU

16th-c inn in horse-racing country with lots of horse talk, a bustling atmosphere, first class service, good food and well kept beer; bedrooms

Once again, reports from readers on this particularly well run pub are consistently enthusiastic. The hands-on landlord and his courteous, efficient staff offer a cheerful welcome to all, and the atmosphere is chatty and easy-going. The beamed and stripped-stone bar has racing prints and photos on the walls (many customers belong to the racing fraternity and a well known racehorse trainer's yard is opposite), old settles and benches around big tables on uneven flagstones, oak tables in a snug alcove, and open fires and woodburning stoves. Darts, TV (for the races) and background music. Donnington BB and SBA on handpump, seven wines by the glass and a dozen malt whiskies. There are picnic-sets under parasols and pretty hanging baskets at the front of the stone building, and a large back garden with a children's play fort. Cotswold Farm Park is nearby. Bedrooms are comfortable (the quietest ones are away from the pub) and there are views of the gallops. It gets packed on race days.

Using local meat and seasonal game, the highly thought-of food includes lunchtime baguettes, duck liver pâté with home-made chutney, seared scallops with cauliflower purée, a pie of the day, brie, beetroot and wild mushroom tart, chicken curry, pheasant, rabbit and venison casserole with dumplings, and puddings such as passion-fruit crème brûlée and chocolate brownie in chocolate sauce. *Benchmark main dish: half crispy gressingham duck with orange sauce £17.95. Two-course evening meal £18.95.*

Donnington ~ Tenant Craig Brown ~ Real ale ~ (01386) 584215 ~ Open 9am-11pm ~ Bar food 12-2, 6-9; all day Fri-Sun ~ Restaurant ~ Children welcome ~ Dogs welcome ~ Wi-fi ~ Bedrooms: £60/£80 ~ www.theploughinnatford.co.uk *Recommended by Guy Vowles, K H Frostick, D L Frostick, Richard Tilbrook, Mike and Mary Carter, Chris and Val Ramstedt*

GLOUCESTER
Café René

SO8318 Map 4

Southgate Street; best to park in Blackfriars car park (Ladybellegate Street) and walk through passageway – pub entrance is just across road; GL1 1TP

Unusual and interestingly placed bar with good value food all day, and good choice of drinks

Even at peak times when they're really busy, the helpful staff in this interesting bar remain friendly and efficient. Reached via a flagstoned passageway beside the partly Norman church of St Mary de Crypt, the place dates from the 17th c and has some stripped brick and timbering. It has an internal floodlit well, with water trickling down into its depths, and a very subterranean feel – no windows, black beams, dim lighting. The long bar counter is made of dozens of big casks, and they keep four changing real ales tapped from the cask, from breweries such as Freeminer, Stroud and Wickwar, plus farm ciders and a good choice of wines by the glass (decoration consists mainly of great banks of empty wine bottles). One antique panelled high-backed settle joins the usual pub tables and wheelback chairs on carpet, and there's a sizeable dining area on the right. Well reproduced background music, a silenced games machine and big-screen TV. There are plenty of picnic-sets under parasols out by the churchyard. They hold a popular rhythm and blues festival at the end of July.

Some sort of good food is served all day: lunchtime sandwiches and wraps, organic chicken liver pâté, creamy garlic mushrooms, stuffed roasted peppers, trio of sausages with mustard mash and red onion gravy, fish pie, curried caribbean lamb, popular chargrilled dishes such as cajun chicken, rack of ribs with barbecue sauce and steaks, and puddings including cheesecake of the day and lemon tart. *Benchmark main dish: burger with cheese, bacon, egg, onions, gherkins and choice of potatoes £8.50. Two-course evening meal £16.00.*

Free house ~ Licensee Paul Soden ~ Real ale ~ (01452) 309340 ~ Open 11am-midnight (later Fri, Sat); 12-12 Sun ~ Bar food 12-10 ~ Restaurant ~ Well behaved children allowed until 7pm ~ Wi-fi ~ Live music Weds, Fri ~ www.caferene.co.uk *Recommended by Ruth May, Chris and Angela Buckell, R T and J C Moggridge*

Pubs close to motorway junctions are listed at the back of the book.

GREAT RISSINGTON
SP1917 Map 4

Lamb 🍷 🛏

*Turn off A40 W of Burford to the Barringtons; keep straight on past
Great Barrington until Great Rissington is signed on left; GL54 2LN*

**Pleasant old bar in Cotswold-stone pub with well liked bar food,
changing real ales and seats in the sheltered garden; bedrooms**

A wellington bomber crashed in the garden here in 1943, with just one
survivor, and you can see a plaque he donated on the wall; other
interesting things to look at include parts of a propeller and assorted
artefacts in display cases. The two-roomed bar has high-backed leather
and farmhouse chairs around polished tables on red carpet, a woodburning
stove in the stone fireplace, and bar chairs at the counter where they
serve Brakspears Double Drop, Wychwood Hobgoblin and a guest such
as Ringwood Best Bitter on handpump; also, ten wines by the glass and
14 malt whiskies. The restaurant has another woodburning stove and old
agricultural tools on the walls; background music, TV, board games and
books for sale (in aid of guide dogs for the blind). You can sit outside on
the front terrace or in the sheltered, well kept hillside garden. A local
circular walk takes in part of the idyllic village, church, River Windrush and
stunning countryside surrounding the pub.

Quite a choice of food includes lunchtime sandwiches, ham hock and black
pudding terrine, quail with puy lentils, chorizo and sweetcorn and onion muffin,
gnocchi with girolles, butternut squash and truffle, pheasant and bacon pie, burger
with bacon, cheese and triple-cooked chips, line-caught bass with crab and braised
fennel, and puddings such as baked duck egg custard with rhubarb sorbet and sticky
toffee pudding with banana ice-cream. *Benchmark main dish: local lamb rump
with salsa verde and sautéed potatoes £16.00. Two-course evening meal £20.00.*

Free house ~ Licensees Paul and Jacqueline Gabriel ~ Real ale ~ (01451) 820388 ~
Open 12-11.30 (midnight Sat, 11 Sun) ~ Bar food 12-2.30 (3 weekends), 6.30-9
(9.30 Fri, Sat) ~ Restaurant ~ Children welcome ~ Dogs allowed in bar ~ Wi-fi ~
Bedrooms: £55/£80 ~ www.thelambinn.com *Recommended by Neil and Angela Huxter*

GRETTON
SP0130 Map 4

Royal Oak 🍺

Off B4077 E of Tewkesbury; GL54 5EP

**Golden-stone pub with light, airy rooms, open fires, six real ales,
popular food and friendly atmosphere; good surrounding walks**

The flower-filled terrace behind this carefully refurbished pub has
plenty of seats with fine views over the village and across the valley
to Dumbleton Hills and the Malverns; as well as a neat lawn, there's a
children's play area and a bookable tennis court. Inside, there's a light and
airy feel and an easy-going atmosphere; the bar rooms have white-painted
kitchen chairs and leather tub chairs around pale wood-topped tables
on bare boards or flagstones, open fires, and animal paintings and farm
tools on pale walls above a grey dado. The dining room and conservatory
are stylish with high-backed chairs around big, chunky tables, antlers on
one wall, a big central woodburning stove and candelabras and evening
candlelight. Cotswold Spring Stunner, Jennings Bitter and Cocker Hoop,
Prescott Grand Prix, Ramsbury Gold and Wye Valley HPA on handpump,
a dozen wines by the glass and summer farm cider. Bantams roam freely,
and in summer the steam trains from the Great Western Railway run along
the bottom of the garden.

🍴 Attractively presented and very popular, the food includes sandwiches, thai-spiced duck with pancakes and sweet chilli dip, breaded brie with spicy tomato chutney, beef, lamb, pork and bean burgers with toppings and fries, wild mushroom risotto, steak and mushroom in ale pie, salmon with spanish-style potatoes and lemon dressing, and puddings such as dark chocolate cheesecake and treacle tart. *Benchmark main dish: beer-battered haddock and chips £12.00. Two-course evening meal £20.00.*

Free house ~ Licensee Rob Owen ~ Real ale ~ (01242) 604999 ~ Open 11-11 (10 Sun) ~ Bar food 12-2.30, 6-9 ~ Restaurant ~ Children welcome ~ Dogs allowed in bar ~ Wi-fi ~ www.royaloakgretton.co.uk *Recommended by Martin and Pauline Jennings, Theocsbrian*

KILCOT
SO6925 Map 4
Kilcot Inn 🛏️
2.3 miles from M50 junction 3; B4221 towards Newent; GL18 1NG

Attractively reworked small country inn, kind staff, enjoyable local food and drink; bedrooms

This is a nice place to stay (and handy for the M50) with light, airy, comfortable bedrooms; breakfasts are good with local bacon and free-range eggs. It's a carefully restored, open-plan inn with stripped beams, bare boards and dark flagstones, sunny bay-window seats, homely armchairs by one of the two warm woodburning stoves, tables with padded dining chairs, and daily papers. Weston's Old Rosie, Rosie's Pig and Perry on handpump, with more cider by the bottle, as well as Hook Norton Lion, Marstons EPA and Wye Valley Butty Bach also on handpump, local wine and organic fruit juice; staff are courteous and friendly. Big-screen TV, maybe background music. The front terrace has picnic-sets under cocktail parasols, with more out behind. There's a smart shed for bicycles.

🍴 Using local produce, the seasonally changing food includes breakfasts (9-11am), lunchtime sandwiches, a charcuterie platter, deep-fried camembert with tomato relish, wild boar meatballs with a tomato and basil sauce on pasta, gloucester old spot sausages with red wine sauce and onion jam, butternut squash and goats cheese risotto, chicken with gorgonzola, pancetta, cauliflower purée and sherry sauce, and puddings such as chocolate and almond cake with white chocolate ice-cream and chocolate 'soil' and vanilla crème brûlée. *Benchmark main dish: duck breast with potato, sage and bacon gratin with butternut purée and red wine sauce £15.95. Two-course evening meal £20.50.*

Free house ~ Licensee Mark Lawrence ~ Real ale ~ (01989) 720707 ~ Open 11am-midnight (10 Sun) ~ Bar food 12-2.30, 6-9.30; 12-3, 5-8 Sun ~ Restaurant ~ Children welcome ~ Dogs allowed in bar ~ Wi-fi ~ Bedrooms: $50/$75 ~ www.kilcotinn.com *Recommended by Comus and Sarah Elliott*

LEIGHTERTON
ST8290 Map 2
Royal Oak 🍴⭐ ♀
Village signposted off A46 S of Nailsworth; GL8 8UN

Handsome country pub elegantly refurbished, good choice of drinks, imaginative food and kind staff

Handy for Westonbirt Arboretum and walks near the quiet village, this is a well run country inn with chatty, welcoming staff. The rambling bar has plenty of nice touches, from the pair of log fireplaces facing each other (you have to look twice to be sure it's not a mirror) to the splendid heavy low-loading antique trolley holding the daily papers. Part parquet, part broad boards, with some stripped stone and some pastel paintwork, and carefully chosen furniture from stylish strung-seat dining chairs to soft sofas. Bath Gem and Hook Norton Old Hooky on handpump, ten interesting wines by the glass and farm cider. A sheltered side courtyard has teak and metal tables and chairs. Good disabled access.

 Making their own bread, ketchup and pickles and offering a two- and three-course set lunch (Tuesday-Friday), the creative food includes lunchtime sandwiches, ham hock and foie gras terrine with spiced pear chutney, barbecue sticky chicken with noodle salad, buttermilk-battered cauliflower with aubergine chutney and saffron potatoes, moules marinière with chips, calves liver with parmesan polenta, crispy bacon and onions, and puddings such as dark chocolate and beetroot cake with red wine syrup and baked egg custard tart. *Benchmark main dish: slow-roasted pork belly with chorizo and white bean sauce £15.95. Two-course evening meal £21.00.*

Free house ~ Licensees Paul and Antonia Whitbread ~ Real ale ~ (01666) 890250 ~ Open 12-3, 5.30-11; 12-11 Sat; 12-9 Sun; closed Mon ~ Bar food 12-2 (3 Sun), 6-9; 12-2.30, 6-9.30 Sat ~ Restaurant ~ Children welcome ~ Dogs allowed in bar ~ Wi-fi ~ www.royaloakleighterton.co.uk *Recommended by Mike Longman, Dr and Mrs A K Clarke, Chris and Angela Buckell, Tom and Ruth Rees*

LOWER SLAUGHTER
SP1622 Map 4
Slaughters Country Inn ♀ 🛏
Village signposted off A429 Bourton-on-the-Water to Stow-on-the-Wold; GL54 2HS

Comfortable streamside inn in beautiful Cotswold village, enjoyable country food in attractive dining bar; comfortable bedrooms

With the little River Eye flowing slowly past the front of this much-extended stone-built inn and on through the village, this is a very appealing place where walkers and other visitors mix contentedly. The spreading bar has several low-beamed linked rooms with well spaced tables on polished limestone flagstones, and a variety of seats from simple chairs to heavy settles and soft sofas. Log fires, medieval-motif curtains for the mullioned windows, shelves of board games, a few carefully placed landscapes or stuffed fish on the cream or puce walls add up to understated refinement, and what really sets the style of the place is the thoroughly professional and efficient service. They keep Brakspears and Wychwood Hobgoblin on handpump, and a good choice of wines by the glass. The evening restaurant, refurbished in 2014, looks over a sweep of lawn and the sheep pasture beyond.

Excellent food from a thoughtful menu includes sandwiches, devilled cornish sardines with new potato and chive salad, chicken liver pâté with madeira jelly, thick-cut ham and eggs, pumpkin, chestnut and sage risotto, venison and root vegetable pie, confit duck leg with red wine sauce and apple and red cabbage, skate wing with caper, shallot and shrimp sauce, and puddings such as espresso tiramisu and double chocolate crémeux. *Benchmark main dish: beer-battered fish and chips £12.50. Two-course evening meal £21.50.*

Free house ~ Licensee Stuart Hodges ~ Real ale ~ (01451) 822143 ~ Open 11-11; 12-10.30 Sun ~ Bar food 12-3, 6.30-9; afternoon tea 3-5.30 ~ Restaurant ~ Children welcome ~ Dogs allowed in bar and bedrooms ~ Wi-fi ~ Bedrooms: £95/£105 ~ www.theslaughtersinn.co.uk *Recommended by Richard Tilbrook, David Fowler*

We accept no free drinks or meals and inspections are anonymous.

NAILSWORTH   ST8699 Map 4

Weighbridge

B4014 towards Tetbury; GL6 9AL

Super two-in-one pies served in cosy old-fashioned bar rooms, a fine choice of drinks, friendly service and a sheltered garden

The famous two-in-one pies here are so popular that they're now offering pudding versions too. Our readers enjoy all aspects of this well run pub. The relaxed bar has three cosily old-fashioned rooms with open fires, stripped-stone walls and antique settles, country chairs and window seats. The black beamed ceiling of the lounge bar is thickly festooned with black ironware – sheep shears, gin traps, lamps and a large collection of keys, many from the old Longfords Mill opposite the pub. Upstairs is a raftered hayloft with an engaging mix of rustic tables. No noisy games machines or background music. Uley Old Spot and Wadworths 6X and a couple of guest beers such as Black Sheep and Palmers Dorset Gold on handpump, 18 wines (and champagne and prosecco) by the glass, Weston's cider and 14 malt whiskies. A sheltered landscaped garden at the back has picnic-sets under umbrellas. Good disabled access and facilities.

 The two-in-one pies (also available for home baking) come in a divided bowl: one half contains the filling of your choice (perhaps steak, kidney and stout, salmon in cream sauce, or root vegetables with beans and pulses in tomato sauce) with a pastry topping, the other half has home-made cauliflower cheese (or broccoli mornay or root vegetables). Also, lunchtime baguettes, home-cooked ham with duck egg and chips, beef hotpot, and puddings including a two-in-one pudding (half blueberry custard crumble, half pear and blackberry pie). *Benchmark main dish: two-in-one pies £11.90. Two-course evening meal £17.00.*

Free house ~ Licensee Howard Parker ~ Real ale ~ (01453) 832520 ~ Open 12-11 (10.30 Sun) ~ Bar food 12-9.30 ~ Restaurant ~ Children allowed away from the bars ~ Dogs welcome ~ Wi-fi ~ www.2in1pub.co.uk *Recommended by Tom and Ruth Rees, Michael Snelgrove*

NETHER WESTCOTE   SP2220 Map 4

Feathered Nest ★ ★ ♀ 🛏

Off A424 Burford to Stow-on-the-Wold; OX7 6SD

Gloucestershire Dining Pub of the Year

Caring service, a happy atmosphere, attractive surroundings and beautifully presented, inventive food and drink; lovely bedrooms

'This has just about everything that makes a pub more than an ordinary experience,' says one happy reader after a visit to this first class and rather special place. The softly lit, largely stripped-stone bar is companionable, with real saddles as bar stools (some of the country's best racehorse trainers live locally), a carved settle among other carefully chosen seats, dark flagstones and low beams. They have 25 wines by the glass from an impressive list, and three beers on handpump such as Prescott Hill Climb, Purity Pure Ubu and Ringwood Boondoggle; service is exemplary. The bar opens into an ochre-walled high-raftered room with deeply comfortable sofas by a vast log fire; background music, board games and TV. Two attractively decorated dining rooms, both on two levels, have a pleasing mix of antique tables in varying sizes, and a lively, up-to-date atmosphere. A flagstoned terrace and heated shelter have teak tables and wicker armchairs, and a spreading lawn bounded by floodlit trees has groups of rustic seats, with the Evenlode Valley beyond. This is a lovely place to stay, with individually decorated, well equipped rooms and delicious breakfasts.

Exceptional modern food from a highly creative kitchen includes lunchtime sandwiches, duck liver, smoked eel, apple, dandelions and tamarind, potted brown shrimps with soda bread, beef in ale pie, roe deer crépinette with parsnip, gin, blackcurrant, chestnut and cocoa bean crumble, salmon and pike mousse en croûte with dill butter sauce and salsify, 16oz chargrilled barbecue pork ribs, and puddings such as banana parfait with Amarula, peanut butter and caramel or blood orange and fennel soufflé. *Benchmark main dish: seasonal suckling pig (pie, loin and head terrine in calvados sauce) £26.50. Two-course evening meal £30.00.*

Free house ~ Licensee Amanda Timmer ~ Real ale ~ (01993) 833030 ~ Open 11-11 (9 Sun); closed Mon except bank holidays ~ Bar food 12-2.30, 6.30-9; 12-3.30 Sun ~ Restaurant ~ Children welcome ~ Dogs allowed in bar ~ Wi-fi ~ Bedrooms: £150/£180 ~ www.thefeatherednestinn.co.uk *Recommended by Michael Doswell, Martin and Karen Wake, Liz Bell*

NEWLAND
Ostrich 🏆

SO5509 Map 4

Off B4228 in Coleford; or can be reached from the A466 in Redbrook by turning off at the England–Wales border – keep bearing right; GL16 8NP

Super range of beers in welcoming country pub, with spacious bar, open fire and good interesting food

This partly 13th-c pub, in a picturesque village close to the River Wye, is particularly popular with walkers and their dogs; Alfie the pub lurcher might be there to greet them. You can be sure of a warm welcome from the landlady and her helpful staff, as well as a chatty and relaxed atmosphere and a fine choice of six real ales on handpump from breweries such as Bath, Otter, RHC, Wye Valley and a couple of changing guests. Also, several wines by the glass and a couple of farm ciders; newspapers to read, perhaps quiet background jazz and board games. The low-ceilinged bar is spacious but cosily traditional, with creaky floors, window shutters, candles in bottles on the tables, miners' lamps on the uneven walls, and comfortable furnishings such as cushioned window seats, wall settles and rod-backed country kitchen chairs. There are picnic-sets in a walled garden behind and more out in front; the church, known as the Cathedral of the Forest, is worth a visit.

Using seasonal local produce, the interesting food includes duck and caramelised kumquat terrine with mandarin jelly, sardines in herb butter on rustic toast, pasta with fresh tomato and basil sauce, chicken with saffron and sherry cream sauce, steak in ale pie, venison and wild mushroom tortellini in a port and porcini jus, sizzling ribs in tangy sauce, and puddings. *Benchmark main dish: salmon and spinach fishcakes with parsley sauce £12.00. Two-course evening meal £20.00.*

Free house ~ Licensee Kathryn Horton ~ Real ale ~ (01594) 833260 ~ Open 12-3, 6.30-11; 12-3, 6-midnight Sat; 12-4, 6.30-10.30 Sun ~ Bar food 12-2.30, 6.30 (6 Sat)-9.30 ~ Restaurant ~ Children welcome ~ Dogs allowed in bar ~ www.theostrichinn.com *Recommended by Phil and Augustine Sullivan*

Real ale may be served from handpumps, electric pumps (not just the on-off switches used for keg beer) or – common in Scotland – tall taps called founts (pronounced 'fonts') where a separate pump pushes the beer up under air pressure.

NORTH CERNEY
SP0208 Map 4

Bathurst Arms ♀ ⇔

A435 Cirencester–Cheltenham; GL7 7BZ

Bustling inn with beamed bar, open fires, fine wines, real ales and interesting food; comfortable bedrooms

Our readers enjoy staying in the comfortably refurbished bedrooms in this handsome 17th-c inn, and the breakfasts are excellent. The heart of the place remains the original beamed and panelled bar with its convivial atmosphere, flagstones, attractive mix of old tables, nicely faded chairs, old-fashioned window seats and a fireplace at each end – one is huge and houses an open woodburner. An oak-floored room off here has country tables, winged high-backed settles forming a few booths; background music, flat-screen TV and board games. The restaurant has leather sofas and another woodburning stove. Hook Norton Bitter and Cotswold Lion, Ramsbury Gold and a changing guest on handpump, and also a wine room where you can choose from 20 by the glass or your own bottle; local soft drinks and juices too. The pleasant riverside garden has picnic-sets sheltered by trees and shrubs. Cerney House Gardens are worth a visit and there are lots of surrounding walks in lovely countryside.

 Good food from a varied menu includes ciabattas, pheasant pâté with onion marmalade, mussels in cider, cream and mustard sauce, gloucester old spot sausages with onion gravy, shallot tarte tatin with creamy pearl barley cassoulet, hake fillet with cheese and herb crumble and a shrimp and chive cream sauce, duck breast with a sweet orange sauce, and puddings such as orange and almond polenta cake and black cherry parfait with sable noir; they also offer a very good value two- and three-course set menu (before 7pm). *Benchmark main dish: burger with bacon, cheese, onion rings and chips £12.00. Two-course evening meal £18.50.*

Free house ~ Licensee James Walker ~ Real ale ~ (01285) 831281 ~ Open 12-11 (10.30 Sun) ~ Bar food 12-2, 6-9; 12-2.30, 6-9.30 Fri, Sat; 12-2.30, 7-9 Sun ~ Restaurant ~ Children welcome ~ Dogs allowed in bar and bedrooms ~ Wi-fi ~ Bedrooms: £65/£85 ~ www.bathurstarms.com *Recommended by Peter and Heather Elliott, Steve Whalley, Di and Mike Gillam, Tom and Ruth Rees, Lisa Kehoe, Giles and Annie Francis, Neil and Anita Christopher, Richard and Patricia Jefferson, Richard Tilbrook*

NORTHLEACH
SP1114 Map 4

Wheatsheaf ⭐ ♀ ⇔

West End; the inn is on your left as you come in following the sign off A429, just SW of the junction with A40; GL54 3EZ

Attractive stone inn with contemporary food, real ales, candles, fresh flowers and a relaxed atmosphere; stylish bedrooms

A former 17th-c coaching inn in a lovely little market town, this civilised place appeals as much to locals as it does to visitors staying overnight. The airy, big-windowed, linked rooms have high ceilings, antique and contemporary artwork, church candles and fresh flowers, an attractive mix of dining chairs, big leather button-back settles and stools around wooden tables, flagstones in the central bar, wooden floors laid with turkish rugs in the airy dining rooms, and three open fires. Bath, Barnsley and Wye Valley HPA on handpump, several wines by the glass from a fantastic list of around 300 and local cider; background music, TV and board games. There are seats in the pretty back garden and they can arrange fishing on the River Coln. This is an enjoyable place to stay, with comfortable, individually styled bedrooms (though our readers suggest asking for the

larger rooms); lovely breakfasts. Dogs are genuinely welcomed and they
even keep a jar of pigs' ears behind the bar for them.

Making impressive use of the best local produce, the accomplished cooking is
offered all day from 8am (breakfasts for non-residents): crab, chilli, garlic and
cherry tomato linguine, steak tartare, aubergine, chickpea and apricot tagine with
bulgar wheat and mint yoghurt, braised lamb shank with soft polenta, olives, rosemary
and garlic, calves liver with beetroot, smoked bacon and balsamic, and puddings such
as chocolate 'balthazar' with crème fraîche; they also offer a two- and three-course
weekday set lunch. *Benchmark main dish: confit duck leg cassoulet £16.50.
Two-course evening meal £19.50.*

Free house ~ Licensees Sam and Georgina Pearman ~ Real ale ~ (01451) 860244 ~
Open 8am-11pm (midnight Sat) ~ Bar food 12-3, 6-10.30; 12-4, 6-10 Sun ~
Children welcome ~ Dogs allowed in bar ~ Wi-fi ~ Bedrooms: /£150 ~
www.cotswoldswheatsheaf.com *Recommended by Simon J Barber, Rod Stoneman,
Martin and Pauline Jennings, Richard Tilbrook, Tony and Rachel Schendel, Guy Vowles,
Fiona Smith, Tracey and Stephen Groves*

OLDBURY-ON-SEVERN
ST6092 Map 2

Anchor ♀ 🍴 £

Village signposted from B4061; BS35 1QA

**Friendly country pub with tasty bar food, a fine choice of drinks,
and a pretty garden with hanging baskets**

With four real ales, very fairly priced food and a warm welcome from
cheerful staff, this well run pub remains a favourite with many. The
neatly kept lounge has modern beams and stonework, a variety of tables
including an attractive oval oak gateleg, cushioned window seats, winged
seats against the wall, oil paintings by a local artist and a big log fire.
The bar has old photographs and farming and fishing bric-a-brac on the
walls. Diners can eat in the lounge or bar area or in the dining room at the
back (good for larger groups); the menu is the same everywhere. Bass,
Butcombe Bitter, St Austell Trelawny and a changing guest from Great
Western or Wye Valley on handpump, well priced for the area; 80 malt
whiskies (the tasting notes are really helpful), a dozen wines by the glass
and three farm ciders. You can eat in the pretty garden in summer, when
the hanging baskets and window boxes are lovely; boules. They have
wheelchair access and a disabled lavatory. Plenty of walks to the River
Severn and along numerous footpaths and bridleways; nearby St Arilda's
church is interesting, on an odd little knoll with wild flowers (the primroses
and daffodils make quite a show in spring) among the gravestones.

Fairly priced and using produce from local farms and estates, the thoughtful
choice of food includes ciabattas, seared scallops and pancetta with lemon and
thyme, home-baked ham and free-range eggs, aubergine and mushroom lasagne, beef
in ale pie, slow-roasted pork belly with apple and sage and mustard mash, lamb curry,
and puddings such as chocolate brownie with chocolate sauce and crème brûlée; they
also offer a two- and three-course set menu (not weekend lunchtimes or Friday or
Saturday evenings). *Benchmark main dish: smoked haddock and salmon fish pie
£9.95. Two-course evening meal £16.00.*

Free house ~ Licensees Michael Dowdeswell and Mark Sorrell ~ Real ale ~ (01454)
413331 ~ Open 11.30-2.30, 6-11; 11.30am-midnight Fri, Sat; 12-11 Sun ~ Bar food 12-2
(2.30 Sat, 3 Sun), 6-9 ~ Restaurant ~ Children in dining room only ~ Dogs allowed in bar
~ www.anchorinnoldbury.co.uk *Recommended by Chris and Angela Buckell, Alan Bulley, Barry
and Monica Jones, James Morrell*

SHEEPSCOMBE   SO8910 Map 4

Butchers Arms £

Village signed off B4070 NE of Stroud; or A46 N of Painswick (but narrow lanes); GL6 7RH

Bustling country pub with enjoyable bar food, real ales, friendly young licensees and fine views

This is a thoroughly enjoyable pub with a great deal of character and an easy-going atmosphere helped by chatty locals and cheerful staff. The bustling lounge bar has beams, wheelback chairs, cushioned stools and other comfortable seats around simple wooden tables, built-in cushioned seats in big bay windows, interesting oddments including blowlamps, irons and plates, and a woodburning stove. The restaurant has an open log fire. Butcombe Gold, Otter Bitter and a guest beer on handpump, several wines by the glass and Weston's cider or perry; darts, chess, cribbage and draughts. The view over the lovely surrounding steep beechwood valley is terrific, and the seats outside make the most of it. The area was apparently once a hunting ground for Henry VIII. Good surrounding walks.

Quite a choice of attractively presented, reliably good food includes lunchtime sandwiches, game terrine with plum and apple chutney, cornish sardine fillets on ciabatta, gammon with egg or pineapple, mixed pepper, leek and coriander risotto, steak and mushroom in red wine pie, rare-breed pork and chive sausages with thyme gravy, salmon, cod and dill fishcakes with lemon mayonnaise, and puddings. *Benchmark main dish: burger made with local beef with interesting toppings, coleslaw and chips £10.50. Two-course evening meal £16.00.*

Free house ~ Licensees Mark and Sharon Tallents ~ Real ale ~ (01452) 812113 ~ Open 11.30-3, 6.30-11; 11.30-11.30 Sat; 12-10.30 Sun ~ Bar food 12-2.30, 6.30-9.30; all day Sat; 12-6 Sun ~ Restaurant ~ Children welcome ~ Dogs allowed in bar ~ Wi-fi ~ www.butchers-arms.co.uk *Recommended by Dr and Mrs A K Clarke, GSB, B J Thompson, Mrs P Sumner, Tracey and Stephen Groves, Mr and Mrs J Gittins, Neil and Anita Christopher, Guy Vowles*

SOUTHROP   SP2003 Map 4

Swan

Off A361 Lechlade–Burford; GL7 3NU

Creeper-covered pub with proper village bar, two dining rooms, imaginative food and a fine choice of drinks

This creeper-covered 17th-c inn has a very attractive village-green setting; the surrounding Leach Valley is also pretty and has good walks. The chatty bar has a bustling, informal atmosphere, with stools against the counter, simple tables and chairs, Hook Norton Hooky Bitter, Prescott Hill Climb and Sharps Doom Bar on handpump and 16 wines by the glass from a carefully chosen list. The low-ceilinged front dining rooms have open fires, all manner of leather dining chairs around a nice mix of old tables, cushions on settles, rugs on flagstones, nightlights, candles and lots of fresh flowers. There's a skittle alley, and tables in the sheltered back garden. They have self-catering cottages to let.

Making impressive use of their own vegetables and eggs and other top quality local produce, the delicious food includes open sandwiches, moules marinière, foie gras parfait with sauternes jelly, leek, porcini and watercress risotto, salmon fishcakes with aioli, lamb rump with cannellini beans, spinach, chilli and garlic, duck breast with braised red wine lentils and rosemary jus, and puddings such as peanut butter parfait with praline and moscatel and pedro ximénez sherry ice-cream. *Benchmark main dish: burger with cheese and pancetta in home-made brioche bun £9.50. Two-course evening meal £24.00.*

Free house ~ Licensee Ms Kim Harvey ~ Real ale ~ (01367) 850205 ~ Open 12-3, 6-11; 12-4.30 Sun; closed Sun evenings ~ Bar food 12-3, 6-9 (9.30 Sat); 12-3.30 Sun ~ Restaurant ~ Children welcome ~ Dogs allowed in bar ~ Wi-fi ~ Occasional live music; phone for details ~ www.theswanatsouthrop.co.uk *Recommended by Bernard Stradling, Mr and Mrs A H Young, Tom and Ruth Rees, Richard Tilbrook, Dennis and Doreen Haward, Mike and Mary Carter, Tracey and Stephen Groves*

STANTON
Mount

SP0634   Map 4

Village signposted off B4632 SW of Broadway; keep on past village on no-through road up hill, bear left; WR12 7NE

Bustling pub in a lovely spot with fantastic views, friendly licensees and good, popular food

Set in a picture-postcard village, this friendly 17th-c pub has fantastic views from seats on the terrace down over the honey-coloured stone house and the Vale of Evesham towards the welsh mountains; more seats in the peaceful garden and also boules. The bars have low ceilings, heavy beams and flagstones and a big log fire in an inglenook fireplace. The restaurant's large picture windows make the most of the view. Donnington BB and SBA on handpump, served by cheerful staff, and a good choice of wines by the glass; darts, board games, and dog biscuits behind the bar. The pub is on the Cotswold Way National Trail.

Well thought-of food includes daily specials, lunchtime baguettes, chicken liver foie gras parfait, deep-fried local cheese with cranberry, orange and red wine sauce, gammon and free-range local egg, gloucester old spot sausages with cheddar mash and jus, sirloin steak with café du paris butter, and puddings. *Benchmark main dish: beer-battered fish and chips £12.50. Two-course evening meal £20.00.*

Donnington ~ Tenants Karl and Pip Baston ~ Real ale ~ (01386) 584316 ~ Open 12-3, 6-11; closed winter Mon (best to phone) ~ Bar food 12-2, 6-9 ~ Restaurant ~ Well behaved children welcome ~ Dogs welcome ~ Wi-fi ~ www.themountinn.co.uk *Recommended by Richard Tilbrook, Dennis and Doreen Haward, Guy Vowles*

STOW-ON-THE-WOLD
Coach & Horses

SP1729   Map 4

Ganborough (on A424 about 2.5 miles N); GL56 0QZ

Well run country pub with a warm welcome, neatly kept rooms, local ale and traditional food

You can be sure of a warm welcome from everyone in this neatly kept country pub: the chef/landlord, his wife and their staff and both Pennell the black labrador and Molly the cat. The bar has a winter log fire in the central chimneypiece, cushioned mate's chairs and settles on flagstones, fish prints on the wall (the landlord is a keen fisherman, and Albert the huge stuffed pike was caught by his great-great-grandfather) and magazines. The pub is close to Donningtons Brewery, so the BB and SBA are well kept on handpump, and there are nine wines by the glass. Steps lead up to the stone-walled dining room with high-backed chairs around pale wooden tables on carpet. The skittle alley doubles as a function room, and they hope to add a new conservatory. The big garden has modern red or white chairs and tables under red parasols on decking, and a play area with sandpits and a new wooden playtower.

Using local, seasonal produce, the traditional, well cooked food includes lunchtime sandwiches, chicken liver pâté with red onion marmalade, sausages with wholegrain mustard mash and red onion gravy, pasta with asparagus, leeks, spinach and peas in a parmesan cream sauce, rabbit pie, pork belly with beetroot and tarragon jus, venison casserole, and puddings such as a crumble of the day and sticky toffee pudding; the first Tuesday of the month is curry night. *Benchmark main dish: beer-battered fish and chips £12.95. Two-course evening meal £20.00.*

Donnington ~ Tenants Jonathan and Jane Kerr ~ Real ale ~ (01451) 830208 ~ Open 12-3, 5.30-11; 12-9 Sun; closed Mon ~ Bar food 12-2.30, 6-8.30 (12-2, 6-8 in winter); 12-3 Sun ~ Restaurant ~ Children welcome ~ Dogs allowed in bar ~ www.coachandhorsesganborough.co.uk *Recommended by Edward May*

TETBURY

ST8494 Map 4

Gumstool ⊙ ☕ 🛏

Part of Calcot Manor Hotel; A4135 W of town, just E of junction with A46; GL8 8YJ

Civilised bar with relaxed atmosphere, super choice of drinks and enjoyable food

This isn't a traditional pub, of course – it's a bar/brasserie attached to the very smart Calcot Manor Hotel – but our readers enjoy their visits very much, and it has an informal and relaxed atmosphere and up to four real ales on handpump. The stylish layout is cleverly divided to give a feeling of intimacy without losing the overall sense of contented bustle: flagstones, elegant wooden dining chairs and tables, well chosen pictures and drawings on mushroom-coloured walls, and leather tub armchairs and stools in front of the big log fire. Butcombe Bitter, Blond and Gold and a changing guest, lots of interesting wines by the glass and several malt whiskies; background music. Westonbirt Arboretum is not far away.

Given the civilised setting, the prices are fair and the food is first class: nibbles such as quail scotch eggs, as well as devilled lambs kidneys on toast, cornish fish stew with garlic mayonnaise and croutons, pumpkin risotto with crumbled goats cheese and red onion jam, lamb hotpot with crispy potatoes, corn-fed chicken with mushroom and bacon sauce, salmon with fennel, blood orange and crushed sweet potato, and puddings such as dark chocolate brownie with salted caramel ice-cream and apple and blackberry crumble. *Benchmark main dish: organic rare-breed burger with bacon jam, cheddar and chips £15.00. Two-course evening meal £22.00.*

Free house ~ Licensees Paul Sadler and Richard Ball ~ Real ale ~ (01666) 890391 ~ Open 11-11 ~ Bar food 12-2.30, 5.30-9.30; 12-4, 6-9 Sun ~ Children welcome ~ Dogs allowed in bedrooms ~ Wi-fi ~ Bedrooms: /£280 ~ www.calcotmanor.co.uk *Recommended by Bernard Stradling, Mr and Mrs P R Thomas, Tracey and Stephen Groves, KC*

UPPER ODDINGTON

SP2225 Map 4

Horse & Groom ⊙ ☕

Village signposted from A436 E of Stow-on-the-Wold; GL56 0XH

Pretty 16th-c Cotswold inn with enterprising food, lots of wines by the glass, local beers and comfortable, character bars; lovely bedrooms

Mr Jackson is a genuinely friendly, helpful landlord who cares for both his pub and his customers, and you can be sure of well kept real ales and imaginative food; breakfasts are first class. The bar has pale polished flagstones, a handsome antique oak box settle among other more modern seats, some nice armchairs at one end, oak beams in the ochre ceiling, stripped-stone walls and a log fire in the inglenook fireplace; the comfortable lounge is similarly furnished. North Cotswold Shagweaver, Otter Bitter and Wye Valley Bitter on handpump, 28 wines (including champagne and sweet wines) by the glass, 20 malt whiskies, local apple juice and elderflower pressé, and cider and lager brewed by Cotswold Brewing Company. There are seats and tables under green parasols on the terrace and in the pretty garden.

 With everything from pickles to home-smoked produce and ice-creams made in-house, the highly rewarding food includes sandwiches, spicy three-bean and cod fishcakes with lemon mayonnaise, pork and rosemary meatballs with spicy tomato sauce, goan chicken curry, mushroom, spinach and tarragon cream bruschetta, venison suet pudding, their own hereford burger with crispy bacon, cheese and chips, and puddings such as caramel panna cotta with chocolate 'soil' and coffee ice-cream and lemon posset with blackcurrant sorbet. *Benchmark main dish: pie of the day £14.50. Two-course evening meal £20.50.*

Free house ~ Licensees Simon and Sally Jackson ~ Real ale ~ (01451) 830584 ~ Open 12-3, 5.30-11; 12-3, 6-10.30 Sun ~ Bar food 12-2, 6.30 (7 Sun)-9 ~ Restaurant ~ Children welcome ~ Dogs allowed in bar ~ Wi-fi ~ Bedrooms: £75/£100 ~ www.horseandgroom.uk.com *Recommended by Bernard Stradling, Keith Moss, R T and J C Moggridge, Nigel and Sue Foster, Richard Tilbrook, Michael Doswell, Katharine Cowherd, Theocsbrian*

WESTON SUBEDGE   SP1241   Map 4
Seagrave Arms ⭐ ⬤ ♟ ⬛

B4632; GL55 6QH

Handsome stone inn with several little bars and dining rooms, charming hands-on owner, friendly staff and impressive food; contemporary bedrooms

As this golden-stone Georgian country inn is close to the Cotswold Way and some of the bedrooms allow dogs, it makes a good base for a weekend. Most of the well equipped, modern bedrooms are in the main house, with others in the converted stables; breakfasts are good and hearty. There's a cosy little bar with a chatty atmosphere, an open fire and ancient flagstones, half-panelled walls and padded window seats, Gloucester Gold and Purity Mad Goose on handpump and ten wines (plus prosecco and champagne) by the glass, served by helpful, friendly staff; background music. The two dining rooms have an appealing variety of wooden chairs and tables on floorboards. Outside, there are wicker chairs and tables on neat gravel at the front of the building and more seats in the back garden.

From a seasonally aware menu, the interesting food includes rabbit ravioli and consommé, slow-cooked salmon with beetroot and horseradish, herb-crusted pollack with lemon fregola, chorizo and broccoli, rump of lamb with wild garlic, black olives and potato gnocchi, pigeon with crispy leg, pancetta crumb, leeks, celeriac and thyme sauce, and puddings such as chocolate délice with salted caramel ice-cream and muscovado and star anise parfait with gingerbread ice-cream. *Benchmark main dish: rare-breed local beef with confit shallot, king oyster mushrooms and red wine jus £18.95. Two-course evening meal £25.50.*

Free house ~ Licensee Paul Denton ~ Real ale ~ (01386) 840192 ~ Open 12-11; 12-4 Sun (12-3, 5.30-11; 12-11 Fri, Sat; 12-4 Sun in winter); closed Sun evening, winter Mon ~ Bar food 12-2.30, 6-9; 12-3 Sun ~ Restaurant ~ Children welcome ~ Dogs allowed in bar and bedrooms ~ Wi-fi ~ Bedrooms: £75/£95 ~ www.seagravearms.co.uk
Recommended by Dennis and Doreen Haward

Also Worth a Visit in Gloucestershire

Besides the fully inspected pubs, you might like to try these pubs that have been recommended to us and described by readers. Do tell us what you think of them: feedback@goodguides.com

ALDERTON   SP9933
Gardeners Arms (01242) 620257
Beckford Road, off B4077 Tewkesbury–Stow; GL20 8NL Attractive thatched Tudor pub, well kept Greene King and guests, decent wines by the glass, enjoyable food from bar snacks and tapas up including weekday deals, breakfast from 9am, good welcoming service, various modernised areas, one featuring an old well, log fire; may be background music; children welcome, dogs allowed in some parts, tables on sheltered terrace, good-sized well tended garden with boules, open (and food) all day Sun. *(Dr A J and Mrs B A Tompsett)*

ALMONDSBURY   ST6084
Bowl (01454) 612757
Church Road; 1.25 miles from M5 junction 16; from A38 towards Thornbury, turn left signed Lower Almondsbury, then right down Sundays Hill, then right; BS32 4DT Pretty setting by church and a popular M5 stop; long beamed main bar with traditional settles, cushioned stools and mate's chairs around elm tables, stripped bare stone walls, big winter log fire at one end, woodburner at the other, Brains The Rev James, Butcombe and guests, decent wines by the glass, food from pubby choices up including good burgers, restaurant extension; background music, free wi-fi; children welcome, seats out in front and on back terrace, pretty hanging tubs and window boxes, 11 bedrooms, parking fee refundable at bar, open all day. *(Steve and Liz Tilley, Adrian Buckland)*

AMBERLEY   SO8401
Amberley Inn (01453) 872565
Steeply off A46 Stroud–Nailsworth – gentler approach from N Nailsworth; GL5 5AF Popular old stone inn with two comfortable bars and a snug, well kept Stroud ales, enjoyable food served by friendly helpful staff, beautiful views; children and dogs welcome, side terrace and back garden, good local walks, 11 bedrooms. *(Cath French, Neil and Anita Christopher)*

AMPNEY CRUCIS   SP0701
Crown of Crucis (01285) 851806
A417 E of Cirencester; GL7 5RS Refurbished roadside inn with spacious split-level bar, beams and log fires, good choice of food including competitively priced dish of the day (weekday lunchtimes), a beer named for them from Wickwar and a guest, decent house wines, pleasant efficient service; children and dogs welcome, disabled facilities, lots of tables out on grass by car park, quiet modern bedrooms around courtyard, good breakfast, cricket pitch over stream, open all day. *(R K Phillips, Neil and Anita Christopher)*

AMPNEY ST PETER   SP0801
★ Red Lion (01285) 851596
A417, E of village; GL7 5SL Unspoilt and unchanging country pub under hospitable veteran landlord (only the third here in over a century); two simple chatty little rooms with log fires, very well kept Timothy Taylors Landlord and Golden Best and maybe Hook Norton from the hatch, no food; outside lavatories; open from 6pm Mon-Sat, and Sun lunchtime. *(Mo and David Trudgill, Giles and Annie Francis, Tom McLean, Ian Herdman)*

AUST   ST5788
Boars Head (01454) 632278
0.5 miles from M48 junction 1, off Avonmouth Road; BS35 4AX 16th-c village pub handy for the 'old' Severn bridge, Marstons-related ales and decent house wines, well priced food including deals, good friendly service, linked rooms and alcoves, beams, some stripped stone and huge log fire, old prints and bric-a-brac; background music, free wi-fi; children (in eating area) and dogs (in bar), wheelchair access, attractive sheltered garden, covered area for smokers, open all day Sun with food till 4pm. *(Chris and Angela Buckell, Bruce Horne)*

AYLBURTON   SO6101
Cross (01594) 842823
High Street; GL15 6DE Decent choice of food from sandwiches and pub favourites to daily specials, changing ales such as Bath, Butcombe, Greene King and Wye Valley, several wines by the glass, welcoming helpful staff, open-plan layout with split-level flagstoned bar, beams, modern furniture alongside old high-backed settles, local photos and bric-a-brac, woodburners in large stone fireplaces, high-raftered dining room, some live music; children welcome, wheelchair access from car park, pleasant garden with play area, open all day weekends. *(Anon)*

BIBURY   SP1006
Catherine Wheel (01285) 740250
Arlington; B4425 NE of Cirencester; GL7 5ND Bright cheerful dining pub, enjoyable fresh food from sandwiches up, well kept Hook Norton, Sharps and a guest, friendly attentive service, open-plan main bar and smaller back rooms, low beams, stripped stone, log fires, raftered dining room;

children welcome, picnic-sets in front and in good-sized garden, famously beautiful village, handy for country and riverside walks, four bedrooms, open all day. *(Anon)*

BISLEY SO9006
✶ **Bear** (01452) 770265

Village signed off A419 E of Stroud; GL6 7BD Interesting 17th-c inn with colonnaded front (originally a courthouse), L-shaped bar with low ceiling, old oak settles, brass and copper implements around extremely wide stone fireplace, well kept St Austell, Butcombe and Wells & Youngs, enjoyable pubby food, friendly staff, separate stripped-stone family area; outside gents', ladies' upstairs; dogs welcome, small flagstoned courtyard, stone mounting blocks in garden across quiet road, one bedroom, open all day Sun. *(Anon)*

BLOCKLEY SP1635
Great Western Arms
(01386) 700362 *Station Road (B4479); GL56 9DT* Updated beamed pub with well kept Hook Norton and decent wines by the glass, enjoyable good value home-made food promptly served by friendly staff, dining room, public bar (dogs welcome here) with darts and TV; paved terrace with smokers' shelter, lovely valley view, attractive village, closed Mon lunchtime. *(Guy Vowles)*

BOURTON-ON-THE-WATER SP1620
Duke of Wellington (01451) 820539
Sherbourne Street; GL54 2BY Welcoming stone-built inn, relaxed open-plan carpeted bar with leather sofas, enjoyable fairly standard food, Sun carvery, Courage and Wells & Youngs ales, more formal back dining room, woodburner, darts; background and some live music, machines; children and dogs welcome, riverside decking under willows, five bedrooms, open (and food) all day. *(Will Raiment)*

BRIMPSFIELD SO9413
Golden Heart (01242) 870261
Nettleton Bottom (not shown on road maps, so instead we list the pub under the name of the nearby village); on A417 N of the Brimpsfield turning northbound; GL4 8LA Traditional roadside inn with low-ceilinged bar divided into five cosy areas, log fire in huge inglenook, exposed stone walls and wood panelling, well worn built-in settles and other old-fashioned furnishings, brass items, typewriters and banknotes, parlour on right with decorative fireplace leading into further room, well kept Brakspears, Jennings, Otter and Ringwood, several wines by glass and popular food from fairly extensive blackboard menu, friendly attentive staff; children and dogs welcome, seats and tables on suntrap terrace with pleasant valley views, nearby walks, bedrooms, open all day weekends and school holidays. *(Giles and Annie Francis, Guy Vowles)*

BROAD CAMPDEN SP1537
✶ **Bakers Arms** (01386) 840515
Village signed from B4081 in Chipping Campden; GL55 6UR 17th-c stone pub in delightful Cotswold village; tiny beamed character bar with stripped-stone walls and inglenook, Donnington, Wickwar and guests, simply furnished beamed dining room with small open fire, pubby food (not Sun evening) plus blackboard specials; darts and board games; children (away from bar) and dogs welcome, picnic-sets on terraces and in back garden, nearby walks, open all day Sat, till 8pm Sun, closed Mon lunchtime. *(Anon)*

BROADWELL SP2027
Fox (01451) 870909
Off A429, 2 miles N of Stow-on-the-Wold; GL56 0UF Family-run golden-stone pub above broad village green; traditional furnishings on flagstones in log-fire bar, stripped-stone walls, jugs hanging from beams, well kept Donnington BB and SBA, lots of rums, winter mulled wine, efficient friendly staff, pubby food (not Sun evening), two carpeted dining areas, maybe George the cat; background music, darts, board games; children welcome, dogs in bar, picnic-sets on gravel in sizeable back garden, paddock with horse called Herman, camping. *(Clive and Fran Dutson)*

BROCKWEIR SO5301
Brockweir Inn (01291) 689548
Signed just off A466 Chepstow–Monmouth; NP16 7NG Welcoming country local near the River Wye and doing well under newish licensees (previously at the George in St Briavels); beams and stripped stonework, quarry tiles, sturdy settles and woodburner, nice snug with parquet floor and open fire, four well kept ales including local Kingstone, farm cider, enjoyable food (not Sun evening), small back dining area and room upstairs 'Devil's Pulpit' for private functions; children and dogs welcome, little walled garden with clay oven, good walks, open all day weekends. *(Neil and Anita Christopher, Bob and Margaret Holder)*

CAMBRIDGE SO7403
George (01453) 890270
3 miles from M5 junction 13 – A38 towards Bristol; GL2 7AL Brick-built roadside pub with opened-up linked areas, pubby furniture, some cushioned pews and window seats, lots of bric-a-brac, two woodburners back-to-back, contrasting modern restaurant with light wood-strip floor, enjoyable sensibly priced food from baguettes and pub favourites to grills and specials, well kept Moles and Timothy Taylors, Thatcher's cider, helpful well organised service; background music, no dogs inside; children welcome, picnic-sets in fenced streamside garden with play area, one bedroom, pleasant campsite, handy for

Slimbridge Wetland Centre, open all day from 10am for breakfast. *(Neil and Anita Christopher)*

CAMP   SO9111
★**Fostons Ash** (01452) 863262
B4070 Birdlip–Stroud, junction with Calf Way; GL6 7ES Popular open-plan dining pub, light and airy, with good food including interesting lunchtime sandwiches and imaginative light dishes, real ales such as Goffs, Greene King and Stroud, decent wines by the glass, neat welcoming staff, daily papers, one end with easy chairs and woodburner; background music; rustic tables in attractive garden with heated terrace and play area, good walks. *(Anon)*

CERNEY WICK   SU0796
Crown (01793) 750369
Village signed from A419; GL7 5QH Friendly old village inn with roomy modern lounge bar and comfortable conservatory dining extension, popular inexpensive food, well kept Wadworths 6X, Wells & Youngs Bombardier and a guest, good service, coal-effect gas fires, games in public bar; children welcome, good-sized garden with swings and chickens, ten bedrooms in motel-style extension. *(Anon)*

CHACELEY   SO8530
Yew Tree (01452) 780333
Stock Lane; GL19 4EQ Remote rambling country pub with spacious river-view dining room, good choice of reasonably priced pubby food (not Sun evening, winter Mon) from bar snacks up, welcoming attentive staff, Sharps Doom Bar and a guest, bar in original 16th-c core with log fire, quarry tiles and stripped-stone walls, second bar with pool, skittle alley; children and dogs welcome, wheelchair access, terrace and attractive waterside lawns, summer barbecues and beer festival, own moorings, on Severn Way, open all day summer. *(Anon)*

CHARLTON KINGS   SO9620
Royal (01242) 228937
Horsefair, opposite church; GL53 8JH Big 19th-c pub with clean modern décor, enjoyable realistically priced food (not Sun evening) in bar or dining conservatory, well kept real ales and decent wines, prompt service; children and dogs welcome, picnic-sets in garden overlooking church, open all day. *(John Coatsworth, Guy Vowles)*

CHEDWORTH   SP0608
Hare & Hounds (01285) 720288
Fosse Cross – A429 N of Cirencester, some way from village; GL54 4NN Rambling stone-built restaurant pub with good interesting food, lunchtime set menu, well kept Arkells and nice wines, efficient service, low beams and wood floors, soft lighting, cosy corners and little side rooms, two big log fires, small conservatory; children

---

(away from bar) and dogs welcome, disabled facilities, ten courtyard bedrooms. *(Helene Grygar, Tom and Ruth Rees)*

CHELTENHAM   SO9421
Jolly Brewmaster (01242) 772261
Painswick Road; GL50 2EZ Popular convivial local with open-plan linked areas around big semicircular counter, fine range of changing ales and ciders, friendly obliging young staff, newspapers, log fire; dogs welcome, coachyard tables, open from 2.30pm (midday Sat, Sun). *(Ian and Jane Irving)*

CHELTENHAM   SO9624
★**Plough** (01242) 222180
Mill Street, Prestbury; GL52 3BG Unspoilt convivial thatched village local tucked away behind the church; comfortable front lounge, service from corner corridor hatch in flagstoned back tap room, grandfather clock and big log fire, well kept ales such as Brains, Wye Valley and Wychwood, good value ciders, straightforward home-made food (not Mon, or evenings Sat, Sun), friendly service; lovely big flower-filled back garden with immaculate boules pitch, open all day Fri-Sun. *(John Coatsworth, Guy Vowles)*

CHELTENHAM   SO9321
Royal Union (01242) 224686
Hatherley Street; GL50 2TT Backstreet local with large bar and cosy snug up steps, around eight well kept ales, reasonably priced wines and good range of whiskies, enjoyable good value food including nice steaks, Sun evening jazz and other live music; well behaved children (no under-5s) allowed, courtyard behind, open all day. *(Anon)*

CHELTENHAM   SO9522
Sandford Park (01242) 571022
High Street; GL50 1DZ New pub (previously a nightclub) sympathetically refurbished with three bar areas and upstairs function room, up to eight real ales along with craft and continental beers, several ciders, good value home-cooked food from short menu (not Sun evening, Mon lunchtime), friendly staff, bar billiards, Sun quiz; large back garden, open all day. *(Guy Vowles)*

CHIPPING CAMPDEN   SP1539
★**Kings** (01386) 840256
High Street; GL55 6AW Eclectic décor in 18th-c hotel's bar-brasserie and separate restaurant, cheery helpful service, good food from lunchtime sandwiches and baguettes to pubby dishes and more elaborate meals, well kept Hook Norton and a guest, good choice of wines by the glass, decent coffee, daily papers and nice log fire; secluded back garden with picnic-sets and terrace tables, 12 comfortable bedrooms, open all day Sat. *(Anon)*

CHIPPING CAMPDEN　　　SP1539
Noel Arms　(01386) 840317
High Street; GL55 6AT Handsome 16th-c
inn with beamed and stripped-stone bar,
modern furniture, open fire, nice food from
sandwiches to steaks, some good curries too
from sri lankan chef, well kept Hook Norton
and local guests, good choice of wines by the
glass, coffee bar (from 9am), conservatory,
restaurant, friendly efficient staff; children
and dogs welcome, sunny courtyard tables,
28 well appointed bedrooms, good breakfast,
open all day. *(Jim and Nancy Forbes)*

CHIPPING SODBURY　　　ST7381
Bell　(01454) 325582
Badminton Road (A432); BS37 6LL
Family-run late 18th-c inn, ales such as Bath
Gem, Butcombe Gold and Sharps Doom Bar
from ornate wooden counter, decent choice
of wines, good pub food including set lunch
deal Mon-Fri, friendly efficient young staff,
dining rooms either side of bar area, some
stripped stone and timbering, sofas and
open fires; background music, TV; children
welcome, four bedrooms. *(Roger and Donna
Huggins)*

CIRENCESTER　　　SP0202
Corinium　(01285) 659711
Dollar Street/Gloucester Street; GL7 2DG
Civilised and comfortable Georgian fronted
hotel (originally a 16th-c wool merchant's
house); bar with good mix of tables on wood
or flagstone floors, leather bucket seats by
woodburner in stone fireplace, enjoyable
fairly priced food from sandwiches to daily
specials, three well kept local ales and
decent wines, cheerful helpful young staff,
restaurant; entrance through charming
courtyard, wheelchair access with assistance,
picnic-sets in attractive walled garden,
15 bedrooms. *(Val and Alan Green)*

CIRENCESTER　　　SP0103
Drillmans Arms　(01285) 653892
Gloucester Road, Stratton; GL7 2JY
Unpretentious old two-room local, cheerful
and welcoming, with well kept Sharps Doom
Bar and three quickly changing guests, basic
lunchtime food, low beams and woodburner,
skittle alley; tables out by small car park,
open all day Sat. *(Richard Tilbrook)*

CIRENCESTER　　　SP0201
Marlborough Arms　07748 185261
Sheep Street; GL7 1QW Recently
renovated bare-boards pub with eight
well kept ales and good choice of proper
ciders (mulled cider in winter), friendly
landlord, traditional lunchtime food, brewery
memorabilia and shelves of bottles, live
music and quiz nights; no credit cards; open
all day. *(Giles and Annie Francis)*

COATES　　　SO9600
★Tunnel House　(01285) 770280
*Follow Tarlton signs (right then left)
from village, pub up rough track on
right after railway bridge; OS Sheet 163
map reference 965005; GL7 6PW* Lively
bow-fronted stone house by entrance to
derelict canal tunnel; rambling character
rooms with beams, flagstones and good mix
of furnishings, plenty to look at including
enamel signs, racing tickets and air travel
labels, a stuffed boar's head and owl, even
an upside-down card table (complete with
cards and drinks) fixed to the ceiling, sofas
by log fire, Cotswold Lion, Prescott, Uley
and a guest, two farm ciders and 14 wines by
the glass, wide range of popular food, good
service, more conventional dining extension
and back conservatory; background music,
free wi-fi; children and dogs welcome,
impressive views from front terrace, big
garden down to canal, good nearby walks,
open (and food) all day. *(Ian Herdman, Neil
and Anita Christopher, Alan Bulley, Tom and
Ruth Rees)*

COLD ASTON　　　SP1219
Plough　(01451) 822602
*Aka Aston Blank; off A436 (B4068) or
A429 SW of Stow-on-the-Wold; GL54 3BN*
Attractive little 17th-c village pub
sympathetically restored and updated under
new owners; low beams, stone and wood
floors, inglenook woodburner, emphasis on
enjoyable freshly cooked food using local
suppliers from sandwiches and ciabattas to
charcoal-grilled steaks, regularly changing
beers such as Stanway poured from the
cask; children and dogs welcome, smart teak
tables and chairs on new terraces, three
bedrooms, open all day Fri-Sun, closed Mon
lunchtime. *(Di and Mike Gillam,
P and J Shapley)*

COLEFORD　　　SO5813
Dog & Muffler　(01594) 832444
*Joyford; B4136 at Five Acres, take Park
Road then at Globe pub turn right into
Joyford Hill, then third right at pub
signpost; OS Sheet 162 map reference
580134; GL16 7AS* Prettily located,
extended and modernised 17th-c country
dining pub, carpeted beamed bar with
woodburner in big fireplace, beamed back
part with dining conservatory, enjoyable
pubby food, Sharps Doom Bar, Wye Valley
Butty Bach and a guest, good friendly
service; children and dogs welcome, lovely

views from terrace, garden with old cider press, nice walks, closed Mon. *(Anon)*

COLESBOURNE SO9913
Colesbourne Inn (01242) 870376

A435 Cirencester–Cheltenham; GL53 9NP Civilised 19th-c grey-stone gabled coaching inn, good choice of enjoyable home-made food from baguettes and wraps up, friendly staff, well kept Wadworths ales and lots of wines by the glass, linked partly panelled rooms, log fires, soft lighting, comfortable mix of settles and leather sofas, candlelit back dining room; TV above fireplace; dogs welcome, views from attractive back garden and terrace, nine bedrooms in converted stable block, good breakfast. *(Andrew Quinn, Neil and Anita Christopher)*

COMPTON ABDALE SP0717
★Garniche at the Puesdown
(01451) 860262 *A40 outside village; GL54 4DN* Spacious series of linked stylish bars and eating areas, mainly stripped-stone walls, rafter-effect or beamed ceilings, rugs on bare boards, chesterfield sofas and armchairs, high-backed dining chairs around mix of tables, log fire and woodburner, Hook Norton Hooky, Old Hooky and Sharps Doom Bar, pubby lunchtime food with more elaborate evening choices, breakfast for non-residents, morning coffee and afternoon tea, gift shop; children welcome, dogs in bar, tables in pretty back garden, comfortable ground-floor bedrooms, closed Sun evening, Mon, otherwise open all day. *(Anon)*

CRANHAM SO8912
★Black Horse (01452) 812217
Village signposted off A46 and B4070 N of Stroud; GL4 8HP Popular down-to-earth 17th-c local, cosy lounge, main bar with traditional furniture, window seats and log fire, well kept Hancocks HB, Sharps Doom Bar and a guest, real ciders, good value home-made blackboard food (not Sun evening when pub opens at 8.30pm), two upstairs dining rooms (one with log fire); well behaved children and dogs welcome, tables out in front and to the side, good country views and walks, closed Mon. *(Alan Weedon)*

DIDMARTON ST8187
Kings Arms (01454) 238245
A433 Tetbury road; GL9 1DT Welcoming beamed 17th-c coaching inn reopened after major refurbishment; dark colour scheme and slate floor, leather armchairs by woodburner, ales such as Bath, Fullers and Uley, good food from sandwiches up, restaurant; soft background music; children welcome, pleasant back garden, bedrooms and self-catering cottages, handy for Westonbirt Arboretum. *(Chris and Angela Buckell, Dr and Mrs A K Clarke, Dr and Mrs J D Abell, Simon Collett-Jones, Revd Michael Vockins)*

DUNTISBOURNE ABBOTS SO9709
★Five Mile House (01285) 821432
E of A417 on parallel old Main Road; GL7 7JR 17th-c country pub under new management; pubby seats and tables in friendly drinking bar, flagstoned tap room with two ancient high-backed settles by stove, steps down to snug and down again to small cellar bar, front restaurant extension, Hook Norton Hooky, Shepherd Neame Spitfire and Timothy Taylors Landlord, several wines by glass, well liked food from father-and-son team; children welcome, dogs in bar, gardens with country views, smart smokers' shelter, open all day weekends, closed Mon. *(Giles and Annie Francis, R K Phillips, Tom McLean)*

EASTLEACH TURVILLE SP1905
★Victoria (01367) 850277
Off A361 S of Burford; GL7 3NQ Open-plan low-ceilinged rooms around central servery, attractive seats built in by log fire, unusual Queen Victoria pictures, well kept Arkells and several good value wines by the glass, shortish choice of sensibly priced pub food (not Sun evening) including baguettes, prompt friendly service; background music; children and dogs welcome, small pleasant front garden with picnic-sets overlooking picturesque village (famous for its spring daffodils), good walks, open all day Sat. *(R T and J C Moggridge, Guy Vowles, Neil and Anita Christopher)*

EBRINGTON SP1839
★Ebrington Arms (01386) 593223
Off B4035 E of Chipping Campden or A429 N of Moreton-in-Marsh; GL55 6NH 17th-c Cotswold-stone pub in attractive village by green, character beamed bar with ladder-back chairs and cushioned settles on flagstones, some seats built into airy bow window, fine inglenook fireplace, half a dozen ales such as Crouch Vale, North Cotswold, Stroud and Uley, nine wines by the glass, Weston's cider and a perry, similarly furnished dining room with another inglenook (original ironwork), interesting food; children and dogs (in bar) welcome, arched stone wall sheltering terrace picnic-sets, more on lawn, handy for Hidcote (NT) and Kiftsgate Court gardens, well equipped country-style bedrooms, open all day from 9am. *(Carol and Luke Wilson, P and J Shapley, Simon Collett-Jones, Jean and Douglas Troup, Martin and Pauline Jennings, Richard Tilbrook and others)*

EDGE SO8409
★Edgemoor (01452) 813576
Gloucester Road (A4173); GL6 6ND Spacious modernised 19th-c dining pub with panoramic valley view across to Painswick from picture windows and pretty terrace, good food including deals, friendly efficient service, up to four well kept local ales, nice

coffee, restaurant; no dogs inside; children welcome, good walks nearby, closed Sun evening in winter. *(Anon)*

ELKSTONE   SO9610
★**Highwayman** (01285) 821221
Beechpike; A417 6 miles N of Cirencester; GL53 9PL Interesting rambling 16th-c building, low beams, stripped stone and log fires, cosy alcoves, antique settles among more modern furnishings, good value home-made food, Arkells beers and good house wines, friendly service; free wi-fi; children and dogs welcome, disabled access, outside play area, closed Sun evening. *(Anon)*

EWEN   SU0097
★**Wild Duck** (01285) 770310
Off A429 S of Cirencester; GL7 6BY Unchanging 16th-c inn with stylishly old-fashioned furnishings and pictures in high-beamed log-fire main bar, lounge with handsome Elizabethan fireplace and antique furnishings, enjoyable food (some pricey), half a dozen real ales including Duck Pond badged for them, very good choice of wines by the glass, friendly staff; background music; children welcome, tables in neatly kept heated courtyard (if you eat here they may ask to keep a credit card behind the bar), garden, 12 bedrooms, open all day. *(Anon)*

FAIRFORD   SP1501
★**Bull** (01285) 712535
Market Place; GL7 4AA Civilised stone hotel with comfortably old-fashioned pubby furnishings in bustling main bar, beams, timbering and open fire, Arkells ales and decent fairly straightforward food, friendly service, nice little residents' lounge with big stone fireplace; children and dogs (in bar) welcome, bedrooms, worth visiting the church which has Britain's only intact set of medieval stained-glass windows, open all day. *(P and J Shapley, Neil and Anita Christopher, Harvey Brown, Emma Scofield, Val and Alan Green)*

FORTHAMPTON   SO8731
Lower Lode Inn (01684) 293224
At the end of Bishop's Walk by river; GL19 4RE Brick-built 15th-c coaching inn with River Severn moorings and plenty of waterside tables (prone to winter flooding), beams, flagstones and traditional seating, woodburners, enjoyable pubby food including Sun carvery, half a dozen well kept interesting beers, friendly helpful staff, restaurant, back pool room; children and dogs welcome, disabled facilities, four bedrooms and campsite, open all day. *(Anon)*

FOSSEBRIDGE   SP0711
★**Fossebridge Inn** (01285) 720721
A429 Cirencester to Stow-on-the-Wold; GL54 3JS Up for sale as we went to press; 17th-c former coaching inn with four acres of attractive lawned riverside gardens, two original bar rooms with open fires and candlelight, beams, stripped-stone walls and flagstones, all sorts of chairs, stools and tables, copper implements, North Cotswold, Otter and St Austell ales, several wines by glass and good popular food, two other rather grand dining rooms; children welcome, comfortable bedrooms and self-catering cottage, Chedworth Roman Villa (NT) is nearby. *(John Holroyd, Richard Tilbrook, Giles and Annie Francis, S F Parrinder, Guy Vowles)*

FRAMPTON COTTERELL   ST6681
Globe (01454) 778286
Church Road; BS36 2AB Large knocked-through bar/dining area with black beams and some stripped stone, usual furniture on parquet or carpet, woodburner in old fireplace, well kept ales such as Butcombe, Sharps and Uley, real ciders, modest well chosen wine list, enjoyable pubby food and bar snacks, attentive friendly staff; background music; children welcome, dogs may get a treat, wheelchair access via side door, garden with play area and smokers' gazebo, church next door, on Frome Valley Walkway, open all day. *(Chris and Angela Buckell, Roger and Donna Huggins)*

FRAMPTON COTTERELL   ST6681
Live & Let Live (01454) 772254
Off A432; Clyde Road; BS36 2EF Attractive chatty pub still serving Bath Ales (although no longer owned by them) and other beers such as Timothy Taylors, also good choice of imported bottled beers, real ciders and decent wines by the glass, enjoyable locally sourced home-made food (not Sun evening) from shortish menu, helpful cheerful staff, linked rooms with carpeted bar and bare-boards dining areas; children (away from bar) and dogs welcome, disabled facilities, picnic-sets out in front and in big garden, play area, open all day. *(Chris and Angela Buckell)*

FRAMPTON MANSELL   SO9202
★**Crown** (01285) 760601
Brown sign to pub off A491 Cirencester–Stroud; GL6 8JG Welcoming 17th-c pub (a former cider house) with good choice of enjoyable hearty food including daily specials, well kept Butcombe, Stroud, Uley and a guest, friendly young staff, heavy beams, stripped stone and rugs on bare

boards, two log fires and woodburner, restaurant; children and dogs welcome, disabled access, picnic-sets in sunny front garden, pretty outlook, 12 decent bedrooms in separate block, open all day from midday. *(Anon)*

FRAMPTON-ON-SEVERN   SO7408
Bell   (01452) 740346
The Green (B4071, handy for M5 junction 13, via A38); GL2 7EP
Handsome Georgian inn attractively opened up, enjoyable good value food in extensive all-day family dining area, proper locals' bar with quarry tiles and flagstones, well kept ales such as Butcombe, Moles and Timothy Taylors, real cider, steps up to restaurant, skittle alley; background music; dogs welcome, plenty of seats outside (front and back), good play area and children's farm, stabling, village cricket green opposite, open all day. *(Anon)*

FRAMPTON-ON-SEVERN   SO7407
Three Horseshoes   (01452) 742100
The Green (B4071, handy for M5 junction 13, via A38); GL2 7DY
Cheerfully unpretentious 18th-c pub by splendid green, welcoming staff and locals, well kept Sharps, Timothy Taylors and Uley, very good value home-made food including speciality pies, folk nights; children and dogs welcome, wheelchair access, front beer garden with boules, open all day weekends. *(Anon)*

GLASSHOUSE   SO7121
★ Glasshouse Inn   (01452) 830529
Off A40 just W of A4136; GL17 0NN
Much-extended beamed red-brick pub with series of small linked rooms, ochre walls and boarded ceilings, appealing old-fashioned and antique furnishings, cavernous black hearth, hunting pictures and taxidermy, candles in bottles, big flagstoned conservatory, well kept ales including Butcombe tapped from the cask, Weston's cider, reasonably priced wines and some interesting malt whiskies; decent home-made food from sandwiches and basket meals up (no bookings except Sun lunch), good friendly service; background music, no under-14s in bars; good disabled access, neat garden with rustic furniture, interesting topiary, flower-decked cider presses and lovely hanging baskets, nearby paths up wooded May Hill, closed Sun evening. *(Chris and Angela Buckell)*

GLOUCESTER   SO8318
Fountain   (01452) 522562
Westgate Street; GL1 2NW Tucked-away 17th-c pub off pedestrianised street, well kept ales such as Butcombe, Fullers, Hook Norton, St Austell and Severn Vale, Weston's cider, reasonably priced pubby food from baguettes up, carpeted bar with handsome stone fireplace, some black beams and panelling, pubby furniture and built-in wall benches; background music; children welcome away from bar, disabled access, flower-filled courtyard, handy for cathedral, open all day. *(Neil Griffins, Chris and Angela Buckell)*

GLOUCESTER   SO8318
New Inn   (01452) 522177
Northgate Street; GL1 1SF Actually one of the city's oldest structures, lovely beamed medieval building with galleried courtyard, well kept Butcombe and up to nine guests including smaller local breweries, decent wines, bargain daily carvery and other good value food, pleasant service, coffee shop, restaurant; soft background music (live music Fri, disco Sat), sports TV, free wi-fi; children welcome, no dogs, wheelchair access to restaurant only, 33 affordably priced bedrooms, handy for cathedral, open all day. *(Val and Alan Green)*

GREAT BARRINGTON   SP2013
★ Fox   (01451) 844385
Off A40 Burford–Northleach; pub towards Little Barrington; OX18 4TB
17th-c inn with stripped stone, simple country furnishings and low ceiling, well kept Donnington BB and SBA, farm cider and good apple juice, decent choice of quickly served food (all day weekends including good Sun carvery), big bare-boards river-view dining conservatory with riverbank mural, traditional games, 'Foxstock' folk festival in Aug; background music, TV; children and dogs welcome, two terraces by the River Windrush (swans and private fishing), outside summer bar and barbecue, garden with orchard and ponds, seven bedrooms, open all day and can get very busy. *(Richard Tilbrook, Guy Vowles)*

GUITING POWER   SP0924
★ Farmers Arms   (01451) 850358
Fosseway (A429); GL54 5TZ Nicely old-fashioned with stripped stone, flagstones, lots of pictures and warm log fire, well kept cheap Donnington BB and SBA, wide blackboard choice of enjoyable honest food cooked by landlord including good rabbit pie, welcoming prompt service, carpeted back dining part, games area with darts, dominoes, cribbage and pool, skittle alley; children welcome, garden with quoits, lovely village, good walks, bedrooms. *(Richard Tilbrook)*

GUITING POWER   SP0924
Hollow Bottom   (01451) 850392
Village signposted off B4068 SW of Stow-on-the-Wold (still called A436 on many maps); GL54 5UX Friendly bustle in this old stone cottage popular with racing fraternity; live horse racing on TV and associated memorabilia in beamed bar, log fire in unusual pillared stone fireplace, a beer named for the pub plus two changing guests, several wines by glass and a dozen

malt whiskies, popular all-day food from
good baguettes up, public bar with flagstones
and stripped stone, darts and board
games; background music; children and
dogs welcome, disabled facilities, country
views from pleasant garden, nearby walks,
bedrooms, car park down steep slope, open
9am–midnight. *(Michael and Jenny Back, Colin
McKerrow, Michael Snelgrove, Michael Sargent
and others)*

HAM   ST6898
Salutation (01453) 810284
*On main road through village;
GL13 9QH* Unpretentious welcoming
three-room country local; brasses on beams,
horse and hunt pictures on Artex walls,
pubby furniture including high-backed
settles and bench seats, five well kept local
ales and eight ciders, simple low-priced food
lunchtime and early evening, guest chef
cooks one dish Mon evening, occasional
live music, skittle alley; no credit cards;
wheelchair access, beer garden with views
over the River Severn, open all day weekends,
closed Mon lunchtime. *(Anon)*

HANHAM   ST6470
Elm Tree (0117) 967 5193
*Abbots Road; S, towards Willsbridge
and Oldland Common; BS15 3NR*
Small stone pub on fringe of Bristol;
open-plan bar with carpeted dining area,
woodburner in central fireplace, good fresh
affordably priced food (not Sun evening)
including traditional puddings, enthusiastic
service, well kept Sharps Doom Bar and
Wadworths 6X from brick-faced counter,
decent wines by the glass; background
jazz, fruit machine; level wheelchair
access, picnic-sets in small enclosed back
garden. *(Simon and Mandy King)*

HARTPURY   SO7924
Royal Exchange (01452) 700273
A417 Gloucester–Ledbury; GL19 3BW
Revamped 19th-c country pub, enjoyable
food (not Sun evening) from sharing plates
up, Wye Valley ales and guests, local cider/
perry, friendly young staff; sports TV; children
welcome, fine views from garden with terrace
and covered deck, open all day Fri-Sun,
closed Mon lunchtime. *(Florence Spencer)*

HAWKESBURY UPTON   ST7786
★Beaufort Arms (01454) 238217
High Street; GL9 1AU Unpretentious
17th-c pub in historic village, welcoming
landlord and friendly chatty local
atmosphere, up to five well kept changing
local ales and a proper cider, popular
no-nonsense food (no starters, small helpings
available), extended uncluttered dining
lounge on right, darts in more spartan
stripped-brick bare-boards bar, interesting
local and brewery memorabilia, lots of
pictures (some for sale), skittle alley; well
behaved children allowed, dogs in bar,

disabled access throughout and facilities,
picnic-sets in smallish enclosed garden,
on Cotswold Way and handy for Badminton
Horse Trials, open all day. *(Chris and Angela
Buckell)*

HILLESLEY   ST7689
Fleece (01453) 520003
*Hawkesbury Road/Chapel Lane;
GL12 7RD* Comfortably refurbished
old stone-roofed pub owned by the local
community; well kept changing ales such as
Butcombe, Cotswold Spring and Stroud, local
cider, good wines by the glass and interesting
malt whiskies, ample helpings of enjoyable
good value pub food, friendly chatty staff, bar
with coir flooring and some polished boards,
mix of pubby furniture, cushioned benches
and wall seats, woodburner, steps down to
dining room and snug, fortnightly Sun quiz
and monthly acoustic music, darts; free
wi-fi; children, dogs and walkers welcome,
wheelchair access to main bar only, back
garden with play area and smokers' shelter,
small village in lovely countryside near
Cotswold Way, open all day. *(M G Hart, Martin
and Margaret Thorpe, Chris and Angela Buckell,
Alan Bulley)*

HINTON DYRHAM   ST7376
★Bull (0117) 937 2332
*2.4 miles from M4 junction 18; A46
towards Bath, then first right (opposite
the Crown); SN14 8HG* 17th-c stone
pub in nice setting, main bar with two huge
fireplaces, low beams, oak settles and pews
on ancient flagstones, horsebrasses, stripped-
stone back area and simply furnished
carpeted restaurant (children allowed here
till 7.30), food (all day weekends) from pub
standards to specials including seasonal
game, good value lunchtime and early
evening set menu (not Fri evening), well
kept Wadworths and a guest; background
music; dogs welcome in bar, wheelchair
accessible with help, seats on front balcony
and in sizeable sheltered upper garden with
play equipment, handy for Dyrham Park
(NT), open all day weekends, closed Mon
lunchtime. *(Simon and Mandy King,
Michael Doswell)*

HORSLEY   ST8497
★Tipputs (01453) 832466
*Just off A46 2 miles S of Nailsworth;
Tiltups End; GL6 0QE* Light and airy
L-shaped bar with tall mullioned windows
and raftered ceiling, panelling with arched
bookshelves, boar's head above woodburner,
interesting mix of good solid tables on
broad boards, armchairs and chesterfield
plus variety of dining chairs, enjoyable food
including indian menu, Stroud ales, efficient
staff, big back galleried restaurant with
comfortable anteroom; background music;
teak tables out behind on grass and decking,
attractive countryside, open all day. *(Anon)*

IRON ACTON
ST6783
White Hart (01454) 228382
High Street; BS37 9UG Big open-plan pub
with little snug one end and dining area the
other, enjoyable fairly priced food (all day
Sun till 7pm), Greene King, Butcombe and a
beer named for them from long servery, good
choice of whiskies too, usual pub furniture
including banquettes, white-painted beams
and log fire; background music, free wi-fi;
children and dogs welcome in certain areas,
disabled facilities, garden with play area,
pasture beyond, open all day. *(Roger and
Donna Huggins)*

KEMBLE
ST9899
★Thames Head (01285) 770259
A433 Cirencester–Tetbury; GL7 6NZ
Stripped stone, timberwork, intriguing little
front alcove, pews in cottagey back area with
log-effect gas fire in big fireplace, country-
look dining room with another fire, good
food from sandwiches and baked potatoes
to steaks, good value wines and well kept
Arkells, friendly obliging staff, skittle alley;
TV; children welcome, tables outside, four
bedrooms in converted barn, good breakfast,
walk (crossing railway line) to nearby
Thames source, open all day. *(KC, Heulwen
and Neville Pinfield)*

KILKENNY
SP0118
Kilkeney Inn (01242) 820341
*A436, 1 mile W of Andoversford;
GL54 4LN* Refurbished spacious interior
(originally six stone cottages) with extended
beamed bar, stripped-stone walls and white
plasterwork, wheelbacks around tables on
quarry tiles or carpet, various clocks dotted
about (owner repairs them), open fire and
woodburner, airy conservatory, Courage and
Wells & Youngs ales, real cider and a dozen
wines by the glass, shortish choice of food
from baguettes up, pleasant young staff,
restaurant; background music; children
welcome, dogs in bar, lovely Cotswold
views from tables out at front, white wicker
furniture in back garden, bedrooms, open
all day. *(P and J Shapley, Richard Tilbrook)*

KINETON
SP0926
Halfway House (01451) 850344
*Signed from B4068 and B4077 W of
Stow-on-the-Wold; GL54 5UG* Simple
and welcoming 17th-c beamed village pub,
good food (not Sun evening) from lunchtime
baguettes up, well kept Donnington BB
and SBA, farm cider and decent wines,
restaurant, log fire; pool and darts; children
welcome, picnic-sets in sheltered back
garden, good walks, bedrooms, open all day
weekends. *(Anon)*

KINGSCOTE
ST8196
★Hunters Hall (01453) 860393
A4135 Dursley–Tetbury; GL8 8XZ
Tudor beams, stripped stone, big log fires and

plenty of character in individually furnished
linked rooms, some sofas and easy chairs,
wide choice of good home-made food at
reasonable prices, well kept Greene King and
Uley, friendly attentive service, flagstoned
back bar with darts, pool and TV; children
and dogs welcome, big garden with play area,
13 bedrooms, open all day. *(Anon)*

KNOCKDOWN
ST8388
Holford Arms (01454) 238669
A433; GL8 8QY Spruced up under
welcoming owners, black beams and
stripped-stone walls, flagstone or wood
floors, cushioned wall/window seats, old
dining tables with candles, flowers in
bottles, some leather sofas and armchairs,
woodburner in big old stone fireplace, local
ales such as Bath, Box Steam and Stroud,
Sherston's cider, good well balanced wine
list, food from baguettes up including good
value Sun lunch, skittle alley; background
and live music (bluegrass Fri); children and
dogs welcome, disabled access, side garden,
camping, handy for Westonbirt Arboretum,
open all day except Mon lunchtime.
(Chris and Angela Buckell)

LECHLADE
SU2199
Crown (01367) 252198
High Street; GL7 3AE Friendly old pub
brewing its own Halfpenny ales (six on offer),
busy bar with fire each end, back games room
with pool and table football, no food, quiz and
live music nights; children welcome, three
bedrooms in separate block overlooking beer
garden, open all day. *(Tony Hobden)*

LECHLADE
SU2199
Swan (01367) 253571
Burford Street; GL7 3AP Welcoming
refurbished 16th-c inn, Halfpenny and Old
Forge beers (brewed at their sister pubs) and
good choice of wines by the glass, sensibly
priced bar food (not Sun evening) including
generous sandwiches and range of burgers,
good log fires, restaurant; four bedrooms,
open all day. *(Dr A Y Drummond)*

LITTLE BARRINGTON
SP2012
Inn For All Seasons (01451) 844324
A40 3 miles W of Burford; OX18 4TN
Handsome old coaching inn with attractive
comfortable lounge bar, low beams, stripped
stone and flagstones, old prints, log fire,
good food including fresh fish, Sharps Doom
Bar and Wadworths 6X, lots of wines by the
glass and malt whiskies, friendly service,
restaurant and conservatory; background
music; dogs welcome, garden with aunt sally,
walks from door, bedrooms. *(Anon)*

LITTLETON-
UPON-SEVERN
ST5989
★White Hart (01454) 412275
*3.5 miles from M48 junction 1;
BS35 1NR* Former farmhouse with three
main rooms, log fires and nice mix of country

furnishings, loveseat in inglenook, flagstones at front, huge tiles at back, fine old White Hart Inn Simonds Ale sign, family room and snug, Wells & Youngs ales and guests, good range of ciders (including their own) and of other drinks, well liked fairly traditional food (all day Sun) plus more adventurous specials; dogs welcome, front wheelchair access, tables on front lawn, more behind by orchard, roaming ducks, geese and chickens (eggs for sale), walks from the door, open all day. *(Chris and Angela Buckell)*

LONGBOROUGH   SP1729
Coach & Horses (01451) 830325
Ganborough Road; GL56 0QU Small, friendly 17th-c stone-built local, Donnington ales, Weston's cider and enjoyable wholesome food (not Sun evening, Mon), leather armchairs on flagstones, inglenook woodburner, darts, dominoes and cribbage; background music; children and dogs welcome, tables out at front looking down on stone cross and village, two simple clean bedrooms, open all day weekends, closed Mon evening. *(Alan Weedon, Guy Vowles, Richard Tilbrook)*

LOWER ODDINGTON   SP2326
★ **Fox** (01451) 870555
Signed off A436; GL56 0UR Smart 16th-c creeper-covered inn with emphasis on good food (mix of modern and traditional), Hook Norton and Sharps Doom Bar, little country-style flagstoned rooms with assorted chairs around pine tables, fresh flowers, hunting figures and pictures, inglenook fireplace, elegant red-walled restaurant; background music turned down on request; children welcome, dogs in bar, white tables and chairs on heated terrace in cottagey garden, pretty village, three bedrooms. *(Bernard Stradling, Richard Tilbrook)*

MARSHFIELD   ST7773
★ **Catherine Wheel** (01225) 892220
High Street; signed off A420 Bristol–Chippenham; SN14 8LR High-ceilinged stripped-stone front part with medley of settles, chairs and stripped tables, charming Georgian dining room with open fire in impressive fireplace, cottagey beamed back area warmed by woodburners, friendly staff and chatty locals, well kept Butcombe, Cotswold and Sharps, interesting wines and other drinks, enjoyable sensibly priced food (not Sun evening) from pub favourites up, darts and dominoes; children and dogs (on leads) welcome, wheelchair access with help, flower-decked backyard, unspoilt village, four bedrooms, open all day. *(Dr and Mrs A K Clarke)*

MAYSHILL   ST6882
New Inn (01454) 773161
Badminton Road (A432 Frampton Cotterell–Yate); BS36 2NT Popular largely 17th-c coaching inn with two comfortably

carpeted bar rooms leading to restaurant, good choice of enjoyable generously served food, friendly staff, well kept Timothy Taylors Landlord and a couple of guests, Weston's cider and decent wines by the glass, log fire; children and dogs welcome, garden with play area. *(Roger and Donna Huggins)*

MEYSEY HAMPTON   SU1199
Masons Arms (01285) 850164
Just off A417 Cirencester–Lechlade; High Street; GL7 5JT 17th-c village local with enjoyable simple food and well kept Arkells, friendly considerate staff, longish open-plan beamed bar with big inglenook fire one end, restaurant; background music; tables out on green, pleasant compact bedrooms, good breakfast, parking may be a problem. *(Lesley and Brian Lynn)*

MINCHINHAMPTON   SO8500
Old Lodge (01453) 832047
Nailsworth–Brimscombe – on common, fork left at pub's sign; OS Sheet 162 map reference 853008; GL6 9AQ Welcoming dining pub (part of the Cotswold Food Club group) with civilised bistro feel, wood floors, stripped-stone walls, modern décor and furnishings, good food from pub favourites up, well kept beers and decent wines by the glass; children welcome, tables on neat lawn looking over NT common with grazing cows and horses, six bedrooms. *(David and Stella Martin)*

MINSTERWORTH   SO7515
Severn Bore (01452) 750318
A48 2 miles SW; GL2 8JX In splendid Severn-side position, open layout with central fireplace, usual pubby furniture, ales including Wickwar Severn Bore and a house beer from Church End, local cider, good choice of food (till 6pm Mon, Tues), skittle alley with pool table and darts; children welcome and dogs (ask first though as there are two pub dogs), wheelchair access (low step into bar), big riverside garden with superb views to the Cotswolds, play area, board giving times/heights of Severn Bore, handy for Westbury Court Garden (NT), open all day and for breakfast on Bore days. *(Anon)*

MISERDEN   SO9308
Carpenters Arms (01285) 821283
Off B4070 NE of Stroud; GL6 7JA Country pub with open-plan low-beamed bar, stripped-stone walls, log fire and woodburner, friendly licensees, Wye Valley and a guest ale, good wine list, enjoyable reasonably priced food using local and home-grown produce including good vegetarian choices, charity quiz nights; children and dogs welcome, garden tables, popular with walkers and handy for Miserden Park, open (and food) all day. *(Chris and Val Ramstedt)*

MORETON-IN-MARSH   SP2032
Inn on the Marsh   (01608) 650709
Stow Road; GL56 ODW Interesting 19th-c beamed bar with warm layout including lovely curved sofa, quite a dutch flavour to the bric-a-brac, models, posters etc, inglenook woodburner, dutch chef-landlady cooking national specialities alongside pubby favourites, four well kept Marstons-related ales, modern conservatory restaurant; may be background music, quiz machine; children and dogs welcome, seats at front and in back garden, closed Mon lunchtime. *(JHBS, Richard Tilbrook)*

MORETON-IN-MARSH   SP2032
Redesdale Arms   (01608) 650308
High Street; GL56 OAW Relaxed 17th-c hotel (former coaching inn); alcoves and big stone fireplace in comfortable solidly furnished panelled bar on right, darts in flagstoned public bar, Wickwar ales, decent wines and coffee, enjoyable good value food served by courteous helpful staff, spacious child-friendly back brasserie and dining conservatory; background music, TVs, games machine; heated floodlit courtyard, 34 comfortable bedrooms (newer ones in mews), open all day from 8am. *(George Atkinson)*

MORETON-IN-MARSH   SP2032
White Hart Royal   (01608) 650731
High Street; GL56 OBA Refurbished 17th-c coaching inn with Charles I connection; cosy beamed quarry-tiled bar with fine inglenook and nice old furniture, adjacent smarter panelled room with Georgian feel, separate lounge and restaurant, Hook Norton and a guest ale, good choice of wines, well priced food from sandwiches and pub favourites to more inventive choices, friendly efficient service from smart staff; background music; courtyard tables, bedrooms. *(Richard Tilbrook, Fiona Smith)*

NAILSWORTH   ST8499
Britannia   (01453) 832501
Cossack Square; GL6 ODG Large open-plan pub (part of the small Cotswold Food Club chain) in former manor house; popular bistro food (best to book evenings) including bargain weekday lunch menu, takeaway pizzas, friendly service, well kept Greene King IPA and a couple of local beers, good choice of wines by the glass, big log fire; picnic-sets in front garden, open all day. *(Tom and Ruth Rees)*

NAILSWORTH   ST8499
★ Egypt Mill   (01453) 833449
Off A46; heading N towards Stroud, first right after roundabout, then left;

GL6 OAE Stylishly converted 16th-c mill with working waterwheels; split-level bar with brick and stone floor, beers such as Stroud and Wye Valley, a dozen wines by the glass, comfortable carpeted lounge with stripped beams and some hefty ironwork from old machinery, seating ranging from elegant wooden dining chairs to cushioned wall seats and sofas, good reasonably priced food served by friendly helpful staff; background music, TV; children welcome, plenty of tables in floodlit garden overlooking millpond, well appointed bedrooms (some with fine beams and timbering), open (and food) all day. *(Dr A McCormick, Dr and Mrs A K Clarke, Tom and Ruth Rees)*

NAUNTON   SP1123
★ Black Horse   (01451) 850565
Off B4068 W of Stow-on-the-Wold; GL54 3AD Welcoming local's pub with well kept/priced Donnington BB and SBA, Weston's cider and good food from traditional favourites to specials such as seasonal game, efficient service, black beams, stripped stone, flagstones and log fire, flowers on plain tables, dining room; background music, darts and dominoes; children and dogs welcome, small seating area outside, charming village and fine Cotswold walks (walking groups asked to pre-order food). *(Richard Tilbrook, Lucien Perring, K H Frostick and others)*

NIBLEY   ST6982
Swan   (01454) 312290
Badminton Road; BS37 5JF Light refurbishment by small local pub group, good food from snacks and lunchtime fixed-price choices to daily specials, three changing ales, real cider and over a dozen wines by the glass, fireside leather sofas one side, dining tables the other; children welcome, open all day in summer, all day Thurs-Sun in winter. *(Roger and Donna Huggins)*

NORTH NIBLEY   ST7596
New Inn   (01453) 543659
E of village itself; Waterley Bottom; GL11 6EF Former cider house in secluded rural setting popular with walkers, well kept ales such as Cotleigh, Moles and Wickwar from antique pumps, fine range of ciders and perries (more in bottles), enjoyable bar food from lunchtime sandwiches and good ploughman's up, lounge bar with cushioned windsor chairs and high-backed settles, partly stripped-stone walls, simple cosy public bar with darts (no children here after 6pm), cider festivals and other events; dogs welcome, hitching rail and trough for horses, picnic-sets and swings on lawn, covered decked area with pool table, two bedrooms, open all day weekends, closed Mon lunchtime (evening too in winter). *(Guy Vowles)*

If we know a pub has an outdoor play area for children, we mention it.

OAKRIDGE LYNCH   SO9103
Butchers Arms (01285) 760371
Off Eastcombe–Bisley Road E of Stroud;
GL6 7NZ Welcoming refurbished beamed
pub with emphasis on chef-landlord's
good food, Wadworths ales, open fires and
friendly relaxed atmosphere; tables on lawn
overlooking valley, nice walks. *(David Butcher,*
David and Stella Martin)

OLD DOWN   ST6187
★Fox (01454) 412507
3.9 miles from M5 junction 15/16; A38
towards Gloucester, then Old Down
signposted; turn left into Inner Down;
BS32 4PR Popular low-beamed cottagey
pub, pleasantly unassuming, with warm local
atmosphere, seven ales including Bath and
Butcombe, real cider and several wines by
the glass, good reasonably priced hearty food
with some interesting specials (best to book),
friendly efficient staff, mainly red-carpeted
bar with log fire, chunky pine tables and
traditional pub seating, snug stone-tiled
family room; good disabled access, long
verandah with grapevine, front and back
gardens, play area. *(James Morrell, PL, Chris*
and Angela Buckell)

OLD SODBURY   ST7581
★Dog (01454) 312006
3 miles from M4 junction 18, via A46
and A432; The Hill (a busy road);
BS37 6LZ Welcoming old pub with popular
two-level bar, low beams, stripped stone and
open fire, enjoyable food from sandwiches
and baked potatoes to fresh fish and steaks,
friendly young staff, well kept ales such as
Wickwar, good wine and soft drinks choice;
children and dogs welcome, big garden with
barbecue and play area, bedrooms, open
all day. *(Roger and Donna Huggins)*

PAINSWICK   SO8609
Falcon (01452) 814222
New Street; GL6 6UN Sizeable old
stone-built inn dating from the 16th c;
sympathetically refurbished and comfortable
open-plan layout with bar and two dining
areas, popular above-average food, four
well kept beers including Sharps Doom
Bar, friendly young staff, some live music;
children and dogs welcome, 12 bedrooms,
opposite churchyard famous for its 99 yews.
(Martin and Pauline Jennings, Neil and Anita
Christopher)

PARKEND   SO6107
Fountain (01594) 562189
Just off B4234; GL15 4JD 18th-c village
inn by terminus of restored Lydney–Parkend
steam railway; three well kept ales including
Wye Valley, Stowford Press cider, wines in
glass-sized bottles, home-made traditional
food including bargain OAP lunches (not
Sun), welcoming helpful staff, coal fire,
assorted chairs and settles in two linked

rooms, old tools, bric-a-brac, photographs
and framed local history information, quiz
and live music nights; children and dogs
welcome, wheelchair access, side garden,
eight bedrooms and bunkhouse, open all
day Sat. *(Anon)*

PARKEND   SO6308
Rising Sun (01594) 562008
Off B4431; GL15 4HN Perched on
wooded hillside and approached by roughish
single-track drive – popular with walkers
and cyclists; open-plan carpeted bar with
modern pub furniture, Butcombe and a guest,
real ciders, straightforward generous food
from sandwiches and baked potatoes up,
friendly service, lounge/games area with pool
and machines; children and dogs welcome,
wheelchair access with help, balcony and
terrace tables under umbrellas, big woodside
garden with play area and pond, self-catering
bedroom, open all day weekends
in summer. *(Anon)*

PILNING   ST5684
Plough (01454) 632556
Handy for M5 junction 17 via B4055
and Station Road; Pilning Street;
BS35 4JJ Thriving local atmosphere under
welcoming hard-working licensees, flagstones
and bare boards, some faux beams, plates,
country prints and repro adverts on dark
cream/red dado walls, sofas and armchairs
in small lounge area, newspapers in public
bar, Wadworths ales and real ciders, good
value bar food (something available all
day), bargain OAP weekday lunch, cheerful
efficient staff, live music; children welcome,
wheelchair access to main areas, garden
with large play area overlooking open
country. *(Chris and Angela Buckell)*

POULTON   SP1001
Falcon (01285) 850878
London Road; GL7 5HN Bistro feel with
good food from landlord-chef including set
lunch, well kept local ales and nice wines
by the glass, friendly attentive service; well
behaved children welcome, closed Sun
evening, Mon. *(Giles and Annie Francis)*

QUENINGTON   SP1404
Keepers Arms (01285) 750349
Church Road; GL7 5BL Community
local in pretty Cotswold village, cosy and
comfortable, with stripped stone, low beams
and log fires, friendly landlord and staff,
enjoyable fairly priced food in bar and
restaurant from sandwiches to good Sun
lunch, well kept changing local beers; dogs
welcome, picnic-sets outside, bedrooms.
(Mo and David Trudgill, Tom McLean, Alan
Bulley, Giles and Annie Francis)

SALFORD HILL   SP2629
Greedy Goose (01608) 646551
Junction A44/A436, near Chastleton;
GL56 0SP Old roadside country dining pub

with contemporary interior, enjoyable food from sandwiches and stone-baked pizzas up, friendly enthusiastic staff, three real ales from small bar area; terrace and garden seating, open all day from 9am. *(Martin and Pauline Jennings)*

SAPPERTON   SO9403
Bell (01285) 760298

Village signposted from A419 Stroud–Cirencester; OS Sheet 163 map reference 948033; GL7 6LE 250-year-old pub under new owners, comfortable seating in front of woodburner, two other cosy rooms with beams, flagstones and open fire, ales such as Hook Norton, Otter, Stroud and Uley, nice food; children and dogs welcome, seats on small front terrace, more in back courtyard garden, plenty of surrounding walks, closed Sun evening, Mon. *(David and Sue Atkinson, Bernard Stradling)*

SAPPERTON   SO9303
Daneway Inn (01285) 760297

Daneway; off A419 Stroud–Cirencester; GL7 6LN Quiet tucked-away local in charming wooded countryside, flagstones and bare boards, woodburner in amazing floor-to-ceiling carved oak dutch fireplace, sporting prints, well kept Wadworths ales, farm ciders and generous simple food from filled baps to good Sun lunch, long-serving landlord and friendly staff, small family room, traditional games in inglenook public bar, folk night Tues; no dogs, tricky wheelchair access; terrace tables and lovely sloping lawn, camping possible, good walks by disused canal (some recent renovation) with tunnel to Coates. *(Giles and Annie Francis)*

SELSEY   SO8303
Bell (01453) 753801

Bell Lane; GL5 5JY Attractively updated village pub under newish licensees, enjoyable home-made food (not Sun evening) using own farm produce and local game, ales including Wye Valley and decent wines by the glass, friendly relaxed service, open fire and woodburner, garden room dining extension, farm shop; children, walkers and dogs welcome, views from terrace tables, near Selsley Common and Cotswold Way, comfortable bedrooms, open all day. *(Anon)*

SHIPTON MOYNE   ST8989
Cat & Custard Pot (01666) 880249

Off B4040 Malmesbury–Bristol; The Street; GL8 8PN Popular chatty pub in picturesque village, well kept Bath, Hook Norton and Wickwar, decent wines, good pubby food promptly served by friendly staff, deceptively spacious inside with several dining areas, beams and bric-a-brac, hunting prints, cosy back snug, woodburner; walkers and dogs welcome, wheelchair access, tables out on lawn. *(Neil and Anita Christopher, Chris and Angela Buckell)*

SIDDINGTON   SU0399
Greyhound (01285) 653573

Ashton Road; village signed from A419 roundabout at Tesco; GL7 6HR Beamed village pub with linked rooms, flagstones and carpets, some bare stone walls, big log fires and woodburner, enjoyable good value food, well kept Wadworths ales and plenty of wines by the glass; background music; children welcome, garden tables, open all day weekends. *(Anon)*

SLAD   SO8707
Woolpack (01452) 813429

B4070 Stroud–Birdlip; GL6 7QA Friendly old-fashioned hillside village pub (new owners) with lovely valley views, four little connecting rooms with Laurie Lee and other interesting photographs, some of his books for sale, log fire and nice tables, enjoyable food (not Sun evening), well kept Uley ales and guests, local farm ciders and perry, decent wines by the glass; children and dogs welcome, nice garden, open all day. *(Guy Vowles)*

SLIMBRIDGE   SO7204
Tudor Arms (01453) 890306

Shepherds Patch; off A38 towards Slimbridge Wetland Centre; GL2 7BP Much extended red-brick pub just back from canal swing bridge; welcoming and popular, with several local ales, eight ciders/perries and good wines by the glass, enjoyable food (all day bar meals) from baguettes and baked potatoes to daily specials, prompt friendly service, linked areas with wood, flagstone or carpeted floors, some leather chairs and settles, comfortable dining room, conservatory, darts, pool and skittle alley; children and dogs welcome, disabled facilities, picnic-sets outside (some on covered terrace), boat trips, 12 annexe bedrooms, caravan site off car park, open all day. *(Chris and Angela Buckell, Theocsbrian)*

SNOWSHILL   SP0933
Snowshill Arms (01386) 852653

Opposite village green; WR12 7JU Unpretentious country pub in honeypot village (so no shortage of customers); well kept Donnington ales and reasonably priced straightforward (but tasty) food from sandwiches up, prompt friendly service, log fire, stripped stone and neat array of tables, charming village views from bow windows, local photographs, skittle alley; children welcome if eating, big back garden with little stream and play area, handy for Snowshill Manor (NT), lavender farm and Cotswold Way walks. *(Richard Tilbrook)*

SOMERFORD KEYNES   SU0195
Bakers Arms (01285) 861298

On main street through village; GL7 6DN Pretty little 17th-c stone-built pub with catslide roof, four ales including

Butcombe and Stroud, Addlestone's cider, good house wine, enjoyable traditional food and specials, friendly service, lots of pine tables in two linked areas, fire in big stone fireplace; children and dogs welcome, nice garden with play area, lovely village, handy for Cotswold Water Park, open (and food) all day except Sun when shuts at 6pm. *(Anon)*

ST BRIAVELS   SO5504
George (01594) 530228
High Street; GL15 6TA Old Wadworths pub under new management; their beers and a couple of guests, enjoyable pubby food including OAP lunch deal (Mon-Fri), friendly service, rambling linked black-beamed rooms with attractive old-fashioned décor, woodburner in big stone fireplace, restaurant with another woodburner; can get very busy weekends (booking advised); children and dogs welcome, flagstoned terrace over former moat of neighbouring Norman fortress, four refurbished bedrooms, open all day. *(Lucien Perring, Bob and Margaret Holder)*

STAUNTON   SO7829
Swan (01452) 840323
Ledbury Road (A417); GL19 3QA Nice pubby atmosphere and good choice of enjoyable reasonably priced home-made food (takeaway suppers available Tues-Sat), good friendly service, well kept ales (hundreds of pump clips on beams), interconnecting rooms including spacious restaurant, comfortable sofas by open fire, conservatory; background music; children and dogs welcome, disabled facilities, pretty garden, closed Sun and Mon evenings. *(Neil and Anita Christopher, Glenwys and Alan Lawrence)*

STAUNTON   SO5412
White Horse (01594) 834001
A4136; GL16 8PA Village pub on edge of Forest of Dean close to the welsh border; good freshly made food in bar or restaurant, well kept local ales and ciders, friendly service, two woodburners, café and small shop; dogs and muddy boots welcome, disabled access, picnic-sets in good-sized garden, open all day weekends, closed Mon. *(Anon)*.

STOW-ON-THE-WOLD   SP1925
★Bell (01451) 870916
Park Street; A436 E of centre; GL54 1AJ Dining pub with comfortable homely décor, very good well presented food including fish specials, excellent service from friendly young staff, three local ales and nice wines (champagne happy hour Friday evening), proper beamed and flagstoned bar with

woodburner; under-16s in dining part only, dogs welcome, picnic-sets outside, five bedrooms, open (and some food) all day. *(Richard Tilbrook)*

STOW-ON-THE-WOLD   SP1925
Kings Arms (01451) 830364
The Square; GL54 1AF Refurbished 16th-c coaching inn, black-beamed bar with wood floor, some blue-painted panelling and stripped stone, woodburner, Greene King ales, enjoyable food here or in upstairs Chophouse restaurant with saggy oak floor, leopard-skin bar stools and ink-spot tables, friendly service; children welcome, ten bedrooms including three courtyard 'cottages', open all day. *(Richard Tilbrook, George Atkinson)*

STOW-ON-THE-WOLD   SP1925
★Queens Head (01451) 830563
The Square; GL54 1AB Splendidly unpretentious for this upmarket town; well kept low-priced Donnington ales, good wines by the glass and good value basic pub meals done well including proper steak and kidney pudding, cheerful helpful service, bustling and chatty stripped-stone front lounge, heavily beamed and flagstoned back bar with high-backed settles, horse prints and some interesting bric-a-brac, coal-effect fire; children and dogs welcome, tables in attractive sunny back courtyard, open all day. *(Mitchell Cregor, Richard Tilbrook, Richard Stanfield)*

SWINEFORD   ST6969
Swan (0117) 932 3101
A431, right on the Somerset border; BS30 6LN Popular stone-built pub with well kept Bath Ales and a guest, decent ciders and carefully chosen wines, good selection of spirits too, enjoyable food from bar snacks and pub favourites up, helpful friendly staff, plain furniture on bare boards or tiles, pastel paintwork and panelled dado, big open fire; children welcome, wheelchair access, large garden with play area, open all day. *(Chris and Angela Buckell)*

TETBURY   ST8893
Priory (01666) 502251
London Road; GL8 8JJ More civilised eating house than pub, with central log fire in comfortable if somewhat sombre high-raftered stone-built former stables, enjoyable food with emphasis on interesting local produce, even a local slant to their good wood-fired pizzas, cheerful service, well kept Stroud, Uley and a guest, three proper ciders and decent wines by the glass; comfortable

---

'Children welcome' means the pub says it lets children inside without any special restriction. If it allows them in, but to restricted areas such as an eating area or family room, we specify this. Some pubs may impose an evening time limit. We do not mention limits after 9pm as we assume children are home by then.

coffee lounge, live music Sun; children very welcome, wheelchair access (staff helpful), roadside terrace picnic-sets, 14 bedrooms, open all day. *(Anon)*

TETBURY   ST8993
★ **Snooty Fox**   (01666) 502436
Market Place; GL8 8DD High-ceilinged stripped-stone hotel lounge, unstuffy with well kept local ales and good house wines, friendly young staff, enjoyable all-day bar food from sandwiches up, leather sofas, brass ceiling fans and elegant fireplace, nice side room and anteroom, restaurant; unobtrusive background music, bar can get very busy weekend evenings; children and dogs welcome, large sheltered front terrace, 12 bedrooms. *(Anon)*

TEWKESBURY   SO8931
Gupshill Manor   (01684) 292278
Gloucester Road (off A38 S edge of town); GL20 5SG Old timbered building with Tardis-like series of lounge and dining areas, plenty of easy chairs and sofas, beams and open fires, good choice of enjoyable food including fixed-price menu and other deals, friendly efficient staff, three well kept Greene King ales and a guest, decent wine list; background music, live jazz last Sun of month; children welcome, disabled access, tables out on partly covered terrace and grass, open (and food) all day. *(Rod Stoneman)*

TEWKESBURY   SO8932
Nottingham Arms   (01684) 276346
High Street; GL20 5JU Popular old black and white fronted bare-boards local, well kept ales such as St Austell, Sharps and Wye Valley, Weston's cider, good home-made food at reasonable prices, back dining room, friendly efficient service, music and quiz nights; dogs welcome, open all day. *(Eddie Edwards)*

TEWKESBURY   SO8933
★ **Olde Black Bear**   (01684) 292202
High Street; GL20 5BJ County's oldest pub (early 14th c), well worth a look for its intricately rambling little rooms with ancient tiles, heavy timbering and low beams; up to five real ales, reasonably priced wines, cheap but decent pubby food, well worn furnishings, open fire; background music; children welcome, terrace and play area in nice riverside garden, moorings, open all day. *(Jeremy King)*

TEWKESBURY   SO8932
Royal Hop Pole   (01684) 274039
Church Street; GL20 5RT Wetherspoons conversion of old inn (some parts dating from the 15th c), their usual value-minded all-day food and drink, good service; free wi-fi; terrace seating and lovely garden leading down to river, 28 bedrooms, open all day from 7am. *(Theocsbrian, Roger and Donna Huggins)*

TODENHAM   SP2436
★ **Farriers Arms**   (01608) 650901
Between A3400 and A429 N of Moreton-in-Marsh; GL56 9PF Unspoilt and welcoming old pub with exposed stone and plastered walls in bar, hop-hung beams, polished flagstones by counter, woodburner in big inglenook, cosy room off with old books and photos, neat restaurant, Hook Norton and a couple of guests, several wines by the glass, shortish choice of good value food from changing blackboard menu, darts, board games; background music; children welcome, dogs in bar, country views from walled garden, terrace overlooking quiet village road and church, aunt sally, good surrounding walks. *(Bernard Stradling, Jean and Douglas Troup, Canon Michael Bourdeaux, Alun and Jennifer Evans, D L Frostick, Dennis and Doreen Haward)*

ULEY   ST7998
Old Crown   (01453) 860502
The Green; GL11 5SN Unspoilt 17th-c pub prettily set by village green just off Cotswold Way; long narrow room with settles and pews on bare boards, step up to partitioned-off lounge area, six well kept local ales including Uley, decent wines by the glass and enjoyable reasonably priced pubby food from baguettes up, friendly service, open fire; a few picnic-sets in front and attractive garden behind, four bedrooms, open all day. *(M G Hart, Guy Vowles)*

UPTON CHEYNEY   ST6969
Upton Inn   (0117) 932 4489
Signed off A431 at Bitton; BS30 6LY 18th-c stone-built village pub, bar with old prints on stone and dark panelled walls, old tables and captain's chairs, step up to carpeted/bare-boards dining area with woodburner, good choice of home-made pubby food from sandwiches up, Sun carvery, well kept Badger ales, Weston's Old Rosie cider, modern opulent mock-Regency restaurant with pictures of Bath, friendly helpful service; background music; wheelchair access possible (enter from car park using ramp), children and dogs welcome, picnic-sets on terrace, picturesque spot with Avon Valley views, open all day. *(Chris and Angela Buckell)*

WESTONBIRT   ST8690
Hare & Hounds   (01666) 881000
A433 SW of Tetbury; GL8 8QL Substantial roadside hotel with separate entrance for pub, good food from snacks up, Cotswold Spring and Wickwar, lots of wines by the glass, good selection of malts and other spirits, prompt cheery service, flagstoned bar with another panelled one to the left, series of interconnecting rooms with polished wood or sisal floors, woodburner in two-way fireplace, some leather sofas and banquettes, more formal restaurant; muddy

boots and dogs welcome in bar, wheelchair access throughout, shaded tables out on front paved area, pleasant gardens, 42 bedrooms including some in annexe, handy for Arboretum, open all day and gets very busy (especially weekend lunchtimes). *(Chris and Angela Buckell)*

WHITECROFT   SO6005
Miners Arms (01594) 562483
B4234 N of Lydney; GL15 4PE Friendly unpretentious local with up to five changing ales, farm ciders and perries, sensibly priced food from snacks up including some greek dishes (landlord is cypriot), attentive helpful service, two rooms on either side of bar, slate and parquet floors, pastel walls with old photographs, conservatory, skittle alley; background and some live music; children and dogs welcome, disabled access, good gardens front and back, one with stream, good local walks, handy for steam railway, self-catering cottage, open all day. *(Anon)*

WHITMINSTER   SO7607
Fromebridge Mill (01452) 741796
Fromebridge Lane (A38 near M5 junction 13); GL2 7PD Comfortable mill-based dining pub under newish management; interconnecting rooms, beams, bare brick walls, flagstone and carpeted floors, some tables overlooking river, well kept Greene King and guests, good choice of wines by the glass, food all day including lunchtime carvery (evenings too at weekends), helpful pleasant staff; can get very busy, no dogs inside; children welcome, wheelchair access throughout, picnic-sets in big garden with play area, pretty waterside setting, footbridge from car park. *(Simon J Barber, Chris and Angela Buckell)*

WILLERSEY   SP1039
★ Bell (01386) 858405
B4632 Cheltenham–Stratford, near Broadway; WR12 7PJ Well run neatly modernised stone-built pub, comfortable front dining area with popular home-made food including weekday set lunch deals, Aston Villa memorabilia and huge collection of model cars in back area past big L-shaped bar counter, Flowers, Hook Norton and Wadworths 6X, relaxed atmosphere, quick friendly service, darts; children welcome, overlooks village green and duck pond, lots of tables in big garden (dogs allowed here only), five bedrooms in outbuildings. *(Martin and Pauline Jennings)*

WINCHCOMBE   SP0228
Lion (01242) 603300
North Street; GL54 5PS Stylishly refurbished former coaching inn with plenty of rustic chic, good food in bar or restaurant, well kept ales such as Prescott and Ringwood, friendly helpful staff, newspapers, magazines and board games; background music turned down on request; children welcome, dogs in bar and snug, seven bedrooms, open all day. *(Richard Tilbrook)*

WINCHCOMBE   SP0228
Old Corner Cupboard
(01242) 602303 *Gloucester Street; GL54 5LX* Attractive old golden-stone pub with enjoyable food including range of curries in back dining room, well kept ales such as Hook Norton and Timothy Taylors, decent wines by the glass, good service, comfortable stripped-stone lounge bar with heavy-beamed Tudor core, traditional hatch-service lobby, small side room with woodburner in massive stone fireplace, traditional games; children welcome, tables in back garden, open all day. *(Dr A J and Mrs B A Tompsett, Guy Vowles, Steve Tilley, M G Hart)*

WINCHCOMBE   SP0228
★ White Hart (01242) 602359
High Street (B4632); GL54 5LJ Popular 16th-c inn with big windows looking out over village street, mix of chairs and small settles around pine tables, bare boards, grey-green paintwork, cricket memorabilia, well kept Goffs and other ales such as Prescott, Wadworths and Wickwar, wine shop at back (corkage added if you buy to drink on premises), wide choice by the glass too, specialist sausage menu and other enjoyable food, good service, separate restaurant, log fire; sports TV; children welcome, dogs in bar and bedrooms, open all day from 9am (10am Sun). *(Dr A J and Mrs B A Tompsett, Guy Vowles, Steve Tilley, Dr Peter Crawshaw, Heulwen and Neville Pinfield)*

WINTERBOURNE   ST6678
Willy Wicket (0117) 956 7308
Wick Wick Close, handy for M4 junction 19 via M32, A4174 E; BS36 1DP Vintage Inn family dining pub by roundabout; popular generously served food including fixed-price menu (till 5pm), Butcombe and a couple of other ales, friendly courteous service, two eating areas off big central bar, beams, timbers and stripped stone, picture windows, two log fires; open (and food) all day. *(David and Ruth Shillitoe, Roger and Donna Huggins)*

WITHINGTON   SP0315
Kings Head (01242) 890216
Kings Head Lane; GL54 4BD Old-fashioned rural local (in same family for over 100 years – the friendly veteran landlady was born here), well kept Hook Norton and maybe Wickwar tapped from the cask, pickled eggs (can bring your own food), bar with woodburner, darts, shove-ha'penny, table skittles and pool, partly stripped-stone lounge bar, impromptu music sessions; children and dogs welcome (there's a pub dog), pleasant garden behind, open all day. *(Giles and Annie Francis)*

WITHINGTON   SP0315
Mill Inn (01242) 890204
Off A436 or A40; GL54 4BE Idyllic
streamside setting for this mossy-roofed old
stone inn, some refurbishment but keeping
character with nice nooks and corners,
beams, wood/flagstone floors, two inglenook
log fires and a woodburner, Sam Smiths
beers, reasonably priced food, two dining
rooms; children and dogs welcome, picnic-
sets in good-sized garden, splendid walks,
open all day weekends. *(Guy Vowles)*

WOODCHESTER   SO8403
★ Old Fleece (01453) 872582
*Rooksmoor; A46 a mile S of Stroud;
GL5 5NB* Old wisteria-clad roadside pub,
part of the small Cotswold Food Club chain;
good choice of well presented interesting
food, friendly accommodating staff, well
kept mostly local beers and good wines
by the glass, bar, dining room and snug,
big windows, bare boards and panelling,
stripped-stone or dark salmon pink walls,
modern paintings, large log fire, daily papers;
children welcome, wheelchair access (except
dining area – you can also eat in bar), two
front terraces, open all day. *(Tom and Ruth
Rees)*

WOODCHESTER   SO8302
Ram (01453) 873329
*High Street, South Woodchester; off A46
S of Stroud; GL5 5EL* Bustling country
pub with up to half a dozen well priced
changing ales and three ciders, enjoyable
fairly standard home-made food, L-shaped
beamed bar with bare boards and stripped

stonework, nice mix of traditional furnishings
including several cushioned antique panelled
settles, open fires, maybe live acoustic music
Sun afternoon; children and dogs welcome,
wheelchair access (steep incline from car
park), terrace with lovely valley views, open
all day. *(Chris and Angela Buckell)*

WOODCHESTER   SO8302
Royal Oak (01453) 872735
*Off A46; Church Road, N Woodchester;
GL5 5PQ* Popular and relaxed 17th-c village
pub; comfortable low-beamed bar on right
with oak tables, old-fashioned stripped-stone
area on left with huge fireplace, locally
sourced home-made food (not Sun evening,
Mon, Tues), Stroud, Uley and a guest, regular
live music; children and dogs welcome, a few
seats out at front, more on back terrace, open
all day Fri-Sun, from 5pm other days. *(Anon)*

WOTTON-UNDER-EDGE   ST7593
Swan (01453) 843004
Market Street; GL12 7AE Rambling 17th-c
beamed coaching inn with series of rooms
off central passage, three Butcombe ales
and Ashton Press cider from small timber-
framed servery, several malts and good wine
list (most by the glass), exposed stone and
brickwork, vintage beer ads and photos of
the hotel, high-backed faux leather chairs
at wood topped tables, old fireplaces, lounge
bar with leather armchairs and sofas, more
modern restaurant, generous helpings of
tasty locally sourced food, breakfast (7.30-
11am), cheery attentive staff; monthly live
music, sports TV, free wi-fi; wheelchair access
to bar area only, eight bedrooms, open all day.
(Chris and Angela Buckell)

Post Office address codings confusingly give the impression that some pubs are in
Gloucestershire, when they're really in Warwickshire (which is where we list them).

Hampshire

KEY	★ Star Pub	🍽 Top Quality Food	🍺 Great Beer
	🍷 Good Wines	£ Bargain Meals	🛏 Good Bedrooms	🍴 Serves Food

AMPORT   SU2944 Map 2

Hawk Inn 🛏

Off A303 at Thruxton interchange; at Andover end of village just before Monxton; SP11 8AE

Relaxed rambling old place with comfortable front bar, two dining areas, contemporary furnishings, helpful staff and well thought-of food; bedrooms

Our favourite spot for a relaxed drink and chat in this rambling pub is the comfortable front bar. This has brown leather armchairs and plush grey sofas by a low table with daily newspapers, a log fire in a brick fireplace with a mirror above and sisal matting on bare boards; to the left is a tucked-away room with horse-racing photographs, shelves of books and a TV. Two dining areas have smart window blinds, black leather cushioned wall seats and elegant wooden chairs (some carved) around pale tables, big oil paintings on pale walls above a grey dado, and a woodburning stove. Black-topped stools line the counter, where courteous staff serve Ramsbury Bitter and a guest ale on handpump and quite a few wines by the glass, and there's also a couple of tables, chairs and more wall seating. Bedrooms are up to date and comfortable, and the sunny sandstone terrace has picnic-sets looking across the lane to more seating on grass that leads down to Pill Hill brook. The famous Hawk Conservancy Trust is in the village.

🍴 As well as breakfasts, the good all-day food includes lunchtime sandwiches, crispy squid with smoked paprika aioli, pheasant and hoi sin spring rolls with sweet chilli and lime, wild mushroom risotto, salmon linguine with dill and pink peppercorns, lamb shank with rosemary, tomato and feta mash, pork belly with honey, mustard and beer glaze and sweet potato mash, and puddings such as ginger and cardamom crème brûlée and sticky toffee pudding with salted caramel ice-cream. *Benchmark main dish: burger with smoked cheese, bacon and fries £13.95. Two-course evening meal £21.00.*

Free house ~ Licensee Rupert Fowler ~ Real ale ~ (01264) 710371 ~ Open 7.30am (8.30 weekends)-11pm (10.30 Sun) ~ Bar food 12-2.30, 6.30-9.30 ~ Children welcome ~ Dogs allowed in bar and bedrooms ~ Wi-fi ~ Bedrooms: /£85 ~ www.hawkinnamport.co.uk
Recommended by B J Harding, Katharine Cowherd

BANK   SU2806 Map 2

Oak 🍺

Signposted just off A35 SW of Lyndhurst; SO43 7FE

New Forest pub with a good mix of customers, popular food and interesting décor

Sensibly open all day – which suits the walkers, horse riders and cyclists who stop for refreshment – this bustling pub remains as well run and friendly as ever. The L-shaped bar has bay windows with built-in red-cushioned seats, and a few little pine-panelled booths with small built-in tables and bench seats. The rest of the bare-boarded bar has low beams and joists, candles in brass holders on a row of stripped old and newer blond tables set against the wall, and all manner of bric-a-brac: fishing rods, spears, a boomerang, old ski poles, brass platters, heavy knives and guns. There are cushioned milk churns along the bar counter and little red lanterns among hop bines above the bar. Fullers London Pride, Gales HSB and Seafarers and a changing guest on handpump and 14 wines by the glass; background music. The pleasant side garden has picnic-sets and long tables and benches by big yew trees.

 As well as lunchtime doorstep sandwiches, the highly thought-of food includes monkfish cheek and squid salad with samphire, goats cheese mousse with watermelon and pomegranate salad, meat and seafood platters, honey-glazed ham and free-range eggs, a pie of the day, mushroom risotto, free-range chicken breast with tahini and yoghurt dressing, and puddings. *Benchmark main dish: cider-braised pork belly with butterbean purée and spiced apple compote £13.95. Two-course evening meal £20.00.*

Fullers ~ Manager Martin Sliva ~ Real ale ~ (023) 8028 2350 ~ Open 11.30-3, 5.30-11; 11.30-11 Sat; 12-10.30 Sun ~ Bar food 12-2.30, 6-9.30; all day weekends ~ Children welcome but no under-5s after 6pm ~ Dogs allowed in bar ~ Wi-fi ~ www.oakinnlyndhurst.co.uk *Recommended by JPC, Michael Butler, John Saville, H J Reynolds, Mrs J A Taylar, Katharine Cowherd, Martin and Karen Wake, N R White, Brian Glozier, Phil and Jane Villiers, Adrian Johnson*

BAUGHURST
SU5860   Map 2
Wellington Arms ⭐ ♀ ⇌
Baughurst Road, S of village; RG26 5LP

Hampshire Dining Pub of the Year

Small pretty country pub-with-rooms, exceptional cooking and a friendly welcome; bedrooms

A fourth delightful, comfortable bedroom will have been added to this charming little country inn by the time this *Guide* is published; an Orangery for dining should also have been completed by then. It's an 18th-c building still run with enthusiasm and great care by the friendly licensees – and our readers love it. The dining room is attractively decorated with an assortment of cushioned oak dining chairs around a mix of polished tables on terracotta tiles, pretty blinds, brass candlesticks, flowers and window sills stacked with cookery books. A couple of ales from breweries such as Two Cocks, Wadworths and West Berkshire on handpump, ten wines by the glass and a farm cider, served by courteous, helpful staff; background music. There are picnic-sets in the garden.

They rear sheep and pigs, keep chickens and bees and grow their own vegetables, and the delicious food takes pub cooking to its highest level: rabbit, pheasant and pork terrine, twice-baked cheddar soufflé on braised leeks with cream, free-range moroccan-style chicken, cornish skate with capers and brown butter, confit duck leg with morels, shallots and braised puy lentils, barbecue lamb with baba ganoush and smashed chickpeas, and puddings such as rhubarb and apple jelly with stem ginger ice-cream and sponge pudding topped with home-made marmalade; they also offer a two- and three-course weekday lunch. *Benchmark main dish:*

home-reared roast rack of pork with crackling and apple sauce £14.50. Two-course evening meal £22.00.

Free house ~ Licensees Simon Page and Jason King ~ Real ale ~ (0118) 982 0110 ~ Open 9-3, 6.30 (6 Sat)-11; 9-4 Sun; closed Sun evening ~ Bar food 12-1.30 (4 Sun), 6.30-8.30 (9 Fri, Sat) ~ Children welcome ~ Dogs welcome ~ Wi-fi ~ Bedrooms: /£95 ~ www.thewellingtonarms.com *Recommended by Harvey Brown, Caroline Prescott, John Ames*

BEAULIEU SU3902 Map 2

Montagu Arms
Almost opposite Palace House; SO42 7ZL

Separate Monty's Bar, open all day for both drinks and food; in lovely village

Although Monty's Bar has its own entrance, atmosphere and customers, it is attached to the solidly built and civilised Montagu Arms hotel (do visit the delightful back garden, especially in warm weather). Customers pop in and out all day for drinks and meals in the simply furnished bar with its panelling and bare floorboards. Two red leather chesterfield sofas face each other in front of the log fire, one bow window is set with armchairs and a table, and another big window has a large circular table surrounded by homely red-cushioned dining chairs; one side of the room has a pool table, darts and TV. A few stools line the counter where they keep Ringwood Best and Fortyniner on handpump and several wines by the glass, served by cheerful, helpful bar staff. Across the entrance hall is a smarter panelled dining room. The picturesque village is much visited and at the heart of the New Forest.

Using free-range local produce, the highly thought-of food includes sandwiches, pork scotch egg (from their own hens) with spicy apple sauce, scallops with black pudding purée and wholegrain mustard sauce, a vegetarian risotto of the day, burger with stilton rarebit, bacon and french fries, sausages with onion gravy, a pie of the day, 12-hour braised lamb shank with rosemary roasted root vegetables and minted jus, and puddings. *Benchmark main dish: beer-battered haddock and chips £12.95. Two-course evening meal £21.50.*

Free house ~ Licensee Sunil Kanjanghat ~ Real ale ~ (01590) 612324 ~ Open 11-11 ~ Bar food 12-2.30 (3 weekends), 6.30-9.30 ~ Restaurant ~ Children welcome ~ Dogs allowed in bar ~ Wi-fi ~ Bedrooms: £121/£143 ~ www.montaguarmshotel.co.uk *Recommended by Isobel Mackinlay, Gavin and Helle May*

BENTWORTH SU6740 Map 2

Sun ◖
Sun Hill; from A339 from Alton, the first turning takes you there direct; or in village follow signpost 'Shalden 2¼, Alton 4¼'; GU34 5JT

Smashing choice of real ales and long-serving landlady in popular country pub; nearby walks

Tucked away down a hidden lane just out of the village, this is a 17th-c country tavern with a fine choice of real ales. Kept well on handpump and served by the long-standing landlady, these might include Andwell Resolute Bitter, Bowman Swift One, Dartmoor Jail Ale, Hogs Back TEA, Ringwood Best, Sharps Doom Bar and Timothy Taylors Landlord. There's an easy-going, chatty atmosphere. The two little traditional interlinked rooms have high-backed antique settles, pews and schoolroom chairs, olde-worlde prints and blacksmith's tools on the walls, and bare boards and scrubbed deal tables on the left; three big fireplaces with log fires make it especially snug in winter. An arch leads to a brick-floored room with another open fire. There are seats out in front and in the back garden; pleasant nearby walks.

🍴 Bar food includes sandwiches, field mushrooms topped with ham and stilton, warm chicken, bacon and avocado salad, beer-battered cod and chips, vegetarian curry, half shoulder of lamb with honey and mint gravy, calves liver and bacon, and puddings such as apple and raspberry crumble and sticky toffee pudding. *Benchmark main dish: steak in ale pie £13.95. Two-course evening meal £19.00.*

Free house ~ Licensee Mary Holmes ~ Real ale ~ (01420) 562338 ~ Open 12-3, 6-11; 12-10.30 Sun ~ Bar food 12-2, 7-9 ~ Children welcome ~ Dogs welcome ~ www.thesuninnbentworth.co.uk *Recommended by Isobel Mackinlay, Mike Swan*

BIGHTON
SU6134 Map 2
English Partridge 🍽️ ♀
Bighton Dean Lane; village signed off B3046 N of Alresford; SO24 9RE

Charming country pub with a genuine welcome, much character in three bars, plenty to look at, good wines and beers and highly enjoyable food

This charming little pub is tucked away in quiet countryside, but very well worthwhile seeking out – and you can be sure of a genuine welcome from the landlord and his young staff. The small room to the left of the door is just right for walkers and their dogs (a waterbowl is placed near the open fire), with just a few chairs and tables, and stools against the bar. The characterful main bar has a wonderful ancient parquet floor, a black dado with hunting prints, local shoot photographs and game bird pictures on the walls above, a stuffed pheasant in a glass cabinet, a woodburning stove in a brick inglenook and a fireplace filled with candles, and all sorts of dining chairs and tables. Flowerpots Goodens Gold, Itchen Valley Green Jackets and Triple fff Alton Pride on handpump, ten wines by the glass, eight gins, farm cider and Somerset cider brandy; darts, board games and maybe unobtrusive background music. Through an open doorway, the back dining room has long built-in wall seats with scatter cushions, similar chairs and tables (each set with a candle in a candlestick), a huge deer's head and a boar's head, antlers, shooting and hunting photographs and fish and bird prints. As we went to press, they were redoing the garden.

🌟 Extremely good food includes creamed mushrooms on toast with a poached egg, spiced chicken and bacon salad, steak pie, butternut squash risotto, pulled pork with pan haggerty, cabbage, bacon and meat juices, stuffed chicken leg with braised haricot beans, stone bass fillet with caper and jus vinaigrette, and puddings such as sticky toffee pudding and maraschino cherry jelly with rum and raisin ice-cream. *Benchmark main dish: beer-battered fish and chips £10.00. Two-course evening meal £19.50.*

Free house ~ Licensee Rupert Reeves ~ Real ale ~ (01962) 732859 ~ Open 12-3, 5-11; 12-11 Sat; 12-10.30 Sun; closed winter Sun evening ~ Bar food 12-2.30 (3 Sun), 6.30-9.30 (9 summer Sun) ~ Children welcome ~ Dogs welcome ~ Wi-fi ~ www.englishpartridge.co.uk *Recommended by Tony and Jill Radnor*

Please let us know what you think of a pub's bedrooms: feedback@goodguides.com or (no stamp needed) The Good Pub Guide, FREEPOST RTJR-ZCYZ-RJZT, Perrymans Lane, Etchingham TN19 7DN.

BOLDRE
Red Lion 🏮 🍺
SZ3198 Map 2

Off A337 N of Lymington; SO41 8NE

Friendly pub on the edge of the New Forest, lots of bygones in five beamed rooms, real ales and interesting food and seats outside

Even on a cold, wet Monday in November, this well run pub has a thriving atmosphere and plenty of customers, all welcomed by the friendly, efficient licensees. The five black-beamed rooms reveal an entertaining collection of bygones, with heavy-horse harness, gin traps, ferocious-looking man traps, copper and brass pans and rural landscapes, as well as a dainty collection of old bottles and glasses. Seating is on pews, sturdy cushioned dining chairs and tapestried stools. There's an old cooking range in the cosy little bar, and three good log fires. Brakspears Oxford Gold, Ringwood Best and Fortyniner and a guest such as Jennings Red Rascal on handpump and 17 wines by the glass. The pub is opposite the village green; in summer, there are seats outside among the flowering tubs and hanging baskets, with more tables in the back garden. A sunny self-catering apartment is for rent. Fine nearby walking.

 Interesting and popular food using local, seasonal produce includes lunchtime sandwiches, tea-smoked trout with potato salad, game terrine with gooseberry and ginger chutney, corned beef hash with bubble and squeak topped with an egg, free-range chicken with smoked cheese sauce and crispy bacon, honey-baked root vegetable pudding with creamy roasted shallot sauce, lamb shank with redcurrant, rosemary and honey, and puddings. *Benchmark main dish: duo of pork (slow-roast belly and fruit-stuffed loin wrapped in bacon) with red wine gravy £14.95. Two-course evening meal £18.50.*

Eldridge Pope ~ Lease Alan and Amanda Pountney ~ Real ale ~ (01590) 673177 ~ Open 11-3, 5.30-11; 11-11 Sat; 12-10.30 Sun ~ Bar food 12-2.30, 6-9.30; all day Sun ~ Restaurant ~ Children welcome away from bar ~ Dogs allowed in bar ~ Wi-fi ~ www.theredlionboldre.co.uk *Recommended by Brian Glozier, Mike Swan, Phil and Jane Villiers*

BRANSGORE
Three Tuns 🏮 🍺
SZ1997 Map 2

Village signposted off A35 and off B3347 N of Christchurch; Ringwood Road, opposite church; BH23 8JH

Pretty thatched pub with proper old-fashioned bar and good beers, a civilised main dining area and inventive food

This 17th-c pub is particularly pretty in summer with its neat thatch and lovely hanging baskets, and there are picnic-sets on the attractive, extensive, shrub-sheltered terrace and more tables on grass overlooking pony paddocks; pétanque. Inside, the roomy low-ceilinged and carpeted main area has a fireside 'codgers' corner', as well as a good mix of comfortably cushioned low chairs around a variety of dining tables. On the right is a separate traditional regulars' bar that seems almost taller than it is wide, with an impressive log-effect stove in a stripped-brick hearth, some shiny black panelling and individualistic pubby furnishings. Otter Bitter and Ringwood Best and Fortyniner, plus guests such as Sharps Doom Bar and Skinners Cornish Knocker, on handpump and nine wines by the glass. The Grade II listed barn is popular for parties.

 Imaginative food using local, seasonal produce includes sandwiches, moules marinière, oxtail and snail pie, pumpkin and chervil root risotto, venison casserole pasty, burger with cheese, bacon, pineapple, coleslaw and chips, corn-fed chicken with foie gras rissole, skate in nut brown butter, and puddings such as warm banana tart with chocolate ice-cream and coconut, mango and passion-fruit surprise. *Benchmark main dish: slow-roasted pork with dauphinoise potatoes £13.95. Two-course evening meal £20.50.*

Enterprise ~ Lease Nigel Glenister ~ Real ale ~ (01425) 672232 ~ Open 11-11; 12-10.30 Sun ~ Bar food 12-2.15, 6.30-9.15; all day weekends ~ Restaurant ~ Children welcome but not in lounge after 6pm ~ Dogs allowed in bar ~ Wi-fi ~ www.threetunsinn.com
Recommended by Patrick and Daphne Darley, Colin McKerrow, S Holder, Michael and Sheila Hawkins

CRAWLEY
Fox & Hounds

SU4234   Map 2

Village signed from A272 and B3420 NW of Winchester; SO21 2PR

Attractive building, three roaring winter log fires, several real ales and popular food; bedrooms

This is a solidly constructed mock-Tudor building where each timbered upper storey juts successively further out, with lots of pegged structural timbers in the neat brickwork and elaborately carved steep gable-ends. It's one of the most striking buildings in a village of fine old houses. The neatly linked rooms have brocaded and cushioned dining chairs, settles and wall seats around straightforward pubby tables on parquet flooring or carpet, horse-racing prints on the walls, old jugs, plates and bowls on window sills and three open fires. The traditional bar serves Sharps Doom Bar and Wychwood Hobgoblin plus guests such as Andwell King John and Flack Manor Double Drop on handpump, 16 wines by the glass and a farm cider. Seats outside on grass.

A wide range of popular food includes sandwiches, terrine of ham hock with beetroot jam, king prawn crostini with sesame and soy dressing, smoked haddock fishcakes with creamed leeks and grain mustard sauce, free-range chicken with wild mushroom and onion sauce, root vegetable crumble, slow-braised pork belly with celeriac mash and cider sauce, and puddings such as lemon posset with berry compote and chocolate marquis. *Benchmark main dish: slow-braised lamb shoulder with pesto mash and roasted mediterranean vegetables £15.95. Two-course evening meal £20.00.*

Enterprise ~ Lease Alex and Sally Wood ~ Real ale ~ (01962) 776006 ~ Open 12-3, 6-11; 12-12 (12-3, 6-11 in winter) Sat; 12-8 (6 in winter) Sun ~ Bar food 12-2.30, 6.30-9.30; 12-4 Sun ~ Restaurant ~ Children welcome ~ Dogs allowed in bar ~ Wi-fi ~ Live music last Fri of month ~ Bedrooms: /£79 ~ www.foxandhoundscrawley.co.uk
Recommended by David and Ruth Hollands, R T and J C Moggridge, Phil Bryant, Laurie and Fiona Scott

DROXFORD
Bakers Arms 🏅 🍺

SU6018   Map 2

High Street; A32 5 miles N of Wickham; SO32 3PA

Attractively opened-up and friendly pub with well kept beers, good, interesting cooking and cosy corners

Many customers are here to enjoy the enticing food, of course, but this bustling pub is also popular with those wanting a pint and a chat or a morning coffee with the daily papers. This combined with a warm welcome from the hands-on licensees keeps everything easy-going and friendly. It's attractively laid-out with the central bar as the main focus: Bowman Swift

One and Wallops Wood on handpump, Thatcher's Original cider and a short careful choice of wines by the glass. Well spaced tables on carpet or neat bare boards are spread around the airy L-shaped open-plan bar, with low leather chesterfields and an assortment of comfortably cushioned chairs at one end; a dark panelled dado, dark beams and joists and a modicum of country oddments emphasise the freshness of the crisp white paintwork; good log fire and board games. To one side, with a separate entrance, is the village post office. There are picnic-sets outside.

As well as a two-course menu plus a drink (Mon-Fri lunch, Mon-Thurs evening), the rewarding dishes include snails with bacon and garlic butter, smoked salmon pâté, jerusalem artichoke, sweet potato, mushroom and blue cheese gratin, beef and pork faggots with mash and gravy, chicken with bourguignon sauce and dauphinoise potatoes, wild bass fillet with lemon risotto, and puddings such as crème brûlée and lemon cheesecake with blackcurrant sorbet. *Benchmark main dish: slow-roast lamb shoulder with rösti potatoes £14.95. Two-course evening meal £21.00.*

Free house ~ Licensees Adam and Anna Cordery ~ Real ale ~ (01489) 877533 ~ Open 12-3, 6-11; 12-4 Sun; closed Sun evening ~ Bar food 12-2, 7-9; 12-3 Sun ~ Well behaved children welcome ~ Dogs allowed in bar ~ Wi-fi ~ www.thebakersarmsdroxford.com
Recommended by Henry Fryer, Stephen and Jean Curtis

EAST END   SZ3696   Map 2
East End Arms 🛏
Back road Lymington–Beaulieu, parallel to B3054; SO41 5SY

Determinedly unfussy bar, attractive dining room, a cheerful atmosphere and good food and drink; bedrooms

When John Illsley, former bass guitarist of Dire Straits, bought this unpretentious pub, locals begged him not to change anything. He agreed – and has been true to his word. The bar is as simple as they come, with a brown leather sofa at one end, a settle at the other, kitchen chairs and stools around straightforward pubby tables and a couple of large handsaws pinned to the ceiling; the locals' noticeboard looks well used. Plenty of chatty and friendly regulars greet you as you come in, and the bar staff are helpful; Ringwood Best or Fortyniner on handpump and several wines by the glass. The half-panelled dining room to the left has various cushioned chairs around tables on bare boards, interesting rock and film star photographs on pale walls, and a couple of leather sofas beside a roaring log fire. The terraced garden has picnic-sets, with more out in front. The cottagey bedrooms are pretty.

Using local, seasonal produce the enjoyable food includes lunchtime sandwiches, soft duck egg with serrano ham, asparagus and slow-roast tomatoes, local crab cakes with chilled gazpacho, beer-battered haddock and chips, honey-glazed pork belly with home-made spring rolls, venison loin with beetroot purée and parsnip mash, cod wrapped in pancetta with herby risotto, and puddings. *Benchmark main dish: calves liver with mustard mash, bacon, crispy onion rings and jus £14.95. Two-course evening meal £21.75.*

Free house ~ Licensee John Illsley ~ Real ale ~ (01590) 626223 ~ Open 11.30-11; 12-10 Sun; 11.30-3, 6-11 in winter ~ Bar food 12-2.30, 7-9.30; not Sun evenings ~ Restaurant ~ Children welcome ~ Dogs allowed in bar ~ Wi-fi ~ Bedrooms: £71/£98.50 ~ www.eastendarms.co.uk *Recommended by Emma Scofield, Mike Swan*

If you know a pub is ever open all day, please tell us.

EAST STRATTON
SU5339   Map 2
Northbrook Arms ◖
Brown sign to pub off A33 4 miles S of A303 junction; SO21 3DU

**Attractive brick pub with character bars, lots to look at, six real ales
and highly rated food; bedrooms**

'A five star experience' is how one reader describes this welcoming pub
and the clean, comfortable and quiet bedrooms; breakfasts are good
too. Other readers are equally full of praise, all mentioning the polite,
hard-working staff, interesting ales and enjoyable food. There's a relaxed
traditional tiled-floor bar on the right, with Alfreds Saxon Bronze, Bowman
Swift One, Flack Manor Double Drop, Sharps Cornish Coaster, Three
Daggers Blonde and Wild Weather Big Muddy on handpump and 13 wines
by the glass; also, a mix of pubby chairs around sturdy stripped-top tables,
a big collection of horsebrasses and tack on beams and standing timbers
and shelves of books; background music. On the left. it's carpeted, and
progressively rather more formal, ending in a proper dining room beyond
a little central hall. There are picnic-sets on the green across the quiet
village road, with more in the pretty side garden; the former stables houses
a skittle alley; fine nearby walks.

Creative food includes smoked salmon terrine, crab, cheddar and chive omelette,
wild mushroom and thyme millefeuille with white truffle oil, and chicken with
pomme purée and madeira jus. They also offer pub classics such as interesting
sandwiches, beer-battered fish and chips, cajun chicken fajitas, gammon and egg
with spiced pineapple pickle, and puddings such as apple and blackberry crumble
and banoffi tart. *Benchmark main dish: pie of the day £12.95. Two-course evening
meal £18.00.*

Free house ~ Licensees Jon Coward and Millie Spurr ~ Real ale ~ (01962) 774150
~ Open 11-11 (10.30 Sun) ~ Bar food 12-9.30 ~ Restaurant ~ Children welcome ~
Dogs welcome ~ Wi-fi ~ Poker Weds evening, live music monthly, wine club monthly ~
Bedrooms: £70/£80 ~ www.thenorthbrookarms.com *Recommended by Sara Fulton,
Roger Baker, Tony Fabian, Ann and Colin Hunt*

EASTON
SU5132   Map 2
Chestnut Horse ★◖ ♟
*3.6 miles from M3 junction 9: A33 towards Kings Worthy, then B3047
towards Itchen Abbas; Easton then signposted on right – bear left in village; SO21 1EG*

**Cosy dining pub with log fires, fresh flowers and candles, deservedly
popular food and friendly staff**

The hub of this pretty village of thatched cottages, this is a smart 16th-c
dining pub run by a friendly, hands-on landlady. The interior, although
open-plan, has a pleasantly rustic and intimate feel with a series of cosily
separate areas; the snug décor takes in candles and fresh flowers on the
tables, log fires in cottagey fireplaces and comfortable furnishings. The
black beams and joists are hung with all sorts of jugs, mugs and chamber-
pots, and there are lots of attractive pictures of wildlife and the local area.
Badger First Gold and a guest beer on handpump, a dozen wines by the
glass and 20 malt whiskies; staff are helpful and efficient. There are seats
and tables out on a smallish sheltered decked area with colourful flower
tubs and baskets, and picnic-sets in front. Walks in the nearby Itchen Valley.

Very good food includes sandwiches, potted rabbit with fruit chutney, smoked
trout with pink grapefruit and mango purée, spring onion, butternut and

roasted pepper gnocchi with tarragon cream, casserole of chicken, chorizo and cannellini beans, swordfish with chimichurri sauce, venison lasagne, and puddings such as vanilla crème brûlée and chocolate bread and butter pudding; they also have a two-course set menu (Mon-Sat lunch, Mon-Fri 6-7pm). *Benchmark main dish: beer-battered fish and chips £12.00. Two-course evening meal £21.50.*

Badger ~ Tenant Karen Wells ~ Real ale ~ (01962) 779257 ~ Open 12-4, 5.30-11; 12-11 Fri-Sun ~ Bar food 12-2.30, 6-9.30; 12-8 Sun ~ Restaurant ~ Children welcome ~ Dogs allowed in bar ~ Wi-fi ~ www.thechestnuthorse.com *Recommended by Helen and Brian Edgeley, Michael Butler, Ann and Colin Hunt, Mrs P Sumner, Richard Tilbrook*

FRITHAM
Royal Oak 🍺
SU2314   Map 2

Village signed from M27 junction 1; SO43 7HJ

Rural New Forest spot and part of a working farm; traditional rooms, log fires, seven real ales and simple lunchtime food

A favourite with so many of our readers, this brick and cob thatched pub remains as charming, unspoilt and welcoming as ever. Even when it's packed out with chatty locals, walkers, cyclists and families with dogs and children, the staff remain efficient and genuinely friendly. Three neatly kept black beamed rooms are straightforward but full of proper traditional character, with prints and pictures involving local characters on the white walls, restored panelling, antique wheelback, spindleback and other old chairs and stools with colourful seats around solid tables, oak floors and two roaring log fires. The back bar has quite a few books; darts and board games. Up to seven real ales are tapped from the cask, including one named for the pub (from Bowman), Cottage Dragon Slayer, Flack Manor Double Drop, Milk Street Funky Monkey, Ringwood Best, Sunny Republic Beach Blonde and Weltons Topper Mild. Also, ten wines by the glass (mulled wine in winter), 14 country wines, local apple juice and a September beer festival. Summer barbecues may be held in the neatly kept big garden, which has a marquee for poor weather and a pétanque pitch. They're planning to have three shepherd's huts for overnight stays. This is a lovely spot right in the middle of the New Forest and part of a working farm, so there are ponies and pigs out on the green and plenty of livestock nearby.

🍴 Good value, limited food – lunchtime only – consists of wholesome soup, a particularly good pork pie, ploughman's, quiche and sausages. *Benchmark main dish: cheese ploughman's £8.50.*

Free house ~ Licensees Neil and Pauline McCulloch ~ Real ale ~ No credit cards ~ (023) 8081 2606 ~ Open 11-11; 12-10.30 Sun; 11-3, 5.30-11 weekdays in winter ~ Bar food 12-2.30 (3 weekends) ~ Children welcome ~ Dogs welcome *Recommended by Nick Lawless, N R White, Ann and Colin Hunt*

HOOK
Hogget 🍺
SU7153   Map 2

1.1 miles from M3 junction 5; A287 N, at junction with A30 (car park just before traffic lights); RG27 9JJ

Well run and accommodating, a proper pub moving with the times and giving good value

This well run pub has a comfortable, welcoming atmosphere and plenty of cheerful customers, both locals and visitors. The rooms ramble all the way round the central server so there's plenty of room for all, and the lighting, wallpaper and carpet pattern, plus the leather sofas and tub chairs over on the right at the back, give an easy-going and homely feel – as does the way the layout provides several smallish distinct areas. Marstons Pedigree, Ringwood Best and Wychwood Hobgoblin on handpump, ten wines by the glass, nine different gins and plenty of staff in neat but informal black uniforms; daily papers, background music and wine bottles on shelves. A sizeable terrace has sturdy tables and chairs, including some in a heated covered area.

As well as nibbles such as toasted nuts and scratchings, the enjoyable food includes lunchtime rolls and sandwiches (not Sunday), piri-piri king prawns, creamy stilton mushrooms, chicken and bacon caesar salad, ham and free-range eggs, pork and sage meatballs with tomato sauce and linguine, sausages of the day with spring onion mash and red wine and onion gravy, pork belly on root vegetable mash with wild mushrooms and crackling, and puddings. *Benchmark main dish: steak, chicken and pulled pork burgers with interesting toppings and triple-cooked chips £12.00. Two-course evening meal £18.00.*

Marstons ~ Lease Tom and Laura Faulkner ~ Real ale ~ (01256) 763009 ~ Open 12-3, 5.30-11; 12-11 Sat; 12-10.30 Sun ~ Bar food 12-2.30, 6.30-9; all day Sat; 12-6 Sun ~ Restaurant ~ Children welcome but not after 7pm Fri and Sat evenings ~ Dogs allowed in bar ~ Wi-fi ~ www.thehogget.co.uk *Recommended by Jeremy King, Simon Collett-Jones*

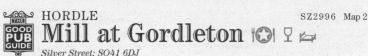

HORDLE   SZ2996   Map 2
Mill at Gordleton 🏵 ♀ ⇔
Silver Street; SO41 6DJ

Charming tucked-away country inn with friendly bar, exceptional food and drink and delightful waterside gardens; comfortable bedrooms

This is a special place: it's civilised without being stuffy and, although it's a small, private hotel (carefully run by green-minded owners), it has a little panelled bar with real ales that's popular with locals (and their dogs). This bar, on the right, has leather armchairs and Victorian-style mahogany dining chairs on parquet flooring, a feature stove, a pretty corner china cupboard, Ringwood Best and a guest such as Sharps Doom Bar on handpump, 18 good wines by the glass, 22 malt whiskies and a rack of daily papers. It overflows into a cosy lounge, and there's also a roomy second bar by the sizeable beamed restaurant extension, which is an attractive room with contemporary art and garden outlook. The bedrooms are comfortable and individual, with excellent breakfasts. The gardens are very special, featuring an extensive series of interestingly planted areas looping about pools and a placid winding stream, dotted with intriguing art objects and with plenty of places to sit, from intimate pairs of seats to teak or wrought-iron tables on the main waterside terrace (which is beautifully lit up at night). The inn is on the edge of the New Forest, with plenty of walks nearby.

Growing their own vegetables, keeping bees, using the best local producers and making absolutely everything in-house, the accomplished food includes sandwiches, twice-baked smoked haddock soufflé, scallops with cauliflower purée and redcurrant and port reduction, burger with cheddar, bacon, onion rings and hand-cut chips, crab platter, breast and confit duck with bubble and squeak, braised fennel and orange jus, and puddings such as baked alaska and Grand Marnier and dark chocolate mousse with crystallised orange; they also offer two- and three-course set menus. *Benchmark main dish: fish pie with organic salmon, smoked haddock and cod in light curry cream with a free-range egg £14.95. Two-course evening meal £23.00.*

Free house ~ Licensee Liz Cottingham ~ Real ale ~ (01590) 682219 ~ Open 11-11
(11.30 Sat); 12-10.30 Sun ~ Bar food 12-2, 7-9; 12-3, 6.15-8.15 Sun ~ Restaurant ~
Children welcome ~ Dogs allowed in bar ~ Wi-fi ~ Bedrooms: £135/£150 ~
www.themillatgordleton.co.uk *Recommended by Leslie and Barbara Owen, N R White*

LISS   SU7826 Map 2
Jolly Drover

London Road, Hill Brow; B2070 S of town, near B3006 junction; GU33 7QL

**Friendly, comfortable pub with plenty of locals and visitors, real ales,
popular food and seats outside; good bedrooms**

The long-serving, enthusiastic licensees work hard to retain traditional
values and create a sense of cheerful enjoyment in their deservedly
busy pub. The neatly carpeted low-beamed bar has leather tub chairs and
a couple of chesterfield sofas in front of the inglenook log fire, daily papers,
board games and Fullers London Pride, Sharps Doom Bar and Timothy
Taylors Landlord on handpump and ten wines by the glass. The several
areas, with understated décor mainly in muted terracotta or pale ochre,
include two back dining sections, one of which opens on to a sheltered
terrace with teak furniture, and a lawn with picnic-sets beyond. The neat
bedrooms are in two barn conversions.

 Good, honest food includes baps and sandwiches, prawn cocktail, garlic
mushrooms, vegetable or meat lasagne, steak and kidney in ale pie, gammon and
free-range eggs, tempura-battered hake and chips, mixed grill, and puddings such as
treacle tart or fruit crumble. *Benchmark main dish: chicken with bacon and stilton
£14.00. Two-course evening meal £18.75.*

Enterprise ~ Lease Barry and Anne Coe ~ Real ale ~ (01730) 893137 ~ Open 10.30-3,
5.30-11; 12-4 Sun; closed Sun evening ~ Bar food 12-2.15, 7-9.30; 12-2.30 Sun ~
Restaurant ~ Children welcome ~ Wi-fi ~ Bedrooms: £70/£90 ~ www.thejollydrover.co.uk
Recommended by Tony and Wendy Hobden

LITTLETON   SU4532 Map 2
Running Horse

Main Road; village signed off B3049 NW of Winchester; SO22 6QS

**Carefully renovated country pub with spreading dining areas,
woodburning stove in bar, enjoyable food and cabana in garden;
pretty bedrooms**

In a country village not far from Winchester, this attractive pub has been
completely refurbished recently. The attractive spreading dining areas
have big flagstones or bare floorboards, a much prized cushioned seat in
a bow window plus wooden armchairs around a table, some wall panelling
beside button-backed banquettes in an alcove, and an appealing variety
of dining chairs around tables (some with barley-twist legs) and polo
photographs on red walls. There are unusual wine-bottle ceiling lights,
old books on rustic bookshelves, antlers and big mirrors and a relaxed,
friendly, chatty atmosphere. A brick fireplace holds a woodburning stove
and leather-topped stools line the counter where they serve Upham Tipster,
Punter and Stakes on handpump, 14 wines by the glass and a farm cider.
The front and back terraces have green metal tables and chairs, and there
are picnic-sets on the back grass by a spreading sycamore and a popular
cabana with cushioned seats. The simply decorated bedrooms are pretty.
This is sister pub to the Thomas Lord in West Meon.

As well as breakfasts for non-residents and sandwiches, food includes duck liver parfait with ale chutney, tomato and goats cheese tart, honey-roasted ham and eggs, smoked chicken caesar salad, chicken tikka masala, beer-battered fish and chips, a pie, pasta dish and fish choice of the day, and puddings such as knickerbocker glory and dark and white chocolate brownie with chocolate sauce. *Benchmark main dish: slow-cooked pork belly with apple purée £13.95. Two-course evening meal £18.00.*

Free house ~ Licensee Becky Anderson ~ Real ale ~ (01962) 880218 ~ Open 11-11 (10.30 Sun) ~ Bar food 12-2.30, 6.30-9.30; 12-3.30, 6.30-9 Sun ~ Restaurant ~ Children welcome ~ Dogs allowed in bar ~ Wi-fi ~ Bedrooms: /£105 ~ www.runninghorseinn.co.uk
Recommended by Isobel Mackinlay, Mike Swan

 LONGSTOCK   SU3537 Map 2
Peat Spade 🌟 ♀
Off A30 on W edge of Stockbridge; SO20 6DR

Former coaching inn with boldly painted rooms, shooting and fishing themed décor, imaginative food and real ales; stylish bedrooms

In a pretty village and right by the River Test, this is a well run pub where locals, diners and residents all mix easily together. The wide mix of customers helps create a cheerful, bustling atmosphere and the hard-working landlady and her diligent young staff offer a warm welcome to all. The bars have a sporting feel, with stuffed fish, lots of hunting pictures and prints on dark red or green walls and even a little fishing shop at the end of the garden (they can arrange fishing and shooting). Both the bar and dining room have pretty windows, an interesting mix of dining chairs around miscellaneous tables on bare boards, standard lamps and candlelight, wine bottles, old stone bottles and soda siphons, a nice display of toby jugs and shelves of books. There's also an upstairs room with comfortable sofas and armchairs. Flack Manor Flack Catcher and Flowerpots Bitter and Goodens Gold on handpump, 11 wines by the glass and 20 malt whiskies; background music. The terrace and garden have plenty of seats for warm weather, and the contemporary bedrooms are stylish and comfortable. The River Test (famous for its fly fishing) is just 100 metres away, and the Test Way footpath is close by.

Highly enjoyable food includes lunchtime sandwiches, nibbles (such as angels and devils on horseback), gin-cured salmon and crispy poached egg, crab with chilli, lime and avocado, butternut squash and sage ravioli, chicken kiev with baked lemon dressing, jacob's ladder beef with garlic and parsley, lemon sole with golden raisins and mixed herb butter, and puddings such as blood orange panna cotta with rhubarb jelly and chocolate and peanut butter tart. *Benchmark main dish: beer-battered haddock and triple-cooked chips £13.00. Two-course evening meal £22.00.*

Free house ~ Licensee Rupert Reeves ~ Real ale ~ (01264) 810612 ~ Open 11-11 ~ Bar food 12-2.30, 6-9.30; 12-4, 7-9 Sun ~ Well behaved children welcome ~ Dogs allowed in bar and bedrooms ~ Wi-fi ~ Bedrooms: /£130 ~ www.peatspadeinn.co.uk
Recommended by Mike Swan, Isobel Mackinlay

 LOWER FROYLE   SU7643 Map 2
Anchor 🌟 ♀ 🛏
Village signposted N of A31 W of Bentley; GU34 4NA

Civilised pub, lots to look at, real ales, good wines and imaginative bar food; comfortable bedrooms

One reader describes this fine old place as 'exemplary in every respect' – and we know just what he means. It's civilised yet informal and friendly, and the various rooms have a good, bustling atmosphere, blazing fires, candlelight, low beams and standing timbers, flagstones in the bar and wood stripped floors elsewhere, sofas and armchairs dotted here and there, and a mix of attractive tables and dining chairs. Throughout are all sorts of interesting knick-knacks, books, lots of copper, horsebrasses, photographs (several of Charterhouse school) and all manner of pictures and prints; the paint colours are fashionable, values traditional. At the counter, where there are high bar chairs, they keep Andwell King John, Flowerport Goodens Gold and Triple fff Altons Pride on handpump, nine wines by the glass (including sparkling wine) and interesting pressés. This is a comfortable and stylish place to stay and the breakfasts are first class too.

Excellent food includes sandwiches, jellied ham hock with piccalilli, treacle-cured salmon and pancetta with a poached egg and honey and mustard dressing, pea and broad bean risotto, lamb and rosemary pie, cod, cockles, clams and samphire with chive butter, seared liver and bacon with red onion marmalade and gravy, and puddings such as sticky date pudding with toffee sauce and strawberry parfait with meringue pieces and strawberry daiquiri sorbet. *Benchmark main dish: local pork four-ways £18.00. Two-course evening meal £21.50.*

Free house ~ Licensee Tracy Levett ~ Real ale ~ (01420) 23261 ~ Open 11-11 (10.30 Sun) ~ Bar food 12-2.30, 6.30-9.30; 12-4, 7-9 Sun ~ Restaurant ~ Children welcome ~ Dogs allowed in bar and bedrooms ~ Wi-fi ~ Bedrooms: /£120 ~ www.anchorinnatlowerfroyle.co.uk *Recommended by Tony and Jill Radnor, John Branston, Dr and Mrs P Truelove*

LOWER WIELD

Yew Tree ⭐ ♀ £

SU6339 Map 2

Turn off A339 NW of Alton at signpost 'Medstead, Bentworth 1', then follow village signposts; or off B3046 S of Basingstoke, signposted from Preston Candover; SO24 9RX

Bustling country pub with an enthusiastic landlord, relaxed atmosphere and super choice of wines and food; sizeable garden and nearby walks

As ever, our readers love this particularly well run pub. Much of this comes down to the genuinely warm welcome from the hard-working, hands-on landlord and his helpful staff, though fair prices for the popular food and drink and the easy-going atmosphere contribute greatly too. A small flagstoned bar area on the left has pictures above a stripped-brick dado, a ticking clock and a log fire. There's carpet round to the right of the serving counter (with a couple of stylish wrought-iron bar chairs); throughout there's a mix of tables, including quite small ones for two, and miscellaneous chairs. Drinks – including 13 wines by the glass from a well chosen list (with summer rosé and Louis Jadot burgundies), and Bowman Yumi, Flowerpots Perridge Pale and a beer from Triple fff named for the pub on handpump – are extremely reasonably priced for the area. There are solid tables and chunky seats out on the front terrace, picnic-sets in a sizeable side garden, pleasant views and a cricket field across the quiet lane; nearby walks.

Very reasonably priced and highly thought of, the good food includes sandwiches, mango and brie parcels on salad, smoked mackerel pâté with lime mayonnaise, chicken or beef burger with toppings and chips, field mushrooms topped with mediterranean vegetable provençale, chicken breast wrapped in parma ham with a sun-dried tomato and red pesto cream, confit duck leg with poached pear and mulled wine jus, and puddings such as gooseberry, apple and berry crumble and chocolate and raisin biscuit cake. *Benchmark main dish: cheesy ham hock, leek and pea pie £9.95. Two-course evening meal £16.95.*

Free house ~ Licensee Tim Gray ~ Real ale ~ (01256) 389224 ~ Open 11-3, 6-11; 12-10.30 Sun; closed Mon, and first two weeks Jan ~ Bar food 12-2, 6.30-9 ~ Restaurant ~ Children welcome ~ Dogs allowed in bar ~ Wi-fi ~ www.the-yewtree.org.uk
Recommended by Tony and Jill Radnor, R Elliott, Teddy O'Connor, Nick Duncan, Andrew Baker, Ann and Colin Hunt, N R White, Martin and Karen Wake

LYMINGTON
Angel & Blue Pig 🛏

SZ3295 Map 2

High Street; SO41 9AP

Bustling and friendly inn with plenty of space in several connected rooms, four real ales, enjoyable food and helpful staff; bedrooms

On the bustling High Street, this busy place has several different seating areas radiating from the central bar – each with its own character. To the right of the door, the cosy front room has comfortable sofas and armchairs around a big chest, rugs on bare boards and an open fire; this leads into a pubby, flagstoned area with high tables and chairs and built-in leather wall seats. The two interconnected dining rooms to the left of the entrance – one carpeted, one with rugs on quarry tiles – have beams and timbers, dining chairs with zigzag backs and grey cushions around a variety of tables, an old range in a brick fireplace, a large boar's head, lots of books on shelves and a bookshelf mural; throughout are numerous hunting prints and porcine bits and pieces. At the back, overlooking the terrace where there are seats and tables under blue parasols, is yet another area with some nice old leather armchairs beside a woodburning stove, and the serving counter where they keep Ringwood Best, a beer named for the pub from Ringwood, and a guest such as Itchen Valley Belgarum on handpump, 16 wines by the glass and a choice of coffees; service is friendly and helpful. The stylish, modern bedrooms are comfortable and well equipped, and breakfasts are good.

Good, enjoyable food includes sandwiches and ciabattas, charcoal-grilled duck skewers with asian salad and sticky plum dressing, crispy crab balls with spicy guacamole, sharing plates, thick-cut ham with free-range eggs, corn-fed, free-range roasted chicken with honey and mustard glaze or piri-piri with chips and paprika slaw, 28-day matured steaks, and puddings such as apple and butterscotch crumble and chocolate brownie with vanilla ice-cream. *Benchmark main dish: roast lamb rump with watercress purée and gratin potatoes £15.95. Two-course evening meal £20.00.*

Free house ~ Licensee Andrew Taylor ~ Real ale ~ (01590) 672050 ~ Open 8.30am-11.30pm (midnight Fri, Sat; 11 Sun) ~ Bar food 8.30am-9.30pm ~ Restaurant ~ Children welcome ~ Dogs allowed in bar ~ Wi-fi ~ Acoustic guitar and singers Fri, jazz Sat evening or Sun lunchtime ~ Bedrooms: £59/£79 ~ www.angel-lymington.com
Recommended by Ruth May, Harvey Brown, J A Goulding, Phil and Jane Villiers

NORTH WALTHAM
Fox 🍴 £

SU5645 Map 2

3 miles from M3 junction 7: A30 southwards, then turn right at second North Waltham turn, just after Wheatsheaf; pub also signed from village centre; RG25 2BE

Traditional flint country pub, very well run, with tasty food and drink and a nice garden

Relaxed and chatty with a good mix of both diners and drinkers, this is a bustling country pub that's also handy for the M3 and A30. The low-ceilinged bar on the left has Brakspears Bitter, Sharps Doom Bar, West Berkshire Good Old Boy and a guest beer such as Exmoor Fox on handpump, lots of bottled ciders plus Aspall's cider on draught, 13 wines by the glass, 22 malt whiskies and quite a collection of miniatures. The big woodburning stove, parquet floor, simple padded country kitchen chairs and 'Beer is Best' and poultry prints above the dark dado – all give a comfortably old-fashioned feel, in which perhaps the vital ingredient is the polite and friendly efficiency of the hands-on landlord; background music, TV. The separate dining room, with high-backed leather chairs on blue tartan carpet, is larger. The garden, colourful in summer with its pergola walkway up from the gate on the lane, and with immaculate flower boxes and baskets, has picnic-sets under cocktail parasols in three separate areas. Walks include a pleasant one to Jane Austen's church at Steventon.

Quite a choice of food includes sandwiches, cheese soufflé, whitebait with aioli, ham and egg, local bangers and mash with onion gravy, provençale vegetable and goats cheese tart, chicken schnitzel with cheese and tomato sauce, and puddings such as pineapple alaska and bread and butter pudding; Monday is curry night, Tuesday is pie evening and Thursday is steak night. *Benchmark main dish: venison haunch with port glaze £16.00. Two-course evening meal £20.75.*

Free house ~ Licensees Rob and Izzy MacKenzie ~ Real ale ~ (01256) 397288 ~ Open 11-11 (midnight Sat, 10.30 Sun) ~ Bar food 12-2.30, 6.30-9; 12-3, 6.30-8.30 Sun ~ Restaurant ~ Children welcome ~ Dogs allowed in bar ~ Wi-fi ~ www.thefox.org
Recommended by Jennifer Banks, Phyl and Jack Street, David Jackman, Jill Hurley

NORTH WARNBOROUGH   SU7352 Map 2
Mill House ⭐ ♀ ◀

A mile from M3 junction 5: A287 towards Farnham, then right (brown sign to pub) on to B3349 Hook Road; RG29 1ET

Converted mill with an attractive layout, inventive modern food, good choice of drinks and lovely waterside terraces

This is a prime example of just how a big, bustling pub should be run. The staff are friendly, efficient and courteous, there's lots to look at, the food and drink are tempting and very good, and the grounds are lovely. Several linked areas on the main upper floor have heavy beams, plenty of well spaced tables in a variety of sizes and styles, rugs on polished boards or beige carpet, coal-effect gas fires in pretty fireplaces, and a profusion of (often interesting) pictures. A section of floor is glazed to show the rushing water and mill wheel below, and a galleried section on the left looks down into a dining room, given a more formal feel by panelling. The well stocked bar has an interesting range of 85 malt whiskies, 14 wines by the glass and a farm cider, as well as Phoenix Brunning & Price Original, Andwell Gold Muddler, Itchen Valley Hampshire Rose, Otter Bitter, Three Castles Saxon Archer, Vale Best Bitter and West Berkshire Swift Pale Ale on handpump. The extensive garden behind the raftered mill building has lots of solid tables and chairs on terraces, even more picnic-sets on grass and attractive landscaping around the sizeable millpond; there's a couple of swings too.

Rewarding food includes sandwiches, smoked haddock arancini with quails egg, char siu pork with pickled ginger, pak choi and radish salad, stilton, wild mushroom and tomato quiche, cumberland sausages with red wine and onion gravy, rosemary and garlic chicken with wild mushrooms, bacon and spinach on pasta, bass fillets with caponata potatoes and tomato pesto, and puddings such as crème brûlée and chocolate brownie. *Benchmark main dish: beer-battered haddock with chips £12.25. Two-course evening meal £17.50.*

Brunning & Price ~ Lease Ian James ~ Real ale ~ (01256) 702953 ~ Open 11.30-11 (10.30 Sun) ~ Bar food 12-10 (9.30 Sun) ~ Restaurant ~ Children welcome ~ Dogs allowed in bar ~ Wi-fi ~ www.millhouse-hook.co.uk *Recommended by Edward Mirzoeff, Ian Herdman, Brian Glozier, M G Hart, B and M Kendall*

PETERSFIELD
SU7423 Map 2

Old Drum

Chapel Street; GU32 3DP

Restored 16th-c inn with friendly staff and atmosphere in bars and dining room, interesting ales and food, and seats in back garden; bedrooms

Carefully and thoughtfully refurbished, this 16th-c town-centre pub offers enjoyable modern food, five local ales and a friendly, easy-going atmosphere. The airy L-shaped bar has all manner of antique dining chairs and tables on bare boards, with a comfortable chesterfield and armchair on a big rug by an open fire (there are three fires in all) and stools against the counter, where they keep Bowman Wallops Wood, Dark Star American Pale Ale, Festival and Hophead, and Suthwyk Liberation on handpump, 16 wines by the glass, ten malt whiskies and farm cider and perry; background jazz and board games. A cosy beamed dining room leads off, with more interesting old cushioned chairs and tables on rug or bare boards, and throughout there are prints and mirrors on pale paintwork or exposed bricks, modern lighting and fresh flowers. The terraced garden has wooden chairs and tables under a gazebo, raised flower beds, firepits and parasols. The two bedrooms are well equipped and comfortable, and the breakfasts good.

 Inventive modern cooking using local, seasonal produce includes lunchtime sandwiches, duck liver parfait with cherry and almond, mackerel fillet with satay sauce, pumpkin, beetroot and pearl barley couscous with goats cheese fritter, smoked haddock fishcake with cider beurre blanc and beef dripping chips, rack of lamb with shoulder ragoût, and puddings such as ginger cake and salted caramel ice-cream affogato and spiced orange baked alaska. *Benchmark main dish: twice-cooked jacob's ladder beef, crispy oxtail, salt-baked carrot and crème fraîche mash £13.95. Two-course evening meal £20.00.*

Free house ~ Licensee Simon Hawkins ~ Real ale ~ (01730) 300544 ~ Open 10-3, 5-11; 10-11 Sat; 12-5 Sun; closed Sun evening ~ Bar food 12-2 (2.30 Sat), 6-9.30; 12-3 Sun ~ Restaurant ~ Children welcome before 9pm but not in evening bar ~ Dogs allowed in bar ~ Wi-fi ~ Bedrooms: £70/£80 ~ www.theolddrum.co.uk *Recommended by Chris Nickson, Val and Alan Green*

PETERSFIELD
SU7227 Map 2

Trooper

From A32 (look for staggered crossroads) take turning to Froxfield and Steep; pub 3 miles down on left in big dip; GU32 1BD

Courteous landlord, popular food, decent drinks, and little persian knick-knacks and local artists' work; comfortable bedrooms

A well run all-rounder and a charming landlord keep our readers coming back here on a regular basis. The bar has all sorts of cushioned dining chairs around dark wooden tables, old film star photos, paintings by local artists (for sale), little persian knick-knacks here and there, several ogival mirrors, lit candles, fresh flowers and a log fire in a stone fireplace; there's also a sun room with lovely downland views, carefully chosen background music, board games, newspapers and magazines. Ringwood Best and Triple fff Altons Pride and Moondance on handpump and several wines by the glass. The attractive raftered restaurant has french windows to a paved terrace with views across the open countryside, and there are lots of picnic-sets on an upper lawn. The horse rail in the car park is reserved 'for horses, camels and local livestock'. This is a comfortable place to stay, with neatly kept bedrooms and good breakfasts. The inn backs on to Ashford Hangers nature reserve.

Good food includes sandwiches, free-range chicken livers with brandy sauce, smoked salmon pâté, home-cooked ham and free-range eggs, mushroom, spinach and chesnut filo tart, steak and kidney pudding, spicy cod, tomato and green olive tagine with herby couscous, beef wellington with wholegrain mustard sauce, and puddings. *Benchmark main dish: slow-roasted lamb shoulder with honey and mint gravy £17.00. Two-course evening meal £21.75.*

Free house ~ Licensee Hassan Matini ~ Real ale ~ (01730) 827293 ~ Open 12-3, 6-11; 12-4 Sun; closed Sun and Mon evenings ~ Bar food 12-3, 6-9.30; 12-3.30 Sun; not Mon ~ Restaurant ~ Children welcome ~ Dogs allowed in bar ~ Wi-fi ~ Bedrooms: £69/£89 ~ www.trooperinn.com *Recommended by Mike Swan, Mike and Mary Carter, Katharine Cowherd*

PETERSFIELD
White Horse

SU7129 Map 2

Up on an old downs road about halfway between Steep and East Tisted, near Priors Dean – OS Sheet 186 or 197 map reference 715290; GU32 1DA

Much-loved old place with a great deal of simple character, friendly licensees and up to ten real ales

As ever, nothing really changes at this unspoilt old pub, which is just how its loyal customers would have it. The two parlour rooms remain charming and idiosyncratic: open fires, oak settles and a mix of dark wooden dining chairs, nice old tables (including some drop-leaf ones), various pictures, farm tools, rugs, a longcase clock, a couple of fireside rocking chairs and so forth. The beamed dining room is smarter, with lots of pictures on the white or pink walls. A fine choice of up to ten ales includes one or two named for the pub, plus Butcombe Bitter, Fullers London Pride, Ringwood Best, Boondoggle and Fortyniner and three quickly changing guests on handpump; lots of country wines. They hold a beer festival in June and a cider festival in September. There are some rustic seats outside and camping facilities.

Favourites on the menu include interesting sausages (such as venison and redcurrant, pork and beetroot, duck with cognac), honey-glazed ham and free-range eggs and steak in ale pie. There are also sandwiches (you can add a mug of soup too), vegetable curry, lambs liver and bacon with onion gravy and mustard mash, and puddings. *Benchmark main dish: smoked fish pie £12.95. Two-course evening meal £18.50.*

Gales (Fullers) ~ Managers Georgie and Paul Stuart ~ Real ale ~ (01420) 588387 ~ Open 12-11.30 ~ Bar food 12-2.30, 6-9.30; all day weekends ~ Restaurant ~ Children welcome ~ Dogs allowed in bar ~ www.pubwithnoname.co.uk
Recommended by Ann and Colin Hunt, Geoff and Linda Payne, Tony and Jill Radnor

---

The star-on-a-plate award, distinguishes pubs where the food is of exceptional quality. The knife-and-fork symbol just means the pub serves food.

PORTSMOUTH
SZ6399 Map 2

Old Customs House 🍴 £

Vernon Buildings, Gunwharf Quays; follow brown signs to Gunwharf Quays car park; PO1 3TY

Well converted historic building in a prime waterfront development with real ales and popular bar food

As this handsome, Grade I listed building is part of the extensive modern waterside shopping complex and usefully open all day, it normally has plenty of customers; there's a lot of space, though, and you can always find somewhere to sit. The big-windowed high-ceilinged rooms have bare boards, nautical prints and photographs on pastel walls, coal-effect gas fires, nice unobtrusive lighting and well padded chairs around sturdy tables of varying sizes; the sunny entrance area has leather sofas. Broad stairs lead up to a carpeted restaurant with similar décor. Fullers ESB, HSB, London Pride and Seafarers and a couple of changing guests on handpump, a decent range of wines by the glass and good coffees and teas. Staff are efficient, the background music well reproduced and the games machines silenced. Picnic-sets out in front are just yards from the water; the bar has disabled access and facilities. The graceful Spinnaker Tower (170 metres tall with staggering views from its observation decks) is just around the corner.

All-day food includes breakfasts until midday, sandwiches, chicken liver pâté with apple and plum chutney, crayfish cocktail, sharing boards, steak in ale pie, grilled artichoke and blue cheese spelt salad with candied walnuts, salt and rosemary roasted chicken with smoked garlic mayonnaise, mussels in cider and bacon with frites, and puddings such as rhubarb trifle and salted caramel and chocolate tart. *Benchmark main dish: beer-battered fish and chips £9.95. Two-course evening meal £15.00.*

Fullers ~ Manager David Hughes ~ Real ale ~ (023) 9283 2333 ~ Open 9am-11pm (midnight Fri, Sat) ~ Bar food all day from 9am ~ Children allowed until 8pm ~ Wi-fi ~ www.theoldcustomshouse.com *Recommended by Paul Rampton, Julie Harding, Brian and Anna Marsden, Ann and Colin Hunt, D J and P M Taylor, Stephen and Jean Curtis*

PRESTON CANDOVER
SU6041 Map 2

Purefoy Arms 🏅 ♀

B3046 Basingstoke–Alresford; RG25 2EJ

First class food and wines in gently upmarket village pub

Customers come from far and wide to enjoy the first class, creative food cooked by the spanish landlord in this smart and civilised dining pub; you'll need to book in advance to be sure of a table. Two pairs of smallish linked rooms have an easy-going country pub feel. On the left, the airy front bar has chunky tables (including tall ones with bar stools) and a corner counter serving a fine changing choice of 15 wines by the glass, a farm cider and Itchen Valley Watercress Line Bitter, Palmers Copper and a guest beer on handpump; this opens into a jute-floored back area with four dining tables and characterful mixed seats including old settles. The right-hand front room has red leather sofas and armchairs by a log fire, and leads back to a bare-boards area with three or four sturdy pale pine tables. The understated contemporary décor in grey and puce goes nicely with the informal friendliness of the service; maybe unobtrusive background music. Don't leave the pub empty-handed: the landlord's father makes delicious chocolates and truffles and there are usually chutneys, ketchup and oils for sale too. The sizeable sloping garden has well spaced picnic-sets, a wendy house and perhaps a big hammock slung between trees; there are teak tables on a terrace sheltered by the pub. This is an attractive village, with nearby snowdrop walks in February.

As well as a two- and three-course set lunch, the delicious food might include appetisers such as manchego cheese and quince and chorizo ibérico, plus rare-breed pork and black pudding terrine with garlic purée, hand-dived scallops and leeks, rare-breed beef and oyster pie, risotto of white truffles and aged parmesan, monkfish, chickpeas, tomato, chorizo and aioli, roast venison with parsnip purée and braised red cabbage, and puddings such as blackberry sponge with duck egg custard. *Benchmark main dish: goose egg, piquillo peppers and hazelnut butter £12.50. Two-course evening meal £22.00.*

Free house ~ Licensees Andres and Marie-Louise Alemany ~ Real ale ~ (01256) 389777 ~ Open 12-3, 6-11; 12-4 Sun; closed Sun evening, all day Mon ~ Bar food 12-3, 6-10; 12-4 Sun ~ Well behaved children welcome until 7pm ~ Dogs allowed in bar ~ Wi-fi ~ www.thepurefoyarms.co.uk *Recommended by Phyl and Jack Street, Isobel Mackinlay, Susan and John Douglas*

ROCKBOURNE

SU1118 Map 2

Rose & Thistle ⬤ ♀

Signed off B3078 Fordingbridge–Cranborne; SP6 3NL

Pretty pub with hands-on landlady and friendly staff, informal bars, real ales, good food and seats in garden

You can be sure of a genuinely warm welcome from the friendly landlady and her helpful staff in this deservedly busy 16th-c thatched village pub. It's all very warm and cosy, and the bar has homely dining chairs, stools and benches around a mix of old pubby tables, Butcombe Gold, Ringwood Best and Sharps Doom Bar on handpump, 13 wines by the glass and Black Rat and Weston's ciders; background music. The restaurant has a log fire in each of its two rooms (one in a big brick inglenook), old engravings and cricket prints and an informal and relaxed atmosphere. There are benches and tables under pretty hanging baskets at the front of the building, with picnic-sets under parasols on the grass; good nearby walks. This is a pretty village on the edge of the New Forest.

Using local, seasonal produce, the well liked food includes lunchtime sandwiches, prawns in piri-piri butter, pulled pork, spring onion and chorizo croquettes with chilli jam, local sausages with onion gravy, vegetarian homity pie with leek sauce, steak and kidney pudding, confit duck with a thyme and honey celeriac purée and orange and Grand Marnier sauce, beef fillet medallions with a port and blue cheese sauce, and puddings. *Benchmark main dish: confit pork belly with ginger beer jus and red onion jam £15.50. Two-course evening meal £22.00.*

Free house ~ Licensee Kerry Dutton ~ Real ale ~ (01725) 518236 ~ Open 11-3, 6-11; 11-11 Sat; 12-10.30 (8 in winter) Sun ~ Bar food 12-2.30, 7-9.30; not Sun evening ~ Restaurant ~ Children welcome ~ Dogs allowed in bar ~ Wi-fi ~ www.roseandthistle.co.uk *Recommended by Mr and Mrs P R Thomas, Stewart Harvey, Peter and Eleanor Kenyon, Fr Robert Marsh*

Real ale to us means beer that has matured naturally in its cask – not pressurised or filtered. We name all real ales stocked. We usually name ales preserved under a light blanket of carbon dioxide too, though purists – pointing out that this stops the natural yeasts developing – would disagree (most people, including us, can't tell the difference!).

SPARSHOLT

SU4331 Map 2

Plough 🎯 ♀

Village signposted off B3049 (Winchester–Stockbridge), a little W of Winchester; SO21 2NW

Neatly kept dining pub with interesting furnishings, an extensive wine list, and highly thought-of bar food; garden with children's play fort

This well run country pub, where the hospitable landlord and his staff offer a warm welcome to all, is so popular that it's best to book a table in advance. The main bar has an interesting mix of wooden tables and farmhouse or upholstered chairs, farm tools, scythes and pitchforks attached to the ceiling, Wadworths IPA, 6X, Bishops Tipple and Horizon on handpump, and quite a few wines and champagne by the glass from an extensive list; the dining tables on the left look over fields and beyond to woodland. Outside, there are plenty of seats on the terrace and lawn and a children's play fort; disabled access and facilities.

The highly rated food includes sandwiches, crayfish and smoked salmon cocktail, goats cheese and pine nut parcel with pickled beetroot, green thai chicken curry, pork and chive sausages with red wine gravy, steak burger and cheese on rosemary focaccia with smoked bacon jam and fries, bass fillet with leeks and balsamic syrup, duck breast with pak choi and honey, soy and ginger jus, and puddings. *Benchmark main dish: slow-cooked pork belly with apple cider and brandy sauce £14.95. Two-course evening meal £20.00.*

Wadworths ~ Tenant Richard Crawford ~ Real ale ~ (01962) 776353 ~ Open 11-3, 6-11; 11-11 Sun ~ Bar food 12-2, 6-9 (8.30 Sun, Mon, 9.30 Fri, Sat) ~ Children welcome ~ Dogs allowed in bar ~ Wi-fi *Recommended by Michael and Susanne Hart, Patrick and Daphne Darley, Peter and Andrea Jacobs, John and Joan Calvert, Neil and Anita Christopher*

STEEP

SU7525 Map 2

Harrow 🍺 £

Take Midhurst exit from Petersfield bypass, at exit roundabout take first left towards Midhurst, then first turning on left opposite garage, and left again at Sheet church; follow over dual carriageway bridge to pub; GU32 2DA

Unchanging, simple place with long-serving landladies, beers tapped from the cask, unfussy food and a big free-flowering garden; no children inside

Many of our readers – like us – have been coming to this delightful little country gem for years. It's been in the same family for 85 years and, thankfully, nothing changes and there's still no pandering to modern methods – no credit cards, no waitress service, no restaurant, no music and the rose-covered loos are outside. Everything revolves around village chat and the friendly locals, who will probably draw you into light-hearted conversation. Adverts for logs sit next to calendars of local views (on sale to support local charities) and news of various quirky competitions. The small public bar has hops and dried flowers (replaced every year) hanging from the beams, built-in wall benches on the tiled floor, stripped-pine wallboards, a good log fire in a big inglenook and wild flowers on scrubbed deal tables; there might be bowls of seasonal walnuts and chestnuts, and dominoes. Bowman Swift One, Dark Star Hophead, Flack Manor Double Drop, Hop Back Citra, Langham Hip Hop and Ringwood Best are tapped straight from casks behind the counter, and they have local wine and apple juice; staff are polite and friendly, even when under pressure. The big garden is left free-flowering so that goldfinches can collect thistle seeds from the grass; there are some seats on paved areas. The Petersfield bypass doesn't intrude much on this idyll, though you'll need to follow the directions above to find the pub. No children inside and dogs must be on leads. They sell honesty-box flowers outside for Macmillan nurses.

🍴 Generously served home-made food includes scotch eggs, sandwiches, hearty soup, ploughman's, quiches and puddings such as treacle tart or seasonal fruit pies. *Benchmark main dish: split pea and ham soup £5.70.*

Free house ~ Licensees Claire and Denise McCutcheon ~ Real ale ~ No credit cards ~ (01730) 262685 ~ Open 12-2.30, 6-11; 11-3, 6-11 Sat; 12-3, 7-10.30 Sun; closed winter Sun evening ~ Bar food 12-2, 7-9; not Sun evening ~ Dogs allowed in bar ~ www.harrow-inn.co.uk *Recommended by Tony and Jill Radnor, Philip and Susan Philcox, Ann and Colin Hunt, Jeremy Whitehorn*

WEST MEON
Thomas Lord
High Street; GU32 1LN

SU6424   Map 2

Cricketing memorabilia in bar rooms of character, a smarter dining room, helpful staff, local beers, well thought-of food and a sizeable garden

There are candles everywhere here – in nice little teacups with saucers, in candlesticks, in silver glassware, in moroccan-style lanterns and in fireplaces. And plenty of cricketing memorabilia too (the pub is named after the founder of Lord's Cricket Ground): cricket bats, gloves, balls, shoes, stumps, photographs and prints – even stuffed squirrels playing the game in a display cabinet above the counter. The relaxed, friendly bar has a leather chesterfield and armchairs beside a log fire, wooden chairs, animal hide stools and corner settles on parquet flooring, Ringwood Best and Upham Punter, Stakes and Tipster on handpump, a dozen wines by the glass and farm cider, served by chatty, helpful staff. A small room leads off here with similar furnishings plus a brace of pheasant in the fireplace and antlers above; background music and board games. The dining room is slightly more formal, with long wide tartan benches beside long tables, green cushioned chairs, a big clock above another fireplace and ruched curtains; another little room has a large button-back banquette, tables and a rustic mural. The sizeable garden has picnic-sets, herbaceous borders, an outdoor pizza oven, a barbecue area, a chicken run and a kitchen garden.

🍴 Using their own eggs and some home-grown produce, the good interesting food includes sandwiches, citrus-cured skate wing with braised chicory and brown butter mayonnaise, lamb terrine with carrot chutney, beer-battered hake and chips, butternut squash tart with crispy chestnuts and chestnut purée, lamb, kale and sweetbread pie, duck breast and faggot with honey parsnip purée and rösti potato, and puddings such as treacle tart and ale ice-cream and blood orange cheesecake with rosemary granola. *Benchmark main dish: dry-aged burger with truffle and parmesan fries £11.50. Two-course evening meal £19.50.*

Free house ~ Licensee Clare Winterbottom ~ Real ale ~ (01730) 829244 ~ Open 12-11 (midnight Sat, 10.30 Sun) ~ Bar food 12-2.30 (3 Sat, 4 Sun), 6-9.30 (10 Fri, Sat, 9 Sun) ~ Restaurant ~ Children welcome ~ Dogs allowed in bar ~ Wi-fi ~ Live music regularly, theatre productions, quiz ~ www.thethomaslord.co.uk *Recommended by Henry Fryer, Isobel Mackinlay*

Places with gardens or terraces usually let children sit there – we note in the text the very few exceptions that don't.

WINCHESTER
GOOD PUB GUIDE

SU4829 Map 2

Wykeham Arms ⭐ ♀

Kingsgate Street (Kingsgate Arch and College Street are now closed to traffic; access is via Canon Street); SO23 9PE

Tucked-away pub with lots to look at, several real ales, many wines by the glass and highly thought-of food; lovely bedrooms

Our readers love this city pub – for a drink and a wander around (there's plenty to look at), for an imaginative meal and as a fine place to stay overnight; some of the individually styled bedrooms have four-posters and the two-level suite has its own sitting room. The series of bustling rooms have all sorts of interesting collections and three log fires, as well as 19th-c oak desks and a pew retired from Winchester College, kitchen chairs, candlelit deal tables and big windows with swagged curtains. A snug room at the back, known as the Jameson Room (after the late landlord, Graeme Jameson), is decorated with a set of Ronald Searle 'Winespeak' prints. A second room is panelled. Fullers HSB, London Pride, Seafarers and a seasonal ale plus a guest such as Flowerpots Goodens Gold and Itchen Valley Belgarum on handpump, 20 wines by the glass, 20 malt whiskies and several ports and sherries; the tea list is pretty special. There are tables on a covered back terrace and in a small courtyard.

Excellent and imaginative, the top class food includes baguettes, ham hock terrine with sweet mustard sabayon, seared scallops with bacon snow and pancetta, beer-battered haddock and triple-cooked chips, guinea fowl breast with braised thigh, salsify and watercress, confit duck leg with braised cassoulet, and puddings such as white chocolate torte, lavender cream and honey ganache and pine nut-crusted buttermilk flan with white chocolate, fennel and sweet carrot. *Benchmark main dish: cheese-topped cottage pie £10.00. Two-course evening meal £23.00.*

Fullers ~ Manager Jon Howard ~ Real ale ~ (01962) 853834 ~ Open 11-11 ~ Bar food 12-3, 6-9.30 ~ Dogs allowed in bar and bedrooms ~ Wi-fi ~ Bedrooms: £99/£149 ~ www.wykehamarmswinchester.co.uk *Recommended by Stephen and Jean Curtis, Martin and Karen Wake, Ann and Colin Hunt, Steve and Liz Tilley, B J Harding, Hugh Roberts, Steve and Claire Harvey, Phil Bryant, Mrs Sally Scott*

Also Worth a Visit in Hampshire

Besides the fully inspected pubs, you might like to try these pubs that have been recommended to us and described by readers. Do tell us what you think of them: feedback@goodguides.com

ALRESFORD SU5832
Bell (01962) 732429
West Street; SO24 9AT Comfortable and welcoming Georgian coaching inn, good popular food including weekday fixed-price menu and plenty of daily specials, friendly attentive service even when busy, five well kept changing ales and good choice of wines, spic-and-span interior with bare boards, scrubbed tables and log fire, daily papers, smallish dining room, occasional live music (mainly jazz); dogs welcome in bar (resident cocker spaniel is Freddie), attractive sunny back courtyard, six bedrooms, closed Sun evening, otherwise open all day. *(David and Judy Robison, Tony and Jill Radnor, Ann and Colin Hunt)*

ALRESFORD SU5831
Cricketers (01962) 732463
Jacklyns Lane; SO24 9LW Large welcoming pebble-dashed corner pub refurbished under newish family management – everything spic and span; good sensibly priced food, well kept local beers, decent wines ad excellent coffee, pleasant staff, separate dining area; children welcome, sizeable garden with covered terrace and good play area. *(Tony and Jill Radnor, Ann and Colin Hunt)*

ALRESFORD   SU5832
Globe (01962) 733118
*Bottom of Broad Street (B3046) where
parking is limited; SO24 9DB* Popular
tile-hung pub reopened summer 2013 under
new management; enjoyable food (all day
Sun) including weekday lunchtime deal,
ales such as Flowerpots, Hogs Back and
Otter, some live music – maybe Mon ukulele
session; children and dogs welcome, garden
overlooking Alresford Pond, good walks, open
all day. *(Ann and Colin Hunt)*

AMPFIELD   SU4023
★White Horse (01794) 368356
A3090 Winchester–Romsey; SO51 9BQ
Snug low-beamed front bar with candles
and soft lighting, inglenook log fire and
comfortable country furnishings, far-
spreading beamed dining area behind, well
kept Greene King ales and guests, good food
including all-day snacks, several nice wines
by the glass, efficient service, locals' bar
with another inglenook; background music;
children and dogs welcome, high-hedged
garden with plenty of picnic-sets, cricket
green beyond, good walks in Ampfield Woods
and handy for Hillier Gardens, open all day.
(Anon)

ARFORD   SU8236
Crown (01428) 712150
Off B3002 W of Hindhead; GU35 8BT
Low-beamed pub with log fires in several
areas from local-feel bar to cosy upper dining
room, well kept changing ales and decent
wines by the glass, good food from pub
favourites to blackboard specials, friendly
staff; children welcome in eating areas,
picnic-sets in peaceful dell by little stream
across the road. *(Tony and Jill Radnor)*

BARTON STACEY   SU4341
Swan (01962) 760470
Village signed off A303; SO21 3RL
Warm friendly atmosphere in beamed former
coaching inn, enjoyable food from pubby
choices up, well kept ales such as Bowman,
Fullers and Otter, good choice of wines,
little lounge area between front log-fire
bar and cosy dining part, back restaurant;
background music; children and dogs
welcome, tables on front lawn and back
terrace, bedrooms, open all day Fri, Sat,
closed Sun evening. *(Anon)*

BASING   SU6653
Millstone (01256) 331153
*Bartons Lane, Old Basing; follow brown
signs to Basing House; RG24 8AE* Busy
pub with lots of picnic-sets out by River
Loddon (ducks and swans) looking across
to former viaduct through scrubland, full
Wadworths range kept well, Weston's cider
and several wines by the glass, food can
be good, dark panelling, old prints and
etchings, sturdy pub furnishings; may be
faint background music; children and dogs
welcome, by ruins of Basing House, open
all day. *(Anna McDermott)*

BATTRAMSLEY   SZ3098
Hobler (01590) 623944
*Southampton Road (A337 S of
Brockenhurst); SO41 8PT* Old roadside
pub with several rooms, modern furnishings
and décor contrasting the ancient heavy-
beamed structure, wood and stone floors,
good interesting food from sandwiches up
using fresh local ingredients, well priced
weekday set menu, ales including Ringwood
and good choice of wines, friendly efficient
service; children welcome, nice garden with
some tables under cover, good New Forest
walks, open all day. *(Dennis and Doreen
Haward)*

BEAUWORTH   SU5624
Milbury's (01962) 771248
*Off A272 Winchester-Petersfield;
SO24 0PB* Attractive old tile-hung pub,
beams, panelling and stripped stone, massive
17th-c treadmill for much older incredibly
deep well, galleried area, up to five changing
ales and straightforward reasonably priced
food, efficient service, skittle alley; children
in eating areas, garden with fine downland
views, good walks. *(Anon)*

BISHOP'S WALTHAM   SU5517
Barleycorn (01489) 892712
Lower Basingwell Street; SO32 1AJ
Popular 18th-c two-bar local, enjoyable
generously served pub food at sensible prices,
friendly efficient service, well kept Greene
King ales and a guest, decent wine, beams
and some low ceiling panelling, open fires;
children and dogs welcome, large garden
with back smokers' area, open all day.
(Ann and Colin Hunt, Stephen and Jean Curtis)

BISHOP'S WALTHAM   SU5517
★Bunch of Grapes (01489) 892935
*St Peter's Street – near entrance to
central car park; SO32 1AD* Neat civilised
little pub in quiet medieval street, smartly
furnished keeping individuality and unspoilt
feel (run by same family for a century), good
chatty landlord and regulars, Goddards and
guests tapped from the cask, own wines from
nearby vineyard, no food; charming walled
back garden, opening times may vary.
(Stephen and Jean Curtis, Phil and Jane Villiers)

BISHOP'S WALTHAM   SU5517
Crown (01489) 893350
The Square; SO32 1AF Beamed 16th-c
coaching inn well refurbished by Fullers;
good range of ales including Gales HSB,
popular food from sandwiches and pub
favourites up, helpful staff, bare boards and
log fires; courtyard tables, opposite entrance
to palace ruins, eight bedrooms, open all day
from 8.30am. *(Ann and Colin Hunt, Val and
Alan Green)*

BRAISHFIELD   SU3724
Wheatsheaf (01794) 367737
Village signposted off A3090 on NW edge of Romsey; SO51 0QE Friendly beamed pub with enjoyable home-made food and well kept beers, cosy log fire, local artwork for sale; background music, sports TV and pool; children and dogs welcome, garden with nice views, woodland walks nearby, close to Hillier Gardens, open all day Fri-Sun. *(Anon)*

BRAMBRIDGE   SU4721
Dog & Crook (01962) 712129
Near M3 junction 12, via B3335; Church Lane; SO50 6HZ Cheerful bustling 18th-c pub with beamed bar and cosy dining room, enjoyable traditional food, Fullers and Ringwood ales, several wines by the glass, friendly speedy service; background music, TV, regular events and summer music nights; dogs welcome, garden with decking and arbour, Itchen Way walks nearby. *(Anon)*

BRAMDEAN   SU6127
Fox (01962) 771363
A272 Winchester–Petersfield; SO24 0LP 17th-c weatherboarded pub under new owners – reports please; open-plan bar with black beams and log fires, local beers and traditional food, fortnightly quiz Mon; children and dogs welcome, walled-in terraced area and spacious lawn under fruit trees, good surrounding walks, open (and food) all day. *(Helen and Brian Edgeley, Richard Tilbrook, John Evans)*

BREAMORE   SU1517
Bat & Ball (01725) 512252
Salisbury Road; SP6 2EA Refurbished village pub with enjoyable reasonably priced food including unusual choices such as kangaroo and crocodile steaks, well kept Ringwood ales, friendly service, two linked bar areas and restaurant; pleasant side garden, bedrooms in two apartments, Avon fishing and walks (lovely ones up by church and stately Breamore House), open (and food) all day. *(Barrie and Mary Crees)*

BROCKENHURST   SU3000
Filly (01590) 623449
Lymington Road (A337 Brockenhurst–Lymington); SO42 7UF Popular roadside pub with enjoyable reasonably priced home-made food including weekday set lunch deal, quick service from friendly young staff, a house beer from Triple fff and guests such as Itchen Valley, decent wines, interesting beamed front bar with inglenook, nice roomy eating areas; children and dogs welcome,

sheltered tables outside, New Forest walks, five bedrooms, open all day. *(Guy and Caroline Howard)*

BROOK   SU2714
Bell (023) 8081 2214
B3079/B3078, handy for M27 junction 1; SO43 7HE Really a hotel with golf club, but has neatly kept bar with lovely inglenook fire, well kept ales, good cider and plenty of wines by the glass, nice food too from sandwiches to blackboard specials, afternoon teas (perhaps with a glass of house champagne), helpful friendly uniformed staff; children and dogs welcome, big garden, delightful village, 27 comfortable bedrooms. *(Penny and Peter Keevil)*

BROOK   SU2713
★Green Dragon (023) 8081 3359
B3078 NW of Cadnam, just off M27 junction 1; SO43 7HE Immaculate thatched New Forest dining pub dating from 15th c, welcoming helpful staff, good fresh food including plenty of seasonal game and fish as well as pubby favourites, well kept Fullers and Ringwood, daily papers, bright linked areas with stripped pine and other pubby furnishings; disabled access from car park, attractive small terrace, garden with paddocks beyond, picturesque village, self-catering apartment. *(PL, Phil and Jane Villiers)*

BROUGHTON   SU3032
Tally Ho (01794) 301280
High Street, opposite church; signed off A30 Stockbridge–Salisbury; SO20 8AA Welcoming village pub with light airy bar and separate eating area, well kept ales such as Ringwood, Sharps and Timothy Taylors, good food from pub favourites up (more elaborate evening choice), friendly service; children welcome, charming secluded back garden, good walks, open all day. *(Ann and Colin Hunt)*

BUCKLERS HARD   SU4000
★Master Builders House
(01590) 616253 *M27 junction 2, follow signs to Beaulieu, turn left on to B3056, then left to Bucklers Hard; SO42 7XB* Sizeable hotel in lovely spot overlooking river; character main bar with heavy beams, log fire and simple furnishings, rugs on wooden floor, mullioned windows, interesting list of shipbuilders dating from 18th c, Ringwood Best and guests, stairs down to room with fireplace at each end, some sort of food all day, afternoon teas; children welcome, small gate at bottom of garden for waterside walks, summer barbecues, 26 bedrooms, open all day. *(Mrs Sally Scott)*

A few pubs try to make you leave a credit card at the bar, as a sort of deposit if you order food. This is a bad practice, and the banks and credit card firms warn you not to let your card go like this.

BURGHCLERE SU4660
Carpenters Arms (01635) 278251
Harts Lane, off A34; RG20 9JY Small, unpretentious and well run, enjoyable sensibly priced home-made food (not Sun evening) from sandwiches up, Arkells and an occasional guest, friendly helpful staff, good country views (Watership Down) from conservatory and terrace, log fire; background music; children, walkers and dogs welcome, handy for Sandham Memorial Chapel (NT) and Highclere Castle, six comfortable annexe bedrooms, open all day. *(Mrs P Sumner)*

BURITON SU7320
Five Bells (01730) 263584
Off A3 S of Petersfield; GU31 5RX Low-beamed 17th-c pub with big log fire and some ancient stripped masonry, popular food (not Sun evening) from sandwiches to daily specials, Badger ales and good wines by the glass; background music; children and dogs welcome, nice garden and sheltered terraces, pretty village with good local walks, self-catering in converted stables, open all day. *(Anon)*

BURLEY SU2202
White Buck (01425) 402264
Bisterne Close; 0.7 miles E, OS Sheet 195 map reference 223028; BH24 4AZ Recent major refurbishment for this 19th-c mock-Tudor hotel; well kept Fullers ales in long bar with two-way log fires at each end, seats in big bow window, comfortable part-panelled shooting-theme snug with stag's head, spacious well divided dining area on different levels, good choice of enjoyable attractively presented food (not overly expensive) and nice wines, helpful personable staff; background music, free wi-fi; children and dogs welcome, terraces and spacious lawn, lovely New Forest setting with superb walks towards Burley itself and over Mill Lawn, good bedrooms, open all day. *(Sara Fulton, Roger Baker)*

BURSLEDON SU4809
Fox & Hounds (023) 8040 2784
Hungerford Bottom; 2 miles from M27 junction 8; SO31 8DE Popular rambling 16th-c Chef & Brewer pub of unusual character, ancient beams, flagstones and big log fires, linked by pleasant family conservatory area to ancient back barn, lantern-lit side stalls, lots of interesting farm equipment, well kept ales including Ringwood, good choice of wines and reasonably priced food, cheerful obliging staff, daily papers; children allowed, tables outside. *(Anon)*

BURSLEDON SU4909
Jolly Sailor (023) 8040 5557
Off A27 towards Bursledon station, Lands End Road; handy for M27 junction 8; SO31 8DN Beamed Badger dining pub worth knowing for its prime location overlooking yachting inlet, their usual ales and good wine choice, food cooked to order (may be a wait and not particularly cheap), log fires; open all day. *(Anon)*

CADNAM SU2913
Sir John Barleycorn
(023) 8081 2236 *Off Southampton Road; by M27 junction 1; SO40 2NP* Picturesque low-slung thatched dining pub extended from cosy beamed and timbered medieval core, decent choice of fairly standard food including good value weekday two-course menu (till 6pm), friendly helpful service, well kept Fullers ales, two log fires, modern décor and stripped wood flooring; background music; children welcome, no dogs inside, suntrap benches in front and out in colourful garden, open (and food) all day. *(Brian Glozier)*

CHALTON SU7316
★ Red Lion (023) 9259 2246
Off A3 Petersfield–Horndean; PO8 0BG Largely extended thatched dining pub with interesting 16th-c core around ancient inglenook fireplace, wide range of popular food from sandwiches and baguettes up, well kept Fullers/Gales ales and lots of country wines, helpful smart staff; children and dogs allowed, good disabled access and facilities, nice views from neat rows of picnic-sets on rectangular lawn by large car park, good walks, handy for Queen Elizabeth Country Park, open (and food) all day. *(Ian Phillips)*

CHAWTON SU7037
★ Greyfriar (01420) 83841
Off A31/A32 S of Alton; Winchester Road; GU34 1SB Popular flower-decked beamed dining pub opposite Jane Austen's House; enjoyable food (till 7pm Sun) from lunchtime sandwiches and bar snacks up, well kept Fullers ales, decent wines by the glass and good coffee, welcoming relaxed atmosphere with comfortable seating and sturdy pine tables in neat linked areas, open fire in restaurant end; background music; children welcome till 9pm, dogs in bar, small garden with terrace, good nearby walks, open all day. *(B J Harding)*

CHERITON SU5828
★ Flower Pots (01962) 771318
Off B3046 towards Beauworth and Winchester; OS Sheet 185 map reference 581282; SO24 0QQ Unspoilt country local in same family for over 45 years; three or four good value own-brewed beers tapped from the cask (brewery tours by arrangement), reasonably priced food (not Sun evening or bank holiday evenings, and possible restrictions during busy times) including range of casseroles and popular Weds curry night, cheerful welcoming staff, extended plain public bar with covered

well, another straightforward but homely room with country pictures on striped wallpaper and ornaments over small log fire; no credit cards or children; dogs welcome, seats on pretty front and back lawns (some under apple trees), heated marquee, three bedrooms. *(Tony and Jill Radnor, R Elliott, Ann and Colin Hunt, David and Judy Robison and others)*

CHILWORTH   SU4118
Chilworth Arms (023) 8076 6247
Chilworth Road (A27 Southampton–Romsey); SO16 7JZ Stylish modern Mitchells & Butlers dining pub, popular food from sharing plates and home-made pizzas up, weekday fixed-price menu till 7pm, good wine choice, ales such as Robinsons and Sharps Doom Bar, cocktails, neat efficient young staff, chunky furniture including quite a lot of leather, log fires, conservatory-style back restaurant; background music; children welcome, disabled access/facilities, large neat garden with terrace, open all day. *(John Jenkins)*

CHURCH CROOKHAM   SU8151
Tweseldown (01252) 613976
Beacon Hill Road; GU52 8DY Flower-decked 19th-c pub with lounge and public bars plus a sizeable split-level barn restaurant, Courage, Fullers, Triple fff and a guest, good choice of wines by the glass, enjoyable home-cooked food from favourites to specials, cheerful service, horse-racing décor (Tweseldown Racecourse nearby), log fires; pool, darts and fruit machine; children and dogs welcome, garden with heated smokers' shelter, open all day. *(KC)*

COLDEN COMMON   SU4722
Rising Sun (01962) 711954
Spring Lane; SO21 1SB Refurbished 19th-c pub in residential street; reasonably priced tasty food including children's choices, well kept ales, bare boards, half-panelling and painted ceiling joists, leather sofas by open fire, some live music; a few picnic-sets in front behind picket fence, more in garden beyond car park. *(Anon)*

CRONDALL   SU7948
Plume of Feathers (01252) 850245
The Borough; GU10 5NT Attractive smallish 15th-c village pub popular for good range of generous home-made food from standards up, friendly helpful staff, well kept Greene King and some unusual guests, nice wines by the glass, beams and dark wood, red carpet, prints on cream walls, restaurant with log fire in big brick fireplace; children welcome, picturesque village, three bedrooms. *(Anon)*

CROOKHAM   SU7952
Exchequer (01252) 615336
Crondall Road; GU51 5SU Welcoming smartly refurbished dining pub, enjoyable home-made food from lunchtime sandwiches to blackboard specials in bar and restaurant, four local ales and good choice of wines by the glass, also cider and lager from local Hogs Back, daily papers, woodburner; terrace tables, near Basingstoke Canal, open all day Fri-Sun. *(Anon)*

CURDRIDGE   SU5314
Cricketers (023) 8078 4420
Curdridge Lane, off B3035 just under a mile NE of A334 junction; SO32 2BH Popular open-plan low-ceilinged Victorian village pub, cheery welcoming landlady and staff, good well presented food (busy at weekends), reasonably priced wines from short but varied list, well kept Greene King ales, lounge part with banquettes, traditional public area, dining section with large Beryl Cook-inspired mural of the locals, cricketing memorabilia; soft background music; tables on front lawn, pleasant walks. *(Ann and Colin Hunt)*

DROXFORD   SU6118
Hurdles (01489) 877451
Brockbridge, just outside Soberton; from A32 just N of Droxford take B2150 towards Denmead; SO32 3QT Smartly modernised dining pub (a former station hotel) with well thought-of food; high ceilings and stripped floorboards, leather chesterfield and armchairs by log fire in one room, dining areas with stylish wallpaper and stripy chairs around shiny modern tables, well kept Bowmans and a guest, decent wines by the glass and good coffee, friendly if not always speedy service; background music; children and dogs (in bar) welcome, neat terraces (one covered and heated), flight of steps up to picnic-sets on sloping lawn by tall trees, open all day. *(Harvey Brown, Toby Jones, John Evans, Tony and Wendy Hobden, Dave Braisted)*

DUMMER   SU5846
Queen (01256) 397367
Less than a mile from M3 junction 7; take Dummer slip road; RG25 2AD Comfortable beamed pub, well divided with lots of softly lit alcoves, Andwell, Otter and Sharps, decent choice of wines by the glass, popular food from lunchtime sandwiches and light dishes up, friendly service, big log fire, Queen and steeplechase prints; background music; children welcome in restaurant, picnic-sets under parasols on terrace and in extended back garden, attractive village with ancient church. *(B J Thompson)*

DUNBRIDGE   SU3126
Mill Arms (01794) 340401
Barley Hill (B3084); SO51 0LF Much extended 18th-c coaching inn opposite station, friendly informal atmosphere in spacious high-ceilinged rooms, scrubbed pine tables and farmhouse chairs on oak or flagstone floors, several sofas, two log fires, well kept Ringwood and guests, food (all day

Sat) including grills and wood-fired pizzas, dinning conservatory, two skittle alleys; background music; children welcome, dogs in bar, big pretty garden, plenty of walks in surrounding Test Valley, six comfortable bedrooms, open till 4.30pm Sun, closed Mon. *(Anon)*

DUNDRIDGE   SU5718
★**Hampshire Bowman**
(01489) 892940 *Off B3035 towards Droxford, Swanmore, then right at Bishop's Waltham signpost; SO32 1GD* Good chatty mix at this friendly relaxed country tavern, five well kept local ales tapped from casks, summer farm cider, well liked good value food (all day Fri-Sun) from hearty pub dishes to specials using local produce, smart stable bar sitting comfortably alongside cosy and unassuming original one, some colourful paintings, no mobile phones (£1 fine in charity box); children (under-14s in stable bar) and dogs welcome, tables on heated terrace and peaceful lawn, play equipment, hitching post for horses, popular with walkers and cyclists, open all day.
(Henry Fryer, Audrey Dowsett, Ann and Colin Hunt)

DURLEY   SU5116
Farmers Home (01489) 860457
B3354 and B2177; Heathen Street/ Curdridge Road; SO32 2BT Comfortable beamed pub, spacious but cosy, with two-bay dining area and restaurant, enjoyable food including good steaks and popular Sun lunch, friendly service, room for drinkers too with well kept Gales HSB, Ringwood and decent wines, woodburner; children and dogs (in bar) welcome, big garden with play area, nice walks, open (and food) all day.
(Ann and Colin Hunt, Gavin and Helle May)

DURLEY   SU5217
Robin Hood (01489) 860229
Durley Street, just off B2177 Bishop's Waltham–Winchester – brown signs to pub; SO32 2AA Popular open-plan beamed pub with good food from varied blackboard menu (order at bar), Greene King and a guest ale, friendly attentive staff, log fire and leather sofas in bare-boards bar, dining area with stone floors and mix of old pine tables and chairs, bookcase door to lavatories; background music; children and dogs welcome, disabled facilities, decked terrace with barbecue, garden with play area and nice country views, open all day Sun.
(Gavin and Helle May, Phil and Jane Villiers)

EAST BOLDRE   SU3700
Turf Cutters Arms (01590) 612331
Main Road; SO42 7WL Small dim-lit 18th-c New Forest local behind white picket fence, lots of beams and pictures, nicely worn-in furnishings on bare boards and flagstones, log fire, enjoyable home-

made food (worth booking in evening), well kept ales including Ringwood, friendly helpful staff and chatty relaxed atmosphere; children and dogs welcome, large garden, good heathland walks, bedrooms in nearby converted barn, open all day. *(N R White)*

EAST MEON   SU6822
★**Olde George** (01730) 823481
Church Street; signed off A272 W of Petersfield, and off A32 in West Meon; GU32 1NH Relaxing heavy-beamed village inn with enjoyable if not particularly cheap bar and restaurant food, Badger ales, cosy areas around central counter, inglenook log fires; children and dogs welcome, nice back terrace, five bedrooms, good breakfast, pretty village with fine church and nice surrounding walks, open all day Sun.
(Steve and Claire Harvey)

EAST WORLDHAM   SU7438
Three Horseshoes (01420) 83211
Cakers Lane (B3004 Alton–Kingsley); GU34 3AE Welcoming early 19th-c brick and stone roadside pub under newish licensees; comfortable and attractive, with good range of reasonably priced food including daily specials, Fullers/Gales ales and one or two guests, good wines by the glass, friendly efficient staff, log fires; free wi-fi; children and dogs welcome, pleasant secluded garden with lots of picnic-sets, five well appointed bedrooms, open all day weekends (till 6pm Sun). *(Susan Crabbe, Tony and Jill Radnor)*

EASTON   SU5132
Cricketers (01962) 791044
Off B3047; SO21 1EJ Pleasantly smartened-up traditional local; enjoyable well priced home-made pubby food in bar and smallish restaurant, three Marstons-related ales including Ringwood, friendly atmosphere, dark tables and chairs on carpet, bare-boards area with sports TV, fortnightly Sun quiz; background music; children and dogs welcome, front terrace with heated smokers' shelter, handy for Itchen Way walks, two bedrooms, open all day. *(Ann and Colin Hunt)*

ELLISFIELD   SU6345
★**Fox** (01256) 381210
Green Lane; S of village off Northgate Lane; RG25 2QW Simple tucked-away place under friendly licensees; mixed collection of stripped tables, country chairs and cushioned wall benches on bare boards and old floor tiles, some exposed masonry, open fires in plain brick fireplaces, Sharps Doom Bar, Fullers London Pride and a guest or two, enjoyable sensibly priced home-made food; outside gents'; children and dogs welcome, picnic-sets in nice garden, good walking country near snowdrop and bluebell woods, open all day. *(Tony and Jill Radnor)*

EMERY DOWN   SU2808
★ **New Forest** (023) 8028 4690
Village signed off A35 just W of Lyndhurst; SO43 7DY Well run 18th-c weatherboarded village pub in one of the best parts of the Forest for walking; good honest home-made food all day including local venison, popular Sun roasts (should book), friendly helpful uniformed staff, Ringwood and guest ales, real cider, good choice of wines by the glass, coffee and tea; attractive softly lit separate areas on varying levels, each with own character, hunting prints, two log fires; background music; children and dogs welcome, covered heated terrace and pleasant little three-level garden, clean bedrooms, open all day and can get very busy weekends. *(Leslie and Barbara Owen, N R White, David and Sally Frost, Phil and Jane Villiers)*

EMSWORTH   SU7405
Blue Bell (01243) 373394
South Street; PO10 7EG Little 1940s red-brick pub close to the quay, friendly busy atmosphere, lived-in interior with lots of memorabilia, good choice of popular no-nonsense food including local fish, best to book weekends, Sharps Doom Bar and guests such as Hogs Back and Itchen Valley, live music; dogs welcome, small front terrace, Sun market in adjacent car park, open all day. *(Geoff and Linda Payne)*

EMSWORTH   SU7505
Lord Raglan (01243) 372587
Queen Street; PO10 7BJ Friendly 18th-c flint pub with wide choice of enjoyable home-made food and well kept Fullers/Gales beers, log fire, restaurant, live music Sun evening; free wi-fi; pleasant waterside garden behind, open all day weekends. *(Ann and Colin Hunt)*

EVERSLEY   SU7861
Golden Pot (0118) 973 2104
B3272; RG27 0NB The charming licensee at this inviting brick pub (a previous Main Entry) has retired – news please; spreading areas with sofas, cushioned settles and other traditional seating, big mirrors, two-sided woodburner, ales have included Andwell, Bowman, Loddon and Windsor & Eton, restaurant; tables out in front and at back with view over fields, has closed Sun evening. *(Paul and Marion Watts, KC, Mrs P Sumner)*

EVERTON   SZ2994
Crown (01590) 642655
Old Christchurch Road; pub signed just off A337 W of Lymington; SO41 0JJ Quietly set New Forest-edge restaurant/pub with good food cooked by landlord-chef, friendly service, Ringwood and guests, reliable wine choice, two attractive dining rooms off tiled-floor bar, log fires; children welcome, picnic-sets on front terrace and in garden behind, closed Mon. *(Anon)*

EXTON   SU6120
★ **Shoe** (01489) 877526
Village signposted from A32 NE of Bishop's Waltham; SO32 3NT Popular brick-built country pub on South Downs Way; three linked rooms with log fires, good well presented food from traditional favourites to more imaginative restaurant-style dishes using own produce, well kept Wadworths ales and a seasonal guest, good friendly service; children and dogs welcome, disabled facilities, seats under parasols at front, more in garden across lane overlooking River Meon. *(William Ruxton, Richard and Liz Dilnot, Annabel and James Bartle)*

FACCOMBE   SU3958
Jack Russell (01264) 737315
Signed from A343 Newbury–Andover; SP11 0DS Light and airy creeper-covered pub (under new management) in village-green setting, opposite pond and by flint church, enjoyable fairly priced food and well kept ales, good cheerful service, carpeted bar with some old farming tools and other bric-a-brac, log fire, conservatory restaurant; children welcome, lawn by beech trees, good walks, bedrooms. *(Ian Herdman)*

FAREHAM   SU5806
Cams Mill (01329) 287506
Cams Hall Estate, off A27; PO16 8UP Large new Fullers waterside pub (re-creation of former tidal mill); roomy interior including high raftered and galleried eating area, popular food; free wi-fi; children and dogs welcome, open all day. *(Ann and Colin Hunt)*

FAREHAM   SU5806
Cob & Pen (01329) 221624
Wallington Shore Road, not far from M27 junction 11; PO16 8SL Old roadside pub with well kept Otter, Ringwood and St Austell, decent choice of enjoyable fairly standard food (all day weekends), Sun carvery, reasonable prices and cheerful prompt service, separate games room; children welcome, large garden, open all day. *(Ann and Colin Hunt)*

FAREHAM   SU5806
Crown (01329) 241750
West Street; PO16 0JW Bustling Wetherspoons (opened 2009 – their second in Fareham) in pedestrianised street, attractive old building with proper pubby atmosphere, a couple of Greene King ales and three guests, usual well priced food, good friendly service; free wi-fi; children welcome, open all day from 7am. *(Ann and Colin Hunt)*

FAREHAM   SU5806
Golden Lion (01329) 234061
High Street; PO16 7AE Traditional 19th-c town local, clean and welcoming, with well kept Fullers/Gales ales from dark wood servery, dining part to the right with

decent reasonably priced pubby food from baguettes up, charity quiz Thurs; background music; children and dogs welcome (resident retriever is Monty), courtyard garden, open all day (till 3pm Sun, 9pm Mon). *(Val and Alan Green, Ann and Colin Hunt)*

FARNBOROUGH   SU8756
★ **Prince of Wales** (01252) 545578
Rectory Road, near station; GU14 8AL
Up to ten good quickly changing ales in friendly Victorian local, exposed brickwork, carpet or wood floors, open fire, antiquey touches in its three small linked areas, popular lunchtime pubby food (not Sun) including deals, good friendly service; terrace and smokers' gazebo, open all day Fri-Sun. *(Anon)*

FAWLEY   SU4603
Jolly Sailor (023) 8089 1305
Ashlett Creek, off B3053; SO45 1DT
Cottagey waterside pub near small boatyard and sailing club, straightforward good value bar food, Ringwood Best and a guest, cheerful service, mixed pubby furnishings on bare boards, raised log fire, second bar with darts and pool; children welcome, tables outside looking past creek's yachts and boats to busy shipping channel, good shore walks, handy for Rothschild rhododendron gardens at Exbury, open all day. *(Phil and Jane Villiers)*

FLEET   SU8053
Oatsheaf (01252) 819508
Crookham Road/Reading Road; GU51 5DR Smartly refurbished Mitchells & Butlers dining pub with plenty of contemporary touches, enjoyable food, ales such as Timothy Taylors Landlord; tables on front terrace, garden behind, open all day. *(Anon)*

GOODWORTH CLATFORD   SU3642
Royal Oak (01264) 324105
Longstock Road; SP11 7QY Comfortably modern L-shaped bar with welcoming staff, good carefully sourced food from pub staples up, Flack Manor and Ringwood ales, good choice of wines by the glass, Weds quiz night; children welcome, sheltered and very pretty dell-like garden, attractive Test Valley village, good River Anton walks, closed Sun evening. *(Anon)*

GOSPORT   SU6101
Jolly Roger (023) 9258 2584
Priory Road, Hardway; PO12 4LQ
Popular extended waterfront pub with fine harbour views, traditional beamed bar with half a dozen well kept ales and decent house wines, good choice of fairly standard home-made food including good value set deals,

efficient friendly young staff, lots of bric-a-brac, log fire, attractive eating area with conservatory; children welcome, disabled access/facilities, seats outside, open all day. *(Howard and Margaret Buchanan, Ann and Colin Hunt, M G Hart, Val and Alan Green)*

GOSPORT   SZ6100
Queens 07974 031671
Queens Road; PO12 1LG Classic bare-boards local with Oakleaf, Ringwood, Wells & Youngs and guests kept in top condition by long-serving landlady, popular Oct beer festival, three areas off bar with good log fire in interesting carved fireplace, sensibly placed darts, pub dog called Stanley; TV room (children welcome here daytime); closed lunchtimes Mon-Thurs, open all day Sat. *(Ann and Colin Hunt)*

GREYWELL   SU7151
Fox & Goose (01256) 702062
Near M3 junction 5; A287 towards Odiham, then first right to village; RG29 1BY Traditional two-bar pub popular with locals and walkers, country kitchen furniture, open fire, enjoyable home-made pubby food from good lunchtime sandwiches up, Sun roast till 5pm, well kept ales including Sharps Doom Bar, friendly helpful service; children and dogs welcome, good-sized back garden, attractive village, Basingstoke Canal walks, open all day. *(Anon)*

HAMBLE   SU4806
Bugle (023) 8045 3000
3 miles from M27 junction 8; SO31 4HA Chatty and bustling little 16th-c village pub by River Hamble, beamed and timbered rooms with flagstones and polished boards, church chairs, woodburner in fine brick fireplace, bar stools along herringbone-brick and timbered counter, ales such as Bowman and Ringwood, popular food (all day weekends); background music, TV; children welcome, dogs in bar, seats on terrace with view of boats, open all day. *(Anon)*

HAMBLE   SU4806
Olde Whyte Harte (023) 8045 2108
High Street; 3 miles from M27 junction 8; SO31 4JF Welcoming old-fashioned village pub, locally popular, with big inglenook log fire, flagstones and low dark 17th-c beams, small cottagey restaurant area, generous fresh pubby food all day along with specials, Fullers/Gales ales and a guest from stone-faced counter, good wines by the glass; background music; children and dogs welcome, small walled garden, handy for nature reserve, open all day. *(Ann and Colin Hunt)*

If you report on a pub that's not a featured entry, please tell us any lunchtimes or evenings when it doesn't serve bar food.

HAMBLEDON   SU6716
★ **Bat & Ball**   (023) 9263 2692
*Broadhalfpenny Down; about 2 miles
E towards Clanfield; PO8 0UB* Extended
dining pub opposite historic cricket pitch
and with plenty of cricketing memorabilia
(the game's rules are said to have been
written here), log fires and comfortable
modern furnishings in three linked rooms,
Fullers ales, enjoyable food from well priced
snacks up, good friendly service, panelled
restaurant; children and dogs welcome,
tables on front terrace, garden behind with
lovely downs views, good walks, open all day.
(Anon)

HAWKLEY   SU7429
Hawkley Inn   (01730) 827205
*Off B3006 near A3 junction; Pococks
Lane; GU33 6NE* Small traditional village
pub with half a dozen well kept ales from
central bar, real ciders too, enjoyable home-
made food (not Sun evening), Mon steak
night, open fires (large moose head above
one), bare boards, flagstones and well used
carpet, old pine tables and assorted chairs;
children and dogs welcome, covered seating
area at front, big back garden, useful for
walkers on Hangers Way, four comfortable
bedrooms, open all day weekends. *(Anon)*

HAYLING ISLAND   SU7201
Maypole   (023) 9246 3670
Havant Road; PO11 0PS Sizeable two-bar
1930s roadside local, family-run and friendly,
with generous reasonably priced pub food
including good ploughman's (home-made
pickles), fish night Fri, steaks Sat, well
kept Fullers/Gales beers, parquet floors and
polished panelling, plenty of good seating,
open fires; darts, Thurs quiz; children and
dogs welcome, garden picnic-sets and play
equipment, closed Sun evening.
(Robert Brindle)

HECKFIELD   SU7260
New Inn   (0118) 932 6374
*B3349 Hook–Reading (former A32);
RG27 0LE* Well run rambling open-plan
dining pub, good welcoming service, generous
helpings of enjoyable food, well kept Badger
ales and good choice of wines by the glass,
attractive layout with some traditional
furniture in original core, two log fires; quiz
nights; restaurant; good-sized heated terrace,
bedrooms in comfortable and well equipped
extension. *(Darren and Jane Staniforth)*

HERRIARD   SS6744
Fur & Feathers   (01256) 384170
*Pub signed just off A339 Basingstoke–
Alton; RG25 2PN* Victorian pub, clean,
light and airy, with four changing ales and
good choice of wines, popular home-made
blackboard food served by friendly staff,
smallish bar area with stools along counter,
dining areas either side, pine furniture

on stripped-wood flooring, painted half-
panelling, old photographs and farm tools,
two woodburners; background music; garden
behind, open all day Fri and Sat, till 6pm
Sun, closed Mon. *(Comus and Sarah Elliott)*

HIGHCLERE   SU4358
Yew Tree   (01635) 253360
Hollington Cross; RG20 9SE Refurbished
17th-c inn under new owners, enjoyable
interesting food (a little pricey) from
sandwiches up in nicely furnished
comfortable low-beamed eating areas, big
inglenook log fire, Flack Manor and Fullers
ales from copper-top counter, good choice of
wines by the glass, daily newspapers; picnic-
sets under parasols on pleasant terrace, eight
good bedrooms, handy for Highclere Castle,
open all day. *(Ian Herdman)*

HORSEBRIDGE   SU3430
John o' Gaunt   (01794) 388394
*Off A3057 Romsey–Andover, just SW of
Kings Somborne; SO20 6PU* Traditional
River Test village pub improved under
current management; enjoyable good value
home-made food from sensibly short menu,
three ales including Ringwood, real cider,
friendly staff and locals, L-shaped log-fire bar
and small back dining area; seats outside,
popular with walkers. *(Ann and Colin Hunt,
Tony and Wendy Hobden)*

HOUGHTON   SU3432
★ **Boot**   (01794) 388310
*Village signposted off A30 in
Stockbridge; SO20 6LH* Refurbished
country pub with cheery log-fire bar and
more formal dining room, well kept Ringwood
and Sharps, Weston's cider, enjoyable bar and
restaurant food (not Sun evening) including
blackboard specials, friendly helpful staff;
picnic-sets out in front and in spacious
tranquil garden by lovely (unfenced)
stretch of River Test where they have fishing
rights, outside summer grill, good walks,
opposite Test Way cycle path, open all day
Fri-Sun. *(Helen and Brian Edgeley)*

HURSLEY   SU4225
Kings Head   (01962) 775208
A3090 Winchester–Romsey; SO21 2JW
Substantial early 19th-c coaching inn with
good local home-made food, five well kept
changing ales and good choice of ciders,
friendly staff, restaurant, skittle alley;
children and dogs welcome, garden tables,
eight comfortable bedrooms, open all
day. *(June Kershaw, Mrs Julie Thomas)*

KEYHAVEN   SZ3091
★ **Gun**   (01590) 642391
Keyhaven Road; SO41 0TP Busy rambling
17th-c pub looking over boatyard and sea to
Isle of Wight; low-beamed bar with nautical
bric-a-brac and plenty of character (less
in family rooms and conservatory), good
reasonably priced local food including crab,

Ringwood, Sharps, Timothy Taylors and Wells & Youngs tapped from the cask, Weston's cider, lots of malt whiskies, helpful young staff, bar billiards; background music; tables out in front and in big back garden with swings and fish pond, you can stroll down to small harbour and walk to Hurst Castle, open all day Sat, closed Sun evening. *(David and Judy Robison, Neil and Angela Huxter)*

KINGS WORTHY   SU4932
Cart & Horses (01962) 882360
A3090 E of Winchester, just off A33; SO23 7QN Popular revamped 18th-c pub adding modern touches to traditional interior, cosy corners, beams and inglenook, enjoyable food including good value weekday set menu, three Greene King ales and good choice of wines by the glass, friendly obliging staff; free wi-fi; children and dogs (in bar) welcome, tables out at front, open all day. *(Robert Watt)*

KINGSCLERE   SU5258
Swan (01635) 298314
Swan Street; RG20 5PP 15th-c beamed village inn under welcoming long serving licensees, Theakstons XB, Wells & Youngs Bitter and three guests, enjoyable reasonably priced home-made food (not Sun evening), friendly helpful staff, log-fire bar and adjoining restaurant; children and dogs welcome, tables on back terrace, good walks, nine bedrooms. *(Anon)*

LANGSTONE   SU7104
★ Royal Oak (023) 9248 3125
Off A3023 just before Hayling Island bridge; Langstone High Street; PO9 1RY Charmingly placed waterside dining pub overlooking tidal inlet and ancient wadeway to Hayling Island, boats at high tide, wading birds when it goes out; Greene King ales and good choice of wines by the glass, reasonably priced food with all-day sandwiches and snacks, spacious flagstoned bar and linked dining areas, log fire; nice garden and good coast paths nearby, open all day. *(R Elliott)*

LINWOOD   SU1910
High Corner (01425) 473973
Signed from A338 via Moyles Court, and from A31; keep on; BH24 3QY Big rambling pub very popular for its splendid New Forest position up a track, with extensive neatly kept wooded garden and lots for children to do; popular and welcoming with some character in original upper log-fire bar, big back extensions for the summer crowds, nicely partitioned restaurant, verandah lounge, interesting family rooms, wide choice of generous bar snacks and restaurant-style food, well kept Wadworths; welcomes dogs and horses (stables and paddock available), seven bedrooms, open all day summer and weekends. *(N R White, Phil and Jane Villiers)*

LITTLE LONDON   SU6259
Plough (01256) 850628
Silchester Road, off A340 N of Basingstoke; RG26 5EP Tucked-away local, cosy and unspoilt, with log fires, low beams and mixed furnishings on brick and tiled floors (watch the step), well kept Palmers, Ringwood and interesting guests tapped from the cask, good value baguettes, bar billiards and darts; dogs welcome, attractive garden, handy for Pamber Forest and Calleva Roman remains. *(Anon)*

LOCKS HEATH   SU5006
Jolly Farmer (01489) 572500
Fleet End Road, not far from M27 junction 9; SO31 9JH Popular flower-decked pub with relaxing series of softly lit linked rooms, nice old scrubbed tables and masses of bric-a-brac and prints, emphasis on wide choice of enjoyable food (all day weekends), interesting long-serving landlord, Fullers/Gales ales, decent wines including country ones, coal-effect gas fires; two sheltered terraces (one with play area and children's lavatory), dogs allowed in some parts (resident cat), nearby walks, four bedrooms, good breakfast, open all day. *(Anon)*

LONG SUTTON   SU7447
Four Horseshoes (01256) 862488
Signed off B3349 S of Hook; RG29 1TA Welcoming unpretentious country local; open plan with black beams and two log fires, long-serving landlord cooking uncomplicated bargain food such as lancashire hotpot and fish and chips, friendly landlady serving a couple of changing ales such as Palmers, decent wines and country wine, small glazed-in verandah; disabled access, lovely hanging baskets, picnic-sets on grass over road, boules and play area, three good value bedrooms (bunk beds available for cyclists/ walkers). *(Tony and Jill Radnor)*

LONGPARISH   SU4344
Cricketers (01264) 720335
B3048, off A303 just E of Andover; SP11 6PZ Cheerful homely village pub with good chatty landlady, connecting rooms and cosy corners, woodburner, wide choice of carefully cooked food from light snacks to popular Sun lunch, prompt service, well kept Wadworths; sizeable back garden; closed Mon. *(B J Harding)*

LONGPARISH   SU4244
★ Plough (01264) 720358
B3048, off A303 just E of Andover; SP11 6PB Smart Victorian inn with original features mixing well with modern touches and furnishings, various neat rooms with beams, standing timbers, flagstone and oak floors, contemporary paintwork, high-backed dining chairs and pews, working fireplaces (one with woodburner), Ringwood Best,

Sharps Doom Bar and Timothy Taylors Landlord, three ciders and several wines by the glass (there's a walk-in 'wine cellar'), enjoyable food from bar and restauarant menus; background music; children and dogs (in bar) welcome, garden with decking, handy for jam-packed A303 and for walking (Test Way passes through car park), open all day (Sun till 6pm). *(Ann and Colin Hunt, Richard and Patricia Jefferson, Stewart and Elizabeth Harvey, Hugh Roberts, B J Harding)*

LYMINGTON   SZ3295
Kings Head (01590) 672709
Quay Hill; SO41 3AR In steep cobbled lane of smart small shops, friendly dimly lit old pub with well kept Fullers London Pride, Ringwood, Timothy Taylors Landlord and a couple of guests, several wines by the glass, good choice of enjoyable home-made food from sandwiches to specials, pleasant helpful staff, nicely mixed old-fashioned furnishings in rambling beamed and bare-boarded rooms (some refurbishment), log fire and woodburner, good classic yacht photographs, daily papers; background music, can get very busy and they may ask for a credit card if you run a tab; children and dogs welcome, nice little sunny courtyard behind, open all day. *(Steve and Liz Tilley, Tony and Wendy Hobden)*

LYNDHURST   SU2908
Waterloo Arms (023) 8028 2113
Pikes Hill, just off A337 N; SO43 7AS Thatched 17th-c New Forest pub with low beams, stripped brick walls and log fire, good choice of pubby food including blackboard specials, two Ringwood beers and Sharps Doom Bar, friendly staff, comfortable bar and roomy back dining area, Tues quiz and Sun live music; children and dogs welcome, terrace and nice big garden, open (and food) all day. *(R G Stollery)*

MAPLEDURWELL   SU6851
Gamekeepers (01256) 322038
Off A30, not far from M3 junction 6; RG25 2LU Dark-beamed dining pub with good upmarket food (not cheap and they add a service charge) from interesting baguettes up, welcoming landlord and friendly staff, well kept Badger ales, good coffee, a few sofas by flagstoned and panelled core, well spaced tables in large dining room; background music, TV; children welcome, terrace and garden, lovely thatched village with duck pond, good walks, open all day. *(Anon)*

MARCHWOOD   SU3809
Pilgrim (023) 8086 7752
Hythe Road, off A326 at Twiggs Lane; SO40 4WU Popular picturesque thatched

pub (originally three cottages), good choice of enjoyable sensibly priced food, well kept Fullers ales and decent wines, friendly helpful staff, open fires; tree-lined garden with round picnic-sets, 14 stylish bedrooms in building across car park, open all day. *(Martin and Sue Radcliffe)*

MATTINGLEY   SU7357
Leather Bottle (0118) 932 6371
3 miles from M3 junction 5; in Hook, turn right-and-left on to B3349 Reading Road (former A32); RG27 8JU Old red-brick chain pub with enjoyable food from varied menu, three local ales including Andwell and plenty of wines by the glass, well spaced tables in linked areas, black beams, flagstones and bare boards, inglenook log fire, extension opening on to covered terrace; background music; children and dogs (in bar) welcome, disabled facilities, two garden areas, open all day. *(Bronwen Matthews-King)*

MEONSTOKE   SU6120
Bucks Head (01489) 877313
Village signed just off A32 N of Droxford; SO32 3NA Unassuming and welcoming little pub with partly panelled L-shaped dining lounge looking over road to water meadows, log fire, plush banquettes and bare boards, popular food including Sun roasts, well kept Greene King ales, another fire in friendly public bar where dogs allowed; small garden, lovely village setting with ducks on pretty little River Meon, good walks, five bedrooms, hearty breakfast, open all day weekends. *(Anon)*

MICHELDEVER   SU5138
Half Moon & Spread Eagle
(01962) 774339 *Brown sign to pub off A33 N of Winchester; SO21 3DG* Simply furnished 18th-c beamed village local, bare-boards bar with woodburner, horsebrasses and old banknotes pinned overhead, five real ales, ample helpings of enjoyable well priced food in carpeted dining side, steps up to games area with pool and shelves of books, quiz last Sat of month; children and dogs welcome, sheltered back terrace and garden, pleasant walks nearby, open all day Sat, Sun till 8pm, closed Mon. *(Jennifer Banks)*

MILFORD-ON-SEA   SZ2891
Beach House (01590) 643044
Park Lane; SO41 0PT Civilised well placed Victorian hotel/dining pub recently refurbished by Hall & Woodhouse, restored oak-panelled interior, entrance-hall bar with Badger First Gold, Tanglefoot and a guest, enjoyable sensibly priced food from baguettes and sharing boards up, also good value lunchtime set deal, friendly attentive service, magnificent views from dining room

---

There are report forms at the back of the book.

and terrace; children welcome, dogs in bar, grounds down to the Solent looking out to the Needles, 15 bedrooms, open all day. *(David and Sally Frost)*

MINSTEAD SU2810

★ **Trusty Servant** (023) 8081 2137

Just off A31, not far from M27 junction 1; SO43 7FY Attractive 19th-c building in pretty New Forest hamlet with interesting church (Sir Arthur Conan Doyle buried here), wandering cattle and ponies, plenty of easy walks; two-room bar and big dining room, well kept ales and good reasonably priced food including local game, welcoming efficient service even when busy; dogs welcome, terrace and big sloping garden, open all day. *(Revd Michael Vockins, Wendy Breese)*

NEW CHERITON — SU5827

★ **Hinton Arms** (01962) 771252

A272 near B3046 junction; SO24 0NH Neatly kept popular country pub with cheerful accommodating landlord, three or four real ales including Bowman Wallops Wood and a house beer brewed by Hampshire, decent food from sandwiches to daily specials, sporting pictures and memorabilia, relaxing atmosphere and friendly staff; TV lounge; well behaved children and dogs welcome, terrace and big garden, very handy for Hinton Ampner House (NT). *(Stuart Paulley)*

NEWNHAM SU7054

Old House At Home (01256) 807626

Handy for M3 junction 5; A287 then keep on across A30; RG27 9AH Bay-windowed dining pub in secluded hamlet, interesting choice of well liked freshly cooked food (not particularly cheap), real ales and good selection of wines by the glass including champagne, friendly efficient service, bare boards, painted half-panelling, open fire in brick fireplace; seats outside, pleasant walks nearby, closed Sun evening. *(Anon)*

ODIHAM SU7451

Water Witch (01256) 808778

Colt Hill – quiet no-through road signed off main street; RG29 1AL Olde-worlde décor in nicely kept Chef & Brewer by picturesque stretch of Basingstoke Canal (boat hire), big but cosily divided with more formal dining area at back, wide choice of food and three mainstream ales; no dogs inside; children welcome, disabled access and parking, pretty hanging baskets in front, terrace with awning, garden down to the water, open all day. *(Ian Phillips, Barry Collett)*

PETERSFIELD SU7423

George (01730) 233343

The Square; GU32 3HH Old building in square with café-style tables outside, nicely

updated interior, rather long and thin but avoids feeling crowded, enjoyable food from well filled lunchtime sandwiches, home-made burgers and Pieminster pies to evening tapas, three well kept ales such as Bowman Swift One, good choice of wines by the glass and decent coffee, friendly young staff, live music Fri; children welcome, garden with terrace behind, open all day from 9am for breakfast. *(George Atkinson)*

PETERSFIELD SU7423

Good Intent (01730) 263838

College Street; GU31 4AF Homely 16th-c coaching inn, friendly and chatty, with five well kept Fullers/Gales beers and enjoyable fresh pubby food (not Sun evening) including range of O'Hagan's sausages, efficient service, low black beams, pine tables and built-in upholstered benches, separate large restaurant, log fires; background music – live Sun, quiz Mon; children and dogs welcome, seats on front terrace, narrow entrance to small back car park, three bedrooms. *(Val and Alan Green, Lucien Perring)*

PORTSMOUTH SZ6399

Bridge Tavern (023) 9275 2992

East Street, Camber Dock; PO1 2JJ Flagstones, bare boards and lots of dark wood, comfortable furnishings, maritime theme with good harbour views, Fullers ales, plenty of fish dishes; nice waterside terrace, open all day. *(Ann and Colin Hunt)*

PORTSMOUTH SZ6399

Dolphin (023) 9282 3595

High Street, Old Portsmouth opposite cathedral; PO1 2LU Spacious old beamed pub – known as the country pub in town, and furnished accordingly; half a dozen well kept ales (some expensive), enjoyable food including good vegetarian options, friendly staff; children and dogs welcome, small terrace behind. *(Ann and Colin Hunt)*

PORTSMOUTH SU6706

George (023) 9222 1079

Portsdown Hill Road, Widley; PO6 1BE Old-fashioned one-bar Georgian local with village feel, half a dozen well kept ales such as Adnams, Greene King and Ringwood, simple lunchtime food, cheerful staff, live music and quiz nights; dogs welcome, views of Hayling Island, Portsmouth and Isle of Wight, hill walks across the road. *(Val and Alan Green)*

PORTSMOUTH SU6501

George (023) 9275 3885

Queen Street, near dockyard entrance; PO1 3HU Spotless old inn with two rooms, one set for dining, log fire, glass-covered well and maritime pictures, real ales such as Greene King IPA, well priced food (not Sun evening, Mon) from sandwiches up, friendly staff; eight bedrooms, handy for dockyard and HMS *Victory*. *(Ann and Colin Hunt)*

PORTSMOUTH   SU6300
Lady Hamilton   (023) 9287 0505
The Hard, near Gunwharf; PO1 3DT
Longish narrow bar with nautical flavour, pictures of Lady Hamilton and Nelson, fairly priced generous food including daily roast, real ales, nice coffee, friendly staff and atmosphere; clean bedrooms, open all day in summer. *(Ann and Colin Hunt)*

PORTSMOUTH   SZ6399
Pembroke   (023) 9282 3961
Pembroke Road; PO1 2NR Traditional well run corner local with good buoyant atmosphere, comfortable and unspoilt under long-serving licensees, Bass, Fullers London Pride and Greene King Abbot from L-shaped bar, fresh rolls, coal-effect gas fire; open all day (break 5-7pm Sun). *(Ann and Colin Hunt)*

PORTSMOUTH   SZ6299
Spice Island   (023) 9287 0543
Bath Square; Old Portsmouth; PO1 2JL Vast largely Georgian waterside pub, Greene King ales and all-day food, big windows overlooking passing ships in roomy modernised areas, upstairs restaurant; disabled facilities, tables out in harbourside square. *(Ann and Colin Hunt)*

PORTSMOUTH   SZ6299
Still & West   (023) 9282 1567
Bath Square, Old Portsmouth; PO1 2JL Great location with superb views of narrow harbour mouth and across to Isle of Wight, especially from glazed-in panoramic upper family area and waterfront terrace with lots of picnic-sets; nautical bar with fireside sofas and cosy colour scheme, Fullers ales, good choice of wines by the glass, enjoyable food all day including signature fish and chips; background music; children welcome, handy for Historic Dockyard, nearby pay-and-display parking, open all day. *(Ann and Colin Hunt)*

PORTSMOUTH   SZ6399
Wellington   (023) 9281 8965
High Street, off Grand Parade, Old Portsmouth; PO1 2LY Smallish open-plan pub with large Georgian bay window, comfortable old-fashioned feel with drapes and red colour scheme, enjoyable reasonably priced food including fresh fish, three real ales, dining area at back, some live music; children and dogs welcome, attractive little outside seating area, near seafront and historic square tower, open all day summer (all day Fri-Sun winter), closed Mon Jan-Apr. *(Ann and Colin Hunt)*

PORTSMOUTH   SU6400
White Swan   (023) 9289 1340
Guildhall Walk; PO1 2DD Refurbished mock-Tudor former Wetherspoons, now owned by Brewhouse & Kitchen and visibly brewing its own beers, also decent choice of well priced food (all day Fri-Sun) from

sandwiches and sharing boards up including a whole chicken steamed in ale, live jazz Sun lunchtime; open all day. *(Ann and Colin Hunt)*

ROMSEY   SU3523
Dukes Head   (01794) 514450
A3057 out towards Stockbridge; SO51 0HB Attractive 16th-c dining pub with warren of small comfortable linked rooms, big log fire, enjoyable generously served food including daily specials, ales such as Flack Manor, Fullers and Sharps; children welcome, sheltered back terrace and pleasant garden, handy for Sir Harold Hillier Gardens, open all day weekends. *(Anon)*

ROMSEY   SU3521
Old House At Home   (01794) 513175
Love Lane; SO51 8DE Attractive 16th-c thatched pub surrounded by new development; friendly and bustling, with appealingly individual and old-fashioned décor, wide choice of freshly made sensibly priced bar food including popular Sun lunch, well kept Fullers/Gales ales and guests, Aspall's cider, decent coffee, cheerful efficient service, good pubby atmosphere; children's play area. *(John Branston)*

ROMSEY   SU3520
Three Tuns   (01794) 512639
Middlebridge Street (but car park signed straight off A27 bypass); SO51 8HL Welcoming old beamed and bow-windowed pub, well kept Flack Manor and guests, enjoyable fairly traditional food from sandwiches up, flagstones and painted panelling, cases of stuffed animals, log fires; children welcome, open all day. *(Natalie Tanner)*

ROTHERWICK   SU7156
Coach & Horses   (01256) 768976
Signed from B3349 N of Hook; also quite handy for M3 junction 5; RG27 9BG Friendly 17th-c pub with traditional beamed front rooms, good value locally sourced pubby food and well kept Badger ales, log fire and woodburners, newer back dining area; children, dogs and muddy boots welcome, tables out at front and on terrace behind, pretty flower tubs and baskets, good walks, open all day Sat, Sun till 6pm, closed Mon. *(Anon)*

ROTHERWICK   SU7156
Falcon   (01256) 765422
Off B3349 N of Hook, not far from M3 junction 5; RG27 9BL Open-plan country pub with good food freshly made by chef-landlord from sandwiches and light dishes up, friendly efficient service, well kept ales such as Otter and Ringwood, good selection of wines, rustic tables and comfy sofa in bare-boards bar, well laid flagstoned dining area, log fires; free wi-fi; children and dogs welcome, disabled access, tables out in front and in back garden, open all day.
(Barbara Rothwell)

SELBORNE   SU7433
Queens (01420) 511454
High Street; GU34 3JJ Comfortably
refurbished and welcoming, open fires,
interesting local memorabilia, well kept
Hogs Back TEA and Triple fff Alton Pride,
food (not Sun evening) from sandwiches
and pubby standards to french country
dishes, cream teas and nice coffee,
cheerful smartly dressed staff, occasional
jazz; children and dogs welcome, garden
picnic-sets, eight bedrooms, very handy
for Gilbert White's House, open all day.
(Rory and Jackie Hudson)

SELBORNE   SU7433
Selborne Arms (01420) 511247
High Street; GU34 3JR Character tables,
pews and deep settles made from casks on
antique boards, good range of changing
largely local ales and several wines by the
glass, popular food from pubby choices up,
big log fire, daily papers, carpeted dining
room with local photographs; no dogs inside;
children welcome, plenty of garden tables,
arbour and terrace heated by logburner,
orchard and good play area, zigzag path up
Hanger, handy for Gilbert White's House,
open all day weekends. *(N R White)*

SHALDEN   SU7043
Golden Pot (01420) 80655
*B3349 Odiham Road N of Alton;
GU34 4DJ* Airy décor with sage-green
walls, bare boards and log fires, enjoyable
sensibly priced food from baguettes up
including themed nights, friendly service,
several interesting real ales, skittle alley;
background music; children welcome, some
tables out on covered area at front, garden
with play area. *(Martin and Karen Wake,
Tony and Jill Radnor)*

SHEDFIELD   SU5613
Samuels Rest (01329) 832213
*Upper Church Road (signed off B2177);
SO32 2JB* Unspoilt cosy village local under
newish welcoming licensees, straightforward
food and three well kept beers, nice eating
area away from bar; garden with terrace,
lovely church. *(Ann and Colin Hunt)*

SHEDFIELD   SU5513
Wheatsheaf (01329) 833024
A334 Wickham–Botley; SO32 2JG
Friendly no-fuss local with well kept
Flowerpots ales tapped from the cask, farm
cider, short sensible choice of enjoyable
bargain lunches (evening food Tues and
Weds), good service, woodburner in public

bar, smaller lounge, live music Sat; dogs
welcome, garden, handy for Wickham
Vineyard, open all day. *(Stephen and
Jean Curtis)*

SHERFIELD ENGLISH   SU3022
Hatchet (01794) 322487
Romsey Road; SO51 6FP Beamed and
panelled 18th-c pub under new licensees,
good choice of popular fairly priced food
including two-for-one steak deal Tues and
Thurs evenings, four well kept ales such as
Dartmoor, St Austell, Sharps and Timothy
Taylors, good wine choice, friendly hard-
working staff, long bar with cosy area down
steps, woodburner, more steps up to second
bar with darts, TV, juke box and machines;
children and dogs welcome, outside seating
on two levels, play area, open all day
weekends. *(Anon)*

SHIPTON BELLINGER   SU2345
Boot (01980) 842279
High Street; SP9 7UF Village pub with
huge range of enjoyable reasonably priced
food including indian, chinese, thai, italian
and mexican as well as traditional english
dishes, friendly staff; background music
turned down on request; children welcome,
back garden with decked area, open all day
weekends. *(Phil and Jane Hodson, Mrs Zara
Elliott)*

SOPLEY   SZ1596
Woolpack (01425) 672252
B3347 N of Christchurch; BH23 7AX
Pretty thatched dining pub with rambling
open-plan low-beamed bar, enjoyable
traditional food plus daily specials,
Ringwood, Sharps Doom Bar and a guest,
Thatcher's cider and good choice of wines
by the glass, modern dining conservatory
overlooking weir; dogs in eating areas,
dogs in certain parts, terrace and charming
garden with weeping willows, duck stream
and footbridges, open (and food) all day.
(Sue and Mike Todd)

SOUTH WARNBOROUGH   SU7247
Poachers (01256) 862218
Alton Road (A32); RG29 1RP Welcoming
village pub with spotless modernised interior,
leather sofas and easy chairs by brick
fireplace in bare-boards bar, spacious dining
area to right with high-backed chairs at light
wood tables, enjoyable food including pizzas,
pasta and pub favourites, well kept ales such
as Andwell, Fullers and Sharps, good choice
of wines by the glass, friendly helpful staff;
seats out in front and in garden behind, five
bedrooms, open all day. *(Val and Alan Green)*

SOUTHAMPTON SU4111
★ **Duke of Wellington** (023) 8033 9222

Bugle Street (or walk along city wall from Bar Gate); SO14 2AH Striking ancient timber-framed building dating from 14th c, cellars even older, heavy beams and great log fire, well kept Wadworths ales, good choice of wines by the glass and good value traditional pub food (not Sun evening), friendly helpful service; background music (live Fri); children welcome, sunny streetside picnic-sets, handy for Tudor House Museum, open all day. *(Nigel and Sue Foster)*

SOUTHAMPTON SU4313
South Western Arms
(023) 8032 4542 *Adelaide Road, by St Denys station; SO17 2HW* Friendly backstreet local with ten well kept changing ales, also good choice of bottled beers and whiskies, friendly staff and easy-going atmosphere, bare boards and brickwork, lots of woodwork, toby jugs, pump clips and stag's head on beams, old range and earthenware, darts, pool and table football in upper gallery allowing children, some live music, beer festivals; dogs welcome on leads, picnic-sets in walled beer garden, open all day from noon. *(Dr Martin Owton)*

SOUTHAMPTON SU4213
White Star (023) 8082 1990

Oxford Street; SO14 3DJ Smart modern bar, banquettes and open fire, comfortable sofas and armchairs in secluded alcoves by south-facing windows, bistro-style dining area, good up-to-date food from interesting baguettes and light dishes up, efficient attentive service, Flack Manor and Itchen Valley ales, nice wines by the glass and lots of cocktails; they may ask to keep a credit card while you eat; sunny pavement tables on pedestrianised street, 13 boutique bedrooms, open all day. *(Anon)*

SOUTHSEA SZ6699
Artillery Arms (023) 9273 3610

Hester Road; PO4 8HB Proper two-bar Victorian backstreet local, good choice of real ales and decent food, friendly atmosphere. *(Ann and Colin Hunt)*

SOUTHSEA SZ6498
Belle Isle (023) 9282 0515

Osbourne Road; PO5 3LR Popular corner café/bar/restaurant in former shop, unusual interior with continental feel, three real ales, international bottled beers, cocktails and reasonably priced interesting blackboard food, decent coffee; children welcome, some seats out at front, open all day. *(Ann and Colin Hunt)*

SOUTHSEA SZ6499
Eldon Arms (023) 9229 7963

Eldon Street/Norfolk Street; PO5 4BS Rambling backstreet pub under new management, Fullers London Pride, Sharps Doom Bar and a guest, old pictures and advertisements, attractive mirrors, bric-a-brac and shelves of books, darts, bar billiards and pool; children welcome, tables in back garden, open all day (from 3pm Mon-Thurs). *(Ann and Colin Hunt)*

SOUTHSEA SZ6499
★ **Hole in the Wall** (023) 9229 8085

Great Southsea Street; PO5 3BY Friendly unspoilt little local in old part of town, excellent range of well kept/priced ales including Oakleaf Hole Hearted, Thatcher's cider, speciality local sausages, meat puddings and other simple good value food, nicely worn boards, dark pews and panelling, old photographs and prints, hundreds of pump clips on ceiling, little snug behind the bar, daily papers, quiz night Thurs, Oct beer festival; small outside area at front with benches, side garden, opens 4pm (noon Fri, 2pm Sun). *(Ann and Colin Hunt)*

SOUTHSEA SZ6499
King Street Tavern (023) 9287 3307

King Street; PO5 4EH Sympathetically refurbished corner pub in attractive conservation area, spectacular Victorian tiled façade, bare boards and original fittings, four well kept Wadworths ales and guests, Thatcher's cider, good value straightforward home-made food from short menu; background and live music including fortnightly Sat jazz; dogs welcome, courtyard tables, open all day Fri-Sun, closed Mon. *(Ann and Colin Hunt)*

SOUTHSEA SZ6598
Leopold (023) 9282 9748

Albert Road; PO4 0JT Traditional green-tiled corner local with ten well kept ales, good choice of ciders and over 100 bottled beers, bright interior with hundreds of pump clips on the walls and pictures of old Portsmouth, good value rolls; unobtrusive TVs each end, games machines, darts, Mon quiz; walled beer garden behind, open all day. *(Ann and Colin Hunt)*

SOUTHSEA SZ6599
Northcote (023) 9278 9888

Francis Avenue; PO4 0HL Welcoming traditional two-bar pub, ales such as Hop Back and Wadworths, cosy carpeted lounge with Sherlock Holmes memorabilia, public bar with pool and darts; seats outside, open all day. *(Ann and Colin Hunt)*

SOUTHSEA SZ6698
Sir Loin of Beef (023) 9282 0115

Highland Road, Eastney; PO4 9NH Simple spic-and-span one-room corner pub, at least eight well kept frequently changing ales (tasters offered), bottled beers, no food, helpful friendly staff and buoyant atmosphere, interesting ship photographs, parasols suspended from ceiling, bar billiards, juke box, monthly Sun jazz and Thurs quiz; open all day. *(Ann and Colin Hunt)*

SOUTHSEA SZ6499
Wine Vaults (023) 9286 4712
Albert Road, opposite King's Theatre; PO5 2SF Bustling Fullers pub with several chatty rooms on different floors, main panelled bar with long plain counter and pubby furniture, smarter restaurant area, seven well kept ales and decent choice of food including pizzas and range of burgers, good service; background music, sports TV; children welcome, dogs in bar, smokers' roof terrace, open (and food) all day. *(Ann and Colin Hunt)*

SOUTHWICK SU6208
Golden Lion (023) 9221 0437
High Street; just off B2177 on Portsdown Hill; PO17 6EB Friendly two-bar 16th-c beamed pub (where Eisenhower and Montgomery came before D-Day); up to six local ales including two from Suthwyk using barley from surrounding fields, four ciders and a dozen wines by the glass, enjoyable locally sourced home-made food (not Sun or Mon evenings) from snacks up in bar and dining room, lounge bar with sofas and log fire, live music including Tues jazz; good outside lavatories; children and dogs welcome, picnic-sets on grass at side, picturesque Estate village with scenic walks, open all day Sat, till 7pm Sun. *(Val and Alan Green, Ann and Colin Hunt)*

SOUTHWICK SU6208
Red Lion (023) 9237 7223
High Street; PO17 6EF Neatly kept low-beamed village dining pub with good choice of well liked food (best to book), Fullers/Gales and a guest beer, several wines by the glass, efficient friendly service from smartly dressed staff even though busy, popular with older diners; children welcome, nice walks, closed Mon. *(Anon)*

ST MARY BOURNE SU4250
Bourne Valley (01264) 738361
Upper Link (B3048); SP11 6BT Attractively updated old red-brick inn, bar with central servery and log fire, separate raftered restaurant, enjoyable interesting food along with pubby choices (some not cheap and service charge added), Upham Punter and three guests, lots of wines by the glass, deli counter; children and dogs welcome, terrace and nice garden backing on to stream, good walks, nine bedrooms, open all day. *(Jennifer Banks, Mrs Julie Thomas)*

STEEP SU7325
Cricketers (01730) 261035
Church Road; GU32 2DW Light airy refurbishment under present owners; good modern pub food including pizzas from visible oven, welcoming helpful staff, ales such as Bowman, Flowerpots and Langhams, decent wines, log fires in brick fireplaces with old portraits above, stripped floorboards and green half-panelling, chandeliers, candelabra and some cricketing memorabilia, occasional live acoustic music; children welcome, painted picnic-sets on narrow front deck, clean comfortable bedrooms, closed Sun evening, otherwise open (and food) all day. *(David and Carole Kidd)*

STOCKBRIDGE SU3535
Three Cups (01264) 810527
High Street; SO20 6HB Lovely low-beamed building dating from 1500, some emphasis on dining with lots of smartly set pine tables, but also high-backed settles, country bric-a-brac and four well kept ales such as Wells & Youngs, good interesting food along with more pubby choices, amiable service, nice wines by the glass, extended 'orangery' restaurant; children and dogs welcome, vine-covered verandah and charming cottage garden with streamside terrace, eight bedrooms, open all day. *(Conor McGaughey, Geoffrey Kemp)*

STOCKBRIDGE SU3535
★White Hart (01264) 810663
High Street; A272/A3057 roundabout; SO20 6HF Pleasantly busy divided beamed bar, attractive décor with antique prints, oak pews and other seats around pine tables, friendly efficient staff, enjoyable food from bar snacks to substantial daily specials, well kept Fullers/Gales beers, comfortable restaurant with blazing log fire (children allowed); dogs in bar, disabled facilities, terrace tables and nice garden, 14 good bedrooms, open all day. *(Edward Mirzoeff, John and Joan Calvert)*

STRATFIELD TURGIS SU6960
Wellington Arms (01256) 882214
Off A33 Reading–Basingstoke; RG27 0AS Handsome old country hotel dating from the 17th c, restful and surprisingly pubby tall-windowed two-room bar, part flagstoned, part carpeted, with leather chesterfields by open fire, two well kept Badger ales, good food and service; children and dogs welcome, garden, 27 comfortable bedrooms, open all day. *(Jennifer Banks)*

STROUD SU7223
Seven Stars (01730) 264122
Winchester Road; set back from A272 Petersfield–Winchester; GU32 3PG Extended and modernised open-plan flint and brick pub, panelling, beams, wood and flagstone floors, good log fires, separate counter for ordering wide choice of good value food including tasty home-made pies, fast friendly service, well kept Badger ales and good wine list, large restaurant; free wi-fi; children and dogs (in bar) welcome, outside tables, good if strenuous walking, open all day. *(Lucien Perring)*

SWANMORE　　　　　　　SU5716
Brickmakers　(01489) 890954
Church Road; SO32 2PA　Refurbished
1920s pub with friendly relaxed atmosphere,
four well kept ales including Bowman, decent
wines and good interesting food all day (till
7pm Sun) from landlord-chef, early evening
deal Mon-Thurs, leather sofas by log fire,
dining area with local artwork, Tues quiz,
some live music; children and dogs welcome
(pub's dog is Rosie), garden with raised deck,
open all day. *(Di Braund, Ann and Colin Hunt,
Stephen and Jean Curtis)*

SWANMORE　　　　　　　SU5816
Hunters　(01489) 877214
Hillgrove; SO32 2PZ　Popular rambling
old dining pub on edge of village, friendly
long-serving licensees and nice staff, wide
choice of good honest freshly made food,
home-baked bread, well kept Bowman and
a guest tapped from the cask, lots of wines
by the glass, bank notes, carpentry and
farm tools on the walls; background music;
children and dogs welcome, big garden with
play area, nice walks N of village, open all
day weekends (can be very busy then).
(Val and Alan Green)

SWANMORE　　　　　　　SU5815
★Rising Sun　(01489) 896663
*Droxford Road; signed off A32 N of
Wickham and B2177 S of Bishop's
Waltham, at Hillpound E of village
centre; SO32 2PS*　Former coaching inn
with friendly hands-on licensees; easy chairs
and sofa by log fire in low-beamed carpeted
bar, pleasant roomier dining area with
brick barrel vaulting in one part, four ales
including Sharps, 13 wines by the glass and
tasty good value food; children and dogs (in
bar) welcome, picnic-sets on side grass with
a play area, Kings Way long-distance path
nearby. *(Val and Alan Green, Dr and Mrs J D
Abell, Paul Sa, Ann and Colin Hunt)*

SWAY　　　　　　　　　　SZ2898
Hare & Hounds　(01590) 682404
*Durns Town, just off B3055 SW of
Brockenhurst; SO41 6AL*　Bright, airy and
comfortable New Forest family dining pub,
popular generously served food, ales such
as Itchen Valley, Ringwood, St Austell and
Timothy Taylors, good helpful service even at
busy times, low beams and central log fire;
background music; dogs welcome, picnic-sets
and play frame in neatly kept garden, open
all day. *(Anon)*

THRUXTON　　　　　　　SU2945
White Horse　(01264) 772401
*Mullens Pond, just off A303 eastbound;
SP11 8EE*　Attractive old thatched pub
tucked below A303 embankment, comfortably
modernised, with emphasis on enjoyable
fresh food, good friendly service, plenty of
wines by the glass and well kept ales such

as Greene King, spacious interior with very
low beams, woodburner and separate dining
area; good-sized garden and terrace, four
bedrooms, closed Sun evening. *(Tony and
Jill Radnor)*

TICHBORNE　　　　　　　SU5730
★Tichborne Arms　(01962) 733760
Signed off B3047; SO24 0NA
Traditional thatched pub with latticed
windows, panelling, antiques and stuffed
animals, open fire, Palmers and guests
tapped from the cask, local cider, enjoyable
food from baguettes up, evening candlelit
tables, locals' bar, darts, board games
and shove-ha'penny; children and dogs
welcome, big garden in rolling countryside,
Wayfarers Walk and Itchen Way pass close
by, closed Sun evening.
(R Elliott, Tony and Jill Radnor)

TIMSBURY　　　　　　　SU3325
★Bear & Ragged Staff
(01794) 368602　*A3057 towards
Stockbridge; pub marked on OS Sheet
185 map reference 334254; SO51 0LB*
Roadside dining pub with good choice of
popular food including blackboard specials,
friendly service, lots of wines by the glass,
Fullers, Hampshire, Ringwood and Timothy
Taylors, good-sized beamed interior with log
fire; children welcome in eating part, tables
in extended garden with play area, handy
for Mottisfont (NT), good walks, open all
day. *(Val and Alan Green)*

TITCHFIELD　　　　　　　SU5405
Wheatsheaf　(01329) 842965
*East Street; off A27 near Fareham;
PO14 4AD*　Welcoming smartened-up old
place with well kept ales and good popular
food (all day Sun) including small-plate
menu, curry night Mon, steak night Tues,
bow-windowed front bar, back restaurant
extension, log fires; background music;
terrace, open all day. *(Val and Alan Green,
Ann and Colin Hunt)*

TOTFORD　　　　　　　　SU5737
Woolpack　0845 293 8066
B3046 Basingstoke–Alresford; SO24 9TJ
Nicely refurbished roadside inn, clean and
comfortable, with good food from bar snacks
to restaurant dishes, ales including Palmers
and one named for the pub, several wines
by the glass including champagne, italian
coffee, efficient service, raised open fire in
bar, smart split-level dining room; pool; round
picnic-sets outside on gravel, lovely setting in
good walking country, seven bedrooms, open
all day. *(Anon)*

TWYFORD　　　　　　　　SU4824
★Bugle　(01962) 714888
B3355/Park Lane; SO21 1QT　Modern
pub with good enterprising food served by
attentive friendly young staff, well kept
ales from Bowman, Flowerpots and Upham,

woodburner, nice wines by the glass; background music; attractive verandah seating area, good walks nearby, open all day. *(Anon)*

UPHAM   SU5320
★ **Brushmakers Arms** (01489) 860231
Shoe Lane; village signed from Winchester–Bishop's Waltham downs road, and from B2177; SO32 1JJ Plenty of regulars and weekend dog walkers at this cheery low-beamed village pub, L-shaped bar divided by central woodburner, cushioned settles and chairs around mix of tables, lots of brushes and related paraphernalia, little back snug, enjoyable home-made food including range of pies, Fullers, Ringwood, Upham and a guest, decent coffee, Sun bar nibbles; children and dogs welcome (the pub cats are Luna and Baxter), big garden with picnic-sets on sheltered terrace and tree-shaded lawn, good walks nearby, open all day Sun. *(Ann and Colin Hunt, Phil and Jane Villiers)*

UPPER CLATFORD   SU3543
Crook & Shears (01264) 361543
Off A343 S of Andover, via Foundry Road; SP11 7QL Cosy 17th-c thatched pub with friendly relaxing atmosphere, several homely olde-worlde seating areas, bare boards and panelling, well kept ales such as Otter, Ringwood and Sharps, Thatcher's cider, traditional reasonably priced food (not Sun evening) from good baguettes to enjoyable Sun roasts, OAP weekday lunch deal, friendly attentive service, open fires and woodburner, small dining room, back skittle alley with own bar; children and dogs welcome, pleasant secluded garden behind, closed Mon lunchtime. *(Ann and Colin Hunt, Penny Matthews)*

UPPER FARRINGDON   SU7135
Rose & Crown (01420) 588231
Off A32 S of Alton; Crows Lane – follow Church, Selborne, Liss signpost; GU34 3ED Airy 19th-c village pub with L-shaped log-fire bar, well kept local ales such as Triple fff, good reasonably priced food (all day Sun) including some interesting choices, efficient friendly young staff, formal back dining room, jazz last Mon of month; children, walkers and dogs welcome, wide views from attractive back garden, open all day weekends. *(Tony and Jill Radnor, N R White, Corinne Green)*

UPTON GREY   SU6948
Hoddington Arms (01256) 862371
Signed off B3349 S of Hook; Bidden Road; RG25 2RL Nicely refurbished 18th-c beamed pub, good food from varied menu (sometimes themed), local ales such as Andwell along with a beer named for them (Hodd), a dozen wines by the glass, events including live music and beer/cider festivals; children and dogs welcome, big enclosed garden with terrace, quiet pretty village, good walking/cycling, open all day. *(Louise Richards)*

WALHAMPTON   SZ3396
Walhampton Arms (01590) 673113
B3054 NE of Lymington; aka Walhampton Inn; SO41 5RE Large comfortable Georgian-style family roadhouse, popular well priced food including carvery in raftered former stables and two adjoining areas, pleasant lounge, Ringwood ales and nice cider, cheerful helpful staff; attractive courtyard, good walks, open all day and handy for Isle of Wight ferry. *(Penny and Peter Keevil)*

WALTHAM CHASE   SU5614
Black Dog (01329) 832316
Winchester Road; SO32 2LX Old brick-built pub with low-ceilinged carpeted front bar, three well kept Greene King ales and a guest, over a dozen wines by the glass, good choice of enjoyable home-made food including weekday lunch deal, cheerful service, log fires, back restaurant; children and dogs welcome, colourful hanging baskets, tables in good-sized neatly kept garden with play area, open all day weekends in summer. *(Ann and Colin Hunt)*

WELL   SU7646
★ **Chequers** (01256) 862605
Off A287 via Crondall, or A31 via Froyle and Lower Froyle; RG29 1TL Appealing low-beamed and panelled country pub under newish management; very good restaurant style food (some quite pricey) including fresh fish/seafood, also lunchtime sandwiches, Badger ales and good choice of wines, friendly efficient service, wood floors and log fires; free wi-fi; bench seating on vine-covered front terrace, spacious back garden overlooking fields. *(F and N Hatch, Martin and Karen Wake, Tony and Jill Radnor)*

WEST TYTHERLEY   SU2730
Black Horse (01794) 340308
North Lane; SP5 1NF Compact unspoilt beamed village local, welcoming licensees and chatty regulars, traditional bar with a couple of long tables and big fireplace, nicely set dining area off, four real ales, enjoyable reasonably priced food including good Sun roasts, skittle alley, quiz last Weds of month; children and dogs welcome, closed Sun evening and lunchtimes Mon-Weds. *(Anon)*

WHERWELL   SU3839
★ **Mayfly** (01264) 860283
Testcombe (over by Fullerton, not in Wherwell itself); A3057 SE of Andover, between B3420 turn-off and Leckford where road crosses River Test; OS Sheet 185 map reference 382390; SO20 6AX Well run busy pub with decking and conservatory overlooking fast-flowing River Test; spacious beamed and carpeted bar with

fishing paraphernalia, rustic pub furnishings and woodburner, ales such as Adnams, Gales, Hop Back, Palmers and Wickwar, lots of wines by the glass, wide range of good popular bar food all day (must book for a good table), courteous well organised service; background music; well behaved children and dogs welcome. *(Jeremy King, Conor McGaughey, Jill Hurley, Martin Day, Helen and Brian Edgeley)*

WHERWELL   SU3840
White Lion (01264) 860317
B3420; SP11 7JF Popular early 17th-c multi-level beamed village inn, good choice of enjoyable food including speciality pies, Flowerpots, Sharps, Timothy Taylors and two guests, several wines by the glass, very friendly helpful staff, open fire, comfy leather sofas and armchairs, dining rooms either side of bar; background music; well behaved children welcome, dogs on leads, sunny courtyard with good quality furniture, Test Way walks, six bedrooms, open all day from 7.30am (breakfast for non-residents). *(Michael and Jenny Back)*

WICKHAM   SU5711
★ Greens (01329) 833197
The Square, at junction with A334; PO17 5JQ Civilised dining place with clean-cut modern furnishings and décor, small bar with leather sofa and armchairs as well as bar stools, wide wine choice and a couple of real ales, efficient obliging young staff, step down to split-level balustraded dining areas, good food from typical bar lunches to imaginative specials; pleasant lawn overlooking water meadows, closed Sun evening and Mon. *(Val and Alan Green)*

WICKHAM   SU5711
Kings Head (01329) 832123
The Square; PO17 5JN Bustling modernised village pub (former coaching inn), open-plan bar with big windows and open fires, well kept Fullers/Gales ales, enjoyable food from sandwiches and sharing boards up, friendly efficient service, back dining area up some steps, skittle alley/function room; background and some live music, sports TV, free wi-fi; children welcome, tables out on square and in garden behind with play area, open (and food) all day. *(Ann and Colin Hunt)*

WINCHESTER   SU4829
Bishop on the Bridge
(01962) 855111 *High Street/Bridge Street; SO23 9JX* Neat efficiently run red-brick Fullers pub, their well kept beers and decent food from sandwiches up, leather sofas, old local prints; free wi-fi; children and dogs welcome, nice back terrace overlooking River Itchen, open all day. *(Pete Walker, Stephen and Jean Curtis)*

WINCHESTER   SU4828
★ Black Boy (01962) 861754
B3403 off M3 junction 10 towards city, then left into Wharf Hill; no nearby daytime parking – 220 metres from car park on B3403; SO23 9NQ Splendidly eccentric décor at this chatty old-fashioned pub, floor-to-ceiling books, lots of big clocks, mobiles made of wine bottles and spectacles, stuffed animals including a baboon and dachshund, two log fires, orange-painted room with big oriental rugs on red floorboards, barn room with open hayloft, five often local beers kept well, straightforward food (not Sun evening, Mon, Tues lunchtime) including good doorstep sandwiches, friendly service, table football and board games; background music; supervised children and dogs welcome, slate tables out in front and seats on attractive secluded terrace, open all day. *(Phil and Jane Villiers, Ann and Colin Hunt)*

WINCHESTER   SU4829
Eclipse (01962) 865676
The Square, between High Street and cathedral; SO23 9EX Picturesque unspoilt 14th-c local with massive beams and timbers in its two small cheerful rooms, four ales such as Bath Gem and Otter, decent choice of wines by the glass, good value traditional lunchtime food including popular Sun roasts, open fire, oak settles; children in back area, seats outside, handy for cathedral. *(Val and Alan Green, Neil and Anita Christopher)*

WINCHESTER   SU4829
★ Old Vine (01962) 854616
Great Minster Street; SO23 9HA Lively big-windowed town bar with well kept ales such as Bowman, Flowerpots, Ringwood and St Austell, high beams, worn oak boards, smarter and larger dining side with good choice of up-to-date food plus sandwiches and pub staples, efficient service even though busy, modern conservatory; faint background music; by cathedral, with sheltered terrace, partly covered and heated, charming bedrooms, open all day. *(Val and Alan Green, Paul Humphreys)*

WINCHESTER   SU4829
William Walker (01962) 627341
The Square; SO23 9EX Rambling corner pub in Cathedral Close, decent range of food from good sandwiches and baguettes up, Fullers ales, nice coffee, friendly service. *(Paul Humphreys)*

The letters and figures after the name of each town are its Ordnance Survey map reference. 'Using the *Guide*' at the beginning of the book explains how it helps you find a pub, in road atlases or large-scale maps as well as in our own maps.

Herefordshire

CAREY
SO5631 Map 4

Cottage of Content 🌟 🛏

Village signposted from good back road betweeen Ross-on-Wye and Hereford E of A49, through Hoarwithy; HR2 6NG

Country furnishings in a friendly rustic cottage with interesting food, real ales and seats on terraces; quiet bedrooms

This medieval cottage was once three labourers' cottages with its own integral cider and ale parlour. It's in a tucked-away, tranquil spot near the River Wye and our readers enjoy their visits (and staying overnight) very much. The friendly licensees have kept much of the place's character: there's a multitude of beams and country furnishings such as stripped-pine kitchen chairs, long pews by one big table and various old-fashioned tables on flagstones or bare boards. Hobsons Best and Wye Valley Butty Bach on handpump and local cider during the summer; background music. There are picnic-sets on the flower-filled front terrace and in the rural-feeling garden at the back. The bedrooms are quiet and the breakfasts good.

 Popular food includes a charcuterie plate, feta, olive and herb soufflé with tomato and basil sauce, beef and wild mushroom crumble, griddled lamb steak with pea and mint pesto, bacon-wrapped roast hake on tomato and smoked paprika cassoulet, rib-eye steak with mustard mash and green peppercorn sauce, and puddings such as burnt honey and yoghurt panna cotta with cardamom-baked rhubarb and iced banana and pecan parfait with caramelised banana. *Benchmark main dish: griddled pork plate (medallions, cured belly and chorizo) with black pudding crisp and crackling £13.50. Two-course evening meal £18.00.*

Free house ~ Licensees Richard and Helen Moore ~ Real ale ~ (01432) 840242 ~ Open 12-2.30, 6.30-11; 12-2.30 Sun; closed Sun evening, Mon, winter Tues, one week Feb, one week Oct ~ Bar food 12-2, 6.30-9; 12-2 Sun ~ Restaurant ~ Children welcome ~ Dogs allowed in bar ~ Bedrooms: £65/£85 ~ www.cottageofcontent.co.uk
Recommended by Mike and Mary Carter, Barry Collett, Michael and Mary Smith

EARDISLEY
SO3149 Map 6

Tram £

Corner of A4111 and Woodseaves Road; HR3 6PG

Character pub (the village itself is a big draw too) with welcoming licensees, a cheerful mix of customers and good food and beer

This is a proper pub with a cheerful mix of cusomers – some in for a chat and a pint, others to enjoy the popular food – and all are warmly welcomed by the friendly licensees and their smiling staff. The beamed bar on the left has appealing local character, especially in the cosy back section behind sturdy standing timbers. Here, regulars congregate on the bare boards by the counter, which serves Hobsons Best, Ludlow Gold and Wye Valley Butty Bach on handpump and three local organic ciders. Elsewhere, there are antique red and ochre floor tiles, a handful of nicely worn tables and chairs, a pair of long cushioned pews enclosing one much longer table, a high-backed settle, old country pictures and a couple of pictorial Wye maps. There's a small dining room on the right and a games room (with pool and darts) in a converted brewhouse with an attached smokers' area; background music. The outside gents' is one of the most stylish we've ever seen; the sizeable, neatly planted garden has picnic-sets on the lawn; pétanque.

Quite a choice of highly rated food includes sandwiches, quenelles of chicken and duck liver pâté, peat-smoked salmon with capers, moroccan-spiced mixed vegetable tagine with red pepper couscous, honey-roast ham and free-range eggs, chicken, ham, leek and button mushroom pie, steak burger with bacon, cheese, onion rings, coleslaw and chips, local fillet steak with port wine jus and potato fondant, and puddings such as rice pudding with berry compote and boozy banoffi pie with butterscotch ice-cream. *Benchmark main dish: 10oz local sirloin steak £15.50. Two-course evening meal £15.00.*

Free house ~ Licensees Mark and Kerry Vernon ~ Real ale ~ (01544) 327251 ~ Open 12-3, 6-midnight (12.30am Sat); 12-3, 7-10.30 Sun; closed Mon except bank holidays ~ Bar food 12-3, 6-9; 12-3 Sun ~ Restaurant ~ Children welcome ~ Dogs allowed in bar ~ Wi-fi ~ www.thetraminn.co.uk *Recommended by Pip White, John and Jennifer Spinks, Miss B D Picton, Alan Bulley, R T and J C Moggridge*

KILPECK   SO4430   Map 6

Kilpeck Inn ♀

Village and church signposted off A465 SW of Hereford; HR2 9DN

Imaginatively extended country inn in fascinating and peaceful village

A new chef-patron has taken over this neat inn, and the cooking is very good indeed. The beamed bar with dark slate flagstones rambles happily around to provide several tempting corners, with an antique high-backed settle in one and high stools around a matching chest-high table in another. This opens into three cosily linked dining rooms on the left, with high panelled wainscoting. Wye Valley Bitter and Butty Bach and a guest such as Kingstone Challenger on handpump and several wines by the glass; background music, darts and TV. The neat back grass has picnic-sets. The four bedrooms (named after local rivers) are very eco-minded, with a biomass boiler and rainwater recycling system. The nearby castle ruins are interesting and the unique romanesque church even more so.

Cooked by the landlord, the well liked food includes sandwiches, twice-baked cheese soufflé, mussels with pancetta and tarragon cream sauce, mustard-roasted ham and free-range eggs, beer-battered hake and chips, chicken with thyme-roasted root vegetables and parsnip crisps, local venison with beetroot and rosemary dauphinoise and redcurrant jus, and puddings such as warm chocolate fondant and bramley apple, cinnamon and oat crumble; they also offer a two- and three-course set lunch. *Benchmark main dish: slow-roasted pork belly with black pudding-stuffed tenderloin, apple mash and cider gravy £13.95. Two-course evening meal £18.25.*

Free house ~ Licensee Ross Williams ~ Real ale ~ (01981) 570464 ~ Open 12-2.30, 5.30-11; 12-3 Sun ~ Bar food 12-2, 7-9; 12-2 Sun ~ Restaurant ~ Children welcome ~ Dogs allowed in bar ~ Wi-fi ~ Bedrooms: £70/£80 ~ www.kilpeckinn.com *Recommended by R T and J C Moggridge, Richard Tilbrook, Miss B D Picton, Mike and Mary Carter, Robert Parker*

LEDBURY

Feathers 🌟 ♀ 🛏

High Street (A417); HR8 1DS

SO7137   Map 4

Handsome old hotel with chatty relaxed bar, more decorous lounge, good food and friendly staff; comfortable bedrooms

This strikingly timbered 16th-c building is a civilised hotel rather than a pub, but it does still have a convivial back bar/brasserie, with a chatty and cheerful mix of drinkers at one end. In the main part, full of contented diners, there are cosy leather easy chairs and sofas by the fire, flowers and oil lamps on stripped kitchen and other tables, and comfortable bays of banquettes and other seats. The long beams are a mass of hop bines, and prints and antique sale notices decorate the stripped panelling. Fullers London Pride and a couple of guests such as Malvern Hills Black Pear and Sharps Doom Bar on handpump, good wines by the glass from an extensive list and 40 malt whiskies; first class staff. The sedate lounge is just right for afternoon tea, with high-sided armchairs and sofas in front of a big log fire, and daily papers. In summer, the sheltered back terrace has abundant plant pots and hanging baskets.

 Using premium ingredients, the attractively presented food includes sandwiches, moules marinière, ham hock terrine with home-made piccalilli, fennel, leek and courgette risotto, beer-battered haddock and fries, burger with smoked bacon and cheese and spicy tomato relish, trio of pork (belly, cheek and fricadelle) with cider and apple, guinea fowl with pancetta beurre blanc and wild garlic mash, and puddings. *Benchmark main dish: lambs liver, goose-fat potatoes and red wine jus £14.25. Two-course evening meal £22.50.*

Free house ~ Licensee David Elliston ~ Real ale ~ (01531) 635266 ~ Open 11-11 (10.30 Sun) ~ Bar food 12-2 (2.30 weekends), 6.30-9.30 (10 Fri-Sun) ~ Restaurant ~ Children welcome ~ Dogs allowed in bar and bedrooms ~ Wi-fi ~ Bedrooms: £95/£145 ~ www.feathers-ledbury.co.uk *Recommended by Steve and Liz Tilley, N R White*

LITTLE COWARNE

Three Horseshoes ♀

Pub signposted off A465 SW of Bromyard; towards Ullingswick; HR7 4RQ

SO6050   Map 4

Long-serving licensees and friendly staff in bustling country pub, with well liked food using home-grown produce; bedrooms

Our readers return frequently to this friendly, carefully kept place. There's a proper welcome for both regulars and visitors, and the quarry-tiled L-shaped middle bar has upholstered settles, wooden chairs and tables, old local photographs above the woodburning stove, and hop-draped beams and local guidebooks. Opening off one side is the garden room, with wicker armchairs around tables, and views over the terraced seating area and well kept garden; leading off the other side is the games room, with pool, darts, a juke box, a games machine and cribbage. Wye Valley Bitter and Butty Bach and a guest such as Greene King Old Speckled Hen on handpump, local Oliver's cider and perry, a dozen wines by the glass and home-made elderflower cordial. A popular Sunday lunchtime carvery is offered in the stripped-stone, raftered and roomy restaurant extension. There are well sited tables and chairs on the terrace and on the neat, prettily planted lawn. The bedrooms are accessed by outside stairs. Disabled access.

Using some home-grown produce and making their own preserves and chutneys (sold at the bar), the popular food includes sandwiches, prawn and haddock smokies, devilled lambs kidneys, cheese, leek, celery, apple and walnut filo pie, venison faggots with damson gin gravy, local pork with cider sauce, and pheasant on parsnip mash with quince and white wine, and puddings – their home-made ice-creams are popular. *Benchmark main dish: steak in ale pie £13.00. Two-course evening meal £19.50.*

Free house ~ Licensees Norman and Janet Whittall ~ Real ale ~ (01885) 400276 ~ Open 11-3, 6.30-11; 12-4, 7-10.30 Sun; closed Tues all year, Sun evening in winter ~ Bar food 12-2, 7-9 ~ Restaurant ~ Children welcome ~ Wi-fi ~ Bedrooms: £40/£70 ~ www.threehorseshoes.co.uk *Recommended by Martin Day, Ed and Glenda Buck*

ROSS-ON-WYE
SO5924 Map 6
Kings Head 🛏
High Street (B4260); HR9 5HL

Welcoming bar in well run market-town hotel with real ales and tasty food; good bedrooms

With fair value food and a warm welcome, this 14th-c hotel is deservedly popular. The little beamed and panelled bar on the right has traditional pub furnishings, including comfortably padded bar seats and an antique cushioned box settle, stripped floorboards and a couple of black leather armchairs by a log-effect fire. Wye Valley Butty Bach and a guest beer such as Sharps Doom Bar on handpump, three farm ciders and several wines by the glass at sensible prices. The beamed lounge bar on the left, also with bare boards, has some timbering, soft leather armchairs, padded bucket seats and shelves of books; unobtrusive background music. There's a big carpeted dining room and the sheltered back courtyard has contemporary tables and chairs. The bedrooms are comfortable, and they do a good breakfast.

 Reasonably priced and tasty, the food includes sandwiches, mussels in indian spices with cider, black pudding fritters with beetroot relish, open lasagne of roasted squash and celeriac, chicken with mushrooms and tarragon oil, shepherd's pie with local lamb, pork in cured ham with blue cheese and port sauce, salmon with beurre blanc, and puddings such as dark chocolate brownie with chocolate sauce and banoffi pie; they also offer a two-course lunch. *Benchmark main dish: steak in ale pie £10.95. Two-course evening meal £20.00.*

Free house ~ Licensee James Vidler ~ Real ale ~ (01989) 763174 ~ Open 11-11; 12-10.30 Sun ~ Bar food 12-2.15 (3 Sun), 6.30-9 ~ Restaurant ~ Children welcome ~ Dogs allowed in bar and bedrooms ~ Wi-fi ~ Bedrooms: £60/£85 ~ www.kingshead.co.uk *Recommended by Howard and Margaret Buchanan, Lucien Perring, Mike and Mary Carter, Guy Vowles*

SYMONDS YAT
SO5616 Map 4
Saracens Head 🍺 🛏
Symonds Yat E; HR9 6JL

Lovely riverside spot with seats on waterside terraces, a fine range of drinks and interesting food; comfortable bedrooms

If you stay in the bedrooms in the main building of this 17th-c inn, you'll have views over the River Wye; there are two more contemporary rooms in the boathouse annexe. The bustling, flagstoned bar has a buoyant, welcoming atmosphere and plenty of chatty customers – as well as cheerful staff who serve Bespoke Saved by the Bell, Kingstone 1503, Otley O1, Sharps Doom Bar and Wye Valley Butty Bach and HPA from handpump, 11 wines by the glass and a dozen malt whiskies. TV, background music and board games. There's also a cosy lounge and a modernised bare-boards dining room. The waterside terraces have plenty of seats, though you'll need to arrive early in fine weather. One way to reach the inn is on the little hand ferry (pulled by one of the staff). Disabled access to the bar and terrace.

The reliably good food includes sandwiches, baguettes, three-cheese beignets with quince dressing, rope-grown mussels in cider and leek cream sauce, sharing platters, pork and apple sausages with grain mustard mash and onion gravy, squash, sage and potato gratin, lamb and rosemary pudding, chilli and soy corn-fed chicken with lemongrass and coriander noodles, and puddings. *Benchmark main dish: beef and celeriac in ale pie £11.95. Two-course evening meal £21.00.*

Free house ~ Licensees P K and C J Rollinson ~ Real ale ~ (01600) 890435 ~ Open 10.30am-11pm (10.30pm Sun) ~ Bar food 12-2.30, 6.30-9 ~ Restaurant ~ Children welcome except in bedrooms ~ Dogs allowed in bar ~ Wi-fi ~ Bedrooms: £59/£89 ~ www.saracensheadinn.co.uk *Recommended by Dave Webster, Sue Holland, Chris and Angela Buckell, Lois Dyer*

TILLINGTON
Bell

SO4645 Map 6

Off A4110 NW of Hereford; HR4 8LE

Friendly and relaxed, with snug character bar opening into civilised dining areas – good value

Even when this bustling place is at its busiest, you can still be sure of a genuine welcome from the friendly, hands-on landlord. The snug parquet-floored bar on the left has assorted bucket armchairs around low chunky mahogany-coloured tables, brightly cushioned wall benches, team photographs and shelves of books; the black beams are strung with dried hops. Sharps Doom Bar, Wye Valley Bitter and a guest such as Cotleigh Barn Owl on handpump, cider made on site and locally produced spirits from Chase, all served by notably cheerful staff; daily papers, unobtrusive background music. The bar opens into a comfortable bare-boards dining lounge with stripy plush banquettes and a coal fire. Beyond that is a pitched-ceiling restaurant area with more banquettes and big country prints; slatted blinds look out on to a sunken terrace with contemporary tables, and a garden with teak tables, picnic-sets and a play area.

Using local produce and their home-reared pigs, the rewarding food includes open sandwiches and baguettes, fishcake with pickled cucumber and lemon and dill mayonnaise, blue cheese and mushrooms on toast, home-baked honey ham and eggs, meatballs and mozzarella on spaghetti with sweet tomato and chilli sauce, rabbit casserole, peppered duck on lemon thyme potatoes with pea and wild mushroom ragoût, and puddings such as butterscotch tart and apple and rhubarb crumble. *Benchmark main dish: steak in ale pie £11.50. Two-course evening meal £18.00.*

Free house ~ Licensee Glenn Williams ~ Real ale ~ (01432) 760395 ~ Open 11am-midnight; 12-11 Sun ~ Bar food 12-2.30, 6-9.15; all day Sat; 12-3 Sun ~ Restaurant ~ Children welcome ~ Dogs allowed in bar ~ www.thebelltillington.co.uk
Recommended by John and Jennifer Spinks

The ▨ symbol shows pubs that keep their beer unusually well, have a particularly good range or brew their own.

TITLEY

Stag

SO3359 Map 6

B4355 N of Kington; HR5 3RL

Herefordshire Dining Pub of the Year

Terrific food using tip top ingredients served in extensive dining rooms; real ales and a fine choice of other drinks, and seats in the two-acre garden; comfortable bedrooms

As always, real care and thought go into the running of this exceptional place. And despite the obvious emphasis on the delicious food, it remains as it's always been – a proper pub with genuinely welcoming and courteous staff and a really interesting range of drinks. The little bar is comfortably hospitable, with a civilised atmosphere and a fine collection of 200 jugs attached to the ceiling. There's Ludlow Gold and Stairway to Paradise and Wye Valley Butty Bach on handpump, nine house wines by the glass (plus a carefully chosen bin list), Dunkerton's organic and Weston's ciders (plus lots of bottled cider and perry), interesting local vodkas and gin from Chase, and quite a choice of spirits. The two-acre garden has seats on the terrace and a croquet lawn. There are bedrooms above the pub and in a Georgian vicarage four minutes' walk away; super breakfasts. The inn is surrounded by good walking country and is handy for the Offa's Dyke Path.

 They make their own crisps, black pudding and other tasty nibbles to go with a pint and grow their own vegetables and salads. The excellent food includes sandwiches, scallops, celeriac purée and crab bisque, duck liver parfait with smoked duck breast and fig, gnocchi with cherry tomatoes, samphire, spinach and parmesan, pork belly, pig cheek, faggot and crisp potato, ox cheek pie, cod fillet with fennel, apple and parmentier potatoes, and puddings such as chocolate mousse, chocolate sorbet, white chocolate ice-cream and chocolate meringue and carrot cake with marmalade vodka frosting, orange and walnut. *Benchmark main dish: local rump steak with béarnaise sauce £16.90. Two-course evening meal £25.00.*

Free house ~ Licensees Steve and Nicola Reynolds ~ Real ale ~ (01544) 230221 ~ Open 12-3, 6.30-11; 12-4, 7-10.30 Sun; closed Mon, Tues, one week Feb, two weeks Nov ~ Bar food 12-2, 6.30-9 (9.30 Sat); 12-3, 7-8.30 Sun ~ Restaurant ~ Children welcome ~ Dogs allowed in bar and bedrooms ~ Wi-fi ~ Bedrooms: £80/£100 ~ www.thestagg.co.uk
Recommended by Huw S Thomas

UPPER COLWALL

Chase £

SO7643 Map 4

Chase Road, brown sign to pub off B4218 Malvern–Colwall, first left after hilltop on bend going W; WR13 6DJ

Gorgeous sunset views from cheerful country tavern's garden, good drinks and cost-conscious food

Under its new landlord, this traditional pub is both friendly and busy – always a good sign. It's the perfect place to relax after enjoying one of the surrounding walks; the tables on the steep series of small, pretty back terraces look across Herefordshire and, on a clear day, as far as the Black Mountains and even the Brecon Beacons. It's chatty and companionable inside, with an array of gilt cast-iron-framed and treadle sewing tables, a great variety of seats (from a wooden-legged tractor seat to a carved pew), an old black kitchen range and plenty of decorations – china mugs, blue glass flasks, lots of small pictures; bar billiards. Half a dozen changing well kept ales are tapped from the cask, such as Bathams Best, Brentwood Gnome Brew, St Georges Charger, Sadlers Thin Ice, Sharps Doom Bar and Woods Shropshire Lad, and several wines by the glass; friendly, helpful staff.

Fair value food with several main dishes costing under £10 includes sandwiches and crusty rolls, field mushroom topped with parmesan and herbs, smoked salmon salad with pink grapefruit and crème fraîche, a curry of the day, honey-roast ham and eggs, chilli con carne, mediterranean vegetable stack with green pesto sauce, steak and kidney pie, and puddings. *Benchmark main dish: fish and chips £10.50. Two-course evening meal £17.00.*

Free house ~ Licensee Jo Walker ~ Real ale ~ (01684) 540276 ~ Open 12-3, 5-11; 12-11 Sat; 12-10.30 Sun ~ Bar food 12-2 (2.30 weekends), 6-9 ~ Restaurant ~ Children welcome ~ Dogs allowed in bar ~ Wi-fi ~ Live music last Sat of month ~ www.thechaseinnuppercolwall.co.uk *Recommended by Dave Braisted, M G Hart*

WALFORD
SO5820 Map 4
Mill Race ⭐️ 🍷
B4234 Ross-on-Wye to Lydney; HR9 5QS

Contemporary furnishings in uncluttered rooms, emphasis on good quality food ingredients, attentive staff, terrace tables and nearby walks

You can sit on the terrace after a walk (they have leaflets describing pleasant ones nearby) and enjoy the view towards Goodrich Castle; the garden has lots more seats and tables. This pink-washed pub is a stylish, civilised place with a row of strikingly tall arched windows, comfortable leather armchairs and sofas on flagstones, and smaller chairs around broad pedestal tables. Photographs of the local countryside hang on the mainly cream or dark pink walls, and there's good unobtrusive lighting. One wall, stripped back to the stonework, contains a woodburning stove that's open to the comfortable, compact dining area on the other side. The granite-topped modern bar counter has Wye Valley Bitter and a changing guest ale on handpump, three farm ciders and 15 fairly priced wines by the glass; background music and TV.

Cattle, rare-breed pigs, turkeys, geese, pheasants, ducks and vegetables are sourced from their own 1,000-acre farm and woodlands. Food includes sandwiches, chicken and bacon caesar salad, scotch egg with spicy brown sauce, honey-roast ham and free-range eggs, pizzas from their wood oven, chicken with date purée, onion and thyme tart and mushroom sauce, monkfish loin with pigs trotter, puy lentils and lobster sausage, and puddings such as prune and Armagnac tart and rhubarb platter. *Benchmark main dish: slow-roasted and stuffed lamb £22.50. Two-course evening meal £20.00.*

Free house ~ Licensee Luke Freeman ~ Real ale ~ (01989) 562891 ~ Open 11-3, 5-11; 10am-11pm Sat; 12-10.30 Sun ~ Bar food 12-2 (2.30 Sat), 6-9.30; 12-9 Sun ~ Restaurant ~ Children welcome ~ Wi-fi ~ www.millrace.info *Recommended by Mike and Mary Carter, Dr and Mrs A J Edwards*

WALTERSTONE
SO3424 Map 6
Carpenters Arms
Follow Walterstone signs off A465; HR2 0DX

Unchanging country tavern in the same family for many years

Vera Watkins has been running this charming little unspoilt stone cottage for many years since she took over from her mother, and the traditional rooms remain unchanged from year to year. There are beams, a roaring fire in a gleaming black range (complete with hot-water tap, bread oven and salt cupboard), warming ancient settles against stripped-stone walls, broad polished flagstones, and Wadworths 6X and a guest such as Breconshire Brecon County tapped straight from the cask. The snug main dining room has mahogany tables and oak corner cupboards, and another little dining area has old oak tables and church pews on more flagstones. The outside lavatories are cold but in character.

Straightforward food includes sandwiches, a changing soup, pies such as salmon and leek or beef in Guinness, various curries, and popular puddings. *Benchmark main dish: local steak £15.95. Two-course evening meal £18.00.*

Free house ~ Licensee Vera Watkins ~ Real ale ~ No credit cards ~ (01873) 890353 ~ Open 12-11 ~ Bar food 12-2, 7-9 ~ Restaurant ~ Children welcome ~ www.thecarpentersarmswalterstone.com *Recommended by Toby Jones*

WOOLHOPE
 SO6135 Map 4

Butchers Arms
Off B4224 in Fownhope; HR1 4RF

Pleasant country inn in peaceful setting, with an inviting garden, interesting food and a fine choice of real ales

This half-timbered pub set in lovely countryside has a new landlord since our last edition. It's a friendly place and the bar has very low beams, built-in cushioned wall seats, farmhouse chairs and stools around a mix of old tables (some set for dining) on carpet, hunting and horse pictures on cream walls and an open fire in a big fireplace; there's also a little beamed dining room, similarly furnished. Wye Valley Bitter and Butty Bach are kept on handpump alongside a couple of guests such as Ledbury Gold and Mayfields Copper Fox, there's a well annotated wine list, with ten by the glass, and a couple of farm ciders. The pretty garden has picnic-sets beside a stream. To really appreciate the surroundings, turn left as you come out of the pub and take the tiny left-hand road at the end of the car park; this turns into a track and then a path, and the view from the top of the hill is quite something.

Using seasonal local produce, the good food includes lunchtime sandwiches, pigeon with black pudding, apple and bacon, twice-baked goats cheese soufflé, vegetable strudel with tomato sauce, pheasant with basil, cream, mushroom and whisky sauce, rabbit, leek and cider pie, lambs liver with crispy onion rings and bacon, and puddings such as vanilla crème brûlée and Baileys and chocolate cheesecake. *Benchmark main dish: beer-battered haddock and chips £11.95. Two-course evening meal £21.00.*

Free house ~ Licensee Philip Vincent ~ Real ale ~ (01432) 860281 ~ Open 11.30-3, 6-11; 11.30-11 (10.30 Sun) Sat; closed Sun evening in winter, Mon except bank holidays ~ Bar food 12-2.30, 6-9; 12-9 weekends ~ Children welcome ~ Dogs welcome ~ Wi-fi ~ www.butchersarmswoolhope.com *Recommended by Chris and Val Ramstedt, Michael and Mary Smith, R T and J C Moggridge, Barry Collett, David and Stella Martin, Martin Day*

WOOLHOPE
SO6135 Map 4

Crown
Village signposted off B4224 in Fownhope; HR1 4QP

Cheery local with fine range of local ciders and perries, and tasty food

Cider enthusiasts enjoy this busy, cheerful pub where the landlord makes two of the farm ciders he serves and keeps another two guests, as well as more than 20 bottled ciders and perrys from within a 15-mile radius. There's also Hobsons Best Bitter, Wye Valley HPA and a changing guest on handpump. The straightforwardly traditional bar has cream walls, some standing timbers, dark wood pubby furniture and plush built-in banquettes on floorboards, cottagey curtained windows and both a woodburning stove and an open fire; background music, darts and board games. There are marvellous views from the lovely big garden, which also has a particularly comfortable smokers' shelter with cushions, darts and quoits, and a garden bar in summer; disabled access.

The well liked food using local suppliers includes sandwiches, chicken and chorizo salad, crispy chilli beef, beer-battered haddock and chips, chargrilled vegetables with couscous, lamb burger with minted yoghurt and fries, cider-baked ham and free-range eggs, chicken with tomato and chilli dressing on pasta, and puddings. *Benchmark main dish: slow-cooked pork belly with chive mash and perry jus £14.00. Two-course evening meal £17.50.*

Free house ~ Licensees Matt and Annalisa Slocombe ~ Real ale ~ (01432) 860468 ~ Open 12-2.30, 6-11; 12-midnight Sat; 12-11 Sun ~ Bar food 12-2 (3.30 Sun), 6-9; 12-3, 6-10 Sat ~ Restaurant ~ Children welcome ~ Wi-fi ~ www.crowninnwoolhope.co.uk
Recommended by Martin Day, Guy Vowles

Also Worth a Visit in Herefordshire

Besides the fully inspected pubs, you might like to try these pubs that have been recommended to us and described by readers. Do tell us what you think of them: feedback@goodguides.com

ALMELEY SO3351
Bells (01544) 327216
Off A480, A4111 or A4112 S of Kington; HR3 6LF Old country local with original jug-and-bottle entry lobby and carpeted beamed bar with woodburner, second bar has been converted to village shop/deli, Simpsons and another local ale, Weston's cider, food (not evenings) from sandwiches up, obliging landlord; children and dogs welcome, garden with decked area and boules, open all day. *(Guy Vowles)*

ASTON CREWS SO6723
Penny Farthing (01989) 750366
Off B4222, signed to Linton; HR9 7LW Roomy partly 15th-c beamed pub again under new management; traditional home-made food and three real ales including Wye Valley, Weston's cider, friendly helpful service, mix of furniture on tartan carpet, log fire and glass-covered well in bar, separate restaurant with pretty valley and Forest of Dean views; children and dogs welcome, tables in garden with more good views and play area, open all day. *(Anon)*

AYMESTREY SO4265
★ Riverside Inn (01568) 708440
A4110, at N end of village, W of Leominster; HR6 9ST Terrace and tree-sheltered garden making most of lovely waterside spot by ancient stone bridge over the Lugg; cosy rambling beamed interior with

some antique furniture alongside stripped country kitchen tables, warm fires, well kept Hobsons, Wye Valley and a guest, local ciders, good lunchtime bar food and more expensive evening menu using rare-breed meat and own fruit and vegetables, friendly helpful landlord and efficient unobtrusive service; quiet background music; children welcome, dogs in bar, bedrooms (fly-fishing for residents), nice breakfast, closed Sun evening, Mon lunchtime (all day Mon in winter). *(Fiona Smith, Tim and Joan Wright, Ann and David Packman)*

BISHOPS FROME SO6648
Green Dragon (01885) 490607
Just off B4214 Bromyard–Ledbury; WR6 5BP Welcoming pub under newish licensees, half a dozen ales including Timothy Taylors and Wye Valley, real ciders, traditional food Tues-Sat evenings and Sun lunchtime, four linked rooms with unspoilt rustic feel, beams, flagstones and log fires including fine inglenook; children and dogs welcome, tiered garden with smokers' shelter, on Herefordshire Trail, closed weekday lunchtimes, open all day Sat. *(Anon)*

BODENHAM SO5454
Englands Gate (01568) 797286
On A417 at Bodenham turn-off, about 6 miles S of Leominster; HR1 3HU Attractive black and white 16th-c coaching inn, rambling interior with beams and joists

in low ceilings around a vast central stone chimneypiece, sturdy timber props, exposed stonework and well worn flagstones (one or two steps), Hobsons, Wye Valley and a guest, traditional cider, enjoyable food served by friendly staff; background music; children welcome, dogs in bar, tables under parasols on terrace and in pleasant garden, modern bedrooms in converted coach house next door, open all day. *(Michael and Mary Smith)*

BOSBURY   SO6943
Bell (01531) 640285
B4220 N of Ledbury; HR8 1PX
Traditional village pub with log fires in both bars, five well kept ales, Weston's cider and good choice of wines by the glass, dining area serving popular sensibly priced food (not Sun evening, Mon) including home-made pizzas and Sun carvery, friendly attentive staff, pool and darts in public bar; dogs welcome, large garden with covered terrace, open all day weekends, closed Mon and Tues lunchtimes. *(Frank Krinks, John Evans)*

BRINGSTY COMMON   SO6954
★ **Live & Let Live** (01886) 821462
*Off A44 Knightwick–Bromyard
1.5 miles W of Whitbourne turn; take
track southwards at Black Cat inn sign,
bearing right at fork; WR6 5UW* Bustling 17th-c timber and thatch cottage; cosy flagstoned bar with scrubbed or polished tables, cushioned chairs, long stripped pew and high-backed winged settle by log fire in cavernous stone fireplace, earthenware jugs hanging from low beams, old casks built into hop-hung bar counter, Ludlow, Malvern Hills and Wye Valley, local ciders and apple juice, well liked pubby food, two dining rooms upstairs under steep rafters; children and dogs welcome, glass-topped well and big wooden hogshead as terrace tables, peaceful views from picnic-sets in former orchard, handy for Brockhampton Estate (NT), closed Mon and winter afternoons Tues-Thurs, otherwise open all day. *(Anon)*

BROMYARD DOWNS   SO6755
★ **Royal Oak** (01885) 482585
*Just NE of Bromyard; pub signed
off A44; HR7 4QP* Beautifully placed low-beamed 18th-c pub with wide views; open-plan carpeted and flagstoned bar, log fire and woodburner, dining room with huge bay window, enjoyable good value home-made food from varied menu, well kept Malvern Hills, Purity and Woods, real cider, friendly service, pool and darts; background music; children, walkers and dogs welcome, picnic-sets on nice front terrace, swings, open all day weekends in Aug. *(Dave Braisted, Neil and Anita Christopher)*

CANON PYON   SO4648
Nags Head (01432) 830725
A4110; HR4 8NY Old timbered roadside pub under new management; beamed log-fire

bar, flagstoned restaurant and overspill/function room, popular pubby food (not evenings Sun or Mon), well kept ales such as Otter and Wye Valley, friendly service; children welcome, extensive garden with play area. *(Anon)*

CLIFFORD   SO2445
Castlefields (01497) 831554
B4350 N of Hay-on-Wye; HR3 5HB
Newly rebuilt family pub, some old features including a well, good popular fairly priced food, Sharps Doom Bar and Wye Valley Butty Bach, friendly helpful staff, woodburner in two-way stone fireplace, restaurant; lovely country views, camping, closed Mon, otherwise open all day. *(Anon)*

CLODOCK   SO3227
Cornewall Arms
N of Walterstone; HR2 0PD Splendidly old-fashioned and unchanging country local in remote hamlet by historic church and facing Black Mountains, stable-door bar with open fire each end, a few mats and comfortable armchairs on stone floor, lots of ornaments and knick-knacks, photos of past village events, books for sale, games including darts and Devil Among the Tailors, bottled Wye Valley and cider, no food or credit cards; erratic opening times.
(Barry Collett)

COLWALL   SO7440
Wellington (01684) 540269
A449 Malvern–Ledbury; WR13 6HW
Welcoming landlord and friendly staff, good sensibly priced food from standards to more imaginative dishes, well kept Goffs Tournament and a couple of guests, good wines by the glass, comfortably lived-in two-level beamed bar with red patterned carpet and nice fire, spacious relaxed back dining area, newspapers and magazines, some live music; children and dogs welcome, picnic-sets on neat grass above car park, good local walks, closed Sun evening, Mon. *(Anon)*

DORSTONE   SO3141
★ **Pandy** (01981) 550273
*Pub signed off B4348 E of Hay-on-Wye;
HR3 6AN* Ancient timbered inn by village green, homely traditional rooms with low hop-strung beams, stout timbers, upright chairs on worn flagstones and in various alcoves, vast open fireplace, locals by bar with good range of beers including Wye Valley, summer farm cider, quite a few malts and irish whiskeys, good food from baguettes and pubby choices to interesting specials, friendly competent staff, board games; background music; children welcome, dogs in bar (resident red setter called Apache), neat side garden with picnic-sets and play area, five good bedrooms in purpose-built annexe, open all day Sat, closed Mon lunchtime (except summer and bank holidays). *(Anon)*

FOWNHOPE
Green Man
SO5734
(01432) 860243

B4224; HR1 4PE Striking 15th-c black and white inn, wall settles, window seats and leather chairs in one beamed bar, standing timbers dividing another, warm woodburners in old fireplaces, good well presented imaginative food in bar and restaurant, friendly helpful service, three changing ales and Weston's cider, good wines, nice coffee; background music, no dogs; children welcome, attractive quiet garden, 11 bedrooms, open all day. *(Michael and Mary Smith)*

GARWAY
Garway Moon
SO4622
(01600) 750270

Centre of village, opposite the green; HR2 8RQ Attractive 18th-c pub in pretty location overlooking common, new licensees and some refurbishment; good locally sourced food served by friendly staff, well kept ales such as Butcombe, Kinstone and Wye Valley, local ciders, beams and exposed stonework, woodburner, restaurant, quiz last Sun of month; children, dogs and muddy boots welcome, garden with new play area, three bedrooms, open all day weekends, closed lunchtimes Mon and Tues. *(John and Nan Hurst)*

GORSLEY
★ Roadmaker
SO6726
(01989) 720352

0.5 miles from M50 junction 3; village signposted from exit – B4221; HR9 7SW Popular 19th-c village pub run well by group of retired gurkhas; large carpeted lounge bar with central log fire, very good nepalese food here and in evening restaurant, also Sun roasts, well kept Brains and Butcombe, efficient courteous service; no dogs; children welcome, terrace with water feature, open all day. *(Anon)*

HAMPTON BISHOP
Bunch of Carrots
SO5538
(01432) 870237

B4224; HR1 4JR Spacious beamed country pub by River Wye, good daily carvery and choice of other pubby food (all day weekends), cheerful efficient service, well kept ales including one badged for them, local cider and several wines by the glass, traditional dimly lit bar area with wood and flagstone floors, logburner, airy restaurant; children and dogs welcome, garden with play area, open all day. *(Diana Hill and Brian Sturgess)*

HAREWOOD END
Harewood End Inn
SO5227
(01989) 730637

A49 Hereford to Ross-on-Wye; HR2 8JT Interesting old inn with comfortable panelled dining lounge and separate restaurant, good choice of enjoyable home-made food, well kept ales such as Black Sheep and Wychwood, decent wines, welcoming attentive staff; nice garden and walks, five bedrooms, closed Mon. *(Barry Collett)*

HEREFORD
Barrels
SO5139
(01432) 274968

St Owen Street; HR1 2JQ Friendly 18th-c coaching inn and former home to the Wye Valley brewery, their very well kept, keenly priced ales from barrel-built counter (beer festival end Aug), Thatcher's cider, no food, cheerful efficient staff and good mix of customers (very busy weekends); pool room, big-screen sports TV, background and some live music; partly covered courtyard behind, open all day. *(Reg Fowle, Helen Rickwood)*

HEREFORD
★ Lichfield Vaults
SO5039
(01432) 266821

Church Street; HR1 2LR A pub since the 18th c (the Dog, then) in picturesque pedestrianised area near cathedral; dark panelling, some stripped brick and exposed joists, impressive plasterwork in big-windowed front room, traditionally furnished with dark pews, padded pub chairs and a couple of heavily padded benches, hot coal stove, charming greek landlord and friendly staff, five well kept ales such as Adnams, Caledonian and Sharps, enjoyable food from sandwiches up including greek dishes, good Sun roasts, daily papers; faint background music, live blues/rock last Sun of month, games machines; children welcome, no dogs, picnic-sets in pleasant back courtyard. *(Richard Tilbrook)*

HEREFORD
Vaga Tavern
SO4939

Vaga Street; HR2 7AT Traditional pub tucked away in residential area, well kept Wye Valley ales and simple snacks, music and quiz nights, skittle alley, pool and darts; open all day Fri-Sun, from 3pm other days. *(Robert W Buckle)*

HOARWITHY
New Harp
SO5429
(01432) 840900

Off A49 Hereford to Ross-on-Wye; HR2 6QH Refurbished open-plan village dining pub with cheerful bustling atmosphere, enjoyable well presented local food from chef-landlord, friendly helpful service, Wye Valley ales and Weston's cider (maybe their own organic cider in summer), pine tables on slate tiles, two woodburners, darts; background and some live music; children, walkers and dogs welcome, pretty tree-sheltered garden with

---

Half pints: by law, a pub should not charge more for half a pint than half the price of a full pint, unless it shows that half-pint price on its price list.

stream, picnic-sets and decked area, little shop and Mon morning post office, unusual italianate Victorian church, open all day Fri-Sun. *(Barry Collett, Dennis and Doreen Haward)*

KENTCHURCH   SO4125
★ **Bridge Inn** (01981) 240408
B4347 Pontrilas–Grosmont; HR2 OBY Ancient attractively refurbished rustic pub, big log fire, good reasonably priced home-made food including weekday set lunch deal, well kept ales such as Otley, Otter and Wye Valley, small pretty back restaurant overlooking River Monnow (two miles of trout fishing), friendly licensees and staff, warm local atmosphere; terrace and waterside garden with pétanque, handy for Herefordshire Trail, closed Mon lunchtime, Tues. *(Alex and Hazel Evans, Theocsbrian, R T and J C Moggridge)*

KINGSLAND   SO4461
Angel (01568) 709195
B4360; HR6 9QS Traditional 16th-c beamed and timbered dining pub, good home-made food (not Mon or Tues lunchtimes) including deals, four well kept changing ales and a dozen wines by the glass, helpful friendly staff, comfortable open-plan interior with open fires, upstairs function/overspill area; sports TV; picnic-sets on front grass, garden behind, best to check opening times. *(Anon)*

KINGSLAND   SO4461
★ **Corners** (01568) 708385
B4360 NW of Leominster, corner of Lugg Green Road; HR6 9RY Comfortably updated, partly black and white 16th-c village inn with snug nooks and corners, log fires, low beams, dark red plasterwork and some stripped brick, comfortable bow-window seat, and group of dark leather armchairs in softly lit carpeted bar, well kept Hobsons and a guest such as Wye Valley, decent selection of wines, airier big raftered side dining room in converted hay loft with huge window, enjoyable reasonably priced food from pubby choices up, cheerful attentive service; children welcome, no garden, comfortable bedrooms in new block behind. *(Peter and Heather Elliott, David M Smith)*

KINGTON   SO3056
★ **Olde Tavern** (01544) 239033
Victoria Road, just off A44 opposite B4355 – follow sign to Town Centre, Hospital, Cattle Market; pub on right opposite Elizabeth Road, no inn sign but Estd 1767 notice; HR5 3BX Gloriously old-fashioned with hatch-served side room opening off small plain parlour and public bar, plenty of dark brown woodwork, big windows, settles and other antique furniture on bare floors, gas fire, old local pictures, china, pewter and curios, well kept Hobsons, Ludlow, Wye Valley and a guest, Weston's

cider, beer festivals, friendly atmosphere, no food; children and dogs welcome, little yard at back, open all day weekends, closed weekday lunchtimes. *(Anon)*

KINGTON   SO2956
Oxford Arms (01544) 230322
Duke Street; HR5 3DR Well worn-in (not to everyone's taste) with woodburners in main bar on left and dining area on right, smaller lounge with sofas and armchairs, well kept local ales and enjoyable reasonably priced food, good friendly service, pool; closed Mon and Tues lunchtimes. *(Reg Fowle, Helen Rickwood)*

KINGTON   SO2956
Royal Oak (01544) 230484
Church Street; HR5 3BE Cheerful two-bar pub with welcoming caring landlord, good value food, well kept Hereford, Ringwood and Sharps, two little open fires, old theatre posters and musical instruments in restaurant, darts and sports TV in public bar; children and dogs welcome, garden with terrace, handy for walkers on Offa's Dyke Path, three neat simple bedrooms, open all day summer, closed weekday lunchtimes in winter. *(Anon)*

LEDBURY   SO7137
★ **Prince of Wales** (01531) 632250
Church Lane; narrow passage from Town Hall; HR8 1DL Friendly family-run local tucked prettily down narrow cobbled alley, seven well kept ales, Weston's cider and foreign bottled beers, knowledgeable staff, simple very good value home-made food from sandwiches up, low beams, shelves of books, long back room; faint background music (live Weds and Sun); a couple of tables in flower-filled backyard, open all day. *(Ken Eames, Dave Braisted, N R White)*

LEDBURY   SO7137
Seven Stars (01531) 635800
Homend (High Street); HR8 1BN Convivial 16th-c beamed and timbered pub rebuilt after recent fire, pleasant bar area with comfortable seating and large farm table, cosy open fire, dining room behind, interesting choice of good well presented food from sensibly short menu, three well kept ales, friendly helpful staff; free wi-fi; children and dogs welcome, walled terrace, three bedrooms. *(Martin and Pauline Jennings)*

LEDBURY   SO7137
Talbot (01531) 632963
New Street; HR8 2DX 16th-c black and white fronted coaching inn; log-fire bar with Wadworths ales and plenty of wines by the glass, good fairly traditional food from sharing boards and lunchtime sandwiches up, friendly efficient service, oak-panelled dining room; courtyard tables, bedrooms, open all day. *(Dr A J and Mrs B A Tompsett)*

LEINTWARDINE   SO4073
Lion (01547) 540203
High Street; SY7 0JZ Nicely restored inn
beautifully situated by packhorse bridge
over River Teme; helpful efficient staff and
friendly atmosphere, good well presented
food from varied if not especially cheap menu
including some imaginative choices, popular
two-room restaurant, well kept local beers;
children welcome, safely fenced riverside
garden with play area, eight attractive
bedrooms, fishing trips arranged, open all
day (till 8pm Sun). *(Gordon and Margaret
Ormondroyd)*

LEINTWARDINE   SO4073
★Sun (01547) 540705
Rosemary Lane, just off A4113; SY7 0LP
Fascinating 19th-c time warp; bare benches
and farmhouse tables by coal fire in
wallpapered brick-floored front bar (dogs
welcome here), well kept Hobsons tapped
from the cask and an occasional guest (Aug
beer festival), another fire in snug carpeted
parlour, pork pies and perhaps a lunchtime
ploughman's (can bring food from adjacent
fish and chip shop), friendly staff, open mike
night last Fri of month; new pavilion-style
building with bar and garden room, closed
Mon lunchtime. *(Peter Thornton)*

LEOMINSTER   SO4959
Grape Vaults (01568) 611404
Broad Street; HR6 8BS Compact well
preserved two-room pub, friendly and
popular, with well kept ales including Ludlow,
good value pubby food, coal fire, beams and
panelling, original dark high-backed settles,
old local prints and posters, bottle collection,
shelves of books in snug; tiny gents'; dogs
welcome, open all day. *(Guy Vowles)*

LINTON   SO6525
Alma (01989) 720355
On main road through village; HR9 7RY
Cheerful unspoilt local in small village, up
to six well kept/priced changing ales such as
Butcombe, Ludlow and Malvern Hills, no food
(may be free Sun nibbles), homely carpeted
front room with sleepy cats by good fire,
small back room with pool, three-day summer
charity music festival; children very welcome,
good-sized garden behind with nice view,
closed weekday lunchtimes. *(Anon)*

MICHAELCHURCH
ESCLEY   SO3133
★Bridge Inn (01981) 510646
*Off back road SE of Hay-on-Wye, along
Escley Brook Valley; HR2 0JW* Black-
beamed riverside inn restored by current
hard-working licensees and delightfully
tucked away in attractive valley; popular
home-made food including some unusual
choices, well kept Wye Valley beers and local
farm cider, friendly atmosphere; children
welcome, seats out on waterside terrace,

field for camping (also a yurt), good walks,
closed Mon lunchtime, otherwise open all
day. *(Neil Hogg, MJVK)*

MUCH DEWCHURCH   SO4831
Black Swan (01981) 540295
*B4348 Ross-on-Wye to Hay-on-Wye;
HR2 8DJ* Roomy and attractive beamed
and timbered local, partly 14th-c, with well
kept Timothy Taylors Landlord and three
local guests, decent wines and enjoyable
straightforward food (no credit cards), log
fires in cosy well worn bar and lounge with
eating area, welcoming helpful landlord,
Thurs folk night; pool room with darts, TV,
juke box; children and dogs welcome, seats
on front terrace, open all day weekends.
(Bob and Angie Farmer)

MUCH MARCLE   SO6634
Royal Oak (01531) 660300
*On A449 Ross-on-Wye to Ledbury;
HR8 2ND* Superb rural spot with
magnificent views, pleasant lounge with open
fire, good reasonably priced food using meat
from local farms, prompt friendly service,
well kept ales such as Jennings, Marstons
and Wye Valley, large back dining area;
garden, two bedrooms. *(Jason Bevan)*

ORLETON   SO4967
★Boot (01568) 780228
Off B4362 W of Woofferton; SY8 4HN
Popular pub with beams, timbering, even
some 16th-c wattle and daub, inglenook
fireplace in charming cosy traditional bar,
steps up to further bar area, good-sized
two-room dining part, varied choice of
interesting well presented food, friendly
quick service, Hobsons, Wye Valley and a
local guest (July beer and music festival),
real ciders; children and dogs welcome, seats
in garden under huge ash tree, fenced-in play
area, open all day weekends. *(Ann and Tony
Bennett-Hughes)*

PEMBRIDGE   SO3958
New Inn (01544) 388427
Market Square (A44); HR6 9DZ
Timeless ancient inn overlooking
small black and white town's church,
unpretentious three-room bar with antique
settles, beams, worn flagstones and
impressive inglenook log fire, well kept
changing ales, farm cider and big helpings
of popular good value plain food, friendly
service, traditional games, quiet little
family dining room; downstairs lavatories;
simple bedrooms. *(Anon)*

ROSS-ON-WYE   SO5924
Mail Rooms (01989) 760920
Gloucester Road; HR9 5BS Open
modern Wetherspoons conversion of
former post office, their usual well priced
food and up to five ales including Greene
King, Weston's cider and good choice of
wines, friendly service; silent TV; children

welcome till 8pm, decked back terrace, open all day from 8am. *(Reg Fowle, Helen Rickwood, Mike and Mary Carter)*

ROSS-ON-WYE SO6024
White Lion (01989) 562785
Wilton Lane; HR9 6AQ Friendly riverside pub dating from 1650, well kept Wye Valley and a couple of guests, enjoyable traditional food at reasonable prices, good service, big fireplace in carpeted bar, stone-walled gaol restaurant (building once a police station); free wi-fi; children welcome, lots of tables in garden and on terrace overlooking the Wye and historic bridge, bedrooms and camping, open all day. *(Anon)*

SELLACK SO5526
★Lough Pool (01989) 730888
Off A49; HR9 6LX Black and white timbered cottage surrounded by bridleways and walks, simple bars with beams and standing timbers, flagstones, rustic furniture and two woodburners, well kept Wye Valley ales and a guest, farm ciders/perries and several wines by the glass, enjoyable locally sourced home-made food, restaurant with garden views; children welcome, dogs allowed in bar, opening times may vary according to season – best to check first. *(Barry Collett, Mike and Mary Carter, Guy Vowles)*

STAPLOW SO6941
Oak (01531) 640954
Bromyard Road (B4214); HR8 1NP Popular roadside village pub, friendly bustle in comfortable beamed bar, restaurant with open kitchen producing enjoyable food from sandwiches and sharing boards up, ales such as Bathams, Brains and Wye Valley, Weston's cider and good choice of wines, cheerful quick service; bedrooms. *(Anon)*

STIFFORDS BRIDGE SO7348
Red Lion (01886) 880318
A4103 3 miles W of Great Malvern; WR13 5NN Refurbished beamed roadside pub under welcoming newish management; good choice of tasty well priced pubby food (not Sun evening), Greene King, Malvern Hills and Wye Valley, real ciders, friendly helpful staff; children welcome and dogs (theirs is called Max), tables in nicely kept garden, farmers' market first Sat of month, open all day Fri-Sun. *(Anon)*

STOCKTON CROSS SO5161
★Stockton Cross Inn (01568) 612509
Kimbolton; A4112, off A49 just N of Leominster; HR6 0HD Cosy half-timbered 16th-c drovers' inn under new ownership; heavily beamed interior with huge log fire and woodburner, handsome antique settle, old leather chairs and

brocaded stools, cast-iron-framed tables, well kept Wye Valley ales and guests, Robinson's cider, enjoyable pub food and good friendly service; children and dogs welcome, pretty garden, handy for Berrington Hall (NT), open all day. *(Anon)*

SUTTON ST NICHOLAS SO5345
Golden Cross (01432) 880274
Corner of Ridgeway Road; HR1 3AZ Thriving modernised pub with enjoyable food including deals, Wye Valley Butty Bach and two regularly changing guests from stone-fronted counter, good service, clean décor, some breweriana, relaxed upstairs restaurant, pool and darts, live music Fri; children and dogs welcome, disabled facilities, pretty village and good walks. *(Reg Fowle, Helen Rickwood)*

SYMONDS YAT SO5515
Old Ferrie (01600) 890232
Ferrie Lane, Symonds Yat West; HR9 6BL Unpretentious old inn in picturesque spot by the River Wye with its own hand-pulled ferry; enjoyable pub food, Wye Valley ales and local cider, friendly helpful staff, games room; riverside terrace, canoeing and good walks, bedrooms and two bunkhouses. *(Anon)*

TRUMPET SO6639
Trumpet Inn (01531) 670277
Corner A413 and A438; HR8 2RA Modernised black and white timbered pub dating from 15th c, well kept Wadworths ales and good food (all day Fri-Sun) from sandwiches to specials, efficient service, beams, stripped brickwork and log fires, dining room, quiz and live music nights; children welcome, tables in big garden behind, campsite with hard standings, open all day. *(David and Julie Glover)*

UPTON BISHOP SO6326
Moody Cow (01989) 780470
B4221 E of Ross-on-Wye; HR9 7TT Refurbished dining pub, L-shaped bar with sandstone walls, slate floor and woodburner, biggish raftered restaurant and second more intimate eating area, good freshly made food, well kept ales and decent wines (including local ones), friendly efficient service; children, dogs and boots welcome, garden with fruit/vegetable beds, courtyard bedroom up spiral staircase, closed Sun evening, Mon. *(Guy Vowles)*

WELLINGTON SO4948
Wellington (01432) 830367
Village signed off A49 N of Hereford; HR4 8AT Red-brick Victorian pub-restaurant; bar with big high-backed settles, antique farm and garden tools, historical photographs of the village, and woodburner

in brick fireplace, Butcombe Wye Valley and a guest, enjoyable fairly traditional food (not Sun evening) cooked by chef-landlord, candlelit stable restaurant and conservatory; background music; children welcome, dogs in bar, nice back garden. *(Anon)*

WELLINGTON HEATH   SO7140
Farmers Arms (01531) 634776
Off B4214 just N of Ledbury – pub signed right, from top of village; Horse Road; HR8 1LS Roomy open-plan pub refurbished under new management, enjoyable food including daily specials, Otter, Wye Valley Butty Bach and a guest, friendly staff; free wi-fi; children and dogs welcome, terrace picnic-sets, good walking country, open all day. *(Anon)*

WEOBLEY   SO4051
Salutation (01544) 318443
Off A4112 SW of Leominster; HR4 8SJ Old beamed and timbered inn at top of delightful village green, good food cooked by chef-landlord from bar snacks up including set lunch, well kept ales such as Otter, Thwaites and Wye Valley, Robinson's cider, pleasant helpful service, two bars and restaurant, log fires; children welcome, sheltered back terrace, three bedrooms, good breakfast. *(Anon)*

WHITNEY-ON-WYE   SO2447
★ Rhydspence (01497) 831262
A438 Hereford–Brecon; HR3 6EU Splendid half-timbered inn (part dates from 1380) on the border with Wales; rambling rooms with heavy beams and timbers, attractive old-fashioned furnishings, log fire in fine big stone fireplace in central bar, well kept Bass, Otter and Robinsons, real cider, good sensibly priced wholesome food cooked by newish landlady, restaurant; children welcome, no dogs while food is being served, garden with views to the Black Mountains, six bedrooms, open all day. *(Anon)*

WINFORTON   SO2946
Sun (01544) 327677
A438; HR3 6EA Friendly unpretentious village pub with enjoyable freshly cooked food all sourced locally, Wye Valley Butty Bach, real ciders, country-style beamed areas either side of central servery, stripped stone and woodburners; background music; children and dogs welcome, garden picnic-sets, closed Sun evening, Mon (also Tues in winter). *(Anon)*

Post Office address codings confusingly give the impression that a few pubs are in Herefordshire when they're really in Gloucestershire or even Wales (which is where we list them).

Hertfordshire

KEY  Star Pub | Top Quality Food | Great Beer | Good Wines | £ Bargain Meals | Good Bedrooms | Serves Food

ALDBURY   SP9612   Map 4
Valiant Trooper ◀

Trooper Road (towards Aldbury Common); off B4506 N of Berkhamsted; HP23 5RW

Cheery, traditional all-rounder with appealing interior, five real ales, generous helpings of pubby food and garden

With well kept ales, highly thought-of food and friendly, courteous staff, this appealing country pub gets warm praise from our readers. The first of the unpretentious and appealing rooms is beamed and has red and black tiles, built-in wall benches, a pew and small dining chairs around attractive country tables, and an inglenook fireplace. Further in, the middle bar has spindleback chairs around tables on a wooden floor and some exposed brickwork. The far room has nice country kitchen chairs around a mix of tables, and a woodburning stove, and the back barn has been converted to house a restaurant; background music. Chiltern Beechwood Bitter, Fullers London Pride, Tring Side Pocket for a Toad and a couple of guests on handpump, five farm ciders and several wines by the glass. The enclosed garden has a wooden adventure playground, and the pub is well placed for walks through the glorious beechwoods of the National Trust's Ashridge Estate.

Promptly served food includes weekend breakfasts (10am-midday), lunchtime sandwiches, crispy oriental duck and orange, smoked haddock fishcakes with sorrel sauce, free-range sausages with bubble and squeak and home-made baked beans, roasted beetroot risotto with goats cheese, burger with coleslaw, tomato relish and chips, cod loin with parsley sauce, and puddings. *Benchmark main dish: steak in ale pie £10.50. Two-course evening meal £16.75.*

Free house ~ Licensee Wendy Greenall ~ Real ale ~ (01442) 851203 ~ Open 11-11; 10am-11pm Sat; 10am-10.30pm Sun ~ Bar food 12-3, 6-9; 12-9 Sat; 12-4 Sun; not Sun or Mon evenings ~ Restaurant ~ Children welcome ~ Dogs allowed in bar ~ Wi-fi ~ www.valianttrooper.co.uk *Recommended by Dennis Jones, Ross Balaam, Tracey and Stephen Groves*

ASHWELL   TL2739   Map 5
Three Tuns ♀

Off A505 NE of Baldock; High Street; SG7 5NL

Bustling inn with a fair choice of drinks, good food served by helpful staff and substantial garden; attractive bedrooms

Three completely refurbished, attractive and comfortable bedrooms have been opened in this pretty red-brick inn; breakfasts are tasty. The airy bar has an open fire, a long settle and cushioned wooden dining chairs around tables (each set with a flowering plant in a small flowerpot), bare floorboards, a few high chairs around equally high tables and pictures on pale walls above a blue dado. The atmosphere is friendly and relaxed. Bath Gem, Greene King IPA and Leeds Best on handpump and 13 wines by the glass; background music. The long Victorian-style dining room has a woodburning stove, built-in wall seats and more cushioned wooden dining chairs around a mix of tables, and rugs on floorboards. There are seats on the terrace and in the substantial garden with apple trees. This is a charming village.

Rewarding food includes sandwiches, smoked haddock carpaccio, goats cheese, beetroot and walnut roulade with balsamic syrup, sausages with onion gravy and mash, chargrilled burger with bacon, cheese and fries, bubble and squeak potato cake with parma ham crisp, fried duck egg and hollandaise, mushroom, chestnut and tarragon wellington with stilton sauce, duck with caramelised parsnip purée and french-style peas, and puddings such as orange drizzle cake and sticky toffee pudding. *Benchmark main dish: slow-cooked pork belly, pig cheeks, black pudding and croquette potato £15.95. Two-course evening meal £20.00.*

Greene King ~ Lease Tim Lightfoot ~ Real ale ~ (01462) 743343 ~ Open 10am-11pm; 12-10.30 Sun ~ Bar food 12-3 (4 Sat), 6-10; 12-5 Sun ~ Restaurant ~ Children welcome ~ Dogs allowed in bar and bedrooms ~ Wi-fi ~ Bedrooms: /£100 ~ www.thethreetunsashwell.co.uk *Recommended by Martin and Alison Stainsby*

BARNET   TQ2599   Map 5

Duke of York ♀
Barnet Road (A1000); EN5 4SG

Big place with reasonably priced bistro-style food and nice garden

Although large and rather grand, this bustling place has been cleverly and attractively divided inside using stairs and open doorways – but there are some cosy, more intimate areas too. Big windows and plenty of mirrors keep everything light and airy, the atmosphere is relaxed and friendly and there are hundreds of prints and photos on cream walls, an eclectic mix of furniture on tiled or wooden flooring, fireplaces and thoughtful touches such as table lamps, books, rugs, fresh fowers and pot plants. Stools line the impressive counter where friendly staff serve Phoenix Brunning & Price Original plus Adnams Mosaic, Growler Bitter, Oakham JHB and Tring Kotuku on handpump, 20 wines by the glass, 70 whiskies and farm cider; background music. The garden is particularly attractive, with plenty of seats, tables and picnic-sets on a tree-surrounded terrace and lawn, and a tractor in the good play area.

The well presented food includes sandwiches, duck liver parfait with rhubarb, apple and ginger chutney, char siu pork belly with pickled ginger salad, mussels with leeks in cider and bacon sauce, mushroom, goats cheese and tarragon quiche, calves liver with celeriac, black pudding and madeira sauce, beer-battered haddock and chips, steak and kidney pie, and puddings such as cherry eton mess and crème brûlée. *Benchmark main dish: braised lamb shoulder with dauphinoise potatoes and rosemary gravy £16.95. Two-course evening meal £18.00.*

Brunning & Price ~ Manager Matthew Daniels ~ Real ale ~ (020) 8449 0297 ~ Open 11.30-11; 12-10.30 Sun ~ Bar food 12-10 (9.30 Sun) ~ Children welcome ~ Dogs allowed in bar ~ Wi-fi ~ www.dukeofyork-barnet.co.uk *Recommended by Isobel Mackinlay, Edward May*

EPPING GREEN
TL2906 Map 5

Beehive

Off B158 SW of Hertford, via Little Berkhamsted; back road towards Newgate Street and Cheshunt; SG13 8NB

Cheerful bustling country pub, popular for its good value food

As ever, the enjoyable fish dishes remain quite a draw to this weatherboarded country pub. The traditional, low-ceilinged bar has a friendly, informal atmosphere and a woodburning stove in a panelled corner, and serves Greene King IPA, Abbot and a changing guest on handpump alongside a good range of wines by the glass; background music. Between the low building and quiet country road is a neat lawn and decked area, with plenty of tables for enjoying the summer sunshine; good woodland walks nearby.

The fish dishes (with daily deliveries from Billingsgate) are very good: skate with caper butter, cod with bacon and mushroom sauce, battered plaice, crab and mango salad and fresh tuna; there are also sandwiches, baguettes and daily specials. *Benchmark main dish: beer-battered fresh cod and chips £10.00. Two-course evening meal £16.50.*

Free house ~ Licensee Martin Squirrell ~ Real ale ~ (01707) 875959 ~ Open 11.30-3, 5.30-11; 12-10.30 Sun ~ Bar food 12-2.30, 6-9.30; 12-4, 6-8.30 Sun ~ Restaurant ~ Children welcome ~ Wi-fi *Recommended by John Branston, Ross Balaam, Anthony and Marie Lewis, Gordon Neighbour*

FLAUNDEN
TL0101 Map 5

Bricklayers Arms ⭐ ♀

4 miles from M25 junction 18; village signposted off A41 – from village centre follow Boxmoor, Bovingdon road and turn right at Belsize, Watford signpost into Hogpits Bottom; HP3 0PH

Cosy country restaurant with fairly elaborate food; very good wine list

The excellent food is the main draw to this civilised and tucked-away 18th-c pub – our readers enjoy their meals here very much. But they also keep Sharps Doom Bar and guest ales from breweries such as Chiltern, Rebellion and Tring on handpump, and an extensive wine list with 25 by the glass. Stubs of knocked-through oak-timbered wall indicate the original room layout of the now fairly open-plan interior, and the well refurbished low-beamed bar is snug and comfortable, with a roaring log fire in winter. This is a lovely peaceful spot in summer, when the terrace and beautifully kept old-fashioned garden with its foxgloves against sheltering hedges comes into its own. Just up the Belsize road, a path on the left leads through delightful woods to a forested area around Hollow Hedge.

Using home-smoked meat and fish, the imaginative food includes king scallops with parsnip purée, dry smoked bacon and hazelnut oil, mushroom feuilletée in calvados cream, local sausages with chive mash and red wine gravy, ox cheek in ale and honey with champ, duck breast with duck leg confit and sweet and sour cranberry juice, bass with samphire pesto cream, 21-day aged beef fillet with green peppercorn-flavoured brandy cream, and puddings such as bourbon vanilla crème brûlée and chocolate and honey fondant with pistachio ice-cream. *Benchmark main dish: steak and kidney in ale pie £13.95. Two-course evening meal £25.00.*

Free house ~ Licensee Alvin Michaels ~ Real ale ~ (01442) 833322 ~ Open 12-11 ~ Bar food 12-2.30, 6.30-9.30; 12-3.30, 6.30-8.30 Sun ~ Restaurant ~ Children welcome ~

Dogs allowed in bar ~ Wi-fi ~ www.bricklayersarms.com *Recommended by Peter and Jan Humphreys, Alex and Hazel Evans, John and Penny Wheeler*

FRITHSDEN
TL0109   Map 5

Alford Arms ⭐ ♀

A4146 from Hemel Hempstead to Water End, then second left (after Red Lion) signed Frithsden, then left at T junction, then right after 0.25 miles; HP1 3DD

Hertfordshire Dining Pub of the Year

Thriving dining pub with a chic interior, good food from imaginative menu, and a thoughtful wine list

The food in this pretty Victorian pub is very good and extremely popular – it's certainly worth booking a table in advance. The elegant, understated interior has simple prints on pale cream walls, with blocks picked out in rich Victorian green or dark red, and an appealing mix of antique furniture (from Georgian chairs to old commode stands) on bare boards and patterned quarry tiles; it's all pulled together by luxuriously opulent curtains. Despite the emphasis on dining, they consider themselves a proper pub and you'll certainly find a few locals chatting at the bar. Sharps Doom Bar, a couple of guests such as Chiltern Beechwood and Tring Side Pocket for a Toad on handpump, plus 24 wines by the glass from a european list (quite a few sweet wines too); background jazz and darts. There are plenty of tables outside and, as the pub is on the Ashridge Estate (National Trust), many customers combine a visit here with a walk.

 Imaginative food includes bubble and squeak with smoked bacon and free-range poached egg, pork and thyme rillettes with roast garlic relish, local sausages of the day, haricot bean, courgette and red onion burger with feta, sweet potato chips and chilli mayonnaise, whole sea bream with beetroot, spinach and broccoli salad and chermoula yoghurt, and puddings such as clove rice pudding with caramelised orange and dark chocolate and salted peanut torte with real ale ice-cream. *Benchmark main dish: coq au vin and parsley mash £14.75. Two-course evening meal £21.00.*

Salisbury Pubs ~ Lease Darren Johnston ~ Real ale ~ (01442) 864480 ~ Open 11-11; 12-10.30 Sun ~ Bar food 12-2.30 (3 Sat), 6.30-9.30 (10 Fri, Sat); 12-9 Sun ~ Restaurant ~ Children welcome ~ Dogs allowed in bar ~ Wi-fi ~ www.alfordarmsfrithsden.co.uk
Recommended by John and Joyce Snell, Simon and Mandy King, Alex and Hazel Evans, Richard Kennell

HARPENDEN
TL1312   Map 5

White Horse

Redbourn Lane, Hatching Green (B487 just W of A1081 roundabout); AL5 2JP

Smart up-to-date dining pub with civilised bar side

This is an attractive, extended, white-weatherboarded pub with a huge sunny terrace and plenty of contemporary seats and tables under parasols. Inside, the chatty bar is split-level (one part was once the stable) with prints on burnt orange-painted plank panelling, stools around tables with taller ones against the counter, and an open fire. Sharps Doom Bar and Tring Bring Me Sunshine and Side Pocket for a Toad on handpump and several wines by the glass, served by friendly, helpful staff; background music and board games. The airy, stylish dining room has tartan-upholstered dining chairs, cushioned wall seats and settles around pale wooden tables on floorboards, and black and white photographs on the walls. As they're usefully open all day from 9.30am, there's a steady stream of customers wanting breakfast, morning coffee or afternoon tea as well as lunch and evening diners.

In addition to breakfasts and a two- and three-course set menu, the good, modern food includes sandwiches, sharing boards, duck liver pâté with blood orange compote, crab mayonnaise with cucumber and fennel salsa, smoked haddock kedgeree with poached free-range egg, wild garlic gnocchi with creamed leeks and broad beans, ox cheek pie in ale gravy, free-range chicken with tomato and basil pasta, and puddings. *Benchmark main dish: lobster shepherd's pie with lobster sauce £20.00. Two-course evening meal £21.50.*

Peach Pub Company ~ Tenant Steve Elliott ~ Real ale ~ (01582) 469290 ~ Open 9.30am-11pm (midnight Sat, 10.30 Sun) ~ Bar food 12-3, 6-10; 12-6 Sun ~ Restaurant ~ Children welcome ~ Dogs allowed in bar ~ Wi-fi ~ www.thewhitehorse-harpenden.co.uk
Recommended by John and Joyce Snell

HERTFORD HEATH   TL3510   Map 5
College Arms
London Road; B1197; SG13 7PW

Light and airy rooms with contemporary furnishings, friendly service, good interesting food and real ales; seats outside

Deservedly popular, this civilised, light and airy place is somewhere our readers come back to repeatedly. The bar has high chairs around equally high tables, long cushioned wall seats and pale leather dining chairs around tables on rugs or wooden floorboards, and a modern bar counter where they serve Sharps Doom Bar and a guest such as Crouch Vale Brewers Gold on handpump and 26 wines by the glass; background jazz. Another area has long button-back wall seats, an open fireplace piled with logs and a doorway that leads to a charming little room with brown leather armchairs, a couple of cushioned pews, a woodburning stove in an old brick fireplace, hunting-themed wallpaper and another rug on floorboards. The elegant, partly carpeted dining room contains a real mix of antique dining chairs and tables, and a couple of large house plants. There are tables, seats and a long wooden bench among flowering pots on the back terrace and a children's play house. It's on the edge of a village and backed by woodland – handy for walks.

The highly rated food includes sandwiches, pigeon pasty with jerusalem artichoke purée and pickled turnips, beetroot-cured salmon fillet with a duo of horseradish, stone-baked pizzas, crab, chorizo, king prawn and chilli linguine, red onion tarte tatin with goats cheese, duck with hoi sin, won ton, pak choi and five-spice jus, herb-crusted cod with bacon caesar salad, and puddings such as treacle tart with pumpkin ice-cream and popcorn fudge and rum and pistachio crème brûlée. *Benchmark main dish: beer-battered fish and chips £11.95. Two-course evening meal £22.00.*

Punch ~ Lease Merissa Tharby ~ Real ale ~ (01992) 558856 ~ Open 12-10 (11 Sat); 12-7 Sun ~ Bar food 12-3, 6-9; 12-4, 6-10 Sat; 12-5 Sun ~ Restaurant ~ Children welcome ~ Dogs allowed in bar ~ Wi-fi ~ www.thecollegearmshertfordheath.com
Recommended by David Hunt, Mrs Margo Finlay, Jörg Kasprowski, David Jackson, Chris and Angela Buckell

> People named as recommenders after the full entries have told us that the pub should be included. But they have not written the report – we have, after anonymous on-the-spot inspection.

NORTHAW
Sun 🏮 ⛾

TL2702   Map 5

B156; on green opposite the church; EN6 4NL

Appealing décor in several little rooms, local ales, helpful service and delicious food

To be sure of a table you must book in advance at this civilised and attractively refurbished 16th-c pub – their imaginative food is extremely popular. The opened-up bar has a curved counter with a stained-glass gantry, some green-painted panelling, an open fire in a little brick fireplace, big boxes of vegetables dotted about (it sounds odd but looks fun) and Buntingford Highwayman, Growler Priory Mild and Red Squirrel Conservation on handpump, 13 wines by the glass and a farm cider, served by friendly staff. The snug has another fireplace and the two dining rooms have exposed brick walls. Throughout, there's a happy mix of antique dining chairs and tables on bare boards or old brick floors, fresh flowers and various china items. The back terrace has picnic-sets beneath parasols, with more on the grass. The pub overlooks the church.

 Using seasonal local and organic produce, the appealing food includes sandwiches, wild mushrooms on toast with sea arrowgrass, asparagus, shrimps and a poached egg, crispy duck, beetroot tops and black pudding, burger with cheddar and triple-cooked chips, guinea fowl with 'pigs in blankets', wild garlic and broad beans, venison loin with red cabbage and prunes and sloe gin, and puddings such as chocolate and orange eton mess and sea buckthorn and raspberry panna cotta with a mini doughnut; they also offer a two- and three-course set lunch (not Sunday). *Benchmark main dish: fillet of hare with smoked bacon, scottish girolles and radishes £16.20. Two-course evening meal £23.50.*

Free house ~ Licensee Oliver Smith ~ Real ale ~ (01707) 655507 ~ Open 12-4, 5-11; 12-11 Sat; 12-5 Sun; closed Sun evening, Mon except bank holidays (when they close Tues instead) ~ Bar food 12-3, 6-10; 12-4 Sun ~ Restaurant ~ Children welcome ~ Dogs allowed in bar ~ Wi-fi ~ www.thesunatnorthaw.co.uk *Recommended by Harvey Brown, Pip White, David Jackson*

POTTERS CROUCH
Holly Bush 🍺 £

TL1105   Map 5

2.25 miles from M25 junction 21A: A405 towards St Albans, then first left, then after a mile turn left (ie away from Chiswell Green), then at T junction turn right into Blunts Lane; can also be reached fairly quickly, with a good map, from M1 exits 6 and 8; AL2 3NN

Well tended cottage with gleaming furniture, fresh flowers and china, well kept Fullers beers, good value food and an attractive garden

Remote in feel though handily just a few minutes' drive from the centre of St Albans and a couple of miles from the M25, this spotlessly kept pub remains on top form. It has highly polished dark wood furnishings, quite a few antique dressers (several filled with plates), a number of comfortably cushioned settles, a fox's mask, some antlers, a fine old clock with a lovely chime, daily papers and (on the right as you enter) a big fireplace. In the evening, neatly placed candles cast glimmering light over darkly varnished tables, all sporting fresh flowers. The long, stepped bar has particularly well kept Fullers ESB, London Pride, Seafarers and a Fullers seasonal beer on handpump, served by helpful staff who remain friendly even when pushed. The fenced-off back garden has plenty of sturdy picnic-sets on a lawn surrounded by handsome trees. Please note that children and dogs aren't allowed.

🍽 As well as lunchtime sandwiches and toasties, the fairly priced food includes prawn and egg mayonnaise, baked camembert with red onion marmalade, deli platters, chilli con carne, lamb koftas with tzatziki, smoked haddock fishcakes with poached egg and spinach, beef and root vegetable casserole with dumplings, and puddings such as treacle tart and chocolate mud cake. *Benchmark main dish: cumberland sausages £10.50. Two-course evening meal £16.50.*

Fullers ~ Tenants Steven and Vanessa Williams ~ Real ale ~ (01727) 851792 ~ Open 12-2.30, 6-11; 12-3, 7-10.30 Sun ~ Bar food 12-2 (2.30 Sun), 6-9; not Sun-Tues evenings ~ www.thehollybushpub.co.uk *Recommended by Sarah Bennett, Tina and David Woods-Taylor*

PRESTON
TL1824 Map 5

Red Lion 🍺 £

Village signposted off B656 S of Hitchin; The Green; SG4 7UD

Homely village local with changing beers, fair-priced food and neat colourful garden

This well run, cheerful place, which claims to be the first community-owned pub in the country, always has plenty of customers. The main room on the left, with grey wainscot, has sturdy, well varnished pub furniture including padded country kitchen chairs and cast-iron-framed tables on patterned carpet, a generous window seat, a log fire in a brick fireplace and fox hunting prints. The somewhat smaller room on the right has steeplechase prints, varnished plank panelling and brocaded bar stools on flagstones around the servery; darts and dominoes. Fullers London Pride and Wells & Youngs on handpump with guests such as Mighty Oak Captain Bob and Oscar Wilde and Oakham Scarlet Macaw; also, farm cider, several wines by the glass (including an english house wine), a perry and winter mulled wine. A few picnic-sets on the front grass face lime trees on the peaceful village green, while the pergola-covered back terrace and good-sized sheltered garden with its colourful herbaceous border have seats and picnic-sets (some shade is provided by a tall ash tree).

🍽 Reasonably priced food includes sandwiches, stilton-stuffed mushrooms, garlic and chilli prawns, pumpkin and goats cheese tart, chilli crab spaghetti, rabbit and cider casserole, beer-battered fish and chips, lamb rogan josh, liver and bacon, and puddings such as chocolate fudge cake and bakewell tart. *Benchmark main dish: fish pie £9.95. Two-course evening meal £14.00.*

Free house ~ Licensee Raymond Lambe ~ Real ale ~ (01462) 459585 ~ Open 12-2.30, 5.30-11; 12-3.30, 5.30-midnight Sat; 12-3.30, 7-10 Sun ~ Bar food 12-2, 6.30-8.30; not Sun evening, Mon ~ Children welcome ~ Dogs welcome ~ www.theredlionpreston.co.uk *Recommended by Ross Balaam*

REDBOURN
TL1011 Map 5

Cricketers 🍺

3.2 miles from M1 junction 9; A5183 signed Redbourn/St Albans, at second roundabout follow B487 for H Hempstead, first right into Chequer Lane, then third right into East Common; AL3 7ND

Good food and beer in a nicely placed and attractively updated pub with a bar and two restaurants

'This ticks all the boxes,' says one reader enthusiastically after a recent visit to this friendly, well run heart-of-the-village pub. The relaxed front bar has country-style decor of comfortable tub chairs, cushioned bench seating and high-backed bar stools on a pale brown carpet, and a woodburning stove. They serve a Greene King beer and four quickly changing ales on handpump, three ciders, an extensive wine list and good coffee; well reproduced background music. This bar leads back into an attractive, comfortably refurbished and unusually shaped modern restaurant; there's also an upstairs contemporary restaurant for private parties or functions. The side garden has plenty of seating and summer barbecues, and the pub is surrounded by numerous walking and cycling routes – Redbourn Common is opposite. Free maps are available, as is information on the museum next door.

Highly enjoyable food using seasonal local produce includes weekday sandwiches, chicken liver parfait with sweet tomato chutney, ham hock with bubble and squeak cake and a poached egg, vegetable and wild garlic risotto with asparagus fritter, cheeseburger with bacon and chips, corn-fed guinea fowl with pancetta, wild mushrooms and marsala cream, cassoulet of confit duck, pork belly and toulouse sausage, and puddings. *Benchmark main dish: slow-braised ox cheek with bourguignon sauce £16.95. Two-course evening meal £22.00.*

Free house ~ Licensees Colin and Debbie Baxter ~ Real ale ~ (01582) 620612 ~ Open 12-11 (midnight Sat, 10.30 Sun) ~ Bar food 12-3, 6-9; 12-4 Sun ~ Restaurant ~ Children welcome ~ Dogs allowed in bar ~ Wi-fi ~ www.thecricketersofredbourn.co.uk
Recommended by David Fowler, Mrs Margo Finlay, Jörg Kasprowski, Edward Mirzoeff

SARRATT
Cock

TQ0498   Map 5

Church End: a very pretty approach is via North Hill, a lane N off A404, just under a mile W of A405; WD3 6HH

Plush pub with friendly staff and a wide choice of drinks and food – good for families outside on summer weekends

Our readers really enjoy their visits to this genuinely friendly and comfortably traditional 17th-c pub. It's nicely positioned too. The latched back door opens straight into the homely tiled snug with its cluster of bar stools, vaulted ceiling and original bread oven. Through an archway, the partly oak-panelled cream-walled lounge has a lovely log fire in an inglenook, pretty Liberty-style curtains, red plush chairs at oak tables, lots of interesting artefacts and several namesake pictures of cockerels. Badger Best and Tanglefoot and a seasonal guest on handpump; background music. The restaurant is in an attractively converted barn. In summer, children can amuse themselves in the bouncy castle and play area, leaving parents to take in the open country views from picnic-sets on the appealing sheltered lawn and terrace. Additional picnic-sets in front look out across a quiet lane towards the churchyard.

Popular food includes sandwiches, crispy whitebait with lemon mayonnaise, home-made pâté, pork and leek sausages with red wine and onion gravy, creamed leeks and mushrooms in a filo basket, a changing curry, liver and bacon casserole, piri-piri chicken with sour cream, crab cakes, and puddings. *Benchmark main dish: steak in ale pie £12.25. Two-course evening meal £19.50.*

Badger ~ Tenants Brian and Marion Eccles ~ Real ale ~ (01923) 282908 ~ Open 12-10.30 (11.30 Sat, 9 Sun) ~ Bar food 12-2.30, 6-9; 12-5 Sun ~ Restaurant ~ Children welcome ~ Dogs allowed in bar ~ Wi-fi ~ www.cockinn.net
Recommended by Paul Humphreys, Dr Kevan Tucker, Roy Hoing, Mrs P J Pearce, David Jackson

SARRATT

Cricketers ♀ ⌷
TQ0499 Map 5

The Green; WD3 6AS

Plenty to look at in rambling rooms, up to six real ales, nice wines, enjoyable food and friendly staff; seats outside

Made up of three charming old cottages next to the village green and duck pond, this is a cleverly refurbished pub with lots of different seating areas. The interlinked rooms have numerous little snugs and alcoves – perfect for a quiet drink – and throughout there's all manner of antique dining rooms and tables on rugs or stripped floorboards, comfortable armchairs or tub seats, cushioned pews, wall seats and two open fires in raised fireplaces. Also, cricketing memorabilia, fresh flowers, large plants and church candles, Phoenix Brunning & Price Original and guests such as Adnams Ghost Ship, Growler Priory Mild, Tring Kotuku and Vale Best Bitter on handpump, good wines by the glass and 50 whiskies; background music and board games. Several sets of french windows open on to the terrace where there are tables and chairs, with picnic-sets on grass next to a colourfully painted tractor.

 Interesting food includes sandwiches, scallops with crispy bacon and garlic-sage butter, a sharing charcuterie board, mussel and prawn pasta with tomato and white wine, honey-roast ham and free-range eggs, caribbean chicken with pineapple salsa and coconut rice, spicy vietnamese king prawn and rice noodle salad with toasted cashew nuts, lime and chilli, and puddings such as banana and honeycomb eton mess and crème brûlée. *Benchmark main dish: slow-roasted lamb shank with mustard mash £16.95. Two-course evening meal £21.00.*

Brunning & Price ~ Licensee David Stowell ~ Real ale ~ (01923) 270877 ~ Open 11.30-11; 12-10.30 Sun ~ Bar food 12-10 (9.30 Sun) ~ Restaurant ~ Children welcome ~ Dogs allowed in bar ~ Wi-fi ~ www.cricketers-sarratt.co.uk
Recommended by Brian Glozier, John Boothman, Barry Collett

WATTON-AT-STONE
Bull
TL3019 Map 5

High Street; SG14 3SB

Bustling old pub with beamed rooms, candlelight and fresh flowers, real ales served by friendly staff and enjoyable food

Usefully open all day, this is a 15th-c pub with much character. At its heart is a huge inglenook fireplace with a leather button-back chesterfield and armchairs on either side (much prized on chilly days), a leather banquette beside a landscape-patterned wall, and solid dark wooden dining chairs and plush-topped stools around all sorts of tables on bare boards. The atmosphere is relaxed and friendly, there are fresh flowers and friendly staff serve Adnams Bitter, Sharps Doom Bar and St Austell Tribute on handpump and good wines by the glass. Near the entrance are some high bar chairs along counters by the windows; from here, it's a step up to a charming little room with just four tables, wooden dining chairs, a wall banquette, decorative logs in a fireplace, books on shelves, board games and an old typewriter. At the other end of the building is an elegantly furnished dining room with carpet and a slate floor. Paintwork throughout is contemporary. Outside, there are church chairs and tables on a covered terrace, picnic-sets on grass, and a small, well equipped play area.

🍴 Good tempting food includes breakfasts and morning coffee with croissants and cakes, lunchtime sandwiches (the soup and sandwich deal is popular), various tapas, earl grey-cured smoked venison, a pie of the day, sweet potato and blue cheese cobbler, braised beef cheek and fillet with horseradish mash, seared cod with chicken oysters and smoked roe, and puddings such as lemon meringue posset and dark chocolate tart with rosemary and orange. *Benchmark main dish: pie of the day £10.50. Two-course evening meal £20.00.*

Punch ~ Licensee Alastair and Anna Bramley ~ Real ale ~ (01920) 831032 ~ Open 9.30am-11pm; 12-6 Sun; closed Sun evening ~ Bar food 12-3, 6-9.30 ~ Restaurant ~ Children welcome ~ Wi-fi ~ www.thebullwatton.co.uk *Recommended by Mrs Margo Finlay, Jörg Kasprowski*

Also Worth a Visit in Hertfordshire

Besides the fully inspected pubs, you might like to try these pubs that have been recommended to us and described by readers. Do tell us what you think of them: feedback@goodguides.com

ALDBURY   SP9612
★**Greyhound** (01442) 851228
Stocks Road; village signed from A4251 Tring–Berkhamsted, and from B4506; HP23 5RT Picturesque village pub with some signs of real age inside, copper-hooded inglenook in cosy traditional beamed bar, more contemporary area with leather chairs, airy oak-floored back restaurant with wicker chairs at big new tables, Badger ales, traditional food (all day weekends) from sandwiches up; children welcome, dogs in bar, front benches facing green with whipping post, stocks and duck pond, suntrap gravel courtyard, eight bedrooms (some in newer building behind), open all day.
(David Jackson)

ALDENHAM   TQ1498
Round Bush (01923) 855532
Roundbush Lane; WD25 8BG Cheery and bustling village pub with plenty of atmosphere, two front rooms and back restaurant, popular generously served food from baguettes to specials, four well kept ales including St Austell, friendly efficient staff, darts, live music and quiz (first Weds of month); children and dogs welcome, big garden, good walks. *(Ross Balaam, Nigel and Sue Foster)*

ASHWELL   TL2639
Bushel & Strike (01462) 742394
Off A507 just E of A1(M) junction 10, N of Baldock, via Newnham; Mill Street opposite church, via Gardiners Lane (car park down Swan Lane); SG7 5LY Smartly modernised village dining pub with enjoyable interesting food (not Sun evening) including good value weekday set menu, Wells & Youngs ales and good choice of other drinks, good service; picnic-sets on lawn and small terrace, open all day. *(Martin and Alison Stainsby)*

AYOT GREEN   TL2213
Waggoners (01707) 324241
Off B197 S of Welwyn; AL6 9AA Former 17th-c coaching inn under french owners; good food from snacks and pubby choices in cosy low-beamed bar to more upmarket french cooking in comfortable restaurant extension, friendly attentive staff, good wine list, real ales; attractive and spacious suntrap back garden with sheltered terrace – some A1(M) noise, wooded walks nearby.
(James Luke)

AYOT ST LAWRENCE   TL1916
Brocket Arms (01438) 820250
Off B651 N of St Albans; AL6 9BT Attractive 14th-c low-beamed inn with enjoyable interesting food (not Sun evening) in bar and restaurant, six real ales including Black Sheep, Greene King and one badged for the pub from Nethergate, wide choice of wines by the glass, inglenook log fires; children welcome, dogs in bar, nice suntrap walled garden with play area, handy for Shaw's Corner (NT), George Bernard Shaw's house, six refurbished bedrooms, open all day.
(Matthew Salisbury)

BALDOCK   TL2433
Orange Tree (01462) 892341
Norton Road; SG7 5AW Old two-bar pub with up to 13 well kept ales including Buntingford and Greene King, local ciders such as Apple Cottage and large selection of whiskies, good value locally sourced home-made food (all day Fri and Sat, till 6pm Sun) including range of pies and blackboard specials, games room with bar billiards, quiz Tues, club folk club Weds; children welcome and dogs (theirs is called Arthur), garden with play area and chickens, open all day Thurs-Sun.
(Stuart Gideon, Mrs Catherine Simmonds)

BARKWAY   TL3834

★ Tally Ho   (01763) 848389

London Road (B1368); SG8 8EX Quirky little local with inviting old sofa, armchairs, horsebrasses and log fire in relaxed cottagey bar, extraordinary range of drinks including 60 malt whiskies and over 200 other spirits, Buntingford, Rebellion and a guest ale (apparently tapped from big casks behind bar, but actually gently pumped), Aspall's cider, fresh flowers and silver candelabra, old-fashioned prints on brown ply panelling, another log fire in old-world dining area serving fairly traditional food; children welcome, dogs in bar, well spaced picnic-sets, weeping willow in garden behind car park, closed Sun evening, otherwise open all day; changing hands as we went to press, so things may change. *(Anon)*

BATFORD   TL1415

★ Gibraltar Castle   (01582) 460005

Lower Luton Road; B653, S of B652 junction; AL5 5AH Traditional long carpeted bar with impressive military memorabilia – everything from rifles and swords to uniforms and medals (plenty of captions to read), also historical pictures of Gibraltar; area with low beams giving way to soaring rafters, comfortably cushioned wall benches, snug window alcoves and nice old fireplace, board games on piano, Fullers London Pride and ESB, popular home-made food (not Sun evening, Mon), friendly service; background music; children and dogs welcome, seats on front terrace looking over road to nature reserve, more tables behind on large decked area with lots of flowers, open all day. *(Anon)*

BERKHAMSTED   SP9907

Rising Sun   (01442) 864913

George Street; HP4 2EG Victorian canalside pub with five well kept ales including one badged for them by Tring, good range of ciders (three beer/cider festivals a year), interesting range of spirits, two very small traditional rooms with a few basic chairs and tables, coal fire, snuff and cigars for sale, no food apart from ploughman's, friendly service; background music; children and dogs welcome, chairs out by canal and well worn seating in covered side beer garden, colourful hanging baskets, open all day in summer, closed lunchtimes Mon-Thurs in winter. *(N R White)*

BISHOP'S STORTFORD   TL5021

Nags Head   (01279) 654553

Dunmow Road; CM23 5HP Well restored 1930s art deco pub (Grade II listed), McMullens ales from island servery and plenty of wines by the glass, wide choice of enjoyable reasonably priced food, lots of smallish well spaced tables, good service; children welcome, garden seating, open all day. *(Mrs K Hooker)*

BOURNE END   TL0206

★ Three Horseshoes   (01442) 862585

Winkwell; just off A4251 Hemel–Berkhamsted; HP1 2RZ Renovated 16th-c pub in charming setting by unusual swing bridge over Grand Union Canal, low-beamed three-room core with inglenooks, traditional furniture including settles, a few sofas, three well kept ales and enjoyable straightforward food (good burgers), efficient uniformed staff (may ask to keep a credit card while you eat), bay-windowed extension overlooking canal; comedy and quiz nights; children welcome, picnic-sets out by the water, open (and food) all day. *(Dennis Jones)*

BRAUGHING   TL3925

Axe & Compass   (01920) 821610

Just off B1368; The Street; SG11 2QR Nice country pub in pretty village with ford; good home-prepared food from traditional to more creative dishes, own-baked bread, well kept ales and several wines by the glass, friendly uniformed staff, mix of furnishings on wood floors in two roomy bars, log fires, restaurant; well behaved children and dogs welcome, garden overlooking playing field, outside bar. *(Mrs Margo Finlay, Jörg Kasprowski, Anthony and Marie Lewis)*

BRAUGHING   TL3925

Golden Fleece   (01920) 823555

Green End (B1368); SG11 2PE 17th-c dining pub with good freshly made food (all day Sun till 6pm) including some imaginative choices, special diets catered for, Adnams and guests, plenty of wines by the glass including champagne, cheerful service, bare-boards bar and two dining rooms, beams and timbers, good log fire; circular picnic-sets out in front, back garden with metal furniture on paved terrace. *(Anon)*

BUSHEY   TQ1394

Horse & Chains   (020) 8421 9907

High Street; WD23 1BL Comfortably modernised dining pub with woodburner in big inglenook, good choice of wines by the glass, real ales and enjoyable bar food from sandwiches and sharing plates up, separate restaurant menu, kitchen view from compact dining room, good friendly service; children welcome, open (and food) all day. *(Anon)*

CHORLEYWOOD   TQ0395

★ Black Horse   (01923) 282252

Dog Kennel Lane, The Common; WD3 5EG Welcoming old country pub popular for its good value generous food (smaller helpings available) from good sandwiches up, bargain OAP meals, well kept ales including Adnams, Wadworths and Wells & Youngs, decent wines, tea and coffee, good cheery service even when busy, low dark beams and two log fires in thoroughly traditional rambling bar, daily papers; big screen TV; children, walkers and dogs welcome, picnic-sets overlooking common, open all day. *(Roy Hoing, Anthony and Marie Lewis)*

CHORLEYWOOD   TQ0396
Gate (01923) 282053
Rickmansworth Road (A404), handy for M25 junction 18; WD3 5SQ Open-plan restaurant pub with bar and two dining areas, clean contemporary décor, enjoyable up-to-date food including sharing plates and good value weekday set menu (till 6pm), ales such as Brakspears, Cropton and Sharps, plenty of wines by the glass, helpful genial staff; background music; children welcome, lots of tables outside, open all day. *(Richard Kennell, Brian Glozier)*

CHORLEYWOOD   TQ0294
⋆ Land of Liberty Peace & Plenty
(01923) 282226 *Long Lane, Heronsgate, just off M25 junction 17; WD3 5BS* Traditional 19th-c pub in leafy outskirts, half a dozen well kept interesting ales and good choice of cider/perry, small range of enjoyable all-day snacks, nice cafetière coffee, good friendly service, simple layout, darts, skittles and board games; background jazz, TV (on request), no mobile phones or children inside; dogs on leads welcome, garden with pavilion, open all day. *(Richard Kennell)*

CHORLEYWOOD   TQ0295
Stag (01923) 282090
Long Lane/Heronsgate Road; WD3 5BT Refurbished open-plan Edwardian dining pub, decent choice of food from sandwiches and light meals up, weekday set lunch, McMullens ales and good choice of wines by the glass, friendly attentive service, bar and eating areas extending into conservatory, woodburner in raised hearth; free wi-fi; children welcome, tables on back lawn, closed Mon, otherwise open all day from 9am (10am weekends), Sun till 7pm. *(Jean Plant)*

COLNEY HEATH   TL2007
Plough (01727) 823720
Sleapshyde; handy for A1(M) junction 3; A414 towards St Albans, double back at first roundabout, then turn left; AL4 0SE Cosy 18th-c low-beamed thatched local, chatty atmosphere, good value generous home-made standard food (not Sun-Tues evenings) from lunchtime baguettes and baked potatoes up, well kept Greene King IPA and Abbot, St Austell Tribute and a guest, friendly efficient staff, big log fire, small brighter back dining area, charity quiz (first Tues of month); sports TV; children welcome, no dogs during food times, front and back terraces, picnic-sets on lawn overlooking fields, open all day weekends. *(Anon)*

COTTERED   TL3229
Bull (01763) 281243
A507 W of Buntingford; SG9 9QP Friendly well run dining pub with airy low-beamed front lounge, good furniture on stripped wood floors, log fire, very well liked if not cheap food from sandwiches up, Greene King ales and decent wines; unobtrusive background music; no prams, no under-7s Mon-Sat, big garden with tables beneath majestic old trees, open all day Sun. *(Anon)*

ELSTREE   TQ1797
Waggon & Horses (020) 8953 1406
Watling Street (A5183 towards Radlett); WD6 3AA Interesting old roadside pub with low black beams and inglenook fires, good choice of enjoyable freshly made food all day (Sun till 6pm) including range of home-made pies and own-smoked fish/meat, well kept ales such as Sharps, Timothy Taylors and Theakstons Old Peculier, several wines by the glass, library with books for sale (proceeds to charity); background and live music, TV; children welcome, garden with play area, outside bar, stage and smokers' shelter, open all day. *(Anon)*

ESSENDON   TL2608
Candlestick (01707) 261322
West End Lane; AL9 6BA Peacefully located country pub under same ownership as the nearby Woodman at Wildhill; emphasis on dining but also well kept local beers and several wines by the glass, relaxed friendly atmosphere, good value freshly prepared bar and restaurant food, comfortable clean interior with faux black timbers, log fires; children and dogs welcome, plenty of seats outside, good walks, closed Mon, otherwise open all day (till 8pm Sun). *(Martin Gough)*

FLAUNDEN   TL0100
Green Dragon (01442) 832269
Flaunden Hill; HP3 0PP Comfortable and chatty 17th-c beamed pub with partly panelled extended lounge, back restaurant and traditional little tap bar, log fire, popular good value food with emphasis on thai dishes, Fullers, St Austell and Wells & Youngs, friendly service, darts and other pub games; background music; children and dogs welcome, hitching rail for horses, well kept garden with smokers' shelter, pretty village, only a short diversion from Chess Valley Walk. *(Richard Kennell, N R White)*

GOSMORE   TL1827
Bull (01462) 440035
High Street; SG4 7QG Welcoming 17th-c village pub, fresh décor with beams and open fires, enjoyable good value food cooked by chef-landlord, Fullers, Sharps and a guest;

It's very helpful if you let us know up-to-date food prices when you report on pubs.

no under-14s in bar after 6pm or on Sun lunchtime, closed Sun evening, Mon. *(Stuart Gideon, Mrs Catherine Simmonds)*

GREAT HORMEAD — TL4030
Three Tuns (01763) 289405
B1038/Horseshoe Hill; SG9 0NT
Old thatched and timbered country pub in lovely surroundings, enjoyable good value food, Greene King IPA and a guest, small linked areas, huge inglenook with another great hearth behind, big back conservatory extension; children and dogs welcome, nice quiet garden, closed Sun evening. *(Anon)*

HATFIELD — TL2308
Horse & Groom (01707) 264765
Park Street, Old Hatfield; AL9 5AT
Friendly old town local with up to half a dozen well kept ales, good value pubby lunchtime food (free Tues, Sat nights if you buy a pint), dark beams and good winter fire, old local photographs, darts and dominoes; sports TV; a few tables out behind, handy for Hatfield House, open all day. *(Anon)*

HEMEL HEMPSTEAD — TL0411
Crown & Sceptre (01442) 234660
Bridens Camp; leaving on A4146, right at Flamstead/Markyate sign opposite Red Lion; HP2 6EY Traditional rambling pub, welcoming and relaxed, with well kept Greene King ales and up to six guests, local cider, generous helpings of good reasonably priced pubby food (not Sun evening), cheerful efficient staff, dining room with woodburner, quiz nights (not during the summer) and beer festivals; children welcome, outside bar/games room (dogs welcome here), picnic-sets out at front and in pleasant garden, good walks, open all day weekends. *(Peter and Jan Humphreys, Dennis Jones, Ross Balaam)*

HEMEL HEMPSTEAD — TL0604
Paper Mill (01442) 288800
Stationers Place, Apsley; HP3 9RH
Recently built canalside pub on site of former paper mill; spacious open-plan interior with upstairs restaurant, Fullers ales and a couple of guests (usually local), sensibly priced food from sandwiches and light dishes up, basket meals too, friendly staff, candles on tables, log fire, comedy, quiz and live music nights; children welcome, tables out on balcony and by the water, open all day. *(Tony and Wendy Hobden)*

HERTFORD — TL3008
Baker Arms (01992) 511235
Ashendene Road; SG13 8PX Nicely set village pub in row of former farm workers' cottages, traditionally refurbished with pubby furniture on wood floors, green wainscoting, enjoyable home-made food from daily changing menu, McMullens ales, helpful friendly staff, restaurant; children welcome, dogs in bar, garden with deck and play area,

clean comfortable bedrooms, open all day in summer (till 6pm Sun, from 3pm Mon). *(Mrs Margo Finlay, Jörg Kasprowski)*

HIGH WYCH — TL4614
Rising Sun (01279) 724099
Signed off A1184 Harlow–Sawbridgeworth; CM21 0HZ Refurbished and opened-up 19th-c red-brick local, well kept Courage Best, Oakham and guests tapped from the cask, friendly staff and locals, woodburner, no food; well behaved children and dogs welcome, small side garden. *(Anon)*

HITCHIN — TL1828
Bricklayers Arms (01462) 422700
Queen Street; SG4 9TP Town local taken over by twin sisters and refurbished, opened-up room with collection of breweriana, a dozen well kept ales including Banks & Taylor and Wells & Youngs, live music; good fish and chip shop next door. *(Stuart Gideon, Mrs Catherine Simmonds)*

HITCHIN — TL1828
Half Moon (01462) 452448
Queen Street; SG4 9TZ Tucked-away open-plan local, friendly and welcoming, with well kept Adnams, Wells & Youngs and half a dozen often local guests, real cider and perry, plenty of wines by the glass, good value traditional food (all day Fri, Sat) along with tapas, some themed nights, two beer festivals; open all day Fri-Sun. *(Stuart Gideon, Mrs Catherine Simmonds)*

HITCHIN — TL1929
Pitcher & Piano (01462) 434396
Market Place; SG5 1DY Light and spacious conversion of the old Corn Exchange, good variety of food and drinks, friendly staff; children welcome, open all day (till 1am Fri, Sat). *(David Hunt)*

HITCHIN — TL1929
Radcliffe Arms (01462) 456111
Walsworth Road; SG4 9ST Busy modernised Victorian pub/restaurant with good freshly made food (some quite pricey), local Buntingford ales, extensive wine list with many by the glass, decent coffee, friendly staff, bar area with central servery, conservatory; children welcome, terrace tables, open all day from 8am (9am weekends) for breakfast, closed Sun evening. *(M and J White, Stuart Gideon, Mrs Catherine Simmonds)*

HITCHIN — TL5122
Victoria (01462) 432682
Ickleford Road, at roundabout; SG5 1TJ Welcoming wedge-shaped Victorian corner local, Greene King ales and a guest, Aspall's cider, enjoyable reasonably priced home-cooked food, events including live music, barn function room; children welcome, seats in sunny beer garden, open all day. *(Stuart Gideon, Mrs Catherine Simmonds)*

HUNSDON   TL4114
Fox & Hounds (01279) 843999
High Street; SG12 8NJ Village dining pub
with chef-landlord cooking good enterprising
seasonal food (some quite pricey), weekday
set menu, friendly efficient service, Adnams
Southwold and a local guest, wide choice
of wines by the glass, organic fruit juices,
beams, panelling and fireside leather sofas,
more formal restaurant with chandelier
and period furniture, bookcase door to
lavatories; children welcome, dogs in bar,
heated covered terrace, closed Sun evening,
Mon. *(Mrs Margo Finlay, Jörg Kasprowski)*

LEMSFORD   TL2112
Crooked Chimney (01707) 397021
*Cromer Hyde Lane (B653 towards
Wheathampstead); AL8 7XE* Big
old building (originally a farmhouse)
refurbished as Vintage Inn dining pub,
popular food including fixed-price menu
(till 5pm Mon-Sat), friendly efficient
service, three well kept mainstream ales
and good choice of wines by the glass,
beams and timbers, central feature
fireplace and two further log fires; children
welcome, pleasant garden by fields, play
area, open all day. *(Ross Balaam)*

LITTLE HADHAM   TL4322
Nags Head (01279) 771555
*Hadham Ford, towards Much Hadham;
SG11 2AX* Popular and welcoming 16th-c
country dining pub with small linked heavily
black-beamed rooms, enjoyable sensibly
priced food from snacks up including good
Sun roasts, small bar with three Greene King
beers and decent wines, restaurant down
a couple of steps; children in eating areas,
tables in pleasant garden. *(Michael Domeney)*

LONG MARSTON   SP8915
Queens Head (01296) 668368
Tring Road; HP23 4QL Refurbished
beamed village local with well kept Fullers
beers, Weston's cider and enjoyable
traditional food including deals; dogs
welcome, seats on terrace, good walks
nearby, two bedrooms in separate annexe,
open all day. *(Anon)*

MUCH HADHAM   TL4219
★Bull (01279) 842668
High Street; SG10 6BU Neatly kept old
dining pub with good home-made food from
sandwiches to daily specials, nice choice
of wines by the glass including champagne,
well kept Brakspears and guests, cheerful
efficient service even at busy times,
inglenook log fire in unspoilt bar with locals
and their dogs, roomy civilised dining lounge

and back dining room; children welcome,
good-sized garden, Henry Moore Foundation
nearby, open all day weekends (food till
6.30pm Sun). *(Mrs Margo Finlay, Jörg
Kasprowski)*

NUTHAMPSTEAD   TL4134
★Woodman (01763) 848328
Off B1368 S of Barkway; SG8 8NB
Tucked-away thatched and weatherboarded
village pub with comfortable unspoilt core,
17th-c low beams/timbers and nice inglenook
log fire, plainer dining extension, good
home-made food (not Sun evening, Mon)
from traditional choices up, home-baked
bread, ales such as Adnams, Buntingford and
Greene King tapped from the cask, friendly
service, interesting USAF memorabilia
and outside memorial (near World War II
airfield); benches out overlooking tranquil
lane, two comfortable bedrooms, open all day
(Sun till 6.30pm, Mon 5-8pm). *(Mrs Margo
Finlay, Jörg Kasprowski)*

PERRY GREEN   TL4317
Hoops (01279) 843568
*Off B1004 Widford–Much Hadham;
SG10 6EF* Refurbished 19th-c pub/
restaurant in grounds of the Henry Moore
Foundation (the sculptor in evidence through
posters, photographs, prints and even the
cushion covers), airy open-plan interior with
beams and standing timbers, spindleback
chairs around rustic tables on tiled floor,
green banquettes, inglenook woodburner,
good reasonably priced locally sourced food
including some unusual choices, Adnams
Best; no dogs inside; children welcome,
garden with large covered terrace, open
all day Weds-Sat, till 6pm Sun, closed Mon,
evening Tues (winter hours may vary).
(Grahame Brooks)

RICKMANSWORTH   TQ0594
Feathers (01923) 770081
Church Street; WD3 1DJ Quietly set off
the high street, beams, panelling and soft
lighting, well kept Fullers London Pride,
Tring and two guests, good wine list, varied
choice of freshly prepared seasonal food
(all day) from sandwiches up including
lunchtime deal, good friendly young staff
coping well when busy; children till 5pm,
picnic-sets out behind. *(Brian Glozier)*

RIDGE   TL2100
Old Guinea (01707) 660894
Crossoaks Lane; EN6 3LH Welcoming
refurbished country pub with pizzeria
alongside traditional bar, open fire, enjoyable
food all day at reasonable prices, St Austell
Tribute; children welcome, dogs in bar, large
garden with far-reaching views. *(Anon)*

Virtually all pubs in this book sell wine by the glass. We mention wines if
they are a cut above the average.

ROYSTON TL3540
Old Bull (01763) 242003

High Street; SG8 9AW Chatty and relaxed coaching inn dating from the 16th c with bow-fronted Georgian façade; roomy high-beamed bar, exposed timbers and handsome fireplaces, wood flooring, easy chairs, papers and magazines, dining area with wall-sized photographs of old Royston, decent choice of food from ciabattas up, good value Sun carvery, Greene King ales and a guest, several wines by the glass, helpful pleasant service; background music and monthly live folk; children welcome, dogs in bar, suntrap courtyard, 11 bedrooms, open all day from 8am. *(Conor McGaughey)*

SARRATT TQ0499
★ Boot (01923) 262247

The Green; WD3 6BL Early 18th-c dining pub with good food (all day Sat, not Sun evening) from lunchtime sandwiches and sharing plates up, weekend breakfast from 9.30am, also tapas and pizzas Fri and Sat evenings, efficient service from friendly young staff, four well kept ales and good choice of wines by the glass, rambling bar with unusual inglenook, restaurant extension; children and (in some parts) dogs welcome, good-sized garden with polytunnel growing own produce, pleasant spot facing green, handy for Chess Valley walks, open all day. *(Ross Balaam, Jacquie Green)*

ST ALBANS TL1406
Fighting Cocks (01727) 869152

Abbey Mill Lane; through abbey gateway – you can drive down; AL3 4HE Ancient octagonal-shaped building (former dovecote) by River Ver; enjoyable food (not Sun evening) from enthusiastic chef-landlord including good Sun lunch, ales such as Leeds, Moles, Purity and Rudgate, friendly helpful service, sunken Stuart cockfighting pit (now a dining area), low heavy beams and panelling, copper-canopied inglenook fire, weekend live music, darts; children and dogs welcome, attractive public park beyond garden, open all day. *(Mrs Sally Scott)*

ST ALBANS TL1406
Garibaldi (01727) 894745

Albert Street; left turn down Holywell Hill past White Hart – car park left at end; AL1 1RT Busy little Victorian backstreet local with well kept Fullers/Gales beers and a guest, good wines by the glass and reasonably priced tasty food (all day weekends – till 7pm Sat, 5pm Sun), friendly staff; sports TV, free wi-fi; children and dogs welcome, garden tables, open all day. *(Nathan Gainford)*

ST ALBANS TL1805
★ Plough (01727) 857777

Tyttenhanger Green, off A414 E; AL4 0RW 18th-c village pub with up to ten well kept ales including Fullers, friendly efficient staff, low-priced straightforward food (not Sun or Mon evenings) from filled pittas and panini up, good log fire and woodburner, interesting old beer bottles and mats, longcase clock, back conservatory, board games and daily newspapers; children welcome, tables on raised front terrace, big garden with play area, open all day Fri-Sun. *(Alan Weedon)*

ST ALBANS TL1307
★ Six Bells (01727) 856945

St Michaels Street; AL3 4SH Rambling old pub popular for its good generous home-made food (not Sun evening), five well kept beers including Timothy Taylors and Tring, cheerful helpful staff, low beams and timbers, log fire, quieter panelled dining room, some live music; children and dogs welcome, occasional barbecues in small back garden, handy for Verulamium Museum, open all day. *(Stephen and Jean Curtis, David and Sue Atkinson)*

ST ALBANS TL1406
White Hart Tap (01727) 860974

Keyfield, round corner from Garibaldi; AL1 1QJ Friendly 19th-c corner local with half a dozen well kept ales (summer beer festivals), decent choice of wines by the glass and reasonably priced fresh food (all day Sat, not Sun evening) including good fish and chips Fri, some live music, Weds quiz; tables outside, open all day. *(Stephen and Jean Curtis)*

ST ALBANS TL1406
White Lion (01727) 850540

Sopwell Lane; AL1 1RN 16th-c local under new management; small friendly front bar and roomy linked lounge areas, enjoyable fairly priced food (not Sat or Sun evenings) from snacks to daily blackboard specials, up to seven well kept ales, Weston's cider, darts, live music Tues; no children inside; dogs welcome, big enclosed garden, open all day. *(Anon)*

THERFIELD TL3337
Fox & Duck (01763) 287246

Signed off A10 S of Royston; The Green; SG8 9PN Open-plan 19th-c bay-windowed pub, country chairs and sturdy stripped-top tables on stone flooring, enjoyable food (not Sun evening) from pub favourites up, Greene King and a couple of guests, friendly helpful staff, smaller boarded area on left with darts, carpeted back restaurant; children welcome, garden behind with gate to park (play equipment), more picnic-sets out on front green, quiet village, pleasant walks nearby, open all day weekends, closed Mon. *(Anon)*

TITMORE GREEN TL2126
Hermit of Redcoats (01438) 747333

Redcoates Green; SG4 7JR Large attractively refurbished red-brick Victorian pub, enjoyable food (not Sun evening, Mon) from light lunchtime choices up, Greene King ales, good service; children, dogs and muddy boots welcome, spacious garden, open all day Fri-Sun. *(Paul Humphreys)*

TRING   SP9211
Akeman (01442) 826027
Akeman Street; HP23 6AA Popular Oakman Inn (their first – opened in 2007), good choice of interesting food with some mediterranean influences from bar snacks and sharing plates up, open kitchen, three well kept ales including Tring, plenty of wines by the glass, cocktails and good coffee, open-plan layout with leather sofas by log fire, afternoon acoustic music first Sun of month; children welcome, nice garden area, open all day from 8am (breakfast till noon). *(Taff Thomas)*

TRING   SP9211
★ Kings Arms (01442) 823318
King Street; by junction with Queen Street (which is off B4635 Western Road – continuation of High Street); HP23 6BE Spic-and-span backstreet pub with lots of cheerful customers and relaxed atmosphere, well kept Wadworths 6X and four quickly changing guests such as Tring, real cider, hearty helpings of good value food including blackboard specials, efficient service, cushioned pews and wooden tables, stools around cast-iron tables, carpeted floors, old brewery advertisements on green-painted or pine panelled walls, two warm winter coal fires; free wi-fi; dogs welcome, children till 8.30pm, tables and heaters in attractive side wagon yard. *(Malcolm and Sue Scott)*

TRING   SP9211
★ Robin Hood (01442) 824912
Brook Street (B486); HP23 5ED Welcoming traditional local with enjoyable good value pubby food (all day Sat, not Sun evening), half a dozen Fullers ales in good condition, homely atmosphere and genial service, several well cared for smallish linked areas, main bar has banquettes and standard pub chairs on bare boards or carpet, conservatory with vaulted ceiling and woodburner; background music; children welcome, dogs in bar (resident yorkshire terrier and westie), small back terrace, public car park nearby, open all day Fri-Sun. *(Anon)*

WARESIDE   TL3915
Chequers (01920) 467010
B1004; SG12 7QY Proper old-fashioned country local with down-to-earth landlady,

three well kept ales such as Buntingford, good straightforward home-made food at reasonable prices including vegetarian options, friendly staff, log fire; children, dogs and walkers welcome. *(Anon)*

WATTON-AT-STONE   TL3019
George & Dragon (01920) 830285
High Street (B1001); SG14 3TA Appealing and welcoming candlelit country dining pub; enjoyable food from sandwiches up using local produce (gluten-free diets catered for), Greene King and guests, interesting mix of antique and modern prints on partly timbered walls, big inglenook fireplace, daily papers; no dogs; children in eating areas, pretty shrub-screened garden with heaters, boules, open all day. *(Stephen and Jean Curtis)*

WELWYN   TL2315
Steamer (01438) 715933
London Road; AL6 9DP Family-friendly pub refurbished under new management, enjoyable reasonably priced pubby lunchtime food, full indian menu evenings and all day Sun, well kept McMullens ales, good coffee; free wi-fi; open all day from 9am for breakfast. *(Jason Hobbs)*

WHEATHAMPSTEAD   TL1712
★ Wicked Lady (01582) 832128
Nomansland Common; B651 0.5 miles S; AL4 8EL Chain dining pub with clean contemporary décor, wide range of good well presented food including weekday fixed-price menu till 6pm, well kept Adnams, Fullers London Pride and Timothy Taylors Landlord, plenty of wines by the glass, cocktails, friendly attentive young staff, various rooms and alcoves, low beams and log fires, conservatory; garden with pleasant terrace, open (and food) all day. *(Anon)*

WIGGINTON   SP9310
Greyhound (01442) 824631
Just S of Tring; HP23 6EH Friendly village pub with four well kept ales including Tring, enjoyable food from pubby choices to daily specials, cheerful efficient service, restaurant; children and dogs welcome, back garden with fenced play area, good Ridgeway walks, three bedrooms, open (and food) all day. *(Ross Balaam)*

WILDHILL   TL2606
Woodman (01707) 642618
Off B158 Brookmans Park–Essendon; AL9 6EA Simple tucked-away country local with friendly staff and regulars, well kept Greene King and four guests, open-plan

---

Post Office address codings confusingly give the impression that some pubs are in Hertfordshire, when they're really in Bedfordshire, Buckinghamshire or Cambridgeshire (which is where we list them).

bar with log fire, two smaller back rooms (one with TV), straightforward weekday bar lunches, darts; plenty of seating in big garden. *(David Jackson)*

WILLIAN   TL2230
★ **Fox** (01462) 480233
A1(M) junction 9; A6141 W towards Letchworth then first left; SG6 2AE .
Civilised contemporary dining pub, comfortable pale wood tables and chairs on stripped boards or big ceramic tiles, paintings by local artists, good inventive food along with more traditional choices, Adnams, Brancaster, Dark Star, Sharps and Woodfordes, good wine list with 14 by the glass, attentive, friendly young staff; background music, TV; children and dogs (in bar) welcome, side terrace with smart tables under parasols, picnic-sets in good-sized back garden below handsome 14th-c church tower, open all day (no food Sun evening). *(Ross Balaam, Brian Glozier, Pat and Graham Williamson)*

WILLIAN   TL2230
Three Horseshoes (01462) 685713
Baldock Lane, off Willian Road, handy for A1(M) junction 9; SG6 2AE
Welcoming traditional village local, enjoyable home-made pubby food generously served and reasonably priced, well kept Greene King and guests, log fires; children and dogs welcome, lots of colourful hanging baskets, small sunny garden, open (and food) all day. *(Pat and Graham Williamson)*

WILSTONE   SP9014
Half Moon (01442) 826410
Tring Road, off B489; HP23 4PD
Traditional old village pub, clean and comfortable, with good value reliable pubby food and well kept ales such as Adnams and Sharps Doom Bar, friendly efficient staff, big log fire, low beams, old local pictures and lots of brasses; may be background radio; handy for Grand Union Canal walks. *(John Kaye, Ross Balaam)*

'Children welcome' means the pub says it lets children inside without any special restriction. If it allows them in, but to restricted areas such as an eating area or family room, we specify this. Places with separate restaurants often let children use them, and hotels usually let children into public areas such as lounges. Some pubs impose an evening time limit – let us know if you find one earlier than 9pm.

Isle of Wight

 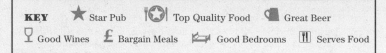
 ## BEMBRIDGE
SZ6587 Map 2

Crab & Lobster ⭐

Foreland Fields Road, off Howgate Road (which is off B3395 via Hillway Road); PO35 5TR

Clifftop views from terrace and delicious seafood; bedrooms

The wonderful view from the coastal bluff over the Solent alone justifies the search for this obscurely located clifftop pub, and the terrace, bedrooms and window seats make the most of this. In summer, the picnic-sets get bagged pretty quickly, so do arrive early. The interior is roomier than you might expect and decorated in a parlour-like style, with lots of yachting memorabilia, old local photographs and a blazing winter fire; darts, dominoes and cribbage. Helpful, cheerful staff serve Goddards Fuggle-Dee-Dum, Greene King IPA and Sharps Doom Bar on handpump, a dozen wines by the glass, 16 malt whiskies and good coffee. The shore is just a stroll away.

⭐ As well as smashing seafood – crab and prawn cocktail, moules marinière, crab and lobster or hot seafood platters, seafood mixed grill – the good food includes lunchtime sandwiches and baguettes, sharing boards, vegetarian, chicken or beef burger with various toppings, ham and egg, a pie of the day, all-day breakfast, and puddings such as banana eton mess with toffee sauce and chocolate brownie; afternoon teas 3-5pm. *Benchmark main dish: crab cakes with tartare sauce £11.75. Two-course evening meal £19.00.*

Enterprise ~ Lease Caroline and Ian Quekett ~ Real ale ~ (01983) 872244 ~ Open 11-11; 12-10.30 Sun ~ Bar food 12-2.30, 6-9 (9.30 Fri, Sat); limited menu 2.30-5.30 weekends and holidays ~ Restaurant ~ Children welcome ~ Dogs allowed in bar ~ Wi-fi ~ Bedrooms: $75/$95 ~ www.crabandlobsterinn.co.uk *Recommended by Michael Tack, Brian Glozier, Adrian Johnson, B J Harding*

 ## FISHBOURNE
SZ5592 Map 2

Fishbourne Inn

From Portsmouth car ferry turn left into Fishbourne Lane (no through road); PO33 4EU

Attractively refurbished pub with a contemporary feel, real ales, plenty of wines by the glass and all-day food; bedrooms

Handy for the Wightlink ferry terminal, this is an attractive half-timbered pub with real ales and well liked food. The open-plan rooms are connected by knocked-through doorways and there's a mix of wooden and high-backed dining chairs around square tables on the slate floor, a red-painted area off the bar with a big model yacht and two leather sofas facing each other, and a woodburning stove in a brick fireplace with an ornate mirror above. The smart dining room has leather high-backed chairs around circular tables on wood flooring and another model yacht on the window sill; one comfortable room has huge brown leather sofas, and throughout there are country pictures on the partly panelled walls. Goddards Fuggle-Dee-Dum, Ringwood Best and Sharps Doom Bar on handpump and 11 wines by the glass from a good list; background music. This is sister pub to the Horse & Groom in Ningwood, Boathouse in Seaview and New Inn at Shalfleet.

Good all-day food includes breakfasts until 11am, lunchtime sandwiches and baguettes, ham and free-range egg, chicken caesar salad, a pie of the day, home-made lentil sausages with vegetarian onion gravy, a pint of shell-on prawns with mayonnaise, rump steak with peppercorn sauce or melted blue cheese, crab and lobster salads, daily specials, and puddings such as rhubarb crumble and dark chocolate and orange mousse. *Benchmark main dish: beer-battered fresh fish and chips £10.95. Two-course evening meal £17.00.*

Enterprise ~ Lease Martin Bullock ~ Real ale ~ (01983) 882823 ~ Open 9am-11pm (10.30pm Sun) ~ Bar food 12-9.30; breakfasts 9-11am ~ Children welcome ~ Dogs allowed in bar ~ Wi-fi ~ Bedrooms: £75/£120 ~ www.thefishbourne.co.uk
Recommended by Adrian Johnson, Ian Phillips

FRESHWATER
SZ3487 Map 2

Red Lion ♀

Church Place; from A3055 at E end of village by Freshwater Garage mini-roundabout follow Yarmouth signpost, then take first real right turn signed to Parish Church; PO40 9BP

Good mix of customers, enjoyable food and beer and a composed atmosphere

Consistently maintaining its high standards, this red-brick pub on a quiet village street remains extremely popular with both locals and visitors – and it's kept an atmosphere that customers without smaller children tend to appreciate. The food is quite a draw, but you're likely to find a row of chatty regulars occupying stools along the counter, enjoying the Goddards Fuggle-Dee-Dum, Sharps Doom Bar and West Berkshire Good Old Boy on handpump and 11 wines by the glass. The comfortably furnished open-plan bar has a winter woodburning stove and country-style furnishings on mainly flagstoned floors and bare boards. Outside, there are tables in a carefully tended garden beside the kitchen's herb and vegetable patch. A couple of picnic-sets in a quiet square at the front have pleasant views of the church. Good walking on the nearby Freshwater Way.

Listed on boards behind the bar, the food includes a cross section of dishes such as field mushrooms with spinach and goats cheese, crab and avocado cocktail, calves liver with bacon and onion gravy, several fresh fish dishes, steak in ale pie, a changing curry, lamb shank with minted gravy, and puddings. *Benchmark main dish: home-made fishcakes £11.50. Two-course evening meal £18.50.*

Enterprise ~ Lease Michael Mence ~ Real ale ~ (01983) 754925 ~ Open 11.30-3 (4 Sat), 5.30-11; 12-3, 6-10.30 Sun ~ Bar food 12-2, 6-9 ~ Children under 10 at the landlord's discretion ~ Dogs welcome ~ www.redlion-freshwater.co.uk *Recommended by John Jenkins*

We checked prices with the pubs as we went to press in summer 2014.
They should hold until around spring 2015.

NINGWOOD
Horse & Groom

SZ3989 Map 2

A3054 Newport–Yarmouth, a mile W of Shalfleet; PO30 4NW

Spacious family dining pub with fairly priced all-day food, excellent play area and crazy golf

Families with children will find plenty to keep them occupied outdoors here – there are ample tables in the garden, a bouncy castle, crazy golf and a fully equipped play area. Inside, you can be sure of a friendly welcome from the licensee and his staff in this neatly kept, carefully extended pub, where the atmosphere is warm and easy-going. The roomy interior has been thoughtfully arranged, with comfortable leather sofas grouped around low tables on flagstones, a nice mix of sturdy tables and chairs well spaced for a relaxing meal, and a winter log fire. Ringwood Best and a couple of guests such as Goddards Scrumdiggity Bitter and Sharps Doom Bar on handpump and a dozen wines by the glass; background music, games machine and board games. There's a good circular walk from the pub's front door; muddy boots and dogs are welcome in the bar. This is sister pub to the Fishbourne Inn at Fishbourne, Boathouse in Seaview and New Inn at Shalfleet.

Fair value and enjoyable, the food includes sandwiches, creamy garlic and brandy button mushrooms, deep-fried whitebait with home-made tartare sauce, fishcakes of the day, chicken topped with melted brie, bacon and tomato chutney, pork loin with mustard sauce and cheese mash, and puddings such as steamed strawberry jam sponge and custard and rocky road with fudge ice-cream. *Benchmark main dish: steak in ale pie £11.50. Two-course evening meal £16.50.*

Enterprise ~ Lease Steve Gilbert ~ Real ale ~ (01983) 760672 ~ Open 9am-11pm ~ Bar food 9am-11pm ~ Children welcome ~ Dogs allowed in bar ~ Wi-fi ~ www.horse-and-groom.com *Recommended by Penny and Peter Keevil, Guy and Caroline Howard*

NITON
Buddle

SZ5075 Map 2

St Catherine's Road, Undercliff; off A3055 just S of village, towards St Catherine's Point; PO38 2NE

Stone pub with sea views from seats in clifftop garden, five real ales and tasty food

Surrounded by National Trust land and handy for the coast path, this 16th-c former smugglers' haunt keeps five real ales on handpump, such as Goddards Ale of Wight, Island Nipper Bitter, Sharps Doom Bar, Yates Dark Side of the Wight and Youngs Best; also, 11 wines by the glass and a couple of farm ciders. The traditional bar rooms have plenty of character: heavy black beams, captain's chairs and wheelbacks or cushioned wall seats around solid wooden tables on big flagstones or carpet, and an open fire in a broad stone fireplace with a massive black oak mantelbeam; background music. Picnic-sets on both stone terraces and on the grass in the neatly kept garden look down to the sea.

All-day food includes sandwiches and baguettes, moules marinière, spicy moroccan lamb skewers with minted yoghurt, aubergine parmigiana, a pie and a curry of the day, chicken or beef burger with toppings and chips, crab salad, seafood risotto, duck stir-fry with noodles, and puddings. *Benchmark main dish: beer-battered fish and chips £10.95. Two-course evening meal £16.50.*

Character Group ~ Lease Mandi O'Reilly ~ Real ale ~ (01983) 730243 ~ Open 11-10.30 (11 Weds, 11.30 Fri, Sat); 12-10.30 Sun ~ Bar food 12-9 ~ Children welcome ~ Dogs welcome ~ Wi-fi ~ Live music Weds, Fri, Sat evenings ~ www.buddleinn.co.uk
Recommended by Edward May, William Wright

SEAVIEW
Boathouse 🛏

SZ5992   Map 2

On B3330 Ryde–Seaview; PO34 5BW

Contemporary décor in well run pub by the beach, real ales, quite a choice of food, a friendly welcome and seats outside; bedrooms

If you stay in the comfortable bedrooms at this extended blue-painted Victorian pub, you can look out to the sea; the picnic-sets and white tables and chairs, some under parasols, have the same view. The interior is appealing: the bar has sturdy leather stools and blue tub-like chairs around circular wooden tables, a large model yacht on the mantelpiece above the open fire with a huge neat stack of logs beside it, fresh flowers and candles, and Fullers Seafarers and Sharps Doom bar on handpump from the pale wooden counter and 11 wines by the glass. In another room a dinghy (complete with oars) leans against the wall. The dining room has elegant dining chairs, more wooden tables, portraits on pale blue walls and an ornate mirror over another open fire; background music. Throughout, the paintwork is light and fresh and there's a mix of polished bare boards, flagstones and carpet. This is sister pub to the Fishbourne Inn at Fishbourne, Horse & Groom in Ningwood and New Inn at Shalfleet.

Food is usefully served all day at weekends (and daily April to October), including sandwiches and baguettes, smoked mackerel pâté with sweet and sour cucumber, local clams steamed in ale, slow-vegetarian frittata, roast pork belly with apple and celeriac mash, duck leg in walnut and pomegranate sauce, crab and lobster salads, and puddings such as chocolate brownie with chocolate sauce and tiramisu cheesecake. *Benchmark main dish: fish pie £10.95. Two-course evening meal £16.50.*

Punch ~ Tenant Martin Bullock ~ Real ale ~ (01983) 810616 ~ Open 9am-11pm (10.30pm Sun) ~ Bar food 9am-11pm ~ Children welcome ~ Dogs allowed in bar ~ Wi-fi ~ Bedrooms: £75/£125 ~ www.theboathouseiow.co.uk *Recommended by John Jenkins*

SHALFLEET
New Inn ⭐ ♀

SZ4089   Map 2

A3054 Newport–Yarmouth; PO30 4NS

Isle of Wight Dining Pub of the Year

Popular pub with seafood specialities, and good beers and wines

How apt that this former fishermen's pub should specialise in fresh fish and shellfish – and it's just a stroll from the quay. The rambling rooms have plenty of character, with warm fires, yachting photographs and pictures, boarded ceilings and scrubbed-pine tables on flagstone, carpet and slate floors. Goddards Fuggle-Dee-Dum, Ringwood Best and Sharps Doom Bar on handpump, 11 wines by the glass and farm cider; background music. There may be double sittings in summer; dogs are only allowed in areas with stone floors. This is sister pub to the Fishbourne Inn at Fishbourne, Horse & Groom in Ningwood and Boathouse in Seaview.

🔟 Food is usefully served all day, starting with breakfasts at 10am: there might be
sandwiches and baguettes, potted crab, wild mushrooms on toasted brioche,
blue cheese dumplings in tomato and garlic sauce, lamb and coriander sausages with
red wine and mint gravy, a trio of daily changing fish with creamy mussels, corn-fed
chicken with chorizo and butterbean cassoulet, big platters of fresh and smoked fish
and shellfish, and puddings. *Benchmark main dish: seafood royale (big platter of
fresh and smoked fish plus hot and cold shellfish) for two people £60.00. Two-course
evening meal £18.50.*

Enterprise ~ Lease Martin Bullock ~ Real ale ~ (01983) 531314 ~ Open 9am-11pm
(10.30pm Sun) ~ Bar food 10-9.30 ~ Children welcome ~ Dogs allowed in bar ~ Wi-fi ~
www.thenew-inn.co.uk *Recommended by Penny and Peter Keevil, B J Harding*

SHORWELL   SZ4582   Map 2
Crown 🍺
B3323 SW of Newport; PO30 3JZ

**Popular pub with an appealing streamside garden and play area,
pubby food and several real ales**

Despite the holidaymakers that frequent this attractive village nestled
beneath the downs, this charming, partly 17th-c pub still has the
character of a proper local. Four opened-up rooms spread around a central
bar with carpet, tiles or flagstones, and there's a warm welcome for all.
Adnams Broadside, Goddards Fuggle-Dee-Dum, St Austell Tribute and
Sharps Doom Bar on handpump, 11 wines by the glass and a farm cider.
The beamed knocked-through lounge has blue and white china on an
attractive carved dresser, old country prints on stripped-stone walls and
a winter log fire with a fancy tile-work surround. Black pews form bays
around tables in a stripped-stone room off to the left, with another log fire;
background music and board games. The tree-sheltered garden has a little
stream that broadens into a small trout-filled pool, plenty of closely spaced
picnic-sets and white garden chairs and tables on grass, and a decent
children's play area.

🍴 Tasty pubby food includes sandwiches, garlic mushrooms, home-made pâté, pizzas,
omelettes, beef, chicken or vegetarian burger with various toppings, a curry of the
day, beer-battered fish and chips, daily specials, and puddings. *Benchmark main
dish: steak in ale pie £12.00. Two-course evening meal £16.00.*

Enterprise ~ Lease Nigel and Pam Wynn ~ Real ale ~ (01983) 740293 ~ Open 10.30am
(11.30am Sun)-11pm~ Bar food 12-9.30 ~ Children welcome ~ Dogs welcome ~ Wi-fi ~
www.crowninnshorwell.co.uk *Recommended by C and R Bromage, Susan Martin Jones*

Also Worth a Visit on the Isle of Wight

Besides the fully inspected pubs, you might like to try these pubs that
have been recommended to us and described by readers. Do tell us what
you think of them: feedback@goodguides.com

ARRETON   SZ5386
★ **White Lion** (01983) 528479
A3056 Newport–Sandown; PO30 3AA
Old white-painted village pub refurbished

under new management; lightened-up
beamed interior (less cluttered than before),
bar with stripped wood floor and comfortable
seats by log fire, Sharps Doom Bar and
Timothy Taylors Landlord, good choice of

We say if we know a pub has background music.

enjoyable fairly priced food, restaurant, friendly helpful staff; children and dogs welcome, pleasant garden, open all day. *(Michael Tack, A N Bance)*

BEMBRIDGE   SZ6488
Pilot Boat (01983) 872077
Station Road/Kings Road; PO35 5NN Welcoming little harbourside pub with ship-like interior, good food from sandwiches to local seafood, well kept Goddards and guests; tables out overlooking water or in pleasant courtyard behind, well placed for coast walks, open all day. *(A N Bance)*

BINSTEAD   SZ5792
Fleming Arms (01983) 563415
Binstead Road; PO33 3RD Spacious roadside pub with wide choice of enjoyable reasonably priced food, Greene King Abbot and Sharps Doom Bar, friendly service; children and dogs welcome, disabled access/facilities, garden, open all day. *(Anon)*

BONCHURCH   SZ5778
★**Bonchurch Inn** (01983) 852611
Bonchurch Shute; from A3055 E of Ventnor turn down to Old Bonchurch; opposite Leconfield Hotel; PO38 1NU Quirky former stables with restaurant run by welcoming italian family; congenial bar with narrow-planked ship's decking and old-fashioned steamer-style seats, Courage ales tapped from the cask, bar food and good italian dishes, charming helpful service, fairly basic family room, darts, shove-ha'penny and other games; background music; dogs welcome, delightful continental-feel central courtyard (parking here can be tricky), holiday flat. *(Anon)*

CARISBROOKE   SZ4687
★**Blacksmiths Arms** (01983) 529263
B3401 1.5 miles W; PO30 5SS Friendly family-run hillside pub, scrubbed tables in neat beamed and flagstoned front bars, superb Solent views from airy bare-boards family dining extension, ales such as Adnams, Island and Timothy Taylors, decent wines and cider, good food including fresh fish; children, dogs and walkers welcome (Tennyson Trail nearby), terrace tables and smallish back garden with same view, play area, open all day. *(Penny and Peter Keevil)*

COWES   SZ5092
★**Folly** (01983) 297171
Folly Lane signed off A3021 just S of Whippingham; PO32 6NB Glorious Medina estuary views from bar and waterside terrace of this cheery laid-back place, timbered ship-like interior with simple wood furnishings, wide range of sensibly priced food from breakfast on, Greene King, Goddards and a guest; background and live music, TV, fruit machine, children and dogs

welcome, showers, long-term parking and weather forecasts for sailors, water taxi, open (and food) all day. *(Anon)*

COWES   SZ4996
Union (01983) 293163
Watch House Lane, in pedestrian centre; PO31 7QH Old-town inn tucked back from seafront with good value freshly made food and well kept Fullers/Gales beers, friendly helpful young staff, cosy areas around central bar, log fire, dining room and conservatory; children and dogs welcome, tables outside, six comfortable clean bedrooms. *(John Jenkins)*

DOWNEND   SZ5387
Hare & Hounds (01983) 523446
A3056; PO30 2NU Thatched family dining pub (bigger inside than it looks) with good choice of enjoyable food including set menu deal, friendly staff, ales such as Goddards and Sharps, lots of beams and stripped brickwork, cosy alcoves in original part, more room in airy barn-type extension; wide views from terrace, nice spot by Robin Hill Adventure Park. *(Ian Phillips)*

GODSHILL   SZ5281
★**Taverners** (01983) 840707
High Street (A3020); PO38 3HZ Welcoming 17th-c pub with good seasonal food from landlord-chef, emphasis on fresh local produce (some home-grown), booking advised weekends, well kept Fullers London Pride, a house beer from Yates and a guest, plenty of wines by the glass, good friendly service, spacious bar and two front dining areas, beams, bare boards and slate floors, woodburner; children and dogs welcome in certain areas, garden with terrace and play area, own shop, limited parking, open all day, closed Sun evening (except bank/school summer holidays). *(B J Harding)*

GURNARD   SZ4796
Woodvale (01983) 292037
Princes Esplanade; PO31 8LE Large 1930s inn with picture-window Solent views, friendly staff, good choice of real ales and plenty of wines by the glass, enjoyable food including good fish/seafood specials, weekend live music, Mon quiz; children welcome, garden with terrace and summer barbecues, refurbished bedrooms, open all day. *(Anon)*

HAVENSTREET   SZ5590
White Hart (01983) 883485
Off A3054 Newport–Ryde; Main Road; PO33 4DP Updated old red-brick village pub with good choice of popular food (all day Sun) including daily specials, Ringwood and Goddards ales, cosy log-fire bar and carpeted dining area; children and dogs welcome, tables in secluded garden behind, open all day. *(Anon)*

HULVERSTONE SZ3984
★ **Sun** (01983) 741124
B3399; PO30 4EH Picture-book thatched
country pub in charming peaceful setting
with lovely views over the Channel, low-
ceilinged bar with regularly changing ales,
nice mix of old furniture on flagstones
and floorboards, brick and stone walls,
horsebrasses and ironwork around fireplace,
large windows in traditionally decorated
newer dining area, all-day pubby food
including local meat, darts and board
games; background music (live Sat evening);
children welcome, dogs in bar (menu for
them), secluded split-level cottagey garden,
open all day. *(Guy and Caroline Howard)*

NEWCHURCH SZ5685
★ **Pointer** (01983) 865202
High Street; PO36 0NN Well run old
two-room pub by Norman church, good
fairly priced local food including blackboard
specials (booking advised in season), well
kept Fullers and a guest ale, friendly service;
children and dogs welcome, views from
pleasant back garden, boules, open (and
food) all day. *(S Holder)*

NORTHWOOD SZ4983
Travellers Joy (01983) 298024
Off B3325 S of Cowes; PO31 8LS
Friendly pub refurbished under new
licensees; eight well kept ales including
locals such as Island Wight Gold (tasters
offered), enjoyable reasonably priced food
from sandwiches and pubby choices to
daily specials, long bar with log fire, dining
conservatory, pool room, Sun quiz and some
live music; children, dogs and walkers
welcome, garden with pétanque and play
area, open (and food) all day. *(Anon)*

RYDE SZ5992
S Fowler & Co (01983) 812112
Union Street; PO33 2LF Wetherspoons in
split-level former department store, plenty
of seating including upstairs family area,
a dozen real ales and good choice of other
drinks including decent coffee, their usual
food and affordable prices, friendly staff; TVs
for subtitled news, free wi-fi; open all day
from 7am. *(Ian Phillips)*

SEAVIEW SZ6291
★ **Seaview Hotel** (01983) 612711
*High Street; off B3330 Ryde–Bembridge;
PO34 5EX* Small gently civilised but
relaxed hotel, traditional wood furnishings,
seafaring paraphernalia and log fire in pubby
bare-boards bar, comfortable more refined
front bar, well kept Goddards, Yates and a
guest, good wine list including some local
ones, good well presented pub food (smaller
helpings available) and more elaborate
restaurant menu using produce from their
farm, friendly interested staff; may ask for
a credit card if you run a tab, background

music, TV; children welcome, dogs in bar,
glimpses of sea from tables on tiny front
terrace, six nice bedrooms (some with sea
views), open all day. *(Anon)*

SHANKLIN SZ5881
★ **Fishermans Cottage** (01983) 863882
Bottom of Shanklin Chine; PO37 6BN
Thatched cottage in terrific setting tucked
into the cliffs on Appley beach, steep zigzag
walk down beautiful chine; low-beamed little
flagstoned rooms refurbished after recent
flood, stripped-stone walls, old local pictures
and some bric-a-brac, Island and Yates beers,
good value pub food including lots of fish;
background and some live music; wheelchair
access, children and dogs welcome,
sun-soaked terrace, lovely seaside walk to
Luccombe, open all day (closed weekdays
end of Oct to early March). *(Adrian Johnson,
Mrs Sally Scott)*

SHANKLIN SZ5881
Steamer (01983) 862641
Esplanade; PO37 6BS Nautical-theme
bar, fun for holiday families, with good range
of real ales and enjoyable food including
local seafood, cheery staff, live music most
weekends; fine sea views from covered
floodlit terrace, eight bedrooms, open all day.
(A N Bance)

ST HELENS SZ6289
Vine (01983) 872337
Upper Green Road; PO33 1UJ Victorian
pub overlooking cricket green, enjoyable
range of food (all day Sat, Sun) including
stone-baked pizzas, ales such as Island and
Ringwood, friendly staff, weekend live music,
quiz Weds; free wi-fi; children and dogs
welcome, play area across the road, open
all day. *(Anon)*

VENTNOR SZ5677
Perks (01983) 857446
High Street; PO38 1LT Little bar packed
with interesting memorabilia behind
shop-window front, well kept ales including
Bass, good range of wines, popular well
priced home-made food from sandwiches
and baked potatoes up, bargain OAP two-
course lunch, fast friendly service. *(Liz and
John Soden)*

VENTNOR SZ5677
★ **Spyglass** (01983) 855338
*Esplanade, SW end; road down is very
steep and twisty, and parking nearby
can be difficult – best to use pay-and-
display (free in winter) about 100
metres up the road; PO38 1JX* Perched
above the beach with a fascinating jumble
of seafaring memorabilia in snug quarry-
tiled interior (anything from ship's wheels
to wrecked rudders to stuffed seagulls),
Ringwood ales and guests, popular food
including fish dishes; background music,
live bands every day in summer (Weds–Sun

in winter); children welcome, dogs in bar, sea-wall terrace with lovely views, coast walk towards the Botanic Garden, heftier hikes on to St Boniface Down and towards the eerie shell of Appuldurcombe House, bedrooms, open all day. *(Penny and Peter Keevil, Adrian Johnson)*

WHITWELL   SZ5277

White Horse (01983) 730375

High Street; PO38 2PY Popular updated and extended old pub, wide range of good value food from pub staples up, well kept ales such as Goddards and Yates, good friendly service, carpeted beamed bar with exposed stonework, restaurant; may be background music, Mon quiz, darts and pool; children and dogs welcome, picnic-sets among fruit trees in big garden with play area, open (and food) all day. *(Guy and Caroline Howard)*

YARMOUTH   SZ3589

Wheatsheaf (01983) 760456

Bridge Road, near ferry; PO41 0PH Modernised opened-up Victorian pub with good well priced food, cheerful service, Goddards, Ringwood and a guest, glazed extension, pool; children and dogs welcome, handy for the harbour, open (and food) all day. *(Anon)*

A star symbol before the name of a pub shows exceptional character and appeal. It doesn't mean extra comfort. Even quite a basic pub can win a star, if it's individual enough.

Kent

BIDDENDEN

TQ8238 Map 3

Three Chimneys 🍴 🍷

A262, a mile W of village; TN27 8LW

Kent Dining Pub of the Year

Pubby beamed rooms of considerable individuality, log fires, imaginative food and pretty garden

As ever, our readers love this informally civilised old pub, which is also handy for nearby Sissinghurst Castle (National Trust). The small low-beamed rooms have plenty of character – they're simply done out with plain wooden furniture and old settles on flagstones and coir matting, some harness and sporting prints on the stripped-brick walls and good log fires. The public bar on the left is quite down to earth, with darts, dominoes and cribbage. Well trained, attentive staff serve Adnams Best, Old Dairy Blue Top and Sarah Hughes Good Shepherd Ale tapped from the cask, 15 wines by the glass, local Biddenden cider and 13 malt whiskies. A candlelit bare-boards restaurant has rustic décor and french windows that open into a conservatory; seats in the garden.

🍴 Excellent food includes ploughman's, deep-fried breadcrumbed brie with apple and celery salad, smoked haddock and salmon fishcakes with tartare sauce, pork and sage sausages with port and red onion gravy, fresh herb and pine nut pesto couscous with grilled goats cheese on roasted vegetables with tomato sauce, guinea fowl with baby onions, mushrooms and pancetta, parmentier potatoes and rich jus, and puddings such as amaretto parfait with fresh berry compote and mississippi mud cake with hot chocolate sauce and honeycomb ice-cream. *Benchmark main dish: smoked haddock on creamed leeks with bacon, spring onions and chive velouté £18.95. Two-course evening meal £24.50.*

Free house ~ Licensee Craig Smith ~ Real ale ~ (01580) 291472 ~ Open 11.30-3, 5.30-11; 11.30-11 Sat; 11.30-10.30 Sun ~ Bar food 12-2 (2.30 Sat, Sun), 6.30-9 (9.30 Fri, Sat) ~ Restaurant ~ Children welcome ~ Dogs allowed in bar ~ www.thethreechimneys.co.uk
Recommended by John Thompson, Mrs J Ekins-Daukes, J R Osborne, John Evans, Martin Day, S F Parrinder, Richard Kennell

BROOKLAND

TQ9724 Map 3

Woolpack £

On A259 from Rye, about a mile before Brookland, take the first right turn signposted Midley where the main road bends sharp left, just after the expanse of Walland Marsh; OS Sheet 189 map reference 977244; TN29 9TJ

15th-c pub with simple furnishings, massive inglenook fireplace, big helpings of tasty food and large garden

This crooked old cottage is popular all year. In winter the massive inglenook fireplace is a big draw (though you may have to share it with the pub cats, Liquorice and Charlie Girl) and in summer it's liked by beach lovers from nearby Camber Sands. The ancient entrance lobby has a lovely uneven brick floor and black-painted pine-panelled walls; to the right, the simple quarry-tiled main bar has basic cushioned plank seats in a fireplace and a painted wood-effect bar counter hung with lots of water jugs. Low-beamed ceilings incorporate some very early ships' timbers, thought to have come from local wrecks. A long elm table has shove-ha'penny carved into one end and there are other old and newer wall benches, chairs at mixed tables with flowers and candles, and photographs of locals. The traditional dining room to the left has carpets and dark wheelback chairs; background music and games machine. Shepherd Neame Master Brew and Spitfire and a seasonal brew on handpump and several wines by the glass. There are plenty of picnic-sets beneath parasols in the garden, which is nicely lit up in the evening.

Good, popular food includes sandwiches, battered brie with redcurrant jelly, prawn cocktail, ham and eggs, vegetable lasagne, rack of barbecue ribs, fish pie, chicken curry, mixed grill, and puddings such as banana split and warm chocolate brownie. *Benchmark main dish: steak in ale pie £10.95. Two-course evening meal £18.00.*

Shepherd Neame ~ Tenant Scott Balcomb ~ Real ale ~ (01797) 344321 ~ Open 11-3, 6-11; 12-11 Sat, Sun, bank and school holidays ~ Bar food 12-2.30, 6-9; all day Sat, Sun, bank and school holidays ~ Restaurant ~ Children welcome ~ Dogs welcome
Recommended by Conrad Freezer, Richard Tilbrook

CHIPSTEAD
TQ5056 Map 3
George & Dragon ★ ♀
Near M25 junction 5; TN13 2RW

Excellent food in popular village dining pub with three real ales, friendly, efficient service and seats in garden

Deservedly popular and very well run, this 16th-c dining pub is at the heart of a pretty village. The opened-up bar has heavy black beams and standing timbers, grey-green panelling, framed articles on the walls about their suppliers, and an easy-going, friendly atmosphere. In the centre, a comfortable sofa and table sit in front of a log fire, with a tiny alcove to one side housing a built-in wall seat and just one table and chair. Westerham Goldings, Grasshopper and Georges Marvellous Medicine on handpump and 21 wines by the glass. Up a step to each side are two small dining areas with more panelling, an attractive assortment of nice old chairs around various tables on bare floorboards and two more (unused) fireplaces. Upstairs is a sizeable timbered dining room with similar furnishings and a cosy room just right for a private party. The back garden has benches, modern chrome and wicker chairs and tables under parasols, as well as raised beds for flowers, herbs and vegetables.

Naming local suppliers and using organic, free-range meat, the imaginative food includes lunchtime sandwiches, monkfish liver pâté with beetroot and dill relish, pork tenderloin rolled in purple mustard and herbs with apple fondant and celeriac rémoulade, caramelised onion, roasted vegetable and goats cheese tart, sea bream with peperonata, courgette ribbons and green salsa, lamb skewers with quinoa salad and spiced coleslaw, and puddings such as toffee apple sponge with pear and ginger sorbet and chocolate and amaretto torte with chocolate mousse and chocolate truffle. *Benchmark main dish: local pork belly with bubble and squeak and apple sauce £14.25. Two-course evening meal £20.00.*

Free house ~ Licensee Ben James ~ Real ale ~ (01732) 779019 ~ Open 11-11 ~ Bar food 12-3 (4 weekends), 6-9.30 (8.30 Sun) ~ Restaurant ~ Children welcome ~ Dogs allowed in bar ~ Wi-fi ~ www.georgeanddragonchipstead.com *Recommended by Simon Pyle, Derek Thomas, Gordon and Margaret Ormondroyd, Colin McLachlan, Tina and David Woods-Taylor*

GOUDHURST   TQ7037 Map 3
Green Cross

East off A21 on to A262 (Station Road); TN17 1HA

Down-to-earth bar with real ales and more formal back restaurant

The little two-roomed front bar is properly pubby and easy-going, though most customers are here to enjoy the fresh seafood and fish. There are stripped wood floors, dark wood furnishings, wine bottles on window sills, hop-draped beams, brass jugs on the mantelshelf above the fire, and a few plush bar stools by the counter; background music. Harveys Best and half a dozen wines by the glass. Attractive in an old-fashioned sort of way, the back dining room is a little more formal with flowers on tables, dark beams in cream walls and country paintings for sale. You can sit out on a small terrace at the side of the pub.

The excellent fresh fish and shellfish dishes include a proper fish soup, linguine with queen scallops, vermouth, tarragon and cream, irish rock oysters on crushed ice and lemon, huge Cornish cock crab salad, halibut with spinach and creamy cheese sauce, and seafood paella; also, non-fishy items such as baguettes, bangers and mash with onion gravy, moroccan-style lamb, and puddings such as apple and mulberry crumble and sticky toffee pudding. *Benchmark main dish: moules frites £10.80. Two-course evening meal £25.00.*

Free house ~ Licensees Lou and Caroline Lizzi ~ Real ale ~ (01580) 211200 ~ Open 12-3, 6-11; closed Sun evening ~ Bar food 12-2.30, 7-9.30 ~ Restaurant ~ Children welcome ~ Wi-fi ~ www.greencrossinn.co.uk *Recommended by Harvey Brown, Emma Scofield*

HOLLINGBOURNE   TQ8354 Map 3
Windmill ★☆

M20 junction 8: A20 towards Lenham then left on to B2163 – Eyhorne Street; ME17 1TR

Excellent food and thoughtful drinks in professionally run dining pub

The creative food remains the star turn here, though the little back bar is used by customers popping in for just a drink and a chat: it has a woodburning stove, an armchair, cushioned settle and high tables and chairs to one side, with Musket Flintlock and Sharps Doom Bar on handpump and 15 wines by the glass. The light and airy main room has white-painted beams, a log fire in a low inglenook fireplace with beribboned antlers above, a couple of armchairs and a table with daily papers, heavy settles with scatter cushions against one wall and a long red leather button-back banquette along the opposite one, and dark wood

---

We mention bottled beers and spirits only if there is something unusual about them – imported belgian real ales, say, or dozens of malt whiskies; so do please let us know about them in your reports.

dining chairs and tables on bare floorboards topped with an antelope skin. Up some steps to the right is a small dining room, while leading off the main room at the other end is a second little room, both with similar furnishings and decorative fireplaces; various deer skulls, a shelf of riding gear, candles and flowers here and there, and background pop music. A back terrace has wooden tables and chairs.

 Impressive and attractively presented, the food includes lunchtime sandwiches, seared tuna carpaccio with pickled vegetables, locally foraged mushroom tart with goats cheese crumb and truffle dressing, slow-cooked pork belly with cider and grain mustard sauce and caramelised apples, coq au vin, dover sole with cockle, clam and seaweed brown butter, and puddings such as chocolate pudding with caramelised clementines and marmalade ice-cream and lemon parfait with poached cranberries; they also offer a two- and three-course set lunch. *Benchmark main dish: lamb shank with rosemary, garlic and red wine £16.95. Two-course evening meal £24.00.*

Enterprise ~ Lease Richard Phillips ~ Real ale ~ (01622) 889000 ~ Open 12-11; 12-9 Sun ~ Bar food 12-2.30, 5.30-9.30; 12-7 Sun ~ Restaurant ~ Children welcome ~ Wi-fi ~ Live music Weds evening ~ www.thewindmillbyrichardphillips.co.uk
Recommended by Jeff Roberts, Christian Mole

ICKHAM — Duke William
TR2258 Map 3

Off A257 E of Canterbury; The Street; CT3 1QP

Relaxing village pub with airy bar, dining conservatory, enjoyable bar food and plenty of seats outside; bedrooms

This friendly village pub attracts plenty of customers, a good mix of both drinkers and diners. The big spreading bar has huge oak beams and stripped joists, a fine mix of seats from settles to high-backed cushioned dining chairs, dark wheelback and bentwood chairs around all sorts of wooden tables on a stripped-wood floor, and a log fire with a couple of settles and a low barrel table in front of it. A central bar counter with high stools and brass coat hooks offers Old Dairy Gold Top, Sharps Doom Bar, Shepherd Neame Whitstable Bay Pale Ale and a guest beer on handpump and a dozen wines by the glass served by chatty, attentive staff. A separate snug little area has one long table, black leather high-backed dining chairs, a flat-screen TV and a computer; daily papers, quiet background music, cheerful modern paintings and large hop bines. Off to the left is a low-ceilinged dining room with plenty of paintings and mirrors and, at the back, an airy dining conservatory with interesting paintings, prints and heraldry. Doors lead from here to a big terrace with wooden and metal tables and chairs and a covered area to one side; picnic-sets on the lawn, swings and a slide.

Good food includes lunchtime sandwiches, chicken liver and brandy pâté with red onion chutney, seared scallops with black pudding, pasta with pesto and chorizo, vegetable curry, beef in ale pie, pork medallions with creamy apricot sauce, halibut fillet with dill and Pernod, and puddings such as chocolate fondant and mixed berry crumble. *Benchmark main dish: pork belly with port, rhubarb and ginger jus £13.95. Two-course evening meal £20.00.*

Free house ~ Licensees Kate and Ryan Coleman ~ Real ale ~ (01227) 721308 ~ Open 12-11 (midnight Fri, Sat); 12-10 Sun ~ Bar food 12-3 (4 Sat), 7-10; 12-8 Sun ~ Restaurant ~ Live bands monthly ~ Dogs allowed in bar ~ Wi-fi ~ Bedrooms: /£70 ~ www.dukewilliam.biz *Recommended by John Saville, Sara Fulton, Roger Baker, R and S Bentley*

IDEN GREEN   TQ8031 Map 3

Woodcock ◖

*Not the Iden Green near Goudhurst; village signed off A268 E of Hawkhurst
and B2086 at W edge of Benenden; in village follow Standen Street sign, then fork left
into Woodcock Lane; TN17 4HT*

**Simple country local with friendly staff and regulars, a relaxed
atmosphere, four real ales and well liked food**

On a tiny Wealden lane, this is an informal and friendly little local in a
quiet spot by woodland – it's good walking country. The low-ceilinged
bar has a woodburning stove in a fine old inglenook fireplace with a
comfortable sofa in front of it, stripped brick walls hung with horse tack, a
couple of big standing timbers, more seating to one side of the counter and
plenty of chatty locals. Greene King Abbot, Morland Original and Ruddles
Best and guests such as Old Dairy Red Top and Ramsgate Gadds No 7 on
handpump and 11 wines by the glass. There's also a small panelled dining
room, and the pretty back garden has seats and tables. The car park is just
along the lane from the pub.

Tasty food includes lunchtime sandwiches, moules marinière, chicken goujons
on avocado and walnut salad, corned beef hash with egg and baked beans,
steak and kidney pie, fish of the day, chargrilled chicken with chorizo, mushrooms,
brandy and cream, salmon with crayfish, grapes, dill and white wine sauce, and
puddings. *Benchmark main dish: beer-battered cod and chips £12.50. Two-course
evening meal £18.00.*

Greene King ~ Lease Andrew Hemmings ~ Real ale ~ (01580) 240009 ~ Open 12-11;
closed Mon except bank holidays ~ Bar food 12-2.15, 6-8.45; 12-3 Sun ~ Restaurant ~
Children welcome ~ Dogs allowed in bar ~ Wi-fi ~ www.thewoodcockinn.com
Recommended by Rob Newland, M P Mackenzie

IVY HATCH   TQ5854 Map 3

Plough ⬤◖ ♀

High Cross Road; village signed off A227 N of Tonbridge; TN15 0NL

**Country pub with first class food, real ales and seats in
landscaped garden**

Rewarding walks surround this tile-hung village pub through woodland
and along the greensand escarpment near One Tree Hill, and at
weekends in particular cyclists and walkers stop here for refreshment – so
it's best to book a table in advance. The various rooms have light wooden
floors, leather chesterfields grouped around an open fire, quite a mix of
cushioned dining chairs around assorted tables, and high bar chairs by the
wooden-topped bar counter where they keep Mad Cat Meaneys Golden
India Pale Ale, Old Dairy Red Top and Ringwood Best on handpump, 12
wines by the glass and farm cider. There's also a conservatory; background
music and board games. Seats in the landscaped garden are surrounded by
cob trees; pétanque. Ightham Mote (National Trust) is close by.

 Cooked by the landlord and his team, the tempting food (starting with
breakfasts except on Sunday) includes lunchtime sandwiches, duck confit with
pomegranate, pine nuts and quinoa, salt and pepper squid with aioli, honey-roasted
ham and eggs, wild boar and apple sausages with mash and red onion marmalade, puy
lentils with halloumi, roasted squash, wild mushrooms and croutons, beef and venison
bourguignon with juniper and herb dumplings, and puddings such as bakewell tart
with chantilly cream and chocolate délice with white chocolate fudge and honeycomb

ice-cream. *Benchmark main dish: rump burger with home-made brioche bun, coleslaw, barbecue sauce and chips £10.00. Two-course evening meal £19.50.*

Free house ~ Licensee Miles Medes ~ Real ale ~ (01732) 810100 ~ Open 9am-11pm; 10am-11pm Sat; 10am-6pm Sun; closed Sun evening ~ Bar food 12-2.45, 6-9.30; 12-5.30 Sun ~ Restaurant ~ Children welcome ~ Wi-fi ~ www.theploughivyhatch.co.uk
Recommended by Mrs D Crew, Bob and Margaret Holder

 ## LANGTON GREEN

TQ5439 Map 3

Hare 🌟 ♀

A264 W of Tunbridge Wells; TN3 0JA

Interestingly decorated Edwardian pub with a fine choice of drinks and imaginative, bistro-style food

Despite the emphasis on the enjoyable food, this roomy mock-Tudor place remains the beating heart of the village, attracting plenty of friendly, chatty regulars. The high-ceilinged rooms are light and airy, with dark-painted dados below pale-painted walls covered in old photographs and prints, 1930s oak furniture, light brown carpet and turkish-style rugs on bare boards, old romantic pastels and a huge collection of chamber-pots hanging from beams. Greene King Abbot, IPA and Yardbird, Morland Old Golden Hen and a guest from a brewer such as Bath Ales on handpump, 27 wines by the glass, 30 malt whiskies and a farm cider; board games. French windows open on to a big terrace with pleasant views of the tree-ringed village green. Parking in front of the pub is limited, but you can park in the lane to one side.

 Good contemporary food includes sandwiches, pigeon breast with beetroot risotto and game reduction, scallops with pea purée, crispy parma ham and herb dressing, various platters, sweet potato, aubergine and spinach malaysian curry, smoked haddock and salmon fishcakes with tomato salad, rosemary and garlic chicken breast with wild mushrooms, bacon and spinach pasta, and puddings such as mixed berry crumble and chocolate brownie with chocolate sauce. *Benchmark main dish: crispy beef salad with cashew nuts, chilli and wasabi £11.75. Two-course evening meal £18.00.*

Brunning & Price ~ Manager Tina Foster ~ Real ale ~ (01892) 862419 ~ Open 12-11 (midnight Fri, Sat, 10 Sun) ~ Bar food 12-9.30 (10 Fri, Sat, 9 Sun) ~ Restaurant ~ Children welcome ~ Dogs allowed in bar ~ Wi-fi ~ www.hare-tunbridgewells.co.uk
Recommended by Richard and Penny Gibbs, Alan Franck

NEWNHAM

TQ9557 Map 3

George

The Street; village signed from A2 W of Ospringe, outside Faversham; ME9 0LL

Old-world village pub with open-plan rooms, a fair choice of drinks and food, and seats in spacious garden

Good walks surround this attractive and tile-hung 16th-c pub in its remote-feeling part of the North Downs; walkers can cool off at picnic-sets in the spacious tree-sheltered garden. Inside, the spreading series of open-plan rooms have hop-strung beams, polished floorboards, stripped brickwork, candles and lamps on handsome tables, a mix of dining chairs and settles, and two inglenook fireplaces (one with a woodburning stove). Shepherd Neame Master Brew, Spitfire and a seasonal guest on handpump, ten wines by the glass and a farm cider. This is the village where James Pimm was born (he invented the fruit cup Pimms).

🍴 Well liked food includes baguettes, chicken liver parfait with home-made onion chutney, thai-spiced mussels with coriander and coconut, thyme mushrooms on toast with slow-roasted tomatoes, ham and free-range eggs, burger with cheese, bacon, spiced tomato mayonnaise and chips, bass on puy lentils with roasted vegetables and topped with prawns in a dill and lemon dressing, herbed lamb rump on crushed new potatoes with rosemary jus, and puddings. *Benchmark main dish: steak in ale pie £9.95. Two-course evening meal £15.00.*

Shepherd Neame ~ Tenants Paul and Lisa Burton ~ Real ale ~ (01795) 890237 ~ Open 11.30-3, 6.30-11; 11.30-6.30 Sun; closed Sun evening ~ Bar food 12-2.30, 7-9.30; 12-4.30 Sun ~ Restaurant ~ Children welcome ~ Live music monthly ~ www.georgeinnewnham.co.uk *Recommended by N R White, Dave Braisted*

PENSHURST   TQ5142 Map 3
Bottle House ⍟ �

Coldharbour Lane; leaving Penshurst SW on B2188 turn right at Smarts Hill signpost, then bear right towards Chiddingstone and Cowden; keep straight on; TN11 8ET

Country pub with connected low-beamed areas, friendly service, chatty atmosphere, real ales, decent wines, popular bar food and sunny terrace; nearby walks

Our readers enjoy their visits to this reliable cottagey pub very much and advise booking a table in advance. The open-plan rooms are split into cosy areas by numerous standing timbers and there are all sorts of joists and beams (a couple of the especially low ones are leather padded). Pine wall boards and bar stools are ranged along the timber-clad copper-topped counter, where they keep Harveys Best and Larkins Traditional on handpump and 19 wines by the glass from a good list. There's also a nice hotchpotch of wooden tables (with fresh flowers and candles), fairly closely spaced chairs on dark boards or coir, a woodburning stove and photographs of the pub and local scenes; background music. Some of the walls are of stripped stone. The sunny, brick-paved terrace has teak chairs and tables under parasols, and olive trees in white pots; parking is limited. Good surrounding walks in this charming area of rolling country.

🌟 Usefully served all day, the highly thought-of food includes slow-braised pig cheeks with apple purée and caramelised leeks, ham hock terrine with pineapple chutney, chilli con carne with sour cream, falafel burger with fennel coleslaw and sweet potato wedges, chargrilled chicken with crispy pancetta and cashew nut salad, beef in Guinness pudding with horseradish mash, bass with chorizo, basil and red pepper salsa and tempura courgettes, and puddings such as rhubarb and blueberry crumble and sticky toffee and almond pudding. *Benchmark main dish: slow-roast pork belly with butternut squash mash, cabbage and bacon and apple and cider sauce £14.75. Two-course evening meal £20.00.*

Free house ~ Licensee Paul Hammond ~ Real ale ~ (01892) 870306 ~ Open 11-11 (10.30 Sun) ~ Bar food 12-10 (9 Sun) ~ Restaurant ~ Children welcome ~ Dogs allowed in bar ~ www.thebottlehouseinnpenshurst.co.uk *Recommended by Tina and David Woods-Taylor, Martin Day, Christian Mole, Brian Dawes, Bob and Margaret Holder*

PLUCKLEY   TQ9243 Map 3
Dering Arms ⍟ ♦ 🛏

Pluckley station, which is signposted from B2077; or follow Station Road (left turn off Smarden Road in centre of Pluckley) for about 1.3 miles S, through Pluckley Thorne; TN27 0RR

Handsome building with stylish main bar, carefully chosen wines, three ales, good fish dishes and roaring log fire; comfortable bedrooms

The rooms in this former hunting lodge have plenty of character, and it's a striking building with an imposing frontage, mullioned arched windows and dutch gables. The high-ceilinged, stylishly plain main bar has a solid country feel with a variety of wooden furniture on flagstones, a roaring log fire in a great fireplace, country prints and some fishing rods. The smaller half-panelled back bar has similar dark wood furnishings, plus an extension with a woodburning stove, comfortable armchairs, sofas and a grand piano; board games. Goachers Gold Star and Old 1066 and a beer named for the pub from Goachers on handpump, eight good wines by the glass from a fine list, 40 malt whiskies and 20 cognacs. Classic car meetings (the landlord James has a couple of classic motors) are held here on the second Sunday of the month. Readers very much enjoy staying here – and the breakfasts are smashing.

 Majoring on local fish and using home-grown herbs, the food includes fish soup with rouille and croutons, sardines with rosemary butter, irish oysters, fillet of hake with crayfish and black butter, and fruits de mer special (24 hours' notice); also non-fishy dishes such as duck rillettes with orange vinaigrette, lamb steak with olives and saffron on couscous, rib-eye steak with horseradish cream, and puddings such as oranges in caramel and Grand Marnier and lemon posset. *Benchmark main dish: bass with minted leeks and bacon and red wine sauce £14.95. Two-course evening meal £20.00.*

Free house ~ Licensee James Buss ~ Real ale ~ (01233) 840371 ~ Open 11-3.30 (4 Sat), 6-11; 12-5 Sun; closed Sun evening ~ Bar food 12-2.30, 6.30-9; 12-4 Sun ~ Restaurant ~ Children welcome ~ Dogs allowed in bar ~ Wi-fi ~ Bedrooms: £85/£95 ~ www.deringarms.com *Recommended by David and Ruth Hollands*

SEVENOAKS   TQ5352   Map 3
White Hart ⭐ ♀
Tonbridge Road (A225 S, past Knole); TN13 1SG

Well run and civilised coaching inn with many interesting rooms, a thoughtful choice of drinks and food, and friendly helpful staff

This refurbished coaching inn is consistently well run and always deservedly busy – our readers continue to greatly enjoy their visits here. Open doorways and steps connect the many rooms, and there are several open fires and woodburning stoves. All manner of nice wooden dining chairs around tables of every size sit on rugs or bare floorboards, the cream walls are hung with lots of prints and old photographs (many of local scenes or schools) and there are fresh flowers and plants, daily papers, board games and a bustling, chatty atmosphere. Phoenix Brunning & Price Original, Exmoor Gold, Growler Hound Dog, Harveys Best, Hepworth Sussex Bitter, Old Dairy Blue Top and Westerham British Bulldog on handpump, 20 good wines by the glass, 50 malt whiskies and a farm cider. It's all very civilised. At the front of the building there are picnic-sets under parasols.

Interesting food includes sandwiches, duck liver parfait with peach jelly, a sharing charcuterie plate, sausages with buttered mash, soy-poached salmon with pak choi, chargrilled tandoori halloumi with fresh pineapple, toasted coconut and lime and mint salad, steak burger with cheese, bacon and chips, king prawn curry with green tomato chutney, and puddings such as crème brûlée and bread and butter pudding with apricot sauce. *Benchmark main dish: home-smoked duck breast with anchovy and pancetta salad £14.95. Two-course evening meal £20.00.*

Brunning & Price ~ Manager Chris Little ~ Real ale ~ (01732) 452022 ~ Open 12-11
(10.30 Sun) ~ Bar food 12-10 (9 Sun) ~ Children welcome away from bar until 7pm
~ Dogs allowed in bar ~ Wi-fi ~ www.bandp.co.uk/whitehart *Recommended by David
Jackman, Mrs Margo Finlay, Jörg Kasprowski, Colin McLachlan, Martin Day, Gordon and
Margaret Ormondroyd, Alan Cowell*

SISSINGHURST   TQ7937   Map 3

Milk House

The Street; TN17 2JG

**Bustling village inn of character, with well kept ales, enjoyable food
and seats in big garden; restful bedrooms**

After a visit to historic Sissinghurst Castle (National Trust) and its
beautiful gardens, this 16th-c inn is just the place to head for. After
a notable entrance hall, the bustling bar is on the right: it has a relaxed
atmosphere, grey-painted beams, wheelback and high-backed dark
grey dining chairs around various pine tables on floorboards and sisal
matting, grey plush sofas facing one another across a simple table in front
of a handsome Tudor fireplace, and candles in hurricane jars; unusual
touches include the book mural wallpaper, milk churns on window sills,
wickerwork used on the bar counter and for lampshades, and a wire cow.
Daily papers, board games and background music. Harveys Best, Musket
Fife & Drum and Old Dairy Red Top on handpump, eight wines by the
glass and several malt whiskies, all served by friendly, helpful staff. The
restaurant to the left is similarly furnished and there's also a small room
leading off, just right for a private party. The big garden has picnic-sets and
a fenced-in pond.

Good, interesting food includes sandwiches, crab and crayfish with avocado
and green apple salad, home-cured beetroot and vodka salmon gravadlax with
horseradish celeriac rémoulade, courgette, feta and mint fritter with capsicum sauce,
pork and herb sausages with red onion marmalade and red wine jus, lemon thyme-
crumbed rose veal escalope with spring onion mash and roast tomato coulis, and
puddings such as bitter chocolate tart with kirsch-soaked cherries and candied ginger
and orange salad with citrus curd. *Benchmark main dish: burger with bacon,
cheese, tomato chutney and fries £12.00. Two-course evening meal £21.50.*

Enterprise ~ Lease Sarah and Dane Allchorne ~ Real ale ~ (01580) 720200 ~
Open 9am-11pm (midnight Sat) ~ Bar food 12-3, 6-9 ~ Restaurant ~ Children
welcome ~ Dogs allowed in bar ~ Wi-fi ~ Bedrooms: /£95 ~ www.themilkhouse.co.uk
Recommended by Martin Jones, Toby Jones

SPELDHURST   TQ5541   Map 3

George & Dragon

Village signed from A264 W of Tunbridge Wells; TN3 0NN

**Fine old pub with beams, flagstones and huge fireplaces, local beers,
good food and attractive outside seating areas**

Although most customers come to this fine half-timbered building
to enjoy the rewarding food, there are ales from breweries such as
Brakspears, Harveys and Larkins on handpump, 16 wines by the glass
and a farm cider, served by friendly, efficient staff. To the right of the
rather splendid entrance hall (where there's a water bowl for thirsty
dogs), a half-panelled room is set for dining with a mix of old wheelback
and other dining chairs and a cushioned wall pew around several tables,
small pictures on the walls, horsebrasses on one great beam, and a huge

inglenook fireplace. A doorway leads to another dining room with similar furnishings and another big inglenook. Those wanting a drink and a chat tend to head to the room on the left of the entrance (though you can eat in here too), where there's a woodburning stove in a small fireplace, high-winged cushioned settles and various wooden tables and dining chairs on a wood-strip floor; background music. There's also an aged-feeling upstairs restaurant. Teak tables, chairs and benches sit on a nicely planted gravel terrace in front of the pub, while at the back is a covered area with big church candles on wooden tables and a lower terrace with seats around a 300-year-old olive tree; more attractive planting here and some modern garden design.

Using local, seasonal produce, the highly rated food includes sandwiches, chicken livers on toast, ham hock terrine with piccalilli, pork sausages with onion gravy, broad bean and pea risotto, black bream fillets with samphire and lemon cockle butter, confit duck leg with fennel, haricot bean and chickpea cassoulet, saddle of rabbit with wild mushroom stuffing, and puddings such as salted caramel and dark chocolate tart and rhubarb panna cotta with vanilla syrup. *Benchmark main dish: slow-cooked pork belly with bubble and squeak £15.50. Two-course evening meal £21.50.*

Free house ~ Licensee Julian Leefe-Griffiths ~ Real ale ~ (01892) 863125 ~ Open 12-11 (10.30 Sun) ~ Bar food 12-2.30 (3 Sat), 7 (6.30 Sat)-9.30; 12-3.30 Sun ~ Restaurant ~ Children welcome ~ Dogs allowed in bar ~ Wi-fi ~ www.speldhurst.com
Recommended by Derek Thomas, Martin Day, Tracey and Stephen Groves

STALISFIELD GREEN
Plough 🍺 🍷
Off A252 in Charing; ME13 0HY

TQ9552   Map 3

Ancient country pub with rambling rooms, open fires, interesting local ales and good bar food

Since our last edition, new licensees have taken over this ancient country pub. It's popular with both diners and drinkers and the several hop-draped rooms are relaxed and easy-going. They ramble around, up and down, with open fires in brick fireplaces, interesting pictures, books on shelves, farmhouse and other nice old dining chairs around a mix of pine or dark wood tables on bare boards, and the odd milk churn dotted about. Goody Good Health, Musket Flintlock and Whitstable Renaissance on handpump, 16 wines by the glass and farm cider. The pub appears to perch on its own amid downland farmland, and picnic-sets on a simple terrace overlook the village green below. They have a site for caravans.

As well as lunchtime sandwiches and a two- and three-course set lunch, the well presented food includes gin-cured salmon with horseradish cream, chicken terrine with truffle mayonnaise, crottin of goats cheese with braised chicory and caramelised pear, local sausages with braised red cabbage, lamb rump with parsnip purée and sautéed potatoes, halibut with chorizo mash, red pepper and fennel, and puddings such as seasonal fruit crumble and chocolate mousse with sea salt caramel and blood orange sorbet. *Benchmark main dish: slow-cooked pork belly with wild garlic croquette, pea purée and sage sauce £13.50. Two-course evening meal £23.00.*

Free house ~ Licensees Richard and Marianne Baker ~ Real ale ~ (01795) 890256 ~ Open 12-3, 6-11; 12-11.30 Sat; 12-6 Sun; closed Sun evening, Mon ~ Bar food 12-2 (3.30 Sat), 6-9; 12-4 Sun ~ Restaurant ~ Children welcome away from main bar ~ Dogs welcome ~ Live music every two months ~ www.stalisfieldgreen.co.uk
Recommended by Mr and Mrs P R Thomas

STODMARSH

TR2160 Map 3

Red Lion 🛏

High Street; off A257 just E of Canterbury; CT3 4BA

Interesting country pub with lots to look at, good choice of drinks and well liked food

Handy for Stodmarsh National Nature Reserve, this bustling country pub has kept some of its quirky charm under newish licensees. The hop-hung rooms have country kitchen chairs (some painted) and tables, books on window sills, shelves and the floor, tankards hanging from beams, various old stone bottles and lamps dotted about, full and empty wine bottles, a big log fire and plenty of candles and fresh flowers. Goody Genesis, Greene King IPA and Sharps Cornish Coaster tapped from the cask, eight wines by the glass and a farm cider; background music. The bedrooms are comfortable and the breakfasts hearty.

 Using local, seasonal produce, the popular food includes sandwiches, pork terrine with pickles, sloe gin-cured salmon with dill cream, ham and eggs, pork and leek sausages with onion gravy, breadcrumbed lamb with white onion purée and redcurrant sauce, chicken, leek and prune pie, fish dish of the day, slow-cooked oxtail with horseradish mash, and puddings. *Benchmark main dish: rib-eye steak with peppercorn sauce and chips £20.00. Two-course evening meal £25.00.*

Free house ~ Licensees Richard and Carol Vale ~ Real ale ~ (01227) 721339 ~ Open 11.30-11 (11.30 Sat); 12-5 Sun; closed Sun evening ~ Bar food 11.30-2.30, 6.30-9; 12-3 Sun ~ Children welcome ~ Dogs allowed in bar ~ Wi-fi ~ Occasional live jazz ~ Bedrooms: /£75 ~ www.theredlionstodmarsh.com *Recommended by Pip White, Caroline Prescott*

STONE IN OXNEY

TQ9428 Map 3

Ferry ◀

Appledore Road; N of Stone-cum-Ebony; TN30 7JY

Bustling small cottage with character rooms, candlelight, open fires, real ales and popular food

In warm weather, the tables and benches on the terrace in front of this pretty little 17th-c pub and the seats in the back garden, which leads down to the river, are much prized; the sunsets here can be lovely. Inside, it's very easy-going and chatty. The main bar has hop-draped painted beams, a green dado, stools against the counter where they serve a beer named for the pub (from Westerham), Hopdaemon Golden Braid, Sharps Doom Bar and a changing guest on handpump, 14 wines by the glass and farm ciders. To the right is a cosy eating area with wheelback chairs and a banquette around a few long tables, a log fire in the inglenook and candles in wall sconces on either side. To the left of the main door is a dining area, with big blackboards on red walls, a woodburning stove beneath a large bressumer beam and high-backed light wooden dining chairs around assorted tables; up a couple of steps is a smarter dining area with modern chandeliers. Background music, TV, games machine, darts and pool in the games room. Throughout there are wooden floors, all sorts of pictures and framed maps, a stuffed fish, beer flagons, an old musket and various brasses. Disabled access in the bar and on the terrace.

All *Guide* inspections are anonymous. Anyone claiming to be a *Good Pub Guide* inspector is a fraud. Please let us know.

🍴 Good, attractively presented food includes sandwiches, moules marinière, pigeon with berries, almonds and soft-boiled quail eggs, various sharing boards, honey and mustard-glazed ham with eggs and beef dripping chips, steak in ale pudding, beef tagine with dates, figs, lemon couscous, a fish dish of the day, and puddings such as black cherry trifle and crème brûlée. *Benchmark main dish: local lamb three-ways with caramelised onion potato cake £20.95. Two-course evening meal £20.50.*

Free house ~ Licensee Paul Wither Green ~ Real ale ~ (01233) 758246 ~ Open 11-11; 12-10 Sun ~ Bar food 12-3, 6-9; 12-8 Sun ~ Restaurant ~ Children welcome ~ Dogs allowed in bar ~ Wi-fi ~ www.oxneyferry.com *Recommended by Caroline Prescott, Pip White, Stuart Paulley, B and M Kendall*

STOWTING

TR1241 Map 3

Tiger 🍺

3.7 miles from M20 junction 11; B2068 N, then left at Stowting signpost, straight across crossroads, then fork left after 0.25 miles and pub is on right; coming from N, follow Brabourne, Wye, Ashford signpost to right at fork, then turn left towards Posting and Lyminge at T junction; TN25 6BA

Peaceful pub with helpful staff, traditional furnishings, well liked food, several real ales and open fires; good walking country

Warm praise again this year from our readers for this well run and friendly pub. The traditionally furnished bars, dating from the 17th c, have warming woodburning stoves and all sorts of wooden tables and chairs and built-in cushioned wall seats on floorboards. There's an unpretentious array of books, board games, candles in bottles, brewery memorabilia and paintings, lots of hops and some faded rugs on the stone floor towards the back of the pub. Shepherd Neame Master Brew and three or four guests from local brewers such as Gravesend, Harveys and Old Dairy on handpump, plenty of malt whiskies, several wines by the glass, local Biddenden cider and local fruit juice. Staff are helpful with wheelchairs. On warmer days you can sit out on the front terrace, and there are plenty of nearby walks along the Wye Downs and North Downs Way.

🍴 Good, enjoyable food includes sandwiches, lightly battered salt and pepper squid with chilli and mango dip, smoked fish and meat platter, burger with all the trimmings and chips, vintage parmesan soufflé with wild mushroom cream, chicken, leek and honey-roasted ham pie, smoked haddock with a poached local duck egg, and puddings such as rhubarb, stem ginger and stout crumble and caramel cheesecake. *Benchmark main dish: free-range pork belly with creamed smoked bacon and leeks and caramelised apples £15.00. Two-course evening meal £20.50.*

Free house ~ Licensees Emma Oliver and Benn Jarvis ~ Real ale ~ (01303) 862130 ~ Open 12-11 (10 Sun); closed Mon, Tues ~ Bar food 12-9.30 ~ Restaurant ~ Children welcome ~ Dogs allowed in bar ~ Wi-fi ~ www.tigerinn.co.uk *Recommended by Rob Newland, Evelyn and Derek Walter, Bernard Stradling, Alan Cowell, Richard Tilbrook*

TUNBRIDGE WELLS

TQ5839 Map 3

Sankeys 🍴 🍷 🍺

Mount Ephraim (A26 just N of junction with A267); TN4 8AA

Pubby street-level bar, informal downstairs brasserie (wonderful fish and shellfish), real ales and good wines, a chatty atmosphere and seats on sunny back terrace

The relaxed street-level bar here is light and airy with comfortably worn, informal leather sofas and pews around all sorts of tables on bare boards. There's also a fine collection of rare enamel signs and antique brewery mirrors, as well as old prints, framed cigarette cards and lots of old wine bottles and soda siphons. A changing beer from Goachers and guests such as BrewDog Dead Pony Club, Quaffing Gravy Pale Ale, Magic Rock Ringmaster and Tonbridge Coppernob on handpump are served by the cheerful landlord, who also keeps fruit beers, a good choice of american and british craft beers and several wines by the glass from a good list; big flat-screen TV for sports (not football – it's very busy for major rugby matches) and background music. Downstairs is the chatty and informal fish restaurant with bistro-style décor; from here, french windows lead on to an inviting suntrap deck with wicker and chrome chairs around wooden tables.

Food in the upstairs bar includes sandwiches, tortilla wraps, ham and eggs, steak, crab or cajun chicken burgers with fries, mussels done several ways, salads such as chicken caesar or oriental duck, and puddings. The excellent à la carte fish and shellfish menu is only served downstairs – our Food Award is for this. *Benchmark main dish: Cornish cock or spider crab salad £18.50. Two-course evening meal £17.50.*

Free house ~ Licensee Matthew Sankey ~ Real ale ~ (01892) 511422 ~ Open 12-midnight (1am Thurs, 3am Fri, Sat); 12-11 Sun ~ Bar food 12-3 (4 Sun), 6-8 ~ Restaurant ~ Children welcome before 6pm ~ Dogs allowed in bar ~ Wi-fi ~ www.sankeys.co.uk *Recommended by Edward May, Harvey Brown*

ULCOMBE   TQ8550 Map 3
Pepper Box

Fairbourne Heath; signposted from A20 in Harrietsham, or follow Ulcombe signpost from A20, then turn left at crossroads with sign to pub, then right at next minor crossroads; ME17 1LP

Friendly country pub with lovely log fire, well liked food, fair choice of drinks, and seats in a pretty garden

The hop-covered terrace and shrub-filled garden look out over a great plateau of rolling arable farmland; the Greensand Way footpath runs close by. Inside, the homely bar has standing timbers and a few low beams (some hung with hops), copper kettles and pans on window sills, and two leather sofas by the splendid inglenook fireplace with its lovely log fire (nice horsebrasses on the bressumer beam). A side area, furnished more functionally for eating, extends into the opened-up beamed dining room, with a range in another inglenook and more horsebrasses. Attentive and convivial licensees serve Shepherd Neame Master Brew and Spitfire and a seasonal beer on handpump and 15 wines by the glass; background music. The two cats are called Murphy and Jim. The village church is worth a look.

Highly enjoyable food includes lunchtime sandwiches, tiger prawns in garlic, chilli and ginger butter, chicken liver and brandy parfait with apricot chutney, potato gnocchi with asparagus, courgette and baby sweetcorn in wild garlic pesto cream, home-cooked ham or local sausages with egg and chips, pork tenderloin with maple syrup and mustard and balsamic sauce, chicken in a morel mushroom and sherry cream sauce, and puddings such as white chocolate and Baileys cheesecake and salted caramel and chocolate tart. *Benchmark main dish: moules marinière £11.00. Two-course evening meal £20.00.*

Shepherd Neame ~ Tenant Sarah Pemble ~ Real ale ~ (01622) 842558 ~ Open 11-3, 6-midnight; 11-11 Sat (11-3, 6-11 in winter); 12-4 Sun ~ Bar food 12-2.15, 6.45-9.45; 12-3 Sun ~ Restaurant ~ Children lunchtimes only (no babies) ~ Dogs allowed in bar ~ www.thepepperboxinn.co.uk *Recommended by Andrew White, Martin Day*

WHITSTABLE
Pearsons Arms ♀

TR1066 Map 3

Sea Wall off Oxford Street after road splits into one-way system;
public parking on left as road divides; CT5 1BT

Seaside pub with an emphasis on interesting food, several local ales and good mix of customers

Our readers enjoy this beachside, weatherboarded pub very much – both for the good, interesting food and as a relaxing place for a quiet pint and newspaper. The two front bars, divided by a central chimney, have cushioned settles, captain's chairs and leather armchairs on a stripped-wood floor, driftwood walls, and big flower arrangements on the bar counter where they serve Gadds Seasider, Thwaites Wainwright and Timothy Taylors Landlord on handpump, 14 wines by the glass and an extensive choice of cocktails; background music. A cosy lower room has trompe l'oeil bookshelves, a couple of big chesterfields and dining chairs around plain tables on a stone floor. Up a couple of flights of stairs, the restaurant has sea views, mushroom-coloured paintwork, contemporary wallpaper, more driftwood and church chairs and pine tables on nice wide floorboards.

As well as lots of interesting nibbles, the rewarding food includes sandwiches, venison faggots wrapped in savoy cabbage with chestnut cream, potted shrimps on melba toast, burger with bacon, blue cheese and triple-cooked chips, smoked haddock with bubble and squeak, caramelised cauliflower, a poached egg and light curry sauce, chicken in red wine with smoked bacon, mushrooms and onions, and puddings such as lemon posset with kumquat compote and apple tarte tatin with calvados caramel; they also offer a two- and three-course set lunch. *Benchmark main dish: beer-battered fish and chips £14.95. Two-course evening meal £25.00.*

Enterprise ~ Lease Jake Alder ~ Real ale ~ (01227) 773133 ~ Open 12-midnight (11 Sun) ~ Bar food 12-2.30, 6.30-9.30; 12-8 Sun ~ Restaurant ~ Children welcome ~ Dogs allowed in bar ~ Wi-fi ~ Live music Tues and Sun evenings ~ www.pearsonsarmsbyrichardphillips.co.uk *Recommended by B and M Kendall, Adrian Johnson, C and R Bromage, Eddie Edwards*

Also Worth a Visit in Kent

Besides the fully inspected pubs, you might like to try these pubs that have been recommended to us and described by readers. Do tell us what you think of them: feedback@goodguides.com

ADDINGTON TQ6559
Angel (01732) 842117
Just off M20 junction 4; Addington Green; ME19 5BB 14th-c pub in classic village-green setting, beams, scrubbed tables and big fireplaces, enjoyable food (all day Fri-Sun) from sandwiches/ciabattas and traditional choices up, fair choice of beers from barrel-fronted counter, lots of wines by the glass, good friendly service, stables restaurant, events including live music Fri,

charity quiz nights and monthly MG/Midget & Sprite car club meetings; tables out at front and back, two bedrooms. *(Anon)*

APPLEDORE TQ9529
Black Lion (01233) 758206
The Street; TN26 2BU Compact 1930s village pub with bustling atmosphere, very welcoming helpful staff, good generous food all day from simple sandwiches to imaginative dishes, lamb from Romney Marsh and local fish, three or four well kept

---

We say if we know a pub allows dogs.

changing ales, Biddenden farm cider, log fire, partitioned back eating area; background music; tables out on green, attractive village, good Military Canal walks. *(Peter Meister)*

BADLESMERE   TR0154
Red Lion (01233) 740320
A251, S of M2 junction 6; ME13 0NX Spacious partly 16th-c roadside country pub run by mother and daughter team, friendly local atmosphere, Gadds and two or three guests from hop-strung bar (Easter and Aug bank holiday beer festivals), enjoyable well priced home-made food (not Sun evening) using local produce, weekday early-bird deals, beams, bare boards and stripped brickwork, books and board games, monthly live music and quiz nights; background music, free wi-fi; children and dogs welcome, large garden with camping in paddock, open all day (till 7pm Sun, 9pm Mon). *(N R White)*

BARHAM   TR2050
Duke of Cumberland
(01227) 831396 *The Street; CT4 6NY* Open-plan pub close to village green, enjoyable home cooking including good Sun roasts, three or four well kept ales such as Harveys, Greene King and Timothy Taylors, friendly staff, bare boards or flagstones, plain tables and chairs, hops and log fire, board games, darts, live music and quiz nights; children welcome, garden with boules and play area, three bedrooms, handy for A2, open all day weekends. *(Peter Smith and Judith Brown)*

BEARSTED   TQ7956
Bell (01622) 738021
Ware Street; by railway bridge, W of centre; ME14 4PA Friendly old local with well kept Greene King IPA and a guest, ample helpings of enjoyable competitively priced food including blackboard specials; can get busy; garden and heated terrace. *(Michael Tack)*

BEARSTED   TQ8055
Oak on the Green (01622) 737976
The Street; ME14 4EJ Two hop-festooned bar areas with bare boards and half-panelling, bustling friendly atmosphere, wide choice of home-made food including mexican dishes and tapas, a house beer from 1648, Fullers London Pride and two local guests, restaurant (they also own the smaller fish restaurant next door); dogs allowed in bar, disabled access, seats out at front under big umbrellas, open (and food) all day. *(Anon)*

BENENDEN   TQ8032
★ Bull (01580) 240054
The Street; by village green; TN17 4DE Relaxed informal atmosphere in bare-boards or dark terracotta tiled rooms, pleasing mix of furniture, church candles on tables, hops, fire in brick inglenook, friendly hands-on licensees, ales such as Dark Star, Harveys, Larkins and Old Dairy from carved wooden counter, Biddenden cider, more formal dining room, tasty generously served food (not Sun evening) including speciality pies and popular Sun carvery, various offers; background music (live most Sun afternoons); children and dogs (in bar) welcome, picnic-sets out in front behind white picket fence, back garden, open all day. *(N R White, Mrs T A Bizat, Conrad Freezer)*

BENENDEN   TQ8032
Kitty Fisher (01580) 240636
The Street; TN17 4DJ Former King William IV refurbished and under same ownership as the Bull on other side of village green; upmarket food including seafood in bar or more formal restaurant, Shepherd Neame and a couple of local guests, good wines, beams and inglenook log fire; pleasant back garden, open all day in summer. *(Anon)*

BIDBOROUGH   TQ5643
Kentish Hare (01892) 525709
Bidborough Ridge; TN3 0XB Refurbished dining pub (former Hare & Hounds) under new owners, conservatory-style restaurant with open-view kitchen and two bars, very good food including set menu (Tues-Thurs), local ales (one badged for them) and excellent choice of wines by the glass, courteous helpful young staff; children (under-5s eat free) and dogs (in public bar) welcome, landscaped garden with decking, open all day Sat, till 5pm Sun, closed Mon. *(Anon)*

BOTOLPHS BRIDGE   TR1233
Botolphs Bridge Inn
(01303) 267346 *W of Hythe; CT21 4NL* Edwardian red-brick country pub on edge of marshes; decent choice of good generous home-made food including fresh fish and Sun roasts, friendly service, well kept Greene King IPA, Sharps Doom Bar and a guest, airy and open-plan with tables laid for dining, carpets or bare boards, two log fires; background music, free wi-fi; children and dogs welcome, nice little garden with marshland view, open all day till 10pm (11pm Fri, Sat), closed Mon. *(Eddie Edwards)*

BOYDEN GATE   TR2265
★ Gate Inn (01227) 860498
Off A299 Herne Bay–Ramsgate – follow Chislet, Upstreet sign opposite Roman Gallery; Chislet also signed off A28 Canterbury–Margate at Upstreet – after turning right into Chislet main street, keep right on to Boyden; CT3 4EB Delightfully unpretentious rustic pub with comfortably worn traditional quarry-tiled rooms, cushioned pews around character tables, hop-strung beams, attractively etched windows, inglenook log fire, Shepherd Neame and a couple of guests from tap room casks, interesting bottled beers, sensibly priced pubby food including signature Gatewich

sandwich, quiz and music nights; children and dogs welcome, sheltered garden bounded by two streams with ducks and geese, open all day Sun. *(Anon)*

BRABOURNE   TR1041
Five Bells (01303) 813334
East Brabourne; TN25 5LP Friendly 16th-c inn at foot of North Downs; opened-up interior with hop-draped beams, standing timbers and ancient brick walls, all manner of dining chairs and tables on stripped boards, wall seats here and there, two log fires, quirky decorations including candles in upturned bottles on the walls and a garland-draped mermaid figurehead, Dark Star, Goachers and Redemption, selection of kentish wines, well liked food from varied menu, shop selling local produce, live music evenings and monthly arts and crafts market; unisex loos; children and dogs welcome, comfortable if eccentric bedrooms, open all day from 9am for breakfast. *(Anon)*

BRASTED   TQ4654
Stanhope Arms (01959) 561970
Church Road; TN16 1HZ Traditional old pub under welcoming new licensees, Greene King ales and enjoyable food (not Sun evening, Mon, Tues), cosy bar, homely log-fire dining room; children and dogs welcome, back garden with bat and trap, closed Mon lunchtime, otherwise open all day. *(Gwyn Jones)*

BRASTED   TQ4755
White Hart (01959) 569457
High Street (A25); TN16 1JE Stylishly refurbished Mitchells & Butlers Country Pub & Eating House, wide choice of food including sharing plates, pizzas and grills, weekday fixed-price menu till 7pm, real ales and plenty of wines by the glass, cocktails, conservatory; terrace and garden tables, open all day. *(B J Harding, Derek Thomas)*

BRENCHLEY   TQ6841
★Halfway House (01892) 722526
Horsmonden Road; TN12 7AX Beamed 18th-c inn with attractive mix of rustic and traditional furnishings on bare boards, old farm tools and other bric-a-brac, two log fires, cheerful staff and particularly friendly landlord, up to a dozen well kept changing ales tapped from the cask, enjoyable traditional home-made food including popular Sun roasts, two eating areas; children and dogs welcome, picnic-sets and play area in big garden, summer barbecues and beer festivals, two bedrooms, open all day (no food Sun evening). *(Alan Franck, Phil and Jane Hodson)*

BROADSTAIRS   TR3967
Charles Dickens (01843) 600160
Victoria Parade; CT10 1QS Refurbished pub centrally placed with view of sea, big busy bar with good selection of beers and wines, wide choice of food including good fish and chips, weekend breakfast from 9am, friendly efficient service, upstairs restaurant, live music Fri, Sat; children welcome, tables out overlooking Viking Bay, almost next door to Dickens House Museum. *(Nigel and Jean Eames, John Wooll)*

BROADSTAIRS   TR3868
Four Candles 07947 062063
Sowell Street; CT10 2AT Quirky one-room micropub in former shop, good selection of local beers chalked on blackboard and tapped from the cask, kentish wines, high tables and stools on sawdust floor, pitchfork handles on the walls (Ronnie Barker's famous sketch inspired by nearby ironmongers), local cheese and pork pies, charming chatty service; closed weekday lunchtimes. *(Malcolm)*

BURMARSH   TR1032
Shepherd & Crook (01303) 872336
Shear Way, next to church; TN29 0JJ Traditional 16th-c local with smuggling history in marshside village; well kept Adnams and a guest beer, Weston's cider, good straightforward home-made food at low prices, prompt friendly service, interesting photographs and blow lamp collection, open fire, bar games; children and dogs welcome, seats on side terrace, closed Tues and Sun evenings, otherwise open all day. *(Eddie Edwards)*

CANTERBURY   TR1458
Dolphin (01227) 455963
St Radigunds Street; CT1 2AA Modernised busy dining pub with plenty of tables in spacious bar, enjoyable generous home-made pubby food from baguettes up, Sharps Doom Bar, Timothy Taylors Landlord and guests such as Gadds, nice wines including country ones, friendly staff, bric-a-brac on delft shelf, board games, flagstoned conservatory, pianist Sun evening, quiz first Mon of month; free wi-fi; children welcome, no dogs, disabled access, good-sized back garden with heaters, open all day. *(Ian Herdman, Peter Smith and Judith Brown)*

CANTERBURY   TR1457
Foundry (01227) 455899
White Horse Lane; CT1 2RU Pub in former 19th-c iron foundry, light and airy interior on two floors, six Canterbury Brewers beers from visible microbrewery plus local guests, craft lagers and kent cider, enjoyable well presented pubby food till 6pm including good sandwiches, helpful cheerful staff; disabled access, small courtyard area, open all day (till late Fri, Sat). *(Tony and Wendy Hobden, Peter Smith and Judith Brown)*

CANTERBURY   TR1458
Millers Arms (01227) 456057
St Radigunds Street/Mill Lane; CT1 2AA Shepherd Neame pub in quiet street near

river, enjoyable well priced food and good wine choice, friendly helpful staff, flagstoned front bar, bare-boards back area, traditional solid furniture, newspapers and log fire, small conservatory; unobtrusive background music; children and dogs welcome, good seating in attractive part-covered courtyard, handy for Marlowe Theatre and cathedral, 11 comfortable bedrooms, ample breakfast, open all day. *(Ian Phillips)*

CANTERBURY   TR1558
New Inn (01227) 464584
Havelock Street; CT1 1NP Friendly and relaxed Victorian terraced local, Adnams, Greene King and up to four guests, Biddenden cider, no food, modern back conservatory; nearby parking can be difficult, open all day Fri, Sat. *(Anon)*

CANTERBURY   TR1457
Parrot (01227) 454170
Church Lane – the one off St Radigunds Street, 100 metres E of St Radigunds car park; CT1 2AG Ancient pub with heavy beams, wood and flagstone floors, stripped masonry, dark panelling and big open fire, Shepherd Neame ales and well liked food, upstairs vaulted restaurant; nicely laid out courtyard with central wood-burning barbecue, open all day. *(Anon)*

CAPEL   TQ6444
Dovecote (01892) 835966
Alders Road; SE of Tonbridge; TN12 6SU Cosy beamed pub with some stripped brickwork and open fire, pitched-ceiling dining end, enjoyable well priced food (not Sun evening, Mon) from sandwiches to Sun roasts, up to six ales tapped from the cask including Harveys, Weston's cider, friendly helpful staff; well behaved children allowed, no dogs inside, lots of picnic-sets in back garden with terrace and play area, nice country surroundings, open all day Sun. *(Terry)*

CHARTHAM   TR1054
Artichoke (01227) 738316
Rottington Street; CT4 7JQ Attractive timbered pub dating from the 15th c, enjoyable reasonably priced traditional food from sandwiches and baked potatoes up, well kept Shepherd Neame ales, good service, carpeted log-fire bar, glass-topped well in dining area, bat and trap and darts; children welcome, picnic-sets in small back garden. *(Peter Smith and Judith Brown)*

CHIDDINGSTONE   TQ5045
Castle Inn (01892) 870247
Off B2027 Tonbridge–Edenbridge; TN8 7AH Rambling traditional old pub in pretty NT village, handsome beamed bar, settles and sturdy wall benches, attractive mullioned window seat, woodburners, brick-floor snug, well kept Harveys and Larkins including winter Porter (brewed in the

village), good choice of food from sandwiches to blackboard specials, friendly helpful staff; children and dogs welcome, tables out at front and in nice secluded garden with own bar and summer barbecues, circular walks from village, handy for Chiddingstone Castle, open all day. *(Pete Walker, Brian Glozier, John Coatsworth, Mrs Sally Scott)*

CHIDDINGSTONE
CAUSEWAY   TQ5247
Greyhound (01892) 870275
Charcott, off back road to Weald; TN11 8LG Updated red-brick village local with good food from landlord-chef, Harveys and a couple of guests, friendly staff, log fire; children and dogs welcome, picnic-sets out in front and in garden, useful for walkers, open all day weekends. *(John Webb)*

CHIDDINGSTONE
CAUSEWAY   TQ5146
Little Brown Jug (01892) 870318
B2027; TN11 8JJ Open-plan Whiting & Hammond pub next to Penshurst station, comfortable bar and big dining extension, enjoyable food at sensible prices from sandwiches and deli plates to full meals, well kept Greene King, Larkins and a guest, good wine list, smiling responsive service, lots of pictures and prints, bookshelves, bare boards and log fires, some live music; children welcome, disabled access/facilities, attractive big garden with play area, open (and food) all day. *(Tina and David Woods-Taylor, Christian Mole)*

CHILHAM   TR0653
★ White Horse (01227) 730355
The Square; CT4 8BY Newish management for this 15th-c pub in picturesque village square; handsome ceiling beams and massive fireplace with lancastrian rose carved on mantel beam, chunky light oak furniture on pale wood flooring and more traditional pubby furniture on quarry tiles, four well kept ales including a house beer from Canterbury Brewers, enjoyable food (all day Sat, not Sun evening) with more adventurous evening choices, friendly helpful service; children welcome, dogs in bar (pub dog is Sean), handy for the castle, open all day. *(Anon)*

CHILLENDEN   TR2653
★ Griffins Head (01304) 840325
SE end of village; 2 miles E of Aylesham; CT3 1PS Attractive beamed and timbered 14th-c pub with two bar rooms and flagstoned back dining room, gently upscale local atmosphere, big log fire, full range of Shepherd Neame ales and decent choice of popular home-made food, good wine list, attentive service; no children, dogs welcome in some parts, pretty garden surrounded by wild roses, summer Sun barbecues, nice countryside, open all day. *(Anon)*

CHIPSTEAD   TQ4956
Bricklayers Arms (01732) 743424
Chevening Road; TN13 2RZ Attractive
busy place overlooking lake and green,
wide choice of good fairly priced pub food
(not Sun evening), well kept Harveys from
casks behind long counter, efficient cheerful
service and relaxed chatty atmosphere,
heavily beamed bar with open fire and fine
racehorse painting, larger back restaurant,
various events including Tues quiz; children
and dogs welcome, seats out in front, open all
day. *(Stephen Funnell, Alan Cowell, B J Harding,
Pete Walker, Nigel and Jean Eames)*

CONYER QUAY   TQ9664
Ship (01795) 520881
Conyer Road; ME9 9HR Well renovated
18th-c creekside pub owned by adjacent
Swale Marina; bare boards and open fires,
good home-cooked food including set lunch
(Mon-Sat), weekend breakfast from 10am,
Adnams Southwold, Shepherd Neame Master
Brew and guests, live folk first and third
Tues of month; children and dogs welcome,
useful for boaters, walkers (on Saxon Way)
and birders, open all day weekends (Sun till
9.30pm). *(Anon)*

COWDEN   TQ4640
Fountain (01342) 850528
*Off A264 and B2026; High Street;
TN8 7JG* Good sensibly priced blackboard
food (not Sun evening) in attractive tile-
hung beamed village pub, steep steps up
to unpretentious dark-panelled corner bar,
well kept Harveys and decent wines by the
glass, old photographs on cream walls, good
log fire, mix of tables in adjoining room,
woodburner in small back dining area with
one big table; background music; children,
walkers and dogs welcome, picnic-sets on
small terrace and lawn, pretty village, open
all day Sun. *(Graham and Carol Parker)*

COWDEN   TQ4642
★ Queens Arms
*Cowden Pound; junction B2026 with
Markbeech Road; TN8 5NP* Friendly
two-room country pub like something from
the 1930s, known locally as Elsie's after long-
serving landlady (no longer in attendance
– pub currently run by volunteers), well kept
Adnams Southwold, no food, coal fire, darts,
occasional folk music and morris dancers;
dogs welcome, closed lunchtimes Mon-Sat,
Sun evening. *(David Jackman)*

CROCKHAM HILL   TQ4450
Royal Oak (01732) 866335
Main Road; TN8 6RD Cosy and chatty old
village pub owned by Westerham brewery,
their ales kept well, popular good value
home-made food (best to book), friendly
hard-working staff, mix of furniture including
comfy leather sofas on stripped-wood floor,
painted panelling, original Tottering-by-
Gently cartoons and old local photographs,
good log fire in right-hand bar, quiz nights
and live folk; walkers (remove muddy boots)
and dogs welcome, small garden, handy for
Chartwell (NT). *(Pauline Fellows and Simon
Robbins, Martin Day, Nick Lawless, Tina and
David Woods-Taylor)*

CRUNDALE   TR0949
Compasses (01227) 700300
Sole Street; CT4 7ES Welcoming country
pub under newish management, good
locally sourced food from landlord-chef
including some imaginative choices, well
kept Shepherd Neame ales and maybe a
guest; children, walkers and dogs welcome,
big garden with play equipment, closed Mon,
otherwise open all day (till 9pm Sun).
(Roz and Richard Goodenough)

DARGATE   TR0761
Dove (01227) 751360
*Village signposted from A299;
ME13 9HB* Tucked-away 18th-c restauranty
pub with rambling rooms, good food (some
quite expensive), Shepherd Neame ales and
guests, nice wines by the glass, plenty of
stripped-wood tables, woodburner, live music
last Fri of month; children, walkers and dogs
welcome, sheltered garden with bat and trap,
open all day Fri, Sat. *(Anon)*

DEAL   TR3751
Berry (01304) 362411
Canada Road; CT14 7EQ Small friendly
no-frills local opposite old Royal Marine
barracks, welcoming enthusiastic landlord,
well kept Dark Star, Harveys and several
changing microbrews including local Time &
Tide (tasting notes on slates, beer festivals),
kent farm cider and perry, no food, L-shaped
carpeted bar with coal fire, newspapers, quiz
and darts teams, pool, live music Thurs; dogs
welcome, small vine-covered back terrace,
open all day, closed Tues till 5.30pm.
(N R White)

DEAL   TR3752
Bohemian (01304) 361939
Beach Street opposite pier; CT14 6HY
Seafront bar fully refurbished after Nov 2012
fire; five ales including Sharps Doom Bar,
around 70 bottled beers and huge selection of
spirits, home-made traditional food including
Sun roasts, friendly helpful staff, L-shaped
room with mismatched furniture (some
découpage tables), polished wood floor, lots
of pictures, mirrors, signs and other odds

We include some hotels with a good bar that offers facilities comparable
to those of a pub.

and ends (customers encouraged to donate items), sofas and weekend papers, similar décor in upstairs cocktail bar with good sea views; background music; children and dogs welcome, sunny split-level deck behind and heated smokers' gazebo, open all day (from 9am Sun) and can get very busy, especially weekends. *(N R White)*

DEAL TR3752
Just Reproach 07432 413226
King Street; CT14 6HX Popular genuinely welcoming micropub in former corner shop; simple drinking room with sturdy tables on bare boards, stools and cushioned benches, friendly knowledgeable service from father-and-daughter team, three or four changing small brewery ales from Kent and further afield poured from the cask, also local ciders and some organic wines, locally made cheese, friendly chatty atmosphere, no mobile phones; dogs welcome, closed Sun evening, Mon. *(N R White)*

DEAL TR3753
Prince Albert (01304) 375425
Middle Street; CT14 6LW Little 19th-c corner pub in conservation area, bowed entrance doors, etched-glass windows and fairly ornate interior with assorted bric-a-brac, three changing ales such as Gadds, Old Dairy and Wantsum, popular food (not Mon, Tues) especially Sun carvery in back dining area, friendly staff; small garden behind, bedrooms, closed lunchtimes except Sun. *(N R White)*

DEAL TR3753
Ship (01304) 372222
Middle Street; CT14 6JZ Dimly lit traditional two-room local in historic maritime quarter; five well kept ales including Caledonian Deuchars IPA, Dark Star and Gadds, friendly landlord, bare boards and lots of dark woodwork, stripped brick and local ship and wreck pictures, evening candles, cosy panelled back bar, piano, open fire and woodburner; no food; dogs welcome, small pretty walled garden, open all day. *(N R White)*

DOVER TR3241
Blakes (01304) 202194
Castle Street; CT16 1PJ Small flagstoned cellar bar down steep steps, brick and flint walls, dim lighting, woodburner, Adnams and six changing guests, farm ciders and perries, over 50 malt whiskies and several wines by the glass, enjoyable lunchtime bar food from sandwiches up, panelled carpeted upstairs restaurant (food all day), friendly enthusiastic landlord, daily papers; well behaved children welcome, dogs in bar,

side garden and suntrap back terrace, four bedrooms, open all day. *(N R White)*

DUNGENESS TR0916
Pilot (01797) 320314
Battery Road; TN29 9NJ Single-storey, mid 20th-c seaside café-bar by shingle beach, well kept Adnams, Courage, Harveys and a guest, decent choice of good value food from nice sandwiches to fish and chips, OAP lunch deal Mon, open-plan interior divided into three areas, dark plank panelling including the slightly curved ceiling, lighter front part overlooking beach, prints and local memorabilia, books for sale (proceeds to Lifeboats Assoc), quick friendly service (even when packed); background music, free wi-fi; children welcome, picnic-sets in side garden, open all day till 10pm (9pm Sun). *(Paul Humphreys)*

DUNKS GREEN TQ6152
★**Kentish Rifleman** (01732) 810727
Dunks Green Road; TN11 9RU Popular Tudor pub restored in modern rustic style, well kept ales such as Harveys and Westerham, enjoyable reasonably priced food (service charge added) including good Sun roasts, friendly efficient staff, bar and two dining areas, rifles on low beams, cosy log fire; children and dogs welcome, tables in pretty garden with well, good walks, open all day weekends (no food Sun evening). *(Gordon and Margaret Ormondroyd, Bob and Margaret Holder, Christian Mole)*

EYNSFORD TQ5365
Malt Shovel (01322) 862164
Station Road; DA4 0ER Traditional dark-panelled pub near church, black beams, patterned carpet and copper kettles, well kept changing ales, good choice of wines by the glass, reasonably priced fairly pubby food (all day weekends) including daily specials, themed nights and popular Sun lunch, prompt friendly service, restaurant; background and some live music, silent sports TV, Tues quiz; children welcome, no dogs, beer garden behind and a few tables out by pavement, car park across busy road, handy for castles and Roman villa, open all day. *(A N Bance, N R White)*

FAVERSHAM TR0161
Anchor (01795) 536471
Abbey Street; ME13 7BP New management for this character beamed pub in attractive 17th-c street near historic quay; sensibly priced traditional food (not Sun or Mon evenings) from baguettes up, some meat from own farm, well kept Shepherd Neame range, friendly service, dimly lit bare-boards bar, frosted windows, panelling and woodburner,

---

If you stay overnight in an inn or hotel, they are allowed to serve you an alcoholic drink at any hour of the day or night.

second room with wood and brick floors and good inglenook log fire, restaurant with white-painted floorboards and large anchor; background music (live Sun – fortnightly in winter); children and dogs welcome, tables in pretty enclosed back garden, open all day. *(N R White)*

FAVERSHAM TR0161
Bear (01795) 532668
Market Place; ME13 7AG Traditional late Victorian Shepherd Neame pub (back part from 16th c), their ales kept well and occasional guests, locals' front bar, snug and back dining lounge with open fire, all off side corridor, pubby lunchtime food (evenings Tues-Thurs); friendly service and relaxed atmosphere; couple of pavement tables, open all day. *(Anon)*

FAVERSHAM TR0160
Elephant (01795) 590157
The Mall; ME13 8JN Well run dimly lit traditional town pub, friendly and chatty, with four or five well kept changing ales mainly from smaller kent breweries such as Hopdaemon, a local cider too, no food (can bring your own), single bare-boards bar with central log fire and cosy seating areas; juke box and some live music, games machine; children and dogs welcome, peaceful suntrap back garden with pond, open all day Sat, till 7pm Sun, from 3pm weekdays, closed Mon. *(N R White)*

FAVERSHAM TR0161
Phoenix (01795) 591462
Abbey Street; ME13 7BH Historic town pub with heavy low beams and stripped stone walls, six well kept beers including Harveys and Timothy Taylors, food from pubby choices up (all day Fri and Sat, not Sun evening), friendly service, leather chesterfields by inglenook log fire, restaurant, various events including live music, charity quiz nights and poetry reading; children and dogs welcome, back garden, open all day. *(Anon)*

FAVERSHAM TR0161
Sun (01795) 535098
West Street; ME13 7JE Rambling old-world 15th-c pub in pedestrianised street, good unpretentious atmosphere with small low-ceilinged partly panelled rooms, scrubbed tables and big inglenook, well kept Shepherd Neame ales from nearby brewery, enjoyable bar food, smart restaurant attached, friendly efficient staff; unobtrusive background music; wheelchair access possible (small step), pleasant back courtyard, eight bedrooms, open all day. *(Anon)*

FINGLESHAM TR3353
★ **Crown** (01304) 612555
Just off A258 Sandwich–Deal; The Street; CT14 0NA Popular neatly kept low-beamed country local dating from 16th c, good value generous home-made food from

usual pub dishes to interesting specials, friendly helpful service, well kept local ales such as Ramsgate, Biddenden cider, softly lit carpeted split-level bar with stripped stone and inglenook log fire, two other attractive dining rooms; children and dogs welcome, lovely big garden with play area, bat and trap, field for caravans, open all day Fri-Sun. *(N R White)*

FRITTENDEN TQ8141
Bell & Jorrocks (01580) 852415
Corner of Biddenden Road/The Street; TN17 2EJ Welcoming simple 18th-c tile-hung and beamed local, well kept Harveys, Woodfords and guests (Apr beer festival), Weston's and Thatcher's ciders, good home-made food (not Sun evening, Mon, Tues), open fire with propeller from german bomber above, hops over bar, kentish darts, live music and other events; sports TV, pool; children and dogs welcome, farmers' market third Sat of month (breakfast available then), open all day. *(Conor McGaughey)*

GOODNESTONE TR2554
★ **Fitzwalter Arms** (01304) 840303
The Street; NB this is in E Kent, not the other Goodnestone; CT3 1PJ Old lattice-windowed beamed village pub, rustic bar with wood floor and open fire, Shepherd Neame ales and local wine, carpeted dining room with another fire, enjoyable reasonably priced home-made food (Weds-Sun), shove-ha'penny and bar billiards; well behaved children and dogs welcome, terrace with steps up to peaceful garden, lovely church next door and close to Goodnestone Park Gardens, open all day Fri-Sun, closed Mon, lunchtime Tues. *(Anon)*

GOUDHURST TQ7237
Star & Eagle (01580) 211512
High Street; TN17 1AL Striking medieval building, now a small hotel, next to the church; settles and Jacobean-style seats in heavily beamed open-plan areas, intriguing smuggling history, log fires, good choice of enjoyable food (some prices on the high side), well kept Brakspears, Harveys and Wychwood from fairly modern bar with lovely views, friendly helpful staff, restaurant; children welcome, no dogs inside, tables outside with same views, attractive village, 11 character bedrooms, good breakfast, open all day. *(Dr and Mrs J D Abell)*

GROOMBRIDGE TQ5337
★ **Crown** (01892) 864742
B2110; TN3 9QH Charming tile-hung wealden inn with snug low-beamed bar, old tables on worn flagstones, panelling, bric-a-brac, fire in sizeable brick inglenook, Harveys, Larkins and a guest, enjoyable fairly traditional food (all day Fri and Sat, till 6pm Sun), good service, recently decorated dining area; children welcome, dogs in bar, narrow old brick terrace overlooking steep

green, back garden, four bedrooms, handy for
Groombridge Place Gardens, open all day.
(B J Harding, Wendy Breese)

HALSTEAD   TQ4861
Rose & Crown (01959) 533120
Otford Lane; TN14 7EA Friendly 19th-c
flint village local, well kept Larkins and four
guest beers, enjoyable good value home-
made food including popular Sun roasts,
welcoming staff, log fire, two bars with lots of
village photographs, darts, stables tearoom/
restaurant; children and dogs welcome,
wheelchair access, garden behind with play
area, summer bat and trap, barbecues, open
all day. *(David Jackman)*

HAWKHURST   TQ7529
★ Black Pig (01580) 752306
Moor Hill (A229); TN18 4PF Bustling
pleasantly refurbished open-plan pub,
L-shaped bar and eating areas on different
levels, all manner of nice old dining chairs
and tables, church candles, interesting
old stove, lots of pictures on bare brick or
painted walls, well kept Dark Star, Harveys,
Larkins and a guest, decent wines by the
glass, good food from lunchtime sandwiches
up, friendly attentive service; plenty of seats
in surprisingly big back garden.
(Peter Meister)

HAWKHURST   TQ7531
★ Great House (01580) 753119
*Gills Green; pub signed off A229 N;
TN18 5EJ* Busy, stylish, white
weatherboarded restauranty pub (part of
the Elite group), well liked if pricey food
(all day weekends), ales such as Harveys,
Old Dairy and Sharps from marble counter,
polite efficient service, sofas, armchairs and
bright scatter cushions in chatty bar, stools
against counter used by locals, dark wood
dining tables and smartly upholstered chairs
on slate floor beside log fire, steps down to
airy dining room with attractive tables and
chairs, working Aga (they cook on it) and
doors out to terrace with plenty of furniture;
background music; children welcome, dogs in
bar, open all day. *(Anon)*

HEADCORN   TQ8344
George & Dragon (01622) 890239
High Street; TN27 9NL Welcoming mock-
Tudor pub with good range of enjoyable
home-made food, Shepherd Neame Master
Brew and guests such as Whitstable, local
cider, open fires, separate dining room with
candlelit tables; background music, free wi-fi;
children and dogs welcome, fenced terrace
with painted wooden furniture, open all day.
(Stuart Paulley)

HEAVERHAM   TQ5758
Chequers (01732) 763968
Watery Lane; TN15 6NP Attractive
15th-c beamed country pub, enjoyable nicely
presented food (not Sun evening) from bar

snacks up, well kept Shepherd Neame and
a dozen wines by the glass, friendly locals'
bar, inglenook woodburner in dining area,
raftered barn restaurant with Cavalier ghost,
some live music; children and dogs welcome,
big garden with play area, good North Downs
walks, open all day Fri and Sat, till 7pm Sun,
closed Mon. *(Pauline Fellows and Simon
Robbins, Martin Day)*

HERNE   TR1865
Butchers Arms (01227) 371000
Herne Street (A291); CT6 7HL Opened
2005 as Britain's first micropub (previously
a butcher's), up to half a dozen well kept
changing ales (mainly local) tapped from
the cask, friendly and knowledgeable former
motorcycle-racing landlord, just a couple of
benches and butcher's-block tables (seats
about ten), bric-a-brac collection, good local
cheeses; dogs welcome, disabled access,
tables out under awning, closed Sun evening,
Mon, short lunchtime opening and shuts
around 9pm. *(Peter Meister)*

HERNE BAY   TR1768
Old Ship (01227) 366636
Central Parade; CT6 5HT Old white
weatherboarded pub with window tables
looking across road to sea, well kept beers
such as Otter and Sharps, popular pub food,
comfortable beamed and carpeted interior;
children welcome till 6pm, sea-view deck.
(N R White)

HERNE BAY   TR1768
Rose (01227) 375081
Mortimer Street; CT6 5ER Traditional
Victorian corner pub, cosy and welcoming,
with well kept Shepherd Neame ales; tables
out on pedestrianised street, open all day.
(Eddie Edwards)

HERNHILL   TR0660
Red Lion (01227) 751207
*Off A299 via Dargate, or A2 via
Boughton Street and Staplestreet;
ME13 9JR* Pretty Tudor community pub by
church and attractive village green, densely
beamed and quite dark inside with pine
tables and chairs on flagstones, log fires, good
choice of enjoyable generously served food at
sensible prices, OAP lunch deal Weds, well
kept Adnams Lighthouse, Sharps Doom Bar,
Shepherd Neame Master Brew and guests,
decent wines, friendly helpful staff, upstairs
restaurant; soft background music; children
and dogs welcome, seats in front and in big
garden with play area, open all day.
(Simon Collett-Jones)

HEVER   TQ4744
Henry VIII (01732) 862457
By gates of Hever Castle; TN8 7NH
Predominantly 17th-c with some fine oak
panelling, wide floorboards and heavy beams,
inglenook fireplace, Henry VIII touches
to décor, emphasis on enjoyable mainly

traditional food from baguettes up, well kept Shepherd Neame ales, friendly efficient staff, restaurant; no dogs even in garden; outside covered area with a couple of leather sofas, steps down to deck and pond-side lawn, handy for Hever Castle, bedrooms, open all day. *(R and S Bentley, B J Harding)*

HODSOLL STREET   TQ6263
★ **Green Man** (01732) 823575
Signed off A227 S of Meopham; turn right in village; TN15 7LE Bustling friendly village pub with neatly arranged traditional furnishings in big airy carpeted rooms, old photographs, plates and hops, log fire, Greene King, Harveys, Timothy Taylors and maybe a local guest, decent choice of enjoyable generously served food including good baguettes and popular two-course weekday lunch deal; background music – live Sun, quiz Mon; children and dogs welcome, tables and climbing frame on back lawn, also seats out at front overlooking green, open (and food) all day Fri-Sun. *(Dave Braisted, N R White)*

HOLLINGBOURNE   TQ8455
Dirty Habit (01622) 880880
B2163, off A20; ME17 1UW Dim-lit ancient beamed pub in Elite Pubs group (Great House in Hawkhurst, Gun at Gun Hill etc); ales including Harveys and Shepherd Neame, several wines by the glass, popular food (all day weekends) and friendly service, main bar area with various armchairs and stools, panelled end room with mix of tables and chairs on animal skin covering wooden boards, panelled dining room under a low beam with similar mix of furniture, antlers here and there, another area with some timbering and open woodburner; children welcome, good outside shelter with armchairs and sofas, on North Downs Way (leaflets for walkers) and handy for Leeds Castle, open all day. *(N R White)*

IDE HILL   TQ4851
Cock (01732) 750310
Off B2042 SW of Sevenoaks; TN14 6JN Pretty village-green local dating from the 15th c, chatty and friendly, with two dimly lit bars (steps between), Greene King ales and enjoyable well priced traditional food (not evenings Sun, Tues), cosy in winter with good inglenook log fire; well behaved children and dogs welcome, picnic-sets out at front, handy for Chartwell (NT) and nearby walks. *(Anon)*

IDEN GREEN   TQ7437
Peacock (01580) 211233
A262 E of Goudhurst; TN17 2PB Weatherboarded village local dating from the 14th c; blazing inglenook log fire in low-beamed main bar, quarry tiles and old sepia photographs, well kept Shepherd Neame ales and enjoyable pubby food (all day Sat), helpful service, dining room and public bar with fire; well behaved children and dogs

welcome, no muddy boots, attractive good-sized garden, closed Sun evening. *(Paul Humphreys)*

IGHTHAM   TQ5956
★ **George & Dragon** (01732) 882440
The Street, A227; TN15 9HH Ancient timbered pub, popular and stylish, with good reasonably priced food from generous snacks up (all day till 6.30pm, not Sun), plenty of friendly smartly dressed staff, well kept Shepherd Neame ales, decent wines, sofas among other furnishings in long sociable main bar, heavy-beamed end room, woodburner and open fires, restaurant; children and dogs welcome, back terrace, handy for Ightham Mote (NT), good walks, open all day. *(Martin Day, Bob and Margaret Holder)*

IGHTHAM COMMON   TQ5855
★ **Harrow** (01732) 885912
Signposted off A25 just W of Ightham; pub sign may be hard to spot; TN15 9EB Smart yet comfortably genial with emphasis on good imaginative food from daily changing menu, also some traditional choices and Sunday roasts, relaxed cheerful bar area to the right with candles and fresh flowers, dining chairs on herringbone wood floor, winter fire, charming little antiquated conservatory and more formal dining room, ales such as Gravesend Shrimpers and Loddon Hoppit; background music; children welcome (not in dining room on Sat evening), pretty little pergola-enclosed back terrace, handy for Ightham Mote (NT), open Thurs-Sun lunchtimes. *(Nick Lawless, Derek Thomas)*

IGHTHAM COMMON   TQ5955
Old House (01732) 886077
Redwell, S of village; OS Sheet 188 map reference 591559; TN15 9EE Basic two-room country local tucked down narrow lane, no inn sign, bare bricks and beams, huge inglenook, half a dozen interesting changing ales from tap room casks, no food, darts; closed weekday lunchtimes, opens 7pm and may shut early if quiet. *(Anon)*

KENNINGTON   TR0245
Old Mill (01223) 737976
Mill Lane; TN25 4DZ Refurbished and much extended dining pub (same owners as the Oak on the Green at Bearsted); good choice of generously served food (some quite expensive), a house beer from 1648, Fullers London Pride and guests such as Goachers and Old Dairy; children welcome, plenty of terrace and garden seating, open all day. *(Tony and Wendy Hobden)*

KILNDOWN   TQ7035
Globe & Rainbow (01892) 890803
Signed off A21 S of Lamberhurst; TN17 2SG Welcoming well cared for pub with small cheerful bar, Harveys and guests

such as Westerham in good condition, decent wines, simple bare-boards dining room with imaginative attractively presented food (shorter lunchtime menu), some themed evenings, friendly young staff; background music; country views from decking out by cricket pitch, closed Mon and Tues, otherwise open all day (till 7pm Sun). *(Martin Day, Conrad Freezer)*

KINGSDOWN   TR3748
Kings Head (01304) 373915
Upper Street; CT14 8BJ Chatty tucked-away split-level local with two cosy bars and recently extended L-shaped area (children welcome here), black timbers, lots of old local photographs on faded cream walls, a few vintage amusement machines, woodburner, Greene King IPA and two mainly local guests, popular reasonably priced food including blackboard specials, friendly landlord and staff, darts; soft background music and occasional live; dogs welcome, garden with skittle alley, open all day Sun, closed weekdays till 5pm. *(N R White)*

LADDINGFORD   TQ6848
Chequers (01622) 871266
The Street; ME18 6BP Friendly old beamed and weatherboarded village pub with good sensibly priced food from sandwiches and sharing boards up (restricted choice Mon lunchtime), well kept Adnams Southwold and three guests (April beer festival); children and dogs welcome, big garden with play area, shetland ponies in paddock, Medway walks nearby, one bedroom, open all day weekends. *(Anon)*

LAMBERHURST   TQ6735
Vineyard (01892) 890222
Lamberhurst Down; S of village signed off A21; TN3 8EU Pretty dining pub by green and vineyards, same ownership as the Great House in Hawkhurst (Elite Pubs); main bar has most character with a few stools by counter serving Harveys, Sharps and a guest, log fire in brick fireplace with boar's head above, wall banquette draped with animal hide, cushioned leather armchairs and mix of dining furniture on flagstones or bare boards, enjoyable bistro-style food, long narrow room off with similar tables and chairs, equestrian pictures and antlers over fireplace, large ham for carving, sketched wallpaper of local landmarks, more formal panelled restaurant; seats and tables on terrace by car park, new bedroom extension. *(Anon)*

LINTON   TQ7550
Bull (01622) 743612
Linton Hill (A229 S of Maidstone); ME17 4AW Comfortably modernised 17th-c dining pub; good choice of food from sandwiches and light dishes to pub favourites and grills, popular carvery (Sun, Thurs evening), fine fireplace in nice old beamed bar, carpeted restaurant area, well

kept Shepherd Neame ales, friendly efficient service; children welcome, dogs in bar, side garden overlooking church, splendid far-reaching views from back decking, two gazebos, open all day. *(Michael Tack, N R White)*

LITTLE CHART   TQ9446
Swan (01233) 840702
The Street; TN27 0QB Attractive 15th-c beamed village pub with notable arched Dering windows, open fires in simple unspoilt front bar and good-sized dining area, enjoyable fairly traditional food (smaller appetites catered for), three well kept beers and decent wines, friendly staff, pool; children welcome, nice riverside garden, closed Mon and Tues, otherwise open all day till midnight (9pm Sun). *(Anon)*

LOWER HARDRES   TR1453
★**Granville** (01227) 700402
Faussett Hill, Street End; B2068 S of Canterbury; CT4 7AL Spacious airy interior with contemporary furnishings, unusual central fire with large conical hood and glimpses of kitchen, proper public bar with farmhouse chairs, settles and woodburner, good popular food (not Sun evening - booking advised) including cheaper weekday set lunch, fine choice of wines from blackboard, Shepherd Neame Master Brew and a seasonal beer, efficient service, daily papers, artwork for sale; background music; children and dogs welcome, french windows to garden with large spreading tree and small sunny terrace, open all day Sun, closed Mon. *(Alan Cowell, Bernard Stradling)*

LUDDESDOWNE   TQ6667
★**Cock** (01474) 814208
Henley Street, N of village – OS Sheet 177 map reference 664672; off A227 in Meopham, or A228 in Cuxton; DA13 0XB Early 18th-c country pub with friendly long-serving no-nonsense landlord, at least six ales including Adnams, Goachers and Shepherd Neame, german beers too, good value straightforward lunchtime food from large filled rolls and basket meals up, rugs on polished boards in pleasant bay-windowed lounge, beams and panelling, quarry-tiled locals' bar, woodburners, pews and other miscellaneous furnishings, aircraft pictures, masses of beer mats and bric-a-brac from stuffed animals to model cars, bar billiards and darts, back dining conservatory, Tues quiz; no children inside or on part-covered heated back terrace, dogs welcome, big secure garden, good walks, open all day. *(N R White)*

LYDDEN   TR2645
Bell (01304) 830296
Canterbury Road (B2060 NW of Dover); CT15 7EX Welcoming busy dining pub with good choice of well cooked interesting food along with pub favourites (good fish and

chips), meal deals, well kept ales such as Sharps and Wantsum, friendly attentive staff, carpeted beamed bar with scrubbed pine tables, woodburner in large brick fireplace, restaurant, skittle alley; children welcome, picnic-sets in sloping garden with play equipment, handy for A2, open (and food) all day Sun. *(Keith and Gillian Duerden, David and Lesley Elliott)*

MAIDSTONE TQ7655
Rifle Volunteers (01622) 758891
Wyatt Street/Church Street; ME14 1EU Quiet old-fashioned backstreet corner pub tied to local Goachers, three of their ales and good value simple home-made food, friendly long-serving landlord, two gas fires, darts; tables outside. *(Anon)*

MARDEN TQ7547
Stile Bridge (01622) 831236
Staplehurst Road (A229); TN12 9BH Friendly roadside pub/restaurant with five well kept ales and lots of bottled beers, proper ciders too, good traditional food (till 5pm Sun), events including beer festivals, live music and comedy nights; dogs welcome in bar, back garden, open all day (till 8pm Sun). *(Steve and Claire Harvey)*

MARGATE TR3570
Lifeboat 07837 024259
Market Street; CT9 1EU Corner ale and cider house (opened 2010) with pleasant cosy atmosphere, small front bar with barrel tables on sawdust floor, dim lighting, larger back room with open fire, up to six well kept local beers and excellent choice of kent ciders/perries served from stillage casks, locally sourced cheeses, sausages, pies and seafood, friendly helpful service, live folk Thurs, jazz Sun afternoon; handy for Turner Contemporary, open all day. *(N R White)*

MARTIN TR3347
Old Lantern (01304) 852276
Off A258 Dover–Deal; The Street; CT15 5JL Pretty 17th-c pub (originally two farmworker cottages), low beams, stripped brick and cosy corners in small neat bar with dining tables, well cooked food from traditional choices up, friendly quick service, one or two Shepherd Neame ales and decent wines, soft lighting, open fire; quiet background music; children welcome, some tables out at front, more in good-sized back garden with big wendy house, beautiful setting, self-catering apartment, in winter closed Sun and Tues evenings, all Mon. *(Paul Rampton, Julie Harding)*

MATFIELD TQ6642
Poet at Matfield (01892) 722416
Maidstone Road; TN12 7JH Refurbished 17th-c beamed pub/restaurant (former Standings Cross) named for Siegfried Sassoon who was born nearby; good well presented food (not Sun evening) from

pubby choices to more expensive restauranty dishes, friendly efficient service, ales such as Old Dairy and Tonbridge, nice wines and kentish gins, some live music; open all day from 9am for breakfast. *(Anon)*

MATFIELD TQ6541
★Wheelwrights Arms (01892) 722129
The Green; TN12 7JX Attractive old weatherboarded pub on edge of village green, sensibly short choice of good imaginative food cooked by landlord-chef along with some pub favourites and nice sandwiches, Shepherd Neame and guests, good wines and freshly ground coffee, friendly attentive service, hop-strung beams, bare boards and woodburner in brick fireplace; children and dogs welcome, picnic-sets out in front, open all day Fri-Sun. *(Mrs L McDermott, Sara Price)*

MEOPHAM TQ6364
Cricketers (01474) 812163
Wrotham Road (A227); DA13 0QA Bustling Whiting & Hammond pub in nice spot overlooking cricket green, popular reasonably priced food, decent wines and four changing ales, friendly staff; children and dogs welcome, disabled facilities, tables out at front and in back garden, open (and food) all day. *(Tina and David Woods-Taylor, Gordon and Margaret Ormondroyd)*

MERSHAM TR0438
Farriers Arms (01233) 720444
The Forstal/Flood Street; TN25 6NU Large opened-up beamed pub owned by the local community, beers from own microbrewery, pubby food from sandwiches and baked potatoes up, children's menu, restaurant, charity quiz Sun; pretty streamside garden behind, pleasant country views, open all day (till 1am Fri, Sat). *(Anon)*

NEWENDEN TQ8327
White Hart (01797) 252166
Rye Road (A268); TN18 5PN Popular 16th-c weatherboarded local; long low-beamed bar with big stone fireplace, dining areas off with enjoyable good value pub food including lunchtime set menu, well kept Harveys and guests, friendly helpful young staff; back games area with pool, sports TV, background music; children welcome, boules in large garden, near river (boat trips to NT's Bodiam Castle), six bedrooms, open all day. *(Paul Humphreys, Conrad Freezer)*

NORTHBOURNE TR3352
Hare & Hounds (01304) 369188
Off A256 or A258 near Dover; The Street; CT14 0LG Chatty 17th-c village pub under newish management; more emphasis now on popular freshly made food from pub favourites up (all day Sun till 6pm), friendly helpful service, well kept ales such as Dark Star, Harveys and Sharps, good choice of wines, clean refurbished interior with polished wood floors and exposed brick,

log fire, quiz third Tues of month; children welcome, garden with marquee and play area, open all day. *(N R White)*

OARE   TR0163

★**Shipwrights Arms** (01795) 590088

S shore of Oare Creek, E of village; signed from Oare Road/Ham Road junction in Faversham; ME13 7TU Remote and ancient marshland tavern with plenty of character, up to six kentish beers tapped from the cask (pewter tankards over counter), enjoyable traditional food (not Sun evening or Mon), three dark simple little bars separated by standing timbers, wood partitions and narrow door arches, medley of seats from tapestry-cushioned stools to black panelled built-in settles forming booths, flags and boating pennants on ceiling, wind gauge above main door (takes reading from chimney); background local radio; children (away from bar area) and dogs welcome, large garden, path along Oare Creek to Swale estuary, lots of surrounding birdlife, closed Mon. *(Colin and Angela Boocock, N R White)*

OLD ROMNEY   TR0325

Rose & Crown (01797) 367500

Swamp Road off A259; TN29 9SQ Friendly bay-windowed pub with good value tasty food and well kept Greene King ales, Biddenden cider, helpful staff, dining conservatory; TV, pool and darts; children welcome, pretty garden with boules, chalet bedrooms, Romney Marsh view, closed Sun evening and Mon, otherwise open all day. *(Alan Cowell)*

OTFORD   TQ5259

Crown (01959) 522847

High Street, pond end; TN14 5PQ Well managed 16th-c local opposite village duck pond, pleasantly chatty beamed lounge with woodburner in old fireplace, unpretentious public bar, well kept ales such as Millis, Tonbridge and Westerham, friendly staff and forthright landlord (ex-army chef), popular food (not Sun-Weds nights) including thai on Fri and Sat evenings, monthly folk club and other live music, darts; tree-shaded seats in back garden, walkers and dogs welcome, closed Mon lunchtime in winter, otherwise open all day. *(N R White)*

PENSHURST   TQ4943

★**Rock** (01892) 870296

Hoath Corner, Chiddingstone Hoath, on back road Chiddingstone–Cowden; OS Sheet 188 map reference 497431; TN8 7BS Tiny welcoming cottage with undulating brick floor, simple furnishings and woodburner in fine brick inglenook, well kept

Larkins and good simple food, large stuffed bull's head for ring the bull, up a step to smaller room with long wooden settle by nice table; walkers and dogs welcome, picnic-sets out in front and on back lawn. *(Martin Day, Alan Franck)*

PENSHURST   TQ5241

★**Spotted Dog** (01892) 870253

Smarts Hill, off B2188 S; TN11 8EP Quaint old weatherboarded pub under welcoming family, heavy low beams and timbers, attractive moulded panelling, rugs and tiles, antique settles, inglenook log fire, Black Cat, Harveys, Larkins and a guest, local cider, good mostly traditional food (all day weekends) including weekday lunch deals, friendly caring service; children and dogs welcome, tiered back terrace (they may ask for a credit card if you eat here), open all day (till 9pm Sun), closed Mon evening. *(Malcolm, Alan Franck, Mrs T A Bizat)*

PETTERIDGE   TQ6640

Hopbine (01892) 722561

Petteridge Lane; NE of village; TN12 7NE Small unspoilt cottage in quiet little hamlet, two small rooms with open fire between, traditional pubby furniture on red patterned carpet, hops and horsebrasses, well kept Badger ales, enjoyable good value home-made food, friendly staff, steps up to simple back part with piano and darts, flagons in brick fireplace; outside gents'; seats in side garden. *(Anon)*

PLAXTOL   TQ6054

★**Golding Hop** (01732) 882150

Sheet Hill (0.5 miles S of Ightham, between A25 and A227); TN15 0PT Secluded old-fashioned country local with hands-on plain-talking landlord; simple dimly lit two-level bar, cask-tapped Adnams and guests kept well, local farm ciders (sometimes their own), short choice of basic good value bar food (not Mon or Tues evenings), old photographs of the pub, woodburners, bar billiards; portable TV for big sports events; no children inside; suntrap streamside lawn and well fenced play area over lane, good walks. *(Alan Franck, Pete Walker)*

PLUCKLEY   TQ9245

Black Horse (01233) 841948

The Street; TN27 0QS Attractive medieval pub behind Georgian façade (the Hare & Hounds in TV series *The Darling Buds of May*); five log fires including vast inglenook, bare boards, beams and flagstones, dark half-panelling, ales such as Greene King, Harveys and Shepherd Neame, enjoyable traditional food from good baguettes up

---

Ring the bull is an ancient pub game – you try to lob a ring on a piece of string over a hook (occasionally a bull's horn) on a wall or ceiling.

(just roasts on Sun), friendly staff, roomy carpeted dining areas, various ghosts; background and live music; children and dogs welcome, spacious informal garden by tall sycamores, play area, good walks, open all day. *(Paul Humphreys)*

RAMSGATE TR3764
Conqueror 07890 203282
Grange Road/St Mildred's Road; CT11 9LR Cosy single-room micropub in former corner shop, welcoming enthusiastic landlord serving three changing ales straight from the cask, also local cider and apple juice, friendly chatty atmosphere, large windows (may steam up when busy) and old photos of the cross-channel paddle steamer the pub is named after; dogs welcome, closed Sun evening, Mon. *(N R White)*

RAMSGATE TR3664
Sir Stanley Gray (01843) 599590
Pegwell Road; CT11 0NJ Over the road from the Pegwell Bay Hotel and connected by a tunnel; fine sea and coastline views from carpeted bar with plush seating and mock beams, open fire, wide choice of popular food all day, friendly service, ales including local Gadds; children welcome, terrace tables. *(N R White)*

ROCHESTER TQ7468
Coopers Arms (01634) 404298
St Margaret's Street; ME1 1TL Jettied Tudor building behind cathedral, cosily unpretentious with two comfortable beamed bars, low-priced pub food and well kept beers (range split between the bars), live music (Sun) and quiz nights, ghost of a monk who was reputedly walled-up here (a mannequin marks the spot); tables in attractive courtyard, open all day. *(Anon)*

ROCHESTER TQ7467
Man of Kent 07772 214315
John Street; ME1 1YN Small basic backstreet corner pub with impressive range of well kept local ales including Goachers, Hopdaemon, Kent and Ramsgate, also draught and bottled continental beers, kentish wines and ciders, friendly knowledgeable staff, no-frills L-shaped bar with well worn seating, log fire and resident dog called Dude, newspapers and board games, some live music; decked back garden, open all day from 2pm weekdays (3pm Mon), noon Sat, Sun. *(N R White)*

ROLVENDEN TQ8431
Bull (01580) 241212
Regent Street; TN17 4PB Welcoming small tile-hung cottage with woodburner in fine brick inglenook, high-backed leather dining chairs around rustic tables on stripped boards, built-in panelled wall seats, fresh flowers, Harveys and a couple from Old Dairy, enjoyable food (not Sun evening in winter) from favourites up, pale oak tables

in dining room, friendly helpful service; soft background music; children welcome, dogs allowed in bar, a few picnic-sets in front, more seats in sizeable back garden, open all day. *(Alec and Joan Laurence)*

SANDWICH TR3358
George & Dragon (01304) 613106
Fisher Street; CT13 9EJ Open-plan 15th-c beamed dining pub in quiet backstreet location popular with locals; enjoyable often interesting food from open-view kitchen, Wantsum, Shepherd Neame and a guest ale, good choice of wines by the glass, friendly obliging staff, warm fire; children and dogs allowed, pretty back terrace, open all day Sat, closed Sun evening. *(William and Ann Reid, Guy Vowles)*

SARRE TR2564
Crown (01843) 847808
Ramsgate Road (A253) off A28; CT7 0LF Historic 15th-c inn (Grade I listed) sandwiched between two main roads; front bar and other rambling rooms including restaurant, beams and log fires, well kept Shepherd Neame ales and decent wines, own cherry brandy (the pub is known locally as the Cherry Brandy House), enjoyable locally sourced food from nicely presented sandwiches up, good friendly service; children welcome, side garden (traffic noise), bedrooms, open all day. *(C and R Bromage)*

SEASALTER TR0864
★Sportsman (01227) 273370
Faversham Road, off B2040; CT5 4BP Restauranty dining pub just inside seawall and rather unprepossessing from outside; imaginative contemporary cooking using plenty of seafood (not Sun evening, Mon, must book and not cheap), home-baked breads, good wine choice including english, a couple of well kept Shepherd Neame ales, knowledgeable landlord and friendly staff, two plain linked rooms and long conservatory, pine tables, wheelback and basket-weave dining chairs on wood floor, local artwork; plastic glasses for outside; children welcome, open all day Sun. *(Nick Roberts, Christian Mole, Martin Day)*

SELLING TR0455
★Rose & Crown (01227) 752214
Follow Perry Wood signs; ME13 9RY Tucked-away 16th-c country pub with hop-strung beams and two inglenook log fires, well kept Adnams, Harveys and a guest, several ciders, generous pub food from sandwiches up, friendly service, games such as cribbage and shut the box, quiz first Weds of month; background music; children welcome, dogs on leads in bar, cottagey back garden with play area and bat and trap, nice walks (Pulpit viewing platform nearby), open all day Sun, closed Mon evening. *(N R White)*

SELLING TR0356
White Lion (01227) 752211
Off A251 S of Faversham (or exit roundabout, M2 junction 7); The Street; ME13 9RQ Cleanly refurbished early 18th-c brick-built coaching inn, popular locally sourced food cooked by irish landlord (best to book weekends, no food Sun evening, Mon), Shepherd Neame ales from unusual semicircular counter, friendly helpful staff, main bare-boards bar with log fire (working spit), another fire in small lower lounge, back restaurant/function room with exposed brickwork and woodburner; background and occasional live music, free wi-fi; children and dogs welcome, tables out at front and in side garden with smokers' shelter, open all day weekends, closed Mon in winter. *(N R White)*

SEVENOAKS TQ5354
Black Boy (01732) 452192
Bank Street; TN13 1UW Centrally placed Shepherd Neame pub in pedestrianised area, bare boards, open fire and some comfortable sofas, their well kept ales and decent wines by the glass, lunchtime pubby food from sandwiches up (just snacks in the evening), good friendly service, live acoustic music first Tues of month; free wi-fi; nice covered seating area outside, open all day (closed Sun in winter). *(David Hunt)*

SEVENOAKS TQ5555
★ Bucks Head (01732) 761330
Godden Green, just E; TN15 0JJ Welcoming and relaxed flower-decked pub with neatly kept bar and restaurant area, good freshly cooked blackboard food from sandwiches up, roast on Sun, well kept Shepherd Neame and a guest, beams, panelling and splendid inglenooks; children and dogs welcome, front terrace overlooking informal green and duck pond, pretty back garden with mature trees, pergola and views over quiet country behind Knole (NT), popular with walkers. *(B J Harding)*

SEVENOAKS TQ5355
Halfway House (01732) 463667
2.5 miles from M25 junction 5; TN13 2JD Nicely updated old roadside pub under new management, friendly staff and regulars, good competitively priced food from sensibly short menu, real ales including Harveys, upper bar with record player and collection of LPs (can bring your own discs); handy for the station, parking can be tricky, open all day (no food weekend evenings or Mon). *(Anon)*

SEVENOAKS TQ5055
Kings Head (01732) 452081
Bessels Green; A25 W, just off A21; TN13 2QA Village-green pub taken over by Whiting & Hammond and extensively refurbished – reports please. *(Taff Thomas)*

SHIPBOURNE TQ5952
★ Chaser (01732) 810360
Stumble Hill (A227 N of Tonbridge); TN11 9PE Comfortably opened up Whiting & Hammond pub with civilised linked rooms converging on large central island, stripped-wood floors, frame-to-frame pictures on deep red and cream walls, pine wainscoting, candles on mix of old solid wood tables, shelves of books and open fires, well kept Greene King, Larkins and guests, good wine and malt whisky choice, also good range of popular well executed food (breakfast Thurs, Sat and Sun), helpful friendly staff, dark panelling and high timber-vaulted ceiling in striking chapel-like restaurant; background music; children welcome, dogs in bar, courtyard and small side garden, good local walks, Thurs morning farmers' market, open (and food) all day, can get very busy. *(Christian Mole, Dave Braisted, Derek Thomas, Tina and David Woods-Taylor, Bob and Margaret Holder and others)*

SHOREHAM TQ5162
Crown (01959) 522903
High Street; TN14 7TJ Homely family-run village pub with two bars and separate dining areas, three or more well kept ales such as Harveys and Sharps Doom Bar, good fairly traditional food cooked to order including daily specials, reasonable prices, open fires; children, walkers and dogs welcome, nice garden, open all day Fri-Sun. *(Anon)*

SHOREHAM TQ5261
Olde George (01959) 522017
Church Street; TN14 7RY Refurbished 16th-c pub in picturesque village opposite church, low beams, uneven floors and a cosy fire, friendly staff and chatty atmosphere, changing real ales and decent food, carpeted dining area to one side; children, walkers and dogs welcome, picnic-sets by road, open all day. *(N R White)*

SHOREHAM TQ5161
Two Brewers (01959) 522800
High Street; TN14 7TD Two softly lit refurbished beamed rooms, back part more restauranty, popular freshly made food from sandwiches up, well kept Greene King and Wells & Youngs, friendly helpful staff,

---

'Children welcome' means the pub says it lets children inside without any special restriction. If it allows them in, but to restricted areas such as an eating area or family room, we specify this. Some pubs may impose an evening time limit. We do not mention limits after 9pm as we assume children are home by then.

snug areas with comfortable seating, two woodburners; handy for walkers, closed Mon and Tues. *(Pauline Fellows and Simon Robbins)*

SNARGATE   TQ9928
★ **Red Lion** (01797) 344648

B2080 Appledore–Brenzett; TN29 9UQ Unchanging 16th-c pub in same family for over 100 years, simple old-fashioned charm in three timeless little rooms with original cream wall panelling, heavy beams in sagging ceilings, dark pine Victorian farmhouse chairs on bare boards, an old piano and coal fire, local cider and four or five ales including Goachers tapped from casks behind unusual free-standing marble-topped counter, no food, traditional games like toad in the hole, nine men's morris and table skittles; children in family room, dogs in bar, outdoor lavatories, cottage garden, closed Mon evening. *(Anon)*

ST MARGARET'S BAY   TR3744
★ **Coastguard** (01304) 853176

Off A256 NE of Dover; keep on down through the village to the bottom of the bay, pub off on right by the beach; CT15 6DY At bottom of a steep windy road with lovely sea views (France visible on a clear day) from prettily planted balcony and beachside seating, nautical décor in carpeted wood-clad bar, four changing ales, bottled continentals, over 40 whiskies and a carefully chosen wine list (some kentish ones), enjoyable fairly priced food from shortish menu, friendly efficient service, more fine views from restaurant with close-set tables on wood-strip floor; background music, free wi-fi (mobile phones pick up french signal); children and dogs allowed in certain areas, good walks, open all day. *(Michael Tack, John Wooll, Peter Smith and Judith Brown, N R White)*

STAPLEHURST   TQ7846
Lord Raglan (01622) 843747

About 1.5 miles from town centre towards Maidstone, turn right off A229 into Chart Hill Road opposite Chart Cars; OS Sheet 188 map reference 785472; TN12 0DE Country pub with cosy chatty area around narrow bar counter, hop-covered low beams, big log fire and woodburner, mix of comfortably worn dark wood furniture, good reasonably priced home-cooked food, Goachers, Harveys and a guest, farm cider and perry, good wine list; children and dogs welcome, reasonable wheelchair access, tables on terrace and in side orchard, Aug onion festival, closed Sun. *(Anon)*

STONE IN OXNEY   TQ9327
★ **Crown** (01233) 758302

Off B2082 Iden–Tenterden; TN30 7JN Smart country dining pub with friendly landlord and staff, very good food from landlady-chef including some imaginative choices, also wood-fired pizzas Fri evening, Sat (takeaways available), well kept Larkins tapped from the cask, light airy open feel with lots of wood, red walls and big inglenook log fire; no under-12s in the evening, rustic furniture on terrace, two refurbished bedrooms. *(Toby Boyle, Alec and Joan Laurence, Peter Meister, Stuart Paulley)*

STONE STREET   TQ5755
Padwell (01732) 761532

Off A25 E of Sevenoaks, on Seal–Plaxtol by-road; OS Sheet 188 map reference 569551; TN15 0LQ Traditional country pub under enthusiastic newish management; cosy convivial atmosphere in L-shaped bar with beams, panelling and log fire, ales such as Larkins and Tonbridge, generous helpings of tasty good value food (not Mon, 10% OAP discount Tues-Fri), friendly helpful staff, more modern back dining area, Weds quiz; children and dogs welcome, front terrace and pleasant garden behind, good walks, open all day weekends. *(N R White)*

TENTERDEN   TQ8833
Vine (01580) 762718

76 High Street; TN30 6AU Welcoming 19th-c Shepherd Neame pub with bistro feel and food to match, airy entrance lobby with comfortable chairs and woodburner, steps down to bar, large back flagstoned restaurant and conservatory; background music, quiz nights Thurs/Sun; children welcome, sunny terrace, open all day. *(Steve and Liz Tilley)*

THURNHAM   TQ8057
★ **Black Horse** (01622) 737185

Not far from M20 junction 7; off A249 at Detling; ME14 3LD Large busy dining pub with enjoyable food all day, children's menu, three well kept ales including Westerham, farm ciders and country wines, friendly efficient uniformed staff, alcove seating, timbers and hop-strung beams, bare boards and log fires, back restaurant area; dogs and walkers welcome, pleasant garden with partly covered terrace, nice views, by Pilgrims Way, comfortable modern bedroom block, hearty breakfast. *(Sara Fulton, Roger Baker, Martin Day, Lee and Liz Potter)*

TOYS HILL   TQ4752
★ **Fox & Hounds** (01732) 750328

Off A25 in Brasted, via Brasted Chart and The Chart; TN16 1QG Traditional country pub with plain tables and chairs on dark boards, leather sofa and easy chair by log fire, hunting prints, old photographs, plates and copper jugs, modern carpeted dining extension with big windows overlooking tree-sheltered garden, enjoyable well presented food (not Sun evening), well kept Greene King ales and several wines by the glass, traditional games; background music, free wi-fi; children (no buggies inside) and dogs welcome, roadside verandah used by smokers, good local walks and views, handy for Chartwell and Emmetts Garden (both NT), open all day Sat, till 6pm Sun, closed Mon; licensees planning to retire, so things may change. *(Anon)*

TUNBRIDGE WELLS   TQ5638
Beacon (01892) 524252
Tea Garden Lane, Rusthall Common; TN3 9JH Cheery Victorian pub with Harveys, Timothy Taylors and Wells & Youngs, lots of wines by the glass, good coffee, airy interior with fireside sofas, stripped panelling, bare boards and ornate wall units, linked dining areas; children welcome, tables on decking with fine view, paths between lakes and springs, three bedrooms, open all day. *(Anon)*

TUNBRIDGE WELLS   TQ5837
Bull (01892) 536526
Frant Road; TN2 5LH Friendly refurbished local with two linked areas, neatly set dining part with well spaced pine tables and chunky chairs on stripped wood, similar bar area, corner black sofa, well kept Shepherd Neame ales and decent wine, generous helpings of enjoyable reasonably priced food, daily papers; background music, TV, pool, free wi-fi; dogs allowed, outside seats for smokers, open all day weekends. *(Tony Hobden)*

UNDERRIVER   TQ5552
★White Rock (01732) 833112
SE of Sevenoaks, off B245; TN15 0SB Welcoming village pub, attractive and relaxed, with good food from pubby choices up (all day weekends, best to book), well kept Harveys, Westerham and a guest, decent wines, beams, bare boards and stripped brickwork in cosy original part with adjacent dining area, another bar in modern extension with woodburner, pool; background and some live music; children welcome, dogs may be allowed (ask first), small front garden, back terrace and large lawn with boules and bat and trap, pretty churchyard and walks nearby, open all day in summer and at weekends. *(Martin Day, Tina and David Woods-Taylor)*

WEST MALLING   TQ6857
Bull (01732) 842753
High Street; ME19 6QH Friendly old pub with good selection of mainly local ales and reasonably priced traditional home-made food (not Sun-Weds evenings), hop-strung beams, bare boards and big log fire, refurbished restaurant, Mon quiz, live music first Sat of month; dogs welcome, open all day Fri-Sun. *(Ross Barnes)*

WESTBERE   TR1862
Old Yew Tree (01227) 710501
Just off A18 Canterbury–Margate; CT2 0HH Heavily beamed early 14th-c pub in pretty village, simply furnished bare-boards bar, inglenook log fire, good reasonably priced food from varied menu, Shepherd Neame Master Brew and a guest, friendly helpful staff, quiz first Weds of month; picnic-sets in garden behind, open all day weekends, closed Mon. *(Joan and Alec Lawrence)*

WESTERHAM   TQ4453
General Wolfe (01959) 562104
High Street, W side of village; TN16 1RQ Attractive 16th-c white weatherboarded pub, recently refurbished but keeping character, one long cottagey room with old beams and woodburner, also a snug, Greene King ales and a local guest, popular sensibly priced food (not Sun-Tues evenings) including one or two unusual dishes; seats out on raised back deck, open all day. *(N R White)*

WESTERHAM   TQ4454
Grasshopper on the Green
(01959) 562926 *The Green; TN16 1AS* Old black-beamed pub (small former coaching house) overlooking village green, three linked bar areas with log fire at back, ales including Westerham, decent pubby food, upstairs restaurant; free wi-fi; children and dogs welcome, seating out at front and in back garden with play area, open all day. *(Martin Day)*

WESTGATE-ON-SEA   TR3270
Bake & Alehouse 07581 468797
Off St Mildred`s Road down alley by cinema; CT8 8RE Former bakery converted to micropub; simple little drinking room with a few tables (expect to share when busy) on bare boards, collages on walls, around four well kept interesting cask-tapped ales, real ciders from the barrel including a warm winter one (Monks Delight), kentish wines, local cheese, sausage rolls and pork pies, friendly chatty atmosphere; closed Sun evening, Mon. *(N R White)*

WHITSTABLE   TR1167
Continental (01227) 280280
Beach Walk; CT5 2BP Mix of 19th-c seafront hotel, pub-café and brasserie restaurant, full range of Whitstable ales, friendly relaxed atmosphere, large windows looking over Thames estuary (can see Southend on a clear day); children welcome, metal tables and chairs outside, 23 bedrooms, more in converted fishermen's huts. *(N R White)*

WHITSTABLE   TR1066
Old Neptune (01227) 272262
Marine Terrace; CT5 1EJ Great view over Swale estuary from this popular unpretentious weatherboarded pub set right on the beach (rebuilt after being washed away in 1897 storm); Harveys, Whitstable and a guest, lunchtime food from shortish menu including seafood specials, friendly young staff, weekend live music; children and dogs welcome, picnic-sets on the shingle (plastic

glasses out here and occasional barbecues), fine sunsets, can get very busy in summer, open all day. *(John Wooll, N R White, Adrian Johnson)*

WICKHAMBREAUX   TR2258
Rose (01227) 721763
The Green; CT3 1RQ Attractive 16th-c and partly older pub under newish management; enjoyable traditional home-made food (not Sun evening), friendly helpful staff, Greene King IPA and three guests (May/Aug beer festivals), real ciders, small bare-boards bar with log fire in big fireplace, dining area beyond standing timbers with woodburner, beams, panelling and stripped brick, quiz third Tues of month; children and dogs welcome, enclosed side garden and small courtyard, nice spot across green from church and watermill, open all day. *(Mr and Mrs Mike Pearson)*

WOODCHURCH   TQ9434
Six Bells (01233) 860246
Front Road, opposite churchyard; TN26 3QQ Attractive weatherboarded village pub behind white picket fence, traditional beamed interior with two bars and dining area, log fires, Fullers, Harveys, Hopdaemon, Timothy Taylors and guests (regular beer festivals), real ciders and good choice of wines, enjoyable reasonably priced pubby food (Sun till 6pm) from sandwiches and baguettes up, friendly helpful staff and good local atmosphere, quiz and music

nights; dogs welcome, tables out in front under wisteria, big garden behind, open all day. *(Paul and Karen Cornock)*

WYE   TR0546
New Flying Horse (01233) 812297
Upper Bridge Street; TN25 5AN 17th-c Shepherd Neame inn with beams and inglenook, enjoyable food including fixed-price menu in bar and restaurant, friendly accommodating staff, Sun quiz, live music last Thurs of month; children welcome, good-sized pretty garden with play area and miniature thatched pub (former Chelsea Flower Show exhibit), nine bedrooms (some in converted stables), open all day. *(Peter Smith and Judith Brown)*

YALDING   TQ6950
★**Walnut Tree** (01622) 814266
B2010 SW of Maidstone; ME18 6JB Timbered village pub with split-level main bar, fine old settles, a long cushioned mahogany bench and mix of dining chairs on brick or carpeted floors, chunky wooden tables with church candles, interesting old photographs, big inglenook log fire, well kept Black Sheep, Harveys and Skinners, good bar food and more inventive restaurant menu, attractive raftered dining room with high-backed leather dining chairs on parquet flooring, lots of local events; background and occasional live music, TV; a few picnic-sets out at front by road. *(Nigel and Jean Eames, Steve and Claire Harvey)*

Lancashire

with Greater Manchester, Merseyside and Wirral

KEY ★ Star Pub ⭐ Top Quality Food 🍺 Great Beer
🍷 Good Wines £ Bargain Meals 🛏 Good Bedrooms 🍴 Serves Food

BASHALL EAVES SD6943 Map 7
Red Pump 🍺 🛏
NW of Clitheroe, off B6478 or B6243; BB7 3DA

Cosy bar, highly thought-of food in more contemporary dining rooms and changing beers in a beautifully placed country inn; bedrooms

This former farmhouse is a comfortable place to stay and makes a handy base for exploring the Forest of Bowland; breakfasts are good and generous and residents can fish in the nearby river. A cheerful place with a chatty, helpful landlord, it has two pleasantly up-to-date dining rooms and a traditional, cosy central bar: bookshelves, cushioned settles, wheelbacks and other nice old chairs on flagstones and a log fire. The quickly changing range of three regional beers on handpump might include Hawkshead Windermere Pale, Moorhouses Pendle Witches Brew and a guest, and they also keep ten wines by the glass and a good range of malt whiskies; board games. You can enjoy the splendid views from seats in the terraced gardens.

🍴 Good food using home-grown herbs includes chicken liver pâté with chutney, crab cakes with aioli, tempura fish and chips, vegetarian wellington, rabbit or venison casserole, a daily fresh fish dish, sirloin steak with a choice of sauces, and puddings such as chocolate mousse with amaretto and blackcurrant sponge with blackcurrant compote and liquorice ice-cream. *Benchmark main dish: slow-roasted pork belly £14.00. Two-course evening meal £17.50.*

Free house ~ Licensees Jonathan and Martina Myerscough ~ Real ale ~ (01254) 826227 ~ Open 12-2.30, 5.45-11; 12-3, 5.30-11 Sat; 12-7 Sun; closed Mon, Tues, two weeks Jan ~ Bar food 12-2.30, 6-9 ~ Restaurant ~ Children welcome ~ Dogs allowed in bar and bedrooms ~ Bedrooms: £65/£95 ~ www.theredpumpinn.co.uk *Recommended by Steve Whalley, Dr Peter D Smart*

BISPHAM GREEN SD4813 Map 7
Eagle & Child ⭐ 🍷 🍺
Maltkiln Lane (Parbold–Croston road, off B5246); L40 3SG

Successful all-rounder with antiques in stylishly simple interior, enterprising food, an interesting range of beers and appealing rustic garden

With its warmly friendly service and highly enjoyable food, this striking red-brick pub wins high praise from our readers. The largely open-plan bar is carefully furnished with a lovely mix of small old oak chairs, an attractive oak coffer, several handsomely carved antique oak settles (the finest made in part, it seems, from a 16th-c wedding bedhead), old hunting prints and engravings and low hop-draped beams. Also, red walls, coir matting, oriental rugs on ancient flagstones in front of the fine old stone fireplace and counter; the pub's dogs are called Betty and Doris. Friendly young staff serve Thwaites Original and Wainwright on handpump alongside guests such as Cross Bay Aurora, Cumberland Corby Ale, Southport Golden Sands and Wells & Youngs Eagle IPA, farm cider, decent wines and around 30 malt whiskies. A popular beer festival is usually held on the early May Bank Holiday weekend. The spacious, gently rustic garden has a well tended but unconventional bowling green; beyond is a wild area that's home to crested newts and moorhens. The shop in the handsome side barn sells interesting wines and pottery and includes a proper butcher and a deli. This is part of the Ainscoughs group.

Rewarding food includes lunchtime sandwiches, warm crab and saffron tart with spiced tomato relish, ham hock and lancashire cheese terrine with home-made piccalilli, various platters, steak and mushroom in ale pie, chargrilled gammon with fried duck egg and pineapple relish, burger with bacon, cheese and mushrooms, spicy tomato relish and triple-cooked chips, changing daily specials, and puddings such as lemon posset with thyme meringue and lemonade jelly and chocolate mousse with rum and raisin ice-cream. *Benchmark main dish: slow-braised beef hotpot with red wine sauce £14.95. Two-course evening meal £19.00.*

Free house ~ Licensee Janine Winward Jones ~ Real ale ~ (01257) 462297 ~ Open 12-11 (10.30 Sun) ~ Bar food 12-2.30, 6-9.30; 12-9.30 weekends ~ Children welcome ~ Dogs welcome ~ www.ainscoughs.co.uk *Recommended by Robert Wivell, Richard Kennell, Alison Ball, Ian Walton, Dr Kevan Tucker*

BLACKBURN
SD6525 Map 7
Oyster & Otter ⭐ ♀
1.8 miles from M65 junction 3: A674 towards Blackburn, turn right at Feniscowles mini-roundabout, signposted to Darwen and Tockholes, into Livesey Branch Road; BB2 5DQ

Contemporary informal bar-restaurant with good food, especially fresh fish and seafood

This is a distinctive clapboard and stone building perched above the road, with an appealing modern layout. Well cushioned dining booths line big windows on one side, and further comfortable table seating is divided into cosy areas by shoulder-high walling and a big stone central hearth with a woodburning stove. If you just want a chat and a drink or coffee, there are high suede seats by a couple of tall tables, plaid bar stools by the serving counter, and an end area with squishy leather sofas, a plaid sofa and library chairs – with a view of the kitchen to tempt you to change your mind and have some food too. Thwaites Wainwright and a guest ale on handpump and ten wines by the glass. Helpful young staff wear neat black aprons, and the piped rock music suits the style of the place. There are teak tables out on a deck above the road.

As well as specials such as smoked haddock and skate fishcakes, chargrilled chilli and lime squid, roast red fish with braised pear and bacon sauce, and persian spiced chicken with saffron chilli rice and lemon yoghurt, the interesting food includes lunchtime sandwiches, baby back ribs with orange, rosemary and chilli, crispy katsu prawns with japanese curry dip, sausages with sticky onion gravy, jerk-spiced sweet potato and black bean curry, and puddings such as chocolate and cherry mousse and steamed syrup pudding with custard. *Benchmark main dish: hake with bacon and brioche crumb, dauphinoise potatoes and red wine shallots £14.95. Two-course evening meal £20.00.*

Free house ~ Licensee Joycelyn Neve ~ Real ale ~ (01254) 203200 ~ Open 12-11
(midnight Fri, Sat); 12-10.30 Sun ~ Bar food 12-9 (10 Fri, Sat, 8.30 Sun) ~ Children
welcome ~ Wi-fi ~ Live music third Fri of month ~ www.oysterandotter.co.uk
Recommended by W K Wood

 DOWNHAM   SD7844   Map 7

Assheton Arms ★ ⚲

Off A59 NE of Clitheroe, via Chatburn; BB7 4BJ

Lancashire Dining Pub of the Year

**Fine old inn with plenty of dining and drinking space, a friendly
welcome, several real ales and creative food**

Named after local landowners, this handsome stone pub is in a very
pretty setting at the top of a steep hill and opposite a lovely church.
It's a genuinely friendly place with helpful staff and an easy-going
atmosphere. A small front bar, with a hatch to the kitchen, has tweed-
upholstered armchairs and stools on big flagstones around just one table,
a woodburning stove surrounded by logs, and drawings of dogs and hunting
prints on grey-green walls. Off to the right, a wood-panelled partition
creates a cosy area where there are similarly cushioned pews and nice old
chairs around various tables on a rug-covered wooden floor, and a couple
of window chairs. The main bar, up a couple of steps, has more tweed-
upholstered seating and dark wooden tables and chairs, old photographs
of the pub and the village on pale walls, and a marble bar counter where
they serve Moorhouses Pride of Pendle, Thwaites Wainwright and Timothy
Taylors Landlord on handpump, a dozen wines by the glass and farm cider;
background music. Two restaurants, on different levels, have an attractive
assortment of dining chairs and tables on a wooden floor or carpeting,
and hunting prints on cream-painted walls; one has a woodburning stove,
the other has a lovely old black kitchen range. Outside at the front of the
building are picnic-sets and tables and chairs.

 Extremely good food includes sticky chicken skewers with cucumber and
peanut sauce, salt and pepper squid with rice wine and ginger dipping sauce,
persian chicken with pomegranate, almond and coriander rice with yoghurt dressing,
goan king prawn curry with coconut rice, szechuan monkfish with chinese sherry,
crispy shallots and ginger, 28-day aged steaks with scrumpy battered onion rings
and chips, and puddings such as vanilla crème brûlée and chocolate and cherry
mousse. *Benchmark main dish: herb-crumbed haddock and chips £10.50.
Two-course evening meal £20.00.*

Free house ~ Licensee Jocelyn Neve ~ Real ale ~ (01200) 441227 ~ Open 10am-
midnight ~ Bar food 12-9 (10 Fri, Sat, 8 Sun) ~ Restaurant ~ Children welcome ~
Dogs allowed in bar ~ Wi-fi ~ www.asshetonarms.com *Recommended by John and Eleanor
Holdsworth, Steve Whalley*

FORMBY   SD3109   Map 7

Sparrowhawk ⚲ ◧

*Southport Old Road; brown sign to pub just off A565 Formby bypass,
S edge of Ainsdale; L37 0AB*

**Light and airy newly converted pub with all the traditional virtues,
in wooded grounds**

Following the usual Brunning & Price layout of linked areas looping
comfortably and extensively around a feature central bar, this has a

good atmosphere at any time of day – it's still chatty and lively at teatime when most pubs are either very quiet or, more likely, closed. There's plenty of variation, from snug leather fireside armchairs in library corners, through tables with rugs on dark boards by big bow windows, to a comfortably carpeted conservatory dining room. The choice of drinks is very wide too: 21 wines by the glass, 69 malt whiskies, Cornish Orchards and Weston's farm ciders, changing ales such as Burscough Mere Blonde, Hawkshead Windermere Pale, Titanic Anchor, Weetwood Cheshire Cat and the Original house beer, brewed for them by Phoenix. They have daily papers, and throughout there are attractive prints on pastel walls, church candles and flowers – and the sense of contented well-being brought by good staff and service. A flagstoned side terrace has sturdy tables, and several picnic-table sets are nicely spread on the woodside lawns by a set of swings and an old Fergie tractor (painted green instead of the usual grey). A walk from the pub to coastal nature reserves might just yield red squirrels, still hanging on in this area.

Good brasserie-style food includes sandwiches, scallops with spiced butter bean purée, crispy chorizo and herb dressing, tandoori chicken with fresh pineapple, coconut and mango, sharing platters, cauliflower and chickpea tagine with date and apricot couscous, pork schnitzel in gremoulata crumb with cheshire cheese potato cake, malaysian chicken curry, hot lamb salad with rösti potato and roast tomato jus, and puddings such as peach bakewell tart and sticky toffee pudding with toffee sauce. *Benchmark main dish: braised lamb shoulder with dauphinoise potatoes £16.95. Two-course evening meal £20.00.*

Brunning & Price ~ Manager Iain Hendry ~ Real ale ~ (01704) 882350 ~ Open 10.30am-11pm; 10.30-10.30 Sun ~ Bar food 12-10 (9.30 Sun) ~ Children welcome ~ Dogs allowed in bar ~ Wi-fi ~ www.sparrowhawk-formby.co.uk *Recommended by John and Hazel Sarkanen, Peter Pilbeam*

GREAT MITTON
Aspinall Arms ♀ 🍺
SD7138   Map 7

B6246 NW of Whalley; BB7 9PQ

Cleverly refurbished and extended pub by a wide expanse of river, with all manner of furnishings and fixtures, cheerful, friendly service and fine choice of drinks and food

The garden to the side of this newly opened and completely renovated pub is beside a great sweep of the River Ribble and picnic-sets look over the water; there's also a terrace with good quality seats and tables under parasols. Inside, the atmosphere throughout the various rambling rooms and snugger corners is easy-going and chatty, and a wide mix of customers drop in and out all day. Seating ranges from attractively cushioned old-style dining chairs through brass-studded leather ones to big armchairs and sofas around an assortment of dark tables; floors are flagstoned, carpeted or wooden and topped with rugs; and the pale-painted or bare stone walls are hung with a big collection of prints and local photographs. Dotted about are large mirrors, house plants, stone bottles and bookshelves and there are both open fires and a woodburning stove. From the central servery, young, friendly and helpful staff serve Phoenix Brunning & Price Original, Bowland Gold, Brightside Odin, Copper Dragon Cobblers Cask, Kelham Island Pale Rider and Moorhouses Black Cat on handpump, 15 wines by the glass, an amazing 150 malt whiskies and a farm cider.

Rewarding food includes sandwiches, rabbit and prune suet pudding, crab, dill and spring onion quiche, puy lentil and aubergine balls with tomato, chilli and pasta, thyme-roast chicken with bacon and red wine jus, seared duck breast with duck hash cake, kumquats and madeira jus, bass fillets with mussels, clams and samphire in white wine, and puddings such as crème brûlée and ginger parkin with cider jelly and apple pie ice-cream. *Benchmark main dish: steak burger with bacon, cheddar, coleslaw and chips £12.45. Two-course evening meal £20.00.*

Brunning & Price ~ Manager Chris Humphries ~ (01254) 826555 ~ Open 10.30am-11pm; 10.30-10.30 Sun ~ Bar food 12-10 ~ Restaurant ~ www.brunningandprice.co.uk/aspinallarms *Recommended by William Wright, Peter Pilbeam, Steve Whalley*

 GREAT MITTON   SD7139   Map 7

Three Fishes 🏅 🍷 ◖

Mitton Road (B6246, off A59 NW of Whalley); BB7 9PQ

Contemporary and stylish pub with tremendous attention to detail, excellent regional food given a modern touch and interesting drinks

Our readers continue to enjoy their visits to this thoughtfully and imaginatively converted place; it's cleverly laid out and, despite its size, has plenty of cosy corners. The areas closest to the bar are elegantly traditional with a couple of big stone fireplaces, rugs on polished floors and upholstered stools. Then there's a series of individually furnished and painted rooms with exposed stone walls, careful spotlighting and wooden slatted blinds, ending with another impressive fireplace. To get a seat, write your name on a blackboard when you arrive and they'll find you when a table becomes free – the system works surprisingly well. Staff are young and friendly and there's a good chatty atmosphere. The long bar counter (with elaborate floral displays) serves Bowland Hen Harrier, Moorhouses Black Cat and Thwaites Wainwright on handpump, farm cider, a dozen wines by the glass and 15 malt whiskies. There are seats and tables on the terrace and in the garden, which overlooks the Ribble Valley.

 Good, popular food includes sandwiches, potted shrimps, twice-baked cheese soufflé, various platters, cheese and onion pie, lancashire hotpot, dripping chips and battered onion rings with beer-infused chicken, free-range pork chop and burger with lots of toppings, fish pie topped with lancashire cheese, bass fillet with yellow beetroots and caesar salad, and puddings such as lemon meringue pie and apple crumble. *Benchmark main dish: lancashire hotpot £12.00. Two-course evening meal £17.50.*

Free house ~ Licensee Andy Morris ~ Real ale ~ (01254) 826888 ~ Open 12-11 (10 Sun) ~ Bar food 12-8.30 (9 Fri, Sat) ~ Children welcome ~ Dogs allowed in bar ~ Wi-fi ~ www.thethreefishes.com *Recommended by John and Sylvia Harrop, Robert Wivell, Roger and Anne Newbury, Ken Richards*

LATHOM   SD4510   Map 7

Ring o' Bells ◖ £

In Lathom, turn right into Ring o' Bells Lane; L40 5TE

Bustling family-friendly canalside pub, interconnected rooms with antique furniture, six real ales, some sort of food all day and children's play areas inside and out

Some kind of food, starting with breakfast, is served all day in this red-brick Victorian pub – it's a handy spot for travellers on the nearby M6. Several interlinked rooms lead off from the handsome central bar counter with its pretty inlaid tiles; throughout are all manner of antique dining chairs and carved settles around some lovely old tables, comfortable sofas, rugs on flagstones, lots of paintings and prints of the local area, sporting activities and plants, and large mirrors, brass lanterns and standard lamps; staffordshire dogs and decorative plates sit on mantelpieces above open fires. Prospect Pioneer and Thwaites Wainwright plus six guests from breweries such as Cumbrian Legendary, Derwent, Hart, Pennine, Prospect and George Wright on handpump, good wines by the glass and over 25 whiskies; background music, TV, darts, board games. Downstairs, there's a more plainly furnished room and indoor and outdoor children's play areas. Plans for their four acres of land include a football pitch, vegetable garden and cider orchard – and, of course, seats and tables by the canal. This is part of the Ainscoughs group.

Very good value food includes lunchtime sandwiches, black pudding potato cake with caramelised onions and fried egg, prawn cocktail, goats cheese and spinach lasagne, steak in ale pudding, cumberland sausages and onion gravy, butterfly chicken topped with bacon, mozzarella and barbecue sauce, and puddings such as banana split and profiteroles with chocolate sauce. *Benchmark main dish: confit pork belly with caramelised cauliflower and baked apple £11.95. Two-course evening meal £15.00.*

Free house ~ Licensee Rebecca Grace ~ Real ale ~ (01704) 893157 ~ Open 11-11 (midnight Sat) ~ Bar food 12-2.30, 5-9; 12-9 Sat; 12-8 Sun ~ Children welcome ~ Dogs allowed in bar ~ Wi-fi ~ www.ringobellspub.com *Recommended by Emma Scofield, Phil and Jane Hodson*

LITTLE ECCLESTON
Cartford
SD4240   Map 7

Cartford Lane, off A586 Garstang–Blackpool, by toll bridge; PR3 0YP

Prettily placed 17th-c coaching inn on riverbank, attractively refurbished and with a thoughtful choice of drinks and food; waterside bedrooms

Nestled on the bank of the River Wyre, this 17th-c coaching inn has extensive views of the surrounding countryside, Trough of Bowland and the peaks of the Lake District; the individually styled bedrooms all have tranquil river views. The unusual four-level layout blends both traditional and contemporary elements with an appealing mix of striking colours, natural wood and polished floors, while the log fire and eclectic choice of furniture creates a comfortable and relaxed feel in the bar lounge; background music. Hawkshead Lakeland Gold, Moorhouses Pride of Pendle, Theakston Old Peculier and a guest from Bowland on handpump alongside speciality bottled beers and Weston's cider; several wines by the glass. There's also another cosy lounge and a new riverside restaurant. In warm weather, the seats in the garden overlooking the water are much prized.

Good, popular food includes lunchtime sandwiches, moules frites, pigeon with puy lentils, chargrilled courgettes and grain mustard dressing, fruit and vegetable curry, burger with bacon, cheese and chunky chips, cajun chicken with honey and ginger sauce, oxtail in ale pudding, pork belly with apple and black pudding fritters, fish pie and puddings such as crème brûlée of the day and chocolate fondant with hazelnut crunch. *Benchmark main dish: venison wellington £16.50. Two-course evening meal £19.00.*

Free house ~ Licensees Patrick and Julie Beaume ~ Real ale ~ (01995) 670166 ~ Open 12-11 (11.30 Sat); 12-10 Sun; closed Mon lunchtime ~ Bar food 12-2, 5.30-9 (10 Fri, Sat); 12-8.30 Sun ~ Restaurant ~ Children welcome until 8.30pm ~ Wi-fi ~ Bedrooms: £70/£110 ~ www.thecartfordinn.co.uk *Recommended by Gordon and Margaret Ormondroyd, Peter Harrison*

MANCHESTER

SJ8297 Map 7

Wharf ♀ ◆

Blantyre Street/Slate Wharf; M15 4SW

Big wharf-like pub with large terrace overlooking canal basin, all manner of furnishings and wall prints, six real ales and a fine choice of other drinks, and good bistro-like food

Although this is a huge place there are cosy alcoves and rooms away from the cheerful buzz of the main open-plan areas, and it's on several levels. Downstairs is more informal and pub-like, with groups of high tables and chairs; upstairs is restauranty with table service. Throughout there's an appealing variety of pre-war-style dining chairs around quite a choice of dark wooden tables on rugs and shiny floorboards, hundreds of interesting prints and posters on bare brick or painted walls, old stone bottles, church candles, house plants and fresh flowers on window sills and tables, bookshelves and armchairs here and there, and large mirrors over open fires. Despite the crowds of happy customers, staff remain unfailingly friendly and helpful. Brunning & Price Original (from Phoenix) and guests from breweries such as Beartown, Conwy, Thwaites, Titanic and Weetwood on handpump, 19 wines by the glass and lots of whiskies. The large front terrace has plenty of wood and chrome tables and chairs around a fountain, and picnic-sets overlooking the canal basin.

 From a brasserie-like menu, the enterprising food includes sandwiches, pigeon breast on shallot and wild mushroom tarte tatin, tempura monkfish cheeks with pea purée and chorizo crisps, smoked haddock with spinach, poached egg and hollandaise sauce, stuffed aubergine with olives and sun-dried tomato couscous and tomato sauce, southern thai sea trout curry, tarragon and white wine chicken with boulangère potatoes, and puddings such as dark chocolate brownie and crème brûlée. *Benchmark main dish: roast beef with all the trimmings £12.95. Two-course evening meal £19.50.*

Brunning & Price ~ Manager Siobhan Youngs ~ Real ale ~ (0161) 220 2960 ~ Open 11-11 (midnight Fri, Sat) ~ Bar food 12-10 (9.30 Sun) ~ Restaurant ~ Children welcome ~ Dogs allowed in bar ~ Wi-fi ~ Live acoustic music Fri evening ~ www.brunningandprice.co.uk/thewharf *Recommended by Mike and Wena Stevenson, Ruth May*

MELLOR

SD6530 Map 7

Millstone ◆ ⇦

The Mellor near Blackburn; Mellor Lane; BB2 7JR

Smart and popular dining pub run by an enthusiastic chef-patron, serving four real ales and rewarding hearty food; comfortable bedrooms

This extended stone former coaching inn has extensive panelling and comfortable seats around polished tables in dining rooms on both sides of the central bar. At busy mealtimes, the whole space is opened into one big happy eating area around the bar itself, which has a handful of tables, settles, housekeeper's chair and rugs on bare boards. Thwaites Original, Lancaster Bomber, Nutty Black and Wainwright on handpump, and decent wines by the glass; log fires. Service, informally friendly and helpful, is normally quite quick; maybe faint piped music. There are seats and tables under parasols on a side terrace. The bedrooms, some in a separate block across the car park, are comfortable and well equipped, and the breakfasts good.

🍴 Using local produce, the wide choice of food includes sandwiches, duck spring rolls with plum sauce, chicken and pulled pork rillette with apple compote, various deli boards, steak and kidney in ale pudding, gammon and poached egg, chicken with bacon in a creamy grain mustard sauce, lamb shank with bubble and squeak, fish curry, and puddings such as hot chocolate fondant and vanilla crème brûlée. *Benchmark main dish: beer-battered haddock and chips £12.50. Two-course evening meal £19.00.*

Thwaites ~ Managers Anson and Sarah Bolton ~ Real ale ~ (01254) 813333 ~ Open 11-11 ~ Bar food 12-9.30 ~ Restaurant ~ Children welcome ~ Wi-fi ~ Bedrooms: £70/£80 ~ www.millstonehotel.co.uk *Recommended by W K Wood, Dave Webster, Sue Holland, Steve Whalley*

NETHER BURROW   SD6175 Map 7

Highwayman 🌟 ♀

A683 S of Kirkby Lonsdale; LA6 2RJ

Substantial and skilfully refurbished old stone house with country interior serving carefully sourced food; lovely gardens

They seem to have got everything just right in this welcoming and very well run 17th-c inn. Although large, the stylishly simple flagstoned interior is nicely divided into intimate corners, with a couple of big log fires and informal wooden furnishings. Black and white wall prints and placemats show the local farmers and producers used, with a map on the menu locating these 'regional food heroes'. Thwaites Lancaster Bomber, Original and Wainwright on handpump, 14 wines by the glass, around a dozen whiskies and a particularly good range of soft drinks; service is friendly and efficient. French windows open out to a big terrace and lovely gardens.

🍴 Impressive food includes duck terrine with citrus jelly, Whitby crab with devilled mayonnaise, cheese and onion pie, burger with local cheese, bacon, piccalilli and spicy tomato relish, smoked fish pie with free-range egg, chicken with avocado, organic curd cheese and tarragon dressing on salad, braised ox cheek with horseradish mash and honey and worcester sauce carrots, and puddings such as apple pie and custard and baked alaska. *Benchmark main dish: lancashire hotpot £12.00. Two-course evening meal £19.50.*

Thwaites ~ Lease Andy Morris and Craig Bancroft ~ Real ale ~ (01524) 273338 ~ Open 12-10 (11 Sat) ~ Bar food 12-2, 5.30-8.30 (9 Fri, Sat, 8 Sun) ~ Children welcome ~ Dogs allowed in bar ~ Wi-fi ~ www.highwaymaninn.co.uk *Recommended by Ray and Winifred Halliday, Caroline Prescott*

PLEASINGTON   SD6528 Map 7

Clog & Billycock 🌟 ♀

Village signposted off A677 Preston New Road on W edge of Blackburn; Billinge End Road; BB2 6QB

Carefully sourced local food in appealingly modernised stone-built village pub

Our readers visit this carefully modernised village pub on a regular basis and always give positive feedback. Run by friendly and efficient licensees and their attentive staff, the place has the feel of an upmarket barn conversion and is light and airy with flagstoned floors and pale grey walls; a cosier room has high-backed settles and a fireplace at the end. The whole pub is packed with light wooden tables – even if they're full when you arrive, such is the size of the place you probably won't have to wait long in the little bar area for a table to become free. Thwaites Original, Coiled Spring, Nutty Black and Wainwright on handpump, 11 wines by the glass, 14 malt whiskies and a farm cider; background music. There are some tables outside, beside a small garden.

 Reliably good food includes potted chicken livers with cumberland sauce, treacle-cured salmon with oriental salad, sharing platters, blue cheese, pear and walnut salad, chicken kebab with onion fritter, curried lentil sauce and coconut rice, free-range pork chop with dripping chips and mushrooms, smoked fish pie with free-range egg, and puddings such as knickerbocker glory and chocolate and orange pudding with chocolate sauce. *Benchmark main dish: lancashire hotpot £12.00. Two-course evening meal £19.50.*

Thwaites ~ Lease Andy Morris and Craig Bancroft ~ Real ale ~ (01254) 201163 ~ Open 12-11 (10.30 Sun) ~ Bar food 12-8.30 (9 Fri, Sat) ~ Children welcome ~ Dogs allowed in bar ~ Wi-fi ~ www.theclogandbillycock.com *Recommended by Graham and Jane Bellfield, W K Wood*

SAWLEY
SD7746 Map 7

Spread Eagle

Village signed just off A59 NE of Clitheroe; BB7 4NH

Nicely refurbished pub with quite a choice of food, riverside restaurant and four real ales; bedrooms

There's a pleasing mix of nice old and quirky modern furniture in this attractive coaching inn – anything from an old settle and pine tables to new low chairs upholstered in animal print fabric, all set off well by the grey rustic stone floor. Low ceilings, cosy sectioning, a warming fire and cottagey windows keep it all feeling intimate. The dining areas are more formal, with modern stripes and (as a bit of a quip on the decorative trend for walls of unread books) a bookshelf mural (much easier to keep dust free); background music. Dark Horse Hetton Pale Ale, Moorhouses Pride of Pendle and White Witch, and Thwaites Wainwright on handpump and several wines by the glass. They have two porches for smokers, and individually furnished, comfortable bedrooms. The pub is handy for exhilarating walks in the Forest of Bowland and close to the substantial ruins of a 12th-c cistercian abbey.

A wide choice of food includes sandwiches, chicken liver pâté with onion jam, twice-baked cheese soufflé, fish or meat sharing platters, a pie of the day, spiced cauliflower and chickpea tagine, steak burger with cheese, bacon and toasted muffin, lamb casserole with dumplings, smoked haddock with poached free-range egg and mustard cream, and puddings such as cherry bakewell tart and chocolate torte; they also offer a two- and three-course set menu (12-2, 5.30-7.30). *Benchmark main dish: slow-cooked lamb shank with pickled cucumber and caper gravy £14.50. Two-course evening meal £20.00.*

Individual Inns ~ Managers Greg and Natalie Barns ~ Real ale ~ (01200) 441202 ~ Open 11-11 (10.30 Sun) ~ Bar food 12-2, 5.30-9; 12-2, 6-9.30 Sat; 12-7.30 Sun ~ Restaurant ~ Children welcome ~ Dogs allowed in bar ~ Wi-fi ~ Live events through the year; phone for details ~ Bedrooms: £92/£110 ~ www.spreadeaglesawley.co.uk *Recommended by Simon and Mandy King, Steve Whalley, John and Sylvia Harrop, W K Wood*

STALYBRIDGE

SJ9598 Map 7

Station Buffet 🍺 £

The Station, Rassbottom Street; SK15 1RF

Classic Victorian station buffet bar with eight quickly changing beers and tasty home-cooked meals

A charming elaboration of what remains firmly a working station buffet, this unpretentious place has been slightly smartened up recently. But the fine range of eight changing beers on handpump remains: Timothy Taylors Landlord and a beer from Millstone, plus six quickly rotating guests from breweries such as Acorn, Bradfield, Magic Rock, Marble, Moorhouses and Sportsman; also, seven wines by the glass, ten malt whiskies and a couple of farm ciders. The bar has a welcoming fire below an etched-glass mirror, period advertisements, photographs of the station and other railway memorabilia on cosy wood-panelled and red walls, and there's a conservatory. An extension along the platform leads into what was the ladies' waiting room and part of the stationmaster's quarters, featuring original ornate ceilings and Victorian-style wallpaper.

Incredibly good value food includes hot paninis, cold muffins and toasties, all-day breakfast, freshly baked pies, chargrilled chicken caesar salad, pork and leek sausage casserole with herb mash, chicken wrapped in bacon with barbecue sauce and cheese, and home-made burger with onion relish, coleslaw and chips; spice night on Wednesdays, monthly greek evening and Sunday afternoon teas. *Benchmark main dish: pie, peas and gravy £3.95.*

Free house ~ Licensee Sam Smith ~ Real ale ~ No credit cards ~ (0161) 303 0007 ~ Open 11-11; 12-10.30 Sun ~ Bar food 11 (12 Sun)-4, 5-7 (9 Weds); not weekend evenings ~ Children welcome ~ Dogs welcome ~ Wi-fi ~ Live folk Sat evening ~ www.stalybridgebuffetbar.co.uk *Recommended by Andy and Jill Kassube, John Fiander*

UPPERMILL

SD0006 Map 7

Church Inn 🍺 £

From the main street (A607), look out for the sign for Saddleworth Church, and turn off up this steep narrow lane – keep on up!; OL3 6LW

Community pub with big range of own-brew beers at unbeatable bargain prices and tasty food; children very welcome

L ively and always packed, this cheerful local pub brews up to 11 of its own, very good value Saddleworth beers – though, if the water levels from the spring aren't high enough for brewing, they bring in guests such as Black Sheep and Copper Dragon. Some of their own seasonal ales are named after the licensee's children, only appearing around their birthdays; two home-brewed lagers on tap too. The big unspoilt L-shaped main bar has high beams and some stripped stone, settles, pews, a good individual mix of chairs, lots of attractive prints and staffordshire and other china on a high delft shelf, jugs, brasses and so forth. TV (when there's sport on) and unobtrusive background music. There's a conservatory that opens on to the terrace. On Wednesdays the local bellringers arrive to practise with a set of handbells kept here; and anyone can join in the morris dancers on Thursdays. Children enjoy all the animals, including rabbits, chickens, dogs, ducks, geese, alpacas, horses, 14 peacocks in the next-door field and some cats that live in an adjacent barn; dogs are made to feel very welcome. It's next to an isolated church, with fine views down the valley.

🍴 A big choice of very good value food includes sandwiches, pâté and toast, spicy chicken wings with a dip, steak and mushroom in ale pie, vegetable fajita sizzler, full english breakfast, gammon with egg or pineapple, lamb shank in minted gravy, mixed grill, and puddings such as chocolate fudge cake and apple crumble. *Benchmark main dish: deep-fried cod and chips £8.25. Two-course evening meal £15.00.*

Own brew ~ Licensee Christine Taylor ~ Real ale ~ (01457) 820902 ~ Open 12-midnight (1am Sat) ~ Bar food 12-3, 5-9; 12-9 Fri-Sun and bank holidays ~ Restaurant ~ Children welcome ~ Dogs allowed in bar ~ Wi-fi ~ www.churchinnsaddleworth.co.uk
Recommended by James Dean, Sharon Jacques, Andrew Laurence, John Fiander

 WADDINGTON   SD7243   Map 7
Lower Buck
Edisford Road; BB7 3HU

Hospitable village pub with reasonably priced, tasty food and five real ales

This cosy, friendly little place is just right for a break after walking in the nearby Ribble Valley. The several small, neatly kept cream-painted bars and dining rooms, each with a warming coal fire, have plenty of chatty customers, good solid chairs and settles on carpet or stripped wooden floors and lots of paintings on the walls. Welcoming staff serve up to five real ales on handpump, such as Bowland Hen Harrier, Moorhouses Premier Bitter, Reedley Hallows Filly Close Blonde and Timothy Taylors Landlord, and ten wines by the glass; darts and pool. There are picnic-sets out on cobbles at the front and in the sunny back garden.

🍴 Popular food includes sandwiches, duck terrine with toast, potted Morecambe Bay shrimps, vegetable lasagne, cottage pie, cumberland sausages with onion gravy, plaice with a creamy prawn sauce, mixed grill, and puddings. *Benchmark main dish: steak and mushroom pie £10.95. Two-course evening meal £18.50.*

Free house ~ Licensee Andrew Warburton ~ Real ale ~ (01200) 423342 ~ Open 11-11 (midnight Sat); 12-11 Sun ~ Bar food 12-2.30, 6-9; 12-9 Sat, Sun and bank holidays ~ Children welcome ~ Dogs allowed in bar ~ Wi-fi ~ www.lowerbuckinn.co.uk
Recommended by Caroline Prescott, Isobel Mackinlay

 WHITEWELL   SD6546   Map 7
Inn at Whitewell ★ 🎖️ ♈ 🍺 🛏️
Most easily reached by B6246 from Whalley; road through Dunsop Bridge from B6478 is also good; BB7 3AT

Elegant manor house with smartly pubby atmosphere, top quality food, exceptional wine list, three ales and professional, friendly service; luxury bedrooms

This civilised and elegant old manor house has been a firm favourite with our readers – and us – for years. It's in a fantastic spot with plenty of surrounding walks and they own several miles of trout, salmon and sea trout fishing on the Hodder; picnic hamper on request. There's an idyllic view from the riverside bar and adjacent terrace. Rooms have handsome old wood furnishings, including antique settles, oak gate-leg tables and sonorous clocks, set off beautifully against powder blue walls neatly hung with big appealing prints. The pubby main bar has roaring log fires in attractive stone fireplaces and heavy curtains on sturdy wooden rails; one area has a selection of newspapers and magazines, local maps and guidebooks. There's a piano for anyone who wants to play, and board games. Early evening sees a cheerful bustle that later settles to a more tranquil and relaxing atmosphere. Drinks include a marvellous wine list of around 230 wines with 16 by the glass (reception has a good wine shop), organic ginger beer, lemonade and fruit juices and up to five real ales on handpump, which might come from Bowland, Copper Dragon, Hawkshead, Timothy Taylors and Tirril. The bedrooms are lovely (several have open fires) and they also have a self-catering holiday house.

Using top quality local produce, the rewarding food includes lunchtime sandwiches, grilled home-made black pudding with cheese mash and apple purée, potted crab with pickled cucumber and avocado purée, cheese and onion pie, spicy cumberland sausages with an egg or onion sauce, chicken in chilli, lime and coconut milk with spicy peanut sauce, slow-roast lamb with hotpot potatoes and carrot purée, and puddings such as sticky toffee pudding with butterscotch sauce and a cheesecake of the day. *Benchmark main dish: poached haddock and creamy prawn pie £11.25. Two-course evening meal £21.00.*

Free house ~ Licensee Charles Bowman ~ Real ale ~ (01200) 448222 ~ Open 10am-11pm ~ Bar food 12-2, 7.30-9.30 ~ Restaurant ~ Children welcome ~ Dogs allowed in bar and bedrooms ~ Wi-fi ~ Bedrooms: £90/£125 ~ www.innatwhitewell.com
Recommended by Barry Collett, David and Sue Atkinson, John and Sylvia Harrop, W K Wood, Roger and Anne Newbury

WORSLEY
Old Hall ♀ ◄

SD7401   Map 7

A mile from M60 junction 13: A575 Walkden Road, then after roundabout take first left into Worsley Park; M28 2QT

Very handsomely converted landmark building, now a welcoming pub scoring high on all counts

This grand timbered mansion, rebuilt and extended in the 18th and 19th centuries, was a seat of the Duke of Bridgewater (for whom James Brindley planned the UK's first proper canal, to transport coal from his mines here). It recently spent some time as a Brewers Fayre chain pub before being taken in hand, in 2013, by Brunning & Price, and restored to make the most of some handsome architectural features. As is usual with B&P, the relaxed and chatty main area spreads generously around the feature central bar, where they serve 17 good wines by the glass, 123 malt whiskies, 38 gins and changing ales on handpump such as Brightside Brindley Blonde, Castle Rock Harvest Pale, Conwy Honey Fayre, Gwynt y Ddraig Black Dragon, Hobsons Mild, and the Original and Black Bee beers brewed for them by Phoenix. There's also the usual abundance of well chosen prints, as well as fireside armchairs, rugs on oak parquet, daily papers, board games, unobtrusive piped music and the good team of well trained staff that B&P aficionados have come to expect. We particularly like the gracefully arched inglenook and matching window alcove, the handsome staircase, the glowing mahogany panelling and the elegant roof lanterns. A big flagstoned terrace has heavy teak tables, and the neat lawn beyond has a fountain among the picnic-table sets; a belt of trees separates it from the golf course of the neighbouring Marriott Hotel.

Good, well presented food includes sandwiches, rabbit and tarragon faggot with carrot purée, char siu pork belly with pak choi and pickled ginger, butternut squash risotto with blue cheese, rosemary and garlic chicken with wild mushroom, bacon and spinach pasta, smoked haddock and salmon fishcakes, trio of duck with plum and ginger rillette and candied kumquats, and puddings such as bread and butter pudding with apricot sauce and raspberry bakewell with pistachio ice-cream. *Benchmark main dish: braised lamb shoulder with dauphinoise potatoes and red wine gravy £16.95. Two-course evening meal £20.00.*

Brunning & Price ~ Manager David Green ~ Real ale ~ (0161) 703 8706 ~ Open 10.30am-11pm (10.30 Sun) ~ Bar food 12-10 (9.30 Sun) ~ Restaurant ~ Children welcome ~ Dogs allowed in bar ~ Wi-fi ~ www.brunningandprice.co.uk/worsleyoldhall *Recommended by Peter Pilbeam, William Wright*

Also Worth a Visit in Lancashire

Besides the fully inspected pubs, you might like to try these pubs that have been recommended to us and described by readers. Do tell us what you think of them: feedback@goodguides.com

ARKHOLME   SD5872

★ **Redwell** (01524) 221240

B6254 Over Kellet–Arkholme; LA6 1BQ Nicely renovated 17th-c country pub-restaurant, spacious interior with wooden tables and chairs on flagstones, also some easy chairs, woodburners, newspapers and magazines, very good individual cooking from landlord-chef including ingredients from next-door smokehouse, home-baked bread, well kept beers, friendly attentive service; background music; tables outside, closed Sun evening, all Mon-Weds. *(Graham and Jane Bellfield, John and Sylvia Harrop, Diane Fairhall, Fay Craddock)*

BARLEY   SD8240

Pendle (01282) 614808

Barley Lane; BB12 9JX Friendly 1930s stone pub in shadow of Pendle Hill, three cosy rooms, two log fires, and five well kept regional ales, simple substantial food (all day weekends) using local produce including good sandwiches, conservatory; garden, lovely village and good walking country, self-catering accommodation, open all day Fri-Sun. *(Dr Kevan Tucker)*

BARNSTON   SJ2783

★ **Fox & Hounds** (0151) 648 7685

3 miles from M53 junction 3: A552 towards Woodchurch, then left on A551; CH61 1BW Well run pub with a cheerful welcome; Brimstage, Theakstons and guests, 60 malt whiskies and good value traditional lunchtime food, roomy carpeted bay-windowed lounge with built-in banquettes and plush-cushioned captain's chairs around solid tables, old local prints and collection of police and other headgear, charming old quarry-tiled corner with antique range, copper kettles, built-in pine kitchen cupboards, enamel food bins and earthenware, small locals' bar (worth a look for its highly traditional layout and collection of horsebrasses and metal ashtrays), snug where children allowed; dogs welcome in bar, picnic-sets at back among colourful tubs and hanging baskets, open all day. *(Tony Tollitt)*

BAY HORSE   SD4952

★ **Bay Horse** (01524) 791204

1.2 miles from M6 junction 33: A6 southwards, then off on left; LA2 0HR Civilised country dining pub (a useful motorway stop); cosily pubby bar with good log fire, cushioned wall banquettes and fresh flowers, ales such as Black Sheep, Lancaster and Moorhouses, 15 wines by the glass, smarter restaurant with cosy corners, another log fire and carefully presented innovative food (not Sun evening and not especially cheap), friendly efficient service; children welcome, garden tables, two bedrooms in converted barn over road, closed Mon. *(Hugh Roberts)*

BELMONT   SD6715

Black Dog (01204) 811218

Church Street (A675); BL7 8AB Nicely set Holts pub with enjoyable food all day (till 6pm Sun), well kept beers and friendly service, cheery small-roomed traditional core, coal and gas fires, picture-window dining extension; children and dogs welcome, seats outside with moorland views above village, attractive part-covered smokers' area, good walks, three decent well priced bedrooms, open all day. *(Anon)*

BLACKO   SD8641

Rising Sun (01282) 612173

A682 towards Gisburn; BB9 6LS Welcoming traditional village pub tied to Moorhouses, four of their ales kept well plus an interesting guest, enjoyable low-priced pubby food including local dish 'stew-and-hard', tiled entry, open fires in three rooms off main bar; walkers and dogs welcome, tables on front terrace with Pendle Hill view, open all day Fri-Sun, from 5pm other days. *(Dr Kevan Tucker)*

BLACKPOOL   SD3035

Pump & Truncheon (01253) 624099

Bonny Street; FY1 5AR Old real-ale pub tucked away behind the Golden Mile opposite police HQ; Moorhouses and guests, good choice of bottled beers too, bargain food, bare boards and stone floors, coal fire; open all day. *(Sam White)*

BLACKSTONE EDGE   SD9617
★**White House** (01706) 378456

A58 Ripponden–Littleborough, just W of B6138; OL15 0LG Beautifully placed moorland dining pub with remote views, emphasis on good value hearty food from sandwiches up (all day Sun), prompt friendly service, Black Sheep, Theakstons and a couple of regional guests, belgian bottled beers, cheerful atmosphere, carpeted main bar with fire, other areas off, most tables used for food; children welcome. *(Anon)*

BOLTON   SD7112
Brewery Tap (01204) 302837

Belmont Road; BL1 7AN Tap for Bank Top, their full range kept well and a guest, knowledgeable friendly staff, no food; dogs welcome, seats outside, open all day. *(Anon)*

BOLTON   SD6809
Victoria (01204) 849944

Markland Hill; BL1 5AG Refurbished and extended family-run pub known locally as Fannys, good choice of enjoyable food including some regional dishes, plenty of wines by the glass, well kept ales such as Jennings and Marstons, good service; children welcome, seats outside on decking, open all day. *(W K Wood)*

BOLTON   SD6913
Wilton Arms (01204) 303307

Belmont Road, Horrocks Fold; BL1 7BT Friendly roadside pub on edge of West Pennine Moors, reasonably priced fresh food and four well kept regional ales including Bank Top Flat Cap, open fires, conservatory; children welcome, valley views and good walks, open all day. *(Dr and Mrs A K Clarke, W K Wood)*

BOLTON BY BOWLAND   SD7849
Coach & Horses (01200) 447202

Main Street; BB7 4NW Stone-built beamed pub-restaurant, strikingly modernised, with black chandeliers, bold fabric wall hangings and big mirrors, enjoyable food from pub favourites to more unusual choices, a couple of ales such as Bowland and Moorhouses, good choice of wines, open fires; children welcome, tables out at back, lovely streamside village with interesting church, three bedrooms, open all day weekends (food till 7pm Sun), closed Mon, Tues. *(Phil Denton)*

BRINDLE   SD5924
★**Cavendish Arms** (01254) 852912

3 miles from M6 junction 29, by A6 and B5256 (Sandy Lane); PR6 8NG Traditional village pub dating from the 15th c, welcoming and popular, with good inexpensive home-made food (all day weekends) from sandwiches up, Banks's, Marstons and two guest ales, beams, cosy

---

snugs with open fires, stained-glass windows, carpets throughout; children welcome, dogs in tap room, heated canopied terrace with water feature, more tables in side garden, good walks, open all day. *(Anon)*

BROUGHTON   SD4838
★**Plough at Eaves** (01772) 690233

A6 N through Broughton, first left into Station Lane under a mile after traffic lights, then left after 1.5 miles, Eaves Lane; PR4 0BJ Pleasantly unpretentious old country tavern with two beamed homely bars, well kept Thwaites ales, good choice of enjoyable food (all day Sun), friendly service, lattice windows and traditional furnishings, old guns over woodburner in one room, Royal Doulton figurines above log fire in dining bar with conservatory; quiet background music, games machine; children welcome, front terrace and spacious side/back garden, well equipped play area, open all day weekends (till 1am Sat), closed Mon except bank holidays. *(Anon)*

BURNLEY   SD8432
Bridge Bier Huis (01282) 411304

Bank Parade; BB11 1UH Open-plan town-centre pub with five well kept/priced ales including Moorhouses, lots of foreign beers on tap and by the bottle, real cider, bargain straightforward food till 7pm (5pm Sun), friendly atmosphere, Weds quiz and some live music; open all day (till 1am Fri, Sat), closed Mon, Tues. *(Anon)*

BURY   SD8313
Trackside (0161) 764 6461

East Lancashire Railway Station, Bolton Street; BL9 0EY Welcoming busy station bar by East Lancs steam railway, bright, airy and clean with nine changing ales, bottled imports, real ciders and great range of whiskies, enjoyable home-made food (not Mon, Tues), fine display of beer labels on ceiling; children welcome till 7.30pm, platform tables, open all day. *(Anon)*

CARNFORTH   SD5173
Longlands (01524) 781256

Tewitfield, about 2 miles N; A6070, off A6; LA6 1JH Family-run village inn with well liked food in bar and restaurant from pizzas and pub favourites up, four good local beers, friendly helpful staff, live music Mon; children and dogs welcome, bedrooms and self-catering cottages, Lancaster Canal nearby, open all day. *(Anon)*

CHEADLE HULME   SJ8785
Church Inn (0161) 485 1897

Ravenoak Road (A5149 SE); SK8 7EG Popular old family-run pub with good interesting food (Sun till 7.30pm) including deals, well kept Robinsons beers and nice selection of wines by the glass, gleaming brass on panelled walls, warming coal fire, friendly staff and locals, back restaurant, live music most Sun evenings; children welcome, seats outside (some under cover), car park across road, open all day. *(Mike and Wena Stevenson)*

CHIPPING   SD6141
★ **Dog & Partridge**   (01995) 61201
Hesketh Lane; crossroads Chipping–Longridge with Inglewhite–Clitheroe; PR3 2TH Comfortable old-fashioned and much-altered 16th-c dining pub in grand countryside, enjoyable food (all day Sun) served by friendly staff, ales such as Thwaites and Tetleys, beams, exposed stone walls and good log fire, small armchairs around close-set tables in main lounge, restaurant; free wi-fi; children welcome, no dogs inside, open all day Sun, closed Mon, Tues evening. *(Anon)*

CHORLEY   SD5817
Yew Tree   (01257) 480344
Dill Hall Brow, Heath Charnock – out past Limbrick towards the reservoirs; PR6 9HA Attractive tucked-away restaurany pub, modernised interior with open-view kitchen, good food from bar snacks and sharing plates up, Tues tapas, Blackedge ales including one badged for them, plenty of wines by the glass, friendly helpful staff; background and some live music; children and dogs (in one part) welcome, picnic-sets out on decked area, open all day Sat, till 8.30pm Sun, closed Mon. *(Anon)*

CHORLTON CUM HARDY   SJ8193
Horse & Jockey   (0161) 860 7794
Chorlton Green; M21 9HS Refurbished low-beamed pub with mock-Tudor façade, own-brewed Bootleg ales and guests, knowledgeable chatty staff and good mix of customers, all-day bar food, more restaurany menu in high-ceilinged evening/weekend dining room (part of former Victorian brewery); children allowed till 9pm, dogs very welcome (a non-alcoholic beer for them), picnic-sets on front terrace looking across to green, open all day. *(Pat and Graham Williamson)*

CLAUGHTON   SD5666
Fenwick Arms   (01524) 221157
A683 Kirkby Lonsdale–Lancaster; LA2 9LA Old black and white dining pub recently refurbished by small local group (Seafood Pub Co); good food (all day Sun) with emphasis on fish, daily specials and weekday set lunch deal, real ales and good choice of wines by the glass, friendly accommodating staff, beams and oak floorboards, painted panelling, fireplaces with black ranges; children welcome, seats outside, open all day. *(Anon)*

COLNE   SD8940
Black Lane Ends   (01282) 863070
Skipton Old Road, Foulridge; BB8 7EP Country pub in quiet lane with good

sensibly priced food from large menu, well kept Copper Dragon and Timothy Taylors Landlord, cheerful attentive staff, two massive fires, small restaurant; children and dogs welcome, garden with play area, good Pennine views, handy for canal and reservoir walks. *(John and Eleanor Holdsworth)*

CONDER GREEN   SD4556
Stork   (01524) 751234
Just off A588; LA2 0AN Fine spot where River Conder joins the Lune estuary among bleak marshes, two blazing log fires in rambling dark-panelled rooms, good reasonably priced food with south african influences, friendly efficient staff, real ales such as Black Sheep and Lancaster; children welcome, handy for Glasson Dock, bedrooms, open all day. *(Anon)*

CROSBY   SJ3100
Crows Nest   (0151) 924 6953
Victoria Road, Great Crosby; L23 7XY Old-fashioned tile-fronted local with cosy front bar, snug and hatch-served back rooms, five well kept ales including Caledonian, friendly staff; open all day. *(Anon)*

DENSHAW   SD9710
Printers Arms   (01457) 874248
Oldham Road; OL3 5SN Above Oldham in shadow of Saddlesworth Moor, modernised interior with small log-fire bar and three other rooms, popular good value food all day including OAP menu (till 6pm, not Sun), Timothy Taylors Golden Best and a beer brewed for them by Bazens, several wines by the glass, friendly efficient young staff; lovely views from two-tier beer garden, open all day. *(Stuart Paulley)*

DENSHAW   SD9711
★ **Rams Head**   (01457) 874802
2 miles from M62 junction 22; A672 towards Oldham, pub N of village; OL3 5UN Sweeping moorland views from inviting dining pub with four thick-walled traditional little rooms, good variety of food (all day weekends) including seasonal game and seafood, well kept ales such as Marstons and Timothy Taylors, efficient friendly service, beam-and-plank ceilings, panelling, oak settles and built-in benches, log fires, tearoom and adjacent delicatessen selling local produce; soft background music; children welcome (not Sat evening), closed Mon except bank holidays. *(Michael Butler, M C and S Jeanes)*

DENTON   SJ9395
Lowes Arms   (0161) 336 3064
Hyde Road (A57); M34 3FF Thriving 19th-c family-run pub with up to four well kept ales such as local Hornbeam and Phoenix (the on-site brewery remains closed), jovial community-spirited landlord and helpful friendly staff, wide choice of good bargain food including daily specials,

bar with pool and darts, restaurant; tables outside, smokers' shelter, open all day. *(Dennis Jones)*

DIGGLE   SE0007
Diggle (01457) 872741
Village signed off A670 just N of Dobcross; OL3 5JZ Sturdy four-square hillside inn overlooking west end of Standedge Canal tunnel; good value all-day food (till 7.30pm Sun) from snacks up, well kept ales such as Black Sheep, Copper Dragon, Millstone and Timothy Taylors, helpful staff; picnic-sets among trees, quiet spot just below the moors, four bedrooms, open (and food) all day. *(Tony Hobden)*

DOBCROSS   SD9906
Swan (01457) 873451
The Square; OL3 5AA Unspoilt low-beamed 18th-c pub sympathetically refurbished by present licensees, three areas off small central bar, all with open fires, flagstones and upholstered bench seating, five Marstons-related beers and enjoyable home-made food including specials, friendly atmosphere, folk, theatre and comedy evenings in upstairs function room; children and dogs welcome, tables out at front, attractive village below moors, open all day weekends, closed Mon lunchtime. *(Tricia Curley)*

DUNHAM TOWN   SJ7488
Axe & Cleaver (01619) 283391
School Lane; WA14 4SE Big 19th-c country house knocked into spacious open-plan Chef & Brewer, well liked food from light lunchtime choices and sharing plates up, friendly service; children welcome, garden picnic-sets, handy for nearby Dunham Massey Hall (NT), open all day. *(Hilary Forrest)*

EGERTON   SD7014
Thomas Egerton (01204) 301774
Blackburn Road; BL7 9SR Friendly village pub (part of the small Welcome Taverns group), freshly made traditional food (all day Sat, till 7pm Sun), good choice of wines and rotating ales including own Dunscar Bridge, efficient service, log fire, quiz Weds and live music Fri; landscaped garden, open all day. *(Sophie McManus)*

EUXTON   SD5318
Travellers Rest (01257) 451184
Dawbers Lane (A581 W); PR7 6EG Refurbished 18th-c roadside dining pub with several connecting rooms (originally three cottages), good varied range of popular food

(all day Sat, till 6pm Sun) including daily specials, organised friendly staff, well kept Black Sheep and four guests, Thurs quiz; children welcome, dogs allowed in part of back bar, nice side garden, open all day. *(Michael Butler)*

FENCE   SD8237
Fence Gate (01282) 618101
2.6 miles from M65 junction 13; Wheatley Lane Road, just off A6068 W; BB12 9EE Imposing recently refurbished 17th-c dining pub; good choice of enjoyable if not cheap food, real ales and several wines by the glass, bar with timbers and big fire, separate champagne/prosecco bar, contemporary brasserie; background music; children welcome, open all day. *(Anon)*

FENCE   SD8237
White Swan (01282) 611773
Wheatley Lane; BB12 9QA Comfortably refurbished village pub under friendly new management; well kept Timothy Taylors and enjoyable blackboard food including popular Sun lunch, open fires; sports TV; covered and heated outside seating area, closed Mon lunchtime, otherwise open all day. *(Dr Kevan Tucker)*

GARSTANG   SD4945
Th'Owd Tithebarn (01995) 604486
Off Church Street; PR3 1PA Creeper-clad tithe barn with big terrace overlooking Lancaster Canal marina and narrow boats; linked high-raftered rooms with red patterned carpet or flagstones, upholstered stools, armchairs and leather tub seats around assorted shiny tables, lots of cartwheels, rustic lamps, horse tack and a fine old kitchen range, ales from Coniston, Kirkby Lonsdale, Lancaster and York, fair value wines by the glass, popular all-day food served by friendly staff; children welcome, dogs in bar. *(Pip White, Emma Scofield)*

GOOSNARGH   SD5738
★**Horns** (01772) 865230
On junction of Horns Lane and Inglewhite Road; pub signed off B5269, towards Chipping; PR3 2FJ Plush early 18th-c inn with relaxed atmosphere, neatly kept carpeted rooms with log fires, popular food from pub standards to local duck and pheasant, Bowland and guest ales, plenty of wines by the glass and good choice of malts, friendly helpful service; background music; children welcome, garden, six bedrooms (some with road noise), caravan park, not far from M6. *(Ray and Winifred Halliday)*

GREAT ECCLESTON   SD4240
Farmers Arms (01995) 672018
Halsall Square (just off A586); PR3 0YE
Attractively refurbished pub-restaurant,
part of small local group since 2013; good
interesting food (all day Sun) with emphasis
on fish/seafood and grills, daily specials, four
ales including Black Sheep and good choice
of wines, friendly helpful staff, upstairs
dining room, open fires; children welcome,
paved outside area with teak furniture, open
all day. *(Anon)*

GREENFIELD   SD9904
Railway Hotel (01457) 872307
*Shaw Hall Bank Road, opposite
station; OL3 7JZ* Friendly four-room pub
with half a dozen well kept mainly local
ales, no food, live music Thurs, Fri and Sun,
log fire, games bar with darts and pool; on
the Transpennine Rail Ale Trail, open all
day. *(Tony Hobden)*

GRINDLETON   SD7646
Buck (01200) 441768
Sawley Road; BB7 4QS
Friendly 19th-c bay-windowed pub in nice
village, decent good value food (all day
Fri-Sun) and three well kept changing
ales, open fire, pool; children and walkers
welcome, beer garden, open all day. *(Brian
and Anna Marsden)*

GRINDLETON   SD7545
★Duke of York (01200) 441266
*Off A59 NE of Clitheroe, either via
Chatburn, or off A671 in W Bradford;
Brow Top; BB7 4QR* Welcoming chef-
landlord and neat helpful staff in comfortable
civilised dining pub, really good imaginative
food with plenty of attention to detail, set
deals too, nice wines and coffee, well kept
Black Sheep and Copper Dragon, various
areas (one with open fire), views over Ribble
Valley to Pendle Hill; tables out on raised
deck and in garden behind, closed Mon.
(Steve Whalley)

HAWKSHAW   SD7515
Red Lion (01204) 856600
Ramsbottom Road; BL8 4JS Pub-hotel
owned by Lees, their ales, enjoyable
reasonably priced food and good service;
children welcome, bedrooms, quiet spot by
River Irwell. *(John and Sylvia Harrop)*

HESKIN GREEN   SD5315
Farmers Arms (01257) 451276
*Wood Lane (B5250, N of M6 junction 27);
PR7 5NP* Popular redecorated country
pub under long-serving family, good choice
of well priced home-made food in two-level
dining area, cheerful helpful staff, ales such
as Jennings, Prospect, Timothy Taylors and
Thwaites, heavy black beams, sparkling
brasses, china and stuffed animals, darts in
public bar, Thurs quiz; background music,

Sky TV; children welcome, dogs in bar/lounge,
picnic-sets in big colourful garden with play
area, more tables front and side, five good
value bedrooms, open all day. *(Anon)*

HEST BANK   SD4766
★Hest Bank Inn (01524) 824339
*Hest Bank Lane; off A6 just N of
Lancaster; LA2 6DN* Good choice of
enjoyable food in picturesque three-
bar coaching inn, nice setting close to
Morecambe Bay, well kept ales such as Black
Sheep and Thwaites, decent wines, friendly
helpful young staff, separate restaurant
area with pleasant conservatory; children
welcome, plenty of tables out by Lancaster
Canal, open all day. *(Clive and Fran Dutson)*

HORNBY   SD5868
Castle (01524) 221204
Main Street; LA2 8JT Nicely restored
sizeable village inn; bar with sofas and open
fires, bistro and restaurant, enjoyable food
from sandwiches, pub favourites and pizzas
up, Black Sheep, Bowland and guests, good
selection of other drinks, friendly helpful
staff; six bedrooms, open all day. *(Anon)*

HURST GREEN   SD6837
★Shireburn Arms (01254) 826678
*Whalley Road (B6243 Clitheroe–
Goosnargh); BB7 9QJ* Welcoming 17th-c
hotel; peaceful Ribble Valley views from big
light and airy restaurant and lovely neatly
kept garden with attractive terrace, good
food (all day weekends) from sandwiches
through traditional dishes with a modern
twist to daily specials, armchairs, sofas and
log fire in beamed and flagstoned lounge
bar with linked dining area, two well kept
ales such as Moorhouses and Thwaites,
several wines by the glass, friendly helpful
service, daily papers; children welcome,
dogs too (may get a treat), pretty Tolkien
walk from here, 22 comfortable bedrooms,
open all day (from 9am for coffee).
(Steve Whalley)

HYDE   SJ9495
Cheshire Ring 07917 055629
*Manchester Road (A57, between M67
junctions 2 and 3); SK14 2BJ* Welcoming
refurbished drinkers' pub tied to Beartown
brewery, their good value ales kept well
along with guests, also imports (draught and
bottled), farm ciders/perries and good house
wines, Thurs curries, quiz Weds; background
music; open all day weekends, closed
weekday lunchtimes. *(Dennis Jones)*

HYDE   SJ9493
Joshua Bradley (0161) 406 6776
Stockport Road, Gee Cross; SK14 5EZ
Former mansion handsomely converted to
pub-restaurant keeping panelling, moulded
ceilings and imposing fireplaces, good range
of well priced popular food, Hydes and a
couple of guest beers in fine condition,

friendly efficient staff; children welcome, heated terrace, play area. *(Dennis Jones)*

HYDE · SJ9595
Sportsman *(0161) 368 5000*
Mottram Road; SK14 2NN Bright cheerful Victorian local, Pennine, Rosendale and lots of changing guests (frequent beer festivals), welcoming licensees, bargain bar food, popular upstairs cuban restaurant, bare boards and open fires, pub games; children and dogs welcome, back terrace with heated smokers' shelter, open all day (from 1pm weekdays). *(Dennis Jones)*

IRBY · SJ2586
Irby Mill *(0151) 604 0194*
Mill Lane, off Greasby Road; CH49 3NT Converted miller's sandstone cottage (original windmill demolished 1898), friendly and welcoming, with well kept Greene King IPA, Wells & Youngs Bombardier and at least four guests, good choice of wines by the glass, ample helpings of popular reasonably priced food all day (till 6pm Sun) from sandwiches up, friendly efficient service, two low-beamed traditional flagstoned rooms and extended carpeted dining area, log fire, interesting old photographs and history; tables on terraces and revamped side area, good local walks, open all day and gets crowded evenings/weekends when parking limited. *(Mark Delap, Paul Humphreys, Tony Tollitt)*

LANCASTER · SD4761
★Borough *(01524) 64170*
Dalton Square; LA1 1PP Popular city-centre pub, stylish and civilised, with chandeliers, dark leather sofas and armchairs, lamps on antique tables, high stools and elbow tables, seven ales including Bowland, Hawkshead and Lancaster, lots of bottled beers, big dining room with central tables and booths along one side, enjoyable food with much emphasis on local suppliers, daily specials and meal deals, jams and local produce for sale, upstairs comedy night Sun; children and dogs welcome, lovely tree-sheltered garden, open all day. *(Anon)*

LANCASTER · SD4761
★Sun *(01524) 66006*
Church Street; LA1 1ET Both traditional and comfortably contemporary, good range of customers, five well kept Lancaster ales and guests, plenty of continental beers and good choice wines by the glass, enjoyable food from pub staples up using local suppliers, beamed bar with panelling, chunky modern tables, several fireplaces, conservatory, Tues quiz; background music and TV; children welcome away from bar, terrace, 16 comfortable bedrooms, open all day. *(David Aston)*

LANCASTER · SD4761
★Water Witch *(01524) 63828*
Parking in Aldcliffe Road behind Royal Lancaster Infirmary, off A6; LA1 1SU Attractive conversion of 18th-c canalside barge-horse stabling, flagstones, stripped stone, rafters and pitch-pine panelling, seven well kept changing ales (third-of-a-pint glasses available) from mirrored bar, enjoyable good value food all day including specials, prompt pleasant service, upstairs restaurant; children in eating areas, tables outside. *(Anon)*

LANESHAW BRIDGE · SD9141
Alma *(01282) 857830*
Emmott Lane, off A6068 E of Colne; BB8 7EG Renovated pub with wide choice of good well priced food, real ales and several wines by the glass, friendly efficient service, large garden room extension; background music; children and dogs welcome, clean comfortable bedrooms. *(John and Eleanor Holdsworth)*

LITTLEBOROUGH · SD9517
Moor Cock *(01706) 378156*
Halifax Road (A58); OL15 0LD Long roadside inn high on the moors with far-reaching views, friendly and popular, with wide range of good value food (all day weekends) from sandwiches and pub favourites up in flagstoned bar or restaurant, four well kept beers; Sky TV, Tues quiz; terrace seating, seven comfortable reasonably priced bedrooms, open all day. *(Simon Le Fort)*

LIVERPOOL · SJ3489
Baltic Fleet *(0151) 709 3116*
Wapping, near Albert Dock; L1 8DQ Unusual bow-fronted pub with six interesting beers including Wapping (brewed in the cellar), several wines by the glass, enjoyable straightforward well priced food (not Sat lunchtime) such as traditional scouse, weekend breakfasts, bare boards, big arched windows, simple mix of furnishings and nautical paraphernalia, upstairs lounge; background music, TV; children welcome in eating areas, dogs in bar, back terrace, open all day. *(Claes Mauroy)*

LIVERPOOL · SJ3589
Belvedere *(0151) 709 0303*
Sugnall Street; L7 7EB Unspoilt 19th-c two-room pub with friendly chatty atmosphere, original fittings including etched glass, coal fires, four well kept ales such as Liverpool Craft and Liverpool Organic, good selection of bottled beers and fine choice of gins (excellent gin and tonic); open all day. *(Anon)*

Virtually all pubs in this book sell wine by the glass. We mention wines if they are a cut above the average.

LIVERPOOL   SJ3589
Cracke (0151) 709 4171
Rice Street; L1 9BB Friendly unsmart local
popular with students; Liverpool Organic,
Thwaites, and several guests, farm cider,
sandwiches till 6pm, small unspoilt bar with
bare boards and bench seats, snug and bigger
back room with unusual Beatles diorama, lots
of posters for local events; juke box, sports
TV; picnic-sets in sizeable back garden, open
all day. *(Claes Mauroy)*

LIVERPOOL   SJ3589
Dispensary (0151) 709 2160
Renshaw Street; L1 2SP Small busy
central pub worth knowing for its very well
kept local beers (up to ten), good choice of
bottled imports too, no food, bare boards
and polished panelling, wonderful etched
windows, comfortable raised back bar with
coal fire, Victorian medical artefacts; notices
on house rules, service mostly friendly,
background music, silent TVs; open all day.
(Claes Mauroy)

LIVERPOOL   SJ3589
Fly in the Loaf (0151) 708 0817
Hardman Street; L1 9AS Former bakery
with smart gleaming bar serving Okells
and up to seven ales from smaller brewers,
foreign beers too, enjoyable simple home-
made food (not Mon) at low prices, friendly
service, long room with panelling, some
raised sections, even a pulpit; background
music, sports TV, upstairs lavatories, open all
day, till midnight weekends. *(Claes Mauroy)*

LIVERPOOL   SJ3490
Globe (0151) 707 0067
Cases Street, opposite station; L1 1HW
Popular little local in busy shopping area,
friendly staff, good selection of well kept
ales, sloping floor to quieter cosy back room;
background music; open all day. *(Anon)*

LIVERPOOL   SJ3490
Hole In Ye Wall (0151) 227 3809
Off Dale Street; L2 2AW Well restored
18th-c pub with thriving local atmosphere in
high-beamed panelled bar, seven changing
ales fed by gravity from upstairs (no cellar
as pub is on Quaker burial site), sandwiches
and basic food till 5pm, free chip butties Sun
when there's a traditional sing-along, friendly
staff, plenty of woodwork, stained glass and
old Liverpool photographs, coal-effect gas fire
in unusual brass-canopied fireplace; no dogs;
children allowed till 5pm, open all day.
(Claes Mauroy)

LIVERPOOL   SJ3490
Hub (0151) 709 2401
Hanover Street; L1 4AA Bar-bistro in
bow-fronted corner building, light modern

interior with wood flooring and big windows,
decent choice of food from sandwiches and
stone-baked pizzas up, reasonably priced
wines, five ales including Liverpool Organic;
children welcome, open all day and can get
very busy. *(Anon)*

LIVERPOOL   SJ3490
Lion (0151) 236 1734
Moorfields, off Tithebarn Street; L2 2BP
Beautifully preserved ornate Victorian
tavern, great changing beer choice and
over 80 malt whiskies, good value simple
lunchtime food including home-made
pork pies, friendly staff, sparkling etched
glass and serving hatches in central bar,
unusual wallpaper and matching curtains,
big mirrors, panelling and tilework, two
small back lounges, one with fine glass
dome, coal fire; open all day. *(Claes Mauroy,
C A Bryson)*

LIVERPOOL   SJ3489
Monro (0151) 707 9933
Duke Street; L1 5AG Stylish gastropub,
popular, comfortable and well run, with
good choice of interesting food including
vegetarian options, lunchtime/early evening
deals (not Sun), well kept Marstons and
guests from small bar, good friendly service;
courtyard tables, open all day. *(Anon)*

LIVERPOOL   SJ3589
Peter Kavanaghs (0151) 709 3443
*Egerton Street, off Catherine Street;
L8 7LY* Shuttered Victorian pub with
interesting décor in several small rooms
including old-world murals, stained glass and
all manner of bric-a-brac (lots hanging from
ceiling), piano, wooden settles and real fires,
well kept Greene King Abbot and guests,
friendly licensees, popular with locals and
students; open all day (till 1am Fri, Sat).
(Claes Mauroy)

LIVERPOOL   SJ3589
Philharmonic Dining Rooms
(0151) 707 2837 *36 Hope Street; corner
of Hardman Street; L1 9BX* Beautifully
preserved Victorian pub with wonderful
period detail; centrepiece mosaic-faced
counter, heavily carved and polished
mahogany partitions radiating out under
intricate plasterwork ceiling, main hall with
stained glass of Boer War heroes Baden-
Powell and Lord Roberts, rich panelling,
mosaic floor and copper panels of musicians
above fireplace, other areas including two
side rooms called Brahms and Liszt, the
original Adamant gents' is also worth a look,
ten real ales, several wines by the glass and
decent choice of malt whiskies, enjoyable
fair-priced food, good service; background
music and machines; children welcome till
7pm, open (and food) all day. *(Mike and Wena*

There are report forms at the back of the book.

Stevenson, Canon Michael Bourdeaux, C A Bryson, Dr Kevan Tucker, Susan and John Douglas, Tom and Jill Jones and others)

LIVERPOOL SJ3490
Richmond (0151) 709 2614
Williamson Street; L1 1EB Popular small corner pub in pedestrianised area, changing ales with support for smaller brewers such as Burscough, Liverpool Organic, Southport and George Wright, over 50 malt whiskies; sports TVs; tables out in front, four bedrooms, open all day. *(Anon)*

LIVERPOOL SJ3589
Roscoe Head (0151) 709 4365
Roscoe Street; L1 2SX Unassuming old local with cosy bar, snug and two other spotless unspoilt little rooms, friendly long-serving landlady, well kept Jennings, Tetleys and four guests, inexpensive home-made lunches (not weekends), interesting memorabilia, traditional games including crib, quiz Tues and Thurs; open all day till midnight. *(Claes Mauroy, C A Bryson)*

LIVERPOOL SJ3490
Ship & Mitre (0151) 236 0859
Dale Street; L2 2JH Friendly local with fine art deco exterior and ship-like interior, popular with university people, up to a dozen changing unusual ales (many beer festivals), real ciders and over 70 bottled continentals, good value basic food (all day Fri-Sun), upstairs function room with original 1930s décor; well behaved children (till 7pm) and dogs welcome, open all day. *(C A Bryson, Kerry Law)*

LIVERPOOL SJ3589
Swan (0151) 709 5281
Wood Street; L1 4DQ Busy unsmart three-floor pub with bare boards and dim lighting, up to eight ales including good value Hydes, bottled belgian beers and a real cider, well priced cobs and weekday lunches, friendly staff; loud rock juke box, silent fruit machine; open all day (till 2am Thurs-Sat). *(Anon)*

LIVERPOOL SJ3490
★Thomas Rigbys (0151) 236 3269
Dale Street; L2 2EZ Spacious beamed and panelled Victorian pub, mosaic flooring, old tiles and etched glass, Okells and three changing guests from impressively long bar, also good range of imported draught and bottled beers, steps up to main area, table service from attentive staff, reasonably priced hearty home-made food (all day till 7pm); disabled access, seats in big courtyard, open all day. *(Claes Mauroy)*

LIVERPOOL SJ3490
White Star (0151) 231 6861
Rainford Gardens, off Matthew Street; L2 6PT Lively traditional local dating from the 18th c, cosy bar, lots of woodwork,

boxing photographs, White Star shipping line and Beatles memorabilia (they used to rehearse in back room), well kept ales such as Bowland and Caledonian Deuchars IPA, basic lunchtime food, friendly staff; sports TVs; open all day. *(Claes Mauroy)*

LONGRIDGE SD6037
New Drop (01254) 878338
Higher Road, Longridge Fell, parallel to B6243 Longridge–Clitheroe; PR3 2YX Popular modernised dining pub in lovely moors-edge country overlooking Ribble Valley, good reasonably priced food, decent wines and three well kept ales (usually have Bowland Hen Harrier), friendly helpful service; children welcome, open all day Sun, closed Mon. *(David Heath)*

LYDGATE SD9704
★White Hart (01457) 872566
Stockport Road; Lydgate not marked on some maps and not the one near Todmorden; take A669 Oldham–Saddleworth, right at brow of hill to A6050 after almost 2.5 miles; OL4 4JJ Smart up-to-date dining pub overlooking Pennine moors, mix of locals in bar or simpler end rooms, and diners in elegant brasserie with smartly dressed staff, high quality food (not cheap), Lees, Timothy Taylors and a guest beer, 16 wines by the glass, old beams and exposed stonework contrasting with deep red or purple walls and modern artwork, open fires, newspapers; TV in lounge; children welcome, dogs in bar, picnic-sets on back lawn making most of position, 12 bedrooms, open all day. *(Anon)*

LYTHAM SD3627
★Taps (01253) 736226
A584 S of Blackpool; Henry Street – in centre, one street in from West Beach; FY8 5LE Cheerful town pub a couple of minutes from the beach; around ten real ales (view-in cellar) including Greene King IPA, proper cider, simple lunchtime food (not Sun); open-plan Victorian-style bar with bare boards and stripped-brick walls, nice old chairs in bays around sides, open fires and a coal-effect gas fire between built-in bookcases, plenty of stained glass; quiz Mon; children allowed till 7.30pm, heated canopied area outside, parking nearby difficult – best to use West Beach car park on seafront (free Sun), open all day. *(Anon)*

MANCHESTER SJ8498
Angel (0161) 833 4786
Angel Street, off Rochdale Road; M4 4BR Good value home-made food (not Sun evening), ten well kept changing ales including Bobs, bottled beers, real cider and perry, bare-boards bar with piano, smaller upstairs restaurant with two log fires and local artwork; children and dogs welcome, back beer garden, open all day. *(Anon)*

MANCHESTER SJ8398
Ape & Apple (0161) 839 9624
John Dalton Street; M2 6HQ Large
recently refurbished open-plan pub, five
well kept good value Holts beers plus guests,
hearty traditional bar food including deals,
comfortable seating, bare boards, carpet
and tiles, lots of old prints and posters,
upstairs restaurant/function room, friendly
atmosphere, Weds comedy night; juke box,
games machines; heated central courtyard,
open all day (till 9pm Sun). *(Jeremy King)*

MANCHESTER SJ8498
Bar Fringe (0161) 835 3815
Swan Street; M4 5JN Long bare-boards
bar specialising in continental beers, also five
changing ales from smaller breweries and
real cider, friendly staff, basic snacks till 4pm
(no food weekends), daily papers, shelves
of empty beer bottles, cartoons, posters,
motorcycle hung above door, rock juke box;
no children or dogs; tables out behind, open
all day, till late Sat, Sun. *(Anon)*

MANCHESTER SJ8397
★ Britons Protection (0161) 236 5895
*Great Bridgewater Street, corner of
Lower Mosley Street; M1 5LE* Lively
unpretentious pub with rambling rooms
and notable tiled murals of 1819 Peterloo
Massacre (took place nearby); plush little
front bar with fine chequered tile floor, glossy
brown and russet wall tiles, solid woodwork
and elaborate plastering, two cosy inner
lounges, both served by hatch, with attractive
brass wall lamps and solidly comfortable
furnishings, coal-effect gas fire in simple art
nouveau fireplace, Coach House, Jennings,
Robinsons and a Tetleys beer named for
the pub from massive counter with heated
footrail, also some 330 malt whiskies,
straightforward food, occasional storytelling,
music and silent film shows; children till
5pm, tables in back garden, open all day
(very busy lunchtime and weekends), may
close early on match days. *(Andy Lickfold,
Dave Webster, Sue Holland, Derek Wason)*

MANCHESTER SJ8498
Castle (0161) 237 9485
*Oldham Street, about 200 metres from
Piccadilly, on right; M4 1LE* Restored
18th-c pub well run by former *Coronation
Street* actor; simple traditional front bar,
small snug, Robinsons ales and guests from
fine bank of handpumps, Weston's Old Rosie
cider, back room for live music and other
events, overspill upstairs room; nice tilework
outside, open all day till late. *(Anon)*

MANCHESTER SJ8497
Circus (0161) 236 5818
Portland Street; M1 4GX Traditional little
bare-boards local with particularly well kept
Tetleys from minute corridor bar (or may be
table service), friendly staff, walls covered
with photos of regulars and local celebrities,
football memorabilia, leatherette banquettes
in panelled back room; often looks closed but
normally open all day (you may have to knock),
can get crowded. *(Martin and Sue Radcliffe)*

MANCHESTER SJ8398
City Arms (0161) 236 4610
*Kennedy Street, off St Peters Square;
M2 4BQ* Busy little pub with eight quickly
changing real ales, belgian bottled beers
and bargain bar lunches, friendly service,
coal fires, bare boards and banquettes,
prints, panelling and masses of pump
clips, handsome tiled façade and corridor;
background music, TV, games machine;
wheelchair access but steps down to back
lounge, open all day. *(Anon)*

MANCHESTER SJ8397
★ Dukes 92 (0161) 839 8642
*Castle Street, below the bottom end of
Deansgate; M3 4LZ* Cleverly converted
former stables looking over canal basin,
cheerful informal atmosphere, with old
and modern furnishings including chaise
longues and deep armchairs, whitewashed
or red walls hung with photos and paintings,
stylish gallery bar accessed by elegant spiral
staircase, three real ales, decent wines and
wide choice of spirits from handsome granite-
topped counter, bar food including pizzas and
deli boards, also a grill menu in one specific
area; background music; children welcome,
waterside tables on big terrace, open all day
(till 1am Fri, Sat). *(Jeremy King)*

MANCHESTER SJ8498
Hare & Hounds (0161) 832 4737
Shudehill, behind Arndale; M4 4AA
Old-fashioned 18th-c local with long narrow
bar linking front snug and comfortable back
lounge, notable tilework, panelling and
stained glass, low-priced Holts beer, friendly
staff; background music, TV; open all day.
(Anon)

MANCHESTER SJ8397
Knott (0161) 839 9229
Deansgate; M3 4LY Friendly modern
glass-fronted café-bar under railway arch
by Castlefield heritage site; seven well kept
ales including Castle Rock and Marble
Manchester, lots of continental imports,
good value food with emphasis on greek
dishes, upstairs smokers' balcony overlooking
Rochdale Canal, open (and food) all day.
(Bob and Tanya Ekers)

MANCHESTER SJ8499
★ Marble Arch (0161) 832 5914
*Rochdale Road (A664), Ancoats; centre
of Gould Street, just E of Victoria
Station; M4 4HY* Cheery own-brew pub
with fine Victorian interior, wonderful lightly
barrel-vaulted high ceiling, extensive marble
and tiling, look out for sloping mosaic floor
and frieze advertising various spirits, their

own good beers plus guests (brewery visible from windows in back dining room – tours by arrangement), enjoyable home-made food; background music, Laurel and Hardy Preservation Society meetings showing old films (third Weds of month); children welcome, small garden, open all day (till midnight Fri, Sat). *(Nick Lawless)*

MANCHESTER SJ8398
Mark Addy (0161) 834 7553
Stanley Street, off New Bailey Street, Salford; M3 5EJ New owners and emphasis no longer on food; unusual converted waiting rooms for boat passengers, barrel-vaulted red sandstone bays with wide glassed-in brick arches, cast-iron pillars and flagstones, views over river, several real ales including local microbrews; background and live music, weekend DJs, sports TV; waterside terrace, open all day (till 2am Fri, Sat). *(Anon)*

MANCHESTER SJ8398
★ Mr Thomas Chop House
(0161) 832 2245 *Cross Street; M2 7AR* Interesting late 19th-c pub, tall and narrow, with well preserved features; good generous freshly made food including some unusual choices, friendly staff coping well when busy, ales such as Holts and Lees and good wines by the glass, front bar with panelling, original gas lamp fittings and framed cartoons, stools at wall and window shelves, back green-tiled eating areas with rows of tables on black and white Victorian tiles, archways and high ceilings; seats out at back, open all day.
(Bob and Tanya Ekers, Jeremy King)

MANCHESTER SJ8298
New Oxford (0161) 832 7082
Bexley Square, Salford; M3 6DB At least eight well kept changing ales plus a good range of draught and bottled continental beers, real ciders too, friendly staff, light and airy café-style feel in small front bar and back room, coal fire, low-priced basic food till 6pm; juke box; seats outside, open all day. *(Anon)*

MANCHESTER SJ8398
Oast House (0161) 829 3830
Crown Square, Springfields; M3 3AY Quirky mock-up of kentish oast house surrounded by modern high-rise, rustic lofty interior with bare boards, timbers and plenty of tables, real ales and good selection of bottled beers and wines, enjoyable fairly priced food from deli boards to grills, friendly helpful young staff, lively atmosphere; prominent background music; children welcome, spacious outside seating area, open all day (till 2am Fri, Sat). *(John Wooll)*

MANCHESTER SJ8284
Parkfield (0161) 766 3923
Park Lane; M45 7GT Refurbished dining pub with good variety of food from sandwiches and pub staples to restaurant

choices, all-day Sun roasts, ales such as Jennings, Moorhouses and Timothy Taylors, freshly ground coffee, cocktails and good wine list; children welcome. *(Anon)*

MANCHESTER SJ8397
★ Peveril of the Peak (0161) 236 6364
Great Bridgewater Street; M1 5JQ Vivid art nouveau external tilework and three sturdily furnished old-fashioned bare-boards rooms, interesting pictures, lots of mahogany, mirrors and stained or frosted glass, log fire, ales such as Caledonian Deuchars IPA, Copper Dragon, Everards and Jennings from central servery, cheap basic lunchtime food; pool, table football, background music, TV; children welcome, pavement tables, closed weekend lunchtimes. *(Jeremy King)*

MANCHESTER SJ8498
Port Street Beer House
(0161) 237 9949 *Port Street; M1 2EQ* Fantastic range of beers from all over the world on draught and in bottles including 12 well kept real ales, good service from knowledgeable staff, no food, can get very busy but more room upstairs, events such as 'meet the brewer' evenings; open all day weekends, from 2pm Fri, 4pm Tues-Thurs, closed Mon. *(Vikki and Matt Wharton)*

MANCHESTER SJ8397
Rain Bar (0161) 235 6500
Great Bridgewater Street; M1 5JG Bare boards and lots of woodwork in former umbrella works, well kept Lees ales and plenty of wines by the glass, enjoyable good value pubby food, friendly efficient staff, relaxed atmosphere, nooks and corners, coal fire in small snug, large upstairs bar-function room, Weds quiz; background music; good back terrace overlooking spruced-up Rochdale Canal, handy for Bridgewater Hall, open (and food) all day. *(Anon)*

MANCHESTER SJ8398
Rising Sun (0161) 834 1193
Queen Street, off Deansgate; also Lloyd Street entrance; M2 5HX Refurbished old city-centre pub, clean and well looked after, with one long opened-up room, dark tables on polished wood floors, old pictures, eight pumps serving good changing ales and real cider, low-priced food weekday lunchtimes, convivial atmosphere; background music, sports TV, games machine and free wi-fi; open all day (1-7pm Sun). *(Jeremy King)*

MANCHESTER SJ8398
★ Sams Chop House (0161) 834 3210
Back Pool Fold, Chapel Walks; M2 1HN Thriving downstairs dining pub, offshoot from Mr Thomas Chop House, with original Victorian décor, generous helpings of good plain english food including weekend brunch, formal waiters, well kept beers and good wine choice, a former haunt of L S Lowry whose statue sits thoughtfully at the bar,

back restaurant with black and white tiled floor; background music, sports TV; some pavement tables, open all day. *(Bob and Tanya Ekers, Jeremy King)*

MANCHESTER   SJ8398

⋆**Sinclairs** (0161) 834 0430

Cathedral Gates, off Exchange Square; M3 1SW Charming low-beamed and timbered 18th-c Sam Smiths pub (rebuilt here in redevelopment), all-day food including fresh oysters, brisk friendly service, bustling atmosphere, quieter upstairs bar with snugs and Jacobean fireplace; tables out in Shambles Square (plastic glasses), open all day. *(Anon)*

MARPLE   SJ9389

Hare & Hounds (0161) 427 0293

Dooley Lane (A627 W); SK6 7EJ Dining pub above River Goyt, modern layout and décor, decent choice of all-day food at reasonable prices, Hydes ales and three interesting guests from stainless servery, brisk friendly service; background and some live music, Weds quiz, sports TV, no dogs; well behaved children welcome, open all day. *(Dennis Jones)*

MARPLE   SJ9588

Ring o' Bells (0161) 427 2300

Church Lane; by Macclesfield Canal, Bridge 2; SK6 7AY Popular old-fashioned local with assorted memorabilia in four linked rooms, well kept Robinsons ales and decent food at reasonable prices, darts, quiz nights and some live music including brass bands in the waterside garden, own narrowboat, one bedroom, open all day. *(Anon)*

MARPLE BRIDGE   SJ9889

Hare & Hounds (0161) 427 4042

Mill Brow: from end of Town Street in centre turn left up Hollins Lane and keep on uphill; SK6 5LW Comfortable and civilised stone-built country pub in lovely spot, smallish and can get crowded, really good attractively presented food (not Mon, Tues) from short modern menu, well kept Robinsons ales and good wines, log fires; garden behind, open all day weekends, closed Mon-Thurs lunchtimes. *(Anon)*

MELLOR   SJ9888

Devonshire Arms (0161) 427 2563

This is the Mellor near Marple, S of Manchester; heading out of Marple on the A626 towards Glossop, Mellor is the next road after the B6102, signposted off on the right at Marple Bridge; Longhurst Lane; SK6 5PP Under friendly new management; front bar with old leather-seated settles and open fire, two small back rooms with Victorian fireplaces, well kept Robinsons and enjoyable reasonably priced home-made food, quiz every other Tues, bank holiday jazz; children and dogs welcome,

garden with waterfall tumbling into fish pond crossed by japanese bridge, large pergola, play area on small tree-sheltered lawn, open all day weekends. *(Anon)*

MORECAMBE   SD4264

Midland Grand Plaza

(01524) 424000 *Marine Road W; LA4 4BZ* Classic art deco hotel in splendid seafront position, comfortable if unorthodox contemporary furnishings in spacious seaview Rotunda Bar, rather pricey but enjoyable food from interesting lancashire tapas to restaurant meals, good service; children welcome, 44 bedrooms, open all day. *(J F M and M West)*

MORECAMBE   SD4364

Palatine (01524) 410503

The Crescent; LA4 5BZ Comfortable Edwardian seafront pub, enjoyable reasonably priced food including deli boards, pizzas and pubby standards, four Lancaster ales and guests, good friendly staff, leather armchairs and some high tables with stools on wood floor, upstairs panelled sea-view dining lounge; seats out in front, open all day (till 1am Fri, Sat). *(Steve and Liz Tilley)*

NEWTON   SD6950

⋆**Parkers Arms** (01200) 446236

B6478 7 miles N of Clitheroe; BB7 3DY Friendly welcome and very good locally sourced food (suppliers listed) from lunchtime sandwiches to imaginative specials, you can eat in the bar or restaurant, four real ales including Bowland, good range of wines, nice coffee and afternoon tea, log fires; children welcome, garden with lovely views, four bedrooms, pretty spot. *(John and Sylvia Harrop)*

PARBOLD   SD4911

Windmill (01257) 462935

Mill Lane; WN8 7NW Nicely modernised beamed pub with opened-up interior, good coal fire, mix of furniture including settles and some interesting carved chairs, candles on tables laid for the popular well executed food (pub favourites to more adventurous specials), six well kept ales and eight wines by the glass, good friendly service from young staff; downstairs gents'; seats out in front and behind, next to village windmill and facing Leeds & Liverpool Canal, good local walks, open all day (food all day Sun). *(Clive and Fran Dutson, Mike and Wena Stevenson)*

PRESTON   SD5329

Black Horse (01772) 204855

Friargate; PR1 2EJ Friendly pub in pedestrianised street with up to eight well kept Robinsons ales, unusual ornate curved and mosaic-tiled Victorian main bar, panelling, stained glass and old local photographs, two quiet cosy snugs, mirrored back area, open fires, upstairs bar serving inexpensive food (not evenings or Sun); no children, open all day from 10.30am. *(Jim and Maggie Cowell)*

RABY   SJ3179
★ **Wheatsheaf** (0151) 336 3416
Raby Mere Road, The Green; from A540 heading S from Heswall, turn left into Upper Raby Road, village about a mile further; CH63 4JH Up to nine well kept real ales in pretty thatched black and white pub, simply furnished rambling rooms with homely feel, cosy central bar and nice snug formed by antique settles around fine old fireplace, small coal fire in more spacious room, well liked reasonably priced bar food (not Sun or Mon evenings) including huge range of sandwiches, à la carte menu in large former cowshed restaurant (Tues-Sat evenings), conservatory; children welcome, dogs in bar, picnic-sets on terrace and in pleasant back garden, open all day and gets very busy at weekends. *(Claes Mauroy, Mike and Shirley Stratton, C A Bryson, Paul Humphreys)*

RAMSBOTTOM   SD8016
Eagle & Child (01706) 557181
Whalley Road, A56; BL0 0DL Friendly well run pub with good freshly made food (booking advised) using locally sourced produce including own vegetables, well kept Thwaites ales, real cider and decent choice of wines by the glass, good service; children welcome, interesting revamped garden, valley views over rooftops to Holcombe Moor and Peel Tower, open all day Fri and Sat, till 7pm Sun. *(Tom Hardcastle, Glenasdias)*

RAMSBOTTOM   SD8017
★ **Fishermans Retreat** (01706) 825314
Twine Valley Park/Fishery signed off A56 N of Bury at Shuttleworth; Bye Road; BL0 0HH Remote yet busy pub-restaurant, generous all-day food (some quite pricey) using produce from surrounding Estate and trout lakes (they can arrange fishing), also have own land where they raise cattle, mountain lodge-feel bar with beams and bare stone walls, five well kept ales including Copper Dragon, Moorhouses, Timothy Taylors and Thwaites, over 500 malt whiskies (also sold in shop), good wine list, small family dining room and restaurant/function room extension, helpful friendly staff; a few picnic-sets with lovely valley views, closed Mon, otherwise open all day. *(Anon)*

RILEY GREEN   SD6225
★ **Royal Oak** (01254) 201445
A675/A6061; PR5 0SL Cosy low-beamed four-room pub (former coaching inn) extended under present owners; good freshly

made food and friendly efficient service, four Thwaites ales and maybe a guest from long back bar, ancient stripped stone, open fires, seats from high-backed settles to red plush armchairs on carpet, lots of nooks and crannies, soft lighting, impressive woodwork and some bric-a-brac, comfortable dining rooms; children and dogs welcome, picnic-sets at front and in side beer garden, short walk from Leeds & Liverpool Canal, footpath to Hoghton Tower, open all day weekends. *(W K Wood)*

ROCHDALE   SD8913
Baum (01706) 352186
Toad Lane (off Hunters Lane) next to the Rochdale Pioneers (Co-op) Museum; OL12 0NU In surviving cobbled street and plenty of old-fashioned charm, seven well kept changing ales and lots of bottled beers, good value food all day (Sun till 6pm) from sandwiches and tapas up including daily roast, cheerful young staff, bare boards, old advertising signs, conservatory; garden with pétanque, open all day (till midnight Fri, Sat). *(Nigel and Jean Eames)*

ROMILEY   SJ9390
Duke of York (0161) 406 9988
Stockport Road; SK6 3AN Popular former coaching inn refurbished (keeping character) and doing well under present licensees; five well kept beers including Thwaites and Wells & Youngs (Oct beer festival), good food at reasonable prices in beamed bar and upstairs restaurant, friendly efficient staff and warm intimate atmosphere; seats out at front behind white picket fence. *(Dennis Jones, Stuart Paulley)*

ROMILEY   SJ9390
Platform 1 (0161) 406 8686
Stockport Road next to the station; SK6 4BN Popular pub revamped in modern/traditional style, open and airy with tiled floor, some high tables and chairs, six mostly local ales including a well priced house beer, enjoyable good value pubby food from sandwiches up, bargain OAP lunch, good friendly service, carpeted upstairs restaurant called Platform 2; small outside seating area, open all day. *(Dennis Jones)*

ROUGHLEE   SD8440
Bay Horse (01282) 696558
Blacko Bar Road; handy for M65 junction 13; BB9 6NP Old village pub reopened 2013 after long closure; modern renovation with slate floor bar/dining area to the right, leather sofas and light open feel, carpeted dining room to the left with view into back kitchen, good food (all day weekends) including interesting daily specials and good value lunchtime/early

---

evening set menu (not Sat, Sun), short well priced wine list, four local ales, friendly competent staff; children welcome, pretty village in beautiful valley near Pendle Hill, good walking country. *(Dr Kevan Tucker)*

RUFFORD   SD4615
Hesketh Arms (01704) 821009
Junction of Liverpool Road (A59) and Holmeswood Road (B5246); L40 1SB Old beamed pub with modernised open-plan interior arranged into distinct areas, pictures and bric-a-brac, good choice of well kept ales including Moorhouses and Tetleys, enjoyable fairly traditional food along with some interesting specials, early-bird deal 5-7pm Mon-Fri; short walk from Leeds & Liverpool Canal, and handy for Rufford Old Hall (NT), open all day. *(Clive and Fran Dutson)*

SLAIDBURN   SD7152
Hark to Bounty (01200) 446246
B6478 N of Clitheroe; BB7 3EP Attractive old stone-built pub with homely linked rooms, enjoyable fresh food (all day Sun) from sandwiches and light dishes up, friendly young staff, four real ales including Theakstons, decent wines and whiskies, comfortable chairs by open fire, games room one end, restaurant the other; pleasant back garden, charming Forest of Bowland village, good walks, nine bedrooms, open all day. *(Anon)*

STALYBRIDGE   SJ9896
Waggon & Horses (01457) 764837
Mottram Road; SK15 2SU Popular family-run pub-restaurant with wide choice of enjoyable reasonably priced food, four well kept Robinsons ales and plenty of wines by the glass, good attentive service, Thurs quiz; children welcome. *(Dennis Jones)*

STOCKPORT   SJ8990
★ Arden Arms (0161) 480 2185
Millgate Street/Corporation Street, opposite pay car park; SK1 2LX Cheerful and thriving Victorian pub in handsome dark-brick building, several well preserved high-ceilinged rooms off island bar (one tiny old-fashioned snug accessed through servery), tiling, panelling and two coal fires, good sensibly priced food (not Mon or Tues evenings) from lunchtime sandwiches to interesting specials, half a dozen well kept Robinsons ales, friendly efficient service; background music; tables in sheltered courtyard with much-used smokers' shelter, open all day. *(Brian and Anna Marsden, Dennis Jones, Steve Hampson and others)*

STOCKPORT   SJ8990
Crown (0161) 480 5850
Heaton Lane, Heaton Norris; SK4 1AR Busy but welcoming partly open-plan Victorian pub popular for its well kept changing ales (up to 16), also bottled beers and real cider, three cosy lounge areas

off bar, spotless stylish décor, wholesome bargain lunches, darts; frequent live music; tables in cobbled courtyard, huge viaduct above, open all day. *(Dennis Jones)*

STOCKPORT   SJ8890
Magnet (0161) 429 6287
Wellington Road North; SK4 1HJ Over half a dozen well kept ales including own Cellar Rat beers, pool and juke box in one of the five rooms, regular events such as comedy and quiz nights; open all day Fri-Sun, from 4pm other days. *(Dennis Jones, Helen McGlasson)*

STOCKPORT   SJ8990
Queens Head (0161) 480 0725
Little Underbank (can be reached by steps from St Petersgate); SK1 1JT Splendid Victorian restoration, long and narrow, with charming separate snug and back dining area, rare brass cordials fountain, double bank of spirits taps and old spirit lamps, old posters and adverts, reasonably priced lunchtime snacks, bargain Sam Smiths, good friendly bustle, bench seating and bare boards; tiny gents' upstairs; open all day, till 7pm Sun. *(Anon)*

STOCKPORT   SJ8990
Railway (0161) 429 6062
Avenue Street (just off M63 junction 13, via A560); SK1 2BZ Bright and airy L-shaped corner bar with up to 15 ales (always a mild), lots of foreign beers and a real cider, friendly staff, no food, old Stockport and railway photographs, bar billiards; tables out behind, open all day. *(Dennis Jones)*

STOCKPORT   SJ8990
Red Bull (0161) 480 1286
Middle Hillgate; SK1 3AY Steps up to friendly well run pub, beamed bar with dark panelling and wood floor, various areas off, well kept Robinsons ales and good value home-cooked food; background and some live music, Weds quiz; four bedrooms, open all day. *(Anon)*

STOCKPORT   SJ8990
Swan With Two Necks
(0161) 480 2341 *Princes Street; SK1 1RY* Traditional narrow pub with welcoming local atmosphere, front panelled bar, back room with button-back wall benches, stone fireplace and skylight, drinking corridor, lunchtime food (not Sun, Mon) from sandwiches up, Robinsons ales; small outside area, open all day till 7pm (6pm Sun). *(Anon)*

STRINES   SJ9686
Sportsmans Arms (0161) 427 2888
B6101 Marple–New Mills; SK6 7GE Comfortable roadside local with panoramic Goyt Valley view from picture-window lounge bar, good changing ale range, enjoyable

well priced home-made food including specials board, small separate bar, log fire, folk night first Weds of month; children and dogs welcome, tables out on side decking, heated smokers' shelter, open all day weekends. *(Anon)*

TATHAM   SD6169
Tatham Bridge Inn (01524) 221326
B6480, off A683 Lancaster–Kirkby Lonsdale; LA2 8NL Busy old pub with cosy low-beamed bar, well kept ales and good range of enjoyable food, friendly staff, dining room along corridor; bedrooms. *(Vicki Trowler)*

TOCKHOLES   SD6623
Black Bull (01254) 581381
Between Tockholes and Blackburn; BB3 0LL Welcoming tucked-away country pub home to the Three B's Brewery, their full range including Black Bull Bitter (tasting trays available), no food; seats outside with nice views, open all day weekends, from 4pm weekdays. *(Nige Collighan)*

TUNSTALL   SD6073
Lunesdale Arms (01524) 274203
A683 S of Kirkby Lonsdale; LA6 2QN Welcoming new people and redecoration for this attractive 18th-c dining pub; opened-up bare-boards interior, good mix of stripped tables and chairs, woodburner in solid stone fireplace, snugger little flagstoned back part and games section with pool, Black Sheep and a couple of guests, enjoyable sensibly priced food from weekly changing menu; children and dogs (in bar) welcome, pretty Lune Valley village, church has Brontë associations, closed Mon. *(John Evans, John and Sylvia Harrop)*

WADDINGTON   SD7243
★Waddington Arms (01200) 423262
Clitheroe Road (B6478 N of Clitheroe); BB7 3HP Character inn with friendly landlord and staff; four linked bars, left one cosiest with blazing woodburner in huge fireplace, other low-beamed rooms have lots to look at including antique and modern prints and vintage motor-racing posters, fine oak settles and chunky stripped-pine tables, generous helpings of popular tasty food, well kept Moorhouses and four guests, good choice of wines by the glass and a dozen malt whiskies; children and dogs welcome, wicker chairs on sunny front terrace looking over to village church, more seats on two-level back terrace and neat tree-sheltered lawn, comfortable bedrooms, good walks in nearby Forest of Bowland, open all day. *(Steve Whalley, John and Eleanor Holdsworth, David Jackman, Brian and Anna Marsden and others)*

WEST BRADFORD   SD7444
Three Millstones (01200) 443339
Waddington Road; BB7 4SX Attractive old building, but more restaurant than pub with all tables laid for dining; popular food from owner-chef including set deals and daily specials in four comfortable linked areas, beams, timbers and two grand fireplaces, ales such as Bowland and Moorhouses, good choice of wines, friendly efficient service; closed Sun evening, Mon, Tues. *(John and Eleanor Holdsworth, Steve Whalley)*

WEST KIRBY   SJ2186
White Lion (0151) 625 9037
Grange Road (A540); CH48 4EE Friendly proper pub in interesting 18th-c sandstone building, several small beamed areas on different levels, Black Sheep, Courage Directors and a couple of quickly changing guests, good value simple bar lunches (not Sun), coal stove; no children; attractive secluded back garden up steep stone steps, fish pond, open all day. *(C A Bryson, Tony Tollitt)*

WHALLEY   SD7336
★Swan (01254) 822195
King Street; BB7 9SN 17th-c former coaching inn with friendly staff and good mix of customers in big bar decorated in beige and cream, modern artwork, dark leather dining chairs around deco-look pedestal tables, ales from Bowland and Timothy Taylors, fair-priced fairly standard food (not Sun evening), further room with leather sofas and armchairs on bare boards; loud background music, games machine; children and dogs (in bar) welcome, picnic-sets on back terrace and on grass strips by car park, bedrooms named after nearby rivers and attractions, open all day. *(Gordon and Margaret Ormondroyd, Steve Whalley, Brian and Anna Marsden)*

WHEATLEY LANE   SD8338
★Sparrowhawk (01282) 603034
Wheatley Lane Road; towards E end of village road, which runs N of and parallel to A6068; one way of reaching it is to follow Fence signpost, then turn off at Barrowford signpost; BB12 9QG Comfortably civilised 1930s feel in imposing black and white pub with quirky domed stained-glass skylight, oak panelling, parquet flooring and leather tub chairs, well kept ales such as Bass, Bank Top, Bowland and Thwaites, nice wines by the glass from cushioned leatherette counter, good food (all day weekends) including sandwiches and light lunches, friendly young staff; background and live music, comedy nights;

children welcome, dogs in bar, heavy wooden tables on spacious front terrace with good views to the moors beyond Nelson and Colne, open all day. *(Dr Kevan Tucker, Jeremy King, Roger and Donna Huggins)*

WISWELL
SD7437
★ **Freemasons Arms** (01254) 822218
Village signposted off A671 and A59 NE of Whalley; pub on Vicarage Fold,
a gravelled pedestrian passage between Pendleton Road and Old Back Lane in village centre (don't expect to park very close); BB7 9DF Civilised dining place with informal feel of an upmarket pub; rugs on polished flagstones, carved oak settles and attractive mix of chairs around handsome stripped or salvaged tables (all beautifully laid), lots of sporting antique prints on cream or pastel walls, open fires and woodburner, more rooms upstairs, really good food from lunchtime sandwiches to beautifully presented restauranty dishes (not Sun evening or Mon and not cheap), competent service from neatly uniformed young staff, well kept ales and excellent choice of wines by the glass from good list; dogs allowed in bar, candlelit tables under awning on heated front terrace, open all day weekends, closed first two weeks Jan. *(Dr Kevan Tucker)*

WRIGHTINGTON
SD5011
Rigbye Arms (01257) 462354
3 miles from M6 junction 27; off A5209 via Robin Hood Lane and left into High Moor Lane; WN6 9QB 17th-c dining pub in attractive moorland setting, welcoming and relaxed, with wide choice of good sensibly priced food (all day Sun) including game menu, hot and cold sandwiches too, friendly prompt service even when busy, well kept Black Sheep, Tetleys and Timothy Taylors, decent wines, several carpeted rooms including cosy tap room, open fires, separate evening restaurant (Weds-Sat); free wi-fi; children welcome, garden, bowling green, regular car club meetings, open all day Sun. *(Will Hancox)*

WRIGHTINGTON BAR
SD5313
Corner House (01257) 451400
B5250, N of M6 junction 27; WN6 9SE Restaurant pub with good food (all day weekends) from traditional to more upscale choices, light lunch menu and daily specials, a couple of real ales and good quality wines, plenty of tables in different refurbished areas; children welcome, seats outside, closed Mon, otherwise open all day. *(Margaret and Jeff Graham)*

Post Office address codings confusingly give the impression that some pubs are in Lancashire when they're really in Cumbria or Yorkshire (which is where we list them).

Leicestershire
and Rutland

 BREEDON ON THE HILL   SK4022   Map 7
Three Horse Shoes 🔘
Main Street (A453); DE73 8AN

Comfortable pub with friendly licensees and emphasis on popular food

Most customers come to this carefully run pub to enjoy the good, interesting food, but they do keep Marstons Pedigree on handpump and decent house wines served by chatty and helpful staff. The clean-cut central bar has a stylishly simple feel with heavy worn flagstones, green walls and ceilings, a log fire, pubby tables and a dark wood counter. Beyond is a dining room with maroon walls, dark pews and tables. The two-room dining area on the right has a comfortably civilised and chatty feel with big antique tables set quite closely together on seagrass matting, and colourful modern country prints and antique engravings on canary yellow walls. Even at lunchtime there are lit candles in elegant modern holders. Their farm shop sells their own and other local produce: eggs, jams, meat, smoked foods and chocolates. Look out for the quaint conical village lock-up opposite.

 Good, enjoyable food includes sandwiches, fish and spinach pancake, smoked salmon with lemon mayonnaise, sausages with onion gravy, beef hotpot, roast vegetable casserole, chicken breast with beetroot sauce, lamb rump with parsnip mash, duck with cabbage and whiskey, and puddings such as treacle tart and lemon cheesecake. *Benchmark main dish: beer-battered fish and chips £10.75. Two-course evening meal £19.50.*

Free house ~ Licensees Ian Davison, Jennie Ison, Stuart Marson ~ Real ale ~ (01332) 695129 ~ Open 11.30-2.30, 5.30-11; 12-3.30 Sun; closed Sun evening, Mon ~ Bar food 12-2, 5.30-9; 12-3.30 Sun ~ Restaurant ~ Children welcome ~ Dogs allowed in bar ~ Wi-fi ~ www.thehorseshoes.com *Recommended by Dr Brian and Mrs Anne Hamilton, Mike and Mary Carter, GSB, Peter J and Avril Hanson, R T and J C Moggridge*

 CLIPSHAM   SK9716   Map 8
Olive Branch ★ 🔘 🍷 ☕ 🛏
Take B668/Stretton exit off A1 N of Stamford; Clipsham signposted E from exit roundabout; LE15 7SH

An exceptional place for a drink, a meal or an overnight stay

Civilised and exceptionally well run, this lovely place remains a favourite with many of our readers. The various small and charmingly attractive rooms have a relaxed country cottage atmosphere, with dark joists and beams, rustic furniture, an interesting mix of pictures (some by local artists), candles on tables and a cosy log fire in a stone inglenook fireplace. Many of the books dotted around were bought at antiques fairs; background music. A carefully chosen range of drinks includes a beer named for the pub and a couple of guests from Grainstore or Sharps on handpump, an enticing wine list (with 17 by the glass), a thoughtful choice of spirits and cocktails, and several british and continental bottled beers. Outside, there are tables, chairs and big plant pots on a pretty little terrace, with more seating on the neat lawn, sheltered in the crook of the two low buildings. The restful bedrooms (in a renovated Georgian house across the road) are extremely comfortable and the breakfasts are delicious. It can get pretty busy at peak times. The wine shop also sells their own jams and chutneys, you can order individual dishes to take away and they can even organise food for a dinner party at home.

 Cooked by one of the chef-patrons, the first class food includes sandwiches, twice-baked cheese soufflé with poached pear and walnut salad, coffee-marinated pigeon breast with celeriac rémoulade, truffle potato gnocchi with wild mushrooms and roasted butternut squash, steak, kidney and bone marrow pie, pheasant breast with puy lentils and honey-roast parsnips, gilt head bream with potato terrine and thyme and lime jus, venison casserole and tarragon dumpling, and puddings such as kaffir lime panna cotta with pineapple carpaccio and coconut ice-cream and cranberry treacle tart with yoghurt ice-cream; they also offer two- and three-course set menus. *Benchmark main dish: lamb chump with mediterranean vegetable tumbet £18.75. Two-course evening meal £22.50.*

Free house ~ Licensees Sean Hope and Ben Jones ~ Real ale ~ (01780) 410355 ~ Open 12-3, 6-11; 12-11 Sat; 12-10.30 Sun ~ Bar food 12-2 (2.30 Sat), 6.30 (7 Fri, Sat)-9.30; 12-3, 7-9 Sun ~ Restaurant ~ Children welcome ~ Dogs allowed in bar and bedrooms ~ Wi-fi ~ Bedrooms: $97.50/$115 ~ www.theolivebranchpub.com *Recommended by Michael Doswell, M and GR, Bob and Tanya Ekers, Derek and Sylvia Stephenson, P Dawn, matt gutteridge, Nick and Gillian Harrison, Richard Kennell, J F M and M West*

COLEORTON
George
SK4117 Map 7

Loughborough Road (A512 E); LE67 8HF

Attractively traditional homely pub with dining area, honest food and drink and large garden

Our readers are very much enjoying their visits to this comfortable pub under its current licensees. There's a good welcoming atmosphere, and the bar on the right is nicely laid out to give the feel of varied and fairly small separate areas: dark leather sofa and tub chairs by a woodburning stove in front, scatter-cushioned pews and mixed chairs below shelves of books in one corner, and mixed seating elsewhere. This room has lots of local photographs on ochre or dove-grey walls, black beams and joists and a dark panelled dado. A bigger room on the left, broadly similar and again with plenty to look at and a woodburning stove, has more of a dining-room feel. Bass, Burton Bridge Bitter and Marstons Pedigree on handpump served by cheerful, efficient staff; background music. The spreading garden behind has sturdy wooden furniture among sizeable trees, and a play area.

Fair value food includes lunchtime ciabattas, field mushroom topped with stilton, bacon and herb crust, smoked trout and potato salad, mixed mushroom lasagne, fresh fish and chips, chicken wrapped in parma ham with garlic and cream cheese, lambs liver and bacon, bass with lemon yoghurt dressing and crushed new potatoes, and puddings. *Benchmark main dish: steak in ale pie £10.95. Two-course evening meal £17.00.*

Free house ~ Licensees Mark and Janice Wilkinson ~ Real ale ~ (01530) 834639 ~ Open 12-3, 5.30-11; 12-11 Fri, Sat; 12-3 Sun; closed Sun evening, Mon ~ Bar food 12-2.30, 6-9 (9.30 Fri, Sat); 12-2 Sun ~ Restaurant ~ Well behaved supervised children welcome ~ Dogs allowed in bar ~ Wi-fi ~ www.georgeinncoleorton.co.uk *Recommended by Lucien Perring, Michael Butler, Comus and Sarah Elliott*

 EXTON   SK9211   Map 7

Fox & Hounds 🌟 🛏

The Green; signed off A606 Stamford–Oakham; LE15 8AP

Well run, friendly inn with comfortable lounge bar, real ales, popular food and quiet garden; bedrooms

There's always a good crowd of customers in this handsome village inn, so it's wise to book a table in advance. It's a friendly place with courteous staff and a genteel atmosphere, and the comfortable high-ceilinged lounge bar has traditional dark red plush easy chairs and wheelback seats around lots of pine tables, maps and hunting prints on the walls, fresh flowers and a winter log fire in a large stone fireplace. Grainstore Ten Fifty, Greene King IPA and a guest beer such as St Austell Tribute on handpump, and eight wines by the glass; TV and background music. The lovely sheltered walled garden has seats among large rose beds overlooking pretty paddocks. If you stay in the spotlessly clean bedrooms, the breakfasts are very good. The inn is handy for Rutland Water and the gardens at Barnsdale.

🌟 Cooked by the landlord, the good, well thought-of food includes lunchtime sandwiches, chicken liver pâté with red onion chutney, avocado and crayfish salad, pizzas with 13 toppings, sharing platters, pasta with gorgonzola, walnut, cream sauce and parmesan, salmon and cod fishcake with wilted spinach and poached egg, breaded veal escalope with chips, and puddings such as tiramisu and lemon tart. *Benchmark main dish: chicken wrapped in parma ham filled with spinach and mozzarella with mushroom sauce £13.95. Two-course evening meal £20.00.*

Free house ~ Licensees Valter and Sandra Floris ~ Real ale ~ (01572) 812403 ~ Open 11-3, 6-11; 11-11 Sat, Sun ~ Bar food 12-2, 6-9; 12-4, 6-8 weekends, bank holidays ~ Restaurant ~ Children welcome ~ Dogs allowed in bar ~ Wi-fi ~ Bedrooms: £55/£80 ~ www.foxandhoundsrutland.co.uk *Recommended by M Mossman, Mrs S Hewitt, Lois Dyer, Dr A J and Mrs B A Tompsett, Barry Collett, Gordon and Margaret Ormondroyd, David and Shelagh Monks*

 GREETHAM   SK9314   Map 7

Wheatsheaf 🌟 🍷

B668 Stretton–Cottesmore; LE15 7NP

Busy, warmly friendly stone pub with interesting food, real ales and a dozen wines, and seats in front and back gardens

Located just a mile from the busy A1, this attractive old stone-built pub is just the place for a lunch break – but it's very popular locally so you'll need to book ahead. The linked L-shaped rooms have both a log fire and a blazing open stove, traditional settles and cushioned captain's chairs around dark tables on blue patterned carpeting, and Greene King IPA, Oakham Inferno and Oldershaw Old Boy on handpump and a dozen wines by the glass, served by genuinely welcoming and helpful licensees; background music. A games room has TV, darts, pool and board games.

The pub dogs are a dachshund and a labradoodle, and visiting dogs are welcome in the bar. There are chunky picnic-sets on the front lawn and more seats on a back terrace by a pretty stream with a duck house; pétanque. They sell their own pickles, chutneys and chocolates; ramp for wheelchairs.

 Very good, highly thought-of food featuring home-made bread and ice-cream includes lunchtime sandwiches, mussels with shallots, white wine and cream, grilled quail and crispy bacon salad, roast butternut squash, red onion and goats cheese tart, line-caught cod with brown shrimp butter sauce, rack of lamb with merguez sausage, spiced aubergine, chilli and rosemary, confit duck leg with puy lentils, bacon, spinach and horseradish, and puddings such as treacle tart with clotted cream and sticky ginger pudding with toffee sauce. *Benchmark main dish: bavette steak with chips £14.50. Two-course evening meal £21.50.*

Punch ~ Lease Scott and Carol Craddock ~ Real ale ~ (01572) 812325 ~ Open 12-3, 6-11; 12-midnight Sat; 12-11 Sun; closed Mon except bank holidays, two weeks Jan ~ Bar food 12-2 (2.15 Sat), 6.30-9; 12-3 Sun ~ Restaurant ~ Children welcome ~ Dogs allowed in bar ~ Wi-fi ~ www.wheatsheaf-greetham.co.uk *Recommended by Michael and Jenny Back, Colin McKerrow, Gordon and Margaret Ormondroyd*

LEICESTER
SK5804 Map 4
Rutland & Derby Arms £
Millstone Lane; nearby metered parking; LE1 5JN

Neatly kept modern town bar with interesting food, impressive drinks range, sheltered courtyard and grassed roof terrace

There's a fine range of drinks at this city-centre bar, served by bright, pleasant young staff: Adnams Broadside, three beers from Everards and a guest such as York Decade on handpump, a farm cider, 20 wines by the glass, 20 malt whiskies and an impressive array of spirits and cocktails. The open-plan interior has a pleasing clean-cut modernity, with comfortable bar chairs by the long counter, padded high seats including one unusual high banquette by chunky tall tables, and a few small prints of classic film posters and the like; apart from some stripped brick, décor is in shades of ochre and coffee; well reproduced background music. The sunny courtyard shelters some chunky garden furniture under parasols and there are seats and tables on an upper terrace.

Popular food, served all day, includes sandwiches using home-baked bread, chilli and coriander tempura squid with kimchi mayonnaise, sticky chicken wings with blue cheese sauce, flatbreads with various toppings, macaroni cheese, beef in ale pie, burger with bacon, cheese and frites, Whitby scampi with tartare sauce, and just one pudding – home-made chocolate brownie with vanilla pod ice-cream; they offer two-for-one flatbreads on Monday, two-for-one burgers on Tuesday and a sandwich and drink deal on Wednesday. *Benchmark main dish: pizza topped with british chorizo and smoked cheddar £8.95. Two-course evening meal £14.00.*

Everards ~ Tenant Samuel Hagger ~ Real ale ~ (0116) 262 3299 ~ Open 12-11 (1am Fri, Sat); closed Sun ~ Bar food 12-8 (9 Fri) ~ Children welcome ~ Wi-fi ~ Acoustic music last Fri of month ~ www.therutlandandderby.co.uk *Recommended by Emma Scofield, Harvey Brown*

If a compulsory service charge is mentioned prominently on a menu or accommodation terms, you must pay it if service was satisfactory. If service is really bad, you are legally entitled to refuse to pay some or all of the service charge as compensation for not getting the service you might reasonably have expected.

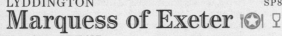

LYDDINGTON

SP8797 Map 4

Marquess of Exeter 🏅 ♀

Main Street; LE15 9LT

Stone inn with contemporary décor, real ales and excellent food cooked by the landlord

With a warm welcome and interesting food, this handsome place is extremely popular. The spacious open-plan areas are laid out with understated but stylish furnishings – the fine flagstone floors, thick walls, beams and exposed stonework are left to speak for themselves. There's a mix of old tables and chairs, smart fabrics, leather sofas, pine chests and old barrels that might always have been here. In winter, it's all warmed by several open fires – one a quite striking piece in dark iron. There's Brakspears Bitter and Ringwood Fortyniner on handpump and around a dozen wines by the glass. Outside is a terrace with seats, and picnic-sets in tree-sheltered gardens that seem to merge with the countryside beyond. The pub is named after the Burghley family, which has long owned this charming village (Burghley House is about 15 miles away).

 Cooked by the landlord, the imaginative food includes lunchtime sandwiches, chicken liver parfait with fig chutney, salt and chilli squid with thai salad, ricotta and spinach stuffed chicken breast with tomato and tarragon sauce, bouillabaisse with saffron aioli, calves liver with crispy parma ham, duck breast with honey parsnips, braised shallots and soya and ginger dressing, and puddings such as plum almond tart with fruit coulis and white chocolate ice-cream and baked egg custard tart with poached rhubarb. *Benchmark main dish: sharing dish for two of beef rib with frites and béarnaise sauce £44.50. Two-course evening meal £23.00.*

Marstons ~ Lease Brian Baker ~ Real ale ~ (01572) 822477 ~ Open 11am-11.30pm; 11.30-11 Sun ~ Bar food 12-2.30, 6.30-9.30; 12-3, 6-9 Sun ~ Restaurant ~ Children welcome but not in bar after 7pm ~ Dogs allowed in bar and bedrooms ~ Bedrooms: £79.50/£99.50 ~ www.marquessexeter.co.uk *Recommended by Mike and Margaret Banks, Dr A J and Mrs B A Tompsett, Colin McLachlan, Michael Sargent*

OADBY

SK6202 Map 4

Cow & Plough 🍺

Gartree Road (B667 N of centre); LE2 2FB

Fantastic collection of brewery memorabilia, seven real ales and good bar food

The seven real ales on handpump in these interestingly converted farm buildings include Steamin' Billy Bitter and Skydiver plus guest beers such as Abbeydale Moonshine, Dark Star Hophead, Fullers London Pride, Rudgate Ruby Mild and Shipstones Bitter; also, a couple of farm ciders, 12 wines by the glass and a dozen malt whiskies. Two of the original dark back rooms, known as the Vaults, contain an extraordinary collection of brewery memorabilia (almost every piece has a story behind it): enamel signs and mirrors advertising long-forgotten brews, an aged brass cash register, and furnishings and fittings salvaged from pubs and even churches (there's some splendid stained-glass behind the counter). The long, light front extension has plenty of plants and fresh flowers, and a real mix of traditionally pubby tables and chairs, with lots of green leatherette sofas and small round cast-iron tables. The conservatory also has a fine collection of brewery and pub signs and the like, and a very eclectic mix of chairs and tables; TV, darts, board games and background music. There are picnic-sets outside in the old yard.

¶↓ Popular food includes sandwiches, mussels in white wine, cream and garlic, pheasant, hare and rabbit terrine with apple and apricot chutney, honey-roast ham and eggs, pork belly with bubble and squeak and cider gravy, chicken with bacon, cabbage and sautéed potatoes, liver and crispy bacon with mustard mash and peppercorn sauce, braised shin of beef with dauphinoise potatoes and gravy, and puddings such as chocolate muffin and vanilla brûlée and walnut brittle; Thursday is pie night. *Benchmark main dish: beef in ale pie £8.00. Two-course evening meal £21.00.*

Free house ~ Licensee Barry Lount ~ Real ale ~ (0116) 272 0852 ~ Open 12-11 ~ Bar food 12-3, 6-9; 12-4 Sun ~ Restaurant ~ Children welcome ~ Dogs welcome ~ Wi-fi ~ Live jazz Weds lunchtime ~ www.steamin-billy.co.uk *Recommended by Barry Collett, Harvey Brown, Dr D J and Mrs S C Walker*

OAKHAM   SK8509   Map 4

Grainstore ▧ £

Station Road, off A606; LE15 6RE

Super own-brewed beers in a converted railway grain warehouse, cheerful customers and pubby food

It's the own-brewed beers in this former Victorian grain store that customers are here to try, and the staff will usually offer a sample or two to help you decide. The ten beers are served traditionally at the left end of the bar counter, and through swan necks with sparklers on the right. As per the traditional tower system of production, the beer is brewed on the upper floors of the building directly above the down-to-earth bar; during working hours, you'll hear the busy noises of the brewery rumbling overhead. Takeaways are offered and a beer festival with over 80 real ales and live music is held during the August Bank Holiday weekend; there's also a farm cider, several wines by the glass and 15 malt whiskies. Décor is plain and functional, with well worn wide floorboards, bare ceiling boards above massive joists supported by red metal pillars, a long brick-built bar counter with cast-iron bar stools, tall cask tables and simple elm chairs; games machine, darts, board games, giant Jenga and bottle-walking. In summer, the huge glass doors are pulled back, opening on to a terrace with picnic-sets (often stacked with barrels). The brewery tours are popular but must be booked in advance. Disabled access.

¶↓ As well as weekend breakfasts (9-11.30am), the tasty, straightforward food includes sandwiches and rolls, gruyère and beer croquettes with ale chutney, chorizo, bacon and black pudding salad, thai green vegetable curry, twice-cooked sticky beef, home-made pork and ale sausages with onion gravy, and puddings such as sticky toffee pudding and bread and butter pudding with custard. *Benchmark main dish: slow-roast pork belly £8.95. Two-course evening meal £11.00.*

Own brew ~ Licensee Peter Atkinson ~ Real ale ~ (01572) 770065 ~ Open 11-11 ~ Bar food 11-9; 9-9 Sat; 9-6 Sun ~ Children welcome ~ Dogs welcome ~ Wi-fi ~ Live music monthly, comedy evening monthly ~ www.grainstorebrewery.com *Recommended by Andy Lickfold, David Jackman, J F M and M West, Barry Collett, P Dawn*

OAKHAM   SK8608   Map 4

Lord Nelson ★ ♀ ▧

Market Place; LE15 6DT

Splendidly restored as proper relaxed grown-up pub, full of interest; open all day, real ales and ciders and enjoyable food

More than half a dozen rooms are spread over two floors in this carefully restored, handsome place and it's worth having a wander around before you decide where to sit. You can choose from cushioned church pews, leather elbow chairs, long oak settles, sofas, armchairs – or, to watch the passing scene, a big bow window seat; carpet, bare boards, or ancient red and black tiles; paintwork in soft shades of ochre, canary yellow, sage or pink, or William Morris wallpaper. There's plenty to look at too, from intriguing antique Police News and other prints – plenty of Nelson, of course – to the collections of mullers, copper kettles and other homely bric-a-brac in the heavy-beamed former kitchen with its Aga. But the main thing is simply the easy-going, good-natured atmosphere. Fullers London Pride, Castle Rock Harvest Pale and guests such as Lancaster Black and Amber and Navigation Pale Ale on handpump; also two farm ciders, 17 wines by the glass and ten malt whiskies. Staff are helpful and efficient; background music and TV.

🍴 Interesting food includes lunchtime sandwiches and wraps (till 5pm Sunday), honey and smoked bacon dough balls, sharing antipasti plates, burger with indian spices, sag aloo and sweet onion bhaji, lamb kofta or halloumi cheese kebabs with meze, chicken with chargrilled baby gem lettuce, smoked bacon, pickled free-range egg, parmesan rarebit and caesar dressing, beef bourguignon pie, and puddings such as apple and cinnamon crumble and treacle tart. *Benchmark main dish: stone-baked pizzas with various toppings £7.95. Two-course evening meal £16.00.*

Free house ~ Licensee Adam Dale ~ Real ale ~ (01572) 868340 ~ Open 10am-11pm; 12-11 Sun ~ Bar food 12-2.30 (5 Sat), 6-9; not Sun evening ~ Children welcome ~ Dogs allowed in bar ~ Wi-fi ~ www.thelordnelsonoakham.com *Recommended by J F M and M West, John and Sylvia Harrop, Barry Collett*

PEGGS GREEN
SK4117 Map 7

New Inn £

Signposted off A512 Ashby–Shepshed at roundabout, then turn immediately left down Zion Hill towards Newbold; pub is 100 metres down on the right, with car park on opposite side of road; LE67 8JE

Intriguing bric-a-brac in unspoilt pub, friendly welcome, good value food and drinks; cottagey garden

The diverting collection of old bric-a-brac that covers almost every inch of the walls and ceilings in the two cosy tiled front rooms of this cheerful pub are worth close inspection. The little room on the left, a bit like an old kitchen parlour (called the Cabin), has china on the mantelpiece, lots of prints and photographs and little collections of this and that, three old cast-iron tables, wooden stools and a small stripped kitchen table. The room to the right has attractive stripped panelling and more appealing bric-a-brac. The small back 'Best' room, with a stripped-wood floor, has a touching display of old local photographs including some colliery ones. Bass, Marstons Pedigree and a guest beer such as Hook Norton Cotswold Lion on handpump; background music and board games. There are plenty of seats in front of the pub, with more in the peaceful back garden. Do check the unusual opening times carefully.

🍴 Incredibly cheap food includes hot and cold cobs, chunky soup, faggots and peas, sausages in onion gravy, corned beef hash, ham and eggs, steak pie and smoked haddock. *Benchmark main dish: steak in ale pie £5.95.*

Enterprise ~ Lease Maria Christina Kell ~ Real ale ~ (01530) 222293 ~ Open 12-2.30, 5.30-11; 12-3, 6.30-11 Sat; 12-3, 7-10.30 Sun; closed Tues-Thurs lunchtimes ~ Bar food

12-2, 6-8 Mon; 12-2 Fri, Sat; filled rolls might be available at other times ~ Well behaved children welcome ~ Dogs welcome ~ Wi-fi ~ Live folk club second Mon of month ~ www.thenewinnpeggsgreen.co.uk *Recommended by Michael Butler, Adrian Johnson*

SILEBY
SK6015 Map 7

White Swan £

Off A6 or A607 N of Leicester; in centre turn into King Street (opposite church), then after mini roundabout turn right at Post Office signpost into Swan Street; LE12 7NW

Exemplary town local, a boon to its chatty regulars, with fair value home cooking luring others from further afield

Mrs Miller has been running this honest local for over 30 years now and it remains popular with regulars – and visitors too – for its good value food and particularly helpful, thoughtful service. It's got all the touches that marked the best of between-the-wars estate pub design, such as an art deco-tiled lobby, polychrome-tiled fireplaces, shiny red Anaglypta ceiling and a comfortable layout of linked but separate areas including a small restaurant (now lined with books). Packed with bric-a-brac from bizarre hats to decorative plates and lots of prints, it quickly draws you in with its genuinely bright and cheerful welcome. Bass, Greene King Ruddles Bitter and a guest beer on handpump, and good value house wines.

 With some dishes costing under £10, the menu includes sandwiches, black pudding and apple fritters, pasta with sunblush tomatoes and feta, gammon with egg or pineapple, chicken in creamy stilton and leek sauce, chilli beef with rice, salmon and prawn pancake with creamy cheese sauce, and puddings such as profiteroles with chocolate sauce and lemon tart; they also offer food specials like pie and pastry or sausage and burger evenings. *Benchmark main dish: beef in Guinness and mushrooms with stilton scone topping £11.95. Two-course evening meal £17.50.*

Free house ~ Licensee Theresa Miller ~ Real ale ~ (01509) 814832 ~ Open 12-2, 6-11; 12-3 Sun; closed Sat lunchtime, Sun evening, Mon, Tues lunchtime ~ Bar food 12-1.30, 6-8.30 ~ Restaurant ~ Children welcome ~ Wi-fi ~ www.whiteswansileby.co.uk
Recommended by Harvey Brown, Emma Scofield

STATHERN
SK7731 Map 7

Red Lion ⭐ ♀ ◖

Off A52 W of Grantham via the brown-signed Belvoir road (keep on towards Harby; Stathern is signposted on left); or off A606 Nottingham–Melton Mowbray via Long Clawson and Harby; LE14 4HS

Leicestershire Dining Pub of the Year

Country-style dining pub with fine range of drinks, imaginative food and lovely service; good garden with a play area

Impeccable, friendly service, delicious food and an interesting range of drinks – it's not surprising that this well run place is so very popular. It's decorated in a charming rustic style and the yellow room on the right, with its collection of wooden spoons and lambing chairs, has a simple country-pub feel. The lounge bar has sofas, an open fire and a big table with books, newspapers and magazines; it leads to a smaller, more traditional flagstoned bar, with terracotta walls, another fireplace and lots of beams and hops. A little room with tables set for eating connects to a long, narrow, main dining room and out to a nicely arranged suntrap lawn and terrace with good hardwood furnishings; background music and TV.

Red Lion Ale (from Grainstore) and guests such as Brewsters Aromantica, Castle Rock Harvest Pale and Fullers London Pride on handpump, with a lager from Brewsters, lots of bottled craft beers, cocktails and 12 wines by the glass. Behind the car park is an unusually big play area with swings and climbing frames. Sister pub is the first class Olive Branch in Clipsham.

Using the best local, seasonal produce, the impressive food includes lunchtime sandwiches, scallops with spicy dhal and coconut, chicken liver parfait with smoked popcorn, sausages with onion jus, spinach pasta with earl grey smoked cherry tomatoes and wild mushrooms, prosciutto roast cod with grilled fennel and chorizo, pork belly with cabbage parcel of brawn, butternut squash and dates, and puddings such as panfruttone and butter pudding with custard and iced chocolate parfait with honeycomb; they also offer two- and three-course set menus. *Benchmark main dish: braised shoulder of lamb £15.50. Two-course evening meal £20.50.*

Free house ~ Licensees Sean Hope and Ben Jones ~ Real ale ~ (01949) 860868 ~ Open 12-3, 6-11; 12-11 Sat; 12-7.30 Sun; closed Mon ~ Bar food 12-2, 6.30-9; 12-3 Sun ~ Restaurant ~ Children welcome ~ Dogs allowed in bar ~ Wi-fi ~ Jazz last Sun evening of month ~ www.theredlioninn.co.uk *Recommended by Michael Doswell, P Dawn*

STRETTON
SK9415 Map 8
Jackson Stops

Rookery Lane; a mile or less off A1, at B668 (Oakham) exit; follow village sign, turning off Clipsham Road into Manor Road, pub on left; LE15 7RA

Attractive thatched former farmhouse with good food, just off A1

This 16th-c thatched stone inn is a place of great character, with warmly welcoming licensees. The meandering rooms are filled with lots of lovely period features; the black-beamed country bar on the left has wall timbering, an elderly settle on the worn tile and brick floor, a couple of bar stools, a cushioned wall pew and a coal fire in one corner. Grainstore Ten Fifty and Cooking on handpump, alongside eight wines by the glass and ten malt whiskies. The smarter main room on the right is light and airy with a nice mix of ancient and modern tables on dark blue carpet, and another coal fire in a stone corner fireplace. Past the bar is the dining room with stripped-stone walls, a tiled floor and an old open cooking range, and there's a second smaller dining room; background music. The pub has one of the only two nurdling benches (a game involving old pennies) left in Britain.

Enjoyable food includes prawn and kiln roast salmon timbale with dill mayonnaise, chicken and duck liver parfait with red onion and cranberry marmalade, emmental, shallot and leek tortellini with sautéed wild mushrooms, spinach and parmesan, beer-battered haddock, french-style peas and chips, lamb rump with black pudding, colcannon, redcurrant and merlot jus, and puddings such as coffee panna cotta with rum-soaked amaretti biscuits and espresso parfait and trio of chocolate (warmed brownie, double chocolate ice-cream, praline profiteroles). *Benchmark main dish: burgundy beef pie £16.00. Two-course evening meal £20.00.*

Free house ~ Licensee Robert Reid ~ Real ale ~ (01780) 410237 ~ Open 12-3, 6-10 (11 Fri, Sat); 12-4 Sun; closed Sun evening, Mon ~ Bar food 12-2.30, 6-9 (9.30 Fri, Sat); 12-4 Sun ~ Restaurant ~ Children welcome ~ Dogs allowed in bar ~ www.thejacksonstops.com *Recommended by Andy Lickfold, Mike and Margaret Banks, G Jennings, Barry Collett, John and Sylvia Harrop, Ian Prince*

If we know a pub has an outdoor play area for children, we mention it.

SWITHLAND
Griffin ◖

SK5512 Map 7

Main Street; between A6 and B5330, between Loughborough and Leicester; LE12 8TJ

A good mix of cheerful customers and well liked food in a well run, busy pub

There's always a warm welcome for visitors in this friendly country pub, although many of the cheerful customers are clearly regulars. The three beamed communicating rooms are cosy and traditional with some panelling, leather armchairs and sofas, cushioned wall seating, a woodburner, a nice mix of wooden tables and chairs, and stools at the counter where Adnams Bitter, Everards Original and Tiger and guests such as Courage Directors and Titanic English Glory are kept on handpump; also, a couple of farm ciders, several malt whiskies and wines by the glass from a good list; background music. The terrace, screened by plants, has wicker seats, and there are more seats in the streamside garden overlooking open fields, as well as painted picnic-sets outside the Old Stables. The pub is in a quiet tucked-away village in the heart of Charnwood Forest and is handy for Bradgate Country Park and walks in Swithland Woods. Good wheelchair access and disabled facilities.

 Good, tasty food includes baguettes, battered king prawns with chilli, creamy garlic mushrooms, ham and eggs, pork sausages with creamy mash and gravy, wild mushroom and parmesan risotto, grilled tuna steak niçoise, thai green chicken curry, moroccan-style lamb with couscous, and puddings such as raspberry and vanilla panna cotta and blueberry sponge with maple syrup; they also offer a two- and three-course set menu. *Benchmark main dish: chicken ballotine stuffed with tomatoes, basil and mozzarella £12.95. Two-course evening meal £21.00.*

Everards ~ Tenant John Cooledge ~ Real ale ~ (01509) 890535 ~ Open 9am-11pm (10.30 Sun) ~ Bar food 12-2.30, 5.30-9; 12-2, 6-8.30 Mon; all day Fri-Sun ~ Restaurant ~ Children welcome ~ Wi-fi ~ www.griffininnswithland.co.uk *Recommended by Simon and Mandy King, Comus and Sarah Elliott, Robert Wivell*

THRUSSINGTON
Star 🛏

SK6415 Map 7

Village signposted off A46 N of Syston; The Green; LE7 4UH

Neatly refurbished 18th-c inn overlooking small village green, usefully open all day from breakfast on; comfortable bedrooms

There's always something happening in this bustling village pub, whether it's live music events, quiz nights, special themed food evenings – or even a magician. The friendly L-shaped bar has heavy low stripped beams and broad floorboards plus stylish contemporary versions of those good-pub staples, the inglenook fireplace and the high-backed settle. One of two cast-iron stoves has above it an inn-side horse print by the early 19th-c sporting painter John Ferneley, who was born nearby, and there are a couple of hunting cartoons on the cream walls. Belvoir Star Bitter, Rugby Egg Chaser and Timothy Taylors Landlord on handpump and ten wines by the glass are served by welcoming efficient staff. The skylit dining room, up a few steps from the bar (with separate level access too), is similar in mood and décor; well reproduced background music. The side garden and flagstoned terrace have seats and tables under parasols.

🍴 Quite a choice of good food includes lunchtime sandwiches, venison terrine with home-made piccalilli, salmon and prawn fishcakes, honey-roast ham and eggs, open ravioli with wild mushrooms, shallots and asparagus, burger with cheddar, bacon, coleslaw and chips, chicken ballotine with rösti potatoes and bacon, a fish dish of the day, and puddings such as lemon curd meringue tart and chocolate and rum torte. *Benchmark main dish: lemon battered fresh haddock and chips £11.95. Two-course evening meal £21.00.*

Free house ~ Licensee Robert Smith ~ Real ale ~ (01664) 424220 ~ Open 8am-11pm (midnight Fri, Sat); 9am-11.30pm Sun ~ Bar food 8am-9.30pm; 12-8 Sun ~ Restaurant ~ Children welcome ~ Dogs allowed in bar ~ Wi-fi ~ Bedrooms: £65/£86 ~ www.thestarinn1744.co.uk *Recommended by Comus and Sarah Elliott, Pip White, Emma Scofield, SAB and MJW*

WING
Kings Arms 🏵 ♀ 🛏

SK8902   Map 4

Village signposted off A6003 S of Oakham; Top Street; LE15 8SE

Nicely kept old pub with big log fires, super choice of wines by the glass, good modern cooking and smokehouse

They take great care with their cooking in this civilised former farmhouse, using the best local producers, running their own smokehouse, baking fresh bread daily and making conserves, pickles, chutneys and so forth. It's best to book a table in advance. The attractive long bar is neatly kept and inviting, with two large log fires (one in a copper-canopied central hearth), various nooks and crannies, nice old low beams and stripped stone, and flagstone or wood-strip floors. Friendly, helpful staff serve almost three dozen wines by the glass, as well as Black Sheep, Grainstore Cooking and a seasonal ale from Grainstore and Marstons Pedigree on handpump, six farm ciders, several grappas and a dozen malt whiskies; board games. There are seats out in front, and more in the sunny yew-sheltered garden; the car park has plenty of space. You'll find a medieval turf maze just up the road and it's a couple of miles to one of England's two osprey hotspots.

🏵 The rewarding food includes sandwiches, lightly battered black pudding fritters, scallops with cauliflower purée, pancetta and grated egg yolk, a smokehouse platter, a choice of frittata, steak burger with bacon, cheese, sweet chilli ketchup and dripping chips, home-smoked honey and cider ham and eggs, gamebird hotpot, halibut with crab bisque and linguine, lamb with confit tongue, lamb jus and dauphinoise potatoes, and puddings such as chocolate mousse and fruit crumble with cinnamon yoghurt ice-cream. *Benchmark main dish: beer-battered fish and chips £12.50. Two-course evening meal £23.00.*

Free house ~ Licensee David Goss ~ Real ale ~ (01572) 737634 ~ Open 12-3, 6.30-11; closed Sun evening, Mon lunchtime; in winter all day Mon, Tues lunchtime ~ Bar food 12-2, 6.30-8.30 (9 Fri, Sat) ~ Restaurant ~ Children welcome away from bar ~ Dogs allowed in bar and bedrooms ~ Wi-fi ~ Bedrooms: £75/£100 ~ www.thekingsarms-wing.co.uk *Recommended by Colin McKerrow, Alan Johnson, R L Borthwick, Pat and Stewart Gordon*

'Children welcome' means the pub says it lets children inside without any special restriction. If it allows them in, but to restricted areas such as an eating area or family room, we specify this. Places with separate restaurants often let children use them, and hotels usually let children into public areas such as lounges. Some pubs impose an evening time limit – let us know if you find one earlier than 9pm.

WOODHOUSE EAVES

SK5313 Map 7

Wheatsheaf 🍴✶ 🛏

Brand Hill; turn right into Main Street, off B591 S of Loughborough;
LE12 8SS

Bustling and friendly country pub with interesting things to look at, good bistro-type food and a fair choice of drinks; well equipped bedrooms

They manage to strike an easy balance at this hospitable, very well run pub between the chatty bar side and the interlinked dining rooms. The beamed bar areas are traditionally furnished (wheelback chairs, open fires, daily papers and the like) and full of interesting motor-racing and family RAF and flying memorabilia. A cosy dining area (called The Mess) even has an RAF Hurricane propeller, and other dining rooms have high-backed chairs around all sorts of tables and prints on pale green walls. It's all very cheerful and easy-going and the kind staff will help with wheelchair access. Adnams Broadside, Greene King Old Speckled Hen and Seafarers and Timothy Taylors Landlord on handpump and around 17 wines by the glass (including champagne) from a thoughtfully compiled list. There's plenty of seating outside among the bright window boxes and tubs. The bedrooms are in a cottage annexe where there's a lounge/dining room for breakfast. They have a disabled parking space in the car park.

 Highly thought-of food includes a daily sandwich and specials board, chicken liver pâté with red onion chutney, twice-baked blue cheese and walnut soufflé with pear and fig dressing, mushroom tagliatelle with parmesan in crème fraîche and madeira sauce, pork and leek sausages with onion and rosemary sauce, salmon, spit-roast chicken (piri-piri or garlic and herb) with fries, smoked haddock and spring onion fishcakes with lemon hollandaise, and puddings such as key lime pie and apple flapjack crumble. *Benchmark main dish: gourmet burger with stilton, bacon, onion rings and fries £11.95. Two-course evening meal £18.50.*

Free house ~ Licensees Richard and Bridget Dimblebee ~ Real ale ~ (01509) 890320 ~ Open 12-3 (4 Sat), 6-11; 12-5 Sun; closed Sun evening ~ Bar food 12-2.30; 6.30-9.15; 12-3.15 Sun ~ Restaurant ~ Children welcome ~ Dogs allowed in bar ~ Bedrooms: £70/£80 ~ www.wheatsheafinn.net *Recommended by David Jackman, Michelle Gallagher, Simon and Mandy King, Dr Martin Owton, SAB and MJW, Gordon and Jenny Quick*

WYMONDHAM

SK8518 Map 7

Berkeley Arms

Main Street; LE14 2AG

Well run village pub with interesting food, inter-linked beamed rooms, a relaxed atmosphere and sunny terrace

Mr Hitchen cooks the good food in this friendly golden-stone inn, while Mrs Hitchen and her helpful staff keep everything running smoothly front of house. There's a welcoming, relaxed atmosphere, helped by knick-knacks, magazines, table lamps and cushions, and at one end two wing chairs are set on patterned carpet beside a low coffee table and a cosy log fire. The red-tiled or wood-floored dining areas, dense with stripped beams and standing timbers, are furnished in a kitchen style with light wood tables and red-cushioned chunky chairs. Marstons Pedigree and guests such as Batemans XB, Castle Rock Harvest Pale and Grainstore Cooking on handpump, 11 wines by the glass and local cider. Outside, on small terraces to either side of the front entrance, picnic-sets get the sun nearly all day long. This is a pretty village surrounded by footpaths and walkways.

🍴 Attractively presented, the interesting food includes sandwiches, scallops and chorizo with fennel and orange purée, potted confit duck leg with pickles and toasted sourdough, wild mushroom and tarragon risotto with poached egg, beer-battered haddock and chips, fillet of pork and black pudding with apple cider sauce, venison loin with caramelised walnuts and poached pear, and puddings such as warm chocolate fondant with cherry ice-cream and lemon verbena and blackberry posset; they also offer a two- and three-course set dinner. *Benchmark main dish: loin of rabbit stuffed with sun-dried tomatoes wrapped in spinach and pancetta with a creamy sauce £14.95. Two-course evening meal £21.00.*

Free house ~ Licensee Louise Hitchen ~ Real ale ~ (01572) 787587 ~ Open 12-3, 6-11; 12-5 Sun; closed Sun evening, Mon, first two weeks Jan, two weeks summer ~ Bar food 12-1.45, 6.30-9; 12-3 Sun ~ Restaurant ~ Children welcome ~ Dogs allowed in bar ~ www.theberkeleyarms.co.uk *Recommended by R L Borthwick*

Also Worth a Visit in Leicestershire

Besides the fully inspected pubs, you might like to try these pubs that have been recommended to us and described by readers. Do tell us what you think of them: feedback@goodguides.com

BARKBY — SK6309
Malt Shovel (0116) 269 2558
Main Street; LE7 3QG Popular and welcoming old family-run village pub, enjoyable good value food (till 6pm Sun) including offers such as two-for-one Mon steak night, four well kept Thwaites ales and a couple of guests (beer festivals), good choice of wines by the glass, U-shaped carpeted bar with fire, small dining room (was the local jail), monthly live music; children and dogs welcome, garden with partly covered heated terrace, open all day weekends. *(Phil and Jane Hodson)*

BLABY — SP5697
Bakers Arms (0116) 278 7253
Quite handy for M1 junction 21; The Green; LE8 4FQ Tucked-away thatched pub (dates from 1485) with lots of low beams, nooks and crannies in linked rooms, wide choice of good interesting food from sandwiches and bar snacks up, Everards ales, restored 19th-c bakery (the pub still does bread-making courses); children welcome, garden picnic-sets. *(Anon)*

BOTCHESTON — SK4804
Greyhound (01455) 822355
Main Street, off B5380 E of Desford; LE9 9FF Beamed village pub under new management; good freshly cooked food at reasonable prices, friendly attentive service, Marstons-related ales, pine tables in two light and airy dining rooms; children welcome, garden with play area, open all day Sat from 8am for breakfast. *(SAB and MJW)*

BRANSTON — SK8129
★**Wheel** (01476) 870376
Main Street; NG32 1RU Beamed 18th-c stone-built village pub with stylishly simple open-plan décor, good country food cooked by chef-landlord, three well kept changing ales from central servery (could be Batemans, Brewsters and Oldershaws – festival early Sept), friendly smartly dressed staff, woodburner and open fires; background and occasional live music; children welcome, dogs in bar, attractive garden, next to church, splendid countryside near Belvoir Castle, closed Mon. *(Phil and Jane Hodson)*

BRAUNSTON — SK8306
Blue Ball (01572) 722135
Off A606 in Oakham; Cedar Street; LE15 8QS Pretty thatched and beamed dining pub with good food (not Sun evening) including deals, well kept Marstons-related ales, decent wines, log fire, leather furniture and country pine in linked rooms, small conservatory, local art for sale, monthly jazz Sun lunchtime; free wi-fi; children welcome, painted furniture outside, attractive village, open all day Sat, till 8pm Sun. *(Barry Collett)*

BRAUNSTON — SK8306
Old Plough (01572) 722714
Off A606 in Oakham; Church Street; LE15 8QT Comfortably opened-up black-beamed village local, Fullers London Pride, Grainstore and a couple of guests, pleasant attentive service, log fire, back dining conservatory; tables in small sheltered garden, open all day weekends. *(Barry Collett)*

Though we don't usually mention it in the text, most pubs will now make coffee or tea – it's always worth asking.

BRUNTINGTHORPE SP6089
⋆**Joiners Arms** (0116) 247 8258
Off A5199 S of Leicester: Church Walk/
Cross Street; LE17 5QH More restaurant
than pub with most of the two beamed rooms
set for eating, drinkers have area by small
light oak bar with open fire; an ale such
as Greene King or Sharps, plenty of wines
by the glass including champagne, first
class imaginative food served by friendly
efficient staff, cheaper set lunch menu,
candles on tables, elegant dining chairs, big
flower arrangements, civilised but relaxed
atmosphere; picnic-sets in front, closed Sun
evening, Mon. *(Keith and Sandra Ross, SAB and
MJW, G Jennings)*

BUCKMINSTER SK8822
⋆**Tollemache Arms** (01476) 860477
B676 Colsterworth–Melton Mowbray;
Main Street; NG33 5SA Stylish dining pub
with linked areas including elegant corner
library room with log fire, other bare-boards
parts with mix of wheelback, dining and
stripped kitchen chairs and some specially
made small pews, daily newspapers by
leather chesterfield, fresh flowers, Oakham,
Tring and nice choice of wines by the glass,
good popular food; background music;
children and dogs welcome, teak furniture
on back grass, small herb and salad garden,
swing, closed Sun evening, Mon. *(Martin
Jones, Toby Jones, Barry Collett)*

BURTON OVERY SP6797
Bell (0116) 259 2365
Main Street; LE8 9DL Good interesting
choice of food from lunchtime sandwiches
up in L-shaped open-plan bar and dining
room (used mainly for larger parties),
log fire, comfortable sofas, ales such as
Langton and Timothy Taylors Landlord,
good helpful service; children welcome,
nice garden, lovely village, open all day
weekends. *(Duncan Cloud, SAB and MJW)*

CALDECOTT SP8693
Plough (01536) 770284
Main Street; LE16 8RS Welcoming pub
in attractive ironstone village; carpeted bar
with banquettes and small tables leading to
spacious eating area, well kept Langton and
a guest, wide range of enjoyable inexpensive
food including blackboard specials, prompt
service; children welcome, garden at back.
(Sue Kidd)

CHURCH LANGTON SP7293
Langton Arms (01858) 545181
*B6047 about 3 miles N of Market
Harborough; just off A6; LE16 7SY*
Extended old village dining pub with
enjoyable sensibly priced home-made food
(Sun till 7pm) including specials, helpful
chatty staff, well kept Greene King ales and
decent wines by the glass, clean modernised
interior, bar to the left, small eating
area on right with open fire, restaurant
behind; background music, TV; children
welcome, garden with heated shelter and
maybe summer bouncy castle, open all
day Fri-Sun. *(Veronica Brown, Phil and Jane
Hodson)*

COLEORTON SK4016
Angel (01530) 834742
The Moor; LE67 8GB Friendly homely
pub with good range of enjoyable reasonably
priced food including Sun carvery, well kept
beers such as Marstons Pedigree, hospitable
attentive staff, beams and open fire; tables
outside, open all day Sun. *(Paul and Karen
Cornock)*

COLEORTON SK4016
Kings Arms (01530) 815435
The Moor (off A512); LE67 8GD
Refurbished village pub with its own good
value Tap House ales along with Bass and a
changing guest, enjoyable reasonably priced
food (not Sun evening, Mon) including daily
carvery, friendly staff, pool room with TV, live
music last Sun of month; children and dogs
welcome, garden with pétanque and play
area, open all day; for sale last we heard –
so things may change. *(Anon)*

COTTESMORE SK9013
Sun (01572) 812321
B668 NE of Oakham; LE15 7DH 17th-c
thatched stone-built village pub under new
owners – reports please. *(Pat and Stewart
Gordon, Gordon and Margaret Ormondroyd,
Barry Collett)*

CROPSTON SK5510
Badgers Sett (0116) 236 7999
Reservoir Road; LE7 7GQ Rambling rustic
Vintage Inn family dining pub, popular place
with their usual good value food, friendly
if not always speedy service, ales such as
Everards and lots of wines by the glass, daily
papers, log fires; nice garden and views over
Cropston Reservoir, open all day. *(Phil and
Jane Hodson)*

DADLINGTON SP4097
Dog & Hedgehog (01455) 213151
The Green, opposite church; CV13 6JB
Popular red-brick village dining pub with
good choice of well liked food, friendly staff
and hands-on owners, ales such as Quartz
and Tunnel, nice wines, restaurant; children
welcome, garden looking down to Ashby de
la Zouch Canal. *(Mike and Margaret Banks,
Gordon and Jenny Quick)*

DISEWORTH SK4524
Plough (01332) 810333
*Near East Midlands Airport and M1
junction 23A; DE74 2QJ* Extended and
recently refurbished 16th-c beamed pub, bar
and spacious dining room, well kept Bass,
Greene King, Marstons and guests, low-
priced traditional food (not Sun evening);

dogs welcome, paved terrace with steps up to lawn, handy for Donington Park race track, open all day. *(Phil and Jane Hodson)*

EAST LANGTON   SP7292
★ **Bell** (01858) 545278

Off B6047; Main Street; LE16 7TW
Appealing creeper-clad beamed country inn buzzing with locals and families, well kept Fullers, Greene King, Langton and a guest, nice wines, good well presented food including daily specials and popular Sun carvery, friendly efficient staff, long low-ceilinged stripped-stone bar, spacious restaurant, modern pine furniture, log fires; picnic-sets on sloping front lawn, bedrooms. *(John Saville, Gerry and Rosemary Dobson, Maurice and Janet Thorpe, Ron Corbett)*

FOXTON   SP6989
★ **Foxton Locks** (0116) 279 1515

Foxton Locks, off A6 3 miles NW of Market Harborough (park by bridge 60/62 and walk); LE16 7RA Popular place in great canalside setting at foot of spectacular flight of locks; large comfortably reworked L-shaped bar, pubby food including winter fixed-price menu, converted boathouse does snacks, friendly service (may slow at busy times), half a dozen well kept ales such as Caledonian Deuchars IPA, Fullers London Pride and Theakstons; children welcome, large raised terrace and covered decking, steps down to fenced waterside lawn, good walks. *(Dr Kevan Tucker, Gerry and Rosemary Dobson, G Jennings)*

GADDESBY   SK6813
Cheney Arms (01664) 840260

Rearsby Lane; LE7 4XE Refurbished red-brick village pub; bar with bare-boards and terracotta-tiled floor, well kept Everards and a guest from brick-faced servery, open fires including inglenook in more formal dining room, big helpings of popular reasonably priced food from good lunchtime baguettes up; free wi-fi; children welcome, walled back garden with smokers' shelter, lovely medieval church, four bedrooms, closed Mon lunchtime. *(R T and J C Moggridge, Phil and Jane Hodson)*

GILMORTON   SP5787
Grey Goose (01455) 552555

Lutterworth Road; LE17 5PN Popular bar-restaurant with good range of enjoyable freshly made food from lunchtime sandwiches up, early-bird weekday deals and Sun carvery, ales such as Grainstore, several wines by the glass including champagne, good friendly service coping well at busy times, light contemporary décor, stylish wood and metal bar stools mixing with comfortable

sofas and armchairs, woodburner in stripped-brick fireplace with logs stacked beside; modern furniture on terrace. *(R L Borthwick)*

GLOOSTON   SP7495
Old Barn (01858) 545884

Off B6047 in Tur Langton; LE16 7ST
Beamed 16th-c village pub refurbished under current hard-working licensees, enjoyable fairly priced food (not Sun evening) including home-made pizzas, daily specials and good value set menu, ales such as Langton and Wells & Youngs, pleasant service and atmosphere; tables out in front, open all day Fri-Sun. *(R L Borthwick)*

GREAT BOWDEN   SP7488
Red Lion (01858) 463106

Off A6 N of Market Harborough; Main Street; LE16 7HB Attractively modernised place with good well presented food, carefully chosen wines and three real ales including a house beer from Langton, friendly helpful staff; background music; children welcome, tables in good-sized garden, open all day, no food Sun evening, Mon. *(Anon)*

GREETHAM   SK9214
Plough (01572) 813613

B668 Stretton–Cottesmore; LE15 7NJ
Traditional village pub, comfortable and welcoming, with good home-made food and five well kept ales including Grainstore and Timothy Taylors, fire dividing cosy lounge from eating area, afternoon teas; children and dogs welcome, garden behind, good local walks and not far from Rutland Water, open all day Thurs-Sun. *(Martin and Alison Stainsby)*

GUMLEY   SP6890
Bell (0116) 279 0126

NW of Market Harborough; Main Street; LE16 7RU Friendly beamed village local under new owners; four ales including Timothy Taylors Landlord, home-cooked food from blackboard menu, carpeted bar with small open fire; sports TV, live music; children welcome and dogs (theirs are Rhum and Islay), pond in terrace garden, open all day weekends. *(Gerry and Rosemary Dobson)*

HALLATON   SP7896
Bewicke Arms (01858) 555217

On Eastgate, opposite village sign; LE16 8UB Extensive refurbishment for this attractive old thatched pub; Fullers London Pride and a local house beer, all-day food from pub favourites up, three bar dining areas, restaurant with scrubbed pine tables, log fires and woodburners, memorabilia from ancient inter-village bottle-kicking match (still held on Easter Mon), upstairs room

---

If you report on a pub that's not a featured entry, please tell us any lunchtimes or evenings when it doesn't serve bar food.

with darts and sports TV; children welcome, no dogs inside, disabled facilities, big terrace overlooking paddock, play area, three bedrooms in converted stables, tearoom and shop, open all day. *(Ian Herdman)*

HINCKLEY   SP4092
Lime Kilns (01455) 631158
Watling Street (A5); LE10 3ED Red-brick roadside pub by the Ashby Canal; decent reasonably priced pubby food (not Sun evening), well kept Marstons-related ales and traditional ciders, friendly staff, small bar and compact upstairs lounge overlooking canal, dominoes, monthly quiz; downstairs lavatories; waterside garden, some moorings, annual boat race, open all day weekends. *(Phil and Jane Hodson)*

HINCKLEY
Railway (01455) 612399
Station Road; LE10 1AP Friendly chatty pub owned by the Steamin' Billy Brewing Company, their ales (contract brewed nearby by Belvoir) and guests from seven pumps, also draught continentals and real cider, sensibly priced food including Thurs steak night, friendly young staff, open fires, darts; dogs welcome, beer garden behind, handy for station. *(Phil and Jane Hodson)*

HOBY   SK6717
Blue Bell (01664) 434247
Main Street; LE14 3DT Attractive rebuilt thatched pub, well run, with good range of enjoyable realistically priced food (all day weekends – best to book) including popular three-course deal Mon, friendly attentive uniformed staff, four well kept Everards ales, Adnams and a guest, good choice of wines by the glass, teas/coffees, open-plan and airy with beams, comfortable traditional furniture, old local photographs, skittle alley and darts; background music; children, dogs and walkers welcome, valley view garden with picnic-sets and boules, open all day. *(Phil and Jane Hodson, R L Borthwick)*

HOSE   SK7329
Rose & Crown (01949) 869458
Bolton Lane; LE14 4JE Modernised 200-year-old beamed village pub, good selection of well kept beers, real cider and several wines by the glass, nice food from pub staples up (not Sun evening, Mon or Tues), small raised dining area and steps up to intimate restaurant; tables on back decking, open all day weekends, closed Mon and Tues lunchtimes. *(Anon)*

HOTON   SK5722
Packe Arms (01509) 889106
A60; LE12 5SJ Spacious old Vintage Inn with sturdy beams and open fires, their usual choice of enjoyable food including good value fixed-price menu, well kept ales such as Batemans, Black Sheep and Everards, realistically priced wines, prompt friendly service from uniformed staff; children welcome, tables outside, open all day. *(Mike and Mary Carter, Phil and Jane Hodson)*

HOUGHTON ON THE HILL   SK6703
Old Black Horse (0116) 241 3486
Main Street (just off A47 Leicester–Uppingham); LE7 9GD Welcoming village pub with enjoyable home-made food (not Sun evening, Mon lunchtime), well kept Everards and a guest and decent wines by the glass, bare-boards dining area with lots of panelling; background music; attractive big garden, boules. *(Barry Collett)*

HUNGARTON   SK6907
Black Boy (0116) 259 5410
Main Street; LE7 9JR Large open-plan partly divided restaurant bar with open fire, good well priced food cooked to order by landlord-chef (weekend booking advised), changing ales such as Greene King, Fullers and Wells & Youngs, cheerful welcoming staff; background music; picnic-sets out on deck, closed Sun evening. *(Anon)*

ILLSTON ON THE HILL   SP7099
★ Fox & Goose (0116) 259 6340
Main Street, off B6047 Market Harborough–Melton Mowbray; LE7 9EG Individual two-bar local, simple, comfortable and friendly, with hunting pictures and assorted oddments including stuffed animals, woodburner and good coal fire, well kept Everards and a guest, enjoyable home-made food (Weds-Sat); children and dogs welcome, closed weekday lunchtimes, open all day weekends. *(Anon)*

KIBWORTH BEAUCHAMP   SP6894
Coach & Horses (0116) 279 2247
A6 S of Leicester; LE8 0NN 16th-c beamed local under newish friendly management; carpeted bar area and refurbished restaurant, enjoyable well priced traditional food along with occasional tapas, ales such as Fullers, Greene King, Marstons and Thwaites; background music; children welcome, no dogs, disabled access, some outside seating at front and side, open all day weekends (food till 7pm Sun), closed Mon lunchtime. *(Anon)*

KIRBY MUXLOE   SK5104
Royal Oak (0116) 239 3166
Main Street; LE9 2AN Recently refurbished modernish pub with good food from sandwiches and pub favourites to more inventive dishes, lunchtime/early-evening set deal, Adnams, Everards and a guest ale, good wine choice, sizeable restaurant, some live jazz; disabled facilities, picnic-sets outside, nearby 15th-c castle ruins. *(Anon)*

KNIPTON   SK8231
Manners Arms (01476) 879222
Signed off A607 Grantham–Melton Mowbray; Croxton Road; NG32 1RH

Handsome Georgian hunting lodge reworked as comfortable country inn, bare-boards bar with log fire, four well kept ales and good choice of wines by the glass, enjoyable food here or in sizeable restaurant with attractive conservatory; background music; terrace with ornamental pool, lovely views over pretty village, ten comfortable individually furnished bedrooms, open all day. *(Anon)*

KNOSSINGTON
SK8008
Fox & Hounds (01664) 452129
Off A606 W of Oakham; Somerby Road; LE15 8LY Attractive 18th-c ivy-clad village pub refurbished by present landlady and emphasis on dining, beamed bar with log fire, cosy eating areas, nice food from traditional choices to blackboard specials, Fullers London Pride, attentive friendly service; no children under 8; dogs welcome, big back garden, closed Mon, lunchtimes Tues-Thurs and Sun evening. *(Anon)*

LEICESTER
SK5804
Ale Wagon (0116) 262 3330
Rutland Street/Charles Street; LE1 1RE Basic 1930s two-room corner local with nine real ales including its own Hoskins Brothers beers, a traditional cider, no food apart from baps, coal fire, upstairs function room; background music; handy for Curve Theatre and station, open all day, closed Sun lunchtime. *(P Dawn)*

LEICESTER
SK5804
Criterion (0116) 262 5418
Millstone Lane; LE1 5JN 1960s building with dark wood and carpeted main room, Oakham ales and up to ten guests at weekends, 100 bottled beers and a couple of real ciders, good value stone-baked pizzas (not Sun) plus some other snacky food, room on left with games and old-fashioned juke box, regular live music and quiz nights, annual comedy festival; picnic-sets outside, open all day. *(P Dawn)*

LEICESTER
SK5804
★ Globe (0116) 253 9492
Silver Street; LE1 5EU Refurbished but keeping original character, lots of woodwork in partitioned areas off central bar, bare boards and some Victorian mosaic floor tiles, mirrors and working gas lamps, four Everards ales along with three guests, two real ciders and over a dozen wines by the glass, friendly staff, enjoyable well priced food (till 6pm Sun) from bar snacks up, good upstairs evening bistro (Thurs-Sat); background music (not in snug); children and dogs welcome, metal café-style tables out in front, open all day. *(Val and Alan Green, P Dawn)*

LEICESTER
SK5803
Kings Head (0116) 254 8240
King Street; LE1 6RL Small drinkers' pub with good atmosphere and helpful friendly staff, three well kept Black Country ales and five regularly changing guests, proper cider, can bring your own food, log fire; no children or dogs, raised back terrace, near rugby ground and busy on match days, open all day. *(Andrew Bosi)*

LEICESTER
SK5803
★ Swan & Rushes (0116) 233 9167
Oxford Street/Infirmary Square; LE1 5WR Triangular-shaped pub with up to nine well kept ales including Batemans and Oakham, over 100 bottled beers, real cider, welcoming staff and thriving local atmosphere in two rooms with big oak tables, low-priced home-made food (not Sun) including stone-baked pizzas, bar billiards and darts, themed beer and cider festivals, Thurs quiz, maybe Sat live music; very busy on match days; dogs welcome, sunny back terrace, open all day. *(Anon)*

LOUGHBOROUGH
SK5319
★ Swan in the Rushes (01509) 217014
The Rushes (A6); LE11 5BE Bare-boards town local with three smallish high-ceilinged rooms, good value Castle Rock and plenty of interesting changing guests, real cider and over 40 malt whiskies, well priced food (not Sun evenings) including vegetarian options, open fire and daily papers, good juke box, refurbished upstairs craft/world beer bar, occasional live music and theatre nights; free wi-fi; children welcome in eating areas, tables outside, open all day. *(P Dawn)*

LOUGHBOROUGH
SK5319
Tap & Mallet (01509) 210028
Nottingham Road; LE11 1EU Basic friendly pub with well kept Abbeydale, Batemans, Oakham and interesting microbrews, also foreign beers and Weston's cider, coal fire, darts and pool, juke box; children welcome, walled back garden with play area and pets corner, open all day Sat, closed lunchtime other days. *(P Dawn)*

LYDDINGTON
SP8796
★ Old White Hart (01572) 821703
Village signed off A6003 N of Corby; LE15 9LR Popular welcoming old inn, softly lit front bar with heavy beams in low ceiling, just a few tables, glass-shielded log fire, Greene King IPA and a guest, good food (not Sun evening in winter) including own sausages and cured meats (landlord is a butcher), half-price offer Mon-Thurs,

---

We mention bottled beers and spirits only if there is something unusual about them – imported belgian real ales, say, or dozens of malt whiskies; so do please let us know about them in your reports.

efficient obliging service, attractive restaurant, further tiled-floor room with rugs, lots of fine hunting prints and woodburner; children welcome, seats by heaters in pretty walled garden, eight floodlit boules pitches, handy for Bede House and good nearby walks, ten bedrooms. *(Tracey and Stephen Groves, Howard and Margaret Buchanan)*

MANTON   SK8704
Horse & Jockey (01572) 737335
St Mary's Road; LE15 8SU Welcoming early 19th-c stone pub with updated low-beamed interior, modern furniture on wood or stone floors, woodburner, well kept ales such as Grainstore and Greene King plus a house beer (Fall at the First), decent fairly priced food from baguettes to blackboard specials, good cheery service; background music; children and dogs welcome, colourful tubs and hanging baskets, terrace picnic-sets, maybe the Rutland Morris Men, nice location – on Rutland Water cycle route (racks provided), open all day in summer (all day Fri, Sat, till 7pm Sun in winter). *(Lois Dyer, Barry Collett, John and Sylvia Harrop)*

MARKET HARBOROUGH   SP7387
Sugar Loaf (01858) 469231
High Street; LE16 7NJ Popular Wetherspoons, smaller than many, attracting an eclectic mix of customers, half a dozen well priced ales (frequent beer festivals), usual value food all day; children welcome. *(Gerry and Rosemary Dobson)*

MARKET OVERTON   SK8816
Black Bull (01572) 767677
Opposite the church; LE15 7PW Attractive thatched and low-beamed stone-built pub (dating from the 17th c) in pretty village well placed for Rutland Water, welcoming licensees and staff, good home-made food (booking advised) from pub staples up in long carpeted bar and two separate dining areas, well kept Black Sheep and a couple of guests, woodburner, banquettes and sofas, newspapers; some background and live music; children and dogs welcome, tables out in front by small carp pool, five bedrooms (the two in the pub are ensuite), open all day Sun till 6pm, closed Mon. *(Phil and Jane Hodson)*

MEDBOURNE   SP7992
★ Nevill Arms (01858) 565288
B664 Market Harborough–Uppingham; LE16 8EE Handsome stone-built Victorian inn nicely located by stream and footbridge, wide range of good bar and restaurant food including vegetarian choices, pleasant helpful uniformed staff, well kept ales such as Bass, Adnams and Sharps, beams and mullion windows, log fires, modern artwork,

stylish restaurant; no dogs; back terrace with stable-conversion café (8am-4pm), streamside picnic-sets, 11 refurbished bedrooms, good breakfast, open all day. *(Barry Collett, Ian Herdman)*

MELTON MOWBRAY   SK7519
Anne of Cleves (01664) 481336
Burton Street, by St Mary's Church; LE13 1AE Monks' chantry dating from the 14th c and gifted to Anne of Cleves by Henry VIII; chunky tables, character chairs and settles on flagstones, heavy beams and latticed mullioned windows, tapestries on burnt orange walls, well kept Everards and guests, decent wines and ample helpings of above average food, small end dining room; background music; tables in pretty little walled garden with flagstone terrace, open all day. *(P and D Carpenter)*

MELTON MOWBRAY   SK7518
Boat (01664) 500969
Burton Street; LE13 1AF Chatty and welcoming one-room local with four well kept ales and lots of malt whiskies, no food, panelling and open fire, darts; dogs welcome, open all day Fri, Sat. *(Glenn Upton, Phil and Jane Hodson)*

MELTON MOWBRAY   SK7519
Crown (01664) 564682
Burton Street; LE13 1AE Handy two-room central pub with well kept Everards and a guest, low priced lunchtime food (also Fri, Sat evenings), friendly staff and customers, skittle alley; children and dogs welcome, disabled access, beer garden behind, open all day. *(Phil and Jane Hodson)*

MOUNTSORREL   SK5715
Swan (0116) 230 2340
Loughborough Road, off A6; LE12 7AT Log fires, old flagstones and stripped stone, friendly staff and locals, enjoyable well priced food from baguettes and light dishes to generous full meals (best to book evenings), well kept ales including Theakstons, Weston's cider and good choice of wines, pine tables and gingham cloths in neat dining area and restaurant; dogs welcome in bar, pretty walled back garden down to canalised River Soar, self-contained accommodation, open all day weekends. *(Anon)*

MOWSLEY   SP6488
Staff of Life (0116) 240 2359
Village signposted off A5199 S of Leicester; Main Street; LE17 6NT Some refurbishment at this well run high-gabled little village pub; roomy fairly traditional bar, high-backed settles on flagstones, wicker chairs on shiny wood floor and stools lined up along unusual circular counter, woodburner,

---

Pubs close to motorway junctions are listed at the back of the book.

Sharps Doom Bar and guests, half a dozen wines by the glass, well liked interesting mid-priced food (not Sun or Mon evenings), set deal (Tues, Weds), good service; background music; well behaved children welcome (no under-12s Fri and Sat nights), seats out in front and on nice leaf-shaded deck, open all day Sun, closed Mon-Fri lunchtimes. *(Nigel and Sue Foster, SAB and MJW)*

OAKHAM   SK8508
Three Crowns (01572) 757441
Northgate, next to methodist church; LE15 6QS Friendly pub serving full range of Steamin' Billy ales, spacious L-shaped bar with mix of tables and chairs, comfortable sofas, no food apart from lunchtime cobs. *(Barry Collett)*

OLD DALBY   SK6723
Crown (01664) 823134
Debdale Hill; LE14 3LF Creeper-clad early 16th-c pub with intimate farmhouse rooms up and down steps, black beams, antique oak settles among other seats, rustic prints and open fires, five real ales including Belvoir and plenty of wines by the glass, enjoyable well presented food from traditional choices up (not Sun evening, Mon), extended dining room opening on to terrace; background music; children and dogs welcome, disabled facilities, attractive garden with boules, open all day weekends, closed Mon lunchtime. *(Anon)*

QUORNDON   SK5516
Manor House (01509) 413416
Woodhouse Road; LE12 8AL Sizeable late Victorian pub with good if not especially cheap food from interesting menu (cheaper set options), ales such as Bass, Belvoir, Greene King, Theakstons and Timothy Taylors, friendly staff; free wi-fi; children welcome, good outside areas, next door to Quorn & Woodhouse heritage railway station, open all day. *(Mike and Mary Carter)*

REDMILE   SK7935
★ **Windmill** (01949) 842281
Off A52 Grantham–Nottingham; Main Street; NG13 0GA Snug low-beamed bar with sofas, easy chairs and log fire in large raised hearth, comfortable roomier dining areas with woodburners, wide choice of good generous home-made food from sandwiches and tapas to game from local Belvoir Estate, meal deals and Sun roasts too, well kept Adnams and Timothy Taylors Landlord, good wines by the glass, local cordials, neat friendly young staff; children welcome, sizeable well furnished front courtyard, open all day. *(Anon)*

ROTHLEY   SK5812
Woodmans Stroke (0116) 230 2785
Church Street; LE7 7PD Immaculate family-run thatched pub with good value weekday lunchtime bar food from sandwiches

up, well kept changing ales, good wines by the glass including champagne, friendly service, beams and settles in front rooms, open fire, old local photographs plus rugby and cricket memorabilia; sports TV; pretty front hanging baskets, cast-iron tables in attractive garden with heaters, pétanque, open all day Sat. *(Gordon and Jenny Quick)*

RYHALL   TF0310
Wicked Witch (01780) 763649
Bridge Street; PE9 4HH Refurbished dining pub with good upmarket food including set deals, main bar, lounge and restaurant; children welcome, tables in back garden, open all day Sat, till 7pm Sun. *(Mike and Margaret Banks)*

SADDINGTON   SP6591
Queens Head (0116) 240 2536
S of Leicester between A5199 (ex A50) and A6; Main Street; LE8 0QH Welcoming village pub with well kept Everards, nice wines and good well presented food, attractively updated interior on different levels, country and reservoir views from dining conservatory and sloping terrace; free wi-fi; children welcome, farm shop, open all day Weds-Sun. *(Veronica Brown)*

SHAWELL   SP5480
White Swan (01788) 860357
Main Street; village signed down declassified road (ex A427) off A5/A426 roundabout – turn right in village; not far from M6 junction 1; LE17 6AG Attractive little beamed 17th-c dining pub cleanly modernised by present owners; good interesting food all day (till 6pm Sun) from landlord-chef along with some pub staples, local Dow Bridge ales and guests, lots of wines by the glass, champagne breakfast Sat, restaurant; children welcome, open all day. *(Anon)*

SHEARSBY   SP6290
Chandlers Arms (0116) 247 8384
Fenny Lane, off A50 Leicester–Northampton; LE17 6PL Comfortable old creeper-clad pub in attractive village, four well kept ales including Dow Bridge (tasting trays, July beer festival), Weston's cider, good value pubby food (not Sun evening), wall seats and wheelback chairs, table skittles; background music, Weds quiz night (Sept-May); tables in secluded raised garden overlooking green, open all day Sun, closed Mon. *(Anon)*

SILEBY   SK6015
Horse & Trumpet (01509) 812549
Barrow Road, opposite church; LE12 7LP Friendly beamed village pub renovated by the Steamin' Billy group, their beers and guests kept well, real cider, fresh cobs, darts, some live music; well behaved dogs welcome, terrace picnic-sets, open all day. *(Anon)*

SOMERBY SK7710

★**Stilton Cheese** (01664) 454394

High Street; off A606 Oakham–Melton Mowbray, via Cold Overton, or Leesthorpe and Pickwell; LE14 2QB Good friendly staff in enjoyable ironstone pub with beamed bar/lounge, comfortable furnishings on red patterned carpets, country prints, plates and copper pots, stuffed badger and pike, Grainstore, Marstons, Tetleys and two guests, 30 malt whiskies, good reasonably priced pubby food along with daily specials, restaurant; children welcome, seats on terrace, peaceful setting on edge of pretty village. *(Mike and Margaret Banks, Alan Bulley)*

SOUTH CROXTON SK6810

Golden Fleece (01664) 840275

Main Street; LE7 3RL Restaurant more than pub; clean minimalist feel with comfortable modern furniture, good choice of popular food including cheaper weekday lunchtime/early evening set menu, Tues italian night and Sun carvery (till 7pm), friendly helpful service, ales such as Adnams and Wells & Youngs, good house wine, log fire; children welcome, lovely area. *(SAB and MJW)*

SOUTH LUFFENHAM SK9401

★**Coach House** (01780) 720166

Stamford Road (A6121); LE15 8NT Nicely reworked old inn with flagstoned bar, stripped stone or terracotta walls, bright scatter cushions on small pews, church candles and log fire, Adnams, Greene King and Timothy Taylors, decent wines by the glass, good well priced food served by friendly efficient staff, neat built-in seating in separate snug, smarter more modern feeling back dining room; children welcome, dogs in bar, small deck behind, seven bedrooms, open all day Sat, closed Sun evening, Mon lunchtime. *(Anon)*

SPROXTON SK8524

Crown (01476) 861608

Coston Road; LE14 4QB Friendly fairly compact 19th-c stone-built inn with spotless well laid-out interior, good reasonably priced food from bar snacks to restaurant dishes cooked by landlord-chef, well kept changing ales, good wines and coffee, light airy bar with woodburner, lounge and restaurant with glassed-off wine store; children welcome, dogs in bar, lovely sunny courtyard, attractive village and nice local walks, three bedrooms, closed Mon. *(Phil and Jane Hodson)*

THORPE LANGTON SP7492

★**Bakers Arms** (01858) 545201

Off B6047 N of Market Harborough; LE16 7TS Civilised thatched restauranty pub; consistently good imaginative food from regularly changing menu (must book), cottagey beamed linked areas and stylishly simple country décor, well kept local Langton ale and good choice of wines by the glass, friendly efficient staff, maybe a pianist; no under-12s or dogs; picnic-sets in back garden with country views, closed weekday lunchtimes, Sun evening, Mon. *(SAB and MJW, R L Borthwick)*

UPPER HAMBLETON SK8907

★**Finchs Arms** (01572) 756575

Off A606; Oakham Road; LE15 8TL Friendly 17th-c stone inn with outstanding views over Rutland Water, four log fires, beamed and flagstoned bar, Black Sheep, Timothy Taylors Landlord and a guest, several wines by the glass including champagne, elegant restaurant with decorative bay trees and modern seating, second newly built dining room, well liked food including set menus, afternoon teas; no dogs; children welcome, suntrap hillside terrace, good surrounding walks, ten bedrooms, open all day. *(Colin McKerrow, Colin McLachlan)*

UPPINGHAM SP8699

Crown (01572) 822302

High Street East; LE15 9PY Welcoming refurbished 18th-c town inn, half a dozen or so well kept ales including Everards (beer festivals), decent reasonably priced home-made food (not Sun evening) including range of pies, back restaurant; background and some live music; bedrooms, open all day. *(D Goodger, Barry Collett)*

UPPINGHAM SP8699

Falcon (01572) 823535

High Street East; LE15 9PY Relaxed and quietly refined old coaching inn, oak-panelled bar and spacious nicely furnished lounge with roaring fire, big windows overlooking market square, enjoyable food (not Sun evening) from bar snacks up, three Grainstore ales, good friendly service; children welcome, dogs in bar, back garden with terrace, bedrooms, open all day. *(Michael Doswell, Barry Collett)*

UPPINGHAM SP8699

Vaults (01572) 823259

Market Place; LE15 9QH Attractive old pub next to church, enjoyable reasonably priced traditional food, friendly helpful staff,

---

Post Office address codings confusingly give the impression that some pubs are in Leicestershire, when they're really in Cambridgeshire (which is where we list them).

Adnams Broadside, Marstons Pedigree, a house beer from Grainstore and a guest, several wines by the glass, comfortable banquettes, pleasant upstairs dining room; background music, sports TVs; children and dogs welcome, some tables out overlooking picturesque square, four bedrooms (bookings from nearby Falcon Hotel), open all day. *(Barry Collett)*

WALTHAM ON THE WOLDS SK8024
Royal Horseshoes (01664) 464289
Melton Road (A607); LE14 4AJ Attractive smartly refurbished stone and thatch pub in centre of village, extensive choice of generous affordably priced food, ales such as Fullers and Greene King, over 20 gins, two main rooms with beams and open fires; tables outside, annexe bedrooms. *(Adrian Johnson)*

WHITWICK SK4316
Three Horseshoes (01530) 837311
Leicester Road; LE67 5GN Unpretentious unchanging local with long quarry-tiled bar, old wooden benches and open fires, tiny snug to the right, well kept Bass and Marstons Pedigree, piano, darts, dominoes and cards, newspapers, no food; outdoor lavatories, no proper pub sign so easy to miss. *(Anon)*

WOODHOUSE EAVES SK5214
Curzon Arms (01509) 890377
Maplewell Road; LE12 8QZ Cheerful old beamed pub in pretty Charnwood Forest village; enjoyable food (not Sun evening) from lunchtime sandwiches and pub favourites up, also good value weekday set menu, ales such as Caledonian Deuchars IPA, Hook Norton Hooky, Sharps Doom Bar and Timothy Taylors Landlord, good friendly service, attractive up-to-date décor,

interesting collection of wall clocks, carpeted dining room; background music, free wi-fi; children, walkers and dogs welcome, ramp for disabled access, good-sized front lawn and terrace, open all day weekends. *(R L Borthwick)*

WOODHOUSE EAVES SK5214
Old Bulls Head (01509) 890255
Main Street; LE12 8RZ Big open-plan contemporary Mitchells & Butlers dining pub, clean and tidy, with good choice of food including pizzas, pasta and grills, fixed-price menu (lunchtime till 7pm weekdays), good wine list and well kept ales such as Timothy Taylors Landlord, friendly staff in black; well behaved children welcome, outside tables, nice village setting and handy for Charnwood Forest and Bardon Hill, open all day. *(Phil and Jane Hodson)*

WYMESWOLD SK6023
Three Crowns (01509) 880153
Far Street (A6006); LE12 6TZ Snug chatty 18th-c local in attractive village, good friendly staff, Adnams, Bass, Sharps and a guest, decent reasonably priced pubby food, pleasant character furnishings in beamed bar and lounge, open fire, lots of atmosphere; picnic-sets out on decking, open all day. *(Comus and Sarah Elliott)*

WYMESWOLD SK6023
Windmill (01509) 881313
Brook Street; LE12 6TT Bustling side-street village pub with enjoyable good value home-made food from lunchtime snacks up, ales such as Castle Rock, Langton and Sharps Doom Bar, good cheerful service even though busy; children welcome, dogs in bar, back garden, open all day weekends. *(Mike and Mary Carter, Comus and Sarah Elliott)*

Lincolnshire

BARNOLDBY LE BECK
TA2303 Map 8

Ship 🍽 🍷

Village signposted off A18 Louth–Grimsby; DN37 0BG

Tranquil refined dining pub with Edwardian and Victorian bric-a-brac

A delightful pub in a charming village with a warm welcome for all. Many customers are here for the good, popular food, but drinkers also pop in and the helpful staff keep Black Sheep and Tom Woods on handpump, up to a dozen malt whiskies and wines by the glass from a good list. It's all neatly kept with an interesting collection of Edwardian and Victorian bric-a-brac: stand-up telephones, violins, a horn gramophone, a bowler and top hats, old racquets, riding crops and hockey sticks. Heavy dark-ringed drapes swathe the windows, with plants in ornate china bowls on the sills. Furnishings include comfortable dark green wall benches with lots of pretty propped-up cushions, heavily stuffed green plush Victorian-looking chairs on a green fleur de lys carpet and a warming winter coal fire; background music. A fenced-off sunny area behind has hanging baskets and a few picnic-sets under parasols.

🍽 Food is especially good and includes sandwiches, cod cheeks with chorizo and pea purée, goats cheese, tomato and pine nut tart with basil oil and red onion marmalade, ballotine of chicken with tomatoes and pesto wrapped in pancetta with celeriac parmentier, pork tenderloin and slow-roast belly with butternut squash purée, leeks and saffron demi-glaze, duck with roast jerusalem artichokes and rhubarb compote, halibut fillet with mini stuffed peppers and pimento sauce, and puddings. *Benchmark main dish: skate wing with parsley butter £14.95. Two-course evening meal £21.00.*

Free house ~ Licensee Michele Hancock ~ Real ale ~ (01472) 822308 ~ Open 12-3, 6-11 (midnight Sat); 12-5 Sun; closed Sun evening ~ Bar food 12-2, 6-9; 12-5 Sun ~ Restaurant ~ Children welcome ~ Wi-fi ~ www.the-shipinn.com
Recommended by Paul Valentine, Michael Butler

DRY DODDINGTON
SK8546 Map 8

Wheatsheaf

Main Street; 1.5 miles off A1 N of Grantham; NG23 5HU

Friendly pub with popular food and drink; handy for A1

New licensees have taken over this friendly old pub and, happily, little has changed. The front bar is basically two rooms, with a woodburning stove, a variety of settles and chairs enlivened by bold patterned scatter cushions, and tables in the windows looking across to the green and the lovely 14th-c church with its crooked tower. The serving bar on the right has Batemans XB, Greene King Abbot, Timothy Taylors Landlord and a guest such as Poachers Billy Boy on handpump, and a nice choice of over a dozen wines by the glass. A slight slope leads down to the extended carpeted and comfortable dining room. Once a cow byre, this part is even more ancient than the rest of the building, perhaps dating from the 13th c; background music. The front terrace has neat tables under cocktail parasols, among tubs of flowers; disabled access at the side.

 Cooked by the landlady, the food includes sandwiches, smoked salmon with capers, black pudding and poached egg salad, home-baked honey-glazed ham and eggs, toad in the hole with cabbage and mash, chicken balti, wild mushroom risotto, lamb with bordelaise sauce and dauphinoise potatoes, salmon with beetroot and orange oil dressing, and puddings such as apple and blackberry crumble and vanilla crème brûlée. *Benchmark main dish: cod and twice-fried chips £12.95. Two-course evening meal £18.00.*

Free house ~ Licensees Steven and Joanne McLeod ~ Real ale ~ (01400) 281458 ~ Open 12-2.30, 5-11; 12-11 Sat, Sun; closed Mon except bank holidays ~ Bar food 12-2.30, 7-9 ~ Restaurant ~ Children welcome ~ Dogs allowed in bar ~ www.wheatsheaf-pub.co.uk
Recommended by Michael and Jenny Back, Ryta Lyndley, Michael Doswell, T E Stone, Gordon and Margaret Ormondroyd

GEDNEY DYKE
Chequers ★ ♀
TF4125 Map 8

Off A17 Holbeach–Kings Lynn; PE12 0AJ

Smart dining pub with small bar, stylish restaurant rooms and imaginative food

This is a stylish and friendly fenland village pub that's popular with both drinkers and diners. The beamed bar has seats against the counter where they serve Woodfordes Wherry on handpump, 15 wines and champagne by the glass and a wide range of spirits. There are several high chairs around equally high tables and an open fire. The smart, interconnected, carpeted dining rooms and conservatory have high-backed cream or black dining chairs around white-clothed tables, and throughout there's bare brick here and there and good lighting; service is helpful and courteous. There are seats on the back terrace and in the fenced-off garden.

As well as a two- and three-course set menu (Wednesday-Saturday lunch, Wednesday-Friday dinner), the high class food includes terrine of confit rabbit and foie gras with pickled cauliflower and hazelnut dressing, gratin of Cornish cock crab, chargrilled chicken caesar salad, feuilletée of baby vegetables with butternut squash purée and sautéed morels, cheese or bacon burger with triple-cooked chips, sea trout with cockle and pancetta linguine and fish velouté, and puddings such as dark chocolate marquise and vanilla cheesecake with pineapple, chilli and lime. *Benchmark main dish: slow-roast pork belly with black pudding croquettes and cider jus £17.95. Two-course evening meal £21.00.*

Free house ~ Licensee Gareth Franklin ~ Real ale ~ (01406) 366700 ~ Open 11.30-3, 5-11.30 (midnight Sat); 12-10 Sun; closed Mon, first two weeks Jan ~ Bar food 12-2.30, 6-9; 12-3 Sun ~ Restaurant ~ Children welcome ~ Dogs allowed in bar ~ Wi-fi ~ www.the-chequers.co.uk *Recommended by Ken Marshall*

If we know a featured-entry pub does sandwiches, we always say so – if they're not mentioned, you'll have to assume you can't get one.

HEIGHINGTON
Butcher & Beast 🍴 £

TF0369 Map 8

High Street; LN4 1JS

Traditional village pub with terrific range of drinks, pubby food and a pretty garden by stream

By the time this edition is published, the hard-working, hands-on licensees will have extended the restaurant here. It's a cheerful and bustling village pub with lots going on – weekly themed food evenings, quizzes and beer festivals – and half a dozen real ales on handpump such as Batemans Black & White, XB, XXXB and a seasonal guest, with another guest from breweries such as Theakstons, Thornbridge or Welbeck Abbey; also two farm ciders, eight wines by the glass, 30 gins and 20 malt whiskies. The simply furnished bar has button-back wall banquettes, pubby furnishings and stools along the counter; occasional TV. The Snug has red-cushioned wall settles and high-backed wooden dining chairs, and the beamed dining room is neatly set with proper tablecloths and napkins; throughout, the cream walls are hung with old village photos and country pictures. A lawn, with picnic-sets, runs down to a stream and the award-winning hanging baskets and tubs are very pretty in summer.

Tasty, good value food includes sandwiches, deep-fried brie with onion relish, salt and pepper squid with garlic mayonnaise, chicken wrapped in pancetta with tomato and basil sauce, mushroom stir-fry, chilli con carne, burger with several toppings and chips, beef and mushroom stroganoff, lambs liver and bacon, and puddings such as chocolate fudge cake and apple crumble. *Benchmark main dish: steak in ale pie £9.25. Two-course evening meal £15.00.*

Batemans ~ Tenants Mal and Diane Gray ~ Real ale ~ (01522) 790386 ~ Open 12-11 (10.30 Sun) ~ Bar food 12-2, 5.30-8; 12-3 Sun ~ Restaurant ~ Children welcome away from bar ~ Dogs allowed in bar ~ Wi-fi ~ www.butcherandbeast.co.uk
Recommended by Paul Strange, Chris Johnson

HOUGH-ON-THE-HILL
Brownlow Arms ⭐🍴 ♟ 🛏

SK9246 Map 8

High Road; NG32 2AZ

Lincolnshire Dining Pub of the Year

Refined country house with beamed bar, real ales, imaginative food and graceful terrace; bedrooms

Our readers very much enjoy staying overnight in this smart old stone inn: the bedrooms are warm, well equipped and have modern bathrooms, and breakfasts are very good. The comfortable, welcoming beamed bar has plenty of panelling, some exposed brickwork, local prints and scenes, a large mirror, and a pile of logs beside the big fireplace. Seating is on elegant, stylishly mismatched upholstered armchairs, and the carefully arranged furnishings give the impression of several separate and cosy areas. Served by impeccably polite staff, the ales on handpump are Black Sheep and Timothy Taylors Landlord, there are ten wines by the glass and up to 20 malt whiskies; easy-listening background music. Do check the limited opening times – and note you'll probably need to book a table in advance.

 Particularly high quality food includes seared scallops, crispy breaded pigs ear, parsnip and apple purée and honey mustard vinaigrette, twice-baked soufflé with goats cheese and roasted red onions, aubergine and plantain curry, coconut and wild rice served on a banana leaf, cottage pie in rich sauce with rosemary and parmesan mash, hake fillet with sorrel and saffron new potatoes, langoustine bisque and nasturtiums, and puddings such as dark chocolate and pistachio baked alaska and apricot and mascarpone crème brûlée with apricot pastilles. *Benchmark main dish: rib-eye steak with truffle butter and chips £24.95. Two-course evening meal £25.00.*

Free house ~ Licensee Paul L Willoughby ~ Real ale ~ (01400) 250234 ~ Open 6-11; 12-4 Sun; closed Sun evening, Mon, lunchtimes Tues-Sat ~ Bar food 6.30-9 (9.30 Fri, Sat); 12-2.30 Sun; see opening hours ~ Restaurant ~ Children over 8 allowed ~ Bedrooms: £65/£110 ~ www.thebrownlowarms.com *Recommended by Lisa Robertson, William and Ann Reid*

INGHAM SK9483 Map 8
Inn on the Green
The Green; LN1 2XT

Nicely modernised place serving thoughtfully prepared food; chatty atmosphere

The locals' bar in this friendly dining pub, with attractive views across the village green, has a relaxed, pubby feel and is liked by those just wanting a chat and a drink beside the log fire – though several tables are occupied by those enjoying the tasty food. The beamed and timbered dining room is spread over two floors, with lots of exposed brickwork, a mix of brasses and copper, local prints and a warm winter fire; the lounge between these rooms has leather sofas and background music and from the bar counter here you can buy home-made jams, marmalade and chutney. There's Sharps Doom Bar and two guests such as Adnams Explorer and Wadworths 6X on handpump, ten wines by the glass and farm cider. Service is good.

 Good, highly thought-of food using home-baked bread includes sandwiches, rabbit terrine with home-made chutney, fishcakes with sweet chilli jam, sharing platters, a pie of the day, vegetable curry, chicken breast with crispy wings, parsley dumplings and onion purée, cod loin in chorizo and mussel sauce, treacle-marinated pork with mustard mash, black pudding and cider jus, and puddings such as plum, cinnamon and brown sugar eton mess and treacle tart and custard. *Benchmark main dish: braised lamb shoulder with spring onion mash £10.95. Two-course evening meal £18.00.*

Free house ~ Licensees Andrew Cafferkey and Sarah Sharpe ~ Real ale ~ (01522) 730354 ~ Open 11.30-3, 6-11; 11.30-11 Sat in summer; 12-10.30 Sun; closed Mon ~ Bar food 12-2 (3.45 Sun), 6-9 ~ Restaurant ~ Children welcome ~ www.innonthegreeningham.co.uk *Recommended by Paul Humphreys, Stephen Woad*

KIRKBY LA THORPE TF0945 Map 8
Queens Head
Village and pub signposted off A17, just E of Sleaford, then turn right into Boston Road cul-de-sac; NG34 9NU

Reliable dining pub very popular for its good food and helpful, efficient service

'What a pity this is so far from home,' says one reader wistfully. The sort of place that customers return to regularly, it's neatly comfortable and gently traditional with plenty of dark-waistcoated staff, open fires and elaborate flower arrangements, and a carpeted bar with stools along the counter, button-back banquettes, sofas and captain's chairs around shiny dark tables. The linen-set beamed restaurant was being refurbished as we went to press. Nice decorative touches take in thoughtful lighting, big prints, china plates on delft shelves and handsome longcase clocks (it's quite something when they all chime at midday). Batemans XB and a guest or two such as Black Sheep and a very local ale on handpump; background music. Easy disabled access.

A wide choice of thoughtful and interesting food includes sandwiches, salmon and coriander fishcakes with sweet chilli jam, smoked duck, chicken and avocado salad with hazelnut vinaigrette, beer-battered haddock and chips, toad in the hole with onion gravy, vegetable wellington with tomato sauce, corn-fed chicken with sage, onion and sausage stuffing with madeira wine gravy, king scallops with cream chive sauce and crispy bacon and leek topping, and puddings such as dark cherry crumble with vanilla custard and home-grown apple and marmalade tart with cheese. *Benchmark main dish: steak and kidney pudding £13.95. Two-course evening meal £22.50.*

Free house ~ Licensee John Clark ~ Real ale ~ (01529) 305743 ~ Open 12-3, 6-11; 12-10.30 Sun ~ Bar food 12-2.30, 6-9.30; 12-8.30 Sun ~ Restaurant ~ Children welcome until 7pm ~ Wi-fi ~ www.thequeensheadinn.com *Recommended by WAH, James Stretton, Dr and Mrs R G J Telfer, David Jackman,*

STAMFORD   TF0306 Map 8
George of Stamford

High Street, St Martins (B1081 S of centre, not the quite different central pedestrianised High Street); PE9 2LB

Handsome coaching inn, civilised but relaxed, with traditional bar, several dining areas and lounges, excellent staff and top class food and drink; lovely bedrooms

As always, this civilised yet informal and rather lovely old place receives warm praise from our readers on all aspects. The various areas are furnished with all manner of seats from leather, cane and antique wicker to soft sofas and easy chairs, and there's a room to suit all occasions. The central lounge is particularly striking with sturdy timbers, broad flagstones, heavy beams and massive stonework. The properly pubby little front York Bar has plenty of relaxed character, Adnams Bitter, Fullers London Pride and Grainstore Triple B on handpump alongside 20 wines from an exceptional list and 30 malt whiskies. There's an amazing panelled restaurant (jacket or tie required) and a less formal Garden Room Restaurant, which has well spaced furniture on herringbone glazed bricks around a central tropical planting. Staff are professional and friendly, with table drinks service in the charming cobbled courtyard. The immaculately kept walled garden is beautifully planted and there's also a sunken lawn with croquet.

Quality as high as this does come at a price; the simplest option is the York Bar snack menu with sandwiches, toasties, chicken liver pâté and smoked salmon plate. First class food in the restaurants includes crab and brown shrimp fishcake, gruyère cheese fritters with thai jelly, aubergine and roasted pepper pasta, free-range chicken with chimichurri sauce and watercress salad, calves liver with parsley mash and red onion marmalade, and lamb cutlets with a ragu of mediterranean vegetables; their morning coffee and afternoon teas are popular. *Benchmark main dish: beef roasted on the bone with yorkshire pudding and hot horseradish sauce £23.75. Two-course evening meal £24.00.*

Free house ~ Licensee Chris Pitman ~ Real ale ~ (01780) 750750 ~ Open 11-11; 12-10.30 Sun ~ Bar food 12-11 ~ Restaurant ~ Children must be over 8 in Oak Panelled Restaurant ~ Dogs allowed in bar and bedrooms ~ Wi-fi ~ Bedrooms: £95/£165 ~ www.georgehotelofstamford.com *Recommended by Barry Collett, Bill Oliver, Roy Hoing*

WOOLSTHORPE

SK8334 Map 8

Chequers

*Woolsthorpe near Belvoir, signposted off A52 or A607 W of Grantham;
NG32 1LU*

**Interesting food at comfortably relaxed inn with good drinks
and appealing castle views from outside tables; bedrooms**

You can be sure of a friendly welcome from the hands-on licensees and
their staff in this 17th-c former coaching inn. Our readers like the heavy-
beamed main bar with its two big tables (one a massive oak construction),
comfortable mix of seating including some handsome leather chairs and
banquettes, and huge boar's head above a good log fire in the big brick
fireplace. Among cartoons on the wall are some of the illustrated claret
bottle labels from the series commissioned from famous artists. There are
more leather seats in a dining area on the left in what was once the village
bakery. A corridor leads to the light and airy main restaurant, decorated
with contemporary pictures, and another bar; background music and board
games. Wentworth Bumble Bee, Tom Woods Best Bitter and a couple of
guests on handpump, around 35 wines by the glass, 50 malt whiskies, 20
gins, a seasonal cocktail list and a farm cider. There are good quality teak
tables, chairs and benches outside and, beyond these, some picnic-sets on
the edge of the pub's cricket field, with views of Belvoir Castle.

Highly enjoyable food includes sandwiches, seared scallops with cauliflower
purée, black pudding and apricots, chicken and stuffing terrine with red
onion marmalade, sausages with onion gravy, a pie of the day, butternut squash
and aubergine tagine with spicy couscous, sea bream with pasta and pesto cream,
pheasant with pearl barley risotto and roasted root vegetables, and puddings such as
lemon meringue pie with raspberry sorbet and dark chocolate and hazelnut marquise
with confit kumquats. *Benchmark main dish: rib of beef with béarnaise sauce for
two people £40.00. Two-course evening meal £22.00.*

Free house ~ Licensee Justin Chad ~ Real ale ~ (01476) 870701 ~ Open 12-11
(midnight Sat); 12-10.30 Sun ~ Bar food 12-2.30, 6-9.30; 12-4, 6-8.30 Sun ~ Restaurant ~
Children welcome ~ Dogs allowed in bar and bedrooms ~ Wi-fi ~ Bedrooms: £50/£70 ~
www.chequersinn.net *Recommended by Vikki and Matt Wharton, Ron Corbett, Ian Herdman*

Also Worth a Visit in Lincolnshire

Besides the fully inspected pubs, you might like to try these pubs that
have been recommended to us and described by readers. Do tell us what
you think of them: feedback@goodguides.com

ALLINGTON

SK8540

★ Welby Arms (01400) 281361
*The Green; off A1 at N end of Grantham
bypass; NG32 2EA* Friendly, well run
and well liked inn with helpful staff, large
simply furnished bar divided by stone
archway, beams and joists, log fires (one
in an attractive arched brick fireplace),
comfortable plush wall banquettes and
stools, up to six changing ales, over 20 wines
by the glass and plenty of malt whiskies,
good popular bar food including blackboard
specials, civilised back dining lounge;
background music; children welcome,
tables in walled courtyard with pretty
flower baskets, picnic-sets on front lawn,
comfortable bedrooms, open all day Sun.
*(M J Daly, Mike and Margaret Banks, Philip and
Susan Philcox, Michael and Jenny Back)*

ASLACKBY

TF0830

Robin Hood & Little John
(01778) 440681 *A15 Bourne–Sleaford;
NG34 0HL* Nicely renovated old mansard-
roofed country pub, split-level bar with
beams, flagstones and woodburners,
mix of seating including a chesterfield
in former inglenook, good choice of food
(not Sun evening) from pub favourites up,
Batemans, Greene King and guests, friendly
staff, separate more modern oak-floored

restaurant; discreet background music, difficult wheelchair access; three-level terrace with pergola and smokers' shelter, closed Mon. *(Anon)*

BASSINGHAM   SK9160
Five Bells (01522) 788269

High Street; LN5 9JZ Cheerful old country pub with good choice of well kept ales and well liked fairly traditional food including good value set menu (booking advised), efficient friendly service, bare-boards interior with hop-strung beams and lots of brass and bric-a-brac, some quotations on the walls, cosy log fires, a well in one part; children and dogs welcome, open all day Sun till 7pm. *(Tony and Maggie Harwood, Ross Balaam)*

BASTON   TF1113
White Horse (01778) 560923

Church Street; PE6 9PE Popular newly renovated 18th-c village pub (was the Spinning Wheel) with spacious bar and restaurant, four mainly local changing ales and several wines by the glass, good reasonably priced food (best to book) from lunchtime hot or cold sandwiches up, friendly efficient staff; children (till 8.30pm) and dogs welcome (the resident springer is Audrey), closed lunchtimes Mon and Tues, otherwise open all day (food till 6pm Sun). *(Elizabeth Tofts)*

BECKINGHAM   SK8753
Pack Horse (01636) 627053

Sleaford Road, off A17; LN5 0RF Welcoming village local with enjoyable home-made food and four well kept ales, open fires; pleasant beer garden. *(Anon)*

BELCHFORD   TF2975
★Blue Bell (01507) 533602

Village signed off A153 Horncastle–Louth; LN9 6LQ 18th-c dining pub with cosy comfortable bar, Batemans, Worthington and guests, Thatcher's cider, good traditional and modern food, efficient friendly service, restaurant; children and dogs welcome, picnic-sets in terraced back garden, good base for Wolds walks and Viking Way (remove muddy boots), may close second and third weeks in Jan. *(Anon)*

BILLINGBOROUGH   TF1134
★Fortescue Arms (01529) 240228

B1177, off A52 Grantham–Boston; NG34 0QB Popular country local with old stonework, exposed brick, wood panelling, beams and big see-through fireplace in carpeted rooms, well kept Greene King and guests, generous helpings of enjoyable pubby food, good friendly service, Victorian prints, brass and copper, a stuffed badger and pheasant, attractive flagstoned dining

rooms each end and another fire; children welcome, no dogs inside, picnic-sets and rattan-style furniture in sheltered courtyard with flowering tubs, open (and food) all day weekends. *(Anon)*

BOSTON   TF3244
Mill (01205) 352874

Spilsby Road (A16); PE21 9QN Popular roadside pub under newish management; enjoyable reasonably priced food (not Tues) including some italian choices, Batemans XB and guest, friendly italian landlord and staff; children welcome, tables out in front. *(Anon)*

BURTON COGGLES   SK9725
Cholmeley Arms (01476) 550225

Village Street; NG33 4JS Well kept ales such as Fullers London Pride, Grainstore and Greene King Abbot in small beamed pubby bar with warm fire, generous helpings of good reasonably priced home-made food (not Sun evening), friendly efficient service, restaurant; farm shop, handy for A1, open all day weekends, closed lunchtimes Mon, Tues. *(M and GR)*

CAYTHORPE   SK9348
Red Lion (01400) 272632

Signed just off A607 N of Grantham; High Street; NG32 3DN Popular village pub with good fairly traditional home-made food (booking advised) including early-bird deal, friendly helpful staff, well kept Adnams and Everards, good sensibly priced wine, bare-boards bar with light wood counter, black beams and roaring fire, carpeted restaurant; back terrace by car park. *(David Howe)*

CHAPEL ST LEONARDS   TF5672
Admiral Benbow (01754) 871847

The Promenade; PE24 5BQ Small beach bar serving three real ales and good choice of foreign bottled beers, ciders too, sandwiches and snacks, bare boards, cushioned bench seats and stools, barrel tables, lots of bric-a-brac and nautical memorabilia on planked walls and ceiling; children and dogs welcome, picnic-sets out on mock-up galleon, great sea views, open all day summer, all Fri-Sun winter. *(Adrian Johnson)*

CLAYPOLE   SK8449
Five Bells (01636) 626561

Main Street; NG23 5BJ Brick-built village pub with good-sized beamed bar and smaller dining area beyond servery, well kept Greene King IPA and three mainly local guests, a couple of ciders, good choice of home-made food, pool and darts; children welcome, grassy back garden with play area, four bedrooms, closed Mon lunchtime, otherwise open all day. *(Anon)*

We say if we know a pub allows dogs.

CLEETHORPES TA3009
No 2 Refreshment Room
07905 375587 *Station Approach;
DN35 8AX* Comfortably refurbished
carpeted platform bar, friendly staff, well
kept Hancocks HB, M&B Mild, Sharps Doom
Bar and three guests (June festival), real
cider, interesting old pictures of the station,
historical books on trains and the local area,
no food but a free Sun night buffet, Thurs
quiz; tables out under heaters, open all day
from 7.30am. *(Lisa Robertson)*

CLEETHORPES TA3108
★Willys (01472) 602145
*Highcliff Road; south promenade;
DN35 8RQ* Popular open-plan bistro-style
seafront pub with panoramic Humber views,
café tables, tiled floor and painted brick
walls; visibly brews its own good ales, also
changing guests and belgian beers, good
home-made bargain bar lunches (evening
food Mon-Thurs), friendly fast service, nice
mix of customers from young and trendy to
weather-beaten fishermen; quiet juke box;
a few tables out on the promenade, open all
day (till late Fri, Sat). *(Derek Wason)*

COLEBY SK9760
Bell (01522) 813778
*Village signed off A607 S of Lincoln,
turn right and right into Far Lane at
church; LN5 0AH* Refurbished restaurant
pub with wide variety of top-notch food
including set lunch and early-bird menus,
good humoured owner-chef and friendly
staff, well kept Timothy Taylors and several
wines by the glass (not cheap) including
champagne, bar and three dining areas;
children over 8 welcome, terrace tables,
village on Viking Way with lovely fenland
views, open only evenings Weds-Sat and
lunchtimes Fri-Sun. *(David Hunt)*

CONINGSBY TF2458
Leagate Inn (01526) 342370
*Leagate Road (B1192 southwards, off
A153 E); LN4 4RS* Heavy-beamed 16th-c
Fenland pub with three cosy linked rooms,
medley of furnishings including high-backed
settles around the biggest of three log
fires, dim lighting, ancient oak panelling,
attractive dining room, even a priest hole;
enjoyable food (all day Sun) from extensive
menu, Adnams, Batemans and Wells &
Youngs, good helpful staff; children welcome,
dogs in bar, pleasant garden, site of old
gallows at front, eight motel bedrooms, open
all day Sun. *(Anon)*

FOSDYKE TF3132
Ship (01205) 260764
Moulton Washway; A17; PE12 6LH
Useful roadside pub with popular reasonably
priced food from varied menu, Sun carvery,
two Adnams beers and Batemans XB,
friendly staff, simple pine and quarry tile

décor, woodburner; children welcome,
garden tables, open all day. *(Derek and Sylvia
Stephenson)*

FULBECK SK9450
Hare & Hounds (01400) 272322
*The Green (A607 Leadenham–
Grantham); NG32 3JJ* Converted 17th-c
maltings overlooking attractive village green,
modernised linked areas, log fire, good
fresh food from ciabattas and pub favourites
up, well kept ales such as Brakspears and
Marstons Pedigree, affordable wine list,
friendly well dressed aware staff, raftered
upstairs function room; terrace seating,
eight bedrooms in adjacent barn conversion,
closed Sun evening. *(Maurice and Janet
Thorpe, David Hunt)*

GAINSBOROUGH SK8189
Eight Jolly Brewers
Ship Court, Silver Street; DN21 2DW
Small drinkers' pub in former warehouse,
eight interesting real ales, traditional cider
and plenty of bottled beers, friendly staff
and locals, beams and bare brick, more room
upstairs and live music Thurs; seats outside,
open all day. *(Anon)*

GRANTHAM SK9136
Blue Pig (01476) 563704
Vine Street; NG31 6RQ Cosy three-
bar Tudor pub, well kept ales and decent
reasonably priced pubby food, friendly staff,
low beams, panelling, stripped stone and
flagstones, open fire; dogs welcome; tables
out behind, open all day. *(Anon)*

GRIMSTHORPE TF0423
Black Horse (01778) 591093
A151 W of Bourne; PE10 0LY Handsome
grey-stone coaching inn under newish couple,
long narrowish modernised bar and four
separate connecting dining areas, open fires,
a couple of ales from local Star and good
realistically priced home-made food, friendly
staff; children and dogs welcome, picnic-sets
in good-sized garden, two bedrooms, handy
for Grimsthorpe Castle, closed Sun evening,
Mon. *(Phil and Jane Hodson)*

IRNHAM TF0226
Griffin (01476) 550201
Bulby Road; NG33 4JG Welcoming old
stone-built inn with generous home-made
food including good value set lunch, ales such
as Navigation and Oakham, three rooms (two
for dining), log fires, warm friendly atmosphere;
background music; children welcome, no dogs
inside, classic car meet first Weds of month
(spring/summer), four bedrooms, nice village
setting, closed Mon, Tues. *(Anon)*

KIRKBY ON BAIN TF2462
★Ebrington Arms (01526) 354560
Main Street; LN10 6YT Popular village
pub with good value traditional food (booking
advised), half a dozen well kept changing

ales and friendly service, beer mats on low 16th-c beams, carpets and banquettes, open fire, restaurant behind; background music, darts; children and dogs welcome, wheelchair access, tables out in front by road, lawn to the side with play equipment, campsite next door, closed Mon lunchtime. *(Anon)*

KIRMINGTON   TA1011
Marrowbone & Cleaver
(01652) 688335 *High Street; DN39 6YZ*
Friendly local with enjoyable good value home-made food (all day Sun) including bargain weekday set lunch, well kept rotating ales, carpeted bar with log fire, snug, dining conservatory, Thurs quiz, darts; TV; children welcome, picnic-sets on side lawn, open all day. *(Anon)*

LINCOLN   SK9871
Dog & Bone (01522) 522403
John Street; LN2 5BH Comfortable and welcoming backstreet local with well kept Batemans and guests, real cider, food Sat and every third Sun (lunchtime), log fires, exchange library of recent fiction; background and live music; dogs welcome (they have their own), picnic-sets on gravel terrace, open all day Fri-Sun, from 4.30pm other days. *(Anon)*

LINCOLN   SK9771
Jolly Brewer (01522) 528583
Broadgate; LN2 5AQ Popular no-frills pub with art deco interior, good choice of well kept ales and ciders, no food, regular live music; back courtyard with covered area, open all day (till 8pm Sun). *(Anon)*

LINCOLN   SK9771
Strugglers (01522) 535023
Westgate; LN1 3BG Cosily worn-in beer lovers' haunt, built in 1841 and once run by local hangman (sign shows man being led to the gallows), half a dozen or more well kept ales including Bass and Timothy Taylors, lots of knick-knacks and pump clips, two open fires (one in back snug), some live acoustic music; no children inside; dogs welcome, steps down to sunny back courtyard with heated canopy, open all day (till 1am Fri, Sat). *(Anon)*

LINCOLN   SK9771
★ Victoria (01522) 541000
Union Road; LN1 3BJ Main draw to this old-fashioned backstreet local are the eight real ales (including Batemans), foreign draught and bottled beers and farm cider (summer and Halloween beer festivals); simply furnished tiled front lounge with pictures of Queen Victoria, coal fire, basic lunchtime food, friendly staff and good mix of customers (gets especially busy lunchtime and later in evening), live music Sat; children and dogs welcome, seats on heated terrace, castle views, open all day till midnight (1am Fri, Sat). *(Sean Finnegan, Chris Johnson)*

LINCOLN   SK9771
Widow Cullens Well (01522) 523020
Steep Hill; just below cathedral; LN2 1LU Ancient revamped building on two floors, cheap Sam Smiths beers and enjoyable food including children's choices, chatty mix of customers, good service, beams, stone walls and open fire, back extension with namesake well; terrace seating, open all day. *(Anon)*

LINCOLN   SK9771
★ Wig & Mitre (01522) 535190
Steep Hill; just below cathedral; LN2 1LU Civilised café-style dining pub with plenty of character and attractive period features over two floors; big-windowed downstairs bar, beams and exposed stone walls, pews and Gothic furniture on oak boards, comfortable sofas in carpeted back area, quieter upstairs dining room with views of castle walls and cathedral, antique prints and caricatures of lawyers/clerics, all-day food from breakfast on including good value set menus and some interesting seasonal dishes, extensive choice of wines by the glass from good list, well kept Black Sheep, Everards and Oakham; children and dogs welcome, open 8am-midnight. *(Val and Alan Green, Ryta Lyndley, Mrs Sally Scott)*

LONG BENNINGTON   SK8344
★ Reindeer (01400) 281382
Just off A1 N of Grantham – S end of village, opposite school; NG23 5DJ Intimate atmosphere in attractively traditional low-beamed pub with popular long-serving landlady, consistently good food (fair value considering the quality) from sandwiches up in bar and more formal restaurant, can get very busy so best to book, John Smiths, Timothy Taylors Landlord and one or two guests, nice wines, good friendly service, coal-effect stove in stone fireplace; background music; picnic-sets under parasols in small front courtyard, closed Sun evening, Mon. *(Brian and Janet Ainscough, Gordon and Margaret Ormondroyd, M and GR)*

LONG BENNINGTON   SK8344
Royal Oak (01400) 281332
Main Road; just off A1 N of Grantham; NG23 5DJ Popular local with enthusiastic welcoming licensees; good-sized bar serving well kept Marstons and Mansfield ales, several wines by the glass and good sensibly priced home-made food including specials, friendly helpful staff; children welcome, seats out in front and in big back garden with play area, path for customers to river, open all day. *(Adrian Finn)*

LOUTH   TF3287
Wheatsheaf (01507) 606262
Westgate, near St James Church; LN11 9YD Cheerful 17th-c low-beamed pub under welcoming newish landlady, well kept Bass, Greene King, Tom Woods and a guest, real cider, enjoyable pubby food served by

friendly young staff, coal fires in all three bars, old photographs; tables outside, open all day and can get busy. *(Anon)*

MINTING
TF1873
Sebastopol (01507) 578577
Off A158 Lincoln–Horncastle; LN9 5RT Refurbished 19th-c red-brick village pub; good home-made food from traditional choices up using Lincolnshire suppliers, well kept Batemans and a local guest, nine wines by the glass, friendly staff, quiz first Weds of month; children welcome, picnic-sets on front terrace, self-catering barn conversion, closed Sun evening, Mon. *(Andy Brown)*

NORTH THORESBY
TF2998
New Inn (01472) 840270
Station Road; DN36 5QS Popular and friendly village pub, good reliable home-made food, well kept Marstons Pedigree, Theakstons and a guest, nice fire in bar, roomy restaurant; disabled facilities, terrace, open all day weekends. *(Anon)*

NORTON DISNEY
SK8859
Green Man (01522) 789804
Main Street, off A46 Newark–Lincoln; LN6 9JU Old beamed village pub-restaurant with opened-up modernised interior; good reasonably priced food from sandwiches and traditional dishes up including some interesting specials, bargain early-evening weekday deal, three well kept ales from central bar, friendly young staff, high-backed dining chairs on wood floor; TV; tables out behind. *(Paul Humphreys, Tony and Maggie Harwood)*

REDBOURNE
SK9799
Red Lion (01652) 648302
Main Road (B1206 SE of Scunthorpe); DN21 4QR Welcoming and comfortable 17th-c coaching inn with good home-made food from changing menu, also good value two-course menu till 7pm (not Sun) and other deals, helpful staff, three well kept ales, open fire, flagstones and polished panelling, garden room restaurant; free wi-fi; children welcome, no dogs, old fire station preserved at one end, attractive village, eight bedrooms, open all day. *(Kay and Alistair Butler)*

SCAMPTON
SK9579
Dambusters (01522) 731333
High Street; LN1 2SD Several beamed rooms around central bar with masses of interesting Dambusters and other RAF memorabilia, reasonably priced straightforward food (not Sun evening), also home-made chutneys, pâté and biscuits for sale, five interesting real ales including own microbrews (ceiling covered in beer mats from past guest beers), pews and chairs around tables on wood floor, log fire in big two-way brick fireplace, more formal seating at back; children and dogs welcome

(their black labrador is Bomber), very near Red Arrows runway viewpoint, open all day Fri, Sat, till 6pm Sun, closed Mon lunchtime. *(Paul Humphreys)*

SKILLINGTON
SK8925
Cross Swords (01476) 861132
The Square; NG33 5HB Traditional 19th-c stone pub in delightful village, welcoming and homely, with good food cooked by landlord-chef from bar snacks to restaurant dishes, a couple of ales such as Bass and Grainstore; background music, no under-10s or dogs; three annexe bedrooms, closed Sun evening, Mon lunchtime. *(Anon)*

SOUTH RAUCEBY
TF0245
Bustard (01529) 488250
Main Street; NG34 8QG Modernised 19th-c stone-built pub with good food from varied menu, well kept ales and plenty of wines by the glass, friendly staff, restaurant; children welcome, attractive sheltered garden, closed Sun evening, Mon. *(Anon)*

STAMFORD
TF0207
All Saints Brewery – Melbourn Brothers (01780) 752186
All Saints Street; PE9 2PA Nicely reworked old building (core is a medieval hall) with warren of rooms on three floors; friendly enthusiastic licensees, upstairs bar serving bottled fruit beers from adjacent early 19th-c brewery and low-priced Sam Smiths on handpump, enjoyable food from pub favourites up including set deals, ground-floor dining area with log fire and woodburner, top floor with leather sofas and wing chairs, board games; children and dogs welcome, picnic-sets in cobbled courtyard, brewery tours, open all day. *(John Coatsworth)*

STAMFORD
TF0306
Bull & Swan (01780) 766412
High Street, St Martins; PE9 2LJ Traditional old inn with three low-beamed connecting rooms, log fires, good often imaginative food from sandwiches and sharing plates up, ales such as Adnams, Grainstore and Oakham, plenty of wines by the glass; children and dogs welcome, tables out in former back coachyard, seven individually styled bedrooms named after animals (some road noise), open all day. *(Richard and Penny Gibbs)*

STAMFORD
TF0207
★ Crown (01780) 763136
All Saints Place; PE9 2AG Substantial well modernised stone-built hotel with emphasis on good seasonal country cooking using local produce (some from their own farm), friendly helpful staff, well kept ales such as Adnams, decent wines, whiskies and coffee, spacious main bar with long leather-cushioned counter, substantial pillars, step up to more traditional flagstoned area with stripped stone

and lots of leather sofas and armchairs, civilised dining room; back courtyard, 28 comfortable bedrooms (some in separate townhouse), good breakfast, open all day. *(Les and Sandra Brown)*

STAMFORD TF0207

Jolly Brewer (01780) 755141

Foundry Road; PE9 2PP Welcoming 19th-c stone-built pub with half a dozen well kept ales, traditional ciders/perries and wide range of interesting whiskies (some from india and japan), low-priced simple food, regular beer festivals and quiz & curry nights, pub games, nice open fire; sports TV, pool and darts; open all day. *(Anon)*

STAMFORD TF0307

⋆**Tobie Norris** (01780) 753800

St Pauls Street; PE9 2BE Centuries old, lovingly restored and full of character; worn flagstones, stripped stonework and open fires, several linked rooms including handsomely panelled shrine to Nelson and Battle of Trafalgar, also an upstairs room with steeply pitched rafters, Adnams, Castle Rock and three guests, lots of 'compile your own' pizzas and other food (not Sun evening), relaxed easy-going atmosphere; children over 10 allowed at lunchtime, dogs in bar, enclosed terrace, open all day. *(Michael Doswell, John Coatsworth)*

SURFLEET TF2528

Mermaid (01775) 680275

B1356 (Gosberton Road), just off A16 N of Spalding; PE11 4AB Welcoming and traditional with two high-ceilinged carpeted rooms, huge sash windows, banquettes, captain's chairs and spindlebacks, up to four changing ales, good choice of fairly standard food including a monthly themed night, friendly fast service, restaurant; background music; pretty terraced garden with bar and seats under thatched parasols, children's play area walled from River Glen, moorings, four bedrooms, open all day Sat in summer, closed Sun evening. *(Colin McIlwain, Michael and Jenny Back)*

TATTERSHALL THORPE TF2159

Blue Bell (01526) 342206

Thorpe Road; B1192 Coningsby–Woodhall Spa; LN4 4PE Ancient low-beamed pub (said to date from the 13th c) with friendly cosy atmosphere, RAF memorabilia including airmen's signatures on the ceiling (pub was used by the Dambusters), big open fire, four well kept ales such as Shepherd Neame Spitfire and Wadworths 6X, some nice wines and enjoyable well priced pubby food, small dining room; garden tables, bedrooms. *(Barry Collett)*

TETFORD TF3374

White Hart (01507) 533255

East Road, off A158 E of Horncastle; LN9 6QQ Friendly bay-windowed village pub dating from the 16th c, Brains Rev James and a couple of guests, good value generous pubby food, pleasant inglenook bar with old-fashioned curved-back settles and slabby elm tables on red tiles, other areas including pool room, regular live music; children and dogs welcome, sheltered back lawn with guinea pigs and rabbits, pretty countryside, bedrooms, closed Mon. *(Anon)*

THEDDLETHORPE ALL SAINTS TF4787

⋆**Kings Head** (01507) 339798

Pub signposted off A1031 N of Maplethorpe; Mill Road; LN12 1PB Long 16th-c thatched pub with cheerful helpful landlord; carpeted two-room front lounge with very low ceiling, brass platters on timbered walls, antique dining chairs and tables, easy chairs by log fire, central bar (more low beams) with well kept ales such as Batemans and a local cider, coal fire with side oven, shelves of books, stuffed owls and country pictures, long dining room, good local food from sandwiches and sharing plates to steaks and fresh Grimsby fish, Sun carvery; one or two picnic-sets in front area, more on lawn, open all day Sat, closed Sun evening, Mon. *(Anon)*

THREEKINGHAM TF0836

Three Kings (01529) 240249

Just off A52 12 miles E of Grantham; Saltersway; NG34 0AU Big entrance hall (former coaching inn), beamed and dark panelled bar with coal fire and pubby furniture including banquettes, compact restaurant plus bigger dining/function room, good choice of enjoyable home-made food, Timothy Taylors Landlord and guests, friendly efficient staff; children and dogs welcome, terrace with covered smokers' area, various car club meetings, closed Mon. *(Anon)*

WAINFLEET TF5058

⋆**Batemans Brewery** (01754) 882009

Mill Lane, off A52 via B1195; PE24 4JE Circular bar in brewery's ivy-covered windmill tower, Batemans ales in top condition, czech and belgian beers on tap too, ground-floor dining area with cheap food including baguettes and a few pubby dishes, plenty of old pub games (more outside), lots of brewery memorabilia and plenty for families to enjoy; entertaining brewery tours and shop, tables on terrace and grass, open 11.30am-4pm (2.30pm in winter), closed Mon, Tues. *(Anon)*

WEST DEEPING   TF1009
Red Lion   (01778) 347190
King Street; PE6 9HP Welcoming stone-built family-run pub with long low-beamed bar, four well kept usually local beers, popular freshly made food (not Sun evening) from baguettes up, back dining extension, stripped stone and open fire, some live music including monthly folk club, Sun quiz; free wi-fi; children welcome, no dogs inside, tables in back garden with terrace and fenced play area, open all day Sat in summer. *(Anon)*

WOODHALL SPA   TF1963
Village Limits   (01526) 353312
Stixwould Road; LN10 6UJ Modernised country pub with good local food cooked by landlord-chef, well kept ales such as Batemans and Tom Woods, friendly service, smallish bar with banquettes, dining room, wood-strip floors and light wood furniture; children welcome, nine courtyard bedrooms, closed Mon lunchtime. *(David H Bennett)*

Post Office address codings confusingly give the impression that a few pubs are in Lincolnshire, when they're really in Cambridgeshire (which is where we list them).

Norfolk

BAWBURGH
Kings Head ♀ 🍺   TG1508   Map 5

Harts Lane; A47 just W of Norwich then B1108; NR9 3LS

Busy, small-roomed pub with five real ales, good wines by the glass, interesting food and friendly service

'A lovely place with everything done well,' one of our readers tells us – and others agree. There's a cheerful atmosphere in the small rooms and, since it dates from the 17th c, plenty of low beams and standing timbers. Also, leather sofas and an attractive assortment of old dining chairs and tables on wood-strip floors, a knocked-through open fire and a couple of woodburning stoves in the restaurant areas. Adnams Bitter, St Austell Tribute and Woodfordes Wherry plus two guest beers on handpump, 11 wines by the glass and 14 malt whiskies; service is friendly and helpful. There are seats in the garden and the pub is opposite a little green.

🍴 Good, rewarding food (with suppliers listed on the menu) includes sandwiches, scallops with coconut and butternut squash purée and chilli oil, twice-baked cheese soufflé with apple and walnut salad, steak burger with red cabbage coleslaw, onion relish and chips, slow-braised beef cheeks with horseradish pomme purée and onion jus, line-caught cod with mussel velouté, gressingham duck with sticky red cabbage and confit leg croquette, and puddings such as dark chocolate and caramel tart with peanut butter parfait and brittle and gingerbread with vanilla panna cotta. *Benchmark main dish: fish and skin-on chips £12.00. Two-course evening meal £20.00.*

Free house ~ Licensee Anton Wimmer ~ Real ale ~ (01603) 744977 ~ Open 11-11; 12-10.30 Sun; closed winter Sun evening ~ Bar food 12-2, 5.30-9; 12-3, 6-9 Sun ~ Restaurant ~ Children welcome ~ Dogs allowed in bar ~ www.kingshead-bawburgh.co.uk
Recommended by Chris Price, David Jackman, Gordon and Margaret Ormondroyd, John Millwood

BURNHAM MARKET
Hoste 🍽️ ♀ 🛏️   TF8342   Map 8

The Green (B1155); PE31 8HD

Civilised and stylish with excellent food and drinks, a proper bar plus several lounge areas and dining rooms, and pretty little garden; luxurious bedrooms

This is by no means a pub – it's a luxury hotel with all the facilities that go with that, but at the front they've kept the historic bar that remains the old soul of the place. Here, as always, you'll find chatty local drinkers and those enjoying morning coffee, plus an informal relaxed atmosphere, stripy cushioned settles, leather dining chairs and armchairs (note the glass-topped suitcase table), rugs on wood-effect flooring, farming implements and bookshelves, cartoons on one wall and a woodburning stove. Professional, courteous staff serve Greene King Abbot and Woodfordes Nelsons Revenge and Wherry on handpump, 19 wines by the glass from an extensive and carefully chosen list with helpful notes, 18 malt whiskies and farm cider. There are also two elegant dining rooms (one panelled, one with contemporary green paintwork), a busy two-roomed conservatory with armchairs and sofas and, throughout, stylish artwork and sculptures; the art gallery is up some stairs. A smart and airy new back restaurant has high-backed beige wicker dining chairs around pale tables, a long wall bench along one side with cheerful scatter cushions and huge glass ceiling lamps; sliding glass doors open on to the pretty garden, which has seats and tables. The lovely bedrooms are deeply comfortable and well equipped and the breakfasts delicious; Admiral Lord Nelson stayed here.

Imaginative, modern food using the best local suppliers includes lunchtime sandwiches, dressed crab with toasted sourdough, lobster risotto, burger with gruyère, bacon and chips, corn-fed chicken with crisp pancetta and artichoke, slow-roast pork belly with prunes, bubble and squeak and crackling, duck breast with parsnip purée and rösti potato, bass with pak choi, chilli, soy and sesame, and puddings such as treacle tart with orange cream and dark chocolate fondant with white chocolate parfait. *Benchmark main dish: rib-eye steak with garlic butter or peppercorn sauce and chips £24.00. Two-course evening meal £25.00.*

Free house ~ Licensee Rob Williamson ~ Real ale ~ (01328) 738777 ~ Open 9am-11pm (midnight Fri, Sat, 10.30 Sun) ~ Bar food 12-2.30, 6-9.30; light snacks 2.30-6 ~ Restaurant ~ Children welcome ~ Dogs allowed in bar ~ Wi-fi ~ Bedrooms: £110/$130 ~ www.thehoste.com *Recommended by James Stretton, W K Wood, David Carr, Roy Hoing, Tracey and Stephen Groves, Michael Sargent*

BURSTON
Crown 🍺

TM1383 Map 5

Village signposted off A140 N of Scole; Mill Road; IP22 5TW

Friendly, relaxed village pub usefully open all day, with a warm welcome, real ales and well liked bar food

In chilly weather, the best place to sit in this bustling village pub is the heavy-beamed, quarry-tiled room, where there are comfortably cushioned sofas in front of a woodburning stove in a huge brick fireplace; there are also stools by a low chunky wooden table and newspapers and magazines to read. Locals tend to gather in an area by the bar counter where they serve Adnams Bitter, Greene King Abbot and guests from breweries such as Growlers and Woodfordes on handpump or tapped from the cask, a farm cider and half a dozen wines by the glass. The public bar on the left has a nice long table and panelled settle on an old brick floor in one alcove, straightforward tables and chairs on carpet by the pool table and, up a step, more tables and chairs. Both of these cream-painted rooms are hung with cheerful, naïve, local character paintings; background music and board games. The simply furnished, beamed dining room has another big brick fireplace. Outside is a smokers' shelter, a couple of picnic-sets in front of the old brick building and more seats in a hedged-off area with a barbecue.

Well liked food includes sandwiches, moules marinière, chicken liver parfait with red onion marmalade, ham and free-range eggs, chicken stuffed with goats cheese and rosemary, butternut squash, caramelised onion and feta strudel, steak and kidney pie, beer-battered fish and chips, lamb shank in red wine and redcurrant with garlic mash, and puddings. *Benchmark main dish: rump steak with mushrooms, onion rings and chips £14.00. Two-course evening meal £17.50.*

Free house ~ Licensees Bev and Steve Kembery ~ Real ale ~ (01379) 741257 ~ Open 12-11 (10.30 Sun) ~ Bar food 12-2, 6.30-9; 12-4 Sun; not Mon ~ Restaurant ~ Children welcome ~ Dogs allowed in bar ~ Live music Thurs evening and every second Sun ~ www.burstoncrown.com *Recommended by Ruth May, Evelyn and Derek Walter, Philip and Susan Philcox*

CASTLE ACRE
Ostrich
Stocks Green; PE32 2AE

TF8115 Map 8

Friendly old village pub with original features, fine old fireplaces, real ales and tasty food

You can still see some of the original masonry and the beams and trusses in the lofty ceilings of this 16th-c inn, although the place was largely rebuilt in the 18th c. The L-shaped, low-ceilinged front bar (on two levels) has a woodburning stove in a huge old fireplace, lots of wheelback chairs and cushioned pews around pubby tables on a wood-strip floor and gold patterned wallpaper; a step leads up to an area in front of the bar counter where there are similar seats and tables and a log fire in a brick fireplace. Greene King IPA, Abbot and Old Speckled Hen and a beer named for the pub on handpump, around a dozen wines by the glass and several malt whiskies. There's a separate dining room with another brick fireplace. The sheltered garden has picnic-sets under parasols and the inn faces the tree-lined village green; the village contains the remains of a Norman castle and a Cluniac monastery.

As well as sandwiches and paninis, the well liked food includes game pâté with caramelised onions, smoked duck on lentils and spinach, blue cheese, roasted cashew nut with chestnut and fennel velouté on pasta, beer-battered cod and chips, gammon, egg and chips with honey and mustard sauce, toad in the hole with gravy, chicken with creamy leek mash and vermouth sauce, beef goulash with bacon dumpling, and puddings. *Benchmark main dish: steak burger with smoked bacon, cheddar and chips £13.50. Two-course evening meal £20.00.*

Greene King ~ Tenant Tiffany Turner ~ Real ale ~ (01760) 755398 ~ Open 10am-11pm (midnight Sat) ~ Bar food 12-3, 6-9 ~ Restaurant ~ Children welcome ~ Dogs allowed in bar ~ Wi-fi ~ Bedrooms: £75/£85 ~ www.ostrichcastleacre.com
Recommended by Dr and Mrs R G J Telfer, Colin McKerrow, Maureen Wood, Nigel and Sue Foster

CLEY-NEXT-THE-SEA
George 🍷 🛏
Off A149 W of Sheringham; High Street; NR25 7RN

TG0443 Map 8

Pubby bar and two dining rooms in sizeable inn, with real ales, good choice of wines and popular food; bedrooms

Bird-watchers have loved the salt marshes around this village inn for years and its little public bar is just the place for sustenance. There's a long leather settle and sturdy dark wooden chairs by a couple of green-topped tables on carpeting, photographs of Norfolk wherries and other local scenes on cream walls, a huge candle in a big glass jar on one window sill, a table of newspapers and a stained-glass window depicting St George and the dragon. Greene King Abbot, Winters Cloudburst, Woodfordes Wherry and Yetmans Red on handpump and 13 wines by the glass. The dining rooms are similarly furnished with pale wooden cushioned chairs and tables, and evening candlelight. Across a lane is a small garden with some seats and tables. The bedrooms are warm and comfortable and a few overlook the marshes. This is a charming and peaceful brick and flint village.

🍴 Popular food includes sandwiches, tempura tiger prawns with sweet chilli dipping sauce, game terrine with home-made pickle, wild mushroom risotto, steak burger with local cheese, smoked bacon and chips, fish dish of the day, chicken with pancetta, savoy cabbage and red wine jus, and puddings such as tangy lemon tart with raspberry coulis, triple chocolate brownie with banana ice-cream and crumble with custard. *Benchmark main dish: beer-battered haddock and chips £13.95. Two-course evening meal £21.00.*

Free house ~ Licensee Stephen Cleeve ~ Real ale ~ (01263) 740652 ~ Open 11-11 ~ Bar food 12-9; 12-2.30, 6-9 (8.30 Sun) in winter ~ Restaurant ~ Children welcome ~ Dogs allowed in bar and bedrooms ~ Wi-fi ~ Bedrooms: /£110 ~ www.thegeorgehotelatcley.co.uk *Recommended by John Evans, Tracey and Stephen Groves, Dennis and Doreen Haward*

EAST RUDHAM   TF8228   Map 8
Crown 🌟 🍷 🛏
A148 W of Fakenham; The Green; PE31 8RD

Neat and smart with attractive open-plan seating areas, cosy back sitting room, very good food, real ales and friendly atmosphere; bedrooms

This is a stylish place under new ownership since it was last in these pages. Open-plan and contemporary in design, it has several distinct seating areas all with a relaxed, friendly atmosphere. One end of the main room has wood and brown leather dining chairs around a mix of tables (including a huge round one), rugs on stripped floorboards, and a log fire flanked by a grandfather clock and bookshelves. The other end is slightly more informal, with another bookshelf beside a second fireplace, a pubby part with white-painted, cushioned built-in seats, and high chairs against the handsomely slate-topped counter where they keep Black Sheep, Woodfordes Wherry and guests such as Adnams Ghost Ship and Norfolk Brewhouse Moon Gazer Amber Ale on handpump and 20 wines by the glass. There's also a cosy lower area to the back of the building, with comfortable leather sofas and armchairs and a flat-screen TV, as well as an upstairs dining room with a high-pitched ceiling and woodburning stove. The front gravelled area has seats under parasols. The bedrooms are comfortable and the breakfasts hearty.

🌟 Imaginative and very good, the food includes pigeon breast with pancetta, pickled beetroot and horseradish cream, salt and pepper calamari, sausages and mash with red onion gravy, vegetable, chicken or king prawn madras, venison meatballs with smoked tomato sauce on pasta, duo of duck (roasted breast and confit leg spring roll) with sesame, peanut and soy noodles and pak choi, and puddings such as triple chocolate mousse and sticky toffee pudding. *Benchmark main dish: burger with smoked bacon, mature cheddar and chips £11.95. Two-course evening meal £21.00.*

Free house ~ Licensee Philip Parker ~ Real ale ~ (01485) 528530 ~ Open 11-11 (midnight Sat) ~ Bar food 12-2.30 (3 Sun), 6-9 ~ Children welcome ~ Dogs welcome ~ Bedrooms: /£80 ~ www.crowninnnorfolk.co.uk *Recommended by Mr and Mrs D J Nash, Edward Mirzoeff, Tracey and Stephen Groves*

GREAT BIRCHAM   TF7632 Map 8
Kings Head 🛏

B1155, S end of village (called and signed Bircham locally); PE31 6RJ

Cheerful little bar in relaxed hotel, comfortable seating areas, four real ales, enjoyable food and seats outside; bedrooms

This handsome Edwardian place is not a straightforward pub – it's more of a hotel – but the attractively contemporary small bar has plenty of regulars and up to four real ales on handpump: Adnams Broadside, Greene King Old Speckled Hen and Ale Fresco, and Woodfordes Wherry. Also, 15 good wines by the glass, 18 malt whiskies and a fine choice of over 50 gins. There are comfortable sofas and tub chairs, a few high chairs against the counter and a log fire – as well as lounge areas and a light and airy modern restaurant; staff are friendly and helpful. There are plenty of tables and chairs outside, both in front and at the back with country views. Overnight guests enjoy comfortable bedrooms and good breakfasts.

 Good food from a varied menu includes lunchtime sandwiches, goats cheese panna cotta with honey-roasted beetroot and orange syrup, truffled scrambled eggs on toasted brioche with chicken liver pâté and smoked pancetta, burger with melted cheese, bacon and chips, parmesan and garlic polenta with roasted mediterranean vegetables and spicy tomato sauce, chicken schnitzel with fried egg, caper parsley butter and fritters, pork fillet with grain mustard sauce and roasted cider apples, and puddings. *Benchmark main dish: 24-day matured fillet steak with choice of sauce and chips £23.50. Two-course evening meal £22.50.*

Free house ~ Licensee Craig Jackson ~ Real ale ~ (01485) 578265 ~ Open 7am-11pm (midnight Fri, Sat) ~ Bar food 7.30am-10, 12-2.30 (3 Sun), 6.39-9 ~ Restaurant ~ Children welcome ~ Dogs welcome ~ Wi-fi ~ Bedrooms: £99/£109 ~ www.the-kings-head-bircham.co.uk *Recommended by Pip White, Toby Jones, Derek Stafford, Mrs V Moody*

GREAT MASSINGHAM   TF7922 Map 8
Dabbling Duck 🏅 🍺

Off A148 King's Lynn–Fakenham; Abbey Road; PE32 2HN

Unassuming from the outside but with a friendly atmosphere, character bars and warm fires, real ales and interesting food; comfortable bedrooms

Our readers enjoy their visits to this bustling pub very much – in all its aspects. The attractively furnished and relaxed bars have leather sofas and armchairs by woodburning stoves (they have three), a mix of antique wooden dining tables and chairs on flagstones or stripped wooden floors, a very high-backed settle, 18th- and 19th-c quirky prints and cartoons, and plenty of beams and standing timbers. At the back of the pub is the Blenheim room, just right for a private group, and there's also a candlelit dining room. Adnams Broadside, Beestons Worth the Wait, Woodfordes Wherry and a guest beer on handpump, served from a bar counter made of great slabs of polished tree trunk; background music, TV, darts and board games. There are tables and chairs on a front terrace overlooking the sizeable village green with its big duck ponds, and more seats in the enclosed back garden with a play area. The bedrooms are named after famous local sportsmen and airmen from the World War II air base in Massingham.

 Highly thought-of food includes sandwiches, gin-cured salmon with salmon roe, juniper, cucumber and fennel, local mussels with root vegetables, beer and crème fraîche, pearl barley and beetroot risotto with blue cheese and candied walnuts, beer and treacle-roasted ham and duck egg with pineapple pickle, salt cod kedgeree with puffed rice and crispy egg, open venison lasagne with truffle honey and salami salad, and puddings such as bread and butter pudding with beer caramel and apple pie with cheese pastry and cinnamon toast ice-cream. *Benchmark main dish: beer-battered and triple-cooked chips £12.50. Two-course evening meal £19.50.*

Free house ~ Licensee Dominic Symington ~ Real ale ~ (01485) 520827 ~ Open 12-11 (10.30 Sun) ~ Bar food 12-2.30, 6.30-9 (9.30 Fri, Sat) ~ Restaurant ~ Children welcome ~ Dogs allowed in bar ~ Wi-fi ~ Bedrooms: £65/£90 ~ www.thedabblingduck.co.uk
Recommended by R C Vincent, Derek and Sylvia Stephenson, Mike and Shelley Woodroffe, Nigel and Sue Foster, Michael Sargent, R T and J C Moggridge, M and GR

HOLKHAM
Victoria ♀ 🛏
TF8943   Map 8

A149 near Holkham Hall; NR23 1RG

Handsome, smart inn with pubby bar, plenty of character dining space, thoughtful choice of drinks, friendly staff and enjoyable food

With the vast stretch of Holkham Sands backed by pine woods just a few minutes away, this upmarket but informal small hotel (owned by the Holkham Estate) makes an excellent base. Some of the stylish bedrooms have views of the sea and breakfasts are good and generous. The proper bare-boards bar to the left is popular with locals, while a spreading dining and sitting area has an appealing variety of antique-style dining chairs and tables on rugs and stripped floorboards, antlers and antique guns, and sofas by a big log fire. There's also a small drawing room to the right of the main entrance (for guests only) with homely furniture, an open fire and an honesty bar. Adnams Bitter, Woodfordes Wherry and a guest on handpump, 20 wines by the glass, good coffee and efficient, polite service. An airy conservatory dining room, decorated in pale beige, leads out to a back courtyard with green-painted furniture; a second sizeable seating area has its own bar.

 Some kind of good, interesting food is served all day (breakfast for non-residents too) and includes buttered herring roes on toast, venison carpaccio with beetroot rémoulade, sausage and mash with onion gravy, vegetable cassoulet and goats cheese croquettes, seasonal local crab salad, coq au vin, game pudding, hake with shrimp beurre blanc, and puddings such as apple crumble and flourless chocolate tart with candied orange. *Benchmark main dish: venison burger with smoked cheddar and chips £12.75. Two-course evening meal £22.00.*

Free house ~ Licensee Lord Coke ~ Real ale ~ (01328) 711008 ~ Open 11-11 (10.30 Sun) ~ Bar food 12-2.30, 6.30-9 ~ Restaurant ~ Children welcome ~ Dogs welcome ~ Wi-fi ~ Bedrooms: £120/£180 ~ www.victoriaatholkham.co.uk
Recommended by David Carr, Peter Sutton

KING'S LYNN
Bank House ♀ 🛏
TF6119   Map 8

Kings Staithe Square via Boat Street and along the quay in one-way system; PE30 1RD

Georgian bar-brasserie with plenty of history and character, airy rooms, real ales and some sort of interesting food all day; bedrooms

In a splendid quayside spot, this civilised place was Barclays Bank's first opening in 1780 and the big-windowed bar was once the bank manager's office. It's now an elegant room with pastel paintwork, sofas, armchairs and some dining tables. There's also a restaurant with fine antique chairs and tables on bare boards, an airy brasserie with sofas and armchairs around low tables and a big brick fireplace, and two further areas – one with fine panelling and an open fire, the other with a half-size antique billiards table disguised as a dining table; background music, TV. The atmosphere throughout is bustling and friendly, with customers popping in and out all day; service is helpful and courteous. Adnams Bitter and Fullers London Pride on handpump, ten wines by the glass, farm cider, organic fruit juices and cocktails. The west-facing riverside terrace has seats and tables, and the bedrooms (most of which look over the river) are stylish and thoughtfully decorated. The Corn Exchange theatre and arts centre is just five minutes away. This is sister pub to the Rose & Crown in Snettisham.

Enjoyable brasserie-style food includes lunchtime sandwiches, ham hock terrine with piccalilli, poached duck egg with pancetta crisp and roast pumpkin, sharing platters, butternut squash and pepper risotto, pork and fennel polpette with tagliatelle, coq au vin, tiger prawn, avocado and pineapple salad, and puddings; they also offer very popular 'carve your own Sunday roasts' and proper afternoon teas. *Benchmark main dish: steak burger with cheese, gherkins, onion rings and chips £10.75. Two-course evening meal £21.00.*

Free house ~ Licensee Anthony Goodrich ~ Real ale ~ (01553) 660492 ~ Open 11-11 ~ Bar food 12-2.30 (5.30 Fri, Sat), 6.30-9 (9.30 Fri, Sat); ~ Restaurant ~ Children welcome ~ Wi-fi ~ Live jazz monthly Sun evening; best to phone ~ Bedrooms: £80/£110 ~ www.thebankhouse.co.uk *Recommended by John Wooll, Tracey and Stephen Groves*

LARLING
TL9889 Map 5

Angel

From A11 Thetford–Attleborough, take B1111 turn-off and follow pub signs; NR16 2QU

Good-natured chatty atmosphere in busy pub with several real ales and tasty bar food; bedrooms

Handy for the busy A11, this well run inn is popular with customers keen on the fine surrounding walks; they also have secure cycle storage. The comfortable 1930s-style lounge on the right has squared panelling, cushioned wheelback chairs, a nice long cushioned and panelled corner settle and some good solid tables for eating; plus, a collection of whisky-water jugs on a delft shelf over the big brick fireplace, a woodburning stove, a couple of copper kettles and some hunting prints. The same friendly family have run the inn since 1913 and they still have the original visitors' books from 1897 to 1909. Adnams Bitter and four guests from breweries such as Crouch Vale, Fat Cat, Hop Back and Orkney on handpump, 100 malt whiskies and ten wines by the glass; they hold an August beer festival with more than 100 real ales and ciders, live music and barbecues. The quarry-tiled black-beamed public bar has a good local feel with darts, juke box, games machine, board games and background music. There's a neat grass area behind the car park with picnic-sets around a big fairy-lit apple tree and a fenced play area. The four-acre meadow is a caravan and camping site from March to October.

Tasty food includes sandwiches and toasties, home-made pâté, crispy whitebait, ham and egg, vegetable balti, burgers with lots of toppings and chips, chicken and bacon pasta with mushrooms and cheese, smoked haddock mornay, mixed grill, and puddings such as chocolate fudge cake and treacle and ginger sponge. *Benchmark main dish: steak and kidney pie £10.95. Two-course evening meal £18.25.*

Free house ~ Licensee Andrew Stammers ~ Real ale ~ (01953) 717963 ~ Open 10am-11pm ~ Bar food 12-9.30 (10 Fri, Sat) ~ Restaurant ~ Children welcome ~ Wi-fi ~ Bedrooms: £50/£80 ~ www.angel-larling.co.uk *Recommended by Ruth May, Emma Scofield, J F M and M West, R C Vincent, Alex and Hazel Evans*

 ## MORSTON
Anchor
TG0043 Map 8

A149 Salthouse–Stiffkey; The Street; NR2 7AA

Quite a choice of rooms filled with bric-a-brac and prints, real ales and some sort of food all day

The surrounding area is wonderful for bird-watching and walking, and you can book seal-spotting trips from this bustling pub. Three traditional rooms on the right have straightforward seats and tables on original wooden floors, coal fires, local 1950s beach photographs and lots of prints and bric-a-brac. Adnams Bitter, local Winters Golden and Woodfordes Wherry on handpump, 18 wines by the glass; background music, darts and board games. The contemporary airy extension on the left, with comfortable benches and tables, leads into the more formal restaurant where local art is displayed on the walls. You can sit outside at the front of the building. If parking is tricky at the pub, there's an overflow around the corner off-road and a National Trust car park five minutes' walk away.

Thursday is curry night, and the menu also offers sandwiches, smoked haddock chowder, mackerel pâté, honey-roast ham and free-range eggs, tartiflette of shiitake mushrooms, spinach and duck egg, burger with cheese, bacon and triple-cooked chips, confit duck with celeriac purée, venison with cheese and potato pie, carrot purée and jus, and puddings such as vanilla crème brûlée and sticky toffee pudding. *Benchmark main dish: chicken with local black pudding, bubble and squeak and rich jus £13.00. Two-course evening meal £18.50.*

Free house ~ Licensees Harry Farrow and Rowan Glennie ~ Real ale ~ (01263) 741392 ~ Open 9am-11pm (10.30pm Sun) ~ Bar food 12-3, 6-9 ~ Restaurant ~ Children welcome ~ Dogs allowed in bar ~ Wi-fi ~ www.morstonanchor.co.uk *Recommended by David Jackman, R C Vincent, David Carr, Roy Hoing*

 ## NORTH CREAKE
Jolly Farmers
TF8538 Map 8

Burnham Road; NR21 9JW

Friendly village local with three cosy rooms, open fires and woodburners, well liked food and several real ales

Enjoyable food and real ales, a relaxed, friendly atmosphere and helpful service – all confirm our readers' enthusiasm for this well run former coaching inn. It has three cosy and relaxed rooms; the main bar has a large open fire in a brick fireplace, a mix of pine farmhouse and high-backed leather dining chairs around scrubbed pine tables on quarry tiles and pale yellow walls. Beside the wooden bar counter are some high bar chairs, and they keep Woodfordes Nelsons Revenge and Wherry on handpump or tapped from the cask, ten wines by the glass and a dozen malt whiskies. There's also a cabinet of model cars. A smaller bar has pews and a woodburning stove, while the red-walled dining room has similar furniture to the bar and another woodburner. There are seats outside on the terrace.

🍴 Good food includes sandwiches, crab and cheese pot, stilton and pear salad with candied walnuts, stilton macaroni, ham and egg, moules frites, lasagne, prawn and coconut curry, lambs liver and bacon, and puddings such as dark chocolate and cherry tart and orange and Cointreau bread and butter pudding. *Benchmark main dish: slow-braised lamb breast with a mint and redcurrant glaze £13.50. Two-course evening meal £19.00.*

Free house ~ Licensees Adrian and Heather Sanders ~ Real ale ~ (01328) 738185 ~ Open 12-2.30, 7-11; 12-7 Sun; closed Mon, Tues ~ Bar food 12-2, 7-9; 12-5.30 Sun ~ Children welcome ~ Dogs allowed in bar ~ www.jollyfarmersnorfolk.co.uk
Recommended by Derek and Sylvia Stephenson, Linda Miller and Derek Greentree, Philip and Susan Philcox

NORWICH

Fat Cat 🍺
TG2109   Map 5

West End Street; NR2 4NA

A place of pilgrimage for beer lovers and open all day; lunchtime rolls and pies

An extraordinary range of up to 32 quickly changing real ales are on offer in this lively, cheerful pub, and the knowledgeable landlord and his helpful staff cope well with the crowds. On handpump or tapped from the cask in a stillroom behind the bar – big windows reveal all – are their own beers (Fat Cat Brewery Tap Bitter, Hell Cat, Honey Ale, Marmalade Cat, Meow Mild and Wild Cat), as well as Adnams Bitter, Dark Star American Pale Ale, Fullers ESB, Green Jack Mahseer IPA, Hop Back Summer Lightning, Kelham Island Pale Rider, Late Knights Worm Catcher IPA, Oakham Inferno, Timothy Taylors Landlord, Woodfordes Once Bittern and guests from all over the country. You'll also find imported draught beers and lagers, over 50 bottled beers from around the world and 20 ciders and perries. The no-nonsense furnishings include plain scrubbed pine tables and simple solid seats, lots of brewery memorabilia, bric-a-brac and stained glass. There are tables outside.

🍴 Bar food consists of rolls and good pies at lunchtime (not Sunday).

Own brew ~ Licensee Colin Keatley ~ Real ale ~ No credit cards ~ (01603) 624364 ~ Open 12-11 (midnight Fri); 11-midnight Sat ~ Bar food filled rolls available until sold out; not Sun ~ Children allowed until 6pm ~ Dogs allowed in bar ~ Wi-fi ~ www.fatcatpub.co.uk *Recommended by Colin and Ruth Munro, David Carr*

SALTHOUSE
Dun Cow 🌟 🍺
TG0743   Map 8

A149 Blakeney–Sheringham (Purdy Street, junction with Bard Hill); NR25 7XA

Relaxed seaside pub, a good all-rounder and with enterprising food

The very high standards of service, food and drink at this smashing pub are consistently praised by our readers. The flint-walled bar consists of a pair of high-raftered rooms opened up into one area, with stone tiles around the counter where regulars congregate, and a carpeted seating area with a fireplace at each end. Also, scrubbed tables, one very high-backed settle as well as country kitchen chairs and elegant little red-padded dining chairs, with big sailing ship and other prints. With Adnams Southwold, Woodfordes Wherry and changing guests on handpump, 19 wines by the glass, 14 malt whiskies and quick service by friendly helpful staff, it has a good relaxed atmosphere. Picnic-sets out on the front grass look across the bird-filled salt marshes towards the sea, and there are more tables in a sheltered back courtyard and an orchard garden beyond. The bedrooms are self-catering.

Using local, seasonal produce and usefully served all day, the good, enjoyable food includes ciabattas (until 5pm), herring roes on toast, curried potted prawns and shrimps, wild mushroom risotto, lamb faggots in madeira and onion sauce, pigs cheeks in ginger and soy with fennel, pak choi and crispy noodles, fresh tuna niçoise, fish pie, and puddings such as treacle tart and pear and almond frangipane. *Benchmark main dish: burger in organic bun with fries, monterey jack cheese and home-made relish £11.00. Two-course evening meal £19.00.*

Punch ~ Lease Daniel Goff ~ Real ale ~ (01263) 740467 ~ Open 11-11 ~ Bar food 12-9 ~ Children welcome ~ Dogs welcome ~ Wi-fi ~ Live music monthly ~ www.salthouseduncow.com *Recommended by Philip and Susan Philcox, Neil and Angela Huxter, Linda Miller and Derek Greentree, Brian Glozier, Mrs Margo Finlay, Jörg Kasprowski, Michael and Jenny Back*

SNETTISHAM   TF6834 Map 8
Rose & Crown 🍽️ ⭐ 🍷 🛏️

Village signposted from A149 King's Lynn–Hunstanton just N of Sandringham; coming in on the B1440 from the roundabout just N of village, take first left turn into Old Church Road; PE31 7LX

Particularly well run inn with log fires and interesting furnishings, imaginative food, a fine range of drinks, and stylish seating on heated terrace; well equipped bedrooms

Our readers enjoy staying in the spacious, well appointed bedrooms in this first class pub – and the breakfasts are very good. The smallest of the three bars is pale grey in colour with coir flooring and old prints of King's Lynn and Sandringham. The other two bars each have a distinct character: an old-fashioned beamed front room with hessian cushions on black settles and a big log fire, and a back bar with another large log fire, the landlord's sporting trophies, old sports equipment and photos of the pub's cricket team. There's also the newly and appealingly refurbished Garden Room and residents' lounge with tweed-covered sofas, armchairs and pouffes interspersed with freshly painted wooden farmhouse chairs and tables, some interesting wallpaper and careful lighting. Adnams Bitter, Fullers London Pride, Greene King Old Speckled Hen and Woodfordes Wherry on handpump, 12 wines by the glass, a dozen malt whiskies and local cider and fruit juices; staff are neatly dressed and courteous. In warm weather, the garden is a lovely place for a drink or a meal with stylish café-style blue chairs and tables under cream parasols on a terrace, outdoor heaters and colourful herbaceous borders; there's also a wooden galleon-shaped climbing fort for children. Disabled lavatories and wheelchair ramp. This is sister pub to the Bank House in King's Lynn.

Using the best local produce, the excellent food includes lunchtime sandwiches (not Sunday), lobster and scallop ravioli with fennel and chilli mussels, devilled lambs kidneys, roast red pepper risotto with ricotta and basil beignets, sausages with ale gravy and mash, chicken suet pudding with smoked bacon potatoes, mallard a l'orange with goose fat potatoes, ray wing with caper and dill gnocchi and roast vine cherry tomatoes, and puddings such as hot chocolate mousse with marshmallows and pear and frangipane tart with madeira syrup. *Benchmark main dish: beer-battered haddock and chips £12.75. Two-course evening meal £19.00.*

Free house ~ Licensee Anthony Goodrich ~ Real ale ~ (01485) 541382 ~ Open 11-11 ~
Bar food 12-2 (5.30 weekends), 6.30-9 (9.30 Fri, Sat) ~ Restaurant ~ Children welcome
~ Dogs welcome ~ Wi-fi ~ Bedrooms: £80/£100 ~ www.roseandcrownsnettisham.co.uk
*Recommended by Sally Anne and Peter Goodale, Mike and Shirley Stratton, M J Daly, John Wooll,
Tracey and Stephen Groves, Dr Peter Crawshaw, R C Vincent, Sara Fulton, Roger Baker, Dennis and
Doreen Haward*

STANHOE
TF8037 Map 8
Duck 🌟 ♀ 🛏

B1155 Docking–Burnham Market; PE31 8QD

**Smart candlelit country dining pub with popular food, real ales
and appealing layout; bedrooms**

Past the village duck pond and surrounded by quiet farmland, this neatly
kept place has a wide mix of both drinking and dining customers.
The original bar is lively and chatty and there are three cosy dining areas
with beams, country kitchen chairs and pews around wooden tables on
bare boards or black slate flooring, and a couple of woodburning stoves.
Elgoods Cambridge and Golden Newt on handpump from a fine slab-
topped counter and 11 wines by the glass. The garden room is candlelit,
and there are seats under apple trees in the pretty garden, with more tables
and seats on the front gravel. The bedrooms are well appointed.

 Generous helpings of highly rated food includes lunchtime open sandwiches,
seared squid, confit pork belly and soy and basil mayonnaise, foie gras
ballotine, sautéed duck hearts and pickled cranberries, honey-roast ham and
free-range eggs, pumpkin risotto with white truffle oil, beer-battered haddock and
chips, rump of local lamb with moroccan-spiced shoulder, quinoa and labneh, and
puddings such as apple and cinnamon crumble and triple chocolate brownie with salt
caramel. *Benchmark main dish: rib-eye pork with braised cheek, sage onion, apple
and vanilla and celeriac purée £15.50. Two-course evening meal £23.00.*

Elgoods ~ Tenants Sarah and Ben Handley ~ Real ale ~ (01485) 518330 ~ Open 11-11;
12-9.30 Sun ~ Bar food 12-2.30, 6-9; 12-8 Sun ~ Restaurant ~ Children welcome ~
Dogs allowed in bar ~ Wi-fi ~ Bedrooms: £85/£125 ~ www.duckinn.co.uk
Recommended by David and Sue Medcalf, R C Vincent, Edward Mirzoeff, Tracey and Stephen Groves

STOKE HOLY CROSS
TG2302 Map 5
Wildebeest Arms ♀

Village signposted off A140 S of Norwich; turn left in village; NR14 8QJ

**Stylish restaurant pub with good enterprising food, thriving relaxed
atmosphere and attractive terrace**

Most people come to this interestingly decorated place to enjoy the
particularly good food, but you can just drop in for a drink – there are
several bar stools by the sleek semicircular bar, and a few casual chairs
as well as tables outside. The long room has an understated african theme
with carefully placed carvings and hangings on the dark sandy walls.
On the polished boards, unusual dark leather chairs are grouped around
striking tables consisting of heavy slabs of well grained wood on elegant
wrought-iron supports. Adnams Southwold and Ringwood Fortyniner
on handpump and several wines by the glass; the neatly dressed staff
are helpful and efficient. The subtly lit front terrace is a great asset, well
sheltered from the road by tall woven willow hurdles, with comfortable
wicker armchairs or cushioned benches around glass-topped tables, most
under big heated canvas parasols.

🍴 Enticing food includes seared scallops with pork belly rillette and bacon crumb, pigeon breast wellington with puy lentils and pickled shiitake mushrooms, herb potato gnocchi with roast butternut squash, jerusalem artichokes and wild mushrooms, pistachio-stuffed pork tenderloin wrapped in parma ham with apricot and thyme purée, chicken with sautéed leeks and peppers, and puddings such as baked apple crumble cheesecake with toffee sauce and cinnamon doughnuts and crème brûlée; they also offer a two- and three-course set lunch. *Benchmark main dish: whole plaice with wilted greens and wild garlic and lemon butter £14.95. Two-course evening meal £23.00.*

Animal Inns ~ Manager Rouve Elvin ~ Real ale ~ (01508) 492497 ~ Open 11.30-3, 6-11 (midnight Fri); 11.30am-midnight Sat; 11.30-10 Sun ~ Bar food 12-2.30, 6.30-9.30; 12-8 Sun ~ Restaurant ~ Children welcome ~ Dogs allowed in bar ~ Wi-fi ~ www.thewildebeest.co.uk *Recommended by Toby Jones, Ben and Ros Goodfellow, Isobel Mackinlay*

THORNHAM
Lifeboat 🍴 🛏

TF7343 Map 8

A149 by Kings Head, then first left; PE36 6LT

Lots of character in traditional inn, plenty of space for eating and dining, real ales and super surrounding walks; bedrooms

The two rooms of the pubby main bar in this neatly kept inn have as much atmosphere as ever, full of chatty customers of all ages. There are beams, open doorways, lots of horse tack and farming implements, big lamps, brass measuring jugs, and chairs and settles around dark sturdy tables on quarry tiles; each fireplace has a woodburning stove, and one bench has an antique penny-in-the-hole game. The adjacent two-level conservatory has chairs around pine-topped tables; steps lead up to the garden with its green-painted furniture under green parasols and good play area for children. The little tap bar is genuine and cosy, and a small eating room off here has a big model train on the mantelpiece. The spreading restaurant is smart and more formal. Adnams Bitter, Greene King Abbot and IPA, Woodfordes Wherry and a seasonal guest from Woodfordes on handpump, nine wines by the glass and several malt whiskies. At the front of the building are some modern grey seats and tables, and picnic-sets under parasols. There are walks around the salt marshes about a mile away. The bedrooms are warm and simply furnished and the breakfasts good.

🍴 Enjoyable food includes lunchtime sandwiches, corned beef hash with poached duck egg and béarnaise sauce, salt and pepper calamari, barbecue ribs with coleslaw and chips, calves liver with smoked bacon and sage, roast cod with garlic mash and red wine sauce, braised beef brisket with Guinness and prunes, and puddings such as sticky toffee pudding and apple and blackberry crumble with sauce anglaise. *Benchmark main dish: roast rump of lamb with dauphinoise potatoes £18.50. Two-course evening meal £24.00.*

Free house ~ Licensee Helen Stafford ~ Real ale ~ (01485) 512236 ~ Open 11-11 (midnight Sat) ~ Bar food 12-9.30; 12-2.30, 6-9 in winter ~ Restaurant ~ Children welcome ~ Dogs allowed in bar and bedrooms ~ Wi-fi ~ Bedrooms: $70/$100 ~ www.lifeboatinnthornham.com *Recommended by Marianne and Peter Stevens, James Stretton, Tracey and Stephen Groves, Derek and Sylvia Stephenson, Mr and Mrs P R Thomas, David and Ruth Hollands, John Wooll, Peter Sutton, David Carr, Dennis and Doreen Haward, J R Wildon*

The letters and figures after the name of each town are its Ordnance Survey map reference. 'Using the *Guide*' at the beginning of the book explains how it helps you find a pub, in road atlases or large-scale maps as well as in our own maps.

THORNHAM
Orange Tree ⭐ ♀ 🛏
TF7343 Map 8

Church Street/A149; PE36 6LY

● ●

Norfolk Dining Pub of the Year

Nice combination of friendly bar and good contemporary dining; suntrap garden; bedrooms

In warm weather the garden in front of this genuinely welcoming inn is much in demand, so it's best to arrive early to bag a seat: lavender beds and climbing roses, lots of picnic-sets under parasols, outdoor heaters and a smart small corner pavilion. At the back of the building is a second outside area with children's play equipment. The sizeable bar is bustling and friendly, with red leather chesterfield sofas in front of a log fire, flowery upholstered or leather and wood dining chairs and red or stripy plush wall seats around a mix of tables on wood or quarry-tiled floors, and white painted beams; background music, board games and flat-screen TV. Helpful, attentive staff serve Adnams Bitter, Woodfordes Wherry and a guest such as Bays Up and Under on handpump and 29 wines by the glass. A little dining room leads off here with silver décor, buddha heads and candles, and the two-part restaurant is simple and contemporary in style. The courtyard bedrooms make a good base for this lovely stretch of the north Norfolk coast and the breakfasts are very good. They're kind to dogs and have a doggie menu plus snacks.

 The beautifully presented, imaginative food includes duck, goose and pork belly yuk sung with kimchi salad and roasted peanuts, scallops with crispy pigs cheek, vanilla and tonka bean panna cotta and golden raisin purée, slow-roast pork belly and barbecue loin with smoked potato pie, poached egg, caramelised onion purée and truffle jus, seafood spaghetti, venison and parsley root faggot with carrot and vanilla purée, sloe gin and hot chocolate sauce, and puddings such as pear, caramel and chocolate brownie and crème caramel with mascarpone sorbet. *Benchmark main dish: rare-breed burger with cheese, smoked bacon, thyme and mustard coleslaw, and bucket of chips £12.85. Two-course evening meal £21.50.*

Punch ~ Lease Mark Goode ~ Real ale ~ (01485) 512213 ~ Open 11-11 (midnight Sat); 12-10.30 Sun ~ Bar food 12-9.30 ~ Restaurant ~ Children welcome ~ Dogs allowed in bar and bedrooms ~ Wi-fi ~ Bedrooms: $80/$89 ~ www.theorangetreethornham.co.uk
Recommended by David Jackman, Derek and Sylvia Stephenson, Mr and Mrs P R Thomas, Tracey and Stephen Groves, David Carr, J R Wildon

THORPE MARKET
Gunton Arms
TG2434 Map 8

Cromer Road; NR11 8TZ

Impressive place with an easy-going atmosphere, open fires and antiques in bar and dining rooms, real ales, interesting food and friendly staff; bedrooms

Grand and rather interesting, this country house-cum-pub is surrounded by a 1,000-acre deer park. The large entrance hall sets the scene; throughout, the atmosphere is informal and relaxed but definitely gently upmarket. The simply furnished bar has dark pubby chairs and tables on a wooden floor, a log fire, a long settle beside a pool table, and high stools against the mahogany counter where they serve Adnams Bitter and Broadside, Wolf Lavender Honey and Woodfordes Wherry on handpump, 13 wines by the glass, 16 malt whiskies and two ciders; staff are chatty and friendly. Heavy curtains line the open doorway that leads into a dining room with vast antlers on the wall above a big log fire (they often cook over this) and straightforward chairs around scrubbed tables on stone tiles. There's also a lounge with comfortable old leather armchairs and a sofa on a fine rug in front of yet another log fire, some genuine antiques, big house plants and standard lamps, plus a more formal restaurant with candles and napery, and two homely sitting rooms for hotel residents. Many of the walls are painted dark red and hung with assorted artwork and big mirrors; background music, darts, TV and board games. The bedrooms have many original fittings, but no TV or tea-making facilities. They hold a wild honey festival in spring and a beer and music festival in August.

Using Estate produce, the hearty rustic food includes sandwiches (until 5pm), jellied ham hock with piccalilli, whipped butternut squash with feta and flatbread, crab pasta with chilli, chicken, bacon and leek pie, pollack fish fingers with chips, roast suckling pig with rainbow chard, venison sausages with onion gravy, slip soles with brown shrimp and sea purslane, and puddings such as cinnamon doughnuts with chocolate sauce and blood orange posset. *Benchmark main dish: loin of fallow deer with morels £18.50. Two-course evening meal £22.50.*

Free house ~ Licensee Simone Baker ~ Real ale ~ (01263) 832010 ~ Open 12-11 (10.30 Sun) ~ Bar food 12-3, 6-10 (9 Sun) ~ Restaurant ~ Children welcome ~ Dogs allowed in bar and bedrooms ~ Wi-fi ~ Bedrooms: /£120 ~ www.theguntonarms.co.uk
Recommended by Paul Humphreys, N R White

WIVETON

Wiveton Bell

TG0442 Map 8

Blakeney Road; NR25 7TL

Busy, open-plan dining pub, drinkers welcomed too, local beers, consistently enjoyable food and seats outside; bedrooms

Although many customers are here to enjoy the imaginative food, there's a cheerful, pubby feel and a good mix of both drinkers and diners. Mainly open-plan, it has some fine old beams, an attractive mix of dining chairs around wooden tables on a stripped-wood floor, a log fire and prints on the yellow walls. The sizeable conservatory has smart beige dining chairs around wooden tables on the coir flooring. Friendly, attentive staff serve Humpty Dumpty Ale, Norfolk Brewhouse Moon Gazer Amber Ale, Woodfordes Wherry and Yetmans Blue on handpump, and 13 wines by the glass. Outside, at the front, picnic-sets on grass look across to the church; at the back, stylish wicker tables and chairs on several decked areas are set among decorative box hedging. The bedrooms are comfortable and they also have a self-catering cottage.

Using local, seasonal produce, the attractively presented, impressive food includes smoked ham hock terrine with their own soft-boiled free-range egg, smoked haddock and leek fishcake with horseradish cream, petit pois, baby spinach and blue cheese risotto, chicken with butternut squash fondant and smoked bacon jus, hake fillet with a herb crust, saffron parmentier potatoes and hazelnut and brown caper butter, venison loin with sweet potato purée and braised venison shoulder kromeski (croquettes), and puddings such as bread and butter pudding with crème anglaise. *Benchmark main dish: slow-braised local pork belly with bourbon glaze and root vegetable dauphinoise £14.95. Two-course evening meal £22.00.*

Free house ~ Licensee Berni Morritt ~ Real ale ~ (01263) 740101 ~ Open 12-11 (10.30 Sun) ~ Bar food 12-2.15 (3 Sun), 6-9.15 (9 Sun) ~ Children welcome ~ Dogs allowed in bar ~ Wi-fi ~ Bedrooms: /£140 ~ www.wivetonbell.co.uk *Recommended by Barrie Fischer, Neil and Angela Huxter, Brian Glozier, David Carr, John Millwood, Roy Hoing, Derek and Sylvia Stephenson, R L Borthwick, Revd Michael Vockins, John Wooll, Stephen Burrows, Michael Sargent*

WOLTERTON
TG1732 Map 8

Saracens Head 🛏

Wolterton; Erpingham signed off A140 N of Aylsham, on through Calthorpe; NR11 7LZ

Remote inn with stylish bars and dining room and seats in courtyard; good bedrooms

Friendly and civilised, this Georgian inn is doing especially well under its present owners; our readers enjoy their visits here very much. The two-room bar is simple but stylish with high ceilings, light terracotta walls and cream and gold curtains at its tall windows – all lending a feeling of space, though it's not large. There's a mix of seats from built-in wall settles to wicker fireside chairs, as well as log fires and flowers, and the windows look on to a charming old-fashioned gravel stableyard with plenty of chairs, benches and tables. A pretty six-table parlour on the right has another big log fire. Woodfordes Wherry and Once Bittern on handpump, several wines by the glass and local soft drinks. The bedrooms are comfortable and up to date.

🍴 Using seasonal, local ingredients (they list the exact mileage the produce has travelled) such as lamb and pork from nearby farms and seafood from the north Norfolk coast, the menu offers rewarding choices such as lunchtime sandwiches (not Sunday), rabbit terrine with spicy apricot chutney, crab with spring onions, mushrooms and cheese, green pea and wild garlic ricotta cake with tomato and basil salad, skate wing with fennel, baby capers and crayfish tails, duck with pineapple, chilli and soy sauce, and puddings such as treacle tart and white chocolate and raspberry cheesecake; they also have a two-course set lunch (Wednesday-Saturday). *Benchmark main dish: slow-cooked pork belly with chorizo, chickpea and tomato sauce £14.50. Two-course evening meal £22.00.*

Free house ~ Licensees Tim and Janie Elwes ~ Real ale ~ (01263) 768909 ~ Open 11.30-2.30, 6-11; 12-2, 6.30-9 Sun; closed Mon except bank holidays, Oct-June Tues lunchtime ~ Bar food 12-2.30, 6.30-9; 12-2, 6-8.30 in winter ~ Restaurant ~ Children welcome ~ Dogs allowed in bar and bedrooms ~ Wi-fi ~ Bedrooms: £70/£100 ~ www.saracenshead-norfolk.co.uk *Recommended by Paul Humphreys, Philip and Susan Philcox, John Wooll*

WOODBASTWICK
TG3214 Map 8

Fur & Feather 🍺

Off B1140 E of Norwich; NR13 6HQ

Full range of first class beers from next-door Woodfordes brewery, friendly service and popular bar food

This thatched, cottagey pub is right next door to Woodfordes brewery and its beers, tapped from the cask, are notably well kept: Bure Gold, Mardlers, Nelsons Revenge, Once Bittern, Sundew and Wherry. You can also visit the brewery shop. Efficient, helpful staff also serve a dozen wines by the glass and ten malt whiskies. The style and atmosphere are not what you'd expect of a brewery tap – it's set out more like a comfortable and roomy dining pub with wooden chairs and tables on tiles or carpeting and sofas and armchairs; background music. There are seats and tables in the pleasant garden. This is a lovely Estate village.

🍴 Generous helpings of well liked food includes baguettes, mussels in ale and cream, game terrine with port jelly, ham and free-range eggs, burger with coleslaw, chips and lots of toppings, roasted vegetable crumble, steak and kidney pudding, pheasant and bacon pie, seafood medley, and puddings such as Malteser marshmallow sundae and baked lemon cheesecake. *Benchmark main dish: steak and kidney pudding £13.00. Two-course evening meal £19.00.*

Woodfordes ~ Tenant Tim Ridley ~ Real ale ~ (01603) 720003 ~ Open 10-10 (9.30 Sun) ~ Bar food 10-9 ~ Restaurant ~ Children welcome ~ Wi-fi ~ www.thefurandfeatherinn.co.uk
Recommended by Mrs D Barrett, Mrs Margo Finlay, Jörg Kasprowski, Tracey and Stephen Groves, N R White, Roy Hoing, Stephen and Jean Curtis, R C Vincent

Also Worth a Visit in Norfolk

Besides the fully inspected pubs, you might like to try these pubs that have been recommended to us and described by readers. Do tell us what you think of them: feedback@goodguides.com

AYLMERTON   TG1840
Roman Camp (01263) 838291
Holt Road (A148); NR11 8QD Large late 19th-c mock-Tudor roadside inn; comfortable panelled bar, cosy sitting room off with warm fire, and light airy dining room, decent choice of enjoyable sensibly priced food, well kept Adnams, Greene King and a guest, friendly helpful service from uniformed staff; children welcome, attractive sheltered garden behind with sunny terraces and pond, 15 bedrooms. *(John Wooll, David Carr)*

AYLSHAM   TG1926
★ **Black Boys** (01263) 732122
Market Place; off B1145; NR11 6EH Small hotel with imposing Georgian façade and informal open-plan bar, popular generously served food (all day) from snacks up including good value Sun roasts, Adnams and guests such as Timothy Taylors, Woodfordes and Wychwood, decent wines, comfortable seats and plenty of tables, high beams, part carpet, part bare boards, helpful young uniformed staff coping well at busy times; children and dogs welcome, seats in front by marketplace, more behind, bedrooms, big cooked breakfast, open all day. *(Dr and Mrs R G J Telfer, John Wooll, Alex and Hazel Evans, David Carr)*

BANNINGHAM   TG2129
★ **Crown** (01263) 733534
Colby Road; opposite church by village green; NR11 7DY Welcoming and popular 17th-c beamed pub in same family for 23 years and recently refurbished; good choice of enjoyable affordably priced food (they're helpful with gluten-free diets), well kept Greene King and local guests, decent wines, good quick service, log fires and woodburners; TV, free wi-fi; children and dogs welcome, disabled access, garden jazz festival Aug, open (and food) all day weekends. *(Julie Hobday, M J Bourke, R C Vincent, Brian Nicholson)*

BARTON BENDISH   TF7105
Berney Arms (01366) 347995
Off A1122 W of Swaffham; Church Road; PE33 9GF Attractive dining pub in quiet village, good freshly made food from sandwiches and pub favourites to more inventive dishes, good value set menu too, service prompt and welcoming, Adnams beers and good choice of wines by the glass, afternoon teas, restaurant; children welcome, pleasant garden, good bedrooms in converted stables and forge, open all day. *(Anon)*

BERNEY ARMS   TG4607
Berney Arms
Accessible only on foot, by rail from Great Yarmouth or by boat; NR30 1SB Extremely remote late 18th-c pub overlooking River Yare and surrounded by RSPB marshland; unpretentious and unsmart (not to everyone's taste) with panelling, tiled flooring and old seating, local ales such as Humpty Dumpty from small brick-faced bar, pubby food; painted picnic-sets outside and expansive views, moorings, short walk to seven-floor windmill, Berney Arms station about 0.75 miles across fields, 5-mile riverside hike to Great Yarmouth, open all day. *(N R White)*

BLAKENEY   TG0244
Blakeney Hotel (01263) 740376
The Quay; NR25 7ND Pleasant flint hotel nicely set near bird marshes, elegant harbour-view bar with good sensibly priced home-made food, friendly attentive staff, well kept Adnams and Woodfordes, games room, restaurant; 37 bedrooms. *(David Carr)*

BLAKENEY   TG0243
Kings Arms (01263) 740341
West Gate Street; NR25 7NQ A stroll from the harbour to this 18th-c pub, friendly and chatty, with Adnams, Greene King Old Speckled Hen, Marstons Pedigree and guests, decent pub food all day from breakfast on,

---

You can send reports directly to us at feedback@goodguides.com

three simple linked low-ceilinged rooms and airy garden room; children and dogs welcome, big garden, bedrooms, open from 9.30am (midday Sun). *(Mr and Mrs D J Nash)*

BLAKENEY   TG0243
White Horse (01263) 740574

Off A149 W of Sheringham; High Street; NR25 7AL Friendly inn popular with both locals and holidaymakers, informal long bar with cream-coloured walls, fine-art equestrian prints and paintings, high-backed brown leather dining and other chairs around light oak tables on black and white striped carpet, Adnams Bitter, Broadside, Explorer and seasonal guest, a dozen wines by the glass, well liked food including local fish and shellfish, airy conservatory; children and dogs welcome, seats in suntrap courtyard and pleasant paved garden, short stroll to harbour, bedrooms, open all day. *(Mike and Shirley Stratton, Revd Michael Vockins, David Carr)*

BLICKLING   TG1728
Buckinghamshire Arms

(01263) 732133 *B1354 NW of Aylsham; NR11 6NF* Handsome Jacobean inn now owned by Colchester Inns and some refurbishment; small proper bar, lounge set for eating with woodburner, smarter more formal dining room with another fire, Adnams, Grain and Woodfordes ales, good choice of wines by the glass, generally well liked food, pleasant attentive young staff; background music; children and dogs welcome, tables out on lawn, well placed by gates to Blickling Hall (NT), lovely walks nearby, three bedrooms, open all day (food all day Sun). *(Dennis and Doreen Haward)*

BRAMERTON   TG2905
Woods End (01508) 538005

N of village, towards river; NR14 7ED Clean modern refurbishment for this pub-restaurant in great spot overlooking bend of River Yare, good food from lunchtime ciabattas and sharing plates up, ales such as Greene King and Woodfordes, efficient friendly service; children welcome, wheelchair access, picnic-sets on waterside deck, moorings, open all day (Fri, Sat till 1am, Sun till 9pm). *(Robert Watt)*

BRANCASTER   TF7743
★**Ship** (01485) 210333

London Street (A149); PE31 8AP Bustling roadside inn, part of the small Flying Kiwi chain; compact bar with built-in cushioned and planked wall seats, Adnams Bitter and Jo C's Norfolk Ale, nice wines by the glass, several dining areas with woodburner in one and neatly log-piled fireplace in another, contemporary paintwork throughout, pale settles and nice mix of other furniture on rugs and bare boards, bookcases, shipping memorabilia and lots of prints, good modern food, daily papers and friendly,

helpful service; background music, TV; children and dogs welcome, gravelled seating area with round picnic-sets out by car park, attractive well equipped bedrooms, open all day. *(David Jackman, P and J Shapley, Tracey and Stephen Groves)*

BRANCASTER STAITHE   TF7944
★**Jolly Sailors** (01485) 210314

Main Road (A149); PE31 8BJ Unpretentious pub set in prime bird-watching territory on edge of NT dunes and salt flats, chatty mix of locals and visitors in simply furnished bars, wheelbacks, settles and cushioned benches around mix of tables on quarry tiles, photographs and local maps on the walls, woodburner, their own Brancaster ales (brewery not on site) and guests, several wines by the glass, sizeable back dining room with popular food including pizzas; children and dogs welcome, plenty of picnic-sets and play equipment in peaceful back garden, ice-cream hut in summer, vine-covered terrace, open all day (food all day summer). *(R C Vincent, James Stretton, Philip and Susan Philcox, Tracey and Stephen Groves, Derek and Sylvia Stephenson and others)*

BRANCASTER STAITHE   TF8044
★**White Horse** (01485) 210262

A149 E of Hunstanton; PE31 8BY Very popular place – restaurant but does have proper informal front locals' bar; own Brancaster ales with guests such as Adnams and Woodfordes, lots of wines by the glass, log fire, pine furniture, historical photographs and bar billiards, middle area with comfortable sofas and newspapers, big airy dining conservatory overlooking tidal marshes, good bar and restaurant food including 'tapas' and plenty of fish, they ask to keep a credit card while you run a tab; children welcome, dogs in bar, seats on sun deck with fine views, more under cover on heated terrace, nice bedrooms, coast path at bottom of garden, open (and food) all day. *(Marianne and Peter Stevens, James Stretton, John Wooll, Tracey and Stephen Groves)*

BROOKE   TM2899
Kings Head (01508) 550335

Norwich Road (B1332); NR15 1AB Welcoming 17th-c village pub with enjoyable food from traditional choices up, good service, four real ales and excellent choice of wines by the glass, maybe a norfolk whisky, light and airy bare-boards bar with log fire, eating area up a step; quiz last Sun of month, free wi-fi; children welcome, tables in sheltered garden, open all day (from 9.30am weekends for breakfast). *(Anon)*

BROOME   TM3591
Artichoke (01986) 893325

Yarmouth Road; NR35 2NZ Unpretentious split-level roadside pub with up to eight well kept ales (some from tap room casks) including Adnams and Elgoods, belgian fruit beers and excellent selection of whiskies too, enjoyable traditional home-made food in bar or dining room, friendly helpful staff, wood and flagstone floors, log fire in big fireplace; dogs welcome, garden picnic-sets, smokers' shelter, closed Mon otherwise open all day. *(Anon)*

**BURNHAM OVERY
STAITHE** TF8444
Hero (01328) 738334

A149; PE31 8JE Spacious modernised roadside pub, good variety of well liked and fairly priced food from baguettes up, cheerful young staff, Adnams and Woodfordes, two dining areas, woodburner; children welcome, no dogs inside, picnic-sets out on gravel. *(Anon)*

BURNHAM THORPE TF8541
★ **Lord Nelson** (01328) 738241

Off B1155 or B1355, near Burnham Market; PE31 8HL Neatly kept 17th-c pub with lots of Nelson memorabilia (he was born in this sleepy village); antique high-backed settles on worn red tiles in small bar, smoke ovens in original fireplace, little snug leading off, two dining rooms one with flagstones and open fire, good bar food, Greene King, Woodfordes and a guest tapped from the cask, several wines by the glass, secret rum-based recipes (Nelson's Blood and Lady Hamilton's Nip); children and dogs welcome, good-sized play area and pétanque in long back garden, open all day in summer, closed Mon evening (except school/bank holidays). *(Rita Scarratt, Sheila Topham, David Carr)*

CHEDGRAVE TM3699
White Horse (01508) 520250

Norwich Road; NR14 6ND Welcoming pub with Timothy Taylors Landlord and four other well kept ales (festivals Apr and Nov), decent wines by the glass, good choice of enjoyable sensibly priced food from lunchtime baguettes up, friendly attentive young staff, log fire and sofas in bar, restaurant, regular events including monthly quiz, pool, darts; children and dogs welcome, garden picnic-sets. *(Richard Ball)*

CLEY-NEXT-THE-SEA TG0443
★ **Three Swallows** (01263) 740526

Holt Road off A149; NR25 7TT Busy refurbished local, log fires in bar and dining room, stripped-pine tables, enjoyable reasonably priced pubby food (all day Sun) from sandwiches up, well kept Adnams, Greene King and Woodfordes from unusual richly carved bar, cheerful hard-working staff; children and dogs welcome, disabled access, metal tables and chairs out at front facing green, big garden with surprisingly grandiose fountain, aviary and heated smokers' shelter,

four annexe bedrooms, good breakfast, handy for the salt marshes, open all day. *(Neil and Angela Huxter, M and GR)*

COCKLEY CLEY TF7904
Twenty Churchwardens
(01760) 721439 *Off A1065 S of Swaffham; PE37 8AN* Friendly nicely informal pub in converted former school next to church, three linked beamed rooms, good open fire, popular food including good home-made pies, well kept Adnams Southwold; no credit cards; children and dogs welcome, tiny unspoilt village. *(Anon)*

COLTISHALL TG2719
Kings Head (01603) 737426

Wroxham Road (B1354); NR12 7EA Popular dining pub close to River Bure and moorings, imaginative food from owner-chef (especially fish/seafood), also bar snacks and lunchtime set menu, well kept Adnams, nice wines by the glass, open fire, fishing nets and stuffed fish including a monster pike, also the bill from a marlin caught by the landlord, cookery school; background music; seats outside (noisy road), four bedrooms. *(Philip and Susan Philcox)*

CONGHAM TF7123
Anvil (01485) 600625

St Andrews Lane; PE32 1DU Tucked-away modern country pub with welcoming licensees, wide choice of enjoyable home-made food from light choices up, Sun carvery, quick friendly service, three well kept ales such as Batemans, reasonable prices, live music and quiz nights; children welcome, picnic-sets in small walled front garden, campsite, open all day weekends, closed Mon. *(R C Vincent)*

CROMER TG2242
Red Lion (01263) 514964

Off A149; Tucker Street/Brook Street; NR27 9HD Substantial refurbished Victorian hotel with elevated sea views, original features including panelling and open fires, five well kept ales in bare-boards flint-walled bar, enjoyable food from sandwiches and ciabattas up including good local mussels, efficient friendly service, restaurant and conservatory; background music; children and dogs welcome, disabled facilities, tables in back courtyard, 14 bedrooms, open all day. *(David Carr, Adrian Johnson, N R White)*

DERSINGHAM TF6930
Feathers (01485) 540768

B1440 towards Sandringham; Manor Road; PE31 6LN Refurbished Jacobean carrstone inn once part of the Sandringham Estate; two adjoining bars (main one with big open fire), well kept Adnams, Woodfordes

---

If you know a pub is ever open all day, please tell us.

and a guest, enjoyable food emphasising local produce and fish, friendly accommodating service, back dining room, function room in converted stables; background music; children and dogs welcome, large garden with play area, five bedrooms, open all day. *(Tracey and Stephen Groves)*

DOWNHAM MARKET   TF6003
Railway Arms (01366) 386636
At railway station, Railway Road; PE38 9EN Cosy station bar with tiny adjoining rooms, one with glowing coal fire, another with second-hand bookshop, real ales tapped from the cask and a couple of ciders, teas, coffee and some snacky food, model train sometimes running around; best to check opening times. *(Anon)*

EAST BARSHAM   TF9133
White Horse (01328) 820645
B1105 3 miles N of Fakenham; NR21 0LH Extended 17th-c inn refurbished under present management, big log fire in beamed bar with adjoining dining area, step up to more formal restaurant, good range of well liked home-made food, Greene King ales, friendly helpful staff; children and dogs (in bar) welcome, new decked area out behind with barbecue, three updated bedrooms and two self-catering cottages, open all day. *(Anon)*

EDGEFIELD   TG0934
★**Pigs** (01263) 587634
Norwich Road; B1149 S of Holt; NR24 2RL Friendly bustling pub with carpeted bar, Adnams, Greene King, Woodfordes and a house beer from Wolf tapped from casks, arches through to simply furnished area with mixed chairs and pews on broad pine boards, airy dining extension in similar style split into stalls by standing timbers and low brick walls, nice variety of good quality food including Norfolk tapas, games room with bar billiards, also children's playroom; background music; dogs allowed in bar, good wheelchair access, rustic seats and tables on big covered front terrace, adventure playground, boules (some with spa facilities), open all day Sun – food all day then too. *(Dr and Mrs R G J Telfer, Tracey and Stephen Groves, Roy Hoing)*

FAKENHAM   TF9229
Limes (01328) 850050
Bridge Street; NR21 9AZ New Wetherspoons, clean, light and spacious, with good choice of beers, enjoyable food and usual value, separate coffee corner; TVs, free wi-fi; plenty of seats outside, open all day from 8am. *(Edna Jones, David Carr)*

GAYTON   TF7219
Crown (01553) 636252
Lynn Road (B1145/B1153); opposite church; PE32 1PA Low-beamed village pub with plenty of character, unusual old features

and charming snug as well as three main areas, good choice of popular sensibly priced food from sandwiches up, Sun carvery, well kept Greene King ales, friendly service, sofas and good log fire, games room; dogs welcome in bar, tables in attractive sheltered garden, four bedrooms. *(Paul Thompson, Tony Westhead)*

GELDESTON   TM3990
★**Locks** (01508) 518414
Off A143/A146 NW of Beccles; off Station Road S of village, obscurely signed down long rough track; NR34 0HW Remote candlelit pub at navigable head of River Waveney; ancient tiled-floor core with beams and big log fire, good Green Jack ales and guests tapped from casks, enjoyable food including burgers, vegetarian dishes and Fri curry night, large extension for summer crowds, regular live music; no credit cards; children welcome, riverside garden, moorings, open all day in summer, closed Mon-Thurs in winter. *(Mrs D Barrett)*

GREAT CRESSINGHAM   TF8401
★**Windmill** (01760) 756232
Village signed off A1065 S of Swaffham; Water End; IP25 6NN Interesting pictures and bric-a-brac in warren of rambling linked rooms, plenty of cosy corners, good value fresh bar food from baguettes to steak and Sun roasts, half a dozen ales including Adnams, Greene King and house beer called Windy Miller Quixote, decent wines, 60 malt whiskies and good coffee, cheery staff, well lit pool room, pub games; background music (live country & western Tues), big sports TV in side snug; children and dogs welcome, large garden with picnic-sets and good play area, caravan parking, bedroom extension. *(R C Vincent)*

GREAT RYBURGH   TF9627
Blue Boar (01328) 829212
Station Road; NR21 0DX Rambling 17th-c beamed pub in nice setting opposite church, good locally sourced food from landlord-chef, can eat in bar or restaurant, a house beer from Winters plus guests such as Adnams and Yetmans, inglenook woodburner; children welcome, garden with enclosed play area, pleasant local walks, five bedrooms, closed Tues and lunchtimes (except Sun). *(George Atkinson)*

GREAT YARMOUTH   TG5207
Mariners (01493) 332299
Howard Street S; NR30 1LN Dutch-gabled two-room pub popular for its excellent range of real ales and ciders (regular festivals), bargain food from sandwiches to specials, efficient staff; open all day. *(Dennis Jones)*

GREAT YARMOUTH   TG5207
St Johns Head (01493) 843443
North Quay; NR30 1JB Friendly traditional flintstone pub, well kept ales

including bargain Elgoods; pool, sports TV; open all day. *(David Carr, Dennis Jones)*

HARPLEY TF7825
Rose & Crown (01485) 521807
Off A148 Fakenham–Kings Lynn; Nethergate Street; PE31 6TW Old village pub continuing well under present welcoming licensees; good choice of enjoyable food from varied menu, Adnams and Woodfordes ales, Aspall's cider, modernised interior with open fires; children and dogs welcome, garden picnic-sets, closed Sun evening, all Mon and lunchtime Tues. *(Anon)*

HEYDON TG1127
★ Earle Arms (01263) 587376
Off B1149; NR11 6AD Nice old dutch-gabled pub overlooking green and church in delightfully unspoilt estate village; well kept Adnams, Woodfordes and a guest, enjoyable food from varied if not extensive menu using local fish and meat (gluten-free choices marked), decent wine list, friendly efficient service, racing prints, some stuffed animals and good log fire in old-fashioned candlelit bar, more formal dining room; children welcome, dogs in bar, picnic-sets in small cottagey back garden, open all day Sun (no evening food then), closed Mon. *(John Wooll)*

HICKLING TG4123
Greyhound (01692) 598306
The Green; NR12 0YA Small busy pub with welcoming open fire, good choice of enjoyable food in bar and neat restaurant, well kept local ales and ciders, friendly long-serving landlord; well behaved children welcome, pretty back garden with terrace tables, bedroom annexe. *(Roy Hoing)*

HINGHAM TG0202
★ White Hart (01953) 850214
Market Place, just off B1108 W of Norwich; NR9 4AF Friendly and civilised Flying Kiwi Inn with character rooms arranged over two floors, beams and standing timbers, stripped floorboards with oriental rugs, attractive mix of furniture including comfortable sofas in quiet corners, lots of prints and photographs on mushroom walls, several woodburners, galleried long room up steps from main bar with egyptian frieze, own-brewed Jo C's Norfolk Kiwi plus Adnams Bitter, lots of wines by glass, good interesting food (all day Sun till 8pm); children and dogs (in bar) welcome, modern benches and seats in gravelled courtyard, pretty village with huge 14th-c church, open all day. *(Evelyn and Derek Walter, Alcuin Bramerton)*

HOLME-NEXT-THE-SEA TF7043
White Horse (01485) 525512
Kirkgate Street; PE36 6LH Attractive old-fashioned place, cosy and rambling, with warm log fires, ample choice of food including local fish and specials, fair prices, friendly efficient service, Adnams, Greene King and decent wines, refurbished side extension; children and dogs welcome (they have a friendly dog and cat), small back garden, seats out in front and on lawn opposite, play area. *(John Wooll, Richard and Liz Thorne)*

HOLT TG0738
Feathers (01263) 712318
Market Place; NR25 6BW Relaxed hotel with popular locals' bar comfortably extended around original panelled area, open fire, antiques in attractive entrance/reception area, good choice of enjoyable fairly priced food including blackboard specials, friendly helpful service, Greene King ales and decent wines, good coffee, restaurant and dining conservatory; background music, no dogs; children welcome, 13 comfortable bedrooms, open all day. *(John Wooll, John Evans, David Carr)*

HOLT TG0738
Kings Head (01263) 712543
High Street/Bull Street; NR25 6BN Bustling rustic public bar, two roomy back bars and conservatory, enjoyable food including charcoal-grilled steaks, prompt friendly service, beers such as Adnams, Humpty Dumpty and Woodfordes, fair choice of wines; some live music, sports TV, pool; children welcome, back terrace with heated smokers' shelter, good-sized garden, three stylish bedrooms, open all day. *(Anon)*

HORSTEAD TG2619
Recruiting Sergeant (01603) 737077
B1150 just S of Coltishall; NR12 7EE Light, airy and roomily set out roadside pub, enjoyable generously served food from fresh panini and wraps up, including good fish choice, efficient friendly service even though busy, up to half a dozen changing ales such as Adnams, Greene King, Timothy Taylors and Woodfordes, plenty of wines by the glass, big open fire; children welcome, terrace and garden tables, bedrooms, open all day. *(Alex and Hazel Evans)*

HUNSTANTON TF6740
Honeystone (01485) 534463
Southend Road; PE36 5AW Newly built Marstons family pub on outskirts, modern décor and furnishings, good choice of food from well priced menu including deals, at least four real ales, good service, children's play areas inside and out; free wi-fi; dogs outside only, open all day. *(S Holder)*

HUNSTANTON TF6740
Waterside (01485) 535810
Beach Terrace Road; PE36 5BQ Former station buffet just above prom, now bar-restaurant with great sea views from popular conservatory (children welcome here), Adnams, Greene King and good value wines, straightforward inexpensive tasty food all day from sandwiches up, quick service by

friendly uniformed staff, Fri quiz; dogs allowed on the lead. *(John Wooll)*

HUNWORTH   TG0735
Hunny Bell   (01263) 712300
Signed off B roads S of Holt; NR24 2AA
Welcoming 18th-c beamed pub, neat bar with nice mix of cushioned dining chairs around wooden tables, stone floor and woodburner, cosy snug with homely furniture on old worn tiles, original stripped-brick walls, another woodburner in high-raftered dining room, good variety of food from bar snacks and pizzas up, ales such as Adnams, Greene King and Woodfordes, good informal service from young staff; children and dogs welcome, picnic-sets on terrace overlooking village green, more seats in garden among fruit trees, open all day weekends (food all day Sun till 8pm). *(Anon)*

INGHAM   TG3926
★ Swan   (01692) 581099
Off A149 SE of North Walsham; signed from Stalham; NR12 9AB Smart 14th-c thatched dining pub nicely placed for Broads and coast; rustic main area divided by massive chimneybreast with woodburner on each side, low beams and hefty standing timbers, bare boards or parquet, some old farm tools, quieter small brick-floored part with leather sofas, good well presented restaurant-style food including set menu choices, home-baked bread, well kept Woodfordes, local cider and good selection of wines, friendly service; children welcome, picnic-sets on sunny back terrace, more at side, five comfortable bedrooms in converted stables, good breakfast. *(David Carr, Roy Hoing, Revd R P Tickle, M and GR, Tom and Ruth Rees)*

ITTERINGHAM   TG1430
★ Walpole Arms   (01263) 587258
Village signposted off B1354 NW of Aylsham; NR11 7AR Beamed 18th-c pub close to Blickling Hall (NT); good modern cooking using fresh local ingredients (some from own farm) along with more traditional choices, efficient friendly service, well kept Adnams and Woodfordes, nice wines by the glass, sizeable open-plan bar with woodburner, stripped-brick walls and dark wood dining tables on red carpet, light airy restaurant opening on to vine-covered terrace, Weds quiz; children welcome, dogs in bar, two-acre landscaped garden open all day Sat, closed Sun evening. *(Paul and Linda Aquilina, Paul McIntyre, Alan and Angela Scouller)*

KING'S LYNN   TF6120
Crown & Mitre   (01553) 774669
Ferry Street; PE30 1LJ Old-fashioned pub in great riverside spot, lots of interesting naval and nautical memorabilia, up to six well kept ales such as Cambridge and Humpty Dumpty – the long-serving no-nonsense landlord is still hoping to brew his own beers, good value straightforward home-made food, river-view back conservatory; no credit cards; well behaved children and dogs welcome, quayside tables. *(John Wooll, Pete Walker, Lawrence Pearse)*

KING'S LYNN   TF6120
Dukes Head   (01553) 774996
Tuesday Market Place; PE30 1JS Imposing Georgian hotel overlooking market square; good food in comfortable modernised lounge bar, Adnams ales and nice selection of wines, elegant restaurant (quite pricey), cheerful attentive service; children welcome, good bedrooms (some in back extension), open all day. *(P and D Carpenter)*

KING'S LYNN   TF6220
Lattice House   (01553) 769585
Corner of Market Lane, off Tuesday Market Place; PE30 1EG Old beamed and raftered Wetherspoons with good choice of ales, reasonably priced food and friendly speedy service, several well divided areas including upstairs bar; children welcome, open all day from 9am (till 1am Fri, Sat). *(Pete Walker)*

KING'S LYNN   TF6119
Marriotts Warehouse
(01553) 818500   *South Quay; PE30 5DT* Bar/restaurant/café in converted 16th-c brick and stone warehouse; food from lunchtime sandwiches and light dishes up, wider evening choice, good range of wines, beers such as Sharps Doom Bar and Woodfordes Wherry, cocktails, small upstairs bar with river views; children welcome, quayside tables, open all day from 10am. *(John Wooll)*

LETHERINGSETT   TG0638
★ Kings Head   (01263) 712691
A148 (Holt Road) W of Holt; NR25 7AR Civilised country house-style inn under new management; small bar on right, main bar to the left with leather armchairs and sofas, rugs on quarry tiles, hunting and coaching prints on mushroom-painted walls, daily papers and open fire, well kept Adnams, Woodfordes Wherry and guest, plenty of wines by the glass and decent coffee, good food served by friendly helpful young staff, bare-boards dining room with mix of furniture including built-in wall seats, some old farm tools, back dining area with painted rafters; background music; children and dogs (in bar) welcome, picnic sets under parasols on front gravel, more on side lawn, play area, four new bedrooms, open all day. *(Brian Glozier, Alex and Hazel Evans)*

LITTLE PLUMSTEAD   TG3112
Brick Kilns   (01603) 720043
Norwich Road (B1140); NR13 5JH Pink-painted beamed country dining pub, wide choice of enjoyable fairly priced food including fish menu and plenty of vegetarian/

vegan options, well kept Adnams and a guest, good friendly service, bare-boards bar area, carpeted restaurant and flagstoned conservatory overlooking paddock with horses, goats and donkeys; children welcome, three new bedrooms, open all day. *(Alex and Hazel Evans)*

MARSHAM   TG1924
Plough (01263) 735000
Old Norwich Road; NR10 5PS Welcoming 18th-c inn with split-level open-plan bar, enjoyable food using local produce including good value set lunch, Adnams and Greene King ales, friendly helpful staff; free wi-fi; children welcome, comfortable bedrooms, open all day. *(David Carr)*

MUNDFORD   TL8093
Crown (01842) 878233
Off A1065 Thetford–Swaffham; Crown Road; IP26 5HQ Unassuming old pub, warmly welcoming, with heavy beams and huge fireplace, interesting local memorabilia, Courage Directors and one or two guests, over 50 malt whiskies, enjoyable generously served food at sensible prices, spiral iron stairs to two restaurant areas (larger one has separate entrance accessible to wheelchairs), locals' bar with sports TV; children and dogs welcome, back terrace and garden with wishing well, Harley-Davidson meeting first Sun of month, bedrooms (some in adjoining building), also self-catering accommodation, open all day. *(Anon)*

NORTHREPPS   TG2439
Foundry Arms (01263) 579256
Church Street; NR27 0AA Welcoming village pub with good reasonably priced traditional food (not Sun evening, Mon), well kept Adnams and Woodfordes, decent choice of wines, woodburner, smallish restaurant; pool and darts; children and dogs welcome, picnic-sets in back garden, open all day. *(Anon)*

NORWICH   TG2309
★Adam & Eve (01603) 667423
Bishopgate; follow Palace Street from Tombland, N of cathedral; NR3 1RZ Ancient pub dating from at least 1241 when used by workmen building the cathedral, has Saxon well beneath the lower bar floor and striking dutch gables (added in 14th and 15th c); old-fashioned small bars with tiled or parquet floors, cushioned benches built into partly panelled walls and some antique high-backed settles, Adnams, Theakstons, Wells & Youngs and a guest, Aspall's cider and 40 malt whiskies, traditional pubby food (not Sun evening); background music; children allowed in snug till 7pm, outside seating with award-winning tubs and hanging baskets,

open all day, closed 25, 26 Dec, 1 Jan. *(Marianne and Peter Stevens, David Carr)*

NORWICH   TG2408
Coach & Horses (01603) 477077
Thorpe Road; NR1 1BA Light and airy tap for Chalk Hill brewery (tours available), friendly staff, good value generous home-made food including all-day breakfast, L-shaped bare-boards bar with open fire, pleasant back dining area; sports TVs, gets very busy on home match days; disabled access possible (not to lavatories), front terrace, open all day. *(David Carr)*

NORWICH   TG2210
Duke of Wellington (01603) 441182
Waterloo Road; NR3 1EG Friendly rambling local with up to 21 well kept quickly changing ales including Oakham and Wolf, many served from tap room casks, foreign bottled beers too, no food apart from sausage rolls and pies (can bring your own), real fire, traditional games, folk music Tues evening, Aug beer festival; nice back terrace, open all day. *(David Carr)*

NORWICH   TG2207
★Eagle (01603) 624173
Newmarket Road (A11, between A140 and A147 ring roads); NR2 2HN Sizeable Georgian red-brick pub under new management; main bar with comfortable sofas and armchairs by open fire in ornate fireplace, white-painted chairs around pine tables on tiled or stripped-wood flooring, also cosy end room, low-ceilinged dining room and spiral staircase to further area, four ales including a house beer from Norfolk Brewhouse, decent wines and enjoyable food from sandwiches up; background music; children and dogs welcome, sunny terrace with picnic-sets and barbecue, more seats on grass, play area. *(Emma Scofield, David Carr)*

NORWICH   TG2310
Fat Cat Brewery Tap
(01603) 413153 *Lawson Road; NR3 4LF* This 1970s shed-like building is home to the Fat Cat brewery (and sister to the Fat Cat – see Main Entries); their beers and up to 12 guests along with draught continentals, 30 bottled beers and eight or more local ciders/perries, no food apart from rolls and pork pies, live music Fri night and Sun afternoon; children (till 6pm) and dogs welcome, seats out in front and behind, open all day. *(David Carr)*

NORWICH   TG2309
★Kings Head (01603) 620468
Magdalen Street; NR3 1JE Traditional Victorian local with friendly licensees and good atmosphere in two simply furnished

---

It's very helpful if you let us know up-to-date food prices when you report on pubs.

bare-boards bars, up to 18 very well kept changing regional ales, good choice of imported beers and a local cider, no food except pork pies, bar billiards in bigger back bar; open all day. *(David Carr)*

NORWICH   TG2208
Plough (01603) 661384
St Benedicts Street; NR2 4AR Friendly little city-centre pub owned by Grain, their ales and guests kept well, good wines, knowledgeable staff, comfortable seating and open fire; good spacious beer garden behind, open all day. *(Anon)*

NORWICH   TG2308
Ribs of Beef (01603) 619517
Wensum Street, S side of Fye Bridge; NR3 1HY Welcoming and comfortable with nine real ales including Adnams, Fullers, Wolf and Woodfordes, traditional cider and good wine choice, deep leather sofas and small tables upstairs, attractive smaller downstairs room with river view, generous well priced pubby food (till 5pm weekends), quick cheerful service, monthly quiz; children welcome, tables out on narrow waterside walkway, open all day. *(David Carr)*

NORWICH   TG2308
Take Five (01603) 763099
Opposite cathedral gate; NR3 1HF Old black and white timber-fronted building, a mix of wine bar, pub and restaurant; four or five mainly local ales and decent wines, enjoyable well priced home-made food with good vegetarian choice, friendly efficient service from aproned staff, good open fire; children welcome, closed Sun, otherwise open all day. *(John Wooll)*

NORWICH   TG2309
Wig & Pen (01603) 625891
St Martins Palace Plain; NR3 1RN Friendly and relaxed 17th-c beamed pub opposite cathedral close, lawyer and judge prints, woodburner, good value generous food with regularly changing specials, prompt service, six ales including Adnams, Fullers and Oakham, good value wines; background music, sports TVs; tables out at front, open all day (till 6pm Sun). *(Anon)*

OLD BUCKENHAM   TM0691
★Gamekeeper (01953) 860397
B1077 S of Attleborough; The Green; NR17 1RE Pretty 16th-c pub with civilised beamed bar, leather armchairs and sofa in front of big inglenook woodburner, nice mix of old wooden seats and tables on fine flagstones or wood floor, local watercolours and unusual interior bow window, well kept Adnams, Timothy Taylors and Woodfordes, Aspall's cider, quite a few wines by glass and several malt whiskies, good food from sandwiches to daily specials, comfortable main back dining area plus a small room for private dining; children welcome away from

bar, dogs allowed, sunny back garden with terrace, closed Sun evening. *(Sheila Topham)*

OVERSTRAND   TG2440
Sea Marge (01263) 579579
High Street; NR27 0AB Substantial sea-view hotel (former Edwardian country house) with separate entrance to spacious bar area, enjoyable food from ciabattas up, restaurant; five-acre grounds with terraced lawns down to coast path and beach, 25 comfortable bedrooms. *(David Carr)*

OVERSTRAND   TG2440
White Horse (01263) 579237
High Street; NR27 0AB Comfortably modernised and stylish, with good choice of enjoyable food in bar, dining room or barn restaurant, at least three well kept local ales, friendly staff, pool room; background music, silent sports TV; children and dogs welcome, picnic-sets in front, more in garden behind with play equipment, eight bedrooms, open all day from 8am. *(John Millwood)*

OXBOROUGH   TF7401
Bedingfeld Arms (01366) 328300
Near church; PE33 9PS Comfortably refurbished late 18th-c coaching inn peacefully set opposite Oxburgh Hall (NT); good food (not Mon) from bar and restaurant menus, well kept ales such as Adnams, Wells & Youngs and Woodfordes, Weston's and Aspall's ciders, friendly helpful staff; background music, TV for major sporting events; children welcome, dogs on the lead in bar, garden with terrace, nine bedrooms (five in separate coach house), open all day. *(Colin McKerrow, Chris Price, Rita Scarratt, P and J Shapley, Edward Mirzoeff)*

POTTER HEIGHAM   TG4119
Falgate (01692) 670003
A1062 Ludham Road; NR29 5HZ Cosy 17th-c family-run inn with well priced generous food (special diets catered for), Greene King, John Smiths, Tetleys and Woodfordes, friendly service, restaurant, pool and darts; background music; children and dogs (in bar) welcome, handy for the river and popular with boaters, three bedrooms, open all day summer. *(John Evans, Brenda Adams)*

RINGSTEAD   TF7040
★Gin Trap (01485) 525264
Village signed off A149 near Hunstanton; OS Sheet 132 map reference 707403; PE36 5JU Attractive well run 17th-c coaching inn with friendly helpful licensees, two bar areas, original part with beams, woodburner and pubby furniture, well kept Adnams and Woodfordes, nicely presented tasty home-made food from changing blackboard menu, airy dining conservatory; background and monthly live acoustic music, fortnightly Sun quiz; children and dogs welcome, tables out in front and

in walled garden, Peddars Way walks, three bedrooms, open all day in summer when can get very busy. *(Linda Miller and Derek Greentree, David and Ruth Hollands, Roy Hoing, Tracey and Stephen Groves)*

SCULTHORPE   TF8930
Hourglass (01328) 856744
The Street; NR21 9QD Restauranty place with long open room combining light modern style with some dark beams, good choice of enjoyable fairly priced food including OAP lunch deal (Mon, Tues), Adnams Broadside and Woodfordes Wherry, quick friendly service. *(M and J White, George Atkinson)*

SCULTHORPE   TF8930
★Sculthorpe Mill (01328) 856161
Inn signed off A148 W of Fakenham, opposite village; NR21 9QG Welcoming dining pub in rebuilt 18th-c mill, appealing riverside setting, seats out under weeping willows and in attractive garden behind; light, airy and relaxed with leather sofas and sturdy tables in bar/dining area, good reasonably priced food from sandwiches to daily specials, attentive service, Greene King ales and good house wines, upstairs restaurant; background music; six comfortable bedrooms, open all day in summer (all day weekends winter). *(John Wooll, Roy Hoing, George Atkinson)*

SEDGEFORD   TF7036
King William IV (01485) 571765
B1454, off A149 Kings Lynn–Hunstanton; PE36 5LU Homely inn handy for beaches and bird-watching; bar and dining areas decorated with paintings of north Norfolk coast and migrating birds, high-backed dark leather dining chairs around pine tables on slate tiles, log fires, Adnams, Greene King and Woodfordes, ten wines by the glass, straightforward food; children welcome (no under-4s in main restaurant after 6.30pm), dogs allowed in bar and a couple of the bedrooms, seats on terrace and under parasols on grass, also an attractive covered dining area surrounded by flowering tubs, closed Mon lunchtime, otherwise open all day. *(David Jackman, Tracey and Stephen Groves, Roy Hoing)*

SHERINGHAM   TG1543
Lobster (01263) 822716
High Street; NR26 8JP Busy pub almost on seafront, friendly panelled bar with old sewing-machine tables and warm fire, seafaring décor, wide range of well kept changing ales (bank holiday festivals), bottled belgian beers and real ciders, decent well priced wines by the glass, good value generous bar meals quickly served, restaurant with seafood including fresh lobster (get there early) and good crab, games in public bar including pool, maybe live music Weds; dogs welcome, two courtyards, heated marquee, open all day.

(Mr and Mrs D J Nash, Adrian Johnson, David Carr, N R White)

SHERINGHAM   TG1543
Two Lifeboats (01263) 823144
High Street/Promenade; NR26 8JR Cleanly refurbished open-plan seafront inn, enjoyable well priced pubby food from baguettes up, Adnams, Nethergate and Woodfordes, good choice of other drinks, friendly staff; background music; children welcome, no dogs in summer, picnic-sets on small terrace overlooking beach, six bedrooms (some with sea view), good breakfast, parking can be tricky. *(David Carr, Dennis and Doreen Haward)*

SHERINGHAM   TG1543
Windham Arms (01263) 822609
Wyndham Street; NR26 8BA Dutch-gabled brick and cobble pub with well kept Woodfordes and other ales, enjoyable sensibly priced food (not Sun) with greek influences (chef is greek), cheerful efficient service, woodburner and tightly packed dining tables in carpeted beamed lounge, separate public bar with pool; dogs welcome, picnic-sets outside, sizeable car park (useful here), open all day but may not serve food weekday lunchtimes out of season. *(Adrian Johnson, Dennis and Doreen Haward)*

SMALLBURGH   TG3324
★Crown (01692) 536314
A149 Yarmouth Road; NR12 9AD Thatched and beamed village inn dating from the 15th c, friendly proper landlord and nice old-fashioned pub atmosphere, well kept Adnams, Greene King, Woodfordes and guests, good choice of wines by the glass, enjoyable home-made pub food in bar and upstairs dining room, prompt service, log fire, daily papers, darts; no dogs or children inside; picnic-sets in pretty back garden, bedrooms, closed Sun evening, Mon lunchtime. *(Philip and Susan Philcox, Roy Hoing)*

SOUTH LOPHAM   TM0481
White Horse (01379) 688579
A1066 Diss–Thetford; The Street; IP22 2LH Beamed village pub under friendly family management, well kept Buffys Mucky Duck, Greene King IPA and Woodfordes Wherry, enjoyable food including deals and Sun carvery, log fires; TV, fruit machine; children welcome, big garden with play area, handy for Bressingham Gardens. *(Anon)*

SOUTH WOOTTON   TF6422
Swan (01553) 672084
Nursery Lane; PE30 3NG Friendly local overlooking village green, duck pond and bowling green, popular reasonably priced food (not Sun or Mon evenings – booking advised) in lounge bar and conservatory restaurant, Thurs curry night, four well kept

changing ales, quieter public bar to the side; children and dogs (in some areas) welcome, small enclosed garden, open all day. *(John Wooll)*

SOUTHREPPS   TG2536
★ Vernon Arms (01263) 833355
Church Street; NR11 8NP Popular old-fashioned brick and cobble village pub, welcoming and relaxed, with good food running up to steaks and well priced crab (must book weekend evenings), friendly helpful staff, well kept Adnams, Greene King, Woodfordes and a guest, good choice of wines and malt whiskies, big log fire; darts and pool; tables outside, children, dogs and muddy walkers welcome, open all day. *(Anon)*

SPOONER ROW   TM0997
Boars (01953) 605851
Just off A11 SW of Wymondham; NR18 9LL Interesting 1920s pub-restaurant in tiny village, good variety of enjoyable locally sourced food from light meals to more expensive (though not pretentious) choices including some good vegetarian options, well kept Adnams and nice range of wines, friendly staff and pub dog, amazing collection of food/wine books; children welcome, tables in well tended pretty garden. *(N R White)*

SPORLE   TF8411
Peddars Inn (01760) 788101
The Street; PE32 2DR Refurbished beamed pub with inglenook bar, dining room and little conservatory, good sensibly priced food from pub favourites to specials, Adnams and a couple of local guests, Aspall's cider, occasional live music and charity quiz nights; children and dogs welcome, a few seats outside on grass, well placed for Peddars Way walkers, open all day Sat, closed Sun evening, all Mon and Tues lunchtime. *(Anon)*

STIFFKEY   TF9643
Red Lion (01328) 830552
A149 Wells–Blakeney; NR23 1AJ Cheerful interesting old pub, front bar with inglenook fireplace, cushioned pews and other pubby seats, local landscape photos, room off with scatter cushions on settles, another room with dark panelling and splendid winged settle, Greene King and Woodfordes ales, food (all day Sun) from pubby choices to local fish/shellfish (local mussels a speciality), two back dining rooms, one a flint-walled conservatory; children and dogs welcome, big partly covered gravelled courtyard, more tables on covered deck, ten bedrooms in modern block with own balconies or terraces, nearby coastal walks, open all day. *(John Wooll,*

David Jackman, Ian Herdman, David Carr, Alison Ball, Ian Walton, Roy Hoing)

STOW BARDOLPH   TF6205
Hare Arms (01366) 382229
Just off A10 N of Downham Market; PE34 3HT Cheerful bustling village pub under long-serving licensees; bar with traditional pub furnishings and interesting bric-a-brac, log fire, Greene King ales and a couple of guests, nine wines by glass and several malt whiskies, well liked food (all day Sun), refurbished dining room and family conservatory; plenty of seats in front and back gardens, maybe some wandering fowl, Church Farm Rare Breeds Centre nearby. *(Anon)*

SWANTON MORLEY   TG0217
Darbys (01362) 637647
B1147 NE of Dereham; NR20 4NY New owner for this cosy unspoilt local, half a dozen real ales tapped from the cask such as Adnams, Beeston, Humpty Dumpty and Woodfordes, fair value food, long bare-boards country-style bar with gin traps and farming memorabilia, log fire and bread oven, step up to attractive dining room, another small room with glassed-over well; children and dogs welcome, TV and board games; back garden with picnic-sets and play area, campsite, open all day Fri-Sun. *(Peter Brix, Pip White)*

TACOLNESTON   TM1495
★ Pelican (01508) 489521
Norwich Road (B1113 SW of city); NR16 1AL Former 17th-c coaching inn, chatty timbered bar with relaxed comfortable atmosphere, good log fire, sofas, armchairs and old stripped settle on quarry tiles, candles and flowers on tables, some booth seating, four well kept ales including one badged for them from Brandon, Aspall's cider and 36 malt whiskies, restaurant area with high-backed leather chairs around oak tables, good choice of food from pub favourites up, friendly service, shop selling local produce and bottled Norfolk/Suffolk ales; background music (live Sun); plenty of tables on decking behind, sheltered lawn beyond, bedrooms, open (and food) all day Sun. *(N R White)*

THETFORD   TL8782
Dolphin (01842) 762406
Old Market Street; IP24 2EQ Refurbished 17th-c beamed pub with good food including signature steaks (not cheap), Adnams, Sharps, Wells & Youngs and a house beer from Tetleys, Aspall's cider, friendly staff; children welcome, nice walled garden with gate to Castle Park, open from 9am for breakfast. *(Anon)*

Half pints: by law, a pub should not charge more for half a pint than half the price of a full pint, unless it shows that half-pint price on its price list.

THOMPSON   TL9296
Chequers (01953) 483360
Griston Road, off A1075 S of Watton;
IP24 1PX Long, low and picturesque
16th-c thatched dining pub tucked away in
attractive spot, enjoyable food including
bargain weekday lunch offer, real ales,
helpful staff and friendly atmosphere, series
of quaint rooms with low beams, inglenooks
and some stripped brickwork; children
welcome, dogs allowed in bar, some seats
out in front and in back garden with swing,
bedroom block, open (and food) all day Sun.
(Anon)

WALSINGHAM   TF9336
Bull (01328) 820333
Common Place/Shire Hall Plain;
NR22 6BP Rather quirky pub in pilgrimage
village; bar with various odds and ends
including half-size statue of Charlie Chaplin,
pictures of archbishops and clerical visiting
cards, typewriter in snug, welcoming landlord
and friendly efficient staff, three well kept
changing ales, tasty food (not Sat and Sun
evenings) from shortish inexpensive menu,
log fire, old-fashioned cash register in gents';
free wi-fi; children welcome, picnic-sets in
courtyard and on attractive flowery terrace
by village square, dovecote stuffed with
plastic lobsters and crabs, outside games
room, bedrooms, snowdrop walk in nearby
abbey garden, open all day. *(John Wooll)*

WARHAM   TF9441
★**Three Horseshoes** (01328) 710547
Warham All Saints; village signed from
A149 Wells-next-the-Sea to Blakeney, and
from B1105 S of Wells; NR23 1NL
Old-fashioned pub with gas lighting in simple
rooms looking unchanged since the 1920s
(parts date back to 1720); stripped-deal or
mahogany tables (one marked for shove-
ha'penny) on stone floor, red leatherette
settles built around partly panelled walls of
public bar, royalist photographs, longcase
clock with a clear piping strike, twister on
ceiling to show whose round it is, open fires
in Victorian fireplaces, well kept Woodfordes
and guests (some cask tapped), local cider,
generous home-made food including range
of pies, friendly unhurried service; dogs
welcome (menu for them), children away
from bar, seats in courtyard garden with
flower tubs and well, five basic bedrooms
in next-door post office. *(Philip and Susan
Philcox, Tracey and Stephen Groves, Derek and
Sylvia Stephenson, Roy Hoing, Nick Clare and
others)*

WEASENHAM ST PETER   TF8522
Fox & Hounds (01328) 838868
A1065 Fakenham–Swaffham; The Green;
PE32 2TD Traditional 18th-c beamed local
with bar and two dining areas (one with
inglenook woodburner), spotless and well
run by friendly family, three changing ales,

good honest home-made food at reasonable
prices including Sun roasts, pubby furniture
and carpets throughout, brasses and lots of
military prints; children welcome, big well
kept garden and terrace, closed Mon. *(Anon)*

WELLS-NEXT-THE-SEA   TF9143
Albatros 07979 087228
The Quay; NR23 1AT Bar on 1899
quayside clipper, charts and other nautical
memorabilia, Woodfordes beers served from
the cask, speciality pancakes, good views
of harbour and tidal marshes, live weekend
music; children and dogs welcome, not good
for disabled, cabin accommodation with
shared showers, open all day. *(John Millwood,
Chris Johnson)*

WELLS-NEXT-THE-SEA   TF9143
Bowling Green (01328) 710100
Church Street; NR23 1JB Welcoming
17th-c pub, Greene King IPA and Woodfordes
Wherry, generous helpings of reasonably
priced traditional food, L-shaped bar with
corner settles, flagstone and brick floor, two
woodburners, raised dining end; children
and dogs welcome, back terrace, two
bedrooms in converted barn, quiet spot on
outskirts. *(John Wooll)*

WELLS-NEXT-THE-SEA   TF9143
Edinburgh (01328) 710120
Station Road/Church Street; NR23 1AE
Traditional 19th-c pub near main shopping
area, enjoyable home-made food and three
well kept ales including Woodfordes, open
fire, sizeable restaurant, also 'lifeboat' dining
room decorated in RNLI colours; background
music, free wi-fi; children and dogs welcome,
disabled access, courtyard with heated
smokers' shelter, three bedrooms, open
all day. *(David Carr, Brian and Jean Hepworth)*

WELLS-NEXT-THE-SEA   TF9143
★**Globe** (01328) 710206
The Buttlands; NR23 1EU Handsome
recently refurbished Georgian inn a short
walk from the quay; plenty of space in
opened-up contemporary rooms, tables on
oak boards, big bow windows, well kept
Adnams beers, thoughtful wine choice and
enjoyable food, evening jazz third Sun of
month; background music; children and
dogs welcome, attractive courtyard with pale
flagstones, more seats at front overlooking
green, seven bedrooms (more planned),
open all day. *(Mr and Mrs D J Nash, Tracey
and Stephen Groves, David Carr, Brian and
Jean Hepworth)*

WEST ACRE   TF7815
Stag (01760) 755395
Low Road; PE32 1TR Small family-run
local with three or more well kept changing
ales in appealing unpretentious bar, obliging
cheerful staff, good value home-made food,
neat dining room; attractive spot in quiet
village, closed Mon. *(Alan Weedon)*

WEST BECKHAM   TG1439
Wheatsheaf   (01263) 822110
Church Road; off A148 Holt–Cromer;
NR25 6NX Traditional brick-built pub in
quiet village, beamed bars with standing
timbers, cottagey doors, horsebrasses
and roaring winter fire, pleasantly
straightforward tables, chairs and wall seats,
Woodfordes ales and quite a few wines by the
glass, reasonably priced food; children and
dogs welcome, charming garden and terrace,
closed Sun evening, Mon. *(Peter Brix, Pip
White, Michael Sargent)*

WEYBOURNE   TG1143
Ship   (01263) 588721
A149 W of Sheringham; The Street;
NR25 7SZ Popular village pub refurbished
under present management; Woodfordes
Wherry and two local guests such as Grain
and Humpty Dumpty, big bar with pubby
furniture and woodburner, two dining rooms,
good reasonably priced home-made food
(not Mon, should book weekends), pleasant
service; background music; well behaved
children welcome, dogs in bar, seats out
at front and in nice side garden handy for

Muckleburgh Military vehicle museum, open
all day in season. *(S Holder, M and GR)*

WORTWELL   TM2784
Bell   (01986) 788547
High Road; IP20 0HH Welcoming
beamed village pub, clean and tidy,
with well kept ales such as Adnams and
Brakspears, enjoyable food including daily
specials, helpful staff; children and dogs
welcome. *(Michael and Jenny Back)*

WYMONDHAM   TG1001
★Green Dragon   (01953) 607907
Church Street; NR18 0PH Picturesque
heavily timbered medieval pub with plenty
of character, small beamed bar and snug,
bigger dining area, interesting pictures, log
fire under Tudor mantelpiece, four well kept
changing ales and over 50 whiskies, winter
mulled wine, plentiful helpings of popular
good value food including daily specials
(best to book), friendly helpful staff, upstairs
function room – acoustic music third Sun of
month; children and dogs welcome, garden
behind with raised deck, near glorious 12th-c
abbey church, open all day (food all day
Fri-Sun). *(Lucien Perring, N R White)*

Post Office address codings confusingly give the impression that a few pubs
are in Norfolk, when they're really in Cambridgeshire or Suffolk (which is
where we list them).

Northamptonshire

ASHBY ST LEDGERS   SP5768   Map 4

Olde Coach House 🛏

*Main Street; 4 miles from M1 junction 18; A5 S to Kilsby, then A361
S towards Daventry; village also signed off A5 N of Weedon; CV23 8UN*

**Carefully modernised former farmhouse with lots of different bar
areas, real ales, good wines, friendly staff and plenty of outside
seating; well appointed bedrooms**

In an attractive little village of thatched houses, this handsome creeper-
clad inn is the sort of place customers return to regularly. There's some
original charm to the opened-up bar on the right, which has stools against
the counter where they keep Brains White Out and Wells & Youngs Bitter
and Bombardier on handpump and eight wines by the glass, served by
friendly staff. Several dining areas, all very relaxed, take in paintwork
ranging from white and light beige to purple, and flooring that includes
stripped wooden boards, original red and white tiles and beige carpeting.
All manner of pale wooden tables are surrounded by an assortment of
church chairs, high-backed leather dining chairs and armchairs, with
comfortable squashy leather sofas and pouffes in front of a log fire. There
are hunting pictures, large mirrors, an original old stove and oven and
fresh flowers; background music and TV. The back garden has picnic-sets
among shrubs and trees, modern tables and chairs out in front under
pretty hanging baskets, and a dining courtyard. Some of the well equipped,
contemporary bedrooms are in converted stables. The church nearby
is interesting.

🍴 Enjoyable food includes sandwiches, chicken terrine wrapped in parma ham
with apricot chutney, local partridge with apple and black pudding salad, lots
of grazing boards and pizzas, barbecue ribs with coleslaw, beef, chicken, pork and
apple and vegetarian burgers with six toppings and chips, liver, bacon and red wine
baby onions, steak in ale pie, rack of lamb with redcurrant jus, and puddings such
as rhubarb tarte tatin and warm chocolate brownie; they also offer a two-course set
menu (before 7.30 Mon-Thurs, 12-2.30 Fri). *Benchmark main dish: grazing boards
£13.00. Two-course evening meal £21.00.*

Quicksilver Management ~ Lease Mark Butler ~ Real ale ~ (01788) 890349 ~
Open 12-11 ~ Bar food 12-2.30, 6-9.30; 12-8 Sun ~ Restaurant ~ Children welcome ~
Dogs allowed in bar ~ Wi-fi ~ Bedrooms: /£75 ~ www.oldecoachhouse.co.uk
Recommended by George Atkinson

BULWICK
SP9694   Map 4

Queens Head 🗨
Off A43 Kettering–Duddington; NN17 3DY

Honey-coloured 17th-c stone pub with five ales, good interesting food and friendly licensees

A mong the things that make this old stone cottage so special are the genuinely welcoming licensees and their helpful staff – nothing is too much trouble. The beamed bar, traditional in feel, has a woodburning stove, exposed stone walls, contemporary paintwork, cushioned wall seats, wooden dining chairs and stone floors; the bellringers still pop in after their Wednesday practice. The dining room has high-backed black or brown leather dining chairs around light wooden tables on floor tiles, another fireplace and quite a few interesting little knick-knacks. Digfield Barnwell, Oakham JHB and guest beers from Church End, Kings Cliffe and Latimer on handpump, ten wines by the glass, several malt whiskies and a farm cider. Outside, there are rattan tables and chairs under a pergola and on the terrace and a pizza oven; this is a lovely spot, with the summer sounds of swallows and house martins, and sheep in the adjacent field.

 Impressive food includes warm ciabatta sandwiches, crispy duck egg, ibérico pancetta and chive hollandaise, scallops with black pudding and caramelised mandarin, toad in the hole with onion gravy, thai red beef curry, corn-fed chicken with risotto of chanterelles, broad beans and truffle, smoked aubergine, spinach and chickpea dhal with puff pastry bouchée and tomato and red onion relish, halibut with spring onion croquettes and cockle sauce, and puddings such as hot chocolate fondant with red cherry ice-cream and prune, almond and cognac tart; they also offer a two- and three-course set menu. *Benchmark main dish: beer-battered fish and chips £10.95. Two-course evening meal £17.50.*

Free house ~ Licensees Julie Barclay and Robert Windeler ~ Real ale ~ (01780) 450272 ~ Open 12-3, 6-11; 12-7 Sun; closed Sun evening, Mon ~ Bar food 12-2, 6-9; 12-3 Sun ~ Restaurant ~ Well behaved children welcome ~ Dogs allowed in bar ~ Wi-fi ~ www.thequeensheadbulwick.co.uk *Recommended by Michael and Jenny Back, M Ross-Thomas, Michael Doswell, Colin McLachlan, Howard and Margaret Buchanan, George Atkinson*

FARTHINGHOE
SP5339   Map 4

Fox
Just off A422 Brackley–Banbury; Baker Street; NN13 5PH

Golden-stone pub, carefully spruced up, with popular food and well kept ales

T here's plenty to look at in this well run stone pub and lots of space for eating and drinking, both inside and out. The pastel walls are hung with small landscapes, old country photographs and framed period advertisements plus a striking triptych of a prowling fox. Seating ranges from dark leather tub chairs, green-padded seats, wall banquettes and neatly built-in traditional wall seats to well cushioned ladder-back and other dining chairs in the eating area, which has quite a low plank-panelled ceiling in one part. The dark-beamed front bar has a log fire in a great stripped-stone fireplace with a side salt cupboard, lighting is sympathetic, and flooring includes some attractively coloured slate tiling. Courage Directors and Wells & Youngs Bitter on handpump, nine good wines by the glass and cocktails; background music, TV, board games and cards by local artists for sale. Behind is a sheltered terrace with teak tables, with picnic-sets under cocktail parasols in the neatly kept garden beyond. The comfortable bedrooms are in the adjoining barn conversion.

As well as lunchtime sandwiches and wraps, the tasty food includes pork, mushroom and apple terrine with chutney, chicken and bacon salad with caesar dressing, sharing boards, spicy moroccan lamb tagine, liver and bacon with bubble and squeak and caramelised onion gravy, moules marinière, burger with bacon, cheese, coleslaw and chips, chicken stuffed with cream cheese and herbs with pancetta mash and roasted tomato and garlic sauce, and puddings such as apple fritters with caramel sauce and lemon posset. *Benchmark main dish: beer-battered haddock and chips £11.50. Two-course evening meal £18.00.*

Charles Wells ~ Lease Mark Higgs ~ Real ale ~ (01295) 713965 ~ Open 12-3, 6-11; 12-11 Sat; 12-9 (6 in winter) Sun ~ Bar food 12-2.30, 6-9.30; 12-4 Sun ~ Restaurant ~ Children welcome ~ Dogs allowed in bar ~ Wi-fi ~ Bedrooms: £65/£75 ~ www.foxatfarthinghoe.co.uk *Recommended by Ian Herdman, JPC, George Atkinson*

FARTHINGSTONE SP6155 Map 4
Kings Arms ◖ £
Off A5 SE of Daventry; village signed from Litchborough; NN12 8EZ

Individual place with cosy traditional interior, carefully prepared food and lovely garden

The handsome gargoyled stone exterior of this traditional little 18th-c country pub is nicely weathered, and very pretty in summer, when the hanging baskets are at their best; there are seats on a tranquil terrace among plant-filled painted tractor tyres and recycled art. The cosy flagstoned bar has a cheerful, bustling atmosphere and plenty of chatty customers, a huge log fire, comfortable homely sofas and armchairs near the entrance, whisky-water jugs hanging from oak beams, and lots of pictures and decorative plates on the walls. A games room at the far end has darts, dominoes, cribbage, table skittles and board games. St Austell Tribute, Thwaites Original and Wadworth 6X on handpump and a short but decent wine list. Look out for the interesting newspaper-influenced décor in the outside gents'. This is a picturesque village and there are good walks nearby including the Knightley Way. It's worth ringing ahead to check the opening and food serving times.

Using some home-grown produce, food (available weekend lunchtimes only) includes sandwiches, british cheese platters, beef in Guinness, pork stew, loch fyne salmon, game casserole, and puddings such as gingerbread pudding and meringues. *Benchmark main dish: yorkshire pudding filled with steak and kidney £8.45.*

Free house ~ Licensees Paul and Denise Egerton ~ Real ale ~ (01327) 361604 ~ Open 6.30-11.30 (midnight Fri); 12-midnight Sat; 12-11 Sun; closed Mon, weekday lunchtimes ~ Bar food 12-2.30 weekends ~ Children welcome ~ Dogs allowed in bar ~ Wi-fi *Recommended by George Atkinson, S F Parrinder*

FOTHERINGHAY TL0593 Map 5
Falcon ◉ ♀
Village signposted off A605 on Peterborough side of Oundle; PE8 5HZ

Northamptonshire Dining Pub of the Year

Upmarket dining pub with good range of drinks and modern british food from snacks up, and attractive garden

At lunchtime, in particular, this appealing pub fills up fast with people keen to enjoy the tempting food – do book a table in advance. There are winter log fires in stone fireplaces, fresh flowers, cushioned slatback armchairs and bucket chairs and comfortably cushioned window seats, and bare floorboards. The Orangery restaurant opens on to a charming lavender-surrounded terrace with lovely views of the vast church behind, and of the attractively planted garden; plenty of seats under parasols. Surprisingly, given the emphasis on dining, there's a thriving little locals' tap bar and a darts team, and a fine choice of drinks including Digfield Fools Nook, Fullers London Pride and Greene King IPA on handpump, 16 good wines by the glass and several malt whiskies; darts and board games. This is a lovely village (Richard III was born here) with plentiful River Nene moorings, and the ruins of Fotheringhay Castle, where Mary Queen of Scots was executed, is nearby.

Interesting food includes sandwiches, twice-baked cheese soufflé with chicory, pear, stilton and walnut salad, spaghetti with cashew nut and rocket pesto, corn-fed chicken with baby leeks and red wine gravy, scottish salmon with sauce vierge, lamb rump with liver, tomato fondue and onion purée, chargrilled pork chop with bacon, cabbage and apple tarte tatin, and puddings such as chocolate nemesis with amaretti cream and spotted dick and custard; they also offer a two- and three-course set menu (not Sat evening or Sun lunchtime). *Benchmark main dish: crispy duck salad with asian slaw and coriander dressing £11.50. Two-course evening meal £19.50.*

Free house ~ Licensee Sally Facer ~ Real ale ~ (01832) 226254 ~ Open 12-11; closed Sun evening Oct-Easter ~ Bar food 12-2, 6-9; 12-3, 6-8.30 (in summer) Sun ~ Restaurant ~ Children welcome ~ Dogs allowed in bar ~ Wi-fi ~ www.thefalcon-inn.co.uk
Recommended by Derek and Sylvia Stephenson, Tracey and Stephen Groves, Michael Sargent, Howard and Margaret Buchanan

GREAT BRINGTON
Althorp Coaching Inn
SP6664 Map 4

Off A428 NW of Northampton, near Althorp Hall; until recently known as the Fox & Hounds; NN7 4JA

Friendly golden-stone thatched pub with great choice of real ales, some fine architectural features, tasty popular food and sheltered garden

With up to nine real ales on handpump served by cheerful staff, it's not surprising that this 16th-c coaching inn is so very busy. As well as Fullers London Pride, Greene King IPA, Hook Norton Old Hooky and St Austell Tribute, there are four or five quickly changing guests; the extended dining area gives views of the 30 or so casks racked in the cellar. Also, eight wines by the glass and a dozen malt whiskies. The ancient bar has all the traditional features you'd wish for, from a dog or two sprawled out by the huge log fire, to old beams, sagging joists and a pleasing mix of country chairs and tables (maybe with fresh flowers) on broad flagstones and bare boards. There are snug alcoves, nooks and crannies with some stripped-pine shutters and panelling, two fine log fires and an eclectic medley of bric-a-brac from farming implements to an old clocking-in machine and country pictures. A converted stable block – now a function room – is next to the lovely cobbled and paved courtyard (also accessible by the old coaching entrance) which has sheltered tables and tubs of flowers; more seating in the charming garden.

Well liked food includes sandwiches and baguettes, ham hock terrine, herring fillets in mustard sauce, wild mushroom and asparagus risotto, chicken with smoked bacon and leek stuffing with a creamy wild mushroom sauce, pork fillet in apple and cider sauce, sea bream fillet on samphire, and puddings such as fruit crumble or chocolate brownies. *Benchmark main dish: local rib-eye steak with onion rings, mushrooms and chips £18.25. Two-course evening meal £18.50.*

Free house ~ Licensee Michael Krempels ~ Real ale ~ (01604) 770651 ~ Open 11am–midnight; 12-11 Sun ~ Bar food 12-3, 6.30-9.30 (10 Fri, Sat); 12-4.30, 5.30-8.30 Sun ~ Restaurant ~ Children welcome ~ Dogs allowed in bar ~ Wi-fi ~ www.althorp-coaching-inn.co.uk *Recommended by Gerry and Rosemary Dobson, Jim and Nancy Forbes, Ron Corbett, George Atkinson*

LOWICK
SP9780   Map 4
Snooty Fox
Off A6116 Corby–Raunds; NN14 3BH

Bustling village pub with plenty of seating space, real ales, quite a choice of food and friendly staff

A t the heart of a peaceful village, this 17th-c solidly built pub is popular for its highly thought-of food. The spacious lounge bar has a woodburning stove in a sizeable fireplace, handsomely moulded dark oak beams, leather sofas and stools and bucket armchairs on the big terracotta tiles, and stripped stonework. A formidable carved counter serves Digfield Fools Nook and Nene Valley OZP on handpump, 22 wines by the glass and a farm cider. The more formal dining rooms have high-backed leather and other dining chairs around quite a choice of chunky tables on pale wooden floorboards; background music. There are picnic-sets under parasols on the front grass and a children's play area.

Tasty food includes lunchtime sandwiches, potted mackerel, breaded brie with red onion chutney, smoked cheddar and red onion marmalade tart, burger with relish and chips, sausages with sage and onion gravy, parma ham-wrapped chicken stuffed with blue cheese with a cream sauce, slow-cooked pork loin with creamy wholegrain mustard sauce, and puddings such as crème brûlée and chocolate and walnut brownie. *Benchmark main dish: duck with brandy and raspberry sauce and potato gratin £16.95. Two-course evening meal £21.00.*

Free house ~ Licensee Aran Biris ~ Real ale ~ (01832) 733434 ~ Open 12-3, 5-11; 12-11 Sat, Sun; closed Mon ~ Bar food 12-2 (3 Sun), 6-9 (9.30 Sat) ~ Restaurant ~ Children welcome ~ Dogs allowed in bar ~ Wi-fi ~ www.thesnootyfoxlowick.com *Recommended by Pip White, Emma Scofield*

NETHER HEYFORD
SP6658   Map 4
Olde Sun £
1.75 miles from M1 junction 16; village signposted left off A45 westbound; Middle Street; NN7 3LL

Unpretentious place with diverting bric-a-brac, reasonably priced pubby bar food and garden with play area

T he several small linked rooms in this mainly 18th-c pub have all manner of entertaining bric-a-brac hanging from the ceilings and packed into nooks and crannies. It includes brassware (one fireplace is a grotto of large brass animals), colourful relief plates, 1930s cigarette cards, railway memorabilia and advertising signs, World War II posters and rope fancywork. The nice old cash till on one of the two counters is wishfully stuck at one and a ha'penny: Banks's Bitter, Greene King Ruddles, Marstons Pedigree and a guest such as Jennings Lakeland Stunner on handpump. Most of the furnishings are properly pubby, with the odd easy chair. There are beams and low ceilings (one painted with a fine sunburst), partly glazed dividing panels, steps between some areas, rugs on parquet, red tiles or flagstones, a big inglenook log fire and (up on the left) a room with full-sized hood skittles, a games machine, darts, cribbage and dominoes; background music. In the garden you'll find antiquated hand-operated farm machines, some with plants in their hoppers. The first thing that will catch your eye when you arrive will probably be a row of brightly coloured grain kibblers along the edge of the fairy-lit front terrace (with picnic-sets).

As well as sandwiches, the newish chef offers fish dishes such as cajun salmon, sea bream with caper sauce and smoked haddock fishcakes, plus chicken, ham and leek pie, goats cheese and onion tart, gammon with pineapple, and puddings such as sticky toffee pudding and apple crumble with custard. *Benchmark main dish: steak pie £8.95. Two-course evening meal £16.00.*

Free house ~ Licensees P Yates and Alan Ford ~ Real ale ~ (01327) 340164 ~ Open 12-2.30, 5-11; 12-midnight Fri, Sat; 12-11 Sun ~ Bar food 12-2, 6.30-9; 12-4 Sun ~ Restaurant ~ Children welcome ~ Dogs welcome *Recommended by Brian and Anna Marsden, Paul Humphreys, George Atkinson, Steve and Sue Griffiths, Phil and Jane Hodson, Gerry and Rosemary Dobson, Edward Mirzoeff*

NORTHAMPTON
Malt Shovel £   SP7559 Map 4

Bridge Street (approach road from M1 junction 15); no parking in nearby street, best to park in Morrisons central car park, far end – passage past Europcar straight to back entrance; NN1 1QF

Friendly, well run real ale pub with bargain lunches and over a dozen varied beers

Our readers enjoy their visits to this cheerful tavern very much – for its atmosphere, bargain food and, of course, the amazing choice of up to 13 real ales. From a battery of handpumps lined up on the long counter there might be Byatts Urban Red, Church End Vicars Ruin, Elgoods Black Dog, Fullers London Pride, Hook Norton Cotswold Lion, Nobbys Best and T'owd Navigation, Oakham Bishops Farewell and JHB, Oldershaw Grantham Stout, Phipps NBC IPA, and RCH Old Slug Porter and PG Steam. They also stock belgian draft and bottled beers, 50 malt whiskies, 17 rums, 17 vodkas and 17 gins, and Cheddar Valley farm cider; regular beer festivals. This is home to quite an extensive collection of carefully chosen brewing memorabilia – look out for the rare Northampton Brewery Company star, displayed outside the pub, and some high-mounted ancient beer engines. Staff are enthusiastic and helpful; darts, daily papers and background music. The secluded backyard has tables and chairs and a smokers' shelter; disabled facilities.

Lunchtime-only food includes filled rolls, fish pie, spinach and ricotta cannelloni, gammon and egg, lambs liver and bacon casserole with mash and onion gravy, and braised pork belly with spring onion mash, red cabbage and parsnip chips. *Benchmark main dish: goat curry £6.00.*

Free house ~ Licensee Mike Evans ~ Real ale ~ (01604) 234212 ~ Open 11.30-3, 5-11; 11.30-11 Thurs-Sat; 12-10.30 Sun ~ Bar food 12-2; not Sun ~ Well behaved children welcome in bar ~ Dogs allowed in bar ~ Blues Weds evening ~ www.maltshoveltavern.com *Recommended by George Atkinson, Dr J Barrie Jones, Richard Kennell*

People named as recommenders after the full entries have told us that the pub should be included. But they have not written the report – we have, after anonymous on-the-spot inspection.

OUNDLE
TL0388 Map 5

Ship £

West Street; PE8 4EF

Bustling down-to-earth town pub with interesting beers and good value pubby food

There's an easy-going, companionable feel and plenty of chatty regulars in this unpretentious local. Off to the left of the central corridor, the heavily beamed lounge (watch your head if you're tall) consists of three cosy areas with a mix of leather and other seats, sturdy tables and a warming log fire in a stone inglenook. A charming little panelled snug at one end has button-back leather seats. The wood-floored public bar has poker evenings on Wednesdays, while the terrace bar has pool and table football; darts, TV, board games and background music. Friendly staff serve Brewsters Hophead, changing ales from Digfield and Phipps, and Sharps Doom Bar on handpump, plus a good range of malt whiskies, seven wines by the glass and two farm ciders. The wooden tables and chairs out on the series of small sunny, covered terraces are lit at night.

Good value traditional food includes baguettes and rolls, smoked mackerel pâté, home-cooked ham and eggs, bangers and mash with onion gravy, burger with cheese, bacon, coleslaw and fries and specials like steak and mushroom in ale pie, tagliatelle carbonara, and haddock parcel with white wine and parsley. *Benchmark main dish: chilli con carne with sour cream and cheese £8.50. Two-course evening meal £17.00.*

Free house ~ Licensees Andrew and Robert Langridge ~ Real ale ~ (01832) 273918 ~ Open 11am-11.45pm ~ Bar food 12-3, 6-9; 12-6 Sun ~ Children welcome ~ Dogs welcome ~ Wi-fi ~ Live bands monthly Sat, open mike first Fri of month ~ Bedrooms: £39/£69 ~ www.theshipinn-oundle.co.uk *Recommended by Richard and Penny Gibbs*

SPRATTON
SP7170 Map 4

Kings Head ♀

Brixworth Road, off A5199 N of Northampton; NN6 8HH

Welcoming family service in enterprising combination of pub, brasserie and relaxed coffee/wine bar

Old pale flagstones and ancient stripped stonework mix nicely here with handsome new wood flooring and up-to-date pastel paintwork in shades of grey and palest fawn – as do the leather chesterfield and antique settle with the metal-braced bentwood café chairs around the stripped brasserie-style tables. The brick counter dispenses changing ales such as Nobbys Guilsborough Gold and Sharps Doom Bar from handpump, and ten decent wines by the glass; good informal service, darts in a side room, nostalgic background pop music. The back cafeteria is similar in style, with sofas and armchairs giving a leisurely feel, plus a tempting cake counter and a glass wall overlooking teak and metal tables in a modern courtyard. The church spire opposite, rebuilt in the 19th c, is a fine sight.

A thoughtful choice of food includes sandwiches, a proper welsh rarebit, duck liver parfait with onion jam, seared scallops with crispy bacon and celeriac purée, wild mushroom and tarragon risotto, honey and mustard-glazed ham and egg, chicken with cauliflower cheese purée and cabbage, confit duck leg with onions four-ways, duck croquette and wilted spinach, and puddings such as a seasonal crumble and banana tarte tatin with coconut ice-cream. *Benchmark main dish: fish of the day with dill mash and red wine butter sauce £15.25. Two-course evening meal £20.50.*

Free house ~ Licensee Duncan Kennedy ~ Real ale ~ (01604) 847351 ~ Open 12-3, 6-11; 12-11.30 Fri, Sat; 12-10.30 Sun ~ Bar food 12-2.30, 6-9.30; 12-5 Sun; cakes and pastries all day ~ Restaurant ~ Children welcome ~ Dogs allowed in bar ~ Wi-fi ~ www.kingsheadspratton.co.uk *Recommended by Gerry and Rosemary Dobson, Paul Dickinson*

SULGRAVE
Star

SP5545 Map 4

Manor Road; E of Banbury, signed off B4525; OX17 2SA

Handsome old inn, carefully refurbished recently, with comfortable bar, Aga-cooked food, real ales and neat garden; bedrooms

Just a stone's throw from the grounds of Sulgrave Manor (the ancestral home of George Washington), this is a carefully renovated and creeper-covered former farmhouse. The comfortably sized bar area is furnished with a cosy selection of chairs, tables and cushioned window seats on polished flagstones, and they keep Hook Norton Cotswold Lion, Old Hooky and a seasonal guest on handpump and six wines by the glass. The restaurant has an Aga-style cooker at one end, where the chef prepares your food in front of you while you sit at brightly coloured, hand-painted chairs and tables, in a room decorated with bunting from painted beams and little contemporary block paintings on grey walls above a pine dado. The neatly kept back garden has a vine-covered trellis, and plenty of space and outdoor games for children.

From a seasonally changing menu, the very good food includes lunchtime sandwiches, pork, plum and brandy pâté with calvados glaze, hot bacon and goats cheese salad, burger with mushrooms, cheese, stilton and chips, frittata with red onion, cheese, mushrooms and peppers, a pie of the day, cajun chicken with cream, gressingham duck with redcurrant, orange and port sauce, and puddings such as iced lemon cheesecake with champagne drizzle and blueberries and apple and rhubarb pie; they hold regular themed food evenings. *Benchmark main dish: turkey, ham and tarragon pie £10.50. Two-course evening meal £15.00.*

Hook Norton ~ Tenant Sue Hilton ~ Real ale ~ (01295) 760389 ~ Open 12-11; 12-9 Sun; 11-3, 6-11 weekdays, 11-11 Sat, 12-5 Sun in winter; closed Mon except bank holidays ~ Bar food 12-9 (7 Sun, 4 winter Sun) ~ Restaurant ~ Children welcome ~ Dogs welcome ~ Wi-fi ~ Bedrooms: /£69 ~ www.thestarinnsulgrave.com *Recommended by R L Borthwick*

Also Worth a Visit in Northamptonshire

Besides the fully inspected pubs, you might like to try these pubs that have been recommended to us and described by readers. Do tell us what you think of them: feedback@goodguides.com

ABTHORPE   SP6446
⋆ **New Inn** (01327) 857306
Signed from A43 at first roundabout S of A5; Silver Street; NN12 8QR Traditional partly thatched country local run by cheery farming family, fairly basic rambling bar with dining area down a couple of steps, four well kept Hook Norton beers and Stowford Press cider, good pubby food (not Sun evening) using their own meat and home-grown herbs, beams, stripped stone and inglenook woodburner, darts and table skittles; quiz last Sun of month, occasional live music, free wi-fi; children, dogs and muddy boots welcome, garden tables, bedrooms in converted barn (short walk across fields), open all day Fri-Sun, closed Mon, lunchtime Tues. *(George Atkinson)*

APETHORPE   TL0295
Kings Head (01780) 470627
Kings Cliffe Road; PE8 5DG Roomy stone-built pub in conservation village, cosy right-hand bar with window seating, log fire in comfortable lounge to the left, Fullers London Pride and three guests, sensibly short choice of enjoyable food including bar snacks and daily specials, friendly efficient service, big dining area; TV; children, dogs

and walkers welcome, some seats out at front and in nice sheltered courtyard behind, open all day Sat, till 7pm Sun. *(Anon)*

AYNHO   SP5133
Cartwright (01869) 811885
Croughton Road (B4100); handy for M40 junction 10; OX17 3BE Spotless 16th-c coaching inn with linked areas, contemporary furniture on wood or tiled floors, some exposed stone walls, leather sofas by big log fire in small bar, ales such as Black Sheep and Hook Norton, nice wines and coffee, good well presented food including set deals, efficient uniformed staff, daily papers; background music, TV, free wi-fi; children welcome, a few seats in pretty corner of former coachyard, 21 bedrooms, good breakfast, pleasant village with apricot trees growing against old cottage walls, open all day. *(George Atkinson)*

AYNHO   SP4932
★ Great Western Arms
(01869) 338288 *On B4031 1.5 miles E of Deddington, 0.75 miles W of Aynho, adjacent to Oxford Canal and Old Aynho station; OX17 3BP* Attractive old pub with series of linked cosy rooms; fine solid country tables on broad flagstones, golden stripped-stone walls, warm cream and deep red plasterwork, fresh flowers and candles, log fires, well kept Hook Norton and guests, good wines by the glass and enjoyable pubby food served by friendly attentive young staff, elegant dining area on right, extensive GWR collection including lots of steam locomotive photographs, daily papers and magazines, skittle alley, pool; background music; children and dogs welcome, white cast-iron furniture in back former stable courtyard, moorings on Oxford Canal and nearby marina, bedrooms (may ask for payment on arrival), open (and food) all day. *(M O S Hawkins, Mike and Margaret Banks, Tony Hobden, Michael Sargent, Phil and Jane Hodson)*

BADBY   SP5659
Maltsters (01327) 702905
The Green; NN11 3AF Refurbished stone-built village pub under newish ownership, long beamed room with fire at each end, enjoyable well priced home-made food including weekday lunchtime/early evening set deal, Steak House restaurant, three well kept ales such as local Gun Dog and Hoggleys, attentive friendly service; children welcome, pleasant side garden and courtyard, well placed for walks on nearby Knightley Way, bedrooms, open all day. *(Roy Shutz)*

BADBY   SP5558
Windmill (01327) 311070
Village signposted off A361 Daventry–Banbury; NN11 3AN Attractive refurbished 17th-c thatched and beamed pub, flagstoned bar area with woodburner

in huge inglenook, up to five changing ales, enjoyable varied choice of good value home-made food from lunchtime sandwiches up, welcoming helpful staff, restaurant extension; background and occasional live music; children and dogs welcome, terrace out by pretty village green, nice walks, eight good bedrooms, open all day. *(George Atkinson)*

BRAUNSTON   SP5465
Admiral Nelson (01788) 891900
Dark Lane, Little Braunston, overlooking Lock 3 just N of Grand Union Canal tunnel; NN11 7HJ 18th-c ex-farmhouse in peaceful setting by canal and hump bridge, good range of sensibly priced food (not Sun evening, Mon) from sandwiches and baguettes up, four changing ales, canal pictures, smallish log-fire bar, carpeted restaurant area with fairly modern pastel décor and brick pillars, games section with hood skittles and darts, some live music including Aug festival; well behaved children and dogs welcome, lots of waterside picnic-sets, may close Mon lunchtime in winter, otherwise open all day. *(George Atkinson)*

BRAYBROOKE   SP7684
Swan (01858) 462754
Griffin Road; LE16 8LH Nicely kept thatched pub with good drinks choice including Everards ales, popular sensibly priced food (not Sun evening) from sandwiches and pub favourites up, friendly staff, fireside sofas, soft lighting, beams and some exposed brickwork, restaurant; quiet background music; children and dogs welcome, disabled facilities, pretty hedged garden with covered terrace, open all day weekends, closed Mon. *(Anon)*

BRIXWORTH   SP7470
Coach & Horses (01604) 880329
Harborough Road, just off A508 N of Northampton; NN6 9BX Welcoming 17th-c stone-built beamed pub, enjoyable good value food including popular Sun lunch, well kept Marstons-related ales, prompt friendly service, log-fire bar with small dining area off, back lounge; tables on gravelled terrace behind, bedrooms in converted outbuildings, charming village with famous Saxon church. *(George Atkinson, Gerry and Rosemary Dobson)*

BROUGHTON   SP8375
Red Lion (01536) 790239
High Street; NN14 1NF Large welcoming stone-built village local with half a dozen well kept ales, farm cider and good choice of wines by the glass from central bar, enjoyable competitively priced home-made food (not Sun evening), bargain OAP lunch Tues and Thurs, Sun carvery, good attentive service, comfortable lounge and dining room, plainer public bar with games, events including beer festivals, live music, poker and quiz nights; background music; children welcome, small

pleasant garden with water feature, open all day Fri-Sun, closed Mon lunchtime. *(Paul Gordon)*

BUCKBY WHARF   SP6066
New Inn   (01327) 844747
A5 N of Weedon; NN6 7PW Canalside pub improved under present licensees; reasonably priced pubby food from baguettes and baked potatoes up, Marstons-related beers, quick cheerful service, several rooms radiating from central servery including a small dining room with fire, games area with table skittles; children welcome, dogs outside only, plenty of picnic-sets by busy Grand Union Canal Lock 7, very popular with summer boaters, open all day. *(George Atkinson)*

BUGBROOKE   SP6756
Wharf Inn   (01604) 832585
The Wharf; off A5 S of Weedon; NN7 3QB Super spot by Grand Union Canal, plenty of tables on big lawn with moorings, large beamed water-view restaurant, bar/lounge with small informal raised eating area either side, lots of stripped brickwork, enjoyable food (all day weekends) from fairly imaginative menu, prompt cheerful service, three well kept ales, lots of wines by the glass, woodburner; background music; children welcome, dogs in garden only, disabled facilities, heated smokers' shelter, open all day. *(Dr Kevan Tucker, George Atkinson)*

CHACOMBE   SP4943
George & Dragon   (01295) 711500
Handy for M40 junction 11, via A361; Silver Street; OX17 2JR Welcoming pub dating from the 17th c with beams, flagstones, panelling and bare stone walls, two inglenook woodburners and deep glass-covered well, good popular food (not Sun evening) in three dining areas from lunchtime sandwiches and traditional choices up, vegetarian options, good service, Everards and a couple of guests from brass-topped counter, several wines by the glass and decent coffee; background music, darts; children and dogs (in bar) welcome, picnic-sets on suntrap terrace, pretty village with interesting church, open all day. *(Ian and Suzy Masser, George Atkinson)*

CHAPEL BRAMPTON   SP7366
★Brampton Halt   (01604) 842676
Pitsford Road, off A5199 N of Northampton; NN6 8BA Well laid out McManus pub on Northampton & Lamport Railway (which is open some weekends) in much-extended former stationmaster's house, large restaurant, railway memorabilia

and train theme throughout, wide choice of enjoyable generous food (smaller helpings available) from sandwiches and meal deals Mon-Fri, good choice of well kept ales (beer festivals) and several wines by the glass, cheerful attentive service even when busy, games and TV in bar; background music; children welcome, lots of tables in big garden with awnings and heaters, summer barbecues and maybe marquee, pretty views over small lake, Nene Way walks. *(George Atkinson, Gerry and Rosemary Dobson)*

CHAPEL BRAMPTON   SP7366
Spencer Arms   (01604) 842237
Northampton Road; NN6 8AE Comfortable Chef & Brewer family dining pub, plenty of tables in long timber-divided L-shaped bar, good choice of sensibly priced food including a tasty fish pie, well kept ales such as Fullers, Sharps and Wells & Youngs, several wines by the glass, friendly generally efficient service, beams and two log fires; soft background music; tables outside, open (and food) all day. *(Gerry and Rosemary Dobson)*

CLIPSTON   SP7181
Bulls Head   (01858) 525268
B4036 S of Market Harborough; LE16 9RT Welcoming bustling village pub with enjoyable good value food, Everards ales and up to five guests, log fire and heavy beams, with coins in the cracks put there by World War II airmen; background music, TV, Tues quiz and curry night; children and dogs welcome, terrace tables, three comfortable bedrooms, open all day weekends. *(Mike and Margaret Banks)*

COLLINGTREE   SP7555
Wooden Walls of Old England
(01604) 760641   *1.2 miles from M1 junction 15; High Street; NN4 0NE* Cosy thatch and stone village pub dating from the 15th c and named as a tribute to the navy; friendly newish management, four well kept Marstons-related ales and good choice of wines by the glass, interesting food (not Sun evening), beams and open fire, table skittles; free wi-fi; big back garden with terrace, open all day Fri-Sun, closed Mon. *(Keith and Sue Campbell)*

COLLYWESTON   SK9902
★Collyweston Slater   (01780) 444288
The Drove (A43); PE9 3PQ Roomy 17th-c main road inn with enjoyable generously served pub food (all day Sun when can get very busy), well kept Everards ales and decent wines, friendly service, surprisingly contemporary with brown leather easy chairs and sofas, smart modern two-part dining room (log fire) and two or three more

---

Real ale to us means beer that has matured naturally in its cask – not pressurised or filtered.

informal areas, one with a raised stove in dividing wall, beams, stripped stone and mix of dark flagstones, bare boards and carpeting; background music, darts; children welcome, teak seats on flagstoned terrace, boules, three bedrooms, open all day. *(Brian and Janet Ainscough)*

COSGROVE   SP7942
Barley Mow (01908) 562957

The Stocks; MK19 7JD Friendly old village pub by Grand Union Canal, well kept Everards ales and enjoyable reasonably priced home-made food, lounge/dining area with dark furniture, small public bar, darts and skittles; children and dogs welcome, tables on terrace and lawn down to canal, open all day. *(Anon)*

CRICK   SP5872
★**Red Lion** (01788) 822342

1 mile from M1 junction 18; in centre of village off A428; NN6 7TX Nicely worn-in stone and thatch coaching inn run by same family since 1979, traditional low-ceilinged bar with lots of old horsebrasses (some rare) and tiny log stove in big inglenook, straightforward low-priced lunchtime food, more elaborate evening menu (not Sun) including popular steaks, plenty for vegetarians too, Adnams Southwold, Greene King Old Speckled Hen, Wells & Youngs Bombardier and a guest, good friendly service; children allowed (under-12s lunchtime only), dogs welcome, picnic-sets on terrace and in Perspex-covered coachyard with pretty hanging baskets. *(Ted George)*

DUDDINGTON   SK9800
Royal Oak (01780) 444267

High Street, just off A43; PE9 3QE Stone-built inn on edge of pretty village; modern bar area with leather sofas and chairs on flagstones, panelling and log fire, three Grainstore ales from brick servery, restaurant with stone walls, oak floor and light oak furniture, enjoyable food from pub favourites up including set lunch deal Mon-Fri; background music; children welcome, disabled facilities, tables on small grassy area at front, six bedrooms, open all day Fri-Sun. *(Ray and Winifred Halliday)*

EAST HADDON   SP6668
★**Red Lion** (01604) 770223

High Street; village signposted off A428 (turn right in village) and off A50 N of Northampton; NN6 8BU Substantial and elegant golden-stone thatched hotel with sizeable dining room, log-fire lounge and bar, emphasis on well presented imaginative food and most tables set for dining, but they do keep Wells & Youngs ales in good condition and offer over a dozen wines by the glass, efficient friendly service; background music; children welcome, attractive grounds including walled side garden, cookery school, seven comfortable bedrooms and

two-bed cottage, good breakfast, closed Sun evening. *(Ron Corbett, Gerry and Rosemary Dobson)*

EASTON-ON-THE-HILL   TF0104
★**Exeter Arms** (01780) 756321

Stamford Road (A43); PE9 3NS Nicely renovated 18th-c pub run by brother and sister team; snug candlelit country-feel bar with traditional furniture on stone floor, well kept ales such as Black Sheep and Oakham, Aspall's cider and plenty of wines by the glass, wide choice of good food (must book weekends) from sandwiches, pizzas and pub favourites to more enterprising dishes, cheerful efficient service, restaurant and new orangery with modern wicker furniture; background music; sunny split-level terrace, paddock, five bedrooms, good breakfast, closed Sun evening. *(Michael Doswell)*

EYDON   SP5450
★**Royal Oak** (01327) 263167

Lime Avenue; village signed off A361 Daventry–Banbury, and from B4525; NN11 3PG Interestingly laid-out 300-year-old ironstone inn, some lovely period features including fine flagstone floors and leaded windows, cosy snug on right with cushioned benches built into alcoves, seats in bow window, cottagey pictures and inglenook log fire, long corridor-like central bar linking three other small characterful rooms, four real ales including Fullers, Hook Norton and Timothy Taylors Landlord, good food (takeaway only Mon evening), friendly staff and lively atmosphere, table skittles in old stable; background music, charity quiz first Sun of month; children and dogs welcome, terrace seating (some under cover), open all day weekends, closed Mon lunchtime. *(Mick Coles, Gene and Kitty Rankin)*

GRAFTON REGIS   SP7546
★**White Hart** (01908) 542123

A508 S of Northampton; NN12 7SR Thatched dining pub with several linked rooms, good pubby food (not Sun evening) including range of home-made soups and popular well priced Sun roasts (best to book) using local meat, Greene King ales and Aspall's cider, good wines by the glass, friendly helpful staff coping well when busy, african grey parrot (can be very vocal), restaurant with open fire and separate menu; background music; children and dogs welcome (they have a couple of boxers), terrace tables and gazebo in good-sized garden, closed Mon. *(George Atkinson)*

GREAT BILLING   SP8162
Elwes Arms (01604) 407521

High Street; NN3 9DT Thatched stone-built 16th-c village pub, two bars (steps between), wide choice of good value tasty food (all day weekends) including weekday lunchtime deal, Black Sheep, Wadworths 6X and Shepherd Neame Spitfire, friendly staff, pleasant dining room (children allowed); background music, TVs, darts, quiz Thurs/Sun, no dogs; garden tables and nice covered decked terrace, play area, open all day Weds-Sun. *(Alan and Shirley Sawden)*

GREAT CRANSLEY SP8276
Three Cranes (01536) 790287
Loddington Road; NN14 1PY Small stone-built village pub run by same family for over 25 years; small bar with dining area to right leading to little conservatory, well kept Banks's Bitter, enjoyable reasonably priced home-made food, prompt friendly service; free wi-fi; two bedrooms, closed weekday lunchtimes. *(Gerry and Rosemary Dobson)*

GREAT DODDINGTON SP8864
Stags Head (01933) 222316
High Street (B573 S of Wellingborough); NN29 7TQ Old stone-built pub with pleasant bar and split-level lounge/dining room, Black Sheep and a house beer from Caledonian, nice wines and good soft drinks range, varied choice of fairly priced food from sandwiches up, special diets catered for, smart cheery service, also separate barn restaurant extension, public bar with pool and games; background music, quiz and poker nights; children and dogs welcome, picnic-sets out in front and in garden, open all day Sun. *(Anon)*

GREAT EVERDON SP5957
Plough (01327) 361606
Next to church; NN11 3BL Small fairly simple bare-boards pub in tucked-away village; bar with a couple of steps down to lounge/dining area, open fire and woodburner, Sharps Doom Bar and a couple of guests such as Gun Dog Jack's Spaniels, short choice of enjoyable reasonably priced lunchtime food cooked by landlady (more substantial meals Fri evening and Sun lunchtime), fortnightly quiz Tues; some seats out in front, more in spacious garden behind, shop (the Furrow) selling vintage furniture, collectables and plants, good walks nearby. *(George Atkinson)*

GREAT OXENDON SP7383
★George (01858) 465205
A508 S of Market Harborough; LE16 8NA Elegant 16th-c dining inn with comfortable convivial bar, well kept ales such as Marstons Pedigree and Shepherd Neame Spitfire, plenty of wines by the glass and good sensibly priced food from light choices up, friendly attentive staff, green leatherette bucket chairs around small tables, brown panelled dado with wallpaper or dark painted walls above, big log fire,

tiled-floor entrance lobby with easy chairs and former inn sign, carpeted conservatory; background music; children welcome, big shrub-sheltered garden, bedrooms, closed Sun evening; for sale last we heard, so things may change. *(George Atkinson, Gerry and Rosemary Dobson)*

GREENS NORTON SP6649
Butchers Arms (01327) 350488
High Street; NN12 8BA Comfortable welcoming village pub with enjoyable straightforward food from sandwiches and pizzas up, lunchtime carvery Weds and Sun, reasonable prices, St Austell, Sharps, Timothy Taylors and a guest, bar and games room with pool, darts and skittles; background and some live music, fortnightly quiz Sun; children (till 9pm) and dogs allowed, disabled access, picnic-sets and play area outside, pretty village near Grafton Way walks, closed lunchtimes Mon and Tues. *(Anon)*

GUILSBOROUGH SP6772
Ward Arms (01604) 740265
High Street; NN6 8PY Small 17th-c thatched and beamed pub in historic village, entrance lobby with stained-glass panels, bar and lounge/dining area with open fire, Nobbys ales (brewed in adjacent stables) and guests, hearty good value food (more extensive evening choice), friendly chatty staff, pool, darts and table skittles; tables outside, open all day Fri-Sun, closed Mon lunchtime. *(George Atkinson)*

HACKLETON SP8054
White Hart (01604) 870271
B526 SE of Northampton; NN7 2AD Comfortably traditional 18th-c country pub; wide choice of enjoyable food from sandwiches and baked potatoes up, friendly helpful staff, Fullers London Pride, Greene King IPA and a guest, decent choice of wines and other drinks, dining area up steps with flame-effect fire, beams, stripped stone and brickwork, illuminated well, split-level flagstoned bar with log fire, pool and hood skittles; background music, TV; children (not in bar after 5pm) and dogs welcome, disabled access, picnic-sets in sunny garden, open all day. *(W J Callis)*

HARRINGTON SP7780
★Tollemache Arms (01536) 710469
High Street; off A508 S of Market Harborough; NN6 9NU Pretty thatched Tudor pub in lovely quiet ironstone village; very low ceilings in compact bar with log fire and in pleasant partly stripped-stone dining room, enjoyable generous food from

---

sandwiches up, well kept Wells & Youngs ales and a guest, friendly attentive staff, table skittles; children welcome, nice back garden with country views, handy for Carpetbagger Aviation Museum, open all day in summer. *(Gerry and Rosemary Dobson, George Atkinson)*

HELLIDON   SP5158
Red Lion (01327) 261200
Stockwell Lane, off A425 W of Daventry; NN11 6LG Welcoming wisteria-clad inn on edge of village opposite small green; bar with woodburner, cosy lounge and softly lit low-ceilinged stripped-stone dining area, enjoyable home-made food served by helpful friendly staff, four changing ales, hood skittles and pool in back games room; children and dogs welcome, a few picnic-sets on front grass, windmill vineyard and pleasant walks nearby, six bedrooms, open all day weekends. *(Anon)*

HIGHAM FERRERS   SP9668
Griffin (01933) 312612
High Street; NN10 8BW 17th-c pub/restaurant (bigger than it looks) with good food including fresh fish and popular Sun carvery (till 5pm), five well kept rotating ales and good selection of wines and malt whiskies, comfortable front bar, large back restaurant and dining conservatory, good service; free wi-fi; tables on heated terrace, open all day Fri-Sun. *(Guy and Caroline Howard)*

HINTON-IN-THE-HEDGES   SP5536
Crewe Arms (01280) 705801
Off A43 W of Brackley; NN13 5NF Welcoming 17th-c extended stone-built village pub under newish management, well kept Hook Norton and guests, enjoyable home-made food from bar snacks up; background music; two bothy bedrooms, open all day. *(Anon)*

KETTERING   SP8778
Alexandra Arms (01536) 522730
Victoria Street; NN16 0BU Backstreet real ale pub with up to 14 changing quickly, hundreds each year, also Julian Church beers brewed in the cellar, knowledgeable landlord, basic opened-up bar with pump clips covering walls and ceiling, back games room with darts, hood skittles and TV, some snacky food; a couple of picnic-sets out in front, small beer garden behind, open all day (from 2pm Mon-Thurs). *(George Atkinson)*

KILSBY   SP5671
★**George** (01788) 822229
2.5 miles from M1 junction 18: A428 towards Daventry, left on to A5 – pub off on right at roundabout; CV23 8YE Popular pub (handy for motorway) with friendly hard-working landlady, proper old-fashioned public bar, wood-panelled lounge with plush banquettes and coal-effect gas

stove opening into smarter area with solidly comfortable furnishings, well kept Adnams, Fullers, Timothy Taylors and a guest, splendid range of malt whiskies, enjoyable good value pubby food, speedy service; live jazz first Sun of month, quiz nights, darts, free-play pool tables, TV; children welcome if dining, dogs in bar, garden picnic-sets, six bedrooms. *(Ted George, Andy and Jill Kassube, Dr Martin Owton)*

KISLINGBURY   SP6959
★**Cromwell Cottage** (01604) 830288
High Street; NN7 4AG Sizeable Mitchells & Butlers family dining pub tucked away near the River Nene; bar/lounge with open fire and some beams, smart bistro dining area with candles on tables, good popular food from snacks to set choices and specials, well kept changing ales and nice wines, efficient service from neat cheerful staff; no dogs; terrace tables, open all day. *(Mike and Margaret Banks, Jim and Nancy Forbes, George Atkinson, Gerry and Rosemary Dobson)*

KISLINGBURY   SP6959
Sun (01604) 833571
Off A45 W of Northampton; Mill Road; NN7 4BB Welcoming 17th-c thatch and ironstone village pub under new local ownership; ales such as Greene King, Hogglgeys, St Austell and Sharps, enjoyable fairly traditional food (all day Sat, not Sun evening), popular with locals and visitors alike, L-shaped bar/lounge and small separate dining area; TV, free wi-fi; a few picnic-sets out in front, open all day weekends. *(George Atkinson)*

LITCHBOROUGH   SP6353
Old Red Lion (01327) 830064
Banbury Road, just off former B4525 Banbury–Northampton; NN12 8JF Attractive beamed pub owned by local farming family and doubling as village shop; four rooms including cosy flagstoned bar with woodburner in big inglenook, Hogglgeys (brewed in the village) and a couple of guests, shortish choice of generously served food (not Sun evening) from sandwiches and baguettes up, pleasant laid-back atmosphere, barn-conversion restaurant at back, skittles and pool; popular with walkers, terrace seating, open all day. *(George Atkinson)*

LITTLE BRINGTON   SP6663
★**Saracens Head** (01604) 770640
4.5 miles from M1 junction 16, first right off A45 to Daventry; also signed off A428; Main Street; NN7 4HS Friendly old village pub with good competitively priced food (not Sun evening, Mon) from interesting menu (smaller helpings available), well kept Greene King IPA, Timothy Taylors Landlord and a guest, several wines by the glass, roomy U-shaped beamed lounge with woodburner, flagstones, chesterfields and lots of old prints, book-lined dining room (proper

napkins); gentle background music; plenty of tables out on gravel/paved area, walks nearby and handy for Althorp House and Holdenby House. *(Sue Kidd, Gerry and Rosemary Dobson, George Atkinson, Dennis and Doreen Haward and others)*

LITTLE HARROWDEN   SP8671
Lamb (01933) 673300
Orlingbury Road/Kings Lane – off A509 or A43 S of Kettering; NN9 5BH Popular pub in delightful village, split-level carpeted lounge with log fire and brasses on 17th-c beams, dining area, good promptly served bargain food, Wells & Youngs Eagle and a couple of guests, short sensibly priced wine list, good coffee, games bar with darts, hood skittles and machines, resident cocker spaniel called Rio; background music; children welcome, small raised terrace and garden, open all day weekends. *(Gerry and Rosemary Dobson)*

MAIDWELL   SP7477
★ Stags Head (01604) 686700
Harborough Road (A508 N of Northampton); a mile from A14 junction 2; NN6 9JA Comfortable dining pub with woodburner in pubby part by bar, extensive eating areas, good value traditional food including evening deals, helpful friendly staff and cheery locals, interesting range of well kept beers from small and large breweries, good choice of other drinks; background and some live music, monthly quiz, free wi-fi; disabled facilities, picnic-sets on back terrace (dogs on leads allowed here), good-sized sheltered sloping garden beyond, summer barbecues, five bedrooms, not far from splendid Palladian Kelmarsh Hall and park. *(Mike and Margaret Banks, Gerry and Rosemary Dobson)*

MOULTON   SP7866
Telegraph (01604) 648228
West Street; NN3 7SB Spacious old stone-built village pub, friendly and popular, with enjoyable promptly served food (not Sun evening) including some interesting specials and weekday lunch deal, well kept ales such as Fullers, Greene King and Sharps, maybe an american craft beer on tap, log fire in bar, back restaurant extension; open all day Fri-Sun. *(G Jennings, Mr and Mrs D J Nash, Gerry and Rosemary Dobson, George Atkinson)*

NASSINGTON   TL0696
Queens Head (01780) 784006
Station Road; PE8 6QB Refurbished stone dining inn, softly lit beamed bar with mix of old tables and chairs, large oriental rug in front of roaring fire, good reasonably priced food from traditional choices to imaginative restaurant dishes using local ingredients,

pleasant helpful uniformed staff, nice choice of wines by the glass, ales such as Greene King, Nene Valley and Oakham, good coffee, separate restaurant; pretty garden by River Nene, delightful village, nine chalet bedrooms. *(Anon)*

NORTHAMPTON   SP7261
Hopping Hare (01604) 580090
Harlestone Road (A428), New Duston; NN5 6DF Edwardian pub/restaurant/hotel on edge of housing estate, contemporary, stylish and comfortable, with good food from lunchtime sandwiches and pub favourites to sharing boards and up-to-date restauranty dishes, Adnams, Black Sheep and some own-label beers, good choice of wines by the glass including champagne, competent friendly service, daily newspapers; background music, free wi-fi; tables out on deck, 19 modern bedrooms, open all day. *(G Jennings)*

NORTHAMPTON   SP7560
Lamplighter (01604) 631125
Overstone Road; NN1 3JS Popular Victorian corner pub in the Mounts area, friendly and welcoming, with wide choice of draught and bottled beers and good value generously served food including range of burgers, regular live music, quiz Weds; children welcome if eating, picnic-sets in heated courtyard, open all day (till 1am Fri, Sat). *(Anon)*

NORTHAMPTON   SP7661
Old England 07742 069768
Kettering Road, near the racecourse; NN1 4BP Quirky conversion of Victorian corner shop over three floors (steepish stairs to upper level and down to cellar bar), ground-floor room with assorted tables and chairs on bare boards, 15 well kept changing ales and a dozen or so ciders from hatch at top of stairs, lots of pictures with medieval or Arthurian themes, plus the odd banner, flag and suit of armour, bargain food including lunchtime set deal, more extensive choice evenings and weekends (when pub is at its busiest), friendly staff and broad mix of customers, cards and board games, folk music, quiz nights and poetry readings; children welcome, closed Mon lunchtime, otherwise open all day (no food Sun evening). *(George Atkinson)*

NORTHAMPTON   SP7560
Wig & Pen (01604) 622178
St Giles Street; NN1 1JA Long L-shaped beamed room with bar running most of its length, a dozen well kept quickly changing ales including Fullers London Pride and Greene King IPA, good choice of bottled beers too, enjoyable nicely presented food (not weekend evenings) from sandwiches

---

Tipping is not normal for bar meals, and not usually expected.

and deli boards up, efficient friendly young staff, live music including Tues jazz; sports TV; split-level walled garden, open all day. *(George Atkinson, Richard Tilbrook)*

OLD SP7873
White Horse (01604) 781297
Walgrave Road, N of Northampton between A43 and A508; NN6 9QX Refurbished village pub with good freshly made food including some interesting choices, three well kept changing ales and decent wines by the glass, friendly efficient staff, quiz night first Thurs of month, live music last Fri; free wi-fi; well behaved children and dogs welcome, garden overlooking 13th-c church, open all day Sat, till 7pm Sun, closed Mon. *(R L Borthwick)*

PAULERSPURY SP7245
Barley Mow (01327) 811086
High Street; NN12 7NA Welcoming 18th-c beamed village pub, various rooms including inglenook bar and raftered bare-stone dining room, ales such as Adnams, Greene King and York, good value fairly standard food from ciabattas up, table skittles and pool, Tues quiz, fortnightly live music Thurs; sports TV; picnic-sets on back lawn, closed lunchtimes Mon and Tues, open all day weekends (till 9pm Sun), no food weekday lunchtimes or Sun evening. *(George Atkinson)*

RUSHDEN SP9566
Station Bar (01933) 318988
Station Approach; NN10 0AW Not a pub, part of station HQ of Rushden Historical Transport Society (non-members can sign in for £1); bar in former ladies' waiting room with gas lighting, enamel signs and railway memorabilia, seven well kept ales including Oakham and Phipps, tea and coffee, filled rolls and perhaps some hot food, friendly staff; also museum and summer train rides, table skittles in a Royal Mail carriage; open all day weekends, closed weekday lunchtimes. *(Anon)*

RUSHTON SP8483
Thornhill Arms (01536) 710251
Station Road; NN14 1RL Rambling family-run dining pub opposite lovely village's cricket green, popular food including keenly priced set menu (weekday evenings, Sat lunchtime) and carvery (Sun, Mon evening), prompt friendly service, usually three well kept ales such as Fullers, Hook Norton and Shepherd Neame, several neatly laid out dining areas including smart high-beamed back restaurant, open fire; children welcome, garden with decked area, open all day Sun. *(Gerry and Rosemary Dobson)*

SLIPTON SP9579
★ Samuel Pepys (01832) 731739
Off A6116 at first roundabout N of A14 junction, towards Twywell and Slipton; NN14 3AR Old reworked stone pub under new management (some redecoration); long modernised bar with heavy low beams, wood flooring, log fire and great central pillar, up to five ales including local Digfield and decent choice of wines by the glass, good variety of popular food including daily specials, OAP weekday lunch deal, friendly attentive service, dining room extending into roomy conservatory with country views; background music; children welcome, dogs in bar, wheelchair access from car park using ramp, well laid-out sheltered garden with heated terrace, open all day weekends (till 7pm Sun in winter). *(Michael and Jenny Back)*

STAVERTON SP5461
Countryman (01327) 311815
Daventry Road (A425); NN11 6JH Beamed and carpeted dining pub with popular food including good value two-course menu, Wells & Youngs Bombardier and a couple of local ales, good friendly service even when busy; background music; children welcome, disabled access, some tables outside and in small garden, open all day Sun. *(George Atkinson)*

STOKE BRUERNE SP7449
Boat (01604) 862428
3.5 miles from M1 junction 15 – A508 towards Stony Stratford, then signed on right; Bridge Road; NN12 7SB Old-world flagstoned bar in picturesque canalside spot by restored lock, more modern central-pillared back bar and bistro, half a dozen Marstons-related ales and maybe a local guest, Thatcher's cider, fairly standard food from baguettes up including deals, friendly efficient young staff, comfortable upstairs bookable restaurant with more elaborate menu, shop for boaters (nice ice-creams); background music, can get busy in summer especially weekends and parking nearby difficult; welcomes dogs and children, disabled facilities, tables out by towpath opposite canal museum, trips on own narrowboat, open all day. *(George Atkinson)*

STOKE DOYLE TL0286
★ Shuckburgh Arms (01832) 272339
Village signed (down Stoke Hill) from SW edge of Oundle; PE8 5TG Attractively reworked relaxed 17th-c pub in quiet hamlet, four traditional rooms with some modern touches, low black beams in bowed ceilings, pictures on pastel walls, lots of pale tables on wood or carpeted floors, stylish art deco seats and elegant dining chairs, inglenook woodburner, ales such as Black Sheep and Nene Valley from granite-top bar, well selected wines, good food served by helpful attentive staff; faint background music; children welcome, garden with decked area and play frame, bedrooms in separate modern block, closed Sun evening. *(Anon)*

SUDBOROUGH SP9682
Vane Arms (01832) 730033
Off A6116; Main Street; NN14 3BX
Refurbished thatched pub with low
beams, stripped stonework and inglenook
fires, enjoyable freshly cooked food, well
kept Everards and guests, friendly staff,
restaurant; tables out on terrace, pretty
village. *(Anon)*

THORNBY SP6675
Red Lion (01604) 740238
*Welford Road; A5199 Northampton–
Leicester; NN6 8SJ* Popular old country
pub with interesting choice of up to four well
kept changing ales, enjoyable home-made
food (not Mon) from standards up including
popular steak and stilton pie, prompt friendly
service, beams and log fire, back dining area;
children and dogs welcome, garden picnic-
sets, open all day weekends when it can
be busy (booking advised Sat evening).
(Gerry and Rosemary Dobson, C A Bryson)

THORPE MANDEVILLE SP5344
★ Three Conies (01295) 711025
Off B4525 E of Banbury; OX17 2EX
Attractive and welcoming 17th-c pub with
wide choice of enjoyable food from good
value sandwiches up, well kept Hook Norton
ales and a guest, beamed bare-boards
bar with some stripped stone, mix of old
dining tables, three good log fires, large
dining room; background and some live
music; children and dogs welcome, disabled
facilities, tables out in front and behind on
decking and lawn, open all day (from 10am
for breakfast). *(Michael Butler)*

THRAPSTON SP9978
Kings Arms (01832) 733911
High Street; NN14 4JJ Welcoming
traditional pub dating from the 18th-c,
mix of furniture on wood or tiled floors in
L-shaped bar, well kept Sharps Doom Bar
and guests such as local Nene Valley, good
affordably priced food (not Sun evening) in
bar or newly modernised upstairs restaurant,
prompt friendly service; background music,
sports TV; children welcome, closed Mon
lunchtime. *(Dennis and Doreen Haward)*

TOWCESTER SP7047
Folly (01327) 354031
A5 S, opposite racecourse; NN12 6LB
Black-beamed 18th-c thatched pub opposite
racecourse, enjoyable sensibly priced food,
local ales and plenty of wines by the glass,
friendly helpful staff, steps up to dining
area; children welcome till 8pm, dogs in bar,
picnic-sets outside, open all day Sun till 8pm,
closed Mon. *(Darren and Jane Staniforth)*

TURWESTON SP6037
Stratton Arms (01280) 704956
*E of crossroads in village; pub itself just
inside Buckinghamshire; NN13 5JX*
Friendly chatty local in picturesque village,
well kept Courage, Shepherd Neame, John
Smiths, Timothy Taylors and a guest, good
choice of other drinks, enjoyable reasonably
priced traditional food (not Sun evening,
Mon or Tues), low ceilings and two log
fires, small restaurant; background music,
sports TV; children and dogs welcome,
large pleasant garden by Great Ouse with
barbecue and play area, camping, open
all day. *(George Atkinson)*

TWYWELL SP9578
Old Friar (01832) 732625
*Lower Street, off A14 W of Thrapston;
NN14 3AH* Well run popular pub with
enjoyable good value food including deals,
carvery all day Sun and Tues-Sat evenings,
Mon curry night, Greene King and a couple
of guests, cheerful attentive service,
modernised split-level interior with beams
and some exposed stonework; children and
dogs welcome, garden with good play area,
open all day Fri-Sun. *(George Atkinson)*

UPPER BODDINGTON SP4853
Plough (01327) 260364
Warwick Road; NN11 6DH Welcoming
18th-thatched village inn recently renovated
keeping much of its original character, small
beamed and flagstoned bar, lobby with old
local photos, Greene King IPA, Shepherd
Neame Spitfire and a guest, good value
traditional food (curry night Tues, fish Weds)
in restaurant, snug or intimate Doll's Parlour
(named after former veteran landlady),
woodburners, quiz first Sun of month,
occasional live music and beer festivals;
free wi-fi; children and dogs welcome, five
bedrooms (some sharing bathroom), usually
closed weekday lunchtimes, open all day
weekends, no food Sun evening, Mon.
(R Anderson)

WADENHOE TL0183
★ Kings Head (01832) 720024
*Church Street; village signposted
(in small print) off A605 S of Oundle;
PE8 5ST* Beautifully placed 17th-c country
pub with picnic-sets on sun terrace and
among trees on grassy stretch by River Nene
(moorings); uncluttered partly stripped-stone
bar with woodburner in fine inglenook, pale
pine furniture and a couple of cushioned wall
seats, simple bare-boards public bar, games
room with darts, dominoes and table skittles,
and attractive little beamed dining room
with more pine furniture, three changing
ales and several wines by the glass, good well
presented food, friendly efficient service;
children and dogs welcome, open all day in
summer, all day Fri, Sat and till 6pm Sun
in winter. *(Ryta Lyndley, R L Borthwick)*

WALGRAVE SP8072
Royal Oak (01604) 781248
*Zion Hill, off A43 Northampton–
Kettering; NN6 9PN* Welcoming old

stone-built village local, good choice of reasonably priced food including fish dishes, popular two-for-one evening deal on main courses (Tues and maybe Sun), well kept Adnams, Greene King and three interesting guests, decent wines, friendly prompt service, long three-part carpeted beamed bar, small lounge, restaurant extension behind; children welcome, small garden with play area, open all day Sun. *(Gerry and Rosemary Dobson)*

WEEDON   SP6359

Crossroads (01327) 340354

3 miles from M1 junction 16; A45 towards Daventry; High Street, on A5 junction; NN7 4PX Spacious Chef & Brewer with beamed bar and dining area, lots of nooks and crannies, comfy sofas, log fires, changing ales and enjoyable food including set deals, friendly attentive staff; children welcome, disabled facilities, tables on terrace and in delightful gardens down to river, comfortable Premier Inn bedroom block, open (and food) all day. *(George Atkinson)*

WEEDON   SP6458

★ Narrow Boat (01327) 340333

3.9 miles from M1 junction 16; A45 towards Daventry, left on to A5, pub then on left after canal, at Stowe Hill – junction Watling Street/Heyford Lane; NN7 4RZ Big draw for this neatly refurbished relaxed pub is its Grand Union Canal position – plenty of seats on covered deck and in garden sloping down to the water, summer bar out here and children's play trail; rambling bar with comfortable dark banquettes and padded chairs around neat tables, woodburner, a couple of Wells & Youngs ales and several wines by the glass, wide choice of enjoyable food (all day weekends), carpeted conservatory with heavy curtains for cooler nights; children and dogs (in bar) welcome, background music; disabled facilities, well equipped comfortable bedrooms in separate block, open all day. *(Dr Kevan Tucker, Brian and Anna Marsden, Mike and Margaret Banks, George Atkinson)*

WELFORD   SP6480

Wharf Inn (01858) 575075

Pub just over Leicestershire border; NN6 6JQ Castellated Georgian folly in delightful setting by two Grand Union Canal marinas, Marstons, Oakham and three guests in unpretentious bar, popular straightforward pubby food, pleasant dining section; children and dogs welcome, big waterside garden, open all day. *(Dr Kevan Tucker)*

WESTON BY WELLAND   SP7791

Wheel & Compass (01858) 565864

Valley Road; LE16 8HZ Old stone-built country pub with wide choice of enjoyable generous food at good prices, Bass, Marstons Pedigree and three changing guests, friendly staff, good wine and soft drinks choice, comfortable bar, nice old-fashioned snug and plenty of dining space; children welcome, open all day. *(Howard and Margaret Buchanan)*

YARDLEY HASTINGS   SP8656

★ Rose & Crown (01604) 696276

Just off A428 Bedford–Northampton; NN7 1EX Spacious and popular 18th-c dining pub in pretty village; flagstones, beams, stripped stonework and quiet corners, step up to big comfortable dining room, flowers on tables, good well presented interesting food from daily changing menu, efficient friendly young staff, six real ales, four ciders and decent range of wines, newspapers; background music; children welcome till 9pm, dogs in bar, picnic-sets in small courtyard and good-sized garden, open all day (from 5pm Mon). *(G Jennings, George Atkinson)*

Northumbria

(County Durham, Northumberland and Tyneside)

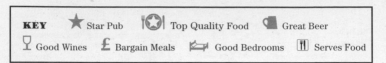

KEY ★ Star Pub | 🔯 Top Quality Food | 🍺 Great Beer
🍷 Good Wines | £ Bargain Meals | 🛏 Good Bedrooms | 🍴 Serves Food

---

ALNMOUTH | NU2410 Map 10
Red Lion 🍺 🛏
Northumberland Street; NE66 2RJ

Friendly former coaching inn, character bar, neat contemporary restaurant, thoughtful choice of drinks and food, and fine views; comfortable bedrooms

In warm weather, the seats in the neat sheltered garden – reached through an ancient stone arch at the back of the yard – are a peaceful place to sit, and a raised deck gives a wide view out over the anchorage of the Aln estuary. This is a friendly 18th-c coaching inn, and the bar has heavy black beams, classic leather wall banquettes, stools and window seats, old local photographs on dark mahogany brown panelling, cheerful fires and a relaxed atmosphere. Helpful staff serve Black Sheep, Roosters Yankee, Tempest RyePA and Tyne Bank Silver Dollar from handpumps and half a dozen wines by the glass. The stripped-brick restaurant has high-backed leather dining chairs around polished tables on a flagstone floor and a woodburning stove; quiet background music. Bedrooms are well equipped and comfortable.

🍴 As well as lunchtime sandwiches and baguettes, the popular food includes pigeon breast with raspberry vinaigrette, smoked salmon tagliatelle in lemon cream, sausages in black pudding and onion gravy, vegetarian patties with sweet potato chips, barbecue pork belly with apple cider rösti, slow-cooked chicken with lime, chilli and coriander, coconut rice and asian slaw, and puddings such as warm chocolate brownie and sticky toffee pudding. *Benchmark main dish: steak in ale pie £10.50. Two-course evening meal £17.00.*

Free house ~ Licensees Jane and Mac McHugh ~ Real ale ~ (01665) 830584 ~ Open 9.30am-11.30pm (10.30pm Sun) ~ Bar food 12-9 (8 Sun) ~ Restaurant ~ Children welcome ~ Dogs allowed in bar ~ Wi-fi ~ Live music monthly ~ Bedrooms: /£95 ~ www.redlionalnmouth.com *Recommended by Comus and Sarah Elliott, Alistair Forsyth*

ANICK | NY9565 Map 10
Rat 🔯 🍷 🍺
Village signposted NE of A69/A695 Hexham junction; NE46 4LN

Views over North Tyne Valley from terrace and garden, refurbished bar and lounge, lots of interesting knick-knacks, half a dozen mainly local real ales and interesting bar food

'This is all that an English country pub should be,' says one reader with enthusiasm, and plenty of others agree. The traditional bar is snug and welcoming with a coal fire in a blackened kitchen range, lots of cottagey knick-knacks from antique floral chamber-pots hanging from the beams to china and glassware on a delft shelf, and little curtained windows that allow in a soft and gentle light; background music, daily papers and magazines. The enthusiastic licensees keep Allendale Curlews Return, Geltsdale Cold Fell, High House Farm Nels Best, Hexhamshire Shire Bitter, Timothy Taylors Landlord and Wylam Red Kite on handpump, a dozen wines by the glass (including champagne), a local gin and farm cider. The conservatory has pleasant views and the garden is quite charming with its dovecote, statues, pretty flower beds and North Tyne Valley views from seats on the terrace. Parking is limited, but you can park around the village green.

Good, interesting food includes sandwiches, local game terrine with fig chutney, kipper rillette with horseradish and potato salad, pan haggerty of parsnips and wild mushrooms topped with cheese, sausages with leek and potato cake and onion gravy, coley with creamed samphire, lemon and capers, rack of lamb with olives, rosemary and oven-dried tomatoes, and puddings such as apple and blueberry crème brûlée and chocolate and coconut bread and butter pudding. *Benchmark main dish: roast rib of beef with béarnaise sauce for two people £45.00. Two-course evening meal £18.00.*

Free house ~ Licensees Phil Mason and Karen Errington ~ Real ale ~ (01434) 602814 ~ Open 12-11 (10.30 Sun) ~ Bar food 12-2 (3 Sun), 6-9 ~ Restaurant ~ Children welcome ~ Wi-fi ~ Live folk first Thurs of month ~ www.theratinn.com *Recommended by Michael Doswell, Comus and Sarah Elliott, Mike and Lynn Robinson, Dr Kevan Tucker*

AYCLIFFE
County 🌟 🍴 🛏️

NZ2822   Map 10

The Green, Aycliffe; just off A1(M) junction 59, off A167 at West Terrace and then right to village green; DL5 6LX

Friendly, well run pub with four real ales, good wines and popular, interesting food; bedrooms

Recently refurbished, this remains a smart and very well run place with an emphasis on the particularly good food. That said, locals still like to pop in for a chat at one of the high bar chairs by the counter, where they keep Black Paw IPA, Just a Minute IPA, Marstons EPA and Thwaites Wainwright on handpump, ten wines by the glass and eight malt whiskies. More or less open-plan throughout, it's warmly decorated with red, green or cream paintwork, striped carpeting, contemporary lighting and candlelight. There are painted ceiling joists, a woodburner and open fires, an assortment of chairs from tartan banquettes and dining chairs to cushion-seated wooden ones around a mix of light or dark wood tables and tartan curtains. The wood-floored restaurant is minimalist with high-backed black leather dining chairs and dark window blinds. There are some metal tables and chairs out in front. The bedrooms are individually designed and attractive.

Lovely, well presented food includes sandwiches, asparagus spears with serrano ham and a poached egg, ham hock and rabbit terrine with sorrel vinaigrette, spicy chickpea tagine, beer-battered haddock and chips, pork medallions with black pudding and creamed leeks, chicken with tagliatelle, black trumpet mushrooms, smoked bacon and cheese shavings, king prawns in garlic butter with lemon, and puddings such as passion-fruit cheesecake with mango foam and honeycomb and chocolate parfait with blackberry purée, popcorn and popcorn tuile. *Benchmark main dish: steak in ale pie £12.50. Two-course evening meal £21.00.*

Free house ~ Licensee Colette Farrell ~ Real ale ~ (01325) 312273 ~ Open 11.30-3,
5-midnight; 11am-midnight Sat, Sun ~ Bar food 12-2, 5.30-9; 12-9 Sun ~ Restaurant ~
Children welcome ~ Bedrooms: £49/£70 ~ www.thecountyaycliffevillage.com
Recommended by Pat and Tony Martin, Mike and Lynn Robinson

BLANCHLAND   NY9650 Map 10

Lord Crewe Arms ★ 🎗 ♀ 🍺 🛏

B6306 S of Hexham; DH8 9SP

**Wonderful old building, full of history, with unique Crypt bar, cosy
sitting rooms and big, spacious character restaurant; comfortable,
well equipped bedrooms**

The history and tremendous age of this fine old hotel are reason enough
to visit: it was originally a guesthouse built in 1235 for the neighbouring
Premonstratensian monastery. But the unique Crypt bar is another draw – a
medieval vaulted room sculpted by thick stone walls, lit by candlelight and
popular with local villagers, it has family crests on the ceiling, high wooden
stools by wall shelves and against the armour-plated counter, cushioned
settles and plush stools around a few little tables, and Allendale Golden
Plover, Hadrian & Border Tyneside Blonde, Wylam Red Kite and a beer
named for the inn (Lord Crewe Brew) on handpump, several wines by
the glass, 20 malt whiskies and a farm cider; darts and board games. One
character sitting area has a leather sofa and two big tartan armchairs on
flagstones in front of a big open fire, while the grandly informal restaurant
features a fine old wooden floor, cushioned wall seating and leather-
cushioned dining chairs around oak-topped tables, fresh flowers, antlers
on the walls and a big central candelabra. The bedrooms are lovely.

 Using home-grown produce and their own smokehouse, the delicious food
includes duck egg with spiced buttered shrimps, eggs benedict and cheddar
with mustard mayonnaise on toast, home-cured smoked salmon, barbecue duck salad
with sweet radish and pea shoots, lunchtime burger with toppings and chips, whole
chicken spit-roasted over the open fire with straw chips, veal rump with sage butter,
pork loin chop and cheek with roasted squash, haddock with Morecambe Bay shrimps,
and puddings such as sea buckthorn posset and bakewell pudding with almond
ice-cream. *Benchmark main dish: steak with herb-baked bone marrow £14.75.
Two-course evening meal £16.00.*

Free house ~ Licensee Tommy Mark ~ Real ale ~ (01434) 675469 ~ Open 11-11 ~
Bar food 12-9 ~ Restaurant ~ Children welcome ~ Dogs allowed in bar and bedrooms ~
Wi-fi ~ Bedrooms: £110/£140 ~ www.lordcrewearmsblanchland.co.uk
Recommended by Martin Jones, Toby Jones, Michael Doswell

CARTERWAY HEADS   NZ0452 Map 10

Manor House Inn 🍺

A68 just N of B6278, near Derwent Reservoir; DH8 9LX

**Handy after a walk, with a traditional bar, comfortable lounge,
bar food and five real ales; bedrooms**

If you've been walking around the nearby Derwent Valley and Reservoir,
head to this genuinely friendly and simple slate-roofed stone house for
a rest. Homely and old-fashioned, the locals' bar has an original boarded
ceiling, pine tables, chairs and stools, old oak pews and a mahogany
counter. The carpeted lounge bar (warmed by a woodburning stove) and
restaurant are comfortably pubby with wheelback chairs, stripped-stone
walls and picture windows that make the most of the lovely setting.

There's Copper Dragon Golden Pippin, Greene King Old Speckled Hen and Thwaites Wainwright on handpump alongside ten wines by the glass, 20 malt whiskies and Weston's Old Rosie cider; darts, board games and background music. There are stunning views over the reservoir and beyond from picnic-sets on the terrace.

 Using local suppliers and seasonal game, some kind of food is served all day: sandwiches, tempura prawns with sweet chilli dip, a changing pâté with red onion marmalade, omelettes, cajun-spiced salmon supreme with red wine glaze, cumberland sausages with rich onion gravy, beer-battered cod and chips, chicken stuffed with chorizo mousse and spring onion mash, daily specials, and puddings. *Benchmark main dish: burger with bacon, cheese, chilli, relish and chips £9.95. Two-course evening meal £17.50.*

Enterprise ~ Licensee Chris Baxter ~ Real ale ~ (01207) 255268 ~ Open 11 (12 Mon)-11; 12-10.30 Sun ~ Bar food 12-9 (8 summer Sun, 7 winter Sun) ~ Restaurant ~ Children welcome ~ Dogs allowed in bar and bedrooms ~ Wi-fi ~ Bedrooms: £60/£80 ~ www.themanorhouseinn.com *Recommended by Mike and Lynn Robinson, Michael Doswell*

COTHERSTONE
NZ0119 Map 10
Fox & Hounds 🛏
B6277; DL12 9PF

Bustling 18th-c inn with cheerful beamed bar, good bar food and quite a few wines by the glass; bedrooms

This Georgian country inn occupies an attractive spot by the village green and makes an excellent focal point for walks along the dramatic wooded Tees Valley from Barnard Castle. There's a cheerful, simply furnished beamed bar with a partly wooden floor (elsewhere it's carpeted), a good winter log fire, thickly cushioned wall seats and local photographs and country pictures on the walls of its various alcoves and recesses. Black Sheep and Ringwood Best Bitter on handpump alongside eight wines by the glass and a dozen malt whiskies from smaller distilleries. Don't be surprised by the unusual loo attendant – an african grey parrot called Reva. There are seats outside on a terrace and quoits.

 The well liked food includes sandwiches, wensleydale cheese and hazelnut pâté with caramelised onion relish, smoked mackerel, prawn and salmon fishcake, vegetable bake, steak and black pudding in ale pie, lambs liver with crispy bacon with mustard mash, gammon with tomato and cheese melt, and puddings such as chocolate cheesecake with chocolate cream crunch and sticky toffee pudding. *Benchmark main dish: chicken stuffed with cheese in a creamy leek sauce and wrapped in bacon £10.85. Two-course evening meal £15.50.*

Free house ~ Licensee Ian Swinburn ~ Real ale ~ (01833) 650241 ~ Open 12-3, 6-11 (10.30 Sun) ~ Bar food 12-2, 6-9 ~ Restaurant ~ Children welcome ~ Dogs allowed in bedrooms ~ Wi-fi ~ Bedrooms: £47.50/£75 ~ www.cotherstonefox.co.uk
Recommended by Isobel Mackinlay

DIPTONMILL
NY9261 Map 10
Dipton Mill Inn 🍷 🍴 £
S of Hexham; off B6306 at Slaley; NE46 1YA

Own-brew beers, good value bar food and waterside terrace

With very reasonably priced food and home-brewed beers, this quaint little isolated pub is a winner with our readers. The neatly kept snug bar has genuine character, dark ply panelling, low ceilings, red furnishings, a dark red carpet and two welcoming open fires. All six of the nicely named beers from the family-owned Hexhamshire Brewery are well kept here on handpump: Blackhall English Stout, Devils Elbow, Devils Water, Old Humbug, Shire Bitter and Whapweasel. Also, 14 wines by the glass, more than 20 malt whiskies, Weston's Old Rosie and a guest cider. The garden is peaceful and pretty with its sunken crazy-paved terrace by the restored mill stream and attractive planting; Hexham Racecourse is not far away.

 Incredible value meals includes lots of sandwiches, steak and kidney pie, tomato, bean and vegetable casserole, chicken breast in sherry sauce, duck with orange and cranberries, haddock with tomatoes and basil, beef braised in red wine, and puddings such as creamy lemon tart and fruit crumble. *Benchmark main dish: mince and dumplings £7.50. Two-course evening meal £12.20.*

Own brew ~ Licensee Geoff Brooker ~ Real ale ~ No credit cards ~ (01434) 606577 ~ Open 12-2.30, 6-11; 12-3 Sun; closed Sun evening ~ Bar food 12-2, 6.30-8.30 ~ Children welcome ~ www.diptonmill.co.uk *Recommended by Claes Mauroy, Dr Kevan Tucker, Andy and Jill Kassube, Mike and Lynn Robinson*

DURHAM   NZ2742 Map 10
Victoria ◀
Hallgarth Street (A177, near Dunelm House); DH1 3AS

Unchanging and neatly kept Victorian pub with royal memorabilia, cheerful locals and well kept regional ales; bedrooms

Delightfully unspoilt, this immaculately kept little brick-built local retains its original layout and has been run by the same friendly family for well over 30 years; it's changed little since it was built. Three little rooms lead off a central bar, with typical Victorian décor that takes in mahogany, etched and cut glass and mirrors, colourful William Morris wallpaper over a high panelled dado, some maroon plush seats in little booths, leatherette wall seats and long narrow drinkers' tables. Also, coal fires in handsome iron and tile fireplaces, photographs and articles showing a real pride in the pub, lots of period prints and engravings of Queen Victoria, and staffordshire figurines of her and the Prince Consort. Coniston Bluebird Bitter, Big Lamp Bitter, Saltaire Blonde, Wylam Gold Tankard and a guest from Jarrow on handpump, over 30 irish whiskeys, 50 scottish malts and cheap house wines; dominoes. Credit cards are accepted only for accommodation. No food.

Free house ~ Licensee Michael Webster ~ Real ale ~ No credit cards ~ (0191) 386 5269 ~ Open 12-11; 12-2, 7-10.30 Sun ~ Children welcome ~ Dogs welcome ~ Bedrooms: £55/£78 ~ www.victoriainn-durhamcity.co.uk *Recommended by Richard Tilbrook, Roger and Donna Huggins, Alan and Jane Shaw, Eric Larkham, Edward Leetham, Comus and Sarah Elliott, David Storey*

HALTWHISTLE   NY7166 Map 10
Milecastle Inn £
Military Road; B6318 NE – OS Sheet 86 map reference 715660; NE49 9NN

Cosy little rooms warmed by winter log fires, real ales and straightforward bar food; fine views and walled garden

Just the sort of place in which to warm up after a blowy walk, this solitary 17th-c pub is close to Hadrian's Wall and some wild scenery. The snug little rooms of the beamed bar have two log fires and are decorated with brasses, horsey and local landscape prints and attractive fresh flowers; at lunchtime, the small comfortable restaurant is used as an overflow space. Big Lamp Bitter and Prince Bishop Ale on handpump, a few wines by the glass and a dozen malt whiskies. There are tables and benches in the big sheltered walled garden, with a dovecote and rather stunning views; two self-catering cottages and a large car park. No dogs inside.

🍴 Pubby food includes sandwiches, game pâté, prawn cocktail, lasagne, beer-battered haddock, wild boar and duck pie, gammon with egg and chips, and steaks. *Benchmark main dish: venison casserole £11.95. Two-course evening meal £16.00.*

Free house ~ Licensees Clare and Kevin Hind ~ Real ale ~ (01434) 321372 ~ Open 12-11; 12-3, 6-11 in winter ~ Bar food 12-8.30; 12-2.30, 6-8.30 in winter ~ Restaurant ~ Children welcome ~ Wi-fi ~ www.milecastle-inn.co.uk *Recommended by Martin Jones*

HEDLEY ON THE HILL NZ0759 Map 10

Feathers 🏵 ♀ ◖

Village signposted from New Ridley, which is signposted from B6309 N of Consett; OS Sheet 88 map reference 078592; NE43 7SW

Northumbria Dining Pub of the Year

Imaginative food, interesting beers from small breweries and friendly welcome in quaint tavern

Overlooking the Cheviots, this 200-year-old hilltop tavern is very much the heart of the local community – and much enjoyed by our readers too. The three neat, homely bars are properly pubby with their open fires, tankard-hung beams, stripped stonework, solid furniture including settles, and old black and white photographs of local places and farm and country workers. Friendly knowledgeable staff serve quickly changing local beers such as Allendale Tar Bar'l, Hexhamshire Devils Elbow and Mordue Northumbrian Blonde and Workie Ticket on handpump, as well as six farm ciders, 23 wines by the glass and 30 malt whiskies. They hold a beer and food festival at Easter with over two dozen real ales, a barrel race on Easter Monday and other traditional events; darts, bar billiards, board games and dominoes. The picnic-sets in front are a nice place to sit and watch the world drift by.

🏵 Top class food using the best local produce (rare-breed beef, game from local shoots, carefully sourced fish) includes sandwiches, roe deer and rare-breed pork pâté with pickles, oysters with shallot vinegar, Tabasco and lemon, roast chestnut and leek pie with mushroom gravy, sausages with ale gravy, lamb with provençale-style stuffed tomatoes and marinated roasted peppers, line-caught bass with lobster sauce and fennel salad, and puddings such as gooseberry posset with gooseberry shortbread and dark chocolate brownie with home-made vanilla ice-cream. *Benchmark main dish: haunch of local roe deer with redcurrant jelly £16.00. Two-course evening meal £20.00.*

Free house ~ Licensees Rhian Cradock and Helen Greer ~ Real ale ~ (01661) 843607 ~ Open 6-10.30 Mon; 12-11 (10.30 Sun); closed Mon lunchtime except bank holidays, closed first two weeks Jan ~ Bar food 12-2 (4.30 Sun), 6-8.30; not Mon ~ Children welcome ~ Wi-fi ~ www.thefeathers.net *Recommended by Dr Kevan Tucker, Peter and Eleanor Kenyon, Comus and Sarah Elliott, Mike and Lynn Robinson*

The star-on-a-plate award, 🏵, distinguishes pubs where the food is of exceptional quality. The knife-and-fork symbol just means the pub serves food.

NEWTON
NZ0364 Map 10

Duke of Wellington ♀ 🍺 🛏

Off A69 E of Corbridge; NE43 7UL

Attractively refurbished and extensive old stone pub with modern and traditional furnishings, five real ales, good wines by the glass and highly thought-of food; bedrooms

In an attractive farming hamlet, this extensively refurbished old stone pub has seats on a back terrace with lovely views across the Tyne Valley. Inside, the bustling bar has leather chesterfields, built-in cushioned wall seats, farmhouse chairs and tables on honey-coloured flagstones, a woodburning stove with a shelf of books to one side, and rustic stools against the counter where they keep Consett Ale Works White Hot, Cumberland Corby Ale, Hadrian & Border Tyneside Blonde, Timothy Taylors Landlord and Wylam Collingwood Festival on handpump, a dozen wines by the glass and 12 malt whiskies; TV, darts, dominoes and daily papers. The L-shaped restaurant has elegant tartan and wood dining chairs around pale tables on bare boards, modern art on exposed stone walls, and french windows that lead on to the terrace. Paintwork throughout is contemporary. The bedrooms are well equipped, warm and comfortable. They hold regular wine tasting evenings, and quiz and music nights.

 Using local, seasonal produce, the enjoyable food includes chicken liver foie gras terrine with confit shallots, honey-roast duck salad with pomegranate, orange and pine nut dressing, sausage and mash with rich onion gravy, a pie of the day, twice-baked parmesan and cauliflower soufflé, smoked salmon fishcakes with a poached egg and lemon, chive butter sauce, guinea fowl with sage, onion and parma ham potato cake and tarragon cream sauce, and puddings such as Baileys crème brûlée and dark chocolate cake with kirsch cherries; they also offer a set lunch and an early-bird menu (6-7pm). *Benchmark main dish: beer-battered fish and chips £11.95. Two-course evening meal £20.00.*

Free house ~ Licensee Rob Harris ~ Real ale ~ (01661) 844446 ~ Open 11-11 ~ Bar food 12-9 ~ Restaurant ~ Children welcome ~ Dogs allowed in bar ~ Wi-fi ~ Bedrooms: £95/£120 ~ www.thedukeofwellingtoninn.co.uk *Recommended by Pat and Stewart Gordon, Andy and Jill Kassube, GSB, Dr Peter D Smart*

NEWTON-BY-THE-SEA
NU2424 Map 10

Ship 🍺

Village signed off B1339 N of Alnwick; NE66 3EL

In a charming square of fishermen's cottages close to the beach, good simple food and own-brew beers; best to check winter opening times

'As good as ever,' says a reader who regularly visits this row of converted fishermen's cottages. Their own-brew ales on handpump remain a big draw; these usually include five at any one time from a choice of 20: maybe Ship Inn Dolly Daydream, Hop Ale, Red Herring, Sea Dog and Squid Ink. The plainly furnished but cosy bare-boards bar on the right has nautical charts on dark pink walls, while another simple room on the left has beams, hop bines, some bright modern pictures on stripped-stone walls and a woodburning stove in a stone fireplace; darts, dominoes. It can get extremely busy at peak times, so it's best to book in advance – and there might be a queue for the bar. Tables outside look across the sloping village green to the massive stretch of empty beautiful beach. There's no nearby parking from May to September, but there's a car park up the hill.

🍴 Generous helpings of simple food includes lunchtime sandwiches, kipper pâté, fennel salami and chorizo (made from rare-breed, free-range and local pigs) with home-made piccalilli, moroccan-roasted vegetable tagine with lemon couscous, whole mackerel stuffed with pesto with tomato, basil and garlic salad, local crab on a herb and olive crouton, sirloin steak with onion marmalade, and puddings such as lemon tart with mixed berries and chocolate and pannetone butter pudding. *Benchmark main dish: monkfish with lemon mash and an olive and chilli salsa £14.50. Two-course evening meal £18.50.*

Own brew ~ Licensee Christine Forsyth ~ Real ale ~ No credit cards ~ (01665) 576262 ~ Open 11-11; 12-10.30 Sun; phone for seasonal opening hours in winter ~ Bar food 12-2.30, 7-8; not Sun-Tues evenings ~ Children welcome ~ Dogs welcome ~ Live folk last Mon of month ~ www.shipinnnewton.co.uk *Recommended by David Eberlin, Pat and Tony Martin, Penny and Peter Keevil, Sheila Topham, Comus and Sarah Elliott, P Dawn, Mike and Lynn Robinson, Colin McLachlan, Dr Kevan Tucker*

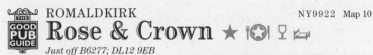

ROMALDKIRK NY9922 Map 10
Rose & Crown ★ 🍴 ♀ 🛏
Just off B6277; DL12 9EB

A civilised base for the area, with accomplished cooking, attentive service and a fine choice of drinks; bedrooms

This handsome 18th-c inn is a lovely place to stay, with plenty to see in the surrounding area. The cosily traditional beamed bar area has lots of brass and copper, old-fashioned seats facing a warming log fire, a Jacobean oak settle, a grandfather clock, and gin traps, old farm tools and black and white pictures of Romaldkirk on the walls. Black Sheep and Thwaites Original and Wainwright on handpump, ten wines by the glass, 14 malt whiskies and organic fruit juices. The hall has farm tools, wine maps and other interesting prints, along with a photograph (taken by a customer) of the Hale-Bopp comet over the interesting old village church. There's also a cosy little snug with sofas and armchairs around a woodburning stove, and an oak-panelled restaurant. Pleasantly positioned tables outside look out to the village green with its original stocks and water pump. The exceptional Bowes Museum and High Force waterfall are nearby, and the owners provide an in-house guide for days out in the area, and a *Walking in Teesdale* book.

🍴 From a seasonally influenced menu, the notably good food includes sandwiches, salt and pepper squid with crispy panko coating and dijon cream, chicken liver parfait with fig and apple chutney, ham hock terrine with a fried duck egg and triple-cooked chips, burger with blue cheese rarebit and chunky ketchup, confit duck leg with apples and a green pepper sauce, trio of lamb (roasted neck end, braised shoulder and kidneys) with pea purée, thai-spiced cod with red curry sauce, and puddings such as salted chocolate tart with chantilly cream and cherry and almond clafoutis with balsamic cream. *Benchmark main dish: beer-battered fish of the day and triple-cooked chips £12.50. Two-course evening meal £20.00.*

Free house ~ Licensee Cheryl Robinson ~ Real ale ~ (01833) 650213 ~ Open 11-11 ~ Bar food 12-2.30, 6.30-9 ~ Restaurant ~ Children welcome but no under-7s after 8pm ~ Dogs allowed in bar and bedrooms ~ Wi-fi ~ Bedrooms: $95/$140 ~ www.rose-and-crown.co.uk *Recommended by Pat and Stewart Gordon, Mr and Mrs P R Thomas, Gordon and Margaret Ormondroyd, Comus and Sarah Elliott*

A star after the name of a pub shows exceptional quality. It means most people (after reading the report to see just why the star has been won) would think a special trip worthwhile.

SEAHOUSES
NU2232 Map 10

Olde Ship ★ ◧ £ ⇌

Just off B1340, towards harbour; NE68 7RD

Lots of atmosphere and maritime memorabilia in busy little inn; views across harbour to Farne Islands; bedrooms

Even at peak times when really busy, the friendly staff in this harbourside stone inn remain helpful and efficient, and our readers enjoy their visits here very much. It's been owned by the same family since it was first licensed in 1812 and the old-fashioned bar has seen a rich assemblage of nautical bits and pieces growing ever since – even the floor is made of scrubbed ship's decking. As well as lots of shiny brass fittings, ship's instruments and equipment, and a knotted anchor made by local fishermen, there are sea pictures and model ships, including fine ones of the North Sunderland lifeboat and the Seahouses' Grace Darling lifeboat. There's also a model of the *Forfarshire*, the paddle steamer that local heroine Grace Darling went to rescue in 1838 (you can read more of the story in the pub), and even the ship's nameboard. An anemometer takes wind speed readings from the top of the chimney. It's all gently lit by stained-glass sea-picture windows, lantern lights and a winter open fire. Simple furnishings include built-in leatherette pews around one end, stools and cast-iron tables. Black Sheep Best, Courage Directors, Greene King Old Speckled Hen and Hadrian & Border Farne Island on handpump, a good wine list and several malt whiskies; background music and TV. The battlemented side terrace (you'll find fishing memorabilia out here too) and one window in the sun lounge look across the harbour to the Farne Islands; if you find yourself here as dusk falls, the light of the Longstones lighthouse shining across the fading evening sky is a charming sight. It's not really suitable for children, though there is a little family room, and they're welcome (as are walkers) on the terrace. You can book boat trips to the Farne Islands at the harbour, and there are bracing coastal walks, particularly to Bamburgh, Grace Darling's birthplace.

The sensibly short choice of food includes sandwiches, duck and orange pâté, prawn cocktail, chicken and mushroom casserole, steak in ale pie, vegetable lasagne, barbecue spare ribs and chips, gammon with pineapple and egg, and puddings such as ginger trifle and strawberry cheesecake. *Benchmark main dish: fresh crab salad £10.75. Two-course evening meal £16.50.*

Free house ~ Licensees Judith Glen and David Swan ~ Real ale ~ (01665) 720200 ~ Open 11-11; 12-11 Sun ~ Bar food 12-2.30, 7-8.30; no evening food Dec-late Jan ~ Restaurant ~ Children allowed in lounge and dining room if eating, but must be over 10 if staying ~ Wi-fi ~ Bedrooms: £47/£94 ~ www.seahouses.co.uk *Recommended by Pat and Tony Martin, Comus and Sarah Elliott, Penny and Peter Keevil, Dr Kevan Tucker, Derek and Sylvia Stephenson, P Dawn, Mike and Lynn Robinson, Colin McLachlan*

STANNERSBURN
NY7286 Map 10

Pheasant £ ⇌

Kielder Water road signposted off B6320 in Bellingham; NE48 1DD

Friendly village inn with quite a mix of customers and homely bar food; streamside garden; bedrooms

Family-run and with the character of an old coaching inn, this is a nice, recently refurbished farmhouse close to Kielder Water. It's cosy and traditional inside; the comfortable, low-beamed lounge has ranks of old local photographs on stripped stone and panelling, brightly polished surfaces, shiny brasses, dark wooden pubby tables and chairs, and upholstered stools ranged along the counter; there are several open fires, darts, TV and background music. The separate public bar is simpler and opens into a further snug seating area with beams and panelling. The friendly licensees and courteous staff serve Timothy Taylors Landlord and a changing guest from Wylam on handpump, half a dozen wines by the glass and 34 malt whiskies. There are picnic-sets in the streamside garden, and a pony paddock too.

Using home-grown and local produce, the popular food includes sandwiches, twice-baked cheese soufflé, chicken liver parfait, game and mushroom pie, fresh crab salad, confit duck breast with berry sauce, salmon with a creamy hot pepper and marmalade sauce, bass with prawn sauce, and puddings such as steamed ginger pudding and brioche and sticky toffee pudding; they can also provide packed lunches. *Benchmark main dish: slow-roasted local lamb with rosemary and redcurrant jus £13.95. Two-course evening meal £18.00.*

Free house ~ Licensees Walter and Robin Kershaw ~ Real ale ~ (01434) 240382 ~ Open 11 (12 Sun)-3, 6-midnight; closed Mon, Tues Nov-Mar ~ Bar food 12-2.30, 6.30-8.30 ~ Restaurant ~ Children welcome ~ Dogs allowed in bedrooms ~ Wi-fi ~ Bedrooms: £70/£90 ~ www.thepheasantinn.com *Recommended by Pat and Stewart Gordon*

WARK
Battlesteads 🍺 🛏
NY8676 Map 10

B6320 N of Hexham; NE48 3LS

Eco pub with good local ales, fair value interesting food and a relaxed atmosphere; comfortable bedrooms

The welcoming owners of this particularly well run inn are extremely conscientious about the environment and gently weave their beliefs into every aspect of their business. They grow their own produce, have a charging point in the car park for electric cars and run a biomass boiler. The nicely restored carpeted bar has a woodburning stove with a traditional oak surround, low beams, comfortable seats including some deep leather sofas and easy chairs, and old *Punch* country life cartoons on the terracotta walls above a dark dado. As well as a dozen or so wines by the glass and a farm cider, they keep five good changing local ales such as Cullercoats Lovely Nelly, Durham Magus, Mordue Workie Ticket and a couple of changing guests on handpump at the heavily carved dark oak bar counter; service is excellent; background music. There's also a restaurant and spacious conservatory, and tables on a terrace. Some of the ground-floor bedrooms have disabled access, and they're licensed to hold civil marriages.

Using carefully sourced local produce (as well as their own), the very good food includes sandwiches, own-made salmon gravadlax with dill cream, pear, walnut and blue cheese salad, deli boards, a pie of the day, wild mushroom and halloumi stack with ginger and chilli oil, sausages with bubble and squeak and onion gravy, dry-cured gammon steak with a free-range egg and pease pudding, chicken, king prawn or vegetable fajitas, and puddings such as gooseberry and apple crumble tart and cheesecake of the day. *Benchmark main dish: cajun salmon with sweet chilli sauce £11.50. Two-course evening meal £18.50.*

Free house ~ Licensees Richard and Dee Slade ~ Real ale ~ (01434) 230209 ~ Open 11-11 ~ Bar food 12-3, 6.30-9 ~ Children welcome ~ Dogs allowed in bar and bedrooms ~ Wi-fi ~ Bedrooms: £70/£115 ~ www.battlesteads.com *Recommended by R L Borthwick, Mike and Lynn Robinson*

It's very helpful if you let us know up-to-date food prices when you report on pubs.

WELDON BRIDGE

NZ1398 Map 10

Anglers Arms

B6344, just off A697; village signposted with Rothbury off A1 N of Morpeth; NE65 8AX

Large helpings of food in appealing bar, real ales and a friendly welcome; bedrooms

'This traditional coaching inn is as enjoyable as ever,' one reader tells us, and others agree. It's always busy with a wide mix of customers – all of whom get a friendly welcome from the helpful staff. The bar is divided into two parts: cream walls on the right; oak panelling, shiny black beams hung with copper pans, and a mantelpiece with staffordshire cats on the left. There's also a grandfather clock, a sofa by a coal fire, old fishing and country prints, a profusion of fishing memorabilia and some taxidermy. Some of the tables are lower than you'd expect for eating, but the chairs have short legs to match (which is different and rather engaging); background music. Shepherd Neame Spitfire, Timothy Taylors Landlord and Wells & Youngs Bitter on handpump, around 36 malt whiskies and decent wines. The attractive garden has tables and a good play area with an assault course. The pub is beside a bridge over the River Coquet and they have fishing rights to a mile of riverbank. The bedrooms are comfortable.

Generously served and well liked, the food includes sandwiches and wraps, kipper salad with a poached egg and caesar dressing, terrine with tomato and onion chutney, chicken with cracked peppercorn sauce, goats cheese risotto, steak in ale pie, salmon fillet with a lemon hollandaise sauce, mixed grill, lambs liver with bacon and gravy, and puddings. *Benchmark main dish: beer-battered cod and chips £11.95. Two-course evening meal £18.00.*

Enterprise ~ Lease John Young ~ Real ale ~ (01665) 570271 ~ Open 11-11; 12-10.30 Sun ~ Bar food 12-9.30 ~ Restaurant ~ Children welcome ~ Dogs allowed in bar and bedrooms ~ Wi-fi ~ Bedrooms: $47.50/$95 ~ www.anglersarms.com *Recommended by WAH, Ian Herdman, Pat and Tony Martin, Mike and Lynn Robinson, Comus and Sarah Elliott*

WINSTON

NZ1416 Map 10

Bridgewater Arms

B6274, just off A67 Darlington–Barnard Castle; DL2 3RN

Carefully renovated former schoolhouse with quite a choice of appealing food, three real ales and seats outside

After a major refurbishment, this converted Victorian schoolhouse is a friendly and relaxed place for both a drink and a meal. The high-ceilinged bar has an open log fire, cushioned settles and chairs, a wall lined with bookcases, and high chairs against the counter where they keep Jennings Cumberland, Timothy Taylors Landlord and a changing guest from Mithril on handpump, a dozen wines by the glass and a dozen malt whiskies. The two rooms of the restaurant have high-backed black leather dining chairs around clothed tables on stripped wooden flooring or tartan carpet, wine bottles lining a delft shelf and various prints and pictures on pale yellow walls. There are some picnic-sets at the front, and the fine old bridge across the River Tees is just a stroll away.

As well as lunchtime sandwiches, the interesting food (with a strong emphasis on fish and shellfish) includes warm duck breast, pancetta and mango salad, queenie scallops with lemon, shallot, basil and parmesan, sausage and mash, rack of lamb with a leek and potato cake and rosemary gravy, cod on spring onion mash with mussels and a curry cream, stir-fried beef with sweet chilli sauce and noodles, bacon-wrapped monkfish on curried prawn risotto, and puddings such as turkish delight ice-cream with chocolate sauce and vanilla panna cotta with roast figs. *Benchmark main dish: bass and king scallops on stir-fried vegetables with lime crème fraîche £23.00. Two-course evening meal £30.00.*

Free house ~ Licensee Paul Grundy ~ Real ale ~ (01325) 730302 ~ Open 12-2.30, 6-11; closed Sun, Mon ~ Bar food 12-2, 6-9 ~ Restaurant ~ Well behaved children welcome ~ Wi-fi ~ www.thebridgewaterarms.com *Recommended by Isobel Mackinlay, Edward May*

Also Worth a Visit in Northumbria

Besides the fully inspected pubs, you might like to try these pubs that have been recommended to us and described by readers. Do tell us what you think of them: feedback@goodguides.com

ACOMB   NY9366
Miners Arms (01434) 603909
Main Street; NE46 4PW Friendly little 18th-c village pub with three real ales and good value traditional food (not Sun evening, Mon) including popular Sun roasts, comfortable settles in carpeted bar, huge fire in stone fireplace, back dining area, folk night first Mon of month, quiz last Thurs; children and dogs welcome, a couple of tables out in front, more in back courtyard, open all day weekends, closed weekday lunchtimes. *(Claes Mauroy, Comus and Sarah Elliott)*

ALLENDALE   NY8355
Golden Lion (01434) 683225
Market Place; NE47 9BD Friendly 18th-c two-room pub with enjoyable good value traditional food, well kept Wylam, Timothy Taylors and three guests, games area with pool and darts, upstairs weekend restaurant, occasional live music; children and dogs welcome, Allendale Fair first weekend June, New Year's Eve flaming barrel procession, open all day. *(Mike and Lynn Robinson)*

ALNMOUTH   NU2410
Sun (01665) 830983
Northumberland Street; NE66 2RA Comfortable banquettes in long low-beamed bar with open fire one end, woodburner the other, carpet or bare boards, decorations made from driftwood, small contemporary dining area, good value traditional food from sandwiches and hot baguettes up, ales such as Black Sheep and Mordue, good coffee, friendly chatty staff; background music; children welcome, attractive seaside village, four bedrooms. *(Comus and Sarah Elliott)*

ALNWICK   NU1911
Hogs Head (01665) 606576
Hawfinch Drive; turn right at BP petrol station; NE66 2BF Newly built pub-hotel

just off the A1 south of Alnwick; large open-plan high-ceilinged interior with exposed brickwork and restful colours, mix of dark wood tables and chairs on light wood floor, some easy chairs and banquettes, plants dotted about, enjoyable fairly traditional food (all day from 7.30am) including specials, children's menu and Sun carvery, well kept local beers such as Hadrian & Border, good attentive young staff; spacious terrace with teak tables under large white parasols, 53 bedrooms. *(Michael Doswell)*

ALNWICK   NU1813
John Bull (01665) 602055
Howick Street; NE66 1UY Popular chatty drinkers' pub, essentially front room of early 19th-c terraced house, good selection of well kept changing ales, real cider, extensive choice of bottled belgian beers and well over 100 malt whiskies; closed weekday lunchtimes. *(Comus and Sarah Elliott)*

ALNWICK   NU1813
Plough (01665) 602395
Bondgate Without; NE66 1PN Smart contemporary pub-boutique hotel in Victorian stone building (now under same management as the Jolly Fisherman at Craster), well kept Timothy Taylors Landlord and a guest in lively front bar, several wines by the glass, good food in bar, bistro or upstairs restaurant, friendly helpful staff; pleasant streetside raised terrace, seven bedrooms, open all day. *(Pat and Tony Martin)*

ALNWICK   NU1813
Tanners Arms (01665) 602553
Hotspur Place; NE66 1QF Welcoming little drinkers' pub with three well kept local ales and a decent glass of wine, flagstones and stripped stone, warm woodburner, plush stools and wall benches, small tree in the centre of the room; juke box and some live acoustic music, TV; dogs welcome, closed lunchtime. *(John Cook)*

AMBLE   NU2604
Wellwood Arms (01665) 714646
High Street, off A1068; NE65 0LD
Refurbished dining pub with good value food
including pub favourites, evening carvery
(all day Sun) and indian menu, ales such as
Timothy Taylors Landlord; children welcome,
four bedrooms, open all day. *(Anon)*

BAMBURGH   NU1834
★Castle (01668) 214616
Front Street; NE69 7BW Clean
comfortably old-fashioned pub with friendly
landlord and staff, well kept ales such as
Hadrian & Border, decent house wines,
winter mulled wine, wide choice of enjoyable
reasonably priced food all day including
good Craster kippers and nice fish and chips,
expanded dining area to cope with summer
visitors, local artwork for sale, open fires;
big courtyard, garden. *(Derek and Sylvia
Stephenson, Comus and Sarah Elliott,
Dennis Jones)*

BAMBURGH   NU1834
Lord Crewe Arms (01668) 214243
Front Street; NE69 7BL Small early 17th-c
hotel prettily set in charming coastal village
dominated by Norman castle; refurbished bar
and restaurant (Wynding Inn) with painted
joists and panelling, bare stone walls and
light wood floor, warm woodburner, beers
from Northumberland and Wells & Youngs,
good food from varied menu including some
interesting choices; sheltered garden with
castle view, short walk from splendid sandy
beach, 17 comfortable bedrooms, good
breakfast. *(Comus and Sarah Elliott, Barry
Collett, Mike and Lynn Robinson)*

BARDON MILL   NY7566
Twice Brewed (01434) 344534
*Military Road (B6318 NE of Hexham);
NE47 7AN* Large busy inn well placed for
fell walkers and major Wall sites, half a dozen
ales including local microbrews and two
badged for them by Yates, 50 rums and
20 malt whiskies, reasonably priced wines,
good value hearty pub food from baguettes
up, quick friendly staff, local photographs
and art for sale; quiet background music,
no dogs; children welcome, picnic-sets in
back garden, 14 bedrooms, open all day.
(Mike and Lynn Robinson)

BARRASFORD   NY9173
★Barrasford Arms (01434) 681237
*Village signposted off A6079 N of
Hexham; NE48 4AA* Highly regarded
cooking from owner-chef at this bustling
sandstone inn including good value set
lunch, nice staff and genuinely local
atmosphere, traditional log-fire bar with
old local photographs and bric-a-brac from
horsebrasses to antlers, up to three ales such
as Sharps and Wylam, two dining rooms, one
with wheelback chairs around neat tables

and stone chimneybreast hung with guns and
copper pans, the second with comfortably
upholstered dining chairs; background music,
TV, darts; children welcome, plenty of nearby
walks and handy for Hadrian's Wall, 11
bedrooms plus a well equipped bunkhouse,
open all day weekends, closed Mon lunchtime
(no food Sun evening). *(Mike and Lynn
Robinson, Michael Doswell)*

BEADNELL   NU2229
Beadnell Towers (01665) 721211
The Wynding, off B1340; NE67 5AY
Large slightly old-fashioned pub-hotel with
unusual mix of furnishings, good food in
bar or restaurant including local game and
fish, two well kept ales such as Allendale
and Hadrian & Border, reasonably priced
wines by the glass and nice coffee, some live
music; can get busy with summer tourists
and booking advised; seats outside, ten
bedrooms. *(Derek and Sylvia Stephenson, John
and Sylvia Harrop, Comus and Sarah Elliott)*

BEADNELL   NU2229
Craster Arms (01665) 720272
The Wynding, off B1340; NE67 5AX
Roomy neatly kept old building with modern
fittings, red banquettes, stripped-brick
and stone walls, popular pubby food and
blackboard specials including local fish/
seafood, well kept Black Sheep and a local
guest, friendly efficient staff, pictures
for sale, July beer and music festival;
background music, TV; children welcome,
dogs in one area, picnic-sets and decking in
big enclosed garden, three good bedrooms,
open all day in summer. *(Derek and Sylvia
Stephenson)*

BEAMISH   NZ2153
★Beamish Mary (0191) 370 0237
*Off A693 signed No Place and
Cooperative Villas, S of museum;
DH9 0QH* Friendly down-to-earth former
pit village inn, eight well kept mainly local
ales, farm cider, big helpings of good home-
made pubby food at bargain prices, coal fires,
two bars with 1960s-feel mix of furnishings,
bric-a-brac, 1920s/30s memorabilia and Aga
with pots and pans, regular live music in
converted stables; sports TV; children till
early evening, bedrooms. *(Mike and Lynn
Robinson, Peter Smith and Judith Brown)*

BEAMISH   NZ2154
Sun (0191) 370 2908
*Far side of Beamish Open Air Museum
– paid entry; DH9 0RG* Edwardian pub
moved from Bishop Auckland as part of the
museum; small front bar with larger back
seating area, authentic period décor and
cheery costumed staff, Stables Beamish
Hall Bitter and one or two guests such as
Theakstons Old Peculier, pickled eggs and
pork pies, big coal fires; children welcome,
lavatories a few yards down the street, open
till 5pm (4pm winter). *(Dennis Jones)*

BERWICK-UPON-TWEED NT9952
Barrels (01289) 308013
Bridge Street; TD15 1ES Small friendly pub with interesting collection of pop memorabilia and other bric-a-brac, eccentric furniture including barber's chair in bare-boards bar, red banquettes in back room, well kept Jarrow Rivet Catcher and four guests, foreign bottled beers, live music (Fri) and DJs (Sat) in basement bar, good quality background music; open all day, from 2pm Jan, Feb. *(Comus and Sarah Elliott, Mike and Lynn Robinson)*

BLYTH NZ2779
Three Horseshoes (01670) 822410
Just off A189, W of town; NE24 4HF Isolated and much-extended building (dates from 1780) perched above dual carriageway, various rooms off central bar (some with view to coast), front conservatory, good reasonably priced often imaginative food (all day Fri-Sun) from sandwiches up, well kept ales such as Adnams, Greene King, High House Farm and Wylam, efficient friendly service; children welcome, covered area outside and good play area, open all day. *(Michael Doswell)*

CATTON NY8257
★ Crown (01434) 683447
B6295, off A686 S of Haydon Bridge; NE47 9QS Friendly 19th-c pub in good walking country; inner bar with stripped stone and bare boards, dark tables, mate's chairs and a traditional settle, coloured lanterns and good log fire, well kept Allendale beers and reasonably priced food (not Sun evening), efficient staff, partly carpeted, lighter extension, interesting local photographs; children and dogs (in bar) welcome, picnic-sets on side terrace and neat small lawn, open all day Fri-Sun, closed Mon. *(Comus and Sarah Elliott)*

CHESTER-LE-STREET NZ2753
Lambton Worm (0191) 387 1162
North Road; DH3 4AJ Interesting building on outskirts with striking union jack front door, spacious bare-boards bar with dark walls and heavily draped windows, comfortable button-back banquettes and some intimate candlelit booths, plenty to look at including pictures fixed to the ceiling and tale of the giant Lambton Worm that once terrorised the area, own Sonnet 43 beers (brewed at sister pub the Clarence Villa at Coxhoe), enjoyable well priced bar food along with à la carte choices, friendly service, large more formal back restaurant with dark half-panelling, ornate gilt ceiling and pictures of film stars and former prime ministers on red walls; live acoustic music Fri; children welcome, open all day. *(Michael Doswell, Comus and Sarah Elliott)*

CHOPPINGTON NZ2583
Swan (01670) 826060
A1068 by level crossing; NE62 5TG Substantial open-plan roadside pub run by hospitable licensees, wholesome carefully prepared food from extensive menu including lunchtime sandwiches and good value deals, well kept Allendale beers from island servery, immaculate interior with padded dining chairs around circular tables on patterned carpet, one or two banquettes and some button-back wing chairs in one corner; bedrooms. *(Michael Doswell)*

CORBRIDGE NY9964
★ Angel (01434) 632119
Main Street; NE45 5LA Imposing coaching inn at end of a broad street facing handsome Tyne bridge; sizeable modernised main bar with light wood tables and chairs and leather wall benches, blue-grey walls, up to six ales such as Allendale, Hadrian & Border and Wylam, Weston's cider, a dozen wines by the glass and 30 malts, popular all-day food (not Sun evening) including interesting specials, efficient uniformed staff, separate oak-panelled lounge with button-back armchairs, sofa and big stone fireplace, daily papers, stripped masonry in raftered back restaurant, evening cocktail bar; children welcome, seats on front cobbles below wall sundial, fine 17th-c arched doorway in left-hand porch, bedrooms, open all day from 7.30am for breakfast (8.30am Sun). *(Eric Larkham, Comus and Sarah Elliott, Mike and Lynn Robinson, Dr Kevan Tucker, GSB and others)*

CORBRIDGE NY9864
★ Black Bull (01434) 632261
Middle Street; NE45 5AT Rambling 18th-c beamed pub with four linked rooms, mix of traditional pub furniture including leather banquettes, wood, flagstone or carpeted floors, log fires (one in open hearth with gleaming copper canopy), ceramic collection in front room and information about Hadrian's Wall, enjoyable pubby food, three Greene King ales and a guest such as Black Sheep, good choice of wines by the glass, efficient friendly service; children welcome, seats out on two-level terrace, open all day. *(Peter and Eleanor Kenyon, Comus and Sarah Elliott, R Anderson)*

CORBRIDGE NY9863
Dyvels (01434) 633633
Station Road; NE45 5AY Comfortable traditional stone inn, friendly and well run, with good value pub food (lunchtime only) from sandwiches up, three or four changing ales and decent wines by the glass; children welcome, no dogs inside, picnic-sets on side terrace and lawn, three bedrooms, open all day. *(Comus and Sarah Elliott)*

CORBRIDGE NY9868
★**Errington Arms** (01434) 672250
About 3 miles N of town; B6318, on A68 roundabout; NE45 5QB Busy 18th-c stone-built pub by Hadrian's Wall attracting good mix of diners and walkers, beamed bars with pine panelling, stone and burgundy walls, farmhouse and other chairs around pine tables on strip-wood flooring, log fire and woodburner, plenty of friendly helpful staff, good choice of well liked fresh food from interesting sandwiches up, Jennings and Wylam ales, several wines by the glass; background music; children welcome, a few picnic-sets out in front, closed Sun evening, Mon. *(Pat and Stewart Gordon)*

CRAMLINGTON NZ2373
Snowy Owl (01670) 736111
Just off A1/A19 junction via A1068; Blagdon Lane; NE23 8AU Large Vintage Inn, relaxed and comfortable, with their usual all-day food, friendly efficient young staff, Black Sheep and a couple of guests, beams, flagstones, stripped stone, soft lighting and an interesting mix of furnishings and decorations, three log fires; background music; disabled access, bedrooms in adjoining Innkeepers Lodge, open all day. *(Comus and Sarah Elliott, Mike and Lynn Robinson)*

CRASTER NU2519
★**Jolly Fisherman** (01665) 576461
Off B1339, NE of Alnwick; NE66 3TR Refurbished and improved under present welcoming management; great spot, long a favourite for its lovely sea and coast views, good food with emphasis on fish/seafood including local crab and good value mixed fishboard, also produce from smokehouse opposite, well kept Black Sheep, Mordue, Timothy Taylors and a guest, good wine list, main bar area with nice open fire, snug, steps up to extended restaurant with picture-window views and seats out on balcony; children and dogs (in bar) welcome, disabled facilities and parking (small car park), beer garden, open all day. *(Janet and Peter Race, Pat and Tony Martin, Comus and Sarah Elliott, Penny and Peter Keevil, John and Sylvia Harrop and others)*

CROOKHAM NT9138
Blue Bell (01890) 820252
Pallinsburn; A697 Wooler–Cornhill; TD12 4SH Welcoming 18th-c roadside country pub with tasty freshly prepared food and well kept ales such as Fyne and Greene King, friendly attentive service; comfortable clean bedrooms, good breakfast. *(Les and Sandra Brown)*

DARLINGTON NZ2814
Number Twenty 2 (01325) 354590
Coniscliffe Road; DL3 7RG Long Victorian pub with bistro feel, high ceiling, bare boards and exposed brickwork, up to

13 quickly changing ales including own Village Brewer range (supplied by Hambleton), draught continentals too, decent food (not Fri and Sat evenings) in compact panelled back room, good friendly service; closed Sun, otherwise open all day. *(WAH)*

DINNINGTON NZ2073
White Swan (01661) 872869
Prestwick Road; NE13 7AG Large open-plan pub very popular for its wide range of competitively priced food including a gluten-free menu, well kept Black Sheep and reasonably priced wines, efficient friendly service even under pressure; children welcome, disabled facilities, new orangery and attractive back garden, handy for Newcastle Airport, open Sun till 6pm, closed Mon evening. *(Michael Doswell)*

DUNSTAN NU2419
Cottage (01665) 576658
Off B1339 Alnmouth–Embleton; NE66 3SZ Comfortable single-storey beamed inn with reasonably priced fairly standard food (smaller helpings available), good service, three well kept ales, restaurant and conservatory; live music and quiz nights, free wi-fi; children and dogs welcome, terrace tables and attractive garden with play area, ten bedrooms, open all day weekends. *(Derek and Sylvia Stephenson)*

DURHAM NZ3136
Clarence Villa (0191) 377 3773
B6291; DH6 4HX Refurbished 19th-c pub back to its original name (was the Kicking Cuddy), own Sonnet 43 beers brewed next door and generous helpings of freshly made pub food including good burgers (try the venison ones), also sandwiches and sharing boards, interesting interior with polished tables, hanging hops and tankards, old bottles and books, a stuffed fish, chainsaw and collection of antlers, snippets of poetry painted on dark green walls, restaurant at back, Fri acoustic music, Sun quiz; open all day. *(Michael Doswell)*

DURHAM NZ2642
Colpitts (0191) 386 9913
Colpitts Terrace/Hawthorn Terrace; DH1 4EG Comfortable two-bar traditional backstreet pub, friendly landlady and locals, cheap well kept Sam Smiths, open fires and original Victorian fittings, back pool room; seats in yard, open all day (from 2pm Mon-Wed). *(Eric Larkham)*

DURHAM NZ2742
Court (0191) 384 7350
Court Lane; DH1 3AW Comfortable 19th-c town pub near law courts; generous helpings of good home-made food from sandwiches and sharing plates to steaks and blackboard specials, two changing local ales, friendly helpful staff, extensive stripped-brick eating area, no mobile phones; background music;

children and dogs welcome, seats outside, smokers' shelter, open (and food) all day. *(Roger and Donna Huggins, Alan and Jane Shaw, Eric Larkham)*

DURHAM NZ2742
★ **Dun Cow** (0191) 386 9219
Old Elvet; DH1 3HN Unchanging backstreet pub in pretty 16th-c black and white timbered cottage, tiny chatty front bar with wall benches, corridor to long narrow back lounge with banquettes, well kept Black Sheep, Camerons and Jennings, good value basic lunchtime snacks, friendly staff; background music; children and dogs welcome, open all day except Sun in winter. *(Eric Larkham)*

DURHAM
Head of Steam (0191) 386 6060
Reform Place, North Road; DH1 4RZ Hidden-away pub close to the river, modern open-plan interior, good range of well kept changing ales, real ciders and plenty of bottled continental beers, competitively priced food till early evening (4pm Sun) including hot dogs and pizzas; background music (live upstairs); outside tables, open all day (till 1am Fri, Sat). *(Peter Smith and Judith Brown, Eric Larkham)*

DURHAM NZ2742
Market Tavern (0191) 386 2069
Market Place; DH1 3NJ Refurbished Taylor Walker pub with decent choice of pubby food, six changing ales and a proper cider, friendly efficient service, popular with students (university folk music night Weds); looks out on marketplace at front and to indoor market at back, open all day. *(Roger and Donna Huggins, Alan and Jane Shaw, Dennis Jones)*

DURHAM NZ2642
Old Elm Tree (0191) 386 4621
Crossgate; DH1 4PS Comfortable friendly old pub on steep hill across from castle, two-room main bar and small lounge, four well kept ales (occasional beer festivals), reasonably priced home-made food, open fires, folk and quiz nights; dogs welcome, small back terrace, open all day. *(Richard Tilbrook, Eric Larkham, Peter Smith and Judith Brown)*

DURHAM NZ2742
Shakespeare (0191) 340 9438
Saddler Street; DH1 3NU Small early 19th-c brick pub retaining some of its original character; compact front bar incorporating the former snug, larger back lounge, Caledonian Deuchars IPA, Fullers London Pride and two guests, friendly staff and locals; children (till 6pm) and dogs welcome, convenient for castle, cathedral and river, can get crowded, usually open all day. *(Dennis Jones)*

DURHAM NZ2742
Swan & Three Cygnets
(0191) 384 0242 *Elvet Bridge; DH1 3AG* Victorian pub in good bridge-end spot high above river, city views from big windows and terrace, bargain lunchtime food and Sam Smiths ales, helpful friendly young staff, popular with locals and students; open all day. *(Mike and Lynn Robinson, Peter Smith and Judith Brown)*

EGGLESCLIFFE NZ4213
Pot & Glass (01642) 651009
Church Road; TS16 9DQ Friendly little village pub with Bass, Black Sheep, Caledonian Deuchars IPA and three guests kept well by enthusiastic landlord, good value straightforward food, folk club and quiz nights; tables on back terrace, lovely setting behind church, open all day Sun, closed Mon lunchtime. *(Taff Thomas)*

EGLINGHAM NU1019
★ **Tankerville Arms** (01665) 578444
B6346 Alnwick–Wooler; NE66 2TX Traditional pub with contemporary touches, cosy friendly atmosphere, beams, bare boards, some stripped stone, banquettes and warm fires, a couple of well kept local ales such as Hadrian & Border, good wines, imaginative nicely presented food from shortish changing menu, raftered split-level restaurant; children and dogs welcome, country views from garden, attractive village, three bedrooms, closed lunchtimes Mon, Tues. *(Comus and Sarah Elliott, John and Sylvia Harrop)*

EMBLETON NU2322
Greys (01665) 576983
Stanley Terrace off W T Stead Road, turn at the Blue Bell; NE66 3UY Warmly welcoming pub with carpeted main front bar, more lived-in part with old photographs and cuttings, cottagey back dining room, open fires, well priced home-made food from sandwiches to local fish, interesting choice of well kept local beers; dogs welcome, small walled back garden, raised decking with village views, open all day. *(David Eberlin, Derek and Sylvia Stephenson, P Dawn)*

ESH NZ1944
Cross Keys (0191) 373 1279
Front Street; DH7 9QR Friendly old village local with hearty helpings of good value freshly made food, half a dozen well kept ales such as Big Lamp, Black Sheep and Shepherd Neame; colourful hanging baskets at front, good country views from behind. *(Michael Doswell)*

FELTON NU1800
Northumberland Arms
(01670) 787370 *West Thirston; B6345, off A1 N of Morpeth; NE65 9EE* Newish owners and stylish refurbishment for this 19th-c inn across road from River

Coquet; beams, stripped stone/brickwork and woodburner in roomy open-plan lounge bar, flagstones and nice mix of furnishings including big sofas, restaurant with mix of light wood tables on bare boards, good sensibly priced food from bar snacks and standard dishes up (best to book), bread from their own bakery, three or four mainly local beers and nice wines by the glass from short well chosen list, efficient friendly service; Thurs quiz, monthly folk night (fourth Tues); children welcome, dogs in bar, six good bedrooms, open (and food) all day. *(Comus and Sarah Elliott, Michael Doswell)*

FROSTERLEY   NZ0236
★ **Black Bull** (01388) 527784
Just off A689 W of centre; DL13 2SL
The only pub we know to have its own peal of bells (licensee is a campanologist); great atmosphere in three interesting traditional beamed and flagstoned rooms with coal fires, landlord's own fine photographs and three grandfather clocks, four well kept local ales, farm cider and perry, carefully chosen wines and malt whiskies, good food using local and organic ingredients (best to book evenings), popular Sun lunch, occasional acoustic live music; well behaved children and dogs welcome, attractive no-smoking terrace with wood-fired bread oven and old railway furnishings (opposite steam station), closed Sun evening to Weds, otherwise open all day. *(John Coatsworth)*

GATESHEAD   NZ2563
Central (0191) 478 2543
Half Moon Lane; NE8 2AN Large 19th-c wedge-shaped pub (Grade II listed) renovated by the Head of Steam chain, great choice of changing local ales, lots of bottled beers, real ciders, low-priced food including themed evenings, upstairs function rooms and roof terrace, live music; open all day (till 1am Fri, Sat). *(Eric Larkham, Dave Webster, Sue Holland, P Dawn, Peter Smith and Judith Brown)*

GREAT WHITTINGTON   NZ0070
Queens Head (01434) 672516
Village signed off A68 and B6018 N of Corbridge; NE19 2HP Handsome golden-stone pub under new owners; dark leather chairs around sturdy tables, some stripped-stone walls and soft lighting, nice hunting mural above old fireplace in long narrow bar, ales such as Black Sheep, High House Farm and Wylam, chinese restaurant at back with modern furnishings; background music; children welcome, dogs in bar, picnic-sets under parasols on little front lawn, closed lunchtimes except Sun. *(Michael Doswell, Mike and Lynn Robinson, GSB)*

GRETA BRIDGE   NZ0813
★ **Morritt** (01833) 627232
Hotel signposted off A66 W of Scotch Corner; DL12 9SE Striking 17th-c country house hotel popular for weddings and the like; properly pubby bar with big windsor armchairs and sturdy oak settles around traditional cast-iron-framed tables, open fires and remarkable 1946 mural of Dickensian characters by JTY Gilroy (known for Guinness advertisements), big windows looking on to extensive lawn, Thwaites Major Morritt (named for them) and Timothy Taylors Landlord, 19 wines by the glass from extensive list, food generally well liked, friendly staff, restaurant; background music; children and dogs (in bar and bedrooms) welcome, attractively laid-out split-level garden with teak tables and play area, open all day. *(Comus and Sarah Elliott, Barry Collett, GSB, S G N Bennett, WAH, Peter and Eleanor Kenyon and others)*

HART   NZ4634
White Hart (01429) 265468
Just off A179 W of Hartlepool; Front Street; TS27 3AW Welcoming end of terrace nautical-theme pub with old ship's figurehead outside, fires in both bars, wide choice of popular traditional food cooked by pleasant landlady, ales such as Copper Dragon; children welcome, no dogs inside, open all day. *(Peter Hacker)*

HARTLEPOOL   NZ5132
Rat Race 07889 828648
Hartlepool Station; TS24 7ED Former station newsagents, one small room (no bar), four well kept regularly changing ales, real cider and perry, you can bring your own food, newspapers; open all day Sat till 9pm, closed Sun, Mon. *(JHBS, P Dawn)*

HARTLEPOOL   NZ4834
Tall Ships (01429) 273515
Middle Warren Local Centre, Mulberry Rise; TS26 0BF Newly built Ember Inn (opened 2008) in lofty position with good views of Hartlepool Bay, spacious open-plan interior, five changing ales (try before you buy), decent all-day food including deals, hard-working staff; tables outside. *(Jeremy King)*

HAYDON BRIDGE   NY8364
★ **General Havelock** (01434) 684376
A69 Corbridge–Haltwhistle; NE47 6ER Old stone pub, a short stroll downstream from Haydon Bridge itself; best part of L-shaped bar is the back with interestingly shaped mahogany-topped tables, long pine benches with colourful cushions and pine

---

Real ale to us means beer that has matured naturally in its cask – not pressurised or filtered.

chest of drawers topped with bric-a-brac, good wildlife photographs, ales from Geltsdale and High House Farm, nine wines by the glass, traditional food (not Sun evening), stripped-stone barn dining room and terrace with fine South Tyne river views; children welcome, dogs in bar, closed Mon. *(Anon)*

HEBBURN
White Lead (0191) 489 4656
Blackett Street; NE31 1ST Recently revamped by Sonnet 43, their beers and enjoyable food including good value set menu, friendly staff, live music Sat; children welcome, outside seating on large deck, open all day. *(Gemma Malloy)*

HEDDON-ON-THE-WALL NZ1366
Swan (01661) 853161
The Towne Gate; NE15 0DR Big open-plan stone-built chain dining pub, bar to the left away from two more contemporary dining areas, good choice of food including bargain daily carvery, three real ales (usually one from Wylam), pleasant young staff; free wi-fi; children welcome, large informal garden with Tyne Valley views, open all day. *(Jeremy King)*

HIGH HESLEDEN NZ4538
Ship (01429) 836453
Off A19 via B1281; TS27 4QD Half a dozen good value changing ales from the region, log fire, sailing ship models including big one hanging with lanterns from boarded ceiling, enjoyable bar food cooked by landlady along with some interesting restaurant dishes; yacht and shipping views from car park, six bedrooms in new block, closed Mon. *(JHBS, P Dawn)*

HOLWICK NY9126
Strathmore Arms (01833) 640362
Back road up Teesdale from Middleton; DL12 0NJ Attractive and welcoming old stone-built country pub in beautiful scenery just off Pennine Way, real ales including a house beer (Strathmore Gold) brewed by Allendale, low-priced traditional food all day, home-baked bread, beams, flagstones and open fire, live music Fri, quiz first Weds of month; free wi-fi; well behaved dogs welcome, popular with walkers, four bedrooms and campsite, closed Tues. *(Roxanne Chamberlain)*

HOLY ISLAND NU1241
Crown & Anchor (01289) 389215
Causeway passable only at low tide, check times (01289) 330733; TD15 2RX Comfortably unpretentious pub-restaurant by the priory, enjoyable fairly traditional home-made food including vegetarian choices and specials (maybe local oysters), well kept Caledonian Deuchars IPA and Wells & Youngs Bombardier, welcoming helpful staff, compact bar with open fire, roomy modern back dining room; children and dogs welcome, garden with lovely views

(may ask for a credit card while you eat), four bedrooms. *(Sheila Topham)*

HOLY ISLAND NU1241
Ship (01289) 389311
Marygate; TD15 2SJ Nicely set pub (busy in season), beamed bar with wood floors, stone walls and maritime memorabilia, big stove, steps down to carpeted lounge/dining area, fairly pubby menu including fish/seafood, Hadrian & Border Holy Island Blessed Bitter badged for the pub plus one or two guests, 30 malt whiskies; background music; children welcome and usually dogs (but ask first), sheltered sunny garden, four bedrooms, may close at quiet times. *(Dennis Jones)*

HORSLEY NZ0965
Lion & Lamb (01661) 852952
B6528, just off A69 Newcastle–Hexham; NE15 0NS 18th-c former coaching inn; main bar with scrubbed tables, stripped stone, flagstones and panelling, four changing ales and a real cider (maybe a blackberry one), decent choice of good food from sandwiches and hearty traditional choices up including summer seafood and winter game, also tapas and good value early-bird deal, efficient service, bare-boards restaurant; children and dogs (not evenings) welcome, Tyne views from attractive garden with roomy terrace, good play area, open all day. *(Comus and Sarah Elliott, Michael Doswell)*

HURWORTH-ON-TEES NZ2814
★Bay Horse (01325) 720663
Church Row; DL2 2AQ Popular dining pub (best to book, particularly weekends) with top notch imaginative food, quite pricey but they also do a fixed-price lunch menu, children's choices too, three changing ales, smiling efficient young staff, sizeable bar with good open fire, restaurant; seats on back terrace and in well tended walled garden beyond, charming village by River Tees, open all day. *(Anon)*

HURWORTH-ON-TEES NZ3110
Otter & Fish (01325) 720019
Off A167 S of Darlington; Strait Lane; DL2 2AH Pleasant village setting and up-to-date open-plan layout, comfortable armchairs and sofas by bar, nice mix of dining furniture, some wall banquettes, flagstones and stripped wood, good well presented local food (wise to book especially weekends) including set deals, good wine selection, ales such as Black Sheep, open fires and church candles; closed Sun evening. *(Richard Tilbrook, Comus and Sarah Elliott)*

KENTON BANKFOOT NZ2068
Twin Farms (0191) 286 1263
Main Road; NE13 8AB Good roomy Fitzgerald pub in elegant period-rustic style, recycled stone, timbers etc, real fires, several pleasant softly lit areas off central

bar, enjoyable food from sandwiches to imaginative specials, well kept changing ales (including local ones) and good selection of wines by the glass, quick friendly service; background music; children welcome, disabled facilities, garden and terrace, handy for A1 and airport, open all day. *(Michael Doswell, Comus and Sarah Elliott)*

LANGDON BECK NY8531
Langdon Beck Hotel
(01833) 622267 *B6277 Middleton–Alston; DL12 0XP* Isolated unpretentious inn with two cosy bars and spacious lounge, well placed for walks including Pennine Way, Jarrow and a guest ale (late May beer festival), good choice of enjoyable generous food using local Teesdale beef and lamb, decent coffee, friendly helpful staff; interesting rock collection in 'geology room'; wonderful fell views from garden, seven bedrooms, open all day, closed Mon in winter. *(Roxanne Chamberlain, Comus and Sarah Elliott)*

LANGLEY ON TYNE NY8160
Carts Bog Inn (01434) 684338
A686 S, junction B6305; NE47 5NW Isolated moorside pub with heavy beams and stripped stone walls, old photographs, lovely open fire, good range of enjoyable generous food from sandwiches up including signature Bog Pie and popular Sun lunch (best to book), two or three well kept local ales, friendly efficient young staff, games room with pool and darts; children and dogs welcome, picnic-sets in big garden with views, quoits, open all day weekends, closed Mon. *(Anon)*

LESBURY NU2311
Coach (01665) 830865
B1339; NE66 3PP Picturesque stone pub at heart of pretty village; contemporary paintwork throughout the low-beamed rooms, pubby tables and chairs on tartan carpet, dark leather stools by counter serving Black Sheep, part off to left with sofas and armchairs, small dining room and a further seating area with woodburner and tub-like chairs; background music, TV; children welcome in dining areas till 7.30pm, seats out in front and on neat terrace, pretty flowering tubs and baskets, handy for Alnwick Castle, open all day. *(Comus and Sarah Elliott)*

LONGBENTON NZ2768
Benton Ale House (0191) 266 1512
Front Street; NE7 7XE Friendly two-bar suburban pub with up to nine Marstons-related ales from horseshoe counter, good well priced simple food; background music, TV; children welcome, disabled facilities, open all day. *(Eric Larkham)*

LONGFRAMLINGTON NU1301
Village Inn (01665) 570268
Just off A697; Front Street; NE65 8AD Friendly 18th-c stone inn arranged into

three distinct areas; tasty freshly prepared pub food including good Sun carvery, own-brewed VIP beers along with local guests, good coffee, some live music, Mon quiz; comfortable bedrooms and self-catering cabins (just outside the village), open all day. *(Michael Doswell, Cliff Sparkes)*

MICKLETON NY9724
Crown (01833) 640381
B6277; DL12 0JZ Cleanly refurbished bar area with woodburner and view into kitchen, popular well priced food including specials, up to four real ales and good wines by the glass, friendly staff; children and dogs welcome, garden picnic-sets, self-catering unit and small campsite, good local walks, open (and food) all day. *(Comus and Sarah Elliott)*

MICKLEY NZ0761
Blue Bell (01661) 843146
Mount Pleasant, off A695 Prudhoe–Stocksfield; NE43 7LP Small open-plan pub with good choice of hearty blackboard food, two well kept ales such as Cumberland and Everards, friendly chatty staff and relaxed rural atmosphere (though on edge of built-up area), spic-and-span interior with bold contrasting colours and roaring fire. *(Michael Doswell)*

MIDDLETON NZ0685
Ox (01670) 772634
Village signed off B6343, W of Hartburn; NE61 4QZ Warmly welcoming Georgian country pub in small tucked-away village, a couple of ales such as Acton and Wylam, tasty straightforward home-made food; children and dogs welcome, handy for Wallington (NT), closed weekday lunchtimes. *(Rupert and Joey Stubbs)*

MILFIELD NT9333
Red Lion (01668) 216224
Main Road (A697 Wooler–Cornhill); NE71 6JD Comfortable 17th-c coaching inn with good fairly priced food including popular Sun carvery, OAP lunch Thurs, four well kept ales including Black Sheep, a dozen wines by the glass and decent coffee, friendly helpful service, Weds quiz; children welcome, pretty garden by car park at back, two bedrooms, good breakfast. *(Comus and Sarah Elliott, J F M and M West, John and Sylvia Harrop, Mrs Carolyn Dixon)*

MORPETH NZ1986
★ Tap & Spile (01670) 513894
Manchester Street; NE61 1BH Consistently welcoming, cosy and easy-going two-room pub, up to seven ales such as Caledonian, Everards, Hadrian & Border and Mordue, Weston's Old Rosie cider and country wines, short choice of good value lunchtime food Fri and Sat, traditional pub furniture and interesting old photographs, quieter back lounge (children allowed here)

with coal-effect gas fire, board and other games, good local folk music Sun afternoon, Mon quiz night; unobtrusive background music, sports TV and quiz machine; dogs welcome in front bar, open all day Fri-Sun. *(Eric Larkham, Mike and Lynn Robinson)*

NETHERTON NT9807
Star (01669) 630238
Off B6341 at Thropton, or A697 via Whittingham; NE65 7HD Simple unchanging village local under charming long-serving landlady (licence has been in her family since 1917), friendly regulars, a changing ale served by jug from hatch in small entrance lobby, only bottled beers in winter, large high-ceilinged room with wall benches, many original features; no food, music, children or dogs; open evenings only from 7.30pm, closed Mon and Thurs. *(P Dawn)*

NEW YORK NZ3269
★**Shiremoor Farm** (0191) 257 6302
Middle Engine Lane; at W end of New York A191 bypass turn S into Norham Road, then first right (pub signed); NE29 8DZ Large, interesting pub cleverly converted from former derelict agricultural building; spacious well divided interior with beams and joists (the conical rafters of a former gin-gan in one part), broad flagstones, several kilims and mix of unusual furniture, farm tools, shields, swords and country pictures; extremely popular fair-priced food, quieter bar with ales such as Cullercoats, Mordue and Timothy Taylors, ten wines by the glass; seats outside on covered heated terrace, open all day. *(Toby Jones, Harvey Brown, Mike and Lynn Robinson)*

NEWBIGGIN-BY-THE-SEA NZ3188
Queens Head (01670) 817293
High Street; NE64 6AT Unchanging Edwardian pub with good friendly landlord and thriving local atmosphere, high-ceilinged rooms and cosy back snug, well kept low-priced beers (pump clips displayed from previous guests), original features including curved bar, mosaic floors and etched windows, lots of old local photographs, dominoes; dogs allowed in some parts, open all day. *(Anon)*

NEWBROUGH NY8768
Red Lion (01283) 575785
Stanegate Road; NE47 5AR Light airy refurbishment and buoyant atmosphere, log fire, flagstones and half-panelling, old local photographs plus some large paintings, good locally sourced food (not Sun evening) in bar and two dining areas, bargain OAP meals and popular Sun roasts, well kept ales such as Hadrian & Border and Mordue, friendly staff, games room with pool and darts, some live

music; children welcome, dogs too outside of food times, garden with play area, good local walks (leaflets provided), on NCN cycle route 72, four bedrooms, open all day. *(Comus and Sarah Elliott)*

NEWBURN NZ1665
★**Keelman** (0191) 267 0772
Grange Road: follow Riverside Country Park brown signs off A6085; NE15 8ND Former 19th-c pumping station with eight well kept Big Lamp beers (brewed on site), relaxed atmosphere and good mix of customers in airy high-ceilinged bar with lofty arched windows, well spaced tables and chairs, more seating in upper gallery, fair value traditional food served by friendly staff, modern dining conservatory; background music, free wi-fi; picnic-sets, tables and benches on spacious terraces among flower tubs and shrub beds, good play area, comfortable bedrooms, open all day. *(Eric Larkham, David Heath, P Dawn, Mike and Lynn Robinson, Peter Smith and Judith Brown)*

NEWCASTLE UPON TYNE NZ2464
★**Bacchus** (0191) 261 1008
High Bridge E, between Pilgrim Street and Grey Street; NE1 6BX Smart, spacious and comfortable with ocean liner look, ship and shipbuilding photographs, good value lunchtime food from sandwiches and panini to a few pubby main meals, Sun roasts, nine very well kept changing ales (beer festivals), plenty of bottled imports, farm cider and decent coffee, friendly helpful staff, can get very busy; background music; disabled facilities, handy for Theatre Royal, open all day. *(Comus and Sarah Elliott, Eric Larkham, Gordon, P Dawn, Mike and Lynn Robinson and others)*

NEWCASTLE UPON TYNE NZ2464
Bodega (0191) 221 1552
Westgate Road; NE1 4AG Majestic Edwardian drinking hall next to Tyne Theatre; Big Lamp, Durham and six guest ales, real cider, friendly service, colourful walls and ceiling, bare boards, snug front cubicles, spacious back area with two magnificent stained-glass cupolas; background music, machines, big-screen TV, very busy on match days; open all day. *(Eric Larkham, P Dawn, Mike and Lynn Robinson)*

NEWCASTLE UPON TYNE NZ2468
Brandling Arms (0191) 285 4023
High Street, Gosforth; NE3 1HD Relaxed modernised place attracting broad mix of customers and at its busiest evenings and weekends, good range of real ales and other drinks, enjoyable food from open-view kitchen including sharing boards and home-made burgers, good value weekday set menu, board games such as 'Gosworth Monopoly',

There are report forms at the back of the book.

Weds quiz; TV, free wi-fi; children welcome till 8pm, tables out in front, no-smoking beer garden behind, open all day. *(Eric Larkham)*

NEWCASTLE UPON TYNE NZ2563
Bridge (0191) 261 9966
Under the Tyne bridge; NE1 3UF Newly opened conversion of the old Newcastle Arms – same owners as the Town Wall; airy interior with brick walls and lots of wood, industrial-style ceiling, view into back microbrewery (joint venture with Wylam), ten ales including guests (sampling trays available), affordable all-day food (till 7pm Fri-Sun) including some imaginative choices; well behaved children and dogs welcome before 7pm, heated terrace, open all day (till 1am Fri, Sat). *(Michael Doswell, Comus and Sarah Elliott, Eric Larkham)*

NEWCASTLE UPON TYNE NZ2563
★ Bridge Hotel (0191) 232 6400
Castle Square, next to high-level bridge; NE1 1RQ Big, well divided, high-ceilinged bar around servery with replica slatted snob screens, Black Sheep, Caledonian Deuchars IPA and seven guests kept well, real cider, friendly staff, bargain generous lunchtime food (not weekends), magnificent fireplace, great river and bridge views from raised back area, live music upstairs including long-standing Mon folk club; background music, sports TV, games machines; flagstoned back terrace overlooking part of old town wall, open all day. *(Eric Larkham, Derek Wason, P Dawn, Mike and Lynn Robinson, Peter Smith and Judith Brown, Roger and Donna Huggins and others)*

NEWCASTLE UPON TYNE NZ2563
Broad Chare (0191) 211 2144
Broad Chare, just off quayside opposite law courts; NE1 3DQ Traditional feel although only recently converted to a pub (was a café), british-leaning food from bar snacks such as crispy pigs ears and Lindisfarne oysters to venison and trotter pie and steaks, four real ales including a house beer from Wylam (Writer's Block), good choice of bottled beers, wines and whiskies, bare-boards bar and snug, old local photographs, upstairs dining room; background music; children welcome till 7pm (later upstairs), no dogs, next door to the Live Theatre, open all day (no food Sun evening). *(Eric Larkham, Andy and Jill Kassube, Comus and Sarah Elliott, Roger and Donna Huggins)*

NEWCASTLE UPON TYNE NZ2464
Centurion (0191) 261 6611
Central Station, Neville Street; NE1 5HL Glorious high-ceilinged Victorian décor with tilework and columns in former first-class waiting room, well restored with comfortable leather seats giving club-like feel, Black Sheep, Caledonian Deuchars IPA , Jarrow Rivet Catcher and a couple of guests, farm

cider, friendly staff; background music, big-screen sports TV; useful café/deli next door, open all day. *(Eric Larkham)*

NEWCASTLE UPON TYNE NZ2664
★ Cluny (0191) 230 4474
Lime Street; NE1 2PQ Bar-café-music venue in interesting 19th-c mill/warehouse (part of the Head of Steam group); good value home-made food all day from massive sandwiches up, cheerful staff, up to eight well kept ales, some exotic beers and rums, sofas in comfortable raised area with daily papers and art magazines, back gallery featuring local artists; background music and regular live bands (also in Cluny 2 next door); children welcome till 7pm, picnic-sets out on green, striking setting below Metro bridge, parking nearby can be difficult, open all day. *(Eric Larkham, Comus and Sarah Elliott)*

NEWCASTLE UPON TYNE NZ2563
★ Crown Posada (0191) 232 1269
The Side; off Dean Street, between and below the two high central bridges (A6125 and A6127); NE1 3JE City's oldest pub, just a few minutes' stroll from the castle; long narrow room with elaborate coffered ceiling, stained-glass counter screens and fine mirrors with tulip lamps on curly brass mounts (matching the great ceiling candelabra), long green built-in leather wall seat flanked by narrow tables, old photos of Newcastle and plenty of caricatures, Allendale, Hadrian & Border, Highland, Titanic and Wylam, may do sandwiches, heating from fat low-level pipes, music from vintage record player; no credit cards; well behaved children in front snug till 6pm, open all day (midnight Fri, Sat) and can get packed at peak times. *(Eric Larkham, Dave Webster, Sue Holland, P Dawn, Peter Smith and Judith Brown, Roger and Donna Huggins)*

NEWCASTLE UPON TYNE NZ2664
Cumberland Arms (0191) 265 6151
James Place Street; NE6 1LD Friendly, unspoilt and traditional, seven particularly well kept mainly local ales including a house beer from Wylam, six farm ciders/perries, two annual beer festivals, limited choice of good value pubby food, obliging staff, open fires, events most nights including live music (regular ukulele band); dogs welcome, tables out overlooking Ouseburn Valley, four bedrooms, open all day weekends, from 3pm other days. *(Eric Larkham, Mike and Lynn Robinson)*

NEWCASTLE UPON TYNE NZ2470
Falcons Nest (0191) 236 7078
Rotary Way, Gosforth (handy for racecourse); NE3 5EH Roomy Vintage Inn with comfortable traditional-style linked rooms, their usual food from sandwiches up including good value weekday set menu till 5pm, pleasant staff, good choice of wines by

the glass, well kept Black Sheep and a couple of guests; children welcome, tables out on terrace and lawn, open all day. *(Gerry and Rosemary Dobson, Mike and Lynn Robinson)*

NEWCASTLE UPON TYNE NZ2664
Free Trade (0191) 265 5764
St Lawrence Road, off Walker Road (A186); NE6 1AP Splendidly basic unpretentious pub with outstanding views up river from big windows, terrace tables and seats on grass, up to nine ales including Mordue, real ciders and plenty of bottled beers and whiskies, good sandwiches/pasties, original Formica tables and coal fire, free juke box, warm friendly atmosphere; steps down to back room and lavatories; open all day. *(Eric Larkham, Mike and Lynn Robinson, Peter Smith and Judith Brown, Roger and Donna Huggins, Comus and Sarah Elliott)*

NEWCASTLE UPON TYNE NZ2463
Town Wall (0191) 232 3000
Pink Lane; across from Central Station; NE1 5HX Newish pub in handsome listed building, warm friendly welcome, spacious bare-boards interior with dark walls, button-back banquettes and mix of well spaced tables and chairs, pictures in heavy gilt frames, up to 12 ales including one badged for them, good choice of bottled beers and wines by the glass, fairly simple well priced food including burgers and pub favourites, all day brunch, basement overspill/function room; background music; well behaved children and dogs welcome, open all day (till 1am Fri, Sat). *(Eric Larkham, Andy and Jill Kassube, Mike and Lynn Robinson, Peter Smith and Judith Brown, Roger and Donna Huggins)*

NEWCASTLE UPON TYNE NZ2068
Twin Farms (0191) 286 1263
Main Road, Kenton Bank Foot; NE13 8AB Comfortable Fitzgerald pub in former stone farmhouse, good choice of beers including Black Sheep and Caledonian Deuchars IPA, enjoyable food from sharing boards to blackboard specials, open fires; Mon quiz; children welcome, disabled facilities, picnic-sets on sunny terrace, open (and food) all day. *(Eric Larkham)*

NEWTON ON THE MOOR NU1705
★ Cook & Barker Arms
(01665) 575234 *Village signed from A1 Alnwick–Felton; NE65 9JY* Nicely traditional stone-built country inn, beamed bar with stripped-stone and partly panelled walls, broad-seated settles around oak-topped tables, horsebrasses, coal fires, Black Sheep, Timothy Taylors and a guest beer, extensive wine list, good popular food using meat from own farm (set deals Mon, Tues lunchtime, early evenings Weds and Thurs), friendly staff, separate restaurant with french windows opening on to terrace; background music, TV, no dogs; children welcome, 18 comfortably refurbished

bedrooms, Boxing Day hunt starts here, open all day. *(Les and Sandra Brown, Comus and Sarah Elliott)*

NEWTON-BY-THE-SEA NU2325
★ Joiners Arms (01665) 576112
In village by turning to Linkhouse; NE66 3EA Refurbished open-plan village pub-restaurant run by enthusiastic couple; flagstoned bar with big front windows and open fire, dining area behind, good imaginative well presented food all day from interesting sandwiches and sharing plates up, takeaway fish and chips too, real ales such as Hadrian & Border and Mordue plus carefully chosen wines, cheerful helpful service from uniformed staff; children and dogs welcome, picnic-sets out in front and behind, good coastal walks, five stylish bedrooms, open all day. *(Frances Gill, Comus and Sarah Elliott, GSB, Emma Beacham)*

NORTH SHIELDS NZ3568
Quay Taphouse (0191) 259 2023
Bell Street; NE30 1HF Clean and airy quayside pub with good value food including sharing platters and tapas, a couple of changing ales, several wines by the glass and decent coffee, quick friendly service; children welcome, open all day. *(Eric Larkham)*

NORTH SHIELDS NZ3668
Staith House (0191) 270 8441
Fish Quay/Union Road; NE30 1JA Newly opened dining pub (former Dolphin), relaxed and comfortable, with good food cooked by chef-owner from sensibly short menu including some interesting takes on familiar dishes, well kept Caledonian Deuchars IPA and Theakstons, friendly enthusiastic staff, attractive interior blending stripped wood, brickwork and stone, deep button-back banquettes and assorted tables and chairs, ships' lamps and old photos of the Tyne, woodburner; picnic-sets outside, open all day, no food Sun evening. *(Michael Doswell)*

PONTELAND NZ1771
Badger (01661) 867931
Street Houses; A696 SE, by garden centre; NE20 9BT Refurbished early 18th-c Vintage Inn with warren of rooms and alcoves, good log fire, well kept beers such as Black Sheep and Timothy Taylors, decent range of wines by the glass, their usual all-day food; background music; children welcome. *(Peter and Eleanor Kenyon, Martin Day)*

PONTELAND NZ1773
Blackbird (01661) 822684
North Road opposite church; NE20 9UH Imposing ancient stone pub refurbished under new management; open-plan interior with mix of furniture including several high tables, button-back banquettes, wood, slate and tartan-carpeted floors, striking old map of Northumberland and etching of

Battle of Otterburn either side of fireplace, larger stone fireplace in unusual Tunnel Room, generous good value pubby food from sandwiches and wraps up, well kept ales including one badged for them, friendly service, Weds quiz; TVs; children welcome, picnic-sets out in front, open all day (till midnight Fri, Sat). *(Michael Doswell, Mike and Lynn Robinson)*

RENNINGTON NU2118
★ **Horseshoes** (01665) 577665
B1340; NE66 3RS Comfortable family-run pub with nice local feel (may be horses in car park), well kept ales including Hadrian & Border and decent wines by the glass, ample helpings of enjoyable locally sourced food, friendly efficient service, simple neat bar with flagstones and woodburner, carpeted restaurant, darts; children welcome, tables out in front, attractive quiet village near coast, Aug scarecrow competition, closed Mon. *(P Dawn)*

SHINCLIFFE NZ2940
Seven Stars (0191) 384 8454
High Street N (A177 S of Durham); DH1 2NU Comfortable and welcoming 18th-c village inn, varied choice of good generous food from pub favourites up including deals, three well kept ales, coal-effect gas fire in lounge bar, panelled dining room; children in eating areas, dogs in bar, some picnic-sets outside, eight bedrooms, open all day. *(John and Sylvia Harrop)*

SLAGGYFORD NY6754
Kirkstyle (01434) 381559
Just N, signed off A689 at Knarsdale; CA8 7PB Welcoming 18th-c country pub in lovely spot looking over South Tyne Valley to hills beyond; good reasonably priced food (not Mon) including some interesting specials, well kept Yates and a guest, dining room, games area with darts and pool; dogs very welcome, quoits team, handy for Pennine Way, Cycle Way, South Tyne Trail and South Tynedale Railway (Lintley terminus), closed Sun evening, Mon lunchtime, and may shut from 9pm if quiet. *(Anon)*

SLALEY NY9757
Rose & Crown (01434) 673996
Church Close; NE47 0AA 17th-c pub now owned by the village, local ales such as Allendale and enjoyable good value home-made food from sandwiches up, beams and log fires; children and dogs welcome, garden with long country views, two bedrooms, open all day in summer. *(Phil and Jane Hodson)*

SLALEY NY9658
★ **Travellers Rest** (01434) 673231
B6306 S of Hexham (and N of village); NE46 1TT Attractive and busy stone-built

country pub, spaciously opened up, with farmhouse-style décor, beams, flagstones and polished wood floors, huge fireplace, comfortable high-backed settles forming discrete areas, friendly uniformed staff, popular good value food (not Sun evening) in bar or quieter dining room, good children's menu, real ales such as Allendale, Black Sheep and Wylam; dogs welcome, tables outside with well equipped adventure play area on grass behind, three good value bedrooms, open all day. *(WAH, Andy and Jill Kassube, Comus and Sarah Elliott)*

SOUTH SHIELDS NZ3567
Alum Ale House (0191) 427 7245
Ferry Street (B1344); NE33 1JR Welcoming traditional 18th-c bow-windowed pub adjacent to North Shields ferry, wide choice of well kept ales, bare boards, coal fire in old range, music and quiz nights; beer garden, handy for marketplace, open all day. *(Eric Larkham)*

SOUTH SHIELDS NZ3566
Steamboat (0191) 454 0134
Mill Dam/Coronation Street; NE33 1EQ Friendly 19th-c corner pub with eight well kept changing ales, lots of nautical bric-a-brac, bar ceiling covered in flags, raised seating area and separate lounge; near river and marketplace, open all day. *(Roger and Donna Huggins, Alan and Jane Shaw)*

STANLEY NZ2054
South Causey (01207) 235555
South Causey Farm, off Causey Road; DH9 0LS Stone-built family-run inn by riding school in 100-acre grounds, beams, oak floors, open fires and eclectic mix of old furniture, wide choice of popular food including very good value weekday lunchtime carvery, Wells & Youngs Bombardier and two local ales kept well, good service; children welcome, dogs allowed in one area, picnic-sets outside, small farm with alpacas, goats etc, 28 bedrooms, open (and food) all day. *(Anon)*

STANNINGTON NZ2179
★ **Ridley Arms** (01670) 789216
Village signed off A1 S of Morpeth; NE61 6EL Extended village pub handy for A1; several separate areas, each with different mood and style, proper front bar area with log fire and cushioned settles, stools along counter serving Anarchy Blonde Star and guests, a dozen wines by the glass, enjoyable reasonably priced pubby food, pleasant helpful staff, several dining areas with comfortable upholstered bucket chairs around dark tables on bare boards or carpet, cartoons and portraits on cream, panelled or stripped-stone walls; background music,

---

We say if we know a pub has background music.

free wi-fi; children welcome, good disabled access, picnic-sets in front and on back terrace, open all day. *(Derek and Sylvia Stephenson, GSB, Comus and Sarah Elliott)*

TYNEMOUTH   NZ3669
Hugos at the Coast (0191) 257 8956
Front Street; NE30 4DZ Popular Sir John Fitzgerald pub with open-plan split-level interior, four changing ales and good choice of wines, bar food from sandwiches up, reasonable prices; TV, darts, Weds quiz; some pavement seats, open all day, food till 6pm (4pm Sun). *(Eric Larkham)*

TYNEMOUTH   NZ3669
Priory (0191) 257 8302
Front Street; NE30 4DX Good friendly atmosphere in this rather quirky place; mismatched furniture including union jack sofas on bare boards, lots of pictures on grey and red walls, various odds and ends including the front of a Mini (working headlights) suspended above the entrance, Black Sheep, Mordue and a house beer from Jarrow, bargain pubby food from sandwiches and baked potatoes up, weekend live music; dogs welcome (treats for good ones), café-style pavement tables, open all day (till 1am Fri, Sat). *(Comus and Sarah Elliott)*

WARENFORD   NU1429
White Swan (01668) 213453
Off A1 S of Belford; NE70 7HY Simply decorated friendly bar with a couple of changing ales such as Greene King and Hadrian & Border, steps down to cosy restaurant with good carefully presented imaginative food, efficient helpful service, warm fires; children and dogs (in bar) welcome, open all day Sun. *(Janet and Peter Race)*

WEST BOLDON   NZ3460
Red Lion (0191) 536 4197
Redcar Terrace; NE36 0PZ Bow-windowed, flower-decked family-run pub, hop-strung beamed bar with open fire, ales such as Black Sheep from ornate wood counter, separate snug and conservatory dining room, good choice of well priced pubby food, friendly smiling service; seats out on back decking, open all day. *(Roger and Donna Huggins)*

WHALTON   NZ1281
Beresford Arms (01670) 775225
B6524; NE61 3UZ Pub-restaurant in attractive village, reliable reasonably priced food including set deals, well kept Timothy Taylors Landlord, friendly helpful staff, high-backed chairs at sturdy candlelit pine tables, tartan carpet, old photographs; children welcome, four comfortable bedrooms, closed Sun evening, Mon (shuts 10pm other days). *(Michael Doswell)*

WHITFIELD   NY7857
Elks Head (01434) 345282
Off A686 SW of Haydon Bridge; NE47 8HD Extended old stone inn attractively set in steep wooded valley, light and spacious, with bar and two dining areas, good value mainly pubby food along with some interesting game dishes, two local ales and several wines by the glass; children welcome, picnic-sets in small pretty front garden by little river, scenic area with good walks, ten bedrooms (some in adjacent cottage). *(Dr Kevan Tucker)*

WHITLEY BAY   NZ3473
Briar Dene (0191) 252 0926
The Links; NE26 1UE Smart brightly decorated two-room pub, fine sea-view spot, up to eight interesting changing ales, good value pubby food till 3pm (4pm weekends) from sandwiches up, friendly efficient staff; children welcome, seats outside, open all day. *(Eric Larkham, Mike and Lynn Robinson)*

WHITLEY BAY   NZ3571
Rockliffe Arms (0191) 253 1299
Algernon Place; NE26 2DT Backstreet Sir John Fitzgerald pub with four well kept changing ales, a good refuge from busy town centre; open all day. *(Eric Larkham)*

WOOLER   NT9928
Tankerville Arms (01668) 281581
A697 N; NE71 6AD Pleasant, if slightly dated, hotel bar in early 17th-c coaching inn, relaxed and friendly, with reasonably priced food including local meat and fish, two changing ales (often Hadrian & Border) and a dozen wines by the glass, jugs of Pimms, small restaurant and larger airy one overlooking nice garden, big log fire; disabled facilities, 16 bedrooms, good local walks, open all day. *(John and Sylvia Harrop)*

WYLAM   NZ1164
★ Boathouse (01661) 853431
Station Road, handy for Newcastle–Carlisle rail line; across Tyne from village (and Stephenson's birthplace); NE41 8HR Convivial two-room pub with a dozen real ales, 15 ciders (some tapped from cellar) and good choice of malt whiskies, some snacky food, helpful young staff, open stove in bright low-beamed bar, fortnightly buskers' night Tues; juke box; children and dogs welcome, seats outside, close to station and river, open all day (evenings can be very busy). *(Eric Larkham, Mike and Lynn Robinson, Comus and Sarah Elliott)*

Nottinghamshire

BLYTH SK6287 Map 7

White Swan

High Street; S81 8EQ

Bustling village pub with both locals and visitors, cosy rooms, real ales and well liked food

Handy for the A1, this is an attractive pub on the edge of a village green. And although this is a proper community pub with plenty of cheerful locals, visitors are also given a warm welcome by the hands-on licensees and their helpful staff. There are beams and exposed brickwork, flagstones and carpeting, and a mix of dining chairs and padded banquettes around an assortment of tables. Adnams Broadside, Fullers London Pride and Theakstons Black Bull on handpump, seven wines by the glass and half a dozen malt whiskies. The live music events are extremely good and popular. There are seats in the little back garden.

🍴 Using local, seasonal produce, the wide choice of good food includes lunchtime sandwiches, warm bacon and stilton salad with cider chutney, calamari with garlic mayonnaise, sharing boards, three cheese and vegetable pie, burgers with salsa and chips, gammon with egg and pineapple, chicken in smoked bacon, mozzarella and barbecue sauce, steaks with a choice of sauces, and puddings. *Benchmark main dish: beef, mushroom and stilton pie £9.95. Two-course evening meal £15.00.*

Enterprise ~ Tenant Adam Kay ~ Real ale ~ (01909) 591222 ~ Open 12-11 ~ Children welcome ~ Wi-fi ~ Live acoustic music monthly Fri; jazz monthly Sun lunch ~ www.whiteswaninnblyth.co.uk *Recommended by Caroline Prescott, Mike Swan*

CAYTHORPE SK6845 Map 7

Black Horse 🍺 £

Turn off A6097 0.25 miles SE of roundabout junction with A612, NE of Nottingham; into Gunthorpe Road, then right into Caythorpe Road and keep on; NG14 7ED

Quaintly old-fashioned little pub brewing its own beer, simple interior and enjoyable homely food; no children, no credit cards

The same friendly family have run this 300-year-old country local for three generations and it remains as popular as ever for their own-brewed ales and good value food. The uncluttered carpeted bar has just five tables, brocaded wall banquettes and settles, decorative plates on a delft shelf, a few horsebrasses on the ceiling joists, and a coal fire. Cheerful regulars might occupy the few bar stools to enjoy the Caythorpe Bitter and seasonal ale that are brewed in outbuildings here, and served alongside a couple of guests such as Bass, Greene King IPA and Sharps Doom Bar on handpump; 11 wines by the glass too. Off the front corridor is a partly panelled inner room with a wall bench running all the way around three unusual long copper-topped tables, and there are several old local photographs; darts and board games. Down on the left, an end room has just one huge round table. There are some seats outside, and the River Trent is fairly close for waterside walks.

 Cooked by the landlady (you need to book a table in advance), the good value food includes sandwiches, plenty of fresh cod, haddock and plaice, omelettes, local sausages with onion gravy, grilled lamb chops, and puddings such as sticky toffee pudding and apple pie. *Benchmark main dish: fresh fish of the day £10.00. Two-course evening meal £15.00.*

Own brew ~ Licensee Sharron Andrews ~ Real ale ~ No credit cards ~ (0115) 966 3520 ~ Open 12-2.30, 5.30-11.30; 12-5, 8-11.30 Sun; closed Mon except bank holidays ~ Bar food 12-1.45, 6-8.30; not Sat evening or Sun ~ Dogs allowed in bar ~ www.caythorpebrewery.co.uk/the_black_horse *Recommended by P Dawn*

COLSTON BASSETT
SK6933   Map 7

Martins Arms ⭐ ♀ ◖

Village signposted off A46 E of Nottingham; School Lane, near market cross in village centre; NG12 3FD

Nottinghamshire Dining Pub of the Year

Smart dining pub with impressive food, good range of drinks including seven real ales and attractive grounds

Most customers in this lovely country pub tend to head to the elegant restaurant to enjoy the top class, imaginatively presented food in civilised surroundings. There's a comfortably relaxed atmosphere, warm log fires in Jacobean fireplaces, fresh flowers and candlelight – and it's all smartly decorated with period fabrics and colours, antique furniture and hunting prints. Neatly uniformed staff serve Bass, Greene King IPA, Marstons Pedigree, Timothy Taylors Landlord and a couple of guests from brewers such as Belhaven and Castle Rock on handpump, as well as 19 wines by the glass or carafe (including prosecco, champagne and sweet wines), Belvoir organic ginger beer and 16 malt whiskies. The lawned garden (summer croquet here) backs on to National Trust parkland, and readers recommend visiting the church opposite and Colston Bassett Dairy, which produces and sells its own stilton cheese, and is just outside the village.

Using the best local produce and game, the excellent food includes sandwiches, duck liver parfait with pear and cinnamon chutney, poached egg royale with smoked salmon, hollandaise and toasted muffin, burger with their own cured bacon, stilton and triple-cooked chips, arancini with mushroom fricassée and quails egg, monkfish with bombay potato terrine, minted yoghurt and aubergine sambal oelek, duck with sweet potato fondant, star anise carrots and coriander caramel, and puddings such as golden syrup sponge with muscovado custard and chocolate torte with frothy hot chocolate mocha. *Benchmark main dish: braised lamb shoulder with crispy sweetbread and hash browns £17.95. Two-course evening meal £20.00.*

Free house ~ Licensees Lynne Strafford Bryan and Salvatore Inguanta ~ Real ale ~ (01949) 81361 ~ Open 12-3, 6-11; 12-4, 7-10.30 Sun ~ Bar food 12-2, 6-9; not Sun evening ~ Restaurant ~ Children welcome ~ Wi-fi ~ Local bands on bank holidays ~ www.themartinsarms.co.uk *Recommended by Mike and Mary Carter, P Dawn, Ian Herdman*

MORTON
Full Moon ◗

SK7251 Map 7

Pub and village signed off Bleasby–Fiskerton back road, SE of Southwell;
NG25 0UT

Five real ales and good food at stylish village local with play area in nice garden

Both the enjoyable food and well kept ales attract customers to this attractive old brick pub tucked away in a remote hamlet not far from the River Trent. There are some comfortable armchairs, two roaring fires, pale cream paintwork and simple furnishings such as an eclectic mix of tables and chairs, with high-backed wooden or upholstered dining chairs around wooden tables in the restaurant. Timothy Taylors Landlord and guests such as Acorn Barnsley Bitter, Dukeries Blonde and Navigation Pale Ale on handpump and nine wines by the glass; background music and board games. There are picnic-sets at the front, more on a peaceful back terrace and sizeable lawn and some sturdy play equipment.

Highly thought-of food includes lunchtime sandwiches, smoked haddock and spring onion soufflé with pea velouté, chicken and leek terrine, sausages with mash and braised onions, goats cheese and pea risotto with lemon oil, steak in ale pie, burger topped with bacon, stilton and red onion marmalade, slow-roast pork belly with sweet potato and roast juices, salmon with beetroot mayonaise and salsa verde, and puddings such as lemon posset with blackcurrant sorbet and warm chocolate fondant pudding with banana ice-cream and chocolate oil. *Benchmark main dish: beer-battered fish and chips £8.95. Two-course evening meal £15.00.*

Free house ~ Licensee David Newby ~ Real ale ~ (01636) 830251 ~ Open 11-3, 5.30-11.30; 10-midnight Sat; 10-10 Sun ~ Bar food 12-2.30, 5.30-9; 12-9 Sat; 12-4 Sun ~ Children welcome ~ Dogs allowed in bar ~ Wi-fi ~ www.thefullmoonmorton.co.uk
Recommended by Margaret Tait, P Dawn

Also Worth a Visit in Nottinghamshire

Besides the fully inspected pubs, you might like to try these pubs that have been recommended to us and described by readers. Do tell us what you think of them: feedback@goodguides.com

AWSWORTH   SK4844
Gate (0115) 932 9821
Main Street, via A6096 off A610 Nuthall–Eastwood bypass; NG16 2RN
Friendly Victorian free house with six well kept ales (usually Blue Monkey and Burton Bridge), cosy bar, coal fire in lounge, small pool room, some snacks, refurbished skittle alley; children welcome till 8pm, dogs in bar, disabled facilities, picnic-sets out in front, near site of once-famous railway viaduct, open all day (till 1am Fri, Sat). *(P Dawn)*

BAGTHORPE   SK4751
Dixies Arms (01773) 810505
A608 towards Eastwood off M1 junction 27, right on B600 via Sandhill Road, left into School Road; Lower Bagthorpe; NG16 5HF Friendly unspoilt 18th-c beamed and tiled-floor local with D H Lawrence

connections, well kept Greene King Abbot, Theakstons Best and a guest, no food, good fire in small part-panelled parlour's fine fireplace, entrance bar with tiny snug, longer narrow room with toby jugs, darts and dominoes, live music Sat, quiz Sun; children and dogs (on leads) welcome, big garden with play area, open all day. *(Anon)*

BEESTON   SK5236
Crown (0115) 925 4738
Church Street; NG9 1FY Owned and sensitively restored by Everards, real ale enthusiast landlord serving up to 14 (some keenly priced), also real ciders, perry and good choice of bottled beers (regular beer festivals), no hot food but fresh cobs and other snacks; front snug and bar with quarry-tiled floor, carpeted parlour with padded wall seats, Victorian décor and new polished bar in lounge, beams, panelling,

bric-a-brac, old red telephone box; terrace tables, open all day. *(P Dawn)*

BEESTON   SK5336
★**Victoria** (0115) 925 4049
Dovecote Lane, backing on to railway station; NG9 1JG Genuine down-to-earth all-rounder attracting good mix of customers, up to 15 real ales (regular beer festivals), two farm ciders, 120 malt whiskies and 30 wines by the glass, good value interesting food (half the menu is vegetarian), friendly efficient service, three fairly simple unfussy rooms with original long narrow layout, solid furnishings, bare boards and stripped woodwork, stained-glass windows, open fires, newspapers and board games, live music (Sun, Mon evening Oct-May); children welcome till 8pm, dogs in bar, seats out on covered heated area overlooking platform (trains pass just a few feet away), limited parking, open all day. *(David Hunt, Derek and Sylvia Stephenson, P Dawn)*

BINGHAM   SK7039
★**Horse & Plough** (01949) 839313
Off A52; Long Acre; NG13 8AF Former 1818 Methodist chapel with low beams, flagstones and stripped brick, prints and old brewery memorabilia, comfortable open-plan seating including pews, well kept Caledonian Deuchars IPA, Thwaites Wainwright and four guests (tasters offered), real cider, good wine choice, enjoyable reasonably priced home-made weekday bar food, popular upstairs grill room (Tues-Sat evenings, all day Sun) with polished boards, hand-painted murals and open kitchen; background music; children and dogs welcome, disabled facilities, open all day. *(P Dawn)*

BLEASBY   SK7149
Waggon & Horses (01636) 830283
Gypsy Lane; NG14 7GG Popular early 19th-c pub with six real ales including Blue Monkey, carpeted lounge/dining room, character bar, snug with leather sofas and armchairs, good value home-made pub food (not Sun evening, Mon, Tues); background music, darts; children, dogs and muddy boots welcome, tables on front terrace and in back garden, good local walks, open all day weekends, closed lunchtimes Mon-Weds. *(Steve and Irene Homer)*

BRAMCOTE   SK5037
White Lion (0115) 925 7841
Just off A52 W of Nottingham; Town Street; NG9 3HH Small 18th-c pub (some recent refurbishment) with well kept Greene King ales from bar serving two split-level adjoining rooms, low-priced pubby food

including Wed curry and Sun roasts, darts and dominoes, quiz nights; children welcome, tables in garden behind, open all day. *(Anon)*

BUNNY   SK5829
Rancliffe Arms (0115) 984 4727
Loughborough Road (A60 S of Nottingham); NG11 6QT Substantial early 18th-c former coaching inn reworked with emphasis on linked dining areas, upscale food from enterprising sandwich range to adventurous dishes, also good carvery (Mon evening, Weds, Sat and Sun), prompt friendly service, chunky country chairs around mixed tables on flagstones or carpet, well kept Marstons-related ales in comfortable log-fire bar with sofas and armchairs; children welcome, decking outside, open all Fri-Sun. *(Gerry and Rosemary Dobson)*

CAR COLSTON   SK7242
Royal Oak (01949) 20247
The Green, off Tenman Lane (off A46 not far from A6097 junction); NG13 8JE Good, well priced, traditional food (not Sun evening) in biggish 19th-c pub opposite one of England's largest village greens, four well kept ales including Marstons and Brakspears, decent choice of wines by the glass, woodburner in lounge bar with tables set for eating, public bar with unusual barrel-vaulted brick ceiling, spotless housekeeping; children welcome, picnic-sets on spacious back lawn, heated smokers' den, camping, open all day Fri-Sun. *(P Dawn)*

CAUNTON   SK7459
★**Caunton Beck** (01636) 636793
Newark Road; NG23 6AE Cleverly reconstructed low-beamed dining pub made to look old using original timbers and reclaimed oak; scrubbed pine tables and country-kitchen chairs, open fire, three ales and over two dozen wines by the glass, well presented popular food from breakfast on, decent coffee and daily papers, relaxed atmosphere with cheerful obliging staff; children welcome, dogs in bar, seats on flowery terrace, open all day from 8.30am, handy for A1. *(David and Ruth Hollands, Ray and Winifred Halliday, G Jennings, W J Taylor)*

EAST BRIDGFORD   SK6943
Reindeer (01949) 829336
Kneeton Road, a mile from A6075, can also be reached from A46; NG13 8PH Village pub under new management, well kept ales such as Batemans, Greene King and Sharps, enjoyable sensibly priced pub food (not Sun evening), beamed main bar and lounge, theatre/cinema and art gallery; children (till 9pm) and dogs welcome,

various pub animals including dogs, horses and chickens, views from garden, open all day. *(Anon)*

EDWINSTOWE SK6266
Forest Lodge (01623) 824443
Church Street; NG21 9QA Friendly 18th-c inn with enjoyable home-made food in pubby bar or restaurant, good service, well kept Wells & Youngs Bombardier and four regularly changing guests (usually one from Welbeck Abbey), log fire; children welcome, 13 bedrooms, handy for Sherwood Forest. *(Derek and Sylvia Stephenson)*

FARNDON SK7652
★ Boathouse (01636) 676578
Off A46 SW of Newark; keep on towards river – pub off Wyke Lane, just past the Riverside pub; NG24 3SX Big-windowed contemporary bar-restaurant overlooking the Trent, emphasis on food but Greene King IPA and a guest served from stylish counter, good choice of wines, main area indeed reminiscent of a boathouse with high ceiling trusses supporting bare ducting and scant modern decoration, second dining area broadly similar, modern cooking along with some pubby dishes, early-bird deal, neat young staff; background and live music (Sun), free wi-fi; children welcome, wicker chairs around teak tables on terrace, own moorings, open all day. *(David Hunt)*

GRANBY SK7436
★ Marquis of Granby (01949) 859517
Off A52 E of Nottingham; Dragon Street; NG13 9PN Popular and friendly 18th-c pub in attractive Vale of Belvoir village, tap for Brewsters with their ales and interesting guests from chunky yew bar counter, no food apart from Fri evening fish and chips, two small comfortable rooms with broad flagstones, some low beams and striking wallpaper, open fire; children and dogs welcome, open from 4pm Mon-Fri, all day weekends. *(Anon)*

GRINGLEY ON THE HILL SK7390
Blue Bell (01777) 816303
High Street, just off A361 Bawtry–Gainsborough; DN10 4RF Open-plan village pub on several levels, pale painted beams, bare boards and striped carpeting, smart high-backed leather dining chairs and wall seats, open fires, good choice of food (not Sun evening, Mon) including so-called 'black rock' grills at your table, Theakstons Best and Wychwood Hobgoblin, Thatcher's cider, live folk and jazz sessions, Tues quiz; children welcome, picnic-sets and play fort in back garden, open all day (from 3pm Mon). *(Anon)*

HARBY SK8870
★ Bottle & Glass (01522) 703438
High Street; village signed off A57 W of Lincoln; NG23 7EB Civilised dining pub with pair of bay-windowed front bars,

attractive pubby furnishings, lots of bright cushions on built-in wall benches, arts-and-crafts chairs, dark flagstones and red walls, log fire, splendid range of wines (big vineyard map of Côte de Beaune in left-hand bar), Black Sheep and a couple of guests such as Tom Woods, good country cooking all day including set menu, friendly attentive service, small area with squashy sofas and armchairs and more formal restaurant; children welcome, dogs in bar, modern wrought-iron furniture on back terrace, picnic-sets on grass beyond, open all day. *(Anon)*

HOCKERTON SK7156
Spread Eagle (01636) 812019
A617 Newark–Mansfield; NG25 0PL Small village pub with linked rooms, well kept Timothy Taylors Landlord and three guests, nine wines by the glass and good pub food including a few daily specials, friendly efficient staff, log fire and woodburner; children welcome, open all day Fri, Sat, till 9pm Sun, closed Mon. *(John Wooll)*

HOVERINGHAM SK6946
Reindeer (0115) 966 3629
Main Street; NG14 7GR Beamed pub with intimate bar and busy restaurant (best to book), good home-made food (not Sun evening) from standards to more enterprising dishes, good value lunchtime set menu, Black Sheep, Castle Rock Harvest Pale and two guests, good wines by the glass, log fire; children welcome, seats outside overlooking cricket pitch, open all day weekends, closed lunchtimes Mon and Tues. *(P Dawn)*

KIMBERLEY SK4944
★ Nelson & Railway (0115) 938 2177
Station Road; handy for M1 junction 26 via A610; NG16 2NR Comfortable beamed Victorian pub in same family for over 40 years; well kept Greene King ales and guests, mix of Edwardian-looking furniture, brewery prints (was tap for defunct Hardys & Hansons Brewery) and railway signs, dining extension, traditional games including alley and table skittles; juke box, games machine; children and dogs allowed, nice front and back gardens, 11 good value bedrooms, open all day. *(Anon)*

KIMBERLEY SK5044
Stag (0115) 938 3151
Nottingham Road; NG16 2NB Friendly 18th-c traditional local spotlessly kept by good landlady, two cosy rooms, small central counter and corridor, low beams, dark panelling and settles, table skittles and working vintage slot machines, old Shipstones Brewery photographs, well kept Adnams, Timothy Taylors Landlord and three guests (May beer festival), no food; children and dogs welcome, attractive back garden with play area, opens 5pm (1.30 Sat, 12 Sun). *(Anon)*

LAMBLEY
SK6345
Woodlark (0115) 931 2535
Church Street; NG4 4QB Welcoming and
interestingly laid-out village local, neatly
furnished bare-brick beamed bar, careful
extension into next house giving comfortable
lounge/dining area, popular good value
freshly made food, downstairs steak bar
(Fri, Sat evenings), well kept Castle Rock,
Sam Smiths, Timothy Taylors Landlord and
a guest, open fire; children and dogs
welcome, tables on side terrace, open all
day. *(Dru and Louisa Marshall)*

LAXTON
SK7266
★ **Dovecote** (01777) 871586
Off A6075 E of Ollerton; NG22 0NU
Red-brick pub handy for A1; cosy country
atmosphere in three traditionally furnished
dining areas, well liked food including
notable steak and ale pie and good value Sun
lunch, Castle Rock, Fullers and a couple of
guests, farm cider and several wines by the
glass, friendly efficient staff; background
music; children welcome, no dogs inside,
small front terrace and sloping garden with
views towards church, interesting village that
still strip farms, two bedrooms, open all day
Sun. *(Margaret Tait, David and Ruth Hollands,
Pat and Stewart Gordon, Howard and Margaret
Buchanan)*

LOWDHAM
SK6646
Worlds End (0115) 966 3857
Plough Lane; NG14 7AT Small 18th-c
village pub with long carpeted beamed
bar/dining room, enjoyable traditional
home-made food (all day Fri, Sat, not Sun
evening), friendly service, three changing
real ales from brick-faced counter, open fire;
background music; children welcome, some
covered seats out at front among colourful
tubs and baskets, picnic-sets on lawned area,
open all day. *(Richard Stanfield)*

MANSFIELD
SK5561
Il Rosso (01623) 623031
Nottingham Road (A60); NG18 4AF
Restaurant pub with enjoyable italian-
influenced food including good fresh fish,
takeaway pizza too, four well kept changing
ales, good service, regular live acoustic
music (Mon jazz); free wi-fi; children
welcome, no dogs inside, terraces front
and back, open all day from 8.30am for
breakfast. *(Anon)*

MANSFIELD
SK5363
Railway Inn (01623) 623086
*Station Street; best approached by
viaduct from near Market Place;
NG18 1EF* Friendly traditional local with
long-serving landlady, three changing ales,
real cider and good bottled beer choice,
bargain home-made food (till 5pm Sun),
two little front rooms leading to main bar,
another cosy room at back, laminate flooring

throughout; children and dogs welcome,
small courtyard and beer garden, handy for
Robin Hood Line station, open all day.
(P Dawn)

MANSFIELD WOODHOUSE SK5463
Greyhound (01623) 464403
High Street; NG19 8BD Friendly 17th-c
village local with up to half a dozen well
kept ales including Adnams and Caledonian
Deuchars IPA (beer festivals), cosy lounge,
darts, dominoes and pool in busy public
bar, regular quiz nights, no food apart from
snacks; dogs welcome, open all day. *(P Dawn)*

MAPLEBECK
SK7160
★ **Beehive**
*Signed down pretty country lanes from
A616 Newark–Ollerton and from A617
Newark–Mansfield; NG22 0BS*
Unpretentious little beamed country tavern
in nice spot, chatty landlady, tiny front bar
with slightly bigger side room, traditional
furnishings and antiques, open fire, well
kept Maypole and guests, no food; tables on
small terrace with flower tubs and grassy
bank running down to stream, summer
barbecues, play area, may be closed weekday
lunchtimes in winter, busy weekends and
bank holidays. *(David and Ruth Hollands)*

NEWARK
SK7954
Castle (01636) 640733
Castle Gate; NG24 1AZ Spotless old low-
ceilinged pub (part of the Yard Glass group),
five or so well kept ales including Sharps
Doom Bar and a house brew from Oldershaw,
bare-boards front room, long panelled and
carpeted back one, old wooden furniture,
lots of mirrors and prints, darts, no food but
can eat in next-door sister pub (the Mayze);
piped and live music, no children; open
all day. *(P Dawn)*

NEWARK
SK8053
Fox & Crown (01636) 605820
Appleton Gate; NG24 1JY Open-plan
bare-boards Castle Rock pub with their
well priced ales and guests from central
servery, four ciders and dozens of whiskies,
vodkas and other spirits, decent wines
by the glass too, friendly obliging staff,
inexpensive food from rolls and baked
potatoes up, several side areas; background
music (live Fri); dogs welcome, children in
dining room, good wheelchair access, open
all day. *(P Dawn)*

NEWARK
SK7953
Just Beer 07983 993747
*Swan & Salmon Yard, off Castle Gate
(B6166); NG24 1BG* Welcoming one-room
micropub tucked down alley, four or five
interesting quickly changing beers from
brick bar, real cider/perry, no other alcoholic
drinks or food apart from cheeseboard,
bright airy minimalist décor with some
brewery memorabilia, half a dozen tables

on stone floor, eclectic mix of customers; dogs welcome, open all day (from 1pm weekdays). *(P Dawn)*

NEWARK SK7953
Prince Rupert (01636) 918121
Stodman Street, off Castle Gate; NG24 1AW Ancient renovated timber-framed pub near market, several small rooms on two floors, beams, exposed brickwork and many original features (some previously covered up), nice old furniture including high-backed settles, conservatory, five real ales such as Blue Monkey, Oakham and Thornbridge, Weston's cider, blackboard choice of wines by the glass, pubby food plus speciality pizzas with some unusual toppings and other imaginative food, friendly staff, live music most weekends; dogs welcome, courtyard with old enamel signs, open all day (till 1am Fri, Sat). *(David and Ruth Hollands, P Dawn)*

NORMANTON ON
THE WOLDS SK6232
Plough (0115) 937 2401
Off A606 5 miles S of Nottingham; NG12 5NN Ivy-clad pub on edge of village, warm and welcoming, with good freshly made food from extensive menu including nice steaks, five real ales such as Fullers London Pride, Theakstons Best and Wells & Youngs Bombardier, friendly uniformed staff, fires in bar and restaurant; soft background music; children welcome, big garden with play area and summer barbecues. *(David and Sue Atkinson, Phil and Jane Hodson)*

NORTH MUSKHAM SK7958
Muskham Ferry (01636) 704943
Ferry Lane, handy for A1 (which has small sign to pub); NG23 6HB Traditional pub in splendid location on River Trent with relaxing views from panelled bar-restaurant, fairly priced food including children's meals and Sun roast, Greene King Abbot, Sharps Doom Bar and a couple of other well kept ales, good wine and soft drinks choice, friendly chatty staff; piped radio, games machine, pool; dogs welcome, terrace overlooking water, moorings, open all day. *(Anon)*

NOTTINGHAM SK5739
Approach (0115) 950 6149
Friar Lane; NG1 6DQ Big open-plan pub attracting younger crowd, wood floor with raised carpeted areas, some high tables and mix of seating including banquettes and leather sofas, Navigation ales and a guest from long wooden servery, good wine range, enjoyable food, comedy and music nights; background music, sports TVs and silent

fruit machine; open all day (till 2am Fri Sat, 6pm Sun). *(P Dawn)*

NOTTINGHAM SK5739
★ Bell (0115) 947 5241
Angel Row; off Market Square; NG1 6HL Deceptively large pub with late Georgian frontage concealing two 500-year-old timber-framed buildings; front Tudor Bar with café feel in summer when french windows open to pavement tables, bright blue walls with glass panels protecting patches of 300-year-old wallpaper; larger low-beamed Elizabethan Bar with half-panelled walls, maple parquet flooring and upstairs Belfry with more heavy panelling and 15th-c crown post; up to a dozen real ales from remarkable deep sandstone cellar, ten wines by the glass, reasonably priced straightforward bar food, welcoming staff; piped and regular live music including trad jazz, TV, silent fruit machine; children welcome in some parts, open all day (till 1am Sat). *(David Hunt, P Dawn)*

NOTTINGHAM SK5843
Bread & Bitter (0115) 960 7541
Woodthorpe Drive; NG3 5JL In former suburban bakery still showing ovens, three bright and airy bare-boarded rooms, around a dozen well kept ales including Castle Rock, farm cider and decent wine choice, reasonably priced pub food from cobs to specials, friendly staff, defunct brewery memorabilia, music and quiz nights, lively weekend atmosphere; well behaved children and dogs welcome, open (and food) all day. *(P Dawn, Dru and Louisa Marshall)*

NOTTINGHAM SK5739
★ Canal House (0115) 955 5060
Canal Street; NG1 7EH Converted wharf building with bridge over indoors canal spur (complete with narrowboat), lots of bare brick and varnished wood, huge joists on steel beams, long bar serving well kept Castle Rock and three guests, 80 or so bottled beers and good choice of wines, enjoyable sensibly priced pubby food (not Sun evening), efficient service; background music; masses of tables out on attractive waterside terrace, open all day. *(David Hunt, P Dawn)*

NOTTINGHAM SK5739
Cock & Hoop (0115) 852 3231
High Pavement; NG1 1HF Tiny bare-boards front bar with fireside armchairs and flagstoned cellar bar attached to decent hotel; characterful décor, reasonably priced fairly traditional food including good Sun roasts, well kept ales such as Amber, Blue Monkey, Flipside and Magpie, attentive friendly service; background music, live jazz last Thurs of month; children and dogs

welcome, disabled facilities, smart bedrooms (ones by the street can be noisy at weekends), open all day. *(P Dawn)*

NOTTINGHAM   SK5739
★**Cross Keys** (0115) 941 7898
Byard Lane; NG1 2GJ Restored Victorian city-centre pub on two levels, lower carpeted part with leather banquettes, panelling and chandeliers, upper area with old wooden chairs and tables on polished boards, interesting prints and pictures and more chandeliers, well kept Navigation ales and a couple of guests, good home-made food from breakfast on, friendly service, upstairs weekend restaurant; sports TV; seats outside, open all day from 9am. *(P Dawn)*

NOTTINGHAM   SK5542
Fox & Crown (0115) 942 2002
Church Street/Lincoln Street, Old Basford; NG6 0GA Range of good Alcazar beers brewed behind this refurbished open-plan pub (window shows the brewery – Sat tours), also guest ales, continentals and good choice of wines, enjoyable thai food; background music, games machines and big-screen sports TV; disabled access, tables on back terrace, beer shop next door, open all day. *(David Hunt, P Dawn)*

NOTTINGHAM   SK5642
Gladstone (0115) 912 9994
Loscoe Road, Carrington; NG5 2AW Welcoming mid-terrace backstreet local with half a dozen well kept ales such as Brewsters, Castle Rock, Oakham and Timothy Taylors, good range of malt whiskies, comfortable lounge with reading matter, basic bar with old sports memorabilia and darts, upstairs folk club Weds, quiz Thurs; background music and sports TV; tables in back garden among colourful tubs and hanging baskets, closed weekday lunchtimes, open all day weekends. *(David Hunt, Jeremy King, P Dawn)*

NOTTINGHAM   SK5640
Hand & Heart (0115) 958 2456
Derby Road; NG1 5BA Unexceptional exterior but unusual inside with bar and dining areas cut deep into back sandstone, a house beer from Dancing Duck, Maypole and guests, two real ciders and good range of whiskies, enjoyable fairly priced traditional food from sandwiches and snacks up, friendly helpful service, upstairs area with glassed-in part overlooking street; background and interesting live music Thurs (jazz, world, klezmer); children welcome till 7pm if eating, dogs in bar, open all day (late licence Fri, Sat). *(Andrew Cooper, P Dawn, Chris Johnson)*

NOTTINGHAM   SK5542
Horse & Groom (0115) 970 3777
Radford Road, New Basford; NG7 7EA Eight good changing ales and a real cider in well run open-plan local by former

Shipstones Brewery, still with their name and other memorabilia, good value fresh straightforward food from sandwiches to Sun lunch, nice snug, some live music; open all day (from 4pm Mon-Weds). *(P Dawn)*

NOTTINGHAM   SK5739
★**Kean's Head** (0115) 947 4052
St Mary's Gate; NG1 1QA Cheery pub in attractive Lace Market area; fairly functional single room with simple wooden café furnishings on wooden boards, some exposed brickwork and red tiling, low sofa by big windows overlooking street, stools by wood counter and small fireplace, Castle Rock and three guests, draught belgian and interesting bottled beers, 20 wines by the glass, around 60 malt whiskies and lots of teas/coffees, tasty fairly traditional food (not Sun evening), friendly service, daily papers; background music; children welcome till 7pm, church next door worth a look, open all day. *(P Dawn)*

NOTTINGHAM   SK5539
King William IV (0115) 958 9864
Manvers Street/Eyre Street, Sneinton; NG2 4PB Two-room Victorian corner local with plenty of character, Oakham and six guests from circular bar, Weston's Old Rosie cider, good fresh cobs, friendly staff, fine tankard collection, pool upstairs, irish music Thurs; silenced sports TV; heated smokers' shelter, handy for cricket, football and rugby grounds, open all day. *(P Dawn)*

NOTTINGHAM   SK5740
★**Lincolnshire Poacher**
(0115) 941 1584 *Mansfield Road; up hill from Victoria Centre; NG1 3FR* Impressive range of drinks at this popular down-to-earth pub (attracts younger evening crowd), 13 well kept ales including Castle Rock, lots of continental draught/bottled beers, half a dozen ciders and over 70 malt whiskies, above average all-day food at reasonable prices; big simple traditional front bar with wall settles, wooden tables and breweriana, plain but lively room on left and corridor to chatty panelled back snug with newspapers and board games, conservatory overlooking tables on large heated back area, live music Sun evening; children (till 8pm) and dogs welcome, open all day (till midnight Sat). *(David Hunt, P Dawn)*

NOTTINGHAM   SK5541
★**Lion** (0115) 970 3506
Lower Mosley Street, New Basford; NG7 7FQ Eleven real ales (tasters available) including regulars Blue Moon, Oakham and Thornbridge from one of the city's deepest cellars (glass viewing panel – can be visited at quiet times), also ten proper ciders; big open-plan room with feel of separate areas, bare bricks and polished dark oak boards, old brewery pictures and posters, open fires, daily papers, regular

live music including popular Sun lunchtime jazz, beer festivals; children welcome till 6pm, no dogs, disabled facilities, garden with terrace and smokers' shelter, open all day summer. *(David Hunt, P Dawn)*

NOTTINGHAM SK5739

Malt Cross (0115) 941 1048

St James's Street; NG1 6FG Former Victorian music hall with vaulted glass roof and gallery looking down on bar area, bare boards and ornate iron pillars, comfortable sofas, good selection of drinks including some interesting real ales, decent well priced food from shortish menu, teas, coffees and daily newspapers, quiz and music nights; plans under way to expand into cellars and ancient caves beneath the building; open all day (till 1am Fri, Sat). *(Chris Johnson)*

NOTTINGHAM SK5739

News House (0115) 952 3061

Canal Street; NG1 7HB Friendly two-room 1950s Castle Rock pub with notable blue exterior tiling, their ales and half a dozen changing guests, belgian and czech imports, decent fresh lunchtime food (Mon-Sat), mix of bare boards and carpet, local newspaper/ radio memorabilia, darts, table skittles and bar billiards, Thurs quiz; big-screen sports TV; a few tables out at front, open all day. *(P Dawn)*

NOTTINGHAM SK5739

★Olde Trip to Jerusalem

(0115) 947 3171 *Brewhouse Yard; from inner ring road follow The North, A6005 Long Eaton signpost until in Castle Boulevard, then right into Castle Road; pub is on the left; NG1 6AD* Unusual rambling pub seemingly clinging to sandstone rock face, largely 17th c and a former brewhouse supplying the hilltop castle; downstairs bar carved into the rock with simple seats built into dark panelling, tables on flagstones, rocky alcoves, Greene King IPA and Hardys & Hansons Olde Trip plus guests, good value food all day, efficient staff dealing well with busy mix of customers; little tourist shop with panelled walls soaring up into dark cavernous heights is very popular; children welcome, seats in snug courtyard and ring the bull, open all day (till midnight Fri, Sat). *(David Hunt, Nigel and Sue Foster, P Dawn, George Atkinson)*

NOTTINGHAM SK5640

Organ Grinder (0115) 970 0630

Alfreton Road; NG7 3JE Homely tap for Blue Monkey with up to nine well kept ales including guests, a couple of ciders and a perry, good local pork pies (some topped with stilton), woodburner; outside seating, open all day. *(Chris Johnson)*

NOTTINGHAM SK5540

Plough (0115) 942 2649

St Peter's Street, Radford; NG7 3EN Friendly 19th-c local brewing its own good value Nottingham ales at the back, also guest beers and farm cider, weekday sandwiches, mosaic floors, old tables and chairs, two coal fires, traditional games and skittle alley, Thurs quiz with free food; dogs welcome (may get a chew), covered smokers' area, open all day. *(P Dawn)*

NOTTINGHAM SK5739

Salutation (0115) 947 6580

Hounds Gate/Maid Marian Way; NG1 7AA Proper pub, low beams, flagstones, ochre walls and cosy corners including two small quiet rooms in ancient lower back part, plusher modern front lounge, up to six real ales and good choice of draught/bottled ciders, quickly served food till 8pm (6pm Sun), helpful friendly staff (ask them to show you the haunted caves below the pub); background music (live band upstairs); open all day (till 3am Fri, Sat). *(P Dawn)*

NOTTINGHAM SK5640

Trent Bridge (0115) 977 8940

Radcliffe Road; NG2 6AA Good fairly new Wetherspoons in sizeable Victorian pub next to the cricket ground (busy on match days), comfortably refurbished linked rooms with panelling and cricketing memorabilia, a dozen well kept ales and decent good value food, efficient friendly staff; sports TVs, free wi-fi; children welcome, open all day from 8am. *(David Hunt)*

NOTTINGHAM SK5838

Trent Navigation (0115) 986 5658

Meadow Lane; NG2 3HS Welcoming tile-fronted Victorian pub close to canal and home to the Navigation brewery, their beers and guests from half a dozen pumps along with ciders/perries, popular food including deals, regular live music (Fri blues) and well attended Sun quiz; sports TV (pub is next to Notts County FC); children welcome, brewery shop at back, open all day. *(P Dawn, Phil and Jane Hodson)*

NOTTINGHAM SK5739

★Vat & Fiddle (0115) 985 0611

Queens Bridge Road; alongside Sheriffs Way (near multi-storey car park); NG2 1NB Plain open-plan brick pub acting as tap for next-door Castle Rock Brewery; unspoilt 1930s feel, varnished pine tables, bentwood chairs and stools on parquet or terrazzo flooring, some brewery memorabilia and interesting photographs of demolished local pubs, a dozen real ales including guests, bottled continentals, farm ciders and 60 malt whiskies, fresh cobs, nice chatty atmosphere; no credit cards; children and dogs welcome, picnic-sets out front by road, open all day (till midnight Fri, Sat). *(David Hunt, P Dawn)*

RADCLIFFE ON TRENT SK6439
Horse Chestnut (0115) 933 1994
Main Road; NG12 2BE Smart pub (under newish management) with plenty of Victorian/Edwardian features, well kept Castle Rock, Fullers, St Austell and three guests, decent wines by the glass and sensibly priced home-made food (not Sun evening) including italian choices, friendly service, two-level main bar, parquet and mosaic floor, panelling, big mirrors and impressive lamps, handsome leather wall benches and period fireplaces, pub dog called Helmsley; disabled access, terrace seating, closed lunchtimes Mon and Tues, otherwise open all day. *(Anon)*

RADCLIFFE ON TRENT SK6439
Manvers Arms (0115) 933 2404
Main Road, opposite church; NG12 2AA Early 19th-c village pub with good nicely presented food (till 7pm Sun) including set menus, prompt friendly service, well kept Caledonian, Castle Rock, Jennings, St Austell and two guests, fairly priced wines, spotless opened-up interior keeping original fireplaces and other features, assorted pubby furniture, some cosy areas with banquettes, pictures and ornaments, chandeliers and potted palms, an old harmonium; mellow background music, live folk/jazz Thurs, quiz Tues and Sun; well behaved children and dogs welcome, plenty of seats in large back garden with trees and shrubs, open all day. *(Anon)*

RUDDINGTON SK5733
Three Crowns 07951 342201
Easthorpe Street; NG11 6LB Open-plan pub known locally as the Top House, well kept Fullers, Nottingham and three guests (beer festivals), good indian food in back Three Spices evening restaurant; open all day weekends, closed lunchtimes Mon and Tues. *(P Dawn)*

SELSTON SK4553
★ Horse & Jockey (01773) 781012
Handy for M1 junctions 27/28; Church Lane; NG16 6FB Interesting pub on different levels dating from the 17th c, low heavy beams, dark flagstones, individual furnishings and good log fire in cast-iron range, friendly staff, Greene King Abbot and Timothy Taylors Landlord poured from the jug and up to four guests, real cider, no food, folk night Weds, quiz Sun; games area with darts and pool; dogs welcome, terrace and smokers' shelter, pleasant rolling country. *(Derek and Sylvia Stephenson)*

SOUTHWELL SK7054
★ Final Whistle (01636) 814953
Station Road; NG25 0ET Railway themed pub commemorating the long defunct Southwell line; ten mainly local ales including Everards and Leatherbritches (beer festivals), real ciders and perries, foreign bottled beers and good range of wines, cheeseboard and some other snacky food, traditional opened-up bar area with tiled or wood floor, settles and armchairs in quieter carpeted room, corridor drinking area, two open fires, panelling, lots of railway memorabilia and other odds and ends; some live music, Tues quiz; children and dogs welcome, back garden with wonderful mock-up of 1920s platform complete with track and buffers, open all day. *(Derek and Sylvia Stephenson, Tony and Maggie Harwood, Dr Brian and Mrs Anne Hamilton, P Dawn)*

SOUTHWELL SK7053
Hearty Goodfellow (01636) 919176
Church Street (A612); NG25 0HQ Welcoming traditional open-plan pub, Everards Tiger and five guests, a couple of traditional ciders and good range of house wines, enjoyable fairly straightforward food (not Sun evening, Mon) at reasonable prices, cheerful young staff, lots of polished wood, two brick fireplaces; background and some live music, sport TVs; children and dogs welcome, covered terrace and nice big tree-shaded garden beyond car park, play area, handy for Southwell Workhouse (NT) and Minster, open all day Fri-Sun, closed Mon lunchtime. *(Pat and Tony Martin, Derek and Sylvia Stephenson, P Dawn)*

THURGARTON SK6949
Red Lion (01636) 830351
Southwell Road (A612); NG14 7GP Cheery 16th-c pub with split-level beamed bars and restaurant, ales such as Black Sheep and Marstons from dark-panelled bar, nice range of enjoyable reasonably priced food (all day weekends and bank holidays), good friendly service, comfortable banquettes and other seating on patterned carpets, lots of nooks and crannies, grandfather clock, open fires, big windows to attractive good-sized back garden on two levels (dogs on leads allowed here); children welcome. *(Derek and Sylvia Stephenson, Margaret Wilson)*

TUXFORD SK7471
Fountain (01777) 872854
Lincoln Road; NG22 0JQ Comfortably updated family dining pub with good range of affordably priced food from sandwiches/ wraps through burgers and pizzas to grills and specials, food challenges including 72oz steak and the 'world's hottest curry' (free if you can finish them), local ales and ciders such as Welbeck Abbey and Scrumpy Wasp, friendly service; free wi-fi; picnic-sets out in fenced area, open all day. *(G L and V Bottomley)*

UNDERWOOD   SK4751
Red Lion (01773) 810482
Off A608/B600, near M1 junction 27;
Church Lane, nearly in Bagthorpe;
NG16 5HD Welcoming 18th-c split-level
beamed village pub, enjoyable sensibly priced
food including set lunch and blackboard
specials, Marstons Pedigree, Sharps Doom
Bar and a couple of guests, good soft drinks
choice, open-plan quarry-tiled bar with
dining area, some cushioned settles, coal-
effect gas fire; background music, games
machine in lobby; children till 7pm away
from bar, dogs welcome, play area in big
woodside garden with terrace, barbecues,
good nearby walks, open all day. *(Anon)*

UPTON   SK7354
★**Cross Keys** (01636) 813269
A612; NG23 5SY 17th-c pub in fine spot
with rambling heavy-beamed bar (some
redecoration by new owners), log fire in
brick fireplace, own Mallard ales (brewed in
Maythorne) and good home-made food (not
Sun evening), friendly staff, back extension;
seats on decked terrace, British Horological
Institute opposite, open all day Fri-Sun,
closed Mon and Tues lunchtimes. *(P Dawn)*

WEST BRIDGFORD   SK5838
Larwood & Voce (0115) 981 9960
Fox Road; NG2 6AJ Well run open-plan
dining pub (part of the small Moleface
group); good locally sourced home-made
food in bar and restaurant area including
some imaginative choices, plenty of wines
by the glass, cocktail menu and three well
kept ales, cheerful staff; sports TV; children
welcome away from bar, seats out on raised
deck with heaters, on the edge of the cricket
ground and handy for Nottingham Forest
FC, open all day, from 9am weekends for
breakfast. *(David Hunt, P Dawn)*

WEST BRIDGFORD   SK5938
Poppy & Pint (0115) 981 9995
Pierrepont Road; NG2 5DX Converted
former British Legion Club backing on to

bowling green and tennis courts; large bar
with raised section and family area, 12 real
ales including Castle Rock, a couple of ciders,
decent food; open all day from 9.30am.
(R Galpin)

WEST BRIDGFORD   SK5837
★**Stratford Haven** (0115) 982 5981
Stratford Road, Trent Bridge; NG2 6BA
Good Castle Rock pub; bare-boards front
bar leading to linked areas including
airy skylit back part with relaxed local
atmosphere, their well kept ales plus
Batemans, Everards and six changing
guests (monthly brewery nights), exotic
bottled beers, farm ciders, ample whiskies
and wines, wide range of good value home-
made food all day, fast friendly service,
daily papers, some live music (nothing
loud); dogs welcome, tables outside, handy
for cricket ground and Nottingham Forest
FC (busy on match days), open all day.
(Andrew Bosi, P Dawn)

WEST STOCKWITH   SK7994
White Hart (01427) 892672
Main Street; DN10 4EY Small refurbished
country pub at junction of Chesterfield Canal
with River Trent, own good Idle beers from
next-door brewery and guests, enjoyable good
value traditional food, friendly atmosphere,
games area with pool, live music Fri, quiz
every other Tues; sports TV; children and
dogs welcome, garden overlooking water,
open all day. *(Anon)*

WYSALL   SK6027
Plough (01509) 880339
Keyworth Road; off A60 at Costock,
or A6006 at Wymeswold; NG12 5QQ
Attractive 17th-c beamed village local;
popular good value lunchtime food from
shortish menu, cheerful staff, Bass, Greene
King Abbot, Timothy Taylors Landlord and
three guests, rooms either side of bar with
nice mix of furnishings, soft lighting, big
log fire; french doors to pretty terrace with
flower tubs and baskets, open all day.
(P Dawn)

Post Office address codings confusingly give the impression that a few pubs are in
Nottinghamshire, when they're really in Derbyshire (which is where we list them).

Oxfordshire

KEY  ★ Star Pub 🎖️ Top Quality Food 🍺 Great Beer

🍷 Good Wines £ Bargain Meals 🛏️ Good Bedrooms 🍴 Serves Food

BANBURY   SP4540   Map 4

Olde Reindeer 🍺 £

Parsons Street, off Market Place; OX16 5NA

Interesting town pub with fine original features, plenty of shoppers and regulars, real ales and simple food

This is a splendid old inn and 'as good as ever' says one reader. There's a friendly welcome from the landlord, a good, bustling atmosphere and plenty of cheerful customers. The front bar has heavy 16th-c beams, very broad polished oak floorboards, a magnificent carved overmantel for one of the two roaring log fires and traditional solid furnishings; some interesting breweriana too. It's worth looking at the handsomely proportioned Globe Room used by Oliver Cromwell as his base during the Civil War. Quite a sight, it still has some very fine carved 17th-c dark oak panelling. Hook Norton Hooky, Lion, Hooky Dark, Old Hooky, Hooky Mild and a changing guest beer on handpump, nine wines by the glass, fruit wines and several malt whiskies. The little back courtyard has tables and benches under parasols, aunt sally and pretty flowering baskets.

🍴 Honest, fair value food includes sandwiches, pâté, beer-battered fish, vegetable lasagne, steak in ale pie, cumberland sausages with gravy in a big yorkshire pudding, daily specials, and puddings. *Benchmark main dish: venison burger with chips £6.95. Two-course evening meal £13.00.*

Hook Norton ~ Tenant Jeremy Money ~ Real ale ~ (01295) 264031 ~ Open 11-11 (midnight Fri, Sat); 12-11 Sun ~ Bar food 12-3, 6-9; 12-3 Sun ~ Children welcome ~ Dogs allowed in bar ~ www.yeoldereindeer.co.uk *Recommended by Ben Weedon, Richard Stanfield, George Atkinson, Barry Collett*

BESSELS LEIGH   SP4501   Map 4

Greyhound 🍷 🍺

A420 Faringdon–Botley; OX13 5PX

**Handsome 400-year-old stone pub with plenty of character
and interest, half a dozen real ales, lots of wines by the glass
and enjoyable interesting food**

Very handy as a break from the busy A420, this handsome former coaching inn looks particularly pretty in summer with its lovely window boxes and hanging baskets. Inside, the knocked-through rooms create plenty of space and interest and the half-panelled walls are covered in all manner of old photographs and pictures. The individually chosen cushioned dining chairs, leather-topped stools and dark wooden tables are grouped on carpeting or rug-covered floorboards, and there are books on shelves, glass and stone bottles on window sills, big gilt mirrors, three fireplaces (one housing a woodburning stove) and sizeable pot plants. Wooden bar stools sit against the counter where they serve Phoenix Brunning & Price Original, Hook Norton Hooky Bitter, White Horse Wayland Smithy and guest beers from breweries such as Loose Cannon and Wychwood on handpump, 14 wines by the glass, 102 malt whiskies and a farm cider. By the back dining extension there's a white picket fence-enclosed garden with picnic-sets under green parasols.

Extremely good food includes sandwiches, baked camembert (for two) with crusty bread, chicken liver pâté with plum and ginger chutney, sharing platters, crab linguine with ginger and chilli, sweet potato and cauliflower curry, pork sausages with onion gravy, braised rabbit, bacon and vegetable broth with tarragon dumplings, sea bream with saffron fondant potato and sauce vierge, and puddings such as coconut-crusted deep-fried ice-cream with dragon fruit carpaccio and tropical fruit salsa and warm sunken chocolate pudding with chocolate sauce. *Benchmark main dish: burger with coleslaw, salsa and chips £11.95. Two-course evening meal £18.00.*

Brunning & Price ~ Manager Peter Palfi ~ Real ale ~ (01865) 862110 ~ Open 11-11; 11.30-10.30 Sun ~ Bar food 12-10 (9.30 Sun) ~ Well behaved children welcome ~ Dogs allowed in bar ~ Wi-fi ~ www.greyhound-besselsleigh.co.uk *Recommended by Derek Goldrei, Taff Thomas, N R White, William Goodhart, Paul Humphreys, S F Parrinder*

BRIGHTWELL BALDWIN SU6594 Map 4
Lord Nelson 🏵 ⌑

Off B480 Chalgrove–Watlington, or B4009 Benson–Watlington; OX49 5NP

Attractive inn with several different character bars, real ales, good wines by the glass and enjoyable well thought-of food; bedrooms

The generously served and very good food at this 300-year-old inn is extremely popular, but there are plenty of cheerful drinkers too, which keeps the atmosphere easy-going and chatty. The bar has wheelback and other dining chairs around assorted dark tables, candles and fresh flowers, wine bottles on window sills, horsebrasses on standing timbers, lots of paintings on the white or red walls and a big brick inglenook fireplace. One cosy room has cushions on comfortable sofas, little lamps on dark furniture, ornate mirrors and portraits in gilt frames; background music. Rebellion IPA, an ale from Loose Cannon and a changing guest on handpump, 14 wines (including champagne) by the glass and winter mulled wine. The back terrace has seats and tables with more in the willow-draped garden; the village church is opposite.

From a thoughtful menu, there might be twice-baked cheese soufflé, crispy duck salad with hoi sin and plum dressing, wild mushroom lasagne, burger with cheese, home-made relish and skinny chips, cod fillet on mixed bean and chorizo cassoulet, pork fillet medallions with creamy leek and apple sauce, specials such as local duck egg, bacon and mushrooms on toast and rack of lamb with rosemary and red wine sauce, and puddings such as plum and almond crumble and chocolate fudge brownie. *Benchmark main dish: beer-battered haddock with triple-cooked chips £14.50. Two-course evening meal £23.00.*

Free house ~ Licensees Roger and Carole Shippey ~ Real ale ~ (01491) 612497 ~ Open 12-3, 6-11; 12-10 Sun ~ Bar food 12-2.30, 6-10 ~ Restaurant ~ Children welcome ~ Dogs allowed in bar ~ Wi-fi ~ Bedrooms: £75/£100 ~ www.lordnelson-inn.co.uk *Recommended by Torrens Lyster, Roy Hoing, Colin McLachlan, Dr W I C Clark, P and J Shapley*

BURFORD
SP2512 Map 4
Highway 🛏
High Street (A361); OX18 4RG

Comfortable old inn overlooking this honeypot village's main street, a good choice of wines and well liked bar food; bedrooms

There are all sorts of interesting touches in this 15th-c town inn, but the main feature in the bar is the pair of big windows overlooking the bustle of the High Street; each consists of several dozen panes of old float glass and has a long cushioned window seat. Also, do notice the stag candlesticks for the rather close-set tables on well worn floorboards, the neat modern dark leather chairs, a nice old station clock above the big log fire in the pleasing simple stone fireplace, and the careful balance of ancient stripped stone with filigree black and pale blue wallpaper. A small corner counter has Hook Norton Best, Prescott Hill Climb and a guest beer on handpump, 16 wines (including champagne) by the glass and 13 malt whiskies; background music, TV and board games. On the right, a second bar room, with another big window seat, is carpeted but otherwise similar in style; there's also a downstairs cellar bar. A few front picnic-sets stand above the pavement. The country house-style bedrooms are all individually decorated and comfortable.

 The popular food includes lunchtime sandwiches, rabbit terrine with fennel chutney, fricassée of wild mushrooms with parsley cream sauce, sharing platters, a pie and a vegetarian dish of the day, local sausages with caramelised onions, chicken with potato galette and blackberries, cider-cured salmon, dressed crab, sea vegetables and lobster bisque, duo of lamb with roasted beetroot and port jus, and puddings. *Benchmark main dish: confit gressingham duck with crispy leeks and balsamic onions £15.95. Two-course evening meal £20.00.*

Free house ~ Licensees Dan, Jane and Michelle Arnell ~ Real ale ~ (01993) 823661 ~ Open 12-11; closed first two weeks Jan ~ Bar food 12-2.30 (3 Sun), 6.30-9 (9.30 Fri, Sat) ~ Children welcome ~ Dogs allowed in bar and bedrooms ~ Wi-fi ~ Bedrooms: £90/£120 ~ www.thehighwayinn.co.uk *Recommended by Martin Jones, Caroline Prescott, George Atkinson*

BURFORD
SP2412 Map 4
Lamb 🍴⭐ � 🛏
Village signposted off A40 W of Oxford; Sheep Street (B4425, off A361); OX18 4LR

Proper pubby bar in civilised inn, real ales and an extensive wine list, interesting bar and restaurant food, and pretty gardens; bedrooms

This is a lovely 15th-c building, peaceful and timeless, with a civilised and friendly atmosphere. The cosy bar remains its heart and has cushioned settles and old chairs on flagstones in front of a log fire, china plates on shelves, Hook Norton Hooky Bitter and Wickwar Cotswold Way on handpump, an extensive wine list with 20 by the glass and 15 malt whiskies. The roomy beamed main lounge is charmingly traditional, with distinguished old seats including a chintzy high-winged settle, ancient cushioned wooden armchairs, and seats built into stone-mullioned windows; fresh flowers on polished oak and elm tables, rugs on wide flagstones and polished oak floorboards, a winter log fire under a fine mantelpiece and plenty of antiques and other decorations including a grandfather clock. Service is impeccable. A pretty terrace with teak furniture leads down to small neatly kept lawns surrounded by flowers, shrubs and small trees. The garden is a real suntrap, enclosed by the warm stone of the surrounding buildings. They're kind to dogs and even have a special menu for them.

Extremely good and highly thought-of, the food includes open sandwiches, deli boards, eggs benedict or royale, scallops with black pudding, local sausages with red onion confit, steak and mushroom in ale pie, crayfish and chive risotto, chicken with olive-crushed potatoes and tomato and basil sauce, cod and prawn fishcakes with red pepper mayonnaise, haunch of venison and spiced venison pie with celeriac spaghetti, and puddings such as lemon posset and baked white chocolate and ginger cheesecake with blackberry compote; they also offer a two- and three-course set evening menu. *Benchmark main dish: dressed crab with skinny chips £12.95. Two-course evening meal £20.50.*

Cotswold Inns & Hotels ~ Manager Bill Ramsay ~ Real ale ~ (01993) 823155 ~ Open 12-11 ~ Bar food 12-9.30 ~ Restaurant ~ Children welcome ~ Dogs allowed in bar and bedrooms ~ Wi-fi ~ Bedrooms: £100/£160 ~ www.cotswold-inns-hotels.co.uk/lamb *Recommended by David Carr, Richard Stanfield, Richard Tilbrook, Michael Sargent, R K Phillips, Martin Cawley*

CHURCHILL
Chequers ◀

SP2824 Map 4

Church Road; B4450 Chipping Norton to Stow-on-the-Wold (and village signed off A361 Chipping Norton–Burford); OX7 6NJ

Bustling village pub with simple furnishings in spacious bars and dining rooms, a friendly, relaxed atmosphere, six ales and popular food

Opposite an impressive church, this busy village pub is Cotswold stone at its most golden. The relaxed and friendly bar has an armchair and other comfortable chairs around an old trunk in front of an inglenook fireplace, some exposed stone walls, cushioned wall seats and a mix of wooden and antique leather chairs around nice old tables on bare floorboards, a few rugs here and there, stools against the counter presided over by a big stag's head, Hook Norton Hooky, Sharps Doom Bar, Shepherd Neame Spitfire, Timothy Taylors Landlord and a couple of guests from breweries such as Cats and Wye Valley on handpump, ten wines by the glass and 11 malt whiskies; darts and background music. At the back is a large extension with soaring rafters, big lantern lights, long button-back leather banquettes and other seating, while upstairs there's another similarly and simply furnished dining area and a room just right for a private party.

Good, interesting food includes devilled kidneys on toast, scallops and crab in mornay sauce, spinach, bacon and avocado salad, spiced chickpea and aubergine tagine, chicken, mushroom and tarragon pie, calves liver and bacon, cod fillet with mussels, leeks and ale, popular steaks with fries and tomatoes, and puddings such as treacle sponge and custard and peanut cookie and salted caramel sundae. *Benchmark main dish: ham hock, leek and cheddar pie £12.00. Two-course evening meal £21.50.*

Free house ~ Real ale ~ (01608) 659393 ~ Open 11am-midnight ~ Bar food 12-3, 6-10 (9 Sun) ~ Restaurant ~ Children welcome ~ Dogs allowed in bar ~ Wi-fi ~ Live music monthly ~ www.thechequerschurchill.com *Recommended by Bernard Stradling, Martin and Pauline Jennings, David Gunn*

The ◀ symbol shows pubs that keep their beer unusually well, have a particularly good range or brew their own.

CLIFTON
SP4931 Map 4

Duke of Cumberlands Head 🍷 🛏

B4031 Deddington–Aynho; OX15 0PE

Cosy bars with beams and a big log fire, good food and short walk to canal; good value bedrooms

This is a family-run, thatched and golden-stone inn close to the Oxford Canal. A friendly place with an easy-going atmosphere, it has beams in low ceilings, rugs on bare boards, an attractive mix of dining chairs and settles around nice old tables, church candles, paintings on exposed stone walls and a good log fire in a vast inglenook fireplace. Hook Norton Lion and guests such as Ramsbury Gold and Sharps Doom Bar on handpump and several wines by the glass; background music. There are a couple of picnic-sets out in front, and good quality seats and tables under parasols on the sunny back terrace. This is an enjoyable place to stay in pretty and reasonably priced bedrooms; breakfasts are continental. They have aunt sally in the garden.

Reliably good food includes lunchtime sandwiches, smoked mackerel pâté, tempura king prawns with sweet chilli sauce, lemon and thyme spatchcock poussin with harissa, couscous and ratatouille, thai green vegetable curry, beer-battered haddock, burger with bacon, cheese, red slaw and chips, duo of lamb (best end and pistachio-crusted shoulder), and puddings such as apple strudel and custard and crumble of the day. *Benchmark main dish: Sunday roast sirloin of beef £13.95. Two-course evening meal £19.50.*

Free house ~ Licensee Alan Newman ~ Real ale ~ (01869) 338534 ~ Open 12-10.30 (10 Sun) ~ Bar food 12-2.30 (3 weekends), 6.30-9 (8.30 Sun) ~ Restaurant ~ Children welcome ~ Dogs welcome ~ Wi-fi ~ Bedrooms: /£75 ~ www.cliftonduke.com
Recommended by David Jackman, N R White

EAST HENDRED
SU4588 Map 2

Eyston Arms

Village signposted off A417 E of Wantage; High Street; OX12 8JY

Attractive bar areas with low beams, flagstones, log fires and candles, imaginative food and helpful service

At this always deservedly busy pub, you'll be welcomed wholeheartedly whether you're dropping in for a chat and a drink or a meal – though it's the inventive food that draws most customers. There are seats at the bar and they do keep a few tables free for drinkers keen to try the Hook Norton Hooky Bitter and Wadworths 6X on handpump, ten wines by the glass and 15 malt whiskies. Several separate-seeming candlelit areas have contemporary paintwork and modern country-style furnishings, low ceilings and beams, stripped timbers and the odd standing timber, nice tables and chairs on flagstones and carpet, some cushioned wall seats and an inglenook fireplace; background music. Picnic-sets outside overlook the pretty lane and there are seats in the back courtyard garden.

Enticing food includes lunchtime sandwiches, asparagus and crispy duck egg with sweet miso dressing, trio of sausages (wild boar, venison, pork and leek) with parsnip mash and gravy, fennel, pear and blue cheese tarte tatin with roasted hazelnut, maple syrup and cider dressing, linguine with king prawns, smoked salmon, cherry tomatoes and chilli oil, lamb rump with bubble and squeak cake, minted pea purée and rosemary and red wine jus, and puddings such as dark chocolate torte with salted caramel sauce and caramel popcorn and lemon and lavender pot with lavender shortbread. *Benchmark main dish: king prawns with lime aioli £14.00. Two-course evening meal £24.00.*

Free house ~ Licensees George Dailey and Daisy Barton ~ Real ale ~ (01235) 833320 ~ Open 11-11; 12-6 Sun ~ Bar food 12-9; 12-4 Sun ~ Restaurant ~ Children welcome ~ Dogs allowed in bar ~ Wi-fi ~ www.eystonarms.co.uk *Recommended by Caroline Prescott, John Oates, Fiona Smith*

HEADINGTON
SP5407 Map 4
Black Boy
Old High Street/St Andrews Road; off A420 at traffic lights opposite B4495; OX3 9HT

Stylish and enterprising dining pub with good, enjoyable food, and useful summer garden

With good, interesting food and weekly changing beers, this modern dining pub is an enjoyable place. It has a cool contemporary look with black leather seating on dark parquet, big mirrors, silvery patterned wallpaper, nightlights in fat opaque cylinders and glittering bottles behind the long bar counter. It's light and airy in feel, particularly at the two tables in the big bay window; just to the side are lower, softer seats beside an open fire. Crisp white tablecloths and bold black and white wallpaper lend the area on the left a touch of formality. Brunswick Midnight Express and Everards Whakatu on handpump, 20 wines by the glass, ten malt whiskies and several coffees and teas. Behind the building is an appealing terrace, with picnic-sets under alternating black and white parasols on smart pale stone chippings, and a central seat encircling an ash tree.

Generous helpings of well executed food include lunchtime sandwiches, little tapas-like dishes, chicken liver and foie gras parfait with sauternes-soaked sultanas and home-made brioche, hot smoked salmon and haddock fishcakes, wild mushroom and champagne lasagne, sausage and mash with onion and ale jus, chicken jambonette with morel and chicken mousse, seafood linguine with white wine and cream, and puddings such as iced white chocolate mousse with home-made raspberry sorbet and sticky toffee pudding. *Benchmark main dish: slow-roast pork belly with garlic and thyme mash and cider jus £14.95. Two-course evening meal £20.00.*

Greene King ~ Lease Abi Rose and Chris Bentham ~ Real ale ~ (01865) 741137 ~ Open 12-3, 5-11 ~ Bar food 12-2.45, 6-9.15 ~ Restaurant ~ Children welcome ~ Wi-fi ~ www.theblackboy.uk.com *Recommended by David Bull, Pam Tomlinson, Wilburoo*

HIGHMOOR
SU6984 Map 2
Rising Sun
Witheridge Hill, signposted off B481; OS Sheet 175 map reference 697841; RG9 5PF

Friendly country village pub with a welcoming landlord, character bars and eating areas, and good food and drink; seats in garden

In a little village in the heart of the Chilterns, this charming 17th-c pub is run by a friendly licensee who welcomes all who walk through his door; it's particularly popular at lunchtime with walkers from nearby Witheridge Hill. The cosy bar has beams, old red and white floor tiles, a comfortable sofa, lots of walking sticks in a pot by the woodburning stove, books on the window sill and leather stools against the counter where they serve Brakspears Bitter and Oxford Gold and a changing guest beer on handpump and a dozen wines by the glass. The three interlinked eating areas have rugs on bare boards, pictures on dark red walls and seating that includes captain's and farmhouse chairs, chunky benches and cushioned wall seats around an assortment of tables; one section has a log fire in a small brick fireplace. There are picnic-sets and white metal chairs and tables in the pleasant back garden.

Very good food includes sandwiches, pâté with chutney, portobello mushrooms with rarebit topping, pork and apple sausages with red onion jus, broccoli, cauliflower and stilton bake, chicken with chorizo and a herb pesto, beef stew with crusty bread, salmon fillet with prawn and caper butter, and puddings. *Benchmark main dish: burger with bacon, cheese, red onion chutney and chips £12.50. Two-course evening meal £19.50.*

Brakspears ~ Tenant Simon Duffy ~ Real ale ~ (01491) 640856 ~ Open 12-3, 5-11; 12-11 Sat; 12-10 Sun ~ Bar food 12-2 (2.30 Sat), 6-9 (9.30 Fri, Sat); 12-3.30 Sun ~ Restaurant ~ Children welcome ~ Dogs allowed in bar ~ Wi-fi ~ www.risingsunwitheridgehill.co.uk
Recommended by Paul Humphreys, Tracey and Stephen Groves, Roy Hoing, Bob and Margaret Holder, Alistair Forsyth, R K Phillips

KINGHAM
Plough ⭐ 🍷 🛏️

SP2624 Map 4

Village signposted off B4450 E of Bledington; or turn S off A436 at staggered crossroads a mile SW of A44 junction – or take signed Daylesford turn off A436 and keep on; The Green; OX7 6YD

Oxfordshire Dining Pub of the Year

Friendly dining pub combining an informal pub atmosphere with upmarket food; bedrooms

It's the exceptional food cooked by Emily Watkins, the chef-patron, that draws most customers to this dining pub-with-rooms. But there's a properly pubby bar with some nice old high-backed settles and brightly cushioned chapel chairs on broad dark boards, candles on stripped tables and cheerful farmyard animal and country prints; at one end is a big log fire, at the other a woodburning stove. A snug one-table area is opposite the servery where they keep Butcombe Bitter, Hook Norton Hooky Bitter and a guest beer on handpump, european wines by the glass, home-made cordials, local cider, some interesting liqueurs and a good choice of teas and coffees; board games. The fairly spacious and raftered two-part dining room is up a few steps. The bedrooms are comfortable and pretty and the breakfasts very good. Smokers get a heated shelter at the back.

Using the best local, seasonal produce, the delicious food includes nibbles such as salt cod brandade with tartar sauce and home-made sausage roll with home-made ketchup, plus squid, mussel and seaweed stew, pressed pork terrine with home-made dijon mustard, chicken supreme with devilled livers sauce, haddock with smoked haddock croquettes and pressed and charred leeks, chargrilled beef rump with bone marrow butter, onion rings and triple-cooked chips, and puddings such as blood orange tart with dark chocolate sorbet and baked custard with poached rhubarb and granita of rhubarb. *Benchmark main dish: pork loin and hodge podge pudding wellington with black cabbage £19.00. Two-course evening meal £26.00.*

Free house ~ Licensees Emily Watkins and Miles Lampson ~ Real ale ~ (01608) 658327 ~ Open 12-11 (midnight Sat, 10 Sun) ~ Bar food 12-2 (3 Sat), 6-9; 12-4, 6-8 Sun ~ Restaurant ~ Children welcome ~ Dogs allowed in bar and bedrooms ~ Wi-fi ~ Bedrooms: £75/£95 ~ www.thekinghamplough.co.uk *Recommended by Bernard Stradling, Colin Flowers*

KINGSTON LISLE

SU3287 Map 4

Blowing Stone ⭐ ◖◉ ♀ ◀

Village signposted off B4507 W of Wantage; OX12 9QL

Easy-going chatty country pub with up-to-date blend of simple comfort, good interesting food and drink

This is a cheerful pub with enjoyable food and drink and a warm welcome from the helpful staff. At its heart is the central bar; as this is racehorse country, they have the *Racing Post* alongside other daily papers, lots of photographs on the pale sage walls of racehorses (often spectacularly coming to grief over jumps), and broad tiles by the log fire which suit the muddy riding boots of the chatty young people in from nearby training stables. Several separate areas radiate off, most of them on the small side, snug and carpeted, though the back dining conservatory is more spacious. Apart from a couple of high-backed winged settles, the furniture is mostly an unfussy mix of country dining tables each with its own set of matching chairs, either padded or generously cushioned. Greene King Morland Original, Purity Pure Ubu, Ramsbury Bitter and Sharps Doom Bar on handpump, 12 decent wines by the glass and ten malt whiskies; background music, TV and board games. There's a couple of picnic-sets under cocktail parasols on the pretty front terrace, with more on the back lawn by a rockery.

 Everything is made from scratch from horseradish up to produce the good, seasonal dishes: lunchtime baguettes, mussels with tomatoes, garlic and white wine, hot sticky chicken wings with fresh mango, spring onion and chilli, steak burger with coleslaw and chips, butternut squash, spinach and chickpea tagine, chicken breast filled with wild mushroom and chicken mousse wrapped in puff pastry with wholegrain mustard sauce, and puddings such as brandy panna cotta with fresh fruit and sticky toffee pudding with toffee sauce. *Benchmark main dish: crispy squid with chilli jam and lime £13.50. Two-course evening meal £21.50.*

Free house ~ Licensees Angus and Steph Tucker ~ Real ale ~ (01367) 820288 ~ Open 12-midnight ~ Bar food 12-2, 6.30-9 ~ Restaurant ~ Children welcome ~ Dogs allowed in bar ~ Wi-fi ~ www.theblowingstone.co.uk *Recommended by Emma Scofield, Martin Jones, Katharine Cowherd, Neil and Angela Huxter*

KIRTLINGTON

SP4919 Map 4

Oxford Arms ◖◉ ♀

Troy Lane, junction with A4095 W of Bicester; OX5 3HA

Civilised and friendly stripped-stone pub with enjoyable food using local produce and good wine choice

'A genteel and friendly old place' is how one reader describes this deservedly popular stone pub – and that seems just right to us. The long line of linked rooms is divided by a central stone hearth with a great round stove, and by the servery itself – where you'll find Brakspears Oxford Gold and St Austell Tribute on handpump, an interesting range of 16 wines in two glass sizes, 15 malt whiskies, farm cider and organic soft drinks. Past the bar area with its cushioned wall pews, creaky beamed ceiling and age-darkened floor tiles, dining tables on parquet have neat red chairs; beyond that, leather sofas cluster round a log fire at the end. Also, church candles, fresh flowers and plenty of stripped stone. A sheltered back terrace has teak tables under giant parasols with heaters, and further off picnic-sets on pale gravel. The geranium-filled window boxes are pretty.

Good, interesting food includes sandwiches, pâté with home-made chutney, potted shrimps, risotto of the day, salmon and prawn fishcakes with sweet chilli sauce, 28-day-aged sirloin steak with mustard and horseradish butter, daily specials, and puddings such as bread and butter pudding and cognac prunes with vanilla ice-cream. *Benchmark main dish: venison burger with triple-cooked chips £14.00. Two-course evening meal £21.00.*

Punch ~ Lease Bryn Jones ~ Real ale ~ (01869) 350208 ~ Open 12-2.30, 6-11; 12-3 Sun ~ Bar food 12-2.30, 6.30-9.30 ~ Restaurant ~ Well behaved children welcome ~ Dogs allowed in bar ~ www.oxford-arms.co.uk *Recommended by Ian Herdman, Val and Alan Green, Ian Wilson, N R White, John Evans, Tony Hobden, Robert Wivell, Brian and Anna Marsden, Simone Barratt, Steve and Liz Tilley, Elena Krasnova*

LANGFORD
Bell ♀

SP2402   Map 4

Village signposted off A361 N of Lechlade, then pub signed; GL7 3LF

Well run, welcoming pub with beams, flagstones and log fires, friendly service, well chosen wines and beer, and good popular food

Tucked away near the village church, this is a bustling 17th-c pub with genuinely friendly licensees. There's a cosy little bar with a couple of high chairs against the counter and a rug on flagstones, plus a larger bar with an open fire, church candles, a mix of stools and dining chairs and Olde Swan Ma Pardoes IPA, Sharps Cornish Coaster and West Berkshire Swift Pale Ale on handpump, 16 wines by the glass, several malt whiskies and a farm cider. The two heavily beamed dining rooms contain more open fires, modern art on the walls, wheelback chairs around dark tables on big flagstones and a couple of cushioned window seats. The small garden has a few seats and tables. This is a quiet and charming village.

The well thought-of food includes sandwiches, chicken liver pâté with cranberry sauce, creamy garlic field mushrooms, chicken in a creamy blue cheese sauce, gammon and free-range eggs, mushroom risotto, lamb shank with rosemary and red wine, smoked haddock with spinach, a poached egg and wholegrain mustard and leek mash, hake fillet with sausage cassoulet, and puddings such as warm chocolate fudge brownie and apple and cinnamon crumble. *Benchmark main dish: crispy pork belly with apple and cider reduction £12.95. Two-course evening meal £19.00.*

Free house ~ Licensee Clive Vasey ~ Real ale ~ (01367) 860249 ~ Open 12-3, 5 (6 in winter)-11; 12-11 (12-3, 6-11 in winter) Sat; 12-3.30 (4 in winter) Sun ~ Bar food 12-2.30, 6-9.30; 12-9.30 Sat ~ Restaurant ~ Children welcome ~ Dogs allowed in bar ~ Wi-fi ~ www.thebellinnlangford.co.uk *Recommended by Mrs Julie Thomas, R K Phillips, Tracey and Stephen Groves*

LONGWORTH
Blue Boar

SU3899   Map 4

Tucks Lane; OX13 5ET

Smashing old pub with a friendly welcome for all, good wines and beer, and fairly priced reliable food; Thames-side walks nearby

Run with thought and care, this old place goes from strength to strength. There's always a good mix of customers and the three low-beamed, characterful small rooms have a bustling but easy-going atmosphere. It's properly traditional, with brasses, hops and assorted knick-knacks (skis, an old clocking-in machine) on the walls and ceilings, scrubbed wooden tables and benches that are properly wooden rather than upholstered, faded rugs and floor tiles, fresh flowers on the bar and two blazing log fires (the one by the bar is noteworthy). The main eating area is the red-painted room at the end and there's a quieter restaurant extension too. Brakspears Bitter, Fullers London Pride and Sharps Doom Bar on handpump, 20 malt whiskies and a dozen wines by the glass. There are tables in front and on the back terrace, and the Thames is a short walk away.

Good, popular food includes chicken liver foie gras, devilled whitebait with aioli, an antipasti sharing board, beer in ale pie, pizzas with lots of toppings, barbecue ribs and chips, lambs liver, smoked bacon and onion gravy, prawn katsu curry, slow-roast pork belly with black pudding, mashed potatoes and apple relish, and puddings such as dark chocolate brownie with marshmallow ice-cream and tiramisu. *Benchmark main dish: burger with cheese, bacon and chips £10.95. Two-course evening meal £20.00.*

Free house ~ Licensee Paul Dailey ~ Real ale ~ (01865) 820494 ~ Open 12-11 (midnight Sat); 12-11 Sun ~ Bar food 12-2.30, 6.30-9.30 (10 Fri, Sat); 12-3, 6.30-9 Sun ~ Restaurant ~ Children welcome ~ Dogs allowed in bar ~ www.blueboarlongworth.co.uk
Recommended by Tim Maddison, Dick and Madeleine Brown, R K Phillips

MINSTER LOVELL
SP3211   Map 4

Old Swan & Minster Mill 🌟 ♀ 🛏

Just N of B4047 Witney–Burford; OX29 0RN

Carefully restored ancient inn with old-fashioned bar, real ales, a fine wine list, pubby and more elaborate food and acres of gardens and grounds; exceptional bedrooms

Much emphasis is placed on the hotel and restaurant side of this civilised and lovely ancient Cotswold inn, but its heart remains in the restful and unchanging little bar. Here you'll find stools at the wooden counter, Brakspears Bitter and Oxford Gold and Wychwood Hobgoblin on handpump, good wines by the glass from a fine list, 23 malt whiskies and quite a choice of teas and coffees. Leading off are several attractive low-beamed rooms with big log fires in huge fireplaces, red and green leather tub chairs, all manner of comfortable armchairs, sofas, dining chairs and wooden tables, rugs on bare boards or ancient flagstones, antiques and prints and lots of horsebrasses, bed-warming pans, swords, hunting horns and even a suit of armour; fresh flowers everywhere, background music and board games. Seats are dotted around the 65 acres of grounds (the white metal ones beside the water are much prized) and they have fishing rights to a mile of the River Windrush, tennis courts, boules and croquet. The bedrooms have plenty of character and the top end ones are luxurious.

The excellent food uses produce from their own kitchen garden: as well as sandwiches, dishes include duck terrine with citrus salad and aged port dressing, king scallop with caramelised white pudding and watercress sauce, trio of local sausages with onion gravy, butternut squash and sage risotto with truffle oil, burger with bacon and cheese and triple-cooked chips, steak in ale pie, and puddings such as warm chocolate fondant and baked alaska with berry coulis. *Benchmark main dish: beer-battered haddock and chips £16.00. Two-course evening meal £24.00.*

Free house ~ Licensee Ian Solkin ~ Real ale ~ (01993) 774441 ~ Open 12 (12.30 weekends)-3, 6.30-11 ~ Bar food 12 (12.30 weekends)-3, 6.30-9 (9.30 Sat) ~ Restaurant ~ Children welcome ~ Dogs allowed in bar and bedrooms ~ Live jazz first Sun of month ~ Bedrooms: £145/£165 ~ www.oldswanandminstermill.com
Recommended by Bernard Stradling, David Carr, Simon and Mandy King, S F Parrinder

OXFORD   SP5106 Map 4
Bear

Alfred Street/Wheatsheaf Alley; OX1 4EH

Delightful pub with friendly staff, two cosy rooms, six real ales and well liked bar food

Dating from 1242, this little local is the oldest pub in the city and was a coaching inn in its heyday. Now it's low-key and rather charming; the two small low-ceilinged, beamed and partly panelled rooms, not over-smart and often packed with students, have a bustling chatty atmosphere, winter coal fires, thousands of vintage ties on the walls and up to six real ales from handpumps on the fine pewter bar counter: Fullers Chiswick, ESB, HSB and London Pride and a guest from Prospect. Staff are friendly and helpful. There are seats under parasols in the terraced back garden where summer barbecues are held.

Bar food includes sandwiches, goats cheese and mushroom parcels, whitebait with paprika mayonnaise, sharing platters, a quiche of the day, beef, chicken or vegetarian burger with toppings and chips, lamb shank with mint sauce, battered haddock and chips, and puddings. *Benchmark main dish: steak in ale pie £12.95. Two-course evening meal £14.00.*

Fullers ~ Manager James Vernede ~ Real ale ~ (01865) 728164 ~ Open 11-11 (midnight Fri, Sat); 11.30-10.30 Sun ~ Bar food 12-9 ~ Children welcome ~ Dogs allowed in bar ~ Live music Weds ~ www.bearoxford.co.uk *Recommended by David Carr*

OXFORD   SP5107 Map 4
Rose & Crown

North Parade Avenue; very narrow, so best to park in a nearby street; OX2 6LX

Long-serving licensees at lively friendly local with a good mix of customers, fine choice of drinks and proper home cooking

With a charming old-fashioned atmosphere and a good mix of customers including undergraduates, this busy local is given a great deal of individuality by its long-serving licensees. The front door opens into a passage with a small counter and bookshelves of reference books for crossword buffs. This leads to two rooms: a cosy one at the front overlooking the street, and a panelled back room housing the main bar and traditional pub furnishings. Adnams Bitter, Hook Norton Old Hooky, Shotover Scholar and a guest beer on handpump, around 30 malt whiskies and quite a choice of wines by the glass (including champagne and sparkling wine). The pleasant walled and heated back courtyard can be covered with a huge awning; at the far end is a 12-seater dining/meeting room. The lavatories are basic.

Honest, traditional and reasonably priced, the food includes sandwiches and baguettes, omelettes, ham, egg and chips, beer-battered fish and chips, pie with mash and gravy, and puddings such as apple pie and a changing hot pudding with custard; Sunday roasts from September to June. *Benchmark main dish: sausages, mash and gravy £7.95. Two-course evening meal £11.50.*

Free house ~ Licensees Andrew and Debbie Hall ~ Real ale ~ No credit cards ~ (01865) 510551 ~ Open 11am-midnight (1am Fri, Sat); closed afternoons (2.30-5.30) Aug, Sept ~ Bar food 12-2.15 (3.15 Sun), 6-9 ~ Well behaved and accompanied children may sit in courtyard until 5pm ~ Wi-fi ~ Occasional live music ~ www.rose-n-crown.com
Recommended by Tony and Jill Radnor

PISHILL
Crown

SU7190   Map 2

B480 Nettlebed–Watlington; RG9 6HH

Fine old inn with attractive beamed bars, winter fires, real ales, several wines by the glass and popular food

Largely rebuilt in the 15th c, this well run, red brick and flint pub is at the heart of the Chilterns with plenty of walks nearby. The friendly, professional licensees offer a warm welcome to all, as do their courteous and efficient staff. The partly panelled walls in the beamed bars are hung with old local photographs and maps, there are nice old chairs around a mix of wooden tables, candles everywhere, Brakspears Bitter and Rebellion IPA on handpump, seven wines by the glass and a dozen malt whiskies. There are standing oak timbers in the knocked-through back area and three roaring log fires in winter; the priest's hole is said to be one of the largest in the country. The beautiful thatched barn is used for parties and functions, and the pretty garden has plenty of seats and tables beneath neat blue parasols. The self-catering cottage can be rented by the night and breakfast can be provided.

Well liked food includes lunchtime sandwiches, potted pork rillettes with apple compote, deep-fried whitebait with aioli, lamb burger with cucumber relish and rosemary fries, butternut squash tart with fennel and walnut crumble, corn-fed chicken with dauphinoise potatoes, brill with pickled cockles, artichoke purée and morel jus, and puddings such as blueberry crème brûlée and dark chocolate mousse with salted caramel and tonka bean tuile. *Benchmark main dish: steak in ale pie £12.50. Two-course evening meal £18.00.*

Free house ~ Licensee Lucas Wood ~ Real ale ~ (01491) 638364 ~ Open 12-3, 6-11; 12-3.30 Sun; closed Sun evening ~ Bar food 12-2.30, 6.30-9 (9.30 Fri, Sat); 12-3 Sun ~ Well behaved children welcome ~ Dogs allowed in bar ~ Wi-fi ~ Bedrooms: /£95 ~ www.thecrowninnpishill.co.uk *Recommended by R T and J C Moggridge, John and Jackie Chalcraft, Di and Mike Gillam*

RAMSDEN
Royal Oak 🍷 ◨

SP3515   Map 4

Village signposted off B4022 Witney–Charlbury; OX7 3AU

Busy pub with long-serving licensees, large helpings of varied food, carefully chosen wines and seats outside; bedrooms

To really appreciate the surrounding countryside and fine walks, it makes sense to stay in the comfortable bedrooms in the converted coach house and stable block. This 17th-c Cotswold stone pub has been run by the same enthusiastic licensees for 27 years, and the unpretentious rooms are relaxed and friendly with all manner of wooden tables, chairs and settles, cushioned window seats, exposed stone walls, bookcases with old and new copies of *Country Life* and, when the weather gets cold, a cheerful log fire. Hook Norton Bitter, Ramsbury Deer Hunter, Wye Valley IPA and a guest beer on handpump, 40 wines by the glass from a carefully chosen list and three farm ciders. Outside, there are tables and chairs in front and on the terrace behind the restaurant (folding doors give easy access). The village church is opposite.

As well as lunchtime sandwiches, the varied menu includes devilled lambs kidneys, baked brie with crudités, vegetable lasagne, burger with bacon, cheese and fries, cod with a tapenade crust and sweet pepper sauce, a pie of the week, free-range poussin in tomato and chorizo sauce, haunch of local venison, and puddings. *Benchmark main dish: steak and kidney pudding £15.00. Two-course evening meal £20.00.*

Free house ~ Licensee Jon Oldham ~ Real ale ~ (01993) 868213 ~ Open 11.30-3.30, 6.30-11; 11.30-11 Sat; 12-10.30 Sun ~ Bar food 12-2, 7-9.30; all day weekends ~ Restaurant ~ Children welcome ~ Dogs allowed in bar ~ Bedrooms: £55/£85 ~ www.royaloakramsden.com *Recommended by David and Sue Atkinson, Richard Stanfield*

 ROTHERFIELD GREYS   SU7282 Map 2

Maltsters Arms ♀

Can be reached off A4155 in Henley, via Greys Road passing Southfields long-stay car park; or follow Greys Church signpost off B481 N of Sonning Common; RG9 4QD

Well run, civilised country pub in the Chilterns with well liked, fairly priced food, nice scenery and walks

As Greys Court (National Trust) is not far away and two good footpaths pass nearby, this civilised and friendly pub is just the place for a break. The maroon-carpeted front room has comfortable wall banquettes and lots of horsebrasses on black beams, Brakspears Bitter and Oxford Gold and a guest beer on handpump, ten wines by the glass and decent coffee; there's a warm open fire in winter and maybe background music. Beyond the serving area, which has hop bines and pewter tankards hanging from its joists, a back room has cricketing prints on dark red walls over a shiny panelled dado, and a mix of furnishings from pink-cushioned pale wooden dining chairs to a pair of leatherette banquettes forming a corner booth. Terrace tables under a big heated canopy are set with linen for meals, and the grass behind has picnic-sets under green parasols, looking out over paddocks to rolling woodland.

🍴 Reasonably priced and popular, the food includes panini, bacon-wrapped egg on french toast, king prawns in herb and garlic butter, steak and kidney pudding, pea and caramelised shallot ravioli in sage butter, slow-roast half shoulder of lamb with red wine jus, daily specials, and puddings. *Benchmark main dish: chicken and mushroom pancake £9.75. Two-course evening meal £18.00.*

Brakspears ~ Tenants Peter and Helen Bland ~ Real ale ~ (01491) 628400 ~ Open 11.45-3, 6-11 (midnight Sat); 12-9 (6 winter) Sun ~ Bar food 12-2.30, 6.15-9.15; 12-2.45 Sun ~ Children welcome ~ Dogs welcome ~ Wi-fi ~ www.maltsters.co.uk *Recommended by Penny and Peter Keevil, DHV, Cliff Sparkes, Roy Hoing*

 SHILTON   SP2608 Map 4

Rose & Crown

Just off B4020 SE of Burford; OX18 4AB

Simple and appealing little village pub, with a relaxed civilised atmosphere, real ales and good food

The friendly, hands-on licensee and his helpful staff will make sure everything runs smoothly when you visit this pretty, 17th-c stone pub. The small front bar has an unassuming but civilised feel, low beams and timbers, exposed stone walls, a log fire in a big fireplace and half a dozen or so farmhouse chairs and tables on the red tiled floor. There are usually a few locals at the planked counter where they serve Hook Norton Old Hooky, Loose Cannon Abingdon Bridge and Wells & Youngs Bitter on handpump, along with ten wines by the glass and six malt whiskies.

A second room, similar but bigger, is used mainly for eating, with flowers on the tables and another fireplace. At the side, an pretty garden has picnic-sets. This is a lovely village.

Cooked by the landlord, the highly thought-of food includes ciabattas, game terrine with red onion marmalade, gravadlax with dill and mustard sauce, ham and egg, chicken ballotine with girolle mushrooms and rainbow chard, smoked haddock, salmon and prawn fish pie, aubergine parmigiana, pork chop with black pudding and champ, and puddings such as chocolate and walnut brownie with chocolate sauce and blackberry and apple crumble. *Benchmark main dish: steak and mushroom in ale pie £12.50. Two-course evening meal £19.50.*

Free house ~ Licensee Martin Coldicott ~ Real ale ~ (01993) 842280 ~ Open 11.30-3, 6-11; 11.30-11 Fri, Sat; 12-10 Sun ~ Bar food 12-2 (2.45 weekends and bank holidays), 7-9 ~ Children welcome until 7pm ~ Dogs allowed in bar ~ www.roseandcrownshilton.com
Recommended by R K Phillips, David Handforth, Mrs V T Bone

SHIPLAKE
SU7779   Map 2

Baskerville 🏵 ⌾ ♟ ◧ 🛏

Station Road, Lower Shiplake (off A4155 just S of Henley); RG9 3NY

Emphasis on imaginative food but a proper public bar too; interesting sporting memorabilia and a pretty garden; bedrooms

Consistently well run and popular, this busy pub is the hub of the village. There are bar chairs around the light, modern counter (used by the chatty locals), a few beams, pale wood dining chairs and tables on floors of light wood or patterned carpet, plush red banquettes by the windows and a couple of log fires in brick fireplaces. Loddon Hoppit, Rebellion IPA, Sharps Doom Bar and Timothy Taylors Landlord on handpump, 15 wines by the glass from a thoughtfully chosen list and 40 malt whiskies, all served by neat staff; they support WaterAid by charging 50p for a jug of iced water and at time of writing have raised £4,300. The red walls are hung with a fair amount of sporting memorabilia and pictures (especially old rowing photos – Henley is very near) as well as signed rugby shirts and photos (the pub has its own rugby club) and maps of the Thames. There are flowers and large house plants dotted about; background music and TV. It feels quite homely in a smart way, with chintzy touches such as a shelf of china cow jugs; there's a separate dining room and a small room for private parties. The pretty garden has a covered barbecue area, smart teak furniture under huge parasols, some rather fun statues cut from box hedging, and a timber play frame. The bedrooms are well equipped and comfortable and the breakfasts extremely good.

Name-checking local producers, the imaginative food includes lunchtime open sandwiches, salt and pepper squid with harissa mayonnaise, crispy pork belly with honey, ginger and chilli dressing, chicken, bacon and mushroom pie, cumin roast rump of lamb with pepper and olive caponata and sweet potato fries, rope-grown mussels with smoked bacon, blue cheese, shallot and cider sauce, and puddings such as lemon posset with raspberry coulis and sticky toffee pudding with toffee sauce. *Benchmark main dish: steak pie £13.50. Two-course evening meal £22.00.*

Free house ~ Licensee Allan Hannah ~ Real ale ~ (0118) 940 3332 ~ Open 11-11; 12-10.30 Sun ~ Bar food 12-9.30 (10 Fri, Sat); 12-3.30 Sun ~ Restaurant ~ Children welcome but not in restaurant after 7pm Fri, Sat ~ Dogs allowed in bar and bedrooms ~ Wi-fi ~ Bedrooms: £89/£99 ~ www.thebaskerville.com *Recommended by Paul Humphreys, John Pritchard*

STANFORD IN THE VALE
SU3393 Map 4

Horse & Jockey ♀ £

A417 Faringdon–Wantage; Faringdon Road; SN7 8NN

Friendly traditional village local with real character, highly thought-of and good value food and well chosen wines

Refurbished after a fire, this is a charming 16th-c pub with a friendly, hard-working landlord. As this is racehorse training country (and given the pub's name) there are big Alfred Munnings' racecourse prints, card collections of Grand National winners and other horse and jockey pictures on the walls. The pub is split into two areas: a contemporary dining area and an older part with flagstones, wood flooring, low beams and raftered ceilings. There are old high-backed settles and leather armchairs, a woodburning stove in a big fireplace and an easy-going and welcoming atmosphere. A beer named for the pub and Cotswold Spring Old Sodbury Mild on handpump, carefully chosen wines by the glass and a dozen malt whiskies. As well as tables under a heated courtyard canopy, there's a separate enclosed and informal family garden with picnic-sets. The bedrooms are comfortable.

As well as sandwiches, the popular food includes duck liver parfait with cranberry and port marmalade, salt and pepper chilli-battered calamari with sweet chilli sauce, sharing boards, lamb rogan josh, sticky barbecue pork ribs, home-baked honey ham and free-range eggs, wild mushroom stroganoff, seafood linguine, and puddings such as toffee apple crumble and new york cheesecake. *Benchmark main dish: steak in ale pie £11.95. Two-course evening meal £17.00.*

Greene King ~ Lease Charles and Anna Gaunt ~ Real ale ~ (01367) 710302 ~ Open 11-3, 5-midnight; 11am-12.30am Fri, Sat; 12-11 Sun ~ Bar food 12-2.30, 6.30-9 (9.30 Fri, Sat) ~ Restaurant ~ Children welcome ~ Dogs allowed in bar ~ Wi-fi ~ Monthly open mike night ~ Bedrooms: £60/£70 ~ www.horseandjockey.org
Recommended by Cliff Sparkes, R K Phillips, Mrs V T Bone

SWERFORD
SP3830 Map 4

Masons Arms ♀

A361 Banbury–Chipping Norton; OX7 4AP

Well liked food and fair choice of drinks in bustling dining pub, relaxed atmosphere and country views

This is an attractive dining pub in the Cotswold hills with a friendly bar. There's a big brown leather sofa facing a couple of armchairs in front of the log fire in a stone fireplace, rugs on pale wooden floors, Brakspears Bitter and Jennings Cumberland on handpump and ten wines by the glass. The light and airy dining extension has pastel-painted dining chairs around nice old tables on beige carpet, and steps lead down to a cream-painted room with chunky tables and contemporary pictures. Around the other side of the bar is another roomy dining room with great views by day, candles at night and a civilised feel; background music. The neat back garden has picnic-sets on grass and pretty views over the Oxfordshire countryside.

Quite a choice of well presented food includes chinese five-spice shredded duck in panko breadcrumbs on stir-fried vegetables with hoi sin sauce, field mushrooms with asparagus and goats cheese rarebit, beer-battered hake and chips, garlic and thyme corn-fed chicken with mango, pineapple and banana sweet curry sauce, beef cobbler with horseradish dumpling, a trio of fish with fennel and potato dauphinoise and lobster bisque, and puddings such as crumble of the day and

chocolate orange tart; they also offer a two- and three-course set lunch.
Benchmark main dish: duo of local pork with creamy white wine and wholegrain mustard sauce £15.95. Two-course evening meal £22.00.

Free house ~ Licensee Louise Davies ~ Real ale ~ (01608) 683212 ~ Open 11-3, 6-11; 11-8 (6 winter) Sun ~ Bar food 12-2.15, 6-9; 12-6 Sun ~ Restaurant ~ Children welcome ~ Wi-fi ~ www.masons-arms.com *Recommended by Ian Herdman, J and S Watkins*

SWINBROOK   SP2812   Map 4

Swan 🌟 ♀ 🛏

Back road a mile N of A40, 2 miles E of Burford; OX18 4DY

Rather smart old pub with handsome oak garden rooms, antiques-filled bars, local beers and contemporary food; bedrooms

When the wisteria is in flower this civilised 400-year-old stone pub looks exceedingly pretty, and the seats and circular picnic-sets make the best of its fine position by a bridge over the River Windrush. The inn is owned by the Dowager Duchess of Devonshire (the last of the Mitford sisters, who grew up in the village) and there are plenty of interesting Mitford family photographs blown up on the walls. The little bar has simple antique furnishings, settles and benches, an open fire and (in an alcove) a stuffed swan; locals drop in here for a pint and a chat. A small dining room leads off from the bar to the right of the entrance, and there are also two green oak garden rooms with high-backed beige and green dining chairs around pale wood tables, and views over the garden and orchard. Hook Norton Hooky Bitter and a couple of changing guest beers on handpump, ten wines by the glass and Weston's organic cider; background music. The elegant bedrooms are in a smartly converted stone barn beside the pub. The Kings Head in Bledington (Gloucestershire) is run by the same first class licensees.

 Using carefully chosen local suppliers, the enterprising seasonal menu includes sandwiches, home-cured bresaola with rocket and parmesan, mackerel with beetroot salad and sweet mustard and dill dressing, saffron risotto with sunblush tomatoes and parmesan, chorizo with sweetcorn pancake and fried egg, corn-fed chicken with walnut pesto, artichoke and olives, shredded venison confit with black pudding, haricots blancs and button onions, and puddings such as rhubarb jelly with chantilly cream and dark chocolate and orange pot with cardamom ice-cream. *Benchmark main dish: whole plaice with crispy pancetta, pea purée and caper and rosemary butter £17.50. Two-course evening meal £22.50.*

Free house ~ Licensees Archie and Nicola Orr-Ewing ~ Real ale ~ (01993) 823339 ~ Open 11.30-11 (11.30 Sat); 12-10.30 Sun; 11-3, 6-11 in winter ~ Bar food 12-2, 7-9 (6.30-9.30 Fri, Sat); 12-3, 6.30-9.30 Sun ~ Restaurant ~ Children welcome ~ Dogs allowed in bar ~ Wi-fi ~ Bedrooms: £100/£120 ~ www.theswanswinbrook.co.uk
Recommended by Bernard Stradling, Dr and Mrs S G Barber, Mike and Mary Carter, Lois Dyer, Richard Stanfield, Michael Sargent

TADPOLE BRIDGE   SP3200   Map 4

Trout 🌟 ♀ 🛏

Back road Bampton–Buckland, 4 miles NE of Faringdon; SN7 8RF

Busy country inn by the River Thames with a fine choice of drinks, popular modern food, and seats in the waterside garden; bedrooms

You'll be warmly welcomed by the courteous, friendly staff in this civilised and busy inn, whether you want just a drink or a full meal or to stay overnight. It remains a favourite with many of our readers. The L-shaped bar has handsome green and red checked chairs around a mix of nice wooden tables, rugs on flagstones, green paintwork behind a modern wooden bar counter, fresh flowers, two woodburning stoves and a large stuffed trout. The airy restaurant is appealingly candlelit in the evenings. Ramsbury Bitter, Siren Undercurrent, Wells & Youngs Bitter and White Horse Wayland Smithy on handpump, 12 wines by the glass from a wide-ranging and carefully chosen list, 14 malt whiskies and two farm ciders. This is a peaceful and picturesque spot by the Thames and there are good quality teak chairs and tables under blue parasols in the pretty garden; arrive early in fine weather as it can get packed. You can hire punts with champagne hampers and there are moorings (book in advance) for six boats. The bedrooms have been refurbished.

 Enjoyable modern cooking includes all-day tapas, goats cheese panna cotta with poached pear, beetroot and hazelnut dressing, scallops with black pudding, cauliflower purée and crispy parma ham, a pie of the day, beer-battered haddock and chips, guinea fowl cooked three ways, roast rack of lamb with red cabbage purée and apricot and rosemary jus, and puddings such as Grand Marnier crème brûlée and white chocolate and hazelnut parfait. *Benchmark main dish: slow-roast suckling pig with sweet potato parmentier £15.95. Two-course evening meal £21.00.*

Free house ~ Licensees Gareth and Helen Pugh ~ Real ale ~ (01367) 870382 ~ Open 11.30-11; 12-10 Sun; 11.30-3, 6-11 Mon-Thurs in winter ~ Bar food 12-2, 7-9; some food all day at weekends ~ Children welcome ~ Dogs welcome ~ Wi-fi ~ Bedrooms: £85/£130 ~ www.troutinn.co.uk *Recommended by R K Phillips, Tony Hobden, Martin and Karen Wake*

WEST HANNEY
Plough
SU4092 Map 2

Just off A338 N of Wantage; Church Street; OX12 0LN

Thatched village pub with tasty, popular food, a good choice of drinks and plenty of seats outside

There's always something going on in this pretty, neatly thatched, early 16th-c village pub – whether book, cricket and golf club meetings, weekly aunt sally tournaments or regular beer festivals. The comfortable, simply furnished bar has horsebrasses on beams, some bar stools, wheelback chairs around wooden tables, a log fire in a stone fireplace and lots of photographs of the pub on the walls. There's Adnams Best, Brains Bitter, Timothy Taylors Landlord and Wadworths 6X on handpump, half a dozen wines by the glass and Thatcher's cider; darts, TV and background music. Outside is a covered seating area, more tables and chairs on a back terrace overlooking the walled garden and plenty of picnic-sets on grass.

The well liked food includes baguettes, garlic mushrooms in sherry and cream, crab and prawn fishcakes with sweet chilli sauce, sharing platters, wild mushroom and blue cheese tart, ham and egg, steak in ale pie, liver, bacon, mash and gravy, lemon and garlic chicken with shallots and cream, a fish dish of the day, and puddings such as banoffi pie and sticky toffee pudding. *Benchmark main dish: beer-battered fish and chips £10.95. Two-course evening meal £18.50.*

Free house ~ Licensee Steve Cadogan ~ Real ale ~ (01235) 868674 ~ Open 12-3, 6-11; 12-midnight Sat, Sun; closed Mon ~ Bar food 12-2.30, 6.30-9.30; 12-5 Sun ~ Children welcome ~ Dogs welcome ~ www.theploughwesthanney.co.uk *Recommended by R K Phillips*

If you know a pub is ever open all day, please tell us.

WOLVERCOTE
SP4809 Map 4

Jacobs Inn .

Godstow Road; OX2 8PG

Informal and friendly place with simple furnishings, some quirky touches, honest, rural cooking and seats in the garden

With brunch served daily (9-5 Monday-Saturday; 9-midday Sunday) using their own eggs, pigs, vegetables and salads, plus cocktails and nibbles, this is a different sort of pub. It's buzzy and informally friendly, with the bar and dining room wrapped around the central bar counter. The simply furnished bar has leather armchairs and chesterfields, some plain tables and benches, wide floorboards, a small open fire, and high chairs at the counter where they keep Brakspears Bitter, Marstons Revisionist Dark IPA, and Ringwood Best and Boondoggle on handpump, 13 wines by the glass and lots of teas and coffees. You can eat at plain wooden tables in a grey panelled area with an open fire, or in the smarter, knocked-through dining room. This has standing timbers in the middle, a fire at each end and dark, shiny wooden chairs and tables on floorboards; there are standard lamps, stags' heads, a reel-to-reel tape recorder, quite a few mirrors and deli items for sale – it's all quite quirky. There are several seating areas outside: good quality tables and chairs under parasols, picnic-sets on decking, and deckchairs and more picnic-sets on grass.

 Brasserie-style food includes daily brunch – eggs royale, benedict or florentine, smoked salmon and scrambled eggs and a meat or vegetarian full breakfast – plus sandwiches, crispy brawn terrine with black pudding and chutney, seafood gratin, bubble and squeak pancakes with crispy egg, toulouse sausages with american mustard and hot dog bun, free-range bacon chop with grilled pineapple and fries, scallops and monkfish skewers with rouille, chilli and dill dressing, and puddings such as chocolate brownie sundae and blood orange cheesecake with orange curd. *Benchmark main dish: braised short rib of beef with house slaw and skinny fries £13.50. Two-course evening meal £19.00.*

Marstons ~ Lease Damion Farah and Johnny Pugsley ~ Real ale ~ (01865) 514333 ~ Open 9am-11pm ~ Bar food 9am-10pm ~ Restaurant ~ Children welcome ~ Dogs allowed in bar ~ Wi-fi ~ www.jacobs-inn.com *Recommended by Phoebe Peacock, Harvey Brown*

WOODSTOCK
SP4416 Map 4

Kings Arms ⭐ £ 🛏

Market Street/Park Lane (A44); OX20 1SU

Stylish town-centre hotel with well liked food, a wide choice of drinks and an enjoyable atmosphere; comfortable bedrooms

Again this year we've had nothing but warm praise from our readers for all aspects of this particularly well run and stylish town-centre inn; the charming, helpful, courteous service and highly enjoyable food have been especially noted. A good mix of customers in the unfussy bar creates a relaxed and informal atmosphere, and there's an appealing variety of old and new furnishings including brown leather furniture on the stripped-wood floor, smart blinds and black and white photographs; at the front is an old wooden settle and an interesting little woodburner. The bar leading to the brasserie-style dining room has an unusual stained-glass structure holding newspapers and magazines, and the attractive restaurant has a fine old fireplace. Brakspears Bitter, Loose Cannon Gunners Gold and North Cotswold Best on handpump, good coffees, 11 wines plus champagne by the glass and 29 malt whiskies. There are seats and tables on the street outside.

As well as a two- and three-course set lunch (Monday-Thursday) plus sandwiches and cream teas (until 6pm), the tempting food includes poached duck egg with spinach and hollandaise, potted mackerel with crispy capers, butter bean and walnut burger with cheese and chips, free-range chicken with minted cracked wheat and pea salad, fillet of bream with lemon and chervil butter, spinach and fennel broth, and puddings such as chocolate and orange brownie with stem ginger ice-cream and nutmeg brûlée with hazelnut brittle. *Benchmark main dish: baked cod with cockles, pea mayonnaise and chips £16.50. Two-course evening meal £20.50.*

Free house ~ Licensees David and Sara Sykes ~ Real ale ~ (01993) 813636 ~ Open 11am-11.30pm (11pm Sun) ~ Bar food 12-2, 6.30-9; some snacks all day ~ Restaurant ~ Children welcome in bar and restaurant but no under-12s in bedrooms ~ Bedrooms: £80/£150 ~ www.kings-hotel-woodstock.co.uk *Recommended by Mike and Shirley Stratton, John Branston, Martin and Pauline Jennings, Neil and Angela Huxter, Mr and Mrs P R Thomas, Richard Tilbrook, Phil and Helen Holt*

Also Worth a Visit in Oxfordshire

Besides the fully inspected pubs, you might like to try these pubs that have been recommended to us and described by readers. Do tell us what you think of them: feedback@goodguides.com

ABINGDON   SU4997
Brewery Tap (01235) 521655
Ock Street; OX14 5BZ Former tap for defunct Morland Brewery but still serving Original along with changing guests, proper ciders and good choice of wines, well priced lunchtime food including popular Sun roasts, stone floors and panelled walls, two log fires, darts, Tues quiz; background and Sun live music, free wi-fi; children and dogs welcome, enclosed courtyard with aunt sally, three bedrooms, open all day (till 1am Fri, Sat). *(Anon)*

ADDERBURY   SP4735
★ Red Lion (01295) 810269
The Green; off A4260 S of Banbury; OX17 3NG Attractive 17th-c stone coaching inn with good choice of enjoyable well priced food (all day weekends) including deals, helpful friendly staff, Greene King ales, good wine range and coffee, linked bar rooms with high stripped beams, panelling and stonework, big inglenook log fire, old books and Victorian/Edwardian pictures, daily papers, games area, more modern back restaurant extension; background music; children in eating areas, picnic-sets out on roadside terrace, 12 character bedrooms, good breakfast, open all day in summer. *(George Atkinson)*

ASTHALL   SP2811
★ Maytime (01993) 822068
Off A40 at W end of Witney bypass, then 1st left; OX18 4HW Refurbished 17th-c Cotswold-stone dining pub; good food from pub favourites to more elaborate restaurant dishes, wide choice of wines by the glass, two or three well kept changing ales and a real cider, lofty main bar with exposed roof trusses and flagstone floor, leather sofas and bar stools, several low beamed cosy dining areas off, one like a library, another with black slate floor and cushioned window seats overlooking lane, woodburner, steps up to conservatory; background music; children and dogs welcome (pub springer is Alfie), picnic-sets out at front with view of Asthall Manor, back terrace overlooking watermeadows, herb garden, enjoyable walks from the door, six well appointed bedrooms (some in courtyard), good breakfast, open all day. *(Laela Guttoriello, Liz Bell)*

ASTON TIRROLD   SU5586
★ Sweet Olive (01235) 851272
Aka Chequers; Fullers Road; village signed off A417 Streatley–Wantage; OX11 9EN Has atmosphere of a rustic french restaurant rather than village pub – but people do pop in for just a drink; main room with wall settles, mate's chairs, a few sturdy tables, grass matting over quarry tiles, small fireplace, good fresh bistro-style food including daily specials, nice french wines by the glass (wine box ends decorate back of servery), Brakspears and Fullers beers, friendly service, smaller room more formally set as restaurant with restrained décor; background music; children welcome, dogs in bar, picnic-sets under parasols in small cottagey garden, aunt sally, closed Sun evening, Weds, all Feb and two weeks in July. *(Colin McLachlan, D C T and E A Frewer)*

BECKLEY   SP5611
★ Abingdon Arms (01865) 351311
Signed off B4027; High Street; OX3 9UU Welcoming old dining pub in lovely unspoilt village; comfortably modernised simple

lounge, smaller public bar with antique carved settles, open fires, well kept Brakspears and guests, fair range of good reasonably priced wines, enjoyable home-made food from pub favourites up including good Sun roasts, friendly efficient service; background and some live music; children and dogs welcome, big garden dropping away from floodlit terrace to trees, summer house, superb views over RSPB Otmoor reserve – good walks, open all day weekends. *(Lesley and Brian Lynn, Martin and Pauline Jennings)*

BEGBROKE   SP4713
Royal Sun (01865) 374718
A44 Oxford–Woodstock; OX5 1RZ Welcoming old stone-built pub with modernised bare-boards interior, wide choice of good value food from snacks to Sun carvery, well kept Hook Norton and a guest, good friendly service, free monkey nuts on the bar; may be background music, big-screen sports TV; children welcome, no dogs inside, tables on terrace and in small garden, open all day from 8.30am for breakfast. *(Anon)*

BLOXHAM   SP4235
★ **Joiners Arms** (01295) 720223
Old Bridge Road, off A361; OX15 4LY Golden-stone 16th-c inn with rambling rooms, white dining chairs around pale tables on wood floor, plenty of exposed stone, open fires, ales such as Brakspears and Marstons, enjoyable traditional food including deals, old well in raftered room off bar; children and dogs welcome, pretty window boxes, seats out under parasols on various levels – most popular down steps by stream (play house there too), open all day. *(Meg and Colin Hamilton)*

BRIGHTWELL   SU5890
Red Lion (01491) 837373
Signed off A4130 2 miles W of Wallingford; OX10 0RT Community village pub still very popular under newish management; four well kept ales with regulars Appleford, Loddon and West Berkshire, wines from nearby vineyard, enjoyable good value home-made food, two-part bar with snug seating by log fire, dining extension; dogs welcome, seats out at front and in back garden, open all day Sun till 9pm. *(John Pritchard)*

BRITWELL SALOME   SU6793
★ **Red Lion** (01491) 613140
B4009 Watlington–Benson; OX49 5LG Interesting food cooked by landlord is main draw to this brick and flint pub; friendly bar with comfortable sofas, pews and assorted tables and chairs, two red-walled dining rooms off, open fires and church candles, West Berkshire Mr Chubbs and Gun Dog Jacks Spaniels kept well, 13 wines by the glass and some unusual gins, good friendly service; children and dogs welcome, seats

in courtyard garden, closed Sun evening, all Mon, Tues lunchtime. *(David and Stella Martin, Torrens Lyster, David Lamb, C A Hall)*

BROUGHTON   SP4238
★ **Saye & Sele Arms** (01295) 263348
B4035 SW of Banbury; OX15 5ED Attractive old stone house part of the Broughton Estate with Castle just five minutes away; sizeable bar with polished flagstones, cushioned window seats and dark wooden furnishings, a few brasses, Adnams, North Cotswold, Sharps and a guest, nine wines by glass and a dozen malt whiskies, good food cooked by landlord, friendly service, two carpeted dining rooms with exposed stone walls, open fires, over 240 ornate water jugs hanging from beams; children welcome, picnic-sets and hanging baskets on terrace, neat lawn with tables under parasols, pergola and smokers' shelter, aunt sally, closed Sun evening. *(P and J Shapley, Martin Jones)*

BUCKLAND   SU3497
★ **Lamb** (01367) 870484
Off A420 NE of Faringdon; SN7 8QN 18th-c stone-built dining pub with good value interesting seasonal food in bar or restaurant, Loose Cannon Abingdon Bridge and a local guest, good choice of wines by the glass; well behaved children and dogs welcome (resident cocker called Oats), pleasant tree-shaded garden, good walks nearby, three comfortable bedrooms, closed Sun evening and Mon. *(William Goodhart)*

BURFORD   SP2512
Angel (01993) 822714
Witney Street; OX18 4SN Long heavy-beamed dining pub in interesting ancient building, warmly welcoming with roaring log fire, popular well cooked brasserie food including set menus, good range of drinks; TV; children welcome, big secluded garden, three comfortable bedrooms, closed Sun evening, Mon. *(Di and Mike Gillam)*

BURFORD   SP2512
★ **Mermaid** (01993) 822193
High Street; OX18 4QF Handsome old dining pub with beams, flagstones, panelling, stripped stone and nice log fire, good food (all day weekends) at sensible prices including local free-range meat and fresh fish, friendly efficient service, well kept Greene King ales and a guest, bay window seating at front, further airy back dining room and upstairs restaurant; background music; children welcome, tables out at front and in courtyard behind, open all day. *(Anon)*

CASSINGTON   SP4510
Chequers (01865) 882620
The Green; OX29 4DG Updated stone-built village pub with welcoming staff, enjoyable good value food from traditional favourites and stone-baked pizzas up, children's

menu too, well kept ales (tasters offered), conservatory dining room; background music, free wi-fi; seats out at front, eight recently refurbished bedrooms. *(Helene Grygar)*

CAULCOTT   SP5024
★ **Horse & Groom** (01869) 343257
Lower Heyford Road (B4030);
OX25 4ND Pretty 16th-c thatched cottage, L-shaped red-carpeted room with log fire in big inglenook (brassware under its long bressumer) and plush-cushioned settles, chairs and stools around a few dark tables at low-ceilinged bar end, White Horse Bitter and a couple of guests, decent house wines, good food (not Sun evening, Mon) including lots of different sausages, dining room at far end with jugs hanging on black joists, decorative plates, watercolours and original drawings, small side sun lounge, shove-ha'penny and board games; well behaved over-5s welcome, picnic-sets on neat lawn, closed Mon evening; for sale as we went to press, so things may change. *(Dave Braisted, Tony Hobden, Sue Callard, Colin McKerrow)*

CHADLINGTON   SP3222
Tite (01608) 676910
Off A361 S of Chipping Norton;
Mill End; OX7 3NY Friendly renovated 17th-c country pub; bar with eating areas either side, beams and stripped stone, pubby furniture including spindleback chairs and settles, flagstones and bare boards, woodburner in large fireplace, well kept Sharps Doom Bar and a couple of guests, a dozen wines by the glass, enjoyable fairly traditional home-cooked food (all day Sat, not Sun evening), winter quiz nights, occasional live music; well behaved children and dogs welcome, split-level terrace and pretty shrub-filled garden, good walks nearby, open all day. *(Richard Stanfield, J C Burgis, Liz Bell)*

CHALGROVE   SU6397
Red Lion (01865) 890625
High Street (B480 Watlington–
Stadhampton); OX44 7SS Attractive and popular beamed village pub, owned by local church trust since 1637; good home-made seasonal food (not Sun evening) from interesting menu, well kept Butcombe, Fullers London Pride, Rebellion Mild and two guests, friendly helpful staff, separate restaurant; nice front and back gardens, open all day Sun. *(Torrens Lyster)*

CHARNEY BASSETT   SU3794
Chequers (01235) 868642
Chapel Lane off Main Street; OX12 0EX
Welcoming 18th-c village-green pub with spacious modernised interior, Brakspears

ales, enjoyable fairly priced food from lunchtime sandwiches and baguettes to steaks; picnic-sets in small garden, three simple bedrooms. *(R K Phillips)*

CHAZEY HEATH   SU6979
Pack Horse (0118) 972 2140
Off A4074 Reading–Wallingford by
B4526; RG4 7UG Attractive 17th-c beamed village dining pub (part of Home Counties group); good choice of enjoyable fairly priced food from sandwiches and light dishes up, four ales including Brakspears and Loddon, plenty of wines by the glass, friendly informal staff, polished tables on wood and rug floors, built-in leatherette banquettes, shelves of books and lots of framed pictures, big log fire in raised hearth; background music; children and dogs (in main bar) welcome, disabled facilities, parasol-shaded tables in back garden, handy for Mapledurham house and watermill, open (and food) all day. *(John Pritchard)*

CHECKENDON   SU6684
★ **Black Horse** (01491) 680418
Village signed off A4074 Reading–
Wallingford; RG8 0TE Charmingly old-fashioned country tavern (tucked into woodland away from main village) kept by same family for 109 years; relaxing and unchanging series of rooms, back one with West Berkshire and White Horse tapped from the cask, one with bar counter has some tent pegs above fireplace (a reminder they used to be made here), homely side lounge with some splendidly unfashionable 1950s-style armchairs and another room beyond that, only baguettes and pickled eggs; no credit cards; children allowed but must be well behaved, seats on verandah and in garden, popular with walkers and cyclists. *(Anon)*

CHECKENDON   SU6682
Four Horseshoes (01491) 680325
Off A4074 Reading–Wallingford;
RG8 0QS Attractive partly thatched two-bar pub refurbished under present licensees; black beams, wood floors and some bare-brick walls, leather sofas by open fires, high-backed dining chairs around light wood tables, some carved bar stools, Brakspears ales and popular well priced traditional food, friendly helpful service, bar billiards; children and dogs welcome, big garden with play area and summer barbecues, good walks, open all day Sat, closed Sun evening, Mon. *(Paul Humphreys, Roy Hoing)*

CHILDREY   SU3687
Hatchet (01235) 751213
B4001/Stowhill; OX12 9UF Beamed village local, friendly and unpretentious,

By law, pubs must show a price list of their drinks. Let us know if you're inconvenienced by any breach of this law.

with half a dozen well kept ales including Greene King Morland Original, enjoyable straightforward food, games area with pool and darts; children and dogs welcome, a few picnic-sets out in front, garden play area, Ridgeway walks, closed Mon, Tues. *(Anon)*

CHIPPING NORTON   SP3127
Blue Boar (01608) 643525
High Street/Goddards Lane; OX7 5NP Spacious stone-built former coaching inn, ample helpings of enjoyable good value food (all day weekends), Marstons-related ales with guests such as local Cats, friendly helpful staff, raftered back restaurant and airy flagstoned garden room, woodburner in big stone fireplace; background and some live music, Thurs quiz, sports TV, fruit machine; children welcome, open all day. *(George Atkinson)*

CHIPPING NORTON   SP3127
★Chequers (01608) 644717
Goddards Lane; OX7 5NP Bustling traditional town pub with three softly lit beamed rooms, no frills but clean and comfortable, low ochre ceilings, log fire and plenty of character, eight well kept Fullers ales including seasonal ones, 15 wines by glass and and good tasty food (not Sun evening), airy conservatory restaurant, friendly efficient staff; children and dogs (in bar) welcome, theatre next door, open all day. *(P and J Shapley, Richard Tilbrook)*

CHISLEHAMPTON   SU5998
Coach & Horses (01865) 890255
B480 Oxford–Watlington, opposite B4015 to Abingdon; OX44 7UX Extended 16th-c coaching inn with two homely and civilised beamed bars, big log fire, sizeable restaurant with polished oak tables and wall banquettes, good choice of well prepared food (not Sun evening), friendly obliging service, three well kept ales usually including Hook Norton; background music; neat terraced gardens overlooking fields by River Thame, some tables out in front, bedrooms in courtyard block, open all day (closed 3-7pm Sun). *(Mr and Mrs P R Thomas, Roy Hoing)*

CHURCH ENSTONE   SP3725
★Crown (01608) 677262
Mill Lane; from A44 take B4030 turn-off at Enstone; OX7 4NN Pleasant uncluttered bar in beamed country pub, straightforward furniture, country pictures on stone walls, some horsebrasses, log fire in large fireplace, well kept Hook Norton and guests, consistently good food from pub favourites up, friendly efficient service, carpeted dining room with red walls, slate-floored conservatory with farmhouse furniture; children welcome, dogs in bar, white metal tables and chairs

on front terrace overlooking lane, picnic-sets in sheltered back garden, closed Sun evening. *(Gerry and Rosemary Dobson, Edward Mirzoeff, Barry Collett)*

COLESHILL   SU2393
Radnor Arms (01793) 861575
B4019 Faringdon–Highworth; village signposted off A417 in Faringdon and A361 in Highworth; SN6 7PR Pub and village owned by NT; bar with cushioned settles, plush carver chairs and woodburner, back alcove with more tables, steps down to main dining area, once a blacksmiths' forge with lofty beamed ceiling, log fire, dozens of tools and smiths' gear on walls, Old Forge ales brewed on site (tasting trays available), well priced traditional food (not Sun evening); children, walkers and dogs welcome, garden with aunt sally and play area, open all day. *(Tom McLean, Phil and Jane Villiers)*

CRAWLEY   SP3412
Lamb (01993) 708792
Steep Hill; just NW of Witney; OX29 9TW 18th-c stone-built dining pub with good imaginative food (daily changing menu) from owner-chef including tapas on Tues evening, friendly attentive service, Brakspears ales, simple beamed bar with polished boards and lovely fireplace, steps up to dining room; views from tables on back terrace and lawn, pretty village, good walks (on Palladian Way), open all day Sat, closed Sun evening, Mon, Tues lunchtime. *(Anon)*

CROPREDY   SP4646
Red Lion (01295) 758680
Off A423 N of Banbury; OX17 1PB Rambling 15th-c thatch-and-stone pub charmingly placed opposite pretty village's churchyard; low beams, inglenook log fire, high-backed settles, brass, plates and pictures, Hook Norton ales and two guests, separate dining room, games room with pool and darts, tiny post office Mon and Weds mornings, also shop at back selling guitars etc; background and some live music, Thurs quiz; children and dogs welcome, picnic-sets in back garden with part-covered terrace, near Oxford Canal (Bridge 152), annual Cropredy folk festival held close by. *(Mike Almond)*

CROWELL   SU7499
Shepherds Crook (01844) 355266
B4009, 2 miles from M40 junction 6; OX39 4RR Reopened and improved under new management, beamed bar with stripped brick and flagstones, woodburner, high-raftered dining area, enjoyable freshly prepared food (not Sun evening) including good value set lunch, ales such as Black Sheep and Rebellion, extensive wine list with

ten by the glass, 25 or so whiskies, 'jazz & dinner' evenings; children and dogs welcome, tables out on front terrace and village green, nice walks, open all day. *(Anon)*

CUMNOR   SP4503
Bear & Ragged Staff
(01865) 862329 *Signed from A420; Appleton Road; OX2 9QH* Extensive restaurant-pub dating from 16th c, contemporary décor in linked rooms with wood floors and painted beams, good food from sandwiches and sharing plates up, friendly efficient service, flagstoned bar with log fire, well kept Greene King ales and good wine choice, airy garden room; background music, TV, free wi-fi; children welcome, decked terrace and fenced play area, nine bedrooms, open (and food) all day. *(David Handforth)*

DEDDINGTON   SP4631
★ Deddington Arms (01869) 338364
Off A4260 (B4031) Banbury–Oxford; Horse Fair; OX15 0SH Beamed and timbered hotel in charming village with lots of antiques shops and good farmers' market fourth Sat of month; very well liked food including set lunchtime/evening menus in sizeable contemporary back dining room, comfortable more traditional bar with mullioned windows, flagstones and log fire, good food here too, Adnams, Black Sheep and a guest, plenty of wines by the glass, attentive friendly service; unobtrusive background music, free wi-fi; children welcome, comfortable chalet bedrooms around courtyard, good breakfast, nice local walks, open all day. *(George Atkinson, R C Vincent)*

DEDDINGTON   SP4631
Unicorn (01869) 338838
Market Place; OX15 0SE Refurbished 17th-c inn again under new management; beamed L-shaped bar, cosy snug with inglenook log fire, candlelit restaurant, good sensibly priced food (not Sun evening) combining traditional and modern cooking, three real ales including Wells & Youngs, good choice of wines by the glass, friendly service; background music (not in snug); well behaved children and dogs welcome, cobbled courtyard leading to long walled back garden, six bedrooms, open all day (all day weekends in winter) and from 9am for good farmers' market (last Sat of month). *(Anon)*

DENCHWORTH   SU3891
Fox (01235) 868258
Off A338 or A417 N of Wantage; Hyde Road; OX12 0DX Comfortable 17th-c thatched and beamed pub in pretty village, enjoyable sensibly priced food from extensive menu, good Sun carvery (best to book), OAP lunch deal Mon-Thurs, friendly efficient staff, well kept Greene King ales, good choice of reasonably priced wines, two log fires and plush seats in low-ceilinged connecting

areas, old prints and paintings, airy dining extension; children and dogs welcome, tables under umbrellas in pleasant sheltered garden with heated terrace. *(N R White, Cliff Sparkes)*

DORCHESTER   SU5794
Fleur de Lys (01865) 340502
Just off A4074 Maidenhead–Oxford; High Street; OX10 7HH Former 16th-c coaching inn opposite abbey, traditional two-level interior with interesting old photographs of the pub, plain wooden tables, open fire and woodburner, good imaginative evening set menu (not Sun), more straightforward lunchtime food, friendly efficient service, three real ales; children (away from bar) and dogs welcome, picnic-sets on front terrace and in back garden with play area and aunt sally, five bedrooms, open all day weekends, closed Mon lunchtime. *(John Pritchard, Paul Humphreys)*

DORCHESTER   SU5794
George (01865) 340404
Just off A4074 Maidenhead–Oxford; High Street; OX10 7HH Handsome 15th-c timbered hotel in lovely village, inglenook log fire in comfortably furnished beamed bar, enjoyable well presented (if not over-generous) food from baguettes up, OAP lunchtime menu, ales such as Hook Norton and Wadworths, cheerful efficient uniformed staff, restaurant; background music; children welcome, 17 bedrooms, open all day. *(R L Borthwick, Simon Collett-Jones, John Pritchard)*

DORCHESTER   SU5794
White Hart (01865) 340074
Now bypassed by A4074; OX10 7HN Hotel and restaurant in former 16th-c coaching inn with smallish beamed bar, Black Sheep and Hook Norton ales, enjoyable food including cheaper set menu, friendly busy staff, impressive raftered dining room; 28 bedrooms, charming village. *(John Pritchard)*

EAST HENDRED   SU4588
Plough (01235) 833213
Off A417 E of Wantage; Orchard Lane; OX12 8JW 16th-c village pub with good choice of home-made food (till 7pm Sun) from traditional choices to specials, Greene King-related ales and decent choice of wines by the glass, efficient friendly service, lofty raftered main room with interesting farming memorabilia, side dining area; background music, sports TV; children and dogs welcome, nice enclosed back garden, attractive village, open all day Fri-Sun, closed Mon. *(Anon)*

EATON   SP4403
Eight Bells (01865) 862261
Signed off B4017 SW of Oxford; OX13 5PR Cosy unpretentious old pub with relaxed local atmosphere, two small low-beamed bars with open fires and a dining area, well kept Loose Cannon ales,

traditional low-priced food served by friendly helpful staff; pleasant garden, nice walks, open all day Fri-Sun, closed Mon. *(Tony Hobden)*

EPWELL   SP3540
★ Chandlers Arms (01295) 780153
Sibford Road, off B4035; OX15 6LH Welcoming little 16th-c stone pub recently renovated and doing well under award-winning licensees Peter and Assumpta Golding; good interesting food (booking advised), well kept Hook Norton ales and proper coffee, bar with country-style furniture, two dining areas; pleasant garden with aunt sally, attractive out-of-the-way village near Macmillan Way long-distance path, open all day. *(Clive and Fran Dutson, P and J Shapley, Colin McKerrow)*

EWELME   SU6491
Shepherds Hut (01491) 836636
Off B4009 about 6 miles SW of M40 junction 6; High Street; OX10 6HQ Extended bay-windowed village pub, beams and bare boards, woodburner, enjoyable home-made food (not Sun evening) from good ciabattas up, Greene King ales and a guest, friendly helpful staff, back dining area, live music and quiz nights; children welcome, terrace picnic-sets with steps up to lawn and play area, open all day. *(Paul Humphreys)*

EXLADE STREET   SU6582
★ Highwayman (01491) 682020
Just off A4074 Reading–Wallingford; RG8 0UA Two beamed bar rooms, mainly 17th-c (parts older), with interesting rambling layout and mix of furniture, good food, well kept beers and plenty of wines by the glass, friendly efficient service, airy conservatory dining room; soft background music; children and dogs welcome, terrace and garden with fine views, closed Sun evening, Mon. *(Colin and Bernardine Perry)*

FERNHAM   SU2991
★ Woodman (01367) 820643
A420 SW of Oxford, then left into B4508 after about 11 miles; village another 6 miles on; SN7 7NX Friendly 17th-c country pub with heavily beamed character main rooms, various odds and ends such as milkmaids' yokes, leather tack, coach horns and an old screw press, original oil paintings and old photographs, cushioned benches, pews and windsor chairs, candlelit tables made from casks and a big open fire, also some comfortable newer areas, Greene King, Oakham, Sharps, Timothy Taylors, Wadworths and White Horse tapped from the cask, several malt whiskies and decent choice of wines by the glass, well thought-of food; background music; children and dogs (in bar) welcome, disabled facilities, terrace seats, good walks below the downs, open all day. *(Brian Glozier)*

FIFIELD   SP2318
Merrymouth (01993) 831652
A424 Burford–Stow; OX7 6HR Simple but comfortable stone inn dating from 13th c, L-shaped bar with bay-window seats, flagstones and low beams, some walls stripped back to old masonry, warm stove, quite dark in places, generous food cooked by landlord including blackboard fish specials, well kept ales such as Brakspears and Hook Norton, decent choice of wines, friendly staff; background music; children and dogs welcome, tables on terrace and in back garden, nice views, nine stable-block bedrooms. *(Stanley and Annie Matthews)*

FILKINS   SP2304
★ Five Alls (01367) 860875
Signed off A361 Lechlade–Burford; GL7 3JQ Carefully refurbished Cotswold-stone inn, beamed bar with leather chesterfields in front of log fire, Brakspears, Wychwood and a beer named for the pub, 16 wines by glass and a dozen malt whiskies, very good bar and restaurant food (not Sun evening) cooked by chef-landlord, dining rooms with stripped-stone walls or half-panelling and variety of tables and chairs on flagstones or floorboards, helpful service; background music; children and dogs welcome, a few picnic-sets out in front, chunky furniture on back terrace, four bedrooms, good breakfast, open all day (till 9pm Sun). *(Mr and Mrs A H Young, Mary Scott-Edeson, Dr and Mrs S G Barber, R K Phillips, Tracey and Stephen Groves)*

FINSTOCK   SP3616
★ Plough (01993) 868333
Just off B4022 N of Witney; High Street; OX7 3BY Thatched low-beamed village pub under welcoming new management; long rambling bar with leather sofas by massive stone inglenook, pictures of local scenes and some historical documents to do with the pub, roomy dining room with candles on stripped-pine tables, popular home-made pubby food (best to book), two or three well kept ales including Adnams Broadside, traditional cider, several wines by the glass and decent choice of whiskies, bar billiards; soft background music; children and dogs (in bar) welcome, seats in neatly kept garden, aunt sally, woodland walks and along River Evenlode, open all day Sat, closed Sun evening. *(P and J Shapley, Michèle Burton)*

FRINGFORD   SP6028
Butchers Arms (01869) 277363
Off A421 N of Bicester; Main Street; OX27 8EB Welcoming partly thatched creeper-clad local in Flora Thompson's 'Candleford' village; enjoyable traditional food including good Sun roasts (three sittings, best to book), well kept Brakspears, Hook Norton and Sharps, charming efficient service, unpretentious interior with L-shaped

bar and back dining room; picnic-sets out at front beside cricket green. *(Clive and Fran Dutson)*

FYFIELD   SU4298
★**White Hart** (01865) 390585

Main Road; off A420 8 miles SW of Oxford; OX13 5LW Grand medieval hall with soaring eaves, huge stone-flanked window embrasures and minstrels' gallery, contrasting cosy low-beamed side bar with large inglenook, fresh flowers and evening candles throughout, civilised friendly atmosphere and full of history; good imaginative modern food (best to book) cooked by licensee using home-grown produce, Hook Norton and a couple of guests (festivals May and Aug bank holidays), around 16 wines by the glass, several malt whiskies and maybe home-made summer elderflower pressé; background music; well behaved children welcome, elegant furniture under umbrellas on spacious heated terrace, lovely gardens, good Thames-side walks, open all day weekends, closed Mon. *(David Handforth, William Goodhart)*

GALLOWSTREE COMMON SU6980
Reformation (0118) 972 3126

Horsepond Road; RG4 9BP Friendly black-beamed village local under newish management, enjoyable home-made food, Brakspears and a couple of Marstons-related guests, open fires, conservatory; events such as tractor runs and log-splitting competitions, some live music; children and dogs welcome, garden with 'shipwreck' play area, closed Sun evening (and Mon in winter). *(Anon)*

GODSTOW   SP4809
★**Trout** (01865) 510930

Off A40/A44 roundabout via Wolvercote; OX2 8PN Pretty 17th-c Mitchells & Butlers dining pub in lovely riverside location (gets packed in fine weather); good choice of food from varied menu including set weekday deal till 6pm (booking essential at busy times), four beamed linked rooms with contemporary furnishings, flagstones and bare boards, log fires in three huge hearths, Brakspears, Sharps and a guest, several wines by the glass; background music; children and dogs (in bar) welcome, plenty of terrace seats under big parasols, footbridge to island (may be closed), abbey ruins opposite, car park fee refunded at bar, open (and food) all day. *(Conor McGaughey, Martin and Alison Stainsby, David Handforth, Peter and DoDo Rawlings)*

GORING   SU5980
★**Catherine Wheel** (01491) 872379

Station Road; RG8 9HB Friendly 18th-c village pub with two neat and cosily traditional bar areas, especially the more individual lower room with its dark beams and inglenook log fire, popular home-made food (not Sun evening) from seasonal menu, well kept Brakspears and guests, Thatcher's

cider, back restaurant, notable doors to lavatories; monthly quiz, TV, free wi-fi; children and dogs welcome, sunny garden and gravel terrace, handy for Thames Path, open all day. *(Anon)*

GOZZARD'S FORD   SU4698
★**Black Horse** (01865) 390530

Off B4017 NW of Abingdon; N of A415 by Marcham–Cothill Road; OX13 6JH Ancient traditional pub in tiny hamlet, good fresh food (all day Sun) especially fish/seafood, well kept Greene King ales and guests, some nice wines, cheerful efficient service, carpeted beamed main bar partly divided by stout timbers and low steps, warming end woodburner, separate plainer public bar with darts and pool; children welcome, pleasant garden, open all day. *(William Goodhart, Neil and Angela Huxter)*

GREAT TEW   SP3929
★**Falkland Arms** (01608) 683653

The Green; off B4022 about 5 miles E of Chipping Norton; OX7 4DB Part-thatched 16th-c golden-stone pub in lovely village, unspoilt partly panelled bar with high-backed settles, diversity of stools and plain tables on flagstones or bare boards, lots of mugs and jugs hanging from beam-and-boards ceiling, interesting brewerania, dim converted oil lamps, shutters for stone-mullioned latticed windows and open fire in fine inglenook, Wadworths and guests, Weston's cider, country wines and 30 malt whiskies, snuff for sale, locally sourced freshly made food, friendly service, separate dining room, live folk Sun evening; children and dogs welcome, tables out at front and under parasols in back garden, six bedrooms and cottage, open all day from 8am (breakfast for non-residents). *(Nancy Weber, Richard Stanfield, Mr and Mrs P R Thomas)*

HAILEY   SU6485
★**King William IV** (01491) 681845

The Hailey near Ipsden, off A4074 or A4130 SE of Wallingford; OX10 6AD Popular fine old pub in lovely countryside, beamed bar with good sturdy furniture on tiles in front of big log fire, three other cosy seating areas opening off, enjoyable reasonably priced food from baguettes to specials, Brakspears and guests tapped from the cask, helpful friendly staff; children and dogs welcome, terrace and large garden enjoying wide-ranging peaceful views, good walking (Chiltern Way and Ridgeway), leave muddy boots in porch, open all day. *(Paul Humphreys, Colin McLachlan, Bob and Margaret Holder)*

HENLEY   SU7682
Anchor (01491) 574753

Friday Street; RG9 1AH Fully refurbished beamed pub with uncluttered gently upmarket feel, wood and stone floors, tall tables, leather sofas and numbered dining tables with flowers, popular food from panini and sharing plates up, Brakspears Bitter and a guest, several wines by the glass; children welcome, smart sunny terrace at back, open all day. *(Paul Humphreys)*

HENLEY   SU7682
Angel on the Bridge (01491) 410678
Thames-side, by the bridge; RG9 1BH
17th c and worth knowing for its prime Thames-side position (packed during the regatta); small front bar with log fire, downstairs back bar and adjacent restaurant, beams, uneven floors and dim lighting, Brakspears ales and maybe a guest such as Ringwood, good choice of wines by the glass, enjoyable food from sandwiches and pubby choices up, cheerful well organised staff, newspapers; nice waterside deck (plastic glasses here), moorings for two boats, open all day at least in summer. *(N R White, Ian Phillips)*

HENLEY   SU7582
★Three Tuns (01491) 410138
Market Place; RG9 2AA Small heavy-beamed front bar with fire, well kept Brakspears and guests such as Ringwood, good attractively presented food from imaginative menu, also good value weekday set lunch, nice wines, friendly helpful service, panelled back dining area with painted timbers and wood floor; monthly comedy and music nights; children welcome, tables in small attractive back courtyard, closed Mon, otherwise open all day (bar snacks only Sun evening). *(Paul Humphreys)*

HOOK NORTON   SP3534
★Gate Hangs High (01608) 737387
N towards Sibford, at Banbury–Rollright crossroads; OX15 5DF Snug tucked-away old stone pub, low-ceilinged bar with traditional furniture on bare boards, attractive inglenook, good reasonably priced home-made food from bar snacks up, well kept Hook Norton ales and a guest, decent wines, friendly helpful service, side dining extension; background music; children and dogs (in bar) welcome, pretty courtyard and country garden, four bedrooms, camping, quite near Rollright Stones, open all day. *(Anon)*

HORNTON   SP3945
Dun Cow (01295) 670524
West End; OX15 6DA Traditional 17th-c thatch and ironstone village pub, friendly and relaxed, with sensibly short choice of good fresh food (not Sun or Mon evenings) from lunchtime sandwiches up using local suppliers, Hook Norton, XT and Wells & Youngs, a dozen wines by the glass; children and dogs welcome, appealing small garden

behind, open all day weekends, closed lunchtimes Mon, Tues (in winter lunchtimes Mon-Thurs). *(Anon)*

KELMSCOTT   SU2499
★Plough (01367) 253543
NW of Faringdon, off B4449 between A417 and A4095; GL7 3HG Well liked country pub with ancient flagstones, stripped stone and log fire, good food from light lunches to more restaurant evening choices, well kept beers such as Hook Norton, Vale, Wickwar and Wye Valley, real cider, helpful friendly staff; children, dogs and boots welcome, tables out in covered area and garden, lovely spot near upper Thames (moorings a few minutes away), eight comfortable bedrooms, good breakfast, no car park, handy for Kelmscott Manor (open Weds and Sat), pub open all day. *(R K Phillips, W M Lien, David and Stella Martin, Tony Hobden, Phil and Jane Villiers)*

KIDMORE END   SU6979
New Inn (0118) 972 3115
Chalkhouse Green Road; signed from B481 in Sonning Common; RG4 9AU Extended black and white pub by village church; beams and big log fire, enjoyable freshly made food, well kept Brakspears ales and decent wines by the glass, pleasant restaurant; children welcome, tables in large sheltered garden with pond, six bedrooms, open all day Thurs-Sat, closed Sun evening. *(Anon)*

KINGHAM   SP2523
★Wild Rabbit (01608) 658389
Church Street; OX7 6YA Major refurbishment for this former 18th-c farmhouse owned by Lady Bamford; plenty of rustic chic with antique country furniture, limestone floors, bare stone walls, beams and huge fireplaces, contemporary artwork and fresh flowers, well priced beers such as Cats, Hook Norton and Prescott, food in bar or more upmarket choices (not cheap) in spacious brasserie-style restaurant with view into kitchen, pleasant young staff in jeans and check shirts; children welcome, dogs in bar, paved front terrace with topiary rabbits, 12 individual and sumptuously appointed bedrooms, open all day. *(Liz Bell)*

LEWKNOR   SU7197
★Olde Leathern Bottel
(01844) 351482 *Under a mile from M40 junction 6; off B4009 towards Watlington; OX49 5TH* Popular and friendly family-run place, two heavy-beamed bars with understated décor and rustic furnishings, open fires, well kept Brakspears and Marstons, several wines by the glass, tasty pub food and specials served quickly,

---

Places with gardens or terraces usually let children sit there – we note in the text the very few exceptions that don't.

family room separated by standing timbers; dogs welcome, splendid garden with plenty of picnic-sets under parasols, play area and boules, handy for walks on Chiltern escarpment. *(R K Phillips, Dave Braisted)*

LONG HANBOROUGH SP4214
★ **George & Dragon** (01993) 881362
A4095 Bladon–Witney; Main Road; OX29 8JX Substantial pub with original two-room bar (17th-c or older), stripped stone, low beams and two woodburners, Courage and Wells & Youngs ales, decent range of wines, roomy thatched restaurant extension with comfortably padded dining chairs around sturdy tables on floorboards, plenty of pictures on plum walls, beams, wide choice of well liked food from lunchtime sandwiches and baked potatoes up, prompt friendly service; background music; children and dogs (in bar) welcome, large back garden with picnic-sets among shrubs, tables beneath canopy on separate sheltered terrace, summer barbecues, closed Sun evening. *(Dennis and Doreen Haward, Dave Braisted)*

LONG WITTENHAM SU5493
Plough (01865) 407738
High Street; OX14 4QH Welcoming 17th-c local continuing well under present licensees; low beams, inglenook fires and lots of brass, three well kept ales including Butcombe, good reasonably priced food (not Sun evening) from sandwiches and traditional choices to interesting specials, friendly helpful young staff, dining room, games in public bar; children welcome, Thames moorings at bottom of nice spacious garden, open all day. *(David Lamb)*

LOWER HEYFORD SP4824
★ **Bell** (01869) 347176
Market Square; OX25 5NY Charming creeper-clad building in small thatched village square, popular with locals and boaters on nearby Oxford Canal, enjoyable fresh food from baguettes to specials, well kept interesting beers including one named for them, good coffee, cheerful quick service, uncluttered pleasantly refurbished rooms around central beamed bar; children welcome, disabled facilities, nice long walled garden with gazebo and aunt sally, canal walks and handy for Rousham Garden. *(Edward Mirzoeff, Tony Hobden)*

MAIDENSGROVE SU7288
Five Horseshoes (01491) 641282
Off B480 and B481, W of village; RG9 6EX Character 16th-c dining pub set high in the Chilterns, rambling bar with low ceiling and log fire, enjoyable food including home-smoked salmon and local game, weekday set menu, friendly service, well kept Brakspears and good choice of wines by the glass, airy conservatory restaurant; children and dogs welcome, plenty of tables in suntrap

garden with lovely views, wood-fired pizzas on summer weekends, good walks, open all day Sat, till 6pm Sun, closed Mon. *(Susan and John Douglas)*

MARSH BALDON SU5699
Seven Stars (01865) 343337
The Baldons signed off A4074 N of Dorchester; OX44 9LP Beamed village-green pub now owned by the local community; refurbished bar areas, seats by corner fire, enjoyable food all day including plenty of gluten-free options, Fullers, Loose Cannon and a couple of local guests, raftered barn restaurant; children and dogs welcome, open all day (till midnight Fri, Sat). *(Jane Taylor and David Dutton)*

MURCOTT SP5815
★ **Nut Tree** (01865) 331253
Off B4027 NE of Oxford, via Islip and Charlton-on-Otmoor; OX5 2RE Beamed and thatched 15th-c dining pub, good imaginative cooking (not cheap) using own produce including home-reared pigs, neat friendly young staff, Vale and two guests, carefully chosen wines; background music; children and dogs (in bar) welcome, terrace and pretty garden, unusual gargoyles on front wall (modelled loosely on local characters), closed Sun evening, Mon. *(Phil and Helen Holt)*

NORTH MORETON SU5689
Bear at Home (01235) 811311
Off A4130 Didcot–Wallingford; High Street; OX11 9AT Dating from the 15th c with traditional beamed bar, cosy fireside areas and dining part with stripped-pine furniture, friendly service from new father and daughter team, sensibly priced home-made pubby food, Timothy Taylors, a beer for the pub from West Berkshire and a couple of local guests (July beer festival), Weston's cider and a dozen wines by the glass; children and dogs welcome, nice back garden overlooking cricket pitch, aunt sally, pretty village, open all day weekends. *(Eddie Edwards)*

NUFFIELD SU6787
Crown (01491) 641335
A4130/B481; RG9 5SJ Friendly newish management at this attractive little brick and flint country pub; good home-made food and well kept Brakspears ales, efficient service, beamed lounge bar with bare boards and inglenook log fire; children and dogs in small garden room, disabled access, tables out at front and in enclosed garden behind, good walks (Ridgeway nearby), closed Sun evening, Mon. *(Ross Balaam)*

OXFORD SP5106
Chequers (01865) 727463
Off High Street; OX1 4DH Narrow 16th-c courtyard pub tucked away down small alleyway, several areas on three floors, interesting architectural features, beams,

panelling and stained glass, eight or so rotating ales and enjoyable good value pubby food (sausage specialities), quick friendly service, games room with balcony; walled garden. *(Roger and Donna Huggins, George Atkinson)*

OXFORD SP5106

★ **Eagle & Child** (01865) 302925

St Giles; OX1 3LU Long narrow Nicholsons pub dating from the 16th c with two charmingly old-fashioned panelled front rooms, well kept Brakspears, Hook Norton and interesting guests, good choice of food from sandwiches to Sun roasts, friendly service and bustling atmosphere, stripped-brick back dining extension and conservatory, Tolkien and C S Lewis connections (the Inklings writers' group used to meet here); games machine; children allowed in back till 8pm, open (and food all day). *(N R White, John Pritchard, Mrs Sally Scott, Neil and Angela Huxter)*

OXFORD SP5105

Head of the River (01865) 721600

Folly Bridge; between St Aldates and Christ Church Meadow; OX1 4LB Civilised well renovated pub by river, boats for hire and nearby walks; spacious split-level downstairs bar with dividing brick arches, flagstones and bare boards, well kept Fullers/Gales beers and good choice of wines by the glass, popular pubby food from sandwiches up, good service, daily papers; background music; tables on stepped heated waterside terrace, 12 bedrooms, open all day. *(Martin Day, Mrs Sally Scott)*

OXFORD SP5203

Isis Farmhouse (01865) 247006

Off Donnington Bridge Road; no car access; OX4 4EL Charming waterside spot for early 19th-c former farmhouse (accessible only to walkers/cyclists), relaxed lived-in interior with two woodburners, short choice of enjoyable home-made food (sensible prices, no credit cards), Appleford and a guest such as Shotover, nice wines and interesting soft drinks, afternoon teas with wonderful home-baked cakes; picnic-sets out on terrace and in garden, aunt sally by arrangement, canoe hire, short walk to Iffley Lock and nearby lavishly decorated early Norman church, open all day Thurs-Sat in summer (Fri-Sun in winter) and all bank holidays including Christmas. *(Martin and Alison Stainsby)*

OXFORD SP5106

★ **Kings Arms** (01865) 242369

Holywell Street; OX1 3SP Dating from the early 17th c, convivial, relaxed and popular with locals and students, quick helpful service, well kept Wells & Youngs range and four guests, fine choice of wines by the glass, eating area with counter servery doing good variety of reasonably

priced food all day, cosy rooms up and down steps, lots of panelling and pictures, daily papers; downstairs lavatories; a few tables outside, open from 10.30am. *(George Atkinson, D J and P M Taylor)*

OXFORD SP5106

Lamb & Flag (01865) 515787

St Giles/Banbury Road; OX1 3JS Old pub owned by nearby college, modern airy front room with light wood panelling and big windows over street, more atmosphere in back rooms with stripped stonework and low-boarded ceilings, a beer by Palmers for the pub (L&F Gold), Shepherd Neame Spitfire, Skinners Betty Stogs and guests, some lunchtime food including sandwiches and tasty home-made pies, Thomas Hardy *Jude the Obscure* connection; open all day. *(Anon)*

OXFORD SP5006

Old Bookbinders (01865) 553549

Victor Street; OX2 6BT Dark and mellow family-run local tucked away in the Jericho area; friendly and unpretentious, with old fittings and lots of interesting bric-a-brac, Greene King ales and three guests, decent choice of whiskies and other spirits, enjoyable french-leaning food including speciality crêpes and some bargain main dishes, board games and shove-ha'penny, Tues quiz, open mike night Sun; amusing touches like multiple door handles to the gents'; children, dogs and students welcome, closed Mon, otherwise open all day. *(Josh Mullett)*

OXFORD SP4907

Perch (01865) 728891

Binsey Lane, on right after river bridge leaving city on A420; OX2 0NG Beautifully set 17th-c thatched limestone building in tiny riverside hamlet, more restaurant than pub with good food from interesting varied menu, efficient friendly young staff, well kept ales such as Hook Norton and good wine list, décor successfully blending new with old beams, flagstones and log fire, Lewis Carroll connection; lovely garden running down to Thames Path, river cruises, open all day. *(Jeremy Whitehorn, Neil and Angela Huxter)*

OXFORD SP5005

★ **Punter** (01865) 248832

South Street, Osney (off A420 Botley Road via Bridge Street); OX2 0BE Friendly relaxed pub overlooking Thames (sister to the Punter in Cambridge); attractive rugs on flagstone or wood floors, nice old dining chairs around interesting tables, paintings for sale, open fire, enjoyable modern food (all day weekends), Greene King, Timothy Taylors and Wadworths, several wines by the glass, friendly service; children and dogs welcome, open all day. *(Susan Loppert, Jane Caplan)*

OXFORD SP5105
Royal Blenheim (01865) 242355
Ebbes Street; OX1 1PT Popular airy 19th-c corner pub, opened by Queen Victoria during her Golden Jubilee, and now the tap for the White Horse Brewery; their range and many interesting guests, good value straightforward food (all day weekends), single room with original tiled floor, raised perimeter booth seating; big-screen sports TV, Weds quiz, Mon knitting club; open all day (till midnight Fri, Sat). *(Peter Martin, Roger and Donna Huggins, Tony Hobden)*

OXFORD SP5106
Turf Tavern (01865) 243235
Bath Place; via St Helen's Passage, between Holywell Street and New College Lane; OX1 3SU Interesting character pub hidden away behind high walls, small dark-beamed bars with lots of snug areas, up to a dozen constantly changing real ales (spring and summer festivals) including Greene King, also Weston's cider and winter mulled wine, reasonably priced fairly standard food, pleasant helpful service; children and dogs welcome, three walled-in courtyards (one with own bar), open (and food) all day. *(Lee Fraser, Martin and Alison Stainsby, Paul Humphreys, David Handforth, David Carr and others)*

OXFORD SP5106
White Horse (01865) 204801
Broad Street; OX1 3BB Bustling and studenty, squeezed between parts of Blackwells bookshop, small narrow bar with snug one-table raised back alcove, low beams and timbers, ochre ceiling, beautiful view of the Clarendon Building and Sheldonian, good choice of ales including Hook Norton, St Austell and Shotover, friendly staff, simple food; open all day. *(Anon)*

PLAY HATCH SU7477
Shoulder of Mutton (0118) 947 3908
W of Henley Road (A4155) roundabout; RG4 9QU Dining pub with low-ceilinged log-fire bar and large back conservatory restaurant, good generous food including signature mutton dishes, well kept Greene King and guests such as nearby Loddon, good value house wines, friendly attentive service; children welcome, picnic-sets in carefully tended walled garden with well, closed Sun evening. *(Paul Humphreys, John Pritchard)*

ROKE SU6293
Home Sweet Home (01491) 838249
Off B4009 Benson–Watlington; OX10 6JD Wadworths country pub with two smallish bars, heavy stripped beams, big log fire and traditional furniture, carpeted room on right leading to restaurant area, enjoyable food served by friendly staff; background music; children welcome and dogs (they have one), low-walled front garden, open all day Sun till 8pm. *(Sharon Oldham, Rob Peacock)*

ROTHERFIELD PEPPARD SU7081
Unicorn (01491) 628674
Colmore Lane; RG9 5LX Attractive country pub in the Chilterns, run by same people as the Little Angel, Henley (see Berkshire) and Cherry Tree, Stoke Row; bustling bar with open fire, real ales and good wines, dining room with high-backed chairs around mix of tables on stripped boards, well liked interesting food including lunchtime sandwiches and daily specials, friendly service; seats out in front and in pretty back garden. *(Anon)*

SANDFORD-ON-THAMES SP5301
Kings Arms (01865) 777095
Church Road; OX4 4YB Delightful lockside spot on Thames with tables on waterside terrace; usual Chef & Brewer menu, well kept ales and good choice of wines by the glass; can get very busy and may be queues; children welcome, moorings, open all day. *(Martin and Alison Stainsby)*

SHENINGTON SP3742
★ Bell (01295) 670274
Off A422 NW of Banbury; OX15 6NQ Good wholesome home cooking in hospitable 17th-c two-room village pub, well kept Hook Norton and maybe a summer guest, decent wine choice, friendly informal service and long-serving licensees, heavy beams, some flagstones, stripped stone and pine panelling, two woodburners; children in eating areas and dogs in bar, picnic-sets out at front, charming quiet village with good walks, three simple bedrooms, generous breakfast, closed Sun evening, Mon. *(Peter J and Avril Hanson, D L Frostick)*

SHIPLAKE SU7476
Flowing Spring (0118) 969 9878
A4155 towards Play Hatch and Reading; RG4 9RB Roadside pub built on bank (all on first floor with slight slope front to back), warm open fires in small two-room bar, assorted bric-a-brac, home-made pubby food (not Sun or Mon evenings) catering for special diets, three Fullers/Gales beers, Aspall's cider, modern dining room with floor-to-ceiling windows, tables out on covered balcony, various events including astronomy nights, beer festivals, comedy and live music; children and dogs welcome, lawned garden bordered by streams (prone to flooding), summer marquee and barbecues, closed Mon, otherwise open all day. *(Paul Humphreys, John Pritchard)*

If we know a pub has an outdoor play area for children, we mention it.

SHIPLAKE
Plowden Arms
SU7678

(0118) 940 2794

Reading Road (A4155); RG9 4BX
Old Brakspears pub on busy road, and
again under new management (some
refurbishment); enjoyable food including
one or two unusual recipes from ancient
cookbooks, good service, four real ales and
extensive wine list (ten by the glass), spacious
knocked-through interior with central log
fire, parts with low beams, plain wooden
tables and chairs on carpeted floors, church
candles; picnic-sets in good-sized garden
(former village bowling green), handy for
Thames walk, closed Mon. *(Marnie Pascoe, John
Pritchard, Paul Humphreys, Eugenie Streather)*

SHIPTON-UNDER-
WYCHWOOD
★ **Lamb**
SP2717

(01993) 830465

*High Street; off A361 to Burford;
OX7 6DQ* Mother and son team at this
handsome stone inn, beamed bar with
oak-panelled settle, farmhouse chairs and
polished tables on wood-block flooring,
stripped-stone walls, church candles and log
fire, three changing ales, good wines (plenty
by the glass) and well liked food, restaurant
area; children welcome, dogs allowed in bar
(they have their own), wheelchair access,
garden with modern furniture on terrace,
five themed bedrooms, open all day. *(Bernard
Stradling, R K Phillips, Simon and Mandy King)*

SHIPTON-UNDER-
WYCHWOOD
Shaven Crown
SP2717

(01993) 830330

High Street (A361); OX7 6BA Ancient
monastic building with magnificent lofty
medieval rafters and imposing double
stairway in hotel part's hall, separate
more down-to-earth back bar with beams,
panelling and booth seating, lovely log fires,
good helpings of enjoyable food, Hook Norton
and a couple of guests, several wines by the
glass, friendly informal service, restaurant;
background music; children and dogs
welcome, peaceful central courtyard with
heaters, bowling green, eight bedrooms
(one in former chapel). *(Richard Stanfield,
N R White)*

SHIPTON-UNDER-
WYCHWOOD
Wychwood Inn
SP2717

(01993) 831185

High Street; OX7 6BA Refurbished former
Red Horse now under same ownership as the
Lamb in same village; contemporary décor
in open-plan bar/dining area, more period
character in flagstoned public bar with black
beams and inglenook, up to eight real ales
including one badged for them and plenty of
wines by the glass, enjoyable food from wraps
to grills, friendly young staff; children and
dogs welcome, picnic-sets on small terrace,
shop in glassed-in coach entrance, five
bedrooms, open all day. *(Liz Bell)*

SHRIVENHAM
Prince of Wales
SU2488

(01793) 782268

*High Street; off A420 or B4000 NE of
Swindon; SN6 8AF* 17th-c stone-built
local doing well under energetic landlord,
good freshly cooked food at fair prices, well
kept Wadworths ales, low-beamed lounge
with log fire, small dining area, side bar with
darts, live jazz and quiz nights; children
welcome, picnic-sets in secluded back garden
overlooking church. *(Dr John Clements)*

SHUTFORD
George & Dragon
SP3840

(01295) 780320

Church Lane; OX15 6PG Ancient stone-
built pub set down from the church; cosy
L-shaped bar with flagstones and impressive
fireplace, five well kept ales including Hook
Norton, decent choice of wines by the glass,
good locally sourced bar and restaurant food
(not Sun evening, Mon), friendly service,
dining room and separate room for sports
TV, darts, quiz every other Sun; children and
dogs welcome, small garden overlooking
village, closed lunchtimes Mon-Thurs, open
all day weekends. *(Anon)*

SIBFORD GOWER
Wykham Arms
SP3537

(01295) 788808

*Signed off B4035 Banbury–Shipston-
on-Stour; Temple Mill Road; OX15 5RX*
Cottagey 17th-c thatched and flagstoned
dining pub, enjoyable food from light
lunchtime menu up, friendly attentive
staff, two well kept changing ales, plenty of
wines by the glass, comfortable open-plan
interior with low-beams and stripped stone,
glass-covered well, inglenook; children
and dogs welcome, country views from big
garden, lovely manor house opposite and
good walks nearby, open all day Sun,
closed Mon. *(Anon)*

SOULDERN
Fox
SP5231

(01869) 345284

Off B4100; Fox Lane; OX27 7JW Pretty
pub set in delightful village, open-plan
beamed layout with woodburner in two-way
fireplace, enjoyable fairly priced food,
friendly attentive service, well kept Hook
Norton and guests, seven wines by the glass;
garden and terrace, four bedrooms, open all
day Sat, till 4pm Sun. *(Anon)*

SOUTH NEWINGTON
Duck on the Pond
SP4033

(01295) 721166

A361; OX15 4JE Roadside dining pub with
tidy modern-rustic décor in small flagstoned
bar and linked carpeted eating areas up
a step, popular food from light dishes to
steak and family Sun lunch, Hook Norton
and a couple of guests, cheerful pleasant
staff, woodburner; background music, no
dogs; spacious grounds with tables on deck
and lawn, aunt sally, pond with waterfowl,
walk down to River Swere, open all day
weekends. *(Anon)*

SOUTH STOKE   SU5983
Perch & Pike   (01491) 872415
Off B4009 2 miles N of Goring; RG8 0JS
Brick and flint pub just a field away from the
Thames, cottagey low-beamed bar with open
fire, well kept beer and good home-made
food, sizeable timbered restaurant extension
where children allowed; may be background
music; tables on terrace and flower-bordered
lawn, four bedrooms. *(Dr and Mrs S G Barber)*

SPARSHOLT   SU3487
Star   (01235) 751873
Watery Lane; OX12 9PL Compact 16th-c
beamed country dining pub with highly
regarded modern food along with cheaper bar
menu, friendly welcoming staff, beers such
as Sharps Doom Bar; dogs welcome in bar
and back garden, pretty village – snowdrops
fill churchyard in spring, eight bedrooms in
converted barn, open all day Fri-Sun,
closed Mon. *(Terry Miller, Andrew Loudon)*

STANTON ST JOHN   SP5709
★Talk House   (01865) 351654
*Middle Road/Wheatley Road (B4027 just
outside village); OX33 1EX* Attractive
part-thatched dining pub; older part on left
with steeply pitched rafters soaring above
stripped-stone walls, mix of old dining
chairs and big stripped tables, large rugs on
flagstones; rest of building converted more
recently but in similar style with massive
beams, flagstones or stoneware tiles, and log
fires below low mantelbeams, popular food
from sandwiches (not Sun) up, three Fullers
ales and several wines by the glass; children
welcome, dogs in bar, inner courtyard with
teak tables and chairs, a few picnic-sets on
side grass, bedrooms, open all day. *(David
Jackman, Martin and Pauline Jennings)*

STEEPLE ASTON   SP4725
★Red Lion   (01869) 340225
*Off A4260 12 miles N of Oxford;
OX25 4RY* Cheerful village pub with neatly
kept beamed and partly panelled bar, antique
settle and other good furnishings, well kept
Hook Norton ales and good choice of wines
by the glass, enjoyable food from shortish
menu including pizzas served by obliging
young staff, back conservatory-style dining
extension; well behaved children welcome
lunchtime and until 7pm, dogs in bar, suntrap
front garden with lovely flowers and shrubs,
parking may be awkward, open all day Sat,
till 5pm Sun. *(M S and M Imhoff)*

STEVENTON   SU4691
North Star
*Stocks Lane, The Causeway, central
westward turn off B4017; OX13 6SG*
Traditional little village pub through yew
tree gateway, tiled entrance corridor, main
area with ancient high-backed settles around
central table, well kept Greene King Morland
Original and guests from side tap room, hatch
service to another room with plain seating,
a couple of tables and coal fire, simple
lunchtime food, friendly staff; dogs welcome,
tables on front grass, aunt sally, open all
day weekends, closed Mon and weekday
lunchtimes. *(Anon)*

STOKE LYNE   SP5628
Peyton Arms   07546 066160
*From minor road off B4110 N of
Bicester, fork left into village; OX27 8SD*
Beautifully situated and largely unspoilt
one-room stone-built alehouse, character
landlord (Mick the Hat) and loyal regulars,
very well kept Hook Norton from casks
behind small corner bar, filled rolls,
inglenook fire, tiled floor and lots of
memorabilia, games area with darts and pool;
no children or dogs; pleasant garden with
aunt sally, open all day weekends till 7pm,
closed Mon, lunchtimes Weds and Thurs (but
best to confirm times by phone). *(Anon)*

STOKE ROW   SU6884
Cherry Tree   (01491) 680430
Off B481 at Highmoor; RG9 5QA
Pub-restaurant with good up-to-date food
including lunchtime set deal, well kept
Brakspears ales, ten wines by the glass, four
linked rooms with stripped wood, heavy low
beams and some flagstones, helpful friendly
staff; background music, TV in bar; well
behaved children and dogs welcome, lots of
tables in attractive garden, nearby walks,
four good bedrooms in converted barn, open
all day (till 5pm Sun). *(Paul Humphreys,
Bob and Margaret Holder)*

STOKE ROW   SU6884
★Crooked Billet   (01491) 681048
*Nottwood Lane, off B491 N of Reading
– OS Sheet 175 map reference 684844;
RG9 5PU* Very nice place, but more
restaurant than pub; charming rustic layout
with heavy beams, flagstones, antique pubby
furnishings and great inglenook log fire,
crimson Victorian-style dining room, wide
choice of competently cooked interesting
food (all day weekends) using local produce,
cheaper set lunches Mon-Fri, helpful friendly
staff, Brakspears Oxford Gold tapped from
the cask (no counter), good wines, relaxed
homely atmosphere; children very welcome,
weekly live music, big garden by Chilterns
beechwoods, open all day. *(Colin McLachlan)*

STONESFIELD   SP3917
White Horse   (01993) 891063
*Village signposted off B4437 Charlbury–
Woodstock; Stonesfield Riding;
OX29 8EA* Attractively upgraded small
country pub; restful colours and well chosen
furniture in cosy bar and dining room, also
little inner room with a single mahogany
table, Ringwood Best, decent wines and good
restaurant-style food; soft background music;
children and dogs (in bar) welcome, neat
walled garden with picnic-sets, skittle alley

in stone barn, good nearby walks and handy for Roman villa at North Leigh, restricted opening/food times – best to phone. *(Dennis and Doreen Haward)*

STONOR   SU7388
Quince Tree   (01491) 639039
B480, off A4130 NW of Henley; RG9 6HE Extensive and stylish revamp of former hotel; bar in modern country style with bleached wood furniture, well kept changing local ales, good food here and in back restaurant (not cheap), friendly prompt service from young staff; children welcome, dogs in bar, landscaped garden and terrace, new barn-like building housing a café on two floors and farm shop/deli, closed Sun evening. *(Susan and John Douglas)*

SUNNINGWELL   SP4900
Flowing Well   (01865) 735846
Just N of Abingdon; OX13 6RB Refurbished timbered pub (former 19th-c rectory) under new management; popular food including british tapas, range of burgers and other pub favourites, a couple of Greene King ales and a guest, good choice of wines; children welcome, dogs in bar, large heated raised terrace, more seats in garden with small well, open (and food) all day. *(Baz Manning)*

SWINFORD   SP4308
Talbot   (01865) 881348
B4044 just S of Eynsham; OX29 4BT Roomy and comfortable 17th-c beamed pub, well kept Arkells direct from cooled cask, good choice of wines and soft drinks, enjoyable reasonably priced pubby food, friendly staff, long attractive flagstoned bar with some stripped stone, cheerful log-effect gas fire, occasional live jazz; may be background music; children and dogs welcome, garden with decked area overlooking Wharf Stream, pleasant walk along lovely stretch of the Thames towpath, moorings quite nearby, 11 bedrooms. *(S F Parrinder)*

THAME   SP7105
Cross Keys   (01844) 218202
Park Street/East Street; OX9 3HP Friendly one-bar 19th-c local, eight well kept ales including own Thame beers (not always available) and six ciders, no food apart from scotch eggs but can bring your own; courtyard garden, open all day weekends. *(Anon)*

THAME   SP7005
James Figg   (01844) 260166
Cornmarket; OX9 2BL Friendly coaching inn, clean and well furnished, with four well kept ales including Purity and Vale, Addlestone's and Aspall's ciders, ten wines by the glass, enjoyable straightforward locally sourced food from sandwiches up, open fire in brick fireplace, portrait of eponymous James

Figg (local 18th-c boxer) and photos of more recent sporting champions, converted stables with own bar for music/functions; busier and noisier evenings; children and dogs welcome, back garden, open all day. *(Anon)*

THAME   SP7006
★Thatch   (01844) 214340
Lower High Street; OX9 2AA Characterful timbered and thatched 16th-c dining pub, cosy bar and nice collection of little higgledy-piggledy rooms, heavy beams, old quarry tiles and flagstones, smart contemporary furnishings and bold paintwork, double-sided inglenook, well kept ales and nice wines by the glass, good interesting food from deli boards to daily specials; children welcome, prettily planted terraced garden with seats and tables under parasols, open (and food) all day. *(Anon)*

THRUPP   SP4815
★Boat   (01865) 374279
Brown sign to pub off A4260 just N of Kidlington; OX5 1JY Attractive 16th-c stone pub set back from the southern Oxford Canal (moorings), low ceilings, bare boards and some ancient floor tiles, log fires and old coal stove, enjoyable well priced home-made food (all day weekends) including vegetarian options, specials and Sun carvery, friendly service, Greene King ales and decent wines; gets busy in summer; children and dogs welcome, fenced garden behind with plenty of tables, open all day. *(Tony Hobden, S F Parrinder)*

TOOT BALDON   SP5600
Mole   (01865) 340001
Between A4074 and B480 SE of Oxford; OX44 9NG Light open-plan restaurantly dining pub with very good if not cheap food (booking advisable), nice wines by the glass, Hook Norton and a guest, leather sofas by bar, neat country furniture or more formal leather dining chairs in linked eating areas including conservatory, stripped 18th-c beams and big open fire; background music; children welcome, no dogs inside, garden tables, open all day. *(Susan Loppert, Jane Caplan)*

WALLINGFORD   SU6089
George   (01491) 836665
High Street; OX10 0BS Handsome extended 16th-c coaching inn, enjoyable food in bistro, restaurant or beamed bar with splendid log fireplace, three Rebellion ales and good choice of other drinks, friendly helpful service; tables in spacious central courtyard, 39 bedrooms, good antiques centre close by. *(George Atkinson)*

WANTAGE   SU3987
King Alfreds Head   (01235) 771595
Market Place; OX12 8AH Recently revamped pub set back from market square, reasonable choice of enjoyable well priced

food including one or two specials, Sun carvery, ales such as St Austell, helpful friendly staff, linked areas, leather sofas by log fire; background music can be loud, sports TV, free wi-fi; children and dogs welcome, sizeable beer garden with summer barbecues and some live music, open all day. *(R K Phillips)*

WANTAGE SU3988
Lamb (01235) 766768

Mill Street, past square and Bell; down hill then bend to left; OX12 9AB Popular 17th-c thatched pub with low beams, log fire and cosy corners, well kept ales including Fullers London Pride from brick-faced bar, good straightforward food at fair prices; children welcome, disabled facilities, garden with play area, open all day. *(Cliff Sparkes)*

WANTAGE SU3987
✱ **Royal Oak** (01235) 763129

Newbury Street; OX12 8DF Popular two-bar corner local with well kept range of West Berkshire ales along with Wadworths 6X and guests, good choice of ciders and perries too, friendly knowledgeable landlord, lots of pump clips, old ship photographs, darts; closed weekday lunchtimes. *(Anon)*

WANTAGE SU3987
Shoulder of Mutton 07870 577742

Wallingford Street; OX12 8AX Victorian pub renovated by enthusiastic landlord keeping character in bar, dining lounge and snug, 11 well kept changing mainly local ales including own Betjeman brews (beer festivals), equally good cider/perry choice, generous vegetarian food, regular folk music and other events; children welcome, dogs allowed in bar, back terrace with hop-covered pergola, four bedrooms, open all day (till midnight Fri, Sat). *(Anon)*

WARBOROUGH SU6093
✱ **Six Bells** (01865) 858265

The Green S; just E of A329, 4 miles N of Wallingford; OX10 7DN Thatched 16th-c pub opposite village cricket green, well kept Brakspears ales and wide choice of good interesting food, friendly attentive staff, appealing country furnishings in small linked areas off bar, low beams, stripped stone and big log fire; tables in pleasant orchard garden. *(Barry Collett, John and Pauline Young, Colin McLachlan)*

WARDINGTON SP4946
Hare & Hounds (01295) 750645

A361 Banbury–Daventry; OX17 1SH Comfortable traditional village local with well kept Hook Norton ales, friendly

welcome, low ceilinged bar leading to dining area, woodburner, enjoyable home-made food, darts and dominoes; children and dogs welcome, garden with aunt sally, open all day Fri, Sat, till 8pm Sun. *(Anon)*

WEST HENDRED SU4489
Extraordinary Hare

(01235) 820383 *A417 Reading Road, outside village; OX12 8RH* Big open-plan village pub refurbished under new management; enjoyable fairly traditional food at sensible prices including daily specials, Greene King and a guest, friendly helpful staff, low-ceilinged main bar with bare boards and terracotta tiles, timber dividers, comfortable parquet-floor dining area, open fire, conservatory; background music; children and dogs welcome, seats on colonnaded verandah, picnic-sets in side garden with covered deck, open all day Fri-Sun. *(R K Phillips, Ema Steed)*

WESTCOTT BARTON SP4325
Fox (01869) 340338

Enstone Road; B4030 off A44 NW of Woodstock; OX7 7BL Spacious 18th-c stone-built village pub again under new management; low beams and flagstones, pews and high-backed settles, well kept ales such as Fullers London Pride, Greene King Old Golden Hen and Hook Norton Hooky, popular food from baguettes up, woodburner in big fireplace, restaurant; background music, steps down to lavatories; children and dogs (not at food times) welcome, pleasant garden with play area and aunt sally, peaceful view. *(Ryan Bass)*

WHITCHURCH SU6377
Ferry Boat (0118) 984 2161

High Street, near toll bridge; RG8 7DB Welcoming comfortably updated 18th-c pub with airy log-fire bar and restaurant, good variety of enjoyable home-made food including stone-baked pizzas, friendly helpful staff, real ales such as Black Sheep and Timothy Taylors Landlord, several wines by the glass; background music, free wi-fi; children (away from bar) and well behaved dogs welcome, café-style seating in courtyard garden, closed Sun evening, Mon. *(Paul Humphreys)*

WHITCHURCH HILL SU6378
Sun (0118) 984 2260

Hill Bottom; signed from B471; RG8 7PG Friendly unassuming brick-built pub in sleepy village, homely L-shaped bar with carpet and bare boards, white textured walls, dark woodwork, plush chairs and wall benches, enjoyable inexpensive home-made food including vegetarian choices,

---

Post Office address codings confusingly give the impression that some pubs are in Oxfordshire, when they're really in Berkshire, Buckinghamshire, Gloucestershire or Warwickshire (which is where we list them).

Brakspears, Hook Norton, Ringwood and a guest; children and dogs welcome, couple of picnic-sets out at front, small side terrace, back lawn with play area, open all day Fri-Sun. *(Paul Humphreys, Richard and Stephanie Foskett, N R White)*

WITNEY SP3509
Angel (01993) 703238
Market Square; OX28 6AL Wide choice of well priced food from good sandwiches up in unpretentious 17th-c town local, a house beer from Wychwood along with Hobgoblin, Brakspears, Marstons and occasional guest, quick friendly service even when packed, daily papers, hot coal fire; background music, big-screen sports TV, pool; lovely hanging baskets, back terrace with smokers' shelter, parking nearby can be difficult, open all day. *(Anon)*

WITNEY SP3509
Fleece (01993) 892270
Church Green; OX28 4AZ Smart civilised town pub (part of the Peach group), popular for its wide choice of good often imaginative food from sandwiches and deli boards up, fixed-price lunchtime deal too, friendly attentive service, Greene King and a couple of guests, leather armchairs on wood floors, daily papers, restaurant; background music; children welcome, café-style tables out at front overlooking green, ten affordable bedrooms, open all day from 9am. *(Jane Taylor and David Dutton, R K Phillips)*

WITNEY SP3510
★ **Horseshoes** (01993) 703086
Corn Street, junction with Holloway Road; OX28 6BS Attractive 16th-c modernised stone-built pub, wide choice of good home-made food from pubby choices to more imaginative restaurary dishes, good value weekday set lunch, Wychwood Hobgoblin and two local guests, decent house wines, friendly accommodating staff, heavy beams, flagstones and comfortable old furniture, log fires, separate back dining room; tables on sunny terrace, open all day. *(Anon)*

WOLVERCOTE SP4909
Plough (01865) 556969
First Turn/Wolvercote Green; OX2 8AH Comfortably worn-in pubby linked areas, armchairs and Victorian-style carpeted bays in main lounge, well kept Greene King ales, farm cider and decent wines by the glass, friendly helpful staff and bustling atmosphere, enjoyable good value usual food in flagstoned former stables dining room and library (children allowed here), traditional snug, woodburner; picnic-sets on front

decking looking over rough meadow to canal and woods, open all day weekends. *(Anon)*

WOODSTOCK SP4417
Black Prince (01993) 811530
Manor Road (A44 N); OX20 1XJ Old pub with one modernised low-ceilinged bar, timbers and stripped stone, suit of armour, log fire one end, good value home-made food from sandwiches to specials, well kept St Austell, Sharps and guests, friendly service, some live music; outside lavatories; children walkers and dogs welcome, tables in pretty garden by small River Glyme, nearby right of way into Blenheim parkland, open all day. *(Anon)*

WOODSTOCK SP4416
Woodstock Arms (01993) 811251
Market Street; OX20 1SX Welcoming 16th-c heavy-beamed stripped-stone pub, enjoyable home-made food (not Sun evening), three well kept Greene King ales and good wine choice, prompt helpful service, log fire in splendid stone fireplace, long narrow bar with end eating area; background music and occasional live jazz; children and dogs welcome, courtyard tables, open all day. *(Anon)*

WOOLSTONE SU2987
White Horse (01367) 820726
Off B4507; SN7 7QL Appealing partly thatched pub with Victorian gables and latticed windows, plush furnishings, spacious beamed and part-panelled bar, two big open fires, Arkells ales and enjoyable good value food from lunchtime sandwiches up, restaurant; free wi-fi; well behaved children and dogs allowed, plenty of seats in front and back gardens, secluded interesting village handy for White Horse and Ridgeway, six bedrooms, open all day. *(R K Phillips, Cliff Sparkes)*

WOOTTON SP4320
Killingworth Castle (01993) 811401
Glympton Road; B4027 N of Woodstock; OX20 1EJ Under same ownership as the Ebrington Arms, Ebrington, Gloucestershire; striking three-storey 17th-c coaching inn with simply furnished candlelit rooms, built-in wall seats and mix of chairs around farmhouse tables on bare boards, woodburner in stone fireplace and another fire, own Yubberton ales along with local guests, cider and lager from Cotswold, good range of spirits featuring smaller british producers, good interesting food (themed evenings), friendly enthusiastic staff; revamped garden with circular picnic-sets under green parasols, five new bedrooms, open all day from 9am. *(Martin and Pauline Jennings)*

Shropshire

KEY  Star Pub · Top Quality Food · Great Beer · Good Wines · £ Bargain Meals · Good Bedrooms · Serves Food

 BISHOP'S CASTLE   SO3288 Map 6
Three Tuns
Salop Street; SY9 5BW

Unpretentious own-brew pub scoring well for food, and for beer from its unique Victorian brewhouse

The four-storey John Roberts brewhouse across the yard from this friendly no-frills pub supplies the well kept beers you'll find here, served from old-fashioned handpumps: Three Tuns Clerics Cure, Mild, Stout, XXX and 1642. You can also buy carry-out kegs and the brewery sells beer by the barrel. They also have eight wines by the glass. The modernised dining room (it's worth booking) is done out in smart oak and glass, while the public, lounge and snug bars with flagstones remain characterfully ungimmicky with a lively bustling atmosphere. Staff are cheery and the pub is genuinely part of the local community – you might chance upon the film club, live jazz, morris dancers, a brass band playing in the garden or the local rugby club enjoying a drink; in July they hold a popular annual beer festival. There are newspapers to read and a good range of board games.

As well as lunchtime sandwiches, the good, popular food includes smoked salmon mousse with pickled cucumber, chicken, thyme and sausage ballotine with sweetcorn purée, roasted tomato and butternut squash sauce with pasta, beer-battered fish and chips, free-range chicken with roasted garlic sauce and braised shallots, lamb rump with sweet potato purée and rosemary jus, and puddings such as ginger cake with chantilly cream and espresso crème brûlée. *Benchmark main dish: rib-eye steak with peppercorn sauce and chips £16.95. Two-course evening meal £17.50.*

Scottish Courage ~ Licensee Tim Curtis-Evans ~ Real ale ~ (01588) 638797 ~ Open 12-11 (10.30 Sun) ~ Bar food 12-2.30, 7-9; 12-3 Sun ~ Restaurant ~ Children welcome ~ Dogs allowed in bar ~ Live music weekends, open mike every second Tues ~ www.thethreetunsinn.co.uk *Recommended by Mike and Eleanor Anderson, Dr Peter Crawshaw, Lois Dyer*

 BRIDGNORTH   SO7192 Map 4
Old Castle £
West Castle Street; WV16 4AB

Traditional town pub, relaxed and friendly, with generous helpings of good value pubby food, well kept ales and good-sized suntrap terrace

'A splendid little town pub' is how a reader described this cheerful place – and many others agree. It's evident from the outside that it was once two knocked-together cottages. The low-beamed open-plan bar is properly pubby with some genuine character: you'll find tiles and bare boards, cushioned wall banquettes and settles around cast-iron-framed tables, and bar stools arranged along the counter where the friendly landlord and his staff serve Hobsons Town Crier, Sharps Doom Bar, Timothy Taylors Landlord and Wye Valley HPA on handpump. A back conservatory extension has darts and pool; background music and big-screen TV for sports events. A big plus is the sunny back terrace with picnic-sets, lovely hanging baskets, big pots of flowers and shrub borders, and decking at the far end that gives an elevated view over the west side of town; children's playthings. Do walk up the street to see the ruined castle – its 20-metre Norman tower tilts at such an extraordinary angle that it makes the leaning tower of Pisa look like a model of rectitude.

🍴 Very fair value food includes lunchtime sandwiches and baguettes, devilled whitebait, cheese and potato pie, burgers with toppings and chips, chicken balti, chilli con carne, beef in Guinness, lambs liver and onions, minted lamb shank, and puddings. *Benchmark main dish: steak in ale pie £9.00. Two-course evening meal £14.00.*

Punch ~ Tenant Bryn Charles Masterman ~ Real ale ~ (01746) 711420 ~ Open 11.30-11 (midnight Sat, 10.30 Sun) ~ Bar food 12-3, 6.30-8.30 ~ Children welcome ~ Dogs welcome ~ Wi-fi ~ www.oldcastlebridgnorth.co.uk *Recommended by Jean and Douglas Troup, David H Bennett, David and Katharine Cooke, Brian and Anna Marsden, R T and J C Moggridge, Robert Parker*

CARDINGTON
Royal Oak
SO5095 Map 4

Village signposted off B4371 Church Stretton–Much Wenlock, pub behind church; also reached via narrow lanes from A49; SY6 7JZ

Lovely country spot, heaps of character inside and seasonal bar food

This is glorious country for walks, such as the one to the summit of Caer Caradoc, a couple of miles to the west (ask for directions at the pub), and the front courtyard makes the most of its beautiful position. Inside, the rambling low-beamed bar is gently frayed around the edges and has a roaring winter log fire, a cauldron, black kettle and pewter jugs in a vast inglenook fireplace, aged standing timbers from a knocked-through wall, and red and green tapestry seats solidly capped in elm; shove-ha'penny and dominoes. Hobsons Best, Ludlow Best, Sharps Doom Bar and Three Tuns XXX on handpump. A comfortable dining area has exposed old beams and studwork. This is said to be Shropshire's oldest continuously licensed pub.

🍴 Generous helpings of food include lunchtime baguettes, black pudding and bacon salad with pepper sauce, stuffed field mushrooms, burgers with chips, chilli con carne, vegetable tagine with rice, specials such as smoked cod, bacon and brie fishcakes and cumberland sausage with onion gravy, and puddings. *Benchmark main dish: fidget pie £10.95. Two-course evening meal £18.00.*

Free house ~ Licensees Steve and Eira Oldham ~ Real ale ~ (01694) 771266 ~ Open 12-2.30, 6-11; 12-11 Sat, Sun; 12-2.30, 6.30-11 in winter; closed winter Sun evening, Mon ~ Bar food 12-2.30, 6 (7 Sun)-9 ~ Restaurant ~ Children welcome ~ Dogs allowed in bar ~ Wi-fi ~ www.at-the-oak.com *Recommended by S and R Dowdy, Dr Peter Crawshaw, Tony Tollitt*

The letters and figures after the name of each town are its Ordnance Survey map reference. 'Using the *Guide*' at the beginning of the book explains how it helps you find a pub, in road atlases or large-scale maps as well as in our own maps.

CHETWYND ASTON

Fox 🏮 ⭐ 🍷 🍺

SJ7517 Map 7

Village signposted off A41 and A518 just S of Newport; TF10 9LQ

Civilised dining pub with generous helpings of well liked food and a fine array of drinks served by ever-attentive staff

Always bustling and friendly, this spotlessly kept 1920s pub is extremely well run. It's a big place but there are cosy corners too, and the courteous staff cope well with the crowds. A series of linked areas, one with a broad arched ceiling, has plenty of tables in all shapes and sizes, some quite elegant, and a loosely matching diversity of comfortable chairs, all laid out in a way that's fine for eating but works equally well for just drinking and chatting. There are masses of interesting prints, three open fires and a few oriental rugs on polished parquet, boards or attractive floor tiling; big windows and careful lighting contribute to the relaxed atmosphere; board games. The handsome bar counter, with a decent complement of bar stools, serves an excellent changing range of about 18 wines by the glass, 40 malt whiskies, 20 gins and Phoenix Brunning & Price Original, Three Tuns XXX, Woods Shropshire Lad and three guests such as Beartown Peach Melbear, Goffs Mordred and Wye Valley Bitter on handpump; good disabled access. The spreading garden is quite lovely, with a sunny terrace, picnic-sets tucked into the shade of mature trees and extensive views across quiet country fields.

 Good, enjoyable food includes sandwiches, smoked salmon roulade with grapefruit, fennel and chicory salad, a charcuterie plate for two, pea, chickpea and coriander cakes with mint yoghurt, chicken, ham hock and leek pie, rare-breed pork, chilli and fennel sausages with onion gravy, duck three-ways (honey-glazed breast, confit leg and faggot) with parsnip purée and port jus, salmon, smoked haddock and prawn pie, and puddings such as waffle with boozy cherries and toffee sauce and crème brûlée. *Benchmark main dish: steak burger with bacon, cheddar, coleslaw and chips £12.45. Two-course evening meal £20.50.*

Brunning & Price ~ Manager Samantha Forrest ~ Real ale ~ (01952) 815940 ~ Open 11-11 ~ Bar food 12-10 (9.30 Sun) ~ Children welcome ~ Dogs allowed in bar ~ www.fox-newport.co.uk *Recommended by Dave Webster, Sue Holland, Brian and Jacky Wilson, Ian Herdman*

CLUN

White Horse 🍺 £

SO3080 Map 6

The Square; SY7 8JA

Bustling local with own brew and guest ales and good value traditional food

There's always a friendly mix of both regulars and visitors in this cheery pub – and a warm welcome for all. Many are here to try the own-brewed Clun beers served by attentive staff: Citadel Strong Ale, Loophole and Pale Ale with guests such as Hobsons Best and Wye Valley Butty Bach on handpump. They also keep five wines by the glass, a few malt whiskies and farm cider. The low-beamed front bar is cosy and friendly and warmed in winter by an inglenook woodburning stove. From the bar, a door leads into a separate little dining room with a rare plank and muntin screen. In the games room at the back you'll find a TV, games machine, darts, pool, juke box and board games; small garden.

🍴 Using locally sourced produce, the good value food includes baguettes, smoked mackerel and horseradish pâté, mushroom stroganoff, gammon with egg or pineapple, beer-battered haddock and chips, sausages with baked beans, cajun chicken with salsa, and puddings. *Benchmark main dish: suet pudding of the day £10.95. Two-course evening meal £16.00.*

Own brew ~ Licensee Jack Limond ~ Real ale ~ No credit cards ~ (01588) 640305 ~ Open 12-midnight ~ Bar food 12-2 (12.30-2.30 Sun), 6.30-8.30 ~ Children welcome ~ Dogs allowed in bar and bedrooms ~ Wi-fi ~ Live music every second Fri of the month ~ Bedrooms: £37.50/£65 ~ www.whi-clun.co.uk *Recommended by David Heath, Dr Peter Crawshaw*

COALPORT
SJ7002 Map 4
Woodbridge 🍷 🍴
Village signposted off A442 1.5 miles S of A4169 Telford roundabout; down in valley, turn left across narrow bridge into Coalport Road, pub then on left; TF8 7JF

Superb Ironbridge Gorge site for extensive handsomely reworked pub, an all-round success

Big windows here look out on a choice section of the wooded gorge, with the many tables and chairs on the big raised deck at first-floor level looking over the River Severn. Inside, it's comfortable and civilised with log fires and Coalport-style stoves, rugs on broad boards as well as tiles or carpet, black beams in the central part, plenty of polished tables and cosy armchair corners – all relaxed and chatty. A mass of mainly 18th- and 19th-c prints – the signature Brunning & Price design feature – decorates the spreading series of many linked rooms; the historic pictures, often of local scenes, are well worth a look. Phoenix Brunning & Price Original, Hobsons Twisted Spire, Ironbridge Gold, Salopian Shropshire Gold, Three Tuns XXX and Woods Shropshire Lad on handpump, 16 wines by the glass, 45 malt whiskies and 15 gins; service is quick and friendly.

🍴 Interesting food includes sandwiches, venison and pork faggot with mushrooms and lentils, roasted red pepper panna cotta with caponata vegetables, sharing platters, bubble and squeak cake with poached duck egg, malaysian chicken curry, butternut squash risotto cakes with tagine sauce, steak and kidney pudding, smoked haddock and salmon fishcakes, and puddings such as raspberry bakewell tart and chocolate and lime cheesecake. *Benchmark main dish: braised shoulder of lamb with dauphinoise potatoes £17.25. Two-course evening meal £20.50.*

Brunning & Price ~ Manager Vrata Krist ~ Real ale ~ (01952) 882054 ~ Open 11.30-11 (midnight Sat, 10.30 Sun) ~ Bar food 12-10 (9.30 Sun) ~ Restaurant ~ Children welcome ~ Dogs allowed in bar ~ Wi-fi ~ www.brunningandprice.co.uk/woodbridge
Recommended by Nick Jenkins, Dr Kevan Tucker, John Oates, Roger and Donna Huggins

IRONBRIDGE
SJ6703 Map 4
Golden Ball 🍴 🛏
Brown sign to pub off Madeley Road (B4373) above village centre – pub behind Horse & Jockey, car park beyond on left; TF8 7BA

Low-beamed, partly Elizabethan pub with good value food and drink; bedrooms

This is a comfortable place to stay overnight and the breakfasts are good. It's a friendly and unassuming inn with worn boards, red-cushioned pews, one or two black beams, a dresser of decorative china and a woodburning stove. Hobsons Town Crier and Wye Valley HPA, plus guests such as Greene King Abbot, St Austell Tribute and Wells & Youngs

Bombardier, on handpump, half a dozen wines by the glass and a couple of farm ciders; background music. There's a pretty fairy-lit pergola path to the door, and a sheltered side courtyard has tables under cocktail parasols. You can walk down to the river, and beyond – but it's steep getting back up.

The tasty food includes sandwiches, chicken liver pâté, smoked salmon and capers, haddock and spring onion fishcakes, cheese and tomato quiche, steak in ale pie, chicken breast wrapped in bacon with stilton sauce, and puddings such as sticky toffee pudding with butterscotch sauce and Baileys chocolate mousse. *Benchmark main dish: steak ciabatta with onions, cheese, mushrooms and chips £7.25. Two-course evening meal £17.00.*

Enterprise ~ Lease Helen Pickerill ~ Real ale ~ (01952) 432179 ~ Open 12-3, 5-11 Mon-Weds; 12-11 Thurs-Sat; 12-10.30 Sun ~ Bar food 12-2.30, 6-9; 12-9 Sat; 12-6 Sun ~ Restaurant ~ Children welcome ~ Dogs allowed in bar ~ Wi-fi ~ Live acoustic music second Sun of month ~ Bedrooms: £55/£65 ~ www.goldenballironbridge.co.uk
Recommended by Roger and Donna Huggins

 LEINTWARDINE   SO4175   Map 6
Jolly Frog
A4113 Ludlow–Knighton, E edge of village; The Toddings; SY7 0LX

Friendly, cheerful bar and good bistro restaurant with fish specials

Just a short drive from Ludlow in glorious countryside, this well run pub is very popular with our readers. The front bar has just a few tables on light oak boards, with red- or blue-check american-cloth covers and red leatherette dining chairs with lion's head knobs. There's a woodburning stove at each end and lightheartedly frenchified décor – kepis and other hats hanging from stripped beams, street signs from Paris, a Metro map. The dining room, up a few steps, is similarly furnished and decorated. Staff are friendly and professional. As well as good wines by the glass (including two champagnes and a prosecco) or in 50cl pitchers, there's Hobsons Best and Three Tuns XXX on handpump and good coffees; unobtrusive, well reproduced jazz. There are one or two tables under a sail canopy in an inner courtyard, and more wicker chairs and tables on an upper deck with wide and peaceful pastoral views.

With home-baked bread and local, seasonal produce, the very good food includes ham hock with pickled quails egg and puy lentils, tempura-battered squid with chilli jam, vegetable risotto, pizzas from a wood-burning oven, chicken with parsley cream sauce and boulangère potatoes, braised lamb shoulder with chilli and salsa verde, halibut with samphire and white wine sauce, and puddings such as tiramisu and caramel panna cotta with praline; they also offer a fixed-price menu (lunch, 6-7pm). *Benchmark main dish: Brixham plaice with white wine and parsley butter £17.00. Two-course evening meal £25.00.*

Free house ~ Licensee Tracey Cooper ~ Real ale ~ (01547) 540298 ~ Open 12-3, 6-11; closed Mon ~ Bar food 12-2, 6-9 ~ Restaurant ~ Children welcome ~ Wi-fi ~ www.thejollyfrog.co.uk *Recommended by David Aston, W M Lien, Gordon and Margaret Ormondroyd*

 LUDLOW   SO5174   Map 6
Charlton Arms
Ludford Bridge, B4361 Overton Road; SY8 1PJ

Fine position for bustling pub near town centre, plenty of space for both drinking and dining, and extensive terraces overlooking the water; bedrooms

Just a short walk from the town centre and overlooking the River Teme, this bustling place has big windows that look down on the massive medieval bridge; two balconies on different levels have seats and tables with the same view – as do the well equipped and cosy refurbished bedrooms. The character bar has proper pubby tables and chairs on tiled and bricked floors, gluggle jugs along the gantry, a double-sided woodburning stove and stools against the hop-hung counter where they keep Hobsons Bitter and Twisted Spire, Ludlow Gold and Wye Valley Butty Bach on handpump and ten wines by the glass or carafe. The two rooms (one has the other side of the woodburning stove) of the lounge are comfortable and chatty, with tub and armchairs on pale wood flooring as well as high-backed black leather dining chairs around tables for eating, and pictures on pale yellow walls. The dining room, with striped high-backed chairs around attractive tables, looks over the fine bridge. Good, friendly service; background music and board games.

Using the best local, seasonal produce, the well presented food includes lunchtime wraps, braised oxtail tortellini with cracked pepper butter, tiger prawns with chorizo, white wine, chilli and parsley, butternut squash pasta with parmesan and sage butter, cumberland sausage with mustard mash and bourguignon sauce, lamb rump with white beans, mint and coriander, pork belly with colcannon mash, a stuffed apple and cider sauce, and puddings. *Benchmark main dish: burger with swiss cheese, home-made pickles and skinny fries £11.50. Two-course evening meal £19.00.*

Free house ~ Licensee Cedric Bosi ~ Real ale ~ (01584) 872813 ~ Open 11-11; 12-10 Sun ~ Bar food 12-3, 6-9.30; 12-3.30, 5.30-8.30 Sun ~ Restaurant ~ Children welcome ~ Dogs allowed in bar ~ Wi-fi ~ Bedrooms: £60/£90 ~ www.thecharltonarms.co.uk
Recommended by Robert W Buckle

 LUDLOW   SO5174   Map 4

Church Inn ⊴ £
Church Street, behind Butter Cross; SY8 1AW

Splendid range of real ales in characterful town-centre inn

With a fine range of ten real ales on handpump and quite a choice of home-made pies, this lively town-centre pub is always full of cheerful customers. Changing regularly, the ales might include Hobsons Town Crier and Mild, Ludlow Boiling Well and Gold, and Wye Valley Bitter and HPA, with guests such as Box Steam Tunnel Vision, Brecon Red Beacons, Mayfields Auntie Myrtles and Woods Shropshire Lad; also, 30 malt whiskies, seven wines by the glass and a farm cider. The ground floor is divided into three appealingly decorated areas, with hops hanging from heavy beams, comfortable banquettes in cosy alcoves off the island counter (part of it is a pulpit), and pews and stripped stonework from the nearby church. There are displays of old photographic equipment, plants on window sills and church prints in the side room. A long central area has a fine stone fireplace and old black and white photos of the town; daily papers and background music. The civilised upstairs lounge bar has good views of the church and surrounding countryside, vaulted ceilings, a display case of glass, china and old bottles, and musical instruments on the walls. The bedrooms are simple but comfortable.

The fairly priced popular food includes sandwiches, chicken liver pâté with onion marmalade, crispy whitebait, vegetable frittata, cajun chicken with sweet potato chips, several different pies, tuna steak with stir-fried vegetables, bacon chop with free-range eggs, and puddings such as raspberry swirl cheesecake and pecan and treacle pie. *Benchmark main dish: steak in ale pie £8.95. Two-course evening meal £15.00.*

Free house ~ Licensee Graham Willson-Lloyd ~ Real ale ~ (01584) 872174 ~ Open 10 (11 Sun)-midnight (1am Fri, Sat) ~ Bar food 12.30-2.30, 6.30-9 (8.30 Sun) ~ Restaurant ~ Children welcome ~ Dogs allowed in bar ~ Wi-fi ~ Guitarist monthly Weds ~ Bedrooms: £50/£80 ~ www.thechurchinn.com *Recommended by Dr Kevan Tucker, David Buffham, Ken Richards*

 MAESBURY MARSH   SJ3125   Map 6

Navigation

Follow Maesbury Road off A483 S of Oswestry; by canal bridge; SY10 8JB

Versatile and friendly canalside pub with cosy bar and local seasonal produce in a choice of dining areas

On the banks of the Montgomery Canal – the terrace has picnic-sets safely fenced off – this is a friendly pub with a book exchange, a shop where you can buy fresh local produce and a two-pint takeaway service. The quarry-tiled bar on the left has squishy brown leather sofas by a traditional black range blazing in a big red fireplace, little upholstered cask seats around three small tables, and dozens of wrist- and pocket-watches hanging from the beams. A couple of steps lead up to a carpeted area beyond a balustrade, with armchairs and sofas around low tables, and a piano; off to the left is a dining area with cheerful prints. The main beamed dining room, with some stripped stone, is beyond another small bar with a coal fire – and an amazing row of cushioned carved choir stalls complete with misericord seats. Sharps Doom Bar and Stonehouse Cambrian Gold on handpump, 11 wines by the glass and a farm cider; quiet background music and board games.

As well as a two- and three-course set menu, the well liked food includes lunchtime sandwiches, potted shrimp with beetroot chutney, smoked salmon parcel with rocket and pine nut salad, faggots with Bovril gravy, outdoor-reared ham with parsley sauce, local game casserole, pork wellington with black pudding mash and mustard cream, and puddings such as chocolate panna cotta with orange jelly and sorbet and syrup sponge with chantilly cream and home-made fudge. *Benchmark main dish: free-range pork sausage with bubble and squeak £10.50. Two-course evening meal £17.00.*

Free house ~ Licensees Brent Ellis and Mark Baggett ~ Real ale ~ (01691) 672958 ~ Open 12-2, 6-11; 12-6 Sun; closed Sun evening, Mon and Tues lunchtimes, first two weeks Jan ~ Bar food 12-2, 6-8.30 ~ Restaurant ~ Children welcome ~ Dogs allowed in bar ~ Wi-fi ~ Folk music third Fri of month ~ www.thenavigation.co.uk *Recommended by Pat and Tony Martin, Steve Whalley*

MUCH WENLOCK   SO6299   Map 4

George & Dragon  £

High Street (A458); TF13 6AA

Bustling and atmospheric with reasonably priced food and good beer selection; usefully open all day

There's so much to look at in this friendly little place as it's filled with a fascinating collection of pub paraphernalia – old brewery and cigarette advertisements, bottle labels, beer trays and George and the dragon pictures, as well as 200 jugs hanging from the beams. The front door takes you straight into a beamed and quarry-tiled room with wooden chairs and tables and antique settles around the walls, with a couple of open fires in attractive Victorian fireplaces. At the back is a timbered dining room. Greene King Abbot, Hobsons Best, St Austell Tribute, Shepherd Neame Spitfire and Thwaites Wainwright on handpump, six wines by the glass and 15 malt whiskies. Background music, dominoes, cards, board games and daily newspapers. There's a pay-and-display car park behind the pub.

Good, tasty food includes sandwiches, blue cheese and walnut pâté, black pudding with red cabbage, vegetable lasagne, home-baked ham with parsley sauce, fidget pie, local steaks, and puddings such as fruit crumble and bread and butter pudding. *Benchmark main dish: beef in ale pie £8.95. Two-course evening meal £11.00.*

Punch ~ Tenant James Scott ~ Real ale ~ (01952) 727312 ~ Open 12-11 (midnight Sat) ~ Bar food 12-2.30, 6-9; not Weds or Sun evenings ~ Restaurant ~ Children welcome ~ Dogs allowed in bar ~ Live music twice a month ~ www.thegeorgedragon.co.uk
Recommended by James Stretton, Mike and Wena Stevenson, David H Bennett, C A Bryson, Patrick and Daphne Darley, Dr Kevan Tucker, Robert Parker, Di and Mike Gillam

NORTON
Hundred House 🍷 🛏
SJ7200 Map 4
A442 Telford–Bridgnorth; TF11 9EE

Family-run inn with rambling rooms, open fires and quite a choice of drinks and good food; comfortable large bedrooms

This carefully kept, family-run inn is a fine place to stay: the bedrooms have antique four-posters or half-testers, Victorian-style baths and rain showers, and their trademark velvet-cushioned swing. In the rambling bar rooms you'll find log fires in handsome fireplaces (one has a great Jacobean arch with fine old black cooking pots) and a variety of interesting chairs and settles with long colourful patchwork leather cushions around sewing machine tables. Hops and huge bunches of dried flowers and herbs hang from beams, and bunches of fresh flowers brighten the tables and counter in the neatly kept bar. Steps lead up past a little balustrade to a partly panelled eating area, where the stripped brickwork looks older than it does elsewhere. Ironbridge Best Bitter and Three Tuns XXX on handpump, 13 wines by the glass and two farm ciders; background music. The lovely garden has old-fashioned roses, herbaceous plants and a big working herb garden (with over 100 varieties) that supplies the kitchen.

Using home-grown herbs and other local produce, the attractively presented, enjoyable food includes sandwiches, seafood platter with fennel salad, potted rabbit with prune purée, chicken stuffed with ricotta, spinach and pine nuts in red pepper and basil sauce, rack of lamb on creamed garlic mash with braised shank in red wine and olive sauce, mixed game pudding with juniper sauce, whole lemon sole with lime, chilli and coriander butter, and puddings. *Benchmark main dish: crispy local pork belly with real ale sauce £13.95. Two-course evening meal £21.00.*

Free house ~ Licensees Henry, Stuart and David Phillips ~ Real ale ~ (01952) 730353 ~ Open 11am-11.15pm (10.30pm Sun) ~ Bar food 12-2.30, 6-9.30; 12-9 Sun ~ Restaurant ~ Children welcome ~ Dogs welcome ~ Wi-fi ~ Bedrooms: £60/£69 ~ www.hundredhouse.co.uk *Recommended by Alfie Bayliss, Charlie May*

If a compulsory service charge is mentioned prominently on a menu or accommodation terms, you must pay it if service was satisfactory. If service is really bad, you are legally entitled to refuse to pay some or all of the service charge as compensation for not getting the service you might reasonably have expected.

SHIPLEY

SO8095 Map 4

Inn at Shipley ♀ ◀

Bridgnorth Road; A454 W of Wolverhampton; WV6 7EQ

Light and airy country pub, good all-rounder

Rambling around the central bar, this well preserved 18th-c brick house has several woodburning stoves and log fires – one in a big inglenook in a cosy, traditionally tiled black-beamed end room, another by a welcoming set of wing and other leather armchairs. It's all very civilised, with mixed dining chairs around a variety of well buffed tables, rugs on polished boards, attractive pictures, big windows letting in plenty of daylight, plus church candles, careful spotlighting, picture-lights and even chandeliers at night. The various areas are interconnected but manage to also feel distinct and individual; upstairs is a separate private dining room with a big round table suitable for eight to perhaps a dozen people. There are changing beers such as Phoenix Brunning & Price Original, Coach House Honeypot, Joules Slumbering Monk, Rudgate Ruby Mild, Salopian Oracle and Stonehouse Station Bitter on handpump, 17 wines by the glass, 82 malt whiskies and a farm cider; good neatly dressed staff, piped music, daily papers, board games. There are plenty of sturdy tables outside, some on a sizeable terrace with a side awning, others by weeping willows on the main lawn behind the car park, more on smaller lawns around the building.

Tempting food includes sandwiches, home-smoked duck with quince jelly, scallops with cauliflower purée and curry oil, pork sausages with onion gravy, rosemary and garlic chicken with wild mushroom and bacon pasta, teriyaki salmon and king prawn salad with crispy wasabi rice balls and pak choi, sweet potato, aubergine and spinach malaysian curry, and puddings such as blackberry and orange cheesecake and bread and butter pudding. *Benchmark main dish: braised shoulder of lamb with dauphinoise potatoes £16.95. Two-course evening meal £20.50.*

Brunning & Price ~ Manager Rachel Lloyd ~ Real ale ~ (01902) 701639 ~
Open 10.30am-11pm ~ Bar food 12-10 (9.30 Sun) ~ Restaurant ~ Children welcome ~
Dogs allowed in bar ~ Wi-fi ~ www.brunningandprice.co.uk/innatshipley
Recommended by Isobel Mackinlay

SHREWSBURY

SJ4812 Map 6

Armoury ⊕ ♀ ◀

Victoria Quay, Victoria Avenue; SY1 1HH

Vibrant atmosphere in interestingly converted riverside warehouse, with enthusiastic young staff, good tempting all-day food and excellent choice of drinks

In summer, the massive red-brick frontage of this 18th-c former warehouse looks pretty with its hanging baskets and smart coach lights. The spacious open-plan interior has long runs of big arched windows with views across the broad River Severn – but it has a personal feel helped by the eclectic décor, furniture layout and lively bustle, despite its size. A variety of wood tables and chairs are grouped on stripped-wood floors, the huge brick walls display floor-to-ceiling books or masses of old prints mounted edge to edge, and there's a grand stone fireplace at one end. Colonial-style fans whirr away on the ceilings, which are supported by green-painted columns, and small wall-mounted glass cabinets display smokers' pipes. The long bar counter has a terrific choice of drinks including Phoenix Brunning & Price Original, Hobsons Twisted Spire and Salopian Shropshire Gold with guests such as Dickensian Ale of Two Cities

Bitter Vol 1, Joules Slumbering Monk, Montys Mischief and Purple Moose Ysgawen on handpump, a great wine list (with 17 by the glass), 100 malt whiskies, a dozen gins, lots of rums and vodkas, a variety of brandies and a farm cider. The pub doesn't have its own car park, but there are plenty of parking places nearby.

 Rewarding food includes sandwiches, rabbit faggot with wild mushrooms, smoked salmon with horseradish panna cotta, beetroot, courgette and goats cheese risotto, honey-roast ham and free-range eggs, steak burger with bacon, cheddar, coleslaw and chips, moroccan chicken with apricot couscous, whole plaice with lemon and caper butter, and puddings such as chocolate orange bread and butter pudding with marmalade glaze and crème brûlée. *Benchmark main dish: beer-battered fish and chips £12.25. Two-course evening meal £20.00.*

Brunning & Price ~ Manager Emily Waring ~ Real ale ~ (01743) 340525 ~ Open 12-11 (10.30 Sun) ~ Bar food 12-10 (9.30 Sun) ~ Children welcome ~ Dogs allowed in bar ~ Wi-fi ~ www.armoury-shrewsbury.co.uk *Recommended by David Aston, David H Bennett, John Oates, Brian and Anna Marsden*

SHREWSBURY
Lion & Pheasant 🏮🍷🛏️
SJ4912 Map 6

Follow City Centre signposts across the English Bridge; SY1 1XJ

Civilised bar and upstairs restaurant in comfortable, neatly updated and well placed inn

A good range of 14 wines by the glass (in three glass sizes) complements the more local Ludlow Gold, Salopian Oracle and Woods Shropshire Lad on handpump in the big-windowed bar. The lowest of the three linked levels has armchairs on dark flagstones by a big inglenook; elsewhere there's a cushioned settee, but most of the seats are at sturdy stripped tables on dark floorboards. A few modern paintings, plentiful flowers and church candles brighten up the restrained cream and grey décor, as do the friendly staff and background music. Off quite a warren of corridors, the restaurant (you can eat from its menu in the bar too) is in the older back part of the building, probably 16th-c, with heavy beams and timbering. Some of the bedrooms provide glimpses of the River Severn below the nearby English Bridge; they do a good breakfast.

 Imaginative food includes sandwiches, peppered venison carpaccio with plum jelly and horseradish cream, baby squid with morcilla, chickpeas, salt cod and piquillo peppers, ham and free-range eggs, wild mushroom risotto, seafood stew with mussel and saffron sauce and aioli, roast fillet of beef, Guinness and beef pie, tempura oyster, salsify and root vegetable purée, and puddings such as hot chocolate fondant with white chocolate parfait and vanilla crème brûlée. *Benchmark main dish: free-range chicken with wild garlic and crispy pancetta £21.00. Two-course evening meal £27.50.*

Free house ~ Licensee Jim Littler ~ Real ale ~ (01743) 770345 ~ Open 11-11 ~ Bar food 12-9.30 (9 Sun) ~ Restaurant ~ Children welcome ~ Wi-fi ~ Bedrooms: £99/£119 ~ www.lionandpheasant.co.uk *Recommended by Isobel Mackinlay, Edward May*

'Children welcome' means the pub says it lets children inside without any special restriction. If it allows them in, but to restricted areas such as an eating area or family room, we specify this. Places with separate restaurants often let children use them, and hotels usually let children into public areas such as lounges. Some pubs impose an evening time limit – let us know if you find one earlier than 9pm.

Also Worth a Visit in Shropshire

Besides the fully inspected pubs, you might like to try these pubs that have been recommended to us and described by readers. Do tell us what you think of them: feedback@goodguides.com

ADMASTON   SJ6313
Pheasant (01952) 251989
Shawbirch Road; TF5 0AD Red-brick Victorian pub with good locally sourced food (all day Sat, till 7pm Sun), three or four well kept ales including Salopian and Woods, pleasant staff, Thurs quiz; garden with play area, open all day. *(Mrs Sally Evans)*

ALBRIGHTON   SJ8104
Shrewsbury Arms (01902) 373003
High Street; WV7 3LA Brick and timber dining pub recently reopened after major refurbishment, good food from light dishes and sharing plates up, real ales, live music Fri; children and dogs welcome. *(John Oates)*

BISHOP'S CASTLE   SO3288
Boars Head (01588) 638521
Church Street; SY9 5AE Comfortable beamed and stripped-stone bar with mix of furniture including pews and settles on bare boards, woodburner in big inglenook, welcoming efficient young staff, well kept ales and enjoyable good value pub food, family room with TV and another inglenook, some live music; free wi-fi; no dogs inside; picnic-sets on back terrace, three roomy high-raftered bedrooms in converted barn, open (and food) all day. *(Anon)*

BISHOP'S CASTLE   SO3288
★**Castle Hotel** (01588) 638403
Market Square, just off B4385; SY9 5BN Substantial coaching inn at top of lovely market town, clubby little beamed and panelled bar with log fire, larger rooms off with big Victorian engravings and another fire, well kept Clun, Hobsons, Six Bells and Three Tuns, farm cider, ten wines by the glass and 30 malt whiskies, handsome panelled dining room, popular food served by friendly staff, darts and board games; background music; children and dogs welcome, pretty hanging baskets at front, garden behind with terrace seating, pergolas and climbing plants, surrounding walks, spacious bedrooms, good breakfast, open all day. *(Mike and Eleanor Anderson, A N Bance)*

BISHOP'S CASTLE   SO3288
★**Six Bells** (01588) 630144
Church Street; SY9 5AA 17th-c pub with own-brew beers the main draw (brewery tours available); smallish no-frills bar with mix of well worn furniture, old local photographs and prints, bigger room with stripped-stone walls, benches around plain tables on bare boards and inglenook woodburner, country wines and summer

farm cider, July beer festival, basic food (not Sun or Tues evenings or Mon); no credit cards; well behaved children and dogs welcome, open all day Sat, closed Mon lunchtime. *(Anon)*

BRIDGES   SO3996
★**Bridges** (01588) 650260
Bridges, W of Ratlinghope; SY5 0ST Old renovated beamed country pub, now the Three Tuns tap with their full range in excellent condition, bare-boards bar to right, large dining room to left, woodburner, decent fairly traditional home-made food (not Sun evening, winter Mon), helpful staff, regular live music; children welcome, dogs in room off bar, tables out by the little River Onny (some on raised deck), bedrooms, also camping and youth hostel nearby, great walking country, open all day. *(C A Bryson, Dr Kevan Tucker, D W Stokes, Dr Peter Crawshaw)*

BRIDGNORTH   SO6890
★**Down** (01746) 789539
The Down; B4364 Ludlow Road 3 miles S; WV16 6UA Good value roadside dining pub overlooking rolling countryside, enjoyable food including popular daily carvery, efficient service, a house beer (Down & Out) from Three Tuns and a couple of local guests; background music; children welcome, nine comfortable bedrooms, open all day. *(David Aston)*

BRIDGNORTH   SO7193
Kings Head (01746) 762141
Whitburn Street; WV16 4QN 17th-c timbered coaching inn with high-raftered back stable bar, good food here from 5pm (all day weekends) or in all-day restaurant with separate menu, Hobsons and a couple of guests, friendly staff, log fires, beams and flagstones, pretty leaded windows; children and dogs welcome, courtyard picnic-sets, open all day. *(Anon)*

BRIDGNORTH   SO7192
★**Railwaymans Arms** (01746) 764361
Severn Valley Station, Hollybush Road (off A458 towards Stourbridge); WV16 5DT Bathams, Hobsons and plenty of other good value local ales kept well in chatty old-fashioned converted waiting room at Severn Valley steam railway terminus, bustling on summer days; old station signs and train nameplates, superb mirror over fireplace, may be simple summer snacks, Sept beer festival; children welcome, wheelchair access with help, tables out on platform the train to Kidderminster

(station bar there too) has an all-day bar and bookable Sun lunches, open all day. *(Anon)*

BROMFIELD   SO4877
★ **Clive** (01584) 856565
A49 2 miles NW of Ludlow; SY8 2JR
Sophisticated minimalist bar-restaurant taking its name from Clive of India who once lived here; emphasis mainly on top notch imaginative food but also Hobsons and Ludlow ales, several wines by the glass and various teas and coffees, welcoming well trained staff, dining room with light wood tables, door to sparsely furnished bar with metal chairs, glass-topped tables and sleek counter, step down to room with soaring beams and rafters, exposed stonework and woodburner in huge fireplace; background jazz; children welcome, tables under parasols on secluded terrace, fish pond, 15 stylish bedrooms, good breakfast, open all day.
(Gordon and Margaret Ormondroyd)

BUCKNELL   SO3574
Baron (01547) 530549
Chapel Lawn Road; just off B4367 Knighton Road; SY7 0AH Modernised family-owned country inn, friendly and efficiently run, with enjoyable home-made food from panini and pizzas up, well kept Ludlow and Wye Valley ales, log fire in carpeted front bar, back dining room with old cider press and grindstone, conservatory; children welcome, lovely views from big garden, five bedrooms, camping field, open all day Sat, closed Sun evening and lunchtimes Mon-Thurs. *(Malcolm and Pauline Pellatt)*

BURLTON   SJ4526
Burlton Inn (01939) 270284
A528 Shrewsbury–Ellesmere, near B4397 junction; SY4 5TB Attractive 18th-c pub under welcoming new management; enjoyable good value food and two well kept Robinsons ales, friendly helpful staff, beams, timbers and log fires, comfortable snug, restaurant with garden room; children welcome, disabled facilities, teak furniture on pleasant terrace, comfortable well equipped bedrooms, good breakfast. *(Anon)*

BURWARTON   SO6185
★ **Boyne Arms** (01746) 787214
B4364 Bridgnorth–Ludlow; WV16 6QH
Handsome Georgian coaching inn with welcoming cheerful staff, enjoyable generous food (not Sun evening, Mon) including good value deals, three Hobsons ales and a guest, Robinson's cider, decent coffee, separate restaurant and public bar (dogs allowed here), function room with pool and other games; children welcome, good timber adventure playground in pretty garden, hitching rail for horses, open all day weekends, closed Mon lunchtime. *(Anon)*

CHURCH STRETTON   SO4593
Bucks Head (01694) 722898
High Street; SY6 6BX Old town pub with several good-sized modernised areas including restaurant, four well kept Marstons ales, decent good value pubby food plus vegetarian options, friendly attentive staff, black beams and timbers, mixed dark wood tables and chairs; four bedrooms, open all day. *(David Aston)*

CHURCH STRETTON   SO4593
Housmans (01694) 724441
High Street; SY6 6BX Buzzing and welcoming restaurant-bar with two well kept ales from Three Tuns and good wine and cocktail lists, food mainly tapas-style sharing plates but also good value two-course weekday lunch deal, local art on walls, occasional jazz and acoustic music; children welcome, open all day weekends. *(Kim Skuse)*

CLUN   SO3080
Sun (01588) 640559
High Street; SY7 8JB Beamed and timbered 15th-c pub with enormous open fire in traditional flagstoned public bar (dogs welcome here), larger carpeted lounge bar, enjoyable home-made food (not Sun evening) from lunchtime sandwiches up, four well kept Three Tuns ales; children welcome, paved back terrace, peaceful village and lovely rolling countryside, bedrooms (some in converted outbuildings), closed Mon lunchtime, otherwise open all day.
(A N Bance)

CLUNTON   SO3381
Crown (01588) 660265
B4368; SY7 0HU Cosy old country local, welcoming and friendly, with good choice of well kept changing ales and enjoyable generous food (Thurs-Sat evenings), also Weds fish and chips and good value Sun lunch, log fire in small flagstoned bar, dining room, games room, folk night third Weds of month; open all day Fri-Sun, closed lunchtimes other days. *(Anon)*

COALPORT   SJ6903
Half Moon (01952) 884443
Off Salthouse Road; TF8 7LP
Reopened 2012 and extensively refurbished after 18-year closure; lovely Severn-side position, three local ales and good choice of fairly priced food including home-made pizzas and basket meals, some live music; children welcome, picnic-sets out overlooking river, four bedrooms, open all day summer. *(Adrian Johnson)*

COALPORT   SJ6902
Shakespeare (01952) 580675
High Street; TF8 7HT Relaxing early 19th-c inn by pretty Severn gorge park, timbering, bare stone walls and tiled floors, well kept Everards, Hobsons,

Ludlow and guests, good value food from sandwiches through pub standards to mexican specialities; children welcome, picnic-sets in tiered garden with play area, handy for China Museum, four bedrooms, open all day weekends, closed weekday lunchtimes. *(Anon)*

CORFTON   SO4985
Sun (01584) 861239
B4368 Much Wenlock–Craven Arms; SY7 9DF Lived-in unchanging three-room country local, own good Corvedale ales (including an unfined beer), friendly long-serving landlord (often busy in back brewery), decent well presented pubby food from baguettes to steaks, lots of breweriana, basic quarry-tiled public bar with darts, pool and juke box, quieter carpeted lounge, dining room with covered well, tourist information; children welcome, dogs in bar, good wheelchair access throughout and disabled lavatories, tables on terrace and in large garden with good play area. *(Anon)*

CRAVEN ARMS   SO5485
Tally Ho (01584) 841811
Bouldon; SY7 9DP Welcoming tucked-away pub reopened by a group of villagers a couple of years ago; local beers and big helpings of enjoyable freshly made pubby food at very reasonable prices, service with a smile; dogs welcome, country views from nice garden. *(David Buffham, Brian and Jacky Wilson)*

FORD   SJ4013
Olde Cross Gates (01743) 851252
A458; SY5 9LH Large brick-built former coaching inn with enjoyable home-cooked food including Sun carvery, local ales and good choice of other drinks (some unusual ones), friendly staff happy to chat; children welcome, outside fenced seating area, open all day Sun. *(Phil and Jane Hodson)*

GRINDLEY BROOK   SJ5242
Horse & Jockey (01948) 662723
A41; SY13 4QJ Extended 19th-c pub with enjoyable good value food from varied menu (all day Fri-Sun), friendly helpful service, eight well kept ales including a house beer from Phoenix named after resident chocolate labrador Blaze, teas and coffees, well divided open-plan interior with mix of furniture on wood or carpeted floors, some interesting bits and pieces, woodburners; sports TV, pool; children, dogs and muddy boots welcome, big play area, handy for Sandstone Trail and Llangollen Canal, open all day. *(Mike and Wena Stevenson, Ann and Tony Bennett-Hughes, Robert W Buckle)*

GRINSHILL   SJ5223
★**Inn at Grinshill** (01939) 220410
Off A49 N of Shrewsbury; SY4 3BL Civilised early Georgian country inn, comfortable 19th-c panelled bar with log fire in raised two-way hearth, Greene King and a couple of local guests, spacious modern restaurant with view into kitchen, good food and friendly competent service; background music, TV; children and dogs welcome, pleasant back garden with plenty of tables and chairs, comfortable clean bedrooms, closed Sun evening, Mon, Tues. *(Anon)*

HIGHLEY   SO7483
Ship (01746) 861219
Severnside; WV16 6NU Refurbished 18th-c inn in lovely riverside location, good choice of enjoyable food (although not much for vegetarians), bargain OAP weekday lunch and early-bird deals, Sun carvery, five real ales; children welcome, tables on raised front deck, handy for Severn Way walks (and Severn Valley Railway), fishing rights, bedrooms. *(Anon)*

HINDFORD   SJ3333
Jack Mytton (01691) 679861
Village and pub signed from A495; SY11 4NL Friendly pub with pleasant rustic bar, log fire, four well kept changing ales and enjoyable food from bar snacks up, airy raftered dining room; children and dogs welcome, picnic-sets in appealing canalside garden, good-sized courtyard with summer bar and carved bear (pub is named after an eccentric squire who rode a bear), moorings; character landlord is planning to retire by end of 2014, and pub is up for sale. *(Mike and Wena Stevenson, Mr and Mrs J J A Davis)*

HODNET   SJ6128
★**Bear** (01630) 685214
Drayton Road (A53); TF9 3NH Old village inn under new management since 2013; very good affordably priced food (all day Fri, Sat, till 6pm Sun, booking advised) from well executed pub favourites to more creative restaurant dishes, four well kept changing ales and 14 wines by the glass, friendly helpful staff, rambling open-plan main area, snug end alcoves with heavy 16th-c beams and timbers, small beamed quarry-tiled bar, woodburners, quiz second Mon of the month; children welcome, dogs in one area (the resident jack russell is Jack), picnic-sets in garden with play area, seven refurbished bedrooms (two more in annexe), opposite Hodnet Hall Gardens and handy for Hawkstone Park, open all day. *(James Austin, Jo Weller)*

Please tell us if any pub deserves to be upgraded to a featured entry – and why: feedback@goodguides.com, or (no stamp needed) The Good Pub Guide, FREEPOST RTJR-ZCYZ-RJZT, Perrymans Lane, Etchingham TN19 7DN.

HOPE SJ3401
Stables (01743) 891344
*Just off A488 3 miles S of Minsterley;
SY5 0EP* Hidden-away little 17th-c beamed
country pub (former drovers' inn), a couple
of ales such as Six Bells and Wye Valley
Butty Bach, enjoyable home-made food,
newspapers, log fires; dogs welcome (their
irish wolfhound is Murphy) fine views from
garden, two bedrooms and a newly built
'shepherd's hut' for the glamping enthusiast,
closed weekday lunchtimes. *(Anon)*

HOPTON WAFERS SO6376
Crown (01299) 270372
A4117; DY14 0NB Attractive 16th-c
creeper-clad inn, light comfortable décor and
furnishings, beams and big inglenook, good
food (all day Sun) in three separate dining
areas, weekday set deal lunchtime/early
evening, ales such as Ludlow and Wye Valley,
good choice of wines and decent coffee,
cheerful efficient staff, relaxed atmosphere;
children and dogs welcome, inviting garden
with terraces, duck pond and stream,
18 bedrooms (11 in new adjoining building),
open all day. *(Dave Braisted, Ryta Lyndley,
Robert Parker)*

IRONBRIDGE SJ6603
★ Malthouse (01952) 433712
*The Wharfage (bottom road alongside
Severn); TF8 7NH* Converted 18th-c
malthouse wonderfully located in historic
gorge, spacious bar with iron pillars
supporting heavy pine beams, lounge/
dining area, up to three well kept changing
ales, good reasonably priced food all day
from baguettes up, live music Fri, Sat;
children and dogs welcome, terrace tables,
11 individually styled bedrooms and self-
catering cottage. *(David H Bennett)*

LEEBOTWOOD SO4798
★ Pound (01694) 751477
*A49 Church Stretton–Shrewsbury;
SY6 6ND* Thatched cruck-framed building
dating from 1458 – thought to be oldest in
the village; stylishly modern bar rooms with
minimalist fixtures and wooden furnishings,
good interesting food cooked by chef-owner
from light meals up, also pub favourites,
a couple of real ales and nice wines by the
glass, friendly efficient service; background
music; seats on flagstoned terrace; disabled
parking spaces (level access to bar), closed
Sun evening, Mon. *(Neil and Anita Christopher)*

LEIGHTON SJ6105
Kynnersley Arms (01952) 510233
B4380; SY5 6RN Victorian building built
on remains of an ancient corn mill; coal fire
and woodburner in main opened-up area,

armchairs and sofas in back part with stairs
to lower level containing mill machinery
(there's also a 17th-c blast furnace), five well
kept mainly local ales including Salopian
Shropshire Gold, traditional food along
with pizzas and pasta dishes, Sun carvery;
background and occasional live music, sports
TV, pool; children and dogs welcome, good
walks nearby, open all day. *(John Oates)*

LITTLE STRETTON SO4491
Green Dragon (01694) 722925
*Village well signed off A49 S of Church
Stretton; Ludlow Road; SY6 6RE* Cleanly
refurbished village pub at the foot of Long
Mynd; popular good value food in bar or
adjacent dining area (well behaved children
allowed here), well kept Wye Valley beers and
guests, friendly efficient young staff, warm
woodburner, stone-floored area for booted
walkers; tables outside and play area, handy
for Cardingmill Valley (NT). *(David Aston,
S and R Dowdy, D W Stokes, Robert W Buckle)*

LITTLE STRETTON SO4492
★ Ragleth (01694) 722711
*Village well signed off A49 S of Church
Stretton; Ludlow Road; SY6 6RB*
Characterful cleverly opened-up 17th-c
dining pub; light and airy bay-windowed
front bar with eclectic mix of old tables and
chairs, some exposed brick and timber work,
huge inglenook in heavily beamed brick- and
tile-floored public bar, four mainly local beers
such as Hobsons, very good food with plenty
of fish dishes, cheerful attentive owners and
staff; background music, TV, darts and board
games; children welcome, dogs in bar, lovely
garden with tulip tree-shaded lawn and good
play area, thatched and timbered church
and fine hill walks nearby, open all day Sat
(summer) and Sun. *(Bernard Stradling, David
Aston, Clive Watkin, John Oates, Dave Webster,
Sue Holland and others)*

LITTLE WENLOCK SJ6507
Huntsman (01952) 503300
Wellington Road; TF6 5BH Welcoming
recently modernised village pub, good food
(something all day) from lunchtime ciabattas
and pub standards up, four well kept
changing ales, beamed stone-floor bar with
central log fire, carpeted restaurant with
high-backed upholstered chairs by light wood
tables, woodburner in big fireplace; terrace
seating, bedrooms, handy for Wrekin walks,
open all day. *(John Oates, S Holder)*

LUDLOW SO5174
Queens (01584) 879177
Lower Galdeford; SY8 1RU Family-run
19th-c pub with good food concentrating
heavily on fresh local produce, four well kept
ales including Hobsons, Ludlow and Wye

Tipping is not normal for bar meals, and not usually expected.

Valley, long narrow oak-floor bar, pine tables in vaulted-ceiling dining area, good friendly service, popular monthly charity quiz, some live music; children welcome (not in bar after 6pm), dogs allowed in one area, open all day. *(Anon)*

LUDLOW
SO5174

Rose & Crown (01584) 872098
Off Church Street, behind Buttercross; SY8 1AP Small unpretentious pub with 13th-c origins and recently taken over by Joules, their beers, real cider and enjoyable food all day, friendly staff, comfortably lived-in L-shaped bar with hops and mugs hanging from black beams, open brick fireplace, separate dining area; children and dogs welcome, approached through passageway with a few courtyard seats at front, pretty spot, three bedrooms. *(Dave Braisted, Dr Kevan Tucker)*

MAESBURY
SJ3026

Original Ball (01691) 654880
Maesbury Road; SY10 8HB Refurbished old brick-built pub, hefty beams, woodburner in central fireplace, Marstons Pedigree and Stonehouse Station Bitter, decent wines and enjoyable reasonably priced pub food, pool area, some live music; TV; children and dogs welcome, open all day weekends, from 4pm other days. *(Jill Sparrow)*

MARKET DRAYTON
SJ6734

Red Lion (01630) 652602
Great Hales Street; TF9 1JP Extended 17th-c coaching inn now tap for Joules Brewery; back entrance into attractive modern bar with light wood floor and substantial oak timbers, traditional dark-beamed part to the right, updated but keeping original features, with pubby furniture on flagstones, brewery mirrors and signs, woodburner, more breweriana in dining/function room to left featuring 'Mousey' Thompson carved oak panelling and fireplace; Joules Pale Ale, Blonde, Slumbering Monk and a seasonal beer (tasting trays available), good selection of wines, fairly straightforward food including range of pies and Sun carvery till 4pm, some live music; picnic-sets outside, brewery tours first Weds of the month, open all day. *(Clive and Fran Dutson, Barry Collett)*

MARTON
SJ2802

★ Sun (01938) 561211
B4386 NE of Chirbury; SY21 8JP Warmly inclusive family-run pub with well liked food including seasonal game and good fresh fish, light and airy black-beamed bar with comfortable sofa and traditional pub furnishings, woodburner in big stone fireplace, Hobsons Best and a guest, chunky pale tables and tall ladder-back chairs in restaurant; children welcome, dogs in bar (but ask first), front terrace, closed Sun evening, Mon and lunchtime Tues. *(Anon)*

MUCH WENLOCK
SO6299

Gaskell Arms (01952) 727212
High Street (A458); TF13 6AQ 17th-c coaching inn with comfortable old-fashioned lounge divided by brass-canopied log fire, enjoyable straightforward bar food at fair prices, friendly attentive service, three well kept ales such as Ludlow, Salopian and Wye Valley, brasses and prints, civilised beamed restaurant, locals' public bar; background music; no dogs; well behaved children allowed, disabled facilities, roomy neat back garden with terrace, 16 bedrooms, open all day. *(Jean and Douglas Troup)*

MUNSLOW
SO5287

★ Crown (01584) 841205
B4368 Much Wenlock–Craven Arms; SY7 9ET Former courthouse with imposing exterior and pretty back façade showing Tudor origins; lots of nooks and crannies, split-level lounge bar with old-fashioned mix of furnishings on broad flagstones, old bottles, country pictures, bread oven by log fire, traditional snug with another fire, eating area with tables around central oven chimney, more beams, flagstones and stripped stone, good imaginative food (local suppliers listed) including popular Sun lunch (must book), ales such as Ludlow, Otter and Three Tuns, local bottled cider, nice wines, helpful efficient staff and friendly bustling atmosphere; background music; children welcome, level wheelchair access to bar only, bedrooms, closed Sun evening, Mon. *(David and Katharine Cooke, Glenwys and Alan Lawrence)*

NESSCLIFFE
SJ3819

Old Three Pigeons (01743) 741279
Off A5 Shrewsbury–Oswestry (now bypassed); SY4 1DB Friendly 16th-c beamed pub with good fairly priced food including fresh fish, three well kept local ales, nice wines by the glass, two bar areas and appealing restaurant, wood floors and warm log fires; children and dogs welcome, picnic-sets in garden with fountain and covered area, opposite Kynaston Cave, good cliff walks, open all day Sun, closed Mon lunchtime. *(Anon)*

PICKLESCOTT
SO4399

Bottle & Glass (01694) 751252
Off A49 N of Church Stretton; SY6 6NR Remote 17th-c rambling country pub with friendly landlord; plenty of character in quarry-tiled bar and lounge/dining areas, low black beams, oak panelling and log fires, assortment of old tables and chairs, traditional home-made food (not Sun evening) from baps up, well kept ales such as Hobsons and Woods; TV; children welcome, seats out on raised front area, bedrooms, open all day weekends (till 7pm Sun). *(Gordon and Margaret Ormondroyd)*

PORTH-Y-WAEN   SJ2623
Lime Kiln (01691) 839599
A495, between village and junction with A483, S of Oswestry; SY10 8LX Beamed roadside pub with very good affordably priced food (not Sun evening) cooked by owner-chef, welcoming service, dining area and small quarry-tiled bar with cushioned wall benches and sofa by open fire, well kept beers, organic cider and a local lager, nice wines too; children welcome, closed Mon, lunchtime Tues. *(Jill Sparrow)*

SHAWBURY   SJ5621
Fox & Hounds (01939) 250600
Wytheford Road; SY4 4JG Built in 1966 and fully renovated in 2007 after long closure; light and spacious with rugs on wood floor, various areas including book-lined dining room with woodburner, lots of pictures on the walls, good fairly priced food from light lunches and sharing boards to daily specials, four or five well kept ales and good choice of wines, efficient helpful service; children welcome, picnic-sets on terrace and lawn, open (and food) all day. *(Mr and Mrs David Horton)*

SHIFNAL   SJ74508
White Hart (01952) 461161
High Street; TF11 8BH Eight well kept interesting ales in chatty 17th-c timbered pub, quaint and old-fashioned with separate bar and lounge, good home-made lunchtime food (not Sun), several wines by the glass, welcoming staff; couple of steep steps at front door, back terrace and beer garden, open all day. *(John Oates)*

SHREWSBURY   SJ4912
Admiral Benbow (01743) 244423
Swan Hill; SY1 1NF Great choice of mainly local ales, also ciders and bottled belgian beers, darts; no children, seats out at back, closed lunchtimes except Sat. *(David Aston)*

SHREWSBURY   SJ4812
Boat House Inn (01743) 231658
New Street/Quarry Park; leaving centre via Welsh Bridge/A488 turn into Port Hill Road; SY3 8JQ Refurbished pub in lovely position by footbridge to Severn park, river views from long lounge bar and terrace tables, well kept ales and enjoyable food including grills, friendly staff; background music; children welcome, no dogs inside, outside summer bar, open all day. *(Duncan Kirkby, Brian Glozier)*

SHREWSBURY   SO4912
Coach & Horses (01743) 365661
Swan Hill/Cross Hill; SY1 1NF Friendly and relaxed beamed local with panelled main bar, cosy little side room and back dining lounge, enjoyable fresh food, well kept Salopian, Stonehouse and guests, real

cider, happy hour (5-7pm Mon-Fri, 7-10pm Sun), friendly helpful staff dressed in black, interesting Guinness prints; background music (maybe live Sun); children allowed in dining room, dogs in bar, disabled facilities (other lavatories up spiral staircase), smokers' roof terrace, open all day. *(Brian and Anna Marsden)*

SHREWSBURY   SJ4913
Dolphin (01743) 247005
A49 0.5 mile N of station; SY1 2EZ Traditionally refurbished little 19th-c pub (reopened 2013), friendly welcoming staff, well kept Joules beers and a couple of guests, short choice of good bar snacks and simple meals, reasonable prices, original features including gas lighting, log fires, music and charity quiz nights; seats on sunny back deck, open all day. *(Keith Fawcett, Robert W Buckle)*

SHREWSBURY   SJ4912
Loggerheads (01743) 360275
Church Street; SY1 1UG Chatty old-fashioned local with panelled back room, flagstones, scrubbed-top tables, high-backed settles and coal fire, three other rooms with lots of prints, bare boards and more flagstones, quaint linking corridor and hatch service of five Marstons-related ales, short choice of bargain pub food, friendly prompt service, live folk Thurs and Sun; open all day. *(David H Bennett)*

SHREWSBURY   SJ4912
Nags Head (01743) 362455
Wyle Cop; SY1 1XB Attractive old two-room pub, small, unpretentious and welcoming, with good range of well kept beers, no food; TV, juke box; area for smokers at back, open all day (till 1am Fri, Sat). *(Kerry Law)*

SHREWSBURY   SJ4911
Prince of Wales (01743) 343301
Bynner Street; SY3 7NZ Traditional backstreet pub popular for its good range of well kept ales (always a mild), friendly atmosphere, Shrewsbury Town FC memorabilia, darts; children and dogs welcome, sunny back deck overlooking own bowling green, open all day Fri-Sun when lunchtime food is served, from 5pm other days. *(John Neal)*

SHREWSBURY   SJ4912
Salopian Bar (01743) 351505
Smithfield Road; SY1 1PW Modernised pub facing river; eight well kept ales including Bathams, Oakham and Stonehouse, good choice of belgian beers and real ciders (regular beer/cider festivals), cheap sandwiches and pies, friendly staff; open mike and quiz nights, sports TV, fruit machine; open all day. *(David Aston, D Weston, David H Bennett)*

SHREWSBURY   SJ4812
Shrewsbury Hotel (01743) 236203
Mardol; SY1 1PU Recently refurbished
partly open-plan Wetherspoons (former
coaching inn) opposite the river, good choice
of food and real ales, low prices, friendly
service; TVs for subtitled news, free wi-fi;
children welcome, tables out in front,
22 bedrooms, open all day from 8am.
(Dave Braisted)

SHREWSBURY   SJ4912
★ Three Fishes (01743) 344793
Fish Street; SY1 1UR Well run timbered
and heavily beamed 16th-c pub in quiet
cobbled street, small tables around
three sides of central bar, flagstones, old
pictures, half a dozen well kept changing
beers from mainstream and smaller
brewers, good value wines, fairly priced
food (not Sun) including blackboard
specials ordered from separate servery,
good friendly service even if busy, no
mobiles; open all day Fri, Sat. *(A N Bance)*

STIPERSTONES   SJ3600
★ Stiperstones Inn (01743) 791327
*Village signed off A488 S of Minsterley;
SY5 0LZ* Cosy traditional pub useful for
a drink after walking (some stunning hikes
on Long Mynd or up dramatic quartzite
ridge of the Stiperstones); small modernised
lounge with comfortable leatherette wall
banquettes and lots of brassware on ply-
panelled walls, plainer public bar with TV,
games machine and darts, a couple of real
ales such as Hobsons and Three Tuns, good
value bar food usefully served all day, friendly
service; background music; children and dogs
welcome, two comfortable bedrooms, open
all day (till 2am Fri, Sat). *(Anon)*

STOTTESDON   SO6782
Fighting Cocks (01746) 718270
High Street; DY14 8TZ Welcoming old
half-timbered community pub in unspoilt
countryside, low ceilings and log fire, good
hearty home-made food using local produce,
well kept Hobsons and a couple of guests,
live music and occasional quiz nights; small
shop behind; nice views from garden tables,
good walks, open all day weekends, closed
weekday lunchtimes. *(Anon)*

TELFORD   SJ6910
Crown (01952) 610888
*Market Street, Oakengates (off A442,
handy for M54 junction 5); TF2 6EA*
Bright 19th-c local (list of licensees to
1835), Hobsons Best and many changing
guests, May and Oct beer festivals with up

to 60 ales, draught continentals and lots of
foreign bottled beers, a real cider or perry,
helpful knowledgeable staff, simple snacky
food (can bring your own), bustling front
bar with light oak flooring and woodburner,
small sky-lit side room and quarry-tiled back
room; regular live music and comedy nights;
suntrap courtyard, handy for station, open
all day. *(Anon)*

WELLINGTON   SJ6511
Cock (01952) 244954
*Holyhead Road (B5061 – former A5);
TF1 2DL* 18th-c coaching inn popular for
its friendly real ale bar, Hobsons and five
well kept quickly changing guests usually
from small breweries, farm cider, separate
bar specialising in belgian beers, friendly
knowledgeable staff, big fireplace; beer
garden with covered area, refurbished
bedrooms, closed lunchtime Mon-Weds, open
all day Thurs-Sat. *(Mark Sykes, D Weston)*

WELLINGTON   SJ6410
Old Orleton (01952) 255011
*Holyhead Road (B5061, off M54
junction 7); TF1 2HA* Modernised 17th-c
coaching inn with restaurant and bar, good
interesting and well presented food, two
well kept Hobsons beers, Weston's cider;
nice view of the Wrekin, ten bedrooms.
(Nick Jenkins)

WELLINGTON   SJ6511
William Withering (01952) 642800
New Street; TF1 1LU Comfortable and
reliable Wetherspoons named after 18th-c
local physician, half a dozen real ales, usual
good value food till 10pm, friendly landlord
and staff, interesting pictures of historic
Wellington; handy for station. *(D Weston,
Mrs Sally Evans)*

WELSHAMPTON   SJ4335
Sun (01948) 710847
A495 Ellesmere–Whitchurch; SY12 0PH
Friendly refurbished village pub with good
choice of reasonably priced food, real ales;
dogs welcome, big back garden, 15-minute
walk to Llangollen/Shropshire Union Canal.
(Anon)

WHITCHURCH   SJ5441
Anchor (01948) 663806
Pepper Street; SY13 1BG Modernised
backstreet pub, with bare-boards bar and
flagstoned restaurant, Sharps Doom Bar
and several well kept guests, enjoyable
reasonably priced food including vegetarian
choices, friendly helpful staff; free wi-fi,
children welcome, courtyard tables, open
all day. *(Jennifer Banks)*

We mention bottled beers and spirits only if there is something unusual about them –
imported belgian real ales, say, or dozens of malt whiskies; so do please
let us know about them in your reports.

WHITCHURCH   SJ5345
Willey Moor Lock (01948) 663274
Tarporley Road; signed off A49 just under 2 miles N; SY13 4HF Large opened-up pub in picturesque spot by Llangollen Canal; two log fires, low beams and countless teapots and toby jugs, cheerful chatty atmosphere, half a dozen changing local ales and around 30 malt whiskies, good value quickly served pub food from sandwiches up; background music, games machine, no credit cards (debit cards accepted); children welcome away from bar, no dogs inside, terrace tables, secure garden with big play area. *(Mike and Wena Stevenson)*

WHITTINGTON   SJ3231
White Lion (01691) 662361
Castle Street; SY11 4DF Sizeable pub just below castle, tasty good value food including early-bird deal, cheerful attentive young staff, two well kept ales and decent wines by the glass, light wood tables in front bar, smaller area with leather sofas, dining room and conservatory; free wi-fi; children welcome, plenty of tables in good outdoor space. *(Anon)*

WISTANSTOW   SO4385
Plough (01588) 673251
Off A49 and A489 N of Craven Arms; SY7 8DG Welcoming village pub adjoining the Woods brewery, their beers in peak condition and enjoyable home-made food (not Mon evening, Tues) including good fresh fish, OAP lunch Mon, friendly efficient service, smallish bar, airy high-ceilinged modern restaurant, games part with darts, dominoes and pool; background music, sports TV, free wi-fi; children and dogs welcome, some tables outside, open all day Fri-Sun, closed Tues lunchtime. *(Patrick and Daphne Darley, Glenwys and Alan Lawrence, Ken Richards)*

Post Office address codings confusingly give the impression that some pubs are in Shropshire, when they're really in Cheshire (which is where we list them).

Somerset

KEY ★ Star Pub    Top Quality Food   Great Beer

⚘ Good Wines   £ Bargain Meals   Good Bedrooms   Serves Food

ASHCOTT   ST4337   Map 1
Ring o' Bells
High Street; pub well signed off A39 W of Street; TA7 9PZ

Friendly village pub with homely décor in several bars, separate restaurant, tasty bar food and changing local ales

Handy for Ham Wall Nature Reserve, this traditional 18th-c pub remains well run and friendly and under the same long-serving family. The three main bars, on different levels, are all comfortable: maroon plush-topped stools, cushioned mate's chairs and dark wooden pubby tables on patterned carpet, horsebrasses along the bressumer beam above the big stone fireplace and a growing collection of hand bells. Ordnance City Detonator, RCH IPA and Teignworthy Gun Dog on handpump, eight wines by the glass and local farm and bottled cider. There's also a separate restaurant, a skittle alley/function room, and plenty of picnic-sets on the terrace and in the garden.

Good, reasonably priced food includes sandwiches, deep-fried mushrooms stuffed with stilton, crab cakes with sweet chilli dip, cheesy leek and broccoli roly-poly with fresh tomato sauce, home-cooked ham and egg, faggots with mash and gravy, hake with spinach, tomato and cheese sauce, chicken breast with apricot stuffing, and puddings such as lemon meringue pie and bread and butter pudding with custard. *Benchmark main dish: home-made pies £9.95. Two-course evening meal £15.50.*

Free house ~ Licensees John and Elaine Foreman and John Sharman ~ Real ale ~ (01458) 210232 ~ Open 12-3, 7-11 (10.30 Sun) ~ Bar food 12-2, 7-10 ~ Restaurant ~ Children welcome ~ Dogs allowed in bar ~ Wi-fi ~ www.ringobells.com
Recommended by John and Nan Hurst, M G Hart, Jenny and Brian Seller

---

ASHILL   ST3116   Map 1
Square & Compass £
Windmill Hill; off A358 between Ilminster and Taunton; up Wood Road for a mile behind Stewley Cross service station; OS Sheet 193 map reference 310166; TA19 9NX

Simple pub with local ales, tasty food and good regular live music in separate sound-proofed barn; comfortable bedrooms

Not easy to find among the Blackdown Hills, this traditional country pub has long-serving owners and draws plenty of locals. The small beamed bar has a winter log fire, hand-made heavy furniture and upholstered window seats that take in the fine view over rolling pastures. Exmoor Ale, St Austell Tribute and a couple of guest ales on handpump, six wines by the glass and a farm cider; classical background music. The pub cat, Lily, may put in an appearance. There's a garden with picnic-sets and a large glass-covered walled terrace. The bedrooms are spacious and comfortable and two have full disabled facilities. The sound-proofed barn, rural-theme in style, is popular for weddings, parties and live music events.

The generous helpings of fair value food include baguettes and sandwiches, garlic king prawns, pâté and toast, chilli with tortillas and sour cream, mushroom stroganoff, local sausages with onion gravy, steak in ale pie, duck with port and cranberry sauce, mixed grill, and puddings such as banoffi pie and apple and blackberry crumble. *Benchmark main dish: chicken with stilton and bacon £12.95. Two-course evening meal £16.00.*

Free house ~ Licensees Chris and Janet Slow ~ Real ale ~ (01823) 480467 ~ Open 12-3, 6.30 (7 Sun)-11.30; 12-3, 7-11.30 Sun; closed lunchtimes Tues-Thurs ~ Bar food 12-2, 7-9 ~ Children welcome ~ Dogs welcome ~ Wi-fi ~ Regular country music in barn behind pub ~ Bedrooms: £65/£85 ~ www.squareandcompasspub.com
Recommended by Nick and Sylvia Pascoe, Roy Hoing

BABCARY
ST5628 Map 2
Red Lion 🌟 Ⓨ 🛏

Off A37 S of Shepton Mallett; 2 miles or so N of roundabout where A37 meets A303 and A372; TA11 7ED

Thatched pub with comfortable rambling rooms, interesting daily changing food and local beers; good bedrooms

As well as a new kitchen, there's been some gentle refurbishment at this bustling thatched inn – a lick of paint here and there, and new curtains and bench and seat covers. Several distinct areas work their way around the bar; to the left is a longish room with dark red walls, a squashy leather sofa and two housekeeper's chairs around a low table by a woodburning stove, and a few well spaced tables and captain's chairs. There are elegant rustic wall lights, clay pipes in a cabinet, local papers or magazines to read and board games. A more dimly lit public bar with lovely dark flagstones has a high-backed old settle and other more straightforward chairs; table skittles and background music. In the good-sized dining room there's a large stone lion's head on a plinth above an open fire, and tables and chairs on a big rug and polished boards. Otter Amber and Teignworthy Reel Ale on handpump, a dozen wines by the glass and two farm ciders. The Den, in the pretty courtyard, has light modern furnishings, a wood-fired pizza oven (used at weekends) and a brasserie-style menu, and doubles as a party, wedding and conference venue. There are picnic-sets and a play area in the long informal garden. The bedrooms are comfortable and well equipped and the pub is handy for the Fleet Air Arm Museum at Yeovilton, the Haynes Motor Museum in Sparkford and for shopping at Clarks Village in Street. Wheelchair access.

Good, enjoyable food includes sandwiches, pulled ham hock, crispy egg and pea purée, mussels in white wine, garlic and parsley cream, an antipasti plate to share, leek, feta and pea risotto, beer-battered haddock and triple-cooked chips, burger with smoked cheese, bacon and pickles, bream with saffron potatoes, samphire and clam cream broth, and puddings such as dark chocolate and beetroot brownie with warm chocolate sauce and coconut panna cotta with chilli, pineapple and mango salsa. *Benchmark main dish: slow-roast pork belly with mustard mash and apple sauce £15.50. Two-course evening meal £21.50.*

Free house ~ Licensee Charles Garrard ~ Real ale ~ (01458) 223230 ~ Open 12-3,
6-midnight; 12-4, 6-11 Sun ~ Bar food 12-2.30 (3 Sun), 7-9.30 (10 Fri, Sat) ~ Restaurant
~ Children welcome ~ Dogs allowed in bar ~ Wi-fi ~ Live music monthly Fri evenings
~ Bedrooms: £90/£110 ~ www.redlionbabcary.co.uk *Recommended by M G Hart, Chris and
Angela Buckell, D and K, Bob and Margaret Holder, Mike and Mary Carter*

 **BATH** ST7465 Map 2

Chequers
Rivers Street; BA1 2QA

**City-centre pub with friendly staff, pretty upstairs restaurant,
and enjoyable food and beers**

Just a short walk from the Circus and Royal Crescent, this 18th-c pub
is a popular spot for a meal or a drink. The two bar rooms have tartan-
cushioned wall pews, chapel, farmhouse and kitchen chairs around all
sorts of tables (each set with flowers) on parquet flooring, wedgwood blue
paintwork with some fine plasterwork, and a coal fire in a white-painted
fireplace. Bath Gem and Butcombe Bitter on handpump and several wines
by the glass. The attractive little restaurant upstairs has high-backed pale
lilac suede dining chairs around candlelit tables, a wooden floor, a large
wall mirror and a huge glass window into the kitchen. In warm weather,
there are picnic-sets under awning on the pavement.

 Good, enterprising food includes salt and pepper squid with aioli, ham hock
terrine with piccalilli, beer-battered haddock and chips, burger with bacon,
cheese, coleslaw and fries, mushroom lasagne with aubergine, figs and rocket, lamb
rump with sweetbreads, curried lentils, bombay potatoes and fennel, pork fillet,
cheek, oyster and belly with black pudding, pickled apple and celeriac, 35-day
dry-aged steaks, and puddings. *Benchmark main dish: duck breast, confit leg
and duck fat chips £21.95. Two-course evening meal £23.00.*

Bath Pub Company ~ Lease Joe Cussens ~ Real ale ~ No credit cards ~ (01225) 360017
~ Open 12-11 ~ Bar food 12-2.30, 6-9.30; 12-3, 6-10 Sat; 12-9 Sun ~ Restaurant ~
Children welcome ~ Dogs allowed in bar ~ Wi-fi ~ www.thechequersbath.com
Recommended by Dr and Mrs A K Clarke, Mr and Mrs A H Young

BATH ST7467 Map 2

Hare & Hounds
Lansdown Road, Lansdown Hill; BA1 5TJ

**Lovely views from back terrace with plenty of seating, relaxed bar
areas, real ales, nice food and helpful staff**

From the decked terrace at the back of this little stone house you can
look down across fields and villages for miles, and there are plenty of
seats and tables for a drink or meal; the same view is visible from the stone
windows in the bar. The atmosphere in the single long room is relaxed
and friendly, helped along by cheerful staff. There are chapel chairs and
long cushioned wall settles around pale wood-topped tables on bare
boards, minimal decoration on pale walls above a blue-grey dado and an
attractively carved counter where they serve a beer named for the pub
(from Caledonian) and St Austell Tribute on handpump and several wines
by the glass; background music. There's a bronze hare and hound at one
end of the mantelpiece above the log fire, and a big mirror above. A little
conservatory to one side is similarly furnished, with dark slate flagstones.
The neat small garden has seats beneath a gazebo.

The good, popular food includes breakfasts (from 8am, weekends 9am), sandwiches, duck terrine with fig chutney, scallops with crispy pork belly, cauliflower, caper and raisin dressing, vegetarian, beef or venison burger with toppings and skinny fries, braised ox cheek with horseradish mash, smoked haddock on leek risotto with poached egg and hollandaise, and puddings such as white chocolate parfait with cardamom anglaise and salted caramel tart with mandarin gel. *Benchmark main dish: beer-battered line-caught cod and chips £13.50. Two-course evening meal £21.00.*

Bath Pub Company ~ Lease Joe Cussens ~ Real ale ~ (01225) 482682 ~ Open 8.30am-11pm (10.30pm Sun) ~ Bar food 8.30am-9.30pm (9pm Sun) ~ Children welcome ~ Dogs welcome ~ Wi-fi ~ www.hareandhoundsbath.com *Recommended by Dr and Mrs A K Clarke, Richard Mason, Mr and Mrs A H Young*

BATH   ST7465   Map 2
Marlborough
35 Marlborough Buildings; BA1 2LY

Open all day and with plenty of customers, candles and fresh flowers, cheerful staff and good food

The little courtyard garden to the side of this bustling pub is a suntrap in summer and there are benches and chairs around tables among the various plantings. Inside, the U-shaped bar is busy throughout the day and the cheerful staff keep the atmosphere easy-going and friendly. There are bare boards throughout, church candles in sizeable jars on the window sills and on the mantelpiece above a fireplace strung with fairy lights, plenty of nightlights, and each table has a single flower in a vase. Seating ranges from thick button-back wall seating to chapel, kitchen and high-backed cushioned dining chairs. Above the green-grey dado on wallpaper or pale painted walls are some cow and parrot paintings; background music. Chunky bar stools line the counter, where they serve Butcombe Bitter and Cotswold Spring Old Sodbury Mild on handpump and several wines by the glass.

As well as a two- and three-course set lunch, the interesting food includes sandwiches, trio of crab (bisque, chilli cake with salsa, rillette and crab mayonnaise), duck liver parfait with red onion, ginger and orange marmalade and ginger brioche, pearl barley, spring onion, pea and mint risotto with crispy duck egg, beer-battered haddock and triple-cooked chips, duo of venison with squash purée and pickled blackberries, and puddings such as dark and white chocolate brownie with orange purée and raspberry and rhubarb trifle with caramel custard. *Benchmark main dish: burger with relish, coleslaw and fries £10.95. Two-course evening meal £22.00.*

Free house ~ Licensees Joe Cussens and Justin Sleath ~ Real ale ~ (01225) 423731 ~ Open 8am (9am weekends)-11pm (10.30pm Sun) ~ Bar food 12-2.30, 6-9.30; 12-3, 6-10 Sat; 12-8 Sun ~ Children welcome ~ Dogs welcome ~ Wi-fi ~ www.marlborough-tavern.com *Recommended by Richard Mason, N R White, Dr and Mrs A K Clarke*

BATH   ST7564   Map 2
Old Green Tree
Green Street; BA1 2JZ

Tiny, unspoilt local with six real ales and lots of cheerful customers

Said to be the oldest pub in the city, this tiny 18th-c tavern remains unspoilt and unchanging and full of a wide mix of chatty and cheerful customers. The three small rooms, with oak panelling and low wood and plaster ceilings, include a comfortable lounge on the left as you go in, its walls decorated with wartime aircraft pictures (in winter) and local artists' work (in spring and summer), and a back bar; the big skylight lightens things up attractively. Green Tree Bitter (named for the pub by Blindmans Brewery), Butcombe Bitter and RCH Pitchfork, with guests such as Cottage Southern Bitter, Sarah Hughes Dark Ruby Mild and Stonehenge Sign of Spring on handpump, seven wines by the glass from a nice little list with helpful notes, 36 malt whiskies and a farm cider. The gents' is basic and down steep steps. No children.

Lunchtime-only food includes sandwiches, soup, pâté, sausages with beer and onion gravy, vegetable curry, steak in ale pie, and chicken korma. *Benchmark main dish: rare roast beef platter £9.00.*

Free house ~ Licensees Nick Luke and Tim Bethune ~ Real ale ~ No credit cards ~ (01225) 448259 ~ Open 11-11; 12-10.30 Sun ~ Bar food 12-4.30; not evenings or Mon
Recommended by Taff Thomas, N R White, Dr J Barrie Jones, Roger and Donna Huggins

BATH
Star
ST7565 Map 2

Vineyards; The Paragon (A4), junction with Guinea Lane; BA1 5NA

Quietly chatty and unchanging old town local, the brewery tap for Abbey Ales; filled rolls only

Loved by loyal locals and many visitors, this charming unspoilt pub is the brewery tap for Abbey Ales. You get a real sense of the past in the four small linked rooms (served from a single bar) and the many original features include traditional wall benches (one is known as Death Row), panelling, dim lighting and open fires. Abbey Bellringer plus guests such as Bass, Dartmoor Jail Ale, Lancaster Black and St Austell Proper Job on handpump, several wines by the glass, 30 malt whiskies and Cheddar Valley cider; darts, shove-ha'penny, board games – and complimentary snuff. It gets particularly busy at weekends and is a bit of a walk from the centre.

Food consists of filled rolls.

Punch ~ Lease Paul Waters and Alan Morgan ~ Real ale ~ (01225) 425072 ~ Open 12-2.30, 5.30-midnight; noon-1am Fri, Sat; 12-midnight Sun ~ Children welcome ~ Dogs welcome ~ Wi-fi ~ www.star-inn-bath.co.uk *Recommended by Dr and Mrs A K Clarke, Taff Thomas, Dr J Barrie Jones, N R White*

BISHOPSWOOD
Candlelight
ST2512 Map 1

Off A303/B3170 S of Taunton; TA20 3RS

Friendly, hard-working licensees in neat dining pub, candlelight and fresh flowers, real ales and farm cider, enjoyable imaginative food and seats in the garden

Our readers return often to this extremely well run and friendly pub. The neatly kept, more-or-less open-plan rooms are separated into different areas by standing stone pillars and open doorways – throughout there's a relaxed, welcoming atmosphere. The beamed bar has high chairs by the counter where they serve Bass, Branscombe Vale Summa That, Otter Bitter and Skinners Cornish Knocker Ale tapped from the cask, nice wines by the glass, a couple of farm ciders and winter drinks such as hot Pimms, whisky toddies and hot chocolate; also, captain's chairs, pews and cushioned window seats around a mix of wooden tables on sanded boards, and a small ornate fireplace. To the left is a comfortable area with a button-back sofa beside a big woodburner, wheelback chairs and cushioned settles around wooden tables set for dining, and country pictures, photos, a hunting horn and bugles on the granite walls; background music and shove-ha'penny. On the other side of the bar is a similarly furnished dining room. Outside, there's a decked area with picnic-sets and a neatly landscaped garden with a paved path winding through low walls set with plants.

 Using their own vegetables and ice-cream, the imaginative food includes home-cured ham, salami and pickled vegetables, home-smoked trout wrapped around smoked salmon terrine with pepper syrup, chicken supreme stuffed with sun-dried tomato mousse, dauphinoise potatoes and basil cream sauce, duck leg bourguignon with glazed shallots, bacon lardons and garlic mash and puddings such as vanilla panna cotta with rapsberry coulis and prune and Armagnac tart with chantilly cream; they also offer a three-course set weekday lunch. *Benchmark main dish: pork tenderloin wellington, roasted root vegetables and sage jus £15.00. Two-course evening meal £21.00.*

Free house ~ Licensees Tom Warren and Debbie Lush ~ Real ale ~ (01460) 234476 ~ Open 12-2.30 (3 Sat), 6-11; 12-11 Sun; closed Mon, first week Nov ~ Bar food 12-2 (2.30 weekends), 7-9 (9.30 Fri, Sat) ~ Well behaved children welcome ~ Dogs allowed in bar ~ Wi-fi ~ www.candlelight-inn.co.uk *Recommended by Ian Herdman, Bob and Margaret Holder, Michael and Diana Clatworthy*

BRISTOL ST5873 Map 2
Highbury Vaults 🍺 £
St Michael's Hill, Cotham; BS2 8DE

Cheerful town pub with up to eight real ales, good value tasty bar food and friendly atmosphere

In Georgian times, this was a lock-up for condemned men (the bars can still be seen on some windows), but today it's full of hustle and bustle and a wide mix of customers. It remains friendly and unpretentious. The little front bar, with a corridor beside it, leads through to a series of small rooms: wooden floors, green and cream paintwork and old-fashioned furniture and prints (including plenty of royal family period engravings and lithographs in the front room). A model railway runs on a shelf the full length of the pub, with tunnels through the walls. Wells & Youngs Bitter, Special and Highbury Gold plus guests such as Bath Gem, Courage Directors, St Austell Tribute, Teignworthy Gun Dog and Towles Ma Beeses Chocolate Stout on handpump and several malt whiskies; bar billiards, TV and board games. The pleasant back terrace has tables built into a partly covered flowery arbour; disabled access to main bar (but not the loos).

Good value food includes filled rolls, burger with cheese, bacon and coleslaw, meat or vegetarian chilli, lasagne, fish pie, and puddings such as chocolate brownie and sticky toffee pudding. *Benchmark main dish: lasagne £8.85. Two-course evening meal £11.00.*

Youngs ~ Manager Bradd Francis ~ Real ale ~ No credit cards ~ (0117) 973 3203 ~ Open 12-midnight (11 Sun) ~ Bar food 12-2 (3 Sun), 5.30-8.30 ~ Children welcome ~ Wi-fi ~ www.highburyvaults.co.uk *Recommended by Taff Thomas*

The star-on-a-plate award, distinguishes pubs where the food is of exceptional quality. The knife-and-fork symbol just means the pub serves food.

CHARLTON HORETHORNE
Kings Arms 🏅🍴 🛏

ST6623 Map 2

B3145 Wincanton–Sherborne; DT9 4NL

Bustling inn with relaxed bars and more formal restaurant, plenty of drinkers and diners, good ales and wines, and enjoyable food; comfortable bedrooms

As well as being a comfortable place to stay with well equipped, contemporary bedrooms, what shines through at this rather smart Edwardian inn is the warm and genuine welcome from the helpful staff. The main bar has an appealing assortment of local art (all for sale) on dark mulberry or cream walls, nice old carved wooden dining chairs and pine pews around a mix of tables, a slate floor and a woodburning stove. Leading off is a cosy room with sofas, and newspapers on low tables. Butcombe Bitter, Sharps Doom Bar and a changing guest such as Wadworths 6X on handpump are served from the rather fine granite bar counter; they also keep 13 wines by the glass, nine malt whiskies and local draught cider. To the left of the main door is an informal dining room with Jacobean-style chairs and tables on a pale wooden floor and more local artwork. The back restaurant (past the open kitchen which is fun to peek into) has decorative wood and glass mirrors, wicker or black leather high-backed dining chairs around chunky polished pale wooden tables on coir carpeting, and handsome striped curtains. At the back of the building is an attractive courtyard with chrome and wicker chairs around teak tables under green parasols, and a smokers' shelter overlooking a croquet lawn.

 Making their own bread, pasta and ice-cream, the rewarding food includes smoked haddock kedgeree, duck, chicken and prosciutto terrine with home-made chutney, butternut squash and goats cheese risotto, free-range confit duck leg with pancetta, baby onions and raspberry vinegar jus, crab tagliatelle with shiitake mushrooms, spring onions and coriander, outdoor-reared pork belly with black pudding fritter, apple terrine and celeriac purée, and puddings such as key lime pie with vanilla crème fraîche and chocolate fudge cake with stem ginger ice-cream. *Benchmark main dish: free-range chicken from their Josper oven with pesto cream sauce £17.00. Two-course evening meal £22.50.*

Free house ~ Licensee Tony Lethbridge ~ Real ale ~ (01963) 220281 ~ Open 7.30am (8.30am Sat)-11pm ~ Bar food 12-2.30, 7-9.30 (9 Sun) ~ Restaurant ~ Children welcome ~ Dogs allowed in bar ~ Wi-fi ~ Bedrooms: /£135 ~ www.thekingsarms.co.uk
Recommended by B J Thompson, Harvey Brown, Mike and Mary Carter, John Chambers, Chris and Angela Buckell

CHURCHILL
Crown 🍺 £

ST4459 Map 1

The Batch; in village, turn off A368 into Skinners Lane at Nelson Arms; BS25 5PP

Unspoilt and unchanging small cottage with friendly customers and staff, super range of real ales and homely lunchtime food

The fantastic range of beers continues to draw locals and visitors to this untouched and simple old pub. The small and rather local-feeling stone-floored and cross-beamed room on the right has a wooden window seat, an unusually sturdy settle, built-in wall benches, a log fire and chatty, friendly customers. The left-hand room has a slate floor, and steps that lead past the big log fire in its large stone fireplace to more sitting space. There's no noise from music or games (except perhaps dominoes). Eight real ales tapped from the cask: Bath Gem, Bass, Butcombe Bitter, Cotleigh Barn Owl, Palmers IPA, RCH IPA, St Austell Tribute and Twisted Oak Old Barn; several wines by the glass and local ciders. The outside lavatories are basic. There are garden tables at the front, more seats on the back lawn and hill views; the Mendip morris men visit in summer and some of the best walking on the Mendips is nearby. There's no pub sign outside, but no one seems to have a problem finding it.

The traditional, reasonably priced food – served at lunch only – includes sandwiches, cauliflower cheese, chilli with rustic bread, beef casserole, and puddings such as spotted dick with custard and chocolate pudding. *Benchmark main dish: rare roast beef sandwich £5.25.*

Free house ~ Licensee Brian Clements ~ Real ale ~ No credit cards ~ (01934) 852995 ~ Open 11 (12 Sun)-11 ~ Bar food 12-2.30; not evenings ~ Children welcome away from bar ~ Dogs allowed in bar ~ Wi-fi *Recommended by Debs Kelly, Adrian Johnson, Taff Thomas, Hugh Roberts*

CLAPTON-IN-GORDANO   ST4773   Map 1

Black Horse ▄ £

4 miles from M5 junction 19; A369 towards Portishead, then B3124 towards Clevedon; in North Weston opposite school, turn left signposted Clapton, then in village take second right, may be signed Clevedon, Clapton Wick; BS20 7RH

Unpretentious old pub with lots of cheerful customers, friendly service, real ales and cider, and simple lunchtime food; pretty garden

'A must go-and-see pub,' says one reader enthusiastically – and so many agree. This place remains, as it has for years, an unspoilt 14th-c local that appeals to customers of all ages who enjoy its old-fashioned charm. The partly flagstoned, partly red-tiled main room has winged settles and built-in wall benches around narrow, dark wooden tables, window seats, a big log fire with stirrups and bits on the mantelbeam, and amusing cartoons and photographs of the pub. A window in an inner snug retains bars from the days when this room was the petty sessions gaol; also, high-backed settles – one with a marvellous carved and canopied creature, another with an art nouveau copper insert reading 'East, West, Hame's Best' – lots of mugs hanging from black beams and plenty of little prints and photographs. There's also a simply furnished room, which is the only place families are allowed; background music. Bath Gem, Brains SA, Butcombe Bitter, Courage Best and Otter Ale on handpump or tapped from the cask, several wines by the glass and two farm ciders. There are old rustic tables and benches in the garden, with more to one side of the car park – the summer flowers are quite a sight. Paths from the pub lead up Naish Hill or to Cadbury Camp (NT) and there's access to local cycle routes.

Traditional, lunchtime-only food includes baguettes and baps with lots of hot and cold fillings, pork in cider, lamb tagine, lasagne and paprika chicken. *Benchmark main dish: beef goulash £7.95.*

Enterprise ~ Lease Nicholas Evans ~ Real ale ~ (01275) 842105 ~ Open 11-11; 12-10 Sun ~ Bar food 12-2.30; not evenings or Sun ~ Children in family room only ~ Dogs allowed in bar ~ Wi-fi ~ www.thekicker.co.uk *Recommended by Paul Humphreys, Tom Evans, Guy Vowles, Dr and Mrs A K Clarke, Roy Hoing, Taff Thomas, Comus and Sarah Elliott, Chris and Angela Buckell*

The details at the end of each featured entry start by saying whether the pub is a free house, or if it belongs to a brewery or pub group (which we name).

COMBE HAY ST7359 Map 2

Wheatsheaf

Village signposted off A367 or B3110 S of Bath; BA2 7EG

Smart and cheerful country dining pub with first class food using locally foraged produce; attractive bedrooms

All the awards we've given this well run dining pub are highly deserved, and it's very much a place for all seasons. In colder weather there's a big log fire and plenty of seasonal game (some caught by the landlord), while in summer picnic-sets on the two-level front garden offer a fine view over the church and valley. It dates partly from the 16th c, and much of the space is devoted to eating; the exception is a central area by a big fireplace, which has sofas on dark flagstones, with daily papers and current issues of *The Field* and *Country Life* on a low table. Other areas have stylish high-backed grey wicker dining chairs around chunky modern dining tables, on parquet or coir matting. It's fresh and bright, with block-mounted photo-prints, contemporary artwork and mirrors with colourful ceramic mosaic frames (many for sale) on white-painted stonework or robin's egg-blue plaster walls. The sills of the many shuttered windows house anything from old soda siphons to a stuffed kingfisher and a Great Lakes model tugboat, and glinting glass wall chandeliers (as well as nightlights in entertaining holders) supplement the ceiling spotlights. There's a very good, if not cheap choice of 16 wines by the glass, 15 malt whiskies, a farm cider, and Butcombe Bitter and Otter Bitter on handpump served by friendly and informal staff; background music and a cheerful springer spaniel. The bedrooms are stylishly simple and spacious. There are walks from the pub.

 They keep chickens, ducks and bees and grow some of their own produce. The delicious food includes scallops with fennel bhaji and fennel purée, rabbit ravioli with carrot and star anise, cottage pie using rare-breed beef, beer-battered fish with skinny chips, guinea fowl poached in sauternes with wild mushroom cassoulet and truffle mash, cannon of lamb with sun-blush tomatoes and black olives, bream with celeriac, braised red cabbage and balsamic, and puddings such as dark chocolate délice with coconut crisp and exotic fruit salad and caramelised banana with toffee and banana sorbet; they also offer a two- and three-course set menu. *Benchmark main dish: daily fresh fish dish £16.00. Two-course evening meal £25.00.*

Free house ~ Licensee Ian Barton ~ Real ale ~ (01225) 833504 ~ Open 10.30-3, 6-11; closed Sun evening, Mon except bank holidays ~ Bar food 12-2.30, 6.30-9 ~ Restaurant ~ Children welcome ~ Dogs welcome ~ Wi-fi ~ Bedrooms: /£120 ~ www.wheatsheafcombehay.co.uk *Recommended by Taff Thomas*

CORTON DENHAM ST6322 Map 2

Queens Arms

Village signposted off B3145 N of Sherborne; DT9 4LR

Civilised stone inn with super choice of drinks, interesting food and a sunny garden; comfortable, stylish bedrooms

Set in lovely countryside with fine surrounding walks, this welcoming inn serves a good choice of drinks and excellent food. The bustling, high-beamed bar has rugs on flagstones and two big armchairs in front of an open fire, some old pews, barrel seats and a sofa, church candles and big bowls of flowers. There's also a couple of separate restaurants – one with cushioned wall seating and chunky leather chairs around dark wooden tables, mirrors down one side and a drop-down cinema screen (screenings are held twice a month). Bath Barnsey, Exmoor Fox, Moor Revival and

Timothy Taylors Landlord on handpump, 16 wines (including champagne) by the glass from a carefully chosen list, 53 malt whiskies, 13 gins, six ciders, unusual bottled beers from Belgium, Germany and the US, and eight local apple juices. A south-facing back terrace has teak tables and chairs under parasols (or heaters, if it's cool) and colourful flower tubs. The comfortable bedrooms have lovely country views and the breakfasts are extremely good.

 Sourcing produce from their own farm and the village, the accomplished food includes sandwiches, whipped beetroot with goats cheese, walnut and beetroot crisp salad, rabbit loin with black pudding bonbon with caramelised quince and plum gel, wild mushroom risotto with truffle oil, honey-roast ham with pineapple salsa and eggs, venison burger with chips, pickles and salad, braised ox cheek, tongue and roasted sirloin with confit shallots and roasted carrot, and puddings such as chocolate marquise with hazelnut butter, barley malt ice-cream and Grand Marnier jelly and plum tarte tatin, panna cotta and sorbet. *Benchmark main dish: beer-battered fish and chips £12.95. Two-course evening meal £23.00.*

Free house ~ Licensees Jeanette and Gordon Reid ~ Real ale ~ (01963) 220317 ~ Open 8am-11.30pm (midnight Sat, 11 Sun) ~ Bar food 12-3, 6-10 (9 Sun) ~ Restaurant ~ Children welcome ~ Dogs allowed in bar and bedrooms ~ Wi-fi ~ Bedrooms: $80/$110 ~ www.thequeensarms.com *Recommended by M G Hart, Lesley and Brian Lynn, S G N Bennett, Colin Honey, Mike and Mary Carter*

CROSCOMBE
ST5844 Map 2

George 🍺 🛏

Long Street (A371 Wells–Shepton Mallet); BA5 3QH

Carefully renovated, warmly welcoming and family-run coaching inn with informative canadian landlord, enjoyable food, good local beers and pretty garden; bedrooms

Mr and Mrs Graham run a very tight ship here and the welcome is second to none. It's always lively and busy with a good mix of locals and visitors. In the main bar there's stripped stone, dark wooden tables and chairs and more comfortable seats, a settle by one of the log fires in inglenook fireplaces, and the family's grandfather clock; a snug area has a woodburning stove. The attractive dining room has more stripped stone, local artwork and family photographs on burgundy walls and high-backed cushioned dining chairs around a mix of tables. The back bar has canadian timber and a pew reclaimed from the local church, and there's a family room with games and books for children. King George the Thirst (from Blindmans), Arbor Beech Blonde, Exmoor Gold, Palmers Best and Yeovil Posh IPA on handpump or tapped from the cask, four farm ciders, ten wines by the glass and home-made elderflower cordial. Darts, a skittle alley, board games, shove-ha'penny and a canadian wooden table game called crokinole. The friendly pub dog is called Tessa, and the cats, DJ and Cookie. The attractive, sizeable garden has seats on a heated and covered terrace, flower borders, a grassed area, a wood-fired pizza oven (used on Fridays) and chickens; children's swings.

Using home-grown and other local produce, the highly thought-of food includes baguettes, smoked mackerel pâté, sharing platters, honey-roast ham and eggs, vegetable lasagne, smoked haddock fishcakes, chicken breast stuffed with prunes and bacon on a chicken liver crouton with dauphinoise potatoes and port gravy, green thai tiger prawn curry, lamb rump with wild mushroom sauce, and puddings such as chocolate truffle mousse and plum and apple crumble; steak night is Wednesday, curry night the last Thursday of the month. *Benchmark main dish: steak in ale pie £11.00. Two-course evening meal £17.00.*

Free house ~ Licensees Peter and Veryan Graham ~ Real ale ~ (01749) 342306 ~
Open 10-3 (4 weekends), 6 (5 Fri)-11 (midnight Fri, Sat) ~ Bar food 12-2.30, 6-9; 12-3,
6-8 Sun ~ Restaurant ~ Children welcome ~ Dogs allowed in bar ~ Wi-fi ~ Acoustic
singers third Sat of month ~ Bedrooms: £45/£80 ~ www.thegeorgeinn.co.uk
Recommended by Mrs P Bishop, Jenny and Brian Seller, Kim Skuse, Dr J Barrie Jones

 DULVERTON   SS9127 Map 1
Woods ★ ⍟ ♀
Bank Square; TA22 9BU

**Smartly informal place with exceptional wines, real ales, first rate
food and a good mix of customers**

Standards here remain consistently high and our readers love their
visits. The charming Mr Groves and his helpful, courteous staff keep
everything running smoothly, no matter how busy the pub gets, and all are
ensured of a genuinely warm welcome. Many customers come for the top
class food, but they keep local beers and, in particular, exceptional
wines – if you want just a glass, they'll open any of their 400 wines from
an extraordinarily good list, and there's also an unlisted collection of about
500 well aged, new world wines that the landlord will happily chat about.
Otter Head, St Austell Dartmoor Best and a changing guest tapped from
the cask, a farm cider, many sherries and some unusual spirits. The pub is
on the edge of Exmoor, so there are plenty of good sporting prints on the
salmon pink walls, antlers and other hunting trophies, stuffed birds and a
couple of salmon rods. There are bare boards on the left by the bar counter,
daily papers, tables partly separated by stable-style timbering and masonry
dividers, and a carpeted area on the right with a woodburning stove in a
big fireplace; maybe unobjectionable background music. Big windows look
on to the quiet town centre (or you can sit on the pavement at a couple of
metal tables) and a small suntrap back courtyard has a few picnic-sets.

 Using their own pigs and chickens, the top class food includes ciabatta rolls,
chicken liver parfait with red onion marmalade, bresaola with mustard ice-
cream, wild mushroom linguine, beef in ale pie, guinea fowl on puy lentils with confit
garlic and red wine sauce, bass, razor clam and scallop with celeriac and truffle purée
and sauce vierge, confit duck leg and breast with port wine sauce, and puddings such
as chocolate brownie with coffee ice-cream and lemon tart with blood orange posset
and Pimms and elderflower sorbet. *Benchmark main dish: seared steak and salad
£13.50. Two-course evening meal £19.50.*

Free house ~ Licensee Patrick Groves ~ Real ale ~ (01398) 324007 ~ Open 11-3, 6-11;
12-3, 7-11 Sun ~ Bar food 12-2, 7-9.30 (9 Sun) ~ Restaurant ~ Children welcome ~
Dogs welcome ~ www.woodsdulverton.co.uk *Recommended by Lynda and Trevor Smith,
Jeremy Whitehorn, Richard and Penny Gibbs, Sheila Topham, Matias Ramon Mendiola,
Keith Stevens, Richard and Patricia Jefferson*

DUNSTER   SS9943 Map 1
Luttrell Arms ♀ ⇌
High Street; A396; TA24 6SG

**Fine old stone building with a great deal of character in several bar
rooms, good choice of drinks, enjoyable food, and seats in courtyard
and garden; bedrooms**

This civilised hotel is on the site of three ancient houses mentioned in
records in 1443 and has some lovely medieval features. The bar that
our readers enjoy is the Old Kitchen Bar, which has the old workings of

the former kitchen, meat hooks on the beamed ceiling, a huge log fire and bread oven, and high chairs at the counter where they keep Exmoor Ale, Otter Amber and Sharps Doom Bar on handpump and several good wines by the glass from an extensive list. Locals tend to head for the simple front bar, and there's also a comfortable lounge with armchairs, sofas, a cushioned window seat and a woodburning stove. Throughout are panelled and cushioned wall seats, old settles and handsome carved dining chairs around an assortment of wooden tables, rugs on tiles, antlers, bed-warmers and old prints, and ancient timber uprights. There are plenty of seats in the back garden, plus metalwork chairs and tables in a galleried courtyard. The newly refurbished bedrooms are well equipped and comfortable and some have antique four-poster beds. The town, on the edge of Exmoor National Park, is pretty and full of interest.

Enjoyable food includes sandwiches (until 6pm), ham hock terrine with pineapple relish, moules marinière, a curry of the day, home-cooked honey-glazed ham and eggs, seafood linguine, steak and kidney pie, corn-fed chicken with crispy pancetta and creamy white wine sauce, bass with coconut, basil and chilli linguine, and puddings such as banoffi pie and fig frangipane with clotted cream. *Benchmark main dish: slow-braised pork belly £14.95. Two-course evening meal £20.00.*

Free house ~ Licensee Tim Waldren ~ Real ale ~ (01643) 821555 ~ Open 10am-11pm ~ Bar food 10-9.30 ~ Restaurant ~ Children welcome ~ Dogs allowed in bar ~ Wi-fi ~ Bedrooms: £100/£140 ~ www.luttrellarms.co.uk *Recommended by Richard and Penny Gibbs*

EXFORD
SS8538   Map 1

Crown
The Green (B3224); TA24 7PP

17th-c coaching inn in pretty moorland village, with friendly character bar with hunting-theme decor, real ales, enjoyable food and big back garden; comfortable bedrooms

As this family-run former coaching inn is in the middle of Exmoor, it makes a good base for exploring the area, and the bedrooms are warm and comfortable. The two-room bar with its easy-going atmosphere is very much the hub of village life, with a log fire in a big stone fireplace, plenty of stuffed animal heads and hunting prints on the cream walls, some hunting-themed plates and old photographs of the area, cushioned benches and other traditional pubby tables and chairs on bare boards. There are stools against the counter where they serve Exmoor Ale and Gold and St Austell Trelawny on handpump, a dozen wines by the glass, 15 malt whiskies and three farm ciders; TV and board games. The dining room is rather smart. There are tables and chairs at the front of the inn and more on a back terrace, as well as three acres of garden with a stream threading its way past gently sloping lawns. They're very dog-friendly, have stabling for horses and can arrange riding, fishing, shooting, hunting, wildlife-watching, cycling and trekking.

Using local organic produce and making everything in-house, the enjoyable food includes baguettes, mussels in cider, garlic and cream, twice-baked cheese soufflé with red onion jam, beer-battered cod with triple-cooked chips, wild mushroom risotto, wild boar and apple sausages with caramelised onion gravy, a curry of the day, lamb shoulder with cauliflower purée and dauphinoise potatoes, and puddings such as sticky toffee pudding and white chocolate mousse. *Benchmark main dish: steak in ale pie £12.50. Two-course evening meal £21.50.*

Free house ~ Licensees Sara and Dan Whittaker ~ Real ale ~ (01643) 831554 ~ Open 12-11 ~ Bar food 12-2.30, 6-9.30 ~ Restaurant ~ Children allowed in eating area of bar, but over-7s only in restaurant ~ Dogs allowed in bar and bedrooms ~ Bedrooms: £65/£115 ~ www.crownhotelexmoor.co.uk *Recommended by Emma Scofield, Martin Jones*

HINTON ST GEORGE   ST4212 Map 1
Lord Poulett Arms

Off A30 W of Crewkerne and off Merriott road (declassified – former A356, off B3165) N of Crewkerne; TA17 8SE

• •

Somerset Dining Pub of the Year

Thatched 17th-c stone inn with antique-filled rooms, top class food using home-grown vegetables, good choice of drinks and a pretty garden; attractive bedrooms

Once again, we've had nothing but warm praise from our readers for this first class, civilised inn – and it makes the perfect break from the traffic-snarled A30. Several charming and cosy linked areas have hop-draped beams, walls of honey-coloured stone or painted in bold Farrow & Ball colours, rugs on bare boards or flagstones, open fires (one in an inglenook, another in a raised fireplace that separates two rooms), antique brass candelabra, fresh flowers and candles, and some lovely old farmhouse, windsor and ladderback chairs around fine oak or elm tables. There's Branscombe Bitter and Branoc, and Otter Ale on handpump, 11 wines by the glass, jugs of Pimms and home-made cordial, some interesting whiskies and local bottled cider and perry; the pub cat is called Honey. Outside, beneath a wisteria-clad pergola, are white metalwork tables and chairs in a mediterranean-style lavender-edged gravelled area, and picnic-sets in a wild flower meadow; boules. The bedrooms are pretty and cottagey and breakfasts very good. This is a peaceful and appealing village with nice surrounding walks.

 Delicious food using home-grown and other local, organic produce includes partridge, black pudding, marinated red cabbage and truffle dressing, Otter ale cured salmon with celeriac rémoulade, burger with blue cheese, bacon and chips, chestnut mushroom fricassée, crisp puff pastry and madeira cream, corn-fed chicken with bubble and squeak, tandoori-dusted hake with kedgeree fritters, venison and bacon meatloaf with soft parmesan polenta, and puddings such as pumpkin crème brûlée mousse with toffee ice-cream and blood orange and brown sugar baked alaska; they also have a supper club menu (5-7pm). *Benchmark main dish: cider-battered fish and triple-cooked chips £14.50. Two-course evening meal £23.00.*

Free house ~ Licensees Steve Hill and Michelle Paynton ~ Real ale ~ (01460) 73149 ~ Open 12-11 ~ Bar food 12-2.30, 5-9.15 ~ Restaurant ~ Children welcome ~ Dogs allowed in bar ~ Wi-fi ~ Live music and barbecue Sun afternoons in summer ~ Bedrooms: £60/£85 ~ www.lordpoulettarms.com *Recommended by R T and J C Moggridge, Gene and Tony Freemantle, Bob and Margaret Holder, John Chambers, Patrick and Daphne Darley*

HOLCOMBE   ST6649 Map 2
Holcombe Inn

Off A367; Stratton Road; BA3 5EB

Friendly inn with far-reaching views, cosy bars, open woodburners, a wide choice of drinks and enjoyable food; comfortable bedrooms

The stylish bedrooms here are individually decorated and well equipped and some have views over peaceful farmland to Downside Abbey's school; they make a good base for exploring the area. To the right of the main entrance is a cosy room with sofas around a central table and an open woodburning stove. To the left is the bar: fine old flagstones, window seats and chunky captain's chairs around pine-topped tables, and a carved wooden counter where they serve Bath Gem and Otter Ale on handpump, 25 wines and champagne by the glass, 25 malt whiskies, cocktails and a thoughtful choice of local drinks (cider, vodka, sloe gin and various juices). Service is friendly and chatty. A two-way woodburning stove also warms the dining room, which is partly carpeted and partly flagstoned with partitioning creating snug seating areas, a mix of high-backed patterned or leather and brass-studded dining chairs around all sorts of tables, and daily newspapers; a little sitting area with a TV leads off here. There are picnic-sets on a terrace and side lawn, and the sunsets can be stunning.

Good food using home-grown herbs includes sandwiches, eggs benedict, royale and florentine, crab fritters with guacamole and pink grapefruit, trio of sausages with crispy pancetta and red wine gravy, provençale vegetable polenta cake, a pie of the day, lager-battered haddock and chips, duck breast with braised chicory wrapped in parma ham and blackberry jus, and puddings such as raspberry eton mess and chocolate nemesis. *Benchmark main dish: pork tenderloin, braised pig cheek, parisienne potatoes and apple and cider jus £16.95. Two-course evening meal £21.00.*

Free house ~ Licensee Julie Berry ~ Real ale ~ (01761) 232478 ~ Open 12-3, 6-11; 12-11 Sat, Sun ~ Bar food 12-2.30, 6-9; 12-9 Fri-Sun ~ Restaurant ~ Children welcome ~ Dogs allowed in bar ~ Wi-fi ~ Bedrooms: £75/£120 ~ www.holcombeinn.co.uk
Recommended by Isobel Mackinlay, Martin Jones, Tony Tollitt

HUISH EPISCOPI   ST4326 Map 1
Rose & Crown 🍺 £
Off A372 E of Langport; TA10 9QT

17th-c pub in the same family for over a century, local cider and real ales, simple food and a friendly welcome

The same friendly family have run this quite unchanging village inn for more than 140 years. There's no bar as such, just a central flagstoned still room where drinks are served: Teignworthy Reel Ale and a couple of guests such as Cheddar Potholer and Plain Inn The Sun, local farm cider and Somerest cider brandy. The casual little front parlours, with their unusual pointed-arch windows, have family photographs, books, cribbage, dominoes, shove-ha'penny, bagatelle and a good mix of both locals and visitors. A much more orthodox big back extension has pool, a games machine and a juke box. There are plenty of seats and tables in the big outdoor eating area and two lawns – one is enclosed and has a children's play area; you can camp (free by arrangement to pub customers) on the adjoining paddock. There's also a separate skittle alley, a big car park, morris men (in summer) and fine nearby river walks; the site of the Battle of Langport (1645) is nearby.

Reasonably priced food includes sandwiches, ploughman's, pork, apple and cider cobbler, chicken in tarragon sauce, stilton and broccoli tart, cottage pie, and puddings such as apple crumble and bread and butter pudding. *Benchmark main dish: steak in ale pie £8.45. Two-course evening meal £12.00.*

Free house ~ Licensees Maureen Pittard, Stephen Pittard and Patricia O'Malley ~ Real ale ~ No credit cards ~ (01458) 250494 ~ Open 11.30-3, 5.30-11; 11.30-11.30 Fri, Sat; 12-10.30 Sun ~ Bar food 12-2, 5.30-7.30; not Sun evening ~ Children welcome ~ Dogs allowed in bar ~ Music and quiz evenings; phone for details
Recommended by Mr Yeldahn, Peter Meister

KINGSDON   ST5126 Map 2
Kingsdon Inn ♀
Off B3151; TA11 7LG

Charming old cottage with low-ceilinged rooms, west country beers, friendly staff and well thought-of food

This charming thatched cottage is just the place to escape from the crowded A303 and also handy for the Fleet Air Arm Museum. It's an easy-going, enjoyable pub with friendly, efficient staff and plenty of room for both drinking and dining. The main bar has a woodburning stove, built-in wooden and cushioned wall seats with pretty scatter cushions, farmhouse and wheelback chairs around scrubbed kitchen tables set with candles and fresh flowers, and red quarry tiles; background classical music. Some steps lead up to a carpeted dining area with a few low sagging beams, half-panelled walls and similar furnishings; one table is snugly set into a former inglenook fireplace. Stools on pale tiles against the counter are popular with locals and there's Butcombe Bitter and St Austell Tribute on handpump and 18 wines by the glass. There's a second dining area plus an attractive separate restaurant with another woodburning stove. The garden has picnic-sets on grass and a small path leading to the front door.

Good food includes lunchtime sandwiches, goats cheese mousse with crisp parma ham and almond and apple salad, butternut squash and blue cheese cannelloni, sausages and mash with port and red onion gravy, free-range chicken with pearl barley, ceps and spinach risotto, fishcakes with triple-cooked chips, venison and kidney pudding, and puddings such as sticky toffee pudding with home-made ginger ice-cream and hazelnut crème brûlée. *Benchmark main dish: slow-cooked pork belly with carrot and anise purée and caramelised apple £13.00. Two-course evening meal £21.00.*

~ Licensee Adam Cain and Cinzia Lezzi ~ Real ale ~ (01935) 840543 ~ Open 12-3, 6-11 (10.30 Sun); closed evening 25 Dec ~ Bar food ~ Children welcome ~ Dogs allowed in bar ~ Wi-fi ~ Bedrooms: £65/£95 ~ www.kingsdoninn.co.uk *Recommended by Alfie Bayliss, Martin Jones*

MELLS   ST7249 Map 2
Talbot 🌟 ♀ 🛏
W of Frome, off A362 or A361; BA11 3PN

Substantial, careful refurbishment for interesting old coaching inn, real ales and good wines, inventive food and seats in courtyard; lovely bedrooms

In an interestingly preserved feudal village, this handsome former coaching inn makes a good base for the area; its smart bedrooms are stylish, comfortable and well equipped and the breakfasts particularly good. The bustling candlelit bar is nicely informal with various wooden tables and chairs on big quarry tiles, a woodburning stove in a stone fireplace, and stools (much used by locals) against the counter where friendly, helpful staff serve Butcombe Bitter, a changing guest from Millstone and a beer named for the pub (from Keystone) on handpump, several good wines by the glass and a farm cider. The two linked dining rooms have brass-studded leather chairs around more wooden tables, a log fire with candles in fine clay cups on the mantelpiece above and lots of coaching prints on the walls; quiet background music. The courtyard with its pale green wirework chairs and tables has a mediterranean feel. Off here, in separate buildings, are the enjoyable, rustic-feeling sitting room with sofas, chairs and tables, smart magazines, a huge mural and vast glass bottles (free films or popular TV programmes are shown here on Sunday evenings); and the grill room, where food is cooked simply on a big open fire and served at shared refectory tables looked down on by 18th-c portraits. Do wander into the walled gardens opposite the inn and visit the lovely church where Siegfried Sassoon is buried. This is sister pub to the Beckford Arms at Fonthill Gifford (Wiltshire).

Extremely good food includes lunchtime sandwiches, treacle-cured local salmon with pickled cucumber and sour cream, chicken liver parfait with caramelised quince, caerphilly-stuffed courgette flower with polenta, globe artichoke and marjoram, burger with bacon, cheddar and chips, crispy pig cheek fritter with jerusalem artichokes, roasted onions and hazelnut, cornish hake with egg, prawns, chard and horseradish, and puddings such as honey and walnut tart with sheep's milk sorbet and damson jelly with a coconut macaroon. *Benchmark main dish: rump steak with roasted beetroot, hay-smoked bone marrow and wild garlic butter £17.50. Two-course evening meal £23.00.*

Free house ~ Licensee Matt Greenlees ~ Real ale ~ (01373) 812254 ~ Open 11-11 (10.30 Sun) ~ Bar food 12-3, 6-9.30; breakfasts 8-10am ~ Restaurant ~ Children welcome ~ Dogs allowed in bar ~ Wi-fi ~ Bedrooms: /£95 ~ www.talbotinn.com *Recommended by Lois Dyer, Ruth May, B and F A Hannam, S G N Bennett, Heulwen and Neville Pinfield*

MIDFORD
ST7660 Map 2
Hope & Anchor
Bath Road (B3110); BA2 7DD

Friendly, partly 17th-c pub with popular food and several real ales

Just ten minutes from Bath and with walks nearby on the disused Somerset and Dorset rail track, this neat, open-plan dining pub is just right for lunch. There's a civilised bar plus a heavy-beamed restaurant with a long cushioned settle against red-patterned wallpaper, a mix of dark wooden dining chairs and tables on flagstones and a woodburning stove. The back conservatory is stylish, modern and popular with families. Box Steam Tunnel Vision, Otter Amber and Sharps Doom Bar on handpump, 11 wines by the glass and a farm cider served by the friendly, long-serving owners. Outside, there are seats on the sheltered back terrace with an upper tier beyond. The pub is on the newish Colliers Way cycle/walking path.

Popular food includes lunchtime baguettes, deep-fried camembert with onion marmalade, smoked salmon and prawn salad, pork and leek sausages with mushroom and onion cream sauce, duck with stir-fried vegetables and plum sauce on noodles, pork fillet with leeks, stilton and smoked paprika, rosemary-marinated venison with sloe gin and blueberry sauce, and puddings such as chocolate and Baileys cheesecake and apple and mixed berry crumble. *Benchmark main dish: steak in ale pie £11.50. Two-course evening meal £17.50.*

Free house ~ Licensee Richard Smolarek ~ Real ale ~ (01225) 832296 ~ Open 11.30-3, 6-11; 11.30-11 Sat, Sun ~ Bar food 12-2 (3 weekends), 6-9.30 ~ Restaurant ~ Children welcome ~ Wi-fi ~ www.hopeandanchormidford.co.uk *Recommended by Harvey Brown, Pip White, M G Hart*

MONKSILVER
ST0737 Map 1
Notley Arms ♀ ⇐
B3188; TA4 4JB

Friendly, busy pub in lovely village with beamed rooms, good food and drink, and neat streamside garden; pretty bedrooms

On the edge of Exmoor National Park, this is a friendly pub in a lovely village. It's been carefully refurbished throughout and the open-plan rooms each have their own atmosphere. There are two open fires plus a woodburning stove, cushioned window seats and settles, an appealing collection of old dining chairs around mixed wooden tables on slate tiles or flagstones, original paintings on cream coloured walls and panelling, and fresh flowers, church candles and big stone bottles; background music. Tractor seats line the bar where they keep Exmoor Ale, St Austell Tribute and Sleaford Pleasant Pheasant on handpump, 12 wines by the glass, 14 malt whiskies and farm cider; staff are courteous and helpful. At the bottom of the neat garden is a swift clear-running stream, there are plenty of picnic-sets on grass and a heated, circular wooden pavilion where a party of 12 could dine; the tethering rail for horses is much used. Bedrooms, in the former coach house, are attractive and comfortable and one is suitable for disabled customers.

Well thought-of food includes lunchtime sandwiches, whipped goats cheese mousse with beetroot, candied walnuts and pressed apples, crab and prawn salad, home-roasted ham with a duck egg, shallot, almond and salsify tarte tatin with truffle oil, beer-battered fish and triple-cooked chips, pork and parmesan meatballs with neapolitan sauce and linguine, and puddings such as warm pear tart with chocolate sauce and vanilla and raspberry mousse with lemon sorbet. *Benchmark main dish: line-caught bass with bombay potatoes and saffron sauce £17.00. Two-course evening meal £18.50.*

Free house ~ Licensees Simon and Caroline Murphy ~ Real ale ~ (01984) 656217 ~ Open 8am-11pm ~ Bar food 12-2.30, 6-9.30 ~ Restaurant ~ Children welcome ~ Dogs welcome ~ Wi-fi ~ Bedrooms: /£75 ~ www.notleyarmsinn.co.uk
Recommended by Richard and Penny Gibbs

MONKTON COMBE
ST7761 Map 2
Wheelwrights Arms
Just off A36 S of Bath; Church Cottages; BA2 7HB

Relaxed and friendly bar/dining room in stone-built pub, cheerful mix of customers, helpful landlord and staff, good food and seats outside; quiet, comfortable bedrooms

This compact old stone-built pub is in a peaceful village surrounded by picturesque hills and valleys on the edge of Bath. A good mix of customers dropping in and out means you must book to be sure of a table in the bar-cum-dining room, and the atmosphere is relaxed, friendly and chatty. At one end, an open fire in a raised fireplace has logs piled on each side and there are cushioned and wooden-planked built-in wall seats, high-backed rush-seated or cushioned dining chairs around tables each set with a small lamp, parquet flooring or carpet, and old photographs and oil paintings (the one above the fireplace of a dog is particularly nice). The middle room has some pretty frieze work, a high shelf of wooden wader birds, and stools against the green-painted counter where they keep Butcombe Bitter and Otter Bitter on handpump, 12 wines by the glass and farm cider; background jazz and board games. A small end room is just right for a group. The gravelled terraces have wood and metal tables and chairs and picnic-sets. The bedrooms in a restored annexe are quiet, well equipped and comfortable.

Good, interesting food includes ciabatta sandwiches, smoked salmon and gravadlax with celeriac rémoulade, fritto misto and aioli, tagliatelle with artichokes, sun-dried tomatoes and wild garlic, daube of beef with thyme polenta, dijon mustard burger with cheese, bacon and chips, and puddings such as sticky toffee pudding with butterscotch sauce and thyme panna cotta with crème fraîche sorbet and honey sponge; they also offer a two- and three-course set weekday menu and maybe themed evenings. *Benchmark main dish: beer-battered fish and chips £13.00. Two-course evening meal £20.00.*

Free house ~ Licensee David Munn ~ Real ale ~ (01225) 722287 ~ Open 8am-11pm ~ Bar food 12-2, 6-10 ~ Children welcome ~ Wi-fi ~ Bedrooms: $85/$125 ~ www.wheelwrightsarms.co.uk *Recommended by Taff Thomas, Alistair Holdoway*

 ODCOMBE   ST5015   Map 2

Masons Arms ◖ ⇦

Off A3088 or A30 just W of Yeovil; Lower Odcombe; BA22 8TX

Own-brew beers and tasty food in pretty thatched cottage; bedrooms

To be sure of a table you must book in advance at this pretty thatched cottage as both the own-brew beers and the food are extremely popular. The simple little bar has joists and a couple of standing timbers, a mix of cushioned dining chairs around all sorts of tables on cream and blue patterned carpet and a couple of tub chairs and a table in the former inglenook fireplace. Up a step is a similar area, while more steps lead down to a dining room with a squashy brown sofa and a couple of cushioned dining chairs in front of a woodburning stove; the sandstone walls are hung with black and white local photographs and country prints. Friendly, chatty staff serve their own-brewed Odcombe No 1, Roly Poly and seasonal beers on handpump, they make their own sloe and elderflower cordials, have 11 wines by the glass and keep farm cider. There's a thatched smokers' shelter and picnic-sets in the garden, plus a vegetable patch and chicken coop. Bedrooms are well equipped and comfortable, and the breakfasts good and hearty; there's also a campsite.

Using home-grown and other local produce, the well liked food includes breakfasts until 11am, lunchtime sandwiches and paninis, crab panna cotta with chilled watercress soup, warm scotch egg with piccalilli, spinach and ricotta tortellini with parmesan cream and truffle toast, corned beef hash with duck egg and grain mustard and bacon sauce, triple-cooked chips with burger or barbecue ribs, baked cod with black olive mash and buttered samphire, and puddings such as lemon curd and clotted cream brûlée and banana and chocolate bread and butter pudding with cinnamon custard. *Benchmark main dish: lambs liver and bacon with bubble and squeak and gravy £14.50. Two-course evening meal £20.00.*

Own brew ~ Licensees Drew Read and Paula Tennyson ~ Real ale ~ (01935) 862591 ~ Open 10-3.30, 6-midnight ~ Bar food 12-2, 6.30-9.30 ~ Children welcome ~ Dogs welcome ~ Wi-fi ~ Bedrooms: $55/$85 ~ www.masonsarmsodcombe.co.uk *Recommended by Michael Doswell, Mike and Mary Carter*

 PITNEY   ST4527   Map 1

Halfway House ◖ £

Just off B3153 W of Somerton; TA10 9AB

Bustling, friendly local with up to ten real ales, local ciders and good simple food

A good cross-section of cheerful customers can always be found in this reliably idiosyncratic and unpretentious village local. The atmosphere remains chatty and easy-going, and the three old-fashioned rooms have communal tables, roaring log fires and a homely feel underlined by a profusion of books, maps and newspapers. The fine range of up to ten regularly changing beers tapped from the cask might include Butcombe Bitter, Dark Star Hophead, Forge Litehouse, Hop Back Summer Lightning, Moor Amoor, Otter Bitter and Bright, Plain Inn the Sun and Teignworthy Reel Ale; also, four farm ciders, a dozen malt whiskies and several wines by the glass; board games. There are tables outside.

As well as lunchtime sandwiches, simple food served in generous helpings includes soup of the day, french onion tart, sausage and mash with onion gravy, beef in ale casserole, lots of different curries, and chilli con carne. *Benchmark main dish: beer-battered fish and chips £9.50. Two-course evening meal £16.00.*

Free house ~ Licensee Mark Phillips ~ Real ale ~ (01458) 252513 ~ Open 11.30-3, 4.30-11 (midnight Fri); 11.30-midnight Sat; 12-11 Sun ~ Bar food 12-2.30, 7-9.30; 1-5 Sun ~ Children welcome ~ Dogs welcome ~ Wi-fi ~ www.thehalfwayhouse.co.uk
Recommended by Richard and Penny Gibbs, Bob and Margaret Holder, S G N Bennett

PRIDDY
ST5250   Map 2
Queen Victoria £
Village signed off B3135; Pelting Drove; BA5 3BA

Stone-built country pub with lots of interconnecting rooms, open fires and woodburners, friendly atmosphere, real ales and honest food; seats outside

The various dimly lit rooms and alcoves in this creeper-clad pub have a lot of character and plenty of original features. One room leading off the main bar has a log fire in a big old stone fireplace with a huge cauldron to one side, and there are flagstoned or slate floors, bare stone walls (the smarter dining room is half panelled and half painted), horse tack, farm tools, photos of Queen Victoria, and chatty, cheerful customers. Furniture is traditional: cushioned wall settles, farmhouse and other solid chairs around all manner of wooden tables, a nice old pew beside a screen settle making a cosy alcove, and high chairs next to the bar counter where they serve Butcombe Bitter and a seasonal guest and Fullers London Pride on handpump, two farm ciders, 15 malt whiskies and ten wines by the glass; shove-ha'penny. There are seats in the front courtyard and more across the lane where there's also a children's playground. Dogs are very welcome and there are walks nearby.

Reasonably priced food includes baguettes, chicken liver and bacon pâté, creamy garlic mushrooms, ham and eggs, brie and beetroot tart, a curry of the day, beef or lamb and mint burger with chips, and puddings such as chocolate fudge cake and tiramisu. *Benchmark main dish: beef in ale pie £9.95. Two-course evening meal £14.00.*

Butcombe ~ Manager Mark Walton ~ Real ale ~ (01749) 676385 ~ Open 12-11 (10.30 Sun) ~ Bar food 12-2, 6-9; 12-9 weekends; all day all week June-Aug ~ Children welcome ~ Dogs welcome ~ Wi-fi ~ www.queenvictoria.butcombe.com
Recommended by Taff Thomas, Mr and Mrs P R Thomas, Chris and Angela Buckell

SOMERTON
ST4828   Map 2
White Hart ♀ ⇦
Market Place; TA11 7LX

Attractive old place in lovely village, several bars with open fires, church candles and big mirrors, simple dining room and enjoyable food; comfortable bedrooms

This handsome stone inn in the market square has been serving customers since the 16th c and, after a recent refurbishment, people are flooding back in again. The main bar has long wall seats with scatter cushions, stools around small tables, big mirrors on the wall, Bath Gem, Cheddar Potholer and Goats Leap, and a guest from Bath on handpump, farm ciders and 14 wines by the glass served by friendly staff. A doorway leads to a cosy room with a leather sofa, armchairs, a chest table and an open fire. Another snug bar has comfortable sofas and armchairs, a cushioned window seat and more chest tables, while a simpler room has straightforward wooden dining chairs and tables, a little brick fireplace and some stained glass. Throughout there are rugs on parquet flooring (some plain bare boards too), church candles, contemporary paintwork and interesting lighting – look out for the antler 'chandelier' with its pretty hanging lampshades; background music and board games. Outside, the flower-filled terrace has tables and chairs under parasols with more on grass. Some of the airy, well equipped bedrooms overlook the square and church.

🍴 Usefully serving breakfast (9-11am) and all-day bar snacks, the interesting food includes cider-cured ham and leek terrine with piccalilli, beef carpaccio with preserved lemon, sharing platters, rare-breed burger with cheese and chips, wood-roasted plaice with dill and caper butter, cauliflower and chickpea salad with pickled raisins and sumac dressing, and puddings such as vanilla and rhubarb parfait with chocolate honeycomb and rocky road sundae with chocolate sauce. *Benchmark main dish: pork ragu with spinach and potato dumplings £16.00. Two-course evening meal £22.00.*

Free house ~ Licensee Natalie Patrick ~ Real ale ~ (01458) 272273 ~ Open 9am-11pm (10pm Sun) ~ Bar food 12-3, 6-10; 12-9 Sun; some kind of food all day ~ Children welcome ~ Dogs allowed in bar and bedrooms ~ Wi-fi ~ Bedrooms: /£85 ~ www.whitehartsomerton.com *Recommended by Edward May, Isobel Mackinlay*

STANTON WICK   ST6162 Map 2

Carpenters Arms 🍽️ ⭐ ♀ 🛏️

Village signposted off A368, just W of junction with A37 S of Bristol; BS39 4BX

Bustling, warm-hearted dining pub in country setting with enjoyable food, friendly staff and fine choice of drinks; comfortable bedrooms

The bedrooms here are quiet and comfortable and our readers enjoy staying in this delightful little stone inn very much; you can also be sure of a warm welcome from the landlord and his helpful staff. Coopers Parlour on the right has a couple of beams, seats around heavy tables on a tartan carpet and attractive curtains; in the angle between here and the bar area is a wide woodburning stove in an opened-through corner fireplace. The bar has wood-backed wall settles with cushions, stripped-stone walls and a big log fire in an inglenook. There's also a snug inner room (brightened by mirrors in arched recesses) and a restaurant with leather sofas, easy chairs and a lounge area at one end. Butcombe Bitter and Sharps Doom Bar and a seasonal ale on handpump, ten wines by the glass (and some interesting bin ends) and several malt whiskies; TV in the snug. There are picnic-sets on the front terrace along with pretty flower beds, hanging baskets and tubs. Nearby walks.

 Enjoyable food includes sandwiches, duck confit with orange and maple-glazed walnut salad, salmon goujons with sweet chilli mayonnaise, beer-battered fish and chips, chicken, leek and ham in a cheese sauce topped with puff pastry, linguine with tomatoes, garlic, chilli and rocket, lamb rump with rosemary sauce and roasted vegetables, and puddings such as chocolate and hazelnut brownie with café latte ice-cream and vanilla panna cotta with passion fruit and mint salsa. *Benchmark main dish: local steaks £18.95. Two-course evening meal £20.00.*

Buccaneer Holdings ~ Manager Simon Pledge ~ Real ale ~ (01761) 490202 ~ Open 11-11; 12-10.30 Sun ~ Bar food 12-2.30, 6-9.30 (10 Fri, Sat); 12-9 Sun; sandwiches all afternoon Sat ~ Restaurant ~ Children welcome ~ Dogs allowed in bar ~ Wi-fi ~ Bedrooms: £72.50/£105 ~ www.the-carpenters-arms.co.uk *Recommended by Chris and Val Ramstedt, Julian and Jennifer Clapham, Mike and Mary Carter, Hugh Roberts, M G Hart, Taff Thomas, Phil and Helen Holt*

STOKE ST GREGORY   ST3527 Map 1
Rose & Crown

Woodhill; follow North Curry signpost off A378 by junction with A358 – keep on to Stoke, bearing right in centre, passing church and follow lane for 0.5 miles; TA3 6EW

Friendly, family-run pub with quite a choice of popular food and a fine choice of drinks; comfortable bedrooms

'Top marks in all respects,' says one reader and many others are just as enthusiastic. It's been run by the same friendly family for more than 34 years and they remain just as hands-on and helpful as ever. The interior is more or less open-plan, and the bar area has wooden stools by a curved brick and pale wood-topped counter with Exmoor Ale, Otter Bright and a guest beer on handpump, local farm cider and eight wines by the glass. This leads into a long, airy dining room with all manner of light and dark wooden dining chairs and pews around a mix of tables under a high-raftered ceiling; background music. There are two other beamed dining rooms with similar furnishings and photographs of the village and pub; one room has a woodburning stove and another has an 18th-c glass-covered well in one corner. Throughout are flagstoned or wooden floors. The sheltered front terrace has plenty of seats. They have three ensuite bedrooms, two of which can connect to make a family room.

As well as lunchtime sandwiches, the wide choice of reliably good food includes mussels in cider, cream and garlic, deep-fried brie with cumberland sauce, meat or vegetarian burger with toppings, coleslaw and chips, lambs liver with crispy bacon and onion gravy, sizzling tandoori chicken with onions and bell peppers, cornish hake with parsley butter, and puddings. *Benchmark main dish: home-made pies £9.95. Two-course evening meal £19.00.*

Free house ~ Licensees Stephen, Sally, Richard and Leonie Browning ~ Real ale ~ (01823) 490296 ~ Open 11-3, 6-11; 12-3, 6-10 Sun ~ Bar food 12-2, 7-9 ~ Restaurant ~ Children welcome ~ Dogs allowed in bar ~ Wi-fi ~ Bedrooms: £65/£85 ~ www.browningpubs.com *Recommended by Adrian Johnson, Wendda and John Knapp, Stan Lea*

WATERROW   ST0525 Map 1
Rock

B3227 Wiveliscombe–Bampton; TA4 2AX

Handsome inn with local ales, interesting food and a nice mix of customers; comfortable bedrooms

Standards remain high at this striking timbered inn built into the rockface on the edge of Exmoor National Park. The relaxed and informal bar area has wheelback and other dining chairs and cushioned window seats around scrubbed kitchen tables on a new tartan carpet, sympathetic lighting and a log fire in a stone fireplace. There's a good mix of customers. High black leather bar chairs line the copper-topped bar counter where they serve Cotleigh Tawny Owl and St Austell Proper Job and Tribute on handpump, several wines by the glass and farm cider. The heavily beamed restaurant is up some steps from the bar, and there's also a private dining room. The cottagey, warm bedrooms have been recently refurbished. There are seats under umbrellas out in front.

Rewarding food using the best local produce and cooked by the landlord includes deep-fried whitebait with paprika mayonnaise, ham hock terrine with fig chutney, gnocchi with roasted red onion, wild mushrooms and creamed cauliflower, hare braised in a peppery red wine sauce with black truffle mash, herb-stuffed chicken breast on rösti potatoes, lamb hotpot, calves liver with caramelised onions on bubble and squeak, and puddings such as rhubarb crumble with home-made ice-cream and iced dark chocolate tiffin with Baileys cream. *Benchmark main dish: beer-battered fish and chips £12.50. Two-course evening meal £21.50.*

Free house ~ Licensees Daren and Ruth Barclay ~ Real ale ~ (01984) 623293 ~ Open 12-3, 6-11; closed Mon and Tues lunchtime except bank holidays ~ Bar food 12-2 (2.30 Sun), 6.30-9 ~ Restaurant ~ Children welcome ~ Dogs allowed in bar and bedrooms ~ Wi-fi ~ Bedrooms: £60/£75 ~ www.rockinn.co.uk *Recommended by Kim Skuse, Bob and Margaret Holder*

WEDMORE
Swan

ST4348 Map 1

Cheddar Road, opposite Church Street; BS28 4EQ

Bustling place with a friendly, informal atmosphere, lots of customers, efficient service and enjoyable food and drinks

There's a really good buoyant atmosphere in this café-like place, with people dropping in and out all day. Bath Gem, Cheddar Potholer, Otter Bitter and a guest from Ordnance City on handpump and nine good wines by the glass are served by quick, friendly staff – though in the morning and afternoon the various coffees, teas and hot chocolate are much in demand. The layout is open-plan, with mirrors everywhere to give the feeling of even more space. The main bar has all sorts of wooden tables and chairs on polished floorboards, a wall seat with attractive scatter cushions, a woodburning stove, suede stools against the panelled counter, and a rustic central table with daily papers. At one end, a step leads down to an area with rugs on huge flagstones, a leather chesterfield, armchairs and brass-studded leather chairs, then down another step to more sofas and armchairs. The airy dining room has high-backed pretty chairs, tables set with candles in glass jars and another woodburner, and off here is the former skittle alley. There are plenty of seats and tables on the terrace and lawn, and at the front of the building the metal furniture among flowering tubs gives a continental feel. The contemporary bedrooms are well equipped and comfortable.

With some sort of imaginative food available all day and using home-baked bread and cakes and home-cured hams and bacon, the highly enjoyable food includes breakfast until 11am, sandwiches, cornish crab and sorrel tart with celeriac rémoulade, duck salad with rhubarb chutney, lamb ragu with mint, chilli and herby spaetzle, tomato, mozzarella and beetroot falafel salad with yoghurt dressing, burger with relish, cheese and chips, cider-battered hake and chips, and puddings such as lemon posset with candied rhubarb and chocolate and pistachio terrine with Frangelico cream. *Benchmark main dish: gloucester old spot pork with leek and spring onion champ and parsley sauce £16.00. Two-course evening meal £22.00.*

Free house ~ Real ale ~ (01934) 710337 ~ Open 9am-11pm (10.30pm Sun) ~ Bar food
9am-10pm; snacks during afternoon ~ Restaurant ~ Children welcome ~ Dogs allowed in
bar ~ Wi-fi ~ Live music, open mike nights, comedy evenings ~ Bedrooms: /£100 ~
www.theswanwedmore.com *Recommended by Michael Doswell, Mr Yeldahn*

WRINGTON   ST4762   Map 2
Plough

2.5 miles off A370 Bristol–Weston, from bottom of Rhodiate Hill; BS40 5QA

**Welcoming, popular pub with bustling bar and two dining rooms,
good food using local produce and well kept beer, and seats outside**

As this neatly kept and well run village pub is so popular – the friendly
staff cope well with the crowds – it's best to book a table in advance.
There's a chatty bar with stools against the counter where they serve
Butcombe Bitter (the brewery is in the village), St Austell Tribute and
Wells & Youngs Special on handpump and 18 wines by the glass, and two
distinct dining rooms – the one at the back has plenty of big windows
overlooking the gazebo and garden. Open doorways link the rooms,
and throughout you'll find (three) winter fires, slate or wooden floors,
beams and standing timbers, plenty of pictures on the planked, red or
yellow walls and all manner of high-backed leather or wooden dining or
farmhouse chairs around many different sizes of table; fresh flowers, a
games chest, table skittles and helpful service. There are picnic-sets at
the front and on the back grass; boules. They hold a farmers' market on
the second Friday of the month, and the pub is handy for both Cheddar
Gorge and Bristol Airport. This is tied in with the Rattlebone at Sherston
(Wiltshire). Disabled access.

Well presented and interesting, the food includes sandwiches and ciabattas,
crispy pork belly with asian slaw, peanuts, chilli and coriander, roasted figs,
parma ham and goats cheese with rocket and pine nut salad, sausages with grain
mustard mash and onion gravy, trout fillets with roasted peppers, tomatoes and
pesto cream, beef, chicken or vegetable burger with interesting toppings, coleslaw
and chips, slow-roasted lamb shoulder with butternut squash and chilli jam, and
puddings such as chocolate and orange mousse and yoghurt panna cotta with saffron
pears. *Benchmark main dish: smoked haddock with creamy spinach, cheddar
and poached egg £12.50. Two-course evening meal £18.00.*

Youngs ~ Tenant Jason Read ~ Real ale ~ (01934) 862871 ~ Open 12-3, 5-11;
12-midnight Fri, Sat; 12-11 Sun ~ Bar food 12-2.30, 6-9.30; 12-9 Sun ~ Restaurant ~
Children welcome ~ Dogs allowed in bar ~ Wi-fi ~ Live irish folk music every fortnight
~ www.theploughatwrington.co.uk *Recommended by John and Gloria Isaacs, Dr and Mrs A K
Clarke, Taff Thomas, M G Hart, Bob and Margaret Holder, Hugh Roberts, Chris and Angela Buckell*

Also Worth a Visit in Somerset

Besides the fully inspected pubs, you might like to try these pubs that
have been recommended to us and described by readers. Do tell us what
you think of them: feedback@goodguides.com

ABBOTS LEIGH   ST5473
George (01275) 376985
*A369, between M5 junction 19 and
Bristol; BS8 3RP* Main-road dining pub
with decent choice of food (all day Sat, not
Sun evening) from lunchtime sandwiches
and pubby choices up, good value weekday
lunchtime/early evening set menu, Bath
Gem, Sharps Doom Bar and a couple of
guests, log fires; free wi-fi; children and
dogs welcome, pleasant enclosed garden
with play castle, open all day.
(Taff Thomas)

APPLEY ST0721
★**Globe** (01823) 672327
*Hamlet signposted from the network
of back roads between A361 and
A38, W of B3187 and W of Milverton
and Wellington; OS Sheet 181 map
reference 072215; TA21 0HJ* Friendly
unspoilt 15th-c pub liked by walkers and
cyclists; entrance corridor with serving
hatch, simple pubby furnishings in beamed
front room, second room with 1930s
railway posters and GWR bench, further
room with easy chairs, Cotleigh Harrier
and a guest, traditional cider, good value
straightforward local food including
popular Sun lunch; children welcome, no
dogs inside, seats in garden, path opposite
leading to River Tone, closed Mon (and Sun
evening in winter). *(S G N Bennett, Peter
Thornton, R T and J C Moggridge)*

AXBRIDGE ST4354
Lamb (01934) 732253
*The Square; off A371 Cheddar–
Winscombe; BS26 2AP* Big rambling
carpeted pub with heavy 15th-c beams and
timbers, stone and roughcast walls, large
stone fireplaces, old settles, unusual bar
front with bottles set in plaster, Butcombe
and guests, well chosen wine and good coffee,
enjoyable food (all day weekends) including
vegetarian and children's, OAP lunch deal
(Tues, Thurs), board games, table skittles
and alley; they ask for a credit card if you
run a tab; dogs allowed, pretty and sheltered
small back garden, medieval King John's
Hunting Lodge (NT) opposite, open all day.
(Anon)

BACKWELL ST4969
George (01275) 462770
*Farleigh Road; A370 W of Bristol;
BS48 3PG* Modernised and extended main
road dining pub (former coaching inn),
welcoming landlord and friendly efficient
staff, popular food in bar and restaurant from
sandwiches and sharing boards up, well kept
Bath, Butcombe, St Austell and a guest, good
choice of wines; background music in some
areas; children and dogs welcome, gravel
terrace and lawn behind, seven bedrooms,
open all day. *(Taff Thomas, Steve and Liz Tilley)*

BARROW GURNEY ST5367
Princes Motto (01275) 472282
B3130, just off A370/A38; BS48 3RY
Cosy and welcoming, with unpretentious
local feel in traditional tap room, long
lounge/dining area up behind, four
Wadworths ales with Butcombe as a guest,
modestly priced simple lunchtime food (also
Fri evening), log fire, some panelling, cricket

team photographs, jugs and china; dogs
welcome, pleasant garden with terrace, open
all day. *(Taff Thomas, Comus and Sarah Elliott)*

BARTON ST DAVID ST5432
Barton Inn (01458) 850451
Main Street; TA11 6BZ Unpretentious
lived-in and locally well loved brick pub,
open-plan bar with bare boards and quarry
tiles, old pews and battered tables, rough
pine panelling, well kept constantly changing
cask-tapped ales, real ciders, simple food
such as pizzas and baguettes (no menu),
lots of pictures, posters and bric-a-brac, live
music and movie nights; big-screen TV for
rugby; wet dogs and muddy walkers welcome,
wheelchair accessible (friendly locals
may also lend a hand), pub sign in mirror
writing, events such as frog racing and worm
charming, open all day weekends, from 5pm
other days; still up for sale. *(Anon)*

BATCOMBE ST6839
★**Three Horseshoes** (01749) 850359
*Village signposted off A359 Bruton–
Frome; BA4 6HE* Handsome honey-
coloured stone inn with long narrow
main room, beams, local pictures, built-in
cushioned window seats and nice mix of
tables, woodburner one end, open fire the
other, Exmoor, Plain Ales and Wild Beer,
around a dozen wines by the glass and
several malt whiskies, very good food (best to
book, especially weekends), efficient service,
attractive stripped-stone dining room;
open mike night last Thursday of month;
children and dogs welcome, simple but pretty
bedrooms, lovely church next door, open all
day weekends. *(S G N Bennett, Steve and Irene
Homer, Steve and Liz Tilley)*

BATH ST7464
Bath Brew House (01225) 805609
James Street W; BA1 2BX Recently
opened conversion of the Metropolitan,
interesting interior visibly brewing its
own James Street beers, all-day food
from open kitchen; good sized split-level
beer garden. *(Taff Thomas)*

BATH ST7565
Bell (01225) 460426
Walcot Street; BA1 5BW Long narrow
split-level pub, co-operatively owned since
2013; nine real ales from local independent
brewers and farm cider, some basic good
value food, lots of pump clips and gig
notices, a couple of fires (one gas), bar
billiards and table football; packed and
lively evenings with regular live music and
DJ sets, free wi-fi; canopied garden, even
has its own laundrette, open all day.
(Dr and Mrs A K Clarke)

We checked prices with the pubs as we went to press in summer 2014. They should
hold until around spring 2015.

BATH　　　　　　　　　　　　ST7165
Boathouse (01225) 482584
Newbridge Road; BA1 3NB Large
light and airy pub in fine riverside spot
near Kennet & Avon marina; food from
club sandwiches and sharing boards up,
efficient courteous young staff, well kept
Brains and guests along with a beer named
for them, decent house wines, lower level
conservatory, newspapers; free wi-fi; children
very welcome, boat views from garden tables
and raised deck, nine bedrooms some with
balconies overlooking the river, open all day.
(Steve and Liz Tilley)

BATH　　　　　　　　　　　　ST7564
★Coeur de Lion (01225) 463568
*Northumberland Place, off High Street
by W H Smith; BA1 5AR* Tiny stained-
glass-fronted single-room pub, perhaps Bath's
prettiest, simple, cosy and jolly, with candles
and log-effect gas fire, well kept Abbey ales
and guests, good well priced food from huge
baps to roasts (vegetarian options too), good
Christmas mulled wine; may be background
music, stairs to lavatories; tables out in
charming flower-filled flagstoned pedestrian
alley, open all day. *(Dr and Mrs A K Clarke,
N R White)*

BATH　　　　　　　　　　　　ST7564
Cosy Club (01225) 464161
Southgate Place; BA1 1AP Newish place
with emphasis on eating, but you can just
have a drink; large upstairs split-level room
(lift or stairs) with wood flooring, assorted
tables and chairs, cushioned stools, sofas and
armchairs, lots of pictures and mirrors, high
ceiling with exposed ducting, wide choice
of food from sandwiches to steaks and good
range of drinks including wines by the glass,
changing real ales, cocktails and various
coffees; tables out on balcony overlooking
shopping centre. *(Roger and Donna Huggins)*

BATH　　　　　　　　　　　　ST7564
★Crystal Palace (01225) 482666
Abbey Green; BA1 1NW Good spacious
two-room pub with dark panelling and tiled
floors, popular sensibly priced food from
lunchtime sandwiches to specials, speedy
friendly service, four well kept Fullers ales,
log fire, family room and conservatory;
background music; sheltered heated
courtyard, handy for Roman Baths and main
shopping areas, open (and food) all day.
(Dr and Mrs A K Clarke, Roger and Donna Huggins)

BATH　　　　　　　　　　　　ST7464
★Garricks Head (01225) 318368
*St Johns Place/Westgate, beside Theatre
Royal; BA1 1ET* Civilised relaxed place
with high-windowed bar, gingham-covered
wooden armchairs by gas-effect coal fire,
church candles on mantelpiece and fine
silver meat domes on wall above, wheelback
and other dining chairs around wooden

tables on bare boards, big black squashy
sofa and more armchairs at far end, sizeable
brass chandeliers, ales such as Palmers,
Otter and Stonehenge, real ciders and decent
wines by the glass, proper cocktails, good
food including pre-theatre set meals,
separate smartly set dining room; may be
soft background jazz; children welcome,
dogs in bar, pavement tables, open all day.
(Dr and Mrs A K Clarke)

BATH　　　　　　　　　　　　ST7766
George (01225) 425079
*Bathampton, E of Bath centre, off A36
or (via toll bridge) off A4; Mill Lane;
BA2 6TR* Beautifully placed old canalside
Chef & Brewer, busy and buzzy, with popular
well priced food all day including offers,
Bath, Wells & Youngs and three guests,
good choice of wines by the glass, young
well organised staff, good-sized bar opening
into cosy beamed rooms with three log
fires, contemporary décor and furnishings;
background music; children welcome, no
dogs inside, wheelchair access, enclosed
suntrap terrace and waterside tables.
(Ian and Rose Lock)

BATH　　　　　　　　　　　　ST7564
Graze (01225) 429392
Behind Bath Spa station; BA1 1SX
Spacious Bath Ales bar-restaurant (part
of the city's Vaults development) arranged
over upper floor and served by lift; modern
steel and glass construction with leather
chairs and benches on wood-strip flooring,
slatted ceiling with exposed air conditioning
and pendant lighting, good selection of
beers (some from onsite microbrewery)
and extensive range of wines and spirits,
enjoyable food cooked in open kitchen
including dry-aged steaks and good value
weekday set lunch, helpful cheery staff
coping well at busy times; children welcome,
two sizeable terraces overlooking Bath one
side, the station the other, life-size models
of cows, pigs and chickens, open all day from
8am (9am Sun) for breakfast. *(Dr and Mrs
A K Clarke, Chris and Angela Buckell, Roger and
Donna Huggins)*

BATH　　　　　　　　　　　　ST7465
Hall & Woodhouse (01225) 469259
Old King Street; BA1 2JW Conversion of
stone-fronted warehouse/auction rooms; big
open-plan interior on two floors, steel girders
and glass, palms and chandeliers, mix of
modern and traditional furniture including
old-fashioned iron-framed tables with large
candles and some simple bench seating,
parquet and slate floors, Badger ales from
full-length servery on the right, sweeping
stairs up to another bar and eating area
(disabled access via lift), roof terrace,
decent choice of food from pub favourites
to specials, helpful chatty staff; gets very
busy with after-work drinkers (standing
room only). *(Chris and Angela Buckell)*

BATH   ST7465

★ **Hop Pole** (01225) 446327

*Albion Buildings, Upper Bristol Road;
BA1 3AR* Bustling family-friendly Bath
Ales pub, their ales and guests kept well,
decent wines by the glass and good choice
of whiskies and other spirits such as Chase
vodkas, good food (not Sun evening, Mon
lunchtime) from traditional favourites up
in bar and former skittle alley restaurant,
efficient interested staff, settles and
other pub furniture on bare boards in four
tastefully reworked linked areas, lots of
black woodwork, ochre walls, some bric-a-
brac, board games and daily papers, Mon
quiz; background music, discreet sports TV;
wheelchair access to main bar area only,
pleasant two-level back courtyard with
boules, fairy-lit vine arbour and heated
summer houses, opposite Victoria Park
(great kids' play area), open all day.
*(Dr and Mrs A K Clarke, Roger and Donna
Huggins, Chris and Angela Buckell)*

BATH   ST7565

King William (01225) 428096

*Thomas Street/A4 London Road;
BA1 5NN* Small corner dining pub with
chunky old tables on bare boards, a few
lighted church candles and perhaps a big
bunch of flowers on counter, well cooked food
from short daily changing menu, four local
ales and good choice of wines by the glass,
steep stairs to simple attractive dining
room; background music; children and
dogs welcome, open all day weekends.
(Bernard Sulzmann)

BATH   ST7464

Market (01225) 330009

Saw Close; BA1 1EY Relaxed bar/
restaurant across from Theatre Royal, on two
floors (upstairs is split level), ales such as
Bristol Beer Factory, enjoyable food including
burgers and pizzas, good coffee, friendly staff;
background music; children welcome, seats
outside. *(Roger and Donna Huggins)*

BATH   ST7565

Pig & Fiddle (01225) 460868

Saracen Street; BA1 5BR Lively place with
half a dozen good sensibly priced local ales,
friendly staff, two big open fires, bare boards
and bright paintwork, clocks on different
time zones, steps up to darker bustling
servery and little dining area, games part
and several TVs for sport; lots of students
at night; picnic-sets on big heated front
terrace, open all day. *(Dr and Mrs A K Clarke,
Martin Cawley)*

BATH   ST7565

Pulteney Arms (01225) 463923

Daniel Street/Sutton Street; BA2 6ND
Cosy and cheerful 18th-c pub, Fullers London
Pride, Otter, Timothy Taylors Landlord and
guests, Thatcher's cider, enjoyable well

priced fresh food including Fri fish night,
lots of Bath RFC memorabilia, traditional
furniture on wooden floors, old gas lamps,
woodburner; background music, sports TV;
pavement tables and small back terrace,
handy for Holburne Museum, open all day
Fri-Sun. *(Dr and Mrs A K Clarke)*

BATH   ST7464

Raven (01225) 425045

Queen Street; BA1 1HE Small buoyant
18th-c city-centre free house, two well kept
ales for the pub from Blindmans and four
guests, craft beers and a changing cider,
decent wines by the glass too, limited choice
of food (good reasonably priced pies), quick
friendly service, bare boards, some stripped
stone and an open fire, newspapers, quieter
upstairs bar, storytelling evenings and
monthly talks on science and the arts; no
under-14s or dogs; open all day. *(N R White,
Dr and Mrs A K Clarke)*

BATH   ST7466

Richmond Arms (01225) 316725

*Richmond Place, off Lansdown Road;
BA1 5PZ* Small welcoming 18th-c bow-
windowed house in unusual quiet setting off
the tourist track; good modern leaning food
(not Mon-Weds), nice choice of wines with
10 by the glass, Butcombe, Sharps Doom
Bar and two local ciders, mix of tables and
chairs on bare boards, local artwork for sale;
children and dogs welcome, enclosed pretty
front garden, open all day weekends (till 7pm
Sun), closed Mon and weekday lunchtimes;
plans for community buyout so may be
changes. *(Richard Mason)*

BATH   ST7364

Royal Oak (01225) 481409

Lower Bristol Road; BA2 3BW Friendly
bare-boards pub with Butts ales and guests,
four ciders, local artwork, regular live music
including Weds folk night; popular with Bath
Rugby supporters – busy on match days; open
all day Fri-Sun, from 4pm other days.
(Taff Thomas)

BATH   ST7464

Salamander (01225) 428889

John Street; BA1 2JL Busy city local tied
to Bath Ales, their full range and a guest kept
well, good choice of wines by the glass, bare
boards, black woodwork and ochre walls,
popular food from sandwiches up including
some unusual choices, friendly helpful young
staff, two rooms downstairs, open-kitchen
restaurant upstairs, daily papers; background
music; children till 8pm, no dogs, open all
day (till 1am Fri, Sat). *(Steve and Liz Tilley,
Taff Thomas, Richard Mason, Dr and Mrs A K
Clarke, Roger and Donna Huggins and others)*

BATH   ST7564

Sam Weller (01225) 474910

Upper Borough Walls; BA1 1RH Fairly
simple pub with Bath Ales and decent choice

of wines by the glass, sensibly priced food, friendly service, small and cosy with big window for watching the world go by. *(Roger and Donna Huggins)*

BATH ST7564
Volunteer Riflemans Arms
(01225) 425210 *New Bond Street Place; BA1 1BH* Friendly little city-centre pub-café with leather sofas and just four close-set tables, wartime posters, open fire, well kept ales including a beer named for them, a couple of draught ciders, upstairs restaurant and roof terrace; pavement tables. *(Dr and Mrs A K Clarke, Roger and Donna Huggins, Andrew Gardner, N R White)*

BATH ST7564
White Hart (01225) 313985
Widcombe Hill; BA2 6AA Bare-boards bistro-style pub popular for its food, quick friendly service even when busy, well kept Butcombe from attractive panelled bar, farm cider, fresh flowers; children and dogs welcome, pretty beer garden, bedrooms and self-catering hostel. *(Dr and Mrs A K Clarke)*

BATHFORD ST7866
Crown (01225) 852426
Bathford Hill, towards Bradford-on-Avon, by Batheaston roundabout and bridge; BA1 7SL Welcoming bistro pub with good blackboard food including weekday set deals, ales such as Bath and Timothy Taylors Landlord, nice wines, charming french landlady; children and dogs welcome, tables out in front and in back garden with pétanque, open all day. *(Dr and Mrs A K Clarke, Taff Thomas)*

BECKINGTON ST8051
Woolpack (01373) 831244
Warminster Road, off A36 bypass; BA11 6SP Old village inn with welcoming helpful staff, enjoyable home-made food from sandwiches up, Greene King ales and a guest, real cider and decent wines, big log fire and chunky candlelit tables in flagstoned bar, attractive oak-panelled dining room (separate menu), conservatory; children and dogs welcome, terrace tables, 11 bedrooms, open all day. *(Anon)*

BLAGDON ST5058
★New Inn (01761) 462475
Signed off A368; Park Lane/Church Street; BS40 7SB Lovely view over Blagdon Lake from seats in front of this friendly pub; well kept Wadworths and guests, decent wines, reasonably priced home-made food, bustling bars with two inglenook log fires, heavy beams hung with horsebrasses and tankards, comfortable antique settles and mate's chairs among more modern furnishings, old prints and photographs, plainer side bar; children (over 10) and dogs welcome, wheelchair access best from front. *(Dr and Mrs A K Clarke)*

BLAGDON ST5059
Queen Adelaide (01761) 463926
High Street; BS40 7RA Cosy unpretentious village pub, Butcombe, Sharps and guests, nice wines and good pubby food, friendly welcoming staff; view of Blagdon Lake from the back, closed Mon. *(Taff Thomas)*

BLAGDON ST5059
Seymour Arms (01761) 462279
Bath Road (A368); BS40 7TH Recently refurbished sister pub to the Albion in Clifton village – reports please. *(Taff Thomas)*

BLAGDON HILL ST2118
Blagdon Inn (01823) 421296
4 miles S of Taunton; TA3 7SG Refurbished village pub under new ownership, imaginative well presented food from co-owner/chef using local and own produce, good wine list, ales such as Butcombe, open fire in bar, well divided dining area; children welcome, adjoining fields with pigs, sheep and chickens, farm shop planned, open all day Sat, closed Sun evening, Mon. *(Patrick and Daphne Darley)*

BLAGDON HILL ST2118
Lamb & Flag (01823) 421736
4 miles S of Taunton; TA3 7SL Atmospheric country pub with 16th-c beams, mixed traditional furniture, woodburner in double-sided fireplace and unusual red and green colour scheme, four well kept west country ales, good value traditional food (not Mon lunchtime) with small helpings available, games room/skittle alley, some live music; children and dogs welcome, picnic-sets in nice garden with Taunton Vale views, shop and post office, open all day Fri, Sat, till 6pm Sun; up for sale as we went to press. *(Patrick and Daphne Darley, Mr Yeldahn)*

BLEADON ST3457
★Queens Arms (01934) 812080
Just off A370 S of Weston; Celtic Way; BS24 0NF Popular 16th-c beamed village pub with informal chatty atmosphere in carefully divided areas, generous reasonably priced food (not Sun evening) from lunchtime baguettes to steaks, friendly service, well kept Butcombe and guests tapped from the cask, local cider and decent wines by the glass, flagstoned restaurant and stripped-stone back bar with woodburner, sturdy tables and winged settles, old hunting prints and some pictures by local artists for sale; children (away from bar) and dogs (away from diners) welcome, partial wheelchair access, picnic-sets on pretty heated terrace, open all day. *(Dr Martin Owton, Taff Thomas, Chris and Angela Buckell)*

BRISTOL ST5773
★Albion (0117) 973 3522
Boyce's Avenue, Clifton; BS8 4AA Bustling 18th-c dining pub down cobbled

alley in Clifton village; entrance with open kitchen, jars of pickles/chutneys on dresser for sale, L-shaped bar with chapel chairs around oak tables on wood floor, leather armchairs in front of woodburner, end room up a step with long high-backed settle; all-day tapas and other imaginative if not cheap food (not Sun evening, Mon), friendly service, St Austell ales and guests such as Dartmouth and Otter, decent wines by the glass, 30 whiskies; children welcome, dogs allowed in bar, picnic-sets under fairy lights on covered and heated front terrace, open all day, closed Mon till 5pm. *(Peter Meister, Taff Thomas)*

BRISTOL ST5773

Alma (0117) 973 5171

Alma Vale Road, Clifton; BS8 2HY
Two-bar pub with good choice of real ales, proper cider and several wines by the glass, well priced food from lunchtime sandwiches up, sofas and armchairs as well as plain tables and chairs, thriving upstairs theatre Tues-Sat; background music, popular with students evenings; easy wheelchair access, small back terrace (not late evening), open all day. *(Taff Thomas, Chris and Angela Buckell)*

BRISTOL ST5873

Bank (0117) 930 4691

John Street; BS1 2HR Small proper single-bar pub, centrally placed (but off the beaten track) and popular with office workers; four changing local ales (may include a porter), real ciders, well priced hearty food till 4pm, comfortable bench seats, newspapers, books on shelf above fireplace, blackboard for quirky facts (not all verified) like 'there are more plastic flamingos than real ones'; background and live music, free wi-fi; dogs welcome, wheelchair access, tables under umbrellas in paved courtyard, open all days. *(Jeremy King, Taff Thomas)*

BRISTOL ST5972

Barley Mow (0117) 930 4709

Barton Road; The Dings; BS2 0LF Late 19th-c Bristol Beer Factory pub in the old industrial area close to floating harbour; their well kept ales and guests, proper ciders, slightly limited choice of other drinks, good filling pub food (not Sun evening) from shortish but well thought-out menu, cheerful chatty landlord, simple uncluttered interior with wood floors, off-white walls and dark green panelled dados, cushioned wall seats and pubby furniture, tables with fresh flowers in beer bottles, some old photographs of the pub, open fire in brick fireplace; sports TV; disabled access, open all day Fri and Sat, till 8pm Sun. *(Chris and Angela Buckell, Mike and Eleanor Anderson, Taff Thomas)*

BRISTOL ST5872

Beer Emporium (0117) 379 0333

King Street; BS1 4EF New cellar bar-restaurant with two vaulted rooms; long stone-faced counter with stained-glass skylight above, 12 regularly changing ales/craft beers (tasters offered) plus over 150 in bottles from around the world, good selection of malt whiskies and other spirits, interesting wine list, coffees and teas, food from british tapas to steaks, cheerful helpful staff, some live music; disabled facilities and access via lift, opposite the Old Vic (pre-theatre menu), open all day till 2am (midnight Sun), can get crowded. *(Roger and Donna Huggins, Chris and Angela Buckell)*

BRISTOL ST5774

Blackboy (0117) 973 5233

Whiteladies Road; BS8 2RY Refurbished dining pub with good uncomplicated food from chef-owner, relaxed friendly atmosphere, back eating area with light wood furniture, small front bar with sewing-machine tables, armchairs and open fire, Butcombe Bitter, St Austell Tribute and Timothy Taylors Landlord, several draught continental lagers. *(Geof Cox)*

BRISTOL ST5872

BrewDog (0117) 927 9258

Baldwin Street, opposite church; BS1 1QW Revamped corner bar owned by BrewDog with their beers and guests from other craft breweries (draught and bottled), limited but interesting selection of substantial bar snacks, happy willing young staff, starkly modern feel with exposed brick, stainless-steel furniture and granite surfaces; can get noisily busy; wheelchair access, open all day till midnight. *(Chris and Angela Buckell, Taff Thomas)*

BRISTOL ST5873

Colston Yard (0117) 376 3232

Upper Maudlin Street/Colston Street; BS1 5BD Popular nicely updated Butcombe pub (site of the old Smiles Brewery), their ales and guests kept well, interesting bottled beers and good choice of wines and whiskies (two from japan), bare-boards front bar split into two, leather stools and banquettes, brewery mirrors, newspapers and board games, larger dining room, good quality pub food all day from lunchtime sandwiches to grills and evening restaurant menu, friendly staff; background music; children welcome, disabled access/facilities (other lavatories downstairs), a few pavement tables, open all day (till 1am Fri, Sat). *(Taff Thomas, Jeremy King, Chris and Angela Buckell, Roger and Donna Huggins)*

BRISTOL ST5872

Commercial Rooms (0117) 927 9681

Corn Street; BS1 1HT Spacious colonnaded Wetherspoons conversion (former merchants' club) with lofty stained-glass domed ceiling, gas lighting, comfortable quieter back room with ornate balcony; wide changing choice of real ales, nice chatty bustle (busiest weekend evenings), their

usual food all day and low prices; ladies'
with chesterfields and open fire; children
welcome, no dogs, side wheelchair access
and disabled facilities, good location, open
all day from 8am and till late Fri-Sun.
(Roger and Donna Huggins, Taff Thomas)

BRISTOL   ST5872
Cornubia (0117) 925 4415
Temple Street; BS1 6EN Tucked-away
18th-c real ale pub with up to 12 including
a seasonal house beer from Arbor, interesting
bottled beers, farm ciders and perry, snacky
food such as pasties and pork pies, friendly
service, walls and ceilings covered in pump
clips, live music including Thurs acoustic
night; can be crowded evenings, not for
wheelchairs; dogs welcome, picnic-sets
in secluded front beer garden (summer
barbecues), boules pitch, closed Sun and
bank holidays. *(Dr and Mrs A K Clarke,
Taff Thomas)*

BRISTOL   ST5772
Cottage (0117) 921 5256
*Baltic Wharf, Cumberland Road;
BS1 6XG* Converted stone-built harbour
master's office on wharf near Maritime
Heritage Centre, comfortable and roomy
with fine views of Georgian landmarks and
Clifton suspension bridge, popular generous
pub food from sandwiches up at reasonable
prices, well kept Butcombe ales and a guest,
real cider and nice wines, good service even
when busy; background music; children
welcome, portable ramps for wheelchairs,
waterside terrace tables, access through
sailing club, on foot along waterfront,
or by round-harbour ferry, open all day.
(Ian Herdman, Peter Meister, Taff Thomas)

BRISTOL   ST5772
Grain Barge (0117) 929 9347
Hotwell Road; BS8 4RU Floating 100-ft
barge owned by Bristol Beer Factory, their
ales kept well, good freshly made food at fair
prices including Sun roasts, friendly staff,
seats out on top deck, sofas and tables on
wood floor below, art exhibitions, live music
Fri night; open all day. *(Taff Thomas, Tony and
Wendy Hobden, Peter Meister)*

BRISTOL   ST5872
Gryphon
Colston Road; BS1 5AP Wedge-shaped
heavy metal/real ale pub with loyal following,
half a dozen well kept quickly changing
beers served by friendly staff, background
music from the likes of AC/DC, Iron Maiden,
Metallica and Napalm Death, live bands
upstairs; handy for Colston Hall, open all day
(till 1.30am Fri, Sat). *(Taff Thomas)*

BRISTOL   ST5772
★ Hope & Anchor (0117) 929 2987
Jacobs Wells Road, Clifton; BS8 1DR
Friendly 18th-c pub with half a dozen
changing ales from central bar, nice wines

and good choice of malts, tables of various
sizes (some shaped to fit corners) on bare
boards, darker back area, flowers and candles,
sensibly priced hearty food all day including
daily specials, friendly staff; soft background
music (occasional live), can get crowded late
evening; children welcome, disabled access,
barbecues in good-sized tiered back garden
with interesting niches, parking nearby can
be tricky, open all day. *(Anon)*

BRISTOL   ST5873
Horts City Tavern (0117) 925 2520
Broad Street; BS1 2EJ Refurbished open-
plan 18th-c pub with well kept Bath Gem
and Wells & Youngs ales, good all-day food
including burgers and pizzas, big windows
overlooking street, 26-seat cinema at back
(free entry if you have a meal); background
music, sports TV; tables in cobbled courtyard,
open all day. *(Roger and Donna Huggins)*

BRISTOL   ST5874
Kensington Arms (0117) 944 6444
Stanley Road; BS6 6NP Dining pub in
the centre of Redland with well liked if not
particularly cheap food from light lunches
up, good buoyant atmosphere and cheerful
accommodating staff, well kept Greene King
ales and a guest, several wines by the glass;
may be background music; children and dogs
welcome, disabled facilities (no wheelchair
access to dining room, but can eat in bar),
heated terrace, open all day. *(Chris and
Val Ramstedt)*

BRISTOL   ST5972
★ Kings Head (0117) 929 2338
Victoria Street; BS1 6DE Friendly and
relaxed 17th-c pub, big front window and
splendid mirrored bar-back, corridor to cosy
panelled snug with serving hatch, four well
kept ales including Butcombe and Sharps
Doom Bar, toby jugs on joists, old-fashioned
local prints and photographs, reasonably
priced wholesome food weekday lunchtimes
(get there early for a seat); background
music, no credit cards; pavement tables,
open all day (closed Sun afternoon).
(Dr and Mrs A K Clarke, Taff Thomas)

BRISTOL   ST5673
Mall (0117) 974 5318
The Mall, Clifton; BS8 4JG Relaxed
corner pub with well kept changing ales,
interesting continental beers and lots of
wines by the glass, enjoyable modern pub
food, tall windows ornate ceiling, some
panelling and mix of old furniture on wood
floors, downstairs bar; Thurs quiz, free
wi-fi; small garden behind, open all day
till midnight. *(Roger and Donna Huggins)*

BRISTOL   ST5772
Merchants Arms (0117) 904 0037
Merchants Road, Hotwells; BS8 4PZ
Tiny two-room pub close to historic dockside,
welcoming landlord and friendly locals, well

kept Bath Ales and their Bounders cider, modest choice of well chosen wines, limited food, open fire; popular Thurs quiz, karaoke/sing-alongs, sports TV; wheelchair access with help (narrow door and steps). *(Taff Thomas, Chris and Angela Buckell)*

BRISTOL   ST5772
Nova Scotia (0117) 929 7994
Baltic Wharf, Cumberland Basin; BS1 6XJ Old local on S side of floating harbour, views to Clifton and Avon Gorge; Courage Best and guests, a real cider and generous helpings of enjoyable pub food, four linked areas, snob screen, mahogany and mirrors, nautical charts as wallpaper, welcoming atmosphere and friendly regulars; wheelchair access with help through snug's door, plenty of tables out by water, bedrooms sharing bathroom. *(Chris and Angela Buckell, Peter Meister, Taff Thomas)*

BRISTOL   ST5872
Old Duke (0117) 927 7137
King Street; BS1 4ER Named after Duke Ellington and festooned with jazz posters, plus one or two instruments, good bands nightly and Sun lunchtime, usual pub furnishings, real ales and simple food; in interesting cobbled area between docks and Bristol Old Vic, gets packed evenings, open all day (till 1am Fri, Sat). *(Taff Thomas)*

BRISTOL   ST5872
Old Fish Market (0117) 921 1515
Baldwin Street; BS1 1QZ Imposing building (former fish market), lots of dark wood including handsome counter, high tables and stools on parquet floor, relaxed friendly atmosphere, comprehensive range of well kept Fullers beers with Butcombe as guest, thai food all day (till 7pm Sun); quiet background music, big-screen sports TVs; open all day. *(Taff Thomas)*

BRISTOL   ST5772
Orchard no phone
Hanover Place, Spike Island; BS1 6XT Friendly unpretentious one-room corner local; half a dozen well kept ales from stillage behind bar and great choice of ciders (perhaps a winter mulled one), good sandwiches and other snacky food, woodburner, live music including Tues jazz; sports TV – pub gets busy on match days; tables out in front, handy for SS *Great Britain*, open all day. *(Taff Thomas)*

BRISTOL   ST5672
Portcullis (0117) 908 5536
Wellington Terrace; BS8 4LE Compact two-storey pub in Georgian building close to Clifton bridge with spectacular views, well kept Dawkins and several changing guests, farm ciders, fine range of wines by the glass and spirits, tapas-style food, good friendly staff, flame-effect gas fire, dark wood and usual pubby furniture; free wi-fi; dogs welcome, tricky wheelchair access, closed weekday lunchtimes, open all day weekends. *(Roger and Donna Huggins, Trevor Graveson)*

BRISTOL   ST5772
Pump House (0117) 927 2229
Merchants Road; BS8 4PZ Spacious nicely converted dockside building (former 19th-c pumping station); charcoal-grey brickwork, tiled floors and high ceilings, good food in bar and smart candlelit mezzanine restaurant, ales such as Bath, Butcombe and St Austell, decent wines from comprehensive list and huge choice of gins, friendly staff, cheerful atmosphere; waterside tables. *(Taff Thomas)*

BRISTOL   ST5872
Royal Naval Volunteer
(0117) 316 9237 *King Street; BS1 4EF* Modernised 17th-c pub in cobbled street, wide range of british beers including real ale, craft and excellent bottled choice, ciders/perries too and a dozen wines by the glass, friendly knowledgeable staff, good interesting food in back restaurant; weekend live music, sports TV; dogs welcome, terrace seating. *(Anon)*

BRISTOL   ST5972
Seven Stars (0117) 927 2845
Thomas Lane; BS1 6JG Unpretentious one-room real ale pub near harbour (and associated with Thomas Clarkson and slave trade abolition), much enjoyed by students and local office workers, eight well kept changing ales (20 from a featured county on first Mon-Weds of month), some interesting malts and bourbons, dark wood and bare boards, old local prints and photographs, no food but can bring in takeaways, weekend folk music; juke box, pool, games machine; disabled access (but narrow alley with uneven cobbles and cast-iron kerbs). *(Taff Thomas, Chris and Angela Buckell, Dr Kevan Tucker)*

BRISTOL   ST5771
Spotted Cow (0117) 963 4433
North Street; BS3 1EZ Modernised early 19th-c pub with open-plan split-level bar, beers from Bath and Butcombe, good choice of sensibly priced food including popular Sun lunch with live jazz (suckling pig first Sun of month); DJ and open mike nights; good-sized enclosed garden behind, open all day (till 1am Thurs-Sat). *(Taff Thomas)*

BRISTOL   ST5872
Three Tuns (0117) 926 8434
St Georges Road; BS1 5UR Owned by local Arbor with their ales and guests, also interesting selection of US beers, Thatcher's cider and decent choice of wines, cheerful knowledgeable staff, extended bar area with mix of pubby furniture on bare boards, a couple of armchairs in alcoves, open fire, lunchtime rolls; very busy weekends when

live music; garden with smokers' area, near cathedral. *(Taff Thomas)*

BRISTOL ST5773
Victoria (0117) 974 5675
Southleigh Road, Clifton; BS8 2BH Modest little two-room pub, popular and can get crowded, with half a dozen or more changing small brewery ales including a couple from Dawkins, interesting bottled belgian beers, local cider and good selection of malt whiskies and wines by the glass, cheerful knowledgeable staff, basic snacks such as pies and sausage rolls, big mirrors and open fire, cards and board games, old silent movies some winter evenings; free wi-fi; dogs welcome, disabled access (a few low kerbs/steps), open all day weekends, from 4pm Mon-Fri. *(Chris and Angela Buckell)*

BRISTOL ST5773
W G Grace (0117) 946 9780
Whiteladies Road; BS8 2NT Popular newish Wetherspoons with rather austere dark frontage – tables and chairs on front terrace; small lounge areas either side of entrance with upholstered chairs, sofas and low tables, grey stone tiles in bar area, wood elsewhere, some alcove seating, Greene King and four local guests from long chrome-topped servery, usual food and value, bare-brick and mock-stone walls in much higher ceilinged eating area at back, history of W G Grace, old Bristol photos and mirrored Betjeman poems on walls; sports TVs, fruit machines, free wi-fi; wheelchair access throughout, open all day from 8am. *(Chris and Angela Buckell)*

BRISTOL ST5976
Wellington (0117) 9513022
Gloucester Road, Horfield (A38); BS7 8UR Lively and roomy 1920s red-brick pub refitted in traditional style, well kept Bath Ales and guests, good choice of bottled beers and other drinks, enjoyable food till 10pm including 28-day dry-aged steaks, pleasant efficient service, large horseshoe bar, sofas and low tables in extended lounge with dining area overlooking sunny terrace; very busy on Bristol RFC or Rovers match days; children welcome, disabled access/facilities, refurbished boutique bedrooms (best to book early), open all day, from 9am weekends for breakfast. *(Chris and Angela Buckell)*

BRISTOL ST5873
White Lion (0117) 927 7744
Quay Head, Colston Avenue; BS1 1EB Small friendly city-centre pub with simple bare-boards bar, four Wickwar ales a guest, range of Pieminster pies, good coffee, daily newspapers and free wi-fi; spiral stairs down to lavatories; café-style pavement tables under awning. *(Taff Thomas)*

BRISTOL ST5873
Zero Degrees (0117) 925 2706
Colston Street; BS1 5BA Converted Victorian tramshed with large industrial-style bar, own beers brewed behind glass walls, cocktails and good choice of other drinks, enjoyable food from open kitchen including wood-fired pizzas and mussel dishes, cheerful helpful staff, upper gallery; loud background music; good disabled facilities, rooftop views from terrace tables, open all day. *(Taff Thomas, Kathrine Haddrell)*

BROADWAY ST3215
Bell (01460) 52343
Broadway Lane; TA19 9RG Comfortably refurbished village pub with flagstones and open fires, innovative well priced food (not Sun evening) along with more traditional choices, also OAP lunch and set menus, Courage Directors and Wells & Youngs Bombardier, skittle alley, quiz second Tues of month; children and dogs welcome, seats out in front and on back terrace, good value bedrooms, open all day Fri-Sun. *(Martin and Alison Stainsby)*

CHEDDAR ST4653
White Hart (01934) 741261
The Bays; BS27 3QN Welcoming village local with well kept beers, traditional ciders and enjoyable fairly priced home-made food including Sun carvery, log fire; live music and quiz nights, free wi-fi; children welcome, picnic-sets out in front and in back garden with play area, open (and food) all day. *(Eddie Edwards)*

CHEW MAGNA ST5763
Pelican (01275) 331777
South Parade; BS40 8SL Refurbished village pub with friendly welcome and buzzy atmosphere; opened-up modern interior with polished wood flooring, candles on chunky tables, some old pew chairs and high-backed settles, leather armchairs by woodburners in stone fireplaces, fresh flowers, well kept changing ales such as Butcombe, Otter and St Austell, good choice of wines by the glass, good food including daily specials; children and dogs welcome, wheelchair access from back courtyard, grassy beer garden, open all day (Sun till 6pm). *(Chris and Angela Buckell, Taff Thomas, Dr and Mrs A K Clarke, Comus and Sarah Elliott and others)*

CHEW MAGNA ST5861
★ Pony & Trap (01275) 332627
Knowle Hill, New Town; from B3130 in village, follow Bishop Sutton, Bath signpost; BS40 8TQ Michelin star dining pub in nice rural spot near Chew Valley Lake; really good imaginative food from sandwiches through to beautifully presented restaurant dishes (must book), good friendly service, two Butcombe ales and a guest, front bar with cushioned wall seats and

built-in benches on parquet, old range in snug area on left, dark plank panelling and housekeeper's chair in corner, lovely pasture views from two-level back dining area with white tables on slate flagstones; children welcome, dogs in bar, modern furniture on back terrace, picnic-sets on grass with chickens in runs below, front smokers' shelter, good walks, closed Mon (apart from Dec). *(David and Jenny Billington, David Wyatt, Taff Thomas, Dr and Mrs A K Clarke, Comus and Sarah Elliott and others)*

CHILCOMPTON ST6451
Somerset Wagon (01761) 232732
B3139; Broadway; BA3 4JW Cosy and welcoming 19th-c pub (former railway inn), well liked good value food, Wadworths ales with Butcombe as a guest, Thatcher's and Weston's ciders, good service even when packed, pleasant olde-worlde areas off central bar, lots of settles, log fire, some live music; children welcome, small front garden, open all day Sun. *(Ian Phillips)*

CHILTHORNE DOMER ST5219
Carpenters Arms (01935) 840770
Tintinhull Road/Vagg Lane; BA21 3PX Opened up and modernised country pub on crossroads, popular locally, with good sensibly priced home-made food and well kept ales such as Otter and Sharps Doom Bar, narrow recently added front conservatory; free wi-fi; children and dogs welcome, terrace with circular picnic-sets, open all day Fri-Sun. *(Anon)*

CHISELBOROUGH ST4614
Cat Head (01935) 881231
Cat Street; leave A303 on A356 towards Crewkerne; take the third left (at 1.4 miles) signed Chiselborough, then left after 0.2 miles; TA14 6TT 16th-c hamstone pub refurbished under newish family owners; bar and three dining areas, flagstones and mullioned windows, woodburner in fine fireplace, home-cooked food from lunchtime sandwiches up, Butcombe, Otter and a guest, Ashton's cider and nine wines by the glass, skittle alley; background music; children and dogs welcome (there are three pub dogs), seats on terrace and in pretty garden, open all day Sat, closed Sun evening and Tues. *(Anon)*

COMBE FLOREY ST1531
★ Farmers Arms (01823) 432267
Off A358 Taunton–Williton, just N of main village turn-off; TA4 3HZ Pretty thatched and beamed village pub, small bar with log fire in big stone fireplace, cushioned pubby chairs and settle on flagstones, stools by counter serving Cotleigh and Exmoor

ales, eight wines by the glass, food has been good (up for sale), cosy dining room with heavy beams and traditional furniture on red patterned carpet; free wi-fi; children and dogs welcome, charming cottagey garden with picnic-sets and flowering tubs, Taunton–Minehead steam line nearby, open all day, no food Sun evening. *(Richard and Penny Gibbs, Bob and Margaret Holder)*

COMPTON DANDO ST6464
Compton Inn (01761) 490321
Court Hill; BS39 4JZ Welcoming two-bar stone-built village pub in lovely setting; enjoyable food from sandwiches up (not particularly cheap), well kept Bath, Butcombe and Sharps, open fire; garden. *(Taff Thomas)*

COMPTON MARTIN ST5457
★ Ring o' Bells (01761) 221284
A368 Bath–Weston; BS40 6JE Old beamed village pub with traditional flagstoned front bar, big inglenook log fire, steps up to spacious back area with oak boards and stripped stone, various odds and end including a bulls head, stuffed fish and a hare called Wally, gold discs and signed celebrity photos, Butcombe and a guest, Ashton's and Thatcher's ciders, good wine and whisky choice, enjoyable freshly made interesting food from lunchtime sandwiches up, good friendly service, traditional pub games, live music including folk night first Thurs of month, quiz last Thurs, May cider and cheese fair with bell ringers and morris men; children and dogs welcome, big garden with play area, two bedrooms, open all day weekends. *(Zoe Garside, Edward Mirzoeff)*

CONGRESBURY ST4363
Plough (01934) 877402
High Street (B3133); BS49 5JA Old-fashioned traditional local – a pub since the 1800s; five well kept changing west country ales such as Butcombe, RCH and St Austell, ciders from Moles and Thatchers, quick smiling service, generous helpings of well cooked pub food and daily specials, several small interconnecting rooms off flagstoned main bar, mix of furniture old and new, built-in pine wall benches, old prints, photos, farm tools and sporting memorabilia, log fire; Sun quiz; dogs welcome, wheelchair access from car park, garden with rustic furniture and boules. *(Chris and Angela Buckell)*

CORFE ST2319
White Hart (01823) 421388
B3170 S of Taunton; TA3 7BU Friendly 17th-c village pub, enjoyable sensibly priced pubby food (not Mon, Tues) including some

---

vegetarian options, well kept ales, hot woodburner and open fire, bar billiards, skittle alley; dogs welcome, open all day Sat, closed Tues lunchtime. *(Patrick and Daphne Darley, Bob and Margaret Holder)*

CRANMORE   ST6643
Strode Arms (01749) 880450
West Cranmore; signed with pub off A361 Frome–Shepton Mallet; BA4 4QJ Pretty dining pub (former 15th-c farmhouse) under new management; rambling redecorated beamed rooms with country furnishings, carpeted or flagstones floors, grandfather clock and some local artwork, old locomotive engineering drawings in public bar, log fires in handsome fireplaces, enjoyable food (not Sun evening) from snacks up including themed nights, Wadworths ales and several wines by the glass; children and dogs welcome, front terrace, more seats in back garden with play area, handy for East Somerset Light Railway, open all day weekends. *(M G Hart, Graham Bennett)*

CULBONE HILL   SS8247
Culbone (01643) 862259
Culbone Hill; A39 W of Porlock, opposite Porlock Weir Toll Road; TA24 8JW More restaurant-with-rooms than pub, set high on the moors and refurbished by present owner; good food including themed nights and set deals, a couple of well kept beers and decent choice of malt whiskies, good friendly service, events such as star-gazing, cookery school; children welcome, terrace with wonderful views over Lorna Doone valley, five well appointed bedrooms, open (and food) all day. *(Richard and Penny Gibbs)*

DINNINGTON   ST4013
Dinnington Docks (01460) 52397
NE of village; Fosse Way; TA17 8SX Good cheery atmosphere in large old-fashioned country local, unspoilt and unfussy, with good choice of inexpensive genuine home cooking including fresh fish Fri, well kept Butcombe and guests, farm ciders, log fire, friendly attentive staff, memorabilia to bolster myth that there was once a railway line and dock here, sofas in family room, skittle alley in adjoining building, some live music; large garden behind, good walks, open all day Fri-Mon. *(S Holder)*

DITCHEAT   ST6236
★Manor House (01749) 860276
Signed off A37 and A371 S of Shepton Mallet; BA4 6RB Pretty 17th-c red-brick village inn, buoyant atmosphere and popular with jockeys from nearby stables, enjoyable home-made food from sandwiches and pubby bar meals to more sophisticated choices, Butcombe and guests, unusual arched doorways linking big flagstoned bar to comfortable lounge and restaurant, open fires, skittle alley; children welcome, tables on back grass,

handy for Royal Bath & West showground, three mews bedrooms, open all day. *(Carey Smith)*

DOWLISH WAKE   ST3712
New Inn (01460) 52413
Off A3037 S of Ilminster, via Kingstone; TA19 0NZ Comfortable and welcoming dark-beamed village pub, decent home-made food including blackboard specials, well kept Butcombe and Otter, local cider, woodburners in stone inglenooks, pleasant dining room; dogs welcome, attractive garden and village, Perry's cider mill and shop nearby, four bedrooms. *(Anon)*

DULVERTON   SS9127
Bridge Inn (01398) 324130
Bridge Street; TA22 9HJ Welcoming unpretentious little pub next to River Barle; reasonably priced food using local suppliers, up to four ales including Exmoor, some unusual imported beers, Addlestone's cider and 30 malt whiskies, comfortable sofas, woodburner, folk night third Sat of month, fortnightly quiz Sun; children and dogs welcome (pub dogs Milly and Molly), two terraces, open all day summer (all day Fri-Sun, closed Mon evening winter). *(Peter Thornton, Richard and Penny Gibbs, Peter and Teresa Blackburn, Eddie Edwards)*

DUNDRY   ST5666
Carpenters (0117) 964 6423
Wells Road; BS41 8NE Reopened 2013 after extensive renovation, good generously served food and well kept ales such as Bath and Butcombe, Thatcher's cider, helpful friendly staff; children welcome, picnic-sets on lawn, may close Sun evening, Mon in winter. *(Taff Thomas, Comus and Sarah Elliott, David and Jill Wyatt)*

DUNDRY   ST5666
Dundry Inn (0117) 964 1722)
Church Road off A38 SW of Bristol; BS41 8LH Refurbished roomy village pub under newish management; half-panelled bar with cushioned window seats and comfy armchairs on oak floor, steps up to stone-tiled dining area with open fire, Bath, Butcombe and Sharps, enjoyable imaginative food along with pubby choices; children welcome, no wheelchair access, picnic-sets in enclosed church-side garden with outstanding views over Bristol and beyond, two bedrooms, handy for airport, closed Mon, otherwise open all day (Sun till 5pm). *(Chris and Angela Buckell, Comus and Sarah Elliott)*

DUNSTER   SS9843
★Stags Head (01643) 821229
West Street (A396); TA24 6SN Friendly helpful staff in unassuming 16th-c roadside inn, enjoyable good value food, Exmoor and a guest ale, candles, beams, timbers and inglenook log fire, steps up to small back dining room; dogs welcome, comfortable

simple bedrooms, good breakfast, closed Weds lunchtime. *(John Chambers)*

EAST HARPTREE   ST5453
Castle of Comfort (01761) 221321
B3134, SW on Old Bristol Road; BS40 6DD Welcoming family management and some recent refurbishment for this former coaching inn set high in the Mendips (last stop before the gallows for some past visitors); hefty timbers and exposed stonework, pubby furniture including cushioned settles on carpet, log fires, Butcombe, Sharps and a guest, good choice of reasonably priced traditional food including nice steaks, friendly staff; children (away from bar) and dogs welcome, wheelchair access, big garden with raised deck and play area, fine walks nearby. *(Taff Thomas)*

EAST HARPTREE   ST5655
Waldegrave Arms (01761) 221429
Church Lane; BS40 6BD Welcoming old pub keeping local feel although largely set out for chef-landlord's good food (not Sun evening, Mon), cheerful young staff, well kept Butcombe and guests, small beamed bar and two dining areas, eclectic mix of furniture and plenty of things to look at, log fires; children and dogs welcome, picnic-sets in attractive sheltered garden, delightful village, closed Mon lunchtime. *(Ian and Rose Lock, Taff Thomas)*

EAST LAMBROOK   ST4218
Rose & Crown (01460) 240433
Silver Street; TA13 5HF Stone-built dining pub spreading extensively from compact 17th-c core with inglenook log fire, friendly staff and relaxed atmosphere, decent choice of freshly made food using local supplies, Palmers ales and nine wines by the glass, restaurant extension with old glass-covered well, skittle alley; picnic-sets on neat lawn, opposite East Lambrook Manor Garden, closed Sun evening, Mon. *(Anon)*

EAST WOODLANDS   ST7944
★ Horse & Groom (01373) 462802
Off A361/B3092 junction; BA11 5LY Small pretty pub (aka the Jockey) tucked away down country lanes, friendly and relaxed, with good choice of enjoyable well priced food (not Sun evening) including some bargain offers, quickly changing ales and real ciders, pews and settles in flagstoned bar, woodburner in comfortable lounge, big dining conservatory, traditional games; children welcome in eating areas, dogs away from restaurant, disabled access, tables out in nice front garden with more seats behind, handy for Longleat. *(Anon)*

ENMORE   ST2434
Tynte Arms (01278) 671351
Enmore Road; TA5 2DP Open-plan low-beamed pub with wide choice of good generous food including lots of fish, home-made puddings and good value set menus, friendly service, west country ales from long bar, plenty of dining tables, chesterfields and settles, end inglenook, china collection; no dogs; car park over road, good walking country. *(Bob and Margaret Holder)*

EVERCREECH   ST6336
Natterjack (01749) 860253
A371 Shepton Mallet–Castle Cary; BA4 6NA Former Victorian station hotel (line closed 1966), good choice of popular generous food at reasonable prices, Butcombe and a couple of guests, real cider and good range of wines, welcoming landlord and cheerful efficient staff, long bar with eating areas off; lots of tables under parasols in big neatly kept garden, five bedrooms in restored cider house. *(Anon)*

EXEBRIDGE   SS9324
Anchor (01398) 323433
B3222 S of Dulverton; pub itself actually over the river, in Devon; TA22 9AZ Idyllically placed Exmoor-edge inn with good food using local suppliers, some emphasis on fresh fish/shellfish, friendly service, Exmoor and Greene King ales, Thatcher's cider, seven wines by the glass, spacious lounge/restaurant area; children welcome, dogs in bar, nice big riverside garden with plenty of tables, six bedrooms (fishing rights for residents), open (and food) all day weekends. *(Taff Thomas)*

EXFORD   SS8538
★ White Horse (01643) 831229
B3224; TA24 7PY Popular and welcoming three-storey creeper-clad inn, more or less open-plan bar, high-backed antique settle among more conventional seats, scrubbed deal tables, hunting prints and local photographs, good log fire, Exmoor ales and Sharps Doom Bar, over 100 malt whiskies, Thatcher's cider, enjoyable hearty food from sandwiches to good value Sun carvery; children and dogs welcome, tables outside and play area, pretty village, Land Rover Exmoor safaris, comfortable bedrooms, open all day from 8am. *(Lynda and Trevor Smith)*

FAULKLAND   ST7555
★ Tuckers Grave (01373) 834230
A366 E of village; BA3 5XF Unspoilt, unchanging and absolutely tiny cider house with friendly locals and charming landlady, flagstoned entrance opening into simple room with casks of Butcombe, Fullers London Pride and Thatcher's Cheddar Valley cider in alcove on left, perhaps lunchtime sandwiches, two high-backed settles facing each other across a single table on right, side room with shove-ha'penny, open fires, daily papers, skittle alley; children welcome in one area, lots of tables and chairs on attractive back lawn, good views, closed Mon lunchtime (except bank holidays). *(Roger and Donna Huggins)*

FRESHFORD ST7960
Inn at Freshford (01225) 722250
Off A36 or B3108; BA2 7WG Roomy
beamed stone-built pub in lovely spot
near river, enjoyable food from lunchtime
sandwiches up, more evening choice, well
kept Box Steam ales and guests, real ciders/
perries, decent wines by the glass and good
choice of gins and malts, helpful attentive
staff; wheelchair access from car park,
pretty hillside garden. *(Taff Thomas,
Chris and Angela Buckell)*

FROME ST7748
Griffin (01373) 467766
Milk Street; BA11 3DB Unpretentious
bare-boards bar with etched glass and open
fires, long counter serving good Milk Street
beers brewed here by the friendly landlord,
hot food Sun, easy-going mixed crowd, quiz
and live music nights; small garden, closed
lunchtimes, open till 1am Fri, Sat, 1-9pm
Sun. *(Anon)*

GLASTONBURY ST5039
Who'd A Thought It (01458) 834460
Northload Street; BA6 9JJ Interesting
pub filled with oddments and memorabilia
including enamel signs and old photographs,
even a red phone box (complete with
mannequin) and bicycle chained to the
ceiling, beams, flagstones, stripped brick
and pine panelling, coal fire in old range,
well kept Palmers ales and decent wines by
the glass, enjoyable freshly cooked food; free
wi-fi; children and dogs welcome, terrace
picnic-sets, five comfortable bedrooms,
open all day. *(Chris and Angela Buckell)*

HALLATROW ST6357
★Old Station (01761) 452228
A39 S of Bristol; BS39 6EN Friendly
former station hotel with extraordinary
collection of bric-a-brac including railway
memorabilia, musical instruments, china
cows, post boxes from sailing boats, even
half an old Citroen, wide mix of furnishings,
Brains Rev James and Butcombe Bitter,
popular food, Pullman carriage restaurant;
children and dogs (in bar) welcome, modern
furniture on decking, picnic-sets on grass,
bedrooms in converted outbuilding (no
breakfast), open all day Fri-Sun. *(Anon)*

HARDWAY ST7234
★Bull (01749) 812200
*Off B3081 Bruton–Wincanton at brown
sign for Stourhead and King Alfred's
Tower; Hardway; BA10 0LN* Charming
beamed 17th-c country dining pub, good
popular food (not Sun evening, Mon) in
comfortable bar and character dining rooms,
well kept Butcombe and Otter, farm cider and
nice wines by the glass, good informal service,
log fire; unobtrusive background music; tables
and barbecues in garden behind, more seats
in rose garden over road. *(Anon)*

HILLFARANCE ST1624
Anchor (01823) 461334
*Oake; pub signed off Bradford-on-Tone to
Oake road; TA4 1AW* Comfortable village
pub with dining area off attractive two-part
bar, good choice of enjoyable food including
Sun carvery, nice atmosphere, three local
ales; children welcome, garden with play
area, bedrooms and holiday apartments.
(Bob and Margaret Holder)

HINTON BLEWETT ST5956
★Ring o' Bells (01761) 452239
Signed off A37 in Clutton; BS39 5AN
Charming low-beamed stone-built country
local opposite village green, old-fashioned
bar with solid furniture including pews,
log fire, good value food (not Sun evening)
cooked by landlady, obliging service,
Butcombe, Fullers and guests, good wines
by the glass, dining room; children, walkers
and dogs welcome, nice view from tables
in sheltered front yard, open all day in
summer. *(Taff Thomas)*

HINTON CHARTERHOUSE ST7758
★Rose & Crown (01225) 722153
B3110 about 4 miles S of Bath; BA2 7SN
Friendly 18th-c village pub with partly
divided bar, fine panelling, cushioned wall
seats and bar stools, farmhouse chairs around
chunky tables on red carpeting, woodburner
in ornate carved stone fireplace (smaller
brick one on other side), Butcombe, Fullers
and a seasonal guest, several wines by glass,
tasty good value food from baguettes to grills,
long dining room and steps to lower area with
unusual beamed ceiling; background music,
TV; children and dogs welcome, picnic-sets
under parasols in terraced garden, pretty
window boxes, monthly summer live music
and barbecue, bedrooms, open all day
Weds-Sun. *(David Heath)*

HOLCOMBE ST6648
Duke of Cumberland
(01761) 233731 *Edford Hill; BA3 5HQ*
Popular modernised pub with good
competitively priced food including
home-made pizzas, local ales such as Bath,
Butcombe and Milk Street, ciders from Long
Ashton and Thatcher's, friendly helpful staff,
log fires, skittle alley; background and some
live music, sports TV; children and dogs
welcome, riverside garden with picnic-sets,
open all day from 10am. *(Ian Phillips)*

HOLTON ST6826
Old Inn (01963) 32002
Off A303 W of Wincanton; BA9 8AR
Refurbished and extended 16th-c dining pub
under new welcoming owners; enjoyable
food from 'tapas' up, well kept local beers,
painted beams, ancient flagstones and big
woodburner, lots of button-back leather
banquettes, raftered restaurant with pale
green and cherry pink walls, charity quiz and

music evenings; children welcome, picnic-sets in front, sheltered garden up steps, open all day Sun. *(Michael Doswell, Ian Jenkins)*

HORTON
ST3214
★**Five Dials** (01460) 55359
Hanning Road; off A303; TA19 9QH
Cleanly updated village pub run by friendly helpful couple, popular reasonably priced home-made food including good steaks and fish, Otter, Sharps Doom Bar and a guest, local ciders and good choice of wines by the glass, restaurant; children and dogs welcome, five bedrooms, open all day Fri-Sun, closed Mon. *(Patrick and Daphne Darley, Evelyn and Derek Walter)*

KELSTON
ST7067
Old Crown (01225) 423032
Bitton Road; A431 W of Bath; BA1 9AQ
17th-c creeper-clad inn with four small traditional rooms, beams and polished flagstones, carved settles and cask tables, logs burning in ancient open range, two more coal-effect fires, well kept Butcombe ales and real cider, enjoyable fairly priced food in bar and small restaurant, good value lunchtime set menu and other deals, Tues quiz; children and dogs welcome, wheelchair access with help, picnic-sets under apple trees in sheltered sunny back garden, play area, barbecues, four bedrooms in converted outbuildings, open all day. *(M G Hart, Dr and Mrs A K Clarke)*

KEYNSHAM
ST6669
★**Lock-Keeper** (0117) 986 2383
Keynsham Road (A4175 NE of town); BS31 2DD Friendly riverside pub with plenty of character, bare boards and relaxed worn-in feel, simple left-hand bar with big painted settle, cushioned wall benches, trophy cabinet and old local photographs, two more little rooms with assorted cushioned dining chairs, more photographs and rustic prints, Wells & Youngs and guests, good choice of wines and coffees, popular reasonably priced bar food, cheerful young staff, light modern conservatory (quite different in style), live music Fri, Sat; children welcome, dogs in bar, disabled access/facilities, teak furniture and giant parasols on big heated deck overlooking water, steps down to picnic-sets on grass, outside bar and barbecue, pétanque, open all day. *(Taff Thomas, Chris and Angela Buckell, Dr and Mrs A K Clarke)*

KILVE
ST1442
Hood Arms (01278) 741210
A39 E of Williton; TA5 1EA Welcoming 18th-c beamed country pub, good interesting food from bar snacks up including popular Sun lunch, well kept Exmoor, Otter, and a guest, warm woodburner in bar, cosy plush lounge, restaurant, skittle alley; children and dogs welcome, nice back garden with tables on sheltered terrace, play area, 12 bedrooms

(two in back lodge); for sale as we went to press. *(Bob and Margaret Holder)*

KINGSTON ST MARY
ST2229
Swan (01823) 451383
Lodes Lane, in centre of village; TA2 8HW Cosy 17th-c roadside village pub, very neat and tidy, with long knocked-through panelled bar, modern furniture on carpets, rough plastered walls with local artwork for sale and lots of signed cricket bats, fresh flowers, big stone fireplaces, home-made mostly pubby food (not Sun evening), well kept ales such as Dartmoor, Exmoor and Sharps, Thatcher's cider, well priced wines, pleasant helpful staff; unobtrusive jazz-based background music; children and dogs welcome, front disabled access, garden with play area, handy for Hestercombe Gardens. *(Giles and Annie Francis, Chris and Angela Buckell)*

KNAPP
ST3025
Rising Sun (01823) 491027
Village W of North Curry (pub signed from here); TA3 6BG Tucked-away 15th-c longhouse surrounded by lovely countryside; handsome beams, flagstones and two inglenooks with woodburners, Exmoor and Sharps Doom Bar, proper cider, good food with emphasis on fish/seafood, seasonal game too, friendly helpful staff; children and dogs welcome, sunny little front terrace, open all day Sat, closed Sun evening (except first Sun of month when there's a quiz) and Mon. *(Kerry Law, Jo Furley, Mr Yeldahn)*

KNOLE
ST4825
Lime Kiln (01458) 241242
A372 E of Langport; TA10 9JH Creeper-clad beamed 17th-c country pub set back from the road, good range of well priced traditional food including children's menu, ales such as Butcombe, Otter and Ringwood, Thatcher's Cheddar Valley cider, friendly attentive staff, flagstoned bar and large carpeted dining room, inglenook log fire; pleasant garden with southerly views, open all day weekends. *(Helen and Brian Edgeley)*

LANGFORD BUDVILLE
ST1122
★**Martlet** (01823) 400262
Off B3187 NW of Wellington; TA21 0QZ Cosy, comfortable and cottagey with friendly landlady and staff, good generously served food (becomes more restaurranty in evenings with fewer drinkers), popular OAP lunch deal Weds-Fri, well kept/priced local ales including Exmoor, inglenook, beams and flagstones, central woodburner, steps up to carpeted lounge with another woodburner; skittle alley. *(S G N Bennett, Patrick and Daphne Darley)*

LANGLEY MARSH
ST0729
Three Horseshoes (01984) 623763
Just N of Wiveliscombe; TA4 2UL Traditional red sandstone pub with well kept beers tapped from the cask and enjoyable

pubby food in bar and dining area, low modern settles in back bar, stone fireplace; background music; seats on verandah and in sloping back garden, monthly vintage car meetings, closed Sun evening, Mon and lunchtimes apart from Sun. *(Richard and Penny Gibbs)*

LANGPORT ST4625
★ **Devonshire Arms** (01458) 241271
B3165 Somerton–Martock, off A372 E of Langport; TA10 9LP Handsome gabled inn (former hunting lodge) with civilised atmosphere; simple back bar with modern metal and leather bar stools, rush-seated high-backed chairs around dark tables on flagstones, up to three west country ales tapped from the cask, local cider brandy and several wines by the glass, stylish main room with comfortable leather sofas and glass-topped log table by fire, scatter cushions on long wall bench, church candles, elegant dining room with brown wicker chairs around pale wood tables on broad boards, good interesting food (local suppliers listed) from lunchtime sandwiches up, charming efficient service, evening pianist; wheelchair access from car park, teak furniture out at front, pretty box-enclosed courtyard with unusual water-ball feature, more seats on raised terraces, nice bedrooms, good breakfast. *(Hugh Roberts, M G Hart, Ian Herdman, Richard and Penny Gibbs, B and F A Hannam and others)*

LONG ASHTON ST5370
Bird in Hand (01275) 395222
Weston Road; BS41 9LA Refurbished stone-built dining pub with good locally sourced food (not Sun evening) from bar meals to imaginative restaurant dishes, well kept Bath, Butcombe, St Austell, Sharps and a guest, Ashton Press cider, nice wines, spindleback chairs and blue-painted pine tables on wood floors, open fire and woodburner; children and dogs welcome, side terrace, parking may be tricky, open all day. *(Roger and Anne Newbury)*

LONG ASHTON ST5370
Miners Rest (01275) 393449
Providence Lane; BS41 9DJ Welcoming three-room country pub, comfortable and unpretentious, with well kept Butcombe, Fullers London Pride and a guest tapped from casks, three or four good farm ciders, generous helpings of inexpensive simple food, cheerful prompt service, local mining memorabilia, log fire, darts; no credit cards; well behaved children and dogs welcome, wheelchair access with some heroics, vine-covered verandah and suntrap terrace, open all day. *(Taff Thomas, Chris and Angela Buckell)*

LOVINGTON ST5831
★ **Pilgrims** (01963) 240597
B3153 Castle Cary–Keinton Mandeville; BA7 7PT More of a restaurant but does have a pubby corner serving a local ale, farm cider and plenty of wines by the glass, good imaginative food (not cheap) using local produce, efficient friendly service, cosy flagstoned inner area with modern prints, bookshelves, china and some sofas by big fireplace, compact eating area with candles on tables and more formal carpeted dining room; children welcome, dogs in bar, decked terrace in enclosed garden, car park exit has own traffic lights, bedrooms (no children), closed Sun evening, Mon and lunchtime Tues. *(Anon)*

LOWER GODNEY ST4742
Sheppey Inn (01458) 831594
Tilleys Drove; BA5 1RZ Revamped character pub attracting good mix of customers; at least six local ciders (one for them) tapped from the barrel along with local ales and craft beers, imaginative choice of well liked food, some cooked in charcoal oven, plain furniture on bare boards, black beams, stripped-stone walls and open fire, stuffed animals and old local photographs, long simply furnished pitched-ceilinged dining area, art exhibitions and live music; children welcome, seats on deck overlooking small river. *(Peter Meister)*

MARK ST3747
Pack Horse (01278) 641209
B3139 Wedmore–Highbridge; Church Street; TA9 4NF Attractive traditional 16th-c village pub run by welcoming greek-cypriot family, good choice of enjoyable home-made food including Sun roasts and fresh Brixham fish (prices can be on the high side), well kept Butcombe and guests, good friendly service, log fire; next to church. *(Richard Wyld)*

MILVERTON ST1225
Globe (01823) 400534
Fore Street; TA4 1JX Popular smartly reworked coaching inn – more restaurant than pub now; much liked mainly local food from interesting lunchtime baguettes and ciabattas up, good value Sun roasts and occasional themed nights, well kept Exmoor, Otter and nice choice of wines by the glass, cheerful helpful staff and friendly labrador, local art for sale; children welcome, terrace tables, bedrooms. *(Giles and Annie Francis, Bob and Margaret Holder, Patrick and Daphne Darley)*

MINEHEAD SS9746
Old Ship Aground (01643) 703516
Quay West; TA24 5UL Harbourside Edwardian pub reopened after revamp by local farming family; three real ales and traditional cider, food using own produce, faux black beams, pubby furniture and window-seat views; background music, free wi-fi; children and dogs welcome, wheelchair access via side door, disabled lavatory, outside tables overlooking harbour, 12 bedrooms, open all day. *(Anon)*

NAILSEA   ST4469
Blue Flame (01275) 856910
Netherton Wood Lane, West End;
BS48 4DE Small friendly 19th-c farmers'
local with two unchanging lived-in rooms,
coal fire, well kept ales from casks behind
bar, traditional ciders, fresh rolls, pub
games; outside lavatories including roofless
gents', limited parking (may be filled with
Land Rovers and tractors); children's room,
sizeable informal garden, open all day
weekends, closed lunchtimes Mon, Tues.
(Taff Thomas)

NEWTON ST LOE   ST7065
Globe (01225) 872891
A4/A36 roundabout; BA2 9BB Popular
17th-c Vintage Inn, large and rambling, with
pleasant décor and dark wood partitions,
pillars and timbers giving secluded feel, their
usual food all day including fixed-price menu
(Mon-Sat till 5pm), well kept Butcombe,
St Austell Tribute and a guest, prompt
friendly service from uniformed staff, good
atmosphere; children welcome, nice back
terrace, open all day. *(Taff Thomas)*

NORTH CURRY   ST3125
Bird in Hand (01823) 490248
Queens Square; off A378 (or A358) E of
Taunton; TA3 6LT Friendly village pub,
cosy main bar with old pews, settles, benches
and yew tables on flagstones, some original
beams and timbers, good inglenook log
fire, well kept ales and decent wines by the
glass, enjoyable food in separate dining part;
background music; children, dogs and muddy
boots welcome, open all day Sun. *(Barry*
Collett, Bob and Margaret Holder)

NORTON ST PHILIP   ST7755
★George (01373) 834224
A366; BA2 7LH Wonderful building full
of history and interest – an inn for over
700 years; big heavy beams, timbering,
stonework and panelling, vast open fires
(not always blazing), distinctive furnishings,
plenty of 18th-c pictures, fine pewter and
heraldic shields, Wadworths ales, enjoyable
fairly straightforward food, friendly staff;
children and dogs (in bar) welcome,
appealing flagstoned courtyard, atmospheric
bedrooms (some reached by Norman turret),
worth strolling over meadow to attractive
churchyard, open all day. *(David Heath,*
John Coatsworth, Roger and Donna Huggins,
Taff Thomas)

NUNNEY   ST7345
George (01373) 836458
Church Street; signed off A361 Shepton
Mallet–Frome; BA11 4LW Comfortable
smartly reworked 17th-c coaching inn,
open-plan lounge with beams, stripped stone
and woodburner in big fireplace, good bar
and restaurant food including Sun roasts,
Wadworths ales and a guest, nice wines

by the glass and decent coffee, separate
restaurant, daily newspapers; children
welcome, dogs in bar, attractive walled
garden, rare 'gallows' inn-sign spanning
road, quaint village with ruined castle,
nine bedrooms, open all day. *(Heulwen and*
Neville Pinfield, Ian Phillips)

OAKHILL   ST6347
Oakhill Inn (01749) 840442
A367 Shepton Mallet–Radstock; BA3 5HU
Dining pub with sofas and easy chairs
among candlelit tables around bar, friendly
atmosphere and welcoming staff, decent
if not particularly cheap food including
some interesting choices, ales such as
Butcombe, dining extension in former skittle
alley, rugs on bare boards, wall of clocks,
log fires; background music; nice views
from garden, five bedrooms, open all day
weekends. *(Anon)*

OVER STRATTON   ST4315
★Royal Oak (01460) 240906
Off A303 via Ilminster turn at S
Petherton roundabout; TA13 5LQ
Friendly thatched family dining pub,
enjoyable reasonably priced food including
bargain two-course lunch (Tues-Sat), well
kept Badger ales, attractive line of linked
rooms, flagstones and thick stone walls,
prettily stencilled beams, scrubbed kitchen
tables, pews, settles etc, log fires and rustic
décor; tables outside, secure play area,
closed Mon. *(Bob and Margaret Holder)*

PITMINSTER   ST2219
Queens Arms (01823) 421529
Off B3170 S of Taunton (or reached
direct); near church; TA3 7AZ Friendly
village pub-restaurant with good imaginative
seasonal food, well kept Otter and a guest,
decent wines, pleasant staff, downstairs skittle
alley; children and dogs welcome, closed Sun
evening. *(Patrick and Daphne Darley)*

PORLOCK   SS8846
★Ship (01643) 862507
High Street; TA24 8QD Picturesque
old thatched pub with beams, flagstones
and big inglenook log fires, enjoyable food
from sandwiches up, well kept ales such
as Cotleigh, Exmoor, Otter and St Austell,
good friendly service, back dining room,
small locals' front bar with games; children
welcome, attractive split-level sunny garden
with decking and play area, nearby nature
trail to Dunkery Beacon, five bedrooms, open
all day; known as the Top Ship to distinguish
it from the Ship at Porlock Weir. *(Anon)*

PORLOCK WEIR   SS8846
★Ship (01643) 863288
Porlock Hill (A39); TA24 8PB
Unpretentious thatched pub in wonderful
spot by peaceful harbour – can get packed;
long and narrow with dark low beams,
flagstones and stripped stone, simple pub

furniture, woodburner, west country ales
including Exmoor, real ciders and a perry,
good whisky and soft drinks choice, enjoyable
pubby food served promptly by friendly staff,
games rooms across small backyard, tea
room; background music and big-screen TV;
children and dogs welcome, sturdy picnic-
sets in front and at side, good coast walks,
three decent bedrooms, limited free parking
but pay & display opposite; calls itself the
Bottom Ship avoiding confusion with the Ship
at Porlock. *(Taff Thomas, Mr and Mrs D J Nash)*

PORTBURY   ST4975
★ **Priory** (01275) 376307
*Station Road, 0.5 miles from A369
(just S of M5 junction 19); BS20 7TN*
Spreading early 19th-c Vintage Inn dining
pub, lots of linked beamed areas, appealing
mix of comfortable furnishings in alcoves,
tartan carpets, log fire, well kept Butcombe,
St Austell and a guest, good range of wines
by the glass and popular sensibly priced food,
friendly enthusiastic young staff; background
music; children welcome, no dogs inside,
pleasant front and back gardens, open (and
food) all day. *(Steve and Claire Harvey)*

PORTISHEAD   ST4576
★ **Windmill** (01275) 843677
*M5 junction 19; A369 into town, then
follow Sea Front sign and into Nore
Road; BS20 6JZ* Busy dining pub making
most of terrific panorama over Bristol
Channel; completely restyled with curving
glass frontage rising two storeys (adjacent
windmill remains untouched), contemporary
furnishings, Bass, Butcombe, Courage and
local guests, plenty of wines by the glass,
good range of enjoyable food including daily
specials and early-bird deal, efficient well
organised staff; children welcome in lower
family floor, dogs allowed in bar, disabled
access including lift, picnic-sets on tiered
lantern-lit terraces and decking, open all
day. *(R T and J C Moggridge, Dr and Mrs A K
Clarke, P and J Shapley, John Pritchard,
Steve and Claire Harvey)*

PRIDDY   ST5450
★ **Hunters Lodge** (01749) 672275
*From Wells on A39 pass hill with TV
mast on left, then next left; BA5 3AR*
Welcoming and unchanging farmers', walkers'
and potholers' pub above Ice Age cavern,
in same family for generations, well kept
local beers tapped from casks behind bar,
Thatcher's and Wilkin's ciders, simple cheap
food, log fires in huge fireplaces, low beams,
flagstones and panelling, old lead mining
photographs, perhaps live folk music; no
mobiles or credit cards; children and dogs
in family room, wheelchair access, garden
picnic-sets. *(Taff Thomas)*

PRISTON   ST6960
Ring o' Bells (01761) 471467
Village SW of Bath; BA2 9EE
Unpretentious old stone pub with large
knocked-through bar, good reasonably priced
traditional food cooked by licensees using
nearby farm produce, real ales from small
local brewers including a house beer from
Blindmans, quick friendly service, flagstones,
beams and good open fire, skittle alley;
children, dogs and muddy boots welcome,
benches out at front overlooking little
village green (maypole here on May Day),
good walks, two bedrooms, closed
Mon lunchtime. *(Taff Thomas)*

PURITON   ST3141
Puriton Inn (01278) 683464
*Just off M5 junction 23; Puriton Hill;
TA7 8AF* Character pub well screened
from motorway, clean and tidy, with ample
straightforward food and well kept ales,
warmly welcoming service even when busy,
pool; children allowed, good disabled access,
front terrace and back garden with play area.
(MP)

RICKFORD   ST4859
Plume of Feathers (01761) 462682
Very sharp turn off A368; BS40 7AH
Cottagey 17th-c local with enjoyable
reasonably priced home-made food in bar
and dining room, friendly service, well kept
Butcombe and guests, local cider and good
choice of wines, black beams and half-
panelling, mix of furniture including cast-iron
tables and settles, log fires, table skittles,
darts and pool; well behaved children and
dogs welcome, rustic tables on narrow front
terrace, pretty streamside hamlet, bedrooms,
open all day. *(Taff Thomas)*

RIMPTON   ST6021
White Post Inn (01935) 851525
Rimpton Hill, B3148; BA22 8AR Small
pub straddling Dorset border (boundary
actually runs through the bar) and recently
refurbished by new chef-owner; good well
presented imaginative food from reworked
pub favourites up, local ales and ciders,
friendly helpful staff, cosy bar with sofas
and woodburner, fine country views from
restaurant and back terrace; children
welcome, three bedrooms, open all day Sat,
closed Sun evening. *(Anon)*

RODE   ST8054
Mill (01373) 831100
NW off Rode Hill; BA11 6AG Popular
pub in beautifully set former watermill,
restauranty layout and up-to-date décor, well
liked food from lunchtime sandwiches up,
Butcombe ales; comedy night second Thurs

Pubs close to motorway junctions are listed at the back of the book.

of month; children welcome, garden and decks overlooking River Frome, play area, open all day. *(John Coatsworth)*

ROWBERROW ST4458
⋆**Swan** (01934) 852371
Off A38 S of A368 junction; BS25 1QL
Neat and spacious dining pub opposite pond, olde-worlde beamery and so forth, good log fires, friendly atmosphere especially in nicely unsophisticated old bar part, good reasonably priced food (small helpings available), prompt pleasant service, well kept Butcombe ales and a guest like Wadworths 6X, Thatcher's cider, decent choice of wines by the glass, live music first Sun of month; children welcome, good-sized garden over road, open all day weekends. *(Taff Thomas, Nigel Long)*

RUMWELL ST1923
Crown (01823) 461662
A38 Taunton–Wellington, just past Stonegallows; TA4 1EL Roomy family-run roadside pub with old beams, cosy corners and roaring log fire, good choice of enjoyable fairly priced food including daily carvery, well kept ales such as Otter, friendly staff; free wi-fi; children welcome, tables in nice garden, handy for Sheppy's Cider. *(Bob and Margaret Holder, Tina and David Woods-Taylor)*

SALTFORD ST6968
Jolly Sailor (01225) 873002
Off A4 Bath–Keynsham; Mead Lane; BS31 3ER Worth knowing for its great River Avon setting by lock and weir; pubby food all day including weekday OAP lunch, Wadworths ales and guests, flagstones, low beams and two log fires, daily papers, conservatory dining room; background music; children allowed, disabled facilities. *(Dr and Mrs A K Clarke)*

SHEPTON MONTAGUE ST6731
⋆**Montague Inn** (01749) 813213
Village signed off A359 Bruton–Castle Cary; BA9 8JW Simply but tastefully furnished dining pub with welcoming licensees, popular for a civilised meal or just a drink, stripped-wood tables and kitchen chairs, inglenook log fire, interesting nicely presented food from lunchtime ciabattas up, well kept Bath, Wadworths and a local guest tapped from the cask, farm ciders, good wine and whisky choice, charming young staff, bright spacious restaurant extension behind; children welcome, dogs in bar (biscuit for good ones), garden and big terrace with teak furniture, maybe summer Sun jazz, peaceful farmland views, closed Sun evening. *(Mrs Blethyn Elliott, Hugh Roberts, Edward Mirzoeff)*

SIMONSBATH SS7739
⋆**Exmoor Forest Inn** (01643) 831341
B3223/B3358; TA24 7SH Beautifully placed in remote countryside and run by friendly licensees; split-level bar with

circular tables by counter, larger area with cushioned settles, upholstered stools and mate's chairs around mix of dark tables, hunting trophies, antlers and horse tack, woodburner, good reasonably priced traditional food alongside more imaginative choices including local game, well kept ales such as Cotleigh, Dartmoor and Exmoor, real cider, good choice of wines by the glass and malt whiskies, residents' lounge, airy dining room; children and dogs welcome, seats in front garden, fine walks along River Barle, own trout and salmon fishing, ten comfortable bedrooms, open all day in high season. *(Richard and Penny Gibbs, Bob and Margaret Holder, Sheila Topham)*

SOMERTON ST4928
Globe (01458) 272474
Market Place; TA11 7LX Old stone-built local with good reasonably priced food and friendly attentive staff, well kept Butcombe, Sharps Doom Bar and a couple of guests, two spacious bars with flagstones and bare boards, inglenook log fire, dining conservatory, pool in back games room, skittle alley; children welcome, garden with summer marquee, open all day. *(Bob and Margaret Holder)*

STAPLE FITZPAINE ST2618
Greyhound (01823) 480227
Off A358 or B3170 S of Taunton; TA3 5SP Rambling country pub with generally good food from varied menu (best to book evenings), well kept Badger ales and good wines by the glass, welcoming helpful staff, flagstones and inglenooks, nice mix of settles and chairs, olde-worlde pictures, farm tools and so forth; children and dogs welcome, comfortable well equipped bedrooms, good breakfast, open all day. *(Sara Fulton, Roger Baker, Guy Vowles)*

STOGUMBER ST0937
White Horse (01984) 656277
Off A358 at Crowcombe; TA4 3TA Friendly old village local with well kept ever-changing west country ales, food can be good especially the home-made fish pie and steak and kidney pudding, carpeted beamed bar with raised end section, old local photographs, log fire, separate restaurant, games room with pool; quiet back terrace, two bedrooms accessed by external staircase, open all day (discounted drinks weekday afternoons). *(Richard and Penny Gibbs, Bob and Margaret Holder)*

TARR SS8632
⋆**Tarr Farm** (01643) 851507
Tarr Steps – narrow road off B3223 N of Dulverton; deep ford if you approach from the W (inn is on E bank); TA22 9PY Lovely Exmoor setting above River Barle's medieval clapper bridge for this 16th-c inn; compact unpretentious bar rooms with good views, stall seating, wall seats and

leather chairs around slabby rustic tables, game bird pictures on wood-clad walls, three woodburners, Exmoor ales and several wines by the glass, good food, residents' end with smart evening restaurant (mix of bar or restaurant choices using local produce), friendly service, pleasant log-fire lounge with dark leather armchairs and sofas; children and dogs welcome, slate-topped stone tables outside making most of setting, extensive grounds, good bedrooms (no under-10s), open all day but closed 1-10 Feb. *(Lynda and Trevor Smith, Bob and Margaret Holder)*

TAUNTON   ST2525
★ **Hankridge Arms** (01823) 444405
Hankridge Way, Deane Gate (near Sainsbury's); just off M5 junction 25 – A358 towards city, then right at roundabout, right at next roundabout; TA1 2LR Interesting nicely restored Badger dining pub based on 16th-c former farmhouse – quite a contrast to the modern shopping complex around it; different-sized linked areas, big log fire, popular generous food from interesting sandwiches through pubby choices to restaurant dishes, set lunch deal, well kept ales and decent wines by the glass, quick friendly young staff; background music; dogs welcome, plenty of tables in pleasant outside area. *(Taff Thomas, Bob and Margaret Holder, R T and J C Moggridge, Dr and Mrs A K Clarke)*

TAUNTON   ST2225
Plough (01823) 324404
Station Road; TA1 1PB Small welcoming pub under new landlord; four well kept local ales including Otter tapped from cooled casks, up to ten racked ciders with more on draught, also Otter Tarka lager and seven wines by the glass, simple food all day till 10pm, bare boards, panelling, candles on tables, cosy nooks and open fire, hidden door to lavatories; background music (live weekends), popular quiz Tues; dogs welcome, open all day (till 2am Fri, Sat). *(Kerry Law, Simon Matthews, Phil and Jane Hodson)*

TAUNTON   ST2223
Vivary Arms (01823) 272563
Wilton Street; across Vivary Park from centre; TA1 3JR Popular low-beamed 18th-c local (Taunton's oldest), good value fresh food from light lunches up in snug plush lounge and small dining room, friendly helpful young staff, well kept ales including Butcombe, decent wines, interesting collection of drink-related items; lovely hanging baskets and flowers. *(Bob and Margaret Holder)*

TINTINHULL   ST5019
★ **Crown & Victoria** (01935) 823341
Farm Street, village signed off A303; BA22 8PZ Handsome golden-stone inn, carpeted throughout, with high bar chairs by new oak counter, well kept Butcombe,

Cheddar, Sharps and Yeovil, farmhouse furniture and big woodburner, good popular food (best to book weekends) including blackboard specials, efficient friendly service, dining room with more pine tables and chairs, former skittle alley also used for dining, end conservatory; children welcome, disabled facilities, big garden with play area, five bedrooms, handy for Tintinhull Garden (NT). *(Mrs T A Bizat, Simon Whitaker, Patrick and Daphne Darley)*

TRISCOMBE   ST1535
Blue Ball (01984) 618242
Village signed off A358 Crowcombe– Bagborough; turn off opposite sign to youth hostel; OS Sheet 181 map reference 155355; TA4 3HE Smartly revamped old thatched inn tucked beneath the Quantocks; all on first floor of original stables sloping down gently on three levels, each with own fire and divided by hand-cut beech partitions, local ales and ciders, several wines by the glass and interesting food; background music; children and dogs welcome, chair lift for disabled customers, decking at top of woodside terraced garden making most of views, two cottage bedrooms, closed Sun evening, Mon lunchtime. *(Rich Frith, Bob and Margaret Holder)*

TRULL   ST2122
Winchester Arms (01823) 284723
Church Road; TA3 7LG Cosy streamside village pub with good value food including popular Sun lunch, west country ales and ciders, friendly attentive staff, small dining room, skittle alley; garden with decked area, six bedrooms. *(Neil and Heather Cross)*

UPTON   ST0129
Lowtrow Cross Inn (01398) 371220
A3190 E of Upton; TA4 2DB Welcoming old pub with character low-beamed bar, log fire and woodburner, bare boards and flagstones, two carpeted country-kitchen dining areas, one with enormous inglenook, generous helpings of tasty home-made food (not Mon, lunchtime Tues), Cotleigh and a couple of guests, good mix of locals and diners; children and dogs welcome, lovely surroundings, camping nearby, closed Mon lunchtime. *(Anon)*

VOBSTER   ST7049
★ **Vobster Inn** (01373) 812920
Lower Vobster; BA3 5RJ Roomy old stone-built dining pub with popular reasonably priced food including fresh fish daily from Cornwall, good friendly service, Butcombe, Ashton Press cider and nice wines by the glass, three comfortable open-plan areas with antique furniture, plenty of room for just a drink; children and dogs (in bar) welcome, side lawn, peaceful views, boules, adventure playground and chickens behind, four bedrooms, closed Sun evening, Mon. *(M G Hart)*

WAMBROOK ST2907
Cotley Inn (01460) 62348
Off A30 W of Chard; don't follow the small signs to Cotley itself; TA20 3EN Refurbished old stone-built pub under welcoming licensees; light and airy beamed bar with flagstones and double-sided woodburner, carpeted dining areas off, two further fires, well kept Otter ales and a guest tapped from the cask, enjoyable reasonably priced traditional food, evening linen napkins, friendly attentive service, skittle alley; background music; children and dogs welcome, lovely view from terrace tables, nice garden below, quiet spot with plenty of surrounding walks, tethering for horses, closed Sun evening, Mon lunchtime. *(PLC, Gerry Price, Bob and Margaret Holder)*

WANSTROW ST7141
Pub (01749) 850455
A359 Frome–Bruton; BA4 4SZ Friendly village local with four well kept beers including Bass and Blindmans, proper cider, flagstone bar with open fire, dining room, bar billiards and other traditional games; closed Mon lunchtime. *(Dr and Mrs A K Clarke)*

WASHFORD ST0440
White Horse (01984) 640415
Abbey Road/Torre Rocks; TA23 0JZ Welcoming and popular old local, good selection of real ales and enjoyable pubby food including daily specials and deals, can eat in bar or separate restaurant area, log fires; large smokers' pavilion over road next to trout stream, bedrooms, good traditional breakfast. *(Richard and Penny Gibbs, Robert Ensor)*

WATCHET ST0643
Star (01984) 631367
Mill Lane (B3191); TA23 0BZ Late 18th-c pub near seafront, main flagstoned bar with other low-beamed side rooms and nooks and crannies, pubby furniture including oak settles, window seats, lots of bric-a-brac, ornate fireplace with woodburner, popular food cooked to order including fresh fish/seafood, four well kept mainly local ales, Thatcher's cider, some interesting whiskies, cheerful efficient staff; children and dogs welcome, wheelchair access, picnic-sets out in front and in beer garden behind. *(Eddie Edwards)*

WELLOW ST7358
Fox & Badger (01225) 832293
Signed off A367 SW of Bath; BA2 8QG Opened-up village pub (some recent refurbishment) with good mix of customers, flagstones one end, bare boards the other, some snug corners, woodburner in massive hearth, Butcombe, Fullers, Greene King and Sharps, four ciders including Thatcher's, wide range of enjoyable bar food from doorstep sandwiches and generous ploughman's up, good Sun lunch, friendly accommodating service; children and dogs welcome, picnic-sets in covered courtyard, open all day Fri, Sat. *(Meg and Colin Hamilton, Nigel Long)*

WELLS ST5445
★City Arms (01749) 673916
High Street; BA5 2AG Bustling town-centre pub with up to seven well kept ales, three ciders and decent reasonably priced food from breakfast on; main bar with leather sofas and chairs around assorted tables, plenty of prints and paintings, gas-effect log fire, upstairs restaurant with vaulted ceiling, red walls and chandeliers; background music; children and dogs welcome, cobbled courtyard and some reminders that the building was once a jail, first-floor terrace, open all day. *(Dr J Barrie Jones)*

WELLS ST5445
Crown (01749) 673457
Market Place; BA5 2RF Former 15th-c coaching inn overlooked by cathedral, various bustling areas with light wooden flooring, plenty of matching chairs and cushioned wall benches, Butcombe and Sharps Doom Bar, enjoyable good value food from sandwiches up in bar and bistro including early-evening deal, competent helpful service; background music, TV and games machine; no dogs; children until 8pm, small heated courtyard, 15 bedrooms, open all day. *(David Carr, Stan Lea)*

WELLS ST5546
★Fountain (01749) 672317
St Thomas Street; BA5 2UU Interesting place, they think of themselves as more of a restaurant now, with customers popping in and out all day, big comfortable bar with bric-a-brac and large fire, quite a choice of food here or in upstairs dining room, Butcombe Bitter and Sharps Doom Bar, several wines by the glass; unobtrusive background music; pretty in summer with window boxes and blue shutters, handy for cathedral and moated Bishop's Palace. *(R K Phillips, Jenny and Brian Seller, Hugh Roberts)*

WEST BAGBOROUGH ST1733
★Rising Sun (01823) 432575
Village signed off A358 NW of Taunton; TA4 3EF Charming village pub lit up with evening candles; small flagstoned bar to right of massive main door with settles and carved dining chairs around polished tables, daily papers on old-fashioned child's desk, fresh flowers and some quirky ornaments dotted about, well kept west country ales, good if not cheap food, friendly service, smart cosy dining room with nice mix of chippendale and other chairs around a few dark wood tables, big modern photographs and coal-effect gas fire in pleasant back snug, upstairs room with trusses in high pitched ceiling, refectory tables and oriental rug on wood

floor, large prints of cathedral cities; children and dogs welcome, teak seats outside by lane, two bedrooms, no car park, closed Sun evening (and Mon in winter). *(Bob and Margaret Holder)*

WEST HATCH   ST2719
Farmers Arms (01823) 480980
Slough Green, W of village; TA3 5RS Welcoming tucked-away country pub (former farmhouse) with four linked rooms, beams, some exposed stone and stripped boards, woodburner, four well kept ales and good choice of wines by the glass, popular home-made food from bar and restaurant menus, afternoon teas, Tues quiz; children welcome, terrace and small lawn, good local walks, five bedrooms. *(John Chambers)*

WEST HUNTSPILL   ST3145
Crossways (01278) 783756
A38, between M5 junctions 22 and 23; TA9 3RA Rambling 17th-c tile-hung pub with six well kept mostly local ales (tasting trays available), good choice of enjoyable generously served food at reasonable prices, friendly efficient staff (they ask for a credit card if you run a tab), split-level carpeted areas with beams and log fires, skittle alley; pool, TV; children and dogs welcome, disabled facilities, garden with play area and heated smokers' shelter, seven bedrooms, open all day. *(Robert Ravenscroft, R K Phillips, Brian and Anna Marsden)*

WEST MONKTON   ST2628
★ Monkton (01823) 412414
Blundells Lane; signed from A3259; TA2 8NP Popular and welcoming village dining pub improved under present licensees; good choice of freshly made food including some south african influences (best to book weekends), bare-boards bar with central woodburner, snug off, separate carpeted restaurant, Exmoor, Otter and Sharps Doom Bar, Aspall's and Thatcher's ciders, several wines by the glass, good service; children and dogs welcome, wheelchair access from car park, lots of tables in big garden bounded by stream, play area. *(Bob and Margaret Holder)*

WEST PENNARD   ST5438
Lion (01458) 832941
A361 E of Glastonbury; Newtown; BA6 8NH Traditional stone-built 16th-c village inn; bar and dining areas off small flagstoned black-beamed core, enjoyable pubby food plus daily specials, Butcombe, Otter and Sharps Doom Bar, inglenook woodburner and open fires; background music; children and dogs welcome, tables on big forecourt, good nearby walks, seven bedrooms in converted side barn. *(Anon)*

WINCANTON   ST7028
Nog Inn (01963) 32998
South Street; BA9 9DL Welcoming split-level pub with Otter, Sharps and a couple of guests, real cider and continental beers, reasonably priced traditional food including Sun carvery (not summer), bare boards, carpet and flagstones, pump clips on ceiling, log fires, darts, charity quiz (last Thurs of month); well behaved children and dogs welcome, pleasant back garden with heated smokers' shelter, open (and food) all day. *(Anon)*

WINFORD   ST5262
Crown (01275) 472388
Crown Hill, off Regil Road; BS40 8AY Old pub in deep country with linked beamed rooms, mix of pubby furniture including settles on flagstones or quarry tiles, old pictures and photographs on rough walls, copper and brass, leather sofas in front of big open fire, enjoyable generous home-made food (all day Sun) at very reasonable prices, Butcombe, Wadworths 6X and a guest, good choice of wines by the glass, friendly attentive landlord and staff, table skittles and skittle alley; children and dogs welcome, wheelchair access with help, tables out in front and in back garden, closed Mon lunchtime, otherwise open all day. *(Taff Thomas)*

WINSFORD   SS9034
Royal Oak (01643) 851455
Off A396 about 10 miles S of Dunster; TA24 7JE Prettily placed thatched and beamed Exmoor inn, good choice of enjoyable local food including daily specials, Exmoor ales and west country ciders, friendly helpful staff, carpeted bar with woodburner in big stone fireplace, large bay window seat looking across towards village green and foot and packhorse bridges over River Winn, restaurant and other lounge areas; children and dogs (in bar) welcome, disabled facilities, eight good bedrooms some with four-posters. *(Geof Cox, Bob and Margaret Holder)*

WITHAM FRIARY   ST7440
★ Seymour Arms (01749) 850742
Signed from B3092 S of Frome; BA11 5HF Well worn-in unchanging flagstoned country tavern, in same friendly family since 1952; two simple rooms off 19th-c hatch-service lobby, one with darts and bar billiards, other with central table skittles, well kept Cheddar Potholer and an occasional guest, Rich's local cider tapped from back room, low prices, open fires, panelled benches, cards and dominoes, no food (can bring your own); children and dogs welcome, garden by main rail line, cricket pitch over the road. *(Anon)*

WITHYPOOL   SS8435
★ Royal Oak (01643) 831506
Village signed off B3233; TA24 7QP Prettily placed country inn – where R D Blackmore stayed while writing *Lorna Doone*; lounge with raised working fireplace,

comfortably cushioned wall seats and slat-backed chairs, sporting trophies, paintings and copper/brass ornaments, enjoyable food here and in restaurant, well kept Exmoor ales, friendly helpful service, character locals' bar; walkers and dogs welcome (leave muddy boots in porch), children in eating areas, wooden benches on terrace, attractive riverside village with lovely walks, grand views from Winsford Hill just up the road, eight bedrooms (twisting staircase to top floor), open all day, but may close for a week in Feb. *(Stephen Shepherd, J V Dadswell, Lynda and Trevor Smith, Richard and Penny Gibbs, Sheila Topham and others)*

WOOKEY ST5245
⋆**Burcott** (01749) 673874
B3139 W of Wells; BA5 1NJ Cheerful beamed roadside pub with two simply furnished old-fashioned front bar rooms, flagstones, some exposed stonework and half-panelling, lantern wall lights, old prints, woodburner, three changing ales and a proper cider, enjoyable food (not Sun, Mon evenings, or Mon lunchtime in winter) from snacks up in bar and restaurant (children allowed here), good service, small games room with built-in wall seats; soft background music, no dogs; wheelchair access, front window boxes and tubs, picnic-sets in sizeable garden with Mendip Hills views, four self-catering units in converted stables. *(Anon)*

WOOKEY HOLE ST5347
Wookey Hole Inn (01749) 676677
High Street; BA5 1BP Usefully placed open-plan family pub, welcoming and relaxed, with idiosyncratic contemporary décor, two eating areas and bar, wood floors and good log fire, three changing local ales, several belgian beers, ciders and perry, good food from pub favourites up, tables with paper cloths for drawing on (crayons provided), efficient friendly staff; background music; dogs allowed in bar, pleasant garden with various sculptures, five individually styled bedrooms, open all day apart from Sun evening. *(Anon)*

WOOLVERTON ST7954
Red Lion (01373) 830350
Set back from A36 N of village; BA2 7QS Roomy refurbished pub, beams, panelling and lots of stripped wood, candles and log-effect fire, well kept Wadworths, decent wines by the glass, good choice of enjoyable food from baguettes up including children's meals, friendly quick service, locals' bar with

fire (dogs allowed here); background music, free wi-fi, plenty of tables outside, play area, open all day Fri-Sat. *(Dave Braisted)*

WRAXALL ST4971
Battleaxes (01275) 857473
Bristol Road B3130, E of Nailsea; BS48 1LQ Interesting stone-built Victorian pub nicely refurbished by the small Flatcappers group; well kept local ales including one badged for them by Three Castles, good choice of wines and other drinks, imaginative food from snacks up as well as pub favourites (they may ask for a credit card if you run a tab), spacious interior split into two main areas, polished boards, painted panelling and good mix of old furniture; children and dogs welcome, wheelchair access using ramps, six bedrooms, handy for Tyntesfield (NT), open all day. *(Steve and Liz Tilley, Taff Thomas)*

WRAXALL ST4971
⋆**Old Barn** (01275) 819011
Just off Bristol Road (B3130) in grounds of Wraxall House; BS48 1LQ Idiosyncratic gabled barn conversion, scrubbed tables, school benches and soft sofas under oak rafters, stripped boards and flagstones, welcoming atmosphere and friendly service, well kept Butcombe, Fullers, Otter, Sharps and a guest tapped from the cask, farm ciders, good wines by the glass, simple sandwiches, unusual board games; occasional background music and sports TV; children and dogs welcome, nice garden with terrace barbecue (bring your own meat) and smokers' shelter, closed Mon lunchtime, otherwise open all day. *(Steve and Liz Tilley, Taff Thomas)*

YARLINGTON ST6529
Stags Head (01963) 440393
Pound Lane; BA9 8DG Old low-ceilinged and flagstoned country pub tucked away in rustic hamlet; Bass, Greene King IPA and a local guest from small central bar, woodburner, chapel chairs and mixed pine tables on left, carpeted dining area on right with big log fire, modern landscape prints and feature cider-press table, second dining room with doors on to terrace, enjoyable food from traditional choices up including bargain OAP lunch, good service; background music; well behaved children welcome, dogs in bar, picnic-sets in sheltered back garden, maybe summer morris men, three bedrooms, closed Sun evening. *(M G Hart, John and Gloria Isaacs, Stan Lea, Robert Watt)*

Staffordshire

CAULDON
SK0749 Map 7

Yew Tree ★★ £

Village signposted from A523 and A52 about 8 miles W of Ashbourne;
ST10 3EJ

Treasure trove of fascinating antiques and dusty bric-a-brac,
simple good value snacks and bargain beer; very eccentric

For over 50 years the jovial Alan East (helped now by his stepson, Dan) has run this extraordinary roadside local with warmth and friendliness – don't let the unassuming exterior put you off the curiosities inside. The most impressive pieces are perhaps the working polyphons and symphonions – 19th-c developments of the musical box, some taller than a person, each with quite a repertoire of tunes and elaborate sound-effects. But there are also two pairs of Queen Victoria's stockings, an amazing collection of ceramics and pottery including a Grecian urn dating back almost 3,000 years, penny-farthing and boneshaker bicycles and the infamous Acme Dog Carrier. Soggily sprung sofas mingle with 18th-c settles, plenty of little wooden tables and a four-person oak church choir seat with carved heads that came from St Mary's church in Stafford. As well as all this, there's an array of musical instruments ranging from a one-string violin (phonofiddle) through pianos and sousaphones to the aptly named serpent. Drinks are very reasonably priced, so it's no wonder the place is popular with locals. You'll find Burton Bridge Bitter, Rudgate Ruby Mild and a guest or two on handpump, ten interesting malt whiskies, eight wines by the glass and farm cider; darts, table skittles, dominoes and cribbage. There are seats outside the front door and in the cobbled stable yard, and they hold vintage car and motorcyle meetings. The pub is tucked unpromisingly between enormous cement works and quarries and almost hidden by a towering yew tree.

🍴 Available during opening hours, the simple good value tasty snacks include cornish pasties, large sausage rolls and local pies.

Free house ~ Licensee Alan East ~ Real ale ~ (01538) 309876 ~ Open 12-3.30, 6-11; 12-midnight Sat; 12-11 Sun; closed winter weekday lunchtimes ~ Bar food available while open ~ Children in polyphon room ~ Dogs welcome ~ Live regular music evenings ~ www.yewtreeinncauldon.co.uk *Recommended by Emma Scofield, Paul Goldman*

A star symbol after the name of a pub shows exceptional character and appeal.
It doesn't mean extra comfort. And it's nothing to do with exceptional food quality,
for which there's a separate star-on-a-plate symbol. Even quite a basic pub can win
a star, if it's individual enough.

CHEADLE

SK0342 Map 7

Queens at Freehay

A mile SE of Cheadle; take Rakeway Road off A522 (via Park Avenue or Mills Road), then after 1 mile turn into Counslow Road; ST10 1RF

Friendly dining pub with a couple of local beers and a decent garden

Our readers really enjoy their visits to this particularly well run dining pub, where you can be sure of a warm welcome from the friendly landlord. The neatly kept interior has one or two cottagey touches that blend well with the modern refurbishments, and the atmosphere is relaxed and friendly. The comfortable lounge bar has pale wood tables on stripped wood floors, small country pictures, and curtains with matching cushions, and opens through an arch into a simple light and airy dining area with elegant chairs and tables on light blue carpet. Helpful staff serve Peakstones Rock Alton Abbey and Chained Oak and a guest beer on handpump; some seating is set aside for those who want just a drink and a chat. The attractive little back garden with its mature shrubs and picnic-sets is kept in immaculate condition.

Enjoyable food includes sandwiches, local black pudding topped with crispy bacon and melted cheese, crispy chicken strips in sweet chilli dip, battered fish and chips, three-mushroom stroganoff, gammon steak with pineapple and cheese, smoked haddock crumble in creamy white wine sauce, chargrilled chicken with a choice of sauces, moroccan lamb tagine, teriyaki pork steak, and puddings. *Benchmark main dish: beef in merlot pie £12.95. Two-course evening meal £17.50.*

Free house ~ Licensee Adrian Rock ~ Real ale ~ (01538) 722383 ~ Open 12-3, 6-11; 12-3, 6.30-10.30 Sun ~ Bar food 12-2, 6-9.30; 12-2.30, 6.30-9.30 Sun ~ Restaurant ~ Children welcome ~ www.queensatfreehay.co.uk *Recommended by Mr and Mrs J Morris, R L Borthwick*

HOAR CROSS

SK1323 Map 7

Meynell Ingram Arms ♀

Abbots Bromley Road; village signposted off A515 just over 3 miles N of Kings Bromley (brown sign to pub too); DE13 8RB

Friendly and civilised, well refurbished recently as a comfortable dining pub

This 17th-c country dining pub has a couple of fireside leather armchairs in the panelled bar, and the airy big-windowed back area has leather settees by another raised fireplace; otherwise, seating is mainly an informal mix of dining chairs around cast-iron-framed and other very solid tables on bare boards. A dining room with a smart dark red Anaglypta dado and matching frieze has more uniformly restaurenty furnishings. There's Burton Bridge Golden Delicious, Marstons Pedigree, Sharps Doom Bar and Timothy Taylors Landlord on handpump, 11 wines by the glass and a few malt whiskies, bunches of flowers in the windows, and friendly, neatly uniformed staff; unobtrusive background music. A sheltered side courtyard has wicker armchairs under an extendable and heated high awning, and unusual picnic-sets stand on individual terraces set into the neatly planted small lawn; more unusual still are the two futuristic glass spheres out here, with in-built seats and tables. There are woodland walks nearby.

Interesting food includes lunchtime sandwiches, duck liver parfait with madeira jelly, sashimi-style tuna with nori and chilli dressing, interesting pizzas, salmon fishcake with mustard-creamed leeks and a poached egg, burger with bacon, gouda and chips, pork belly with anise-glazed carrots, pavé of peppered roe deer with cabbage and chocolate sauce, and puddings such as sherry trifle and treacle tart with clotted cream; they also offer a two- and three-course set menu. *Benchmark main dish: chicken, ham and wholegrain mustard pie £14.00. Two-course evening meal £23.00.*

Free house ~ Licensee Warren Bailey ~ Real ale ~ (01283) 575988 ~ Open 12-11 (midnight Sat); 12-10.30 Sun ~ Bar food 12-2.30, 6.30-9 (9.30 Fri, Sat); 12-4.45, 6-9 Sun ~ Restaurant ~ Children welcome ~ Wi-fi ~ www.themeynell.co.uk *Recommended by Alfie Bayliss, Phoebe Peacock*

SALT   SJ9527 Map 7

Holly Bush £

Village signposted off A51 S of Stone (and A518 NE of Stafford); ST18 0BX

Delightful medieval pub with all-day food

Even when really busy – which this thatched pub often is – the friendly and efficient staff manage to keep things running smoothly. Several cosy areas spread out from the standing-only serving section, with high-backed cushioned pews, old tables and more conventional seats. The oldest part has a heavy-beamed and planked ceiling (some of the beams are attractively carved), a woodburning stove and a salt cupboard built into a big inglenook, with other nice old-fashioned touches including copper utensils, horsebrasses and an ancient pair of riding boots on the mantelpiece. A modern back extension, with beams, stripped brickwork and a small coal fire, blends in well. Adnams Bitter, Marstons Pedigree and a guest ale on handpump, alongside a dozen wines by the glass. They operate a secure locker system for credit cards, which they'll ask to keep if you run a tab. The back of the pub outside is beautifully tended and filled with flowers, with rustic picnic-sets on a big lawn. This is a pretty village.

 Fair value hearty food includes lunchtime sandwiches and toasties, duck liver pâté with beetroot and orange chutney, corned beef hash with spinach and poached egg, burger with bacon, cheese, coleslaw and chips, steak and kidney pudding, a fresh fish dish of the day, venison casserole and puddings. *Benchmark main dish: steak in ale pie £9.95. Two-course evening meal £15.00.*

Admiral Taverns ~ Licensees Geoffrey and Joseph Holland ~ Real ale ~ (01889) 508234 ~ Open 12-11 (10.30 Sun) ~ Bar food 12-9.30 (9 Sun) ~ Children welcome ~ Wi-fi ~ www.hollybushinn.co.uk *Recommended by Dennis Jones, Brian and Anna Marsden, Stephen Shepherd*

WRINEHILL   SJ7547 Map 7

Hand & Trumpet 🏆 ♀ 🍴

A531 Newcastle–Nantwich; CW3 9BJ

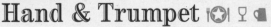

Staffordshire Dining Pub of the Year

Big attractive dining pub with good food all day, professional service, nice range of real ales and wines; appealing garden

Even though this is a substantial and stylish dining pub, there's still an intimate feel to the linked, open-plan areas. These, working their way around the long, solidly built counter, have a gentle mix of dining chairs and sturdy tables on polished tiles or stripped-oak boards and several warming oriental rugs that soften the acoustics. There are nicely lit prints and mirrors on cream walls between a mainly dark dado, plenty of house plants, open fires and deep red ceilings. Original bow windows and a large skylight keep the place light and airy, and french windows open on to a spacious balustraded deck with teak tables and chairs, which look down over ducks swimming on a big pond in the sizeable garden. Friendly attentive staff serve Phoenix Brunning & Price Original, Caledonian Deuchars IPA and Salopian Oracle with guests such as Black Sheep Golden Sheep, Merlin Dragon Slayer and Stonehouse Station Bitter on handpump, as well as 16 wines by the glass and about 70 whiskies; good disabled access and facilities; board games.

Enjoyable food from an interesting menu includes sandwiches, seared carpaccio of lamb with feta and mint panna cotta, prawn salad with pink grapefruit, guacamole and bloody mary sauce, wild mushroom, spinach, hazelnut and blue cheese pasta with truffle oil, beer-battered haddock and chips, pork tenderloin and belly with butternut squash purée, crackling and pickled apple sauce, creole-spiced chicken with roasted red pepper, sweet potato, coconut and pineapple salad, and puddings such as dark chocolate and Baileys torte and lemon tart with roasted fruit compote. *Benchmark main dish: braised lamb shoulder with dauphinoise potatoes £17.25. Two-course evening meal £20.00.*

Brunning & Price ~ Manager John Unsworth ~ Real ale ~ (01270) 820048 ~ Open 11.30-11 (10.30 Sun) ~ Bar food 12-10 ~ Children welcome ~ Dogs allowed in bar ~ Wi-fi ~ www.handandtrumpet-wrinehill.co.uk *Recommended by Mrs G Marlow, Dave Webster, Sue Holland, Steve and Liz Tilley*

Also Worth a Visit in Staffordshire

Besides the fully inspected pubs, you might like to try these pubs that have been recommended to us and described by readers. Do tell us what you think of them: feedback@goodguides.com

ABBOTS BROMLEY   SK0824
Coach & Horses (01283) 840256
High Street; WS15 3BN Refurbished village pub with good choice of enjoyable home-made food including weekday tapas, beamed bar with stone floor, carpeted restaurant, log fire, three or four mainstream ales and several wines by the glass, friendly helpful staff; children and dogs (in bar) welcome, pleasant garden with circular picnic-sets, open all day Sun (food till 7pm), closed Mon lunchtime. *(Anon)*

ABBOTS BROMLEY   SK0824
★ **Goats Head** (01283) 840254
Market Place; WS15 3BP Beamed and timbered village pub with friendly local atmosphere, half a dozen well kept ales including St Austell and Timothy Taylors (May beer festival), lots of wines by the glass, enjoyable home-made food (not Sun evening) served by attentive helpful staff, opened-up cream-painted interior, unpretentious but comfortable, with oak floors, traditional furnishings and fire in big inglenook; juke box and TV; children and dogs welcome,

teak furniture on sheltered lawn looking up to church tower, open all day. *(Clifford Blakemore)*

ALSAGERS BANK   SJ8048
Gresley Arms (01782) 722469
High Street; ST7 8BQ At the top of Alsagers Bank with wonderful far-reaching views; eight or more interesting ales from smaller breweries and several real ciders, good value pubby food (not lunchtimes apart from Sun), traditional slate-floor bar with beams and open fire, comfortable lounge, picture-window dining room taking in the view, and a lower family room, monthly folk night and regular beer festivals; walkers and dogs welcome, garden tables, open all day Thurs-Sun, from 3pm other days. *(Dave Webster, Sue Holland)*

ALSTONEFIELD   SK1355
★ **George** (01335) 310205
Village signed from A515 Ashbourne–Buxton; DE6 2FX Welcoming stone-built pub overlooking small village green, straightforward bar with low beams, old Peak District photographs and pictures, warming

---

If you stay overnight in an inn or hotel, they are allowed to serve you an alcoholic drink at any hour of the day or night.

fire, well kept Marstons-related beers from copper-topped counter, a dozen wines by the glass, farmhouse furniture and woodburner in neat dining room, good locally sourced food cooked to order from shortish menu (some prices on the high side); children welcome, dogs in bar, seats out in front or in big sheltered back stableyard, open all day Fri-Sun. *(Jill and Julian Tasker)*

ALSTONEFIELD SK1255
Watts Russell Arms (01335) 310126
Hopedale; DE6 2GD Nicely placed 18th-c stone-built beamed pub, three well kept Thornbridge ales, Ashover cider, fairly short menu including lunchtime wraps and perhaps lobby (a local stew), tapas Fri evening, two lived-in carpeted rooms with pubby furniture and banquettes, stone fireplace; children and dogs welcome (Hector is the large pub dog), picnic-sets on sheltered tiered terrace and in garden, open all day, closed Mon evening. *(Dennis Jones)*

BLACKBROOK SJ7638
Swan With Two Necks
(01782) 680343 *Nantwich Road (A51); ST5 5EH* Country pub-restaurant with smart contemporary décor in civilised open-plan dining areas, good well presented food (booking advised) from sharing boards up, ales such as Purity, Timothy Taylors and Titanic, nice wines by the glass including champagne, efficient friendly service (they may ask to keep a credit card while running a tab); background music; children welcome, comfortable tables out on decking, open (and food) all day. *(Anon)*

BLITHBURY SK0819
Bull & Spectacles (01889) 504201
Uttoxeter Road (B5014 S of Abbots Bromley); WS15 3HY Friendly 17th-c pub with good choice of enjoyable food including bargain lunchtime Hot Table (half a dozen or so generous main dishes with help-yourself vegetables, and some puddings), an ale from Greene King and a guest; children and dogs welcome, next door to reindeer farm, open all day Sun. *(David Green)*

BOBBINGTON SO8190
Red Lion (01384) 221237
Six Ashes Road, off A458 Stourbridge– Bridgnorth; DY7 5DU Friendly family-run pub popular for its good choice of enjoyable food and well kept ales (Enville, Hobsons, Holdens and Wye Valley), drinking and eating areas well separated, games part with darts, table football and pool; children welcome, good-sized garden with robust play area, 17 comfortable bedrooms in modern block, good breakfast, open all day weekends. *(Anon)*

BREWOOD SJ8808
Swan (01902) 850330
Market Place; ST19 9BS Former coaching inn with two low-beamed bars, Caledonian, Courage, Theakstons and some more local beers, good selection of whiskies, no food apart from lunchtime baguettes, inglenook log fire, upstairs skittle alley; open all day. *(Anon)*

BURSLEM SJ8649
Leopard (01782) 819644
Market Place; ST6 3AA Traditional Victorian city-centre pub with three rooms including a snug, good choice of enjoyable home-made food (Tues-Sun lunchtimes, Fri and Sat evenings), Bass and at least three changing guests, well priced wines, friendly helpful service, live music, ghost tours in derelict hotel part; open all day. *(Jeremy King)*

BURTON UPON TRENT SK2523
★Burton Bridge Inn (01283) 536596
Bridge Street (A50); DE14 1SY Genuinely friendly down-to-earth local with own good Burton Bridge ales from brewery across old-fashioned brick yard; simple little front area leading into adjacent bar with pews, plain walls hung with notices, awards and brewery memorabilia, 20 malt whiskies and lots of country wines, small beamed and oak-panelled lounge with simple furniture and flame-effect fire, panelled upstairs dining room, short choice of low-priced lunchtime food Weds-Sat, skittle alley; no credit cards; children welcome, dogs in bar, open all day Fri, Sat. *(David H Bennett)*

BURTON UPON TRENT SK2423
★Coopers Tavern (01283) 532551
Cross Street; DE14 1EG Old-fashioned 19th-c backstreet local tied to Joules – was tap for the Bass brewery and still has some glorious ephemera including mirrors and glazed adverts; homely and warm with coal fire, straightforward front parlour with pleasant jumble of furniture, back bar doubling as tap room, up to half a dozen guest ales including Bass and good selection of ciders/perries, friendly landlady, pork pies only but can bring your own food (or take beer to next-door curry house), live music Sun; children and dogs welcome, small back garden, open all day Thurs-Sun, from 5pm Mon, 3pm Tues and Weds. *(David H Bennett)*

BURTON UPON TRENT SK2423
Old Cottage Tavern (01283) 511615
Rangemoor Street/Byrkley Street; DE14 2EG Friendly corner local with well kept Burton Old Cottage beers and guests, two bars, snug and compact back restaurant, upstairs games room with skittle alley, folk nights; three bedrooms, open all day. *(Anon)*

CANNOCK WOOD SK0412
Park Gate (01543) 682223
Park Gate Road, S side of Cannock Chase; WS15 4RN Large red-brick dining pub with popular food including various deals and children's menu, ales such as Holdens, St Austell and Sharps, comfortably

modernised interior, conservatory; background music; dogs allowed in bar, secluded nice back garden with plenty of picnic-sets and play area, by Castle Ring Iron Age fort, good Cannock Chase walks. *(Brian and Anna Marsden)*

CODSALL   SJ8603
Codsall Station (01902) 847061
Chapel Lane/Station Road; WV8 1BY
Simply restored vintage waiting room and ticket office of working station, comfortable and welcoming, with well kept Holdens ales and a couple of guests, good value food (sandwiches only Sun) including blackboard specials, lots of railway memorabilia, open fire, conservatory; terrace seating, open all day Fri-Sun. *(Tony Hobden)*

CONSALL   SK0049
★ **Black Lion** (01782) 550294
Consall Forge, OS Sheet 118 map reference 000491; best approach from Nature Park, off A522, using car park 0.5 miles past Nature Centre; ST9 0AJ
Traditional take-us-as-you-find-us local tucked away in rustic old-fashioned canalside settlement by restored steam railway station, generous helpings of enjoyable unpretentious food cooked by landlord, wide range of well kept mostly local ales (tasting trays available), several ciders, flagstones and good coal fire; background music, can get very busy weekend lunchtimes; children welcome, seats outside overlooking canal, area for campers and store for boaters, good walks, open all day. *(Anon)*

COPMERE END   SJ8029
Star (01785) 850279
W of Eccleshall; ST21 6EW Friendly two-room 19th-c country local with well kept Bass, Joules, Titanic, Wells & Youngs and a guest, good variety of reasonably priced food from sandwiches up, open fire and woodburner, piano; children and dogs welcome, tables and play area in back garden overlooking mere, good walks, open all day weekends, closed Mon. *(Margaret and Peter Staples)*

DENSTONE   SK0940
Tavern (01889) 590847
College Road; ST14 5HR Welcoming stone-built village pub, comfortable lounge with antiques, good food (not Mon evening) including freshly made pizzas Fri, Sat evenings, pleasant service, well kept Marstons ales and good choice of wines by the glass, dining conservatory; children welcome, picnic-sets out in front, lovely church and well stocked farm shop.
(Brian and Jacky Wilson)

DRAYCOTT IN THE MOORS   SJ9840
Draycott Arms (01782) 395595
Cheadle Road; ST11 9RQ Family-run village pub, traditional bar and snug with

original floor tiles and woodwork, a beer for them from Marstons (Draycott Crusader) along with Pedigree and well kept guests, good food in restaurant including meat from own farm, friendly staff, Mon quiz; open all day. *(George Peacock)*

ECCLESHALL   SJ8329
Old Smithy (01785) 850564
Castle Street; ST21 6DF Refurbished pub-restaurant with comfortable clean modern décor, popular freshly made food (all day Sun) at fair prices including decent vegetarian options, five mainstream ales and good choice of other drinks, friendly helpful staff, Mon evening pianist; children welcome, open all day. *(Mr and Mrs J Morris)*

ECCLESHALL   SJ8329
Royal Oak (01785) 859065
High Street; ST21 6BW Old colonnaded coaching inn lovingly restored by Joules Brewery and run by father-and-son team; their well kept ales and enjoyable locally sourced food including Mon and Tues bargains, welcoming chatty staff; beer garden, open all day. *(Kerry Law, Robert W Buckle)*

ELLASTONE   SK1143
Duncombe Arms (01335) 324275
Main Road; DE6 2GZ Refurbished village dining pub with good food (all day Sun) in bar and restaurant including daily specials, Marstons Pedigree, a house beer brewed by Banks's and guests, wide choice of wines by the glass including champagne, friendly staff; children welcome, good-sized garden with own bar, open all day. *(Anon)*

FLASH   SK0267
Travellers Rest/Knights Table
(01298) 236695 *A53 Buxton–Leek; SK17 0SN* Isolated main-road pub and one of the highest in Britain, clean and friendly, with good reasonably priced traditional food (not Sun evening), four well kept ales and good selection of wines, beams, bare stone walls and open fires, medieval knights' theme; free wi-fi; children welcome, great Peak District views from back terrace, classic car meet last Thurs of month, bedrooms, closed Mon, otherwise open all day.
(Clive Dennis, John Woolf)

FRADLEY   SK1414
★ **White Swan** (01283) 790330
Fradley Junction; DE13 7DN Perfect canalside location at Trent & Mersey and Coventry junction, well kept Black Sheep, Greene King Abbot, Marstons Pedigree and three guests, cheery traditional public bar with two fires, quieter plusher lounge and lower vaulted room (former stable), food including Sun carvery, cribbage and dominoes, Thurs folk night, open mike Sun; children (not in bar) and dogs welcome, waterside tables, classic car/motorbike meetings, open all day. *(S J and C C Davidson)*

GAILEY SJ9010
Spread Eagle (01902) 790212
A5/A449; ST19 5PN Spacious Marstons
roadhouse, variety of separate areas
including relaxing sofas and family area with
toys, good value usual food, daily carvery,
efficient helpful service; good disabled access
and facilities, big terrace, lawn with play
area, open all day. *(Anon)*

GNOSALL SJ8120
Navigation (01785) 822327
Newport Road; ST20 0EQ Relaxed
two-bar pub with dining conservatory and
terrace overlooking Shropshire Union Canal
(moorings), good friendly service, popular
reasonably priced traditional food and
specials, well kept Banks's ales, good value
wines, live music Thurs, pool and darts;
children welcome, dogs in bar, disabled
facilities. *(Anon)*

HANLEY SJ8847
Coachmakers Arms (01782) 262158
Lichfield Street; ST1 3EA Chatty
traditional 19th-c town local with four small
rooms and drinking corridor, half a dozen
well kept ales including Bass, farm cider,
darts, cards and dominoes, original seating
and local tilework, open fire; children
welcome, open all day (but under threat of
demolition). *(Dave Webster, Sue Holland)*

HAUGHTON SJ8620
Bell (01785) 780301
A518 Stafford–Newport; ST18 9EX
19th-c village pub with good value popular
pub food (not Sun or Mon evenings, best to
book), well kept Banks's, Marstons, Timothy
Taylors and a guest, friendly attentive service
even when busy, restaurant behind; sports
TV in bar; children welcome, no dogs inside,
picnic-sets in back garden, open all day
Fri-Sun. *(Anon)*

HIGH OFFLEY SJ7725
Anchor (01785) 284569
*Off A519 Eccleshall–Newport; towards
High Lea, by Shropshire Union Canal
Bridge 42; Peggs Lane; ST20 0NG*
Real boaters' pub on Shropshire Union Canal,
little changed in the century or more this
family have run it; two small simple front
rooms, Marstons Pedigree and Wadworths
6X, Weston's farm cider, sandwiches on
request, owners' sitting room behind bar,
occasional weekend sing-alongs; no children
inside; outbuilding with semi-open lavatories
(swallows may fly through), lovely garden
with great hanging baskets and notable
topiary anchor, caravan/campsite, closed
Mon-Thurs in winter. *(S J and C C Davidson)*

HIMLEY SO8990
★Crooked House (01384) 238583
*Signed down long lane from B4176
Gornalwood–Himley, OS Sheet 139 map
reference 896908; DY3 4DA* Extraordinary
sight, building thrown wildly out of kilter by
mining subsidence, one side 4-ft lower than
the other and slopes are so weird that things
appear to roll uphill; public bar (dogs allowed
here) with grandfather clock and hatch
serving Banks's and other Marstons-related
ales, lounge bar, good food from bar snacks
and pub standards to more unusual creative
choices, cheery service, some local antiques
in level extension, conservatory; children
welcome in eating areas, big outside
terrace, closed Mon, otherwise open all day
(till 8pm Sun). *(Anon)*

HOPWAS SK1704
Tame Otter (01827) 53361
*Hints Road (A51 Tamworth–Lichfield);
B78 3AT* Popular Vintage Inn by
Birmingham & Fazeley Canal (moorings),
refurbished beamed interior on different
levels, cosy corners, their usual fairly priced
food all day, friendly efficient service, ales
such as Banks's, Bass and Marstons, decent
choice of wines, nice mixed furnishings,
old photographs and canalia, three fires;
children welcome, large garden with plenty
of seating. *(Mike and Mary Carter, David Green)*

KIDSGROVE SJ8354
★Blue Bell (01782) 774052
*Hardingswood; off A50 NW edge of
town; ST7 1EG* Simple friendly pub
(looks more like a house) with half a
dozen thoughtfully chosen and constantly
changing ales from smaller breweries,
around 30 bottled continentals, up to three
draught farm ciders and a perry, filled rolls
weekends only; four small, carpeted rooms,
unfussy and straightforward, with blue
upholstered benches, basic pub furniture,
gas-effect coal fire; may be background
music, no credit cards; dogs and well
behaved children welcome, tables in front
and on little back lawn, close to Trent &
Mersey and Macclesfield Canal junction,
open all day Mon and weekday
lunchtimes. *(Dave Webster, Sue Holland)*

KINGS BROMLEY SK1216
Royal Oak (01543) 473980
Manor Road (A515); DE13 7HZ Village
pub thriving under present management;
enjoyable good value food including OAP
weekday lunch and Sun carvery, well kept
Marstons-related ales, friendly staff, music
and quiz nights; children and dogs welcome,
big garden, open all day. *(David M Smith)*

KNIGHTON SJ7240
White Lion (01630) 647300
B5415 Woore–Market Drayton; TF9 4HJ
Welcoming unpretentious local with well kept
changing ales and enjoyable food (not Sun
or Mon evenings), nice bar areas with open
fires, more formal conservatory restaurant;
open all day Sun, from 5pm other days.
(Richard and Penny Gibbs)

LEEK   SJ9856
Den Engel (01538) 373751
Stanley Street; ST13 5HG Relaxed
belgian-style bar in high-ceilinged Jacobean
building, great selection of bottled and
draught continental beers, three dozen
genevers, plus four changing real ales (always
one from Titanic), knowledgeable landlord,
enjoyable food (not Mon, Tues) in upstairs
restaurant such as moules frites; background
classical music, can get packed weekends;
dogs welcome, tables on back terrace, closed
lunchtimes, open all day weekends, from 4pm
other days. *(Anon)*

LEEK   SJ9856
★Wilkes Head
St Edward Street; ST13 5DS Friendly
three-room local dating from the 18th c (still
has back coaching stables), owned by Whim
with their ales and interesting guests, real
ciders and good choice of whiskies, filled
rolls, gas fire and lots of pump clips, pub
games, juke box in back room, regular live
music (landlord is a musician); children
allowed in one room (not really a family
pub), dogs welcome but ask first, fair
disabled access, garden with stage, open
all day except Mon lunchtime. *(Anon)*

LICHFIELD   SK0705
★Boat (01543) 361692
*From A5 at Muckley Corner, take A461
signed Walsall; pub is on right just
before M6 Toll; WS14 0BU* Efficiently
run dining pub, handy break for a meal
off M6 toll; most emphasis on food with
huge floor-to-ceiling menu boards, views
into kitchen and dishes ranging from
lunchtime sandwiches through light snacks
to interesting main choices, cheery café
atmosphere, bright plastic flooring, striking
photo-prints, leather club chairs and sofas
around coffee tables and potted palms, more
conventional and comfortable dining areas
with sturdy modern pine furniture on carpet
and views of disused canal, three well kept
changing ales, ten wines by the glass, friendly
old chocolate lab called Harvey; background
music; children welcome, good wheelchair
access, seats on raised decking, open (and
food) all day Sun. *(David Green, Richard
Kennell, Phil and Jane Hodson)*

LICHFIELD   SK1109
Duke of York (01543) 300386
Greenhill/Church Street; WS13 6DY
Old beamed pub with split-level front
bar, cosy carpeted lounge and converted
back stables bar, inglenook woodburners,
well kept Joules ales and guests, simple
lunchtime food (not Sun), pleasant staff;

no children but dogs allowed, terrace
picnic-sets behind and own bowling green,
open all day. *(George Atkinson)*

LICHFIELD   SK1308
Horse & Jockey (01543) 262924
*Tamworth Road (A51 Lichfield–
Tamworth); WS14 9JE* Cosy old-fashioned
pub with wide range of popular freshly
prepared food including fish specials
(booking advisable), ales such as Castle
Rock, Marstons and Sharps, good friendly
service; darts; children welcome if eating,
no dogs, open all day Sun. *(David Green)*

LITTLE BRIDGEFORD   SJ8727
Mill (01785) 282710
*Worston Lane; near M6 junction 14;
turn right off A5013 at Little Bridgeford;
ST18 9QA* Useful sensibly priced dining pub
in attractive 1814 watermill, enjoyable food
in bar and restaurant including Sun carvery,
ales such as Greene King and Marstons,
good friendly service, Thurs quiz; children
welcome, pleasant grounds with adventure
playground and nature trail (lakes, islands
etc); open all day. *(Anon)*

LONGNOR   SK0965
Old Cheshire Cheese (01298) 83218
High Street; SK17 0NS Welcoming and
relaxed 17th-c village pub, three well kept
Robinsons ales and decent good value
food including blackboard specials, open
fire, bric-a-brac and pictures in traditional
main bar, two dining rooms, pool and TV in
separate rooms; free wi-fi; children, walkers
and dogs welcome, tables out in front, four
bedrooms in converted stables over road,
open (and food) all day (may close Mon in
winter). *(Brian and Anna Marsden)*

MEERBROOK   SJ9960
Lazy Trout (01538) 300385
Centre of village; ST13 8SN Popular and
welcoming country pub with good generous
food from imaginative menu, attentive
friendly service, four well kept changing
beers, cosily old-fashioned bar, comfortable
lounge with log fire and dining area; children
welcome, dogs and muddy boots in bar, pretty
garden behind, appealing setting and good
walks. *(Dr D J and Mrs S C Walker, Michael
Mellers)*

ONECOTE   SK0455
Jervis Arms (01538) 304206
B5053; ST13 7RU Busy country pub,
black-beamed main bar with inglenook
woodburner, well kept Titanic, Wadworths
6X and guests, reasonably priced pub food,
separate dining and family rooms; dogs
welcome in bar, attractive streamside (River

Though we don't usually mention it in the text, most pubs will now make
coffee or tea – it's always worth asking.

Hamps) garden with footbridge to car park, play area, open all day in summer, all day Sun winter; up for sale last we heard. *(Anon)*

PENKRIDGE   SJ9214
Littleton Arms (01785) 716300
St Michaels Square/A449 – M6 detour between junctions 12 and 13; ST19 5AL
Cheerfully busy dining pub-hotel (former coaching inn) with contemporary open-plan layout, varied choice of enjoyable food (some quite pricey), good wines by the glass and five well kept changing ales from island servery, friendly accommodating staff; background music; children and dogs (in bar area) welcome, ten bedrooms, open all day. *(Stuart Paulley)*

RUSHTON SPENCER   SJ9362
Knot Inn (01260) 226238
Station Lane; SK11 0QU Sizeable red-brick pub opposite former railway and station, enjoyable hearty home-made food including good value two-course deal, well kept changing beers, friendly staff and locals; children welcome, large area out at back with play area, good walks (on Staffordshire Way). *(Dr D J and Mrs S C Walker)*

SEIGHFORD   SJ8725
Holly Bush (01785) 281644
3 miles from M6 junction 14 via A5013/B5405; ST18 9PQ Refurbished beamed pub village owned and leased to Titanic, their ales and guests, good value locally sourced pub food (all day Fri, Sat, till 7pm Sun) from lunch-time sandwiches and light choices up, weekend live music and monthly charity quiz; beer garden, open all day Fri-Sun. *(Mike Walker)*

SHEEN   SK1160
Staffordshire Knot (01298) 84329
Off B5054 at Hulme End; SK17 0ET Welcoming traditional 17th-c stone-built village pub, nice mix of old furniture on flagstones or red and black tiles, stag's head and hunting prints, two log fires in hefty stone fireplaces, good interesting food cooked by landlady, well kept local Whim Hartington and reasonably priced wines, friendly helpful staff; closed Mon. *(Anon)*

STAFFORD   SJ9323
Swan (01785) 258142
Greengate Street; ST16 2JA Modernised coaching inn with two bars, well kept Marstons-related ales and guests such as Joules and Purity, good sensibly priced bar and brasserie food including Tues evening vegetarian/vegan night, coffee shop, friendly helpful staff; courtyard with rattan-style furniture, 31 bedrooms. *(Robert W Buckle)*

STOKE-ON-TRENT   SJ8649
Bulls Head (01782) 834153
St Johns Square, Burslem; ST6 3AJ Old-fashioned two-room tap for Titanic with up to ten ales (including guests) from horseshoe bar, also good selection of belgian beers, ciders and wines, well cared for interior with varnished tables on wood or carpeted floors, coal fire; bar billiards, table skittles and good juke box; drinking area outside (may be barbecue if Port Vale are at home), open all day Fri-Sun, closed till 3pm Mon, Tues. *(Jeremy King)*

STOKE-ON-TRENT   SJ8745
Glebe (01782) 860670
35 Glebe Street, by the Civic Centre; ST4 1HG Well restored 19th-c Joules corner pub, their ales and good choice of ciders and wines from central mahogany counter, William Morris leaded windows, bare boards and panelling, some civic portraits and big fireplace with coat of arms above, wholesome bar food (not Sun, Mon evening), friendly staff; quite handy for station, open all day. *(Susan and Nigel Brookes)*

STONE   SJ8933
Wayfarer (01785) 811023
The Fillybrooks (A34 just N); ST15 0NB Fresh contemporary décor (sister pub to the Swan With Two Necks at Blackbrook), good food from varied menu including sharing plates and stone-baked pizzas, beers such as Fullers, Sharps and Timothy Taylors, lots of wines by the glass, friendly staff; terrace seating, open all day. *(Dave Webster, Sue Holland, Susan and Nigel Brookes)*

STOWE   SK0027
★ **Cock** (01889) 270237
Off A518 Stafford–Uttoxeter; ST18 0LF Popular bistro-style conversion of old village pub (calls itself Bistro le Coq), good competently cooked french food (not Sun evening) from sensibly short fixed-price menus, some reasonably priced wines, small bar area serving real ale, friendly efficient service; well behaved children welcome, closed Mon lunchtime. *(Susan and Nigel Brookes)*

TRYSULL   SO8594
Bell (01902) 892871
Bell Road; WV5 7JB Extended and recently redecorated 19th-c village pub next to church, cosy bar, inglenook lounge and large back dining area with conservatory, well kept/priced Holdens, Bathams and a guest, popular good value food from cobs up including meal deals, friendly helpful service; dogs

---

Post Office address codings confusingly give the impression that some pubs are in Staffordshire, when they're really in Cheshire or Derbyshire (which is where we list them).

welcome in bar, front terrace, open all day weekends. *(Robert Parker, Paul Humphreys)*

TUTBURY   SK2128
Olde Dog & Partridge
(01283) 813030 *High Street; off A50 N of Burton; DE13 9LS* Chef & Brewer in handsome Tudor inn, rambling extensively back with heavy beams, timbers, various small rooms, nooks and corners, good choice of ales such as Jaipur and plenty of wines by the glass, their usual all-day food including deals and children's meals, prompt friendly service, good log fire; free wi-fi; nine comfortable bedrooms, open from 7am (8.30am weekends). *(John Saville, David M Smith)*

WETTON   SK1055
★ **Olde Royal Oak** (01335) 310287
Village signed off Hulme End– Alstonefield road, between B5054 and A515; DE6 2AF Welcoming old stone-built pub in lovely NT countryside – a popular stop for walkers; traditional bar with white ceiling boards above black beams, small dining chairs around rustic tables, oak corner cupboard, open fire in stone fireplace, more modern-feeling area leading to carpeted sun lounge, four changing ales and some 30 malt whiskies, well cooked good value pubby food, darts and shove-ha'penny; background music, TV; children and dogs welcome, picnic-sets in shaded garden, self-catering cottage and paddock for caravans/tents, closed Mon, Tues. *(R L Borthwick, MP)*

WHITTINGTON   SK1608
Dog (01543) 432601
The one near Lichfield; Main Street; WS14 9JU Beamed 18th-c village inn with good freshly made food (not Sun evening, Mon) from sensibly short menu, three well kept ales including Black Sheep and decent choice of wines by the glass, pleasant efficient service; small terrace, bedrooms, open all day Fri-Sun, closed Mon lunchtime. *(Anon)*

YOXALL   SK1418
Golden Cup (01543) 472295
Main Street (A515); DE13 8NQ Friendly well run village inn dating from the early 18th c, reasonably priced traditional home-made food from sandwiches to good value three-course Sun lunch, well kept Marstons Pedigree and a guest, lounge bar, games and sports TV in public bar; cheery window boxes and hanging baskets, nice garden down to small river, reasonably priced bedrooms, camping, open all day weekends. *(Anon)*

Suffolk

ALDEBURGH

TM4656 Map 5

Cross Keys
Crabbe Street; IP15 5BN

16th-c pub with seats outside near the beach, chatty atmosphere, friendly licensee and local beers; bedrooms

Its seafront position makes this traditional old pub a favourite spot in summer – there are views across the promenade and shingle to the water from the seats on the sheltered back terrace. Inside, the cheery, bustling atmosphere is helped along by the obliging licensee and his staff, and the low-ceilinged interconnecting bars have antique and other pubby furniture, miscellaneous paintings on the walls and log fires in two inglenook fireplaces. Adnams Bitter, Broadside and Ghost Ship on handpump, decent wines by the glass and several malt whiskies; background music and games machine. The bedrooms are attractively furnished.

🍽 Tasty food includes lunchtime sandwiches, devilled whitebait, pâté of the day, ham and eggs, steak and kidney pie, whole grilled plaice, braised oxtail, summer dressed crab salad, skate wing in black butter, and puddings. *Benchmark main dish: beer-battered cod and chips £10.25. Two-course evening meal £18.00.*

Adnams ~ Tenants Mike and Janet Clement ~ Real ale ~ (01728) 452637 ~ Open 11am (12 Sun)-midnight ~ Bar food 12-2 (3 weekends), 7-9; no food Sun evening ~ Children welcome ~ Dogs allowed in bar ~ Bedrooms: £65/£85 ~ www.aldeburgh-crosskeys.co.uk
Recommended by Andrew Gardner, Sheila Topham, C A Bryson, Pat and Graham Williamson, MDN, N R White

BOXFORD

TL9640 Map 5

Fleece ⭐ 🍺
Broad Street (A1071 Sudbury–Ipswich); CO10 5DX

Attractively restored, partly 15th-c pub flourishing under current ownership, good food and splendid beer range

Our readers love their visits to this particularly well run pub of real character, and both the own-brewed ales and the food are highly enjoyable. As well as genuinely welcoming licensees and a chatty, companionable atmosphere, what is really special is the Corder Room. It's beautifully done out, with dark panelled wainscoting, handsome William Morris wallpaper under a high delft shelf, sweeping heavy red curtains and a handful of attractive period dining tables with good chairs and a built-in wall settle. The beamed bar on the left has a woodburning stove in the terracotta-tiled front part, a big fireplace beneath a wall hanging at the back, a couple of rugs on the boards there, and a mix of pews, a winged settle and other seats around old stripped tables. Centre of attraction is the serving counter, with local farm cider, and changing ales on handpump: their own Mill Green White Horse Bitter, Mawkin Mild and a couple of changing guests plus a seasonal guest from Adnams and Crouch Vale Brewers Gold; also, 11 wines by the glass, several malt whiskies and their own cider. This is sister pub to the White Horse, Edwardstone.

Very good food includes lunchtime sandwiches, spicy crab fritters with sweet chilli sauce, caesar salad with herb croutons, sausages with mash and onion gravy, steak or vegetable burger with toppings and sweet potato fries or skinny chips, chicken in a champagne cream sauce, beer-battered fish and chips, and puddings such as crème brûlée and apple crumble. *Benchmark main dish: slow-roasted pork belly £12.50. Two-course evening meal £18.00.*

Free house ~ Licensees Jarred and Clare Harris ~ Real ale ~ (01787) 211183 ~ Open 12-3, 5-11; 12-midnight Fri, Sat; 12-11 Sun ~ Bar food 12-2 (2.30 weekends), 6-9; not Sun evening or Mon ~ Restaurant ~ Children welcome away from bar ~ Dogs welcome ~ Wi-fi ~ Live folk third Fri of month ~ www.boxfordfleece.com *Recommended by Mrs Margo Finlay, Jörg Kasprowski, Giles and Annie Francis*

BURY ST EDMUNDS
Old Cannon 🍺 🛏

TL8564   Map 5

Cannon Street, just off A134/A1101 roundabout at N end of town; IP33 1JR

Busy own-brew town pub with local drinks and interesting bar food; bedrooms

The brewery in this Victorian townhouse is actually in the bar. There are two huge gleaming stainless-steel brewing vessels and views up to a steel balustraded open-plan malt floor above the counter, where they serve their own Old Cannon Best, Gunner's Daughter and seasonal ales such as Blonde Bombshell, Brass Monkey and Hornblower, plus guests such as Adnams Bitter, Calvors Smooth Hoperator and Marstons EPA on handpump; also, ten wines by the glass and carefully chosen spirits. A row of chunky old bar stools line the ochre-painted counter, and there's an appealing assortment of old and new chairs and tables and upholstered banquettes on well worn bare boards; background music. The comfortable bedrooms are in the old brewhouse across the courtyard. Behind, through the old coach arch, is a good-sized cobbled courtyard with hanging baskets and stylish metal tables and chairs.

Rewarding food includes lunchtime sandwiches, potato, spring onion and tarragon hash with a fried duck egg, grilled sardines and tapenade on toast, broccoli and roasted red peppers in a lemon cream sauce with cashews and pasta, a proper fish pie with cheddar mash, beer-battered fish and chips, sweet chilli chicken stir-fry, and puddings such as a cheesecake of the day and dark chocolate mousse with white chocolate cookie; they also offer a good value three-course set menu (not Sunday). *Benchmark main dish: toad in the hole with colcannon and onion gravy £13.75. Two-course evening meal £19.00.*

Own brew ~ Licensee Garry Clark ~ Real ale ~ (01284) 768769 ~ Open 12-11 (10.30 Sun) ~ Bar food 12-9; 12-3 Sun ~ Restaurant ~ Children in restaurant but only if eating ~ Wi-fi ~ Bedrooms: £90/£120 ~ www.oldcannonbrewery.co.uk *Recommended by PL, Barry Collett*

The 🍺 symbol shows pubs that keep their beer unusually well, have a particularly good range or brew their own.

 CHELMONDISTON   TM2037   Map 5

Butt & Oyster

Pin Mill – signposted from B1456 SE of Ipswich; continue to bottom of road; IP9 1JW

Chatty old riverside pub with pleasant views, good food and drink and seats on the terrace

'We've been coming here for 30 years and still love it,' says one reader, and you can't get better praise than that. A simple old bargeman's pub (named for the flounders and oysters that used to be caught here), it has fine views over the bustling River Orwell from seats on the terrace or by the windows in the bar. The half-panelled little smoke room is pleasantly worn and unfussy with high-backed and other old-fashioned settles on the tiled floor. There's also a two-level dining room with country kitchen furniture on bare boards and pictures and boat-related artefacts on the walls above the dado. Adnams Southwold and Lighthouse and guests tapped from the cask by friendly, efficient staff, several wines by the glass and local cider; board games. The annual Thames Barge Race (end June/early July) is fun. The car park can fill up pretty quickly.

With an emphasis on fresh fish, the enjoyable food includes lunchtime sandwiches, scallops and chorizo with salad, king prawns in garlic butter, seafood risotto and fish stew, but they also offer non-fishy dishes such as vegetable, chicken, pork or beef burger with toppings and chips, local sausages with mash and gravy and chicken marinated in lemon and rosemary, plus puddings such as lemon tart and sticky toffee pudding. *Benchmark main dish: beer-battered cod and chips £10.95. Two-course evening meal £17.00.*

Adnams ~ Lease Steve Lomas ~ Real ale ~ (01473) 780764 ~ Open 11 (9am weekends)-11 ~ Bar food 12-9.30 ~ Restaurant ~ Children welcome in dining rooms ~ Dogs allowed in bar ~ Wi-fi ~ www.debeninns.co.uk/buttandoyster *Recommended by Mrs Carolyn Dixon, Roger and Anne Newbury, Steve and Irene Homer, Pat and Tony Martin, Dennis and Doreen Haward, Mrs Margo Finlay, Jörg Kasprowski*

 DUNWICH   TM4770   Map 5

Ship

St James Street; IP17 3DT

Friendly, well run and pleasantly traditional pub in a coastal village, tasty bar food and local ales; bedrooms

Just a stone's throw from the sea, this informal and relaxed pub is handy for some of the best coast paths in Suffolk; you'll get a warm welcome from the licensee and his friendly staff and dogs may be given a treat and a bowl of water. The traditionally furnished main bar has benches, pews, captain's chairs and wooden tables on a tiled floor, a woodburning stove (left open in cold weather) and lots of sea prints. Adnams Bitter and a couple of changing guests are served from antique handpumps at the handsomely panelled bar counter, as well as several wines by the glass; board games. A simple conservatory looks on to a back terrace, and the large garden is very pleasant, with well spaced picnic-sets, two large anchors and an enormous fig tree (they may have Shakespeare performances here in August). Our readers enjoy staying here and the breakfasts are hearty. The RSPB reserve at Minsmere and nearby Dunwich Museum are worth visiting and there's more walking in Dunwich Forest.

🍴 Interesting, well liked food includes ham hock terrine with pickled courgettes and a free-range egg, home-smoked duck breast, thyme shallots and apple and celeriac coleslaw, cranberry and nut roast with roasted root vegetables and baked field mushroom, pork sausages with crispy onion rings, gravy and mash, slow-braised ox cheeks and bone marrow fritter with cauliflower cheese, bass fillet with home-made pasta and pickled vegetables, and puddings such as knickerbocker glory and chocolate torte. *Benchmark main dish: slow-cooked pork belly with date and apple purée £13.95. Two-course evening meal £18.50.*

Free house ~ Licensee Matt Goodwin ~ Real ale ~ (01728) 648219 ~ Open 7.30am-11pm; 12-10.30 Sun ~ Bar food 12-3, 6-9; 12-9 Fri-Sun ~ Restaurant evening only ~ Children welcome away from bar ~ Dogs allowed in bar and bedrooms ~ Wi-fi ~ Live music last Thurs of month ~ Bedrooms: £65/£97.50 ~ www.shipatdunwich.co.uk
Recommended by David and Judy Robison

EASTBRIDGE
TM4566 Map 5

Eels Foot 🛏
Off B1122 N of Leiston; IP16 4SN

Country local with hospitable atmosphere, fair value food using their own eggs, and Thursday evening folk sessions; bedrooms

Our readers enjoy staying in the comfortable, attractive and quiet bedrooms in the separate building here (one room has wheelchair access); the breakfasts are very good too. It's a friendly, simple pub: the upper and lower parts of the bar have light modern furnishings on stripped wood floors, a warming fire, Adnams Southwold, Broadside, Ghost Ship and Lighthouse and a changing guest on handpump, 11 wines by the glass, several malt whiskies and a farm cider; darts in a side area, board games, cribbage and a neat back dining room. There are seats on the terrace and benches out in the lovely big back garden. RSPB Minsmere is nearby and the inn borders the freshwater marshes where there's an abundance of birds and butterflies; a footpath leads directly to the sea. It does get busy in summer.

🍴 Enjoyable food includes lunchtime sandwiches, ham and egg, beef or vegetarian cannelloni, local sausages with mash and gravy, winter casseroles, various pies, beer-battered line-caught fish and chips, and puddings such as rhubarb crumble and sticky toffee pudding. *Benchmark main dish: lasagne with garlic bread £9.95. Two-course evening meal £16.50.*

Adnams ~ Tenant Julian Wallis ~ Real ale ~ (01728) 830154 ~ Open 12-3, 6-11; 12-11 Fri; 11.30-11 Sat; 12-10.30 Sun ~ Bar food 12-2.30, 6.30-9 ~ Children welcome ~ Dogs welcome ~ Wi-fi ~ Live folk music Thurs evening and last Sun of month ~ Bedrooms: £80/£99 ~ www.theeelsfootinn.co.uk *Recommended by Anthony Barnes, Roy Hoing, Peter Meister, Pat and Alan Timmon, Giles and Annie Francis*

EDWARDSTONE
TL9542 Map 5

White Horse 🍺
Mill Green, just E; village signed off A1071 in Boxford; CO10 5PX

Own-brew pub with traditional furnishings in simple rooms, hearty food, self-catering and a campsite

The own-brewed Mill Green ales served in this unpretentious village local continue to draw in cheerful customers. On handpump or tapped from the cask, these might include White Horse Bitter, Green Goose and Mawkin Mild with guest ales such as Dark Star American Pale Ale and Woodfordes

Wherry; also, several wines by the glass and malt whiskies. Several bar rooms of various sizes include a tiny one with just one table and lots of beer mats on the walls. The floors are bare boards throughout, the cream walls above a pink dado are hung with rustic prints and photographs, and there's a mix of second-hand tables and chairs including an old steamer bench and panelled settle, and both a woodburner and an open fire; background music, darts, bar billiards, ring the bull, quoits, dominoes, cards and board games. Outside, there are sturdy teak tables and seats on an end terrace, an attractive smokers' shelter with green panelled seating, and some makeshift picnic-sets on a grassy area. The self-catering 'cottages' are rather scandinavian in style, and there's a campsite with shower block. This is sister pub to the Fleece at Boxford.

🍴 Well liked food includes lunchtime sandwiches, lemon sole goujons with sweet chilli dip, smoked duck and bacon salad, honey-roast ham and eggs, broad bean, pea and rocket risotto, local pheasant in cider with wholegrain mustard mash and celeriac purée, pike fillet with pickled shiitake mushrooms and roasted rosemary potatoes, and puddings such as triple- chocolate brownie and sugar and spice crème brûlée. *Benchmark main dish: rare-breed burger with chutney and chips £9.95. Two-course evening meal £15.00.*

Own brew ~ Licensee Natasha Long ~ Real ale ~ (01787) 211211 ~ Open 12-midnight (11 Sun, Mon); 12-3, 5-11 Mon-Thurs in winter ~ Bar food 12-3, 6-9; 12-3.30 Sun; not Mon ~ Restaurant ~ Children welcome in bar until 6pm ~ Dogs welcome ~ Wi-fi ~ Live folk and blues sessions monthly ~ Bedrooms: /£90 ~ www.edwardstonewhitehorse.co.uk
Recommended by Giles and Annie Francis

IPSWICH   TM1844 Map 5

Fat Cat 🍺

Spring Road, opposite junction with Nelson Road (best bet for parking is up there); IP4 5NL

Fantastic range of changing real ales in a well run town pub; garden

As ever, the fantastic range of up to 16 real ales on handpump or tapped from the cask in this warmly friendly and cheerful town pub continues to draw the crowds. Coming from across the country, the ales might include Adnams Southwold, Broadside and Old, Crouch Vale Brewers Gold and Yakima Gold, Earl Soham Victoria, Elgoods Black Dog, Fat Cat Mocha Moggy Stout and Wild Cat, Green Jack Orange Wheat Beer and Old Cock Old Ale, Hop Back Summer Lightning, Oakham Inferno, Sharps Doom Bar and Woodfordes Wherry. They also stock quite a few belgian bottled beers, farm cider and seven wines by the glass. The bars have bare floorboards, a mix of café and bar stools, unpadded wall benches and cushioned seats around cast-iron and wooden pub tables, and lots of enamel brewery signs and posters on canary-yellow walls; board games and shove-ha'penny. There's also a spacious back conservatory and several picnic-sets on the terrace and lawn. Very little nearby parking. Well behaved dogs are welcome but must be kept on a lead.

🍴 They keep a supply of baguettes, spicy scotch eggs and pasties made in their small kitchen and are happy for you to bring in takeaway food (not Friday or Saturday).

Free house ~ Licensees John and Ann Keatley ~ Real ale ~ No credit cards ~ (01473) 726524 ~ Open 12 (11 Sat)-11 ~ Bar food all day while it lasts ~ www.fatcatipswich.co.uk
Recommended by Richard Kramer, Edward May, Mike Swan, Peter Brix

LINDSEY TYE

TL9846   Map 5

Red Rose ♀

Village signposted off A1141 NW of Hadleigh; IP7 6PP

15th-c hall house with a couple of neat bars, enjoyable popular food, real ales and plenty of outside seating

A firm favourite with both locals and visitors, this handsome hall house remains as consistently well run and friendly as ever. The neatly kept main bar has low beams, some standing timbers and an assortment of wooden tables and chairs. In front of a splendid log fire in an old brick fireplace are a couple of squashy red leather sofas, a low table and some brass measuring jugs. A second room is furnished in a similar way and also has a big brick fireplace, but is much simpler in feel and perhaps quieter. Adnams Southwold and Ghost Ship and Mauldons Bitter on handpump and 11 wines by the glass. There are flowering tubs and a few picnic-sets in front, with more picnic-sets at the back – where there's also a children's play area and a football pitch.

 Using their own meat and other local ingredients, the good, popular food includes lunchtime sandwiches, garlic mushrooms with blue cheese, thai fishcakes with sweet chilli sauce, vegetable curry, cumberland sausage with rosemary mash and red wine jus, beer-battered haddock and chips, duck breast with thyme mash and shallot purée, and puddings such as treacle tart with custard and sticky toffee pudding; they offer a two- and three-course set menu on Sunday. *Benchmark main dish: rare-breed burger with blue cheese, bacon and chips £12.00. Two-course evening meal £19.00.*

Free house ~ Licensee Peter Miller ~ Real ale ~ (01449) 741424 ~ Open 11-3, 5-11; 11-11 Sat; 11-10.30 Sun; 11-3, 5-11 weekends in winter ~ Bar food 12-2.30, 6-9.30; 12-3, 7-9 Sun; 12-4 Sun in winter ~ Children welcome ~ Dogs welcome ~ Wi-fi ~ www.thelindseyrose.co.uk *Recommended by Steve Stagg, Mrs Carolyn Dixon*

LONG MELFORD

TL8646   Map 5

Black Lion ✪ ♀ 🛏

Church Walk; CO10 9DN

Well appointed hotel with relaxed and comfortable bar, modern bar food, attentive staff and seats in pretty garden; bedrooms

This is a comfortable and civilised hotel rather than a straightforward pub – but our readers enjoy their visits here very much. The back bar, where locals tend to drop in for just a drink and a chat, has two comfortable sofas and leather winged armchairs, an open fire and serves Adnams Southwold on handpump and 18 wines by the glass; background music. The red-walled dining room has attractive chairs around handsome candlelit tables on tartan carpet, another open fire and heavy swagged curtains; the windows overlook the village green. You can take afternoon tea in the appealing Victorian walled garden and the individually decorated bedrooms are appealing and well equipped; breakfasts are particularly good.

Interesting food includes open sandwiches, potted Estate rabbit with pickled mushrooms, cod cheek fritters with saffron aioli, free-range chicken kiev with parsley sauce, cannelloni of spinach, ricotta and nutmeg butter, rack of lamb with rosemary potatoes and red wine sauce, rainbow trout with brown shrimp butter and seaweed, and puddings such as chocolate marquise with white chocolate sauce and caramelised lemon tart; they also offer a two- and three-course set menu. *Benchmark main dish: beer-battered fish and chips £14.00. Two-course evening meal £24.00.*

Ravenwood Group ~ Licensee Craig Jarvis ~ Real ale ~ (01787) 312356 ~ Open 7.30am (8.30am weekends)-11pm ~ Bar food 7.30am (8.30am weekends)-9.30am, 12-2, 7-9.30 (10 Fri, Sat, 9 Sun) ~ Restaurant ~ Children welcome ~ Dogs allowed in bar and bedrooms ~ Wi-fi ~ Bedrooms: £113/£150 ~ www.blacklionhotel.net
Recommended by Paul and Marion Watts, Mrs Carolyn Dixon, Mrs Margo Finlay, Jörg Kasprowski

 MIDDLETON   TM4267   Map 5

Bell ⚐ £

Off A12 in Yoxford via B1122 towards Leiston, also signposted off B1125 Leiston–Westleton; The Street; IP17 3NN

Thatch and low beams, friendly chef-landlord, good beer and popular good value food – a peaceful spot

In a quiet village location overlooked by the church's grand flint tower, this is a cheerful, bustling pub with a warm welcome from the character landlord. On the left, the traditional bar has a log fire in a big hearth, old local photographs, a low plank-panelled ceiling, bar stools and pew seating, Adnams Southwold, Broadside and Ghost Ship tapped from the cask and nine wines by the glass. On the right, an informal two-room carpeted lounge/dining area has padded mate's and library chairs around dark tables under low black beams, with pews by a big woodburning stove and modern seaside brewery prints. Dogs are welcomed with treats and a bowl of water. It's a pretty cream-washed building, with picnic-sets under cocktail parasols out in front, and camping available in the broad meadow behind. The RSPB Minsmere reserve is nearby, as are walks along the coast.

🍴 Generous helpings of good value food includes lunchtime sandwiches, sausages and mash, ham and egg, liver and bacon, a vegetarian dish, confit duck leg and breast with roast pear and sweet orange gravy, and daily specials. *Benchmark main dish: beer-battered cod and chips £9.50. Two-course evening meal £15.00.*

Adnams ~ Tenants Nicholas and Trish Musgrove ~ Real ale ~ (01728) 648286 ~ Open 12-3, 6-11; 12-midnight Sat; 12-10.30 Sun; closed Mon lunchtime ~ Bar food 12-2.15, 6-9.15; 12-5 Sun; not Mon ~ Restaurant ~ Well behaved children allowed away from bar ~ Dogs allowed in bar *Recommended by Stephen and Jean Curtis, R L Borthwick, Peter Meister*

 PETTISTREE   TM2954   Map 5

Greyhound

The Street; brown sign to pub off B1438 S of Wickham Market, 0.5 miles N of A12; IP13 0HP

Neatly kept village pub with enjoyable food and drink

This enjoyable pub run by hard-working, friendly licensees has just two smallish rooms, so it's worth booking in advance to be sure of a table. They keep Earl Soham Victoria Bitter and guests such as Adnams Ghost Ship and Earl Soham Brandeston Gold on handpump, several wines by the glass and quite a few malt whiskies, and there are open fires, some rather low beams, chunky farmhouse chairs and cushioned settles around dark wooden tables on the bare floorboards and candlelight. The well kept side garden has picnic-sets under parasols, with more beside the gravelled front car park; the village church is next door.

🍴 Cooked by the landlady using local, seasonal produce, the highly thought-of food includes ciabattas, pheasant and black pudding terrine with beetroot relish, crab and prawn cocktail, basil gnocchi with sun-dried tomato pesto and roasted peppers, gammon and egg, hake and salmon fishcake with roasted fennel, wild scottish venison sausages with onion gravy, and puddings such as chocolate brownie with chantilly cream and lemon posset with poached rhubarb. *Benchmark main dish: slow-roasted pork belly in cider with black pudding, bubble and squeak and cider gravy £12.95. Two-course evening meal £18.00.*

Free house ~ Licensees Stewart and Louise McKenzie ~ Real ale ~ (01728) 746451 ~ Open 12-3, 6-11; 12-4, 7-10.30 Sun; closed Mon and two weeks Jan ~ Bar food 12-3, 6-9; not Sun evening or Mon ~ Restaurant ~ Children welcome ~ Dogs allowed in bar ~ www.greyhoundinnpettistree.co.uk *Recommended by Paul Whayman, Richard Kevern*

REDE
Plough
TL8055 Map 5

Village signposted off A143 Bury St Edmunds–Haverhill; IP29 4BE

Well liked and promptly served food in a 16th-c pub, several wines by the glass and friendly service

At the end of a quiet green in a tucked-away village is this quaint, partly thatched pink-washed pub. The pretty bar is traditional with low beams, comfortable seating and a solid-fuel stove in a brick fireplace, and they keep Fullers London Pride, Harveys Best, Sharps Doom Bar and Timothy Taylors Landlord on handpump and several wines by the glass; background music. There are picnic-sets in the sheltered cottagey garden and at the front near the green.

 Well liked food includes a changing pâté, black pudding fritters with onion chutney, carpaccio of wild boar topped with parmesan, honey-roast vegetables with puy lentil casserole, ham, egg and chips, chicken and porcini mushrooms with pasta, calves liver and bacon, moroccan-spiced lamb tagine, and puddings such as blueberry and apple tart and vanilla panna cotta with rhubarb compote. *Benchmark main dish: monkfish creole £12.95. Two-course evening meal £18.00.*

Admiral Taverns ~ Tenant Brian Desborough ~ Real ale ~ (01284) 789208 ~ Open 11-3, 6.30-11.30; 12-3, 7-11 Sun ~ Bar food 12-2, 7-9; 12-3 Sun ~ Restaurant ~ Children welcome until 8pm *Recommended by Mrs Margo Finlay, Jörg Kasprowski, Mike and Lynne Steane*

SIBTON
White Horse 🌟 ⌷ 🛏
TM3570 Map 5

Halesworth Road/Hubbard's Hill, N of Peasenhall; IP17 2JJ

Suffolk Dining Pub of the Year

Particularly well run inn with nicely old-fashioned bar, good mix of customers, real ales and imaginative food

As well as being a proper village pub with a good local following, run by genuinely friendly, hands-on licensees, this place offers first class food and comfortable bedrooms. The appealing bar has a roaring log fire in a large inglenook fireplace, horsebrasses and tack on the walls, old settles and pews, and they serve Adnams Southwold, Green Jack Trawlerboys Best Bitter and Woodfordes Nelsons Revenge on handpump, nine wines by the glass and 15 malt whiskies from an old oak-panelled counter. They hold beer festivals in June and August, and a viewing panel reveals the working cellar and its ancient floor. Steps lead up past an ancient partly knocked-through timbered wall into a carpeted gallery, and there's a smart dining room and a secluded (and popular) dining terrace. The big garden has plenty of seats.

Using produce from their kitchen garden, the appealing food includes sandwiches, eggs benedict, chicken and chorizo terrine with roasted red pepper and balsamic salsa, caramelised potato, apricot and onion tagine with cucumber and yoghurt, steak and kidney pudding, red mullet fillets with mediterranean vegetable ratatouille and basil pesto, pork belly with madeira cream sauce and dauphinoise potatoes, and puddings such as toffee apple crumble and chocolate and hazelnut meringue with raspberry coulis; they also offer a two- and three-course set lunch (Tuesday-Saturday). *Benchmark main dish: beer-battered fresh cod and chips £11.95. Two-course evening meal £21.00.*

Free house ~ Licensees Neil and Gill Mason ~ Real ale ~ (01728) 660337 ~ Open 12-3, 6.30 (6 Sat)-11; 12-3.30, 6.45-10.30 Sun; closed Mon lunchtime ~ Bar food 12-2, 6.30-9; 12-2.30, 7-8.30 Sun ~ Restaurant ~ Well behaved children welcome but must be over 6 in evening and over 12 for accommodation ~ Dogs allowed in bar ~ Wi-fi ~ Bedrooms: $80/$90 ~ www.sibtonwhitehorseinn.co.uk *Recommended by R L Borthwick, Mark Barker, M and J White, Simon Rodway, David Jackman, Robert Turnham*

SOUTHWOLD
Crown 🌟 🍷 🍺 🛏

TM5076 Map 5

High Street; IP18 6DP

Comfortable hotel with relaxed bars, a fine choice of drinks, excellent imaginative food and seats outside; lovely bedrooms

Busy and friendly all day from 8am for breakfast, this remains a smart and civilised hotel and 'as excellent as always' according to one reader. You can be sure of a courteous welcome from the staff. Although there are plenty of seating areas, many customers are very fond of the cosy, oak-panelled back locals' bar (reserved for drinkers and where dogs are allowed) with its proper pubby atmosphere and red leatherette wall benches on red carpeting. Also, Adnams Southwold, Broadside and Ghost Ship on handpump, 14 wines by the glass from a splendid list, ten malt whiskies and several hand-crafted spirits. The elegant beamed front bar has a relaxed, informal atmosphere, a stripped curved high-backed settle and other dark varnished settles, kitchen and other chairs, and a carefully restored rather fine carved wooden fireplace; maybe newspapers to read. The outdoor tables in a sunny sheltered corner are very pleasant and this is a special place to stay, with delicious breakfasts.

 First class food includes lunchtime sandwiches, confit duck terrine with cucumber and soy, vodka gravadlax with pickled clams and grapefruit salad, sharing boards, chargrilled spiced vegetables with moroccan-style couscous, prawn spaghetti with tomato, lemon and chilli, fishcake with a poached egg and beurre blanc, beer-battered plaice and chips, corn-fed chicken supreme with blue cheese, garlic and bacon, and puddings such as chocolate and banana brûlée and lemon and ricotta tart with honey and thyme ice-cream. *Benchmark main dish: rump of beef with dripping chips and béarnaise sauce £19.95. Two-course evening meal £24.00.*

Adnams ~ Manager Jenny Knights ~ Real ale ~ (01502) 722275 ~ Open 8am-11pm (10.30pm Sun) ~ Bar food 12-2 (2.30 weekends), 6.30 (6 Sat)-9 ~ Children welcome ~ Dogs allowed in bar ~ Wi-fi ~ Bedrooms: $135/$205 ~ www.adnams.co.uk/hotels/the-crown *Recommended by Colin McLachlan, W K Wood, David Carr, Roger Fox, M and GR, Sheila Topham, Ian Herdman*

People named as recommenders after the full entries have told us that the pub should be included. But they have not written the report – we have, after anonymous on-the-spot inspection.

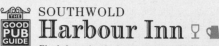 SOUTHWOLD TM4975 Map 5

Harbour Inn ♀ ◖

Blackshore, by the boats; from A1095, turn right at the Kings Head, and keep on past the golf course and water tower; IP18 6TA

Great spot down by the boats, lots of outside tables – interesting interior too; popular food with emphasis on local seafood

No matter how deservedly busy this old fisherman's pub is, service remains friendly and efficient. It's in a fine location overlooking the boats on the Blyth estuary and the picnic-sets on the front terrace, by a big cannon, make the most of this view; there are also seats and tables behind the pub, looking over the marshy commons to the town. The back bar is nicely nautical, with dark panelling and built-in wall seats around scrubbed tables; the low ceiling is draped with ensigns, signal flags, pennants and a line strung with ancient dried fish, and there's a quaint old stove, rope fancywork, a plethora of local fishing photographs and even portholes with water bubbling behind them. Cheerful staff serve 16 wines by the glass, along with Adnams Southwold, Broadside, Ghost Ship and Mosaic on handpump. They have their own weather station for walkers and sailors. The lower front bar, with a tiled floor and panelling, is broadly similar, while the large, elevated dining room has panoramic views of the harbour, lighthouse, brewery and churches beyond the marshes. You can walk from here along the estuary to Walberswick (where the Bell is under the same good management as this pub) via a footbridge and return by the one-man ferry.

 Good, enjoyable food includes lunchtime sandwiches, numerous little tapas-style dishes such as thai-style whelks, home-made scotch quails eggs and sticky pork ribs, as well as vegetarian moussaka, clam, king prawn and smoked haddock chowder, pizzas from the wood-fired oven, dressed Cromer crab, half a grilled chicken with coleslaw and chips, skate wing with caper and almond butter, moroccan-style lamb curry, and puddings such as bakewell tart and knickerbocker glory. *Benchmark main dish: beer-battered fresh cod and chips £11.00. Two-course evening meal £16.00.*

Adnams ~ Tenant Nick Attfield ~-Real ale ~ (01502) 722381 ~ Open 11-11 ~ Bar food 12-9 ~ Children welcome away from top bar ~ Dogs allowed in bar ~ Folk singers second Thurs of month, shindig first and third Sun of month ~ www.harbourinnsouthwold.co.uk
Recommended by Martin and Pauline Jennings, Rita Scarratt, Peter Meister, Pat and Tony Martin, Ian Herdman

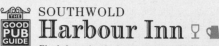 SOUTHWOLD TM5076 Map 5

Lord Nelson ◖ £

East Street, off High Street (A1095); IP18 6EJ

Bow-windowed town pub with long-serving owners, well liked pubby food and a good choice of drinks; seats outside

As ever, this well run, seafront pub remains incredibly busy at any time of the year. The cheerful crowd of customers (often with their dogs) are quickly served by the efficient staff, and the partly panelled traditional bar and its two small side rooms are kept spotless. There's good lighting, a small but extremely hot coal fire, light wood furniture on a tiled floor, lamps in nice nooks and corners and some interesting Nelson memorabilia, including interesting nautical prints and a fine model of HMS *Victory*. They serve the whole range of Adnams beers alongside 12 wines by the glass and several malt whiskies; board games. There are seats out in front with a sidelong view of the sea, and more in a sheltered (and heated) back garden, with the Adnams brewery in sight (and often the appetising fragrance of brewing in progress). Disabled access is not perfect but is possible.

🍴 Very fairly priced and tasty, the food includes lunchtime sandwiches, chicken liver pâté with redcurrant jam, cod fishcakes with sun-dried tomato mayonnaise, chicken caesar salad, rump burger with bacon, cheese and chips, vegetable thai green curry, lamb tagine with saffron rice, bass with chive and brown shrimp butter, and puddings such as apple crumble and maple and walnut bread and butter pudding. *Benchmark main dish: beer-battered cod and chips £10.25. Two-course evening meal £16.00.*

Adnams ~ Tenants David and Gemma Sanchez ~ Real ale ~ (01502) 722079 ~ Open 10.30am-11pm; 12-10.30 Sun ~ Bar food 12-2, 6.30-9 ~ Children welcome in snug and family room ~ Dogs welcome ~ www.thelordnelsonsouthwold.co.uk
Recommended by R J Herd, Sheila Topham, Conrad Freezer, David Carr, C A Bryson, Richard Symonds, Barry Collett, Roger and Anne Newbury, Rita Scarratt, Pat and Tony Martin, Tracey and Stephen Groves, MDN, David Jackman, Ian Herdman, N R White

STOKE-BY-NAYLAND
TL9836   Map 5

Crown ★ 🎖 � 🛏

Park Street (B1068); CO6 4SE

Smart dining pub with attractive modern furnishings, imaginative food using local produce, real ales and a great wine choice; good bedrooms

There's always a good mix of both drinkers and diners in this civilised pub and the atmosphere is relaxed and chatty. The extensive open-plan dining bar is well laid out to give several distinct-feeling areas: a sofa and easy chairs on flagstones near the serving counter, a couple more armchairs under heavy beams by the big woodburning stove, one sizeable table tucked nicely into a three-sided built-in seat and a lower side room with more beams and cheerful floral wallpaper. Tables are mostly stripped veterans, with high-backed dining chairs, but there are more modern chunky pine tables at the back; contemporary artworks (mostly for sale) and daily papers. Friendly and informally dressed staff bustle happily about, and they keep Adnams Southwold, Crouch Vale Brewers Gold, Dark Star American Pale Ale and Woodfordes Wherry on handpump and Aspall's cider. Wine is a big plus, with three dozen by the glass and hundreds more from the glass-walled 'cellar shop' in one corner – you can buy there to take away too. The sheltered flagstoned back terrace has comfortable teak furniture, with heaters, big terracotta-coloured parasols and a peaceful view over rolling, lightly wooded countryside. Beyond is the very well equipped separate bedroom block (breakfasts are first class); good disabled access. The pretty village is worth exploring.

🎖 Excellent food includes pigeon, bacon, shallot and pistachio salad, twice-baked cheese soufflé, chicken and chestnut pie, crab, leek and crème fraîche tart with saffron aioli, cod fillet with mussels, wild garlic and lemon cream, venison and prune casserole with herb dumplings, lamb rump with cockles and port sauce, and puddings such as profiteroles with chocolate and orange sauce and lemon panna cotta with lemon curd doughnuts. *Benchmark main dish: beer-battered haddock and chips £13.95. Two-course evening meal £20.00.*

Free house ~ Licensee Richard Sunderland ~ Real ale ~ (01206) 262001 ~ Open 11-11; 12-10.30 Sun ~ Bar food 12-2.30, 6-9.30 (10 Fri, Sat); all day Sun ~ Children welcome ~ Dogs allowed in bar ~ Wi-fi ~ Bedrooms: £95/£130 ~ www.crowninn.net
Recommended by J F M and M West, N R White, Mrs Carolyn Dixon, Gerry and Rosemary Dobson, Mrs Margo Finlay, Jörg Kasprowski, Jocelyn Matheson, MDN

WALBERSWICK

TM4974 Map 5

Anchor ♀ ⇐

The Street (B1387); village signed off A12; IP18 6UA

Friendly, bustling pub with plenty of space for both drinking and dining, particularly good food and thoughtful choice of drinks; bedrooms

Although many customers come to this 1920s place to enjoy the highly thought-of food, it also has a simply furnished front bar where they keep Adnams Southwold, Broadside, Ghost Ship and a changing guest on handpump, 40 bottled beers and a fine choice of wines by the glass. This room, divided into snug halves by a two-way open fire, has big windows, heavy stripped tables on original oak flooring, sturdy built-in green leather wall seats and nicely framed black and white fishermen photographs on colourwashed panelling; daily papers and board games. The extensive dining area stretches back from a small more modern-feeling lounge. There are plenty of seats in the pretty garden and an outdoor bar serving the flagstoned terrace. As well as the coast path there's a pleasant walk across to Southwold. There are bedrooms in the main house and six spacious chalet-style rooms in the garden with sea or beach hut and sand dune views.

Using local, seasonal produce, the rewarding food includes game, pistachio and prune terrine with apple chutney, beetroot-cured gravadlax with celeriac rémoulade and horseradish mousse, beer-battered cod and chips, slow-roasted lamb shoulder with gnocchi, asparagus and mint, crab linguine with chilli, rib-eye steak with green peppercorn sauce, and puddings such as chocolate fondant with salted caramel ice-cream and banana fritters with toffee sauce. *Benchmark main dish: fishcakes with aioli £14.75. Two-course evening meal £21.00.*

Adnams ~ Lease Mark and Sophie Dorber ~ Real ale ~ (01502) 722112 ~ Open 11-11 ~ Bar food 12-3, 6-9 ~ Restaurant ~ Children welcome ~ Dogs allowed in bar and bedrooms ~ Bedrooms: £120/£145 ~ www.anchoratwalberswick.com *Recommended by David Howe, Alan Cowell, Andrew Gardner, Ryta Lyndley, John Warbey, Tracey and Stephen Groves*

WALBERSWICK

TM4974 Map 5

Bell 🏮 ♀ ◖ ⇐

Just off B1387; IP18 6TN

Interesting and thriving 16th-c inn with good food and drinks choice, friendly atmosphere and nice garden; cosy bedrooms

With a lovely, chatty atmosphere and plenty of customers, this well run inn is much enjoyed by our readers. The charming rambling bar has antique curved settles, cushioned pews and window seats, scrubbed tables and two huge fireplaces (one with an elderly woodburning stove watched over by a pair of staffordshire china dogs); fine old flooring encompasses sagging ancient bricks, broad boards, flagstones and black and red tiles. Friendly staff serve 16 good wines by the glass, several malt whiskies and Adnams Southwold, Broadside, Ghost Ship and Mosaic on handpump; background music. Don't miss the classic *New Yorker* wine cartoons in the lavatories. The Barn Café is open during the school holidays for light snacks, cakes, teas and so forth. A big, neatly planted sheltered garden behind has smart oak tables and chairs under blue parasols and a view over the dunes to the sea; the rowing-boat ferry to Southwold is nearby (there's a footbridge a bit further away). The bedrooms, some with sea or harbour views, are attractively decorated, and breakfasts are good. This is sister pub to the Harbour Inn in Southwold.

Using local fish and free-range meat, the rewarding food includes lunchtime sandwiches, smoked haddock in cheese sauce, baked camembert with rosemary, garlic and sea salt and cranberry sauce, a pie and a curry of the week, rump burger with cheese, tomato chutney and chips, mediterranean-style fish stew, confit duck leg with cock-a-leekie-style potato bake, and puddings such as baked alaska with pistachio ice-cream and warm chocolate and walnut brownie with cinnamon ice-cream. *Benchmark main dish: steak in ale pie £12.00. Two-course evening meal £18.50.*

Adnams ~ Tenant Nick Attfield ~ Real ale ~ (01502) 723109 ~ Open 11-11 ~ Bar food 12-2.30, 6-9 ~ Children welcome away from bar ~ Dogs allowed in bar and bedrooms ~ Wi-fi ~ Bedrooms: £80/£95 ~ www.bellinnwalberswick.co.uk
Recommended by Conrad Freezer, R L Borthwick, Tracey and Stephen Groves, N R White

WALDRINGFIELD
Maybush £

TM2844 Map 5

Off A12 S of Martlesham; The Quay, Cliff Road; IP12 4QL

Busy pub with tables outside by the riverbank; nautical décor and a fair choice of drinks and good value traditional bar food

With access to a sandy beach and lovely views over the River Deben, it makes sense for this busy family pub to be open – and serve food – all day; plenty of picnic-sets look over the water and, if you arrive early enough, you might be lucky to get a window table inside. The spacious knocked-through bar is divided into separate areas by fireplaces or steps. There's a nautical theme, with an elaborate ship's model in a glass case and a few more in a light, high-ceilinged extension – as well as lots of old lanterns, pistols and aerial photographs; background music and board games. Adnams Southwold, Broadside and Ghost Ship on handpump and a fair choice of wines by the glass. River cruises are available nearby, though you have to pre-book; this is a haven for bird-watchers and ramblers.

Popular food includes sandwiches, shredded gressingham duck pancakes with hoi sin sauce, cucumber and spring onions, breaded garlic mushrooms with garlic mayonnaise dip, sharing platters, lamb, pork, cajun chicken, beef or vegetarian burger with toppings and chips, barbecue chicken with bacon and cheese, gammon and free-range egg, bass fillets topped with garlic prawns, and puddings such as chocolate brownie and lemon lush. *Benchmark main dish: beer-battered fresh cod and chips £10.95. Two-course evening meal £18.00.*

Adnams ~ Lease Steve and Louise Lomas ~ Real ale ~ (01473) 736215 ~ Open 9am-11pm ~ Bar food 9am-9.30pm ~ Restaurant ~ Children welcome ~ Dogs allowed in bar ~ Wi-fi ~ www.debeninns.co.uk/maybush *Recommended by Margaret and Peter Staples*

WESTLETON
Crown 🌟 🍷 🛏

TM4469 Map 5

B1125 Blythburgh–Leiston; IP17 3AD

Bustling old inn with a cosy chatty bar, plenty of dining areas, carefully chosen drinks and interesting food; comfortable modern bedrooms

This is a comfortable and stylish old coaching inn with plenty of seats and tables in the charming terraced garden. Inside, the heart of the place remains the attractive little bar with a lovely log fire and plenty of original features. Locals tend to drop in here for a pint and a chat, which keeps the atmosphere informal and relaxed, and they serve Adnams

Southwold and Broadside, Brandon Rusty Bucket and Green Jack Orange
Wheat Beer on handpump and a dozen wines by the glass from a thoughtful
list; background music and board games. There's also a parlour, a dining
room and a conservatory, all manner of wooden dining chairs and tables
and historic photographs on some fine old bare-brick walls. The spotless,
comfortable bedrooms are either in the main inn itself (some are up steep
stairs) or in converted stables and cottages.

 Well presented and impressive, the food includes lunchtime sandwiches,
rabbit and ham hock terrine with piccalilli, tempura tiger prawns with asian
vegetables, peanut, chilli and sesame salad, beer-battered fish and chips, sweet potato
and aubergine tagine with lemon and almond couscous, pork fillet, belly and cheek,
potato and ham hock boulangère, apple purée and cider gravy, chicken breast with
stuffed thigh, shiitake and oyster mushrooms, mushroom and soy broth and won ton
crisp, and puddings such as knickerbocker glory and glazed lemon tart with raspberry
sorbet; they also offer a two- and three-course set lunch (and Thurs evening)
menu. *Benchmark main dish: spicy bass with curried cockle and coconut cream
and onion bhaji £17.50. Two-course evening meal £21.50.*

Free house ~ Licensee Gareth Clarke ~ Real ale ~ (01728) 648777 ~ Open 11-11;
12-10.30 Sun ~ Bar food 12-2.30, 6.30-9.30 ~ Restaurant ~ Children welcome ~ Dogs
allowed in bar and bedrooms ~ Wi-fi ~ Bedrooms: £90/£95 ~ www.westletoncrown.co.uk
Recommended by R L Borthwick, Richard Seal, Tracey and Stephen Groves

WHEPSTEAD
White Horse 🏆 ☆ ♀

TL8258 Map 5

Off B1066 S of Bury; Rede Road; IP29 4SS

**Charmingly reworked country pub with attractively furnished rooms
and well liked food and drink**

This well run place has been carefully refurbished recently and the
garden has been replanted. Originally 17th-c, the building has had
several Victorian additions and there's plenty of space for both drinkers
and diners. The dark-beamed bar has a woodburning stove in a low
fireplace, stools around pubby tables on the tiled floor, and boards listing
the menu. Linked rooms have sturdy, country kitchen tables and chairs
on striped carpeting or antique floor tiles, with some nicely cushioned
traditional wall seats and some rather fine old farmhouse chairs. Oil
paintings of food by a local artist (for sale) and old prints decorate walls
painted in Farrow & Ball burnt orange; the bookshelves have books
that are actually worth reading. Adnams Southwold and Broadside on
handpump and eight wines by the glass, served by attentive, friendly staff.
A tuck shop sells sweets, chocolates and ice-creams; the resident westie
is called Skye. A neat sheltered back terrace is brightened up by colourful
oilcloth tablecloths, and birdsong, heard at the picnic-sets on the grass,
emphasises what a peaceful spot this is.

The extremely popular and interesting food includes mixed hors d'oeuvres to
share, ham hock terrine with home-made piccalilli, open pie with chicken,
mushrooms, tarragon and wine, sausages with cider and leeks on spring onion mash,
roast pumpkin risotto with pine nuts, slow-braised lamb shoulder with olives and
herbs, and puddings such as spotted dick with golden syrup and crème anglaise and
chocolate and orange panna cotta. *Benchmark main dish: madras-style fish curry
with naan bread £14.95. Two-course evening meal £19.00.*

Free house ~ Licensees Gary and Di Kingshott ~ Real ale ~ (01284) 735760 ~
Open 12-3, 7-11; 12-3 Sun ~ Bar food 12-2, 7-9 ~ Children welcome ~ Dogs allowed in bar
~ www.whitehorsewhepstead.co.uk *Recommended by Lucien Perring, Mike and Mary Carter*

Also Worth a Visit in Suffolk

Besides the fully inspected pubs, you might like to try these pubs that
have been recommended to us and described by readers. Do tell us what
you think of them: feedback@goodguides.com

ALDEBURGH TM4656
White Hart (01728) 453205
High Street; IP15 5AJ Friendly one-room
local in former reading room, panelling,
stained-glass windows and high ceiling, four
Adnams ales and guests, decent wines by the
glass, summer pizzas in back courtyard, open
fire; no children inside, dogs welcome, open
all day. *(Giles and Annie Francis)*

ALDRINGHAM TM4461
Parrot & Punchbowl
(01728) 830221 *B1122/B1353 S
of Leiston; IP16 4PY* Attractive and
welcoming beamed country pub with good
fairly priced standard food (not Sun evening),
well kept Greene King and Woodfordes,
two-level restaurant; dogs welcome, nice
sheltered garden, also family garden with
adventure play area. *(Anon)*

BADINGHAM TM3068
White Horse (01728) 638280
A1120 S of village; IP13 8JR Welcoming
16th-c low-beamed pub refurbished under
new owners; enjoyable traditional food
including themed nights, four changing
ales and three ciders, inglenook log fire
and two woodburners; quiz first Tues of
month, local band last Tues; children, dogs
and muddy boots welcome, neat bowling
green and nice rambling garden, open all
day Sun. *(Anon)*

BARHAM TM1251
Sorrel Horse (01473) 830327
Old Norwich Road; IP6 0PG Friendly
open-plan country inn with good log fire
in central chimneybreast, dark beams and
timbers, well kept Adnams and Woodfordes,
popular pubby food; free wi-fi; children and
dogs welcome, disabled facilities, picnic-sets
on side grass with big play area, bedrooms in
converted barn, open all day Weds-Sun.
(Anon)

BARTON MILLS TL72173
Olde Bull (01638) 711001
*Just S of Mildenhall; The Street;
IP28 6AA* Revamped former coaching
inn with good food (not especially cheap)
from lunchtime sandwiches and pubby
dishes to interesting restaurant choices,
Adnams Broadside and a couple of guests,
decent wine list and coffee, friendly staff;
background and some live music; well
behaved children welcome, no dogs inside,
15 individually styled bedrooms (plenty of
quirky touches), open all day. *(D and M T
Ayres-Regan)*

BILDESTON TL9949
Crown (01449) 740510
B1115 SW of Stowmarket; IP7 7EB
Picturesque and impressively refurbished
15th-c timbered country inn, smart beamed
main bar with leather armchairs and
inglenook log fire, more intimate back area
with contemporary art, ales such as Greene
King and nice choice of wines by the glass,
good food (not cheap) from reworked pub
favourites to upmarket choices including
tasting menu in more formal dining room;
children welcome, disabled access and
parking, tables laid for eating in appealing
central courtyard, more in large beautifully
kept garden with decking, quiet comfortable
bedrooms. *(Anon)*

BILDESTON TL9949
Kings Head (01449) 741434
High Street; IP7 7ED Small beamed
16th-c village pub brewing its own good beers
(brewery tours), also local microbrewery
guests, well priced home-made food (Fri
evening, Sat, Sun lunchtime), pleasant
chatty staff, wood-floored bar with inglenook
woodburner, darts; children welcome, back
garden with terrace and play equipment,
open all day weekends, closed Mon, Tues
and lunchtimes Weds-Fri. *(Jeremy King,
Iain Lister)*

BLAXHALL TM3656
Ship (01728) 688316
*Off B1069 S of Snape; can be reached
from A12 via Little Glemham; IP12 2DY*
Charming country setting for this popular
and friendly low-beamed 18th-c pub; good
reasonably priced traditional food in bar
and restaurant, well kept Adnams Bitter,
Woodfordes Wherry and guests, some live
music including folk in side room with piano;
children in eating areas, dogs in bar, eight
refurbished chalet bedrooms, good breakfast,
open all day weekends. *(R J Herd, Pat and
Alan Timmon)*

BRAMFIELD TM3973
★**Queens Head** (01986) 784214
*The Street; A144 S of Halesworth;
IP19 9HT* Village pub next to interesting
church; various rooms with heavy beams,
timbering and exposed brickwork, country
kitchen-style furniture on carpet, local
artwork on walls, high-raftered lounge with
log fire in impressive fireplace, separate
bar also with open fires, Adnams ales and
enjoyable home-made food (not Sun evening
in winter), good friendly service; regular
live music; children away from main bar

area and dogs welcome, picnic-sets in tiered garden. *(Caroline Prescott, Gavin and Helle May, Simon Rodway)*

BRENT ELEIGH   TL9348
✶ **Cock** (01787) 247371
A1141 SE of Lavenham; CO10 9PB
Timeless and friendly thatched country pub, Adnams, Greene King Abbot and a guest, organic farm cider, enjoyable traditional food cooked by landlady, cosy ochre-walled snug and second small room, antique floor tiles, lovely coal fire, old photographs of village (church well worth a look), darts, shove-ha'penny and toad in the hole; well behaved children and dogs welcome, picnic-sets up on side grass with summer hatch service, one bedroom, open all day Fri-Sun. *(Anon)*

BROCKLEY GREEN   TL7247
✶ **Plough** (01440) 786789
Hundon Road; CO10 8DT Friendly neatly kept knocked-through bar, beams, timbers and stripped brick, scrubbed tables and open fire, good food from lunchtime sandwiches and deli boards up, cheerful efficient staff, three changing ales and good choice of wines by the glass, several malt whiskies too, restaurant; children and dogs welcome, attractive grounds with peaceful country views, comfortable bedrooms, open all day weekends. *(Robert Turnham)*

BROMESWELL   TM3050
British Larder (01394) 460310
Orford Road, Bromeswell Heath; IP12 2PU Neat beamed restaurant pub with good if not cheap food from chef-licensees using local seasonal produce, well kept ales such as Woodfordes Wherry and nice wines by the glass in separate bar, pleasant service, home-made jams etc for sale (they've also written a cookbook); children welcome, plenty of tables outside, big play area, open all day weekends. *(J F M and M West, Nick and Gillian Harrison)*

BUNGAY   TM3389
Castle (01986) 892283
Earsham Street; NR35 1AF Pleasantly informal 16th-c dining inn with good interesting food from chef-owner; opened-up beamed interior with restaurant part at front, two open fires, friendly efficient staff, Earl Soham Victoria Bitter and a guest, Aspall's cider, nice choice of wines by the glass, afternoon teas, french windows to pretty courtyard garden, occasional live acoustic music; children welcome, dogs in bar area, four comfortable bedrooms, open all day in summer. *(Anon)*

BURY ST EDMUNDS   TL8463
Dove (01284) 702787
Hospital Road; IP33 3JU Friendly 19th-c alehouse with rustic bare-boards bar and separate parlour, half a dozen well kept mostly local beers, quiz and

folk nights, maybe a local morris troupe; closed weekday lunchtimes. *(Anon)*

BURY ST EDMUNDS   TL8564
Fox (01284) 705562
Eastgate Street; IP33 1XX Attractive ancient beamed pub (Olde English Inns group) with informal bustling atmosphere, enjoyable pubby food from sandwiches and wraps up, well kept Greene King ales, plenty of wines by the glass, cocktails, efficient friendly staff, Sun evening jazz; bedrooms in converted barn behind, open all day from 7am (breakfast for non-residents). *(John Saville)*

BURY ST EDMUNDS   TL8564
✶ **Nutshell** (01284) 764867
The Traverse, central pedestrian link off Abbeygate Street; IP33 1BJ Tiny simple local with timeless interior (can be a crush at busy times), lots of interest such as a mummified cat (found walled up here) hanging from dark brown ceiling along with companion rat, bits of a skeleton, vintage bank notes, cigarette packets, military and other badges, spears and a great metal halberd, one short wooden bench along shopfront corner windows, a cut-down sewing-machine table and an elbow rest running along a rather battered counter, Greene King ales, no food; background music, steep narrow stairs up to lavatories; children (till 7pm) and dogs welcome, open all day. *(Barry Collett)*

BURY ST EDMUNDS   TL8563
✶ **Rose & Crown** (01284) 755934
Whiting Street; IP33 1NP Cheerful black-beamed corner local with long-serving affable licensees, bargain simple lunchtime home cooking (not Sun), particularly well kept Greene King ales (including XX Mild) and guests, pleasant lounge with lots of piggy pictures and bric-a-brac, good games-oriented public bar, rare separate off-sales counter; piped radio, no credit cards or under-14s; pretty back courtyard, open all day weekdays. *(Anon)*

BUXHALL   TM9957
Crown (01449) 736521
Off B1115 W of Stowmarket; Mill Road; IP14 3DW Cosy and welcoming low-beamed bar with inglenook woodburner, well kept Greene King ales and nice choice of wines by the glass, good well presented food (not particularly cheap), airy dining room; children and dogs welcome, plenty of tables on terrace with views over open country (ignore the pylons), herb garden, closed Sun evening, Mon. *(Anon)*

CAVENDISH   TL8046
Bull (01787) 280245
A1092 Long Melford–Clare; CO10 8AX Well looked after old inn with heavy beams, timbers and fine fireplaces, Adnams ales

and enjoyable reasonably priced pub food, attentive friendly service; regular events including live music and quiz first Sun of month; children in eating areas, garden tables, car park (useful in this honeypot village), three bedrooms, closed Sun evening, Mon, Tues. *(Anon)*

CAVENDISH   TL8046
★ **George** (01787) 280248

A1092; The Green; CO10 8BA 16th-c dining inn with contemporary feel in two bow-windowed front areas, beams and timbers, big woodburner in stripped-brick fireplace, generally very well liked food from interesting varied menu including set deals, two Growler ales and plenty of wines by the glass, Aspall's cider, back servery and further eating area, charming young staff, daily newspapers; children and well behaved dogs welcome, stylish furniture on sheltered back terrace, tree-shaded garden with lovely village church behind, five bedrooms up rather steep staircase, good breakfast, open all day except Sun evening. *(Robert and Sarah Milne)*

CHELSWORTH   TL9848
Peacock (01449) 740758

B1115 Sudbury–Needham Market; IP7 7HU Prettily set old dining pub with lots of Tudor brickwork and exposed beams, separate pubby bar with big inglenook, local ales and fairly standard food (not Sun evening), friendly service; dogs welcome (resident greyhounds), four bedrooms, attractive small garden and village. *(Mrs Carolyn Dixon)*

CHILLESFORD   TM3852
★ **Froize** (01394) 450282

B1084 E of Woodbridge; IP12 3PU Restaurant rather than pub (open only when they serve food, so not Mon or evenings Sun-Weds), pleasant bar and restaurant, reliably good if not cheap buffet-style food from owner-chef using carefully sourced local produce including game, nice wines by the glass and well kept Adnams, warmly welcoming service, little deli next to bar; no dogs inside. *(Mike and Linda Hudson)*

CRETINGHAM   TM2260
Bell (01728) 685419

The Street; IP13 7BJ Attractive old pub recently refurbished by friendly new owners; good home-made food and well kept ales such as Adnams and Earl Soham, nice wines by the glass, bare-boards bar, dining tables in tiled second room, beams and timbers, leather sofa and armchairs by woodburner; garden picnic-sets. *(J F M and M West)*

DENNINGTON   TM2867
★ **Queen** (01728) 638241

A1120; The Square; IP13 8AB Beamed and timbered Tudor pub restaurant prettily placed by church, L-shaped main bar, Adnams and maybe a guest, Aspall's cider, enjoyable food (best to book weekends) including some interesting specials, friendly service; background music; children in family room, side lawn by noble lime trees, decked area behind and pond with ducks and carp, backs on to Dennington Park with swings etc. *(Margaret Tait)*

EARL SOHAM   TM2263
Victoria (01728) 685758

A1120 Yoxford–Stowmarket; IP13 7RL Simple pub with own brewery nearby: Earl Soham Victoria Bitter, Brandeston Gold, Sir Rogers Porter and seasonal beers, some refurbishment (and free wi-fi) under new licensees, but bar has had kitchen chairs and pews, scrubbed country tables, tiled or bare board floors, panelling and open fires, also some interesting pictures of Queen Victoria, bar food including Sun roasts; outside gents'; children and dogs welcome, seats out in front and on raised back lawn, handy for working windmill at Saxted. *(Colin and Ruth Munro, Sheila Topham, Pat and Tony Martin, J F M and M West)*

EASTON   TM2858
★ **White Horse** (01728) 746456

N of Wickham Market on back road to Earl Soham and Framlingham; IP13 0ED Attractive early 18th-c pub with three smart but simple rooms, farmhouse tables, country kitchen chairs, pews and settles, open fires, Adnams Southwold and two local guests, ten wines by the glass, good locally sourced food including blackboard specials, friendly staff, restaurant; background music; children and dogs welcome, seats out at front and in back garden, good local walks, open (and food) all day weekends. *(Anthony Barnes, Ian Phillips, J F M and M West)*

FELIXSTOWE FERRY   TM3237
Ferry Boat (01394) 284203

Off Ferry Road, on the green; IP11 9RZ Much modernised 17th-c pub tucked between golf links and dunes near harbour, martello tower and summer rowing-boat ferry; enjoyable fair value pub food including good fish dishes, friendly efficient service, well kept Adnams and Woodfordes Wherry, decent coffee, warm log fire; background music, busy on summer weekends, and they may ask to keep a credit card while you eat; dogs welcome, tables out in front, on green opposite and in fenced garden, good coast walks. *(J F M and M West)*

FRAMLINGHAM   TM2863
Crown (01728) 723521

Market Hill; IP13 9AP Stylishly refurbished 16th-c beamed coaching inn, good food from lunchtime sandwiches and pizzas up (more restaurant evening choice), Greene King and guests, several wines by the glass, open fires; background and some live acoustic music; children and dogs welcome, tables in back courtyard, 14 bedrooms, open all day. *(David and Sue Atkinson)*

FRAMLINGHAM   TM2862
Station Hotel (01728) 723455
Station Road (B1116 S); IP13 9EE Simple high-ceilinged big-windowed bar with scrubbed tables on stripped boards, candles in bottles, well kept Earl Soham ales and good choice of house wines, popular freshly cooked food from interesting menu, friendly staff and relaxed atmosphere, back snug with tiled floor; children and dogs welcome, picnic-sets in pleasant garden. *(J F M and M West)*

FRESSINGFIELD   TM2677
★ Fox & Goose (01379) 586247
Church Street; B1116 N of Framlingham; IP21 5PB Relaxed dining pub in beautifully timbered 16th-c building next to church, very good food in cosy informal heavy-beamed rooms with log fire, upstairs restaurant, friendly efficient service, good wines by the glass, Adnams and a guest tapped from the cask in side bar; faint background music; children welcome, downstairs disabled facilities, tables out by duck pond, closed Mon. *(W K Wood)*

GREAT BRICETT   TM0450
Red Lion (01473) 657799
B1078, E of Bildeston; IP7 7DD Old extended beamed pub serving really good interesting vegetarian and vegan food at competitive prices (nothing for meat eaters), children's menu and takeaways too; dogs welcome in bar, garden with deck and play equipment, closed Mon. *(Maggie Woolley, Mrs Carolyn Dixon)*

GREAT GLEMHAM   TM3461
Crown (01728) 663693
Between A12 Wickham Market– Saxmundham and B1119 Saxmundham–Framlingham; IP17 2DA Early 19th-c pub reopened after two-year closure by beer enthusiast landlord; traditionally restored interior with wood and tiled floors, two big fireplaces, well kept local beers from old brass handpumps, food Thurs-Sat and Sun lunchtime; disabled access, garden. *(Nick Clare)*

GRUNDISBURGH   TM2250
★ Dog (01473) 735267
The Green; off A12 via B1079 from Woodbridge bypass; IP13 6TA Friendly pink-washed pub with villagey public bar, log fire, settles and dark wooden carvers around pubby tables on tiles, Adnams, Earl Soham, Woodfordes and a guest, half a dozen wines by the glass, well liked good value food including set lunch Tues-Sat, relaxing carpeted lounge linking to bare-boards dining room; children and dogs (in bar) welcome, picnic-sets out in front by flowering tubs, more seats in wicker-fenced

mediterranean-feel back garden, play area, open all day Fri-Sun, closed Mon. *(J F M and M West, Pat and Alan Timmon)*

HADLEIGH   TM0242
Kings Head (01473) 828855
High Street; IP7 5EF Modernised old pub with popular food from daily changing menu, also good wood-fired pizzas, Adnams, Greene King, Crouch Vale and guests, Aspall's cider, friendly staff; open all day (Sun till 5pm). *(Mrs Carolyn Dixon)*

HADLEIGH   TM0242
Ram (01473) 822880 .
Market Place; IP7 5DL Popular smartly refurbished bar-restaurant (sister to the Swan at Long Melford) facing Georgian corn exchange; good well presented food (not Sun evening) including fixed-price menu, plenty of wines by the glass from extensive list, cocktails and Greene King IPA, efficient service; children welcome, small courtyard garden behind, open all day (Sun till 7pm). *(Mrs Carolyn Dixon)*

HAUGHLEY   TM0262
Kings Arms (01449) 614462
Off A45/B1113 N of Stowmarket; Old Street; IP14 3NT 16th-c extended timbered pub, horsebrasses and other bits and pieces, big brick fireplace, enjoyable fairly traditional pub food cooked to order and reasonably priced, well kept Greene King beers (Abbot ale was named here by a landlord in 1950), also a guest such as Thwaites and good choice of wines, busy public bar with pool, darts and trophies above TV, dining area with tablecloths; background music, no dogs inside; children welcome, tables and play area in back garden, nice village, open all day Fri-Sun. *(Jeremy King)*

HAWKEDON   TL7953
★ Queens Head (01284) 789218
Off A143 at Wickham Street, NE of Haverhill; and off B1066; IP29 4NN Flint Tudor pub in pretty setting looking down broad peaceful green to interesting largely Norman village church; quarry-tiled bar with dark beams and ochre walls, plenty of pews and chapel chairs around scrubbed tables, elderly armchairs by antique woodburner in huge fireplace, cheerful licensees and staff, Adnams, Woodfordes and guests, farm cider/perry and nice choice of wines, good popular food (not Mon, Tues) using home-reared meat, dining area stretching back with country prints and a couple of tusky boars' heads, some live music; picnic-sets out in front, more on back terrace overlooking rolling country, little shop (Fri and Sat mornings) selling carefully chosen meats as well as their own bacon, pies, casseroles etc; tables out front and back, open all day Fri-Sun, closed lunchtimes Mon-Thurs. *(Lucien Perring, R A P Cross)*

HENLEY   TM1552
Cross Keys (01449) 761958
Main Road/Clay Lane; IP6 0QP Roadside
country pub redecorated under welcoming
new licensees, enjoyable good value home-
made food served by friendly staff, real ales
such as Greene King and good wines by the
glass; children and dogs welcome, nice back
garden, open all day Sat, closed Sun evening,
Mon. *(J F M and M West)*

HITCHAM   TL9851
White Horse (01449) 740981
*The Street (B1115 Sudbury–
Stowmarket); IP7 7NQ* Friendly 16th-c
village pub, a former staging post for
travellers between London and Norfolk,
two bars with ales such as Adnams, Earl
Soham and Greene King, log fire, beams
and timbering, dark wooden chairs around
clothed tables in restaurant, honest
pubby dishes plus more elaborate evening
choices, obliging service; children and dogs
welcome, nice bedrooms in separate barn
conversion. *(Sarah Pawsley)*

HOXNE   TM1877
⋆Swan (01379) 668275
*Low Street; off B1118, signed off A140
S of Diss; IP21 5AS* Timber-framed 15th-c
pub under newish management; pubby
bar with two solid oak counters, broad oak
floorboards and deep-set inglenook, Adnams,
Woodfordes and a guest tapped from the
cask, several wines by the glass, good fairly
traditional food (all day weekends), friendly
attentive staff, restaurant; children and dogs
(in bar) welcome, seats under parasols on
two sheltered terraces and in lovely spacious
garden extending to stream, nearby tree that
King Edmund was tied to at his execution,
open all day. *(Anon)*

IPSWICH   TM1644
Dove Street (01473) 211270
St Helen's Street; IP4 2LA Over 20 well
kept quickly changing ales including their
own brews (regular beer festivals), farm
ciders, bottled beers and good selection
of whiskies, low priced simple home-made
food, hot drinks, bare-boards bar, carpeted
snug and back conservatory; dogs welcome,
children till 7pm, terrace seating, two
bedrooms and brewery shop across the road,
open all day. *(Anon)*

IPSWICH   TM1645
Greyhound (01473) 252862
Henley Road/Anglesea Road; IP1 3SE
Popular 19th-c pub close to Christchurch
Park; cosy front bar, corridor to larger

lounge/dining area, five well kept Adnams
ales and a couple of guests, good substantial
home cooking including bargain weekday
lunch, quick service; sports TV, free wi-fi;
children welcome, picnic-sets under parasols
on back terrace, open all day Fri-Sun
(breakfast Sun from 10am). *(Anon)*

IPSWICH   TM1747
Railway Inn (01473) 252337
Westerfield Road; IP6 9AA Refurbished
pub, now lighter and brighter with more
of a bistro feel; very popular locally with
enjoyable reasonably priced food including
set menus, well kept Sharps Doom Bar,
pleasant attentive service; children and dogs
(in bar area) welcome, tables outside.
(J F M and M West)

KESGRAVE   TM2346
Kesgrave Hall (01473) 333741
Hall Road; IP5 2PU Country hotel with
comfortably contemporary bare-boards bar,
Adnams and a couple of guests from granite-
topped servery, several wines by the glass and
cocktails, popular often imaginative food in
open-kitchen brasserie (no booking so best
to arrive early), efficient young staff; children
and dogs welcome, attractive heated terrace
with huge retractable awning, 23 stylish
bedrooms, open (and food) all day.
(J F M and M West)

LAVENHAM -   TL9149
Angel (01787) 247388
Market Place; CO10 9QZ Handsome Tudor
building with firm emphasis on dining (part
of Marco Pierre White's Wheelers group);
long bar with inglenook log fire and some
fine 16th-c ceiling plasterwork, further
dining areas with elegant chairs around
white-clothed tables, more heavy beams and
panelling, grill-based menu, ales such as
Adnams Southwold and Sharps; children and
dogs (in bar) welcome, sizeable back garden,
bedrooms, delightful small town, open all day.
(Toby Jones, Emma Scofield)

LAVENHAM   TL9149
Swan (01787) 247477
High Street; CO10 9QA Smart, well
equipped and by no means cheap hotel
incorporating handsome medieval buildings,
well worth a look for its appealing network
of beamed and timbered alcoves and
more open areas, including peaceful little
tiled-floor inner bar with leather chairs and
memorabilia of its days as the local for US
48th Bomber Group, well kept Adnams and
a guest beer, wide choice of consistently
good food in informal brasserie or lavishly
timbered restaurant, efficient young staff;

Post Office address codings confusingly give the impression that some pubs
are in Suffolk, when they're really in Cambridgeshire, Essex or Norfolk
(which is where we list them).

children and dogs welcome, sheltered courtyard garden, 45 bedrooms, open all day. *(Mrs Carolyn Dixon, Ian and Rose Lock)*

LAXFIELD   TM2972
⋆ **Kings Head** (01986) 798395

Gorams Mill Lane, behind church; IP13 8DW Unspoilt thatched pub with no bar counter – instead, Adnams range and a guest poured in tap room; interesting little chequer-tiled front room dominated by a three-sided booth of high-backed settles in front of old range fire, two other equally unspoilt rooms with pews, old seats and scrubbed deal tables, well liked tasty bar food including good home-made pies served by friendly helpful staff; children and dogs welcome, neatly kept garden with arbour and small pavilion for cooler evenings, boules played on Sun, bedrooms and self-catering apartment, open all day in summer. *(Margaret Tait, Tim Maddison, Sheila Topham, Roger Fox)*

LAXFIELD   TM2972
Royal Oak (01986) 798666

High Street; IP13 8DH Extended Tudor pub next to 14th-c church; beams, old quarry tiles and inglenook, well kept Adnams and Woodfordes ales, good value food including some themed evenings, friendly staff, quiz and music nights; children welcome, tables out in front. *(Rita Scarratt)*

LEVINGTON   TM2339
Ship (01473) 659573

Gun Hill; from A14/A12 Bucklesham roundabout take A1156 exit, then first left into Felixstowe Road, after nearly a mile the village and pub are signed to the right; IP10 0LQ Charming old Adnams pub with plenty of nautical trappings and character, settles and built-in wall benches, big black circular stove, flagstoned dining room with more nautical bric-a-brac; beside little lime-washed church and has views (if a little obscured) over River Orwell estuary. *(Bill and Marian de Bass, Mrs Carolyn Dixon)*

LONG MELFORD   TL8645
⋆ **Bull** (01787) 378494

Hall Street (B1064); CO10 9JG Small 15th-c hotel in good location and full of character; old-fashioned timbered front lounge with beautifully carved beams, antique furnishings, log fire in huge fireplace, more spacious back bar with sporting prints, well kept Greene King ales and a guest, Aspall's cider, decent wines, reasonably priced standard Old English Inns menu, good helpful service from cheerful staff, daily papers, restaurant; children welcome, tables in attractive courtyard, comfortable

bedrooms and substantial breakfast, open all day weekends. *(Ron Corbett)*

LONG MELFORD   TL8645
Crown (01787) 377666

Hall Street; CO10 9JL Friendly partly 17th-c family-run inn, changing ales such as Adnams, Greene King, Humpty Dumpty and Mauldons from central servery with unusual bar chairs, log fire, some stripped brickwork and tartan carpet, oak-floored restaurant with high-backed chairs and vibrant red walls, good locally sourced food from bar snacks up, friendly helpful service; attractive terrace with big awnings and small pond, 12 well equipped bedrooms, open all day. *(Alan Thwaite)*

LONG MELFORD   TL8645
Swan (01787) 464545

Hall Street; CO10 9JQ Beamed dining pub run well by brother and sister team, good daily changing up-to-date food (not Sun evening, best to book) using local seasonal produce, set-menu choices lunchtimes (not Sun) and Mon-Thurs evenings, well selected wines, cocktails and a couple of real ales, obliging service, pastel grey-green décor with high backed dining chairs on bare boards, modern artwork; unobtrusive background music; tables outside, open all day (till 7pm Sun). *(Alan Thwaite)*

LOWESTOFT   TM5593
Triangle (01502) 582711

St Peter's Street; NR32 1QA Popular two-bar tap for Green Jack ales, guest beers too and real cider, regular beer festivals, breweriana, open fire; pool and TV in back bar, live music Fri; open all day (till 1am Fri, Sat). *(Anon)*

MELTON   TM2850
Olde Coach & Horses
(01394) 384851 *Melton Road; IP12 1PD* Attractively modernised beamed former staging inn, good choice of enjoyable fairly priced food from sandwiches, snacks and sharing plates up (special diets catered for), Adnams and decent wines by the glass, good friendly service; free wi-fi; children welcome, dogs in wood-floored area, tables outside under parasols, colourful hanging baskets and planters, open all day from 9am for breakfast. *(Nick and Gillian Harrison)*

MONKS ELEIGH   TL9647
Swan (01449) 741391

A1141 NW of Hadleigh; IP7 7AU Taken over by owners of the Angel at Stoke-by-Nayland (Exclusive Inns) and being refurbished as we went to press – reports please. *(Mrs Carolyn Dixon)*

We include some hotels with a good bar that offers facilities comparable to those of a pub.

MOULTON   TL6964
Packhorse (01638) 751818
Bridge Street; CB8 8SP Stylishly revamped
under new management and now more
restaurant with rooms than pub; good
popular (if pricey) food from chef-owner
including some inventive choices (must
book), carve your own Sun roast at the table,
well kept ales such as Adnams, Purity and
Woodfordes, good wines by the glass, pleasant
attentive service; dogs welcome, adjacent to
delightful 15th-c bridge across the Kennett,
handy for Newmarket races, four bedrooms,
open all day. *(J F M and M West)*

NAYLAND   TL9734
★Anchor (01206) 262313
*Court Street; just off A134 – turn-off S
of signposted B1087 main village turn;
CO6 4JL* Friendly pub by River Stour under
same ownership as the Angel at Stoke-by-
Nayland; bare-boards bar with assorted
wooden dining chairs and tables, big gilt
mirror on silvery wallpaper one end, another
mirror above pretty fireplace at the other,
five changing ales and several wines by the
glass, interesting food (some home-smoked)
along with more standard dishes, Fri tapas,
two other rooms behind and steep stairs up
to cosy restaurant; children welcome, dogs in
bar, terrace tables overlooking river, open all
day (no food Sun evening). *(Brian and Anna
Marsden)*

NEWBOURNE   TM2743
★Fox (01473) 736307
*Off A12 at roundabout 1.7 miles N
of A14 junction; The Street; IP12 4NY*
Pink-washed 16th-c pub decked with summer
flowers, low-beamed bar with slabby elm and
other dark tables on tiled floor, stuffed fox in
inglenook, comfortable carpeted dining room
with modern artwork and various mirrors,
Adnams Southwold and guests, decent wines
by the glass, good variety of well liked food
(all day weekends) including reasonably
priced Sun roasts, good service; background
music; children and dogs (in bar) welcome,
wheelchair access, attractive grounds with
rose garden and pond, open all day. *(Anon)*

NEWMARKET   TL6464
Bedford Lodge (01638) 663175
Bury Road; CB8 7BX 18th-c hotel's bar
(used by locals) with well kept Adnams,
plenty of wines by the glass including
champagne and good food from snacks up,
attentive young staff, log fire, restaurant;
seats on terrace overlooking gardens, 77
bedrooms, open all day. *(J F M and M West)*

ORFORD   TM4249
★Jolly Sailor (01394) 450243
Quay Street; IP12 2NU Friendly old
pub under new mother and daughter team;
several snug rooms with exposed brickwork,
boating pictures and other nautical

memorabilia, four well kept Adnams beers
and popular sensibly priced food from
lunchtime sandwiches up, unusual spiral
staircase in corner of flagstoned main bar
by brick inglenook, horsebrasses and local
photographs, two cushioned pews and long
antique stripped deal table, maybe local
sea shanty group; free wi-fi; children and
dogs welcome, tables on back terrace and
lawn with views over marshes, popular with
walkers and bird-watchers, bedrooms, open
all day weekends. *(Anon)*

POLSTEAD   TL9938
Cock (01206) 263150
*Signed off B1068 and A1071 E of
Sudbury, then pub signed; Polstead
Green; CO6 5AL* Welcoming beamed
and timbered 16th-c village local; bar with
woodburner, Greene King and guests, good
choice of wines, enjoyable reasonably priced
home-made food from lunchtime sandwiches
up, helpful friendly staff, light and airy barn
restaurant; background music; children
and dogs welcome, disabled facilities,
picnic-sets overlooking small green, open all
day weekends, closed Mon and winter Sun
evening. *(Carol and Luke Wilson)*

RAMSHOLT   TM3041
Ramsholt Arms (01394) 411229
Signed off B1083; Dock Road; IP12 3AB
Lovely isolated spot overlooking River Deben
and now under same management as the
Crown at Ufford; refurbished open-plan bar
busy on summer weekends and handy for
bird walks and Sutton Hoo (NT), good food
from lunchtime sandwiches, sharing plates
and pub favourites to local seafood, Adnams
and a couple of guests, decent wines by the
glass, log fire; children welcome, plenty of
tables outside taking in the view, open all
day weekends. *(N R White, Nick and Gillian
Harrison)*

RATTLESDEN   TL9758
Brewers Arms (01449) 736377
*Lower Road; off B1115 via Buxhall or
A45 via Woolpit, W of Stowmarket;
IP30 0RJ* 16th-c beamed village pub under
new management; bar on right serving three
real ales and Aspall's cider, lounge on left
winding back through standing timbers to
restaurant area with flint walls and ancient
bread oven, good range of food including
tapas; children welcome, dogs in bar, french
windows into walled garden with plenty of
seats, open all day weekends. *(J F M and
M West)*

RENDHAM   TM3564
White Horse (01728) 663497
*B1119 Framlingham–Saxmundham;
IP17 2AF* Partly divided open-plan pub
with good reasonably priced home-made food
using local suppliers, ales including Earl
Soham and Mauldons (Aug beer festival),
friendly service, two open fires, quiz and

music nights; well behaved dogs welcome, garden tables, lovely spot opposite 14th-c church, good local walks, closed weekday lunchtimes. *(Anon)*

REYDON
TM4977
★ Randolph (01502) 723603
Wangford Road (B1126 just NW of Southwold); IP18 6PZ Stylish inn with quite an emphasis on dining and bedroom side; bar with high-backed leather dining chairs around chunky wooden tables on parquet floor, sofa and a couple of comfortable armchairs, prints of pub from 1910 and photographs of Southwold beach, Adnams beers, dining room with more high-backed chairs on red carpet, pretty little Victorian fireplace filled with candles, nicely varied menu including children's choices, pleasant staff; background music, TV, games machine; dogs welcome in small back bar, wheelchair access, picnic-sets on decked area and grass, ten bedrooms, good breakfast, open all day. *(N R White)*

RINGSFIELD
TM4187
Horseshoes (01502) 713114
Cromwell Road off A145; NR34 8LR Revamped pub with clean modern interior, enjoyable good value pub food, OAP deal Weds, three well kept changing ales, back dining room; children welcome. *(Anon)*

ROUGHAM
TL9063
★ Ravenwood Hall (01359) 270345
Off A14 E of Bury St Edmunds; IP30 9JA Country-house hotel with two compact bar rooms, tall ceilings, patterned wallpaper and big heavily draped windows overlooking sweeping lawn with stately cedar, back area set for eating with upholstered settles and dining chairs, sporting prints and log fire, very good well presented food (own smoked meats and fish), well kept Adnams, good choice of wines and malt whiskies, pleasant attentive staff, comfortable lounge area with horse pictures, a few moulded beams and early Tudor wall decoration above big inglenook, separate more formal restaurant; background music; children and dogs welcome, teak furniture in garden, swimming pool, croquet, geese and pygmy goats in big enclosures, 14 bedrooms, open 9am-midnight. *(J F M and M West, Mr and Mrs M Walker, Ryta Lyndley)*

SAXTEAD GREEN
TM2564
Old Mill House (01728) 685064
B1119; The Green; IP13 9QE Roomy dining pub across green from windmill, beamed carpeted bar, neat country-look flagstoned restaurant extension, wooden tables and chairs, good choice of generous well priced fresh food (all day Sun) including daily carvery, good friendly service, well kept Greene King, decent

wines; discreet background music; children very welcome, attractive sizeable garden with terrace and good play area, open all day Sun. *(J F M and M West)*

SHOTTISHAM
TM3244
Sorrel Horse (01394) 411617
Hollesley Road; IP12 3HD Charming 15th-c thatched community-owned local; ales such as Earl Soham and Woodfordes tapped from the cask, decent choice of home-made traditional food including deals, attentive helpful young staff, good log fire in tiled-floor bar with games area (bar billiards), woodburner in appealing dining room, fortnightly quiz Weds; children and dogs welcome, tables out on sloping front lawn and in small garden behind, open all day weekends. *(Brian and Anna Marsden)*

SNAPE
TM3958
★ Crown (01728) 688324
Bridge Road (B1069); IP17 1SL Small well laid out 15th-c beamed pub with brick floors, inglenook log fire and fine double suffolk settle, well kept Adnams ales, good fresh food using local ingredients including own meat (reared behind the pub), reasonable prices, efficient friendly young staff, folk night last Thurs of month, darts; children and dogs welcome, garden, two bedrooms. *(Edward Mirzoeff, R J Herd, Conrad Freezer, C A Bryson, Pat and Alan Timmon)*

SNAPE
TM4058
★ Golden Key (01728) 688510
Priory Lane; IP17 1SA Traditionally furnished village pub with low-beamed lounge, old-fashioned settle and straightforward tables and chairs on chequerboard tiled floor, log fire, small snug and two dining rooms, Adnams ales, local cider and a dozen wines by the glass, enjoyable food from monthly changing menu, friendly attentive staff; children and dogs welcome, two terraces with pretty hanging baskets and seats under large parasols, handy for the Maltings, comfortable bedrooms, open all day weekends. *(Anthony Barnes, Tracey and Stephen Groves, Susan and Jeremy Arthern)*

SNAPE
TM3957
★ Plough & Sail (01728) 688413
The Maltings, Snape Bridge (B1069 S); IP17 1SR Nicely placed dining pub (part of the Maltings complex) airily extended around original 16th-c core, mostly open-plan with good blend of traditional and modern furnishings, Adnams Bitter, Woodfordes Wherry and guests, a dozen wines by the glass including champagne, good bistro-style food (pre- and post-concert menus), spacious dining room and upstairs restaurant, efficient well organised service; background music; children and dogs (in bar) welcome, teak

---

If we know a pub has an outdoor play area for children, we mention it.

furniture on flower-filled terrace, picnic-sets at front, open all day. *(Tracey and Stephen Groves, N R White)*

SOUTH COVE   TM4982
Five Bells (01502) 675249
B1127 Southwold–Wrentham; NR34 7JF Spacious old creeper-clad pub set back from the road, friendly and well run, with three well kept Adnams ales and Aspall's cider from thatched servery, good pubby blackboard food in bar, side room with settles or back restaurant, good service; tables out in front, play area, quiet caravan site in back paddock, bedrooms. *(Robert Turnham)*

SOUTHWOLD   TM5076
★ Red Lion (01502) 722385
South Green; IP18 6ET Cheerful pubby front bar with big windows looking over green towards the sea, sturdy wall benches and bar stools on flagstones, well kept Adnams including seasonals, quieter back room with mate's chairs, cushioned pews and polished dark tables on pale woodstrip flooring, seaside cartoons by Giles, Mac and the like, good range of popular reasonably priced food served by friendly neatly dressed staff, three linked dining rooms; background music (live Sun afternoon); tables out in front and in small sheltered back courtyard, right by the Adnams retail shop. *(Anon)*

SOUTHWOLD   TM5076
Sole Bay (01502) 723736
East Green; IP18 6JN Busy pub near Adnams Brewery, their full range kept well and good wine choice, cheerful efficient staff, enjoyable reasonably priced simple food (not Sun evening) including good fish and chips, airy interior with well spaced tables, conservatory; sports TV; children and dogs welcome, disabled facilities, picnic-sets outside, moments from sea and lighthouse, open all day. *(W K Wood, David Carr, N R White)*

SOUTHWOLD   TM5076
★ Swan (01502) 722186
Market Place; IP18 6EG Relaxed comfortable back bar in smart Adnams-owned hotel, their full range kept well and bottled beers, fine wines and malt whiskies, good bar food including lunchtime set menu (Mon-Sat), cheerful competent staff, coffee and teas in luxurious chintzy front lounge, restaurant; nice garden, 42 bedrooms – some in separate block where (by arrangement) dogs can stay too, good breakfast. *(Richard Symonds, M and GR, David Carr, Ian Herdman)*

STANSFIELD   TL7851
Compasses (01284) 789263
High Street; CO10 8LN Simply refurbished little country pub under newish ownership; locally sourced food (much from next door farm), Adnams, Growler and Woodfordes ales (plans for own microbrewery), Aspall's cider and good range of wines, beams, bare

boards and large woodburner; children and dogs welcome, tables outside with lovely rural views, good walks, open all day Fri, Sat (till 10pm), closed Sun evening, Mon, Tues lunchtime. *(Anon)*

STOKE ASH   TM1170
White Horse (01379) 678222
A140/Workhouse Road; IP23 7ET Sizeable 17th-c roadside coaching inn, beams and inglenook fireplaces, generous helpings of good reasonably priced pub food all day from 8am, well kept Adnams, Greene King and Woodfordes, local Calvors lager and Aspall's cider, prompt friendly service from young staff; children welcome, bedrooms in modern annexe. *(J F M and M West, Mr and Mrs M Walker, Robert and Sarah Milne)*

STOKE-BY-NAYLAND   TL9836
★ Angel (01206) 263245
B1068 Sudbury–East Bergholt; CO6 4SA Elegant and comfortable 17th-c inn; lounge with handsome beams, timbers and stripped brickwork, leather chesterfields and wing armchairs around low tables, pictures of local scenes, more formal room with deep glass-covered well, chatty bar with straightforward furniture on red tiles, well kept Banks's Mansfield and a guest, ten wines by the glass, wide range of enterprising food (all day weekends) served promptly by friendly uniformed staff; children and dogs (in bar) welcome, seats on sheltered terrace, six individually styled bedrooms, open all day from 8am (noon Sun). *(Brian and Anna Marsden, MDN, Gerry and Rosemary Dobson, N R White and others)*

STOWMARKET   TW0558
Kings Arms (01449) 675232
Station Road East; IP14 1RQ Friendly double-fronted Victorian pub with three rooms, half a dozen mainly local ales including Woodfordes Wherry, Weston's cider, straightforward food; pool, TV; dogs welcome when not too busy, back terrace and a room for occasional live music, also beer festivals and barbecues, open all day and handy for station. *(Tony and Wendy Hobden)*

STOWMARKET   TM0457
Magpie (01449) 612727
Combs Ford; IP14 2AP Friendly local, lots of old beams, traditional home-made food including good value Sun carvery, five well kept ales such as Hancocks, Sharps Doom Bar and bargain Greene King IPA, pleasant conservatory; darts, pool, sports TV, fruit machine; closed Tues. *(John Middlemiss)*

STRATFORD ST MARY   TM0434
Swan (01206) 321244
Lower Street; CO7 6JR Cosy 16th-c timbered coaching inn (sister pub to the Anchor at Walberswick – see Main Entries), welcoming and friendly, with good upmarket food, two or three changing ales and

extensive range of imported draught and bottled beers, proper ciders too and over 20 wines by the glass from good list, two beamed bars, log fire in Tudor brick fireplace in one, coal fire in the other, eclectic mix of old furniture, compact back restaurant; cribbage and other games; children and dogs welcome, terrace and garden behind, more seats across road overlooking River Stour and canoe landing stage, open all day. *(Anon)*

STUTTON   TM1434
Gardeners Arms (01473) 328868
Manningtree Road, Upper Street (B1080); IP9 2TG Cottagey roadside pub on edge of small village, well kept Adnams and guests, enjoyable home-made food including daily specials and OAP meals, friendly helpful landlord, cosy L-shaped bar with log fire, side dining room and larger area stretching to the back, lots of bric-a-brac, film posters and musical instruments; children and dogs (on leads) welcome, two-tier back garden with pond, open all day weekends. *(N R White)*

SUDBURY   TL8741
Brewery Tap (01787) 370876
East Street; CO10 2TP Corner tap for Mauldons brewery, their range and guests kept well, good choice of malt whiskies, bare boards and scrubbed tables, some food (can bring your own), darts, cribbage and bar billiards, live music including jazz; dogs welcome, open all day. *(Anon)*

SWILLAND   TM1852
Moon & Mushroom (01473) 785320
Off B1078; IP6 9LR Popular 16th-c country local serving East Anglian beers from racked casks behind long counter, old tables and chairs on quarry tiles, log fire, good value home-made food such as venison and ale steamed pudding; children and dogs welcome, heated terrace with grapevines and roses, closed Sun evening, Mon. *(David M Smith)*

THORNDON   TM1469
Black Horse (01379) 678523
Off A140 or B1077, S of Eye; The Street; IP23 7JR Friendly 17th-c village pub with enjoyable food including good value lunchtime carvery, three well kept local ales, beams, lots of timbering, stripped brick and big fireplaces; well behaved children welcome, tables on lawn, country views behind, open all day Sun. *(Malcolm)*

THORPENESS   TM4759
★ Dolphin (01728) 454994
Just off B1353; Old Homes Road; village signposted from Aldeburgh; IP16 4FE Neatly kept extended pub in interesting seaside village (all built in the early 1900s);

main bar with scandinavian feel, pale wooden tables and pleasing assortment of old chairs on broad modern quarry tiles, log fire, Adnams, Woodfordes and a guest, several wines by the glass, more traditional public bar with pubby furniture on stripped-wood floor, built-in cushioned wall seats and old local photographs, airy dining room with country kitchen-style furniture, good food and friendly service; background music, TV; children and dogs welcome, good sized garden with terrace, bedrooms, open all day July, Aug. *(Mike and Linda Hudson, Anthony Barnes, J F M and M West, David Jackman)*

THURSTON   TL9165
Fox & Hounds (01359) 232228
Barton Road; IP31 3QT Quite an imposing building, welcoming inside, with well kept Adnams, Greene King and guests such as Woodfordes, pubby furnishings in neatly kept carpeted lounge (back part set for dining), lots of pump clips, ceiling fans, big helpings of reasonably priced pubby food (not Sun evening or Mon), bare-boards public bar with pool, darts and machines; background music and quiz nights; dogs welcome, picnic-sets on grassed area by car park and on small covered side terrace, pretty village, two bedrooms, open all day Fri-Sun. *(Jeremy King)*

TUDDENHAM   TM1948
★ Fountain (01473) 785377
The Street; village signed off B1077 N of Ipswich; IP6 9BT Buzzy well run dining pub in nice village, several linked café-style rooms (minimal décor) with heavy beams and timbering, stripped floors, wooden dining chairs around light tables, open fire, lots of prints (some by cartoonist Giles who spent time here after World War II), wide choice of well cooked food (all day Sun till 7pm) including set menus, Adnams Bitter and good selection of wines by the glass, decent coffee, pleasant helpful service; background music; no under-10s in bar after 6.30pm, wicker and metal chairs on covered heated terrace, more seats under huge parasols on sizeable lawn, closed first week Jan. *(J F M and M West, Nick Clare, Ryta Lyndley)*

UFFORD   TM2952
Crown (01394) 461030
High Street; IP13 6EL Welcoming family-run pub-restaurant, Adnams and a seasonal guest, Aspall's cider and a dozen wines by the glass, good well presented food from varied menu (changes daily), good service, newspapers; children welcome, garden picnic-sets and play area, open all day weekends (till 9pm Sun), closed Tues. *(Pat and Graham Williamson, Nick and Gillian Harrison)*

It's very helpful if you let us know up-to-date food prices when you report on pubs.

UFFORD
TM2952

White Lion (01394) 460770

Lower Street (off B1438, towards Eyke); IP13 6DW Home to the Uffa Brewery with Gold, Tipple, Pride and Punch plus guests from Adnams, Earl Soham and Woodfordes in 16th-c village pub near quiet stretch of River Deben; captain's chairs and wheelbacks around simple tables, central woodburning stove, enjoyable generous home-made food (they raise their own pigs, free-range hens and bees), shop/deli ; nice views from outside tables, may be summer barbecues, closed Mon lunchtime and Sun evening. *(Brian and Anna Marsden, Pat and Graham Williamson)*

WANGFORD
TM4679

Angel (01502) 578636

Signed just off A12 by B1126 junction; High Street; NR34 8RL Handsome old village coaching inn with airy beamed and carpeted bar, enjoyable good value food from sandwiches up, pleasant efficient service, Adnams, Black Sheep, Brakspears and Greene King, decent wines, family dining room; dogs welcome, seven comfortable bedrooms (the church clock sounds on the quarter), good breakfast. *(Annamstorey)*

WESTLETON
TM4469

White Horse (01728) 648222

Darsham Road, off B1125 Blythburgh–Leiston; IP17 3AH Friendly and relaxed traditional pub with generous home-made food and well kept ales from Adnams, unassuming high-ceilinged bar with central fire, steps down to stone-floored back dining room; children welcome, picnic-sets in cottagey garden with climbing frame, more out by village duck pond, four bedrooms, open (and food) all day Fri-Sun. *(Peter Meister)*

WITNESHAM
TM1850

Barley Mow (01473) 785395

Mow Hill; IP6 9EH Friendly old two-bar beamed local with enthusiastic community-spirited landlord, well kept ales such as Woodfordes Wherry, decent wines by the glass and reasonably priced tasty pub food (not Mon, Sat lunchtime, Sun evening) including specials, Giles cartoons dotted about (he used to drink here); quiz, bingo and music nights; children and dogs welcome, back garden (summer barbecues), open all day except Mon lunchtime. *(Paul Rampton, Julie Harding, J F M and M West)*

WOODBRIDGE
TM2648

Cherry Tree (01394) 384627

Opposite Notcutts Nursery, off A12; Cumberland Street; IP12 4AG 17th-c open-plan pub (bigger than it looks) with well kept Adnams and guests, good wines by the glass and ample helpings of reasonably priced tasty food including specials, friendly service, beams and two log fires, mix of pine furniture, old local photographs; children welcome, dogs in bar, garden with play area, three bedrooms in converted barn, good breakfast (for non-residents too), open all day. *(Nick and Gillian Harrison, MDN)*

WOODBRIDGE
TM2748

Crown (01394) 384242

Thoroughfare/Quay Street; IP12 1AD Stylishly refurbished 17th-c dining inn, well kept Adnams and Meantime from glass-roofed bar (boat suspended above counter), lots of wines by the glass, good imaginative food including fixed-price menu, pleasant young staff, various eating areas with contemporary furnishings, live jazz last Thurs of month; children and dogs (in bar) welcome, courtyard tables, ten well appointed bedrooms, open all day. *(Anon)*

WOODBRIDGE
TM2749

Olde Bell & Steelyard

(01394) 382933 *New Street, off Market Square; IP12 1DZ* Ancient and unpretentious timber-framed pub with two smallish beamed bars and compact dining room, lots of brassware, log fire, Greene King ales and guests from canopied servery, real ciders, enjoyable home-made food from bar snacks up, friendly welcoming staff, traditional games including bar billiards, live music; well behaved children and dogs welcome, back terrace, steelyard still overhanging street, open till late Fri and Sat. *(Simon Tucker)*

WOOLPIT
TL9762

Swan (01359) 240482

The Street; IP30 9QN Welcoming old coaching house pleasantly situated in village square, heavy beams and painted panelling, mixed tables and chairs on carpet, roaring log fire one end, very good inventive food from daily changing blackboard menu, prompt friendly service, well kept Adnams from slate-top counter and lots of wines by the glass; soft background music; walled garden behind, four bedrooms in converted stables. *(Michael and Mary Smith)*

Cribbage is a card game using a block of wood with holes for matchsticks or special pins to score with; regulars in cribbage pubs are usually happy to teach strangers how to play.

Surrey

KEY  ★ Star Pub 🍽️ Top Quality Food 🍺 Great Beer

🍷 Good Wines £ Bargain Meals 🛏️ Good Bedrooms 🍴 Serves Food

BRAMLEY
Jolly Farmer 🍷 🍺

TQ0044   Map 3

High Street; GU5 0HB

Relaxed village inn near Surrey Hills with great selection of beers

---

They keep a fine range of eight real ales on handpump in this warm and welcoming family-run pub: Wells & Youngs Original, plus guests that might include Bowman Swift One and Wallops Wood, Dove Street Bitter, Irving Invincible, Long Man Golden Tipple, Otley Hop Angeles and York Centurions Ghost Ale. Also, 18 wines by the glass, ten malt whiskies and two farm ciders. The traditional interior is filled with a homely miscellany of wooden tables and chairs, with collections of plates, enamel advertising signs, sewing machines, antique bottles, prints and old tools filling the walls and surfaces. Timbered semi-partitions, a mix of brick and timbering and an open fireplace give the place a snug, cosy feel; background music and board games. There are tables out by the car park, and the village is handy for Winkworth Arboretum (National Trust) and walks up St Martha's Hill.

🍴 Quite a choice of food includes lunchtime baguettes, devilled whitebait with home-made tartare sauce, baked field mushrooms with toppings, honey-glazed mustard ham and eggs, rack of barbecue pork ribs with fries, local sausages with red wine and onion gravy, chicken with sweet red peppers, cheese and cream sauce, braised lamb shank and mash, and puddings such as crème brûlée and pecan pie. *Benchmark main dish: burger with toppings, dips and chips £8.00. Two-course evening meal £18.00.*

Free house ~ Licensees Steve and Chris Hardstone ~ Real ale ~ (01483) 893355 ~ Open 11 (12 Sun)-11 ~ Bar food 12-2.30, 6 (7 Sun)-9.30 ~ Restaurant ~ Children welcome ~ Dogs allowed in bar ~ Wi-fi ~ Bedrooms: £90/£100 ~ www.jollyfarmer.co.uk
Recommended by Patrick Hamblin, John Thompson

BUCKLAND
Jolly Farmers 🍽️

TQ2250   Map 3

Reigate Road (A25 W of Reigate); RH3 7BG

Unusual place that serves and sells a wide range of local produce; fun to eat or shop in and atmospheric too

---

Some kind of food is served all day in this unusual pub-eatery-cum-farm shop: breakfast, morning coffee, lunch, afternoon tea and supper. The flagstoned bar, with beams and timbers, has an informal, relaxed atmosphere, brown leather sofas and armchairs, Hogs Back Fresh Spring

Ale and Pilgrim Progress on handpump, 13 wines by the glass and several malt whiskies. A small brick fireplace separates the bar from the wooden-floored dining room. The shop, stretching across three little rooms, stocks fresh vegetables, deli meats, cheeses, cakes, chocolates and their own range of preserves; they hold a weekly food market with stalls outside (Saturdays 9am-3pm) and organise several food festivals and events throughout the year. There are tables out on a back terrace overlooking the car park; children's play area.

 Using some home-grown produce, the interesting food includes lunchtime sandwiches, potted pig cheeks, truffled wild mushrooms on toast, sharing platters, steak and kidney pudding, leek and blue cheese tart, beef or spiced chicken burger with toppings, seared tuna steak with salad, a fish dish of the day, steaks with a sauce of choice, and puddings. *Benchmark main dish: beer-battered fish and chips £8.50. Two-course evening meal £19.00.*

Free house ~ Licensees Jon and Paula Briscoe ~ Real ale ~ (01737) 221355 ~ Open 8am (9am weekends)-11.30pm (10pm Sun) ~ Bar food 8am (9.15am weekends)-9.30pm (8pm Sun) ~ Restaurant ~ Children welcome ~ Dogs allowed in bar ~ Wi-fi ~ www.thejollyfarmersreigate.co.uk *Recommended by John Faircloth, Ian Herdman*

CHIPSTEAD
THE GOOD PUB GUIDE
White Hart 🏵 ♟

TQ2757 Map 3

Hazelwood Lane; CR5 3QW

Plenty to look at in open-plan rooms, thoughtful choice of drinks, interesting food and friendly staff

This is a neatly kept 18th-c pub opposite rugby playing fields and with distant views. The open-plan rooms are informal and friendly and there's lots to look at. A raftered dining room to the right has elegant metal chandeliers, rough-plastered walls, an open fire in a brick fireplace and a couple of carved metal standing uprights. The central bar has stools at the panelled counter where helpful staff serve Phoenix Brunning & Price Original, Pilgrim Surrey Bitter, Sharps Doom Bar, Tonbridge Coppernob and Westerham Hop Rocket India Pale Ale on handpump, 20 wines by the glass and up to 80 malt whiskies; background music and board games. The long room to the left is light and airy, with wall panelling at one end, a woodburning stove and numerous windows overlooking the seats on the terrace. Throughout, there's a fine mix of antique dining chairs and settles around all sorts of tables (each set with a church candle), rugs on bare boards or flagstones, hundreds of interesting cartoons, country pictures, cricketing prints and rugby team photographs, large ornate mirrors and, on the window sills and mantelpieces, old glass and stone bottles, clocks, books and plants.

 Rewarding food includes sandwiches, scallops with creamed leeks and pancetta, pork and black pudding fritters with piccalilli, poached egg muffin with wilted spinach and hollandaise, honey-glazed ham and free-range eggs, spicy peanut curry with okra, aubergine and red peppers, calves liver and crispy bacon with red wine gravy, smoked haddock and salmon fishcakes, slow-braised lamb shoulder with dauphinoise potatoes, and puddings such as warm chocolate brownie with boozy cherries and hot waffle with butterscotch sauce. *Benchmark main dish: chicken, ham and leek pie £13.95. Two-course evening meal £20.00.*

Brunning & Price ~ Manager Damian Mann ~ Real ale ~ (01737) 554455 ~ Open 11.30-11; 12-10.30 Sun ~ Bar food 12-10 (9.30 Sun) ~ Restaurant ~ Children welcome ~ Dogs allowed in bar ~ Wi-fi ~ www.brunningandprice.co.uk/whitehartchipstead
Recommended by Fiona Smith, John Branston

CLAYGATE

TQ1563 Map 3

Foley ♀

Hare Lane; KT10 0LZ

Carefully refurbished spreading place with lots of interesting drinking and dining areas, a thoughtful choice of drinks, wide range of snacks and full meals and efficient service; attractive bedrooms

Youngs have owned this pub for 126 years and have done a magnificent job of restoring and updating it. The most pubby part is at the front, where there's an assortment of wooden dining chairs and tables on bare boards, stools against the counter and leather armchairs and sofas by a Victorian fireplace: Wells & Youngs Bitter, Bombardier and Special and a changing guest ale on handpump, 30 wines by the glass, interesting spirits and quite a choice of coffees and teas. Leading off here are lots of interconnected but separate sitting and dining areas, with more armchairs, sofas, settles, long cushioned wall benches, an appealing variety of upholstered and wooden dining chairs around every size and style of table on floorboards or slate tiles, a glass-fronted, two-way open fire, candles in glass jars, and plenty of modern artwork; it's fun to sit and watch the action in the open kitchen. Also, background music, board games and daily papers. There's plenty of room for drinking and dining outside on the two-level terraces. The bedrooms are well equipped and comfortably contemporary.

As well as breakfasts, nibbles such as scotch eggs or sausage rolls and sandwiches, the highly thought-of food includes potted crab with samphire and capers, ham hock terrine with apple and piccalilli, sharing boards, sausages with ale-battered onion rings, provençale vegetable pancakes, burger with cheddar, bacon and chips, a pie of the day, salmon with roast fennel and fennel cream, and puddings. *Benchmark main dish: local rib-eye steak with peppercorn sauce and chips £19.95. Two-course evening meal £20.00.*

Wells & Youngs ~ Manager Nick Brookes ~ Real ale ~ (01372) 462021 ~ Open 11-11; 12-10.30 Sun ~ Bar food 7.30am-9.30am, 12-10; 8.30am-10.30am, 12-9 Sun ~ Restaurant ~ Children welcome ~ Dogs allowed in bar ~ Wi-fi ~ Bedrooms: $145/$155 ~ www.thefoley.co.uk *Recommended by Caroline Prescott, Martin Jones*

CRANLEIGH

TQ0539 Map 3

Richard Onslow

High Street; GU6 8AU

Busy pub with a good mix of customers in several bar rooms, four real ales and interesting all-day food; bedrooms

Open from 7.30am for breakfast and serving some kind of food all day every day, this bustling town-centre pub has a cheerful atmosphere and customers constantly dropping in and out. The little public bar has stools by the counter, leather tub chairs and a built-in sofa, and a slate-floored drinking area where they keep Adnams Lighthouse, Firebird Heritage XX, Sharps Doom Bar and Surrey Hills Shere Drop on handpump, ten wines by the glass, a few malt whiskies and a farm cider. Two dining rooms have a mix of tartan tub chairs around wooden tables, a rather fine long leather-cushioned church pew, local photographs on mainly pale paintwork and a couple of open fires, one in a nice brick fireplace. The sizeable restaurant, with pale tables and chairs on the wooden floor and modern flowery wallpaper, has big windows overlooking the street; background music and board games. There are a few tables and chairs in the terraced back garden and on the front pavement. The bedrooms are smart and well equipped.

🍴 From a well judged menu, the extremely good food includes sandwiches, queenie scallops with bacon and sweetcorn purée, lambs kidneys with grilled field mushroom, deli boards, a roast of the day, chestnut and artichoke pithivier with taleggio cream, smoked haddock kedgeree with a free-range poached egg, chicken with broad bean and pearl barley risotto and tarragon dressing, and puddings such as baked alaska using home-made Guinness ice-cream and chocolate millionaire's shortcake with salted caramel ice-cream. *Benchmark main dish: rump steak with béarnaise sauce and chips £18.50. Two-course evening meal £18.00.*

Peach Pub Company ~ Licensee John Taylor ~ Real ale ~ (01483) 274922 ~ Open 11-midnight ~ Bar food 7.30am-10pm ~ Restaurant ~ Children welcome ~ Dogs allowed in bar and bedrooms ~ Wi-fi ~ Bedrooms: /£90 ~ www.therichardonslow.co.uk
Recommended by David Jackman

ELSTEAD   SU9044   Map 2
Mill at Elstead

Farnham Road (B3001 just W of village, which is itself between Farnham and Milford); GU8 6LE

Fascinating building with big attractive waterside garden, Fullers beers and well liked food

Rising four storeys, this sensitively converted, largely 18th-c watermill is in a rather special setting above the prettily banked River Wey. Picnic-sets are dotted about by the water with its lovely millpond, swans and weeping willows, and it's charmingly floodlit at night. Big windows throughout make the most of the delightful surroundings. A series of rambling linked bar areas on the spacious ground floor, and a restaurant upstairs, change in mood from one part to the next. You'll find brown leather armchairs and antique engravings by a longcase clock, neat modern tables and dining chairs on dark woodstrip flooring, big country tables on broad ceramic tiles, iron pillars, stripped masonry and a log fire in a huge inglenook. Fullers London Pride, ESB, Seafarers and a guest ale on handpump and a good range of wines by the glass; background music.

🍴 The reliably good food includes sandwiches (until 6pm), smoked mackerel and potato terrine with horseradish dressing, black pudding and chorizo croquettes with confit tomato sauce, courgette, fennel, feta, mint, quinoa and nut salad, chicken, ham and leek pie, ballotine of chicken with mushroom sauce and fondant potato, pork wellington with ham and apple crumble and cider sauce, and puddings. *Benchmark main dish: provençale-style fish stew £14.95. Two-course evening meal £19.50.*

Fullers ~ Managers Jeff and Georgia Watts ~ Real ale ~ (01252) 703333 ~ Open 11-11; 11.30-10.30 Sun ~ Bar food 12-9 (8 Sun) ~ Restaurant ~ Children welcome ~ Dogs allowed in bar ~ Wi-fi ~ www.millelstead.co.uk   *Recommended by John Beeken*

ESHER   TQ1566   Map 3
Marneys

Alma Road (one-way), Weston Green; heading N on A309 from A307 roundabout, after Lamb & Star pub turn left into Lime Tree Avenue (signposted to All Saints Parish Church), then left at T junction into Chestnut Avenue; KT10 8JN

Country-feeling pub with good value traditional food and attractive garden

Handy for Hampton Court Palace, this rather charming little pub is just the place for lunch. There are just two rooms. The small snug bar with its low-beamed ceiling has Fullers London Pride, Sharps Doom Bar and Wells & Youngs Bitter on handpump, 16 wines by the glass, ten malt whiskies and perhaps horse racing on the unobtrusive corner TV. To the left, past a little cast-iron woodburning stove, the dining area has big pine tables, pews, pale country kitchen chairs and cottagey blue-curtained windows; background music. There are seats and wooden tables on the front terrace, which has views over the wooded common, village church and duck pond, and more seats on the decked area in the pleasantly planted sheltered garden.

 Very fairly priced for the area, the well thought-of food includes lunchtime sandwiches, box-baked camembert with chutney, deep-fried whitebait with tartare sauce, a pie of the week, thai-style salmon fishcakes with sweet chilli sauce, lamb and rosemary burger topped with goats cheese, minute steak and fries, and puddings such as crème brûlée and sticky toffee pudding. *Benchmark main dish: steak in ale pie £11.95. Two-course evening meal £20.00.*

Free house ~ Licensee Thomas Duxberry ~ Real ale ~ (020) 8398 4444 ~ Open 11am-11.30pm; 12-11 Sun ~ Bar food 12-2.30, 6-9; 12-4 Sun; not Fri-Sun evenings ~ Restaurant ~ Children welcome away from bar ~ Dogs allowed in bar ~ Wi-fi ~ www.marneys.com
Recommended by Ian Phillips, C and R Bromage, Simon Rodway

LEIGH
TQ2147 Map 3

Seven Stars ♀
Dawes Green, south of A25 Dorking–Reigate; RH2 8NP

Popular country dining pub with enjoyable food and good wines

On a sunny day, take advantage of the plentiful outside seating around this pretty tile-hung pub – in the beer garden at the front, on the terrace and in the side garden. Inside, it's neatly kept and homely with a properly traditional atmosphere. The comfortable saloon bar has fine flagstones, beams, dark wheelback chairs and a 1633 inglenook fireback showing a royal coat of arms. The public bar is plainer. They keep Fullers London Pride, Sharps Doom Bar, Wells & Youngs Bitter and a guest such as Surrey Hills Ranmore Ale on handpump on the glowing copper counter, alongside several wines by the glass. The sympathetic restaurant extension at the side incorporates 17th-c floor timbers from a granary.

 Well liked food includes lunchtime baguettes, deep-fried whitebait with spicy mayonnaise, prawn and crayfish cocktail, home-cooked ham and egg, butternut squash risotto, rump burger with interesting toppings and chips, chicken kiev with chasseur sauce, fish pie, and puddings such as mint chocolate mousse and apple and toffee crumble. *Benchmark main dish: burger with brie, caramelised onion and home-made mayonnaise £11.50. Two-course evening meal £18.00.*

Punch ~ Lease James Slayford ~ Real ale ~ (01306) 611254 ~ Open 12-11 (10 Sun) ~ Bar food 12-9.30; 12-6 Sun ~ Restaurant ~ Children welcome in restaurant only ~ Dogs allowed in bar ~ Wi-fi ~ www.7starsleigh.co.uk *Recommended by Nick Lawless, Michael and Margaret Cross, John Saville, R K Phillips*

MICKLEHAM
TQ1753 Map 3

Running Horses 🌟 ♀ 🛏
Old London Road (B2209); RH5 6DU

Upmarket pub with elegant restaurant and comfortable bar, and a wide choice of imaginative food

The terrace in front of this extremely popular and well run pub is a fine place to sit on a warm day among lovely flowering tubs and hanging baskets, and there's a peaceful view of the old church with its strange stubby steeple. The stylish and spacious bar has a cheerfully smart atmosphere, hunting pictures, racing cartoons and Hogarth prints, lots of race tickets hanging from a beam, fresh flowers or a fire in an inglenook at one end, cushioned wall settles and other dining chairs around straightforward pubby tables and bar stools. Brakspears Bitter, Oxford Gold and Special, Fullers London Pride and a seasonal guest from Brakspears on handpump, alongside 15 good wines by the glass; background music. The extensive restaurant is open to the bar and, although set out fairly formally with crisp white cloths and candles on each table, shares the same relaxing atmosphere. Parking is in a narrow lane (you can also park on the main road). A notice by the door asks walkers to remove or cover their boots.

First class food includes lunchtime sandwiches, ham hock terrine with piccalilli, chicken caesar salad, brie and mushroom risotto, moules frites, smoked haddock and salmon fishcakes with shallot and parsley sauce, a pie of the day, braised pork belly with sticky red cabbage, champ mash and cider sauce, calves liver with bacon and a rich onion jus, and puddings such as white chocolate and strawberry cheesecake and sticky toffee pudding. *Benchmark main dish: bubble and squeak with an egg and mornay sauce £12.95. Two-course evening meal £21.00.*

Brakspears ~ Manager Robin Taylor ~ Real ale ~ (01372) 372279 ~ Open 12-11 (10.30 Sun) ~ Bar food 12-2.30 (3 Sat), 7-9.30; 12-6 Sun ~ Restaurant ~ Children welcome but must be over 10 in bar area ~ Dogs allowed in bar ~ Wi-fi ~ Bedrooms: £95/£110 ~ www.therunninghorses.co.uk *Recommended by Sheila Topham, Mike Rothwell, John Evans*

MILFORD
Refectory 🍷 ◖
SU9542   Map 2

Portsmouth Road; GU8 5HJ

Lots of interest and space in beamed and timbered rooms, fine stone fireplaces, six real ales and other thoughtful drinks and well liked food

This is a handsome place with golden stone and timbers, and has, as one reader put it, 'a natural warmth and welcoming charm about it'. The L-shaped, mainly open-plan rooms are spacious and extremely interesting: there are strikingly heavy beams, exposed stone walls, stalling and standing timbers creating separate seating areas, and a couple of big log fires in handsome stone fireplaces. A two-tiered and balconied part at one end has a wall covered with huge brass platters; elsewhere, there are nice old photographs and a variety of paintings. Dining chairs and dark wooden tables are grouped on wooden, quarry-tiled or carpeted flooring, and there are also rugs, bookshelves, big pot plants, stone bottles on window sills and fresh flowers. High wooden bar stools line the long counter where they serve Phoenix Brunning & Price Original, Hogs Back TEA, Dark Star Hophead and guests such as Andwell Gold Muddler, Bowman Elderado and Hepworth Dark Horse on handpump, a dozen wines by the glass, around 80 malt whiskies and two farm ciders. There are teak tables and chairs in the back courtyard adjacent to the characterful pigeonry. Facilities for wheelchair users are outstandingly good and there are disabled parking spaces.

Quite a choice of food includes sandwiches, chicken liver pâté, tempura cauliflower fritters with chilli caponata relish, prawn and spinach linguine with white wine and cream, pork and leek sausages with wholegrain mustard mash and onion gravy, steak burger with bacon, cheese, coleslaw and chips, beef and mushroom in ale pie, braised lamb shoulder with dauphinoise potatoes and redcurrant gravy, and puddings such as crème brûlée and sticky toffee pudding with toffee sauce. *Benchmark main dish: beer-battered fish and chips £12.75. Two-course evening meal £19.00.*

Brunning & Price ~ Manager Katie Dallyn ~ Real ale ~ (01483) 413820 ~ Open 12-11; 12-10.30 Sun ~ Bar food 12-10 (9.30 Sun) ~ Restaurant ~ Children welcome ~ Dogs allowed in bar ~ Wi-fi ~ www.brunningandprice.co.uk/refectory *Recommended by Simon and Mandy King, Phil Bryant, Martin and Alison Stainsby, Mrs Sally Scott*

 OUTWOOD   TQ3246   Map 3
Bell
Outwood Common, just E of village; off A23 S of Redhill; RH1 5PN

An attractive, extended 17th-c dining pub on the outskirts of a village

Try to arrive early in warm weather so you can sit in the well managed garden, with its sheltered lawn among flowers and shrubs, and look past the surrounding pine trees to rolling fields and woods; it's very peaceful. The softly lit, smartly rustic beamed bar is warm and cosy, with oak and elm tables and chairs (some Jacobean in style), low beams and a vast stone inglenook fireplace. An enormous bell sits in a bar alcove. If you want to eat, it's best to book in advance, especially in the evening (when drinking-only space is limited). There's Fullers London Pride, ESB and a changing guest on handpump, plus 20 wines by the glass and a large range of spirits; background music.

Good, popular food includes lunchtime sandwiches, pigeon breast with red onion chutney, breaded whitebait with lemon aioli, sharing boards, butternut squash with feta, spinach and warm potato salad, burger with lots of toppings and chips, sea bream fillets with thai-style chutney, glazed ham hock with pineapple and a duck egg, and puddings such as crumble of the day and chocolate brownie with salted caramel ice-cream. *Benchmark main dish: liver and bacon with spring onion and pea mash £14.25. Two-course evening meal £21.00.*

Fullers ~ Managers Jason and Sian Smith ~ Real ale ~ (01342) 842989 ~ Open 12-11 (10.30 Sun) ~ Bar food 12-2.30, 6-9.30; 12-9 Sun ~ Restaurant ~ Children welcome ~ Dogs allowed in bar ~ Wi-fi ~ www.belloutwood.co.uk *Recommended by Geoffrey Kemp, John Branston*

 SHAMLEY GREEN   TQ0343   Map 3
Red Lion
The Green; GU5 0UB

Pleasant dining pub with popular tasty food and nice gardens

Looking over the village green and cricket pitch, this well run pub has helpful, friendly staff and enjoyable food. The two connected bars are fairly traditional with a mix of new and old wooden tables, chairs and cushioned settles on bare boards and red carpet, stripped standing timbers, fresh white walls and deep red ceilings and open fires; background music. Wells & Youngs IPA and a couple of guests such as Hogs Back TEA and Sharps Doom Bar on handpump, and 11 wines by the glass. There are plenty of hand-made rustic tables and benches outside, both at the front and the back – which is more secluded and has seats on a heated, covered terrace overlooking a pond and grassed dining areas.

Good food includes sandwiches, crispy duck salad with oranges and hoi sin dressing, king prawns in garlic butter, steak in ale pie, chilli con carne with sour cream, salmon in white wine topped with caramelised scallops, chicken stuffed with feta, sun-dried tomatoes, lemon and rosemary with fries, and puddings such as ginger pudding with ginger and brandy sauce and fruit crumble. *Benchmark main dish: veal schnitzel in lemon and garlic butter with a fried egg and fries £14.95. Two-course evening meal £19.00.*

Punch ~ Lease Debbie Ersser ~ Real ale ~ (01483) 892202 ~ Open 11.30-11; 12-10 Sun (12-8 in winter) ~ Bar food 12-2.30 (3 weekends), 6.30-9.30 (8.30 summer Sun); not winter Sun evening ~ Restaurant ~ Children welcome ~ Dogs allowed in bar ~ Wi-fi ~ www.redlionshamleygreen.com *Recommended by Emma Scofield, Tony and Rachel Schendel, C Merritt*

SUNBURY
TQ1068   Map 3
Flower Pot 🍴

1.6 miles from M3 junction 1; follow Lower Sunbury sign from exit roundabout, then at Thames Street turn right; pub on next corner, with Green Street; TW16 6AA

Former coaching inn with appealing, contemporary bar and dining room, real ales and all-day food; bedrooms

In a villagey area with waterside walks, this is a handsome pub with elegant wrought-iron balconies; it's just across the road from a lovely reach of the Thames. The airy bar has leather tub chairs around copper-topped tables, high chairs upholstered in brown and beige tartan around equally high tables in pale wood, attractive flagstones, contemporary paintwork and stools against the counter; there's also a couple of comfortably plush burgundy armchairs. The bar leads into the dining area, which has duck egg blue-painted and dark wooden cushioned dining chairs around an assortment of partly painted tables on wooden flooring, all manner of artwork on wallpapered walls and a large gilt-edged mirror over an open fireplace; candles in glass jars, fresh flowers, background music and newspapers. Brakspears Bitter and a guest beer on handpump and 15 wines by the glass. A side terrace has wood and metal tables and chairs. The bedrooms are smart and comfortable.

The well liked food includes spiced crab salad, chicken liver pâté with crab apple and grape jam, sharing boards, spinach and feta cannelloni with basil and tomato sauce, stone-baked pizzas, lamb shank with sweet potato mash and rosemary broth, piri-piri free-range chicken with coleslaw and fries, cod fillet with shrimps and asparagus and broad bean risotto, and puddings such as seasonal crumble and chocolate brownie. *Benchmark main dish: pie of the day £13.50. Two-course evening meal £18.00.*

Brakspears ~ Tenant Simon Bailey ~ Real ale ~ (01932) 780741 ~ Open 7am-11pm; 8am-midnight Sat, Sun ~ Bar food 7-3, 6-9 (10 Fri, Sat); 8am-9pm Sun ~ Restaurant ~ Children welcome ~ Dogs allowed in bar ~ Wi-fi ~ Bedrooms: /£109 ~ www.theflowerpothotel.co.uk *Recommended by Martin Jones, Isobel Mackinlay, Ron Corbett*

SUTTON GREEN
TQ0054   Map 2
Olive Tree ♀

Sutton Green Road; GU4 7QD

A good mix of drinkers and diners in sizeable country pub with plenty of fish dishes and wines by the glass

This is a big rambling dining pub in quiet countryside with walks nearby. The bar area has leather sofas by an open fire and stools against the counter where they keep Sharps Doom Bar and Timothy Taylors Landlord on handpump, 18 wines by the glass and seasonal home-made drinks such as elderflower cordial. The spreading dining room leads off from here, with cushions on settles, leather-seated high-backed dining chairs around an assortment of tables, wooden floors, clean-cut pastel décor and a relaxing atmosphere. There are seats and tables under parasols on the back terrace.

🍴 With quite an emphasis on fish, the highly thought-of food includes smoked salmon pâté, tiger prawn and roasted red pepper risotto, pancetta-wrapped monkfish with mustard seed and tarragon sauce, a platter of mixed roast shellfish and scallops with cream and Cointreau – as well as open sandwiches, wild mushrooms in garlic butter on toasted sourdough with a poached egg, chicken, mushroom and ham pie, beef stroganoff, lamb tagine, and puddings such as treacle tart and banoffi pie. *Benchmark main dish: beer-battered cod and chips £13.80. Two-course evening meal £19.00.*

Mitchells & Butlers~ Lease Gill and Rupert Ponsonby ~ Real ale ~ (01483) 729999 ~ Open 12-3, 6-11; 12-4 Sun; closed Sun evening, Mon ~ Bar food 12-2.30, 7-9.30 ~ Restaurant ~ Children welcome ~ Dogs allowed in bar ~ Wi-fi ~ www.theolivetreesuttongreen.com *Recommended by Peter Sutton, Peter Brix*

THAMES DITTON
Olde Swan 🍺
Summer Road; KT7 0QQ

TQ1667   Map 12

Fine spot by the Thames with terraced seating outside, character bars, several ales and tasty pubby food

On a warm day, our readers enjoy sitting at the smart wooden tables and chairs under blue parasols that overlook a quiet Thames backwater and across to Ditton Island. It's best to arrive early to be sure of finding somewhere to park just down the road. The long bar area has wood and flagstone flooring, dark farmhouse and other dining chairs around all sorts of tables, and comfortable leather sofas in front of a big brick fireplace with an open log fire. There's Greene King IPA and Abbot with guests such as Ascot Posh Pooch, Cottage Golden Arrow, Surrey Hills Shere Drop and Theakstons Black Bull on handpump, 18 wines by the glass and ten malt whiskies. The carpeted dining rooms are similarly furnished and have more open fires (one in a Tudor fireplace), standing timbers, bare brick (or interestingly wallpapered) walls, and various prints and paintings.

🍴 From a wide menu, the well liked food includes sandwiches and wraps, ham hock and black pudding hash with a poached egg and creamy mustard sauce, barbecue chicken wings, red pepper and cheese burger with sweet potato and mozzarella, half a roast chicken with coleslaw and chips, hickory and maple salmon fillet with edamame beans and salad, mixed grill with a free-range egg, and puddings such as gooseberry crumble and chocolate brownie. *Benchmark main dish: beer-battered fish and chips £9.49. Two-course evening meal £15.00.*

Greene King ~ Manager Mike Dandy ~ Real ale ~ (020) 8398 1814 ~ Open 11-11 (10.30 Sun) ~ Bar food 11-10; 12-9 Sun ~ Restaurant ~ Children welcome ~ Dogs allowed in bar ~ Wi-fi ~ Live jazz third Sun afternoon of month; disco last Fri of month ~ www.yeoldeswan-thames-ditton.co.uk *Recommended by Neil Muscroft*

'Children welcome' means the pub says it lets children inside without any special restriction. If it allows them in, but to restricted areas such as an eating area or family room, we specify this. Some pubs may impose an evening time limit. We do not mention limits after 9pm as we assume children are home by then.

THURSLEY
SU9039 Map 2

Three Horseshoes

Dye House Road, just off A3 SW of Godalming; GU8 6QD

Surrey Dining Pub of the Year

Civilised country village pub with a broad range of good food

Well placed for bracing heathland walks over Thursley Common (they keep walking maps by the bar), this is a pretty tile-hung pub owned by a consortium of villagers who rescued it from closure. It has the feel of a gently upmarket country local; the convivial beamed front bar has a winter log fire, Hogs Back TEA and guests such as Langham Hip Hop and Tillingbourne AONB on handpump, 12 wines by the glass, a few malt whiskies and a farm cider; background music. The art displayed in the dining room is for sale. Tables in the delightful two-acre garden take in pleasant views over the Common and Thursley's 1,000-year-old Saxon church. On the terrace are smart comfortable chairs around tables with parasols. A separate area has a big play fort, a barbecue and a charcoal spit-roast that is used on bank holidays. Visiting dogs and horses might get offered a biscuit or carrot.

 Very good food using local produce includes lunchtime sandwiches, rabbit, pigeon, bacon and mushroom terrine with piccalilli, trout with brown shrimps, caper, seaweed and potato salad and horseradish and raspberry vinegar, artichoke, rocket and pecorino risotto, chargrilled free-range chicken caesar with fresh anchovies, pollack with pea purée and avocado oil, confit duck leg with black pudding, goose fat beans and dauphinoise potatoes, and puddings such as wild strawberry and Pimms sorbet and triple chocolate brownie. *Benchmark main dish: pork and leek sausages with spring greens and fried onions £11.50. Two-course evening meal £22.00.*

Free house ~ Licensees David Alders and Sandra Proni ~ Real ale ~ (01252) 703268 ~ Open 12-3, 5.30-11; 12-11 Sat; 12-8 Sun ~ Bar food 12.30-2.15, 7-9.15; 12-3 Sun ~ Restaurant ~ Well behaved children welcome ~ Dogs allowed in bar ~ Wi-fi ~ www.threehorseshoesthursley.com *Recommended by Hunter and Christine Wright, N R White, Martin and Karen Wake, Tony and Jill Radnor*

WEST END
SU9461 Map 2

Inn at West End

Just under 2.5 miles from M3 junction 3; A322 S, on right; GU24 9PW

Clean-cut dining pub with prompt friendly service, excellent wines, popular inventive food using village-reared pork, game shot by the landlord and their own vegetables, and pretty terrace

By the time this *Guide* is published, the hard-working and enthusiastic licensees hope to have opened 12 comfortable and well equipped bedrooms here. Wine continues to play an important role, with 16 served in three sizes of glass from a list of around 500 (Iberia is the speciality), and several sherries, sweet wines and port. They plan to start a wine club offering wines by the case at importer prices. It's an open-plan place with attractive modern prints on canary-yellow walls above a red dado, bare floorboards and, on the left, a row of dining tables set with crisp white linen over pale yellow tablecloths. The bar counter – where you'll find Fullers London Pride and guests such as Andwell Resolute and Fullers Seafarers on handpump, and around 30 whiskies – is straight ahead as you come in, with chatting regulars perched on the comfortable bar stools.

The area on the right has a pleasant relaxed atmosphere, blue-cushioned wall benches and dining chairs around solid pale wood tables, broadsheet daily papers, magazines and a row of reference books on the brick chimneybreast above an open fire. This leads into a garden room, which in turn opens on to a terrace shaded by a grape- and clematis-covered pergola, and a very pleasant garden; boules.

They open at 9am (not Sunday) for coffee and cake, and use game from local shoots (some retrieved by Sunny the pub dog), village-reared pork and lamb and home-grown vegetables. The nicely presented and very good food includes sandwiches, goats cheese and rosemary bonbons with poached pear and walnut dressing, fritto misto with aioli and rouille, red onion, mushroom and kale risotto with basil oil, game casserole, calves liver, crispy bacon and roasted garlic mash, fish pie, shredded venison and caramelised onion filo parcel with red wine jus, and puddings such as passion-fruit panna cotta with blood orange, and fruit and nut brownie with dark chocolate sauce; they also offer a two-course set lunch (not Sunday). *Benchmark main dish: smoked haddock kedgeree and poached egg £12.00. Two-course evening meal £25.00.*

Free house ~ Licensees Gerry and Ann Price ~ Real ale ~ (01276) 858652 ~ Open 9am-11pm; 12-10.30 Sun ~ Bar food 12-2.30, 6-9.30 ~ Restaurant ~ Children welcome if seated and dining ~ Dogs allowed in bar ~ Wi-fi ~ www.the-inn.co.uk
Recommended by Ian Wilson, Edward Mirzoeff, S F Parrinder, Susan and John Douglas

Also Worth a Visit in Surrey

Besides the fully inspected pubs, you might like to try these pubs that have been recommended to us and described by readers. Do tell us what you think of them: feedback@goodguides.com

ABINGER COMMON   TQ1146
Abinger Hatch (01306) 730737
Off A25 W of Dorking, towards Abinger Hammer; RH5 6HZ
Modernised dining pub in beautiful woodland spot, spacious interior with heavy beams and log fires, good food from ciabattas and sharing plates up, plenty of wines by the glass, Ringwood Best, friendly attentive staff; children and dogs (in one area) welcome, some disabled access, picnic-sets in side garden with boules, summer barbecues, near pretty church and pond. *(Anon)*

ALBURY   TQ0447
★ **Drummond Arms** (01483) 202039
Off A248 SE of Guildford; The Street; GU5 9AG Smartened pub in pretty village; Adnams, Courage, Fullers and a guest such as Hogs Back TEA, good choice of wines, food from sandwiches and light dishes up, cheerful courteous service, opened-up bar with leather chesterfields, log fire and newspapers, parquet-floored dining room, conservatory; good-sized pretty back garden by little River Tillingbourne, duck island, summer barbecues and hog roasts, pleasant walks nearby, nine bedrooms, open all day weekends. *(Ian Phillips, John Branston)*

ALFOLD   TQ0435
Alfold Barn (01403) 752288
Horsham Road, A281; GU6 8JE
Beautifully preserved 16th-c building with bar and restaurant, good locally sourced home-made food including weekday lunch deal, friendly attentive service, up to three well kept ales from nearby breweries, beams and rafters, mixed furniture on flagstones or carpet, warming log fires; children welcome, garden with play area and animals including Rosie the goat, closed Sun evening, Mon. *(Anon)*

ALFOLD   TQ0334
Three Compasses (01483) 275729
Dunsfold Road; GU6 8HY Reworked 400-year-old pub with interesting 1940s theme (plenty to look at); well kept Otter, Sharps Doom Bar and a guest, enjoyable freshly made food (not Sun evening, Mon) in bar and restaurant area, games room with darts, table

skittles and bar billiards, Mon swing/jive classes; children and dogs welcome, good-sized garden with play area, on back lane to former Dunsfold Aerodrome (now Dunsfold Park with little museum, and home to *Top Gear*'s test track), Wey & Arun Canal nearby, open all day in summer, closed Sun evening, Mon in winter. *(Tony and Wendy Hobden)*

ASH VALE   SU8952
Swan (01252) 325212
Hutton Road, off Ash Vale Road (B3411) via Heathvale Bridge Road; GU12 5HA Three-room Chef & Brewer on Basingstoke Canal, wide choice of popular well priced food all day including specials, ales such as Fullers London Pride and Surrey Hills Shere Drop, good value wines by the glass, mix of furniture on tiles or carpet, large log fires; background music; children welcome, attractive garden, neat heated terraces and window boxes, open all day. *(Anon)*

BANSTEAD   TQ2559
Woolpack (01737) 354560
High Street; SM7 2NZ Open-plan pub with well kept Shepherd Neame ales and a couple of interesting guests, enjoyable home-made food from standard dishes up (some available in smaller helpings), friendly helpful service, restaurant, Thurs quiz, live music including afternoon trad jazz (first Tues of month), buoyant local atmosphere evenings; plenty of seats in big garden, open all day. *(Conor McGaughey, Sue and Mike Todd)*

BETCHWORTH   TQ1950
Arkle Manor (01737) 842110
Reigate Road; RH3 7HB Smart Mitchells & Butlers restaurant pub with good choice of popular food including weekday fixed-price offer till 6pm, friendly efficient service (they may ask for a credit card if running a tab), appealing rambling layout with easy chairs and so forth, real ales and lots of wines by the glass, cocktails; children welcome, steps up to back terrace and leafy garden, open all day. *(John Evans)*

BETCHWORTH   TQ2149
Dolphin (01737) 842288
Off A25 W of Reigate; The Street; RH3 7DW Beamed 16th-c village pub on Greensand Way, plain tables on ancient flagstones in neat front bar with inglenook log fire, snug and a further panelled bar with chiming grandfather clock, nice old local photographs, well kept Wells & Youngs ales and guests such as Hogs Back, enjoyable fairly priced traditional food (all day weekends) including daily specials, friendly efficient young staff, restaurant; children and dogs welcome, front and side terraces, back garden, picturesque village (fine Pre-Raphaelite pulpit in church), open all day. *(John Evans)*

BLETCHINGLEY   TQ3250
Red Lion (01883) 743342
Castle Street (A25), Redhill side; RH1 4NU Modernised beamed village dining pub, mix of tables and chairs, lots of racing prints, good reasonably priced mainly traditional food all day (till 8pm Sun), friendly staff, well kept Greene King ales and good choice of wines by the glass; monthly quiz, some live music including tribute bands; children welcome (under-10s till 7pm), tables on heated terrace by car park, secret garden, open all day. *(Geoffrey Kemp, David Jackman)*

BLETCHINGLEY   TQ3250
Whyte Harte (01883) 743231
2.5 miles from M25 junction 6, via A22 then A25 towards Redhill; RH1 4PB Low-beamed Tudor inn doing well under current management; good well presented food served by friendly staff, three changing ales and plenty of wines by the glass, big inglenook log fire in extensive open-plan bar, separate dining area; background music; lovely beer garden, eight bedrooms, good breakfast, attractive village street (shame about the traffic), open all day. *(Nick Lawless, Fiona Smith)*

BLINDLEY HEATH   TQ3645
★ Red Barn (01342) 830820
Tandridge Lane, just off B2029, which is off A22; RH7 6LL Splendid farmhouse/ barn conversion; contemporary furnishings mixing with 17th-c beams and timbers, central glass-sided woodburner (its flue soaring up into the roof), large model plane hanging from rafters, one wall with shelves of books, another hung with antlers, clever partitioning creating cosier areas too; red cooking range and big wooden tables in farmhouse-style room, adjacent bar with sofas by large fireplace, one or two real ales and good wine list, well liked food served by efficient smart staff; background and some live music, bar billiards; children and dogs (in bar) welcome, solid granite tables on lawn, farmers' market first Sat of month, open all day. *(Derek Thomas, Mrs Sally Scott)*

BROCKHAM   TQ1949
Inn on the Green (01737) 845101
Brockham Green; RH3 7JS Comfortably refurbished dining pub facing village green, enjoyable if not cheap food from traditional choices up including steaks cooked on a hot stone, well kept Adnams, Black Sheep and Fullers London Pride, conservatory; children welcome, picnic-sets out at front, garden behind. *(Anon)*

BROCKHAM   TQ1949
Royal Oak (01737) 843241
Brockham Green; RH3 7JS Nice spot on charming village green below North Downs; bare boards bar and light airy

dining area, well kept Sharps and Wells & Youngs, enjoyable freshly cooked pub food at reasonable prices, good service from warmly welcoming staff; children and dogs allowed, tables out in front looking across to fine church, more seats in back garden, handy for Greensand Way. *(C and R Bromage, Peter Hailey)*

BYFLEET — TQ0661
Plough (01932) 354895

High Road; KT14 7QT Small friendly local with some refurbishment under present licensees; eight real ales including Sharps Doom Bar and Wells & Youngs Bombardier, traditional food, beams and two open fires, rustic furnishings, farm tools, brass and copper, more modern back area, crib and dominoes, charity quiz second Tues of month; children (away from bar) and dogs welcome, terrace and shady back garden, open all day. *(Ian Phillips)*

CARSHALTON — TQ2764
Hope (020) 8240 1255

West Street; SM5 2PR Friendly community pub saved from closure by local consortium; Downton, Windsor & Eton and five guests, also craft beers, real cider/perry and over 50 bottled beers, generous low-priced pubby food (limited evening choice), 1950s feel with a room either side of bar, lots of pump clips on walls, open fire, larger back room with bar billiards, some live mainly acoustic music, regular beer and cider festivals; garden, open all day. *(Conor McGaughey, Tony Hobden)*

CATERHAM — TQ3254
Harrow (01883) 343260

Stanstead Road, Whitehill; CR3 6AJ Beamed 16th-c pub high up in open country by North Downs Way; L-shaped bare-boards bar and carpeted back dining area, several real ales (sometimes straight from the cask), enjoyable food (not Sun evening) including daily specials, good local atmosphere and friendly service; children and dogs welcome, garden picnic-sets, popular with walkers and cyclists, open all day. *(Tim Everitt)*

CHARLESHILL — SU8844
Donkey (01252) 702124

B3001 Milford–Farnham near Tilford; coming from Elstead, turn left as soon as you see pub sign; GU10 2AU Old-fashioned beamed dining pub with nice landlady and prompt friendly service, enjoyable home-made food, well kept ales such as Fullers, Greene King and Harveys, good choice of wines by the glass, conservatory restaurant, traditional games; children and dogs welcome, attractive garden

with wendy house, much-loved donkeys Pip and Dusty, good walks, open all day Sun. *(Mrs P Sumner, Tony and Jill Radnor)*

CHERTSEY — TQ0566
Kingfisher (01932) 579811

Chertsey Bridge Road (Shepperton side of river); KT16 8LF Big Vintage Inn in good Thames-side spot by 18th-c bridge; repro period décor and furnishings in series of small intimate areas, ales such as Fullers, Hogs Back and Timothy Taylors, good choice of wines by the glass, their usual menus from sandwiches up including fixed-price offer till 5pm, friendly service, log fires, daily papers, large-scale map for walkers, interesting old pictures; soft background music; families welcome if eating, roadside terrace looking over to river, open all day. *(Ian Phillips, Eddie Edwards)*

CHERTSEY — TQ0466
Thyme at the Tavern
(01932) 429667 *London Street; KT16 8AA* Busy local with Courage Best, Marstons Pedigree and two guests from nearby breweries (regular festivals), well priced pubby food (not Mon, Sat or evenings Fri, Sun) from sandwiches and sharing plates up, popular Sun lunch (must book), live music Fri; dogs welcome, bedrooms, open all day (from 5pm Mon, 4pm Sat). *(Hunter and Christine Wright)*

CHIDDINGFOLD — SU9635
★ Crown (01428) 682255

The Green (A283); GU8 4TX Lovely 700-year-old timbered building with strong sense of history; bar and connected dining rooms with massive beams (some over 2-ft thick), oak panelling, fine stained-glass windows and magnificently carved fireplace, mate's and other pubby chairs, cushioned wall seats and some fine antique tables, lots of portraits, simple split-level back public bar with open fire, Fullers, Hogs Back, Ringwood and Sharps, several wines by the glass, enjoyable often interesting food (all day weekends); children (there's a playroom) and dogs welcome in some areas, seats outside looking across village green to interesting church, more tables in sheltered central courtyard, character bedrooms, open all day from 7am (8am Sun) for breakfast. *(Richard and Penny Gibbs, David H T Dimock)*

CHILWORTH — TQ0347
Percy Arms (01483) 561765

Dorking Road; GU4 8NP Partly 18th-c inn with south african influences in décor and food, good choice of wines by the glass, Greene King ales and a beer named for the pub, front bar and lounge with steps down to dining area, efficient service despite being busy, newspapers and background jazz; children welcome, garden tables with pretty views over Vale of Chilworth to St Martha's Hill, good walks, five bedrooms. *(Anon)*

CHIPSTEAD TQ2555
Well House (01737) 830640
Chipstead signed with Mugswell off A217, N of M25 junction 8; CR5 3SQ Cottagey 16th-c pub with log fires in all three rooms, well kept Adnams, Fullers, Surrey Hills and local guests, Millwhites cider, food from baguettes up (not Sun evening), friendly staff, bric-a-brac above bar, pewter tankards hanging from ceiling, conservatory, resident ghost called Harry the Monk; dogs allowed (they have cats), large pleasing hillside garden with ancient well (reputed to be mentioned in the Domesday Book), delightful setting, open all day. *(Conor McGaughey, N R White)*

CHURT SU8538
Crossways (01428) 714323
Corner of A287 and Hale House Lane; GU10 2JE Friendly down-to-earth local, quarry-tiled public bar and carpeted saloon with panelling and plush banquettes, busy evenings for great changing beer range at reasonable prices, also four or more real ciders, good well priced home-made pub lunches (not Sun) including nice pies, evening food Weds only, cheerful young staff; TVs and machines; dogs welcome, garden, open all day Fri-Sun. *(Tony and Jill Radnor)*

CLAYGATE TQ1563
Hare & Hounds (01372) 465149
The Green; KT10 0JL Renovated flower-decked Victorian/Edwardian village pub with small restaurant, good sensibly priced french food, nice wines and well kept ales, competent friendly service; outside seating at front and in small back garden. *(Geoffrey Kemp)*

COBHAM TQ1159
Running Mare (01932) 862007
Tilt Road; KT11 3EZ Attractive old flower-decked pub overlooking green (can get very busy); well kept Fullers, Hogs Back and Wells & Youngs, good food including popular Sun lunch, efficient friendly service, two timbered bars and restaurant, some refurbishment; children very welcome, a few tables out at front and on rose-covered back terrace, open all day. *(Shirley Mackenzie, Geoffrey Kemp, C and R Bromage)*

COLDHARBOUR TQ1544
Plough (01306) 711793
Village signposted in the network of small roads around Leith Hill; RH5 6HD Cosy two-bar pub with own-brewed Leith Hill ales and guests, proper cider and several wines by the glass, open fires, light beams

and timbering, food in bar or restaurant (not always open) including range of home-made burgers, pleasant service, snug games room with darts, board games and cards; background music, TV; children (if eating) and dogs welcome, front terrace and quiet back garden overlooking fields, five bedrooms (ones above bar noisy), open all day. *(Richard Stanfield)*

COMPTON SU9546
Harrow (01483) 810594
B3000 towards Godalming off A3; GU3 1EG 18th-c roadside pub with emphasis on enjoyable good value pub food (not Sun evening), three real ales and good choice of wines by the glass, friendly attentive service, split-level bar with log fire, beamed dining area; children welcome, back terrace and streamside garden, open all day. *(Anon)*

COMPTON SU9646
★ ## Withies (01483) 421158
Withies Lane; pub signed from B3000; GU3 1JA Carefully altered 16th-c pub, charmingly civilised and gently old-fashioned, with low-beamed bar, some 17th-c carved panels between windows, splendid art nouveau settle among old sewing-machine tables, log fire in massive inglenook, well kept Adnams, Greene King IPA, Hogs Back TEA and Sharps Doom Bar, popular (not cheap) bar food served by efficient bow-tied staff; children welcome, seats on terrace, under apple trees and creeper-hung arbour, flower-edged neat front lawn, on edge of Loseley Park and close to Watts Gallery, closed Sun evening. *(Conor McGaughey, Colin McKerrow, Dr and Mrs J D Abell, Helen and Brian Edgeley, Geoffrey Kemp)*

DORMANSLAND TQ4042
Old House At Home (01342) 836828
West Street; RH7 6QP Friendly 19th-c village pub, beamed bar with open fire and traditional furniture on parquet floor, horsebrasses above unusual barrel-fronted counter serving Shepherd Neame ales, enjoyable well priced food (not Sun evening) cooked by landlady-chef including some good vegetarian options and fresh pizzas, carpeted restaurant and plainer room with darts and TV, some live music; children and dogs welcome, a few picnic-sets in front, beer garden behind. *(Anon)*

DORMANSLAND TQ4042
Plough (01342) 832933
Plough Road, off B2028 NE; RH7 6PS Friendly traditional old pub in quiet village, well kept Fullers, Harveys and Sharps, Weston's cider, decent wines, good choice of enjoyable bar food including specials board, thai restaurant, log fires and original features; children welcome, disabled facilities, good-sized garden. *(R and S Bentley, David Jackman)*

DUNSFOLD TQ0036
Sun (01483) 200242
Off B2130 S of Godalming; GU8 4LE
Old double-fronted pub with four rooms
(brighter at the front), beams and some
exposed brickwork, scrubbed pine furniture
and two massive log fires, ales such as
Adnams, Harveys and Sharps, decent wines,
enjoyable home-made pub food at reasonable
prices including popular Sun lunch (best to
book), good friendly service; Sun quiz, darts;
children and dogs welcome, seats on terrace
and common opposite, good walks.
(Ian Phillips)

EASHING SU9543
★ Stag (01483) 421568
*Lower Eashing, just off A3 southbound;
GU7 2QG* Civilised, gently upmarket
riverside pub with Georgian façade masking
much older interior; attractively opened-up
rooms including charming old-fashioned
locals' bar with armchairs on red and black
quarry tiles, cosy log-fire snug beyond, Hogs
Back TEA, a house beer from Marstons and
two guests, Hazy Hog cider, good choice of
enjoyable food served by attentive courteous
staff, several linked dining areas including
river room up a couple of steps looking out on
to mature trees by millstream; dogs allowed
in bar, extensive terrace with wicker and
wooden furniture under parasols (some by
weir), picnic-sets on grass, seven bedrooms,
open all day. *(Martin and Karen Wake, Sheila
Topham)*

EAST CLANDON TQ0551
★ Queens Head (01483) 222332
*Just off A246 Guildford–Leatherhead;
The Street; GU4 7RY* Popular refurbished
dining pub in same small group as Duke of
Cambridge at Tilford, Stag at Eashing and
Wheatsheaf at Farnham, good food from light
dishes up including set lunch (Mon-Thurs),
well kept Hogs Back, Ringwood and Surrey
Hills from fine elm-topped counter, also Hazy
Hog cider, good friendly service, comfortable
linked rooms, log fire in big inglenook, daily
newspapers; children welcome, tables out
in front and on new side terrace, handy for
Clandon Park and Hatchlands (both NT),
open all day Fri, Sat, till 9pm Sun.
(John Saville, John Evans)

EFFINGHAM TQ1153
★ Plough (01372) 458121
Orestan Lane; KT24 5SW Popular
refurbished Youngs pub with well kept ales
and enjoyable home-made food including
good Sun roasts and proper children's
menu, plenty of wines by the glass, friendly
efficient staff, open interior around central
bar, grey painted beams, delft shelving and
half-panelling, wood floors, two coal-effect
gas fires; plenty of tables on forecourt and
in pretty garden with fruit trees, disabled
access and parking, handy for Polesden Lacey

(NT), open all day Sun till 7pm. *(Shirley
Mackenzie, Alan and Shirley Sawden, Simon and
Mandy King)*

ENGLEFIELD GREEN SU9771
Sun (01784) 432515
Wick Lane, Bishopsgate; TW20 0UF
Friendly lived-in beamed local with well kept
Courage Best, Greene King and Sharps Doom
Bar, good blackboard wine choice, generous
inexpensive pubby food from sandwiches
up, pleasant attentive service, small wooden
tables with banquettes and low stools, lots
of pub bric-a-brac including interesting beer
bottle collection, log fire, conservatory; soft
background music and silent games machine;
children welcome, biscuits and water for
dogs, a few tables out at front and in quiet
little garden, handy for Windsor Great Park
and Savill Garden. *(Simon Collett-Jones)*

EPSOM TQ2158
Derby Arms (01372) 722330
Downs Road, Epsom Downs; KT18 5LE
Comfortably reworked Mitchells & Butlers
dining pub, their usual popular food, good
range of wines by the glass and two real ales,
efficient courteous staff, open contemporary
feel in bar and restaurant with horse-racing
theme, two-way log fire; picnic-sets outside,
good views – opposite racecourse grandstand,
open all day. *(P and J Shapley)*

EPSOM TQ2160
Rising Sun (01372) 740809
Heathcote Road; KT18 5DX Friendly well
restored Victorian backstreet pub, open-
plan but with well defined cosy front bar,
Wells & Youngs and a couple of mainstream
guests, several wines by the glass, enjoyable
home-made food (till 10pm Sat) with
some imaginative additions to traditional
menu, efficient courteous service, open
fire; disabled access/facilities, nice garden
with covered area, barbecues, open all
day. *(Stephen O'Neill, Simon and Mandy King)*

EPSOM TQ2158
Rubbing House (01372) 745050
*Langley Vale Road (on Epsom Downs
Racecourse); KT18 5LJ* Restauranty
dining pub popular for its fantastic
racecourse views – can get very busy but
staff cope well; attractive modern décor,
good value promptly served food including
children's menu, tables perhaps a little
close together, Greene King and Sharps ales,
serious wine list, upper balcony for Derby
days; background music; seating out by
course, open all day. *(P and J Shapley,
C and R Bromage, N R White)*

ESHER TQ1264
Prince of Wales (01372) 465483
*West End Lane; off A244 towards
Hersham, by Princess Alice Hospice;
KT10 8LA* Busy Victorian dining pub (Chef
& Brewer) in nice village setting on edge of

green; wide choice of reasonably priced food all day including children's menu, well kept Adnams, Fullers and Rebellion, good wine choice, friendly efficient service, log fires and newspapers; background music; disabled access, big garden, old brewery building next door (now staff accommodation), open all day. *(Ian Phillips, Geoffrey Kemp, Tom and Ruth Rees)*

FARNHAM   SU8346
Wheatsheaf (01252) 717135
West Street; GU9 7DR Stylishly refurbished old pub in same group as the Queens Head at East Clandon, Stag at Eashing and Duke of Cambridge at Tilford; good food (all day Fri-Sun) from open kitchen including grills, gluten-free diets catered for, local ales such as Hogs Back, craft beers and good choice of wines and whiskies, friendly helpful staff; free wi-fi; children welcome, seats in back courtyard, open all day (from 9am weekends for breakfast). *(Anon)*

FICKLESHOLE   TQ3960
White Bear (01959) 573166
Featherbed Lane/Fairchildes Lane; off A2022 just S of A212 roundabout; CR6 9PH Long 16th-c country dining pub with lots of small rooms, beams, flagstones and open fires, popular good value food (all day Fri, Sat from breakfast on), orders taken from the bar (they ask for a credit card if you run a tab), Brakspears, Pilgrim and a couple of guests; children and well behaved dogs welcome, picnic-sets and stone bear on front terrace, sizeable back garden with summer 'kitchen', open all day. *(Mrs Elizabeth Hough, C and R Bromage, Alec and Joan Laurence, David Jackman)*

FOREST GREEN   TQ1241
★ **Parrot** (01306) 621339
B2127 just W of junction with B2126, SW of Dorking; RH5 5RZ Cheerful old tile-hung village pub, heavy beams, timbers, flagstones and nooks and crannies, inglenook log fire, popular food (not Sun evening) using produce from own farm, five well kept changing ales including Ringwood, 16 wines by the glass, local fruit juices, efficient friendly service; shop selling own meat, cheeses, cured hams, pies and so forth; dogs welcome in bar, disabled facilities, attractive gardens with lovely country views, good walks nearby, open all day (till midnight Sat). *(Richard Stanfield, Guy Vowles, P and J Shapley)*

GODALMING   SU9643
Star (01483) 417717
Church Street; GU7 1EL Friendly 17th-c local in cobbled pedestrian street, cosy low-beamed and panelled L-shaped bar, up to eight well kept changing ales (four tapped from the cask) including Greene King, five proper ciders/perries, lunchtime bar food, more modern back room, regular events including Mon folk night, Weds knitting

(Stitch n' Bitch), chess and book clubs; heated back terrace, open all day. *(George Batty)*

GODSTONE   TQ3551
White Hart (01883) 743216
Handy for M25 junction 6; High Street; RH9 8DU Beamed and timbered Mitchells & Butlers pub (former coaching inn) opposite pretty village pond, emphasis on food side with good choice in bar and restaurant including fixed-price menu, Fullers London Pride and a guest, decent choice of wines by the glass, friendly staff, conservatory; children welcome, suntrap back courtyard, open all day. *(Phil and Jane Hodson, Ian Phillips)*

GOMSHALL   TQ0847
Compasses (01483) 202506
Station Road (A25); GU5 9LA Popular village pub with plain bar and much bigger comfortable dining room, also café and post office, good value home-made food (all day except Sun evening), well kept Surrey Hills ales, decent wines by the glass, friendly helpful service; background music (live Fri) – also Aug 'Gomstock' festival; children and dogs welcome, pretty garden sloping down to roadside mill stream, two bedrooms, open all day. *(Alan and Shirley Sawden)*

GOMSHALL   TQ0847
Gomshall Mill (01483) 203060
Station Road; GU5 9LB Timber-framed medieval mill by River Tillingbourne, part of the Home Counties group and quite restauranty, although does serve four well kept ales and several wines by the glass, good sensibly priced food including sandwiches and children's meals, friendly staff, interesting multi-level interior; terrace seating, open all day. *(Hunter and Christine Wright)*

GRAYSWOOD   SU9134
Wheatsheaf (01428) 644440
Grayswood Road (A286 NE of Haslemere); GU27 2DE Welcoming family-run dining pub with light airy décor, enjoyable freshly made food in bar and restaurant, good range of well kept beers, friendly helpful staff; front verandah, side terrace, seven bedrooms in extension, good breakfast. *(Anon)*

GUILDFORD   SU9949
Kings Head (01483) 575004
Quarry Street; GU1 3XQ Dating from the 16th c with lots of beams and stripped brickwork, cosy corners with armchairs, stylish oval tables, inglenook log fire, well kept Hogs Back and guests, decent wines, enjoyable reasonably priced food (not Sun evening) including variety of burgers and pizzas, bargain lunch deal Mon-Thurs, quiz-and-curry night Mon, friendly young staff; background music (live Sun), fruit machine,

sports TV, no dogs inside; picnic-sets in pleasant back courtyard with roof terrace giving castle views, open all day (till 2.30am Fri, Sat). *(Phil and Jane Villiers)*

GUILDFORD   SU9948
Olde Ship (01483) 575731
Portsmouth Road (St Catherine's, A3100 S); GU2 4EB Three cosy areas around central bar, ancient beams, bare boards and flagstones, roaring log fire in big fireplace, woodburner the other end, comfortable mix of furniture, enjoyable food including good wood-fired pizzas, well kept Greene King ales and a guest, decent wines, friendly staff and locals; dogs welcome, open all day weekends. *(Anon)*

GUILDFORD   SU9949
Three Pigeons (01483) 575728
High Street; GU1 3AJ Nicholsons pub with good beer range, pleasant panelled décor, spiral stairs to upper bar; background music; open all day (till midnight Fri, Sat). *(Ian Phillips)*

GUILDFORD   SU9949
Weyside (01483) 568024
Shalford Road, Millbrook; across car park from Yvonne Arnaud Theatre, beyond boatyard; GU1 3XJ Big riverside pub (former Boatman) recently refurbished by Youngs, their ales and enjoyable food from sharing dishes and pub favourites up, friendly service, large split-level bar dropping down to back dining conservatory, also barn-room restaurant; children and dogs welcome, terrace overlooking River Wey, open all day. *(Anon)*

HAMBLEDON   SU9639
Merry Harriers (01428) 682883
Off A283; just N of village; GU8 4DR Beamed 16th-c country local with huge inglenook log fire and pine tables on bare boards, five well kept ales including Pilgrim, Surrey Hills and Tillingbourne, decent wines, generally well liked pub food from sandwiches up, all home-made and sourced locally, friendly staff, occasional live music and beer festivals; children welcome, seats out in front and in big garden with boules, llamas in adjacent fields, good walking country near Greensand Way, three bedrooms in converted barn, campsite, open all day weekends in summer. *(N R White)*

HORLEY   TQ2742
Olde Six Bells (01293) 825028
Quite handy for M23 junction 9, off Horley turn from A23; Church Road – head for the church spire; RH6 8AD Ancient stone-roofed Vintage Inn – part of heavy-beamed open-plan bar was probably a medieval chapel and some masonry may date from 9th c; their usual good value food including fixed-price menu, Fullers London Pride, Sharps Doom Bar and a guest, log

fires, upstairs overflow raftered dining room, conservatory; children welcome, tables out by bend in River Mole, open all day. *(Tony Scott)*

HORSELL   SU9859
Cricketers (01483) 762363
Horsell Birch; GU21 4XB Country pub popular for its good sensibly priced food including Sun carvery, cheerful efficient service, Shepherd Neame ales and plenty of wines by the glass, quietly comfortable sections and extended back eating area, log fires, newspapers, live jazz Mon; no dogs inside; children welcome, wheelchair access, picnic-sets out at front overlooking Horsell Common, big back garden with barbecue and play area. *(Ian Phillips)*

HORSELL   SU9959
Plough (01483) 714105
Off South Road; Cheapside; GU21 4JL Small friendly local overlooking wooded heath, relaxed atmosphere, well kept Dartmoor, Sharps and a guest, reasonably priced home-made food (not Sun or Mon evenings) including daily specials and weekday set-menu, L-shaped bar with woodburner; Weds quiz; families and dogs welcome (theirs is Buddy), tables in pretty garden with play area, open all day. *(Ian Phillips)*

HORSELL   SU9959
★ **Red Lion** (01483) 768497
High Street; GU21 4SS Large and very popular with light airy feel, split-level bar with comfortable sofas and easy chairs, clusters of pictures on cream-painted walls, Fullers London Pride, St Austell Tribute and a guest from long wooden servery, a dozen wines by the glass, back dining room with exposed brick walls, old pews and blackboards listing the good bistro-style food, efficient service; children allowed till early evening, ivy-clad passage to garden and comfortable tree-sheltered terrace, good walks, open all day. *(Ian Phillips, Phil Bryant)*

HORSELL COMMON   TQ0160
★ **Sands at Bleak House**
(01483) 756988 *Chertsey Road, The Anthonys; A320 Woking–Ottershaw; GU21 5NL* Smart contemporary pub-restaurant, grey sandstone for floor and face of bar counter, brown leather sofas and cushioned stools, two dining rooms with dark wood furniture, good if not cheap food, Andwell, Hogs Back and Sharps, friendly attentive uniformed staff, woodburners, daily newspapers; background music, TV; smokers' marquee in courtyard with picnic-sets, good shortish walk to sandpits that inspired H G Wells's *The War of the Worlds*, seven bedrooms, open all day, till 6pm Sun. *(Anon)*

IRONS BOTTOM   TQ2546
Three Horseshoes (01293) 862315
Sidlow Bridge, off A217; RH2 8PT Welcoming roadside pub with good

reasonably priced home-made food from pub favourites up, well kept Dark Star, Fullers, Pilgrim, Surrey Hills and guests, quick friendly service, traditional furnishings including upholstered banquettes, dark wood and patterned carpet, some barrel tables, darts; tables outside, summer barbecues, handy for Gatwick Airport. *(C and R Bromage)*

LALEHAM TQ0568
★**Three Horseshoes** (01784) 455014
Shepperton Road (B376); TW18 1SE
Bustling smartened-up pub near pleasant stretch of Thames, spacious airy bar with white walls and contrasting deep-blue woodwork, easy-going mix of tables and chairs on bare boards, log fire fronted by armchairs and squashy sofa, Fullers beers and plenty of wines by the glass, popular sensibly priced food served by efficient friendly staff, dining areas with assorted tables and chairs, pictures and mirrors on grey walls; background music; children welcome in restaurant till 7.30pm, attractive flagstoned terrace, picnic-sets on grass, open (and food) all day. *(Ian Phillips, Ron Corbett, Hunter and Christine Wright, Eddie Edwards and others)*

LIMPSFIELD CHART TQ4251
Carpenters Arms (01883) 722209
Tally Road; RH8 0TG Friendly open-plan pub refurbished by Westerham, their full range kept well (tasting trays available), popular home-made food (not Sun evening) from light lunches up, friendly helpful staff, garden room; free wi-fi; tables on terrace and lawn, delightful setting by village common, lovely walks and handy for Chartwell (NT), open all day weekends. *(John Branston, Nick Lawless, B J Harding)*

LINGFIELD TQ3844
★**Hare & Hounds** (01342) 832351
Turn off B2029 N at Crowhurst/ Edenbridge signpost; RH7 6BZ Smallish open-plan bar with bare boards and flagstones, mixed seating including leather chesterfield, dining area, very good food from wide-ranging menu cooked and beautifully presented by adventurous french chef-owner, efficient friendly service, well kept Harveys and Sharps Doom Bar, good wines by the glass; children and dogs welcome, tables in pleasant split-level garden with decking, nice walking country (leave boots in porch), open all day, closed Sun evening. *(David Alexander)*

MICKLEHAM TQ1753
King William IV (01372) 372590
Just off A24 Leatherhead–Dorking; Byttom Hill; RH5 6EL Steps up to small nicely placed country pub, well kept Hogs Back TEA, Surrey Hills Shere Drop and Triple fff Altons Pride, wide choice of enjoyable

food including blackboard specials and good vegetarian options, friendly attentive service, pleasant outlook from snug plank-panelled front bar; background music, outside gents'; children welcome, plenty of tables (some in heated open-sided timber shelters) in lovely terraced garden with great valley views, closed Sun and Mon evenings. *(Matthew Salisbury)*

MOGADOR TQ2453
Sportsman (01737) 246655
From M25 up A217 past second roundabout, then Mogador signed; KT20 7ES Modernised and extended low-ceilinged pub on edge of Walton Heath (originally 16th-c royal hunting lodge), well kept ales including Sharps and Wells & Youngs, good food from varied interesting menu, friendly attentive service, restaurant with raised section, Mon quiz; children welcome (no pushchairs), dogs in bar, picnic-sets out on common and on back lawn, more seats on front verandah, popular with walkers and riders, open all day. *(Brian Glozier)*

NUTFIELD TQ3050
Queens Head (01737) 823619
A25 E of Redhill; RH1 4HH Very welcoming three-room pub under newish licensees, good locally sourced food (not Sun evening) from sandwiches and pub favourites to one or two unusual dishes, four well kept ales such as Harveys, Hogs Back, Pilgrim and Surrey Hills, plenty of wines by the glass; regular live music, Sun quiz; picnic-sets on side lawn, summer barbecues, open all day. *(David and Sally Cullen, Caroline Hoyle, Mrs S Slater)*

OCKLEY TQ1337
★**Punchbowl** (01306) 627249
Oakwood Hill, signed off A29 S; RH5 5PU Attractive 16th-c tile-hung country pub with Horsham slab roof; friendly landlord and welcoming relaxed atmosphere, wide choice of good value generously served food (all day weekends), Badger ales, central bar with huge inglenook, polished flagstones and low beams, collections of brass spiles, horsebrasses and cigarette lighters, restaurant area to left and another bar to right with sofas, armchairs and TV, daily papers; children welcome and dogs (water bowl and biscuits), picnic-sets in pretty garden, smokers' awning, quiet spot with good walks including Sussex Border Path, open all day (till 6.30pm Sun). *(Anon)*

OTTERSHAW TQ0263
Castle (01932) 872373
Brox Road, off A320 not far from M25 junction 11; KT16 0LW Two-bar early Victorian local with big crackling log fires, country paraphernalia on black ceiling joists

---

Tipping is not normal for bar meals, and not usually expected.

and walls, beers (not cheap) from Harveys, Hogs Back, Sharps and Timothy Taylors, Addlestone's cider, enjoyable bar food (not Sun evening); background music, TV, free wi-fi; children welcome in conservatory till 7pm, dogs in bar, tables on terrace and grass, open all day. *(Ian Phillips)*

OUTWOOD   TQ3146
Dog & Duck (01342) 842964
Prince of Wales Road; turn off A23 at station sign in Salfords, S of Redhill – OS Sheet 187 map reference 312460; RH1 5QU Unhurried beamed country pub with good fairly priced home-made food in bar or restaurant, friendly service, well kept Badger ales from brick-faced bar, decent wines, warm winter fires; monthly quiz and live music nights; children welcome, garden with duck pond and play area. *(Richard Tilbrook, Mrs Sally Scott)*

OXTED   TQ4048
Royal Oak (01883) 722207
Caterfield Lane, Staffhurst Wood, S of town; RH8 0RR Popular well managed country pub, cheerful and comfortable, with ales such as Adnams, Greene King and Larkins, also good range of ciders including Biddenden and Weston's, enjoyable locally sourced home-made food (not Sun or Mon evenings), back dining room, open fire; dogs welcome, nice garden with lovely views across fields, open all day Fri-Sun. *(David Jackman, Simon Rodway, R and S Bentley)*

PUTTENHAM   SU9347
Good Intent (01483) 810387
Signed off B3000 just S of A31 junction; The Street/Seale Lane; GU3 1AR Well worn-in convivial beamed village local, Otter, Sharps, Timothy Taylors and three guests, popular reasonably priced traditional food (not Sun, Mon), log fire in cosy front bar with alcove seating, newspapers, old photographs of the pub, simple dining area; well behaved children and dogs welcome, small sunny garden, good walks, open all day weekends. *(Anon)*

PYRFORD LOCK   TQ0559
Anchor (01932) 342507
3 miles from M25 junction 10 – S on A3, then take Wisley slip road and go on past RHS Wisley garden; GU23 6QW Light and airy Badger family dining pub (can get very busy and may be queues), enjoyable food all day with small helpings available, lunchtime sandwiches too, good service, simple tables on bare boards, quieter more comfortable panelled back area, narrowboat memorabilia, pleasant oak-framed conservatory, daily papers; dogs allowed in some areas, splendid terrace by bridge and locks on River Wey Navigation, fenced-off play area, large car park across road, handy for RHS Wisley. *(Susan and John Douglas, Katharine Cowherd, Colin McKerrow)*

REDHILL   TQ2750
Garland (01737) 760377
Brighton Road; RH1 6PP Friendly 19th-c Harveys corner local, their full range including seasonals in good condition, well priced simple food (weekday lunchtimes, Fri evening, Sun till 4pm), dim lighting, darts and bar billiards, regular quiz nights; children and dogs welcome, open all day. *(Tony Hobden)*

REDHILL   TQ2850
Home Cottage (01737) 762771
Redstone Hill; RH1 4AW Stylishly updated 19th-c Youngs pub with their ales and guests, good variety of enjoyable food all day in bar and restaurant; seats outside including raised deck, open (and food) all day. *(Anon)*

REDHILL   TQ2749
Plough (01737) 766686
Church Road, St Johns; RH1 6QE Friendly early 17th-c beamed pub, lots of bits and pieces to look at including copper and brass hanging from ceiling, Fullers, Wells & Youngs and a couple of guests, enjoyable sensibly priced blackboard food (not Sun evening), open fire, Weds quiz; no under-10s inside, dogs welcome, back garden with terrace, open all day. *(Tony Scott)*

REIGATE HEATH   TQ2349
Skimmington Castle (01737) 243100
Off A25 Reigate–Dorking via Flanchford Road and Bonny's Road; RH2 8RL Nicely located small country pub, emphasis on enjoyable home-made food (can get very busy, best to book), ales such as Black Sheep, Harveys, Hogs Back and St Austell, friendly helpful service, panelled beamed rooms, big working fireplace; children, dogs and muddy boots welcome. *(C and R Bromage, Ian Phillips, Brian Glozier, Mrs Sally Scott, Tony Scott)*

RIPLEY   TQ0456
Seven Stars (01483) 225128
Newark Lane (B367); GU23 6DL Neat 1930s family-run pub, enjoyable food from extensive menu, Brakspears, Fullers, Sharps and Shepherd Neame, good wines and coffee, snug areas, red patterned carpet, gleaming brasses and open fire; quiet background music; picnic-sets and heated wooden booths in tidy garden, river and canalside walks, closed Sun evening. *(Ian Phillips, Tom and Ruth Rees)*

SEND   TQ0156
New Inn (01483) 762736
Send Road, Cartbridge; GU23 7EN Well placed old pub by River Wey Navigation, long bar and dining room, Adnams, Fullers, Greene King, Ringwood and a weekly guest, good choice of nicely presented generous food (all day weekends) from sandwiches to blackboard specials, friendly service, beams and log-effect gas fires; children and

dogs welcome, large waterside garden with moorings and smokers' shelter. *(Anon)*

SEND MARSH — TQ0455
Saddlers Arms (01483) 224209
Send Marsh Road; GU23 6JQ Friendly unpretentious low-beamed local, homely and warm, with Fullers London Pride, Sharps Doom Bar and a couple of guests, good value home-made food (Sun till 4pm) from lunchtime sandwiches up, log-effect gas fire, sparkling brassware, toby jugs etc, live music and quiz nights; children and dogs welcome, picnic-sets out in front and behind, open all day. *(Ian Phillips)*

SHALFORD — SU9946
Parrot (01483) 561400
Broadford Road; GU4 8DW Big welcoming inn with wide range of popular freshly made food, Fullers London Pride, Sharps Doom Bar and Surrey Hills Shere Drop, good friendly service, rows of neat pine dining tables, some easy chairs around low tables, pleasant conservatory; free wi-fi; children welcome till 8pm, attractive garden, four bedrooms, handy for Loseley Park. *(David M Smith)*

SHALFORD — TQ0047
Seahorse (01483) 514350
A281 S of Guildford; The Street; GU4 8BU Gently upmarket Mitchells & Butlers dining pub with wide range of food including popular set menu (weekday lunchtimes, early evenings), friendly young staff, Adnams and Sharps Doom Bar, good choice of wines and other drinks, contemporary furniture and artwork, double-sided log fire, smart dining room, comfortable part near entrance with sofas and huge window; picnic-sets in big lawned garden, covered terrace, handy for Shalford Mill (NT), open all day. *(Ian Phillips)*

SHEPPERTON — TQ0765
Thames Court (01932) 221957
Shepperton Lock, Ferry Lane; turn left off B375 towards Chertsey, 100 metres from Square; TW17 9LJ Huge Vintage Inn dining pub in great Thames-side location; plenty of wines by the glass, well kept Fullers, Sharps and a guest, their usual food all day from sandwiches to good Sun roasts, friendly efficient service, galleried central atrium with attractive panelled areas up and down stairs, comfortable armchairs, newspapers and two good log fires; can get very busy weekends; children welcome, modern furniture on large tree-shaded terrace with heaters, open all day. *(Ian Phillips, Eddie Edwards)*

SHERE — TQ0747
William Bray (01483) 202044
Shere Lane; GU5 9HS Emphasis on well presented locally sourced food (not particularly cheap), ales such as Surrey Hills and decent choice of wines and whiskies,

roomy contemporary bar with stone floor and woodburner, more formal airy restaurant with comfortable leather chairs and large F1 racing photographs (owner was driver for Tyrrell and Lotus); background music; dogs welcome, tables on front split-level terrace, pretty landscaped garden, useful car park, open all day. *(Anon)*

SOUTH GODSTONE — TQ3549
Fox & Hounds (01342) 893474
Tilburstow Hill Road/Harts Lane, off A22; RH9 8LY Pleasant old tile-hung country pub with woodburner in low-beamed bar, good value home-cooked food, well kept Greene King ales from tiny bar counter, inglenook restaurant; free wi-fi; children and dogs welcome, garden, open all day. *(Wendy Breese)*

STAINES — TQ0371
Bells (01784) 454240
Church Street; TW18 4ZB Comfortable and sociable Youngs pub in old part of town, their well kept ales and a guest, decent choice of wines and good promptly served fresh food (special diets catered for), central fireplace; dogs allowed in bar, tables in nice back garden with heated terrace, limited roadside parking, open all day Fri-Sun (no food Sun evening). *(Ron Corbett)*

STAINES — TQ0371
Swan (01784) 452494
The Hythe; south bank, over Staines Bridge; TW18 3JB Splendid Thames-side setting with good tables on verandah and terrace overlooking the water, big conservatory, several distinctly different areas including river-view upstairs restaurant, enjoyable food from sandwiches up, prompt friendly service, well kept Fullers ales; can be very busy Sun lunchtime and on summer evenings; 11 comfortable bedrooms, moorings, open all day. *(Anon)*

STOKE D'ABERNON — TQ1259
★ Old Plough (01932) 862244
Station Road, off A245; KT11 3BN Popular nicely updated 300-year-old pub under same ownership as the Red Lion at Horsell and Three Horseshoes at Laleham; good freshly made food, Fullers and a guest such as Surrey Hills, plenty of wines by the glass, competent friendly staff, restaurant with various knick-knacks; newspapers and free wi-fi; children welcome in restaurant till 7.30pm, dogs in bar, seats out under pergola and in attractive garden, open (and food) all day. *(Martin Shorrock, Lorry Spooner, Kim Judge, Shirley Mackenzie, C and R Bromage)*

SUTTON ABINGER — TQ1045
Volunteer (01306) 730985
Water Lane; just off B2126 via Raikes Lane, 1.5 miles S of Abinger Hammer; RH5 6PR Picturesque family-run pub in delightful setting above clear stream, low-

ceilinged linked rooms, log fires, Badger ales, enjoyable standard food from sandwiches up, good friendly service, restaurant; terrace and sun-trap lawns stepped up behind, nice walks, closed Sun evening, otherwise open all day. *(Tom and Ruth Rees)*

TADWORTH   TQ2355
★**Dukes Head** (01737) 812173
Dorking Road (B2032 opposite common and woods); KT20 5SL Roomy and comfortably refurbished 19th-c pub, popular for its good varied choice of well priced food (all day except Sun evening, booking advised) from generous sandwiches up, five well kept ales including a house beer (KT20) brewed by Morlands, Aspall's cider, good choice of wines by the glass, helpful cheery staff, three dining areas and two big inglenook log fires; background music, Weds quiz; lots of hanging baskets and plenty of tables in well tended back garden, open all day (till 8pm Sun).
(C and R Bromage, John Branston)

TANDRIDGE   TQ3750
Barley Mow (01883) 713770
Tandridge Lane, off A25 W of Oxted; RH8 9NJ Three decent sized bars, front ones carpeted, beams, exposed brick and stonework, enjoyable food all day with fresh fish specials alongside pub staples, well kept Badger ales, good wines by the glass, friendly helpful service; background and Fri live music including jazz; children welcome till 9pm, dogs in bar, pleasant garden (summer barbecues) with heated smokers' shelter, three bedrooms, good breakfast.
(Ross Balaam)

THAMES DITTON   TQ1567
Albany (020) 8972 9163
Queens Road, signed off Summer Road; KT7 0QY Mitchells & Butlers bar-with-restaurant in lovely Thames-side position, light airy modern feel, with good variety of food from sharing plates and pizzas to more upscale dishes, weekday lunchtime and early evening fixed-price menu, good choice of wines by the glass, cocktails and a couple of ales such as Sharps and Timothy Taylors, cheerful service, log fire, river pictures, daily papers; nice balconies and river-view terrace, moorings, open all day. *(John Branston)*

THAMES DITTON   TQ1667
Red Lion (020) 8398 8662
High Street; KT7 0SF Revamped (not smart) and extended pub with enjoyable home-made food from regularly changing menu, decent wines and coffee, ales such as Surrey Hills and Twickenham from servery clad with reclaimed doors, cheerful young staff; children welcome, seats on split-level terrace with Lego wall, open all day.
(Tom and Ruth Rees)

TILFORD   SU8742
Duke of Cambridge (01252) 792236
Tilford Road; GU10 2DD Civilised smartly done pub in same small local group as Queens Head at East Clandon, Stag at Eashing and Wheatsheaf at Farnham; enjoyable food with emphasis on local ingredients from varied interesting menu, children's meals too, good choice of wines, ales such as Hogs Back TEA and Surrey Hills Shere Drop, helpful service; May charity music festival; part covered terrace and garden with outside bar/grill, good play area, open all day. *(Anon)*

TONGHAM   SU8848
White Harte (01252) 782419
The Street; GU10 1DH Large welcoming corner pub very popular locally; bar, dining lounge and back games room with pool and darts, carpets and faux beams, good choice of beers including Hogs Back (brewery nearby), enjoyable straightforward food (not Mon) at reasonable prices, good considerate service, quiz and music nigts; sports TV; children and dogs welcome, outside seating front and back including raised deck, open all day.
(Tony Hobden)

VIRGINIA WATER   SU9968
Rose & Olive Branch
(01344) 843713 *Callow Hill; GU25 4LH*
Small unpretentious red-brick pub, with good choice of popular food including speciality pies, gluten-free and children's choices too, three Greene King ales, decent wines, friendly busy staff; background music; tables on front terrace and in garden behind, good walks. *(D J and P M Taylor)*

WALLISWOOD   TQ1138
Scarlett Arms (01306) 627243
Signed from Ewhurst–Rowhook back road, or off A29 S of Ockley; RH5 5RD
Cottagey 16th-c village pub with low beams and flagstones, simple furniture and two log fires (one in big inglenook), Badger ales, well priced traditional food (not Sun evening) including malaysian and indian evenings, friendly helpful staff, dining room behind; background music; children and dogs welcome, tables out at front and in garden under parasols, good walks, open all day Fri, Sat, till 9.30pm Sun, closed Mon lunchtime. *(Anon)*

WALTON-ON-THAMES   TQ1068
Weir (01932) 784530
Towpath, Waterside Drive, off Sunbury Lane; KT12 2JB Edwardian pub in nice Thames-side spot with big terrace overlooking river, weir and steel walkway, decent choice of food all day (till 7.30pm Sun) from snacks up, ales such as Greene

---

We say if we know a pub allows dogs.

King, Sharps and Woodfordes, traditional décor, river pictures, newspapers; children and dogs welcome, lovely towpath walks, six bedrooms. *(Anon)*

WARLINGHAM   TQ3955
Botley Hill Farmhouse
(01959) 577154 *S on Limpsfield Road (B269); CR6 9QH* Busy country pub dating from the 16th c with low-ceilinged linked rooms up and down steps, enjoyable reasonably priced food (till 6.30pm Sun) from standards up, well kept Greene King Abbot and local guests, decent choice of wines by the glass, good friendly staff, soft lighting, spreading carpet, quite close-set tables, big log fireplace in one attractive flagstoned room; marquee for weekend entertainment including tribute bands and discos; children and dogs welcome, disabled access, side and back terraces, neat garden with fine view, play area and aviary, open all day. *(Anon)*

WEST CLANDON   TQ0451
★ Bulls Head (01483) 222444
A247 SE of Woking; GU4 7ST
Comfortable, spotless and unchanging, based on 1540s timbered hall house, popular especially with older people lunchtime for good value straightforward food (not Sun evening) including proper home-made pies, friendly helpful staff, ales from Sharps, Surrey Hills and Wells & Youngs, good coffee, small lantern-lit beamed front bar with open fire and some stripped brick, old local prints, bric-a-brac and hops, simple raised back inglenook dining area, games room with darts and pool; children and dogs on leads welcome, disabled access from car park, good play area in neat little garden, nice walks, handy for Clandon Park (NT). *(Ron Corbett, Ian Phillips)*

WEST CLANDON   TQ0452
Onslow Arms (01483) 222447
A247 SE of Woking; GU4 7TE Busy pub with heavily beamed rambling rooms leading away from central bar; wooden dining chairs and tables on wide floorboards, built-in cushioned window seats, all sorts of copper implements, hunting horns and china in cabinets, leather sofas by woodburner, Sharps Cornish Coaster, Surrey Hills Shere Drop, a beer named for the pub from Caledonian and a guest, good popular food from traditional choices up, efficient friendly staff, big back restaurant with rugs on bare boards and chesterfields in front of open fire; live music Weds; children (till early evening) and dogs welcome, courtyard garden with tables under parasols, pretty pots and huge stone dog. *(Alan Bowker)*

WEST HORSLEY   TQ0853
★ Barley Mow (01483) 282693
Off A246 Leatherhead–Guildford at Bell & Colvill garage roundabout; The Street; KT24 6HR Welcoming tree-shaded traditional pub, low beams, mix of flagstones, bare boards and carpet, two log fires, well kept ales such as Fullers London Pride, Surrey Hills and Wells & Youngs, decent wines, enjoyable traditional food (not Sun evening) and thai menu (not Sun lunchtime), barn function room; background music; children welcome, dogs on leads, picnic-sets in good-sized garden, open all day. *(Anon)*

WEST HORSLEY   TQ0752
King William IV (01483) 282318
The Street; KT24 6BG Comfortable and welcoming early 19th-c village pub, low entrance door to front and side bars, beams, flagstones and log fire, back conservatory restaurant, good variety of enjoyable food (all day Sat, not Sun evening) including some mexican dishes and daily specials board, three or four changing ales, decent choice of wines by the glass and good coffee, newspapers and board games; background music, free wi-fi; children and dogs welcome, good disabled access, small sunny garden with deck and play area. *(Richard Stanfield, Ian Phillips)*

WEYBRIDGE   TQ0763
Hand & Spear (01932) 828063
Old Heath Road/Station Road; KT13 8TX Large stylishly refurbished Youngs pub (former station hotel), good food from pub favourites to more unusual choices, efficient friendly staff, quiz and comedy nights; seats outside, open all day. *(John Coatsworth, Ian Phillips)*

WEYBRIDGE   TQ0765
Minnow (01932) 831672
Thames Street/Walton Lane; KT13 8NG Busy bay-windowed Mitchells & Butlers dining pub; contemporary pastel décor and unusual decorative panels, chunky tables and chairs on gleaming flagstones, some sofas and armchairs, two-way log fire in raised hearth, popular food including fixed-price weekday menu till 6pm, ales such as Fullers, Timothy Taylors and Wells & Youngs, good wines by the glass, friendly staff; children welcome, big front terrace with heaters, open all day. *(Ron Corbett, Katharine Cowherd)*

WEYBRIDGE   TQ0965
Oatlands Chaser (01932) 253277
Oatlands Chase; KT13 9RW Big attractively modernised building in quiet residential road, rambling bar with stylish contemporary décor, pastels and unusual wallpaper, glazed panels, flagstones and painted boards, feature central fireplace, carefully mismatched furnishings mainly laid out for the wide range of good all-day food from sharing plates and light lunches to Sun roasts and proper children's meals, three well kept changing ales, good wine choice, newspapers; disabled access, lots of tables out at front (some under trees), 19 bedrooms. *(Minda and Stanley Alexander, Ian Phillips)*

WEYBRIDGE   TQ0765
★ **Old Crown** (01932) 842844
Thames Street; KT13 8LP Comfortably
old-fashioned three-bar pub dating from
the 16th c, good value traditional food (not
Sun-Tues evenings) from sandwiches to fresh
fish, Courage, Wells & Youngs and a guest
kept well (not cheap), good choice of wines
by the glass, friendly efficient service, family
lounge and conservatory, coal-effect gas fire;
may be sports TV in back bar with Lions RFC
photographs, silent fruit machine; children
welcome, secluded terrace and smokers'
shelter, steps down to suntrap garden
overlooking Wey/Thames confluence, mooring
for small boats, open all day. *(Ian Phillips,
John Millwood)*

WEYBRIDGE   TQ0664
Queens Head (01932) 839820
Bridge Road; KT13 8XS Refurbished
18th-c pub owned by Raymond Blanc's
White Brasserie Company, emphasis on
dining but also a proper bar serving Fullers,
Sharps and Thwaites, plenty of wines by the
glass including champagne, friendly staff,
newspapers; soft background music; under-6s
eat free, a couple of picnic-sets outside, open
(and food) all day. *(John Millwood, Ian Phillips)*

WINDLESHAM   SU9464
Brickmakers (01276) 472267
*Chertsey Road (B386, W of B383
roundabout); GU20 6HT* Refurbished red-
brick country dining pub, linked areas with
pastel and more vibrant colours, light wood
furniture on flagstone or wood floors, two-way
woodburner, good freshly prepared food (all
day Fri-Sun, when best to book) using local
suppliers, Courage Best, Fullers London
Pride and Sharps Doom Bar, good choice
of wines by the glass and decent coffee,
efficient friendly service, conservatory; well
behaved children allowed, appealing garden
with pergola, open all day from 9am for
breakfast. *(Geoffrey Kemp, D J and P M Taylor,
Phil Bryant)*

WOKING   TQ0058
Herbert Wells (01483) 722818
Chertsey Road; GU21 5AJ Corner
Wetherspoons named after H G Wells, busy
with shoppers yet with lots of cosy areas and
side snugs, eight or so well kept ales, three
ciders and their usual competitively priced
all-day food including Tues steak night,
friendly helpful staff, daily papers, old local
pictures; free wi-fi; pavement tables, open
from 8am. *(Ian Phillips, Tony Hobden)*

WOOD STREET   SU9550
Royal Oak (01483) 235137
Oak Hill; GU3 3DA Popular 1920s village
local, comfortably unpretentious, with
well kept Ringwood and four guests, local
cider, good value traditional home-cooked
lunchtime food, friendly staff; dogs welcome,
good-sized garden. *(Anon)*

WORPLESDON   SU9854
Jolly Farmer (01483) 234658
*Burdenshott Road, off A320 Guildford–
Woking, not in village; GU3 3RN*
Old pub in pleasant country setting, dark-
beamed bar with small log fire, well kept
Fullers/Gales beers, stripped-brick dining
extension with rugs on bare boards, good
traditional food from lunchtime sandwiches
up (they may want to swipe your credit
card if running a tab); background music;
children and dogs welcome, garden tables
under parasols and pergola, open all day.
(Edward and Jill Wilson)

WRECCLESHAM   SU8344
Bat & Ball (01252) 792108
*Bat & Ball Lane, South Farnham;
approach from Sandrock Hill and Upper
Bourne Lane, then narrow steep lane
to pub; GU10 4SA* Fairly traditional pub
tucked away in hidden valley, decent range
of food (all day weekends) from pubby
choices up including good puddings display,
six well kept local ales (June beer and music
festival), plenty of wines by the glass, friendly
efficient staff; children and dogs welcome,
disabled facilities, tables out on attractive
heated terrace with vine arbour and in
garden with substantial play fort, open
all day. *(Anon)*

WRECCLESHAM   SU8244
Royal Oak (01252) 728319
The Street; GU10 4QS Black beamed
17th-c village pub with good value fairly
straightforward home-made food (smaller
helpings available), Greene King IPA and
a couple of guests, friendly helpful staff,
log fire; Sun quiz; children and dogs
welcome, big garden with play area, open
all day. *(Patric Curwen, Tony and Jill Radnor)*

Post Office address codings confusingly give the impression that some pubs are in
Surrey when they're really in Hampshire or London (which is where we list them).
And there's further confusion from the way the Post Office still talks about Middlesex
– which disappeared in local government reorganisation nearly 50 years ago.

Sussex

ALCISTON
TQ5005   Map 3

Rose Cottage

Village signposted off A27 Polegate–Lewes; BN26 6UW

Old-fashioned cottage with cosy fires and country bric-a-brac, several wines by the glass, well liked food and local beers; bedrooms

This is a very enjoyable village pub with a long-serving, character landlord – and plenty to look at. There are half a dozen tables with cushioned pews, winter log fires and quite a forest of harness, traps, a thatcher's blade and lots of other black ironware, plus more bric-a-brac on the shelves above the stripped pine dado or on the sills of the etched-glass windows; Jasper the talkative parrot is in the bar at lunchtimes only (he gets too noisy in the evenings). Note that you can't book tables in the bar at lunchtime. Burning Sky Plateau and Harveys Best on handpump, eight wines by the glass and a farm cider; darts, background music and board games. There are heaters outside for cooler evenings, and the garden has ducks and chickens. You can walk straight up the South Downs from here – head along the winding village street, past a huge, ancient tithe barn and to the foot of the steep escarpment – and there's also fishing and shooting nearby. Bookings in the self-catering bedrooms are for a minimum of two nights.

Enjoyable food includes smoked salmon cornet filled with prawns, pâté with plum chutney, lunchtime ploughman's, local sausages with onion gravy, vegetable lasagne, chicken curry, steak in ale pie, rabbit casserole with bacon and cream, half a crispy gressingham duck with a sauce of the day, plaice in lemon and parsley butter, and puddings. *Benchmark main dish: fish pie £11.50. Two-course evening meal £18.00.*

Free house ~ Licensee Ian Lewis ~ Real ale ~ (01323) 870377 ~ Open 11.30-3, 6.30-11; 12-3 Sun ~ Bar food 12-2, 6.30-9.30; 12-3 Sun ~ Restaurant ~ Children aged 10 and over welcome ~ Dogs allowed in bar ~ Wi-fi ~ Bedrooms: £35/£60 ~ www.therosecottageinn.com *Recommended by Peter and Jan Humphreys, R and S Bentley, Richard Tilbrook, Tom and Jill Jones, Alan Cowell, Phil and Jane Villiers*

ALFRISTON
TQ5203   Map 3

George ♀

High Street; BN26 5SY

Venerable 14th-c timbered inn in lovely village with comfortable, heavily beamed bars, good wines and several real ales; fine nearby walks; bedrooms

After wandering around the lovely village, this fine old inn is just the place for a drink or a meal. The long bar, dominated by a huge stone inglenook fireplace with a log fire (or summer flower arrangement), has massive hop-hung low beams, soft lighting, lots of copper and brass, and settles and chairs around sturdy stripped tables. Greene King Abbot, Dark Star Hophead and St Austell Proper Job on handpump, ten wines by the glass (including champagne and a pudding wine), ten gins, board games and background music; good service. The lounge has comfortable sofas, standing timbers and rugs on the wooden floor, and the restaurant is cosy and candlelit. There are seats in the spacious flint-walled garden, and the beamed bedrooms are comfortable; there's no car park but you can park a couple of minutes away. Two long-distance paths, the South Downs Way and Vanguard Way, cross here and the quietly beautiful Cuckmere Haven is nearby.

Usefully served all day, the popular food includes lunchtime sandwiches and toasties, honey-roast ham hock terrine with pickled vegetables, mussels in bacon, leek and cider, sharing boards, ham and free-range eggs, thai red vegetable curry, corn-fed chicken supreme stuffed with spinach, feta and pine nuts on wild mushroom linguine, trout fillets on red lentils with chorizo and vegetables, braised fennel and saffron sauce, and puddings such as banoffi pie and crème brûlée with berry compote. *Benchmark main dish: honey-spiced bass fillets with celeriac purée and roasted new potatoes £16.00. Two-course evening meal £20.75.*

Greene King ~ Lease Roland and Cate Couch ~ Real ale ~ (01323) 870319 ~ Open 11 (12 weekends)-11 ~ Bar food 12-9 ~ Restaurant ~ Children welcome ~ Dogs welcome ~ Wi-fi ~ Bedrooms: £75/£120 ~ www.thegeorge-alfriston.com
Recommended by Richard Tilbrook, Fr Robert Marsh

 CHARLTON   SU8812   Map 2
Fox Goes Free ♀
Village signposted off A286 Chichester–Midhurst in Singleton, also from Chichester–Petworth via East Dean; PO18 0HU

Comfortable old pub with beamed bars, popular food and drink, and big garden; bedrooms

This friendly old pub is handy for Goodwood and always busy (it gets pretty crowded on race days). The attractive back garden has the Downs as a backdrop and is just the spot to while away a warm lunchtime; there are also rustic benches and tables on the gravelled front terrace. The bar, the first of a dark, cosy series of separate rooms, has old irish settles, tables and chapel chairs and an open fire. Standing timbers divide up a larger beamed bar, which has a huge brick fireplace with a woodburning stove and old local photographs on the walls. A dining area with house plants in the windows overlooks the garden. The family extension is a clever conversion from horse boxes and the stables where the 1926 Goodwood winner was housed; darts, TV, games machine, background music and board games. Ballards Best, Otter Bitter, a beer named for the pub brewed by Arundel, and a guest such as Harveys Best on handpump, 15 wines by the glass and Addlestone's cider. You can walk up to Levin Down nature reserve, or stroll around the Iron Age hillfort on the Trundle, with huge views to the Isle of Wight; the Weald & Downland Open Air Museum and West Dean Gardens are nearby too.

Nicely presented food includes lunchtime ciabatta sandwiches (not Sunday), duck spring rolls with ginger and apricot sauce, smoked pigeon breast with pancetta and white bean cassoulet, cumberland sausages with caramelised onion and wholegrain mustard mash, spinach pancakes filled with sweet potato, beetroot and rosemary with a parmesan and nutmeg cream sauce, chorizo, scallop and spinach risotto, braised shoulder of lamb with balsamic, mint and lyonnaise potatoes, and puddings such as passion-fruit mousse and treacle sponge with custard. *Benchmark main dish: pie of the day £12.50. Two-course evening meal £20.00.*

Free house ~ Licensee David Coxon ~ Real ale ~ (01243) 811461 ~ Open 11am-11.30pm; 12-10.30 Sun ~ Bar food 12-2.30, 6.15-9.45; 12-10 weekends ~ Restaurant ~ Children welcome ~ Dogs allowed in bar ~ Wi-fi ~ Live music Weds ~ Bedrooms: £65/£90 ~ www.thefoxgoesfree.com *Recommended by J A Snell, Steve and Irene Homer, C and R Bromage, Roy Hoing, Richard Tilbrook, Tracey and Stephen Groves*

CHIDDINGLY TQ5414 Map 3
Six Bells £
Village signed off A22 Uckfield–Hailsham; BN8 6HE

Lively, unpretentious village local with good live music at weekends, bargain bar food and a friendly, long-serving landlord

Even when this well run local is at its busiest (usually at weekends), the welcoming landlord and his staff keep things running smoothly. There's a great deal of unpretentious character in the many small interconnected bars with their interesting bric-a-brac, local pictures, photographs and posters, as well as solid old wood pews, antique chairs and tables and cushioned window seats; log fires too. A sensitive extension provides some much-needed family space; board games. Courage Directors, Harveys Best and a guest beer such as York Final Whistle on handpump, decent wines by the glass and a farm cider. Outside at the back, there are tables beyond a big raised goldfish pond and a boules pitch; the church opposite has the interesting Jefferay Monument. The weekend live music is popular, and vintage and kit-car meetings are held outside the pub every month. This is a pleasant area for walks.

Exceptionally good value and well liked, the food includes lunchtime rolls and baked potatoes, garlic prawns, farmhouse pâté, mushroom stroganoff, crispy pork belly ribs, smoked haddock and prawns, ham hock with french bread and salad, and puddings such as banoffi pie and raspberry pavlova. *Benchmark main dish: steak and kidney pie £4.40. Two-course evening meal £10.50.*

Free house ~ Licensee Paul Newman ~ Real ale ~ (01825) 872227 ~ Open 11-3, 6-11; 11am-midnight Fri, Sat; 12-10.30 Sun ~ Bar food 12-2.30, 6-9.30; all day Fri-Sun ~ Children allowed away from main bar ~ Dogs allowed in bar ~ Wi-fi ~ Live music Fri-Sun evenings, Sun lunchtime *Recommended by Jason Caulkin, Ann and Colin Hunt, Tom and Jill Jones*

CHILGROVE SU8116 Map 2
Royal Oak £
Off B2141 Petersfield–Chichester, signed Hooksway; PO18 9JZ

Unchanging and peaceful country pub with welcoming licensees, honest food and big pretty garden

Many of the customers here are walkers – often with their dogs – as this friendly pub is tucked away in an isolated wooded location amid the South Downs. The two simple, cosy bars have huge log fires, plain country kitchen tables and chairs, cottagey knick-knacks and Bowman Wallops Wood, Fullers HSB and Seafarers and a guest from Weltons on handpump. There's also a homely dining room with a woodburning stove and a plainer family room; background music, cribbage, dominoes and shut the box. Twiglet and Amber are the pub staffies and the parrot is called Gilbert. The big, pretty garden has picnic-sets under parasols.

🍴 Unpretentious food includes lunchtime rolls, creamy garlic mushrooms, duck and orange pâté, vegetable lasagne, tuna pasta bake, burger of the day with coleslaw and fries, chicken with bacon, mushroom and onion sauce, rib-eye steak with onion rings and chips, and puddings. *Benchmark main dish: venison pie £10.95. Two-course evening meal £16.00.*

Free house ~ Licensee Dave Jeffery ~ Real ale ~ (01243) 535257 ~ Open 11.30-2.30, 6-11; 12-3 Sun; closed Sun evening, Mon and first two weeks Nov ~ Bar food 12-2, 7-9 ~ Restaurant ~ Children in family room ~ Dogs allowed in bar ~ Wi-fi ~ Live music last Fri evening of month ~ www.royaloakhooksway.co.uk *Recommended by Ann and Colin Hunt*

DANEHILL TQ4128 Map 3
Coach & Horses ⭐ 🍷
Off A275, via School Lane towards Chelwood Common; RH17 7JF

Well run dining pub with bustling bars, welcoming staff, very good food and ales and a big garden

This highly enjoyable pub serves first class food but has a welcome for drinkers too. The little bar to the right has half-panelled walls, simple furniture on polished floorboards, a small woodburner in a brick fireplace and a big hatch to the bar counter: Harveys Best and a guest such as Long Man Best Bitter on handpump, local Black Pig farmhouse cider and 11 wines by the glass including prosecco and Bluebell sparkling wine from Sussex. A couple of steps lead down to a half-panelled area with a mix of dining chairs around characterful wooden tables (set with flowers and candles) on a fine brick floor, and artwork on the walls that changes every couple of months; cribbage, dominoes and cards. Down another step is a dining area with stone walls, beams, flagstones and a woodburning stove. There's an adult-only terrace beneath a huge maple tree, and picnic-sets and a children's play area in the big garden, which has fine views of the South Downs.

⭐ As well as pubby staples such as lunchtime baguettes, local game pâté and ham and eggs, the imaginative food includes ham hock terrine with potted brawn and apple and celeriac rémoulade, roasted gnocchi romana with smoked aubergine, wild mushrooms and mushroom and chervil velouté, moules frites, guinea fowl with curried courgette risotto, braised beef cheeks with smoked bacon and celeriac, and puddings. *Benchmark main dish: duck breast and confit leg with black pepper purée £16.00. Two-course evening meal £21.00.*

Free house ~ Licensee Ian Philpots ~ Real ale ~ (01825) 740369 ~ Open 12-3, 5.30-11; 12-11 Sat; 12-10.30 Sun ~ Bar food 12-2 (2.30 Sat), 6.30-9 (9.30 Fri, Sat); 12-3 Sun ~ Restaurant ~ Well behaved children welcome but not on adult terrace ~ Dogs allowed in bar ~ Wi-fi ~ www.coachandhorses.co *Recommended by Steve and Irene Homer, Alan Bowker, R and S Bentley, Pete Walker, Alan Cowell, Martin and Karen Wake, Duane Lawrence*

DIAL POST TQ1519 Map 3
Crown
Worthing Road (off A24 S of Horsham); RH13 8NH

Tile-hung village pub with interesting food and a good mix of drinkers and diners

The bustling atmosphere, friendly staff and enjoyable food at this pleasantly spacious village pub continue to attract warm and enthusiastic reports from our readers. The beamed bar has a couple of standing timbers, brown squashy sofas, pine tables and chairs, a stone floor, a small woodburning stove in a brick fireplace, and Harveys Best and two changing guest beers from breweries such as Bedlam and Kissingate on handpump, served from the attractive herringbone brick counter; ten wines by the glass. To the right of the bar, the restaurant (with more beams) has an ornamental woodburner in a brick fireplace, a few photographs, chunky pine tables, chairs, a couple of cushioned pews and a shelf of books; steps lead down to an additional dining room; board games. The pub dog is called Chops. The straightforwardly furnished dining conservatory, facing the village green, is light and airy. There are picnic-sets in the garden behind the pub.

Using seasonal, local produce, the extremely popular food includes lunchtime sandwiches (not Sunday), devilled whitebait with spicy aioli, chicken liver and pork pâté, ham and free-range eggs, goats cheese salad with jerusalem artichoke, beetroot and honey-roasted walnuts, battered fish and chips, free-range chicken tikka masala, steak, Guinness and oyster pie, and puddings such as sticky toffee pudding with home-made vanilla ice-cream and rhubarb, peach and ginger crumble. *Benchmark main dish: steak burger with interesting toppings and chips £11.00. Two-course evening meal £19.50.*

Free house ~ Licensees James and Penny Middleton-Burn ~ Real ale ~ (01403) 710902 ~ Open 12-3, 6-11; 12-4 Sun; closed Sun evening ~ Bar food 12-2.15, 6-9 (9.30 Fri, Sat); 12-3 Sun ~ Restaurant ~ Children welcome but for dining only after 7pm ~ Dogs allowed in bar ~ Wi-fi ~ www.crowninndialpost.co.uk *Recommended by Geoffrey Taylor, Ron Corbett, Sara Fulton, Roger Baker, Tony and Wendy Hobden, Tracey and Stephen Groves, Martin Stafford*

DITCHLING
Bull 🍺 🛏

TQ3215 Map 3

High Street (B2112); BN6 8TA

Ancient local in centre of village with busy main bar, two smaller rooms, a good choice of ales and popular food; bedrooms

In summer, the window boxes at the front of this village inn are very pretty and there are plenty of picnic-sets in the garden and on the little terrace. In colder weather, the beamed main bar is a cosy haven with its log fire in a sizeable inglenook fireplace and candles on each table. Friendly, helpful young staff greet you at the bar counter where they keep Harveys Best and four changing guest beers from small breweries on handpump, 20 wines by the glass and a good choice of spirits; daily newspapers and background music. There are benches, high-backed dark leather dining chairs, a nicely carved settle beside the fire, an assortment of wooden tables, bare boards and a few photos of the pub; you need to book to be sure of a table. To the left of the door is a simpler, smaller bar with another log fire, a few chunky pine tables on old parquet flooring and hatch service, and a further room with a big chesterfield sofa and one long table (just right for a private party). The contemporary bedrooms are comfortable.

As well as offering breakfasts to non-residents at weekends, the highly thought-of food includes lunchtime sandwiches, venison carpaccio, crab ravioli with tomato and chilli sauce, wild mushroom risotto with truffle oil, chicken and ham hock pie, lamb stew with thyme dumplings, cod with french bean fricassée and mango salsa, rosemary braised rabbit with pea pasta, and puddings. *Benchmark main dish: beer-battered haddock and chips £14.00. Two-course evening meal £21.00.*

Free house ~ Licensee Dominic Worrall ~ Real ale ~ (01273) 843147 ~ Open 11 (8am weekends)-11 (10.30 Sun) ~ Bar food 12-2.30, 6-9.30; all day from 8.30am weekends ~ Restaurant ~ Children welcome ~ Dogs allowed in bar ~ Wi-fi ~ Bedrooms: /£100 ~ www.thebullditchling.com *Recommended by Harvey Brown, Tony Scott*

DUNCTON
SU9517 Map 3

Cricketers

Set back from A285; GU28 0LB

Charming old coaching inn with friendly licensees, real ales, popular food and suntrap back garden

Handy for Goodwood, this 17th-c inn got its present name from its 19th-c owner John Wisden, the cricketer who published the famous *Wisden Cricketers' Almanack*. Accordingly, there's a display of cricketing memorabilia in the friendly, traditional bar, which has a few standing timbers, simple seating and an open woodburning stove in the inglenook fireplace. Steps lead down to a dining room furnished with farmhouse chairs around wooden tables. Dark Star Partridge, Langhams Hip Hop and Triple fff Moondance on handpump, nine wines by the glass and two farm ciders. There are picnic-sets out in front beneath the flowering window boxes and more on decked areas and under parasols on the grass in the picturesque back garden, which make the most of the pub's hilly position.

 Using local meat and game, the good food includes lunchtime sandwiches (not Sunday), sticky duck salad, baked goats cheese crostini, ham and eggs, chips with beer-battered fresh haddock and with bacon- and brie-topped burger, chicken stuffed with mediterranean tapenade, sizzling pork, parsnip and pear skillet, steaks with a choice of sauces, and puddings. *Benchmark main dish: steak in ale pie £10.95. Two-course evening meal £19.00.*

Inn Company ~ Manager Martin Boult ~ Real ale ~ (01798) 342473 ~ Open 11-11; 12-10.30 Sun ~ Bar food 12-2.30, 6-9; 12-9 Fri-Sun; also, brunch 11-midday, hot snacks 3-6 ~ Children welcome ~ Dogs allowed in bar ~ www.thecricketersduncton.co.uk
Recommended by Steve and Irene Homer, Colin McKerrow, David Jackman

EAST CHILTINGTON
TQ3715 Map 3

Jolly Sportsman ⭐️🍴 ♀

2 miles N of B2116; Chapel Lane – follow sign to 13th-c church; BN7 3BA

Inventive modern food in civilised, rather smart place, small bar for drinkers with real ales, fine wines and huge range of malt whiskies; pleasant garden

The bar here may be small – this is, after all, a first class dining pub with excellent, accomplished food – but it's light and full of character. There's a roaring winter fire, a mix of furniture on the stripped wood floors and Dark Star Hophead and Harveys Best tapped from the cask. They also have a remarkably good wine list with around 15 by the glass, over 80 malt whiskies, farm cider, an extensive list of cognacs, Armagnacs and grappa and quite a choice of bottled Belgian beers. The larger restaurant is smart but cosy and welcoming, with contemporary light wood furniture and modern landscapes on coffee-coloured walls; there's also a garden room. The inviting cottagey front garden has rustic tables and benches under gnarled trees on a terrace and on a bricked area, and more on a large back lawn; views extend towards the Downs and there's a play area for children. From here you can stroll or cycle past the church through the trees along an unmade track (on the course of a Roman road).

Cooked by the chef-patron, the exceptional food includes lunchtime ploughman's and charcuterie plates as well as bass mousseline with pea velouté, goats cheese parfait with tapenade, butternut squash thai green curry and stir-fried pak choi, guinea fowl breast with fresh morels and asparagus, stone bass fillet with saffron, fennel, orange and spinach, angus rib-eye with béarnaise sauce and chips, and puddings such as grilled spiced fruit kebab with coconut ice-cream and chocolate tart with crème fraîche; the two- and three-course set lunch is fantastic value given the quality. *Benchmark main dish: rump of organic salt marsh lamb with dauphinoise potatoes £18.50. Two-course evening meal £24.00.*

Free house ~ Licensee Bruce Wass ~ Real ale ~ (01273) 890400 ~ Open 12-3, 6-11; 12-11 Sat; 12-4 Sun; closed Mon ~ Bar food 12.15-2.30, 6-9 (10 Fri, Sat); 12.15-3.30 Sun ~ Restaurant ~ Children welcome ~ Dogs allowed in bar ~ Wi-fi ~ www.thejollysportsman.com *Recommended by Steve and Irene Homer, N R White, Nick Lawless*

EAST DEAN
TV5597 Map 3

Tiger ♀ ⌂

Off A259 Eastbourne–Seaford; BN20 0DA

Pretty old pub with two little bars and a dining room, an informal and friendly atmosphere, own-brewed beers and tasty food; bedrooms

This is a charming inn with comfortable bedrooms and good breakfasts, set in an idyllic spot by a secluded sloping village green lined with similar cottages. It's extremely popular with both chatty drinkers and those eating, so do arrive early to be sure of a seat; they only take table reservations from October to March. The focal point of the little beamed main bar is the open woodburning stove in a brick inglenook, surrounded by polished horsebrasses; there are just a few rustic tables with benches, simple wooden chairs, a window seat and a long cushioned wall bench. The walls are hung with fish prints and a stuffed tiger's head, and a couple of hunting horns hang above the long bar counter. Friendly, attentive staff serve Harveys Best, their own-brewed Beachy Head Legless Rambler (brewery tours available on request) and a guest beer on handpump, and nine wines by the glass. Down a step on the right is a small room with an exceptionally fine high-backed curved settle and a couple of other old settles, nice old chairs and wooden tables on coir carpeting, and on the walls an ancient map of Eastbourne and Beachy Head and photographs of the pub; the dining room, to the left of the main bar, has a cream woodburner and hunting prints. There are picnic-sets on the terrace among the window boxes and flowering climbers, or you can sit on the village green itself. The pub is well positioned for walks to the coast and along the clifftops of the Seven Sisters and up to Belle Tout Lighthouse and Beachy Head.

As well as offering breakfasts to non-residents until 10am, the much liked food includes lunchtime ploughman's, pâté of the day with home-made chutney, sausages with wholegrain mustard mash and roasted red onion gravy, barbecue chicken topped with bacon and cheese, a seasonal risotto of the day, duck breast with a sauce of the day, slow-roasted pork belly with black pudding mash, and puddings such as a cheesecake of the day and sticky toffee pudding. *Benchmark main dish: burger with bacon, cheese and chips £10.95. Two-course evening meal £18.50.*

Free house ~ Licensee Janice Avis ~ Real ale ~ (01323) 423209 ~ Open 10am-11.30pm; 8am-12.30am Fri, Sat ~ Bar food 12-3, 6-9 ~ Restaurant ~ Children welcome ~ Dogs allowed in bar ~ Wi-fi ~ Bedrooms: /£130 ~ www.beachyhead.org.uk
Recommended by Jason Caulkin, Ron Corbett, Steve and Irene Homer, Pete Walker, Simon Rodway, Emma Scofield, Mrs Sally Scott, Phil and Jane Villiers

EAST LAVANT

SU8608 Map 2

Royal Oak 🌟 ♀ 🛏

Pook Lane, off A286; PO18 0AX

Bustling and friendly dining pub with proper drinking area, excellent food, extensive wine list and real ales; super bedrooms

This pretty little white house, handy for Goodwood and some pleasant walks, has a proper drinking area despite its emphasis on food. It's open-plan in design, with low beams, exposed brickwork, crooked timbers, winter log fires and church candles. The much-used drinking part at the front has wall seats and sofas, Long Man American Pale Ale and Copper Hop and Sharps Doom Bar tapped from the cask, 22 wines by the glass from an extensive list, 20 malt whiskies. The attentive staff provide a friendly welcome. The attached seating area, focused on dining, is sensitively furnished with brown suede and leather dining chairs around scrubbed pine tables, and pictures of motor sport and local scenes on the walls; background music and board games. Outside, there are cushioned seats and tables under green parasols on the flagstoned front terrace with far-reaching views to the Downs; rambling around the side and back are terraced, brick and grass areas with more seats and attractive tubs and baskets. The bedrooms are stylish and well equipped and they also have self-catering cottages. The car park is across the road.

 Imaginative food using fresh local produce includes lunchtime sandwiches, confit chicken and ham hock terrine with chutney, potted crab with mizuna and avocado, steak burger with cheese, red onion jam and skinny fries, pea, broad bean and asparagus risotto, cider-battered cod and chips, corn-fed chicken with tomato, chorizo and bean cassoulet, a fresh fish dish of the day, and puddings such as seasonal crumble and treacle tart with clotted cream; they also offer a two- and three-course set lunch. *Benchmark main dish: trio of pork with marmalade and crackling £16.90. Two-course evening meal £23.40.*

Free house ~ Licensee Charles Ullmann ~ Real ale ~ (01243) 527434 ~ Open 7.30am-10.30pm ~ Bar food 12-2.30, 6-9 (9.30 Fri, Sat); 12-3, 6.30-9 Sun ~ Restaurant ~ Children welcome ~ Dogs allowed in bar ~ Wi-fi ~ Bedrooms: £85/£125 ~ www.royaloakeastlavant.co.uk *Recommended by John Evans, Tony and Jill Radnor, Tracey and Stephen Groves*

ERIDGE GREEN

TQ5535 Map 3

Nevill Crest & Gun ♀

A26 Tunbridge Wells–Crowborough; TN3 9JR

Handsome old building with lots of character, beams and standing timbers, hundreds of pictures and photographs, six real ales, enjoyable modern food and friendly, efficient staff

This 500-year-old former farmhouse has been cleverly and carefully opened up inside, with standing timbers and doorways keeping some sense of separate rooms. The civilised, easy-going atmosphere is helped by the wide mix of customers. Throughout, there are heavy beams (some carved), panelling, rugs on wooden floors, and woodburning stoves and an open fire in three fireplaces (the linenfold carved bressumer above one is worth seeking out). Also, all manner of individual dining chairs around dark wood or copper-topped tables, lots of pictures, maps and photographs to do with the local area, and window sills crammed with toby jugs, stone and glass bottles and plants. Phoenix Brunning & Price Original plus Adnams Southwold, Harveys Best, Hepworth Prospect, Larkins Traditional,

Long Man Long Blonde and Wells & Youngs Original on handpump, a farm cider, 15 wines by the glass and 100 malt whiskies; daily papers, board games and background music. There are a few picnic-sets in front of the building, and teak furniture on the back terrace next to the recently built dining extension with its large windows, light oak rafters, beams and coir flooring.

🍴 The nicely presented, interesting food includes sandwiches, crab and samphire tartlet with chive crème fraîche, chicken liver and thyme parfait with apple and date chutney, pork and leek sausages with red wine and onion gravy, potato gnocchi with tarragon cream sauce, confit duck leg with tomato, chorizo and mixed beans, thai-style fish stew with noodles and wasabi fritter, and puddings such as baked cherry and amaretti cheesecake and chocolate truffle torte with raspberry coulis. *Benchmark main dish: slow-cooked lamb shoulder with dauphinoise potatoes £16.95. Two-course evening meal £20.00.*

Brunning & Price ~ Manager Adam Holland ~ Real ale ~ (01892) 864209 ~ Open 12-11 (10.30 Sun) ~ Bar food 12-9.30 (10 Fri, Sat) ~ Children welcome ~ Dogs allowed in bar ~ Wi-fi ~ www.nevillcrestandgun.co.uk *Recommended by Nigel and Jean Eames*

EWHURST GREEN   TQ7924 Map 3

White Dog

Turn off A21 to Bodiam at S end of Hurst Green, cross B2244, pass Bodiam Castle, cross river then bear left uphill at Ewhurst Green sign; TN32 5TD

Welcoming village pub with a nice little bar, several real ales and popular food; bedrooms

An inviting pub on a winter's day with a roaring log fire in the inglenook fireplace, this family-run place is also lovely in summer when you can sit in the back garden with views over Bodiam Castle (National Trust). The bar on the left has a fine inglenook fireplace, hop-draped beams, wood-panelled walls, farm implements and horsebrasses, a few tables with high-backed, rush-seated dining chairs and red plush-topped bar stools on the old brick or flagstoned floor. There's also a high-backed cushioned settle by the counter where they serve Dark Star Hophead, Harveys Best and a beer named for the pub (from Old Dairy) on handpump and several wines by the glass. To the right of the door is the dining room with sturdy wooden tables and chairs on more flagstones, and a railway station mural; background music. A games room has darts, pool and board games.

🍴 The well liked food, using local produce, includes ciabatta sandwiches, potted shrimps, ham hock terrine with piccalilli, crayfish, crab and chilli linguine, porcini, sage and cheese risotto, cannon of lamb with port wine jus and couscous, guinea fowl with tarragon cream, and puddings. *Benchmark main dish: plaice on the bone £13.95. Two-course evening meal £20.00.*

Free house ~ Licensees Harriet and Dale Skinner ~ Real ale ~ (01580) 830264 ~ Open 12-11; 12-3, 6-11 in winter ~ Bar food 12-2, 6-9 ~ Restaurant ~ Children welcome ~ Dogs allowed in bar and bedrooms ~ Wi-fi ~ Live music monthly ~ Bedrooms: /£85 ~ www.thewhitedogewhurst.co.uk *Recommended by Rob Newland, Mrs Blethyn Elliott, B and M Kendall, Roger White, Kevin Streeter, John Wideman, Paul Austin*

If a compulsory service charge is mentioned prominently on a menu or accommodation terms, you must pay it if service was satisfactory. If service is really bad, you are legally entitled to refuse to pay some or all of the service charge as compensation for not getting the service you might reasonably have expected.

FIRLE

Ram

TQ4607 Map 3

Village signed off A27 Lewes–Polegate; BN8 6NS

Bustling country pub with three open fires, character rooms, helpful friendly service, a good choice of drinks, enjoyable food and seats in garden; comfortable bedrooms

Tucked beneath the Downs in a small village, this friendly old inn dates back in part some 500 years, and is full of walkers, riders and countryfolk. The main bar has captain's and mate's chairs and a couple of gingham armchairs around dark pubby tables on bare boards or quarry tiles, a log fire, gilt-edged paintings on dark brown walls, Harveys and a couple of guest beers on handpump, 20 wines by the glass and a thoughtful choice of spirits; service is welcoming and helpful. A cosy bar leads off here with another log fire, olive-green built-in planked and cushioned wall seats and more dark chairs and tables on parquet flooring; throughout there are various ceramic ram's heads or skulls, black and white photos of the local area, candles in hurricane jars and daily papers. Also, darts and board games. The back dining room is up some steps and overlooks the garden, where there are tables and chairs on a terrace and picnic-sets on grass; more picnic-sets under parasols at the front. The bedrooms are comfortable and the breakfasts feature local bacon, eggs and sausages.

Using local meat, game and fish, the enjoyable food includes lunchtime sandwiches, confit rabbit and ham hock terrine with chutney, crayfish, avocado and sun-blush tomato salad, sharing boards, pea, broad bean and feta risotto, twice-cooked pork belly with chive mash and red wine jus, black bream fillets with roast lemon oil and samphire, gressingham duck breast with mustard cream and lyonnaise potatoes, and puddings such as roast pear crème brûlée and dark chocolate brownie. *Benchmark main dish: beer-battered fish and chips £13.95. Two-course evening meal £19.50.*

Free house ~ Licensee Hayley Bayes ~ Real ale ~ (01273) 858222 ~ Open 11.30 (9am weekends)-11 ~ Bar food 12-3, 6.30-9; 9am-9pm weekends ~ Restaurant ~ Children welcome in snug and family room ~ Dogs welcome ~ Wi-fi ~ Folk music first Mon of month ~ Bedrooms: £70/£90 ~ www.raminn.co.uk *Recommended by Alfie Bayliss, Harvey Brown*

FLETCHING

Griffin

TQ4223 Map 3

Village signposted off A272 W of Uckfield; TN22 3SS

Busy, gently upmarket inn with a fine wine list, real ales and bistro-style bar food, and a big garden with far-reaching views; bedrooms

On a warm summer Sunday this civilised inn really comes into its own. The two-acre back garden is appealing and very spacious, and there are plenty of seats (on grass and a sandstone terrace) where you can enjoy the top class barbecues featuring fresh fish and shellfish and spit-roasts; readers tell us they make a mean Pimms too. Inside, the beamed and quaintly panelled bar rooms have blazing log fires, old photographs and hunting prints, straightforward close-set furniture including some captain's chairs and china on a delft shelf. There's a small bare-boarded serving area off to one side and a snug separate bar with sofas and a TV. The place gets pretty packed at weekends. Harveys Best, Hogs Back TEA, Kings Horsham Best and a guest beer on handpump, plus 20 wines by the glass from a good list (including champagne and sweet wine). The bright and pretty bedrooms are comfortable and the breakfasts good. There are ramps for wheelchairs.

Using local and organic produce, the impressive food includes mediterreanean fish soup with croutons, aioli and gruyère, rabbit and mascarpone pasta with tarragon and truffle oil, fresh crab linguine with chilli, fennel and white wine, organic chicken and mushroom pie, slow-roasted pork belly with caramelised apples and pears and red wine jus, duck breast with sweet potato fondant and thyme and orange jus, and puddings such as dark chocolate brownie with strawberry ice-cream and plum frangipane with plum compote. *Benchmark main dish: beer-battered cod and chips £14.00. Two-course evening meal £22.00.*

Free house ~ Licensees James Pullan and Samantha Barlow ~ Real ale ~ (01825) 722890 ~ Open 12-midnight (11 Sun) ~ Bar food 12-3, 7-9.30 ~ Restaurant ~ Children welcome ~ Dogs allowed in bar ~ Wi-fi ~ Live pianist Fri evening, Sun lunch ~ Bedrooms: £70/£100 ~ www.thegriffininn.co.uk *Recommended by Barry Haynes, Mrs J Ekins-Daukes, Nick Lawless, Sheila Topham, John Ralph, Christopher and Elise Way*

HEATHFIELD

TQ5920 Map 3

Star ◀

Church Street, Old Heathfield, off A265/B2096 E; TN21 9AH

Pleasant old pub with bustling, friendly atmosphere, good mix of customers, well liked food and decent choice of drinks; pretty garden

Tucked below the Early English tower of the church next door, this is a handsome 14th-c pilgrims' inn. There are ancient heavy beams, built-in wall settles and window seats, panelling, inglenook fireplaces and a roaring winter log fire; a doorway leads to a similarly decorated room set up more for eating with wooden tables and chairs (one table has high-backed white leather dining chairs) and a woodburning stove. An upstairs dining room has a striking barrel-vaulted ceiling (it was originally a dormitory for masons working on the reconstruction of the church after a fire in 1348). Harveys Best and guests such as Shepherd Neame Master Brew and Wells & Youngs Special on handpump, and an extensive wine list with 11 by the glass; background music. The very prettily planted garden has rustic furniture under smart umbrellas and lovely views of rolling pasture dotted with sheep and lined with oak trees.

Popular food using local, seasonal produce includes moules marinière, devilled kidneys on toast, home-cooked gammon and free-range eggs, beer-battered fresh fish and chips, asparagus risotto with garlic pesto, free-range chicken stuffed with mushrooms and wrapped in parma ham with a tomato dressing, free-range pork and Harveys ale sausages with balsamic onion gravy, and puddings such as plum and almond tart and tequila, lime and mint panna cotta. *Benchmark main dish: beef in ale pie £11.95. Two-course evening meal £19.00.*

Free house ~ Licensees Mike and Sue Chappell ~ Real ale ~ (01435) 863570 ~ Open 11-11; 12-10 Sun ~ Bar food 12-2.30, 6.30-9; 12-3, 6-8.30 Sun ~ Restaurant ~ Children welcome ~ Wi-fi ~ www.starinnoldheathfield.co.uk *Recommended by Nick Lawless, Mrs Blethyn Elliott, Martin Day*

HIGH HURSTWOOD

TQ4925 Map 3

Hurstwood ◉ ♀

Hurstwood Road off A272; TN22 4AH

Friendly, bustling dining pub with chatty bar area, real ales and good wines by the glass, excellent food and seats in the garden

Opposite the village green, this is a well run, friendly pub with a bustling, chatty atmosphere. The U-shaped open-plan interior is beamed and has a central bar where helpful, attentive young staff serve Harveys and maybe a local guest on handpump, 11 good wines by the glass, a fair choice of spirits and cocktails; good coffees. There are spindleback bar chairs against the counter (full of cheerful locals on our visit) and an area beside the log fire in the tiled Victorian fireplace that has a couple of leather sofas, armchairs and two tables – perfect for a drink and a chat. Many people are here for the particularly good food and the happy mix of tables are set with red gingham napkins, little chilli plants and church candles in rustic ironwork candlesticks. Chairs range from farmhouse to captain's to cushioned dining ones on bare boards, there's a grey dado topped with pale painted walls hung with hunting prints and other artwork, various lamps and lanterns, a piano (which does get used) and some twig decorations. French windows at one end open on to decking with seats and tables, which leads down to a grassed area with more seats.

Accomplished, interesting food using local game and fish includes lunchtime open sandwiches, salt and pepper squid with saffron aioli, peppered beef carpaccio with cornichon and caper salsa, toasted pine nuts, rocket and shaved parmesan, roast vegetable, ricotta and feta tart, crab linguine with tomato, chilli, samphire and white wine, lamb chop with lemon and fennel seed rösti, butternut squash purée and lamb jus, and puddings such as dark chocolate nemesis and orange polenta cake with orange syrup and mascarpone; they also offer a two- and three-course set menu. *Benchmark main dish: beer-battered fresh fish and chips £13.20. Two-course evening meal £21.00.*

Free house ~ Licensees Martin and Lenka Spanek ~ Real ale ~ (01825) 732257 ~ Open 12-11; 12-5.30 Sun; closed Sun evening except bank holiday weekends ~ Bar food 12-2.30, 7-9.30 ~ Children welcome ~ Dogs allowed in bar ~ Wi-fi ~ www.thehurstwood.com *Recommended by Edward May*

HORSHAM
Black Jug ♀
North Street; RH12 1RJ

TQ1730 Map 3

Lively town pub with wide choice of drinks, efficient staff and freshly produced bar food

Bustling and friendly, this well run town pub has helpful, attentive staff and a wide mix of customers. The single large early 20th-century room has a long central bar, a nice collection of sizeable dark wood tables and comfortable chairs on the stripped-wood floor, bookcases and interesting old prints and photographs above a dark wood-panelled dado on cream walls; board games. A spacious, bright conservatory has similar furniture and lots of hanging baskets. Phoenix Brunning & Price Original, Caledonian Deuchars IPA, Harveys Best and guests such as Castle Rock Harvest Pale, Timothy Taylors Landlord and Wychwood Hobgoblin on handpump, 20 wines by the glass, 150 malt whiskies and farm cider. The pretty flower-filled back terrace has plenty of garden furniture; parking is in the council car park next door as the small one by the pub is for staff and deliveries only.

A thoughtful choice of enticing food includes sandwiches, saffron and lemon panna cotta with mediterranean vegetables, tomato pesto and toasted croutons, sticky sesame pork belly with ginger and orange dressing, steak burger with bacon, cheese, coleslaw and chips, crispy beef salad with chilli and cashew nuts, braised shoulder of lamb with dauphinoise potatoes, rosemary and garlic chicken with wild mushrooms, spinach, bacon and pasta, and puddings such as bread and butter pudding with apricot sauce and dark chocolate truffle torte. *Benchmark main dish: beer-battered fish and chips £12.75. Two-course evening meal £20.00.*

Brunning & Price ~ Tenant Alastair Craig ~ Real ale ~ (01403) 253526 ~ Open 11.30am-
11pm; 12-10.30 Sun ~ Bar food 12-10 (9.30 Sun) ~ Children welcome till 5pm ~ Dogs
allowed in bar ~ Wi-fi ~ www.blackjug-horsham.co.uk *Recommended by Edward May,
Tony Scott, Elliot Baker*

LURGASHALL

SU9327   Map 2

Noahs Ark

Off A283 N of Petworth; GU28 9ET

**Busy old pub in nice spot with neatly kept rooms, real ales
and pleasing food using local produce**

Full of happy chatter from the varied customers – walkers, cricketers
and plenty of diners – this neatly kept pub has an idyllic position by
the village green. The simple, traditional bar, popular with locals, has
leather-topped bar stools by the counter where they serve Greene King
IPA and Abbot and a guest such as Skinners Betty Stogs on handpump
and ten wines by the glass. There are also beams, a mix of wooden chairs
and tables, parquet flooring and an inglenook fireplace. Open to the top
of the rafters, the dining room is spacious and airy with church candles
and fresh flowers on light wood tables; a couple of comfortable sofas
face each other in front of an open woodburning stove; background
music. The pub's border terrier is called Gillie and visiting dogs may get
a dog biscuit. Picnic-sets make the most of the setting, overlooked by
Blackdown Hill and with views of the village green and cricket pitch;
there are more tables in a large side garden.

Using local produce, the enjoyable food includes lunchtime sandwiches, scotch
egg with spicy apple sauce, twice-baked cheese soufflé, creamy wild mushroom
risotto, tempura-battered haddock and chips, free-range chicken with leeks and
pancetta, rib-eye steak with peppercorn sauce, and puddings. *Benchmark main
dish: burger with cheese, bacon, mushroom and chips £12.50. Two-course evening
meal £21.00.*

Greene King ~ Lease Henry Coghlan and Amy Whitmore ~ Real ale ~ (01428) 707346 ~
Open 11-11 (midnight Sat); 12-10.30 (8 in winter) Sun ~ Bar food 12-2.30, 7-9.30;
12-3.30 Sun ~ Restaurant ~ Children welcome ~ Dogs allowed in bar ~ Wi-fi ~
www.noahsarkinn.co.uk *Recommended by Richard Tilbrook, Tony and Rachel Schendel,
Ian Phillips, John Millwood*

MAYFIELD

TQ5927   Map 3

Rose & Crown

Fletching Street; TN20 6TE

**Pretty weatherboarded cottage with unspoilt bars, relaxed
atmosphere, local beers and popular bar food**

Once the village brewhouse, this pretty weatherboarded 16th-c inn is
down a lane in one of the most beautiful villages of the Weald. Several
bars wander round the little central server, but the two cosy front rooms
have the most character: low ceiling boards with coins embedded in the
glossy paintwork, bench seats built into partly panelled walls, pewter
tankards hanging above the bar and along a beam, and a mix of simple
dining chairs around wooden tables on stripped floorboards. There are
candles in a brick fireplace, a big log fire in the inglenook, Harveys Best
and a changing guest such as Westerham Summer Perle on handpump
and a dozen wines by the glass. Down some steps to the left is a larger
carpeted room with a comfortable cushioned sofa, similar tables and

chairs, a woodburning stove and several mirrors; steps at the other end lead up to a less used back area. There are picnic-sets under parasols on the front terrace and in the decked back garden.

 Food includes ciabatta sandwiches, whole baked camembert with garlic and thyme, whitebait with mayonnaise, a seasonal risotto, wild boar and apple sausages with red onion gravy, burger with cheese, bacon and chips, daily specials, and puddings such as treacle sponge with custard and lemon crème brûlée. *Benchmark main dish: home-cooked gammon with triple-cooked chips and eggs £9.95. Two-course evening meal £16.50.*

Mitchells & Butlers ~ Lease Liz Maltman ~ Real ale ~ (01435) 872200 ~ Open 11-11 (midnight Fri, Sat); 12-10.30 Sun ~ Bar food 12-9 (9.30 Fri, Sat; 7 Sun) ~ Children welcome until 8.30pm ~ Dogs welcome ~ Wi-fi ~ Live music Sat evenings ~ www.roseandcrownmayfield.co.uk *Recommended by Isobel Mackinlay*

OVING
SU9005   Map 2
Gribble Inn ◖
Between A27 and A259 E of Chichester; PO20 2BP

Own-brewed beers in bustling 16th-c thatched pub with beamed and timbered linked rooms, well liked bar food and pretty garden

With some interesting names, the own-brew beers on handpump in this thatched pub are quite a draw: Fuzzy Duck, Gribble Ale, Pigs Ear, Plucking Pheasant, Regs Tipple and three seasonal ales, such as CHI.P.A, Sussex Quad Hopper or strong Wobbler Ale. The chatty bar features lots of heavy beams and timbering, old country kitchen furnishings and pews, while the various linked rooms have a cottagey feel and huge winter log fires. Also, board games and a skittle alley with its own bar. There are seats outside in a covered area and more chairs and tables in the pretty garden with its apple and pear trees. The pub also contains a village shop that sells local and pub-produced items and serves breakfasts (9.30-11.30am) and cakes and hot drinks (all day).

 Using yeast from the brewery for the home-baked bread, the food includes lunchtime sandwiches, chicken liver pâté with chutney, beer-battered haddock and chips, a pie of the day, spinach and mushroom roulade with tarragon sauce, venison burger with black pudding, bacon, mushroom and egg, rib-eye steak with a choice of sauces, and puddings such as lemon crème brûlée with elderflower ice-cream and 'beeramisu' (chocolate ale cake). *Benchmark main dish: pork belly in cider with creamed cabbage and bacon £14.95. Two-course evening meal £17.00.*

Badger ~ Licensees Simon Wood and Nicola Tester ~ Real ale ~ (01243) 786893 ~ Open 11-11; 12-10 Sun ~ Bar food 12-2.30, 6-9; 12-3 Sun ~ Restaurant ~ Children welcome away from bar ~ Dogs allowed in bar ~ www.gribbleinn.co.uk
Recommended by Nigel and Sue Foster, David H T Dimock, Tony Hobden

PETWORTH
SU9721   Map 2
Angel ⭐ ♈ ⛏
Angel Street; GU28 0BG

Medieval building with an 18th-c façade, a chatty atmosphere in opened-up beamed bars, log fires, friendly service and good, interesting food; bedrooms

In a market town famed for its antiques shops, this is a carefully renovated inn with plenty of loyal customers. There's an easy-going and friendly atmosphere and the interconnected rooms have kept many of their original features. The front bar has beams, a log fire in an inglenook fireplace and an appealing variety of old wooden and cushioned dining chairs and tables on wide floorboards. It leads through to the main room with high chairs by the counter where they keep Langham Best alongside a couple of guests from breweries such as Dark Star and Firebird on handpump, 22 wines by the glass from an extensive list and 26 malt whiskies; board games. There are also high-backed brown leather and antique chairs and tables on pale wooden flooring, the odd milk churn and french windows to a sizeable three-level back garden. The cosy and popular back bar is similarly furnished, with a second log fire. The bedrooms are comfortable and breakfasts good.

Rewarding food using locally sourced ingredients includes lunchtime sandwiches, chicken, chorizo and liver parfait, chilli and garlic tiger prawns, sausages with onion gravy, chicken with bacon, brie and brandy in a creamy mushroom and tarragon sauce, steak and kidney in ale pudding, thai green vegetable curry, confit crispy duck leg with noodles and stir-fried vegetables, fish pie, and puddings such as chocolate brownie with hot fudge sauce. *Benchmark main dish: beer-battered fresh haddock and chips £12.95. Two-course evening meal £21.00.*

Free house ~ Licensee Murray Inglis ~ Real ale ~ (01798) 342153 ~ Open 10.30am-11pm; 11.30-10.30 Sun ~ Bar food 12-2.30, 6.30-9.30; Sun 12-2.30, 6-9 ~ Children welcome ~ Dogs allowed in bar and bedrooms ~ Wi-fi ~ Bedrooms: £90/£100 ~ www.angelinnpetworth.co.uk *Recommended by Martin Jones, Toby Jones, Tony and Wendy Hobden, Michael and Sheila Hawkins*

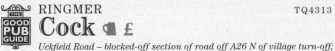

RINGMER
Cock 🍺 £

TQ4313 Map 3

Uckfield Road – blocked-off section of road off A26 N of village turn-off; BN8 5RX

16th-c country pub with a wide choice of popular bar food, real ales in character bar, and plenty of seats in the garden

'As good as ever,' says one reader with enthusiasm after another enjoyable visit to this friendly former coaching inn. The unspoilt bar has traditional pubby furniture on flagstones, heavy beams, Harveys Best and a couple of guests from breweries such as Arundel, Hammerpot, Hogs Back and Long Man on handpump, 12 wines by the glass and a dozen malt whiskies; good service and a blazing winter log fire. There are also three dining areas; background music. Outside, on the terrace and in the garden, are lots of picnic-sets with views across open fields to the South Downs. Visiting dogs are offered a bowl of water and a chew, and the owners' dogs are called Bailey and Tally.

Quite a choice of popular, fair value food includes lunchtime sandwiches (not Sunday), deep-fried camembert with cranberry sauce, egg and prawn mayonnaise, home-cooked ham and free-range eggs, mushroom and red pepper stroganoff, local venison burger with spicy relish and chips, chicken with barbecue sauce and mozzarella, salmon fillet with cream and watercress sauce, and puddings such as jam roly-poly with custard and banoffi pie. *Benchmark main dish: steak in ale pie £11.25. Two-course evening meal £18.00.*

Free house ~ Licensees Ian, Val, Nick and Matt Ridley ~ Real ale ~ (01273) 812040 ~ Open 11-3, 6-11.30; 11-11.30 Sun ~ Bar food 12-2.15 (2.30 Sat), 6-9.30; 12-9.30 Sun ~ Restaurant ~ Well behaved children welcome (no toddlers) ~ Dogs allowed in bar ~ Wi-fi ~ www.cockpub.co.uk *Recommended by Tony and Wendy Hobden, Ann and Colin Hunt*

ROBERTSBRIDGE
TQ7323   Map 3

George 🛏
High Street; TN32 5AW

Friendly former coaching inn with local beers in bustling bar, tasty food using seasonal produce in dining room, and seats outside; good bedrooms

Offering a warm welcome to all their customers – dogs included – this handsome old place is run by hard-working, friendly licensees. There's a log fire in the brick inglenook fireplace with a leather sofa and a couple of armchairs in front of it – just right for a quiet pint and a chat – plus high bar stools by the counter where they serve Harveys Best, Sharps Doom Bar and a guest such as Hastings Blonde on handpump, 20 wines by the glass and a farm cider; helpful staff and an easy-going atmosphere. Leading off from here is the refurbished dining area, with elegant high-backed beige tartan or leather chairs around a mix of tables (each with fresh flowers and a tea-light) on stripped floorboards and tea-lights in a small fireplace; background music. In warm weather there are plenty of seats and tables on the outdoor back terrace. The bedrooms are comfortable and the breakfasts good.

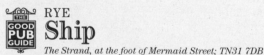 Using free-range, local and seasonal produce, the tasty food includes lunchtime baguettes, twice-baked goats cheese soufflé, locally smoked fish platter, chicken on smoked bacon and savoy cabbage with cream sauce, tempura local cod and chips (available to take away most evenings too), calves liver with bubble and squeak and roasted onion gravy, chargrilled bass with ginger and chilli, rib-eye steak with peppercorn sauce, and puddings. *Benchmark main dish: slow-roast pork belly with apple rösti £14.50. Two-course evening meal £19.50.*

Free house ~ Licensees John and Jane Turner ~ Real ale ~ (01580) 880315 ~ Open 11-11; 12-8 Sun; closed Mon ~ Bar food 12-2.30, 6.30-9; 12-3 Sun ~ Children welcome but must be accompanied by adult at all times ~ Dogs allowed in bar ~ Wi-fi ~ Bedrooms: £83/£100 ~ www.thegeorgerobertsbridge.co.uk *Recommended by B and M Kendall, Pete Walker, Tom and Jill Jones*

RYE
TQ9120   Map 3

Ship
The Strand, at the foot of Mermaid Street; TN31 7DB

Informal and prettily set old inn with a relaxed atmosphere, straightforward furnishings, local ales and often inventive food; bedrooms

At the bottom of the famous Mermaid Street, this 16th-c inn was once used as a warehouse for storing goods seized from smugglers. It has an easy-going atmosphere and décor that's a successful blend of quirkiness and comfort. The ground floor is all opened up, from the sunny big-windowed front part to a snugger section at the back, with a log fire in the stripped-brick fireplace below a stuffed boar's head. Flooring varies from one area to the next: composition, stripped boards, flagstones, a bit of carpet in the armchair corner. There are beams and timbers, a mixed bag of rather second-hand-feeling furnishings – a cosy group of overstuffed leather armchairs and sofa, random stripped or Formica-topped tables and various café chairs – that suit it nicely, as do the utilitarian bulkhead wall lamps. Harveys Best and a couple of guests such as Old Dairy Gold Top and Rother Valley Hoppers Ale on handpump, local farm cider and perry, and several wines by the glass; board games. In addition to the simply furnished

SUSSEX | 777

but comfortable bedrooms, the pub rents out a 300-year-old single-storey cottage and 500-year-old house. There are picnic-sets and a couple of cheerful oilcloth-covered tables out by the quiet lane.

 The short menu of interesting food using local, seasonal produce includes weekday lunchtime sandwiches, devilled kidneys on toasted brioche, chorizo, black pudding, broad bean and soft-boiled egg salad, chicken and mushroom pie, cheeseburger with onion rings, bacon, barbecue relish and fries, pink-cooked lamb with medjool dates, olives and feta, fish curry, and puddings. *Benchmark main dish: fish pie £13.00. Two-course evening meal £19.25.*

Enterprise ~ Lease Karen Northcote ~ Real ale ~ (01797) 222233 ~ Open 8am-11pm (10.30 Sun) ~ Bar food 8.30-11.30am (breakfast); 12-3 (3.30 weekends), 6-10 ~ Children welcome ~ Dogs welcome ~ Wi-fi ~ Bedrooms: $100/$110 ~ www.theshipinnrye.co.uk
Recommended by Guy Vowles, Simon Rodway, Mike and Eleanor Anderson, Anthony Barnes

RYE   TQ9220 Map 3
Ypres Castle
Gun Garden; steps up from A259, or down past Ypres Tower; TN31 7HH

Traditional pub with several real ales, quite a choice of bar food and seats in sheltered garden

This unpretentious, pleasantly traditional pub is usefully open all day and has views down over the River Rother. In the main bar there are wall banquettes with pale blue cushions, an open fire in a stone fireplace with a mirror above and easy chairs in front, assorted chairs and tables (each set with a modern oil lamp) and local artwork. Stools line the blue-panelled counter where they keep five real ales from breweries such as Adnams, Harveys, Larkins, Old Dairy and Rother Valley on handpump, several wines by the glass and farm cider; background music and board games. The back dining room has paintings and pictures of Rye and similar furnishings to the bar; there's another dining room at the front. The sheltered garden is a tempting place to sit.

 As well as lunchtime baguettes, the well liked food includes prawn cocktail, chicken liver pâté with chutney, local ham and egg, sausages and mash with red onion gravy, vegetarian chilli, local lamb rump with ratatouille and dauphinoise potatoes, slow-roast pork belly with roasted garlic mash and red wine sauce, and puddings such as apple crumble and chocolate fudge cake. *Benchmark main dish: beer-battered fresh local fish and chips £10.50. Two-course evening meal £18.00.*

Free house ~ Licensee Garry Dowling ~ Real ale ~ (01797) 223248 ~ Open 12-11 ~ Bar food 12-3, 6-9 (8 Fri); 12-3 Sun ~ Children welcome ~ Dogs welcome ~ Wi-fi ~ Live music Fri and Sun evenings ~ www.yprescastleinn.co.uk *Recommended by Peter Meister, Quentin and Carol Williamson, Joanne Owen, Bill Adie, Peter Smith and Judith Brown, Anthony Barnes*

SALEHURST   TQ7424 Map 3
Salehurst Halt £
Village signposted from Robertsbridge bypass on A21 Tunbridge Wells–Battle; Church Lane; TN32 5PH

Relaxed small local in quiet hamlet with chatty atmosphere, real ales, well liked and reasonably priced bar food, and seats in pretty back garden

'A cracking little pub' is how one of our readers describes this very well run, friendly local – and we agree. It's in a small hamlet near the church and surrounded by pretty countryside, and customers come from far and wide. To the right of the door is a small stone-floored area with a couple of tables, a settle, a TV and an open fire. Furniture includes a nice long scrubbed pine table, a couple of sofas and a mix of more ordinary pubby tables and wheelback and mate's chairs on the wood-strip floor; occasional background music, board games and highbrow books on the shelves. Dark Star American Pale Ale, Harveys Best and a guest such as Old Dairy Red Top on handpump, farm cider, several malt whiskies and eight wines by the glass. The cottagey and charming back garden has views over the Rother Valley and the summer barbecues and pizzas from the wood-fired oven are extremely popular; there's also a terrace with metal chairs and tiled tables, and outdoor table tennis as well as other garden games.

As well as lunchtime baguettes, the well liked food using local produce includes chicken and prune terrine with chutney, salt and pepper squid, a changing vegetarian pasta dish, beer-battered local cod and chips, pork and hop sausages with onion gravy, jerk chicken, lamb kofta kebab with couscous and tzatziki, and puddings such as white chocolate and strawberry mousse and fruit crumble. *Benchmark main dish: changing curries £11.00. Two-course evening meal £15.00.*

Free house ~ Licensee Andrew Augarde ~ Real ale ~ (01580) 880620 ~ Open 12-11 (10.30 Sun); closed Mon ~ Bar food 12-2.30, 7-9; not Sun evening, Mon, Tues evening ~ Children welcome ~ Dogs welcome ~ Wi-fi ~ www.salehursthalt.co.uk
Recommended by Peter Meister

TICEHURST
Bell 🛏

TQ6830   Map 3

High Street; TN5 7AS

Extensively but carefully restored old inn with heavily beamed rooms, real ales and good wines by the glass, popular food and friendly service; bedrooms

Much of the character of this sensitively renovated old coaching inn has been kept, and the two main rooms still display their heavy beams and timbering. The bar has rugs on bare boards, an inglenook fireplace, tables surrounded by a mix of cushioned wooden dining chairs, some quirky decorations such as a stuffed owl in a niche, a rug in the shape of a tiger skin and fez or top-hat lightshades hanging from the ceiling, and sizeable stools beside the wooden counter where they serve Harveys Best and guests such as Long Man Long Blonde and Tonbridge Alsace Gold on handpump, 16 wines by the glass and a dozen malt whiskies. The dining room continues from the bar and is similarly furnished, with the addition of cushioned wall settles and an eclectic choice of paintings on the red walls; service is helpful and friendly. A separate room has comfortable sofas grouped around a low table in front of another open fire, interesting wallpaper, a large globe, an ancient typewriter and various books and pieces of china. What was the carriage room holds a long, sunken table with benches on either side (perfect for an informal party) and there's an upstairs function room too. The gents' are well worth a peek for their highly unusual urinals. Each of the comfortable, well equipped bedrooms has a silver birch tree and other rustic décor. Outside, solid modern wooden chairs and tables and picnic-sets sit on the back terrace and on gravel.

Popular modern food includes lunchtime baps, crab pâté, crispy fried monkfish cheeks with gribiche sauce, spinach and honeyed goats cheese wrapped in filo pastry on ratatouille, burger with relish and triple-cooked chips, hake fillet with braised lettuce and maple-cured bacon, home-smoked and roasted pork loin with apple mash and cider and chilli jus, and puddings such as frozen berries with hot white chocolate sauce and custard tart with poached rhubarb; they also offer a two- and three-course set lunch. *Benchmark main dish: local steak with chips £21.50. Two-course evening meal £30.00.*

Free house ~ Licensee Jhonnie de Oliveira ~ Real ale ~ (01580) 200234 ~ Open 9am-11pm (midnight Fri, Sat, 10.30 Sun) ~ Bar food 12-3, 6-9.30; 12-4, 6-9 Sun ~ Restaurant ~ Children welcome ~ Dogs allowed in bar and bedrooms ~ Live music last Sun of the month ~ Bedrooms: /£95 ~ www.thebellinticehurst.com *Recommended by Richard and Penny Gibbs, Charles and Gillian Van Der Lande, Peter Meister*

TILLINGTON
SU9621   Map 2
Horse Guards
Off A272 Midhurst–Petworth; GU28 9AF

Sussex Dining Pub of the Year

300-year-old inn with beams, panelling and open fires in rambling rooms, inventive food and a thoughtful choice of drinks; cottagey bedrooms

Our readers love this inn and several have described it as 'a gem'. In warm weather the leafy, lush and sheltered garden has picnic-sets, day beds, deck chairs and even a hammock, and there's also a charming terrace. But it's just as enticing in cold weather too, thanks to the open fires and cosy bars. With a gently civilised, friendly atmosphere and a good mix of both locals and visitors, the neatly kept, beamed front bar has some good country furniture on bare boards, a chesterfield in one corner and a lovely view beyond the village to the Rother Valley from a seat in the big panelled bow window. High bar chairs line the counter where they keep Harveys Best and Langham Hip Hop on handpump, 14 wines by the glass, home-made sloe gin and local farm juices. Other rambling beamed rooms have similar furniture on brick floors, rugs and original panelling and there are fresh flowers throughout. The cosy country bedrooms are comfortable and breakfasts are good. The medieval church with its unusual spire was painted by Constable and Turner; Petworth House (National Trust) is close by.

From the small, seasonal menu (using some of their own and foraged produce) the delicious food includes lunchtime sandwiches, ham and egg, and beer-battered whiting with chips, as well as potted shrimps, potato and pine nut croquettes with local cheese fondue, beetroot tatin with confit garlic, feta, pumpkin seed oil and crème fraîche, barbary duck with dauphinoise potatoes and blood orange sauce, bream fillet with ratatouille and anya potatoes, and puddings such as chocolate and almond terrine with hazelnut pralines and pistachio, rosewater and cardamom iced parfait with candied almonds and poached pear. *Benchmark main dish: local venison haunch with heart ragu, potato gnocchi and truffle oil £16.50. Two-course evening meal £23.50.*

Enterprise ~ Lease Sam Beard ~ Real ale ~ (01798) 342332 ~ Open 12-midnight ~ Bar food 12-2.30 (3 Sat), 6.30-9 (9.30 Fri, Sat); 12-3.30, 6.30-9 Sun ~ Children welcome ~ Dogs allowed in bar and bedrooms ~ Wi-fi ~ Bedrooms: £85/£95 ~ www.thehorseguardsinn.co.uk *Recommended by Ann and Colin Hunt, Tracey and Stephen Groves, John Evans, Derek Thomas, Sheila Topham, Christopher and Elise Way, Richard Tilbrook*

The star-on-a-plate award, distinguishes pubs where the food is of exceptional quality. The knife-and-fork symbol just means the pub serves food.

WARNINGLID
TQ2425 Map 3

Half Moon 🍴⭐ 🍷

B2115 off A23 S of Handcross or off B2110 Handcross–Lower Beeding; RH17 5TR

Good modern cooking in simply furnished pub with an informal chatty atmosphere, real ales, lots of wines by the glass and seats in sizeable garden

Whether it's a drink or a meal you want, the friendly staff here are always welcoming. There's a proper pubby atmosphere and the lively locals' bar has straightforward wooden furniture on bare boards and a small Victorian fireplace; a room just off here has oak beams and flagstones. A couple of steps lead down to the dining areas with a happy mix of wooden chairs, cushioned wall settles and nice old tables on floorboards, plank panelling and bare brick, and old village photographs; there's also another open fire and a glass-covered well. Bedlam Golden Ale, Greene King Old Speckled Hen, Harveys Best and Hurst Founders Best Bitter on handpump, around 18 wines by the glass, several malt whiskies and a farm cider. There are quite a few picnic-sets on the lawn in the sheltered, sizeable garden, which has a most spectacular avenue of trees, with uplighters that glow at night.

 The enjoyable, interesting food includes lunchtime sandwiches, wild sea trout and dill tartlet with spinach and crayfish cream, cheddar, parmesan and chive beignets with cauliflower purée, local sausages with onion gravy, chicken, beef, pork, venison or vegetarian burger with several toppings and chips, beer-battered cod and chips, Estate venison duo (roasted loin and braised shoulder) with rosemary and potato terrine and Calvados jus, and puddings such as double chocolate brownie with white chocolate ice-cream and warm bakewell tart with raspberry sorbet. *Benchmark main dish: calves liver with spring greens and onion gravy £16.00. Two-course evening meal £20.00.*

Free house ~ Licensees Jonny Lea and James Amico ~ Real ale ~ (01444) 461227 ~ Open 11.30-3, 5.30-11; 11.30-11 Sat; 12-9 Sun ~ Bar food 12-2, 6-9.30; 12-3 Sun ~ Restaurant ~ Children welcome ~ Dogs allowed in bar ~ Wi-fi ~ www.thehalfmoonwarninglid.co.uk *Recommended by Conor McGaughey, Guy Vowles, Derek Thomas*

WARTLING
TQ6509 Map 3

Lamb 🍷

Village signed with Herstmonceux Castle off A271 Herstmonceux–Battle; BN27 1RY

Friendly family-owned country pub, comfortable seating areas, cosy little bar, changing real ales, modern food and seats on pretty back terrace; bedrooms

You can be sure of a genuinely friendly welcome at this easy-going and rather civilised place, which is extremely popular for a drink and a chat or a leisurely meal. The little entrance bar on the right has a few dining chairs with arms around a rustic circular table on wide floorboards, an open fireplace, grey-green paintwork and tapestry curtains. The two-level beamed and timbered dining room leading off here has similar furnishings on more wide boards, a couple of armchairs in front of a woodburning stove in an inglenook fireplace and a handsome settle against a panelled end wall; plenty of candles in brass sticks. At the back is a larger bustling bar with sheepskins draped over built-in panelled and cushioned benches on a raised area, another woodburner fronted by armchairs and a sofa, and a vinyl record player (in working order). French windows open to steps that lead up to the terraced garden where there are chunky green-painted seats and benches among flowering tubs. Harveys Best, Old Dairy Spring Top and Pig & Porter Crab & Winkle on handpump and eight wines by the glass. The sizeable restaurant right at the back of the building has animal and country paintings on the walls, antiques and large flower arrangements. The sussex spaniel is called Maude.

Good, interesting food from a sensibly shortish menu backed up by daily specials includes goats cheese and thyme panna cotta with confit onion marmalade, smoked ham hock and leek terrine with chutney, sweet potato gnocchi with sage and garlic butter and parmesan, lamb burger with apple coleslaw and fries, seared monkfish with basil pesto potatoes and lemon butter sauce, and puddings such as strawberry cheesecake and lemon drizzle cake with chantilly cream. *Benchmark main dish: haddock, leek and paprika fishcakes with home-made sweet chilli sauce £12.00. Two-course evening meal £20.00.*

Free house ~ Licensee Charlie Braxton ~ Real ale ~ (01323) 832116 ~ Open 11.30-11 (5 Sun); closed Sun evening ~ Bar food 12-3, 6-9; 12-2.30 Sun ~ Children welcome ~ Dogs allowed in bar ~ Wi-fi ~ Bedrooms: /£85 ~ www.lambinnwartling.co.uk
Recommended by Caroline Prescott, Isobel Mackinlay, Steve and Liz Tilley

WEST HOATHLY
Cat 🏅 🛏

TQ3632 Map 3

Village signposted from A22 and B2028 S of East Grinstead; North Lane; RH19 4PP

Popular 16th-c inn with old-fashioned bar, airy dining rooms, local real ales, tempting food and seats outside; lovely bedrooms

There's lots to see and do nearby, so the comfortable and very pretty bedrooms (with coffee machines and goose-down duvets) make a good base for the area – and are highly thought-of by our readers; the breakfasts are top notch too. Downstairs, the lovely old bar has a bustling, friendly atmosphere, beams, proper pubby tables and chairs on an old wooden floor, and a fine log fire in an inglenook fireplace. With a focus on local breweries, Harveys Best and Larkins Traditional Ale are available alongside a couple of guests such as Black Cat and a seasonal Harveys on handpump, as well as local cider and apple juice and several wines by the glass; look out for the glass cover over the 75-ft deep well. The light and airy dining rooms have a nice mix of wooden dining chairs and tables on pale wood-strip flooring, and throughout there are hops, china platters, brass and copper ornaments and a gently upmarket atmosphere. The contemporary-style garden room has glass doors that open on to a terrace with teak furniture. The cocker spaniel is called Harvey. Steam train enthusiasts can visit the Bluebell Railway, and the Priest House in the village is a fascinating museum in a cottage endowed with an extraordinary array of ancient anti-witch symbols. Parking is limited.

Using very carefully sourced local and organic produce, the rewarding and well presented food includes lunchtime sandwiches, venison and pistachio terrine with quince jelly, smoked haddock, cod and prawn fishcake with wholegrain mustard cream, squash, goats cheese and chard pastilla (a sweet and savoury north african pie), prosciutto-wrapped chicken with red wine sauce and dauphinoise potatoes, slow-cooked pork belly with black pudding mash and caramelised apple, and puddings such as orange and almond cake with rosemary syrup and Valrhona chocolate brownie with salt caramel and honeycomb ice-cream.

Benchmark main dish: steak and mushroom in ale pie £14.50. Two-course evening meal £22.00.

Free house ~ Licensee Andrew Russell ~ Real ale ~ (01342) 810369 ~ Open 12-11; 12-5 Sun ~ Bar food 12-2, 6-9; 12-2.30, 6-9.30 Fri, Sat; 12-2.30 Sun ~ Well behaved children welcome if over 7 ~ Dogs allowed in bar and bedrooms ~ Wi-fi ~ Pianist last Fri evening of month and every other Sun lunch ~ Bedrooms: £80/£110 ~ www.catinn.co.uk
Recommended by Nick Lawless, Bernard Stradling, Grahame Brooks, Martin and Karen Wake, Steve and Irene Homer, Hunter and Christine Wright, J A Snell, Wendy Breese, Mrs Sally Scott, Sheila Topham

Also Worth a Visit in Sussex

Besides the fully inspected pubs, you might like to try these pubs that have been recommended to us and described by readers. Do tell us what you think of them: feedback@goodguides.com

ALFOLD BARS   TQ0333
Sir Roger Tichborne (01403) 751873
B2133 N of Loxwood; RH14 0QS
Renovated and extended beamed country pub keeping original nooks and crannies, good well presented food (not Sun evening) from varied reasonably priced menu, friendly prompt service, five well kept ales including Wells & Youngs and one for the pub from local Firebird, flagstones and log fires; children and dogs welcome, back terrace and sloping lawn with lovely rural views, good walks, open all day. *(Tony and Wendy Hobden)*

ALFRISTON   TQ5203
Olde Smugglers (01323) 870241
Waterloo Square; BN26 5UE Charming 14th-c inn, low beams and panelling, brick floor, sofas by huge inglenook, masses of bric-a-brac and smuggling mementoes, various nooks and crannies, wide range of popular bar food from sandwiches to specials, Harveys and guests, real cider and good choice of wines by the glass; background music; children in eating area and conservatory, dogs welcome, tables on well planted back suntrap terrace and lawn, three bedrooms, open all day and can get crowded – lovely village draws many visitors. *(Anon)*

ALFRISTON   TQ5203
Star (01323) 870495
High Street; BN26 5TA Fair-sized hotel with fine painted medieval carvings outside, heavy-beamed old-fashioned bar with some interesting features including a sanctuary post, antique furnishings and big log fire in Tudor fireplace, comfortable lounge with easy chairs, more space behind for eating, enjoyable reasonably priced bar food (pricey restaurant menu), ales such as Beachy Head and Long Man, efficient polite service; monthly quiz; children welcome, dogs in bar, 37 bedrooms (most in 1960s part behind), open all day in summer. *(John Warner, Tom and Jill Jones)*

AMBERLEY   TQ0211
Bridge (01798) 831619
Houghton Bridge, off B2139; BN18 9LR Popular and welcoming open-plan dining pub, comfortable and relaxed, with pleasant bar and two-room dining area, candles on tables, log fire, wide range of reasonably priced generous food (not Sun evening) from good sandwiches up, well kept ales including Harveys, cheerful efficient service; children and dogs welcome, seats out in front, more tables in enclosed side garden, handy for station, open all day. *(Ann and Colin Hunt)*

AMBERLEY   TQ0313
★**Sportsmans** (01798) 831787
Crossgates; Rackham Road, off B2139; BN18 9NR Popular pub with good fairly priced food and well kept ales such as Harveys, Hammerpot, Kings and Langhams (Aug festival), friendly efficient young staff, three bars including brick-floored one with darts, great views over Amberley Wildbrooks from pretty back conservatory restaurant and tables outside; dogs welcome, good walks, neat bedrooms. *(Pete Walker)*

ANGMERING   TQ0604
Lamb (01903) 774300
The Square; BN16 4EQ Airy up-to-date revamp for this village coaching inn, enjoyable food (not Sun evening) from varied menu including good value two-course lunch, ales such as Fullers and Harveys from light wood servery, good choice of wines by the glass, friendly service, half-panelling and wood-strip floors, inglenook log fire in bar, woodburner on raised plinth in restaurant; children welcome, refurbished bedrooms, open all day. *(Tom and Ruth Rees)*

ANGMERING   TQ0704
Spotted Cow (01903) 783919
High Street; BN16 4AW Six well kept ales including Fullers, Harveys, Skinners and Timothy Taylors, decent wines by the glass, smallish bar on left, long dining extension

with large conservatory on right, popular food from sandwiches up, good friendly service, two fires, sporting caricatures, smuggling history; children welcome, disabled access, big garden with boules and play area, lovely walk to Highdown Hill fort, open all day weekends. *(Peter Meister)*

ARDINGLY   TQ3430

★ **Gardeners Arms** (01444) 892328

B2028 2 miles N; RH17 6TJ Reliable food from sandwiches and pub favourites up in old linked rooms, Badger beers, pleasant efficient service, standing timbers and inglenooks, scrubbed pine on flagstones and broad boards, old local photographs, mural in back part, lighted candles and nice relaxed atmosphere; children and dogs welcome, disabled facilities, café-style furniture on pretty terrace and in side garden, opposite South of England showground and handy for Borde Hill and Wakehurst Place (NT), open all day. *(Grahame Brooks)*

ARLINGTON   TQ5507

★ **Old Oak** (01323) 482072

Caneheath; off A22 or A27 NW of Polegate; BN26 6SJ 17th-c former almshouse with open-plan L-shaped bar, beams, log fires and comfortable seating, well kept Harveys and a guest tapped from the cask, traditional bar food (all day weekends), toad in the hole played here; background music; children and dogs welcome, round picnic-sets in quiet garden, play area, walks in nearby Abbots Wood, open all day. *(Fr Robert Marsh, Alan Weedon)*

ARLINGTON   TQ5407

Yew Tree (01323) 870590

Off A22 near Hailsham, or A27 W of Polegate; BN26 6RX Neatly modernised Victorian village pub popular for its wide range of good value generous home-made food (booking advised), well kept Harveys and Long Man, decent wines, prompt friendly service even when busy, log fires, hop-covered beams and old local photographs, darts in thriving bare-boards bar, plush lounge, comfortable conservatory; children welcome, nice big garden with play area, paddock with farm animals, good walks. *(John Beeken)*

ARUNDEL   TQ0208

★ **Black Rabbit** (01903) 882828

Mill Road, Offham; keep on and don't give up!; BN18 9PB Refurbished riverside pub in lovely spot near wildfowl reserve with timeless views of water meadows and castle – well organised for families and can get very busy; long bar with eating areas at either end, good choice of enjoyable food all day from baguettes and sharing boards up, well kept Badger ales and decent wines by

the glass, good service, log fires, newspapers; background music; dogs welcome, covered tables and pretty hanging baskets out at front, extensive terrace across road overlooking river, play area, boat trips and good walks. *(Peter Meister, John Beeken, Tony Scott)*

ARUNDEL   TQ0107

Swan (01903) 882314

High Street; BN18 9AG Smart but comfortably relaxed open-plan L-shaped bar with attractive woodwork and matching fittings, efficient young staff, well kept Fullers ales and occasional guests, enjoyable fairly priced food from baguettes to blackboard specials, sporting bric-a-brac and old photographs, open fire, restaurant; 15 bedrooms, no car park (pay-and-display opposite), open all day. *(Nigel and Sue Foster, Alan Bulley)*

ASHURST   TQ1816

★ **Fountain** (01403) 710219

B2135 S of Partridge Green; BN44 3AP Appealing 16th-c country pub; rustic tap room on right with log fire in brick inglenook, country dining chairs around polished tables on flagstones, Harveys Best and guests, several wines by the glass, well liked food (all day weekends) from varied menu, opened-up snug with heavy beams and another inglenook, skittle alley/function room; children (not in front bar) and dogs welcome, seats on front brick terrace, pretty garden with raised herb beds, young orchard and duck pond, summer barbecues, open all day. *(Steve and Irene Homer, Pete Walker, Tom and Jill Jones, Nick Lawless)*

BALLS CROSS   SU9826

★ **Stag** (01403) 820241

Village signed off A283 at N edge of Petworth; GU28 9JP Unchanging and cheery 17th-c country pub, fishing rods and country knick-knacks, tiny flagstoned bar with log fire in huge inglenook, a few seats and bar stools, Badger beers, summer cider and several wines by the glass, second tiny room and appealing old-fashioned restaurant with horse pictures, enjoyable pubby food (not Sun evening), good service, bar skittles, darts and board games in separate carpeted room; veteran outside lavatories; well behaved children allowed away from main bar, dogs welcome, seats in front under parasols, more in pretty back garden, bedrooms, open all day weekends. *(Colin McKerrow)*

BARCOMBE   TQ4416

Anchor (01273) 400414

Barcombe Mills; BN8 5BS Lots of lawn tables by winding River Ouse (boat hire), two beamed bars, well kept ales including

---

Harveys Best, friendly smartly dressed staff, restaurant and small front conservatory; open all day. *(Mrs Sally Scott)*

BARCOMBE CROSS　　　　TQ4212
Royal Oak　(01273) 400418
Off A275 N of Lewes; BN8 5BA
Refurbished red-brick village pub continuing well under present family owners; good mix of locals and visitors, up to five well kept Harveys ales and reasonably priced wines, enjoyable generously served food cooked by landlord-chef from bar snacks up, friendly helpful service, beams, bare boards and open fire, skittle alley; a few tables out in front and in small tree-shaded garden, open all day. *(John Beeken)*

BARNS GREEN　　　　TQ1227
Queens Head　(01403) 730436
Chapel Road; RH13 0PS Welcoming traditional village pub, extensive blackboard choice of good generous home-made food, Kings ales along with Fullers London Pride and Sharps Doom Bar, a couple of real ciders, reasonable prices, regular quiz nights; children welcome, tables out at front and in back garden with play area. *(Anon)*

BECKLEY　　　　TQ8423
Rose & Crown　(01797) 252161
Northiam Road (B2088); TN31 6SE
Popular village local with five or so well kept ales including Harveys, generous pub food from baguettes up, cosy lower eating area with log fire; children welcome, views from pleasant garden. *(Anon)*

BEPTON　　　　SU8620
Country Inn　(01730) 813466
Severals Road; GU29 0LR Popular old-fashioned country local, well kept ales such as Sharps Doom Bar and Wells & Youngs, hearty helpings of good value bar food (not Sun evening), friendly helpful staff, heavy beams, stripped brickwork and welcoming log fire, darts, quiz nights; background music, TV; children welcome, tables out at front and in big garden with shady trees and play area, quiet spot, open all day Fri-Sun.
(John Beeken, Tony and Wendy Hobden)

BERWICK　　　　TQ5105
★**Cricketers Arms**　(01323) 870469
Lower Road, S of A27; BN26 6SP
Charming flint local with three small unpretentious bars, huge supporting beam in each low ceiling, simple country furnishings on quarry tiles, cricketing pictures and bats, two log fires, friendly staff, four Harveys ales tapped from the cask, country wines and good coffee, popular bar food (all day weekends and summer weekdays), old Sussex coin game toad in the hole; children in family room only, dogs welcome, delightful cottagey front garden with picnic-sets among small brick paths, more seats behind, Bloomsbury Group wall

paintings in nearby church, good South Downs walks. *(John Beeken, Alec and Joan Laurence, Pete Walker, Mrs Sally Scott, Tony Scott)*

BILLINGSHURST　　　　TQ0830
Blue Ship　(01403) 822709
The Haven; hamlet signposted off A29 just N of junction with A264, then follow signpost left towards Garlands and Okehurst; RH14 9BS Unspoilt pub in quiet country spot, beamed and brick-floored front bar, scrubbed tables and wall benches, inglenook woodburner, ales such as K&B Sussex tapped from the cask and served from hatch, good home-made food (not Mon) from pub favourites up, two small carpeted back rooms, darts, bar billiards, shove-ha'penny, cribbage and dominoes; children and dogs welcome, tables out at front and in side garden with play area, local produce for sale, camping, closed Sun evening, Mon lunchtime. *(Ian Phillips, Mrs Sally Scott)*

BILLINGSHURST　　　　TQ0725
Limeburners　(01403) 782311
Lordings Road, Newbridge (B2133/A272 W); RH14 9JA Friendly characterful pub in converted row of cottages, three Fullers ales and enjoyable fairly priced food (not Sun evening) from snacks up, good friendly service, open fires, quiz nights; children welcome, pleasant front garden, play area behind. *(Ian Phillips, Tony and Wendy Hobden)*

BLACKBOYS　　　　TQ5220
★**Blackboys Inn**　(01825) 890283
B2192, S edge of village; TN22 5LG
Old weatherboarded inn set back from road; main bar to the right with beams, timbers, dark wooden furniture and log fire, locals' bar to left with lots of bric-a-brac, Harveys ales including seasonals, several wines by the glass, wide choice of enjoyable food (all day Sat, till 7pm Sun), panelled dining areas; background and some live music; children and dogs (in bar) welcome, sizeable garden with seats under trees, on terrace and under cover by duck pond, good walks (Vanguard Way passes the pub, Wealdway close by), open all day. *(Isobel Mackinlay, Edward May)*

BOGNOR REGIS　　　　SZ9201
Royal Oak　(01243) 821002
A259 Chichester Road, North Bersted; PO21 5JF Old-fashioned two-bar beamed local (aka the Pink Pub), well kept Long Man, food till 6.30pm (not Sun evening), friendly service; bar billiards, darts, sports TV; children and dogs welcome (pub boxer is Alfie). *(Eddie Edwards)*

BOLNEY　　　　TQ2623
Bolney Stage　(01444) 881200
London Road, off old A23 just N of A272; RH17 5RL Sizeable well refurbished 16th-c timbered dining pub (part of the Home Counties group), enjoyable varied choice of food all day, three or four changing ales

(usually local Bedlam) and good selection of wines by the glass, friendly service, low beams and polished flagstones, nice mix of old furniture, woodburner and big two-way log fire; children welcome, dogs in main bar, disabled facilities, tables on terrace and lawn, play area, handy for Sheffield Park (NT) and Bluebell Railway. *(Anon)*

BOLNEY TQ2622
Eight Bells (01444) 881396
The Street; RH17 5QW Well managed village pub with wide food choice from ciabattas and light dishes to enjoyable specials, bargain OAP lunch Tues and Weds, efficient friendly service, well kept Harveys and guests, decent choice of wines including some from local vineyard, brick-floored bar with eight handbells suspended from ceiling, good log fire, timbered dining extension; children welcome, disabled facilities, tables under big umbrellas on outside deck with neatly lit steps, play area, pram race Easter Mon, three bedrooms in separate cottage. *(Tony and Wendy Hobden)*

BOSHAM SU8003
★**Anchor Bleu** (01243) 573956
High Street; PO18 8LS Waterside inn overlooking Chichester Harbour; two simple bars with some beams in low ochre ceilings, worn flagstones and exposed timbered brickwork, lots of nautical bric-a-brac, robust furniture (some tables very close together), up to six real ales and popular bar food, efficient friendly staff (they ask for a credit card if you run a tab), new upstairs dining room; children and dogs welcome, seats on back terrace overlooking ducks and boats on sheltered inlet, huge wheel-operated bulkhead door wards off high tides, church up lane in Bayeux Tapestry, village and shore are worth exploring, open all day in summer and can get very busy. *(R L Borthwick, Roy Hoing, B and M Kendall, Dr and Mrs J D Abell, Mrs Sally Scott, J A Snell and others)*

BOSHAM SU8105
White Swan (01243) 578917
A259 roundabout; Station Road; PO18 8NG Refurbished dining pub with enjoyable sensibly priced food (not Sun evening) including offers and themed nights, three well kept ales such as Dark Star, Hop Back and Langhams, good sized bar area with bucket chairs on flagstones, restaurant beyond, darts in snug, regular quiz; open all day. *(J A Snell, Ann and Colin Hunt, Tony and Wendy Hobden)*

BREDE TQ8218
Red Lion (01424) 882188
A28 opposite church; TN31 6EJ Relaxed beamed village pub with plain tables and chairs on bare boards, candles, inglenook log fire, good fairly priced food including local fish, Sun carvery (should book), well kept Sharps Doom Bar, Wells & Youngs and

two local guests, friendly swift service, back dining area decorated with sheet music and musical instruments; children and dogs welcome, a few picnic-sets out at front, garden behind with roaming chickens (eggs for sale), narrow entrance to car park, open all day Fri-Sun. *(Peter Meister, Alec and Joan Laurence, Conrad Freezer)*

BRIGHTON TQ3104
★**Basketmakers Arms**
(01273) 689006 *Gloucester Road – the E end, near Cheltenham Place; off Marlborough Place (A23) via Gloucester Street; BN1 4AD* Cheerful bustling backstreet local with eight pumps serving Fullers/Gales beers and guests, decent wines by the glass, over 100 malt whiskies and quite a choice of other spirits, enjoyable very good value bar food all day (till 6pm weekends), two small low-ceilinged rooms, lots of interesting old tins, cigarette cards on one beam, whisky labels on another, also beer mats, old advertisements, photographs and posters; background music; children welcome till 8pm, dogs on leads, a few pavement tables, open all day (till midnight Fri, Sat). *(Tony and Wendy Hobden, Pete Walker)*

BRIGHTON TQ3004
Brighton Beer Dispensary
(01273) 205797 *Dean Street; BN1 3EG* Former Prince Arthur now jointly owned by Brighton Bier and Late Knights Brewery; wide choice of ales and craft beers with a further 60 in bottles, four hand-pulled ciders too, bar snacks and burgers, quiz nights and storytelling evenings; open all day. *(Anon)*

BRIGHTON TQ3104
Colonnade (01273) 328728
New Road, off North Street; by Theatre Royal; BN1 1UF Small richly restored Edwardian bar, with red plush banquettes, velvet swags, shining brass and mahogany, gleaming mirrors, interesting pre-war playbills and signed theatrical photographs, well kept Fullers London Pride and Harveys Best, lots of lagers, bar snacks, daily papers; downstairs lavatories; tiny front terrace overlooking Pavilion gardens. *(Anon)*

BRIGHTON TQ3004
Craft Beer Company
Upper North Street; BN1 3FG Corner pub refurbished by this small growing company (their first outside London); simple L-shaped bar with raised back section, fine choice of interesting draught and bottled beers from UK and international brewers, friendly knowledgeable staff, food limited to pork pies and scotch eggs; open all day. *(N R White)*

BRIGHTON TQ3104
★**Cricketers** (01273) 329472
Black Lion Street; BN1 1ND Proper town pub, friendly bustle at busy times, nice relaxed atmosphere when quieter, cosy

and darkly Victorian with lots of interesting bric-a-brac including a stuffed bear, well kept Fullers, Kings, Theakstons and Wells & Youngs tapped from the cask, decent coffee, well priced pubby food (till 8pm weekends) from sandwiches up, attentive service, tables in covered former stables courtyard, upstairs bar with Graham Greene memorabilia (pub features in *Brighton Rock*); background and live music; children allowed till 8pm, tall tables out in front, open all day. *(Pete Walker, N R White)*

BRIGHTON TQ3004
★ Evening Star (01273) 328931

Surrey Street; BN1 3PB Popular chatty drinkers' pub with good mix of customers, simple pale wood furniture on bare boards, up to four well kept Dark Star ales (originally brewed here) and lots of changing guest beers including continentals (in bottles too), traditional ciders and perries, country wines, lunchtime baguettes, friendly staff coping well when busy; background and some live music; pavement tables, open all day. *(N R White, Pete Walker, Peter Meister)*

BRIGHTON TQ2804
★ Ginger Pig (01273) 736123

Hove Street; BN3 2TR Bustling place just minutes from the beach; informal bare-boards bar with plush stools and simple wooden dining chairs around mixed tables, armchairs and sofas here and there, Harveys Best and a guest, nice wines by the glass and interesting local spirits and soft drinks, raised restaurant part with long button-back wall seating and more wooden tables and chairs, contemporary cow paintings, enterprising modern food served by friendly competent staff; background jazz; children welcome, open all day. *(Val and Alan Green)*

BRIGHTON TQ3104
Prince George (01273) 681055

Trafalgar Street; BN1 4EQ Three linked rooms (front ones are best) off main bar, mix of furnishings on stripped floor, some bare brick walls and several big mirrors, six well kept changing local ales and lots of wines by the glass, inexpensive popular organic and vegetarian/vegan food, friendly helpful staff; Sun quiz; children (till 7pm) and dogs welcome, small heated back courtyard, open (and food) all day. *(Anon)*

BRIGHTON TQ3004
Pub du Vin (01273) 718588

Ship Street; BN1 1AD Next to Hotel du Vin; long narrow stripped-boards bar with comfortable wall seating one end, bay window the other, soft lighting and local photographs, five well kept ales including Arundel and Dark Star from ornate pewter counter, good choice of wines by the glass, enjoyable pubby food served by friendly staff, modern leather-seated bar chairs and light oak tables, flame-effect fire, small cosy

coir-carpeted room opposite with squashy black armchairs and sofas; splendid gents' with original marble fittings; 11 comfortable bedrooms, open all day. *(N R White)*

BROWNBREAD STREET TQ6714
Ash Tree (01424) 892104

Off A271 (was B2204) W of Battle; 1st northward road W of Ashburnham Place, then 1st fork left, then bear right into Brownbread Street; TN33 9NX Tranquil 17th-c country local tucked away in isolated hamlet, enjoyable affordably priced home-made food including specials, good choice of wines and well kept ales including Harveys Best, cheerful service, cosy beamed bars with nice old settles and chairs, stripped brickwork, interesting dining areas with timbered dividers, good inglenook log fires, quiz first Tues of month; children (in eating area) and dogs welcome, pretty garden, open all day. *(R D Skibinski)*

BURPHAM TQ0308
George (01903) 883131

Off A27 near Warningcamp; BN18 9RR Refurbished 17th-c beamed pub under community ownership; four ales including Greene King, Harveys and a house beer from Arundel, interesting choice of freshly made food, friendly service; drop-down sports TV, free wi-fi; children and dogs welcome, picnic-sets out in front, hilltop village and short walk from door gives splendid views down to Arundel Castle and river, open all Sat, till 6.30pm Sun. *(John Davis)*

BURWASH TQ6724
Rose & Crown (01435) 882600

Inn sign on A265; TN19 7ER Low-beamed timbered local tucked away down lane in pretty village, enjoyable food, well kept Harveys and decent wines, inglenook log fire in bar, pleasant restaurant area with woodburner, glass-covered well just inside front door; tables out in small quiet garden, bedrooms. *(Colin McKerrow)*

BURY TQ0013
Squire & Horse (01798) 831343

Bury Common; A29 Fontwell–Pulborough; RH20 1NS Smart roadside dining pub with good imaginative food from australian chef, friendly efficient service, well kept Harveys and a guest, good choice of wines, several attractive partly divided beamed areas, plush wall seats, hunting prints and ornaments, log fire; no dogs; children welcome, pleasant garden and pretty terrace (some road noise), open all day Sun. *(Ann and Colin Hunt, Michael and Sheila Hawkins)*

BYWORTH SU9821
★ Black Horse (01798) 342424

Off A283; GU28 0HL Popular and chatty country pub with smart simply furnished bar, pews and scrubbed tables on bare boards, pictures and old photographs, daily papers and open fires, ales including Flowerpots and Fullers, decent food (not Sun evening) from light lunchtime dishes up, children's menu, nooks and crannies in back restaurant, spiral staircase to heavily beamed function/dining room, games room with pool; dogs allowed in bar, attractive garden with tables on steep grassy terraces, lovely Downs views, open all day. *(Tony and Wendy Hobden)*

CHAILEY   TQ3919
Horns Lodge (01273) 400422
A275; BN8 4BD Traditional former coaching inn, heavily timbered inside, with settles, horsebrasses and local prints, log fires at each end of longish front bar, well kept Dark Star, Harveys and two guests, real cider, good range of fairly priced bar food (not Tues) from sandwiches up, obliging staff, brick-floored restaurant, games area with bar billiards, darts and toad in the hole, cribbage, dominoes and board games too; background music; children and dogs welcome, tables in garden with sandpit, bedrooms, open all day weekends; still for sale (but business as usual) as we went to press. *(John Beeken, Steve and Irene Homer, Paul Lucas)*

CHALVINGTON   TQ5209
Yew Tree Inn (01323) 811326
Chalvington Road, between Chalvington and Golden Cross; BN27 3TB Isolated 17th-c country pub with low beams, stripped brick, flagstones and inglenook, enjoyable well priced home-made food (not Sun evening) from lunchtime baguettes and ciabattas up, Harveys ales with guests such as Long Man and Wells & Youngs, conservatory; children and dogs welcome, good-sized terrace, extensive grounds with play area, own cricket pitch and camping, good walks, open all day (till 6pm Sun). *(Anon)*

CHICHESTER   SU8605
Chichester Inn (01243) 783185
West Street; PO19 1RP Georgian pub (quieter than the city-centre ones) with half a dozen local ales such as Dark Star, Irving and Langhams, bargain pubby food all day from snacks up, friendly service, smallish front lounge with plain wooden tables and chairs, sofas by open fire, larger back public bar, live music Weds, Fri and Sat; pool and sports TV; courtyard garden with smokers' shelter, two bedrooms, open all day summer, all day Fri-Sun winter. *(Tony and Wendy Hobden, B and M Kendall)*

CHICHESTER   SU8604
Eastgate (01243) 774877
The Hornet (A286); PO19 7JG Friendly town pub with reasonably priced straightforward food, three Fullers ales and

a guest beer, light airy interior extending back, darts, pool and cribbage; background and weekend live music; children and dogs welcome, small heated terrace behind, open all day. *(Tony and Wendy Hobden)*

CHICHESTER   SU8504
Fountain (01243) 781352
Southgate; PO19 1ES Attractive two-room front bar with beams, painted panelling, stone floor and open fire, dining room behind incorporating part of Roman wall, enjoyable sensibly priced food (not Sun evening) from pub standards to more adventurous choices, Badger ales, friendly helpful staff, live music and quiz nights; children and dogs welcome, tables in side courtyard, open all day. *(Nigel and Sue Foster, B and M Kendall)*

CHICHESTER   SU8605
Park Tavern (01243) 785057
Priory Road, opposite Jubilee Park; PO19 1NS Friendly lively pub in pleasant spot opposite Priory Park, good choice of Fullers/Gales beers and enjoyable reasonably priced home-made food, smallish front bar and extensive back eating area, quiz Tues, live music Sun; dogs welcome (resident bulldog and whippet). *(Phil and Jane Villiers)*

CHIDHAM   SU7804
Old House At Home (01243) 572477
Off A259 at Barleycorn pub in Nutbourne; Cot Lane; PO18 8SU Neat cottagey pub in remote unspoilt farm-hamlet; good choice of popular food including local fish specials, friendly efficient service, five real ales and decent wines, low beams and timbering, log fire; children allowed in eating areas, tables in nice garden, nearby walks by Chichester Harbour, open all day. *(R L Borthwick, J A Snell, Tony and Jill Radnor, Michael and Sheila Hawkins)*

CLIMPING   TQ0001
Black Horse (01903) 715175
Climping Street; BN17 5RL Extended 18th-c country pub under newish management; enjoyable reasonably priced food from snacks up, two well kept ales such as Fullers and Sharps Doom Bar, decent wines by the glass, good friendly service, L-shaped interior with dining part at front, log fires, darts and skittle alley; children welcome, tables out in front and on back decking, short walk to the beach. *(Colin McKerrow, Tony and Wendy Hobden, John Beeken)*

COCKING CAUSEWAY   SU8819
Greyhound (01730) 814425
A286 Cocking–Midhurst; GU29 9QH Pretty 18th-c tile-hung pub, enjoyable good value home-made food (should book weekends), Sharps Doom Bar and two

---

If you know a pub is ever open all day, please tell us.

or three local beers such as Downland, friendly prompt service, open-plan but cosy beamed and panelled bar with alcoves, log fire, pine furniture in big new dining conservatory; children welcome, grassed area at front with picnic-sets and huge eucalyptus, sizeable garden and play area behind, open all day Sun. *(Tony and Wendy Hobden, John Beeken)*

COLEMANS HATCH   TQ4533
★ **Hatch** (01342) 822363

Signed off B2026, or off B2110 opposite church; TN7 4EJ Quaint and appealing little weatherboarded Ashdown Forest pub dating from 1430, big log fire in quickly filling beamed bar, small back dining room with another fire, good generous home-made food, well kept Harveys, Larkins and one or two guest beers, quick service from friendly young staff, good mix of customers including families and dogs; not much parking so get there early; picnic-sets on front terrace and in beautifully kept big garden, open all day Sun, and Sat in summer. *(Pete Walker)*

COMPTON   SU7714
Coach & Horses (02392) 631228

B2146 S of Petersfield; PO18 9HA Welcoming 17th-c two-bar local in charming downland village, not far from Uppark (NT), beams, panelling, shuttered windows and log fires, up to five changing ales, good food cooked by landlord-chef including daily specials, bar billiards; children and dogs welcome, tables out by village square, nice surrounding walks, closed Mon. *(Geoff and Linda Payne)*

COOKSBRIDGE   TQ4014
Rainbow (01273) 400334

Junction A275 with Cooksbridge and Newick Road; BN8 4SS Attractive 18th-c flint dining pub (same owners as the Fountain in Ashurst and Royal Oak at Poynings), good locally sourced food from sandwiches to specials, helpful friendly service, nice choice of wines and three well kept ales, small bar area with open fire, restaurant; children welcome, large garden with terrace. *(John Beeken)*

COOLHAM   TQ1423
George & Dragon (01403) 741320

Dragons Green, Dragons Lane; pub signed off A272; RH13 8GE Tile-hung cottage with cosy chatty bar, massive unusually low black beams (date cut into one could be 1677 or 1577), timbered walls and log fire in big inglenook, Harveys, Kings, Sharps and a guest, good food from pub standards up, friendly staff, smaller back bar

(dogs allowed here), separate restaurant; children welcome, picnic-sets in pretty orchard garden. *(Anon)*

COOTHAM   TQ0714
Crown (01903) 742625

Pulborough Road (A283); RH20 4JN Extended village pub with L-shaped bar on two levels, well kept Bass, Harveys and a guest, wide choice of food from bar snacks up (smaller helpings available), also set menus, friendly service, two open fires, large back dining area, games room (darts and pool); children and dogs welcome, big garden with play area and goats, handy for Parham House, open all day Sun. *(Tony and Wendy Hobden)*

COUSLEY WOOD   TQ6533
★ **Old Vine** (01892) 782271

B2100 Wadhurst–Lamberhurst; TN5 6ER Popular 16th-c weatherboarded pub with linked, uncluttered rooms, heavy beams and open timbering, candles on nice old pine tables surrounded by farmhouse chairs, several settles (one by big log fire has an especially high back), wood or brick flooring (restaurant area is carpeted), well kept Harveys Best and a guest from attractively painted servery, several good wines by the glass, tasty food served by friendly helpful staff; dogs welcome, picnic-sets on front terrace, three bedrooms, open all day weekends (food till 6.30pm Sun). *(Alec and Joan Laurence, Nigel and Jean Eames)*

COWBEECH   TQ6114
★ **Merrie Harriers** (01323) 833108

Off A271; BN27 4JQ White clapboarded 16th-c village local, beamed public bar with inglenook log fire, high-backed settle and mixed tables and chairs, old local photographs, carpeted dining lounge with small open fire, well kept Harveys Best and a guest, winter mulled wine, good food from nice bar snacks up, friendly service, brick-walled back restaurant; occasional background music; rustic seats in terraced garden with country views, open all day Fri-Sun. *(Anon)*

COWFOLD   TQ2122
Hare & Hounds (01403) 865354

Henfield Road (A281 S); RH13 8DR Small friendly village pub with well kept Dark Star, Harveys and a guest (July beer festival), good value traditional home-made food including Thurs OAP lunch, flagstoned bar with log fire, little room off to the right, carpeted dining room to the left, some bric-a-brac; a couple of picnic-sets out in front, back terrace, open all day weekends. *(Tony and Wendy Hobden)*

The letters and figures after the name of each town are its Ordnance Survey map reference. 'Using the *Guide*' at the beginning of the book explains how it helps you find a pub, in road atlases or large-scale maps as well as in our own maps.

CRAWLEY DOWN   TQ3437
Dukes Head (01342) 712431
A264/A2028 by roundabout; RH10 4HH
Big refurbished dining pub with large lounge
bar and three differently styled eating areas,
log fires, good choice of well liked food all
day including fixed-price menu and popular
Sun roasts, decent wines, ales such as Fullers
London Pride and Harveys, quick service
from nice staff; can get very busy weekends;
lots of space outside, handy for Gatwick.
(Gene and Tony Freemantle, Judy and Paul Cove)

CUCKFIELD   TQ3024
Talbot (01444) 455898
High Street; RH17 5JX Thriving pub
under same management as the Half Moon
at Warninglid (see Main Entries) and
due major refurbishment as we went to
press; imaginative food in bar and upstairs
restaurant, real ales, good service; open
all day. *(Anon)*

DALLINGTON   TQ6619
★ Swan (01424) 838242
Woods Corner, B2096 E; TN21 9LB
Popular old local with cheerful chatty
atmosphere, well kept Harveys and a
guest, decent wines by the glass, enjoyable
blackboard food including deals, takeaway
fish and chips (Tues), efficient friendly
service, bare-boards bar divided by standing
timbers, mixed furniture including cushioned
settle and high-backed pew, candles in
bottles and fresh flowers, big woodburner,
simple back restaurant with far-reaching
views to the coast; background music;
children and dogs welcome, steps down to
lavatories and garden. *(Anon)*

DENTON   TQ4502
Flying Fish (01273) 515440
Denton Road; BN9 0QB Welcoming
17th-c flint village pub, enjoyable food from
baguettes up, well kept Shepherd Neame ales
and guests including Harveys, friendly helpful
staff; picnic-sets out by road and on back
deck looking up to sloping garden, handy for
South Downs Way, open all day. *(Anon)*

DEVILS DYKE   TQ2511
Devils Dyke (01273) 857256
Devils Dyke Road; BN1 8YJ Vintage Inn
set alone on Downs above Brighton and worth
visiting for the spectacular views night and
day; well kept ales such as Harveys, Shepherd
Neame and Timothy Taylors, their usual food,
clean and tidy with cheerful helpful staff;
children welcome, tables outside, NT pay
car park, open all day and can get very busy
summer weekends. *(Keith Stevens)*

DONNINGTON   SU8501
Blacksmiths (01243) 785578
B2201 S of Chichester; PO20 7PR Small
roadside pub renovated by new owners;
fresh modern décor with white walls and

light wood floors, one or two beams, modern
artwork and some quirky touches, interesting
food from sensibly short menu, local ales and
mainly organic wines, open fire; children
welcome, big back garden with terrace, herb
garden and chickens, three bedrooms, open
all day Fri, Sat, closed Sun evening, Mon,
Tues. *(Anon)*

EARTHAM   SU9309
★ George (01243) 814340
*Signed off A285 Chichester–Petworth,
from Fontwell off A27, from Slindon
off A29; PO18 0LT* Welcoming village pub
with enjoyable locally sourced food, up to
five real ales and decent wines including
english ones, good friendly service even
when busy, log fires in comfortable lounge
and flagstoned public bar (dogs allowed on
leads), restaurant and café; background
music; children welcome in eating areas, easy
disabled access, large garden and attractive
surroundings, lovely walks, closed Mon,
otherwise open all day. *(Mrs T A Bizat)*

EAST ASHLING   SU8207
★ Horse & Groom (01243) 575339
B2178; PO18 9AX Busy country pub with
well kept Hop Back Summer Lightning,
Sharps Doom Bar and Wells & Youngs Bitter,
decent choice of wines by the glass, enjoyable
food from good sandwiches up, reasonable
prices and helpful service, unchanging
front drinkers' bar with old pale flagstones
and inglenook woodburner, carpeted area
with scrubbed trestle tables, fresh and airy
extension with solid pale country kitchen
furniture on neat bare boards; children and
dogs allowed in some parts, garden picnic-
sets under umbrellas, 11 bedrooms, open all
day Sat, closed Sun evening. *(J A Snell)*

EAST DEAN   SU9012
Star & Garter (01243) 811318
*Village signed with Charlton off A286
in Singleton; also signed off A285;
PO18 0JG* Airy dining pub in peaceful
village-green setting; pleasant bar and
restaurant with exposed brickwork, panelling
and oak floors, furnishings from sturdy
stripped tables and country kitchen chairs
through chunky modern to antique carved
settles, Arundel ales tapped from the cask
and several wines by the glass, good food
from burgers to fish specials, friendly service;
background music; children and dogs (in
bar) welcome, teak furniture on heated
terrace, smokers' shelter, steps down to
walled lawn with picnic-sets, near South
Downs Way, bedrooms, open (and food) all
day weekends. *(Anon)*

EAST GRINSTEAD   TQ3936
★ Old Mill (01342) 326341
*Dunnings Road, S towards Saint Hill;
RH19 4AT* Interesting 16th-c mill cottage
over stream reworked as spacious informal
Whiting & Hammond dining pub; lots of

panelling, old photographs and pictures, carpeted main dining area with mix of old tables (each with church candle), steps down to ancient very low-ceilinged part with fine timbers and inglenook woodburner, sizeable bar with long curved counter, library dining area off, enjoyable freshly made food all day, Harveys ales including seasonals and good choice of wines by the glass, friendly efficient service; background music; children welcome, picnic-sets in front garden, covered deck next to working waterwheel, handy for Standen (NT), open all day from 9am (breakfast Fri-Sun). *(Tony Scott)*

EAST GRINSTEAD   TQ3938
Ship (01342) 312089
Ship Street (centre); RH19 4EG Large open-plan Youngs pub with their Bitter, Special, Bombardier and a guest such as St Austell Tribute, good range of competitively priced mainly pubby food, friendly staff; background music, sports TV; children welcome, tiered decking behind, bedrooms, open (and food) all day. *(Tony and Wendy Hobden)*

EAST HOATHLY   TQ5216
★ Kings Head (01825) 840238
High Street/Mill Lane; BN8 6DR Well kept 1648 ales (brewed here) and Harveys Best in long comfortably worn-in open-plan bar, some dark panelling and stripped brick, upholstered settles, old local photographs, log fire, wide choice of enjoyable generously served food at sensible prices, friendly staff and locals, daily papers, restaurant; TV; dogs welcome in bar, steps up to walled back garden, safe for children, open all day. *(John Beeken, Ann and Colin Hunt)*

EASTBOURNE   TV6098
Bibendum (01323) 735363
Grange Road/South Street opposite Town Hall; BN21 4EU Roomy 19th-c corner place with bit of a wine bar feel, good choice of beers and consistent good value food, friendly helpful staff, restaurant; seats out in front, open (and food) all day. *(Tom and Jill Jones)*

EASTBOURNE   TV6199
Marine (01323) 720464
Seaside Road (A259); BN22 7NE Spacious comfortable pub near seafront run by welcoming long-serving licensees, panelled bar, lounge with sofas and tub chairs, log fire, three well kept ales and good choice of wines, whiskies and brandies, good freshly made food from sandwiches to daily specials, back conservatory; children welcome, terrace and covered smokers' area. *(Alan Johnson)*

EASTERGATE   SU9405
Wilkes Head (01243) 543380
Just off A29 Fontwell–Bognor; Church Lane; PO20 3UT Small friendly red-brick local with two bars and back dining extension, beams, flagstones and inglenook log fire, enjoyable reasonably priced blackboard food from sandwiches up, Adnams and four guest ales, proper cider, darts; tables in big garden with play area, open all day weekends. *(Nigel and Sue Foster, Tony Hobden, John Beeken)*

ELSTED   SU8320
Elsted Inn (01730) 813662
Elsted Marsh; GU29 0JT Attractive and welcoming Victorian country pub, enjoyable reasonably priced food from shortish menu, real ales such as Gales and Otter, friendly accommodating service, two log fires, nice country furniture on bare boards, old Goodwood racing photos (both horses and cars), dining area at back; plenty of seating in lovely enclosed Downs-view garden with big terrace, four bedrooms, open all day in summer. *(John Beeken)*

ELSTED   SU8119
★ Three Horseshoes (01730) 825746
Village signed from B2141 Chichester–Petersfield; from A272 about 2 miles W of Midhurst, turn left heading W; GU29 0JY A congenial bustle at this pretty white-painted old pub, beamed rooms, log fires and candlelight, ancient flooring, antique furnishings, fresh flowers and interesting prints and photographs, four changing ales tapped from the cask, summer cider, really good attractively presented food, friendly service; well behaved children allowed, dogs in bar, two delightful connecting gardens with plenty of seats and fine Downs views, good surrounding walks. *(Tony and Jill Radnor, John Beeken, Stephen and Jean Curtis, Gordon Stevenson and others)*

ERIDGE STATION   TQ5434
★ Huntsman (01892) 864258
Signed off A26 S of Eridge Green; TN3 9LE Country local with two opened-up rooms, pubby furniture on bare boards, some tables with carved/painted board games including own 'Eridgeopoly', hunting pictures, three Badger ales and over a dozen wines by the glass, popular bar food (not Sun evening, Mon) including fresh fish, seasonal game and home-grown produce, friendly staff; children and dogs welcome, picnic-sets and heaters on decking, outside bar, more seats on lawn among weeping willows, open all day weekends, closed Mon lunchtime. *(Claire Millar)*

Places with gardens or terraces usually let children sit there – we note in the text the very few exceptions that don't.

FAYGATE
Cherry Tree (01293) 851305

TQ2134

A264; RH12 4SA Old pub in lay-by off dual carriageway; reasonably priced food, ales such as K&B Sussex, friendly helpful staff; nice back garden with gate to bridleway. *(Ian Phillips)*

FERRING
Henty Arms (01903) 241254

TQ0903

Ferring Lane; BN12 6QY Six well kept changing ales and generous well priced food (can get busy so best to book), breakfast from 9am Tues-Fri, neat friendly staff, opened-up lounge/dining area, log fire, separate bar with games and TV; garden tables. *(Tony and Wendy Hobden)*

FINDON
Gun (01903) 873206

TQ1208

High Street; BN14 0TA Low-beamed pub with opened-up bar area and restaurant, enjoyable food including good value french night (Tues) and popular Sun lunch, four well kept Marstons-related beers, friendly staff, log fire; free wi-fi; children and dogs (in bar) welcome, sheltered garden, pretty village below Cissbury Ring (NT), Sept sheep fair. *(J A Snell, Tony and Wendy Hobden)*

FISHBOURNE
Bulls Head (01243) 839895

SU8304

Fishbourne Road (A259 Chichester–Emsworth); PO19 3JP Former 17th-c farmhouse with traditional interior, copper pans on black beams, some stripped brick and panelling, good log fire, well kept Fullers/Gales beers and popular home-made food; background music; children welcome, tables on heated covered deck, four bedrooms in former skittle alley, handy for Roman villa. *(John Beeken, David H T Dimock)*

FITTLEWORTH
Swan (01798) 865429

TQ0118

Lower Street (B2138, off A283 W of Pulborough); RH20 1EL Pretty tile-hung dining inn doing well under newish management; beamed main bar with windsor chairs and bar stools on wood floor, big inglenook log fire, Harveys, Sharps Doom Bar and a guest, several wines by the glass, good food from pubby choices up in bar and separate panelled restaurant, set lunch deal Mon-Fri, efficient friendly staff; background music, free wi-fi, children and dogs welcome, big back lawn with plenty of tables, good walks nearby, 14 comfortable well priced bedrooms, open all day weekends. *(Chris Wall, John Davis)*

FULKING
Shepherd & Dog (01273) 857382

TQ2411

Off A281 N of Brighton, via Poynings; BN5 9LU 17th-c bay-windowed pub in beautiful spot below Downs, low beams, panelling and inglenook, their own Downland

beers (brewed a couple of miles away) and guests, traditional food from baguettes up (fish Fri), friendly efficient service; children and dogs welcome, terrace and pretty streamside garden, straightforward climb to Devils Dyke, open all day till 10.30pm (8pm Sun). *(John Beeken, Keith Stevens)*

FUNTINGTON
★ **Fox & Hounds** (01243) 575246

SU7908

Common Road (B2146); PO18 9LL Old bay-windowed pub with updated beamed rooms in grey/green shades, welcoming log fires, good food all day from open sandwiches and snacks up, popular Sun carvery, booking advised weekends, well kept Dark Star, Timothy Taylors and guests, lots of wines by the glass and good coffee, comfortable spacious dining extension; free wi-fi; children welcome, tables out in front and in walled back garden, pair of inn signs – one a pack of hounds, the other a family of foxes, open all day (from 9am weekends for breakfast). *(Lawrence Pearse, Tim and Joan Wright, Nigel and Sue Foster, J A Snell)*

GLYNDE
Trevor Arms (01273) 858208

TQ4508

Over railway bridge, S of village; BN8 6SS Fine downland views from character brick and flint village pub (same management as the Ram at Firle – see Main Entries); main opened-up bar with two boar's heads, piano and large woodburner, church pews and wheelbacks around dark tables on bare boards, daily papers, trivia machine, well kept Harveys Best and local guests, small simply furnished tap bar with chatty regulars, dining area with mix of high-backed settles, pews and cushioned chairs around assorted tables, toad in the hole and darts, old local photos including Harveys brewery, popular fairly traditional home-made food (all day weekends); children and dogs welcome, big back garden with wendy house, swings and picnic-sets (more in front), popular with walkers, station next door, open all day. *(Ann and Colin Hunt)*

GRAFFHAM
Foresters Arms (01798) 867202

SU9218

Village off A285; GU28 0QA Popular 16th-c pub; main bar with heavy beams, log fire in huge brick fireplace, pews, wheelback and old-fashioned school chairs around antique pine tables, two other areas, ales such as Dark Star and Harveys, good food from ciabattas up, friendly attentive service, monthly live jazz; children and dogs welcome, attractive sunny back garden and good local walks, some classic car meetings, three bedrooms. *(Roger and Val, Colin McKerrow)*

GUN HILL
★ **Gun** (01825) 872361

TQ5614

Off A22 NW of Hailsham, or off A267; TN21 0JU Big 15th-c country dining pub with good popular bistro-style food and efficient friendly service; large central bar with nice old brick floor, stools against counter, Aga in corner, small grey-panelled room off with rugs on bare boards, animal skins on cushioned wall benches and mix of scrubbed and dark tables, logs piled into tall fireplace, well kept Harveys and Timothy Taylors Landlord, decent wines by the glass, close-set tables in two-room cottagey restaurant, beams and open fires, old bottles and glasses along gantry, gun prints and country pictures; background jazz; children welcome, picnic-sets in garden and on lantern-lit front terrace, Wealden Way walks, open all day Sun. *(Tom and Jill Jones)*

HALNAKER   SU9008
★**Anglesey Arms** (01243) 773474
A285 Chichester–Petworth; PO18 ONQ
Georgian pub belonging to the Goodwood Estate; bare boards, settles and log fire, well kept Black Sheep, Wells & Youngs and a couple of guests, decent wines, good varied if not particularly cheap food including local organic produce and Selsey fish, friendly accommodating service, simple but smart L-shaped dining room (children allowed) with woodburners, stripped pine and some flagstones, traditional games; dogs welcome in bar, tables in big tree-lined garden, good nearby walks, open all day Fri, Sat. *(Anon)*

HAMMERPOT   TQ0605
★**Woodmans Arms** (01903) 871240
On N (eastbound) side of A27;
BN16 4EU Pretty thatched pub with beams, timbers and inglenook woodburner, good choice of enjoyable food from sandwiches up (smaller helpings available) including popular Sun lunch, three or four well kept Fullers/Gales beers, nice wines by the glass, efficient service from friendly neat staff, comfortable bar with snug to the left and restaurant to right, occasional live music; no dogs inside; children welcome if eating, tables in nice garden, open all day Sat, till 5pm Sun. *(Val and Alan Green, David Holmes, Tony and Wendy Hobden)*

HANDCROSS   TQ2328
Wheatsheaf (01444) 400472
B2110 W; RH13 6NZ Welcoming country pub with good range of generous home-made food using local produce, Badger ales, efficient staff (they will ask to swipe a card if running a tab), two simply furnished bars with lots of horse tack and farm tools, log fires, caged parrot; children welcome, garden with covered terrace and play area, handy for Nymans (NT), open all day (till 7pm Sun). *(Tony and Wendy Hobden)*

HARTFIELD   TQ4735
Haywaggon (01892) 770252
High Street (A2026); TN7 4AB Sizeable 16th-c dining pub in centre of village, two big log fires, pews and lots of large tables in spacious low-beamed bar, good varied choice

of food in former bakehouse restaurant, cheerful helpful staff, well kept Harveys with guests such as Black Cat and Larkins, reasonably priced wines, live jazz second Mon of month, quiz second Sun; tables outside, three bedrooms in converted stable block, open all day. *(R and S Bentley, Wendy Breese, Alan Cowell)*

HENLEY   SU8925
★**Duke of Cumberland Arms**
(01428) 652280 *Off A286 S of Fernhurst;*
GU27 3HQ Wisteria-clad 15th-c stone-built pub with log fires in two small rooms, low ceilings, scrubbed oak furniture on brick or flagstoned floors, rustic decorations, well kept Harveys and a couple of guests tapped from the cask, good food (not Sun or Mon evenings) from well executed pub favourites to interesting restaurant-style dishes using home-grown produce, separate tiled-floor dining room with more modern feel, friendly staff; well behaved children and dogs welcome, deck with lovely hill views, charming sloping garden and trout ponds, open all day. *(Conor McGaughey, Christopher and Elise Way)*

HERMITAGE   SU7505
★**Sussex Brewery** (01243) 371533
A259 just W of Emsworth; PO10 8AU
Bustling little pub with some redecoration under present management; small bare-boards bar with good fire in brick inglenook, simple furniture, flagstoned snug, Wells & Youngs and four guest ales, ten wines by the glass, hearty food including speciality sausages (including vegetarian ones), small upstairs restaurant; children and dogs welcome, picnic-sets in back courtyard, open all day. *(Anon)*

HOUGHTON   TQ0111
★**George & Dragon** (01798) 831559
B2139 W of Storrington; BN18 9LW
13th-c beams and timbers in attractive spic-and-span bar rambling up and down steps, note the elephant photograph above the fireplace, good Arun Valley views from back extension, well liked reasonably priced food, Marstons-related ales and decent wines by the glass, good friendly service; background music; children and dogs welcome, seats on decked terrace and in charming sloping garden, good walks, open all day Fri-Sun. *(Ann and Colin Hunt, Mrs T A Bizat, Tony Scott)*

HUNSTON   SU8601
Spotted Cow (01243) 786718
B2145 S of Chichester; PO20 1PD
Friendly flagstoned pub with big log fires and up-to-date décor, good choice of enjoyable food (not Sun, Mon evenings) including specials, Fullers/Gales beers, small front bar, roomier side lounge with armchairs, sofas and low tables, airy high-ceilinged restaurant; may be background music; children (if eating) and dogs welcome,

good disabled access, pretty garden, handy for towpath walkers, open all day. *(David H T Dimock)*

HURSTPIERPOINT   TQ2816
★**New Inn** (01273) 834608
High Street; BN6 9RQ Popular 16th-c beamed pub under same management as Bull in Ditchling, well kept ales including Harveys, good wines by the glass, enjoyable food with plenty for vegetarians, friendly attentive young staff, contrasting linked areas including dimly lit oak-panelled back part (children allowed here) with bric-a-brac and open fire, and smart apple-green dining room; sports TV; dogs welcome, garden tables, open all day. *(Conor McGaughey)*

ICKLESHAM   TQ8716
★**Queens Head** (01424) 814552
Off A259 Rye–Hastings; TN36 4BL Friendly well run country pub, extremely popular locally (and at weekends with cyclists and walkers), open-plan areas around big counter, high timbered walls, vaulted roof, shelves of bottles, plenty of farming implements and animal traps, pubby furniture on brown pattered carpet, other areas with inglenooks and a back room with old bicycle memorabilia, up to eight well kept ales including Greene King and Harveys, local cider, several wines by the glass, good choice of reasonably priced home-made food (all day weekends); well behaved children allowed away from bar till 8.30pm, dogs welcome, picnic-sets, boules and play area in peaceful garden with fine Brede Valley views, you can walk to Winchelsea, open all day. *(Martin Day, Lucien Perring, Mrs Sally Scott, Tony Scott, Tom and Jill Jones)*

ICKLESHAM   TQ8716
★**Robin Hood** (01424) 814277
Main Road; TN36 4BD Friendly no-frills beamed pub with enthusiastic landlord and cheerful helpful staff, great local atmosphere, good value unpretentious home-made food including blackboard specials, nine well kept changing ales and three real ciders, hops overhead, lots of copper bric-a-brac, log fire, games area with pool, back dining extension; big garden with Brede Valley views. *(Anon)*

ISFIELD   TQ4417
Laughing Fish (01825) 750349
Station Road; TN22 5XB Nicely old-fashioned opened-up Victorian local with affable landlord and cheerful staff, good value home-made bar food (not Sun evening) including specials board and some good vegetarian dishes, well kept Greene King with guests such as Dark Star and Isfield, open fire, bar billiards and other traditional games, events including entertaining beer race Easter Mon; children and dogs welcome, disabled access, small pleasantly shaded walled garden with enclosed play area, field

for camping, right by Lavender Line railway (pub was station hotel), open all day. *(John Beeken, Ann and Colin Hunt)*

KINGSTON   TQ3908
★**Juggs** (01273) 472523
Village signed off A27 by roundabout W of Lewes; BN7 3NT Popular tile-hung village pub with heavy 15th-c beams and very low front door, lots of neatly stripped masonry, sturdy wooden furniture on bare boards and stone slabs, log fires, smaller eating areas including a family room, variety of enjoyable reasonably priced food from sandwiches and pub standards up (some interesting choices), well kept Harveys and Shepherd Neame, good wines and coffee, friendly helpful young staff; background music, fortnightly quiz; dogs welcome, disabled access/facilities, outside tables including covered area with heaters (they ask to swipe a credit card if you eat here), lots of tubs and hanging baskets, play area, nice walks, open all day. *(Conor McGaughey, Tony and Wendy Hobden, Keith Stevens, Mrs Sally Scott, John Beeken)*

LANCING   TQ1704
Crabtree (01903) 755514
Crabtree Lane; BN15 9NQ Friendly 1930s pub with Fullers London Pride and three changing guests, bargain lunches including Sun carvery, comfortable lounge with wood floor, unusual domed ceiling and art deco lights, games area in large public bar, quiz nights; children and dogs welcome, garden with Downs views and play area. *(Tony and Wendy Hobden)*

LEWES   TQ4210
Gardeners Arms (01273) 474808
Cliffe High Street; BN7 2AN Unpretentious little bare-boards local opposite brewery shop, lots of beer mats on gantry, homely stools, built-in wall seats and plain scrubbed tables around three narrow sides of bar, dog water bowl by blocked-up fireplace, Harveys and five interesting changing guests, farm ciders, some lunchtime food including sandwiches, pasties and pies, bar nibbles on Sun, photos of Lewes bonfire night; background music, TV, darts; no children; open all day. *(Anon)*

LEWES   TQ4210
★**John Harvey** (01273) 479880
Bear Yard, just off Cliffe High Street; BN7 2AN Bustling tap for nearby Harveys brewery, four of their beers including seasonals kept perfectly, some cask tapped, good well priced food (not Sun evening) from lunchtime sandwiches, baked potatoes and ciabattas up, friendly efficient young staff, flagstoned bar with one great vat halved to make two towering 'snugs' for several people, lighter room on left, woodburner, upstairs restaurant/function room, live music including Tues folk and Weds jazz;

a few tables outside, open all day. *(Ann and Colin Hunt, Pete Walker, Tony and Wendy Hobden, Phil and Jane Villiers)*

LEWES   TQ4110
★ **Lewes Arms**   (01273) 473152
Castle Ditch Lane/Mount Place – tucked behind castle ruins; BN7 1YH Cheerful unpretentious little local with five well kept Fullers ales and two guests, 30 malt whiskies and plenty of wines by the glass, good reasonably priced generous bar food, tiny front bar on right with stools along nicely curved counter and bench window seats, two other simple rooms hung with photographs and information about the famous Lewes bonfire night, beer mats pinned over doorways, poetry and folk evenings and more obscure events like pea throwing and dwyle flunking; background music; children away from front bar and dogs welcome (there are two pub dogs), picnic-sets on attractive split-level back terrace, open all day (till midnight Fri, Sat). *(Conor McGaughey, Tony Scott, Tony and Wendy Hobden)*

LEWES   TQ4110
★ **Pelham Arms**   (01273) 476149
At top of High Street; BN7 1XL Popular 17th-c beamed pub, good well presented food (booking advised) including some interesting vegetarian choices, friendly staff, three Badger ales, character rambling interior with inglenook, live swing first Thurs of month; children till 8pm, dogs in bar areas, small courtyard garden, open all day. *(Anon)*

LEWES   TQ4110
Rights of Man   (01273) 486894
High Street; BN7 1YE New Harveys pub close to the law courts, five of their beers kept well and enjoyable food including tapas, spruced-up Victorian-style décor with a series of booths, legal-theme pictures, another bar at the back and roof terrace; background music, free wi-fi; open all day. *(Tony and Wendy Hobden)*

LEWES   TQ4210
★ **Snowdrop**   (01273) 471018
South Street; BN7 2BU Welcoming pub tucked below the chalk cliffs; narrowboat theme with brightly painted servery and colourful jugs, kettles, lanterns etc hanging from curved planked ceiling, wide mix of simple furniture on parquet flooring, old sewing machines and huge stone jars, slightly bohemian atmosphere; well kept ales such as Dark Star, Harveys, Hogs Back and Rectory, hearty helpings of enjoyable good value local food including good vegetarian choice, nice coffee, friendly efficient staff (may ask for a credit card if running a tab), more tables in upstairs room (spiral stairs) with bar

billiards and darts; background music – live jazz Mon; dogs very welcome (menu for them), outside seating on both sides with pretty hanging baskets, open all day. *(Steve and Irene Homer, Ann and Colin Hunt)*

LEWES   TQ4009
Swan   (01273) 480211
Southover High Street; BN7 1HU Popular traditional local with well kept Harveys and enjoyable reasonably priced home-made food, friendly efficient service, open fires; background music (on vinyl) and some live music; walled garden behind. *(R T and J C Moggridge)*

LINDFIELD   TQ3425
Bent Arms   (01444) 483146
High Street; RH16 2HP Recently refurbished 16th-c coaching inn, black beams and timbers, some stained glass, popular affordably priced home-made food (evening set menu), Badger ales, friendly service; children welcome, back garden with covered area, nine bedrooms and cottage. *(Mrs P R Sykes)*

LITTLEHAMPTON   TQ02020
★ **Arun View**   (01903) 722335
Wharf Road; W towards Chichester; BN17 5DD Airy appealing 18th-c pub in lovely harbour spot with busy waterway directly below windows, very popular lunchtimes with older people (younger crowd evenings) for its enjoyable interesting food (all day Sun) from sandwiches to good fresh fish, well kept Arundel, Fullers London Pride and Ringwood, 20 wines by the glass, cheerful helpful staff, lots of drawings, caricatures and nautical collectables, flagstoned and panelled back bar with banquettes and dark wood tables, large conservatory; background and some live music, TVs, pool; disabled facilities, flower-filled terrace, summer barbecues, interesting waterside walkway to coast, four bedrooms, open all day. *(Anon)*

LITTLEHAMPTON
Steam Packet   (01903) 715994
River Road; BN17 5BZ Recently renovated corner pub just across from the Arun View; open-plan interior providing several separate seating areas, ales such as Courage Directors, Langhams Hip Hop and a guest, shortish menu of snacks and light meals augmented by good specials board; quiz Thurs; seats out in small area facing river, raised back garden, open all day. *(Tony and Wendy Hobden)*

LODSWORTH   SU9321
Halfway Bridge Inn   (01798) 861281
Just before village, on A272 Midhurst– Petworth; GU28 9BP Restaurantly 17th-c coaching inn, various character rooms with

---

We include some hotels with a good bar that offers facilities comparable to those of a pub.

SUSSEX | 795

good oak chairs and individual mix of tables, log fires (one in polished kitchen range), interconnecting restaurant areas with beams and wooden floors, generally well liked food (all day weekends) including daily specials, Langhams and Sharps Doom Bar, wide range of wines by the glass; background music, free wi-fi, daily newspapers; children and dogs (in bar) welcome, small back terrace, stylish bedrooms in former stable yard, open all day. *(Peter Loader)*

LODSWORTH   SU9223
★ **Hollist Arms** (01798) 861310
Off A272 Midhurst–Petworth; GU28 9BZ
In lovely spot by village green, small snug room on right with open fire, public bar on left serving Langhams, Skinners and Timothy Taylors, decent wines, popular french-influenced food (not Sun evening, Mon), friendly attentive service, L-shaped dining room with sofas by inglenook, elegant dining chairs and wheelbacks on wood-strip floor, interesting prints and paintings; background music; children and dogs welcome, steps up to pretty cottagey back garden, picnic-sets on terrace or you can sit under a huge horse chestnut on the green, good walks nearby, open all day. *(Martin and Karen Wake)*

LOWER BEEDING   TQ2225
Crabtree (01403) 892666
Brighton Road; RH13 6PT Family run pub with Victorian façade but much older inside with Tudor beams and huge inglenook (dated 1537), simple light modern décor, dining room in converted barn, good interesting food (all day Sun till 7pm) using genuinely local seasonal produce including daily changing set lunchtime menu, friendly service, well kept Badger beers and good selection of wines by the glass (including english ones); children welcome, dogs in bar, landscaped garden, with fine country views, handy for Nymans (NT), open all day. *(Martin and Karen Wake, Tony and Wendy Hobden, Alan Cowell)*

LYMINSTER   TQ0204
Six Bells (01903) 713639
Lyminster Road (A284), Wick; BN17 7PS Unassuming 18th-c flint pub with open bar area and separate dining room, well kept Fullers London Pride and Sharps Doom Bar, good house wine, generous helpings of enjoyable home-cooked food including lunchtime offers (best to book weekends), friendly efficient staff, low black beams, wood floor and big inglenook with horsebrasses, pubby furnishings; background music, free wi-fi; dogs on leads welcome, terrace and garden seating. *(Dr and Mrs R E S Tanner, Tony and Wendy Hobden, John Beeken)*

MARK CROSS   TQ5831
★ **Mark Cross Inn** (01892) 852423
A267 N of Mayfield; TN6 3NP Big Whiting & Hammond pub with linked areas on varying levels, well kept Fullers, Harveys, Sharps and

a guest, good wines by the glass and decent coffee, varied choice of enjoyable food (all day) served by friendly efficient young staff, real mix of dark wood tables and cushioned dining chairs, walls crowded with prints, old photographs and postcards, books, church candles, working Victorian fireplace; children welcome, wheelchair access, decking with teak furniture, picnic-sets out on grass, broad Weald views, open all day (from 9am for weekend breakfast). *(Nigel and Jean Eames, Gerry and Rosemary Dobson)*

MAYFIELD   TQ5826
Middle House (01435) 872146
High Street; TN20 6AB Handsome 16th-c timbered inn, L-shaped beamed bar with massive fireplace, several well kept ales including Harveys, local cider and decent wines, quiet lounge area with leather chesterfields around log fire in ornate carved fireplace, good choice of enjoyable food, friendly staff coping well at busy times, attractive panelled restaurant; background music; children welcome, terraced back garden with lovely views, five bedrooms, open all day. *(Martin and Alison Stainsby, Tony Scott, R and S Bentley)*

MID LAVANT   SU8508
Earl of March (01243) 533993
A286 Lavant Road; PO18 0BQ Updated and extended with emphasis on eating, but seats for drinkers in flagstoned log-fire bar serving well kept ales such as Ballards, Harveys and Hop Back, good if pricey food with much sourced locally, nice wines including nearby Tinwood (sparkling) and other english choices, plush dining area and conservatory with seafood bar, pleasant staff; delightful location with view up to Goodwood from neatly kept garden, local walks. *(Tracey and Stephen Groves)*

MILLAND   SU8328
Rising Sun (01428) 741347
Iping Road junction with main road through village; GU30 7NA Three linked rooms including cheery log-fire bar and bare-boards restaurant, Fullers/Gales beers and good choice of well cooked nicely presented food, attentive amiable staff, live music first Mon of month; children welcome (popular with families at weekends), garden, heated terrace and smokers' gazebo, good walking area, open all day weekends. *(Anon)*

MILTON STREET   TQ5304
★ **Sussex Ox** (01323) 870840
Off A27 just under a mile E of Alfriston roundabout; BN26 5RL Extended country pub (originally a 1900s slaughterhouse) with magnificent Downs views; bar area with a couple of high tables and chairs on bare boards, old local photographs, three real ales including Harveys and good choice of wines by the glass, lower brick-floored room with farmhouse furniture and woodburner,

similarly furnished dining room (children allowed here), further two-room front eating area with high-backed rush-seated chairs, popular food from traditional choices up, friendly service; dogs welcome in bar, teak seating on raised back deck taking in the view, picnic-sets in garden below and more under parasols at front. *(John Beeken, Tom and Jill Jones, Tony Scott)*

NETHERFIELD   TQ7118
Netherfield Arms (01424) 838282
Just off B2096 Heathfield–Battle; TN33 9QD Low-ceilinged 18th-c country dining pub with wide choice of enjoyable food including good specials, friendly attentive service, decent wines and a well kept ale such as Long Man, inglenook log fire, cosy restaurant; lovely back garden, far reaching views from front, closed Sun evening, Mon. *(Mr and Mrs J Mandeville)*

NEWHAVEN   TQ4500
Hope (01273) 515389
Follow West Beach signs from A259 westbound; BN9 9DN Big-windowed pub overlooking busy harbour entrance, long bar with raised area, open fires and comfy sofas, upstairs dining conservatory and breezy balcony tables with even better view towards Seaford Head, well kept ales such as Dark Star and Harveys, good choice of generous realistically priced food, friendly staff and pub dog (Pip); tables on grassed waterside area. *(John Beeken)*

NUTBOURNE   TQ0718
Rising Sun (01798) 812191
Off A283 E of Pulborough; The Street; RH20 2HE Unspoilt creeper-clad village pub dating partly from the 16th c, beams, bare boards and scrubbed tables, friendly helpful licensees (same family ownership for over 30 years), well kept Fullers London Pride and guests, good home-made food including some unusual choices, big log fire, daily papers, enamel signs and 1920s fashion and dance posters, cosy snug, attractive back family room; live music last Tues of month; dogs welcome, garden with small back terrace under apple tree, smokers' shelter, listed outside lavatory, closed Sun evening. *(Tony and Wendy Hobden)*

NUTHURST   TQ1926
Black Horse (01403) 891272
Off A281 SE of Horsham; RH13 6LH Convivial 17th-c country pub with low black beams, flagstones/bare boards, inglenook log fire and plenty of character in its several small rooms, decent bistro-style food (some prices on the high side), attentive uniformed staff, ales such as Dark Star, Long Man, Sharps and Wells & Youngs, several wines by the glass, charity quiz Weds; children and dogs welcome, pretty streamside back garden, more seats on front terrace, open all day Sat, till 8.30 Sun. *(Ian Phillips)*

OFFHAM   TQ3912
★**Blacksmiths Arms** (01273) 472971
A275 N of Lewes; BN7 3QD Civilised open-plan dining pub, comfortable and welcoming, with good food from chef-owner including seafood and some nice vegetarian choices, well kept Harveys Best and a seasonal beer, good wines, efficient friendly service from uniformed staff, huge end inglenook; french windows to terrace with picnic-sets, four bedrooms. *(Christine and Andy Farley)*

OFFHAM   TQ4011
★**Chalk Pit** (01273) 471124
Offham Road (A275 N of Lewes); BN7 3QF Former late 18th-c chalk pit building on three levels, well kept Harveys and a guest, decent wines by the glass, wide choice of popular home-made food including OAP bargains, attentive cheerful staff, neat restaurant extension, skittle alley, toad in the hole played Mon nights; children welcome, garden with terrace seating, smokers' shelter with pool table, three bedrooms, open (and usually food) all day Fri-Sun. *(John Beeken)*

PARTRIDGE GREEN   TQ1819
★**Green Man** (01403) 710250
Off A24 just under a mile S of A272 junction – take B2135 at West Grinstead signpost; pub at Jolesfield, N of Partridge Green; RH13 8JT Relaxed gently upmarket dining pub with popular enterprising food, several champagnes by the glass and other good wines, Dark Star and Harveys Best, excellent service; unassuming front area by counter with bentwood bar seats, stools and library chairs around one or two low tables, old curved high-back settle, main eating area widening into back part with pretty enamelled stove and pitched ceiling on left, more self-contained room on right with stag's head, minimal decoration but plenty of atmosphere; cast-iron seats and picnic-sets under parasols in neat back garden. *(Val and Alan Green)*

PARTRIDGE GREEN   TQ1819
Partridge (01403) 710391
Church Road/High Street; RH13 8JS Spaciously renovated village pub acting as tap for Dark Star, full range and maybe a guest, real cider, enjoyable home-made food (not Sun, Mon evenings) at sensible prices, friendly atmosphere, darts and pool; children and dogs welcome, garden with play equipment and large terrace, open all day. *(Colin Gooch)*

PATCHING   TQ0705
Fox (01903) 871299
Arundel Road; signed off A27 eastbound just W of Worthing; BN13 3UJ Generous good value home-made food including popular Sun roasts (best to book), quick friendly service even at busy times, two or

three well kept changing ales, large dining area off roomy panelled bar, hunting pictures; quiet background music; children and dogs welcome, disabled access, good-sized tree-shaded garden with play area, open all day weekends. *(Tony and Wendy Hobden)*

PETT   TQ8713
Royal Oak   (01424) 812515
Pett Road; TN35 4HG Light and airy pub under same ownership as the Queens Head at Icklesham; roomy main bar with big open fire, well kept Harveys and a couple of changing guests, good popular home-made food including plenty of fish and decent vegetarian options, two dining areas, efficient friendly service, monthly live music and quiz nights; dogs welcome (maybe a biscuit), small garden behind, open all day.
(Peter Meister, Lucien Perring)

PETT   TQ8613
Two Sawyers   (01424) 812255
Pett Road, off A259; TN35 4HB Meandering low-beamed rooms including bare-boards bar with stripped tables, tiny snug, passage sloping down to restaurant allowing children, popular good value freshly made food, friendly service, well kept Harveys with guests like Dark Star, Ringwood and Wells & Youngs, local farm cider and perry, wide range of wines; background music; dogs allowed in bar, suntrap front courtyard, back garden with shady trees and well spaced tables, three bedrooms, open all day.
(Peter Meister, Lucien Perring)

PETWORTH   SU9719
Badgers   (01798) 342651
Station Road (A285 1.5 miles S); GU28 0JF Restauranty dining pub with good up-to-date food including tapas, seasonal game and seafood, can eat in bar areas or restaurant, friendly helpful staff, a couple of changing ales such as Wells & Youngs and good choice of wines, cosy fireside area with sofas; free wi-fi; over-5s allowed in bar's eating area, stylish tables and seats on terrace by water lily pool, summer barbecues, three well appointed bedrooms with own Nespresso machines, good breakfast, closed winter Sun evenings. *(Colin McKerrow)*

PETWORTH   SU9721
Star   (01798) 342569
Market Square; GU28 0AH Airy open-plan pub in centre with seats out in front, well kept Fullers ales and decent wines, enjoyable fairly priced food (not Sun evening), good coffee, leather armchairs and sofa by open fire, friendly atmosphere; free wi-fi; open all day. *(Ann and Colin Hunt)*

PETWORTH   SU9722
Stonemasons   (01798) 342510
North Street; GU28 9NL Attractive low-beamed 17th-c inn refurbished under new owners; enjoyable freshly made food at

fair prices, Sharps Doom Bar and a couple of guests, helpful efficient staff, opened-up areas in former adjoining cottages, inglenook log fires; children and dogs welcome, picnic-sets in pleasant sheltered back garden, five bedrooms, opposite Petworth House (NT) so can get busy, open all day. *(Ian Phillips)*

PLAYDEN   TQ9121
Playden Oasts   (01797) 223502
Rye Road; TN31 7UL Converted three-roundel oast with comfortable bar and restaurant, helpful chatty landlord, enjoyable food from well filled baguettes up, Harveys Best, friendly homely atmosphere; eight bedrooms. *(Paul Humphreys)*

PLUMPTON   TQ3613
★ Half Moon   (01273) 890253
Ditchling Road (B2116); BN7 3AF Enlarged beamed and timbered dining pub with good locally sourced food including midweek set lunch, also children's menu and traditional Sun roasts, local ales and plenty of wines by the glass, good friendly service, log fire with unusual flint chimneybreast; background music; dogs welcome in bar, tables in wisteria-clad front courtyard and on back terrace, big Downs-view garden with picnic area, summer family days (last Sun of July and Aug) with face painting and bouncy castle, good walks, open all day (till 6pm Sun).
(Steve and Irene Homer, Roger and Val)

POYNINGS   TQ2611
Royal Oak   (01273) 857389
The Street; BN45 7AQ Well run 19th-c pub with large beamed bar, good food from sandwiches and sharing plates up, helpful efficient service, real ales including Harveys from three-sided servery, leather sofas and traditional furnishing, woodburner; children and dogs welcome, big attractive garden with country/Downs views. *(R Anderson)*

RINGMER   TQ4512
Green Man   (01273) 812422
Lewes Road; BN8 5NA Doing well under present landlord; welcoming bar with busy mix of locals and visitors, six real ales from brick-faced counter, log fire, wide choice of keenly priced hearty food, good service, restaurant area; children and dogs welcome, terrace tables, more on lawn under trees, play area. *(John Beeken)*

ROWHOOK   TQ1234
★ Chequers   (01403) 790480
Off A29 NW of Horsham; RH12 3PY Attractive and welcoming 16th-c pub, beamed and flagstoned front bar with portraits and inglenook log fire, step up to low-beamed lounge, well kept Harveys and guests, decent wines by the glass, good cooking from chef-landlord using local ingredients including home-grown vegetables, separate restaurant; background music; children and dogs welcome, tables out

on front terraces and in pretty garden behind with good play area, attractive surroundings, closed Sun evening. *(Anon)*

RUSHLAKE GREEN   TQ6218
★ **Horse & Groom** (01435) 830320
Off B2096 Heathfield–Battle; TN21 9QE
Cheerful little village-green pub; L-shaped low-beamed bar with brick fireplace and local pictures, small room down a step with horsey décor and local artwork, simple beamed restaurant, good food cooked by chef-landlord from pub favourites to more elaborate daily changing choices, maybe lunchtime deal, Harveys, Shepherd Neame and a dozen wines by the glass; children and dogs welcome, charming cottagey garden with pretty country views, nice walks, open all day weekends. *(Anon)*

RUSPER   TQ1836
★ **Royal Oak** (01293) 871393
Friday Street, towards Warnham – back road N of Horsham, E of A24 (OS Sheet 187 map reference 185369); RH12 4QA
Old-fashioned and well worn-in tile-hung pub in very rural spot on Sussex Border Path, small carpeted top bar with leather sofas and armchairs, log fire, steps down to long beamed main bar with plush wall seats, pine tables and chairs and homely knick-knacks, well kept Surrey Hills Ranmore and six changing guests, farm ciders and perries, short choice of enjoyable low-priced lunchtime food (evenings and Sun lunch by pre-arrangement), plain games room with darts; no children inside, a few picnic-sets on grass by road and in streamside garden beyond car park, roaming chickens (eggs for sale), bedrooms, closes at 9pm (4pm Sun). *(Anon)*

RYE   TQ9220
★ **George** (01797) 222114
High Street; TN31 7JT Sizeable hotel with popular beamed bar, mix of furniture including settles on bare boards, log fire, ales such as Dark Star, Franklins, Harveys and Old Dairy, continental beers on tap too, good friendly service from neat staff, interesting bistro-style food, big spreading restaurant to right of main door; may be background jazz; children and dogs welcome, attractive bedrooms, open all day. *(Anon)*

RYE   TQ9220
★ **Mermaid** (01797) 223065
Mermaid Street; TN31 7EY Lovely old timbered inn on famous cobbled street (cellars date from 12th c, although pub was rebuilt in 1420); civilised antiques-filled bar, Victorian gothick carved chairs, older but plainer oak seats, huge working inglenook with massive bressumer, Fullers, Greene King and Harveys, good selection of wines and malt whiskies, short bar menu, more elaborate and expensive restaurant choices, good friendly service, reputedly haunted

by five ghosts; background music; children welcome, seats on small back terrace, bedrooms (most with four-posters), open all day. *(Richard Tilbrook, Pete Walker)*

RYE HARBOUR   TQ9419
Inkerman Arms (01797) 222464
Rye Harbour Road; TN31 7TQ Friendly plain pub near nature reserve, large helpings of enjoyable food including good fish and chips, a couple of changing local ales; tables out in small sheltered back area, open all day Fri-Sun. *(Rob Newland)*

SCAYNES HILL   TQ3824
Sloop (01444) 831219
Sloop Lane, Freshfield Lock; RH17 7NP Traditional tucked-away country pub, main bar with wood floors, painted panelling and woodburner, fresh flowers and daily papers, linked dining area to the right and public bar with old photographs, good fairly standard food (not Sun evening) including a weekday lunchtime menu for smaller appetites, well kept Dark Star, Harveys, a beer for the pub from Hurst and local guests, several wines by the glass, friendly staff, Sun live acoustic music; picnic-sets in sheltered garden, open all day weekends. *(Steve and Irene Homer)*

SEDLESCOMBE   TQ7817
Queens Head (01424) 870228
The Green; TN33 0QA Attractive heavily beamed tile-hung village-green pub refurbished under present management; main bar on right with mixed tables and wheelback chairs on wood floor, church candles and fresh flowers, a huge cartwheel and some farming odds and ends, Harveys and Sharps Doom Bar from plank-fronted servery, side room laid for dining with brick fireplace, sofas in back lounge, another dining room to left of entrance with sisal flooring and huge working inglenook, good popular food (best to book) from shortish menu; quiet background music; children and dogs welcome, garden picnic-sets. *(Caroline Prescott)*

SELSEY   SZ8593
Seal (01243) 602461
Hillfield Road; PO20 0JX Modernised late 19th-c pub under same family ownership since 1971; seven well kept changing ales, enjoyable nicely presented food (all day Fri-Sun) including local fish and good value two-course menu (Sun-Weds), friendly service, old lifeboat and other photographs, restaurant, some live music, quiz first Weds of month; a few tables out in front, 13 bedrooms, nearby caravan parks, open all day. *(Tony and Wendy Hobden)*

SHOREHAM-BY-SEA   TQ2105
Red Lion (01273) 453171
Upper Shoreham Road; BN43 5TE Modest dimly lit low-beamed and timbered 16th-c pub with settles in snug alcoves, well

kept Harveys and changing guests such as Adur, Arundel and Hepworth (Easter beer festival), traditional summer ciders and decent wines, pubby food from sandwiches up, log fire in unusual fireplace, another open fire in dining room, further bar with covered terrace; dogs welcome, pretty sheltered garden behind, old bridge and lovely Norman church opposite, good Downs views, popular with walkers and cyclists (on Downs Link trail), open all day. *(John Coatsworth, Tony and Wendy Hobden)*

SHORTBRIDGE   TQ4521
★**Peacock** (01825) 762463
Piltdown; OS Sheet 198 map reference 450215; TN22 3XA Civilised and welcoming country dining pub with two fine yew trees flanking entrance, beams, timbers and big inglenook, some nice old furniture on parquet floors, good food from light dishes up, two or three well kept ales and nice wines by the glass, friendly attentive staff, restaurant; children welcome, back garden and terrace. *(Mrs Sally Scott)*

SIDLESHAM   SZ8697
★**Crab & Lobster** (01243) 641233
Mill Lane; off B2145 S of Chichester; PO20 7NB Restaurant-with-rooms rather than pub but walkers and bird-watchers welcome in small flagstoned bar for light meals, Harveys and Sharps, 17 wines by the glass including champagne (also interesting selection of 50cl carafes), stylish, upmarket restaurant with good imaginative (and pricey) food including excellent local fish, competent friendly young staff; background music; children welcome, tables on back terrace overlooking marshes, smart bedrooms, self-catering cottage, open all day (food all day weekends). *(Paddy and Annabelle Cribb, John Wooll, Tracey and Stephen Groves)*

SINGLETON   SU8713
★**Partridge** (01243) 811251
Just off A286 Midhurst–Chichester; PO18 0EY Pretty 16th-c pub handy for Weald & Downland Open Air Museum; all sorts of light and dark wood tables and dining chairs on polished wooden floors, flagstones or carpet, some country knick-knacks, open fires and woodburner, Fullers London Pride, Harveys Best and a summer guest, several wines by the glass, well liked food from good lunchtime sandwiches up, friendly service, daily papers and board games, maybe summer table tennis; background music; children welcome, plenty of seats under parasols on terrace and in walled garden. *(Richard Tilbrook, Val and Alan Green, Martin and Karen Wake, Nigel and Sue Foster)*

SLAUGHAM   TQ2528
Chequers (01444) 400239
Off A23 S of Handcross; RH17 6AQ Modernised hilltop village pub looking across to 12th-c church; leather sofas, bare boards and soft lighting, good well presented food including children's choices, Laines Best and decent wines, open fire, newspapers and magazines; children welcome, sloping garden behind with lovely country views, lakeside walks, six bedrooms, open all day and handy for Gatwick. *(Ian Phillips)*

SLINDON   SU9708
Spur (01243) 814216
Slindon Common; A29 towards Bognor; BN18 0NE Roomy 17th-c pub with welcoming licensees and efficient friendly staff, wide choice of popular carefully cooked food from bar snacks to more upmarket (but good value) restaurant dishes, Courage Directors and Sharps Doom Bar, pine tables and two big log fires, large panelled restaurant with linen table cloths, games room with darts and pool, skittle alley; children welcome, dogs in bar, pretty garden (traffic noise), good local walks, open all day Sun. *(M G Hart, Nigel and Sue Foster, David H T Dimock, Tony and Wendy Hobden)*

SLINFOLD   TQ1131
Red Lyon (01403) 790339
The Street; RH13 0RR Red-brick village pub with friendly accommodating landlord, ales such as Badger K&B, Fullers, Sharps and Timothy Taylors, enjoyable freshly made food, restaurant, two coal fires; some live music, TV; children and dogs welcome, big garden with terrace, summer barbecues, bedrooms. *(Ian Phillips)*

SOMPTING   TQ1605
Gardeners Arms (01903) 233666
West Street; BN15 0AR 19th-c pub run by friendly licensees, just off main coast road (the famous Saxon church is unfortunately on the far side of the dual carriageway), generous helpings of tasty low-priced pub food including some real bargains (railway-carriage restaurant no longer in use), Bass, Harveys, Sharps Doom Bar and a guest, log fire; background music, Tues quiz; children and dogs welcome, seats on raised terrace, open all day. *(Tony and Wendy Hobden)*

SOUTH HARTING   SU7819
White Hart (01730) 825124
B2146 SE of Petersfield; GU31 5QB Welcoming old beamed pub sympathetically renovated under new owners; well kept Upham ales and good interesting food from sourdough baguettes up, lunchtime set menu,

---

By law, pubs must show a price list of their drinks. Let us know if you're inconvenienced by any breach of this law.

split-level bare-boards interior, inglenook log fires; children, dogs and walkers welcome, terrace and garden with spectacular Downs views, handy for Uppark (NT), open all day. *(Val and Alan Green)*

SOUTHWATER   TQ1528
Bax Castle (01403) 730369
Two Mile Ash, a mile or so NW;
RH13 0LA Early 19th-c country pub with well liked traditional home-made food including popular Sun roasts, three Marstons-related ales, friendly staff, sofas next to big log fire, barn restaurant; background music (live Fri); children and dogs welcome, pleasant garden with play area, near Downs Link path on former railway track, open all day (till 9pm Sun). *(Mrs Sally Scott)*

STAPLEFIELD   TQ2728
Jolly Tanners (01444) 400335
Handcross Road, just off A23;
RH17 6EF Neatly kept split-level local by cricket green, welcoming landlord and pub dogs, two good log fires, padded settles, lots of china, brasses and old photographs, well kept Fullers London Pride, Harveys and guests (beer festivals), real ciders, pubby food including good Sun roasts, friendly chatty atmosphere; background and weekend live music including jazz; children and dogs welcome, attractive suntrap garden, quite handy for Nymans (NT), open all day Fri-Sun. *(Anon)*

STAPLEFIELD   TQ2728
Victory (01444) 400463
Warninglid Road; RH17 6EU Pretty little shuttered dining pub overlooking cricket green (and London to Brighton veteran car run, first Sun in Nov), friendly staff, good choice of popular home-made food, smaller helpings for children, well kept Harveys Best from zinc-topped counter, local cider and decent wines, beams and woodburner; nice tree-shaded garden with play area. *(C and R Bromage)*

STEDHAM   SU8522
Hamilton Arms (01730) 812555
School Lane (off A272); GU29 0NZ Village local run by friendly thai family, standard pub food as well as good thai bar snacks and restaurant dishes (you can buy ingredients in their little shop), good value Sun buffet, reasonably priced wines and four or more well kept ales, games room; unobtrusive background music, muted TV; pretty hanging baskets on front terrace overlooking small green, good nearby walks, closed Mon, otherwise open all day. *(J A Snell)*

STEYNING   TQ1711
Chequer (01903) 814437
High Street; BN44 3RE Two-bar low-beamed Tudor coaching inn, four or so well kept ales including Dark Star, good

choice of wines, well priced usual food (not Sun evening) from generous baguettes up including breakfast from 10am, log fire, antique snooker table, large painting featuring the locals, some live music; smokers' shelter, bedrooms, open all day. *(Pete Walker, Val and Alan Green)*

STOPHAM   TQ0318
★**White Hart** (01798) 873321
Off A283 E of village, W of Pulborough;
RH20 1DS Fine old pub by medieval River Arun bridge, heavy beams, timbers and panelling, log fire and sofas in one of its three snug rooms, well kept ales such as Arundel, Langhams and Kings, good generous food (all day weekends) from baguettes and pizzas up, friendly efficient service, some interesting bric-a-brac, Thurs quiz night; children and dogs welcome, waterside tables, some under cover, open all day. *(Jay Marsh)*

STOUGHTON   SU8011
Hare & Hounds (02392) 631433
Signed off B2146 Petersfield–Emsworth;
PO18 9JQ Airy pine-clad country dining pub with good reasonably priced fresh food from sandwiches to Sun roasts, up to six well kept ales and Weston's cider, flagstones and big open fires, public bar with darts, quiz nights; children in eating areas, dogs welcome, tables on pretty front terrace and grass behind, lovely setting near Saxon church, good local walks, open all day Fri-Sun. *(Geoff and Linda Payne)*

SUTTON   SU9715
★**White Horse** (01798) 869221
The Street; RH20 1PS Opened-up country inn close to Bignor Roman Villa; bar with open brick fireplaces at each end, tea-lights on mantelpieces, cushioned high bar chairs, Wadworths 6X and a guest, good wines by the glass, two-room barrel-vaulted dining area with minimalist contemporary décor and another little fire, well thought-of food, friendly young staff; children welcome, dogs in bar, steps up to lawn with plenty of picnic-sets, more seats in front, good surrounding walks, bedrooms, closed Sun evening, Mon. *(Glenwys and Alan Lawrence, Martin and Karen Wake)*

THAKEHAM   TQ1017
White Lion (01798) 813141
Off B2139 N of Storrington; The Street;
RH20 3EP Tile-hung 16th-c two-bar village pub, good food (not Sun evening) from open kitchen, friendly informal service, real ales such as Arundel, Fullers, Harveys and St Austell, nice wines by the glass, heavy beams, panelling, bare boards and traditional furnishings including settles, pleasant dining room with inglenook woodburner, fresh flowers, newspapers; dogs welcome, sunny terrace tables, more on small lawn, pretty village, open all day. *(Anon)*

TICEHURST
TQ6831

Bull (01580) 200586

*Three Legged Cross; off B2099 towards
Wadhurst; TN5 7HH* Attractive 14th-c
pub with big log fires in two heavy-beamed
old-fashioned bars, well kept Harveys and a
guest, contemporary furnishings and flooring
in light airy dining extension serving good
food; children and dogs welcome, charming
front garden (busy in summer), bigger back
one with play area, four bedrooms. *(Anon)*

TICEHURST
TQ6930

Cherry Tree (01580) 200337

*B2087 towards Flimwell, on short
one-way stretch near Dale Hill golf club;
TN5 7DG* Refurbished family-run pub with
both drinkers and diners in bar to left, mix
of wooden dining chairs and tables, nice
log fire, high chairs against counter serving
Harveys Best and a guest, decent wines by
the glass, good food from snacks up and
popular Sun lunch, restaurant area to right
with similar furnishings, small end room for
private parties; picnic-sets on front deck,
tepee in top garden. *(Anon)*

TURNERS HILL
TQ3435

Crown (01342) 715218

East Street; RH10 4PT Refurbished village
pub dating from the 16th c, low-beamed
bar with sofas by big log fire, steps down
to high-raftered dining area with parquet
floor and another fire, decent food from
sandwiches and pubby choices up, well kept
ales including Harveys and St Austell, good
service; children welcome, picnic-sets out in
front, sheltered back garden with terrace and
enjoyable valley views, open all day.
(C and R Bromage)

TURNERS HILL
TQ3435

★Red Lion (01342) 715416

Lion Lane, just off B2028; RH10 4NU
Old-fashioned, unpretentious and welcoming
country local, snug parquet-floored bar with
plush wall benches and small open fire, steps
up to carpeted dining area with inglenook log
fire, cushioned pews and settles, old photos
and brewery memorabilia, well kept Harveys
ales and good home-made food (lunchtime
only – must book Sun); background and some
summer live music, quiz nights; children
(away from bar) and dogs welcome, picnic-
sets on side grass overlooking village, open
all day, Sun till 10pm (8pm winter). *(William
Ruxton, Nick Lawless, Pete Walker, Mrs P R Sykes,
Tony and Wendy Hobden)*

UDIMORE
TQ8818

Plough (01797) 223381

*Cock Marling (B2089 W of Rye);
TN31 6AL* Popular 17th-c beamed roadside
pub with enjoyable freshly made food
including tapas, well kept Harveys, Old Dairy
and a guest, good choice of wines by the
glass, friendly service, front bar and carpeted
dining area, some bric-a-brac, local artwork
and photographs, two woodburners; children
and dogs welcome, tables on good-sized
sunny back terrace, nice views, open all day
Fri, Sat, closed Sun evening, Mon. *(Anon)*

UPPER DICKER
TQ5409

Plough (01323) 844859

Coldharbour Road; BN27 3QJ Extended
17th-c pub improved under current licensees;
small central beamed bar with seats by
inglenook, two dining areas off to left and
step up to larger dining bar on right with
raised area, well kept Shepherd Neame with
Harveys as guest, good choice of enjoyable
food; background music, Tues quiz; children
and dogs welcome, good-sized garden with
raised deck and play area, open (and food)
all day. *(Fr Robert Marsh, Mike and Shelley
Woodroffe, Nigel and Jean Eames)*

WALDERTON
SU7910

Barley Mow (02392) 631321

*Stoughton Road, just off B2146
Chichester–Petersfield; PO18 9ED*
Country pub with good value generous food
from lunchtime sandwiches up including
Sun carvery, well kept ales such as Arundel,
Harveys and Ringwood, good wine choice,
friendly service even on busy weekends, two
log fires and rustic bric-a-brac in U-shaped
bar with roomy dining areas, live jazz suppers
(third Tues of month), popular skittle alley;
children welcome, big pleasant streamside
back garden, good walks (Kingley Vale
nearby), handy for Stansted Park, open all
day weekends. *(Lawrence Pearse, Tim and
Joan Wright)*

WALDRON
TQ5419

★Star (01435) 812495

Blackboys–Horam side road; TN21 0RA
Pretty pub in quiet village, beamed main
bar with settle next to good log fire in brick
inglenook, wheelbacks around pubby tables
on old quarry tiles, several built-in cushioned
wall and window seats, old local pictures
and photographs, high stools by central
counter serving a couple of Harveys ales and
a guest like Dark Star Hophead, maybe own
apple juice, good food including lunchtime
sandwiches and platters, pubby dishes and
specials, dining areas with painted chairs
around pine-topped tables on parquet or bare
boards, bookshelf wallpaper, chatty local
atmosphere and friendly staff, music and quiz
nights; picnic-sets in pleasant back garden,
wassailing on Twelfth Night, small café
and shop next door. *(PL, Mike and Eleanor
Anderson, Paul Lucas)*

WARBLETON
TQ6018

★Black Duck (01435) 830636

S of B2096 SE of Heathfield; TN21 9BD
Friendly licensees at this small renovated
pub tucked down from church; L-shaped
main room with pale oak flooring, cushioned
leather sofas in front of roaring inglenook,

beams and walls hung with horsebrasses, tankards, musical instruments, farm tools, even an old typewriter, high-backed dining chairs around mix of tables, enjoyable pubby food including daily specials, bar area up a step with stools along counter, Harveys, Sharps Doom Bar and nice wines by the glass, cabinet of books and board games, perky pub dog; background music; picnic-sets in back garden with sweeping valley views, more on front grass. *(Anon)*

WEST ASHLING   SU8007
Richmond Arms   (01243) 572046
Just off B2146; Mill Road; PO18 8EA
Village dining pub in quiet pretty setting near big millpond with ducks and geese, good interesting food (quite pricey), Harveys ales and plenty of wines by the glass, competent staff; no dogs; children welcome, two nice bedrooms, closed Sun evening, Mon and Tues. *(Ann and Colin Hunt)*

WEST WITTERING   SZ8099
Lamb   (01243) 511105
Chichester Road; B2179/A286 towards Birdham; PO20 8QA Welcoming 18th-c tile-hung country pub, enjoyable food including blackboard specials, Badger ales, friendly staff coping well during busy summer months, rugs and mix of furniture on wood floor, blazing fire; children and dogs welcome, tables out in front and in small sheltered back garden with terrace. *(Nigel and Sue Foster, David H T Dimock)*

WEST WITTERING   SZ7798
Old House At Home   (01243) 511234
Cakeham Road; PO20 8AD Roomy and cheerfully brightened up with three bar areas on two levels, wood floors and modern décor, local artwork for sale, well kept ales including Otter and Fullers London Pride, enjoyable traditional food along with daily specials, friendly staff, log fires; children and dogs (in bar) welcome, garden with covered deck and play area, handy for the beach, three bedrooms. *(Anon)*

WILMINGTON   TQ5404
★ Giants Rest   (01323) 870207
Just off A27; BN26 5SQ Busy country pub continuing well under present management; long wood-floored bar, adjacent open areas with simple furniture, log fire, good value Long Man ales and enjoyable food including daily specials and gluten-free options; children and dogs welcome, lots of seats in front garden, surrounded by South Downs walks and village famous for chalk-carved Long Man, two comfortable bedrooms up narrow stairs sharing bathroom, open all day weekends (food all day Sun). *(John Warner, John Beeken, Fr Robert Marsh, Tom and Jill Jones)*

WINCHELSEA   TQ9017
New Inn   (01797) 226252
German Street; just off A259; TN36 4EN
Attractive 18th-c pub with L-shaped front bar mainly laid for dining, good fair-value food from sandwiches to local fish, well kept Greene King and guests, friendly helpful staff, some slate flagstones, blackened beams and log fire, separate back bar with darts and TV; background music; children welcome, pleasant tree-shaded walled garden, delightful setting opposite church (Spike Milligan buried here), comfortable bedrooms, good breakfast. *(Lucien Perring, Peter Meister, John Beeken, Peter Smith and Judith Brown)*

WINEHAM   TQ2320
★ Royal Oak   (01444) 881252
Village signposted from A272 and B2116; BN5 9AY Splendidly old-fashioned local with log fire in enormous inglenook, Harveys Best and guests tapped from casks in still room, enjoyable seasonal food (not Sun evening), jugs and ancient corkscrews on very low beams, collection of cigarette boxes, a stuffed stoat and crocodile, more bric-a-brac in back parlour with views of quiet countryside; children away from bar and dogs welcome (they have a bearded collie and a staffie), picnic sets outside, closed evenings 25 and 26 Dec, 1 Jan. *(Anon)*

WISBOROUGH GREEN   TQ0626
Bat & Ball   (01403) 700676
Newpound Lane; RH14 0EH 18th-c red-brick Badger pub set in 6-acre site, their ales and short choice of food including home-made pizzas, bar and two side rooms, beams, flagstones and bare boards, inglenook fire, shop selling local produce; children welcome, camping facilities including two shepherd's huts, handy for Fishers Farm Park, open (and food) all day. *(Tony and Wendy Hobden)*

WISBOROUGH GREEN   TQ0526
Cricketers Arms   (01403) 700369
Loxwood Road, just off A272 Billingshurst–Petworth; RH14 0DG
Attractive old pub with well kept Fullers and Harveys, good choice of food including specials, cheerful staff, open-plan with two big woodburners, pleasing mix of country furniture, stripped-brick dining area on left; live music nights; tables out on terrace, across lane from green. *(Tony Scott, John Davis)*

WISBOROUGH GREEN   TQ0525
Three Crowns   (0333) 700 7333
Billingshurst Road (A272); RH14 0DX
Well looked after beamed pub with good freshly made food (not Sun evening) from pub favourites to daily specials, prompt

---

We say if we know a pub has background music.

friendly service, three well kept ales including Harveys, extensive choice of wines by the glass including champagne; children welcome, sizeable tree-shaded back garden, open all day. *(Val and Alan Green)*

WITHYHAM   TQ4935
Dorset Arms (01892) 770278
B2110; TN7 4BD Recently revamped 16th-c pub handy for Forest Way walks – reports please. *(Anon)*

WOODMANCOTE   SU7707
Woodmancote (01243) 371019
The one near Emsworth; Woodmancote Lane; PO10 8RD Well run village pub with interesting contemporary décor – plenty of quirky touches; good popular food from sandwiches and sharing boards up (best to book), ales such as Brains, Courage and Hogs Back, several wines by the glass, restaurant; dogs welcome in bar, outside seating, open all day. *(Wendda and John Knapp)*

WORTHING   TQ1404
Cricketers (01903) 233369
Broadwater Street W, Broadwater Green (A24); BN14 9DE Extended panelled local with well kept ales such as Fullers, Greene King, Harveys and Sharps, enjoyable reasonably priced lunchtime food (also Thurs-Sat evenings), friendly staff, old photographs, prints and copper knick-knacks, steps down to small lounge area with

dining room beyond, log fires, quiz evenings; children and dogs welcome, good-sized garden with play area, open all day. *(Tony and Wendy Hobden)*

WORTHING   TQ1502
Selden Arms (01903) 234854
Lyndhurst Road, between Waitrose and hospital; BN11 2DB Friendly chatty backstreet local opposite the gasworks, welcoming long-serving licensees, well kept Dark Star Hophead and several changing guests, several continental bottled beers and farm cider, bargain lunchtime food (not Sun) including doorstep sandwiches, comfortably worn interior with lots of old local photographs, log fire, occasional live music; dogs welcome, open all day. *(Tony and Wendy Hobden, N R White)*

WORTHING   TQ1502
Swan (01903) 232923
High Street; BN11 1DN Villagey atmosphere with good mix of customers in U-shaped bar, four well kept ales such as Arundel, Harveys, Hogs Back and Otter, reasonably priced pubby lunchtime food (also early Fri evening), friendly welcoming staff, old-fashioned carpeted interior with lots of odds and ends hanging from beams, some stained glass, bar billiards, live music and quiz nights; children welcome, small back terrace used by smokers, open all day. *(Tony and Wendy Hobden)*

Warwickshire
with Birmingham and West Midlands

KEY	★ Star Pub	⭐ Top Quality Food	🍺 Great Beer
♉ Good Wines	£ Bargain Meals	🛏 Good Bedrooms	🍴 Serves Food

ALCESTER
Holly Bush 🍺

SP0957 Map 4

Henley Street (continuation of High Street towards B4089; not much nearby parking); B49 5QX

Traditional inn with timeless appeal, nine real ales and well liked food

With tasty food and a fine choice of nine real ales on handpump, this unpretentious 17th-c pub is very much enjoyed by our readers. Several small rooms have a variety of simple furniture on bare boards or flagstones, stripped masonry and dark board panelling, some antique prints and open fires. The chatty heart of the place is at the back on the left, with a few big Victorian lithographs and a warm woodburning stove in a capacious fireplace. The hard-working landlady and her friendly staff serve Black Sheep, Hobsons Best and Town Crier, Hook Norton Lion, Marstons Pedigree and Purity Pure Gold with guests from breweries such as Banks's, North Cotswold and Wye Valley on handpump, plus eight wines by the glass and a couple of farm ciders. Outside, there are seats in a pretty little garden with a sheltered side terrace; good disabled access.

🍴 Popular dishes include lunchtime sandwiches, potted crab and smoked fish mousse, chicken liver parfait with whisky, beef, chicken or vegetarian burger with toppings, coleslaw and chips, old spot sausages with champ mash and rich gravy, gammon and eggs, free-range chicken with fricassée of wild mushrooms with vermouth sauce, cod loin with warm salad of potatoes and chorizo, and puddings such as black cherry and rum roulade and mango and passion-fruit cheesecake. *Benchmark main dish: beer-battered fish and chips £9.00. Two-course evening meal £14.00.*

Free house ~ Licensee Teej Deffley ~ Real ale ~ (01789) 762482 ~ Open 12-11 ~ Bar food 12-2.30, 6-9 (9.30 Fri, Sat); 12-3 Sun; not Sun evening, Mon or Tues ~ Restaurant ~ Children welcome ~ Dogs allowed in bar ~ Wi-fi ~ www.thehollybushalcester.co.uk
Recommended by Paul Humphreys, Roger and Donna Huggins

ALDERMINSTER
Bell ⭐ ♉ 🛏

SP2348 Map 4

A3400 Oxford–Stratford; CV37 8NY

Handsome coaching inn with a smart but easy-going atmosphere, real ales, a good choice of wines, excellent modern cooking and helpful service; comfortable bedrooms

Just a few miles from Stratford, this is a civilised Georgian coaching inn in the middle of an attractive village surrounded by lovely countryside.

The open-plan rooms cleverly manage to create a contemporary feel that goes well with the many original features: beams, standing timbers, flagstoned or wooden floors, fresh flowers and candles. A small, bustling bar – with Alscot Ale (from the Warwickshire Beer Co) and a changing guest beer on handpump, a dozen wines by the glass and proper cocktails (including a special bloody mary) – has comfortable brown leather armchairs in front of an open fire, high bar chairs by the blue-painted counter and daily papers; background music. The restaurant has an eclectic mix of furniture including painted dining chairs and tables, and leads into the conservatory, which shares the same Stour Valley views as the appealing courtyard with its modern chairs and tables. The nine boutique-style bedrooms are individually decorated and comfortable.

Using Alscot Estate produce, the good, interesting food includes lunchtime sandwiches, slow-cooked pork belly with a barbecue glaze and water melon and chorizo salad, mussels and prawns in romesco sauce, lamb in honey and mustard with a greek salad and minty yoghurt, chicken in a white wine and wild mushroom sauce with tarragon polenta, and puddings such as chocolate and hazelnut cheesecake and sticky toffee pudding; they also offer a two- and three-course lunch and three-course evening meal (not weekends). *Benchmark main dish: burger with toppings and chips £12.25. Two-course evening meal £20.00.*

Free house ~ Licensee Emma Holman-West ~ Real ale ~ (01789) 450414 ~ Open 9.30-3, 5.30-11; 9.30-11 Sat; 9.30am-9pm Sun ~ Bar food 12-2, 6.30-9; 12-3, 6.30-9.30 (8.30 Sun) Fri, Sat ~ Restaurant ~ Children welcome ~ Dogs allowed in bar ~ Wi-fi ~ Bedrooms: £70/£110 ~ www.thebellald.co.uk *Recommended by P and J Shapley*

ARDENS GRAFTON   SP1153   Map 4
Golden Cross
Off A46 or B439 W of Stratford, corner of Wixford Road/Grafton Lane; B50 4LG

Friendly, relaxed beamed bar and attractive dining room in bustling country dining pub with well thought-of food

With a genuinely warm welcome and appealing furnishings, this bustling pub gets warm praise from our readers. There are character seats among the chapel chairs around country kitchen tables, rugs on ancient dark flagstones, buff-coloured walls hung with contemporary local photographs and a woodburning stove in a large old fireplace. There's Wells & Youngs IPA and Eagle, Purity UBU and a guest beer on handpump, ten wines by the glass and, next to a fine antique curved-back settle, a table of daily papers including the *Racing Post*. The carpeted dining room has local prints, an unusual coffered ceiling and a big mullioned bay window; background music. There are picnic-sets in the good-sized, neatly planted back garden, with big canopied heaters on the terrace and a pleasant country outlook.

As well as lunchtime sandwiches, the enjoyable food includes plenty of tapas such as garlic tiger prawns, spicy meatballs in tomato sauce, and roasted red peppers and artichoke hearts, as well as chicken liver pâté with onion marmalade, chicken or beef burger with cheese, bacon, tomato and pepper relish and chips, chicken with chorizo mash and herb oil, whole trout with an almond and honey crust, pork medallions with red wine gravy and lyonnaise potatoes, and puddings. *Benchmark main dish: gammon with bubble and squeak, roasted root vegetables, poached egg and parsley sauce £12.95. Two-course evening meal £19.00.*

Charles Wells ~ Lease Debbie Honychurch ~ Real ale ~ (01789) 772420 ~ Open 12-3, 5-midnight; 12-midnight Sat, Sun ~ Bar food 12-2.30, 5-9; 12-9 Sat; 12-8 Sun ~

Restaurant ~ Children welcome ~ Dogs allowed in bar ~ Wi-fi ~ Live acoustic music
Thurs evenings ~ www.thegoldencross.net *Recommended by Martin and Pauline Jennings,
Clive and Fran Dutson, Dave Braisted, Mrs Blethyn Elliott, R T and J C Moggridge, Michael Butler*

BARFORD   SP2660   Map 4
Granville ♀

1.7 miles from M40 junction 15; A429 S (Wellesbourne Road); CV35 8DS

**Bustling friendly pub with a welcome for all, enjoyable food
and drink, and seats outside under cover**

The perfect break from the M40, this warmly friendly pub has highly
thought-of food and drink. It's attractively decorated with sage-green
paintwork, pale wooden tables and chairs on floorboards, and comfortable
leather sofas by an open fire with a big ornate mirror above. The more
formal restaurant has high rafters, stripped-brick walls and quite an
assortment of dining chairs and tables, and there's a good mix of both
diners and chatty drinkers. Fullers London Pride, Hook Norton Hooky
Bitter and Purity UBU on handpump and 13 wines by the glass. On the
floodlit back terrace are seats and tables under huge retractable awnings;
disabled parking (wheelchair access from side entrance).

Rewarding food includes lunchtime sandwiches, black pudding with poached egg
and crispy pancetta, cornish sardines on toast, burger with cheese, mushroom,
bacon and chips, wild mushroom risotto with white truffle oil, salmon, cod and
smoked haddock fishcakes with a chive beurre blanc, chicken supreme with red
pepper and cream cheese stuffing and potato rösti, stone bass with sautéed samphire
and lemon butter sauce, and puddings. *Benchmark main dish: beer-battered
haddock and chips £11.95. Two-course evening meal £16.00.*

Enterprise ~ Lease Amanda Lake ~ Real ale ~ (01926) 624236 ~ Open 12-3, 5-11;
12-11.30 Sat, Sun ~ Bar food 12-2.30, 6-9; 12-9.30 Sat (snacks in afternoon);
12-4 Sun ~ Restaurant ~ Children welcome ~ Dogs allowed in bar ~ Wi-fi ~
www.granvillebarford.co.uk *Recommended by David M Smith, Simon and Mandy King*

BARSTON   SP1978   Map 4
Malt Shovel ⭐ ♀

*3 miles from M42 junction 5; A4141 towards Knowle, then first left
into Jacobean Lane/Barston Lane; B92 0JP*

**Well run country dining pub full of happy customers, with an
attractive layout, good service and seats in sheltered garden**

Our readers love this pub. It's a thoroughly enjoyable all-rounder
with plenty of drinkers and diners and a warm welcome for all from
the friendly, hands-on landlady. The light and airy bar, its big terracotta
floor tiles neatly offset by dark grouting, rambles extensively around
the zinc-topped central counter, which is painted blue to match the
dado and other panelling; 15 wines are served by the glass, plus Black
Sheep, Oakham JHB and Sharps Doom Bar on handpump. Furnishings
are comfortable, with informal dining chairs and scatter-cushioned
pews around stripped-top tables of varying types and sizes. Cheerful
fruit and vegetable paintings decorate the cream walls and, at one end,
brown slatted blinds give a glimpse of the kitchen; efficient service by
neat young staff. The sheltered back garden with its weeping willow has
picnic-sets, and the terrace and verandah tables have cushions on the
teak seats in summer.

Excellent food from a well judged menu includes summer lunchtime sandwiches, chicken and chorizo patties with guacamole, sour cream and tortilla chips, chinese-spiced confit duck leg with vermicelli noodles and hoi sin sauce, ricotta and spinach tortelloni, steak in ale pudding, corn-fed chicken with melted brie, smoked bacon and raspberry vinegar, delicious fish such as grilled plaice and roasted sweet potato, crab and black tuscan olive dressing or wild turbot with mussels, crayfish, samphire and saffron broth, and puddings such as white chocolate and passion-fruit mousse with candied carrot and mango sorbet, and banana cheesecake with coconut sorbet. *Benchmark main dish: salmon fishcakes with spinach, egg and tarragon hollandaise £13.95. Two-course evening meal £21.00.*

Free house ~ Licensee Helen Somerfield ~ Real ale ~ (01675) 443223 ~ Open 12-11.30 (midnight Sat) ~ Bar food 12-2.30, 6-9.30; 12-4 Sun ~ Restaurant ~ Children welcome ~ Dogs allowed in bar ~ Wi-fi ~ www.themaltshovelatbarston.com *Recommended by Ian Herdman, Di and Mike Gillam, P A Rowe, Roy Shutz, Mike and Mary Carter, Susan and John Douglas*

BIRMINGHAM
Old Joint Stock ♦ £
SP0686 Map 4

Temple Row West; B2 5NY

Big bustling Fullers pie-and-ale pub with impressive Victorian façade and interior, and a small back terrace

To find this extraordinary place, just head for the cathedral – the pub is opposite. The interior is impressively flamboyant: chandeliers hang from the soaring pink and gilt ceiling, gently illuminated busts line the top of the ornately plastered walls and there's a splendid, if well worn, cupola above the centre of the room. Big portraits and smart long curtains create an air of unexpected elegance. Around the walls are plenty of tables and chairs, some in cosy corners, with more on a big dining balcony that overlooks the bar and is reached by a grand staircase. A separate room, with panelling and a fireplace, has a more intimate, clubby feel. As far as we know, this is the northernmost venue to be owned by London brewer Fullers and they keep the full range of Fullers beers on handpump, alongside up to four local guests such as Byatts Urban Red, Castle Rock Harvest Pale, Heritage Revolution and Hook Norton Hooky, 13 wines by the glass and a decent range of malt whiskies, all served from a handsome dark wood island bar counter; daily papers, background music and board games. Most nights see something on in the smart purpose-built little theatre on the first floor, and a small back terrace has some cast-iron tables and chairs and wall-mounted heaters.

Well liked food includes sandwiches, snacks such as beer-battered cod goujons, piri-piri chicken skewers and barbecue pork ribs, plus burger with bacon, smoked cheddar, relish and chips, quinoa, aubergine and feta salad with saffron yoghurt, pork and cider sausages with onion rings and gravy, rump steak and stilton salad, and puddings such as chocolate brownie and vintage ale and molasses sticky toffee pudding. *Benchmark main dish: steak in ale pie £12.75. Two-course evening meal £17.00.*

Fullers ~ Manager Paul Bancroft ~ Real ale ~ (0121) 200 1892 ~ Open 11-11; 12-5 Sun ~ Bar food 12-10; 12-4 Sun ~ Restaurant ~ Children welcome in dining area only ~ Wi-fi ~ Jazz in bar Weds evening, Sun lunchtime ~ www.oldjointstocktheatre.co.uk
Recommended by Andy Dolan, Dave Webster, Sue Holland, Susan and John Douglas, Alan Johnson, Mrs Julie Thomas, Theocsbrian, Barry Collett, Ross Balaam

Pubs close to motorway junctions are listed at the back of the book.

ETTINGTON
Chequers ⭐🍷

SP2748 Map 4

Banbury Road (A422); CV37 7SR

Good enterprising food the main attraction; good drinks too and pretty floodlit garden

This has some of the most comfortable bar chairs we've come across lately, set around one high tripod table and at the counter itself, which has well kept Butcombe Bitter, Greene King IPA and Purity Mad Goose on handpump, and a good choice of wines by the glass. The bar and restaurant areas both have a variety of comfortable and rather elegant dining chairs; big mirrors, a piano and richly figured velvet curtains and wall hangings add to the pampered feeling. On a weekday lunchtime the atmosphere is relaxed and companionable, with unobtrusive nostalgic background music – it's busier at weekends, of course. Service is attentive and personal, and the sheltered garden behind has picnic-table sets on the lawn and stylish terrace tables.

 The very good food, using their own herbs and served in sensibly sized helpings, includes enterprising sandwiches, goats cheese, red onion and rosemary tart with fig salad, an antipasti sharing board, sweet potato gnocchi with butternut squash, cherry tomatoes and stilton sauce, seared hake with wild mushroom linguine and parmesan cream, a pie of the day, a particularly good chicken and chorizo risotto, confit pork belly with tuscan sausage and mixed bean ragoût, and hard-to-resist puddings. Fish night is Tues evening once a month (phone for details). *Benchmark main dish: battered fresh fish and chips £12.50. Two-course evening meal £20.00.*

Free house ~ Licensees James and Kirstin Viggers ~ Real ale ~ (01789) 740387 ~ Open 12-3, 5-11; 12-11 Sat; 12-6 Sun; closed Sun evening, Mon ~ Bar food 12-2.30, 6.30-9.30; 12-3.30 Sun ~ Restaurant ~ Children welcome ~ Dogs allowed in bar ~ Wi-fi ~ www.the-chequers-ettington.co.uk *Recommended by Steve Wilkes, Emma Scofield, Caroline Prescott, Martin and Pauline Jennings*

FARNBOROUGH
Inn at Farnborough ⭐🍷

SP4349 Map 4

Off A423 N of Banbury; OX17 1DZ

Snug bar in civilised dining pub with wide choice of interesting food, both traditional and more elaborate

Surrounded by lovely walks, this golden-stone 16th-c pub is tucked away in a National Trust village. The cosy bar on the right has dark beams and flagstones, some honey-coloured stripped stone, bucket armchairs with scatter cushions and matching window seats, racing car pictures, and a log fire in a big stone fireplace. Purity Gold and UBU on handpump, 19 wines by the glass and several malt whiskies; background music and board games. A second fireplace, open on two sides, with a seat built in around it, divides off a compact two-room dining area with sturdy stripped kitchen tables and high-backed leather chairs; the carpeted inner room has wallpaper imitating shelves of books. There are blue picnic-sets and other seats in the neat sloping garden, which has a big yew tree and a canopied deck. Not a lot of nearby parking.

Highly enjoyable food includes nibbles such as skinny fries with basil aioli, honey and mustard sausages and crudités with harissa hummus, as well as ciabatta sandwiches, shellfish bisque, thai grilled chicken and pawpaw salad, dry-cured ham with free-range eggs and beef dripping chips, angus burgers with toppings and skinny fries, chicken curry, slow-cooked free-range pig cheeks puttanesca with crackling, monkfish, crayfish and saffron risotto, and puddings such as dark chocolate and salted caramel tart with orange blossom ice-cream and lemon crème brûlée with gin and tonic granita. *Benchmark main dish: shin of beef with confit potatoes and blue cheese £17.95. Two-course evening meal £24.00.*

Free house ~ Licensees Anthony and Jo Robinson ~ Real ale ~ (01295) 690615 ~ Open 10-3, 6-11; 10-midnight Sat, Sun ~ Bar food 12-2.45 (3 Sat), 6-10; 12-10 Sun ~ Restaurant ~ Children welcome ~ Dogs allowed in bar ~ Wi-fi ~ www.innatfarnborough.co.uk
Recommended by Michael Tack, R Anderson, Geoff and Linda Payne

---

GAYDON   SP3654   Map 4
Malt Shovel ◗

Under a mile from M40 junction 12; B4451 into village, then over roundabout and across B4100; Church Road; CV35 0ET

Bustling pub in a quiet village with a nice mix of pubby bar and smarter restaurant

With a fine range of drinks and tasty food cooked by the landlord, this cheerful village pub draws a good mix of regulars and visitors. Mahogany-varnished boards through to bright carpeting link the entrance and the bar counter to the right, with a woodburning stove on the left. The central area has a high-pitched ceiling, milk churns and earthenware containers in a loft above the bar, and three steps lead up to a space with comfortable sofas overlooked by a big stained-glass window; reproductions of classic posters line the walls. Adnams Southwold and Broadside, Sharps Doom Bar, Timothy Taylors Landlord and Wells & Youngs Bombardier on handpump, with 11 wines by the glass and two farm ciders. The busy eating area has fresh flowers on a mix of kitchen, pub and dining tables; background music, darts. The jack russell is called Mollie.

Cooked by the landlord, the popular food includes lunchtime sandwiches and baguettes, pâté with plum and apple chutney, smoked haddock welsh rarebit, three-cheese vegetable lasagne, a big breakfast, wild boar and apple sausages in calvados and cider, slow-braised beef in red wine sauce, beer-battered haddock and chips, and puddings such as apple and raspberry pie and bread and butter pudding. *Benchmark main dish: pie of the day £10.95. Two-course evening meal £19.00.*

Enterprise ~ Lease Richard and Debi Morisot ~ Real ale ~ (01926) 641221 ~ Open 11-3, 5-11; 11-11 Fri, Sat; 12-10.30 Sun ~ Bar food 12-2, 6.30-9 ~ Restaurant ~ Children welcome ~ Dogs allowed in bar ~ Wi-fi ~ www.maltshovelgaydon.co.uk
Recommended by George Atkinson, Piotr Chodzko-Zajko, Paul Humphreys, Dave Braisted, David and Shelagh Monks

---

HAMPTON-IN-ARDEN   SP2080   Map 4
White Lion ◗

High Street; handy for M42 junction 6; B92 0AA

Useful village local with six real ales; bedrooms

Opposite a church mentioned in the Domesday Book, this former farmhouse has a good choice of ales. The carpeted bar is nice and relaxed, with assorted furniture trimly laid out, neatly curtained small windows, low-beamed ceilings and some local memorabilia on the fresh cream walls. Banks's Sunbeam, Castle Rock Harvest Pale, Hobsons Best, M&B Brew XI, Purity UBU and Sharps Doom Bar on handpump from the timber-planked bar; background music, TV and board games. The modern dining areas are fresh and airy with light wood and cane chairs on stripped floorboards. The pub is in an attractive village and handy for the NEC. The bedrooms are quiet and comfortable.

🍴 Traditional food includes a wide choice of sandwiches, whitebait with tartare sauce, terrine with crusty bread, beef or chicken burger with cheese, sweet onion jam, coleslaw and chips, coq au vin, a quiche and pie of the day, moules frites, and puddings such as a crumble of the day and chocolate brownie. *Benchmark main dish: pork belly £13.95. Two-course evening meal £18.00.*

Free house ~ Licensee Chris Roach ~ Real ale ~ (01675) 442833 ~ Open 12-11 (midnight Sat); 12-10.30 Sun ~ Bar food 12-2.30, 6-9.30; 12-4 Sun ~ Restaurant ~ Children welcome ~ Dogs welcome ~ Wi-fi ~ Bedrooms: £75/£85 ~ www.thewhitelioninn.com *Recommended by Sara Fulton, Roger Baker, Dr and Mrs A K Clarke, Dr D J and Mrs S C Walker*

HUNNINGHAM
Red Lion
SP3768 Map 4

Village signposted off B4453 Leamington–Rugby just E of Weston, and off B4455 Fosse Way 2.5 miles SW of A423 junction; CV33 9DY

Fine riverside spot for civilised but friendly pub, good range of drinks and well liked food

Light, airy and open-plan, yet cleverly sectioned, in layout, this attractive pub is appealingly furnished. There are pews with scatter cushions, an assortment of antique dining chairs and stools around nice polished tables on bare boards (a few big rugs here and there), contemporary paintwork and walls hung with film and rock star photographs (one long wall is a papered mural of bookshelves); a cosy room has tub armchairs around an open coal fire. Greene King IPA, Old Speckled Hen and a guest beer on handpump, ten wines by the glass and 40 malt whiskies; background music. Windows at one end take in views of the garden, which looks across to the charmingly arched 14th-c bridge over the River Leam; there's plenty of picnic-sets here and at the front and they have a basket of rugs for customers to take outside to sit on – a lovely idea for a warm day.

🍴 Interesting food includes lunchtime sandwiches, sharing boards, pea, ham and mint arancini with apple salad, twice-baked cheese and asparagus soufflé, a pie of the day, chickpea fritters with courgette salad and fig and balsamic dressing, whole rack of Jack Daniels-marinated sticky ribs with coleslaw and chunky chips, chicken and bacon lasagne, confit lamb with celeriac mash, bacon and red wine and mint sauce, king prawn, salmon and garlic risotto, and puddings such as 'New York Rumble' (marshmallows, chocolate brownie, ice-cream, meringue and chocolate sauce) and apple and blackberry crumble. *Benchmark main dish: burger with bacon, cheese and chips £12.00. Two-course evening meal £18.50.*

Greene King ~ Lease Mercedes Grayshon ~ Real ale ~ (01926) 632715 ~ Open 12-11 (10.30 Sun) ~ Bar food 12-9 (8 Sun); also breakfast 11am-midday ~ Restaurant ~ Children welcome ~ Dogs allowed in bar ~ Wi-fi ~ www.redlionhunningham.co.uk *Recommended by Dru and Louisa Marshall, George Atkinson*

ILMINGTON
Howard Arms
SP2143 Map 4

Village signed with Wimpstone off A3400 S of Stratford; CV36 4LT

Lovely mellow-toned interior, lots to look at and enjoyable food and drink; appealing bedrooms

Right by the village green this is a charming golden-stone inn with pretty window boxes in summer. The new licensees have kept the décor much as it was; the attractive beamed rooms have a civilised but easy-going feel and a pleasing variety of furniture ranging from leather or high-backed wooden dining chairs through pews and rustic stools around all manner of tables on rugs, bare boards and some fine, worn flagstones. Also, quite a few prints on gold-painted walls, shelves of books, candles and a log fire in a huge stone inglenook. High stools and chairs line the counter where they keep Hook Norton Hooky, North Cotswold Shagweaver, Timothy Taylors Landlord and Wye Valley Butty Bach on handpump, 30 wines by the glass and a dozen malt whiskies; background music. The big back garden has picnic-sets under parasols and a colourful herbaceous border. The bedrooms are comfortable and the breakfasts good; there are walks on the nearby hills.

Imaginative food includes lunchtime sandwiches, sharing boards, tempura king prawns with oriental salad, corn-fed chicken and leek terrine with tarragon jelly, aubergine parmigiana, burger with cheese, bacon, pickles, home-made relish and chips, lamb rump with ratatouille timbale and port reduction, a fresh fish dish of the day, slow-roasted honey pork belly with pea and potato purée and red onion and apple jus, and puddings such as frozen orange and espresso mousse and chocolate truffle cake with spiced raspberries and rum sauce. *Benchmark main dish: light battered fish and chips £13.50. Two-course evening meal £20.50.*

Free house ~ Licensee Grant Owen ~ Real ale ~ (01608) 682226 ~ Open 11-11; 12-10.30 Sun ~ Bar food 12-3, 6-9.30; 12-8 Sun ~ Restaurant ~ Children welcome ~ Dogs allowed in bar ~ Wi-fi ~ Bedrooms: $90/$120 ~ www.howardarms.com
Recommended by Clive and Fran Dutson, N R White, Mr and Mrs A H Young

LONG COMPTON   SP2832 Map 4
Red Lion
A3400 S of Shipston-on-Stour; CV36 5JS

Traditional character and contemporary touches in comfortably furnished coaching inn; good bedrooms

A firm favourite with both locals and visitors, this is a lovely old coaching inn that gets warm praise year after year. It's also a charming place to stay, with pretty bedrooms, and readers have told us dogs are welcomed too. The spacious, charmingly furnished lounge bar has some exposed stone and beams and nice rambling corners with cushioned settles among pleasantly assorted and comfortable seats and leather armchairs; there are tables on flagstones and carpet, animal prints on warm paintwork and both an open fire and a woodburning stove. Hook Norton Hooky Bitter and a guest such as Wickwar Cotswold Way on handpump and a dozen wines by the glass; the chocolate labrador is called Cocoa. The simple public bar has darts, pool and TV; background music. There are tables and a play area in the big back garden.

Rewarding food includes lunchtime sandwiches, free-range pork and chicken terrine with apple chutney, smoked haddock and sweetcorn chowder, vegetable and lentil cottage pie, battered cod with chips, local sausages with confit onions and smoked bacon gravy, herb-crusted rack of lamb with tomato provençale and rosemary jus, gressingham duck with creamed parsnips and spiced orange and cranberry sauce, and puddings such as blackberry and vanilla crème brûlée and sticky toffee pudding with banana ice-cream. *Benchmark main dish: steak in ale pie £13.95. Two-course evening meal £20.00.*

Cropthorne Inns ~ Manager Lisa Phipps ~ Real ale ~ (01608) 684221 ~ Open 10-2.30, 6-11; 10am-11pm Sat, Sun ~ Bar food 12-2.30, 6-9; 12-9.30 Fri, Sat; 12-9 Sun ~ Restaurant ~ Children welcome ~ Dogs welcome ~ Wi-fi ~ Bedrooms: £60/£90 ~ www.redlion-longcompton.co.uk *Recommended by Bernard Stradling, Barry Collett, J R and P D Holt, Alun and Jennifer Evans, K H Frostick, Clive and Fran Dutson, Lesley Finch, Martin Cawley, P and J Shapley, Sarah Williamson*

LOWER BRAILES
SP3139 Map 4
George

B4035 Shipston–Banbury; OX15 5HN

Handsome stone-built inn dating from 14th c, cheerful landlord and customers and well liked food

Stonemasons working on the interesting church in this lovely village were housed here, so parts of the bar are ancient. This back bar is beamed and panelled and has a cheerful atmosphere helped along by chatty locals. There's also a roomy front bar with dark oak chairs and tables on flagstones and an inglenook fireplace, and a separate restaurant. Hook Norton Hooky, Old Hooky and Lion and a guest such as Wadworths St George & the Dragon on handpump, nine wines by the glass and farm cider; background music, TV, games machine, darts, pool, juke box and board games. Outside there's aunt sally, and picnic-sets (some blue-painted) in the sizeable and sheltered back garden and on the terrace; a few tables and chairs out in front. Good walking nearby.

 The tasty food includes lunchtime sandwiches, chicken liver pâté, platter of smoked fish with cucumber and lime dressing, a pie of the day, broad beans and asparagus risotto, lambs liver and bacon on bubble and squeak, honey-glazed confit duck leg with marmalade sautéed potatoes, beer-battered haddock and chips, and puddings such as hot chocolate fondant and lemon posset. *Benchmark main dish: 8-hour braised lamb shoulder £12.95. Two-course evening meal £17.00.*

Free house ~ Licensee Baggy Saunders ~ Real ale ~ (01608) 685788 ~ Open 12-11 (midnight Fri); 11am-midnight Sat ~ Bar food 12-2.30 (3.30 Sun), 6-9; not Sun evening or Mon ~ Restaurant ~ Children welcome but not in bar after 8pm Fri, Sat ~ Dogs allowed in bar and bedrooms ~ Wi-fi ~ Live music monthly Sat evening ~ Bedrooms: £60/£80 ~ www.thegeorgeatbrailes.co.uk *Recommended by Phoebe Peacock, Peter Brix*

PRESTON BAGOT
SP1765 Map 4
Crabmill

A4189 Henley-in-Arden to Warwick; B95 5EE

Comfortable décor, open fires and particularly good food and drink in mill conversion

Attractively decorated inside, this rambling old cider mill has a civilised but relaxed atmosphere. There are contemporary furnishings and warm colour combinations, and the smart two-level lounge area has comfortable sofas and chairs, low tables, big table lamps and one or two rugs on bare boards. The elegant, low-beamed dining section is roomy with caramel leather banquettes and chairs at pine tables, and a beamed and flagstoned bar area has some stripped-pine country tables and chairs and snug corners; open fires. From the gleaming metal bar they serve Purity UBU, Sharps Doom Bar and Whale Pale Whale on handpump and nine wines by the glass; background music. There are lots of tables (some under cover) in the large, pleasant, decked garden.

Impressive food includes lunchtime sandwiches, twice-baked gruyère with apple, chicory, candied walnuts and cider honey dressing, crab with guacamole, tomato, prawns and bloody mary mayonnaise, vegetarian cannelloni with parmesan topping, a pie of the day, bass fillets and king prawn curry with coconut and mango sambal, three-way duck (breast, liver and mini shepherd's pie) with thyme and honey sauce, and puddings. *Benchmark main dish: pork belly with truffle mash, black pudding and toffee apples £15.95. Two-course evening meal £22.00.*

Free house ~ Licensee Sally Coll ~ Real ale ~ (01926) 843342 ~ Open 11-11; 12-6 Sun ~ Bar food 12-2.30 (3 Fri, Sat), 6.30-9.30; 12-4 Sun ~ Restaurant ~ Children welcome ~ Dogs allowed in bar ~ Wi-fi ~ www.thecrabmill.co.uk *Recommended by Dr Brian Hands, Clive and Fran Dutson, Mrs Blethyn Elliott, Ian Herdman*

 STRATFORD-UPON-AVON   SP2055   Map 4

Bear ♀ ◗ ⛵

Swan's Nest Hotel, just off A3400 Banbury Road, by bridge; CV37 7LT

Great real ale choice in properly pubby bar of large comfortable riverside hotel

Separate and yet part of the Swan's Nest hotel complex, this is an extremely popular, cosy and friendly place. Many are drawn by the fine choice of ales from an impressive row of handpumps on the pewter-topped counter: Bear Bitter (named for them by North Cotswold), Church End Grave Diggers Ale, Everards Tiger, Hook Norton Old Hooky, North Cotswold Best, Wood Farm No 8 and Wye Valley Butty Bach and HPA. Also, 26 wines by the glass and several malt whiskies. The two linked rooms are thoroughly traditional with china and other bric-a-brac on the delft shelf above panelling, a couple of wing armchairs by a fire, a variety of other carefully chosen seats including sofas and scatter-cushioned banquettes, a character settle and a splendid long bench with baluster legs. Big windows look out at the swans on a reach of river between two bridges, and in summer there are teak tables on a waterside lawn beyond the service road. Service is thoroughly professional.

Good value popular food includes lunchtime sandwiches, chicken liver parfait with spiced plum chutney, smoked salmon with beetroot and horseradish quenelle, chicken caesar salad, wild mushroom risotto, fishcakes with tomato provençale, shepherd's pie, beer-battered haddock and chips, and puddings such as warm chocolate cake and caramelised lemon tart. *Benchmark main dish: burger with toppings and chips £8.95. Two-course evening meal £15.00.*

Free house ~ Licensee Simon Taylor ~ Real ale ~ (01789) 265540 ~ Open 12-11 (midnight Fri, Sat) ~ Bar food 12-3, 5-10; all day weekends ~ Restaurant ~ Children welcome ~ Dogs welcome ~ Wi-fi ~ www.thebearfreehouse.co.uk *Recommended by Val and Alan Green, N R White, JHBS*

WELFORD-ON-AVON   SP1452   Map 4

Bell ⭐ ♀ ◗

Off B439 W of Stratford; High Street; CV37 8EB

Warwickshire Dining Pub of the Year

Enjoyably civilised pub with appealing ancient interior, good carefully sourced food, a great range of drinks and seats on pretty terrace

Once they've discovered it, customers tend to come back on a regular basis to this particularly well run 17th-c pub and we hear nothing but

praise for the way the charming licensees and their staff look after them.
The attractive interior – with plenty of signs of the building's venerable age
– is divided into five comfortable areas, each with its own character, from
the cosy terracotta-painted bar to a light and airy gallery room with antique
wood panelling, solid oak floor and contemporary Lloyd Loom chairs.
Flagstone floors, stripped or well polished antique or period-style furniture
and three good fires (one in an inglenook) add warmth and cosiness.
Hobsons Best, Purity Pure Gold and UBU and a guest on handpump and
18 wines (including prosecco and champagne) by the glass; background
music. In summer, the virginia creeper-covered exterior is festooned with
colourful hanging baskets. The lovely garden has solid teak furniture,
a vine-covered terrace, water features and gentle lighting. This riverside
village has a handsome church and pretty thatched black and white
cottages and is certainly worth exploring.

Using the best local produce and listing their suppliers on the menu, the
highly enjoyable food includes lunchtime sandwiches, crayfish, prawn and
melon cocktail, chicken liver pâté with red onion and redcurrant marmalade,
brunch (not Sunday), chicken and crispy bacon caesar salad, faggots with sage
and onion gravy, spinach and ricotta tortellini with tomato and basil sauce,
garlic-roasted chicken with wild mushroom and madeira sauce, bass wrapped
in prosciutto on crispy potato and chives with a sun-dried tomato dressing, and
puddings such as chocolate pot with chantilly cream and morello cherry steamed
pudding with custard; they hold regular themed food evenings. *Benchmark main
dish: pie of the day £13.75. Two-course evening meal £19.50.*

Laurel (Enterprise) ~ Lease Colin and Teresa Ombler ~ Real ale ~ (01789) 750353 ~
Open 11.30-3, 6-11; 11.30-11.30 Sat; 11.45-10.30 Sun ~ Bar food 11.45-2.30, 6-9.30 (10
Fri); 11.45-10 Sat; 11.45-9.30 Sun ~ Children welcome ~ www.thebellwelford.co.uk
*Recommended by Mike and Mary Carter, Sarah Everson, Mrs D L Wilson, Beryl Chisholm,
P B Smith, Kim Andrews, Peter Elliott, Ron Corbett, Susan and John Douglas, Hugh Roberts*

Also Worth a Visit in Warwickshire

Besides the fully inspected pubs, you might like to try these pubs that
have been recommended to us and described by readers. Do tell us what
you think of them: feedback@goodguides.com

ALDRIDGE   SK0900
Old Irish Harp (01922) 455968
*Chester Road, Little Aston (A452 over
Staffordshire border); WS9 0LP* Popular
modernised pub with good choice of
enjoyable food including speciality rotisserie
chicken, set deals Mon-Fri, Banks's Bitter,
Jennings Cumberland and Marstons
Pedigree, extensive dining area; free wi-fi;
children welcome (they eat for free 3-7pm
weekdays when adults buy food), plenty
of seats outside, open all day. *(Clifford
Blakemore)*

ALVESTON   SP2356
Ferry (01789) 269883
*Ferry Lane; end of village, off B4086
Stratford–Wellesbourne; CV37 7QX*
Comfortable and stylish beamed dining
pub, good imaginative food along with pub
favourites, reasonable prices, ales such as

Hook Norton, Sharps and Wells & Youngs,
friendly staff; nice spot with seats out in
front, open all day Sat, closed Sun evening
and first Mon of month. *(R J Herd)*

ARMSCOTE   SP2444
★ **Fuzzy Duck** (01608) 682635
*Off A3400 Stratford–Shipston;
CV37 8DD* Stylishly reworked former 18th-c
coaching inn; beams, flagstones and fine
fireplaces mixing with modern furnishings
in bar and restaurant, well kept ales such
as Purity Mad Goose and nice wines by the
glass, good well presented food using local
produce, efficient friendly staff; children
welcome and dogs (get a special pack if
staying overnight), wicker seats under
parasols on deck, four pretty bedrooms
named after ducks and stocked with Baylis
& Harding toiletries (the family own the
pub), open all day Fri and Sat, closed Sun
evening, Mon. *(Anon)*

AVON DASSETT   SP4049
Avon Inn (01295) 690036
Off B4100 Banbury–Warwick; CV47 2AS
Double-fronted mellow-stone village pub
refurbished and given italian theme,
welcoming helpful staff, good italian food,
decent wines and a couple of real ales;
background and some live music; children
welcome, picnic-sets out in front by quiet
road, small side garden, charming village on
slopes of Burton Dassett Hills Country Park,
open all day. *(Anon)*

BARSTON   SP2078
★Bulls Head (01675) 442830
*From M42 junction 5, A4141 towards
Warwick, first left, then signed down
Barston Lane; B92 0JU* Unassuming and
unspoilt partly Tudor village pub, four well
kept ales such as Adnams, Purity, Woodfordes
and Wye Valley, popular traditional home-
made food from sandwiches to specials,
friendly helpful staff, log fires, comfortable
lounge with pictures and plates, oak-beamed
bar and separate dining room; children
and dogs allowed, good-sized secluded
garden alongside pub and barn, open all day
Fri-Sun. *(Clive and Fran Dutson)*

BAXTERLEY   SP2796
Rose (01827) 713939
Main Road; CV9 2LE Welcoming pub
opposite village pond in former coal mining
country, Bass, St Austell Tribute, Wells &
Youngs Bombardier and a guest, fairly priced
traditional food including Sun carvery, open
fires; dogs welcome in bar, good-sized garden,
open all day Fri-Sun. *(Anon)*

BINLEY WOODS   SP3977
Roseycombe (024) 7654 1022
Rugby Road; CV3 2AY Warm and friendly
1930s pub with wide choice of bargain home-
made food, Bass and Theakstons, Weds quiz
night, some live music; children welcome,
big garden. *(Alan Johnson, Roger and Donna
Huggins)*

BIRMINGHAM   SP0788
★Bartons Arms (0121) 333 5988
High Street, Aston (A34); B6 4UP
Magnificent Edwardian landmark, an oasis
in a rather daunting area, impressive linked
richly decorated rooms from the palatial to
the snug, original tilework murals, stained
glass and mahogany, decorative fireplaces,
sweeping stairs to handsome upstairs rooms,
well kept Oakham ales and a guest from
ornate island bar with snob screens in one
section, interesting imported bottled beers
and frequent mini beer festivals, nice choice
of well priced thai food, good young staff;
open all day. *(Andy Dolan)*

BIRMINGHAM   SP0688
Lord Clifden (0121) 523 7515
*Great Hampton Street (Jewellery
Quarter); B18 6AA* Fairly traditional
with leather banquettes and padded stools
around dimpled copper-top tables, bustling
atmosphere, wide choice of good value
generous food from sandwiches to daily specials,
Wye Valley and guests, continental beers,
prompt friendly service, interesting collection
of street art including Banksy's, darts in front
bare-boards section; sports TVs (outside too),
Thurs quiz night and weekend DJs; plenty of
seats in enclosed part-covered beer garden
with table tennis and table football, open all
day (till late Fri, Sat). *(Anon)*

BIRMINGHAM   SP0786
Old Contemptibles (0121) 236 5264
Edmund Street; B3 2HB Spacious well
restored Edwardian corner pub with lofty
ceiling and lots of woodwork, decent choice
of real ales (customers vote for guest beers),
enjoyable well priced food including range
of sausages and pies, friendly efficient young
staff; upstairs lavatories; no children, handy
central location, popular at lunchtime
with office workers, open all day (till 6pm
Sun). *(Andy Dolan, Alan Johnson)*

BIRMINGHAM   SP0784
Old Moseley Arms (0121) 440 1954
Tindal Street; B12 9QU Tucked-away
Victorian pub with four well kept ales
including Enville and Wye Valley (regular
festivals), keenly priced indian snacks and
full meals (all day Sun); juke box; outside
seating area, handy for Edgbaston cricket
ground, open all day. *(Chris and Angela
Buckell)*

BIRMINGHAM   SP0686
Pennyblacks (0121) 632 1460
*Mailbox shopping mall, Wharfside
Street; B1 1RQ* Recently revamped
contemporary bar in good canalside spot;
spacious well divided interior including
some booth seating, wall paintings and
neon, several real ales (third of a pint
glasses available), extensive wine range and
cocktails, enjoyable food; DJ nights, Sky
Sports, free wi-fi; seats out by water, open
all day till late. *(Andy Dolan)*

BIRMINGHAM   SP0686
Post Office Vaults (0121) 643 7354
New Street/Pinfold Street; B2 4BA
Two entrances to this simple downstairs bar
with 13 interesting ciders/perries, eight real

A star symbol before the name of a pub shows exceptional character and appeal.
It doesn't mean extra comfort. Even quite a basic pub can win a star,
if it's individual enough.

ales including Hobsons and Salopian and over 300 international bottled beers, friendly knowledgeable staff, no food; handy for New Street station, open all day. *(Mike and Eleanor Anderson)*

BIRMINGHAM SP0586
Prince of Wales (0121) 643 9460
Cambridge Street; B1 2NP Traditional 19th-c pub behind the repertory theatre and symphony hall; L-shaped bar with friendly mix of customers, eight well kept beers such as Enville, Purity, Timothy Taylors and Tetleys, bargain straightforward food (not Sun, Mon), friendly service; may be background music (live Thurs, Sun); popular with Grand Union Canal users in summer, open all day (till 2am Fri, Sat). *(Stephen and Jean Curtis)*

BIRMINGHAM SP0687
Rose Villa (0121) 236 7910
By clock in Jewellery Quarter (Warstone Lane/Vyse Street); B18 6JW Listed 1920s building with panelled front saloon leading through to small but magnificent bar, floor-to-ceiling green tiles and massive tiled arch over fireplace, original parquet flooring and impressive stained glass, quirky touches such as antler chandeliers and a red phone box, four or five well kept ales including Sharps Doom Bar, cocktails, reasonably priced food from american diner menu; live music and DJs Fri, Sat till late – can get very busy; open all day, from 11am weekends for brunch. *(Anon)*

BIRMINGHAM SP0686
★ Wellington (0121) 200 3115
Bennetts Hill; B2 5SN Old-fashioned high-ceilinged pub with superb range of changing beers (listed on TV screens – order by number), most from small breweries and always one from Black Country Ales, also farm ciders, experienced landlord, friendly staff and nice pub cat, no food but plates and cutlery if you bring your own, regular beer festivals and quiz nights, can get very busy; tables out behind, open all day. *(Andy Dolan, Eddie Gallacher, Dr and Mrs A K Clarke, Dave Webster, Sue Holland, Alan Johnson)*

BLOXWICH SJ9902
★ Turf (01922) 407745
Wolverhampton Road, off A34 just S of A4124; WS3 2EZ Affectionately known as Tinky's, this unchanging terraced pub has been run by the same family for 140 years; entrance hall like a 1930s home, public bar through door on right (reminiscent of a waiting room) with wooden slatted wall benches and three small tables on fine tiled floor, William Morris curtains and wallpaper and simple fireplace, more comfortable old smoking room and tiny back parlour, friendly landladies and chatty locals, Holdens, Oakham, Otter and a couple of guests, no

food; lavatories at end of simple garden; closed Mon-Thurs lunchtimes. *(Anon)*

BRIERLEY HILL SO9286
★ Vine (01384) 78293
B4172 between A461 and (nearer) A4100; immediately after the turn into Delph Road; DY5 2TN Popular Black Country pub (aka the Bull & Bladder) offering a true taste of the West Midlands; down-to-earth welcome and friendly chatty locals in meandering series of rooms, each different in character, traditional front bar with wall benches and simple leatherette-topped oak stools, comfortable extended snug with solidly built red plush seats, tartan-decorated back bar with brass chandeliers, well kept and priced Bathams from brewery next door, a couple of simple very cheap lunchtime dishes (no credit cards); TV, games machine, darts and dominoes; children and dogs welcome, tables in backyard, open all day. *(Anon)*

BROOM SP0853
Broom Tavern (01789) 773666
High Street; off B439 in Bidford; B50 4HL Refurbished 16th-c brick and timber village pub, relaxed and welcoming, with good interesting food from chef-owners, three real ales, black beams and log fire, Mon quiz; children welcome, tables out on grass either side, handy for Ragley Hall, open all day weekends. *(Anon)*

CLAVERDON SP2064
★ Red Lion (01926) 842291
Station Road; B4095 towards Warwick; CV35 8PE Popular beamed Tudor dining pub with good food (all day Sun) from pub favourites up, friendly attentive service, decent wines and well kept Purity Mad Goose, log fires, linked rooms including back dining area with country views over sheltered heated deck and gardens; open all day. *(Ian Herdman)*

COVENTRY SP3279
Old Windmill (024) 7625 1717
Spon Street; CV1 3BA Timber-framed 15th-c pub with lots of tiny rooms (known locally as Ma Brown's), exposed beams in uneven ceilings, carved oak seats on flagstones, inglenook woodburner, half a dozen well kept ales along with traditional ciders and a perry, pubby food till 6pm (not Sun, Mon); popular with students and busy at weekends, games machines and juke box, darts, no credit cards; closed Mon lunchtime, otherwise open all day. *(Anon)*

COVENTRY SP3379
Town Wall (024) 7622 0963
Bond Street, among car parks behind Belgrade Theatre; CV1 4AH Busy Victorian city-centre local with half a dozen real ales including Bass in top condition, farm cider, food from lunchtime doorstep

sandwiches to hearty dishes such as rabbit pie, unspoilt basic front bar and tiny snug, engraved windows, bigger back lounge with actor/playwright photographs and pictures of old Coventry, open fires; big-screen sports TV; open all day. *(Howard and Margaret Buchanan, Alan Johnson, Ian Barritt)*

COVENTRY   SP3378
Whitefriars (024) 7625 1655
Gosford Street; CV1 5DL Pair of well preserved medieval townhouses, three old-fashioned rooms on both floors, lots of ancient beams, timbers and furniture, flagstones, cobbles and coal fire, five well kept changing ales, daily papers, bar lunches (not weekends); some live music, no children inside unless eating; smokers' shelter on good-sized terrace behind, open all day (1am Fri, Sat). *(Alan Johnson)*

DUDLEY   SO9591
Bottle & Glass
Black Country Museum, Tipton Road; DY1 4SQ Reconstructed alehouse moved here as were other buildings in this extensive open-air working museum (well worth a visit for its re-created period village complete with shops, fairground, school, barge wharf and tram system); friendly staff in costume, three well kept local beers, chunky filled rolls, front parlour and back room with piano, wall benches, sawdust on old boards, two fires. *(George Atkinson)*

DUNCHURCH   SP4871
Green Man (01788) 810210
Daventry Road; CV22 6NS Small beamed village pub with enjoyable home-made food at reasonable prices, four well kept beers such as Greene King, St Austell, Timothy Taylors and Wells & Youngs, decent wines by the glass, good friendly service, open fire, pool; children welcome, picnic-sets and play area on back lawn, bedrooms. *(P M Newsome)*

EASENHALL   SP4679
★ Golden Lion (01788) 833577
Main Street; CV23 0JA Spotless bar in 16th-c part of busy comfortable hotel, low beams, dark panelling, settles and inglenook log fire, well kept changing ales such as Wells & Youngs, enjoyable food including good Sun carvery, friendly helpful service; background music; children welcome, disabled access, tables out at side and on spacious lawn, 20 well equipped bedrooms, attractive village, open all day. *(Gerry and Rosemary Dobson, M J Winterton)*

EDGE HILL   SP3747
★ Castle (01295) 670255
Off A422; OX15 6DJ Curious crenellated octagonal tower built 1742 as gothic folly (it marks where Charles I raised his standard at start of Battle of Edgehill); major revamp under new owners creating bar and four dining areas, plenty of original features including arched windows and doorways, beams and stone fireplaces, fantastic views (some floor-to-ceiling windows), good food (not Sun evening), deli bar for sandwiches, coffee and afternoon teas, well kept Hook Norton ales, friendly enthusiastic young staff; downstairs lavatories; children welcome, seats in lovely big garden with more outstanding views, beautiful Compton Wynyates nearby, open all day Sat, till 7pm Sun. *(G Jennings, Susan and John Douglas)*

FENNY COMPTON   SP4152
Merrie Lion (01295) 771134
Brook Street; CV47 2YH Refurbished early 18th-c beamed village pub; three well kept beers including one badged for them, decent range of wines and good freshly made food from pubby choices up, friendly welcoming atmosphere; tables outside, handy for Burton Dassett Hills Country Park, open all day weekends. *(Mr and Mrs Miles and Tracey Forsyth, John and Sharon Hancock)*

FILLONGLEY   SP2787
Cottage (01676) 540599
Black Hall Lane; CV7 8EG Popular country dining pub on village outskirts, wholesome good value food including early bird and OAP deals, beers such as Marstons, St Austell and Timothy Taylors, friendly caring service; back terrace and lawn overlooking fields, closes Sun evening at 6pm. *(Graham and Elizabeth Hargreaves)*

FIVE WAYS   SP2270
★ Case is Altered (01926) 484206
Follow Rowington signs at junction roundabout off A4177/A4141 N of Warwick, then right into Case Lane; CV35 7JD Convivial unspoilt old cottage licensed for over three centuries; Old Pie Factory ales and three guests served by friendly landlady, no food, simple small main bar with fine old poster of Lucas, Blackwell & Arkwright Brewery (now flats), clock with hours spelling out Thornleys Ale (another defunct brewery), and just a few sturdy old-fashioned tables and couple of stout leather-covered settles facing each other over spotless tiles, modest little back room with old bar billiards table (it takes sixpences); no children, dogs or mobiles; full disabled access, stone table on little brick courtyard. *(Kerry Law)*

FLECKNOE   SP5163
Old Olive Bush (01788) 891134
Off A425 W of Daventry; CV23 8AT Unspoilt little Edwardian pub in quiet photogenic village, friendly chatty atmosphere, enjoyable traditional food cooked by landlady, well kept changing ales and decent wines, open fire in bar with stripped-wood floor, steps up to games room with table skittles, small dining room with etched glass windows and another fire;

children welcome, pretty garden, closed Mon, weekday lunchtimes. *(George Atkinson)*

FRANKTON   SP4270
Friendly (01926) 632430
Just over a mile S of B4453 Leamington Spa–Rugby; Main Street; CV23 9NY
This popular old low-ceilinged village pub lives up to its name, also serves good home-made food such as rabbit pie and four real ales, wines in mini bottles, two neat rooms, open fire. *(Ted George)*

GREAT WOLFORD   SP2434
★Fox & Hounds (01608) 674220
Village signed on right on A3400, 3 miles S of Shipston-on-Stour; CV36 5NQ
Delightful unspoilt 16th-c inn with helpful friendly staff; inglenook log fire with bread oven, low hop-strung beams, appealing collection of old furniture including tall pews on flagstones, motley assortment of antique hunting prints, vintage photographs and so on, Hook Norton, Purity and a guest from old-fashioned tap room, good creative cooking using local ingredients (not Sun evening or two weeks in Jan), home-baked bread; outside lavatories; children and dogs welcome, terrace with solid wooden furniture and a well, three bedrooms, closed Sun evening, Mon. *(M Mossman, Clive and Fran Dutson)*

HALFORD   SP2645
Halford (01789) 748217
A429 Fosse Way; CV36 5BN Cotswold-stone inn handy if walking Fosse Way; pastel-walled bar on right of cobbled entry with lattice-decorated dining chairs around chunky tables, bay window seats and leather sofa by woodburner, Hook Norton Old Hooky and St Austell Tribute, well liked generously served food, unusual rustic benches and table in back room, partly flagstoned restaurant on left with dark wooden tables and chairs and another fire; background music; teak furniture in spacious old coachyard, water feature and contemporary ironwork, 11 comfortable modern bedrooms, open all day. *(Richard Tilbrook, K H Frostick)*

HAMPTON LUCY   SP2557
Boars Head (01789) 840533
Church Street, E of Stratford; CV35 8BE
Roomy two-bar local next to lovely church, changing real ales and enjoyable good value pubby food, friendly service, low beams and log fire; soft background music; secluded back garden, pretty village near Charlecote House (NT). *(Anon)*

HARBORNE   SP0384
Plough (0121) 427 3678
High Street; B17 9NT Popular quirky place with enjoyable range of food including stone-baked pizzas and chargrilled burgers, regular offers, well kept Purity, Wye Valley and a guest, plenty of wines by the glass and some

50 whiskies, good coffee too; background music; well behaved children welcome, garden with covered area, open all day from 8am (9am weekends) for breakfast. *(Anon)*

HARBOROUGH MAGNA   SP4779
Old Lion (01788) 833238
3 miles from M6 junction 1; B4112 Pailton Road; CV23 0HQ Welcoming village pub stylishly refurbished with emphasis on good food, friendly attentive staff, good choice of wines, Greene King ales; closed Mon lunchtime, otherwise open all day. *(Anon)*

HATTON   SP2367
★Falcon (01926) 484281
Birmingham Road, Haseley (A4177, not far from M40 junction 15); CV35 7HA
Smartly refurbished dining pub with relaxing rooms around island bar, lots of stripped brickwork and low beams, tiled and oak-planked floors, good moderately priced food (not Sun evening) from sandwiches and pub favourites up, friendly service, nice choice of wines by the glass, well kept Marstons-related ales, barn-style back restaurant; children welcome, disabled facilities, garden (dogs allowed here) with heated covered terrace, eight bedrooms in converted barn, open all day. *(Andy Dolan)*

HENLEY-IN-ARDEN   SP1566
★Bluebell (01564) 793049
High Street (A3400, off M40 junction 16); B95 5AT Impressive timber-framed dining pub with fine coach entrance, emphasis on imaginative food (not Sun evening) from sandwiches to restaurant-style dishes, cheaper lunchtime/early evening set menu (Tues-Fri), cheerful helpful staff, rambling old beamed and flagstoned interior with contemporary furnishings creating a stylish but relaxed atmosphere, big fireplace, well kept ales such as Church End and Purity, 20 wines by the glass, good coffee and afternoon teas, daily papers; may be background music; children welcome if eating, dogs allowed, tables on back decking, closed Mon, otherwise open all day. *(R J Herd, Ian Herdman)*

ILMINGTON   SP2143
Red Lion (01608) 682366
Front Street; CV36 4LX Popular stone-built village pub, flagstoned bar with fire on one side of central servery, dining room the other, well kept Hook Norton and good food cooked by landlady; secluded garden. *(K H Frostick)*

KENILWORTH   SP2872
Clarendon Arms (01926) 852017
Castle Hill; CV8 1NB Busy pub opposite castle and under same ownership as next door Harringtons restaurant; well kept Hook Norton, Sharps, Wye Valley and a local guest, tasty reasonably priced pub food,

several rooms off long bare-boards bustling bar, largish peaceful upstairs dining room, cheerful young staff; children welcome, dogs in bar, metal tables on small raised terrace, daytime car park fee deducted from food bill, open all day Fri-Sun. *(Andy Dolan, Alan Johnson)*

KENILWORTH SP2872
Cross (01926) 853840
New Street; CV8 2EZ Smart 19th-c restaurant-pub under newish ownership, good enterprising food (not cheap), 18 wines by the glass and a couple of ales such as Caledonian and Wells & Youngs, open-plan split-level interior with view into kitchen; terrace and small garden, closed Mon. *(Clive and Fran Dutson)*

KENILWORTH SP2871
Queen & Castle (01926) 852661
Castle Green; CV8 1ND Modernised beamed Mitchells & Butlers dining pub opposite castle, good range of enjoyable food including weekday set menu (till 6pm), plenty of wines by the glass; children welcome, open all day. *(Dr D J and Mrs S C Walker)*

KENILWORTH SP2872
★Virgins & Castle (01926) 853737
High Street; CV8 1LY Maze of intimate rooms off inner servery, small snugs by entrance corridor, flagstones, heavy beams, lots of woodwork including booth seating, coal fire, four well kept Everards ales and a couple of guests, good food at reasonable prices, friendly service, games bar upstairs, restaurant; children in eating areas, disabled facilities, tables in sheltered garden, parking can be a problem, open all day. *(Roger and Donna Huggins, Dr D J and Mrs S C Walker)*

KNOWLE SP1875
Kings Arms (01564) 771177
Warwick Road, A4110, about a mile S; B93 0EE Popular beamed Mitchells & Butlers dining pub, recently refurbished but keeping character, extensive choice of enjoyable food including good value weekday set menu till 6pm, Brakspears Oxford Gold, Marstons Pedigree and a couple of guests, plenty of wines by the glass (taster sets of three 50ml glasses available), smart efficient young staff, attractive interesting décor, big dining room overlooking Grand Union Canal; lots of tables out by the water, moorings, Innkeeper's Lodge bedrooms, open all day. *(David Green, Dennis and Doreen Haward)*

LADBROKE SP4158
Bell (01926) 811224
Signed off A423 S of Southam; CV47 2BY Refurbished beamed country pub set back from the road, smallish bar with tub chairs by log fire, snug off with library wallpaper and another fire in little brick fireplace, three ales including Ringwood and plenty of wines by the glass, enjoyable food from pub favourites and grills up, weekday set menu, airy restaurant with light oak flooring; background music, free wi-fi; children and dogs (in bar) welcome, a few picnic-sets out in front and on side grass, pleasant surroundings, closed Sun evening, Mon. *(John Marshall)*

LAPWORTH SP1871
★Boot (01564) 782464
Old Warwick Road; B4439 Hockley Heath–Warwick – 2.8 miles from M40 junction 1, but from southbound carriageway only, and return only to northbound; B94 6JU Popular upmarket dining pub near Stratford Canal, good range of food from interesting menu including weekday fixed-price offer, efficient cheerful young staff, upscale wines, Purity UBU and St Austell Tribute, stripped beams and dark panelling, big antique hunting prints, cushioned pews and bucket chairs on ancient quarry tiles and bare boards, warm fire, charming low-raftered upstairs dining room; background music; children and good-natured dogs welcome, teak tables, some under extendable canopy on side terrace, and picnic-sets on grass beyond, nice walks, open all day. *(W M Lien)*

LAPWORTH SP1970
Navigation (01564) 783337
Old Warwick Road (B4439 SE); B94 6NA Refurbished beamed pub by the Grand Union Canal; slate-floor bar with woodburner, bare-boards snug and restaurant, well kept ales such as Banks's, Byatts, Purity, Timothy Taylors and Wadworths, unusually Guinness also on handpump, decent wines and enjoyable good value food (all day Fri-Sun) from sandwiches and other bar choices up, charming staff; children welcome, dogs in bar, covered terrace and waterside garden, handy for Packwood House and Baddesley Clinton (both NT), open all day. *(W M Lien)*

LAPWORTH SP1872
Punch Bowl (01564) 784564
Not far from M42 junction 4, off old Warwick–Hockley Heath Road; B94 6HR Completely reconstructed using old beams etc, main emphasis on dining with good range of well presented interesting food from lunchtime sandwiches/panini and light dishes up, stools along bar for drinkers, Greene King IPA and Wells & Youngs Bombardier, friendly efficient staff; garden picnic-sets, open all day. *(R J Herd)*

LEAMINGTON SPA SP3165
Benjamin Satchwell (01926) 883733
The Parade; CV32 4AQ Spacious Wetherspoons stretching back to street behind, tidy and airy, with a dozen ales from long servery, their usual affordably priced food, quick friendly service, two levels

with some cosy seating; children welcome, disabled facilities, open all day from 7am. *(George Atkinson)*

LEAMINGTON SPA   SP3165
Cricketers Arms (01926) 881293
Archery Road; CV31 3PT Friendly town local opposite bowling greens; enjoyable fairly priced food using meat from good local butcher, popular Sun roasts (till 6pm), also nice home-made sausage rolls and scotch eggs, well kept Slaughterhouse and a couple of guests such as Timothy Taylors from central bar, Weston's cider, comfortable banquettes, some panelling and cricketing memorabilia, open fires; darts, sports TV, fortnightly quiz Mon; children and dogs welcome, heated back terrace, open all day. *(Lee Fraser, Geoffrey and Penny Hughes, Tony and Wendy Hobden)*

LEEK WOOTTON   SP2868
Anchor (01926) 853355
Warwick Road; CV35 7QX Neat and well run dining lounge popular for its good fresh food including fish specials, well kept Bass, Hook Norton Old Hooky and two guests, good selection of affordably priced wines and soft drinks, attentive friendly service, lots of close-set tables, smaller overflow dining area; background music, sports TV; children welcome, no dogs inside, long garden behind with play area, open all day Sun. *(Ian Herdman)*

LIGHTHORNE   SP3455
Antelope (01926) 651188
Old School Lane, Bishops Hill; a mile SW of B4100 N of Banbury; CV35 0AU Attractive early 18th-c stone-built pub in pretty village setting, two neatly kept comfortable bars (one old, one newer), separate dining area, beams, flagstones and big open fire, well kept ales such as Greene King IPA, Sharps Doom Bar, Slaughterhouse and Warwickshire, enjoyable food from good sandwiches up, friendly effective service; children welcome, picnic-sets out by well and on small grassy area, open all day. *(Clive and Fran Dutson)*

LITTLE COMPTON   SP2530
★ Red Lion (01608) 674397
Off A44 Moreton-in-Marsh to Chipping Norton; GL56 0RT Low-beamed 16th-c Cotswold-stone inn, enjoyable good value food cooked by landlady from pubby choices up, Donnington ales and good choice of wines by the glass, snug alcoves, inglenook woodburner; darts and pool in public bar; well behaved children and dogs welcome,

pretty side garden with aunt sally, two nice bedrooms. *(Bernard Stradling, R K Phillips, Grahame Brooks)*

LONG ITCHINGTON   SP4165
Buck & Bell (01926) 811177
A423 N of Southam; The Green; CV47 9PH Attractively laid-out dining pub with plenty of character in several linked rambling areas, good choice of food including lunchtime set menu, decent wines by the glass and well kept ales such as Banks's, Holdens, Marstons and Sharps, efficient staff, big log fireplaces, hunting prints and interesting variety of seating around cast-iron-framed tables, elegantly furnished flagstoned restaurant, stairs up to carpeted gallery; background music; tables on back verandah, more in front looking across village green and rookery, open all day. *(Dr Kevan Tucker, Andy Dolan, Clive and Fran Dutson, Dru and Louisa Marshall, George Atkinson and others)*

LOWER GORNAL   SO9191
Fountain (01384) 242777
Temple Street; DY3 2PE Lively two-room local with eight well kept ales including Greene King, Hobsons and RCH, draught continentals, real ciders and country wines too, enjoyable inexpensive food (not Sun evening), back dining area, pigs-and-pen skittles; background music; garden behind, open all day. *(Anon)*

LYE   SO9284
★ Windsor Castle (01384) 895230
Stourbridge Road (corner A458/A4036; car park in Pedmore Road just above traffic lights – don't be tempted to use the next-door restaurant's parking!); DY9 7DG Focus on the interesting well kept beers from impressive row of ten handpumps including own Sadlers ales (brewery tours available); central flagstoned part is functionally furnished with bar stools by counter and by cask table, a tall tripod table and a window-shelf overlooking the road, several snugger rooms off with bare boards or carpet, some brewing memorabilia, enjoyable food (not Sun evening) using free-range and local produce; children welcome, disabled facilities, picnic-sets on side terrace plus some verandah seating, handy for Lye station, open all day. *(Anon)*

MONKS KIRBY   SP4682
Bell (01788) 832352
Just off B4027 W of Pailton; CV23 0QY Popular pub run by hospitable long-serving spanish landlord, lived-in interior with

dark beams, timber dividers, flagstones and cobbles, wide choice of good spanish food including starters doubling as tapas, fine range of spanish wines and of brandies and malt whiskies, two well kept Greene King ales, relaxed informal service; appropriate background music; children and dogs welcome, streamside back terrace with country view, closed Mon. *(Susan and John Douglas)*

NAPTON   SP4560
Folly (01926) 815185
Off A425 towards Priors Hardwick; Folly Lane, by locks; CV47 8NZ Beamed brick pub in lovely spot on Oxford Canal by Napton locks and Folly Bridge (113): three bars on different levels, mix of furnishings and two big log fires, lots of pictures, old framed photographs and other memorabilia, enjoyable home-made food (not Sun evening), well kept ales including Hook Norton, friendly happy staff; children and dogs welcome. *(Anon)*

NETHER WHITACRE   SP2292
Gate (01675) 481292
Gate Lane; B46 2DS Warmly welcoming traditional community pub with well kept Marstons-related ales and guests, good honest local food, different rooms reflecting generations of expansion and change, conservatory, games room with pool; no credit cards; children welcome, garden picnic-sets, open all day. *(David M Smith)*

NETHERTON   SO9488
★ **Old Swan** (01384) 253075
Halesowen Road (A459 just S of centre); DY2 9PY Victorian tavern full of traditional character and known locally as Ma Pardoe's after a former long-serving landlady; wonderfully unspoilt front bar with big swan centrepiece in patterned enamel ceiling, engraved mirrors, traditional furnishings and old-fashioned cylinder stove, other rooms including cosy back snug and more modern lounge, good value own-brewed ales, wholesome bar food (not Sun evening), upstairs restaurant; no under-16s; dogs allowed in bar, open all day (Sun break 4-7pm). *(Anon)*

NEWBOLD ON STOUR   SP2446
White Hart (01789) 450205
A3400 S of Stratford; CV37 8TS Welcoming dining pub in same family for many years, proper pubby atmosphere, with good varied home-made food (not Sun evening) including specials board, Adnams Southwold and Purity Mad Goose, nice wines, long airy beamed bar with good log fire in large stone fireplace, flagstones and big bay windows, roomy back bar and separate dining room, ring the bull; children and dogs welcome, picnic-sets out at front and on back lawned area, open all day weekends. *(JHBS, Lois Dyer)*

NUNEATON   SP3790
Attleborough Arms (024) 7638 3231
Highfield Road, Attleborough; CV11 4PL Large fairly recently rebuilt pub, nicely open, modern and comfortable, with wide choice of enjoyable low-priced food including Thurs grill night, good range of Marstons-related beers and a dozen wines by the glass, helpful attentive service; disabled access, open all day. *(David Green)*

OFFCHURCH   SP3665
★ **Stag** (01926) 425801
N of Welsh Road, off A425 at Radford Semele; CV33 9AQ Refurbished 16th-c thatched and beamed village pub, oak-floored bar with log fires and buoyant atmosphere, Purity and Warwickshire ales, a dozen wines by the glass, good interesting food served by friendly efficient young staff, more formal cosy restaurant areas with bold wallpaper, striking fabrics, animal heads and big mirrors; children and dogs (in bar) welcome, nice garden with black furniture on terrace, open all day. *(W M Lien, Roy Shutz)*

OXHILL   SP3149
★ **Peacock** (01295) 688060
Off A422 Stratford–Banbury; CV35 0QU Popular pleasantly upgraded stone-built country pub, good varied menu including special offers, friendly attentive young staff, three well kept ales including a house beer from Wychwood (May, Aug beer festivals), good selection of wines by the glass, cosy beamed bar with big solid tables and woodburner, half-panelled bare-boards dining room; light background music; children welcome, dogs in bar (friendly resident retriever), nice back garden, pretty village, open all day. *(K H Frostick, George Atkinson, JHBS)*

PRINCETHORPE   SP4070
Three Horseshoes (01926) 632345
High Town; junction A423/B4453; CV23 9PR Friendly old beamed village pub with Marstons EPA and Pedigree and Wells & Youngs Bombardier, enjoyable traditional food including children's choices, good service, decorative plates, pictures, comfortable settles and chairs, two restaurant areas, pub cat; free wi-fi; big garden with terrace and play area, five bedrooms, open all day Fri-Sun. *(Alan Johnson, Shaun Mahoney)*

PRIORS MARSTON   SP4857
Holly Bush (01327) 260934
Off A361 S of Daventry; Holly Bush Lane; CV47 7RW 16th-c pub with beams, flagstones and lots of stripped stone in rambling linked rooms, log fire and woodburners, above-average well presented food (not Sun evening, Mon), ales such as Hook Norton, friendly efficient young staff, darts; free wi-fi; children welcome, terrace

and sheltered garden (summer barbecues), open all day weekends, closed Mon lunchtime. *(Andy Dolan, Alan Johnson)*

RATLEY   SP3847
★ **Rose & Crown** (01295) 678148
Off A422 NW of Banbury; OX15 6DS
Ancient golden-stone village pub under new management, charming and cosy, with well kept Cats, Purity, Sharps, St Austell and Whale, enjoyable good value food from ciabattas up, friendly helpful staff, carpeted black-beamed bar with woodburner each end, traditional furniture and window seats, little snug, darts; background and some live music; children, walkers and dogs welcome, tables on sunny split-level terrace, aunt sally, near lovely church in sleepy village, handy for Upton House (NT), closed Mon lunchtime. *(Susan and John Douglas)*

RUGBY   SP5075
Merchants (01788) 571119
Little Church Street; CV21 3AN Open-plan pub tucked away near main shopping area, cheerfully busy, with nine quickly changing ales, real ciders and lots of continental bottled beers (regular beer/cider festivals), low priced pubby food and pizzas, quite dark inside with bare boards, mat-covered flagstones, beams and lots of breweriana; background music (live Tues), sports TVs; open all day, till 1am Fri, Sat. *(Andy Dolan, George Atkinson)*

RUGBY   SP5075
Seven Stars (01788) 546611
Albert Square; CV21 2SH Traditionally refurbished 19th-c red-brick local with great choice of ales including B&T and Everards, personable landlord and friendly staff, main bar, lounge, snug and conservatory; some outside seating, open all day. *(Anon)*

RUSHALL   SK03001
Manor Arms (01922) 642333
Park Road, off A461; WS4 1LG Interesting low-beamed 18th-c pub (on much older foundations) by Rushall Canal, three rooms in contrasting styles, one with big inglenook, good value simple food including generous sandwiches, friendly staff, well kept Banks's ales from pumps fixed to the wall (there's no counter); waterside garden, by Park Lime Pits nature reserve. *(James Simister)*

SALFORD PRIORS   SP0751
Bell (01789) 772112
Evesham Road (B439); WR11 8UU Welcoming modernised roadside pub; bucket chairs and leather sofas in log-fire bar, separate dining room, changing choice of enjoyable freshly cooked food including good value lunchtime set menu, special diets catered for and local suppliers listed, well kept Sharps Doom Bar, Wickwar BOB and Wye Valley HPA, real cider and decent wines,

friendly service, Sun quiz; outside eating and drinking areas, self-catering apartment, open all day. *(Clive and Fran Dutson)*

SAMBOURNE   SP0561
Green Dragon (01527) 892465
Village signed off A448; B96 6NU Early 18th-c pub opposite village green, low-beamed rooms with flagstones and open fires, enjoyable fairly straightforward food (not Sun evening) including weekday lunchtime deal, well kept Hobsons, Purity and a guest; children welcome, seats in courtyard, six bedrooms. *(Clive and Fran Dutson, Dave Braisted)*

SEDGLEY   SO9293
★ **Beacon** (01902) 883380
Bilston Street; A463, off A4123 Wolverhampton–Dudley; DY3 1JE Plain old brick pub with own good Sarah Hughes ales from traditional Victorian tower brewery behind; cheery locals in simple quarry-tiled drinking corridor, little snug on left with wall settles, imposing green-tiled marble fireplace and glazed serving hatch, old-fashioned furnishings such as velvet and net curtains, mahogany tables on patterned carpet, small landscape prints, sparse tap room on right with blackened range, dark-panelled lounge with sturdy red leather wall settles and big dramatic sea prints, plant-filled conservatory (no seats), little food apart from cobs; no credit cards; children allowed in some parts including garden with play area. *(Anon)*

SHIPSTON-ON-STOUR   SP2540
Black Horse (01608) 238489
Station Road (off A3400); CV36 4BT Ancient stone and thatch pub doing well under present management, ales including Purity and Wye Valley, Hogan's cider, good authentic thai food, friendly service, low-beamed rooms off central entrance passage, inglenook log fire; darts, free wi-fi; enclosed back garden, closed Mon lunchtime. *(JHBS)*

SHIPSTON-ON-STOUR   SP2540
★ **Horseshoe** (01608) 662190
Church Street; CV36 4AP Pretty 17th-c timbered coaching inn, friendly and relaxed, with open-plan carpeted bar, big fireplace, refurbished restaurant, three ales such as Lancaster, Sharps and Wye Valley, Hogan's cider, good reasonably priced food (not Sun evening), live folk second Tues of month, pub games including aunt sally; free wi-fi; children and dogs welcome, sunny back terrace with heated smokers' shelter, open all day. *(JHBS, Martin and Pauline Jennings)*

SHUSTOKE   SP2290
★ **Griffin** (01675) 481205
Church End, a mile E of village; 5 miles from M6 junction 4; A446 towards Tamworth, then right on to B4114

straight through Coleshill; B46 2LB
Unpretentious country local with a dozen changing ales including own Griffin (brewed in next-door barn), farm cider and country wines, may be winter mulled wine, standard lunchtime bar food (not Sun); cheery low-beamed L-shaped bar with log fires in two stone fireplaces (one a big inglenook), fairly simple décor including cushioned café seats, elm-topped sewing trestles and a nice old-fashioned settle, beer mats on ceiling, conservatory (children allowed here); games machine; dogs welcome, old-fashioned seats on back grass with distant views of Birmingham, large terrace, play area and summer marquee (live music), camping field, open all day Sun. *(M S and M Imhoff)*

SHUSTOKE   SP2290
Plough (01675) 481557
B4114 Nuneaton–Coleshill; B46 2AN
Old-fashioned feel with a number of rooms around the bar, well kept Bass, Black Sheep, Everards and a guest, good choice of fairly straightforward food served by friendly helpful staff, separate dining room, black beams, open fire and gleaming brass; seats out at back along with caged rabbits and exotic birds. *(Clive and Fran Dutson)*

STRATFORD-UPON-AVON SP2054
★ Encore (01789) 269462
Bridge Street; CV37 6AB More modern bar than traditional pub; main beamed area with big windows, well spaced cast-iron tables, bucket armchairs and square stools on broad oak boards or pale flagstones, large charcoal sketches of local scenes, softly lit dark-walled back area with barrel and other rustic tables, stairs up to long comfortable dining room with river views, log fire, Purity, Robinsons and Sharps, plenty of wines by the glass and good coffee, popular food including fixed-price weekday menu; background music; children welcome, dogs in bar, open (and food) all day from 9.30am, can get very busy weekends. *(N R White, Hugh Roberts)*

STRATFORD-UPON-AVON SP2054
★ Garrick (01789) 292186
High Street; CV37 6AU Ancient bustling pub with heavy beams and timbers in irregularly shaped rooms, simple furnishings on bare boards or flagstones, enjoyable fairly priced food from sandwiches and light dishes up, well kept Greene King ales and decent wines by the glass, friendly helpful staff, small air-conditioned back dining area; background music, TV, games machine; children welcome, open (and food) all day. *(N R White, Alan Johnson)*

STRATFORD-UPON-AVON SP1955
Old Thatch (01789) 295216
Rother Street/Greenhill Street; CV37 6LE Cosy and welcoming thatched pub dating from the 15th c on corner of market square,

well kept Fullers ales, nice wines, popular fairly priced food including Sun carvery, rustic décor, beams, slate or wood floors, sofas and log fire, back dining area; covered tables outside. *(Val and Alan Green, N R White, Alan Johnson)*

STRATFORD-UPON-AVON SP1954
Windmill (01789) 297687
Church Street; CV37 6HB Ancient black and white pub (with town's oldest licence) beyond the striking Guild Chapel, very low beams, panelling, mainly stone floors, big fireplace (gas fire), enjoyable good value food (till 8pm) from varied menu including deals, friendly efficient staff, Greene King, Purity UBU and guests; background music, sports TV, games machines; courtyard tables, open all day. *(George Atkinson)*

STRETTON-ON-FOSSE   SP2238
★ Plough (01608) 661053
Just off A429; GL56 9QX Popular and unpretentious little 17th-c village local; central servery separating small bar and snug dining area, good choice of food from pubby choices up, friendly service, Wickwar BOB and three guests, stripped brick/stone walls and some flagstones, low oak beams, inglenook log fire, dominoes and cribbage; children welcome, no dogs, a few tables outside, smokers' shelter. *(Guy Vowles, JHBS, K H Frostick)*

TANWORTH-IN-ARDEN   SP1170
★ Bell (01564) 742212
The Green; B94 5AL Restauranty pub with contemporary bar-style décor, nice food from light dishes such as british tapas to full meals, good choice of wines by the glass and a couple of well kept ales, friendly staff; free wi-fi; children in eating areas, outlook on pretty village's green and lovely 14th-c church, back terrace with alloy planters, nine stylish modern bedrooms (good base for walks), also has a post office/shop, open all day. *(Andy Dolan)*

TANWORTH-IN-ARDEN   SP1071
Warwickshire Lad (01564) 742346
Broad Lane; B94 5DP Beamed country pub with good reasonably priced food all day including lunchtime bargains, a local Whitworths ale brewed for them along with Robinsons, St Austell and Wye Valley, quick service; popular with walkers (bridleway opposite). *(Dave Braisted, Clive and Fran Dutson)*

TEMPLE GRAFTON   SP1355
Blue Boar (01789) 750010
A mile E, towards Binton; off A422 W of Stratford; B49 6NR Welcoming stone-built dining pub with good choice of enjoyable food from bar snacks up, four well kept ales, beams, stripped stonework and log fires, glass-covered well with goldfish, smarter dining room up a couple of steps; big-screen

TVs; children and dogs welcome, picnic-sets outside, bedrooms. *(Grahame Brooks)*

TIPTON SO9492
Pie Factory (0121) 557 1402
Hurst Lane, Dudley Road towards Wednesbury; A457/A4037; DY4 9AB Eccentric décor and quirky food – the mixed grill comes on a shovel, and you're awarded a certificate if you finish their massive Desperate Dan Cow Pie (comes with pastry horns) – other pies and good value food including Sun carvery, well kept Lump Hammer house ales brewed by Enville plus a guest; background music (live weekends), TV; children welcome, bedrooms. *(Anon)*

UPPER BRAILES SP3039
Gate (01608) 685212
B4035 Shipston-on-Stour to Banbury; OX15 5AX Traditional low-beamed village local, well kept Hook Norton and a guest, Weston's cider, enjoyable food (not Sun evening, Mon) including good fish and chips, efficient friendly service, coal fire; TV, darts; children welcome, tables in extensive back garden with play area and aunt sally, pretty hillside spot with lovely walks, two comfortable bedrooms, good breakfast, closed Mon lunchtime. *(Stephen and Jean Curtis, JHBS)*

UPPER GORNAL SO9292
★ Britannia (01902) 883253
Kent Street (A459); DY3 1UX Popular old-fashioned 19th-c local with friendly chatty atmosphere (known locally as Sally's after former landlady), particularly well kept/priced Bathams, three coal fires in front bar and time-trapped little back room with its wonderful wall-mounted handpumps, some bar snacks including good local pork pies; sports TV; dogs welcome, nice flower-filled backyard, open all day Sat, till 4pm Sun. *(Anon)*

WALSALL SP0198
Black Country Arms
(01922) 640588 *High Street; WS1 1QW* Imposing old town pub on three levels, a dozen well kept ales including Black Country, decent home-made pubby food at bargain prices till 4pm (6pm Sat), good friendly service; background and live music, quiz nights; no dogs, small side terrace, open all day (till midnight Fri, Sat). *(Pat and Tony Martin, Theocsbrian)*

WARMINGTON SP4147
Plough (01295) 690666
Just off B4100 N of Banbury; OX17 1BX Attractive and welcoming old stone-built pub under brother and sister team, some refurbishment but keeping character and good local atmosphere, low heavy beams, comfortable chairs by inglenook woodburner, well kept Greene King and guests, enjoyable home-made food (not Mon), extended dining room; background music; children welcome, tables on back terrace, delightful village with interesting church, closed Sun evening. *(Nigel and Sue Foster)*

WARWICK SP2864
★ Rose & Crown (01926) 411117
Market Place; CV34 4SH Up-to-date uncluttered décor, bustling and friendly, with big leather sofas and low tables by open fire, dining area with large modern photographs, good choice of sensibly priced interesting food all day, well kept Purity and Sharps Doom Bar, plenty of fancy keg dispensers, good wines and coffee, cheerful efficient service, newspapers; background music; tables out under parasols, comfortable good-sized bedrooms, open all day from 8am for breakfast. *(Alan Johnson, Christopher and Elise Way)*

WARWICK SP2967
★ Saxon Mill (01926) 492255
Guys Cliffe, A429 just N; CV34 5YN Mitchells & Butlers dining pub in charmingly set converted mill; beams and log fire, smart contemporary chairs and tables on polished boards and flagstones, cosy corners with leather armchairs and big rugs, mill race and turning wheel behind glass, enjoyable food in bar and (best to book) upstairs family restaurant, good choice of wines by the glass and some local beers, friendly service; background music; tables out on terraces by broad willow-flanked river, more over bridge, delightful views across to Guys Cliffe House ruins, open all day. *(Nigel and Sue Foster)*

WHICHFORD SP3134
Norman Knight (01608) 684621
Ascott Road, opposite village green; CV36 5PE Sympathetically extended beamed and flagstoned pub, good Patriot ales from own microbrewery and changing guests, traditional ciders and perry, enjoyable freshly made food (not Sun and Mon evenings) from favourites up, friendly helpful service, live music including monthly folk club; children and dogs welcome (resident pugs – a beer named after them), tables out by lovely village green, aunt sally, site at back for five caravans, classic car/bike meetings third Thurs of month in summer, good walks, open all day weekends. *(Anon)*

WILLEY SP4885
Wood Farm (01788) 833469
Coalpit Lane; CV23 0SL Modern visitor centre attached to (and with views into) Wood Farm Brewery, eight of their ales and occasional guests, good choice of enjoyable reasonably priced food including Sun carvery, upstairs galleried function/overflow room; children welcome, no dogs, picnic-sets outside with country views, camping, brewery tours (must pre-book, not Sun), open all day (till 6pm Sun). *(Alan Johnson, George Atkinson)*

WILLOUGHBY SP5267
Rose (01788) 891180
Just off A45 E of Dunchurch; Main Street; CV23 8BH Neatly decorated old beamed and thatched dining pub; soft lighting, wood or tiled floors, some panelling and inglenook woodburner, good range of food cooked well by italian chef-landlord, Hook Norton and Sharps Doom Bar, reasonably priced house wines, friendly attentive young staff; children and dogs, welcome, disabled facilities, seating in side garden with gate to park and play area. *(M C and S Jeanes, Liane, George Atkinson)*

WOLVERHAMPTON SO9298
★ ### Great Western (01902) 351090
Corn Hill/Sun Street, behind railway station; WV10 0DG Cheerful pub hidden away in cobbled lane down from mainline station; Holdens and guest beers kept well, real cider, bargain home-made food (not Sun), helpful friendly staff, traditional front bar, other rooms including neat dining conservatory, interesting railway memorabilia, open fires; background radio, TV; children and dogs welcome, yard with summer barbecues, open all day. *(Anon)*

WOOTTON WAWEN SP1563
Bulls Head (01564) 795803
Stratford Road, just off A3400; B95 6BD Attractive 17th-c black and white building, more restaurant than pub but does serve a couple of Marstons-related ales; good food from snacks and light dishes up including seafood/fish specials, extensive wine list, friendly helpful staff, log fires, low Elizabethan beams and timbers; children welcome, dogs in snug, outside tables front and back, handy for one of England's finest churches and Stratford Canal walks, open all day Fri, Sat and till 6pm Sun. *(Mrs B H Adams)*

Real ale to us means beer that has matured naturally in its cask – not pressurised or filtered. We name all real ales stocked. We usually name ales preserved under a light blanket of carbon dioxide too, though purists – pointing out that this stops the natural yeasts developing – would disagree (most people, including us, can't tell the difference!)

Wiltshire

ALDBOURNE
Blue Boar ■ £
SU2675   Map 2

The Green (off B4192 in centre); SN8 2EN

Busy local in pretty village green setting, simple pubby furnishings in bar, cottagey restaurant and seats outside

Picnic-sets in front of this popular village pub make the most of the charming setting opposite a pretty, cottage-lined green, and the window boxes are lovely. Inside, the heavily beamed bar has much local atmosphere, a noticeboard with news of beer festivals and live music events, a woodburning stove in an inglenook fireplace with a stuffed boar's head and large clock above it, horsebrasses on the bressumer beam, built-in wooden window seats, tall farmhouse chairs and other red-cushioned pubby chairs on flagstones or bare boards. There are stools by the counter where they keep Wadworths IPA and 6X plus guests such as Batemans XXXB and Wadworths Bishops Tipple and Swordfish on handpump, eight wines by the glass, 17 malt whiskies and a farm cider. The back restaurant is beamed and cottagey with standing timbers, dark wooden chairs and tables on floorboards and rugs, and plates on a dresser.

 Well liked food at fair prices includes sandwiches and baguettes, breaded whitebait, smoked mackerel pâté, pumpkin and parmesan ravioli, ham and free-range eggs, steak and kidney pie, beer-battered cod and chips, chicken in white wine and tarragon, liver and bacon, salmon in lemon and parsley butter, and puddings such as banoffi pie and lemon tart. *Benchmark main dish: steak and kidney pie £9.50. Two-course evening meal £15.00.*

Wadworths ~ Tenants Michael and Joanne Hehir ~ Real ale ~ (01672) 540237 ~ Open 11.30-3, 5.30-11.30; 11.30am-midnight Fri, Sat; 12-11 Sun ~ Bar food 12-2 (2.30 Fri, Sat), 6.30-9; 12-4 Sun ~ Restaurant ~ Children welcome ~ Dogs allowed in bar ~ Wi-fi ~ Live music regularly (best to phone) ~ www.theblueboarpub.co.uk
Recommended by Edward May

BRINKWORTH
Three Crowns
SU0184   Map 2

The Street; B4042 Wootton Bassett–Malmesbury; SN15 5AF

Popular village pub with bar and spreading dining areas, real ales, well liked food and seats on terrace and in garden

Back in these pages under new licensees, the most pubby part here is the traditional bar liked by locals for a pint and a chat. There are beams and partitioning, cushioned wall settles and sturdy mate's chairs around shiny tables on green and pink patterned carpet, horsebrasses, jugs and mugs, and a fireplace at each end; background music and TV. Fullers London Pride, Sharps Doom Bar and a guest such as Otter Bitter on handpump, 18 wines by the glass and a farm cider. There's a conservatory-style flagstoned restaurant to one side with flowers on tables, big ceiling fans and brass, glass and china objects on the window sills. Other spreading dining areas have hunting horns on stone walls, bottles along shelves, all sorts of chairs and settles, shells in hanging nets and a giant pair of bellows. There are seats and tables under parasols on the terrace, and more tables in the garden looking across to the church and farmland.

As well as a two- and three-course set menu (not Sunday), the tasty food includes confit chicken leg and ham terrine with pickles, crab tian with smoked salmon mousse, chicken caesar salad, sausages and onion gravy, prawn or vegetable curry, monkfish with samphire and smoked bacon cream, lamb rump with gratin potatoes and mint jus, and puddings such as lemon tart with passion-fruit mousse and vanilla crème brûlée. *Benchmark main dish: beer-battered fish and chips £12.00. Two-course evening meal £19.50.*

Enterprise ~ Lease Andrew Hughes ~ Real ale ~ (01666) 510366 ~ Open 10am-11pm (midnight Sat); 12-11 Sun ~ Bar food 12-2.30, 6-9.30; 12-8 Sun ~ Restaurant ~ Children welcome ~ Dogs allowed in bar ~ Wi-fi ~ www.threecrowns.co.uk
Recommended by Ian Herdman, Kristin Warry

BROAD HINTON
Barbury ♀
SU1176 Map 2
On A4361 Swindon–Devizes, E of village; SN4 9PF

Friendly roadside pub with an easy-going atmosphere, enjoyable food, comfortable and contemporary furnishings, and a good balance between eating and drinking

Handy for junction 16 of the M4 and for ramblers on the Ridgeway, this well run roadside pub attracts a cheerful mix of customers. The long bar room has a comfortable sofa and two stumpy armchairs in pale brown leather beside a woodburner at one end, a few high-backed wicker armchairs around a couple of tables on bare boards, and game, hunting, shooting and fishing prints. The area around the dark grey-painted counter has Regency-striped modern armchairs and tables, St Austell Proper Job and Trelawny and a guest beer on handpump and 30 good wines by the glass, served by helpful, willing staff. Next to a second woodburner at the other end of the room are leather-cushioned chairs around polished tables (set for dining); a step up leads to a carpeted dining room. Throughout there are cream altar candles, basketweave lampshades, ornate mirrors and planked ceilings; daily papers and background music. Outside, there are seats and tables on a partly covered back terrace. This is sister pub to the Vine Tree in Norton.

Enjoyable food includes lunchtime sandwiches, pork rillettes with dill pickle, poached pear, chicory and blue cheese salad and candied walnuts, home-cooked ham and free-range eggs with triple-cooked chips, honey-roast squash with wild mushrooms and spinach, wild boar and black pudding sausages with redcurrant jus, salmon fillet with roasted peppers and basil pesto, venison liver with pancetta and red wine sauce, and puddings such as treacle tart and dark belgian chocolate tart. *Benchmark main dish: sirloin steak with fries £17.95. Two-course evening meal £22.00.*

Free house ~ Licensees Charles Walker and Tiggi Wood ~ Real ale ~ (01793) 731510 ~ Open 11-11 (midnight Fri, Sat); 11-10.30 Sun ~ Bar food 12-2.30, 7-9.30 (9.45 Fri, Sat);

12-3.15 Sun ~ Children welcome ~ Dogs welcome ~ Wi-fi ~ www.thebarburyinn.co.uk
Recommended by Isobel Mackinlay, Martin Jones, Tony Baldwin

BROUGHTON GIFFORD

Fox 🏵 ▢ Ⴘ

ST8763   Map 2

Village signposted off A365 to B3107 W of Melksham; The Street; SN12 8PN

Comfortably stylish pub with good, interesting food, real ales and several wines by the glass, and a nice garden

It's best to book in advance for this civilised and friendly pub with its highly thought-of food and four real ales – tables do get snapped up quickly. Each of the interconnected areas has a chatty atmosphere, and the big bird and plant prints, attractive table lamps and white-painted beams contrast nicely with the broad dark flagstones. You can sink into sofas or armchairs by a table of daily papers (another has magazines and board games), take one of the padded stools by the pink-painted bar counter, or go for the mix of gently old-fashioned dining chairs around the unmatched stripped dining tables, adorned with candles in brass sticks. There's also a warm log fire in a stone fireplace. Courteous, helpful staff serve Bath Gem, Butcombe Bitter, Fullers London Pride and a guest beer on handpump, a dozen wines by the glass, 15 malt whiskies and a good choice of spirits; background music. The terrace behind has picnic-sets and leads out on to a good-sized sheltered lawn.

Using home-grown produce, raising pigs for cured hams, charcuterie and so forth, baking bread daily and offering a two- and three-course set lunch, the tempting food includes lunchtime sandwiches, chicken liver parfait with home-made chutney, scallops with courgette linguine, cauliflower purée and bacon, sausages and buttery mash, cornish fish and chips, spinach and ricotta tortellini with warm tomato vinaigrette, chicken supreme with consommé, braised venison pie, and puddings such as chocolate and peanut butter pudding with toffee nuts. *Benchmark main dish: fillet of beef with bacon, fondant potato and mini yorkshire pudding £27.95. Two-course evening meal £22.00.*

Free house ~ Licensee Derek Geneen ~ Real ale ~ (01225) 782949 ~ Open 12-11.30 (midnight Sat); 12-10 Sun; closed Mon ~ Bar food 12-2.30, 6-9.30; 12-5.30 Sun ~ Children welcome ~ Dogs welcome ~ www.thefox-broughtongifford.co.uk
Recommended by Mr and Mrs A H Young, Mr and Mrs P R Thomas

CHICKSGROVE

Compasses ★ 🏵 Ⴘ ⮑

ST9729   Map 2

From A30 5.5 miles W of B3089 junction, take lane on N side signposted Sutton Mandeville, Sutton Row, then first left fork (small signs point the way to the pub, in Lower Chicksgrove; look out for the car park); can also be reached off B3089 W of Dinton, passing the glorious spire of Teffont Evias church; SP3 6NB

Excellent all-rounder with enjoyable food, a genuine welcome, four real ales and seats in the quiet garden; attractive bedrooms

Whether you're just dropping in for a friendly, chatty pint or staying overnight in the comfortable bedrooms, this 14th-c thatched inn has got things exactly right and our readers thoroughly enjoy their visits here. The unchanging bar has plenty of real character: old bottles and jugs hanging from beams above the roughly timbered counter, farm tools and traps on the part-stripped stone walls, high-backed wooden settles forming snug booths around tables on the mostly flagstoned floor and a log fire. Butcombe Bitter, Plain Inntrigue and Waylands Sixpenny Addlestone Ale on handpump, nine wines by the glass and nine malt whiskies. The quiet garden, terraces and flagstoned courtyard all have seating, and there are pleasant walks in the surrounding countryside.

 Good interesting food includes potted rabbit and pancetta with pear and apple chutney, scallops with courgette spaghetti and ginger beurre blanc, roasted butternut squash with red peppers, cannellini beans and goats cheese, wild boar sausages with onion gravy, minted lamb pie, free-range chicken stuffed with sunblush tomato and basil with parmentier potatoes, duck breast with plum brandy jus, and puddings such as bread and butter pudding with marmalade ice-cream and white chocolate and raspberry cheesecake. *Benchmark main dish: slow-cooked pork belly with wholegrain mustard mash, glazed apricots and cider jus £15.50. Two-course evening meal £22.50.*

Free house ~ Licensee Alan Stoneham ~ Real ale ~ (01722) 714318 ~ Open 12-3, 6-11; 12-3, 7-10.30 Sun; closed Mon lunch Jan-Easter ~ Bar food 12-2, 6.30-9 ~ Children welcome ~ Dogs welcome ~ Wi-fi ~ Bedrooms: £65/£85 ~ www.thecompassesinn.com
Recommended by Simon Lindsey, Rose Rogers, Phil and Jane Hodson, Tony and Rachel Schendel, Wendy Breese, Ian Herdman, Howard and Margaret Buchanan

COMPTON BASSETT
White Horse 🍴⭐ 🍷 🛏

SU0372 Map 2

At N end of village; SN11 8RG

Bustling, refurbished village pub with four ales, good wines by the glass, inventive food and seats in big garden; pretty bedrooms

'A very special place' and 'the perfect bolthole' are just two comments from enthusiastic readers on this warmly friendly village pub. The simply furnished, bustling bar has some homely upholstered chairs and a nice carved settle around assorted tables on parquet flooring, a woodburning stove and bar stools against the counter where they keep Bath Gem, Sharps Doom Bar, Shepherd Neame Spitfire and Wadworths 6X on handpump, 16 wines by the glass, 18 malt whiskies, a good range of spirits and farm cider. Staff are lovely. The dining room has red walls and carpet at one end and bare floorboards and pale paintwork at the other; throughout there are beams, joists and miscellaneous antique tables and chairs, and there's another woodburning stove here too. Background music and board games. The large, neatly kept garden has picnic-sets and other seats and a boules pitch, and the paddock holds pigs, sheep and geese. The comfortable bedrooms are in a separate building and look over the grounds; good walking nearby.

 Impressive food includes lunchtime sandwiches, seared scallop with cauliflower beignet and red pepper sauce, guinea fowl and smoked bacon scotch egg, roasted mediterranean vegetable risotto, home-made sausages with red wine and shallot jus, teriyaki corn-fed chicken with herb gnocchi, creamed leeks and carrot purée, bass fillet with pak choi, roasted red peppers and sauce nero, and puddings such as Baileys brûlée with pistachio biscotti and raspberry parfait with pear, honeycomb and ginger crumb. *Benchmark main dish: fillet of local beef wrapped in mushroom mousse with fondant potato and wild mushroom sauce £19.95. Two-course evening meal £22.50.*

Free house ~ Licensees Danny and Tara Adams ~ Real ale ~ (01249) 813118 ~ Open 12-11; 12-4 Sun; closed Sun evening, Mon ~ Bar food 12-2.30, 6-9 ~ Restaurant ~ Children welcome ~ Dogs allowed in bar ~ Wi-fi ~ Bedrooms: £85/£95 ~ www.whitehorse-comptonbassett.co.uk *Recommended by Alastair Muir, Michael Doswell*

There are report forms at the back of the book.

CORSHAM   ST8670   Map 2

Methuen Arms 🏵 🛏

High Street; SN13 0HB

Bustling hotel with character bars, friendly staff, imaginative food, good wines and ales, and seats outside; comfortable bedrooms

Civilised yet informal and run by professional, hands-on licensees, this is a handsome Georgian inn with first class food and well equipped, comfortable bedrooms. But the little front bar also attracts those who just want a chat and a drink and is much favoured locally. Snug in the evening with candlelight, it has a log fire, a big old clock under a sizeable mirror, an assortment of antique dining chairs and tables, rugs on elm floorboards, Bath SPA, Otter Amber and Moles Landlords Choice on handpump, 12 wines by the glass and ten malt whiskies. Across the green-painted bar counter is a second small bar, with similar furnishings, bare boards and rugs and a couple of armchairs. The dining room has settles (carved and plain), high-backed wooden armed dining chairs around old sewing machine treadle tables, an open fire with tea-lights, fine black and white photographs of large local houses on pale sage green paintwork and swagged curtains. Another room leads off here, and there's also a back restaurant. The side garden has seats and tables.

🏵 As well as a two- and three-course set menu, the delicious food includes sandwiches, duck confit and mushrooms on toasted sourdough, ham hock and leek terrine with beetroot relish, beer-battered haddock and chips, aubergine, spinach and feta torte with tomato and black olive sauce, saddleback pork chop with sardalaise potatoes and salsa verde, roasted cod with leek, pea and chorizo risotto with gremolata, and puddings such as warm chocolate fudge cake with salted caramel ice-cream and apple and blackberry crumble tart with marsala ice-cream. *Benchmark main dish: lambs liver with soft polenta, pancetta and roasted onions £15.95. Two-course evening meal £23.00.*

Free house ~ Licensees Martin and Debbie Still ~ Real ale ~ (01249) 717060 ~ Open 12-11 ~ Bar food 12-3, 6-10 (9 Sun) ~ Restaurant ~ Children welcome ~ Dogs allowed in bar ~ Wi-fi ~ Bedrooms: £85/£140 ~ www.themethuenarms.com
Recommended by Mr and Mrs P R Thomas, Michael Doswell

CRICKLADE   SU1093   Map 4

Red Lion 🏵 🍺 🛏

Off A419 Swindon–Cirencester; High Street; SN6 6DD

16th-c inn with imaginative food in two dining rooms, nine real ales, friendly, relaxed atmosphere and big garden; bedrooms

With ten real ales on handpump (including their own-brews), lots to look at and attractive, comfortable bedrooms, this very well run former coaching inn is a big hit with our readers. The bar has a good community atmosphere, stools by the nice old counter, wheelbacks and other chairs around dark wooden tables on red-patterned carpet, an open fire and all sorts of bric-a-brac on the stone walls including stuffed fish and animal heads and old street signs. You can eat here or in the slightly more formal dining room, furnished with pale wooden farmhouse chairs and tables, beige carpeting and a woodburning stove in a brick fireplace; background music. They serve their own Hop Kettle North Wall and Tricerahops, plus guests such as Arbor Blue Sky Drinking, Brewsters Hophead, Hop Kettle Old Ale and Tiny Rebel/Dark Star Rebel Alliance, 60 bottled beers, three farm ciders, eight wines by the glass, 20 malt whiskies and 20 gins (gin hour is 5.30-6.30). There are plenty of picnic-sets in the big back garden. You can walk along the nearby Thames Path or through the pretty historic town.

 From a thoughtful menu using their own hand-reared pork, home-baked bread and hand-churned butter (and listing other local producers), the good food includes lunchtime sandwiches, air-dried veal with pickled vegetables, haddock and fennel fishcake, home-cooked honey and mustard ham, free-range eggs and triple-cooked chips, pork and ale sausages with caramelised onion gravy, wild-mushroom tart with tempura shimeji mushroom and madeira jelly, free-range pork T-bone, bacon and leek croquettes with braised red cabbage, and puddings. *Benchmark main dish: burger with bacon, cheese and triple-cooked chips £12.50. Two-course evening meal £20.50.*

Free house ~ Licensee Tom Gee ~ Real ale ~ (01793) 750776 ~ Open 12-11 (midnight Sat); 12-10.30 Sun ~ Bar food 12-2.30 (3 weekends), 6.30-9 (9.30 Fri, Sat) ~ Restaurant ~ Children welcome ~ Dogs welcome ~ Wi-fi ~ Bedrooms: /£80 ~ www.theredlioncricklade.co.uk *Recommended by Simon Daws, Michael Doswell, Ian Herdman, Paul Moss, Mrs Margo Finlay, Jörg Kasprowski, Giles and Annie Francis, Lesley Dick, Simon Collett-Jones, Guy Vowles, Phil and Jane Villiers*

CRUDWELL
ST9592 Map 4

Potting Shed 🏮 🍷 🍺

A429 N of Malmesbury; The Street; SN16 9EW

Civilised but relaxed dining pub with low-beamed rambling rooms, friendly, helpful staff, an interesting range of drinks and creative cooking; seats in the big garden

Everything here is first class, from the genuine welcome to the carefully chosen drinks and the imaginative food using home-grown produce. Reader reports remain as enthusiastic as ever. Low-beamed rooms ramble around the bar with mixed plain tables and chairs on pale flagstones, log fires (one in a big worn stone fireplace), some homely armchairs in one corner and daily papers. Four steps take you up into a high-raftered area with wood flooring, and there's another smaller separate room that's ideal for a lunch or dinner party. The quirky, rustic decorations are not overdone: a garden-fork door handle, garden-tool beer pumps, rather witty big black and white photographs. A fine range of drinks includes Bath Gem, Butcombe Gold, Sharps Doom Bar, Timothy Taylors Landlord and a beer named for them from Malmesbury on handpump, as well as 25 wines and champagne by the glass, three farm ciders, home-made seasonal cocktails using local or home-grown fruit, local fruit liqueurs, good coffees and popular winter mulled cider; well chosen background music and board games. Barney, Rubble and Tilly are the pub dogs. There are sturdy teak seats around cask tables as well as picnic-sets out on the side grass among weeping willows. The pub's two acres of gardens supply many of the ingredients used in the food; they've also developed ten raised beds and donated them to local villagers – these are pleasant to wander through. Good access for those in need of extra assistance. They also own the hotel across the road.

 The enterprising and extremely good food includes lunchtime sandwiches, braised goose thigh with honey-glazed chestnuts, beetroot purée and port reduction, scallops with apple purée, lardons, chilli and herb butter, vegetable cannelloni with spicy tomato sauce and parmesan, bream with fennel and chive sauce, guinea fowl leg stuffed with bacon, onion and tarragon with madeira jus, rack of rabbit with rabbit croquettes, french-style petit pois and rabbit jus, and puddings such as dark chocolate and peanut ice-cream cake and blueberry and redcurrant parfait with blueberry syrup and toasted nut praline. *Benchmark main dish: beer-battered haddock and triple-cooked chips £13.25. Two-course evening meal £21.00.*

Enterprise ~ Lease Jonathan Barry and Julian Muggridge ~ Real ale ~ (01666) 577833 ~ Open 11-11 (midnight Sat) ~ Bar food 12-2.30, 7-9.30; 12-3, 7-9 Sun ~ Restaurant ~ Children welcome ~ Dogs welcome ~ Wi-fi ~ www.thepottingshedpub.com
Recommended by Michael Doswell, Maureen Wood, Paul Goldman, Mr and Mrs P R Thomas, Dr and Mrs A K Clarke, Leslie and Barbara Owen, M G Hart, Di and Mike Gillam, Phil and Jane Villiers, Michael Sargent

EAST CHISENBURY
SU1352 Map 2

Red Lion

At S end of village; SN9 6AQ

Country inn in peaceful village run by hard-working chef-owners, contemporary décor, an informal atmosphere and excellent food; bedrooms

The River Avon is just a few yards from the private deck of your lovely, well equipped bedroom if you're staying at this thatched country inn, and breakfasts are delicious; bloody marys and bucks fizz are complimentary. Mr and Mrs Manning are both top chefs and the food is exceptional, using home-grown produce, their own sausages and smoked meats and freshly baked bread. The emphasis is therefore very much on dining, but they do keep Andwell Resolute and Bath Gem on handpump, ten wines by the glass, home-made cordial and quite a range of gins and malt whiskies. One long room is split into different areas by brick and green-planked timbers. One end has a big woodburner in a brick inglenook, the other a comfortable black leather sofa and armchairs; in between are painted or wooden dining chairs around chunky pale oak tables on bare boards or stone, with wine bottles and candles on the window sills. Drinkers tend to congregate at the high chairs by the bar counter. There's an additional dining room too; background music. Outside, there are picnic-sets on a terrace, and tables and chairs on the grass above; you can also go into the upper garden where they keep chickens. They make their own dog treats.

Naming their local suppliers, the first class creative food includes sandwiches, warm cornish crab tart, tagliarini of rabbit with broad beans, lovage, lemon and parmesan, goats cheese and wild herb risotto, cheeseburger with chips, guinea fowl breast with polenta, asparagus and roasting juices, hake with mussels, peas, bacon and a chive beurre blanc, duck with farfalle, baby leeks, shiitake mushrooms and meat juices, and puddings such as lemon tart with pine nut crumb and thyme crème fraîche and mango with pistachio and toasted rice ice-cream. *Benchmark main dish: rib of beef for two people with chips and béarnaise sauce £60.00. Two-course evening meal £27.00.*

Free house ~ Licensees Britt and Guy Manning ~ Real ale ~ (01980) 671124 ~ Open 9am-11pm (10pm Sun) ~ Bar food 12-2.15, 6-8.30; 12-2.30, 6-7.45 Sun ~ Restaurant ~ Children welcome ~ Dogs allowed in bar and bedrooms ~ Wi-fi ~ Bedrooms: /£150 ~ www.redlionfreehouse.com *Recommended by Val and Alan Green, Mrs Zara Elliott*

'Children welcome' means the pub says it lets children inside without any special restriction. If it allows them in, but to restricted areas such as an eating area or family room, we specify this. Places with separate restaurants often let children use them, and hotels usually let children into public areas such as lounges. Some pubs impose an evening time limit – let us know if you find one earlier than 9pm.

EAST KNOYLE
Fox & Hounds 🍷

ST8731 Map 2

Village signposted off A350 S of A303; The Green (named on some road atlases), a mile NW at OS Sheet 183 map reference 872313; or follow signpost off B3089, about 0.5 miles E of A303 junction near Little Chef; SP3 6BN

Pretty thatched village pub with splendid views, welcoming service, good beers and popular enjoyable food

On a clear day, from the picnic-sets facing the green in front of this partly thatched old place, you can enjoy remarkable views over into Somerset and Dorset. Inside, the three linked areas – on different levels around the central horseshoe-shaped servery – have big log fires, plentiful oak woodwork and flagstones, comfortably padded dining chairs around big scrubbed tables, and a couple of leather sofas; the furnishings are all very individual and uncluttered. There's also a small light-painted conservatory restaurant. Hop Back Summer Lightning, Palmers Copper Ale and Plain Sheep Dip on handpump, several wines by the glass and farm cider; background music. The nearby woods are good for a stroll and the Wiltshire Cycleway passes through the village.

🍴 Quite a choice of food includes a terrine of the week, nachos with melted cheese, guacamole and sour cream, home-made sausages and gravy, steak and kidney pudding, chicken wrapped in bacon with pesto cream sauce, a vegetarian curry, and puddings such as raspberry and white chocolate cheesecake and fruit crumble. *Benchmark main dish: fish of the day with chips £12.00. Two-course evening meal £19.00.*

Free house ~ Licensee Murray Seator ~ Real ale ~ (01747) 830573 ~ Open 11.30-3, 5.30-11 (10 Sun) ~ Bar food 12-2.30, 6-9.30 ~ Children welcome ~ Dogs welcome ~ www.foxandhounds-eastknoyle.co.uk *Recommended by Mr and Mrs J Davis, Paul Goldman, Ian Herdman, Roy Hoing, Martin and Karen Wake*

EDINGTON
Three Daggers

ST9353 Map 2

Westbury Road (B3098); BA13 4PG

Rejuvenated village pub, open fires, beams and candlelight, modern conservatory, helpful staff, enjoyable food and own-brew beers; bedrooms

You can spend a happy couple of hours browsing in the separate farm shop of this appealing brick-built pub, and then pop across the car park for lunch. An open-plan and heavily beamed place, it's been carefully refurbished, and the bar is easy-going and friendly: leather sofas and armchairs at one end in front of a woodburning stove, kitchen and chapel chairs and built-in planked wall seats with scatter cushions, leather-topped stools against the counter, and a cosy nook with just one table. A two-way fireplace opens into the candlelit restaurant, which has lots of photos of local people and views, and similar tables and chairs on a dark slate floor; stairs lead up to another dining room with beams in a high apex roof and some unusual large wooden chandeliers. Their own hand-pumped beers, Daggers Ale, Blonde and Edge, are brewed in the farm shop building and they also have 14 wines by the glass, ten malt whiskies and a couple of farm ciders; background music, darts, TV and board games. The airy conservatory has tea-lights or church candles on scrubbed kitchen tables and wooden dining chairs. Just beyond this are picnic-sets on grass plus a fenced-off, well equipped children's play area. The three bedrooms are pretty.

Open from 8am for breakfast, the good, interesting food includes sandwiches, mussels in cider broth, pork rillette with apple jelly, hot seared beef salad with deep-fried noodle nest and honey and soy dressing, wild mushroom and thyme tart with chive sauce, calves liver and oak-smoked bacon, roasted cod with blackened spices, chorizo and white bean cassoulet, chicken two-ways (spring onion and ginger ballotine and sticky wings), and puddings such as chocolate torte with morello cherries and rhubarb tart with mascarpone. *Benchmark main dish: steak in ale pie £14.75. Two-course evening meal £20.50.*

Free house ~ Licensee Jackie Cosens ~ Real ale ~ (01380) 830940 ~ Open 8am-11pm; 9am-10.30 Sun ~ Bar food 12-2.30, 6-9 (9.30 Fri, Sat); 12-8.30 Sun; breakfast 8.30 11.30am; 9-11am Sun; ~ Restaurant ~ Children welcome ~ Dogs allowed in bar ~ Wi-fi ~ Live music first Fri of month ~ Bedrooms: £85/£95 ~ www.threedaggers.co.uk
Recommended by N R White, John Matthews

FONTHILL GIFFORD
Beckford Arms 🌟 � 🛏

ST9231   Map 2

Off B3089 W at Fonthill Bishop; SP3 6PX

Wiltshire Dining Pub of the Year

18th-c coaching inn with character bar and restaurant, unfailingly good food, thoughtful drinks choice and an informal but civilised atmosphere; bedrooms

This is a lovely place to stay (with wonderful walks nearby) and some of the comfortable, well equipped bedrooms overlook the one-acre garden; breakfasts are generous and very good. An elegant Georgian coaching inn, it has a civilised but informal atmosphere, a good mix of both locals and visitors and a warm welcome for all. The main bar has a huge fireplace, bar stools beside the counter and various old wooden dining chairs and tables on parquet flooring. To drink: Bath Gem, Butcombe Bitter and Keystone Phoenix (brewed especially for them) on handpump, 15 wines by the glass, 20 malt whiskies, winter mulled wine and cider, and cocktails such as a bellini using locally produced peach liqueur and a bloody mary using home-grown horseradish; service is friendly and helpful. The stylish, cosy sitting room has comfortable sofas facing one another across a low table of newspapers, a nice built-in window seat among other chairs and tables, and an open fire in a stone fireplace with candles in brass candlesticks and fresh flowers on the mantelpiece. There's also a separate restaurant and charming private dining room. Much of the artwork on the walls is by local artists. They host film nights on occasional Sundays and will provide water and bones for dogs (the pub dog is called Elsa). The mature rambling garden has seats on a brick terrace, hammocks under trees, games for children, a dog bath and boules.

Making their own chutneys and jams, using local (and some home-grown) produce and home-smoking meat and fish, the excellent food includes lunchtime sandwiches, scallops with avocado, chilli, red pepper purée and Pernod, guinea fowl and black pudding terrine with shallot purée and quail egg, omelette arnold bennett, a proper niçoise salad, goats cheese in filo pastry with basil pesto and sunblush tomato couscous, veal schnitzel with a fried duck egg, sautéed potatoes and sage butter, and puddings such as dark chocolate fondant with raspberry sorbet and sticky toffee pudding with popcorn ice-cream. *Benchmark main dish: beef and marrow burger with bacon, cheddar, pickle and chips £11.50. Two-course evening meal £21.00.*

Free house ~ Licensees Dan Brod and Charlie Luxton ~ Real ale ~ (01747) 870385 ~
Open 11-11 (10.30 Sun) ~ Bar food 12-3, 7-9 ~ Children welcome ~ Dogs welcome ~
Wi-fi ~ Bedrooms: /£100 ~ www.beckfordarms.com *Recommended by B J Thompson,*
Richard and Penny Gibbs, Gerry Price, Ian Herdman, Michael Sargent, Michael Doswell

FORD   ST8474 Map 2

White Hart 🛏

Off A420 Chippenham–Bristol; SN14 8RP

**16th-c inn with attractively refurbished rooms, good choice of food
and drink, helpful staff and seats beside trout stream; bedrooms**

The carefully refurbished beamed rooms in this handsome country inn
are painted in bold, contemporary colours, and the atmosphere is
relaxed and friendly. There's an appealing variety of dining and tub chairs,
cushioned wall seats, leather-padded benches, button-back sofas and both
high and low stools around all sizes of wooden tables on bare floorboards
or quarry tiles, and lots of wall prints, candles in glass lanterns and books
on shelves. For cooler weather, there's both a woodburning stove and an
open log fire. A beer named for the pub (from Ringwood), Bath Gem, Box
Steam Tunnel Vision and Brakspears Oxford Gold on handpump, 22 wines
by the glass and a dozen malt whiskies. The front courtyard and terrace
have plenty of solid tables and chairs under parasols, with picnic-sets next
to a trout stream by a small stone bridge. The bedrooms are comfortable
and the breakfasts good.

 Rewarding food using local produce includes sandwiches and ciabattas, crispy
crab balls with spicy guacamole, mussels in creamy white wine sauce, sharing
platters, asparagus and watercress tart, steak burger with bacon, a choice of cheeses
and burger sauce, chicken with chorizo, spinach and wild mushroom sauce, beer-
battered fish and chips, and puddings such as lemon meringue pie and chocolate
brownie. *Benchmark main dish: 28-day-aged rib-eye steak with a choice of side
dishes £23.95. Two-course evening meal £18.00.*

Revere Pub Company ~ Manager Adam Ford ~ Real ale ~ (01249) 782213 ~
Open 12-11 (10.30 Sun) ~ Bar food 12-10 (9.30 Sun) ~ Restaurant ~ Children welcome
~ Dogs allowed in bar ~ Wi-fi ~ Bedrooms: /£80 ~ www.whitehart-ford.com
Recommended by John and Gloria Isaacs, Jim and Maggie Cowell, Mr and Mrs D J Nash

GREAT BEDWYN   SU2764 Map 2

Three Tuns ♀

*Village signposted off A338 S of Hungerford, or off A4 W of Hungerford
via Little Bedwyn; High Street; SN8 3NU*

**Carefully refurbished village pub with simple furnishings and original
features, a friendly welcome, three real ales and highly rated food**

This neatly kept 18th-c village pub is on the edge of the Savernake Forest
and there are lovely walks nearby. Run with enthusiasm by the chef-
owner and his wife, it was once a bakery – you can still see the bread oven.
The beamed front bar is traditional and simply furnished with pubby stools
and chairs on bare floorboards, and has an open fire, artwork by local
artists on the walls and plenty of original features. Butcombe Bitter, Otter
Bitter and Ramsbury Gold on handpump, 13 wines including champagne
and prosecco by the glass, local soft drinks and several malt whiskies.
French windows in the back dining room lead into the garden (which has
undergone a lot of work) where there are new tables and chairs and a new

outdoor grill. Renovations to turn the barn into bedrooms had just started as we went to press.

🍴 Cooked by the landlord using seasonal produce, the interesting food includes braised rabbit and chorizo on toast with a poached egg, chicken liver and foie gras parfait with rhubarb jelly, wild mushroom risotto, burger with smoked cheddar and beef dripping chips, calves liver with caramelised onion mash and roasted baby beetroot, rib-eye steak with bone marrow and a choice of sauces, and puddings such as warm chocolate pudding with salted caramel ice-cream and maple syrup crème brûlée. *Benchmark main dish: cod with smoked bacon, duck confit and lentils £18.00. Two-course evening meal £23.00.*

Free house ~ Licensees James and Ashley Wilsey ~ Real ale ~ (01672) 870280 ~ Open 10-3, 6-11; 10am-11pm Sat; 10-6 Sun; closed Mon except bank holidays ~ Bar food 12.30-2.30, 6-9.30 ~ Children welcome ~ Dogs welcome ~ Wi-fi ~ Live jazz last Sun of month in summer ~ www.threetunsbedwyn.co.uk *Recommended by Mr and Mrs P R Thomas*

GRITTLETON
ST8680 Map 2

Neeld Arms 🍺 🛏

From M4 junction 17, follow A429 to Cirencester and immediately left, signed Stanton St Quintin and Grittleton; SN14 6AP

Bustling village pub with popular food and beer and friendly staff; comfortable bedrooms

'This seems to get better every time we stay here,' says one reader with enthusiasm – the bedrooms do have a lot of character and the welcome is genuinely friendly. Dating from the 17th c, its rooms are largely open-plan with Cotswold-stone walls, contemporary colours on wood panelling and a pleasant mix of seating ranging from bar stools and a traditional settle to window seats and pale wooden dining chairs around an assortment of tables – each set with fresh flowers. The little brick fireplace houses a woodburning stove and there's an inglenook fireplace on the right. Otter Bitter, St Austell Tribute, Sharps Doom Bar and a changing guest on handpump, served from the blue-painted panelled and oak-topped bar counter. The back dining area has another inglenook with a big woodburning stove; even back here, you still feel thoroughly part of the action. There's an outdoor terrace with a pergola.

🍴 The highly thought-of and fairly priced food includes lunchtime ciabatta sandwiches, moules marinière, local wild boar salami and parma ham, goats cheese, tomato and basil tart, ham and egg, local sausages and mash, pork medallions with apple and calvados sauce, calves liver with black pudding on a potato rösti, and puddings such as fresh mango crème brûlée and crêpe suzette in an orange liqueur sauce. *Benchmark main dish: pie of the day £10.95. Two-course evening meal £17.00.*

Free house ~ Licensees Charlie and Boo West ~ Real ale ~ (01249) 782470 ~ Open 12-3, 5.30 (7 Sun)-11.30 ~ Bar food 12-2, 6.30-9.30; 12-2, 7-9 Sun ~ Restaurant ~ Children welcome ~ Dogs welcome ~ Wi-fi ~ Bedrooms: £50/£80 ~ www.neeldarms.co.uk
Recommended by P M Newsome, Mike and Mary Carter, Sara Fulton, Roger Baker

HOLT
ST8561 Map 2

Toll Gate 🛏

Ham Green; B3107 W of Melksham; BA14 6PX

Friendly 16th-c pub with cheerful staff, character bar and dining room, woodburning stoves, real ales and popular food; pretty bedrooms

You can be sure of a warm reception from the friendly landlord and his staff in this former weavers' shed. Pulling in plenty of local customers, the relaxed little bar has real character, a group of comfortable armchairs near the woodburning stove, a nice mix of seats and tables on pale floorboards, a cushioned corner settle, large flowery wallpaper or pale green walls above a dark green dado and paintings for sale. High chairs line the counter where they keep Box Steam Golden Bolt, Butcombe Bitter, Dorset Piddle Bitter and Sharps Doom Bar on handpump, 16 wines by the glass and three farm ciders; games and newspapers. The dining room leads off here with another woodburner, high-backed black leather and other cushioned chairs around a medley of tables, fresh flowers and neat cream blinds. Up a few steps, the high-raftered restaurant is similarly furnished, with white-painted deer heads on a dark blue wall and church windows (this used to be a workers' chapel). The heated back terrace has seats, tables and a wishing well and there's a wendy house. The bedrooms have open fires.

Using local seasonal produce, the popular food includes lunchtime sandwiches (not Sunday), duck spring roll with chilli and mint, blue cheesecake with pear and walnuts, a risotto and a pie of the day, burger with bacon, smoked cheese, coleslaw and chips, fish of the day en papillote, pork belly with apple and rosemary compote, and puddings such as lemon mousse meringue and chocolate, orange and hazelnut torte. *Benchmark main dish: haunch of beef £14.75. Two-course evening meal £18.00.*

Free house ~ Licensees Laura and Mark ~ Real ale ~ (01225) 782326 ~ Open 11-11; 11-4 Sun; closed Sun evening, Mon ~ Bar food 12-2, 6.30-9 ~ Restaurant ~ Children welcome ~ Wi-fi ~ Bedrooms: /£70 ~ www.tollgateholt.co.uk *Recommended by Pip White, Toby Jones*

LACOCK

Rising Sun
ST9367 Map 2

Bewley Common, Bowden Hill – out towards Sandy Lane, up hill past abbey; OS Sheet 173 map reference 935679; SN15 2PP

Unassuming stone pub with welcoming atmosphere, well liked food and wonderful views from garden

From the big two-level terrace here with its modern steel and wood tables and chairs you can see up to 25 miles across the Avon Valley; the sunsets can be glorious. Inside, three welcoming little rooms have been knocked together to form one simply furnished area with a mix of wooden chairs and tables on stone floors, country pictures and open fires; there's also a conservatory with the same fantastic view as the terrace. Moles Best Bitter, Barleymole and Mole Catcher on handpump, 19 wines by the glass and farm cider; friendly, helpful service and background music. Disabled access is tricky.

Pubby food includes deep-fried brie with cranberry sauce, garlic mushrooms, ham and free-range eggs, burger with cheese, bacon and chips, vegetable lasagne, a pie of the day, beer-battered fish with tartare sauce, and puddings. *Benchmark main dish: salmon and prawns in a creamy spicy cajun sauce £14.95. Two-course evening meal £16.00.*

Moles ~ Managers Roger Cox and Kay Thomas ~ Real ale ~ (01249) 730363 ~ Open 12-11 (10 Sun) ~ Bar food 12-2.30, 6-9; all day summer Sat; 12-6 (4 in winter) Sun ~ Restaurant ~ Well behaved children welcome ~ Dogs allowed in bar ~ Wi-fi ~ www.therisingsunlacock.co.uk *Recommended by Simon and Mandy King, Mrs M Chater, Chris and Angela Buckell*

LOWER CHUTE

SU3153 Map 2

Hatchet

The Chutes well signposted via Appleshaw off A342, 2.5 miles W of Andover; SP11 9DX

Unchanging and neatly kept old country inn with a friendly welcome for all, four beers and enjoyable food; comfortable bedrooms

The convivial landlord in this charming pub, tucked away in a pretty hamlet, offers a genuine welcome to all. There's a peaceful local feel to the very low-beamed bar with its splendid 16th-c fireback in a huge fireplace (and a roaring winter log fire) and various comfortable seats around oak tables; there's also an extensive restaurant. Bowmans Swift One, Otter Bitter, Sharps Doom Bar and Timothy Taylors Landlord on handpump, ten wines by the glass, 25 malt whiskies and several farm ciders; board games, cribbage and background music. There are seats out on a terrace and the side grass and a safe play area for children. The snug bedrooms make this a fine place to stay (dogs are welcome in one room); breakfasts are hearty.

 The highly rated food includes chicken liver pâté with apricot chutney, scallops with chorizo and black pudding, spinach and red pepper lasagne, lamb shank in redcurrant and rosemary sauce, liver and bacon with onion gravy, fish pie, chicken in bacon, leek and stilton sauce, and puddings such as apple pie and chocolate brownie. *Benchmark main dish: steak in ale pie £10.95. Two-course evening meal £18.00.*

Free house ~ Licensee Jeremy McKay ~ Real ale ~ (01264) 730229 ~ Open 11.30-3, 6-11; 12-3, 7-10.30 Sun ~ Bar food 12-2.15, 6.30-9.45; 12-3, 7-9.30 Sun ~ Restaurant ~ Children welcome ~ Dogs welcome ~ Wi-fi ~ Bedrooms: /£80 ~ www.thehatchetinn.com
Recommended by Ian Herdman, N R White

MANTON

SU1768 Map 2

Outside Chance ♀

Village (and pub) signposted off A4 just W of Marlborough; High Street; SN8 4HW

Popular dining pub, civilised and traditional, nicely reworked with sporting theme; interesting modern food

There are plenty of walks and things to see and do around this rather civilised village pub, so it's helpful that they're open all day. The three small linked rooms have flagstones or bare boards, hops on beams and mainly plain pub furnishings such as chapel chairs and a long-cushioned pew; one room has a more cosseted feel, with panelling and a comfortable banquette. The décor celebrates unlikely horse-racing winners, such as 100-1 Grand National winners Caughoo and Foinavon, Mr Spooner's Only Dreams (a 100-1 winner at Leicester in 2007), or the odd-gaited little Seabiscuit who cheered many thousands of americans with his dogged pursuit of victory during the Depression. There's a splendid log fire in the big main fireplace and maybe fresh flowers and candlelight; background music and board games. Wadworths IPA and 6X and a guest such as St George & the Dragon on handpump, 13 good wines by the glass, nicely served coffees; neatly dressed young staff. A suntrap side terrace has contemporary tables with metal frames and granite tops, while the good-sized garden has sturdy rustic tables and benches under ash trees; they have private access to the local playing fields and children's play area.

Interesting food includes ham terrine with red onion jam, smoked haddock fishcake with chowder, butternut squash, chive and pecorino risotto, a pie of the week, beer-battered fish with triple-cooked chips, pork chops with black pudding mash and apple purée, gressingham duck breast with shiitake mushrooms and thyme and banana shallot, and puddings such as vanilla panna cotta with berries and warm chocolate brownie. *Benchmark main dish: burger with bacon, cheese, home-made coleslaw and onion jam and fries £12.95. Two-course evening meal £20.00.*

Wadworths ~ Tenant Howard Spooner ~ Real ale ~ (01672) 512352 ~ Open 12-11; 12-3, 5.30-11 weekdays in winter ~ Bar food 12-2.30 (3 Sat), 6-9; 12-3.30, 7-9 Sun ~ Restaurant ~ Children welcome ~ Dogs welcome ~ Wi-fi ~ Open mike last Fri of month ~ www.theoutsidechance.co.uk *Recommended by Edward May, Toby Jones, Michael Doswell*

 MARLBOROUGH SU1869 Map 2
Lamb ◨ £
The Parade; SN8 1NE

Friendly former coaching inn with big helpings of popular food, real ales, plenty of customers and traditional pubby furnishings; comfortable bedrooms

This is a proper family-run local with a bustling, friendly atmosphere and our readers enjoy their visits here; plenty of chatty regulars too. The L-shaped bar has lots of hop bines, wall banquettes, wheelback chairs around wooden tables on parquet flooring, Cecil Aldin prints on red walls, candles in bottles and a two-way log-effect woodburning stove; the easy-going bulldog may be poddling about. Wadworths IPA, 6X, Horizon and Swordfish tapped from the cask and several wines by the glass; games machine, juke box, darts and TV. There are picnic-sets and modern alloy and wicker seats and tables in the attractive back courtyard. The bedrooms are light and cottagey (some are in a former stable block) and breakfasts hearty. In summer, the window boxes are very pretty.

 Good popular food cooked by the landlady includes lunchtime sandwiches and toasties, eggs benedict, whitebait with garlic mayonnaise, corned beef hash and egg, local free-range sausages, a full breakfast (lunchtime only), butternut squash and chickpea tagine, goan chicken curry, herb-battered cod and chips, and puddings such as fruit crumble and treacle tart with clotted cream ice-cream. *Benchmark main dish: fish pie £11.50. Two-course evening meal £16.00.*

Wadworths ~ Tenant Vyv Scott ~ Real ale ~ (01672) 512668 ~ Open 11-11 (11.30 Sat); 12-10.30 Sun ~ Bar food 12-2.30, 6.30-9; not Fri-Sun evenings ~ Children welcome ~ Dogs allowed in bar ~ Wi-fi ~ Live music monthly ~ Bedrooms: £55/£80 ~ www.thelambinnmarlborough.com *Recommended by D and M T Ayres-Regan, Tony Baldwin*

MARSTON MEYSEY SU1297 Map 4
Old Spotted Cow ♀
Off A419 Swindon–Cirencester; SN6 6LQ

An easy-going atmosphere in cottagey bar rooms, friendly young staff, lots to look at, well kept ales and enjoyable food

With a charming atmosphere, plenty of interesting knick-knacks and enjoyable food and drink, this is a friendly pub with a country outlook. The main bar has high-backed cushioned dining chairs around chunky pine tables on wooden floorboards or parquet, a few rugs here and there, an open fire at each end of the room (with comfortable sofas in front of one), fresh flowers and brass candlesticks with candles. There are indeed cows of some sort all around: paintings, drawings, postcards, all manner and colour of china ones – some actually are spotted – and embroidery and toy ones too; also has lots of beer mats and bank notes pinned to beams. Butcombe Gold, Moles Tap and Otter Amber on handpump, a dozen wines by the glass, farm cider, a proper bloody mary and home-made cordials served by helpful staff. Two cottagey dining rooms lead off here with similar tables and chairs, a couple of long pews and a big bookshelf. There are seats and picnic-sets on the front grass and a children's play area beyond a big willow tree. A classic car show is held here on the first May bank holiday.

Cooked by the landlady, the interesting food includes lunchtime sandwiches, pork terrine with home-made chutney, chicken livers with sage cream, pancetta and mushrooms, tomato risotto with black olives and feta, sea bream with harissa and coconut rice, slow-roasted lamb shoulder with yoghurt and cardamom crust and lemon couscous, linguine with king prawns and roasted salmon in saffron cream sauce, and puddings. *Benchmark main dish: bacon, poached egg, bubble and squeak and mustard cream sauce £8.00. Two-course evening meal £18.00.*

Free house ~ Licensee Anna Langley-Poole ~ Real ale ~ (01285) 810264 ~ Open 11-11; 11-sunset Sun; 11-6.30 Sun in winter ~ Bar food 12-2 (3.30 Sun), 7-9 ~ Restaurant ~ Children welcome but must be over 10 in bar ~ Dogs allowed in bar ~ Wi-fi ~ www.theoldspottedcow.co.uk *Recommended by Gavin and Helle May, Isobel Mackinlay, David Fowler*

NEWTON TONY
Malet Arms 🌟 🔖   SU2140   Map 2
Village signposted off A338 Swindon–Salisbury; SP4 0HF

Smashing village pub with no pretensions, a good choice of local beers and highly thought-of food

'It's a shame I don't live closer – but then I'd probably move in!' says one reader wistfully. We always receive high praise from our contributors for this fine old coaching inn, with warm comments specifically for the charming landlord and his friendly, efficient staff. The low-beamed interconnecting rooms have nice furnishings, including a mix of tables of different sizes with high-winged wall settles, carved pews, chapel and carver chairs, and lots of pictures of local scenes and from imperial days. The main front windows are said to be made from the stern of a ship, and there's a log and coal fire in a huge fireplace. The snug is noteworthy for its fantastic collection of photographs and prints celebrating the local aviation history of Boscombe Down, alongside archive photographs of Stonehenge festivals of the 1970s and '80s. At the back is a homely, red-painted dining room. Four real ales on handpump come from breweries such as Butcombe, Fullers, Hop Back, Itchen Valley, Ramsbury, Salisbury, Stonehenge and Triple fff and they also keep 40 malt whiskies, eight wines by the glass and Weston's Old Rosie cider. There are seats on the small front terrace with more on grass and in the back garden. The road to the pub goes through a ford – it may be best to use an alternative route in winter, as the water can be quite deep. There's an all-weather cricket pitch on the village green.

 Using seasonal game from local shoots (bagged by the landlord), lamb raised in the surrounding fields and free-range local pork, the enjoyable food includes a popular spicy rarebit, chicken liver pâté with home-made onion bread, mackerel with gremolata and parsley potatoes, venison en croûte with port jus, breast of lamb stuffed with spicy sausage with rosemary gravy, and puddings such as spiced pear crumble cake and devon fudge cheesecake. *Benchmark main dish: burger with chips £9.95. Two-course evening meal £17.50.*

Free house ~ Licensees Noel and Annie Cardew ~ Real ale ~ (01980) 629279 ~ Open 11-3, 6-11; 12-4, 7-10.30 Sun ~ Bar food 12-2.30, 6.30-9.30; 12-2.30, 6-9 Sun ~ Restaurant ~ Children allowed in restaurant or snug only ~ Dogs allowed in bar ~ www.maletarms.com
Recommended by Tony and Rachel Schendel, S G N Bennett, Howard and Margaret Buchanan, Pat and Tony Martin, David Silk

NORTON
ST8884 Map 2
Vine Tree 🌟🍷

4 miles from M4 junction 17; A429 towards Malmesbury, then left at Hullavington, Sherston signpost, then follow Norton signposts; in village turn right at Foxley signpost, which takes you into Honey Lane; SN16 0JP

Civilised dining pub with beams and candlelight, big choice of first class food, super wines and a sizeable garden

A wide mix of customers – both loyal regulars and newcomers – create a lively, bustling atmosphere here and all are keen to sample the exceptional drinks and food. The three neatly maintained small rooms open into one another, with aged beams, some old settles and unvarnished wooden tables on flagstone floors, big cream church altar candles, a woodburning stove at one end of the restaurant and a large open fireplace in the central bar, and limited edition and sporting prints; look out for Clementine, the friendly and docile black labrador. St Austell Tribute and a guest beer on handpump, 40 wines by the glass (including sparkling wines and champagne) and quite a choice of malt whiskies and Armagnacs, as well as mulled wine in winter and award-winning bloody marys year round. There are picnic-sets and a children's play area in the two-acre garden, plus a pretty suntrap terrace with teak furniture under big cream umbrellas, and an attractive smokers' shelter. Pets (including horses!) are welcomed and provided for. Look out for the two ghosts that some visitors have spotted. The licensees also run the Barbury at Broad Hinton.

🌟 Using local producers and seasonal ingredients, the impressive food includes duck and chicken liver pâté with orange and tarragon chutney, yellowfin tuna carpaccio with soft-boiled quails eggs, olives and capers, a changing vegetarian risotto, home-roasted honey and mustard ham and free range eggs, pork and sage burger with smoked cheese, apple and thyme compote and chips, rabbit and chicken meatballs on home-made linguine with smoked bacon sauce, lamb chump with salsa verde, and puddings such as sticky toffee pudding and eton mess. *Benchmark main dish: sirloin steak with fries £17.95. Two-course evening meal £22.00.*

Free house ~ Licensees Charles Walker and Tiggi Wood ~ Real ale ~ (01666) 837654 ~ Open 12-3, 6-midnight; 12-4 Sun ~ Bar food 12-2.30, 7-9.30 (9.45 Fri, Sat); 12-3.15 Sun ~ Children welcome ~ Dogs welcome ~ Wi-fi ~ www.thevinetree.co.uk
Recommended by David Jackman, Edward May, Mike and Mary Carter

PITTON
SU2131 Map 2
Silver Plough 🍷 🛏

Village signed from A30 E of Salisbury (follow brown signs); SP5 1DU

Bustling country dining pub with popular, reasonably priced bar food, good drinks and nearby walks; bedrooms

There's always a cheerful crowd of customers here, both locals and visitors of all ages – and dogs are welcomed in the snug where they keep biscuits on the bar. There's plenty to look at in the comfortable, nicely kept front bar: the black beams are strung with hundreds of antique boot-warmers and stretchers, pewter and china tankards, copper kettles, toby jugs, earthenware and glass rolling pins, and so forth. Seats include half a dozen cushioned antique oak settles (one elaborately carved, next to a very fine reproduction of an Elizabethan oak table) around rustic pine tables. They keep Badger Bitter, Sussex and Tanglefoot on handpump and 13 wines by the glass served from a bar made from a hand-carved Elizabethan overmantel. The back bar is simpler, but still has a big winged high-backed settle, cases of antique swords and some substantial pictures; there are two woodburning stoves for winter warmth; background music. The skittle alley is for private use only. The quiet south-facing lawn has picnic-sets and other tables beneath cocktail parasols and there are more seats on the heated terrace; occasional barbecues. If you stay overnight and don't have breakfast, prices are cheaper than those given below. There are plenty of walks in the surrounding woodland and on downland paths.

🍴 Popular food includes lunchtime sandwiches, ham hock terrine with piccalilli, garlic and herb king prawns, chickpea and lentil curry with vegetable bhaji, chargrilled lemon thyme chicken caesar salad, burger with tomato and onion chutney, bacon and cheese, beer-battered hake and chips, chicken and bacon pie, maple-roasted pork belly with bubble and squeak and cider sauce, daily specials, and puddings. *Benchmark main dish: steak in ale pie £11.95. Two-course evening meal £18.00.*

Badger ~ Tenants Stephen and Susan Keyes ~ Real ale ~ (01722) 712266 ~ Open 12-3, 6-11; 12-9.30 Sun ~ Bar food 12-2, 6-9; 12-8 Sun ~ Restaurant ~ Children welcome ~ Dogs allowed in bar ~ Wi-fi ~ Bedrooms: $60/$70 ~ www.silverplough-pitton.co.uk
Recommended by Edward Mirzoeff, Conor McGaughey, George Atkinson, N R White, Fr Robert Marsh, Helen and Brian Edgeley, Norman Patterson, Peter Andrews

POULSHOT
ST9760   Map 2
Raven 🍺
Off A361; SN10 1RW

Pretty village pub with friendly licensees, enjoyable beer and food (cooked by the landlord) and seats in a walled back garden

The professional and welcoming licensees take great care of both their pretty half-timbered pub and their loyal customers – and it shows. The two cosy black-beamed rooms are spotless, with comfortable banquettes, pubby chairs and tables and an open fire. Wadworths IPA and 6X plus a weekend guest beer tapped from the cask and 13 wines by the glass; background music in the dining room only. The jack russell is called Faith and the doberman, Harvey. There are picnic-sets under parasols in the walled back garden and the pub is just across from the village green; good nearby walks.

🍴 The tasty, popular food, cooked by the landlord, includes baguettes, prawn and crayfish cocktail, chicken liver pâté with apple chutney, ham and free-range eggs, vegetarian cajun burger with coleslaw and chips, steak and kidney pie, caribbean jerk chicken with pineapple salsa, free-range pork belly with red wine gravy and apple sauce, bass with salsa verde, and puddings such as pear and almond tart and dark chocolate, coffee and whisky mousse. *Benchmark main dish: fish crumble £11.95. Two-course evening meal £18.00.*

Wadworths ~ Tenants Jeremy and Nathalie Edwards ~ Real ale ~ (01380) 828271 ~ Open 11.30-3, 6.30-11; 12-3.30, 7-10.30 Sun; closed Sun evening, Mon Oct-Easter ~ Bar food 12-2 (2.30 Sun), 7-9 ~ Restaurant ~ Children welcome ~ Dogs allowed in bar ~ Wi-fi ~ www.ravenpoulshot.co.uk *Recommended by Mr and Mrs P R Thomas, Toby Jones*

RAMSBURY

Bell 🍽 🛏

Off B4192 NW of Hungerford, or A4 W; SN8 2PE   SU2771   Map 2

Lovely old inn with beams and timbering, contemporary paintwork and plenty of comfort, a civilised and relaxed atmosphere, efficient staff, thoughtful drinks choice and excellent food; spotless bedrooms

This handsome and civilised 300-year-old former coaching inn has been thoughtfully refurbished and brought up to date with contemporary paintwork and décor blending well with heavy beams and timbering. It brings in a good mix of both locals and visitors, and a friendly welcome is guaranteed. The two rooms of the bar both have a woodburning stove, tartan cushioned wall seats and pale wooden dining chairs around assorted tables, country and wildlife paintings, interesting stained-glass windows and stools against the counter, where efficient, black-clothed staff keep Ramsbury Belapur IPA, Bitter and Gold and a guest from Coastal on handpump, a dozen wines by the glass and 20 malt whiskies. A cosy room between the bar and restaurant has much-prized armchairs and sofas before an open fire, a table of magazines and papers, a couple of portraits, stuffed birds and squirrel, books on shelves and patterned wallpaper. The restaurant, smart but relaxed, is similarly furnished to the bar with white-clothed tables on bare boards or rugs, oil paintings and winter-scene photographs on beige walls; fresh flowers decorate each table. A nice surprise is the charming back café with white-painted farmhouse, tub and wicker chairs on floorboards, where they offer toasties, buns, cakes and so forth – it's very popular for morning coffee and afternoon tea. The garden has picnic-sets on a lower terrace and raised lawn, with more on a little terrace towards the front. The restful, well equipped bedrooms are named after game birds or fish.

 Well presented and using home-grown and Estate produce, the first class food includes lunchtime sandwiches, ballotine of partridge with pear gel, tagliatelle with mushrooms, thyme and crème fraîche, burger of the day with cheese, bacon and excellent triple-cooked chips, gammon with cajun fries, an egg and pineapple, fish pie, venison with celeriac and carrot rösti and parsnip purée, bass with caper and lemon beurre noisette, and puddings such as cherry chocolate torte with cherry ice-cream and plum sponge with ginger crème anglaise. *Benchmark main dish: beer-battered haddock and triple-cooked chips £11.95. Two-course evening meal £25.00.*

Free house ~ Licensee Alistair Ewing ~ Real ale ~ (01672) 520230 ~ Open 12-11 (10 Sun) ~ Bar food 12-2.30, 6-9; 12-3, 6-8 Sun ~ Restaurant ~ Children welcome ~ Dogs allowed in bar ~ Wi-fi ~ Bedrooms: /£110 ~ www.thebellramsbury.com
Recommended by Alfie Bayliss, Edward May

SALISBURY

Haunch of Venison £

Minster Street, opposite Market Cross; SP1 1TB   SU1429   Map 2

Ancient pub oozing history, with tiny beamed rooms, unique fittings and a famous mummified hand

Both the tiny downstairs rooms here have a great deal of character and atmosphere and date from 1320, when the place was used by craftsmen working on the spire of Salisbury Cathedral. There are massive beams in the white ceiling, stout oak benches built into timbered walls, black and white floor tiles and an open fire. A tiny snug (popular with locals, but historically said to be where the ladies drank) opens off the entrance lobby.

Courage Best, Hop Back GFB and Summer Lightning, Ringwood Fortyniner and Salisbury English Ale on handpump from a unique pewter bar counter – there's also a rare set of antique taps for gravity-fed spirits and liqueurs, 60 malt whiskies and a dozen wines by the glass; background music and board games. Halfway up the stairs is a panelled room they call the House of Lords, which has a small-paned window looking down to the main bar and a splendid fireplace that dates from the building's early years; behind glass in a small wall slit is the smoke-preserved mummified hand of an 18th-c card sharp still clutching his cards.

Bar food includes lunchtime sandwiches, ham hock terrine with piccalilli, creamy garlic wild mushrooms on toast, ham and free-range eggs, smoked haddock and salmon fishcakes, venison burger with pickles and chips, chicken in lemon thyme butter with dauphinoise potatoes, pork belly with cider and mustard sauce, and puddings. *Benchmark main dish: venison and smoked bacon casserole £10.95. Two-course evening meal £17.50.*

Scottish Courage ~ Lease Alex Marshall ~ Real ale ~ (01722) 411313 ~ Open 11-midnight; 12-8 Sun ~ Bar food 12-2.30, 5-9.30; all day weekends ~ Restaurant ~ Children welcome ~ Dogs allowed in bar ~ Wi-fi ~ www.restaurant-salisbury.com
Recommended by Giles and Annie Francis, Paul Humphreys, Tony and Rachel Schendel, Mrs Sally Scott

SHERSTON ST8585 Map 2
Rattlebone ♀
Church Street; B4040 Malmesbury–Chipping Sodbury; SN16 0LR

Village pub with lots of atmosphere in rambling rooms, real ales and good bar food using local and free-range produce; friendly staff

This 17th-c village pub has great character, a varied mix of customers and a bustling atmosphere in its softly lit rambling rooms – it's beautiful inside and out. There's a public bar and a long back dining room; throughout you'll find beams, standing timbers and flagstones, pews, settles and country kitchen chairs around an assortment of tables, and armchairs and sofas by roaring fires. Butcombe Bitter, St Austell Tribute and Wells & Youngs Bitter on handpump, 16 wines by the glass from a thoughtful list, local cider and home-made lemonade; background music, board games, TV and games machine. Outside is a skittle alley and three boules pitches, often in use by one of the many pub teams; a boules festival is held in July, as well as mangold hurling (similar to boules, but using cattle-feed turnips) and other events. The two pretty gardens include an extended terrace where they hold barbecues and spit roasts. Wheelchair access.

Using local, seasonal ingredients the good food includes lunchtime sandwiches, potted smoked haddock with cream, cheddar and poached egg, chicken liver parfait, ham and free-range eggs, leek and blue cheese linguine, beer-battered haddock and chips, chicken curry, a pie of the day, pork steak with pear tarte tatin and stilton sauce, and puddings such as raspberry and vodka terrine with raspberry sorbet and white chocolate and pistachio cheesecake. *Benchmark main dish: burger with stilton and skinny fries £10.50. Two-course evening meal £17.50.*

Youngs ~ Tenant Jason Read ~ Real ale ~ (01666) 840871 ~ Open 12-3, 5-11 (midnight Fri); 12-midnight Sat; 12-11 Sun ~ Bar food 12-2.30, 6-9.30; 12-3, 6-8.30 Sun ~ Restaurant ~ Children welcome ~ Dogs allowed in bar ~ Wi-fi ~ Live music last weekend of month ~ www.therattlebone.co.uk *Recommended by Tom and Ruth Rees, David Jackman, Michael Snelgrove, Chris and Angela Buckell*

SOUTH WRAXALL

ST8364 Map 2

Longs Arms 🌟

Upper S Wraxall, off B3109 N of Bradford-on-Avon; BA15 2SB

Friendly licensees for well run old stone inn with plenty of character, real ales and first class food using local seasonal produce

A ppealing to customers of all ages, this handsome stone inn remains as popular as ever with our readers. With a warm and friendly atmosphere, the bar has windsor and other pubby chairs around wooden tables on flagstones, a woodburning stove in the fireplace and high chairs by the counter where they keep Wadworths IPA and 6X on handpump and ten wines by the glass. Another room has cushioned and other dining chairs, a nice old settle and a wall banquette around a mix of tables on carpeting, fresh flowers and lots of prints and paintings; board games and skittle alley. There are tables and chairs in the pretty walled back garden, which also has raised beds and a greenhouse for salad leaves and herbs. Dog biscuits are kept behind the bar.

 Cooked by the landlord, the inventive food includes lunchtime sandwiches, potted Morecambe Bay shrimps on squid toast, twice-baked cheese soufflé, crispy liver with black pudding and pickles, black bream with squid ink tagliatelle, cockles and spider crab sauce, pedigree saddleback pork shoulder with chive mash and crab apple jelly, beef and rabbit pie, duck breast with duck scratchings, beetroot and jersey royals, and puddings such as chocolate tart with pistachios and bakewell tart with cherry sorbet. *Benchmark main dish: lemon sole with pine nuts, baby fennel and lobster sauce £18.00. Two-course evening meal £21.50.*

Wadworths ~ Tenants Rob and Liz Allcock ~ Real ale ~ (01225) 864450 ~ Open 12-3.30, 5.30-11.30; 12-11.30 Fri-Sun; closed Mon and three weeks Jan/Feb ~ Bar food 12-3, 5.30-9.30; 12-9.30 Fri, Sat; 12-5 Sun ~ Restaurant ~ Children welcome ~ Dogs allowed in bar ~ www.thelongsarms.com *Recommended by D P and M A Miles, R L Borthwick, Pete Flower, Priscilla Bishop, David and Jill Wyatt*

SWINDON

SU1384 Map 2

Weighbridge Brewhouse 🍺

Penzance Drive; SN5 7JL

Stunning building with stylish modern décor, own microbrewery ales, a huge wine list, a big range of popular food and helpful staff

E ven though this is a huge place, it does get packed out – so you should book ahead to be sure of a table. The fantastic-looking, stylishly modern dining room is open-plan with a steel-tensioned high-raftered roof – the big central skylight adds even more light. Much emphasis is placed on the highly popular food, but this really is a brewhouse (you can peek through a glass viewing panel to see the equipment) and they keep six own-brewed ales at any one time: Weighbridge Brewhouse Aunt Sallys, Best, Brinkworth Village, Crystal Galaxy, Pooleys Golden and Rock On Ruby. Also, 23 wines by the glass, 25 malt whiskies, and a cocktail menu. The bar area has comfortable brown leather chesterfields and wood and leather armchairs around a few tables on dark flagstones, much-used blue bar chairs against the long dimpled and polished steel counter and a sizeable carved wooden eagle on a stand. The dining room features attractive high-backed striped chairs and long wall banquettes, bare brick walls, candles in red glass jars on the window sills and a glass cabinet at the end displaying about 1,000 bottled beers from around the world. Metal stairs lead up to an area with big sofas and chairs beside a glass piano that overlooks the dining room below; another room up here is used for smaller parties and private functions. There are seats on an outside terrace.

🍴 Highly enjoyable food includes lunch dishes (all at £12.50) such as bubble and squeak with crispy bacon and free-range eggs, vegetarian mexican tagliatelle, sausages of the day with spring onion mash and onion gravy, and seafood in a creamy white wine and dill sauce in a filo basket, as well as pricier options such as crispy duck with redcurrant jelly and cherry wine sauce, pork tenderloin with mushrooms, bacon and baby onions in red wine and cream with cheese dumplings, excellent steaks with several sauces, and puddings such as banoffi pie and honeycomb cheesecake with toffee sauce. *Benchmark main dish: kangaroo, venison and wild boar fillets on wild mushrooms in marsala sauce £25.00. Two-course evening meal £28.00.*

Free house ~ Licensees Anthony and Allyson Windle ~ Real ale ~ (01793) 881500 ~ Open 11-11; 12-10.30 Sun ~ Bar food 12-2, 6-9.30; 12-8 Sun ~ Restaurant ~ Children welcome before 8pm ~ Dogs allowed in bar ~ Wi-fi ~ Live music Thurs-Sat evenings ~ www.weighbridgebrewhouse.co.uk *Recommended by Ruth May, Emma Scofield, Pat and Tony Martin, Roger and Donna Huggins*

TOLLARD ROYAL
King John 🏅 ⇌

ST9317 Map 2

B3081 Shaftesbury–Sixpenny Handley; SP5 5PS

Pleasing contemporary furnishings in carefully opened-up pub, courteous helpful service, a good choice of drinks and excellent food; pretty bedrooms

Most people come to this elegantly furnished pub to enjoy the delicious food, but there's a genuinely warm welcome from the friendly staff and a good choice of drinks too. The L-shaped, open-plan bar has a log fire, a civilised yet informal feel and nice little touches such as a rosemary plant and tiny metal buckets of salt and pepper on scrubbed kitchen tables, dog-motif cushions, a screen made up of the sides of wine boxes, and candles in big glass jars. An appealing mix of seats takes in spindlebacks, captain's and chapel chairs (some built into the bay windows) plus the odd cushioned settle, and there are big terracotta floor tiles, lantern-style wall lights, hound, hunting and other photographs, a master of hounds picture and prints of early 19th-c scientists. A second log fire has fender seats to each side and leather chesterfields in front, and there's also a stuffed heron and grouse and daily papers. Butcombe Bitter and Adam Hensons Rare Breed and Flack Manor Double Drop on handpump and good wines by the glass; you can buy wine from their shop too. Outside the front of the building are seats and tables beneath parasols, with more up steps in the raised garden where there's also an outdoor kitchen pavilion. The bedrooms are comfortable and pretty and there's a self-catering cottage opposite.

🍽 Using the best local produce, the inventive food includes numerous lunchtime dishes that can be ordered as small plates for sharing: rock oysters, lobster gnocchi, devilled duck livers on toast, gruyère fondue with grissini, and pigs head hash with parsley sauce and an egg. Evening choices include portland crab on toast, pigeon salad with bacon, warm fallow deer salad with greens, cod fillet with roast fennel gnocchi, rose veal chops with béarnaise sauce, and puddings such as chocolate and orange terrine and apple doughnuts with toffee sauce and mulled cider. *Benchmark main dish: twice-baked cheddar cheese soufflé and salad £14.95. Two-course evening meal £27.00.*

Free house ~ Licensees Alex and Gretchen Booj ~ Real ale ~ (01725) 516207 ~ Open 8am-midnight ~ Bar food 12-2.30, 7-9.30; 12-3, 7-9 Sun ~ Restaurant ~ Children welcome but over-5s only in evening ~ Dogs welcome ~ Wi-fi ~ Bedrooms: £130/£140 ~

www.kingjohninn.co.uk *Recommended by Lesley and Brian Lynn, Mr and Mrs J J A Davis,*
Peter and Eleanor Kenyon, Michael Doswell

UPTON LOVELL
ST9441   Map 2

Prince Leopold

Up Street, village signed from A36; BA12 0JP

**Snug little rooms, a friendly atmosphere, welcoming licensees
and enjoyable food and drink; bedrooms**

Run by charming licensees, this is a prettily tucked away and neatly modernised Victorian pub. The simply furnished bar – busy with chatty, cheerful locals – has two farmhouse tables with sturdy chairs, well used bar stools against the hand-crafted elm counter, wooden floorboards and an easy-going atmosphere. Butcombe Bitter, Plain Arty Farty and Sharps Doom Bar on handpump and interesting wines and spirits. A cosy little snug to the right of the door has bookshelves on either side of an open fire, comfortable sofas around a table with daily papers, rugs and a few settles with tapestry and other cushions. Two linked rooms lead off the bar with a mix of high-backed leather or wooden dining chairs, more rugs on floorboards and some country prints on the pale green panelled walls. The back room is a semi-private dining room. The light and airy restaurant is more formal and overlooks the River Wylye – as do some outdoor balcony tables. There are water bowls for dogs and seats in the terraced, riverside garden. The cottagey bedrooms are comfortable and well equipped.

A wide choice of good food includes lunchtime sandwiches, sardines with chilli, lemon and garlic, cajun chicken with coriander and yoghurt dip, sharing platters, wild mushroom and spinach risotto, sausage and mash with onion gravy, burger with onion rings, pickles and chips, duck breast with pak choi, rösti potato and redcurrant sauce, salmon fillet with salsa verde, and puddings such as key lime pie and apple and berry crumble. *Benchmark main dish: 21-day-aged rib-eye steak with a choice of sauce and chips £19.95. Two-course evening meal £20.00.*

Free house ~ Licensee Liza Kearney ~ Real ale ~ (01985) 850460 ~ Open 12-3, 6-11 (midnight Fri, Sat); 12-3, 6-10 Sun ~ Bar food 12-2.30, 6-9.30 ~ Restaurant ~ Children welcome ~ Dogs welcome ~ Wi-fi ~ Bedrooms: £60/£75 ~ www.princeleopoldinn.co.uk
Recommended by John and June Freeman

WEST LAVINGTON
SU0052   Map 2

Bridge Inn ⭐

Church Street (A360); SN10 4LD

**Friendly dining pub with good bar food cooked by the landlord,
real ales and a light, comfortable bar**

With an easy-going atmosphere and accomplished cooking, this quietly civilised village pub is enjoyed by locals and visitors. The comfortable, spacious bar mixes contemporary features with firmly traditional fixtures such as the enormous brick inglenook with its roaring log fire; at the opposite end is a smaller modern fireplace, in an area set mostly for eating. The cream-painted or exposed brick walls are hung with local pictures of the Lavingtons and there are fresh flowers and evening candlelight; timbers and the occasional step divide the various areas. Sharps Doom Bar and Wadworths IPA on handpump, ten wines by the glass and half a dozen malt whiskies; background music and board games. The raised lawn at the back is a pleasant place to spend a summer's afternoon, and there are large vegetable patches for home-grown produce and chickens; boules.

Cooked by the landlord, the rewarding food includes lunchtime ciabatta sandwiches, malaysian prawn laksa with noodles, rabbit rillettes with apple chutney, brie, sweet potato and red onion frittata, burger with pulled barbecue pork, red cabbage slaw and fries, beer-battered fish and chips, bass fillet with niçoise salad, sirloin steak with peppercorn sauce, and puddings such as buttermilk panna cotta with poached rhubarb, and banana and peanut butter sponge with toffee sauce, peanut brittle and banana and rum ice-cream. *Benchmark main dish: venison haunch with rhubarb purée and blackcurrant jus £16.50. Two-course evening meal £20.00.*

Enterprise ~ Lease Emily Robinson and James Stewart ~ Real ale ~ (01380) 813213 ~ Open 12-3, 6-10; 12-4 Sun; closed Sun evening, Mon ~ Bar food 12-2.30, 6.30-9 ~ Children welcome ~ Dogs welcome ~ Wi-fi ~ www.the-bridge-inn.co.uk
Recommended by Verity Wills, Mrs Blethyn Elliott

Also Worth a Visit in Wiltshire

Besides the fully inspected pubs, you might like to try these pubs that have been recommended to us and described by readers. Do tell us what you think of them: feedback@goodguides.com

ALDBOURNE   SU2675
Crown (01672) 540214
The Square; SN8 2DU Old local overlooking pretty village's pond, good value enjoyable food including pizzas and Sun carvery, Sharps Doom Bar, Shepherd Neame Spitfire and guests, friendly helpful staff, comfortable two-part beamed lounge with sofas by log fire in huge brick inglenook linking to public bar, old tables and bare boards, small nicely laid out dining room; background music and some live music, Mon movie night, Tues quiz; children and dogs welcome, courtyard tables, Early English church nearby, four bedrooms, open (and food) all day. *(Anon)*

ALVEDISTON   ST9723
Crown (01722) 780335
Off A30 W of Salisbury; SP5 5JY Cosy 15th-c thatched inn with three very low-beamed, partly panelled rooms, two inglenooks, good choice of enjoyable fairly priced home-made food, four well kept ales including Sixpenny, Wessex cider, pleasant service; children and dogs welcome, pretty views from attractive garden with terrace, good local walks, three bedrooms, open all day Sat, till 9pm Sun. *(David and Judy Robison)*

BADBURY   SU1980
★ **Plough** (01793) 740342
A346 (Marlborough Road) just S of M4 junction 15; SN4 0EP Country pub well placed for M4 with good choice of enjoyable fairly priced food (all day weekends), friendly helpful staff, well kept Arkells and decent wines, large rambling bar with log fire, light airy dining room; background music; children and dogs welcome, tree-shaded garden with downs views, open all day. *(Giles and Annie Francis, R T and J C Moggridge)*

BARFORD ST MARTIN   SU0531
★ **Barford Inn** (01722) 742242
B3089 W of Salisbury (Grovely Road), just off A30; SP3 4AB Welcoming 16th-c coaching inn, dark-panelled front bar with big log fire, other interlinking rooms, old utensils and farming tools, beamed bare-brick restaurant, wide choice of enjoyable reasonably priced food including deals, prompt friendly service, well kept Badger ales and decent wines by the glass; children welcome, dogs in bar, disabled access (not to bar) and facilities, terrace tables, more in back garden, four comfortable annexe bedrooms, good walks, open all day. *(Wendy Breese)*

BECKHAMPTON   SU0868
★ **Waggon & Horses** (01672) 539418
A4 Marlborough–Calne; SN8 1QJ Handsome stone and thatch former coaching inn; generous fairly priced food cooked to order from varied menu in open-plan beamed bar or separate dining area, well kept Wadworths ales, good cheerful service; background music; children and dogs welcome, pleasant raised garden with play area, handy for Avebury (NT). *(P A Rowe, Sheila and Robert Robinson, David Crook)*

BERWICK ST JAMES   SU0739
★ **Boot** (01722) 790243
High Street (B3083); SP3 4TN Welcoming flint and stone pub not far from Stonehenge, good locally sourced food from daily changing blackboard menu, friendly efficient staff, well kept Wadworths ales and a guest, huge log fire in inglenook at one end, sporting prints over brick fireplace at other, lit candles, small back dining room with collection of celebrity boots; children and dogs welcome, sheltered side lawn. *(Gavin McLauchlan, Simon Elwood)*

BERWICK ST JOHN   ST9422

★**Talbot**   (01747) 828222

*Village signed from A30 E of
Shaftesbury; SP7 0HA* Unspoilt 17th-c
pub in attractive village, simple furnishings
and big inglenook in heavily beamed bar,
Ringwood Best, Wadworths 6X and a guest
such as Sixpenny IPA, several wines by the
glass, good choice of popular home-made
food including decent vegetarian options,
friendly service, restaurant, darts; free wi-fi;
children welcome and dogs (pub has its
own), seats outside, good local walks, closed
Sun evening, Mon. *(B J Thompson, Pip White,
Toby Jones)*

BIDDESTONE   ST8673

Biddestone Arms   (01249) 714377

*Off A420 W of Chippenham; The Green;
SN14 7DG* Welcoming spacious pub mostly
set out for its well liked food from standards
to specials, good vegetarian options and Sun
carvery too, friendly helpful service, well kept
ales such as Wadworths, games in compact
public bar, nice open fire; children and dogs
(in bar areas) allowed, tables in pretty back
garden, pretty village with lovely pond.
*(Cane family, Jenny Hughes, Mr and Mrs
A H Young)*

BOX   ST8168

Northey Arms   (01225) 742333

A4, Bath side; SN13 8AE Stone-built
19th-c dining pub with good choice
of enjoyable food all day, Wadworths
ales, decent wines by the glass, fresh
contemporary décor with chunky modern
tables and high-backed rattan chairs;
background music; children welcome, garden
tables, five new bedrooms, open all day from
8am for breakfast. *(Mr and Mrs P R Thomas,
Taff Thomas)*

BOX   ST8369

★**Quarrymans Arms**   (01225) 743569

*Box Hill; from Bath on A4 right into
Bargates 50 metres before railway
bridge, left up Quarry Hill at T junction,
left again at grassy triangle; from
Corsham, left after Rudloe Park Hotel
into Beech Road, third left on to Barnetts
Hill, and right at top of hill; OS Sheet
173 map reference 834694; SN13 8HN*
Enjoyable unpretentious pub with friendly
staff and informal relaxed atmosphere,
plenty of mining-related photographs and
memorabilia dotted around (once the local
of Bath-stone miners – you can hire a key to
visit the extensive mines), well kept
Butcombe, Moles, Wadworths and guests,
60 malt whiskies and several wines by the
glass, decent choice of enjoyable fairly
priced food including daily specials;
children and dogs welcome, picnic-sets on
terrace with sweeping views, popular with
walkers and potholers, four bedrooms,
open all day. *(MJVK, Dr and Mrs A K Clarke,*

*Roger and Donna Huggins, Alan and Jane Shaw,
Taff Thomas)*

BRADFORD-ON-AVON   ST8260

Barge   (01225) 863403

Frome Road; BA15 2EA Large modernised
open-plan pub set down from canal, well kept
ales such as Brakspears, Fullers, Marstons
and Ringwood, nice wines by the glass,
enjoyable pub food including children's
choices, good service and happy atmosphere,
stripped stone and flagstones, solid furniture,
woodburners; wheelchair access, garden
with smokers' pavilion, steps up to canalside
picnic-sets, moorings, five bedrooms.
(J D O Carter, John Coatsworth, Taff Thomas)

BRADFORD-ON-AVON   ST8261

★**Castle**   (01225) 865657

*Mount Pleasant, by junction with A363,
N edge of town; extremely limited pub
parking, spaces in nearby streets;
BA15 1SJ* Imposing stone pub owned by
Flatcappers; unspoilt bar with individual
atmosphere, wide range of seating on dark
flagstones, church candles, daily papers and
good log fire, a house beer from Vale along
with guests such as Bath, Glastonbury, Milk
Street and Three Castles, farm cider and
well chosen wines chalked on blackboard,
good all-day food from breakfast on including
sandwiches and baguettes, cheerful helpful
service, bare-boards rooms on right similar
in style; background music, board games;
children welcome, wheelchair access, long
tables and benches on sunny front terrace
with sweeping town views, comfortable
boutique bedrooms, limited parking, open all
day. *(Chris and Angela Buckell, Mr and Mrs P R
Thomas, Hugh Roberts, Carol and Luke Wilson)*

BRADFORD-ON-AVON   ST8060

Cross Guns   (01225) 862335

*Avoncliff, 2 miles W; OS Sheet 173 map
reference 805600; BA15 2HB* Congenial
bustle on summer days with swarms of
people in partly concreted areas steeply
terraced above the bridges, aqueducts and
river; appealingly quaint at quieter times,
with stripped-stone low-beamed bar, 16th-c
inglenook, full Box Steam range kept well
and a guest, several ciders, lots of malt
whiskies and interesting wines by the glass
including country ones, decent choice of food
from baguettes up, good friendly service,
upstairs river-view restaurant; children
and dogs welcome, wheelchair accessible,
bedrooms, open (and food) all day. *(Anon)*

BRADFORD-ON-AVON   ST8161

Dog & Fox   (01225) 862137

Ashley Road; BA15 1RT Well run
traditional pub on country outskirts, three
well kept ales and three good ciders,
enjoyable straightforward low-priced
food (not Sun or Mon evenings); children
welcome, garden with play area, open all
day weekends. *(Taff Thomas)*

BROMHAM ST9665
Greyhound (01380) 850241
Off A342; High Street; SN15 2HA
Popular old beamed dining pub with light modern décor, comfortable sofas and log fires, walk-across well in back bar, wide choice of good reasonably priced home-made food including weekday set lunch, efficient friendly service, well kept Wadworths ales and wide choice of wines, upstairs skittle alley/restaurant; background music; children welcome, no dogs inside, pretty hanging baskets in front, big enclosed garden with decking and boules, open (and food) all day. *(Sue Vince, Mr and Mrs P R Thomas)*

BULKINGTON ST9458
★ Well (01380) 828287
High Street; SN10 1SJ Roomy and attractively modernised open-plan pub, good food from traditional favourites to interesting well presented restaurant-style dishes, theme night first Mon of month, efficient friendly service, ales such as Butcombe, Sharps, Timothy Taylors and Wadworths, well priced wines; closed Mon lunchtime. *(Anon)*

BURCOMBE SU0631
★ Ship (01722) 743182
Burcombe Lane; brown sign to pub off A30 W of Salisbury, then turn right; SP2 0EJ Busy pub and most customers here for the food – pubby dishes through to more elaborate restaurant-style meals, also a good value lunchtime/early evening set menu (Mon-Thurs); area by entrance with log fire, beams and leather-cushioned wall and window seats on dark slate tiles, steps up to spreading area of pale wood dining chairs around bleached tables on neat dark brown wood-strip floor, more beams (one supporting a splendid chandelier), small modern pictures and big church candles, Butcombe, Ringwood and Wadworths, good choice of wines by the glass and whiskies; background music; children welcome, dogs in bar, picnic-sets in informal back garden sloping down to willows by fenced-off River Nadder. *(Anon)*

BURTON ST8179
Old House At Home (01454) 218227
B4039 Chippenham–Chipping Sodbury; SN14 7LT Spacious ivy-clad stone dining pub, popular food including fresh fish and game, friendly efficient service, a couple of well kept ales and good choice of wines by the glass, log fire; children welcome, six bedrooms, open (and food) all day. *(Roger and Donna Huggins)*

CASTLE COMBE ST8477
Castle Inn (01249) 783030
Off A420; SN14 7HN Handsome inn centrally placed in this remarkably preserved Cotswold village; beamed bar with big inglenook, padded bar stools and fine old settle, hunting and vintage motor racing pictures, Butcombe and Great Western, decent wines by the glass, well liked bar food and more restauranty evening menu, friendly attentive service, two snug lounges, formal dining rooms and big upstairs eating area opening on to charming little roof terrace; no dogs; children welcome, tables out at front looking down idyllic main street, fascinating medieval church clock, 11 bedrooms, limited parking, open all day. *(Anon)*

CHILMARK ST9732
Black Dog (01722) 716344
B3089 Salisbury–Hindon; SP3 5AH 15th-c beamed village pub with several cosy linked areas, cushioned window seats, inglenook woodburner, a suit of armour in one part, black and white film star pictures in another, enjoyable home-made food from lunchtime sandwiches and pizzas up, Wadworths ales, friendly service; Mon quiz, free wi-fi; children and dogs welcome, good-sized roadside garden, closed Sun evening, also Tues Oct-March. *(Mr and Mrs J Davis)*

CHIRTON SU0757
Wiltshire Yeoman (01380) 840665
Andover Road (A342 SE of Devizes); SN10 3QN Welcoming 19th-c red-brick pub, bare-boards bar with log-fire, separate carpeted dining room, enjoyable home-made food including blackboard specials, Wadworths ales, skittle alley/function area; background music; children and dogs welcome, back garden with heated gazebo, closed Sun evening, Mon. *(Anon)*

CHITTERNE ST9843
Kings Head (01985) 850770
B390 Heytesbury–Shrewton; BA12 0LJ Attractive traditional pub refurbished after flooding, welcoming landlord, slate-floor bar with woodburner, two dining areas, well kept Flowers and Plain, home-made pubby food (Tues-Sat evenings, Sun lunchtime); children and dogs welcome, side garden, pretty village, handy for Salisbury Plain walks. *(Hugh Roberts)*

CORSHAM ST8670
Hare & Hounds (01249) 701106
Pickwick (A4 E); SN13 0HY Friendly old pub by mini roundabout, popular well priced food (smaller helpings available), well kept ales such as Bath Gem and Caledonian Deuchars IPA, plenty of wines by the glass, log fire, Tues quiz; children (if eating) and dogs welcome, picnic-sets on strip of lawn between car park and road, open (and food) all day. *(Roger and Donna Huggins, Alan and Jane Shaw)*

CORSHAM ST8670
★ Two Pigs (01249) 712515
Pickwick (A4); SN13 0HY Friendly and cheerfully eccentric little beer lovers' pub run by individualistic landlord – most lively on Mon evenings when there's live music;

collection of bric-a-brac in narrow dimly lit flagstoned bar, enamel signs on wood-clad walls, pig-theme ornaments and old radios, Stonehenge ales including Pigswill and a couple of guests; background blues, no food or under-21s; covered yard outside called the Sty, closed lunchtimes except Sun. *(Dr and Mrs A K Clarke, Roger and Donna Huggins, Alan and Jane Shaw)*

CORTON   ST9340
★**Dove**   (01985) 850109

Off A36 at Upton Lovell, SE of Warminster; BA12 0SZ Popular well prepared food from baguettes and pub favourites to more enterprising dishes, good service, at least three well kept ales such as Otter, Salisbury and Sharps, nice wines by the glass and good choice of other drinks, opened-up rooms with flagstones, oak boards, magnolia walls and pale green dados, lots of animal pictures/sculptures, flowers on good quality dining tables, newspapers and woodburner in the bar, sunny conservatory; can get very busy; children and dogs welcome, wheelchair access/facilities, rustic furniture in garden, lovely valley, five comfortable bedrooms in courtyard annexe, open all day Sun. *(Chris and Angela Buckell)*

CROCKERTON   ST8642
★**Bath Arms**   (01985) 212262

Off A350 Warminster–Blandford; BA12 8AJ Welcoming old dining pub, bar with plush banquettes and matching chairs, well spaced tables on parquet, beams in whitewashed ceiling, crackling log fire, three Wessex ales, real cider and several wines by the glass, generally well liked food including some interesting modern dishes, cheerful staff, two formal dining rooms with chunky pine furniture; background music; children and dogs welcome, several garden areas with plenty of picnic-sets, gets crowded during school holidays (Longleat close by), bedrooms, open all day weekends. *(Anon)*

DEVIZES   SU0061
Bear   (01380) 722444

Market Place; SN10 1HS Refurbished ancient coaching inn, big carpeted main bar with log fires, winged wall settles and upholstered bucket armchairs, steps up to room named after portrait painter Thomas Lawrence with oak-panelled walls and big open fireplace, well kept Wadworths and extensive choice of wines by the glass, enjoyable food from sandwiches and light dishes up, Bear Grills bistro, cellar bar with live music (Fri) and comedy night first Thurs of month; children welcome, dogs in

front bar, wheelchair access throughout, mediterranean-style courtyard, 25 bedrooms, open all day. *(Anon)*

DEVIZES   SU0061
British Lion   (01380) 720665

A361 Swindon roundabout; SN10 1LQ Chatty little beer lovers' pub with four well kept quickly changing ales, bare-boards bar with brewery mirrors, gas fire, back part with pool and darts, no food; garden behind, open all day. *(Anon)*

DINTON   SU0131
Penruddocke Arms   (01722) 716253

Hindon Road; SP3 5EL Roadside country pub under friendly new licensees (formerly at the Bell in Wylye), spacious and comfortable, with good reasonably priced home-made food and well kept changing ales, games room (pool and darts); bedrooms. *(Anon)*

DONHEAD ST ANDREW   ST9124
★**Forester**   (01747) 828038

Village signposted off A30 E of Shaftesbury, just E of Ludwell; Lower Street; SP7 9EE Attractive 14th-c thatched restaurant-pub in charming village; relaxed atmosphere in nice bar, stripped tables on wood floors, log fire in inglenook, alcove with sofa and magazines, Butcombe Bitter and a guest, 15 wines by the glass including champagne, very good well presented food from bar tapas up with much emphasis on fresh fish/seafood, good service, comfortable main dining room with well spaced country kitchen tables, second cosier dining room; children and dogs welcome, seats outside on good-sized terrace with country views, can walk up White Sheet Hill and past the old and 'new' Wardour castles, closed Sun evening, Mon. *(David and Judy Robison, Edward Mirzoeff)*

EBBESBOURNE WAKE   ST9924
★**Horseshoe**   (01722) 780474

On A354 S of Salisbury, right at signpost at Coombe Bissett; village about 8 miles further; SP5 5JF Unspoilt country pub in pretty village with plenty of regular customers, welcoming long-serving licensees and friendly staff, well kept Bowman, Otter, Palmers and guests tapped from the cask, farm cider, good traditional food (not Mon) with lots of accompanying vegetables, neatly kept and comfortable character bar, collection of farm tools and bric-a-brac on beams, conservatory extension and small restaurant; children (away from bar) and dogs welcome, seats in pretty little garden with views over River Ebble valley, play area,

---

Please tell us if the décor, atmosphere, food or drink at a pub is different from our description. We rely on readers' reports to keep us up to date: feedback@goodguides.com, or (no stamp needed) The Good Pub Guide, FREEPOST RTJR-ZCYZ-RJZT, Perrymans Lane, Etchingham TN19 7DN.

chickens and a goat in paddock, good nearby walks, one bedroom, closed Sun evening, Mon lunchtime. *(Phil and Jane Villiers, Michael and Mary Smith)*

ENFORD   SU14351
Swan (01980) 670338
Long Street, off A345; SN9 6DD
Attractive and welcoming thatched village pub with comfortable beamed interior, good range of beers and enjoyable well presented food from baguettes to daily specials; seats out on small front terrace. *(David Wiltshire, Hugh Roberts)*

FOXHAM   ST9777
Foxham Inn (01249) 740665
NE of Chippenham; SN15 4NQ Small remote country dining pub with simple traditional décor, enterprising food strong on local produce along with more straightforward bar meals, well kept ales such as Bath and Wadworths, good choice of wines by the glass and nice coffee, woodburner, more contemporary back restaurant, own bread, chutneys, jams etc for sale; children and dogs welcome, disabled access and facilities, terrace tables with pergola, extensive views from front, peaceful village, two bedrooms, closed Mon. *(Alastair Muir, Mr and Mrs A H Young)*

FROXFIELD   SU2968
Pelican (01488) 682479
Off A4; SN8 3JY Modernised 17th-c coaching inn, good choice of enjoyable home-made food served by helpful friendly young staff, local ales, comfortable relaxed atmosphere; pleasant streamside garden with terrace and duck pond, Kennet & Avon Canal walks, bedrooms, open all day. *(David and Judy Robison)*

HAMPTWORTH   SU2419
Cuckoo (01794) 390302
Hamptworth Road; SP5 2DU 17th-c thatched New Forest pub, peaceful and unspoilt, with friendly mix of customers from farmers to families in four compact rooms around tiny servery, ales such as Bowman, Hop Back and Ringwood tapped from the cask, real ciders/perry, simple food like pasties and pies, mugs and jugs hanging from ceiling, beer memorabilia, basic wooden furniture and open fire; dogs welcome, big garden with view of golf course, open all day Fri-Sun. *(Anon)*

HANNINGTON   SU1793
Jolly Tar (01793) 762245
Off B4019 W of Highworth; Queens Road; SN6 7RP Relaxing beamed bar with big log fire, steps up to flagstoned and stripped-stone dining area, good reasonably priced home-made food from ciabattas up, well kept Arkells ales, friendly helpful service; children welcome, picnic-sets on front terrace and in big garden with play

area, four comfortable bedrooms, good breakfast, pretty village. *(Ross Balaam)*

HEDDINGTON   ST9966
Ivy (01380) 859652
Off A3102 S of Calne; SN11 0PL Picturesque thatched 15th-c village local under welcoming licensees; good inglenook log fire in L-shaped bar, heavy low beams, timbered walls, assorted furnishings on parquet floor, cask-tapped Wadworths ales, pubby food (not Sun evening, Mon), back dining room; children and dogs welcome, disabled access, picnic-sets in small side garden, open all day weekends, closed weekday lunchtimes. *(Anon)*

HEYTESBURY   ST9242
Angel (01985) 840330
Just off A36 E of Warminster; High Street; BA12 0ED Beamed 16th-c coaching inn in quiet village just below Salisbury Plain, spacious and comfortably modernised, with good food (not Sun evening, must book weekends), Greene King ales, friendly helpful staff, log fire; children and dogs (in bar) welcome, bedrooms, open all day (till 8pm Sun). *(Hugh Roberts)*

HINDON   ST9032
Angel (01747) 820696
B3089 Wilton–Mere; SP3 6DJ Modernised dining pub with big log fire, flagstones and other coaching-inn survivals, good food from pub favourites through grills to specials, friendly efficient service, nice choice of wines, ales such as Otter, Sharps and Timothy Taylors, daily newspapers; children welcome, dogs in bar, courtyard tables, nine comfortable bedrooms (named after game birds), open all day. *(Anon)*

HINDON   ST9132
Lamb (01747) 820573
B3089 Wilton–Mere; SP3 6DP Attractive old hotel with long roomy log-fire bar, two flagstoned lower sections with very long polished table, high-backed pews and settles, up steps to a third, bigger area, well kept ales including Wells & Youngs, several wines by the glass and around 100 malt whiskies, cuban cigars, enjoyable bar and restaurant food, friendly helpful service from smartly dressed staff; can get very busy, service charge added to bill; children and dogs welcome, tables on roadside terrace and in garden across road with boules, 19 bedrooms, good breakfast, open all day from 7.30am. *(Anon)*

HONEYSTREET   SU1061
Barge (01672) 851705
Off A345 W of Pewsey; SN9 5PS Early 19th-c stone pub in nice setting by Kennet & Avon Canal, open-plan bar with wood floor and dark walls, good Honeystreet beers (brewed by Stonehenge) including 1810, Croppie and Alien Abduction,

traditional cider, tasty reasonably priced traditional food, friendly service, pool room with painted ceiling of local area, occasional magic shows, live music Sat; children, dogs, crop-circle and UFO enthusiasts welcome, waterside picnic-sets, camping field, good walks, open all day summer. *(N R White)*

HORNINGSHAM   ST8041
Bath Arms (01985) 844308

By tradesmen's entrance to Longleat House; BA12 7LY Handsome old stone-built inn on pretty village's sloping green, stylishly opened up as welcoming dining pub with several linked areas including a proper bar, polished wood floors and open fires, good generous local food from bar snacks up, well kept Wessex ales and a guest, Weston's cider, good choice of wines and other drinks, charming efficient staff, side restaurant and conservatory; can get very busy; wheelchair access to bars via side door, attractive garden with neat terraces, smokers' gazebo, 15 bedrooms. *(Mark Flynn, Chris and Angela Buckell)*

HORTON   SU0363
Bridge Inn (01380) 860273

Horton Road; village signed off A361 London Road, NE of Devizes; SN10 2JS Former flour mill and bakery by Kennet & Avon Canal, carpeted log-fire area on left with tables set for dining, more pubby part to right of bar with some stripped brickwork and country kitchen furniture on reconstituted flagstones, old bargee photographs and rural pictures, Wadworths ales, good value food including Weds curry buffet and Sun carvery, friendly service; background music, TV; well behaved children welcome, dogs in bar, disabled facilities, safely fenced garden with picnic-sets, original grinding wheel, canal walks and moorings, bedrooms, closed Mon. *(Anon)*

KILMINGTON   ST7835
Red Lion (01985) 844263

B3092 Mere–Frome, 2.5 miles S of Maiden Bradley; 3 miles from A303 Mere turn-off; BA12 6RP NT-owned country pub with low-beamed flagstoned bar, cushioned wall and window seats, curved high-backed settle, log fires in big fireplaces (fine iron fireback in one), well kept ales including Butcombe and traditional ciders such as Lilley's, lunchtime bar food and more elaborate evening menu, newer big-windowed dining area with modern country feel; children and dogs (in bar) welcome, picnic-sets in large attractive garden with smokers' shelter, White Sheet Hill (hang-gliding) and Stourhead gardens (NT) nearby. *(Chris and Angela Buckell, Pete Walker, Edward Mirzoeff)*

LACOCK   ST9268
Bell (01249) 730308

E of village; SN15 2PJ Extended cottagey pub with warm welcome, Bath, Palmers,

Great Western and guests kept well (winter beer festival), traditional ciders, decent wines by the glass and lots of malt whiskies, good choice of popular food, linked rooms off bar including pretty restaurant and conservatory; children welcome away from bar, disabled access, sheltered well tended garden, open (and food) all day weekends. *(Dr and Mrs A K Clarke, N R White)*

LACOCK   ST9168
★ George (01249) 730263

West Street; village signed off A350 S of Chippenham; SN15 2LH Rambling inn at centre of busy NT tourist village; low-beamed bar with upright timbers creating cosy corners, armchairs and windsor chairs around close-set tables, seats in stone-mullioned windows, some flagstones, dog treadwheel in outer breast of central fireplace, lots of old pictures and bric-a-brac, souvenirs from filming *Cranford* and *Harry Potter* in the village, Wadworths beers and Weston's cider, bar food from snacks up; background music; children and dogs welcome, tricky wheelchair access, picnic-sets on grass and in appealing courtyard with pillory and well, open all day in summer. *(Roger and Donna Huggins, Alan and Jane Shaw, Adrian Johnson)*

LACOCK   ST9168
★ Red Lion (01249) 730456

High Street; SN15 2LQ Popular NT-owned Georgian inn, sizeable opened-up interior with log fire in big stone fireplace, bare boards and flagstones, roughly carved screens here and there and some cosy alcoves, well kept Wadworths ales, Thatcher's and Weston's ciders, enjoyable food from sandwiches and sharing plates up, pleasant attentive service; background music; children and dogs welcome, wheelchair access to main bar area only, picnic-sets out on gravel, four modern bedrooms, open (and food) all day. *(J D O Carter, Steve Whalley)*

LIDDINGTON   SU2081
Village Inn (01793) 790314

Handy for M4 junction 15, via A419 and B4192; Bell Lane; SN4 0HE Comfortable and welcoming with enjoyable good value food from varied menu including early-bird bargains and daily specials, well kept Arkells ales; linked bar areas, stripped-stone and raftered back dining extension, conservatory, log fire in splendid fireplace; well behaved children over 8 allowed in restaurant area, disabled facilities, terrace tables. *(Ian Herdman, KC, R K Phillips)*

LITTLE SOMERFORD   .   ST9784
Somerford Arms (01666) 826535

Signed off B4042 Malmesbury–Brinkworth; SN15 5JP Modernised village pub with nice welcoming atmosphere, easy chairs in front of bar's woodburner, green-painted half-panelling and stone flooring, linked restaurant with good food – all home-made including some inventive dishes, well kept changing ales and lots of wines by the glass, pub dog (boxer called Nutmeg) and parrot; children, other dogs and muddy boots welcome, open all day. *(MJVK)*

LONGBRIDGE DEVERILL ST8640
George (01985) 840396
A350/B3095; BA12 7DG Popular extended roadside inn recently refurbished by Upham, their beers kept well and plentiful helpings of enjoyable freshly made food, Sun carvery, friendly enthusiastic staff, conservatory; children welcome, big riverside garden with play area and maybe summer marquee, 12 bedrooms, open all day (breakfast from 8am). *(Edward Mirzoeff, Comus and Sarah Elliott)*

LOWER WOODFORD SU1235
★Wheatsheaf (01722) 782203
Signed off A360 just N of Salisbury; SP4 6NQ Updated and extended 18th-c Badger dining pub, open airy feel, with good choice of fairly priced traditional food from sharing boards up (booking advised weekends), well kept beers, good wines and coffee, well trained genial staff, beams, panelling and exposed brickwork, mix of old furniture, log fire and woodburner; background music, free wi-fi; children welcome, dogs in bar, disabled access and parking, tree-lined fenced garden with play area, pretty setting, open (and food) all day. *(Robert Watt, Mrs Zara Elliott)*

LUCKINGTON ST8384
★Old Royal Ship (01666) 840222
Off B4040 SW of Malmesbury; SN14 6PA Friendly pub by village green, opened up inside with one long bar divided into three areas, Bass, Stonehenge, Wadworths and Wickwar from central servery, also farm cider and several wines by the glass, good range of well liked food including vegetarian, decent coffee, prompt service, neat tables, spindleback chairs and small cushioned settles on dark boards, some stripped masonry and small open fire, skittle alley; background music – live jazz second Weds of month, games machine; children welcome, garden (beyond car park) with boules, play area and plenty of seats, Badminton House close by, open all day Sat. *(John and Gloria Isaacs, Guy Vowles)*

MALMESBURY ST9287
Smoking Dog (01666) 825823
High Street; SN16 9AT Old mid-terrace stone local with two cosy flagstoned front bars, well kept ales and several wines by the glass, decent choice of food in back dining

area, log fire; children and dogs welcome, small secluded garden up steep steps, spring sausage and beer festival, bedrooms, open all day. *(Jim and Maggie Cowell)*

MARLBOROUGH SU1869
Castle & Ball (01672) 515201
High Street; SN8 1LZ Popular refurbished coaching inn dating from the 15th c (Old English Inn); spacious interior with lounge bar and restaurant, wide choice of enjoyable food including deals, Greene King ales and nice range of well listed wines by the glass, good attentive service; background music; children and dogs (in bar) welcome, seats out under projecting colonnade and in back walled garden, 37 bedrooms, open all day. *(George Atkinson, Susan and Nigel Brookes)*

MONKTON FARLEIGH ST8065
Muddy Duck (01225) 858705
Signed off A363 Bradford–Bath; BA15 2QH Imposing 17th-c stone pub-restaurant in lovely village; bare-boards bar with leather armchairs by inglenook woodburner, Butcombe, St Austell and a guest from zinc-topped counter, good wine and whisky choice, parquet-floored restaurant with low pendant lighting and open fire, good variety of enjoyable food (all day weekends, till 7.30pm Sun), efficient friendly service; background music; children welcome, dogs in bar, seats in front courtyard and two-tier back garden with country views, five bedrooms (three with log fires), open all day. *(Anon)*

NESTON ST8668
Neston Country Inn (01225) 811694
Pool Green; SN13 9SN Welcoming village pub with good reasonably priced food cooked to order from varied menu, well kept ales such as Fullers, Milk Street and Plain, friendly helpful staff; four bedrooms, open all day weekends (till 9pm Sun), closed Mon lunchtime (and Tues lunchtime after bank holiday). *(Jenny and Brian Seller)*

NETHERHAMPTON SU1129
★Victoria & Albert (01722) 743174
Just off A3094 W of Salisbury; SP2 8PU Cosy black-beamed bar in simple thatched cottage, good generous food from sandwiches up, sensible prices and local supplies, three well kept changing ales, farm cider and decent wines, welcoming helpful staff, old-fashioned cushioned wall settles on ancient floor tiles, log fire, restaurant; children and dogs welcome, hatch service for sizeable terrace and garden behind, handy for Wilton House and Nadder Valley walks. *(Anon)*

The letters and figures after the name of each town are its Ordnance Survey map reference. 'Using the *Guide*' at the beginning of the book explains how it helps you find a pub, in road atlases or large-scale maps as well as in our own maps.

OGBOURNE ST ANDREW SU1871

Silks on the Downs (01672) 841229

A345 N of Marlborough; SN8 1RZ
Popular civilised restauranty pub with
horse-racing theme, good variety of enjoyable
food (best to book), ales such as Adnams,
Ramsbury and Wadworths, decent wines by
the glass, good friendly service, stylish décor
with mix of dining tables on polished wood
floors, some good prints and photographs
as well as framed racing silks; well behaved
children allowed, small decked area and
garden, closed Sun evening. *(Ross Balaam)*

PEWSEY SU1561

French Horn (01672) 562443

*A345 towards Marlborough; Pewsey
Wharf; SN9 5NT* Pleasant red-brick
roadside pub; two-part back bar with steps
down to more formal front dining area
(children allowed here), flagstones and
woodburners, wide choice of enjoyable fairly
priced blackboard food, well kept Wadworths
ales, fast friendly service; background music;
dogs welcome in bar, picnic-sets out behind,
walks and moorings by Kennet & Avon
Canal below, closed Tues. *(Sheila and Robert
Robinson)*

REDLYNCH SU2021

Kings Head (01725) 510420

Off A338 via B3080; The Row; SP5 2JT
Refurbished early 18th-c pub on edge of
New Forest; three well kept ales including
Ringwood Best, decent house wines and
coffee, good value home-made food including
OAP weekday lunch deal for two, beamed and
flagstoned main bar with woodburner in large
brick fireplace, small conservatory, live folk
Weds; free wi-fi; children, dogs and muddy
boots welcome, picnic-sets out in front and in
side garden, nice Pepperbox Hill (NT) walks
nearby, shuts 3-6pm. *(Anon)*

ROWDE ST9762

★George & Dragon (01380) 723053

A342 Devizes–Chippenham; SN10 2PN
Lots of character in this welcoming and well
run 16th-c coaching inn, two low-beamed
rooms with large open fireplaces, wooden
dining chairs around candlelit tables, antique
rugs and walls covered with old pictures and
portraits, Butcombe and guests, good food
including plenty of fresh fish, not cheap but
they do have a good value set menu (Mon-Sat
lunch, Mon-Thurs evenings); background
music; children and dogs welcome, seats
in pretty back garden, Kennet & Avon
Canal nearby, three bedrooms, closed Sun
evening. *(Patrick Hunt, Mr and Mrs A H Young)*

SALISBURY SU1430

Avon Brewery (01722) 416184

Castle Street; SP1 3SP Long narrow city
bar with frosted and engraved bow window,
dark mahogany and two open fires, friendly
staff and regulars, well kept Ringwood Best

and a couple of other Marstons-related
beers, reasonably priced pubby food from
sandwiches up, small back dining room;
sheltered courtyard garden overlooking
river, open all day (till 5pm Sun). *(Paul
Humphreys)*

SALISBURY SU1429

Kings Head (01722) 342050

Bridge Street; SP1 2ND Corner
Wetherspoons in nice spot by river (site of
former hotel), variety of seating in large
relaxed bar with separate TV area, upstairs
gallery, two Greene King ales and four quickly
changing guests, low-priced menu including
breakfast, log fire; good value bedrooms,
open all day from 7am (till 1am Thurs-Sat).
(Jim and Maggie Cowell)

SALISBURY SU1429

New Inn (01722) 326662

New Street; SP1 2PH Much extended old
building with massive beams and timbers,
good choice of enjoyable home-made food
from pub staples up, well kept Badger ales
and decent house wines, cheerful service,
flagstones, floorboards and carpet, quiet cosy
alcoves, inglenook log fire; children welcome,
pretty walled garden with striking view of
nearby cathedral spire, three bedrooms,
open all day. *(Paul Humphreys, Michael and
Mary Smith)*

SALISBURY SU1329

★Old Mill (01722) 327517

Town Path, West Harnham; SP2 8EU
Charming 17th-c pub-hotel in tranquil
setting, unpretentious beamed bars with
prized window tables, decent choice of
enjoyable fair value food from sandwiches
up, well kept local ales, good wines and
malt whiskies, friendly service, attractive
restaurant showing mill race; children
welcome, small floodlit garden by duck-filled
millpond, delightful stroll across water
meadows from cathedral (classic view of it
from bridge beyond garden), 11 bedrooms,
open all day. *(Paul Wilson, Paul Humphreys,
Mr and Mrs J J A Davis, Mrs Sally Scott, Phil and
Jane Villiers)*

SALISBURY SU1429

Village (01722) 329707

Wilton Road; SP2 7EF Friendly corner
pub popular for its interesting range of real
ales including Downton, railway memorabilia
(near the station); sports TV, free wi-fi; open
all day (from 3pm Mon-Thurs). *(Steve Curtis,
Phil and Jane Villiers)*

SALISBURY SU1430

Wyndham Arms (01722) 331026

Estcourt Road; SP1 3AS Corner local
with unpretentious modern decor, popular
and friendly, with full Hop Back range
(brewery was based here) and a guest such
as Downton, bottled beers and country wines,
no food, small front and side rooms, longer

main bar, darts and board games; children and dogs welcome, open all day Thurs-Sun, from 4.30pm other days. *(N R White, Tony and Rachel Schendel, Phil and Jane Villiers)*

SANDY LANE ST9668
★ George (01380) 850403
A342 Devizes–Chippenham; SN15 2PX Handsome Georgian pub with neat cosy bar, straightforward seats and tables on wooden flooring, open fire, Wadworths and a guest, plenty of wines by the glass, popular food, back dining room and wood-framed conservatory; children and dogs (in bar) welcome, terrace with rattan furniture, more seats on lawn, charming thatched village, Bowood walks, closed Sun evening, Mon, otherwise open all day. *(David Crook, Caroline Prescott)*

SEEND ST9361
Barge (01380) 828230
Seend Cleeve; signed off A361 Devizes–Trowbridge; SN12 6QB Busy waterside pub with plenty of seats in garden making most of boating activity on Kennet & Avon Canal (moorings), some unusual seating in bar including painted milk churns, pretty Victorian fireplace, Wadworths ales and extensive range of wines by the glass, decent choice of food, friendly service; background music, free wi-fi; children and dogs welcome, summer barbecues, open all day. *(J D O Carter)*

SEEND ST9562
Three Magpies (01380) 828389
Sells Green – A365 towards Melksham; SN12 6RN Traditional partly 18th-c pub with well kept Wadworths and decent choice of wines by the glass, enjoyable home-made pubby food including bargain two-course lunch (Mon and Weds), good friendly service, two warm fires; free wi-fi; children welcome, dogs allowed in bar, big garden with play area, campsite next door, open all day. *(John Allman)*

SEMINGTON ST9259
★ Lamb (01380) 870263
The Strand; A361 Devizes–Trowbridge; BA14 6LL Refurbished dining pub with various eating areas including bar with wood-strip floor and log fire, good food from pub favourites to specials, beers such as Bath and Box Steam, friendly staff; background music; children and dogs welcome, pleasant garden with views to the Bowood Estate, self-catering cottages. *(Anon)*

SHALBOURNE SU3162
Plough (01672) 870295
Off A338; SN8 3QF Low-beamed traditional village pub on green, good choice

of enjoyable fairly priced blackboard food including vegetarian options, Butcombe and Wadworths, friendly helpful landlady and staff, neat tiled-floor bar with sofa and armchairs in snug; disabled access, small garden with play area. *(R Elliott)*

SHAW ST8765
Golden Fleece (01225) 702050
Folly Lane (A365 towards Atworth); SN12 8HB Attractive former coaching inn with low-ceilinged L-shaped bar and long front dining extension, good reasonably priced food including blackboard specials, weekday OAP lunch, ales such as Bath, Dartmoor and St Austell, pleasant welcoming staff; background music; children allowed, back terrace with steps up to lawn, open all day Sun. *(Maureen Wood)*

SOUTH MARSTON SU1987
Carpenters Arms (01793) 822997
Just off A420 E of Swindon; SN3 4ST Roomy old Arkells local with warm friendly atmosphere, good choice of enjoyable well priced food (not Sun evening, Mon lunchtime) including fixed-price menu, beamed bar with open fire, separate carpeted restaurant, pool room; background music; children and dogs welcome, big back garden with terrace and play area, nine motel bedrooms (some train noise), caravan parking, open all day. *(Anon)*

STEEPLE ASHTON ST9056
Longs Arms (01380) 870245
High Street; BA14 6EU Spotless 17th-c coaching inn with friendly local atmosphere, well kept Sharps and Wadworths, plenty of wines by the glass, good choice of fresh locally sourced food including lunchtime sandwiches, bar with lots of pictures and old photos, adjacent dining area, woodburner; quiz Mon, free wi-fi; children and dogs welcome, big garden with play area, adjoining self-catering cottage, delightful village, open all day weekends if busy. *(Michael Doswell)*

STOURTON ST7733
★ Spread Eagle (01747) 840587
Church Lawn; follow Stourhead brown signs off B3092, N of junction with A303 W of Mere; BA12 6QE Busy Georgian inn at entrance to Stourhead Estate; old-fashioned, rather civilised interior with antique panel-back settles, solid tables and chairs, sporting prints and log fires in handsome fireplaces, room by entrance with armchairs, longcase clock and corner china cupboard, well kept Butcombe and a guest, interesting wines by the glass and popular home-made food served by efficient helpful staff, cream teas, restaurant; background music; children welcome, wheelchair access

---

We say if we know a pub allows dogs.

(step down to dining areas), smart back courtyard, five bedrooms (guests can wander freely around famous NT gardens outside normal hours), open all day. *(Di and Mike Gillam, S J and C C Davidson, Sheila Topham, Dave Braisted)*

SUTTON BENGER ST9478
Wellesley Arms (01249) 721721
Handy for M4 junction 17, via B4122 and B4069; High Street; SN15 4RD Beamed 15th-c Cotswold stone pub with pleasant bar areas and restaurant, good pubby food (not Sun evening) including lunchtime set menu, Wadworths ales, efficient friendly service; background music, TV; children and dogs welcome, garden with play area, paddock, open all day weekends, closed Mon lunchtime. *(Anon)*

SUTTON VENY ST8941
Woolpack (01985) 840834
High Street; BA12 7AW Small well run village local pleasantly refurbished by present licensees, good blackboard food including some inventive dishes cooked by landlord-chef (best to book), Marstons and Ringwood ales, sensibly priced wines by the glass, charming service, compact side dining area; closed Sun evening, Mon lunchtime. *(Anon)*

TISBURY ST9429
Boot (01747) 870363
High Street; SP3 6PS Unpretentious ancient village local with long-serving and welcoming licensees, up to four well kept changing ales tapped from the cask, cider/ perry, range of pizzas and reasonably priced pubby food, notable fireplace; dogs welcome, tables in good-sized back garden, closed Sun evening, Tues lunchtime. *(Anon)*

UPAVON SU1355
Ship (01980) 630313
High Street; SN9 6EA Large thatched pub with welcoming local atmosphere, good choice of enjoyable home-made food including wood-fired pizzas, friendly helpful service, well kept changing ales and a couple of traditional ciders, decent range of wines and whiskies too, some interesting nautical memorabilia, occasional live acoustic music; parking can be tricky; dogs welcome, picnic-sets in front and on small side terrace. *(John and Nan Hurst, Phil and Jane Villiers)*

UPTON SCUDAMORE ST8647
★Angel (01985) 213225
Off A350 N of Warminster; BA12 0AG Stylish contemporary dining pub in former 16th-c coaching inn, airy upper part leading down to bar area with sofas and armchairs by open fire, mixed traditional pine furniture on wood floor, good choice of popular modern food (not particularly cheap) served by competent friendly staff, well kept ales including Butcombe, decent wines by the

glass; background music; children welcome, dogs on leads in bar, sheltered back terrace, ten bedrooms in house across car park; for sale as we went to press. *(N R White)*

WARMINSTER ST8644
Fox & Hounds (01985) 216711
Deverill Road; BA12 9QP Friendly two-bar community local, Wessex beers and at least one guest, six ciders, skittle alley; TV, pool; open all day. *(Dr and Mrs A K Clarke)*

WARMINSTER ST8745
Organ (01985) 211777
49 High Street; BA12 9AQ Sympathetic restoration of former 18th-c inn (reopened 2006 after 93 years as a shop), front bar, snug and traditional games room, welcoming owners and chatty regulars, local beers including one named for them, real ciders/ perries, good cheap lunchtime cheeseboard, skittle alley, local art in upstairs gallery; no under-21s, open 4pm-midnight, all day Sat. *(Anon)*

WARMINSTER ST8745
★Weymouth Arms (01985) 216995
Emwell Street; BA12 8JA Charming backstreet pub with snug panelled entrance bar, log fire in fine stone fireplace, ancient books on mantelpiece, leather tub chairs around walnut and satinwood table, more seats against the walls, daily papers, Butcombe and Wadworths 6X, nice wines by the glass, second heavily panelled room with wide floorboards and smaller fireplace, candles in brass sticks, split-level dining room stretching back to open kitchen, good interesting food, friendly service; children welcome, dogs in bar, seats in flower-filled back courtyard, six well equipped comfortable bedrooms, closed Mon lunchtime. *(S G N Bennett)*

WEST OVERTON SU1368
Bell (01672) 861099
A4 Marlborough–Calne; SN8 1QD Refurbished former coaching inn with good traditional and more upmarket food cooked by owner-chef using fresh local ingredients, bar with woodburner and spacious restaurant beyond, Wadworths and other local beers, attentive friendly uniformed staff; background music; disabled access, nice secluded back garden with terrace and own bar, country views, good walks nearby, closed Mon, no food Sun evenings. *(Michael Doswell, P A Rowe, Mr and Mrs P R Thomas, Mr and Mrs A H Young)*

WESTWOOD ST8159
★New Inn (01225) 863123
Off B3109 S of Bradford-on-Avon; BA15 2AE Traditional 18th-c country pub with several linked rooms, beams and stripped stone, scrubbed tables on slate floor, lots of pictures, imaginative good value food (not Sun evening) cooked by chef-owner

together with pub staples, generous Sun lunch and a monthly themed night, well kept Wadworths, cheerful buzzy atmosphere; children and dogs welcome, tables in paved garden behind, pretty village with good surrounding walks, Westwood Manor (NT) opposite. *(Michael Doswell, Mark Flynn)*

WHITEPARISH   SU2423
Fountain (01794) 884266
The Street; SP5 2SG Friendly little green-shuttered 17th-c beamed inn, enjoyable well priced traditional food in log-fire bar or restaurant, Sharps Doom Bar and guests such as Downton and Flack Manor; free wi-fi; a few seats out at back, six bedrooms, open all day Fri-Sun, closed lunchtimes Mon-Weds. *(Colin McKerrow)*

WILTON   SU2661
★ Swan (01672) 870274
The village S of Great Bedwyn; SN8 3SS Popular light and airy 1930s pub, good well presented seasonal food (not Sun evening) including daily specials, two Ramsbury ales and a local guest, farm ciders and good value wines from extensive list, friendly efficient staff, stripped pine tables, high-backed settles and pews on bare boards, woodburner; children and dogs welcome, disabled access, front garden with picnic-sets, picturesque village with windmill, open all day weekends. *(JPC, Alan and Audrey Moulds)*

WINGFIELD   ST8256
★ Poplars (01225) 752426
B3109 S of Bradford-on-Avon (Shop Lane); BA14 9LN Appealing country pub with beams and log fires, very popular (especially with older people at lunchtime) for its sensibly priced food from pub staples to interesting specials, Wadworths ales and Weston's cider, friendly fast service even when busy, warm atmosphere, light and airy family dining extension; nice garden, own cricket pitch. *(Mrs P Bishop, Taff Thomas)*

WINSLEY   ST7960
★ Seven Stars (01225) 722204
Off B3108 bypass W of Bradford-on-Avon (pub just over Wiltshire border); BA15 2LQ Handsome bustling inn with low-beamed linked areas, light pastel paintwork and stripped-stone walls, farmhouse chairs

around candlelit tables on flagstones or coir, woodburner, very good freshly made food using local suppliers, friendly helpful service, changing ales such as Bath, Moles, Palmers and Skinners, Thatcher's and Weston's ciders, nice wines by the glass; background music; children and dogs (in bar) welcome, disabled access with ramp, tables under parasols on terrace and neat grassy surrounds, bowling green opposite, closed Sun evening. *(Michael Doswell, Mr and Mrs P R Thomas, Taff Thomas, Dr Matt Burleigh, Chris and Angela Buckell, Howard and Margaret Buchanan and others)*

WINTERBOURNE
BASSETT   SU1075
White Horse (01793) 731257
Off A4361 S of Swindon; SN4 9QB Roadside dining pub with gently old-fashioned feel, carpeted bar with plenty of wood, wrought-iron plush-topped stools and cushioned dining chairs, Wadworths ales and quite a few wines by the glass, enjoyable home-made food including daily specials (seasonal game), dining rooms with country kitchen furniture on light wood floors, old prints and paintings, woodburner in little brick fireplace, conservatory; background music; children welcome, dogs in bar, tables on good-sized lawn, closed Sun evening, Mon lunchtime. *(Anon)*

WOOTTON RIVERS   SU1963
Royal Oak (01672) 810322
Off A346, A345 or B3087; SN8 4NQ Cosy 16th-c beamed and thatched pub, good food from lunchtime sandwiches to nice fish dishes, ales such as Ramsbury and Wadworths 6X, plenty of wines by the glass, friendly competent service, comfortable L-shaped dining lounge with woodburner, timbered bar and small games area; children and dogs welcome, tables out in yard, pleasant village, bedrooms in adjoining building. *(Guy Vowles)*

ZEALS   ST7831
Bell & Crown (01747) 840404
A303; BA12 6NJ Nicely laid out beamed dining pub, warm and friendly, with good food cooked by chef-landlord, efficient service, ales such as Butcombe, Palmers and Wadworths, nice wines by the glass, big log fire in bar, restaurant; closed Sun evening. *(Hugo Jeune)*

Worcestershire

BRANSFORD
SO8052 Map 4

Bear & Ragged Staff  ♟

Off A4103 SW of Worcester; Station Road; WR6 5JH

Cheerfully run dining pub with pleasant places to sit both inside and out, and well liked food and drink

The hard-working licensees in this civilised dining pub offer a warm welcome to all their customers – locals and visitors alike. The relaxed bar has Hobsons Twisted Spire and Sharps Doom Bar on handpump, ten wines by the glass, several malt whiskies and quite a few brandies and liqueurs. The restaurant is more formal, with upholstered dining chairs, proper tablecloths and linen napkins. These interconnecting rooms give fine views of attractive rolling country (as do the pretty garden and terrace). In winter there's a warming open fire; background music and darts. Good disabled access and facilities.

Making everything in-house and growing some of their own produce, the particularly rewarding food includes lunchtime sandwiches, king scallops with crispy bacon and smoked paprika sauce, pork brawn terrine with minted baba ganoush dressing on spinach salad, home-baked honey roast gammon and eggs, seafood and leek risotto, lamb shank with apricots, prunes and toasted almonds, stone bass with artichokes, capers and broad beans in mint nut brown butter, chicken on field mushroom with truffle-scented cream and cheese flaky pastry, and puddings. *Benchmark main dish: beer-battered cod and chips £12.95. Two-course evening meal £20.00.*

Free house ~ Licensee Lynda Williams ~ Real ale ~ (01886) 833399 ~ Open 11.30-2, 6-11; 12-2.30 Sun ~ Bar food 12-2, 6-9; 12-2.30 Sun ~ Restaurant ~ Children welcome ~ Dogs allowed in bar ~ www.bear.uk.com *Recommended by Dave de Santis, Melanie Dawson, Tricia Rawlings, Norman and Barbara Kay, Mike and Mary Carter*

BRETFORTON
SP0943 Map 4

Fleece ★ 🍴 £

B4035 E of Evesham: turn S off this road into village; pub is in central square by church; there's a sizeable car park at one side of the church; WR11 7JE

Marvellously unspoilt medieval pub owned by the National Trust

Before becoming a pub in 1848, this medieval and partly thatched building was a farm owned by the same family for nearly 500 years; they left it to the National Trust in 1977. Many of the furnishings, such as the great oak dresser that holds a priceless 48-piece set of Stuart pewter, are heirlooms passed down through the generations. The little rooms are atmospherically dim with massive beams, exposed timbers and marks scored on the worn and crazed flagstones to keep out demons. There are two fine grandfather clocks, ancient kitchen chairs, curved high-backed settles, a rocking chair and a rack of heavy pointed iron shafts (probably for spit roasting) in one of the huge inglenook fireplaces, and two other log fires. Plenty of oddities include a great cheese-press and set of cheese moulds and a rare dough-proving table; a leaflet details the more bizarre items. Uley Pigs Ear, Wye Valley Bitter and guests such as Celt Experience Iron Age and Gloucester Dockside Dark on handpump, 20 wines by the glass, a similar number of malt whiskies and four farm ciders; board games. They hold an asparagus auction at the end of May, as part of the Vale of Evesham Asparagus Festival, and also host the village fête on August Bank Holiday Monday. Their calendar of events also includes morris dancing and the village silver band plays here regularly too. The lawn, with fruit trees around a beautifully restored thatched and timbered barn, is a lovely place to sit, and there are more picnic-sets and a stone pump-trough in the front courtyard. If you're visiting to enjoy the famous historic interior, best to go midweek as it can be very busy at weekends.

Bar food includes lunchtime sandwiches, organic brie, shallot and asparagus tart, cheese and meat platter, vegetable curry, beer-battered cod with triple-cooked chips, gammon and eggs, pork fillet stuffed with asparagus and wrapped in bacon with saffron sauce, lemon and garlic roasted chicken breast with shredded asparagus and spring onion salad, a pie of the day, and puddings such as triple chocolate brownie and lemon meringue sundae. *Benchmark main dish: trio of local sausages with red onion marmalade £8.95. Two-course evening meal £15.00.*

Free house ~ Licensee Nigel Smith ~ Real ale ~ (01386) 831173 ~ Open 11-11 ~ Bar food 12-2.30, 6.30-9; 12-4, 6.30-8.30 Sun ~ Restaurant ~ Children welcome ~ Dogs allowed in bar ~ Wi-fi ~ Live folk music weekly (see website) ~ Bedrooms: /£97.50 ~ www.thefleeceinn.co.uk *Recommended by Torrens Lyster, K H Frostick, Philip Meek*

BROADWAY
SP0937   Map 4

Crown & Trumpet ⍟ £
Church Street; WR12 7AE

Unreconstructed honest local with good real ale and decent food; bedrooms

This is a handsome, much-visited little town and this unpretentious, old-fashioned local gets many visitors. There's a friendly welcome for all and the atmosphere is cheerful and easy-going. The bustling beamed and timbered bar has antique dark high-backed settles, large solid tables and a blazing log fire. Butcombe Bitter, Cotswold Spring Codrington Codger, Stanway Cotteswold Gold and Stroud Tom Long on handpump, alongside two local farm ciders, nine wines by the glass, ten malt whiskies, hot toddies, mulled wine and a good range of soft drinks. There's an assortment of pub games, including darts, cribbage, shut the box, dominoes, bar skittles and ring the bull, as well as a games machine, TV and background music. The hardwood tables and chairs outside, among flowers on a slightly raised front terrace, are popular with walkers – even in adverse weather.

Very good value food includes baguettes, faggots or beer-battered fish with chips, vegetable lasagne, duck and apricot or venison sausages, gammon and egg, pies such as steak and kidney and beef in plum gravy, and puddings such as spotted dick with custard and treacle tart; they also do pie and pint evenings and early bird choices (6-7.15pm). *Benchmark main dish: pie of the day £8.95. Two-course evening meal £16.00.*

Laurel (Enterprise) ~ Lease Andrew Scott ~ Real ale ~ (01386) 853202 ~ Open 11-11 (midnight Sat) ~ Bar food 12-2.30, 5.45-9.30; 12-9.30 weekends ~ Children welcome ~ Dogs allowed in bar ~ Wi-fi ~ Live jazz/blues Thurs evening, 1960s-'80s music Sat evening ~ Bedrooms: /£68 ~ www.cotswoldholidays.co.uk *Recommended by Ian and Jane Irving, Lucien Perring, Mark Delap, Dave Braisted, Theocsbrian, Guy Vowles*

CHILDSWICKHAM

SP0738 Map 4

Childswickham Inn

Off A44 NW of Broadway; WR12 7HP

Bustling dining pub with highly thought-of food, good drinks choice, attentive staff and seats in neat garden

Most customers are here to enjoy the interesting food, but there's a locals' lounge bar with leather sofas and armchairs (dogs are allowed here), and they keep Hook Norton Old Hooky, Sharps Doom Bar and Timothy Taylors Landlord on handpump, several wines by the glass, malt whiskies and farm cider; background music. There are two dining areas, one with high-backed dark leather chairs on terracotta tiles, the other with country kitchen chairs on bare floorboards; both have contemporary artwork on part-timbered walls painted cream or pale violet. There's an open fire and a woodburning stove. Outside the neat garden has rush-seated chairs and tables on decking and on separate areas under parasols; disabled facilities.

 From a thoughtful menu, the food includes pork, leek and apricot terrine with fruit chutney, bubble and squeak with a poached egg, crispy pancetta and mustard dressing, feta and basil roulade with red pepper and sunblush tomato coulis, a pie of the day, local sausages with onion gravy, rosemary and garlic lamb with pea and mint risotto, cod loin with chilli and crab linguine, and puddings such as rhubarb and custard pot and chocolate and orange torte with chocolate and orange ice-cream. *Benchmark main dish: gressingham duck with sweet potato fondant and onion purée £15.95. Two-course evening meal £21.00.*

Punch ~ Tenant Carol Marshall ~ Real ale ~ (01386) 852461 ~ Open 12-3, 5.30-11; 12-11 Sat, Sun ~ Bar food 12-2, 6-9; 12-6 Sun; Restaurant not Sun evening or Mon lunch ~ Children welcome ~ Dogs allowed in bar ~ Wi-fi ~ www.childswickhaminn.co.uk *Recommended by Dr A J and Mrs B A Tompsett, Bernard Stradling*

CLENT

SO9279 Map 4

Fountain ⭐🍴 ♀

Adams Hill/Odnall Lane; off A491 at Holy Cross/Clent exit roundabout, via Violet Lane, then right at T junction; DY9 9PU

Restaurany pub often packed to overflowing, with imaginative dishes and good choice of drinks

Attentive staff, well kept ales and impressive food – it's not surprising our readers enjoy their visits here so much. The long, spotlessly kept and carpeted dining bar (consisting of three knocked-together areas) is fairly traditional, with teak chairs and pedestal tables and some comfortably cushioned brocaded wall seats. There are nicely framed local photographs on the rag-rolled pinkish walls above a dark panelled dado, pretty wall lights and candles on the tables (flowers in summer). The changing real ales include Marstons Burton Bitter and Pedigree and Wychwood Hobgoblin on handpump and most of their wines are available by the glass; also speciality teas, good coffees and freshly squeezed orange juice. Background music and skittle alley. There are tables out on a decked area.

Consistently top quality food includes lunchtime sandwiches, very popular mini loaves with garlic, parsley butter and toppings, avocado and prawns, chicken liver pâté with onion marmalade, twice-cooked pork belly with spring onion mash and cider and wholegrain mustard sauce, chicken with smoked sausage and black pudding on mushroom and tarragon sauce, goats cheese and red onion marmalade wellington with creamy tomato sauce, thai-style king prawn, king scallop and monkfish with rice noodles and coconut liquor, and puddings such as white chocolate crème brûlée and sticky toffee pudding with toffee sauce; they also offer a two- and three-course set menu. *Benchmark main dish: half shoulder lamb pot roast £18.50. Two-course evening meal £22.00.*

Marstons ~ Lease Richard and Jacque Macey ~ Real ale ~ (01562) 883286 ~ Open 11-11; 12-9 Sun ~ Bar food 12-2, 6-9 (9.30 Fri, Sat); 12-6 Sun ~ Children welcome ~ Wi-fi ~ www.thefountainatclent.co.uk *Recommended by Ian Herdman, S Holder*

CUTNALL GREEN
Chequers ⭐ ☆ 🍷
Kidderminster Road; WR9 0PJ

SO8868   Map 4

Bustling roadside pub with plenty of drinking and dining space in interesting rooms and rewarding food

Many customers are here for the very good food cooked by the former England football team chef, Roger Narbett. It's an interesting pub, built some 90 years ago on the site of an old coaching inn, and is a clever mix of ancient and modern: red-painted walls between beams and timbering, broad floorboards and weathered quarry tiles, and warm winter fires. There are leather sofas and tub chairs, high-backed purple and red or ladderback dining chairs around all sorts of tables, plenty of mirrors giving the impression of even more space, brass plates and mugs, candles and fresh flowers. Banks's Sunbeam, Marstons Pedigree New World and Wye Valley HPA on handpump and a dozen wines by the glass. One elegant but cosy room, known as the Players Lounge, has photographs of Mr Narbett's football chef days and overlooks the pretty terrace and garden equipped with heaters and parasols. This is sister pub to the Bell & Cross at Holy Cross.

As well as serving weekend breakfasts (9-11am), the wide choice of inventive food includes lunchtime sandwiches, lamb koftas with tzatziki, pomegranate and cashew nut salad and flatbread, oriental chicken with frazzled noodles and soy dip, a pie of the day, honey and lemon thyme chicken with crispy pancetta, avocado, quail's egg and skinny fries, beer-battered cod and chips, calves liver with bubble and squeak, smoked bacon and red onion confit, angus steak with garlic and herb butter and truffled parmesan chips, and puddings such as coconut and pineapple tart with coconut ice-cream and banana daiquiri crème brûlée. *Benchmark main dish: slow-cooked lamb shoulder with sweet potato and chorizo dauphinoise and pea and mint purée £16.75. Two-course evening meal £20.00.*

Free house ~ Licensees Roger and Jo Narbett ~ Real ale ~ (01299) 851292 ~ Open 12-11 (10.30 Sun) ~ Bar food 12-9 (9.30 Fri, Sat, 8.30 Sun) ~ Restaurant ~ Children welcome ~ Dogs allowed in bar ~ Wi-fi ~ www.chequerscutnallgreen.co.uk
Recommended by Dave Braisted, Phil and Helen Holt

A star symbol after the name of a pub show exceptional character and appeal. It doesn't mean extra comfort. And it's nothing to do with exceptional food quality, for which there's a separate star-on-a-plate symbol. Even quite a basic pub can win a star, if it's individual enough.

HOLY CROSS
SO9278 Map 4

Bell & Cross ★ 🏵 ♀

2 miles from M5 junction 3: A491 towards Stourbridge, then follow Clent signpost off on left; DY9 9QL

A delightful old interior, particularly good food, staff with a can-do attitude and a pretty garden

If you're fed up with the M5, this charming dining pub will make the perfect break. It has a cosy bar and four attractively decorated dining rooms with a choice of carpet, bare boards, lino or nice old quarry tiles, and a variety of moods from snug and chatty to bright and airy. Décor includes theatrical engravings on red walls, nice sporting prints on pale green walls, and racing and gundog pictures above a black panelled dado; most room have coal fires. Neatly dressed, courteous staff serve Enville Ale, Marstons Burton Bitter, Purity Pure Gold and Timothy Taylors Landlord on handpump and 12 wines by the glass. The lovely garden has a spacious lawn, and the terrace offers pleasant views. This is sister pub to the Chequers at Cutnall Green.

 Imaginative food includes lunchtime sandwiches, confit duck rillette with pineapple salsa, king prawns and chorizo skewer with catalan salad and aioli, burger with cheese, relish, lots of toppings and skinny fries, beer-battered cod and chips, a pie of the day, slow-cooked lamb shoulder with chorizo and sweet potato dauphinoise and pea and mint purée, free-range pork belly with griddled apricots and port wine jus, and puddings such as salted caramel and pecan cheesecake and warm toffee apple and frangipane tart; they also offer a two and three-course set menu (not Friday evening or weekends). *Benchmark main dish: honey and lemon thyme chicken with crispy pancetta, avocado, quail egg and fries £14.95. Two-course evening meal £20.00.*

Enterprise ~ Lease Roger and Jo Narbett ~ Real ale ~ (01562) 730319 ~ Open 12-3, 6-11; 12-10.30 Sun ~ Bar food 12-2, 6-9 (9.30 Sat); 12-7 Sun ~ Restaurant ~ Children welcome ~ Dogs allowed in bar ~ Wi-fi ~ www.bellandcrossclent.co.uk
Recommended by Andy Dolan, David Heath, Dr D J and Mrs S C Walker, Steve Whalley, Dennis and Doreen Haward, David and Katharine Cooke, Roger and Donna Huggins, R T and J C Moggridge

KNIGHTWICK
SO7355 Map 4

Talbot 🏵 ♀ ▢ ▭

Knightsford Bridge; B4197 just off A44 Worcester-Bromyard; WR6 5PH

Interesting old coaching inn with good beer from its own brewery, and riverside garden; comfortable bedrooms

'This fine old place is as enjoyable as ever,' says a reader with enthusiasm – and many others agree. A rambling country hotel with long-serving licensees, it attracts a good mix of visitors and locals keen to enjoy the own-brew beers and inventive food. The heavily beamed and extended traditional lounge bar has a warm winter log fire, a variety of seats from small carved or leatherette armchairs to winged settles by the windows, and a vast stove in a big central stone hearth. The bar opens into a light and airy garden room. The well furnished back public bar has pool on a raised side area, TV, darts, juke box and cribbage. In contrast, the dining room is a sedate place for a quiet meal. Their Teme Valley microbrewery uses locally grown hops to produce That, This, T'Other and a seasonal ale that are served alongside Hobsons Best and a changing guest, a dozen wines by the glass and 16 malt whiskies; they hold regular beer festivals. A farmers' market takes place here on the second Sunday of the month. In warm weather, it's lovely to use the tables on the lawn beside the River Teme (it's across the lane but they serve out here too) or you can sit in front of the building on old-fashioned seats.

 Making their own preserves, bread and black pudding and growing organic salads and vegetables, the highly thought-of food includes lunchtime sandwiches, pork, orange and cognac pâté with chutney, moules marinière, vegetarian quiche, pork, rabbit and beef burger with coleslaw and chips, chicken and mushroom pie, cottage pie, slow-cooked mutton with braised oxtail and wild garlic and nettle-top gnocchi, and puddings such as apple crumble and custard; they also offer a weekly two- and three-course set menu. *Benchmark main dish: raised pork and game pie with chips £14.00. Two-course evening meal £22.00.*

Own brew ~ Licensee Annie Clift ~ Real ale ~ (01886) 821235 ~ Open 8am-11pm (midnight Fri, 10.30pm Sun) ~ Bar food 12-9 ~ Restaurant ~ Children welcome ~ Dogs allowed in bar and bedrooms ~ Wi-fi ~ Bedrooms: £65/£110 ~ www.the-talbot.co.uk
Recommended by Patrick and Daphne Darley, Pat and Tony Martin, Tony and Wendy Hobden

MALVERN SO7845 Map 4
Nags Head ◖
Bottom end of Bank Street, steep turn down off A449; WR14 2JG

Remarkable range of real ales, delightfully eclectic layout and décor, tasty lunchtime bar food and warmly welcoming atmosphere

Quite simply, our readers love this pub, from its fine range of beers to the interesting food and the genuine welcome for all from the cheerful, professional staff. A series of snug, individually decorated rooms, with one or two steps between and two open fires, have an easy-going chatty atmosphere. Each is filled with all sorts of chairs including leather armchairs, pews sometimes arranged as booths and a mix of tables with sturdy ones stained different colours. There are bare boards here, flagstones there, carpet elsewhere and plenty of interesting pictures and homely touches such as house plants, shelves of well thumbed books and broadsheet newspapers; board games. If you struggle to choose from the 15 beers on handpump, you'll be offered a taster: Banks's Bitter, Bathams Best Bitter, Otter Bitter, St Georges Charger, Dragons Blood and Friar Tuck, Ringwood Fortyniner and Woods Shropshire Lad plus seven changing guests. Also, two farm ciders, 30 malt whiskies, ten gins, ten bottled craft ales and lagers and ten wines by the glass including dessert ones. The front terrace and garden have picnic-sets, benches and rustic tables as well as parasols and heaters.

Popular lunchtime food includes sandwiches, honey-roast ham and eggs, courgette, squash and pepper curry, beer-battered cod and chips and chicken, mushroom and tarragon pie; evening meals (served in the barn extension dining room only) include smoked duck terrine with pear chutney, piri-piri king prawns with aioli, five-spice crispy duck with pak choi, corn-fed chicken with broad bean and tomato confit, duo of pork (belly and cheek) with bubble and squeak and cider apple sauce, and whole lemon sole with roasted fennel, parsley and caper butter. *Benchmark main dish: venison and bacon pie £13.90. Two-course evening meal £21.00.*

Free house ~ Licensees Clare Keane and Alex Whistance ~ Real ale ~ (01684) 574373 ~ Open 11am-11.15pm (11.30pm Fri, Sat); 12-11 Sun ~ Bar food 12-2, 6.30-8.30; 12-2.30, 7-8.30 Sun ~ Restaurant ~ Children welcome ~ Dogs welcome ~ Wi-fi ~ www.nagsheadmalvern.co.uk *Recommended by Paul Humphreys, Torrens Lyster, Jean and Douglas Troup, Pat and Tony Martin, Chris and Angela Buckell, Barry Collett*

NEWLAND

SO7948 Map 4

Swan

Worcester Road (set well back from A449 just NW of Malvern); WR13 5AY

Popular, interesting pub with six real ales and seats in the big garden

It's worth looking closely at the comfortable and clearly individually chosen seats in the dimly lit and dark beamed bar here for their carving – the wall tapestries are interesting too. Traditionally furnished, with a forest canopy of hops, whisky-water jugs, beakers and tankards, the place has a lot of character. The carved counter has St Georges Dragons Blood and Friar Tuck, Ringwood Fortyniner, Sharps Doom Bar and a couple of guests such as Adnams Broadside and Shepherd Neame New World Pale Ale on handpump, plus several wines, malt whiskies and four farm ciders. On the right is a broadly similar red-carpeted dining room and, beyond it, in complete contrast, an ultra-modern glass garden room; background music and board games. The garden itself is as individual as the pub, with a cluster of huge casks topped with flowers, even a piano doing flower-tub duty, and a set of stocks on the pretty front terrace.

Quite a choice of food includes scotch quail eggs with piccalilli, honey and ale chicken skewers with peanut and coriander salsa, wild mushroom lasagne, beer-battered cod and chips, faggots and mash with rich gravy, spatchcock guinea fowl with chilli polenta chips and smoked green onion relish, beef bourguignon, gilt-head bream with mint, salad and yoghurt dressing, and puddings. *Benchmark main dish: crispy pork belly with apple and thyme mash and lavender and clove cream £13.80. Two-course evening meal £20.00.*

Free house ~ Licensee Nick Taylor ~ Real ale ~ (01886) 832224 ~ Open 12-11.30 ~ Bar food 12-2.30, 6.30-9; 12-3, 7-9 Sun ~ Restaurant ~ Children welcome ~ Dogs allowed in bar ~ Wi-fi ~ www.theswaninnmalvern.co.uk *Recommended by Paul Humphreys, P and J Shapley, M G Hart*

TENBURY WELLS

SO6468 Map 4

Talbot ♀ ⇦

Newnham Bridge; A456; WR15 8JF

Carefully refurbished Victorian coaching inn with plenty of character in bar and dining rooms, real ales, good wines and highly rated food; bedrooms

This is a substantial former coaching inn with a civilised but informal atmosphere and a friendly welcome from the landlord and his staff. There are nice old red and black and original quarry tiles, bare floorboards, open fires and candlelight, with the bar and dining rooms being quite different in style: an assortment of dark pubby, high-backed painted wooden and comfortably upholstered dining chairs around a variety of tables, leather tub chairs and sofas here and there, bookshelves, old photographs of the local area, table lights and standard lamps, some elegant antiques dotted about and pretty arrangements of fresh flowers. It gets pretty busy at weekends, when you'll need to book a table in advance. Hobsons Best Bitter and Wye Valley HPA on handpump, local cider and nine wines by the glass from a good list. The bedrooms are thoughtfully decorated and well equipped.

Enjoyable food includes lunchtime sandwiches, crayfish and mango cocktail, corned beef hash with a poached egg and sweetcorn fritter, asparagus and garlic tagliatelle with white wine and cream, chicken with creamed broad beans and dauphinoise potatoes, beer-battered fish of the day with lemon caper compote, duck with pancetta and thyme potato cake and parsnip purée, and puddings such as apple crumble with cinnamon ice-cream and vanilla crème brûlée. *Benchmark main dish: steak burger with coleslaw and triple-cooked chips £11.95. Two-course evening meal £18.00.*

Free house ~ Licensee Ian Dowling ~ Real ale ~ (01584) 781941 ~ Open 10am-11pm (11.30 Sat); 12-7 Sun ~ Bar food 12-2.30, 6-9; 12-5 Sun ~ Restaurant ~ Children welcome ~ Dogs allowed in bar ~ Wi-fi ~ Bedrooms: £75/£85 ~ www.talbotinnnewnhambridge.co.uk *Recommended by Gavin and Helle May, Isobel Mackinlay*

WELLAND   SO8039   Map 4
Inn at Welland 🍽️ ☆ ♟

Drake Street; A4104 W of Upton upon Severn; WR13 6LN

Worcestershire Dining Pub of the Year

Stylish contemporary country dining bar with good food and wines, and nice tables outside

Offering tranquil views of the Malvern Hills, the good-sized neat garden has tables with comfortable teak or wicker chairs, some on a biggish sheltered deck, others on individual separate terraces set into lawn; it's handy for the Three Counties showground. Inside, cool grey paintwork, a few carefully chosen modern prints and attractive seat fabrics give a feeling of unobtrusive good taste, with beige flagstones in the central area, good new wood flooring to the sides and a woodburning stove at one end. The lively buzz of conversation is gently underscored by barely perceptible background music. They have Malvern Hills Black Pear, Otter Bitter and Wye Valley Butty Bach on handpump, 18 wines by the glass including an unusually wide range of pudding wines, and two farm ciders; plenty of efficient neatly dressed staff.

As well as lunchtime sandwiches, the imaginative food includes scallops with slow-roast pork belly and apple and fennel salad, chicken liver, chorizo and beetroot salad, omelette arnold bennett, pork and leek sausages with cabbage and bacon and caramelised onion gravy, spit-roast herb-marinated poussin with poultry jus, salmon fillet with tartare croquette and sauce vierge, lamb steak with boulangère potatoes, pea purée and mint jus, and puddings such as caramelised banana and toffee eton mess with butterscotch sauce and espresso crème brûlée with blood orange sorbet and Cointreau syrup; they provide a good cheese board. *Benchmark main dish: cider and home-cured treacle roast ham and free-range eggs £10.50. Two-course evening meal £20.00.*

Free house ~ Licensees David and Gillian Saxon ~ Real ale ~ (01684) 592317 ~ Open 12-4, 6-11; 12-3 Sun; closed Sun evening, Mon ~ Bar food 12-2.30, 6-9.30; 12-3 Sun ~ Restaurant ~ Children welcome ~ Wi-fi ~ www.theinnatwelland.co.uk *Recommended by Alfie Bayliss, Phoebe Peacock*

> Real ale to us means beer that has matured naturally in its cask – not pressurised or filtered. We name all real ales stocked. We usually name ales preserved under a light blanket of carbon dioxide too, though purists – pointing out that this stops the natural yeasts developing – would disagree (most people, including us, can't tell the difference!)

Also Worth a Visit in Worcestershire

Besides the fully inspected pubs, you might like to try these pubs that have been recommended to us and described by readers. Do tell us what you think of them: feedback@goodguides.com

ABBERLEY   SO7567
Manor Arms (01299) 890300
Netherton Lane; WR6 6BN Recently revamped country inn tucked away in quiet village backwater opposite fine Norman church; changing ales and good selection of wines, enjoyable if not particularly cheap food from pub favourites up, friendly service; two-level deck with lovely valley views, good walks (on Worcestershire Way), six refurbished bedrooms. *(Anon)*

ALVECHURCH   SP0172
Weighbridge (0121) 445 5111
Scarfield Wharf; B48 7SQ Converted little house by Worcester & Birmingham Canal marina, bar and a couple of small rooms, five well kept ales such as Kinver Bargee Bitter and Weatheroak Tillermans Tipple, simple low-priced food (not Tues, Weds); tables outside. *(Anon)*

ASHTON UNDER HILL   SO9938
Star (01386) 881325
Elmley Road; WR11 7SN Smallish pub perched above road in quiet village at foot of Bredon Hill; linked beamed rooms around bar, one with flagstones and log fire, steps up to pitch-roofed dining room with woodburner, good choice of well liked food (not Sun or Mon evenings) from fresh baguettes to specials, real ales such as Gresham and Greene King IPA, friendly staff; background music, TV and games machine; children and dogs welcome, picnic-sets in pleasant garden, good walks. *(Dave Braisted)*

ASTON FIELDS   SO9669
Ladybird Inn (01527) 878014
Finstall Road (B184 just S of Bromsgrove); B60 2DZ Light and airy red-brick Edwardian pub adjoining hotel (next to station), panelled bar and comfortable lounge, reasonably priced pub food along with separate italian restaurant, own Birds ales and guests such as Bathams and Wye Valley, good service (may ask for a credit card if running a tab); children welcome, open all day. *(Dave Braisted)*

BARNARDS GREEN   SO7945
Bluebell (01684) 575031
Junction B4211 to Rhydd Green with B4208 to Malvern Show Ground; WR14 3QP Chain dining pub nicely set back from the road, comfortable and reliable, with good choice of enjoyable well priced food,

children eat free 3-7pm weekdays, Marstons-related ales, friendly staff coping well at busy times, quiz first Weds of month; free wi-fi; dogs welcome in one part of the bar, disabled facilities, nice outside seating areas, open (and food) all day. *(Paul Humphreys, S F Parrinder)*

BECKFORD   SO9835
Beckford Inn (01386) 881532
A435; GL20 7AN Sizeable 18th-c roadside inn, beams, log fires and some stripped stone, four well kept ales and good range of wines by the glass, enjoyable food from traditional choices up, two bar areas and good-sized carpeted restaurant, friendly helpful staff; children welcome, wheelchair access, picnic-sets in large garden, eight comfortable bedrooms. *(Roger and Donna Huggins)*

BELBROUGHTON   SO9177
Queens (01562) 730276
Queens Hill (B4188 E of Kidderminster); DY9 0DU Refurbished old red-brick pub by Belne Brook, several linked rooms including beamed slate-floor bar, good modern food alongside pub standards, also set menu choices, three well kept beers and nice selection of wines, friendly staff coping well at busy times; disabled facilities, small roadside terrace, pleasant village and handy for M5 (junction 4), open all day weekends. *(W M Lien)*

BERROW   SO7835
Duke of York (01684) 833449
Junction A438/B4208; WR13 6JQ Bustling old country pub with two spic-and-span linked rooms, beams, nooks and crannies and log fire, welcoming friendly staff, good food from baguettes up including daily fresh fish, well kept Wye Valley and a guest ale, restaurant; big garden behind, handy for Malvern Hills. *(Geoffrey and Penny Hughes)*

BERROW GREEN   SO7458
★Admiral Rodney (01886) 821375
B4197, off A44 W of Worcester; WR6 6PL Light and roomy high-beamed 17th-c dining pub, big stripped kitchen tables and two woodburners, popular reasonably priced food from varied menu (should book Fri, Sat evenings), friendly fast service, well kept Birds, Wye Valley and guests, real cider/perry, charming end restaurant in rebuilt barn, folk music third Weds of month, skittle alley; well behaved children and dogs welcome, disabled

---

We say if we know a pub has background music.

facilities, tables outside with pretty view and heated covered terrace, good walks, three bedrooms, closed Mon lunchtime, open all day weekends. *(Neil and Anita Christopher)*

BEWDLEY   SO7775
Hop Pole (01299) 401295
Hop Pole Lane; DY12 2QH Friendly refurbished family-run pub with good choice of enjoyable food (booking advised) from pub classics up, OAP lunchtime deal Mon-Sat, three or four well kept Marstons-related ales and several wines by the glass, walls decorated with old tools etc, cast-iron range in dining area, live music Weds; free wi-fi; children and dogs (not during food times) welcome, front garden with scarecrow and vegetable patch, open all day (afternoon break Mon). *(Ron and Sue Gilbert)*

BEWDLEY   SO7875
★ Little Pack Horse (01299) 403762
High Street; no nearby parking – best to use main car park, then cross B4190 (Cleobury Road) and keep walking on down narrowing High Street; DY12 2DH Friendly town pub tucked away in side street with nicely timbered rooms, reclaimed oak panelling and floorboards, woodburner, tasty food including good pies and suet puddings, ales such as Bewdley, Holdens, Hobsons and Wye Valley, selection of bottled ciders and perries and almost two dozen wines, cheerful helpful service, restaurant; background music (live last Fri of month), TV; children and dogs (in bar) welcome, heated outside area, no parking, open all day weekends; may have changed hands by the time you read this. *(Mike Tippins)*

BEWDLEY   SO7875
Mug House (01299) 402543
Severn Side North; DY12 2EE 18th-c bay-windowed pub in charming Severn-side spot, enjoyable traditional food and five well kept ales including local Bewdley, Timothy Taylors and Wye Valley, log fire, restaurant with lobster tank; children (till 8pm) and dogs welcome, disabled access, glass-covered terrace behind, seven river-view bedrooms, open all day. *(Anon)*

BIRLINGHAM   SO9343
Swan (01386) 750485
Church Street; off A4104 S of Pershore, via B4080 Eckington Road, turn off at sign to Birlingham with integral 'The Swan Inn' brown sign (not the 'Birlingham (village only)' road), then left; WR10 3AQ Pretty thatched and timbered cottage, beamed quarry-tiled bar with copper-topped tables, darts, woodburner in big stone fireplace, snug inner carpeted area by smallish counter, Wye Valley Bitter and three guests, real ciders, beer festivals May and Sept, cribbage, dominoes, poker; simple back dining conservatory, reasonably priced straightforward food (not Sun

evening) including fresh fish, well trained friendly staff; children welcome, dogs in bar, pretty back garden divided by shrubs, seats and tables under parasols. *(Martin and Pauline Jennings)*

BISHAMPTON   SO9445
Dolphin (01386) 462343
Main Street; WR10 2LX Comfortably updated village pub under new owners, good standard and variety of reasonably priced food cooked by landlord-chef including daily specials, beers such as Hook Norton and Sharps, well chosen wines by the glass, efficient friendly young staff; children and dogs welcome, seats on paved terrace and small raised deck, open all day Sat, till 9pm Sun, closed Mon lunchtime. *(Martin and Pauline Jennings)*

BREDON   SO9236
★ Fox & Hounds (01684) 772377
4.5 miles from M5 junction 9; A438 to Northway, left at B4079, in Bredon follow sign to church; GL20 7LA Cottagey 16th-c thatched pub with open-plan carpeted bar, low beams, stone pillars and stripped timbers, central woodburner, traditional furnishings including upholstered settles, a variety of wheelback, tub and kitchen chairs around handsome mahogany and cast-iron-framed tables, elegant wall lamps, smaller side bar, Banks's, Greene King and a guest, nice wines by the glass, wide choice of food including specials, fast friendly service; background music; children and dogs (in bar) welcome, outside picnic-sets (some under cover), handy M5 break. *(R J Herd, Dr A J and Mrs B A Tompsett, Dr D J and Mrs S C Walker, Martin and Pauline Jennings)*

BROADWAS-ON-TEME   SO7555
Royal Oak (01886) 821353
A44; WR6 5NE Red-brick roadside pub with various areas including unusual lofty-raftered medieval-style dining hall, good value daily carvery and other popular food, well kept ales and decent wines by the glass, friendly helpful service; free wi-fi; children welcome, disabled access, garden with play area, open all day weekends. *(Denys Gueroult)*

CALLOW END   SO8349
Blue Bell (01905) 830261
Upton Road; WR2 4TY Marstons local with two bars and dining area, wide variety of enjoyable food including lots of specials, well kept beers and friendly welcoming staff, open fire; children allowed, dogs in garden only, open all day weekends. *(Dave Braisted)*

CALLOW HILL   SO7473
Royal Forester (01299) 266286
Near Wyre Forest visitor centre; DY14 9XW Dining pub dating in part from the 15th c, good food and friendly helpful service, relaxed lounge bar with two well kept ales such as Wye Valley, Robinson's

cider, restaurant; children and dogs welcome, seats outside, seven contemporary bedrooms, open all day. *(Anon)*

CAUNSALL
SO8480
Anchor (01562) 850254
Caunsall Road, off A449; DY11 5YL
Traditional unchanging two-room pub (in same family since 1927), friendly atmosphere and can get busy, half a dozen well kept ales including Hobsons, Holdens and Wye Valley, traditional ciders and generously filled cobs, friendly efficient service; dogs welcome, tables outside, near canal. *(Anon)*

CHADDESLEY CORBETT
SO8973
Fox (01562) 777247
A448 Bromsgrove–Kidderminster; DY10 4QN Friendly pub popular for its good value food including daily carvery and grills, Wye Valley and a couple of guests, several wines by the glass, pleasant attentive service; children welcome, open all day. *(Dave Braisted)*

CLAINES
SO8558
Mug House (01905) 456649
Claines Lane, off A449 3 miles W of M5 junction 3; WR3 7RN Fine views from ancient country tavern in unique churchyard setting by fields below the Malvern Hills; several small rooms around central bar, low doorways and heavy oak beams, well kept Banks's and other Marstons-related beers, simple lunchtime pub food (not Sun); no credit cards, outside lavatories; children allowed away from servery, open all day weekends. *(Anon)*

CROWLE
SO9256
Old Chequers (01905) 381275
Crowle Green, not far from M5 junction 6; WR7 4AA Civilised 17th-c dining pub mixing traditional and contemporary décor; oak beams and log fires, leather sofas, modern tables and chairs in bar and restaurant, friendly prompt service, good variety of enjoyable home-made food from pub favourites up including fixed-price menu, three real ales and nice choice of wines by the glass, baby grand piano, some live jazz; children and dogs (in bar) welcome, disabled facilities, picnic-sets in garden behind, open all day, closed Sun evening. *(Martin and Pauline Jennings, Alan Weedon)*

DEFFORD
SO9042
★ Monkey House (01386) 750234
A4104, after passing Oak pub on right, it's the last of a small group of cottages; WR8 9BW Tiny black and white cider house, a wonderful time warp and in the same family for over 150 years; drinks limited to cider and a perry tapped from barrels into pottery mugs and served by landlady from a hatch, no food (can bring your own); children welcome, no dogs (resident rottweilers), garden with caravans, sheds and Mandy

the horse, small spartan outbuilding with a couple of plain tables, settle and fireplace, open Fri and Sun lunchtimes, Weds and Sat evenings. *(Anon)*

DEFFORD
SO9042
Oak (01386) 750327
Woodmancote (A4104); WR8 9BW Modernised 17th-c beamed country pub with two front bars and back restaurant, well kept Sharps Doom Bar and Wye Valley ales, Thatcher's cider, enjoyable fairly priced food from ciabattas up, friendly staff; children welcome, vine-covered front pergola, garden with chickens and orchard. *(Paul Humphreys)*

DODFORD
SO9372
Dodford Inn (01527) 875074
Whinfield Road; B61 9BG Welcoming unpretentious country pub in quiet spot overlooking wooded valley, traditional décor and simple furnishings, up to five well kept changing local ales, good value pub food cooked to order from baps up, central fire; children, walkers and dogs welcome, terrace and good sized garden, camping. *(Nigel and Sue Foster)*

DRAYTON
SO9075
Robin Hood (01562) 730526
Off B4188; DY9 0BW Refurbished early 19th-c dining pub, inglenook log fire, low beams and lovely stained glass in large lounge, good food from sensibly priced menu, also themed evenings such as seafood and japanese, well kept Enville, Holdens and Wye Valley, Thatcher's cider; can get very busy weekends; children welcome, terrace and garden tables, play area, attractive surroundings and good walks, open all day. *(Dave Braisted)*

DROITWICH
SO8963
Gardeners Arms (01905) 772936
Vines Lane; WR9 8LU Individual place on the edge of town; cosy traditional bar to the right, bistro-style restaurant to the left with red gingham tablecloths and lots of pictures (mostly for sale), four Marstons-related ales, well priced food from varied menu including range of good local sausages, friendly attentive service, events such as live music, quiz nights, themed food evenings, whisky tastings and cigar club; children and dogs welcome, outside seating areas on different levels below railway embankment with quirky mix of furniture, play area, camping, close to Droitwich Canal, open all day. *(Clive and Fran Dutson, Dave Braisted, John and Hazel Sarkanen)*

DROITWICH
SO9063
Hop Pole (01905) 770155
Friar Street; WR9 8ED Heavy-beamed local with panelled rooms on different levels, friendly staff, well kept Enville, Malvern Hills, Wye Valley and a guest, bargain home-made lunchtime food including doorstep sandwiches, dominoes, darts and pool, live

music first Sun of month; children welcome, partly canopied back garden, open all day. *(Alan Weedon, Dave Braisted)*

ELDERSFIELD   SO8131

★ **Butchers Arms** (01452) 840381

Village signposted from B4211; Lime Street (coming from A417, go past the Eldersfield turn and take the next one), OS Sheet 150 map reference 815314; also signposted from B4208 N of Staunton; GL19 4NX Pretty cottage with deliberately simple unspoilt little locals' bar, ales such as St Austell, Wickwar and Wye Valley tapped from the cask, a farm cider and short but well chosen wine list, just a dozen seats in candlelit dining room, good carefully prepared, well presented food (not cheap) using ingredients from named local farms, booking essential lunchtimes and advisable evenings; no under-10s, garden picnic-sets, nice surroundings, closed Sun evening, Mon, ten days in Jan and the latter part of Aug, food served lunchtime Fri-Sun, evening Tues-Sat. *(Anon)*

EVESHAM   SP0344

Evesham Hotel (01386) 765566

Coopers Lane; WR11 1DA Idiosyncratic hotel's busy bar with amazing range of malt whiskies and spirits, a beer from Teme Valley and good if quirky wine list, interesting menu including good value lunchtime buffet (no tips or service charge), elegant dining room; remarkable lavatories with talking mirrors; children welcome (toys for them), indoor swimming pool, 39 comfortable bedrooms, open all day. *(Miss B D Picton)*

FECKENHAM   SP0061

Forest (01527) 894422

B4090 Droitwich–Alcester; B96 6JE Contemporary revamp for this village dining pub; good interesting food, freshly made and well presented, from lunchtime sandwiches and sharing boards up, Hook Norton Hooky and Old Hooky and St Austell Tribute, oak-floored bar with light wood stools at high tables and some other more comfortable seating, panels of bookshelf wallpaper dotted about, woodburner, adjoining restaurant with upholstered booth seats, conservatory; children welcome, disabled access/facilities, rattan furniture on block-paved terrace with big outdoor fireplace, more tables on raised lawn, open all day. *(Dave Braisted)*

FLADBURY   SO9946

Chequers (01386) 861854

Chequers Lane; WR10 2PZ Refurbished old pub (new management) in peaceful village; long beamed bar with log fire in old-fashioned range, ales such as Sharps Doom Bar and Wye Valley, Aspall's and Weston's ciders, enjoyable sensibly priced home-made food, timbered back restaurant with conservatory; background music, free wi-fi; children welcome, steps up to walled terrace, play area on lawn, eight bedrooms in extension. *(Dave Braisted)*

GRIMLEY   SO8359

Camp House (01905) 640288

A443 5 miles N from Worcester, right to Grimley, right at village T junction; WR2 6LX Simple unspoilt old pub in same family since 1939, appealing Severn-side setting (prone to flooding) with own landing stage, generous home-made food at bargain prices, well kept Bathams and guests, Thatcher's and Robinson's ciders, friendly laid-back atmosphere; no credit cards; children and well behaved dogs welcome, attractive lawns (maybe wandering peacocks), small campsite, open all day. *(Anon)*

GUARLFORD   SO8245

Plough & Harrow (01684) 310453

B4211 E of village; WR13 6NY Country pub with contemporary feel despite low beams in bar, enjoyable home-made pubby food, Wadworths ales, airy two-level restaurant; Thurs quiz and some live music; children welcome, hedged back garden, own pigs and vegetables in adjacent field, closed Wed. *(Anon)*

HADLEY   SO8662

Bowling Green (01905) 620294

Hadley Heath; off A4133 Droitwich–Ombersley; WR9 0AR Friendly 16th-c inn with beams and big log fire, sofas in back lounge, well kept Wadworths range and decent wines by the glass, good food (all day weekends) from sandwiches to daily specials, attractive restaurant; children welcome, tables out overlooking own bowling green (UK's oldest), eight comfortable bedrooms, nice walks (footpath starts from car park), open all day. *(M Ross-Thomas, M C and S Jeanes)*

HANBURY   SO9662

Vernon (01527) 821236

Droitwich Road (B4090); B60 4DB 18th-c former coaching inn, contemporary refurbishment and calls itself a country restaurant with rooms, but still serves real ales such as Wye Valley and Sharps in beamed bar with woodburner, nice food from light choices to more enterprising restaurant-style dishes, set menu too, good friendly service; modern terrace seating, five stylish bedrooms, open all day (till 2am Fri, Sat). *(Dave Braisted)*

HANLEY CASTLE   SO8342

★ **Three Kings** (01684) 592686

Church End, off B4211 N of Upton upon Severn; WR8 0BL Timeless, hospitable and by no means smart – in same family for over 100 years and a favourite with those who put unspoilt character and individuality first; cheerful homely tiled-floor tap room separated from entrance corridor by monumental built-in settle, equally vast inglenook fireplace, room on left with darts and board games, separate entrance to timbered lounge with second inglenook and neatly blacked kitchen range, leatherette armchairs, spindleback chairs and antique winged settle, well kept Butcombe, Hobsons and three guests from smaller brewers, Weston's cider and around 75 malt whiskies, simple snacks, occasional live music; old-fashioned wood and iron seats on front terrace looking across to great cedar shading tiny green. *(Joan and Tony Walker, M G Hart, Barry Collett)*

HIMBLETON   SO9458
Galton Arms (01905) 391672
Harrow Lane; WR9 7LQ Friendly old black and white bay-windowed country pub, enjoyable food in split-level beamed bar or restaurant, well kept ales such as Bathams, St Austell and Wye Valley, woodburner; picnic-sets in small garden, local walks. *(Dave Braisted)*

KEMPSEY   SO8548
Walter de Cantelupe
(01905) 820572 *3.7 miles from M5 junction 7: A44 towards Worcester, left on to A4440, then left on A38 at roundabout; Main Road; WR5 3NA* Traditional carpeted bar with inglenook log fire, ales such as Cannon Royall, Cotleigh and Timothy Taylors, summer farm cider and maybe locally pressed apple juice, enjoyable home-made food, table skittles; background music, sports TV; children in dining area till 8.15pm, dogs in bar and bedrooms, pretty suntrap walled garden, closed Mon. *(Anon)*

KIDDERMINSTER   SO8376
★ King & Castle (01562) 747505
Railway Station, Comberton Hill; DY10 1QX Bustling and neatly re-created Edwardian refreshment room suiting its setting in Severn Valley Railway terminus, steam trains outside and railway memorabilia and photographs inside, simple furnishings, Bathams, very good value Wyre Piddle and guests, reasonably priced straightforward food in adjacent dining room (9am-3pm), cheerful staff coping well on busy bank holidays and railway gala days; little museum close by, open all day. *(Roger and Donna Huggins)*

LULSLEY   SO7354
Fox & Hounds (01886) 821228
Signed a mile off A44 Worcester–Bromyard; WR6 5QT Pleasant tucked-away country pub with well kept Greene King, Hobsons, Otter and a guest (May beer festival), Robinson's cider and nice wines, good choice of enjoyable reasonably priced food (not evenings Sun, Mon or Weds), friendly staff and locals, smallish parquet-floored bar with open fire, steps down to lounge area, sizeable dining conservatory,

Tues jazz night; children welcome, dogs in bar, colourful side rose garden and separate enclosed play area, nice walks (near Worcestershire Way), open all day Fri-Sun. *(Anon)*

MALVERN   SO7746
Foley Arms (01684) 573397
Worcester Road; WR14 4QS Substantial Georgian hotel owned by Wetherspoons, usual good value; splendid views from sunny terrace and back bedrooms, open all day from 7am. *(Torrens Lyster, Alan Weedon, Dave Braisted)*

MALVERN   SO7640
Malvern Hills Hotel (01684) 540690
Opposite British Camp car park, Wynds Point; junction A449/B4232 S; WR13 6DW Big comfortable dark-panelled lounge bar, very popular weekends, enjoyable food from baguettes up, well kept changing ales such as local Malvern Hills and Wye Valley, quite a few malt whiskies and good coffee, friendly service, woodburner, downstairs pool room, smart more expensive restaurant; background music; dogs welcome, great views from terrace, bedrooms small but comfortable, open all day. *(David Edwards)*

MALVERN   SO7746
Red Lion (01684) 564787
St Ann's Road; WR14 4RG Enjoyable food (all day weekends) from substantial sandwiches and baguettes up, also adjacent thai restaurant (asian fusion buffet Sun), well kept Marstons-related ales, cheerful prompt service, airy modern décor with stripped pine, bare boards, flagstones and pastel colours; background and live music; attractive partly covered front terrace, well placed for walks, open all day weekends, closed Mon-Thurs lunchtimes. *(Paul Humphreys)*

MALVERN   SO7643
Wyche (01684) 575396
Wyche Road; WR14 4EQ Comfortable busy pub near top of Malvern Hills, splendid views and popular with walkers, five local ales and affordable pubby food; children and dogs welcome, four bedrooms, open all day. *(Guy Vowles)*

OMBERSLEY   SO8463
★ Cross Keys (01905) 620588
Just off A449; Main Road (A4133, Kidderminster end); WR9 0DS Carpeted bar with easy-going atmosphere, archways opening into several separate areas – nicest on left with attractive Bob Lofthouse animal etchings, hop-strung beams and some horse tack on dark varnished country panelling, ales such as Timothy Taylors Landlord and Wye Valley HPA, good value wines by the glass and decent coffee, comfortable back room with softly upholstered sofas and armchairs leading to dining conservatory, nice food from

baguettes to enterprising daily specials (good fish choice), friendly helpful service; unobtrusive background music; children welcome if eating, terrace with alloy furniture under big heated canopy. *(M and GR, David Edwards)*

OMBERSLEY   SO8463
★ Kings Arms (01905) 620142
Main Road (A4133); WR9 0EW Imposing beamed and timbered Tudor pub, spotless rambling rooms with nooks and crannies, three splendid fireplaces, low-ceilinged quarry-tiled bar with dark wood pew and stools around cast-iron tables, three dining areas, one room with Charles II coat of arms decorating its ceiling, ales such as Jennings and Marstons, good food popular with older diners; background music; children and dogs welcome, seats on tree-sheltered courtyard, colourful hanging baskets and tubs, open all day. *(Dr and Mrs A K Clarke, E Clark, Richard and Penny Gibbs, David and Stella Martin)*

PENSAX   SO7368
★ Bell (01299) 896677
B4202 Abberley–Clows Top, Snead Common part of village; WR6 6AE Mock-Tudor roadside pub with good local atmosphere and welcoming landlord, half a dozen changing ales such as Hobsons (festival last weekend of June), also cider and perry, well liked pubby food (not Sun evening) from sandwiches up, L-shaped main bar with traditional décor, cushioned pews and pubby tables on bare boards, vintage beer ads and wartime front pages, two open fires and woodburner, dining room with french windows opening on to deck; children welcome, dogs in bar, country-view garden, open all day summer weekends, closed Mon. *(Lynda and Trevor Smith)*

PEOPLETON   SO9350
Crown (01905) 840222
Village and pub signed off A44 at Allens Hill; WR10 2EE Cosy village pub with friendly mix of drinkers and diners, beamed bar with big inglenook, well laid out eating area, good generous food (must book) from sandwiches up including set deals, plenty of freshly cooked vegetables, Fullers and Hook Norton ales, nice wines by the glass, efficient pleasant service; surcharge added if paying by credit card; flower-filled back garden. *(Martin and Pauline Jennings)*

PERSHORE   SO9545
★ Brandy Cask (01386) 552602
Bridge Street; WR10 1AJ Plain high-ceilinged bow-windowed bar, own good ales from courtyard brewery and guests, friendly helpful service, coal fire, reasonably priced generous food from sandwiches to steaks, quaintly decorated dining room; well behaved children allowed, no dogs inside, terrace and koi pond in long attractive garden down to river. *(Joan and Tony Walker)*

SEVERN STOKE   SO8544
Rose & Crown (01905) 371249
A38 S of Worcester; WR8 9JQ Attractive 16th-c black and white pub, low beams, knick-knacks and good fire in character bar, some cushioned wall seats and high-backed settles among more modern pub furniture, well kept Marstons-related ales, decent choice of enjoyable sensibly priced food including vegetarian, good friendly service, carpeted back restaurant, music and quiz nights; dogs welcome, wheelchair access with help, picnic-sets in big garden with play area, Malvern Hills views and good walks, open (and food) all day. *(R L Borthwick)*

SHATTERFORD   SO7981
Bellmans Cross (01299) 861322
Bridgnorth Road (A442); DY12 1RN Welcoming dining pub with good nicely presented food cooked by french chef-landlord, restaurant with kitchen view, pleasant service, real ales and good choice of wines from neat timber-effect bar, teas and coffees; children welcome, picnic-sets outside, handy for Severn Woods walks, open all day weekends. *(Anon)*

STOKE POUND   SO9667
Queens Head (01527) 557007
Sugarbrook Lane, by Bridge 48, Worcester & Birmingham Canal; B60 3AU Smartly refurbished by the small Lovely Pubs group; fairly large bar with comfortable seating area, dedicated dining part beyond, good choice of enjoyable food including sharing plates, wood-fired pizzas and charcoal spit-roasts, early evening discount Mon-Fri, well kept ales such as Greene King, Purity and Wye Valley, large selection of wines from glass fronted store, helpful pleasant young staff; children welcome, waterside garden with tepee, moorings, good walk up the 36 locks of the Tardebigge Steps, quite handy for Avoncroft Museum, open all day. *(Clive and Fran Dutson, Helene Grygar, Dave Braisted)*

STOKE WORKS   SO9365
Bowling Green (01527) 861291
A mile from M5 junction 5, via Stoke Lane; handy for Worcester & Birmingham Canal; B60 4BH Friendly comfortable pub with enjoyable straight-forward food at bargain prices (not Sun), Banks's and Marstons EPA; children welcome, big garden with play area and neat bowling green, open all day. *(Dave Braisted)*

TIBBERTON   SO9057
Bridge Inn (01905) 345874
Plough Road; WR9 7NQ By Worcester & Birmingham Canal (Bridge 25); two comfortable dining sections with central fireplace, separate public bar, enjoyable reasonably priced traditional food, Banks's ales and a Marstons guest, friendly staff,

some live music; children, dogs and muddy boots welcome, picnic-sets by water and in garden with secure play area, moorings, open all day. *(Dave Braisted)*

UPHAMPTON   SO8464
Fruiterers Arms (01905) 620305
Off A449 N of Ombersley; WR9 0JW
Homely country local (looks like a private house, and has been in the same family for over 160 years), good value Cannon Royall ales brewed at the back of the pub and guest beers, farm cider and perry, simple rustic Jacobean panelled bar and lounge with comfortable armchairs, beams and log fire, lots of photographs and memorabilia, no food except filled rolls Fri-Sun; children till 9pm, back terrace and some seats out in front, open all day. *(Anon)*

WEATHEROAK HILL   SP0574
★ Coach & Horses (01564) 823386
Icknield Street – coming S on A435 from Wythall roundabout, filter right off dual carriageway a mile S, then in village turn left towards Alvechurch; not far from M42 junction 3; B48 7EA Roomy country pub (in same family since 1968) brewing its own good Weatheroak beers, well kept guests too and farm ciders, enjoyable choice of fairly priced home-cooked food (not Sun evening); proper old-fashioned tiled-floor bar with log fire (dogs allowed here), lounge bar with steps up to comfortably furnished high-raftered room with another fire, modern barn-style restaurant; children welcome, plenty of seats out on lawns and terrace, open all day. *(Anon)*

WEST MALVERN   SO7645
★ Brewers Arms (01684) 568147
The Dingle, signed off B4232; WR14 4BQ
Attractive and friendly little two-bar beamed country local down steep path, Malvern Hills, Marstons, Wye Valley and up to five guests (Oct beer festival); good value home-made food, neat airy dining room; children, walkers and dogs welcome, glorious view from small garden, smokers' folly, open all day Fri-Sun. *(Anon)*

WILDMOOR   SO9675
Wildmoor Oak (0121) 453 2696
A mile from M5 junction 4 – first left off A491 towards Stourbridge; Top Road; B61 0RB Busy country local with good choice of enjoyable food including caribbean dishes cooked by landlord, changing real ales, ciders and perries, friendly atmosphere; live jazz last Sun of month, funk/soul disco first Fri, free wi-fi; small sloping terrace and garden, closed Mon lunchtime, otherwise open all day. *(Sarah Rees)*

WILLERSEY   SP1039
New Inn (01386) 853226
Main Street; WR12 7PJ Friendly and attractive old stone-built local in lovely village, generous good value pub food all day from sandwiches up, prompt service, well kept Donnington ales, ancient flagstones, darts and raised end area in traditional main bar with woodburner, pool in separate public bar, skittle alley; background music, TV; tables outside, good local walks, open all day. *(Alan Weedon, Martin and Pauline Jennings)*

WORCESTER   SO8554
Cardinals Hat (01905) 724006
Friar Street; just off A44 near cathedral; WR1 2NA Dating from the 14th c with three recently restored small character rooms (one with fine oak panelling), half a dozen changing ales, real ciders and plenty of bottled beers, good bar snacks and cheese/meat platters, friendly well informed staff; free wi-fi; children welcome, pleasant little brick-paved terrace behind, closed Mon lunchtime, otherwise open all day. *(Lesley and Brian Lynn)*

WORCESTER   SO8455
Dragon (01905) 25845
The Tything (A38); WR1 1JT Simply furnished open-plan alehouse with six well kept interesting beers from smaller brewers including own Little Ale Cart, bottled belgians and Thatcher's cider too, friendly staff; dogs welcome, partly covered back terrace, open all day Fri and Sat (lunchtime food then, roasts on Sun), closed Mon and Tues lunchtimes. *(Giles and Annie Francis)*

WORCESTER   SO8454
Farriers Arms (01905) 27569
Fish Street; WR1 2HN Welcoming and relaxed old timbered pub rambling through pleasant lounge/dining area and public bar, enjoyable inexpensive food, well kept ales such as Wells & Youngs Bombardier and decent house wines, good cheerful service; TV, pool, darts; beer garden, handy for cathedral, open all day. *(George Atkinson)*

WORCESTER   SO8455
★ Marwood (01905) 330460
The Tything (A38); some nearby parking; WR1 1JL Easy to miss this old building; quirky and civilised with a long narrow series of small linked areas, dark flagstones and broad floorboards, stripped or cast-iron-framed tables, the odd chandelier, a few italian deco posters, open fires, upstairs room looking across to law courts, well kept

We include some hotels with a good bar that offers facilities comparable to those of a pub.

Butcombe, Purity, Sharps Doom Bar and guests, enjoyable food (not Sun evening) from sandwiches and tapas up, friendly service; background music; children (in bar till 7.30pm) and dogs welcome, sunny flagstoned courtyard, open all day (till late Sat). *(Anon)*

WORCESTER   SO8555
Plough   (01905) 21381
Fish Street; WR1 2HN Traditional corner pub with two simple rooms off entrance lobby, six interesting ales usually including Hobsons and Malvern Hills, farm cider and perry, good whisky choice, coal-effect gas fire; outside lavatories; small back terrace with cathedral view, open all day, closed Thurs lunchtime. *(Anon)*

WORCESTER   SO8455
Postal Order   (01905) 22373
Foregate Street; WR1 1DN Popular Wetherspoons in former sorting office, wide range of well kept beers, Weston's cider and their usual good value food; open all day from 8am. *(Anon)*

WORCESTER   SO8554
Swan With Two Nicks
(01905) 28190 *New Street/Friar Street; WR1 2DP* Rambling town pub dating from the early 16th c, plenty of character in bare-boards low-ceilinged front rooms, four changing local ales and some interesting bottled ciders, good value lunchtime food including specials, friendly atmosphere, other areas – one for Fri live music; open all day apart from Sun evening. *(Robert W Buckle, Phil and Jane Hodson)*

WYRE PIDDLE   SO9647
Anchor   (01386) 641510
Off A4538 NW of Evesham; WR10 2JB Great position by River Avon with moorings, decking on three levels, floodlit lawn and view from airy back dining room; some refurbishment by new owners, enjoyable well priced home-made food (not Sun evening) from baguettes up, beers such as Wye Valley in beamed and flagstoned bar with inglenook stove, good friendly service; children welcome, open all day. *(Dave Braisted)*

Post Office address codings confusingly give the impression that some pubs are in Worcestershire, when they're really in Gloucestershire, Herefordshire, Shropshire or Warwickshire (which is where we list them).

Yorkshire

ADDINGHAM   SE0749   Map 7
Fleece 🍽 ☖
Main Street (B6160, off A65); LS29 0LY

Enterprising management with strong sense of style; good food cooked by the landlord and his team using local produce

Always deservedly busy, this is a creeper-covered pub for all seasons. In warm weather, you can sit beneath giant parasols on the flagstoned front terrace; another dining terrace looks out over the garden. In winter, you can have a drink or meal beside the roaring log fire in its high-manteled fireplace. The smart bar on the right has cool décor of dark flagstones, polished floorboards, crisp cream paintwork and wallpaper based on antique fish prints above a charcoal-grey high dado. A pair of grey plaid tub armchairs stand by a great arched stone fireplace, and down a few steps is the civilised dining room (occasionally given over to cookery classes). The interesting black-beamed village bar on the left, with broad floorboards, has comfortably worn easy chairs as well as cushioned wall benches and window seats, and some very unusual substantial tables. Nicely framed local photographs include a series devoted to former landlord 'Heapy', hero survivor of a 1944 torpedoing. A good range of carefully chosen drinks includes Black Sheep Best, Copper Dragon Best, Saltaire Blonde and a guest beer on handpump and 15 wines (including champagne and rosé) by the glass; background music and board games. They have a deli next door.

🍽 Using the best local produce and baking their own bread twice-daily, the enticing food includes sandwiches, ham hock terrine with piccalilli, prawn and crayfish cocktail, wild mushroom, chestnut and cavolo nero risotto with pink grapefruit salad, toad in the hole with onion gravy, spiced lamb and chickpea curry with coconut milk, dry-cured gammon with poached egg and pineapple pickle, pig on a plate (pork fillet wrapped in parma ham, black pudding, twice-cooked old spot belly), and puddings such as stem ginger crème brûlée with rhubarb compote and chocolate and kirsch mousse with chocolate 'soil' and cherry sorbet; they also offer a weekday two- and three-course set menu (lunchtime, 6-7pm). *Benchmark main dish: salmon, haddock and coley pie in tarragon cream £14.00. Two-course evening meal £19.50.*

Punch ~ Lease Craig Minto ~ Real ale ~ (01943) 830491 ~ Open 12-11 (midnight Sat, 10 Sun) ~ Bar food 12-2, 6 (5 Fri, Sat)-9; 12-6 Sun ~ Restaurant ~ Children welcome ~ Dogs allowed in bar ~ Wi-fi ~ www.fleeceinnaddingham.co.uk *Recommended by Dave Braisted, Tina and David Woods-Taylor*

ASENBY
SE3975 Map 7
Crab & Lobster ★ ♀ 🛏
Dishforth Road; village signed off A168 – handy for A1; YO7 3QL

Interesting furnishings and décor in rambling bar, inventive restauranty food, good drinks choice and seats on attractive terrace; smart bedrooms

The rambling L-shaped bar in this smart, handsome place does attract customers dropping in for a drink and a chat and they do keep Copper Dragon Best and Golden Pippin on handpump – but the main emphasis is on the hotel and restaurant side. This bustling bar has an interesting jumble of seats, from antique high-backed and other settles through sofas and wing armchairs heaped with cushions to tall and rather theatrical corner seats; the tables are almost as much of a mix. The walls and available surfaces are a jungle of bric-a-brac including lots of race tickets, while standard and table lamps and candles keep even the lighting pleasantly informal. There's also a cosy main restaurant and a dining pavilion with big tropical plants, nautical bits and pieces and Edwardian sofas; background music. The gardens have bamboo and palm trees lining the path, which leads to a gazebo; there are seats on a mediterranean-style terrace. The opulent bedrooms (based on famous hotels around the world) are in the nearby Crab Manor, which has seven acres of mature gardens and a 180-metre golf hole with full practice facilities.

Impressive – if not cheap – food includes a fish club sandwich (not Sunday), spare ribs with Jack Daniels and treacle, mussels in ale with smoked bacon and shallots, twice-baked spinach and cheese soufflé, beer-battered haddock and chips, confit shoulder of local pork with roast apples and wholegrain mustard mash, loin of venison with juniper and redcurrant and pear and ginger jelly, and puddings such as Baileys white chocolate cheesecake and knickerbocker glory; they also offer a two- and three-course set menu. *Benchmark main dish: half lobster thermidor £22.50. Two-course evening meal £28.00.*

Vimac Leisure ~ Licensee Mark Spenceley ~ Real ale ~ (01845) 577286 ~ Open 11am-11.30pm ~ Bar food 12-2.30, 7 (6.30 Sat)-9 (9.30 Sat) ~ Restaurant ~ Children welcome ~ Live jazz Weds evening ~ Bedrooms: £110/£160 ~ www.crabandlobster.co.uk
Recommended by Henry Curran

BECK HOLE
NZ8202 Map 10
Birch Hall
Off A169 SW of Whitby, from top of Sleights Moor; YO22 5LE

Extraordinary place in lovely valley with friendly landlady, real ales and simple snacks

This is a tiny pub-cum-village-shop in stunning surroundings. The two unchanging rooms (the shop sells postcards, sweets and ice-creams) have simple furnishings, built-in cushioned wall seats, wooden tables (one embedded with 136 pennies), flagstones or composition flooring, unusual items such as french breakfast cereal boxes, a tube of toothpaste priced 1/-3d, and a model train running around a head-height shelf. Milton Minerva and two guests on handpump and several malt whiskies and wines by the glass. There are benches outside in a streamside garden and wonderful surrounding walks (one along a disused railway). They have a self-catering cottage for hire.

Bar snacks only, such as local pork pie, butties, scones and their famous beer cake.

Free house ~ Licensee Glenys Crampton ~ Real ale ~ No credit cards ~ (01947) 896245 ~ Open 11-11; 11-3, 7.30-11 Weds-Sun in winter; closed Mon evening winter, all day Tues Nov-April ~ Bar food available during opening hours ~ Children in small family room ~ Dogs welcome ~ www.beckhole.info/bhi.htm *Recommended by William Wright, Toby Jones*

BLAKEY RIDGE   SE6799   Map 10
Lion 🍺 🛏

From A171 Guisborough–Whitby follow Castleton, Hutton-le-Hole signposts; from A170 Kirkby Moorside–Pickering follow Keldholm, Hutton-le-Hole, Castleton signposts; OS Sheet 100 map reference 679996; YO62 7LQ

Extended pub in fine scenery and open all day; popular food; bedrooms

There's always a good crowd of customers here despite it being so remote, and as it's 404 metres above sea level, the views over the valleys of Rosedale and Farndale are breathtaking. The surrounding hikes and the nearby Coast to Coast path also make it popular with walkers. The low-beamed rambling bars have open fires, a few big high-backed rustic settles around cast-iron-framed tables, lots of small dining chairs, a nice leather sofa and stone walls hung with some old engravings and photographs of the pub under snow (it can easily get cut off in winter – 40 days is the record so far). The fine choice of beers on handpump might include Black Sheep Best, Copper Dragon Golden Pippin, Theakstons Best, Masham Ale and Old Peculier, Thwaites Wainwright and York Guzzler and they have 13 wines by the glass and several malt whiskies; background music and games machine. If you're thinking of staying over, book well in advance; they offer good value midweek winter deals. This is a regular stop-off for coach parties.

Tasty food includes lunchtime sandwiches, giant yorkshire pudding with gravy, deep-fried brie with cranberry sauce, home-cooked ham and egg, vegetarian nut roast, chicken curry, steak and stilton burger, beer-battered haddock and chips, pork fillet with leek and bacon sauce, fillet steak tornedo rossini, and puddings such as jam roly-poly with custard and a cheesecake of the day. *Benchmark main dish: steak and mushroom pie £11.50. Two-course evening meal £17.00.*

Free house ~ Licensees Barry, Diana, Paul and David Crossland ~ Real ale ~ (01751) 417320 ~ Open 10am-11pm (midnight Sat) ~ Bar food 12-10 ~ Restaurant ~ Children welcome ~ Dogs allowed in bar and bedrooms ~ Wi-fi ~ Bedrooms: $48.50/$82 ~ www.lionblakey.co.uk *Recommended by WAH, Stephen Funnell, Richard Cole, Dr J Barrie Jones, Tina and David Woods-Taylor*

BOROUGHBRIDGE   SE3966   Map 7
Black Bull £

St James Square; B6265, just off A1(M); YO51 9AR

Bustling town pub with real ales, several wines by the glass and traditional bar food; bedrooms

Very popular locally, but with a warm welcome for visitors too, this attractive inn dates from the 13th c. It makes a good lunchtime break from the A1 and there are lots of separate drinking and eating areas where plenty of cheerful regulars drop in for a pint and a chat. The main bar area has a big stone fireplace and comfortable seats and is served through an old-fashioned hatch; there's also a cosy snug with traditional wall settles, and a tap room, lounge bar and restaurant. John Smiths Cask, Rudgate Viking and a changing guest from Timothy Taylors on handpump, eight

wines by the glass and 19 malt whiskies; dominoes. The borzoi dog is called
Spot and the two cats Kia and Mershka. The hanging baskets are lovely.

Fair-priced bar snacks (the Bargain Meals award is for these dishes) include
hot and cold sandwiches, battered haddock and chips, and pork sausages with
onion gravy; there are also daily specials such as duck stir-fry, pork tenderloin with
pink peppercorn sauce, salmon steak on noodles with oriental sauce, and venison
steak on bacon and blue cheese with a berry glaze, plus puddings such as chocolate
fudge cake and jam sponge with custard. *Benchmark main dish: pie of the day
£8.50. Two-course evening meal £19.00.*

Free house ~ Licensee Anthony Burgess ~ Real ale ~ (01423) 322413 ~
Open 11-11 (midnight Fri, Sat); 11.30-11 Sun ~ Bar food 12-2, 6-9 (9.30 Fri, Sat) ~
Restaurant ~ Children welcome ~ Dogs welcome ~ Wi-fi ~ Bedrooms: £50/£75 ~
www.blackbullboroughbridge.co.uk *Recommended by Roger and Donna Huggins, Martin Day,
John and Eleanor Holdsworth*

BRADFIELD
Strines Inn £ 🛏

SK2290 Map 7

*From A57 heading E of junction with A6013 (Ladybower Reservoir) take
first left turn (signposted with Bradfield) then bear left; with a map can also be
reached more circuitously from Strines signpost on A616 at head of Underbank
Reservoir, W of Stocksbridge; S6 6JE*

**Surrounded by fine scenery with quite a mix of customers and
traditional beer and bar food; bedrooms**

Although there's a 16th-c coat of arms over the door of this moorland
inn, the place probably dates back 300 years before that. It's popular
with walkers and their dogs as the Peak District National Park is on the
doorstep and the surrounding scenery is superb. The main bar has black
beams liberally decked with copper kettles and so forth, quite a menagerie
of stuffed animals, homely red plush-cushioned traditional wooden wall
benches and small chairs, and a coal fire in a rather grand stone fireplace.
Two other rooms, to the right and left, are similarly furnished. Acorn
Yorkshire Pride, Bradfield Farmers Blonde, Jennings Cocker Hoop and
Marstons Pedigree on handpump and ten wines by the glass. There are
plenty of picnic-sets outside, as well as swings, a play area and peacocks,
geese and chickens. The bedrooms have four-poster beds and a dining table
(they serve breakfast in your room); the front room overlooks the reservoir.

Good traditional food includes sandwiches, giant yorkshire pudding with onion
gravy, game pâté, vegetable lasagne, burger with chips, liver and onions, chilli
con carne, a huge mixed grill, and puddings such as caramel apple pie and chocolate
fudge cake. *Benchmark main dish: steak in ale pie £9.50. Two-course evening
meal £14.00.*

Free house ~ Licensee Bruce Howarth ~ Real ale ~ (0114) 285 1247 ~
Open 10.30am-11pm; 10.30-3, 5.30-11 Mon-Thurs in winter ~ Bar food 12-9; 12-2.30,
5.30-9 weekdays in winter ~ Children welcome ~ Dogs welcome ~ Bedrooms: £65/£85 ~
www.thestrinesinn.webs.com *Recommended by Mr and Mrs N Davies, Robert Parker*

BROUGHTON
Bull ⭐ ▽

SD9450 Map 7

A59; BD23 3AE

**Handsome, carefully refurbished inn making good use of pale oak and
contemporary paintwork, fine choice of drinks and enjoyable bar food**

There's a lot to do and see close to this handsome stone inn – including walking through Broughton Estate's 3,000 acres of beautiful countryside and parkland. In warm weather you can sit at the solid chairs and tables on the attractive terrace in front of the building. Inside, the various carefully furnished rooms have lots of pale oak, handsome flagstones, exposed stone walls, built-in wall seats and a mix of dining chairs around polished tables, contemporary paintwork hung with photographs of local suppliers and open log fires. Dark Horse Hetton Pale Ale, Moorhouses Pride of Pendle and Thwaites Best on handpump, several malt whiskies, ten wines by the glass and a couple of farm ciders.

From a modern brasserie-style menu with interesting touches, the food includes lunchtime sandwiches, Whitby crab with devilled mayonnaise, twice-baked wensleydale cheese soufflé, sharing platters, curried leek and potato hash with sweet onion fritters, pork and beef sausage with chilli cheese, crispy onions, pickles, relish and dripping chips, beer-battered line-caught haddock and chips, duck breast with a spicy honey glaze and rhubarb sauce, and puddings such as duck alaska and filled pancakes. *Benchmark main dish: mutton hotpot £12.00. Two-course evening meal £19.50.*

Ribble Valley Inns ~ Manager Craig Bancroft ~ Real ale ~ (01756) 792065 ~ Open 12-11 (10.30 Sun) ~ Bar food 12-2, 5.30-8.30 (9 Fri, Sat); 12-8.30 Sun ~ Children welcome ~ Dogs allowed in bar ~ www.thebullatbroughton.com *Recommended by Graham and Jane Bellfield, Dr Kevan Tucker*

CONSTABLE BURTON
Wyvill Arms ⭐ ♈ 🍺 🛏 SE1690 Map 10
A684 E of Leyburn; DL8 5LH

Well run, friendly dining pub with interesting food, a dozen wines by the glass, real ales and efficient helpful service; bedrooms

'We were so impressed with our stay here that we booked another one as soon as we'd left,' is a typical comment from several of our readers after enjoying the comfortable bedrooms in this 18th-c former farmhouse; the hearty breakfasts also come in for warm praise (you can buy their home-made marmalade as a souvenir). The small bar area has a mix of seating, a finely worked plaster ceiling with the Wyvill family's coat of arms and an elaborate stone fireplace with a warm winter fire. The second bar has a lower ceiling with fans, leather seating, old oak tables, various alcoves and a model train on a railway track running around the room; the reception area includes a huge leather sofa that can seat up to eight people, another carved stone fireplace and an old leaded stained-glass church window partition. Both rooms are hung with pictures of local scenes. The three real ales on handpump are Theakstons Best, Wensleydale Coverdale Gamekeeper and a guest beer, and they have nine wines by the glass and nine malt whiskies; chess, backgammon and dominoes. There are several large wooden benches under sizeable white parasols for outdoor dining and picnic-sets by a well. Do pay a visit to the Constable Burton Hall opposite.

From a varied menu using local and regional produce backed up by home-grown herbs and vegetables, the seriously good food includes lunchtime sandwiches, duck liver pâté with chutney, king scallops with pea purée and café de paris butter, wild mushroom risotto, steak and onion pie, half duck confit with plum sauce, herb-crusted lamb with parsnip purée, dauphinoise potatoes and rosemary jus, steaks with interesting sauces, and puddings such as mascarpone cheesecake with lemon curd topping and pecan pie. *Benchmark main dish: cod with king scallops, tiger prawns and chorizo cream £16.50. Two-course evening meal £19.50.*

Free house ~ Licensee Nigel Stevens ~ Real ale ~ (01677) 450581 ~ Open 11-3, 5.30
(6 Sun)-11; closed Mon ~ Bar food 12-2.15, 5.30-9 ~ Restaurant ~ Children welcome until
8.30 ~ Dogs allowed in bar ~ Wi-fi ~ Bedrooms: £65/£85 ~ www.thewyvillarms.co.uk
Recommended by Janet and Peter Race, Michael Doswell

COXWOLD
SE5377   Map 7

Fauconberg Arms 🌟 � 🛏

Off A170 Thirsk–Helmsley, via Kilburn or Wass; easily found off A19 too;
YO61 4AD

**Family-run inn with highly popular food, a good range of drinks
and seats in the back garden; comfortable bedrooms**

Run by a family who care about their customers, this nicely updated old
inn is named after Lord Fauconberg who married Oliver Cromwell's
daughter Mary. The heavily beamed and flagstoned bar has log fires in both
linked areas (one in an unusual arched fireplace in a broad low inglenook),
muted contemporary colours, some attractive oak chairs by local
craftsmen alongside more usual pub furnishings, carefully chosen old local
photographs and other pictures, and copper implements and china. Rudgate
Jorvik Blonde, Theakstons Best and a changing guest on handpump, a
thoughtful choice of around 30 wines by the glass, farm cider and 30 malt
whiskies. The candlelit dining room is quietly elegant with a gently upmarket
yet relaxed atmosphere. The pub dogs are called Bramble and Phoebe. The
garden behind has seats and tables on the terrace and views across the fields
to the ruins of Byland Abbey; picnic-sets and teak benches on the front
cobbles look along this charming village's broad tree-lined verges, bright
with flower tubs. This is an attractive place to stay – super breakfasts too.

Using local and regional produce including lots of winter game, the classic food
cooked by the landlord includes lunchtime sandwiches, seasonal pâté with
preserves, black pudding, smoked bacon and red onion salad, sharing platters,
a changing vegetarian frittata, burger with bacon, cheese, coleslaw and chips, beer-
battered fresh haddock and chips, 28-day-aged steaks, and puddings such as fruit
crumble and sticky toffee pudding. *Benchmark main dish: pie of the day £12.50.*
Two-course evening meal £19.00.

Free house ~ Licensee Simon Rheinberg ~ Real ale ~ (01347) 868214 ~ Open 11am-
midnight ~ Bar food 12-2.30 (3 weekends), 6-9 ~ Restaurant ~ Children welcome ~ Dogs
welcome ~ Wi-fi ~ Live music regularly; check website for details ~ Bedrooms: £75/£85 ~
www.fauconbergarms.com *Recommended by John Oates*

CRAYKE
SE5670   Map 7

Durham Ox 🌟 ♀ 🛏

Off B1363 at Brandsby, towards Easingwold; West Way; YO61 4TE

**Well run and friendly inn with interesting décor in old-fashioned,
relaxing rooms, fine drinks and smashing food; lovely views and
comfortable bedrooms**

You can be sure of an enjoyable all-round experience in this civilised,
well run inn. The old-fashioned lounge bar has an enormous inglenook
fireplace, pictures and photographs on the dark red walls, interesting satirical
carvings in the panelling (Victorian copies of medieval pew ends), polished
copper and brass, and venerable tables, antique seats and settles on the
flagstones. In the bottom bar is a framed illustrated account of local history
(some of it gruesome) dating back to the 12th c, and a large framed print
of the famous Durham Ox which weighed 171 stone. The Burns Bar has

a woodburning stove, exposed brickwork and large french windows that open on to a balcony area. Black Sheep Best, Timothy Taylors Landlord and a changing guest such as York Guzzler on handpump, 14 wines by the glass and ten malt whiskies; background music. There are seats in the courtyard garden and fantastic views over the Vale of York on three sides; on the fourth side is a charming view to the medieval church on the hill – supposedly the very hill up which the Grand Old Duke of York marched his men. Interesting regular events include a Meet the Brewers evening hosted by Timothy Taylors and cookery demonstrations from the head chef. The bedrooms, in the main building or renovated farm cottages (dogs allowed here), are well equipped, spacious and comfortable; breakfasts are very good. The nearby A19 leads straight to a Park & Ride for York. The pub is part of Provenance Inns.

The imaginative menu celebrates the best of the local produce (particularly game and fish) and they make their own bread and petits fours: lunchtime sandwiches and eggs benedict, ham hock terrine with piccalilli, queen scallops baked with garlic butter and gruyère, sweet-cured bacon steak with fried egg and skinny fries, moroccan vegetable tagine, slow-braised lamb shoulder with herb dumpling and red wine jus, bass fillets with crab and pea risotto and crispy arancini, and puddings such as rhubarb bakewell tart with rhubarb jelly and chocolate fondant with black cherry ice-cream; they still offer some dishes for £7 before 7pm. *Benchmark main dish: beer-battered fish and chips £11.95. Two-course evening meal £20.00.*

Free house ~ Licensee Michael Ibbotson ~ Real ale ~ (01347) 821506 ~ Open 11-11; 12-11 Sun ~ Bar food 12-2.30, 5.30-9.30; 12-3, 5.30-8.30 Sun ~ Restaurant ~ Children welcome ~ Dogs allowed in bedrooms ~ Wi-fi ~ Live music Thurs evenings ~ Bedrooms: £80/£120 ~ www.thedurhamox.com *Recommended by David Jackman, Janet and Peter Race, Walter and Susan Rinaldi-Butcher*

CROPTON
SE7588 Map 10
New Inn
Village signposted off A170 W of Pickering; YO18 8HH

Genuinely warm welcome in a modernised village pub with own-brew beers, traditional furnishings and brewery tours; bedrooms

Beers from both the Cropton Brewery and Great Yorkshire Brewery are produced here and the brewery tours are fun; the £6 fee includes a pint of one of the brews. They keep Cropton Monkmans Slaughter and Yorkshire Warrior and Great Yorkshire Pale and Classic, plus a guest from each, on handpump; also, an own-brew cider, eight wines by the glass and ten malt whiskies. The traditional village bar has wood panelling, plush seating, lots of brass and a small fire. A local artist has designed the historical posters lining the downstairs conservatory, which doubles as a visitor centre at busy times. The elegant restaurant features locally made furniture and paintings by local artists; background music, TV, games machine, darts, pool and a juke box. There's a neat terrace, a garden with a pond and a brewery shop.

Bar food includes sandwiches, blue cheese, bacon and black pudding tart, corn-fed chicken with savoy cabbage and potato rösti, cheese, leek and potato pie, lager-battered cod and chips, 21-day-aged sirloin steak with ale butter, and puddings such as apple and plum tart and espresso crème brûlée. *Benchmark main dish: steak in ale pie £10.50. Two-course evening meal £16.00.*

Own brew ~ Licensee Philip Lee ~ Real ale ~ (01751) 417330 ~ Open 11-11 (midnight Sat) ~ Bar food 12-2.30, 5.30-9; 12-3, 5.30-8 Sun ~ Restaurant ~ Well behaved children welcome ~ Dogs allowed in bar ~ Wi-fi ~ Bedrooms: £60/£85 ~ www.croptonbrewery.com *Recommended by P Dawn*

DOWNHOLME
Bolton Arms

SE1197 Map 10

Village signposted just off A6108 Leyburn–Richmond; DL11 6AE

Tasty food in unusual village's cosy country pub; bedrooms

In summer, the hanging baskets in front of this welcoming little pub are very pretty and the views from the neat garden (on the same level as the dining room and sharing the views) are magnificent; there are also picnic-sets and benches on a lower level, and quoits. The softly lit, carpeted and black-beamed bar is down a few steps and has two smallish linked areas off the servery where they keep Black Sheep Best and Timothy Taylors Landlord on handpump, ten wines by the glass and ten malt whiskies. There are comfortable plush wall banquettes, a log fire in a neat fireplace, quite a lot of gleaming brass, a few small country pictures and drinks' advertisements on pinkish rough-plastered walls; background music and dominoes. There's also a conservatory.

🍴 Popular food cooked by the landlord includes sandwiches and baguettes, tempura king prawns with sweet chilli dip, black pudding stack with cheese and bacon, thai stir-fry vegetables, cumberland sausage with onion gravy, lambs liver and bacon, fresh seafood tagliatelle, mixed grill, and puddings; there's also an early-bird menu (6-7pm Mon-Thurs). *Benchmark main dish: kleftico (slow-cooked lamb greek-style) £14.75. Two-course evening meal £20.00.*

Free house ~ Licensees Steve and Nicola Ross ~ Real ale ~ (01748) 823716 ~ Open 11-3, 6-11.30 (midnight weekends); closed Tues lunchtime ~ Bar food 12-2, 6-9.30 ~ Restaurant ~ Children welcome ~ Bedrooms: £45/£70 ~ www.boltonarmsdownholme.com
Recommended by WAH, Ryta Lyndley

EAST WITTON
Blue Lion

SE1486 Map 10

A6108 Leyburn–Ripon; DL8 4SN

Civilised dining pub with interesting rooms, daily papers, real ales, delicious food and courteous service; comfortable bedrooms

A perfect base for exploring the fine surroundings of the Yorkshire Dales National Park, this delightful Georgian coaching inn, run by the same charming couple for over 20 years now, remains a firm favourite with our readers. You can drop in for a drink beside the log fire or stay longer for an excellent meal – you'll be warmly welcomed by the courteous staff whichever you choose; they're kind to dogs too. The big squarish bar is civilised but informal with soft lighting, high-backed antique settles and old windsor chairs on turkish rugs and flagstones, ham hooks in the high ceiling decorated with dried wheat, teazles and so forth, a delft shelf filled with appropriate bric-a-brac, plus several prints, sporting caricatures and other pictures; daily papers. Black Sheep Best and Golden Sheep and Theakstons Best on handpump, an impressive wine list including a dozen (plus champagne) by the glass and 17 malt whiskies. The candlelit high-ceilinged dining room has another open fire. Picnic-sets on the gravel outside look beyond the stone houses on the far side of the village green to Witton Fell, and there's a big attractive back garden. The comfortable bedrooms with pretty country furnishings are either in the main house or in converted stables across the courtyard (where dogs are welcome).

🌟 Top class local and regional produce is at the heart of the seriously good, imaginative food that includes lunchtime sandwiches, roasted whole quail with confit leg and quail egg, Whitby crab and spinach raviolone with shellfish bisque, chicken breast with truffled leeks, fondant potato and tarragon sauce, steak and kidney pudding, slow-roasted venison with juniper sauce, halibut with celeriac purée, caper, raisin and brown shrimp sauce, and puddings such as mandarin cheesecake with orange and mint salad and dark chocolate terrine with candied hazelnuts and hazelnut cream; they also offer a two- and three-course set lunch. *Benchmark main dish: smoked haddock, mushroom and leek cream with a soft poached egg and gruyère £17.95. Two-course evening meal £25.00.*

Free house ~ Licensee Paul Klein ~ Real ale ~ (01969) 624273 ~ Open 11-11 ~ Bar food 12-2, 7-9 ~ Restaurant ~ Children welcome ~ Dogs allowed in bar and bedrooms ~ Wi-fi ~ Bedrooms: £69.50/£94 ~ www.thebluelion.co.uk *Recommended by Neil and Angela Huxter, Janet and Peter Race, J R Wildon, Michael Doswell*

 ELSLACK   SD9249   Map 7

Tempest Arms

Just off A56 Earby–Skipton; BD23 3AY

Friendly inn with three log fires in stylish rooms, six real ales, good wines and popular food; bedrooms

What makes this carefully run 18th-c stone inn special is that, despite having 21 well equipped and warm bedrooms, the atmosphere throughout remains that of a friendly local pub. And the wide mix of happy customers stands testament to that. It's stylish but understated and cosy with plenty of character in the bar and surrounding dining areas: cushioned armchairs, built-in wall seats with comfortable cushions, stools and lots of tables and three log fires – one greets you at the entrance and divides the bar and restaurant. There's quite a bit of exposed stonework, amusing prints on cream walls, half a dozen real ales such as Dark Horse Hetton Pale Ale, Ilkley Mary Jane and Thwaites Wainwright on handpump, 12 wines by the glass and 20 malt whiskies; limited background music. The tables outside are largely screened from the road by a raised bank. The beautiful scenery and walks of the Yorkshire Dales are close by.

 As well as open sandwiches and interesting platters, the wide choice of enterprising food includes queenie scallops and tiger prawns in a creamy white wine sauce with swiss cheese, pork, sage and apple meatballs with pasta in a rich tomato sauce, venison and wild boar sausage on bean and pancetta stew, steak and mushroom pudding, onion and cheese pie on bubble and squeak in creamy asparagus sauce, seafood pancake, lamb curry, mixed grill, and puddings. *Benchmark main dish: slow-cooked lamb shoulder with redcurrant and mint sauce £14.95. Two-course evening meal £19.50.*

Individual Inns ~ Managers Martin and Veronica Clarkson ~ Real ale ~ (01282) 842450 ~ Open 11-11; 12-10.30 Sun ~ Bar food 12-2.30, 6-9 (9.30 Fri, Sat); 12-7.30 Sun ~ Restaurant ~ Children welcome ~ Dogs allowed in bar and bedrooms ~ Wi-fi ~ Bedrooms: £75/£100 ~ www.tempestarms.co.uk *Recommended by Glenn Foard, Claes Mauroy, Les and Sandra Brown, Christopher Mobbs, Gordon and Margaret Ormondroyd*

FELIXKIRK   SE4684   Map 10

Carpenters Arms

Village signed off A170 E of Thirsk; YO7 2DP

Pretty village pub, carefully refurbished, with opened-up rooms, beams and candlelight, friendly service, real ales and highly thought-of food; lodge-style bedrooms

This friendly, enjoyable pub makes a good base for both short walks and long-distance hikes (the Cleveland Way is in the locality). The opened-up bars are spacious with a pubby feel and a warm welcome for both drinkers and diners, with dark beams and joists, candlelight and fresh flowers, stools against the panelled counter where they keep Black Sheep Best, Timothy Taylors Landlord and a changing guest from Theakstons on handpump, 19 wines by the glass and 18 malt whiskies, and a mix of chairs and tables on big flagstones; there's also a snug seating area with tartan armchairs in front of a double-sided woodburning stove. The red-walled dining room has a mix of antique and country kitchen chairs around scrubbed tables. Throughout the walls are hung with traditional prints, local pictures and maps; background music and board games. The front of the pub enjoys all-day sunshine and is a fine spot in warm weather. The ultra-modern and well equipped bedrooms, arranged around the landscaped garden behind the inn, come with a drying wardrobe for wet days and a log-effect gas fire; dogs are welcome. The pub belongs to the Provenance Inns group.

Diligently using a network of local suppliers, the contemporary food includes lunchtime sandwiches, confit chicken and duck liver terrine with piccalilli, crisp crab arancini and prawn cocktail, sharing platters, burger with cheese, bacon, beer-battered onion rings and chips, chicken filled with cheese, wrapped in dried ham with skinny fries, halibut with pea and lemon risotto and shrimp butter sauce, and puddings such as chocolate and hazelnut arctic roll with black cherry sauce and spicy pear tarte tatin. *Benchmark main dish: lamb rump with sun-dried tomato crumb and tapenade dressing £16.50. Two-course evening meal £21.00.*

Free house ~ Licensee Michael Ibbotson ~ Real ale ~ (01845) 537369 ~ Open 12-11 ~ Bar food 12-2.30, 5.30-9.30; 12-3, 5.30-8.30 Sun ~ Children welcome ~ Dogs allowed in bar and bedrooms ~ Wi-fi ~ Live music monthly Sun evening ~ Bedrooms: /£120 ~ www.thecarpentersarmsfelixkirk.com *Recommended by Clive and Fran Dutson*

GRANTLEY
Grantley Arms ⭑🍷   SE2369 Map 7
Village signposted off B6265 W of Ripon; HG4 3PJ

Relaxed and interesting dining pub with good food

'An inviting, comfortable and spotless pub – very Yorkshire,' says one of our readers with warm enthusiasm; we absolutely agree. This creeper-clad 17th-c country inn has plenty of local atmosphere, a lovely welcome and excellent food. In the front bar there's a huge fireplace built of massive stone blocks that houses a woodburning stove, brown beams supporting shiny cream ceiling planks and traditional furnishings: green wall banquettes, comfortable dining chairs, tea-lights on polished tables (some cast-iron-framed) and flowery carpet, with some of the landlady's own paintings of ponies and dogs above the green dado. The back dining room has crisp linen tablecloths, decorative plates and more paintings, mainly landscapes. Great Yorkshire Classic and Theakstons Best on handpump, nine wines by the glass, eight malt whiskies, a farm cider and attentive friendly service. Teak tables and chairs on the flagstoned front terrace have a pleasant outlook, and Fountains Abbey and Studley Royal Water Garden (National Trust) are nearby.

With their own-made breads and chutney, the highly satisfying food includes open sandwiches, black pudding with truffled scrambled egg, prawn cocktail with cucumber sorbet, a pie of the week, a vegetarian dish of the day, gammon with an egg and grilled pineapple, ling fillet with parmesan cheese risotto and nut pesto, confit lamb with peppers, olives and red wine sauce, and puddings such as apple and rhubarb pie and coconut panna cotta with mango sorbet; they also offer a two- and three-course set menu (not Sunday). *Benchmark main dish: chicken, ham and leek pie £13.95. Two-course evening meal £19.00.*

Free house ~ Licensees Valerie Sails and Eric Broadwith ~ Real ale ~ (01765) 620227 ~ Open 12-3, 5.30-10.30; 12-3, 5-11 Fri, Sat; 12-10.30 Sun; closed Mon except bank holidays ~ Bar food 12-2, 5.30-9 (9.30 Sat); 12-3.30, 5.30-8 Sun ~ Restaurant ~ Well behaved children welcome ~ Wi-fi ~ www.grantleyarms.com *Recommended by James Naylor, Michael Doswell, Janet and Peter Race, Walter and Susan Rinaldi-Butcher, Gordon and Margaret Ormondroyd*

GRINTON
SE0498   Map 10

Bridge Inn

B6270 W of Richmond; DL11 6HH

Bustling pub with traditional, comfortable bars, log fires, several real ales and malt whiskies, and tasty bar food; neat bedrooms

This warmly welcoming old Swaledale pub in a pretty village is opposite a lovely church known as the Cathedral of the Dales. It has a relaxing, comfortable atmosphere, bow-window seats and a pair of stripped traditional settles among more usual pub seats (all well cushioned), a good log fire, and Jennings Cumberland and Lakeland Stunner, Marstons Revisionist Dark IPA and a guest ale on handpump; also, eight wines by the glass and 25 malt whiskies. On the right, a few steps head down into a room with darts and ring the bull. On the left, past leather armchairs and a sofa next to a second log fire (and a glass chess set), is an extensive two-part dining room with décor in cream and shades of brown, and a modicum of fishing memorabilia. The bedrooms are neat, simple and comfortable, and breakfasts good. There are picnic-sets outside and some fine surrounding walks.

Using game shot by the landlord and other local produce, the good, often interesting food is served all day: baguettes (until 5.30pm), smoked ham hock terrine, rabbit kebabs with smoked red onion mayonnaise, nut and pumpkin seed roast with mushroom and tomato sauce, chicken stuffed with mascarpone and basil, wrapped in bacon with pasta, duck breast with chinese five spice and noodles, tuna steak with salsa verde, and puddings such as chocolate pear pudding with chocolate sauce and lemon cheesecake with plum and blackberry sauce. *Benchmark main dish: steak in ale pie £9.95. Two-course evening meal £17.50.*

Jennings (Marstons) ~ Lease Andrew Atkin ~ Real ale ~ (01748) 884224 ~ Open 12-11 (midnight Sat) ~ Bar food 12-9 ~ Restaurant ~ Children welcome ~ Dogs allowed in bar and bedrooms ~ Wi-fi ~ Bedrooms: £51/£82 ~ www.bridgeinngrinton.co.uk
Recommended by Duncan, Carol and Alistair Hallows, Geoff and Linda Payne

HALIFAX
SE1027   Map 7

Shibden Mill

Off A58 into Kell Lane at Stump Cross Inn, near A6036 junction; keep on, pub signposted from Kell Lane on left; HX3 7UL

300-year-old mill with a cosy rambling bar, four real ales and inventive, top class bar food; comfortable bedrooms

'If I could move in, I would,' says one reader with enthusiasm about this hidden-away country gem. The rambling bar is full of nooks and crannies and the bustling atmosphere is helped along by a good mix of locals and visitors. Some cosy side areas have banquettes heaped with cushions and rugs, well spaced attractive old tables and chairs, and candles in elegant iron holders, which give a feeling of real intimacy; also, old hunting prints, country landscapes and so forth, and a couple of big log fires. A beer named for them (from Moorhouses), Black Sheep Best, Copper Dragon and Little Valley on handpump and 21 wines by the glass from a wide list. There's also an upstairs restaurant; background music and TV. Outside on the pleasant heated terrace are plenty of seats and tables, and the building is prettily floodlit at night. The bedrooms are stylish and well equipped, and there are some lovely walks nearby.

Highly accomplished food from a seasonally aware menu includes lunchtime sandwiches, roasted quail with white polenta and parmesan, grape jelly and black won tons, crispy duck eggs with sweet cauliflower purée and truffle, shallot tarte tatin with goats cheese, pear and pickled walnuts, rare-breed pork and apple sausages with onion chutney and bourguignon sauce, cod, wild salmon, mackerel, crab and langoustine open fish pie with citrus purée and thermidor sauce, and puddings such as caramelised lemon tart and burnt meringue and creamy rice pudding with poached local rhubarb; they also have a fine list of artisan cheeses and a two- and three-course set menu (lunchtime and early evening). *Benchmark main dish: local rabbit with air-dried ham, pearl barley risotto, wild mushrooms and rabbit leg pie £18.00. Two-course evening meal £26.00.*

Free house ~ Licensee Glen Pearson ~ Real ale ~ (01422) 365840 ~ Open 12-11 (10.30 Sun) ~ Bar food 12-2 (2.30 Fri, Sat), 5.30-9 (9.30 Fri, Sat); 12-7.30 Sun ~ Restaurant ~ Children welcome ~ Dogs allowed in bar ~ Wi-fi ~ Bedrooms: £95/£117 ~ www.shibdenmillinn.com *Recommended by Dr Kevan Tucker, Stanley and Annie Matthews*

HARTSHEAD
Gray Ox 🍴 ♀

SE1822 Map 7

3.5 miles from M62 junction 25; A644 towards Dewsbury, left on to A62, next left on to B6119, then first left on to Fall Lane; left into Hartshead Lane; pub on right; WF15 8AL

Handsome dining pub with cosy beamed bars, inventive cooking, real ales, several wines by the glass and fine views

A lone on a moorland road, this smart, bustling dining pub with its roaring log fire is a welcome respite from the M62. The main bar has beams and flagstones, bentwood chairs and leather stools around stripped-pine tables, and leading off from here the comfortable carpeted dining areas have bold paintwork and leather dining chairs around polished tables; the hunting-theme wallpaper is interesting and unusual. There's also a private dining room. Jennings Cumberland and Cocker Hoop on handpump, 15 wines by the glass and a cocktail menu; background music. There are picnic-sets outside, and fine views through the latticed pub windows across the Calder Valley to the distant outskirts of Huddersfield – the lights are pretty at night.

Using premium local ingredients and listing their food heroes on a board, the assured cooking includes lunchtime sandwiches, king scallops with thai salad, duck rillette with caper, gherkin and shallot salad and mustard hollandaise, pork sausages with apple fritter and red wine jus, butternut squash gnocchi with pesto and pine nuts, chicken with leek and potato rösti, goats cheese and red onion spring roll and wholegrain mustard cream, moules marinière with fries and aioli, and puddings such as iced white chocolate and coconut parfait with milk chocolate sauce and key lime pie with vanilla and mint ice-cream. They also offer a two- and three-course weekday menu (12-2, 6-7). *Benchmark main dish: beer-battered fish and chips £11.00. Two-course evening meal £20.50.*

Banks's (Marstons) ~ Lease Bernadette McCarron ~ Real ale ~ (01274) 872845 ~ Open 12-3, 6-midnight; 12-midnight Sat; 12-11 Sun ~ Bar food 12-2, 6-9 (9.30 Sat);

12-7 Sun ~ Restaurant ~ Children welcome ~ www.grayoxinn.co.uk *Recommended by Gordon and Margaret Ormondroyd, Pat and Tony Martin, Keith Moss, Brian and Anna Marsden, John and Eleanor Holdsworth*

HELPERBY   SE4370 Map 7
Oak Tree �⭐ 🍷 🛏
Raskelf Road; YO61 2PH

Attractive pub with real ales in friendly bar, fine food in elegant dining rooms, bold paintwork and seats on terrace; comfortable bedrooms

Our readers love visiting this pretty and carefully renovated pub where you can be sure of a genuine welcome from the friendly staff. The informal bar has church chairs and elegant wooden dining chairs around a mix of wooden tables on old quarry tiles, flagstones and oak floorboards, prints and paintings on bold red walls, and open fires; background music. Stools line the counter where they keep Black Sheep Best, Timothy Taylors Landlord and a guest such as Timothy Taylors Golden Best on handpump and a dozen wines by the glass. The main dining room has a large woodburner in a huge brick fireplace, a big central flower arrangement, high-backed burgundy and graceful wooden chairs around nice old tables on oak flooring, ornate mirrors and some striking artwork on the turquoise or exposed brick walls. French windows lead out to the terrace where there are plenty of seats and tables for summer dining. Upstairs, a private dining room has a two-way woodburner, a sitting room, and doors to a terrace. The bedrooms are comfortable and well equipped. The pub is part of Provenance Inns.

From a wide and interesting menu featuring plenty of local produce, the attractively presented food includes breakfasts (8-11am), morning pastries, lunchtime sandwiches, Whitby crab with tomato jelly, mango and chilli, pressed duck leg with beetroot and orange, sharing platters, pizzas from their wood-fired oven (also available to take away), burger with bacon, smoked cheese, coleslaw and skinny fries, aubergine moussaka, free-range chicken with coq au vin sauce, pancetta and wild mushrooms, lamb rump with ratatouille, and puddings such as apple strudel crumble tart; they also offer a two- and three-course set lunch (not Sunday). *Benchmark main dish: beer-battered fish and chips £12.95. Two-course evening meal £20.00.*

Free house ~ Licensee Michael Ibbotson ~ Real ale ~ (01423) 789189 ~ Open 11-11 ~ Bar food 12-2.30, 5.30-9.30; 12-3, 5.30-8.30 Sun ~ Restaurant ~ Children welcome ~ Dogs allowed in bar and bedrooms ~ Wi-fi ~ Bedrooms: £80/£120 ~ www.theoaktreehelperby.com *Recommended by Walter and Susan Rinaldi-Butcher, Michael Butler, Michael Doswell, John and Eleanor Holdsworth*

ILKLEY   SE1347 Map 7
Wheatley Arms 🍷 🍴 🛏
Wheatley Lane, Ben Rhydding; LS29 8PP

Smart stone inn with plenty of room in boldly decorated dining rooms, cosy bar, professional service and good food and drink; comfortable bedrooms

Near Ilkley Moor and some wonderful walks, this substantial stone inn is just the place for a break, with individually decorated, well equipped and comfortable bedrooms (some with a private roof terrace); breakfasts are good. The interconnected dining rooms have all manner of nice antique and upholstered chairs and stools and prettily cushioned wooden or rush-seated settles around assorted tables, rugs on bare boards, some bold wallpaper, various prints and two log fires; our readers like the smart garden room. One half of the locals' bar has tub armchairs and other comfortable seats, the other has tartan-cushioned wall seats and mate's chairs, with classic wooden stools against the counter where they keep a fine range of six ales on handpump: Ilkley Joshua Jane and Mary Jane, Kirkstall Three Swords, Thwaites Original and Wharfedale Black and Blonde. Also, 23 wines by the glass (including prosecco and champagne), a dozen malt whiskies and a farm cider; background music and TV. There are seats and tables on the terrace.

A wide choice of enjoyable food includes sandwiches (until 5.30pm), thai-style fishcakes with chilli dipping sauce and wasabi mayonnaise, chicken liver parfait with red onion marmalade, sharing boards, brie and red onion vol-au-vent-style tart, beer-battered haddock and chips, chicken stuffed with sage and sausage meat with masala cream sauce, duck breast with tarragon roast carrots, wild mushrooms and madeira jus, game pie, and puddings such as rum and raisin cheesecake and pear frangipane with pear sorbet; they serve proper afternoon teas (not Sunday) and a two- and three-course set menu (not weekends). *Benchmark main dish: daube of beef £12.45. Two-course evening meal £20.50.*

Free house ~ Licensee Steve Benson ~ Real ale ~ (01943) 816496 ~ Open 11-11 (midnight Fri, Sat); 11-10.30 Sun ~ Bar food 12-2, 5.30-9 (9.30 Sat); 12-7.30 ~ Restaurant ~ Children welcome ~ Dogs allowed in bar ~ Wi-fi ~ Live jazz lunchtime first Sun of month ~ Bedrooms: $85/$100 ~ www.wheatleyarms.co.uk
Recommended by Gordon and Margaret Ormondroyd

KIRKBY FLEETHAM   SE2894 Map 10

Black Horse

Village signposted off A1 S of Catterick; Lumley Lane; DL7 0SH

Attractively reworked country inn with good enterprising food, a good choice of drinks and a cheerful atmosphere; bedrooms are stylish and comfortable

Although this carefully run village pub is very popular with locals (who tend to congregate around the leather bar stools by the counter), there are always plenty of warmly welcomed visitors too. The long softly lit beamed and flagstoned bar on the right has cushioned wall seats, some little settles and high-backed dining chairs by the log fire at one end (blazing even for breakfast), and wrought-iron chairs that are a good deal more comfortable than they look at the other; the cosy snug has darts. As well as 11 wines by the glass, there's Black Sheep Best, Ossett Yorkshire Blonde and Timothy Taylors Landlord on handpump. The dining room towards the back is light and open, with big bow windows each side and a casual contemporary look thanks to loose-covered dining chairs or pastel garden settles with scatter cushions around tables painted pale green. There's also a dark and intimate private dining room. Service is friendly and very attentive; maybe background pop music. The neat sheltered back lawn and flagstoned side terrace have teak seats and tables, and there are picnic-sets at the front; quoits. The comfortable and stylish bedrooms have a lot of antique charm and the breakfasts are excellent – though they don't start till 9am (if you can't wait, you can get good continental hampers).

Enjoyable food with some interesting touches and using prime local ingredients includes lunchtime sandwiches, chicken liver parfait with clementine marmalade, salmon and prawn fishcakes with lemon and dill hollandaise, pea and mint risotto, dry-cured bacon chop with duck egg, chicken wrapped in parma ham with cheese and wild mushroom sauce, shepherd's pie, duo of lamb (confit shoulder and rack) with baby root vegetables and red wine jus, and puddings such as sticky toffee pudding with toffee sauce and irish cream crème brûlée. *Benchmark main dish: steak pie £13.50. Two-course evening meal £20.00.*

Free house ~ Licensee Philip Barker ~ Real ale ~ (01609) 749011 ~ Open 12-11.30 (midnight Sat, 10.30 Sun) ~ Bar food 12-2, 6-9 (9.30 Fri, Sat); 12-8 Sun ~ Restaurant ~ Children welcome ~ Dogs allowed in bar and bedrooms ~ Wi-fi ~ Bedrooms: /£120 ~ www.blackhorsekirkbyfleetham.com *Recommended by Toby Jones, Martin Jones*

 LEDSHAM   SE4529   Map 7
Chequers
1.5 miles from A1(M) junction 42: follow Leeds signs, then Ledsham signposted; Claypit Lane; LS25 5LP

Friendly village pub with hands-on landlord, log fires in several beamed rooms, real ales and interesting, very popular food; pretty back terrace

Creeper-covered and spotlessly kept, this well run pub is in a charming village and handy for the A1 – and you can be sure of a friendly welcome from the landlord and his helpful staff. The several small, individually decorated rooms have plenty of character, with low beams, lots of cosy alcoves, toby jugs and all sorts of knick-knacks on the walls and ceilings (cricketing enthusiasts will be interested to see a large photo in one of the rooms of four yorkshire heroes) and log fires. From the old-fashioned little central panelled-in servery, they offer Brass Castle Cliffhanger, Leeds Best, Theakstons Best, Timothy Taylors Landlord and a guest on handpump and eight wines by the glass. The lovely sheltered two-level terrace at the back has plenty of tables among roses, and the hanging baskets and flowers are very pretty. RSPB Fairburn Ings reserve is not far and the ancient village church is worth a visit.

As well as sandwiches and baguettes, the inventive food includes duck liver pâté with tomato chutney, scallops with garlic and chilli, corned beef hash with caramelised onions, wild mushroom and feta tart, steak and mushroom pie, halibut with herb and garlic crust and mussel and dill cream sauce, noisettes of lamb with redcurrant jus, and puddings such as fresh fruit crème brûlée trifle and chocolate chip fudge brownie. *Benchmark main dish: steak pie £11.95. Two-course evening meal £22.00.*

Free house ~ Licensee Chris Wraith ~ Real ale ~ (01977) 683135 ~ Open 11-11; 12-6 Sun ~ Bar food 12-9; 12-5 Sun ~ Restaurant ~ Children until 8pm ~ Dogs allowed in bar ~ Wi-fi ~ www.thechequersinn.f9.co.uk *Recommended by Dr D J and Mrs S C Walker, Tony Middis, Michael Butler, Pat and Stewart Gordon, B and M Kendall*

LEVISHAM   SE8390   Map 10
Horseshoe
Off A169 N of Pickering; YO18 7NL

Friendly village pub run by two brothers (one cooks the good popular food), neat rooms, real ales and seats on the village green; bedrooms

The wonderful scenery of the North York Moors National Park surrounds this traditional family-run inn and our readers enjoy using the comfortable bedrooms here as a base; breakfasts are hearty. The bustling bars have beams, blue banquettes, wheelback and captain's chairs around a variety of tables on polished wooden floors, vibrant landscapes by a local artist on the walls and a log fire in the stone fireplace; an adjoining snug has a woodburning stove, comfortable leather sofas and old photographs of the pub and the lovely village. Black Sheep Best and a couple of guests such as Brass Castle Cliffhanger and Wold Top Headland Red on handpump, half a dozen wines by the glass and 15 malt whiskies; background music. There are seats on the attractive green, with more in the back garden. The historic church is worth a visit. This is sister pub to the Fox & Rabbit in Lockton.

Using local, seasonal produce (the pigs are raised next door) and cooked by one of the landlords, the generously served and very good food might include lunchtime sandwiches, creamy garlic mushrooms, grilled black pudding wrapped in bacon with sautéed potatoes, sausages with onion gravy, ratatouille with a cheese and herb crust, beef stroganoff, lamb shank with minted gravy, Whitby haddock and chips, and puddings such as lime cheesecake and sticky toffee pudding. *Benchmark main dish: venison pie £10.95. Two-course evening meal £17.50.*

Free house ~ Licensees Toby and Charles Wood ~ Real ale ~ (01751) 460240 ~ Open 10am-11.30pm ~ Bar food 12-2, 6-8.30 ~ Children welcome ~ Dogs allowed in bar ~ Wi-fi ~ Bedrooms: £45/£60 ~ www.horseshoelevisham.co.uk *Recommended by Simon and Mandy King, Comus and Sarah Elliott, Peter and Anne Hollindale, David Heath, Sara Fulton, Roger Baker*

LEYBURN
Sandpiper 🌟 ⏣ ⛉
SE1190   Map 10

Just off Market Place; DL8 5AT

Appealing food and cosy bar for drinkers in 17th-c cottage, real ales and impressive choice of whisky; bedrooms

'We could not have asked for anything more,' says one reader after staying in the comfortable, well equipped bedrooms in this attractive 17th-c inn; the breakfasts are excellent too. There's always a good mix of both locals and visitors and a friendly welcome for all from the landlord and his staff. The cosy bar has a couple of black beams in the low ceiling, a log fire and wooden or cushioned built-in wall seats around a few tables; the back snug, up three steps, features lovely Dales photographs – get here early if you want a seat. There are photographs and a woodburning stove in a stone fireplace by the linenfold panelled bar counter; to the left is the attractive restaurant, with dark wooden tables and chairs on bare boards and fresh flowers. Black Sheep Best and a guest from breweries such as Rudgate and York on handpump, up to 75 malt whiskies and a decent wine list with ten by the glass; background music and dominoes. In good weather, you can enjoy a drink on the front terrace among the pretty hanging baskets and flowering climbers.

Using a network of local suppliers, the chef-patron cooks the tempting food, including lunchtime sandwiches, caramelised pork belly with queenie scallops, old spot terrine with warm black pudding, omelette arnold bennett, mixed mushroom risotto, rib burger and skinny fries, sausages and mash with onion gravy, coq au vin, brill topped with smoked salmon, tiger prawns and leeks, gressingham duck with dauphinoise potatoes and marmalade sauce, and puddings such as peanut and hazelnut blondie and knickerbocker glory. *Benchmark main dish: venison with home-made chorizo and mushrooms £18.75. Two-course evening meal £25.00.*

Free house ~ Licensee Jonathan Harrison ~ Real ale ~ (01969) 622206 ~ Open 10.30-3, 6.30 (6 Sat)-11; closed Mon and some winter Tues ~ Bar food 12-2.30, 6.30-9 ~ Restaurant ~ Children welcome ~ Dogs allowed in bar and bedrooms ~ Wi-fi ~ Bedrooms: £80/£90 ~ www.sandpiperinn.co.uk *Recommended by Robert Wivell, Penny and Peter Keevil, J R Wildon, Simon Hand, WAH, Lynda and Trevor Smith, Pat and Graham Williamson, Geoff and Linda Payne*

LINTON IN CRAVEN
SD9962 Map 7

Fountaine

Off B6265 Skipton–Grassington; BD23 5HJ

Neatly kept pub in charming village, attractive furnishings, open fires, five real ales and popular food; bedrooms

Always bustling and friendly, this civilised inn has plenty of customers keen to enjoy the wide choice of reliably good food. There are beams and white-painted joists in the low ceilings, log fires (one in a beautifully carved, heavy wooden fireplace), attractive built-in cushioned wall benches and stools around a mix of copper-topped tables, little wall lamps and quite a few prints on the pale walls. As well as a beer named for the pub from Bridestones, they keep Tetleys Bitter, Thwaites Original and guests from Dark Horse and Ilkley on handpump, 17 wines by the glass and a dozen malt whiskies served by efficient staff; background music, darts and board games. The teak benches and tables under green parasols on the terrace look across the road to the duck pond, and there are attractive hanging baskets. The well equipped bedrooms are in a converted barn behind the pub. This is a pretty hamlet, with fine walks in the beautiful Dales countryside.

Popular and highly rated, the food includes sandwiches, black pudding and cheese stack with apple fritter and mustard drizzle, potted trout and prawns, salad boards, a pie of the day, feta and spinach filo tart, corn-fed chicken stuffed with cream cheese and sunblush tomatoes, and wrapped in bacon with a tomato and chorizo sauce, smoked haddock on mash and spinach with a curry sauce, half roast duck with apple and calvados gravy, and puddings such as chocolate fudge brownie and white chocolate cheesecake. *Benchmark main dish: brisket of beef with yorkshire pudding and rich gravy £13.50. Two-course evening meal £16.00.*

Individual Inns ~ Manager Christopher Gregson ~ Real ale ~ (01756) 752210 ~ Open 11-11; 12-10.30 Sun ~ Bar food 12-9 ~ Restaurant ~ Children welcome ~ Dogs allowed in bar ~ Wi-fi ~ Bedrooms: £75/£99 ~ www.individualinns.co.uk *Recommended by John and Eleanor Holdsworth, Lynda and Trevor Smith, Peter Smith and Judith Brown, John and Sylvia Harrop*

LOCKTON
SE8488 Map 10

Fox & Rabbit

A169 N of Pickering; YO18 7NQ

Neatly kept pub with fine views, a friendly atmosphere in bars and restaurant, real ales and popular food

Two brothers – one is also the chef – have run this attractive pub for ten years now, and they remain as enthusiastic as ever. The interconnected rooms have beams and panelling, some exposed stonework, wall settles and banquettes, dark pubby chairs and tables on the tartan carpet, a log fire and a warm inviting atmosphere; fresh flowers, brasses, china plates, prints and old local photographs too. The locals' bar is busy and cheerful and the views from the comfortable restaurant are panoramic – it's worth arriving early to bag a window seat. Black Sheep Best, Cropton Yorkshire Moors and Wold Top Spring Fling on handpump, a dozen wines by the glass, 12 malt whiskies and home-made seasonal elderflower cordial; background music, games machine, pool, juke box and board games. Outside are seats under parasols and some picnic sets; as the inn is in the North York Moors National Park, there are plenty of surrounding walks. They have a caravan site. This is sister pub to the Horseshoe in Levisham.

🍴 Using local, seasonal produce, the hearty food includes sandwiches, chicken liver pâté with apple and tomato chutney, prawn cocktail, sausages with red onion gravy, butternut squash and pea risotto, deep-fried Whitby haddock and chips, slow-roasted pork belly with caramelised shallots, cider jus and apple sauce, sirloin steak with onion rings and peppercorn sauce, and puddings. *Benchmark main dish: steak in ale pie £11.50. Two-course evening meal £18.50.*

Free house ~ Licensees Toby and Charles Wood ~ Real ale ~ (01751) 460213 ~ Open 10am-11.30pm ~ Bar food 12-4 (2 in winter), 5-8.30; 12-8.30 Sun ~ Restaurant ~ Children welcome ~ Dogs allowed in bar ~ Wi-fi ~ www.foxandrabbit.co.uk
Recommended by Comus and Sarah Elliott

 **LOW CATTON**   SE7053   Map 7
Gold Cup
Village signposted with High Catton off A166 in Stamford Bridge or A1079 at Kexby Bridge; YO41 1EA

Friendly, pleasant pub with attractive bars, real ales, decent dependable food, seats in garden and ponies in paddock

The amiable hands-on licensees have been here for 25 years and, thankfully, it remains a proper village pub. The neatly kept beamed bars have a bustling atmosphere with chatty locals, plenty of smart tables and chairs on the stripped wooden floors, quite a few pictures, an open fire at one end opposite a woodburning stove and coach lights on the rustic-looking walls. The spacious restaurant, with solid wooden pews and tables (said to be made from a single oak tree), has pleasant views of the surrounding fields. Theakstons Black Bull on handpump; background music and pool. There's a grassed area in the garden for children and the back paddock houses two ponies, Cinderella and Polly. The pub has fishing rights on the adjacent River Derwent.

🍴 As well as a two- and three-course evening menu (not weekends), the tasty food includes lunchtime sandwiches (not Sunday), beer-battered mushrooms with garlic mayonnaise, breaded brie wedges with cranberry and orange dip, three-egg omelettes, steak burger topped with stilton and chips, loin of pork with yorkshire pudding, salmon fillet with asparagus and lemon hollandaise, steak in ale pie, and puddings. *Benchmark main dish: spicy cajun chicken £9.95. Two-course evening meal £18.00.*

Free house ~ Licensees Pat and Ray Hales ~ Real ale ~ (01759) 371354 ~ Open 12-2.30, 6-11; 12-11 Sat; 12-10.30 Sun; closed Mon lunchtime ~ Bar food 12-2, 6-9; 12-9 weekends ~ Restaurant ~ Children welcome ~ Dogs allowed in bar ~ www.goldcuplowcatton.com
Recommended by Dave Newton

 **MARTON CUM GRAFTON**   SE4263   Map 7
Punch Bowl 🌟 �
Signed off A1 3 miles N of A59; YO51 9QY

Refurbished old inn in lovely village, with beams and standing timbers, character bar and dining rooms, real ales, interesting food using seasonal local produce, and seats outside

Dating in part from the 16th c, this handsome inn has kept many original features. The main bar is beamed and timbered with a built-in window seat at one end, lots of red leather-topped stools, cushioned settles and church chairs around pubby tables on flagstones or bare floorboards, Black Sheep Best, Great Yorkshire Classic and Timothy Taylors Golden Best and

Landlord on handpump, 23 wines by the glass and a dozen malt whiskies, served by friendly staff. Open doorways lead to five separate dining areas, each with an open fire, heavy beams, red walls covered with photographs of vintage car races and racing drivers, sporting-themed cartoons and old photographs of the pub and village, and an attractive mix of cushioned wall seats and wooden or high-backed red dining chairs around antique tables on oak floors. Up a swirling staircase is a coffee loft and a private dining room. There are seats and tables on the back courtyard where they hold summer barbecues. The pub belongs to Provenance Inns.

Using local and regional produce, the imaginative food includes sandwiches, pigeon and mushroom fricassée, smoked chicken, white truffle and leek terrine with apple and raisin chutney, various platters, creamy garlic gnocchi with parmesan, chargrilled burger with cheese, bacon and beer-battered onion rings, harissa chicken kebabs with minted yoghurt, aioli dips and flatbread, bacon steak with eggs and fries, steak in ale pie, sea trout with spring onion and asparagus risotto, and puddings such as iced nougatine parfait with passion-fruit and banana sorbet and gooseberry crumble. *Benchmark main dish: local pork ribs in sticky barbecue sauce with slaw salad and fries £14.95. Two-course evening meal £20.00.*

Free house ~ Licensee Michael Ibbotson ~ Real ale ~ (01423) 322519 ~ Open 12-3, 5-11; 12-11 Sat, Sun ~ Bar food 12-2.30 (3 Sun), 5.30-9.30 (8.30 Sun) ~ Children welcome ~ Dogs allowed in bar ~ Wi-fi ~ Live music Thurs evening ~ www.thepunchbowlmartoncumgrafton.com *Recommended by Walter and Susan Rinaldi-Butcher, Peter and Anne Hollindale, Michael Doswell*

MASHAM
SE2281 Map 10
Black Sheep Brewery
Brewery signed off Leyburn Road A6108; HG4 4EN

Lively place with friendly staff, quite a mix of customers, unusual décor in big warehouse room, well kept beers and popular food

Even though this sizeable brewery is more of a bistro than a pub, the beers are, not surprisingly, very well kept. A huge upper warehouse room has a bar serving Black Sheep Best, Ale, Golden Sheep Ale, Riggwelter and a couple of changing guests on handpump, several wines by the glass and a fair choice of soft drinks. Most of the good-sized tables have cheery gingham tablecloths and brightly cushioned green café chairs, and there are some modern pubbier tables near the bar. It's partly divided by free-standing partitions and there's a good deal of bare woodwork, with some cream-painted rough stonework and green-painted steel girders and pillars; background music and friendly service. There are interesting brewery tours and a shop selling beers and mainly beer-related items from pub games and T-shirts to pottery and fudge. A glass wall lets you see into the brewing exhibition centre. Picnic-sets out on the grass.

As well as scones, cakes and traybakes, the popular food includes lunchtime sandwiches, chicken liver parfait with ale chutney, queen scallops and prawns in smoked bacon and cheese sauce, mediterranean vegetable tart, pork and ale sausages on sage mash with onion gravy, beef in ale pie, burger with cheese, bacon and onion marmalade, beer-battered haddock and chips, and puddings such as black cherry frangipane and apple crumble. *Benchmark main dish: beef in ale casserole £12.95. Two-course evening meal £17.95.*

Free house ~ Licensee Paul Casterton ~ Real ale ~ (01765) 680100 ~ Open 10.30-4.30 Mon-Weds, Sun; 10.30am-11pm Thurs-Sat ~ Bar food 12-2.30 Mon-Weds, Sun; 12-2.30, 6.30-8.45 Thurs-Sat ~ Children welcome ~ Wi-fi ~ www.blacksheepbrewery.co.uk
Recommended by Gavin and Helle May, Isobel Mackinlay, Janet and Peter Race

PICKHILL

SE3483 Map 10

Nags Head ⭐ ♀ 🛏

A1 junction 50 (northbound) or junction 51 (southbound), village signed off A6055, Street Lane; YO7 4JG

Neatly kept dining pub with consistently good food, a fine choice of carefully chosen drinks, a tap room, smarter lounge and friendly service; comfortable bedrooms

Whether you're dropping in for a pint and a chat, a leisurely meal or an overnight stay, you'll be well looked after by the hard-working and hands-on licensee Mr Boynton, who's been here for over 40 years. Many of the tables are laid for eating, so if it's just a drink you're after, head to the bustling tap room on the left, where the beams are decorated with jugs, coach horns, ale-yards and so forth, and masses of neckties hang as a frieze from a rail around the red ceiling. The smarter lounge bar has deep green plush banquettes on a matching carpet, pictures (for sale) on the neat cream walls and an open fire. There's also a library-themed restaurant. Black Sheep Best, Rudgate Mild, Theakstons Best and a guest beer on handpump, 30 malt whiskies, vintage Armagnacs and a carefully chosen wine list with ten by the glass. One table is inset with a chessboard; darts, TV and background music. There's a front verandah, a boules and quoits pitch and a nine-hole putting green. The bedrooms are comfortable and well equipped, and the buffet-style breakfasts enjoyable.

Rewarding food using local, seasonal produce includes lunchtime sandwiches, omelettes, cottage pie and bacon chop with a free-range fried egg, as well as more elaborate choices such as ham terrine with apple jelly, thai-style tiger prawns with broth and won tons, red lentil and coconut dhal with pickles, chutney and naan bread, slow-braised lamb shoulder with pearl barley, salted beetroot and sweetbreads, free-range chicken with braised baby gem, wild mushrooms and red onions, cod loin with lime and shrimp butter and herb mash, and puddings such as dark chocolate and cherry mousse with cherry sorbet and iced earl grey tea parfait with banana won tons and boozy prunes. *Benchmark main dish: steak in ale pie £12.95. Two-course evening meal £18.00.*

Free house ~ Licensee Edward Boynton ~ Real ale ~ (01845) 567391 ~ Open 11-11; 12-10.30 Sun ~ Bar food 12-2, 5.30-9.30; 12-2.30, 5.30-8 Sun ~ Restaurant ~ Well-behaved children welcome until 7.30pm (after 7.30pm in dining room only) ~ Dogs allowed in bar ~ Wi-fi ~ Bedrooms: £65/£87 ~ www.nagsheadpickhill.co.uk *Recommended by Ian Malone, Les and Sandra Brown, Michael Doswell, Pat and Tony Martin, David and Ruth Hollands*

RIPPONDEN

SE0419 Map 7

Old Bridge ♀ 🍺

From A58, best approach is Elland Road (opposite the Golden Lion), park opposite the church in pub's car park and walk back over ancient hump-back bridge; HX6 4DF

Pleasant old pub by medieval bridge with relaxed communicating rooms and well liked food

A comment from one of our readers sums up this well run, 14th-c inn very aptly: 'This is a place to visit and then leave with a smile on your face. And then visit again.' The welcome from the third generation of the family to run the place is genuinely warm, and it somehow manages to be both a locals' pub and a dining pub, which keeps the atmosphere bustling and easy-going. The three communicating rooms, each on a slightly different level, have oak settles built into window recesses in the thick stone walls, antique oak tables, rush-seated chairs and comfortably cushioned free-standing settles, a few well chosen pictures and prints on the panelled or painted walls and a big woodburning stove. Timothy Taylors Best, Dark Mild, Golden Best and Landlord and a couple of guests such as Oates Wild Oates and Phoenix Navvy on handpump, quite a few foreign bottled beers, a dozen wines by the glass, 30 malt whiskies and farm cider; quick, efficient service. The pub is next to a beautiful medieval packhorse bridge over the little River Ryburn and seats in the pub garden overlook the water. If you have trouble finding the pub (there's no traditional pub sign outside), just head for the church.

 The ever-popular weekday lunchtime cold meat and salad buffet has been running since 1963 (they also offer soup and sandwiches at lunch); evening and weekend choices include sandwiches, stilton cheesecake with pickled pear and walnut salad, potted crab with toast soldiers, spinach, red pepper, feta and pine nut tart, toulouse sausages on mustard mash with cabbage and bacon and red wine gravy, corn-fed chicken on chorizo, red onion and sweet pepper cassoulet, and puddings. *Benchmark main dish: steak in ale pie £10.00. Two-course evening meal £15.50.*

Free house ~ Licensees Tim and Lindsay Eaton Walker ~ Real ale ~ (01422) 822595 ~ Open 12-3, 5.30-11; 12-11 Fri, Sat; 12-10.30 Sun ~ Bar food 12-2, 6.30-9.30; 12-4 Sun ~ Children allowed until 8pm but must be seated away from bar ~ www.theoldbridgeinn.co.uk *Recommended by Mike Samuels, Dr Kevan Tucker, Richard Kennell*

 ROBIN HOOD'S BAY   NZ9505 Map 10
Laurel
Bay Bank; village signed off A171 S of Whitby; YO22 4SE

Delightful little pub in unspoilt fishing village, neat friendly bar and real ales; no food

Thankfully, this little local remains quite unchanged and the charming landlord is welcoming to all his customers. It's at the bottom of a row of fishermen's cottages in one of the prettiest and most unspoilt fishing villages on the north-east coast. The neatly kept beamed main bar has an open fire and is decorated with old local photographs, Victorian prints and brasses and lager bottles from all over the world. There's Adnams Southwold and Theakstons Best and Old Peculier on handpump; darts, board games and background music. In summer, the hanging baskets and window boxes are lovely. They rent out a self-contained apartment for two people. There's no food, but you can bring in sandwiches from the tea shop next door and eat them in the pub.

Free house ~ Licensee Brian Catling ~ Real ale ~ No credit cards ~ (01947) 880400 ~ Open 12-11 (10.30 Sun); 3-11 Mon-Thurs in winter ~ Children in snug bar only ~ Dogs welcome *Recommended by Harvey Brown, Toby Jones, David Carr*

ROECLIFFE   SE3765 Map 7
Crown
Off A168 just W of Boroughbridge; handy for A1(M) junction 48; YO51 9LY

Smartly updated and attractively placed pub with a civilised bar, excellent enterprising food and a fine choice of drinks; charming bedrooms

Reports from our readers remain as warmly enthusiastic as ever about this lovely inn – 'it deserves every award you could give it,' says one. There's always a cheerful crowd of locals and visitors, and everyone is made welcome by the friendly, hard-working Mainey family. The bar has a contemporary colour scheme of dark reds and near whites with pleasant prints carefully grouped and lit; one area has chunky pine tables on flagstones, while another, with a log fire, has dark tables on plaid carpet. Theakstons Best, Timothy Taylors Landlord and a couple of guests such as Ilkley Gold and Yorkshire Heart Silverheart IPA on handpump, 40 wines by the glass and 15 malt whiskies. For meals, you can choose between a small candlelit olive-green bistro with nice tables, a longcase clock and a couple of paintings, and a more formal restaurant. This is a very nice place to stay, with cosy, country-style bedrooms. The village green is opposite.

Using only small local suppliers for produce and making their own bread, jams, chutneys and cakes, the delicious food includes lunchtime sandwiches, king scallops with home-made black pudding, pea and rocket purée and crispy shallots, twice-baked cheddar soufflé, steak in ale pie, gressingham duck with honey and balsamic reduction on pak choi, slow-braised ox cheek with crispy pancetta and mash, bass fillet with roasted scallops, crispy chorizo and pepper and basil risotto, venison loin on rösti potato with blackberry jus, and puddings such as belgian chocolate fondant with home-made double chocolate ice-cream and lemon honeycomb iced parfait, lemon shortbread and lemon possett shot. *Benchmark main dish: smoked haddock, salmon, king prawn and mussel pie £13.95. Two-course evening meal £23.00.*

Free house ~ Licensee Karl Mainey ~ Real ale ~ (01423) 322300 ~ Open 12-11 ~ Bar food 12-2.30, 6-9.15; 12-7 Sun ~ Restaurant ~ Children welcome ~ Dogs allowed in bar and bedrooms ~ Wi-fi ~ Bedrooms: £80/£100 ~ www.crowninnroecliffe.com
Recommended by Les and Sandra Brown, David Jackman, Janet and Peter Race, C A Hall, Nick and Gillian Harrison, Alistair Forsyth, Dave Newton

SANCTON
SE9039   Map 7
Star 🍴 ♀ 🍺
King Street (A1034 S of Market Weighton); YO43 4QP

Cheerful bar with four real ales, more formal dining rooms with accomplished food, and a friendly, easy-going atmosphere

In a farming village surrounded by lovely countryside, this is a carefully extended 800-year-old pub run by enthusiastic and hard-working licensees. There's a bar with a woodburning stove, traditional red plush stools around a mix of tables, a cheerful atmosphere helped along by locals and walkers, beers from breweries such as Black Sheep, Copper Dragon, Great Newsome and Wold Top served on handpump from the brick counter, 18 wines by the glass including prosecco and champagne, and friendly, helpful service. The more formal (though still relaxed) dining rooms have comfortable high-backed dark leather dining chairs around wooden tables on carpeting, and prints on red- or cream-painted walls. There are picnic-sets outside at the back.

Using local producers, village allotments and growing their own, the exceptional food includes lunchtime sandwiches, scallops with crispy quail egg, tarragon and hazelnut, yorkshire pudding with braised oxtail, red wine meat juices and sage crisp, lunchtime sausage and mash with roast shallot gravy, potato and spring onion scone with butternut squash, chanterelles and baby leeks and port reduction, and beer-battered haddock and chips, with evening choices such as line-caught wild bass with pak choi and blood orange salad with sauternes velouté, rosemary and juniper marinated venison loin with beetroot fondant, glazed carrots and red onion tarte tatin, and duck breast with orange and port wine jus with fondant potato, and puddings such as glazed lemon tart with raspberry meringue and raspberry sorbet and chocolate fondant with white chocolate fudge, malt ice-cream and salted hazelnuts. *Benchmark main dish: pork belly with black pudding, potato rösti, rhubarb, apple gel and cider £18.95. Two-course evening meal £23.00.*

Free house ~ Licensees Ben and Lindsey Cox ~ Real ale ~ (01430) 827269 ~
Open 12-3, 6-11; 12-11 Sun; closed Mon ~ Bar food 12-2, 6-9.30; 12-3, 6-8 Sun ~
Restaurant ~ Children welcome ~ www.thestaratsancton.co.uk
Recommended by John and Eleanor Holdsworth

SANDHUTTON   SE3882 Map 10

Kings Arms 🍺

A167, 1 mile N of A61 Thirsk–Ripon; YO7 4RW

**Cheerful pub with friendly service, interesting food and beer,
and comfortable furnishings; bedrooms**

Run by a father and son, this bustling village pub is very popular locally – but there's a hearty reception for visitors too. The bar has a traditional pubby atmosphere, an unusual circular woodburner in one corner, a high central table with four equally high stools, high-backed brown leather-seated dining chairs around light pine tables, a couple of cushioned wicker armchairs, some attractive modern bar stools and photographs of the pub in years gone by. Black Sheep Best, Rudgate Viking, Village Brewer White Boar Bitter and Walls Gun Dog Bitter on handpump, nine wines by the glass and efficient, friendly service. The two connecting dining rooms have similar furnishings to the bar (though there's also a nice big table with smart high-backed dining chairs), arty flower photographs on cream walls and a shelf above a small woodburning stove with more knick-knacks and some candles; background music, darts, board games and TV. They have a shop selling their own ready meals as well as sausages, pies and sandwiches.

🍴 Using local, seasonal produce, the well thought-of food includes lunchtime sandwiches, chicken liver pâté with plum and ginger chutney, black pudding topped with bacon and a poached egg, vegetarian haggis pudding with roast organic vegetables, burger with toppings and chips, pie of the day, cajun chicken with black bean pasta, pheasant breast with black pudding, apple and calvados sauce, beer-battered fish and chips, duck with hoi sin sauce, and puddings. *Benchmark main dish: salmon, cod and prawn fishcake with sweet chilli sauce £9.95. Two-course evening meal £17.00.*

Free house ~ Licensees Raymond and Alexander Boynton ~ Real ale ~
(01845) 587887 ~ Open 11-11 (midnight Sat, 10 Sun) ~ Bar food 12-2.30, 5.30-9; 12-7 (5 in winter) Sun ~ Restaurant ~ Children welcome ~ Wi-fi ~ Bedrooms: £45/£70 ~
www.thekingsarmssandhutton.co.uk *Recommended by Ian Wilson, Janet and Peter Race, Brian and Jean Hepworth*

SHEFFIELD   SK4086 Map 7

Kelham Island Tavern 🍺 £

Kelham Island; S3 8RY

**Busy little local with 13 changing real ales, basic but decent lunchtime
pub food, a friendly welcome and pretty back garden**

The fantastic choice of real ales here attracts beer lovers in droves – there's usually up to 13 interesting brews on handpump (always a mild and a stout or porter), served by well organised, knowledgeable and friendly staff. Their regulars are Abbeydale Deception, Acorn Barnsley Bitter, Bradfield Farmers Blonde and Pictish Brewers Gold ,with guests from breweries such as North Riding, Rudgate, Thwaites, Wentworth,

Wold Top and Yorkshire Dales; also, 40 malt whiskies and farm cider.
It's a busy backstreet local with a wide array of cheerful customers and
pubby furnishings. The flower-filled and unusual back courtyard garden
has plenty of seats and tables and a woodburning stove for chilly evenings.
The front window boxes regularly win awards.

🍴 The tasty and very good value pubby food – lunchtime only – includes sandwiches
and toasties, burgers with chips, liver and onions, chilli prawns, mushroom and
red pepper stroganoff, and lamb curry. *Benchmark main dish: steak pie £5.50.*

Free house ~ Licensee Trevor Wraith ~ Real ale ~ (0114) 272 2482 ~ Open 12-midnight
~ Bar food 12-3; not Sun ~ Children allowed in back room ~ Dogs welcome ~ Live folk
Sun evenings ~ www.kelhamislandtavern.co.uk *Recommended by Toby Jones, Edward May*

SOUTH DALTON

SE9645 Map 8

Pipe & Glass 🍺 🍷 🛏

West End; brown sign to pub off B1248 NW of Beverley; HU17 7PN

Yorkshire Dining Pub of the Year

**Attractive dining pub with a proper bar area, real ales, interesting
modern cooking, good service, garden and front terrace; stylish
bedrooms**

It's the wonderful food that draws most customers to this attractive
white-washed dining pub, but there's still a proper bustling bar area and
they do keep Black Sheep Best, Cropton Two Chefs (named for them) and
guests from Great Newsome and Wold Top on handpump, 15 wines by the
glass, 40 malt whiskies and a farm cider; service is prompt and friendly.
The beamed and bow-windowed bar has copper pans hanging above the
log fire in the sizeable fireplace, some old prints, and cushioned window
seats and high-backed wooden dining chairs around a mix of tables
(each set with a church candle). Beyond that, all is airy and comfortably
contemporary, angling around past some chunky button-back leather
chesterfields into a light restaurant area overlooking Dalton Park, with
high-backed stylish dining chairs around well spaced country tables on
bare boards. The decorations – a row of serious cookery books and framed
big-name restaurant menus – show how high the licensee aims; background
music. There are tables on the garden's peaceful lawn and picnic-sets on
the front terrace; the yew tree is said to be some 500 years old. The two
suites, stylish and well equipped, have views over Dalton Park. The village
is charming and its elegant Victorian church spire, 62 metres tall, is visible
for miles around.

 Beautifully presented, the confident, contemporary food is cooked by the
landlord using top quality local produce: lunchtime sandwiches, hot and
cold cured salmon tartare, hot smoked salmon scotch egg, warm gravadlax with
compressed cucumber, fennel seed grissini and coriander, old spot potted pork with
sticky apple and crackling salad and spelt toast, celeriac with wild mushrooms, baby
leeks, crispy poached duck egg and hazelnut milk, guinea fowl with crispy leg parcel,
devils on horseback and sherry cream, fillet of beef with ox tongue and parsley fritter,
horseradish hollandaise and chips, and puddings such as liquorice panna cotta
with mulled fruits and little doughnuts and a trio of apples (crumble, sticky sponge,
sorbet). *Benchmark main dish: local sausages with bubble and squeak and ale
gravy £10.95. Two-course evening meal £30.00.*

Free house ~ Licensees Kate and James Mackenzie ~ Real ale ~ (01430) 810246 ~
Open 12-11 (10.30 Sun); closed Mon except bank holidays ~ Bar food 12-9.30; 12-4 Sun ~
Restaurant ~ Children welcome ~ Wi-fi ~ Bedrooms: /£170 ~ www.pipeandglass.co.uk
Recommended by Dr Kevan Tucker

THORNTON WATLASS
SE2385 Map 10

Buck

Village signposted off B6268 Bedale–Masham; HG4 4AH

Honest village pub with five real ales, traditional bars, well liked food and popular Sunday jazz; bedrooms

Very much the heart of the local community, this popular village pub has been run by the hard-working and hands-on licensees for 28 years. The pleasantly traditional bar on the right has upholstered old-fashioned wall settles on carpet, a fine mahogany bar counter, a high shelf packed with ancient bottles, several mounted fox masks and brushes and a brick fireplace. The Long Room (overlooking the cricket green) has large prints of old Thornton Watlass cricket teams, signed bats, cricket balls and so forth. Hop Studio Dark Rose, Theakstons Best, Walls County Best and Gun Dog Bitter and a guest from Theakstons on handpump, several wines by the glass, their acclaimed bloody mary and over 40 interesting malt whiskies; darts. The sheltered garden has a well equipped play area and summer barbecues, and they have their own cricket team; quoits. The bedrooms are clean and comfortable and the breakfasts excellent.

Good, well liked food includes lunchtime sandwiches, chicken liver parfait, king scallops with garlic and gruyère, their famous rarebit with chutney, wild mushroom stroganoff, burger with cheese, red onion marmalade and chips, chicken stuffed with blue cheese and wrapped in smoked bacon with red wine jus, crisp salmon fillet with herb oil, duck breast with stir-fried vegetables, and puddings. *Benchmark main dish: steak in ale pie £11.00. Two-course evening meal £17.00.*

Free house ~ Licensees Michael and Margaret Fox ~ Real ale ~ (01677) 422461 ~ Open 11-11 ~ Bar food 12-2, 6-9; 12-3, 6-8.30 Sun ~ Restaurant ~ Children welcome ~ Dogs allowed in bedrooms ~ Wi-fi ~ Live trad jazz Sun lunchtimes ~ Bedrooms: £70/£90 ~ www.buckwatlass.co.uk *Recommended by Brian and Audrey Goodson*

WASS
SE5579 Map 7

Wombwell Arms

Back road W of Ampleforth; or follow brown sign for Byland Abbey off A170 Thirsk–Helmsley; YO61 4BE

Consistently enjoyable village pub with a friendly atmosphere, good mix of locals and visitors, interesting bar food and real ales; bedrooms

In a pretty village below the Hambleton Hills and with fine walking nearby, this is a bustling 17th-c inn with plenty of customers. The two bars are carefully looked after, with simple character, pine farmhouse chairs and tables, some exposed stone walls and log fires; the walls of the Poacher's Bar (dogs are welcome here) are hung with brewery memorabilia. From the panelled bar counter, friendly staff serve Black Sheep Best, Great Newsome Pricky Back Otchan and Pennine Best Bitter on handpump, ten wines by the glass (quite a few from Mrs Walker's native South Africa) and ten malt whiskies; darts and board games. The two restaurants are incorporated into a former granary and there are seats outside. Byland Abbey is nearby.

Cooked by the landlady and with some south african touches, the food includes lunchtime sandwiches, trio of smoked fish, black pudding nuggets with smoked bacon and chives, rooibos tea-smoked chicken and chorizo salad, bobotie (a mild, fruity curry), pork fillet with mushrooms and baby onions in a brandy and mustard sauce, salmon with a poached egg and hollandaise sauce, and puddings; there's also a very good value three-course set menu (Monday-Thursday). *Benchmark main dish: steak in Guinness pie £12.95. Two-course evening meal £19.00.*

Free house ~ Licensees Ian and Eunice Walker ~ Real ale ~ (01347) 868280 ~ Open 12-3, 6-11; 12-11 Sat; 12-10.30 Sun ~ Bar food 12-2 (2.30 Sat), 6-8.30 (9 Fri, Sat); 12-3, 6-8 Sun ~ Restaurant ~ Children welcome ~ Dogs allowed in bar ~ Wi-fi ~ Bedrooms: £75/£99 ~ www.wombwellarms.co.uk *Recommended by Dr D J and Mrs S C Walker, Dr Peter Crawshaw*

WIDDOP   SD9531   Map 7
Pack Horse 🍺 £

The Ridge; from A646 on W side of Hebden Bridge, turn off at Heptonstall signpost (as it's a sharp turn, coming out of Hebden Bridge the road signs direct you around a turning circle), then follow Slack and Widdop signposts; can also be reached from Nelson and Colne, on high, pretty road; OS Sheet 103 map reference 952317; HX7 7AT

Friendly pub up on the moors and liked by walkers for generous tasty honest food, five real ales and lots of malt whiskies; bedrooms

Considering its isolated setting high up on the moors, this traditional pub is surprisingly busy. The bar has welcoming winter fires, window seats cut into the partly panelled stripped-stone walls that take in the beautiful views, sturdy furnishings and horsey mementoes. Black Sheep Best, Copper Dragon Golden Pippin, Thwaites Bitter and a guest ale on handpump, around 140 single malt whiskies and some irish ones, and a dozen wines by the glass. The friendly golden retrievers are called Padge and Purdey, the alsatian is Holly. There are seats outside in the cobblestoned beer garden, and pretty summer hanging baskets. As well as comfortable bedrooms (the breakfasts are very good), they also offer a smart self-catering apartment.

 Hearty food at reasonable prices includes lunchtime sandwiches, garlic mushrooms, a changing pâté, vegetable gratin, chilli con carne, giant burger with cheese, lambs liver and bacon, fish pie, daily specials, and puddings. *Benchmark main dish: rack of lamb with mint sauce £13.95. Two-course evening meal £15.50.*

Free house ~ Licensee Andrew Hollinrake ~ Real ale ~ (01422) 842803 ~ Open 12-3, 7-11; 12-11 Sun; closed Mon ~ Bar food 12-2, 7-9; 12-8 Sun ~ Children welcome ~ Dogs allowed in bar ~ www.thepackhorse.org *Recommended by Emma Scofield, Toby Jones*

YORK   SE5951   Map 7
Maltings 🍺 £

Tanners Moat/Wellington Row, below Lendal Bridge; YO1 6HU

Bustling, friendly city pub with cheerful landlord, interesting real ales and other drinks, plus good value standard food

There's always a cheerful atmosphere here helped along by the jovial landlord, plus a fine choice of up to seven real ales on handpump such as Black Sheep Bitter, one each from Roosters and York and four that change daily. They also keep six continental beers on tap, two craft beers, lots of bottled beers, four farm ciders, 15 country wines and 25 whiskies from all over the world. The tricksy décor is strong on salvaged, somewhat quirky junk: old doors for the bar front and much of the ceiling, a marvellous collection of railway signs and amusing notices, an old chocolate dispensing machine, cigarette and tobacco advertisements alongside cough and chest remedies, what looks like a suburban front door for the entrance to the ladies', partly stripped orange brick walls and even a lavatory pan in one corner; games machine. The day's papers are framed in the gents. Nearby parking is difficult; the pub is very handy for the National Railway Museum and the station. Please note that dogs are allowed in only after food service has finished.

🍴 Incredibly good value pubby food includes sandwiches and toasties, chips done all sorts of ways with numerous dips, baked potatoes, vegetarian lasagne, ham and eggs, and sausage and beans. *Benchmark main dish: beef in ale pie £6.75.*

Free house ~ Licensee Shaun Collinge ~ Real ale ~ No credit cards ~ (01904) 655387 ~ Open 11-11; 12-10.30 Sun ~ Bar food 12-2 weekdays; 12-4 weekends ~ Children allowed only during meal times ~ Dogs allowed in bar ~ Live music Mon and Tues evenings ~ www.maltings.co.uk *Recommended by David H Bennett, Ryta Lyndley, Eric Larkham, G Jennings, Pat and Graham Williamson, Phil Bryant, Dr J Barrie Jones*

Also Worth a Visit in Yorkshire

Besides the fully inspected pubs, you might like to try these pubs that have been recommended to us and described by readers. Do tell us what you think of them: feedback@goodguides.com

AINTHORPE NZ7007
Fox & Hounds (01287) 660218
Brook Lane; YO21 2LD Traditional beamed moorland inn dating from the 16th c, tranquil setting with sheep grazing freely and wonderful views; nice open fire in unusual stone fireplace, comfortable seating, well kept Theakstons ales and good choice of wines by the glass, generous fairly priced food including daily specials, friendly staff, restaurant, games room; free wi-fi; dogs welcome, great walks from the door, seven bedrooms and attached self-catering cottage, open all day. *(Paul and Karen Cornock, Rod Lambert)*

ALDBOROUGH SE4166
Ship (01423) 322749
Off B6265 just S of Boroughbridge, close to A1; YO51 9ER Attractive 14th-c beamed village dining pub, good food from sandwiches and pub standards up, cheerful service, well kept ales including Theakstons, extensive wine list, some old-fashioned seats around cast-iron-framed tables, lots of copper and brass, inglenook fire, restaurant; children and dogs welcome, a few picnic-sets outside, handy for Roman remains and museum, bedrooms, open all day Sun, closed Mon lunchtime. *(Peter Hacker)*

AMPLEFORTH SE5878
★**White Swan** (01439) 788239
Off A170 W of Helmsley; East End; YO62 4DA Attractively decorated pub with plum-coloured beamed lounge, slate or carpeted floors, sporting prints and two-way woodburner, locals' bar with beams and standing timbers, red patterned wall seating and log fire, more formal dining area has plush furnishings and

linen-clothed tables, enjoyable food from traditional choices up, Black Sheep and Theakstons, good wines by the glass and ten malt whiskies, friendly service; background music, pool, darts and dominoes; children welcome, back terrace overlooking valley, open all day weekends. *(Pat and Stewart Gordon, Debi Henson)*

APPLETON-LE-MOORS SE7388
★**Moors** (01751) 417435
N of A170, just under 1.5 miles E of Kirkby Moorside; YO62 6TF Traditional stone-built village pub, beamed bar with built-in high-backed settle next to old kitchen fireplace, plenty of other seating, some sparse decorations (a few copper pans, earthenware mugs, country ironwork), three changing regional ales and over 50 malt whiskies, popular good value home-made food (something all day) using vegetables from own allotment, friendly helpful staff; background music, darts; children and dogs welcome, tables in lovely walled garden with quiet country views, walks to Rosedale Abbey or Hartoft End, seven good bedrooms, open all day. *(T E Stone)*

APPLETREEWICK SE0560
★**Craven Arms** (01756) 720270
Off B6160 Burnsall–Bolton Abbey; BD23 6DA Character creeper-covered 17th-c beamed pub, comfortably down-to-earth settles and rugs on flagstones, oak panelling, fire in old range, good welcoming service, up to eight well kept ales including a house beer from Dark Horse, good choice of wines by the glass, enjoyable home-made food from baguettes up, small dining room and splendid thatched and raftered cruck barn with gallery; children, dogs and boots welcome (plenty of surrounding walks),

wheelchair access, nice country views from front picnic-sets, more seats in back garden, open all day Weds-Sun. *(Claes Mauroy, Simon and Mandy King, Lawrence Pearse, Lynda and Trevor Smith, Pat and Graham Williamson)*

APPLETREEWICK   SE0560
New Inn   (01756) 720252
W end of main village; BD23 6DA
Unpretentious warmly welcoming country local with lovely views, six well kept ales including Black Sheep and Daleside, good choice of continental bottled beers, generous tasty home cooking, distinctive décor and interesting old local photographs; children and dogs welcome, three garden areas, good walks, five bedrooms and nearby camping, open all day. *(Claes Mauroy, Pat and Graham Williamson)*

ARNCLIFFE   SD9371
★Falcon   (01756) 770205
Off B6160 N of Grassington; BD23 5QE
Basic no-frills country tavern under friendly new management; lovely setting on village green, coal fire in small bar with elderly furnishings, well kept Timothy Taylors Landlord and a guest either from handpump or tapped from cask to stoneware jugs in central hatch-style servery, inexpensive simple lunchtime food, attractive watercolours, sepia photographs and humorous sporting prints, back sunroom overlooking pleasant garden; children till 9pm and dogs welcome, four miles of trout fishing, nice walks, five bedrooms (two with own bathroom), breakfast and evening meal for residents. *(Claes Mauroy, B and M Kendall)*

ASKRIGG   SD9491
Crown   (01969) 650387
Main Street; DL8 3HQ
Friendly open-plan local in James Herriot village, three areas off main bar, open fires including old-fashioned range, buzzy atmosphere, enjoyable pub food at reasonable prices, Black Sheep, Theakstons and a guest; children, walkers and dogs welcome, tables outside, open all day. *(Geoff and Linda Payne)*

ASKRIGG   SD9491
Kings Arms   (01969) 650113
Signed from A684 Leyburn–Sedbergh in Bainbridge; DL8 3HQ Popular 18th-c coaching inn (the Drovers in TV's *All Creatures Great and Small*) and under same ownership as the Charles Bathurst at Langthwaite; flagstoned high-ceilinged main bar with good log fire, traditional furnishings and décor, well kept Black Sheep, Theakstons, a house beer from Yorkshire Dales and two guests, 13 wines by the glass, enjoyable reasonably priced food and friendly efficient service, restaurant with inglenook, games room in former barrel-vaulted beer cellar; background music; children welcome, pleasant side courtyard, bedrooms run

separately as part of Holiday Property Bond complex behind. *(Janet and Peter Race, Comus and Sarah Elliott, Mrs Carolyn Dixon)*

AUSTWICK   SD7668
★Game Cock   (01524) 251226
Just off A65 Settle–Kirkby Lonsdale; LA2 8BB Quaint civilised place in pretty spot below Three Peaks; good log fire in old-fashioned beamed bare-boards back bar, cheerful efficient staff and friendly locals, well kept Thwaites and a guest, winter mulled wine and nice coffee, most space devoted to the food side, with good fairly priced choice from french chef-landlord, pizzas and children's meals as well, two dining rooms and modern conservatory-type extension at front; walkers and dogs welcome, garden with play equipment, four neat bedrooms, closed Mon, otherwise open all day (till 1am if busy). *(Christopher Mobbs, M and GR)*

AYSGARTH   SE0188
Aysgarth Falls   (01969) 663775
A684; DL8 3SR Moorland hotel refurbished and doing well under present licensees, comfortable eating areas, some interesting ancient masonry at the back recalling its days as a pilgrims' inn, good food and welcoming accommodating service, ales such as Black Sheep, Theakstons and Wensleydale in log-fire bar (dogs welcome); great scenery near broad waterfalls, 11 bedrooms, camping (adults only). *(Lynda and Trevor Smith, John Gosling)*

AYSGARTH   SE0088
George & Dragon   (01969) 663358
Just off A684; DL8 3AD Welcoming 17th-c posting inn with emphasis on good value pubby food from sandwiches up, two big dining areas, small beamed and panelled bar with log fire, well kept ales including Black Sheep Bitter, Theakstons Best and a house beer from Yorkshire Dales, good choice of wines by the glass; may be background music; children and dogs (in bar) welcome, nice paved garden, lovely scenery and walks, handy for Aysgarth Falls, seven bedrooms, open all day. *(Geoff and Linda Payne, Stuart Paulley)*

BAINBRIDGE   SD9390
Rose & Crown   (01969) 650225
A684; DL8 3EE Inn's old-fashioned front bar overlooking moorland village green, beams, oak panelling, old settles and big log fire, several well kept ales including Black Sheep, back restaurant; children welcome, plenty of good walks, bedrooms, open all day. *(Comus and Sarah Elliott)*

BARKISLAND   SE0419
★Fleece   (01422) 820687
B6113 towards Ripponden; HX4 0DJ
Well renovated and extended 18th-c beamed moorland dining pub, very good food (all day

from breakfast on, till 7pm Sun) including weekday set menu, efficient friendly uniformed staff, well kept Timothy Taylors Landlord and a couple of guests, popular comedy club last Sun of month; background music; children welcome, lovely Pennine views from first-floor terrace and garden, five bedrooms, handy for M62, open all day from 9am. *(Gordon and Margaret Ormondroyd, Pat and Tony Martin, John and Eleanor Holdsworth)*

BARMBY ON THE MARSH   SE6828
Kings Head   (01757) 630705
High Street; DN14 7HT Renovated and extended early 19th-c beamed village pub, good locally sourced food including some imaginative choices, Yorkshire tapas, Sun lunchtime carvery, four well kept local ales, bar, lounge and restaurant, deli (home-baked bread to order); children welcome, disabled facilities, open all day weekends, closed Mon and Tues lunchtimes. *(John and Eleanor Holdsworth)*

BARNSLEY   SE3203
Strafford Arms   (01226) 287488
Near Northern College, about 2.5 miles NW of M1 junction 36; S75 3EW Pretty stone-built village pub recently revamped by Fine & Country Inns, enjoyable food (some cooked in Josper grill), Timothy Taylors ales and good range of wines, open fires including one in big Yorkshire range; free wi-fi; children, dogs and muddy boots welcome, on Trans Pennine Trail and by entrance to Wentworth Castle, open (and food) all day. *(Anon)*

BEDALE   SE2688
Old Black Swan   (01677) 422973
Market Place; DL8 1ED Thriving old pub with attractive façade, generous helpings of good value popular food, friendly efficient staff, well kept ales including Theakstons, log fire, darts, pool; sports TV; children welcome, disabled facilities, small covered back terrace, Tues market, open all day. *(Janet and Peter Race)*

BEVERLEY   TA0339
White Horse   (01482) 861973
Hengate, off North Bar; HU17 8BN Carefully preserved Victorian interior with basic little rooms huddled around central bar, brown leatherette seats (high-backed settles in one little snug) and plain chairs and benches on bare boards, antique cartoons and sentimental engravings, gas-lit chandelier, open fires, games room, upstairs family room, bargain Sam Smiths and guest beers, basic food; children till 7pm, no dogs, open all day. *(Anon)*

BEVERLEY   TA0239
Woolpack   (01482) 867095
Westwood Road, W of centre; HU17 8EN Small proper pub in pair of 19th-c cottages kept spotless by welcoming landlady, good

traditional food at reasonable prices and seven well kept Marstons-related beers, cosy snug, open fires, simple furnishings, brasses, knick-knacks and prints; Thurs quiz; beer garden, open all day weekends, closed Mon lunchtime. *(C A Hall)*

BINGLEY   SE1039
Brown Cow   (01274) 564345
Ireland Bridge; B6429 just W of junction with A650; BD16 2QX Comfortable open-plan pub in pleasant spot by the river, Timothy Taylors range and good choice of enjoyable food including burgers and stone-baked pizzas, popular live music Sat, quiz Tues; children and dogs welcome, tables on sheltered terrace, open all day Fri-Sun. *(Anon)*

BINGLEY   SE1242
Dick Hudsons   (01274) 552121
Otley Road, High Eldwick; BD16 3BA Good Vintage Inn family dining pub, Black Sheep, Marstons and Timothy Taylors, lots of wines by the glass, their usual food done well, quick service; tables out by cricket field, great views, open all day. *(Pat and Graham Williamson)*

BINGLEY   SE1039
Glen   (01274) 563589
Gilstead Lane, Gilstead; BD16 3LN Recently renovated (Pickles Pubs) on leafy outskirts; good choice of popular fairly traditional food (all day Sun) from hot or cold sandwiches up, reasonable prices, six real ales, conservatory dining area; free wi-fi; children and dogs welcome, garden with play area and outside bar, open all day. *(John and Eleanor Holdsworth)*

BIRSTWITH   SE2459
★Station Hotel   (01423) 770254
Off B6165 W of Ripley; HG3 3AG Welcoming immaculately kept stone-built Dales pub; bar, log-fire restaurant and garden room, good sensibly priced home-made food from extensive menu including lunchtime/ early evening set deal, four local ales and 14 wines by the glass, friendly efficient staff; tables in landscaped garden with heated smokers' shelter, picturesque valley, five refurbished bedrooms, open all day (till 9.30pm Sun). *(M S Catling, Gordon and Jenny Quick, John and Eleanor Holdsworth)*

BLAXTON   SE6700
Blue Bell   (01302) 773195
Thorne Road (A614); DN9 3AL Friendly roadside pub under new management, good home-made blackboard food and well kept ales, conservatory; children and dogs welcome, a few seats outside. *(Anneliese Hall)*

BOLTON ABBEY   SE0754
Devonshire Arms   (01756) 710441
B6160; BD23 6AJ Comfortable and elegant 18th c hotel in wonderful position on edge of

Bolton Abbey Estate; good if pricey food from light meals up in bright modern brasserie-bar, contemporary paintings (some for sale) on roughcast walls, colourful armchairs around cast-iron-framed tables on pale wood floor, four well kept Copper Dragon ales and good wines by the glass, afternoon teas, more formal restaurant; tables in spacious courtyard with extensive views, Estate and Strid River valley walks, bedrooms in old and new wings. *(Richard Kennell)*

BRADFORD   SE1533
Fighting Cock (01274) 726907
Preston Street (off B6145); BD7 1JE Busy bare-boards alehouse by industrial estate, a dozen well kept changing ales, foreign draught/bottled beers and real ciders, friendly staff and lively atmosphere, all-day sandwiches plus good simple lunchtime hot dishes (not Sun), may be free bread and dripping on the bar, low prices, coal fires; open all day. *(Anon)*

BRADFORD   SE1533
New Beehive (01274) 721784
Westgate; BD1 3AA Robustly old-fashioned five-room Edwardian inn, plenty of period features including gas lighting, big mirrors, interesting paintings and coal fires, changing ales (mostly from smaller brewers) along with continental bottled beers, welcoming staff and friendly atmosphere, pool room, weekend live music in cellar bar; children welcome, nice back courtyard, 17 bedrooms, open all day (till 1am Fri, Sat), from 6pm Sun. *(Anon)*

BRADFORD   SE1633
Sparrow Bier Café (01677) 470411
North Parade; BD1 3HZ Bare-boards bar with great selection of bottled beers, draught continentals and local real ales, friendly knowledgeable staff, good deli platters and pies, local artwork, more tables in cellar bar; background music; open all day, closed Sun. *(Pat and Tony Martin)*

BRADFORD   SE1938
Stansfield Arms (0113) 250 2659
Apperley Lane, Apperley Bridge; off A658 NE; BD10 0NP Popular ivy-clad pub dating from 16th c, family-run and friendly, with enjoyable food including early evening deal, well kept Black Sheep, Timothy Taylors Landlord and a guest, beams, stripped stone and dark panelling, restaurant; children welcome, tables out on front decking, pleasant setting, open all day and can get very busy. *(John and Eleanor Holdsworth)*

BRANDESBURTON   TA1147
Dacre Arms (01964) 542392
Signed off A165 N of Beverley and Hornsea turn-offs; YO25 8RL Modernised old pub popular for its good value generously served food from lunchtime sandwiches and grills, also bargain OAP two-course deal and

children's meals, friendly young staff, well kept ales such as John Smiths, Theakstons and Wold Top, restaurant; picnic-sets out in small fenced area, open (and food) all day Fri-Sun. *(C A Hall)*

BREARTON   SE3260
★ Malt Shovel (01423) 862929
Village signposted off A61 N of Harrogate; HG3 3BX New licensees for this 16th-c dining pub; heavily beamed rooms with two open fires and woodburner, attractive mix of dining chairs around tables on wood or slate floors, some partitioning separating several eating areas, good food from light lunches up, Black Sheep, Timothy Taylors Landlord and a guest from linenfold oak counter, plenty of wines by the glass, airy conservatory; occasional opera evenings with dinner, and maybe a jazz pianist Sun; children welcome, tables under parasols in garden and pretty summer hanging baskets, closed Sun evening, Mon. *(Ryan Green, Dennis Jones, Derek and Sylvia Stephenson)*

BRIDGE HEWICK   SE3370
Black-a-moor (01765) 603511
Boroughbridge Road (B6265 E of Ripon); HG4 5AA Roomy family-run dining pub with wide choice of popular home-cooked food including good value early-bird deal (lunchtime and evening), well kept local beers and good selection of wines, friendly young staff, sofas and woodburner in bar area; free wi-fi; children welcome, refurbished bedrooms. *(Duncan, Carol and Alistair Hallows, Janet and Peter Race)*

BRIGHOUSE   SE1325
Sun (01422) 202230
N, on A649; Wakefield Road, Lightcliffe; HX3 8TH Extended and renovated 18th-c stone-built dining pub, good choice of reasonably priced pubby food including Sun carvery, Timothy Taylors Landlord, Copper Dragon and a guest, plenty of wines by the glass, friendly staff; free wi-fi; open all day. *(Gordon and Margaret Ormondroyd)*

BURN   SE5928
★ Wheatsheaf (01757) 270614
Main Road (A19 Selby–Doncaster); YO8 8LJ Welcoming busy mock-Tudor roadside pub, comfortable seats and tables in partly divided open-plan bar with masses to look at: gleaming copper kettles, black dagging shears, polished buffalo horns, cases of model vans and lorries, decorative mugs above one bow-window seat, a drying rack over the log fire; John Smiths, Timothy Taylors and guests, 20 malt whiskies, good value straightforward food (not Sun-Weds evenings), roast only on Sun; pool table, games machine, TV and maybe unobtrusive background music; children and dogs welcome, picnic-sets on heated terrace in small back garden, open all day till midnight. *(Anon)*

BURNSALL   SE0361
★ **Red Lion** (01756) 720204
B6160 S of Grassington; BD23 6BU
Family-run 16th-c inn in lovely spot by
River Wharfe, attractively panelled, sturdily
furnished front dining rooms with log fire,
more basic back public bar, good imaginative
food (all day weekends), well kept ales such
as Copper Dragon and Timothy Taylors, nice
wines, efficient friendly service, conservatory;
children welcome, tables out on front cobbles
and on big back terrace, views across to
Burnsall Fell, comfortable bedrooms (dogs
allowed in some and in bar), fishing permits
available, open all day. *(M J Daly)*

BURTON LEONARD   SE3263
★ **Hare & Hounds** (01765) 677355
*Off A61 Ripon–Harrogate, handy for
A1(M) junction 48; HG3 3SG* Civilised
and welcoming 19th-c village dining pub,
good popular food served promptly from
lunchtime sandwiches up, well kept ales
such as Black Sheep and Timothy Taylors
from long counter, large carpeted main area
divided by log fire, traditional furnishings,
bright small side room; children in eating
areas, pretty little back garden, closed Mon.
(Robert Wivell, Michael Butler, Peter Hacker)

BURYTHORPE   SE7964
Bay Horse (01653) 658302
*Off A64 8.5 miles NE of York ring road,
via Kirkham and Westow; 5 miles S of
Malton, by Welham Road; YO17 9LJ*
Welcoming dining pub with linked rooms,
good choice of reasonably priced food from
blackboard menu, Black Sheep, Copper
Dragon and several wines by the glass,
main bar has carved antique pews and
old hunting prints, end dining room with
attractive farmyard animal paintings, also
a snug with sofa and log fire and red-walled
room with rugs on flagstones; unobtrusive
background music; children welcome, dogs
in bar, flat disabled access from car park,
contemporary furniture on terrace under
parasols, nice Wolds-edge village with
fine surrounding walks, open all day Sun,
closed Mon. *(Simon and Mandy King, Pat and
Graham Williamson)*

CARLTON   SE0684
Foresters Arms (01969) 640272
Off A684 W of Leyburn; DL8 4BB
Old stone pub owned by local co-operative;
log fire bar with dark low beams and
flagstones, four well kept local ales and
good range of popular affordably priced
food, carpeted restaurant, events such as
book club, children's cookery classes and
fortnightly Tues quiz; disabled access, a
few picnic-sets out at front, pretty village
in heart of Yorkshire Dales National Park,
lovely views, three bedrooms, open all day
weekends, closed Mon lunchtime. *(Dr Peter
Crawshaw, Gordon and Jenny Quick)*

CARLTON HUSTHWAITE   SE4976
Carlton Inn (01845) 501265
Butt Lane; YO7 2BW Cosy modernised
beamed dining pub; good fairly priced food
cooked by landlady including daily specials
and lunchtime/early evening set menu,
cheerful helpful service, John Smiths and
Theakstons, local cider, mix of country
furniture including some old settles, open
fire; children welcome, dogs in back bar area,
garden picnic-sets, open all day Sun, closed
Mon. *(Walter and Susan Rinaldi-Butcher,
Dr Peter Crawshaw)*

CARTHORPE   SE3083
★ **Fox & Hounds** (01845) 567433
*Village signed from A1 N of Ripon, via
B6285; DL8 2LG* Welcoming neatly kept
dining pub with emphasis on good well
presented food, attractive high-raftered
restaurant with lots of farm and smithy tools,
Black Sheep and Worthington in L-shaped
bar with two log fires, plush seating, plates
on stripped beams and evocative Victorian
photographs of Whitby, some theatrical
memorabilia in corridors, good friendly
service; background classical music; children
welcome, handy for A1, closed Mon and first
week Jan. *(Janet and Peter Race)*

CATTAL   SE4455
Victoria (01423) 330249
Station Road; YO26 8EB Bustling
Victorian-themed dining pub, good nicely
presented food (should book) from extensive
menu including specials, charming attentive
service, well kept ales with one from local
Rudgate named for the landlord, good value
wines; children welcome, picnic-sets in
gravelled back garden, closed lunchtime
(except Sun) and all day Mon, handy for
station. *(Les and Sandra Brown, Brian and
Janet Ainscough)*

CAWOOD   SE5737
Ferry (01757) 268515
*King Street (B1222 NW of Selby), by
Ouse swing bridge; YO8 3TL* Interesting
16th-c inn with several comfortable areas,
enjoyable unpretentious food and well
kept ales, log fire in massive inglenook, low
beams, stripped brickwork and bare boards;
nice flagstone terrace and lawn down to river,
bedrooms, open all day (from 3pm Mon).
(Pat and Graham Williamson)

CHAPEL-LE-DALE   SD7477
★ **Hill Inn** (01524) 241256
*B5655 Ingleton–Hawes, 3 miles N
of Ingleton; LA6 3AR* Former farmhouse
with fantastic views to Ingleborough and
Whernside, a haven for weary walkers
(wonderful remote surrounding walks);
lived-in interior with beams, log fires
and bare-stone recesses, straightforward
furniture on stripped wooden floors, nice
pictures and some interesting local artefacts,

Black Sheep, Dent and Theakstons, enjoyable wholesome food, separate dining room and sun lounge, relaxed chatty atmosphere; children welcome, dogs in bar, two bedrooms and space for five caravans, open all day Sat, closed Mon. *(David Heath)*

CLAPHAM
SD7469
New Inn (01524) 251203

Off A65 N of Settle; LA2 8HH Recently renovated 18th-c riverside inn in famously pretty village, local ales and good well presented food in bar or restaurant including some interesting vegetarian options, friendly staff; children and dogs welcome, tables outside, handy for walk to Ingleborough Cave and more adventurous hikes, 20 refurbished bedrooms. *(Anon)*

CLIFTON
SE1622
★**Black Horse** (01484) 713862

Westgate/Coalpit Lane; signed off Brighouse Road from M62 junction 25; HD6 4HJ Friendly 17th-c inn-restaurant, pleasant décor, front dining rooms with good interesting food including a few pubby dishes, can be pricey, efficient uniformed service, open fire in back bar with beam-and-plank ceiling, well kept Timothy Taylors Landlord and a house beer brewed by Brass Monkey, decent wines; appealing courtyard, 21 comfortable bedrooms, pleasant village, open all day. *(Michael Butler)*

CLOUGHTON NEWLANDS
TA0195
Bryherstones (01723) 870744

Newlands Road, off A171 in Cloughton; YO13 0AR Traditional stone pub with several interconnecting rooms including dining room up on right and flagstoned stable-theme bar on left, lighter bare-boards back room with open fire, enjoyable popular food using locally sourced meat, Timothy Taylors and a house beer from Wold Top, good friendly service, games room (pool and darts); children and dogs welcome, picnic-sets and play area in sheltered back garden, closed lunchtimes Mon-Weds. *(Robin Constable)*

COLTON
SE5444
★**Old Sun** (01904) 744261

Off A64 York–Tadcaster; LS24 8EP Top notch cooking at this refurbished and extended 18th-c beamed dining pub, good wine list with plenty available by the glass, well kept Black Sheep and Cropton (proper bar area), friendly competent staff; cookery demonstrations and little shop selling home-made and local produce; children welcome, seats out on front terrace, bedrooms in separate building, open all

day Sun (food till 7pm then). *(Gordon and Margaret Ormondroyd, Dave Newton)*

CONEYTHORPE
SE3958
★**Tiger** (01423) 863632

2.3 miles from A1(M) junction 47; A59 towards York, then village signposted (and brown sign to Tiger Inn); bear left at brown sign in Flaxby; HG5 0RY Spreading red-carpeted bar with hundreds of pewter tankards hanging from ochre-painted joists, olde-worlde prints, china figurines in one arched alcove, padded grey wall seats, pews and settles around sturdy scrubbed tables, open fire, more formal back dining area, sensibly priced food from lunchtime sandwiches through pubby favourites, also set deals, Black Sheep, Copper Dragon and Timothy Taylors Landlord, friendly helpful staff; nostalgic background music; picnic-sets on front gravel terrace and on small green opposite, open all day. *(Pat and Graham Williamson)*

CRAY
SD9479
White Lion (01756) 760262

B6160 N of Kettlewell; BD23 5JB Highest Wharfedale pub (again under new licensees) in lovely countryside and popular with walkers; simple bar with open fire and flagstones, ales such as Copper Dragon, Sharps, Tetleys and Theakstons, tasty good value pub food, bar and two snugs, original bull 'ook game; children and dogs welcome, picnic-sets above quiet steep lane or can sit on flat limestone slabs in shallow stream opposite, ten bedrooms, open all day, closed Mon in winter. *(Lawrence Pearse, Peter Smith and Judith Brown)*

CRIGGLESTONE
SE3217
Red Kite (01924) 251542

Denby Dale Road, Durkar (A636, by M1 junction 39); WF4 3BB Vintage Inn by busy roundabout, built to look like a Georgian house adjoining a cottage row, their usual food including good value set menu, well kept Black Sheep, York and a guest, plenty of wines by the glass, good friendly service, log fire; children welcome, disabled facilities, lots of tables outside, bedrooms in adjacent Premier Inn, open all day from 8am for breakfast. *(Derek and Sylvia Stephenson)*

CULLINGWORTH
SE0636
George (01535) 275566

Station Road; BD13 5HN Own Old Spot beers brewed in the village and enjoyable reasonably priced home-made food from light lunchtime choices up, good service; children welcome till 9pm, open all day. *(John and Eleanor Holdsworth)*

A star symbol before the name of a pub shows exceptional character and appeal. It doesn't mean extra comfort. Even quite a basic pub can win a star, if it's individual enough.

DACRE BANKS　　　　　　SE1961

★ **Royal Oak**　(01423) 780200

B6451 S of Pateley Bridge; HG3 4EN
Popular solidly comfortable 18th-c pub with
Nidderdale views, good traditional food
(not Sun evening) along with daily specials
and events such as summer crab festival,
attentive friendly staff, well kept Greene King
ales and good choice of wines by the glass,
interesting selection of gins too, beams and
panelling, log-fire dining room, games room
with darts, dominoes and pool; background
music, TV; children welcome in eating areas,
terrace and informal back garden, three
bedrooms, big breakfast, open all day.
(Claes Mauroy)

DALTON　　　　　　　　SE4476

Moor & Pheasant　(01845) 577756

Dalton Moor, E of village; YO7 3JD
Smartly modernised beamed pub serving
good food (all day Sun till 7pm) including
daily specials and lunchtime/early evening
set deal, very popular with older customers,
ales such as Copper Dragon and Theakstons;
garden with rattan furniture on paved terrace,
heated smokers' shelter, open all day.
(John and Eleanor Holdsworth)

DANBY　　　　　　　　　NZ7008

Duke of Wellington　(01287) 660351

West Lane; YO21 2LY 18th-c creeper-clad
inn overlooking village green, usually four
Yorkshire ales such as Copper Dragon and
Daleside, enjoyable home-made food; clean
comfortable bedrooms. *(JHBS)*

DARLEY　　　　　　　　SE1961

Wellington Arms　(01423) 780362

B6451; Darley Head; HG3 2QQ Roadside
stone inn with fine Nidderdale views, beams
and big open fire, good freshly made food
(same menu lunchtime and evening), well
kept Black Sheep, Copper Dragon, Timothy
Taylors and Tetleys, helpful friendly staff;
children welcome, seats on large grassed
area, bedrooms, good breakfast, open
all day. *(Stanley and Annie Matthews)*

DEWSBURY　　　　　　　SE2622

Huntsman　(01924) 275700

*Walker Cottages, Chidswell Lane, Shaw
Cross – pub signed; WF12 7SW* Cosy
low-beamed converted cottages alongside
urban-fringe farm, lots of agricultural bric-a-
brac, blazing log fire, small front extension,
Timothy Taylors Landlord and three guests
such as Old Mill, well priced home-made food
(lunchtimes Tues-Sat, evenings Thurs, Fri till
7.30pm), quiet relaxed atmosphere; open all
day weekends, closed Mon. *(Michael Butler)*

DEWSBURY　　　　　　　SE2420

Leggers　(01924) 502846

*Robinsons Boat Yard, Savile Town
Wharf, Mill Street East (SE of B6409);
WF12 9BD* Hayloft conversion above former

stables by Calder & Hebble Navigation
marina, well kept Everards Tiger and five
guests, bottled belgian beers, real cider
and perry, good value straightforward food,
friendly staff, assorted memorabilia; pool;
picnic-sets outside, boat trips, open all day.
(Anon)

DEWSBURY　　　　　　　SE2421

★ **West Riding Licensed
Refreshment Rooms**　(01924) 459193

Station, Wellington Road; WF13 1HF
Convivial three-room early Victorian station
bar, eight well kept changing ales such as
Black Sheep, Oakham, Timothy Taylors and
Sportsman (brewed at their sister pub in
Huddersfield), foreign bottled beers and
farm ciders, bargain generous lunchtime food
on scrubbed tables, popular pie night Tues,
curry night Weds and Yorkshire tapas night
Thurs, good weekend breakfast too, friendly
staff, lots of steam memorabilia including
paintings by local artists, coal fire, daily
papers, impressive juke box and some live
music; children till 6pm in two end rooms,
disabled access, open all day. *(Andy and Jill
Kassube, Jim and Sheila Wilson)*

DONCASTER　　　　　　SE5702

Corner Pin　(01302) 340670

*St Sepulchre Gate West, Cleveland Street;
DN1 3AH* Plush beamed lounge with old
local pub prints, welsh dresser and china,
York Guzzler and interesting guests kept well
(beer festivals), good value traditional home-
made food including popular Sun lunch,
friendly landlady, cheery public bar with
darts, games machine and TV; back decking,
open all day. *(P Dawn)*

DONCASTER　　　　　　SE5703

Plough　(01302) 738310

*West Laith Gate, by Frenchgate shopping
centre; DN1 1SF* Small old-fashioned
local with friendly long-serving licensees
and chatty regulars, Acorn Barnsley Bitter
and guests, bustling front room with darts,
dominoes and sports TV, old town maps,
quieter back lounge; tiny central courtyard,
open all day (Sun afternoon break).
(Peter F Marshall, P Dawn)

DUNNINGTON　　　　　　SE6751

Windmill　(01904) 481898

Hull Road (A1079); YO19 5LP Welcoming
dining pub, large and fairly modern, with
popular home-made food served by friendly
staff, good range of beers, back conservatory,
quieter small raised dining area; ten
bedrooms, open all day Sun. *(David H Bennett)*

EASINGWOLD　　　　　　SE5270

★ **George**　(01347) 821698

Market Place; YO61 3AD Neat, bright
and airy market town hotel (former 18th-c
coaching inn), quiet corners even when
busy, helpful cheerful service, well kept
Black Sheep, Moorhouses and a guest, good

sensibly priced food in bar and restaurant, beams, horsebrasses and warm log fires, slightly old-fashioned feel and popular with older customers; pleasant bedrooms, good breakfast. *(Robert Turnham)*

EAST MARTON   SD9050
Cross Keys   (01282) 844326
A59 Gisburn–Skipton; BD23 3LP
Comfortable and welcoming 18th-c pub behind small green near Leeds & Liverpool Canal (and Pennine Way), heavy beams and big open fire, good freshly cooked food (all day Sun) from shortish menu supplemented by interesting blackboard specials, well kept ales including Copper Dragon and Theakstons, friendly service, more restaurant-y dining room; background music; children and dogs welcome, tables on front deck, open all day. *(Richard and Karen Holt, Brian and Janet Ainscough)*

EAST MORTON   SE0941
Busfeild Arms   (01274) 563169
Main Road; BD20 5SP Attractive 19th-c stone-built village pub (originally a school), traditionally furnished beamed and flagstoned bar with woodburner, four ales including Tetleys and Timothy Taylors Landlord, good range of enjoyable well priced food, weekday early-bird deal (5.30-6.30pm), efficient cheerful service, restaurant; quiz Thurs, live music Sat, sports TV; children welcome, picnic-sets on front terrace, open all day. *(John and Eleanor Holdsworth)*

EAST WITTON   SE1487
★ Cover Bridge Inn   (01969) 623250
A6108 out towards Middleham; DL8 4SQ
Cosy and welcoming 16th-c flagstoned country local, good choice of well kept Yorkshire brewed ales and enjoyable generous pub food at sensible prices, small restaurant, roaring fires; children and dogs welcome, riverside garden with play area, three bedrooms, open all day. *(Anon)*

EGTON   NZ8006
Wheatsheaf   (01947) 895271
Village centre; YO21 1TZ 19th-c village pub of real character, interesting pictures and collectables in small bare-boards bar with fire in old range, good generously served food including fresh fish and seasonal game, friendly service, Black Sheep, Timothy Taylors Landlord and a summer guest, several wines by the glass, restaurant; four bedrooms in adjacent cottage, open all day weekends, closed Mon. *(P Dawn)*

EGTON BRIDGE   NZ8005
Horseshoe   (01947) 895245
Village signed off A171 W of Whitby; YO21 1XE Attractively placed 18th-c stone inn with some refurbishment under present landlord; open fire, high-backed built-in winged settles, wall seats and spindleback chairs, various odds and ends including a

big stuffed trout (caught nearby in 1913), Theakstons Best and a couple of guests, traditional food; background music; children welcome, dogs in side bar during mealtimes, seats on quiet terrace in nice mature garden by small River Esk, good walks (on Coast to Coast path), six bedrooms, open all day weekends. *(P Dawn, Vikki and Matt Wharton)*

EGTON BRIDGE   NZ8005
★ Postgate   (01947) 895241
Village signed off A171 W of Whitby; YO21 1UX Moorland village pub next to station; good imaginative food at fair prices including fresh local fish, friendly staff, well kept Black Sheep and a guest, traditional quarry-tiled bar with beams, panelled dado and coal fire in antique range, elegant restaurant; children and dogs welcome, walled front garden with picnic-sets either side of brick path, three nice bedrooms. *(Dr and Mrs R G J Telfer, P Dawn, Tina and David Woods-Taylor)*

ELLAND   SE1021
Barge & Barrel   (01422) 371770
Quite handy for M62 junction 24; Park Road (A6025, via A629 and B6114); HX5 9HP Large roadside pub by Calder & Hebble Navigation, own-brew beers along with plenty of guests including regulars Abbeydale, Black Sheep, Milltown and Timothy Taylors, pubby food, lounge bar, snug with open fire and games room, Thurs quiz and occasional live music; children welcome, waterside seats and moorings, limited parking, open all day. *(Tony Hobden)*

ELLAND   SE1019
Golden Fleece   (01422) 372704
Lindley Road, handy for M62 junction 24; HX5 0TE Comfortably refurbished country pub next to cricket field; good home-made food at reasonable prices including daily specials, well kept local ales, cheerful helpful service (can slow at busy times); also own nearby farm shop, closed Mon lunchtime, otherwise open all day. *(Gordon and Margaret Ormondroyd)*

ETTON   SE9743
Light Dragoon   (01430) 810282
3.5 miles N of Beverley, off B1248; Main Street; HU17 7PQ Roomy country local improved under present landlord, enjoyable good value food, two real ales and several wines by the glass, cheerful staff, inglenook fireplace; children and muddy walkers welcome, small back garden with swings and slide, nice village on Wolds cycle route, open all day Sun, closed Mon. *(Dr Kevan Tucker, C A Hall)*

FERRENSBY   SE3660
★ General Tarleton   (01423) 340284
A655 N of Knaresborough; HG5 0PZ
Carefully renovated 18th-c coaching inn, more restaurant-with-rooms than pub,

but there's an informal bar with sofas and woodburner serving Black Sheep, Timothy Taylors Landlord and a dozen wines by the glass, other open-plan rooms with low beams, brick pillars creating alcoves, exposed stonework and dark leather high-backed dining chairs around wooden tables, first class modern cooking from owner-chef along with more traditional food and children's menu, good well trained staff; seats in covered courtyard and tree-lined garden, pretty country views, 13 stylish bedrooms, good breakfast. *(Janet and Peter Race, Dr P Brown, Pat and Graham Williamson, Richard Cole)*

FILEY   TA1180
Bonhommes (01723) 514054
The Crescent; YO14 9JH Friendly busy bar with several well kept ales including one badged for them, live music and quiz nights; children and dogs welcome, open all day till late. *(Anon)*

FINGHALL   SE1889
★ **Queens Head** (01677) 450259
Off A684 E of Leyburn; DL8.5ND Welcoming comfortable dining pub, log fires either end of low-beamed bar with stone archway, settles making stalls around big tables, Theakstons, and guests, good food from sandwiches, deli boards and traditional favourites up, midweek deals and Sat brunch, extended back dining room with Wensleydale view; children welcome, no dogs inside, disabled facilities, back garden with decking sharing same view, three bedrooms, open all day weekends in summer. *(Anon)*

FIXBY   SE1119
Nags Head (01727) 871100
New Hey Road, by M62 junction 24 south side, past Hilton; HD2 2EA Spacious ivy-covered chain dining pub, appealing outside and comfortable in, pubby bar with four well kept ales, enjoyable fairly priced food including carvery and OAP deals, friendly helpful service, linked areas with wood and slate floors, restaurant on two levels; garden tables, bedrooms in adjoining Premier Inn, open all day. *(Gordon and Margaret Ormondroyd, John and Eleanor Holdsworth)*

GARGRAVE   SD9253
Masons Arms (01756) 749510
Church Street/Marton Road (off A65 NW of Skipton); BD23 3NL Welcoming beamed pub with friendly local atmosphere, open interior divided into bar, lounge and restaurant, log fire, ample helpings of enjoyable home-made food at very fair prices, well kept ales such as Black Sheep, Copper Dragon, Tetleys and Timothy Taylors from ornate counter, live acoustic music first Fri of month in winter, darts; children and dogs welcome, tables out behind overlooking own bowling green, charming village on Pennine

Way and not far from Leeds & Liverpool Canal, six bedrooms in converted barn, open (and food) all day. *(Michael Butler)*

GIGGLESWICK   SD8164
★ **Black Horse** (01729) 822506
Church Street – take care with the car park; BD24 0BE Hospitable licensees in 17th-c village pub prettily set by church; cosy bar with gleaming brass, copper and bric-a-brac, coal-effect fire, good value generous food, well kept Timothy Taylors, Tetleys and guests, intimate dining room, good service, piano (often played), monthly quiz; children welcome till 9pm, no dogs, sheltered heated back terrace, smokers' shelter, three reasonably priced comfortable bedrooms and good breakfast, open all day weekends; still for sale as we went to press, but business as usual. *(Dr and Mrs Leach, M and GR)*

GIGGLESWICK   SD8164
Harts Head (01729) 822086
Belle Hill; BD24 0BA Cheerful bustling 18th-c village inn, comfortable carpeted bar/lounge with well kept Caledonian, Kirkby Lonsdale, Tetleys and three guests, good choice of enjoyable reasonably priced food, restaurant, residents' snooker room; sports TV; picnic-sets on sloping lawn, ten bedrooms, open all day Fri-Sun, closed lunchtimes Tues, Thurs. *(Anon)*

GILLAMOOR   SE6890
★ **Royal Oak** (01751) 431414
Off A170 in Kirkbymoorside; YO62 7HX Stone-built 18th-c dining pub (some recent refurbishment) with interesting locally sourced food at sensible prices including specials and good vegetarian choice, friendly staff, ales such as Black Sheep and Copper Dragon, reasonably priced wines, roomy bar with heavy dark beams, log fires in two tall stone fireplaces (one with old kitchen range), overspill dining room (dogs allowed here); children welcome, eight comfortable modern bedrooms, good breakfast, attractive village handy for Barnsdale Moor walks. *(Stanley and Annie Matthews)*

GILLING EAST   SE6176
★ **Fairfax Arms** (01439) 788212
Main Street (B1363, off A170 via Oswaldkirk); YO62 4JH Smartly refurbished country inn, beamed bar with bare boards by handsome oak counter, carpeted area with woodburner, Black Sheep, Tetleys and some interesting wines by the glass, daily newspapers, two-part carpeted dining room with big hunting prints on red walls, nicely old-fashioned floral curtains and some padded oak settles, enjoyable modern food plus pub favourites, friendly black-aproned staff; picnic-sets out in front by floodlit roadside stream, pleasant village well placed for Howardian Hills and North York Moors, comfortable up-to-date bedrooms, good breakfast, open all day weekends. *(Anon)*

GLUSBURN　　　　　　　SD9944
Dog & Gun　(01535) 633855
*Colne Road (A6068 W) opposite Malsis
School; BD20 8DS* Sizeable stone-built
pub, attractive inside and out, and very
popular for its wide choice of enjoyable good
value food, attentive cheerful service, well
kept Timothy Taylors ales; children welcome,
tables out in front and on small roof terrace,
open (and food) all day. *(Gordon and Margaret
Ormondroyd)*

GOATHLAND　　　　　　NZ8200
Mallyan Spout Hotel　(01947) 896486
Opposite church; YO22 5AN Old creeper-
clad stone hotel with three spacious lounges
and traditional bar, open fires and fine
views, good fairly priced bar food and Sun
lunchtime carvery, three real ales, good malt
whiskies and wines, friendly helpful staff,
smart restaurant; well behaved children in
eating areas, handy for namesake waterfall,
comfortable bedrooms and good buffet
breakfast, open all day. *(Comus and Sarah
Elliott)*

GOMERSAL　　　　　　　SE2026
Wheatsheaf　(01274) 878638
Upper Lane, Little Gomersal; BD19 4JF
Popular village pub with dining areas either
side of bar, big helpings of enjoyable good
value food, four ales including Greene King
Abbot, John Smiths and Timothy Taylors
Landlord, friendly welcoming staff; front
garden. *(Michael Butler)*

GOODMANHAM　　　　　SE8943
★Goodmanham Arms　(01430) 873849
Main Street; YO43 3JA Welcoming little
red-brick country pub with three traditional
linked areas, beam-and-plank ceilings,
some red and black floor tiles, good mix
of furniture and lots of interesting odds
and ends, even a Harley Davidson, good
wholesome food from italian chef-owner (no
starters) including a winter casserole cooked
over the open fire, evening meals served
5-7pm Mon and Fri only, seven real ales –
three from on-site All Hallows microbrewery,
reasonable prices, occasional acoustic music;
children and dogs welcome, good walks (on
Wolds Way), open all day. *(Pat and Graham
Williamson, John and Eleanor Holdsworth,
David Heath, P Dawn, R Anderson)*

GRANGE MOOR　　　　SE2215
Kaye Arms　(01924) 848385
Wakefield Road (A642); WF4 4BG
Smartly refurbished dining pub under
welcoming new management, enjoyable
good value food, well kept ales such as
Ossett and plenty of wines by the glass,
efficient polished service; handy for
National Coal Mining Museum, open all day
weekends. *(Gordon and Margaret Ormondroyd)*

GRASSINGTON　　　　　SE0064
★Devonshire　(01756) 752525
The Square; BD23 5AD Handsome old
stone hotel, reliably run, with cheerful
bustling atmosphere, good window seats and
tables outside overlooking sloping village
square, decent pubby food from sandwiches
up, Fri fish night, well kept Black Sheep,
Copper Dragon, Moorhouses and Tetleys,
plenty of wines by the glass, bar, snug and
spacious restaurant, interesting pictures
and ornaments, beams and open fires;
children and dogs (in bar) welcome, seven
comfortable bedrooms, open (and food)
all day. *(Michael Butler, Dr Kevan Tucker)*

GRASSINGTON　　　　　SE0064
Foresters Arms　(01756) 752349
Main Street; BD23 5AA Comfortable
opened-up old coaching inn with friendly
bustling atmosphere, good reasonably priced
generous food, well kept ales including Black
Sheep, cheerful helpful service, log fires,
dining room off on right, pool and sports TV
on left, popular Mon quiz; children welcome,
outside tables, 14 affordable bedrooms (ones
over bar noisy), good breakfast, fine walking
country, open all day. *(Michael Butler)*

GREAT BROUGHTON　　NZ5405
Bay Horse　(01642) 712319
High Street; TS9 7HA Big creeper-clad
dining pub in attractive village, wide choice
of food including blackboard specials and
good value set lunch, friendly attentive
service, real ales such as Camerons and
Jennings, restaurant; children welcome,
seats outside, open (and food) all day
weekends. *(Stephen Funnell)*

GREAT HABTON　　　　SE7576
★Grapes　(01653) 669166
*Corner of Habton Lane and Kirby
Misperton Lane; YO17 6TU* Traditionally
refurbished beamed dining pub in small
village, homely and cosy, with good cooking
including fresh local fish and game, home-
baked bread, Marstons-related ales, open
fire, small public bar with darts and TV;
background music; a few roadside picnic-sets
(water for dogs), nice walks, open all day
Sun, closed Mon, lunchtime Tues. *(Anon)*

GREAT OUSEBURN　　　SE4461
Crown　(01423) 330013
*Off B6265 SE of Boroughbridge;
YO26 9RF* Steps up to welcoming 18th-c
pub with some refurbishment under present
owner, enjoyable food from traditional

By law, pubs must show a price list of their drinks. Let us know if you're
inconvenienced by any breach of this law.

choices up and good value early-bird menu, Black Sheep, Copper Dragon and Timothy Taylors Landlord, various areas including back dining extension; children and dogs welcome, garden with terrace tables, open all day. *(Anon)*

GUISELEY   SE1941
Coopers (01943) 878835

Otley Road; LS20 8AH Market Town Taverns conversion of former Co-operative store, open-plan bare-boards bar with good range of food from lunchtime sandwiches up, eight real ales including Black Sheep and Timothy Taylors, music nights in upstairs function/dining room; open all day. *(Anon)*

HALIFAX   SE0924
Three Pigeons (01422) 347001

Sun Fold, South Parade; off Church Street; HX1 2LX Carefully restored, four-room 1930s pub (Grade II listed), art deco fittings, ceiling painting in octagonal main area, original flooring, panelling and tiled fireplaces with log fires, usually six Ossett ales along with Fernandes and Rat, good Robinson's pies, friendly chatty staff; tables outside, handy for Eureka! Museum and Shay Stadium (pub very busy on match days), open all day Fri-Sun, from 4pm other days. *(Eric Larkham, Pat and Tony Martin)*

HAWDRAW   SD8691
★ Green Dragon (01969) 667392

Village signed off A684; DL8 3LZ Friendly traditional Dales pub dating from 13th c and full of character; stripped stone, antique settles on flagstones, lots of bric-a-brac, low-beamed snug with fire in old iron range, another in big main bar, five well kept ales including one badged for them from Yorkshire Dales, enjoyable generous food, small neat restaurant, annual brass band competition; children and dogs welcome, bedrooms, next to Hardraw Force – England's highest single-drop waterfall. *(Comus and Sarah Elliott, J R Wildon)*

HAROME   SE6482
★ Star (01439) 770397

High Street; village signed S of A170, E of Helmsley; YO62 5JE Restaurant-with-rooms in pretty 14th-c thatched building, but bar does have informal feel, bowed beam-and-plank ceiling, plenty of bric-a-brac, interesting furniture including 'Mousey' Thompson pieces, log fire and well polished tiled kitchen range, three changing ales and plenty of wines by the glass, home-made fruit liqueurs, snacks served in cocktail bar, coffee loft in the eaves, inventive ambitious cooking from chef-owner (not cheap), well trained helpful staff; background music; children welcome, seats on sheltered front terrace, more in garden, open all day Sun, closed Mon lunchtime. *(Ryta Lyndley, Barbara and Peter Kelly, Geoff and Linda Payne, J F M and M West)*

HARPHAM   TA0961
St Quintin Arms (01262) 490329

Main Street; YO25 4QY Comfortable old village pub with enjoyable reasonably priced home-made food (not Sun evening) including plenty of specials, well kept Tetleys and Wold Top, friendly landlord and staff, small dining room; sheltered garden with pond, on National Cycle Route 1, three bedrooms, open all day Sun, closed lunchtimes Mon and Tues. *(Dr Kevan Tucker)*

HARROGATE   SE3155
Coach & Horses (01423) 561802

West Park; HG1 1BJ Very friendly bustling pub with half a dozen good Yorkshire brewed ales and over 80 malt whiskies, enjoyable lunchtime food at bargain prices, obliging service, nice interior with booth seating; no children, dogs allowed after 4pm, open all day. *(Anon)*

HARROGATE   SE2955
★ Hales (01423) 725570

Crescent Road; HG1 2RS Classic Victorian décor in 18th-c gas-lit local close to Pump Rooms, leather seats in alcoves, stuffed birds, comfortable saloon and tiny snug, half a dozen ales including Daleside, simple good value lunchtime food, friendly helpful staff; can get lively weekend evenings, open all day. *(Anon)*

HARROGATE   SE2955
★ Old Bell (01423) 507930

Royal Parade; HG1 2SZ Thriving Market Town Tavern with eight mainly local beers from handsome counter, lots of bottled continentals and impressive choice of wines by the glass, friendly helpful staff, lunchtime snacks including sandwiches (interesting choice of breads), more elaborate evening meals upstairs, bare boards and panelling, old sweet shop ads and breweriana, daily newspapers; no children; dogs welcome, open all day. *(Michael Butler, Steve Ickringill)*

HARROGATE   SE3055
Swan on the Stray (01423) 524587

Corner Devonshire Place and A59; HG1 4AA Market Town Tavern with enjoyable reasonably priced food from shortish menu plus a few specials, eight mostly local ales, good range of imported beers and several ciders, cheerful efficient service, daily newspapers; dogs welcome, open all day (food till 6pm Sun). *(Brian and Janet Ainscough, Steve Ickringill)*

HARROGATE   SE3155
Winter Gardens (01423) 877010

Royal Baths, Crescent Road; HG1 2RR Interesting Wetherspoons transformation of former ballroom in landmark building, well kept ales, generous usual good value food, many original features, comfortable sofas in lofty hall, upper gallery; very busy late

evening; attractive terrace, open all day.
(Ryta Lyndley, B and M Kendall, Brian and Anna Marsden)

HAWNBY · SE5489
Inn at Hawnby (01439) 798202

Aka Hawnby Hotel; off B1257 NW of Helmsley; YO62 5QS Pleasantly situated inn with good local food including some interesting choices, helpful welcoming service, Black Sheep, Great Newsome and Timothy Taylors, good choice of wines by the glass; children and dogs (in bar) welcome, lovely views from restaurant and garden tables, pretty village in walking country (packed lunches available), nine bedrooms (three in converted stables over road), open all day Fri-Sun. *(Anon)*

HEADINGLEY · SE2736
Arcadia (0113) 274 5599

Arndale Centre; LS6 2UE Small Market Town Tavern in former bank, good choice of changing regional ales kept well, lots of continental bottled beers and good range of wines, knowledgeable staff, bar food (Thurs-Sun), stairs to mezzanine; no children; open all day. *(Peter Smith and Judith Brown)*

HEATH · SE3520
Kings Arms (01924) 377527

Village signposted from A655 Wakefield–Normanton – or, more directly, turn off to the left opposite Horse & Groom; WF1 5SL Old-fashioned gas-lit pub with genuine character, fire in black range (long row of smoothing irons on the mantelpiece), plain elm stools, built-in oak settles and dark panelling, Clarks, Ossett and several guest ales, decent food (all day Fri and Sat, till 5pm Sun), more comfortable extension carefully preserving the original style, two other small flagstoned rooms and a conservatory; summer folk events; children and dogs (in bar) welcome, benches out at front facing village green (surrounded by fine 19th-c stone merchants' houses), picnic-sets on side lawn and in nice walled garden, open all day.
(John and Eleanor Holdsworth, Michael Butler, Derek and Sylvia Stephenson, Richard Cole)

HEBDEN · SE0263
Clarendon (01756) 752446

B6265; BD23 5DE Pleasant well cared-for pub surrounded by wonderful moorland walking country; bar, snug and dining area, open fire, Thwaites and good variety of enjoyable plentiful food including blackboard choices, cheerful relaxed atmosphere; children welcome, farm shop, three updated bedrooms, open all day weekends.
(Claes Mauroy, Robert Wivell, B and M Kendall)

HEBDEN BRIDGE · SD9927
Old Gate (01422) 843993

Oldgate; HX7 8JP Smartly refurbished bar-restaurant with buzzy atmosphere, wide choice of good all-day food (till 7pm Sun), nine well kept ales and plenty of bottled beers, lots of wines by glass including champagne, bar popular with young people, upstairs room for comedy club and other events; children welcome, tables outside, open all day. *(Pat and Tony Martin, Pauline Fellows and Simon Robbins, Jim and Sheila Wilson)*

HEBDEN BRIDGE · SD9827
Stubbings Wharf (01422) 844107

About a mile W; HX7 6LU Friendly pub in good spot by Rochdale Canal with adjacent moorings, popular good value food (all day weekends, booking advised) from sandwiches and light meals up, half a dozen well kept regional ales, proper ciders; children and dogs welcome, boat trips, open all day.
(Jim and Sheila Wilson)

HEBDEN BRIDGE · SD9927
★White Lion (01422) 842197

Bridge Gate; HX7 8EX Solid stone-built 17th-c inn with spacious refurbished interior, good choice of enjoyable sensibly priced food from sandwiches and deli boards up, five well kept ales including Black Sheep and Timothy Taylors, friendly service; children welcome, dogs in snug, disabled facilities, attractive secluded riverside garden, ten good bedrooms (four in courtyard), open (and food) all day. *(Anon)*

HELMSLEY · SE6183
Feathers (01439) 770275

Market Place; YO62 5BH Substantial stone inn with sensibly priced generous food from sandwiches to good seasonal crab, popular Sun carvery, well kept Black Sheep, Tetleys and a guest, good friendly service, several rooms with comfortable seats, oak and walnut tables (some by Robert 'Mouseman' Thompson – as is the bar counter), flagstones or tartan carpet, heavy medieval beams and huge inglenook log fire, panelled corridors; children welcome in eating area, tables out in front, 22 clean comfortable bedrooms, open all day. *(Anon)*

HEPWORTH · SE1606
Butchers Arms (01484) 687147

Village signposted off A616 SE of Holmfirth; Towngate; HD9 1TE Old country dining pub under new licensees; enjoyable french-influenced food (till 7pm Sun, not Mon evening) including good value set menu, three well kept Yorkshire ales and decent wines by the glass, friendly staff, flagstones by counter, bare boards elsewhere, log fire, low beams (handsomely carved in room on right - a particularly nice beam-and-plank ceiling); children, walkers and dogs welcome, terrace seating, open all day. *(Karen Percival)*

HETTON · SD9658
★Angel (01756) 730263

Off B6265 Skipton–Grassington; BD23 6LT Busy dining pub with three neatly kept timbered and panelled rooms mainly set for their highly rated imaginative food (all day Sun), good friendly service, main bar with farmhouse range in stone fireplace, well kept Black Sheep, Dark Horse and a guest, 20 wines by the glass, lots of nooks and alcoves, country kitchen and dining chairs, plush seats, all sorts of tables, Ronald Searle wine-snob cartoons along with older engravings and photographs, log fires; children welcome, smart furniture on two covered terraces, good bedrooms, closed Jan. *(M J Daly, B and M Kendall, W K Wood, Peter Smith and Judith Brown, Ray and Winifred Halliday)*

HOLMFIRTH   SD1408
Nook (01484) 681568
Victoria Square/South Lane; HD9 2DN Friendly tucked-away 18th-c stone local (aka Rose & Crown) with own-brew beers and guests, no-frills bar areas with flagstones and quarry tiles, big open fire, low-priced home-made pubby food including good burgers, adjoining tapas bar; juke box and some live music, pool; heated streamside terrace, new bedrooms, open (and food) all day. *(Anon)*

HORBURY   SE2918
Boons (01924) 277267
Queen Street; WF4 6LP Lively, chatty and comfortably unpretentious flagstoned local, Clarkes, John Smiths, Timothy Taylors Landlord and up to four quickly changing guests, pleasant young staff, no food, rugby league memorabilia, warm fire, back tap room with pool; TV, no children; courtyard tables, open all day Fri-Sun. *(Michael Butler)*

HORBURY   SE2917
Bulls Head (01924) 265526
Southfield Lane; WF4 5AR Large open-plan pub popular locally for its food, smart attentive staff, Black Sheep and Tetleys, lots of wines by the glass; front picnic-sets. *(Michael Butler)*

HORBURY   SE2918
Cricketers (01924) 267032
Cluntergate; WF4 5AG Welcoming refurbished Edwardian pub, Black Sheep, Timothy Taylors and six local guests such as Five Towns, Tigertops and Sportsman (brewed at their sister pub in Huddersfield), also craft beers such as BrewDog, real cider and good selection of spirits, reasonably priced cheeseboards and meze platters, regular beer festivals, Weds quiz and monthly acoustic night; open all day Fri-Sun, from 4pm other days. *(Andy and Jill Kassube)*

HORSFORTH   SE2438
Brownlee Arms (0113) 258 1608
Long Row; LS18 5AA Stone-built dining pub recently taken over and comfortably refurbished by Greencliffe Taverns, good choice of enjoyable food, Timothy Taylors Landlord and guests, pleasant efficient

staff; children welcome, open (and food) all day. *(Gordon and Margaret Ormondroyd)*

HORSFORTH   SE2438
Town Street Tavern (0113) 281 9996
Town Street; LS18 4RJ Market Town Tavern with eight well kept ales and lots of draught/bottled continental beers, good generous food in small bare-boards bar and upstairs evening bistro (closed Sun), good service; children and dogs welcome, small terrace, open all day. *(Anon)*

HUBBERHOLME   SD9278
★ George (01756) 760223
Dubbs Lane; BD23 5JE Small beautifully placed ancient Dales inn under friendly newish owners; heavy beams, flagstones and stripped stone, enjoyable fairly priced home-made food including good steak and ale pie, four well kept beers such as Black Sheep and Tetleys, open fire, perpetual candle on bar; outside lavatories; children allowed in dining area, dogs usually welcome (but ask first), terrace seating, River Wharfe fishing rights, six comfortable clean bedrooms (three in annexe), good breakfast, closed Mon lunchtime, Tues, otherwise open all day. *(M J Daly, Steve Lumb)*

HUDDERSFIELD   SE1416
Grove (01484) 430113
Spring Grove Street; HD1 4BP Friendly two-bar pub with huge selection of bottled beers, 18 well kept/priced ales including Magic Rock, Timothy Taylors and Thornbridge, 120 malt whiskies and 60 vodkas, also real cider, knowledgeable staff, no food but choice of snacks from dried crickets to biltong, traditional Irish music (Thurs evening), art gallery; children and dogs welcome, back terrace, open all day. *(Anon)*

HUDDERSFIELD   SE1416
Head of Steam (01484) 454533
St Georges Square, part of the station (direct access to platform 1); HD1 1JF Railway memorabilia and old advertising signs, model trains, cars, buses and planes for sale, long bar with up to ten changing ales, lots of bottled beers, farm ciders and perry, good choice of enjoyable well priced food, black leather easy chairs and sofas, hot coal fire, back buffet, some live jazz and blues nights in lounge; unobtrusive background music, can be very busy; open all day. *(Jim and Sheila Wilson)*

HUDDERSFIELD   SE1416
Kings Head (01484) 511058
Station, St Georges Square; HD1 1JF Victorian station building housing friendly well run pub (perhaps more utilitarian than the alternative Head of Steam); large open-plan room with original tiled floor, two smaller rooms off, ten well kept beers, good sandwiches and cobs, some live afternoon/

evening music, Jimi Hendrix pub sign; disabled access via platform 1, open all day. *(Anon)*

HUDDERSFIELD   SE1416
Rat & Ratchet (01484) 542400
Chapel Hill; HD1 3EB Split-level flagstone and bare-boards local with its own-brew beers and several guests such as Fullers, Pictish and Ossett, good range of farm ciders/ perries too, pork pies and sausage rolls, friendly staff, some brewery memorabilia and music posters, pinball machine; open all day Fri-Sun, from 3pm other days. *(Anon)*

HUDDERSFIELD   SE1417
Slubbers Arms (01484) 429032
Halifax Old Road; HD1 6HW Friendly V-shaped traditional three-room pub, good range of beers including Timothy Taylors from horseshoe bar, pie-and-peas menu, black and white photographs and old wartime posters, warm fire, games room; well behaved dogs welcome, terrace for smokers, open all day and busy on match days. *(Jeremy King)*

HUDDERSFIELD   SE1417
Sportsman 07766 131123
St Johns Road; HD1 5AY Same owners as the West Riding Licensed Refreshment Rooms at Dewsbury; eight real ales including Black Sheep, Timothy Taylors and their own beers (brewed in the cellar), regular beer festivals, good value food such as meat and cheese boards, hot lunchtime food Fri-Sun (bargain roast), comfortable lounge and two cosy side rooms; handy for station, open all day. *(Andy and Jill Kassube, Tony Hobden)*

HUDDERSFIELD   SE1415
Star (01484) 545443
Albert Street, Lockwood; HD1 3PJ Unpretentious friendly local with excellent range of competitively priced ales kept well by enthusiastic landlady, continental beers and farm cider, beer festivals in back marquee, open fire; open all day weekends, closed Mon and lunchtimes Tues-Fri. *(Anon)*

HUDSWELL   NZ1400
George & Dragon (01748) 518373
Hudswell Lane; DL11 6BL Popular community-owned pub run by mother and daughter, good choice of well priced food (must book) including vegetarian and gluten-free options, well kept Black Sheep and guests, friendly atmosphere; children and dogs welcome, panoramic Swaledale views from back terrace, open all day weekends, closed Mon lunchtime. *(Ms S Young)*

HUGGATE   SE8855
Wolds Inn (01377) 288217
Driffield Road; YO42 1YH Traditional 16th-c village pub cheerfully blending locals' bar and games room with civilised and comfortable panelled dining room, enjoyable food including substantial mixed grill and

good fish pie, well kept Black Sheep, Timothy Taylors and guests, good range of wines; benches out in front, pleasant garden behind with delightful views, lovely village and good walks, handy for Wolds Way, three bedrooms, open all day Sun, closed Mon. *(Dr Kevan Tucker)*

HULL   TA0929
Hop & Vine 07500 543199
Albion Street; HU1 3TG Small basement bar with two or three interesting changing ales, good range of continental beers and farm ciders/perry, friendly knowledgeable staff, sandwiches (home-baked breads) and bargain basic specials; closed Sun, Mon and lunchtime Tues, otherwise open all day. *(Anon)*

HULL   TA1028
★ Olde White Harte (01482) 326363
Passage off Silver Street; HU1 1JG Ancient pub with Civil War history, carved heavy beams, attractive stained glass and two big inglenooks with frieze of delft tiles, well kept Caledonian, Theakstons and guests from copper-topped counter, 80 or so malt whiskies; old skull in a Perspex case (found here in the 19th c); children welcome, dogs in bar, heated courtyard, open all day. *(Anon)*

HULL   TA0929
Whalebone (01482) 226648
Wincolmlee; HU2 0PA Friendly local brewing its own good value ales such as Neckoil, also Copper Dragon, Tetley, Timothy Taylors Landlord and other guests, real ciders and perry, no food, old-fashioned décor and plenty of memorabilia including Hull City AFC and black and white photos of closed local pubs; open all day. *(Anon)*

HUTTON-LE-HOLE   SE7089
Crown (01751) 417343
The Green; YO62 6UA Overlooking pretty village green with wandering sheep in classic coach-trip country; enjoyable home-made pubby food (not Sun evening), Black Sheep, Tetleys and a guest, decent wines by the glass, cheerful efficient service, opened-up bar with varnished woodwork, dining area; quiz first Sun of month; children and clean dogs welcome, small site for caravans behind, Ryedale Folk Museum next door and handy for Farndale walks, open all day Sun till 6pm, closed winter Mon, Tues. *(Anon)*

ILKLEY   SE1147
Ilkley Moor Vaults (01943) 607012
Stockeld Road/Stourton Road, off A65 Leeds–Skipton; LS29 9HD Atmospheric flagstoned pub with good home-made food including own-smoked fish and meats, well kept Caledonian Deuchars IPA, Theakstons Black Bull, Timothy Taylors Landlord and a guest, decent wines by the glass, friendly helpful service, log fire; children welcome, open all day weekends, closed Mon. *(John and Eleanor Holdsworth)*

KEIGHLEY   SE0641
Boltmakers Arms (01535) 661936
East Parade; BD21 5HX Small open-plan
split-level character local, friendly and
bustling, with full Timothy Taylors range and
a guest kept well, keen prices, limited food,
lots to look at including brewing pictures
and celebrity photos, coal fire; Tues quiz,
some live music, sports TV; short walk from
Keighley & Worth Valley Railway, open all day.
(Anon)

KELD   NY8900
Keld Lodge (01748) 886259
Butthouse Rigg (B6270); DL11 6LL
Remote former youth hostel now serving as
village inn, three well kept Black Sheep ales
and tasty sensibly priced food, good service,
various rooms including conservatory-style
restaurant with superb Swaledale views;
children and dogs welcome, popular with
Coast to Coast walkers, 11 bedrooms, open
all day. *(Ian Collyer, Stephen Funnell)*

KETTLESING   SE2257
★ Queens Head (01423) 770263
*Village signposted off A59 W of
Harrogate; HG3 2LB* Popular stone pub
with good well priced traditional food,
L-shaped carpeted main bar with lots of
close-set cushioned dining chairs and tables,
open fires, little heraldic shields on walls,
19th-c song sheet covers and lithographs of
Queen Victoria, delft shelf of blue and white
china, smaller bar on left with built-in red
banquettes and cricketing prints, life-size
portrait of Elizabeth I in lobby, well kept
Black Sheep, Roosters and Theakstons, good
friendly service; background radio; children
welcome, seats in neatly kept suntrap back
garden, benches in front by lane, eight
bedrooms, open all day Sun. *(Margaret and
Peter Staples, John and Eleanor Holdsworth)*

KETTLEWELL   SD9672
Blue Bell (01756) 760230
Middle Lane; BD23 5QX Roomy knocked-
through 17th-c coaching inn, Copper Dragon
ales kept well and enjoyable home-made food
using local ingredients, low beams and snug
simple furnishings, old country photographs,
daily newspapers, woodburner, restaurant;
Sun quiz, TV and free wi-fi; children welcome,
shaded picnic-sets on cobbles facing bridge
over the Wharfe, six annexe bedrooms, open
(and food) all day. *(M J Daly)*

KETTLEWELL   SD9772
★ Kings Head (01756) 761600
The Green; BD23 5RD Recently
refurbished old pub tucked away near
church, flagstoned main bar with log fire
in big stone inglenook, three local ales and
well chosen wines, good affordably priced
food (all day Sun till 7pm) cooked by chef-
landlord from pub favourites to imaginative
restaurant dishes, efficient friendly service;

children welcome, no dogs inside, six
renovated bedrooms, attractive village
and good surrounding walks, closed Mon,
otherwise open all day. *(B and M Kendall)*

KETTLEWELL   SD9672
★ Racehorses (01756) 760233
B6160 N of Skipton; BD23 5QZ
Comfortable, civilised and friendly two-bar
inn with dining area, enjoyable sensibly
priced food, well kept Timothy Taylors ales,
good log fire; children welcome, dogs in bar
areas, front and back terrace seating, pretty
village well placed for Wharfedale walks,
parking can be difficult, 13 good bedrooms,
open all day. *(Anon)*

KILBURN   SE5179
Forresters Arms (01347) 868386
*Between A170 and A19 SW of Thirsk;
YO61 4AH* Welcoming beamed inn next to
Robert Thompson furniture workshops (early
examples of his work in both bars); roaring
fires, well kept local ales and good choice
of food including home-made ice-cream and
cakes, lounge and restaurant; background
music, TV; children welcome, dogs in some
areas, suntrap seats out in front, smokers'
shelter at back, ten bedrooms, open all day.
(Dr D J and Mrs S C Walker)

KILDWICK   SE0145
White Lion (01535) 632265
A629 Keighley–Skipton; BD20 9BH
Old two-bar stone pub near Leeds &
Liverpool Canal, enjoyable food (not Sun
evening) including good value theme nights,
Copper Dragon, Ilkley, Tetleys and Timothy
Taylors; children and dogs welcome, next to
ancient church in attractive village with nice
walks, two bedrooms, open all day. *(Dr Kevan
Tucker, Pat and Graham Williamson)*

KIRKBY OVERBLOW   SE3249
Shoulder of Mutton (01423) 871205
Main Street; HG3 1HD 19th-c village
pub with three linked areas, bare boards or
flagstones, comfortable banquettes, two open
fires, well kept ales such as Black Sheep and
Timothy Taylors Landlord and plenty of wines
by the glass, good freshly prepared food (all
day Sun till 7pm) including early-bird menu,
friendly attentive service, Sun quiz; picnic-
sets in back garden, shop, closed Mon.
(Margaret and Peter Staples)

KIRKBYMOORSIDE   SE6986
George & Dragon (01751) 433334
Market Place; YO62 6AA 17th-c coaching
inn, front bar with beams and panelling,
tub seats around wooden tables on carpet
or stripped wood, log fire, good choice of
well kept ales and several malt whiskies,
enjoyable generous bar food including
good value lunchtime set deal and Sun
carvery, afternoon teas, good service; also
a snug, bistro and more formal restaurant;
background music; children welcome, seats

and heaters on front and back terraces,
20 bedrooms, Weds market day, open all day.
(Peter Smith and Judith Brown)

KNARESBOROUGH   SE3556
⋆ **Blind Jacks** (01423) 869148

Market Place; HG5 8AL Simply done
multi-floor tavern in 18th-c building (pub
since 1990s), old-fashioned traditional
character with low beams, bare brick and
floorboards, cast-iron-framed tables, pews
and stools, brewery mirrors etc, ales from
on-site microbrewery along with changing
guests and draught continentals, friendly
helpful staff, limited food (cheese and pâté),
two small downstairs rooms, quieter upstairs;
well behaved children allowed away from bar,
dogs welcome, open all day weekends, from
4pm other days; shop next door sells all sorts
of rare bottled beers. *(Anon)*

KNARESBOROUGH   SE3457
Mitre (01423) 868948

Station Road; HG5 9AA Red-brick
1920s Market Town Tavern by the station,
clean fresh décor and friendly staff, up to
eight regional ales including Black Sheep,
Hawkshead and Roosters, interesting
continental beers, enjoyable sensibly priced
food (not Sun evening) in bar, side dining
room and evening brasserie (Fri, Sat),
live music Sun evening; children and dogs
welcome, terrace tables under parasols, four
bedrooms, open all day. *(B and M Kendall,
Roger and Donna Huggins)*

LANGTHWAITE   NY0002
⋆ **Charles Bathurst** (01748) 884567

*Arkengarthdale, a mile N towards Tan
Hill; DL11 6EN* Welcoming busy country
inn (worth checking no corporate events/
weddings on your visit) with strong emphasis
on dining and bedrooms, but pubby feel in
long bar; scrubbed pine tables and country
chairs on stripped floors, snug alcoves, open
fire, some stools by counter, Black Sheep,
Theakstons and Timothy Taylors, several
wines by the glass, popular often interesting
food, dining room with views of Scar House,
Robert 'Mousey' Thompson furniture, several
other dining areas; background music,
TV, pool, darts and other games; children
welcome, lovely walks from the door and
views over village and Arkengarthdale,
smart bedrooms (best not above dining
room), open all day. *(Anthony Barnes, WAH,
David and Ruth Hollands)*

LANGTHWAITE   NZ0002
⋆ **Red Lion** (01748) 884218

*Just off Reeth–Brough Arkengarthdale
Road; DL11 6RE* Proper pub dating from
17th c, homely and relaxing, in beguiling
Dales village with ancient bridge; friendly
and welcoming with character landlady,
lunchtime sandwiches, pasties and sausage
rolls, a couple of well kept Black Sheep
ales, Thatcher's cider, country wines, tea

and coffee, well behaved children allowed
lunchtime in low-ceilinged side snug,
newspapers and postcards; the ladies' is a
genuine bathroom; no dogs inside, good walks
including circular ones from the pub – maps
and guides for sale. *(Anthony Barnes, Comus
and Sarah Elliott)*

LASTINGHAM   SE7290
⋆ **Blacksmiths Arms** (01751) 417247

Off A170 W of Pickering; YO62 6TL
Popular old beamed pub opposite beautiful
Saxon church in charming village, log fire
in open range, traditional furnishings,
Theakstons and other regional ales, several
wines by the glass, good generously served
home-made food (not Sun evening),
friendly prompt service, darts, board games;
background music; children and walkers
welcome, seats in back garden, three
bedrooms, open all day in summer. *(Anon)*

LEALHOLM   NZ7607
⋆ **Board** (01947) 897279

Off A171 W of Whitby; YO21 2AJ
In wonderful moorland village spot by wide
pool of River Esk; homely bare-boards bar
on right with squishy old sofa and armchairs
by big black stove, local landscape
photographs on stripped-stone or maroon
walls, china cabinet and piano, left-hand bar
with another fire, traditional pub furniture,
darts and a stuffed otter, carpeted dining
room, four well kept changing ales, five
ciders (maybe a raspberry one) and dozens
of whiskies, good seasonal food using meat
from own farm and other local produce,
friendly helpful staff; children, dogs and
muddy boots welcome, secluded waterside
garden with decking, bedrooms (good
breakfast) and self-catering cottage,
open all day. *(Comus and Sarah Elliott,
Vikki and Matt Wharton)*

LEAVENING   SE7863
Jolly Farmers (01653) 658276

Main Street; YO17 9SA Bustling village
local, friendly and welcoming, with four
changing ales and popular good value
traditional food (not Mon, Tues), front bar
with eating area behind, separate dining
room; some live music; open all day weekends,
closed weekday lunchtimes. *(Anon)*

LEEDS   SE2932
Cross Keys (0113) 243 3711

Water Lane, Holbeck; LS11 5WD
Revamped early 19th-c pub; flagstones and
bare boards, stripped brick, original tiling
and timbers, old prints and photographs,
a collection of clocks in one part, four
interesting Yorkshire ales and imported
bottled beers, shortish choice of good well
prepared food (not Sun evening), winding
stairs up to function/dining room, newspapers
and board games; children welcome,
tables under big parasols in sheltered back
courtyard, open all day. *(Jeremy King)*

LEEDS SE3131
Garden Gate (0113) 277 7705
Whitfield Place, Hunslet; LS10 2QB
Impressive Edwardian pub (Grade II* listed)
owned by Leeds Brewery (closed for
maintenance as we went to press but should
have reopened by the time you read this);
their well kept ales from rare curved ceramic
counter, a wealth of other period features in
rooms off central drinking corridor including
intricate glass and woodwork, art nouveau
tiling, moulded ceilings and mosaic floors;
tables out in front. *(Anon)*

LEEDS SE2932
★ Grove (0113) 243 9254
Back Row, Holbeck; LS11 5PL Unspoilt
and lived-in 1930s-feel local overshadowed
by towering office blocks, tables and stools
in main bar with marble floor, panelling and
original fireplace, large back room and snug
off drinking corridor, good choice of well kept
ales including Daleside and Moorhouses,
Weston's cider, lunchtime food (not Sat),
friendly staff, regular live music; open all day.
(Anon)

LEEDS SE2932
Midnight Bell (0113) 244 5044
Water Lane, Holbeck; LS11 5QN Leeds
Brewery pub on two floors in Holbeck Urban
Village, three of their ales and guests kept
well, enjoyable home-made food (all day
weekends), friendly staff, light contemporary
décor mixing with original beams and
stripped brickwork; families welcome,
courtyard beer garden, open all day.
(Dr Kevan Tucker, Jeremy King)

LEEDS SE3037
Mustard Pot (0113) 269 5699
*Strainbeck Lane, Chapel Allerton;
LS7 3QY* Friendly management in relaxed
easy-going dining pub, enjoyable food (all day
Sun) from lunchtime sandwiches to daily
specials, Marstons-related ales, decent wines
by the glass, mix of furniture from farmhouse
tables and chairs to comfortable banquettes
and leather chesterfields, half-panelling and
open fire; background music; children welcome,
pleasant front garden, open all day. *(Anon)*

LEEDS SE2236
Palace (0113) 244 5882
Kirkgate; LS2 7DJ Traditional Nicholsons
pub with stripped boards and polished
panelling, friendly helpful staff, good choice
of reasonably priced food, Bass, Fullers,
Tetleys and six guests; no dogs inside, tables
out in front and in small back courtyard,
open (and food) all day from 10am. *(Anon)*

LEEDS SE2933
Pour House 07816 481492
Canal Wharf, Holbeck; LS11 5PS
Refurbished canalside pub in old granary
building, good value food from sandwiches
and sharing plates up, friendly service, two
Wharfe Bank ales and good choice of bottled
beers and other drinks, seating on two levels;
Mon quiz; open (and food) all day. *(Andy and
Jill Kassube)*

LEEDS SE2236
Railway Hotel (0113) 257 6603
*Calverley Bridge, Rodley; off A6120
Horsforth ring road; LS13 1NR* Friendly
straightforward pub by Leeds & Liverpool
Canal, enjoyable simple food, well kept Leeds
ales; children and dogs welcome, towpath
walks/cycling. *(Dr Kevan Tucker, John and
Eleanor Holdsworth)*

LEEDS SE3033
Victoria (0113) 245 1386
Great George Street; LS1 3DL Opulent
early Victorian pub with grand cut and
etched mirrors, impressive globe lamps
extending from majestic bar, carved
beams, leather-seat booths with working
snob screens, smaller rooms off, eight real
ales, friendly efficient service, standard
Nicholsons food in separate room with
serving hatch; open all day. *(Anon)*

LEEDS SE3033
★ Whitelocks (0113) 245 3950
*Turks Head Yard, off Briggate;
LS1 6HB* Classic Victorian pub, a
little worn around the edges but full of
character; long narrow bar with tiled
counter, grand mirrors, mahogany and glass
screens, heavy copper-topped tables and
red leather, well kept Theakstons ales and
enjoyable generous food, friendly hard-
working young staff; crowded at lunchtime;
children welcome, tables in narrow
courtyard, open (and food) all day.
(Eric Larkham, Kay and Alistair Butler)

LEYBURN SE1190
Black Swan (01969) 623131
Market Place; DL8 5AS Attractive old
creeper-clad hotel with chatty locals and
character landlord in cheerful open-plan
bar, decent range of food including
popular Sun carvery, quick service,
well kept Black Sheep Timothy Taylors,
Theakstons and a guest, good wines by the
glass; no credit cards; children welcome,
dogs before 6pm, disabled access, tables
on cobbled terrace, seven bedrooms, open
all day. *(Anon)*

Cribbage is a card game using a block of wood with holes for matchsticks or
special pins to score with; regulars in cribbage pubs are usually happy to teach
strangers how to play.

LEYBURN   SE1190
Bolton Arms (01969) 623327
Market Place; DL8 5BW Substantial
18th-c stone-built inn at top of marketplace,
well priced pub food including popular
Sun carvery, Black Sheep, Richmond and
Wensleydale, enjoyable mix of customers;
sports TV; seats outside, four bedrooms.
(Robert Wivell)

LINTHWAITE   SE1014
★ Sair (01484) 842370
Lane Top, Hoyle Ing, off A62; HD7 5SG
Old-fashioned four-room pub brewing its own
good value Linfit beers, pews and chairs on
rough flagstones or wood floors, log-burning
ranges, dominoes, cribbage and shove-
ha'penny, piano and vintage rock juke box; no
food or credit cards; dogs welcome, children
till 8pm, plenty of tables out in front with
fine Colne Valley views, restored Huddersfield
Narrow Canal nearby, open all day weekends,
from 5pm weekdays. *(Tony Hobden)*

LINTON   SE3846
★ Windmill (01937) 582209
Off A661 W of Wetherby; LS22 4HT
Welcoming upmarket pub on different levels,
beams and stripped stone, antique settles
around copper-topped tables, log fires, good
food including lunchtime bargains, more
expensive evening menu (not Sun), John
Smiths, Theakstons Best and guests, several
wines by the glass, fast friendly service,
restaurant and conservatory; background
music; children and dogs welcome, sunny
back terrace and sheltered garden with pear
tree raised from seed brought back from
Napoleonic Wars, two bedrooms in annexe,
open all day weekends. *(Margaret Tait,
Ray and Winifred Halliday, Robert Watt)*

LITTON   SD9074
Queens Arms (01756) 770096
Off B6160 N of Grassington; BD23 5QJ
Beautifully placed 17th-c Dales pub with
some redecoration under present owner;
main bar with stone floor and beam-and-
plank ceiling, old photographs on rough
stone walls, coal fire, plainer carpeted
dining room with woodburner and pictures
of local scenes, Black Sheep, Goose Eye and
Thwaites, enjoyable freshly made food from
baguettes up, friendly staff; children and
dogs welcome, plenty of seats in two-tier
garden, country views and good surrounding
walks, six bedrooms, open all day weekends,
closed Mon. *(Michael Doswell)*

LOFTHOUSE   SE1073
Crown (01423) 755206
*Pub signed from main road; Nidderdale;
HG3 5RZ* Prettily placed Dales pub,
friendly and relaxed, with hearty simple food
from good proper sandwiches up, well kept
Black Sheep and Theakstons, small public
bar, eating extension where children allowed;

no credit cards, outside gents'; dogs welcome,
good walks from the door, bedrooms.
(B and M Kendall)

LOW BRADFIELD   SK2691
Plough (0114) 285 1280
*Village signposted off B6077 and B6076
NW of Sheffield; New Road; S6 6HW*
Traditionally refurbished pub ideally placed
for some of South Yorkshire's finest scenery;
L-shaped bar with stone walls, comfortable
wall banquettes and captain's chairs, big
arched inglenook log fire, well kept Bradfield,
Thwaites and a guest, good value food from
sandwiches and baked potatoes to grills, two-
for-one deals weekday lunchtimes and Sun
carvery; background music, sports TV, Weds
quiz; children and dogs welcome, seats on
back verandah, terrace and lawn, good walks,
Damflask and Agden Reservoirs close by,
open (and food) all day. *(Peter F Marshall)*

LOW ROW   SD9898
★ Punch Bowl (01748) 886233
B6270 Reeth–Muker; DL11 6PF
17th-c country inn under same ownership
as the Charles Bathurst at Langthwaite;
long bare-boards bar with peaceful view
over Swaledale, stripped kitchen tables and
a variety of seats, armchairs and sofa by
woodburner at one end, pastel walls, good
food (menu on huge mirror) including some
interesting choices, nice wines by the glass,
well kept Black Sheep ales and a guest,
cheerful efficient staff, separate dining room
similar in style; wide views from terrace set
above road, comfortable bedrooms, good
breakfast, open all day. *(John Coatsworth,
Comus and Sarah Elliott, Michael Doswell,
Derek and Sylvia Stephenson)*

LUND   SE9748
★ Wellington (01377) 217294
Off B1248 SW of Driffield; YO25 9TE
Smart busy pub with cosy Farmers Bar,
beams, well polished wooden banquettes and
square tables, quirky fireplace, plainer side
room with flagstones and wine-theme décor,
Yorkstone walkway to room with village's
Britain in Bloom awards, highly rated well
presented food (not Sun evening and not
cheap) in restaurant and bistro dining area,
well kept ales including Timothy Taylors and
Theakstons, good wine list, 25 malt whiskies,
friendly efficient staff; background music,
TV; children welcome, benches in pretty
back courtyard, open all day Sun, closed Mon
lunchtime. *(Michael Butler, Pat and Stewart
Gordon, Roger A Bellingham, Dr Kevan Tucker,
P Dawn and others)*

MALHAM   SD9062
Lister Arms (01729) 830330
Off A65 NW of Skipton; BD23 4DB
Friendly creeper-clad stone-built inn tied
to Thwaites, their well kept ales (tasting
trays available) and lots of bottled imports,
enjoyable food including lunchtime

sandwiches, deli boards and daily specials, steps down to bare-boards dining room with stripped-pine tables, woodburners; children and dogs welcome, seats out overlooking small green, more in back garden, lovely spot by river and good walking country, nine comfortable clean bedrooms, open all day. *(Anon)*

MANFIELD NZ2213
Crown (01325) 374243
Vicars Lane; DL2 2RF Traditional unpretentious village local, friendly and welcoming, with eight interesting regularly changing ales including own Village Brewer beers (brewed by Hambleton), enjoyable simple home-made food, two bars and games room with pool; dogs welcome, garden, good walks nearby. *(Anon)*

MARSDEN SE0411
★ Riverhead Brewery Tap
(01484) 841270 *Peel Street, next to Co-op; just off A62 Huddersfield–Oldham; HD7 6BR* Owned by Ossett with up to ten well kept ales including Riverhead range (microbrewery visible from bare-boards bar), bustling friendly atmosphere, airy upstairs beamed restaurant with stripped tables (moors view from some) and open kitchen, good choice of enjoyable food including set menu; unobtrusive background music; dogs welcome, wheelchair access, some riverside tables, open all day. *(Tony Hobden)*

MASHAM SE2280
Kings Head (01765) 689295
Market Place; HG4 4EF Handsome 18th-c stone inn (Chef & Brewer), two modernised linked bars with stone fireplaces, well kept Black Sheep and Theakstons, nice choice of wines, good food served by friendly helpful staff, part-panelled restaurant; background music, TV; children welcome, tables out at front and in sunny back courtyard, 27 bedrooms, open all day. *(Dr and Mrs R G J Telfer)*

MASHAM SE2281
White Bear (01765) 689227
Wellgarth, Crosshills; signed off A6108 opposite turn into town; HG4 4EN Comfortably updated stone-built beamed inn, small public bar with full range of Theakstons ales kept well, larger lounge with welcoming coal fire, good choice of enjoyable food from sandwiches up (not Sun evening), decent wines by the glass, friendly efficient staff, restaurant extension; background music; children and dogs welcome, terrace tables, 14 bedrooms, open all day. *(Janet and Peter Race)*

MAUNBY SE3586
Buck (01845) 587777
Off A167 S of Northallerton; YO7 4HD Refurbished dining pub in out-of-way village by River Swale, interesting highly regarded food (not Sun evening, Mon) cooked by

owner-chef, also traditional choices and good value set menu, ales such as Rudgate and Theakstons, friendly helpful service, beamed bar with two log fires, more contemporary restaurant and conservatory with one huge table; children welcome, dogs in bar. *(Anon)*

MENSTON SE1744
Fox (01943) 873024
Bradford Road (A65/A6038); LS29 6EB Contemporary Mitchells & Butlers dining pub in former coaching inn on busy junction, good choice of popular fairly priced food, efficient friendly staff, Black Sheep, Timothy Taylors Landlord and a guest, Aspall's cider, big fireplace, flagstones and polished boards in one part; background music; two terraces looking beyond car park to cricket field, open all day. *(Lucien Perring, Gordon and Margaret Ormondroyd)*

MIDDLEHAM SE1287
★ White Swan (01969) 622093
Market Place; DL8 4PE Extended coaching inn opposite cobbled market town square, beamed and flagstoned entrance bar with built-in window pew and pubby furniture, open woodburner, well kept Theakstons ales, several wines by the glass and malt whiskies, enjoyable bistro-style food, friendly efficient staff, modern spacious dining room, large fireplace and small area with contemporary leather seats and sofa, more dining space in back room; background music; children welcome, comfortable bedrooms. *(WAH)*

MIDDLETON TYAS NZ2205
Shoulder of Mutton (01325) 377271
Just E of A1 Scotch Corner roundabout; DL10 6QX Welcoming old pub with three softly lit low ceilinged rooms on different levels, good freshly made food from snacks to appealing specials, well kept Adnams, Black Sheep and a guest, prompt friendly service; a useful A1/A66 stop. *(Gerry and Rosemary Dobson, Michael Doswell)*

MILLINGTON SE8351
Gait (01759) 302045
Main Street; YO42 1TX Friendly and popular 16th-c beamed local, well kept ales such as Haworth Steam, Titanic and Wold Top, enjoyable straightforward home-made food (maybe beef from own herd), nice mix of old and newer furnishings, large map of Yorkshire on the ceiling, big inglenook log fire, live music or quiz Weds; children and dogs welcome, garden picnic-sets, appealing village in good Wolds walking country, closed Mon and lunchtimes Tues-Thurs. *(Robert Wivell)*

MIRFIELD SE2017
Hare & Hounds (01924) 493814
Liley Lane (B6118 2 miles S); WF14 8EE Popular well cared-for Vintage Inn, attractive open-plan interior with several distinct areas (some down steps),

their usual good choice of reasonably priced food including fixed-price menu till 5pm (not Sun), well kept ales such as Black Sheep and Timothy Taylors, cheerful helpful staff, roaring log fire; children welcome, tables outside with good Pennine views, open (and food) all day. *(Gordon and Margaret Ormondroyd)*

MOULTON   NZ2303
⋆**Black Bull**   (01325) 377556
Just E of A1, a mile E of Scotch Corner; DL10 6QJ Recently refurbished village pub (part of Provenance Inns group), good food including charcoal-cooked steaks and plenty of fish/seafood, three real ales and decent choice of wines by the glass, flagstoned bar with woodburner in brick fireplace, scatter cushions on leather wall benches, dining area with attractive mix of antique-style chairs around dark pubby tables, also smart new dining extension with glass walls and doors leading on to big terrace; open all day.
(Anon)

MUKER   SD9097
⋆**Farmers Arms**   (01748) 886297
B6270 W of Reeth; DL11 6QG Small unpretentious walkers' pub in beautiful valley village, four well kept local ales, wines, teas and coffees, enjoyable straightforward good value food, warm fire, simple modern pine furniture, flagstones and panelling, darts and dominoes; soft background music; children and dogs welcome, hill views from terrace tables, stream across road, open all day. *(Anon)*

MYTHOLMROYD   SD9922
Hinchcliffe Arms   (01422) 883256
Off B6138 S at Cragg Vale; HX7 5TA Tucked-away old stone-built pub with really good food from traditional choices to more enterprising restaurant dishes (everything home-made), four well kept ales including a house beer from Ilkley, friendly staff, open fires; well behaved dogs allowed in bar, lovely setting near village church on road leading only to reservoir, popular with walkers, open all day weekends (Sun till 9pm), closed Mon and lunchtime Tues.
(John and Eleanor Holdsworth)

MYTHOLMROYD   SE0125
Shoulder of Mutton   (01422) 883165
New Road (B6138); HX7 5DZ Comfortable fairly basic local with popular low-priced home cooking, friendly efficient service, family dining areas and cosy child- and food-free parts, well kept Black Sheep, Copper Dragon, Timothy Taylors and guests, toby jugs and other china; sports

TV; streamside back terrace, open all day weekends. *(Tony Hobden)*

NAFFERTON   TA0559
Cross Keys   (01377) 256349
North Street; YO25 4JW Friendly corner pub in pretty Wolds village, enjoyable food including pub standards, pizzas, pasta and a few greek dishes (owner is greek), well kept John Smiths and Wold Top, some live music; children welcome, on National Cycle Route 1, open all day (from 3.30pm Mon). *(Dr Kevan Tucker)*

NEWTON-ON-OUSE   SE5160
⋆**Dawnay Arms**   (01347) 848345
Off A19 N of York; YO30 2BR 18th-c inn with two bars and airy river-view dining room, low beams, stripped masonry, open fire and inglenook woodburner, chunky pine tables and old pews on bare boards and flagstones, fishing memorabilia, highly regarded original food (till 6pm Sun), also good lunchtime sandwiches (home-baked bread), interesting vegetarian menu and children's choices, ales such as Tetleys and Timothy Taylors, good range of wines by the glass, friendly efficient service; terrace tables, lawn running down to Ouse moorings, handy for Beningbrough Hall (NT), closed Mon. *(Pat and Graham Williamson)*

NORLAND   SE0521
Moorcock   (01422) 832103
Moor Bottom Lane; HX6 3RP Modernised old building with fairly simple L-shaped bar and beamed restaurant, enjoyable food including set menus, friendly service, well kept Timothy Taylors and Thwaites; children welcome, fine valley views from village, popular scarecrow festival early Sept, open all day Fri-Sun, closed Mon and lunchtimes Tues-Thurs. *(Pat and Tony Martin)*

NORTH DALTON   SE9352
Star   (01377) 217688
B1246 Pocklington–Driffield; YO25 9UX Picturesque 18th-c inn next to village pond, good range of changing ales and man-sized helpings of well cooked food including blackboard specials, open-fire in pubby bar, restaurant; children welcome, bedrooms. *(C A Hall)*

NORTH RIGTON   SE2749
Square & Compass   (01423) 733031
Hall Green Lane/Rigton Hill; LS17 0DJ Substantial stone building recently reopened after refurbishment; beamed bar with Copper Dragon, Leeds and Theakstons, plenty of wines by the glass, good choice of food from

---

sandwiches and sharing boards up, pleasant service by aproned staff, restaurant; well behaved children and dogs (in bar) welcome, tables on tiered terrace, peaceful village, open all day from 10am. *(Revd R P Tickle)*

NORTH STAINLEY   SE2876
Staveley Arms (01765) 635439
A6108 Ripon–Masham; HG4 3HT Welcoming refurbished village pub, good food (not Sun evening, Mon) with some italian influences, early-bird menu and Sun carvery, well kept ales including Black Sheep and Theakstons; children welcome, garden seating, handy for Lightwater Valley.
(Janet and Peter Race)

NORTHALLERTON   SE3794
Tithe Bar (01609) 778482
Friarage Street; DL6 1DP Market Town Tavern with half a dozen good mainly local ales along with plenty of continental beers, tasty food including set deals, friendly young staff, three traditional bar areas, bare boards and brewery posters, upstairs evening brasserie; children and dogs welcome, open all day. *(Richard Tilbrook)*

NORWOOD GREEN   SE1326
Old White Beare (01274) 676645
Signed off A641 in Wyke, or off A58 Halifax–Leeds just W of Wyke; Village Street; HX3 8QG Nicely renovated and extended 16th-c pub named after ship whose timbers it incorporates; well kept Copper Dragon, Timothy Taylors and a guest, decent choice of food (all day weekends) including weekday fixed-price menu, bar with steps up to dining area, small character snug, imposing galleried flagstoned barn restaurant, some live music; children and dogs welcome, a few tables out in front and in back garden, Calderdale Way and Brontë Way pass the door, open all day. *(John and Eleanor Holdsworth, Gordon and Margaret Ormondroyd)*

NUNNINGTON   SE6679
Royal Oak (01439) 748271
Church Street; at back of village, which is signposted from A170 and B1257; YO62 5US Neatly refurbished old pub under new owners, bar with high beams and some old farm tools on a bare-stone wall, nice mix of furniture, dining area linked by double-sided woodburner, enjoyable food with tuscan influences, ales such as Theakstons and York, nice wines and italian coffee, bar billiards; children and dogs welcome, terrace seating, handy for Nunnington Hall (NT). *(Anon)*

OAKWORTH   SE0138
Grouse (01535) 643073
Harehills, Oldfield; 2 miles towards Colne; BD22 0RX Comfortable old pub with enjoyable food from light lunches to good steaks and daily specials, well kept Timothy Taylors ales, friendly service;

children and dogs (in snug) welcome, undisturbed hamlet in fine moorland surroundings, picnic-sets on terrace with lovely Pennine views, open (and food) all day. *(Anon)*

OLDSTEAD   SE5380
★ Black Swan (01347) 868387
Village signed off Thirsk Bank, W of Coxwold; YO61 4BL Tucked-away 16th-c restaurant with rooms in beautiful surroundings; bar with beams, flagstones and 'Mousey' Thompson furniture, log fire, lots of wines by the glass and well kept Black Sheep, attractive back dining rooms serving first class food (not cheap, but bar food and sandwiches available lunchtime), friendly attentive staff; children welcome, picnic-sets out in front, four comfortable well equipped bedrooms with own terrace, good breakfast, fine surrounding walks, closed lunchtimes Mon-Weds, two weeks in Jan. *(Hunter and Christine Wright)*

OSMOTHERLEY   SE4597
★ Golden Lion (01609) 883526
The Green, West End; off A19 N of Thirsk; DL6 3AA Attractive busy old stone pub with friendly welcome, Timothy Taylors and guests, around 50 malt whiskies, roomy beamed bar on left with old pews and a few decorations, similarly unpretentious well worn-in eating area on right, weekend dining room, well liked pubby food and good service; background music; children welcome, dogs in bar, seats in covered courtyard, benches out front looking across village green, 44-mile Lyke Wake Walk starts here and Coast to Coast one nearby, comfortable bedrooms, closed Mon and Tues lunchtimes, otherwise open all day. *(Anon)*

OSSETT   SE2719
★ Brewers Pride (01924) 273865
Low Mill Road/Healey Lane (long cul-de-sac by railway sidings, off B6128); WF5 8ND Friendly local with Bobs White Lion (brewed at back of pub), Rudgate Ruby Mild and seven guests, cosy front rooms and flagstoned bar, open fires, brewery memorabilia, good well priced food (not Sun evening), back dining extension and small games room, live music first Sun of month; well behaved children welcome, big back garden, near Calder & Hebble Navigation, open all day. *(Michael Butler)*

OSSETT   SE2719
Tap (01924) 272215
The Green; WF5 8JS Basic décor with flagstones and open fire, pleasant relaxed atmosphere, Ossett ales and guests (usually Fullers London Pride), decent wines by the glass, friendly staff and locals, photos of other Ossett pubs; small car park (parking elsewhere nearby can be difficult); open all day Thurs-Sun, from 3pm other days. *(Michael Butler)*

OTLEY SE2045
Chevin (01943) 876109
West Chevin Road, off A660; LS29 6BE
Well maintained pub largely rebuilt after fire, good home-made food including seasonal game and early evening deal, Timothy Taylors Landlord and a guest, friendly young staff; children and dogs welcome, garden with splendid Wharfedale views, open (and food) all day. *(John and Eleanor Holdsworth)*

OTLEY SE1945
Fleece (01943) 465034
Westgate (A659); LS21 3DT Smartly refurbished stone-built pub keeping original layout, full range of Wharfe Bank ales and three changing guests, good food (all day weekends) including early-bird deal Mon-Fri, dining room at back with fine views over River Wharfe, open fires; free wi-fi; children and dogs (in snug) welcome, front disabled access, garden sloping down to river, open all day. *(Gordon and Margaret Ormondroyd)*

OTLEY SE2045
Horse & Farrier (01943) 468400
Bridge Street; LS21 1BQ Modernised Market Town Tavern with five real ales and good reasonably priced food (all day weekends) including particularly well liked fish, most main courses available in smaller helpings, friendly young staff; disabled facilities, four bedrooms, nice outside seating area. *(Pat and Tony Martin)*

OTLEY SE2045
Old Cock (01943) 464424
Crossgate; LS21 1AA Traditional drinkers' pub with good choice of mainly local ales and a couple of ciders, some foreign beers too, no cooked food but good pies and sausage sandwiches; open all day. *(Pat and Tony Martin)*

OTLEY SE2047
Roebuck (01943) 463063
Roebuck Terrace; LS21 2EY Low-beamed pub refurbished to a high standard, good freshly made food from sandwiches and sharing plates up including range of hearty pies, Black Sheep, Saltaire, Tetleys and a guest, plenty of wines by the glass, good helpful service, log fire; children welcome, wheelchair access, tables out in neat garden, open 11am-10.45pm, food all day weekends. *(John and Eleanor Holdsworth)*

OXENHOPE SE0434
★ Dog & Gun (01535) 643159
Off B6141 towards Denholme; BD22 9SN Beautifully placed roomy 17th-c moorland pub, smartly extended, comfortable and often very busy, wide choice of good generously served food (best to book) from sandwiches up, attentive friendly staff and ebullient landlord, full Timothy Taylors range kept well, good selection of malts, beamery, copper, brasses, plates and jugs, big log fire

each end, padded settles and stools, glass-covered well in one dining area, wonderful views; five bedrooms in adjoining hotel, open all day weekends. *(Gordon and Margaret Ormondroyd, John and Eleanor Holdsworth)*

PICKERING SE7984
White Swan (01751) 472288
Market Place, just off A170; YO18 7AA Civilised and welcoming 16th-c coaching inn with cosy properly pubby bar, sofas and a few tables, panelling and log fire, Black Sheep, Timothy Taylors Landlord and a dozen wines by the glass, second bare-boards room with big bow window and handsome art nouveau iron fireplace, extremely good food in flagstoned restaurant and next-door deli, efficient friendly staff, residents' lounge in converted beamed barn; children and dogs (in bar) welcome, bedrooms, open all day from 7.30am. *(Dr D J and Mrs S C Walker, Comus and Sarah Elliott, Ian Herdman, Barbara and Peter Kelly, Janet and Peter Race and others)*

POOL SE2445
White Hart (0113) 203 7862
Just off A658 S of Harrogate, A659 E of Otley; LS21 1LH Light and airy Mitchells & Butlers dining pub (bigger inside than it looks), well liked food all day from sharing plates and pizzas to more restauranty dishes, fixed-price menu too, good service from friendly young staff, nice choice of wines by the glass, Leeds and Timothy Taylors, stylishly simple bistro eating areas, armchairs and sofas on bar's flagstones and bare boards; plenty of tables outside, open all day. *(Michael Butler)*

POTTO NZ4703
Dog & Gun (01642) 700232
Cooper Lane; DL6 3HQ Tucked-away modern bar-restaurant-hotel, clean contemporary décor, well liked food from varied menu, a house beer brewed by local Wainstones, Black Sheep and a guest, good choice of wines, friendly attentive service; tables under parasols on front decking, five bedrooms, closed lunchtimes Mon and Tues, otherwise open (and food) all day. *(Anon)*

REDMIRE SE0491
Bolton Arms (01969) 624336
Hargill Lane; DL8 4EA Friendly village pub under welcoming licensees, popular promptly served food, well kept Black Sheep, Theakstons, Thwaites and a guest, comfortable carpeted bar, attractive dining room; free wi-fi; disabled facilities, small garden, handy for Wensleydale Railway and Bolton Castle, good walks, five courtyard bedrooms, open all day. *(WAH)*

REETH SE0499
Buck (01748) 884210
Arkengarthdale Road/Silver Street; DL11 6SW Beamed 18th-c coaching inn by village green, Black Sheep, Caledonian,

Copper Dragon, Timothy Taylors and a guest, pizzas and other enjoyable home made food, regular live music including name bands; free wi-fi; children welcome, dogs in bar, a few tables out in front, also a secret walled garden, good walking country, ten bedrooms, open all day. *(Stephen Funnell)*

RIBBLEHEAD   SD7678

Station Inn (01524) 241274

B6255 Ingleton–Hawes; LA6 3AS
Great spot up on the moors by Ribblehead Viaduct (Settle to Carlisle trains), generous helpings of enjoyable home-made food (all day weekends), half a dozen well kept local ales and good value wines, tea and coffee, simple public bar with woodburner, dining room with open fire, viaduct and train pictures; background music, TV, darts and pool; children welcome, muddy boots and paws allowed in the bar, picnic-sets outside, refurbished bedrooms, bunkhouse and camping, open all day. *(Claes Mauroy)*

RICHMOND   NZ1701

Black Lion (01748) 826217

Finkle Street; DL10 4QB Family-run Georgian coaching inn with enjoyable good value food including lunchtime sandwiches/light meals and weekday early-bird deal (5-7pm), can eat in bar or upstairs restaurant, well kept Black Sheep, St Austell Tribute and Timothy Taylors Landlord, good friendly service, log fires; TV; dogs welcome in bar, comfortable reasonably priced bedrooms. *(Derek and Sylvia Stephenson)*

RIPLEY   SE2860

★ Boars Head (01423) 771888

Off A61 Harrogate–Ripon; HG3 3AY
Smart old hotel with informal relaxed atmosphere, long bar-bistro with nice mix of dining chairs and tables, warm yellow walls hung with golf clubs, cricket bats, some jolly cricketing/hunting drawings, a boar's head and an interesting religious carving, Black Sheep, Daleside and Theakstons, 20 wines by the glass and several malt whiskies, popular food (all day Sun) using produce from the Estate (the Ingilby family have lived in next-door Ripley Castle for over 650 years); children welcome, dogs in bar and bedrooms, pleasant little garden, open all day summer. *(Mr and Mrs P R Thomas, Janet and Peter Race)*

RIPON   SE3171

★ One-Eyed Rat (01765) 607704

Allhallowgate; HG4 1LQ Friendly little bare-boards pub with numerous well kept ales (occasional festivals), farm cider, draught continentals and lots of bottled beers, country wines too, long narrow bar with roaring fire, cigarette cards, framed beer mats, bank notes and old pictures, no food but may be free black pudding; pool;

children welcome, nice outside seating area, open all day Sat, closed weekday lunchtimes. *(Paul Humphreys, Paul Bromley)*

RIPON   SE3171

Royal Oak (01765) 602284

Kirkgate; HG4 1PB Centrally placed 18th-c coaching inn on pedestrianised street; smart modern refurbishment by Timothy Taylors with their ales and guests kept well and good choice of wines, dining area on two levels and much emphasis on good food (all day weekends) from sandwiches and pub staples to more enterprising dishes, lunchtime and early evening deals, good service; background music; children welcome, no dogs inside, teak furniture on courtyard terrace, six updated bedrooms, open all day. *(Paul Humphreys, Brian and Anna Marsden)*

RIPON   SE3171

Turf (01765) 602172

Ripon Spa Hotel, Park Street; HG4 2BU
Hotel's civilised racing theme bar/bistro, spacious and popular, with good food and friendly atmosphere, open fires; terrace tables. *(Janet and Peter Race)*

RIPON   SE3170

Water Rat (01765) 602251

Bondgate Green, off B6265; HG4 1QW
Small pub on two levels, prettily set by footbridge over River Skell and near restored canal basin; well kept ales including Black Sheep, a real cider and keenly priced wines, decent straightforward food, friendly service, conservatory; charming view of cathedral, ducks and weir from riverside terrace. *(M and J White, Paul Humphreys, Pat and Graham Williamson)*

RIPPONDEN   SE0319

Fox (01422) 825880

Oldham Road; just off M62 junction 22; HX6 4DP Modern timber-fronted pub-restaurant with wide choice of good food cooked by landlord-chef including fresh fish/seafood, efficient service, well kept Copper Dragon Golden Pippin and Thwaites Wainwright, live acoustic music last Thurs of month; children welcome, seats outside, open (and food) all day weekends, closed Mon-Thurs lunchtimes. *(Pat and Tony Martin)*

RISHWORTH   SE0316

Booth Wood (01422) 825600

Oldham Road (A672); HX6 4QU
Recently refurbished beamed and flagstoned country pub; local Oates beers and guests, good range of enjoyable well priced food from sandwiches to blackboard specials, lunchtime/early evening bargains, friendly staff, some leather sofas and wing-back chairs, woodburners, live music including folk nights; children welcome, open all day (from 9.30 Sun for breakfast). *(Jim and Sheila Wilson, Gordon and Margaret Ormondroyd)*

ROBIN HOOD'S BAY NZ9504
Bay Hotel (01947) 880278
The Dock, Bay Town; YO22 4SJ Friendly old village inn at end of the 191-mile Coast to Coast path – so popular with walkers; fine sea views from cosy picture-window upstairs bar (Wainwright bar downstairs open too if busy), ales including Caledonian Deuchars IPA and Theakstons, reasonably priced home-made food in bar and separate dining area from sandwiches up, young staff coping well, log fires; background music; dogs welcome, lots of tables outside, steep road down and no parking at bottom, open all day. *(Stephen Funnell, Barbara and Peter Kelly)*

ROBIN HOOD'S BAY NZ9505
Victoria (01947) 880205
Station Road; YO22 4RL Clifftop Victorian hotel with great bay views, good choice of beers from curved counter in traditional carpeted bar, enjoyable fresh food here, in restaurant or large family room, also a coffee shop/tea room; dogs welcome, useful car park, play area in big garden overlooking sea and village, comfortable bedrooms, good breakfast. *(Stephen Funnell)*

SALTBURN-BY-THE-SEA NZ6621
Ship (01287) 622361
A174 towards Whitby; TS12 1HF Beautiful setting among beached fishing boats, sea views from nautical-style black-beamed bars and big dining lounge, real ales, decent choice of wines by the glass and generous fairly priced food, friendly helpful service, restaurant and family room; tables outside, open all day in summer and can get very busy. *(Barbara and Peter Kelly)*

SANDSEND NZ8612
Hart (01947) 893304
East Row; YO21 3SU Shoreside pub with good choice of generously served traditional food including fish/seafood, well kept ales such as Black Sheep, prompt friendly service, log fire in beamed and flagstoned bar, upstairs dining room; dogs welcome, picnic-sets on small side terrace, open all day (till 6pm Sun). *(Stephen Woad)*

SAWDON TA9484
★Anvil (01723) 859896
Main Street; YO13 9DY Pretty high-raftered former smithy with good locally sourced food from chef-landlord, well kept ales including Black Sheep and nice range of wines, friendly attentive staff, feature smith's hearth, anvil and old tools, woodburner, lower-ceilinged second bar leading to small neat dining room; terrace seating, two self-catering cottages, closed Mon, Tues. *(Stanley and Annie Matthews, Garth and Lyn Lewis)*

SCARBOROUGH TA0588
Golden Ball (01723) 353899
Sandside, opposite harbour; YO11 1PG Mock-Tudor seafront pub with good harbour and bay views from highly prized window seats (busy in summer), panelled bar with some nautical memorabilia, well kept low-priced Sam Smiths; family lounge upstairs, tables out in yard, open all day. *(David Carr)*

SCARBOROUGH TA0387
Valley (01723) 372593
Valley Road; YO11 2LX Family-run Victorian pub with basement bar, up to six well kept changing ales and eight ciders/perries, excellent choice of bottled belgian beers too, friendly staff, no food, more seats upstairs and pool room; bedrooms, open all day. *(Anon)*

SCAWTON SE5483
★Hare (01845) 597769
Off A170 Thirsk–Helmsley; YO7 2HG Attractive quietly placed dining pub with really good imaginative food (not cheap) cooked by landlord-chef, nice wines by the glass and well kept ales such as Black Sheep, stripped-pine tables, heavy beams and some flagstones, open fire and woodburner, pub ghost called Bob; children and dogs (in bar) welcome, garden tables, closed Sun evening, Mon. *(Anon)*

SCORTON NZ2500
Farmers Arms (01748) 812533
Northside; DL10 6DW Comfortably refurbished little pub in terrace of old cottages overlooking green, well kept Black Sheep, Copper Dragon and Courage Directors, decent wines and enjoyable food including good rabbit pie, fresh Whitby fish and popular Sun lunch (till 3pm), friendly accommodating staff, bar with open fire, darts and dominoes, restaurant; background music, fortnightly quiz; children and dogs welcome, open all day Fri-Sun, closed Mon lunchtime. *(Pat and Stewart Gordon, Dr Brian Hands)*

SETTLE SD8163
Lion (01729) 822203
B6480 (main road through town), off A65 bypass; BD24 0HB Refurbished market-town inn with grand staircase sweeping down into baronial-style high-beamed hall bar, lovely log fire, second bar with bare boards and dark half-panelling, lots of old local photographs and another open fire, enjoyable all-day food including deli boards and specials, well kept Thwaites and occasional guests, decent wines by the glass, helpful welcoming staff, restaurant; Tues jazz, monthly quiz, silent TV and games

---

There are report forms at the back of the book.

machine; children and dogs welcome, courtyard tables, 14 bedrooms. *(Anon)*

SHEFFIELD SK3487
Bath (0114) 249 5151
Victoria Street, off Glossop Road; S3 7QL
Victorian corner pub with well restored 1930s interior, two rooms and a drinking corridor, friendly staff, well kept Thornbridge and guests, simple lunchtime bar food (sandwiches only Sat), live music Sun and Weds with some emphasis on jazz/blues; open all day (from 4pm Sun). *(Martin Day)*

SHEFFIELD SK3687
Beauchief (0114) 262 0500
Abbeydale Road South; S7 2QW Former railway hotel with good all-day food in bar and brasserie including Sun carvery, Thornbridge ales and nice choice of wines, friendly service; children welcome (under-8s eat free Mon-Fri), large garden, six bedrooms, open all day from 7am (happy hour 5-7pm). *(Tom and Ruth Rees)*

SHEFFIELD SK3687
★**Fat Cat** (0114) 249 4801
23 Alma Street; S3 8SA Deservedly busy town local with own Kelham Island ales and plenty of changing guests, draught and bottled belgian beers, real cider/perry and country wines, low-priced mainly vegetarian bar food (not Sun evening), friendly staff, two small downstairs rooms with coal fires, simple wooden tables and cushioned seats, brewery-related prints, jugs, bottles and advertising mirrors, upstairs overspill room; children away from main bar and dogs welcome, picnic-sets in back courtyard with heated smokers' shelter, new brewery shop/visitor centre (book tours on 0114 249 4804), open all day. *(Anon)*

SHEFFIELD SK3687
Gardeners Rest (0114) 272 4978
Neepsend Lane; S3 8AT Welcoming beer-enthusiast landlord serving his own good Sheffield ales from light wood counter, also several changing guests tapped from the cask, farm cider and continental beers, no food, old brewery memorabilia and changing local artwork, daily papers, games including bar billiards, live music and popular Sun quiz; well behaved children (till 9pm) and dogs welcome, disabled facilities, back conservatory and tables out overlooking River Don, open all day Thurs-Sun, from 3pm other days. *(Anon)*

SHEFFIELD SK3588
Harlequin (0114) 275 8195
Nursery Street; S3 8GG Welcoming open-plan corner pub owned by nearby Brew Company, their well kept ales and great selection of changing guests, also bottled imports and real ciders/perries, straightforward cheap lunchtime food including Sun roasts, beer festivals, weekend live music,

Weds quiz; children till 7pm and dogs welcome, outside seating, open all day. *(Anon)*

SHEFFIELD SK3687
★**Hillsborough** (0114) 232 2100
Langsett Road/Wood Street; by Primrose View tram stop; S6 2UB Chatty and friendly pub-in-hotel, own microbrews (brewed in cellar) along with four quickly changing guests, good choice of wines and soft drinks, generous well priced food including Sun roasts, daily papers, open fire, bare-boards bar, lounge, views to ski slope from attractive back conservatory and terrace tables; silent TV; children and dogs welcome, six good value bedrooms, covered parking, open all day. *(Anon)*

SHEFFIELD SK3290
★**New Barrack** (0114) 234 9148
601 Penistone Road, Hillsborough; S6 2GA Friendly lively pub with nine ales including Castle Rock and lots of bottled belgian beers, good choice of whiskies too, tasty unusual bar food (Fri, Sat light suppers till midnight), Sun carvery, comfortable front lounge with log fire and upholstered seats on old pine floors, tap room with another fire, back room for small functions, daily papers, bar billiards, regular events including chess club, live music and comedy nights; TV; children (till 9pm) and dogs welcome, attractive little walled garden, difficult local parking, closed lunchtimes Mon, Tues, otherwise open all day. *(Anon)*

SHEFFIELD SK3186
Ranmoor (0114) 230 1325
Fulwood Road (across from church); S10 3GD Comfortable and neat open-plan Victorian local, five well kept ales including Abbeydale, Bradfield and Timothy Taylors, good value home cooking (not Sun, Mon), leather sofas by etched bay windows, big mirrors and period fireplaces, well varnished tables, china display cabinet, piano (often played), newspapers; dogs welcome, two outside seating areas, open all day. *(Jeremy King)*

SHEFFIELD SK3185
Rising Sun (0114) 230 3855
Fulwood Road; S10 3QA Friendly drinkers' pub with 13 ales including seven from Abbeydale (July beer festival), plenty of bottled beers too, two rooms, one with raised back area, some leather sofas and other well worn furniture, prints and black and white photos, shelves of books, simple lunchtime food; soft background music (live Mon), quiz Weds and Sun; dogs welcome, a few tables out in front, more on back terrace, open all day. *(Jeremy King)*

SHEFFIELD SK3586
Sheffield Tap (0114) 273 7558
Station, platform 1B; S1 2BP Busy station bar in restored Edwardian refreshment room,

popular for its huge choice of world beers on draught and in bottles, also own Tapped ales from visible microbrewery and plenty of guests including Thornbridge, knowledgeable helpful staff, snacky food, tiled interior with vaulted roof; open all day. *(Anon)*

SHEFFIELD   SK3687
⋆**Wellington** (0114) 249 2295

Henry Street; by Shalesmoor tram stop; S3 7EQ Unpretentious relaxed corner pub with up to ten changing beers including own bargain Little Ale Cart brews, bottled imports, real cider, coal fire in lounge, photographs of old Sheffield, daily papers and pub games, friendly staff; tables out behind, open all day with afternoon break on Sun. *(Anon)*

SHELF   SE1127
Duke of York (01422) 203615

West Street; A644 Brighouse– Queensbury; HX3 7LN Traditional early 19th-c ivy-clad dining pub, three rooms with bar at back, enjoyable generously served food (all day weekends, till 7pm Sun) including lunchtime/early evening set menu, chiefly Timothy Taylors ales, beams, mullioned windows and open fires; children and dogs welcome, open all day. *(Gordon and Margaret Ormondroyd, John and Eleanor Holdsworth)*

SHELLEY   SE2112
⋆**Three Acres** (01484) 602606

Roydhouse (not signed); from B6116 towards Skelmanthorpe, turn left in Shelley (signposted Flockton, Elmley, Elmley Moor), go up lane for 2 miles towards radio mast; HD8 8LR Civilised former coaching inn with emphasis on hotel and dining side; roomy lounge with leather chesterfields, old prints and so forth, tankards hanging from main beam, well kept Copper Dragon, 40 malt whiskies and up to 17 wines by the glass from serious (not cheap) list, several formal dining rooms, wide choice of good if expensive food from lunchtime sandwiches up, competent friendly service; conferences, weddings and events; children welcome, fine moorland setting and lovely views, smart well equipped bedrooms. *(Gordon and Margaret Ormondroyd, Michael Butler)*

SHEPLEY   SE1809
Farmers Boy (01484) 605355

Marsh Lane, W of village – off A629 at Black Bull (leads on past pub to A635); HD8 8AP Smart stone-built dining pub, small traditional beamed public bar on right, Black Sheep, Bradfield and Copper Dragon, bare-boards area on left with coal fire and sturdy country tables, carpeted part rambling back through plenty of neat linen-set dining tables, barn restaurant with own terrace, popular often imaginative food, not cheap but good value set menu (weekday lunchtime, Mon-Thurs 6-7pm), friendly service;

unobtrusive background music; picnic-sets out in front, open all day. *(Anon)*

SHIPLEY   SE1437
Fannys Ale House (01274) 591419

Saltaire Road; BD18 3JN Cosy and friendly bare-boards alehouse on two floors, gas lighting, log fire and woodburner, brewery memorabilia, up to ten real ales including Timothy Taylors and Theakstons in top condition, bottled beers and farm ciders, back extension; can be crowded weekend evenings; dogs welcome, open all day, closed Mon lunchtime. *(James Stretton)*

SINNINGTON   SE7485
⋆**Fox & Hounds** (01751) 431577

Off A170 W of Pickering; YO62 6SQ Pretty village's popular 18th-c coaching inn, carpeted beamed bar with woodburner, various pictures and old artefacts, comfortable seats, imaginative well presented food, particularly friendly and helpful staff, well kept ales such as Black Sheep, Copper Dragon and Wold Top, several wines by the glass and some rare whiskies, lounge and smart separate restaurant; background music; children and dogs welcome, picnic-sets in front, more in garden, ten good comfortable bedrooms. *(Pat and Stewart Gordon)*

SKIPTON   SD9849
Copper Dragon Brewery
(01756) 7045560 *Snaygill Industrial Estate, Keighley Road; BD23 2QR* Visitor centre's modern bar/bistro across road from brewery, perhaps more canteeny than pubby, with full range of Copper Dragon ales, good plentiful food at realistic prices including daily specials, friendly efficient staff; brewery tours and shop, open all day Fri and Sat, till 4pm Sun, 3pm other days. *(Gordon and Margaret Ormondroyd)*

SKIPTON   SD9851
⋆**Narrow Boat** (01756) 797922

Victoria Street; pub signed down alley off Coach Street; BD23 1JE Lively extended pub down cobbled alley, eight well kept ales, draught and bottled continental beers, farm cider and perry, dining chairs, pews and stools around wooden tables on bare boards, various breweriana, upstairs galleried area with interesting canal mural, decent reasonably priced bar food (not Sun evening) including sausage menu, folk club Mon evening, quiz Weds; children allowed if eating, dogs welcome, picnic-sets under front colonnade, Leeds & Liverpool Canal nearby, open all day. *(David Jackman, Dr Kevan Tucker)*

SKIPTON   SD9851
Woolly Sheep (01756) 700966

Sheep Street; BD23 1HY Bustling narrow pub with full Timothy Taylors range kept well and a guest, prompt friendly enthusiastic service, two beamed bars off flagstoned passage, exposed brickwork, stone fireplace, lots of sheep prints and bric-a-brac, daily papers, attractive and comfortable raised lunchtime dining area at back, good value and variety of enjoyable food (plenty for children); wheelchair access with help, covered decked terrace behind, six good value bedrooms, good breakfast, open all day. *(Simon and Mandy King, B and M Kendall, M and J White, Dr Kevan Tucker, JHBS)*

SKIPTON SD9851
Yorkshire Rose (01756) 793884
Coach Street; BD23 1LH Former Rose & Crown under new owners, comfortable modern refurbishment with rugs on wood floors, some easy chairs and scatter-cushion wall benches, high chairs on flagstones around bar serving five real ales, good value pubby food including early-bird deal (Mon-Thurs), open fire in tartan carpeted part; Thurs quiz, sports TVs, games machine, free wi-fi; children and dogs welcome, beer garden, open (and food) all day. *(Anon)*

SLAITHWAITE SE0813
Commercial (01484) 846258
Carr Lane; HD7 5AN Centrally placed corner pub with eight real ales including two low-priced ones from local Empire, farm cider, some snacky food; dogs welcome, near the station and on the Transpennine Real Ale Trail, open all day. *(Tony Hobden)*

SLEDMERE SE9364
★ Triton (01377) 236078
B1252/B1253 junction, NW of Great Driffield; YO25 3XQ Handsome old inn by Sledmere House, open-plan bar with old-fashioned atmosphere, dark wooden furniture on red patterned carpet, 15 clocks ranging from grandfather to cuckoo, lots of willow pattern plates, all manner of paintings and pictures, open fire, Greene King, Timothy Taylors, Tetleys and Wold Top, 50 different gins, well liked freshly cooked food (only take bookings in separate restaurant), friendly helpful staff; children welcome till 8pm, five good bedrooms, massive breakfast, open all day Sun till 9pm, closed winter Mon lunchtime. *(Dennis Jones, Stanley and Annie Matthews)*

SNAINTON TA9182
Coachman (01723) 859231
Pickering Road W (A170); YO13 9PL More restaurant-with-rooms but also a small lively bar serving local ales, good well presented food in smart white-tableclothed dining room, friendly service, comfortable lounge with squashy sofas; well tended gardens, three bedrooms, good breakfast. *(Sara Fulton, Roger Baker)*

SNAITH SE6422
Brewers Arms (01405) 862404
Pontefract Road; DN14 9JS Georgian inn tied to local Old Mill brewery, their distinctive range from brick and timber-fronted servery, decent home-made food including fresh fish/seafood, friendly helpful staff, open-plan carpeted interior, old well complete with skeleton; children welcome in eating areas, refurbished bedrooms. *(Anon)*

SNAPE SE2684
★ Castle Arms (01677) 470270
Off B6268 Masham–Bedale; DL8 2TB Welcoming homely pub in pretty village, flagstoned bar with open fire, horsebrasses on beams, straightforward pubby furniture, Banks's, Jennings and Marstons, well liked bar food, dining room (also flagstoned) with dark tables and chairs and another fire; children and dogs welcome, picnic-sets out at front and in courtyard, fine walks in Yorkshire Dales and on North York Moors, nine bedrooms. *(John and Eleanor Holdsworth)*

SOUTH KILVINGTON SE4284
Old Oak Tree (01845) 523276
Stockton Road (A61); YO7 2NL Spacious low-ceilinged pub with three linked rooms and long back conservatory, good food and well kept beers served by friendly staff; tables on sloping lawn. *(Tina and David Woods-Taylor)*

SOWERBY BRIDGE SE0623
Jubilee Refreshment Rooms
(01422) 648285 *Sowerby Bridge Station; HX6 3AB* Refurbished 19th-c station building run by two railway-enthusiast brothers, up to six real ales, bottled continentals, ciders and perries, simple food including breakfast, good pies and home-made cakes, railway memorabilia, old enamel signs, art deco ceiling lamps and feature jeweller's clock; open all day from 9.30am (12 Sun). *(Pat and Tony Martin, Tony Hobden)*

SOWERBY BRIDGE SE0523
Works (01422) 834821
Hollins Mill Lane, off A58; HX6 2QG Big airy bare-boards pub in converted joinery workshop by Rochdale Canal, seating from pews to comfortable sofas, nine well kept ales and a couple of ciders, good bargain home-made food from sandwiches and pub favourites to vegetarian choices, Weds curry night, Sun brunch, comedy and music nights in big upstairs room; children and dogs welcome, backyard (covered in poor weather), disabled facilities, open all day. *(Anon)*

We accept no free drinks or meals and inspections are anonymous.

STAMFORD BRIDGE SE7055
★**Three Cups** (01759) 375901
A166 W of town; YO41 1AX Vintage Inn
family dining pub with popular food all day
including fixed-price menu till 5pm, plenty of
wines by the glass, ales such as Black Sheep
and Leeds, friendly helpful staff, pleasant
rustic décor with two blazing fires, glass-
topped well in bar; disabled access, play area
behind, river walks nearby. *(Margaret and Jeff
Graham, Roger A Bellingham, Pat and Graham
Williamson, Michael Butler)*

STANBURY SE0037
Old Silent (01535) 647437
Hob Lane; BD22 0HW Friendly
moorland dining pub under new ownership,
enjoyable reasonably priced home-made
food, Timothy Taylors Landlord, Theakstons
Old Peculier and guests, attentive helpful
service, character linked rooms with
beams, flagstones, mullioned windows and
open fires, restaurant and conservatory;
free wi-fi; children and dogs welcome,
bedrooms, open all day till 9pm (8pm Sun).
(Anon)

STAVELEY SE3662
Royal Oak (01423) 340267
*Signed off A6055 Knaresborough–
Boroughbridge; HG5 9LD* Popular
welcoming pub in village conservation area;
beams and panelling, open fires, broad bow
window overlooking front lawn, well kept
Black Sheep, Timothy Taylors and a guest,
several wines by the glass, good choice
of enjoyable food in bar and restaurant.
(David Battle)

STILLINGTON SE5867
Bay Tree (01347) 811394
*Main Street; leave York on outer ring
road (A1237) to Scarborough, first exit
on left signposted B1363 to Helmsley;
YO61 1JU* Cottagey pub-restaurant in
pretty village's main street, contemporary
bar areas with civilised chatty atmosphere,
comfortable cushioned wall seats and
leather/bamboo tub chairs around mix
of tables, church candles and lanterns,
central gas-effect coal fire, real ales such
as Black Sheep, several wines by the glass
and enjoyable bistro-style food including
blackboard specials, steps up to cosy
dining area, larger conservatory-style back
restaurant; background music; seats in
garden and a couple of picnic-sets at front,
closed Mon. *(Michael Butler)*

STOKESLEY NZ5208
★**White Swan** (01642) 710263
West End; TS9 5BL Good Captain Cook
ales brewed in this attractive flower-clad
pub, L-shaped bar with three relaxing
seating areas, log fire, lots of brass on elegant
dark panelling, lovely bar counter carving,
assorted memorabilia and unusual clock,

good lunchtime ploughman's (Weds-Sat), live
music and beer festivals; no children, dogs
welcome, open all day. *(Anon)*

SUTTON UPON DERWENT SE7047
★**St Vincent Arms** (01904) 608349
*Main Street (B1228 SE of York);
YO41 4BN* Enjoyable cheerful pub with
Fullers and up to seven guests, lots of wines
by the glass, good popular bar food (more
elaborate evening meals – need to book
weekends), bustling parlour-style front bar
with panelling, traditional high-backed
settles, windsor chairs, cushioned bow-
window seat and gas-effect coal fire, another
lounge and separate dining room open off
here; children welcome, dogs in bar, garden
tables, handy for Yorkshire Air Museum.
(Kay and Alistair Butler)

SWANLAND SE9928
Swan & Cygnet (01482) 634571
Main Street; HU14 3QP Modernised
open-plan village pub, clean and bright, with
good home-cooked food including monthly
changing set menus, well kept Marstons-
related beers, good service. *(C A Hall)*

TAN HILL NY8906
Tan Hill Inn (01833) 628246
*Arkengarthdale Road, Reeth–Brough,
at junction Keld/West Stonesdale Road;
DL11 6ED* Basic old pub (Britain's highest)
in wonderful bleak setting on Pennine
Way, full of bric-a-brac and interesting
photographs, simple sturdy furniture,
flagstones, ever-burning big log fire (with
prized stone side seats), chatty atmosphere,
five well kept ales including one badged for
them from Dent, good cheap pubby food,
family room, live weekend music; can get
overcrowded, often snowbound; children and
dogs welcome, seven bedrooms, bunk rooms
and camping, ducks and chickens, Swaledale
sheep show here last Thurs in May, open
all day. *(Comus and Sarah Elliott)*

THIRSK SE4282
Golden Fleece (01845) 523108
Market Place; YO7 1LL Comfortable
bustling old coaching inn with enjoyable bar
food, Black Sheep ales and good friendly
service, restaurant, view across marketplace
from bay windows; dogs welcome, 23
bedrooms, good breakfast. *(Dr D J and
Mrs S C Walker)*

THIXENDALE SE8461
Cross Keys (01377) 288272
*Off A166 3 miles N of Fridaythorpe;
YO17 9TG* Unspoilt welcoming country
pub in deep valley below the rolling Wolds
and popular with walkers; cosy and relaxed
L-shaped bar with fitted wall seats, well kept
Tetleys and a couple of guests, generous
uncomplicated blackboard food; no children
inside; big garden behind with views, handy
for Wharram Percy earthworks, comfortable

bedrooms in converted stables, good breakfast, closed Mon lunchtime (Mon-Thurs lunchtimes winter). *(Brian and Anna Marsden)*

THOLTHORPE SE4766
New Inn (01347) 838329
Flawith Road; YO61 1SL Cleanly updated beamed village-green pub with log-fire bar and candlelit restaurant, good locally sourced food (not Tues lunchtime) including early-bird deal, allergies catered for, John Smiths and a local guest; children welcome, closed Mon. *(John and Eleanor Holdsworth)*

THORNTON SE0933
Ring o' Bells (01274) 832296
Hill Top Road, W of village, and N of B6145; BD13 3QL Hilltop dining pub under long-serving owners, cosy series of linked rooms with dark beams and panelling, plush seating for glass-topped tables on red carpeting, old local photographs at one end, more modern restaurant the other, Black Sheep Best, Copper Dragon Golden Pippin and Saltaire Blonde, nine wines by the glass and 20 malt whiskies, quite a range of food from pubby dishes up; background music; high position gives long views towards Shipley and Bingley. *(John and Eleanor Holdsworth)*

THORNTON SE0832
White Horse (01274) 834268
Well Heads; BD13 3SJ Deceptively large country pub popular for its wide choice of good food including an early-bird menu, five well kept Timothy Taylors ales, pleasant helpful staff, four separate areas, two with log fires; upstairs lavatories (disabled ones on ground level), also disabled space in car park. *(Gordon and Margaret Ormondroyd, John and Eleanor Holdsworth)*

THORNTON-LE-CLAY SE6865
White Swan (01653) 618286
Off A64 SW of Malton, via Foston; Low Street; YO60 7TG Refurbished 19th-c family-run village pub; Black Sheep, Moorhouses and a beer named for the pub, nice wines by the glass and generous well priced home-made food including daily specials, friendly helpful young staff, some local chutneys, preserves etc for sale; children welcome, large garden (maybe summer bouncy castle), attractive countryside nearby and Castle Howard, closed Mon, Tues. *(Gordon and Margaret Ormondroyd)*

THORP ARCH SE4346
Pax (01937) 843183
The Village; LS23 7AR 19th-c village pub continuing well under present welcoming licensees, enjoyable home-made food

(notable steak and ale pie) at sensible prices, changing ales such as Abbeydale, Moorhouses and Roosters, friendly helpful service, two bar areas, open fire, back dining area; children and dogs welcome, useful for A1, open all day weekends, closed Mon. *(Les and Sandra Brown)*

THRESHFIELD SD9863
Old Hall Inn (01756) 752441
B6160/B6265 just outside Grassington; BD23 5HB Popular old village inn with well cooked attractively presented food from landlord-chef, good choice of beers and wines, linked rooms including smart dining room, open fires (one in fine blacked kitchen range), high beam-and-plank ceiling, cushioned wall pews; neat garden and pretty hanging baskets, comfortable bedrooms, self-catering cottage, open (and food) all day. *(Pat and Stewart Gordon, T Peter Wall)*

TIMBLE SE1852
★ **Timble Inn** (01943) 880530
Off Otley–Blubberhouses moors road; LS21 2NN Smartly restored 18th-c inn tucked away in quiet farmland hamlet, good food from pub favourites up including well aged Nidderdale beef (booking advised), Timothy Taylors Landlord, Theakstons and a guest; children welcome, no dogs at food times, good walks from the door, seven well appointed bedrooms, closed Sun evening, Mon and Tues. *(Janet and Peter Race)*

TOCKWITH SE4652
Spotted Ox (01423) 358387
Westfield Road, off B1224; YO26 7PY Traditional beamed village local, friendly and relaxed, with well served ales including Tetleys, good choice of enjoyable sensibly priced home-made food, attentive staff, three areas off central bar, interesting local history; open all day Fri-Sun. *(Les and Sandra Brown)*

TONG SE2230
Greyhound (0113) 285 2427
Tong Lane; BD4 0RR Traditional low-beamed and flagstoned local by village cricket field, distinctive areas including cosy dining room, generous helpings of enjoyable good value food, ales including Black Sheep, Leeds, Timothy Taylors and Tetleys, several wines by the glass, good friendly service; tables outside, open all day (food till 5.45pm Sun). *(Gordon and Margaret Ormondroyd)*

TOPCLIFFE SE4076
Angel (01845) 578000
Off A1, take A168 to Thirsk, after 3 miles follow signs for Topcliffe; Long Street; YO7 3RW Part of the growing West Park Inns group; bare-boards bar with log fire, real ales and good choice of wines by the glass,

---

If we know a pub has an outdoor play area for children, we mention it.

enjoyable food in carpeted grill restaurant, weekday early-bird deal (5-6pm), pleasant helpful service; background music, comedy night first Tues of month; children welcome, nice garden, 16 bedrooms, open all day. *(John and Eleanor Holdsworth)*

TOTLEY   SK3080
Cricket (0114) 236 5256
Signed from A621; Penny Lane; S17 3AZ Tucked-away 19th-c stone-built pub (part of the BrewKitchen group) beside rustic cricket field, much focus on dining but still a friendly local atmosphere, pews, mixed chairs and pine tables on bare boards and flagstones, log fires, good quality blackboard food from sandwiches and pub staples to more unusual choices including portuguese dishes and own-smoked fish/meats, cheaper lunchtime/early evening set menu (Mon-Fri), Thornbridge ales and good choice of wines from extensive list, friendly service; children and dogs welcome, outside tables and summer barbecues, Peak District views, open (and food) all day. *(Mrs Jo Rees)*

TOWTON   SE4839
Rockingham Arms (01937) 530948
A162 Tadcaster–Ferrybridge; LS24 9PB Comfortably refurbished roadside village pub, enjoyable home-made food including early-bird menu (5-7pm Tues-Thurs), friendly attentive service, ales such as Black Sheep and Theakstons, back conservatory; garden tables, handy for Towton Battlefield, closed Sun evening, Mon, otherwise open all day. *(Robert Wivell, Revd R P Tickle)*

WAKEFIELD   SE3320
Bull & Fairhouse (01924) 362930
George Street; WF1 1DL Welcoming chatty 19th-c pub, well kept Bobs White Lion, Great Heck Golden Bull and four other changing ales (beer festivals), bare-boards bar with comfortable rooms off, open fire, no food, live music weekends, quiz Thurs; children welcome till 8pm, dogs on leads, open all day Fri-Sun, from 4pm other days. *(Anon)*

WAKEFIELD   SE3417
Castle (01924) 256981
Barnsley Road, Sandal; WF2 6AS Popular refurbished dining pub with good affordably priced food cooked to order, well kept beers such as York, friendly staff and pleasant relaxed atmosphere; unobtrusive background music. *(Michael Butler, John and Eleanor Holdsworth)*

WAKEFIELD   SE3320
Fernandes Brewery Tap
(01924) 386348 *Avison Yard, Kirkgate; WF1 1UA* Owned by Ossett but still brewing Fernandes ales in cellar, interesting guest beers, bottled imports and traditional ciders, newish ground-floor bar with flagstones, bare brick and panelling, original raftered top-floor bar with unusual breweriana;

dogs welcome, open all day Fri-Sun (when some lunchtime food available), from 4pm other days. *(Anon)*

WAKEFIELD   SE3220
Harrys Bar (01924) 373773
Westgate; WF1 1EL Cheery little one-room local with well kept Leeds, Ossett and guests, stripped-brick walls, open fire, live music Weds; small back garden, open all day Sun, closed lunchtime other days. *(Anon)*

WALKINGTON   SE9937
Dog & Duck (01482) 423026
B1230, East End; HU17 8RX Comfortably modernised pub with enjoyable generously served food including blackboard specials, four well kept Marstons-related beers, friendly helpful service; sports TV; children welcome, garden and terrace with pizza oven and barbecue, charming village, open (and food) all day. *(Michael Butler)*

WALKINGTON   SE9937
Ferguson-Fawsitt Arms
(01482) 882665 *East End; B1230 W of Beverley; HU17 8RX* Named after two important local families and known as the 'Fergie'; wide choice of popular reasonably priced food including carvery (all day Sun), good friendly service, real ales and decent wines, interesting mock-Tudor bars; children welcome, tables out on terrace, ten good value bedrooms in modern annexe, delightful village. *(Michael Butler)*

WALTON   SE4447
Fox & Hounds (01937) 842192
Hall Park Road, off back road Wetherby–Tadcaster; LS23 7DQ Welcoming dining pub with good reasonably priced food from sandwiches to specials (should book Sun lunch), well kept Black Sheep, John Smiths and a guest, friendly thriving atmosphere; children welcome, handy A1 stop. *(Robert Wivell, Malcolm and Pauline Pellatt)*

WALTON   SE3517
New Inn (01924) 255447
Shay Lane; WF2 6LA Refurbished open-plan village pub with several well kept beers including Ossett, Theakstons and Timothy Taylors, good helpings of tasty well priced food, friendly staff and buoyant atmosphere, split-level back dining extension; quiz and music nights; children welcome, dogs in bar, open (and food) all day. *(Michael Butler)*

WATH   SE3277
George (01765) 641324
Main Street; village N of Ripon; HG4 5EN Friendly refurbished village pub with good range of enjoyable traditional food (not Sun evening), Rudgate, Theakstons and a guest, decent choice of wines; five comfortable bedrooms, open all day weekends closed lunchtimes Mon, Tues. *(Andy and Jill Kassube)*

WATH-IN-NIDDERDALE   SE1467
⋆ **Sportsmans Arms** (01423) 711306
Nidderdale road off B6265 in Pateley Bridge; village and pub signposted over hump-back bridge, on right after a couple of miles; HG3 5PP Civilised, beautifully located restaurant with rooms run by long-serving owner, most emphasis on the excellent food and bedrooms but has proper welcoming bar with open fire (a highly rated ploughman's here), Black Sheep and Timothy Taylors Landlord, Thatcher's cider, 20 wines by the glass from extensive list and 40 malt whiskies, helpful hospitable staff; background music; children welcome, dogs in bar, benches and tables outside and seats in pretty garden with croquet, own fishing on River Nidd. *(Janet and Peter Race, Stephen Woad, M and J White, Hunter and Christine Wright, Gordon and Margaret Ormondroyd, Lynda and Trevor Smith)*

WEAVERTHORPE   SE9670
Blue Bell (01944) 738204
Main Road; YO17 8EX Upscale country dining pub, quite ornate in parts, with good attractively presented food and fine choice of wines (many by the glass including champagne), well kept Tetleys and Timothy Taylors Landlord, cosy cheerful bar with unusual collection of bottles and packaging, open fire, intimate back restaurant, friendly attentive staff; 12 bedrooms (six in annexe), interesting village, closed Sun evening, Mon. *(R G Stollery)*

WELBURN   SE7168
⋆ **Crown & Cushion** (01653) 618777
Off A64; YO60 7DZ Welcoming much-refurbished and extended 18th-c village pub (part of the Provenance Inns group), beams and log fires, exposed stone walls and good mix of furniture including cushioned settles on red and black tiles or bare boards, collections of stone bottles and copper cooking implements, well kept Black Sheep, Golden Sheep and a guest, enjoyable good value food (all day Sun) from bar snacks up including set lunch and early-bird deals, friendly helpful staff; children and dogs welcome, attractive small back garden with modern furniture on paved terrace, handy for Castle Howard, open all day Fri-Sun. *(Dr and Mrs J D Abell)*

WENSLEY   SE0989
Three Horseshoes (01969) 622327
A684; DL8 4HJ Simple little beamed and flagstoned country pub, friendly staff and regulars, warm woodburner, good selection of local ales and tasty straightforward food; outside lavatories; dogs welcome, lovely views from garden, popular with walkers, open all day. *(Anon)*

WEST TANFIELD   SE2678
Bruce Arms (01677) 470325
Main Street (A6108 N of Ripon); HG4 5JJ Comfortable and welcoming with good affordably priced food from landlord-chef, well kept Black Sheep and Copper Dragon, nice wines, flagstones and log fires; two bedrooms, good breakfast, closed Mon. *(Anon)*

WEST TANFIELD   SE2678
Bull (01677) 470678
Church Street (A6108 N of Ripon); HG4 5JQ Open-plan with slightly raised dining area to the left and flagstoned bar on right, popular fairly standard food (all day Sat, not Sun evening), well kept Black Sheep and Theakstons, friendly service; background and occasional live music; children (away from bar) and dogs welcome, tables on terraces in attractive garden sloping steeply to River Ure and its old bridge, five bedrooms, open all day weekends, closed Tues. *(Anon)*

WEST WITTON   SE0588
Wensleydale Heifer (01969) 622322
A684 W of Leyburn; DL8 4LS Stylish restaurant-with-rooms rather than pub, but can pop in just for a drink; excellent food with emphasis on fish/seafood and grills (not cheap), also lunchtime 'tapas' and good value set menu (lunchtime/early evening), good wines, cosy informal upmarket food bar with Black Sheep and a house beer brewed by Yorkshire, extensive main formal restaurant, attentive helpful service; saucy seaside postcards in gents', 13 good bedrooms (back ones quietest), big breakfast, open all day. *(Geoff and Linda Payne, Comus and Sarah Elliott)*

WESTOW   SE7565
Blacksmiths Arms (01653) 619606
Off A64 York–Malton; Main Street; YO60 7NE 18th-c pub with attractive beamed bar, woodburner in brick inglenook, original bread oven, beers such as Copper Dragon, Tetleys and Thwaites, home-made food from sandwiches and pub favourites up, restaurant; picnic-sets on side terrace, closed Mon, otherwise open all day. *(Michael Butler)*

WETHERBY   SE4048
Swan & Talbot (01937) 582040
Handy for A1; North Street; LS22 6NN Comfortable traditional town pub (a former posting inn) with large bar area and restaurant, good generous food including deals and daily specials, well kept ales such

---

A few pubs try to make you leave a credit card at the bar, as a sort of deposit if you order food. This is a bad practice, and the banks and credit card firms warn you not to let your card go like this.

as Black Sheep, Fullers and John Smiths, busy friendly staff; children welcome, courtyard tables, open all day. *(Gordon and Jenny Quick)*

WHITBY   NZ9011
Black Horse (01947) 602906
Church Street; YO22 4BH Small traditional two-room pub, much older than its Victorian frontage, and previously a funeral parlour and brothel; friendly and down to earth with well kept Adnams, Black Dog, Timothy Taylors and a couple of guests, Yorkshire 'tapas', tins of snuff for sale; dogs welcome, four cosy bedrooms open all day. *(Sarah Marriott, David Carr)*

WHITBY   NZ9011
Board (01947) 602884
Church Street; YO22 4DE Busy pub in good spot opposite fish quay, faux-beamed bar with nice old range in one part, banquettes and other pubby furniture on patterned carpet, modern dining room downstairs with fine harbour view from big windows, well kept Caledonian Deuchars IPA and Theakstons, good value pub food, friendly staff; background and live music, Weds quiz, TV and games machine; bedrooms. *(Stanley and Annie Matthews)*

WHITBY   NZ9011
Dolphin (01947) 602197
Bridge Street, just over bridge to E/Old Whitby; YO22 4BG Well positioned inn with good harbour views, enjoyable home-made food from lunchtime sandwiches up, friendly service, ales such as Black Sheep, Copper Dragon and Timothy Taylors, various linked areas on different levels; TV, games machine, darts; children and dogs welcome, seats out in front by swing bridge, six bedrooms (five with views). *(David Carr)*

WHITBY   NZ9011
★ ## Duke of York (01947) 600324
Church Street, Harbour East Side; YO22 4DE Busy pub in fine harbourside position, good views and handy for the famous 199 steps leading up to abbey; comfortable beamed lounge bar with fishing memorabilia, Black Sheep, Caledonian and three guests, decent wines and several malt whiskies, enjoyable straightforward bar food, attentive service; background music, TV, games machine; children welcome, bedrooms overlooking water, no nearby parking, open (and food) all day. *(Comus and Sarah Elliott, Pat and Graham Williamson, David Carr)*

WHITBY   NZ8911
Station Inn (01947) 603937
New Quay Road; YO21 1DH Friendly three-room bare-boards drinkers' pub across from the station and harbour, clean and comfortable, with good mix of customers, seven well kept ales including a house beer brewed by Whitby, Weston's cider and

good wines by the glass, traditional games; background and regular live music; dogs welcome, open all day. *(Anon)*

WIGGLESWORTH   SD8056
Plough (01729) 840243
B6478, off A65 S of Settle; BD23 4RJ Light, airy and comfortable old inn with good elegantly presented modern food (all day Sun till 7pm), friendly efficient service, local ales and decent wines by the glass, cosy log fire, panoramic Dales views; bedrooms. *(Anon)*

WIGHILL   SE4746
White Swan (01937) 832217
Main Street; LS24 8BQ Updated fairly modern village pub with two cosy front rooms and larger side extension, enjoyable traditional home-cooked food, well kept Black Sheep, a house brew from Moorhouses and a guest, tea room; children welcome, no dogs inside, wheelchair access with help (steps down to lavatories), picnic-sets on side lawn, closed Mon, Tues. *(Simon and Mandy King)*

WOMBLETON   SE6683
Plough (01751) 431356
Main Street; YO62 7RW Welcoming village local with good home-made food including blackboard specials, ales such as Black Sheep, John Smiths, Tetleys and Theakstons, bar eating area and restaurant; tables outside. *(Stanley and Annie Matthews)*

WORTLEY   SK3099
Wortley Arms (0114) 288 8749
A629 N of Sheffield; S35 7DB 18th-c stone-built coaching inn with beams, panelling and large inglenook, good food and well kept ales such as Bradfield, Stancill and Wentworth; children and dogs (in bar) welcome, about ten minutes from M1, open all day (till 8.30pm Sun). *(Fiona Thomas)*

YORK   SE6051
★ ## Black Swan (01904) 686910
Peaseholme Green (inner ring road); YO1 7PR Striking timbered and jettied Tudor building, compact panelled front bar, crooked-floored central hall with fine period staircase, vast inglenook in black-beamed back bar, good choice of real ales, decent wines and reasonably priced pubby food from sandwiches up; background music; children welcome, useful car park behind, bedrooms, open all day. *(Anon)*

YORK   SE6051
★ ## Blue Bell (01904) 654904
Fossgate; YO1 9TF Delightfully old-fashioned little Edwardian pub, very friendly and chatty, with well kept Bradfield, Rudgate, Timothy Taylors Landlord and three guests (a dark mild always available), good value lunchtime sandwiches (not Sun), daily papers, tiny tiled-floor front bar with roaring fire, panelled ceiling and stained glass,

corridor to small back room with hatch service, lamps and candles, pub games; soft background music; no children, dogs welcome, open all day (but maybe just for locals on busy nights). *(David H Bennett, Eric Larkham)*

YORK SE5951

★**Brigantes** (01904) 675355

Micklegate; YO1 6JX Refurbished Market Town Taverns bar-bistro with shop-style frontage, wooden table and chairs on bare boards, blue-painted half-panelling and screens forming booths, eight well kept mainly Yorkshire ales (York Brewery is in street behind), good range of bottled beers, Broadoak's cider, decent wines and coffee, enjoyable brasserie food all day from snacks and sandwiches to good fish and chips, quick cheerful service, upstairs function room. *(Eric Larkham, Brian and Janet Ainscough, GSB, Pat and Tony Martin)*

YORK SE6051

Golden Ball (01904) 652211

Cromwell Road/Victor Street; YO1 6DU Friendly well preserved four-room Edwardian corner pub owned by local co-operative, five well kept changing ales, no food apart from bar snacks, bar billiards, cards and dominoes, live music Thurs; TV; lovely small walled garden, open all day weekends, closed weekday lunchtimes. *(Simon and Mandy King)*

YORK SE6051

Golden Fleece (01904) 625171

Pavement; YO1 9UP Popular little city-centre pub with good value generously served food, well kept beers from Copper Dragon, Timothy Taylors, Theakstons and Wychwood, long corridor from bar to comfortable back dining room (sloping floors – it dates from 1503), interesting décor with quite a library, lots of pictures and ghost stories; background music and occasional folk evenings; children allowed if eating, no dogs, four bedrooms, open all day. *(Chris and Jenny Howland-Harris, Robert Lester)*

YORK SE6052

Golden Slipper (01904) 651235

Goodramgate; YO1 7LG Dating from 15th c with unpretentious bar and three comfortably old-fashioned small rooms, one lined with books, cheerful efficient staff, simple low-priced lunchtime food (till 6pm Thurs-Sun) from sandwiches up, five changing ales, Weds quiz, Sun live music; TV, free wi-fi; children welcome, tables in back courtyard. *(Eric Larkham)*

YORK SE6052

Guy Fawkes (01904) 466674

High Petergate; YO1 7HP Friendly pub in splendid spot next to the Minster, dark panelled interior with small bar to the left, half a dozen real ales including a house beer from Great Heck, enjoyable sensibly

priced food (not Sun evening) from shortish menu plus blackboard specials, good helpful service, dining rooms lit by gas wall-lights and candles, open fires; courtyard tables, 13 bedrooms, open all day. *(Eric Larkham, M and J White, Paul Humphreys, Phil Bryant)*

YORK SE6051

Harkers (01904) 672795

St Helens Square; YO1 8QN Handsome late Georgian building (basement has part of Roman gateway) converted by Nicholsons, spacious split level bar with high ceilings and columns, a couple of smaller rooms off, half a dozen ales including Rudgate, John Smiths and York from long counter, their usual good value food; open all day. *(Theocsbrian)*

YORK SE6052

House of Trembling Madness (01904) 640009

Stonegate; YO1 8AS Unusual place above own off-licence; impressive high-raftered medieval room with collection of stuffed animal heads from moles to lions, eclectic mix of furniture including cask seats and pews on bare boards, lovely old brick fireplace, real ales and craft beers from pulpit servery, also huge selection of bottled beers (all available to buy downstairs), good knowledgeable staff, hearty reasonably priced food including various platters; two self-catering apartments in ancient courtyard behind, open (and food) all day. *(Eric Larkham)*

YORK SE6052

Lamb & Lion (01904) 612078

High Petergate; YO1 7EH Sparse furnishings and low lighting including candles giving a spartan Georgian feel, friendly helpful service, four well kept ales including Black Sheep and a locally brewed house beer, enjoyable simple bar food plus more elaborate evening set menu (Tues-Sat), no food Sun evening, compact rooms off dark corridors; steep steps up to small attractive garden below city wall and looking up to the Minster, 12 bedrooms, open all day. *(Eric Larkham, Paul Humphreys, John T Ames)*

YORK SE6051

Lendal Cellars (01904) 623121

Lendal; YO1 8AA Split-level ale house in broad-vaulted 17th-c cellars, stripped brickwork, stone floor, linked rooms and alcoves, good choice of changing ales and wines by the glass, foreign bottled beers, farm cider and decent coffee, enjoyable generous pubby food, friendly helpful staff; background music; children allowed if eating, no dogs, open (and food) all day. *(Eric Larkham)*

YORK SE6052

Old White Swan (01904) 540911

Goodramgate; YO1 7LF Bustling spacious Nicholsons pub with Victorian, Georgian and Tudor-themed bars, popular good value food, eight well kept ales and good whisky choice, central glass-covered courtyard (dogs allowed here); background and monthly live music, big-screen sports TV, games machines; children welcome (till 9pm if eating), open all day. *(Eric Larkham, Phil Bryant)*

YORK   SE6051
Phoenix (01904) 656401
George Street; YO1 9PT Friendly little pub next to city walls, proper front public bar and comfortable back horseshoe-shaped lounge, five well kept ales from Yorkshire brewers, decent wines and simple food, live jazz two or three times a week, bar billiards; beer garden, handy for Barbican, open all day Sat, closed lunchtimes other days. *(Anon)*

YORK
Pivni (01904) 635464
Patrick Pool; YO1 8BB Old black and white pub close to the Shambles, extensive range of foreign draught and bottled beers (some unusual choices), also good selection of local ales, friendly knowledgeable staff, small narrow bar, more seats upstairs, snacky food and good coffee; open all day. *(Phil Bryant)*

YORK   SE6051
Punch Bowl (01904) 655147
Stonegate; YO1 8AN Bustling old black and white fronted pub with small panelled rooms off corridor, good choice of well kept beers, decent wines and sensibly priced Nicholsons menu, efficient friendly service; background music; open (and food) all day. *(Eric Larkham)*

YORK   SE6052
Snickleway (01904) 656138
Goodramgate; YO1 7LS Interesting little open-plan pub behind big shop-front window, lots of antiques, copper and brass, cosy fires, five well kept ales, some lunchtime food (not

Sun) including good sandwiches, cheery landlord and prompt friendly service, Tues quiz, various ghosts including Mrs Tulliver and her cat; open all day. *(Paul Humphreys)*

YORK   SE6051
Swan (01904) 634968
Bishopgate Street, Clementhorpe; YO23 1JH Unspoilt 1930s pub (Grade II listed), hatch service to lobby for two small rooms off main bar, several changing ales and ciders, friendly knowledgeable staff may offer tasters; small pleasant walled garden, near city walls, open all day weekends, closed weekday lunchtimes. *(Anon)*

YORK   SE6052
★Three Legged Mare (01904) 638246
High Petergate; YO1 7EN Bustling light and airy modern café-bar with York Brewery's full range and guests kept well (12 handpumps), plenty of belgian beers too, quick friendly young staff, interesting sandwiches and some basic lunchtime hot food, back conservatory; no children; disabled facilities (other lavatories down spiral stairs), back garden with replica gallows after which pub is named, open all day till midnight (11pm Sun). *(Eric Larkham, Theocsbrian)*

YORK   SE5951
York Tap (01904) 659009
Station Road; YO24 1AB Restored Edwardian bar at York Station, high ceiling with feature stained-glass dome, columns and iron fretwork, bentwood chairs and stools on terrazzo floor, button-back banquettes, period fireplaces, great selection of real ales from circular counter with brass footrail, also bottled beers listed on blackboard, good pork pies (three types); open all day from 10am. *(David Heath, Dave Braisted)*

LONDON

KEY ★ Star Pub 🌟 Top Quality Food 🍺 Great Beer

♀ Good Wines £ Bargain Meals 🛏 Good Bedrooms 🍴 Serves Food

CENTRAL LONDON   Map 13

Bountiful Cow

Eagle Street; ⊖ Holborn; WC1R 4AP

Bustling and informal place popular with those wanting either a chat at the bar or a meaty meal

The informal street-level bar in this pub-cum-grill house has chrome and beige leatherette bar stools against the counter (grabbed quickly by those wanting a chat and a pint), a raised area by the windows with booth seating, and a smallish upper room with red wicker dining chairs around oak tables on oak floorboards, and beef-related prints and posters on the painted brick walls; piped jazz. Adnams Best and Dark Star Hophead on handpump and ten wines by the glass. There's also a larger downstairs dining room with cow prints on the walls. This is sister pub to the Seven Stars, also in Holborn.

🍴 As well as big steaks and burgers, the food includes duck rillettes, octopus salad, a charcuterie plate and tapas board, linguine with artichoke hearts and peas, corn-fed chicken with couscous, chargrilled sea bream, and puddings such as panna cotta with raspberry coulis and belgian apple tart. *Benchmark main dish: rump steak £19.00. Two-course evening meal £21.00.*

Free house ~ Licensee Cveta Dukovska ~ Real ale ~ (020) 7404 0200 ~ Open 11-11; 12-11 Sat; closed Sun ~ Bar food 12-10.30 ~ Children welcome ~ Wi-fi ~ www.thebountifulcow.co.uk *Recommended by Phil Bryant*

CENTRAL LONDON   TQ2781   Map 13

Grazing Goat ♀ 🛏

New Quebec Street; ⊖ Marble Arch; W1H 7RQ

A good mixed crowd of customers for this enjoyable place, restful pale décor, a thoughtful choice of drinks and good, interesting food; bedrooms

This is just the place to escape the hustle and bustle of Oxford Street and Marble Arch. A stylish pub with a rustic feel, it has a cosy area with brown leather armchairs and a big gilt-edged mirror above an open fire, and plenty of spreading dining space with white cushioned and beige dining chairs around pale tables on bare boards, sage green or light oak-panelled walls, hanging lamps and lanterns and some goat memorabilia dotted about. Stools line the long solid counter where efficient, friendly staff serve Florence A Head in a Hat Topee and Capper on handpump, over 20 wines by the glass and plenty of cocktails. The upstairs restaurant is more formal.

Glass doors open on to the street where there are a few wooden-slatted chairs and tables. The bedrooms are modern and well equipped, with good bathrooms. This is sister pub to the Orange, Pantechnicon and Thomas Cubitt.

 Starting with breakfasts, the modern bistro-style food includes venison and smoked bacon pâté with toasted potato and rosemary sourdough, warm root vegetable, squash and barley salad with cheese, spinach and smoked tomato dressing, rare-breed burger with mushroom and three-cheese sauce and green peppercorn mayonnaise, line-caught cod fillet with crab and tarragon croquette and truffle cream, beef, stilton and ale pie, and puddings such as clementine and almond syrup cake with pomegranate syrup and treacle tart with vanilla custard. *Benchmark main dish: beer-battered fish and chips £13.50. Two-course evening meal £25.00.*

Free house ~ Real ale ~ (020) 7724 7243 ~ Open 7.30am-11.30pm (10.30pm Sun) ~ Bar food 7.30am-9.30pm ~ Restaurant ~ Children welcome ~ Dogs allowed in bar ~ Wi-fi ~ Bedrooms: /£205 ~ www.thegrazinggoat.co.uk *Recommended by Mike Swan, Emma Scofield*

CENTRAL LONDON   Map 13
Lamb & Flag 🍺 £
Rose Street, off Garrick Street; ⊖ *Leicester Square, Covent Garden;*
WC2E 9EB

Historic yet unpretentious, full of character and atmosphere and with eight real ales and pubby food; especially busy in the evening

This pub has a lively and well documented history: Dryden was nearly beaten to death by hired thugs outside, and Dickens made fun of the Middle Temple lawyers who frequented it when he was working in nearby Catherine Street. It's an unspoilt and, in places, rather basic old tavern: the more spartan front room leads into a cosy, atmospheric, low-ceilinged back bar with high-backed black settles and an open fire. The pub is owned by Fullers, so they keep around half a dozen of their beers plus guests such as Adnams Ghost Ship and Butcombe Bitter on handpump, as well as 12 wines by the glass and 25 malt whiskies. The pub cat is called Beautiful. The upstairs Dryden Room is often less crowded and has more seats (though fewer beers).

 Tasty bar food, served upstairs, includes sandwiches, whitebait with smoked paprika, chargrilled courgette and fennel salad with goats cheese and cherry tomatoes, sausages with mash and onion gravy, parmesan-coated chicken with pesto, a pie of the day, gammon and egg, and puddings such as apple crumble and chocolate brownie. *Benchmark main dish: beer-battered fish and chips £9.95. Two-course evening meal £15.00.*

Fullers ~ Manager Christopher Buckley ~ Real ale ~ (020) 7497 9504 ~ Open 11-11 (11.30 Fri, Sat); 12-10.30 Sun ~ Bar food 12-8 (5 Fri, Sat); 12-8 Sun ~ Restaurant ~ Children in upstairs dining room only ~ Dogs allowed in bar ~ Wi-fi ~ Live jazz first Sun evening of month ~ www.lambandflagcoventgarden.co.uk *Recommended by Pete Walker*

CENTRAL LONDON   Map 13
Old Bank of England � 🍺
Fleet Street; ⊖ *Chancery Lane (not Sundays), Temple (not Sundays)*
⊖ ⇌ *Blackfriars; EC4A 2LT*

Dramatically converted former bank building, with gleaming chandeliers in impressive, soaring bar, well kept Fullers beers and good pies

This Grade I-listed Italianate building will amaze you. It's a former subsidiary branch of the Bank of England with a quite astounding interior. The soaring spacious bar has three gleaming chandeliers hanging from an exquisitely plastered ceiling that's high above an unusually tall island bar counter crowned with a clock. The end wall has huge paintings and murals that look like 18th-c depictions of Justice, but in fact feature members of the Fuller, Smith and Turner families, who run the brewery that owns the pub. There are well polished dark wooden furnishings, luxurious curtains swagging massive windows, plenty of framed prints and, despite the grandeur, some surprisingly cosy corners, with screens between some tables creating an unexpectedly intimate feel. The quieter galleried section upstairs offers a bird's-eye view of the action, and some smaller rooms (used mainly for functions) open off. Seven Fullers beers are on handpump alongside a good choice of malt whiskies and a dozen wines by the glass. At lunchtimes the background music is generally classical or easy listening; it's louder and livelier in the evenings. There's also a garden with seats (one of the few pubs in the area to have one).

Pies have a long if rather dubious pedigree in this area: it was in the vaults and tunnels below the Old Bank and the surrounding buildings that Sweeney Todd butchered the clients destined to provide the fillings at his mistress Mrs Lovett's nearby pie shop. Well, somehow or other, good home-made pies have become a speciality on the menu here too: steak in ale, cock-a-leekie, smoked fish, homity. Also, sandwiches, sharing platters, beer-battered hake and chips, curried sweet potato and lentil stew, corn-fed chicken with a creamy wild mushroom sauce, and puddings such as chocolate brownie and apple and blackberry pie. *Benchmark main dish: pie of the day £11.00. Two-course evening meal £16.00.*

Fullers ~ Manager Jo Farquhar ~ Real ale ~ (020) 7430 2255 ~ Open 11-11; closed weekends and bank holidays ~ Bar food 12-9 Mon-Fri ~ Children welcome until 5pm ~ Wi-fi ~ www.oldbankofengland.co.uk *Recommended by Conor McGaughey, Barry Collett, Dr and Mrs A K Clarke, Taff Thomas*

CENTRAL LONDON   Map 13
Olde Mitre ◀ £

Ely Place; the easiest way to find it is from the narrow passageway beside 8 Hatton Garden; ⊖ Chancery Lane (not Sundays); EC1N 6SJ

Hard to find but well worth it – an unspoilt old pub with lovely atmosphere, unusual guest beers and bargain toasted sandwiches

'You feel like you've stepped back in time,' says one reader and, indeed, it's hard to believe you're so close to Holborn and the edge of the City. The cosy small rooms have lots of dark panelling as well as antique settles and – particularly in the popular back room, where there are more seats – old local pictures and so forth. It gets good-naturedly packed with the City suited-and-booted between 12.30pm and 2.15pm, filling up again in the early evening, but in the early afternoon and by around 8pm is a good deal more tranquil. An upstairs room, mainly used for functions, may double as an overflow area at peak periods. Served by the proper hands-on licensee, the well kept ales on handpump include Adnams Broadside, Fullers London Pride and Seafarer and four quickly changing guests, and they hold three beer festivals a year; farm cider and several wines by the glass. No music, TV or machines – the only games here are cribbage and dominoes. There's some space for outside drinking by the pot plants and jasmine in the narrow yard between the pub and St Ethelreda's Church (which is worth a look). Note the pub doesn't open on weekends or bank holidays. The iron gates that guard one entrance to Ely Place are a reminder of the days when the law in this district was administered by the Bishops of Ely. The best approach is from Hatton Garden, walking up the right-hand side away from Chancery Lane; an easily missed sign on a lamp post points the way down a narrow alley. No children.

🍴 Served all day, bar snacks are limited to scotch eggs, pork pies and sausage rolls, and really good value toasties.

Fullers ~ Managers Eamon and Kathy Scott ~ Real ale ~ (020) 7405 4751 ~ Open 11-11; closed weekends and bank holidays ~ Bar food 11.30-9.30 ~ Wi-fi ~ www.yeoldemitreholborn.co.uk *Recommended by Martin and Sue Radcliffe, Conor McGaughey, Mrs Sally Scott*

 CENTRAL LONDON Map 13

Orange 🛏

Pimlico Road; ⊖ Sloane Square; SW1W 8NE

Buzzy, carefully restored pub with simply decorated rooms, a thoughtful choice of drinks, good modern cooking and easy-going atmosphere; bedrooms

Right in the heart of Pimlico, this restored Georgian inn is a fine place to stay with well equipped, comfortable bedrooms and first class breakfasts. The two floors of the pub itself have huge sash windows on all sides, making the interconnected rooms light and airy; throughout, the décor is shabby chic and simple and the atmosphere easy-going and chatty. The high-ceilinged downstairs bar has wooden dining chairs around pale tables on bare boards, an open fire at one end and a big carved counter where they keep Adnams Jack Brand Mosaic Pale Ale and a couple of guests on handpump, 20 wines by the glass and a lengthy cocktail list. The dining room to the right, usually packed with cheerful customers, is decorated with prints, glass bottles and soda siphons, big house plants and a few rustic knick-knacks. Upstairs, the linked restaurant rooms are similarly furnished with old french travel posters and circus prints on cream walls, more open fireplaces, big glass ceiling lights and chandeliers and quiet background jazz. Service is courteous and friendly. This is sister pub to the Grazing Goat, Pantechnicon and Thomas Cubitt.

🍴 As well as wood-fired pizzas, the good modern food includes breakfasts (for non-residents too, until 11.30am), smoked mackerel pâté with spiced rhubarb compote, mussels with bloody mary sauce, chargrilled corn-fed chicken with roasted butternut and wheat grain salad, rabbit ragoût with black olive gnocchi, fish of the day, outdoor-reared pork with cider-braised red cabbage, and puddings such as apple and cherry crumble and chocolate espresso tart. *Benchmark main dish: hake fillet with celeriac, broad beans and tomatoes £18.50. Two-course evening meal £25.00.*

Free house ~ Real ale ~ (020) 7881 9844 ~ Open 8am-11.30pm (midnight Fri, Sat); 8am-10.30pm Sun ~ Bar food 8am-9.30pm ~ Restaurant ~ Children welcome ~ Dogs allowed in bar ~ Wi-fi ~ Bedrooms: /£205 ~ www.theorange.co.uk *Recommended by Peter Sutton, Charlie May*

 CENTRAL LONDON Map 13

Pantechnicon 🍷

Motcomb Street; ⊖ Knightsbridge; SW1X 8LA

Bustling and civilised with good drinks choice, rewarding food and friendly, helpful service

Located in a quiet residential area, this civilised place is named after
the 1830s landmark building just up the road. It's all very relaxed,
with customers drinking and chatting, working at laptops or enjoying
the interesting, good quality food. Apart from one table surrounded by
stools beside the bar counter, there are high-backed upholstered dining
chairs around wooden tables on parquet flooring, comfortable leather wall
seats and eclectic décor that ranges from 19th-c postcards to nobility and
envelopes displayed address-side out to Edward Lear illustrations and
World War II prints – plus antique books on window sills. Friendly, helpful
staff serve Florence A Head In A Hat Topee on handpump, cocktails and
quite a few wines by the glass. The upstairs restaurant has leather chairs
and wooden tables on more parquet and a huge mirror above an open fire.
Above that is a room for private hire, and up again a cosy loft used for
monthly events such as cheese tastings. The front pavement has tables and
chairs beneath a striped awning. This is sister pub to the Grazing Goat,
Orange and Thomas Cubitt.

The enterprising food includes crispy squid, prawns, lemon and artichokes with a
smoked chilli dressing, smoked ham hock, leek and parsley terrine with quail egg,
beef, tomato and rosemary pie, burger with Guinness ketchup and green peppercorn
mayonnaise, corn-fed chicken with girolles and mint dressing, hake with leeks, fennel,
broad beans and a citrus butter sauce, pork shoulder with cabbage rémoulade and
braised haricot beans, rose veal chop with truffle mash and a choice of sauces, and
puddings such as chocolate truffle tart and orange almond cake. *Benchmark main
dish: daily changing fish dish £17.50. Two-course evening meal £23.50.*

Free house ~ Real ale ~ (020) 7730 6074 ~ Open 12-11; 9am-11pm Sat; 9am-10.30pm
Sun ~ Bar food 12-10; 9-4 weekend brunch ~ Children welcome ~ Dogs allowed in bar ~
www.thepantechnicon.com *Recommended by Harvey Brown, Caroline Prescott*

CENTRAL LONDON   Map 13
Running Horse 🍷 🍺

Corner of Davies Street and Davies Mews; ⊖ *Bond Street; W1K 5JE*

**Friendly, bustling Mayfair pub with four ales, good wines
and tasty food**

A pub since 1738 and refurbished by Chase Distillery, this place has a
bustling, friendly atmosphere. The open-plan bar has an appealing
collection of wooden dining chairs and cushioned settles around a mix
of tables on bare boards, tartan armchairs beside a blanket-box table in
front of the green-tiled fireplace, and high chairs against the counter where
they keep Rebellion IPA, Mutiny and Smuggler and Wye Valley HPA on
handpump and lots of good wines by the glass. There are horse-racing
prints on plain wooden or navy-painted wall panelling, and a projector
shows live televised horse racing. Upstairs feels more Mayfair than cheery
pub, with plenty more horsey prints on racing colours wallpaper, club-
like button-back leather or upholstered and painted chairs, and brass
chandeliers. There are contemporary wicker seats and tables on the
pavement outside.

Popular food includes diver-caught scallops with pea purée and ham crisps,
ham hock terrine with home-made piccalilli, wild boar sausages in cider,
scottish smoked salmon and crab salad, free-range chicken burger with wild garlic
mayonnaise, mature cheddar, leek and potato pie, shepherd's pie, and puddings such
as rhubarb trifle and toffee banana pudding. *Benchmark main dish: chopped rump
burger with triple-cooked chips and onion marmalade £16.00. Two-course evening
meal £22.00.*

Free house ~ Licensee James Chase ~ Real ale ~ (020) 7493 1275 ~ Open 12-midnight; closed Sun evening ~ Bar food 12-3, 6-10; 12-10 Sat ~ Children welcome ~ Dogs welcome ~ Wi-fi ~ www.therunninghorselondon.co.uk *Recommended by Stuart Gideon, Mrs Catherine Simmonds*

CENTRAL LONDON
Seven Stars ◀

Map 13

Carey Street; ⊖ *Temple (not Sundays), Chancery Lane (not Sundays), Holborn; WC2A 2JB*

Quirky pub with cheerful staff, an interesting mix of customers and a good choice of drinks and food

This cosy and unchanging little pub faces the back of the Law Courts and is a favourite with lawyers, Church of England music directors and choir singers; numerous caricatures of barristers and judges line the red-painted walls of the two main rooms. Also, posters of legal-themed british films, big ceiling fans and a relaxed, intimate atmosphere; checked tablecloths add a quirky, almost continental touch. A third area, in what was once a legal wig shop next door, still retains the original frontage, with a neat display of wigs in the window. It's worth getting here early as they don't take bookings and tables get snapped up quickly. There's Adnams Best and Broadside and a couple of guests such as Sambrooks Wandle and Sharps Cornish Coaster on handpump, and six wines by the glass (they import wine from France); they do a particularly good dry martini. On busy evenings customers overflow to the quiet road in front; things generally quieten down after 8pm and there can be a nice, sleepy atmosphere some afternoons. The Elizabethan stairs up to the loos are rather steep, but there's a good strong handrail. The pub cat, who wears a ruff, is called Ray Brown. The licensees also run the Bountiful Cow on Eagle Street, near Holborn tube station. No children.

 Cooked according to the landlady's fancy, the good, interesting food includes duck rillettes on toast, leek, pea and garlic leaf linguine, calves brains with scrambled egg, hot german sausages with sautéed potatoes, tuna kedgeree biriyani, rabbit stew, and ice-creams served in a small kilner jar. *Benchmark main dish: chicken and pheasant pie £11.50. Two-course evening meal £16.00.*

Free house ~ Licensee Roxy Beaujolais ~ Real ale ~ (020) 7242 8521 ~ Open 11 (12 Sat)-11; 12-10.30 Sun; closed some bank holidays ~ Bar food 12 (1pm weekends)-9.30 ~ Wi-fi ~ www.thesevenstars1602.co.uk *Recommended by Conor McGaughey, N R White, Phil Bryant*

CENTRAL LONDON
Star ◀

Map 13

Belgrave Mews West, behind the German Embassy, off Belgrave Square; ⊖ *Knightsbridge, Hyde Park Corner; SW1X 8HT*

Bustling local with restful bar, upstairs dining room, Fullers ales, well liked bar food and colourful hanging baskets

In summer, this pub tucked away in a cobbled mews is covered with an astonishing array of hanging baskets and flowering tubs – but it's popular in winter too, when there's a warm open fire. The small bar is a pleasant place, with sash windows, a wooden floor, stools by the counter and Fullers ESB, London Pride and Seafarers and a guest such as Trumans Lazarus on handpump, nine wines by the glass and a few malt whiskies. An arch leads to the main seating area with well polished tables and chairs, and good lighting; there's also an upstairs dining room. Outside peak times it has a restful local feel. It's said that this is where the Great Train Robbery was planned.

🍴 Well liked food includes lunchtime sandwiches, whitebait with aioli, field mushrooms on toasted brioche with a fried duck egg, smoked trout with broccoli and spelt salad, dill and yoghurt, sharing platters, scallop, sorrel and spinach risotto, three-cheese ravioli with roasted butternut squash, spinach and hazelnut butter, burger with cheddar, bacon and chips, lamb, feta and pomegranate salad with mint, hazelnuts and cucumber, and puddings such as lemon and poppyseed cake with sweet mascarpone and banoffi pie with toffee sauce. *Benchmark main dish: beer-battered fish and chips £11.00. Two-course evening meal £17.00.*

Fullers ~ Manager Marta Lemieszewska ~ Real ale ~ (020) 7235 3019 ~ Open 11 (12 Sat)-11; 12-10.30 Sun ~ Bar food 12-3, 5-9; 12-5 Sun ~ Restaurant ~ Children welcome ~ Dogs welcome ~ Wi-fi ~ www.star-tavern-belgravia.co.uk
Recommended by Dr and Mrs A K Clarke, N R White, Susan and John Douglas, Mike and Jayne Bastin, Phil Bryant

CENTRAL LONDON
Thomas Cubitt ♀

Map 13

Elizabeth Street; ⊖ *Sloane Square* ⊖ ⇌ *Victoria; SW1W 9PA*

Belgravia pub named after the legendary builder, a civilised but friendly atmosphere and enjoyable food and drink

In warm weather, the floor-to-ceiling glass doors of the bar are pulled back to open on to well-heeled Elizabeth Street, where there are cordoned-off tables and chairs on the pavement. The busy bar has miscellaneous Edwardian-style cushioned dining chairs around wooden tables on stripped parquet flooring, architectural prints and antlers on panelled or painted walls, open fires and lovely flower arrangements. Attentive staff serve Florence A Head In A Hat Topee and Capper on handpump, cocktails and quite a few wines by the glass. The more formal dining room upstairs has smart upholstered wooden chairs around white-clothed tables, candles in wall holders, a few prints, house plants and window blinds. This is sister pub to the Grazing Goat, Orange and Pantechnicon.

🍴 Enterprising food includes crispy squid, prawns, lemon and artichokes with a smoked chilli dressing, smoked ham hock, leek and parsley terrine with quail egg, beef, tomato and rosemary pie, corn-fed chicken with girolles and mint dressing, hake with leeks, fennel, broad beans and a citrus butter sauce, pork shoulder with cabbage rémoulade and braised haricot beans, rose veal chop with truffle mash and a choice of sauces, and puddings such as chocolate truffle tart and orange almond cake. *Benchmark main dish: rare-breed burger with Guinness ketchup and green peppercorn mayonnaise £14.50. Two-course evening meal £23.50.*

Free house ~ Real ale ~ (020) 7730 6060 ~ Open 12-11 (10.30 Sun) ~ Bar food 12-10.30 (10 Sun) ~ Restaurant ~ Children welcome ~ Dogs allowed in bar ~ www.thethomascubitt.co.uk *Recommended by Peter Loader*

NORTH LONDON
Drapers Arms 🍽️⭐ ♀

Map 13

Far west end of Barnsbury Street; ⊖ ⇌ *Highbury & Islington; N1 1ER*

Streamlined place with good mix of customers, a thoughtful choice of drinks, imaginative modern food, and seats in attractive back garden

This well run pub has many attributes, but the one we hear most praise for is the first class modern cooking. A simply furnished Georgian townhouse, it has a spreading bar with a mix of elegant dark wooden tables and dining chairs on bare boards, an arresting bright green-painted counter that contrasts with soft duck-egg blue walls, gilt mirrors over smart fireplaces, a sofa and some comfortable chairs. Harveys Best, Windsor & Eton Knight of the Garter and a guest from London Fields on handpump, 17 carefully chosen wines by the glass and british draught lagers. Upstairs, the stylish dining room has similar tables and chairs on a striking chequerboard-painted wooden floor; background music and board games. In warm weather, the lovely back terrace is a real bonus, with white or green benches and chairs around zinc-topped tables – each set with a church candle in a hurricane lamp – flagstones and large parasols.

Using seasonal produce, the impressive food includes cuttlefish with orange and fennel salad, home-smoked cured salmon with pickled cucumber and horseradish cream, globe artichoke, green beans, chard, peas and garlic butter with tomato salsa, lemon sole with brown shrimps, capers and brown butter, spiced quail with carrot, coriander and saffron mayonnaise, a proper kedgeree, grilled fore-rib chop with marrow butter and chips, and puddings such as peach and custard tart and chocolate brownie sundae. *Benchmark main dish: lamb rump with glazed carrots, crushed potatoes and lamb sauce £17.00. Two-course evening meal £22.00.*

Free house ~ Licensee Nick Gibson ~ Real ale ~ (020) 7619 0348 ~ Open 12-11 ~ Bar food 12-3, 6-10.30; 12-4, 7-10.30 Sat; 12-8.30 Sun ~ Restaurant ~ Children welcome but must be seated and dining after 6pm ~ Dogs allowed in bar ~ Wi-fi ~ www.thedrapersarms.com *Recommended by Fr Robert Marsh*

NORTH LONDON   Map 12

Holly Bush ♀ ⬤

Holly Mount; ⊖ Hampstead; NW3 6SG

Unique village local, with good food and drinks and lovely unspoilt feel

You can be sure of a warm welcome at this charming old place, which has plenty of atmosphere even when quiet. The old-fashioned front bar has a dark sagging ceiling, brown and cream panelled walls (decorated with old advertisements and a few hanging plates), open fires, bare boards and secretive bays formed by partly glazed partitions. The slightly more intimate back room, named after the painter George Romney, has an embossed red ceiling, panelled and etched glass alcoves, and ochre-painted brick walls covered with small prints; lots of board and card games. Fullers Chiswick Bitter, Fools Gold, London Pride and Seafarers on handpump, as well as 15 malt whiskies and 14 wines by the glass from a good wine list. The upstairs dining room has table service at the weekend, as does the rest of the pub on Sundays. There are benches on the pavement outside.

As well as snacks such as chorizo scotch egg and ox cheek pasty, the interesting food includes lunchtime sandwiches, salmon carpaccio with pink berries, cucumber and citrus salad, rope-grown mussels, crayfish broth and fregola, chermoula aubergine with bulgar and date salad, yoghurt and zhoug (green chilli sauce), rump of lamb with roasted butternut squash, leek and flageolet bean ragoût, cod loin with sun-blush tomato and prawn crust, spring green croquettes and saffron sauce, beef in ale pie, and puddings such as dark chocolate and amaretto torte and cardamom and rosewater crème brûlée. *Benchmark main dish: sirloin steak with peppercorn sauce and chips £21.50. Two-course evening meal £20.00.*

Fullers ~ Manager Ben Ralph ~ Real ale ~ (020) 7435 2892 ~ Open 12-11 (10.30 Sun) ~ Bar food 12-3 (4 Sat), 6-10; 12-8 Sun ~ Restaurant ~ Children welcome ~ Dogs welcome ~ Wi-fi ~ www.hollybushhampstead.co.uk *Recommended by Phil Bryant, N R White, Di and Mike Gillam*

NORTH LONDON   Map 12

Princess of Wales ♀

Fitzroy Road/Chalcot Road; ⊖ Chalk Farm via Regent's Park Road and footbridge; NW1 8LL

Friendly, buzzy place with three different seating areas to choose from, enjoyable food, wide choice of drinks and funky garden

Spread over three floors, this bustling and welcoming pub usefully serves some kind of food all day. The main bar, at ground level, is open-plan and light with big windows looking out to the street, wooden tables and chairs on bare boards and plenty of high chairs against the counter where they keep By the Horns The Mayor of Garratt and a couple of quickly changing guests on handpump, 16 wines by the glass, 11 malt whiskies and good cocktails. Upstairs, the smarter dining room has beige and white-painted chairs, leather sofas and stools around wooden tables on more bare boards, big gilt-edged mirrors and chandeliers; two TVs. Orange and green plush banquettes create a diner-like feel in the colourful Garden Room downstairs, and doors lead out to the suntrap garden with its Bansky-style mural, framed wall mirrors and picnic-sets (some painted pink and purple) under parasols.

The good food includes a highly rated breakfast and brunch, lunchtime sandwiches, parma ham with roasted figs, baby buffalo mozzarella and aged balsamic, crispy squid with chilli salt, burger topped with blue cheese, bacon, garlic mushrooms and chips, sausages with mash and onion gravy, half roast chicken with coleslaw and fries, a pie of the day, slow-roast pork belly with scallops and teriyaki sauce, and puddings such as double chocolate and peanut butter brownie with salted caramel ice-cream and apple and raspberry crumble. *Benchmark main dish: duck breast with dauphinoise potatoes and black cabbage £12.50. Two-course evening meal £19.00.*

Free house ~ Licensee Lawrence Santi ~ Real ale ~ (020) 7722 0354 ~ Open 9am-midnight (11.30 Sun) ~ Bar food 9am-3.30, 6-10; all day weekends ~ Children welcome ~ Dogs allowed in bar ~ Live jazz Sun (best to phone) ~ www.lovetheprincess.com
Recommended by Edward May, Harvey Brown

SOUTH LONDON   Map 12

Earl Spencer

Merton Road; ⊖ Southfields; SW18 5JL

Good, interesting food and six real ales in busy but friendly pub

This is a sizeable Edwardian pub with a lively, bustling atmosphere and plenty of cheerful customers. There are cushioned wooden, farmhouse and leather dining tables around all sorts of tables on bare boards, standard lamps, modern art on the walls and an open fire; the back bar has long tables, pews and benches. Stools line the U-shaped counter where efficient, friendly staff serve six ales on handpump: Adnams Broadside, Harveys Best, Otter Amber, Sambrooks Wandle, Sharps Cornish Coaster and Timothy Taylors Landlord. Also, 20 wines by the glass and 20 malt whiskies; they also sell 14 kinds of cigar. There are picnic-sets out on the front pavement.

Tasty food includes sandwiches, brown and white crab pâté, pea, mascarpone and chilli fritters with pesto, roast butternut squash risotto, chicken, apricot and mint tagine with couscous and yoghurt, lamb curry, fillet of cod with cherry tomato, lemon and pepper salsa, rack of pork with braised red cabbage and apple sauce, roast skate wing with brown caper butter, and puddings such as crème caramel and chocolate pot. *Benchmark main dish: bavette steak with watercress, parsley and garlic butter and fries £16.00. Two-course evening meal £21.00.*

Enterprise ~ Lease Michael Mann ~ Real ale ~ (020) 8870 9244 ~ Open 4-11 Mon-Thurs; 11am-midnight Fri, Sat; 12-10.30 Sun ~ Bar food 7-10 Mon-Thurs; 12.30-3.30, 7-10 Fri, Sat; 12.30-4, 7-9.30 Sun ~ Children welcome ~ Dogs allowed in bar ~ Wi-fi ~ www.theearlspencer.co.uk *Recommended by Mrs G Marlow*

SOUTH LONDON
Fox & Grapes

Map 12

Camp Road; ⊖ Wimbledon; SW19 4UN

Wide mix of customers for very popular pub, friendly, efficient staff and enjoyable drink and food

This 18th-c pub is ideally placed on the edge of Wimbledon Common and is extremely popular with walkers (often with dogs in tow). It's a friendly, busy place with efficient, helpful staff and always a good mix of drinkers and diners. The spacious main bar – with a step between its two halves – has high ceilings with unusual chandeliers, green leather and all sorts of wooden dining chairs around an assortment of tables on parquet flooring, built-in wall seats and settles with pretty scatter cushions, a couple of large cartwheels, and high chairs against the counter where they keep Adnams Southwold, Sharps Doom Bar and Wye Valley HPA on handpump and nine wines by the glass. There's also a cosy area with green-painted plank walls and an ornately carved mirror. The three bedrooms are light, airy and pretty; continental breakfasts. This is sister pub to the Malt House in Fulham.

Imaginative food includes game terrine with redcurrant gel, tandoori pigeon with dhal and raisins, casserole of mussels and clams with chilli broth, burger with cheese, chard, shiitake mushroom and sushi rice hotpot, caramelised onions and triple-cooked chips, steak and Guinness pie, braised shoulder of lamb with artichoke, feta and onion, and puddings such as blood orange posset and chocolate and whisky pot. *Benchmark main dish: turbot with crab butter and sea greens £29.50. Two-course evening meal £21.00.*

Enterprise ~ Manager Jessica Chanter ~ Real ale ~ (020) 8619 1300 ~ Open 11-11 (10.30 Sun) ~ Bar food 12-3, 6-9.30; 12.30-8.30 ~ Children welcome ~ Dogs welcome ~ Wi-fi ~ Bedrooms: /£125 ~ www.foxandgrapeswimbledon.co.uk *Recommended by Susan and John Douglas, Peter Sutton*

SOUTH LONDON
Greenwich Union ◀

Map 12

Royal Hill; ⊖⇄ Greenwich; SE10 8RT

Enterprising pub with distinctive beers from the small Meantime Brewery plus other interesting drinks, and good, popular food

This friendly, nicely renovated pub is a tap for the small local Meantime Brewery and stocks all their distinctive unpasteurised beers. The range includes a traditional pale ale (served cool, under pressure), a mix of proper pilsners, lagers, porters and wheat beers, and a stout; the knowledgeable, helpful staff will usually offer small tasters to help you choose. They also have a helpfully annotated list of around 150 bottled beers, a good choice of unusual spirits, a thoughtful wine list, carefully chosen teas and coffees and fresh, daily squeezed orange juice. Feeling a bit more like a bar than a pub, the long, narrow stone-flagged room has several different parts: a simple area at the front with a few wooden chairs and tables, a stove and newspapers; then, past the counter with its headings recalling the branding of the brewery's first beers, several brown leather cushioned pews and armchairs beneath framed editions of *Picture Post* on the yellow walls; background music, TV. Beyond here, a much lighter, more modern-feeling conservatory has comfortable brown leather wall benches, a few original pictures and paintings, and white fairy lights under a glass roof. This leads to an appealing terrace with green picnic-sets and a couple of old-fashioned lamp posts; the fence at the end is painted to resemble a poppy field, the one at the side a wheat field. Although there are plenty of tables out here, it does get busy in summer (as does the whole pub on weekday evenings). There's also a couple of tables outside the front next to the street. The pub is slightly removed from Greenwich's key attractions – as you walk towards it, look out for the particularly good traditional cheese shop.

As well as sandwiches, the good food includes devilled kidneys on toasted sourdough, calamari with garlic and squid ink aioli, beef, lamb or vegetarian burger with toppings and chips, fresh fish and chips, steak and kidney pie, herrings with potato and broccoli salad and soft-boiled egg, and puddings such as sticky toffee pudding and chocolate mousse; they also do Saturday brunch (until 1.30pm). *Benchmark main dish: angus burger with watercress aioli and chips £12.50. Two-course evening meal £25.00.*

Free house ~ Licensee Daniel Persson ~ (020) 8692 6258 ~ Open 12-11; 10am-11pm Sat; 10am-10.30pm Sun ~ Bar food 12-10; 10-10 Sat; 10-9 Sun ~ Well behaved children welcome ~ Dogs allowed in bar ~ Wi-fi ~ www.greenwichunion.com *Recommended by Ian Phillips, Simon Pyle, John Fiander*

SOUTH LONDON   Map 13

Royal Oak

Tabard Street/Nebraska Street; ⊖ ⇄ *Borough, London Bridge; SE1 4JU*

Old-fashioned corner house with particularly well kept beers and honest food

This was the first London pub for Sussex brewery Harveys (they now also run the Cats Back in Wandsworth); they transformed it by painstakingly re-creating the look and feel of a traditional London alehouse – you'd never imagine it had been any different. The place is always packed with customers of all ages, all keen to enjoy the full range of Harveys ales, plus a guest from Fullers on handpump and Thatcher's cider. The two busy little L-shaped rooms meander around the central wooden servery, which has a fine old clock in the middle. They're done out in a cosy, traditional style with patterned rugs on the wooden floors, plates running along a delft shelf, black and white scenes or period sheet music on the red-painted walls, and an assortment of wooden tables and chairs. There's a disabled access ramp at the Nebraska Street entrance.

Tasty food includes lunchtime sandwiches, duck liver pâté, deep-fried camembert, rabbit casserole, goats cheese and beetroot salad, scallops and bacon, half roast duck with vegetables, and puddings such as sherry trifle and treacle tart. *Benchmark main dish: bubble and squeak with black pudding, bacon and duck egg £9.25. Two-course evening meal £16.50.*

Harveys ~ Tenants John Porteous, Frank Taylor ~ Real ale ~ (020) 7357 7173 ~ Open 11-11; 12-9 Sun ~ Bar food 12-2.45, 5-9.15; 12-8 Sun ~ Children welcome until 9pm ~ Dogs welcome ~ www.harveys.org.uk *Recommended by Giles and Annie Francis, Comus and Sarah Elliott, Pete Walker, B and M Kendall, Phil Bryant, N R White*

Anglesea Arms ▾ ◀

Selwood Terrace; ⊖ South Kensington; SW7 3QG

Five changing ales on handpump, interesting food, plenty of customers and heated front terrace

This is a very busy Victorian pub, well run and friendly, with a good mix of both regulars and visitors. There are cast-iron tables on wood-strip flooring, a few central elbow tables, panelling and heavy portraits, large brass chandeliers hanging from dark ceilings, and big windows with swagged curtains; several booths at one end have partly glazed screens. Adnams Broadside, Greene King IPA, Sambrooks Wandle, Trumans Lazarus and a beer named for the pub (from Greene King) on handpump, 15 wines by the glass and 13 malt whiskies. Steps lead down to a leather-seated dining room with more wooden flooring, portraits and candles in bottles. In warm weather, there are plenty of good quality tables and chairs outside on the heated front terrace, with more to the side on the pavement. Charles Dickens lived at No.11.

Interesting food includes lunchtime sandwiches, confit guinea fowl and duck ballotine, mussels in garlic, cream and cider, puff pastry tart with spinach, mushrooms and gruyère, beer-battered cod and chips, calves liver and bacon with onion purée, corn-fed chicken with spring onion mash and thyme gravy, chargrilled swordfish steak with ratatouille and couscous, and puddings such as pecan tart and eton mess. *Benchmark main dish: chicken and ham pie £13.00. Two-course evening meal £20.00.*

Free house ~ Licensee Ben Coles ~ Real ale ~ (020) 7373 7960 ~ Open 11-11; 12-10.30 Sun ~ Bar food 12-3 (5 Sat), 6-10; 12-9.30 Sun ~ Restaurant ~ Children welcome ~ Dogs allowed in bar ~ Wi-fi ~ www.angleseaarms.com *Recommended by Peter Sutton*

Bell

Thames Street, Hampton; ⇌ Hampton; TW12 2EA

Bustling pub by the Thames with seats outside, real ales, popular food and friendly service

With amiable, helpful service and an easy-going feel, this is a well liked pub that our readers enjoy. The interconnected rooms have wooden dining and tub chairs around copper-topped or chunky wooden tables, comfortably upholstered wall seats with scatter cushions, mirrors, old photographs and plenty of church candles. From the long panelled counter they serve Sambrooks Wandle, Sharps Doom Bar and Twickenham Naked Ladies on handpump, 20 wines by the glass and speciality teas and coffees. There are plenty of seats and tables in the refurbished garden, which now has heaters, lighting and booth seating; summer barbecues.

Using carefully sourced produce, the enjoyable food includes lunchtime sandwiches, chicken liver pâté with chutney, potted prawns in chilli and tarragon butter, sharing boards, beef, mushroom or thai-spiced chicken burger with toppings and chips, indian barbecued spatchcocked chicken with coleslaw and skinny fries, a pie of the day, pork cutlet with chorizo and borlotti beans and apple and cider gravy, and puddings such as seasonal crumble and sticky toffee pudding. *Benchmark main dish: beer-battered fish and chips £11.50. Two-course evening meal £18.50.*

Absolute Pubs ~ Lease Simon Bailey ~ Real ale ~ (020) 8941 9799 ~ Open 11-11 (midnight Fri, Sat) ~ Bar food 12-3, 6-10; 12-10 Sat; 12-9 Sun ~ Restaurant ~ Children

welcome ~ Dogs allowed in bar ~ Wi-fi ~ Live acoustic music Sat evening, comedy
first Weds of month ~ www.thebellinnhampton.co.uk *Recommended by Emma Scofield,
Caroline Prescott*

WEST LONDON   Map 12
Churchill Arms ♀ ◖ £
Kensington Church Street; ⊖ *Notting Hill Gate, Kensington High Street;*
W8 7LN

**Cheery irish landlord at bustling and friendly local with very well
kept beers and popular thai food; even at its most crowded, it stays
relaxed and welcoming**

M r O'Brien has been running this busy local for 30 years and remains
as enthusiastic and friendly as ever. He's a great collector and loves
butterflies – you'll see a variety of prints and books on the subject dotted
around the bar. He doesn't stop there, though: the pub is filled with
countless lamps, miners' lights, horse tack, bedpans and brasses hanging
from the ceiling, a couple of interesting carved figures and statuettes
behind the central bar counter, prints of american presidents and lots of
Churchill memorabilia. Well kept Fullers Chiswick, ESB, London Pride
and Fullers seasonal beers on handpump and 18 wines by the glass. The
spacious and rather smart plant-filled dining conservatory may be used
for hatching butterflies, but is better known for its wide range of excellent
thai food. They have their own cricket and football teams and hold regular
special events. The pub façade is quite a sight in summer when it almost
disappears behind the glorious display of 85 window boxes and 42 hanging
baskets. There are some chrome tables and chairs outside.

The splendid value thai food ranges from a proper thai curry to various rice,
noodle and stir-fry dishes. At lunchtimes there's usually a few traditional
dishes such as fish and chips or sausage and chips, and they do a good value Sunday
roast. *Benchmark main dish: stir-fried chicken with cashew nuts £7.50.
Two-course evening meal £19.00.*

Fullers ~ Manager Gerry O'Brien ~ Real ale ~ (020) 7727 4242 ~ Open 11-11 (midnight
Thurs-Sat); 12-10.30 Sun ~ Bar food 12-10 ~ Restaurant ~ Children welcome ~ Dogs
welcome ~ Wi-fi ~ www.churchillarmskensington.co.uk *Recommended by Edward Mirzoeff*

WEST LONDON   Map 12
Crown & Sceptre
Holland Road; ⊖ *Earl's Court* ⊖ ⇄ *Kensington (Olympia) (*⊖ *weekends
only); W14 8BA*

**Friendly corner pub with an easy-going atmosphere, attentive staff
and a good choice of both food and drinks**

O n the doorstep of Olympia exhibition centre, this is a civilised Victorian
corner pub with an attractively refurbished interior. Light and airy,
it has sofas, antique-style dining chairs and leather cube stools around
wooden tables, rugs on bare boards, an open gas fire, fresh flowers and
papers to read; staff are friendly and helpful and it's all very relaxed.
Courage Directors, Wells & Youngs London Gold and a guest from
Theakstons on handpump, a dozen wines by the glass and 22 malt whiskies;
background music, TV and board games. There's also a cosy cellar bar
with banquette seating, big prints on rough wood walls, some leather cube
stools, candles in bottles and a roulette wheel carved into one large table.
On the pavement outside are a few tables and chairs. The bedrooms are up
to date and comfortable.

🍴 Good food includes lunchtime sandwiches, Sunday brunch, bubble and squeak with a poached egg and bacon, beef carpaccio with thai sauce, wild mushroom and tarragon pasta with madeira reduction, beer-battered fish and chips, jerk chicken with paprika sweet potato wedges and pineapple, cheeseburger with bacon, aioli, coleslaw and fries, bass with squid ink risotto and salsa verde, and puddings. *Benchmark main dish: rotisserie chicken with red peppers and chilli and truffle sauce £12.00. Two-course evening meal £19.00.*

Free house ~ Licensee Freddie Van Hagen ~ Real ale ~ (020) 7603 2007 ~ Open 7.30am-11.30pm ~ Bar food 12-3, 6-9; 12-7 Sun ~ Restaurant ~ Children welcome ~ Dogs allowed in bar ~ Wi-fi ~ Bedrooms: £90/£100 ~ www.crownandsceptrepub.com
Recommended by Ian Phillips

WEST LONDON
Map 12
Dove 🍺

Upper Mall; ⊖ Ravenscourt Park; W6 9TA

One of London's best known pubs, with a lovely riverside terrace, cosily traditional front bar and an interesting history

Head down the steps at the back of this 17th-c pub to reach the verandah with its highly prized tables looking over the low river wall to the Thames Reach just above Hammersmith Bridge; a tiny exclusive area can be reached up a spiral staircase, a prime spot for watching the rowing crews on the water. The front snug is in the Guinness World Records for having the smallest bar room (a mere 1.3 metres by 2.4 metres) and is cosy, traditional and unchanging, with black panelling and red leatherette cushioned built-in wall settles and stools around assorted tables. It leads to a bigger, similarly furnished back room that's more geared to eating, which in turn leads to a conservatory. Fullers ESB, HSB and London Pride plus a guest or two on handpump and 19 wines by the glass including champagne and sparkling wine. The pub has played host to many writers, actors and artists over the years (there's a fascinating framed list of them all on a wall); it's said to be where 'Rule Britannia' was composed and was a favourite with Turner, who painted the view of the Thames from the delightful back terrace, and with Graham Greene. The street itself is associated with the foundation of the arts and crafts movement – William Morris's old residence (open certain afternoons) is nearby.

🍴 Tasty food includes crispy pig cheeks with chervil sauce, chicken liver parfait with ruby port reduction, sharing boards, chestnut mushroom and cheese macaroni with truffle oil, corn-fed chicken ballotine with smoked bacon stuffing and mustard sauce, a trio of sausages with bubble and squeak and caramelised onion jus, steak in ale pie, and puddings such as dark chocolate tart and summer pudding. *Benchmark main dish: beer-battered fish and chips £11.95. Two-course evening meal £19.00.*

Fullers ~ Manager Rob Collett ~ Real ale ~ (020) 8748 9474 ~ Open 11-11; 12-10.30 Sun ~ Bar food 12-10 (8 Sun) ~ Children welcome ~ Dogs welcome ~ Wi-fi ~ Live irish folk Mon evening ~ www.dovehammersmith.co.uk *Recommended by N R White*

Please keep sending us reports. We rely on readers for news of new discoveries, and particularly for news of changes – however slight – at the fully described pubs: feedback@goodguides.com, or (no stamp needed) The Good Pub Guide, FREEPOST RTJR-ZCYZ-RJZT, Perrymans Lane, Etchingham TN19 7DN.

WEST LONDON Map 12
Duke of Sussex ⭐ ♀ 🍺

South Parade; ⊖ Chiswick Park ⇌ South Acton; W4 5LF

Attractively restored Victorian local with interesting bar food, a good choice of drinks and a lovely big garden

On a sunny day, try to arrive early if you want a seat in the unexpectedly big garden as it does get packed out. There are tables under parasols, nicely laid out plants, heaters and carefully positioned lighting. Inside, the classy, simply furnished bar has some original etched glass, chapel and farmhouse chairs around scrubbed pine and dark wood tables, and huge windows overlooking Acton Green. The big horseshoe-shaped counter, lined with high bar stools, is where they serve St Austells Proper Job, Titanic Steerage and Trumans Runner on handpump, 30 wines by the glass and 15 malt whiskies. Off here is a dining room, again with plenty of simple wooden furnishings on parquet, but also six-seater booths, chandeliers, antique lamps, a splendid skylight framed by colourfully painted cherubs, and a couple of big mirrors, one above a small tiled fireplace.

The likeable and interesting food includes lots of tapas such as razor clams with chorizo, garlic and chilli, ham croquettes and spanish cured meats, plus more substantial choices such as lamb rump with tabbouleh and harissa, pork, chorizo and bean stew, skirt steak with aioli and chips, chicken pie, skate wing with capers, fennel and samphire, and puddings such as chocolate brownie and lemon meringue pie. *Benchmark main dish: seafood paella £14.50. Two-course evening meal £20.00.*

Greene King ~ Manager Matt Mullett ~ Real ale ~ (020) 8742 8801 ~ Open 12-11 (11.30 Fri, Sat); 12-10.30 Sun ~ Bar food 12-10.30 (9.30 Sun) ~ Restaurant ~ Children welcome ~ Dogs allowed in bar ~ Wi-fi ~ www.thedukeofsussex.co.uk
Recommended by N R White, Simon Rodway

WEST LONDON TQ2577 Map 12
Malt House 🛏

Vanston Place; ⊖ Fulham Broadway; SW6 1AY

Refurbished pub with plenty of room, Brakspears ales, enjoyable food and hidden-away garden; bedrooms

Dating from 1729, this large corner pub has been totally refurbished but still retains some original features. The light U-shaped bar has big windows and high ceilings, contemporary dark wooden dining chairs and a long wall banquette, pale-topped tables, groups of sofas and armchairs and a wooden floor. Paintwork is pale grey and the planked walls are hung with watercolours. High chairs line the counter, where they serve Brakspears Bitter and Oxford Gold and Marstons Pedigree on handpump and several decent wines by the glass; background music. The little tucked-away back garden has pretty hanging baskets, orange stripey-cushioned benches, tables and chairs on flagstones and a gazebo with fairy lights. The bedrooms are airy and well equipped, and the breakfasts very good. This is sister pub to the Fox & Grapes in Wimbledon.

Popular food includes sandwiches, pork belly, snails and celeriac purée, mussels with fennel and wild garlic, beer-battered fish and chips, lemon and thyme-marinated poussin, lamb shoulder with wild garlic, rib-eye steak with béarnaise sauce and chips, and puddings such as chocolate brownie and prune and almond tart with buttermilk sorbet. *Benchmark main dish: burger with welsh rarebit and caramelised onions £14.25. Two-course evening meal £22.00.*

Brakspears ~ Lease Jessica Chanter ~ Real ale ~ (020) 7084 6888 ~ Open 11-11 ~
Bar food 12-3, 6-10; 12-9 Sun ~ Restaurant ~ Children welcome ~ Dogs welcome ~
Wi-fi ~ Bedrooms: /£135 ~ www.malthousefulham.co.uk *Recommended by Mike Swan,
Richard Tilbrook*

WEST LONDON   TQ1568   Map 12
Mute Swan ♀ ◀

Palace Gate, Hampton Court Road; ⇌ Hampton Court; KT8 9BN

**Handsome, refurbished pub close to the Thames with sunny seats
outside, an airy relaxed bar, an upstairs dining room, a thoughtful
choice of drinks and imaginative food**

Right opposite the gates to Hampton Court Palace, this carefully
refurbished pub is also just yards from the River Thames; the sunny
front terrace has plenty of seats and tables, so in good weather it's best
to get here early to bag one. The light and airy bar has four big leather
armchairs grouped together around a low table in the centre, while the
rest of the room has brown leather wall seating, high-backed Edwardian-
style cushioned dining chairs around dark tables, rugs on bare boards,
walls covered in interesting photographs, maps, prints and posters,
sizeable house plants, glass and stone bottles on the window sills and a
woodburning stove; the atmosphere is informal and relaxed. A fine range
of drinks includes Brunning & Price Phoenix Original, Hogs Back TEA,
Twickenham Naked Ladies and three guests on handpump, 19 wines by
the glass, a farm cider and 75 malt whiskies; staff are friendly, efficient
and helpful. A metal spiral staircase – presided over by an elegant metal
chandelier – leads up to the dining area where there are caramel-leather,
brass-studded chairs around well spaced tables on bare boards or
carpeting, and numerous photographs and prints. Dogs get a water bowl
on the ground floor. There are a few parking spaces in front, but you'll
probably have to park elsewhere.

 Attractively presented, the enjoyable food includes sandwiches, cured salmon
with cucumber and fennel salad, cucumber sorbet and tonic jelly, pigeon breast
with beetroot risotto and game jus, sharing platters, open vegetable samosa with
tandoori paneer cheese, crab linguine with ginger and chilli, venison, pork and prune
pudding, chicken, leek and ham hock pie, and puddings such as crème brûlée and
lemon and passion-fruit meringue pie. *Benchmark main dish: steak burger with
bacon, cheese, coleslaw and chips £12.95. Two-course evening meal £20.00.*

Brunning & Price ~ Manager Sal Morgan ~ Real ale ~ (020) 8941 5959 ~ Open 11-11
(midnight Fri, Sat); 11-9.30 Sun ~ Bar food 12-10 ~ Children welcome only in upstairs
restaurant ~ Dogs welcome ~ Wi-fi ~ www.muteswan.co.uk *Recommended by Harvey
Brown, Toby Jones*

WEST LONDON   Map 3
Old Orchard ◉ ♀

Off Park Lane; Harefield; ⇌ Denham (some distance away); UB9 6HJ

**Wonderful views from the garden in front of this Edwardian house,
a good choice of drinks, friendly staff and well liked, interesting,
brasserie-style food**

The position here is very special. Tables on the front terrace have a
stunning view down to the longboats on the canal and across to the
lakes that are part of the conservation area known as the Colne Valley
Regional Park; it's a haven for wildlife. The seats in the gazebo and the

picnic-sets in the garden have the same fantastic view. Inside, the open-plan rooms have an attractive mix of cushioned dining chairs around all sizes and shapes of dark wooden tables, lots of prints, maps and pictures covering the walls, books on shelves, old glass bottles on window sills and rugs on wood or parquet flooring. One room is hung with a sizeable rug and some tapestry. There are daily papers to read, three cosy coal fires, big pot plants and fresh flowers. Half a dozen real ales on handpump served by friendly, efficient staff include Phoenix Brunning & Price Original, Mighty Oak Oscar Wilde and Tring Side Pocket for a Toad alongside guests such as Binghams Vanilla Stout, Buntingford Highway Man and Cotleigh Harrier; also, 17 wines by the glass, 140 malt whiskies and two farm ciders. The atmosphere is civilised and easy-going.

 Rewarding food includes lunchtime sandwiches, tempura-battered cod cheeks with caper, parsley and lemon salad, beetroot-cured salmon with salmon mousse, crab linguine, vietnamese pork belly with mango and papaya salad, sweet potato, spinach and goats cheese lasagne, chicken, ham and leek pie, braised lamb shoulder with dauphinoise potatoes and redcurrant gravy, sea bream with cucumber salsa and prawn croquette, and puddings such as chocolate brownie and lemon posset. *Benchmark main dish: beer-battered fish and chips £12.75. Two-course evening meal £18.00.*

Brunning & Price ~ Manager Dan Redfern ~ Real ale ~ (01895) 822631 ~ Open 11.30-11; 12-10.30 Sun ~ Bar food 12-10 (9.30 Sun) ~ Children welcome ~ Dogs welcome ~ Wi-fi ~ www.oldorchard-harefield.co.uk *Recommended by M J Daly, Ross Balaam, David Jackman, Brian Glozier*

WEST LONDON
Portobello Gold ♀
Map 12

Portobello Road, opposite Denbigh Terrace; ⊖ Notting Hill Gate; W11 2QB

Engaging combination of pub, hotel and restaurant with a relaxed atmosphere, enjoyable food (especially in attractive dining conservatory) and excellent range of drinks; bedrooms

Almost bohemian and certainly enterprising, this fun place holds a monthly art and photographic exhibition and regular live music, and usefully opens early for breakfast, morning coffee, pastries and the papers. Our favourite part is the exotic-seeming dining room with its big tropical plants, photographs of famous singers and bands on the red or green walls, and contemporary high-backed wicker dining chairs around polished wooden tables of all sizes; a cage of vocal canaries adds to the outdoor effect and in summer they open up the sliding roof. The smaller front bar has a nice old fireplace and cushioned banquettes, and there's a new oyster bar. It's very relaxed, cheerful and informal, but can get a bit rushed when busy in the evening. Harveys Best and Wells & Youngs Bitter on handpump, 18 wines by the glass from a thoughtfully chosen list, 'as many quality tequilas as are imported into the UK' and classic cocktails. They also have a cigar menu, an eclectic choice of background music, TV, chess and backgammon. The back garden has seats and tables for dining, and there are a couple of tables and chairs on the pretty street outside. Some bedrooms are small, but there's a spacious apartment with a rooftop terrace and putting green. Although parking nearby is restricted, you can usually find a space (except on Saturdays).

Good, interesting food includes a breakfast menu (10am-12pm), oysters, sashimi of salmon with wasabi and sushi ginger, thai-style mussels, vegetarian fajitas, chicken caesar salad, wild boar and apple sausages on parsley mash with onion gravy, pork chop with cider apple sauce, seafood linguine, tempura-battered fish and chips, minute rib-eye steak with fries, and puddings such as pecan pie and chocolate and amaretti torte. *Benchmark main dish: burger with cheese, bacon, onions and chips £13.00. Two-course evening meal £20.00.*

Enterprise ~ Lease Michael Bell and Linda Johnson-Bell ~ Real ale ~ (020) 7460 4910 ~ Open 10am-midnight; 9am-12.30am Sat; 10am-11.30pm Sun ~ Bar food 10-10; 10-5, 7-10 Sat; 10-9 Sun ~ Restaurant ~ Children welcome ~ Dogs allowed in bar ~ Wi-fi ~ Live music Sun evening ~ Bedrooms: /£75 ~ www.portobellogold.com
Recommended by Martin Jones, Harvey Brown

WEST LONDON Map 12
Scarsdale

Edwardes Square; ⊖ *High Street Kensington; W8 6HE*

Kensington pub with winter fires and summer terrace, an easy-going atmosphere and good food and drink

In a lovely leafy square, this busy Georgian pub remains as relaxed and friendly as ever. It's all very easy-going with straightforward furniture: scrubbed pine tables, simple cushioned dining chairs, pews and built-in wall seats on bare boards, oil paintings in fancy gilt frames, old local photographs, coal-effect gas fires and heavily swagged curtains. Adnams Broadside, Fullers London Pride and Seafarers and a guest such as Liberation Ale on handpump, 16 wines by the glass and a dozen malt whiskies. The attractive front terrace has seats and tables under big parasols.

 The highly thought-of food includes duck and apricot terrine with apple chutney, salmon and broccoli fishcake with chilli and lemon mayonnaise, a pie of the day, cumberland sausages with herb mash and onion gravy, chargrilled chicken salad with honey and grain mustard dressing, spinach and ricotta tortellini with sun-blush tomato sauce, rib-eye steak with wedges, and puddings such as sticky toffee pudding and eton mess. *Benchmark main dish: slow-roasted lamb shoulder with garlic and rosemary sauce £16.95. Two-course evening meal £21.00.*

Fullers ~ Managers Raymond and Sarah Dodgson ~ Real ale ~ (020) 7937 1811 ~ Open 11-11; 12-10.30 Sun ~ Bar food 12-10 (9.30 Sun) ~ Restaurant ~ Children welcome in dining area only ~ Dogs welcome ~ Wi-fi ~ www.scarsdaletavern.co.uk
Recommended by Emma Scofield, Mike Swan

WEST LONDON Map 12
White Horse 🌟 ♈ ◧

Parsons Green; ⊖ *Parsons Green; SW6 4UL*

London Dining Pub of the Year

Cheerfully relaxed local with big terrace, an excellent range of carefully sourced drinks and imaginative food

Even when really pushed, the well trained and friendly staff remain as efficient as ever in this extremely popular pub. The stylishly modernised U-shaped bar has a gently upmarket and chatty atmosphere, plenty of chesterfield leather sofas and wooden tables, huge windows with slatted wooden blinds, wood and flagstone floors, and winter coal and log fires (one in an elegant marble fireplace); there's also an upstairs dining room with its own bar. The impressive range of drinks takes in regular real ales such as Adnams Broadside, Harveys Best, Oakham JHB and guests such as Shamblemoose Wyoming and West Berkshire Maggs Mild on handpump, imported keg beers from overseas (usually belgian and german but occasionally from further afield), six of the seven trappist beers, around 140 other foreign bottled beers, several malt whiskies and 20 good wines by the glass. They hold quarterly beer festivals, often spotlighting regional breweries. On summer evenings and weekends, the front terrace – which overlooks Parsons Green itself – has something of a continental feel with its many seats and tables; there are barbecues most sunny evenings.

 Interesting food includes lunchtime sandwiches, pork and rabbit terrine with piccalilli, crab, avocado, celeriac and apple coleslaw, chicken caesar salad, gnocchi with wild mushrooms, spinach and truffle cream, free-range sausages with mash, smoked haddock, salmon and cod pie, lamb rump with fennel purée, beetroot and watercress, and puddings. *Benchmark main dish: burger with bacon jam, cheese, relish and chips £15.50. Two-course evening meal £21.00.*

Mitchells & Butlers ~ Manager Jez Manterfield ~ Real ale ~ (020) 7736 2115 ~ Open 9.30am-midnight ~ Bar food 12-10.30 ~ Restaurant ~ Children welcome ~ Dogs allowed in bar ~ Wi-fi ~ www.whitehorsesw6.com *Recommended by Phil Bryant*

WEST LONDON
Map 12
Windsor Castle

Campden Hill Road; ✆ Notting Hill Gate; W8 7AR

Genuinely unspoilt, with lots of atmosphere in tiny, dark rooms and lovely summer garden; good beers and reliable food

With one of London's best pub gardens, this place feels secluded thanks to the high ivy-covered sheltering walls – there are lots of tables and chairs on flagstones, as well as a summer bar (and heaters for cooler evenings). The interior has a great deal of character and genuine old-fashioned charm, with a wealth of dark oak furnishings, sturdy high-backed built-in elm benches, time-smoked ceilings, soft lighting and a coal-effect fire. Three of the tiny unspoilt rooms have their own entrance from the street, but it's much more fun trying to navigate through the minuscule doors between them inside. Usually fairly quiet at lunchtime, it tends to be packed most evenings. The panelled and wood-floored dining room at the back overlooks the garden. Timothy Taylors Landlord and Windsor & Eton Knight of the Garter on handpump alongside eight guests from breweries such as Batemans, Ilkley, Sambrooks, Shepherd Neame and Triple fff; also, farm ciders, decent house wines, malt whiskies and jugs of Pimms.

The good, interesting food includes sandwiches, home-made scotch egg, pork, apple and leek terrine with piccalilli, smoked duck breast with artichoke purée, date purée and blood orange jelly, cherry tomato tarte tatin, free-range sausages with shallot crisps and red wine gravy, cider and tarragon battered cod with twice-cooked chips, chicken hotpot with bacon and cider, rabbit and crayfish pie, and puddings such as white chocolate and strawberry mousse and sticky toffee pudding with toffee sauce. *Benchmark main dish: burger with bacon jam, cheddar, relish and fries £16.00. Two-course evening meal £23.00.*

Mitchells & Butlers ~ Manager Suzanne Grantham ~ Real ale ~ (020) 7243 8797 ~ Open 12-11 (10.30 Sun) ~ Bar food 12-10 (9 Sun) ~ Restaurant ~ Children welcome till 7pm ~ Dogs welcome ~ Wi-fi ~ www.thewindsorcastlekensington.co.uk
Recommended by Conor McGaughey

The star-on-a-plate award, ⬤, distinguishes pubs where the food is of exceptional quality. The knife-and-fork symbol just means the pub serves food.

Also Worth a Visit in London

Besides the fully inspected pubs, you might like to try these pubs that have been recommended to us and described by readers. Do tell us what you think of them: feedback@goodguides.com

CENTRAL LONDON

EC1

Bishops Finger (020) 7248 2341
West Smithfield; EC1A 9JR Welcoming little pub close to Smithfield Market, Shepherd Neame ales including seasonal brews, good range of sausages and other food in bar or upstairs room; children welcome, seats out in front, closed weekends and bank holidays, otherwise open all day. *(Anon)*

Butchers Hook & Cleaver
(020) 7600 9181 *West Smithfield; EC1A 9DY* Fullers conversion of bank and adjoining butcher's, pleasant relaxed atmosphere, their full range kept well and enjoyable pubby food including various pies, spiral stairs to mezzanine; background music, free wi-fi; open all day, closed weekends. *(John and Gloria Isaacs)*

Craft Beer Company
Leather Lane; EC1N 7TR Corner drinkers' pub with excellent selection of real ales and craft beers plus an extensive bottled range (some real rarities), good choice of wines and spirits too, high stools and tables on bare boards, big chandelier hanging from mirrored ceiling, can get very busy but service remains efficient and friendly, food limited to snacks, upstairs room; open all day. *(N R White)*

Fox & Anchor (020) 7250 1300
Charterhouse Street; EC1M 6AA Beautifully restored late Victorian pub by Smithfield Market, welcoming staff, long slender bar with unusual pewter-topped counter, lots of mahogany, green leather and etched glass, small back snugs, ales such as Adnams, Harviestoun and Purity served in pewter tankards plus a house beer from Nethergate, oyster bar and good range of freshly cooked food including popular home-made pies and a daily roast carved at your table, tempting traditional puddings too; six individual well appointed bedrooms, open all day from 7am (8.30am weekends). *(N R White)*

Gunmakers (020) 7278 1022
Eyre Street Hill; EC1R 5ET Popular little Victorian pub with four interesting changing ales, friendly knowledgeable landlord, enjoyable and often individual food from daily blackboard, back conservatory and more room upstairs; dogs welcome, open all day weekdays, closed weekends. *(Anon)*

★**Jerusalem Tavern** (020) 7490 4281
Britton Street; EC1M 5UQ Convincing and atmospheric re-creation of a dark 18th-c tavern (1720 merchant's house with shopfront added 1810), tiny dimly lit bar, simple wood furnishings on bare boards, some remarkable old wall tiles, coal fires and candlelight, stairs to a precarious-feeling (though perfectly secure) balcony, plainer back room, St Peters beers tapped from the cask, short choice of lunchtime food, friendly attentive young staff; can get very crowded at peak times, no children; dogs welcome, seats out on pavement, open all day during the week, closed weekends, bank holidays and 24 Dec-2 Jan. *(Phil Bryant, Roger and Donna Huggins, Tom McLean, N R White)*

Old Fountain (020) 7253 2970
Baldwin Street; EC1V 9NU Popular traditional old pub in same family since 1964; long bar serving two rooms, up to eight real ales chalked up on board including Fullers London Pride, pubby food from sandwiches up (not Sat lunchtime), main carpeted part with wooden tables and chairs, padded stools and fish tank, darts, roof terrace and function room for live music; open all day. *(Roger and Donna Huggins, Dave G)*

Old Red Cow (020) 7726 2595
Long Lane; EC1A 9EJ Cheerful little corner pub with five changing ales from smaller brewers and a good range of other draught and bottled beers, nice food from home-made pies to steak tartare, Sun roasts, second bar upstairs; open all day. *(John and Gloria Isaacs, N R White)*

EC2

★**Dirty Dicks** (020) 7283 5888
Bishopsgate; EC2M 4NR Olde-worlde re-creation of traditional City tavern, busy and fun for foreign visitors, booths, barrel tables, exposed brick and low beams, interesting old prints, Wells & Youngs ales, good variety of enjoyable well priced food from sandwiches up, pleasant service, calmer cellar wine bar with wine racks overhead in brick barrel-vaulted ceiling, further upstairs area too; background music, games machines and TV; closed weekends. *(Anon)*

Hamilton Hall (020) 7247 3579
Bishopsgate; also entrance from Liverpool Street Station; EC2M 7PY Showpiece Wetherspoons with flamboyant Victorian baroque décor, plaster nudes and fruit mouldings, chandeliers, mirrors, good-sized comfortable mezzanine, lots of real ales

including interesting guests, decent wines and coffee, their usual food (all day) and competitive pricing, friendly staff; silenced machines, free wi-fi; good disabled access, café-style furniture out in front, open all day from 7am, can get very crowded after work. *(Claes Mauroy)*

Lord Aberconway (020) 7929 1743

Old Broad Street; EC2M 1QT Victorian feel with high moulded ceiling, dark panelling and some red leather bench seats, six well kept ales such as Adnams, Fullers and Lancaster, reasonably priced, typical Nicholsons menu from sandwiches up, wrought-iron-railed upper dining gallery; silent fruit machine, gets busy with after-work drinkers; handy for Liverpool Street Station, closed Sat evening, Sun. *(Jeremy King)*

EC3

East India Arms (020) 7265 5121

Fenchurch Street; EC3M 4BR Standing-room Victorian corner pub popular with City workers, well kept Shepherd Neame ales, good service, small single room with wood floor, old local photographs and brewery mirrors; tables outside, closed weekends. *(Taff Thomas)*

Hoop & Grapes (020) 7481 4583

Aldgate High Street; EC3N 1AL Originally 17th-c (dismantled and rebuilt 1983) and much bigger inside than it looks; long partitioned bare-boards bar with beams, timbers and panelling, furniture more modern including sofas, good range of real ale, Shepherd Neame ales and standard all-day (though till 6pm weekends) Nicholsons menu (very popular lunchtime); a few seats in front, closed weekends, otherwise open all day. *(Phil Bryant)*

Jamaica Wine House

(020) 7929 6972 *St Michael's Alley, Cornhill; EC3V 9DS* 19th-c pub on the site of London's first coffee house, in a warren of small alleys; traditional Victorian décor with ornate ceilings, oak-panelled bar, booths and bare boards, Shepherd Neame ales and wide choice of wines, food in downstairs lunchtime dining area, friendly helpful service, bustling atmosphere (quietens after 8pm); closed weekends. *(Ross Balaam)*

Lamb (020) 7626 2454

Leadenhall Market; EC3V 1LR Well run stand-up bar, staff always polite and efficient even when very busy with sharp City lads, Wells & Youngs ales, good choice of wines by the glass, panelling, engraved glass, plenty of ledges and shelves, spiral stairs up to tables and seating in small light and airy carpeted gallery overlooking market's central crossing, corner servery doing lunchtime carvery and other food, separate stairs to nice bright dining room (not cheap), also basement bar with shiny wall tiling and own entrance;

tables out under splendid Victorian market roof – crowds here in warmer months, open all day, closed weekends. *(N R White)*

Ship (020) 7929 3903

Talbot Court, off Eastcheap; EC3V 0BP Interesting pub tucked down alleyway; busy bare-boards bar with soft lighting and ornate decor, quieter upstairs carpeted bar usually set for dining, friendly efficient staff, several well kept ales including a house beer from St Austell, good value Nicholsons food; open all day weekdays, closed weekends. *(N R White)*

Ship (020) 7702 4422

Hart Street; EC3R 7NB Tiny one-room City pub with ornate flower-decked façade; friendly landlady and staff, Caledonian ales and two well kept changing guests, some food including sandwiches and burgers, limited seating; spiral stairs down to lavatories; closed weekends. *(Taff Thomas)*

Simpsons Tavern (020) 7626 9985

Just off Cornhill; EC3V 9DR Pleasingly old-fashioned place founded in 1757; rather clubby small panelled bar serving five real ales including a guest, stairs down to another bar with snacks, traditional chophouse with upright stall seating (expect to share a table) and similar upstairs restaurant, good value straightforward food from sandwiches and snacks up; open weekday lunchtimes and from 8am Tues-Fri for breakfast. *(Anon)*

Swan (020) 7929 6550

Ship Tavern Passage, off Gracechurch Street; EC3V 1LY Traditional Fullers pub with bustling narrow flagstoned bar, their ales kept well, generous lunchtime sandwiches and snacks, friendly efficient service, neatly kept Victorian panelled décor, low lighting, larger more ordinary carpeted bar upstairs; silent corner TV; covered alley used by smokers, open all day Mon-Fri (may be closed by 8.30pm), shut at weekends. *(N R White)*

EC4

★ Black Friar (020) 7236 5474

Queen Victoria Street; EC4V 4EG An architectural gem (some of the best Edwardian bronze and marble art nouveau work to be found anywhere) and built on site of 13th-c Dominican priory; inner back room (the Grotto) with low vaulted mosaic ceiling, big bas-relief friezes of jolly monks set into richly coloured florentine marble walls, gleaming mirrors, seats built into golden marble recesses and an opulent pillared inglenook, tongue-in-cheek verbal embellishments such as Silence is Golden and Finery is Foolish, and try to spot the opium-smoking hints modelled into the front room's fireplace; six ales including Fullers, Sharps and St Austell Nicholsons, plenty of wines by the glass, sound traditional all-day food (speciality pies); children welcome if quiet, plenty of room on wide forecourt, handy for new Blackfriars Station. *(Phil Bryant, G Jennings, N R White, Pete Walker, Sue and Mike Todd and others)*

Castle (020) 7405 5470

Castle Street/Furnival Street; EC4A 1JS A pub has existed here since the 16th c – although present building dates from 1901; traditional bare-boards bar with dark panelling, mirrors and minimal furnishings (window ledges and stools), eight ales including house Red Car with many from smaller breweries, several wines by the glass, limited lunchtime bar food such as steak and stilton pie and a daily roast, friendly staff, upstairs dining area; background music, TV; open all day weekdays, closed weekends. *(Phil Bryant)*

Centre Page (020) 7236 3614

Aka the Horn; Knightrider Street near Millennium Bridge; EC4V 5BH Modernised pub with window booths or 'traps' in narrow entrance room, more space beyond, traditional style with panelling and subdued lighting, chatty atmosphere, mix of after-work drinkers and tourists, friendly efficient young staff, simple reasonably priced bar menu (from 9am for breakfast), downstairs dining room, well kept Fullers ales, tea and coffee; background music; tables outside with good view of St Paul's. *(John Jenkins, David Jackman)*

Cockpit (020) 7248 7315

St Andrews Hill/Ireland Place, off Queen Victoria Street; EC4V 5BY Plenty of atmosphere in this little corner pub near St Paul's; as name suggests, a former cockfighting venue with surviving spectators' gallery; good selection of ales such as Adnams, Black Sheep, Dartmoor and Timothy Taylors, lunchtime food. *(Richard Tilbrook)*

Old Bell (020) 7583 0216

Fleet Street, near Ludgate Circus; EC4Y 1DH Dimly lit 17th-c tavern backing on to St Bride's; stained-glass bow window, heavy black beams, bare boards and flagstones, half a dozen or more well kept changing ales from island servery (can try before you buy, tasting trays available), usual Nicholsons food, friendly helpful young staff and cheery atmosphere, various seating nooks, brass-topped tables, coal fire; background music; covered and heated outside area, open all day (may close early weekend evenings). *(Conor McGaughey, N R White, David M Smith)*

★ Olde Cheshire Cheese

(020) 7353 6170 *Wine Office Court, off 145 Fleet Street; EC4A 2BU* Best to visit this 17th-c former chophouse outside peak times when it can be packed (early evening especially); soaked in history with warmly old-fashioned unpretentious rooms, high beams, bare boards, old built-in black benches, Victorian paintings on dark brown walls, big open fires, tiny snug and steep stone steps down to unexpected series of cosy areas and secluded alcoves, Sam Smiths, all-day pubby food; look out for the famous parrot (now stuffed) that entertained princes and other distinguished guests for over 40 years; children allowed in eating area lunchtime only, closed Sun evening. *(N R White)*

Olde Watling (020) 7248 8935

Watling Street; EC4M 9BR Heavy-beamed and timbered post-blitz replica of pub built by Wren in 1668; interesting choice of well kept beers, standard Nicholsons menu, good service, quieter back bar and upstairs dining room; open all day. *(Phil Bryant)*

SW1

Albert (020) 7222 5577

Victoria Street; SW1H 0NP Busy open-plan airy bar with cut and etched windows, gleaming mahogany, ornate ceiling and solid comfortable furnishings, enjoyable pubby food all day from sandwiches up, well kept Fullers London Pride, Wells & Youngs Bombardier and guests, 24 wines by the glass, efficient cheerful service, handsome staircase lined with portraits of prime ministers leading up to carvery/dining room; background music, games machine, lavatories down steep stairs; children welcome if eating, open all day from 8am (breakfast till noon). *(Anon)*

Antelope (020) 7824 8512

Eaton Terrace; SW1W 8EZ Pretty little flower-decked Belgravia pub, traditional interior with snug seating areas, bare boards and panelling, mix of old and new furniture including leather bucket chairs, interesting prints, gas-effect coal fire in tiled Victorian fireplace, Fullers ales from central servery and decent house wines, upstairs dining room (children allowed) serving reasonably priced pubby food; TVs, free wi-fi, daily papers; dogs welcome, open all day and can get crowded in the evening. *(Anthony and Marie Lewis)*

Buckingham Arms (020) 7222 3386

Petty France; SW1H 9EU Welcoming and relaxed bow-windowed early 19th-c local, Wells & Youngs ales and a guest from long curved bar, good range of wines by the glass, reasonably priced pubby food from back open kitchen, elegant mirrors and dark woodwork, stained-glass screens, stools at modern high tables, some armchairs and upholstered banquettes, unusual side corridor with elbow ledge for drinkers; background music, TV; dogs welcome, handy for Buckingham Palace, Westminster Abbey and St James's Park, open all day, till 6pm weekends. *(Conor McGaughey, Phil Bryant)*

Cask & Glass (020) 7834 7630

Palace Street; SW1E 5HN Snug one-room traditional pub with good range of Shepherd Neame ales, friendly staff and atmosphere, good value lunchtime sandwiches, old prints and shiny black panelling; quiet corner TV; hanging baskets and a few tables outside, handy for Queen's Gallery, open all day, till 8pm Sat, closed Sun. *(Anon)*

Cask Pub & Kitchen

(020) 7630 7225 *Charlwood Street/ Tachbrook Street; SW1V 2EE* Modern and spacious with simple furnishings, excellent choice of real ales and craft beers, also over 500 in bottles, decent range of wines too, friendly knowledgeable staff, good burgers (roasts on Sun), chatty atmosphere – can get packed evenings and noisy, regular beer-related events such as 'Meet the Brewer'; downstairs gents'; some outside seating, open all day. *(Richard Tilbrook, N R White)*

Clarence (020) 7930 4808

Whitehall; SW1A 2HP Civilised beamed corner pub (Geronimo Inn), Wells & Youngs and guests, decent wines by the glass and popular food from snacks up, friendly chatty staff, well spaced tables and varied seating including tub chairs and banquettes, upstairs dining area; pavement tables, open (and food) all day. *(Anon)*

★ Fox & Hounds (020) 7730 6367

Passmore Street/Graham Terrace; SW1W 8HR Small convivial Wells & Youngs local, warm red décor with big hunting prints, old sepia photographs and toby jugs, wall benches and sofas, book-lined back room, hanging plants under attractive skylight, coal-effect gas fire, some low-priced pubby food; can get crowded with after-work drinkers. *(Claes Mauroy)*

★ Grenadier (020) 7235 3074

Wilton Row; the turning off Wilton Crescent looks prohibitive, but the barrier and watchman are there to keep out cars; SW1X 7NR Steps up to cosy old mews pub with lots of character and military history, but not much space (avoid 5-7pm); simple unfussy panelled bar, stools and wooden benches, changing ales such as Fullers, Timothy Taylors, Wells & Youngs and Woodfordes from rare pewter-topped counter, famous bloody marys, bar food on blackboard, intimate back restaurant, no mobiles or photography; children over 8 and dogs allowed, sentry box and single table outside, open all day. *(Conor McGaughey, Phil Bryant)*

Jugged Hare (020) 7828 1543

Vauxhall Bridge Road/Rochester Row; SW1V 1DX Popular Fullers Ale & Pie pub in former colonnaded bank; pillars, dark wood, balustraded balcony, large chandelier, busts and sepia London photographs, smaller back dining room, six well kept ales, reasonably

priced food from sandwiches up including pie range, good friendly service; background music, TVs, silent fruit machine; open all day. *(Anon)*

★ Lord Moon of the Mall

(020) 7839 7701 *Whitehall; SW1A 2DY* Wetherspoons bank conversion with elegant main room, big arched windows looking over Whitehall, old prints and a large painting of Tim Martin (founder of the chain), through an arch the style is more recognisably Wetherspoons with neatly tiled areas, bookshelves opposite long bar, up to nine real ales and their good value food (from breakfasts up); silent fruit machines, cash machine; children allowed if eating, dogs welcome, open all day from 8am (till midnight Fri, Sat). *(Pete Walker)*

Morpeth Arms (020) 7834 6442

Millbank; SW1P 4RW Victorian pub facing Thames, roomy and comfortable, with fine view across river from upstairs room, some etched and cut glass, lots of mirrors, paintings, prints and old photographs, well kept Wells & Youngs and a guest, decent choice of wines, fair value food served all day, welcoming staff, reputedly haunted (built on site of Millbank Prison, some cells remain below); background music; seats outside (a lot of traffic), handy for Tate Britain and Thames Path walkers. *(Anon)*

Nags Head (020) 7235 1135

Kinnerton Street; SW1X 8ED Unspoilt little mews pub, low-ceilinged panelled front room with unusual sunken counter, log-effect gas fire in old range, narrow passage down to even smaller bar, Adnams from 19th-c handpumps, all-day no-frills food, theatrical mementoes, old what-the-butler-saw machine and one-armed bandit, no mobiles; individual background music; well behaved children and dogs allowed, a few seats outside, open all day. *(Claes Mauroy, Conor McGaughey)*

Red Lion (020) 7930 5826

Parliament Street; SW1A 2NH Recently refurbished Victorian pub by Houses of Parliament, used by Foreign Office staff and MPs, divided bare-boards bar with showy chandeliers suspended from fine moulded ceiling, parliamentary cartoons and prints, Fullers/Gales beers and decent wines from long counter, good range of food, efficient staff, also clubby cellar bar and upstairs panelled dining room; free wi-fi; children welcome, outside bench seating, open all day (till 9pm Sun). *(Anon)*

★ Red Lion (020) 7321 0782

Duke of York Street; SW1Y 6JP Pretty little Victorian pub, remarkably preserved and packed with customers often spilling out on to pavement by mass of foliage and flowers; series of small rooms with lots of polished mahogany, a gleaming profusion of mirrors, cut/etched windows and chandeliers, striking ornamental plaster ceiling, Fullers/Gales beers, simple good value bar food (all day weekdays, snacks evening, diners have priority over a few of the front tables); no children; dogs welcome, closed Sun and bank holidays, otherwise open all day. *(Anon)*

Speaker (020) 7222 1749

Great Peter Street; SW1P 2HA Bustling chatty atmosphere in unpretentious smallish corner pub (can get packed at peak times), well kept Timothy Taylors, Wells & Youngs and guests, bottled beers and lots of whiskies, limited simple but well liked food, friendly staff, panelling, political cartoons and prints, no mobiles or background music; open all day weekdays, closed Sat, Sun. *(Anon)*

★ St Stephens Tavern (020) 7925 2286

Parliament Street; SW1A 2JR Victorian pub opposite Houses of Parliament and Big Ben (so quite touristy), lofty ceilings with brass chandeliers, tall windows with etched glass and swagged curtains, gleaming mahogany, charming upper gallery bar (may be reserved for functions), four well kept Badger ales from handsome counter with pedestal lamps, friendly efficient staff, enjoyable good value food from sandwiches up, division bell for MPs and lots of parliamentary memorabilia; open all day. *(Ross Balaam, Dave Braisted, Paul Humphreys)*

Wetherspoons (020) 7931 0445

Victoria Station; SW1V 1JT Modern pub up escalators on mezzanine with glass wall overlooking main concourse and platform indicators, good value changing ales, plenty of wines by the glass and a couple of real ciders, reasonably priced food, prompt friendly service; free wi-fi; children welcome, some tables outside, open all day from 7am. *(Tony and Wendy Hobden)*

White Swan (020) 7821 8568

Vauxhall Bridge Road; SW1V 2SA Roomy corner pub handy for Tate Britain, lots of dark dining tables on three levels in long room, well cooked reasonably priced pubby food, six or more ales including Adnams, Fullers, Portobello and Timothy Taylors, decent wines by the glass, quick helpful uniformed staff; background music, can get very busy at peak times; open all day. *(Dr and Mrs J D Abell)*

SW3

★ Coopers Arms (020) 7376 3120

Flood Street; SW3 5TB Useful bolthole for King's Road shoppers (so can get busy); comfortable dark-walled open-plan bar with mix of good-sized tables on floorboards, pre-war sideboard and dresser, railway clock, moose head, Wells & Youngs ales and good all-day bar food; well behaved children till 7pm, dogs allowed in bar, courtyard garden. *(Richard and Penny Gibbs)*

Pigs Ear (020) 7352 2908

Old Church Street; SW3 5BS Civilised L-shaped corner pub, friendly and relaxed, with short interesting choice of bar food and more elaborate evening menu, lots of wines by the glass including champagne and good Ridgeview english sparkling wine, three changing ales such as Caledonian Deuchars IPA , Uley Pigs Ear and Wandle, good coffee and service, tables and benches on wood floors, butterflies and 1960s posters on grey/green panelling, large mirrors and huge windows, open fire, upstairs restaurant; background music; children and dogs (in bar) welcome, open all day. *(Richard and Penny Gibbs)*

Surprise (020) 7351 6954

Christchurch Terrace; SW3 4AJ Late Victorian Chelsea pub revamped by Geronimo Inns and popular with well heeled locals, Wells & Youngs, Sharps and a house beer (HMS Surprise) from light wood servery, champagne and plenty of other wines by the glass, interesting food including british tapas-style choices, canapé boards and set menu, friendly service, soft grey décor and comfortable furnishings with floral sofas and armchairs on sturdy floorboards, stained-glass partitioning, upstairs dining room, daily papers; open all day. *(Susan and John Douglas)*

W1

★ Argyll Arms (020) 7734 6117

Argyll Street; W1F 7TP Popular and unexpectedly individual pub with three interesting little front cubicle rooms (essentially unchanged since 1860s), wooden partitions and impressive frosted and engraved glass, mirrored corridor to spacious back room, good choice of beers including Brains, Nicholsons, Fullers and Sharps, well liked reasonably priced food in bar or upstairs dining room overlooking pedestrianised street, teas and coffees, theatrical photographs; background music, fruit machine; children welcome till 8pm, open (and food) all day. *(Ian Phillips, Tracey and Stephen Groves)*

★ Audley (020) 7499 1843

Mount Street; W1K 2RX Classic late Victorian Mayfair pub, opulent red plush, mahogany panelling and engraved glass, chandeliers and clock in extravagantly carved bracket hanging from ornately corniced ceiling, Fullers London Pride, Sharps Doom Bar, Taylor Walker 1730 and guests from long polished bar, good choice of pub food (reasonably priced for the area), friendly efficient service, upstairs panelled dining room, wine bar in the cellar; quiet background music, TV, pool; children till 6pm, pavement tables, open (and food) all day. *(Anon)*

Crown & Two Chairmen

(020) 7437 8192 *Bateman Street/Dean Street; W1D 3SB* Large main room with smaller area off to the right, different height tables on bare boards, Sharps, Windsor & Eton and three guests, also craft beers such as Camden Town, decent food from bar snacks up including set menu and Sun roasts, upstairs dining room, good mix of customers (gets busy with after-work drinkers); free wi-fi; open (and food) all day. *(Jeremy King)*

De Hems (020) 7437 2494

Macclesfield Street; W1D 5BW Nicholsons dutch bar (some recent refurbishment), panelled walls, mixed tables on bare boards, big continental founts and good range of interesting bottled beers, dutch-influenced food as well as more traditional choices, friendly service, smaller upstairs area; background music; open all day and can get very busy. *(Mrs Sally Scott)*

★Dog & Duck (020) 7494 0697

Bateman Street/Frith Street; W1D 3AJ Bags of character in this tiny Soho pub – best enjoyed in the afternoon when not so packed; unusual old tiles and mosaics (the dog with tongue hanging out in hot pursuit of a duck is notable), heavy old advertising mirrors and open fire, Fullers London Pride and guests from unusual little counter and quite a few wines by the glass, enjoyable well-priced food in cosy upstairs dining room; background music drowned out by cheerful chatter; children allowed upstairs, dogs in bar, open (and food) all day. *(Richard and Penny Gibbs, Jeremy King, David Jackman, Dr and Mrs A K Clarke)*

French House (020) 7437 2477

Dean Street; W1D 5BG Small character Soho pub with impressive range of wines and bottled beers, other unusual drinks, some draught beers (no real ales or pint glasses), lively chatty atmosphere – mainly standing room, theatre memorabilia, shortish choice of reasonably priced food (Mon-Fri till 4pm) in bar or upstairs restaurant, efficient staff; no music or mobile phones, can get very busy evenings with customers spilling on to the street, open all day. *(Jeremy King)*

★Grapes (020) 7493 4216

Shepherd Market; W1J 7QQ Genuinely old-fashioned pub with dimly lit bar, plenty of well worn plush red furnishings, stuffed birds and fish in display cases, wood floors, panelling, coal fire and snug back alcove, six ales including Fullers, Sharps and a house beer from Brains, good choice of authentic thai food (not Sun evening), english food too, lots of customers (especially early evening) spilling out on to square; children till 6pm weekdays (anytime weekends), open all day. *(Dr Matt Burleigh, Ian Phillips, Iain Clark)*

★Guinea (020) 7409 1728

Bruton Place; W1J 6NL Lovely hanging baskets and chatty customers outside this tiny 17th-c mews pub, standing room only at peak times, a few cushioned wooden seats and tables on tartan carpet, side elbow shelf and snug back area, old-fashioned prints, planked ceiling, Wells & Youngs and a guest from striking counter, famous steak and kidney pie, grills and some sandwiches (no food weekends), smart Guinea Grill restaurant; no children; closed Sat lunchtime, Sun and bank holidays. *(Dr Matt Burleigh)*

Prince Regent (020) 7486 7395

Marylebone High Street; W1U 5JN Victorian corner pub in Marleybone village, flamboyant (if slightly worn) bare-boards interior with richly coloured furnishings, large gilt mirrors and opulent chandeliers, four changing ales, sensibly priced home-made food including good value weekday set menu and Sat brunch, upstairs 'Opium Room'; free wi-fi; open all day. *(John Voos)*

Three Tuns (020) 7408 0330

Portman Mews S; W1H 6HP Large bare-boards front bar and sizeable lounge/ dining area with beams and nooks and crannies, Greene King, Timothy Taylors and Wells & Youngs, enjoyable reasonably priced pubby food, good friendly staff and vibrant atmosphere; street benches. *(Phil and Jane Hodson)*

Tottenham (020) 7636 8324

Oxford Street, near junction with Tottenham Court Road; W1D 1AN Ornate late Victorian pub with long narrow bar, old tiling, mirrors, mahogany fittings and so forth, also three notable murals behind glass of voluptuous nymphs, dark floorboards and leather banquettes, extensive range of reasonably priced beers, enjoyable all-day food from Nicholsons menu, friendly service, dining room downstairs; background music and fruit machine; can get very busy at lunchtime. *(Susan and John Douglas, Comus and Sarah Elliott)*

W2 TQ2680

Leinster Arms (020) 7402 4670

Leinster Terrace; W2 3EU Flower-decked Bayswater pub close to Hyde Park, friendly and busy, with good range of beers and well liked food; sports TV, free wi-fi; children and dogs welcome, open (and food) all day. *(Dr and Mrs A K Clarke)*

Mad Bishop & Bear

(020) 7402 2441 *Paddington Station; W2 1HB* Up escalators from concourse, full Fullers range kept well and a guest beer, good wine choice, reasonably priced standard food quickly served including breakfast from 8am (10am Sun), ornate plasterwork, etched mirrors and fancy lamps, parquet, tiles and

carpet, booths with leather banquettes, lots of wood and prints, train departures screen; background music, TVs, games machine; tables out overlooking station, open all day till 11pm (10.30pm Sun). *(Dr and Mrs A K Clarke, Pete Walker)*

★**Victoria** (020) 7724 1191
Strathearn Place; W2 2NH Well run bare-boards pub with lots of Victorian pictures and memorabilia, cast-iron fireplaces, gilded mirrors and mahogany panelling, brass mock-gas lamps above attractive horseshoe bar serving Fullers ales and guests from smaller breweries, several wines by the glass and reasonably priced popular food, friendly service and chatty relaxed atmosphere; upstairs has small library/snug and replica of Gaiety Theatre bar (mostly for private functions now); quiet background music, TV; pavement tables, open all day. *(Phil Bryant, Dr and Mrs A K Clarke)*

WC1

Calthorpe Arms (020) 7278 4732
Grays Inn Road; WC1X 8JR Friendly early Victorian corner local with well kept Wells & Youngs ales and guests, enjoyable low-priced pub food including good Sun roasts, free bar nibbles too on Sun, carpeted bar with plush wall seats, upstairs overspill dining/function room; sports TV; dogs welcome, pavement tables, open all day. *(Anon)*

★**Cittie of Yorke** (020) 7242 7670
High Holborn; WC1V 6BN Splendid back bar rather like a baronial hall with extraordinarily extended bar counter, 1,000-gallon wine vats resting above gantry, big bulbous lights hanging from soaring raftered roof, intimate ornately carved booths, triangular fireplace with grates on all three sides, smaller comfortable panelled room with lots of little prints of York, cheap Sam Smiths beers and reasonably priced bar food, lots of students, lawyers and City types but plenty of space to absorb crowds; fruit machine; children welcome, open all day, closed Sun. *(Barry Collett, Pete Walker, Phil Bryant, Mrs Sally Scott)*

★**Lamb** (020) 7405 0713
Lamb's Conduit Street; WC1N 3LZ Famously unspoilt Victorian pub with bank of cut-glass swivelling snob screens around U-shaped counter, sepia photographs of 1890s actresses on ochre panelled walls, traditional cast-iron-framed tables, snug little back room, Wells & Youngs and guests, good choice of malt whiskies, straightforward pubby food including good baguettes, can get very busy but staff cope well; children welcome till 5pm, slatted wooden seats out in front, more in small courtyard, Foundling Museum nearby, open all day (till midnight Thurs-Sat). *(Roy Hoing, Tracey and Stephen Groves)*

Museum Tavern (020) 7242 8987
Museum Street/Great Russell Street; WC1B 3BA Traditional high-ceilinged ornate Victorian pub facing British Museum, busy lunchtime and early evening, but can be quite peaceful other times, half a dozen ales and several wines by the glass, straightforward Taylor Walker menu, friendly helpful staff; one or two tables out under gas lamps, open all day. *(Eric Larkham)*

Norfolk Arms (020) 7388 3937
Leigh Street; WC1H 9EP Atmospheric tile-fronted pub with ornate ceiling and other high-Victorian features, very good tapas, a couple of well kept changing ales and nice wines, close-set tables in bustling U-shaped bar, friendly efficient service; handy for British Museum. *(Richard Tilbrook, Tracey and Stephen Groves)*

Penderels Oak (020) 7242 5669
High Holborn; WC1V 7HJ Vast Wetherspoons with attractive décor and woodwork, lots of books, pew seating around central tables, their well priced food and fine choice of good value real ales, efficient friendly staff, cellar bar; pavement seating, open all day from 8am. *(Anon)*

Plough (020) 3582 3812
Museum Street/Little Russell Street; WC1A 1LH Popular and welcoming Bloomsbury local, with longish bar and upstairs drinking/dining room, well kept ales and enjoyable fairly priced food from short menu, quick service; a few tables out in front. *(Eric Larkham)*

★**Princess Louise** (020) 7405 8816
High Holborn; WC1V 7EP Splendid Victorian gin palace with extravagant décor – even the gents' has its own preservation order; gloriously opulent main bar with wood and glass partitions, fine etched and gilt mirrors, brightly coloured and fruit-shaped tiles, slender Portland stone columns soaring towards the lofty and deeply moulded plaster ceiling, open fire, cheap Sam Smiths from long counter, competitively priced pubby food (not Fri-Sun) in quieter upstairs room; gets crowded early weekday evenings, no children; open all day. *(Giles and Annie Francis, Phil Bryant, Barry Collett, Ian Phillips)*

Queens Larder (020) 7837 5627
Queen Square; WC1N 3AR Small character pub on corner of traffic-free square and cobbled Cosmo Place, also known as Queen Charlotte (where she stored food for her mad husband George III who was being cared for nearby); circular cast-iron tables, wall benches and stools around attractive U-shaped bar, theatre posters on dark panelled walls, Greene King ales, decent choice of fairly priced pubby food, upstairs function room; background jazz; dogs welcome, picnic-sets and heater outside. *(John Wooll, Phil Bryant)*

★**Skinners Arms** (020) 7837 5621
Judd Street; WC1H 9NT Richly decorated,
with glorious woodwork, marble pillars, high
ceilings and ornate windows, lots of London
prints on busy wallpaper, interesting layout
including comfortable back seating area,
Greene King Abbot and guests from attractive
long bar, decent home-made food (very popular
burgers and fish and chips), unobtrusive
background music, muted corner TV; pavement
picnic-sets, handy for British Library, open all
day, closed Sun. *(Andy Lickfold)*

WC2
Angel (020) 7240 2876
St Giles High Street; WC2H 8LE
Interesting Victorian pub with warren of
little rooms including comfortable upstairs
sitting room, cheap Sam Smiths Old
Brewery tapped from the cask, welcoming
landlord. *(Richard Tilbrook)*

Bear & Staff (020) 7930 5261
Bear Street; WC2H 7AX Traditional
Nicholsons corner pub with six well kept
changing ales, standard pubby food from
sandwiches and sharing platters up, upstairs
dining room named after Charlie Chaplin
who used the pub; open all day. *(Anon)*

★**Chandos** (020) 7836 1401
St Martin's Lane; WC2N 4ER Busy
bare-boards bar (can get packed early
evening) with snug cubicles, lots of theatre
memorabilia on stairs up to smarter more
comfortable lounge with opera photographs,
low wooden tables, panelling, leather sofas
and coloured windows, cheap Sam Smiths
and reasonably priced food; background
music and games machines; children upstairs
till 6pm, note the automaton on the roof
(working 10am-2pm, 4-9pm), open all day
from 9am (for breakfast). *(Anon)*

Cheshire Cheese (020) 7836 2347
*Little Essex Street/Milford Lane;
WC2R 3LD* Small cosy panelled pub with
leaded bow windows, beams and high-backed
settles, well kept St Austell Tribute, Sharps
Doom Bar and Wells & Youngs Bombardier,
decent wines, low-priced pubby food served
by friendly staff; background music; closed
weekends. *(Anon)*

Coal Hole (020) 7379 9883
Strand; WC2R 0DW Well preserved
Edwardian pub adjacent to the Savoy;
original leaded windows, classical wall
reliefs, mock-baronial high ceiling and raised
back gallery, ten changing ales from central
servery, standard Nicholsons menu, wine bar
downstairs; sports TV; open all day. *(Dr and
Mrs A K Clarke, N R White)*

★**Cross Keys** (020) 7836 5185
Endell Street/Betterton Street; WC2H 9EB
Foliage-covered Covent Garden pub with
fascinating interior, masses of photographs,

pictures and posters including Beatles
memorabilia, all kinds of brassware and
bric-a-brac from stuffed fish to musical
instruments, three well kept Brodies ales
and couple of guests (usually smaller London
brewers), decent wines by the glass, good
lunchtime sandwiches and a few bargain
hot dishes; fruit machine, gents' downstairs;
sheltered outside cobbled area with flower
tubs, open all day. *(Anon)*

Edgar Wallace (020) 7353 3120
Essex Street; WC2R 3JE Simple spacious
open-plan pub dating from 18th c, eight
well kept ales including some unusual
ones and a beer badged for them from
Nethergate, enjoyable good value food all
day from sandwiches up, friendly efficient
service, half-panelled walls and red ceilings,
interesting Edgar Wallace memorabilia
(pub renamed 1975 to mark his centenary)
and lots of old beer and cigarette adverts,
upstairs dining room; a few high tables in
side alleyway, closed weekends. *(N R White)*

George (020) 7353 9638
Strand; WC2R 1AP Timbered pub near
the law courts, long narrow bare-boards
bar, nine real ales and a dozen wines by the
glass, lunchtime food from sandwiches to
good value weekday carvery in upstairs bar,
separate evening menu, comedy club Sat
night; sports TVs; open all day. *(N R White)*

★**Harp** (020) 7836 0291
47 Chandos Place; WC2N 4HS Friendly
unpretentious pub with long narrow bar, high
stools and elbow tables, much prized window
seats, big mirrors on red walls, some lovely
stained glass and quirkily executed celebrity
portraits, up to ten real ales including Dark
Star, Harveys and Sambrooks, good choice
of traditional ciders/perries and quite a few
malt whiskies, range of lunchtime sausages
served in baguettes, quieter little upstairs
room; open all day. *(Brian and Anna Marsden,
Comus and Sarah Elliott, Pete Walker, N R White)*

Knights Templar (020) 7831 2660
Chancery Lane; WC2A 1DT Reliable
Wetherspoons in big-windowed former
bank, marble pillars, handsome fittings and
plasterwork, good bustling atmosphere on
two levels, some interesting real ales at
bargain prices, good wine choice and usual
well priced food, friendly staff; remarkably
handsome lavatories; free wi-fi; open all
day Mon-Fri, till 5pm Sat, closed Sun.
(Ian Herdman, Taff Thomas)

Lady Ottoline (020) 7831 0008
Northington Street; WC1N 2JF Restored
Bloomsbury pub with real mix of antique-
style wooden dining chairs and tables on bare
boards, enjoyable food from short menu, four
real ales and good wines, friendly service,
upstairs dining rooms; peaceful atmosphere
despite TV; open all day. *(Tom and Ruth Rees)*

Nell of Old Drury (020) 7836 5328

Catherine Street; WC2B 5JS Small friendly bow-windowed pub, lots of theatrical posters, soft lighting and comfortable seats, real ales such as Sharps Doom Bar, no food, chatty atmosphere (but can get packed), room upstairs; open all day Sat, closed Sun. *(Taff Thomas)*

Porterhouse (020) 7379 7917

Maiden Lane; WC2E 7NA Good daytime pub (can be packed evenings), London outpost of Dublin's Porterhouse microbrewery, their interesting beers along with guests and lots of bottled imports, good choice of wines by the glass, reasonably priced food from sandwiches up, shiny three-level labyrinth of stairs (lifts for disabled), galleries and copper ducting and piping, some nice design touches, sonorous open-work clock, neatly cased bottled beer displays; background and live music, sports TV (repeated in gents'); tables on front terrace, open all day. *(Anon)*

Salisbury (020) 7836 5863

St Martin's Lane; WC2N 4AP Gleaming Victorian pub in the heart of the West End, a wealth of cut-glass and mahogany, curved upholstered wall seat creating impression of several distinct areas, wonderfully ornate bronze light fittings, lots of mirrors, back room popular with diners (can be closed for private functions) and separate small side room, some interesting photographs including Dylan Thomas enjoying a drink here in 1941, lots of theatre posters, up to six well kept ales, bar food (from sharing platters up) all day, coffees and cheerful staff; steep stairs down to lavatories; children allowed till 5pm, fine details on building exterior, seats in pedestrianised side alley, open till midnight Fri, Sat. *(Michael Butler, B and M Kendall, Susan and John Douglas, Pete Walker)*

Ship (020) 7405 1992

Gate Street; WC2A 3HP Tucked-away bare-boards pub with roomy minimally furnished bar, some booth seating, chesterfields by open fire, quite dark with leaded lights, panelling and plaster relief ceiling, six well kept changing ales, enjoyable bar food (all day weekends), upstairs restaurant with separate menu, friendly service; background music. *(John Evans)*

★ Ship & Shovell (020) 7839 1311

Craven Passage, off Craven Street; WC2N 5PH Well kept Badger ales and a guest, good friendly staff, decent reasonably priced food including wide range of baguettes, bar snacks and pubby choices; brightly lit with dark wood, etched mirrors and interesting mainly naval pictures, plenty of tables, some stall seating, open fire, compact back section, separate partitioned bar across 'Underneath the Arches' alley; TV; open all day, closed Sun. *(Taff Thomas)*

EAST LONDON

E1

★ Prospect of Whitby (020) 3603 4041

Wapping Wall; E1W 3SH Claims to be oldest pub on the Thames dating from 1520 (although largely rebuilt after much later fire), was known as the Devil's Tavern and has a colourful history (Pepys and Dickens used it regularly and Turner came for weeks at a time to study the river views) – tourists love it; L-shaped bare-boards bar with plenty of beams, flagstones and panelling, ales such as Adnams, Fullers, Wells & Youngs and Woodfordes from fine pewter counter, good choice of wines by the glass, bar food and more formal restaurant upstairs; children welcome (only if eating after 5.30pm), unbeatable views towards Docklands from tables on waterfront courtyard, open all day. *(N R White, Phil and Jane Hodson, Paul Rampton, Julie Harding, Taff Thomas and others)*

Town of Ramsgate (020) 7481 8000

Wapping High Street; E1W 2PN Interesting old-London Thames-side setting affording a restricted but evocative river view from small back floodlit terrace with mock gallows (hanging dock was nearby), long narrow chatty bar with squared oak panelling, Fullers London Pride, Sharps Doom Bar and a guest, friendly helpful service, good choice of generous standard food and daily specials, various deals; background music, Mon quiz; open all day. *(Brian and Anna Marsden, N R White)*

Water Poet (020) 7426 0495

Folgate Street; E1 6BX Big rambling Spitalfields pub with bohemian feel and ornate touches, enjoyable food in bar and dining room including good Sun roasts, real ales such as Dark Star, London Fields, Meantime and Trumans, decent wines, friendly staff and good mix of customers, comfortable leather sofas and armchairs on wood floor, basement bar/function room, comedy club, separate pool room with two tables; sports TV; large enclosed outside area with 'barn' room and barbecue, open all day. *(Tom and Ruth Rees)*

E3

★ Crown (020) 8880 7261

Grove Road/Old Ford Road; E3 5SN Stylish dining pub (Geronimo Inn) with relaxed welcoming bar, faux animal hide stools and chunky pine tables on polished boards, big bay window with comfortable scatter cushion seating area, books etc on open shelves, well kept Wells & Youngs and guests, good choice of wines by the glass, friendly chatty young staff, three individually decorated upstairs dining areas overlooking Victoria Park, imaginative food (all day Sun); background music; children and dogs welcome, open all day. *(Anon)*

Palm Tree (020) 8980 2918
Haverfield Road; E3 5BH Lone survivor of
blitzed East End terrace tucked away in Mile
End Park by Regent's Canal; two Edwardian
bars around oval servery, old fashioned and
unchanging under long-serving licensees,
a couple of well kept ales, lunchtime
sandwiches, good local atmosphere with
popular weekend jazz; no credit cards; open
all day (till late Sat). *(Anon)*

E10
King William IV (020) 8556 2460
High Road Leyton; E10 6AE Imposing
flower-decked Victorian building, home to
Brodies brewery; up to 20 well kept low-
priced ales including guests, beer festivals,
enjoyable bargain food, darts and bar
billiards; big-screen sports TV; six bedrooms.
(Anon)

E11
Red Lion (020) 8988 2929
High Road Leytonstone; E11 3AA Large
friendly 19th-c corner pub revamped by the
Antic group with plenty of quirky character,
high-ceilinged open-plan interior with lots
of pictures, mirrors, books and general
bric-a-brac, ten changing ales, real ciders
(festivals), enjoyable, interesting food, bar
billiards and table football; weekend DJs
and live music, quiz night Mon, summer craft
fair; children welcome, back garden, open all
day. *(Phil Bryant)*

E14
★**Grapes** (020) 7987 4396
Narrow Street; E14 8BP Relatively
unchanged since Charles Dickens used it as
a model for his Six Jolly Fellowship Porters
in Our Mutual Friend; a proper traditional
tavern with friendly atmosphere and good
mix of customers, partly panelled bar with
lots of prints of actors, old local maps and the
pub itself, elaborately etched windows, plates
along a shelf, daily papers, larger back area
leading to small deck with views over river
towards Canary Wharf, Adnams, Marstons,
Timothy Taylors and a guest, good value tasty
bar food, upstairs restaurant with fine views;
no children, dogs on the lead welcome, can
catch Canary Wharf ferry and enter pub via
steps from foreshore, open all day. *(Claes
Mauroy, John Wooll, Victoria Cotton, Phil Bryant,
N R White)*

★**Gun** (020) 7515 5222
Coldharbour; E14 9NS Top notch
gastropub with great views from riverside
terrace of the O2 centre; smart front
restaurant and two character bars – busy
flagstoned drinkers' one with antique guns
and log fire, cosy red-painted next-door room
with leather sofas and armchairs, stuffed
boar's head and modern prints, Adnams
Bitter and guests, several wines by the
glass and very well liked contemporary food
(not cheap), efficient service from friendly

staff; background music; children welcome
till 8pm, open all day. *(Dave Snowden, Taff
Thomas)*

Narrow (020) 7592 7950
Narrow Street; E14 8DJ Popular stylish
dining pub (owned by Gordon Ramsay) with
great Thames views from window seats and
covered terrace, simple but smart bar with
white walls and blue woodwork, mosaic-tiled
fireplaces and colourful striped armchairs,
Adnams, Greene King and a guest, good
wines, food from bar snacks to pricier
restaurant meals, dining room also white
with matching furnishings, local maps, prints
and a suspended boat; background music
(live Weds); children welcome, open all day.
(N R White)

NORTH LONDON

N1
Albion (020) 7607 7450
Thornhill Road; N1 1HW Charming
wisteria-clad Georgian building in Islington
conservation area; attractive bare-boards
interior with minimalist front bar and
spacious back lounge/dining room,
interesting choice of good mid-priced home-
made food, a couple of well kept ales such
as Caledonian Deuchars IPA and Ringwood
Best, helpful cheerful service; tables out at
front and in impressive walled back garden
with pergola, open all day. *(Phil Bryant)*

Charles Lamb (020) 7837 5040
Elia Street; N1 8DE Small friendly
backstreet corner pub, four well kept ales
such as Dark Star and Windsor & Eton,
interesting bottled beers and decent choice
of wines by the glass including own-label,
good blackboard food (french and english),
big windows, polished boards and simple
traditional furniture; background jazz;
pavement tables, closed Mon and Tues
lunchtimes, otherwise open all day.
(N R White)

Duke of Cambridge (020) 7359 3066
St Peter's Street; N1 8JT Well established
as London's first organic pub, simply
decorated busy main room with chunky
wooden tables, pews and benches on bare
boards, corridor past open kitchen to more
formal dining room and conservatory, ales
such as Little Valley, Pitfield and St Peters,
also organic draught lagers, ciders, spirits
and wines, interesting bar food using
seasonal produce but not cheap and they add
a service charge, teas and coffees; children
welcome, dogs in bar, open all day. *(Anon)*

Earl of Essex (020) 7424 5828
Danbury Street; N1 8LE One-room
Islington pub brewing its own Earl ales, great
choice of other beers too on draught and in
bottles, straightforward home-made food
with beer recommendations listed on menu;

back walled garden, open all day (from 1pm Mon, 2pm Tues). *(Anon)*

Hemingford Arms (020) 7607 3303

Hemingford Road; N1 1DF Ivy-clad Metropolitan (formerly Capital) pub filled with bric-a-brac, good choice of real ales from central servery, traditional food alongside thai restaurant and popular Sunday roasts, open fire, upstairs bar, live music and Weds quiz night; sports TV, machines; picnic-sets outside. *(Perry Benson)*

★ Island Queen (020) 7354 8741

Noel Road; N1 8HD Fine high-ceilinged Victorian pub handy for Camden Passage antiques area, Fullers London Pride, a guest ale, lots of imported beers and good value wines from island bar, sensibly short choice of brasserie-style food including Sun brunch and fixed-price menu, pleasant staff and laid-back atmosphere, dark wood and big decorative fairy light-edged mirrors, intimate back area, upstairs room; popular weekend evenings with young crowd; children welcome, café-style pavement tables, open all day. *(John Wooll)*

Marquess Tavern (020) 7359 4615

Canonbury Street/Marquess Road; N1 2TB Imposing recently refurbished Victorian pub, bare boards and a mix of furniture including sofas around big horseshoe servery, a couple of fireplaces and lots of prints (some recalling George Orwell who used to drink here), Wells & Youngs beers and good selection of wines, traditional and more adventurous food in bar or back skylit room with classical wall columns, big mirrors and modern lights dangling from the high ceiling; background music, TV; children and dogs welcome, a few seats out behind front railings, open (and food) all day. *(Anon)*

★ Parcel Yard (020) 7713 7258

King's Cross Station, N end of new concourse, up stairs (or lift); N1C 4AH Impressive restoration of listed Victorian parcel sorting office, lots of interesting bare-boards rooms off corridors around airy central atrium, pleasing old-fashioned feel with exposed pipework and ducting adding to the effect, back bar serving full range of well kept Fullers beers plus guests from long modern counter, plenty of wines by the glass, similar upstairs area with old and new furniture including comfortable sofas, railway memorabilia and some nice touches like Victorian envelope wallpaper, good imaginative food from bar snacks up, breakfast till 11.45am, prompt smiling service, power points to recharge phones/laptops, platform views; open all day from 8am (9am Sun). *(Susan and John Douglas, David and Sue Smith, Peter Wright, Pete Walker and others)*

Wenlock Arms (020) 7608 3406

Wenlock Road; N1 7TA Corner local with friendly service and excellent choice of real ales and craft beers, half a dozen ciders and foreign bottled beers too from central servery, simple food, alcove seating, coal fires, darts; open all day. *(Anon)*

N6

★ Flask (020) 8348 7346

Highgate West Hill; N6 6BU Comfortable traditional Georgian pub owned by Fullers; intriguing up-and-down layout, sash-windowed bar hatch, panelling and high-backed carved settle in snug lower area with log fire, enjoyable food from pub favourites to more elaborate dishes, efficient friendly service; picnic-sets out in front courtyard, handy for strolls around Highgate village or Hampstead Heath, open all day. *(John and Gloria Isaacs, Phil Bryant, N R White, Roger and Donna Huggins)*

Prince of Wales (020) 8340 0445

Highgate High Street; N6 5JX Small unpretentious bare-boards local with bench seats, stools and old wooden tables, two coal-effect gas fires, well kept Butcombe and up to three guests from horseshoe bar, decent choice of blackboard wines, food from thai dishes to Sun roasts, friendly prompt service; background music, TV, Tues quiz; tables on small terrace behind, open all day. *(John and Sarah Webb)*

Victoria (020) 8341 3290

North Hill; N6 4QA Tucked-away traditional Victorian pub in tree-lined street, Harveys, Timothy Taylors Landlord and Wells & Youngs, good food including popular Sun lunch, themed nights, Mon quiz; children and dogs welcome. *(Anon)*

N8

Kings Head (020) 8340 1028

Crouch End Hill/Broadway; N8 8AA Victorian corner pub with open-plan bar, cushioned window seats, leather banquettes, high stools and elbow tables on bare boards, well kept ales such as Sambrooks and Sharps, good choice of other drinks, enjoyable food including set menu, friendly helpful staff, downstairs comedy club (Thurs, Sat, Sun); background music, TV; open all day (till 2am Fri, Sat). *(John Wooll)*

NW1

Albert (020) 7722 1886

Princess Road; NW1 8JR Welcoming split-level Victorian corner pub tucked away in residential street; partly green-tiled exterior, roomy U-shaped bar with corniced ceiling, bare boards and cast-iron fireplace, some old photographs, decent selection of fairly priced pubby food from panini and baked potatoes up including good fish and chips, well kept Greene King and Timothy Taylors Landlord, obliging friendly staff, conservatory, live music and quiz nights; children welcome, attractive back garden. *(Phil Bryant)*

Bree Louise (020) 7681 4930
Cobourg Street/Euston Street; NW1 2HH Determinedly no-frills corner pub with wide selection of real ales on handpump and gravity, good choice of ciders too, food emphasising pies (Mon-Thurs bargains), basic décor and well worn furnishings; can get very busy early evening; pavement tables, handy for Euston Station, open all day. *(Eric Larkham, Richard Tilbrook)*

★ Chapel (020) 7402 9220
Chapel Street; NW1 5DP Busy and noisy in the evening (quieter during the day), this corner dining pub attracts an equal share of drinkers; spacious rooms dominated by open kitchen, smart but simple furnishings, sofas at lounge end by big fireplace, good choice of wines by the glass, Adnams and Greene King, several coffees and teas, good food from shortish blackboard menu, brisk friendly service; children and dogs welcome, picnic-sets in sizeable back garden, more seats on decking under heated parasols, covered smokers' area, open all day. *(Jeremy King, Tracey and Stephen Groves)*

★ Doric Arch (020) 7388 2221
Eversholt Street; NW1 2DN Virtually part of Euston Station, up stairs from bus terminus with raised back part overlooking it, well kept Fullers ales and guests, Weston's cider, friendly prompt service (even when busy), enjoyable well priced pubby food lunchtime and from 4pm weekdays (12-5pm weekends), pleasantly nostalgic atmosphere and some quiet corners, intriguing train and other transport memorabilia including big clock at entrance, downstairs restaurant; discreet sports TV, machines; open all day. *(Dennis Jones, Dr and Mrs A K Clarke, N R White, Eric Larkham, Pete Walker)*

Engineer (020) 7483 1890
Gloucester Avenue; NW1 8JH High-ceilinged Mitchells & Butlers pub with L-shaped panelled bar, dining room and more ornate upstairs restaurant/function area, good choice of popular food, Sharps Doom Bar and a guest, plenty of wines by the glass; TV for major sporting events; children welcome, attractive secluded garden (some tables set for dining), handy for Primrose Hill, open all day from 9am for breakfast. *(Taff Thomas, Jeremy King)*

Euston Flyer (020) 7383 0856
Euston Road, opposite British Library; NW1 2RA Big welcoming open-plan pub, Fullers/Gales beers and enjoyable fairly standard food including Weds curry night, relaxed lunchtime atmosphere (can get packed evenings), plenty of light wood, mix

of furniture on carpet or boarded floors, mirrors, photographs of old London, smaller raised areas and private corners, big doors open to street in warm weather; background music, Sky TV, silent games machine; open (and food) all day. *(Eric Larkham, Pete Walker)*

Euston Tap (020) 3137 8837
Euston Road; NW1 2EF Small 19th-c neoclassical lodge in front of Euston Station, good selection of ever-changing real ales and other beers from around the world including huge bottled range, friendly knowledgeable staff, evening pizzas Tues-Sat, more space and lavatory up spiral staircase; outside seating, open all day from noon; identical building opposite dedicated to ciders/perries (open from 3.30pm, closed Sun). *(Eric Larkham, N R White, Claes Mauroy)*

Lansdowne (020) 7483 0409
Gloucester Avenue; NW1 8HX Tile-fronted 19th-c corner pub, dark Anaglypta ceiling and dado, wooden tables and chairs on varnished boards, open fire with picture of the pub above, candles on shelves, ales such as Wells & Youngs Bombardier, enjoyable mediterranean-influenced food from open kitchen, pizzas and snacks available all day, also weekend breakfasts; children welcome, street tables. *(Jeremy King)*

Metropolitan (020) 7486 3489
Baker Street Station, Marylebone Road; NW1 5LA Wetherspoons in impressively ornate Victorian hall, large with lots of tables on one side, very long bar the other, leather sofas and some elbow tables, ten or more real ales, good coffee, their usual inexpensive food; games machines; family area, open all day. *(Tony Hobden)*

★ Queens Head & Artichoke
(020) 7916 6206 *Albany Street; NW1 4EA* Corner pub-restaurant near Regent's Park with good very fairly priced modern food (all day Sun) including tapas, blackboard sherries and good choice of wines by the glass, well kept Adnams, Marstons, Sharps and Timothy Taylors from Edwardian counter, bare boards and panelling, large leaded windows, upstairs dining room; may be background music; pavement picnic-sets under awning. *(Jeremy King)*

NW3

★ Flask (020) 7435 4580
Flask Walk; NW3 1HE Bustling local with two traditional front bars divided by unique Victorian screen, smart banquettes, panelling and lots of little prints, attractive fireplace, Wells & Youngs and a guest, plenty of wines by the glass and maybe winter mulled wine, popular all-day food, good friendly service, dining conservatory; background music, TV; children (till 8pm) and dogs welcome, seats and tables in alley, open all day. *(Tom McLean, N R White)*

Magdala (020) 7435 2503

South Hill Park; NW3 2SB Where Ruth Ellis (the last woman to be hanged in England) shot her lover – the bullet holes are still visible outside; bar with minimal decoration and a piano, three real ales, dining lounge with leather chesterfields by open fire, second more formal dining room, good variety of food from sharing plates up, bar snacks including home-made crisps (meals all day weekends), friendly staff; seats under giant parasol on side terrace; open all day. *(Roger and Donna Huggins, Tom McLean)*

★Spaniards Inn (020) 8731 8406

Spaniards Lane; NW3 7JJ Busy 16th-c pub right next to Hampstead Heath with charming big garden split up into areas by careful planting, flagstoned walk among roses, side arbour with climbing plants and plenty of seats on crazy-paved terrace (arrive early weekends as popular with dog walkers and families); attractive and characterful low-ceilinged rooms with oak panelling, antique winged settles, snug alcoves and open fires, up to five real ales, two ciders, continental draught lagers and several wines by glass, popular pubby food with a few twists, upstairs dining room; car park fills fast and nearby parking is difficult, open (and food) all day. *(N R White)*

NW5   TQ2886

★Bull & Last (020) 7267 8955

Highgate Road; NW5 1QS Traditional décor with a stylish twist and liked by customers of all ages; single room with big windows, colonial-style fans in planked ceiling, collection of tankards, faded map of London, stuffed bulls' heads and pheasants, good imaginative food (not cheap), takeaway tubs of home-made ice-cream and picnic hampers for Hampstead Heath, four well kept changing ales, nice selection of wines and plenty of whiskies and gins (maybe own sloe gin), friendly enthusiastic staff; quiz Sun evening; children (away from bar) and dogs welcome, hanging baskets and picnic-sets by street, open all day. *(Gerry Price)*

Junction Tavern (020) 7485 9400

Fortess Road; NW5 1AG Victorian corner pub with good fresh italian and british food (service charge added) including Sat brunch, dining room and back conservatory, modern décor, St Austell, Sambrooks, Shepherd Neame and Thwaites (beer festivals), good choice of wines by the glass, friendly staff; background music; no children after 7pm, picnic-sets in back garden, open all day Fri-Sun, closed lunchtimes Mon-Thurs. *(Phil Bryant)*

Southampton Arms

Highgate Road; NW5 1LE Nicely restored and handy for the Heath; well run little pub with impressive range of small-brewery beers, ciders and perries, snacky food including good filled rolls, sausage rolls and scotch eggs, can get crowded with wide mix of customers. *(Gerry Price)*

SOUTH LONDON

SE1

Anchor (020) 7407 1577

Bankside; SE1 9EF In great Thames-side spot with river views from upper floors and roof terrace, beams, stripped brickwork and old-world corners, well kept Fullers London Pride and Wells & Youngs, good choice of wines by the glass, popular fish and chip bar (takeaways available) and other good value all-day food, breakfast/tea room, can get very busy and service may slow; background music; provision for children, disabled access, more tables under big parasols on raised riverside terrace, bedrooms in Premier Inn behind. *(N R White, Pete Walker, Mrs Sally Scott)*

Anchor & Hope (020) 7928 9898

The Cut; SE1 8LP Informal bare-boards gastropub, food from changing menu can be good (and prices can be high), well kept Wells & Youngs and guests, sensibly priced wines by tumbler or carafe, plain bar with big windows and mix of furniture including elbow tables, curtained-off dining part with small open kitchen, tight-packed scrubbed tables and contemporary art; children and dogs welcome, on same street as Young and Old Vics, closed Sun evening and Mon lunchtime, otherwise open all day. *(John Saville, Gerry Price)*

Dean Swift (020) 7357 0748

Gainsford Street; SE1 2NE One-room pub tucked away behind Tower Bridge, good selection of cask and craft beers such as Moor, London Fields, Kernel, Magic Rock and Redwell, several wines by the glass, friendly well informed staff, enjoyable food from bar snacks to Sun roasts; sports TV, Sun quiz; open (and food) all day. *(Stuart Warmsley)*

Fire Station (020) 7620 2226

Waterloo Road; SE1 8SB Unusual fire station conversion, busy and noisy, with two huge knocked-through tiled rooms, lots of wooden tables and mix of chairs, pews and worn leather armchairs, distinctive box-shaped floral lampshades, sizeable plants, back bar with red fire buckets on shelf, smarter dining room, good modern food, Marstons-related ales and plenty of wines by the glass including champagne, prices on the high side; background music; children welcome, tables out in front, picnic-sets in scruffy side alley, handy for Old Vic, open (and food) all day from 9am for breakfast. *(Ian Phillips, Phil Bryant)*

★Founders Arms (020) 7928 1899

Hopton Street; SE1 9JH Modern building with glass walls in superb location – outstanding terrace views along Thames and handy for South Bank attractions; plenty of customers (City types, tourists, theatre- and gallery-goers) spilling on to pavement and river walls, Wells & Youngs and a guest, lots of wines by the glass, extensive choice of well priced bar food all day (weekend breakfasts from 9am), tea and coffee from separate servery, cheerful service; background music; children welcome away from bar, open till midnight Fri, Sat. *(Pete Walker, Jeremy King, Phil and Jane Villiers)*

★ **George** (020) 7407 2056

Off 77 Borough High Street; SE1 1NH Tucked-away 16th-c coaching inn (mentioned in *Little Dorrit*), owned by the National Trust and beautifully preserved; lots of tables in bustling cobbled courtyard with views of the tiered exterior galleries, series of no-frills ground-floor rooms with black beams, square-latticed windows and some panelling, plain oak or elm tables on bare boards, old-fashioned built-in settles, dimpled glass lanterns and a 1797 Act of Parliament clock, impressive central staircase up to series of dining rooms and balcony, well kept Greene King ales and a beer badged for the pub, good value traditional food all day (not Sun evening), friendly staff; children welcome away from bar, open all day. *(Michael Butler, B and M Kendall, Pete Walker, Roger and Donna Huggins, N R White)*

Horniman (020) 7407 1991

Hays Galleria, off Battlebridge Lane; SE1 2HD Spacious bright and airy Thames-side drinking hall with lots of polished wood, comfortable seating including a few sofas, upstairs seating, several real ales with unusual guests (may offer tasters), lunchtime food from soup and sandwiches up, snacks other times, efficient bar staff coping with large numbers after work; unobtrusive background music; fine river views from outside picnic-sets, open all day. *(Phil and Jane Villiers)*

★ **Kings Arms** (020) 7207 0784

Roupell Street; SE1 8TB Proper corner local, bustling and friendly, with curved servery dividing traditional bar and lounge, bare boards and attractive local prints, open fire, nine well kept changing ales, good wine and malt whisky choice, welcoming efficient staff, enjoyable food from thai dishes to Sun roasts, big back extension with conservatory/courtyard dining area; background music; open all day. *(Anon)*

Mad Hatter (020) 7401 9222

Stamford Street, Blackfriars Road end; SE1 9NY Fullers pub-hotel in former hat factory; smartly Edwardianised bar with booth seating, etched glass, lots of prints and collection of hats in glass cases, enjoyable traditional food including pies, four well kept beers and fine choice of whiskies, helpful staff; clean bedrooms, open all day. *(Claes Mauroy, David Jackman)*

★ **Market Porter** (020) 7407 2495

Stoney Street; SE1 9AA Properly pubby no-frills place opening at 6am weekdays for workers at neighbouring market, up to ten unusual real ales (over 60 guests a week) often from far-flung brewers and in top condition, particularly helpful friendly service, bare boards and open fire, beams with barrels balanced on them, simple furnishings, food in bar and upstairs lunchtime restaurant; background music; children allowed weekends till 7pm, dogs welcome, gets very busy with drinkers spilling on to the street, open all day. *(Comus and Sarah Elliott, Pete Walker, Jeremy King, Phil and Jane Villiers)*

Old Thameside (020) 7403 4243

Pickfords Wharf, Clink Street; SE1 9DG Nicholsons pastiche of ancient tavern in former warehouse beside dock with replica *Golden Hind*; on two floors with splendid river view upstairs and from waterside terrace, hefty beams and timbers, flagstones and exposed brickwork, several changing ales and tasty pub food; background music, sports TV downstairs (spiral stairs); open all day. *(John and Gloria Isaacs, Roger and Donna Huggins)*

Rake (020) 7407 0557

Winchester Walk; SE1 9AG Tiny discreetly modern Borough Market bar with amazing bottled beer range in wall-wide cooler, also half a dozen continental lagers on tap and three real ales, good friendly service; fair-sized covered and heated outside area. *(Comus and Sarah Elliott, Jeremy King)*

Roebuck (020) 7357 7324

Great Dover Street; SE1 4YG Victorian pub with open-plan bar, big windows and high ceilings, a mix of wooden chairs and tables and leather chesterfields on bare boards, ales from Meantime, Sam Brookes and Trumans, farm cider and several wines by the glass, good interesting food (all day Sun); upstairs lounge with own bar (Charlie Chaplin is said to have performed here as a boy), Tues rock quiz, Thurs poetry readings; picnic-sets outside, open all day. *(Anon)*

Wheatsheaf (020) 7407 9934

Southwark Street; SE1 1TY In cellars beneath the Hop Exchange, brick vaulted ceilings and iron pillars, high stools around elbow tables, traditional wooden tables and chairs, ten real ales, decent pubby food; sports TV; open all day. *(Pete Walker)*

Wheatsheaf (020) 7940 3880

Stoney Street; opposite Borough Market main entrance under new railway bridge; SE1 9AA Youngs pub with comfortably refurbished interior, three of their well kept beers and a guest, 'street food with style' from side campervan kitchen, heated back garden; open all day from 9am (12 Sun). *(Comus and Sarah Elliott)*

White Hart (020) 7928 9190

*Cornwall Road/Whittlesey Street;
SE1 8TJ* Backstreet corner local near
Waterloo Station, friendly community bustle,
comfortable sofas, stripped boards and
so forth, real ales, craft beers and artisan
spirits, lots of bottled beers, good range of
ciders and wines, sensibly priced up-to-date
blackboard food as well as pub standards,
Sunday bloody marys and newspapers,
helpful efficient staff; background music;
open all day. *(Adam Gordon)*

SE5

★ **Crooked Well** (020) 7252 7798

Grove Lane; SE5 8SY Popular early 19th-c
restauranty pub with really good imaginative
food including two-course lunch deal (Tues-
Fri), nice wines and cocktails, Sharps Doom
Bar, welcoming helpful staff; seats outside,
closed Mon lunchtime, otherwise open all day.
(Jeremy Bennett, John Saville, Matthew Read)

SE8

Dog & Bell (020) 8692 5664

Prince Street; SE8 3JD Friendly old-
fashioned local tucked away on Thames
Path, wood benches around bright cheerfully
decorated L-shaped bar, open fire, up to half
a dozen well kept ales including Fullers,
bottled belgians, prompt friendly service,
reasonably priced pub food from good
sandwiches up, dining room, bar billiards; TV;
tables in yard, open all day. *(Anon)*

SE9

Park Tavern (020) 8850 8919

Passey Place; SE9 5DA Traditional
Victorian corner pub off Eltham High Street,
half a dozen well kept ales including Wells
& Youngs and 14 wines by the glass, log
fire, friendly easy-going atmosphere; soft
background music; pleasant little garden
behind, open all day. *(Taff Thomas)*

SE10

Cutty Sark (020) 8858 3146

*Ballast Quay, off Lassell Street;
SE10 9PD* Great Thames views from this
early 19th-c Greenwich tavern, genuinely
unspoilt old-fashioned bar, dark flagstones,
simple furnishings including barrel seats,
open fires, narrow openings to tiny side
snugs, upstairs room (reached by winding
staircase) with ship deck-feel and prized
seat in big bow window, up to five well kept
changing ales, organic wines, malt whiskies
and enjoyable all-day bar food; background
music; children and dogs welcome, busy
riverside terrace across narrow cobbled
lane, limited parking (but free if you get
a space). *(Taff Thomas)*

Old Brewery (020) 3327 1280

*Pepys Building, Old Royal Naval College;
SE10 9LW* Modernised 19th-c building
in grounds of Old Royal Naval College and
a stone's throw from the *Cutty Sark*; front
bar with Meantime beers (some brewed
here) and guests plus many more in bottles,
gleaming brewery equipment in separate
back hall acting as café/evening restaurant;
nice courtyard garden, open (and food)
all day. *(Anon)*

Trafalgar (020) 8858 2909

Park Row; SE10 9NW Substantial 18th-c
building with splendid river views from big
windows directly above water in four elegant
rooms, oak panelling and good maritime
and local prints, three real ales and decent
house wines, enjoyable if pricey food (not
Sun evening) including signature whitebait
and massive ciabattas; background music;
children welcome, tables out by Nelson
statue, handy for Maritime Museum, open
all day (can get packed Fri, Sat evenings).
(Paul Humphreys)

Yacht (020) 7858 0175

Crane Street; SE10 9NP Neatly
modernised with great river views from
spacious room up a few steps from bar, four
well kept ales and wide choice of reasonably
priced food, friendly attentive staff, cosy
banquettes, light wood panelling, portholes
and yacht pictures; children welcome,
cheerful hanging baskets in front, open
(and food) all day. *(Mrs Sally Scott)*

SE12   TQ3974

Lord Northbrook (020) 8318 1127

Burnt Ash Road; SE12 8PU Opened-up
Victorian corner pub with armchairs, wooden
dining tables and chairs on bare boards,
contemporary paintwork, welcoming friendly
staff, enjoyable brasserie-style food from
sharing plates up (all day weekends), five
interesting ales; tables and chairs in back
garden; open all day. *(Jason Wollington,
Kath Butler)*

SE15   TQ3575

Ivy House (020) 7277 8233

Stuart Road; SE15 3BE Co-operatively
owned pub with excellent range of changing
ales and craft beers, well priced food
including burgers and hot dogs, old-fashioned
panelled interior, stage in back room for live
music, comedy and theatre nights; children
(till 8pm) and dogs welcome, rack for
cyclists, open all day. *(Anon)*

Old Nuns Head (020) 7639 4007

Nunhead Green; SE15 3QQ Open-plan
1930s brick and timber pub on edge of
small green, popular locally, four well kept
changing ales and enjoyable food from
standards up including some interesting
choices, roasts only on Sun, cheerful efficient
staff, Thurs quiz; children welcome, back
garden and a few seats out in front, handy
for the fascinating Nunhead Cemetery.
(John Wooll)

SE16
★ **Mayflower** (020) 7237 4088
Rotherhithe Street; SE16 4NF Unchanging cosy old riverside pub in unusual street with lovely early 18th-c church; good generous bar food including more upmarket daily specials, Greene King and guests, good value wines and decent coffee, obliging service, black beams, panelling, nautical bric-a-brac, high-backed settles and coal fires, good Thames views from upstairs evening restaurant; background music; children welcome, fun jetty/terrace over water (barbecues), open all day. *(Anon)*

SE19
TQ3370
Westow House (020) 8670 0654
Westow Hill; SE19 1TX Character local with eight well kept beers and interesting modern all-day cooking, chesterfield sofas, cushioned wall seating and a mix of wooden dining chairs and tables, artwork on walls, lots of books on shelves, busy convivial atmosphere, table football and pinball, regular live music Thurs evenings, open all day. *(Brian and Anna Marsden)*

SE21
Crown & Greyhound
(020) 8299 4976 *Dulwich Village; SE21 7BJ* Big busy (especially evenings) Victorian pub with cosy period interior, traditional upholstered settles and stripped kitchen tables on bare boards, big back dining room, conservatory, Harveys, Sharps Doom Bar and a couple of guests (Easter beer festival and summer cider festival), just under two dozen wines by the glass, straightforward bar food (all day), popular Sun carvery, helpful friendly service; background music; children and dogs welcome, summer barbecues in pleasant back garden, open (and food) all day.
(Giles and Annie Francis, B and M Kendall)

SE22
Clockhouse (020) 8693 2901
Peckham Rye/Barry Road; SE22 9QA Light and airy restyled Victorian pub, well kept Wells & Youngs and guests, decent wines and cocktail list, enjoyable fairly priced bar food; background music, Weds quiz; children and dogs welcome, tables on front terrace looking across to Peckham Rye, open (and food) all day. *(Paul Humphreys)*

SE24
Florence (020) 7326 4987
Dulwich Road; SE24 0NG Tile-fronted Victorian pub brewing its own beers, guest ales and traditional cider on offer too, enjoyable sensibly priced food from interesting varied menu, friendly busy

atmosphere, open contemporary décor, children's play room; a few tables out in front under awning, more on back terrace, open all day (till 1am Fri, Sat). *(Anon)*

SW4
Bobbin (020) 7738 8953
Lillieshall Road; SW4 0LN Tucked-away 19th-c pub in Clapham Old Town, unpretentious opened-up front bar with blue walls and blue-painted chairs on bare boards, upholstered wall benches, ales such as Harveys and Sambrooks, enjoyable reasonably priced food (some italian influences), flagstoned back conservatory; background music, darts and board games; sunny walled beer garden, open all day Fri-Sun, from 5pm other days. *(Anon)*

Windmill (020) 8673 4578
Clapham Common South Side; SW4 9DE Big bustling pub by the common, contemporary front bar, quite a few original Victorian features, pillared dining room leading through to conservatory-style eating area, popular, varied choice of food all day (good breakfasts, too), Wells & Youngs ales and decent wines by the glass, background music, Sun quiz; children welcome, bar, tables under red umbrellas along front, also seats in side garden area, good bedrooms, open all day. *(Anon)*

SW11
Eagle Ale House (020) 7228 2328
Chatham Road; SW11 6HG Attractive unpretentious backstreet local, seven changing ales including southern brewers like Harveys, Surrey Hills and Westerham, welcoming efficient service, worn leather chesterfield in fireside corner of L-shaped bar; big-screen sports TV; dogs welcome, back terrace with heated marquee, small front terrace too, open all day weekends, from 3pm other days. *(Anon)*

Falcon (020) 7228 2076
St John's Hill; SW11 1RU Lively Victorian pub with ten well kept beers from remarkably long light oak counter, period partitions, cut-glass and mirrors, subdued lighting, quieter back dining area serving good value pub food, friendly service; TV; handy for Clapham Junction Station, open all day. *(Ross Balaam)*

Fox & Hounds (020) 7924 5483
Latchmere Road; SW11 2JU Victorian pub with good mediterranean food (all day Sun, not Mon-Thurs lunchtimes), four real ales and several wines by glass, spacious straightforward bar with big windows overlooking street, bare boards, mismatched tables and chairs, photographs on walls, fresh flowers, daily papers, view of kitchen

---

If you know a pub is ever open all day, please tell us.

behind; background music, TV; children (till 7pm) and dogs welcome, garden seats under big parasols, open all day Fri-Sun, closed Mon lunchtime. *(Anon)*

Prince Albert (020) 7228 0923
Albert Bridge Road; SW11 4PF Large modernised Victorian pub (Geronimo Inn) popular with young professionals, raised dining area, mix of wooden dining and armchairs around pale wooden tables, plenty of space, open fire, good range of beers, quite a choice of popular food and efficient friendly staff; regular backgammon tournaments; seats and heaters out in front overlooking Battersea Park, garden behind; dogs welcome. *(Richard and Penny Gibbs)*

Westbridge (020) 7228 6482
Battersea Bridge Road; SW11 3AG Interesting ever-changing choice of real ales, craft beers and ciders, above average food from open kitchen particularly hot dogs and steaks, can eat in bar or back restaurant, friendly staff; background music may be loud, popular with art students early evening; seats for smokers out at front and back, open all day. *(Richard and Penny Gibbs)*

Woodman (020) 7228 2968
Battersea High Street; SW11 3HX Sensitively refurbished by welcoming young couple (he's the chef), good seasonal food from bar snacks and sharing platters up, Badger ales, Weston's cider and several wines by the glass, good friendly service, has village local-feel and can get very busy (particularly in summer); dogs welcome, garden. *(Richard and Penny Gibbs)*

SW12
Avalon (020) 8675 8613
Balham Hill; SW12 9EB Part of the Renaissance group, popular often interesting food including weekend brunch, well kept changing ales and good choice of wines by the glass, plenty of room in split-level bar and back dining area, big murals, stuffed animals and coal fires; sports TV; children welcome, front terrace and nice sunny garden behind, open all day (till 1am Fri, Sat). *(Anon)*

★Nightingale (020) 8673 1637
Nightingale Lane; SW12 8NX Cosy and civilised early Victorian local, small woody front bar opening into larger back area and attractive family conservatory, well kept Wells & Youngs ales, enjoyable sensibly priced bar food, friendly service, board games; sports TV; small secluded back garden with smokers' shelter. *(Anon)*

SW13
White Hart (020) 8876 5177
The Terrace; SW13 0NR Newly revamped open-plan dining pub with fine river views, well kept Wells & Youngs ales along with craft beers from Camden Town and Meantime,

good selection of wines by the glass, food in bar or upstairs restaurant with open kitchen and balcony; open (and food) all day. *(Anon)*

SW14
Victoria (020) 8876 4238
West Temple Sheen; SW14 7RT Contemporary styling with emphasis on conservatory restaurant, good if not particularly cheap food including breakfast from 8.30am (not Sun), friendly service, well kept Fullers London Pride and Timothy Taylors Landlord in small wood-floored bar with leather sofas and woodburners; background music; children and dogs welcome, play area in nice garden, barbecues, comfortable bedrooms, open all day. *(Simon Rodway, Colin McLachlan)*

SW15
★Telegraph (020) 8788 2011
Telegraph Road; SW15 3TU Big pub on Putney Heath, two attractively modernised rooms with bold décor, leather armchairs and sofas, rugs on polished wood, grand dining table, six real ales including house Semaphore brewed by Weltons, bistro-style food all day, good attentive service, newspapers and board games; background music and live blues/jazz nights, sports TV, occasional quiz; children and dogs welcome, great garden with rural feel, busy outside with families and dogs in summer. *(Colin McKerrow)*

SW16
Earl Ferrers (020) 8835 8333
Ellora Road; SW16 6JF Opened-up Streatham corner local, Sambrooks and several other well kept ales (tasters offered), interesting food along with pub standards, good friendly service, mixed tables and chairs, sofas, old photographs; pool and darts, music Mon and Thurs, quiz Weds plus other events such as book and knitting clubs; children welcome, some tables outside with tractor-seat stools, open all day weekends, from 5pm weekdays. *(Anon)*

Railway (020) 8769 9448
Greyhound Lane, Streatham; SW16 5SD Busy Streatham corner local with two big rooms (back one for families), rotating ales from London brewers such as Meantime, Redemption, Sambrooks and Trumans, enjoyable freshly made food, friendly staff, events including Tues quiz and monthly farmers' market; walled back garden, open all day (till 1am Fri, Sat). *(Anon)*

SW18
Alma (020) 8870 2537
York Road; SW18 1TF Corner Victorian pub-hotel with well kept Wells & Youngs ales and good choice of wines from island bar, sofas and informal mix of tables and chairs on wood floor, mosaic plaques and painted mirrors, good food in back restaurant,

friendly helpful staff; 23 bedrooms, open all day. *(Anon)*

Cats Back (020) 8617 3448

Point Pleasant; SW18 1NN Traditionally refurbished 19th-c corner pub, Harveys first in SW London, four of their ales along with bottled beers, enjoyable food including tapas, friendly staff, regular blues bands; partially covered beer garden with heaters, open all day weekends, closed Mon lunchtime. *(Anon)*

Ship (020) 8870 9667

Jews Row; SW18 1TB Popular riverside pub by Wandsworth Bridge; light and airy conservatory-style décor, mix of furnishings on bare boards, church candles on tables, basic public bar, well kept Wells & Youngs, Sambrooks and a guest, freshly cooked interesting bistro food (not especially cheap) in extended restaurant with own garden; children and dogs welcome, good-sized terrace with barbecue and outside bar, open all day. *(Anon)*

SW19

Alexandra (020) 8947 7691

Wimbledon Hill Road; SW19 7NE Busy Youngs pub with their well kept beers and guests from central bar, good wine choice, enjoyable well priced food from sandwiches to good Sun roasts, friendly alert service, comfortably up-to-date décor in linked rooms; sports TVs; tables out in mews and on attractive roof terrace. *(Colin McKerrow)*

Crooked Billet (020) 8946 4942

Wimbledon Common; SW19 4RQ Busy 18th-c pub popular for its position by common (almost next door to the Hand in Hand); Wells & Youngs ales and guests, good choice of wines and enjoyable food in bar or dining room, friendly helpful staff, clean traditional interior with high-backed settles and scrubbed pine tables on oak boards, some interesting old prints, winter fire, board games and Mon quiz; children (away from bar) and dogs welcome, plastic glasses for outside, open (and food) all day. *(Tony Swindells)*

Hand in Hand (020) 8946 5720

Crooked Billet; SW19 4RQ Friendly Youngs local on edge of Wimbledon Common, their ales and guests kept well, enjoyable home-made pubby food, several areas off central bar including family room with games, log fire; front courtyard, benches out by common, open all day. *(Paul Bonner, Tony Swindells)*

Sultan (020) 8544 9323

Norman Road; SW19 1BN Red-brick 1930s drinkers' pub owned by Hop Back and

hidden in a tangle of suburban roads; their ales and maybe a guest in top condition (carry-outs available), friendly locals, big scrubbed tables, darts in public bar; nice walled beer garden with summer barbecues, open all day. *(John Coatsworth)*

WEST LONDON

SW6

★Atlas (020) 7385 9129

Seagrave Road; SW6 1RX Busy tucked-away pub with long simple bar, plenty of panelling and dark wall benches, mix of old tables and chairs, brick fireplaces, good italian-leaning food (all day Sun), well kept Fullers, St Austell, Sharps and a guest, lots of wines by the glass and decent coffee, friendly service; they may ask for a credit card while you run a tab, background music; children (till 7pm) and dogs welcome, seats under awning on heated and attractively planted side terrace, open all day. *(Alistair Forsyth)*

Brown Cow (020) 7384 9559

Fulham Road; SW6 5SA Former restaurant imaginatively reworked as popular rustic-style dining pub (same owner as nearby Sands End), assortment of old furniture on bare boards including butcher's block table, pendant lighting, Victorian prints of prize cows, one wall clad in distressed mirrored glass, enjoyable if not especially cheap modern pub food from bar snacks up, ales such as Greene King and Trumans; dogs welcome, benches and milk churns outside, open all day. *(Susan and John Douglas)*

Harwood Arms (020) 7386 1847

Walham Grove; SW6 1QP Bare-boards gastropub with good food from bar snacks to enterprising pricey full meals, extensive wine list, a couple of well kept changing ales, bar area with leather sofas, young lively atmosphere; closed Mon lunchtime, otherwise open all day. *(Anon)*

Sands End (020) 7731 7823

Stephendale Road; SW6 2PR Fulham dining pub with a mix of wooden chairs around a medley of tables on bare boards, open fire, particularly good, modern british food including weekend brunch, real ales such as Black Sheep, Hook Norton and Sharps Doom Bar; attracts upmarket crowd and can be very busy. *(Susan and John Douglas)*

SW7

Queens Arms (020) 7823 9293

Queen's Gate Mews; SW7 5QL Popular Victorian corner pub with open-plan bare-boards bar, generous helpings of enjoyable good value home-made food, decent wines by the glass and good selection of beers, friendly

---

We say if we know a pub has background music.

helpful service; TV; children welcome, disabled facilities, handy for Albert Hall, open all day. *(John Branston, N R White)*

SW10

Chelsea Ram · (020) 7351 4008
Burnaby Street; SW10 0PL Corner Geronimo Inn, mix of furniture on bare boards or stripy carpet including farmhouse tables, padded stools around an old workbench, cushioned wall seats, shelves of books and some striking artwork, tiled Victorian fireplace, Wells & Youngs and guests, good food including daily specials and popular Sun roasts, friendly service, board games; pavement picnic-sets, open all day. *(Anon)*

W4

★ Bell & Crown (020) 8994 4164
Strand on the Green; W4 3PF Well run Fullers local with enjoyable sensibly priced food and good friendly staff, panelling and log fire, great Thames views from back bar and conservatory, lots of atmosphere and can get very busy weekends; dogs welcome, terrace and towpath area, good walks, open all day. *(Ian Herdman, Phil Bryant, N R White)*

★ Bulls Head (020) 8994 1204
Strand on the Green; W4 3PQ Refurbished old Thames-side pub (served as Cromwell's HQ during Civil War), seats by windows overlooking the water in beamed rooms, steps up and down, ales such as Fullers and Wells & Youngs, several wines by the glass, decent all-day pubby food served by friendly helpful staff; background music; seats out by river, pretty hanging baskets, part of Chef & Brewer chain. *(Anon)*

City Barge (020) 8994 2148
Strand on the Green; W4 3PH Recent extensive refurbishment for this old riverside pub; light modern split-level interior keeping a few original features such as Victorian panelling and open fires, good choice of ales/craft beers and wines by the glass (prosecco on tap), popular food from open kitchen such as soft-shell crab burger and signature oxtail cottage pie, weekend brunch, friendly young staff; background music; children and dogs welcome, waterside picnic-sets facing Oliver's Island, deckchairs on grass and more formal terrace, open (and food) all day. *(Jeremy King, Gordon and Jenny Quick)*

Roebuck (020) 8995 4392
Chiswick High Road; W4 1PU Popular relaxed Victorian dining pub with high ceilings and bare boards, front bar and roomy back dining area opening on to delightful paved garden, enjoyable well presented food (all day Sun) from open kitchen, daily changing menu, four real ales and good choice of wines by the glass; dogs welcome, open all day. *(N R White, Simon Rodway)*

Swan (020) 8994 8262
Evershed Walk, Acton Lane; W4 5HH Cosy well supported 19th-c local with good mix of customers and convivial atmosphere, nice food (not weekday lunchtimes, all day Sun) including some interesting choices, friendly staff, a dozen or so wines by the glass, Sharps Doom Bar and guests, two bars with wood floors and panelling, leather chesterfields by open fire; dogs very welcome, children till 7.30, picnic-sets on good spacious terrace, open all day weekends, from 5pm other days. *(N R White, Simon Rodway)*

Tabard (020) 8994 3492
Bath Road; W4 1LW Roomy Chiswick pub built in 1880, pleasant chatty atmosphere, up to ten changing ales, decent choice of wines and all-day pubby food, friendly efficient staff, arts and crafts interior with lots of nooks and corners, period mirrors and high frieze of William de Morgan tiles, fringe theatre upstairs; well behaved children welcome, disabled access, terrace tables by busy road, open all day. *(N R White)*

W6

Black Lion (020) 8748 2639
South Black Lion Lane; W6 9TJ Welcoming old pub set back from the river; helpful friendly staff, well kept Thwaites, Wells & Youngs Bombardier and three guests, good choice of wines by the glass and nice coffee, enjoyable food including New Zealand influences and tapas, L-shaped interior with bare boards, half-panelling and some high tables and stools, skittle alley; children and dogs welcome, tables on heated terrace with table tennis, garden, open all day. *(Michael Butler, Phil Bryant, Simon Rodway)*

Blue Anchor (020) 8748 5774
Lower Mall; W6 9DJ Right on the Thames (first licensed 1722), a short walk from Hammersmith Bridge; two traditional linked areas with oak floors and panelling, good value enjoyable bar lunches including daily specials, a house beer from Nelsons and guests, friendly helpful service, pleasant river-view room upstairs; busy at weekends; disabled facilities, waterside tables. *(Phil Bryant, N R White)*

Carpenters Arms (020) 8741 8386
Black Lion Lane; W6 9BG Good imaginative cooking at this relaxed corner dining pub, fine for just a drink too with plenty of wines by the glass and Adnams Bitter, friendly staff, simple bare-boards interior with open fire; dogs welcome, attractive garden, open all day. *(Simon Rodway)*

Crabtree (020) 7385 3929
Rainville Road; W6 9HA Well placed Victorian pub backing on to the river, airy high-ceilinged front bar with restaurant behind, four changing ales and good range of

wines by the glass, food from sharing plates up (not the cheapest and they add a service charge); spacious split-level waterside terrace with plenty of shrubbery, outside bar/barbecue, handy for Thames Path and Bishop's Park, open (and food) all day. *(Anon)*

Latymers (020) 8748 3446

Hammersmith Road; W6 7JP Big lively bar with mirrored ceiling, well kept Fullers ales and friendly bar staff, sports TVs, good reasonably priced thai food in spacious back restaurant. *(Susan and John Douglas)*

Queens Head (020) 7603 3174

Brook Green; W6 7BL Big Fullers pub dating from early 18th c with cosy linked rooms, beams, open fires, country furniture and pictures in keeping with period, good, interesting menu from sandwiches up, four well kept beers and nice wines, attentive service; tables out in front overlooking green with tennis courts, pleasant garden behind. *(Edward Mirzoeff)*

W7

Fox (020) 8567 4021

Green Lane; W7 2PJ Friendly open-plan 19th-c local in quiet cul-de-sac near Grand Union Canal, several real ales including Fullers London Pride, Sharps Cornish Coaster and Timothy Taylors Landlord, decent wines by the glass and well priced food including popular Sun lunch, panelling and stained glass, farm tools hung from ceiling; children and dogs welcome, small side garden, horse and donkey in pub's field across road, food/crafts market last Sat of month, towpath walks, open all day. *(Susan and John Douglas)*

W8

Britannia (020) 7937 6905

Allen Street, off Kensington High Street; W8 6UX Popular Wells & Youngs pub closed for major refurbishment as we went to press – reports please. *(Anon)*

W9

Prince Alfred (020) 7286 3287

Formosa Street; W9 1EE Well preserved austerely ornate Victorian pub with five separate bars (lots of mahogany), snob screens and duck-through doors, beautiful etched-glass bow window, Wells & Youngs ales, enjoyable all-day food including some imaginative choices in airy modern dining room with large centre skylight, cellar function rooms; background music; open all day. *(Anon)*

Warwick Castle (020) 7266 0921

Warwick Place; W9 2PX Popular character pub in narrow street near Little Venice, open-fronted with a few pavement tables, unspoilt rooms with comfortable lived-in feel, etched windows, panelling, open fires

and some striking light fittings, real ales such as Greene King, Sambrooks and Sharps, blackboard food from sandwiches and pub standards up. *(Phil Bryant, Susan and John Douglas)*

W12

★ **Princess Victoria** (020) 8749 5886

Uxbridge Road; W12 9DH Imposing Victorian gin palace with carefully restored rather grand bar, oil paintings on slate-coloured walls, a couple of stuffed animal heads, comfortable leather wall seats, parquet flooring, small fireplace, Fullers and Timothy Taylors, 36 wines by the glass and lots of spirits from handsome marble-topped horseshoe counter, particularly good, imaginative modern bar food, large dining room with plenty of original features and more paintings, wine and cigar shop; children allowed if eating, dogs in bar, white wrought-iron furniture on pretty terrace, popular artisan market in front (Sat), open all day. *(Anon)*

W13

Duke of Kent (020) 8991 7820

Scotch Common; W13 8DL Large recently refurbished open-plan pub with lots of interesting discrete areas, coal fires, several Fullers ales and guests, good food from pub standards up, friendly staff; live music Sun, free wi-fi; children welcome, big garden with part covered terrace and play area, open all day. *(Revd R P Tickle)*

W14   TQ2477

★ **Colton Arms** (020) 7385 6956

Greyhound Road; W14 9SD Unspoilt little gem, like an old-fashioned country tavern and in same family for over 40 years; main U-shaped front bar with log fire, polished brasses, fox mask, hunting crops and hunting-scene plates, fine collection of handsomely carved antique oak furniture, two tiny back rooms with own serving counters (ring bell for service), Fullers London Pride, Sharps Doom Bar and a guest, old-fashioned brass till; no food or credit cards; children (over 4) till 7pm, dogs allowed in bar, charming back terrace with neat rose arbour, next to the Queen's Club tennis courts and gardens. *(Emma Scofield)*

★ **Havelock Tavern** (020) 7603 5374

Masbro Road; W14 0LS Popular gastropub in former shop, light airy L-shaped bar with plain unfussy décor, second small room with pews, good imaginative freshly prepared food from daily changing menu, home-baked bread, Sambrooks Wandle, Sharps Doom Bar and guests, wide choice of interesting wines by the glass, swift friendly service; free wi-fi; children and dogs welcome, picnic-sets on small paved terrace, open all day. *(Anon)*

OUTER LONDON

BECKENHAM BR3   TQ3769
George (020) 8663 3468
High Street; BR3 1AG Busy weatherboarded pub with friendly efficient staff,
half a dozen real ales and good value food
including deals; children welcome, side
garden with terrace, open all day. *(Eddie
Edwards)*

Jolly Woodman (020) 8663 1031
Chancery Lane; BR3 6NR Welcoming
old-fashioned local in conservation area,
cosy chatty atmosphere in L-shaped bar with
woodburner, five or so well kept changing
ales such as Harveys and Timothy Taylors
Landlord, good choice of whiskies, reasonably
priced home-made food (weekday lunchtimes
only) including sandwiches; dogs welcome,
pavement tables and sunny flower-filled back
courtyard, open all day (from 4pm Mon).
(N R White)

BEXLEYHEATH DA6   TQ4875
Robin Hood & Little John
(020) 8303 1128 *Lion Road; DA6 8PF*
Small 19th-c family-run local in residential
area, welcoming and spotless, with eight
well kept ales such as Adnams, Brains,
Fullers and Sharps, popular bargain pubby
lunchtime food (not Sun) including an italian
daily special (landlady is from Italy); well
behaved children allowed away from the bar
till 8.30pm, garden. *(Casey Fleming)*

BIGGIN HILL TN16   TQ4359
★ Old Jail (01959) 572979
*Jail Lane; (E off A233 S of airport and
industrial estate, towards Berry's Hill
and Cudham); TN16 3AX* Big family
garden with picnic-sets, substantial trees
and good play area for this popular country
pub (on fringe of London); traditional
beamed and low-ceilinged rooms with
RAF memorabilia, two cosy small areas
to right divided by timbers, one with big
inglenook, other with cabinet of Battle
of Britain plates, Fullers, Harveys and
Shepherd Neame, standard fairly priced
food (not Sun evening) from sandwiches
up, friendly service, step up to dining room
with more wartime prints/plates and small
open fire; discreet background music; dogs
welcome, nice hanging baskets, open all day
weekends. *(Pete Walker, Alan Weedon)*

BOTANY BAY EN2   TQ2999
Robin Hood (020) 8363 3781
*2 miles from M25 junction 24; Ridgeway
(A1005 Enfield Road); EN2 8AP* Roomy
open-plan Edwardian roadhouse, enjoyable
home-made pub food including daily specials,
well kept McMullens ales, decent wines,
friendly uniformed staff; free wi-fi; good-sized
garden with roses and weeping willow, open
all day. *(Nigel and Sue Foster)*

BROMLEY BR1   TQ4069
Red Lion (020) 8460 2691
North Road; BR1 3LG Chatty well
managed backstreet local in conservation
area, traditional dimly lit interior with wood
floor, tiling, green velvet drapes and shelves
of books, well kept Greene King, Harveys
and guests, lunchtime food, good friendly
service; tables out in front, open all day.
(N R White)

BR2   TQ4265
Two Doves (020) 8462 1627
Oakley Road (A233); BR2 8HD Popular,
comfortable and unpretentious, and notable
for its lovely garden; friendly staff and locals,
well kept St Austell Tribute, Wells & Youngs
and a guest, no hot food but ploughman's and
snacks, modern back conservatory, open all
day Fri-Sun. *(N R White)*

CHELSFIELD BR6   TQ4864
Five Bells 821044
*Church Road; just off A224 Orpington
bypass; BR6 7RE* Chatty 17th-c white
weatherboarded village local, two separate
bars and dining area, settle by inglenook,
friendly staff, well kept Courage, Harveys and
guests, reasonably priced food from snacks
up (evening food Thurs-Sat only), live music
including jazz, Tues quiz; sports TV; children
welcome, picnic-sets among flowers out in
front, open all day. *(Conor McGaughey)*

CHISLEHURST BR7   TQ4469
Crown (020) 8467 7326
School Road; BR7 5PQ Imposing
Victorian pub overlooking common, simple
attractive interior with flagstoned bar and
several dining areas, well kept Shepherd
Neame ales and good quality food with
dishes such as sea bream and guinea fowl,
friendly helpful service; terrace tables,
pétanque, seven bedrooms, open all day.
(B and M Kendall)

COCKFOSTERS EN4   TQ2796
Cock & Dragon (020) 8449 7160
Chalk Lane/Games Road; EN4 9HU
Roomy bar with mix of tables, pews and
sofas, well kept ales and good range of wines,
popular back thai restaurant; handy for Trent
Country Park. *(Nigel and Sue Foster)*

EASTCOTE HA5   TQ1089
Case is Altered (020) 8866 0476
High Road/Southill Lane; HA5 2EW
Attractive 17th-c pub in quiet setting adjacent
to cricket ground; main bar, flagstoned snug
and barn dining area, Brakspears, Sharps
Doom Bar and three guests, good choice
of tasty generously served food all day
(Sun till 6pm), lunchtime deal Mon-Thurs,
friendly efficient staff; children and dogs
welcome, nice front garden (very popular
in fine weather), handy for Eastcote House
Gardens. *(Brian Glozier)*

HAMPTON COURT KT8   TQ1668

★ **Kings Arms**   (020) 8977 1729

*Hampton Court Road, by Lion Gate;
KT8 9DD* Civilised well run pub by Hampton
Court itself (so popular with tourists),
comfortable furnishings including sofas in
back area, attractive Farrow & Ball colours,
good open fires, lots of oak panelling,
beams and some stained glass, well kept
Badger beers, good choice of wines by the
glass, friendly service, enjoyable food from
sandwiches up, restaurant too (food all day
weekends); background music; children and
dogs welcome, picnic-sets on roadside front
terrace, limited parking, 13 bedrooms, open
all day. *(Anon)*

HARROW HA1   TQ1587
Castle   (020) 8422 3155
West Street; HA1 3EF Edwardian Fullers
pub in picturesque part, their ales and guests
kept very well, enjoyable food from lunchtime
sandwiches to full meals, several rooms
around central servery, open fires, rugs on
bare boards and lots of panelling, collection
of clocks in cheery front bar, more sedate
back lounge; children welcome, steps up from
street, nice garden behind, open (and food)
all day. *(Linda Miller and Derek Greentree, Phil
Bryant, Brian Glozier)*

ISLEWORTH TW7   TQ1675
London Apprentice   (020) 8560 1915
Church Street; TW7 6BG Large Thames-
side Taylor Walker pub, reasonably priced
food from sandwiches up, well kept ales such
as Adnams, Fullers, Hook Norton, Sharps and
Wells & Youngs, good wine choice, log fire,
pleasant friendly service, upstairs river-view
restaurant; may be background music; children
welcome, attractive riverside terrace with
good quality benches, chairs and tables under
parasols, open all day. *(Susan and John Douglas)*

KEW TW9   TQ1977
Coach & Horses   (020) 8940 1208
Kew Green; TW9 3BH Refurbished
coaching inn overlooking green, Wells &
Youngs ales and a guest, enjoyable food
from sandwiches and traditional choices
up, friendly young staff, relaxed open-plan
interior with armchairs, sofas and log fire,
shelves of books, restaurant with kitchen view;
background music, sports TV; children and
dogs welcome, teak tables on front terrace,
secret garden behind with chickens, nice
setting handy for Kew Gardens and National
Archive (beware of parking restrictions), 31
bedrooms, buffet breakfast, open all day.
(Susan and John Douglas, N R White)

KINGSTON KT2   TQ1869
Boaters   (020) 8541 4672
*Canbury Gardens (park in Lower Ham
Road if you can); KT2 5AU* Family-
friendly pub by the Thames in small park, half
a dozen ales such as Hogs Back, Twickenham

and Sambrooks, good wines from reasonably
priced list, well prepared/presented food
including weekend breakfast from 10am,
efficient staff, comfortable banquettes in
charming bar, newspapers, Sun evening jazz,
quiz Mon; smart riverside terrace, parking
nearby can be difficult, open all day. *(David
and Sally Frost, Tom and Ruth Rees)*

Canbury Arms   (020) 8255 9129
Canbury Park Road; KT2 6LQ Open-plan
pub with simple contemporary décor, bare
boards and big windows, relaxed friendly
atmosphere, good up-to-date food including
breakfast from 9am (not Sun), helpful young
staff, five well kept ales and good wine choice,
nice coffee, stone-floor side conservatory,
regular events such as quiz and music nights,
wine tasting and camera club; children and
dogs welcome, tables out at front under
parasols, open all day. *(Meg and Colin Hamilton)*

ORPINGTON BR6   TQ4963
★ **Bo-Peep**   (01959) 534457
*Hewitts Road, Chelsfield; 1.7 miles from
M25 junction 4; BR6 7QL* Useful M25
country-feel dining pub, old low beams and
enormous inglenook in carpeted bar, two
cosy candlelit dining rooms, airy side room
overlooking lane, Sharps Doom Bar, Wells
& Youngs Bombardier and a changing beer
from Westerham, cheerful helpful staff, good
helpings of enjoyable food (all day Sat, not
Sun evening) from traditional choices up;
background music; children welcome, dogs
in bar, picnic-sets on big brick terrace, open
all day. *(Pete Walker, Alan Cowell)*

OSTERLEY TW7   TQ1578
Hare & Hounds   (020) 8560 5438
*Windmill Lane (B454, off A4 – called
Syon Lane at that point); TW7 5PR*
Roomy carefully refurbished Fullers pub, wide
choice of food from sandwiches to reasonably
priced main dishes, pleasant dining extension,
interesting local wartime photographs;
children and dogs welcome, disabled facilities,
spacious terrace and big floodlit mature
garden, nice setting opposite beautiful
Osterley Park (NT), open all day. *(Susan and
John Douglas)*

PINNER HA5   TQ1289
Queens Head   (020) 8868 4607
High Street; HA5 5PJ Traditional beamed
and panelled local dating from the 16th c,
welcoming bustle and interesting décor, seven
well kept ales including Adnams Southwold,
Greene King Abbot and Wells & Youngs
Bombardier, simple good value lunchtime bar
food; no children inside; dogs welcome (not
during lunch), small back terrace for evening
sun, open all day. *(Brian Glozier)*

RICHMOND TW9   TQ1774
Princes Head   (020) 8940 1572
The Green; TW9 1LX Large open-plan pub
overlooking cricket green near theatre, clean

and well run, with low-ceilinged panelled areas off big island bar, well kept Fullers ales, popular sensibly priced pub food from sandwiches up, friendly young staff and chatty locals, coal-effect fire; over-21s only, dogs welcome, circular picnic-sets outside, open all day. *(Anon)*

Watermans Arms (020) 8940 2893

Water Lane; TW9 1TJ Friendly old-fashioned Youngs local with their well kept Bitter and a couple of guests from Twickenham, enjoyable thai food, traditional layout with open fire, red banquettes and model of a Thames barge, upstairs restaurant; handy for the river. *(Claes Mauroy, Ian Phillips)*

★**White Cross** (020) 8940 6844

Water Lane; TW9 1TH Lovely garden with terrific Thames views, seats on paved area, outside bar and boats to Kingston and Hampton Court; two chatty main rooms with local prints and photographs, three log fires (one unusually below a window), well kept Wells & Youngs and guests from old-fashioned island servery, a dozen wines by the glass, decent bar food all day, bright and airy upstairs room (children welcome here till 6pm) with pretty cast-iron balcony for splendid river view, good mix of customers; background music, TV; dogs welcome, tides can reach the pub entrance (wellies provided). *(N R White, Simon Collett-Jones, Gordon and Jenny Quick, Tom and Ruth Rees and others)*

White Swan (020) 8940 0959

Old Palace Lane; TW9 1PG Small 18th-c cottagey pub, civilised and relaxed, with rustic dark-beamed open-plan bar, well kept Otter, St Austell, Sharps and Timothy Taylors, popular freshly made food, coal-effect fires, back dining conservatory and upstairs restaurant; soft background music; children allowed, some seats on narrow paved area at front, more in pretty walled back terrace below railway, open all day. *(Claes Mauroy, N R White, Ian Phillips)*

RICHMOND TW10   TQ1874
White Horse (020) 8940 2418

Worple Way, off Sheen Road; TW10 6DF Large open-plan pub, their ales and good choice of wines from long aluminium counter, airy interior with pastel shades, exposed brickwork and mix of old and new furniture on bare boards including some easy chairs, enjoyable food from traditional favourites up, friendly helpful service; free wi-fi; children welcome (playground next door), two-level back terrace, open all day. *(Phil Bryant)*

ROMFORD RM1   TQ5188
Golden Lion (01708) 740081

High Street; RM1 1HR Popular former coaching inn with spacious beamed interior, ten real ales and good value pubby food, good

mix of age groups, friendly staff, weekend live music; open all day. *(Robert Lester)*

ROMFORD RM2   TQ5188
Ship (01708) 741571

Main Road; RM2 5EL 17th-c black and white pub, panelling, low beams and woodburner in fine brick fireplace, Adnams, Courage, Fullers, Sharps and guests, all-day food from sandwiches and sharing boards up (till 5pm Fri-Sun), live weekend music; children and dogs welcome, picnic-sets in back garden under parasols. *(Robert Lester)*

TEDDINGTON TW11   TQ1770
Lion (020) 8977 4779

Wick Road; TW11 9DN Backstreet pub extended to include french restaurant, good food including well priced set choices, nice selection of wines and well kept beers such as Fullers and Sharps; outside seating, open all day. *(Tom and Ruth Rees)*

TWICKENHAM TW1   TQ1673
Crown (020) 8892 5896

Richmond Road, St Margarets; TW1 2NH Refurbished Georgian pub with emphasis on good food (several large dining areas), but also well kept ales, nice wines by the glass and decent coffee, friendly efficient staff; daily newspapers, free wi-fi; children welcome, picnic-sets in sunny courtyard garden, open (and food) all day. *(Hunter and Christine Wright)*

White Swan (020) 8892 2166

Riverside; TW1 3DN Refurbished 17th-c Thames-side pub up steep anti-flood steps, bare-boards L-shaped bar with cosy log fire, river views from prized bay-window, changing ales such as Hogs Back, Sambrooks, Sharps and Twickenham, enjoyable food (all day weekends) including deals, friendly local atmosphere, board games; children welcome, tranquil setting opposite Eel Pie Island with well used balcony and waterside terrace across quiet lane, open all day. *(Phil Bryant, Edward Mirzoeff)*

TWICKENHAM TW2   TQ1572
Sussex Arms (020) 8894 7468

Staines Road; TW2 5BG Traditional bare-boards pub with 18 handpumps plus ciders and perries from long counter, plenty in bottles too, simple food including good home-made pies, walls and ceilings covered in beer mats and pump clips, open fire, some live acoustic music; large back garden with boules, open all day. *(Mark Percy, Lesley Mayoh)*

UXBRIDGE UB8   TQ0582
Malt Shovel (01895) 812797

Iver Lane, Cowley (B470); UB8 2JE Vintage Inn by Grand Union Canal, their usual fair-priced food including set deal, ales such as Caledonian, Fullers and Greene King; children welcome, seats outside, open (and food) all day. *(Barrie and Mary Crees)*

SCOTLAND

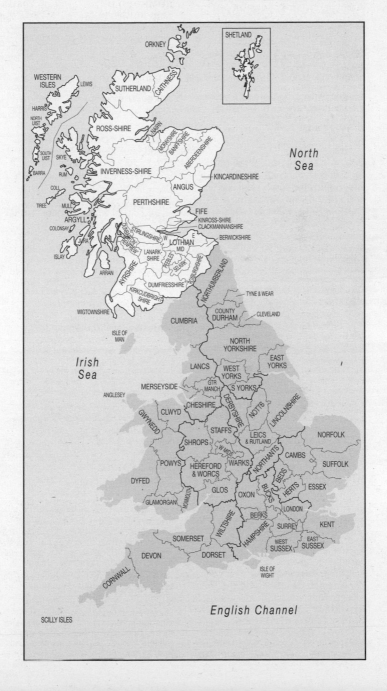

ORKNEY

SHETLAND

WESTERN ISLES
LEWIS
HARRIS
NORTH UIST
SOUTH UIST
BARRA
SKYE
RUM
COLL
TIREE
MULL
COLONSAY
JURA
ISLAY
ARRAN

SUTHERLAND
CAITHNESS
ROSS-SHIRE
NAIRN
MORAYSHIRE
BANFFSHIRE
ABERDEENSHIRE
INVERNESS-SHIRE
KINCARDINESHIRE
ANGUS
PERTHSHIRE
FIFE
KINROSS-SHIRE
CLACKMANNANSHIRE
STIRLINGSHIRE W
DUMBARTON
RENFREW
LANARK-SHIRE
LOTHIAN
MID
E
BERWICKSHIRE
PEEBLES
SELKIRK
ROXBURGHSHIRE
AYRSHIRE
DUMFRIESSHIRE
KIRKCUDBRIGHTSHIRE
WIGTOWNSHIRE

North Sea

NORTHUMBERLAND
TYNE & WEAR
CUMBRIA
COUNTY DURHAM
CLEVELAND
ISLE OF MAN
NORTH YORKSHIRE
LANCS
WEST YORKS
EAST YORKS
MERSEYSIDE
GTR MANCH
S YORKS
ANGLESEY
CHESHIRE
DERBYSHIRE
NOTTS
LINCOLNSHIRE
GWYNEDD
CLWYD
STAFFS
LEICS & RUTLAND
NORFOLK
SHROPS
W MIDS
WARKS
NORTHANTS
CAMBS
SUFFOLK
POWYS
HEREFORD & WORCS
BEDS
DYFED
MONMOUTH
GLOS
OXON
BUCKS
HERTS
ESSEX
GLAMORGAN
BERKS
LONDON
WILTSHIRE
HAMPSHIRE
SURREY
KENT
SOMERSET
WEST SUSSEX
EAST SUSSEX
DEVON
DORSET
ISLE OF WIGHT
CORNWALL

Irish Sea

English Channel

SCILLY ISLES

KEY ★ Star Pub   ⊚ Top Quality Food   ◀ Great Beer

♈ Good Wines   £ Bargain Meals   ⇌ Good Bedrooms   ⊞ Serves Food

APPLECROSS   NG7144   Map 11

Applecross Inn ★ ⇌

Off A896 S of Shieldaig; IV54 8LR

Wonderfully remote pub on famously scenic route on west coast; particularly friendly welcome, real ales and good seafood; bedrooms

Our readers love this inn, and judging by the surprising number of visitors (given its lonely position), so does everyone else. It's reached by driving through miles of spectacularly wild, unpopulated scenery and over the famous Pass of the Cattle (Bealach na Bà), and it looks across the water to the Cuillin Hills on Skye. The no-nonsense, welcoming bar has a woodburning stove, exposed stone walls, upholstered pine furnishings and a stone floor; An Teallach Ale and Isle of Skye Skye Light on handpump, over 50 malt whiskies and a good, varied wine list; pool (winter only), TV and board games. The tables in the shoreside garden enjoy magnificent views. If you wish to stay here you must book some months ahead. The alternative route, along the single-track lane winding around the coast from just south of Shieldaig, has equally glorious sea loch (and then sea) views nearly all the way. Some disabled facilities.

⊞ Emphasis is on the top quality local fish and seafood dishes – squat lobsters, oysters, fresh haddock, a seafood platter, king scallops and dressed crab with smoked salmon – but they also serve haggis in Drambuie with cream, gammon and eggs, chicken green thai curry, local venison casserole, sirloin steak with pepper sauce and chips, and puddings such as hot chocolate fudge cake and raspberry cranachan. *Benchmark main dish: local langoustines in garlic butter £18.50. Two-course evening meal £25.00.*

Free house ~ Licensee Judith Fish ~ Real ale ~ (01520) 744262 ~ Open 11am-11.30pm (midnight Sat); 12-11 Sun ~ Bar food 12-9 ~ Children welcome till 8.30pm ~ Dogs welcome ~ Wi-fi ~ Bedrooms: $85/$130 ~ www.applecross.uk.com *Recommended by Tom Jensen, Richard and Penny Gibbs, Barry Collett, John and Pauline Cope, Ken Richards, Edna Jones, Roy Payne*

DALKEITH   NR3264   Map 11

Sun ⊚ ♈ ⇌

A7 S; EH22 4TR

Family-run inn with charming bar and restaurant, open fires, leafy garden, local ale and delicious food; comfortable, airy bedrooms

Close to the River Esk and surrounded by five acres of wooded grounds, this former coaching inn is very much a family-run business. It's been carefully renovated with walls stripped back to the original stone (or with hunting-theme wallpaper), bare floorboards and refurbished fireplaces. There are cushioned built-in settles, all sorts of wooden dining chairs around an appealing collection of tables, gilt-edged mirrors and high stools against the counter where friendly staff serve Stewart Pentland IPA and a guest beer on handpump and good wines by the glass; background music. Seats on the covered courtyard overlook the garden where they hold popular summer barbecues. The stylish bedrooms are thoughtfully equipped and comfortable and breakfasts are highly rated. Edinburgh is just 20 minutes away.

From an inventive menu using the best Scottish produce, cooked by the landlord and his son, the enticing modern food includes lunchtime sandwiches, thai-spiced crab claw timbale with lemongrass, coriander, lime broth and crispy crab won ton, oat-crusted haggis bonbons, bashed carrot and swede and whisky cream, artichoke heart, pine nut and parmesan pasta, lambs liver with crispy bacon and onion gravy, seared pork fillet with bubble and squeak potato cake, black pudding, twice-cooked pork belly, apple purée and red wine jus, shellfish marinière plates, and puddings such as rocky road brownie slice and cherry purée with vanilla ice-cream; they also offer a two- and three-course early-bird set menu. *Benchmark main dish: pork platter (smoked ham haunch pie, fillet wrapped in ham, black pudding croquette, cheek) £15.00. Two-course evening meal £21.00.*

Free house ~ Licensee Bernadette McCarron ~ Real ale ~ (0131) 663 2456 ~ Open 12-11 ~ Bar food 12-9 weekdays; 12-2, 6-9 Sat; 12-3.30, 5-7 Sun ~ Children welcome ~ Wi-fi ~ Bedrooms: £75/£95 ~ www.thesuninnedinburgh.co.uk *Recommended by Edward May*

EDINBURGH
Abbotsford ◙ £
Rose Street; E end, beside South St David Street; EH2 2PR

NT2574 Map 11

Busy city pub with period features, changing beers, and bar and restaurant food

There's a fine choice of real ales in this handsome Edwardian pub with its lively atmosphere and unchanging feel. Perched at the centre, on red flooring, is a hefty Victorian island bar ornately carved from dark spanish mahogany and highly polished, serving up to six changing beers (on handpump and air pressure) such as Fyne Ales Jarl, Cromarty Happy Chappy, Harviestoun Bitter & Twisted, Highland Dark Munro, Inveralmond Ossian and Oakham Bishops Farewell; also, a selection of bottled american craft beers and around 70 malt whiskies. At lunchtime you'll usually find an eclectic mix of business people and locals occupying stools around the bar and long wooden tables, and leatherette benches running the length of the high-panelled dark wood walls. High above all this is a rather handsome green and gold plaster-moulded ceiling. The smarter upstairs restaurant, with white tablecloths, black walls and high ornate white ceiling, looks impressive too.

Bar food includes haggis, neeps and tatties with thyme jus, roasted red pepper stuffed with thai-spiced couscous and feta cheese, burger with lots of toppings, basil coleslaw and chips, coq au vin, smoked cod with chorizo and tomato, chickpea and french bean cassoulet, steak in ale pie, and puddings such as ginger and date pudding with butterscotch sauce and strawberry tart. *Benchmark main dish: battered haddock and chips £9.95. Two-course evening meal £17.00.*

Stewart ~ Licensee Daniel Jackson ~ Real ale ~ (0131) 225 5276 ~ Open 11-11 (midnight Fri, Sat) ~ Bar food 12-3, 5.30-10; 12-10 Fri, Sat ~ Restaurant 12-2.15, 5.30-9.30 ~ Children over 5 allowed in restaurant ~ www.theabbotsford.com *Recommended by John Beeken, Eric Larkham, the Dutchman*

EDINBURGH
Bow Bar ◙
West Bow; EH1 2HH

NT2574 Map 11

Cosy, enjoyably unpretentious backstreet pub with an excellent choice of well kept beers

The splendid range of real ales – and the way they're served – is one of the main draws to this cheerfully traditional alehouse. The rectangular bar has an impressive carved mahogany gantry, and from the tall 1920s founts on the bar counter, knowledgeable staff dispense eight well kept real ales such as Alechemy Bowhemia Pale, Cromarty Red Rocker, Fyne Ales Hurricane Jack and Jarl, Great Heck Yakima IPA, Moor Dark Alliance, Stewart Edinburgh Number 3 and Tyne Bank Mocha Milk Stout; regular beer festivals. Also on offer are some 260 malts, including five 'malts of the moment', a good choice of rums, 40 international bottled beers and 20 gins. The walls are covered with a fine collection of enamel advertising signs and handsome antique brewery mirrors, and there are sturdy leatherette wall seats and café-style bar seats around heavy narrow tables on the wooden floor. No children allowed. Food is limited to pies and soup.

Free house ~ Licensee Mike Smith ~ Real ale ~ (0131) 226 7667 ~ Open 12-midnight; 12.30-11.30 Sun ~ Bar food 12-3 ~ Dogs welcome ~ Wi-fi *Recommended by R T and J C Moggridge, Eric Larkham*

 EDINBURGH   NT2574   Map 11

Guildford Arms 🍺 £

West Register Street; EH2 2AA

Busy and friendly, with spectacular Victorian décor, a marvellous range of real ales and good food

A big part of this bustling pub's appeal is the array of ten well kept real ales, but its chief glory is the splendid Victorian décor. Opulently excessive, this features ornate painted plasterwork on the lofty ceiling, heavy swagged velvet curtains, dark mahogany fittings and a busy patterned carpet. Tables and stools are lined up along the towering arched windows opposite the bar, where knowledgeable, efficient staff may offer a taste before you select from the quickly changing range of beers: Alechemy Starlaw, Cairngorm Wildcat, Highland Island Hopping, Orkney Dark Island, Stewart Pentland IPA, Wells & Youngs Bombardier, and guests from breweries such as Bristol Beer Factory, Cromarty, Eden, Hawkshead, Revolutions and Wild Beer. Also nine wines by the glass, about 50 malt whiskies, a dozen rums and a dozen gins; TV and background music. The snug little upstairs gallery restaurant, with strongly contrasting modern décor, gives a fine dress-circle view of the main bar (on the way up notice the lovely old mirror decorated with two tigers).

🍴 Tasty food includes open sandwiches, fish chowder, smoked salmon and cream cheese roulade with citrus dressing, haggis with neeps and tatties, mushroom wellington with blue cheese, caramelised onions and cranberries, sausages of the day with onion gravy, chicken wrapped in smoked bacon and stuffed with haggis in whisky sauce, haunch of venison in a red wine, rosemary and mushroom sauce, and puddings. *Benchmark main dish: steak in ale pie £9.95. Two-course evening meal £18.00.*

Stewart ~ Lease Steve Jackson ~ Real ale ~ (0131) 556 4312 ~ Open 11-11 (midnight Fri, Sat) ~ Bar food 12-3, 5-9.30 (10 Fri, Sat); snacks during afternoon ~ Restaurant 12 (12.30 Sun)-2.30, 6-9.30 (10 Fri, Sat) ~ Children welcome in upstairs gallery if dining and over 5 ~ Dogs allowed in bar ~ www.guildfordarms.com *Recommended by John Beeken, Janet and Peter Race, Comus and Sarah Elliott, Eric Larkham, Brian and Anna Marsden*

The letters and figures after the name of each town are its Ordnance Survey map reference. 'Using the *Guide*' at the beginning of the book explains how it helps you find a pub, in road atlases or large-scale maps as well as in our own maps.

EDINBURGH   NT2574   Map 11

Kays Bar 🍺 £

Jamaica Street West; off India Street; EH3 6HF

Cosy, enjoyably chatty backstreet pub with good value lunchtime food and an excellent choice of well kept beers

A ttracting an eclectic mix of customers, this busy and convivial little backstreet pub has a very enjoyable local feel, and is not at all touristy. There are long well worn curving red plush wall banquettes and stools around cast-iron tables on red carpet, and red pillars supporting a red ceiling. It's simply decorated with big casks and vats arranged along the walls, old wine and spirits merchant notices and gas-type lamps. A quiet panelled back room (a bit like a library) leads off, with a narrow plank-panelled pitched ceiling and a collection of books ranging from dictionaries to ancient steam-train books for boys; there's a lovely warming coal fire in winter. The seven real ales include Caledonian Deuchars IPA and 80/- and Theakstons Best, plus guests such as Atom Dark Matter, Courage Directors, Hop Back Crop Circle and Timothy Taylors Landlord on handpump; they also stock more than 70 malt whiskies aged from eight to 50 years, and ten blended whiskies; board games. In days past, the pub was owned by John Kay, a whisky and wine merchant; wine barrels were hoisted up to the first floor and dispensed through pipes attached to nipples visible around the ceiling light rose.

🍴 Very reasonably priced lunchtime food includes pâté, an antipasti platter, baked potatoes, haggis, neeps and tatties, and chicken or beef curry. *Benchmark main dish: chilli mince and potatoes £4.50.*

Free house ~ Licensee Fraser Gillespie ~ Real ale ~ (0131) 225 1858 ~ Open 11am-midnight (1am Fri, Sat); 12.30-11 Sun ~ Bar food 12-2.30; not Sun ~ Wi-fi ~ www.kaysbar.co.uk *Recommended by Peter F Marshall*

GLASGOW   NS5965   Map 11

Babbity Bowster 🍴⭐ 🍷

Blackfriars Street; G1 1PE

A lively mix of traditional and modern with a continental feel too

T his city-centre pub is very much a Glasgow institution, with a thoroughly convivial atmosphere and good mix of locals and visitors. The simply decorated, light-filled interior has fine tall windows, well lit photographs and big pen-and-wash drawings of the city, its people and musicians, dark grey stools and wall seats around dark grey tables on stripped wooden boards and a peat fire. The bar opens on to a pleasant terrace with tables under cocktail parasols, trellised vines and shrubs; they may have barbecues out here in summer. Caledonian Deuchars IPA and a couple of guests such as Fyne Ales Jarl and Williams Brothers May Bee on air-pressure tall fount, and a remarkably sound collection of wines and malt whiskies; good tea and coffee too. On Saturday evenings, the pub has live traditional scottish music, while at other times you may find games of boules in progress outside. Note the bedroom price is for the room only.

🌟 The short menu offers enjoyable food at fair prices: sandwiches, haggis, neeps and tatties, a pie of the day, vegetarian lasagne and daily specials, with more elaborate restaurant choices such as cullen skink, herb-crusted rack of lamb, slow-cooked pork stuffed with black pudding and apple, and puddings such as caramelised lemon tart. *Benchmark main dish: haunch of venison £15.25. Two-course evening meal £20.00.*

Free house ~ Licensee Fraser Laurie ~ Real ale ~ (0141) 552 5055 ~ Open 11am-midnight; 12.30-midnight Sun ~ Bar food 12-10 ~ Restaurant ~ Children welcome if eating ~ Wi-fi ~ Live traditional music Weds afternoon, Sat early evening ~ Bedrooms: £50/£65 ~ www.babbitybowster.com *Recommended by Isobel Mackinlay*

GLASGOW   NS5965 Map 11
Bon Accord ⬤ £
North Street; G3 7DA

Remarkable choice of drinks including an impressive range of whiskies and real ales, a good welcome and bargain food

Glasgow's finest pub for real ales, this friendly alehouse changes its well kept beers so often that they can get through around 1,000 a year. Alongside Caledonian Deuchars, they have nine daily changing guests sourced from breweries around Britain and served from swan-necked handpumps. Also, continental bottled beers, a farm cider and, in a remarkable display behind the counter, 380 malt whiskies and lots of gins, vodkas and rums. Staff are knowledgeable so do ask for help if you need it. The several linked traditional bars are warmly understated with cream or terracotta walls, a mix of chairs and tables, a leather sofa and plenty of bar stools on polished bare boards or carpeting; TV, background music and board games. There are circular picnic-sets on a small terrace, and modern tables and chairs out in front.

 The amazingly cheap food includes baguettes, baked potatoes, giant yorkshire pudding filled with sausages and onion gravy, full breakfast, chilli con carne, cajun chicken, gammon and eggs, burgers with cheese, bacon and fries, and puddings such as clootie dumpling and apple pie with custard. *Benchmark main dish: battered fresh haddock and chips £6.95. Two-course evening meal £9.50.*

Free house ~ Licensee Paul McDonagh ~ Real ale ~ (0141) 248 4427 ~ Open 11am-midnight; 12.30pm-midnight Sun ~ Bar food 11 (12.30 Sun)-8 ~ Children welcome until 8pm ~ Wi-fi ~ Live band Sat evening ~ www.bonaccordweb.co.uk
Recommended by Dr and Mrs A K Clarke

GLENCOE   NN1058 Map 11
Clachaig ⬤
Old Glencoe Road, behind NTS Visitor Centre; PH49 4HX

Climbers' and walkers' haunt with a broad selection of scottish beers and malts

They keep a fantastic choice of up to 15 scottish real ales on handpump here – from a quickly changing choice there might be An Teallach Crofters Pale Ale, Cairngorm Stag, Fraoch Heather Ale and Williams Brothers Kelpie Seaweed Ale; Williams alcoholic ginger beer, around 300 malt whiskies, scottish gins, vodkas and rums and some unusual scottish lagers too. As the inn is surrounded by the majestic mountain scenery of Glencoe, many of the customers are walkers, climbers and mountain bikers who gather beside the log fire in the Boots Bar and swap stories; bands play here on Saturday nights. There's also a whisky barrel-panelled, slate-floored snug and a lounge with a mix of dining chairs and leather sofas, its walls hung with photos signed by famous climbers. Background music and pool. This makes a useful base to stay overnight and they also run self-catering properties in the area.

Hearty food includes venison pastrami, black pudding with local bacon and apple and plum chutney, haggis with neeps and tatties, angus burger with cheese, and puddings such as ecclefechan tart (mixed fruits and nuts). *Benchmark main dish: venison pie £11.95. Two-course evening meal £17.50.*

Free house ~ Licensees Guy and Edward Daynes ~ Real ale ~ (01855) 811252 ~ Open 11-11 (midnight Fri); 11-11.30 Sat ~ Bar food 12-9 ~ Children allowed in lounge ~ Dogs welcome ~ Wi-fi ~ Live music Sat night ~ Bedrooms: £51/£102 ~ www.clachaig.com
Recommended by Pip White

ISLE OF WHITHORN
NX4736 Map 9

Steam Packet ♀ 🛏

Harbour Row; DG8 8LL

Waterside views from friendly, family-run inn with six real ales and tasty pubby food; bedrooms

The big picture windows at this welcoming, family-run inn have fine views over a busy crowd of yachts and fishing boats in the harbour, and then beyond to calmer waters; some bedrooms have the same outlook. The comfortable low-ceilinged bar is split into two: on the right, plush button-back banquettes and boat pictures, and on the left, green leatherette stools around cast-iron-framed tables on big stone tiles, and a woodburning stove in the bare stone wall. There's a lower beamed dining room, which has excellent colour wildlife photographs, rugs on a wooden floor and a solid fuel stove, and also a small eating area off the lounge bar, and a conservatory. Belhaven Best Ale, Fyne Ales Jarl and Timothy Taylors Landlord and guest beers from brewers such as Houston or Orkney on handpump, quite a few malt whiskies and 11 wines by the glass; TV, dominoes and pool. There are white tables and chairs in the garden. You can walk from here up to the remains of St Ninian's kirk, on a headland behind the village.

Quite a choice of food includes wraps and baguettes, chicken liver and whisky pâté, local mussels in chive creamy sauce, field mushrooms stuffed with ratatouille, chicken curry, burger with onion rings, cheese, bacon, egg and chips, slow-cooked pork belly with apple and haggis potato cake and orange and star anise syrup, monkfish and parma ham filo parcel with wild mushroom sauce, and puddings such as Drambuie crème brûlée and a trio of chocolate. *Benchmark main dish: battered fish and chips £10.95. Two-course evening meal £19.00.*

Free house ~ Licensee Alastair Scoular ~ Real ale ~ (01988) 500334 ~ Open 11-11; 12-11 Sun; 11-3, 6-11 Tues-Fri in winter ~ Bar food 12-2, 6.30-9 ~ Restaurant ~ Children welcome except in public bar ~ Dogs allowed in bar and bedrooms ~ Wi-fi ~ Bedrooms: £30/£60 ~ www.steampacketinn.biz *Recommended by Isobel Mackinlay*

KIPPEN
NS6594 Map 11

Cross Keys 🛏

Main Street; village signposted off A811 W of Stirling; FK8 3DN

Cosy 18th-c inn with obliging staff, real ales, tasty food and views of the Trossachs; bedrooms

Very cosy with its dark panelling and subdued lighting, this unpretentious and comfortable early 18th-c inn has a strong local following, but extends a warm welcome to visitors too. The bar has a timeless quality, with attractive bare stone walls and An Teallach Ale and a changing guest on handpump, 20 malt whiskies, a dozen wines by the glass and a farm cider. A straightforward lounge has a log fire and there's a coal fire in the attractive family dining room; background music. Tables in the garden have good views towards the Trossachs.

🍴 Enjoyable food includes lunchtime sandwiches, cullen skink, smoked mackerel rillette with beetroot and lemon crème fraîche, garlic mushroom pie with parsnip mash, steak or pulled pork burger with mustard mayonnaise, coleslaw and fries, steak in ale pie, salmon fillet on a herbed potato cake, carrot and courgette noodles and braised fennel, braised ox cheek with horseradish mash and honey carrots, and puddings such as chocolate and orange parfait with fruit coulis and sticky toffee pudding with toffee sauce. *Benchmark main dish: moroccan lamb with bulgar wheat, flatbread and crème fraîche £14.00. Two-course evening meal £16.50.*

Free house ~ Licensees Debby McGregor and Brian Horsburgh ~ Real ale ~ (01786) 870293 ~ Open 12-3, 5-midnight (1am Fri); 12-1am Sat; 12-midnight Sun ~ Bar food 12-2.30, 5-9; 12-9 Sat; 12-8 Sun ~ Children welcome until 9pm ~ Dogs welcome ~ Wi-fi ~ Folk music first and third Sun of the month ~ Bedrooms: £55/£70 ~ www.kippencrosskeys.com *Recommended by J F M and M West*

MEIKLEOUR
Meikleour Arms 🛏️

NO1539 Map 11

A984 W of Coupar Angus; PH2 6EB

Traditional country inn and part of the Meikleour Estate; a welcoming and well run base for the area; bedrooms

Our readers enjoy staying overnight in this early 19th-c creeper-covered inn where the pretty bedrooms are comfortable, warm and well appointed; good breakfasts too. The main lounge bar is basically two rooms (one carpeted, the other with a stone floor) with comfortable seating, some angling equipment and fishing/shooting pictures, oil-burning fires, Orkney Dark Island, Strathbraan Due South and Look West and a guest from Inveralmond, 50 malt whiskies and nine wines by the glass served by attentive, friendly staff; background music. The panelled and tartan-carpeted dining room is elegant and more formal. The garden has seats on a small colonnaded verandah and sloping lawn with distant Highland views. Do visit the spectacular beech hedge just 300 metres away which was planted over 250 years ago – it's the tallest in the world. The inn is a very good base for rural Perthshire with lots to do and see nearby – including one of the best salmon beats in Scotland.

🍴 Using Estate produce plus more from their own walled garden, the good, sensibly priced food includes lunchtime sandwiches, hazelnut butter grilled scallops, home-smoked venison with creamed horseradish, burger with bacon, cheese, caramelised onions and chilli jam, sun-dried tomatoes, asparagus and broccoli with linguine, slow-roast pork belly with spring onion mash and coarse-grain mustard sauce, bass with lemon and caper dressing, and puddings such as lemon tart with honey cream and chocolate fudge brownie. *Benchmark main dish: beer-battered fish and chips £10.95. Two-course evening meal £23.00.*

Free house ~ Licensee Greg Burgess ~ Real ale ~ (01250) 883206 ~ Open 11-11 (midnight Fri, Sat) ~ Bar food 12-9 ~ Restaurant ~ Children welcome ~ Dogs allowed in bar and bedrooms ~ Wi-fi ~ Bedrooms: £90/£110 ~ www.meikleourarms.co.uk *Recommended by J and S Watkins*

> A star after the name of a pub shows exceptional quality. It means most people (after reading the report to see just why the star has been won) would think a special trip worthwhile.

MELROSE

NT5433 Map 9

Burts Hotel 🍽 🛏

B6374, Market Square; TD6 9PL

Comfortable town-centre hotel with imaginative food and a fine array of malt whiskies; bedrooms

Just a few steps from the abbey ruins in the middle of a beautifully unspoilt small town, this smart, family-run hotel makes a good base for exploring the area. Neat public areas are maintained with attention to detail. The welcoming red carpeted bar has tidy pub tables between cushioned wall seats and windsor armchairs, a warming fire, scottish prints on pale green walls and a long dark wood counter serving Knops Musselburgh Broke, Scottish Borders Game Bird and Timothy Taylors Landlord on handpump, 12 wines by the glass from a good wine list, a farm cider and around 70 malt whiskies. The elegant restaurant with its swagged curtains, dark blue wallpaper and tables laid with white linen offers a smarter dining experience; background music. Service here is helpful and polite and the licensees are very hands-on. The bedrooms, though quite small, are immaculate and comfortably decorated and the breakfasts are well thought-of. In summer you can sit out in the well tended garden.

Good food includes lunchtime sandwiches, confit duck and foie gras roulade with cherry and cranberry compote, scallop and tiger prawn terrine with pickled cucumber and citrus dressing, tomato, mozzarella and basil tart with pesto, burger with bacon, cheese, onions and chutney, chicken supreme with confit leg, stuffing, parsnip purée and gravy, beef bourguignon, lamb curry, bass with sweet potato gnocchi, fennel purée and salsa verde, and puddings such as rhubarb crème brûlée with rhubarb jelly, doughnuts and ginger ice-cream and tiramisu with mocha ice-cream. *Benchmark main dish: beer-battered fish and chips £12.95. Two-course evening meal £19.00.*

Free house ~ Licensees Graham and Nick Henderson ~ Real ale ~ (01896) 822285 ~ Open 11-2.30, 5 (6 Sun)-11 ~ Bar food 12-2, 6-9.30 (10 Fri, Sat) ~ Restaurant ~ Children welcome ~ Dogs allowed in bar and bedrooms ~ Wi-fi ~ Bedrooms: £74/£136 ~ www.burtshotel.co.uk *Recommended by J F M and M West, Comus and Sarah Elliott, William and Ann Reid, Roy Payne, Ian Herdman*

PLOCKTON

NG8033 Map 11

Plockton Hotel ★ 🍽 🛏

Village signposted from A87 near Kyle of Lochalsh; IV52 8TN

Lovely views from this family-run lochside hotel; very good food with emphasis on local seafood and real ales; bedrooms

This is a special place to stay, and it's worth booking well ahead. Half the comfortable bedrooms have extraordinary loch views; the others, some with balconies, look over the hillside garden, and breakfasts are good. The welcoming, comfortably furnished lounge bar has window seats with a view of the harbour boats, as well as antiqued dark red leather seating around neat Regency-style tables on a tartan carpet, three model ships set into the woodwork and partly panelled stone walls. The separate public bar has pool, board games, TV, a games machine, juke box and background music. Cromarty Hit the Lip, Highland Seafire and Scapa Special and Inveralmond Ossian on handpump, 30 malt whiskies and several wines by the glass. Tables in the front garden look out past the village's trademark palm trees and colourfully flowering shrub-lined shore, across the sheltered anchorage to the rugged mountainous surrounds of Loch Carron; a stream runs down the hill into a pond in the attractive back garden. There's a hotel nearby called the Plockton, so don't get the two confused.

Particularly good food includes lunchtime sandwiches, country pâté, haggis and whisky, their own smokies, a vegetarian dish of the day, chargrilled fresh langoustines, chicken stuffed with smoked ham and cheese with sun-dried tomato, garlic and basil sauce, herring in oatmeal, beer-battered fresh haddock and chips, venison casserole, and puddings. *Benchmark main dish: seafood platter £22.95. Two-course evening meal £20.00.*

Free house ~ Licensee Alan Pearson ~ Real ale ~ (01599) 544274 ~ Open 11-midnight (11.30 Sat); 12-11 Sun ~ Bar food 12-2.15, 6-9 ~ Restaurant ~ Children welcome ~ Live music Weds evening ~ Bedrooms: £55/£130 ~ www.plocktonhotel.co.uk
Recommended by M J Winterton, Les and Sandra Brown, Pete Walker, Ken Richards, Barry Collett

SHIELDAIG
NG8153 Map 11
Tigh an Eilean Hotel ⌐
Village signposted just off A896 Lochcarron–Gairloch; IV54 8XN

Separate, contemporary hotel bar memorably placed beneath formidable peaks, with real ales and enjoyable food; tranquil bedrooms

Many of the Scottish pubs we recommend seem to be in lovely countryside with stunning views, but the setting of this friendly hotel easily stands out as one of the best, looking over the forested Shieldaig Island to Loch Torridon and then to the sea beyond. Separate from the hotel, the bright, attractive bar is on two storeys with an open staircase; dining is on the first floor and a decked balcony has a magnificent loch and village view. The place is gently contemporary and nicely relaxed with timbered floors, timber-boarded walls, shiny bolts through exposed timber roof beams, and an open kitchen. A couple of changing ales from An Teallach on handpump (although sometimes in January there may be no real ale on offer) and up to a dozen wines by the glass. Next door, the bedrooms are comfortable and peaceful. The tables outside in a sheltered little courtyard are well placed to enjoy the gorgeous position.

Making the best of the top class local produce, the good food might include hand-dived scallops with cucumber, mango and mint salad and a light curry yoghurt dressing, crab tortellini with squat lobsters and a crustacean 'bisque' butter sauce, venison with honey-roasted pears and celeriac purée, barbary duck with fresh mango, honey and soy sauce, rack of lamb with a herb crust and lamb jus, corn-fed catalan-style chicken, and puddings such as chocolate tart with espresso ice-cream and crème brûlée. *Benchmark main dish: seafood platter £22.00. Two-course evening meal £22.50.*

Free house ~ Licensee Cathryn Field ~ Real ale ~ (01520) 755251 ~ Open 11-11 (1am Fri, Sat) ~ Bar food 12-9; 12-2.30, 6.30-9 in winter ~ Restaurant ~ Children welcome till 10pm ~ Dogs allowed in bar and bedrooms ~ Traditional live folk music in summer ~ Bedrooms: £80/£160 ~ www.tighaneilean.co.uk *Recommended by Steve and Irene Homer, the Dutchman*

'Children welcome' means the pub says it lets children inside without any special restriction. If it allows them in, but to restricted areas such as an eating area or family room, we specify this. Some pubs may impose an evening time limit. We do not mention limits after 9pm as we assume children are home by then.

SLIGACHAN
NG4930   Map 11

Sligachan Hotel 🍺 🛏

A87 Broadford–Portree, junction with A863; IV47 8SW

Mountain hotel (open March-October) with spectacular setting on the Isle of Skye, with walkers' bar and plusher side, food all day, impressive range of whiskies and useful children's play area

Some of the most testing walks in Britain are right on the doorstep of this stunningly set hotel at the foot of the Cuillins. The huge modern pine-clad main bar, falling somewhere between a basic climbers' bar and the plusher, more sedate hotel side, is spaciously open to the ceiling rafters and has geometrically laid-out dark tables and chairs on neat carpets; pool. As well as their own Cuillin Black Face, Pinnacle and Skye they keep a guest such as Orkney Red MacGregor on handpump plus an incredible display of their 400 malt whiskies at one end of the counter. It can get quite lively in here some nights, but there's a more sedate lounge bar with leather bucket armchairs on plush carpets and a coal fire; background highland and islands music. The separate restaurant is in the hotel itself. The interesting little museum, well worth a visit, charts the history of the hotel, its famous climbers, photographs and climbing and angling records. There are tables out in the garden and a big play area for children, which can be seen from the bar. The bedrooms are comfortable, bright and modern and they offer self-catering and have a campsite with caravan hook-ups. Dogs are allowed only in the main bar and not in the hotel's cocktail bar – but may stay in some bedrooms.

Some sort of food is usefully served all day and might include open sandwiches and paninis, venison pâté with red onion marmalade, hand-dived scallops with chorizo butter, wild mushroom risotto with truffle oil, cajun chicken burger with barbecue sauce, coleslaw and fries, haggis, neeps and tatties, bass on sun-dried tomato mash with tapenade, venison casserole, lamb rump with leek fondue, caramelised vegetables and whisky jus, and puddings such as chocolate tart with chantilly cream and iced cranachan parfait with coulis. *Benchmark main dish: beer-battered fish and chips £10.00. Two-course evening meal £16.00.*

Own brew ~ Licensee Sandy Coghill ~ Real ale ~ (01478) 650204 ~ Open 8am-midnight; 11am-midnight Sun; closed Nov-Feb (the hotel side); phone for bar times ~ Bar food 8am-9pm ~ Restaurant ~ Children welcome ~ Dogs allowed in bar and bedrooms ~ Wi-fi ~ Bedrooms: £48/£96 ~ www.sligachan.co.uk   *Recommended by Dave Braisted*

STEIN
NG2656   Map 11

Stein Inn 🛏

End of B886 N of Dunvegan in Waternish, off A850 Dunvegan–Portree; OS Sheet 23 map reference 263564; IV55 8GA

Lovely setting on Skye's northern corner for this welcoming 18th-c inn with good, simple food and lots of whiskies; a rewarding place to stay

Warmly welcoming to all – children and dogs included – this is an inn of great character in a tiny waterside hamlet with classic Hebridean views across Loch Dunvegan; a drink on the benches outside makes the most of this. The unpretentious original public bar makes a particularly inviting retreat from the elements, with sturdy country furnishings, flagstones, beam-and-plank ceiling, partly panelled stripped-stone walls and a warming double-sided stove between the two rooms. There's a games area with pool table, darts, board games, dominoes and cribbage, and maybe background music. Caledonian Deuchars IPA and a couple of local guests such as Cairngorm Trade Winds and Orkney Dark Island on handpump, a dozen wines by the glass and over 135 malt whiskies. Good service from smartly uniformed staff. There's a lively indoor play area for children and showers for yachtsmen. All the bedrooms have views of the sea and breakfasts are good – it's well worth pre-ordering the tasty smoked kippers.

Using local fish and highland meat, the popular food at sensible prices includes chicken liver pâté, peat-smoked scottish salmon, macaroni cheese, venison burger or scampi with fries, steak in ale casserole, langoustine (hot or cold), duck breast with cranberry sauce, and puddings such as key lime pie and apple and blueberry crumble. *Benchmark main dish: beer-battered haddock and chips £10.75. Two-course evening meal £16.50.*

Free house ~ Licensees Angus and Teresa Mcghie ~ Real ale ~ (01470) 592362 ~ Open 11am-midnight; 11.30-11 Sun; 12-11 in winter ~ Bar food 12-4, 6-9.30; 12.30-4, 6-9 Sun ~ Children welcome ~ Dogs allowed in bar and bedrooms ~ Wi-fi ~ Bedrooms: $45/$77 ~ www.steininn.co.uk *Recommended by David and Sue Atkinson, Edna Jones*

SWINTON
Wheatsheaf ♀ 🛏
A6112 N of Coldstream; TD11 3JJ

NT8347   Map 10

Civilised place with small bar for drinkers, comfortable lounges, quite a choice of food and drinks and professional service; appealing bedrooms

Although this is a restaurant-with-rooms and the emphasis is on the food and accommodation, the friendly attentive staff welcome customers in the little bar and informal lounges. Here they keep Belhaven IPA on handpump alongside 50 malt whiskies and 18 wines by the glass. There are comfortable plush armchairs and sofas, several nice old oak settles with cushions, a little open fire, sporting prints and china plates on the bottle-green walls in the bar, and small agricultural prints and a fishing-theme décor on the painted or bare stone walls in the lounges. The dining room and front conservatory with its vaulted pine ceiling have cushioned bamboo and barley-twist dining chairs around pale wood tables, carpet, and fresh flowers on the tables, while the more formal restaurant has black leather high-backed dining chairs around clothed tables; background music. The bedrooms are well equipped and comfortable. This is a pretty village surrounded by rolling countryside and only a few miles from the River Tweed.

Interesting food includes lunchtime sandwiches, home-smoked kangaroo fillet, crayfish and white crab with thermidor sauce and pea and mint coulis, burger with bacon, cheese and chips, corn-fed chicken with tomato and truffle oil cannelloni and cider and balsamic jus, venison loin with smoked pancetta cake, chanterelle jam and juniper berry jus, tiger prawn, smoked haddock, salmon, bass and scallop pie with vanilla cream sauce, and puddings such as bourbon, coffee and cinnamon tiramisu and white chocolate and rhubarb mousse with saffron syrup. *Benchmark main dish: 36-day aged sirloin steak with chips £21.95. Two-course evening meal £23.00.*

Free house ~ Licensees Chris and Jan Winson ~ Real ale ~ (01890) 860257 ~ Open 11-11; 12-3, 6-9 Jan-Mar ~ Bar food 12-2 (3 weekends), 6-9; not lunchtimes Jan-Mar ~ Restaurant ~ Young children allowed in restaurant 6-7pm ~ Dogs allowed in bar ~ Wi-fi ~ Bedrooms: $89/$119 ~ www.wheatsheaf-swinton.co.uk *Recommended by Martin Jones*

THORNHILL
Lion & Unicorn
NS6699 Map 11

Main Street (A873); FK8 3PJ

Busy, interesting pub with emphasis on its home-made food; friendly staff

Dating in part from the 17th-c, this neatly kept and friendly inn is run by helpful, attentive licensees. There's a back bar with a pubby character, some exposed stone walls, wooden flooring and stools lined along the counter where they keep Greene King Ruddles Best on handpump and several wines by the glass; log fires. This opens to a games room with a pool table, juke box, fruit machine, darts, TV and board games. The more restauranty-feeling carpeted front room has pub furniture, usually set for dining, a beamed ceiling and – as evidence of the building's 17th-c past – an original massive fireplace with a log fire in a high brazier, almost big enough to drive a car into; background music. Outside are benches on a gravelled garden and a lawn with a play area.

Popular food includes lunchtime sandwiches, haggis fritters with whisky, honey and grain mustard dip, mussels in white wine and garlic, three-cheese macaroni, beer-battered haddock or scampi with chips, steak burger with cheese and bacon, chicken topped with haggis wrapped in bacon with whisky cream sauce, and puddings such as sticky toffee pudding and ice-cream. *Benchmark main dish: steak in ale pie £9.75. Two-course evening meal £14.00.*

Free house ~ Licensee Fiona Stevenson ~ Real ale ~ (01786) 850204 ~ Open 11am-midnight (1am Fri, Sat); 12-midnight Sun ~ Bar food 12-9 ~ Restaurant ~ Children welcome ~ Dogs allowed in bar ~ Wi-fi ~ Bedrooms: $55/$75 ~ www.lion-unicorn.co.uk
Recommended by Caroline Prescott

ULLAPOOL
Ceilidh Place ♀
NH1293 Map 11

West Argyle Street; IV26 2TY

Bustling, arty place with cosy bar, attractively furnished rooms, an easy-going atmosphere and lots of customers dropping in and out all day; bedrooms

Though its setting in a side street above this small town is quiet, there's usually quite a lot going on at this pretty, rose-draped white house. It's rather like a stylish, arty café/bar – but with a distinctly Celtic character. There's an art gallery, bookshop and café, and regular jazz, folk and classical music. The conservatory-style main area has a mix of dining chairs around dark wooden tables; there's also a cosy bar area, and other rooms filled with all sorts of armchairs, sofas and wall seats with scatter cushions, rugs on floors and a woodburning stove. An Teallach Ale on handpump, 35 wines by the glass and 75 malt whiskies. Tables on the front terrace look over other houses to the distant hills beyond the natural harbour. The bedrooms are comfortable.

Highly thought-of food includes rolls, breakfast items such as french toast with bacon, mushrooms and maple syrup, smoked haddock chowder, haggis with clapshot and onion gravy, pork schnitzel, mussels in cream, white wine and garlic with chips, venison or chickpea, wasabi and sesame burgers with toppings, blackened salmon with roast pepper salad, beef in ale casserole, seafood stew, and puddings such as lime posset and a changing torte. *Benchmark main dish: monkfish with salsa verde £16.00. Two-course evening meal £19.00.*

Free house ~ Licensee Rebecca Urquhart ~ Real ale ~ (01854) 612103 ~ Open 11am-1am (midnight Sat); 12.30-11 Sun; closed Jan ~ Bar food 8-5, 6-9 ~ Restaurant ~ Children welcome but must leave bar by 7pm ~ Dogs allowed in bedrooms ~ Bedrooms: £56/£112 ~ www.theceilidhplace.com *Recommended by Isobel Mackinlay*

WEEM
NN8449   Map 11
Ailean Chraggan ♀
B846; PH15 2LD

Changing range of seasonal food in family-run hotel

Homely and welcoming, this friendly small hotel is popular with both locals and visitors. The busy bar has a chatty feel, Inveralmond Ossian on handpump and over 100 malt whiskies; winter darts. There's also an adjoining neatly old-fashioned dining room and a comfortably carpeted modern lounge. There are great views from the flower-filled, covered terrace and from the garden to the mountains beyond the Tay, and up to Ben Lawers (the highest peak in this part of Scotland); the owners can arrange fishing nearby. The bedrooms are spacious and pleasant.

Well liked food using local game and seafood includes lunchtime sandwiches, venison, prune and pistachio terrine with plum chutney, salmon and smoked haddock fishcakes with chilli sauce, spinach, chestnut, blue cheese and mushroom parcels with spicy sauce, chicken stuffed with haggis with a rich jus, duck breast on a sweet potato rösti with red onion marmalade and celeriac rémoulade, scallops on roast leeks with chilli, garlic and lemongrass butter, fillet steak and local lobster ravioli, and puddings such as orange and cinnamon crème brûlée and white chocolate and raspberry cheesecake. *Benchmark main dish: seafood platter £24.95. Two-course evening meal £20.00.*

Free house ~ Licensee Alastair Gillespie ~ Real ale ~ (01887) 820346 ~ Open 11-11 ~ Bar food 12-2, 5.30-8.30 (9 Sat) ~ Restaurant ~ Children welcome ~ Dogs allowed in bar and bedrooms ~ Wi-fi ~ Bedrooms: £55/£110 ~ www.aileanchraggan.co.uk
Recommended by Isobel Mackinlay, Neil and Angela Huxter

Also Worth a Visit in Scotland

Besides the fully inspected pubs, you might like to try these pubs that have been recommended to us and described by readers. Do tell us what you think of them: feedback@goodguides.com

ABERDEENSHIRE

ABERDEEN
NJ9305

Grill (01224) 573530
Union Street; AB11 6BA Don't be put off by the outside of this 19th-c granite building – the remodelled 1920s interior is well worth a look; long wood-floored bar with fine moulded ceiling, mahogany panelling and original button-back leather wall benches, ornate servery with glazed cabinets housing some of the 500 or so whiskies (including a few distilled in the 1930s and 60 from around the world), five well kept ales including Caledonian 80/- and Harviestoun Bitter & Twisted, basic snacks; no children or dogs; open all day (till 1am Fri, Sat). *(Anon)*

ABERDEEN
NJ9406

★ **Prince of Wales** (01224) 640597
St Nicholas Lane; AB10 1HF Individual and convivial old tavern with eight changing ales from very long counter, bargain hearty food, painted floorboards, flagstones or carpet, pews and screened booths, original tiled spitoon running length of bar; games machines; live music Sun evening, children over 5 welcome if eating, open all day from 10am (11am Sun). *(Pete Walker)*

ABOYNE
NO5298

★ **Boat** (01339) 886137
Charlestown Road (B968, just off A93); AB34 5EL Friendly country inn with fine views across River Dee, partly carpeted bar with model train chugging its way around

just below ceiling height, scottish pictures, brasses and woodburner in stone fireplace, games in public bar end, spiral stairs up to roomy additional dining area, three well kept ales, decent wines and some 30 malts, tasty bar food from sandwiches up, more elaborate seasonal evening menu; background music, games machine; children welcome, dogs in bar, six comfortable well equipped bedrooms, open all day. *(J F M and M West, Robert Watt)*

OLDMELDRUM NJ8127
Redgarth (01651) 872353
Kirk Brae, off A957; AB51 0DJ Good-sized comfortable lounge with traditional décor and subdued lighting, two or three well kept ales and good range of malt whiskies, popular reasonably priced food including authentic goulash from new hungarian chef, friendly attentive service, restaurant; children welcome, lovely views to Bennachie, bedrooms (get booked quickly). *(David and Betty Gittins)*

PENNAN NJ8465
Pennan Inn (01346) 561201
Just off B9031 Banff–Fraserburgh; AB43 6JB Whitewashed building in long row of old fishermen's cottages, wonderful spot right by the sea – scenes from film *Local Hero* (1983) shot here; small bar with simple furniture and exposed stone walls, separate restaurant (more spacious in feel) with wooden tables and upholstered high-backed chairs, pictures on plain painted walls, enjoyable sensibly priced food from shortish menu including some thai dishes, at least one real ale, friendly service; three bedrooms, at foot of steep winding road and parking along front limited, closed Mon, shut out of season. *(GSB)*

ANGUS
BROUGHTY FERRY NO4630
★ Fishermans Tavern (01382) 775941
Fort Street; turning off shore road; DD5 2AD Once a row of fishermen's cottages, this friendly pub is just steps from the beach, up to eight well kept changing ales (May beer festival) and good range of malt whiskies, secluded lounge area with coal fire, small carpeted snug with basket-weave wall panels, another fire in back bar popular with diners for the wide choice of fair priced pubby food (offers available), fiddle music Thurs night, quiz every other Mon; TV, fruit machine; children and dogs welcome, disabled facilities, tables on front pavement, more in secluded little walled garden, 12 bedrooms, open all day (till 1am Thurs-Sat). *(Anon)*

ARGYLL
BRIDGE OF ORCHY NN2939
★ Bridge of Orchy Hotel
(01838) 400208 *A82 Tyndrum–Glencoe; PA36 4AB* Spectacular spot on West Highland Way, very welcoming with good fairly priced all-day food in bar, lounge and smarter restaurant, decent choice of well kept ales, house wines and malt whiskies, interesting mountain photographs; ten good bedrooms, more in airy riverside annexe. *(Anon)*

CAIRNDOW NN1811
Cairndow Stagecoach Inn
(01499) 600286 *Village and pub signed off A83; PA26 8BN* Refurbished 17th-c coaching inn in wonderful position on edge of Loch Fyne, good sensibly priced food including local venison, ales such as Fyne Hurricane Jack and over 40 malt whiskies, friendly accommodating staff; children and dogs welcome, lovely peaceful lochside garden, 14 comfortable bedrooms, six more in modern annexe with balconies overlooking the water, good breakfast (excellent kippers), open (and food) all day. *(Pat and Stewart Gordon)*

CONNEL NM9034
Oyster (01631) 710666
A85, W of Connel Bridge; PA37 1PJ 18th-c pub opposite former ferry slipway, lovely view across the water (especially at sunset), decent-sized bar with friendly highland atmosphere, log fire in stone fireplace, café with cakes, ice-cream and coffees, enjoyable food including delicious local seafood, Caledonian Deuchars IPA, good range of wines and malts, attentive service; sports TV, pool and darts; modern hotel part with 16 attractive bedrooms next door with separate evening restaurant. *(Anon)*

INVERARAY NN0908
★ George (01499) 302111
Main Street East; PA32 8TT Very popular Georgian hotel (packed during holiday times) at hub of this appealing small town; bustling pubby bar with exposed joists, bare stone walls, old tiles and big flagstones, antique settles, carved wooden benches and cushioned stone slabs along the walls, four log fires, a couple of real ales and 100 malt whiskies, good food in bar and smarter restaurant, live entertainment Fri, Sat; children and dogs welcome, well laid-out terraces with plenty of seats, bedrooms, Inveraray Castle and walks close by, open all day till 1am. *(Anon)*

LOCH ECK NS1491
Coylet (01369) 840426
A815, E shore; PA23 8SG Former coaching inn in beautiful lochside setting, simply furnished bar with big stag's head above fireplace, good pubby food, Fyne Highlander on draught; four bedrooms, sells fishing permits and arranges boat trips. *(Dave Braisted)*

OBAN   NM8530
Cuan Mor (01631) 565078
George Street; PA34 5SD Contemporary
quayside bar-restaurant with lots of kitchen-
style chairs and tables on bare boards,
snug bar with open fire, over 100 malts and
their own-brewed real ales, wide choice of
competitively priced food all day, friendly
service; children welcome, some seats
outside. *(Dave Braisted)*

OBAN   NM8529
Lorne (01631) 570020
Stevenson Street; PA34 5NA Nice
Victorian décor including tiles and island bar
with ornate brasswork, well kept Oban Bay
ales, reasonably priced food from ciabattas
and wraps through pizzas to local fish, good
service, live music and DJs at weekends;
children welcome, sheltered beer garden,
open all day till late. *(Carola and Brian Groom,
Jim and Sheila Wilson)*

OTTER FERRY   NR9384
Oystercatcher (01700) 821229
B8000, by the water; PA21 2DH Friendly
family-run pub-restaurant in old building
in outstanding spot overlooking Loch Fyne,
good food using local fish and shellfish, well
kept ales including Fyne from pine-clad bar,
decent wine list; lots of tables out on spit,
free moorings, open all day. *(Anon)*

TARBERT   NR8365
West Loch Hotel (01880) 820283
A83, a mile S; PA29 6YF Friendly
18th-c family-run inn overlooking sea loch,
comfortably updated with exposed stone
walls, pale-topped tables and high-backed
dark dining chairs, comfortable lounges with
fine views or open fire, enjoyable food using
local produce, Belhaven and good selection
of whiskies and gins, helpful cheerful service;
children and dogs welcome, eight bedrooms
some with loch views, handy for ferry terminal.
(Dave Braisted)

TAYVALLICH   NR7487
Tayvallich Inn (01546) 870282
B8025; PA31 8PL Small single-storey
conversion by Loch Sween specialising in
good local seafood; pale pine furnishings
on quarry tiles, local nautical charts, good
range of whiskies and usually a couple of
beers from Loch Ness, friendly atmosphere;
background music (live first Fri of month);
children and dogs welcome, a few picnic-sets
on front deck with lovely views over yacht
anchorage, open all day weekends, closed
Mon. *(Jim and Sheila Wilson)*

AYRSHIRE

AYR   NS3322
Black Bull (01292) 288799
River Street; KA8 0AX Welcoming pub
by the river, well kept beers including

Caledonian, friendly staff and regulars, good
honest food. *(Eddie Edwards)*

AYR   NS3321
West Kirk (01292) 880416
Sandgate; KA7 1BX Wetherspoons
conversion of 19th-c church keeping original
stained glass, pulpit, balconies, doors and so
forth, seven real ales and their usual food;
TVs, free wi-fi; open all day from 8am.
(Dr Peter Crawshaw)

DUNURE   NS2515
Dunure (01292) 500549
Just off A719 SW of Ayr; KA7 4LN
Welcoming place attractively set by
harbourside ruined castle; updated bar,
lounge and restaurant, varied food including
fresh fish/seafood, nice wines; no real ales;
courtyard tables, bedrooms and two cottages,
not far from Culzean Castle (NTS). *(Paul
Bromley)*

SYMINGTON   NS3831
Wheatsheaf (01563) 830307
*Just off A77 Ayr–Kilmarnock; Main
Street; KA1 5QB* Single-storey former
17th-c posting inn, charming and cosy, with
wide choice of good well priced food (must
book weekends) including lunchtime/early
evening set menu, efficient friendly service,
log fire; children welcome, tables outside,
quiet pretty village, open (and food) all day.
(Barry Collett)

BERWICKSHIRE

ALLANTON   NT8654
★ Allanton Inn (01890) 818260
B6347 S of Chirnside; TD11 3JZ
Well run 18th-c stone-built village inn with
attractive bare-boards interior, good fairly
priced food including fresh fish from daily
changing menu, a couple of real ales, good
wine list and speciality gins, friendly efficient
service, log fire in small side dining room;
background music; children welcome, picnic-
sets in sheltered garden behind, nice views,
seven bedrooms, open all day. *(Comus and
Sarah Elliott, John and Sylvia Harrop, Dr Peter
Crawshaw)*

AUCHENCROW   NT8560
Craw (01890) 761253
*B6438 NE of Duns; pub signed off A1;
TD14 5LS* Attractive little 18th-c pub in
row of cream-washed slate-roofed cottages,
friendly and welcoming, with good well
presented food including fresh fish and
seafood, changing ales from smaller brewers
(maybe autumn beer festival), good wines by
the glass, beams decorated with hundreds
of beer mats, pictures on panelled walls,
woodburner, more formal back restaurant;
children welcome, tables on decking behind
and out on village green, three bedrooms
and self-catering apartment, open all day
weekends. *(Anon)*

CAITHNESS

MEY ND2872

Castle Arms (01847) 851244

A836; KW14 8XH 19th-c former coaching
inn, enjoyable home-made food (restaurant
shut winter lunchtimes) including takeaway
fish and chips Weds and Fri from 4.30, friendly
helpful service, plenty of malt whiskies,
views of Dunnet Head and across Pentland
Firth to the Orkneys; pool; seven comfortable
bedrooms and two suites in back extension,
well placed for north coast of Caithness, Gills
Bay ferry and Castle of Mey. *(Anon)*

DUMFRIESSHIRE

BARGRENNAN NX3576

House O' Hill (01671) 840243

*Off A714, road opposite church;
DG8 6RN* Small pub on edge of Galloway
Forest (good mountain biking), enthusiastic
owners, interesting well cooked/priced
food using local, seasonal produce (best to
book), a couple of real ales and good wine
list, friendly helpful staff; two comfortable
bedrooms (good breakfast) and self-catering
cottage, open all day. *(Dr Peter D Smart)*

DUMFRIES NX9776

★ Cavens Arms (01387) 252896

Buccleuch Street; DG1 2AH Good home-
made food all day (not Mon) from pubby
standards up, seven well kept interesting
ales, Aspall's and Stowford Press cider, fine
choice of malts, friendly landlord and good
helpful staff, civilised front part with lots
of wood, drinkers' area at back with bar
stools, banquettes and traditional cast-iron
tables, recently added lounge areas; can get
very busy, discreet TV, no children or dogs;
disabled facilities, small terrace at back,
open all day. *(Eric Larkham, Dr J Barrie Jones)*

DUMFRIES NX9775

Globe (01387) 252335

High Street; DG1 2JA Proper town pub
with strong Burns connections, especially
in old-fashioned dark-panelled 17th-century
snug and little museum of a room beyond;
main part more modern in feel, ales such as
Caledonian Deuchars IPA and Sulwath The
Grace, plenty of whiskies, good value pubby
food (evening by arrangement), friendly
service; live music Mon evening, children
welcome in eating areas, terrace seating,
open all day. *(Anon)*

MOFFAT NT0805

Annandale Arms (01683) 220013

High Street; DG10 9HF 18th-c hotel's
pleasant oak-panelled bar, local Broughton
ales, Weston's cider and around 50 malt
whiskies (including a breakfast one), nice
food served by friendly staff, restaurant; free
wi-fi; 16 bedrooms. *(Johnston and Maureen
Anderson)*

MOFFAT NT0805

Black Bull (01683) 220206

Churchgate; DG10 9EG Attractive small
hotel (former coaching inn), comfortable
dimly lit bar with Burns memorabilia, well
kept Caledonian Deuchars IPA and several
dozen malts, enjoyable food including steaks
and grills, simply furnished carpeted dining
room, friendly public bar across courtyard
with railway memorabilia, pool, darts and
big-screen sports TV; background and live
acoustic music; children welcome, tables in
courtyard, eight small bedrooms in annexe
(dogs welcome), hearty breakfast, no car
park, open all day. *(Johnston and Maureen
Anderson)*

MOFFAT NT0805

Buccleuch Arms (01683) 220003

High Street; DG10 9ET Friendly rather
old-fashioned Georgian coaching inn with
roomy carpeted bar and lounge areas, open
fire, good popular food using local produce
(suppliers listed) from sandwiches and
toasties up, informal upstairs restaurant,
polite quick service, interesting wines by
the glass, over 70 malts and bottled beers,
cocktails; soft background music, Sky TV
(in public bar next door); dogs welcome,
garden (bike storage), 16 bedrooms, open
all day. *(Anon)*

DUNBARTONSHIRE

ARROCHAR NN2903

Village Inn (01301) 702279

*A814, just off A83 W of Loch Lomond;
G83 7AX* Friendly cosy and interesting
with well kept ales such as Caledonian and
Fyne, good hearty home-made food in simple
all-day dining area (gets booked up) with
heavy beams, bare boards, some panelling
and roaring fire, steps down to unpretentious
bar, several dozen malts, good coffee, fine
sea and hill views; background music, juke
box; children welcome in eating areas till
8pm, no dogs, tables out on deck and lawn,
comfortable bedrooms including spacious
ones in former back barn, good breakfast,
open all day. *(Eric Larkham, David and Sue
Atkinson)*

EAST LOTHIAN

GULLANE NT4882

★ Old Clubhouse (01620) 842008

East Links Road; EH31 2AF Single-storey
building overlooking Gullane Links, with cosy
bar and more formal dining room, seating
from wooden dining chairs and banquettes
to big squashy leather armchairs and sofas,
Victorian pictures and cartoons, stuffed
birds, pre-war sheet music, golfing and other
memorabilia, open fires, good choice of food
plus specials, four ales including Belhaven
and Caledonian, nice house wines, fast
friendly service, plenty of seats and tables

on front terrace; children and dogs welcome, open all day. *(Comus and Sarah Elliott)*

HADDINGTON — NT5173
Victoria (01620) 823332
Court Street; EH41 3JD Popular bar-restaurant with a mix of cushioned dining chairs and wall banquettes on wooden flooring or carpets, woodburning stove, good imaginative local food cooked by chef-landlord, a couple of changing real ales, short but decent wine list, prompt friendly service; five bedrooms, open all day.
(Ian Wilson, Comus and Sarah Elliott)

HADDINGTON — NT5173
Waterside (01620) 825674
Waterside; just off A6093, over pedestrian bridge at E end of town; EH41 4AT Attractively set riverside dining pub next to historic bridge, spacious modernised interior with some stylish touches, enjoyable bistro-style food, three real ales from smaller brewers, good wine choice, pleasant friendly staff; children welcome (family room with toys), picnic-sets out overlooking the Tyne. *(Comus and Sarah Elliott)*

FIFE

CULROSS — NS9885
Red Lion (01383) 880225
Low Causeway; KY12 8HN Popular old pub in pretty NTS village, enjoyable good value food, a beer from Inveralmond and several wines by the glass, beams and amazing painted ceilings; seats outside, open (and food) all day. *(Brian and Anna Marsden)*

CUPAR — NO3714
Boudingait (01334) 654681
Bonnygate; KY15 4BU Bustling bar with high-backed, captain's and cushion-seated chairs around dark tables on wooden flooring, open fire, high chairs against the counter, friendly attentive staff, good variety of reasonably priced home-made food (something available all day), live folk and quiz nights; children welcome. *(Anon)*

ELIE — NO4999
★Ship (01333) 330246
The Toft, off A917 (High Street) towards harbour; KY9 1DT Pleasant welcoming seaside inn, very much part of the community, and in good position for enjoying a drink overlooking the sandy bay and on towards the stone pier and old granary; unspoilt beamed nautical-feel bar with old prints and maps on partly panelled walls, coal fires, well kept Caledonian Deuchars IPA, a few malt whiskies and good bar food, simple carpeted back room with board games (children welcome here); dogs allowed in bar, open all day (till 1am Fri, Sat). *(Pat and Stewart Gordon, Brian and Anna Marsden)*

INVERNESS-SHIRE

MALLAIG — NM6796
Steam (01687) 462002
Davies Brae; PH41 4PU Refurbished Victorian inn run by mother and daughter, good choice of food from bar snacks to freshly landed fish (takeaway menu too), speedy service, bar with open fire and pool, split-level restaurant with high-backed dark leather chairs around pale tables on floorboards, live music including traditional at weekends; children and dogs welcome (not in bedrooms), tables in back garden, five bedrooms. *(Mike and Mary Carter)*

ARDGOUR
Inn at Ardgour (01855) 841225
From A82 follow signs for Strontian A861 and take Corran Ferry across loch to the inn; NB ferry does not sail over Christmas period; PH33 7AA Traditional fairly remote roadside inn by Corran Ferry slipway; enjoyable food and decent beer and whisky choice, friendly accommodating staff, restaurant; children welcome, a few tables outside, fine Loch Linnhe views, clean bedrooms, open all day. *(Eddie Edwards)*

AVIEMORE — NH8612
Cairngorm (01479) 810233
Grampian Road (A9); PH22 1PE Large flagstoned bar in traditional hotel, lively and friendly, with prompt helpful service, good value food all day (including afternoon tea and meals on local steam train) from wide-ranging menu using local produce, Cairngorm ales, good choice of other drinks, tartan-walled and carpeted restaurant with skulls and antlers; some live music, sports TV; children welcome, comfortable smart bedrooms (some with stunning views). *(Anon)*

CARRBRIDGE — NH9022
Cairn (01479) 841212
Main Road; PH23 3AS Welcoming tartan-carpeted, traditionally furnished hotel bar, enjoyable pubby food using local produce and well kept ales such as Black Isle, Cairngorm and Highland, old local pictures, warm coal fire, separate more formal dining room; pool and sports TV; children and dogs welcome, white metal seats and tables outside in front, seven comfortable bedrooms, open all day. *(Anon)*

DORES — NH5934
Dores (01463) 751203
B852 SW of Inverness; IV2 6TR Traditional country pub with exposed stone walls and low ceilings in delightful spot on the shore of Loch Ness, splendid views; small attractive bar on right with two or three well kept ales such as Belhaven Black and Cairngorm Trade Winds, daily newspapers, good interesting food (pub favourites too) in

two-part dining area to the left, friendly staff; children and dogs welcome, sheltered front garden, more tables out behind taking in the view. *(the Dutchman)*

FORT WILLIAM   NN1274
Ben Nevis Inn (01397) 701227
N off A82: Achintee; PH33 6TE Roomy, well converted, raftered stone barn in stunning spot by path up to Ben Nevis, good mainly straightforward food (lots of walkers so best to book), ales such as Cairngorm Nessies Monster Mash, prompt cheery service, bare-boards dining area with steps up to bar, live music (Tues in summer, first and third Thurs in winter); seats out at front and back, bunkhouse below, open all day Apr-Oct, otherwise closed Mon-Weds, children welcome, no dogs. *(Michael Peters, M J Winterton)*

GLEN SHIEL   NH0711
⋆Cluanie Inn (01320) 340238
A87 Invergarry–Kyle of Lochalsh, on Loch Cluanie; IV63 7YW Welcoming inn in lovely isolated setting by Loch Cluanie, stunning views, friendly table service for drinks including well kept Isle of Skye, fine malt range, big helpings of enjoyable food (good local game and salmon and home-grown herbs) in three knocked-together rooms with dining chairs around polished tables, overspill into restaurant, warm log fire, chatty parrots in lobby – watch your fingers; children allowed, dogs too (owners have several of their own), big comfortable pine-furnished modern bedrooms, bunkhouse, great breakfasts (non-residents welcome), open all day. *(Anon)*

GLENUIG   NM6576
Glenuig Inn (01687) 470219
A861 SW of Lochailort, off A830 Fort William–Mallaig; PH38 4NG Friendly refurbished bar on picturesque bay, enjoyable locally sourced all-day food including some from next-door smokery, well kept Cairngorm ales and a scottish cider on tap, lots of bottled beers and good range of whiskies, woodburner in dining room; dogs welcome, bedrooms in adjoining block, also bunkhouse popular with walkers and divers, moorings for visiting yachts, open all day. *(David and Sue Atkinson, Dave Braisted)*

INVERIE   NG7500
⋆Old Forge (01687) 462267
Park in Mallaig for ferry; PH41 4PL Utterly remote waterside stone pub with stunning views across Loch Nevis; comfortable mix of old furnishings, lots of charts and sailing prints, open fire, buoyant atmosphere, good reasonably priced bar food including fresh seafood and good venison burgers, two well kept changing ales in season such as local Glenfinnan, lots of whiskies and good wine choice, restaurant extension, occasional live music and ceilidhs

(instruments provided); the snag is getting there – boat (jetty moorings and new pier), Mallaig foot-ferry six times a day (four in winter), or 15-mile walk through Knoydart from nearest road; children and dogs welcome, two bedrooms (get booked early), open all day summer. *(Dave Braisted, David Crook, R Anderson)*

INVERMORISTON   NH4216
Glenmoriston Arms (01320) 351206
A82/A887; IV63 7YA Small civilised hotel dating in part from 1740 when it was a drovers' inn, tartan-carpeted bar with open fire and big old stag's head, neatly laid out restaurant with antique rifles, well kept beer and over 100 malt whiskies, enjoyable food from lunchtime sandwiches up, friendly staff; handy for Loch Ness, ten bedrooms (three in converted outbuilding). *(Anon)*

INVERNESS   NH6645
Kings Highway (01463) 251830
Church Street; IV1 1EN A Wetherspoons Lodge in former 19th-c hotel; plenty of seating in comfortable open-plan interior, up to ten real ales and their usual well priced food including good fish and chips; TVs, free wi-fi; children welcome, 27 bedrooms, open all day from 7am for breakfast, handy for station. *(Dave Braisted, Edna Jones)*

INVERNESS   NH6645
Number 27 (01463) 241999
Castle Street; IV2 3DU Busy pub opposite the castle, cheery welcoming staff, plenty of draught and bottled beers, good choice of well prepared food at reasonable prices, restaurant at back; open all day. *(A J Holland)*

ONICH   NN0263
Four Seasons (01855) 821393
Off A82, signed for Inchree, N of village; PH33 6SE Wooden building – part of Inchree holiday complex; bare-boards bar with cushioned wall benches, dining area with unusual central log fire, up to three scottish ales and decent choice of whiskies, generous varied evening food at reasonable prices, friendly helpful staff, local maps and guidebooks for sale, daily weather forecast and free wi-fi; children (till 8.30) and dogs welcome, hostel, lodge and chalet accommodation, handy for Corran Ferry, open all day in season (when can be very busy), check winter opening. *(Eddie Edwards)*

ROY BRIDGE   NN2781
Stronlossit Inn (01397) 712253
Off A86; PH31 4AG Village inn with three well kept changing ales and over 80 malts, good choice of enjoyable sensibly priced food all day, decent coffee, bar with banquette seating and wooden dining chairs on carpeting, an open fire; seats on terrace in flower-filled garden, good disabled access, ten bedrooms, open all day. *(M J Winterton)*

KINCARDINESHIRE

FETTERCAIRN NO6573

Ramsay Arms (01561) 340334

Burnside Road; AB30 1XX Hotel with
enjoyable pubby food in tartan-carpeted bar
and smart oak-panelled restaurant, friendly
service, well kept ales and several malts
including the local Fettercairn; children
welcome, picnic-sets in garden, attractive
village (liked by Queen Victoria who stayed
at the hotel), 12 comfortable bedrooms,
good breakfast. *(Anon)*

STONEHAVEN NO8785

Marine Hotel (01569) 762155

Shore Head; AB39 2JY Popular
harbourside pub with six well kept ales
including own Dunnottar brews, over 170
bottled belgian beers and plenty of whiskies,
good food especially local fish/seafood,
efficient service, large stripped-stone bar
with log fire in cosy side room, upstairs
sea-view restaurant, live acoustic music last
Thurs of month; children welcome, pavement
tables, updated bedrooms, open all day (till
1am Fri, Sat). *(Robert Watt)*

KIRKCUDBRIGHTSHIRE

GATEHOUSE OF FLEET NX6056

Masonic Arms (01557) 814335

Ann Street; off B727; DG7 2HU Spacious
dining pub with comfortable two-room pubby
bar, traditional seating, pictures on timbered
walls, plates on delft shelf, stuffed fish above
brick fireplace, a couple of real ales and good
choice of malts, enjoyable food in bar and
contemporary restaurant, tapas night Tues,
spanish set menu Fri, attractive terracotta-
tiled conservatory with cane furniture;
background music (live Thurs), quiz Weds,
free wi-fi; children and dogs welcome,
picnic-sets under parasols in neatly kept
sheltered garden, more seats in front, open
all day. *(Anon)*

GATEHOUSE OF FLEET NX5956

Ship (01557) 814217

Fleet Street; DG7 2JT Late Victorian
village inn on the banks of the River Fleet,
enjoyable popular food, Belhaven beers
and good choice of malt whiskies, neatly
kept refurbished interior with woodburner,
welcoming service, restaurant with chairs
and wall banquettes around wooden tables;
waterside garden, comfortable bedrooms
and tasty breakfasts; Dorothy Sayers wrote
Five Red Herrings while staying here in
the 1930s. *(Phil and Jane Hodson)*

HAUGH OF URR NX8066

★Laurie Arms (01556) 660246

*B794 N of Dalbeattie; Main Street;
DG7 3YA* Neatly kept and attractively
decorated 19th-c pub with good local
atmosphere, traditional furnishings in log-fire

bar with steps up to similar area, restaurant
with napery, tasty food from bar snacks to
steaks, good changing real ales and decent
wines by the glass, welcoming attentive
service, games room with darts, pool and juke
box, splendid Bamforth comic postcards in
the gents'; tables out at front and picnic-sets
on sheltered terrace behind, open all day
weekends. *(R J Herd)*

KIRKCUDBRIGHT NX6850

★Selkirk Arms (01557) 330402

High Street; DG6 4JG Comfortable well
run 18th-c hotel in pleasant spot by mouth of
the Dee, simple locals' front bar (own street
entrance), partitioned high-ceilinged and
tartan-carpeted lounge with upholstered
armchairs, wall banquettes and paintings
for sale, ales including a house beer from
local Sulwath, rewarding food in bistro and
restaurant from pub standards up, good
helpful service; background music, TV;
children (not in bar) and dogs welcome,
smart wooden furniture under blue
parasols in neat garden with 15th-c font,
16 comfortable bedrooms, open all day.
(Steve Whalley)

LANARKSHIRE

BALMAHA NS4290

Oak Tree (01360) 870357

B837; G63 0JQ Family-run slate-clad inn
on Loch Lomond's quiet side, beams, timbers
and panelling, pubby bar with lots of old
photographs, farm tools and collection of
grandfather clocks, log fire, good choice of
enjoyable food from sandwiches and snacks
up, scottish ales (own brew-house planned),
good whisky selection, restaurant and new
coffee shop and ice-cream parlour; children
welcome, plenty of tables out around ancient
oak tree, popular with West Highland Way
walkers, seven attractive bedrooms, two
bunkhouses and four cottages.
(Laurence Smith)

BIGGAR NT0437

Crown (01899) 220116

High Street (A702); ML12 6DL Friendly
old pub with enjoyable food all day including
home-made burgers and pizzas, Sun carvery,
two well kept changing ales, open fire in
beamed front bar, panelled lounge with
old local pictures, restaurant; fortnightly
acoustic music, Sat karaoke; children
welcome, open (and food) all day.
(David and Betty Gittins)

GLASGOW NS5965

Counting House (0141) 225 0160

*Corner of St Vincent Place and George
Square; G1 2DH* Impressive Wetherspoons
bank conversion, imposing interior rising
into lofty richly decorated coffered ceiling
culminating in great central dome, big
windows, decorative glasswork, wall-safes,
several areas with solidly comfortable

seating, smaller rooms (once managers' offices) around perimeter, one like a well stocked library, a few themed with pictures and prints of historical characters, real ales from far and wide, bottled beers and lots of malt whiskies, usual good value food all day; children welcome if eating, open 8am–midnight. *(Anon)*

GLASGOW NS5865
Drum & Monkey (0141) 221 6636
St Vincent Street; G2 5TF Lively and busy Nicholsons bank conversion with ornate ceiling, granite pillars and lots of carved mahogany, Caledonian and other beers from island bar, decent range of wines and good value food, pleasant staff, quieter back area; open all day. *(Jeremy King)*

GLASGOW NS5865
Pot Still (0141) 333 0980
Hope Street; G2 2TH Comfortable and welcoming little pub with hundreds of malt whiskies, traditional bare-boards interior with raised area at back, button-back leather bench seats, dark panelling, etched and stained glass, columns up to ornately corniced ceiling, four changing ales and interesting bottled beers from nice old-fashioned servery, knowledgeable friendly staff; silent fruit machine; open all day. *(Jeremy King, Frank Murphy)*

GLASGOW NS5965
★Sloans (0141) 221 8886
Argyle Arcade; G2 8BG Restored Grade A listed building over three floors, many original features including a fine mahogany staircase, etched glass, ornate woodwork and moulded ceilings, Caledonian Deuchars IPA and Kelburn, enjoyable food from sandwiches up in ground-floor bar-bistro and upstairs restaurant, friendly staff, events in impressive barrel-vaulted parquet-floored ballroom; children welcome, tables in courtyard, Sat and Sun all-day market, open all day (till late Fri, Sat). *(Dr and Mrs A K Clarke)*

GLASGOW NS5865
State (0141) 332 2159
Holland Street; G2 4NG High-ceilinged bar with marble pillars, lots of carved wood including handsome oak island servery, half a dozen or so well kept changing ales, bargain basic lunchtime food from sandwiches up, some areas set for dining, good atmosphere and friendly staff, armchairs among other comfortable seats, coal-effect gas fire in big wooden fireplace, old prints and theatrical posters; background music (live weekends and comedy nights), silent sports TVs, games machine. *(Jeremy King)*

GLASGOW NS5666
Tennents (0141) 339 7203
Byres Road; G12 8TN Big busy high-ceilinged Victorian corner pub near

university, ornate plasterwork, panelling and paintings, traditional stools, chairs, tables and wall seating, a dozen well kept ales, wide range of good value food from sandwiches and baked potatoes up including bargain offers and Sunday breakfast, basement bar for weekend DJs and Mon quiz; sports TVs; open all day. *(Dr and Mrs A K Clarke)*

GLASGOW NS5666
Three Judges (0141) 337 3055
Dumbarton Road, opposite Byres Road; G11 6PR Traditional corner bar with up to nine quickly changing real ales from small breweries far and wide (they get through several hundred a year), farm cider, pump clips on walls, friendly staff and locals, live jazz Sun afternoons, no food; dogs welcome, open all day. *(Dr and Mrs A K Clarke)*

MIDLOTHIAN

EDINBURGH
Blue Blazer (0131) 229 5030
Spittal Street/Bread Street; EH3 9DX Traditional two-room bare-boards drinkers' pub with up to eight real ales, good selection of rums, whiskies and gins too, helpful knowledgeable staff, open fire; background and some live acoustic music; dogs welcome, open all day. *(Eric Larkham)*

EDINBURGH NT2574
★Café Royal (0131) 556 1884
West Register Street; EH2 2AA Opulent building's dazzling Victorian baroque interior, floors and stairway laid with marble, chandeliers hanging from magnificent plasterwork ceilings, superb series of Doulton tilework portraits of historical innovators (Watt, Faraday, Stephenson, Caxton, Benjamin Franklin and Robert Peel), substantial island bar serving well kept Caledonian Deuchars IPA and three guests, several wines by the glass and 25 malts, well liked food, good friendly service, the restaurant's stained glass is also worth seeing (children welcome here); background music and games machine; open all day (till 1am Fri, Sat); can get very busy. *(David and Sue Smith, Comus and Sarah Elliott, Barry Collett, Paul Humphreys, Jeremy King and others)*

EDINBURGH NT2471
★Canny Man's (0131) 447 1484
Morningside Road; aka Volunteer Arms; EH10 4QU Utterly individual and distinctive, saloon, lounge and snug with fascinating bric-a-brac, ceiling papered with sheet music, huge range of appetising open sandwiches, lots of whiskies, good wines and well kept ales such as Caledonian and Timothy Taylors Landlord, efficient friendly service; no credit cards, mobile phones or backpackers; children welcome, courtyard tables. *(Pat and Stewart Gordon, Ken Richards)*

EDINBURGH   NT2573
Deacon Brodies (0131) 225 6531
Lawnmarket; EH1 2NT Entertainingly
commemorating the notorious highwayman
town councillor who was eventually hanged
on the scaffold he'd designed; very busy,
ornately high-ceilinged city bar, well
kept Belhaven and Caledonian from long
counter, decent whisky selection, good
choice of reasonably priced food in upstairs
dining lounge, service may struggle at busy
times; background music, TV; pavement
seating. *(John Beeken)*

EDINBURGH   NT2573
Doric (0131) 225 1084
Market Street; EH1 1DE Welcoming 17th-c
pub/restaurant with plenty of atmosphere,
simple furnishings in small bar with wood
floor and lots of pictures, good range of
changing ales and bottled beers, 50 single
malts, friendly young staff, popular food
(must book) in upstairs wine bar (children
welcome) and bistro; handy for Waverley
Station, open all day. *(Dr Peter D Smart)*

EDINBURGH   NT2573
Ensign Ewart (0131) 225 7440
*Lawnmarket, Royal Mile; last pub on
right before castle; EH1 2PE* Charming
dimly lit old-world pub handy for castle (so
gets busy), beams peppered with brasses,
huge painting of Ewart at Waterloo capturing
french banner, assorted furniture including
elbow tables, friendly efficient staff, well
kept Caledonian ales and plenty of whiskies,
straighforward bar food; background music,
games machine, keypad entry to lavatories;
open all day. *(Peter F Marshall)*

EDINBURGH   NT2573
★ Halfway House (0131) 225 7101
*Fleshmarket Close (steps between
Cockburn Street and Market Street,
opposite Waverley Station); EH1 1BX*
Tiny one-room pub off steep steps, part
carpeted, part tiled, with a few small tables
and high-backed settles, lots of prints
(some golf and railway themes), four well
kept scottish ales (third of a pint glasses
available), good range of malt whiskies, short
choice of decent cheap food all day, friendly
staff; dogs welcome, open all day. *(Comus and
Sarah Elliott)*

EDINBURGH   NT2473
Hanging Bat (0131) 229 0759
Lothian Road; EH3 9AB Modern bar on
three levels with own microbrewery, fine
selection of craft beers and real ales, over
100 bottled beers and good range of wines

and gins, barbecue-style food; dogs welcome,
children till 8pm, open (and food) all day.
(Eric Larkham)

EDINBURGH   NT2676
Kings Wark (0131) 554 9260
The Shore, Leith; EH6 6QU Old bare-
boards pub on Leith's restored waterfront;
plenty of atmosphere in stripped-stone
candlelit interior, good selection of well kept
ales, interesting modern cooking including
popular Sunday breakfasts and good value
wines; seats outside, open all day.
(David Hunt)

EDINBURGH   NT1968
Kinleith Arms (0131) 453 3214
Lanark Road (A70); EH14 5EN Friendly
traditional local with well kept Caledonian
ales and enjoyable good value pub food
(seafood chowder recommended); sports TV,
darts; open all day. *(R T and J C Moggridge)*

EDINBURGH   NT2872
Sheep Heid (0131) 661 7974
The Causeway, Duddingston; EH15 3QA
Comfortably refurbished coaching inn (part
of the Village Pub & Kitchen chain) in lovely
spot near King Arthur's Seat, long history,
fine rounded bar counter in main room,
attractive dining rooms, well kept beers and
good, enterprising food (all day) including
children's menu, friendly young staff, skittle
alley; courtyard tables. *(Anthony Jones)*

EDINBURGH   NT2574
Standing Order (0131) 225 4460
George Street; EH2 2LR Grand
Wetherspoons bank conversion in three
elegant Georgian houses, imposing
columns, enormous main room with
elaborate colourful ceiling, lots of tables,
smaller side booths, other rooms including
two with floor-to-ceiling bookshelves,
comfortable clubby seats, Adam fireplace
and portraits, wide range of real ales from
long counter, bar food, gets very busy
(particularly Sat night) but obliging staff
cope well; weekend live music, sports TV,
free wi-fi; children welcome, disabled
facilities, open 8am-1am. *(John Beeken,
R T and J C Moggridge)*

EDINBURGH   NT2574
★ Starbank (0131) 552 4141
*Laverockbank Road, off Starbank Road,
just off A901 Granton–Leith; EH5 3BZ*
Cheerful pub in a fine spot with terrific views
over the Firth of Forth, long light and airy
bare-boards bar, some leather bench and tub
seats, up to eight well kept ales and good
choice of malt whiskies, interesting food

We include some hotels with a good bar that offers facilities comparable
to those of a pub.

(and set menus) in conservatory restaurant; background and some live music, sports TV, fruit machine; children welcome till 9pm if dining, dogs on leads, sheltered back terrace, parking on adjacent hilly street, open all day. *(Anon)*

RATHO   NT1470
Bridge (0131) 333 1320
Baird Road; EH28 8RA Popular extended 18th-c pub with good freshly made food from varied menu using local produce (including some of their own), changing scottish ales such as Cairngorm, Inveralmond and Orkney, good malt whisky choice, friendly staff; children very welcome, garden by Union Canal with wandering ducks, trips on own canal boats, four bedrooms, open (and food) all day. *(Pat and Stewart Gordon)*

PEEBLESSHIRE

INNERLEITHEN   NT3336
★**Traquair Arms** (01896) 830229
B709, just off A72 Peebles–Galashiels; follow signs for Traquair House; EH44 6PD Modernised inn at heart of pretty borders village, one of the few places serving Traquair ale (produced in original oak vessels in 18th-c brewhouse at nearby Traquair House), also Caledonian Deuchars IPA and Timothy Taylors Landlord, 40 malt whiskies, enjoyable italian-influenced food (all day weekends), main bar with warm open fire, another in relaxed bistro-style restaurant, good mix of customers; background music, TV; children welcome, dogs in bar, picnic-sets on neat back lawn, 14 bedrooms and six self-catering cottages, open all day. *(Anon)*

PERTHSHIRE

BLAIR ATHOLL   NN8765
★**Atholl Arms** (01796) 481205
B8079; PH18 5SG Sizeable hotel's cosy two-roomed bar (one beamed and tartan-carpeted) with open fires, armchairs, sofas and traditional tables, chairs and benches, grand dining room with suit of armour and stag's head, four local Moulin ales, good well priced food all day from sandwiches to interesting dishes, local meat and wild salmon, quick friendly service, open fire; 31 good value bedrooms, lovely setting near the castle. *(Lucien Perring)*

BRIG O' TURK   NN5306
★**Byre** (01877) 376292
A821 Callander–Trossachs, just outside village; FK17 8HT Beautifully placed byre conversion with slate-floored log-fire bar and roomier high-raftered restaurant area, popular food including local game and fish and some imaginative dishes (best to book), friendly helpful staff; picnic-sets out on gravel in front and at the back, boules piste, good walks, open all day, closed Jan. *(Anon)*

DUNKELD   NO0243
Atholl Arms (01350) 727219
Atholl Street (A923); PH8 OAQ Sizeable Victorian hotel with comfortably furnished smallish bar and lounge, open fires, good choice of well kept ales such as Inveralmond, enjoyable food from varied menu including cullen skink and beef stovies, friendly service; 17 bedrooms (some with River Tay views). *(Anon)*

DUNNING   NO0114
Kirkstyle (01764) 684248
B9141, off A9 S of Perth; Kirkstyle Square; PH2 0RR Unpretentious 18th-c streamside pub with chatty regulars, log fire in snug bar, up to three real ales from across Britain and good choice of whiskies, enjoyable good value home-made food including some interesting specials (book in season), attentive friendly service, split-level stripped-stone back restaurant; background music; children welcome, dogs allowed in garden only, open all day weekends, closed Mon and Tues lunchtimes. *(Anon)*

KENMORE   NN7745
★**Kenmore Hotel** (01887) 830205
A827 W of Aberfeldy; PH15 2NU Civilised small hotel dating from the 16th c in pretty Loch Tay village; comfortable traditional front lounge with warm log fire and poem pencilled by Burns himself on the chimney breast, dozens of malts helpfully arranged alphabetically, polite uniformed staff, modern restaurant with balcony; back public bar and terrace overlooking River Tay with enjoyable food from lunchtime soup and sandwiches up (especially good grills), Inveralmond Ossian, decent wines by the glass; pool and winter darts, juke box, TV, fruit machine; children and dogs welcome, 40 good bedrooms plus luxury lodges, open all day. *(Anon)*

KILMAHOG   NN6008
★**Lade** (01877) 330152
A84 just NW of Callander, by A821 junction; FK17 8HD Lively place with a strong scottish theme – traditional weekend music, real ale shop with over 190 bottled beers from regional microbreweries and their own-brewed WayLade ales; plenty of character in several cosy beamed areas with panelling and stripped stone, highland prints and works by local artists, 40 malt whiskies, enjoyable home-made food from bar snacks up, big-windowed restaurant, friendly staff; background music; children and dogs (in bar) welcome, terrace tables, pleasant garden with fish ponds, open all day (till 1am Fri, Sat). *(Pat and Stewart Gordon)*

LOCH TUMMEL   NN8160
★**Loch Tummel Inn** (01882) 634272
B8019 4 miles E of Tummel Bridge; PH16 5RP Beautifully placed traditional lochside inn renovated by present owners,

great views over water to Schiehallion, cosy character bar area with woodburner, comfortable lounges, attractive contemporary restaurant, good fresh seasonal food, two changing ales such as Inveralmond and Orkney; children and dogs welcome, lots of walks and wildlife, six bedrooms, closed Mon (and Tues Nov-Mar), shut early Jan to early Feb. *(Anon)*

PITLOCHRY NN9163
★ **Killiecrankie Hotel** (01796) 473220
Killiecrankie, off A9 N; PH16 5LG
Comfortable splendidly placed country hotel with attractive panelled bar and airy conservatory, imaginative food, friendly efficient service, well kept ales, fine range of malts and good choice of wines, restaurant; children in eating areas, extensive peaceful grounds with dramatic views, ten pretty bedrooms. *(Anon)*

PITLOCHRY NN9459
★ **Moulin** (01796) 472196
Kirkmichael Road, Moulin; A924 NE of Pitlochry centre; PH16 5EH Attractive much-extended inn brewing its own good beers in stables across the street, decent wines by the glass too and 45 malt whiskies, lively down-to-earth bar in oldest part with traditional character, smaller bare-boards room and bigger carpeted area with cushioned booths divided by stained-glass country scenes, well liked food served by cheerful helpful staff, separate restaurant; bar billiards and a 1960s one-arm bandit; children and dogs (in bar) welcome, picnic-sets on gravel looking across to village kirk, good nearby walks, 15 comfortable bedrooms and two self-catering cottages, open all day. *(David and Sue Atkinson, Pete Walker, Johnston and Maureen Anderson, Barry Collett)*

PITLOCHRY NN9358
Old Mill (01796) 474020
Mill Lane; PH16 5BH Welcoming family-run inn with enjoyable food from sandwiches and sharing plates up, four real ales and good wine and whisky choice, friendly staff; regular live music, free wi-fi; courtyard tables by Moulin Burn, comfortable bedrooms, open (and food) all day. *(Susan Ingram)*

RENFREWSHIRE
HOUSTON NS4066
★ **Fox & Hounds** (01505) 612448
South Street at junction with Main Street (B789, off B790 at Langbank signpost E of Bridge of Weir); PA6 7EN 18th-c village pub with seven constantly changing own-brew beers, good range of other drinks too including a dozen wines by the glass and 87 malt whiskies, plush hunting-theme lounge with beams, polished brass and open fire, enjoyable food from sandwiches to full meals in upstairs bar-restaurant, younger crowd in separate lively

downstairs bar with large-screen TV, pool, juke box and fruit machines; children and dogs welcome, seats out in covered and heated back area, open all day (till 1am Fri, Sat). *(Anon)*

ROSS-SHIRE
BADACHRO NG7873
★ **Badachro Inn** (01445) 741255
2.5 miles S of Gairloch village turn off A832 on to B8056, then after another 3.25 miles turn right in Badachro to the quay and inn; IV21 2AA Superbly positioned by Loch Gairloch with terrific views from decking down to water's edge, popular (especially summer) with happy mix of sailing visitors (free moorings) and chatty locals; welcoming bar with interesting photographs, An Teallach, Caledonian and a guest ale, about 30 malt whiskies and eight wines by the glass, quieter eating area with big log fire, dining conservatory overlooking bay, good reasonably priced food including locally smoked fish and seafood; background music; children and dogs welcome, one bedroom, open all day. *(the Dutchman, Edna Jones)*

FORTROSE NH7256
★ **Anderson** (01381) 620236
Union Street, off A832; IV10 8TD Friendly enthusiastic american licensees at this seaside hotel with vast selection of international beers (one of the largest collections of bottled belgians in the UK), also four well kept changing ales, Addlestone's cider and 250 malt whiskies, quite a few wines too, good food in homely bar and light airy dining room with open fire, board and puzzle-type games; background and live traditional music (every other Sun), knitting club and monthly quiz; children welcome, dogs in bar (resident dog and cat), seats out behind on gravel, nine bedrooms, open from 4pm (3pm Sun). *(Dr Peter Crawshaw)*

GAIRLOCH NG8075
Old Inn (01445) 712006
Just off A832/B8021; IV21 2BD Quietly positioned old drovers' inn by stream, own-brew beers and guests, decent wines by the glass and 20 malt whiskies, food (not Sun evening) can be good including local fish and game, own smokery, relaxed locals' bar with traditional décor and woodburner, bistro/restaurant; background music (live Fri), TV, fruit machine; children and dogs welcome, picnic-sets out by trees, bedrooms, open all day till 1am (11pm Sun). *(Laurence Smith)*

MELVAIG NG7485
Melvaig (01445) 771212
Aultgrishan (B8021); IV21 2DZ Remotely placed down long track leading to Rua Reidh lighthouse, and with wonderful views across to Skye;

reminiscent of a pebble-dashed bungalow and eccentrically packed with memorabilia including thousands of records (landlord had connection with Pink Floyd), 1960s juke box, old car parts, even a mannequin sitting at a piano, surprisingly good food particularly fish, An Teallach ales, open fire, pool and darts; closed Mon and Tues, only open weekends in winter; still for sale last we heard. *(Richard and Penny Gibbs)*

PLOCKTON NG8033

★ **Plockton Inn** (01599) 544222
Innes Street; unconnected to Plockton Hotel; IV52 8TW Close to the harbour in this lovely village, congenial bustling atmosphere even in winter, good well priced food with emphasis on local fish/seafood (some from own back smokery), well kept changing beers and good range of malts, lively public bar with traditional music Tues and Thurs evenings; seats out on decking, 14 bedrooms (seven in annexe over road), good breakfast. *(Pete Walker)*

SHIEL BRIDGE NG9319
Kintail Lodge (01599) 511275
A87, N of Sheil Bridge; IV40 8HL Lots of varnished wood in large plain bar adjoining hotel, convivial bustle in season, Isle of Skye Red Cuillin and plenty of malt whiskies, particularly good food (making the most of top quality local produce) from same kitchen as attractive restaurant and conservatory with magnificent view down Loch Duich to Skye, friendly efficient service; 12 comfortable bedrooms, bunkhouse, good breakfast, dogs welcome. *(Anon)*

ULLAPOOL NH1294
Morefield Motel (01854) 612161
A835 N edge of town; IV26 2TQ Modern family-run place, clean and bright, with cheerful L-shaped lounge bar, good food including local fish and seafood, well kept changing ales, decent wines and over 50 malt whiskies, large conservatory; background music, pool and darts; children welcome, terrace tables, bedrooms, open all day. *(Anon)*

ROXBURGHSHIRE

KELSO NT7234
Cobbles (01573) 223548
Bowmont Street; TD5 7JH Small comfortably refurbished 19th-c dining pub just off the main square, friendly and well run with good range of food from pub standards to more enterprising dishes, brewery tap for local Tempest ales, decent wines and malts from end bar, open fire and pubby furnishings in bar, elegantly furnished dining room with overspill room upstairs, folk music Fri evening; children welcome, disabled facilities, open all day. *(Anon)*

KIRK YETHOLM NT8328
Border (01573) 420237
Village signposted off B6352/B6401 crossroads, SE of Kelso; The Green; TD5 8PQ Welcoming comfortable hotel facing village green, unpretentious bar with beams, flagstones and log fire, snug side rooms, two or three changing scottish ales, good fairly priced home-made food from snacks up, spacious dining room with fishing theme, lounge with another fire and neat conservatory; background music; children welcome, dogs in bar, sheltered back terrace, five bedrooms, open all day. *(Anon)*

ST BOSWELLS NT5930
Buccleuch Arms (01835) 822243
A68 just S of Newtown St Boswells; TD6 0EW Civilised 19th-c sandstone hotel with bar, comfortable lounge and bistro, good popular food promptly served by friendly staff, real ale, open fires; children and dogs welcome, tables in attractive garden behind, 19 bedrooms. *(Pat and Stewart Gordon, Martin Day)*

SELKIRKSHIRE

MOUNTBENGER NT3324
Gordon Arms (01750) 82261
A708/B709; TD7 5LE Nice old pub with enthusiastic licensees – an oasis in these empty moorlands; simply furnished public bar and lounge area, winter fire, one real ale, good value pubby food, live music; open all day, six bedrooms. *(Comus and Sarah Elliott)*

ST MARY'S LOCH NT2321
Tibbie Shiels (01750) 42231
A708 SW of Selkirk; TD7 5LH In wonderful peaceful setting by beautiful St Marys Loch, handy for Southern Upland Way and Grey Mares Tail waterfall; good food cooked to order and well kept Broughton beers, friendly staff, interesting literary history; background music – live at weekends; children welcome, five comfortable bedrooms, also camping, open all day in season (all day weekends, from 6pm weekdays at other times). *(R T and J C Moggridge)*

STIRLINGSHIRE

DRYMEN NS4788
Winnock (01360) 660245
Just off A811; The Square; G63 0BL Big Best Western's modern split-level stripped-stone and beamed lounge bar, blazing log fires, leather sofas and easy chairs, well kept Caledonian Deuchars IPA and good choice of malt whiskies, wide choice of well thought-of food, quick service from neat helpful young staff, steps down to restaurant area, airy conservatory; background music; big garden, 73 comfortable bedrooms. *(Lucien Perring)*

SUTHERLAND

LAIRG NC5224

★**Crask Inn** (01549) 411241

A836 13 miles N towards Altnaharra; IV27 4AB Remote homely inn on single-track road through peaceful moorland, good simple food cooked by landlady including own lamb (the friendly hard-working licensees keep sheep on this working croft), comfortably basic bar with large peat stove to dry the sheepdogs (other dogs welcome), a summer real ale, Black Isle bottled beers in winter, interesting books, piano, pleasant separate dining room; three bedrooms (lights out when generator goes off), simple nearby bunkhouse. *(Les and Sandra Brown, Dr Peter Crawshaw)*

LOCHINVER NC0922

Caberfeidh (01571) 844321

Culag Road (A837); IV27 4JY Delightful lochside position with lovely views, cosy bar, conservatory and more formal restaurant, shortish menu with emphasis on local seafood (tapas, too), well kept beers including Caledonian, charming landlord and staff; dogs welcome, small harbourside garden, open all day (shut Mon). *(Anon)*

WEST LOTHIAN

BO'NESS NS9981

Corbie (01506) 825307

A904 Corbiehall; EH51 OAS Refurbished pub with up to six well kept local ales including Kinneil (brewed behind), 70 malt whiskies (tasting evenings) and simple reasonably priced food, friendly staff; children welcome, open (and food) all day. *(John Grace)*

LINLITHGOW NS0077

★**Four Marys** (01506) 842171

High Street; 2 miles from M9 junction 3 (and little further from junction 4) – town signposted; EH49 7ED Evocative 16th-c place – named after Mary, Queen of Scots' four ladies-in-waiting – and filled with mementoes of the ill-fated queen including pictures and written records, pieces of bed curtain and clothing, even a facsimile of her death-mask; neatly kept L-shaped room with mahogany dining chairs around stripped period and antique tables, attractive old corner cupboards, elaborate Victorian dresser serving as part of the bar, mainly stripped-stone walls with some remarkable masonry in the inner area, up to nine real ales (May, Oct festivals), good range of malt whiskies, fair value food including good cullen skink, cheery landlord and courteous staff; background music; children in dining area until 9.30pm, heated outdoor smoking area, difficult parking, open all day (till 1am Fri, Sat). *(Peter F Marshall)*

QUEENSFERRY NT1378

Hawes (031) 331 1990

Newhalls Road; EH30 9TA Vintage Inn renovation featured famously in *Kidnapped*, a great spot for tourists with fine views of the Forth bridges (one rail bridge support in the car park); wide choice of enjoyable food in roomy separate dining areas including good value set menu (Mon-Sat till 5pm), friendly efficient staff, plenty of wines by the glass, Caledonian Deuchars IPA and two other ales; children welcome, tables on back lawn with play area, 14 bedrooms, open (and food) all day. *(Barry Collett)*

WIGTOWNSHIRE

BLADNOCH NX4254

Bladnoch Inn (01988) 402200

Corner of A714 and B7005; DG8 9AB Cheerful bar, neat and bright, with eating area, enjoyable well priced pubby food from sandwiches up, Sun carvery, a beer such as Belhaven, friendly obliging service, restaurant; background music; children and dogs welcome, picturesque riverside setting across from Bladnoch distillery (tours), four good value bedrooms, open all day. *(Pat and Stewart Gordon)*

PORTPATRICK NW9954

Crown (01776) 810261

North Crescent; DG9 8SX Popular seafront hotel in delightful harbourside village, enjoyable reasonably priced food all day including notable seafood, friendly prompt service, several dozen malts, decent wines by the glass, warm fire in rambling traditional bar with cosy corners, sewing machine tables, old photographs and posters, attractively decorated early 20th-c dining room opening through conservatory into sheltered back garden; background music, TV; children and dogs welcome, tables out in front. *(R J Herd, Desmond Hall)*

STRANRAER NX0660

Grapes (01776) 703386

Bridge Street; DG9 7HY Popular and welcoming 19th-c local, simple and old-fashioned with 1940s feel, a couple of well kept ales and over 60 malts, regular traditional music in bar or upstairs room; dogs welcome, courtyard seating, open all day. *(Anon)*

Real ale may be served from handpumps, electric pumps (not just the on-off switches used for keg beer) or – common in Scotland – tall taps called founts (pronounced 'fonts') where a separate pump pushes the beer up under air pressure.

Scottish Islands

ARRAN

CATACOL   NR9049
Catacol Bay (01770) 830231
A841; KA27 8HN Unpretentious hotel
rather than pub, run by same family for 30 years
and in wonderful setting yards from the sea
(own mooring) with bay window looking across
to Kintyre – cosy when gales blow; simple bar,
ales from Belhaven, Houston and Timothy
Taylors, pool, all-day good food (Sunday buffet
until 4pm) and hearty breakfasts; tables outside
and children's play area, six simple bedrooms
with washbasins – the ones at the front have
the view. *(Dave Braisted)*

BARRA

CASTLEBAY   NL6698
Castlebay Hotel (01871) 810223
*By aeroplane from Glasgow or ferry
from Oban; HS9 5XD* Big lively bar – once
popular with those in the herring trade –
next to hotel, popular meeting place, regular
local musicians and comedians, comfortable
seating, two-level restaurant (carpeted or
with wooden flooring) with great harbour
view, popular food, pleasant young staff;
decent bedrooms (dogs allowed). *(Steve and
Irene Homer)*

BUTE

PORT BANNATYNE   NS0767
Port Royal (01700) 505073
Marine Road; PA20 0LW Cheerful
stone-built place (more restaurant than pub)
looking across sea to Argyll, interior reworked
as pre-revolution russian tavern with bare
boards, painted timbers and tapestries, food
including russian dishes and good seafood,
choice of russian beers and vodkas too, open
fire, candles and wild flowers; two annexe
bedrooms, substantial breakfast, closed
lunchtimes and all day Tues. *(Anon)*

ROTHESAY   NS0864
Black Bull (01700) 502366
W Princes Street; PA20 9AF Traditional
comfortably furnished pub with enjoyable
reasonably priced food and two well kept
ales, good attentive service, fine display of
old Clyde steamers; opposite pier with its
wonderfully restored Victorian gents', open
all day. *(Dave Braisted, Dennis Jones)*

COLONSAY

SCALASAIG   NR3893
★Colonsay (01951) 200316
W on B8086; PA61 7YP Stylish 18th-c
hotel, a haven for ramblers and birders, with
log fires, interesting old islander pictures,
pastel walls and polished painted boards,
bar with sofas and books and board games,
enjoyable food from lunchtime doorstep
sandwiches to fresh seafood and game (set
price pre-ferry suppers Fri and Sun and
some home-grown produce), good local
Colonsay ale, lots of malt whiskies, informal
restaurant; children and dogs welcome,
pleasant views from gardens, comfortable
bedrooms. *(Anon)*

CUMBRAE

MILLPORT   NS1554
Frasers (01475) 530518
Cardiff Street; KA28 0AS Small pub set
just back from the harbour, bar and lounge
with old paddle steamer pictures, enjoyable
very reasonably priced pubby food, a couple
of beers from Houston, friendly staff; children
welcome, no dogs, tables in yard behind,
open all day. *(Dave Braisted)*

HARRIS

TARBERT   NB1500
★Harris Hotel (01859) 502154
Scott Road; HS3 3DL Large hotel in same
family for over a century, nice small panelled
bar with welcoming feel, local Hebridean
ales, rare malt whiskies, interesting food
with modern touches using best local meat
and shellfish and ranging from lunchtime
baguettes through afternoon teas and
up, smart but relaxed airy restaurant;
23 comfortable bedrooms with sea views.
(Dave Braisted)

ISLAY

BOWMORE   NR3159
★Harbour Inn (01496) 810330
The Square; PA43 7JR Fine inn with
traditional local bar and plenty of regulars,
lovely harbour and loch views from attractive
dining room, good local fish and seafood,
proper afternoon teas, pleasant service, nice
choice of wines and local malts including
attractively priced rare ones, warmly
welcoming service; good value bedrooms
with views. *(Richard J Holloway)*

PORT ASKAIG   NR4369
Port Askaig (01496) 840245
A846, by port; PA46 7RD Family-run inn
on shores of Sound of Islay overlooking ferry
pier; snug, tartan-carpeted original bar with
good range of malt whiskies, local bottled
ales, popular all-day bar food, neat bistro
restaurant with view of the sea and ferries,
traditional residents' lounge; dogs welcome
in bar, plenty of picnic-sets on grass, eight
clean, neat bedrooms plus apartment, open
all day. *(Dave Braisted)*

PORT CHARLOTTE   NR2558
★Port Charlotte Hotel
(01496) 850360 *Main Street; PA48 7TU*
Most beautiful of Islay's Georgian villages
and in lovely position with sweeping views

over Loch Indaal, exceptional collection of about 150 Islay malts including rare ones, two changing local ales, decent wines by the glass, good food using local meat, game and seafood, civilised bare-boards pubby bar with padded wall seats, open fire and modern art, comfortable back bar, neatly kept separate restaurant and roomy conservatory (overlooking beach), regular traditional live music; children (not in bar after 10pm) and well behaved dogs (not in public areas) welcome, garden tables, near sandy beach, ten attractive bedrooms (nine with sea view), open all day till 1am. *(Richard J Holloway)*

PORTNAHAVEN   NN1652
An Tighe Seinnse (01496) 860224
Queen Street; PA47 7SJ Friendly little end-of-terrace harbourside pub tucked away in this remote attractive fishing village, cosy bar with room off, open fire, fair-priced tasty food including local seafood, Belhaven keg beer and bottled Islay ales, good choice of malts; sports TV and occasional live music; can get crowded, open all day. *(Anon)*

JURA
CRAIGHOUSE   NR5266
Jura Hotel (01496) 820243
A846, opposite distillery; PA60 7XU Family-run and in superb setting with view over the Small Isles to the mainland, bar, two lounges and restaurant and good, tasty food; garden down to water's edge, 17 bedrooms, most with sea view; camping by water's edge. *(Anon)*

MULL
DERVAIG   NM4251
★ ## Bellachroy (01688) 400314
B8073; PA75 6QW Island's oldest inn dating from 1608, pub and restaurant food including local seafood, afternoon teas, local ales, good choice of whiskies and wine, traditional bar with darts, attractive dining area, comfortable residents' lounge with games and TV; children and dogs welcome, covered outside area plus plenty of picnic-sets, nice spot in sleepy lochside village, six comfortable bedrooms, open all year. *(Dave Braisted)*

TOBERMORY   NM5055
Macdonald Arms (01688) 302011
Main Street; PA75 6NT Seafront hotel very popular for its tasty low-priced food, well kept Belhaven Best, basic décor and furnishings. *(Anon)*

TOBERMORY   NM5055
Mishnish (01688) 302500
Main Street – the yellow building; PA75 6NU Previously popular and atmospheric place right on the bay, under

new ownership as we went to press and being 'tidied up' – reports please. *(Richard and Penny Gibbs)*

NORTH UIST
CLADDACH KIRKIBOST   NF7766
Westford (01876) 580653
A865; HS6 5EP Bright cheerful place run by young landlady from Kent, welcoming and cosy with woodburner, enjoyable home-made food from shortish menu, well kept Isle of Skye along with bottled beers, lovely scenery and white beaches; dogs welcome, cottage accommodation. *(Mr and Mrs M Wall)*

ORKNEY
DOUNBY   HY3001
Merkister (01856) 771366
Russland Road, by Harray Loch; KW17 2LF Fishing hotel in great location on the loch shore, bar dominated by prize catches, good food here and in evening restaurant including hand-dived scallops and local aberdeen angus steaks, local bottled beers, good friendly service; 16 bedrooms, open all day. *(Anon)*

ST MARY'S   HY4700
Commodore (01856) 781788
A961; KW17 2RU Modern single-storey building with stunning views over Scapa Flow, bar with well kept Orkney beers, pool and darts, enjoyable food using local produce (takeaway dishes Fri, Sat evenings) in contemporary restaurant with high-backed dark leather dining chairs around woodblock tables on pale wooden flooring; open all day. *(Anon)*

WESTRAY   HY4348
Pierowall Hotel (01857) 677472
Centre of Pierowall village, B9066; KW17 2BZ Comfortable pub-hotel near ferry, friendly main bar largely given over to eating, from sandwiches and light snacks up including good freshly landed fish, bottled Orkney beers and good choice of malts, lounge bar with TV, pool room and separate dining area; six bedrooms with bay or hill views. *(Anon)*

SKYE
ARDVASAR   NG6303
Ardvasar Hotel (01471) 844223
A851 at S of island, near Armadale pier; IV45 8RS Wonderful sea and mountain views from this comfortable peacefully placed white stone inn, charming owner (will pick you up from the ferry) and friendly efficient staff, good home-made food using local fish and meat, lots of malt whiskies, real ales including Isle of Skye, two bars and games room; background music, TV; children welcome in eating areas, tables outside, lovely walks, ten bedrooms (front ones overlook the sound), open all day. *(Dave Braisted)*

CARBOST   NG3731
★ **Old Inn** (01478) 640205

B8009; IV47 8SR Little-changed
unpretentious waterside pub with stunning
views, well positioned for walkers and
climbers; simply furnished chatty bar with
exposed stone walls, bare-board or tiled
floors, open fire, Cuillin Pinnacle, Skye Ale
and a guest, traditional cider and quite a few
malt whiskies, tasty fair priced food using
local fish and highland meat; background
music (live Fri), darts and pool; children and
dogs welcome, picnic-sets on terrace by the
water, bedrooms and bunkhouse taking in
the views, Talisker distillery nearby, closed
afternoons in winter, otherwise open all day.
(David and Sue Atkinson)

DUNVEGAN   NG2547
Dunvegan (01470) 521497

A850/A863; IV55 8WA Early 19th-c inn on
the Duirnish peninsula; plenty of tables in
airy lounge bar, good food from baguettes up
including local seafood, evening restaurant
(open Easter-Oct), conservatory with superb
loch and mountain views, friendly service,
live music in cellar bar (Thurs and Sat
evenings) with pool and snooker; waterfront
garden, six bedrooms and bunkhouse.
(M J Winterton)

ISLE ORNSAY   NG7012
★ **Eilean Iarmain** (01471) 833332

Off A851 Broadford–Armadale;
IV43 8QR Small traditional bar at smartly
old-fashioned hotel in beautiful location,
friendly locals and staff, bar food most of the
day from same kitchen as charming sea-view
restaurant, an Isle of Skye real ale, good
choice of vatted (blended) malt whiskies
including their own Gaelic Whisky Collection,
banquettes, open fire; traditional background
music; children welcome, outside tables
with spectacular views, 16 very comfortable
bedrooms, open all day. *(Anon)*

SOUTH UIST

LOCH CARNAN   NF8144
Orasay Inn (01870) 610298

Signed off A865 S of Creagorry;
HS8 5PD Lovely remote spot overlooking
sea, wonderful sunsets, friendly service,
tempting local fish/seafood and beef from
own herd in comfortable modern lounge
and conservatory-style restaurant, pleasant
public bar, straightforward furnishings
and décor; seats outside on raised decked
area, compact comfortable bedrooms – two
with own terrace, open all day at least in
summer. *(Linda Miller and Derek Greentree)*

'Children welcome' means the pub says it lets children inside without any special
restriction. If it allows them in, but to restricted areas such as an eating area or family
room, we specify this. Places with separate restaurants often let children use them,
and hotels usually let children into public areas such as lounges. Some pubs impose
an evening time limit – let us know if you find one earlier than 9pm.

WALES

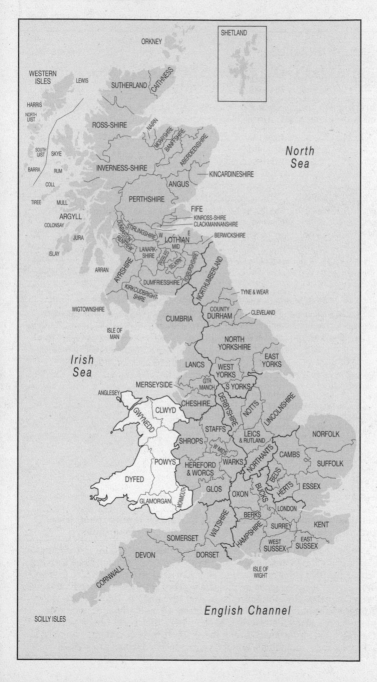

SHETLAND

ORKNEY

North
Sea

WESTERN
ISLES

LEWIS

HARRIS

NORTH
UIST

SUTHERLAND

CAITHNESS

SOUTH
UIST

SKYE

ROSS-SHIRE

BARRA

RUM

COLL

TIREE

MULL

COLONSAY

ARGYLL

JURA

ISLAY

INVERNESS-SHIRE

NAIRN

MORAYSHIRE

BANFFSHIRE

ABERDEENSHIRE

KINCARDINESHIRE

ANGUS

PERTHSHIRE

FIFE

KINROSS-SHIRE

CLACKMANNANSHIRE

STIRLINGSHIRE

DUNBARTON

RENFREW

W

E

LOTHIAN

MID

BERWICKSHIRE

LANARK-
SHIRE

PEEBLES

SELKIRK

ROXBURGHSHIRE

AYRSHIRE

ARRAN

DUMFRIESSHIRE

KIRKCUDBRIGHT-
SHIRE

NORTHUMBERLAND

TYNE & WEAR

WIGTOWNSHIRE

CUMBRIA

COUNTY
DURHAM

CLEVELAND

ISLE OF
MAN

Irish
Sea

NORTH
YORKSHIRE

LANCS

WEST
YORKS

EAST
YORKS

MERSEYSIDE

GTR
MANCH

S YORKS

ANGLESEY

CHESHIRE

DERBYSHIRE

NOTTS

LINCOLNSHIRE

GWYNEDD

CLWYD

STAFFS

SHROPS

LEICS
& RUTLAND

NORFOLK

W MIDS

POWYS

HEREFORD
& WORCS

WARKS

NORTHANTS

CAMBS

SUFFOLK

DYFED

GLOS

OXON

BUCKS

BEDS

HERTS

ESSEX

GLAMORGAN

MONMOUTH

BERKS

LONDON

WILTSHIRE

SURREY

KENT

SOMERSET

HAMPSHIRE

WEST
SUSSEX

EAST
SUSSEX

DEVON

DORSET

ISLE OF
WIGHT

CORNWALL

SCILLY ISLES

English Channel

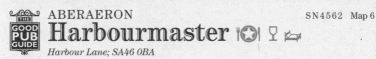

KEY ★ Star Pub 🔘 Top Quality Food 🍺 Great Beer

🍷 Good Wines £ Bargain Meals 🛏 Good Bedrooms 🍴 Serves Food

ABERAERON

SN4562 Map 6

Harbourmaster 🔘 🍷 🛏

Harbour Lane; SA46 0BA

Thriving waterside dining pub/hotel with interesting food and wines and welcoming staff; up-to-date bedrooms

With a prime location on the yacht-filled harbour, among a charming array of colour-washed buildings, this handsome small hotel is extremely well run and deservedly popular. The bar has an assortment of leather sofas, a stuffed albatross reputed to have collided with a ship belonging to the owner's great-grandfather, blue walls, a zinc-clad counter and french windows. A large minimalist dining area has modern light wood furniture on light wood floors against aqua blue walls, and there's also a four-seater cwtch, or snug, within the former porch; TV in the bar for rugby matches. Purple Moose Glaslyn and a beer brewed by them for the pub alongside a guest from a brewer such as Otley on handpump, 14 good wines by the glass and farm cider. The owners are chatty and welcoming, the bedrooms are comfortable and the breakfasts good. You can sit outside on a bench near the road and take in the view. Disabled access.

🔘 Good food includes home-cured salmon with yoghurt and cucumber, salt and pepper squid with chilli jam, excellent crab, chilli and garlic linguine, pork faggots with onion gravy, chicken caesar salad, minute steak with garlic butter, salmon fishcakes with asian slaw and chilli jam, pork chop with sautéed potatoes, black pudding and cider sauce, and puddings such as bakewell tart with amaretto cream and baked alaska with blackberry coulis. *Benchmark main dish: burger with bacon, cheese, cumin ketchup and skinny fries £10.00. Two-course evening meal £20.00.*

Free house ~ Licensees Glyn and Menna Heulyn ~ Real ale ~ (01545) 570755 ~ Open 10am-11.30pm ~ Bar food 12-2.30, 6-9 ~ Restaurant ~ Children over 5 allowed if staying ~ Wi-fi ~ Bedrooms: £65/£110 ~ www.harbour-master.com
Recommended by Lois Dyer, Dr Kevan Tucker, Mr and Mrs P R Thomas

ABERGAVENNY

SO2914 Map 6

Angel 🍷 🛏

Cross Street, by town hall; NP7 5EN

Bustling, friendly hotel with chatty bar, smart dining room, friendly staff and enjoyable food and drink; comfortable bedrooms

Run by a charming, hard-working family, this comfortable, late Georgian coaching inn is the hub of the village. The two-level bar has a thriving local atmosphere, big sofas, armchairs and settles, rugs on flagstones and some lovely bevelled glass behind the servery where they keep Evan Evans Cwrw, Hereford Herefordshire Light Ale, Rhymney Bitter and Wye Valley Bitter on handpump, 11 wines by the glass, 15 malt whiskies and farm cider. There's also an attractive lounge where they serve a very popular afternoon tea, and a smart dining room. The pretty courtyard, candlelit at night, has seats and tables, and the renovated bedrooms are stylish.

Rewarding food includes interesting sandwiches, hand-picked crab with crab toasts, crispy poached egg with smoked bacon and black pudding, spinach, tomato and feta pasta, free-range chicken with wild mushroom sauce, beef braised with red wine, crayfish risotto, gilt-head bream, prawn and potato cake with avocado, olive and tomato sauce, rib-eye steak with horseradish butter and chips, and puddings such as cherry trifle and treacle tart. *Benchmark main dish: roast lamb rump with potato gratin £17.80. Two-course evening meal £22.00.*

Free house ~ Licensee William Griffiths ~ Real ale ~ (01873) 857121 ~ Open 10am-11pm (11.30 Sat) ~ Bar food 12-2.30, 6-9.30 ~ Restaurant ~ Children welcome ~ Dogs allowed in bar and bedrooms ~ Wi-fi ~ Bedrooms: /£111 ~ www.angelabergavenny.com

Recommended by Eryl and Keith Dykes

ANGLE SM8703 Map 6

Old Point House £

Signed off B4320 in village, along long rough waterside track; SA71 5AS

Thoroughly unpretentious, welcoming seafarers' pub on the Pembrokeshire Coast Path, with quite a choice of food and waterside tables

This pub is on the Pembrokeshire Coast Path and you can walk west from here around the peninsula to the beach at West Angle Bay. Known as the 'lifeboatman's local', it's a simple and enjoyable place run by a friendly landlord and his staff, and popular with our readers. The rooms have stacks of seafaring character with lots of photographs and charts, and some of the little windows and picnic-sets on the big gravelled terrace give charming views across the water. Until the 1980s the tiny spartan snug bar was the only public room: it's got a small length of bar in one corner serving Felinfoel Single Dragon and a guest such as Felinfoel IPA, farm cider, several wines by the glass and cheap soft drinks; also, a concrete floor, two simple wood settles and a warming fire in a lovely old fireplace. There's also a lounge bar and a separate dining room; outside lavatories. The road from Angle is unmade, and gets cut off about four times a year for a couple of hours by spring tides.

Likeable pubby food includes excellent fish chowder as well as sandwiches, prawn cocktail, tomato and basil pasta, beer-battered fish and chips, beef curry, chilli con carne, sausages with chips and beans, bass fillet with lemon and herb butter, and puddings such as white chocolate and lemon cheesecake and sticky toffee pudding. *Benchmark main dish: chicken and bacon in barbecue sauce topped with cheese £10.95. Two-course evening meal £25.00.*

Free house ~ Licensee Robert Noble ~ Real ale ~ (01646) 641205 ~ Open 12-10 (11 Sat); 12-3, 6-10 Weds-Sun in winter; closed Mon and Tues in winter, Jan, Nov ~ Bar food 12.30-2.30, 6.30-8.30; no food except for residents Mon-Thurs Nov-Feb ~ Restaurant ~ Children welcome ~ Dogs allowed in bar and bedrooms ~ Wi-fi ~ Bedrooms: £43/£90

Recommended by Stephen and Jean Curtis, David Jackman, DHV, Barry Collett

BEAUMARIS SH6076 Map 6

Olde Bulls Head

Castle Street; LL58 8AP

Interesting historic inn of many faces including a rambling bar, stylish brasserie and restaurant; well equipped bedrooms

Our readers really enjoy eating and staying here. The low-beamed bar is a rambling place with plenty of interesting reminders of the town's past: there's a rare 17th-c brass water clock, a bloodthirsty crew of cutlasses and even an oak ducking stool tucked among the snug alcoves. Also, lots of copper and china jugs, comfortable low-seated settles, leather-cushioned window seats and a good log fire. Kindly staff serve Bass, Hancocks HB and a guest such as Great Orme Celtica on handpump. In contrast, the busy brasserie behind is lively and stylishly modern, with a wine list that includes around 17 by the glass, while the exceptionally good upstairs restaurant is elegantly smart for a more formal meal and has a wine list that runs to 120 bottles; background music. The entrance to the pretty courtyard is closed by a huge simple-hinged door that's an astonishing 3.3 metres wide and 4 metres high. The bedrooms in the inn itself are named after characters in Dickens's novels – the author came here – and are very well equipped; some are traditional, others more contemporary in style. They also have bedrooms in the Townhouse, an adjacent property with disabled access.

Tempting modern food includes lunchtime sandwiches, chicken, pork and bacon terrine with caramelised red onion chutney, moules marinière, bacon chop with grain mustard mash and an egg, potato gnocchi with leeks, goats cheese and cream, cassoulet of white fish, fennel, dill, courgette and saffron, slow-cooked lamb shoulder with mint gravy, chargrilled chicken with roast mediterranean vegetables and basil pesto, and puddings such as belgian chocolate mousse and crème caramel with cinnamon apple compote. *Benchmark main dish: beer-battered hake and chips £14.50. Two-course evening meal £21.00.*

Free house ~ Licensee David Robertson ~ Real ale ~ (01248) 810329 ~ Open 11-11; 12-10.30 Sun ~ Bar food 12-2 (3 Sun), 6-9.30 ~ Restaurant ~ Children welcome in China Bar only till 9pm ~ Dogs allowed in bar and bedrooms ~ Wi-fi ~ Bedrooms: £82.50/£105 ~ www.bullsheadinn.co.uk *Recommended by Martin Jones, Toby Jones*

COLWYN BAY
Pen-y-Bryn 🌟 ♟ 🍴

SH8478 Map 6

B5113 Llanwrst Road, on southern outskirts; when you see the pub, turn off into Wentworth Avenue for the car park; LL29 6DD

Spacious open-plan modern bungalow overlooking the bay, with reliable food all day, good range of drinks and obliging staff

The big windows at the back look over seats and tables on the terraces and in the sizeable garden and then across the sea to the Great Orme; the flowering tubs and hanging baskets at the front are lovely. Although the building might look a tad unprepossessing, don't be put off – inside, it's delightful. Extending around the three long sides of the bar counter you'll find a mix of seating and well spaced tables, oriental rugs on pale stripped boards, shelves of books, welcoming coal fires, a profusion of pictures, big pot plants, careful lighting and dark green old-fashioned school radiators. Interested young staff serve Phoenix Brunning & Price Original, Purple Moose Snowdonia and four changing guests such as Big Hand Little Monkey, Conwy Infusion, Great Orme Celtica and Timothy Taylors Boltmaker on handpump, well chosen good value wines including 19 by the glass and 65 malt whiskies; board games and background music.

Tempting food served all day includes lunchtime sandwiches, red pepper panna cotta with tomato and feta dressing, chicken liver pâté with home-made chutney, slow-cooked duck leg with pea, broad bean, bacon and mint salad, portobello mushroom burger with sweet potato chips and crème fraîche and chive dip, smoked cod with white bean and chorizo cassoulet, minted lamb pudding, chinese-style beef salad with cashew nuts and sweet chilli dressing, and puddings such as lemon posset with chantilly cream and chocolate brownie with chocolate sauce. *Benchmark main dish: braised lamb shoulder with dauphinoise potatoes and rosemary and redcurrant sauce £16.95. Two-course evening meal £21.00.*

Brunning & Price ~ Manager Andrew Grant ~ Real ale ~ (01492) 533360 ~
Open 11.30-11; 12-10.30 Sun ~ Bar food 12-9.30 (9 Sun) ~ Children welcome ~ Wi-fi ~
www.penybryn-colwynbay.co.uk *Recommended by Stuart and Jasmine Kelly, Mike Proctor,*
Clive Watkin, John and Sylvia Harrop, Chris and Val Ramstedt

CRICKHOWELL

SO2118 Map 6

Bear ★ ♀ ⇔

Brecon Road; A40; NP8 1BW

Convivial, interesting and bustling inn with splendid, old-fashioned bar area warmed by a log fire and enjoyable food; comfortable bedrooms

Dogs (who may get titbits) and their owners are warmly welcomed in this charming old inn where there's always a bustling, chatty atmosphere. The heavily beamed lounge has fresh flowers on tables, lots of little plush-seated bentwood armchairs and handsome cushioned antique settles, and a window seat that looks down on the market square. Next to the great roaring log fire are a big sofa and leather easy chairs, on oak parquet flooring with rugs. Other antiques include a fine oak dresser filled with pewter mugs and brassware, a longcase clock and interesting prints. Brains Rev James, Hancocks, Wye Valley Butty Bach and a frequently changing guest such as Theakstons Old Peculier are on handpump, alongside 50 malt whiskies, local ciders, vintage and late-bottled ports and unusual wines (with several by the glass); disabled lavatories. This is a particularly appealing place to stay: the older bedrooms in the main building have antiques while some of the refurbished ones are in a country style, some with jacuzzis and four-poster beds; breakfasts are excellent. Reception rooms, ably hosted by patient staff, are comfortably furnished, and there are seats in the small garden.

Quickly served and notably good, food includes lunchtime sandwiches, duck liver and port parfait with apple and rosemary compote, prawn cocktail, spaghetti with tomato, peppers and capers, chicken and leek pie, beer-battered fish and chips, venison sausages with colcannon mash and onion gravy, jerk pork belly with asian slaw and sweet potato fries, slow-cooked lamb shank with spring onion mash and braising juices, and puddings such as panettone bread and butter pudding with rum, bananas and brown bread ice-cream, and apple and whinberry crumble. *Benchmark main dish: chicken in a mushroom and creamy masala sauce £13.50. Two-course evening meal £17.75.*

Free house ~ Licensee Judy Hindmarsh ~ Real ale ~ (01873) 810408 ~ Open 10am-11pm; 12-10.30 Sun ~ Bar food 12.15-2, 6-10; 12-9.30 Sun ~ Restaurant ~ Children welcome but no under-6s in restaurant areas ~ Dogs allowed in bar and bedrooms ~ Wi-fi ~ Bedrooms: £77/£95 ~ www.bearhotel.co.uk *Recommended by Tom and Ruth Rees, Ron Corbett, Dave Webster, Sue Holland, Mike and Mary Carter, Guy Vowles, S Holder*

CRICKHOWELL

SO1919 Map 6

Nantyffin Cider Mill 🏵

A40/A479 NW; NP8 1SG

Former drovers' inn in the Black Mountains, with interesting drinks and food and a friendly welcome

In beautiful countryside, this handsome L-shaped pink-washed dining pub faces an attractive stretch of the River Usk and has charming views from tables on the lawn. Inside, the bar has good, solid wooden chairs and tables on tiles or carpeting, a big, broad fireplace with a woodburning stove and large wood basket beside it. There's Felinfoel Double Dragon on handpump, two farm ciders from Weston's and several wines by the glass including sweet wines; background music. The open-plan main area has a few beams and standing timbers, similar solid tables and chairs and an open fire in the grey stonework wall. There's an old cider press in the striking, high-raftered restaurant, alongside a mix of wooden furniture and a large rug on pale stripped wooden flooring. Tretower Court and Castle are close by.

Using the best local seasonal produce, including plenty of fresh fish and game, the interesting food from a thoughtful menu includes lunchtime sandwiches, ham hock terrine with piccalilli, hot oak and whisky smoked salmon with potato salad and chive dressing, sharing platters, tempura-battered fish and chips, calves liver with bacon, sage and tarragon and cider gravy, steak burger with cheese, colseslaw, onion rings and chips, barbecue pork ribs, and puddings such as vanilla cheesecake with Grand Marnier-soaked oranges and chocolate torte with white chocolate sauce. *Benchmark main dish: pie of the day £11.00. Two-course evening meal £19.00.*

Free house ~ Licensees Glyn and Jess Bridgeman and Sean Gerrard ~ Real ale ~ (01873) 810775 ~ Open 11.30-3, 5.30-11; 11.30-11.30 Sat; 11.30-4, 6-10.30 Sun; closed Mon except bank holidays, Tues, winter Sun evening ~ Bar food 12-2.30, 5.30-9.30; 12-2.30, 6.30-9 Sun ~ Restaurant ~ Children welcome ~ Dogs allowed in bar ~ Bedrooms: $55/$75 ~ www.cidermill.co.uk *Recommended by B and M Kendall*

EAST ABERTHAW
ST0366 Map 6

Blue Anchor ⚓ £

Village signed off B4265; CF62 3DD

Thatched character pub with cosy range of low-beamed little rooms, making a memorable spot for a drink

All the way round the central servery in this pretty, massive-walled building is a warren of low-beamed rooms that date back 600 years. It's one of the oldest pubs in Wales. There are tiny doorways, open fires (including one in an inglenook with antique oak seats built into the stripped stonework), and other seats and tables worked into a series of chatty little alcoves; the more open front bar still has an ancient lime-ash floor. Brains Bitter, Theakstons Old Peculier, Wadworths 6X and Wye Valley Hereford Pale Ale on handpump, as well as Gwynt y Ddraig farm cider and eight wines by the glass. Rustic seats shelter peacefully among tubs and troughs of flowers outside, with stone tables on a newer terrace. The pub can get very full in the evenings and on summer weekends. A path from here leads to the shingly flats of the estuary.

As well as baked potatoes and baguettes at lunchtime, the rewarding food includes game terrine with parsnip rémoulade, confit duck leg croquettes with onion and orange marmalade, porcini and garlic ravioli with marinated mushrooms and garlic cream, thai green chicken curry, gammon steak with pineapple and fried egg, line-caught deep-fried haddock with chips, pork meatballs with spaghetti and spicy tomato sauce, local pheasant breast with confit leg on bubble and squeak with juniper and port sauce, and puddings. *Benchmark main dish: roasted venison with sweet potato purée and smoked pancetta £12.50. Two-course evening meal £17.00.*

Free house ~ Licensee Jeremy Coleman ~ Real ale ~ (01446) 750329 ~ Open 11-11; 12-10.30 Sun ~ Bar food 12-2, 6-9.30; not Sun evening ~ Restaurant ~ Children welcome ~ Dogs allowed in bar ~ Wi-fi ~ www.blueanchoraberthaw.com *Recommended by Daz Smith, Heulwen and Neville Pinfield*

FELINFACH
Griffin 🏆 ♿

A470 NE of Brecon; LD3 0UB

Wales Dining Pub of the Year

Highly thought-of dining pub with home-grown vegetables among its carefully sourced ingredients, a fine range of drinks and upbeat rustic décor; inviting bedrooms

Contemporary and classy, this well run dining pub is a civilised place for a first class meal – or even better, a relaxing break. The bedrooms are comfortable and tastefully decorated and the hearty breakfasts nicely informal: you make your own toast and help yourself to home-made marmalade and jam. The back bar is quite pubby in an up-to-date way, with four leather sofas around a low table on pitted quarry tiles by a high slate hearth with a log fire; behind are mixed stripped seats around scrubbed kitchen tables on bare boards, and a bright blue and ochre colour scheme with some modern prints. The acoustics are pretty lively, due to so much bare flooring and uncurtained windows; background music, board games and plenty of books. Efficient staff serve a fine choice of drinks, many from smaller, independent suppliers, including a thoughtful choice of wines that varies through the seasons (with 16 by the glass and carafe), welsh spirits, cocktails, local bottled cider, locally sourced apple juice, non-alcoholic cocktails made with produce from their garden, unusual continental and local bottled beers, and a range of sherries. Four real ales such as Celt Experience Golden Age, Tiny Rebel Urban IPA, Wye Valley Butty Bach and a guest from Brecon are on handpump. The two smallish front dining rooms that link through to the back bar are attractive. On the left: mixed dining chairs around mainly stripped tables on flagstones and white-painted rough stone walls, with a cream-coloured Aga in a big stripped-stone embrasure; on the right: similar furniture on bare boards, big modern prints on terracotta walls and smart dark curtains. Children can play with the landlady's dog and visit the chickens in the henhouse. Dogs may sit with owners at certain tables while dining. Seats and tables outside; good wheelchair access.

 Using produce from their own organically certified kitchen garden, other carefully sourced seasonal ingredients, game from local shoots and produce from nearby farms, the accomplished and imaginative food includes potato gnocchi with wild rabbit, corn and pancetta, cured salmon with pea and broad bean caesar salad, pea and feta cheese risotto, duck and pork cassoulet with grilled squash and parmesan, venison haunch with pancetta, black pudding, chanterelles and hazelnut sauce, monkfish with grilled leeks, baby onions, broccoli and peppercorn sauce, and puddings such as treacle tart with milk ice-cream and chocolate marquise with armagnac custard. *Benchmark main dish: rib-eye of welsh beef with onions, béarnaise sauce and chips £17.95. Two-course evening meal £25.00.*

Free house ~ Licensees Charles and Edmund Inkin and Julie Bell ~ Real ale ~ (01874) 620111 ~ Open 11-11 ~ Bar food 12-2.30, 6-9 (9.30 Fri, Sat) ~ Children welcome ~ Dogs welcome ~ Acoustic session lunchtimes first and third Sun of month ~ Bedrooms: £105/£125 ~ www.eatdrinksleep.ltd.uk *Recommended by David Jackman, Taff Thomas, Alex and Hazel Evans, R T and J C Moggridge, Ian and Rose Lock, John Jenkins*

GRESFORD
SJ3453 Map 6

Pant-yr-Ochain ⭐ ♀ ☕

Off A483 on N edge of Wrexham: at roundabout take A5156 (A534) towards Nantwich, then first left towards the Flash; LL12 8TY

Thoughtfully run, gently refined dining pub in the Brunning & Price group, good food all day, a very wide range of drinks and pretty lakeside garden

Set in its own attractive grounds with lovely trees, this elaborately gabled 16th-c place has the feel of an elegant country house. The light and airy rooms are stylishly decorated, with a wide range of interesting prints and bric-a-brac, and a good mix of individually chosen country furnishings, including comfortable seats for relaxing as well as more upright ones for eating. There's a newer conservatory and a good open fire; one area is set out as a library, with floor-to-ceiling bookshelves. The impressive line-up of drinks served by exemplary staff includes Phoenix Brunning & Price Original, Flowers Original and Purple Moose Snowdonia and guests such as Barngates Catnap, Liverpool Organic Best Bitter, Salopian Shropshire Gold, and Timothy Taylors Landlord on handpump, a farm cider, 15 wines by the glass and around 80 malt whiskies. The enchanting garden has herbaceous borders and thriving box-edged herb beds, with solid wooden furniture overlooking a lake frequented by waterfowl. Good disabled access.

⭐ Tempting bistro-style food includes lunchtime sandwiches, scallops with roasted butternut squash purée, crispy bacon and lemon and caper dressing, celeriac and red onion bhajis with pineapple relish, steak in ale pie, teriyaki salmon with noodles, mango and wasabi nut pea salad, pork and leek sausages with mash and onion gravy, malaysian chicken curry with coconut rice, calves liver with roast shallots and madeira sauce, and puddings such as apricot panna cotta and pecan nut tart with butterscotch sauce. *Benchmark main dish: beer-battered haddock and chips £12.75. Two-course evening meal £20.00.*

Brunning & Price ~ Licensee James Meakin ~ Real ale ~ (01978) 853525 ~ Open 11-11; 12-10.30 Sun ~ Bar food 12-9.30 (9 Sun) ~ Children welcome ~ Dogs allowed in bar ~ Wi-fi ~ www.brunningandprice.co.uk/pantyrochain *Recommended by Di and Mike Gillam, Clive Watkin, Roger and Anne Newbury, R T and J C Moggridge, Brian and Anna Marsden*

LLANBERIS
SH6655 Map 6

Pen-y-Gwryd 🛏

Nant Gwynant; at junction of A498 and A4086, ie across mountains from Llanberis; OS Sheet 115 map reference 660558; LL55 4NT

Atmospheric and cheerfully unchanged mountaineers' haunt in the wilds of Snowdonia, run by the same family since 1947; bedrooms

Full of climbers' mementoes, this family-run mountain inn – memorably placed beneath Snowdon and the Glyders – has changed remarkably little over many years. You can still make out the fading signatures scrawled on the ceiling by the 1953 Everest team, who used this as a training base, and on display is the very rope that connected Hillary and Tenzing on top of the mountain. One snug little room in the homely slate-floored log cabin bar has built-in wall benches and sturdy country chairs. From here you can look out to precipitous Moel Siabod beyond the lake opposite. A smaller room has a worthy collection of illustrious boots from famous climbs, and a cosy panelled smoke room has more fascinating climbing mementoes and equipment; darts, pool, board games, skittles, bar billiards and table tennis. Purple Moose Glaslyn and Madogs are on handpump and they have several malts. Staying in the comfortable but basic bedrooms can be quite an experience, and the excellent traditional breakfast is served between 8.30 and 9am (they may serve earlier); dogs £5 a night. The inn has its own chapel (built for the millennium and dedicated by the Archbishop of Wales), sauna and outdoor natural pool, and the garden overlooks a lake.

Ordered through a hatch, the short choice of simple, good-value lunchtime food includes rolls, ploughman's, pies, salads and quiche of the day, as well as daily specials such as roast beef. The three- or five-course hearty fixed-price meal in the evening restaurant is signalled by a gong at 7.30pm – if you're late, you'll miss it; maybe chicken liver pâté or smoked salmon salad followed by beef and Guinness pie, roast loin of pork, chargrilled mediterranean vegetables with halloumi, and sticky toffee pudding. *Benchmark main dish: roast lamb with redcurrant gravy £9.50. Two-course evening meal £25.00.*

Free house ~ Licensee Jane Pullee ~ Real ale ~ (01286) 870211 ~ Open 11-11 (10.30 Sun); closed all Nov, Dec, midweek in Jan and Feb ~ Bar food 12-2, evening meal at 7.30pm ~ Restaurant evening ~ Children welcome ~ Dogs allowed in bar and bedrooms ~ Wi-fi ~ Bedrooms: £43/£86 ~ www.pyg.co.uk *Recommended by Earl and Chris Pick*

LLANDUDNO JUNCTION
SH8180 Map 6

Queens Head 🏅 🍴 ♀

Glanwydden; heading towards Llandudno on B5115 from Colwyn Bay, turn left into Llanrhos Road at roundabout as you enter the Penrhyn Bay speed limit; Glanwydden is signed as the first left turn; LL31 9JP

Consistently good food served all day at comfortably modern dining pub

It's mainly the very good food that draws so many customers to this modest-looking pub tucked away in an isolated village; it's best to book a table in advance. The spacious modern lounge bar – partly divided by a white wall of broad arches – has beams, beige plush wall banquettes, rush-seated wooden and high-backed black leather dining chairs around neat black tables on tartan carpeting, an open woodburning stove and fresh flowers. There's a little public bar too. Adnams Best, Great Orme Best and a guest beer on handpump, 12 decent wines by the glass, several malt whiskies and good coffee; unobtrusive background music. There's a pleasing mix of seats and tables under parasols outside. Northern Snowdonia is within easy reach, and the pretty stone cottage (which sleeps two) across the road is for rent.

Attractively presented and enjoyable, the food includes lunchtime sandwiches, deep-fried brie with cranberry and orange chutney, smoked salmon and trout mousse with melba toast, burger with melted cheese, sticky onions and chunky chips, spinach and ricotta cannelloni, hot and spicy tiger prawns with garlic butter, gammon with egg, mushrooms and pineapple salsa, calves liver with crispy bacon and onion gravy, duck breast with stir-fried oriental vegetables, and puddings. *Benchmark main dish: bass fillet with mussel and leek broth £13.95. Two-course evening meal £19.50.*

Free house ~ Licensees Robert and Sally Cureton ~ Real ale ~ (01492) 546570 ~ Open 11.30-10.30 ~ Bar food 12-9 ~ Restaurant ~ Children welcome ~ Wi-fi ~ www.queensheadglanwydden.co.uk *Recommended by Mike and Mary Carter*

The 🍺 symbol shows pubs that keep their beer unusually well, have a particularly good range or brew their own.

LLANELIAN-YN-RHOS

SH8676 Map 6

White Lion

Signed off A5830 (shown as B5383 on some maps) and B5381,
S of Colwyn Bay; LL29 8YA

**Bustling village local with bar and spacious dining areas,
tasty food, real ales and helpful staff**

Tucked away in a knot of lanes in rolling country above Colwyn Bay, this pleasantly unfussy village local is run by helpful staff. It comprises two distinct parts, each with its own cheery personality, linked by a broad flight of steps. Up at the top is a neat and very spacious dining area, while down at the other end is a traditional old bar with antique high-backed settles angling snugly around a big fireplace, and flagstones by the counter. Marstons Burton Bitter and Pedigree and Purple Moose Glaslyn Ale on handpump, 11 wines by the glass and several malt whiskies. Off to the left is another dining room with jugs hanging from beams and teapots above the windows; background music. There are tables in an attractive courtyard (also used for parking) next to the church.

Quite a choice of food includes lunchtime sandwiches, prawn cocktail, black pudding and smoked bacon salad with honey and mustard dressing, chicken curry, goats cheese, mushroom and leek tart, gammon with egg and pineapple, barbecue spare ribs with chips, lamb hotpot, steak in Guinness pie, fish stew, and puddings such as chocolate fudge cake and apple pie. *Benchmark main dish: roast beef and yorkshire pudding £10.95. Two-course evening meal £17.00.*

Free house ~ Licensee Simon Cole ~ Real ale ~ (01492) 515807 ~ Open 11.30-3.30, 6-11; 12-10.30 Sun; closed Mon except school and bank holidays ~ Bar food 12-2, 6-9; 12-8.30 Sun ~ Restaurant ~ Children welcome ~ Wi-fi ~ Live jazz Tues evening, bluegrass Weds evening ~ www.whitelioninn.co.uk *Recommended by Mr and Mrs J J A Davis, C A Bryson*

LLANGOLLEN

SJ2142 Map 6

Corn Mill 🏵️ ☆ | ♀ 🍺

Dee Lane, very narrow lane off Castle Street (A539) just S of bridge; nearby
parking can be tricky, may be best to use public park on Parade Street/East Street
and walk; LL20 8PN

**Excellent on all counts, with personable young staff, super food all
day, good beers and a fascinating riverside building with fine views**

Deservedly popular, this imaginatively restored mill looks across the River Dee to the Llangollen Canal. A long narrow deck along one side of the building juts out over the water, while the interior has been interestingly refitted with pale pine flooring on stout beams, a striking open stairway with gleaming timber and tensioned steel rails, and mainly stripped stone walls. Quite a lot of the old machinery is still in place, including the huge waterwheel (often turning) and there are good-sized dining tables, big rugs, thoughtfully chosen pictures (many to do with water) and quite a few pot plants. One of the two serving bars, away from the water, has a much more local feel, with regulars sitting on the bar stools, pews on dark slate flagstones and daily papers. Pleasant young staff serve Brunning & Price Phoenix Original and Facers DHB on handpump with three guests such as Conwy Rampart, Plassey Blue Bell Bitter and Weetwood Old Dog; also, farm cider, around 50 sensibly priced malt whiskies and a decent wine choice with around a dozen by the glass.

As well as lunchtime sandwiches, the good, interesting food includes pigeon breast with beetroot risotto and game reduction, char siu pork belly with pak choi, radish and pickled ginger, macaroni cheese, pork and leek sausages with onion gravy, ham and free-range eggs, crab linguine with chilli, ginger and coriander, chicken, ham and leek pie with cider gravy, whole plaice with caper and dill butter, and puddings such as syrup sponge with custard and dark chocolate truffle torte. *Benchmark main dish: slow-braised lamb shoulder with dauphinoise potatoes £16.95. Two-course evening meal £20.00.*

Brunning & Price ~ Manager Andrew Barker ~ Real ale ~ (01978) 869555 ~ Open 11-11 (10.30 Sun) ~ Bar food 12-9.30 (9 Sun) ~ Restaurant ~ Children welcome ~ Dogs allowed in bar ~ www.brunningandprice.co.uk/cornmill *Recommended by Claes Mauroy, Clive Watkin, R Anderson, JPC*

MOLD
Glasfryn 🏅 🍷 🍴
SJ2465 Map 6

N of the centre on Raikes Lane (parallel to the A5119), just past the well signposted Theatr Clwyd; CH7 6LR

Lively open-plan bistro-style pub with inventive all-day food, nice décor and wide choice of drinks

Although perhaps rather unassuming in looks, once you're inside this bistro-style pub the atmosphere is lively and cheerful. The open-plan interior is cleverly laid out to create plenty of nice quiet corners with a mix of informal attractive country furnishings, turkey-style rugs on bare boards, deep red ceilings (some high), a warming fire and plenty of close-hung homely pictures; background music. As well as 22 wines by the glass, local apple juice, farm cider and 40 malt whiskies, there's a wide choice of beers on handpump, with Phoenix Brunning & Price Original, Hobsons Best and Purple Moose Snowdonia alongside several swiftly changing guests such as Adnams Ghost Ship, Purple Moose Dark Side of the Moose and Yorkshire Dales Witch Blonde Ale. On warm days, the wooden tables on the large terrace in front of the pub are an idyllic place to sit, providing sweeping views of the Clwydian Hills. Theatr Clwyd is just over the road.

 Some sort of tempting food is available all day: lunchtime sandwiches, squid and chorizo with roasted tomato salad, goats cheese bonbons with spiced pear and candied walnuts, crispy duck pancakes with hoi sin sauce, braised ox cheek with cauliflower cheese mash, vegetarian sausages with tomato sauce and mediterranean vegetables, malaysian fish stew, steak and kidney pudding, beer-battered haddock and chips, and puddings such as lemon tart and waffle with honeycomb ice-cream and butterscotch sauce. *Benchmark main dish: slow-braised lamb shoulder with dauphinoise potatoes and rosemary and redcurrant gravy £16.95. Two-course evening meal £20.00.*

Brunning & Price ~ Manager Graham Arathoon ~ Real ale ~ (01352) 750500 ~ Open 11.30-11; 12-10.30 Sun ~ Bar food 12-9.30 (9 Sun) ~ Children welcome ~ Dogs allowed in bar ~ Wi-fi ~ www.glasfryn-mold.co.uk *Recommended by Clive Watkin, C A Bryson, Gerry and Rosemary Dobson*

MONKNASH
Plough & Harrow 🍴 £
SS9170 Map 6

Signposted Marcross, Broughton off B4265 St Brides Major–Llantwit Major – turn left at end of Water Street; OS Sheet 170 map reference 920706; CF71 7QQ

Old building full of history and character, with a huge log fire and a good choice of real ales

The eight real ales on handpump or tapped from the cask continue to draw in plenty of customers and might include Bass, Hancocks HB, Wye Valley HPA and four changing guests such as Brains Rev James, Otley O-Mai, Skinners Pennycomequick and Timothy Taylors Landlord; they usually hold beer festivals in June and September. Also, a good range of local farm cider and welsh and scottish malt whiskies. Some of the building dates back 900 years and formed part of a monastic grange, the ruins of which can be seen in adjacent fields. The unspoilt main bar with its massively thick stone walls used to be the scriptures room and mortuary; it has ancient ham hooks in the heavily beamed ceiling, an intriguing arched doorway to the back and a comfortably informal mix of furnishings that includes three fine stripped-pine settles on broad flagstones. There's a log fire in a huge fireplace with a side bread oven large enough to feed a village; background music in the left-hand room. The front garden has some picnic-sets. Dogs are welcome in the bar – but not while food is being served. A path from the pub leads through the wooded valley of Cwm Nash to the coast, revealing a spectacular stretch of cliffs around Nash Point.

Changing food includes ciabatta sandwiches, crispy chilli duck salad, field mushroom stuffed with beetroot and goats cheese with sun-blush tomato and feta salad, salmon wrapped in prosciutto with smoked salmon and crayfish salad, burger with toppings and chips, slow-cooked pork belly with wholegrain mustard mash and apple sauce, and puddings such as apple and seasonal berry crumble and chocolate fudge cake. *Benchmark main dish: steak in ale pie £8.95. Two-course evening meal £13.00.*

Free house ~ Licensee Paula Jones ~ Real ale ~ (01656) 890209 ~ Open 12-11 ~ Bar food 12-2.30 (5 weekends), 6-9; not Sun evening ~ Restaurant ~ No children in bar after 7pm ~ Live music Sat evening ~ www.ploughandharrow.org *Recommended by Harvey Brown, Ruth May*

NEWPORT
SN0539   Map 6

Golden Lion

East Street (A487); SA42 0SY

Nicely redone and friendly local, with tasty food, pleasant staff; well appointed bedrooms

Incredibly popular as a place for a good meal and as a fair value overnight base for exploring northern Pembrokeshire, this place also has a genuinely pubby bar. It's cheerful and well run and some of the cosy series of beamed rooms have distinctive old settles, three changing beers from brewers such as Bluestone, Sharps and Thwaites on handpump, as well as several malt whiskies, wines by the glass and Gwynt y Ddraig cider; pool, juke box, darts, board games, dominoes and games machine. The dining room has elegant blond wood oak furniture, whitewashed walls and potted plants; service is efficient and friendly. There are tables outside at the front and in a side garden; good disabled access and facilities.

Consistently good, enjoyable food includes sandwiches, creamy garlic mushrooms on toasted brioche, mackerel pâté, spicy mixed bean, pepper and chickpea casserole, a pie of the day, free-range chicken in lemon, garlic and chilli, mint and rosemary lamb chops, a fish dish of the day, rib-eye steak with peppercorn and brandy sauce, and puddings such as strawberry cheesecake with passion-fruit cream and banoffi pie with chantilly cream and honeycomb crunch. *Benchmark main dish: beer-battered cod and chips £11.95. Two-course evening meal £18.50.*

Free house ~ Licensee Daron Paish ~ Real ale ~ (01239) 820321 ~ Open 12pm-2am ~ Bar food 12-2.30, 6.30-9 ~ Restaurant ~ Children welcome ~ Dogs allowed in bar and

bedrooms ~ Wi-fi ~ Live music Sat evenings Sept-Mar ~ Bedrooms: £70/£90 ~
www.goldenlionpembrokeshire.co.uk *Recommended by Jen Llywelyn, Tim Arnold and Jim
Wingate, David Jackman, R T and J C Moggridge, Geoff and Linda Payne, J A Snell, Ron Corbett*

OLD RADNOR   SO2459 Map 6

Harp 🏅 🛏

Village signposted off A44 Kington–New Radnor in Walton; LD8 2RH

**Delightfully placed inn with cottagey bar, tasty food and well kept
ales; comfortable bedrooms**

This charming 15th-c hilltop pub is set in perfect walking country
overlooking the heights of Radnor Forest. There's a warm welcome
for all, and the characterful public bar has high-backed settles, an antique
reader's chair and other venerable chairs around a log fire; board games,
cribbage, darts and quoits. The snug slate-floored lounge contains a
handsome curved antique settle, a log fire in a fine inglenook and lots of
local books and guides for residents; a quieter dining area off to the right
extends into another dining room with a woodburning stove. A couple
of changing real ales such as Ludlow Gold and Salopian Oracle are on
handpump, as well as Dunkerton's cider and perry, local cassis and several
malt whiskies, and they hold a beer, cider and perry festival in June. Tables
outside make the most of the view. The impressive village church is worth
a look for its early organ case (Britain's oldest), fine rood screen and
ancient font.

 Using some home-grown and other local, seasonal produce, the popular
food includes lunchtime sandwiches, beetroot and lemon battered tiger
prawns with pea and dill purée, pigeon with roast chicory, grated fennel and
walnut salad, toad in the hole, home-cooked ham and eggs, pork loin wrapped
in prosciutto and stuffed with apple, black pudding and leek with wholegrain
mustard cream sauce, battered cod with chips, and puddings such as rocky road
cheesecake and rhubarb crème brûlée. *Benchmark main dish: rump steak
and chips £15.00. Two-course evening meal £20.00.*

Free house ~ Licensees Chris Ireland and Angela Lyne ~ Real ale ~ (01544) 350655 ~
Open 6-11; 12-3, 6-11 Sat; 12-3, 6-10.30 Sun; closed Mon, weekday lunchtimes ~ Bar food
12-2.30 (weekends); 6-9 Tues-Sat; not Sun evening ~ Children welcome ~ Dogs allowed
in bar and bedrooms ~ Wi-fi ~ Bedrooms: £70/£95 ~ www.harpinnradnor.co.uk
Recommended by Ann and Colin Hunt, Dr Kevan Tucker, Sara Fulton, Roger Baker

OVERTON BRIDGE   SJ3542 Map 6

Cross Foxes 🏅 🍷

A539 W of Overton, near Erbistock; LL13 0DR

**Terrific river views from well run 18th-c coaching inn with tasty
bar food and an extensive range of drinks**

The River Dee sweeps past below this substantial 18th-c coaching inn –
the oak chairs and tables on a raised terrace make the most of this fine
position, while picnic-sets down on a lawn are even closer to the water. The
ancient low-beamed bar, with its red tiled floor, dark timbers, warm fire in
the big inglenook and built-in old pews, is more traditional than most pubs
in the Brunning & Price group, though the characteristic turkey rugs, big
pot plants and frame-to-frame pictures are present, as they are in the dining
areas; board games and newspapers. Big windows all round the walls of the
airy dining conservatory also overlook the river. Friendly, competent staff
serve Brakspear Bitter, Jennings Cumberland and a couple of guests on

handpump, a farm cider, 50 malts, an excellent range of Armagnacs and a changing choice of around 15 wines by the glass.

🎯 Tempting food includes five-spiced pulled pork terrine with plum chutney, tempura prawns with noodle salad and chilli jam, sea trout with warm niçoise salad, sweet potato and aubergine malaysian curry, steak burger with bacon, cheese, coleslaw and chips, moroccan-spiced monkfish with apricot, mint and pomegranate couscous with harissa yoghurt, chicken and ham hock pie with tarragon sauce, and puddings such as white chocolate panna cotta and eton mess. *Benchmark main dish: slow-braised lamb shoulder with dauphinoise potatoes £16.95. Two-course evening meal £20.00.*

Brunning & Price ~ Manager Ian Pritchard-Jones ~ Real ale ~ (01978) 780380 ~ Open 11-11 (10.30 Sun) ~ Bar food 12-9.30 (9 Sun) ~ Children welcome ~ Dogs allowed in bar ~ Wi-fi ~ www.crossfoxes-erbistock.co.uk *Recommended by Mike and Mary Carter, Peter and Josie Fawcett, Roger and Anne Newbury*

PANTYGELLI
GOOD PUB GUIDE
Crown 🎯 ♟ 🍺

SO3017   Map 6

Old Hereford Road N of Abergavenny; off A40 by war memorial via Pen Y Pound, passing leisure centre; Pantygelli also signposted from A465; NP7 7HR

Prettily placed country pub, attractive inside and out, with good food and drinks

Our readers enjoy their visits here very much and the hands-on owners maintain their consistently high standards year after year. The pub is in a quiet spot between the Sugar Loaf and Skirrid mountains and wrought-iron and wicker chairs on the flower-filled front terrace look up from this lush valley to the hills; a smaller back terrace is surrounded by lavender. Inside, the dark flagstoned bar, with sturdy timber props and beams, has a piano at the back, darts opposite, a log fire in the stone fireplace and – served from its slate-roofed counter – well kept Bass, Rhymney Best, Wye Valley HPA and a guest such as Evan Evans Cwrw on handpump, Gwatkin's farm cider, seven good wines by the glass, local organic apple juice and good coffees. On the left are four smallish, linked, carpeted dining rooms, the front pair separated by a massive stone chimneybreast; thoughtfully chosen individual furnishings and lots of attractive prints by local artists make it all thoroughly civilised; background music, darts and board games.

🎯 As well as daily specials, the highly thought-of food includes lunchtime sandwiches, pâté with home-made chutney, prawn cocktail, venison sausages with red onion gravy, goats cheese and cherry tomato tart, steak in ale pie, guinea fowl and chicory wrapped in bacon with a raisin and madeira sauce, wild bass fillet with tagliatelle vongole and tomato and olive tapenade, and puddings such as whisky chocolate pot and rose crème brûlée. *Benchmark main dish: cold roast beef with bubble and squeak £10.25. Two-course evening meal £16.00.*

Free house ~ Licensees Steve and Cherrie Chadwick ~ Real ale ~ (01873) 853314 ~ Open 12-2.30, 6-11; 12-3, 6-11 (10.30 Sun) Sat; closed Mon lunchtime ~ Bar food 12-2, 7-9; not Sun evening or Mon ~ Restaurant ~ Children welcome ~ Dogs allowed in bar ~ Wi-fi ~ www.thecrownatpantygelli.com *Recommended by John Edwell, Trevor Swindells, Heulwen and Neville Pinfield, John Jenkins*

People named as recommenders after the full entries have told us that the pub should be included. But they have not written the report – we have, after anonymous on-the-spot inspection.

PENNAL
Riverside ◖

SH6900 Map 6

A493; opposite church; SY20 9DW

Carefully refurbished pub with tasty food and local beers, and efficient young staff

Very much a dining pub, this is a 16th-c village building in the Dovey Valley with plenty of surrounding walks. There's always a wide mix of customers, children and dogs included, and the neatly refurbished rooms have green and white walls, slate flooring tiles, a woodburning stove, modern light wood dining furniture and some funky fabrics. High-backed stools are lined up along the stone-fronted counter where they serve four changing beers on handpump such as Cwrw Llyn Cochyn, Purple Moose Glaslyn Ale, Thornbridge Jaipur and Tiny Rebel Fubar, 25 malt whiskies, a dozen wines by the glass and farm cider; background music and TV. There are seats and tables in the garden, and they also run a guesthouse at Pennal.

As well as lunchtime rolls, sandwiches and sharing boards, the wide choice of tasty food includes scallops with crispy black pudding and sweet potato purée, chicken skewers with basil aioli and sweet chilli and lime dip, roast peppers stuffed with couscous and grilled halloumi, steak burger with cheese, bacon and skinny fries, pork schnitzel with spicy tomato sauce, loin of venison with caramelised shallots and red wine and thyme sauce, haddock and chips, and puddings such as rice pudding with apricot compote and raspberry ripple cheesecake. *Benchmark main dish: local bass fillet with king prawns and dill hollandaise £16.50. Two-course evening meal £19.50.*

Free house ~ Licensees Glyn and Corina Davies ~ Real ale ~ (01654) 791285 ~ Open 12-11 (midnight Sat); closed Mon Nov-March, two weeks in Jan ~ Bar food 12-2.30, 6-9.30 ~ Restaurant ~ Children welcome ~ Dogs allowed in bar ~ Wi-fi ~ Bedrooms: £55/£75 ~ www.riversidehotel-pennal.co.uk *Recommended by Mike and Mary Carter, Phil and Helen Holt, John Evans, Michael Butler*

PENTYRCH
Kings Arms  ⚑ ♟ ⚐

ST1081 Map 6

Church Road; CF15 9QF

Village pub very much part of the community with a perky bar, civilised lounge and top class food in a bustling dining room

Whether for a pint and a chat or a delicious meal, this 16th-c longhouse is very popular locally (it's in a village on the outskirts of Cardiff) and with visitors too. The cosy bar has a cheerful atmosphere, captain's and other wooden dining chairs and settles around an attractive mix of tables on flagstones and a woodburning stove in a sizeable brick fireplace. There's Brains Bitter and SA, Caledonian Deuchars IPA and Sharps Doom Bar on handpump, 14 wines by the glass and nine malt whiskies, all served by helpful, friendly staff. The comfortable lounge has chesterfield sofas and a log fire, and there's a restaurant as well. Plenty of seats on a terrace and picnic-sets under parasols in the garden. As we went to press, they were hoping to open a deli and greengrocer.

As well as daily specials such as black pudding fritter and bacon salad, wild mushroom risotto and fresh fish gratin, the impressive food includes lunchtime sandwiches, mackerel with black olive tapenade and slow-roast tomatoes, mussels in ale, steak burger with bacon, cheese and chips, chicken and chorizo orzotto with leeks, thyme and garlic, pork saltimbocca with sage and prosciutto and garlic potatoes, lamb fillet with red pepper purée and goats cheese bonbons, and puddings such as sticky toffee pudding and toffee sauce and baked ricotta with fruit and berries; they also offer a good value two- and three-course set menu. *Benchmark main dish: beer-battered fish and chips £10.50. Two-course evening meal £19.00.*

Free house ~ Licensee Andrew Aston ~ Real ale ~ (029) 2089 0202 ~ Open 12-11 (midnight Fri, Sat); 12-8 Sun ~ Restaurant ~ Children welcome ~ Dogs welcome ~ Wi-fi ~ Live bands second Fri of month ~ www.kingsarmspentyrch.co.uk
Recommended by Martin Jones, Toby Jones

PONTYPRIDD

ST0790 Map 6

Bunch of Grapes ⭐ ♀ 🍺

Off A4054; Ynysangharad Road; CF37 4DA

Refurbished pub with a fine choice of drinks in friendly, relaxed bar, delicious inventive food and a warm welcome for all

You'll find a fantastic range of drinks at this 18th-c pub by the defunct Glamorganshire Canal, served by knowledgeable, friendly and efficient staff: their own Otley O2 CroesO and three guest beers plus another four quickly changing guests from other breweries such as Dark Star Hophead, Palmers Tally Ho!, Salopian Oracle and Thornbridge Jaipur on handpump. They hold around six beer and music festivals each year and also keep continental and american ales on draught or in bottles, a couple of local ciders or perrys, eight wines by the glass and good coffee. The cosy bar has an informal, relaxed atmosphere, comfortable leather sofas, wooden chairs and tables, a roaring log fire, newspapers to read and background music. There's also a restaurant with elegant high-backed wooden dining chairs around a mix of tables, and prints on pale contemporary paintwork. A deli offers home-baked bread and chutneys, home-cooked ham, local eggs, quite a choice of welsh cheeses and so forth, and holds cookery classes and regular themed evenings. There are seats outside on decking.

⭐ Excellent, creative food using the best local and seasonal produce includes lunchtime sandwiches, cockles on laver bread with leeks, home-cured pancetta and charred lemon, warm confit duck leg with rhubarb sauce, beetroot and tomato tarte tatin with pine nut, spring onion and broad bean salad, guinea fowl with home-smoked potatoes, caramelised pumpkin and pied de mouton (nicknamed hedgehog) mushrooms, rabbit in ale with black pudding and shoe-string potatoes, grey mullet with wilted spinach, roasted pink fir potatoes and gremolata, and puddings such as lavendar crème brûlée and dark chocolate and yoghurt mousse with meringue and raspberries. *Benchmark main dish: confit pork belly with caramelised apple sauce and black pudding mash £15.50. Two-course evening meal £20.00.*

Free house ~ Licensee Nick Otley ~ Real ale ~ (01443) 402934 ~ Open 11am-11.30pm; 12-11 Sun ~ Bar food 12-9 ~ Restaurant ~ No children after 8pm unless dining in restaurant ~ Dogs allowed in bar ~ Wi-fi ~ www.bunchofgrapes.org.uk
Recommended by Taff Thomas, R T and J C Moggridge, John Jenkins

RAGLAN

SO3609 Map 6

Clytha Arms ⭐ 🍺 🛏

Clytha, off Abergavenny road – former A40, now declassified; NP7 9BW

Fine setting in spacious grounds, a relaxing spot for enjoying good food and impressive range of drinks; comfortable bedrooms

This gracious old country inn combines a civilised atmosphere with a pleasantly pubby feel, and has an attractive setting in spacious grounds on the edge of Clytha Park. It's also a short stroll from the riverside path by the Usk; dogs are made welcome and the pub has its own labrador and collie. With long heated verandahs and diamond-paned windows, the bar and lounge are comfortable, light and airy, with pine settles, window seats with big cushions, a good mix of old country furniture, scrubbed wood floors and a couple of open log fires; there's also a contemporary linen-set restaurant. The notable array of drinks includes Kite Carmarthen Pale Ale and Wye Valley Bitter and four swiftly changing guests on handpump, an extensive wine list with eight by the glass, 20 malt whiskies, three farm ciders, their own perry and various continental beers; they hold occasional cider and beer festivals. Darts, bar skittles, boules, board games and large-screen TV for rugby matches. The bedrooms are comfortable and the welsh breakfasts good.

 As well as a tapas menu (part welsh, part spanish – potted crab, chicken goujons with chilli mayo and smoked duck, orange and onion salad) and sandwiches, the interesting food includes mussels in cider and leeks, pork and wild mushroom faggots with black pudding mash, stuffed ham in cider sauce with garlic and rosemary potatoes, wild sausage, bratwurst and brockwurst with potato pancakes, chicken, fruit and coconut or crayfish curries, fish dishes of the day, a pie of the day, roast quails with apple and calvados, and puddings such as treacle pudding with custard and rhubarb and ginger cheesecake; they also offer a two- and three-course set menu. *Benchmark main dish: leek and laver bread rissoles with beetroot chutney £10.90. Two-course evening meal £22.00.*

Free house ~ Licensees Andrew and Beverley Canning ~ Real ale ~ (01873) 840206 ~ Open 12-3, 6-midnight; 12-midnight Fri, Sat; 12-10.30 Sun; closed Mon lunchtime ~ Bar food 12.30-2.15, 7-9.30; not Sun evening ~ Restaurant ~ Children welcome ~ Dogs allowed in bar and bedrooms ~ Bedrooms: £60/£90 ~ www.clytha-arms.com
Recommended by David Jackman, N R White

ROSEBUSH
Tafarn Sinc

SN0729   Map 6

B4329 Haverfordwest–Cardigan; SA66 7QU

Unique 19th-c curio, a slice of social and industrial history by abandoned slate quarries

This quite extraordinary relic – a maroon-painted corrugated structure – originated in 1876 as a hotel on a long-defunct railway serving the nearby abandoned slate quarries, which now form a dramatic landscape. The halt itself has been more or less recreated, even down to life-size dummy passengers waiting on the platform; the sizeable garden is periodically enlivened by the sounds of steam trains chuffing through – actually broadcast from a replica signal box. The interior resembles a museum of local history, with sawdust on the floor, hams, washing and goodness knows what else hung from the ceiling, and an appealingly buoyant atmosphere; you'll hear Welsh spoken here. The bar has plank panelling, an informal mix of old chairs and pews and a woodburner, with Cwrw Tafarn Sinc (brewed locally for the pub) and Sharps Doom Bar on handpump; background music, darts, games machine, board games and TV.

Basic food includes gammon steak with pineapple, vegetable lasagne, lamb burgers, steaks and puddings; no starters. *Benchmark main dish: faggots and mushy peas £10.50. Two-course evening meal £15.00.*

Free house ~ Licensee Hafwen Davies ~ Real ale ~ (01437) 532214 ~ Open 12-11 (midnight Sun); closed Mon except Aug and bank holidays ~ Bar food 12-2, 6-9 ~ Restaurant ~ Children welcome ~ www.tafarnsinc.co.uk *Recommended by Jen Llywelyn, Tim Arnold and Jim Wingate, Stephen and Jean Curtis, David Jackman, Dr Kevan Tucker*

SKENFRITH
Bell 🏅 ⬤ ♀ 🛏
SO4520 Map 6

Just off B4521, NE of Abergavenny and N of Monmouth; NP7 8UH

Elegant but relaxed inn much praised for classy food and thoughtful choice of drinks; excellent bedrooms

A civilised place for exploring the area, this smart country inn is close to the impressive ruin of Skenfrith Castle (National Trust) and a pretty bridge over the River Monnow; they have leaflets for six circular walks. The flagstoned bar at the back is neat, light and airy with dark wooden country kitchen and rush-seated dining chairs, church candles and fresh flowers on dark tables, canary yellow walls and brocaded curtains. The flagstone bar on the left is similarly decorated, with old local and school photographs, a couple of pews and sofas, dining tables and café chairs, and board games. From the bleached oak counter they serve Wye Valley Bitter and Hereford Pale Ale on handpump, plus bottled local cider and perry, 12 wines by the glass from an impressive list, local sparkling wine, early landed cognacs and a good range of malt whiskies. The lounge bar on the right, opening into the dining area, has an impressive Jacobean-style carved settle and a housekeeper's chair by a log fire in the big fireplace; there's a new sitting room too, with comfortable sofas, daily papers and magazines and a log fire. The terrace has good solid tables under parasols, with steps leading to a sloping lawn and a newly opened orchard area (ideal for families); the kitchen garden is immaculate. The individually decorated bedrooms are named after brown trout fishing flies. Good disabled access.

 Using carefully chosen local (and home-grown) produce, the impressive food includes lunchtime sandwiches, king scallops with samphire and parmesan gratin, goats cheese mousse with roasted beetroot and candied walnuts, steak, thyme and horseradish pie, lamb rump with garlic fondant potatoes and basil olive jus, bream fillet with radish, artichoke and dandelion risotto, duck cooked three-ways with glazed vegetables and red wine jus, and puddings such as vanilla and yoghurt panna cotta with strawberry millefeuille and apple doughnuts with malted cider and toffee sauce. *Benchmark main dish: roast haunch of local venison £18.00. Two-course evening meal £24.00.*

Free house ~ Licensee John van Niekerk ~ Real ale ~ (01600) 750235 ~ Open 11-11; 12-10 Sun ~ Bar food 12-2.30, 7-9.30 (9 Sun) ~ Restaurant ~ Children welcome but not in evening restaurant ~ Dogs welcome ~ Wi-fi ~ Bedrooms: £90/£130 ~ www.skenfrith.co.uk
Recommended by Dr Peter Crawshaw

STACKPOLE
Stackpole Inn 🏅 ⬤ 🛏
SR9896 Map 6

Village signed off B4319 S of Pembroke; SA71 5DF

Usefully placed for exploring the Pembrokeshire Coast Path and the Bosherston Lily Ponds and with enjoyable food and friendly service; good bedrooms

Much enjoyed by climbers, fishermen and bird-watchers, this is a very popular place to stay – the spotless bedrooms are comfortable and the breakfasts enjoyable. The inn is on the National Trust's Stackpole Estate within strolling distance of the coast path and an idyllically secluded beach. An area around the bar has pine tables and chairs, but most of the pub, L-shaped on four different levels, is given over to diners, with neat light oak furnishings, ash beams and low ceilings to match; background music and board games. Brains Rev James, Felinfoel Double Dragon, Gower Gold and

Rhymney Export Ale on handpump, 14 wines by the glass, 15 malt whiskies and two farm ciders. The attractive gardens feature colourful flowerbeds and mature trees and there are plenty of picnic-sets at the front.

 High quality food includes lunchtime sandwiches, pork terrine with home-made piccalilli, prawn cocktail, thai green chicken curry, trio of sausages with garlic mash and onion rings, honey-roasted butternut squash with feta and pine nuts, chicken with butterbean and herb mash and white wine sauce, lots of local fish dishes, and puddings such as almond, lemon and thyme cake with blackberry coulis and chocolate and lavender tart with clotted cream; they also offer afternoon tea. *Benchmark main dish: grilled haddock with chips and minted crushed peas £15.00. Two-course evening meal £20.00.*

Free house ~ Licensees Gary and Becky Evans ~ Real ale ~ (01646) 672324 ~ Open 12-3, 6-11; 12-11 Sat, Sun ~ Bar food 12-2, 6.30-9 ~ Restaurant ~ Children welcome ~ Dogs allowed in bar ~ Wi-fi ~ Bedrooms: £60/£90 ~ www.stackpoleinn.co.uk
Recommended by R T and J C Moggridge, Barry Collett

TY'N-Y-GROES
Groes 🌟 🛏

SH7773   Map 6

B5106 N of village; LL32 8TN

Stacks of character in gracious, antique-laden 15th-c Snowdonia hotel, local beer and lovely garden

This is a lovely place to spend a few days and the well equipped bedroom suites (some with terraces or balconies) have gorgeous views; they also rent out a well appointed wooden cabin and a cottage in the historic centre of Conwy. Past the hot stove in the entrance area, the rambling, low-beamed and thick-walled rooms are nicely decorated with antique settles and an old sofa, old clocks, portraits, hats and tins hanging from the walls and fresh flowers. A fine antique fireback is built into one wall, perhaps originally from the formidable fireplace in the back bar, which houses a collection of stone cats as well as cheerful winter log fires; background music. You might find a harpist playing here on certain days. They keep Groes Ale (brewed for the pub) from the family's own Great Orme brewery a couple of miles away, alongside a guest such as Sharps Doom Bar on handpump, several bottled Great Orme beers, 20 wines by the glass and 20 malt whiskies. Several options for dining include an airy conservatory and a smart restaurant set with white linen. The idyllic back garden has flower-filled hayracks and an enchantingly verdant outlook, and there are more seats on a narrow flower-decked roadside terrace.

 Quite a choice of food using herbs from the hotel garden and other local produce includes lunchtime sandwiches, potted pork and rabbit with peach and ginger chutney, deep-fried whitebait with aioli, chicken wrapped in bacon with creamy wild mushroom sauce, chargrilled aubergine lasagne, gammon and eggs with fresh pineapple, duck breast with rhubarb and gin sauce, plaice with lemon and caper butter, and puddings such as white chocolate and banana brûlée with peanut butter biscuit and waffle with toffee sauce and home-made vanilla ice-cream. *Benchmark main dish: burger with cheddar, onions and their secret sauce £12.25. Two-course evening meal £18.00.*

Free house ~ Licensee Dawn Humphreys ~ Real ale ~ (01492) 650545 ~ Open 12-2.30, 6-11 ~ Bar food 12-2, 6.30-9 ~ Restaurant ~ Children welcome ~ Dogs allowed in bar and bedrooms ~ Wi-fi ~ Bedrooms: £100/£125 ~ www.groesinn.com
Recommended by Mr and Mrs J S Heathcote, Mike Proctor, Dr and Mrs P Truelove, Derek Stafford, Paul and Sonia Broadgate

USK

SO3700 Map 6

Nags Head ♀

The Square; NP15 1BH

Spotlessly kept by the same family for 47 years, traditional in style with a hearty welcome and good food and drinks

'This remains excellent in all respects,' says one of our readers. The long-serving Key family run this beautifully kept coaching inn with as much friendliness and enthusiasm as ever. The traditional main bar is cheerily chatty and cosy, with lots of well polished tables and chairs packed under its beams (some with farming tools, lanterns or horsebrasses and harness attached), as well as leatherette wall benches, and various sets of sporting prints and local pictures – look out for the original deeds to the pub. Tucked away at the front is an intimate little corner with some african masks, while on the other side of the room a passageway leads to a dining area; background music. There may be prints for sale, and perhaps a group of sociable locals. They offer nine wines by the glass, along with Brains Rev James and SA and a guest such as Sharps Doom Bar on handpump. The church here is well worth a look. The pub has no parking and nearby street parking can be limited.

Generously served, the well liked, tasty food includes lunchtime sandwiches, leek and welsh cheddar soup, faggots and gravy, steak pie, sausage and mash, partridge stuffed with apricots, a brace of quail, and puddings such as treacle and walnut tart and sticky toffee pudding. *Benchmark main dish: rabbit pie £10.00. Two-course evening meal £17.00.*

Free house ~ Licensee Key family ~ Real ale ~ (01291) 672820 ~ Open 10.30-3, 5-11 ~ Bar food 11-2, 5.30-9.30 ~ Restaurant ~ Children welcome ~ Dogs allowed in bar ~ Wi-fi
Recommended by Eryl and Keith Dykes, Sue and Ken Le Prevost

Also Worth a Visit in Wales

Besides the fully inspected pubs, you might like to try these pubs that have been recommended to us and described by readers. Do tell us what you think of them: feedback@goodguides.com

ANGLESEY

ABERFFRAW   SH3568
Crown (01407) 840222
Bodorgan Square; LL63 5BX Refurbished pub in small village set back from the coast, well kept Sharps Doom Bar and two local beers, enjoyable competitively priced home-made food, quick friendly service; sports TV; well behaved children and dogs welcome, suntrap beer garden with sturdy furniture and views towards the dunes, closed Mon, Tues, otherwise open all day. *(Michael Butler)*

MENAI BRIDGE   SH5773
Gazelle (01248) 713364
Glyngarth; A545, halfway towards Beaumaris; LL59 5PD Hotel and restaurant rather than pub in outstanding waterside situation looking across to Snowdonia, main bar with smaller rooms off, up to three Robinsons ales and seven

wines by the glass, good reasonably priced food from bar snacks up; children and dogs (in bar) welcome, steep garden behind (and walk down from car park), 11 bedrooms, slipway and mooring for visiting boats, open all day summer, all day Fri-Sun winter.
(Paul and Karen Cornock)

RED WHARF BAY   SH5281
Ship (01248) 852568
Village signed off A5025 N of Pentraeth; LL75 8RJ Whitewashed 18th-c pub worth visiting for position right on Anglesey's east coast (arrive early for a seat with fantastic views of miles of tidal sands); big old-fashioned rooms either side of bar counter, nautical bric-a-brac, long varnished wall pews, cast-iron-framed tables and open fires, three well kept ales including Adnams, 50 malt whiskies and decent choice of wines, enjoyable food; if you run a tab they lock your card in a numbered box and hand you

the key, background Classic FM in lounge; children welcome in room on left, dogs in bar, limited disabled access, numerous outside tables, open all day. *(Michael Butler)*

RHOSCOLYN   SH2675
⋆White Eagle (01407) 860267
Off B4545 S of Holyhead; LL65 2NJ
Remote place rebuilt almost from scratch on site of an old pub; airy modern feel in neatly kept rooms, relaxed atmosphere and nice winter fire, Cobblers Ale (brewed for the pub by Thornbridge), Marstons, Weetwood and a guest from smart oak counter, several wines by the glass, extensive choice of good locally sourced food (all day Sun, and school holidays, best to book), friendly helpful service, restaurant; children welcome, dogs in bar (biscuits for them), terrific sea views from decking and picnic-sets in good-sized garden, lane down to beach, open all day. *(Chris and Val Ramstedt, Howard Drake)*

RHOSNEIGR   SH3272
Oystercatcher (01407) 812829
A4080; LL64 5JP Modern glass-fronted Huf Haus set in dunes close to the sea, under same owners as the White Eagle at Rhoscolyn but not a pub (created as a restaurant/chefs' academy); great views from upstairs restaurant and bar with good range of food including pizzas and grills, ales such as Conwy Honey Fayre and Weetwood Eastgate, decent choice of wines by the glass, ground-floor coffee bar; children welcome, upper terrace with rattan sofas and colourful reproduction beach huts, full wheelchair access, open all day. *(Simon and Mandy King)*

CEREDIGION

ABERAERON   SN4562
Castle (01545) 570205
Market Street; SA46 0AU Red-painted early 19th-c building with popular contemporary and boldly decorated café-bar and elegant wooden-floored restaurant upstairs, good friendly service, wide choice of enjoyable home-cooked food and sensibly priced wine list, ales such as Evan Evans and Tomos Watkins, welsh whisky; six comfortable bedrooms and self-catering apartment. *(Peter Hacker)*

CLWYD

CARROG   SJ1143
Grouse (01490) 430272
B5436, signed off A5 Llangollen–Corwen; LL21 9AT Small unpretentious pub with superb views over River Dee and beyond from bay window and balcony, Lees ales, enjoyable food all day from sandwiches up, reasonable prices, friendly helpful staff, local pictures, pool in games room; background music; children welcome, wheelchair access (side door a bit narrow), tables in pretty walled garden,

covered terrace for smokers, narrow turn into car park, handy for Llangollen steam railway. *(Anon)*

GRAIG FECHAN   SJ1454
Three Pigeons (01824) 703178
Signed off B5429 S of Ruthin; LL15 2EU Extended largely 18th-c pub with enjoyable inexpensive food from sandwiches up (all day Sun, not Mon), friendly licensees, good range of real ales and plenty of wines by the glass, various nooks and corners, interesting mix of furniture and some old signs on the walls, great country views from restaurant; children allowed if eating, big garden with terrace and same views, two self-catering apartments, closed Mon lunchtime, good walks. *(Mike and Wena Stevenson)*

LLANARMON DYFFRYN
CEIRIOG   SJ1532
⋆Hand (01691) 600666
B4500 from Chirk; LL20 7LD Comfortable and welcoming rural hotel at heart of Upper Ceiriog valley set against backdrop of the Berwyn Mountains; low-beamed bar with inglenook log fire, sturdy tables and mix of seating including settles, old prints on cream walls, stools along modern counter serving a couple of ales, several malt whiskies and reasonably priced wines by the glass, largely stripped-stone carpeted dining room with woodburner, good popular food including notable local pies, residents' lounge and games room; no children in dining room after 7.30pm, dogs allowed in bar, tables on crazy-paved front terrace, more in garden, spacious bedrooms, good breakfast, open all day. *(Kim Skuse, Simon and Mandy King, Vikki and Matt Wharton)*

LLANARMON DYFFRYN
CEIRIOG   SJ1532
⋆West Arms (01691) 600665
End of B4500 W of Chirk; LL20 7LD 16th-c beamed and timbered inn in lovely surroundings, cosy atmosphere in picturesque upmarket lounge bar full of antique settles, sofas, even an elaborately carved confessional stall, good original bar food strong on local produce plus evening restaurant (open Sun lunch), friendly staff, good range of wines, malt whiskies and three well kept local ales, more sofas in old-fashioned entrance hall, comfortable back bar too, roaring log fires, good restaurant; children welcome, dogs welcome throughout (including bedrooms), disabled access, pretty lawn running down to River Ceiriog (fishing for residents), good walks, 16 comfortable character bedrooms. *(Anon)*

LLANFERRES   SJ1860
⋆Druid (01352) 810225
A494 Mold–Ruthin; CH7 5SN Extended 17th-c whitewashed inn set in fine walking country along the Alyn Valley towards Loggerheads Country Park, or up Offa's

Dyke Path to Moel Famau; views from broad bay window in civilised plush lounge and from bigger beamed back bar with two handsome antique oak settles, pleasant mix of more modern furnishings and quarry-tiled area by log fire. Marstons-related ales, 30 malt whiskies, decent reasonably priced traditional food plus specials, games room with darts and pool, board games; background music, TV; children welcome, dogs in bar and bedroom, stables outside at the front, open all day Fri, Sat, till 10pm Sun. *(Anon)*

MINERA   SJ2651
Tyn-y-Capel (01978) 269347
Church Road; LL11 3DA Community-owned pub run mainly by volunteers, good locally sourced food (not Sun evening) including ramblers' menu, half a dozen changing ales (one badged for them from Big Hand), local cider, Sun quiz, also traditional music first Sun afternoon of the month; children and dogs (in bar) welcome, lovely hill views from terrace, park opposite with play area, closed Mon, Tues and lunchtime Weds, otherwise open all day. *(Dr David and Mrs Clare Gidlow, Helen Eustace)*

RUABON   SJ3043
Bridge End (01978) 810881
Bridge Street; LL14 6DA Proper old-fashioned pub owned by McGivern, their ales (brewed here) and guests, decent wines, enthusiastic staff and a cheerful atmosphere, basic home-made food, black beams and open fires, Tues quiz, folk music Weds evening, spacious garden; open all day weekends and from 5pm weekdays (4pm Fri). *(Claes Mauroy)*

DYFED

ABERAERON   SN4562
Cadwgan (01545) 570149
Market Street; SA46 0AU Small late 18th-c pub opposite harbour, basic with friendly regulars, well kept Hancocks HB and a guest, some nautical memorabilia and interesting old photographs, open fire, no food; sports TV; children and dogs welcome, pavement seats and little garden behind, open all day (Sun till 5pm). *(Anon)*

ABERCYCH   SN2539
★ **Nags Head** (01239) 841200
Off B4332 Cenarth–Boncath; SA37 0HJ Tucked-away riverside pub with dimly lit beamed and flagstoned bar, stripped wood tables and big fireplace, hundreds of beer bottles, clocks showing time around the world, photographs of locals and a coracle on brick and stone walls, even a large stuffed rat, own-brewed Cych Valley beers, pubby food and specials in two sizeable dining areas; background music, piano; children and dogs welcome (pub yorkie is Scrappy), benches in garden overlooking river (fishing rights), play area with wooden castle,

barbecues, three bedrooms, open all day weekends, closed Mon lunchtime. *(Anon)*

ABERGORLECH   SN5833
★ **Black Lion** (01558) 685271
B4310; SA32 7SN Friendly old coaching inn in fine rural position; traditionally furnished stripped-stone bar with flagstones, coal stove, oak furniture and high-backed black settles, copper pans on beams, old jugs on shelves, local paintings and fresh flowers, dining extension with french windows opening on to enclosed garden, Rhymney and a guest beer, local cider, good varied choice of inexpensive home-cooked food; background music; children and dogs welcome, lovely views of Cothi Valley from riverside garden, self-catering cottage, open all day weekends, closed Mon, good nearby mountain biking. *(Anon)*

BOSHERSTON   SR9694
St Govans Country Inn
(01646) 661311 *Off B4319 S of Pembroke; SA71 5DN* Busy pub with big modernised open-plan bar, cheery and simple, with several changing ales and enjoyable well priced pub food, good climbing photographs and murals of local beauty spots, log fire in large stone fireplace, dominoes, board games, pool (winter only); background music, TV, games machine; children and dogs welcome, picnic-sets on small front terrace, four good value bedrooms (car park if you stay), handy for water-lily lakes, beach and cliff walks, open all day in season (all day weekends at other times). *(Ian and Jane Irving)*

BROAD HAVEN   SM8614
★ **Druidstone Hotel** (01437) 781221
N on coast road, bear left for about 1.5 miles then follow sign left to Druidstone Haven; SA62 3NE Cheerfully informal country house in grand spot above the sea, individual, relaxed and with terrific views, inventive cooking using fresh often organic ingredients (best to book) including good value themed 'feast evening' Tues, helpful efficient service, cellar bar with local ale tapped from the cask, country wines and other drinks, ceilidhs and folk events, friendly pub dogs (others welcome), all sorts of sporting activities from boules to sand-yachting; attractive high-walled garden, spacious homely bedrooms, also an eco-friendly chalet and an apartment built into a hill, closed Jan, Nov, restaurant closed Sun evening. *(Geoff and Linda Payne, Richard and Judy Winn)*

CAIO   SN6739
Brunant Arms (01558) 650483
Off A482 Llanwrda–Lampeter; SA19 8RD Unpretentious and interestingly furnished village pub, comfortable and friendly with helpful staff, nice log fire, a couple of local ales, enjoyable regularly changing home-made food from baguettes up, stripped-stone

public bar with games including pool, some live music; sports TV; children and dogs welcome, small Perspex-roofed verandah and lower terrace, handy for Dolaucothi Gold Mines (NT), open all day. *(Anon)*

CAREW   SN0403
★ **Carew Inn** (01646) 651267

A4075 off A477; SA70 8SL Stone-built pub with appealing cottagey atmosphere, unpretentious small panelled public bar, nice old bentwood stools and mix of tables and chairs on bare boards, small dining area, lounge bar with low tables, warm open fires, Brains, Sharps, Worthington and a guest, enjoyable generously served food, two upstairs dining rooms with black leather chairs at black tables; background music, darts; children and dogs (in bar) welcome, enclosed back garden with play equipment, view of imposing Carew Castle ruins and remarkable 9th-c celtic cross, open all day. *(N R White)*

CILYCWM   SN7540
Neuadd Fawr Arms (01550) 721644

By church entrance; SA20 0ST Former 18th-c drovers' inn, restored by present owners, eclectic mix of old furniture on huge slate flagstones, woodburners, one or two changing local ales, good seasonal food with interesting specials in bar or smaller dining room, friendly helpful service; children and dogs welcome, good spot by churchyard above River Gwenlais, among lanes to Llyn Brianne, open all day weekends, may close weekday lunchtimes in winter. *(Anon)*

COSHESTON   SN0003
Brewery Inn (01646) 686678

Signed E from village crossroads; SA72 4UD Welcoming 17th-c village pub with three well kept ales, good reasonably priced and enjoyable food (not Sun evening, Mon) freshly cooked by landlord, helpful friendly service, quiz and curry Weds; five clean and spacious self-catering apartments at back. *(Anon)*

CRESSWELL QUAY   SN0506
★ **Cresselly Arms** (01646) 651210

Village signed from A4075; SA68 0TE Simple unchanging alehouse overlooking tidal creek, same licensee since 1982 – his predecessor retired aged 92; plenty of local customers in two old-fashioned linked rooms, built-in wall benches, kitchen chairs and plain tables on red and black tiles, open fire in one room, Aga in the other with lots of pictorial china hanging from high beam-and-plank ceiling, a third more conventionally furnished red-carpeted room, Worthington and a winter guest ale served from glass jugs, no food apart from rolls on Sat; no children;

seats outside making most of view, you can arrive by boat if tide is right, open all day weekends. *(Giles and Annie Francis)*

CWM GWAUN   SN0333
★ **Dyffryn Arms** (01348) 881305

Cwm Gwaun and Pontfaen signed off B4313 E of Fishguard; SA65 9SE Classic rural time warp, virtually the social centre for this lush green valley, very relaxed, basic and idiosyncratic, with much-loved veteran landlady (her farming family have run it since 1840, and she's been in charge for well over a third of that time); 1920s front parlour with plain deal furniture and draughts boards inlaid into tables, coal fire, well kept Bass served by jug through sliding hatch, low prices, World War I prints and posters, large collection of banknotes, darts, duck eggs for sale; lovely outside view and walks in nearby Preseli Hills, open more or less all day (may close if no customers). *(Giles and Annie Francis, Dr Kevan Tucker)*

DALE   SM8105
Griffin (01646) 636227

B4327, by sea on one-way system; SA62 3RB Old waterside pub run by friendly couple, two imaginatively decorated cosy rooms, open fires, well kept Brains, Evan Evans and a local guest, nice wines, popular food including good local fish/seafood specials, pleasant attentive service; children welcome, lovely estuary views – can sit out on seawall, open all day summer. *(Alan Bulley, Geoff and Linda Payne, Stephen and Jean Curtis)*

DINAS   SN0139
Old Sailors (01348) 811491

Pwllgwaelod; from A487 in Dinas Cross follow Bryn-henllan signpost; SA42 0SE Shack-like building in superb position, snugged down into the sand by isolated cove below Dinas Head with its bracing walks; specialising in fresh local seafood (usually have crab and lobster), also good snacks, coffee and summer cream teas, well kept Felinfoel Double Dragon, decent wine, maritime bric-a-brac; children welcome, no dogs inside, picnic-sets on grass overlooking beach with views across to Fishguard, closed Mon, open all day rest of week (Tues till 6pm if quiet), shut Jan. *(Dr Kevan Tucker)*

FISHGUARD   SM9537
★ **Fishguard Arms** (01348) 872763

Main Street (A487); SA65 9HJ Tiny unspoilt bay-windowed terrace pub with friendly community atmosphere and character landlord, front bar with unusually high counter serving well kept/priced Bass direct from the cask, rugby photographs and open fire, back snug with woodburner

---

If you have to cancel a reservation for a bedroom or restaurant, please telephone or write to warn them. You may lose your deposit if you've paid one.

and traditional games, no food; sports TV; smokers' area out behind, open all day, closed Weds evening. *(Giles and Annie Francis)*

FISHGUARD
SM9637

Ship (01348) 874033

Newport Road, Lower Town; SA65 9ND
Cheerful atmosphere and charming landlord in softly lit 18th-c pub near old harbour, well kept Felinfoel Double Dragon and Theakstons tapped from the cask, coal fire, lots of boat pictures, model ships and photos of actors such as Richard Burton and Peter O'Toole who drank here while filming locally, no food, piano and occasional live music; TV for rugby; children welcome (toys provided), dogs on leads, open all day weekends, closed Mon (and Tues in winter), shut weekday lunchtimes. *(Giles and Annie Francis)*

JAMESTON
SS0699

Tudor Lodge (01834) 871212

A4139, E of Jameston; SA70 7SS
Friendly family-run inn close to the coast, two character bars with open fire and woodburner, Sharps Doom Bar, a guest ale and several wines by the glass, airy carpeted dining room with pale beams and high-backed chairs around sturdy tables, second dining room with modern art, well liked food; children welcome, play area and plenty of picnic-sets outside, stylishly comfortable bedrooms, good breakfast, open all day in summer. *(Isabel MacKinley, Harvey Brown)*

LITTLE HAVEN
SM8512

★**Castle Inn** (01437) 781445

Grove Place; SA62 3UF Welcoming pub well placed by green looking over sandy bay (lovely sunsets), popular generously served food including pizzas and good local fish, Marstons-related ales, decent choice of wines by the glass, tea and cafetière coffee, bare-boards bar and carpeted dining area with big oak tables, beams, some stripped stone, castle prints, pool in back area; children and dogs welcome, picnic-sets out in front, New Year's Day charity swim, open all day. *(Geoff and Linda Payne)*

LITTLE HAVEN
SM8512

St Brides Inn (01437) 781266

St Brides Road; SA62 3UN
Just 20 metres from Pembrokeshire Coast Path; neat stripped-stone bar and linked carpeted dining area, traditional furnishings, log fire, interesting well in back corner grotto thought to be partly Roman, Banks's, Marstons and a guest, enjoyable bar food; background music and TV; children welcome, dogs in bar, seats in sheltered suntrap terrace garden across road, two bedrooms, open all day summer. *(Stephen and Jean Curtis)*

LLANDDAROG
SN5016

★**Butchers Arms** (01267) 275330

On back road by church; SA32 8NS
Ancient heavily black-beamed local with three intimate eating areas off small central bar, welcoming staff, enjoyable generous home-made food, cask-tapped Felinfoel ales and good wines by the glass, conventional pub furniture, gleaming brass, candles in bottles, open woodburner in biggish fireplace; background music; children welcome, tables outside, nice window boxes, bedroom in converted stables, closed Sun and Mon. *(Anon)*

LLANDDAROG
SN5016

White Hart (01267) 275395

Aka Yr Hydd Gwyn; off A48 E of Carmarthen, via B4310; SA32 8NT
Ancient thatched pub with own-brew beers using water from 90-metre borehole, also own ciders; comfortable lived-in beamed rooms with lots of engaging bric-a-brac and antiques including a suit of armour, 17th-c carved settles by huge log fire, interestingly furnished high-raftered dining room, generous if not cheap food, home-made jams, chutneys and honey for sale; cash or debit cards only, background music, no dogs inside; children welcome, disabled access (ramps provided), picnic-sets on front terrace and in back garden with play area, small farmyard, closed Weds. *(Taff Thomas, Mike and Mary Carter)*

LLANDOVERY
SN7634

Castle (01550) 720343

Kings Road; SA20 0AP Welcoming hotel next to castle ruins, good, attractively presented food from sandwiches and deli boards to charcoal grills and fresh fish specials, courteous efficient service, well kept Brains, Kite and Evan Evans; picnic-sets out in front under parasols, comfortable bedrooms. *(Mo and David Trudgill, Hugh Davies)*

LLANFALLTEG
SN1519

Plash (01437) 563472

Village NE of Whitland; SA34 0UN
Small mid-terrace village local with a warm welcome, beamed bar with piano and open fire, well kept ales such as Purple Moose, Salopian, Three Tuns and Wye Valley, Stowford Press cider, some low-priced bar food along with pizzas; children and dogs welcome, garden tables, self-catering cottage, closed lunchtimes Mon and Tues, otherwise open all day. *(Steve Goymer, David and Julie Glover)*

LLANFIHANGEL-Y-CREUDDYN
SN6676

Y Ffarmers (01974) 261275

Village signed off A4120 W of Pisgah; SY23 4LA Nicely refurbished family-run village pub, good locally sourced seasonal food cooked by landlord-chef (not Sun evening, Mon, Tues lunchtime), well kept Felinfoel with guests such as Purple Moose, friendly helpful service, traditional bar with oak boards and woodburner; children welcome, closed Mon, lunchtime Tues. *(Anon)*

LLWYNDAFYDD SN3755
Crown (01545) 560396
Off A486 S of Newquay; SA44 6BU Traditional village pub, beams, stripped stone, red plush banquettes and copper-topped tables, woodburners, changing ales and well prepared pubby food including Sun carvery, friendly service; children and dogs (in bar) welcome, terrace and pretty garden with play area and some animals, lane down to attractive cove, open all day. *(Kay and Alistair Butler)*

LYDSTEP SS0898
Lydstep Tavern (01834) 871521
A4139, in main village; SA70 7SG Modernised village pub with good range of well priced generously served food including daily specials, beers such as local Preseli, friendly quick service, log fire; children and dogs (in designated area) welcome, picnic-sets in pleasant garden, on National Park coastal path, open (and food) all day in season, best to check other times. *(Ian and Jane Irving)*

NEWCHAPEL SN2239
Ffynnone Arms (01239) 841800
B4332; SA37 0EH 18th-c beamed pub, friendly and welcoming, with tasty traditional food in restaurant (Wed evening to Sun lunchtime) including special dietary requirements and using home-grown produce, Evan Evans and guests, local ciders, afternoon teas in season, two woodburners, darts, pool and table skittles; disabled facilities, picnic-sets in small garden, open all day weekends, closed weekday lunchtimes. *(Barry and Lyn Davis)*

NEWPORT SN0539
Castle (01239) 820742
Bridge Street; SA42 0TB Welcoming old pub with bar, lounge and restaurant, enjoyable fairly priced home-made food, Sun carvery, Felinfoel, Mantle, Wye Valley and guests, pleasant service, some live music; children and dogs welcome, three bedrooms, handy for Parrog Estuary walk (especially for bird-watchers). *(Anon)*

NEWPORT SN0539
Royal Oak (01239) 820632
West Street (A487); SA42 0TA Sizeable pub with good food including lunchtime light dishes, local lamb and lots of authentic curries, Felinfoel Double Dragon and Sharps Doom Bar, friendly helpful staff, children welcome in lounge with eating areas, separate stone and slate bar with pool and games, upstairs dining room; some tables outside, easy walk to beach and coast path, open all day. *(Heulwen and Neville Pinfield)*

PEMBROKE DOCK SM9603
Shipwright (01646) 682090
Front Street; SA72 6JX Little blue-painted end of terrace pub on waterfront overlooking estuary, enjoyable pubby food and well kept Sharps Doom Bar, friendly efficient staff, nautical and other memorabilia; children welcome, five minutes from Ireland ferry terminal. *(Pauline Fellows and Simon Robbins, R T and J C Moggridge)*

PENRHIWLLAN SN3641
Daffodil (01559) 370343
A475 Newcastle Emlyn–Lampeter; SA44 5NG Smart contemporary open-plan dining pub with comfortable welcoming bar (though most there to eat), scatter-cushion sofas and leather tub chairs on pale limestone floor, woodburner, bar chairs by granite-panelled counter serving well kept Evan Evans and Greene King, two lower-ceilinged end rooms with big oriental rugs, steps down to two airy dining rooms, one with picture windows by open kitchen, food can be very good especially puddings and Sun lunch; background music; children welcome, nicely furnished decked area outside with valley views. *(Anon)*

PONTRHYDFENDIGAID SN7366
Black Lion (01974) 831624
Off B4343 Tregaron–Devils Bridge; SY25 6BE Relaxed country inn under friendly landlord, smallish main bar with dark beams and floorboards, lots of stripped stone, old country furniture, woodburner and big pot-irons in vast fireplace, copper, brass and so forth on mantelpiece, historical photographs, Felinfoel Double Dragon and a local guest, seven wines by the glass, enjoyable good value home-cooked food including vegetarian/vegan options, quarry-tiled back dining room, small games room with pool and darts; background music; children and dogs (away from diners) welcome, back courtyard and tree-shaded garden, seven bedrooms (five in converted stables), good walking/cycling country and not far from Strata Florida Abbey, open all day. *(Taff Thomas, B and M Kendall)*

PORTHGAIN SM8132
★ Sloop (01348) 831449
Off A487 St Davids–Fishguard; SA62 5BN Busy tavern (especially holiday times) snuggled down in cove wedged tightly between headlands on Pembrokeshire Coast Path – fine walks in either direction; plank-ceilinged bar with lots of lobster pots and fishing nets, ship clocks and lanterns and even relics from local wrecks, decent-sized eating area with simple furnishings and freezer for kid's ice-creams, well liked bar

---

Tipping is not normal for bar meals, and not usually expected.

food from sandwiches to good steaks and fresh fish (own fishing business), Brains, Felinfoel and Green King, separate games room with juke box; seats on heated terrace overlooking harbour, self-catering cottage in village, open all day from 9.30am for breakfast, cake and coffee all day, till 1am Fri, Sat. *(Geoff and Linda Payne)*

PUMSAINT SN6540
Dolaucothi Arms (01558) 650237
A482 Lampeter–Llandovery; SA19 8UW Welcoming NT-owned pub (part of the Dolaucothi Estate), local beers and hearty home-made food (not Sun evening), flagstoned bar with two woodburners; muddy walkers and dogs welcome (pub cat Lily), garden overlooking Cothi River – pub has 4 miles of fishing rights, two bedrooms, closed Mon and lunchtime Tues, otherwise open all day. *(Anon)*

RHANDIRMWYN SN7843
Royal Oak (01550) 760201
7 miles N of Llandovery; SA20 0NY Friendly 17th-c stone-built inn in remote and peaceful walking country, comfortable traditional bar with log fire, four well kept local ales, ciders and perries, good variety of popular sensibly priced food sourced locally, big dining area, pool room; children and dogs welcome, hill views from garden and cottagey bedrooms, handy for Brecon Beacons. *(Anon)*

ST DOGMAELS SN1646
Ferry (01239) 615172
B4546; SA43 3LF Old stone building with spectacular views of Teifi estuary and hills from picture-window dining extension, popular food from daily changing menu, character bar with pine tables and interesting old photographs, Brains and summer guest ales, several wines by the glass, pleasant attentive staff; background music, monthly quiz; children and dogs welcome, plenty of room outside on linked decked areas, open all day. *(Anon)*

TENBY SN1300
Buccaneer (01834) 842273
St Julian's Street; SA70 7AS Popular place with good affordably priced food, well kept ales and friendly efficient service; live music Weds and Fri; children welcome, sunny beer garden, open (and food) all day. *(Mike and Mary Carter)*

TRESAITH SN2751
★ Ship (01239) 811816
Off A487 E of Cardigan; bear right in village and keep on down – pub's car park fills quickly; SA43 2JL Excellent position beside broad sandy surfing beach (maybe dolphins), seats under glass canopy on heated front decking and picnic-sets on two-level terrace; front dining area with same view plus back room with winter log

fire, sofas and pubby furniture, big local photos, also two appealing back rooms – one with old-fashioned stove and snug alcove, Brains Rev James and SA, food can be good; children welcome, sea-view bedrooms and lovely coastal walks from this steep little village. *(Jen Llywelyn, Tim Arnold and Jim Wingate, Simon Rodway, Lois Dyer, Kay and Alistair Butler)*

GLAMORGAN

BISHOPSTON SS5789
Joiners Arms (01792) 232658
Bishopston Road, just off B4436 SW of Swansea; SA3 3EJ Thriving local brewing its own good value Swansea ales along with well kept guests, quite a choice of reasonably priced food from paninis up (not Sun evening, Mon), friendly staff, unpretentious quarry-tiled bar with massive solid-fuel stove, comfortable lounge; TV for rugby; children welcome, open all day. *(Anon)*

CAERPHILLY ST1484
★ Black Cock (029) 2088 0534
Watford; Tongwynlais exit from M4 junction 32, then right just after church; CF83 1NF Good, friendly new management for beamed country pub (gently refurbished) with series of interconnecting rooms, large back room extension with huge photo of Caerphilly Castle across one wall, good choice of enjoyable pub food all day (book for Sun lunch) including children's, well kept welsh ales, cheerful staff, woodburners; background music; dogs welcome in bar, disabled access, sizeable terraced garden among trees with good play area, in the hills just below Caerphilly Common, popular with walkers and riders (there's a hitching rail), open all day. *(Anon)*

CARDIFF ST1876
City Arms (029) 2064 1913
Quay Street; CF10 1EA City-centre alehouse with four Brains beers and ten regularly changing guests (some cask-tapped), tasting trays available, also plenty of draught/bottled continentals and real cider, friendly knowledgeable staff, no food; free wi-fi; open all day (till 2am Fri, Sat). *(Anon)*

CARDIFF ST1876
Cottage (029) 2033 7195
St Mary Street, near Howells; CF10 1AA 18th-c Brains pub with their full range kept well, long neat bar with narrow frontage and back eating area, lots of polished wood, glass and mirrors, pictures on papered walls, brasserie-style food including sharing platters, good cheerful service and relaxed friendly atmosphere even Fri and Sat when crowded (gets packed on rugby international days); open all day. *(Roger and Donna Huggins)*

CARDIFF · ST1776
Cricketers · (029) 2034 5102
Cathedral Road; CF11 9LL Victorian townhouse in quiet residential area backing on to Glamorgan CC, well kept Evan Evans ales and enjoyable freshly made food (not Sun evening), Thurs jazz supper; children welcome, sunny back garden, open all day. *(Michael Butler)*

CARDIFF · ST1876
Goat Major · (029) 2033 7161
High Street, opposite castle; CF10 1PU Named for Royal Welsh Regiment mascot (plenty of pictures), Victorian-style décor with dark panelling and green leatherette wall seats, shiny floor tiles around bar, carpets beyond, Brains beers kept well, pie-based menu till 6pm (4pm Sun), friendly young staff; background music, silent TVs showing subtitled news; children welcome, open all day. *(Roger and Donna Huggins, Jeremy King)*

CARDIFF · ST1876
Zero Degrees · (029) 2022 9494
Westgate Street; CF10 1DD Lively contemporary two-level place visibly brewing its own interesting beers, good selection of other drinks including cocktails and 'beertails', enjoyable italian-leaning food and mussel dishes, friendly staff; background music, sports TVs, free wi-fi, open all day. *(Berwyn Owen)*

COWBRIDGE · SS9974
★ Bear · (01446) 774814
High Street, with car park behind off North Street; signed off A48; CF71 7AF Busy Georgian coaching inn in smart village, well kept Brains, Hancocks and guests, decent house wines, enjoyable usual food from good sandwiches and wraps up, young uniformed staff, three attractively furnished bars with flagstones, bare boards or carpet, some stripped stone and panelling, big hot open fires, barrel-vaulted cellar restaurant; children and dogs (in one bar) welcome, courtyard tables, comfortable quiet bedrooms, open all day, bike hire, disabled parking. *(Anon)*

COWBRIDGE · SS9974
Duke of Wellington · (01446) 773592
High Street; CF71 7AG Popular 16th-c half-timbered building with wide oak-panelled rooms and airy back conservatory, wooden seats and tables on terrace, good food cooked to order from extensive and imaginative menu, efficient waitress service, five Brains beers; nice one-street Vale of Glamorgan town. *(Peter Hacker)*

GWAELOD-Y-GARTH · ST1183
Gwaelod y Garth Inn
(029) 2081 0408 *Main Road; CF15 9HH* Meaning 'foot of the mountain', this stone-built village pub has wonderful valley views and is popular with walkers on Taff Ely Ridgeway Path; highly thought-of, well presented food (all day Fri and Sat, not Sun evening), friendly efficient service, own-brew beer along with Wye Valley and guests from pine-clad bar, log fires, upstairs restaurant (disabled access from back car park); table skittles, pool, digital juke box; children and dogs welcome, three bedrooms, open all day. *(Anon)*

KENFIG · SS8081
★ Prince of Wales · (01656) 740356
2.2 miles from M4 junction 37; A4229 towards Porthcawl, then right when dual carriageway narrows on bend, signed Maudlam, Kenfig; CF33 4PR Ancient local with plenty of individuality by historic sand dunes, cheerful welcoming landlord, well kept ales tapped from the cask, decent wines and good choice of malts, enjoyable straightforward generous food at low prices (not Mon), chatty panelled room off main bar (dogs allowed here), log fires, stripped stone, lots of wreck pictures, restaurant with upstairs overspill room, several ghosts; TV for special rugby events; children till 9pm, handy for nature reserve (June orchids), open all day. *(Anon)*

LISVANE · ST1883
Ty Mawr Arms · (01222) 754456
From B4562 on E edge turn N into Church Road, bear left into Llwyn y Pia Road, keep on along Graig Road; CF14 0UF Large welcoming country pub with good choice of popular food, well kept Brains and guest ales, decent wines by the glass, teas and coffees, friendly service, great views over Cardiff from spacious bay-windowed dining area off traditional log-fire bar; children welcome, disabled access with help to main bar area, big attractive garden with pond, open all day. *(Roger and Donna Huggins)*

LLANBLETHIAN · SS9873
Cross · (01446) 772995
Church Road; CF71 7JF Former staging inn with friendly owners, well kept Wye Valley and guests (beer festivals), enjoyable freshly made food from pubby choices up in contemporary bar or light airy restaurant, reasonable prices, open fire and woodburner; children and dogs welcome, seats and tables outside on decking, open all day. *(Anon)*

LLANCARFAN · ST0570
Fox & Hounds · (01446) 781287
Signed off A4226; can also be reached from A48 from Bonvilston or B4265 via Llancadle; CF62 3AD Good attractively presented food using local ingredients in neat comfortably modernised village pub, Brains beers kept well and nice choice of wines, friendly staff; unobtrusive background music; tables on covered terrace, pretty

streamside setting by interesting church, eight comfortable and pretty bedrooms, good breakfast, closed Sun evening. *(Anon)*

LLANGENNITH   SS4291
Kings Head   (01792) 386212
Clos St Cenydd, opposite church; SA3 1HX Extended 17th-c stone-built inn with wide choice of popular food promptly served by friendly staff, up to seven ales including own Gower brews and over 100 malt whiskies; pool and juke box in lively public bar; children and dogs welcome, large terrace with village views, good walks, not far from great surfing beach and large campsite, bedrooms in separate buildings to the side and rear, open (and food) all day. *(Canon Michael Bourdeaux)*

LLANGYNWYD   SS8588
Old House   (01656) 733310
Off A4063 S of Maesteg; pub behind church, nearly a mile W of modern village; CF34 9SB Partly thatched and beamed dining pub, well kept Flowers and decent wines by the glass, good malt whiskies, reasonably priced food from pubby choices to specials, nice staff, high-backed black leather dining chairs around pubby tables on wooden flooring, sporting pictures, lots of jugs and brassware, huge fireplace, attractive conservatory extension; children welcome, picnic-sets on terrace, children's play equipment, nearby huge churchyard and valley views worth a look; open all day. *(Ian Phillips)*

LLANMADOC   SS4493
★ Britannia   (01792) 386624
The Gower, near Whiteford Burrows (NT); SA3 1DB Busy summer dining pub out on the peninsula, good freshly made bar and restaurant food including set menus, ales such as Fullers, Gower and Marstons, gleaming copper stove in beamed and tiled bar, steps up to stripped-stone dining area, good service; children and dogs welcome, tables out in front and in nice big garden behind, rabbit hutch and aviary, great estuary views, lovely walks. *(Hugh Roberts, Canon Michael Bourdeaux, Michael Butler)*

LLANSAMLET   SS6897
Plough & Harrow   (01792) 772263
Church Road; SA7 9RL Friendly and cheery open-plan pub with well kept Marstons-related ales such as Banks's Sunbeam and Jennings Cocker Hoop, good value generous pub food including deals, carvery (Weds, Sun), quiz Weds. *(R T and J C Moggridge)*

OGMORE   SS8876
Pelican   (01656) 880049
Ogmore Road (B4524); CF32 0QP Nice spot above ruined castle, beamery, bare boards and welcoming fire, popular all-day food including tapas and afternoon

teas, Sharps Doom Bar and Wye Valley, cheerful service; may try to keep your credit card while you eat; dogs allowed in lounge (flagstone floor), live music weekends, picnic-sets on small front terrace, rather grand smokers' hut, views and handy for beaches. *(Anon)*

OLDWALLS   SS4891
Greyhound   (01792) 391027
W of Llanrhidian; SA3 1HA 19th-c pub with spacious beamed and dark-panelled carpeted lounge bar, well kept ales including own Gower brews, decent wine and coffee, wide choice of popular food from sandwiches up including good Sun roasts, friendly staff, hot coal fires, back dining room and upstairs overspill/function room; children and dogs welcome, picnic-sets in big garden with terrace, play area and good views, open all day. *(Anon)*

PONTNEDDFECHAN   SN8907
Angel   (01639) 722013
Just off A465; Pontneathvaughan Road; SA11 5NR Comfortably opened-up 16th-c pub with friendly staff and atmosphere, well kept ales such as Neath Witch Hunter, enjoyable fairly priced pub food (good lamb cawl), masses of jugs on beams, ancient houseware and old kitchen range, separate flagstoned bar; terrace tables, good walks including the waterfalls. *(R T and J C Moggridge)*

REYNOLDSTON   SS4889
★ King Arthur   (01792) 390775
Higher Green, off A4118; SA3 1AD Cheerful pub-hotel with timbered main bar and hall, country-style restaurant, family summer dining area (games room with pool in winter), good fairly priced all-day food, friendly staff coping well when busy, Felinfoel and guests, country house bric-a-brac, log fire, lively local atmosphere evenings; background music; tables out on green, play area, 19 bedrooms and self-catering cottage, open all day. *(Anon)*

ST HILARY   ST0173
Bush   (01446) 776888
Off A48 E of Cowbridge; CF71 7DP Cosily restored 16th-c thatched and beamed pub, flagstoned main bar with inglenook, snug and bare-boards lounge, good mix of old furniture, Bass, Greene King, Hancocks and a guest, Weston's cider, good choice of wines by the glass, enjoyable food including home-made pies, gluten-free choices too, friendly service, carpeted restaurant with open ceiling; children and dogs (in bar) welcome, some benches out at front, garden behind, open all day Fri-Sun. *(Anon)*

SWANSEA   SS6492
Brunswick   (01792) 465676
Duke Street; SA1 4HS Large rambling local with traditional pubby furnishings, lots

of knick-knacks, artwork and prints for sale, bargain popular weekday food till 7.30pm, Courage, Greene King and a guest (usually local), friendly helpful service, regular live music, quiz night Mon; open all day. *(Jan Masson)*

GWENT

ABERGAVENNY   SO3111
⋆**Hardwick** (01873) 854220
Hardwick; B4598 SE, off A40 at A465/ A4042 exit – coming from E on A40, go right round the exit system, as B4598 is final road out; NP7 9AA Restaurant-with-rooms – you'll need to book for owner-chef's highly regarded imaginative food; drinkers welcome in simple bar with spindleback chairs around pub tables, stripped brickwork by fireplace and small corner counter serving Rhymney and Wye Valley, local perry and a dozen wines by the glass, two dining rooms, one with beams, bare boards and huge fireplace, the other in lighter carpeted extension, friendly service; background music; no under-8s in restaurant after 8pm, teak tables and chairs under umbrellas by car park, neat garden, bedrooms, open all day (till 10pm Sun), closed winter Mon and second week Jan. *(John Jenkins)*

CAERLEON   ST3490
⋆**Bell** (01633) 420613
Bulmore Road; off M4 junction 24 via B4237 and B4236; NP18 1QQ Nicely furnished linked beamed areas in old stone coaching inn, good popular (often imaginative) food using local ingredients (book weekends), well kept Timothy Taylors Landlord, Wye Valley HPA and a guest, over 20 welsh ciders and perries, big open fireplace; unobtrusive background music (live Sun afternoon); children welcome, pretty back terrace with koi tank, open all day. *(Anon)*

CHEPSTOW   ST5394
Three Tuns (01291) 645797
Bridge Street; NP16 5EY Early 17th-c and a pub for much of that time; refurbished bare-boards interior with painted farmhouse pine furniture, couple of mismatched sofas by woodburner, dresser with china plates, local ales and ciders from nice wooden counter at unusual angle, very reasonably priced home-made bar food (not Tues), friendly staff; background music (live Sat); dogs welcome, pretty bedrooms, open all day (till 10pm Mon-Thurs); disabled access (one bedroom suitable). *(Anon)*

GROSMONT   SO4024
Angel (01981) 240646
Corner of B4347 and Poorscript Lane; NP7 8EP Small 17th-c local owned by village co-operative, rustic interior with simple wooden furniture, Fullers, Tomos Watkins and Wye Valley, real ciders, straightforward bar food (not Sun or Mon),

ambitious evening food, pool room with darts, live music (instruments provided); no lavatories – public ones close by; a couple of garden tables and boules behind, seats out by ancient market cross on attractive steep single street in sight of castle, good local walks, open all day Sat, closed Mon lunchtime. *(Guy Vowles)*

LLANDENNY   SO4103
⋆**Raglan Arms** (01291) 690800
Centre of village; NP15 1DL Well run dining pub with interesting fresh food (not Sun evening), Wye Valley Butty Bach and good selection of wines, friendly welcoming young staff, big pine tables and a couple of leather sofas in linked dining rooms leading to conservatory, log fire in flagstoned bar's handsome stone fireplace, relaxed informal atmosphere; children welcome, garden tables, closed Mon. *(Anon)*

LLANGATTOCK LINGOED   SO3620
Hunters Moon (01873) 821499
Off B4521 just E of Llanvetherine; NP7 8RR Family-owned and attractive tucked-away pub dating from 13th c, beams, dark stripped stone and flagstones, woodburner, friendly licensees and locals, welsh ales tapped from the cask, separate dining room, enjoyable straightforward all-day food; children welcome, tables out on deck and in charming dell with ducks, waterfall, four comfortable bedrooms, glorious country on Offa's Dyke Path, open all day. *(Neil and Anita Christopher)*

LLANGYBI   ST3797
White Hart (01633) 450258
On main road; NP15 1NP Friendly village dining pub in delightful 12th-c monastery building, part of Jane Seymour's dowry, pubby bar with roaring log fire, steps up to pleasant light restaurant, good if not particularly cheap food (not Sun evening), afternoon tea (not Sun or Mon), breakfasts Sat morning, several well kept mainly welsh ales, good choice of wines by the glass; children welcome, two nice bedrooms, open all day, closed Mon. *(Anon)*

LLANOVER   SO2907
⋆**Goose & Cuckoo** (01873) 880277
Upper Llanover signed up track off A4042 S of Abergavenny; after 0.5 miles take first left; NP7 9ER Remote single-room pub looking over picturesque valley just inside Brecon Beacons National Park; essentially one small rustically furnished room with woodburner in arched stone fireplace, small picture-window extension makes most of the view, Newmans Stag, Rhymney Bitter and a couple of guests, 80 whiskies, simple tasty food, daily papers, board games, cribbage and darts; no credit cards; children and dogs welcome, picnic-sets out on gravel below, they keep sheep, geese and chickens and may have honey for sale,

bedrooms, open all day weekends, closed Mon. *(Guy Vowles)*

LLANTHONY   SO2827
★**Priory Hotel** (01873) 890487

Aka Abbey Hotel, Llanthony Priory; off A465, back road Llanvihangel Crucorney–Hay; NP7 7NN Magical setting for plain bar in dimly lit vaulted flagstoned crypt of graceful ruined Norman abbey, lovely in summer, with lawns around and the peaceful border hills beyond; well kept ales such as Brains, Felinfoel and Newmans, summer farm cider, good coffee, simple lunchtime bar food (can be long queue on fine summer days, but number system works well), evening restaurant, occasional live music; no dogs; children welcome but not in hotel area with four bedrooms in restored parts of abbey walls, open all day Sat, summer Sun, closed winter Mon-Thurs, Sun evening. *(Taff Thomas)*

LLANTRISANT FAWR   ST3997
Greyhound (01291) 672505

Off A449 near Usk; NP15 1LE Prettily set 17th-c country inn with relaxed homely feel in three linked beamed rooms, steps between two, nice mix of furnishings and rustic decorations, enjoyable home cooking at sensible prices, efficient service, two or more well kept ales, decent wines by the glass, log fires, pleasant panelled dining room; muddy boots/dogs welcome in stable bar, attractive garden with big fountain, hill views, comfortable bedrooms in converted stable block, closed Sun evening. *(Anon)*

MAMHILAD   SO3004
Horseshoe (01873) 880542

Old Abergavenny Road; NP4 8QZ Old beamed country pub, slate-floor bar with traditional pubby furniture, a couple of unusual posts acting as elbow-tables, original Hancocks pub sign, ornate woodburner in stone fireplace, tasty fairly priced food (not Sun evening) from lunchtime baguettes up, Sharps Doom Bar and a local guest, Blaengawney cider; children welcome, dogs away from dining area, lovely views particularly from tables by car park over road, open all day Fri-Sun, closed Mon. *(Mr N and Mr G Webb)*

PENALLT   SO5209
Inn at Penallt (01600) 772765

Village signed off B4293; at crossroads in village turn left; NP25 4SE 17th-c stone pub, imaginative food using local produce including set lunch, also local ales and cider, well priced wine list, courteous efficient service, airy slate-floored bar with woodburner, restaurant and small back conservatory; children and dogs welcome, big garden with terrace and play area, Wye Valley views, four bedrooms, closed Mon, lunchtime Tues (and maybe lunchtimes Weds and Thurs in winter). *(Anon)*

RAGLAN   SO4107
Beaufort Arms (01291) 690412

High Street; NP15 2DY Pub-hotel (former 16th-c coaching inn) with two character beamed bars, one with big stone fireplace and comfortable seats on slate floor, well kept Fullers London Pride and Wye Valley Butty Bach, good varied range of locally sourced food (own-grown produce) including set lunch/early evening menu, light airy brasserie, friendly attentive service; background music; children welcome, terrace tables, 17 good bedrooms. *(Eryl and Keith Dykes)*

REDBROOK   SO5309
★**Boat** (01600) 712615

Car park signed on A466 Chepstow–Monmouth, then 30-metre footbridge over Wye; or very narrow steep car access from Penallt in Wales; NP25 4AJ Beautifully set riverside pub with well kept Wye Valley and guests tapped from the cask, lots of ciders, perries and country wines, enjoyable good value simple food from baguettes and baked potatoes up (nothing fried), helpful staff, unchanging interior with stripped-stone walls, flagstones and roaring woodburner; live bands Thurs evening, children and dogs (on leads) welcome, rough home-built seats in informal tiered suntrap garden with stream spilling down waterfall cliffs into duck pond, open all day. *(Anon)*

TINTERN   SO5300
★**Anchor** (01291) 689582

Off A466 at brown Abbey sign; NP16 6TE Medieval building next to the magnificent abbey ruins; bar was originally the abbey's cider mill with beams, flagstones and bare stone walls, Bath Ales, Otter, Wye Valley and a guest, wide range of farm and local bottled ciders plus several wines by the glass and Penderyn whisky/gin, airy garden room with brightly painted chairs around wooden tables, picture windows making most of the view (abbey floodlit at night), restaurant in former ferryman's cottage, good range of interesting food, pleasant hard-working staff; children and dogs welcome, wheelchair access to bar only, terrace and lawn with picnic-sets, River Wye just behind and lots of surrounding walks, open all day from 9am. *(Harvey Brown, Pip White, Neil and Anita Christopher, Ian and Rose Lock, Chris and Angela Buckell)*

TRELLECK   SO5005
Lion (01600) 860322

B4293 6 miles S of Monmouth; NP25 4PA Open-plan bar with one or two low black beams, nice mix of old furniture, two log fires, ales such as Butcombe, Felinfoel and Wye Valley, wide range of fair-priced traditional food with specials such as ostrich and kangaroo, takeaway pizzas, games such as shove ha'penny, ring the bull and table skittles, background music; children and dogs welcome, picnic-sets on grass, side courtyard overlooking church, self-catering cottage, open all day, closed Sun evening. *(Anon)*

TRELLECK GRANGE   SO5001
Fountain   (01291) 689303
Minor road Tintern–Llanishen, SE of village; NP16 6QW Traditional 17th-c country pub under friendly licensees, enjoyable local food from pub favourites to game specials, three well kept welsh ales, farm cider and perry, roomy low-beamed flagstoned bar with log fire; dogs welcome, small walled garden, peaceful spot on small winding road, comfortable bedrooms (no children), open all day, closed Mon. *(Anon)*

USK   SO3700
Cross Keys   (01291) 672535
Bridge Street; NP15 1BG Small two-bar stone pub dating from 14th c, wide choice of generously served popular food, well kept Brains and Hancocks, good service and friendly atmosphere, woodburning stove in handsome fireplace, oak beams, wall plaques marking past flood levels, daily newspapers; sports TV; children and dogs (not during food times) welcome, seats, tables and benches among hanging baskets on back terrace, disabled access, five comfortable bedrooms, good breakfast, open all day. *(Anon)*

USK   SO3700
Kings Head   (01291) 672963
Old Market Street; NP15 1AL 16th-c family-run inn with chatty relaxed atmosphere, very popular, generously served food and well kept beers, friendly efficient staff, huge log fire in superb fireplace; sports TV; bedrooms, open all day. *(Anon)*

GWYNEDD

ABERDOVEY   SN6196
Britannia   (01654) 767426
Sea View Terrace; LL35 0EF Friendly busting harbourside inn; great estuary and distant mountain views from upstairs restaurant with balcony, good range of enjoyable well priced food including fresh crab and summer afternoon teas with home-made cakes, downstairs locals' bar with real ales, darts and TV, woodburner in cosy back snug; children welcome (not in bar), three bedrooms, open all day. *(Jean and Douglas Troup)*

ABERDOVEY   SN6196
★ Penhelig Arms   (01654) 767215
Opposite Penhelig Station; LL35 0LT Fine harbourside location for this 18th-c hotel, traditional bar with warm fire in central stone fireplace, some panelling, Brains ales and a guest, good choice of wines and malt whiskies, enjoyable food including good fish and chips; children welcome, dogs allowed in bar and comfortable bedrooms

(some have balconies overlooking estuary, ones nearest road can be noisy), open all day. *(Richard Osborne-Fardon, Phil and Helen Holt)*

BETWS-Y-COED   SH7955
★ Ty Gwyn   (01690) 710383
A5 just S of bridge to village; LL24 0SG Family-run restaurant-with-rooms rather than pub (you must eat or stay overnight to be served alcohol), but pubby feel in character beamed lounge bar with ancient cooking range, easy chairs, antiques, silver, cut-glass, old prints and bric-a-brac, really good interesting food using local produce including own fruit and vegetables, beers such as Adnams, Brains and Great Orme, friendly professional service; background music; children welcome, 12 comfortable bedrooms and holiday cottage, closed Mon-Weds in Jan. *(Anon)*

BLAENAU FFESTINIOG   SH7041
Pengwern Arms   (01766) 762200
Church Square, Ffestiniog; LL41 4PB Co-operative-owned village square pub being restored in stages; panelled bar with well kept/priced Llŷn or Purple Moose and a guest, dining area serving standard weekend food including bargain Sun lunch, friendly local atmosphere, Mon quiz; fine views from back garden, bedrooms. *(Mike and Eleanor Anderson)*

CAERNARFON   SH4762
★ Black Boy   (01286) 673604
Northgate Street; LL55 1RW Busy traditional 16th-c inn with cosy beamed lounge bar, sumptuously furnished and packed with tables, additional dining room across corridor and dimly lit atmospheric public bar with well kept Bass, Cwrw Llŷn, Purple Moose and two guests, enjoyable generous food all day from sandwiches up (try the traditional 'lobsgows' stew), good friendly service and lots of welsh chat; soft 1970s background music, TV, free wi-fi; disabled access (ramps) and facilities, a few pavement tables, 26 bedrooms, more in separate townhouse, open (and food) all day. *(Dave Webster, Sue Holland, Simon and Mandy King)*

CAPEL CURIG   SH7257
★ Bryn Tyrch   (01690) 720223
A5 E; LL24 0EL Family-owned roadside inn perfectly placed for mountains of Snowdonia; bare-stone walkers' bar with big communal tables and amazing picture-windows views, two Great Orme ales and a guest beer, quite a few malt whiskies, comprehensive choice of good well presented food including packed lunches and hampers; second bar with big menu boards, leather sofas and mix of tables on floorboards, coal fire; children and dogs welcome, steep little side garden, more seats on terrace and across road by stream, country-style bedrooms, open all day weekends, from 4.30pm weekdays (12pm during holidays). *(Anon)*

CAPEL CURIG   SH7357
Tyn y Coed (01690) 720331
A5 SE of village; LL24 0EE Friendly inn
across road from River Llugwy with stage
coach at entrance; enjoyable good value
home-made food using local produce, well
kept Purple Moose and three guests, pleasant
quick service, log fires, pool room with juke
box; nice side terrace, good surrounding
walks, comfortable bedrooms, cycle storage
and drying room, closed weekday lunchtimes
out of season, otherwise open all day.
(Chris and Val Ramstedt)

CONWY   SH7777
Albion (01492) 582484
Uppergate Street; LL32 8RF Sensitively
restored 1920s pub thriving under collective
ownership of four welsh brewers – Conwy,
Great Orme, Nant and Purple Moose, their
beers and guests kept well, interesting
building with plenty of well preserved
features including stained glass and huge
baronial fireplace, quieter back room with
serving hatch. *(Anon)*

LLANDUDNO   SH7882
Cottage Loaf (01492) 870762
Market Street; LL30 2SR Friendly former
bakery with woodburning stoves, flagstones,
rugs on bare boards and salvaged ship's
timbers, mix of individual tables, benches,
cushioned settles and attractive dining
chairs, big new garden room extension,
enjoyable brasserie-style food (all day), five
well kept local ales such as Great Orme. *(Rod
and Sue Forrester, Roy Bowman, Derek Wason)*

LLANDUDNO   SH7882
Queen Victoria (01492) 860952
Church Walks; LL30 2HD Traditional
Victorian pub away from high-street bustle,
well kept Banks's, Marstons Pedigree and
guests, good choice of enjoyable affordable
pubby food in bar or upstairs restaurant,
congenial atmosphere and good service;
children and dogs welcome, a few seats
out in front, not far from the Great Orme
Tramway, open (and food) all day. *(Adrian
Johnson)*

LLANFAETHLU   SH3286
Black Lion (01407) 730718
A5025; LL65 4NL Renovated 18th-c inn
(was derelict for many years and next-door
cottages still to be restored); slate-floor bar
with exposed stone and woodburner, a few
high-backed stools at oak-topped counter,
Marstons Pedigree and a couple of guests,
room off with pitched roof and another
woodburner, back dining extension, good
food with a modern twist using Anglesey
produce including meat from own farm,
friendly helpful staff; soft background
music; children and dogs (in bar) welcome,
disabled access, facilities and parking,
terrace with views to Snowdonia and of

working windmill, two well appointed
bedrooms, open all day Sat, best to check
other days. *(Simon and Mandy King)*

LLANFROTHEN   SH6141
Brondanw Arms (01766) 770555
*Aka Y Ring; A4085 just N of B4410;
LL48 6AQ* Welsh-speaking village pub at
end of short whitewashed terrace, main bar
with slate floor and woodburner in large
fireplace, pews and window benches, old
farm tools on the ceiling, snug with panelled
booths and potbelly stove, long spacious
dining room behind with contrasting red
walls, good home-cooked food, Robinsons
ales, friendly helpful staff; children welcome,
wheelchair access (two long shallow steps at
front), Snowdonia Park views from garden
with play area, good walking area, camping,
handy for Plas Brondanw Gardens. *(Simon
and Mandy King)*

LLANUWCHLLYN   SH8730
Eagles (01678) 540278
Aka Eryrod; A494/B4403; LL23 7UB
Family-run and welcoming with good
reasonably priced, well thought-of food
(bilingual menu and not Mon lunchtime)
using own farm produce, opened-up
slate-floor bar with log fire, beams and
stripped stone, back picture-window view of
mountains with Lake Bala in distance, ales
such as Purple Moose, limited wine choice in
small bottles; sports TV; children welcome,
metal tables and chairs on flower-filled back
terrace, open all day summer (afternoon
break Mon). *(Anon)*

MAENTWROG   SH6640
Grapes (01766) 590208
*A496; village signed from A470;
LL41 4HN* Handome old inn reopened after
refurbishment, three bars, woodburning
stoves, good-sized conservatory with
views of trains on Ffestiniog Railway,
smiling, helpful staff, traditional plus more
adventurous, highly rated food, seats on
pleasant terrace, boutique-style bedrooms,
open all day weekends, children and dogs
welcome. *(Anon)*

PENMAENPOOL   SH6918
George III (01341) 422525
Just off A493, near Dolgellau; LL40 1YD
Attractive, busy inn dating from 1650, lovely
views over Mawddach estuary from civilised
partly panelled upstairs bar opening into
cosy inglenook lounge, more basic beamed
and flagstoned downstairs bar for peak times,
well kept ale such as Black Sheep, Fullers
and Purple Moose, enjoyable, interesting food
including specials, restaurant; they ask to
keep a credit card if you run a tab; dogs and
children welcome, sheltered terrace,
11 good bedrooms including some in
converted station (line now a walkway),
open all day. *(Phil and Helen Holt)*

PORTH DINLLAEN   SH2741

★**Ty Coch** (01758) 720498

Beach car park signed from Morfa Nefyn, then 15-minute walk; LL53 6DB Former 19th-c vicarage in idyllic location right on beach with great view along coast to mountains, far from roads and only reached on foot; bar crammed with nautical paraphernalia, pewter, old miners' and railway lamps, RNLI memorabilia etc, simple furnishings and coal fire, up to three real ales and a craft beer (served in plastic as worried about glass on beach), short lunchtime bar menu; children and dogs welcome, open all day in season (till 4pm Sun), 12-4pm Oct-Easter (but shut weekdays a fortnight before Easter). *(Matt Williams)*

PORTHMADOG   SH5738

Spooners (01766) 516032

Harbour Station; LL49 9NF Platform café-bar at steam line terminus, lots of railway memorabilia including a former working engine in one corner, Marstons-related ales and welsh guests such as Purple Moose, good value pub food including popular Sun lunch, evening meals Tues-Sat (all week in high season); children welcome, platform tables, open all day. *(Brian and Anna Marsden)*

TREFRIW   SH7863

Old Ship (01492) 640013

B5106; LL27 0JH Well run old pub with nice staff and cheerful local atmosphere, good home-made food from daily changing blackboard menu, particularly well kept Marstons-related ales and local guests, good selection of wines/malt whiskies, log fire and inglenook woodburner; garden with picnic-sets by stream, children welcome, open all day weekends, closed Mon. *(Claes Mauroy, Mike Proctor, Mike and Wena Stevenson, Martin Cawley)*

TREMADOG   SH5640

Union (01766) 512748

Market Square; LL49 9RB Traditional early 19th-c stone-built pub in terrace overlooking square, cosy and comfortable, with quiet panelled lounge on left, carpeted public bar to the right with bare stone walls and woodburner, well kept ales such as Great Orme and Purple Moose, enjoyable fairly priced pubby food including an authentic daily curry, friendly staff, back restaurant; darts and TV; children welcome, paved terrace behind. *(Simon and Mandy King)*

TUDWEILIOG   SH2336

Lion (01758) 659724

Nefyn Road (B4417), Llŷn Peninsula; LL53 8ND Cheerful village inn with enjoyable sensibly priced food from baguettes to blackboard specials, homely furnishings in lounge bar and two dining rooms (one for families, one with woodburning stove), quick friendly service, real ales such as Purple Moose (up to three in summer), dozens of malt whiskies, decent wines, pool table and board games in public bar; pleasant front garden, four bedrooms, open all day in season. *(Anon)*

PEMBROKESHIRE

HERMON   SN2031

Lamb (01239) 831864

Taylors Row; SA36 0DS Friendly family-run pub dating from 17th c, homely and comfortable, with generous food cooked by landlady; well behaved dogs welcome, three bedrooms and caravan pitches. *(Ron Corbett)*

POWYS

BLEDDFA   SO2068

Hundred House (01547) 550441

A488 Knighton–Penybont; LD7 1PA 16th-c pub (former courthouse) opposite village green, friendly licensees, carpeted lounge bar with woodburner in big inglenook, L-shaped room with lower flagstoned bar, another big fireplace in cosy dining room, much liked traditional food, Radnorshire ales; background music; children welcome, tables in side garden with play area, lovely countryside, closed Mon, otherwise open all day. *(Anon)*

CAERSWS   SO0391

Buck (01686) 688267

Main Street; SY17 5EL Friendly extended old inn, welcoming staff, good sensibly priced and very popular home-made food (evenings Thurs-Sat, lunchtime Sun) in bar and restaurant, local ales; bedrooms, open all day weekends, from 5pm weekdays. *(Jean and Douglas Troup)*

CARNO   SN9696

Aleppo Merchant (01686) 420210

A470 Newtown–Machynlleth; SY17 5LL Good choice of reasonably priced pub food from sandwiches up (from 12pm), helpful friendly staff, Boddingtons and a guest, plushly modernised stripped-stone bar, peaceful lounge on right with open fire, restaurant (well behaved children allowed here), back extension with big-screen TV in games room; background music; disabled access, steps up to tables in back garden, bedrooms, nice countryside, open all day. *(Anon)*

CRICKHOWELL   SO2118

Dragon (01873) 810362

High Street; NP8 1BE Welcoming, family-owned old inn (more hotel-restaurant than pub but with small bar) with flagstones, slates and wooden floor, pubby chairs and tables, sofas and armchairs by open fire, enjoyable traditional food with welsh choices (all day), good, prompt friendly service, Rhymney, log fire; 15 bedrooms. *(Eryl and Keith Dykes)*

DERWENLAS SN7299

⋆**Black Lion** (01654) 703913

A487 just S of Machynlleth; SY20 8TN Cosy 16th-c country pub with good range of enjoyable well priced food including children's menu, friendly staff coping well at busy times, Wye Valley Butty Bach and a guest, decent wines, heavy black beams, thick walls and black timbering, attractive pictures, brasses and lion models, tartan carpet over big slate flagstones, good log fire; background music; garden behind with play area and steps up into woods, limited parking, bedrooms, closed Mon. *(B and M Kendall, Lois Dyer)*

DINAS MAWDDWY SH8514

Red Lion (01650) 531247

Dyfi Road; off A470 (N of A458 junction); SY20 9JA Two small traditional front bars and more modern back extension, changing ales including some from small local brewers, good generous home-made food including specials, reasonable prices and friendly efficient service, open fire, beams and lots of brass; children welcome, simple bedrooms, pub named in welsh (Llew Coch). *(Anon)*

GLADESTRY SO2355

Royal Oak (01544) 370669

B4594; HR5 3NR Old-fashioned village pub on Offa's Dyke Path with friendly licensees, simple stripped-stone slate-floored walkers' bar, beams hung with tankards and lanterns, piano, darts, carpeted lounge, open fires, ales from Golden Valley and Wye Valley, uncomplicated home-made food; no credit cards; children welcome, dogs in bar (and bedrooms by arrangement), sheltered back garden, camping, closed Sun and Thurs evenings in summer, all day Tues, Thurs plus mornings Weds, Fri in winter, Mon all year except bank holidays. *(Ann and Colin Hunt)*

GLASBURY SO1839

Harp (01497) 847373

B4350 towards Hay, just N of A438; HR3 5NR Welcoming, relaxed, homely old place with good value pubby food (not Mon) cooked by landlady including proper pies and takeaway pizzas, log-fire lounge with eating areas, airy bar, well kept local ales, picture windows over wooded garden sloping to River Wye, some acoustic music, darts; river views from picnic-sets on terrace and back bedrooms, good breakfast. *(Anon)*

HAY-ON-WYE SO2242

⋆**Blue Boar** (01497) 820884

Castle Street/Oxford Road; HR3 5DF Medieval bar in character pub, cosy corners, dark panelling, pews and country chairs, open fire in Edwardian fireplace, four well kept local ales including a house beer from Hydes, organic bottled cider and several wines by the glass, enjoyable food

(from breakfast on) in quite different long open café/dining room, bright light décor, local artwork for sale and another open fire, friendly efficient service; background music; children and dogs welcome, tables in tree-shaded garden, open all day from 9am. *(John and Bryony Coles, Ian and Rose Lock)*

HAY-ON-WYE SO2342

⋆**Old Black Lion** (01497) 820841

Lion Street; HR3 5AD Comfortable low-beamed bar with original fireplace and old pine tables mostly laid for dining, good bar and restaurant food, Wye Valley Butty Bach (labelled as Old Black Lion) and a guest, friendly helpful service; children over 5 allowed if eating, no dogs, sheltered back terrace, ten bedrooms (some above bar), good breakfast, open all day. *(N R White)*

HAY-ON-WYE SO2242

⋆**Three Tuns** (01497) 821855

Broad Street; HR3 5DB Popular freshly prepared food (all day Sat) including home-baked bread in big pub with low beams and inglenook woodburners, lighter sofa area, ancient stairs to raftered restaurant, well kept ales and good wine choice, prompt helpful service; may ask for a credit card if you run a tab, no dogs; children welcome till 7pm, disabled facilities, seats under big parasols in sheltered courtyard, open all day weekends, closed Mon and Tues out of season. *(Anon)*

KNIGHTON SO2972

George & Dragon (01547) 528532

Broad Street; LD7 1BL Friendly family-run 17th-c inn, dark-panelled back lounge bar with stone fireplace, hanging jugs and mugs, stags' heads and two fine carved settles, front public bar, well kept Brains Rev James, Stonehouse Station Bitter and a summer guest, good choice of reasonably priced pub food, small restaurant; children and dogs welcome, handy stop-off for Offa's Dyke Path, five bedrooms in converted stables, open all day Fri-Sun. *(Phil and Jane Hodson)*

KNIGHTON SO2872

Horse & Jockey (01547) 520062

Wylcwm Place; LD7 1AE Popular old family-run pub with several cosy areas, one with log fire, enjoyable good value food from traditional choices and pizzas up in bar and adjoining restaurant, cheerful service, well kept beers; tables in pleasant medieval courtyard, six bedrooms, handy for Offa's Dyke Path. *(Ann and Colin Hunt, Lois Dyer)*

LLANBEDR SO2320

Red Lion (01873) 810754

Off A40 at Crickhowell; NP8 1SR Quaint, welcoming old local in pretty village in dell, heavy beams, antique settles in lounge and snug, log fires, well kept Rhymney, Wye Valley and a guest ale, front dining area with good value home-made food; good walking country (porch for muddy boots), closed weekday lunchtime (except 2-5pm Weds), open all day weekends. *(Guy Vowles)*

LLANFIHANGEL-NANT-MELAN   SO1958
Red Lion (01544) 350220
A44 10 miles W of Kington; LD8 2TN
Stripped-stone and beamed 16th-c roadside dining pub, roomy main bar with flagstones and woodburner, carpeted restaurant, front sun porch, good reasonably priced home-made food from shortish menu including imaginative vegetarian options, Brains and changing guests, friendly service, back bar with woodburner, pool and darts; children and dogs welcome, country views from pleasant garden, seven bedrooms (three in annexe), handy for Radnor Forest walks and near impressive waterfall, open all day Sun till 9pm, closed Tues. *(Ann and Colin Hunt, Dave Braisted)*

LLANGURIG   SN9079
Blue Bell (01686) 440254
A44 opposite church; SY18 6SG Friendly old-fashioned village inn with well kept Brains Rev James and Wye Valley Butty Bach, Thatcher's cider, ample helpings of enjoyable good value pubby food, comfortable flagstoned bar, games room with darts, dominoes and pool, small dining room; background music, no dogs; children welcome, nine simple bedrooms, open all day. *(Lois Dyer, Kay and Alistair Butler)*

LLANIDLOES   SN9584
Crown & Anchor (01686) 412398
Long Bridge Street; SY18 6EF Friendly unspoilt town-centre pub known locally as Rubys after landlady who has run it for 49 years, well kept Brains Rev James and Worthington Bitter, chatty locals' bar, lounge, snug and two other rooms, one with pool and games machine separated by central hallway; open all day; for sale so things may change. *(Anon)*

LLANWRTYD WELLS   SN8746
Neuadd Arms (01591) 610236
The Square; LD5 4RB Sizeable 19th-c hotel (friendly and by no means upmarket) brewing its own good value Heart of Wales beers in back stable block, enjoyable straightforward home-made food, log fires in lounge and small tiled public bar still with old service bells, restaurant, games room; lots of outdoor events (some rather outré such as bogsnorkelling and man v horse); well behaved dogs welcome in bars, a few tables out in front, 21 bedrooms (front ones can be noisy), engaging very small town in good walking area, open all day. *(Taff Thomas)*

LLOWES   SO1941
Radnor Arms (01497) 847460
A438 Brecon–Hereford; HR3 5JA
Attractive little stone-built country pub, well kept Wye Valley Butty Bach and a guest, extensive choice of bottled beers, good food including tapas and Fri lunchtime beer-battered haddock, children's menu, traditional beamed bar with stripped stone and log fire, two small dining rooms; dogs welcome, tables in garden looking over fields to Black Mountains, small campsite, closed Sun evening, Mon, Tues. *(Anon)*

PAINSCASTLE   SO1646
★ Roast Ox (01497) 851398
Off A470 Brecon–Builth Wells, or from A438 at Clyro; LD2 3JL Well restored pub with beams, flagstones, stripped stone, appropriate simple furnishings and some rustic bric-a-brac, huge antlers above open fire, well kept ales tapped from the cask and good range of farm ciders, popular freshly made food, friendly quick service; children and dogs welcome, picnic-sets outside, attractive hill country, ten comfortable and neat bedrooms. *(Anon)*

PENCELLI   SO0925
Royal Oak (01874) 665396
B4558 SE of Brecon; LD3 7LX
Unpretentious and friendly with two small bars, low beams, assorted pine furniture on polished flagstones, autographed sporting memorabilia, log fires, well kept Brains Rev James and a guest, small blackboard choice of enjoyable home-made food (standard times in summer, Thurs-Sat evenings and weekend lunchtimes in winter), simple modern candlelit dining room; children welcome, terraces backing on to Monmouth & Brecon Canal (nearby moorings), lovely canalside walks and handy for Taff Trail, closed Mon-Weds out of season. *(Anon)*

PEN-Y-CAE   SN8313
Ancient Briton (01639) 730273
Brecon Road (A4067); SA9 1YY Friendly opened-up roadside pub, six or more well kept ales from far and wide, local cider, enjoyable reasonably priced home-made food; outside seats and play area, campsite (good facilities), handy for Dan-yr-Ogof caves, Henrhyd Waterfall and Carig-y-Nos Country Park, open all day. *(Anon)*

PRESTEIGNE   SO3164
Radnorshire Arms (01544) 267406
High Street (B4355 N of centre); LD8 2BE Fine Elizabethan timbered hotel full of rambling individuality and historical charm; relaxed bar, venerable dark oak

Half pints: by law, a pub should not charge more for half a pint than half the price of a full pint, unless it shows that half-pint price on its price list.

panelling, latticed windows, elegantly moulded black oak beams, polished copper pans and measures, a handful of armchairs, lovely dining room, wide choice of enjoyable well priced pubby food including takeaway pizzas, decent choice of real ales and ciders, friendly efficient staff; background music, pool room; children welcome, dogs in some bedrooms, metal seats and tables on covered terrace overlooking children's outside play area, 16 bedrooms (eight in garden lodge), open all day. *(Anon)*

RHAYADER SN9668

★ **Triangle** (01597) 810537

Cwmdauddwr; B4518 by bridge over River Wye, SW of centre; LD6 5AR Interesting mainly 16th-c pub, small and spotless, with buoyant local atmosphere and welcoming helpful staff, shortish choice of good value home-made pubby food (best to book evenings), well kept Brains Rev James and Hancocks HB, small selection

of reasonably priced wines, dining area with nice view over park to Wye, darts and quiz nights; three tables on small front terrace, parking can be difficult. *(Taff Thomas, Lois Dyer)*

TALYBONT-ON-USK SO1122

★ **Star** (01874) 676635

B4558; LD3 7YX Old-fashioned canalside inn with several plainly furnished pubby rooms, open fires (one in splendid stone fireplace), five good changing ales served by enthusiastic landlord, real cider, enjoyable fairly priced bar food (more interesting evening choice), good mix of customers including walkers with dogs; sports TV, juke box, live music last Fri of month, Weds quiz, free wi-fi; children welcome, picnic sets in sizeable tree-ringed garden with path leading to river, lovely village surrounded by Brecon Beacons National Park, two bedrooms, open all day summer (all day Fri-Sun in winter). *(Guy Vowles)*

Post Office address codings confusingly give the impression that some pubs are in Gwent or Powys, Wales, when they're really in Gloucestershire or Shropshire (which is where we list them).

A little further afield

CHANNEL ISLANDS

GUERNSEY

FOREST

Deerhound (01481) 238585
Le Bourg; GY8 0AN Spacious roadside dining pub with modern interior, popular well priced food including summer seafood menu, Liberation ales, friendly helpful service; free wi-fi; children welcome, terrace tables, handy for the airport, open all day. *(Anon)*

KING'S MILLS

★**Fleur du Jardin** (01481) 257996
King's Mills Road; GY5 7JT Lovely country hotel in attractive walled garden with solar-heated swimming pool, relaxing low-beamed flagstoned bar with good log fire, old prints and subdued lighting, good food strong on local produce and seafood, friendly helpful service, several ales such as Adnams Broadside and Liberation, good choice of wines by the glass, local cider, restaurant; background music; children and small dogs welcome, plenty of tables on back terrace, 15 clean comfortable bedrooms, open all day. *(Anon)*

ST PETER PORT

Ship & Crown (01481) 728994
Opposite Crown Pier, Esplanade; GY1 2NB Bustling town pub with bay windows overlooking harbour, very popular with yachting people and smarter locals; interesting photographs (especially of World War II occupation, also boats and local shipwrecks), good value all-day bar food from sandwiches up, three changing ales and a proper cider, welcoming prompt service even when busy, more modern-feel Crow's Nest brasserie upstairs with fine views; sports TVs in bar; open all day from 10am till late. *(Stephen and Jean Curtis)*

VALE

Houmet (01481) 242214
Grande Havre; GY6 8JR Modern building overlooking Grande Havre Bay, front restaurant/bar with conservatory, good choice of reasonably priced popular food (best to book) including fresh local fish and seafood, friendly service, a couple of real ales and several wines by the glass, back public bar with pool, darts and big-screen sports TV (dogs allowed here); children welcome, tables out on decking, open all day (till 6pm Sun). *(Anon)*

JERSEY

GRÈVE DE LECQ

★**Moulin de Lecq** (01534) 482818
Mont de la Grève de Lecq; JE3 2DT Cheerful family-friendly converted mill dating from 12th c with massive waterwheel dominating the softly lit beamed bar, good pubby food, four changing ales and a couple of real ciders, prompt friendly service, lots of board games, pool in upstairs games room, restaurant extension; dogs welcome in bar, terrace picnic-sets and good adventure playground, quiet streamside spot with nice walks, open all day in summer. *(Anon)*

ST AUBIN

Boat House (01534) 747141
North Quay; JE3 8BS Modern steel and timber-clad harbourside building with great views (window tables for diners), bar serving well kept local ales and several wines by the glass, good food ranging from tapas to Josper-grilled steaks, airy upstairs restaurant; balcony and decked terrace, open all day. *(Anon)*

ST AUBIN

★**Old Court House Inn** (01534) 746433 *Harbour Boulevard; JE3 8AB* Pubby low-beamed downstairs bar with open fire, other rambling areas including bistro, food from pubby snacks to lots of good fresh fish, well kept real ales and nice wines by the glass, handsome upstairs restaurant, glorious views across harbour to St Helier; children welcome, front deck overlooking harbour, more seats in floral courtyard behind, ten comfortable bedrooms, open all day (food all day in summer). *(Anon)*

ST BRELADE

Old Smugglers (01534) 741510
Ouaisne Bay; OS map reference 595476; JE3 8AW Happily unpretentious black-

beamed pub just above Ouaisne beach, up to four well kept ales including Bass, farm cider, enjoyable reasonably priced pubby food (good steaks), friendly service, log fires, traditional built-in settles, darts, cribbage and dominoes, restaurant; occasional live music, sports TV; children and dogs welcome, sun porch with interesting coast views, open all day in summer. *(John Evans)*

ST HELIER
★ **Lamplighter** (01534) 723119
Mulcaster Street; JE2 3NJ Small pub with up to eight well kept ales including Liberation, local cider, around 160 whiskies, bargain simple food such as crab sandwiches, heavy timbers, rough panelling and scrubbed pine tables; sports TV, can get very busy; interesting patriotic façade (the only union flag visible during Nazi occupation), open all day. *(Anon)*

ST MARY
St Marys (01534) 482897
La Rue des Buttes; JE3 3DF Old inn opposite attractive church, modern interior with bar and spacious dining area, good choice of popular reasonably priced food from lunchtime sandwiches up, Liberation and guest beers, plenty of wines by the glasss; pool, darts, free wi-fi; children welcome, seats in front garden and back courtyard, open all day. *(Anon)*

ISLE OF MAN

BALDRINE   SC4180
Liverpool Arms (01624) 674787
Main Road; IM4 6AE Former coaching inn with enjoyable choice of reasonably priced pub food (all day Fri-Sun), Okells and guests,

friendly welcoming staff, open fires; sports TV, pool and darts; children allowed, open all day. *(Anon)*

LAXEY   SC4382
Shore (01624) 861509
Old Laxey Hill; IM4 7DA Friendly nautically themed village pub brewing its own Old Laxey Bosun Bitter, good value wines by the glass and enjoyable pubby lunchtime food (also Tues curry and Thurs steak nights); children welcome till 9pm, picnic-sets out by lovely stream, nice walk to Laxey waterwheel, open all day. *(Dr J Barrie Jones)*

PEEL   SC2484
Creek (01624) 842216
Station Place/North Quay; IM5 1AT In lovely setting on the ancient quayside opposite Manannan Heritage Centre, welcoming relaxed atmosphere, wide choice of sensibly priced food including fish, crab and lobsters fresh from the boats, good local kippers too, well kept Okells and nine guest ales, nautical theme lounge bar with etched mirrors and mainly old woodwork, public bar with TVs and weekend live music; children welcome, tables outside overlooking harbour, open (and food) all day. *(Steve and Irene Homer)*

PORT ERIN   SC1969
Falcon's Nest (01624) 834077
Station Road; IM9 6AF Friendly family-run hotel overlooking the bay, good sensibly priced food including local fish/seafood and Sun carvery, five well kept ales (May beer festival) and some 70 malt whiskies, two bars, one with open fire, conservatory and restaurant; children welcome, 39 bedrooms many with sea view, also eight self-catering apartments, handy for steam rail terminus, open all day. *(Dr J Barrie Jones)*

Please tell us if the décor, atmosphere, food or drink at a pub is different from our description. We rely on readers' reports to keep us up to date: feedback@goodguides. com, or (no stamp needed) The Good Pub Guide, FREEPOST RTJR-ZCYZ-RJZT, Perrymans Lane, Etchingham TN19 7DN.

Pubs that serve food all day

We list here all the pubs that have told us they plan to serve food all day, even if it's only one day of the week. The individual entries for the pubs themselves show the actual details.

Bedfordshire

Ireland, Black Horse
Oakley, Bedford Arms
Steppingley, French Horn

Berkshire

Cookham Dean, Chequers
Kintbury, Dundas Arms
Peasemore, Fox
Sonning, Bull
White Waltham, Beehive

Buckinghamshire

Forty Green, Royal Standard of England
Stoke Mandeville, Bell
Wooburn Common, Chequers

Cambridgeshire

Peterborough, Brewery Tap
Stilton, Bell

Cheshire

Aldford, Grosvenor Arms
Allostock, Three Greyhounds
Astbury, Egerton Arms
Aston, Bhurtpore
Bunbury, Dysart Arms
Burleydam, Combermere Arms
Burwardsley, Pheasant
Chester, Architect; Mill; Old Harkers Arms
Cholmondeley, Cholmondeley Arms
Cotebrook, Fox & Barrel
Delamere, Fishpool
Eaton, Plough
Lower Withington, Black Swan
Macclesfield, Sutton Hall
Marton, Davenport Arms
Mobberley, Bulls Head; Church Inn
Mottram St Andrew, Bulls Head
Nether Alderley, Wizard
Spurstow, Yew Tree
Thelwall, Little Manor
Warmingham, Bears Paw

Cornwall

Morwenstow, Bush
Mylor Bridge, Pandora
Porthtowan, Blue

Cumbria

Cartmel Fell, Masons Arms
Crosthwaite, Punch Bowl
Elterwater, Britannia
Ings, Watermill
Levens, Strickland Arms
Ravenstonedale, Black Swan

Derbyshire

Alderwasley, Bear

Chelmorton, Church Inn

Fenny Bentley, Coach & Horses

Hathersage, Plough

Hayfield, Lantern Pike; Royal

Ladybower Reservoir, Ladybower Inn; Yorkshire Bridge

Litton, Red Lion

Repton, Bulls Head

Devon

Cockwood, Anchor

Iddesleigh, Duke of York

Postbridge, Warren House

Sidbury, Hare & Hounds

Dorset

Tarrant Monkton, Langton Arms

Weymouth, Red Lion

Worth Matravers, Square & Compass

Essex

Aythorpe Roding, Axe & Compasses

Feering, Sun

Fyfield, Queens Head

Little Walden, Crown

South Hanningfield, Old Windmill

Gloucestershire

Ford, Plough

Nailsworth, Weighbridge

Sheepscombe, Butchers Arms

Hampshire

Bransgore, Three Tuns

Littleton, Running Horse

Portsmouth, Old Customs House

Hertfordshire

Aldbury, Valiant Trooper

Ashwell, Three Tuns

Barnet, Duke of York

Harpenden, White Horse

Isle of Wight

Fishbourne, Fishbourne Inn

Ningwood, Horse & Groom

Niton, Buddle

Seaview, Boathouse

Shorwell, Crown

Kent

Brookland, Woolpack

Hollingbourne, Windmill

Langton Green, Hare

Penshurst, Bottle House

Sevenoaks, White Hart

Stalisfield Green, Plough

Stowting, Tiger

Lancashire

Bashall Eaves, Red Pump

Bispham Green, Eagle & Child

Blackburn, Oyster & Otter

Formby, Sparrowhawk

Great Mitton, Aspinall Arms; Three Fishes

Manchester, Wharf

Nether Burrow, Highwayman

Pleasington, Clog & Billycock

Stalybridge, Station Buffet

Uppermill, Church Inn

Waddington, Lower Buck

Leicestershire and Rutland

Coleorton, George

Lyddington, Marquess of Exeter

Swithland, Griffin

Woodhouse Eaves, Wheatsheaf

Lincolnshire

Kirkby la Thorpe, Queens Head

Stamford, George of Stamford

Norfolk

King's Lynn, Bank House

Larling, Angel

Morston, Anchor

Salthouse, Dun Cow

Thorpe Market, Gunton Arms

Woodbastwick, Fur & Feather

Northamptonshire

Ashby St Ledgers, Olde Coach House

Oundle, Ship

Northumbria

Alnmouth, Red Lion

Aycliffe, County

Blanchland, Lord Crewe Arms

Carterway Heads, Manor House Inn

Newton, Duke of Wellington

Weldon Bridge, Anglers Arms

Oxfordshire

Kingham, Plough

Oxford, Bear

Wolvercote, Jacobs Inn

Shropshire

Chetwynd Aston, Fox

Shipley, Inn at Shipley

Shrewsbury, Armoury

Somerset

Bath, Marlborough

Dunster, Luttrell Arms

Hinton St George, Lord Poulett Arms

Stanton Wick, Carpenters Arms

Wedmore, Swan

Staffordshire

Salt, Holly Bush

Wrinehill, Hand & Trumpet

Suffolk

Chelmondiston, Butt & Oyster

Southwold, Harbour Inn

Stoke-by-Nayland, Crown

Waldringfield, Maybush

Surrey

Buckland, Jolly Farmers

Elstead, Mill at Elstead

Milford, Refectory

Outwood, Bell

Sussex

Alfriston, George

Charlton, Fox Goes Free

Chiddingly, Six Bells

East Chiltington, Jolly Sportsman

Eridge Green, Nevill Crest & Gun

Horsham, Black Jug

Mayfield, Rose & Crown

Ringmer, Cock

Warwickshire

Barford, Granville

Birmingham, Old Joint Stock

Farnborough, Inn at Farnborough

Hunningham, Red Lion

Long Compton, Red Lion

Welford-on-Avon, Bell

Wiltshire

Brinkworth, Three Crowns

Yorkshire

Beck Hole, Birch Hall

Blakey Ridge, Lion

Bradfield, Strines Inn

Broughton, Bull

Elslack, Tempest Arms

Grinton, Bridge Inn

Halifax, Shibden Mill

Hartshead, Gray Ox

Ledsham, Chequers

Linton in Craven, Fountaine

Widdop, Pack Horse

London

Central London, Bountiful Cow;
Old Bank of England; Olde Mitre;
Seven Stars; Thomas Cubitt

Hampton Court, Mute Swan

North London, Holly Bush

South London, Greenwich Union

West London, Churchill
Arms; Dove; Duke of Sussex;
Old Orchard; Portobello Gold;
Scarsdale; White Horse; Windsor
Castle

Scotland

Applecross, Applecross Inn

Edinburgh, Abbotsford

Glasgow, Babbity Bowster; Bon
Accord

Glencoe, Clachaig

Kippen, Cross Keys

Shieldaig, Tigh an Eilean Hotel

Thornhill, Lion & Unicorn

Scottish Islands

Sligachan, Sligachan Hotel

Wales

Colwyn Bay, Pen-y-Bryn

Gresford, Pant-yr-Ochain

Llandudno Junction, Queens
Head

Llanelian-yn-Rhos, White Lion

Llangollen, Corn Mill

Mold, Glasfryn

Overton Bridge, Cross Foxes

Pontypridd, Bunch of Grapes

Pubs near motorway junctions

The number at the start of each line is the number of the junction.

Detailed directions are given in the main entry for each pub. In this section, to help you find the pubs quickly before you're past the junction, we give the name of the chapter where you'll find the text.

M1

9: Redbourn, Cricketers (Hertfordshire) 3.2 miles

13: Woburn, Birch (Bedfordshire) 3.5 miles

16: Nether Heyford, Olde Sun (Northamptonshire) 1.8 miles

18: Ashby St Ledgers, Olde Coach House (Northamptonshire) 4 miles

M3

1: Sunbury, Flower Pot (Surrey) 1.6 miles

3: West End, Inn at West End (Surrey) 2.4 miles

5: North Warnborough, Mill House (Hampshire) 1 mile; Hook, Hogget (Hampshire) 1.1 miles

7: North Waltham, Fox (Hampshire) 3 miles

9: Easton, Chestnut Horse (Hampshire) 3.6 miles

M4

9: Bray, Hinds Head (Berkshire) 1.75 miles; Bray, Crown (Berkshire) 1.75 miles

13: Peasemore, Fox (Berkshire) 4 miles

14: Shefford Woodlands, Pheasant (Berkshire) 0.3 miles; East Garston, Queens Arms (Berkshire) 3.5 miles

17: Norton, Vine Tree (Wiltshire) 4 miles

M5

4: Holy Cross, Bell & Cross (Worcestershire) 4 miles

10: Dunster, Luttrell Arms (Somerset) miles; Coombe Hill, Gloucester Old Spot (Gloucestershire) 1 mile

13: Eastington, Old Badger (Gloucestershire) 1 mile

19: Clapton-in-Gordano, Black Horse (Somerset) 4 miles

26: Clayhidon, Merry Harriers (Devon) 3.1 miles

30: Woodbury Salterton, Diggers Rest (Devon) 3.5 miles

M6

17: Sandbach, Old Hall (Cheshire) 1.2 miles

18: Allostock, Three Greyhounds (Cheshire) 4.7 miles

19: Mobberley, Bulls Head (Cheshire) 4 miles

36: Levens, Strickland Arms (Cumbria) 4 miles

40: Yanwath, Gate Inn (Cumbria) 2.25 miles; Tirril, Queens Head (Cumbria) 3.5 miles

M11

9: Hinxton, Red Lion (Cambridgeshire) 2 miles; Great Chesterford, Crown & Thistle (Essex) 1.5 miles

10: Duxford, John Barleycorn (Cambridgeshire) 1.8 miles; Whittlesford, Tickell Arms (Cambridgeshire) 2.4 miles

M20

8: Hollingbourne, Windmill (Kent) 1 mile

11: Stowting, Tiger (Kent) 3.7 miles

M25

5: Chipstead, George & Dragon (Kent) 1.25 miles

16: Denham, Swan (Buckinghamshire) 0.75 miles

18: Flaunden, Bricklayers Arms (Hertfordshire) 4 miles

21A: Potters Crouch, Holly Bush (Hertfordshire) 2.3 miles

M27

1: Fritham, Royal Oak (Hampshire) 4 miles

M40

2: Hedgerley, White Horse (Buckinghamshire) 2.4 miles; Forty Green, Royal Standard of England (Buckinghamshire) 3.5 miles

12: Gaydon, Malt Shovel (Warwickshire) 0.9 miles

15: Barford, Granville (Warwickshire) 1.7 miles

M42

5: Barston, Malt Shovel (Warwickshire) 3 miles

6: Hampton in Arden, White Lion (Warwickshire) 1.25 miles

M50

3: Kilcot, Kilcot Inn (Gloucestershire) 2.3 miles

M60

13: Worsley, Old Hall (Lancashire) 1 mile

M62

25: Hartshead, Gray Ox (Yorkshire) 3.5 miles

M65

3: Blackburn, Oyster & Otter (Lancashire) 1.8 miles

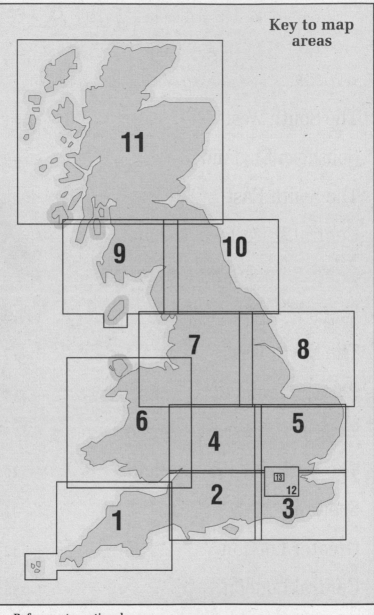

Key to map areas

11

9 **10**

7 **8**

6 **5**

4

2 **13** **12**

3

1

Reference to sectional maps

▦ Motorway	● Main Entry
Major road	◉ Main Entry with accommodation
- - - County boundary	■ Place name to assist navigation

MAPS

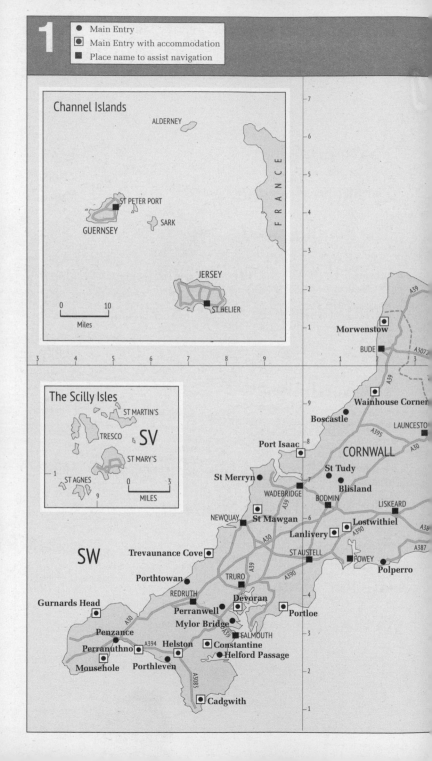

1

- Main Entry
- ● Main Entry with accommodation
- ■ Place name to assist navigation

Channel Islands

ALDERNEY

FRANCE

ST PETER PORT

GUERNSEY

SARK

JERSEY

ST HELIER

0   10
Miles

The Scilly Isles

ST MARTIN'S

TRESCO

SV

ST MARY'S

ST AGNES

0   3
MILES

Morwenstow

BUDE

A39

A3072

Wainhouse Corner

LAUNCESTO

Boscastle

A395

A30

Port Isaac

St Tudy

CORNWALL

St Merryn

WADEBRIDGE

Blisland

BODMIN

LISKEARD

NEWQUAY

St Mawgan

Lanlivery

Lostwithiel

A390

A38

Trevaunance Cove

ST AUSTELL

FOWEY

A387

SW

Porthtowan

TRURO

A390

Polperro

REDRUTH

Devoran

Portloe

Gurnards Head

A30

Perranwell

Penzance

Mylor Bridge

A394

Helston

Constantine

Perranuthnoe

FALMOUTH

Helford Passage

Mousehole

Porthleven

A3083

Cadgwith

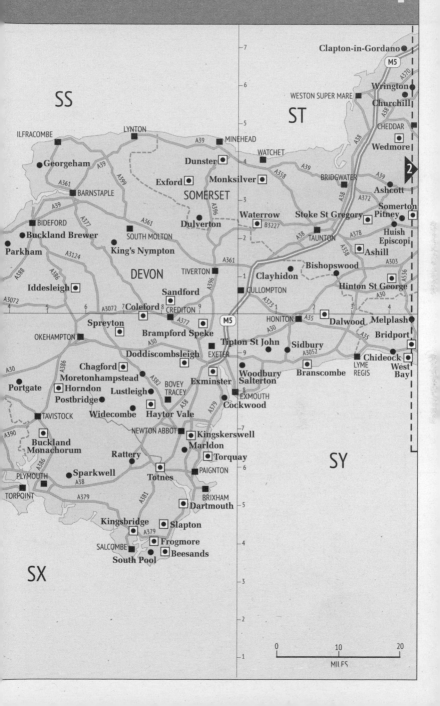

2

- ● Main Entry
- ◉ Main Entry with accommodation
- ■ Place name to assist navigation

GLOUCESTERSHIRE

Oldbury-on-Severn
Tetbury
Crudwell
Cricklade
Leighterton
MALMESBURY
Brinkworth
Sherston
Norton
Swindon
Grittleton
Broad Hinton
Ford
CHIPPENHAM
Compton Bassett
Bristol
Corsham
Lacock
CALNE
Marlborough
South Wraxall
MELKSHAM
Manton
Bath
Holt
Stanton Wick
Monkton Combe
Winsley
Broughton Gifford
Wrington
Midford
BRADFORD-ON-AVON
DEVIZES
Combe Hay
Poulshot
WILTSHIRE
TROWBRIDGE
MIDSOMER NORTON
West Lavington
CHEDDAR
Holcombe
Edington
East Chisenbury
Priddy
Mells
FROME
WELLS
Croscombe
WARMINSTER
SHEPTON MALLET
SOMERSET
Upton Lovell
Newton Tony
GLASTONBURY
WYLYE
AMERSBURY
ST
Somerton
East Knoyle
Fonthill Gifford
Pitton
Babcary
WINCANTON
Chicksgrove
Salisbury
Kingsdon
Buckhorn Weston
Corton Denham
West Stour
Charlton Horethorne
SHAFTESBURY
Rockbourne
Trent
Tollard Royal
FORDINGBRIDGE
YEOVIL
Sherborne
Shroton
Cranborne
Fritham
Odcombe
Farnham
DORSET
Tarrant Monkton
Middlemarsh
BLANDFORD FORUM
RINGWOOD
Evershot
Plush
Wimborne Minster
Cerne Abbas
Bransgore
Melplash
CHRISTCHURCH
Nettlecombe
Askerswell
DORCHESTER
POOLE
Bridport
BOURNEMOUTH
Mudeford
WAREHAM
Weymouth
Church Knowle
SWANAGE
SY
Worth Matravers

M4 M5 M5 M4 M4

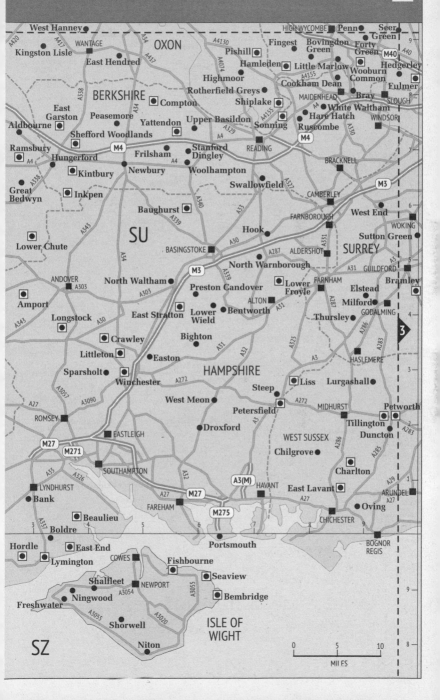

HIGH WYCOMBE   Penn   Seer Green

West Hanney

WANTAGE   OXON

Kingston Lisle

East Hendred

Pishill   Fingest   Bovingdon Green   Forty Green

Hamleden   Little Marlow   Wooburn Common   Hedgerley

Highmoor   Cookham Dean   M40

BERKSHIRE   Rotherfield Greys   MAIDENHEAD   White Waltham   Fulmer

Compton   Shiplake   Bray   SLOUGH

East Garston   Peasemore   Upper Basildon   Sonning   Hare Hatch   WINDSOR

Aldbourne   Yattendon   Ruscombe   M4

Shefford Woodlands   READING

Ramsbury   M4   Stanford Dingley   BRACKNELL

Hungerford   Frilsham   Newbury

Kintbury   Woolhampton   CAMBERLEY   M3

Great Bedwyn   Inkpen   Swallowfield   FARNBOROUGH   West End

Baughurst   WOKING

SU   Sutton Green

Lower Chute   Hook   ALDERSHOT   SURREY

BASINGSTOKE   North Warnborough   GUILDFORD

ANDOVER   M3   FARNHAM   Bramley

North Waltham   Preston Candover   Lower Froyle   Elstead

Amport   ALTON   Milford   GODALMING

Longstock   East Stratton   Lower Wield   Bentworth   Thursley

Crawley   Bighton   HASLEMERE

Littleton   Easton

Sparsholt   HAMPSHIRE   Liss   Lurgashall

Winchester   Steep   MIDHURST   Petworth

West Meon   Petersfield   Tillington

ROMSEY   Droxford   Duncton

EASTLEIGH   WEST SUSSEX

M27   Chilgrove

M271   Charlton

SOUTHAMPTON   A3(M)   HAVANT   East Lavant   ARUNDEL

LYNDHURST   M27   CHICHESTER   Oving

Bank   FAREHAM   M275   BOGNOR REGIS

Beaulieu   Boldre

Hordle   East End   Portsmouth

Lymington   COWES   Fishbourne

Shalfleet   Seaview

Ningwood   NEWPORT   Bembridge

Freshwater

Shorwell   ISLE OF WIGHT

SZ   Niton

0   5   10

MILES

● Main Entry
◉ Main Entry with accommodation
■ Place name to assist navigation

BUCKS

M1

M11

5

GREATER LONDON

Hedgerley
M40
● Harefield (see West London)
● Denham
Fulmer
UXBRIDGE

A127
Horndon-on
-the-Hill ◉
M25
A13
A128

BERKS

M4

TILBURY

M25 A30

■ STAINES

DARTFORD

GRAVESEND

ROCHESTER
A2

M3

◉ Sunbury
Esher ● Thames Ditton
Claygate
A3

M25

M20
A227

M20

A228

M2

WOKING

SURREY
M25
A246
A217

Chipstead

Chipstead
M26
WESTERHAM Sevenoaks
● Ivy Hatch
A26

MAIDSTONE

Sutton Green
● Mickleham
Buckland
DORKING
REIGATE
A25
A25
M25

A24
A25

A21
A227
TONBRIDGE

TQ

GUILDFORD

Bramley ◉
● Shamley Green
A29
Leigh ●
A217
A23

● Outwood
A22

Penshurst
● Speldhurst
Langton Green
Eridge Green
Tunbridge
Wells
Goudhurst
A262

A281

◉ Cranleigh

M23 A264

EAST GRINSTEAD

A267
A21

2

A24

CRAWLEY
A26A

● Horsham

Warninglid

◉ West Hoathly
Danehill
HAYWARDS
HEATH
A272
A275

CROWBOROUGH

A21 A26

High Hurstwood
● Mayfield

Ticehurst ◉

Salehurst
A265
Robertsbridge

A29

◉ Petworth
A283
● Dial Post

A24

A23
A273
■ BURGESS HILL

◉ Fletching
UCKFIELD
A272
A26

Heathfield

EAST
SUSSEX
A271

A29

WEST SUSSEX

◉ East Chiltington
Ditchling
A275
● Ringmer
LEWES

A267
A21
● Chiddingly

ARUNDEL

A27
A259 WORTHING
A283
A27
A273

A27

A259
BRIGHTON

HAILSHAM ■
Firle
Alciston
A26
NEWHAVEN
A259

◉ Wartling
A259

Alfriston ◉

A27
BEXHILL

EASTBOURNE

TV

◉ East Dean

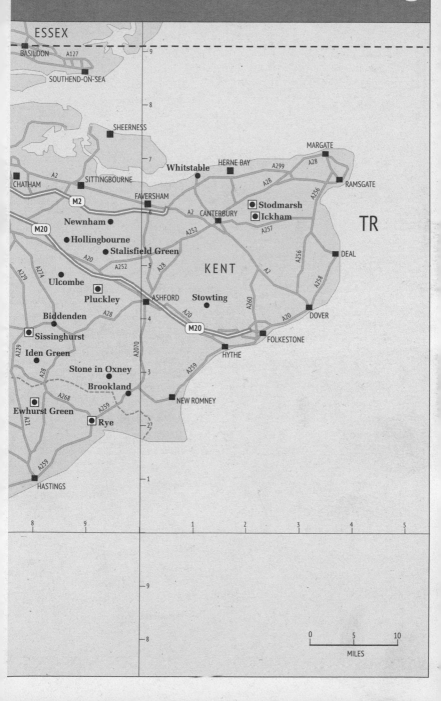

3

ESSEX

BASILDON A127

SOUTHEND-ON-SEA

SHEERNESS

MARGATE

Whitstable HERNE BAY A299

A28

CHATHAM A2 SITTINGBOURNE A28 RAMSGATE

M2 FAVERSHAM A256

Stodmarsh

A2 CANTERBURY **Ickham**

M20 **Newnham** A257

Hollingbourne A252 A256 DEAL

A20 **Stalisfield Green** **KENT**

A274 A252 A28 A258

A279 A1

Ulcombe ASHFORD **Stowting**

Pluckley A260 A20 DOVER

Biddenden A28 A20

A229 A20 FOLKESTONE

Sissinghurst M20

Iden Green A2070 HYTHE

A28 **Stone in Oxney** A259

Brookland

A268 NEW ROMNEY

A259

Ewhurst Green A21

A259

Rye

HASTINGS

TR

8   9   1   2   3   4   5

9

8

0   5   10
MILES

Shrewsbury
A5
TELFORD
STAFFS
M54
M6
LICHFIELD
7
TAMWORTH
M6 Toll
A5
A41
SJ
Ironbridge
A442
A38
Coalport
M42
Norton
A454
WOLVERHAMPTON
8
9
Shipley
Much Wenlock
Cardington
Bridgnorth
A458
SHROPSHIRE
A442
A4123
9
A38(M)
M6
Birmingham
A38
Hampton in Arden
A34
M5
Clent
Barston
M42
Ludlow
A4117
KIDDERMINSTER
A449
A456
Holy Cross
A49
BEWDLEY
M42
A448
7
M40
A456
A4189
Preston
Bagot
A443
Cutnall Green
REDDITCH
A435
A5400
A46
Tenbury Wells
WORCESTERSHIRE
6
Alcester
LEOMINSTER
A38
A46
Stratford-
upon-Avon
A44
Knightwick
WORCESTER
A422
Ardens Grafton
A46
A471
Little Cowarne
Bransford
Welford-on-Avon
B439
A417
Newland
A449
5
Alderminster
A3400
6
HEREFORDSHIRE
A4103
Malvern
Ilmington
HEREFORD
Upper Colwall
A44
A4104
Bretforton
SO
A438
M5
EVESHAM
Weston Subedge
Ledbury
Welland
A46
Childswickham
B4632
Chipping
Campden
Woolhope
A438
Stanton
Broadway
Carey
Bourton-on-the-Hill
A449
TEWKESBURY
A435
Gretton
MORETON-IN-MARSH
A44
M50
3
Ford
Upper
Oddington
Ashleworth
A38
Coombe Hill
Lower Slaughter
Ross-on-Wye
Stow-on-the-Wold
A49
Kilcot
Cheltenham
Brockhampton
A436
Bledington
A424
Clifford's Mesne
A40
Nether Westcote
Walford
Gloucester
Great
Rissington
A466
Symonds Yat
A4136
Blaisdon
Cowley
A429
Burford
MONMOUTH
A46
Northleach
A40
Shilton
GLOUCESTERSHIRE
Sheepscombe
A417
1
North
Cerney
B4425
Newland
STROUD
Langford
Eastington
A419
Barnsley
Southrop
A417
A48
A38
Cirencester
Dursley
A4135
Nailsworth
A433
A429
Marston Meysey
A466
Oldbury-on-
-Severn
M5
Tetbury
A419
CHEPSTOW
Leighterton
Crudwell
Cricklade

MILES
10
5
5
6
8
5
6
8
2

A169
A159
A41
A458

6

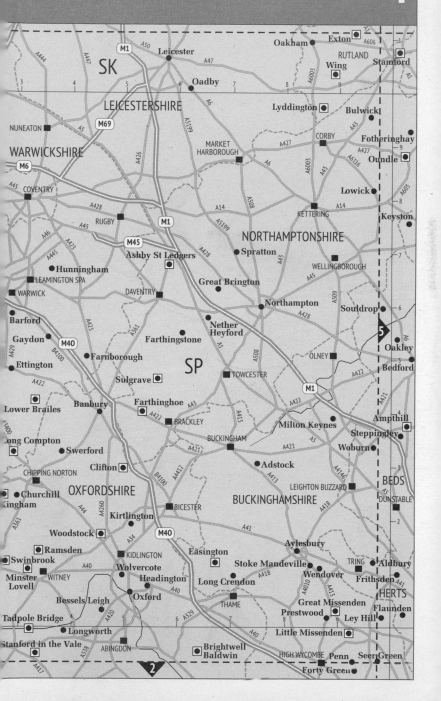

5

- Main Entry
- Main Entry with accommodation
- Place name to assist navigation

LINCS

WISBECH

8

Stamford

DOWNHAM MARKET

A47

A47

TF

A15

A1

1

2

A1122

5

6

7

3

Peterborough

A605

A141

A10

A1101

Elton

Fotheringhay

CAMBRIDGESHIRE

Brandon Creek

NORTHANTS

Stilton

CHATTERIS

A142

Oundle

A1(M)

Sutton Gault

ELY

A142

MILDENHALL

A1123

A1101

A11

A1065

Keyston

A14

Huntingdon

Hemingford Abbots

Hemingford Grey

Fen Drayton

A10

NEWMARKET

Kimbolton

A14

B645

A1

A14

Souldrop

A428

CAMBRIDGE

Great Wilbraham

A11

Oakley

Ravensden

A1198

TL

A143

Bedford

Sutton

Balsham

A1307

BEDFORDSHIRE

Whittlesford

Ireland

A10

Duxford

A1092

Ampthill

A507

ROYSTON

A505

Hinxton

A1017

Flitton

Ashwell

Great Chesterford

Little Walden

Steppingley

A6

A1

A505

SAFFRON WALDEN

A10

Wendens Ambo

A600

Arkesden

M1

HITCHIN

A507

Clavering

M11

ESSEX

A505

PRESTON

STEVENAGE

HERTFORDSHIRE

DUNSTABLE

Luton

A1(M)

A602

Watton-at-Stone

A120

Dunmow

BRAINTREE

A120

Harpenden

BISHOP'S STORTFORD

Hatfield Broad Oak

Litley Green

A151

A1081

A119

HERTFORD

Fuller Street

HEMEL HEMPSTEAD

Redbourn

Hertford Heath

A414

Aythorpe Roding

A1060

A12

Frithsden

ST ALBANS

A1000

HARLOW

Fyfield

CHELMSFORD

Potters Crouch

Epping Green

A10

A414

Flaunden

Northlaw

Mill Green

M25

Sarratt

Barnet

TQ

M25

EPPING

Margaretting Tye

A5183

A1V

A1000

ENFIELD

A12

M25

South Hanningfield

3

BRENTWOOD

4

A5

A6

6

5

9

8

1

2

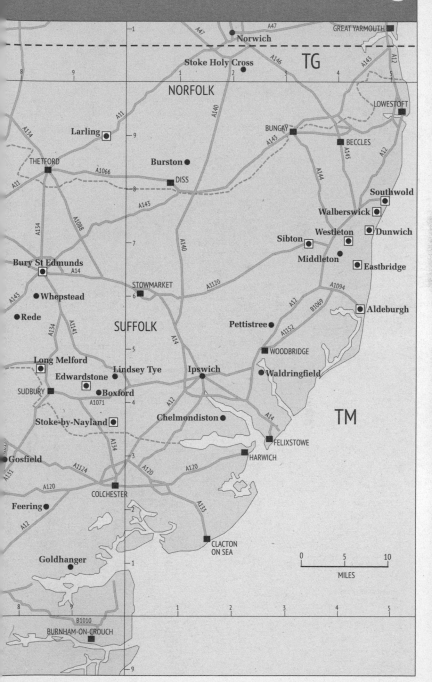

5

A47
Norwich
Stoke Holy Cross
A146
TG
GREAT YARMOUTH

NORFOLK
A140
LOWESTOFT

A11
Larling
BUNGAY
A143
BECCLES
A145
A134
THETFORD
A1066
Burston
DISS
Southwold
A143
Walberswick
A134
A1068
A140
Westleton
Dunwich
Sibton
Middleton
Eastbridge
Bury St Edmunds
A14
STOWMARKET
A1120
A1094
Whepstead
A143
SUFFOLK
A12
B1069
Aldeburgh
Rede
A134
A1141
Pettistree
A1152
Long Melford
A14
WOODBRIDGE
Edwardstone
Lindsey Tye
Ipswich
Waldringfield
SUDBURY
Boxford
A1071
Stoke-by-Nayland
A12
Chelmondiston
A14
TM
Gosfield
A134
FELIXSTOWE
A131
A1124
A120
A120
HARWICH
A120
COLCHESTER
Feering
A12
A133

Goldhanger
CLACTON
ON SEA

0   5   10
MILES

BURNHAM-ON-CROUCH
B1010

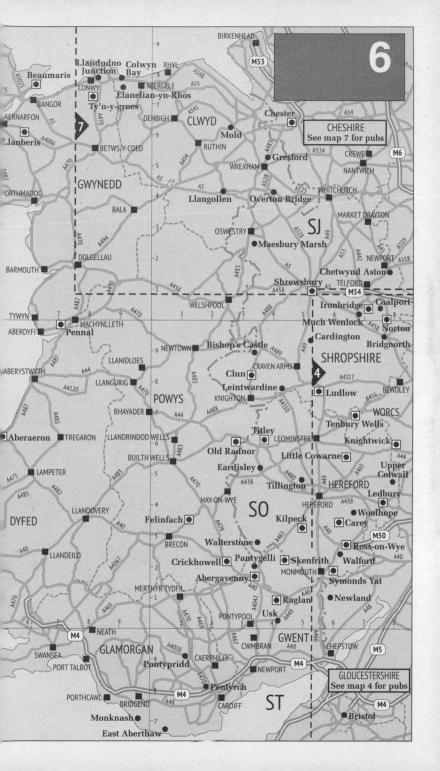

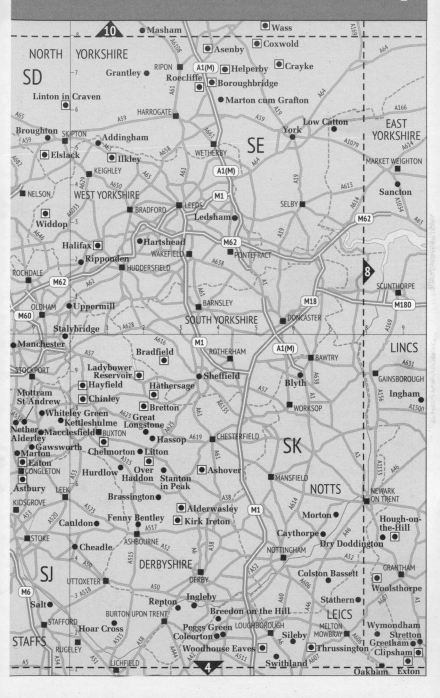

NORTH YORKSHIRE

SD

Masham

Wass

Asenby

Coxwold

Grantley

RIPON

A1(M)

Helperby

Crayke

Roecliffe

Boroughbridge

Linton in Craven

Marton cum Grafton

HARROGATE

A59

Low Catton

York

EAST YORKSHIRE

Broughton

SKIPTON

Addingham

Elslack

Ilkley

KEIGHLEY

WETHERBY

SE

A1(M)

MARKET WEIGHTON

NELSON

WEST YORKSHIRE

A650

LEEDS

M1

SELBY

Sancton

Widdop

BRADFORD

Ledsham

M62

Halifax

Hartshead

WAKEFIELD

PONTEFRACT

SCUNTHORPE

ROCHDALE

Ripponden

HUDDERSFIELD

A638

8

M62

OLDHAM

A62

M18

M180

M60

Uppermill

BARNSLEY

DONCASTER

Stalybridge

SOUTH YORKSHIRE

Manchester

A628

M1

A1(M)

LINCS

Bradfield

ROTHERHAM

BAWTRY

STOCKPORT

Ladybower Reservoir

Sheffield

Blyth

GAINSBOROUGH

Mottram St Andrew

Hayfield

Hathersage

Ingham

Whiteley Green

Chinley

Bretton

WORKSOP

Kettleshulme

Great Longstone

Nether Alderley

Macclesfield

BUXTON

Hassop

CHESTERFIELD

SK

Gawsworth

Chelmorton

Litton

Marton

Eaton

Over Haddon

Stanton in Peak

Ashover

MANSFIELD

NOTTS

CONGLETON

NEWARK ON TRENT

Astbury

LEEK

Hurdlow

Brassington

A38

M1

Alderwasley

Morton

Hough-on-the-Hill

KIDSGROVE

Cauldon

Fenny Bentley

Kirk Ireton

Caythorpe

STOKE

ASHBOURNE

Dry Doddington

Cheadle

A52

NOTTINGHAM

GRANTHAM

SJ

UTTOXETER

DERBYSHIRE

DERBY

Colston Bassett

Woolsthorpe

M6

Ingleby

Stathern

Salt

Repton

Breedon on the Hill

LEICS

Wymondham

STAFFORD

Hoar Cross

BURTON UPON TRENT

Peggs Green

LOUGHBOROUGH

MELTON MOWBRAY

Stretton

STAFFS

Coleorton

Sileby

Greetham

RUGELEY

Woodhouse Eaves

Thrussington

Clipsham

LICHFIELD

4

Swithland

Oakham

Exton

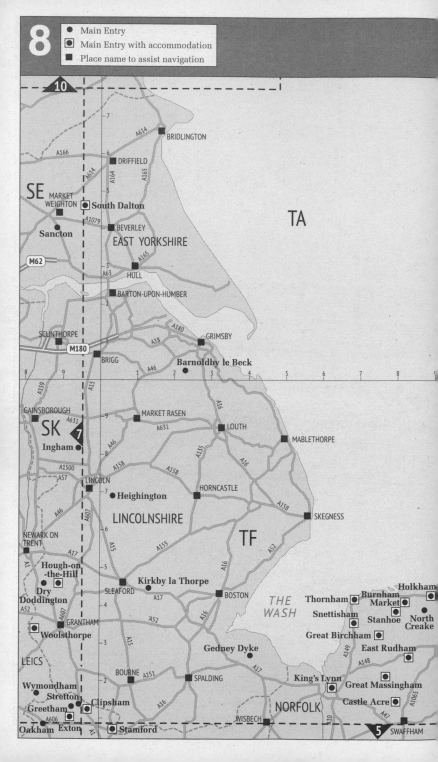

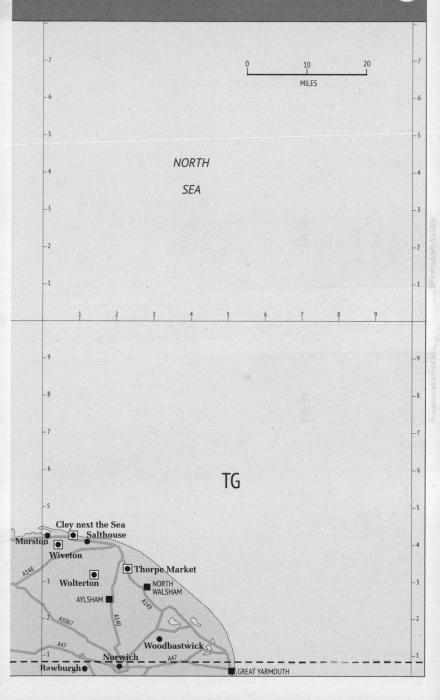

8

0   10   20
MILES

NORTH

SEA

7
6
5
4
3
2
1

1 2 3 4 5 6 7 8 9

9
8
7
6
5
4
3
2
1

TG

Cley next the Sea
Salthouse
Morston
Wiveton

Thorpe Market

Wolterton
NORTH
WALSHAM

AYLSHAM

A148
A1067
A140
A149
A47

Woodbastwick

Rawburgh
Norwich
A47
GREAT YARMOUTH

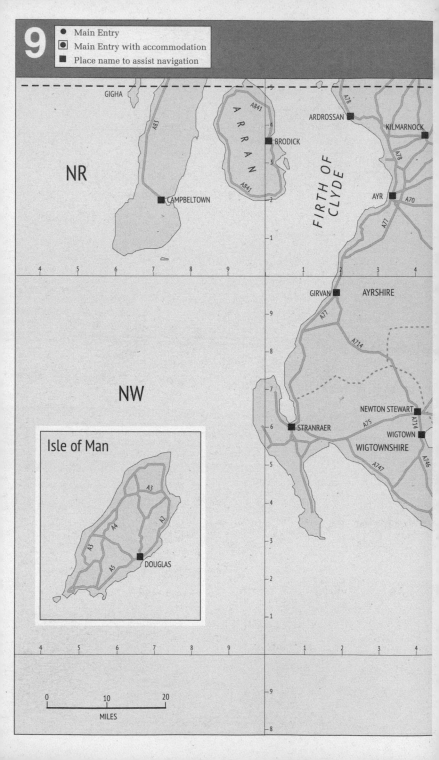

- Main Entry
- Main Entry with accommodation
- Place name to assist navigation

GIGHA

ARRAN

A841

A83

BRODICK

CAMPBELTOWN

A841

NR

FIRTH OF CLYDE

ARDROSSAN

A78

KILMARNOCK

A78

AYR

A70

A77

NW

GIRVAN

AYRSHIRE

A77

A714

NEWTON STEWART

A714

STRANRAER

A75

WIGTOWN

A746

WIGTOWNSHIRE

A747

Isle of Man

A3

A4

A2

A5

A5

DOUGLAS

0   10   20

MILES

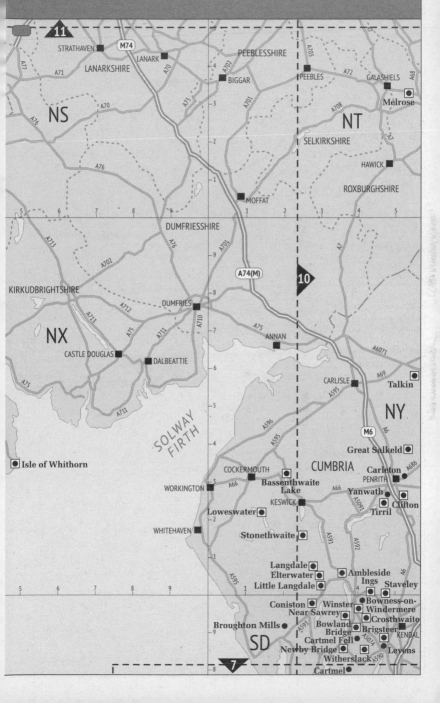

11

STRATHAVEN M74 LANARK
LANARKSHIRE PEEBLESSHIRE
A77 A71 A70 A73 BIGGAR A702 A701 PEEBLES A72 GALASHIELS A68
NS A76 A70 A701 SELKIRKSHIRE Melrose A7
A708 NT
A76 MOFFAT A7 HAWICK ROXBURGHSHIRE
DUMFRIESSHIRE A701
A702 A74(M) 10
KIRKUDBRIGHTSHIRE A712 DUMFRIES A710 A7
A713 A75 DUMFRIES A75 ANNAN
NX A713 A711 A710 A6071
CASTLE DOUGLAS DALBEATTIE
A75 A711 CARLISLE A69 Talkin
SOLWAY FIRTH A595 NY
A596 M6 A6
A595 Great Salkeld
COCKERMOUTH CUMBRIA Carleton A686
WORKINGTON A66 Bassenthwaite Lake A66 PENRITH Yanwath A6091 Clifton
Loweswater KESWICK Tirril
WHITEHAVEN Stonethwaite A591 A592
A595 A591 A6
Langdale Ambleside Staveley
Elterwater Ings
Little Langdale Winster Bowness-on-Windermere
Coniston Near Sawrey Crosthwaite
Broughton Mills Bowland Brigsteer KENDAL
SD Cartmel Fell A5074 Levens
Newby Bridge Witherslack A590
Cartmel

7

Isle of Whithorn

10

- ● Main Entry
- ◉ Main Entry with accommodation
- ■ Place name to assist navigation

11

BERWICKSHIRE

BERWICK-UPON-TWEED

A703

PEEBLES

A72

A6112 Swinton

A697

A68

GALASHIELS

Melrose ◉

A7

A698 COLDSTREAM

KELSO

A698

A1

4

NT

SELKIRKSHIRE

A708

A7

WOOLER

3

Seahouses ◉

A697

Newton-by-the-Sea ◉

JEDBURGH

A68

HAWICK

A6088

ROXBURGHSHIRE

A68

ALNWICK

ALNMOUTH ◉

A1

2

1

3 4 5 6 7 8 9 3

Weldon Bridge ◉

DUMFRIESSHIRE

OTTERBURN

A696

A1068

9

A74(M)

A7

A6071

Stannersburn ◉

A68

MORPETH ■

A1

9

NORTHUMBERLAND

BRAMPTON

Wark ◉

8

A19

HAYDON BRIDGE

Haltwhistle ●

Anick ●

Newton ●

NEWCASTLE UPON TYNE

A69

A69

HEXHAM

CARLISLE

A69

A686

Diptonmill ●

CORBRIDGE

A695

GATESHEAD

7

A395

Talkin ◉

A689

Hedley on the Hill ●

CONSETT

M6

A6

NY

Blanchland ◉

5

A68

Carterway Heads ◉

A1(M)

ALSTON

Durham ◉

A167

A686

A689

DURHAM

Great Salkeld ◉

4

PENRITH

Carleton ●

BISHOP AUCKLAND

3

Aycliffe ◉

Yanwath ◉

Clifton ◉

A66

A688

A167

Tirril ◉

Romaldkirk ◉

KESWICK

2

Winston ●

A67

Cotherstone ●

Stonethwaite ◉

BROUGH

A66

BARNARD CASTLE

DARLINGTON ■

A66

Langdale ◉

CUMBRIA

A685

Ravenstonedale ◉

SCOTCH CORNER ■

1

Elterwater ◉

Ambleside ◉

M6

7

A6

Downholme ●

NORTH

Little Langdale ◉

Ings ◉

Staveley ◉

Grinton ◉

Constable Burton ◉

A684

Winster ◉

Bowness-on-Windermere ◉

A683

Leyburn ●

Kirkby Fleetham ◉

Coniston ◉

Crosthwaite ◉

KENDAL

East Witton ◉

Near Sawrey ◉

Bowland Bridge ◉

9

Thornton Watlass ◉

Cartmel Fell ◉

Brigsteer ◉

SEDBERGH ■

Pickhill ◉

Witherslack ◉

Levens ◉

A684

A1(M)

SD

Newby Bridge ◉

Masham ●

Cartmel ●

8

NU

NORTH

SEA

0   10   20
MILES

SOUTH SHIELDS

SUNDERLAND

NZ

HARTLEPOOL

MIDDLESBROUGH

A174

A171

WHITBY

Robin
Hood's Bay

Beck Hole

A169

A171

YORKSHIRE

Blakey Ridge

SE

Cropton

Levisham
Lockton

TA

Felixkirk

A170

SCARBOROUGH

THIRSK

PICKERING   A170

andhutton   Wass

A169

A165

8

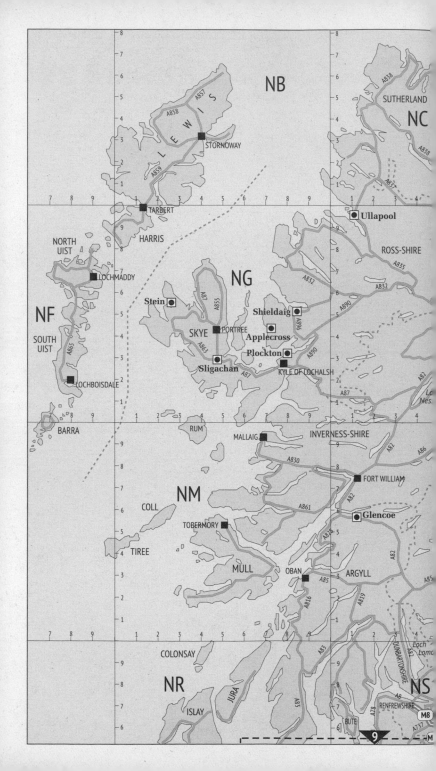

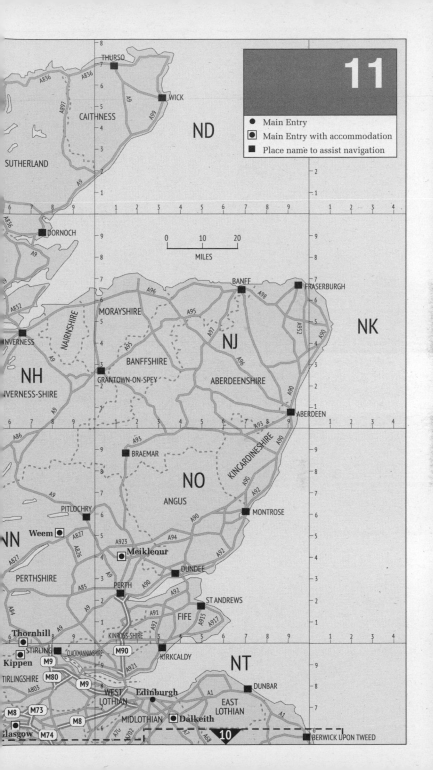

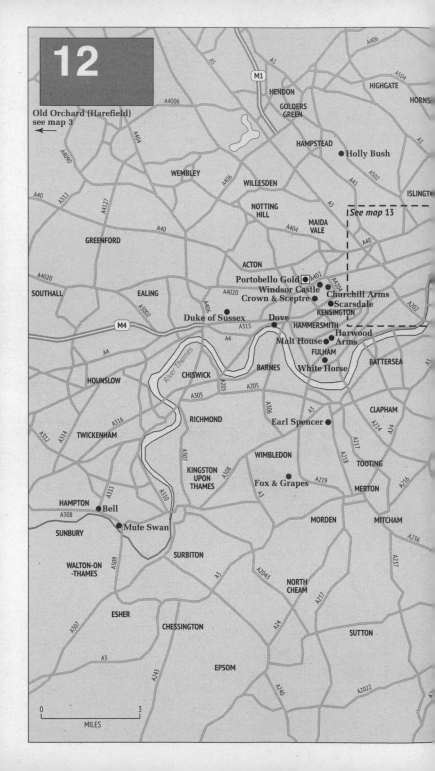

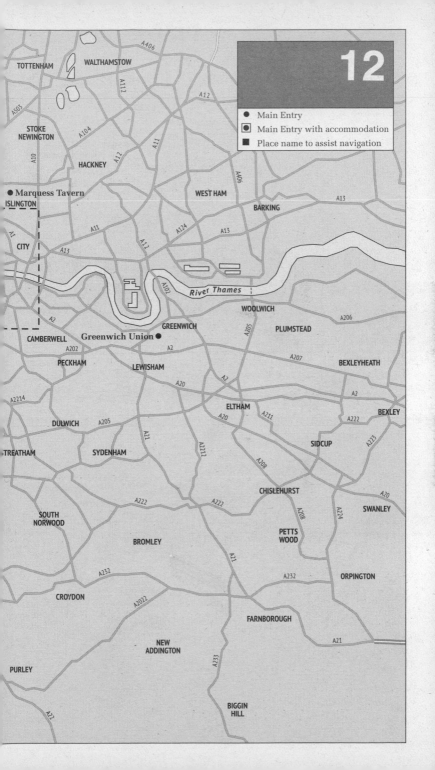

● Main Entry
◉ Main Entry with accommodation
■ Place name to assist navigation

TOTTENHAM
WALTHAMSTOW
A406
A112
A12
A503
STOKE
NEWINGTON
A104
A11
A10
HACKNEY
A12
A406
WEST HAM
BARKING
A13
● Marquess Tavern
ISLINGTON
A11
A124
A13
A1
A12
CITY
A13
River Thames
A102
WOOLWICH
A206
PLUMSTEAD
A205
GREENWICH
CAMBERWELL
Greenwich Union ●
A2
A202
BEXLEYHEATH
PECKHAM
LEWISHAM
A207
A2
A20
A2
A2
A2214
ELTHAM
BEXLEY
DULWICH
A205
A20
A211
A222
A21
A223
TREATHAM
SYDENHAM
A212
SIDCUP
A208
CHISLEHURST
A20
SOUTH
NORWOOD
A222
A222
A208
A224
SWANLEY
BROMLEY
PETTS
WOOD
A232
A21
ORPINGTON
A232
A232
CROYDON
A2022
FARNBOROUGH
A21
NEW
ADDINGTON
A233
PURLEY
A22
BIGGIN
HILL

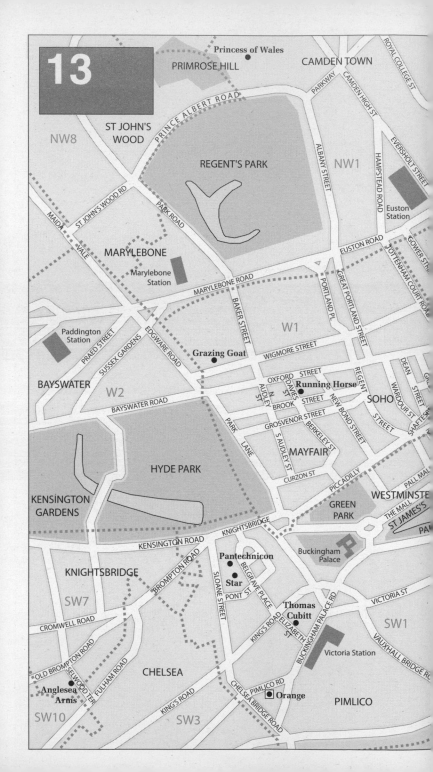

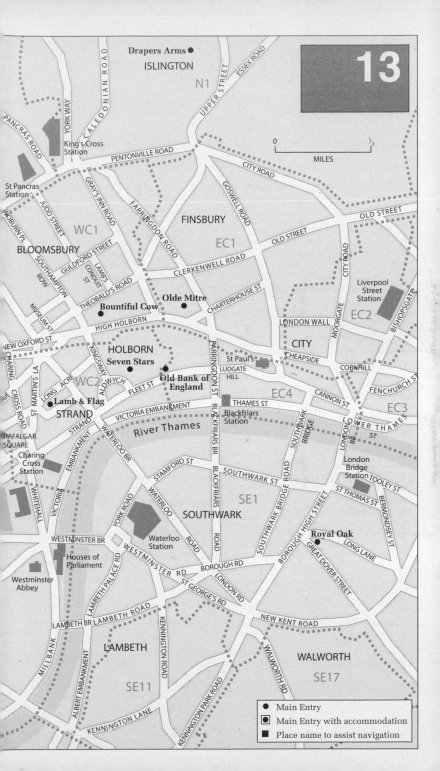

REPORT FORMS

We would very much appreciate hearing about your visits to pubs in this *Guide*, whether you have found them as described and recommend them for continued inclusion or noticed a fall in standards.

We'd also be glad to hear of any new pubs that you think we should know about. Readers' reports are very valuable to us, and sometimes pubs are dropped simply because we have had no up-to-date news on them.

You can use the tear-out forms on the following pages, email us at feedback@goodguides.co.uk or send us comments via our website (www.thegoodpubguide.co.uk) or app. We include two types of forms: one for you to simply list pubs you have visited and confirm that our review is accurate, and the other for you to give us more detailed information on individual pubs. If you would like more forms, please write to us at:

The Good Pub Guide

FREEPOST RTJR-ZCYZ-RJZT, Perrymans Lane, Etchingham TN19 7DN

Though we try to answer all letters, please understand if there's a delay (particularly in summer, our busiest period).

We'll assume we can print your name or initials as a recommender unless you tell us otherwise.

MAIN ENTRY OR 'ALSO WORTH A VISIT'?

Please try to gauge whether a pub should be a Main Entry or go in the Also Worth a Visit section (and tick the relevant box). Main Entries need to have qualities that would make it worth other readers' while to travel some distance to them. If a pub is an entirely new recommendation, the Also Worth a Visit section may be the best place for it to start its career in the *Guide* – to encourage other readers to report on it.

The more detail you can put into your description of a pub, the better. Any information on how good the landlord or landlady is, what it looks like inside, what you like about the atmosphere and character, the quality and type of food, which real ales are available and whether they're well kept, whether bedrooms are available, and how big/attractive the garden is. Other helpful information includes prices for food and bedrooms, food service and opening hours, and if children or dogs are welcome.

If the food or accommodation is outstanding, tick the FOOD AWARD or the STAY AWARD box.

If you're in a position to gauge a pub's suitability or otherwise for disabled people, do please tell us about that.

If you can, give the full address or directions for any pub not currently in the *Guide* – most of all, please give us its postcode. If we can't find a pub's postcode, we don't include it in the *Guide*.

I have been to the following pubs in *The Good Pub Guide 2015* in the last few months, found them as described, and confirm that they deserve continued inclusion:

continued overleaf

Pubs visited continued...........

By returning this form, you consent to the collection, recording and use of the information you submit, by The Random House Group Ltd. Any personal details which you provide from which we can identify you are held and processed in accordance with the Data Protection Act 1998 and will not be passed on to any third parties. The Random House Group Ltd may wish to send you further information on their associated products.

Please tick box if you do not wish to receive any such information. ☐

Your own name and address *(block capitals please)*

....

....

....

Postcode..

In returning this form I confirm my agreement that the information I provide may be used by The Random House Group Ltd, its assignees and/or licensees in any media or medium whatsoever.

Please return to

The Good Pub Guide
FREEPOST RTJR-ZCYZ-RJZT,
Perrymans Lane,
Etchingham
TN19 7DN

IF YOU PREFER, YOU CAN SEND
US REPORTS BY EMAIL:

feedback@goodguides.com

I have been to the following pubs in *The Good Pub Guide 2015* in the last few months, found them as described, and confirm that they deserve continued inclusion:

continued overleaf

PLEASE GIVE YOUR NAME AND ADDRESS ON THE BACK OF THIS FORM

Pubs visited continued..........

Your own name and address *(block capitals please)*

....

....

....

Postcode...

Please return to

The Good Pub Guide
FREEPOST RTJR-ZCYZ-RJZT,
Perrymans Lane,
Etchingham
TN19 7DN

IF YOU PREFER, YOU CAN SEND
US REPORTS BY EMAIL:

feedback@goodguides.com

I have been to the following pubs in *The Good Pub Guide 2015* in the last few months, found them as described, and confirm that they deserve continued inclusion:

continued overleaf

PLEASE GIVE YOUR NAME AND ADDRESS ON THE BACK OF THIS FORM

Pubs visited continued..........

By returning this form, you consent to the collection, recording and use of the information you submit, by The Random House Group Ltd. Any personal details which you provide from which we can identify you are held and processed in accordance with the Data Protection Act 1998 and will not be passed on to any third parties. The Random House Group Ltd may wish to send you further information on their associated products.

Please tick box if you do not wish to receive any such information. ☐

Your own name and address (*block capitals please*)

....

....

....

Postcode...

In returning this form I confirm my agreement that the information I provide may be used by The Random House Group Ltd, its assignees and/or licensees in any media or medium whatsoever.

Please return to

The Good Pub Guide
FREEPOST RTJR-ZCYZ-RJZT,
Perrymans Lane,
Etchingham
TN19 7DN

IF YOU PREFER, YOU CAN SEND
US REPORTS BY EMAIL:

feedback@goodguides.com

Report on (pub's name)

....

Pub's address

....

☐ YES MAIN ENTRY   ☐ YES WORTH A VISIT   ☐ NO don't include

Please tick one of these boxes to show your verdict, and give reasons, descriptive comments, prices and the date of your visit

☐ Deserves **FOOD Award**   ☐ Deserves **STAY Award**   2015:1

PLEASE GIVE YOUR NAME AND ADDRESS ON THE BACK OF THIS FORM

✂ ....

Report on (pub's name)

....

Pub's address

....

☐ YES MAIN ENTRY   ☐ YES WORTH A VISIT   ☐ NO don't include

Please tick one of these boxes to show your verdict, and give reasons, descriptive comments, prices and the date of your visit

☐ Deserves **FOOD Award**   ☐ Deserves **STAY Award**   2015:2

PLEASE GIVE YOUR NAME AND ADDRESS ON THE BACK OF THIS FORM

Your own name and address *(block capitals please)*

In returning this form I confirm my agreement that the information I provide may be used by The Random House Group Ltd, its assignees and/or licensees in any media or medium whatsoever.

DO NOT USE THIS SIDE OF THE PAGE FOR WRITING ABOUT PUBS

By returning this form, you consent to the collection, recording and use of the information you submit, by The Random House Group Ltd. Any personal details which you provide from which we can identify you are held and processed in accordance with the Data Protection Act 1998 and will not be passed on to any third parties. The Random House Group Ltd may wish to send you further information on their associated products. Please tick box if you do not wish to receive any such information.

✂ ....

Your own name and address *(block capitals please)*

In returning this form I confirm my agreement that the information I provide may be used by The Random House Group Ltd, its assignees and/or licensees in any media or medium whatsoever.

DO NOT USE THIS SIDE OF THE PAGE FOR WRITING ABOUT PUBS

By returning this form, you consent to the collection, recording and use of the information you submit, by The Random House Group Ltd. Any personal details which you provide from which we can identify you are held and processed in accordance with the Data Protection Act 1998 and will not be passed on to any third parties. The Random House Group Ltd may wish to send you further information on their associated products. Please tick box if you do not wish to receive any such information.

Report on (pub's name)

....

Pub's address

....

☐ YES MAIN ENTRY ☐ YES WORTH A VISIT ☐ NO don't include

Please tick one of these boxes to show your verdict, and give reasons, descriptive comments, prices and the date of your visit

☐ Deserves **FOOD Award** ☐ Deserves **STAY Award** 2015:3

PLEASE GIVE YOUR NAME AND ADDRESS ON THE BACK OF THIS FORM

✂ ....

Report on (pub's name)

....

Pub's address

....

☐ YES MAIN ENTRY ☐ YES WORTH A VISIT ☐ NO don't include

Please tick one of these boxes to show your verdict, and give reasons, descriptive comments, prices and the date of your visit

☐ Deserves **FOOD Award** ☐ Deserves **STAY Award** 2015:4

PLEASE GIVE YOUR NAME AND ADDRESS ON THE BACK OF THIS FORM

Your own name and address *(block capitals please)*

In returning this form I confirm my agreement that the information I provide may be used by The Random House Group Ltd, its assignees and/or licensees in any media or medium whatsoever.

DO NOT USE THIS SIDE OF THE PAGE FOR WRITING ABOUT PUBS

✂ ···

Your own name and address *(block capitals please)*

In returning this form I confirm my agreement that the information I provide may be used by The Random House Group Ltd, its assignees and/or licensees in any media or medium whatsoever.

DO NOT USE THIS SIDE OF THE PAGE FOR WRITING ABOUT PUBS

By returning this form, you consent to the collection, recording and use of the information you submit, by The Random House Group Ltd. Any personal details which you provide from which we can identify you are held and processed in accordance with the Data Protection Act 1998 and will not be passed on to any third parties. The Random House Group Ltd may wish to send you further information on their associated products. Please tick box if you do not wish to receive any such information.